Karch's Drug Abuse Handbook

Karch's Drug Abuse Handbook

Third Edition

Edited by
Steven B. Karch and Bruce A. Goldberger

CRC Press
Taylor & Francis Group
Boca Raton London New York

CRC Press is an imprint of the
Taylor & Francis Group, an **informa** business

Third edition published 2023
by CRC Press
2 Park Square, Milton Park, Abingdon, Oxon, OX14 4RN

and by CRC Press
6000 Broken Sound Parkway NW, Suite 300, Boca Raton, FL 33487-2742

First edition published by CRC Press 1997
Second edition published by CRC Press 2006

CRC Press is an imprint of Informa UK Limited

British Library Cataloguing-in-Publication Data
A catalogue record for this book is available from the British Library

Library of Congress Cataloging-in-Publication Data

Names: Karch, Steven B., editor. | Goldberger, Bruce A., editor.
Title: Karch's drug abuse handbook / [edited by] Steven B. Karch and Bruce A. Goldberger.
Other titles: Drug abuse handbook
Description: Third edition. | Boca Raton : CRC Press, 2022. | Previous published as: Drug abuse handbook / editor-in-chief, Steven B. Karch. | Includes bibliographical references and index. | Summary: "Packed with the latest information, the book includes tables of all Scheduled Drugs, methods of Quantitative Analysis, and a glossary of forensic toxicology terms. Pictures and diagrams show the effects of drugs and the chemical make-up and breakdown of abused drugs. It includes references to the best sources in legal medicine, pharmacology, and the law"-- Provided by publisher.
Identifiers: LCCN 2020047353 (print) | LCCN 2020047354 (ebook) | ISBN 9781420094992 (hardback) | ISBN 9781315155159 (ebook)
Subjects: LCSH: Drugs of abuse--Handbooks, manuals, etc. | Drug abuse--Handbooks, manuals, etc. | Forensic toxicology--Handbooks, manuals, etc.
Classification: LCC RM316 .D76 2022 (print) | LCC RM316 (ebook) | DDC 616.86--dc23
LC record available at https://lccn.loc.gov/2020047353
LC ebook record available at https://lccn.loc.gov/2020047354

ISBN: 978-1-4200-9499-2 (hbk)
ISBN: 978-1-032-04073-8 (pbk)
ISBN: 978-1-315-15515-9 (ebk)

DOI: 10.4324/9781315155159

Typeset in Times
by Deanta Global Publishing Services, Chennai, India

This book is dedicated to my mentors, Henry Urich, Professor of Neuropathology at the Royal London Hospital and Stanford, and Margaret Billingham, Professor of Pathology at Stanford, and to Boyd Stephens, Chief Medical Examiner, San Francisco. Their deaths all came too early. They taught me to be a good scientist. I like to think they would have been satisfied. It is also dedicated to my wife; not only did she help with the project, but she helped nurse me back to being healthy enough to finally finish the book!

Steven B. Karch, MD

I am eternally grateful for the opportunities to grow, serve, and thrive.
I am humbled by my family, friends, mentors, and colleagues' encouragement, trust, and love.
I am blessed by a lifetime of experiences.

Bruce A. Goldberger, PhD

Contents

Editors

Steven B. Karch received his undergraduate degree from Brown University in Providence, Rhode Island. He attended graduate school in anatomy and cell biology at Stanford University. He received his medical degree from Tulane University in New Orleans and did postgraduate training in neuropathology at the Royal London Hospital and in cardiac pathology at Stanford University. Dr. Karch is a fellow of the Faculty of Forensic and Legal Medicine of the Royal College of Physicians of London and also a fellow of the Forensic Science Society. He served as a cardiac pathologist at the office of the San Francisco Medical Examiner, publishing a number of books and papers when he was serving there.

Dr. Karch is the author of nearly 100 papers and book chapters, most having to do with the effects of drug abuse on the heart. He has published 12 books and is at work on several more, including a novel on the medical legal fallout of Hurricane Katrina. He was a forensic science editor for Humana Press and continues as an associate editor for the *Journal of Cardiovascular Toxicology*.

Dr. Karch was elected as a Wellcome fellow to the Royal Society of Medicine in 1972 and has remained active in the organization ever since. He is best known in the United Kingdom as one of the Crown pathologists who helped build the case against Dr. Harold Shipman and testified against him at trial. He also played a key part in the defense of Dr. David Moor, who had been wrongfully charged with the death of one of his patients. Dr. Karch was hired by the British government to assist in the arrest of Dr. Harold Shipman who fatally poisoned hundreds of his patients. He also testified for the defense of Dr. Anna Pou, the physician who was arrested but not indicted for second degree murder in some of the patient deaths at Memorial Hospital during Hurricane Katrina.

Dr. Bruce A. Goldberger is a Professor and the Chief of the Forensic Medicine Division in the Department of Pathology, Immunology, and Laboratory Medicine in the College of Medicine at the University of Florida in Gainesville. He is the Technical and Administrative Director of the Forensic Toxicology Laboratory. Dr. Goldberger is the Director of UF Health Forensic Medicine, the Program Director of the Florida Emergency Mortuary Operations Response System, and a Co-Investigator of the National Drug Early Warning System. Dr. Goldberger is the Director of the University of Florida Forensic Epidemiology Team.

Dr. Goldberger trained under the direction of Dr. Yale Caplan at the University of Maryland School of Medicine. Dr. Goldberger developed many new and innovative methods to solve a myriad of complex analytical problems. He also trained with Dr. Edward Cone at the Addiction Research Center in Baltimore, performing pivotal research in the detection and disposition of heroin and its metabolites in biological specimens. Dr. Goldberger's work led to the discovery of heroin and 6-acetylmorphine in the hair of heroin users, an accomplishment which directed future work in the analysis of drugs and drug metabolites in hair.

Dr. Goldberger is a consultant for the nation's leading public health institution, the Centers for Disease Control and Prevention, and is a member of the White House Office of National Drug Control Policy Evolving and Emerging Threats Committee. Dr. Goldberger is the Editor-in-Chief of the *Journal of Analytical Toxicology*, the official journal of the Society of Forensic Toxicologists and The International Association of Forensic Toxicologists. The journal is the premier international toxicology journal devoted to the timely dissemination of scientific communications concerning the analysis of impairing and toxic substances in biological matrices.

Dr. Goldberger's career has been unique, merging the academic environment including research and teaching with a service component spanning clinical, forensic, and medical toxicology. He is a recognized leader in the field, serving key forensic organizations including the American Academy of Forensic Sciences, the American Board of Forensic Toxicology, the Forensic Specialties Accreditation Board, and the Society of Forensic Toxicologists.

Dr. Goldberger has been prolific in research and publication in the areas of clinical, medical, and forensic toxicology, as well as in the medicolegal investigation of death including the certification of the cause and manner of death. He has co-edited 5 books, 45 book chapters, and 124 peer-reviewed papers.

Dr. Goldberger has received numerous honors and awards including the American Academy of Forensic Sciences Toxicology Section's Irving Sunshine Award and Alexander O. Gettler Award; the Florida Association of Medical Examiners' Outstanding Achievement Award; the National Safety Council's Robert F. Borkenstein Award; Northeastern University's Richard Saferstein Memorial Award in Forensic Science; and the American Academy of Forensic Science's Distinguished Fellow Award.

Section Editor Biographies

Brandi L. Bellissima received her bachelor's degree in Biology and Chemistry from Florida International University. After serving as a forensic toxicologist at the Miami-Dade Medical Examiner Department, she returned to university and completed her doctorate in Pharmacology at the University of Auckland, where her research focused on drug-induced cardiotoxicity. Currently, she is a clinical research scientist at Syneos Health. Dr. Bellissima is a member of the Society of Toxicology, The International Association of Forensic Toxicologists, and the Society of Forensic Toxicologists. Dr. Bellissima is a peer reviewer for several scientific journals. She currently lives in Florida and spends her free time riding horses.

Elisabetta Bertol received her degree in Biology at the University of Florence, Italy, and did post-graduate training in antidoping and forensic sciences. She has been Professor of Forensic Toxicology at the University of Florence since 1992 and is currently Full Professor and Director of the Forensic Toxicology Unit at Careggi Hospital in Florence. She has managed and coordinated various research projects funded by public authorities (Regional, Ministerial, European) and private institutions (banks, foundations). She is the author of more than 200 papers and book chapters dealing with poisons, drugs of abuse, intoxications, and drug laws. She is the past President of the Italian Forensic Toxicologist Group and a fellow of The International Association of Forensic Toxicologists.

Dennis J. Crouch, before his retirement from the University of Utah, served as a Co-Director of the Center for Human Toxicology, Director of the Sports Medicine Research & Testing Laboratory, and a Research Associate Professor in the College of Pharmacy, Department of Pharmacology and Toxicology. Mr. Crouch is a Diplomate of the American Board of Forensic Toxicology. He has published over 100 peer-reviewed scientific articles and presented over 90 scientific papers nationally and internationally in the areas of point of collection drug testing, mass spectrometry, sports medicine, therapeutic drug monitoring, analytical toxicology, forensic toxicology, drugs and driving, and workplace drug testing. He has also served as an inspector and consultant for multiple laboratory accreditation programs and routinely provides consultation and expert witness services in the various specialties of forensic toxicology.

Donata Favretto received her degree in Pharmaceutical Chemistry and Technologies from the University of Padua, Italy, and did post-graduate training in bioanalytical methodology and forensic sciences at the National Council of Researches. She is currently Associate Professor of Forensic Toxicology at the University of Padua and head of the Laboratory of Legal Medicine and Toxicology at the local hospital. She is the author of more than 200 papers and book chapters dealing with chronic and acute human intoxications, drugs and driving, alcohol abuse, and hair testing. She is the President of the Italian Forensic Toxicologist Group and of the Society of Hair Testing, and a member of the board of The International Association of Forensic Toxicologists.

Fintan Garavan completed his PhD in Toxicology from Trinity College, Dublin, Ireland in 1994. The subject matter was on theories in narcosis. He completed his medical training at Trinity College, Dublin, Ireland in 1999 and his Surgical Pathology training in 2006. He completed Fellowships in Forensic Pathology at the Miami-Dade Medical Examiners Department from 2006 to 2009. He was awarded Fellow of the Royal College of Pathologists, London, by examination in 2010 and became a Fellow of the National Association of Medical Examiners, USA in 2010. He has worked in seven countries around the world and currently works as a forensic pathologist at the Miami-Dade Medical Examiners Department. He provides expert testimony in matters related to death caused by drugs/toxins and or pathology/injuries.

Dimitri Gerostamoulos is currently a toxicologist and pharmacologist and holds a degree of Doctor of Philosophy (Medicine) in the field of Forensic Toxicology and a Bachelor of Science (Honours) degree, both from Monash University, Victoria, Australia. He has published numerous scientific papers and chapters in books and is an active member of The International Association of Forensic Toxicologists. He is also a member of the Society of Forensic Toxicologists, the Society of Hair Testing, and the Forensic and Clinical Toxicology Association of Australasia. Dr. Gerostamoulos is also an approved accreditation assessor for the National Association of Testing Authorities, Australia in Forensic Science. Dr. Gerostamoulos has given evidence in over 150 cases in criminal and civil courts and at coronial inquests in the field of forensic toxicology and pharmacology, and has provided opinions on a number of other cases around Australia in relation to the pharmacology of drugs, effects of drugs in drivers, and analytical and toxicological issues in relation to drugs in hair, blood, urine, and other matrices.

Robert E. Johnston is a partner at the law firm of Hollingsworth LLP in Washington, D.C. An attorney for more than 25 years, his practice focuses on trials and appeals of complex litigation matters, with an emphasis on defending pharmaceutical and pesticide products liability litigation and environmental exposure litigation, and prosecuting insurance coverage disputes for corporate clients. He has served as co-lead trial counsel in multiple pharmaceutical products liability trials. He manages the defense of class action, consolidated, and serial litigations and significant individual matters as well. Mr. Johnston has developed key liability defenses to sweeping allegations of corporate misconduct, and has worked with experts and senior company employees to advance those defenses in depositions and at trial. Mr. Johnston is a member of the Defense Research Institute (DRI) and the National Association of Railroad Trial Counsel (NARTC). He has served on the faculty at NARTC's College of Railroad Trial advocacy – an intensive six-day trial techniques course for young trial attorneys. He is listed in the 2020 edition of *Super Lawyers* and is recognized as an AV Preeminent Lawyer by Martindale-Hubbell. He is a Fellow of the Litigation Counsel of America, which recognizes excellence among U.S. litigation and trial counsel. He is a 1994 graduate of the George Washington University Law School, where he served on the George Washington Law Review (which published his note on *qui tam* litigation) and was awarded the Order of the Coif.

Alan W. Jones was born and educated in Wales (UK), but has spent most of his career living and working in Sweden. He holds three academic degrees; a BSc in chemistry (1969), a PhD in analytical and physiological chemistry (1974) and a senior doctorate degree DSc (1992), all of which were awarded by the University of Wales (Cardiff, UK). In 2013, Dr. Jones retired from his appointment as senior scientist at Sweden's National Laboratory of Forensic Medicine, Division of Forensic Genetics and Forensic Toxicology (Linköping, Sweden). He currently serves as a guest professor in forensic toxicology at the University of Linköping (Sweden), Division of Clinical Chemistry and Pharmacology. Over the past 40 years, Dr. Jones' research interests and activities have focused on the determination of ethanol and other abused drugs in biological specimens from living and deceased persons. The results of his research are documented in about 470 articles appearing in 100 different scientific journals. Furthermore, Dr. Jones has authored scores of book chapters and encyclopedia entries about the forensic pharmacology and toxicology of ethanol and other drugs of abuse. He has served as *ad hoc* peer reviewer for manuscripts submitted for publication to about 80 scientific journals and he belongs to the editorial boards of a dozen others. Dr. Jones has been called to testify as an expert witness in criminal trials involving drug-related crimes in seven different countries as well as hundreds of times in Sweden.

Loralie J. Langman completed her PhD in Laboratory Medicine and Pathology at the University of Alberta, Canada. She completed her Clinical Chemistry training at the University of Toronto, specializing in Forensic Toxicology and Molecular Genetics. She is currently the Director of the Clinical and Forensic Toxicology Laboratory, Clinical Mass Spectroscopy Laboratory, a Consultant for the Personalized Genomics Laboratory, Mayo Clinic Rochester, MN, and Professor of Laboratory Medicine and Pathology, Mayo Clinic College of Medicine.

Eric Lasker is a partner in the law firm Hollingsworth LLP, where he litigates a wide variety of complex civil matters, with a current focus on toxic torts, environmental litigation, and pharmaceutical products liability. Over the past 30 years, Mr. Lasker has focuses on scientific analyses of medical causation issues in connection with a wide variety of products liability claims involving antipsychotic medications, obstetrical drugs, antifungals, antiepileptics, contact and intraocular lenses, cough/cold medicines, and herbicides and in toxics/environmental matters involving ethylene oxide, asbestos, lead, nonionizing radiation, arsenic, and chemical solvents. Along with George Mason University law professor David Bernstein, Mr. Lasker authored "Defending *Daubert*: It's Time to Amend Federal Rule of Evidence 702," 57:1 *William & Mary L. Rev.* (2015), which triggered the Federal Rules of Evidence Advisory Committee review that led to the current proposed amendments to Rule 702 on the standards for admissibility of scientific expert testimony in the courtroom. Mr. Lasker was recognized by *The American Lawyer* as "Litigator of the Week", by *Law360* as a products liability MPV, and as a *Bloomberg News* Rainmaker for his work in securing a victory for Firm client, DynCorp International, where the court dismissed claims brought by 3,200 Ecuadorians for alleged personal injury and property damage in connection with "Plan Colombia" counternarcotics aerial herbicide spraying operations in southern Colombia because plaintiffs failed to present reliable evidence linking those claimed injuries and damage to the spraying operations. Mr. Lasker is a 2022 AV Preeminent Lawyer by ALM Media and Martindale-Hubbell and listed in the 2022 edition of *Super Lawyers*. He is a graduate of the University of Pennsylvania and Yale Law School.

Peter T. Lin completed his MD at the State University of New York at Downstate, residency training in anatomic and clinical pathology at Mayo Clinic in Rochester, Minnesota, and forensic pathology, forensic neuropathology, and cardiovascular pathology fellowships at the Office of Chief Medical Examiner for the City of New York. He previously worked as a senior medical examiner for the City of New York. Currently, he is an Assistant Professor in Laboratory Medicine and Pathology at the Mayo Clinic College of Medicine. He is also co-director of the Mayo Clinic Autopsy Laboratory and Assistant Chief Medical Examiner for the Southern Minnesota Regional Medical Examiner Office. His areas of practice and research include forensic pathology, hospital autopsy pathology, cardiovascular pathology, and thoracic transplant pathology.

Binh T. Ly is a Professor in the Division of Medical Toxicology and the Department of Emergency Medicine at the University of California San Diego School of Medicine. He is currently serving as the departmental Vice Chair for Medical Education and is also the Assistant Medical Director and consultant for the San Diego Division of the California Poison Control System. Previously, Dr. Ly was the Director of the Emergency Medicine Residency and Medical Toxicology Fellowship Training Programs and has personally mentored over 200 physicians enrolled in these programs over the course of his 20-year career. Dr. Ly is active clinically, serving both as an attending physician in the Emergency Department and on the Medical Toxicology Consultation Service at University of California San Diego Health. Academically, Dr. Ly's areas of interest include acute and chronic poisonings from a multiplicity of xenobiotics such as recreational drugs of abuse that include stimulants, central nervous system depressants, and hallucinogens, as well as other psychotropic drugs and chemicals. Dr. Ly also has particular interest in novel, designer drugs that have emerged worldwide, such as synthetic cannabinoids ("spice") and cathinones ("bath salts"). In addition to treating intoxications and overdoses, Dr. Ly has advanced treatment guidelines for drug withdrawal from agents such as opioids, alcohol, gamma-hydroxy-butyrate, and other sedatives. Dr. Ly is a recognized expert in the aforementioned areas, has authored numerous publications, and has also spoken to national and international audiences.

Mario Thevis graduated in organic chemistry and sports sciences in 1998. He earned his PhD in Biochemistry in 2001 and did post-doctoral research at the Department of Chemistry and Biochemistry of the University of California Los Angeles in 2002. After being a senior researcher from 2003 to 2005, he was appointed as Professor for Preventive Doping Research at the German Sport University Cologne in 2006. He further qualified as a forensic chemist, acts as director of the European Monitoring Center for Emerging Doping Agents, and is editor-in-chief of *Drug Testing & Analysis*. In August 2017, he accepted the position of Director of the Institute of Biochemistry of the German Sport University Cologne.

Gary M. Vilke has been a Professor in the Department of Emergency Medicine at the University of California, San Diego since 1996 and is the former Medical Director for the County of San Diego Emergency Medical Services. Dr. Vilke served as the Director for Custody Services at University of California, San Diego for over 15 years and is the Vice Chair for Clinical Operations at University of California, San Diego. His research focus has been in the areas of prehospital care and in-custody deaths, and he has published over 300 original articles and 85 book chapters, including over 70 articles on topics including positional asphyxia, weight force on the back, oleoresin capsicum spray, neck holds, restraint chairs, Excited Delirium Syndrome, and the TASER. He has lectured internationally on these topics. Additionally, he has over 35 grant funded projects, including funding to perform research on in-custody deaths from several national organizations, including the Police Executive Research Forum, the Institute for the Prevention of In-Custody Deaths, and the National Institute of Justice. He is the Co-Editor of the textbook, *Guidelines for Investigating Officer-Involved Shootings, Arrest-Related Deaths and Deaths in Custody*.

Contributor Affiliations

Dunya Nasrallah Alfaraj
Imam Abdulrahman bin Faisal University
Dammam, Saudi Arabia

Tamara F. Barago
Hollingsworth LLP
Washington, DC

Michael R. Baylor
Forensic Science Consultant
Cary, NC

Brandi L. Bellissima
Syneos Health
Miami, FL

Elisabetta Bertol
Forensic Toxicology
University of Florence
Florence, Italy

Jennifer Collins
VP Operations/Discipline Director Forensic Toxicology
Labcorp
St Paul, MN

Bryan Corbett
Division of Medical Toxicology
Department of Emergency Medicine
University of California, San Diego
San Diego, CA

Christopher J Coyne
Associate Professor of Emergency Medicine
Clinical Research Director
Department of Emergency Medicine
University of California San Diego Health System
San Diego, CA

Dennis J. Crouch
Utah Toxicology Expert Services
Sandy, UT

Susan D. Crumpton
RTI International
Research Triangle Park, NC

Michael A. Darracq
UCSF Fresno Medical Education Program
Department of Emergency Medicine
Professor of Clinical Emergency Medicine
Fresno, CA

Josef Dib
Center for Preventive Doping Research-Institute of Biochemistry
German Sport University Cologne
Cologne, Germany

Donata Favretto
Forensic Toxicology
University of Padua
Padua, Italy

Fintan Garavan
Miami-Dade Medical Examiners Department
Miami, FL

Dimitri Gerostamoulos
Victorian Institute of Forensic Medicine
Southbank VIC, Australia

and

Department of Forensic Medicine
Monash University
Melbourne, Australia

Christian Görgens
Center for Preventive Doping Research-Institute of Biochemistry
German Sport University Cologne
Cologne, Germany

Sven Guddat
Center for Preventive Doping Research-Institute of Biochemistry
German Sport University Cologne
Cologne, Germany

Kama Guluma
Department of Emergency Medicine
University of California San Diego
San Diego, CA

Anders Helander
Department of Laboratory Medicine
Karolinska Institutet
Stockholm, Sweden

Kathryn S. Jensen
Hollingsworth LLP
Washington, DC

Robert E. Johnston
Hollingsworth LLP
Washington, DC

Alan W. Jones
Division of Clinical Chemistry and Pharmacology
Department of Biomedical and Clinical Sciences
Linköping University
Linköping, Sweden

Leo J. Kadehjian
Biomedical Consulting
Palo Alto, CA

R. Adam Koch
Department of Emergency Medicine
Naval Medical Center Camp Lejeune
Camp Lejeune, NC

Cynthia Koh
VA Greater Los Angeles Healthcare System
David Geffen School of Medicine at UCLA
Los Angeles, CA

Allyson Kreshak
Division of Medical Toxicology
Department of Emergency Medicine
University of California San Diego
San Diego, CA

Oliver Krug
Center for Preventive Doping Research-Institute of Biochemistry
German Sport University Cologne
Cologne, Germany

Samuel H.F. Lam
Department of Emergency Medicine
Sutter Medical Center Sacramento
Sacramento, CA

Loralie J. Langman
Mayo Clinic College of Medicine
Rochester, MN

Eric Lasker
Hollingsworth LLP
Washington, DC

Daniel R. Lasoff
Division of Medical Toxicology
Department of Emergency Medicine
University of California, San Diego
San Diego, CA

Alexis Lenz
Department of Emergency Medicine
University of California, San Diego
San Diego, CA

Peter T. Lin
Mayo Clinic

and

Southern Minnesota Regional Medical Examiner Office
Rochester, MN

Jessica Lu
O'Melveny & Myers
Washington, DC

Binh T. Ly
Division of Medical Toxicology
Department of Emergency Medicine
University of California, San Diego
San Diego, CA

Christopher S. Martin
Department of Psychiatry
University of Pittsburgh
Pittsburgh, PA

Christine Moore
9-Delta Analytical LLC,
Ontario, CA

Fern P. O'Brian
Bethesda, MD

Thomas Piper
Center for Preventive Doping Research-Institute of Biochemistry
German Sport University Cologne
Cologne, Germany

Derrick J Pounder
Department of Forensic Medicine
University of Dundee
Scotland, UK

Phillipp Reihlen
Center for Preventive Doping Research-Institute of Biochemistry
German Sport University Cologne
Cologne, Germany

Christie Sun
Division of Medical Toxicology
Department of Emergency Medicine
University of California, San Diego
San Diego, CA

Craig A. Sutheimer
Forensic Toxicologist and Consultant
Raleigh, NC

Christopher R. Tainter
Division of Critical Care
Department of Anesthesiology
UC San Diego
San Diego, CA

Mario Thevis
Center for Preventive Doping Research/Institute of Biochemistry, German Sport University Cologne
Cologne, Germany
and
European Monitoring Center for Emerging Doping Agents (EuMoCEDA)
Cologne/Bonn, German

Andreas Thomas
Center for Preventive Doping Research-Institute of Biochemistry
German Sport University Cologne
Cologne, Germany

Stephen Thornton
Medical Director
Kansas Poison Control Center
University of Kansas Health System
Kansas City, KS

Gary M. Vilke
Department of Emergency Medicine
University of California San Diego
San Diego, CA

Katja Walpurgis
Center for Preventive Doping Research-Institute of Biochemistry
German Sport University Cologne
Cologne, Germany

J Michael Walsh
The Walsh Group
Bethany Beach, DE

Gabriel Wardi
Department of Emergency Medicine
University of California San Diego
San Diego, CA

Michael P. Wilson
Department of Emergency Medicine and Psychiatry
University of Arkansas for Medical Sciences
Little Rock, AR

John Robert Zettl
Forensic Consultants, Inc.
Centennial, CO

Preface

The first edition of this Handbook was published in 1998. My intent then, and now, was to inform the forensic community about the details of recent scientific advances, many of which had not yet been incorporated into forensic practice. At the time, I had no idea I would be writing still another preface 20 years later, nor did I suspect there would be so much more material to incorporate. I was equally surprised that so much information, which seemed important then, seems so much less important now.

Readers will note changes in the new Handbook. Additional subjects have been added and some deleted. An explanation is in order. The chapter on Federal Drug Scheduling has been omitted for several reasons, most especially the large number of deaths attributable to analogue drugs, not just fentanyl analogues but new synthetic opiates and benzodiazepines as well. More than 700 analogue drugs are now in circulation. The current law is inadequate to cope with these changes.

Major revisions of The Federal Analogue Act, 21 U.S.C. § 813 (a section of the United States Controlled Substances Act passed in 1988) allowed any chemical "substantially similar to a controlled substance listed in Schedule I or II to be treated as if it were listed in Schedule I." This law will expire in 2020. There is no obvious way that the Act, which was really just a catch-all statute intended to enable prosecutions of crimes involving drugs that are substantially similar to already scheduled drugs, was intended to cope with the massive explosion of the fentanyl analogues; synthetic opiates and cathinones weren't even considered. There seemed little point in publishing a chapter on a law that will change radically in the near future.

The chapter on Workplace Drug Testing was deleted for a mix of technical and political reasons. Except for businesses heavily regulated by the Federal government, such as police and military contractors, where every step of the testing process is tightly regulated, Federal law has little to say about non-Federal drug testing in the so-called Drug Free Workplace. Except for Federally regulated workplaces, no private business is required to do drug testing, though they are free to do so providing that the testing performed conforms to the laws of the state in which it done. More often than not, state laws mirror their Federal counterparts.

Neither state nor Federal laws ever anticipated the legalization of either marijuana use or testing, and even though Federal law is overriding, at this point, regulation is left to the states. Several state statutes authorizing medical marijuana use also contain provisions prohibiting discrimination against employees for testing positive for marijuana. Other states have taken the opposite approach, and given the prolonged excretion times for cannabinoids, it is not at all clear how a positive test in a state with legal marijuana should be managed. Clearly, statutes on workplace drug testing will require extensive revision, but that is simply not going to happen in the near future, and there is little reason for speculating about them in this edition of the Handbook.

If the inadequacy of the law weren't a sufficient reason not to deal with the subject, there is always the issue of how testing is to be done. Oral fluid is not yet approved for regulated drug testing (only urine is permissible). In 2011, an expert committee recommended that mandatory Federal drug testing guidelines be revised to allow lab-based oral fluid testing. In 2015, the Substance Abuse and Mental Health Services Administration (SAMHSA) published a notice to establish the scientific and technical guidelines for the inclusion of oral fluid specimens in the guidelines. These regulations have not been written, or at least, none has been accepted. When the laws and technologies have been harmonized, hopefully before the next edition of this book, Workplace Testing will again be included in this Handbook.

Other noteworthy changes in this edition of the Handbook are the addition of a detailed chapter on the pharmacology and pharmacokinetics of fentanyl and its derivatives. This chapter replaces previous chapters on neurochemistry and addiction. An additional section contains an introduction to the basics of toxicogenetics. That subject was not much in vogue in 2006 at the time the second edition was printed, but it certainly is now, and it is gratifying to see that the subject has come into its own. The chapter on addiction has been deleted. It is now generally agreed that addiction is not simply an issue involving dopamine neurochemistry, but rather, as the American Society of Addiction Medicine (ASAM) puts it:

> Addiction is a treatable, chronic medical disease involving complex interactions among brain circuits, genetics, the environment, and an individual's life experiences. People with addiction use substances or engage in behaviors that become compulsive and often continue despite harmful consequences.

Clearly, the proliferation of both issues and viewpoints, both theoretical and practical, makes it impossible to manage in just one section of this Handbook. A separate book would be required.

Finally, the Legal section has been expanded and now accounts for a very important section of the book. Most forensic practitioners have a general knowledge of Daubert and its progeny, but surprisingly few are aware of the Burrage ruling. In 2014, the United States Supreme Court, in a unanimous ruling written by Antonin Scalia, ruled that a defendant cannot be liable for penalty enhancement under the penalty enhancement provision of the Controlled Substances Act unless such use is a but-for cause of the death or injury, at least when the use of a drug distributed by the defendant is not an independently sufficient cause of the victim's death or serious bodily injury. That ruling was prompted by the death of an addict who bought heroin from two different dealers. Since it could not be proven which dose of heroin caused the death, enhancement provisions could not be applied to either drug dealer. In essence, the ruling makes it almost impossible to rule that in a given case the cause of death was "polypharmacy" and still expect to apply enhancements to the prison term.

As was discussed in the preface to the second edition, doctors have known for years that the courtroom is not the proper venue to seek out scientific truth. Physicians and forensic specialists seem to forget that in the minds of jurors, the opinions of laboratory technicians and the opinions of forensic specialists carry equal weight. Most members of the profession, let alone the public, simply do not have the tools to decide whether a given argument is junk science or evidence-based science. It is my hope that, if nothing else, the material presented here can help the experts decide what is true and what is not, and testify with a degree of certainty that they have correctly explained the facts at issue.

Steven Karch, MD, FFFLM, FCSFS
Berkeley, California
July 1, 2022

1 Clinical Syndromes and Emergency Room Physician and Management Issues

Section Editors: Gary M. Vilke and Binh T. Ly

CONTENTS

DOI: 10.4324/9781315155159-1

1.1 MEDICAL ASPECTS OF DRUG ABUSE

Stephen Thornton and Binh T. Ly

Drug abuse is associated with many medical problems and complications stemming both from regular use and from overdoses. Another serious medical complication arising from drug abuse is the withdrawal syndrome, which manifests during abstinence from the drug (see Chapter 7 for a more detailed discussion of withdrawal syndromes).

Drug abuse affects a number of organ systems. Central nervous system (CNS) symptoms can range from headaches and altered mental status to life-threatening situations like coma and seizures. Cardiovascular manifestations of drug abuse include alterations in blood pressure and heart rate as well as arrhythmias and organ ischemia. Respiratory arrest, pulmonary edema, and pneumothorax may occur. Metabolic effects such as alterations in body temperature, electrolytes, and acid-base disturbances are commonly seen. Reproductive consequences, ranging from impaired fertility to intrauterine growth retardation, premature births, and neonatal syndromes, may also occur.

Infectious complications from intravenous drug use include viral infections such as HIV and hepatitis B as well as bacterial infections including bacterial endocarditis, osteomyelitis, and abscesses.

In this chapter, we describe the specific clinical syndromes associated with drugs of abuse.

1.1.1 STIMULANTS

Stimulant drugs are a diverse group of chemicals that act primarily through activation of the sympathetic nervous system. They are sometimes referred to as sympathomimetics. In small to moderate doses, they result in an elevated mood, increased energy and alertness, and decreased appetite. During intoxication, they have profound CNS, cardiovascular system, and metabolic effects.

1.1.1.1 Cocaine

Cocaine is a classic drug of abuse with a long and sometimes complicated history [1]. It is also one of the most commonly encountered stimulants and is frequently implicated in causing serious medical complications [2–4]. Its primary mechanism of action is the blockade of reuptake of dopamine and other catecholamines by the neurons [5]. It also has pre-serotonin effects along with centrally mediated neural sympathetic activation [5, 6]. In addition to stimulating the sympathetic nervous system, cocaine has a local anesthetic effect and blocks fast sodium channels in neural tissue and the myocardium [7].

Cocaine may be taken orally, injected intravenously, insufflated via the nose, or smoked and inhaled via the lungs. Crack is the anhydrous base of cocaine and the form most frequently smoked. Cocaine's half-life is approximately 60 minutes but may be prolonged in cases of large or chronic dosing [8, 9]. After intravenous injection or inhalation, there is typically rapid onset of CNS and cardiac manifestations [10]. However, effects may be delayed after oral ingestion. The duration of cocaine's effect is dependent on the amount and route of administration but is usually about 1–2 hours after exposure [11]. Acute cocaine intoxication usually resolves after approximately 6 hours, but some vascular manifestations, such as myocardial infarction and stroke, may occur many hours after use, and a poorly understood cocaine "crash" syndrome may last for several days after cocaine binging.

Most of the toxic manifestations of cocaine are due to excessive central and sympathetic nervous system stimulation. CNS stimulation causes behavioral changes, mood alterations, delirium, and psychiatric abnormalities. Sympathetic nervous system stimulation causes cardiovascular system abnormalities, such as alterations in blood pressure, heart rate, arrhythmias, and hyperthermia. The local anesthetic effect can lead to seizures and dysrhythmias. Some of these manifestations, especially in the CNS and the cardiovascular system, can be life-threatening.

1.1.1.1.1 Central Nervous System

In moderate doses, cocaine produces arousal and euphoria but also anxiety and restlessness. Acute intoxication may result in severe psychiatric disturbances, such as acute anxiety, panic attacks, delirium, or acute psychosis [12]. Chronic cocaine intoxication can produce paranoid psychosis similar to schizophrenia [13]. There is evidence suggesting that chronic cocaine use may lead to permanent neurological abnormalities. Brain atrophy, particularly in the frontal cortex and basal ganglia, has been found in chronic cocaine abusers, as well as cerebral blood perfusion deficits in frontal, periventricular, and temporal areas [13, 14]. Abnormalities in cerebral glucose metabolism, as well as reduction in ATP/Pi ratios in cerebral cortex, were found in chronic cocaine addicts. These changes are similar to those observed after cerebral hypoxia [15].

Headache: Headache is common in cocaine users and has been reported in up to 90% of the users surveyed [16]. In some patients, the headaches were triggered by cocaine, whereas others reported them in association with cocaine withdrawal [14, 17]. Both migraine headache and cluster headaches have been associated with cocaine use [18, 19]. In some instances, headaches may be induced by hypertension. Persistent headaches despite normalization of blood pressure should raise concern about intracranial hemorrhage [20].

Cerebrovascular accidents: A variety of neurologic signs have been reported in patients with cocaine intoxication, among them dizziness, vertigo, tremor, and blurred vision. Transient hemiparesis has also been observed and may be the result of cerebral vasospasm [21, 22]. Large systematic reviews have demonstrated that cocaine use is associated with an increased risk for both ischemic and hemorrhagic strokes [23]. This risk appears to be particularly pronounced in younger adults [24]. Among the patients with strokes, about 50% have cerebral hemorrhage, 30% subarachnoid hemorrhage, and 20% ischemic stroke [14, 17, 25]. This distribution differs from the one found in the general population, where ischemia and not hemorrhage accounts for the majority of strokes. The mechanism of cocaine-associated stroke is thought to be an acute elevation of blood pressure induced by increased sympathetic activity, which may cause rupture of a cerebral aneurysm, or vasospasm or cerebral vasoconstriction [26]. Interestingly, anticardiolipin antibodies, which are associated with an increased risk of stroke, were found in 27% of asymptomatic cocaine users and in five of seven cocaine users with thromboembolism [27]. There are also multiple reports of acute spontaneous subdural hematoma associated with cocaine use [28, 29].

Movement disorders: Cocaine use has been associated with acute dystonic reactions, which in some cases have been precipitated by neuroleptics and in others without neuroleptics. Acute dystonia was reported after cocaine use as well as during cocaine withdrawal [30, 31]. Choreoathetoid movements lasting up to 6 days have also been described [32]. This is often referred to as "crack dancing."

Seizures: Seizures are seen in about 1.4% to 2.8% of cocaine abusers admitted to a hospital [14, 17, 30, 33, 34]. They are usually generalized, tonic-clonic in character, and may occur soon after taking cocaine or after a delay of several hours. Seizures may be associated with recreational cocaine use but are more common in intoxication or "body packer" syndrome [14, 33]. Children can have seizures as a first manifestation of cocaine exposure [17]. The mechanism of cocaine-related seizures is not fully elucidated but may be related to its local anesthetic properties.

Excited delirium: Excited delirium is a constellation of delirium, agitation, acidosis, and hyperadrenergic autonomic dysfunction, which can result in significant morbidity and mortality [35]. It is often associated with drug use, including cocaine [36].

Other complications: Cocaine abuse can be associated with frontal sinusitis and brain abscess after chronic cocaine snorting [37]. Cocaine snorting is also associated with atrophy of nasal mucosa, necrosis, and perforation of the nasal septum [30].

1.1.1.1.2 Cardiovascular System

Blood pressure: Intense sympathetic stimulation induced by cocaine results in hypertension and tachycardia. Hypertension is a combined result of increased cardiac output and increased systemic vascular resistance. Hypertension may contribute to stroke, aortic dissection, acute pulmonary edema, and renal injury seen with cocaine use [38].

Myocardial ischemia: Myocardial infarction has been well documented in cocaine abuse. It is the end result of a combination of several factors, including coronary vasospasm, increased myocardial oxygen demand due to increased myocardial workload, and thrombosis [39–42]. Most patients with cocaine-related ischemia present within 1 h of cocaine use, when the plasma concentrations of cocaine are the highest; however, some patients present hours after cocaine use. The late presentation may be caused by delayed coronary vasoconstriction induced by major cocaine metabolites [41, 43]. However, only between 4% and 6% of patients presenting to the emergency room with cocaine-associated chest pain have acute coronary syndrome [41, 44]. Ambulatory electrocardiographic (ECG) monitoring of chronic cocaine users during the first week of cocaine withdrawal demonstrated recurrent episodes of ST segment elevation, probably due to vasospasm [45]. Myocarditis presenting as patchy myocardial necrosis has been observed after acute cocaine intoxication and is believed to result from intense catecholamine stimulation [39, 45]. Clinically, this results in ST segment elevations and/or T wave inversions with elevated CPK-MB fraction. Acutely, a catecholamine-induced or Takusubu cardiomyopathy may be seen with the classic left ventricular ballooning on echocardiogram [46]. In chronic cocaine use, the result may be myocardial fibrosis and cardiomyopathy. The cardiomyopathy is often dilated and may improve with cessation of cocaine [47]. Other organs may be affected by ischemia resulting from vasoconstriction, including renal infarction and ischemic colitis and mesenteric ischemia, which can be life-threatening [48–50]. These patients usually present with intense flank or diffuse abdominal pain.

Aortic dissection: Cocaine use is a known risk factor for aortic dissection [51]. In particular, those with cocaine-associated aortic dissection were significantly younger than those who did not use cocaine.

Arrhythmia: Arrhythmia is common in cocaine intoxication; in acute intoxication, it results from sympathetic stimulation or local anesthetic effect, and later, it may be the result of myocardial ischemia or myocarditis. The most common arrhythmia is sinus tachycardia; other arrhythmias include atrial tachycardia and fibrillation; ventricular tachycardia, including *torsade de pointes*; and conduction disturbances due to local anesthetic effects of cocaine, with wide complex tachycardia [45, 52]. Ventricular fibrillation can be a cause of sudden death, and asystole has also been reported.

QT prolongation was observed in patients after cocaine exposure [53].

Shock: Shock may develop in patients with cocaine intoxication as a result of reduced cardiac output due to myocardial ischemia, direct myocardial depression, myocarditis, or arrhythmia, and as a result of vasodilatation due to either local anesthetic effects of cocaine on blood vessels or its effects on brain stem. Takotsubo cardiomyopathy, an acute cardiomyopathy associated with excessive catecholamines, has been described with cocaine use [46, 54]. The acutely depressed cardiac output caused by the cardiomyopathy could contribute to shock states sometimes seen with cocaine intoxication [55]. In addition, hypovolemia may be present in agitated and/or hyperthermic patients and contribute to shock.

Sudden death: Most deaths occur within minutes to hours of acute cocaine intoxication, and most are the result of arrhythmia due to either massive catecholamine release or ischemia. Many convulse prior to death. Some sudden deaths can be attributed to excited delirium [56]. In others, death is due to medical reasons (*e.g.*, trauma, homicide) related to cocaine intoxication and accounts for about 11% of all cocaine-related deaths [28, 57].

Pulmonary: Pulmonary edema is a common finding at autopsies of victims of cocaine intoxication [58]. It can occur in acute intoxication either because of myocardial dysfunction or as a result of a massive increase in the afterload due to vasoconstriction. Noncardiogenic pulmonary edema has also been reported [39]. A syndrome called "crack lung" has been described, which consists of fever, pulmonary infiltrates, bronchospasm, and eosinophilia [59–61]. Alveolar macrophages from crack cocaine smokers were deficient in cytokine production and in their ability to kill bacteria and tumor cells [62]. Pulmonary vasculitis can be seen and may be due to levamisole-adulterated cocaine [63]. Pneumomediastinum and pneumothorax have been described in patients who snort or smoke cocaine, presumably due to increased airway pressure during a Valsalva maneuver [64, 65].

Metabolic complications: Severe hyperthermia has been described in patients with acute cocaine intoxication; the mechanism probably is muscular hyperactivity due to agitation or seizures and increased metabolic rate. However, cocaine, even in small doses, was shown to impair sweating and cutaneous vasodilatation as well as heat perception [66]. Consistently with these findings, it was found that on hot days (with ambient temperature above 31 °C), the number of deaths from accidental cocaine overdose was 33% higher than on days with lower temperatures [67]. Hyperthermia is also part of the excited delirium syndrome, where it accompanies extremely violent and agitated behavior [36]. Hyperthermia, if untreated, can result in brain damage, rhabdomyolysis with renal failure, coagulation abnormalities, and death. Rhabdomyolysis can be seen with acute cocaine intoxication and is most often the result of muscular hyperactivity and hyperthermia, but it can also be due to muscular ischemia due to vasoconstriction [68]. Lactic acidosis may be a complication of prolonged muscular hyperactivity and is well described in the agitated or restrained cocaine-intoxicated patient [69].

Reproductive/neonatal: Cocaine use during pregnancy can result in an increased incidence of spontaneous abortion, placenta previa, and abruption of the placenta [70]. Placental ischemia results in intrauterine growth retardation [71, 72]. Cocaine intoxication can mimic pre-eclampsia or eclampsia [73]. Neonates born to cocaine-addicted mothers have various neurologic abnormalities, including irritability, tremulousness, poor feeding, hypotonia or hypertonia, and hyperreflexia. This syndrome may last for 8 to 10 weeks [39, 72]. There is a dose–response relationship between adverse neonatal effects and maternal cocaine exposure [72].

Dermatological: The use of cocaine is associated with formication, the perception of insects crawling over or under the skin [74]. This sometimes referred to as "crack bugs." It can result in multiple skin lesions as the users attempt to remove the insects. Cocaine has also been associated with a cutaneous vasculitis, which is now thought to be due to the adulterant levamisole [75].

Withdrawal: Abstinence after prolonged use of cocaine can result in a "cocaine crash," manifesting as anxiety, depression, exhaustion, and craving for cocaine [76]. This is followed days later by a withdrawal phase that is characterized by gradually increasing craving that can last for weeks [76]. Suicidal ideation is common. The symptoms can last for several weeks to several months after the cessation of use [76].

Toxicity of cocaine adulterants: Cocaine is frequently adulterated or "cut" with other substances [77]. The most commonly encountered and most clinically concerning substance is levamisole. Levamisole is an immunomodulating anti-helminthic drug previously used to treat a multitude of conditions, including colon cancer [78]. Some studies suggest that over 70% of cocaine now is adulterated with levamisole [79]. The exact reason why levamisole is being added to cocaine is unclear. However, it has been associated with multiple pathological manifestations, including vasculitis, glomerulonephritis, and agranulocytosis [80]. Levamisole is metabolized to aminorex, which may have some sympathomimetic activity [81]. Though its toxicity is currently unclear, aminorex may be associated with causing pulmonary hypertension [82].

1.1.1.2 Natural Stimulants

Ephedrine and cathinone belong to a group of naturally occurring stimulants that resemble amphetamine in structure. Ephedrine is found in a variety of plants, primarily the *Ephedra* shrubs, commonly known as ma-huang. It is a component of many Chinese medicines, nonprescription decongestants, and previously, dietary supplements [83]. Four different enantiomers of ephedrine can be present in ephedra, with the (–) ephedrine form the most common and clinically important [84]. Cathinone is found in the khat shrub (*Catha edulis*), is which is endemic to parts of eastern Africa. The leaves of the khat shrub contain multiple compounds, but the primary active ingredient is (–) cathinone [85]. Khat leaves are chewed, and the use of khat is widespread in many east African and Middle Eastern countries [30, 86].

1.1.1.2.1 Ephedrine

Ephedrine acts directly on alpha- and beta-adrenergic receptors and also stimulates the release of norepinephrine [87]. It exhibits fewer CNS effects than amphetamine. Pseudoephedrine is a dextro isomer of ephedrine and is less potent [88]. Both drugs are marketed as nonprescription medications for nasal decongestion and are ingredients in many cold medications and bronchodilators. Ephedrine-containing dietary supplements (also known as ma-huang) were widely used for weight loss and energy enhancement until December 2003, when the Food and Drug Administration (FDA) banned the use of ephedrine in dietary supplements due to the risk of cardiovascular complications, including myocardial infarction, sudden death, and stroke [83, 89]. The main manifestations of ephedrine intoxication are cardiovascular, with elevation of blood pressure and heart rate [90]. Hypertension due to ephedrine intoxication, even if moderate, can result in neurologic complications including headache, confusion, seizures, and stroke, both ischemic and hemorrhagic [91]. There have also been reports of intracerebral vasculitis and hemorrhage associated with ephedrine abuse [92]. Severe headache, focal neurologic deficit, or changes in mental status in ephedrine intoxication should raise the possibility of intracerebral hemorrhage or stroke. Psychosis has been associated with ephedrine abuse [93]. Fatalities may result from myocardial infarction, arrhythmia, seizures, or stroke [92].

Another, little-recognized complication of the chronic use of ephedra-containing products is kidney stones, which have been found to contain ephedrine and pseudoephedrine [94].

1.1.1.2.2 Cathinone

Naturally occurring cathinone has CNS effects quite similar to those of amphetamine; but due to the bulkiness of the khat leaves, the actual amount of cathinone ingested is usually not large or rapid. Social use of khat causes increased energy level and alertness but also mood lability, anxiety, and insomnia [95]. Khat abuse may result in mania-like symptoms, paranoia, and acute schizophrenia-like psychosis. Most cases of khat-induced psychosis are self-limiting and preceded by heavy khat consumption [86, 95, 96]. No specific physical withdrawal syndrome is recognized, but there is a psychological withdrawal characterized by depression, hypersomnia, and loss of energy [49, 57, 95, 96].

Khat intoxication may result in cardiovascular toxicity with hypertension and tachycardia, but severe hypertension has not been observed [95, 97]. Khat use is associated with an increased risk of myocardial infarction [98]. Compared with non-chewers, khat chewers presenting with acute myocardial infarction were more likely to be young and without cardiovascular risk factors and to present during or immediately after khat-chewing sessions [99].

There is an association between khat use and gastric ulcers as well as constipation, although the causation is not clear [95].

Babies born to khat-chewing mothers are likely to suffer from intrauterine growth retardation [100]. Long-term chewing of khat (for more than 25 years) was found to be strongly associated with oral cancer [96].

1.1.1.3 Synthetic Stimulants

Classically, amphetamine and its analogs, such as methamphetamine, were the primary synthetic stimulants used [101]. Now, substituted cathinones (i.e., "bath salts") and methylphenidate and its analogs are increasingly being used [102]. All the synthetic stimulants are considered to be primarily indirect sympathomimetics that act by releasing biogenic amines from storage sites in both the CNS and the peripheral nervous system [103]. They may also have some direct alpha and beta receptor agonism [103]. Thus, they create a hyperadrenergic state resulting in CNS stimulation and arousal in lower doses, and serious mental changes and cardiovascular effects during intoxication.

1.1.1.3.1 Amphetamine

Amphetamine is a potent CNS stimulator. Its structure is similar to those of norepinephrine and other naturally occurring catecholamines. It exists as a racemic solution, but dextroamphetamine or the (–) amphetamine isomer is approximately two to three times more potent than levoamphetamine with regard to CNS stimulation [104, 105]. Amphetamine is typically taken orally or injected intravenously but can also be insufflated. The onset of amphetamine's clinical effects is generally rapid, with the exception of lisdexamphetamine, which is a prodrug and must be metabolized to dextroamphetamine. This can result in delayed and prolonged symptoms [106]. The clinical effects of amphetamines are similar to those of cocaine. Amphetamine does have a longer half-life than cocaine (7–14 hours), and the half-life can be greatly influenced by urinary pH [107]. The duration of amphetamine-induced symptoms tends to be longer than for cocaine, and duration will depend on the amount of exposure. There are multiple "designer" amphetamines, which may have different or more severe toxicity than the parent amphetamine compound [108].

CNS effects: During acute intoxication with amphetamines, patients commonly present with euphoria, restlessness, paranoia, agitation, and anxiety [30, 109]. In one sample of drug users, 55% of amphetamine users reported having at least one adverse effect (anxiety, depression, paranoia, or sleep and appetite disturbances) [4]. Seizures may occur in about 3% of the patients presenting in the hospital with amphetamine intoxication [34, 109]. As with any stimulant, excited delirium can occur with severe amphetamine toxicity [110]. Stroke has been reported in patients with amphetamine intoxication; it is usually hemorrhagic and associated with hypertension [111, 112]. There have also been reports of cerebral vasculitis and hemorrhage with chronic abuse of amphetamine [113–115]. Chronic amphetamine abuse may precipitate psychiatric disturbances, such as paranoia and psychosis that can persist for weeks [116, 117].

Movement disorders: Chronic high-dose amphetamine use is associated with stereotypic behavior, dyskinesias, and chorea, especially in patients with preexisting basal ganglia disorders [118]. Amphetamines exacerbate tics in patients who already have them and may induce tics, although the causation is unclear [30].

Cardiovascular effects: The major effects seen during acute intoxication are hypertension and tachycardia [109]. Myocardial ischemia and infarction have been reported; the underlying mechanisms are increased myocardial oxygen demand and/or coronary vasospasm [40, 109, 119, 120]. Both acute and chronic abuse has been reported to result in cardiomyopathy [121, 122]. Systemic necrotizing vasculitis, resembling periarteritis nodosa, has been associated with chronic amphetamine abuse [123].

Metabolic and other effects: Acute amphetamine intoxication can manifest with sweating, tremor, muscle fasciculations, and rigidity. Hyperthermia can develop and may be life-threatening if not treated promptly [124]. The mechanisms underlying hyperthermia are thought to be muscle hyperactivity and CNS dysfunction. The same mechanisms may also cause rhabdomyolysis with attendant renal failure [125]. Chronic amphetamine abuse can result in weight loss of up to 20 to 30 lb and malnutrition [30]. Though well described with methamphetamine use, dental disease does not seem as prevalent with amphetamine use.

Withdrawal: Amphetamine withdrawal is a common but poorly studied process, with most literature concerning methamphetamine withdrawal. Criteria for diagnosing amphetamine withdrawal include dysphoric mood and two or more symptoms: fatigue, vivid or unpleasant dreams, insomnia or hypersomnia, increased appetite, and psychomotor agitation or retardation that occur following discontinuation of amphetamine [126]. Similarly to methamphetamine withdrawal, amphetamine withdrawal is described to start within 24 hours of cessation, peaks in 2 to 4 days, and can last several weeks [127]. The main symptoms are anxiety, craving, and depression, occasionally with suicidal ideation [76].

1.1.1.3.2 Methamphetamine

Methamphetamine is an amphetamine analog and a widely abused drug. It was first synthesized in 1919 and saw widespread use starting in the 1940s [101]. Compared with amphetamine, it is purported to have increased CNS penetration and more potency. However, this has not been demonstrated in human studies [128]. Methamphetamine can be ingested orally or snorted [129]. The crystallized form of methamphetamine hydrochloride, known as "ice" or "crystal," is commonly smoked and inhaled [130]. Methamphetamine's clinical effects can last over 24 hours and reflect its elimination half-life of approximately 10 hours [131]. The clinical effects of methamphetamine are generally similar to those seen with amphetamine. However, there is significantly more experience with methamphetamine toxicity due to its being abused much more frequently than amphetamine [132].

CNS effects: Classically, methamphetamine is thought to produce more CNS stimulation with fewer peripheral effects than amphetamine, but studies have found them to be equipotent [128, 133, 134]. Agitation, paranoia, confusion, and psychosis can all be seen with methamphetamine use [135]. Rarely the psychosis can be chronic [136]. Acutely, large methamphetamine exposures can result in excited delirium [137]. Stroke, both ischemic and hemorrhagic, has been reported with methamphetamine abuse, and in some cases, the stroke was delayed by 10 to 12 h after last use [138, 139]. Older methamphetamine users appear to be at particular risk [140].

Movement disorders: Choreoathetosis is associated with acute methamphetamine use and is likely due to excessive dopaminergic activity [141]. There is evidence to suggest that methamphetamine use can increase the risk of developing Parkinson's disease, though its acute use is not associated with Parkinsonian-like movement disorders [142, 143]. Bruxism is frequently seen with methamphetamine toxicity [144].

Cardiovascular effects: Sinus tachycardia and hypertension are the most common cardiovascular effects seen with methamphetamine use [145]. Not surprisingly, myocardial infarction in the setting of methamphetamine use is well described [146, 147]. In addition, cardiogenic shock and cardiomyopathy can be seen with methamphetamine toxicity [148]. Both an acute Takotsubo cardiomyopathy and a chronic fibrotic cardiomyopathy have been associated with methamphetamine use [149, 150]. Patients who develop methamphetamine cardiomyopathy are often young (average age 30 years old) and manifest severe disease, with over 80% in one study having New York Heart Association functional class III or IV dyspnea [150].

Pulmonary effects: Methamphetamine use has been linked with the development of idiopathic pulmonary arterial hypertension [151, 152]. The mechanism behind the development of this progressive and debilitating disorder is thought to be methamphetamine's serotonergic properties [153]. Surprisingly, few other pulmonary pathologies are attributed to methamphetamine use.

Metabolic and other effects: Rhabdomyolysis has been described in association with methamphetamine abuse, usually in the setting of agitation [154]. Severe dental disease, termed "meth mouth," is widely seen with methamphetamine abuse, and some consider it pathognomonic for methamphetamine abuse [155, 156]. It is thought to be related to the bruxism and xerostomia seen with chronic methamphetamine use. Methamphetamine use is associated with formication and the resultant typical skin lesions [157].

Withdrawal: Methamphetamine withdrawal has the same diagnostic criteria as amphetamine withdrawal. It is characterized by an acute phase that starts within 24 hours of cessation and lasts approximately 7–10 days [127]. Anxiety, depression, and craving are seen during the acute phase. Psychosis has also been reported [158]. There is then a subacute phase, which can last for several weeks and is characterized by gradually decreasing craving.

1.1.1.3.3 Substituted Cathinones

Substituted cathinones are synthetic analogs of the naturally occurring stimulant cathinone. Though some substituted cathinones were synthesized and investigated as far back as the 1930s and 1960s, they were not considered a significant drug of abuse till the early 21st century [159]. Around 2010, starting first in Europe, then in the United States, substituted cathinones emerged as a potent drug of abuse [160, 161]. These substances were often marketed as "bath salts" or "plant foods" and distributed via smoke shops or the internet [162]. Methcathinone and mephedrone (4-methylmethcathinone) were among the first substituted cathinones to emerge, but others rapidly followed, and currently, it is estimated that there may be more than 50 different substituted cathinones available [163]. Structurally, the substituted cathinones are very similar to amphetamine and differ only by the addition of a ketone group [164]. Their mechanism of action can be complex; some promote the release of catecholamines, similarly to amphetamines, while others may inhibit the reuptake of catecholamines, similarly to cocaine [165]. They can be taken orally, inhaled, or injected intravenously [166]. The onset of symptoms is typically rapid, and the duration of the effects can be several hours, up to 24 hours or more, depending on the amount used [167]. The exact half-life of the various substituted cathinones is poorly defined but likely similar to the corresponding amphetamine. The clinical effects of substituted cathinones are also similar to those of amphetamines; though there is evidence that substituted cathinones may be associated with more severe symptoms [168, 169].

CNS effects: Agitation, confusion, hallucinations, and psychosis are commonly described to result from synthetic cathinone use [170]. Similarly to other stimulants, substituted cathinones likely increase the risk of cerebrovascular accidents, but currently, there are no published reports to this effect. A leukoencephalopathy has been attributed to substituted cathinone use, but in this case, the presence of a substituted cathinone was not analytically confirmed, and the patient had multiple other organ derangements [171].

Excited delirium: There are multiple reports of substituted cathinone use being associated with excited delirium, often with severe outcomes [172, 173]. One study suggests that substituted cathinones are associated with more excited delirium than methamphetamine [174].

Movement disorders: Substituted cathinones would be expected to cause similar movement disorders as amphetamines. It is notable that a Parkinsonian syndrome was associated with the intravenous use of the substituted cathinone methcathione [175]. The investigation determined that the methcathinone was contaminated with manganese used in its illicit manufacturing.

Cardiovascular effects: Sinus tachycardia and hypertension are commonly seen with substituted cathinone use [170]. Considering the potent sympathomimetic effects of substituted cathinones, it is reasonable to assume that they will raise the risk of myocardial infarction. However, there is little published evidence in this regard. There is a report of a substituted cathinone–associated acute cardiomyopathy that resolved with abstinence [176].

Pulmonary effects: There is little published literature describing acute or chronic pulmonary effects from substituted cathinones. It is unknown at this time whether substituted cathinone use can also contribute to the development of pulmonary hypertension, similarly to methamphetamine.

Metabolic and other effects: Rhabdomyolysis is commonly seen with substituted cathinone intoxication and appears to be more prominent with substituted cathinones than with other stimulants [169]. Compartment syndrome, usually in the setting of agitation, has also been described with substituted cathinone use [177]. Rarely, hepatotoxicity has been seen with substituted cathinone use. It appears to be related to oxidative stress and mitochondrial dysfunction, and there may be a genetic pre-disposition [178, 179]. Hyponatremia has been described with use of the substituted cathinone methylone, likely due to its structural similarity to MDMA [180].

Withdrawal: Withdrawal from substituted cathinones has not been well described but is likely to be similar to methamphetamine. Neonatal withdrawal has been described in a baby born to a woman who chronically used 4-methylethcathinone, a substituted cathinone [181]. The symptoms of jitteriness and irritability resolved after 12 days.

1.1.1.3.4 Methylphenidate

Methylphenidate is structurally distinct from amphetamines but has similar properties. It blocks the reuptake primarily of dopamine and norepinephrine [182]. It is used clinically for the treatment of attention-deficit disorder and narcolepsy [183]. In therapeutic doses, it is a mild CNS stimulant, with more mental than motor effects, and has minimal peripheral effects [184]. However, it has become a widely misused or abused substance [185]. It is taken orally or insufflated or injected intravenously. When used in high doses, it may cause generalized CNS stimulation, with symptoms similar to those of amphetamine or methamphetamine. These commonly include sinus tachycardia, hypertension, and psychomotor agitation [186]. Seizures or other severe toxicity are rarely reported [187]. Analogs of methylphenidate (ethylphenidate) are also occasionally abused and appear to cause similar symptoms as methylphenidate [188]. However, deaths have been reported with its use [189].

1.1.1.3.5 Other Synthetic Stimulants

1.1.1.3.5.1 Phenylpropanolamine Phenylpropanolamine (PPA) is primarily an alpha-adrenergic agonist, both directly and indirectly through release of norepinephrine [190]. It is structurally related to amphetamine. PPA was previously an ingredient in many cold and anorectic agents but was banned by the FDA in 2000 because of an association with hemorrhagic stroke [191]. It is still occasionally misused. PPA toxicity is associated with severe effects such as strokes and myocardial infarctions [192]. Of note, reflexive bradycardia can be seen with PPA toxicity due to its powerful alpha effects [193].

1.1.1.3.5.2 Dimethylamylamine Dimethylamylamine (DMAA) shares some structural similarity to amphetamine but lacks the benzyl ring. It is an indirectly acting sympathomimetic that was previously used as a decongestant but now is found in dietary supplements [194]. It has abuse potential, and its misuse has been associated with typical stimulant complications such as hypertension, tachycardia, and psychomotor agitation [195]. Occasionally, severe symptoms such as cerebral hemorrhage can be seen [196].

1.1.1.3.5.3 Piperazines Piperazines are a group of compounds that have a six-membered ring containing two nitrogen atoms at opposite positions in the ring. They are indirect sympathomimetics with clinical effects similar to those of cocaine and amphetamines [197]. Some were previously used as anti-helminthic drugs but now are abused as “Party Pills” or “Pep Pills” [198]. Clinically they cause tachycardia, hypertension, and psychomotor agitation [199]. Seizures have been reported with piperazine use [200]. Choreoathetoid movement disorders can also be seen [201].

ACKNOWLEDGMENTS

Shoshana Zevin, M.D. and Neal L. Benowitz, M.D.

REFERENCES

1. Goldstein RA, DesLauriers C, Burda AM. Cocaine: history, social implications, and toxicity--a review. *Dis Mon* 2009;55(1):6–38; Das G. Cocaine abuse in North America: a milestone in history. *J Clin Pharmacol* 1993;33(4):296–310.
2. Gawin FH, Ellinwood EH, Jr. Cocaine and other stimulants. Actions, abuse, and treatment. *N Engl J Med* 1988;318(18):1173–82.
3. Boghdadi MS, Henning RJ. Cocaine: pathophysiology and clinical toxicology. *Heart Lung* 1997;26(6):466–83.
4. Williamson S, Gossop M, Powis B, Griffiths P, Fountain J, Strang J. Adverse effects of stimulant drugs in a community sample of drug users. *Drug Alcohol Depend* 1997;44(2–3):87–94.
5. Fleckenstein AE, Gibb JW, Hanson GR. Differential effects of stimulants on monoaminergic transporters: pharmacological consequences and implications for neurotoxicity. *Eur J Pharmacol* 2000;406(1):1–13.
6. Ramamoorthy S, Blakely RD. Phosphorylation and sequestration of serotonin transporters differentially modulated by psychostimulants. *Science* 1999;285(5428):763–6.
7. O'Leary ME, Chahine M. Cocaine binds to a common site on open and inactivated human heart (Na(v)1.5) sodium channels. *J Physiol* 2002;541(Pt 3):701–16.
8. Jufer RA, Wstadik A, Walsh SL, Levine BS, Cone EJ. Elimination of cocaine and metabolites in plasma, saliva, and urine following repeated oral administration to human volunteers. *J Anal Toxicol* 2000;24(7):467–77.
9. de Prost N, Mégarbane B, Questel F, Bloch V, Bertaux DC, Pourriat JL, Rabbat A. Blood cocaine and metabolite pharmacokinetics after cardiac arrest in a body-packer case. *Hum Exp Toxicol* 2010;29(1):49–53.
10. Jenkins AJ, Keenan RM, Henningfield JE, Cone EJ. Correlation between pharmacological effects and plasma cocaine concentrations after smoked administration. *J Anal Toxicol* 2002 Oct;26(7):382–92.
11. Heard K, Palmer R, Zahniser NR. Mechanisms of acute cocaine toxicity. *Open Pharmacol J* 2008;2(9):70–78.

12. Lowenstein DH, Massa SM, Rowbotham MC, Collins SD, McKinney HE, Simon RP. Acute neurologic and psychiatric complications associated with cocaine abuse. *Am J Med* 1987;83(5):841–6.
13. Majewska MD. Cocaine addiction as a neurological disorder: implications for treatment. *NIDA Res Monogr* 1996;163:1–26.
14. Daras M. Neurologic complications of cocaine. *NIDA Res Monogr* 1996;163:43–65.
15. Christensen JD, Kaufman MJ, Levin JM, Mendelson JH, Holman BL, Cohen BM, et al. Abnormal cerebral metabolism in polydrug abusers during early withdrawal: a 31P MR spectroscopy study. *Magn Reson Med* 1996;35(5):658–63.
16. Fofi L, Orlandi V, Vanacore N, Mizzoni MC, Rosa A, Aurilia C, Egeo G, Casella P, Barbanti P. Headache in chronic cocaine users: a cross-sectional study.*Cephalalgia* 2014;34(9):671–8.
17. Mueller PD, Benowitz NL, Olson KR. Cocaine. *Emerg Med Clin North Am* 1990;8(3):481–93.
18. Satel SL, Gawin FH. Migrainelike headache and cocaine use. *JAMA* 1989;261(20):2995–6.
19. Cafforio G, Morelli N, Rota E, Piane RM, Mazzoni M. Cocaine-induced cluster-like headache. *Neurol Sci* 2014;35(2):319–21.
20. Martin-Schild S, Albright KC, Hallevi H, Barreto AD, Philip M, Misra V, Grotta JC, Savitz SI. Intracerebral hemorrhage in cocaine users. *Stroke* 2010;41(4):680–4.
21. Rowbotham MC. Neurologic aspects of cocaine abuse [clinical conference]. *West J Med* 1988;149(4):442–8.
22. Effiong C, Ahuja TS, Wagner JD, Singhal PC, Mattana J. Reversible hemiplegia as a consequence of severe hyperkalemia and cocaine abuse in a hemodialysis patient. *Am J Med Sci* 1997;314(6):408–10.
23. Sordo L, Indave BI, Barrio G, Degenhardt L, de la Fuente L, Bravo MJ. Cocaine use and risk of stroke: a systematic review. *Drug Alcohol Depend* 2014;142:1–13.
24. Cheng YC, Ryan KA, Qadwai SA, Shah J, Sparks MJ, Wozniak MA, Stern BJ, Phipps MS, Cronin CA, Magder LS, Cole JW, Kittner SJ. Cocaine use and risk of Ischemic stroke in young adults. *Stroke* 2016;47(4):918–22.
25. Tardiff K, Gross E, Wu J, Stajic M, Millman R. Analysis of cocaine-positive fatalities. *J Forensic Sci* 1989;34(1):53–63.
26. Kaufman MJ, Levin JM, Ross MH, Lange N, Rose SL, Kukes TJ, et al. Cocaine-induced cerebral vasoconstriction detected in humans with magnetic resonance angiography. *JAMA* 1998;279(5):376–80.
27. Fritsma GA, Leikin JB, Maturen AJ, Froelich CJ, Hryhorczuk DO. Detection of anticardiolipin antibody in patients with cocaine abuse. *J Emerg Med* 1991;9 (Suppl 1): 37–43.
28. Keller TM, Chappell ET. Spontaneous acute subdural hematoma precipitated by cocaine abuse: case report. *Surg Neurol* 1997;47(1):12–4.
29. Saleh T, Badshah A, Afzal K. Spontaneous acute subdural hematoma secondary to cocaine abuse. *South Med J* 2010;103(7):714–5.
30. Sanchez-Ramos JR. Psychostimulants. *Neurol Clin* 1993;11(3):535–53.
31. Catalano G, Catalano MC, Rodriguez R. Dystonia associated with crack cocaine use. *South Med J* 1997;90(10):1050–2.
32. Daras M, Koppel BS, Atos Radzion E. Cocaine-induced choreoathetoid movements ("crack dancing"). *Neurology* 1994;44(4):751–2.
33. Winbery S, Blaho K, Logan B, Geraci S. Multiple cocaine-induced seizures and corresponding cocaine and metabolite concentrations. *Am J Emerg Med* 1998;16(5):529–33.
34. Zagnoni PG, Albano C. Psychostimulants and epilepsy. *Epilepsia* 2002;43(Suppl 2):28–31.
35. Vilke GM, DeBard ML, Chan TC, Ho JD, Dawes DM, Hall C, Curtis MD, Costello MW, Mash DC, Coffman SR, McMullen MJ, Metzger JC, Roberts JR, Sztajnkrcer MD, Henderson SO, Adler J, Czarnecki F, Heck J, Bozeman WP. Excited Delirium Syndrome (ExDS): defining based on a review of the literature. *J Emerg Med* 2012;43(5):897–905.
36. Ruttenber AJ, Lawler-Heavner J, Yin M, Wetli CV, Hearn WL, Mash DC. Fatal excited delirium following cocaine use: epidemiologic findings provide new evidence for mechanisms of cocaine toxicity. *J Forensic Sci* 1997;42(1):25–31.
37. Naveen RA. Brain abscess: a complication of cocaine inhalation. *NY State J Med* 1988;88:548–50.
38. Thakur V, Godley C, Weed S, Cook ME, Hoffman E. Case reports: cocaine-associated accelerated hypertension and renal failure. *Am J Med Sci* 1996;312(6):295–8.
39. Benowitz NL. Clinical pharmacology and toxicology of cocaine [published erratum appears in *Pharmacol Toxicol* 1993 Jun;72(6):343]. *Pharmacol Toxicol* 1993;72(1):3–12.
40. Ghuran A, Nolan J. Recreational drug misuse: issues for the cardiologist. *Heart* 2000;83(6):627–33.
41. Lange RA, Hillis LD. Cardiovascular complications of cocaine use. *N Engl J Med* 2001;345(5):351–8.
42. Benzaquen BS, Cohen V, Eisenberg MJ. Effects of cocaine on the coronary arteries. *Am Heart J* 2001;142(3):402–10.
43. Mittleman MA, Mintzer D, Maclure M, Tofler GH, Sherwood JB, Muller JE. Triggering of myocardial infarction by cocaine. *Circulation* 1999;99(21):2737–41.
44. Feldman JA, Fish SS, Beshansky JR, Griffith JL, Woolard RH, Selker HP. Acute cardiac ischemia in patients with cocaine-associated complaints: results of a multicenter trial. *Ann Emerg Med* 2000;36(5):469–76.
45. Nademanee K. Cardiovascular effects and toxicities of cocaine. *J Addict Dis* 1992;11(4):71–82.
46. Gill D, Sheikh N, Ruiz VG, Liu K. Case report: cocaine-induced takotsubo cardiomyopathy. *Hellenic J Cardiol* 2017.
47. Cooper CJ, Said S, Alkhateeb H, Rodriguez E, Trien R, Ajmal S, Blandon PA,Hernandez GT. Dilated cardiomyopathy secondary to chronic cocaine abuse: a case report. *BMC Res Notes* 2013;6:536.
48. Boutros HH, Pautler S, Chakrabarti S. Cocaine-induced ischemic colitis with small-vessel thrombosis of colon and gallbladder. *J Clin Gastroenterol* 1997;24(1):49–53.
49. Linder JD, Monkemuller KE, Raijman I, Johnson L, Lazenby AJ, Wilcox CM. Cocaine-associated ischemic colitis. *South Med J* 2000;93(9):909–13.
50. Niazi M, Kondru A, Levy J, Bloom AA. Spectrum of ischemic colitis in cocaine users. *Dig Dis Sci* 1997;42(7):1537–41.
51. Dean JH, Woznicki EM, O'Gara P, Montgomery DG, Trimarchi S, Myrmel T, Pyeritz RE, Harris KM, Suzuki T, Braverman AC, Hughes GC, Kline-Rogers E, Nienaber CA, Isselbacher EM, Eagle KA, Bossone E. Cocaine-related aortic dissection: lessons from the International Registry of Acute Aortic Dissection. *Am J Med* 2014;127(9):878–85.
52. Kalimullah EA, Bryant SM. Case files of the medical toxicology fellowship at the toxikon consortium in Chicago: cocaine-associated wide-complex dysrhythmias and cardiac arrest - treatment nuances and controversies. *J Med Toxicol* 2008;4(4):277–83.
53. Gamouras GA, Monir G, Plunkitt K, Gursoy S, Dreifus LS. Cocaine abuse: repolarization abnormalities and ventricular arrhythmias. *Am J Med Sci* 2000;320(1):9–12.

54. Butterfield M, Riguzzi C, Frenkel O, Nagdev A. Stimulant-related Takotsubo cardiomyopathy. *Am J Emerg Med* 2015;33(3):476.
55. Arora S, Alfayoumi F, Srinivasan V. Transient left ventricular apical ballooning after cocaine use: is catecholamine cardiotoxicity the pathologic link? *Mayo Clin Proc* 2006;81(6):829–32.
56. Ruttenber AJ, Lawler Heavner J, Yin M, Wetli CV, Hearn WL, Mash DC. Fatal excited delirium following cocaine use: epidemiologic findings provide new evidence for mechanisms of cocaine toxicity. *J Forensic Sci* 1997;42(1):25–31.
57. Marzuk PM, Tardiff K, Leon AC, Hirsch CS, Stajic M, Portera L, et al. Fatal injuries after cocaine use as a leading cause of death among young adults in New York City. *N Engl J Med* 1995;332(26):1753–7.
58. Bailey ME, Fraire AE, Greenberg SD, Barnard J, Cagle PT. Pulmonary histopathology in cocaine abusers. *Hum Pathol* 1994;25(2):203–7.
59. Kissner DG, Lawrence WD, Selis JE, Flint A. Crack lung: pulmonary disease caused by cocaine abuse. *Am Rev Respir Dis* 1987;136(5):1250–2.
60. Tashkin DP. Airway effects of marijuana, cocaine, and other inhaled illicit agents. *Curr Opin Pulm Med* 2001;7(2): 43–61.
61. Albertson TE, Walby WF. Respiratory toxicities from stimulant use. *Clin Rev Allergy Immunol* 1997;15(3):221–41.
62. Baldwin GC, Tashkin DP, Buckley DM, Park AN, Dubinett SM, Roth MD. Marijuana and cocaine impair alveolar macrophage function and cytokine production. *Am J Respir Crit Care Med* 1997;156(5):1606–13.
63. Karch SB, Busardò FP, Vaiano F, Portelli F, Zaami S, Bertol E. Levamisole adulterated cocaine and pulmonary vasculitis: presentation of two lethal cases and brief literature review. *Forensic Sci Int* 2016;265:96–102.
64. Soares DS, Ferdman A, Alli R. Subcutaneous emphysema and pneumomediastinum following cocaine inhalation: a case report. *J Med Case Rep* 2015;9:195.
65. Maeder M, Ullmer E. Pneumomediastinum and bilateral pneumothorax as a complication of cocaine smoking. *Respiration* 2003;70(4):407.
66. Crandall CG, Vongpatanasin W, Victor RG. Mechanism of cocaine-induced hyperthermia in humans. *Ann Intern Med* 2002;136(11):785–91.
67. Marzuk PM, Tardiff K, Leon AC, Hirsch CS, Portera L, Iqbal MI, et al. Ambient temperature and mortality from unintentional cocaine overdose. *JAMA* 1998;279(22):1795–800.
68. Horowitz BZ, Panacek EA, Jouriles NJ. Severe rhabdomyolysis with renal failure after intranasal cocaine use. *J Emerg Med* 1997;15(6):833–7.
69. Alshayeb H, Showkat A, Wall BM. Lactic acidosis in restrained cocaine intoxicated patients. *Tenn Med* 2010;103(10):37–9.
70. Mbah AK, Alio AP, Fombo DW, Bruder K, Dagne G, Salihu HM. Association between cocaine abuse in pregnancy and placenta-associated syndromes using propensity score matching approach. *Early Hum Dev* 2012;88(6):333–7.
71. Bateman DA, Chiriboga CA. Dose–response effect of cocaine on newborn head circumference. *Pediatrics* 2000;106 (3):E33.
72. Chiriboga CA, Brust JC, Bateman D, Hauser WA. Dose–response effect of fetal cocaine exposure on newborn neurologic function. *Pediatrics* 1999;103(1):79–85.
73. Towers CV, Pircon RA, Nageotte MP, Porto M, Garite TJ. Cocaine intoxication presenting as preeclampsia and eclampsia. *Obstet Gynecol* 1993;81(4):545–7.
74. Brewer JD, Meves A, Bostwick JM, Hamacher KL, Pittelkow MR. Cocaine abuse: dermatologic manifestations and therapeutic approaches. *J Am Acad Dermatol* 2008;59(3):483–7.
75. Gross RL, Brucker J, Bahce-Altuntas A, Abadi MA, Lipoff J, Kotlyar D, Barland P, Putterman C. A novel cutaneous vasculitis syndrome induced by levamisole-contaminated cocaine. *Clin Rheumatol* 2011;30(10):1385–92.
76. Lago JA, Kosten TR. Stimulant withdrawal. *Addiction* 1994;89(11):1477–81.
77. Broséus J, Gentile N, Esseiva P. The cutting of cocaine and heroin: a critical review. *Forensic Sci Int* 2016;262: 73–83.
78. Mutch RS, Hutson PR. Levamisole in the adjuvant treatment of colon cancer. *Clin Pharm* 1991;10(2):95–109.
79. Buchanan JA, Heard K, Burbach C, Wilson ML, Dart R. Prevalence of levamisole in urine toxicology screens positive for cocaine in an inner-city hospital. *JAMA* 2011;305(16): 1657–8.
80. Nolan AL, Jen KY. Pathologic manifestations of levamisole-adulterated cocaine exposure. *Diagn Pathol* 2015;10:48.
81. Bertol E, Mari F, Milia MG, Politi L, Furlanetto S, Karch SB. Determination of aminorex in human urine samples by GC-MS after use of levamisole. *J Pharm Biomed Anal* 2011;55(5):1186–9.
82. Karch SB, Defraia B, Messerini L, Mari F, Vaiano F, Bertol E. Aminorex associated with possible idiopathic pulmonary hypertension in a cocaine user. *Forensic Sci Int* 2014;240:e7–10.
83. Food and Drug Administration, Public Health Service, U.S. Department of Healthand Human Services. Dietary supplements containing ephedrine alkaloids adulterated because they present an unreasonable risk; final rule. *J Pain Palliat Care Pharmacother* 2004;18(3):95–107.
84. Phinney KW, Ihara T, Sander LC. Determination of ephedrine alkaloid stereoisomers in dietary supplements by capillary electrophoresis. *J Chromatogr A* 2005;1077(1):90–7.
85. Gambaro V, Arnoldi S, Colombo ML, Dell'Acqua L, Guerrini K, Roda G. Determination of the active principles of Catha Edulis: quali-quantitative analysis of cathinone, cathine, and phenylpropanolamine. *Forensic Sci Int* 2012;217(1–3):87–92.
86. Pantelis C, Hindler CG, Taylor JC. Use and abuse of khat (Catha edulis): areview of the distribution, pharmacology, side effects and a description of psychosis attributed to khat chewing. *Psychol Med* 1989;19(3):657–68.
87. Trendelenburg U, Supersensitivity and subsensitivity to sympathomimetic amines. *Pharmacol Rev* 1963;15: 225–76.
88. Drew CD, Knight GT, Hughes DT, Bush M. Comparison of the effects of D-(-)-ephedrine and L-(+)-pseudoephedrine on the cardiovascular and respiratory systems in man. *Br J Clin Pharmacol* 1978;6(3):221–5.
89. Haller CA, Benowitz NL. Adverse cardiovascular and central nervous system events associated with dietary supplements containing ephedra alkaloids. *N Engl J Med* 2000;343(25):1833–8.
90. Battig K. Acute and chronic cardiovascular and behavioural effects of caffeine, aspirin and ephedrine. *Int J Obes Relat Metab Disord* 1993;17 Suppl 1:S61–4.
91. Bruno A, Nolte KB, Chapin J. Stroke associated with ephedrine use. *Neurology* 1993;43(7):1313–6.
92. MMWR. Adverse events associated with ephedrine-containing products — Texas, December 1993–September 1995. *MMWR Morb Mortal Wkly Rep* 1996;45(32):689–93.

93. Kim TJ, LeBourgeois HW 3rd. Banned, but not forgotten: a case of ephedrine-induced psychosis. *Prim Care Companion J Clin Psychiatry* 2004;6(3):136–7.
94. Powell T, Hsu FF, Turk J, Hruska K. Ma-huang strikes again: ephedrine nephrolithiasis. *Am J Kidney Dis* 1998;32(1):153–9.
95. Luqman W, Danowski TS. The use of khat (*Catha edulis*) in Yemen. Social and medical observations. *Ann Intern Med* 1976;85(2):246–9.
96. Yousef G, Huq Z, Lambert T. Khat chewing as a cause of psychosis. *Br J Hosp Med* 1995;54(7):322–6.
97. Hassan NA, Gunaid AA, Abdo Rabbo AA, Abdel Kader ZY, al Mansoob MA, Awad AY, et al. The effect of Qat chewing on blood pressure and heart rate in healthy volunteers. *Trop Doct* 2000;30(2):107–8.
98. Al-Motarreb A, Briancon S, Al-Jaber N, Al-Adhi B, Al-Jailani F, Salek MS, Broadley KJ. Khat chewing is a risk factor for acute myocardial infarction: a case-control study. *Br J Clin Pharmacol* 2005;59(5):574–8.
99. Al Motarreb A, Al Kebsi M, Al Adhi B, Broadley KJ. Khat chewing and acute myocardial infarction. *Heart* 2002;87(3):279–80.
100. Eriksson M, Ghani NA, Kristiansson B. Khat-chewing during pregnancy-effect upon the off-spring and some characteristics of the chewers. *East Afr Med J* 1991;68(2):106–11.
101. Vearrier D, Greenberg MI, Miller SN, Okaneku JT, Haggerty DA. Methamphetamine: history, pathophysiology, adverse health effects, current trends, and hazards associated with the clandestine manufacture of methamphetamine. *Dis Mon* 2012;58(2):38–89.
102. Gunderson EW, Kirkpatrick MG, Willing LM, Holstege CP. Substituted cathinone products: a new trend in "bath salts" and other designer stimulant drug use. *J Addict Med* 2013;7(3):153–62.
103. Sulzer D, Sonders MS, Poulsen NW, Galli A. Mechanisms of neurotransmitter release by amphetamines: a review. *Prog Neurobiol* 2005;75(6):406–33.
104. Sloviter RS, Damiano BP, Connor JD. Relative potency of amphetamine isomers in causing the serotonin behavioral syndrome in rats. *Biol Psychiatry* 1980;15(5):789–96.
105. Smith RC, Davis JM. Comparative effects of d-amphetamine, l-amphetamine, and methylphenidate on mood in man. *Psychopharmacology (Berl)* 1977;53(1):1–12.
106. Ermer JC, Pennick M, Frick G. Lisdexamfetamine dimesylate: prodrug delivery, amphetamine exposure and duration of efficacy. *Clin Drug Investig* 2016;36(5):341–56.
107. Wan SH, Matin SB, Azarnoff DL. Kinetics, salivary excretion of amphetamine isomers, and effect of urinary pH. *Clin Pharmacol Ther* 1978;23(5):585–90.
108. Bost RO. 3,4-Methylenedioxymethamphetamine (MDMA) and other amphetamine derivatives. *J Forensic Sci* 1988;33(2):576–87.
109. Derlet RW, Rice P, Horowitz BZ, Lord RV. Amphetamine toxicity: experience with 127 cases. *J Emerg Med* 1989;7(2):157–61.
110. Stratton SJ, Rogers C, Brickett K, Gruzinski G. Factors associated with sudden death of individuals requiring restraint for excited delirium. *Am J Emerg Med* 2001;19(3):187–91.
111. Agaba EA, Lynch RM, Baskaran A, Jackson T. Massive intracerebral hematoma and extradural hematoma in amphetamine abuse. *Am J Emerg Med* 2002;20(1):55–7.
112. El Omar MM, Ray K, Geary R. Intracerebral haemorrhage in a young adult: consider amphetamine abuse. *Br J Clin Pract* 1996;50(2):115–6.
113. Matick H, Anderson D, Brumlik J. Cerebral vasculitis associated with oral amphetamine overdose. *Arch Neurol* 1983;40(4):253–4.
114. Shaw HE, Jr, Lawson JG, Stulting RD. *Amaurosis fugax* and retinal vasculitis associated with methamphetamine inhalation. *J Clin Neuroophthalmol* 1985;5(3):169–76.
115. Buxton N, McConachie NS. Amphetamine abuse and intracranial haemorrhage. *J R Soc Med* 2000;93(9):472–7.
116. Harris D, Batki SL. Stimulant psychosis: symptom profile and acute clinical course. *Am J Addict* 2000;9(1):28–37.
117. Flaum M, Schultz SK. When does amphetamine-induced psychosis become schizophrenia? *Am J Psychiatry* 1996;153(6):812–5.
118. Downes MA, Whyte IM. Amphetamine-induced movement disorder. *Emerg Med Australas* 2005;17(3):277–80.
119. Costa GM, Pizzi C, Bresciani B, Tumscitz C, Gentile M, Bugiardini R. Acute myocardial infarction caused by amphetamines: a case report and review of the literature. *Ital Heart J* 2001;2(6):478–80.
120. Waksman J, Taylor RN, Jr, Bodor GS, Daly FF, Jolliff HA, Dart RC. Acute myocardial infarction associated with amphetamine use. *Mayo Clin Proc* 2001;76(3):323–6.
121. Smith HJ, Roche AH, Jausch MF, Herdson PB. Cardiomyopathy associated with amphetamine administration. *Am Heart J* 1976;91(6):792–7.
122. Toce MS, Farias M, Bruccoleri R, Brown DW, Burns MM. A case report of reversible takotsubo cardiomyopathy after Amphetamine/Dextroamphetamine ingestion in a 15-year-old adolescent girl. *J Pediatr* 2017;182:385–388.
123. Welling TH, Williams DM, Stanley JC. Excessive oral amphetamine use as a possible cause of renal and splanchnic arterial aneurysms: a report of two cases. *J Vasc Surg* 1998;28(4):727–31.
124. Callaway CW, Clark RF. Hyperthermia in psychostimulant overdose. *Ann Emerg Med* 1994;24(1):68–76.
125. Kendrick WC, Hull AR, Knochel JP. Rhabdomyolysis and shock after intravenous amphetamine administration. *Ann Intern Med* 1977;86(4):381–7.
126. DSM-IV-TR. *Diagnositic and Statistical Manual of Mental Disorders.* 4th Edition. Washington, DC: American Psychiatric Association, 2000.
127. McGregor C, Srisurapanont M, Jittiwutikarn J, Laobhripatr S, Wongtan T, White JM. The nature, time course and severity of methamphetamine withdrawal. *Addiction* 2005;100(9):1320–9.
128. Kirkpatrick MG, Gunderson EW, Johanson CE, Levin FR, Foltin RW, Hart CL. Comparison of intranasal methamphetamine and d-amphetamine self-administration by humans. *Addiction* 2012;107(4):783–91.
129. Albertson TE, Derlet RW, Van Hoozen BE. Methamphetamine and the expanding complications of amphetamines. *West J Med* 1999;170(4):214–9.
130. Schifano F, Corkery JM, Cuffolo G. Smokable ("ice", "crystal meth") and non smokable amphetamine-type stimulants: clinical pharmacological and epidemiological issues, with special reference to the UK. *Ann Ist Super Sanita* 2007;43(1):110–5.
131. Harris DS, Boxenbaum H, Everhart ET, Sequeira G, Mendelson JE, Jones RT. The bioavailability of intranasal and smoked methamphetamine. *Clin Pharmacol Ther* 2003;74(5):475–86.
132. Substance Abuse and Mental Health Services Administration, Office of Applied Studies. Treatment Episode Data Set (TEDS) Highlights - –2007 National Admissions to Substance Abuse Treatment Services. Rockville, MD, 2009. OAS Series #S-45, HHS Publication No. (SMA) 09-4360.

133. Buchanan JF, Brown CR. 'Designer drugs.' A problem in clinical toxicology. *Med Toxicol Adverse Drug Exp* 1988;3(1):1–17.
134. Balster RL, Schuster CR. A comparison of d-amphetamine l-amphetamine, and methamphetamine self-administration in rhesus monkeys. *Pharmacol Biochem Behav* 1973;1: 67–71.
135. Glasner-Edwards S, Mooney LJ. Methamphetamine psychosis: epidemiology and management. *CNS Drugs* 2014;28(12):1115–26.
136. Akiyama K, Saito A, Shimoda K. Chronic methamphetamine psychosis after long-term abstinence in Japanese incarcerated patients. *Am J Addict* 2011;20(3):240–9.
137. Kiely E, Lee CJ, Marinetti L. A fatality from an oral ingestion of methamphetamine. *J Anal Toxicol* 2009;33(8):557–60.
138. Rothrock JF, Rubenstein R, Lyden PD. Ischemic stroke associated with methamphetamine inhalation. *Neurology* 1988;38(4):589–92.
139. Perez JA, Jr, Arsura EL, Strategos S. Methamphetamine-related stroke: four cases. *J Emerg Med* 1999;17(3):469–71.
140. Huang MC, Yang SY, Lin SK, Chen KY, Chen YY, Kuo CJ, Hung YN. Risk of cardiovascular diseases and stroke events in methamphetamine users: a 10-year follow-up study. *J Clin Psychiatry* 2016;77(10):1396–403.
141. Sperling LS, Horowitz JL. Methamphetamine-induced choreoathetosis and rhabdomyolysis. *Ann Intern Med* 1994;121(12):986.
142. Callaghan RC, Cunningham JK, Sajeev G, Kish SJ. Incidence of Parkinson's disease among hospital patients with methamphetamine-use disorders. *Mov Disord* 2010;25(14):2333–9.
143. Curtin K, Fleckenstein AE, Robison RJ, Crookston MJ, Smith KR, Hanson GR. Methamphetamine/amphetamine abuse and risk of Parkinson's disease in Utah: a population-based assessment. *Drug Alcohol Depend* 2015;146:30–8.
144. Rommel N, Rohleder NH, Koerdt S, Wagenpfeil S, Härtel-Petri R, Wolff KD, Kesting MR. Sympathomimetic effects of chronic methamphetamine abuse on oral health: a cross-sectional study. *BMC Oral Health* 2016;16(1):59.
145. Hawley LA, Auten JD, Matteucci MJ, Decker L, Hurst N, Beer W, Clark RF. Cardiac complications of adult methamphetamine exposures. *J Emerg Med* 2013;45(6):821–7.
146. Watts DJ, McCollester L. Methamphetamine-induced myocardial infarction with elevated troponin I. *Am J Emerg Med* 2006;24(1):132–4.
147. Wijetunga M, Bhan R, Lindsay J, Karch S. Acute coronary syndrome and crystal methamphetamine use: a case series. *Hawaii Med J* 2004;63(1):8–13, 25.
148. Stokes MB, Fernando H, Taylor AJ. Cardiogenic shock secondary to methamphetamine induced cardiomyopathy requiring veno-arterial extra-corporeal membrane oxygenation. *Int J Cardiol* 2016;207:134–5.
149. Madias JE. Methamphetamine-triggered Takotsubo syndrome and methamphetamine-associated cardiomyopathy: a continuum? *Intern Med J* 2016;46(6):752–3.
150. Schürer S, Klingel K, Sandri M, Majunke N, Besler C, Kandolf R, Lurz P, Luck M, Hertel P, Schuler G, Linke A, Mangner N. Clinical characteristics, histopathological features, and clinical outcome of methamphetamine-associated cardiomyopathy. *JACC Heart Fail* 2017;5(6):435–45.
151. Chin KM, Channick RN, Rubin LJ. Is methamphetamine use associated with idiopathic pulmonary arterial hypertension? *Chest* 2006;130(6):1657–63.
152. Schaiberger PH, Kennedy TC, Miller FC, Gal J, Petty TL. Pulmonary hypertension associated with long-term inhalation of "crank" methamphetamine. *Chest* 1993.
153. Rothman RB, Baumann MH. Methamphetamine and idiopathic pulmonary arterial hypertension: role of the serotonin transporter. *Chest* 2007;132(4):1412–3; 104(2):614–6.
154. Richards JR, Johnson EB, Stark RW, Derlet RW. Methamphetamine abuse and rhabdomyolysis in the ED: a 5-year study. *Am J Emerg Med* 1999;17(7):681–5.
155. Galloway T. Meth mouth: a modern epidemic. *J Okla Dent Assoc* 2010;101(8):27–8.
156. Brown RE, Morisky DE, Silverstein SJ. Meth mouth severity in response to drug-use patterns and dental access in methamphetamine users. *J Calif Dent Assoc* 2013;41(6):421–8.
157. Yaffee HS. Cutaneous stigmas associated with methedrine (methamphetamine). *Arch Dermatol* 1971;104(6):687.
158. Zorick T, Nestor L, Miotto K, Sugar C, Hellemann G, Scanlon G, Rawson R, London ED. Withdrawal symptoms in abstinent methamphetamine-dependent subjects. *Addiction* 2010;105(10):1809–18.
159. Koppe H, Ludwig G, Zeile K. "US Patent 3478050 - 1-(3',4'-methylenedioxy-phenyl)-2-pyrrolidino-alkanones-(1)". *Boehringer Sohn Ingelheim* 1965, May.
160. Wood DM, Davies S, Puchnarewicz M, Button J, Archer R, Ovaska H, Ramsey J, Lee T, Holt DW, Dargan PI. Recreational use of mephedrone (4-methylmethcathinone, 4-MMC) with associated sympathomimetic toxicity. *J Med Toxicol* 2010;6(3):327–30.
161. Spiller HA, Ryan ML, Weston RG, Jansen J. Clinical experience with and analytical confirmation of "bath salts" and "legal highs" (synthetic cathinones) in the United States. *Clin Toxicol (Phila)* 2011;49(6):499–505.
162. Schneir A, Ly BT, Casagrande K, Darracq M, Offerman SR, Thornton S, Smollin C, Vohra R, Rangun C, Tomaszewski C, Gerona RR. Comprehensive analysis of "bath salts" purchased from California stores and the internet. *Clin Toxicol (Phila)* 2014;52(7):651–8.
163. European Monitoring Centre for Drugs and Drug Addiction (2015) *New Psychoactive Substances in Europe. An Update from the EU Early Warning System (March 2015).* Luxembourg: Publications Office of the European Union.
164. Gerona RR, Wu AH. Bath salts. *Clin Lab Med* 2012;32(3):415–27.
165. Simmler LD, Buser TA, Donzelli M, Schramm Y, Dieu LH, Huwyler J, Chaboz S, Hoener MC, Liechti ME. Pharmacological characterization of designer cathinones in vitro. *Br J Pharmacol* 2013;168(2):458–70.
166. Warrick BJ, Hill M, Hekman K, Christensen R, Goetz R, Casavant MJ, Wahl M, Mowry JB, Spiller H, Anderson D, Aleguas A, Gummin D, Thomas R, Nezlek C, Smolinske S. A 9-state analysis of designer stimulant, "bath salt," hospital visits reported to poison control centers. *Ann Emerg Med* 2013;62(3):244–51.
167. Romanek K, Stenzel J, Schmoll S, Schrettl V, Geith S, Eyer F, Rabe C. Synthetic cathinones in Southern Germany - characteristics of users, substance-patterns, co-ingestions, and complications. *Clin Toxicol (Phila)* 2017;55(6): 573–8.
168. Froberg BA, Levine M, Beuhler MC, Judge BS, Moore PW, Engebretsen KM, Mckeown NJ, Rosenbaum CD, Young AC, Rusyniak DE; ACMT Toxicology Investigators Consortium (ToxIC). Acute Methylenedioxypyrovalerone Toxicity. *J Med Toxicol* 2015;11(2):185–94.

169. O'Connor AD, Padilla-Jones A, Gerkin RD, Levine M. Prevalence of rhabdomyolysis in sympathomimetic toxicity: a comparison of stimulants. *J Med Toxicol* 2015;11(2):195–200.
170. Beck O, Franzen L, Bäckberg M, Signell P, Helander A. Intoxications involving MDPV in Sweden during 2010–2014: results from the STRIDA project. *Clin Toxicol (Phila)* 2015;53(9):865–73.
171. Kramer CL, Wetzel DR, Wijdicks EF. Devastating delayed leukoencephalopathy associated with bath salt inhalation. *Neurocrit Care* 2016;24(3):454–8.
172. Penders TM, Gestring RE, Vilensky DA. Excited delirium following use of synthetic cathinones (bath salts). *Gen Hosp Psychiatry* 2012;34(6):647–50.
173. Kesha K, Boggs CL, Ripple MG, Allan CH, Levine B, Jufer-Phipps R, Doyon S, Chi P, Fowler DR. Methylenedioxypyrovalerone ("bath salts"), related death: case report and review of the literature. *J Forensic Sci* 2013;58(6):1654–9.
174. Ezaki J, Ro A, Hasegawa M, Kibayashi K. Fatal overdose from synthetic cannabinoids and cathinones in Japan: demographics and autopsy findings. *Am J Drug Alcohol Abuse* 2016;42(5):520–9.
175. Stepens A, Logina I, Liguts V, Aldins P, Eksteina I, Platkājis A, Mārtinsone I, Tērauds E, Rozentāle B, Donaghy M. A Parkinsonian syndrome in methcathinone users and the role of manganese. *N Engl J Med* 2008;358(10):1009–17.
176. Sivagnanam K, Chaudari D, Lopez P, Sutherland ME, Ramu VK. "Bath salts" induced severe reversible cardiomyopathy. *Am J Case Rep* 2013;14:288–91.
177. Levine M, Levitan R, Skolnik A. Compartment syndrome after "bath salts" use: acase series. *Ann Emerg Med* 2013;61(4):480–3.
178. Valente MJ, Araújo AM, Bastos Mde L, Fernandes E, Carvalho F, Guedes de Pinho P, Carvalho M. Editor's highlight: characterization of hepatotoxicity mechanisms triggered by designer cathinone drugs (β-Keto Amphetamines). *Toxicol Sci* 2016;153(1):89–102.
179. Luethi D, Liechti ME, Krähenbühl S. Mechanisms of hepatocellular toxicity associated with new psychoactive synthetic cathinones. *Toxicology* 2017.
180. Boulanger-Gobeil C, St-Onge M, Laliberté M, Auger PL. Seizures and hyponatremia related to ethcathinone and methylone poisoning. *J Med Toxicol* 2012;8(1):59–61.
181. Pichini S, Rotolo MC, García J, Girona N, Leal L, García-Algar O, Pacifici R. Neonatal withdrawal syndrome after chronic maternal consumption of 4-methylethcathinone. *Forensic Sci Int* 2014;245:e33–5.
182. Schmeichel BE Berridge CW. Neurocircuitry underlying the preferential sensitivity of prefrontal catecholamines to low-dose psychostimulants. *Neuropsychopharmacol* 2013;38:1079–84.
183. Challman TD, Lipsky JJ. Methylphenidate: its pharmacology and uses. *Mayo Clin Proc* 2000;75(7):711–21.
184. Hysek CM, Simmler LD, Schillinger N, Meyer N, Schmid Y, Donzelli M, Grouzmann E, Liechti ME. Pharmacokinetic and pharmacodynamic effects of methylphenidate and MDMA administered alone or in combination. *Int J Neuropsychopharmacol* 2014;17(3):371–81.
185. Bjarnadottir GD, Haraldsson HM, Rafnar BO, Sigurdsson E, Steingrimsson S, Johannsson M, Bragadottir H, Magnusson A. Prevalent intravenous abuse of methylphenidate among treatment-seeking patients with substance abuse disorders: a descriptive population-based study. *J Addict Med* 2015;9(3):188–94.
186. Hondebrink L, Rietjens SJ, Hunault CC, Pereira RR, Kelleci N, Yasar G, Ghebreslasie A, Lo-A-Foe C, De Vries I, Meulenbelt J. Methylphenidate intoxications in children and adults: exposure circumstances and evidence-based dose threshold for pre-hospital triage. *Clin Toxicol (Phila)* 2015;53(3):168–77.
187. Klein-Schwartz W, McGrath J. Poison centers' experience with methylphenidate abuse in pre-teens and adolescents. *J Am Acad Child Adolesc Psychiatry* 2003;42(3): 288–94.
188. Ho JH, Bailey GP, Archer JR, Dargan PI, Wood DM. Ethylphenidate: availability, patterns of use, and acute effects of this novel psychoactive substance. *Eur J Clin Pharmacol* 2015;71(10):1185–96.
189. Maskell PD, Smith PR, Cole R, Hikin L, Morley SR. Seven fatalities associated with ethylphenidate. *Forensic Sci Int* 2016;265:70–4.
190. Thomas SH, Clark KL, Allen R, Smith SE. A comparison of the cardiovascular effects of phenylpropanolamine and phenylephrine containing proprietary cold remedies. *Br J Clin Pharmacol* 1991;32(6):705–11.
191. Mersfelder TL. Phenylpropanolamine and stroke: the study, the FDA ruling, the implications. *Cleve Clin J Med* 2001;68(3):208–9, 213–9, 22.
192. Oosterbaan R, Burns MJ. Myocardial infarction associated with phenylpropanolamine. *J Emerg Med* 2000;18(1): 55–9.
193. Pentel P, Mikell F. Reaction to phenylpropalamine/chlorpheniramine/belladonna compound in a women with unrecognised autonomic dysfunction. *Lancet* 1982;2(8292): 274.
194. Dolan SB, Gatch MB. Abuse liability of the dietary supplement dimethylamylamine. *Drug Alcohol Depend* 2015;146:97–102.
195. Forrester M. Exposures to 1,3-dimethylamylamine-containing products reported to Texas poison centers. *Hum Exp Toxicol* 2013;32(1):18–23.
196. Gee P, Tallon C, Long N, Moore G, Boet R, Jackson S. Use of recreational drug 1,3 Dimethylamylamine (DMAA) [corrected] associated with cerebral hemorrhage. *Ann Emerg Med* 2012;60(4):431–4.
197. Schep LJ, Slaughter RJ, Vale JA, Beasley DM, Gee P. The clinical toxicology of the designer "party pills" benzylpiperazine and trifluoromethylphenylpiperazine. *C lin Toxicol (Phila)* 2011;49(3):131–41.
198. Antia U, Tingle MD, Russell BR. 'Party pill' drugs--BZP and TFMPP. *N Z Med J* 2009;122(1307):55–68. Review. Erratum in. *N Z Med J* 2010.
199. Wilkins C, Sweetsur P, Girling M. Patterns of benzylpiperazine/trifluoromethylphenylpiperazine party pill use and adverse effects in a population sample in New Zealand. *Drug Alcohol Rev* 2008;27(6):633–9.
200. Wood DM, Dargan PI, Button J, Holt DW, Ovaska H, Ramsey J, Jones AL. Collapse, reported seizure—and an unexpected pill. *Lancet* 2007;369(9571):1490.
201. Gee P, Richardson S, Woltersdorf W, Moore G. Toxic effects of BZP-based herbal party pills in humans: a prospective study in Christchurch, New Zealand. *N Z Med J* 2005;118:U1784.

1.2 HALLUCINOGENS

Daniel R. Lasoff and Binh T. Ly

1.2.1 Hallucinogens

The primary effects of hallucinogenic drugs are altered sensory perception and mood. The effects may differ by class of drug and mechanisms of action. They may also be accompanied by autonomic disturbances. Most hallucinogens do not induce physical dependence. The specific mechanisms of action are not known for many of the drugs, but there is experimental evidence that they act at adrenergic, serotoninergic, opioid, or a combination of receptors. The changes in mood and perception are probably related specifically to serotoninergic activity.[1,2] Depending on the drug, prolonged exposure or high doses may lead to depletion of serotonin and dopamine in the brain. Acute or chronic hallucinogen use may precipitate psychiatric symptoms that can be prolonged long beyond the detectable presence of the drug in the body. Chronic psychiatric impairment and memory disturbances, possibly related to damage to serotoninergic neurons in the brain, may occur.

1.2.1.1 Phenylethylamine Derivatives

1.2.1.1.1 Mescaline

Mescaline is a naturally occurring phenylethylamine derivative. Its use probably dates as far back as 5,700 years ago.[3,4] It is found in peyote cactus and can be ingested orally or intravenously. It shares the phenylethylamine structural backbone found in dopamine and epinephrine. The precise mechanism of action is unknown, but it is thought to alter the activity of serotonin, norepinephrine, and dopamine at their respective receptors.[5] The signs of intoxication usually appear within 1 hour of ingestion, peak at 4 hours, and last 8 to 14 hours. The psychic phase lasts about 6 hours.[3] There are both physiological and psychological manifestations of mescaline.

Physiological effects: These are mainly manifestations of adrenergic activation: dilated pupils, increased sweating, and elevated systolic blood pressure and temperature. Some users may experience nausea, vomiting, or dizziness, which usually resolves within an hour of consumption.[6,7] Other reported causes of fatalities include a case of Mallory–Weiss esophageal lacerations after vomiting associated with ingesting mescaline.[8] Cases of botulism have also occurred due to consumption of peyote-containing ceremonial tea that had been stored for a prolonged time.[9]

Psychological effects: These begin several hours after the ingestion. Typically, there is a feeling of euphoria, a sense of physical power, and distortion of sensation. There is enhanced color perception.[10,11] Hallucinations and agitation are common.[12] Users may also experience feelings of depersonalization, disorientation, anxiety, emotional lability, or emotional outbursts.[6] Fatalities from mescaline have been associated with traumatic injuries associated with misinterpretation of reality. There is no known physical dependence for mescaline.[10,11]

1.2.1.1.2 TMA-2 (2,4,5-Trimethoxyamphetamine)

TMA is a synthetic analogue of mescaline and amphetamine. It is more potent than mescaline but resembles mescaline in its effects.[13] This is a Schedule I drug under the Controlled Substances Act in the United States.

1.2.1.1.3 DOM/STP (4-Methyl-2, 5-Dimethoxyamphetamine)

This is another amphetamine analogue with a narrow window between desired and harmful effects. During the 1960s, it gained popularity under the street name "STP" (Serenity, Tranquility, Peace). Low doses of 2 to 3 mg cause perceptual distortion and mild sympathetic stimulation, but doses two-to-three times higher produce hallucinations and more pronounced sympathetic stimulation.[5,14]

1.2.1.1.4 PMA (para-Methoxyamphetamine)

Known on the street as "Death" or "Dr Death" after a string of fatalities, PMA is a very potent hallucinogen and central nervous system (CNS) stimulant.[15] Overdose may present with severe sympathetic stimulation, including seizures, hyperthermia, coagulopathy, and rhabdomyolysis, similar to intoxication with other amphetamines, and can also result in fatalities.[16–18] PMA is a more potent CNS stimulant than other amphetamines, and there have been reports of fatalities when PMA was substituted for methylenedioxymethamphetamine (MDMA).[18,19]

1.2.1.1.5 DOB (4-Bromo-2,5-Dimethoxyamphetamine)

DOB, otherwise called bromo-DOM, is a potent serotonin agonist phenylethylamine derivative.[20] It is long-acting, with effects starting within an hour, reaching their full strength after 3 to 4 hours, and lasting up to 18 hours.[21] The manifestations of intoxication are mood enhancement with visual distortion. There are case reports of severely intoxicated patients with hallucinations, agitation, and sympathetic stimulation.[22] DOB, when ingested in large doses, can have an ergot-like effect and cause severe generalized peripheral vasospasm, with tissue ischemia likely due to its strong serotonergic acticity.[23] Other fatalities have occurred due to cerebral edema.[24]

1.2.1.1.6 MDMA (3,4-Methylenedioxymethamphetamine)

MDMA is one of the most popular "designer drugs" today and is used recreationally by a large number of young people.[108] It is also known as "Ecstasy," "Adam," "E," "X," and "Molly."[25] It was "rediscovered" in the 1970s as an adjunct to psychotherapy, but its use has been limited by Drug Enforcement Administration (DEA) scheduling and regulation.[26,27]

Psychological effects: After ingestion of 75 to 150 mg, users experience a sense of euphoria, heightened awareness, improved sense of communication, and enhanced sexuality but also experience some impairment in the performance of psychomotor tasks.[10,28] Acute neuropsychiatric complications have been reported and include anxiety, insomnia, depression, paranoia, confusion, panic attacks, and psychosis.[29,30] Adverse effects during the 24 hours following use include lack of energy, restlessness, insomnia, lack of appetite, and difficulty concentrating.[114] Chronic effects of MDMA abuse include depression, drowsiness, anxiety, panic disorder, aggressive outbursts, psychosis, impaired decision making, and memory disturbance.[31–35] The memory disturbance and impaired cognitive function were found in chronic users who were abstinent as well as in former users as long as a year after stopping.[36–39] Although the exact mechanism of action is not known, there is some evidence from animal studies, as well as from human subjects, that MDMA can cause damage to serotoninergic neurons in the brain.[40–42] Chronic users of MDMA were found to have a lower density of serotonin (5-hydroxytryptamine, 5-HT) transporters in cortex compared with nonusers. There was a dose–response relationship associated with the extent of use.[43–45]

Physiological effects: The stimulatory effects of MDMA are apparent even in mild intoxication. Effects include elevated blood pressure and heart rate, increased thirst, dilated pupils, and hyperactivity. Recreational doses of 0.75 mg/kg of MDMA significantly increased heart rate and blood pressure.[46] Also common are nausea, vomiting, bruxism (jaw clenching, teeth grinding), hyperreflexia, muscle aches, hot flushes, and nystagmus.[47] Additional side effects reported include paresthesias, blurred vision, and motor tics. MDMA has been implicated in numerous deaths due to sudden cardiovascular collapse, dysrhythmias, and myocardial ischemia or infarct.[48–51] There are several case reports of hepatotoxicity, including hepatic failure requiring transplantation, following MDMA ingestion.[130–134] Hyponatremia, which can potentiate seizures, is another common finding, which is likely caused by increased thirst resulting in enhanced electrolyte-free water intake and potentially inappropriate vasopressin secretion.[52–55] CNS complications reported include seizures, intracranial hemorrhage, status epilepticus, heat stroke, and cerebral edema.[56–59] A specific syndrome of MDMA intoxication has been reported particularly in the setting of crowding and vigorous dancing, such as in "raves" or clubs. It includes several manifestations: hyperthermia, dehydration, seizures, rhabdomyolysis, disseminated intravascular coagulation, and acute renal failure.[30,60,61] This is thought to be the consequence of a combination of sympathomimetic effects including cutaneous vasoconstriction and extreme physical exertion in hot, poorly ventilated environments, although some features may be on the spectrum of a condition called serotonin syndrome.[141]

Reproductive/neonatal effects: A prospective study following 136 women exposed to MDMA during pregnancy found a significantly increased risk (15.4%) of congenital defects, particularly cardiovascular and musculoskeletal anomalies.[62] Heavier MDMA use by pregnant mothers was also found to predict poorer mental and motor development in infants.[63]

1.2.1.1.7 MDA (3,4-Methylenedioxyamphetamine)

MDA is an amphetamine derivative included in the category of "designer drugs" and is also a metabolite of MDMA. While in small doses it produces mild intoxication with a feeling of euphoria, large doses can cause hallucinations, agitation, and delirium.[5] It also can produce intense sympathetic stimulation with hypertension, tachycardia, seizures, and hyperthermia. Death has been reported after MDA use, usually as a result of seizures or hyperthermia.[64]

1.2.1.1.8 MDEA (3,4-Methylenedioxyethamphetamine)

Otherwise known as "Eve," MDEA is an analogue of MDMA, with effects as well as adverse events similar to those of MDMA.[65]

1.2.1.2 Lysergic Acid Diethylamide

Lysergic acid diethylamide (LSD) is a synthetic lysergamide with potent hallucinogenic properties. Its use has declined steadily due to the increased availability of other hallucinogens.[66] The main site of action of LSD is at a serotonin receptor subtype ($5\text{-HT}_{2\,\text{receptor}}$).[67] The effects of LSD, both psychological and physical, are dose related. With oral doses of 20 to 50 μg, the onset of effects is after 5 to 10 minutes, with peak effects occurring 30 to 90 minutes post ingestion. The duration of the effects may be from 8 to 12 hours, and recovery lasts between 10 and 12 hours, with normal cognition alternating with altered mood and perception. Cognitive effects are dose related, and a more moderate dose of around 75–150 μg will significantly alter the level of consciousness.[68] This dosing range can produce distortions of time and altered visual perception with very vivid color perception. Euphoria and anxiety may be experienced. There are also signs of sympathetic stimulation, with dilated pupils, tachycardia, elevated blood pressure, elevated body temperature, and facial flushing. Tremors and hyperreflexia are also common.[10,69] A "bad trip" may be experienced during LSD intoxication.

These are terrifying hallucinations that may precipitate panic attack, disorientation, delirium, or depression with suicidal ideation. A "bad trip" may occur with first-time use as well as after recurrent use. Five major categories of psychiatric adverse effects have been described: anxiety and panic, self-destructive behavior, such as attempting to jump out of the window, hallucinations, acute psychosis, and major depressive reactions.[69] Patients who have taken very high doses of LSD have presented with manifestations of intense sympathetic stimulation, including hyperthermia, coagulopathy, circulatory collapse, and respiratory arrest.[70] Another danger of LSD abuse is traffic collisions and trauma while trying to drive during acute intoxication or the recovery phase.

There may be chronic toxic effects associated with LSD abuse. Effects that have been described include:

1. Prolonged psychosis, especially among users with preexisting psychiatric conditions
2. Prolonged or intermittent major depression
3. Disruption of personality
4. Flashbacks
5. Hallucinogen Persisting Perception Disorder

The last syndrome is characterized by the recurrence of perceptual symptoms experienced while intoxicated with LSD and leading to functional impairment.[71,72] This can be manifested as abnormalities in color or visual hallucinations and distortions.

Flashbacks may occur months, and even years, after LSD use. It has been reported that 50% of users experienced flashbacks during the 5 years after their last use of LSD.[71,72] In most cases, flashbacks occur after LSD has been used more than ten times.[70] Rarely, the flashbacks may be frightening hallucinations; in extreme cases, these have been associated with homicide or suicide. Flashbacks may be triggered by stress, illness, and marijuana and alcohol use.[10,69]

1.2.1.3 Dissociative Anesthetics

1.2.1.3.1 Phencyclidine

Phencyclidine (PCP) was developed as an anesthetic and has properties similar to those of ketamine, but a high incidence of emergence reactions, including nightmares and hallucinations, limited its clinical use in anesthesia.[73] In the 1960s, PCP became a popular street drug shortly after its clinical use was abandoned. It is most commonly smoked but can also be ingested orally, snorted, or injected. PCP is also commonly used as an additive to other drugs, such as marijuana, mescaline, and LSD. The mechanism of action of PCP is complex but includes the blockade of the cationic calcium channel of the N-methyl-D-aspartate (NMDA) receptor as well as agonism of sigma opioid receptors.[74,75] This produces a dissociated state without causing respiratory depression.[76] It also inhibits the reuptake of dopamine and norepinephrine and has direct alpha-adrenergic effects. The effects of PCP are dose dependent. Smoking causes a rapid onset of effects; the half-life of PCP may range from 11 to 51 hours.[77]

Psychological effects: At low doses of 1 to 5 mg, PCP produces euphoria, relaxation, and a feeling of numbness. There may also be a feeling of altered body image and sensory distortion. At higher doses, there may be agitation, bizarre behavior, and psychosis resembling paranoid schizophrenia. The patients may alternate between agitation and a catatonic-like state. "Out of body" experiences have been described. There is also potent analgesia, which may lead to self-injury.[77,78] Patients who develop an emergence reaction may experience psychiatric effects lasting hours to weeks.[79]

Physiological effects: During mild intoxication, the commonly described sign is nystagmus, which may be horizontal, vertical, or rotary.[80] Individuals may present in a dissociative state in which they are unresponsive but their eyes remain open.[81] One of the more sensationalized effects of PCP intoxication is the individual who requires several people or police officers to restrain them due to superhuman strength.[82] Other rare effects include the development of hyperthermia, encephalopathy, rhabdomyolysis, tachycardia, and hypertension, but this may be associated with prolonged restraint.[83]

1.2.1.4 Indolealkylamines

1.2.1.4.1 Psilocybin

Psilocybin is a hallucinogen found in numerous species of "magic mushrooms." Ingested psilocybin is converted to psilocin, which is psychoactive.[84] Psilocybin and psilocin are structural analogues of serotonin and exhibit their activity at the 5-HT receptor.[85] The mushrooms exist as dried preparations, which are consumed orally. Hallucinations typically occur 1–2 hours after consumption and may be preceded by vomiting. Hallucinations typically last 2–4 hours.

Psychological effects: Psychological effects include distortions in perception of color and shapes (delusions), auditory and visual hallucinations, euphoria, increased openness, and diminished inhibition. Adverse psychological effects include anxiety, panic attacks, psychiatric breaks, and flashbacks.

Physiological effects: Common physical features include mydriasis, hyperreflexia, tachycardia, drowsiness, and vomiting.[86] While there are no cases of fatal hallucinogenic mushroom poisoning, morbidity and mortality can occur due to trauma such as jumping off buildings or out of windows.[87,88] Rare complications that have been reported include hyperthermia, seizures, and status epilepticus.[87] The use of monoamine oxidase

(MAO) inhibitors may increase the risk of adverse events and length of time of intoxication with psilocybin use.[89] MAO inhibitors are an older class of drug used to treat depression that functions by preventing the breakdown of monoamine neurotransmitters such as serotonin, epinephrine, and norepinephrine.

1.2.1.4.2 Dimethyltryptamine

Dimethyltryptamine (DMT) is a naturally occurring alkaloid found in various plants and animals with potent hallucinogenic properties. DMT shares structural similarities with serotonin and psilocybin and acts primarily at the serotonin receptor to produce hallucinations.[90] DMT can be injected, ingested, or smoked. When injected, it produces hallucinations within 90 seconds that resolve within 30 minutes.[91] Smoking has been the most common reported manner of use. One technique of oral ingestion of DMT includes consuming *ayahuasca* tea. Historically, ayahuasca is a traditional spiritual concoction used by indigenous people of northern South America. This tea is made by combining DMT with an MAO inhibitor to significantly increase the duration of action of DMT.[92]

Psychological effects: Reported psychiatric effects of DMT use include experiencing "meaningful and insightful" thoughts, "spiritual experiences," euphoria, visual hallucinations, and the sensation of a dissociated state. Adverse effects reported by users include anxiety, panic attacks, and intense hallucinations.[91,92]

Physiological effects: Users can experience vomiting, coughing, nausea, elevated blood pressure, tachycardia, and elevated temperature.[91]

1.2.1.5 Kratom

Kratom is a plant that occurs naturally in Southeast Asia and is reported to have analgesic and stimulant properties as well as potentially hallucinogenic properties. Mitragynine is an alkaloid found in kratom that has activity at opioid and serotonin receptors.[93,94] It is available in preparations as powders that can be consumed in teas and drinks or smoked, or in capsule forms. *Kratom* is typically ingested for its opioid properties, but users also report euphoria, opioid-like highs, and increased energy.[95] It has been touted as a treatment for chronic pain as well as opioid withdrawal.[96] Hallucinations are unusual and are generally not the intent of use.[97]

1.2.1.6 *Salvia divinorum*

Salvia divinorum is an herb from the mint family. It is widely marketed over the internet as a "legal hallucinogen.[98]" Salvinorin A is a potent hallucinogen present in salvia. Unlike other hallucinogens discussed in this chapter, salvinorin A has no activity on the serotonin receptor but instead acts on the kappa opioid receptor.[99] Salvia is absorbed either buccally by chewing and cheeking or through the lungs by smoking and produces a rapid onset of effects in minutes. Reported effects include vivid hallucinations, synesthesia, enhanced insight, floating sensations, out of body experiences, dissociated states, drowsiness, and anxiety.[100,101] Ingestion does not appear to be effective in producing the desired effects. Symptoms are usually short lived and do not typically last for more than 2 hours.[100,102] To date, no long-term adverse effects have been described with salvia use.[102]

REFERENCES

1. Aghajanian GK, Marek GJ. Serotonin model of schizophrenia: emerging role of glutamate mechanisms. *Brain Res Brain Res Rev* 2000;31(2–3):302–12. Review. PubMed PMID: 10719157.
2. Aghajanian GK, Marek GJ. Serotonin and hallucinogens. *Neuropsychopharmacology* 1999;21(2 Suppl):16S–23S. Review. PubMed PMID: 10432484.
3. Hollister LE, Hartman AM. Mescaline, lysergic acid diethylamide and psilocybin comparison of clinical syndromes, effects on color perception and biochemical measures. *Compr Psychiatry* 1962;3:235–42. PubMed PMID: 13908449.
4. Bruhn JG, De Smet PA, El-Seedi HR, et al. Mescaline use for 5700 years. *Lancet* 2002;359(9320):1866. PubMed PMID: 12044415.
5. Buchanan JF, Brown CR. 'Designer drugs'. A problem in clinical toxicology. *Med Toxicol Adverse Drug Exp* 1988;3(1):1–17. Review. PubMed PMID: 3285124.
6. Reynolds PC, Jindrich EJ. A mescaline associated fatality. *J Anal Toxicol* 1985;9(4):183–4. PubMed PMID: 4033076.
7. Kapadia GJ, Fayez MB. Peyote constituents: chemistry, biogenesis, and biological effects. *J Pharm Sci* 1970;59(12):1699–727. Review. PubMed PMID: 5499699.
8. Nolte KB, Zumwalt RE. Fatal peyote ingestion associated with Mallory-Weiss lacerations. *West J Med* 1999;170(6):328. PubMed PMID: 10443159; PubMed Central PMCID: PMC1305682.
9. Hashimoto H, Clyde VJ, Parko KL. Botulism from peyote. *N Engl J Med* 1998;339(3):203–4. PubMed PMID: 9669923.
10. Leikin JB, Krantz AJ, Zell-Kanter M, et al. Clinical features and management of intoxication due to hallucinogenic drugs. *Med Toxicol Adverse Drug Exp* 1989;4(5):324–50. Review. PubMed PMID: 2682130.
11. Mack RB. Marching to a different cactus: peyote (mescaline) intoxication. *N C Med J* 1986;47(3):137–8. PubMed PMID: 3457285.
12. Carstairs SD, Cantrell FL. Peyote and mescaline exposures: a 12-year review of a statewide poison center database. *Clin Toxicol (Phila)* 2010;48(4):350–3. doi: 10.3109/15563650903586745. PubMed PMID: 20170392.
13. Shulgin, AT. DMT & TMA-2. *J Psychedelic Drugs* 1976;8(2): 167–9.
14. Shulgin, AT. STP. *J Psychedelic Drugs* 1977;9(2):171–2.
15. Caldicott DG, Edwards NA, Kruys A, et al. Dancing with "death": p-methoxyamphetamine overdose and its acute management. *J Toxicol Clin Toxicol* 2003;41(2):143–54. PubMed PMID: 12733852..
16. James RA, Dinan A. Hyperpyrexia associated with fatal paramethoxyamphetamine (PMA) abuse. *Med Sci Law* 1998;38(1):83–5. PubMed PMID: 9481084.
17. Kraner JC, McCoy DJ, Evans MA, Evans LE, Sweeney BJ. Fatalities caused by the MDMA-related drug paramethoxyamphetamine (PMA). *J Anal Toxicol* 2001;25(7):645–8. PubMed PMID: 11599617.

18. Byard RW, Gilbert J, James R, Lokan RJ. Amphetamine derivative fatalities in South Australia--is "Ecstasy" the culprit? *Am J Forensic Med Pathol* 1998;19(3):261–5. PubMed PMID: 9760094.
19. Dams R, De Letter EA, Mortier KA, et al. Fatality due to combined use of the designer drugs MDMA and PMA: a distribution study. *J Anal Toxicol* 2003;27(5):318–22. PubMed PMID: 12908947.
20. Ray TS. Psychedelics and the human receptorome. *PLoS One* 2010;5(2):e9019. doi: 10.1371/journal.pone.0009019. Erratum in: *PLoS One* 2010;5(3). doi: 10.1371/annotation/e580a864-cf13-40c2-9bd9-b9687a6f0fe4. PubMed PMID: 20126400; PubMed Central PMCID: PMC2814854.
21. Shulgin, Alexander T. DOB. *J Psychoactive Drugs* 1981;13(1):99.
22. Buhrich N, Morris G, Cook G. Bromo-DMA: the Australasian hallucinogen? *Aust N Z J Psychiatry* 1983;17(3):275–9. PubMed PMID: 6580896.
23. Bowen JS, Davis GB, Kearney TE, et al. Diffuse vascular spasm associated with 4-bromo-2,5-dimethoxyamphetamine ingestion. *JAMA* 1983;249(11):1477–9. PubMed PMID: 6827726.
24. Winek CL, Collom WD, Bricker JD. A death due to 4-bromo-2,5-dimethoxyamphetamine. *Clin Toxicol* 1981;18(3):267–71. PubMed PMID: 7237958
25. Mishor Z, Ward CJ, Leuenberger D, et al. Street names for commonly encountered psychoactives. 2015.
26. Wagner MT, Mithoefer MC, Mithoefer AT, et al. Therapeutic effect of increased openness: Investigating mechanism of action in MDMA-assisted psychotherapy. *J Psychopharmacol* 2017;31(8):967–74. doi: 10.1177/0269881117711712. Epub 2017 Jun 21. PubMed PMID: 28635375; PubMed Central PMCID: PMC5544120.
27. Nutt DJ, King LA, Nichols DE. Effects of Schedule I drug laws on neuroscience research and treatment innovation. *Nat Rev Neurosci* 2013;14(8):577–85. doi: 10.1038/nrn3530. Epub 2013 Jun 12. Review. PubMed PMID: 23756634.
28. Lamers CT, Ramaekers JG, Muntjewerff ND, et al. Dissociable effects of a single dose of ecstasy (MDMA) on psychomotor skills and attentional performance. *J Psychopharmacol* 2003;17(4):379–87. PubMed PMID: 14870949.
29. Vaiva G, Boss V, Bailly D, et al. An "accidental" acute psychosis with ecstasy use. *J Psychoactive Drugs* 2001;33(1):95–8. PubMed PMID: 11333007.
30. McCann UD, Ricaurte GA. MDMA ("ecstasy") and panic disorder: induction by a single dose. *Biol Psychiatry* 1992;32(10):950–3. PubMed PMID: 1361366.
31. Wunderli MD, Vonmoos M, Fürst M, et al. Discrete memory impairments in largely pure chronic users of MDMA. *Eur Neuropsychopharmacol* 2017;27(10):987–99. doi: 10.1016/j.euroneuro.2017.08.425. Epub 2017 Aug 31. PubMed PMID: 28866005.
32. Betzler F, Viohl L, Romanczuk-Seiferth N. Decision-making in chronic ecstasy users: a systematic review. *Eur J Neurosci* 2017;45(1):34–44. doi: 10.1111/ejn.13480. Epub 2016 Dec 15. Review. PubMed PMID: 27859780.
33. Morgan MJ, McFie L, Fleetwood H, et al. Ecstasy (MDMA): are the psychological problems associated with its use reversed by prolonged abstinence? *Psychopharmacology (Berl)* 2002;159(3):294–303. Epub 2001 Oct 12. PubMed PMID: 11862362.
34. MacInnes N, Handley SL, Harding GF. Former chronic methylenedioxymethamphetamine (MDMA or ecstasy) users report mild depressive symptoms. *J Psychopharmacol* 2001;15(3):181–6. PubMed PMID: 11565625.
35. Gerra G, Zaimovic A, Ampollini R. Experimentally induced aggressive behavior in subjects with 3,4-methylenedioxy-methamphetamine ("Ecstasy") use history: psychobiological correlates. *J Subst Abuse* 2001;13(4):471–91. PubMed PMID: 11775077.
36. Ricaurte GA, McCann UD. Assessing long-term effects of MDMA (Ecstasy). *Lancet* 2001;358(9296):1831–2. PubMed PMID: 11741618.
37. Reneman L, Lavalaye J, Schmand B. Cortical serotonin transporter density and verbal memory in individuals who stopped using 3,4-methylenedioxymethamphetamine (MDMA or "ecstasy"): preliminary findings. *Arch Gen Psychiatry* 2001;58(10):901–6. PubMed PMID: 11576026.
38. Gouzoulis-Mayfrank E, Daumann J, Tuchtenhagen F, et al. Impaired cognitive performance in drug free users of recreational ecstasy (MDMA). *J Neurol Neurosurg Psychiatry* 2000;68(6):719–25. PubMed PMID: 10811694; PubMed Central PMCID: PMC1736948.
39. Parrott AC, Sisk E, Turner JJ. Psychobiological problems in heavy 'ecstasy' (MDMA) polydrug users. *Drug Alcohol Depend* 2000;60(1):105–10. PubMed PMID: 10821995.
40. Anneken JH, Collins SA, Yamamoto BK, et al. MDMA and Glutamate: Implications for Hippocampal Neurotoxicity. *Stimulants, Club and Dissociative Drugs, Hallucinogens, Steroids, Inhalants and International Aspects.* Elsevier Inc., 2016.
41. Steele TD, McCann UD, Ricaurte GA. 3,4-methylenedioxymethamphetamine (MDMA, "Ecstasy"): pharmacology and toxicology in animals and humans. *Addiction* 1994;89(5):539–51. Review. PubMed PMID: 7913850.
42. Kish SJ, Furukawa Y, Ang L, Vorce SP, Kalasinsky KS. Striatal serotonin is depleted in brain of a human MDMA (Ecstasy) user. *Neurology* 2000;55(2):294–6. PubMed PMID: 10908909
43. Bisagno V, Cadet JL. "Methamphetamine and MDMA neurotoxicity: biochemical and molecular mechanisms." *Handbook of Neurotoxicity.* Springer, New York, 2014;347–63.
44. McCann UD, Szabo Z, Scheffel U, Dannals RF, Ricaurte GA. Positron emission tomographic evidence of toxic effect of MDMA ("Ecstasy") on brain serotonin neurons in human beings. *Lancet* 1998;352(9138):1433–7. PubMed PMID: 9807990.
45. Reneman L, Booij J, de Bruin K, et al. Effects of dose, sex, and long-term abstention from use on toxic effects of MDMA (ecstasy) on brain serotonin neurons. *Lancet* 2001;358(9296):1864–9. PubMed PMID: 11741626.
46. Kirkpatrick MG, Lee R, Wardle MC, Jacob S, de Wit H. Effects of MDMA and Intranasal oxytocin on social and emotional processing. *Neuropsychopharmacology* 2014;39(7):1654–63. doi: 10.1038/npp.2014.12. Epub 2014 Jan 22. PubMed PMID: 24448644; PubMed Central PMCID: PMC4023138.
47. Dinis-Oliveira RJ, Caldas I, Carvalho F, et al. Bruxism after 3,4-methylenedioxymethamphetamine (ecstasy) abuse. *Clin Toxicol (Phila)* 2010;48(8):863–4. doi: 10.3109/15563650.2010.489903. Epub 2010 Jun 1. PubMed PMID: 20515398.
48. Cerit L, Duygu H. Myocardial bridging and sudden death. *Int J Cardiol* 2017;229:11. doi: 10.1016/j.ijcard.2016.11.308. Epub 2016 Dec 1. PubMed PMID: 27923515.
49. Henry JA, Jeffreys KJ, Dawling S. Toxicity and deaths from 3,4-methylenedioxymethamphetamine ("ecstasy"). *Lancet* 1992;340(8816):384–7. PubMed PMID: 1353554.

50. McCann UD, Slate SO, Ricaurte GA. Adverse reactions with 3,4-methylenedioxymethamphetamine (MDMA; 'ecstasy'). *Drug Saf* 1996;15(2):107–15. Review. PubMed PMID: 8884162.
51. Henry JA. Ecstasy and the dance of death. *BMJ* 1992;305(6844):5–6. PubMed PMID: 1353390; PubMed Central PMCID: PMC1882471.
52. Maxwell DL, Polkey MI, Henry JA. Hyponatraemia and catatonic stupor after taking "ecstasy". *BMJ* 1993;307(6916):1399. PubMed PMID: 7903884; PubMed Central PMCID: PMC1679614.
53. Baggott MJ, Garrison KJ, Coyle JR, et al. MDMA impairs response to water intake in healthy volunteers. *Adv Pharmacol Sci* 2016;2016:2175896. doi: 10.1155/2016/2175896. Epub 2016 Jun 14. PubMed PMID: 27403159; PubMed Central PMCID: PMC4923534.
54. Wilkins B. Cerebral oedema after MDMA ("ecstasy") and unrestricted water intake. Hyponatraemia must be treated with low water input. *BMJ* 1996;313(7058):689–90; author reply 690. PubMed PMID: 8811776; PubMed Central PMCID: PMC2351978.
55. Henry JA, Fallon JK, Kicman AT, et al. Low-dose MDMA ("ecstasy") induces vasopressin secretion. *Lancet* 1998;351(9118):1784. PubMed PMID: 9635954.
56. Kahn DE, Ferraro N, Benveniste RJ. 3 cases of primary intracranial hemorrhage associated with "Molly", a purified form of 3,4-methylenedioxymethamphetamine (MDMA). *J Neurol Sci* 2012;323(1–2):257–60. doi: 10.1016/j.jns.2012.08.031. Epub 2012 Sep 19. PubMed PMID: 22998806.
57. Cock HR. Drug-induced status epilepticus. *Epilepsy Behav* 2015;49:76–82. doi: 10.1016/j.yebeh.2015.04.034. Epub 2015 Jul 22. Review. PubMed PMID: 26210064.
58. Armenian P, Mamantov TM, Tsutaoka BT. Multiple MDMA (Ecstasy) overdoses at a rave event: a case series. *J Intensive Care Med* 2013;28(4):252–8. doi: 10.1177/0885066612445982. Epub 2012 May 28. PubMed PMID: 22640978.
59. Campbell GA, Rosner MH. The agony of ecstasy: MDMA (3,4-methylenedioxymethamphetamine) and the kidney. *Clin J Am Soc Nephrol* 2008;3(6):1852–60. doi: 10.2215/CJN.02080508. Epub 2008 Aug 6. Review. PubMed PMID: 18684895.
60. Vanden Eede H, Montenij LJ, Touw DJ, et al. Rhabdomyolysis in MDMA intoxication: a rapid and underestimated killer. "Clean" Ecstasy, a safe party drug? *J Emerg Med* 2012;42(6):655–8. doi: 10.1016/j.jemermed.2009.04.057. Epub 2009 Jun 4. PubMed PMID: 19500935.
61. Williams H, Dratcu L, Taylor R, et al. "Saturday night fever": ecstasy related problems in a London accident and emergency department. *J Accid Emerg Med* 1998;15(5):322–6. PubMed PMID: 9785160; PubMed Central PMCID: PMC1343173.
62. McElhatton PR, Bateman DN, Evans C, et al. Congenital anomalies after prenatal ecstasy exposure. *Lancet* 1999;354(9188):1441–2. PubMed PMID: 10543673.
63. Singer LT, Moore DG, Min MO, et al. One-year outcomes of prenatal exposure to MDMA and other recreational drugs. *Pediatrics* 2012;130(3):407–13. doi: 10.1542/peds.2012-0666. Epub 2012 Aug 20. PubMed PMID: 22908109; PubMed Central PMCID: PMC3428761.
64. Simpson DL, Rumack BH. Methylenedioxyamphetamine. Clinical description of overdose, death, and review of pharmacology. *Arch Intern Med* 1981;141(11):1507–9. PubMed PMID: 7283563.
65. Tehan B, Hardern R, Bodenham A. Hyperthermia associated with 3,4-methylenedioxyethamphetamine ('Eve'). *Anaesthesia* 1993;48(6):507–10. Review. PubMed PMID: 8322992.
66. Johnston LD, O'Malley PM, Bachman JG, et al. Monitoring the future national results on adolescent drug use: Overview of key findings, 2012.
67. Jacobs BL. How Hallucinogenic drugs work: hallucinogenic drugs appear to exert their effects by acting on a specific type of serotonin receptor in the brain. *Am Sci* 1987;75(4):386–92.
68. Passie T, Halpern JH, Stichtenoth DO, Emrich HM, Hintzen A. The pharmacology of lysergic acid diethylamide: a review. *CNS Neurosci Ther* 2008;14(4):295–314. doi: 10.1111/j.1755-5949.2008.00059.x. Review. PubMed PMID: 19040555.
69. Schwartz RH. LSD. Its rise, fall, and renewed popularity among high school students. *Pediatr Clin North Am* 1995;42(2):403–13. Review. PubMed PMID: 7724266.
70. Abraham HD, Aldridge AM. Adverse consequences of lysergic acid diethylamide. *Addiction* 1993;88(10):1327–34. Review. PubMed PMID: 8251869.
71. American Psychiatriation Association, ed: "Diagnostic and Statistical Manual of Mental Disorders". 5th ed. Washington, DC: American Psychiatrtic association; 2013.
72. Halpern JH, Pope HG Jr. Hallucinogen persisting perception disorder: what do we know after 50 years? *Drug Alcohol Depend* 2003;69(2):109–19. Review. PubMed PMID: 12609692.
73. Bey T, Patel A. Phencyclidine intoxication and adverse effects: a clinical and pharmacological review of an illicit drug. *Cal J Emerg Med* 2007;8(1):9–14. PubMed PMID: 20440387; PubMed Central PMCID: PMC2859735.
74. Contreras PC, Monahan JB, Lanthorn TH, et al. Phencyclidine. Physiological actions, interactions with excitatory amino acids and endogenous ligands. *Mol Neurobiol* 1987;1(3):191–211. Review. PubMed PMID: 2855791.
75. Sonders MS, Keana JF, Weber E. Phencyclidine and psychotomimetic sigma opiates: recent insights into their biochemical and physiological sites of action. *Trends Neurosci* 1988;11(1):37–40. Review. PubMed PMID: 2469154.
76. Weiner AL, Vieira L, McKay CA, Bayer MJ. Ketamine abusers presenting to the emergency department: a case series. *J Emerg Med* 2000;18(4):447–51. PubMed PMID: 10802423.
77. Brust JC. Other agents. Phencyclidine, marijuana, hallucinogens, inhalants, and anticholinergics. *Neurol Clin* 1993;11(3):555–61. Review. PubMed PMID: 8377742.
78. McCarron MM, Schulze BW, Thompson GA. Acute phencyclidine intoxication: clinical patterns, complications, and treatment. *Ann Emerg Med* 1981;10(6):290–7. PubMed PMID: 7235337.
79. Ly BT, Williams SR. *Hallucinogens. Rosen's Emergency Medicine: Concepts and Clinical Practice.* 8th ed. Philadelphia, PA: Elsevier Mosby. 2014, 2015–2023.
80. Erickson TB, Thompson TM, Lu JJ. The approach to the patient with an unknown overdose. *Emerg Med Clin North Am* 2007;25(2):249–81; abstract vii. Review. PubMed PMID: 17482020.
81. Muetzelfeldt L, Kamboj SK, Rees H. Journey through the K-hole: phenomenological aspects of ketamine use. *Drug Alcohol Depend* 2008;95(3):219–29. doi: 10.1016/j.drugalcdep.2008.01.024. Epub 2008 Mar 19. PubMed PMID: 18355990.

82. Morris H, Wallach J. From PCP to MXE: a comprehensive review of the non-medical use of dissociative drugs. *Drug Test Anal* 2014;6(7–8):614–32. doi: 10.1002/dta.1620. Epub 2014 Mar 26. Review. PubMed PMID: 24678061.
83. Richards JR. Rhabdomyolysis and drugs of abuse. *J Emerg Med* 2000;19(1):51–6. PubMed PMID: 10863119.
84. Lindenblatt H, Krämer E, Holzmann-Erens P, Gouzoulis-Mayfrank E, Kovar KA. Quantitation of psilocin in human plasma by high-performance liquid chromatography and electrochemical detection: comparison of liquid-liquid extraction with automated on-line solid-phase extraction. *J Chromatogr B Biomed Sci Appl* 1998;709(2):255–63. PubMed PMID: 9657222.
85. Aghajanian GK, Marek GJ. Serotonin and hallucinogens. *Neuropsychopharmacology* 21(Suppl, 2):16S–23S.
86. Peden NR, Bissett AF, Macaulay KE, Crooks J, Pelosi AJ. Clinical toxicology of "magic mushroom" ingestion. *Postgrad Med J* 1981;57(671):543–5. PubMed PMID: 7199140; PubMed Central PMCID: PMC2426147.
87. van Amsterdam J, Opperhuizen A, van den Brink W. Harm potential of magic mushroom use: a review. *Regul Toxicol Pharmacol* 2011;59(3):423–9. doi: 10.1016/j.yrtph.2011.01.006. Epub 2011 Jan 21. Review. PubMed PMID: 21256914.
88. Asselborn G, Wennig R, Yegles M. Tragic flying attempt under the influence of "magic mushrooms". *Probl Forensic Sci* 2000;42:41–6.
89. McDonald A. Mushrooms and madness. Hallucinogenic mushrooms and some psychopharmacological implications. *Can J Psychiatry* 1980;25(7):586–94. Review. PubMed PMID: 6777029.
90. Smith RL, Canton H, Barrett RJ, Sanders-Bush E. Agonist properties of N,N-dimethyltryptamine at serotonin 5-HT2A and 5-HT2C receptors. *Pharmacol Biochem Behav* 1998;61(3):323–30. PubMed PMID: 9768567.
91. Strassman RJ, Qualls CR, Uhlenhuth EH, Kellner R. Dose-response study of N,N-dimethyltryptamine in humans. II. Subjective effects and preliminary results of a new rating scale. *Arch Gen Psychiatry* 1994;51(2):98–108. PubMed PMID: 8297217.
92. Cakic V, Potkonyak J, Marshall A. Dimethyltryptamine (DMT): subjective effects and patterns of use among Australian recreational users. *Drug Alcohol Depend* 2010;111(1–2):30–7. doi: 10.1016/j.drugalcdep.2010.03.015. Epub 2010 May 31. PubMed PMID: 20570058.
93. Ward J, Rosenbaum C, Hernon C, et al. Herbal medicines for the management of opioid addiction: safe and effective alternatives to conventional pharmacotherapy? *CNS Drugs* 2011;25(12):999–1007. doi: 10.2165/11596830-000000000-00000. Review. PubMed PMID: 22133323.
94. Warner ML, Kaufman NC, Grundmann O. The pharmacology and toxicology of kratom: from traditional herb to drug of abuse. *Int J Legal Med* 2016;130(1):127–38. doi: 10.1007/s00414-015-1279-y. Epub 2015 Oct 28. Review. PubMed PMID: 26511390.
95. Hassan Z, Muzaimi M, Navaratnam V. From Kratom to mitragynine and its derivatives: physiological and behavioural effects related to use, abuse, and addiction. *Neurosci Biobehav Rev* 2013;37(2):138–51. doi: 10.1016/j.neubiorev.2012.11.012. Epub 2012 Dec 1. Review. PubMed PMID: 23206666.
96. Boyer EW, Babu KM, Adkins JE, et al. Self-treatment of opioid withdrawal using kratom (Mitragynia speciosa korth). *Addiction* 2008;103(6):1048–50. doi: 10.1111/j.1360-0443.2008.02209.x. PubMed PMID: 18482427; PubMed Central PMCID: PMC3670991.
97. Forrester MB. Kratom exposures reported to Texas poison centers. *J Addict Dis* 2013;32(4):396–400. doi: 10.1080/10550887.2013.854153. PubMed PMID: 24325774.
98. Dennehy CE, Tsourounis C, Miller AE. Evaluation of herbal dietary supplements marketed on the internet for recreational use. *Ann Pharmacother* 2005;39(10):1634–9. Epub 2005 Sep 13. PubMed PMID: 16159994.
99. Sheffler DJ, Roth BL. Salvinorin A: the "magic mint" hallucinogen finds a molecular target in the kappa opioid receptor. *Trends Pharmacol Sci* 2003;24(3):107–9. Review. PubMed PMID: 12628350.
100. Siebert DJ. Salvia divinorum and salvinorin A: new pharmacologic findings. *J Ethnopharmacol* 1994;43(1):53–6. PubMed PMID: 7526076.
101. Baggott MJ, Erowid E, Erowid F, Galloway GP, Mendelson J. Use patterns and self-reported effects of Salvia divinorum: an internet-based survey. *Drug Alcohol Depend* 2010;111(3):250–6. doi: 10.1016/j.drugalcdep.2010.05.003. PubMed PMID: 20627425.
102. Babu KM, McCurdy CR, Boyer EW. Opioid receptors and legal highs: Salvia divinorum and Kratom. *Clin Toxicol (Phila)* 2008;46(2):146–52. doi: 10.1080/15563650701241795. Review. PubMed PMID: 18259963.

1.3 CANNABINOIDS

Christie Sun and Binh T. Ly

1.3.1 Natural

Marijuana refers to a mixture of flowers and dried leaves from the *Cannabis sativa* plant. Originally cultivated as a source of fibers, it has had historic therapeutic use as well as more recent recreational use. Historically used for its therapeutic properties, it is a common recreational drug. The major cannabinoids include delta-9-tetrahydrocannabinol (THC), cannabinol, and cannabidiol, though THC is thought to be the major contributor to the psychoactive effects of cannabis. There is a great variability in the amount of THC in different plants, and thus, in different batches of marijuana. For example, hashish oil, the pressed sap of the *Cannabis* plant, can contain up to 50 times the amount of THC compared with an equal weight of marijuana.

Cannabinoid (CB) receptors are linked to G proteins that inhibit adenylate cyclase. THC is thought to exert its effects through binding to CB_1 receptors. Classically, CB_1 receptors were thought to be more centrally located and responsible for the psychogenic effect, while CB_2 receptors were peripherally located and though to be related to immune response. More recent research has identified CB_2 in the brain, though the effects of marijuana are unclear.[1] Endogenous cannabinoids, including anandamide, 2-arachidonylglycerol, 2-arachidonyl glyceryl ether, and N-arachidonoyl dopamine, have been identified, but their rapid hydrolysis *in vivo* likely limits their effects.[2–4] The endogenous cannabinoids produce effects similar to those of THC when administered to animals. Their physiological functions on CB receptors are not yet fully understood but are thought to involve cognition regulation, memory, nociception, or immune response.

Today, marijuana is one of the most commonly ingested illicit drugs in the United States.[5–7] The pharmacokinetics of marijuana is highly variable. Marijuana is usually inhaled; the onset of action is within 3–10 minutes, and the effects last up to 2 to 3 hours.[8] However, during the past 20 years, improved cultivation techniques have resulted in greatly increased potency of cannabis products. Ingestion of cannabis usually manifests symptoms within 1–3 hours, but this is generally less predictable than with the inhaled route. The bioavailability of inhaled marijuana is 10% to 35%, while that of ingested marijuana is 5% to 20%. After absorption, cannabinoids undergo hydroxylation and carboxylation; then, THC is almost completely metabolized by CYP2C9 and CYP 3A4 ultimately to 11-nor-delta-9-THC carboxylic acid, which is the component targeted for detection on most qualitative urine drugs of abuse screens. Unfortunately, with chronic users, this substance may be detected and result in a positive qualitative screen for marijuana even weeks following a period of abstinence.[9] Therefore, a positive qualitative marijuana screen alone cannot be used as evidence to argue acute intoxication.

Acute effects of marijuana include relaxation and sometimes euphoria, and also perceptual changes, such as enhanced vividness of colors, music, emotions, and increased appetite.[4,10] There may be a feeling of depersonalization. These effects may last for hours depending on the dose. There is impairment of concentration, psychomotor performance, and problem solving, which can be variable, depending on tolerance as well as strain of cannabis. While studies that examine the effect of marijuana are heterogeneous, in one systematic review, there was an increased odds ratio of motor vehicle collisions in those under the influence of cannabis compared with those who were unimpaired.[11] High doses of THC may cause hallucinations, anxiety, panic, and psychosis.[8,12,13] These effects may last for several days. Physical effects include impairment of balance, conjunctival infection, increased heart rate, orthostatic hypotension, peripheral vasoconstriction with cold extremities, dry mouth, and increased appetite.[4,10] There are reports of intravenously injected marijuana extract, which results in rapid onset of nausea, vomiting, fever, and diarrhea and is followed by hypotension, acute renal failure, thrombocytopenia, and rhabdomyolysis.[14] With recreational marijuana being legalized in more and more states within the United States, a *per se* standard for a charge of driving under the influence of drug is being considered, similar to the 0.08% standard that has been adopted for ethanol in every state. This *per se* standard for marijuana intoxication will likely include the quantitative analysis of THC concentrations, not just the carboxylic acid metabolite.[15]

Chronic use of marijuana can cause THC deposition in fatty tissues. Chronic users have also been reported to experience an amotivation syndrome, manifesting underachievement, apathy, lack of energy, and loss of motivation persisting for days or longer.[12] Chronic and heavy users of marijuana exhibit impaired performance on tests of memory and attention even after 19hours abstinence.[16–19] The impaired performance was significantly correlated with the duration of cannabis use.[16] However, it is not clear whether there is any permanent neurological damage, a withdrawal effect from the drug, or whether the impairment is due to prolonged release of cannabis from tissues.[18,19]

Chronic use of marijuana may affect the hypothalamic-pituitary-adrenal axis, altering hormone activity and causing impotence in men and menstrual irregularities in women.[20] Decreased birth weights were found after maternal cannabis use during pregnancy, but there was no association with birth defects.[10,21] There is a suggestion that *in utero* exposure to marijuana led to lower verbal and memory scores on testing between ages 4 and 9.[22] Chronic smokers of marijuana are at risk for chronic obstructive lung disease, and marijuana may be associated with the development of respiratory tract carcinoma and head and neck cancer in young adults.[23–29] There are also reports of spontaneous pneumothorax in daily marijuana smokers, although the patients smoked tobacco as well. The mechanism is sustained Valsalva maneuver during forced inhalation.[30]

Chronic cannabis use has been shown to lead to the development of tolerance and dependence, and withdrawal syndrome has been demonstrated. Based on rat studies, this may be related to a down-regulation of CB1 receptor density.[31] About 8% to 10% of cannabis users will develop dependence, but the amount and frequency of use required to develop dependence is not well established.[4,32–35] Although the time of onset and duration are not well qualified, cannabis withdrawal syndrome is characterized by restlessness, anxiety, insomnia, anorexia, muscle tremors, and craving for marijuana.[4,36,37]

1.3.2 Synthetic

Synthetic cannabinoids (SCs) are cannabinoid receptor agonists that have been developed in recent decades. Initial products were semisynthetic compounds that were structurally similar to THC with variable cannabinoid receptor binding affinity. More recent synthetic compounds do not necessarily retain this structural similarity but do bind CB_1 receptors more avidly than THC. SC incense herbal blends have gained popularity, particularly among adolescents, increasing the incidence of exposure and leading to the selection of various SCs for scheduling by the Drug Enforcement Administration. However, laboratories may continually alter these substances, making detection difficult.

SCs are almost uniformly CB_1 receptor agonists but can possess variable agonist and antagonist properties within the endocannabinoid receptor system. It is postulated that because of their greater affinity for CB_1 receptors and the variability of their receptor activity, their clinical effects can be varied and unpredictable. Additionally, inconsistent dosing, potential for adulteration, and active metabolites make it similarly difficult to determine the clinical course and effects. Local outbreaks of similar signs and symptoms can sometimes be linked to a single offending agent but typically require concerted efforts of law enforcement and public health officials as well as laboratory testing.[38]

A wide range of clinical findings has been described in the acute use of SCs. Cohort studies describe heterogeneous clinical outcomes, including tachycardia as well as bradycardia, hypotension, rhabdomyolysis, hyperthermia, psychosis, and delirium.[39,40] There are also reports of myocardial ischemia, acute kidney failure, seizures, and death associated with SCs. However, the effects of chronic SC use are not yet well described.

1.3.3 Treatment

Treatment of both natural and synthetic cannabinoid toxicity is generally supportive. Decontamination is not generally used for oral ingestions, particularly in the setting of altered mental status, which may increase risk of aspiration to the patient. The majority of cases that require treatment appear to be related to SC use, though agitation or transient psychosis can manifest with natural cannabis use. Though a wide range of treatments have been reported to be used, commonly used pharmacological agents include benzodiazepines and antipsychotics. Note that some SC patients require a more intensive level of care, including vasopressors or mechanical ventilation. Co-ingestions are common with SC use and require identification and treatment as needed. There are no specific antidotes of either cannabis or SC toxicity.

Cannabinoid hyperemesis syndrome has also been described in chronic marijuana users. It is a cyclic vomiting syndrome usually associated with regular cannabis use. The syndrome is typically associated with relief of symptoms from bathing or showering in hot water and topical application of capsaicin. While its pathophysiology is not well understood, it is thought to be related to the agonism of CB_1 receptors as well as activation of a transient receptor potential vanilloid 1 (TRPV) receptor, which interacts with the cannabinoid system.[41]

REFERENCES

1. Seely KA, Prather PI, James LP, Moran JH. Marijuana-based drugs: innovative therapeutics or designer drugs of abuse? *Mol Interv* 2011;11:36–51.
2. Martin BR, Mechoulam R, Razdan RK. Discovery and characterization of endogenous cannabinoids. *Life Sci* 1999;65(6–7):573–95.
3. Ameri A. The effects of cannabinoids on the brain. *Prog Neurobiol* 1999;58(4):315–48.
4. Ashton CH. Pharmacology and effects of cannabis: a brief review. *Br J Psychiatry* 2001;178:101–6.
5. Gruber AJ, Pope HG, Jr. Marijuana use among adolescents. *Pediatr Clin North Am* 2002;49(2):389–413.
6. Gledhill Hoyt J, Lee H, Strote J, Wechsler H. Increased use of marijuana and other illicit drugs at US colleges in the 1990s: results of three national surveys. *Addiction* 2000;95(11):1655–67.
7. Harris D, Jones RT, Shank R, Nath R, Fernandez E, Goldstein K, Mendelson J. Self-reported marijuana effects and characteristics of 100 San Francisco medical marijuana club members. *J Addict Dis* 2000;19(3):89–103.
8. Brust JC. Other agents. Phencyclidine, marijuana, hallucinogens, inhalants, and anticholinergics. *Neurol Clin* 1993;11(3):555–61.
9. Ellis GM, Jr, Mann MA, Judson BA, Schramm NT, Tashchian A. Excretion patterns of cannabinoid metabolites after last use in a group of chronic users. *Clin Pharmacol Ther* 1985;38(5):572–8.
10. Hall W, Solowij N. Adverse effects of cannabis. *Lancet* 1998;352(9140):1611–6.
11. Ashbridge M, Hayden JA, Cartwright JL. Acute cannabis consumption and motor vehicle collision risk: systematic review of observational studies and meta-analysis. *BMJ* 2012;344:1–9.
12. Johns A. Psychiatric effects of cannabis. *Br J Psychiatry* 2001;178:116–22.
13. Nunez LA, Gurpegui M. Cannabis-induced psychosis: a cross-sectional comparison with acute schizophrenia. *Acta Psychiatr Scand* 2002;105(3):173–8.
14. Farber SJ, Huertas VE. Intravenously injected marijuana syndrome. *Arch Int Med* 1976;136:337–9.
15. Wong K, Brady JE, Li G. Establishing legal limits for driving under the influence of marijuana. *Inj Epidemiol* 2014;1(1):26.

16. Solowij N, Stephens RS, Roffman RA, Babor T, Kadden R, Miller M, et al. Cognitive functioning of long-term heavy cannabis users seeking treatment. *JAMA* 2002;287(9):1123–31.
17. Pope HG, Jr, Yurgelun Todd D. The residual cognitive effects of heavy marijuana use in college students. *JAMA* 1996;275(7):521–7.
18. Pope HG, Jr, Gruber AJ, Hudson JI, Huestis MA, Yurgelun Todd D. Neuropsychological performance in long-term cannabis users. *Arch Gen Psychiatry* 2001;58(10):909–15.
19. Pope HG, Jr. Cannabis, cognition, and residual confounding. *JAMA* 2002;287(9):1172–4.
20. Hollister LE. Health aspects of cannabis. *Pharmacol Rev* 1986;38(1):1–20.
21. Fergusson DM, Horwood LJ, Northstone K. Maternal use of cannabis and pregnancy outcome. *BJOG* 2002;109(1):21–7.
22. Fried PA, Smith AM. A literature review of the consequences of prenatal marihuana exposure. An emerging theme of a deficiency in aspects of executive function. *Neurotoxicol Teratol* 2001;23(1):1–11.
23. Tashkin DP. Airway effects of marijuana, cocaine, and other inhaled illicit agents. *Curr Opin Pulm Med* 2001;7(2):43–61.
24. Baldwin GC, Tashkin DP, Buckley DM, Park AN, Dubinett SM, Roth MD. Marijuana and cocaine impair alveolar macrophage function and cytokine production. *Am J Respir Crit Care Med* 1997;156(5):1606–13.
25. Taylor FMd. Marijuana as a potential respiratory tract carcinogen: a retrospective analysis of a community hospital population. *South Med J* 1988;81(10):1213–6.
26. Wu TC, Tashkin DP, Djahed B, Rose JE. Pulmonary hazards of smoking marijuana as compared with tobacco. *N Engl J Med* 1988;318(6):347–51.
27. Taylor DR, Poulton R, Moffitt TE, Ramankutty P, Sears MR. The respiratory effects of cannabis dependence in young adults. *Addiction* 2000;95(11):1669–77.
28. Van Hoozen BE, Cross CE. Marijuana. Respiratory tract effects. *Clin Rev Allergy Immunol* 1997;15(3):243–69.
29. Zhang ZF, Morgenstern H, Spitz MR, Tashkin DP, Yu GP, Marshall JR, et al. Marijuana use and increased risk of squamous cell carcinoma of the head and neck. *Cancer Epidemiol Biomarkers Prev* 1999;8(12):1071–8.
30. Feldman AL, Sullivan JT, Passero MA, Lewis DC. Pneumothorax in polysubstance-abusing marijuana and tobacco smokers: three cases. *J Subst Abuse* 1993;5(2):183–6.
31. Lichtman AH, Martin BR. Marijuana withdrawal syndrome in the animal model. *J Clin Pharmacol* 2002;42:20S–27S.
32. von Sydow K, Lieb R, Pfister H, Hofler M, Sonntag H, Wittchen HU. The natural course of cannabis use, abuse and dependence over four years: a longitudinal community study of adolescents and young adults. *Drug Alcohol Depend* 2001;64(3):347–61.
33. Swift W, Hall W, Teesson M. Characteristics of DSM-IV and ICD-10 cannabis dependence among Australian adults: results from the National Survey of Mental Health and Wellbeing. *Drug Alcohol Depend* 2001;63(2):147–53.
34. Rosenberg MF, Anthony JC. Early clinical manifestations of cannabis dependence in a community sample. *Drug Alcohol Depend* 2001;64(2):123–31.
35. Coffey C, Carlin JB, Degenhardt L, Lynskey M, Sanci L, Patton GC. Cannabis dependence in young adults: an Australian population study. *Addiction* 2002;97(2):187–94.
36. Budney AJ, Hughes JR, Moore BA, Novy PL. Marijuana abstinence effects in marijuana smokers maintained in their home environment. *Arch Gen Psychiatry* 2001;58(10):917–24.
37. Kouri EM, Pope HG, Jr. Abstinence symptoms during withdrawal from chronic marijuana use. *Exp Clin Psychopharmacol* 2000;8(4):483–92.
38. Schwartz MD, Trecki J, Edison LA, et al. A common source outbreak of severe delirium associated with exposure to the novel synthetic cannabinoid ADB-PINACA. *JEM* 2015;48(5):573–80.
39. Monte AA, Calello DP, Gerona RR, et al. Characteristics and treatment of patients with clinical illness due to synthetic cannabinoid inhalation reported by medical toxicologists: a ToxIC database study. *J Med Tox* 2017;13:146–52.
40. Monte AA, Bronstein AC, Cao DJ, et al. An outbreak of exposure to a novel synthetic cannabinoid. *N Engl J Med* 2014;370(4):389–90.
41. Sorensen CJ, DeSanto K, Borgelt L, et al. Cannabinoid hyperemesis syndrome: diagnosis, pathophysiology, and treatment – a systematic review. *J Med Tox* 2017;13(1):71–87.

1.4 OPIOIDS

Cynthia Koh and Binh T. Ly

Opioids have been used since ancient times, but today, they have become central in clinical use for pain management, with secondary use as cough suppressants and antidiarrheal agents. Unfortunately, their euphoric effects on mood often lead to abuse, which is then further encouraged by physical and psychological dependence. Opioids are a diverse group of drugs, produced both synthetically (*e.g.*, methadone, fentanyl), naturally as derivatives of opium (*e.g.*, morphine, heroin, codeine), and even endogenously (*e.g.*, enkephalins, endorphins, dynorphins).

Irrespective of their origin, opioids all act to stimulate several subtypes of opiate receptors (mu, delta, and kappa), which differ in their affinity to each opioid and also in their downstream effects. To add further complexity, opiate receptors are present in differing concentrations in different regions of the nervous system. For example, receptors involved in analgesia are located in the periaqueductal gray matter, while receptors believed to be responsible for reinforcing effects are in the ventral tegmental area and the nucleus accumbens. There are also opiate receptors in the locus ceruleus, an important region in the control of autonomic activity that is suppressed in the presence of opioid agonism; in opioid withdrawal, there is therefore an increase in neuronal firing in the locus ceruleus, resulting in the autonomic hyperactivity characteristic of opioid withdrawal. Tolerance develops to many of the opioid effects, but differentially to different effects.[1,2]

In general, opioids cause analgesia and sedation, respiratory depression, and slowed gastrointestinal transit. Severe intoxication results in coma and respiratory depression, which may progress to apnea and death.[3] Even though different opioid drugs have similar effects, cross-tolerance between drugs is not complete, a phenomenon explained by the discovery of subtypes of mu and delta receptors with differential binding of opioid agonists.[4–6]

Regardless, the adverse effects of opioids are particularly worrisome in the face of their increasing use, with prescriptions of opioids in the United States increasing 700% between 1997 and 2007.[7] Perhaps unsurprisingly, the National Poison Data System's 2015 report revealed more than 685,000 exposures to opioids, leading to more than 18,500 admissions to health care facilities.[8] From 2002 to 2013, the rate of opioid overdoses quadrupled.[9] This surge in opioid prescriptions and subsequent heroin addiction has led to the declaration in October 2017 that this opioid epidemic is a national public health emergency in the United States.

1.4.1 Opiate Effects

1.4.1.1 Analgesic Effects

Mu-opioid receptors (mu_1) play a major role in analgesia, which is mediated through central, spinal, and peripheral mechanisms. Analgesia is dose dependent, and in high doses, opioids produce anesthesia. Tolerance to analgesic effects develops less rapidly compared with tolerance to mood or respiratory effects.[1]

1.4.1.2 Mental Effects

Mood: Opioid drugs have reinforcing properties, possibly mediated through activation of dopaminergic neurons in the ventral tegmental area and nucleus accumbens. Usually, the effect on the mood is relaxation and euphoria, although patients who take opiates for pain relief more often report dysphoria after taking the drug. Tolerance to euphoria-inducing effects develops rapidly.

Sedation: Sedation is dose dependent and is often accompanied by stereotypic dreaming.[1] Tolerance develops rapidly. Sedation is a typical first sign of opioid intoxication, and respiratory depression does not occur unless the patient is sedated.

1.4.1.3 Gastrointestinal Effects

Nausea and vomiting: Nausea and vomiting are prominent side effects of opiates, resulting from their actions on the chemoreceptor trigger zone in the medulla. However, tolerance usually develops to these effects. Different opiates have different likelihood for causing nausea.

Constipation: Opioid drugs decrease gastrointestinal motility and peristalsis, acting in the spinal cord and gastrointestinal tract and thus causing constipation. Tolerance does not develop to this effect, so constipation persists even in chronic users, a property that makes opioids useful for symptomatic treatment of diarrhea.[10]

1.4.1.4 Respiratory Effects

Respiratory depression: Dose-dependent respiratory depression is the most serious adverse effect of opioids and almost always the cause of death from overdose, often occurring within minutes of an intravenous dose. Tolerance to respiratory depression develops but is lost rapidly after abstinence. The mechanism is through stimulation of the mu_2-receptor in respiratory centers in the brain stem.[11] Opioids are medically used for the relief of dyspnea in terminally ill patients with cancer; this effect may be also mediated by opioid receptors in the bronchioles and alveolar walls.[3]

Pulmonary edema: Non-cardiogenic pulmonary edema occurs with many opioid drugs. The precise mechanisms are unknown but probably involve hypoperfusion with tissue injury and cytokine-induced pulmonary capillary endothelial injury. Pulmonary edema is particularly common with heroin intoxication, even in the absence of naloxone administration, which was previously implicated in this entity.[7,12]

Cough suppression: Opioids may suppress the coughing reflex by acting in the medulla. The prescribed doses for this indication are usually lower than for analgesia.

1.4.1.5 Other Effects

Pupillary constriction: Miosis is very consistently present in opioid intoxication unless anoxic brain damage is present. Miosis may also not be observed with meperidine intoxication.

Pruritus: Pruritus is very common in patients receiving opioids as well as in addicts. It is caused by histamine release mediated by the mu receptors.[13]

Urinary retention: This effect is mediated through spinal cord opiate receptors.[14]

Individual narcotic agents have specific effects, which are discussed later.

Convulsions: Convulsions have also been reported with both meperidine and tramadol intoxications.

1.4.2 Specific Opioid Agents

Morphine: Available by intravenous, subcutaneous, oral, and rectal routes, morphine has an elimination half-life of about 1.7 hours. Of note, it is converted to a 6-glucuronide metabolite that is also pharmacologically active and has caused death from accumulation in patients with poor renal function. While well absorbed, morphine undergoes significant first-pass metabolism when taken orally and thus requires higher doses than with parenteral administration to achieve the desired effects. Although the oral route is the accepted route of administration for pain control in patients with chronic pain, this route is often not utilized by drug addicts. Neuroexcitatory side effects, not mediated by opioid receptors, including delirium, myoclonus, seizures, hyperalgesia, and allodynia, have occurred with morphine and are probably related to the accumulation of metabolites such as morphine-3-glucuronide.[15,16]

Heroin: Heroin (diacetylmorphine) is a synthetic derivative of morphine. In the body, it is rapidly converted to 6-acetylmorphine and then to morphine. The conversion to morphine occurs within minutes. In addition to the effects common to most opioids, there have been reports of acute rhabdomyolysis with myoglobinuria during heroin intoxication.[17,18] In some cases, the patients have been comatose, lying with pressure on their muscles, but in other cases, rhabdomyolysis occurred with alert patients, accompanied by muscle pains, weakness, and swelling.[19,20] Chronic abuse of heroin has been associated with progressive nephrotic syndrome resulting in renal failure, with histopathology revealing focal segmental glomerulosclerosis.[21]

Additionally, there is a broad spectrum of neuropathological changes in the brains of heroin abusers, some of which are related to prolonged anoxia or vasculitis. Spongiform leukoencephalopathy has been described following inhalation of pre-heated heroin, with two cases having a delay in onset.[22,23] Another report describes extrapyramidal toxicity after recovery from the acute intoxication of an overdose of intranasal heroin.[24]

Codeine: Codeine, one of the substances found in opium, is about 20% as potent as morphine as an analgesic. It is mostly used as a cough suppressant and as an ingredient in pain medications. To be effective as an analgesic, codeine must be converted to morphine. This reaction is performed by the isozyme CYP2D6 of the P450 enzymes and is subject to genetic polymorphisms. About 10% of Caucasians are poor metabolizers, meaning that they do not convert codeine to morphine and thus do not derive therapeutic benefit from codeine. Inhibition of CYP2D6 resulted in diminished effects of codeine and caused codeine-dependent patients to use less codeine.[25,26]

Methadone: Although previously used mainly as a maintenance therapy for heroin addicts, in today's use, it plays a large role in long-term management of chronic pain. A synthetic long-acting opioid agonist, it is well absorbed orally and does not undergo significant first-pass metabolism. Although it provides comparable analgesia to morphine, it differs significantly in the considerable length of its half-life, which ranges from 15 to 55 hours.[27] This long half-life is also what makes appropriate titration of the drug difficult; indeed, many deaths reported in the literature are described during periods of too rapid up-titration of doses.[28] Methadone use has also been demonstrated to cause QT-interval prolongation on electrocardiograms and increases the risk of ventricular dysrhythmias, although this effect is typically only observed in patients receiving very high doses.[29] The clinical significance of this effect is likely minimal.[30]

Buprenorphine: A partial mu-opioid agonist, buprenorphine has become popular as an effective agent to treat opioid withdrawal symptoms while also helping to stem covert abuse of illicit drugs.[31] It exhibits less respiratory depression and has no known cardiotoxicity, properties that make its safety favorable compared with methadone.[32] However, like other opioids, in overdose it may produce significant respiratory depression,[33] and with longstanding use, it has also been demonstrated to produce withdrawal.[34]

Fentanyl: Fentanyl and related analogs (sufentanil, alfentanil, remifentanil, carfentanil) are synthetic opioid agonists structurally related to meperidine. Fentanyl is 50 to 100 times more potent than morphine and has a half-life of about 4 hours. Fentanyl is administered intravenously, transdermally with a patch, or orally with a lozenge, and is used for surgical anesthesia, especially for cardiac surgery; transdermal fentanyl is used for post-operative analgesia and for chronic pain management.[35] Fentanyl derivatives that are "street-synthesized" belong to a group of "designer drugs" and include alpha-methyl-fentanyl ("China White") and 3-methyl-fentanyl (3MF). Due to the very high potency of fentanyl and related drugs, respiratory depression may occur very rapidly. There are some reports of seizures associated with fentanyl anesthesia,[36] and a syndrome of delayed respiratory depression with truncal muscular rigidity occurring after recovery from fentanyl anesthesia has been reported.[37] In March 2016, the County of Sacramento Health Department issued a warning following a cluster of poisonings associated with fentanyl-contaminated street Norco.[38]

Hydromorphone: Hydromorphone is a synthetic derivative of morphine that is seven to ten times more potent compared with morphine.[39] Its half-life is about 2.5 hours. Hydromorphone intoxication presents with all the signs of typical opiate intoxication.[40]

Hydrocodone: Derived from codeine, hydrocodone is mostly converted to an inactive metabolite, norhydrocodone, but through a minor pathway mediated by CYP2D6, it produces a small amount of hydromorphone.[41] It produces more sedation than codeine,[42] and overdoses produce the same effects as other opioids; however, presentations may not be as clear, as it is frequently formulated as a combination drug.

Oxycodone: A semi-synthetic opioid derived from thebaine (a naturally occurring component of opium), its potency and half-life are comparable to those of morphine. It rose to prominence through a swell of abuse and deaths in the northeastern United States during the latter half of the 1990s, a practice of crushing and then snorting it earning it the name of "hillbilly heroin."[43]

Oxymorphone: This compound is approximately ten times more potent than morphine.[44] It produces all the signs of classic opiate intoxication.

Meperidine: Meperidine is a synthetic opioid. Its half-life is about 3 hours, but its metabolite, normeperidine, has a half-life of 15 to 34 hours and thus accumulates in plasma with repeated dosing. In patients with renal failure, the half-life of normeperidine may be as long as 3 to 4 days. Normeperidine is pharmacologically active and has both mu-mediated effects as well as other effects not mediated by opioid receptors. Acute intoxication with meperidine presents like morphine intoxication, with respiratory depression, and can be reversed with naloxone. Patients treated with high doses of meperidine, or patients with renal failure, may accumulate high levels of normeperidine, resulting in a syndrome characterized by irritability, myoclonus, and seizures.[45–48] Because of the side effects, on the one hand, and lack of any specific benefits, on the other, meperidine use has been declining since the 1990s.[5]

Propoxyphene: Propoxyphene is a derivative of methadone, but unlike methadone, it is only a mild analgesic. It has a half-life of about 15 hours but is metabolized to norpropoxyphene, a potentially toxic metabolite with a longer half-life (about 30 hours). Propoxyphene has been associated with a high incidence of toxicity, because in addition to being a respiratory depressant, it also produces sodium-channel blockade, and was thus implicated in seizures and fatal cardiac abnormalities.[49] Fortunately, the wide QRS has been shown to respond to sodium bicarbonate.[50] Although it was once highly abused, the high frequency of dangerous adverse effects led to its removal from the United States market in 2010.

Pentazocine: Pentazocine is both an opiate agonist and an antagonist. It is an agonist for kappa, delta, and sigma receptors[51] but antagonizes mu receptors. This renders pentazocine less likely to be abused. Pentazocine produces analgesia in non-tolerant patients but may produce withdrawal in tolerant individuals. The action on sigma and kappa receptors probably mediates a psychotomimetic reaction.[52] Pentazocine also potentiates the release of catecholamines from adrenal glands, and in high doses, it can cause elevated blood pressure and tachycardia. There are two case reports of fibrous myopathy following intramuscular pentazocine abuse.[53,54]

Tramadol: Tramadol and related synthetic analgesic (tapentadol) effects are mediated through both weak mu-opioid agonism as well as noradrenergic reuptake inhibition. Tramadol rose to prominence in the late 1990s as an analgesic without the dependence noted with other opioids and was thus initially unscheduled.[55] However, after it was brought to market, reports began appearing describing withdrawal symptoms,[56] of which the most dangerous are seizures.[57] Seizures have also been frequently reported with therapeutic use and in toxicity.[58] As it has two separate and contradictory actions, in overdose, it can produce a mixture of opioid-like effects (respiratory depression, coma) and excitatory effects (agitation, hypertension, tachycardia) attributed to its noradrenergic effects. It has also been described as being able to produce serotonin toxicity, particularly in combination with other serotonergic agents;[59–64] however, this may be a manifestation of its monoamine reuptake inhibition. Tramadol was subsequently given a Schedule IV designation in 2014. Tapentadol was listed as a Schedule II agent in 2009.

1.4.3 Opioid Withdrawal

Abstinence after prolonged use of opioids results in a withdrawal syndrome. The severity of the symptoms depends on the duration of use and the daily dose of the opioid taken before the cessation of use; it is usually more severe in drug abusers than in patients taking opioids for pain relief. Opioid withdrawal can be precipitated by naloxone and can occur even after a single dose of an opioid. Acute withdrawal after naloxone usually results in nausea, vomiting, profuse sweating, diarrhea, fatigue, and aches and pains, which may last up to 12 hours.[64] During unassisted opioid withdrawal, the patient will experience craving for the drug, usually 4 to 6 hours after the last administered dose of short-acting opioids such as morphine or heroin but possibly delayed (12 to 24 hours with methadone). If no drug is administered at this point, there will be a feeling of intense discomfort, anxiety, agitation, myalgias, sweating, and increased bowel movement. The symptoms will increase over the next 36 to 48 hours, reach their peak at 36 to 72 hours, and resolve over the next 7 to 10 days. The withdrawal symptoms are not life-threatening, despite the distress they produce, and can be treated specifically with opioid replacement (usually methadone) in doses that will make the patient comfortable, or with supportive treatment including clonidine (a central alpha-agonist) or benzodiazepines for anxiety. These interventions may also be used in combination in the treatment of opioid withdrawal that is refractory to single-agent strategies.

ACKNOWLEDGMENTS

Shoshana Zevin, M.D. and Neal L. Benowitz, M.D.

REFERENCES

1. Foley KM. Opioids. *Neurol Clin* 1993;11(3):503–22.
2. Benowitz NL. Substance abuse: dependence and treatment. In Melmon KL, Morrelli HF, Hoffman BB, Nierenberg DW (Eds.) *Clinical Pharmacology*. 3 ed. New York: McGraw-Hill, 1992, 763–786.
3. Zebraski SE, Kochenash SM, Raffa RB. Lung opioid receptors: pharmacology and possible target for nebulized morphine in dyspnea. *Life Sci* 2000;66(23):2221–31.
4. Pasternak GW. Insights into mu opioid pharmacology: the role of mu opioid receptor subtypes. *Life Sci* 2001;68(19–20):2213–9.
5. Pasternak GW. The pharmacology of mu analgesics: from patients to genes. *Neuroscientist* 2001;7(3):220–31.
6. Zaki PA, Bilsky EJ, Vanderah TW, Lai J, Evans CJ, Porreca F. Opioid receptor types and subtypes: the delta receptor as a model. *Annu Rev Pharmacol Toxicol* 1996;36:379–401.
7. Boyer EW. Management of opioid analgesic overdose. *N Engl J Med* 2012;367(2):146–55.
8. Mowry JB, Spyker DA, Brooks DE, Zimmerman A, Schauben JL. Annual Report of the American Association of Poison Control Centers' National Poison Data System (NPDS): 33rd Annual Report. *Clin Toxicol (Phila)* 2016;54(10):924–1109.
9. Smith D. Medicalizing the opioid epidemic in the U.S. in the era of health care reform. *J Psychoactive Drugs* 2017;49(2):95–101.
10. Pappagallo M. Incidence, prevalence, and management of opioid bowel dysfunction. *Am J Surg* 2001;182(5A Suppl):11s–18s.
11. Ling GS, Spiegel K, Lockhart SH, Pasternak GW. Separation of opioid analgesia from respiratory depression: evidence for different receptor mechanisms. *J Pharmacol Exp Ther* 1985;232(1):149–55.
12. Sporer KA, Dorn E. Heroin-related noncardiogenic pulmonary edema : a case series. *Chest* 2001;120(5):1628–32.
13. Ballantyne JC, Loach AB, Carr DB. Itching after epidural and spinal opiates. *Pain* 1988;33(2):149–60.
14. Dray A. Epidural opiates and urinary retention: new models provide new insights [editorial]. *Anesthesiology* 1988;68(3):323–4.
15. Smith MT. Neuroexcitatory effects of morphine and hydromorphone: evidence implicating the 3-glucuronide metabolites. *Clin Exp Pharmacol Physiol* 2000;27(7):524–8.
16. Mercadante S. Opioid rotation for cancer pain: rationale and clinical aspects. *Cancer* 1999;86(9):1856–66.
17. Richards JR. Rhabdomyolysis and drugs of abuse. *J Emerg Med* 2000;19(1):51–6.
18. Richter RW. Muscle damage in heroin addicts. *N Engl J Med* 1971;284(15):920.
19. Klockgether T, Weller M, Haarmeier T, Kaskas B, Maier G, Dichgans J. Gluteal compartment syndrome due to rhabdomyolysis after heroin abuse. *Neurology* 1997;48(1): 275–6.
20. Rice EK, Isbel NM, Becker GJ, Atkins RC, McMahon LP. Heroin overdose and myoglobinuric acute renal failure. *Clin Nephrol* 2000;54(6):449–54.
21. Dubrow A, Mittman N, Ghali V, Flamenbaum W. The changing spectrum of heroin-associated nephropathy. *Am J Kidney Dis* 1985;5(1):36–41.
22. Niehaus L, Meyer BU. Bilateral borderzone brain infarctions in association with heroin abuse. *J Neurol Sci* 1998;160(2):180–2.
23. Buttner A, Mall G, Penning R, Weis S. The neuropathology of heroin abuse. *Forensic Sci Int* 2000;113(1–3):435–42.
24. Schoser BG, Groden C. Subacute onset of oculogyric crises and generalized dystonia following intranasal administration of heroin. *Addiction* 1999;94(3):431–4.
25. Kathiramalainathan K, Kaplan HL, Romach MK, Busto UE, Li NY, Sawe J, et al. Inhibition of cytochrome P450 2D6 modifies codeine abuse liability. *J Clin Psychopharmacol* 2000;20(4):435–44.
26. Romach MK, Otton SV, Somer G, Tyndale RF, Sellers EM. Cytochrome P450 2D6 and treatment of codeine dependence. *J Clin Psychopharmacol* 2000;20(1):43–5.
27. Baker DD, Jenkins AJ. A comparison of methadone, oxycodone, and hydrocodone related deaths in Northeast Ohio. *J Anal Toxicol* 2008;32(2):165–71.
28. Drummer OH, Opeskin K, Syrjanen M, Cordner SM. Methadone toxicity causing death in ten subjects starting on a methadone maintenance program. *Am J Forensic Med Pathol* 1992;13(4):346–50.
29. Katz DF, Sun J, Khatri V, Kao D, Bucher-Bartelson B, Traut C, Lundin-Martinez J, Goodman M, Mehler PS, Krantz MJ. QTc interval screening in an opioid treatment program. *Am J Cardiol* 2013;112(7):1013–8.
30. Martell BA, Arnsten JH, Ray B, Gourevitch MN. The impact of methadone induction on cardiac conduction in opiate users. *Ann Intern Med* 2003;139:154–5.
31. Greenwald MK, Johanson CE, Moody DE, Woods JH, Kilbourn MR, Koeppe RA, Schuster CR, Zubieta JK. Effects of buprenorphine maintenance dose on

mu-opioid receptor availability, plasma concentrations, and antagonist blockade in heroin-dependent volunteers. *Neuropsychopharmacology* 2003;28(11):2000–9.
32. Walsh SL, Eissenberg T. The clinical pharmacology of buprenorphine: extrapolating from the laboratory to the clinic. *Drug Alcohol Depend* 2003;70(2 Suppl):S13–27.
33. Kintz P. Deaths involving buprenorphine: a compendium of French cases. *Forensic Sci Int* 2001;121(1–2):65–9.
34. Eissenberg T, Greenwald MK, Johnson RE, Liebson IA, Bigelow GE, Stitzer ML. Buprenorphine's physical dependence potential: antagonist-precipitated withdrawal in humans. *J Pharmacol Exp Ther* 1996;276(2):449–59.
35. Yee LY, Lopez JR. Transdermal fentanyl. *Ann Pharmacother* 1992;26(11):1393–9.
36. Sprung J, Schedewie HK. Apparent focal motor seizure with a jacksonian march induced by fentanyl: a case report and review of the literature. *J Clin Anesth* 1992;4(2):139–43.
37. Caspi J, Klausner JM, Safadi T, Amar R, Rozin RR, Merin G. Delayed respiratory depression following fentanyl anesthesia for cardiac surgery. *Crit Care Med* 1988;16(3):238–40.
38. Kasirye O. Drug overdose health alert: fentanyl contaminated street Norco. *County of Sacramento.* Retrieved December 30, 2016, from http://www.dhhs.saccounty.net/PUB/Documents/AZ-Health-Info/ME-20160325-Health+Alert+-+Contaminated+Norco.pdf
39. Keeri-Szanto M. Anaesthesia time/dose curves IX: the use of hydromorphone in surgical anaesthesia and postoperative pain relief in comparison to morphine. *Can Anaesth Soc J* 1976;23(6):587–95.
40. Parab PV, et al. Pharmacokinetics of hydromorphone after intravenous, peroral and rectal administration to human subjects. *Biopharm Drug Dispos* 1988;9(2):187–99.
41. Hutchinson MR, Menelaou A, Foster DJ, Coller JK, Somogyi AA. CYP2D6 and CYP3A4 involvement in the primary oxidative metabolism of hydrocodone by human liver microsomes. *Br J Clin Pharmacol* 2004;57(3):287–97.
42. Thomson PDR, Montvale NJ. *Hycodan | In Physicians' Desk Reference*, 60th ed. 2006, p. 1104.
43. Drummer OH, Syrjanen ML, Phelan M, Cordner SM. A study of deaths involving oxycodone. *J Forensic Sci* 1994;39(4):1069–75.
44. Cone EJ, Darwin WD, Buchwald WF, Gorodetzky CW. Oxymorphone metabolism and urinary excretion in human, rat, guinea pig, rabbit, and dog. *Drug Metab Dispos* 1983;11(5):446–50.
45. Stock SL, Catalano G, Catalano MC. Meperidine associated mental status changes in a patient with chronic renal failure. *J Fla Med Assoc* 1996;83(5):315–9.
46. Hassan H, Bastani B, Gellens M. Successful treatment of normeperidine neurotoxicity by hemodialysis. *Am J Kidney Dis* 2000;35(1):146–9.
47. Kussman BD, Sethna NF. Pethidine-associated seizure in a healthy adolescent receiving pethidine for postoperative pain control. *Paediatr Anaesth* 1998;8(4):349–52.
48. Latta KS, Ginsberg B, Barkin RL. Meperidine: a critical review. *Am J Ther* 2002;9(1):53–68.
49. Lawson AA, Northridge DB. Dextropropoxyphene overdose. Epidemiology, clinical presentation and management. *Med Toxicol Adverse Drug Exp* 1987;2(6):430–44.
50. Stork CM, Redd JT, Fine K, Hoffman RS. Propoxyphene-induced wide QRS complex dysrhythmia responsive to sodium bicarbonate — A case report. *J Toxicol Clin Toxicol* 1995;33(2):179–83.
51. Zabetian CP, Staley JK, Flynn DD, Mash DC. [3H]-(+)-Pentazocine binding to sigma recognition sites in human cerebellum. *Life Sci* 1994;55(20):L389–95.
52. Pfeiffer A, Brantl V, Herz A, Emrich HM. Psychotomimesis mediated by kappa opiate receptors. *Science* 1986;233(4765):774–6.
53. Das CP, Thussu A, Prabhakar S, Banerjee AK. Pentazocine-induced fibromyositis and contracture. *Postgrad Med J* 1999;75(884):361–2.
54. Sinsawaiwong S, Phanthumchinda K. Pentazocine-induced fibrous myopathy and localized neuropathy. *J Med Assoc Thai* 1998;81(9):717–21.
55. Cicero TJ, Adams EH, Geller A, Inciardi JA, Muñoz A, Schnoll SH, Senay EC, Woody GE. A postmarketing surveillance program to monitor Ultram (tramadol hydrochloride) abuse in the United States. *Drug Alcohol Depend* 1999;57(1):7–22.
56. Freye E, Levy J. Acute abstinence syndrome following abrupt cessation of long-term use of tramadol (Ultram): a case study. *Eur J Pain* 2000;4(3):307–11.
57. Ryan NM, Isbister GK. Tramadol overdose causes seizures and respiratory depression but serotonin toxicity appears unlikely. *Clin Toxicol (Phila)* 2015;53(6):545–50.
58. Boostani R, Derakhshan S. Tramadol induced seizure: a 3-year study. *Caspian J Intern Med* 2012;3(3):484–7.
59. Ripple MG, Pestaner JP, Levine BS, Smialek JE. Lethal combination of tramadol and multiple drugs affecting serotonin. *Am J Forensic Med Pathol* 2000;21:370–4.
60. Mason BJ, Blackburn KH. Possible serotonin syndrome associated with tramadol and sertraline coadministration. *Ann Pharmacother* 1997;31:175–7.
61. Garrett PM. Tramadol overdose and serotonin syndrome manifest- ing as acute right heart dysfunction. *Anaesth Intensive Care* 2004;32:575–7.
62. Houlihan DJ. Serotonin syndrome resulting from coadministration of tramadol, venlafaxine, and mirtazapine. *Ann Pharmacother* 2004;38:411–3.
63. Nelson EM, Philbrick AM. Avoiding serotonin syndrome: the nature of the interaction between tramadol and selective serotonin reuptake inhibitors. *Ann Pharmacother* 2012;46:1712–6.
64. Farrell M. Opiate withdrawal. *Addiction* 1994;89(11):1471–5.

1.5 SEDATIVE-HYPNOTICS

Michael Darracq and Binh T. Ly

1.5.1 Benzodiazepines

Benzodiazepines act through potentiation of gamma-aminobutyric acid (GABA) activity in the brain. GABA is an inhibitory neurotransmitter that binds to GABA receptors, opening chloride channels and allowing the influx of chloride ions into neurons. Chloride influx hyperpolarizes the cell membrane and prevents the cell from firing. Benzodiazepines bind to a specific site on the GABA receptor and increase the frequency of GABA channel opening when GABA is present.[1]

While sharing the same pharmacodynamic properties, benzodiazepines are commonly classified according to duration of activity: very short-acting (midazolam), short-acting (triazolam), intermediate-acting (alprazolam), long-acting (diazepam), and very long-acting (flurazepam). With the exception of oxazepam and lorazepam, which are glucuronidated, most benzodiazepines are metabolized by liver cytochrome P450 enzymes and have active metabolites.

The use of sedative-hypnotics, in particular benzodiazepines, is common in the United States. Common uses for benzodiazepines include alcohol withdrawal, generalized anxiety disorder (GAD), panic disorder, insomnia, muscle relaxation, and seizures.[2] Prescriptions for benzodiazepines are also described to be increasing. In 2012, a 17% increase in the number of prescriptions for benzodiazepines since 2006 was reported, with roughly 96 million prescriptions for benzodiazepines having been written in 2012. In 2015, it was estimated that 5.2% of U.S. adults between the ages of 18 and 80 used a benzodiazepine. The use of benzodiazepines is also noted to increase with age: from 2.6% (18–35 years) to 5.4% (36–50 years) to 7.4% (51–64 years) to 8.7% (65–80 years).[3] Prescriptions for alprazolam (Xanax), a benzodiazepine, increased by 23% over the same period of time, making it the most prescribed psychiatric medication and the 11th most commonly prescribed medication overall.[4]

Following acute overdose of benzodiazepines, initial signs and symptoms may manifest as incoordination, ataxia (unsteady gait), slurred speech, and excessive sleepiness. The majority of patients with pure benzodiazepine overdose will usually only manifest with these central nervous system (CNS) symptoms. Gastrointestinal symptoms such as nausea and vomiting, however, have been reported following acute overdose with benzodiazepines.[5] Paradoxical reactions such as increased anxiety, agitation, hallucinations, and delirium may also occur following benzodiazepine routine use or overdose.[6]

More serious and life-threatening toxicity is rare following pure benzodiazepine overdose but may occur when combined with other CNS sedatives such as ethanol and opioids.[7,8] These symptoms and signs include deep and prolonged or cyclical coma, apnea, respiratory depression (both depressed rate and depth of respiration), hypoxia, hypothermia, bradycardia, cardiac arrest, and pulmonary aspiration.[9–13]

The elderly and those with concomitant chronic medical problems are more at risk for lethal overdose from benzodiazepines even at relatively low doses.[5,14–16] Benzodiazepine use in elderly individuals has been associated with falls and hip fractures due to drowsiness and ataxia.[17] Because benzodiazepines cause physical and psychological dependence, they are generally recommended for limited periods of time (several weeks) with carefully titrated doses.[18,19]

Withdrawal may occur after sudden cessation of benzodiazepines; it is usually associated with prolonged use of high doses but may also occur after therapeutic doses when the drug has been used for several months. Symptoms include anxiety, panic attacks, insomnia, irritability, agitation, tremor, and anorexia. Withdrawal from high doses of benzodiazepines and from short-acting benzodiazepines is usually more severe and may result in seizures and psychotic reactions.[20] The time course of the withdrawal syndrome depends on the half-life of the specific compound.

Prolonged use of benzodiazepines may result in tolerance, and cross-tolerance may develop when other sedative-hypnotics, such as ethanol, have been used. While complex, proposed mechanisms for tolerance include downregulation of $GABA_A$ receptors and configurational changes in the $GABA_A$ receptor or in the receptor–agonist complex resulting in diminished sensitivity to agonist activity.[21–23]

1.5.2 Phenazepam

A long-acting and powerful benzodiazepine, phenazepam was first developed in the former Soviet Union in 1974 and is used clinically in the treatment of epilepsy, anxiety, alcohol withdrawal syndrome, and sleep disorders in Russia and the former soviet republics.[24] Typically, phenazepam is prescribed for short courses (less than 2 weeks) due to recognition of risk for abuse and dependency.[25]

In western Europe and the United States, however, phenazepam has been increasingly used for recreational nonmedical purposes and is readily available over the internet.[26] Hospitalizations and fatalities have been reported following overdose and in particular when combined with other medications such as antidepressants, sleep medications, pain medications, or alcohol.[24,26–29]

In the United States, sale for human use remains illegal.[30] Although it is currently unscheduled by the U.S. Drug Enforcement Administration (DEA), individual states including Louisiana and Arkansas have classified phenazepam as a controlled dangerous substance (Schedule 1 Controlled Substance) after several products sold under the guise of air freshener ("Zannie") or similar and claiming not to be for human consumption were associated with serious human morbidity and death.[31]

Clinical effects in both therapeutic use and overdose are similar to those of other benzodiazepines and include loss of coordination, amnesia, and excessive somnolence.

Phenazepam is reported to be ten times as potent as diazepam, another more common benzodiazepine.[27] Withdrawal symptoms may be delayed for 2 or more days due to the long duration of clinical activity of phenazepam.

1.5.3 Barbiturates

Barbiturates are used clinically as sedative-hypnotic drugs. Common uses include in the treatment of epilepsy and in the induction of anesthesia. Barbiturates modulate $GABA_A$ receptor binding sites and increase the duration of $GABA_A$ receptor opening in the presence of the inhibitory neurotransmitter GABA. In high concentrations, barbiturates may enhance chloride ion flux independently of GABA effects at the receptor.[32]

Acute barbiturate intoxication presents with progressive encephalopathy and coma. Mild intoxication may present as over-sedation, slurred speech, ataxia, and nystagmus. Severe intoxication may present with coma, absent reflexes, hypothermia, hypotension, and respiratory depression. Apnea and shock may occur. The time course of intoxication depends on the pharmacokinetics of the specific drug; coma may last for 5 to 7 days following phenobarbital overdose. Barbiturates are usually abused as a "treatment" for unpleasant symptoms of stimulant intoxication; in this context, short-acting drugs, such as pentobarbital and secobarbital, are often used.[33]

Withdrawal symptoms upon cessation of barbiturates may occur after prolonged use even of therapeutic doses, although severe withdrawal is seen most commonly in polysubstance abusers. The presentation of barbiturate withdrawal is similar to that of benzodiazepine withdrawal: symptoms may include anxiety, panic attacks, insomnia, irritability, agitation, tremor, and anorexia.

1.5.4 Gamma Hydroxybutyrate (GHB) and Analogs

Gamma hydroxybutyrate (GHB) is produced in nanomolar quantities in the human brain and acts as a neurotransmitter that modulates the effects of GABA. Until 1990, it was sold at health food stores and was popular among athletes as an alternative to steroids. Because growth hormone is released during sleep, some athletes and bodybuilders took GHB because of its sleep-inducing effects. GHB was thought to indirectly result in increased muscle development.

Sixteen cases of adverse effects due to GHB-containing products were reported to the California Poison Control System (CPCS), San Francisco division between June and October 1990. Four patients presented with coma and two additional patients had tonic-clonic seizures with doses ranging from one-fourth to four tablespoons.[34] As a result of this and other similar cases, the U.S. Federal Drug Administration (FDA) banned over-the-counter sales of GHB in November 1990, and GHB was classified as a Schedule I controlled substance in March 2000.

Clinical effects following oral GHB dosing include euphoria, dizziness, and deepening somnolence at increasing doses.[35] Doses greater than 50 mg/kg produce an anesthetic effect. Typical abuse doses of GHB are greater than 35 mg/kg.[36] Because of its ability to produce moderate to deep unconsciousness, GHB has been used in cases of drug-facilitated sexual assault. Because of laws banning the possession, manufacturing, and consumption of GHB, analogs have appeared that mimic the clinical effects of GHB, including gamma butyrolactone (GBL), 1,4 butanediol (1,4 BD), gamma-hydroxyvaleric acid (GHV), and gamma-valerolactone (GVL). Many of these exist as commercially and legally obtained industrial solvents and may be listed under other pseudonyms. GBL and 1,4 BD are converted endogenously in the human body into GHB. GHV binds directly to GHB sites on the $GABA_B$ receptor. GVL is a precursor to GHV. GVL, like GHB, produces somnolence, ataxia, and catalepsy but at doses larger than those with GHB.[37]

1.5.5 Solvents

Solvents constitute a large class of industrial chemicals that have sedative-hypnotic effects when used inappropriately. Particularly among adolescents, common solvents including glues, paint thinners, nail lacquer removers, lighter fluids, cleaning solutions, aerosols, and gasoline are abused for these sedative-hypnotic effects.[38,39] Methods of abuse include bagging, in which the substance is first placed in a plastic bag from which the user inhales the vapors, huffing, in which the substance is sprayed on a rag or cloth that is placed over the face, and sniffing, in which the solvent vapors are inhaled directly from the container. Solvents are hydrocarbons that are lipid soluble and diffuse freely across the blood brain barrier and through cell membranes.

Clinical effects are similar between various solvent chemicals, including toluene and acetone. These clinical effects occur rapidly following exposure and typically last 15–45 minutes after inhalation. Habitual users may develop a characteristic dermatitis rash around the nose and mouth from use and may have a characteristic solvent odor on their breath.[40] Feelings of euphoria, disinhibition, dizziness, slurred speech, lack of coordination, and impaired judgment may result from use.[40,41] More severe intoxication may present with nausea, vomiting, diarrhea, tremor, ataxia, paresthesias, hallucinations, and muscle aches and pains. Seizures and coma following use have also been reported.[39,42] Toluene in particular has also been associated with renal tubular acidosis, acute tubular necrosis, and severe hypokalemia.[43] Deaths resulting from asphyxiation or from cardiac dysrhythmias are associated with solvent abuse.[41] Chronic abusers may develop cerebellar syndromes, (particularly with toluene) parkinsonism, peripheral neuropathy, and cognitive impairments.[40–42]

Peripheral neuropathies, motor and symmetrical, are associated with n-hexane and naphtha.[42]

1.5.6 Management

Management of acute sedative-hypnotic intoxication is predominantly supportive. As the principal clinical effect of sedative-hypnotic intoxication is CNS and respiratory depression, particular focus should be placed on ensuring adequate oxygenation, ventilation, and circulatory support to the intoxicated patient. The use of activated charcoal is generally discouraged, as CNS depression resulting from sedative-hypnotic intoxication may lead to aspiration of gastric contents, including charcoal, with resultant pulmonary toxicity.

A specific antidote, flumazenil, is available for reversal of the effects of benzodiazepines. It is effective in reversing the sedative and other effects of benzodiazepines but in one study was associated with seizures in 1.4% of patients. (PMID 22766408).[44]

Beta blockers are recommended in the treatment of cardiac dysrhythmias such as ventricular tachycardia resulting from solvent intoxication. Cardiac sensitization to catecholamines is the putative mechanism for this phenomenon.

REFERENCES

1. Tallman JF, Gallager DW, Mallorga P, Thomas JW, Strittmatter W, Hirata F, et al. Studies on benzodiazepine receptors. *Adv Biochem Psychopharmacol* 1980;21:277–83.
2. Anderson L. Benzodiazepines: overview and use. May 4 2014. http://www.drugs.com/article/benzodiazepines.html, Accessed December 4, 2017.
3. Olfson M, King M, Schoenbaum M. Benzodiazepine use in the United States. *JAMA Psychiatry* 2015;72(2):136–42. doi:10.1001/jamapsychiatry.2014.1763.
4. Miller L. Listening to Xanax. March 18 2012. http://nymag.com/news/features/xanax-2012-3/index1.html, Accessed December 4, 2017.
5. Gaudreault P, Guay J, Thivierge RL, Verdy I. Benzodiazepine poisoning. Clinical and pharmacological considerations and treatment. *Drug Saf* 1991;6(4):247–65. doi:10.2165/00002018-199106040-00003. PMID 1888441
6. Garnier R, Medernach C, Harbach S, Fournier E. [Agitation and hallucinations during acute lorazepam poisoning in children. Apropos of 65 personal cases]. *Ann Pediatr (Paris) (in French)* 1984;31(4):286–9.
7. http://www.samhsa.gov/data/sites/default/files/DAWN-SR192-BenzoCombos-2014/DAWN-SR192-BenzoCombos-2014.pdf
8. Dart RC. *Medical Toxicology* (3rd ed.). USA: Lippincott Williams & Wilkins, 2003. p. 811. ISBN 978-0-7817-2845-4
9. Berger R, Green G, Melnick A. Cardiac arrest caused by oral diazepam intoxication. *Clin Pediatr (Phila)* 1975;14(9):842–4. doi:10.1177/000992287501400910. PMID 1157438
10. Welch TR, Rumack BH, Hammond K. Clonazepam overdose resulting in cyclic coma. *Clin Toxicol* 1977;10(4):433–6. doi:10.3109/15563657709046280. PMID 862377
11. Höjer J, Baehrendtz S, Gustafsson L. Benzodiazepine poisoning: experience of 702 admissions to an intensive care unit during a 14-year period. *J Intern Med* 1989;226(2):117–22. doi:10.1111/j.1365-2796.1989.tb01365.x. PMID 2769176
12. Busto U, Kaplan HL, Sellers EM. Benzodiazepine-associated emergencies in Toronto. *Am J Psychiatry* 1980;137(2):224–7. PMID 6101526
13. Greenblatt DJ, Allen MD, Noel BJ, Shader RI. Acute overdosage with benzodiazepine derivatives. *Clin Pharmacol Ther* 1977;21(4):497–514. PMID 14802
14. Sunter JP, Bal TS, Cowan WK. Three cases of fatal triazolam poisoning. *BMJ* 1988;297(6650):719. doi:10.1136/bmj.297.6650.719. PMC 1834083. PMID 3147739
15. Brødsgaard I, Hansen AC, Vesterby A. Two cases of lethal nitrazepam poisoning. *Am J Forensic Med Pathol* 1995;16(2):151–3. doi:10.1097/00000433-199506000-00015. PMID 7572872
16. Reidenberg MM, Levy M, Warner H, Coutinho CB, Schwartz MA, Yu G, Cheripko J. Relationship between diazepam dose, plasma level, age, and central nervous system depression. *Clin Pharmacol Ther* 1978;23(4):371–4. PMID 630787
17. Wysowski DK, Baum C, Ferguson WJ, Lundin F, Ng MJ, Hammerstrom T. Sedative–hypnotic drugs and the risk of hip fracture. *J Clin Epidemiol* 1996;49(1):111–3.
18. Woods JH, Winger G. Current benzodiazepine issues. *Psychopharmacology (Berlin)* 1995;118(2):107–15; discussion 118, 120–1. Ashton H. Guidelines for the rational use of benzodiazepines. When and what to use. *Drugs* 1994;48(1):25–40.
19. Nelson J, Chouinard G. Guidelines for the clinical use of benzodiazepines: pharmacokinetics, dependency, rebound and withdrawal. *Can J Clin Pharmacol* 1999;6(2):69–83.
20. Petursson H. The benzodiazepine withdrawal syndrome. *Addiction* 1994;89(11):1455–9.
21. Miller LG, Greenblatt DJ, Roy RB, Summer WR, Shader RI. Chronic benzodiazepine administration. II. Discontinuation syndrome is associated with upregulation of gamma-aminobutyric $acid_A$ receptor complex binding and function. *J Pharmacol Exp Ther* 1988;246(1):177–82.
22. Lader M. Biological processes in benzodiazepine dependence. *Addiction* 1994;89(11):1413–8.
23. Bateson AN. Basic pharmacologic mechanisms involved in benzodiazepine tolerance and withdrawal. *Curr Pharm Des* 2002;8(1):5–21.
24. Corkery JM, Schifano F, Ghodse AH. Phenazepam abuse in the UK: an emerging problem causing serious adverse health problems, including death. *Hum Psychopharmarmacol* 2012;27(3):254–61.
25. Phenazepam (bromdihydrochlorphenylbenzodiazepine) Tablets. Full Prescribing Information. *Russian State Register of Medicines* (in Russian). Valenta Pharm, JSC. Retrieved 18 January 2016.
26. Bailey K, Richards-Waugh L, Clay D, et al. Fatality involving the ingestion of phenazepam and poppy seed tea. *J Anal Toxicol* 2010;34(8):527–32. [PubMed]
27. Kyle PB, Brown AP, Stevenson JL. Reactivity of commercial benzodiazepine immunoassays to phenazepam. *J Anal Toxicol* 2012;36(3):207–9. [PubMed]
28. The Atlanta Journal-Constitution. *Exotic Drug Leaves Cherokee Teen Dead, 3 Friends Hospitalized.* 22 March 2012. http://www.ajc.com/news/news/local/exotic-drug-leaves-cherokee-teen-dead-3-friends-ho/nQkNR/
29. America Now. *KSLA News 12 Investigates: "Zannie" in the ArkLaTex.* 7 April 2012. http://www.americanownews.com/story/17040198/ksla-news-12-investigates-zannie-in-the-arklatex
30. New York nurse sentenced for selling unapproved "Party Drug" Phenazepam on the Internet. *U.S. Department of Justice.* October 10, 2012. http://www.fda.gov/ICECI/CriminalInvestigations/ucm323965.htm
31. Bill to Ban Zannie Passes. *KSLA* 2012;12.. Retrieved 21 May 2012. http://www.ksla.com/story/18578228/bill-to-ban-zannie-passes

32. Ito T, Suzuki T, Wellman SE, Ho IK. Pharmacology of barbiturate tolerance/dependence: $GABA_A$ receptors and molecular aspects. *Life Sci* 1996;59(3):169–95.
33. Coupey SM. Barbiturates. *Pediatr Rev* 1997;18(8):260–4.
34. Dyer JE. Gamma-hydroxybutyrate: a health food product producing coma and seizure-like activity. *Am J Emerg Med* 1991;9:321–4.
35. Baselt RC, Cravey RC. Gamma-hydroxybutyrate. In *Disposition of Toxic Drugs and Chemicals in Man.* Foster City, CA: Chemical Toxicology, 1995:348–9.
36. *A Health Educator's Guide to Understanding Drugs of Abuse Testing By Dr. Amitava Dasgupta.*
37. Carter LP, Chen W, Wu H, et al. Comparison of the behavioral effects of gamma-hydroxybutyric acid (GHB) and its 4-methyl substituted analog, gamma-hydryoxyvaleric acid (GHV) *Drug Alcohol Depend* 2005;78:91–99.
38. Kurtzman TL, Otsuka KN, Wahl RA. Inhalant abuse by adolescents. *J Adolesc Health* 2001;28(3):170–80.
39. Brouette T, Anton R. Clinical review of inhalants. *Am J Addict* 2001;10(1):79–94.
40. Ron MA. Volatile substance abuse: a review of possible long-term neurological, intellectual and psychiatric sequelae. *Br J Psychiatry* 1986;148:235–46.
41. al-Alousi LM. Pathology of volatile substance abuse: a case report and a literature review. *Med Sci Law* 1989;29(3):189–208.
42. Meadows R, Verghese A. Medical complications of glue sniffing. *South Med J* 1996;89(5):455–62.
43. Crowe AV, Howse M, Bell GM, Henry JA. Substance abuse and the kidney. *QJM* 2000;93(3):147–52.
44. Kreshak AA, Cantrell FL, Clark RF, Tomaszewski CA. A poison center's ten-year experience with flumazenil administration to acutely poisoned patients. *J Emerg Med* 2012;43(4):677–82.

1.6 DECREASED MENTAL STATUS: COMA, STUPOR, AND LETHARGY

Allyson Kreshak

1.6.1 General Comments

In the setting of drug overdose, coma usually reflects global depression of the brain's cerebral cortex. This can be a direct effect of the drug on specific neurotransmitters or receptors or an indirect process such as trauma or asphyxia. Evaluation and treatment are focused largely on maintaining a functional airway and ventilations and the administration of potential antidotes while evaluating for underlying medical conditions. The following section describes the appropriate use of antidotes and the emergent approach to the patient with a decreased level of consciousness from drug use.

Arousal level versus content of consciousness: It is often useful to distinguish between the arousal *level* and the *content* of consciousness. Alertness and wakefulness are a reflection of the arousal level, while content of consciousness refers to perceptions of external stimuli and bodily stimuli, including language, self-awareness, and emotions [1]. In referring to altered mental status characterized by coma, stupor, or lethargy, we address the level of consciousness as it applies to the drug-abusing patient along a clinical spectrum with deep coma on one end, stupor in the middle, and lethargy representing a mildly decreased level of consciousness.

Attributes of a good antidote: The ideal antidote should be safe, effective, rapidly acting, and easy to administer. It should also have low abuse potential and act as long as the intoxicating drug or be amenable to re-dosing. The following antidotes are of potential use for evaluating and treating patients who present with acute altered mental status.

Thiamine: Thiamine is an important cofactor for several metabolic enzymes that are vital for the metabolism of carbohydrates and for the proper function of the pentose phosphate pathway [2]. When thiamine is absent or deficient, Wernicke's encephalopathy, classically described as a triad of oculomotor abnormalities, ataxia, and global confusion, may result. Thiamine administration should be considered for patients with altered mental status who have a suspected history of alcohol abuse or malnutrition [1]. Although Wernicke's is rare, empiric treatment for this disease is safe [3], inexpensive, and cost-effective [4].

Dextrose: Hypoglycemia is a common cause of altered mental status and is characterized by coma, stupor, or lethargy. For this reason, serum glucose concentration should be assessed in all patients with altered mental status. Hypoglycemia or hyperglycemia can mimic stroke [5]; however, the empiric administration of glucose for patients with altered mental status is cautioned against. Among those who have altered mental status due to a stroke, concern about worsened stroke outcomes following empiric treatment of altered mental status with glucose favors checking the blood glucose prior to administration of glucose [6, 7]. Following the administration of a glucose bolus, a transient hyperglycemic state occurs [8], and hyperglycemia is considered a poor prognostic factor in stroke patients [6, 7]. Furthermore, hyperglycemia may potentially decrease any beneficial effect of the administration of tissue plasminogen activator, a treatment for stroke [9].

Naloxone: Naloxone is used as an antidote to opioid overdose. The use of naloxone can provide an effective reversal of signs and symptoms that comprise the opioid toxidrome, which is characterized by stupor, hypoventilation, miosis, and decreased bowel sounds [10, 11]. Death from opioid overdose is predominantly due to respiratory depression [12]. Naloxone should be administered primarily to reverse respiratory depression (respiratory rate <8–12 breaths/minute) and not necessarily dosed to fully arouse the patient due to the risk of inducing significant withdrawal [13, 14]. In addition to reversing respiratory depression and eliminating the need for airway interventions, naloxone may assist in the diagnosis of opioid overdose and potentially eliminate the need for additional diagnostic studies involved in the evaluation of the patient with altered mental status [13].

Overall, the use of naloxone is relatively safe [15]. The main effects of naloxone include the reversal of opioid-induced respiratory depression and altered mental status. Naloxone also reverses opioid-induced analgesia, bradycardia, and gastrointestinal stasis [16]. Pulmonary edema has been associated with the use of naloxone but should not be considered a direct side effect [17–23]. Hypertension [24–26], seizures [27], arrhythmias [28, 29], and cardiac arrest [30] have been described with the use of naloxone. In addition, administration of naloxone may precipitate opioid withdrawal [31], which although it is not life-threatening, can cause the patient to develop nausea, vomiting, diarrhea, yawning, piloerection, and agitation [32]. For this reason, when using naloxone to restore respiratory function, it is prudent to start with administration of a low dose of naloxone, typically 0.04 mg, and increase the dose up to a maximum of 15 mg until sufficient respiratory function is attained [14, 33]. If respiratory function is not restored after maximum dosing of naloxone, opioids are not the likely cause of respiratory depression [34, 35]. An important consideration in naloxone dosing is the duration of action of the opioid to which the patient was exposed. The respiratory depressive effects of an opioid may outlast the effects of a single dose of naloxone, which is commonly 20–90 minutes. In these scenarios, naloxone may be re-dosed or even administered as an infusion to restore ventilations [14, 36]. The decision to administer naloxone should be based on the patient's clinical presentation and not based on a drug screen [37].

Flumazenil: Flumazenil is a highly competitive antagonist of the benzodiazepine receptor at the $GABA_A$ receptor [38]. It reverses benzodiazepine's effects during conscious sedation or general anesthesia [39–51]. Flumazenil use may assist in the diagnostic evaluation of a patient who presents with altered mental status due to a pure benzodiazepine overdose characterized by lethargy, stupor, or coma [52–57]. When effective, its administration may prevent the need for additional diagnostic studies involved in the acute evaluation of patients with altered mental status [58, 59]. The main, considerable potential side effect following flumazenil administration is the development of seizures [60–63]. Patients at risk for the development of flumazenil-induced seizures and in whom flumazenil should not be administered are 1) patients who chronically take benzodiazepines, 2) patients who have co-ingested a pro-convulsant drug, and 3) patients who have a seizure disorder [60]. Other reported adverse effects include agitation due to benzodiazepine withdrawal [64–67], arrhythmia [68, 69], cardiac arrest [70], and death [71].

Flumazenil may be most effectively used to treat a non-benzodiazepine-dependent patient who presents with altered mental status due to a pure benzodiazepine overdose. Prior to the administration of flumazenil, it is important to establish a reliable history that correlates with the patient's clinical presentation consistent with benzodiazepine overdose [72, 73]. Safe administration of flumazenil to the patient with an acute unknown overdose is less clear due to the risk of inducing seizures [60, 63, 71, 74–76]. Recently, a meta-analysis of 13 randomized clinical trials involving the use of flumazenil in suspected both pure benzodiazepine-exposed patients and poly-substance overdose patients reported a higher incidence of serious adverse effects (2.4%) (including seizures, arrhythmia, and hypotension) among those administered flumazenil when compared with those administered placebo (<1%) [77]. While all these data highlight the need for cautious use of this antidote, other studies have reported a low rate of seizures after flumazenil administration to patients with an unknown overdose [78–81]. If the decision is made to administer flumazenil, and seizures occur after the administration, the seizures should be treated with high doses of benzodiazepines or barbiturates [60]. Overall, the decision to use flumazenil in an acute overdose patient should involve a careful assessment of the risks and benefits of its use with the knowledge that benzodiazepine overdose has low morbidity and mortality [82].

Other limited applications of flumazenil use among patients with altered mental status include the temporary reversal of hepatic encephalopathy [83] and the reversal of benzodiazepine-induced delirium among patients being treated for alcohol withdrawal [84].

Physostigmine: Physostigmine is a reversible acetylcholinesterase inhibitor that acts in the peripheral and central nervous systems and can be used in the evaluation and treatment of patients who present with the anticholinergic toxidrome following exposure to an anticholinergic agent [85]. The anticholinergic toxidrome is characterized by altered mental status, elevated temperature, tachycardia, decreased bowel sounds, dry mucous membranes, large pupils, and urinary retention. The primary manifestation of anticholinergic poisoning is altered mental status, which can range from confusion to coma [86]. Physostigmine works to increase synaptic concentrations of acetylcholine and reverse the altered mental status associated with the toxidrome [85, 87]. In this regard, it can be used as a diagnostic agent [88]. When fully effective, its use can eliminate the need for diagnostic tests such as head computed tomography and lumbar puncture as well as interventions such as intubation and thus, can result in lower resource utilization and increased patient safety [85, 88]. In a retrospective analysis of 815 patients with the anticholinergic toxidrome, patients who received only physostigmine as a treatment intervention had a significantly lower rate of intubation when compared with other treatment groups [89]. Side effects associated with physostigmine use include bradycardia or asystole [88, 90], diaphoresis, increased gastrointestinal and respiratory secretions, bronchospasm, and seizures [88]. Physostigmine should not be administered to patients who have intraventricular conduction delays or atrioventricular block on the electrocardiogram, intestinal obstruction, or reversible airway disease [91].

1.6.2 Approach to Management

1.6.2.1 Immediate Interventions

1. **Airway, Breathing, Circulation:** Maintain the airway and assist ventilation if necessary. Administer supplemental oxygen. Treat hypotension, and resuscitate as per standard emergency care.

2. **Thiamine:** Administer thiamine 100 mg intravenously [92] to patients who are suspected of alcohol abuse, Wernicke's encephalopathy, or malnutrition.
3. **Dextrose:**
   a. **Caution:** Perform rapid bedside fingerstick glucose testing in all patients with altered mental status. Hypoglycemia and hyperglycemia can mimic stroke.
   b. **Indications for use:** Hypoglycemia (serum glucose <70 mg/sL) [93].
   c. **Dose:** 25 g of 50% dextrose solution intravenously [93].
4. **Naloxone:**
   a. **Caution:** Be aware of the possibility of the patient developing acute opioid withdrawal.
   b. **Indications for use:** Patients with a respiratory rate <12 breaths per minute and altered mental status should receive naloxone.
   c. **Dose:** Small doses (0.04 mg) should be the initial dose. If no response, repeat by titrating up the dose until 15 mg of naloxone has been given or until respirations have been restored. Naloxone can be administered via the intravenous, intramuscular, or intranasal route [14].

   Comment: Reversal of opioid toxicity, once achieved, will be sustained for approximately 20 to 60 min. Because the duration of action of many opioids exceeds the duration of action of naloxone, the patient may require repeated bolus doses or be administered a continuous infusion at a dose sufficient to prevent the reappearance of respiratory depression [14, 36].
5. **Flumazenil:**
   a. **Caution:** Be aware of the possibility of the patient developing seizures or arrhythmia.
   b. **Indications:** Used for the reversal of benzodiazepine-induced sedation. Use is contraindicated in patients who have ingested pro-convulsant drugs, who have benzodiazepine tolerance, and who have a seizure history [60]. If the patient has no known contraindications to flumazenil use, carefully consider the benefits of flumazenil administration relative to the risks.
   c. **Dose:** Administer flumazenil 0.2 mg intravenously over 30 seconds, to be followed 60 seconds later by 0.3 mg intravenously if the patient's mental status does not improve. Subsequent doses of 0.5 mg administered intravenously at 1-minute intervals may also be given up to a maximum of 3 mg in 1 hour. If needed, a continuous infusion can be given at 0.3–0.5 mg/hour [79].

   Comment: The binding of flumazenil to the benzodiazepine–receptor complex is competitive, and flumazenil has a shorter duration of action, approximately 60 minutes, than most benzodiazepines. For this reason, patients should be closely monitored for re-sedation and the need for re-dosing [79].
6. **Physostigmine:**
   a. **Caution:** Prior to administration, check an electrocardiogram for intraventricular conduction defects or atrioventricular block. If these are present, physostigmine is relatively contraindicated [91]. Anticipate development of possible cholinergic symptoms after administration [88].
   b. **Indications:** Use is intended for reversal of the altered mental status associated with the anticholinergic toxidrome.
   c. **Dose:** Administer a total of 0.5 to 2 mg intravenously at increments of 0.5 mg over 1 to 2 minutes [88].

   Comment: The duration of action of physostigmine is 45–60 minutes. The effects of the anticholinergic agent may outlast the clinical reversal of physostigmine. If needed, physostigmine may be re-dosed [85, 88].

1.6.2.2 Secondary Interventions

1. **Reassess:** If the patient remains comatose, stuporous, or lethargic despite administration of antidotes, reassess for underlying medical causes (meningitis, trauma, status epilepticus, etc.) and consider admission.
2. **Monitor:** Maintain continuous monitoring (oxygen saturation, blood pressure, cardiac monitoring) at all times.

   Comment: This is particularly important since the duration of action of many opioids and benzodiazepines is longer than the duration of action of their respective antidote.
3. **Head computed tomography/lumbar puncture:** Consider head computed tomography and lumbar puncture if the patient has an unexplained persistent altered mental status, is hyperthermic, or has persistent focal neurological findings despite evaluation and interventions as delineated earlier.
4. **Electrocardiogram:** Perform an electrocardiogram on all overdose patients who have altered mental status.
5. **Laboratory data:** For patients who respond to antidotes and return to their baseline mental status within an observation period of several hours, no laboratory testing may be necessary if a return to baseline mental status and physical examination is present on reassessment and if the vital signs are within normal. If the patient remains persistently altered or has significantly abnormal vital signs, check electrolytes, complete blood count, creatine phosphokinase, renal function, hepatic function, and acetaminophen and salicylate concentrations. Toxicology screens are generally over-utilized [94], and they infrequently contribute information

to the acute management of patients with altered mental status [37].

6. **Disposition:**

Admission: Patients who have required more than one dose of antidote or require an infusion of the antidote in order to maintain their respirations and mental status should be considered for admission due to possible recurrence of drug effect and the need for additional antidote dosing. Patients who present with significant hypoxia or respiratory depression should also be considered for admission due to the risk of associated conditions. Patients who are symptomatic after exposure to long-acting opioids should be admitted.

Comment: Antidote infusions should be maintained in a monitored setting, and patients should be closely monitored any time the infusion is stopped. Monitoring for 6 hours after the infusion has been discontinued is usually adequate [14].

Discharge: Stable patients who have returned to baseline mental status and physical exam and have reassuring vital signs and laboratory data may be observed for a period of time, which depends on the drug of exposure, if known, and any underlying conditions. Usually, 6 hours is adequate [95].

ACKNOWLEDGMENTS

Brett A. Roth, M.D., Neal L. Benowitz, M.D., and Kent R. Olson, M.D.

REFERENCES

1. Huff J. Altered mental status and coma. In Tintinalli JE, Stapczynski J, Ma O, Yealy DM, Meckler GD, Cline DM (Eds.) *Tintinalli's Emergency Medicine: A Comprehensive Study Guide, 8ème*. New York: McGraw-Hill, 2016. http://accessmedicine.mhmedical.com/content.aspx?bookid=1658&sectionid=109436746. Accessed June 05, 2017.
2. Guido ME, Brady W, DeBehnke D. Reversible neurological deficits in a chronic alcohol abuser: a case report of Wernicke's encephalopathy. *Am J Emerg Med* 1994;12:238–40.
3. Wrenn KD, Murphy F, Slovis CM. A toxicity study of parenteral thiamine hydrochloride. *Ann Emerg Med* 1989;18:867–70.
4. Centerwall BS, Criqui MH. Prevention of the Wernicke-Korsakoff syndrome: a cost-benefit analysis. *N Engl J Med* 1978;299:285–9.
5. Jauch EC, Saver JL, Adams HP Jr, Bruno A, Connors JJ, Demaerschalk BM, et al. Guidelines for the early management of patient with acute ischemic stroke. A guideline for healthcare professional from the American Heart Association. *Stroke* 2013;44:870–947.
6. Bruno A, Biller J, Adams HP, Clarke WR, Woolson RF, Williams LS, Hansen MD. Acute blood glucose level and outcome from ischemic stroke. Triage of ORG10172 in Acute Stroke Treatment (TOAST) Investigators. *Neurology* 1999;52:280–4.
7. Weir CJ, Murray GD, Dyker AG, Lees KR. Is hyperglycemia an independent predictor of poor outcome after acute stroke? Results of a long-term follow-up study. *BMJ* 1997;314:1303–6.
8. Balentine JR, Gaeta TJ, Kessler D, Bagiella E, Lee T. Effect of 50mL dextrose in water administration on the blood sugar of euglycemic volunteers. *Acad Emerg Med* 1998;5:691–4.
9. Alvarez-Sabin J, Molina CA, Montaner J, Arenillas JF, Huertas R, Ribo M, Codina A, Quintana M. Effects of admission hyperglycemia on stroke outcome in reperfused tissue plasminogen activator-treated patients. *Stroke* 2003;34:1235–41.
10. Kaplan JL, Marx JA, Calabro JJ, Gin Shaw SL, Spiller JD, SpiveyWL, et al. Double-blind, randomized study of malmefene and naloxone in emergency department patients with suspected narcotic overdose. *Ann Emerg Med* 1999;34:42–50.
11. Yealy DM, Paris PM, Kaplan RM, Heller MB, Marini SE. The safety of prehospital naloxone administration by paramedics. *Ann Emerg Med* 1990;19:902–5.
12. Niester M, Overdyk E, Smith T, et al. Opioid-induced respiratory depression in paediatrics: a revew of case reports. *Br J Anaesth* 2013;110:175–82.
13. Nelson LS, Olsen D. Opioids. In: Hoffman RS, Howland MA, Lewin NA, Nelson LS, Goldfrank LR (Eds.) *Goldfrank's Toxicologic Emergencies*, 10th ed. New York: McGraw-Hill, 492–509.
14. Boyer E. Management of opioid analgesic overdose. *N Engl J Med* 2012;367:146–55.
15. Hoffman RS, Goldfrank LR. The poisoned patient with altered consciousness. Controversies in the use of a "coma cocktail". *JAMA* 1995;274:562–9.
16. Nelson LS, Howland MA. Opioid antagonists. In: Hoffman RS, Howland MA, Lewin NA, Nelson LS, Goldfrank LR (Eds.) *Goldfrank's Toxicologic Emergencies*, 10th ed. New York: McGraw-Hill, 510–515.
17. Sporer KA, Dorn E. Heroin-related non-cardiogenic pulmonary edema. A case series. *Chest* 2001;120:1628–32.
18. Osler W. Oedema of left lung-morphia poisoning. *Montreal Gen Hosp Rep* 1880;1:291–2.
19. Schwartz JA, Koenigsberg MD. Naloxone-induced pulmonary edema. *Ann Emerg Med* 1987;16(11):1294–6.
20. Prough DS, Roy R, Bumgarner J, Shannon G. Acute pulmonary edema in healthy teenagers following conservative doses of intravenous naloxone. *Anesthesiology* 1984;60(5):485–6.
21. Smialek JE, Monforte JR, Aronow R, Spitz WU. Methadone deaths in children: a continuing problem. *JAMA* 1977;238:2516–7.
22. Olinger CP, Adams HP Jr, Brott TG, et al. High dose intravenous naloxone for the treatment of acute ischemic stroke. *Stroke* 1990;21:721–5.
23. Groeger JS, Carlon GC, Howland WS. Naloxone in septic shock. *Crit Care Med* 1983;11:650–4.
24. Wasserberger J, Ordog GJ. Naloxone-induced hypertension in patients on clonidine [letter]. *Ann Emerg Med* 1988;17:557.
25. Levin ER, Sharp B, Drayer JI, Weber MA. Severe hypertension induced by naloxone by naloxone. *Am J Med Sci* 1985;290:70–2.
26. Azar I, Turndorf H. Severe hypertension and multiple atrial premature contractions following naloxone administration. *Anesth Analg* 1979;58:524–5.
27. Mariani PJ. Seizure associated with low-dose naloxone. *Am J Emerg Med* 1989;7:127–9.

28. Lameijer H, Azizi N, Ligtenberg JJM, Maaten JCT. Ventricular tachycardia after naloxone administration: a drug related complication? Case report and literature review. *Drug Saf-Case Rep* 2014;1:2.
29. Hunter R. Ventricular tachycardia following naloxone administration in an illicit drug misuse. *J Clin Forensic Med* 2005;12:218–9.
30. Cuss FM, Colaco CB, Baron JH. Cardiac arrest after reversal of effects of opiates with naloxone. *Br Med J (Clin Res Ed)* 1984;288(6414):363–4.
31. Lubman DZ, Koutsogiannis KI. Emergency management of inadvertent accelerated opiate withdrawal in dependent opiate users. *Drug Alcohol Rev* 2003;22:433–6.
32. Chiang WK, Goldfrank LR. Substance withdrawal. *Emerg Clin North Am* 1990;8:613–32.
33. Wermeling DP. Review of naloxone safety for opioid overdose: practical considerations for new technology and expanded public access. *Ther Adv Drug Saf* 2015;6:20–31.
34. Prosser JM, Jones BE, Nelson L. Com- plications of oral exposure to fentanyl transdermal delivery system patches. *J Med Toxicol* 2010;6:443–7.
35. Schumann H, Erickson T, Thompson TM, Zautcke JL, Denton JS. Fentanyl epi- demic in Chicago, Illinois and surrounding Cook County. *Clin Toxicol* 2008;46:501–6.
36. Goldfrank L, Weisman RS, Errick JK, Lo MW. A dosing nomogram for continu- ous infusion of intravenous naloxone. *Ann Emerg Med* 1986;15:566–70.
37. Boyer EW, Shannon MW. Which drug tests in medical emergencies? *Clin Chem* 2003;49:353–4.
38. Hunkeler W, Mohler H, Pieri L, Polc P, Bonetti EP, Cumin R, et al. Selective antagonists of benzodiazepines. *Nature* 1981;290:514–6.
39. Alon E, Baitella L, Hossli G. Double-blind study of the reversal of midazolam supplemented general anesthesia with Ro 15–1788. *Br J Anaesth* 1987;59:455–8.
40. Dimitriou B, Kottis G, Bathrelou S, Triantaphyllidis A. Flumazenil in reversal of central effects of midazolam used as induction agent in general anesthesia. *Drug Res* 1989;39:399–400.
41. Fisher GC, Hutton P. Cardiovascular responses to flumazenil-induced arousal after arterial surgery. *Anesthesiology* 1989;44:104–6.
42. Geller E, Weinbrum A, Schiff B, Speiser Z, Nevo Y, Halpern P, et al. The effects of flumazenil on the process of recovery from halothane anaesthesia. *Eur J Anaesthesiol* 1988;2(Suppl):151–3.
43. Geller E, Niv D, Nevo Y, Leykin Y, Sorkin P, Rudick V. Early clinical experience in reversing benzodiazepine sedation with flumazenil after short procedures. *Resuscitation* 1988;16 Suppl:S49–56.
44. Ghoneim MM, Dembo JB, Block RI. Time course of antagonism of sedative and amnesic effects of diazepam by flumazenil. *Anesthesiology* 1989;70:899–904.
45. Harrop-Griffiths AW, Watson NA, Jewkes DA. Midazolam and flumazenil in the anaesthetic management of trigeminal nerve thermocoagulation. *Br J Anaesth* 1990;64:586–9.
46. Marty J, Nitenberg A, Phillip I, Foult JM, Joyon D, Desmonts JM. Coronary and left ventricular hemodynamic responses following reversal of flunitrazepam-induced sedation with flumazenil in patients with coronary artery disease. *Anesthesiology* 1991;74:71–6.
47. Mora CT, Torjman M, White PF. Effects of diazepam and flumazenil on sedation and hypoxic ventilatory response. *Anesth Analg* 1989;68:473–8.
48. Ricou B, Forster A, Brückner A, Chastonary P, Gemperle M. Clinical evaluation of a specific benzodiazepine antagonist (Ro-15-1788). *Br J Anaesth* 1986;58:1005–11.
49. Rosenbaum NL, Hooper PA. The effects of flumazenil, a new benzodiazepine antagonist, on the reversal of midazolam sedation and amnesia in dental patients. *Br Dent J* 1985;65:400–2.
50. White PF, Shafer A, Boyle WA 3rd, Doze VA, Duncan S. Benzodiazepine antagonism does not provoke a stress response. *Anesthesiology* 1989;70:636–9.
51. Wolff J, Carl P, Clausen TG, Mikkelsen BO. Ro 15–1788 for postoperative recovery. *Anesthesiology* 1986;41:1001–6.
52. Brogden RN, Goa KL. Flumazenil. A reappraisal of its pharmacological properties and therapeutic efficacy as a benzodiazepine antagonist. *Drugs* 1991;42:1061–89.
53. Höjer J, Baehrendtz S. The effect of flumazenil (Ro 15–1788) in the management of self-induced benzodiazepine poisoning. *Acta Med Scand* 1988;224:357–65.
54. Knudsen L, Lonka L, Sørensen H, Kirkegaard L, Jensen OV, Jensen S. Benzodiazepine intoxication treated with flumazenil (Anexate, RO 15–1788). *Anaesthesia* 1988;43: 274–6.
55. Breheny FX. Reversal of midazolam sedation with flumazenil. *Crit Care Med* 1991;20:736–9.
56. Kreshak A, Tomaszewski C, Clark R, Cantrell F. Flumazenil administration to poisoned pediatric patients. *Ped Emerg Care* 2012;28:448–50. doi:10.1097/PEC.0b013e3182531d0d.
57. Jensen S, Kirkegaard L, Anderson BN. Randomized clinical investigation of Ro-15-1788, a benzodiazepine antagonist, in reversing the central effects of flunitrazepam. *Eur J Anaesthesiol* 1987;4:113–8.
58. Höjer J, Baehrendtz S, Matell G, Gustafsson LL. Diagnostic utility of flumazenil in coma with suspected poisoning: a double blind, randomized controlled study. *BMJ* 1990;30:1308.
59. Winkler E, Almog S, Kriger D, Tirosh MS, Halkin H, Ezra D. Use of flumazenil in the diagnosis and treatment of patients with a coma of unknown etiology. *Crit Care Med* 1993;21:538–42.
60. Spivey WH. Flumazenil and seizures: analysis of 43 cases. *Clin Ther* 1992;14(2):292–305.
61. Chern TL, Kwan A. Flumazenil-induced seizure accompanying benzodiazepine and baclofen intoxication [letter]. *Am J Emerg Med* 1996;14(2):231–2.
62. McDuffee AT, Tobias JD. Seizure after flumazenil administration in a pediatric patient. *Pediatr Emerg Care* 1995;11(3):186–7.
63. Mordel A, Winkler E, Almog S, Tirosh M, Ezra D. Seizures after flumazenil administration in a case of combined benzodiazepine and tricyclic antidepressant overdose. *Crit Care Med* 1992;20:1733–4.
64. Amrein R, Hetzel W, Hartmann D, Lorscheid T. Clinical pharmacology of flumazenil. *Eur J Anaesthesiol Suppl* 1988;2:65–80.
65. Amrein R, Leishman B, Bentzinger C, Roncari G. Flumazenil in benzodiazepine antagonism: actions and clinical use in intoxications and anaesthesiology. *Med Toxicol Adverse Drug Exp* 1987;2:411–29.
66. Lader M. Anxiolytic drugs: dependence, addiction and abuse. *Eur Neuro-Psychopharmacol* 1994;4:85–91.
67. Lukes SE, Griffiths RR. Precipitated withdrawal by a benzodiazepine receptor antagonist (Ro-15-1788) after 7 days of diazepam. *Science* 1982;217:1161–3.

68. Soleimanpour H, Ziapour B, Negargar S, Taghizadieh A, Shadvar K. Ventricular tachycardia due to flumazenil administration. *Pak J Biol Sci* 2010;13:1161–3.
69. Herd B, Clarke F. Complete heart block after flumazenil. *Hum Exp Toxicol* 1991;10:289.
70. Katz Y, Boulos M, Singer P, Rosenberg B. Cardiac arrest associated with flumazenil. *BMJ* 1992;304:1415.
71. Haverkos GP, DiSalvo RP, Imhoff TE. Fatal seizures after flumazenil administration in a patient with mixed overdose. *Ann Pharmacother* 1994;28(12):1347–9.
72. Chern TL, et al., Diagnostic and therapeutic utility of flumazenil in comatose patients with drug overdose. *Am J Emerg Med* 1993;11(2):122–4.
73. Weinbroum A, Halpern P, Geller E. The use of flumazenil in the management of acute drug poisoning — a review. *Intensive Care Med* 1991;17 Suppl 1:S32–8.
74. Geller E, Crome P, Schaller MD, Marchant B, Ectors M, Scollo-Lavizzari G. Risks and benefits of therapy with flumazenil (Anexate) in mixed drug intoxications. *Eur Neurol* 1991;31:241–50.
75. Gueye PN, Hoffman JR, Taboulet P, Vicaut E, Baud FJ. Empiric use of flumazenil in comatose patients: limited applicability of criteria to define low risk. *Ann Emerg Med* 1996;27:730–5.
76. L'heureux P, Vranckx M, Leduc D, Askenasi R. Flumazenil in mixed benzodiazepine/tricyclic antidepressant overdose: a placebo controlled study in the dog. *Am J Emerg Med* 1992;10:184–8.
77. Penninga E, Graudal N, Ladekarl MB, Jurgens G. Adverse events associated with flumazenil treatment for the management of suspected benzodiazepine intoxication – a systematic review with meta-analyses of randomized trials. *Basic Clin Pharmacol Toxicol* 2016;118:37–44. doi:10.111/bcpt.12434.
78. Höjer J, Baehrendtz S, Matell G, Gustafsson LL. Diagnostic utility of flumazenil in coma with suspected poisoning: a double blind, randomized controlled study. *BMJ* 1990;301:1308.
79. Weinbroum A, Rudick V, Sorkine P, Nevo Y, Halpern P, Geller E, et al. Use of flumazenil in the treatment of drug overdose: a double-blind and open clinical study in 110 patients. *Crit Care Med* 1996;24:199–206.
80. Kreshak A, Cantrell F, Clark R. Tomaszewski CA A poison center's 10 year experience with flumazenil administration to acutely poisoned adults. *J Emerg Med* 2012;43:667. doi:10.1016/j.jemermed.2012.01.059.
81. Veiraiah A, Dyas J, Cooper G, Routledge PA. Thompson JP Flumazenil use in benzodiazepine overdose in the UK: a retrospective survey of NPIS data. *Emerg Med J* 2012;29:565–9. doi:10.1136/emj.2010.095075.
82. Höjer J, Baehrendtz S, Gustafsson L. Benzodiazepine poisoning: experience of 702 admissions to an intensive care unit during a 14-year period. *J Intern Med* 1989;226:117–22.
83. Barbaro G, Di Lorenzo G, Soldini M, Giancaspro G, Bellomo G, Belloni G. Flumazenil for hepatic encephalopathy grade III and IVa in patients with cirrhosis: an Italian multicenter double-blind, placebo-controlled, cross-over study. *Hepatology* 1998;28:374–8.
84. Moore PW, Donovan JW, Burkhart KK, Waskin JA, Hieger MA, Adkins AR, et al. Safety and efficacy of flumazenil for reversal of iatrogenic benzodiazepine-associated delirium toxicity during treatment of alcohol withdrawal, a retrospective review at one center. *J Med Toxicol* 2014;10:126–32. doi:10.1007/s13181-014-0391-6.
85. Burns MJ, Linden CH, Graudins A, Brown RM, Fletcher KE. A comparison of physostigmine and benzodiazepines for the treatment of anticholingergic poisoning. *Ann Emerg Med* 2000;35:374–81.
86. Curry SC, O'Connor AD, Graeme KA, Mills KC, Skolnik AB. Neurotransmitters and neuromodulators. In Hoffman RS, Howland MA, Lewin NA, Nelson LS, Goldfrank LR (Eds.) *Goldfrank's Toxicologic Emergencies*, 10th ed. New York: McGraw-Hill, 2015, 172–201.
87. Beaver KM, Gavin TJ. Treatment of acute anticholinergic poisoning with physostigmine. *Am J Emerg Med* 1998;16:505–7.
88. Schneir AB, Offerman SR, Ly BT, Davis JD, Baldwin MT, Williams SR, Clark RF. Complications of diagnostic physostigmine administration to emergency department patients. *Annals Emerg Med* 2003;42:14–19.
89. Watkins JW, Schwarz ES, Arroyo-Plasencia AM, Mullins ME. The use of physostigmine by toxicologists in anticholinergic toxicity. *J Med Toxicol* 2015;11:179–84.
90. Pentel P, Peterson CD. Asystole complicating physostigmine treatment in tricyclic antidepressant overdose. *Ann Emerg Med* 1980;9:588–90.
91. *Physostigmine Sulfate. American Hospital Formulary Service (AHFS).* Bethesda, MD, American Society of Health System Pharmacists, 2013.
92. www.pdr.net. Accessed June 10, 2017.
93. Goyal N, Schlichting AB. Type 1 diabetes mellitus. In Tintinalli JE, Stapczynski J, Ma O, Yealy DM, Meckler GD, Cline DM (Eds.) *Tintinalli's Emergency Medicine: A Comprehensive Study Guide, 8ème.* New York: McGraw-Hill, 2016. http://accessmedicine.mhmedical.com/content.aspx?bookid=1658&sectionid=109443541. Accessed June 10, 2017.
94. Olson KR, Pentel PR, Kelley MT. Physical assessment and differential diagnosis of the poisoned patient. *Med Toxicol Adverse Drug Exp* 1987;2:52–81.
95. Hollander JE, McCracken G, Johnson S, Valentine SM, Shih R. Emergency department observation of poisoned patients: how long is necessary? *Acad Emerg Med* 1999;6:887–94.

1.7 AGITATION, DELIRIUM, AND PSYCHOSIS

Michael P. Wilson and Gary M. Vilke

1.7.1 General Comments

Agitation is a large problem nationwide in the field, in the emergency department, and in the outpatient clinic setting. Although precise numbers are hard to determine, it is likely that as many as 1.7 million episodes of acute agitation are treated annually in U.S. emergency departments, with countless more treated in the prehospital setting, clinics, and primary physician offices [1–3].

- Agitation is a nonspecific term that refers to increased motor or verbal activity which disrupts the traditional physician–patient collaboration [4]. Agitation is a syndrome, not a diagnosis, and may or may not require medical therapy. For example, a patient who is angry about their hospital bill likely does not require treatment with antipsychotic medications. Treatment of agitation should focus on the most likely causes (see later).
- Delirium is a state associated with inattention and fluctuating level of consciousness. Like agitation, it has many causes. Treatment should target the most likely cause.
- Psychosis is an abnormal mental condition. In the medical sense, it means that an individual's thinking is so disturbed that they cannot adequately perceive reality in the way that others do.

In clinical practice, management of all three conditions depends on treating the most likely underlying condition.

Over the past several years, modern expert consensus has called for improved humane practices to treat agitated patients [5, 6]. Multiple expert consensus documents have recommended a number of components in the treatment of agitation for optimum care [3, 7]. These include the use of standardized agitation scales to objectively measure agitation; the use of verbal de-escalation to calm the patient when this can be done safely; if needed, the careful use of medication targeted to the specific type of agitation, and particularly the use of oral medicines whenever possible; and the use of second-generation antipsychotics (SGAs) over first-generation antipsychotics (FGAs) in most situations not involving alcohol intoxication. Treatment of agitation may focus more on some techniques, such as verbal de-escalation, in outpatient settings which may not readily stock antipsychotics.

1.7.1.1 Confounders

Although often approached by clinicians without forethought, the rapid treatment of agitation, delirium, or psychosis involves a multitude of legal and ethical issues. The first issue is treatment versus restraint. If medications are being utilized to target the most likely cause of the patient's symptoms, such measures are typically considered therapeutic. If medications, however, are used to prevent movement, commonly referred to as "keeping the patient in the bed," the medications are then considered to be no different from physical restraints [8].

The issue of physical restraint is of paramount importance. Although courts have recognized the authority of physicians to "hold" patients who might be at risk of harming themselves or others, this right is not without limits [9]. Only therapeutic modalities may be used, and restraints such as TASERs or handcuffs are allowed to be used only by security services [10]. Even when medical restraints are used, physicians have been successfully sued for preventing patients who are of sound mind from leaving the hospital [9].

1.7.1.2 Initial Approach to the Agitated Patient

In a word, the initial approach should be made "carefully." No matter which part of the hospital or outpatient clinic the patient is in, the goals of agitation treatment are the same: a) calm and protect the patient; b) calm and protect staff; c) evaluate and appropriately disposition the patient. From this perspective, it should be recognized that the use of medications can often confuse evaluation and delay disposition [11]. This goal of evaluating and dispositioning is an often-overlooked and important goal of agitation treatment. An agitated patient may need transfer to a higher level of care, or may simply be allowed to leave if he or she is capable of making informed decisions and if an effort has been made to resolve the particular situation.

1.7.1.3 Initial Pharmacological Intervention

For those patients whose behavior continues to deteriorate, who cannot be maintained without constant ongoing verbal de-escalation or who refuse medication, a show of force is typically recommended [5]. This is better termed a "show of concern" instead of a "show of force" in order to reinforce the concern for the individual and the caring nature of the intervention. Oral medication is typically offered at this point, with the decision to use intramuscular (IM) medication made with careful consideration as to the type of agitation [12]. Although not well studied, oral medication is thought be as efficacious as IM injections despite differences in time to peak plasma concentration [13, 14]. The challenge is often getting the patient to take oral medications.

The decision to force IM or intravenous (IV) medication implies a determination that a patient lacks the capacity to make safe and appropriate decisions about their own care during the agitation episode, although they may of course regain this capacity later after therapy [15]. These medications are appropriate if a patient cannot appreciate the consequences of a particular decision, such as those patients who are violent or gravely disabled. A patient simply being on a psychiatric hold alone is not generally considered grounds for forcing medication unless there is an emergent reason for doing so.

The type or assumed cause of agitation will most likely guide the best choice of medication (see treatment algorithm later). In an outpatient setting, the need to emergently medicate the patient is often a reliable sign that the patient should be transferred to a higher level of care. If a patient's behavior continues to deteriorate, physical restraints are a last resort [16].

In terms of medication, there a number of different options in the United States, with haloperidol and lorazepam perhaps being the most common combination used in emergency departments [17–19]. Haloperidol, first Food and Drug Administration (FDA) approved in 1967, is a butyrophenone with primary activity at the dopamine 2 (D2) receptor [20]. Although commonly used, haloperidol carries a black-box warning about the risks of use to treat dementia-related psychosis as it lengthens QT intervals and is not FDA approved for IV use. Haloperidol should be used cautiously in patients whose intervals are already prolonged, who are on other QT-prolonging drugs, or who may develop dystonic or other extrapyramidal reactions.

Given the side effects of haloperidol and the need for administration with adjunctive medications, expert consensus documents have recommended atypical or "second-generation" antipsychotics for first-line use in patients who are not intoxicated with alcohol. Typically, the goal of medication should be "calming" rather than outright sedation and putting them to sleep.

Using phenothiazines to treat agitation secondary to substance withdrawal, particularly alcohol withdrawal, has been discouraged because of treatment failure and possibly increased mortality [21]. However, using antipsychotics such as haloperidol to treat substance-induced agitation, often referred to as substance-induced psychosis, is more controversial. Even single doses of amphetamines can induce a transient psychotic reaction, which may be more pronounced in individuals who already have psychotic symptoms [22]. This may be related to changes in both 5-HT and D2 receptors, and symptoms may be less responsive to antipsychotic medication. However, a Cochrane review noted that based on a single randomized controlled trial, olanzapine may be as efficacious as haloperidol but with fewer side effects [23]. Given other beneficial effects of benzodiazepines, this class of medications is likely the continuing first choice for this condition [24].

1.7.2 Stepwise Approach to Management

1.7.2.1 Immediate Interventions: Safety First

"Safety first" starts with the recognition of agitation as compared with aggression. Although agitation does not necessarily lead to aggression, it is thought to make aggression more likely. Patients who are exhibiting threatening behavior directed towards persons or property should only be approached by hospital security or police. If these are not immediately available, maintaining a safe distance and attempting verbal de-escalation should occur until security resources arrive.

When dealing with agitated patients, staff should have a prepared place in a separate room away from potential weapons and sharp objects, and there should be an easy way of notifying security if the need arises. Rooms should ideally have more than one exit to prevent trapping of staff members. If not, staff should attempt to remain between the patient and a safe exit.

Once a patient becomes agitated, if possible, efforts should be made to ensure that they are physically comfortable. External stimuli such as loud noises should be minimized. Staff assigned to the patient should be trained and encouraged to utilize verbal de-escalation techniques. Although there is little experimental evidence, such as what sorts of verbal techniques to employ, there are likely few, if any, negative side effects to patients from being "talked down" as long as this can be done safely [25, 26].

1.7.2.2 ABCs/Assess Underlying Medical Conditions

Once safety is ensured, patients should be assessed for underlying medical conditions. Although antipsychotics may be useful in treating symptoms, they are often not the preferred treatment for medical conditions such as hyperthyroidism, hypoxia, or a variety of other medical conditions. If the most likely cause is substance intoxication or withdrawal, benzodiazepines may be most useful (see Figure 1.7.1).

1.7.2.3 Secondary Interventions

1.7.2.3.1 Physical Restraints

Restraints should be used sparingly, with as little force as possible, and only when necessary to protect the patient or staff from harm. The characteristics of restrained patients are not well studied but appear to depend more on disruptiveness than on patient demographics [27]. In a hospital setting, physical restraint should be performed by trained security personnel with or without the assistance of trained medical staff. Staff members who have not been trained in restraint should not attempt this except under extenuating circumstances.

1.7.2.3.2 IVs, Monitor, Further Evaluation

Patients with severe enough agitation to warrant medication and physical restraint likely will require cardiac and ventilatory monitoring. This will include cardiac monitoring and pulse oximetry once the patient is calmed enough for the monitoring equipment to be placed. Depending on the degree of agitation and preceding physical activity, IV fluids and evaluation of electrolytes and renal function as well as creatine phosphokinase levels to assess for possible rhabdomyolysis may be indicated. While toxicology screens of blood and urine are generally over-utilized, they are recommended if the etiologic diagnosis remains questionable.

1.7.2.3.3 Disposition

Agitation itself does not always require hospital admission, but consequences of such agitation, including electrolyte abnormalities, rhabdomyolysis, or physical injury during

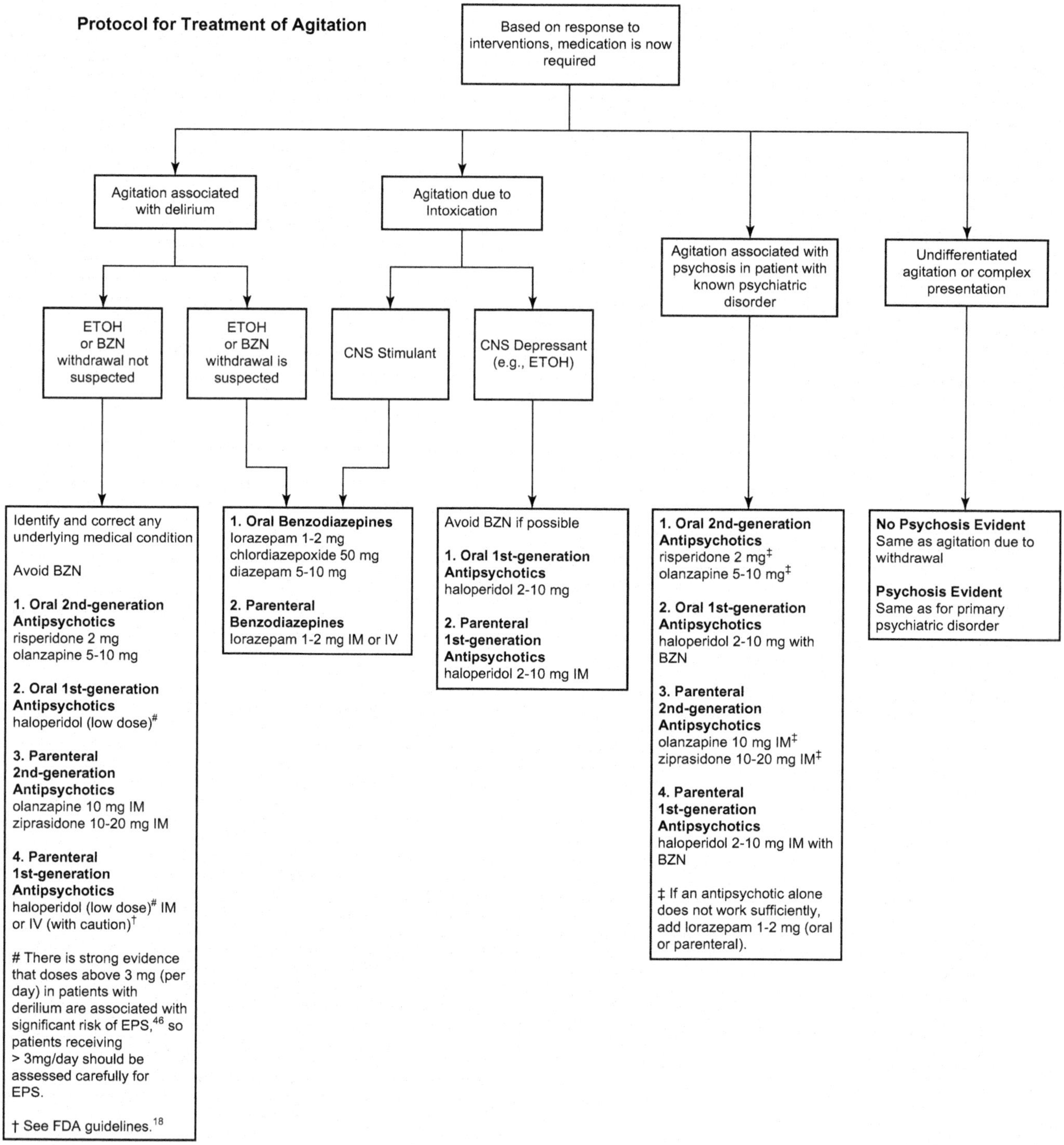

FIGURE 1.7.1 Protocol for treatment of agitation. BZN, benzodiazepine; EPS, extrapyramidal side effects; ETOH, alcohol; IM, intramuscular.

restraint, may prompt admission. Patients with improved symptomatology and who have capacity to make informed decisions and who are not at risk to themselves or others may be considered for discharge with appropriate psychological counseling and follow up. Patients with true delirium, disorganized thinking, or escalating agitation will likely require admission to the hospital or further observation and therapy until demonstration of further improvement.

REFERENCES

1. Zeller SL, Wilson MP. Acute treatment of agitation in schizophrenia. *Drug Discov Today: Therap Strate* 2011;8(1–2):25–9.
2. Zeller SL, Holloman GH, Wilson MP. Management of agitation. In Tasman A, Lieberman J, Kay J, First M, Riba M (Eds.) *Psychiatry*, 4th ed. Oxford: Wiley Publishing, 2014.

3. Zeller SL, Nordstrom KD, Wilson MP. *The Diagnosis and Management of Agitation*. Cambridge: Cambridge University Press, 2017. 281p.
4. Nordstrom K, Zun LS, Wilson MP, Md VS, Ng AT, Bregman B, et al. Medical evaluation and triage of the agitated patient: consensus statement of the american association for emergency psychiatry project Beta medical evaluation workgroup. *West J Emerg Med* 2012;13(1):3–10.
5. Allen MH, Currier GW, Carpenter D, Ross RW, Docherty JP, Expert Consensus Panel for Behavioral E. The expert consensus guideline series. Treatment of behavioral emergencies 2005. *J Psychiatr Pract* 2005;11 Suppl 1:5–108; quiz 10–2.
6. Holloman GH, Jr, Zeller SL. Overview of project BETA: best practices in evaluation and treatment of agitation. *West J Emerg Med* 2012;13(1):1–2.
7. Zeller SL, Rhoades RW. Systematic reviews of assessment measures and pharmacologic treatments for agitation. *Clin Ther* 2010;32(3):403–25.
8. Wilson MP, Sloane C. Chemical restraints, physical restraints, and other demonstrations of force. In Jesus J, Rosen P, Adams J, Derse A, Wolfe R, Grossman S (Eds.) *Ethical Problems in Emergency Medicine: A Discussion-Based Review*. Oxford: Wiley-Blackwell, 2012, 139–148.
9. Annas GJ. The last resort -- the use of physical restraints in medical emergencies. *N Engl J Med* 1999;341:1408–12.
10. State Operations Manual: Appendix A. *Survey Protocol, Regulations, and Interpretive Guidelines for Hospitals*. Accessed July 24, 2017 at: https://www.cms.gov/Regulations-and-Guidance/Guidance/Manuals/downloads/som107ap_a_hospitals.pdf
11. Wilson MP, Brennan JJ, Modesti L, Deen J, Anderson L, Vilke GM, et al. Lengths of stay for involuntarily held psychiatric patients in the ED are affected by both patient characteristics and medication use. *Am J Emerg Med* 2015;33(4):527–30.
12. Wilson MP, Pepper D, Currier GW, Holloman GH, Jr, Feifel D. The psychopharmacology of agitation: consensus statement of the american association for emergency psychiatry project BETA psychopharmacology workgroup. *West J Emerg Med* 2012;13(1):26–34.
13. Mullinax S, Shokraneh F, Wilson MP, Adams CE. Oral medication for agitation of psychiatric origin: a scoping review of randomized controlled trials. *J Emerg Med* 2017;53(4):524–9.
14. Gault TI, Gray SM, Vilke GM, Wilson MP. Are oral medications effective in the management of acute agitation? *J Emerg Med* 2012;43(5):854–9.
15. Pepper D, Wilson MP. The ethics of agitation: when is an agitated patient decisionally capable? In Zeller S, Nordstrom K, Wilson MP (Eds.) *The Diagnosis and Management Of Agitation*. Cambridge: Cambridge Press, 2017.
16. Knox DK, Holloman GH. Use and avoidance of seclusion and restraint: consensus statement of the American association for emergency psychiatry project BETA seclusion and restraint workgroup. *West J Emerg Med* 2012;13(1): 35–40.
17. MacDonald K, Wilson M, Minassian A, Vilke GM, Becker O, Tallian K, et al. A naturalistic study of intramuscular haloperidol versus intramuscular olanzapine for the management of acute agitation. *J Clin Psychopharmacol* 2012;32(3):317–22.
18. Campillo A, Castillo E, Vilke GM, Hopper A, Ryan V, Wilson MP. First-generation antipsychotics are often prescribed in the emergency department but are often not administered with adjunctive medications. *J Emerg Med* 2015;49(6):901–6.
19. Wilson MP, Minassian A, Bahramzi M, Campillo A, Vilke GM. Despite expert recommendations, second-generation antipsychotics are not often prescribed in the emergency department. *J Emerg Med* 2014;46(6):808–13.
20. Wilson MP, Nordstrom K, Vilke GM. The agitated patient in the emergency department. *Current Emergency and Hospital Medicine Reports* 2015;3(4):188–94.
21. Olmedo R, Hoffman RS. Withdrawal syndromes. *Emerg Med Clin North Am* 2000;18(2):273–88.
22. Curran C, Byrappa N, McBride A. Stimulant psychosis: systematic review. *Br J Psychiatry* 2004;185:196–204.
23. Shoptaw SJ, Kao U, Ling W. Treatment for amphetamine psychosis. *Cochrane Database Syst Rev* 2009;1(1):CD003026.
24. Afonso L, Mohammad T, Thatai D. Crack whips the heart: a review of the cardiovascular toxicity of cocaine. *Am J Cardiol* 2007;100(6):1040–3.
25. Marco CA, Vaughan J. Emergency management of agitation in schizophrenia. *Am J Emerg Med* 2005;23(6): 767–76.
26. Richmond JS, Berlin JS, Fishkind AB, Holloman GH, Jr, Zeller SL, Wilson MP, et al. Verbal De-escalation of the agitated patient: consensus statement of the American association for emergency psychiatry project Beta de-escalation workgroup. *West J Emerg Med* 2012;13(1):17–25.
27. Simpson SA, Joesch JM, West, II, Pasic J. Risk for physical restraint or seclusion in the psychiatric emergency service (PES). *Gen Hosp Psychiatry* 2014;36(1):113–8.

1.8 SEIZURES

Samuel H. F. Lam and Gary M. Vilke

1.8.1 General Comments

While most drug-related seizures are self-limited, repeated or prolonged seizure activity may lead to permanent neurological injury or death.[1–8] Primate studies using baboons have shown that 82 minutes of induced status epilepticus produced visible neuropathological injury in non-paralyzed ventilated animals. Results were similar if the baboons were paralyzed and ventilated first.[9] In addition to the potential for direct brain injury, prolonged seizure activity may produce rhabdomyolysis and cause or aggravate hyperthermia, which can further injure the brain.[10]

Mechanisms: Simplistically stated, seizure is the result of imbalance between excitatory and inhibitory pathways in the brain. Gamma aminobutyric acid (GABA) is the primary inhibitory brain neurotransmitter, while glutamate is the primary excitatory brain neurotransmitter. Other neurotransmitters postulated to be involved in seizure pathophysiology include norepinephrine, dopamine, serotonin, acetylcholine, histamine, and adenosine.[11] Drugs may precipitate seizures through several distinct mechanisms (Table 1.8.1). A direct central nervous system (CNS) stimulant effect is probably the mechanism in most cocaine-, phencyclidine-, and amphetamine-induced seizures.[12,13] Seizures from these drugs generally occur *at the time of use*. Seizures associated with other drugs, such as alcohol, benzodiazepines, and barbiturates, generally occur during *a time of withdrawal* from chronic, high doses of the drug due to loss of their inhibitory effects.[12] Other *indirect* causes of seizures exist. Cerebral infarction or hemorrhage may precipitate seizures in patients abusing sympathomimetic drugs.[14,15] Vasculitis has been associated with amphetamine and cocaine abuse and may result in seizures.[16] Intravenous drug–using (IVDU) patients with acquired human immune deficiency (HIV) are susceptible to CNS infections such as toxoplasmosis, cryptococcus, viral encephalitis, syphilis, or lymphoma, which can precipitate seizures. Bacterial endocarditis is a complication of IVDU that can cause septic cerebral emboli leading to seizures. Foreign material (e.g., talc or cotton) emboli and toxic drug byproducts or expanders used in illicit drugs have also been implicated[17] (Tables 1.8.2–1.8.4). Brain trauma or closed head injury resulting in seizures may occur secondary to altered mental status from drug use. Finally, chronic drug or alcohol abuse often leads to systemic medical problems such as hypoglycemia, tissue hypoxia, liver failure, sepsis, or meningitis, all of which may precipitate seizure activity.

Benzodiazepines: Benzodiazepines are the preferred choice for the initial treatment of the actively seizing patient.[11] Their therapeutic effects are mediated via $GABA_A$ receptors.[13] Benzodiazepines are readily available, require no prolonged loading, and are quite safe from a cardiovascular standpoint. The main disadvantages are excessive sedation and ventilatory depression, especially when given with barbiturates such as phenobarbital.

Of the benzodiazepines, lorazepam has the longest anticonvulsant activity, around 4 to 6 hours, and is considered the agent of first choice.[18] Lorazepam has a tendency to persist in the brain, while agents like diazepam and midazolam both redistribute out of the brain more rapidly and thus have a shorter protective effect.[19] However, Leppik et al. found no significant statistical difference between diazepam and lorazepam in clinical efficacy for initial control of convulsive status.[20] On the other hand, a recent Cochrane review and a large randomized controlled trial for status epilepticus of any cause found that intravenous (IV) lorazepam was better than IV diazepam or phenytoin alone in terminating status epilepticus.[21,22] Interestingly, lorazepam is not Food and Drug Administration (FDA) approved for seizure control. Lorazepam is also quite viscous and must be refrigerated and diluted before infusion. Diazepam is irritating to veins, and after intramuscular dosing, absorption is unpredictable. Midazolam may be used alternatively and has the advantage of rapid intramuscular absorption in patients without venous access. Intramuscular midazolam has been proved to be compatible to intravenous lorazepam in terms of effectiveness and safety in a randomized prehospital status epilepticus therapeutic trial.[23]

Barbiturates: Barbiturates exerts their therapeutic effects via binding to the $GABA_A$ receptors as well as directly opening chloride channels at high doses.[11] They are associated with a high incidence of hypotension[24,25] and therefore should not be administered in the hypotensive patient. Furthermore, they require time-consuming loading of 30 minutes or more. Finally, barbiturates frequently cause prolonged sedation, especially after the co-administration of benzodiazepines, thus hindering the ability of the physician to perform serial neurological examinations. Barbiturates do have the advantage of lowering intracranial pressure in the head-injured patient, though their ability to improve outcome has been disputed in a recent Cochrane review, and are helpful for treating withdrawal symptoms in patients with sedative–hypnotic addiction.[25,26] Barbiturates are considered second-line agents after the use of

TABLE 1.8.1
Mechanisms of Drug-Related Seizures

1. Direct CNS toxicity: Cocaine, phencyclidine, amphetamines
2. CNS hyperactivity after cessation of drug: Alcohol, barbiturates, benzodiazepines
3. Indirect CNS toxicity
    a. Trauma: subdural, epidural hematoma due to blunt force
    b. Stroke: cerebral infarct, hemorrhage, or vasculitis
    c. Infection of CNS
    d. Foreign materials (e.g., talc), other drug adulterants (see Tables 1.8.2–1.8.4)
    e. Systemic metabolic problems (e.g., hypoxia, hypoglycemia, liver or renal failure)
    f. Post-traumatic epilepsy, or epilepsy exacerbated by drug abuse
    g. Epilepsy additional to drug use

benzodiazepines for seizures caused by drugs of abuse.

Common barbiturate choices include phenobarbital, propofol, and pentobarbital. Phenobarbital was as effective as lorazepam in terminating status epilepticus in a randomized, double-blind Veterans Affairs study.[22] Although it may be administered at an IV rate of 100 mg/min, requiring only 10 min to fully load a 70-kg patient with 15 mg/kg, most nursing protocols require the physician to institute phenobarbital loading or to give no more than 60 mg/min IV. Phenobarbital also has a half-life of 87–100 hours, which may lead to prolonged drowsiness in patients. Propofol has been shown in limited studies to be effective in terminating refractory status epilepticus.[27–29] It is also advocated by some as a second-line agent for control of drug-induced seizures because of its additional effect as a N-methyl-D-aspartate (NMDA, a subtype of glutamate receptor) antagonist.[30] Disadvantages of propofol include hypertriglyceridemia, respiratory depression, hypotension, involuntary body movements, and propofol infusion syndrome (bradycardia, hypotension, rhabdomyolysis, and metabolic acidosis) after prolonged infusions of 48 hours or more. Pentobarbital has a therapeutic profile similar to that of phenobarbital.

Other drugs: A meta-analysis published in 2014 examined five antiepileptic drugs for treatment of benzodiazepine-resistant status epilepticus and concluded that valproic acid and levetiracetam are as effective as phenobarbital.[31] Both these medications have multiple and incompletely understood mechanisms of action. A systemic review in 2014 found 30 studies (over 800 patients) supporting the effectiveness of valproic acid in benzodiazepine-resistant status epilepticus, including 6 randomized controlled trials.[32] Levetiracetam is a relatively new medication, and evidence supporting its effectiveness has been mostly retrospective or observational in nature.[33] Recently, two small prospective randomized trials have been conducted comparing phenytoin with levetiracetam, with conclusions that both are equally efficacious.[34,35] Based on this evidence, valproic acid and levetiracetam are now recommended as second-line medications in patients with status epilepticus.[33]

Phenytoin/Fosphenytoin: Unlike phenobarbital and benzodiazepines, which elevate the seizure threshold, phenytoin increases the threshold for sodium channel depolarization and exerts its anticonvulsant effects mainly by limiting the spread of seizure activity and reducing seizure propagation. Because phenytoin does not elevate the seizure threshold, it is less effective against drug-induced seizures.[11] Animal models of cocaine-induced seizures and human studies of alcohol withdrawal seizures have supported this claim.[36–39] Although they remain second-line agents for status epilepticus in general, fosphenytoin and phenytoin are not recommended for treatment of drug-induced seizures.[11,30,40]

General anesthesia: Pentobarbital, thiopental, midazolam, or propofol anesthesia may be used as a last resort, usually with the aid of an anesthesiologist, to induce general anesthesia.[41] If paralysis is used, the patient must be intubated and mechanically ventilated. It is important to remember that when patients having seizures are paralyzed with neuromuscular blockers such that seizure activity is not readily apparent, they may continue to have electrical seizure activity, leading to persistent cerebral hypermetabolism and the continued risk of brain injury. An electroencephalogram (EEG) should be used to monitor all patients paralyzed for seizure disorder to determine the need for further anticonvulsant therapy.

1.8.2 Stepwise Approach to Management

1.8.2.1 Immediate Interventions

1. **Airway, Breathing, Circulation:** Maintain the airway and assist ventilation if necessary. Administer supplemental oxygen. Treat hypotension and resuscitate as per previous reviews.[42]

TABLE 1.8.2
Cocaine Additives

Cocaine Additives
Pharmacologically Active
Lidocaine
Cyproheptidine
Methephedrine
Diphenhydramine
Benzocaine
Mepivacaine
Aminopyrine
Methapyrilene
Tetracaine
Nicotinamide
Ephedrine
Phenylpropanolamine
Acetaminophen
Procaine base
Caffeine
Acetophenetidin
1-(1-Phenylcyclohexyl)pyrrolidine
Methaqualone
Dyclonine
Pyridoxine
Codeine
Stearic acid
Piracetam
Rosin (colophonum)
Fencanfamine
Benzoic acid
Phenothiazines
L-Threonine
Heroin
Boric acid
Aspirin
Dibucaine
Propoxyphene
Heroin[a]
Amphetamine[a]
Methamphetamine[a]
Inert
Inositol
Mannitol
Lactose
Dextrose
Starch
Sucrose
Sodium bicarbonate
Barium carbonate
Mannose
Volatile Compounds
Benzene
Methyl ethyl ketone
Ether
Acetone

Source: Shesser, R. et al., *Am. J. Emerg. Med.*, 9, 336, 1991. With permission.

[a] Considered frequent additives/coinjectants; absolute frequency unknown.

TABLE 1.8.3
Phencyclidine Additives

Phencyclidine Additives
Active
Phenylpropanolamine
Benzocaine
Procaine
Ephedrine
Caffeine
Piperidine
PCC (1-piperidinocyclohexanecarbonitrile)
TCP (1-[1-(2-thienyl)cyclohexyl]-piperidine)
PCE (cyclohexamine)
PHP (phenylcyclohexylpyrrolidine)
Ketamine
Inert
Magnesium sulfate
Ammonium chloride
Ammonium hydroxide
Phenyllithium halide
Phenylmagnesium halide
Volatile
Ethyl ether
Toluene
Cyclohexanol
Isopropanol

Source: Shesser, R. et al., *Am. J. Emerg. Med.*, 9, 336, 1991. With permission.

2. **Antidotes:** Administer appropriate antidotes, including 25 g dextrose IV if the patient is hypoglycemic. Give pyridoxine if isoniazid toxicity is suspected. Administer naloxone only if seizures are thought to be caused by hypoxia resulting from narcotic-associated respiratory depression.
3. **Anticonvulsants:** Administer one of the drugs listed in Table 1.8.5.
   Comment: As noted earlier, the authors have a strong preference for benzodiazepines, particularly lorazepam. If lorazepam is used, most seizures stop after 2 to 4 mg, but there is no clear dose–response data available. Some authorities stop if 4 mg is unsuccessful, but some providers consider it reasonable to give up to 10 to 12 mg of lorazepam before switching to an alternative therapy. Neurologists generally recommend the aggressive use of a single medication before switching to another medication, as switching too quickly often results in the under-dosing of both medications. Ventilatory depression should not keep one from using large doses of benzodiazepines, as has been done safely with delirium tremens, especially in the drug-abusing patient with status epilepticus.[43] If large doses of benzodiazepines are used, patients frequently require intubation and mechanical ventilation.

TABLE 1.8.4
Heroin Additives

Alkaloids
Thebaine
Acetylcodeine
Papaverine
Noscapine
Narceine
Active Nonalkaloids
Tolmectin
Quinine
Phenobarbital
Methaqualone
Lidocaine
Phenolphthalein
Caffeine
Dextromoramide
Chloroquine
Diazepam
Nicotinamide
N-Phenyl-2-naphthylamine
Phenacetin
Acetaminophen
Fentanyl
Doxepin
Naproxen
Promazine
Piracetam
Procaine
Diphenhydramine
Aminopyrine
Allobarbital
Indomethacin
Glutethimide
Scopolamine
Sulfonamide
Arsenic
Strychnine
Cocaine[a]
Amphetamine[a]
Methamphetamine[a]
Inert
Starch
Sugar
Calcium tartrate
Calcium carbonate
Sodium carbonate
Sucrose
Dextrin
Magnesium sulfate
Dextrose
Lactose
Barium sulfate
Silicon dioxide
Vitamin C
Volatile
Rosin
Toluene
Methanol
Acetaldehyde
Ethanol
Acetone
Diethyl ether
Chloroform
Acetic Acid

Source: Shesser, R. et al., *Am. J. Emerg. Med.*, 9, 336, 1991. With permission.

[a] Considered frequent additives/coinjectants; absolute frequency unknown.

4. **Reassess temperature:** Immediately check the rectal temperature and cool the patient rapidly if the temperature is above 40 °C (104 °F) (see chapter on hyperthermia).
5. **Lumbar puncture:** Perform lumbar puncture if the patient is febrile to rule out meningitis. Do not wait for computerized tomography (CT) results or laboratory analysis of cerebral spinal fluid (CSF) to initiate therapy with appropriate antibiotics if meningitis is suspected. Perform CT prior to lumbar puncture if the patient is at risk for having a CNS mass lesion.
6. **Gastric decontamination:** Consider gastrointestinal decontamination if the patient is a body packer or stuffer or if the patient has ingested large quantities of drug (see chapter on gastric decontamination).
7. **Laboratory data:** Electrolytes, glucose, calcium, magnesium, and biochemical screens for liver and renal disease are generally recommended.[12] Check creatine kinase levels to detect evidence of rhabdomyolysis. Although urine and blood toxicologic screens are generally overutilized, they are recommended in the case of new-onset seizures to avoid an inappropriate diagnosis of idiopathic epilepsy.[44]

1.8.2.2 Secondary Interventions

1. **Computerized tomography (CT):** Earnest et al. documented a 6.2% incidence of clinically significant intracranial lesions on brain CT scan in a series of 259 patients with first alcohol-related seizures, and Pascual-Leone et al. found clinically significant CT lesions in 16% of 44 patients presenting with cocaine-induced seizures.[45,46] Cocaine-induced thrombosis and hypertension have been implicated as the cause of stroke in patients with seizures.[47,48] On the other hand, Holland et al. performed a retrospective review of 37 cocaine-associated seizures and concluded that CT scanning was not necessary regardless of the patient's previous seizure history if the patient suffered a brief, generalized, tonic–clonic seizure and had normal vital signs and physical examination and a postictal state lasting 30 min or less.[49] Patel et al. prospectively studied 152 patients with mental status change due to poisoning or drug overdose, 13 (9%) of whom presented with seizure.[50] Forty-three of the patients underwent head CT, none of whom had any acute finding. Nevertheless, given the high incidence of traumatic, hemorrhagic, and infectious complications associated with drug abuse, it would be reasonable to obtain a CT of the brain for new-onset seizures or for any high-risk seizures *in drug abuse patients* (Table 1.8.6). The European Federation of Neurological Societies guideline on the diagnosis and management of alcohol-related

TABLE 1.8.5
Medications Used for Seizure Control

Lorazepam	0.05–0.10 mg/kg IV over 2 min (max. 4 mg)	May repeat as necessary, may give intramuscularly (IM) although IV route preferred
Midazolam	0.05–0.10 mg/kg IV over 2 min 0.1–0.2 mg/kg IM (max. 10 mg)	May repeat as necessary
Diazepam	0.10 mg/kg IV over 2 min (max. 10 mg)	May repeat as necessary
Phenobarbital	15–20 mg/kg IV over 20 min	Watch for hypotension, prolonged sedation
Pentobarbital	5–6 mg/kg IV, slow infusion over 8–10 min, then continuous infusion at 0.5–3.0 mg/kg/h titrated to effect	Use as inducing agent for general anesthesia, watch for hypotension, continuous EEG monitoring necessary after general anesthesia
Propofol	1–2 mg/kg IV load dose over 5 min	May repeat as necessary. Watch for hypotension. May need airway protection at higher dose (up to 10–12 mg/kg/h)
Valproic Acid	20–40 mg/kg IV at 5 mg/kg/min	
Levetiracetam	40–60 mg/kg IV over 15 min (max 4,500 mg)	

TABLE 1.8.6
High-Risk Seizures

Neurological deficit
Evidence of head trauma
Prolonged postictal state
Focal seizures or focal onset with secondary generalization[a]
Seizures occurring after a period of prolonged abstinence[a]
Onset of seizures before age 30 if alcohol only involved
Mental illness or inability to fully evaluate the patient's baseline mental function

[a] High risk for having a positive CT result requiring intervention.

seizures also recommends obtaining brain imaging, such as CT or magnetic resonance imaging, in patients with first episodes of alcohol-related seizures.[51]

2. **Monitor:** Monitor neurological and cardiovascular status as well as hydration and electrolyte balance.
3. **Anticonvulsant therapy:** Rarely, chronic anticonvulsant or other specific treatment of alcohol- or drug-related seizures is indicated. For patients who present with multiple seizures, status epilepticus, or high-risk seizures (Table 1.8.6), continued outpatient therapy may be indicated.
4. **Disposition:** Only patients with normal vital signs, mental status, and physical examination; after a brief isolated seizure; with a normal evaluation (i.e., CT scan, laboratory data, etc.) should be considered for discharge from the emergency department.

ACKNOWLEDGMENTS

Brett A. Roth, M.D., Neal L. Benowitz, M.D., and Kent R. Olson, M.D.

REFERENCES

1. Wetli CV, Wright RK. Death caused by recreational cocaine use. *JAMA* 1979;241(23):2519–22.
2. Simpson DL, Rumack BH. Methylenedioxyamphetamine. Clinical description of overdose, death, and review of pharmacology. *Arch Intern Med* 1981;141(11):1507–9.
3. Jonsson S, O'Meara M, Young JB. Acute cocaine poisoning. Importance of treating seizures and acidosis. *Am J Med* 1983;75(6):1061–4.
4. Campbell BG. Cocaine abuse with hyperthermia, seizures and fatal complications. *Med J Aust* 1988;149(7):387–9.
5. Kramer LD, Locke GE, Ogunyemi A, Nelson L. Cocaine-related seizures in adults. *Am J Drug Alcohol Abuse* 1990;16(3–4):307–17.
6. Olson KR, et al. Seizures associated with poisoning and drug overdose [corrected and re published article originally printed in Am J Emerg Med 1993 Nov;11(6):565–8]. *Am J Emerg Med* 1994;12(3):392–5.
7. Thundiyil JG, Kearney TE, Olson KR. Evolving epidemiology of drug-induced seizures reported to a Poison Control Center System. *J Med Toxicol* 2007;3(1):15–9.
8. Walker MC. Pathophysiology of status epilepticus. *Neurosci Lett* 2016. pii: S0304-3940(16)30993-4. [Epub ahead of print]
9. Meldrum BS, Vigouroux RA, Brierley JB. Systemic factors and epileptic brain damage. Prolonged seizures in paralyzed, artificially ventilated baboons. *Arch Neurol* 1973;29(2):82–7.
10. Olson KR, Benowitz NL. Environmental and drug-induced hyperthermia. Pathophysiology, recognition, and management. *Emerg Med Clin North Am* 1984;2(3):459–74.
11. Chen HY, Albertson TE, Olson KR. Treatment of drug-induced seizures. *Br J Clin Pharmacol* 2016;81(3):412–9.
12. Earnest MP. Seizures. *Neurol Clin* 1993;11(3):563–75.

13. Lason W. Neurochemical and pharmacological aspects of cocaine-induced seizures. *Pol J Pharmacol* 2001;53(1):57–60.
14. Jacobs IG, et al. Cocaine abuse: neurovascular complications. *Radiology* 1989;170(1 Pt 1):223–7.
15. Auer J, Berent R, Eber B, Cardiovascular complications of cocaine use. *N Engl J Med* 2001;345(21):1575; author reply 1576.
16. Rumbaugh CL, et al. Cerebral angiographic changes in the drug abuse patient. *Radiology* 1971;101(2):335–44.
17. Neiman J, Haapaniemi HM, Hillbom M. Neurological complications of drug abuse: pathophysiological mechanisms. *Eur J Neurol* 2000;7(6):595–606.
18. Treiman DM. The role of benzodiazepines in the management of status epilepticus. *Neurology* 1990;40(5 Suppl 2):32–42.
19. Kyriakopoulos AA, Greenblatt DJ, Shader RI. Clinical pharmacokinetics of lorazepam: a review. *J Clin Psychiatry* 1978;39(10 Pt 2):16–23.
20. Leppik IE, et al. Double-blind study of lorazepam and diazepam in status epilepticus. *JAMA* 1983;249(11):1452–4.
21. Prasad M, Krishnan PR, Sequeira R, Al-Roomi K. Anticonvulsant therapy for status epilepticus. *Cochrane Database Syst Rev* 2014;9:CD003723.
22. Treiman DM, et al.; Veterans Affairs Status Epilepticus Cooperative Study Group. A comparison of four treatments for generalized convulsive status epilepticus. *N Engl J Med* 1998;339(12):792–8.
23. Silbergleit R, et al.; NETT Investigators. Intramuscular versus intravenous therapy for prehospital status epilepticus. *N Engl J Med* 2012;366(7):591–600.
24. Lee TL. Pharmacology of propofol. *Ann Acad Med Singapore* 1991;20(1):61–5.
25. Roberts I, Sydenham E. Barbiturates for acute traumatic brain injury. *Cochrane Database Syst Rev* 2012;12:CD000033.
26. Santos C, Olmedo RE. Sedative-hypnotic drug withdrawal syndrome: recognition and treatment. *Emerg Med Pract* 2017;19(3):1–20.
27. Rossetti AO, Milligan TA, Vulliémoz S, Michaelides C, Bertschi M, Lee JW. A randomized trial for the treatment of refractory status epilepticus. *Neurocrit Care* 2011;14(1):4–10.
28. Rossetti AO, Reichhart MD, Schaller MD, Despland PA, Bogousslavsky J. Propofol treatment of refractory status epilepticus: a study of 31 episodes. *Epilepsia* 2004;45(7):757.
29. Prasad A, Worrall BB, Bertram EH, Bleck TP. Propofol and midazolam in the treatment of refractory status epilepticus. *Epilepsia* 2001;42(3):380–6.
30. Sharma AN, Hoffman RJ. Toxin-related seizures. *Emerg Med Clin North Am* 2011;29:125–39.
31. Yasiry Z, Shorvon SD. The relative effectiveness of five antiepileptic drugs in treatment of benzodiazepine-resistant convulsive status epilepticus: a meta-analysis of published studies. *Seizure* 2014;23(3):167–74.
32. Trinka E, Höfler J, Zerbs A, Brigo F. Efficacy and safety of intravenous valproate for status epilepticus: a systematic review. *CNS Drugs* 2014;28(7):623–39.
33. Drisland FW. Convulsive status epilepticus in adults: treatment and prognosis. *UpToDate*. www.uptodate.com. Accessed August 5, 2017.
34. Mundlamuri RC, et al. Management of generalised convulsive status epilepticus (SE): a prospective randomised controlled study of combined treatment with intravenous lorazepam with either phenytoin, sodium valproate or levetiracetam--Pilot study. *Epilepsy Res* 2015;114:52–8.
35. Chakravarthi S, Goyal MK, Modi M, Bhalla A, Singh P. Levetiracetam versus phenytoin in management of status epilepticus. *J Clin Neurosci* 2015;22(6):959–63.
36. Derlet RW, Albertson TE. Anticonvulsant modification of cocaine-induced toxicity in the rat. *Neuropharmacology* 1990;29(3):255–9.
37. Alldredge BK, Lowenstein DH, Simon RP. Placebo-controlled trial of intravenous diphenylhydantoin for short-term treatment of alcohol withdrawal seizures. *Am J Med* 1989;87(6):645–8.
38. Chance JF. Emergency department treatment of alcohol withdrawal seizures with phenytoin. *Ann Emerg Med* 1991;20:520–2.
39. Rathlev NK, et al. The lack of efficacy of phenytoin in the prevention of recurrent alcohol-related seizures. *Ann Emerg Med* 1994;23:513–8.
40. Brophy GM, et al.; Neurocritical care society status epilepticus guideline writing committee. guidelines for the evaluation and management of status epilepticus. *Neurocrit Care* 2012;17:3–23.
41. Trinka E, Kälviäinen R. 25 years of advances in the definition, classification and treatment of status epilepticus. *Seizure* 2017;44:65–73.
42. Callaway CW, et al.; Advanced life support chapter collaborators. Part 4: advanced life support: 2015 international consensus on cardiopulmonary resuscitation and emergency cardiovascular care science with treatment recommendations. *Circulation* 2015;132(16 Suppl 1):S84–145.
43. Hayes PC, Faestel PM, Shimamoto PL, Holland C. Alcohol withdrawal requiring massive prolonged benzodiazepine infusion. *Mil Med* 2007;172(5):556–9.
44. Olson KR, Pentel PR, Kelley MT. Physical assessment and differential diagnosis of the poisoned patient. *Med Toxicol* 1987;2(1):52–81.
45. Earnest MP, Feldman H, Marx JA, Harris JA, Biletch M, Sullivan LP. Intracranial lesions shown by CT scans in 259 cases of first alcohol-related seizures. *Neurology* 1988;38:1561–5.
46. Pascual-Leone A, et al. Cocaine-induced seizures. *Neurology* 1990;40(3 Pt 1):404–7.
47. Brown E, et al. CNS complications of cocaine abuse: prevalence, pathophysiology, and neuroradiology. *AJR Am J Roentgenol* 1992;159(1):137–47.
48. Daras M, Tuchman AJ, Marks S. Central nervous system infarction related to cocaine abuse. *Stroke* 1991;22(10):1320–5.
49. Holland RW 3rd, et al. Grand mal seizures temporally related to cocaine use: clinical and diagnostic features [see comments]. *Ann Emerg Med* 1992;21(7):772–6.
50. Patel MM, Tsutaoka BT, Banerji S, Blanc PD, Olson KR. ED utilization of computed tomography in a poisoned population. *Am J Emerg Med* 2002;20(3):212–7.
51. Brathen G et al.; EFNS Task Force on Diagnosis and Treatment of Alcohol-Related Seizures. EFNS guideline on the diagnosis and management of alcohol-related seizures: report of an EFNS task force. *Eur J Neurol* 2005;12(8):575–81.

1.9 HYPERTHERMIA/HEAT STROKE

Gary M. Vilke and Alexis Lenz

1.9.1 General Comments

Hyperthermia is defined when an individual's core temperature is elevated beyond what is normally maintained by the body. This elevation is typically either due to the body's inability to dissipate heat as energy or due to excessive heat production by the body. Fever is not synonymous with hyperthermia. Fever is described as temperature greater than 38 °C due to an increase in the regulatory set point from cytokine release. A temperature above 40 °C is considered severe hyperthermia and is a well-recognized cause of major morbidity and mortality. Above 42 °C, the body can go into multi-organ failure and disseminated intravascular coagulation (DIC) [1]. Classic heat stroke is characterized by hyperthermia with a core temperature of 40 °C (the temperature differs according to different authors) or higher, and severe central nervous system (CNS) dysfunction. It has been associated with mortality rates of up to 80% and a high likelihood of disabling neurologic sequelae [1, 2]. This is different from exertional heat stroke, which is due to exercise and hyperthermia [3].

Drug-induced heat stroke: Drug-induced heat stroke typically falls under the category of classic heat stroke, as it relates to the inability to thermoregulate core temperatures, resulting in hyperthermia with neurologic dysfunction. A variety of drugs and toxins may cause hyperthermia, and this may initially be overlooked while the more familiar manifestations of the intoxication, like altered mental status and seizures, are being managed [4–7]. Although no study has documented the incidence of death as it relates to drug abuse and hyperthermia per se, a case series by Rosenberg et al. described 12 patients who presented with temperatures 40.5 °C or greater for at least 1 hour [8]. Five of the 12 patients died, and 4 had severe permanent neurologic sequelae. Patients with hyperthermia and altered mental status may be diagnosed as having environmental or exertional heat stroke while the potential contribution of drugs is overlooked. It is important for the physician to look for clues of drug-induced hyperthermia from the history and physical examination and to promptly discontinue the offending drug and initiate appropriate treatment.

Mechanisms: Mechanisms of drug-induced hyperthermia are varied. Most commonly, excessive heat production results from muscular hyperactivity due to sympathomimetic and epileptogenic agents or metabolic hyperactivity due to salicylates, pentachlorophenol, or dinitrophenol. In addition, heat dissipation is often impaired by inhibition of sweating due to anticholinergic agents, antihistamines, antidepressants, and antipsychotics or by cutaneous vasoconstriction due to sympathomimetic agents. Lastly, hyperthermia may result from interference with central thermoregulation by phenothiazines, cocaine, and amphetamines [9, 10]. When healthy, cocaine-naive persons are subjected to passive heating, pretreatment with even a small dose of intranasal cocaine impairs sweating and cutaneous vasodilation, the major autonomic adjustments to thermal stress, and heat perception, which is the key trigger for behavioral adjustments [11]. Phencyclidine (PCP) is a sympathetic nervous system stimulant and may also have anticholinergic properties, which inhibit sweating [12]. This property, plus the tendency to generate unrestrained outbursts of violent activity and seizures, has resulted in hyperthermia, rhabdomyolysis, and death. Of 1,000 cases of PCP intoxication reviewed by McCarron et al., 26 had temperatures over 38.9 °C, and 4 had temperatures over 41 °C [13]. A patient restrained in a straitjacket after becoming violent following LSD ingestion developed hyperthermia to 41.6 °C, hypotension, rhabdomyolysis, and renal failure, and ultimately died, although this is uncommon with LSD [14]. This has been suggested to be due to its serotonergic effects and a tendency to provoke panic. Specific mechanisms may dictate the specific form of hyperthermic syndrome, although classically, five syndromes are described: malignant hyperthermia, neuroleptic malignant syndrome, serotonin syndrome (SS), sympathomimetic poisoning, and anticholinergic poisoning.

Malignant hyperthermia: Malignant hyperthermia (MH) is a drug-induced hyperthermia classically associated with exposure to volatile anesthetic agents or depolarizing muscle relaxants and is most commonly seen in the operating room, with the incidence of MH reactions ranging from 1:5,000 to 1:50,000–100,000 anesthesia events [7]. MH has also been associated with cocaine and PCP [15, 16]. The primary defect is felt to be an alteration in cellular permeability, which results in an inability to regulate calcium concentrations within the skeletal muscle fibers. As a result of the accumulation of calcium, muscles sustain contraction, which causes severe muscular rigidity and heat generation. Temperatures greater than 110 °F have been reported. Treatment includes cooling, reversing acidosis and hypercarbia, treating rhabdomyolysis, and correcting any electrolyte dysfunction. Dantrolene is the most effective treatment for MH. While dantrolene has been suggested to diminish hyperthermia associated with amphetamine and ecstasy overdose, it has not been shown in any controlled study to be effective due to the infrequency of these cases, and therefore, confirmation of its usefulness for these indications requires further evaluation [17–20].

Neuroleptic malignant syndrome: Neuroleptic malignant syndrome (NMS) is another cause of drug-induced hyperthermia. It is associated with the use of antipsychotics such as haloperidol or withdrawal of dopaminergic xenobiotics and usually develops over several weeks [21]. NMS is defined by four signs: hyperthermia, muscular rigidity, autonomic dysfunction, and altered consciousness, usually in the form of a catatonic state. The muscular rigidity is classically described as "lead pipe rigidity." Temperature elevation and altered mental state occur after the onset of rigidity. Neuromuscular relaxation with benzodiazepines and routine external cooling measures are generally effective for treatment of the severe rigidity and hyperthermia in this condition. The patient should have all dopamine antagonists, including first-generation antipsychotics, second-generation antipsychotics, or anti-emetics such as metoclopramide, stopped. Although the treatment of NMS is primarily supportive, multiple case reports have documented the successful use of dantrolene [22, 23]. Several reviews of the literature have also shown encouraging results for the use of dantrolene, bromocriptine, and amantadine [24–26]. NMS requires admission to the intensive care unit and typically takes 5–15 days to resolve.

Serotonin syndrome: SS is a clinical syndrome associated with excess free serotonin levels [27]. It arises from the combination of prescription drugs such as selective serotonin-reuptake inhibitors, monoamine oxidase inhibitors, and tricyclic antidepressants together and/or in conjunction with cocaine, MDMA, or amphetamines. Symptoms usually develop over several hours. Muscle rigidity is not as prominent as with NMS, and sweating and gastrointestinal complaints are much more common. Symptoms of autonomic dysfunction are common and include hyperthermia and tachycardia, neuromuscular complaints such as clonus and hyperreflexia, mental status changes such as agitation or anxiety, and an exaggerated tremor. Hunter criteria define SS as serotonergic medications plus one of the following: spontaneous clonus, inducible clonus and agitation or diaphoresis, ocular clonus and agitation or diaphoresis, tremor and hyperreflexia, hypertonia, and temperature >38 °C and ocular clonus or inducible clonus. Initial treatment is aimed at controlling hyperthermia with cooling and benzodiazepines. The role of cyproheptadine, a nonspecific antihistamine with 5-HT2A antagonistic activity, in the treatment of SS has been supported by case studies [28, 29], but there is a lack of evidence in the form of randomized controlled studies. Also, the dose of cyproheptidine may need to be as high as 20–30 mg to ensure blockade of central 5-HT2 receptors [30]. Some antipsychotics with 5-HT2A antagonist effects, such as chlorpromazine, are also options [30, 31]. Antipyretics are typically not useful as the hyperthermia is due to muscle rigidity.

Sympathomimetic: Sympathomimetic toxicity results from drugs such as cocaine, amphetamines, ecstasy, and PCP. Those who present with intoxication may have hyperthermia, tachycardia, hypertension, sweating, and mydriasis on examination. Cocaine intoxication causes psychomotor agitation, which causes an increase of excitatory neurotransmitters, which can cause hyperthermia. Treatment is typically supportive and consists of benzodiazepines for agitation, hyperthermia, and hypertension and intravenous fluids [32, 33].

Anticholinergic: Toxicity from anticholinergics may present very similarly to sympathomimetic poisoning, but in contrast, patients tend to be dry with no evidence of sweating. Although there are reported to be large numbers of exposures to anticholinergics annually, there are few reported major long-term effects [34]. Anticholinergics include antihistamines, tricyclic antidepressants (TCAs), atropine, and sleep aids like doxylamine. Treatment involves cooling for hyperthermia, benzodiazepines for seizures, and general symptomatic treatment. Sodium bicarbonate is used for prolonged QRS complexes and other cardiac rhythm disturbances in overdoses such as a TCA. Some overdoses may benefit from physostigmine, particularly if the diagnosis is in question, although usually, anticholinergic toxicity can be treated symptomatically [35, 36].

Importance of paralysis and cooling: Management of hyperthermia includes removal of the offending agent and rapid cooling to a temperature below 38.9 °C. However, it is important to avoid overcooling, and this must be monitored closely while cooling is taking place. Zalis et al. showed that hyperthermia was directly related to mortality in mongrel dogs with amphetamine overdose [37, 38]. Paralysis was shown to stop muscle hyperactivity, reduce hyperthermia, and decrease mortality. Davis et al. showed that dogs given high doses of PCP exhibited toxicity, which was diminished by paralysis and cooling measures [39]. Animal studies also indicate a key role for hyperthermia in complications associated with cocaine overdose. Catravas and Waters demonstrated that dogs given otherwise lethal cocaine infusions survived if severe hyperthermia was prevented [40]. In this study, temperature correlated better with survival than did pulse or blood pressure. Measures to prevent hyperthermia have included neuromuscular paralysis, sedation with benzodiazepines, and external cooling.

Prognosis: The prognosis for severe hyperthermia depends on the duration of temperature elevation, the maximum temperature reached, and the affected individual's underlying health. Seizures are also associated with a poorer prognosis. This may in part be because they are often resistant to treatment in the hyperthermic individual. Delays in cooling and other treatments have been associated with a significantly increased incidence of mortality, up to 80%, highest in the elderly. But with early diagnosis and treatment, the mortality rate is closer to 10%.

1.9.2 Stepwise Approach to Management

1.9.2.1 Immediate Interventions

Airway, Breathing, Circulation: Maintain the airway and assist ventilation if necessary. Administer supplemental oxygen. Treat hypotension, and use treatments and antidotes depending on the particular causative agent.

Cooling: Evaporative cooling is favored as the technique of choice. Evaporative cooling combines the advantages of simplicity and noninvasiveness [41]. Some authors advocate the use of strategically placed ice packs, although there are no controlled studies demonstrating their effectiveness, and ice packs may contribute to shivering, which may further increase heat generation. Immersion in an ice water bath is also a highly effective measure to reduce core temperatures but limits the health care provider's access to the patient, requires more equipment and preparation, and is unsafe for elderly patients. This has been reported to cool more rapidly than evaporative cooling and may be a better approach [42, 43]. Gastric lavage with cold water or saline is an effective and rapid central cooling technique that can be used in combination with evaporation in severe cases. Neuromuscular paralysis should be considered in severe cases in which temperature is persistently greater than 40 °C. Cooling technique is as follows:

- Completely remove *all* clothing.
- Place cardiac monitor leads on the patient's back so that they adhere to the skin during the cooling process.
- Wet the skin with room temperature tap water with a sponge or spray bottle.
- Position high-speed fans close to the patient.
- Consider placing ice packs to the groin and axillae.
- Treat shivering with lorazepam, 0.1 mg/kg intravenously (IV), or midazolam, 0.1 to 0.2 mg/kg IV.
- Treat continued muscular hyperactivity, such as severe shivering, rigidity, or agitation, with neuromuscular paralysis, endotracheal intubation, and mechanical ventilation.
- Employ fluid replacement to correct volume depletion and to facilitate thermoregulation by sweating.
- Treat known causes. If known MH, give dantrolene, 1 mg/kg rapid IV push. Repeat as necessary up to 10 mg/kg.
- Use Foley catheter to monitor urine output closely.
- Monitor the core temperature and discontinue cooling when the temperature reaches 38.5 °C to avoid overcorrecting and inducing hypothermia.

Thermometry: This is the least invasive, most accurate method available in the emergency department and is recommended for monitoring and tracking the treatment in these patients. Thermistors attached to urinary catheters as well as rectal thermistors are commonly used to monitor core temperature. An esophageal thermistor also closely correlates with core temperature. If the patient has a Swan–Ganz catheter, pulmonary arterial temperature may be measured precisely with a thermistor catheter. Most other standard measurements of body temperature, including oral, tympanic, temporal, and axillary, differ substantially from actual core temperature.

Circulatory support: Insertion of a Swan–Ganz catheter or central venous pressure monitor is indicated whenever necessary to guide fluid therapy. Patients with low cardiac output and hypotension should not be treated with α-adrenergic agents since these drugs promote vasoconstriction without improving cardiac output or perfusion, decrease cutaneous heat exchange, and perhaps enhance ischemic renal and hepatic damage. As fluid shifts occur with sweating losses, monitoring for appropriate urine output as well as electrolytes is critical.

1.9.2.2 Secondary Interventions

Laboratory data: Send blood for complete blood count, platelet count, international normalized ratio, electrolytes, calcium, lactate, troponin, blood urea nitrogen, creatinine, and liver function tests. Also send blood cultures. Check serum creatine phosphokinase and urine for myoglobin to assess for rhabdomyolysis. If rhabdomyolysis is suspected, see section on rhabdomyolysis. Although urine and blood toxicological screens are generally over-utilized, they should be sent if the diagnosis is in question. Salicylate levels should be checked on all cases with an unknown cause of hyperthermia.

Computed tomography (CT): Consider CT of brain for persistently altered mental status or focal neurological deficit.

Lumbar puncture: Perform lumbar puncture and send cerebral spinal fluid for analysis if patient has signs or symptoms of meningitis. If meningitis is suspected, administer empiric antibiotics.

Cardiac evaluation: Electrocardiogram or chest X-ray as indicated clinically.

Disposition: All patients with severe hyperthermia or heat stroke should be admitted to the hospital. Patients with normal or mildly abnormal laboratory values who become normothermic in the emergency department may be admitted to the medical floor on a case by case basis.

ACKNOWLEDGMENTS

Brett A. Roth, M.D., Neal L. Benowitz, M.D., and Kent R. Olson, M.D.

REFERENCES

1. Mechem CC. (2017). Severe nonexertional hyperthermia (classic heat stroke) in adults. Retrieved from uptotdate: https://www.uptodate.com/contents/severe-nonexertional-hyperthermia-classic-heat-stroke-in-adults source=search_result&search=hyperthermia&selectedTitle=2~150.
2. Klenk J, Becker C, Rapp K. Heat-related mortality in residents of nursing homes. *Age Ageing* 2010;39:245.
3. Buchama A, Knochel JP. Heat stroke. *N Engl J Med* 2002;346:1978.
4. Walter FG, et al. Marijuana and hyperthermia. *J Toxicol Clin Toxicol* 1996;34(2):217–21.
5. Hayes BD, Martinez JP, Barrueto F Jr. Drug-induced hyperthermic syndromes: part I. Hyperthermia in overdose. *Emerg Med Clin North Am* 2013;31(4):1019–33.
6. Musselman ME, Saely S. Diagnosis and treatment of drug-induced hyperthermia. *Am J Health Syst Pharm* 2013;70(1):34–42.
7. McAllen KJ, Schwartz DR. Adverse drug reactions resulting in hyperthermia in the intensive care unit. *Crit Care Med* 2010;38(6 Suppl):S244–52.
8. Rosenberg J, et al. Hyperthermia associated with drug intoxication. *Crit Care Med* 1986;14(11):964–9.
9. Halloran LL, Bernard DW. Management of drug-induced hyperthermia. *Curr Opin Pediatr* 2004;16(2):211–5.
10. Hadad E, Weinbroum AA, Ben-Abraham R. Drug-induced hyperthermia. *Curr Opin Pediatr* 2004;16(2):211–5.
11. Crandall CG, Vongpatanasin W, Victor RG. Mechanism of cocaine-induced hyperthermia in humans. *Ann Intern Med* 2001;136(11):785–91.
12. Aniline O, Pitts FN Jr. Phencyclidine (PCP): a review and perspectives. *Crit Rev Toxicol* 1982;10(2):145–77.
13. McCarron MM, Schulze BW, Thompson GA, et al. Acute phencyclidine intoxication: incidence of clinical findings in 1,000 cases. *Ann Emerg Med* 1981;10(5):237–47.
14. Mercieca J, Brown EA. Acute renal failure due to rhabdomyolysis associated with use of a straitjacket in lysergide intoxication. *Br Med J (Clin Res Ed)* 1984;288(6435): 949–50.
15. Loghmanee F, Tobak M. Fatal malignant hyperthermia associated with recreational cocaine and ethanol abuse. *Am J Forensic Med Pathol* 1986;7(3):246–8.
16. Armen R, Kanel G, Reynolds T. Phencyclidine-induced malignant hyperthermia causing submassive liver necrosis. *Am J Med* 1984;77(1):167–72.
17. Duffy MR, Ferguson C. Role of dantrolene in treatment of heat stroke associated with Ecstasy ingestion. *Br J Anaesth* 2007;98(1):148–9.
18. Grunau BE, Wiens MO, Brubacher JR. Dantrolene in the treatment of MDMA-related hyperpyrexia: a systematic review. *CJEM* 2010;12(5):435–42.
19. Krause T, Gerbershagen MU, Fiege M, et al. Dantrolene--a review of its pharmacology, therapeutic use and new developments. *Anaesthesia* 2004;59(4):364–73.
20. Rusyniak DE, Sprague JE. Toxin-induced hyperthermic syndromes. *Med Clin North Am* 2005;89(6):1277–96.
21. Wilson MP, Vilke GM, Hayden SR, Nordstrom K. Psychiatric emergencies for clinicians: emergency department management of neuroleptic malignant syndrome. *J Emerg Med* 2016;51(1):66–9.
22. Kouparanis A, Bozikas A, Spilioti M, et al. Neuroleptic malignant syndrome in a patient on long-term olanzapine treatment at a stable dose: successful treatment with dantrolene. *Brain Inj* 2015;29(5):658–60.
23. Lazarus A. Therapy of neuroleptic malignant syndrome. *Psychiatr Dev* 1986;4(1):19–30.
24. Reulbach U, Dutsch C, Biermann T, et al. Managing an effective treatment for neuroleptic malignant syndrome. *Crit Care* 2007;11:R4.
25. Sakkas P, Davis JM, Janicak PG, et al. Drug treatment of the neuroleptic malignant syndrome. *Psychopharmacol Bull* 1991;27:381–4.
26. Rosenberg MR, Green M. Neuroleptic malignant syndrome: review of response to therapy. *Arch Intern Med* 1989;149(9):1927–31.
27. Nordstrom K, Vilke GM, Wilson MP. Psychiatric emergencies for clinicians: emergency department management of serotonin syndrome. *J Emerg Med* 2016;50(1):89–91.
28. Graudins A, Stearman A, Chan B. Treatment of the serotonin syndrome wih cyproheptidine. *J Emerg Med* 1998;16:615–9.
29. McDaniel WW. Serotonin syndrome: early management with cyproheptidine. *Ann Pharmacother* 2001;35(7–8):870–3.
30. Gillman PK. The serotonin syndrome and its treatment. *J Psychopharmacol* 1999;13(1):100–9.
31. Frank C. Recognition and treatment of serotonin syndrome. *Can Fam Physician* 2008;54:988–92.
32. Richards JR, Garber D, Laurin EG, et al. Treatment of cocaine cardiovascular toxicity: a systematic review. *Clin Toxicol (Phila)* 2016;54(5):345–64.
33. Richards JR, Albertson TE, Derlet RW, et al. Treatment of toxicity from amphetamines, related derivatives, and analogues: a systematic clinical review. *Drug Alcohol Depend* 2015;150:1–13.
34. Mowry JB, Spyker DA, Brooks DE, et al. 2015 Annual Report of the American Association of Poison Control Centers' National Poison Data System (NPDS): 33rd Annual Report. *Clin Toxicol (Phila)* 2016;54:924.
35. Dawson AH, Buckley NA. Pharmacological management of anticholinergic delirium - theory, evidence and practice. *Br J Clin Pharmacol* 2016;81(3):516–24.
36. Arens AM, Shah K, Al-Abri S, Olson KR, Kearney T. Safety and effectiveness of physostigmine: a 10-year retrospective review. *Clin Toxicol (Phila)* 2018;56(2):101–7.
37. Zalis EG, Kaplan G. The effect of aggregation on amphetamine toxicity in the dog. *Arch Int Pharmacodyn Ther* 1966;159(1):196–9.

38. Zalis EG, Lundberg GD, Knutson RA. The pathophysiology of acute amphetamine poisoning with pathologic correlation. *J Pharmacol Exp Ther*, 1967;158(1):115–27.
39. Davis WM, Hacket RB, Obrosky KW, et al. Factors in the lethality of i.v. phencyclidine in conscious dogs. *Gen Pharmacol* 1991;22(4):723–8.
40. Catravas JD, Waters IW. Acute cocaine intoxication in the conscious dog: studies on the mechanism of lethality. *J Pharmacol Exp Ther* 1981;217(2):350–6.
41. Bouchama A, Dehbi M, Chaves-Carballo E. Cooling and hemodynamic management in heatstroke: practical recommendations. *Critical Care* 2007;11(3):1–17.
42. Laskowski LK, Landry A, Vassallo SU, Hoffman RS. Ice water submersion for rapid cooling in severe drug-induced hyperthermia. *Clin Toxicol* 2015;53(3):181–4.
43. Nye EA, Edler JR, Eberman LE, Games KE. Optimizing cold-water immersion for exercise-induced hyperthermia: an evidence-based paper. *J Athl Train* 2016;51(6):500–1.

1.10 RHABDOMYOLYSIS

Gabriel Wardi and Christopher R. Tainter

1.10.1 General Comments

Rhabdomyolysis (literally "dissolution of skeletal muscle") is defined as a syndrome of skeletal muscle injury or necrosis with release of intra-cellular contents into the blood and systemic complications.[1] Although there are many ways of classifying rhabdomyolysis, a well-accepted method classifies eight causes of rhabdomyolysis: trauma, exertion, muscular hypoxia, genetic defects, infection, extremes of temperature, metabolic/electrolyte disorders, drugs/toxins, and idiopathic.[2] Importantly, rhabdomyolysis has been associated with all common drugs of abuse.[3–16] Despite the myriad causes of rhabdomyolysis, the final common pathway is a pathologically high amount of calcium in the cytoplasm of skeletal muscle injury that results in cellular damage and the release of intra-cellular contents.[17] The classic signs and symptoms of nausea, vomiting, myalgias, muscle swelling, tenderness, "tea-colored" urine, and weakness are present in only a minority of cases, 13% in one study.[16] Thus, the diagnosis depends on laboratory evaluation and a high clinical suspicion.

Elevated levels of serum creatine phosphokinase (CK or CPK), in the absence of CK from other sources (brain or heart), are the most sensitive indicator of muscle injury,[1] with most authors recognizing a CK level of more than five-fold that of the upper limit of normal, or greater than 1,000 IU/L, as diagnostic. CK levels tend to increase within the first 12 hours of the insult, peak at days 3–5, and typically return to baseline within 6–10 days.[18] There is a spectrum of severity of rhabdomyolysis ranging from those who are asymptomatic to those in significant multi-organ failure. Patients with less severe rhabdomyolysis, typically from chronic or intermittent mild muscle breakdown, have occasionally been described as having a condition called "hyperCKemia."[2]

Rhabdomyolysis may also be suspected with a positive urine dipstick for heme if no red blood cells are present on the urine microscopic examination. In this case, the positive orthotolidine reaction may be attributed to myoglobin in the absence of hemoglobin. Myoglobin is detectable in the urine when serum levels exceed 0.3 mg/L.[19] Because myoglobin is cleared from the plasma in 1 to 6 hours by renal excretion and by metabolism to bilirubin, the urine dipstick test for myoglobin may occasionally be negative due to rapid clearance.[1,16,20] Gabow et al. reported that in the absence of hematuria, only 50% of patients with rhabdomyolysis had urine that was orthotolidine-positive.[1]

Prompt diagnosis and early aggressive therapy of rhabdomyolysis are important because if untreated, it may produce myoglobinuric renal failure and life-threatening hyperkalemia. Myoglobinuric renal failure may be prevented by prompt identification and aggressive treatment. Compartment syndrome is not uncommon in patients with severe rhabdomyolysis and can occur either primarily from a crush injury or secondary to massive fluid shifts from the extracellular space into skeletal muscle cells due to a rapid increase in intra-cellular osmolarity.[21]

Assessing risk for developing acute renal failure:

Several heterogeneous studies have attempted to identify which patients will progress to myoglobinuric renal failure based on their laboratory values. Unfortunately, there are no prospective studies with standardized treatment regimens to determine which patients are at risk. Risk factors for more severe injury include delay to treatment, acidosis, electrolyte derangements, and level of CK.[22–27]

More recently, McMahon et al. created and validated a prediction rule to identify patients at risk for the development of kidney injury that required renal replacement therapy (RRT) and mortality.[28] They found an association between CK levels > 40,000 U/L and need for renal replacement therapy and mortality, and they also noted that increasing age, female sex, initial creatinine, phosphate, calcium, bicarbonate, and cause of rhabdomyolysis were also predictors in multivariable analysis. Another recent study found no relationship between initial CK levels, kidney injury, and mortality but found that initial creatinine levels were associated with both these outcomes.[29]

Prognosis:

Approximately 10% of patients with rhabdomyolysis presenting to hospitals develop myoglobinuric renal failure,[15] and major reports of patient series indicate that approximately 5% of patients with severe rhabdomyolysis die.[1,6] Death is often due not to rhabdomyolysis or its complications but rather, to the event that caused rhabdomyolysis, such as traumatic injury or sepsis. With temporary support from hemodialysis, acute myoglobinuric renal failure has a good prognosis, and full recovery should be expected, although the underlying insult may still result in death or poor clinical outcome.[2]

Crystalloids:

Aggressive initial fluid resuscitation is the mainstay of therapy for patients with rhabdomyolysis. In reviews of myoglobinuric renal failure,[1,6,18,21,30–33] hypovolemia is a consistent finding among all evaluated risk factors. Myoglobinuric renal failure seen in military recruits and bodybuilders has an especially strong association with dehydration.[34,35] Additionally, patients at risk for capillary damage and fluid leak from tissue injury may develop "relative" hypovolemia. The role of dehydration appears to implicate renal ischemia and perhaps acidosis and/or aciduria as necessary cofactors in the development of myoglobinuric acute renal failure.[36] A recent meta-analysis recommended the administration of intravenous fluid, preferably within 6 hours of the inciting event, to maintain urine output of at least 300 ml/h for the first 24 hours.[37] There has also been no convincing data to suggest that the type of crystalloid fluid administered, whether chloride liberal (e.g., normal saline) or conservative (e.g., lactated Ringer's) has any impact upon long-term outcomes.[38]

Alkalinization:

An acidic urinary environment is poorly tolerated by nephrons and is a well-described risk factor for the development of kidney injury. Thus, the main purpose of alkalinization of urine is to prevent the dissociation of myoglobin into globin and hematin (both significantly nephrotoxic agents),[15] which occurs with a urinary pH below 5.6.[39] The nephrotoxic effect of hematin has been ascribed to the production of free hydroxy radicals.[40] Dog studies have shown that the infusion of free hematin causes significantly greater renal dysfunction than does myoglobin.[41] Furthermore, in urine below pH 5.0, the solubility of myoglobin decreases markedly and results in myoglobin cast formation and an increase in the amount of myoglobin retained in renal tubules. Thus, by alkalinizing urine, this process is theoretically prevented. An acidic urinary pH has been shown to have a high correlation with the development of acute renal failure.[42] Rabbit studies by Perri et al.[43] showed that animals with a urinary pH lower than 6 invariably develop renal failure after infusions of myoglobin, whereas those with a urine pH of more than 6 do not develop renal insufficiency. Despite well-performed animal studies, no controlled human studies have evaluated the effectiveness of alkalinization for rhabdomyolysis. For this reason, as well as certain concerns about hypernatremia, hypervolemia, and hypocalcemia, some authors[44] do not recommend bicarbonate therapy. Furthermore, the risks of paradoxical intra-cellular acidosis due to the generation of carbon dioxide from the metabolism of bicarbonate merit frequent laboratory evaluation to monitor for this.[45,46]

Mannitol:

Several mechanisms have been proposed to explain the protective action of mannitol. Improved diuresis may simply dilute nephrotoxic agents in urine (e.g., myoglobin, hematin, and urate) and "flush out" myoglobin in partially obstructed tubules.[47] This increase in diuresis results in increased renal perfusion, which provides necessary renal blood flow to partially damaged nephrons. In addition, renal tubular oxygen consumption is closely coupled to sodium reabsorption, and by preventing sodium reabsorption, mannitol or furosemide may decrease the oxygen requirements of renal tubules.[48] This may allow the tubules to survive the metabolic insult produced by hematin.[15] Mannitol itself is a free radical scavenger and thus, also has a direct antioxidant effect upon nephrons. Wilson et al.[49] showed that mannitol plus saline almost totally prevented the development of azotemia after glycerol-induced rhabdomyolysis in rats. However, the risks of mannitol include dehydration and hypotension, given its potent diuretic effects, and high levels of mannitol have been associated with renal vasoconstriction and acute injury.[50] As with bicarbonate, mannitol has not been shown to be more effective in prospective, controlled trials than crystalloid alone.[51,52] In selected cases of hemodynamically stable patients with low urine output at risk of developing kidney injury, mannitol administration may be considered for its potential benefits.

Furosemide:

Loop diuretics such as furosemide have also been used in an attempt to prevent acute renal failure. As with mannitol and bicarbonate, no controlled human studies on their efficacy have been done. Furosemide may work similarly to mannitol to decrease sodium reabsorption and thus conserve renal tubule energy expenditure, decreasing the risk of ischemia. It may also simply convert oliguric renal failure to non-oliguric renal failure, which carries a more favorable prognosis.[53,54] Furosemide also does not increase serum osmolality to the extent that mannitol does but may exacerbate hypovolemia if not used with caution.

Renal replacement therapy (RRT):

When patients develop kidney injury from rhabdomyolysis, they are at risk of developing profound metabolic derangements, including life-threatening electrolyte abnormalities, acidosis, or volume overload, and may require RRT. Typically, intermittent hemodialysis (iHD) is used as it can rapidly correct these abnormalities. However, iHD is unable to remove myoglobin. There is some evidence that continuous renal replacement therapy (CRRT) can remove myoglobin, but there has been no evidence that the use of CRRT improves outcomes.[55] It is important to note that there have been no randomized trials evaluating prophylactic dialysis, and thus, this prophylactic approach with CRRT is not recommended at this point.[2]

1.10.2 Stepwise Approach to Management

1.10.2.1 Immediate Interventions

1. **Stabilization:** Maintain the airway and assist ventilation if necessary. Administer supplemental oxygen if appropriate. Treat hypotension and resuscitate as needed.[3] Administer supportive care and antidotes as clinically indicated. Identify the

reasons for rhabdomyolysis and treat the underlying cause. Examine the patient serially for developing signs of compartment syndrome.

2. **Crystalloid:** If the patient is hemodynamically stable, administer intermittent fluid boluses of crystalloid solution until hypovolemia is corrected. Assuming that larger volumes are not needed for other reasons, crystalloid infusion is then administered at a rate of 2.5 ml/kg of total body weight per hour. Monitor urine output closely. In patients with advanced heart failure, pulmonary edema, or other signs of volume overload, a more conservative fluid strategy may be prudent.

1.10.2.2 Secondary Interventions

1. **Reassess:** Check serum sodium and potassium concentrations and urine pH frequently. If large volumes of crystalloid solution are required for resuscitation, or sodium bicarbonate is used, check sodium every 6 to 8 h; otherwise, check every 12 to 24 h. Check serum pH every few hours if the patient is significantly acidotic (pH <7.3) or if large amounts of sodium bicarbonate are used.
2. **Bicarbonate:** If urinary pH is <5.6 (the pH at which myoglobin dissociates into globin and hematin), consider the administration of sodium bicarbonate intravenously (IV) in boluses of 1 mmol/kg body weight until the arterial blood pH is about 7.45 or the urinary pH rises to 6.5. Recently, this approach has fallen out of favor with some authors and experts due to potential harm from hypernatremia and volume overload, and there are no randomized trials that support its use. However, the benefits in serious rhabdomyolysis may outweigh these risks.[2,56] *Urinary* pH, not serum pH, has been found to correlate with precipitation of myoglobin within renal tubules, and as a result, the primary concern should be to increase urinary pH. Because of metabolic complications that may exist at a higher arterial pH (hypokalemia and the shifting of the oxygen-hemoglobin saturation curve to the left), bicarbonate should not be used if serum pH is already >7.45. Furthermore, if urinary pH does not increase within 4–6 hours or the patient develops symptomatic hypocalcemia, bicarbonate therapy should cease, as additional therapy is unlikely to be beneficial.[2]
3. **Avoid nephrotoxic agents:** Secondary insults can significantly worsen renal function and result in acute kidney injury. Non-steroidal anti-inflammatory medications, contrast media, and numerous antibiotics all pose risks of potentially unnecessary and avoidable risks to the kidney. The use of these agents should be carefully weighed against potential harm.
4. **Potassium:** Potassium may help to maintain a more alkaline urine. If urine pH falls below 5.6 in the presence of alkalemia, and serum potassium is low, then consider additional potassium supplementation until the urine pH rises above 6.0 or until the serum potassium concentration reaches 5 mEq/L. Patients with acute kidney injury are at elevated risk for hyperkalemia, and this should be closely monitored and held if the potential for hyperkalemia outweighs the potential benefit of urine alkalinization. The kidney of patients with hypokalemia will spare potassium and excrete hydrogen ions, resulting in a decrease of urinary bicarbonate and thus maintaining aciduria. Acidic urine increases myoglobin precipitation and increases the risk of myoglobinuric renal failure. There are no controlled studies demonstrating the role of potassium in the treatment of rhabdomyolysis, but supplementation into a normal range is unlikely to be harmful and may be beneficial. One study showed that during active work, potassium may act as a vasodilator and increase blood flow to working muscle.[56] Knochel et al.[57] have presented data demonstrating that skeletal muscle of potassium-depleted dogs releases very little potassium during exertion and that exertion is not accompanied by an increase in blood flow. This may result in localized muscle ischemia and persistent rhabdomyolysis.
5. **Acetazolamide:** Carbonic anhydrase inhibitors like acetazolamide may assist in producing a more alkaline urine. If the patient is persistently aciduric despite alkalemia and normal serum potassium concentrations, Curry et al.[15] recommend the use of 250 mg of acetazolamide IV to increase urinary pH. There is, however, no evidence that acetazolamide is efficacious for treatment of rhabdomyolysis. In general, acetazolamide should not be given to a patient suffering from salicylate poisoning, since it acidifies blood and alkalinizes cerebrospinal fluid, increasing the volume of distribution of salicylate and trapping salicylate in the central nervous system.[58–60] In animal models of salicylate poisoning, the administration of acetazolamide markedly increases the mortality rate.[60]
6. **Decreased urine output below 1.5 to 2.0 ml/kg/h with objective hemodynamic parameters of either normovolemia or hypovolemia:** Administer more crystalloid (500 cc fluid bolus) and consider increasing crystalloid infusion rate to 3.5 cc/kg/h.
7. **Decreased urine output below 1.5 to 2.0 ml/kg/h with objective hemodynamic parameters of hypervolemia:** Give a single dose of 1 g/kg body weight of mannitol IV over 30 min and administer any additional doses 0.5 g/kg IV over 15 min. Monitor serum osmolality if repeated doses are required. Mannitol may be administered every 6 h if serum osmolality remains below 300

mOsm/L. Mannitol is also particularly useful if there is potential or evidence of compartment syndrome.[61] Watch for pulmonary edema and monitor serum osmolality. Mannitol should also not be used in the presence of hemorrhagic shock or hypovolemia.

8. **Furosemide:** If urine output does not respond to fluids or mannitol, then administer furosemide. Start with 10 mg IVP.
9. **Discontinuation of therapy:** Continue the treatment protocol described until the urine is consistently orthotolidine-negative, laboratory signs of continued rhabdomyolysis are no longer present, and renal function is improving or normal. Stop fluids, mannitol, and bicarbonate if oliguria or anuria is refractory to therapy.
10. **Hemodialysis:** Those who do go on to develop acute tubular necrosis may require iHD for several days or weeks until renal function returns. Indications for hemodialysis include serious electrolyte abnormalities (e.g., hyperkalemia), clinically significant acidosis resistant to conventional therapy, and volume overload. A moderate elevation of blood urea nitrogen and creatinine levels without other clinical effects is not an indication for dialysis. CRRT should be considered in hemodynamically unstable patients. There is no role for prophylactic CRRT in removing myoglobin.
11. **Hyperkalemia:** Insulin therapy given in combination with dextrose or beta agonists (e.g., albuterol) may lower extracellular potassium levels temporarily. Dialysis may be required for potassium removal in severe cases. Calcium may help stabilize the myocardial depolarization threshold but should be used with caution as it may precipitate with phosphate and worsen renal failure (see later); thus, it should only be given in the presence of arrhythmias from hyperkalemia.
12. **Hypocalcemia:** Hypocalcemia is common in patients with severe rhabdomyolysis.[15] Treatment of asymptomatic hypocalcemia is discouraged due to theoretical concern that it could precipitate with phosphate and increase the resulting deposition of calcium phosphate crystals in the renal tubules, further worsening kidney injury. Patients at risk of hypotension from hypocalcemia-induced vasoplegia or cardiac arrhythmias from hypocalcemia (typically at levels less than or equal to 6 mEq/L), however, will benefit from the administration of calcium.[62]
13. **Hyperphosphatemia:** Elevated phosphate levels are not uncommon in patients with rhabdomyolysis due to release of intra-cellular contents. Patients should receive phosphate binders, which will not only help with hyperphosphatemia but also increase calcium levels.
14. **Disposition:** Patients with drug overdose who present with mild elevations of their CK may be considered for discharge if all the following conditions are met:
    a. The patient must have normal vital signs.
    b. There is no evidence of ongoing muscle injury.
    c. The patient has normal renal function.
    d. The patient is well hydrated and not acidotic, with normal electrolytes.
    e. The patient can take fluids by mouth and is not at risk for dehydration.
    f. Follow up is easily arranged for repeat CK in 12 to 24 h.
    g. A repeat serum CK level 6 to 8 h after the first shows a decreasing trend.

All other patients should be admitted to the hospital for aggressive fluid therapy as described earlier. Those at high risk for decompensation or requiring immediate correction of life-threatening conditions should be admitted to an intensive care unit.

REFERENCES

1. Gabow PA, Kaehny WD, Kelleher SP. The spectrum of rhabdomyolysis. *Medicine* 1982;61:141–52.
2. Bosch X, Poch E, Grau JM. Rhabdomyolysis and acute kidney injury. *N Engl J Med* 2009;361:62–72.
3. Callaway CW, Clark RF. Hyperthermia in psychostimulant overdose. *Ann Emerg Med* 1994;24(1):68–76.
4. Mercieca J, Brown EA. Acute renal failure due to rhabdomyolysis associated with use of a straitjacket in lysergide intoxication. *Br Med J (Clin Res Ed)* 1984;288(6435):1949–50.
5. Akisu M, et al. Severe acute thinner intoxication. *Turk J Pediatr* 1996;38(2):223–5.
6. Akmal M, et al. Rhabdomyolysis with and without acute renal failure in patients with phencyclidine intoxication. *Am J Nephrol* 1981;1(2):91–6.
7. Anand V, Siami G, Stone WJ. Cocaine-associated rhabdomyolysis and acute renal failure. *South Med J* 1989;82(1):67–9.
8. Bakir AA, Dunea G. Drugs of abuse and renal disease. *Curr Opin Nephrol Hypertens* 1996;5(2):122–6.
9. Chan P, et al. Acute heroin intoxication with complications of acute pulmonary edema, acute renal failure, rhabdomyolysis and lumbosacral plexitis: a case report. *Chung Hua I Hsueh Tsa Chih (Taipei)* 1995;55(5):397–400.
10. Chan P, et al. Fatal and nonfatal methamphetamine intoxication in the intensive care unit. *J Toxicol Clin Toxicol* 1994;32(2):147–55.
11. Cogen FC, et al. Phencyclidine-associated acute rhabdomyolysis. *Ann Intern Med* 1978;88(2):210–2.
12. Henry JA, Jeffreys KJ, and Dawling S. Toxicity and deaths from 3,4 methylenedioxymethamphetamine ("ecstasy"). *Lancet* 1992;340(8816):384–7.
13. Melandri R, et al. Myocardial damage and rhabdomyolysis associated with prolonged hypoxic coma following opiate overdose. *J Toxicol Clin Toxicol* 1996;34(2):199–203.
14. Tehan B, Hardern R, Bodenham A. Hyperthermia associated with 3,4 methylenedioxyethamphetamine ("Eve"). *Anaesthesia* 1993;48(6):507–10.

15. Curry SC, Chang D, Connor D. Drug- and toxin-induced rhabdomyolysis. *Ann Emerg Med* 1989;18(10):1068–84.
16. Welch RD, Todd K, Krause GS. Incidence of cocaine-associated rhabdomyolysis. *Ann Emerg Med* 1991;20(2):154–7.
17. Chatzizisis YS, Misirli G, Hatzitolios AI, Giannoglou GD. The syndrome of rhabdomyolysis: complications and treatment. *Eur J Inter Med* 2008;19(8):568–74.
18. Nance JR, Mammen AL. Diagnostic evaluation of rhabdomyolysis. *Muscle Nerve* 2015;51(6):793–810.
19. Giannoglou GD, Chatzizisis YS, Misirli G. The syndrome of rhabdomyolysis: pathophysiology and diagnosis. *Eur J Intern Med* 2007;19(2):90–100.
20. Knochel JP. Rhabdomyolysis and myoglobinuria. *Annu Rev Med* 1982;33:435–43.
21. Better OS, Rubinstein I, Reis DN. Muscle crush compartment syndrome: fulminant local edema with threatening systemic effects. *Kidney Int* 2003;63:1155–7.
22. Knottenbelt JD. Traumatic rhabdomyolysis from severe beating — experience of volume diuresis in 200 patients. *J Trauma* 1994;37(2):214–9.
23. Veenstra J, et al. Relationship between elevated creatine phosphokinase and the clinical spectrum of rhabdomyolysis. *Nephrol Dial Transplant* 1994;9(6):637.
24. Oda J, et al. Analysis of 372 patients with crush syndrome caused by the Hanshin-Awaji earthquake. *J Trauma* 1997;42(3):470–5; discussion 475–6.
25. Eneas JF, Schoenfeld PY, Humphreys MH. The effect of infusion of mannitol-sodium bicarbonate on the clinical course of myoglobinuria. *Arch Intern Med* 1979;139(7):801–5.
26. Feinfeld DA, et al. A prospective study of urine and serum myoglobin levels in patients with acute rhabdomyolysis. *Clin Nephrol* 1992;38(4):193–5.
27. Loun B, et al. Adaptation of a quantitative immunoassay for urine myoglobin. Predictor in detecting renal dysfunction. *Am J Clin Pathol* 1996;105(4):479–86.
28. McMahon GM, Zeng X, Waikar SS. A risk prediction score for kidney failure or mortality in rhabdomyolysis. *JAMA Intern Med* 2013;173(19):1821–7.
29. Baeza-Trinidad R, Brea-Hernando A, Morera-Rodriguez S, Brito-Diaz Y, Sanchez-Hernandez S, El Bikri L, Ramalle-Gomara E, Garcia-Alvarez JL. Creatinine as predictor value of mortality and acute kidney injury in rhabdomyolysis. *Intern Med J* 2015;45(11):1173–8.
30. Knochel JP. Catastrophic medical events with exhaustive exercise: "white collar rhabdomyolysis". *Kidney Int* 1990;38(4):709–19.
31. Kageyama Y. Rhabdomyolysis: clinical analysis of 20 patients. *Nippon Jinzo Gakkai Shi* 1989;31(10):1099–103.
32. Ellinas PA, Rosner F. Rhabdomyolysis: report of eleven cases. *J Natl Med Assoc* 1992;84(7):617–24.
33. Ward MM. Factors predictive of acute renal failure in rhabdomyolysis. *Arch Intern Med* 1988;148(7):1553–7.
34. Gardner JW, Kark JA. Fatal rhabdomyolysis presenting as mild heat illness in military training. *Mil Med* 1994;159(2):160–3.
35. Morocco PA. Atraumatic rhabdomyolysis in a 20-year-old bodybuilder. *J Emerg Nurs* 1991;17(6):370–2.
36. Sinert R, et al. Exercise-induced rhabdomyolysis. *Ann Emerg Med* 1994;23(6):1301–6.
37. Scharman EJ, Troutman WG. Prevention of kidney injury following rhabdomyolysis: a systematic review. *Ann Pharmaco* 2013;47(1):90–105.
38. Cho YS, Lim H, Kim SH. Comparison of lactated Ringer's solution and 0.9% saline in the treatment of rhabdomyolysis induced by doxylamine intoxication. *Emer Med J* 2007;24(4):276–80.
39. Bunn HF, Jandi JH. Exchange of heme analogue hemoglobin molecules. *Proc Natl Acad Sci USA* 1977;56: 974–8.
40. Paller MS. Hemoglobin- and myoglobin-induced acute renal failure in rats: role of iron in nephrotoxicity. *Am J Physiol* 1988;255(3 Pt 2):F539–44.
41. Anderson WAD, Morrison DB, Williams EF. Pathologic changes following injection of ferrihemate (hematin) in dogs. *Arch Pathol* 1942;33:589–602.
42. Garcia G, et al. Nephrotoxicity of myoglobin in the rat: relative importance of urine pH and prior dehydration (abstract). *Kidney Int* 1981;19:200.
43. Perri GC, Gerini P. Uraemia in the rabbit after injection of crystalline myoglobin. *Br J Exp Pathol* 1952;33:440–4.
44. POISONDEX(R) Editorial Staff and Kulig K. Rhabdomyolysis. POISONDEX(R): treatment protocols. 1992.
45. Zutt R, van der Kooi AJ, Linthorst GE, Wanders RJ, de Visser M. Rhabdomyolysis: review of the literature. *Neuromuscul Disord* 2014;24(8):651–9.
46. Berend K, de Vries AP, Gans RO. Physiological approach to assessment of acid-base disturbances. *N Engl J Med* 2015;372(2):195.
47. Eneas JF, Schoenfeld PY, Humphreys MH. The effect of infusion of mannitol-sodium bicarbonate on the clinical course of myoglobinuria. *Arch Intern Med* 1979;139: 801–5.
48. Bragadottir G, Redfors B, Ricksten SE. Mannitol increases renal blood flow and maintains filtration fraction and oxygenation in postoperative acute kidney injury: a prospective interventional study. *Critical Care* 2012;16(4): R159.
49. Lameire N, et al. Pathophysiology, causes, and prognosis of acute renal failure in the elderly. *Renal Fail* 1996;18(3):333–46.
50. Druml W. Prognosis of acute renal failure 1975–1995. *Nephron* 1996;73(1):8–15.
51. Wilson DR, et al. Glycerol induced hemoglobinuric acute renal failure in the rat. 3. Micropuncture study of the effects of mannitol and isotonic saline on individual nephron function. *Nephron* 1967;4(6):337–55.
52. Visweswaran P, Massin EK, Dubose TD Jr. Mannitol-induced acute renal failure. *J Am Soc Nephrol* 1997;8: 1028–33.
53. Homsi E, Barreiro MF, Orlando JM, Higa EM. Prophylaxis of acute renal failure in patients with rhabdomyolysis. *Ren Fail* 1997;19:283–8.
54. Brown CV, Rhee P, Chan L, Evans K, Demetriades D, Velmahos GC. Preventing renal failure in patients with rhabdomyoly- sis: do bicarbonate and mannitol make a difference? *J Trauma* 2004;56:1191–6.
55. Zeng X, Zhang L, Wu T, Fu P. Continuous renal replacement therapy (CRRT) for rhabdomyolysis. *Cochrane Database Syst Rev* 2014;6:CD008566.
56. Altintepe L, Guney I, Tonbul Z, Turk S, Mazi M, Agca E, et al. Early and intensive fluid replacement prevents acute renal failure in the crush cases associated with spontaneous collapse of an apartment in Konya. *Ren Fail* 2007;29(6):737–41.
57. Knochel JP, Schlein EM. On the mechanism of rhabdomyolysis in potassium depletion. *J Clin Invest* 1972;51(7): 1750–8.
58. Temple AR. Acute and chronic effects of aspirin toxicity and their treatment. *Arch Intern Med* 1981;141(3 Spec No):364–9.

59. Javaheri S. Effects of acetazolamide on cerebrospinal fluid ions in metabolic alkalosis in dogs. *J Appl Physiol* 1987;62(4):1582–8.
60. Kaplan SA, Del Carmen FT. Experimental salicylate poisoning. Observation on the effects of carbonic anhydrase inhibitor and bicarbonate. *Pediatrics* 1958;21:762–70.
61. Holt SG, Moore KP. Pathogenesis and treatment of renal dysfunction in rhabdomyolysis. *Intens Care Med* 2001;27:803–11.
62. Gozal Y. Calcium administration in rhabdomyolysis may be detrimental. *Anesth Analg* 1996;82:185–6.

1.11 HYPERTENSIVE EMERGENCIES

Dunya N. Alfaraj and Gary M. Vilke

1.11.1 General Comments

1.11.1.1 Hypertension

A hypertensive crisis is classified as hypertensive emergency (HTN-E) or hypertensive urgency (HTN-U). HTN-E is characterized by a severe elevation of blood pressure (BP; $\geq$180/120 mmHg) with evidence of progressive organ damage or target organ failure. HTN-U is defined as uncontrolled BP without evidence of failure or damage to the target organ (see Figure 1.11.1). Many of these patients have withdrawn from or are noncompliant with antihypertensive therapy. Examples of target organ damage include hypertensive encephalopathy, intracranial hemorrhage, acute ischemic stroke, acute myocardial infarction, acute heart failure with pulmonary edema, unstable angina, aortic dissection, acute renal failure, and eclampsia.[1,2]

In hypertensive emergencies, the choice of the first-line agent is dictated by the affected target organ. The goal is to reduce BP by 25% over a period of 60 minutes or so, then to 160/100–110 for the next 2–6 hours, then to normal over 24–48 hours. Eclampsia, pheochromocytoma, and aortic dissection are exceptional cases, in which BP must be reduced as rapidly as possible within 60 minutes to a target systolic blood pressure (SBP) $\leq$140 mmHg for eclampsia and pheochromocytoma and to a target SBP $\leq$120 mmHg for aortic dissection (see Figure 1.11.1). Direct arteriolar dilating agents such as nitroglycerin or nitroprusside, a pure alpha-adrenergic blocking agent such as phentolamine, or a calcium antagonist such as nicardipine may be used. But beta blockade should precede a vasodilator to prevent reflex tachycardia.[2]

Reducing BP too rapidly in chronically hypertensive patients can lead to organ hypoperfusion, as the body is used to the higher pressure head, which can lead to ischemic damage. Preventing or minimizing end organ damage is a more important goal than lowering the actual BP.[3] With the loss of normal cerebral autoregulation, theoretical concerns are: high BP can lead to cerebral edema, hematoma expansion, or hemorrhagic transformation; and low BP can lead to increased cerebral infarction or perihematomal ischemia.[4] Therefore, in ischemic stroke, current guidelines recommend a 15% reduction within the first 24 hours only in cases where BP exceeds 220/110 mmHg.[2,5]

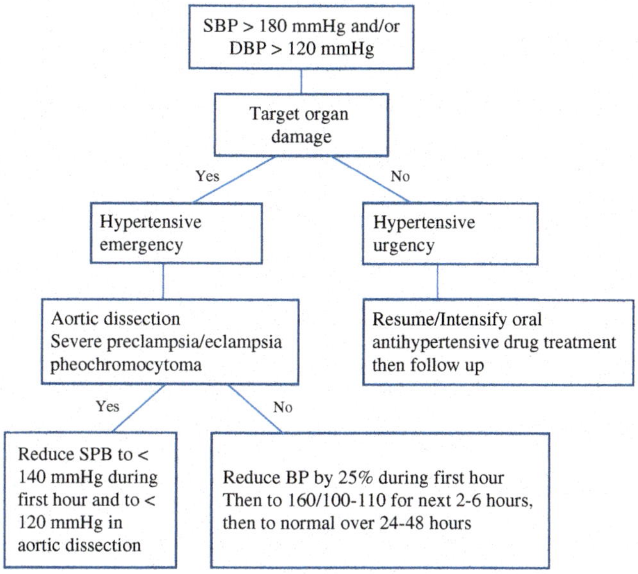

FIGURE 1.11.1 Management of hypertensive crisis.

Based on the half-life time of medication, the emergency physician can choose an appropriate treatment for emergency hypertension depending on the clinical presentation. Esmolol, a cardio-selective β1 receptor blocker, will decrease cardiac output, heart rate, and stroke volume, but its ultra-short action limits its use to intravenous infusion. Labetalol, an α1 and β blocker, has a longer half-life of about 5.5 h, which can create difficulties in titration. Calcium channel blockers are considered a first-line treatment because they are strong vasodilators and have few negative effects on cardiac conduction and contractility when compared with β-blockers. Nicardipine, a second-generation dihydropyridine calcium channel blocker, causes coronary and cerebral artery vasodilation. However, the major disadvantage of these central drugs is their prolonged half-life and the relatively large volumes of solution in which the drugs need to be diluted.[6]

Blood pressure readings higher than 130–139/85–89 mmHg over time are associated with a higher rate of cardiovascular disease, including myocardial infarction and stroke. Drug-induced hypertension is usually short-lived; however, hypertensive emergencies have been reported. Among illicit drugs, cocaine is the leading cause of emergency department visits and mortality due to cardiovascular and cerebrovascular complications. Cocaine is associated with hypertension urgencies and emergencies, as well as ventricular hypertrophy, ischemic heart disease, myocardial infarction, aortic dissection, ventricular arrhythmia, cardiomyopathy, endocarditis, stroke, subarachnoid hemorrhage, intracerebral hemorrhage, and cerebral ischemia.[7–11] A low, non-intoxicating dose of intranasal cocaine (2 mg/kg) has even been shown to decrease both coronary artery diameter and coronary sinus blood flow, an indirect measure of coronary arterial flow in patients undergoing diagnostic cardiac catheterization for the evaluation of chest pain.[12]

Oral phenylpropanolamine (PPA) was commonly used as a decongestant, cough suppressant, and weight control agent. However, it has been noted that PPA can raise blood pressure to dangerous levels that may result in hemorrhagic stroke. In 2003, PPA was actually withdrawn for use in humans by the U.S. Food and Drug Administration (FDA) amidst concerns of the risk for increasing the incidence of hemorrhagic stroke.[13–15]

For cocaine-induced hypertension, non-dihydropyridine calcium channel blockers such as diltiazem and verapamil have been demonstrated to reduce the hypertension but not tachycardia. Dihydropyridine agents such as nifedipine may actually cause reflex tachycardia and should be avoided. The alpha-blocker phentolamine can treat alpha-mediated hypertension but not tachycardia; however, it is rarely used, and most clinicians are unfamiliar with its use. Nitroglycerin and nitroprusside are effective at lowering blood pressure, but reflex tachycardia may occur. The mixed beta/alpha-blocker labetalol has been shown to be safe and effective for treating concomitant cocaine-induced hypertension and tachycardia without "unopposed alpha-stimulation" adverse events. Catecholamine excess may cause cardiac hypertrophy, fibrosis, and myocardial ischemia. These predispose the heart to arrhythmias. Supraventricular tachyarrhythmias could be treated with adenosine or calcium channel blockers. Lidocaine and intravenous lipid emulsion could be used for serious ventricular tachydysrhythmia. Hyperthermia from cocaine toxicity is best treated with external cooling measures using tepid water misting with convection cooling from a fan.[16,17] Thomas et al. studied cocaine toxicity in dogs and found that hospitalization for monitoring and supportive care is recommended given the potential for life-threatening complications such as seizures, hypertensive crisis, and tachyarrhythmias. The prognosis for survival to hospital discharge can be good with the appropriate supportive care.[18]

There is some noted conflict in the literature regarding the effectiveness of benzodiazepines in treating symptoms induced by sympathomimetic drugs like cocaine. Goldstein et al. found that benzodiazepines are the main medication for sympathomimetic drugs; they treat and help prevent seizures, calm the agitated patient, and prevent delirium.[19] The possibility of a diazepam-induced attenuation of sympathetic outflow is supported by the observation that diazepam can reduce the release of plasma catecholamines, especially norepinephrine.[20,21] However, Gomez et al. suggest that benzodiazepines have a dopaminergic component, which may contradict the classic view that benzodiazepines are useful against sympathomimetic drugs that cause dopamine release, such as cocaine, amphetamine, and nicotine.[22] Richard et al. also found that benzodiazepines may not always be effective for tachycardia, hypertension, and vasospasm from cocaine toxicity.[23] Haga and associates reported that cocaine increased heart rate, not blood pressure, after triazolam pretreatment, but this was not statistically significant.[24] Nonetheless, despite these theoretical concerns, benzodiazepines remain the mainstay for treating symptomatic cocaine intoxication.

As an alternative to benzodiazepines, sympathomimetic-induced symptoms can also be managed by other medications such as antipsychotics or diphenhydramine. Korczak et al. demonstrated that antipsychotics or combination therapy of benzodiazepines and antipsychotics were more effective, requiring fewer repeat doses for sedation, and had lower adverse events than benzodiazepines alone.[25] Diphenhydramine has been used to enhance sedation and as prophylaxis against dystonia and akathisia secondary to cocaine.[16] Zhang et al. demonstrated Enzyme-based Novel Therapy, Albu-CocH1 (or TV-1380), as an alternative to diazepam in cocaine toxicity treatment. They found that pretreatment of rats with this novel therapy before administration of cocaine was able to convert cocaine rapidly and completely to a physiologically inactive metabolite. They also indicated from animal data that Albu-CocH1 is much more effective than diazepam in cocaine toxicity treatment.[26]

Beta-blockers are primarily used to treat angina and hypertension related to cocaine toxicity, though they are often used to control anxiety and agitation.[27] Unlike benzodiazepines, β-blockers directly counter the hyperadrenergic effect of cocaine without the risk of over-sedation and respiratory depression.[28] The study by Nguyen and associates, as well as several other recent large studies, confirms that β-blockers represent an important treatment option for patients with cocaine toxicity.[29] Guidelines released in 2008 recommended against using beta-blockers for cocaine toxicity because of the theory that cocaine would potentiate vasospasm secondary to unopposed α-adrenergic effects.[30] It was believed that the hyperadrenergic state stimulates both α-adrenoreceptors (mediating peripheral vasoconstriction) and β2-adrenoreceptors (mediating peripheral vasodilation). Consequently, in treating patients with hypertension and tachycardia, it is important to achieve blockade of both α- and β-adrenoreceptors.[31] Stankowski et al. note that β-blockers should be used with extreme caution in patients with cocaine-associated cardiac disease as there is always a possibility of exacerbating coronary spasms with some, but not all, beta-blockers.[32] Unfortunately, for over three decades, "unopposed alpha-receptor activation" dogma has prevailed, and β-blocker use in cocaine-positive patients has been cited as an absolute contraindication despite limited and inconsistent clinical evidence.[29,33] The evidence against the use of beta-blockers in cocaine toxicity might not be strong enough to withhold these drugs from patients with cocaine toxicity, especially those with ventricular arrhythmias or left ventricular systolic dysfunction.[34]

Subsequently, further evidence and updated guidelines have become available, debunking the claim against using beta-blockers for cocaine toxicity.[30] The study of Espana et al. did not support the presence of an unopposed alpha-adrenergic effect in patients with continuing cocaine-induced chest pain and treated safely with beta-blocker.[35] Fanari et al. found no differences in outcomes between patients treated versus not treated with β-blocker therapy in the setting of cocaine toxicity.[36] Richards and colleagues performed an extensive systematic review on the treatment of cocaine cardiovascular toxicity and concluded that β-blockers were safe and effective, especially for concomitant cocaine-induced hypertension and tachycardia.[37]

Propranolol is a nonselective beta-blocker. Several studies have confirmed that propranolol has a significant hypotensive action both when used alone and as an adjuvant therapy.[38] American Heart Association (AHA) guidelines for cardiopulmonary resuscitation and emergency cardiovascular care advise that although evidence of benefit exists, the current recommendation is that pure beta-blockers are not indicated for the treatment of cocaine-related cardiac toxicity.[39] Richards et al. write that labetalol is an excellent choice for monotherapy of cocaine cardiovascular toxicity when tachycardia is accompanied by hypertension. With its α- and β-blocking properties, labetalol directly antagonizes the hyperadrenergic effects of cocaine and unlike benzodiazepines, does not increase the risk of respiratory depression, over-sedation, and paradoxical agitation.[40] Agrawal et al. note that the role of labetalol in the treatment of cocaine toxicity has been controversial and warrants further investigation.[41] Hamad et al. report an interesting case report describing the association of life-threatening hyperkalemia in a dialysis patient with hypertensive emergency treated with labetalol.[42] Labetalol has an alpha-to-beta blockade ratio of 1:7. Therefore, it may not provide enough protection for cocaine-toxic patients from unopposed alpha stimulation. Labetalol also increased seizures and mortality in animal models.[23]

However, several studies and case reports have documented the safety and usefulness of labetalol in cocaine-intoxicated patients.[43] The 2012 American College of Cardiology Foundation (ACCF)/AHA guidelines on unstable angina and non–ST-segment elevation myocardial infarction recommend that a combined alpha- and beta-blocking agent (e.g., labetalol or carvedilol) may be a reasonable treatment choice for cocaine-related hypertension (SBP >150 mmHg) or sinus tachycardia (pulse >100 beats per min), provided that the patient has received a vasodilator, such as nitroglycerin or a calcium channel blocker, within the past hour.[44] Both carvedilol and labetalol were investigated by Sofuoglu and associates, who reported that pretreatment by either agent successfully attenuated the rise in blood pressure and heart rate associated with smoking cocaine ($p < 0.05$).[45,46] Hoskins et al. demonstrated that labetalol treatment was associated with reduced heart rate, SBP, and diastolic BP ($p < 0.005$) in 60 patients with cocaine-associated acute coronary syndrome, with an added benefit of reducing the inflammatory markers interleukin-6, CD40 ligand, and choline ($p < 0.005$).[47] Richards et al. demonstrated that labetalol represents an effective first-line treatment for topical cocaine complications. Topical cocaine is sometimes used for the treatment of epistaxis, which may result in sudden hypertension, tachycardia, coronary arterial vasoconstriction, and dysrhythmia. They also noted that labetalol, unlike benzodiazepines, has no respiratory or sedative side effects, and labetalol, with its mixed β/α-blocking properties, mitigates the potential for unopposed α-stimulation.[48] In one case report, a patient with a history of hypertension taking oral clonidine presented with headache and resistant hypertension, 230/130, not responding to oral clonidine. The computed tomography (CT) of the brain was normal, and medication history revealed that the patient had recently taken Libido-Max, an over-the-counter supplement for erectile dysfunction. This supplement includes yohimbine, an α-2 antagonist, which counteracts the effects of oral clonidine. His blood pressure was successfully treated with intravenous labetalol, and his symptoms quickly resolved after lowering of his blood pressure.[49] A systematic review of cocaine-related cardiovascular toxicity found that combined alpha/beta-blockers were effective in attenuating both hypertension and tachycardia, with no adverse events reported.[23]

Overall, the conclusions in the study by Stankowski et al. are most reasonable when they note that medications such as labetalol with both alpha- and beta-blocking activity have been proposed to avoid blocking the beta receptor alone. In a single clinical trial, labetalol was found to exacerbate cocaine-induced alpha-adrenergic stimulation and was ineffective at reducing cocaine-induced coronary vasoconstriction.[50]

Esmolol produces early regression of left ventricular hypertrophy and improves coronary artery remodeling, although the impact of short-term treatment with this beta-blocker on remodeling in large arteries has not yet been studied.[51] Arnalich-Montiel et al. found that short-term esmolol therapy improves early coronary artery remodeling in spontaneously hypertensive rats.[52]

In cocaine-induced aortic dissection, beta-adrenergic antagonists (esmolol, metroprolol, or labetalol) represent the first-choice agents along with vasodilators (sodium nitroprusside) and calcium channel antagonists. Vasodilator therapy should not be initiated prior to rate control as these agents are associated with reflex tachycardia that may increase aortic wall stress, leading to expansion of a thoracic aortic dissection, and thus, are relatively contraindicated in patients with acute aortic dissection.[53] For cocaine-induced chest pain, nitroglycerin acts by relaxing smooth muscle and dilating veins, arteries, and coronary arteries. Venodilation lowers preload and therefore reduces wall stress, resulting in a decrease in myocardial oxygen demand. Nitroglycerin could temporarily decrease chest pain by lowering the patient's blood pressure and reducing wall stress. However, as vasodilators may increase the force of left ventricular ejection, nitroglycerin alone must be used with caution.[54]

1.11.2 Stepwise Approach to Management

1.11.2.1 Immediate Interventions

1. **Airway, breathing, circulation:** Maintain the airway and assist ventilation if necessary. Administer supplemental oxygen. Resuscitate as per previous reviews.
2. **Antidotes:** Administer appropriate antidotes, including 25 g dextrose IV if the patient is hypoglycemic, as per Section 8.2.1.
3. **Agitation or seizures:** Administer a benzodiazepine and/or antipsychotic.
4. **Medications:**

   In adults with a hypertensive emergency, admission to an intensive care unit is recommended for continuous monitoring of BP and target organ damage and for intravenous administration of an appropriate drug (see Tables 1.11.1 and 1.11.2 for treatment considerations). Nitroprusside generally requires continuous intra-arterial blood pressure monitoring. The use of oral therapy is discouraged for hypertensive emergencies.[2]

Hypertensive urgency is treated by reinstitution or intensification of antihypertensive drug therapy. There is no indication for referral to the emergency department, immediate reduction in BP in the emergency department, or hospitalization for such patients.[2]

Although oral PPA was withdrawn for use in humans by the U.S. FDA due to concern of increasing incidence of hemorrhagic stroke,[13–15] it may be substituted by illicit drug users with stimulants such as amphetamine and cocaine. PPA is an indirect sympathomimetic and direct alpha agonist. The combination of severe hypertension with reflex bradycardia is a clue to vasoconstriction from direct alpha stimulation by PPA. Hypertension from PPA is usually best treated with phentolamine.

5. **Laboratory data/imaging:** For patients with hypertensive emergencies, electrolytes, CPK, blood urea nitrogen, creatinine, and troponin should be considered to assess for end organ injury. Perform a chest X-ray as clinically indicated. For apparently uncomplicated hypertension without symptoms, laboratory data may be performed at the discretion of the physician. An electrocardiogram is a consideration to rule out silent ischemia.

1.11.2.2 Secondary Interventions

1. **Monitoring:** Continue close monitoring of patient's blood pressure and cardiac status with frequent manual blood pressure readings. Consider placing an arterial line for better monitoring in patients with persistently labile hypertension or for those who have hypertension that is difficult to control.
2. **CT of brain:** Patients with severe headaches that do not resolve after the control of hypertension should undergo CT of the head to rule out intracranial bleeding. Any focal neurologic findings or alterations in the level of consciousness warrant an urgent head CT.
3. **Lumbar puncture:** If CT of head is negative and the patient continues to have symptoms of severe headache or nuchal rigidity, consider performing

TABLE 1.11.1
Management of Hypertensive Emergencies for Patients with Selected Comorbidities

Comorbidity	Preferred Drug(s)	Comments
Acute aortic dissection	Beta-adrenergic antagonists (esmolol, metroprolol, or labetalol) followed by vasodilator (e.g., nitroprusside or nicardipine)	Target SBP ≤120 mmHg within 20 minutes. Control heart rate before vasodilator therapy to avoid reflex tachycardia that may result in expansion of aortic dissection
Acute pulmonary edema	Clevidipine, nitroglycerin, nitroprusside	Beta-blocker contraindicated
Acute coronary syndrome	Esmolol, labetalol, nicardipine, nitroglycerin	Beta-blocker contraindicated in heart failure, heart block, and hyperactive airway disease
Acute renal failure	Clevidipine, fenoldopam, nicardipine	
Eclampsia or preeclampsia	Hydralazine, labetalol, nicardipine	Requires rapid BP lowering if not responsive to magnesium
Perioperative hypertension[a]	Clevidipine, esmolol, nicardipine, nitroglycerin	
Catecholamine excess (pheochromocytoma, interactions between monoamine oxidase inhibitors and other drugs or food, cocaine toxicity, amphetamine overdose, phenylpropanolamine or clonidine withdrawal, post-enterectomy)	Clevidipine, nicardipine, phentolamine	Require rapid BP lowering (benzodiazepine could be given in addition to antihypertensive medication in case of drug overdose)
Acute intracerebral hemorrhage	Nicardipine, labetalol, esmolol	Standard approach: reduction to a target of SBP 140 to 179 mmHg. Intensive approach: BP <140/90 mmHg within 6 hours of an acute intracerebral hemorrhage. Intensive approach may result in greater attenuation of absolute hematoma at 24 hours and better functional recovery
Acute ischemic stroke	Nicardipine, labetalol	Treat when BP >220/110 except with thrombolytics >185/110

[a] Perioperative BP ≥160/90 mmHg or SBP ≥20%of preoperative value persist for ≥15 min.

TABLE 1.11.2
Intravenous Antihypertensive Drugs for the Treatment of Hypertensive Emergencies

Class	Drug	Comments
Calcium channel blocker	Nicardipine	Contraindicated in severe aortic stenosis. Safe in elderly.
	Clevidipine	Contraindicated in patients with allergy to soy or egg products and in patients with defective lipid metabolism. Use low dose for elderly.
Vasodilators	Sodium nitroprusside	Intra-arterial BP monitoring recommended. Dosing adjustment required for elderly. Side effects: Tachyphylaxis, cyanide toxicity, irreversible neurological changes, and cardiac arrest.
	Nitroglycerin	Use only in acute coronary syndrome and/or acute pulmonary edema. Avoid use in patients with dehydration or who recently used erectile dysfunction medications.
	Hydralazine	Unpredictability of response and prolonged duration of action make hydralazine undesirable first-line agent for acute treatment. BP decrease within 10–30 min and lasts 2–4 h.
Beta-blocker	Esmolol (selective beta 1) Labetalol (nonselective beta+alpha)	Should not be given in patients with reactive airways disease, chronic obstructive pulmonary disease, heart failure, or second- or third-degree heart block.
Alpha-blocker	Phentolamine	Used in hypertensive emergencies induced by catecholamine excess.
Dopamine1-receptor selective agonist	Fenoldopam	Contraindicated in patients with increased intraocular pressure (glaucoma) or intracranial pressure and sulfite allergy.
ACE inhibitor	Enalapril	Contraindicated in: pregnancy, acute myocardial infarction, or bilateral renal artery stenosis. Dose not easily adjusted. Relatively slow onset of action (15 min) and unpredictability of BP response.

a lumbar puncture to rule out subarachnoid hemorrhage.

4. **Disposition:** Patients may be considered for discharge from the emergency department if they demonstrate moderate uncomplicated hypertension controlled with sedation or a minimal use of antihypertensive agents without evidence of end organ damage, based on clinical presentation or laboratory studies, and if any associated symptoms have resolved after improvement of the blood pressure. All patients with hypertensive emergencies should be admitted to the hospital regardless of response to initial therapy.

ACKNOWLEDGMENTS

Brett A. Roth, M.D., Neal L. Benowitz, M.D., and Kent R. Olson, M.D.

REFERENCES

1. Dhadke SV, Dhadke VN, Batra DS. Clinical profile of hypertensive emergencies in an intensive care unit. *J Assoc Physicians India* 2017;65(5):18–22.
2. Whelton PK, Carey RM, Aronow WS et al. ACC/AHA/AAPA/ABC/ACPM/AGS/APhA/ASH/ASPC/NMA/PCNA Guideline for the Prevention, Detection, Evaluation, and Management of High Blood Pressure in Adults: a Report of the American College of Cardiology/American Heart Association Task Force on Clinical Practice Guidelines. *Hypertension* 2017 Nov 13.
3. Cheng SL. Treating HTN crisis. How low? How fast? *RN* 2005;68(6):37–41; quiz
4. Appleton JP, Sprigg N, Bath PM. Blood pressure management in acute stroke. *Stroke and Vascular Neurology* 2016;1:e000020.
5. Bowry R, Navalkele DD, Gonzales NR. Blood pressure management in stroke. *Neurol Clin Pract* 2014;4(5): 419–26.
6. Castellon-Larios K, Fiorda-Diaz J, Arias-Morales CE, Bergese SD. Hypertensive emergency: an updated review. *Ann Clin Exp Hypertension* 2015;3(2):1029.
7. Eto M, Okayama M, Takeshima T, Kumada M, Aonuma T, Nakamura Y, et al. Interaction between alcohol habit ad gene polymorphism of beta-2 adrenergic receptor of the risk of high normal blood pressure. *J Am College Cardiol* 2015;65(10):A1468.
8. Grossman A, Messerli FH, Grossman E. Drug induced hypertension – an unappreciated cause of secondary hypertension. *Eur J Pharmacol* 2015.
9. Grasing K, Mathur D, DeSouza C, Newton TF, Moody DE, Sturgill M. Cocaine cardiovascular effects and pharmacokinetics after treatment with the acetylcholinesterase inhibitor donepezil. *Am J Addict* 2016;25(5):392–9.
10. Havakuk O, Rezkalla SH, Kloner RA. The cardiovascular effects of cocaine. *J Am Coll Cardiol* 2017;70:101–13.
11. Stankowski RV, Kloner RA, Rezkalla SH. Cardiovascular consequences of cocaine use. *Trends Cardiovasc Med* 2015;25(6):517–26.

12. Vongpatanasin W, Taylor JA, Victor RG. Effects of cocaine on heart rate variability in healthy subjects. *Am J Cardiol* 2004;93:385–8.
13. Salerno SM, Jackson JL, Berbano EP. The impact of oral phenylpropanolamine on blood pressure: a meta-analysis and review of the literature. *Journal of Human Hypertension* 2005;19(8):643–52.
14. Segev G, Westropp JL, Kulik C, Lavy E. Changes in blood pressure following escalating doses of phenylpropanolamine and a suggested protocol for monitoring. *Can Vet J* 2015;56(1):39–43.
15. Stier BG, Hennekens CH. Phenylpropanolamine and hemorrhagic stroke in the hemorrhagic stroke project: a reappraisal in the context of science, the food and drug administration, and the law. *Ann Epidemiol* 2006;16(1):49–52.
16. Richards JR, Le JK. Toxicity, cocaine. [Updated 2017 Apr 22]. In *StatPearls* [Internet]. Treasure Island, FL: StatPearls Publishing, 2018.
17. Bădilă E, Hostiuc M, Weiss E, Bartoş D. Illicit drugs and their impact on cardiovascular pathology. *Rom J Intern Med* 2015;53(3):218–25.
18. Thomas EK, Drobatz KJ, Mandell DC. Presumptive cocaine toxicosis in 19 dogs: 2004–2012. *J Vet Emerg Crit Care (San Antonio)* 2014;24(2):201–7.
19. Goldstein S, Richard J. *Toxicity Sympathomimetics Chapter, StatPearls Publishing*, April 15, 2017. PMID:28613508.
20. Costa A, Bosone D, Zoppi AD, Angelo A, Ghiotto N, Guaschino E, et al. Effect of diazepam on 24-hour blood pressure and heart rate in healthy young volunteers. *Pharmacology* 2018;101:86–91.
21. Rothman RB, et al. Amphetamine-type central nervous system stimulants release norepinephrine more potently than they release dopamine and serotonin. *Synapse* 2001;39(1):32–41.
22. Gomez-A A, Fiorenza AM, Boschen SL, Sugi AH, Beckman D, Ferreira ST, et al. Diazepam inhibits electrically evoked and tonic dopamine release in the nucleus accumbens and reverses the effect of amphetamine. *ACS Chem Neurosci* 2017;8(2):300–9.
23. Richards JR, Garber D, Laurin EG, Albertson TE, Derlet RW, Amsterdam EA, et al. Treatment of cocaine cardiovascular toxicity: a systematic review. *Clin Toxicol (Phila)* 2016;54(5):345–64.
24. Haga JL, Baker RW, Rush CR. Behavioral and physiological effects of cocaine in humans following triazolam. *Pharmacol Biochem Behav* 2003;76:383–92.
25. Korczak V, Kirby A, Gunja N. Chemical agents for the sedation of agitated patients in the ED: a systematic review. *Am J Emerg Med* 2016;34(12):2426–31.
26. Zhang T, Zheng X, Zhou Z, Chen X, Jin Z, Deng J et al. Clinical potential of an enzyme-based novel therapy for cocaine overdose. *Sci Rep* 2017;7(1):15303.
27. Kampman KM. New medications for the treatment of cocaine dependence. *Psychiatry (Edgmont)* 2005;2(12):44–48.
28. Richards JR. β-blocker treatment of vascular disease in cocaine addiction. *Atherosclerosis* 2017;264:122.
29. Richards JR. Safety and efficacy of beta blockers in cocaine-using patients with heart failure. *Am J Cardiol* 2017;121(3):393.
30. Schurr JW, Gitman B, Belchikov Y. Controversial therapeutics: the β-adrenergic antagonist and cocaine-associated cardiovascular complications dilemma. *Pharmacotherapy* 2014;34(12):1269–81.
31. Richards JR. Beta blockers and the cardiac complications of methamphetamine heart, lung & circulation. *Heart Lung Circ* 2017;26(4):416–7.
32. Stankowski RV, Kloner RA, Rezkalla SH. Letter to the editor response. *Trends Cardiovasc Med* 2016;26(2):203.
33. Richards JR, Hollander JE, Ramoska EA, Fareed FN, Sand IC, Izquierdo Gómez MM, et al. β-Blockers, cocaine, and the unopposed α-stimulation phenomenon. *J Cardiovasc Pharmacol Ther* 2017;22(3):239–49.
34. Haber MA. Should beta-blockers be used in the setting of cocaine-related chest pain? *The NYU Langone Online Journal of Medicine* 2014.
35. Espana Schmidt C, Pastori L, Pekler G, Visco F, Mushiyev S. Early use of beta blockers in patients with cocaine associated chest pain. *Int J Cardiol Heart Vascul* 2015;8:167–9.
36. Fanari Z, Kennedy KK, Lim MJ, Laddu AA, Stolker JM. Comparison of in-hospital outcomes for beta-blocker use versus non-beta blocker use in patients presenting with cocaine-associated chest pain. *Am J Cardiol* 2014;113(11):1802–6.
37. Bachi K, Mani V, Trivieri MG, Jeyachandran D, Fayad ZA, Goldstein RZ, et al. Reply to: "β-blocker treatment of vascular disease in cocaine addiction". *Atherosclerosis* 2017;264:123–4.
38. Constantine GR, Ranasinghe P, Weeratunga P, Weeraratne C, Galappatthy P, Rajapakse S, et al. Addition of Propranolol in Resistant Arterial hypertension Treatment (APROPRIATE study): study protocol for a randomized double-blind placebo-controlled trial. *Trials* 2017;18:124.
39. American Heart Association. Part 10: special circumstances of resuscitation. *Web-based Integrated 2010 & 2015 American Heart Association Guidelines for Cardiopulmonary Resuscitation and Emergency Cardiovascular Care.* Available at https://eccguidelines.heart.org/index.php/circulation/cpr-ecc-guidelines-2/part-10-special-circumstances-of-resuscitation/. October 2010; Accessed June 30, 2016.
40. Richards JR, Laurin EG, Tabish N, Lange RA. Response to β-Blocker in acute cocaine toxicity: is it safe? *J Emerg Med* 2017;53(4):571–2.
41. Agrawal PR, Scarabelli TM, Saravolatz L, Kini A, Jalota A, Chen-Scarabelli C, et al. Current strategies in the evaluation and management of cocaine-induced chest pain. *Cardiol Rev* 2015;23(6):303–11.
42. Hamad A, et al. Life-threatening hyperkalemia after intravenous labetolol injection for hypertensive emergency in a hemodialysis patient. *Am J Nephrol* 2001;21(3):241–4.
43. Subramanian S, Sampathkumar S, Menezes RG, Thirumalaikolundusubramanian P. β-Blocker in acute cocaine toxicity: is it safe? *J Emerg Med* 2017;53(4):570.
44. Anderson JL, Adams CD, Antman EM, Bridges CR, Califf RM, et al. 2012 ACCF/AHA focused update incorporated into the ACCF/AHA 2007 guidelines for the management of patients with unstable angina/non-ST-elevation myocardial infarction: a report of the American College of Cardiology Foundation/American Heart Association Task Force on Practice Guidelines. *J Am Coll Cardiol* 2013;61(23):e179–347.
45. Sofuoglu M, Brown S, Babb DA, et al. Carvedilol affects the physiological and behavioral response to smoked cocaine in humans. *Drug Alcohol Depend* 2000;60:69–76.
46. Sofuoglu M, Brown S, Babb DA, et al. Effects of labetalol treatment on the physiological and subjective response to smoked cocaine. *Pharmacol Biochem Behav* 2000;65:255–9.

47. Hoskins MH, Leleiko RM, Ramos JJ, et al. Effects of labetalol on hemodynamic parameters and soluble biomarkers of inflammation in acute coronary syndrome in patients with active cocaine use. *J Cardiovasc Pharmacol Ther* 2010;15:47–52.
48. Richards JR; Laurin EG; Tabish N; Lange RA. Acute toxicity from topical cocaine for epistaxis: treatment with labetalol. *J Emerg Med* 2017;52(3):311–3.
49. Malaty J, Malaty IA. Hypertensive urgency: an important aetiology of rebound hypertension. *BMJ Case Rep* 2014.
50. Richards JR, Lange RA. Labetalol and cardiovascular consequences of cocaine use. *Trends Cardiovasc Med* 2016;26(2):202–3.
51. Quintana-Villamandos B, González MC, Delgado-Martos MJ, Condezo-Hoyos L, Böger RH, Lüneburg N, et al. Short-term esmolol attenuates remodeling of the thoracic aorta in hypertensive rats by decreasing concentrations of ADMA down-regulated by oxidative stress. *Eur J Pharmacol* 2016;791:502–9.
52. Arnalich-Montiel A, González MC, Delgado-Baeza E, Delgado-Martos MJ, Condezo-Hoyos L, Martos-Rodríguez A et al. Short-term esmolol improves coronary artery remodeling in spontaneously hypertensive rats through increased nitric oxide bioavailability and superoxide dismutase activity. *Biomed Res Int* 2014;2014:531087.
53. Siddiqui S, Kwan CN, Concepcion J, Malik BA, Moskovits N, Hollander GM. A unique case of acute aortic dissection mimicking myocardial infarction. *Case Rep Images Med* 2017;3:53.
54. Kim HJ, Lee H, Cho B. A case of acute aortic dissection presenting with chest pain relieved by sublingual nitroglycerin. *Korean J Fam Med* 2013;34:429–433.

1.12 CARDIAC EFFECTS

R. Adam Koch and Binh T. Ly

In general, the drugs of abuse are a diverse group of xenobiotics that can have multiple effects on the heart. These xenobiotics generally fall into four major categories with some overlap between them and also some heterogeneity within the groups. The major categories are sympathomimetics, sedative-hypnotics, inhalants, and miscellaneous. Synthetic cannabinoids do not fit perfectly into these categories but will be included in the sympathomimetics. The majority of this chapter will focus on the sympathomimetics.

Sympathomimetics generally act through two mechanisms to affect the cardiovascular system. There are direct effects on cardiac physiology and indirect effects through tachycardia, vasospasm, platelet activation, and accelerated atherosclerosis. Cocaine is a classic example of a xenobiotic with direct and indirect effects. Cocaine causes sodium channel blockade, calcium channel effects, human ether-a-go-go (hERG) channel blockade, coronary artery vasospasm, premature atherosclerosis, platelet aggregation, and increased myocardial oxygen demand due to tachycardia [1].

Sedative-hypnotic agents generally have fewer cardiac effects, though there are a number of opioids with known direct cardiac activity [2–4], and recently, some benzodiazepines have been examined for possible calcium channel effects [5, 6]. Ethanol or drinking alcohol has many acute and chronic effects on cardiac tissue but will not be further discussed in this chapter [7].

The major category of inhalants is a diverse category with a long history of known cardiac effects. The classic "sudden sniffing death syndrome" has been documented for years in the literature [8–11]. The cause of this disorder is not completely clear, but it is thought to be sensitization of the myocardium to catecholamines, leading to dysrhythmias [11].

The last major category is hallucinogens. Most of these act through serotonin pathways and have minimal cardiac effects. Some of the drugs included here would be lysergic acid diethylamide (LSD), psilocybin mushrooms, and salvia. The only one with significant cardiac effects would be phencyclidine, but it has been shown that even those cardiac effects are rarely significant and that it could be considered as part of the sympathomimetic group when considering cardiac effects [12].

1.12.1 General Comments

1.12.1.1 Sympathomimetics

1.12.1.1.1 Cocaine

Cocaine has numerous direct effects on cardiac tissue. Cocaine is in the same family of local anesthetics, and one of its effects is to block neuronal and cardiac sodium channels [13]. This is caused by inhibition of rapid inward sodium current due to binding of cocaine to the inner membrane. The binding preferentially occurs during the inactive conformation of the sodium channel [13]. This leads to prolongation of phase zero of the cardiac action potential. Cocaine's slow dissociation from the sodium channel and other characteristics make it most similar to a Vaugh-Williams type 1c antidysrhythmic [1, 13]. Similarly to other type 1c antiarrhythmics, cocaine has been shown to lead to life-threatening dysrhythmias, likely due to reentrant patterns [1]. Cocaine usage has been associated with a Brugada pattern on electrocardiogram (ECG), and this is also likely due to cocaine's sodium channel effects. This is worrisome, as individuals with Brugada are at an increased risk of sudden death from cardiac arrhythmia [1].

A second direct effect of cocaine is to block the potassium channels on cardiac cells. Blockade of potassium channels leads to QT prolongation on ECGs and has been associated with *torsades de pointes* (TdP), which is a nonperfusing rhythm and can degenerate into ventricular fibrillation, leading to sudden death. This blockade of potassium channels seems to be specifically due to cocaine's effects on the hERG channel, which leads to prolongation of rapid delayed rectifier potassium current(I_{Kr}) [1]. This prolongation of the I_{Kr} is what leads to the prolongation of the QT interval. Cocaethylene is a longer-lived metabolite created when cocaine and ethanol are used concurrently and has similar effects on the hERG channel, leading to even longer potassium effects and increased risk of cardiac dysrhythmias [1].

A third direct effect of cocaine is the binding to L-type calcium channels. This has been demonstrated in animal studies and likely is another mechanism for dysrhythmias that can be induced by cocaine use. Cocaine binds to these channels, facilitating their opening and decreasing their closing rates. These two actions cause increased influx of calcium into the cardiac myocytes, which leads to abnormal cardiac conduction. This abnormal conduction leads to an increased likelihood of dysrhythmia generation [1].

Another effect of cocaine toxicity is rhabdomyolysis, which leads to hyperkalemia. The hyperkalemia can be thought of as either a direct cardiac effect of cocaine or an indirect effect. It is indirect in that the cocaine is not directly causing these effects, but the potassium is causing a direct effect on the cardiac tissue. Hyperkalemia causes multiple effects on cardiac tissue, and this is why hyperkalemic solutions are used to effectuate cardiac arrest for cardiac surgery. The elevated serum potassium concentrations raise the resting membrane potential of the cardiac cells, which leads to inactivation of the fast sodium channel and stimulation of calcium channels, causing influx of calcium into the cardiac cell. The elevated serum potassium also inhibits the sodium-potassium ATPase pump, leading to increased sodium levels in the cardiac cell. These elevated myocyte sodium levels cause the sodium-calcium exchanger to run in reverse, leading to a further increase in calcium influx into the cardiac cell [14, 15]. All of this leads to greater cardiac excitability and increased risk of cardiac dysrhythmias. As the potassium continues to rise, there is increasing myocardiocyte depression, which can ultimately lead to asystole [14].

The indirect effect of sympathetic activation by cocaine also leads to significant cardiac effects. Cocaine blocks the reuptake of catecholamines, including dopamine, norepinephrine, and serotonin, which leads to increased activation of adrenergic nerves due to excess catecholamines present in the nerve terminals [16]. This activation leads to increased heart rate, myocardial contractility, blood pressure, and temperature (hyperthermia). These effects cause increased myocardial demand for oxygen, along with the coronary artery vasospasm causing decreased myocardial oxygen supply, leading to acute myocardial infarctions [17]. Activation of the sympathetic system and catecholamine toxicity has been postulated as the cause of Takotsubo cardiomyopathy or broken heart syndrome noted in some cocaine users [18–20].

Another indirect effect of cocaine use is the activation of the platelets and an alteration of the balance of procoagulant and anticoagulant factors, leading to a prothrombotic state [17]. Cocaine also causes premature atherosclerosis in users [1]. These three effects along with the above-mentioned sympathetic stimulation lead to a significant incidence of acute myocardial infarction with cocaine use [21]. The chronic use of cocaine can cause dilated cardiomyopathy, which is thought to be due to repeated subclinical ischemic events over time [22].

1.12.1.1.2 Amphetamines

This group is very diverse, including numerous existing and emerging chemical analogs, but will be discussed as a group due the fact that their mechanisms of action are similar. Amphetamines all have a phenylethylamine backbone with substitutions at different points along the structure. The substitutions cause significant changes in binding affinities for target receptors and also lead to the variability in signs and symptoms seen with this group of drugs of abuse [23]. Novel psychoactive substances such as benzofurans, tryptamines, NBOMe, 2Cs, and many others are included in this group; technically, some of them are not phenylethylamines, but their mechanisms are similar to those of phenylethylamines.

Amphetamines work by increasing endogenous catecholamines (norepinephrine, dopamine, and serotonin) through a couple of mechanisms. First, amphetamines enter the nerve terminal either via passive diffusion or through a reuptake transporter [24]. These amphetamines then interact with neurotransmitter transporters on the vesicular membrane in the nerve terminal to release neurotransmitters into the synapse [25]. Second, amphetamines also competitively block the reuptake of neurotransmitters in the synapse and act as monoamine oxidase inhibitors, causing the slower clearance of the catecholamines in the synapse [26, 27]. All these actions lead to a significant increase in activation of α-adrenergic, β-adrenergic, serotoninergic, and dopaminergic receptors.

Similarly to cocaine, this increase in sympathetic stimulation leads to hypertension, tachycardia, and cardiac dysrhythmias [24, 28, 29]. There have also been reports of Takotsubo cardiomyopathy and acute myocardial infarction with amphetamine usage [30]. This excessive activation of the sympathetic system can also lead to rhabdomyolysis and hyperthermia in a similar fashion to cocaine usage. This can also lead to hyperkalemia with its associated complications [29, 31].

Recently, there has been some work attempting to explain the QT prolongation noted with some amphetamine usage [32, 33]. It was generally accepted that these types of xenobiotics did not have any direct effect on the myocyte channels. New animal research demonstrates that methamphetamine binds potassium channels and L-type calcium channels, inhibiting flow through these channels [34]. The slowing of current through these channels could account for the noted QT prolongation and increasing risk of cardiac dysrhythmias, including *torsades de pointes* and ventricular fibrillation.

1.12.1.1.3 Cannabinoids

The use of marijuana has long been thought to have minimal acute effects on the heart. The introductions of higher-potency marijuana and synthetic cannabinoids have been challenging this view [35]. There are two main cannabinoid receptors identified at this time, and they have been designated cannabinoid receptor 1 (CB_1R) and cannabinoid receptor 2 (CB_2R), but it is suspected that there are more to be discovered [36, 37]. These are G-protein-coupled receptors that perform functions via inhibiting adenylyl cyclase and modulating ion-channel function and have been found throughout the body [38]. CB_1Rs are found in low levels in cardiac and vascular tissue and in peripheral neurons but are mostly found in the brain. The activation of these receptors in brain tissue and peripheral neurons leads to release of catecholamines, which is likely the cause of the cardiovascular symptoms seen in patients [39].

The research into cannabinoids is the most recent of all the sympathomimetics, but there is increasing use of synthetic cannabinoids, and there have been multiple adverse effects associated with their usage [35, 40, 41]. Current research indicates that the synthetic cannabinoids can have much higher affinities for the cannabinoid receptors, thus leading to more pronounced effects with even smaller doses [42]. Increasing activation of cannabinoid receptors leads to elevated heart rate and blood pressure, agitation, and rhabdomyolysis [43–46]. There has also been documented dysrhythmia, acute myocardial infarction, cardiomyopathy, and sudden death associated with high-potency marijuana and synthetic cannabinoids [47–50].

1.12.1.2 Sedative-Hypnotics

1.12.1.2.1 Opioids

With few exceptions, opioids as a class generally do not directly affect cardiac tissue. Opioids act through the μ-receptor in the brain and spinal cord to cause respiratory and mental status depression as well as analgesia. There has been some noted decrease in blood pressure, heart rate, and cardiac output, but this is thought to be due to increased vagal tone [51]. Most cardiac effects are secondary to the respiratory depression and non-cardiogenic pulmonary edema noted with opioid usage and reversal [52].

A prominent exception to this rule is methadone. Methadone has been noted in multiple studies to prolong the QT interval through its inhibition of the hERG channel. The inhibition of the hERG channel leads to prolongation of potassium current via I_{Kr}, which is seen on the electrocardiogram as an increase in the QT interval [2, 53–59]. This puts the patient at risk for *torsades de pointes* and ventricular fibrillation. Recently, it has been noted that loperamide, a peripheral μ-receptor agonist typically used as an antidiarrheal agent that is now being used by addicts to self-treat opioid dependence, has similar QT prolonging effects in very high doses [4, 60–63]. Propoxyphene, an older opioid, was withdrawn from the market in the United States in 2010 due to its severe QT-prolonging effects and association with *torsades de pointes* [3, 64]. This is caused by the usual mechanism of inhibition of the hERG channel, as with methadone and many other QT-prolonging drugs.

Another more recent discovery is that tramadol has been associated with Brugada electrocardiogram pattern [65]. It is generally felt that drugs that induce or unmask Brugada have sodium channel blocking effects. There is experimental evidence that tramadol does inhibit sodium channels, and this is also consistent with a case series of ECG patterns noted in tramadol overdose [66, 67].

1.12.1.2.2 Benzodiazepines

Benzodiazepines are generally not noted to cause significant cardiac effects or dysrhythmias. There is experimental evidence that midazolam and diazepam interact with L-type calcium channels, modifying the flow of calcium across those channels [5, 68]. This interaction with calcium channels could account for the atrioventricular (AV) nodal block noted with these and other benzodiazepines. This AV block is generally first or second degree, temporary, and of unclear clinical significance [6, 69, 70].

1.12.1.3 Inhalants

Volatile hydrocarbons have been known since the 1950s to have significant cardiac effects. The first reports of "sudden sniffing death" originated in the late 1960s [8]. The specific mechanism that causes this has yet to be fully elucidated, but it is generally thought to be much more likely when there is a surge of catecholamines in the setting of myocardium that has been sensitized to catecholamines during and after inhaling hydrocarbons. There are multiple theories attempting to explain the cardiac sensitization phenomena, and it might be one or all of them contributing to this effect. It has been shown that some hydrocarbons inhibit voltage-gated sodium channels, and this occurs preferentially in the inactivated state [71]. This would lead to prolongation of phase zero of the action potential, similarly to cocaine. Other work has shown that hydrocarbons also inhibit potassium channels through the hERG channel [72]. The hERG channel inhibition leads to QT prolongation. Finally, experiments show that calcium influx into the cells is also inhibited by hydrocarbons. Either individually or together, these effects lead to enhanced automaticity and after-depolarizations that have a high likelihood of triggering both lethal and non-lethal dysrhythmias [72].

1.12.1.4 Stepwise Approach to Management

Of the agents discussed in this chapter, cocaine is the most potent cardiac toxin, and the following recommendations are primarily to address cocaine toxicity. Most of the other drugs of abuse have similar cardiac effects but are generally not as potent as cocaine. Based on this concept, treatment of cocaine toxicity should also correct the toxicity from other drugs of abuse. Areas that require different management will be discussed in the special circumstances section.

1.12.1.5 Immediate Interventions

1. **Airway, breathing, circulation:** Maintain the airway and assist ventilation if necessary. Administer supplemental oxygenation for hypoxia. Begin crystalloid infusion and bolus as needed for hypotension. Otherwise, treat hypotension and resuscitate as per standardized guidelines [73].
2. **Intravenous access, oxygen, monitor:** Acquire peripheral intravenous access, provide supplemental oxygen to patients with hypoxia, and continuously monitor cardiac status.
3. **Antidotes:** Administer appropriate antidotes.
   a. Consider naloxone for opioid effects. May require redosing and higher doses depending on opioid involved [74, 75].
   b. Consider flumazenil to reverse benzodiazepine effects on obtunded patients [75].
   c. Dextrose intravenously (IV) if hypoglycemic [75].
4. **Sedative:** Administer a benzodiazepine if the patient is anxious, delirious, psychotic, hyperthermic, hypertensive, or experiencing chest pain or transient dysrhythmias. Treatment may require administering significantly higher than standard doses for symptom control. In experiments in animals, benzodiazepines attenuate the cardiac and central nervous system toxicity of sympathomimetics [76, 77].
5. **Aspirin:** This helps prevent the formation of thrombi in patients with suspected ischemia. This recommendation is based on theoretical considerations [78–80], the drug's good safety profile, and the extensive investigation of aspirin in patients with ischemic heart disease unrelated to cocaine. The use of aspirin in patients with cocaine-associated myocardial ischemia has been shown to be safe [81–83].
6. **Nitroglycerin:** If the patient is hemodynamically stable, but chest pain persists, administer sublingual or transdermal nitroglycerin. Nitroglycerin

is shown to reverse cocaine-associated coronary artery spasm [84], and there are reports of its ability to ameliorate cocaine-associated chest pain [85]. If chest pain persists, and the patient is hemodynamically stable, a nitroglycerin infusion may be used. Titrate upward to control of pain if blood pressure remains stable [86].

7. **Blood pressure control:** Consider the use of a calcium channel blocker such as verapamil, nicardipine, or a nonspecific alpha and beta antagonist such as labetalol [87, 88] for resistant myocardial ischemia or hypertensive emergency. There is some evidence that the combined alpha and beta antagonist may be more effective, as there is not a risk of reflex tachycardia [87, 89]. These medications can decrease the systemic vascular resistance as well as relieving the coronary artery vasospasm [87–89].
8. **Opioids:** Consider administration of opioids like morphine for chest pain if patient is hemodynamically stable and pain is not resolved with the aforementioned interventions. Opioids may also help to alleviate anxiety [90].
9. **Phentolamine:** Use phentolamine, an alpha-adrenergic antagonist for resistant hypertensive crisis as evidenced by chest pain, encephalopathy, intracranial hemorrhage, and other vascular emergencies. This has been shown to reverse coronary artery vasoconstriction in cocaine use [91] and would be as effective for sympathomimetic overdose [92].
10. **Thrombolytics:** These are only to be utilized if the patient is clearly having an acute ST segment elevation myocardial infarction on ECG and percutaneous coronary intervention is not readily available.
11. **Dysrhythmias:**
    a. **Supraventricular arrhythmias:** These are generally paroxysmal supraventricular tachycardia, rapid atrial fibrillation, or atrial flutter [93]. These dysrhythmias are generally short-lived and resolve without treatment if the patient is hemodynamically stable. When these arrhythmias are persistent, then benzodiazepines are the first line of treatment to decrease the catecholamine effects [94]. If the patient is unstable with these rhythms, then they should be treated per the American Heart Association's American Advanced Cardiac Life Support (ACLS) protocols.
    b. **Ventricular dysrhythmias:** Hemodynamically unstable ventricular tachycardia should be treated with immediate cardioversion or defibrillation along with the administration of lidocaine, calcium channel blockers, and benzodiazepines. Patients should be reshocked after each administration of lidocaine or calcium channel blockers [95]. The sodium channel effects are manifested by a wide complex sinus rhythm and frequently respond to boluses of sodium bicarbonate or hypertonic saline solutions. A bicarbonate drip (made by adding 2 to 3 ampoules of sodium bicarbonate in 1 liter of D5W) may be run simultaneously at 200 ml/h. There is good data to show that a combined alpha and beta blocker works at least as well as a calcium channel blocker and would be another option [87]. If the patient is stable, and ventricular tachycardia does not respond to benzodiazepines, calcium channel blocker or lidocaine may be considered [95].
    c. ***Torsades de pointes*:** This generally occurs in self-terminating bursts but should be treated with magnesium sulfate, which is thought to decrease early after-depolarizations and help prevent continued episodes of TdP [96]. If this is not sufficient, and the patient is not already tachycardic, then isoproterenol is a good option to achieve a target heart rate of 90–110 [96]. If neither of these interventions is effective in preventing the patient from having frequent TdP, then the transvenous overdrive pacing should be considered. The patient is usually paced at 100–110 bpm, but rates up to 140 bpm may be needed. If the patient is unstable or has severe hypotension from the TdP, then they need immediate electrical cardioversion [96].

Comment: Caution should be taken to avoid hypernatremia or hypervolemia and resulting pulmonary edema from overaggressive sodium bicarbonate or hypertonic saline administration [97]. Class 1a and 1c antiarrhythmic agents (i.e., procainamide, disopyramide, quinidine, and propafenone) are contraindicated in the setting of drug-induced conduction abnormalities [98].

1.12.1.6 Secondary Interventions

1. **Repeat ECG:** Repeat ECG if chest pain worsens or recurs.
2. **Chest radiograph and ultrasonography:** To further assess for congestive heart failure or evidence of cardiomyopathy. These modalities may also be used to assess for pneumothorax or pneumomediastinum.
3. **Monitoring:** A period of 9 to 12 hours of cardiac monitoring is recommended for patients with chest pain associated with cocaine use (see section on disposition) [1].
4. **Coronary stress testing:** Because patients with cocaine-associated chest pain have a 1-year survival of 98% and an incidence of late myocardial infarction of only 1%, urgent cardiac evaluation is

probably not necessary for patients in whom acute myocardial infarction has been ruled out [99]. However, keep in mind that patients who rule in for cocaine-induced myocardial infarction, despite an average age of 32 to 38 years, have a 31% to 67% incidence of significant underlying coronary artery disease [100].

5. **Laboratory data:** Baseline laboratory data may include a complete blood count, troponin, creatine kinase, and electrolyte panel. Repeat troponin every 3–4 hours during initial management. Comment: Rhabdomyolysis may complicate cocaine intoxication with increased myoglobin, creatine kinase, and potassium from muscle breakdown. If this occurs, then the creatine kinase and potassium will need to be checked every 2–3 hours [45].
6. **Disposition:**
   a. **Intensive care unit:** All patients with evidence of acute myocardial infarction or hypertensive emergency or any unstable patient [82].
   b. **Telemetry monitored bed:** Hemodynamically stable patients without ongoing chest pain, ECG changes, or elevated troponin may be disposed to a monitored observation unit for a minimum of 12 hours of monitoring and serial troponin levels and ECGs. Patients who have no evidence of ongoing chest pain with normal ECG and cardiac enzymes after 12 hours may be discharged [82].
   c. **Home:** Selected patients who have normal ECG and troponin with no evidence of ongoing ischemia or other complications may be discharged after a period of observation [82].

1.12.1.7 Special Circumstances

1. **Drug-induced long QT syndrome:** There is currently no specific treatment for this syndrome other than discontinuation of the causative agent. Magnesium sulfate has not been shown to prophylactically prevent TdP and runs the risk of hypermagnesemia [96].
2. **Rhabdomyolysis:** There is significant risk of this with any of these drugs due to their sympathomimetic effects, delirium, agitation, and some direct myotoxic effects [33, 43, 94, 101, 102].
   a. IV hydration with crystalloid fluids [103]. Consider cooled IV fluids for patients with concomitant hyperthermia.
   b. Mannitol may be considered to maintain urine output but has not been demonstrated to prevent acute renal failure [104].
   c. Dialysis may be utilized if acute renal failure occurs and if hyperkalemia or other significant electrolyte and acid-base disorders occur [103].
3. **Hyperthermia:** Temperature elevations associated with sympathomimetic toxicity are typically modest and respond well to evaporative cooling measures, cooling blankets, and applying ice packs to the neck, axilla, and groin. When hyperthermia is severe, ice water immersion has been shown to be most effective but is impractical in most hospital settings. Other cooling measures include commercially available non-invasive cooling pads and invasive cooling catheters designed for therapeutic hypothermia in post–cardiac arrest patients but can also be used to treat drug-induced hyperthermia. Neuromuscular blockade along with sedatives may also be employed to stop heat production from ongoing agitation and muscular activity.
4. **Inhalant tachydysrhythmias or "sudden sniffing death":** It has been suggested that a beta receptor antagonist such as esmolol would be helpful to blunt the effect of catecholamines and should be considered [11]. This could possibly prevent the degeneration into ventricular fibrillation or other non-perfusing rhythms.

REFERENCES

1. Phillips K, Luk A, Soor GS, Abraham JR, Leong S, Butany J. Cocaine cardiotoxicity: a review of the pathophysiology, pathology, and treatment options. *Am J Cardiovasc Drugs* 2009;9(3):177–96. Epub 2009/05/26. doi: 10.2165/00129784-200909030-00005. PubMed PMID: 19463023.
2. Alinejad S, Kazemi T, Zamani N, Hoffman RS, Mehrpour O. A systematic review of the cardiotoxicity of methadone. *Excli J* 2015;14:577–600. Epub 2016/02/13. doi:10.17179/excli2015-553. PubMed PMID: 26869865; PubMed Central PMCID: PMCPMC4747000.
3. Raffa RB, Burmeister JJ, Yuvasheva E, Pergolizzi JV, Jr. QTc interval prolongation by d-propoxyphene: what about other analgesics? *Expert Opin Pharmacother* 2012;13(10):1397–409. Epub 2012/05/10. doi: 10.1517/14656566.2012.682150. PubMed PMID: 22568597.
4. Eggleston W, Clark KH, Marraffa JM. Loperamide abuse associated with cardiac dysrhythmia and death. *Ann Emerg Med* 2017;69(1):83–6. Epub 2016/05/04. doi: 10.1016/j.annemergmed.2016.03.047. PubMed PMID: 27140747.
5. Kanaya N, Murray PA, Damron DS. Effects of L-type Ca2+ channel modulation on direct myocardial effects of diazepam and midazolam in adult rat ventricular myocytes. *J Anesth* 2006;20(1):17–25. Epub 2006/01/20. doi: 10.1007/s00540-005-0356-7. PubMed PMID: 16421671.
6. Mullins ME. First-degree atrioventricular block in alprazolam overdose reversed by flumazenil. *J Pharm Pharmacol* 1999;51(3):367–70. Epub 1999/05/27. PubMed PMID: 10344640.
7. Piano MR. Alcohol's effects on the cardiovascular system. *Alcohol Res* 2017;38(2):219–41. Epub 2017/10/11. PubMed PMID: 28988575; PubMed Central PMCID: PMCPMC5513687.
8. Bass M. Sudden sniffing death. *Jama* 1970;212(12):2075–9. Epub 1970/06/22. PubMed PMID: 5467774.
9. King GS, Smialek JE, Troutman WG. Sudden death in adolescents resulting from the inhalation of typewriter correction fluid. *Jama* 1985;253(11):1604–6. Epub 1985/03/15. PubMed PMID: 3974043.

10. Meadows R, Verghese A. Medical complications of glue sniffing. *South Med J* 1996;89(5):455–62. Epub 1996/05/01. PubMed PMID: 8638168.
11. Tormoehlen LM, Tekulve KJ, Nanagas KA. Hydrocarbon toxicity: a review. *Clin Toxicol (Phila)* 2014;52(5):479–89. Epub 2014/06/10. doi: 10.3109/15563650.2014.923904. PubMed PMID: 24911841.
12. Dominici P, Kopec K, Manur R, Khalid A, Damiron K, Rowden A. Phencyclidine intoxication case series study. *J Med Toxicol* 2015;11(3):321–5. Epub 2014/12/17. doi: 10.1007/s13181-014-0453-9. PubMed PMID: 25502414; PubMed Central PMCID: PMCPMC4547967.
13. Bauman JL, Grawe JJ, Winecoff AP, Hariman RJ. Cocaine-related sudden cardiac death: a hypothesis correlating basic science and clinical observations. *J Clin Pharmacol* 1994;34(9):902–11. Epub 1994/09/01. PubMed PMID: 7983233.
14. Parham WA, Mehdirad AA, Biermann KM, Fredman CS. Hyperkalemia revisited. *Tex Heart Inst J* 2006;33(1):40–7. Epub 2006/04/01. PubMed PMID: 16572868; PubMed Central PMCID: PMCPMC1413606.
15. Rossignol P, Legrand M, Kosiborod M, Hollenberg SM, Peacock WF, Emmett M, et al. Emergency management of severe hyperkalemia: guideline for best practice and opportunities for the future. *Pharmacol Res* 2016;113(Pt A):585–91. Epub 2016/10/21. doi: 10.1016/j.phrs.2016.09.039. Pub Med PMID: 27693804.
16. Fischbach P. The role of illicit drug use in sudden death in the young. *Cardiol Young* 2017;27(S1):S75–s9. Epub 2017/01/14. doi: 10.1017/s1047951116002274. PubMed PMID: 28084963.
17. Frishman WH, Del Vecchio A, Sanal S, Ismail A. Cardiovascular manifestations of substance abuse part 1: cocaine. *Heart Dis* 2003;5(3):187–201. Epub 2003/06/05. doi: 10.1097/01.hdx.0000074519.43281.fa. PubMed PMID: 12783633.
18. Butterfield M, Riguzzi C, Frenkel O, Nagdev A. Stimulant-related Takotsubo cardiomyopathy. *Am J Emerg Med* 2015;33(3):476.e1–3. Epub 2014/10/14. doi: 10.1016/j.ajem.2014.08.058. PubMed PMID: 25308824.
19. Gill D, Sheikh N, Ruiz VG, Liu K. Case report: cocaine-induced takotsubo cardiomyopathy. *Hellenic J Cardiol* 2017. Epub 2017/06/11. doi: 10.1016/j.hjc.2017.05.008. PubMed PMID: 28600168.
20. Sarkar S, Arguelles E, de Elia C. Takosubo cardiomyopathy presenting as a non-ST segment elevation myocardial infarction in the setting of cocaine use and asthma exacerbation. *Int J Cardiol* 2013;168(1):e1–2. Epub 2013/05/21. doi: 10.1016/j.ijcard.2013.04.191. PubMed PMID: 23684595.
21. Qureshi AI, Suri MF, Guterman LR, Hopkins LN. Cocaine use and the likelihood of nonfatal myocardial infarction and stroke: data from the Third National Health and Nutrition Examination Survey. *Circulation* 2001;103(4):502–6. Epub 2001/02/07. PubMed PMID: 11157713.
22. Lange RA, Hillis LD. Cardiovascular complications of cocaine use. *N Engl J Med* 2001;345(5):351–8. Epub 2001/08/04. doi: 10.1056/nejm200108023450507. PubMed PMID: 11484693.
23. Kleven MS, Seiden LS. Methamphetamine-induced neurotoxicity: structure activity relationships. *Ann N Y Acad Sci* 1992;654:292–301. Epub 1992/06/28. PubMed PMID: 1632588.
24. Seiden LS, Kleven MS. Methamphetamine and related drugs: toxicity and resulting behavioral changes in response to pharmacological probes. *NIDA Res Monogr* 1989;94:146–60. Epub 1989/01/01. PubMed PMID: 2514362.
25. Sulzer D, Chen TK, Lau YY, Kristensen H, Rayport S, Ewing A. Amphetamine redistributes dopamine from synaptic vesicles to the cytosol and promotes reverse transport. *J Neurosci* 1995;15(5 Pt 2):4102–8. Epub 1995/05/01. PubMed PMID: 7751968.
26. Pitts DK, Marwah J. Cocaine and central monoaminergic neurotransmission: a review of electrophysiological studies and comparison to amphetamine and antidepressants. *Life Sci* 1988;42(9):949–68. Epub 1988/01/01. PubMed PMID: 2893968.
27. Groves P, Ryan L, Diana M, Gariano R. Neurophysiological consequences of amphetamine administration. *NIDA Res Monogr* 1988;90:213–22. Epub 1988/01/01. PubMed PMID: 2855854.
28. Bazmi E, Mousavi F, Giahchin L, Mokhtari T, Behnoush B. Cardiovascular complications of acute amphetamine abuse: cross-sectional study. *Sultan Qaboos Univ Med J* 2017;17(1):e31–e7. Epub 2017/04/19. doi: 10.18295/squmj.2016.17.01.007. PubMed PMID: 28417026; PubMed Central PMCID: PMCPMC5380419.
29. Schep LJ, Slaughter RJ, Beasley DM. The clinical toxicology of metamfetamine. *Clin Toxicol (Phila)* 2010;48(7):675–94. Epub 2010/09/21. doi: 10.3109/15563650.2010.516752. PubMed PMID: 20849327.
30. Ghuran A, Nolan J. Recreational drug misuse: issues for the cardiologist. *Heart* 2000;83(6):627–33. Epub 2000/05/18. PubMed PMID: 10814617; PubMed Central PMCID: PMCPMC1760847.
31. Quinton MS, Yamamoto BK. Causes and consequences of methamphetamine and MDMA toxicity. *Aaps J* 2006;8(2):E337–47. Epub 2006/06/27. doi: 10.1208/aapsj080238. PubMed PMID: 16796384; PubMed Central PMCID: PMCPMC3231568.
32. Liang CS, Huang YC. Methamphetamine-associated QTc prolongation in a dose-dependent and reversible manner. *J Neuropsychiatry Clin Neurosci U.S.* 2013;25:E58.
33. Hall AP, Henry JA. Acute toxic effects of 'Ecstasy' (MDMA) and related compounds: overview of pathophysiology and clinical management. *Br J Anaesth* 2006;96(6):678–85. Epub 2006/04/06. doi: 10.1093/bja/ael078. PubMed PMID: 16595612.
34. Liang R, Zhou Y, Wu F, Zhou C, Zhao X, Zhang M, et al. Effect of methamphetamine on potassium and L-type calcium currents in rat ventricular myocytes. *Toxicol Mech Methods* 2010;20(8):458–65. Epub 2010/07/09. doi: 10.3109/15376516.2010.497979. PubMed PMID: 20608758.
35. Monte AA, Calello DP, Gerona RR, Hamad E, Campleman SL, Brent J, et al. Characteristics and treatment of patients with clinical illness due to synthetic cannabinoid inhalation reported by medical toxicologists: a ToxIC database study. *J Med Toxicol* 2017;13(2):146–52. Epub 2017/04/12. doi: 10.1007/s13181-017-0605-9. PubMed PMID: 28397128; PubMed Central PMCID: PMCPMC5440319.
36. Pacher P, Batkai S, Kunos G. The endocannabinoid system as an emerging target of pharmacotherapy. *Pharmacol Rev* 2006;58(3):389–462. Epub 2006/09/14. doi: 10.1124/pr.58.3.2. PubMed PMID: 16968947; PubMed Central PMCID: PMCPMC2241751.
37. Pertwee RG, Howlett AC, Abood ME, Alexander SP, Di Marzo V, Elphick MR, et al. International union of basic and clinical pharmacology. LXXIX. Cannabinoid receptors and their ligands: beyond CB(1) and CB(2). *Pharmacol Rev* 2010;62(4):588–631. Epub 2010/11/17. doi: 10.1124/pr.110.003004. PubMed PMID: 21079038; PubMed Central PMCID: PMCPMC2993256.

38. Soethoudt M, Grether U, Fingerle J, Grim TW, Fezza F, de Petrocellis L, et al. Cannabinoid CB2 receptor ligand profiling reveals biased signalling and off-target activity. *Nat Commun* 2017;8:13958. Epub 2017/01/04. doi: 10.1038/ncomms13958. PubMed PMID: 28045021; PubMed Central PMCID: PMCPMC5216056 Hoffmann-La Roche and P.P. is full time employee of NIH. All academic authors state that they have no conflict of interest.
39. Niederhoffer N, Schmid K, Szabo B. The peripheral sympathetic nervous system is the major target of cannabinoids in eliciting cardiovascular depression. *Naunyn Schmiedebergs Arch Pharmacol* 2003;367(5):434–43. Epub 2003/04/24. doi: 10.1007/s00210-003-0755-y. PubMed PMID: 12709782.
40. Law R, Schier J, Martin C, Chang A, Wolkin A. Notes from the field: increase in reported adverse health effects related to synthetic cannabinoid use - United States, January–May 2015. *MMWR Morb Mortal Wkly Rep* 2015;64(22):618–9. Epub 2015/06/13. PubMed PMID: 26068566.
41. Adams AJ, Banister SD, Irizarry L, Trecki J, Schwartz M, Gerona R. "Zombie" outbreak caused by the synthetic cannabinoid AMB-FUBINACA in New York. *N Engl J Med* 2017;376(3):235–42. Epub 2016/12/16. doi: 10.1056/NEJMoa1610300. PubMed PMID: 27973993.
42. Pacher P, Steffens S, Hasko G, Schindler TH, Kunos G. Cardiovascular effects of marijuana and synthetic cannabinoids: the good, the bad, and the ugly. *Nat Rev Cardiol* 2017. Epub 2017/09/15. doi: 10.1038/nrcardio.2017.130. PubMed PMID: 28905873.
43. Adedinsewo DA, Odewole O, Todd T. Acute rhabdomyolysis following synthetic cannabinoid ingestion. *N Am J Med Sci* 2016;8(6):256–8. Epub 2016/08/09. doi: 10.4103/1947-2714.185038. PubMed PMID: 27500131; PubMed Central PMCID: PMCPMC4960936.
44. Katz KD, Leonetti AL, Bailey BC, Surmaitis RM, Eustice ER, Kacinko S, et al. Case series of synthetic cannabinoid intoxication from one toxicology center. *West J Emerg Med* 2016;17(3):290–4. Epub 2016/06/23. doi: 10.5811/westjem.2016.2.29519. PubMed PMID: 27330661; PubMed Central PMCID: PMCPMC4899060.
45. Sweeney B, Talebi S, Toro D, Gonzalez K, Menoscal JP, Shaw R, et al. Hyperthermia and severe rhabdomyolysis from synthetic cannabinoids. *Am J Emerg Med* 2016;34(1):121.e1–2. Epub 2015/07/06. doi: 10.1016/j.ajem.2015.05.052. PubMed PMID: 26143311.
46. Obafemi AI, Kleinschmidt K, Goto C, Fout D. Cluster of acute toxicity from ingestion of synthetic cannabinoid-laced brownies. *J Med Toxicol* 2015;11(4):426–9. Epub 2015/05/15. doi: 10.1007/s13181-015-0482-z. PubMed PMID: 25967137; PubMed Central PMCID: PMCPMC4675604.
47. Ting JY. Reversible cardiomyopathy associated with acute inhaled marijuana use in a young adult. *Clin Toxicol (Phila)* 2007;45:432–4.
48. Sanchez Lazaro IJ, Almenar Bonet L, Sancho-Tello MJ, Martinez-Dolz L. Ventricular tachycardia due to marijuana use in a heart transplant patient. *Rev Esp Cardiol* 2009;62:459–61.
49. Hartung B, Kauferstein S, Ritz-Timme S, Daldrup T. Sudden unexpected death under acute influence of cannabis. *Forensic Sci Int* 2014;237:e11–3. Epub 2014/03/07. doi: 10.1016/j.forsciint.2014.02.001. PubMed PMID: 24598271.
50. Mir A, Obafemi A, Young A, Kane C. Myocardial infarction associated with use of the synthetic cannabinoid K2. *Pediatrics* 2011;128(6):e1622-7. Epub 2011/11/09. doi: 10.1542/peds.2010-3823. PubMed PMID: 22065271.
51. Brashear RE, Cornog JL, Forney RB. Cardiovascular effects of heroin in the dog. *Anesth Analg* 1973;52(3):323–7. Epub 1973/05/01. PubMed PMID: 4513357.
52. Sporer KA, Dorn E. Heroin-related noncardiogenic pulmonary edema : a case series. *Chest* 2001;120(5):1628–32. Epub 2001/11/20. PubMed PMID: 11713145.
53. Krantz MJ, Lowery CM, Martell BA, Gourevitch MN, Arnsten JH. Effects of methadone on QT-interval dispersion. *Pharmacotherapy* 2005;25(11):1523–9. Epub 2005/10/20. doi: 10.1592/phco.2005.25.11.1523. PubMed PMID: 16232014.
54. Stringer J, Welsh C, Tommasello A. Methadone-associated Q-T interval prolongation and torsades de pointes. *Am J Health Syst Pharm* 2009;66(9):825–33. Epub 2009/04/24. doi: 10.2146/ajhp070392. PubMed PMID: 19386945.
55. Nordt SP, Zilberstein J, Gold B. Methadone-induced torsade de pointes. *Am J Emerg Med* 2011;29(4):476.e1–2. Epub 2010/08/03. doi: 10.1016/j.ajem.2010.04.023. PubMed PMID: 20674223.
56. Thanavaro KL, Thanavaro JL. Methadone-induced torsades de pointes: a twist of fate. *Heart Lung* 2011;40(5):448–53. Epub 2011/03/18. doi: 10.1016/j.hrtlng.2010.12.008. PubMed PMID: 21411146.
57. McNamara JK, Shinkazh N, Rim F, Sunga R, Cristian A. Methadone-associated prolongation of the QTc interval at doses used for chronic pain. 2011;36(2):78–107. Epub 2011/02/01. PubMed PMID: 25873775; PubMed Central PMCID: PMCPMC4386710.
58. Khalesi S, Shemirani H, Dehghani-Tafti F. Methadone induced torsades de pointes and ventricular fibrillation: a case review. *ARYA Atheroscler* 2014;10(6):339–42. Epub 2015/03/31. PubMed PMID: 25815024; PubMed Central PMCID: PMCPMC4354087.
59. Lusetti M, Licata M, Silingardi E, Reggiani Bonetti L, Palmiere C. Therapeutic and recreational methadone cardiotoxicity. *J Forensic Leg Med* 2016;39:80–4. Epub 2016/02/10. doi: 10.1016/j.jflm.2016.01.016. PubMed PMID: 26859696.
60. Upadhyay A, Bodar V, Malekzadegan M, Singh S, Frumkin W, Mangla A, et al. Loperamide induced life threatening ventricular arrhythmia. *Case Rep Cardiol* 2016;2016:5040176. Epub 2016/08/23. doi: 10.1155/2016/5040176. PubMed PMID: 27547470; PubMed Central PMCID: PMCPMC4980497.
61. Rasla S, St Amand A, Garas MK, El Meligy A, Minami T. Unexpected serious cardiac arrhythmias in the setting of loperamide abuse. *R I Med J* 2017;100(4):33–6. Epub 2017/04/05. PubMed PMID: 28375418.
62. Bhatti Z, Norsworthy J, Szombathy T. Loperamide metabolite-induced cardiomyopathy and QTc prolongation. *Clin Toxicol (Phila)* 2017;55(7):659–61. Epub 2017/03/30. doi: 10.1080/15563650.2017.1304555. PubMed PMID: 28349724.
63. Swank KA, Wu E, Kortepeter C, McAninch J, Levin RL. Adverse event detection using the FDA post-marketing drug safety surveillance system: cardiotoxicity associated with loperamide abuse and misuse. *J Am Pharm Assoc* 2017;57(2s):S63–s7. Epub 2017/01/12. doi: 10.1016/j.japh.2016.11.011. PubMed PMID: 28073687.
64. Adler A, Viskin S, Bhuiyan ZA, Eisenberg E, Rosso R. Propoxyphene-induced torsades de pointes. *Heart Rhythm* 2011;8(12):1952–4. Epub 2011/07/19. doi: 10.1016/j.hrthm.2011.07.015. PubMed PMID: 21763256.

65. Cole JB, Sattiraju S, Bilden EF, Asinger RW, Bertog SC. Isolated tramadol overdose associated with Brugada ECG pattern. *Pacing Clin Electrophysiol* 2012;35(8):e219–21. Epub 2010/11/03. doi: 10.1111/j.1540-8159.2010.02924.x. PubMed PMID: 21039643.
66. Hafezi Moghadam P, Zarei N, Farsi D, Abbasi S, Mofidi M, Rezai M, et al. Electrocardiographic changes in patients with tramadol-induced idiosyncratic seizures. *Turk J Emerg Med* 2016;16(4):151–4. Epub 2016/12/21. doi: 10.1016/j.tjem.2016.08.005. PubMed PMID: 27995207; PubMed Central PMCID: PMCPMC5154583.
67. Haeseler G, Foadi N, Ahrens J, Dengler R, Hecker H, Leuwer M. Tramadol, fentanyl and sufentanil but not morphine block voltage-operated sodium channels. *Pain* 2006;126(1–3):234–44. Epub 2006/09/05. doi: 10.1016/j.pain.2006.07.003. PubMed PMID: 16949748.
68. Nonaka A, Kashimoto S, Imamura M, Furuya A, Kumazawa T. Mechanism of the negative inotropic effect of midazolam and diazepam in cultured foetal mouse cardiac myocytes. *Eur J Anaesthesiol* 1997;14(5):481–7. Epub 1997/09/26. PubMed PMID: 9303284.
69. Arroyo Plasencia AM, Ballentine LM, Mowry JB, Kao LW. Benzodiazepine-associated atrioventricular block. *Am J Ther* 2012;19(1):e48–52. Epub 2010/06/11. doi: 10.1097/MJT.0b013e3181dcf572. PubMed PMID: 20535011.
70. Anand K, Kumar M. Benzodiazepine overdose associated atrioventricular block. *Anesth Essays Res* 2013;7(3):419–20. Epub 2013/09/01. doi: 10.4103/0259-1162.123280. PubMed PMID: 25885999; PubMed Central PMCID: PMCPMC4173567.
71. Stadnicka A, Kwok WM, Hartmann HA, Bosnjak ZJ. Effects of halothane and isoflurane on fast and slow inactivation of human heart hH1a sodium channels. *Anesthesiology* 1999;90(6):1671–83. Epub 1999/06/09. PubMed PMID: 10360866.
72. Zhou Y, Wu HJ, Zhang YH, Sun HY, Wong TM, Li GR. Ionic mechanisms underlying cardiac toxicity of the organochloride solvent trichloromethane. *Toxicology* 2011;290(2–3):295–304. Epub 2011/10/26. doi: 10.1016/j.tox.2011.10.009. PubMed PMID: 22024336.
73. Soar J, Callaway CW, Aibiki M, Bottiger BW, Brooks SC, Deakin CD, et al. Part 4: advanced life support: 2015 international consensus on cardiopulmonary resuscitation and emergency cardiovascular care science with treatment recommendations. *Resuscitation* 2015;95:e71–120. Epub 2015/10/20. doi: 10.1016/j.resuscitation.2015.07.042. PubMed PMID: 26477429.
74. Parthvi R, Agrawal A, Khanijo S, Tsegaye A, Talwar A. Acute opiate overdose: an update on management strategies in emergency department and critical care unit. *Am J Ther* 2017. Epub 2017/09/28. doi: 10.1097/mjt.0000000000000681. PubMed PMID: 28952972.
75. Sivilotti ML. Flumazenil, naloxone and the 'coma cocktail'. *Br J Clin Pharmacol* 2016;81(3):428–36. Epub 2015/10/16. doi: 10.1111/bcp.12731. PubMed PMID: 26469689; PubMed Central PMCID: PMCPMC4767210.
76. Guinn MM, Bedford JA, Wilson MC. Antagonism of intravenous cocaine lethality in nonhuman primates. *Clin Toxicol* 1980;16(4):499–508. Epub 1980/06/01. doi: 10.3109/15563658008989979. PubMed PMID: 7408425.
77. Derlet RW, Albertson TE, Rice P. Antagonism of cocaine, amphetamine, and methamphetamine toxicity. *Pharmacol Biochem Behav* 1990;36(4):745–9. Epub 1990/08/01. PubMed PMID: 2217500.
78. Heesch C, Wilhelm C, Ristich J, Adnane J, Bontempo F, Wagner W. Cocaine activates platelets and increases the formation of circulating platelet containing microaggregates in humans. *Heart* 2000;83(6):688–95. doi: 10.1136/heart.83.6.688. PubMed PMID: 10814631; PubMed Central PMCID: PMC1760877.
79. Schnetzer GW, 3rd. Platelets and thrombogenesis--current concepts. *Am Heart J* 1972;83(4):552–64. Epub 1972/04/01. PubMed PMID: 4339454.
80. Togna G, Tempesta E, Togna AR, Dolci N, Cebo B, Caprino L. Platelet responsiveness and biosynthesis of thromboxane and prostacyclin in response to in vitro cocaine treatment. *Haemostasis* 1985;15(2):100–7. Epub 1985/01/01. PubMed PMID: 3924789.
81. Hollander JE. Cocaine intoxication and hypertension. *Ann Emerg Med* 2008;51(Supplement):S18–20.
82. McCord J, Jneid H, Hollander JE, de Lemos JA, Cercek B, Hsue P, et al. Management of cocaine-associated chest pain and myocardial infarction: a scientific statement from the American Heart Association Acute Cardiac Care Committee of the Council on Clinical Cardiology. *Circulation* 2008;117(14):1897–907. Epub 2008/03/19. doi: 10.1161/circulationaha.107.188950. PubMed PMID: 18347214.
83. Weber JE, Shofer FS, Larkin GL, Kalaria AS, Hollander JE. Validation of a brief observation period for patients with cocaine-associated chest pain. *N Engl J Med* 2003;348(6):510–7. Epub 2003/02/07. doi: 10.1056/NEJMoa022206. PubMed PMID: 12571258.
84. Brogan WC, 3rd, Lange RA, Kim AS, Moliterno DJ, Hillis LD. Alleviation of cocaine-induced coronary vasoconstriction by nitroglycerin. *J Am Coll Cardiol* 1991;18(2):581–6. Epub 1991/08/01. PubMed PMID: 1906905.
85. Honderick T, Williams D, Seaberg D, Wears R. A prospective, randomized, controlled trial of benzodiazepines and nitroglycerine or nitroglycerine alone in the treatment of cocaine-associated acute coronary syndromes. *Am J Emerg Med* 2003;21(1):39–42. Epub 2003/02/04. doi: 10.1053/ajem.2003.50010. PubMed PMID: 12563578.
86. Finkel JB, Marhefka GD. Rethinking cocaine-associated chest pain and acute coronary syndromes. *Mayo Clin Proc* 2011;86(12):1198–207. Epub 2011/12/03. doi: 10.4065/mcp.2011.0338. PubMed PMID: 22134939; PubMed Central PMCID: PMCPMC3228621.
87. Hoskins MH, Leleiko RM, Ramos JJ, Sola S, Caneer PM, Khan BV. Effects of labetalol on hemodynamic parameters and soluble biomarkers of inflammation in acute coronary syndrome in patients with active cocaine use. *J Cardiovasc Pharmacol Ther* 2010;15(1):47–52. Epub 2010/02/06. doi: 10.1177/1074248409358409. PubMed PMID: 20133495.
88. Gay GR, Loper KA. The use of labetalol in the management of cocaine crisis. *Ann Emerg Med* 1988;17(3):282–3. Epub 1988/03/01. PubMed PMID: 3345023.
89. Negus BH, Willard JE, Hillis LD, Glamann DB, Landau C, Snyder RW, et al. Alleviation of cocaine-induced coronary vasoconstriction with intravenous verapamil. *Am J Cardiol* 1994;73(7):510–3. Epub 1994/03/01. PubMed PMID: 8141094.
90. Saland KE, Hillis LD, Lange RA, Cigarroa JE. Influence of morphine sulfate on cocaine-induced coronary vasoconstriction. *Am J Cardiol* 2002;90(7):810–1. Epub 2002/10/03. PubMed PMID: 12356410.
91. Lange RA, Cigarroa RG, Yancy CW, Jr, Willard JE, Popma JJ, Sills MN, et al. Cocaine-induced coronary-artery vasoconstriction. *N Engl J Med* 1989;321(23):1557–62. Epub 1989/12/07. doi: 10.1056/nejm198912073212301. PubMed PMID: 2573838.

92. Hollander JE, Carter WA, Hoffman RS. Use of phentolamine for cocaine-induced myocardial ischemia. *N Engl J Med* 1992;327(5):361. Epub 1992/07/30. doi: 10.1056/nejm199207303270517. PubMed PMID: 1620184.
93. Chakko S, Sepulveda S, Kessler KM, Sotomayor MC, Mash DC, Prineas RJ, et al. Frequency and type of electrocardiographic abnormalities in cocaine abusers (electrocardiogram in cocaine abuse). *Am J Cardiol* 1994;74(7):710–3. Epub 1994/10/01. PubMed PMID: 7942531.
94. Richards JR, Garber D, Laurin EG, Albertson TE, Derlet RW, Amsterdam EA, et al. Treatment of cocaine cardiovascular toxicity: a systematic review. *Clin Toxicol (Phila)* 2016;54(5):345–64. Epub 2016/02/27. doi: 10.3109/15563650.2016.1142090. PubMed PMID: 26919414.
95. Hollander JE, Henry TD. Evaluation and management of the patient who has cocaine-associated chest pain. *Cardiol Clin* 2006;24(1):103–14. Epub 2005/12/06. doi: 10.1016/j.ccl.2005.09.003. PubMed PMID: 16326260.
96. Thomas SH, Behr ER. Pharmacological treatment of acquired QT prolongation and torsades de pointes. *Br J Clin Pharmacol* 2016;81(3):420–7. Epub 2015/07/18. doi: 10.1111/bcp.12726. PubMed PMID: 26183037; PubMed Central PMCID: PMCPMC4767204.
97. Beckman KJ, Parker RB, Hariman RJ, Gallastegui JL, Javaid JI, Bauman JL. Hemodynamic and electrophysiological actions of cocaine. Effects of sodium bicarbonate as an antidote in dogs. *Circulation* 1991;83(5):1799–807. Epub 1991/05/01. PubMed PMID: 1850669.
98. Kuczkowski KM. More on the idiosyncratic effects of cocaine on the human heart. *Emerg Med J* 2007;24:147.
99. Hollander JE, Hoffman RS, Gennis P, Fairweather P, Feldman JA, Fish SS, et al. Cocaine-associated chest pain: one-year follow-up. *Acad Emerg Med* 1995;2(3):179–84. Epub 1995/03/01. PubMed PMID: 7497030.
100. Kontos MC, Jesse RL, Tatum JL, Ornato JP. Coronary angiographic findings in patients with cocaine-associated chest pain. *J Emerg Med* 2003;24(1):9–13. Epub 2003/01/30. PubMed PMID: 12554033.
101. Camara-Lemarroy CR, Rodriguez-Gutierrez R, Monreal-Robles R, Gonzalez-Gonzalez JG. Acute toluene intoxication--clinical presentation, management and prognosis: a prospective observational study. *BMC Emerg Med* 2015;15:19. Epub 2015/08/19. doi: 10.1186/s12873-015-0039-0. PubMed PMID: 26282250; PubMed Central PMCID: PMCPMC4539858.
102. Kumar S, Joginpally T, Kim D, Yadava M, Norgais K, Laird-Fick HS. Cardiomyopathy from 1,1-Difluoroethane Inhalation. *Cardiovasc Toxicol* 2016;16(4):370–3. Epub 2015/11/29. doi: 10.1007/s12012-015-9348-5. PubMed PMID: 26613951.
103. Khan FY. Rhabdomyolysis: a review of the literature. *Neth J Med* 2009;67(9):272–83. Epub 2009/10/21. PubMed PMID: 19841484.
104. Torres PA, Helmstetter JA, Kaye AM, Kaye AD. Rhabdomyolysis: pathogenesis, diagnosis, and treatment. *Ochsner J* 2015;15(1):58–69. Epub 2015/04/02. PubMed PMID: 25829882; PubMed Central PMCID: PMCPMC4365849.

The views expressed in this article are those of the author(s) and do not necessarily reflect the official policy or position of the Department of the Navy, Department of Defense, or the United States Government.

I am a military service member (or employee of the U.S. Government). This work was prepared as part of my official duties. Title 17, USC, §105 provides that 'Copyright protection under this title is not available for any work of the U.S. Government.' Title 17, USC, §101 defines a U.S. Government work as a work prepared by a military service member or employee of the U.S. Government as part of that person's official duties.

1.13 EXCITED DELIRIUM SYNDROME

Christopher J. Coyne, Gary M. Vilke and Binh T. Ly

1.13.1 Introduction

Excited delirium syndrome (ExDS) is frequently defined as an alteration in mental status accompanied by severe agitation, hyperactivity, paranoia, and often combativeness. In the absence of appropriate treatment, these cases will typically progress to a sudden cessation of agitation, loss of consciousness, cardiovascular collapse, and death [1]. Although the medical literature has described this clinical entity since the 19th century, there still remains some controversy over the circumstances that surround many of these cases, especially those that end in death. The primary source of this controversy stems from the fact that many cases of ExDS, and the associated deaths, take place while these persons are in the custody of law enforcement. In fact, some have referred to the disease as a "sudden death in custody syndrome" [2, 3]. To add to this controversy, there is still no unifying medical definition of the syndrome, given significant variation in presenting signs, symptoms, and autopsy findings. Some of the presenting characteristics may include elevated temperature, rapid breathing, delusional thoughts, profuse sweating, excessive strength, inappropriate clothing for the environment (naked), glass/mirror attraction, and keening (making animal-like sounds) [4]. None of these findings are pathognomonic, however, and they may or not be present in all patients.

Due to the variation of initial presenting characteristics, many of the initial reports and publications came from the forensic literature. Since this time, the fields of emergency medicine, toxicology, and psychiatry have all published on this disease, and clinical policies have been put forth, supporting the existence of this complicated syndrome [5, 6]. Despite these publications, however, the diagnosis of ExDS remains elusive, in part because the constellation of symptoms overlaps with several other medical conditions, including sepsis, stimulant drug intoxication, trauma, psychiatric disease, hyperthyroidism, and seizure disorders [7]. One must first evaluate and control for these conditions before applying the definition of ExDS.

1.13.2 Historical Context

The medical condition we now know as excited delirium syndrome was first described by Dr Luther Bell in his paper "On a Form of Disease Resembling Some Advanced Stage of Mania and Fever," published in the *American Journal of Insanity* in 1849 [8]. Bell described the disease as an exhaustive mania characterized by severe, refractory agitation that was not amenable to available treatments. Many patients would go days to weeks without sleep before succumbing to cardiovascular collapse and death. Many were noted to be hyperthermic. Out of the 1,700 patients Dr Bell treated as chief psychiatrist at McLean Asylum for the insane, he reported 40 patients who displayed the confusion and agitation that was eventually defined as Bell's Mania. Overall, he documented a mortality rate of approximately 70% for those patients who displayed symptoms of the disease. Fortunately, by the mid-1950s, there was a drastic decline in reports of Bell's Mania. This was likely due to the rise of modern antipsychotics for the treatment of patients with severe agitation. For decades, there were virtually no cases of ExDS reported in the medical literature, until a sudden resurgence of the disease was seen in the 1980s.

Although some of the new cases of ExDS were attributed to untreated, severe psychiatric disease, more often, the new cases were associated with stimulant drug intoxication. Specifically, there appeared to be a direct correlation between rising cases of ExDS and the surge of cocaine use in North America [9, 10]. Several of these initial cases of stimulant-induced ExDS were likely mislabeled as simple cocaine toxicity, while we now know that cocaine-induced ExDS has an associated mortality rate significantly higher than cocaine toxicity alone [11]. Grant et al. researched this epidemic of new cases by investigating medical examiner data in Maryland from 1930 to 2004. Through this study, he identified 202 cases of ExDS, with a significant spike in the mid-1980s, carrying forward into the 2000s. Over 80% of these cases involved middle-aged men who were positive for cocaine on post-mortem toxicology screens [12, 13]. Nearly all these cases involved several characteristics of ExDS, including superhuman strength, imperviousness to pain, hyperthermia, and profuse sweating. Given that many who succumb to ExDS die prior to hospital arrival, it is no surprise that the medical examiner community was the first to accurately identify these deaths as uniquely different from simple stimulant intoxication [14].

1.13.3 Pathophysiology

The exact pathophysiology of ExDS remains debated to this day, but much has been done to describe several potential mechanisms that contribute to stimulant-induced ExDS. Although several illicit drugs can contribute to the development of ExDS, including methamphetamines, phencyclidine (PCP), and hallucinogens, cocaine remains the predominant precipitant of ExDS for several potential reasons related to the effects of the drug on the human body. Cocaine is known to cause aberrations in dopamine processing in the mesolimbic pathway and other critical areas of the brain, resulting in the commonly described hyperactivity and hyperthermia of ExDS [7]. Specifically, cocaine blocks the presynaptic reuptake of adrenergic amines, increasing their availability. This produces the euphoric and addictive effects of the drug through serotonin and dopaminergic effects, respectively. We also see peripheral effects of cocaine though its action on α_1, α_2, β_1, and β_2 adrenergic receptors, resulting in tachycardia, hypertension, and sweating [11]. These mechanisms and the resulting symptoms encapsulate several overlapping symptoms of both simple cocaine intoxication and excited delirium. Although there is no clear physiologic demarcation as one begins to experience ExDS, there are subtle differences in dopamine processing on post-mortem analysis between cases and controls that may shed light on the different pathophysiologic processes at work.

Much of our understanding of the biochemical basis of ExDS comes from the work of Mash et al. In 2003, Mash published her findings, noting that there was an up-regulation of α-synuclein in the midbrain dopamine neurons of chronic cocaine users. Increased binding of this protein to dopamine presynaptic terminals has been shown to increase dopamine reuptake and induce dopamine-related apoptosis. Over time and with chronic use, this leads to irreversible neuroadaptive changes that allow the brains of chronic users to tolerate the dopaminergic and oxidative effects of cocaine abuse. In a comparison of chronic cocaine abusers with controls, researchers found significantly elevated levels of α-synuclein in the ventral tegmental and substantia nigra areas of the midbrain. This is in contrast to those cocaine users who died of ExDS, who had notably decreased levels of α-synuclein in the substantia nigra relative to controls. This suggests that those persons who suffer from ExDS potentially lack the protective up-regulation of α-synuclein and are unable to process the excessive levels of dopamine release and reuptake inhibition [15].

A second maladaptive factor found in ExDS patients involves the D_3 subtype dopamine receptor. In the normal human brain, this receptor is found in the nucleus accumbens and limbic sectors of the caudate and putamen. These areas are involved in the addictive effects as well as the euphoric effects of cocaine. In chronic cocaine users, we find a compensatory up-regulation of D_3 receptors in these brain regions versus controls [16]. This is in contrast to cocaine users who die of ExDS, who display no difference in the density of D_3 receptors versus controls. This may be due to abnormal processing of D_3 receptor mRNA, though the specific underlying mechanism has not yet been discovered [17]. Interestingly, we see similar aberrant D_3 receptor processing in chronic schizophrenics, strengthening the theory that this mechanism may play a significant role in the development of ExDS.

One additional finding suggesting that abnormal dopamine processing plays a role in the development of ExDS involves the activity of dopamine transporters. Chronic cocaine users generally display evidence of increased dopamine transporter function versus controls. This increased activity was not found in post-mortem analysis of patients who died from ExDS, despite their having been chronic cocaine users [18]. This lack of compensatory increase in dopamine transporters results in higher synaptic levels of dopamine and the potential for the toxic effects of dopamine hyper-stimulation.

Overall, the research to date suggests that although cocaine and other stimulants are the primary precipitants of the modern ExDS, there appears to be a genetic predisposing factor that strongly contributes to persons suffering from ExDS. Aberrant dopaminergic processing and maladaptation to increased dopamine levels place these individuals at greater risk of dopamine toxicity and the resultant physiologic effects of autonomic instability and delirium [7].

1.13.4 Diagnosis

1.13.4.1 Pre-Clinical Characteristics

As noted earlier, many of the death from ExDS occur prior to hospital arrival. This means that most of these patients will either be found deceased or encountered by paramedics, emergency medical technicians, or police. Given the aggressive and erratic behavior of ExDS patients, it is no surprise that law enforcement is generally the first to arrive on scene. Often, these patients are quite combative and require many individuals to help in the control and restraint process. Police may have to use less lethal weapons to subdue these individuals, such as a TASER electronic control device, and patients will often be placed in restraint devices for their own and personnel safety.

Given the nature of the disease, the high mortality, and the general difficulty in the restraint process, there has been significant controversy in the legal community regarding ExDS. Not infrequently, these patients will die in custody due to the complex pathophysiologic processes previously described. Unfortunately, when a person dies in the custody of law enforcement, especially after significant force was necessary to subdue the person, the case often results in litigation.

First responders may see any of the following characteristics when they approach a patient with ExDS:

- Extreme agitation or aggressiveness
- Delusional thoughts
- Profuse sweating
- Rapid breathing
- Hot to touch
- Attempted self cooling
- Near constant physical activity
- Lack of fatigue
- High tolerance to pain
- Not responsive to police presence
- Inappropriate clothing for environment/naked
- Excessive/superhuman strength
- Glass attraction/destruction
- Keening (unintelligible animal-like sounds)

A study by Hall et al. found that out of 1,269 consecutive persons whom police used force to subdue and restrain, 1 in 6 displayed 3 or more characteristics of ExDS. The most commonly displayed characteristics were violent behavior (63%), high pain tolerance (20.8%), constant or near constant activity (24.7%), and not responding to police presence (21.7%) [19]. This study suggests that we are likely seeing patients in the emergency department after police altercations who may have subtle signs of ExDS. Obtaining a comprehensive description of events from pre-hospital personnel is of paramount importance, especially in situations where ExDS is on the differential diagnosis.

1.13.4.2 Clinical and Laboratory Characteristics

Although pre-clinical data can be very helpful in the diagnosis of ExDS, there are situations where these data are unavailable, especially in cases where police hand over care to medics, who then transport the patient to the hospital. Luckily, there are several objective findings that can help the clinician diagnose the syndrome. Although no case is the same, patients with ExDS will typically express some of the following characteristics:

- Rapid heart rate
- Elevated blood pressure
- Elevated respiratory rate
- Elevated body temperature
- Dilated pupils
- Profuse sweating
- Elevated serum creatinine phosphokinase (CPK) or myoglobin (rhabdomyolysis)
- Elevated serum creatinine
- Low pH on blood gas testing (metabolic acidosis)
- Urine toxicological screen positive for stimulants (cocaine, methamphetamine, PCP)
- History of antipsychotic or anticholinergic use
- History of schizophrenia or bipolar disorder and not on therapy
- Abnormal heart rhythm or electrocardiogram (ECG) prior to or after cardiac arrest

During the medical workup, one assesses for other potential life-threatening conditions prior to making the diagnosis of ExDS. Sepsis, neuroleptic malignant syndrome, serotonin syndrome, and hyperthyroidism can all cause some of these symptoms and clinical findings and should be excluded through history, physical examination, and laboratory findings. Additionally, each patient should receive a traumatic injury screening examination, given that many arrive at the hospital after a physical altercation with police, emergency medical services, or bystanders.

1.13.5 Treatment

The most important aspect of treatment for patients with ExDS is rapid and complete sedation. This not only helps reduce the catecholamine cascade and autonomic instability but also reduces a very serious threat to personnel safety. Several medications are potentially useful in this situation, including benzodiazepines, neuroleptic antipsychotics, ketamine, and other sedatives.

Benzodiazepines provide sedation through their effect on the inhibitory gamma-aminobutyric acid (GABA) receptor. They are particularly useful when patients present with sympathomimetic toxicity or when the cause of agitation is undetermined [20]. In a head to head trial of intramuscular midazolam, lorazepam, and haloperidol, it was demonstrated that the midazolam group had a quicker time to sedation and shorter duration of sedation. Midazolam was also found to be better at controlling motor agitation than haloperidol [21]. Further studies, however, indicate that midazolam may require multiple doses to obtain desired effect, subsequent repeat doses afterwards to maintain sedation, and worsened respiratory suppression [22], though this is likely due to the need for higher doses of sedation in patients with ExDS compared with other forms of agitation needing medicinal therapy.

First-generation antipsychotics (FGA) are also an option; however, in situations of undifferentiated agitation, this is typically not considered the first choice. If an FGA is used, the current recommended practice is to provide co-administration of a benzodiazepine or anticholinergic to limit the potential for extrapyramidal symptoms and acute dystonic reactions [23–25]. For a small subset of patients, the use of FGAs may exacerbate their agitation and potentially worsen violent behavior [26].

Ketamine has been strongly supported in recent literature for use in highly agitated patients in both the emergency department and pre-hospital settings. In general, ketamine rapidly sedates patients and with few exceptions, does not affect airway control, breathing, heart rate, or blood pressure in an adverse manner [27]. Recent studies, however, provide mixed results. Cole et al. compared ketamine versus haloperidol for use in agitated patients. They found that ketamine had a significantly faster onset of sedation (5 minutes versus 17 minutes with haloperidol), though it was associated with a higher intubation rate at the hospital when used in the pre-hospital setting [28]. This increased intubation rate is likely due to the successful calming and sedative effect on the patient upon arrival to the emergency department. A more recent case series by Scaggs et al. specifically studied the use of ketamine in patients who displayed symptoms of ExDS in the pre-hospital setting. They noted that an intramuscular 5 mg/kg ketamine injection was effective, reliable, and safe [27]. An additional study found that emergency department use of ketamine for agitation was quite effective at achieving initial sedation, though it generally required more repeat dosing than other sedatives [29].

Once adequate sedation is achieved, the following treatments should proceed rapidly and include cooling measures for hyperthermia, intravenous hydration, and diagnostic studies as appropriate. In advanced stages of ExDS, severe hyperthermia may require active cooling measures including cooled intravenous fluids, evaporative cooling, and ice packs, and in some cases, internal cooling measures may be needed. Large volume fluid resuscitation may also be necessary, especially given the potential for rhabdomyolysis compounded by severe dehydration from evaporative and other insensible fluid losses during the acutely agitated state. These patients should remain on cardiac monitoring due to autonomic instability and the potential for cardiac dysrhythmias. Further resuscitative measures, including treatment of traumatic injuries, correction of metabolic acidosis, and correction of electrolyte disturbances, should be guided by the particular findings of each case.

1.13.6 Conclusion

ExDS is a potentially fatal disease characterized by severe agitation, incredible strength, confusion, and combativeness. It is a dangerous disease not only for the patient but also for police, pre-hospital personnel, and hospital staff caring for the individual. Without timely identification and treatment, however, these patients can rapidly decompensate into cardiovascular collapse and death. All patients should receive an expedited assessment for traumatic injuries, cardiac dysrhythmias, rhabdomyolysis, and other metabolic derangements. Once identified, ExDS should be treated with rapid sedation, cooling measures, and intravenous fluids. As more and more illicit sympathomimetic drugs become available, it is likely that we will continue to see more cases of ExDS in the emergency department. It is imperative that we recognize the clinical presentations of these cases early, treat aggressively, and most importantly, take precautions to maintain the safety of the patient and all personnel.

REFERENCES

1. Wetli CV, Mash D, Karch SB. Cocaine-associated agitated delirium and the neuroleptic malignant syndrome. *Am J Emerg Med* 1996;14(4):425–8.
2. Vilke GM, DeBard ML, Chan TC, et al. Excited Delirium Syndrome (ExDS): defining based on a review of the literature. *J Emerg Med* 2012;43(5):897–905.
3. Robinson D, Hunt S. Sudden in-custody death syndrome. *Top Emerg Med* 2005;27(1):36–43.
4. Gill JR. The syndrome of excited delirium. *Forensic Sci Med Pathol* 2014;10(2):223–8.
5. Stephens BG, Jentzen JM, Karch S, et al. National association of medical examiners position paper on the certification of cocaine-related deaths. *Am J Forensic Med Pathol* 2004;25(1):11–3.
6. Vilke GM, Payne-James J, Karch SB. Excited delirium syndrome (ExDS): redefining an old diagnosis. *J Forensic Leg Med* 2012;19(1):7–11.
7. Takeuchi A, Ahern T, Henderson SO. Excited delirium. *West J Emerg Med* 2011;12(1):77–83.
8. Bell L. On a form of disease resembling some advanced stage of mania and fever. *Am J Insanity* 1849;6:97–127.
9. Fishbain DA, Wetli CV. Cocaine intoxication, delirium, and death in a body packer. *Ann Emerg Med* 1981;10(10):531–2.
10. Staley JK, Welti CV, Ruttenber AJ, et al. Altered dopaminergic synaptic markers in cocaine psychosis and sudden death. *NIDA Res Monogr Series* 1995;153:491.
11. Plush T, Shakespeare W, Jacobs D, et al. Cocaine-induced agitated delirium: a case report and review. *J Intensive Care Med* 2015;30(1):49–57.
12. Grant JR, Southall PE, Fowler DR, et al. Death in custody: a historical analysis. *J Forensic Sci* 2007;52(5):1177–81.
13. Southall PE, Pestaner JP. Overwhelming number of AA deaths occur in police custody. *J Natl Med Assoc* 2003;95(8):754–5.
14. Stratton SJ, Rogers C, Green K. Sudden death in individuals in hobble restraints during paramedic transport. *Ann Emerg Med* 1995;25(5):710–2.
15. Mash, DC, Ouyang Q, Pablo J, et al. Cocaine abusers have an overexpression of alpha-synuclein in dopamine neurons. *J Neurosci* 2003;23(7):2564–71.
16. Little KY, McLaughlin DP, Zhang L, et al. Brain dopamine transporter messenger RNA and binding sites in cocaine users: a postmortem study. *Arch Gen Psychiatry* 1998;55(9):793–9.
17. Mash DC, Staley JK. D3 dopamine and kappa opioid receptor alterations in human brain of cocaine-overdose victims. *Ann N Y Acad Sci* 1999;877:507–22.
18. Pitts DK, Marwah J. Cocaine modulation of central monoaminergic neurotransmission. *Pharmacol Biochem Behav* 1987;26(2):453–61.
19. Hall CA, Kader AS, Danielle McHale AM, et al. Frequency of signs of excited delirium syndrome in subjects undergoing police use of force: descriptive evaluation of a prospective, consecutive cohort. *J Forensic Leg Med* 2013;20(2):102–7.
20. Wilson MP, Pepper D, Currier GW, et al. The psychopharmacology of agitation: consensus statement of the american association for emergency psychiatry project beta psychopharmacology workgroup. *West J Emerg Med* 2012;13(1):26–34.
21. Nobay F, Simon BC, Levitt MA, et al. A prospective, double-blind, randomized trial of midazolam versus haloperidol versus lorazepam in the chemical restraint of violent and severely agitated patients. *Acad Emerg Med* 2004;11(7):744–9.
22. Martel M, Sterzinger A, Miner J, et al. Management of acute undifferentiated agitation in the emergency department: a randomized double-blind trial of droperidol, ziprasidone, and midazolam. *Acad Emerg Med* 2005;12(12):1167–72.
23. Battaglia J, Moss S, Rush J, et al. Haloperidol, lorazepam, or both for psychotic agitation? A multicenter, prospective, double-blind, emergency department study. *Am J Emerg Med* 1997;15:335–40.
24. Raveendran NS, Tharyan P, Alexander J, et al. Rapid tranquillisation in psychiatric emergency settings in India: pragmatic randomised controlled trial of intramuscular olanzapine versus intramuscular haloperidol plus promethazine. *BMJ* 2007;335(7625):865.
25. Gillies D, Beck A, McCloud A, *Benzodiazepines Alone or in Combination with Antipsychotic Drugs for Acute Psychosis*. The Cochrane Library, 2005.
26. Herrera JN, Sramek JJ, Costa JF, et al. High potency neuroleptics and violence in schizophrenics. *J Nerv Ment Dis* 1988;176(9):558–61.
27. Scaggs TR, Glass DM, Hutchcraft MG, et al. Prehospital Ketamine is a safe and effective treatment for excited delirium in a community hospital based EMS system. *Prehosp Disaster Med* 2016;31(5):563–9.
28. Cole JB, Moore JC, Nystrom PC, et al. A prospective study of ketamine versus haloperidol for severe prehospital agitation. *Clin Toxicol (Phila)* 2016;54(7):556–62.
29. Hopper AB, Vilke GM, Castillo EM, et al. Ketamine use for acute agitation in the emergency department. *J Emerg Med* 2015;48(6):712–9.

1.14 STROKE WITH DRUG ABUSE

Kama Guluma

1.14.1 General Comments

Illicit drug abuse remains a significant public health issue, with of 30% of adults having used a drug within the prior month and an especially high prevalence of use among the young (NIH National Institute on Drug Abuse 2015, Arria 2017). Young adults with drug abuse have a 6.5-fold increase in risk of hemorrhagic and ischemic stroke (Kaku 1990). In a U.S. study of stroke patients 18 to 44 years old, the use of illicit drugs was found to be the fifth most common cause for ischemic stroke and contributory in 9% of cases, with a marked increase in the rate of use over a decade (3.8% in 1993 versus 19.8% in 2005) (Kissela 2012). In a cross-sectional study, the use of amphetamines increased the risk of hemorrhagic stroke almost fivefold, and cocaine was associated with an over twofold increase in the risk of hemorrhagic and ischemic stroke (Westover 2007, Sordo 2014, Indave 2017). While causation has not been clearly established, and stroke is relatively rare, there appears to be an independent, robust, and temporal association between acute, heavy cannabis use and acute ischemic stroke (Barber 2013, Thomas 2014, Hackam 2015, Rumalla 2016). With any patient presenting with an ischemic or hemorrhagic stroke, a complication of drug abuse should be considered because of specific implications for treatment. Psychomotor stimulants such as amphetamines and cocaine are more commonly associated with stroke than are drugs such as opioids, psychomimetics, and cannabis; even drugs used for doping in sports may be implicated in stroke (Fonseca 2013).

1.14.1.1 Ischemic Stroke as a Complication of Drug Abuse

The drugs most commonly associated with acute ischemic stroke are cocaine and amphetamines, although marijuana and phencyclidine (PCP) have also been implicated. The mechanisms by which these drugs cause an ischemic stroke include vasospasm, vasculitis (which leads to a stroke through either local thromboembolism or dissection of the vessel wall), embolism, and drug-induced prothrombotic state.

1.14.1.1.1 Drug-Induced Vasospasm

The drug most associated with cerebral vasospasm is cocaine. Cocaine (and its much longer-lived metabolite) predisposes to vasospasm by preventing uptake of sympathomimetic neurotransmitters, leading to a sensitization to epinephrine and norepinephrine and accumulation of serotonin (one of the main cerebral vasoconstrictors) that may last – and precipitate acute ischemic stroke – for hours after use (Sáez 2011, Koch 2008, Fonseca 2013). Both cocaine hydrochloride and alkaloid crack (following any method of administration) can cause stroke, and crack cocaine appears to be associated with both ischemic stroke and hemorrhagic stroke, whereas cocaine hydrochloride results more often in hemorrhagic stroke (Fonseca 2013). There is a causal link between acute cocaine use and acute ischemic stroke (Cheng 2016). As many as 25–60% of all cocaine-associated strokes are ischemic (Levine 1990, Fonseca 2013), and a majority (50–80%) involve the middle cerebral artery with a profile that suggests repeated episodes of vasospasm (Bartzokis 1999), although subcortical, cerebellar, brain stem, retinal, and spinal infarcts have been reported (Daras 1991). Patients with cocaine-associated stroke typically do not have classic risk factors for ischemic stroke and tend to be young, in the fourth decade of life (Fonseca 2013).

Ecstasy, which alters brain serotonin concentrations involved in the regulation of brain microvasculature, has also been implicated in vasospastic ischemic strokes occurring within hours of ingestion (Hughes 1993, Gledhill 1993, Manchanda 1993), with cerebral angiography in one case report of a stroke occurring 48 hours after intake of a variant of Ecstasy demonstrating significant vascular abnormalities of large-caliber, medium-caliber, and small-caliber vessels with watershed infarction (Ambrose 2010). Infarcts are frequently seen in brain areas with high expression of serotonin receptors, such as the occipital cortex and globus pallidus (Hagan 2007).

In cannabis-associated strokes, which typically occur in patients without typical risk factors for stroke (Rumalla 2016), angiography reveals a specific pattern of multifocal vasoconstriction involving multiple intracranial arteries that reverses after cannabis withdrawal, with no evidence of structural vasculopathy (Mateo 2005), more frequent in the vertebrobasilar territory (Wolff 2011), with a preponderance of infarcts in the posterior circulation that suggests a susceptibility there (Singh 2012). The presumed mechanism for this large vessel vasoconstriction is hypothesized to be altered cerebral autoregulation, vasospasm, and cerebral vasoconstriction syndrome, possibly compounded by hypotension (Thanvi 2009, Renard 2012).

Lysergic acid diethylamide (LSD) is used far less frequently now than it was in its heyday but is being explored as a psychoactive therapeutic agent (Huestis 2017). It is an ergot derivative and a vasoconstrictor that has been implicated in ischemic stroke from carotid vasoconstriction in a few case reports (Lieberman 1974, Sobel 1971). The last case of ischemic stroke resulting from ingestion of LSD was reported in 1974 (Lieberman 1974).

1.14.1.1.2 Drug-Induced Vasculitis

Vasculitis can in and of itself lead to focal thrombosis and ischemia, but it can also co-exist with (if not underlie) arterial dissections that may also cause a stroke (Tolani 2015). The drugs most associated with vasculitis are amphetamines and possibly cocaine. The use of methamphetamine – the most potent and commonly abused amphetamine – and the derivatives 3,4-methylenedioxyamphetamine and 3,4-methylenedioxymethamphetamine (Ecstasy) increases the odds of having a stroke to almost four times that of non-users (Petitti 1998). Methamphetamine has a direct toxic or immunological effect in the cerebral vessels, causing a histologically evident necrotizing angiitis of small and large cerebral arteries (Shibata 1991, McGee 2004). Cerebral vasculitis is found on neuroimaging of both hemorrhagic and ischemic stroke associated with methamphetamine abuse (McGee 2004). Ecstasy has been hypothesized to also cause cerebral vasculitis (Auer 2002), and ephedrine has been reported to cause a late vasculitis (Wooten 1983) and an increased risk of strokes. Vasculitis has been histologically demonstrated in isolated cases of cocaine-associated stroke (Fredericks 1991), and Moyamoya-like vasculopathy has been reported in cocaine addicts (Storen 2000), but most autopsies have failed to show significant, if any, vasculitis, making vasculitis a controversial cause of stroke in cocaine users (Fonseca 2013). Heroin can also cause stroke from vasculitis (Niehaus 1998). The heroin-induced hypereosinophilia associated with smoking or inhaling heroin (which induces a pulmonary hypereosinophilia; Brander 1993) has been reported to result in ischemic stroke, presumably through local hypercoagulability from eosinophilic granules and endothelial cell damage (Bolz 2015).

1.14.1.1.3 Drug-Induced Embolism

Any drug that is injected may cause an embolic stroke. Most heroin-associated strokes occur after intravenous use (Bartolomei 1992, Adle-Biassette 1996, Benoilid 2013). Almost all heroin-induced strokes are ischemic, resulting from emboli either due to infective endocarditis (Büttner 2000, Hadley 2017) or from solid adulterants (such as aspirin, cleaning powder, starch, sugar, strychnine, and talcum powder) that are co-injected into the vein and then either directly embolize to the brain via a patent foramen ovale or are caught in the lungs, where – through repeated pulmonary insults and chronic granulomatous inflammation over time – they lead to pulmonary hypertension and opening of pulmonary fistulae that enable right-to-left shunting of venous emboli to the brain (Fonseca 2013).

1.14.1.1.4 Drug-Induced Prothrombotic State

Drugs can induce a prothrombotic state by increasing platelet count or activity, augmenting the activity of procoagulant factors, or increasing blood viscosity. Cocaine results in endothelial dysfunction, predisposing to thrombus formation (Sáez 2011), and increases platelet activation (Pereira 2011). Illegal performance-enhancing or doping substances used in sports (such as anabolic–androgenic steroids, corticosteroids, adrenocorticotropic hormone [ACTH], human chorionic gonadotropin [HCG], growth hormone, and erythropoietin) can also lead to a prothrombotic state (Fonseca 2013). Anabolic–androgenic steroids are atherogenic, promote hypertension, increase platelet count and function, increase the activity of pro-coagulants, decrease fibrinolysis, and increase blood viscosity (Fonseca 2013) and have been associated with acute ischemic stroke in bodybuilders (Santamarina 2008, Shimada 2012, Low 2016). Erythropoietin and derivatives are similarly prothrombotic and increase blood viscosity.

1.14.1.1.5 Other Mechanisms

The preceding mechanisms aside, chronic drug use, specifically cocaine and methamphetamine use, can also accelerate cerebrovascular atherosclerosis and endothelial dysfunction, leading to an increased pre-disposition to "run-of-the-mill" ischemic cerebrovascular and cardiovascular events, in some case series associated with ischemic stroke without the vasospasm or vasculitis described earlier (Ho 2009, Toossi 2010). Cocaine leads to accelerated atherosclerosis (Sáez 2011) and induces cerebral microischemia when taken at a typical user's dose, an effect that is exacerbated by repeated use (Fonseca 2013). Heroin can also induce ischemic stroke circumstantially through global brain hypoxia from respiratory depression (Niehaus 1998, Büttner 2000, Daras 2001) or focal compression of the carotid artery from prolonged lateral neck flexion while in an opioid coma (Jensen 1990), resulting in infarcts in the globus pallidus or in the watershed zones between major cerebral arterial territories (Vila 1997, Büttner 2000, Hagan 2007).

1.14.1.2 Hemorrhagic Stroke as a Complication of Drug Abuse

Amphetamines and cocaine are the drugs most associated with hemorrhagic stroke. Amphetamines have been heavily implicated in acute drug-induced hemorrhagic strokes, specifically intraparenchymal hematomas (subcortical and lobar) and subarachnoid hemorrhages (McGee 2004, Ho 2009), even after only a single dose. Amphetamine use has been noted in some case series to confer over twice the risk of hemorrhage as does cocaine use (odds ratio 4.95 versus 2.33) with increased risk of death (Westover 2007). The presumed causes are amphetamine-induced acute hypertension on the background of the cerebral vasculitis described earlier, with frequent reports of underlying aneurysms in those patients presenting with subarachnoid hemorrhage (SAH) (Ho 2009).

Cocaine use is also associated with hemorrhagic stroke (Klonoff 1989), especially in those actively consuming it. Mechanisms include a sudden increase in arterial blood pressure (also often in association with an underlying aneurysm or arteriovenous malformation [Klonoff 1989, Oyesiku 1993] or concurrent vasculitis), hemorrhagic transformation of vasoconstriction-related multifocal ischemic infarcts (Case records of the Massachusetts General Hospital 1993), and acutely disordered cerebrovascular autoregulation with vasodilatation and increased cerebral blood flow (Kibayashi 1995). The acute cocaine-induced elevation in arterial blood pressure may be resolved at the time of presentation due to its short half-life (Daras 1994). Cocaine is associated with intraparenchymal hemorrhage, intraventricular hemorrhage, and SAH (Levine 1990). Case-control studies have shown that cocaine-related intracranial hemorrhage (ICH) patients have higher initial blood pressures, more subcortical and intraventricular hemorrhage, and a poorer prognosis (worse outcome with regard to discharge to home or inpatient rehabilitation, and a threefold higher risk of dying during hospitalization) than those with ICH that is not cocaine-related (Martin-Schild 2010, Bajwa 2013). Aneurysmal SAH patients who use cocaine tend to be younger than their non-cocaine-using counterparts (45.1 years vs. 54.1 years; $p \leq 0.0003$ in one study) (Alaraj 2010), with aneurysms that seem to rupture earlier, at a significantly smaller size (Vannemreddy 2008).

Other drugs of abuse are also associated with ICH. Phencyclidine ("angel dust") is a sympathomimetic vasoconstrictor that can cause acute hypertension and delayed hypertensive crisis days after its use (McCarron 1981), resulting in ICH and SAH (Boyko 1987). Marijuana can affect cerebral autoregulation and vascular tone, leading to a reversible vasoconstriction syndrome and SAH or ICH (Ducros 2007, Esse 2011). Recreational marijuana has been associated with an increased likelihood of aneurysmal SAH (Rumalla 2016 – JSCD). An ICH should be suspected in any patient with a significant acute headache following the use of one of these drugs.

1.14.2 Stepwise Approach to Management

1.14.2.1 Immediate Interventions

1. *Primary stabilization:*
   A patient presenting with a drug-induced stroke should be primarily stabilized like any patient in extremis, with attention to maintaining an airway and adequate ventilation, using ventilator support and reversal agents for opiate overdoses where indicated, and using standard measures outlined elsewhere in this text to address any life-threatening issues with cardiovascular instability, such as a significant cardiac dysrhythmia or hypotension. Issues with stabilization that are paramount in a patient with a stroke are minimizing any episodes of hypoxia or hypotension, as these are significant determinants of outcome. When indicated, intubation for airway protection not only prevents early aspiration but enables mechanical ventilation to treat elevated intracranial pressure (ICP) elevation or malignant brain edema from the stroke should it become necessary (Grotta 1995, Jauch 2013). In normoxic stroke patients not needing intubation or ventilator support, the routine administration of oxygen has not been shown to be of any utility; supplemental oxygen should be reserved for those with pulse oximetry lower than 94% (Jauch 2013).
2. *Control of agitation:*
   The delirium, psychosis, or agitation from an acute stimulant drug ingestion may be particularly harmful in the setting of a stroke due to the tendency to raise ICP and potentially exacerbate ICH where present. Furthermore, it may complicate attempts to obtain the emergent neuroimaging needed to evaluate that stroke. Benzodiazepines should be administered to sedate this type of patient and will be additionally helpful in mitigating the cardiovascular effects of cocaine and methamphetamine intoxication.
3. *Emergent neuroimaging:*
   The patient with a drug-induced stroke will present in a manner in which the type of stroke (hemorrhagic versus ischemic) and its cause (vascular abnormality, thromboembolism, vasospasm, dissection) will be undifferentiated. The emergent neuro-imaging in such a patient therefore involves a multimodal imaging paradigm – utilizing computed tomography (CT) imaging, magnetic resonance imaging (MRI), or both – that addresses three nested clinical questions: 1) Are the patient's stroke symptoms due to an ICH (i.e., is it a hemorrhagic stroke)? … Or due to an ischemic stroke that is already so far along that it would pre-dispose to hemorrhagic conversion if subjected to reperfusion therapy? 2) If not, assuming the stroke is ischemic, is there a causative lesion that can be addressed with endovascular therapy? 3) If this is the case, is there likely to be salvageable brain that would be amenable to endovascular reperfusion?

   A non-contrast CT scan of the brain is typically used to address the first question, although an MRI can also be used (Jauch 2013, Merino 2010, Kurz 2016). If there is a hemorrhagic stroke, the indicated treatment for hemorrhagic stroke can be initiated. If the initial non-contrast head CT reveals frank hypodensity (meaning brain tissue that is already necrotic) in the brain tissue, or a very large volume of edematous change, then reperfusion may be deferred if the risk of hemorrhagic conversion is considered too high. The non-contrast head CT may also reveal an actual clot sitting in a vessel such as the middle cerebral artery, vertebral artery, or basilar artery (a hyperdense artery sign) (Jauch 2013).

   If the initial non-contrast CT reveals neither a hemorrhage nor tissue that will likely hemorrhage, then additional angiographic imaging is obtained to address the second question, identifying an amenable causative lesion. Obtaining anatomic detail of the head and neck vasculature is particularly important in drug-related strokes, since the causative lesion of an ischemic stroke may be not only thromboembolic but also vasospastic or due to a dissection. Arteriography is important even in drug-related hemorrhagic strokes; up to 41% of cocaine-related cerebral hemorrhages have evidence of vascular abnormalities such as aneurysms or arteriovenous malformations (Fonseca 2013). This anatomic information can be obtained with either CT angiography of the brain and neck done simultaneously with the initial non-contrast brain CT, or magnetic resonance angiography (MRA) done simultaneously with initial MRI (Merino 2010, Kurz 2016).

There are a variety of CT and MRI imaging protocols designed to address the third question, as to whether there is salvageable brain tissue. Contrast-enhanced CT imaging or MRI imaging can provide a measure of cerebral perfusion and blood flow so as to assess for a penumbra, i.e., an area of hypoperfused but salvageable tissue surrounding a core of more irreversibly damaged tissue (Merino 2010, Kurz 2016). An Alberta Stroke Program Early CT score (ASPECTS), in which ten specific ganglionic and supraganglionic brain regions are examined for ischemic changes on non-contrast CT and one point subtracted from a total of ten for each region that is affected, can be used as a measure of salvageability (Goyal 2015). There are also additional CT protocols, such as "multiphase CT," that utilize a sequence of "rapid-fire" repeat scans to detect the delayed, penumbra-saving blood flow supplied by collaterals in each cardiac cycle (Menon 2015).

4. *Acute hypertensive crisis:*
The systemic effects of drugs like cocaine and methamphetamine include sympathomimetic elevation of systolic and diastolic blood pressure, tachycardia, cardiac dysrhythmias, and hyperpyrexia (Fonseca 2013, Richards 2016). The clinical priorities in addressing an acute drug-induced elevation in blood pressure become very specific in a patient with coincident ischemic or hemorrhagic stroke. Considerations that come into play include not only the target blood pressure reduction but also the type of blood pressure control agent to be used. The management of acute elevations in blood pressure differs depending on whether the stroke is an ischemic stroke, an ICH, or an SAH.

With an ischemic stroke, residual blood flow to penumbral brain tissue, i.e., the salvageable tissue surrounding a core infarct in which the effects of ischemia are potentially reversible, is exquisitely sensitive to mean arterial pressure. There is a clearly documented U-shaped correlation between admission blood pressure and outcome (neurological deficit, risk of neurological deterioration, death) (Leonardi-Bee 2002, Castillo 2004, Vemmos 2004, Okumura 2005), in which too low a blood pressure presumably results in worsened ischemia, and too high a blood pressure results in complications such as hemorrhagic conversion or cerebral edema, encephalopathy, and organ dysfunction (although the in-hospital correlation between blood pressure and outcome appears more linear; Jauch 2013). In the patient with an acute ischemic stroke, the optimal systolic blood pressure (SBP) is between 121 and 200 mm Hg, and the optimal diastolic blood pressure (DBP) is between 81 and 110 mm Hg (Jauch 2013). These same blood pressure parameters should probably be incorporated into the treatment of a cocaine- or methamphetamine-induced ischemic stroke with elevated blood pressure. In those patients in whom intravenous thrombolysis or endovascular therapy is being considered, the blood pressure should be gently lowered to a target of 185/110 mm Hg, and after thrombolysis, it must be maintained below 180/105 mm Hg to reduce the risk of ICH, keeping in mind that a target SBP of 141 to 150 mm Hg has been shown to be associated with the best outcome after thrombolysis (Ahmed 2009, Jauch 2013).

An ICH, unlike an ischemic stroke, is a space-occupying lesion within the calvarium, subject to the Monro-Kellie doctrine (Mokri 2001), and presents a catch-22 in that high blood pressure potentially results in worsening hematoma expansion, while lower blood pressure presumably results in less perfusion to compressed peri-hematomal brain tissue. Patients with ICH tend to present with elevations in blood pressure that are higher than those seen in ischemic stroke patients, an autoregulatory phenomenon that lasts a few days and then resolves (Qureshi 2007). In the acute phase, hematoma expansion is an issue, with a >33% increase in size occurring in two-thirds of patients within the first hour of presentation (Brott 1997, Davis 2006), associated with a significantly worse outcome and mortality (Moon 2008, Fan 2012). A spate of clinical trials investigating the benefit of intensive blood pressure reduction to a target of 140/90 mm Hg have culminated in two large trials that while showing reductions in hematoma expansion, failed to show an effect on outcome (Anderson 2013, Qureshi 2016). Current guidelines state that an SBP >220 mm Hg should be aggressively treated and that reducing an ICH patient's blood pressure to 140/90 is probably safe and effective (Hemphill 2015).

An SAH is unlike an ischemic stroke or ICH in that the primary consideration is preventing re-bleeding from the ruptured aneurysm that caused it. Re-bleeding – a major source of poor outcome in SAH – occurs in 8–23% of patients in the first 24 hours after SAH, with a peak time of re-bleeding occurring within 2 hours (in 77% of re-bleeds) and with 90% of re-bleeds occurring within 6 hours (Broderick 1994, Ohkuma 2001). While there is no prospective interventional data on blood pressure manipulation and re-bleeding, re-bleeding is associated with an SBP over 160 mm Hg, and therefore, current recommendations are to keep the patient's SBP lower than this (Tang 2014, Etminan 2017).

Compared with the blood pressure elevation in a drug-intoxicated patient who does not have an acute ischemic stroke, ICH, or SAH (in whom oftentimes supportive measures and time will result in a decrease in blood pressure), the blood pressure reduction in a patient with one of the preceding neurovascular catastrophes has to be even more rapidly and definitively controlled, using medications such as labetol or nicardipine (Jauch 2013, Hemphill 2015). Benzodiazepines do not consistently reduce the tachycardia, hypertension, and vasospasm from cocaine toxicity (Richards 2016). Labetalol can be given as a 10-mg bolus intravenously (IV) followed by continuous IV infusion of 2–8 mg/min. Nicardipine can be started as a drip, at 5 mg/hour IV, and titrated up to the desired effect by 2.5 mg/hour every 5–15 minutes, up to a maximum of 15 mg/hour. Sodium nitroprusside can be considered if the blood pressure cannot be controlled or if the DBP is >140 mm Hg. Other agents (hydralazine, enalaprilat, etc.) may be considered when appropriate. A concern when using a beta-blocker such as labetolol to treat a stroke in the setting of acute cocaine intoxication is the possibility of "unopposed alpha-stimulation," but a recent systematic review incorporating 1,744 patients who underwent treatment for cocaine-related tachycardia, dysrhythmia, hypertension, and coronary vasospasm with beta-blockers found that there were only seven putative cases of adverse "unopposed alpha -stimulation," three due to the β1/β2-blocker propranolol, three due to the β1-blocker esmolol, and one due to the β1-blocker metoprolol, with no cases attributed to the use of mixed β1/β2/α1-blockers (Richards 2016). Labetolol is a mixed β1/β2/α1-blocker that has been used safely to ameliorate cocaine-induced cardiovascular effects (Sofuoglu 2000), and the risk of an unopposed alpha effect appears to be low. There is little literature on the effects of nicardipine in the setting of acute cocaine toxicity.

Calcium channel blockers are an attractive agent to consider in this setting because of their ability to vasodilate and treat vasospasm, but a concern here is reflex tachycardia. The dihydropyridine class calcium channel blockers, such as nifedipine and amlodipine, are more likely to result in reflex tachycardia compared with the benzothiazepine phenylalkylamine class agents such as diltiazem and verapamil (Olson 2013). A systematic review of the available literature revealed that when calcium channel blockers are used to treat cocaine-induced cardiovascular toxicity, they reduce blood pressure but not heart rate (Richards 2016).

5. *Laboratories:*
The laboratory data considerations that are specific to a drug-related stroke include a fingerstick glucose to screen for hypoglycemia, a complete blood count (CBC) to screen for thrombocytopenia in those patients at risk for it, coagulation parameters (prothrombin time [PT], international normalized ratio [INR], and activated partial thromboplastin time [aPTT]) in those patients taking anticoagulants, and cardiac enzymes (creatine kinase [CK], CK myocardial band [CK-MB], troponin) and an electrocardiogram to screen for coincident cardiac ischemia, since an ongoing acute myocardial infarction or pericarditis (or recent episode) complicates therapy with thrombolytics (Jauch 2013). In addition, electrolytes with renal function studies are recommended, and a pregnancy test should be obtained in any female patient with child-bearing potential. Apart from a fingerstick glucose, obtaining laboratory tests should not delay treatment with fibrinolytic therapy (Jauch 2013); retrospective studies have shown that there is a very low rate of unsuspected significant coagulopathy or thrombocytopenia in patients who have received IV thrombolysis (Cucchiara 2007, Rost 2009). A urine or serum toxicology test is very helpful in any younger patient presenting with stroke, given the specific considerations that come into play with a drug-induced stroke, as the patient's report of drug use may be unreliable. Blood cultures should be considered in those patients with either an ischemic or a hemorrhagic stroke in whom infectious endocarditis or a mycotic aneurysm is suspected.

6. *Emergent reperfusion for ischemic stroke:*
The mainstay of emergent reperfusion for stroke is thrombolytic therapy with intravenous recombinant tissue plasminogen activator (rt-PA). One retrospective study evaluating the treatment of cocaine-associated stroke with tissue plasminogen activator found that cocaine-positive and cocaine-negative treated patients had stroke severity and safety outcomes that were similar (Martin-Schild 2009). The dosing of intravenous rt-PA is as per standard guidelines, at a weight-based dose of 0.9 mg/kg (to a maximum of 90 mg), with the first 10% of the dose given as a bolus over 1 minute and the remaining 90% given as an infusion over 59 minutes (Jauch 2013). Standard inclusion and exclusion criteria have been published (Jauch 2013). Inclusion criteria for IV thrombolytic therapy include age ≥18 years, defined onset of symptoms within 4.5 hours of onset, and no hemorrhage on non-contrast head CT. Absolute contraindications include an ischemic stroke, serious brain injury, or intracranial surgery within the previous 3 months, prior ICH, SAH, arterial puncture at non-compressible site within the previous 7 days, active bleeding on examination, uncontrollable elevation in blood pressure >185/110 mm Hg, known bleeding diathesis (such as a platelet count <100,000/mm^3, heparin use with an elevated aPTT, or current anticoagulant use with an INR >1.7), blood glucose <50 mg/dL, and hypodensity in over one-third of the cerebral hemisphere on CT. Relative contraindications to IV

thrombolytics (in which the risk should be weighed against the benefit) include a history of major surgery or trauma within the previous 14 days, gastrointestinal or genitourinary bleeding within 21 days, a seizure at the time the stroke was observed, and an acute myocardial infarction within the previous 3 months. For patients presenting between 3 and 4.5 hours of onset, there are additional exclusion criteria, specifically age >80 years, oral anticoagulant use (regardless of INR), NIH Stroke Scale (NIHSS) >25, involvement of hypodensity in over one-third of the MCA territory, and a history of both a previous stroke and diabetes. Other considerations for exclusion, such as extremes of age, rapidly involving symptoms, mild symptoms, and use in pregnancy, have undergone rigorous re-evaluation recently, with assessments in favor of using thrombolysis judiciously (Demaerschalk 2016).

Endovascular therapy has rapidly emerged as a significant therapy for ischemic stroke caused by a large vessel occlusion after five trials (MR CLEAN, ESCAPE, REVASCAT, SWIFT PRIME, and EXTEND IA) done between December 2010 and December 2014 showed benefit of a combination of endovascular therapy with IV thrombolysis over IV thrombolysis alone (Berkhemer 2015, Campbell 2015, Jovin 2015, Goyal 2015, Saver 2015). The patient who warrants serious consideration for (having inclusion criteria for) endovascular therapy is an adult over 18 years of age with a causative large vessel occlusion of either the internal carotid artery or proximal MCA (M1 area), who is receiving IV t-PA within 4.5 hours of onset according to guidelines from professional medical societies, who has a favorable pre-stroke modified Rankin Scale (mRS) score – an assessment of overall neurological function – of 0 to 1, a NIHSS score ≥6, an ASPECTS score ≥6, and for whom treatment can be initiated (i.e., groin puncture attained) within 6 hours of symptom onset (Powers 2015). There is little data on the risk specific to endovascular intervention in patients taking drugs known to cause vasospasm, but one report serves as a caution: García-Bermejo reported two cases of severe iatrogenic occlusive vasospasm during endovascular procedures in chronic cocaine users (García-Bermejo 2015). The decision as to the risks and benefits of endovascular therapy for stroke should be made in concert with neurovascular experts performing the procedure.

7. *Coagulopathy reversal:*
For hemorrhagic strokes such as ICH and SAH, a primary goal of immediate therapy, in addition to blood pressure control, is the emergent institution of coagulopathy reversal measures in patients who either have an inherited coagulation factor deficiency or happen to be taking anticoagulant medications. In patients with a specific coagulation factor deficiency, repletion of that specific factor as per factor-specific guidelines should be initiated. In those who are taking warfarin, protein complex concentrates (PCCs) or activated PCC FEIBA (factor VIII inhibitor bypassing activity), which reduce the associated coagulopathy within minutes of administration, are the first line of treatment (Sarode 2013, Hemphill 2015). Fresh frozen plasma and Vitamin K are also options, but it must be kept in mind that use of the former requires large volumes (on the order of liters) to treat coagulopathy of any significance (Abdel-Wahab 2006, Goodnough 2011, Hemphill 2015), and the latter does not take effect for hours (Watson 2001, Lubetsky 2003). In ICH patients who happen to be taking a novel oral anticoagulant (NOAC) such as apixiban, rivaroxaban, or dabigatran, the options are more limited for rapid coagulopathy reversal. PCCs can be considered, as there is evidence that they have partial physiological action, and dabigatran coagulopathy can be treated with a mono-clonal antibody reversal agent and dialysis out of the blood stream (Eerenberg 2011, Marlu 2012, Ray 2014, Hemphill 2015). For patients taking enoxaparin, protamine can be considered, with the caveat that it only partially reverses activity (Hirsh 2008), but there are specific reversal agents that have recently shown efficacy (Ansell 2016, Huisman 2016). Several studies investigating platelet transfusions for those ICH patients taking antiplatelet agents such as aspirin and clopidogrel have failed to show an effect on hematoma size or outcome (Batchelor 2012, Martin 2013, Leong 2015), and a recent prospective trial of early (<6 hours) transfusion showed that it in fact worsened outcome (Baharoglu 2016); platelet transfusion for ICH in patients taking antiplatelet agents is therefore not currently recommended. In patients with coincident thrombocytopenia, on the other hand, a platelet transfusion as per transfusion guidelines is still indicated. There is little evidence to support the routine use of any of these reversal measures as empiric therapy in patients without coagulopathy.
8. *Acute seizure control and seizure prophylaxis:*
Strokes are frequently associated with seizures (Beghi 2011, De Herdt 2011), with a rate as high as 14% after ICH, with the highest risk being from ICH with cortical involvement. The use of drugs may confer additional risk; cocaine has been shown to independently increase the risk of seizing after aneurysmal SAH (Chang 2016). While prospective and population-based studies have shown no association between clinical seizures and neurological outcome or mortality from stroke (Passero 2002, Szaflarski 2008, De Herdt 2011, Mullen 2013), an ongoing seizure places

severe metabolic demands on injured brain and should be treated with benzodiazepines, with an escalation of therapy, as is standard for the treatment of acute seizures, if there is no response. For the patient who has not seized, on the other hand, prophylactic anticonvulsant medication has not been demonstrated to be beneficial and is thus not recommended (Hemphill 2015).

1.14.2.2 Secondary Diagnostics and Interventions

1. *Intracranial monitoring and treatment:*
   Up to 70% of patients with ICH may have least one episode of intracranial hypertension (defined as an ICP >20 mm Hg) (Kamel 2012). Elevated ICP may decrease cerebral perfusion pressure (CPP) and cerebral blood flow. The usual causes are hydrocephalus from an intraventricular location of the hemorrhage or mass effect from the hematoma (and ICP may be elevated in and around the hematoma but not distant from it; Chambers 2001), and therefore, patients with limited intraventricular involvement and small hematomas typically will not require treatment to lower ICP. Increased ICP is more common in younger patients and those with a supratentorial hemorrhage location (Kamel 2012). Hydrocephalus is associated with worsened outcome in acute ICH (Diringer 1998, Huttner 2006, 2007). There is a paucity of published studies showing that management of elevated ICP has an effect on outcome, but invasive ICP monitoring through insertion of devices inserted into the brain parenchyma or cerebral ventricles, so as to detect and treat elevations in ICP that would decrease CPP and cerebral blood flow, is still advocated in guidelines (Hemphill 2015). ICP monitoring is indicated for patients with a Glasgow Coma Scale (GCS) score of ≤8, patients with clinical evidence of transtentorial herniation, or patients with significant IVH or hydrocephalus, with a goal of maintaining ICP below 20 mm Hg and keeping CPP between 50 and 70 mm Hg (since CPP <70 to 80 mm Hg is associated with brain tissue hypoxia and poor outcome; Hemphill 2015). Methods of treating elevated ICP include elevation of the head of the bed to 30°, sedation (Wolfe 2009), mannitol or hypertonic saline (which may be more effective) (Kamel 2011, Hemphill 2015), and even barbiturate coma or mild hypothermia in refractory cases.
2. *Emergent surgical procedures for stroke:*
   The utility of emergency surgical procedures, such as extracranial-intracranial bypass and carotid endarterectomy, in ischemic stroke has not been well established (Jauch 2013).The role and effectiveness of acute hematoma evacuation for hemorrhagic stroke are still unresolved, despite randomized controlled trials evaluating it (Akhigbe 2017), but literature supports such surgery in patients with cerebellar hemorrhages >3 cm in diameter or in whom cerebellar hemorrhage is associated with brainstem compression or hydrocephalus (Da Pian 1984, Firsching 1991, van Loon 1993). Trials of minimally invasive (endoscopic) surgery have shown promise and are ongoing (Fam 2017, Hanley 2016). In patients with CSF outflow obstruction caused by hydrocephalus or a trapped ventricle, CSF drainage with an intraventricular catheter should be considered, but the role for intraventricular administration of rt-PA or clot evacuation for intraventricular hemorrhage is unclear (Hemphill 2015).
3. *Temperature management:*
   Approximately a third of patients admitted with acute ischemic stroke will have a temperature >37.6 °C within the first hours after stroke onset (Azzimondi 1995, Boysen 2001). This is associated with poor neurological outcome due to increased metabolic demand and enhancement of secondary molecular injury (Azzimondi 1995, Reith 1996, Castillo 1998, Ginsberg 1998, Hajat 2000, Wang 2000, Kammersgaard 2002, Prasad 2010, Saxena 2015). Two large randomized, double-blind, controlled trials found no statistically significant treatment effect on outcome from using acetaminophen to reduce body temperature and prevent fever in stroke patients (den Hertog 2009, de Ridder 2017), and the impact that this literature will have on current guideline-based recommendations to use antipyretic medications to treat hyperthermic patients with ischemic stroke (Jauch 2013) is not known. Fever is not uncommon in patients with ICH, especially those with intraventricular hemorrhage. The duration of fever correlates with outcome and appears to be an independent negative prognostic factor (Schwarz 2000). Fever may also be associated with hematoma growth, albeit without clear causality (Rincon 2013). This being said, maintenance of normothermia in ICH patients has not been clearly demonstrated to effect outcome (Broessner 2009, Middleton 2011, Hemphill 2015).
4. *Nimodipine:*
   The data regarding the occurrence of vasospasm and outcome in patients with SAH associated with cocaine abuse is conflicted, with one study finding no significant difference in hemorrhage severity, short-term outcome, incidence of symptomatic or radiologic vasospasm, stroke, or death between cocaine users and nonusers (Alaraj 2010). Others have found connections to the contrary, with threefold greater risk of developing vasospasm in SAH with cocaine use (Howington 2003, Conway 2001) and a poor outcome related to intravenous cocaine use, presumably due to an increased intensity and duration of vasospasm related to the use of cocaine

(Simpson 1990). Nimodipine is typically given to patients with SAH so as to prevent vasospasm in the ensuing days. In one small study evaluating the ability of nimodipine to attenuate the hemodynamic effects of cocaine deliberately given to patients, the co-administration of the two resulted in no untoward effects (Kosten 1999).

5. *Anticoagulation:*
   IV administered heparin was used for decades as a treatment of patients with acute ischemic stroke but is now used infrequently. Urgent anticoagulation with heparin, low molecular weight heparin, or novel oral anticoagulants to either prevent early recurrent stroke, halt neurological worsening, or try to improve outcome is not supported by evidence and is therefore not recommended in national guidelines, especially given the increased risk of intracranial hemorrhagic complications (Jauch 2013). The effectiveness of urgent anticoagulation in potentially high-risk groups, such as those with stroke presumptively caused by either a severe stenosis of an internal carotid artery, intracardiac or intra-arterial thrombi, arterial dissection, or vertebrobasilar disease, is not well established (Jauch 2013). The use of intravenous antiplatelet agents (such as tirofiban and eptifibatide) and intravenous glycoprotein IIb/IIIa receptor inhibitors is similarly unsupported. The use of orally administered aspirin at an initial dose of 325 mg is, on the other hand, recommended for treatment of most patients with an acute ischemic stroke and should be started within 24 to 48 hours after stroke onset (and only after 24 hours in those patients treated with rt-PA).
6. *Other diagnostics and interventions:*
   In patients for whom a concern for endocarditis or other systemic infection exists, blood cultures can be obtained and appropriate empiric antibiotic therapy administered. Some authors have found methamphetamine-induced vasculitis (Salanova 1984) and heroin-induced vasculitis (Niehaus 1998) – and the associated neurological deficits – to be responsive to steroid immunosuppression, but there is insufficient data to recommend this on an empiric basis.
7. *Disposition:*
   Almost all drug-induced stroke patients should be admitted, given the acuity of disease. Those with large hemorrhages, those with suspicion or evidence of ICP elevation, and those with ischemic strokes having just received intravenous thrombolysis or endovascular reperfusion therapy will require ICU-level care due to the degree of monitoring and frequency of neurological checks indicated. Those with acute strokes not meeting indications for ICU-level care should be admitted into a setting in which neurological checks can be performed frequently and cardiac monitoring instituted as appropriate. Given the complexity and multidisciplinary nature of the care required (spanning the spectrum from acute stabilization, reperfusion therapy, and endovascular intervention to acute stroke rehabilitation), these patients should be admitted to a medical center with dedicated resources and an established track record of caring for patients with acute ischemic and hemorrhagic stroke, such as a Primary Stroke Center or a Comprehensive Stroke Center.

REFERENCES

Abdel-Wahab OI, Healy B, Dzik WH. Effect of fresh-frozen plasma transfusion on prothrombin time and bleeding in patients with mild coagulation abnormalities. *Transfusion* 2006;46(8):1279–85.

Adle-Biassette H, Marc B, Benhaiem-Sigaux N, Durigon M, Gray F. Cerebral infarctions in a drug addict inhaling heroin. *Arch Anat Cytol Pathol* 1996;44(1):12–7.

Ahmed N, Wahlgren N, Brainin M, Castillo J, Ford GA, Kaste M, Lees KR, Toni D; SITS Investigators. Relationship of blood pressure, antihypertensive therapy, and outcome in ischemic stroke treated with intravenous thrombolysis: retrospective analysis from Safe Implementation of Thrombolysis in Stroke-International Stroke Thrombolysis Register (SITS-ISTR). *Stroke* 2009;40(7):2442–9.

Akhigbe T, Zolnourian A. Role of surgery in the management of patients with supratentorial spontaneous intracerebral hematoma: critical appraisal of evidence. *J Clin Neurosci* 2017;39:35–8.

Alaraj A, Wallace A, Mander N, Aletich V, Charbel FT, Amin-Hanjani S. Effect of acute cocaine use on vasospasm and outcome in aneurysmal subarachnoid hemorrhage. *World Neurosurg* 2010;73(4):357–60.

Ambrose JB, Bennett HD, Lee HS, Josephson SA. Cerebral vasculopathy after 4-bromo-2,5-dimethoxyphenethylamine ingestion. *Neurologist* 2010;16(3):199–202.

Anderson CS, Heeley E, Huang Y, Wang J, Stapf C, Delcourt C, Lindley R, Robinson T, Lavados P, Neal B, Hata J, Arima H, Parsons M, Li Y, Wang J, Heritier S, Li Q, Woodward M, Simes RJ, Davis SM, Chalmers J; INTERACT2 Investigators. Rapid blood-pressure lowering in patients with acute intracerebral hemorrhage. *N Engl J Med* 2013;368(25):2355–65.

Ansell JE, Laulicht BE, Bakhru SH, Hoffman M, Steiner SS, Costin JC. Ciraparantag safely and completely reverses the anticoagulant effects of low molecular weight heparin. *Thromb Res* 2016;146:113–8.

Arria AM, Caldeira KM, Allen HK, Bugbee BA, Vincent KB, O'Grady KE. Prevalence and incidence of drug use among college students: an 8-year longitudinal analysis. *Am J Drug Alcohol Abuse* 2017;12:1–8.

Auer J, Berent R, Weber T, Lassnig E, Eber B. Subarachnoid haemorrhage with "Ecstasy" abuse in a young adult. *Neurol Sci* 2002;23(4):199–201.

Azzimondi G, Bassein L, Nonino F, Fiorani L, Vignatelli L, Re G, D'Alessandro R. Fever in acute stroke worsens prognosis. A prospective study. *Stroke* 1995;26(11):2040–3.

Baharoglu MI, Cordonnier C, Al-Shahi Salman R, de Gans K, Koopman MM, Brand A, Majoie CB, Beenen LF, Marquering HA, Vermeulen M, Nederkoorn PJ, de Haan RJ, Roos YB; PATCH Investigators. Platelet transfusion versus standard care after acute stroke due to spontaneous cerebral haemorrhage associated with antiplatelet therapy (PATCH): a randomised, open-label, phase 3 trial. *Lancet* 2016;387(10038):2605–13.

Barber PA, Pridmore HM, Krishnamurthy V, Roberts S, Spriggs DA, Carter KN, Anderson NE. Cannabis, ischemic stroke, and transient ischemic attack: a case-control study. *Stroke* 2013;44(8):2327–9.

Bartolomei F, Nicoli F, Swiader L, Gastaut JL. Ischemic cerebral vascular stroke after heroin sniffing. A new case. *Presse Med* 1992;21(21):983–6.

Batchelor JS, Grayson A. A meta-analysis to determine the effect on survival of platelet transfusions in patients with either spontaneous or traumatic antiplatelet medication-associated intracranial haemorrhage. *BMJ Open* 2012;2(2):e000588.

Benoilid A, Collongues N, de Seze J, Blanc F. Heroin inhalation-induced unilateral complete hippocampal stroke. *Neurocase* 2013;19(4):313–5.

Berkhemer OA, Fransen PS, Beumer D, van den Berg LA, Lingsma HF, Yoo AJ, Schonewille WJ, Vos JA, Nederkoorn PJ, Wermer MJ, van Walderveen MA, Staals J, Hofmeijer J, van Oostayen JA, Lycklama à Nijeholt GJ, Boiten J, Brouwer PA, Emmer BJ, de Bruijn SF, van Dijk LC, Kappelle LJ, Lo RH, van Dijk EJ, de Vries J, de Kort PL, van Rooij WJ, van den Berg JS, van Hasselt BA, Aerden LA, Dallinga RJ, Visser MC, Bot JC, Vroomen PC, Eshghi O, Schreuder TH, Heijboer RJ, Keizer K, Tielbeek AV, den Hertog HM, Gerrits DG, van den Berg-Vos RM, Karas GB, Steyerberg EW, Flach HZ, Marquering HA, Sprengers ME, Jenniskens SF, Beenen LF, van den Berg R, Koudstaal PJ, van Zwam WH, Roos YB, van der Lugt A, van Oostenbrugge RJ, Majoie CB, Dippel DW; MR CLEAN Investigators. A randomized trial of intraarterial treatment for acute ischemic stroke. *N Engl J Med* 2015;372(1):11–20.

Bolz J, Meves SH, Kara K, Reinacher-Schick A, Gold R, Krogias C. Multiple cerebral infarctions in a young patient with heroin-induced hypereosinophilic syndrome. *J Neurol Sci* 2015;356(1–2):193–5..

Boyko OB, Burger PC, Heinz ER. Pathological and radiological correlation of subarachnoid hemorrhage in phencyclidine abuse. Case report. *J Neurosurg* 1987;67(3):446–8.

Boysen G, Christensen H. Stroke severity determines body temperature in acute stroke. *Stroke* 2001;32(2):413–7.

Brander PE, Tukiainen P. Acute eosinophilic pneumonia in a heroin smoker. *Eur Respir J* 1993;6(5):750–2.

Broderick J, Brott T, Duldner J, Tomsick T, Leach A. Initial and recurrent bleeding are the major causes of death following subarachnoid hemorrhage. *Stroke* 1994;25:1342–7.

Broessner G, Beer R, Lackner P, Helbok R, Fischer M, Pfausler B, Rhorer J, Küppers-Tiedt L, Schneider D, Schmutzhard E. Prophylactic, endovascularly based, long-term normothermia in ICU patients with severe cerebrovascular disease: bicenter prospective, randomized trial. *Stroke* 2009;40(12):e657–65.

Brott T, Broderick J, Kothari R, Barsan W, Tomsick T, Sauerbeck L, Spilker J, Duldner J, Khoury J. Early hemorrhage growth in patients with intracerebral hemorrhage. *Stroke* 1997;28:1–5.

Brust JC. Vasculitis owing to substance abuse. *Neurol Clin* 1997;15(4):945–57.

Büttner A, Mall G, Penning R, Weis S. The neuropathology of heroin abuse. *Forensic Sci Int* 2000;113(1–3):435–42.

Campbell BC, Mitchell PJ, Kleinig TJ, Dewey HM, Churilov L, Yassi N, Yan B, Dowling RJ, Parsons MW, Oxley TJ, Wu TY, Brooks M, Simpson MA, Miteff F, Levi CR, Krause M, Harrington TJ, Faulder KC, Steinfort BS, Priglinger M, Ang T, Scroop R, Barber PA, McGuinness B, Wijeratne T, Phan TG, Chong W, Chandra RV, Bladin CF, Badve M, Rice H, de Villiers L, Ma H, Desmond PM, Donnan GA, Davis SM; EXTEND-IA Investigators. Endovascular therapy for ischemic stroke with perfusion-imaging selection. *N Engl J Med* 2015;372(11):1009–18.

Case records of the Massachusetts General Hospital. Weekly clinicopathological exercises. Case 27-1993. A 32-year-old man with the sudden onset of a right-sided headache and left hemiplegia and hemianesthesia. *N Engl J Med* 1993;329(2):117–24.

Castillo J, Dávalos A, Marrugat J, Noya M. Timing for fever-related brain damage in acute ischemic stroke. *Stroke* 1998;29(12):2455–60.

Castillo J, Leira R, García MM, Serena J, Blanco M, Dávalos A. Blood pressure decrease during the acute phase of ischemic stroke is associated with brain injury and poor stroke outcome. *Stroke* 2004;35(2):520–6.

Chambers IR, Banister K, Mendelow AD. Intracranial pressure within a developing intracerebral haemorrhage. *Br J Neurosurg* 2001;15(2):140–1.

Cheng YC, Ryan KA, Qadwai SA, Shah J, Sparks MJ, Wozniak MA, Stern BJ, Phipps MS, Cronin CA, Magder LS, Cole JW, Kittner SJ. Cocaine use and risk of ischemic stroke in young adults. *Stroke* 2016;47(4):918–22.

Conway JE, Tamargo RJ. Cocaine use is an independent risk factor for cerebral vasospasm after aneurysmal subarachnoid hemorrhage. *Stroke* 2001;32(10):2338–43.

Da Pian R, Bazzan A, Pasqualin A. Surgical versus medical treatment of spontaneous posterior fossa haematomas: a cooperative study on 205 cases. *Neurol Res* 1984;6(3):145–51.

Daras MD, Tuchman AJ, Koppel BS, Samkoff LM, Weitzner I, Marc J. Neurovascular complications of cocaine. *Acta Neurol Scand* 1994;90(2):124–9.

Daras MD, Orrego JJ, Akfirat GL, Samkoff LM, Koppel BS. Bilateral symmetrical basal ganglia infarction after intravenous use of cocaine and heroin. *Clin Imaging* 2001;25(1):12–4.

Davis SM, Broderick J, Hennerici M, Brun NC, Diringer MN, Mayer SA, Begtrup K, Steiner T; Recombinant Activated Factor VII intracerebral hemorrhage trial investigators. hematoma growth is a determinant of mortality and poor outcome after intracerebral hemorrhage. *Neurology* 2006;66(8):1175–81.

de Ridder IR, den Hertog HM, van Gemert HM, Schreuder AH, Ruitenberg A, Maasland EL, Saxena R, van Tuijl JH, Jansen BP, Van den Berg-Vos RM, Vermeij F, Koudstaal PJ, Kappelle LJ, Algra A, van der Worp HB, Dippel DW; Trial organization. PAIS 2 (Paracetamol [Acetaminophen] in Stroke 2): results of a randomized, double-blind placebo-controlled clinical trial. *Stroke* 2017;48(4):977–982.

Demaerschalk BM, Kleindorfer DO, Adeoye OM, Demchuk AM, Fugate JE, Grotta JC, Khalessi AA, Levy EI, Palesch YY, Prabhakaran S, Saposnik G, Saver JL, Smith EE; American Heart Association Stroke Council and Council on Epidemiology and Prevention. Scientific rationale for the inclusion and exclusion criteria for intravenous alteplase in acute ischemic stroke: a statement for healthcare professionals from the American Heart Association/American Stroke Association. *Stroke* 2016;47(2):581–641.

den Hertog HM, van der Worp HB, van Gemert HM, Algra A, Kappelle LJ, van Gijn J, Koudstaal PJ, Dippel DW; PAIS Investigators. The Paracetamol (Acetaminophen) in Stroke (PAIS) trial: a multicentre, randomised, placebo-controlled, phase III trial. *Lancet Neurol* 2009;8(5):434–40.

Diringer MN, Edwards DF, Zazulia AR. Hydrocephalus: a previously unrecognized predictor of poor outcome from supratentorial intracerebral hemorrhage. *Stroke* 1998;29(7):1352–7.

Ducros A, Boukobza M, Porcher R, Sarov M, Valade D, Bousser MG. The clinical and radiological spectrum of reversible cerebral vasoconstriction syndrome. A prospective series of 67 patients. *Brain* 2007;130(Pt 12):3091–101.

Eerenberg ES, Kamphuisen PW, Sijpkens MK, Meijers JC, Buller HR, Levi M. Reversal of rivaroxaban and dabigatran by prothrombin complex concentrate: a randomized, placebo-controlled, crossover study in healthy subjects. *Circulation* 2011;124(14):1573–9.

Esse K, Fossati-Bellani M, Traylor A, Martin-Schild S. Epidemic of illicit drug use, mechanisms of action/addiction and stroke as a health hazard. *Brain Behav* 2011;1(1):44–54.

Etminan N, Macdonald RL. Management of aneurysmal subarachnoid hemorrhage. *Handb Clin Neurol* 2017;140:195–228.

Fam MD, Hanley D, Stadnik A, Zeineddine HA, Girard R, Jesselson M, Cao Y, Money L, McBee N, Bistran-Hall AJ, Mould WA, Lane K, Camarata PJ, Zuccarello M, Awad IA. Surgical performance in minimally invasive surgery plus recombinant tissue plasminogen activator for intracerebral hemorrhage evacuation phase III clinical trial. *Neurosurgery* 2017. doi: 10.1093/neuros/nyx123. [Epub ahead of print].

Fan JS, Huang HH, Chen YC, Yen DH, Kao WF, Huang MS, Huang CI, Lee CH. Emergency department neurologic deterioration in patients with spontaneous intracerebral hemorrhage: incidence, predictors, and prognostic significance. *Acad Emerg Med* 2012;19(2):133–8.

Firsching R, Huber M, Frowein RA. Cerebellar haemorrhage: management and prognosis. *Neurosurg Rev* 1991;14(3):191–4.

Fonseca AC, Ferro JM. Drug abuse and stroke. *Curr Neurol Neurosci Rep* 2013;13(2):325.

Fredericks RK, Lefkowitz DS, Challa VR, Troost BT. Cerebral vasculitis associated with cocaine abuse. *Stroke* 1991;22(11):1437–9.

Ginsberg MD, Busto R. Combating hyperthermia in acute stroke: a significant clinical concern. *Stroke* 1998;29(2):529–34.

Gledhill JA, Moore DF, Bell D, Henry JA. Subarachnoid haemorrhage associated with MDMA abuse. *J Neurol Neurosurg Psychiatry* 1993;56(9):1036–7.

Goodnough LT, Shander A. How I treat warfarin-associated coagulopathy in patients with intracerebral hemorrhage. *Blood* 2011;117(23):6091–9.

Goyal M, Demchuk AM, Menon BK, Eesa M, Rempel JL, Thornton J, Roy D, Jovin TG, Willinsky RA, Sapkota BL, Dowlatshahi D, Frei DF, Kamal NR, Montanera WJ, Poppe AY, Ryckborst KJ, Silver FL, Shuaib A, Tampieri D, Williams D, Bang OY, Baxter BW, Burns PA, Choe H, Heo JH, Holmstedt CA, Jankowitz B, Kelly M, Linares G, Mandzia JL, Shankar J, Sohn SI, Swartz RH, Barber PA, Coutts SB, Smith EE, Morrish WF, Weill A, Subramaniam S, Mitha AP, Wong JH, Lowerison MW, Sajobi TT, Hill MD; ESCAPE Trial Investigators. Randomized assessment of rapid endovascular treatment of ischemic stroke. *N Engl J Med* 2015;372(11):1019–30.

Grotta J, Pasteur W, Khwaja G, Hamel T, Fisher M, Ramirez A. Elective intubation for neurologic deterioration after stroke. *Neurology* 1995;45(4):640–4.

Hackam DG. Cannabis and stroke: systematic appraisal of case reports. *Stroke* 2015;46(3):852–6.

Hadley C, Haneef Mohamed AW, Singhal A. Central nervous system fungal infection in a young male with a history of intravenous drug abuse and hepatitis C. *Radiol Case Rep* 2017;12(3):590–6.

Hagan IG, Burney K. Radiology of recreational drug abuse. *Radiographics* 2007;27(4):919–40.

Hajat C, Hajat S, Sharma P. Effects of poststroke pyrexia on stroke outcome : a meta-analysis of studies in patients. *Stroke* 2000;31(2):410–4.

Hanley DF, Thompson RE, Muschelli J, Rosenblum M, McBee N, Lane K, Bistran-Hall AJ, Mayo SW, Keyl P, Gandhi D, Morgan TC, Ullman N, Mould WA, Carhuapoma JR, Kase C, Ziai W, Thompson CB, Yenokyan G, Huang E, Broaddus WC, Graham RS, Aldrich EF, Dodd R, Wijman C, Caron JL, Huang J, Camarata P, Mendelow AD, Gregson B, Janis S, Vespa P, Martin N, Awad I, Zuccarello M; MISTIE Investigators. Safety and efficacy of minimally invasive surgery plus alteplase in intracerebral haemorrhage evacuation (MISTIE): a randomised, controlled, open-label, phase 2 trial. *Lancet Neurol* 2016;15(12):1228–37.

Hemphill JC 3rd, Greenberg SM, Anderson CS, Becker K, Bendok BR, Cushman M, Fung GL, Goldstein JN, Macdonald RL, Mitchell PH, Scott PA, Selim MH, Woo D; American Heart Association Stroke Council; Council on Cardiovascular and Stroke Nursing; Council on Clinical Cardiology. Guidelines for the management of spontaneous intracerebral hemorrhage: a guideline for healthcare professionals from the American Heart Association/American Stroke Association. *Stroke* 2015;46(7):2032–60.

Hirsh J, Bauer KA, Donati MB, Gould M, Samama MM, Weitz JI. Parenteral anticoagulants: American college of chest physicians evidence-based clinical practice guidelines (8th Edition). *Chest* 2008;133(6 Suppl):141S–159S.

Ho EL, Josephson SA, Lee HS, Smith WS. Cerebrovascular complications of methamphetamine abuse. *Neurocrit Care* 2009;10(3):295–305.

Howington JU, Kutz SC, Wilding GE, Awasthi D. Cocaine use as a predictor of outcome in aneurysmal subarachnoid hemorrhage. *J Neurosurg* 2003;99(2):271–5.

Huestis MA, Tyndale RF. Designer drugs 2.0. *Clin Pharmacol Ther* 2017;101(2):152–7.

Hughes JC, McCabe M, Evans RJ. Intracranial haemorrhage associated with ingestion of 'ecstasy'. *Arch Emerg Med* 1993;10(4):372–4.

Huisman MV, Fanikos J. Idarucizumab and factor Xa reversal agents: role in hospital guidelines and protocols. *Am J Emerg Med* 2016;34(11S):46–51.

Huttner HB, Köhrmann M, Berger C, Georgiadis D, Schwab S. Influence of intraventricular hemorrhage and occlusive hydrocephalus on the long-term outcome of treated patients with basal ganglia hemorrhage: a case-control study. *J Neurosurg* 2006;105(3):412–7.

Huttner HB, Nagel S, Tognoni E, Köhrmann M, Jüttler E, Orakcioglu B, Schellinger PD, Schwab S, Bardutzky J. Intracerebral hemorrhage with severe ventricular involvement: lumbar drainage for communicating hydrocephalus. *Stroke* 2007;38(1):183–7.

Indave BI, Sordo L, Bravo MJ, Sarasa-Renedo A, Fernández-Balbuena S, De la Fuente L, Sonego M, Barrio G. Risk of stroke in prescription and other amphetamine-type stimulants use: a systematic review. *Drug Alcohol Rev* 2017 May 8. [Epub ahead of print].

Jauch EC, Saver JL, Adams HP Jr, Bruno A, Connors JJ, Demaerschalk BM, Khatri P, McMullan PW Jr, Qureshi AI, Rosenfield K, Scott PA, Summers DR, Wang DZ, Wintermark M, Yonas H; American Heart Association Stroke Council; Council on Cardiovascular Nursing; Council on Peripheral Vascular Disease; Council on Clinical Cardiology. Guidelines for the early management of patients with acute ischemic stroke: a guideline for healthcare professionals from the American Heart Association/American Stroke Association. *Stroke* 2013;44(3):870–947.

Jensen R, Olsen TS, Winther BB. Severe non-occlusive ischemic stroke in young heroin addicts. *Acta Neurol Scand* 1990;81(4):354–7.

Jovin TG, Chamorro A, Cobo E, de Miquel MA, Molina CA, Rovira A, San Román L, Serena J, Abilleira S, Ribó M, Millán M, Urra X, Cardona P, López-Cancio E, Tomasello A, Castaño C, Blasco J, Aja L, Dorado L, Quesada H, Rubiera M, Hernandez-Pérez M, Goyal M, Demchuk AM, von Kummer R, Gallofré M, Dávalos A; REVASCAT Trial Investigators. Thrombectomy within 8 hours after symptom onset in ischemic stroke. *N Engl J Med* 2015;372(24):2296–306.

Kamel H, Hemphill JC 3rd. Characteristics and sequelae of intracranial hypertension after intracerebral hemorrhage. *Neurocrit Care* 2012;17(2):172–6.

Kamel H, Navi BB, Nakagawa K, Hemphill JC 3rd, Ko NU. Hypertonic saline versus mannitol for the treatment of elevated intracranial pressure: a meta-analysis of randomized clinical trials. *Crit Care Med* 2011;39(3):554–9.

Kammersgaard LP, Jørgensen HS, Rungby JA, Reith J, Nakayama H, Weber UJ, Houth J, Olsen TS. Admission body temperature predicts long-term mortality after acute stroke: the Copenhagen Stroke Study. *Stroke* 2002;33(7):1759–62.

Kibayashi K, Mastri AR, Hirsch CS. Cocaine induced intracerebral hemorrhage: analysis of predisposing factors and mechanisms causing hemorrhagic strokes. *Hum Pathol* 1995;26(6):659–63.

Kissela BM, Khoury JC, Alwell K, Moomaw CJ, Woo D, Adeoye O, Flaherty ML, Khatri P, Ferioli S, De Los Rios La Rosa F, Broderick JP, Kleindorfer DO. Age at stroke: temporal trends in stroke incidence in a large, biracial population. *Neurology* 2012;79(17):1781–7.

Klonoff DC, Andrews BT, Obana WG. Stroke associated with cocaine use. *Arch Neurol* 1989;46(9):989–93.

Koch S, Sacco RL. Cocaine-associated stroke: some new insights? *Nat Clin Pract Neurol* 2008;4(11):579.

Kurz KD, Ringstad G, Odland A, Advani R, Farbu E, Kurz MW. Radiological imaging in acute ischaemic stroke. *Eur J Neurol* 2016;23(Suppl 1):8–17.

Leonardi-Bee J, Bath PM, Phillips SJ, Sandercock PA; IST Collaborative Group.. Blood pressure and clinical outcomes in the International Stroke Trial. *Stroke* 2002;33(5): 1315–20.

Leong LB, David TK. Is platelet transfusion effective in patients taking antiplatelet agents who suffer an intracranial hemorrhage? *J Emerg Med* 2015 Apr 3. pii: S0736-4679(15)0 0151-1.

Levine SR, Brust JC, Futrell N, Ho KL, Blake D, Millikan CH, Brass LM, Fayad P, Schultz LR, Selwa JF, et al. Cerebrovascular complications of the use of the "crack" form of alkaloidal cocaine. *N Engl J Med* 1990;323(11):699–704.

Lieberman AN, Bloom W, Kishore PS, Lin JP. Carotid artery occlusion following ingestion of LSD. *Stroke* 1974;5(2):213–5.

Low MS, Vilcassim S, Fedele P, Grigoriadis G. Anabolic androgenic steroids, an easily forgotten cause of polycythaemia and cerebral infarction. *Intern Med J* 2016;46(4):497–9.

Lubetsky A, Yonath H, Olchovsky D, Loebstein R, Halkin H, Ezra D. Comparison of oral vs intravenous phytonadione (vitamin K1) in patients with excessive anticoagulation: a prospective randomized controlled study. *Arch Intern Med* 2003;163(20):2469–73.

Manchanda S, Connolly MJ. Cerebral infarction in association with Ecstasy abuse. *Postgrad Med J* 1993;69(817):874–5.

Marlu R, Hodaj E, Paris A, Albaladejo P, Cracowski JL, Pernod G. Effect of non-specific reversal agents on anticoagulant activity of dabigatran and rivaroxaban: a randomised crossover ex vivo study in healthy volunteers. *Thromb Haemost* 2012;108(2):217–24.

Martin M, Conlon LW. Does platelet transfusion improve outcomes in patients with spontaneous or traumatic intracerebral hemorrhage? *Ann Emerg Med* 2013;61(1):58–61.

Martin-Schild S, Albright KC, Misra V, Philip M, Barreto AD, Hallevi H, Grotta JC, Savitz SI. Intravenous tissue plasminogen activator in patients with cocaine-associated acute ischemic stroke. *Stroke* 2009;40(11):3635–7.

Martin-Schild S, Albright KC, Hallevi H, Barreto AD, Philip M, Misra V, Grotta JC, Savitz SI. Intracerebral hemorrhage in cocaine users. *Stroke* 2010;41(4):680–4.

Mateo I, Pinedo A, Gomez-Beldarrain M, Basterretxea JM, Garcia-Monco JC. Recurrent stroke associated with cannabis use. *J Neurol Neurosurg Psychiatry* 2005;76(3):435–7.

McCarron MM, Schulze BW, Thompson GA, Conder MC, Goetz WA. Acute phencyclidine intoxication: clinical patterns, complications, and treatment. *Ann Emerg Med* 1981;10(6):290–7.

McGee SM, McGee DN, McGee MB. Spontaneous intracerebral hemorrhage related to methamphetamine abuse: autopsy findings and clinical correlation. *Am J Forensic Med Pathol* 2004;25(4):334–7.

Menon BK, d'Esterre CD, Qazi EM, Almekhlafi M, Hahn L, Demchuk AM, Goyal M. Multiphase CT angiography: a new tool for the imaging triage of patients with acute ischemic stroke. *Radiology* 2015;275(2):510–20.

Merino JG, Warach S. Imaging of acute stroke. *Nat Rev Neurol* 2010;6(10):560–71.

Middleton S, McElduff P, Ward J, Grimshaw JM, Dale S, D'Este C, Drury P, Griffiths R, Cheung NW, Quinn C, Evans M, Cadilhac D, Levi C; QASC Trialists Group. Implementation of evidence-based treatment protocols to manage fever, hyperglycaemia, and swallowing dysfunction in acute stroke (QASC): a cluster randomised controlled trial. *Lancet* 2011;378(9804):1699–706.

Mokri B. The Monro-Kellie hypothesis: applications in CSF volume depletion. *Neurology* 2001;56(12):1746–8.

Moon JS, Janjua N, Ahmed S, Kirmani JF, Harris-Lane P, Jacob M, Ezzeddine MA, Qureshi AI. Prehospital neurologic deterioration in patients with intracerebral hemorrhage. *Crit Care Med* 2008;36:172–5.

Mullen MT, Kasner SE, Messé SR. Seizures do not increase in-hospital mortality after intracerebral hemorrhage in the nationwide inpatient sample. *Neurocrit Care* 2013;19(1):19–24.

Niehaus L, Meyer BU. Bilateral borderzone brain infarctions in association with heroin abuse. *J Neurol Sci* 1998;160(2):180–2.

NIH National Institute on Drug Abuse. *National Survey on Drug Use and Health survey.* 2015. https://www.drugabuse.gov/national-survey-drug-use-health, Accessed July 26, 2017.

Ohkuma H, Tsurutani H, Suzuki S. Incidence and significance of early aneurysmal rebleeding before neurosurgical or neurological management. *Stroke* 2001;32:1176–80.

Okumura K, Ohya Y, Maehara A, Wakugami K, Iseki K, Takishita S. Effects of blood pressure levels on case fatality after acute stroke. *J Hypertens* 2005;23(6):1217–23.

Olson KR. What is the best treatment for acute calcium channel blocker overdose? *Ann Emerg Med* 2013;62:259–61.

Oyesiku NM, Colohan AR, Barrow DL, Reisner A. Cocaine-induced aneurysmal rupture: an emergent negative factor in the natural history of intracranial aneurysms? *Neurosurgery* 1993;32(4):518–25.

Passero S, Rocchi R, Rossi S, Ulivelli M, Vatti G. Seizures after spontaneous supratentorial intracerebral hemorrhage. *Epilepsia* 2002;43(10):1175–80.

Pereira J, Sáez CG, Pallavicini J, Panes O, Pereira-Flores K, Cabreras MJ, Massardo T, Mezzano D. Platelet activation in chronic cocaine users: effect of short term abstinence. *Platelets* 2011;22(8):596–601.

Petitti DB, Sidney S, Quesenberry C, Bernstein A. Stroke and cocaine or amphetamine use. *Epidemiology* 1998;9(6):596–600.

Powers WJ, Derdeyn CP, Biller J, Coffey CS, Hoh BL, Jauch EC, Johnston KC, Johnston SC, Khalessi AA, Kidwell CS, Meschia JF, Ovbiagele B, Yavagal DR; American Heart Association Stroke Council. American Heart Association/American Stroke Association Focused Update of the 2013 Guidelines for the early management of patients with acute ischemic stroke regarding endovascular treatment: a guideline for healthcare professionals from the American Heart Association/American Stroke Association. *Stroke* 2015;46(10):3020–35.

Prasad K, Krishnan PR. Fever is associated with doubling of odds of short-term mortality in ischemic stroke: an updated meta-analysis. *Acta Neurol Scand* 2010;122(6):404–8.

Qureshi AI, Ezzeddine MA, Nasar A, Suri MF, Kirmani JF, Hussein HM, Divani AA, Reddi AS. Prevalence of elevated blood pressure in 563,704 adult patients with stroke presenting to the ED in the United States. *Am J Emerg Med* 2007;25:32–8.

Qureshi AI, Palesch YY, Barsan WG, Hanley DF, Hsu CY, Martin RL, Moy CS, Silbergleit R, Steiner T, Suarez JI, Toyoda K, Wang Y, Yamamoto H, Yoon BW; ATACH-2 trial investigators and the neurological emergency treatment trials network. intensive blood-pressure lowering in patients with acute cerebral hemorrhage. *N Engl J Med* 2016;375(11):1033–43.

Ray B, Keyrouz SG. Management of anticoagulant-related intracranial hemorrhage: an evidence-based review. *Crit Care* 2014;18(3):223.

Reith J, Jørgensen HS, Pedersen PM, Nakayama H, Raaschou HO, Jeppesen LL, Olsen TS. Body temperature in acute stroke: relation to stroke severity, infarct size, mortality, and outcome. *Lancet* 1996;347(8999):422–5.

Renard D, Taieb G, Gras-Combe G, Labauge P. Cannabis-related myocardial infarction and cardioembolic stroke. *J Stroke Cerebrovasc Dis* 2012;21(1):82–3.

Richards JR, Garber D, Laurin EG, Albertson TE, Derlet RW, Amsterdam EA, Olson KR, Ramoska EA, Lange RA. Treatment of cocaine cardiovascular toxicity: a systematic review. *Clin Toxicol (Phila)* 2016;54(5):345–64.

Rincon F, Lyden P, Mayer SA. Relationship between temperature, hematoma growth, and functional outcome after intracerebral hemorrhage. *Neurocrit Care* 2013;18(1):45–53.

Rost NS, Masrur S, Pervez MA, Viswanathan A, Schwamm LH. Unsuspected coagulopathy rarely prevents IV thrombolysis in acute ischemic stroke. *Neurology* 2009;73(23):1957–62.

Rumalla K, Reddy AY, Mittal MK. Recreational marijuana use and acute ischemic stroke: a population-based analysis of hospitalized patients in the United States. *J Neurol Sci* 2016;364:191–6.

Rumalla K, Reddy AY, Mittal MK. Association of recreational marijuana use with aneurysmal subarachnoid hemorrhage. *J Stroke Cerebrovasc Dis* 2016;25(2):452–60.

Sáez CG, Olivares P, Pallavicini J, Panes O, Moreno N, Massardo T, Mezzano D, Pereira J. Increased number of circulating endothelial cells and plasma markers of endothelial damage in chronic cocaine users. *Thromb Res* 2011;128(4):e18–23.

Salanova V, Taubner R. Intracerebral haemorrhage and vasculitis secondary to amphetamine use. *Postgrad Med J* 1984;60(704):429–30.

Santamarina RD, Besocke AG, Romano LM, Ioli PL, Gonorazky SE. Ischemic stroke related to anabolic abuse. *Clin Neuropharmacol* 2008;31(2):80–5.

Sarode R, Milling TJ Jr, Refaai MA, Mangione A, Schneider A, Durn BL, Goldstein JN. Efficacy and safety of a 4-factor prothrombin complex concentrate in patients on vitamin K antagonists presenting with major bleeding: a randomized, plasma-controlled, phase IIIb study. *Circulation* 2013;128(11):1234–43.

Saver JL, Goyal M, Bonafe A, Diener HC, Levy EI, Pereira VM, Albers GW, Cognard C, Cohen DJ, Hacke W, Jansen O, Jovin TG, Mattle HP, Nogueira RG, Siddiqui AH, Yavagal DR, Baxter BW, Devlin TG, Lopes DK, Reddy VK, du Mesnil de Rochemont R, Singer OC, Jahan R; SWIFT PRIME investigators. Stent-retriever thrombectomy after intravenous t-PA vs. t-PA alone in stroke. *N Engl J Med* 2015;372(24):2285–95.

Saxena M, Young P, Pilcher D, Bailey M, Harrison D, Bellomo R, Finfer S, Beasley R, Hyam J, Menon D, Rowan K, Myburgh J. Early temperature and mortality in critically ill patients with acute neurological diseases: trauma and stroke differ from infection. *Intensive Care Med* 2015;41(5):823–32.

Schwarz S, Häfner K, Aschoff A, Schwab S. Incidence and prognostic significance of fever following intracerebral hemorrhage. *Neurology* 2000;54(2):354–61.

Shibata S, Mori K, Sekine I, Suyama H. Subarachnoid and intracerebral hemorrhage associated with necrotizing angiitis due to methamphetamine abuse--an autopsy case. *Neurol Med Chir (Tokyo)* 1991;31(1):49–52.

Shimada Y, Yoritaka A, Tanaka Y, Miyamoto N, Ueno Y, Hattori N, Takao U. Cerebral infarction in a young man using high-dose anabolic steroids. *J Stroke Cerebrovasc Dis* 2012;21(8):906.e9–11.

Simpson RK Jr, Fischer DK, Narayan RK, Cech DA, Robertson CS. Intravenous cocaine abuse and subarachnoid haemorrhage: effect on outcome. *Br J Neurosurg* 1990;4(1):27–30.

Singh NN, Pan Y, Muengtaweeponsa S, Geller TJ, Cruz-Flores S. Cannabis-related stroke: case series and review of literature. *J Stroke Cerebrovasc Dis* 2012;21(7):555–60.

Sobel J, Espinas OE, Friedman SA. Carotid artery obstruction following LSD capsule ingestion. *Arch Intern Med* 1971;127(2):290–1.

Sofuoglu M, Brown S, Babb DA, Pentel PR, Hatsukami DK. Effects of labetalol treatment on the physiological and subjective response to smoked cocaine. *Pharmacol Biochem Behav* 2000;65(2):255–9.

Sordo L, Indave BI, Barrio G, Degenhardt L, de la Fuente L, Bravo MJ. Cocaine use and risk of stroke: a systematic review. *Drug Alcohol Depend* 2014;142:1–13.

Storen EC, Wijdicks EF, Crum BA, Schultz G. Moyamoya-like vasculopathy from cocaine dependency. *AJNR Am J Neuroradiol* 2000;21(6):1008–10.

Szaflarski JP, Rackley AY, Kleindorfer DO, Khoury J, Woo D, Miller R, Alwell K, Broderick JP, Kissela BM. Incidence of seizures in the acute phase of stroke: a population-based study. *Epilepsia* 2008;49(6):974–81.

Tang C, Zhang TS, Zhou LF. Risk factors for rebleeding of aneurysmal subarachnoid hemorrhage: a meta-analysis. *PLoS One* 2014;9(6):e99536.

Thanvi BR, Treadwell SD. Cannabis and stroke: is there a link? *Postgrad Med J* 2009;85(1000):80–3.

Tolani AT, Yeom KW, Elbers J. Focal cerebral arteriopathy: the face with many names. *Pediatr Neurol* 2015;53(3):247–52.

Toossi S, Hess CP, Hills NK, Josephson SA. Neurovascular complications of cocaine use at a tertiary stroke center. *J Stroke Cerebrovasc Dis* 2010;19(4):273–8.

van Loon J, Van Calenbergh F, Goffin J, Plets C. Controversies in the management of spontaneous cerebellar haemorrhage. A consecutive series of 49 cases and review of the literature. *Acta Neurochir (Wien)* 1993;122(3–4):187–93.

Vannemreddy P, Caldito G, Willis B, Nanda A. Influence of cocaine on ruptured intracranial aneurysms: a case control study of poor prognostic indicators. *J Neurosurg* 2008;108(3):470–6.

Vemmos KN, Tsivgoulis G, Spengos K, Zakopoulos N, Synetos A, Manios E, Konstantopoulou P, Mavrikakis M. U-shaped relationship between mortality and admission blood pressure in patients with acute stroke. *J Intern Med* 2004;255(2):257–65.

Vila N, Chamorro A. Ballistic movements due to ischemic infarcts after intravenous heroin overdose: report of two cases. *Clin Neurol Neurosurg* 1997;99(4):259–62.

Wang Y, Lim LL, Levi C, Heller RF, Fisher J. Influence of admission body temperature on stroke mortality. *Stroke* 2000;31(2):404–9.

Watson HG, Baglin T, Laidlaw SL, Makris M, Preston FE. A comparison of the efficacy and rate of response to oral and intravenous Vitamin K in reversal of over-anticoagulation with warfarin. *Br J Haematol* 2001;115(1):145–9.

Westover AN, McBride S, Haley RW. Stroke in young adults who abuse amphetamines or cocaine: a population-based study of hospitalized patients. *Arch Gen Psychiatry* 2007;64(4):495–502.

Wolfe TJ, Torbey MT. Management of intracranial pressure. *Curr Neurol Neurosci Rep* 2009;9(6):477–85.

Wolff V, Lauer V, Rouyer O, Sellal F, Meyer N, Raul JS, Sabourdy C, Boujan F, Jahn C, Beaujeux R, Marescaux C. Cannabis use, ischemic stroke, and multifocal intracranial vasoconstriction: a prospective study in 48 consecutive young patients. *Stroke* 2011;42(6):1778–80.

Wooten MR, Khangure MS, Murphy MJ. Intracerebral hemorrhage and vasculitis related to ephedrine abuse. *Ann Neurol* 1983;13(3):337–40.

1.15 PULMONARY DISEASE

Christopher R. Tainter and Gabriel Wardi

1.15.1 Pulmonary Manifestations of Illicit Drug Use

The alveolar capillary membrane is a unique interface between the environment and the intravascular space, which is commonly exploited as a convenient mechanism for rapid delivery into the bloodstream by smoking and/or inhalation. The distribution, timing, and mechanism for pulmonary complications related to illicit drug use depend on a variety of factors. Smaller inhaled particles (<2.5 μm) may reach the distal airways, while larger particles (2.5–6 μm) may deposit in the larger airways.[1] Some effects are immediate (e.g., bronchoconstriction), while others may develop over time or with repeated exposure (e.g., emphysema). Direct exposure from inhalation or smoking may occur, but injury can also develop through hematogenous exposure or effects secondary to intoxication, such as aspiration injury while unconscious. Barotrauma (most commonly pneumothorax or pneumomediastinum) may occur as a result of dramatic changes in intrathoracic pressure from vigorous coughing, forcible inhalation, or repeated Valsalva maneuvers in an attempt to increase absorption.[2] One series of 241 cases described the following rates of pulmonary complications associated with illicit drugs: acute respiratory depression (56.8%), aspiration pneumonia (12.9%), pulmonary edema (10.0%), bacterial pneumonia (7.5%), lung abscess (5.0%), septic pulmonary emboli (4.6%), atelectasis (2.5%), and pulmonary fibrosis/granulomatosis (0.8%).[3] Table 1.15.1 describes the relative frequency of several complications with more popular inhaled drugs.

The most commonly smoked agents include marijuana, heroin, cocaine, and other stimulants (including methamphetamine and newer engineered psychotropics such as "bath salts"). Marijuana, prepared from the *Cannabis* plant, is increasingly available due in part to its legalization in many states. It may be smoked as a cigarette, from a pipe, or in an electronic vaporizer (vaping). Heroin is usually smoked by heating a mixture of heroin and caffeine on foil and then inhaling the resultant vapor through a straw. Alkyloidal cocaine ("freebase" or "crack") is also heated and the vapors inhaled, as is crystallized methamphetamine. Ascribing a specific pulmonary dysfunction or pathology to a specific drug is difficult, because most drug users consistently use more than one drug, and by the nature of their unregulated production, illegal drugs are

TABLE 1.15.1
Mechanisms of Pulmonary Complications of Common Illicit Drugs (Reproduced)[4]

Pulmonary complications	Mechanisms of injury	Heroin	Cocaine	Amphetamine-type	Marijuana
Aspiration pneumonia	Impairment of consciousness, alteration of gag reflexes	+++	++	+	±
Pulmonary infections	Impaired alveolar macrophages, embolization of valve vegetation or infected thrombi	+++	+	0	0
Cardiogenic pulmonary edema	Cardiac dysfunction, myocardial ischemia, arrhythmia, cardiomyopathy	+	++	++	±
Noncardiogenic pulmonary edema	Alveolar epithelial damage, anaphylactoid mechanisms	++	++	+	+
Excessive bronchial reactivity	Airway mucosal irritation	±	++	±	+
Hypersensitivity pneumonitis	Immunologic response to antigen	+	++	±	±
Bronchiolitis obliterans organizing pneumonia	Inflammatory narrowing of terminal bronchioles	0	+	0	±
Pulmonary granulomatosis	Reaction to foreign bodies	+	++	+	+
Eosinophilic lung disease	Alveolar hemorrhage + hypersensitivity pneumonitis	0	+	0	0
Pulmonary hemorrhage	Mucosal ulceration, pulmonary infarction, diffuse alveolar capillary injury	±	++	+	±
Pulmonary fibrosis	Diffuse interstitial fibrosis	0	+	0	0
Emphysema	Panlobular alveoli destruction, synergism with tobacco and combustion products	+	++	0	++
Pulmonary arterial hypertension	Vasoconstrictor effects on pulmonary circulation, particle embolization, deregulation of mediators of vascular tone	+	+++	++	+
Barotrauma	Deep inspiration, vigorous coughing, Valsalva maneuver	+	+++	++	++

0: absent; ±: possible; +: rare; ++: common; +++: frequent.

often compounded with additional materials, which may cause independent injury.

"Crack lung" is an acute alveolitis occurring after inhalation of freebase ("crack") cocaine.[5] The exact mechanism of injury is not completely understood and is likely multifactorial, including thermal injury, adrenergic stimulation, and inhalation of concomitant impurities. Eosinophilic alveolar pneumonia, as well as peripheral eosinophilia, supports the diagnosis. Supportive care is recommended, and improvement is expected after the first 24 hours. Corticosteroids are recommended when eosinophilic pneumonia is present.

Fatal and nonfatal pulmonary edema (Figure 1.15.1) have been reported in cocaine smokers who have no obvious cardiac or central nervous system disease.[6] Bronchoalveolar lavage fluid may have an elevated protein level, suggesting that the edema is due more to altered alveolar capillary permeability than to hemodynamic changes.[7] Pneumonitis, as defined by widening of the alveolar septae in the presence of a polymorphous infiltrate (lymphocytes, neutrophils, macrophages, and eosinophils) or fibrosis, was seen in one-fourth of the victims studied by Bailey et al.[8]

Noncardiogenic pulmonary edema (NCPE) is a common manifestation of severe opioid overdose.[9] It is controversial whether this is a consequence of negative pressure generated by forced inspiration against a closed glottis, a direct effect of the drug like histamine release, or even an effect of a sympathetic surge induced by a reversal agent, although the last is less likely, based on the presence of NCPE on autopsy of decedents who did not receive a reversal agent.

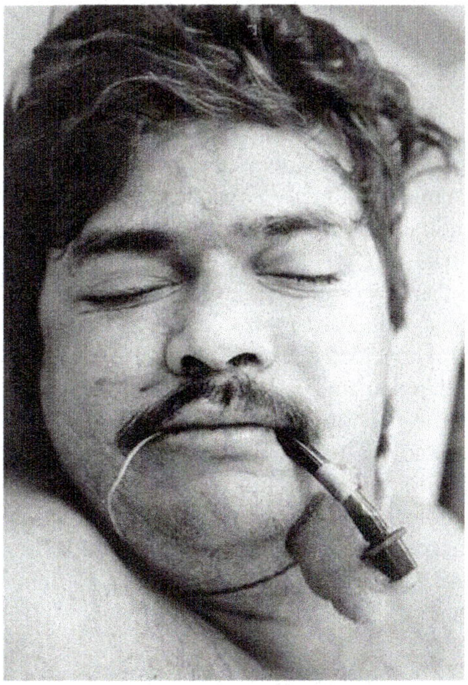

FIGURE 1.15.1 Abundant blood-tinged foam escapes from the end of the endotracheal tube in this drug abuser with pulmonary edema.

Other popular inhaled intoxicants have various adverse effects, which are usually a result of direct tissue injury. These include volatile hydrocarbons (e.g., gasoline, toluene, or solvents), ammonia, and nitrous oxide, which is commonly available as an aerosol propellant. Common symptoms include throat or bronchial irritation, pneumonitis, bronchospasm or reactive airway disease exacerbation, chest pain, and shortness of breath. Specific treatments have not been described, and supportive care is recommended.

1.15.2 Pulmonary Complications of Intravenous Drug Abuse

In addition to contaminants in illicit intravenous drug preparations, abusers may crush oral medications for intravenous injection. Methadone,[10] methylphenidate (Ritalin),[11] and propoxyphene[12] are examples of oral drugs abused in this fashion. Excipient materials from the crushed pills reach the lung and cause thrombosis, granulomatous inflammation, and fibrosis. The granulomas have numerous multinucleated giant cells and contain birefringent foreign material (Figure 1.15.2). The granulomas and foreign material impart a granular texture to the lung and may lead to pulmonary hypertension, cor pulmonale, and sudden death. In nonfatal cases, patients may present with dyspnea, hypoxemia, and diffuse micronodules apparent on their chest radiographs. Patients may demonstrate reduced diffusion across the parenchyma, and serum angiotensin-converting enzyme concentration in the lung is elevated. Macrophage infiltration and digestion of the alveolar architecture may result in a precocious panlobular emphysema, similar to that seen in alpha-1-antitrypsin deficiency.[13]

Vasculitis may occur as a result of local inflammation or hypersensitivity reactions to the drug or its counterparts. The pulmonary arteries may have medial hypertrophy, fibrointimal hyperplasia, and angiomatoid lesions (Figure 1.15.3). Cryptogenic organizing pneumonia (COP, also called bronchiolitis obliterans organizing pneumonia

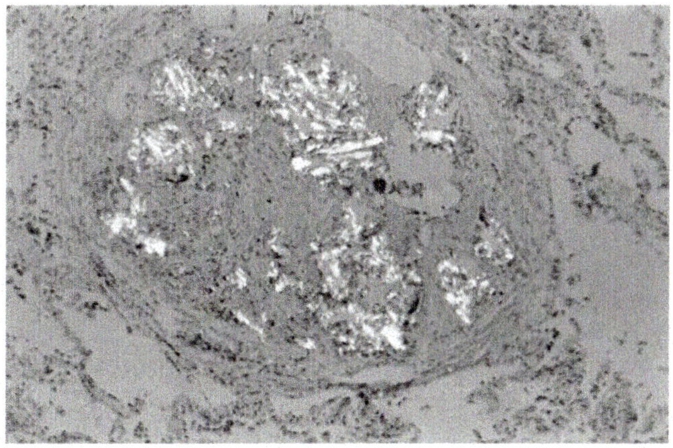

FIGURE 1.15.2 Abundant birefringent material lies within this pulmonary artery thrombus from an intravenous drug abuser (hematoxylin and eosin, polarized light, original magnification 80×).

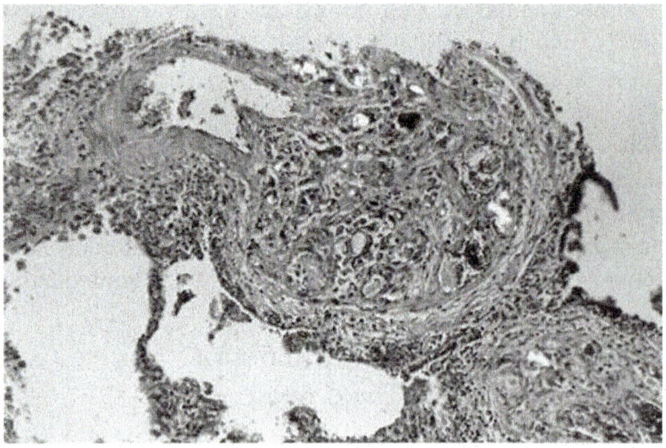

FIGURE 1.15.3 Angiomatoid lesion with birefringent talc in an intravenous drug abuser (hematoxylin and eosin, polarized light, original magnification 80×).

or BOOP) may occur as a result of proliferation of fibrinous connective tissue of the epithelium and resultant narrowing of the bronchioles. More extensive pulmonary fibrosis may also involve the interstitium and alveoli.

1.15.3 Pulmonary Hypertension

Pulmonary hypertension (PH) is defined by a mean pulmonary artery pressure (mPAP) of at least 25 mmHg at rest. The initial classification scheme was first proposed in 1973 following a sharp increase in the incidence of patients with PH, which was related to wide-spread use of an appetite suppressant, aminorex fumarate.[14] Currently, there are five classifications of PH identified by the World Health Organization (WHO), grouped by underlying pathology:[15]

Group 1: Pulmonary arterial hypertension
Group 2: PH secondary to left heart disease
Group 3: PH secondary to chronic hypoxia and/or lung disease
Group 4: PH secondary to chronic thromboembolic disease
Group 5: PH due to multiple pathologies or uncertain mechanism

Of these, only pulmonary arterial hypertension (PAH) has been linked with non-injectable illicit substance and drug use. PAH refers strictly to WHO Group I disease and is characterized by a progressive narrowing and destruction of the smaller pulmonary arteries. It is a rare condition, with an estimated incidence of 5 to 25 cases per 1 million people.[16] PAH is defined by a mPAP of at least 25 mmHg, a pulmonary wedge pressure lower than 15 mm Hg, and a pulmonary vascular resistance greater than 3.0 Wood units.[17]

In PAH, the distal pulmonary arteries (smaller than 50 microns) undergo fibrotic, hypertrophic, and inflammatory changes secondary to abnormal proliferation of fibroblasts, endothelial proliferation, and vascular smooth muscle cell growth that manifest in the deleterious remodeling of the pulmonary arterial tree. Plexiform lesions, characterized by thrombosis and fibrosis of these smaller arteries, are frequently identified at autopsy.[18] There is also a significant imbalance between pulmonary vasodilators (nitric oxide and prostacyclin) and pulmonary vasoconstrictors (endothelin-1), which further exacerbates the development of PH. Ultimately, these patients develop marked increases in pulmonary vascular resistance and a decrease in pulmonary arterial compliance, resulting in right ventricular dilation with eventual hypertrophy, impaired filling of both the left and right ventricles, resultant heart failure, and death.

Identifiable risk factors for the development of PAH include collagen vascular disease, human immunodeficiency virus (HIV) infection, schistosomiasis (the most common cause worldwide), congenital heart disease, and importantly, numerous toxins, drugs of abuse, and medications. Table 1.15.2 shows a list of the medications and toxins and associated risk for the development of PAH. Although the exact mechanism by which these drugs cause PAH is unknown, it is currently thought that alterations in growth factors secondary to use of these substances induce the development of abnormal pulmonary artery smooth muscle. In particular, serotonin and platelet-derived growth factor have been implicated as potential mediators in the pathogenesis of PAH.[19,20]

TABLE 1.15.2
Classification for Drug- and Toxin-Induced PAH (Reproduced)[15]

Definite	Possible
Aminorex	Cocaine
Fenfluramine	Phenylpropanolamine
Dexfenfluramine	Si John's wort
Toxic rapeseed oil	Cliemolherapevtx agents
Benfluorex	**Interferon α and β**
SSRIs[a]	**Amphetamine-like drugs**
Likely	**Unlikely**
Amphetamines	Oral contraceptives
L-Tryptophan	Estrogen
Methamphetamines	Cigarette smoking
Dasautinib	

[a] Selective serotonin reuptake inhibitors (SSRIs) have been demonstrated as a risk factor for the development of persistent pulmonary hypertension the newborn (PPHN) in pregnant women exposed to SSRIs (especially after 20 weeks of gestation). PPHN does not strictly belong to Group 1 (pulmonary arterial hypertension ([PAH]) but to a separated Group 1. Main modifications to the previous Danapoint classification are in **bold**.

1.15.4 Aspiration Injuries

Aspiration of orogastric material (bacteria, acid, food, etc.) can occur in victims rendered unconscious by drugs directly (e.g., opioids) or indirectly (e.g., by drug-induced

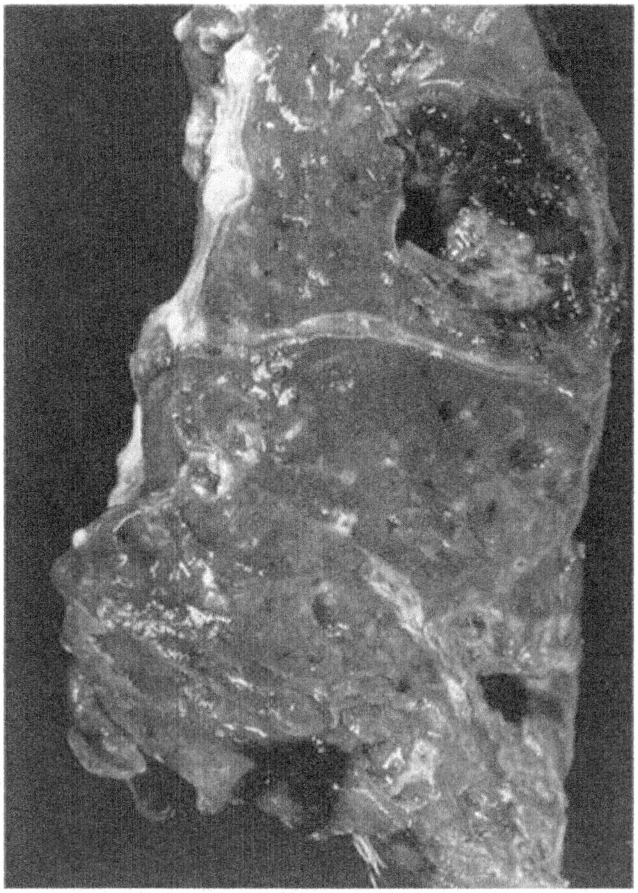

FIGURE 1.15.4 This sectioned lung has multiple abscess cavities. The victim was a 31-year-old cocaine "skin popper."

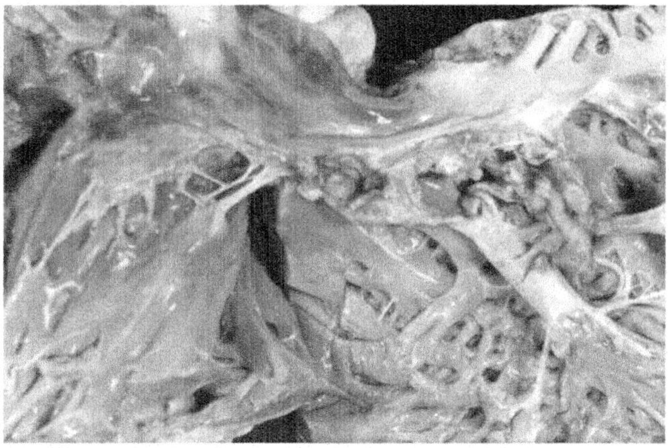

FIGURE 1.15.5 The victim had acute bacterial endocarditis of the tricuspid valve with septic thromboemboli.

seizures). The posterior segments of the upper lobes or the superior segments of the left lower lobe are commonly involved when the victim is recumbent during aspiration. The basal lung segments are affected when the victim is more upright, and the anterior segment of the right middle lobe is involved when the victim is prone or inclined forward. Chemical irritation from gastric acid (Mendelson's syndrome) may produce bronchiolitis, hemorrhagic edema, and diffuse alveolar damage.

Aspiration most commonly results in pneumonitis, although occasionally bacterial pneumonia may result, especially in chronic repeated small-volume aspiration.[21] A broad range of Gram positive and Gram negative organisms may be responsible, and it is notable that anaerobic organisms are very rarely causative, despite a historical misrepresentation.[22] Necrotizing bacteria or septic thromboemboli from tricuspid valve endocarditis can also produce multiple lung abscesses and pneumonia in the intravenous drug abuser (Figures 1.15.4 and 1.15.5).

REFERENCES

1. Pritchard JN. The influence of lung deposition on clinical response. *J Aerosol Med* 2001;14 Suppl 1:S19–26.
2. Seaman ME. Barotrauma related to inhalational drug abuse. *J Emerg Med* 1990;8(2):141–9.
3. Gottlieb LS, Boylen TC. Pulmonary complications of drug abuse. *West J Med* 1974;120(1):8–16.
4. Megarbane B, Chevillard L. The large spectrum of pulmonary complications following illicit drug use: features and mechanisms. *Chem Biol Interact* 2013;206(3):444–51.
5. Forrester JM, Steele AW, Waldron JA, et al. Crack lung: an acute pulmonary syndrome with a spectrum of clinical and histopathologic findings. *Am Rev Respir Dis* 1990;142(2):462–7.
6. Hoffman CK, Goodman PC. Pulmonary edema in cocaine smokers. *Radiology* 1989;172(2):463–5.
7. Cucco RA, Yoo OH, Cregler L, et al. Nonfatal pulmonary edema after "freebase" cocaine smoking. *Am Rev Respir Dis* 1987;136(1):179–81.
8. Bailey ME, Fraire AE, Greenberg SD, et al. Pulmonary histopathology in cocaine abusers. *Hum Pathol* 1994;25(2):203–7.
9. Dinis-Oliveira RJ, Carvalho F, Moreira R, et al. Clinical and forensic signs related to opioids abuse. *Curr Drug Abuse Rev* 2012;5(4):273–90.
10. Lamb D, Roberts G. Starch and talc emboli in drug addicts' lungs. *J Clin Pathol* 1972;25(10):876–81.
11. Stern EJ, Frank MS, Schmutz JF, et al. Panlobular pulmonary emphysema caused by i.v. injection of methylphenidate (Ritalin): findings on chest radiographs and CT scans. *AJR Am J Roentgenol* 1994;162(3):555–60.
12. Butz WC. Pulmonary arteriole foreign body granulomata associated with angiomatoids resulting from the intravenous injection of oral medications, e. g., propoxyphene hydrochloride (Darvon). *J Forensic Sci* 1969;14(3):317–26.
13. Sherman CB, Hudson LD, Pierson DJ. Severe precocious emphysema in intravenous methylphenidate (Ritalin) abusers. *Chest* 1987;92(6):1085–87.
14. Hatano S, Strasser T. *Primary Pulmonary Hypertension. Report on a WHO Meeting October 15–17, 1973.* World Health Organization, 1975.
15. Simonneau G, Gatzoulis MA, Adatia I, et al. Updated clinical classification of pulmonary hypertension. *J Am Coll Cardiol* 2013;62(25 Suppl):D34–41.
16. Humbert M, Sitbon O, Chaouat A, et al. Survival in patients with idiopathic, familial, and anorexigen-associated pulmonary arterial hypertension in the modern management era. *Circulation* 2010;122(2):156–63.
17. Galie N, Humbert M, Vachiery JL, et al. 2015 ESC/ERS Guidelines for the diagnosis and treatment of pulmonary hypertension: the Joint Task Force for the Diagnosis and Treatment of Pulmonary Hypertension of the

European Society of Cardiology (ESC) and the European Respiratory Society (ERS): endorsed by: association for European Paediatric and Congenital Cardiology (AEPC), International Society for Heart and Lung Transplantation (ISHLT). *Eur Heart J* 2016;37(1):67–119.

18. Ranchoux B, Antigny F, Rucker-Martin C, et al. Endothelial-to-mesenchymal transition in pulmonary hypertension. *Circulation* 2015;131(11):1006–18.
19. Eddahibi S, Humbert M, Fadel E, et al. Hyperplasia of pulmonary artery smooth muscle cells is causally related to overexpression of the serotonin transporter in primary pulmonary hypertension. *Chest* 2002;121(3 Suppl):97S–98S.
20. Ren W, Watts SW, Fanburg BL. Serotonin transporter interacts with the PDGFbeta receptor in PDGF-BB-induced signaling and mitogenesis in pulmonary artery smooth muscle cells. *Am J Physiol Lung Cell Mol Physiol* 2011;300(3):L486–497.
21. Marik PE. Aspiration pneumonitis and aspiration pneumonia. *N Engl J Med* 2001;344(9):665–71.
22. Mier L, Dreyfuss D, Darchy B, et al. Is penicillin G an adequate initial treatment for aspiration pneumonia? A prospective evaluation using a protected specimen brush and quantitative cultures. *Intensive Care Med* 1993;19(5):279–84.

1.16 BODY PACKERS AND STUFFERS

Christie Sun and Binh T. Ly

1.16.1 General Comments

Definitions of the terms *packing* and *stuffing* are required to understand the different approaches to decontamination that are available. *Body packing* refers to the use of the human gastrointestinal (GI) tract for purposes of drug smuggling.[1–3] Smugglers or "mules" ingest a drug, usually cocaine or heroin, carefully wrapped in high-grade latex, aluminum foil, or condoms designed to prevent leakage. Case reports even describe the use of children who are forced to consume large numbers of drug-containing packets.[4] There are reports of ingestions of as many as 500 packages. Though the number and size of packets may vary, each packet typically contains 0.5 to 10 g of a drug; each packet may contain potentially fatal amounts, though the type of drug may vary. Rates of complication secondary to rupture were high initially, but recent advances in the packaging have decreased rates of rupture.

Body stuffing refers to the act of swallowing poorly wrapped "baggies," vials, or other packages filled with illegal drugs in an attempt to conceal them from the police. Body stuffers usually present to health care in the custody of law enforcement. Baggies or vials may or may not contain lethal amounts of drug but are generally not well wrapped and may manifest complications from leakage. A variant of body stuffing is the ingestion of drugs to produce an acute medical condition that could necessitate medical intervention, thereby deferring incarceration.[5]

1.16.2 Stepwise Approach to Management

The initial step to management of these patients is obtaining an adequate history and examination. As most patients will present with law enforcement, they may be reluctant to provide an accurate history, but it is important to attempt to obtain the number of packages, their contents, type of wrapping, and time of ingestion. A thorough physical examination is necessary to elucidate whether there are any signs or symptoms consistent with a clinical toxidrome. In addition, other clinical presentations include obstruction due to the packets, gastric perforation, gastric hemorrhage, esophageal obstruction, uterine ischemia, and septic shock.[6–12] Further treatment can be categorized into patients who are symptomatic versus those who are asymptomatic.

Radiographic evaluation can be difficult in both body stuffers and body packers. The sensitivity of plain abdominal radiographs in body packers has been reported to be 75% to 95%, though this is dependent on the number of packets and components of their packaging.[13] There is some suggestion that supine films or oral contrast may improve sensitivity.[14,15] Computed tomography (CT) has increased the reported sensitivity, but there are case reports of retained packets after evaluation with CT.[16–20] Ultrasound is another method that has been evaluated and shown promise, but more investigation is necessary into its utility.[21,22] Magnetic resonance imaging (MRI) is unlikely to add utility in evaluation for packets. Generally, stuffers have low rates of detection with radiographic imaging.[23]

Gastric decontamination is the mainstay of management for body packers in asymptomatic patients, though it is also commonly advocated in body stuffers. Activated charcoal (AC) is relatively safe, although vomiting and diarrhea are seen commonly when cathartics such as sorbitol are added, and constipation can result if cathartics are withheld. Serious adverse effects include pulmonary aspiration of AC along with gastric contents,[24–26] significant morbidity from spillage of AC in the peritoneum after perforation from gastric lavage,[27] and intestinal obstruction and pseudo-obstruction.[28–30] While there are no studies that show clinical benefit in packers or stuffers, treatment with AC is commonly used on the basis that cocaine and heroin are common in drug packets and bind well to AC. The risks and benefits of AC are individual for each patient based on their clinical status and possible downstream effects of the drug ingested as well as available antidotes. Cocaine packers tend to have a higher risk of surgical interventions, while opioid antagonists and mechanical ventilation can be used in heroin packers.

Whole bowel irrigation (WBI) involves the administration of large volumes (2 L/h in an adult, 0.5 L/h in a child) of polyethylene glycol electrolyte lavage solution (PEG-ELS) through a nasogastric tube. WBI is generally accepted as a method to enhance elimination by decreasing the transit time of the packets and potential absorption.[1,31] Because of its balanced electrolyte content and iso-osmolar nature, PEG-ELS use results in minimal net water and electrolyte shifts and is safe and effective under the right circumstances. In the case of body packers, the bowel cleansing from WBI may reduce morbidity should bowel perforation occur or surgery be required.[1] In a case described by Utecht et al.,[31] it was presumed that WBI was effective in completely dissolving the heroin initially wrapped in electrical tape prior to ingestion. Though the studies are not definitive, it is generally accepted to confer benefit in these cases. In body stuffers, it is not likely to offer benefit unless large amounts are ingested. It has been shown that PEG 4000, a water-soluble polymer comparable to the polymer used in PEG-ELS, can increase the dissolution rates of poorly water-soluble drugs,[32] but other studies do not confirm those results. Orogastric lavage is not helpful in these cases, as packets are too large to fit through the tubing.

Cathartics are occasionally used to accelerate the transit time of drug and drug packets but have been shown to cause electrolyte disturbances and are no longer routinely recommended.[33] Additionally, petroleum-based cathartics may compromise the integrity of some packet wrappers.[34] Enemas and manual removal should not be attempted due to the danger of rupture. Promotility agents such as erythromycin or metoclopramide have been used safely[4] but have not been shown to change clinical outcomes.

The end point for asymptomatic patients differs depending on whether patients are stuffers or packers. In body packers, removal of all packets is the goal. There are reports of packets even after treatment with WBI. Thus medical observation in addition to complete GI decontamination is recommended in these patients. Oftentimes, the endpoint for these patients involves multiple packet-free stools and a negative confirmatory imaging study after a prolonged period of observation without symptoms of toxicity. The use of serial urine drug of abuse screens may be helpful with body packers, as these individuals are not necessarily users of the drug. In these circumstances, the drug screen may be negative initially and later become positive, suggestive of loss of integrity of the package, an ominous sign. Body stuffers, on the other hand, generally manifest symptoms quickly, secondary to the poor integrity of their packaging, or do not manifest symptoms at all. A shorter observation period of approximately 6 hours can typically be used for the majority of these patients, though longer periods should be considered in those with potentially large doses. Unlike with packers, urine drug of abuse screens are typically not useful.

Treatment of symptomatic patients depends on the drug contained within the packets, the amount, and availability of a reasonable antidote, such as naloxone for heroin. Surgical decontamination in addition to standard medical therapies may be necessary in those with signs of toxicity, as they may be life-threatening. This is particularly true in those with cocaine or amphetamine toxicity, as benzodiazepines and other sedatives may not be sufficient therapy. Other medical interventions such as vasodilators may be needed to counteract the vasoconstrictive effects of cocaine and amphetamine. Surgical removal may not be definitive in all cases, as there are cases of retained packets even after surgical removal. Endoscopy and proctoscopy have also been reported to be successful in some cases, but rupture can still occur.[35,36]

REFERENCES

1. Hoffman RS, Smilkstein MJ, Goldfrank LR. Whole bowel irrigation and the cocaine body-packer: a new approach to a common problem. *Am J Emerg Med* 1990;8(6):523–7.
2. Duenas-Laita A, Nogue S, Burillo-Putze G. Body packing. *N Engl J Med* 2004;350(12):1260–1; author reply 1260–1.
3. Bulstrode N, Banks F, Shrotria S. The outcome of drug smuggling by 'body packers' — the British experience. *Ann R Coll Surg Engl* 2002;84(1):35–8.
4. Traub SJ, Kohn GL, Hoffman RS, et al. Pediatric "body packing." *Arch Pediatr Adolesc Med* 2003;157(2):174–7.
5. Roberts JR, et al. The bodystuffer syndrome: a clandestine form of drug overdose. *Am J Emerg Med* 1986;4(1):24–7.
6. de Beer SA et al. Surgery for body packing in the Caribbean: a retrospective study of 70 patients. *World J Surg* 2008;32:281–5.
7. Hutchins KD, et al. Heroin body packing: three fatal cases of intestinal perforation. *J Forensic Sci* 2000;45:42–7.
8. Miller JS, et al. Giant gastric ulcer in a body packer. *J Trauma* 1998;45:617–9.
9. Duenas-Laita A et al. Body packing. *N Engl J Med* 2004;350:1260–1.
10. Karkos PD, et al. An unusual foreign body in the oesophagus. The body packer syndrome. *Eur Arch Otorhinolaryngol* 2005;262:154–6.
11. Chaudhary AM et al. Endoscopic removal of a cocaine packet from the stomach. *J Clin Gastroenterol* 1998;27:155–6.
12. Gill JR et al. Ten years of "body packers" in New York City: 50 deaths. *J Forensic Sci* 2002;47:843–6.
13. Caruana DS et al. Cocaine-packet ingestion. Diagnosis, management, and natural history. *Ann Intern Med* 1984;100:73–4.
14. Marc B, Baud FJ, Aelion MJ, et al. The cocaine body-packer syndrome: evaluation of a method of contrast study of the bowel. *J Forensic Sci* 1990;35:345–55.
15. June R, Aka SE, Keys N, Wahl M. Medical outcome of cocaine body stuffers. *J Emerg Med* 2000;18:221–4.
16. Schmidt S, Hugli O, Rizzo E, et al. Detection of ingested cocaine-filled packets - diagnostic value of unxenhanced CT. *Eur J Radiol* 2008;67:133–8.
17. Kersschot EA, Beaucourt LE, Degryse HR, et al. Roentgenographical detection of cocaine smuggling in the alimentary tract. *Rofo* 1985;142:295–8.
18. Flach PM, Ross SG, Ampanozi G et al. "Drug mules" as a radiological challenge: sensitivity and specificity in identifying internal cocaine in body packers, body pushers, and body stuffers by computed tomography, plain radiography and Lodox. *Eur J Radiol* 2012;81:2518–26.
19. Hahn I-H, Hoffman RS, Nelson LS. Contrast CT scan fails to detect the last heroin packet. *J Emerg Med* 2004;27: 279–83.
20. Eng JG, Aks SE, Waldrom R et al. False-negative abdominal CT scan in a cocaine body stuffer. *Am J Emerg Med* 1999;17:702–4.
21. Hierholzer J, Coredes M, Tantow H, et al. Drug smuggling by ingested cocaine-filled packages: conventional x-ray and ultrasound. *Abdom Imaging* 1995;20:333–8.
22. Meijer R, Bots ML. Detection of intestinal drug containers by ultrasound scanning: an airport screening tool? *Eur Radiol* 2003;13:1312–15.
23. Hergan K, Kolfer K, Oser W. Drug smuggling by body packing: what radiologists should know about it. *Eur Radiol* 2004;14:736–42.
24. Pollack MM et al. Aspiration of activated charcoal and gastric contents. *Ann Emerg Med* 1981;10(10):528–9.
25. Menzies DG, Busuttil A, Prescott LF. Fatal pulmonary aspiration of oral activated charcoal. *BMJ* 1988;297(6646):459–60.
26. Givens T, Holloway M, Wason S, Pulmonary aspiration of activated charcoal: a complication of its misuse in overdose management. *Pediatr Emerg Care* 1992;8(3):137–40.
27. Mariani PJ, Pook N. Gastrointestinal tract perforation with charcoal peritoneum complicating orogastric intubation and lavage. *Ann Emerg Med* 1993;22(3):606–9.
28. Ray MJ et al. Charcoal bezoar. Small-bowel obstruction secondary to amitriptyline overdose therapy [published erratum appears in *Dig Dis Sci* 1988 Oct;33(10):1344]. *Dig Dis Sci* 1988;33(1):106–7.
29. Watson WA, Cremer KF, Chapman JA. Gastrointestinal obstruction associated with multiple-dose activated charcoal. *J Emerg Med* 1986;4(5):401–7.
30. Longdon P, Henderson A. Intestinal pseudo-obstruction following the use of enteral charcoal and sorbitol and mechanical ventilation with papaveretum sedation for theophylline poisoning. *Drug Saf* 1992;7(1):74–7.

31. Utecht MJ, Stone AF, McCarron MM. Heroin body packers. *J Emerg Med* 1993;11(1):33–40.
32. Niazi S. Effect of polyethylene glycol 4000 on dissolution properties of sulfathiazole polymorphs. *J Pharm Sci* 1976;65(2):302–4.
33. Barceloux D, McGuigan M, Hartigan-Go K. Position statement: cathartics. American Academy of Clinical Toxicology, European Association of Poison Centers and Clinical Toxicologists. *J Toxicol Clin Toxicol* 1992;35:743–52.
34. Visser L, Stricker B, Hoogendoorn M, et al. Do not give paraffin to packers. *Lancet* 1998;352:1352.
35. Pollack CV, Biggers DW, Carlton FB, et al. Two crack cocaine body stuffers. *Ann Emerg Med* 1992;21:1370–80.
36. Suaraz CA, Arango A, Lester JL. Cocaine - condom ingestion. Surgical treatment. *JAMA* 1977;238:1391–2.

1.17 VASCULAR EFFECTS OF SUBSTANCE ABUSE

R. Adam Koch and Binh T. Ly

Drugs of abuse have been known to cause multiple effects related to vascular system disorders, including hypertension, aortic dissection, vasculitis, premature atherosclerosis, and others [1–7]. In general, these effects have been associated with cocaine, methamphetamines, and other sympathomimetics. There have been some reports of synthetic cannabinoids also causing elevated blood pressure and vasculitis, but in general, the effects are not as severe as those occurring with sympathomimetics and are felt to act through the same mechanism of activation of the sympathetic system [8]. In the following, the separate areas will be discussed with their mechanisms and then a section on immediate management.

1.17.1 General Comments

- **Cocaine**
  Similarly to cardiac effects, cocaine causes prototypical vascular effects that may be applied broadly across most sympathomimetics. All sympathomimetics increase vascular tone through actions on neuronal transmitters, but norepinephrine seems to be the neurotransmitter most closely linked to the blood pressure elevation [9, 10]. Cocaine, specifically, is known to increase the production of endothelin 1 and raises vascular tone through other pathways as well. Endothelin 1 reacts with endothelin receptors to cause calcium release from the sarcoplasmic reticulum of vascular smooth muscle. This leads to significant contraction and vasoconstriction [7, 11]. Cocaine has also been shown to decrease nitric oxide, an endogenous vasodilator, which also leads to vasoconstriction [12]. All these effects in isolation or combination may lead to significant elevations in blood pressure and the risks associated with hypertensive crisis.

  The significant vasospasm can lead to multiple hypertensive disorders. The most significant are aortic and coronary artery dissection, both of which can rapidly lead to death if untreated [13–15]. The vasospasm is mediated through the endothelin receptors and norepinephrine elevations as mentioned earlier. The dissection is also thought to be due to decreased vessel elasticity and increased vascular smooth muscle cell apoptosis [16, 17]. The patient will typically present with severe tearing chest or back pain. With progression of these conditions, involvement of coronary vessels and the aorta may lead to acute myocardial infarction or exsanguination, respectively.

  Vasospasm occurs throughout the body and can lead to effects in any major or minor vessel. In gastrointestinal arteries, this can lead to ischemic bowel with severe abdominal pain and bloody stools [18]. This can progress to intestinal infarction, overwhelming sepsis, and death [19, 20]. A less common abdominal disease process occurs with splenic or renal artery infarctions but can lead to similarly lethal results if not recognized [21–23]. Vasospasm of the retinal vessels can lead to temporary or even permanent visual changes and blindness [24, 25]. Cerebral vessels will be discussed in the section on drug-associated cerebral vasculitis.

  Cocaine is known to enhance coagulation and thrombosis. Cocaine activates platelets via multiple effects. It increases expression of platelet factor 4, thromboglobulin B, and P-selectin [26, 27]. These activated platelets are then more likely to adhere to vascular endothelium and form clots in the absence of endothelial injury. Another effect of cocaine is to elevate levels of C-reactive protein, von Willebrand factor, and fibrinogen, which leads to a prothrombotic state [28]. Cocaine is also known to increase the activity of plasminogen activator inhibitor type 1, which leads to decreased thrombosis breakdown [29]. All these factors lead to significant enhancements in thrombus formation and impaired thrombus breakdown, causing significant risk for infarction throughout the body.

  Cocaine abuse has been correlated in multiple studies with accelerated atherosclerosis [17, 30–33]. This is caused by multiple factors and actions of cocaine toxicity. Cocaine directly increases the permeability of the endothelial wall by altering tight junctions and so allowing lipid to infiltrate the vascular walls [34]. This lipid deposition leads to atherosclerotic plaques, which are at risk for rupture, leading to complete vessel occlusion. Cocaine also elevates the pro-inflammatory cytokines (such as tumor necrosis factor alpha, interleukin 1 beta, and others) and decreases the anti-inflammatory markers (such as interleukin-10). This pro-inflammatory state also contributes to accelerated atherosclerosis [35, 36].

  The atherosclerotic and prothrombotic effects can be especially damaging when combined with the vasospastic effects. In the pulmonary vasculature, the vasospasm and hypercoagulable state can lead to pulmonary embolism and infarction [37]. The cardiac effects seen with vasospasm can be exacerbated by the atherosclerosis and hypercoagulable state and lead to acute plaque rupture and thrombosis [38, 39]. These effects can occur in any vessels and have been reported throughout the body. Some of the more worrisome reports include limb ischemia, likely due to spasm, thrombosis, and atherogenesis [40].

Another major cause of vascular issues with cocaine are the adulterants that are added to cut the cocaine. The most striking example of this is levamisole, which in 2009 was estimated to contaminate 69 percent of U.S. cocaine supply [41]. Levamisole, an antihelminthic immunomodulator, has led to significant vasculitis with areas of purpura and necrotic lesions [42, 43]. The mechanism is not completely elucidated, but it seems to occur in patients predisposed to ANCA production, and the cocaine-levamisole leads to an activation of the immune system with loss of tolerance for self-antigens [44, 45]. This syndrome can usually be identified by high titers of *p*-ANCA, which has become directed at human neutrophilic enolase instead of its usual target, myeloperoxidase [46, 47]. The necrotic lesions resolve with abstinence but recur with repeat exposure.

- **Amphetamines**

This class has significant variability, based on the specific receptors each chemical has greater affinity for, and this affects their vascular effects. Those that have more dopamine and norepinephrine effects lead to greater vascular effects, which are very similar to the vascular effects of cocaine. Some, such as 3,4-methylenedioxymethamphetamine (MDMA), have more serotonin effects and fewer norepinephrine or dopamine effects and so generally have less hypertension, tachycardia, and vascular risk [48]. In very large doses, though, these distinctions can diminish and vascular risks rise [49, 50]. Methamphetamine will be discussed as the class example with some discussion of specific others.

Similarly to cocaine, methamphetamine causes a release of norepinephrine, but through a slightly different mechanism. Instead of blocking reuptake at the nerve terminal, methamphetamine diffuses into the presynaptic nerve terminal and interacts with vesicle membranes, causing release of norepinephrine, dopamine, etc. into the synaptic cleft [51, 52]. These neurotransmitters, especially norepinephrine, activate alpha and beta adrenergic receptors, leading to tachycardia, hypertension, and other hypertensive crises. There is emerging evidence that similarly to cocaine, methamphetamine use leads to increased endothelin 1 release, which causes significant vasoconstriction. This is mediated by endothelin receptors on vascular smooth muscle [53].

Vasospasm with amphetamines can lead to effects similar to those seen with cocaine toxicity. Methamphetamine use has been linked with aortic dissection, coronary artery dissection, ischemic colitis, and others [1, 54–56]. The mechanism is severe vasoconstriction, and there is some evidence of a direct degenerative effect of methamphetamine on the walls of the aorta [1]. Other amphetamines that interact with serotonin receptors more than other receptors, such as bromo-benzodifuranyl-isopropylamine (bromo-dragonFLY), have been associated with cases of necrosis, gangrene, and amputation due to peripheral vasoconstriction. This vasoconstriction seems to be mediated more through agonism of the 5-HT_{2A} and 5-HT_{1B} serotonin receptors than through the effects of alpha or beta adrenergic receptors, though those effects are also felt to be contributory [57, 58].

Methamphetamine and other amphetamines have been linked to multiple cardiovascular deaths and acute myocardial infarction [59, 60]. Some of these deaths may be attributable to the acute coronary artery vasoconstriction, but there is increasing evidence that amphetamines and methamphetamine specifically lead to accelerated atherosclerosis [61]. The exact mechanism has yet to be elucidated, but work is ongoing. The combination of vasospasm with atherosclerotic plaques puts these individuals at much higher risk of acute myocardial infarction compared with age-matched controls.

In addition to the accelerated atherosclerosis, amphetamine abuse has been associated with necrotizing vasculitis of small- and medium-sized arteries. This can be seen on angiography as beading and narrowing of arteries in multiple organ systems, including the cerebral, cardiac, intestinal, and renal [62–64]. The exact mechanism causing this vasculitis is unclear; however, there seems to be a direct effect of amphetamine that is not due to contaminants, based on experiments with animals [65, 66]. This vasculitis leads to cerebral infarctions, cerebral hemorrhage, acute kidney injury, and similar injuries in other affected organs [67].

- **Drug-associated cerebral vasculitis**

Both cocaine and amphetamines are well known for their deleterious cerebrovascular effects [67, 68]. Cocaine causes significant vascular effects within the cerebral vasculature. The actions on cerebral vasculature are the same as discussed earlier. The increased shear forces, early atherosclerosis, and vasospasm lead to increased rates of subarachnoid, intraventricular, and intraparenchymal hemorrhages both with and without vasculitis [69–71]. Cocaine is also associated with significant increases in ruptured intracerebral aneurysms [72]. These effects lead to the classic symptoms of acute strokes, manifesting as weakness, facial droop, etc. Cocaine use is also associated with increased rates of ischemic stroke and transient ischemic attacks [67, 73–75]. Cocaine's vasoconstricting effects, increased thrombosis, and accelerated atherosclerosis lead to the increased rates of ischemic occlusions.

The vasculitis caused by cocaine also leads to increased risk of ischemic stroke and neurologic symptoms. Although the exact cause of the vasculitis remains unclear, the finding has been demonstrated on angiography, biopsy, and multiple autopsy studies [76–78]. The pattern seen on angiography is the finding of arterial beading, and there have been studies showing cocaine use to be associated with inflammatory changes in blood vessels and endothelial dysfunction, which could lead to vasculitis [17, 79]. Cocaine use has also been associated with cases of multifocal inflammatory leukoencephalopathy, and some, but not all, of the cases have been related to cocaine contaminated with levamisole [80, 81]. These patients can present with a multitude of neurologic symptoms depending on where the lesions are located. These lesions are usually most easily seen on magnetic resonance imaging, but the exact cause of the lesions is undetermined at this time.

Amphetamines also have a long history of intracranial hemorrhage and cerebral infarction. The vasculitis seen with amphetamines generally can be seen as beading, narrowing, and irregularity of flow in small- and medium-sized arteries on angiography [62, 82]. Amphetamines use is associated with a 4.95 times increased risk of stroke, and 80 percent of those strokes will be hemorrhagic [83]. Increased risk of stroke from amphetamines is two times the risk conferred by cocaine use [84]. The pathogenesis of the strokes is thought to be due to the acute vasoconstriction combined with the underlying vasculitis [67]. The mechanism of the vasculitis is not fully elucidated but is felt to be due to a direct effect of amphetamine on the vessel wall. This leads to fibrinoid necrosis of the intima and media and destruction of the vascular smooth muscle [85]. This vasculitis has been demonstrated in animal models as well as on human autopsy studies [65, 66].

- **Stepwise approach to management**
  In general, cocaine and amphetamines can be treated similarly when dealing with vascular toxicity. Their mechanisms of action are similar enough in the vascular environment not to require specific modifications in treatment. This is especially helpful, as acutely, it can be difficult to distinguish vascular toxicity from these agents.

1.17.1.1 Immediate Interventions

1. **Airway, breathing, circulation:** Maintain the airway, and assist ventilation if necessary. Administer supplemental oxygen for hypoxia. Treat any hypotension, and resuscitate as per guidelines [86].
2. **Intravenous access, oxygen, monitor:** Acquire peripheral intravenous access, provide supplemental oxygen to patients with hypoxia. Obtain electrocardiogram (ECG) and continuously monitor cardiac status.
3. **Antidotes:** There are no specific antidotes available for cocaine or amphetamine toxicity.
4. **Sedative:** Administer a benzodiazepine if the patient is anxious, delirious, psychotic, hypertensive, or hyperthermic or is experiencing chest pain or transient dysrhythmias. Treatment may require administering significantly higher than standard doses for symptom control. In experiments in animals, benzodiazepines attenuate the cardiac and central nervous system (CNS) toxicity of sympathomimetics. In animal experiments, benzodiazepines attenuated the cardiac and CNS toxicity of amphetamines and cocaine [87–89]. Dexmedetomidine, an alpha-2 adrenergic agonist commonly used for sedation, may offer some advantages, given its negative feedback mechanism on the presynaptic terminal, preventing further release of catecholamines, particularly in the case of amphetamine.
5. **Aspirin:** This may help prevent the formation of thrombi in patients with suspected cardiac or other vessel ischemia [90–92]. The use of aspirin in patients with cocaine-associated myocardial ischemia has been shown to be safe [93–95]. In patients with suspected vascular dissection or intracranial bleeding, aspirin would be contraindicated due to risks of worsening hemorrhage.
6. **Blood pressure control:** Consider the use of a calcium-channel blocker such as verapamil, nicardipine, or a nonspecific alpha and beta antagonist such as labetalol [96, 97] in hypertensive vascular emergencies. There is some evidence that the combined alpha and beta receptor antagonist can be more effective, as there is no risk of reflex tachycardia [96, 98]. These medications can decrease systemic vascular resistance as well as relieving the coronary artery vasospasm [96–98]. For more information about blood pressure control in aortic dissection, see the special section.
7. **Phentolamine:** Consider phentolamine, an alpha-adrenergic antagonist, for resistant hypertensive emergency, as evidenced by chest pain, encephalopathy, etc. This has been shown to reverse coronary artery vasoconstriction in cocaine use [14] and would be as effective for any, such as amphetamines. Low dose may avoid the hypotensive side-effects of the drug while maintaining the anti-ischemic effects [99].
8. **Thrombolytics:**
   a. Ischemic stroke symptoms – At this time, these patients should be treated according to current guidelines for ischemic stroke without a history of sympathomimetic use. One small study showed that patients had no greater risk of hemorrhagic transformation after being

treated with tissue plasminogen activator (tPA) than individuals without a cocaine use history [100]. Blood pressure may need to be controlled with medications prior to thrombolytic treatment. Please see prior section on stroke for complete treatment protocol.

b. Ischemic cardiac symptoms – These patients should be treated similarly to other patients with cardiac ischemia. Thrombolytics are only to be utilized if the patient is clearly having an ST-segment elevation myocardial infarction and percutaneous coronary intervention is not rapidly available. Please see prior section on cardiac effects for complete protocol for treatment.

c. Vascular dissection – Thrombolytics are contraindicated in patients with suspected or confirmed dissection.

1.17.1.2 Secondary Interventions

1. **ECG:** Repeat ECG if chest pain worsens or recurs.
2. **Chest radiography and ultrasonography:** Obtain to further assess for congestive heart failure, signs of aortic dissection, pneumothorax, or pneumomediastinum.
3. **Computed tomography (CT):** A head CT should be obtained to evaluate for acute intracranial pathology for patients with severe headache or neurologic symptoms. If this is negative, then consider CT angiography of the brain to evaluate for large vessel occlusions or other vascular abnormalities (i.e., aneurysms, dissections, etc.). Patients with significant chest pain and symptoms consistent with aortic dissection should get CT angiography of the chest, abdomen, and pelvis to evaluate for aortic dissection.
4. **Magnetic resonance imaging (MRI):** MRI of the brain may be needed to further evaluate neurologic symptoms that do not have clear causation on other testing.
5. **Monitoring:** A period of 9 to 12 hours of cardiac monitoring is recommended for patients with chest pain or other hypertensive crisis associated with sympathomimetic use (see disposition section) [31].
6. **Laboratory data:** Baseline laboratory data should include a complete blood count, prothrombin time and activated partial thromboplastin time, troponin, creatine kinase, and electrolyte panel.
7. **Disposition:**
   a. Intensive care unit: All patients with evidence of acute myocardial infarction, any arterial dissection, other hypertensive emergency, or any unstable patient [94].
   b. Telemetry monitored bed: Hemodynamically stable patients without ongoing chest pain, cardiac ischemia, neurologic deficits, elevated troponin, or rhabdomyolysis. Patients who have no evidence of ongoing chest pain with normal ECG and cardiac enzymes or no neurologic symptoms after 12 hours may be discharged if an appropriate workup has been performed [94].
   c. Home: Selected patients who have normal ECG, troponin, normalized blood pressure, and no evidence of ongoing ischemia, hypertensive, emergency, or other serious complications requiring treatment may be discharged after a period of observation [94].

1.17.1.3 Special Circumstances

1. **Aortic Dissection:** This is an acute surgical emergency, and cardiothoracic surgery should be consulted emergently. Prior to definitive therapy in the operating suite, the patient will need acute control of blood pressure and heart rate to decrease vascular wall stress and help minimize further propagation of the dissection. Generally, heart rate is controlled with a beta-blocking medication such as esmolol, but with the possible risk of unopposed alpha stimulation, a combined alpha and beta blocker such as labetalol is a better initial choice [101]. Following initial efforts, nitroprusside or nicardipine may also be used as needed to lower blood pressure [102]. The patient should also be typed and cross matched for blood.
2. **Hyperthermia:** Temperature elevations associated with sympathomimetic toxicity are typically modest and respond well to evaporative cooling measures, cooling blankets, and applying ice packs to the neck, axilla, and groin. When hyperthermia is severe, ice water immersion has been shown to be most effective but is impractical in most hospital settings. Other cooling measures include commercially available non-invasive cooling pads and invasive cooling catheters, which were designed for therapeutic hypothermia in post–cardiac arrest patients but can also be used to treat drug-induced hyperthermia. Neuromuscular blockade along with sedatives may also be employed to stop heat production due to ongoing agitation and muscular activity.

REFERENCES

1. Swalwell CI, Davis GG. Methamphetamine as a risk factor for acute aortic dissection. *J Forensic Sci* 1999;44(1):23–6. Epub 1999/02/13. PubMed PMID: 9987866.
2. Yu YJ, Cooper DR, Wellenstein DE, Block B. Cerebral angiitis and intracerebral hemorrhage associated with methamphetamine abuse. Case report. *J Neurosurg* 1983;58(1):109–11. Epub 1983/01/01. doi: 10.3171/jns.1983.58.1.0109. PubMed PMID: 6401189.

3. Glick R, Hoying J, Cerullo L, Perlman S. Phenylpropanolamine: an over-the-counter drug causing central nervous system vasculitis and intracerebral hemorrhage. Case report and review. *Neurosurgery* 1987;20(6):969–74. Epub 1987/06/01. PubMed PMID: 2956531.
4. Morrow PL, McQuillen JB. Cerebral vasculitis associated with cocaine abuse. *J Forensic Sci* 1993;38(3):732–8. Epub 1993/05/01. PubMed PMID: 8515225.
5. Merkel PA, Koroshetz WJ, Irizarry MC, Cudkowicz ME. Cocaine-associated cerebral vasculitis. *Semin Arthritis Rheum* 1995;25(3):172–83. Epub 1995/12/01. PubMed PMID: 8650587.
6. McGee SM, McGee DN, McGee MB. Spontaneous intracerebral hemorrhage related to methamphetamine abuse: autopsy findings and clinical correlation. *Am J Forensic Med Pathol* 2004;25(4):334–7. Epub 2004/12/04. PubMed PMID: 15577524.
7. Mo W, Arruda JA, Dunea G, Singh AK. Cocaine-induced hypertension: role of the peripheral sympathetic system. *Pharmacol Res* 1999;40(2):139–45. Epub 1999/08/06. doi: 10.1006/phrs.1999.0503. PubMed PMID: 10433872.
8. Pacher P, Steffens S, Hasko G, Schindler TH, Kunos G. Cardiovascular effects of marijuana and synthetic cannabinoids: the good, the bad, and the ugly. *Nat Rev Cardiol* 2017. Epub 2017/09/15. doi: 10.1038/nrcardio.2017.130. PubMed PMID: 28905873.
9. Whitby LG, Hertting G, Axelrod J. Effect of cocaine on the disposition of noradrenaline labelled with tritium. *Nature* 1960;187:604–5. Epub 1960/08/13. PubMed PMID: 13844323.
10. Muscholl E. Effect of cocaine and related drugs on the uptake of noradrenaline by heart and spleen. *Br J Pharmacol Chemother* 1961;16:352–9. Epub 1961/06/01. PubMed PMID: 13727081; PubMed Central PMCID: PMCPMC1482029.
11. Wilbert-Lampen U, Seliger C, Zilker T, Arendt RM. Cocaine increases the endothelial release of immunoreactive endothelin and its concentrations in human plasma and urine: reversal by coincubation with sigma-receptor antagonists. *Circulation* 1998;98(5):385–90. Epub 1998/08/26. PubMed PMID: 9714087.
12. Mo W, Singh AK, Arruda JA, Dunea G. Role of nitric oxide in cocaine-induced acute hypertension. *Am J Hypertens* 1998;11(6 Pt 1):708–14. Epub 1998/07/10. PubMed PMID: 9657630.
13. Hsue PY, Salinas CL, Bolger AF, Benowitz NL, Waters DD. Acute aortic dissection related to crack cocaine. *Circulation* 2002;105(13):1592–5. Epub 2002/04/03. PubMed PMID: 11927528.
14. Lange RA, Cigarroa RG, Yancy CW, Jr, Willard JE, Popma JJ, Sills MN, et al. Cocaine-induced coronary-artery vasoconstriction. *N Engl J Med* 1989;321(23):1557–62. Epub 1989/12/07. doi: 10.1056/nejm198912073212301. PubMed PMID: 2573838.
15. Steinhauer JR, Caulfield JB. Spontaneous coronary artery dissection associated with cocaine use: a case report and brief review. *Cardiovasc Pathol* 2001;10(3):141–5. Epub 2001/08/04. PubMed PMID: 11485859.
16. Eisenberg MJ, Yakel DL, Mendelson J, Redberg RF, Jones RT, Foster E. Immediate effects of intravenous cocaine on the thoracic aorta and coronary arteries. A transesophageal echocardiographic study. *Chest* 1996;110(1):147–54. Epub 1996/07/01. PubMed PMID: 8681619.
17. Su J, Li J, Li W, Altura B. Cocaine induces apoptosis in primary cultured rat aortic vascular smooth muscle cells: possible relationship to aortic dissection, atherosclerosis, and hypertension. *Int J Toxicol* 2004;23(4):233–7. Epub 2004/09/17. doi: 10.1080/10915810490471361. PubMed PMID: 15371167.
18. Niazi M, Kondru A, Levy J, Bloom AA. Spectrum of ischemic colitis in cocaine users. *Dig Dis Sci* 1997;42(7):1537–41. Epub 1997/07/01. PubMed PMID: 9246060.
19. Hon DC, Salloum LJ, Hardy HW, 3rd, Barone JE. Crack-induced enteric ischemia. *N J Med* 1990;87(12):1001–2. Epub 1990/12/01. PubMed PMID: 2270146.
20. Osorio J, Farreras N, Ortiz De Zarate L, Bachs E. Cocaine-induced mesenteric ischaemia. *Dig Surg* 2000;17(6):648–51. Epub 2001/01/13. doi: 10.1159/000051980. PubMed PMID: 11155017.
21. Dettmeyer R, Schlamann M, Madea B. Cocaine-associated abscesses with lethal sepsis after splenic infarction in an 17-year-old woman. *Forensic Sci Int* 2004;140(1):21–3. Epub 2004/03/12. doi: 10.1016/j.forsciint.2003.11.031. PubMed PMID: 15013162.
22. Edmondson DA, Towne JB, Foley DW, Abu-Hajir M, Kochar MS. Cocaine-induced renal artery dissection and thrombosis leading to renal infarction. *WMJ* 2004;103(7):66–9. Epub 2005/02/09. PubMed PMID: 15696837.
23. Fabbian F, Pala M, De Giorgi A, Tiseo R, Molino C, Mallozzi Menegatti A, et al. Left kidney: an unusual site of cocaine-related renal infarction. A case report. *Eur Rev Med Pharmacol Sci* 2012;16(Suppl 1):30–3. Epub 2012/05/16. PubMed PMID: 22582481.
24. Libman RB, Masters SR, de Paola A, Mohr JP. Transient monocular blindness associated with cocaine abuse. *Neurology* 1993;43(1):228–9. Epub 1993/01/01. PubMed PMID: 8423897.
25. Hoffman RS, Reimer BI. "Crack" cocaine-induced bilateral amblyopia. *Am J Emerg Med* 1993;11(1):35–7. Epub 1993/01/01. PubMed PMID: 8447867.
26. Heesch CM, Wilhelm CR, Ristich J, Adnane J, Bontempo FA, Wagner WR. Cocaine activates platelets and increases the formation of circulating platelet containing microaggregates in humans. *Heart* 2000;83(6):688–95. Epub 2000/05/18. PubMed PMID: 10814631; PubMed Central PMCID: PMCPMC1760877.
27. Kugelmass AD, Shannon RP, Yeo EL, Ware JA. Intravenous cocaine induces platelet activation in the conscious dog. *Circulation* 1995;91(5):1336–40. Epub 1995/03/01. PubMed PMID: 7532553.
28. Siegel AJ, Mendelson JH, Sholar MB, McDonald JC, Lewandrowski KB, Lewandrowski EL, et al. Effect of cocaine usage on C-reactive protein, von Willebrand factor, and fibrinogen. *Am J Cardiol* 2002;89(9):1133–5. Epub 2002/05/04. PubMed PMID: 11988210.
29. Moliterno DJ, Lange RA, Gerard RD, Willard JE, Lackner C, Hillis LD. Influence of intranasal cocaine on plasma constituents associated with endogenous thrombosis and thrombolysis. *Am J Med* 1994;96(6):492–6. Epub 1994/06/01. PubMed PMID: 8017445.
30. Bansal S, Morgan J. Vascular toxicity of cocaine. *Vascular Disease Prevention* 2009;6(1):5. doi: 10.2174/1567270001006010030.
31. Phillips K, Luk A, Soor GS, Abraham JR, Leong S, Butany J. Cocaine cardiotoxicity: a review of the pathophysiology, pathology, and treatment options. *Am J Cardiovasc Drugs* 2009;9(3):177–96. Epub 2009/05/26. doi: 10.2165/00129784-200909030-00005. PubMed PMID: 19463023.
32. Piano MR. Alcohol's effects on the cardiovascular system. *Alcohol Res* 2017;38(2):219–41. Epub 2017/10/11. PubMed PMID: 28988575; PubMed Central PMCID: PMCPMC5513687.

33. Pradhan L, Mondal D, Chandra S, Ali M, Agrawal KC. Molecular analysis of cocaine-induced endothelial dysfunction: role of endothelin-1 and nitric oxide. *Cardiovasc Toxicol* 2008;8(4):161–71. Epub 2008/09/25. doi: 10.1007/s12012-008-9025-z. PubMed PMID: 18813882.
34. Kolodgie FD, Wilson PS, Mergner WJ, Virmani R. Cocaine-induced increase in the permeability function of human vascular endothelial cell monolayers. *Exp Mol Pathol* 1999;66(2):109–22. Epub 1999/07/20. doi: 10.1006/exmp.1999.2253. PubMed PMID: 10409439.
35. Narvaez JC, Magalhaes PV, Fries GR, Colpo GD, Czepielewski LS, Vianna P, et al. Peripheral toxicity in crack cocaine use disorders. *Neurosci Lett* 2013;544:80–4. Epub 2013/04/20. doi: 10.1016/j.neulet.2013.03.045. PubMed PMID: 23597759.
36. Fox HC, D'Sa C, Kimmerling A, Siedlarz KM, Tuit KL, Stowe R, et al. Immune system inflammation in cocaine dependent individuals: implications for medications development. *Hum Psychopharmacol* 2012;27(2):156–66. Epub 2012/03/06. doi: 10.1002/hup.1251. PubMed PMID: 22389080; PubMed Central PMCID: PMCPMC 3674778.
37. Delaney K, Hoffman RS. Pulmonary infarction associated with crack cocaine use in a previously healthy 23-year-old woman. *Am J Med* 1991;91:92–4.
38. Afonso L, Mohammad T, Thatai D. Crack whips the heart: a review of the cardiovascular toxicity of cocaine. *Am J Cardiol* 2007;100(6):1040–3. Epub 2007/09/11. doi: 10.1016/j.amjcard.2007.04.049. PubMed PMID: 17826394.
39. Schwartz BG, Rezkalla S, Kloner RA. Cardiovascular effects of cocaine. *Circulation* 2010;122(24):2558–69. Epub 2010/12/16. doi: 10.1161/circulationaha.110.940569. PubMed PMID: 21156654.
40. Gutierrez A, England JD, Krupski WC. Cocaine-induced peripheral vascular occlusive disease--a case report. *Angiology* 1998;49(3):221–4. Epub 1998/04/02. doi: 10.1177/000331979804900308. PubMed PMID: 9523545.
41. Larocque A, Hoffman RS. Levamisole in cocaine: unexpected news from an old acquaintance. *Clin Toxicol (Phila)* 2012;50(4):231–41. Epub 2012/03/30. doi: 10.3109/15563650.2012.665455. PubMed PMID: 22455354.
42. Fan T, Macaraeg J, Haddad TM, Bacon H, Le D, Mirza M, et al. A case report on suspected levamisole-induced pseudovasculitis. *WMJ* 2017;116(1):37–9. Epub 2017/11/04. PubMed PMID: 29099568.
43. Mohan V, Maiti A, Swaby MG, Cherian SV. Vasculitis due to levamisole-adulterated cocaine. *Postgrad Med J* 2018;94(1107):61. Epub 2017/10/04. doi: 10.1136/postgradmedj-2017-135162. PubMed PMID: 28972099.
44. Khan TA, Cuchacovich R, Espinoza LR, Lata S, Patel NJ, Garcia-Valladares I, et al. Vasculopathy, hematological, and immune abnormalities associated with levamisole-contaminated cocaine use. *Semin Arthritis Rheum* 2011;41(3):445–54. Epub 2011/12/14. doi: 10.1016/j.semarthrit.2011.04.010. PubMed PMID: 22152487.
45. de la Hera I, Sanz V, Cullen D, Chico R, Petiti G, Villar M, et al. Necrosis of ears after use of cocaine probably adulterated with levamisole. *Dermatology* 2011;223(1):25–8. Epub 2011/08/19. doi: 10.1159/000329436. PubMed PMID: 21846960.
46. Trimarchi M, Bussi M, Sinico RA, Meroni P, Specks U. Cocaine-induced midline destructive lesions - an autoimmune disease? *Autoimmun Rev* 2013;12(4):496–500. Epub 2012/09/04. doi: 10.1016/j.autrev.2012.08.009. PubMed PMID: 22940554.
47. Graf J. Rheumatic manifestations of cocaine use. *Curr Opin Rheumatol* 2013;25(1):50–5. Epub 2012/12/01. doi: 10.1097/BOR.0b013e32835b4449. PubMed PMID: 23196324.
48. Callaway CW, Johnson MP, Gold LH, Nichols DE, Geyer MA. Amphetamine derivatives induce locomotor hyperactivity by acting as indirect serotonin agonists. *Psychopharmacology (Berl)* 1991;104(3):293–301. Epub 1991/01/01. PubMed PMID: 1924637.
49. Gill JR, Hayes JA, deSouza IS, Marker E, Stajic M. Ecstasy (MDMA) deaths in New York City: a case series and review of the literature. *J Forensic Sci* 2002;47(1):121–6. Epub 2002/06/18. PubMed PMID: 12064638.
50. Karlovsek MZ, Alibegovic A, Balazic J. Our experiences with fatal ecstasy abuse (two case reports). *Forensic Sci Int* 2005;147 Suppl:S77–80. Epub 2005/02/08. doi: 10.1016/j.forsciint.2004.09.084. PubMed PMID: 15694737.
51. Seiden LS, Kleven MS. Methamphetamine and related drugs: toxicity and resulting behavioral changes in response to pharmacological probes. *NIDA Res Monogr* 1989;94:146–60. Epub 1989/01/01. PubMed PMID: 2514362.
52. Sulzer D, Chen TK, Lau YY, Kristensen H, Rayport S, Ewing A. Amphetamine redistributes dopamine from synaptic vesicles to the cytosol and promotes reverse transport. *J Neurosci* 1995;15(5 Pt 2):4102–8. Epub 1995/05/01. PubMed PMID: 7751968.
53. Seo JW, Jones SM, Hostetter TA, Iliff JJ, West GA. Methamphetamine induces the release of endothelin. *J Neurosci Res* 2016;94(2):170–8. Epub 2015/11/17. doi: 10.1002/jnr.23697. PubMed PMID: 26568405.
54. Wako E, LeDoux D, Mitsumori L, Aldea GS. The emerging epidemic of methamphetamine-induced aortic dissections. *J Card Surg* 2007;22(5):390–3. Epub 2007/09/07. doi: 10.1111/j.1540-8191.2007.00432.x. PubMed PMID: 17803574.
55. Kanwar M, Gill N. Spontaneous multivessel coronary artery dissection. *J Invasive Cardiol* 2010;22(1):E5–6. Epub 2010/01/06. PubMed PMID: 20048405.
56. Holubar SD, Hassinger JP, Dozois EJ, Masuoka HC. Methamphetamine colitis: a rare case of ischemic colitis in a young patient. *Arch Surg* 2009;144(8):780–2. Epub 2009/08/19. doi: 10.1001/archsurg.2009.139. PubMed PMID: 19687384.
57. Dawson P, Moffatt JD. Cardiovascular toxicity of novel psychoactive drugs: lessons from the past. *Prog Neuropsychopharmacol Biol Psychiatry* 2012;39(2):244–52. Epub 2012/05/15. doi: 10.1016/j.pnpbp.2012.05.003. PubMed PMID: 22580238.
58. Hill SL, Thomas SHL. What's new in… Toxicity of drugs of abuse. *Medicine* 2009;37(11):621–6. doi: https://doi.org/10.1016/j.mpmed.2009.08.009.
59. Hoggett K, McCoubrie D, Fatovich DM. Ecstasy-induced acute coronary syndrome: something to rave about. *Emerg Med Australas* 2012;24(3):339–42. Epub 2012/06/08. doi: 10.1111/j.1742-6723.2012.01542.x. PubMed PMID: 22672176.
60. Westover AN, Nakonezny PA, Haley RW. Acute myocardial infarction in young adults who abuse amphetamines. *Drug Alcohol Depend* 2008;96(1–2):49–56. Epub 2008/03/21. doi: 10.1016/j.drugalcdep.2008.01.027. PubMed PMID: 18353567; PubMed Central PMCID: PMCPMC2533107.
61. Akhgari M, Mobaraki H, Etemadi-Aleagha A. Histopathological study of cardiac lesions in methamphetamine poisoning-related deaths. *Daru* 2017;25(1):5. Epub 2017/02/19. doi: 10.1186/s40199-017-0170-4. PubMed PMID: 28212679; PubMed Central PMCID: PMCPMC5316196.

62. Bostwick DG. Amphetamine induced cerebral vasculitis. *Hum Pathol* 1981;12(11):1031–3. Epub 1981/11/01. PubMed PMID: 7319490.
63. Citron BP, Halpern M, McCarron M, Lundberg GD, McCormick R, Pincus IJ, et al. Necrotizing angiitis associated with drug abuse. *N Engl J Med* 1970;283(19):1003–11. Epub 1970/11/05. doi: 10.1056/nejm197011052831901. PubMed PMID: 4394271.
64. Kwon C, Zaritsky A, Dharnidharka VR. Transient proximal tubular renal injury following Ecstasy ingestion. *Pediatr Nephrol* 2003;18(8):820–2. Epub 2003/05/30. doi: 10.1007/s00467-003-1164-7. PubMed PMID: 12774221.
65. Rumbaugh CL, Bergeron RT, Scanlan RL, Teal JS, Segall HD, Fang HC, et al. Cerebral vascular changes secondary to amphetamine abuse in the experimental animal. *Radiology* 1971;101(2):345–51. Epub 1971/11/01. doi: 10.1148/101.2.345. PubMed PMID: 5000427.
66. Rumbaugh CL, Fang HC, Higgins RE, Bergeron RT, Segall HD, Teal JS. Cerebral microvascular injury in experimental drug abuse. *Invest Radiol* 1976;11(4):282–94. Epub 1976/07/01. PubMed PMID: 821897.
67. Brust JC. Vasculitis owing to substance abuse. *Neurol Clin* 1997;15(4):945–57. Epub 1998/03/07. PubMed PMID: 9367974.
68. Buttner A. Neuropathological alterations in cocaine abuse. *Curr Med Chem* 2012;19(33):5597–600. Epub 2012/08/04. PubMed PMID: 22856656.
69. Aggarwal SK, Williams V, Levine SR, Cassin BJ, Garcia JH. Cocaine-associated intracranial hemorrhage: absence of vasculitis in 14 cases *Neurology* 1996;46(6):1741–3. Epub 1996/06/01. PubMed PMID: 8649582.
70. Daras M, Tuchman AJ, Marks S. Central nervous system infarction related to cocaine abuse. *Stroke* 1991;22(10):1320–5. Epub 1991/10/01. PubMed PMID: 1926246.
71. Sordo L, Indave BI, Barrio G, Degenhardt L, de la Fuente L, Bravo MJ. Cocaine use and risk of stroke: a systematic review. *Drug Alcohol Depend* 2014;142:1–13. Epub 2014/07/30. doi: 10.1016/j.drugalcdep.2014.06.041. PubMed PMID: 25066468.
72. Vannemreddy P, Caldito G, Willis B, Nanda A. Influence of cocaine on ruptured intracranial aneurysms: a case control study of poor prognostic indicators. *J Neurosurg* 2008;108(3):470–6. Epub 2008/03/04. doi: 10.3171/jns/2008/108/3/0470. PubMed PMID: 18312093.
73. Jacobs IG, Roszler MH, Kelly JK, Klein MA, Kling GA. Cocaine abuse: neurovascular complications. *Radiology* 1989;170(1 Pt 1):223–7. Epub 1989/01/01. doi: 10.1148/radiology.170.1.2909100. PubMed PMID: 2909100.
74. Levine SR, Brust JC, Futrell N, Ho KL, Blake D, Millikan CH, et al. Cerebrovascular complications of the use of the "crack" form of alkaloidal cocaine. *N Engl J Med* 1990;323(11):699–704. Epub 1990/09/13. doi: 10.1056/nejm199009133231102. PubMed PMID: 2388668.
75. Levine SR, Brust JC, Futrell N, Brass LM, Blake D, Fayad P, et al. A comparative study of the cerebrovascular complications of cocaine: alkaloidal versus hydrochloride--a review. *Neurology* 1991;41(8):1173–7. Epub 1991/08/01. PubMed PMID: 1866000.
76. Klonoff DC, Andrews BT, Obana WG. Stroke associated with cocaine use. *Arch Neurol* 1989;46(9):989–93. Epub 1989/09/01. PubMed PMID: 2673163.
77. Case records of the Massachusetts General Hospital. Weekly clinicopathological exercises. Case 27-1993. A 32-year-old man with the sudden onset of a right-sided headache and left hemiplegia and hemianesthesia. *N Engl J Med* 1993;329(2):117–24. Epub 1993/07/08. doi: 10.1056/nejm199307083290209. PubMed PMID: 8110218.
78. Fredericks RK, Lefkowitz DS, Challa VR, Troost BT. Cerebral vasculitis associated with cocaine abuse. *Stroke* 1991;22(11):1437–9. Epub 1991/11/01. PubMed PMID: 1750054.
79. Ross BM, Moszczynska A, Peretti FJ, Adams V, Schmunk GA, Kalasinsky KS, et al. Decreased activity of brain phospholipid metabolic enzymes in human users of cocaine and methamphetamine. *Drug Alcohol Depend* 2002;67(1):73–9. Epub 2002/06/14. PubMed PMID: 12062780.
80. Vosoughi R, Schmidt BJ. Multifocal leukoencephalopathy in cocaine users: a report of two cases and review of the literature. *BMC Neurol* 2015;15:208. Epub 2015/10/21. doi: 10.1186/s12883-015-0467-1. PubMed PMID: 26482228; PubMed Central PMCID: PMCPMC4615875.
81. Vitt JR, Brown EG, Chow DS, Josephson SA. Confirmed case of levamisole-associated multifocal inflammatory leukoencephalopathy in a cocaine user. *J Neuroimmunol* 2017;305:128–30. Epub 2017/03/13. doi: 10.1016/j.jneuroim.2017.01.018. PubMed PMID: 28284332.
82. Mattson RH, Calverley JR. Dextroamphetamine-sulfate-induced dyskinesias. *Jama* 1968;204(5):400–2. Epub 1968/04/29. PubMed PMID: 5694457.
83. Lappin JM, Darke S, Farrell M. Stroke and methamphetamine use in young adults: a review. *J Neurol Neurosurg Psychiatry* 2017;88(12):1079–91. Epub 2017/08/25. doi: 10.1136/jnnp-2017-316071. PubMed PMID: 28835475.
84. Westover AN, McBride S, Haley RW. Stroke in young adults who abuse amphetamines or cocaine: a population-based study of hospitalized patients. *Arch Gen Psychiatry* 2007;64(4):495–502. Epub 2007/04/04. doi: 10.1001/archpsyc.64.4.495. PubMed PMID: 17404126.
85. Shibata S, Mori K, Sekine I, Suyama H. Subarachnoid and intracerebral hemorrhage associated with necrotizing angiitis due to methamphetamine abuse--an autopsy case. *Neurol Med Chir (Tokyo)* 1991;31(1):49–52. Epub 1991/01/01. PubMed PMID: 1712924.
86. Soar J, Callaway CW, Aibiki M, Bottiger BW, Brooks SC, Deakin CD, et al. Part 4: advanced life support: 2015 International Consensus on Cardiopulmonary Resuscitation and Emergency Cardiovascular Care Science with Treatment Recommendations. *Resuscitation* 2015;95:e71–120. Epub 2015/10/20. doi: 10.1016/j.resuscitation.2015.07.042. PubMed PMID: 26477429.
87. Guinn MM, Bedford JA, Wilson MC. Antagonism of intravenous cocaine lethality in nonhuman primates. *Clin Toxicol* 1980;16(4):499–508. Epub 1980/06/01. doi: 10.3109/15563658008989979. PubMed PMID: 7408425.
88. Derlet RW, Albertson TE, Rice P. Antagonism of cocaine, amphetamine, and methamphetamine toxicity. *Pharmacol Biochem Behav* 1990;36(4):745–9. Epub 1990/08/01. PubMed PMID: 2217500.
89. Richards JR, Albertson TE, Derlet RW, Lange RA, Olson KR, Horowitz BZ. Treatment of toxicity from amphetamines, related derivatives, and analogues: a systematic clinical review. *Drug Alcohol Depend* 2015;150:1–13. Epub 2015/03/01. doi: 10.1016/j.drugalcdep.2015.01.040. PubMed PMID: 25724076.
90. Heesch C, Wilhelm C, Ristich J, Adnane J, Bontempo F, Wagner W. Cocaine activates platelets and increases the formation of circulating platelet containing microaggregates in humans. *Heart* 2000;83(6):688–95. doi: 10.1136/heart.83.6.688. PubMed PMID: 10814631; PubMed Central PMCID: PMC1760877.
91. Schnetzer GW, 3rd. Platelets and thrombogenesis--current concepts. *Am Heart J* 1972;83(4):552–64. Epub 1972/04/01. PubMed PMID: 4339454.

92. Togna G, Tempesta E, Togna AR, Dolci N, Cebo B, Caprino L. Platelet responsiveness and biosynthesis of thromboxane and prostacyclin in response to in vitro cocaine treatment. *Haemostasis* 1985;15(2):100–7. Epub 1985/01/01. PubMed PMID: 3924789.
93. Hollander JE. Cocaine intoxication and hypertension. *Ann Emerg Med* 2008;51(Supplement):S18–20.
94. McCord J, Jneid H, Hollander JE, de Lemos JA, Cercek B, Hsue P, et al. Management of cocaine-associated chest pain and myocardial infarction: a scientific statement from the American Heart Association Acute Cardiac Care Committee of the Council on Clinical Cardiology. *Circulation* 2008;117(14):1897–907. Epub 2008/03/19. doi: 10.1161/circulationaha.107.188950. PubMed PMID: 18347214.
95. Weber JE, Shofer FS, Larkin GL, Kalaria AS, Hollander JE. Validation of a brief observation period for patients with cocaine-associated chest pain. *N Engl J Med* 2003;348(6):510–7. Epub 2003/02/07. doi: 10.1056/NEJMoa022206. PubMed PMID: 12571258.
96. Hoskins MH, Leleiko RM, Ramos JJ, Sola S, Caneer PM, Khan BV. Effects of labetalol on hemodynamic parameters and soluble biomarkers of inflammation in acute coronary syndrome in patients with active cocaine use. *J Cardiovasc Pharmacol Ther* 2010;15(1):47–52. Epub 2010/02/06. doi: 10.1177/1074248409358409. PubMed PMID: 20133495.
97. Gay GR, Loper KA. The use of labetalol in the management of cocaine crisis. *Ann Emerg Med* 1988;17(3):282–3. Epub 1988/03/01. PubMed PMID: 3345023.
98. Negus BH, Willard JE, Hillis LD, Glamann DB, Landau C, Snyder RW, et al. Alleviation of cocaine-induced coronary vasoconstriction with intravenous verapamil. *Am J Cardiol* 1994;73(7):510–3. Epub 1994/03/01. PubMed PMID: 8141094.
99. Hollander JE, Carter WA, Hoffman RS. Use of phentolamine for cocaine-induced myocardial ischemia. *N Engl J Med* 1992;327(5):361. Epub 1992/07/30. doi: 10.1056/nejm199207303270517. PubMed PMID: 1620184.
100. Martin-Schild S, Albright KC, Misra V, Philip M, Barreto AD, Hallevi H, et al. Intravenous tissue plasminogen activator in patients with cocaine-associated acute ischemic stroke. *Stroke* 2009;40:3635–7.
101. Hiratzka LF, Bakris GL, Beckman JA, Bersin RM, Carr VF, Casey DE, Jr, et al. 2010 ACCF/AHA/AATS/ACR/ASA/SCA/SCAI/SIR/STS/SVM Guidelines for the diagnosis and management of patients with thoracic aortic disease. A Report of the American College of Cardiology Foundation/American Heart Association Task Force on Practice Guidelines, American Association for Thoracic Surgery, American College of Radiology,American Stroke Association, Society of Cardiovascular Anesthesiologists, Society for Cardiovascular Angiography and Interventions, Society of Interventional Radiology, Society of Thoracic Surgeons,and Society for Vascular Medicine. *J Am Coll Cardiol* 2010;55(14):e27–e129. Epub 2010/04/03. doi: 10.1016/j.jacc.2010.02.015. PubMed PMID: 20359588.
102. Marik PE, Rivera R. Hypertensive emergencies: an update. *Curr Opin Crit Care* 2011;17(6):569–80. Epub 2011/10/12. doi: 10.1097/MCC.0b013e32834cd31d. PubMed PMID: 21986463.

1.18 VALVULAR HEART DISEASE

Gabriel Wardi and Gary Vilke

1.18.1 Introduction

Infective endocarditis (IE) has remained an elusive diagnosis over the past century and a half. Indeed, Sir William Osler once stated: "few diseases present greater difficulties in the way of diagnosis than malignant endocarditis, difficulties which in many cases are practically insurmountable."[1] It is a rare condition, with an estimated yearly incidence between 3 to 10 per 100,000 people in the United States.[2] Historically, rheumatic heart disease (RHD) was the most prevalent risk factor for IE in developed countries, but since the advent of antibiotic therapy for *Streptococcal* pharyngitis, the incidence of this has significantly decreased. Other risk factors and comorbid conditions, such as intravenous drug use (IVDU), congenital and valvular heart disease, the presence of indwelling cardiac devices and lines, long-term hemodialysis, malignancy, diabetes, advanced age, and poor dental hygiene, are now felt to be responsible for the vast majority of cases of IE. Importantly, the decreased incidence of RHD has changed the average age of diagnosis; patients now typically develop IE much later in life with the exception of patients who abuse IV drugs.

1.18.2 Epidemiology

Although intravenous (IV) drug abuse is a recognized risk factor for IE, this is not a frequent complication among IV drug users. The incidence of IE in IV drug abusers is estimated at 2–4 cases per 1,000 IV drug abusers admitted to the hospital.[3–5] However, as IV heroin use has nearly doubled in the United States in the past decade, there has been an increase in the number of patients with IVDU-associated IE from 6–8% to 12% during this same time period.[6] Recent epidemiologic data found a sharp increase in the number of female IV drug abusers with IE in the past decade, which may now be similar to that of males who abuse IV drugs.[7] There is also a strong association with IE from IVDU and the presence of the human immunodeficiency virus (HIV).[8]

1.18.3 Anatomic Considerations and Pathophysiology

The frequency of underlying heart disease in IV drug abusers with endocarditis is 26% compared with 60% of non-addicts with endocarditis. In a cohort of 85 IV drug abusers, echocardiography failed to detect any valvular vegetation consistent with endocarditis.[9] Eight IV drug abusers had thickened or redundant leaflets (with or without prolapse) of the mitral, aortic, or tricuspid valve. Focally thickened leaflets of the mitral and tricuspid valves have been reported in other series of asymptomatic IV drug abusers who were examined by echocardiography.[10] These subtle morphologic abnormalities may be the stratum upon which endocarditis builds. Most researchers agree that endothelial injury or damage initiates fibrin, platelet, and bacterial depositions that produce endocarditis. In Dressler and Robert's series of 80 autopsied IV drug abusers with IE, the tricuspid valve was involved in half the victims compared with 15% of victims dying of acute endocarditis who did not use IV drugs.[11] More recently, Yuan et al. noted that a history of IVDU was the most prominent risk factor for the development of right-sided endocarditis in a case-series of 262 patients.[12]

Why IV drug users are more likely to develop right-sided endocarditis than non-IV drug users is not known. Postulated factors include physical damage by injected particulate debris, such as talc, especially if pills are crushed and then injected. The physical process of injecting drugs, particularly if done without sterile technique, also may introduce bacteria from the skin or contaminated needles into the circulation. Furthermore, human saliva, either used as a diluent or applied to the skin prior to injection, increases the chance that oral flora can enter the systemic circulation.[13] Drug-induced pulmonary hypertension from methamphetamine or vasospasm from cocaine may cause increased right ventricular pressure and more turbulent flow, resulting in tricuspid valve injury. However, IV drug abusers can, and often do, have left-sided valve involvement. A study of 1,529 patients in Spain with a history of IVDU and endocarditis found that 79% of cases involved the right heart, 16% involved the left heart, and 5% were mixed.[14]

1.18.4 Microbiology

The most common cause of IE is *Staphylococcus aureus*, regardless of risk factor or comorbid condition.[15] Patients who abuse IV drugs were the first group in which methicillin-resistant *S. aureus* (MRSA) was reported, and outbreaks of MRSA endocarditis in IV drug users have been identified worldwide. Importantly, the prevalence of MRSA as causative organism in IE has been increasing, and it is now recognized that there are both community-acquired and hospital-associated strains.[16] *Streptococci* and *Enterococci* species are the next most common microorganisms identified in these patients. Polymicrobial infection is seen in 8% to 9% of cases of IE that involve IV drug abusers. Fungal endocarditis, typically caused by *Candida* species, is usually superimposed on valves previously damaged by an earlier episode of bacterial endocarditis or on prosthetic valves and is associated with poor outcome. Non-pathogenic oral flora, such as *Eikenella corrodens*, *Streptococcus milleri*, and *Haemophilus parainfluenzae*, can cause IE if saliva is used on drug paraphernalia prior to injection or as a diluent.[17] Other unusual pathogens causing endocarditis in IV drug abusers are shown in Table 1.18.1.

1.18.5 Macroscopic and Microscopic Findings

Grossly, IE is characterized by friable, white or tan vegetations found on the valve leaflets along the closure lines. Vegetations may be single or more often, multiple. In one

TABLE 1.18.1
Uncommon Pathogens in Endocarditis of Intravenous Drug Abusers[11]

Group B *Streptococcus* (*Streptococcus agalactiae*)
Coagulase-negative *Staphylococcus*
Gram-negative bacteria (*Pseudomonas*, *Serratia*, *Kingella*, etc.)
Corynebacterium spp., *Neisseria sicca*, *Rothia denticariosua*
Haemophilus spp.
Erysipelothrix
Anaerobic bacteria (*Bacteroides*, *Veillonella*, *Eikenella*, *Fusobacterium* spp., *Clostridium* spp., etc.)
Fungi (*Candida* spp.)

clinical series, the mean vegetation size in IV drug abusers with acute right-sided bacterial endocarditis was 1.5 0.7 cm.[18] The size, color, and appearance of the vegetations can vary, however. Streptococcal vegetations grow more slowly than staphylococcal vegetations but may become larger. Fungal vegetations are usually larger than bacterial vegetations. Vegetations occur more often on the atrial side of the atrioventricular valves and on the ventricular side of the aortic or pulmonic valves. Suppurative bacteria such as *Staphylococcus* may cause valve perforation, resulting in acute valvular insufficiency.

Infection may extend into the adjacent myocardium, producing necrotic fistulas, aneurysms, or ring abscess (usually of the aortic valve). Further extension results in pericarditis, found in 4% to 27% of cases of left-sided IE.[19] Involvement of the chordae tendineae may lead to rupture and valvular insufficiency. Tricuspid and pulmonic vegetations may embolize to the lungs, resulting in the formation of suppurative abscesses (Figures 1.18.1 and 1.18.2). Perforation, indentation, or aneurysm of the valve cusp or chordae tendineae is presumptive evidence of healed endocarditis.

Microscopically, IE is characterized by masses of fibrin, platelets, and polymorphonuclear leukocytes with bacterial colonies on the valve surface. Bacteria are less frequent after antibiotic treatment and may not be demonstrable by Gram stain even if present.[20] Later, the microscopic appearance is characterized by organization with capillary proliferation, a mixed cellular infiltrate, and the formation of granulation tissue. If the individual survives, the lesions eventually heal by fibrosis and re-endothelialization. Calcification may be present in the healed lesions.

1.18.6 Diagnosis

Patients with acute IE typically present with fever, chills, malaise, and heart murmur. Importantly, clinical signs of left- and right-sided endocarditis are different. The

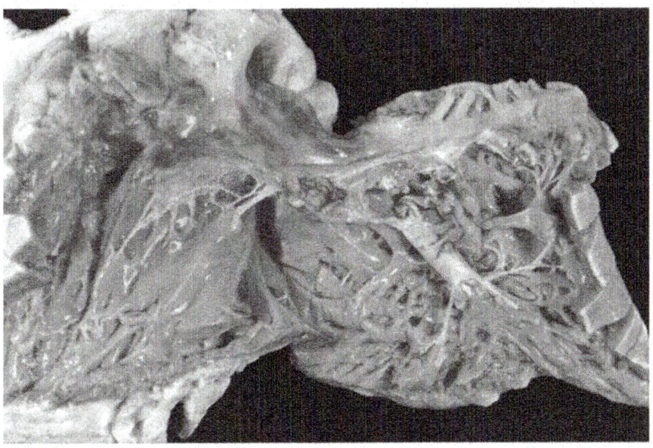

FIGURE 1.18.1 Large necrotizing vegetations on the tricuspid valve of this 31-year-old addict who commonly injected drug subcutaneously ("skin popping"). Blood cultures were positive for *Streptococcus hominus*.

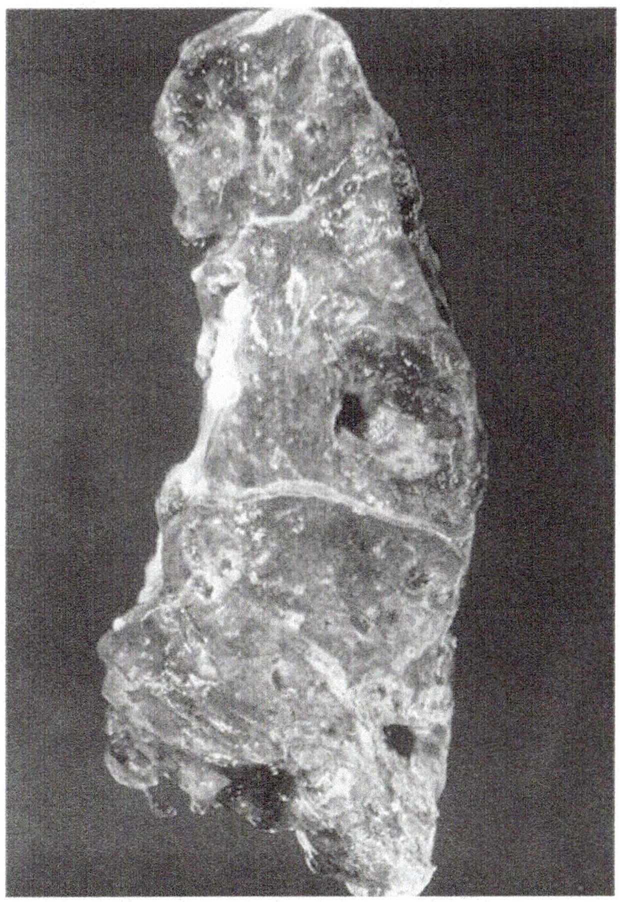

FIGURE 1.18.2 The lung from the victim in Figure 1.18.1 has multiple suppurative abscesses and extensive dark red consolidation.

presence of a new or worsening murmur, appreciated in 48% and 20% of patients, respectively, is typically heard in patients with left-sided IE. Right-sided valve murmurs (as in IV drug abusers) may be less audible than left-sided valve murmurs because the reduced chamber pressures of the right heart produce less turbulence and less noise. Signs of early tricuspid insufficiency may be minimal with only an atrial or ventricular gallop and no murmur. Later, a systolic regurgitant murmur, louder with inspiration, appears. Large "v" waves in the neck veins and a pulsating liver are signs of severe tricuspid regurgitation.[21]

The occurrence of chest pain with dyspnea and hemoptysis, along with characteristic abnormalities of the chest radiograph, including multiple segmental infiltrates with lower lobe predilection, suggests septic pulmonary emboli from a right-sided valvular vegetation. Other findings from right-sided IE include pulmonary abscess, pneumothorax, pleural effusions, and empyema. Rarely, cardiac complications, such as right-sided heart failure due to destruction of the tricuspid valve or conduction abnormalities, may occur as well. Systemic embolization can occur in right-sided endocarditis from septic pulmonary vein thrombi, left-sided valvular involvement, or paradoxical embolization through a patent foramen ovale. Thus, the "classic" findings of Janeway lesions, Osler nodes, and splinter hemorrhages are uncommonly seen in right-sided endocarditis. Table 1.18.2 compares the clinical features of right-sided and left-sided endocarditis.[22]

The source of the infecting organisms is usually from the addict's own body (skin or mouth flora) or soft tissue infection at the injection site, not contaminants in the drugs or the drug paraphernalia.[23] Cultures of heroin samples and drug paraphernalia have failed to demonstrate the presence of common pathogens. Bacteremia is characteristic of endocarditis, and most IV drug abusers with endocarditis have positive blood cultures that persist even after a few days of antibiotic treatment. Both the European Society of Cardiology (ESC) and the American College of Cardiology (ACC) recommend that three blood cultures be drawn if IE is suspected, although they differ on the time interval between draws. The ACC recommends waiting 6 hours, whereas the ESC suggests 30 minutes.[24–25] True culture-negative endocarditis is rare in IV drug abusers, and negative blood cultures suggest another cause for their illness, infection with fastidious organisms, or antibiotic administration prior to drawing of blood cultures. Recent advances in serologic testing have been able to identify the offending microorganism in up to 60% culture-negative cases of IE.[26]

Echocardiography is essential in the diagnosis of IE. Trans-thoracic echocardiogram (TTE) has a sensitivity between 50% and 90% and a specificity of 90% in patients with native valve endocarditis. A trans-esophageal echocardiogram (TEE) is recommended in situations in which a TTE is non-diagnostic and there is significant concern for IE. The presence of prosthetic valves and intracardiac devices lowers the sensitivity of TTE and may necessitate the use of a TEE for diagnosis rather than TTE.[24]

Currently, the ACC recommends that the modified Duke criteria be used to diagnose IE. These criteria are based upon clinical, microbiologic, and echocardiographic findings and are provided in Tables 1.18.3 and 1.18.4.

1.18.7 Prognosis and Outcomes

In-hospital mortality in IV drug abusers with acute right-sided endocarditis varies from 4% to 14%. This is lower than left-sided IE, which has an approximately 20% in-hospital mortality.[27] Unfortunately, recurrent IVDU is the most significant risk factor for recurrent IE, and a significant percentage relapse. Furthermore, surgical intervention in these patients is associated with very poor outcomes (5-year survival approximately 50%) and thus is not routinely recommended.[28]

1.18.8 Fenfluramine-Associated Regurgitant Valve Disease

Fenfluramine is a sympathomimetic amine chemically similar to amphetamine but with lower stimulant activity. It was first approved by the Food and Drug Administration (FDA) in 1973 as a short-term appetite suppressant and was a popular anorectic agent in the 1990s, prescribed alone or in combination with another sympathomimetic amine, phentermine. Prescriptions for these appetite suppressants exceeded 18 million in 1996. The FDA later requested the

TABLE 1.18.2
Comparison of Right-Sided and Left-Sided Endocarditis

Right-Sided	Left-Sided
IV drug abusers most common	Structural heart disease
Staphylococcus aureus most common	*Staphylococcus aureus* most common
Polymicrobial involvement uncommon	Polymicrobial involvement rare
Presents with pleuropneumonic symptoms	Symptoms from distal systemic embolization more common
10% of all infective endocarditis	90% of all infective endocarditis
Heart failure is unusual	Heart failure is common
Good prognosis with frequent cure after medical therapy	Poor prognosis with poor success rate using medical therapy
Surgery usually does not require immediate valve replacement	Surgery usually requires immediate valve replacement

TABLE 1.18.3
Major and Minor Criteria for the Diagnosis of Endocarditis

Major criteria
- Blood culture positive for IE
  - Typical microorganisms consistent with IE from two separate blood cultures:
    - Viridans streptococci, *Streptococcus bovis.* HACEK group, *Staphylococcus aureus;* or
    - Community-acquired enterococci. in the absence of a primary locus, or
  - Microorganisms consistent with IE from persistently positive blood cultures, defined as follows:
    - At least 2 positive cultures of blood samples drawn >12 h apart; or
    - All of 3 or a majority of ≥4 separate cultures of blood (with first and last sample drawn at least 1 h apart)
    - **Single positive blood culture for *Coxiella burnetii* or antiphase I IgG antibody titer >1 : 800**
- Evidence of endocardial involvement
- Echocardiogram positive for IE (**TEE** recommended in patients with prosthetic valves, rated at least "possible **IE**" by clinical criteria, or complicated **IE** [paravalvular abscess]; **TTE** as first test in other patients). defined as follows:
    - Oscillating intracardiac mass on valve or supporting structures, in the path of regurgitant jets, or on implanted material in the absence of an alternative anatomic explanation: or Abscess: or
    - New partial dehiscence of prosthetic valve
- New valvular regurgitation (worsening or changing of pre-existing murmur not sufficient)

Minor criteria
- Predisposition, predisposing heart condition or injection drug use
- Fever, temperature >38 °C
- Vascular phenomena, major arterial emboli, septic pulmonary infarcts, mycotic aneurysm, intracranial hemorrhage, conjunctival hemorrhages, and Janewav's lesions
- Immunologic phenomena: glomerulonephritis. Osier's nodes, Roth's spots, and rheumatoid factor
- Microbiological evidence: positive blood culture but does not meet a major criterion as noted above or serological evidence of active infection with organism consistent with IE

Echocardiographic minor criteria eliminated

Source: Li, JS, et al., *Clin. Infect. Dis.*, 30, 633, 2000.
TTE, trans-thoracic echocardiography, TEE, trans-esophageal echocardiography.

TABLE 1.18.4
Definition of Clinical and Pathologic Infective Endocarditis, as Defined by the Modified Duke Criteria

Definite infective endocarditis

Pathologic criteria

(1) Microorganisms demonstrated by culture or histologic examination of a vegetation, a vegetation that has embolized. or an intracardiac abscess specimen: or
(2) Pathologic lesions, vegetation or intracardiac abscess confirmed by histologic examination showing active endocarditis

Clinical criteria

(1) 2 major criteria; or
(2) 1 major criterion and three minor criteria; or
(3) 5 minor criteria

Possible infective endocarditis

(1) 1 major criterion and one minor criterion; or
(2) 3 minor criteria

Rejected

(1) Firm alternate diagnosis explaining evidence of infective endocarditis: or
(2) Resolution of infective endocarditis syndrome with antibiotic therapy for <4 days; or
(3) No pathologic evidence of infective endocarditis at surgery or autopsy, with antibiotic therapy for ≤4 days; or
(4) Does not meet criteria for possible infective endocarditis, as above

Source: Li, JS, et al., *Clin. Infect. Dis.*, 30, 633, 2000.

removal of fenfluramine-phentermine in 1997 after numerous documented reports of valvular heart disease and pulmonary hypertension. Fenfluramine's anorectic effect is thought to result from its ability to promote serotonin release and decrease brain re-uptake. It is thought that serotonin stimulates fibroblast growth and fibrinogenesis, which in turn causes valvular pathology. Both left- and right-sided valvular pathology has been associated with fenfluramine use, although the mitral valve is most typically and prominently affected.[28]

Connolly et al.[29] described 24 women with regurgitant valve disease that had its onset after they took fenfluramine-phentermine ("fen-phen") for 1 to 28 months. One-fifth of these women required valve surgery, and one-third developed pulmonary hypertension. Macroscopic features in the removed valves from these women included irregular nodular leaflet thickening, thickened and tethered glistening white leaflets, leaflets with "stuck on" or "onlay" plaques, and chordal fusion. Valve vegetations, commissural fusion, and annular dilatation were not seen. Microscopically, fibromyxoid plaques and nodules were seen to lie on top of the affected leaflet or encase the chordae tendinae. Myofibroblasts proliferated in the extracellular matrix. The onlay plaques are usually found to be superficial to the elastic fiber layer in the mitral valve. Ultimately, these pathologic changes result in a thickened immobile regurgitant valve. Other pathologists have confirmed these findings.[30,31] Later case control and meta-analysis studies,[32,33] however, did not demonstrate as much clinically significant mitral valve disease as the original Connolly study, but by then, fenfluramine had already been removed from the U.S. market. A long-term follow-up study of 5,743 users of fenfluramine found that all valves were at risk of developing some type of insufficiency. Female sex, advanced age, and duration of fenfluramine use were all associated with presence of valvular abnormalities.[34]

ACKNOWLEDGMENT

Michael D. Bell, M.D.

REFERENCES

1. Osler W. The Gulstonian lectures, on malignant endocarditis. *BMJ* 1885;1:577–79.
2. Correa de Sa DD, Tleyjeh IM, Anavekar NS, et al. Epidemiological trends of infective endocarditis: a population-based study in Olmsted County, Minnesota. *Mayo Clin Proc* 2010;85:422–26.
3. Weinstein L, Brusch JL. Endocarditis in intravenous drug abusers. In *Infective Endocarditis*, Oxford University Press, New York, 1996, 194–209.
4. Sande MA, Lee BL, Mills J, et al. Endocarditis in intravenous drug users. In *Infective Endocarditis*, Kaye D (Ed), Raven Press, New York City, 1992, 345.
5. Spijkerman IJ, van Ameijden EJ, Mientjes GH, et al. Human immunodeficiency virus infection and other risk factors for skin abscesses and endocarditis among injection drug users. *J Clin Epidemiol* 1996;49:1149.
6. Substance Abuse and Mental Health Services Administration. *Results from the 2013 National Survey on Drug Use and Health: Summary of National Findings. NSDUH Series H-48, HHS Publication No. (SMA) 14–4863.* Substance Abuse and Mental Health Services Administration, Rockville, MD, 2014. https://www.samhsa.gov/data/sites/default/files/NSDUHresultsPDFWHTML2013/Web/NSDUHresults2013.pdf (Accessed May 16, 2017).
7. Wurcel AG, Anderson JE, Chui KK, et al. Increasing infectious endocarditis admissions among young people who inject drugs. *Open Forum Infect Dis* 2016;3:ofw157.
8. Nahass RG, et al. Infective endocarditis in intravenous drug users: a comparison of human immunodeficiency virus type I-negative and-positive patients. *J Infect Dis* 1990;162(4):967–70.
9. Willoughby SB, Vlahov D, Herskowitz A. Frequency of left ventricular dysfunction and other echocardiographic abnormalities in human immunodeficiency virus seronegative intravenous drug abusers. *Am J Cardiol* 1993;71:446–7.
10. Pons-Llado G, Carreras F, Borras X, et al. Findings on Doppler echocardiography in asymptomatic intravenous heroin users, *Am J Cardiol* 1992;69:238–41.
11. Dressler F, Roberts W. Infective endocarditis in opiate addicts: analysis of 80 cases studied at autopsy. *Am J Cardiol* 1989;63:1240–57.
12. Yuan SM. Right-sided infective endocarditis: recent epidemiologic changes. *Int J Clin Exp Med* 2014;7:199–218.
13. Hoen B, Duval X. Infective endocarditis. *N Engl J Med* 2013;368:1425–33.
14. Miró JM, Moreno A, Mestres CA. Infective endocarditis in intravenous drug abusers. *Curr Infect Dis Rep* 2003;5:307–16.
15. Murdoch DR, Corey GR, Hoen B, et al. International Collaboration on Endocarditis-Prospective Cohort Study (ICE-PCS) investigators. Clinical presentation, etiology, and outcome of infective endocarditis in the 21st century: the International Collaboration on Endocarditis-Prospective Cohort Study. Clinical presentation, etiology, and outcome of infective endocarditis in the 21st century. *Arch Intern Med* 2009;169:463–73.
16. Millar BC, Prendergast BD, Moore JE. Community-associated MRSA (CA-MRSA): an emerging pathogen in infective endocarditis. *J Antimicro Chemother* 2008;61(1):1–7.
17. SousaC,BotelhoC,RodriguesD,etal.Infectiveendocarditisin intravenous drug abusers: an update. *Eur J Clin Microbiol Infect Dis* 2012;31:2905–10.
18. Hecht SR, Berger M. Right-sided endocarditis in intravenous drug users: prognostic features in 102 episodes. *Ann Int Med* 1992;117:560–6.
19. Buchbinder NA, Roberts WC. Left-sided valvular active infective endocarditis: a study of forty-five patients. *Am J Med* 1972;53:20–35.
20. McFarland MM. Pathology of infective endocarditis. In *Infective Endocarditis*, 2nd ed., Kaye D (Ed.), Raven Press, New York, 1992, 57–83.
21. Cannon NJ, Cobbs CG. Infective endocarditis in drug addicts. In *Infective Endocarditis*, Kaye D. (Ed.), University Park Press, Baltimore, 1976, 111–127.
22. Chan P, Ogilby JD, Segal B. Tricuspid valve endocarditis. *Am Heart J* 1989;117:1140–6.
23. Wetli CV. *Illicit Drug Abuse in Pathology of Environmental and Occupational Disease*, Craighead JD (Ed.), Mosby-Year Book, St. Louis, 1995, 259–268.

24. Nishimura RA, Otto CM, Bonow RO, et al. American College of Cardiology/American Heart Association Task Force on Practice Guidelines. 2014 AHA/ACC guideline for the management of patients with valvular heart disease: a report of the American College of Cardiology/American Heart Association Task Force on Practice Guidelines. *J Am Coll Cardiol* 2014;63:e57–185.
25. Habib G, Lancellotti P, Antunes MJ, et al. 2015 ESC guidelines for the management of infective endocarditis: the task force for the management of infective endocarditis of the European Society of Cardiology (ESC) Endorsed by: European Association for Cardio-Thoracic Surgery (EACTS), the European Association of Nuclear Medicine (EANM). *Eur Heart J* 2015;36:3075–128.
26. Fournier PE, Thuny F, Richet H, et al. Comprehensive diagnostic strategy for blood culture-negative endocarditis: a prospective study of 819 new cases. *Clin Infect Dis* 2010;51:131–40.
27. Thuny F, Grisoli D, Collart F, Habib G, Raoult D. Management of infective endocarditis: challenges and perspectives. *Lancet* 2012;379(9819):965–75.
28. Rabkin DG, Mokadam NA, Miller DW, Goetz RR, Verrier ED, Aldea GS. Long-term outcome for the surgical treatment of infective endocarditis with a focus on intravenous drug users. *Ann Thorac Surg* 2012;93:51–7.
29. Connolly HM, Crary JL, McGoon MD, Hensrud DD, Edwards BS, Edwards WD, Schaff HV. Valvular heart disease associated with fenfluramine-phentermine. *N Engl J Med* 1997;337:581–8.
30. Volmar KE, Hutchins GM. Aortic and mitral fenfluramine-phentermine valvulopathy in 64 patients treated with anorectic agents. *Arch Pathol Lab Med* 2001;125: 1555–61.
31. Steffee CH, Singh HK, Chitwood WR. Histologic changes in three explanted native cardiac valves following use of fenfluramines. *Cardiovasc Pathol* 1999;8:245–53.
32. Gardin JM, Schumacher D, Constantine G, et al. Valvular abnormalities and cardiovascular status following exposure to dexfenfluramine or phentermine/fenfluramine. *J Am Med Assoc* 2000;283:1738–40.
33. Sachdev M, Miller WC, Ryan T, Jollis JG. Effect of fenfluramine-derivative diet pills on cardiac valves: a meta-analysis of observational studies. *Am Heart J* 2002;144: 1065–73.
34. Allen MR, Urie PM, Hopkins PN. Valvular regurgitation and surgery associated with fenfluramine use: an analysis of 5743 individuals. *BMC Med* 2008;6(1):34.

1.19 DISORDERS OF THE CENTRAL NERVOUS SYSTEM

Bryan Corbett and Binh T. Ly

1.19.1 General Considerations

The central nervous system (CNS) is the target of myriad drugs, and the manifestations are as diverse as there are drugs that affect it. Some drugs are specific for the CNS, while others are not. Mechanisms of toxicity include affecting neurotransmitter release and reuptake, neuroreceptor binding, and more general metabolic derangements, to name a few. A cataloguing of all the drugs, their specific toxicities, or even more broad categories of CNS effects is beyond the scope of this chapter and to some extent has been covered in other sections. Instead, we will focus on CNS disorders related to alcohol, movement, infectious processes secondary to drug use, and heroin spongiform leukoencephalopathy.

1.19.2 Alcohol Related

1.19.2.1 Alcohol Withdrawal

Definition/Presentation: Alcohol withdrawal varies from minor to severe. It can occur as early as 6 hours after cessation of drinking and can occur with measurable ethanol levels. Early findings relate to autonomic hyperactivity and include tachycardia, tremor, hypertension, anxiety, and agitation (Victor 1953). About 10 percent of patients develop a seizure (Victor 1953). Seizures may occur even with otherwise minor alcohol withdrawal (McMicken). Delirium Tremens (DT) is a term frequently used in relation to alcohol withdrawal. Not all patients who undergo withdrawal are in DT or will develop DT. It is defined by an alteration in cognition or consciousness along with the other typical findings of withdrawal, occurs 2–4 days after cessation of drinking, and may last for up 2 weeks (American Psychiatric Association DSM V, Victor 1953).

Pathophysiology: Chronic ethanol use and stimulation of gamma-aminobutyric acid (GABA) receptors leads to downregulation of these receptors as well as a decrease in their sensitivity to activation (Brousse, Kumar S). In addition, N-methyl-D-aspartate (NMDA) receptors (which are inhibited by ethanol) are upregulated (Haugbol). The net effect is a decrease in inhibitory activity and an increase in excitatory activity in the CNS, leading to the aforementioned clinical manifestations.

Diagnosis: Various biochemical tests have been explored to try to identify those at risk for alcohol withdrawal. None have been perfect, and they are not routinely used. In our practice, diagnosis is based on history of ethanol abuse, presence of typical features, and exclusion of other causes of the patients' presentation.

Treatment: Benzodiazepines are the mainstay of treatment for alcohol withdrawal. They have been shown to be superior to various other medications in terms of preventing seizures and DTs (Kaim). Oral administration is reasonable in mild cases of withdrawal, but we recommend the intravenous (IV) route in more significant cases of withdrawal because of the more rapid effect. Various benzodiazepines can be used. The aforementioned study used chlordiazepoxide, but its use is limited in severe withdrawal, as it is only available in an oral formulation in the United States. Other benzodiazepines, including, but not limited to, lorazepam, diazepam, and midazolam, can be used as well. Diazepam has theoretical pharmacokinetic benefits compared with lorazepam and midazolam: specifically, a prolonged half-life and active metabolites that allow sustained effects after a single dose (Writland). We suggest initial dosing with 1–2 mg for lorazepam and 10–20 mg for diazepam (dependent on the severity of the presenting symptoms) with frequent post-dosing reassessment (about 15 minutes) and escalation of dosing by doubling the last dose until adequate control of symptoms occurs. Studies have demonstrated the efficacy of this symptom-based dosing rather than a fixed schedule (Cassidy, Daeppen, Saitz). This approach has been shown to be superior to continuous infusions of benzodiazepines as well (Spies). Occasionally, very high doses of benzodiazepines are needed, or benzodiazepines may even be ineffective in the treatment of alcohol withdrawal. In these cases, we recommend the use of phenobarbital, a barbiturate. Phenobarbital, like benzodiazepines, potentiates the effects of GABA and at high doses, can directly activate GABA receptors. It has a different binding site and mechanism of GABA potentiation than benzodiazepines, allowing synergistic effects as well as activity at certain GABA receptor subtypes that are not as responsive to benzodiazepines (Sieghart). Studies have shown a reduction in the incidence of intubation when phenobarbital has been used in resistant alcohol withdrawal (Gold). In addition, phenobarbital has been shown to be equivalent to benzodiazepines with regard to initial control and subsequent outpatient alcohol withdrawal treatment (Hendey). Other medications such as propofol, beta-antagonists, and dexmedetomidine have been used as well but are not currently routinely recommended (Baumgartner, Gold, Kraus, Rayner). Patients with mild withdrawal that can be controlled in the emergency department or outpatient clinic and with a maintained level of alertness can be safely discharged home. More severe withdrawal necessitating significant repeat dosing of medications or necessitating high enough doses (for control of autonomic dysfunction) to lead to CNS depression warrant admission.

1.19.2.2 Wernicke–Korsakoff Syndrome

Definition/Presentation: Wernicke encephalopathy is a neuropsychiatric disorder classically described as the triad of ataxia, nystagmus or ophthalmoplegia, and confusion (Sanvisens). This triad, however, is present in only about 16–20 percent of patients, and in one study, 12 percent of patients diagnosed with Wernicke encephalopathy had none of these features (Sanvisens, Harper). Wernicke encephalopathy is present in 0.8–2.8 percent of the general population

(Lishman, Charness). Among those with chronic ethanol abuse, the prevalence is higher: around 12–13 percent (Torvik 1982, Torvik 1991). Older studies have reported a 17 percent mortality, whereas a more recent study reported just over 45 percent of patients dying during the follow up period (median of 5.3 years) (Victor 1971, Victor 1989, Sanvisens). In this newer study, 2 of 51 patients died during their initial hospitalization (Sanvisens). Wernicke encephalopathy is reversible with appropriate treatment (see later) (Thomson 2002, Thomson 2009). Untreated, however, it can progress to include Korsakoff syndrome, generally considered irreversible and characterized by anterograde and retrograde amnesia, confabulation, and psychosis (Sanvisens, Latt, Thomson 2012).

Pathophysiology: Chronic alcohol use leads to thiamine deficiency via many mechanisms: specifically, poor nutritional intake, decreased absorption, and impaired utilization (Thomson 2002, Thomson 2009, Sechi, Cook). Thiamine is an essential co-factor for multiple enzymes involved in carbohydrate metabolism, and impairment of such widespread enzymatic processes can be expected to cause myriad effects (Latt, Sanvisens). Exactly how this metabolic insult leads to neurologic injury is still somewhat unclear. Current evidence suggests that increased concentrations of glutamate (presumably secondary to dysfunction of alpha-ketoglutarate dehydrogenase, of which thiamine is an essential co-factor) with subsequent calcium-mediated excitatory amino acid–induced neuronal injury plays a role (Butterworth, Jhala, Langlais, Munujos). This is likely an oversimplification of the true pathophysiology, however, and other mechanisms probably contribute as well.

Diagnosis: The diagnosis of Wernicke–Korsakoff syndrome is generally clinical. Imaging and lab modalities can aid in the diagnosis. For example, magnetic resonance imaging (MRI) is 93 percent specific for the diagnosis but only 53 percent sensitive (Antunez). Blood thiamine levels can be helpful, although Wernicke encephalopathy has been diagnosed with normal values (Davies). In addition, Wernicke encephalopathy has been diagnosed in the setting of normal blood thiamine levels in individuals with mutations in a thiamine transport protein needed for cellular uptake (Kono). The issue seems to be that blood thiamine levels do not necessarily reflect intracellular concentrations where the thiamine is needed for normal enzymatic function.

Treatment: Thiamine repletion is the mainstay of treatment. The optimal dose is unclear. A recent Cochrane review found that a dose of 200 mg per day intravenously (IV) was superior to a 5 mg per day IV dosing schedule. Other intermediate doses were not found to convey a benefit over the 5 mg per day dosing, however. In the end, the authors concluded that there was insufficient data to recommend a specific dose (Day). Although some controversy exists, thiamine should be given prior to glucose, as carbohydrate administration in the setting of thiamine deficiency may precipitate Wernicke encephalopathy (Latt).

1.19.2.3 Vitamin B_{12} (Cobalamin) Deficiency

Definition/Presentation: Vitamin B_{12}, or cobalamin, deficiency can have many manifestations. Particularly well known are the hematologic ones, but given this chapter's focus on the CNS, we will discuss subacute combined degeneration and the neuropathy that complicates deficiency. Subacute combined degeneration is the term given to damage to the posterior columns of the spinal cord, which leads to loss of proprioception and vibration sense in the arms and legs (Xiao). Clinical manifestations include generally symmetric sensorineural abnormalities, which can lead to gait difficulty and ataxia (Xiao). Peripheral sensory nerve and even motor nerve involvement occurs as well (Franques 2013, Sapperstein, De Rosa, Kalita). Presenting complaints typically relate to the sensory component of nerve damage and include numbness and tingling of the extremities as well as gait difficulty (Garakani). Physical exam may demonstrate weakness, hyperreflexia or hyporeflexia, reduced sensation (pinprick, vibration, proprioception), and gait difficulty (Lin, Garakani, Franques, Weimann). Occasionally, bowel and bladder involvement also occur (Garakani). While not the focus of this section, it should be noted that patients with Vitamin B_{12} deficiency may present with various neuropsychiatric manifestations such as dementia, psychosis, emotional lability, and amnesia, to name a few (Rannelli, Stabler). Vitamin B_{12} deficiency is relatively common, and its frequency increases with age. Its prevalence has been estimated at 15 percent in those older than 65, but this does not mean that all these patients had the above-described neurologic findings (Pennypacker). A retrospective study from 2010 assessed vitamin B_{12} levels in patients with megaloblastic anemia who had been admitted. Three of seven (42 percent) alcoholic patients in the study had low B_{12} levels (Fragasso). This may underestimate the prevalence of vitamin B_{12} deficiency in alcoholics, as normal levels do not rule out a functional deficiency (more later), and liver disease is known to falsely increase B_{12} levels (Ermens). Alternatively, this study may overestimate B_{12} deficiency, as megaloblastic anemia is a known result of B_{12} deficiency. Further complicating the interpretation of this data is that this population is unlikely to be generalizable to the overall population of alcoholics. In addition, as mentioned with regard to the whole population and not just alcoholics, a vitamin B_{12} deficiency does not correlate with the presence of neurologic findings. As such, the true incidence and prevalence of the neurologic complications of B_{12} deficiency are unclear.

Pathophysiology: Vitamin B_{12} is a necessary co-factor in the synthesis of methionine from homocysteine, which is important in proper myelin production. This myelin dysfunction is thought to lead to the manifestations of subacute combined degeneration (as well as other peripheral neuropathies), although multiple other metabolic processes are affected as well and may contribute to the disease process (Weimann, Hathout, Waclawik, Jevtovic, Sesso, Stacy). Alcohol consumption is a known risk factor for vitamin B_{12} deficiency (Weimann). Poor nutrition contributes to this deficiency, but there also seems to be a functional deficiency of vitamin B_{12} (i.e., normal circulating vitamin B_{12} levels but elevated levels of homocysteine and methylmalonic acid, which are metabolized by vitamin B_{12}–dependent enzymes) in these patients as well (Klee, Solomon). In addition to elevated levels of homocysteine and methylmalonic acid, a functional deficiency is supported by the fact that many of these patients respond to treatment with vitamin B_{12} despite their normal levels (Solomon, Devalia). The exact mechanism for this functional deficit is unclear, but there is some evidence that oxidant stress plays a role (Solomon).

Diagnosis: Suspicion for vitamin B_{12} deficiency should be prompted when patients present with typical complaints (as described earlier) in the setting of a supporting history and physical examination. Measurement of vitamin B_{12} levels can also be helpful. Normal vitamin B_{12} levels, however, do not rule out a functional deficiency as described earlier. A functional deficiency is supported by elevated levels of homocysteine or methylmalonic acid (Franques, Klee). Macrocytic anemia and hyper-segmented neutrophils may be indications of deficiency as well (Metz). MRI of the spinal cord may identify lesions in the posterior cord, corticospinal tracts, or peripheral nerves, but sensitivity is modest at 50 percent (Xiao). Electrophysiologic studies may be performed to confirm physical examination findings. These typically show a sensorimotor axonopathy (Saperstein).

Treatment: Vitamin B_{12} is available in oral and parenteral (intramuscular and subcutaneous) formulations. Some data shows that oral administration results in higher B_{12} values than intramuscular administration, but clinical outcomes of those patients with neurologic findings were roughly similar (Butler). Other studies have shown conflicting results, and the doses (as well as frequency) of parenteral and oral vitamin B_{12} were not uniform throughout the studies, making definitive conclusions difficult (Parry-Strong, Metaxas). Given current evidence, either high-dose oral (2,000–1,000 microgram doses daily or every other day) or parenteral vitamin B_{12} supplementation seems reasonable, although specific dosing recommendations are unclear.

1.19.3 Movement Disorders

1.19.3.1 Dopamine Receptor Antagonists

Pathophysiology: In discussing dopamine receptor antagonist–related movement disorders, it is prudent to start with the pathophysiology prior to any discussion of definition or presentation. The role of dopamine in movement is demonstrated by the effects of its deficiency, as in Parkinson disease,. in which pigmented cells in the substantia nigra (in the midbrain) are lost. Dopaminergic neurons from the substantia nigra project and synapse on neurons in the caudate and putamen (together the corpus striatum), forming the nigral striatal pathway. Dopamine receptor blockade in the corpus striatum seems to lead to some of the symptoms of decreased movement seen in Parkinson disease (Marsden, Caroff 2011, Sethi, Mehta). Interestingly, blockade takes place rapidly, but symptoms of drug-induced parkinsonism are often delayed days to weeks, suggesting a more complex mechanism (Nordstrom, Farde).

1.19.3.1.1 Akathisia Theory

Blockade of dopamine receptors in the cortex (receiving projections from the midbrain and hence termed the meso-cortical dopamine pathways) results in increased motor activity and may explain the somewhat paradoxical findings of akathisia that often occur in concert with dystonia or drug-induced parkinsonism (Marsden). In contrast, positron emission tomography (PET) studies have shown an association between akathisia and significant dopamine receptor blockade in the striatum. These studies did not assess dopamine receptor blockade in the cortex, however, and concurrent blockade could take place, so it is not possible to conclude that akathisia is only from striatal blockade (Nordstrom, Farde). Arguing against the meso-cortical theory of akathisia is the fact that newer atypical antipsychotics are known to have fewer extra-pyramidal side-effects (EPS) than typical antipsychotics yet have been shown to bind cortical dopamine receptors with similar affinity but striatal dopamine receptors with lower affinity (Xiberas, Kessler, Pierre, Caroff 2011). Further muddying the waters, however, are contradictory studies, which found no difference in striatal versus cortical dopamine blockade with atypical antipsychotics (Agid, Talvik).

1.19.3.1.2 Dystonia Theory

Yet another potential mechanism is suggested by the efficacy of antimuscarinic medications in treating dystonic reactions. As the theory goes, dopamine and acetylcholine balance is important in proper motor function. In the setting of dopamine receptor blockade, there is a relative overactivity of acetylcholine. Antimuscarinic medications may reduce this overactivity and restore some balance to the system (Mehta, Thanvi, Sethi). Further evidence of this theory comes from primate studies in which pre-administration of dopamine agonists prevents development of dystonia after dopamine antagonist administration (Nealer).

1.19.3.1.3 Tardive Movements

Similarly to the preceding discussions, the pathophysiology of tardive movements is incompletely understood. There is some thought that dopamine receptor hypersensitivity causes these movements. This is supported by the fact that discontinuation of dopamine receptor antagonists may precipitate tardive movements, increasing doses of dopamine receptor antagonists or other anti-dopaminergic drugs temporarily improve tardive symptoms, and administration of dopamine agonists in patients with Parkinson disease results in tardive like movements (Mehta, Marsden). Furthermore, a rat study has shown increased number and activity of dopamine receptors after treatment with dopamine receptor antagonists (Hitri). Human studies are less clear, however. One autopsy study demonstrated increased or decreased dopamine receptor concentration (dependent on location in the brain) in patients with a history of tardive symptoms (May Reynolds). A PET study showed no difference in dopamine receptor density between patients with and without tardive symptoms (Anderson).

All these theories are likely an oversimplification but provide some framework for the findings seen in dopamine receptor blockade. Various dopamine receptors exist, which can be stimulatory or inhibitory in response to dopamine. The D_2 subtype of dopamine receptors seems particularly implicated in the motor complications of antipsychotic medications. In addition, these receptors can be pre-synaptic or post-synaptic, adding another layer of complexity (Marsden, Sethi). Furthermore, there is complex interplay between dopamine and various other neurotransmitters, which likely play a role in the pathophysiology of these various movement disorder subtypes. Acetylcholine has already been mentioned, but GABA and serotonin transmission have also been implicated (Meltzer, Andersson 1989, Gunne, Tarsy, Caroff 2011, Sethi).

Definition/Presentation: Manifestations of dopamine receptor blockade exist on a continuum, with milder symptoms including dystonia and akathisia. Dystonia is characterized by involuntary muscle contractions that can be quite painful and occurs in 2–60 percent of individuals taking neuroleptics (Marsden, Pierre). Examples include back arching (opisthotonos) and neck twisting (torticollis) (Mehta), A particularly concerning and life-threatening example is acute laryngeal dystonia or spasmodic dysphonia, in which the vocal cords and laryngeal muscles are affected. The presentation includes stridor and respiratory distress (Burkhard, Mehta). Non-dopamine antagonists may rarely cause dystonic reactions. Examples include serotonin reuptake inhibitors, opioids, methylphenidate, rivastigmine, albendazole, gabapentin, cetirizine, foscarnet, quinine, and general anesthetics (Burkhard). Akathisia is characterized by a subjective sense of restlessness as well as objective findings in which patients fidget, repetitively move their limbs, and generally have difficulty in staying still (Burkhard, Ayd). Its incidence is anywhere from 21 to 75 percent (Cunningham). As with dystonia, occasionally, non-dopamine receptor blocking agents can precipitate akathisia. Examples include selective serotonin reuptake inhibitors (SSRIs), antiepileptics, and cocaine (Burkhard). Both dystonic reactions and akathisia may occur hours or days after initiation of dopamine receptor antagonists (Burkhard, Mehta, Keepers). Dose increases may also be responsible for precipitating dystonia and akathisia (Mehta, Healy). The risk for developing movement disorders, in general, is higher with the typical antipsychotics than with the newer atypical antipsychotics (Pierre, Caroff 2011). Young age and male gender are risk factors as well (Burkhard).

On the more severe spectrum of dopamine receptor blockade is drug-induced or drug-exacerbated parkinsonism (DIP). In DIP, the ultimate manifestations are due entirely to the effects of medications. A subset of patients may have subclinical Parkinson disease, and the addition of anti-dopaminergic medications precipitates or unmasks the underlying disease process. The incidence is reported to be 15–60 percent (Stephen, Mutch, Ayd). Findings include bradykinesia, rigidity, tremor, and gait instability. The tremor and gait difficulty are less prominent than in idiopathic Parkinson disease (Mehta, Lopez-Sendon). The onset is somewhat slower than for the above-mentioned milder symptoms, occurring on the order of weeks to months after drug initiation. Again, increasing doses may precipitate problems (Mehta). In contrast to dystonia and akathisia, the risk is higher in the elderly and females (Lopez-Sendon). As with dystonic reactions and akathisia, a number of non-dopamine antagonists have been associated with DIP. These include calcium channel blockers, phenytoin, valproate, levetiracetam, lithium, monoamine oxidase inhibitors (MAOIs), and SSRIs. Other, less common substances may cause parkinsonism, including organophosphate pesticides, manganese, methanol, cyanide, carbon monoxide, carbon disulfide, and 1-methyl-4-phenyl-1,2,3,6-tetrahydropyridine (MPTP) (Burkhard).

Tardive symptoms are unique in that they do not seem to exist within the continuum of dopamine receptor blockade that has been described earlier in reference to dystonia, akathisia, and DIP. Typically, tardive symptoms involve the orofacial muscles and manifest as repetitive movements such as lip smacking, chewing, and various tongue movements. This is classically referred to as tardive dyskinesia, but other variants exist, including tardive tics, akathisia, dystonia, and myoclonus, to name a few (Mehta, Caroff 2011, Sethi). Tardive symptoms were initially thought to be permanent, but there have been reports of improvement (with drug cessation), although few patients have complete resolution of symptoms (Gardos, Glazer 1984, Glazer 1990).

Diagnosis: There is no laboratory test, biological marker, or gold standard in the diagnosis of drug-induced movement disorders. Diagnosis should be based on history of drug exposure with appropriate clinical findings. Other possible diagnoses should be ruled out as appropriate within the clinical context.

Treatment: Antimuscarinic medications such as diphenhydramine and benztropine are effective in ameliorating dystonic reactions and akathisia. Other antimuscarinics have been reported to be useful as well. Benzodiazepines such as diazepam can also be used (Burkhard, Keepers, Mehta, Waugh). Discontinuation of the offending agent, if possible, is also important. Switching drugs from a typical to an atypical antipsychotic may also help. Other medications, including beta blockers, amantadine, mirtazapine, and clonidine, have also been used for the treatment of akathisia (Burkhard). In DIP, these management strategies have limited usefulness. In addition, typical medications used to treat Parkinson disease have limited efficacy in DIP, and withdrawal of the drug and a trial of a different agent is recommended (Burkhard). With withdrawal of the offending agent, DIP typically resolves over a period of months (Burkhard).

Treatment of tardive symptoms is challenging. As mentioned earlier, discontinuation of dopamine antagonists may eventually lead to improvement, but often symptoms worsen in the short term. Switching from typical to atypical antipsychotics (with less dopamine antagonism) may also help. A litany of other medications has been tried as well and will not be reviewed here (Mehta, Caroff 2011, Sethi).

1.19.3.2 Neuroleptic Malignant Syndrome

Definition/Presentation: Neuroleptic Malignant Syndrome (NMS) is a potentially life-threatening reaction that results from dopamine receptor blockade or withdrawal of dopaminergic medications (Bhanushali, Newman). Mortality was reported as 8.6 percent in one study (Nakamura). The reaction is idiosyncratic in that it can occur in patients on stable long-term dosing regimens of neuroleptics. Higher doses of neuroleptics, frequency of dose increases, relative dose increase, and parenteral administration (depot preparations) increase the risk of developing NMS (Adnet, Berardi, Keck). The risk is also higher with typical versus atypical antipsychotics at 16 versus 3 percent, respectively (Trollor). When the two subtypes of antipsychotics are included together, the incidence has been reported to be 0.07–3.23 percent (Trollor). Drugs other than antipsychotics with dopamine blocking activity may also precipitate NMS (Burkhard). Signs and symptoms typically develop over the course of days to weeks, and recovery is similarly prolonged. The classic description of NMS is that of hyperthermia, altered mental status, autonomic instability (in our experience, hyperactivity), and extremity rigidity ("lead-pipe" rigidity). In clinical practice, however, NMS exists on a continuum of dopamine receptor blockade, with severity and number of symptoms related to more severe receptor blockade. Altered mental status may entail confusion, delirium, or coma. Cardiac and respiratory abnormalities have been described as examples of autonomic instability (Bhanushali). In our experience, patients typically have autonomic hyperactivity, and this typically manifests as tachycardia and hypertension. In addition to rigidity, other motor symptoms related to dopamine blockade may be present, including akinesia, bradykinesia, tremor, and cogwheeling. Rhabdomyolysis may result secondary to muscular rigidity (Bhanushali).

Pathophysiology: NMS is thought to be the result of central dopamine receptor blockade (predominantly, if not completely, the D_2 receptor). The pathophysiology of motor dysfunction and dopamine receptor blockade has been reviewed previously and will not be further discussed here. The hypothalamus is important in thermoregulation, and dopaminergic neurons are known to synapse on the hypothalamus. Some evidence suggests that impairment in proper dopamine-hypothalamic function is important in the development of hyperthermia in NMS (Gurrera 1996). Exactly how dopamine blockade leads to the autonomic dysfunction in NMS is unclear. A role for dopamine in regulation of the sympathetic nervous system is probably related in some degree to dopamine's interaction with the hypothalamus and has been postulated as the cause of the autonomic dysfunction (Gurrera 1999). Altered mental status is likely multifactorial.

Diagnosis: Various diagnostic criteria for NMS have been proposed and will not be reviewed here. A more recent set of consensus criteria was published in 2011 that is worth mentioning (Gurrera 2011). These criteria were externally validated in 2017; however, some critiques bear mentioning (Gurrera 2017). First, there is no agreed-upon gold standard for the diagnosis of NMS; thus, validation of any criteria is inherently difficult. The study was retrospective and based not on bedside assessment of included patients but rather, on phone interview records. In addition, the initially derived criteria to be validated were modified, albeit slightly, from their initial development. Our approach to diagnosis is based on exposure to dopamine receptor antagonists or withdrawal of dopaminergic medications with findings consistent with NMS, and other possible causes are excluded.

Treatment: Treatment revolves around supportive care and withdrawal of culprit medications or reinstitution of dopaminergic medications. We recommend liberal use of benzodiazepines for sedation and to help treat autonomic hyperactivity. Patients with resistant hyperthermia and continued muscular rigidity may warrant neuromuscular blockade and mechanical ventilation. Dantrolene, which prevents release of calcium from sarcoplasmic reticulum, has been used to treat NMS but offers no benefit over paralytics when the concern is extreme rigidity and does not address the pathophysiologic basis of NMS (Bhanushali, Sethi, Paul-Pletzer, Szentesi). Bromocriptine, a dopamine receptor agonist, has also been used for the treatment of NMS. Only oral formulations are available, complicating use in critically ill patients. Intuitively, a dopamine agonist makes sense for the treatment of a condition related to dopamine antagonism. However, randomized controlled trials are lacking, leading to debate over bromocriptine's efficacy compared with supportive care alone. One study found a statistically significant longer length of stay and more complications in patients with NMS treated with supportive care alone versus dantrolene, bromocriptine, or both (Rosebush). This study grouped dantrolene and bromocriptine together, and some patients in this group received both dantrolene and bromocriptine. In addition, this study was not standardized in terms of treatment choice, which was left to physician discretion. These limitations make definitive conclusions about the use of bromocriptine difficult. Finally, electroconvulsive therapy (ECT) has been reported to be beneficial in severe cases of drug-resistant NMS (Nisijima 1999). Its use is rare, and further study is needed to determine efficacy and indications if it is found to be useful.

1.19.3.3 Serotonin Syndrome

Definition/Presentation: Serotonin syndrome (SS) is a potentially life-threatening condition related to excessive serotonergic activity. Manifestations range from mild to severe depending on the level of serotonergic activity. It is classically described as consisting of a triad of altered mental status, neuromuscular abnormalities, and autonomic findings (Sun-Edelstein, Boyer). Not all three findings need be present for the diagnosis. Altered mental status may entail agitation, confusion, or hallucinations. Autonomic findings include tachycardia, diaphoresis, hyperthermia, mydriasis, and hypertension. Rigidity may be present, although hyperreflexia and particularly clonus, while not pathognomonic, is highly suggestive of SS in the right clinical context. Seizures may also occur (Boyer, Sun-Edelstein). SS is generally rapid in onset, occurring within 24 hours of dose escalation or initiation of a new serotonergic agent (Mason). Fatalities are often related to uncontrolled hyperthermia (Nadkarni, Rajapakse, Thanacoody). SS has a reported incidence of 0.4 cases per 1,000 patient months with therapeutic dosing. However, this study only looked at a single drug, nefazodone (Mackay). Among patients who overdose on SSRIs, 14–16 percent develop SS (Isbister). These estimates should be interpreted with caution, given the diagnostic challenges of SS, and many other factors likely play a role in the incidence of SS as well. Examples include whether the patient's presentation is due to an overdose of a single drug or the result of a drug–drug interaction. The specific medication(s) involved also likely plays a role.

Pathophysiology: Serotonergic neurons are found in the median raphe nuclei in the brainstem (Saper, Ivanusa). Serotonin is important to many processes in the CNS, including, but not limited to, wakefulness, emesis, migraine, and thermoregulation (Gillman 2004, Rastogi, Aykroyd, Mills, Saper). Serotonin is also found in the periphery, where it modulates vascular tone and gastrointestinal motility (Van Oekelen, Saper). The pathophysiology of SS is incompletely understood, but evidence points to excessive activity at a specific subtype of serotonin receptor, 5-HT_{2A} (Van Oekelen, Nisijima 2004, Nisijima 2001). This mechanism is supported by the efficacy of 5-HT_{2A} receptor antagonists in ameliorating signs and symptoms of SS (Gillman 1999, Nisijima 2004). Norepinephrine may play a role in the pathophysiology of SS as well. Animal models have shown some correlation between severity of symptoms and CNS norepinephrine levels (Nisijima 2004, Nisijima 2001). SS typically results from mixing of serotonergic drugs but does occur with overdose of single agents (Daniels, Hanekamp, Keltner, Paruchuri). Culprit medications include MAOIs, tricyclic antidepressants, SSRIs, certain opioids and antibiotics, anti-tussive medications (dextromethorphan), as well as a host of others (Sternbach, Gill, Parrott, Lee, Gardner, Giese, DeSilva, Callaway, Izzo, Lange-Asschenfeldt, Turkel, Asch).

Diagnosis: As with NMS, the diagnosis of SS is clinical. There is no pathognomonic finding or laboratory test. Laboratory abnormalities are non-specific and secondary to physiologic and metabolic insults. Diagnosis should be based on exclusion of other causes and the identification of typical findings in the setting of multiple serotonergic agents or overdose. Different diagnostic criteria have been proposed, and although some have been found to have good agreement with a clinical toxicologist, none have been externally validated to our knowledge (Dunkley, Sternbach).

Treatment: General goals of treatment should be to support normal physiologic function. Removal of the offending agent or agents is paramount. Benzodiazepines should be used for sedation and to help mitigate autonomic and muscular hyperactivity. Cooling measures should be instituted for hyperthermia that does not improve with sedation alone. In extreme cases, patients should be paralyzed to prevent muscular hyperactivity and further heat generation. Cyproheptadine is an antihistamine with antagonistic properties at the 5-HT_{2A} receptor (Graudins, Lappin). Animal models have shown benefit in treating or preventing SS (Nisijima 2001, Nisijima 2004). Various human cases have reported promising results as well (Gillman 1999, Graudins, Lappin). Along with rapid onset, many cases of SS resolve rapidly, with resolution within 24 hours. Some drugs with a long half-life or active metabolites may have a more prolonged course (Boyer).

1.19.3.4 Nitrous Oxide (N_2O)

Definition/Presentation: Nitrous oxide (N_2O) is a gas used for anesthesia as well as a propellant for whipped cream (Garakani, Weimann). Individual canisters for use in home whipped cream dispensers are also sold and commonly referred to as "whippits." Recreational abuse for its mind-altering effects is relatively common. Chronic use leads to neurologic damage of the dorsal columns of the spinal cord, responsible for fine touch and proprioception, as well as peripheral nerves, similarly to vitamin B_{12} deficiency (Lin, Blanco, Layzer, Vishnubhakat). This presentation was previously described under Vitamin B_{12} deficiency.

Pathophysiology: The importance of Vitamin B_{12} to proper myelin formation has been discussed previously under vitamin B_{12} deficiency. Rather than a quantitative deficiency in Vitamin B_{12}, N_2O causes a functional deficiency of vitamin B_{12}. N_2O oxidizes the cobalt ion in Vitamin B_{12}, rendering B_{12} inactive. Thus, despite normal levels of vitamin B_{12}, enzymatic function is impaired, and typical manifestations of a quantitative B_{12} deficiency ensue (Garakani, Weimann).

Diagnosis: As mentioned, N_2O causes a functional B_{12} deficit, and measured levels are likely to be within the normal range. As such, diagnosis is based on identification of a functional deficiency. This has been covered under the vitamin B_{12} deficiency section, and the reader is referred there for further information on diagnosing a functional deficiency as well as the use of adjunctive testing.

Treatment: Initial management should be counseling on the discontinuation of N_2O abuse. While vitamin B_{12} supplementation is the treatment of choice in typical vitamin B_{12} deficiency, administration in the setting of continued N_2O abuse will only result in continued vitamin B_{12} oxidation and inactivation. Direct supplementation with methionine (the product of the vitamin B_{12}–dependent enzymatic transformation of homocysteine) circumvents this issue (Stacy). Symptoms generally improve over time, although in some cases they may be permanent (Weimann).

1.19.4 CNS Infections Related to Drug Use

1.19.4.1 Botulism

Definition/Presentation: A brief disclaimer prior to further discussion. Botulism is not technically a disorder of the CNS, as it affects peripheral nerves; however, the connection between wound botulism and IV drug abuse and significant associated morbidity and mortality make it an important topic to discuss in this chapter. *Clostridium botulinum* is a gram-positive, spore-forming, obligate anaerobic bacterium (Sobel, Smith). Multiple forms of botulism exist; foodborne, wound, infant, and adult intestinal toxemia (Brook, Cherington, Sobel). Wound botulism, the form that typically occurs in IV drug users, will be discussed here. While wound botulism is rare, it has been increasing in frequency over the last 25 years or so (Cherington, Sobel). Even among IV drug users, wound botulism is more common in those using "black tar heroin" (Passaro, Werner). Cases have been reported with intranasal cocaine use as well (Kudrow). The disease is a result of the effects of toxin produced by *C. botulinum*, but rare cases secondary to other *Clostridium* species have been reported (Brook, Sobel). The typical presentation is that of a descending, symmetric, flaccid paralysis. Early symptoms are usually bulbar and include ptosis, diplopia (from weakness of ocular muscles), dysarthria, and dysphagia (Brook, Cherington 1974, Shapiro, Hughes). Autonomic involvement can occur, with manifestations such as postural hypotension, decreased sweating (anhidrosis), constipation, urinary retention, and dry mouth (Brook, Cherington, Barnes, Sobel). Diaphragmatic involvement may compromise the patient's respiratory status and may progress to death. Sensory involvement is lacking, and patients maintain an intact mental status. Mydriasis or unresponsive pupils also occurs (Cherington). In contrast to other forms of botulism, gastrointestinal symptoms such as nausea, vomiting, and diarrhea are absent in wound botulism (Werner).

Pathophysiology: As mentioned, botulism results from toxins produced by the bacteria rather than a classic infection. Distinct yet related toxin subtypes A through G cause essentially the same clinical syndrome, some being more potent than others (Brook, Brin, Burningham, Schantz). Contamination of a wound with spores may result in germination (needs anaerobic environment), bacterial replication, and toxin production (Brook). In relation to drug use, this typically occurs in IV drug users or skin poppers who inject "black tar heroin" (Passaro, Werner). The toxin prevents the release of acetylcholine from peripheral cholinergic neurons (Horowitz, Cherington). This binding is irreversible, and the neuron must form a new nerve terminal to regain proper function (Foran, Duchen). Inhibition of release of acetylcholine, the neurotransmitter at the neuromuscular junction, is the basis of the flaccid paralysis that is seen. Acetylcholine is also the neurotransmitter at various peripheral cholinergic neurons of the autonomic nervous system, resulting in those findings as well (Girlanda, Jenzer).

Diagnosis: Wound botulism should be considered if the patient presents with typical symptoms and has a history of IV drug use. The presence of an open wound with typical symptoms may also prompt consideration. The wound may be relatively innocuous or even absent. Identification of the bacteria and/or toxin in the wound may be helpful in the setting of an appropriate presentation. Identification of toxin in serum is diagnostic (Sobel). The botulism subtype can be identified using mouse bioassays (Hayes). Electromyography may be helpful in identifying the neuromuscular junction as the location of pathology (Cherington). This is not pathognomonic for botulism, however, as other disease processes may also act at the neuromuscular junction.

Treatment: Antitoxin may be given to prevent further nerve terminal involvement, but this will not reverse terminals already affected and should be given early (Brook, Cherington, Tacket). Antitoxin consists of equine derived F(ab')2 fragments, but immune reactions do occur (Brook, Cherington, CDC). It is a heptavalent antitoxin with activity against botulism strains A–G (CDC). Antibiotic treatment with penicillin and wound debridement should be considered to treat and remove the infection and prevent further toxin production (Brook, Cherington). Respiratory support with intubation and mechanical ventilation may be necessary in severe cases. Most patients recover completely, but this may be prolonged on the order of weeks to months and in some cases, up to a year (Brook, Cherington, Sobel).

1.19.4.2 Spinal Epidural Abscess

Definition/Presentation: Spinal epidural abscesses (SEAs) are rare, occurring in 0.2–2.8 versus 12.5 cases per 10,000, depending on the study (Martin RJ, Rigamonti). The classic presentation is a triad of back pain, fever, and neurologic deficits. This occurs in only 13–37 percent of patients, however (Rigamonti). Most patients complain of back pain (70–100 percent), about half of fever, and another half of weakness of the extremities (Patel, Darouiche, Thompkins, Adogwa). Multiple risk factors exist, including advanced age, diabetes, alcoholism, immunocompromised states, cancer, and spinal instrumentation or trauma. Most germane to our discussion is the risk with IV drug use (Chao). Most abscesses (about 80 percent) occur in the lumbar and thoracic spine (Kabbara). Complications include permanent neurological injury (30–50 percent) and death (10–20 percent) (Darouiche, Schoenfeld, Reihsaus, Adogwa).

Pathophysiology: In about half of cases, SEA is the result of seeding from another infectious site, although spread from a contiguous site of infection also occurs (Baker, Ericsson, Darouiche). *Staphylococcus aureus* is the most commonly implicated bacterium, being found in 39–90 percent of cases (Tang, Rigamonti, Nussbaum, Sendi, Darouiche). Abscesses also occur secondary to epidural injections (Grewal). In these cases, *S. epidermidis* is more frequently implicated (Soehle). *Pseudomonas* has been isolated from patients with IV drug use (Kaufman). Various other bacteria and fungi have been implicated as well (Reihsaus, Huang).

Diagnosis: Diagnosis is challenging, with anywhere from 11 to 75 percent of cases missed on first presentation (Darouiche, Patel). Another study found that about half of patients have two emergency department visits and a tenth have three or more visits before the definitive diagnosis is made (Davis 2004). Physical examination findings vary and include focal and diffuse back tenderness, motor and sensory deficits, as well as loss of bowel and bladder control (Darouiche, Reihsaus, Rigamonti, Soehle, Tompkins). The erythrocyte sedimentation rate (ESR) is a useful laboratory test to aid diagnosis. One study found that 98 percent of 63 patients had an ESR above 20 (Davis 2004). Another found ESR to be 100 percent sensitive for the diagnosis of SEA although only 67 percent specific (Davis 2011). Conversely, an elevated white blood cell count was present in only two-thirds of patients (Davis 2004, Davis 2011). Imaging is the mainstay of diagnosis. Contrast enhanced MRI with gadolinium is best, with a sensitivity of 90 percent (Teman, Rigamonti). A computed tomography (CT) myelogram can be obtained if MRI contraindications exist (Chima, Defroda) but is invasive, and CT with contrast is also an option (Chima-Melton, Defroda, Sendi, Darouiche).

Treatment: Once the diagnosis has been made or suspicion is high enough, broad-spectrum antibiotics should be initiated until speciation of the culprit organism occurs. Vancomycin plus a third-generation cephalosporin or aminoglycoside for Gram negative coverage is reasonable (Rigamonti). Surgical spine specialists should then be consulted for operative management. Conservative care has been used, but some studies show increased morbidity and mortality with non-operative management (Patel, Adogwa, Savage K, Alton, Epstein).

1.19.5 Heroin Smoker Leukoencephalopathy

Definition/Presentation: Heroin spongiform leukoencephalopathy (HSLE) was first reported by Wolters et al. in 1982 after an outbreak in the Netherlands (Wolters). It is primarily associated with smoking or inhaling heroin vapor (Wolters). This method of heroin administration is also termed "chasing the dragon" and is usually done by heating heroin on a piece of aluminum foil with an open flame (Kass-Hout). There is a diverse clinical presentation, depending upon the areas of the brain involved, and patients can present with inattention, personality changes, dysarthria, ataxia, nystagmus, dementia, coma, and death (Buxton, Kass-Hout). Wolters initially described 3 stages of HSLE among his initial cohort of 47 patients. Patients first presented with speech difficulties, "pronounced motor restlessness," and "cerebellar ataxia" as well as "apathy." After 2-4 weeks, 26 (55 percent) of these patients went on to what Wolters called the intermediate stage. The remainder of the patients had a stable clinical course with some partial improvement. The intermediate stage was characterized by rapid worsening of cerebellar signs, particularly gait. Hemiplegia, quadriplegia, myoclonic jerks, and chorea-athetoid movements also were reported. Of these 26 patients, another 11 (or 23 percent of the original 47) went on to the third or terminal stage of the disease. Again, this progression occurred over 2–4 weeks, and those who did not progress remained stable or had some improvement. This final stage was characterized by central pyrexia, hypotonia, mutism, and death from respiratory failure (Wolters). More recent case reports describe patients whose clinical description was consistent with this final stage yet who made a meaningful recovery (Barnett, Gacouin, Chen, Chang). One possible explanation is an improvement in supportive care since Wolters' initial publication, where only 1 patient of the 11 deaths was mechanically ventilated) (Wolters). Since its initial description, there have been multiple other reports of HSLE from around the globe, including Europe, Asia, and North America (Kass-Hout, Long, Au-Yeung, Bach, Gacouin, Kriegstein 1997, Pirompanich). The presentation and progression or improvement of these cases are, in general, consistent with Wolters' initial description, except for the handful of patients who recovered from the final and supposedly terminal stage.

The specifics regarding frequency of heroin smoking and time since last use are not reported in Wolters' paper, only that epidemiological studies pointed to smoking heroin as the cause. Wolters did state that there was no correlation between disease course and duration or quantity of heroin used. In a case series from Canada, the mean duration of "chasing the dragon" before development of HSLE was 9.5 years (Buxton). In contrast, some publications describe development of HSLE after smoking heroin only one to two times (Kass-Hout, Kriegstein 1997, Vella). Another case series suggested a dose–response relationship with regard to the severity of clinical findings (Kriegstein 1997). While initially associated with "chasing the dragon," HSLE has been reported after IV administration and ingestion as well (Maschke, Perez, Barnett, Pirompanich, Rizzuto, Chen).

Pathophysiology: The pathophysiology of HSLE is incompletely understood. A toxic contaminant in heroin or a toxic byproduct of pyrolysis was initially proposed to be the causative factor. Rat studies, however, were unable to reproduce the disease when exposed to heroin pyrolyzate that caused HSLE in human patients (Wolters). In addition, reports with IV administration argue against the pyrolysis theory. In Wolters' original paper, autopsy of 10 of the 11 patients who died showed white matter edema. Histopathologic examination of a subset of the brains from Wolter's study as well as more recent histopathologic examinations show vacuole formation in myelin, causing a "spongiform myelinopathy" with associated edema (Wolters, Rizzuto, Kriegstein 1997, Yin). Electron microscopy, in line with histopathologic examinations, shows spongiform degeneration of the myelin but also mitochondrial swelling in the associated oligodendrocytes (Wolters, Kriegstein 1997).

Diagnosis: As with most diagnoses, a good history and physical examination are key to correct diagnosis. Patients presenting with some of the above-described neurologic deficits with a history of "chasing of the dragon" should prompt consideration of HSLE. Patients with a history of IV heroin abuse with the proper presentation should still be considered for HSLE, given previous reports mentioned earlier. The diagnosis can be confirmed on MRI, which typically shows increased T2 and DWI signal within white matter of the cerebellum, brainstem, and cerebrum to varying degrees (Kass-Hout, Au-Yeung, Bach, Gacouin, Hagel, Villela). The utility of cerebral spinal fluid (CSF) is unclear. Two cases reported elevated protein, and one of these also had white cells in the CSF; however, the CSF was unremarkable in other reports (Bach, Long, Barnett, Gacouin, Hill, Kriegstein 1997, Pirompanich).

Treatment: Treatment is generally supportive along with cessation of drug use. Radiologic and functional improvement have been reported with long-term supportive care and rehabilitation as mentioned earlier (Barnett, Gacouin). Treatment with coenzyme Q has been associated with good outcomes, but other treatment modalities were employed in these cases, including corticosteroids, vitamin C, and vitamin E in addition to usual supportive care, making definitive conclusions difficult (Kriegstein 1999, Gacouin, Kriegstein).

REFERENCES

Adnet P, Lestavel P, Krivosic-Horber R. Neuroleptic malignant syndrome. *Br J Anaesth* 2000;85:129–35.

Adogwa O, Karikari IO, Carr KR, et al. Spontaneous spinal epidural abscess in patients 50 years of age and older: a 15-year institutional perspective and review of the literature: clinical article. *J Neurosur Spine* 2014;20(3):344–9.

Agid O, Mamo D, Ginovart N, Vitcu I, Wilson AA, Zipursky RB, Kapur S. Striatal vs Extrastriatal Dopamine D_2 Receptors in Antipsychotic Respons-A Double-Blind PET Study in Schizophrenia. *Neuropsychopharmacology* 2007;32:1209–15.

Alton TB, Patel AR, Bransford RJ, Bellabarba C, Lee MJ, Chapman JR. Is there a difference in neurologic outcome in medical versus early operative management of cervical epidural abscesses? *Spine J* 2015;15:10–17.

American Psychiatric Association. *Diagnostic and Statistical Manual of Mental Disorders*, 5th edition, test revision (DSM-V). Washington, DC: American Psychiatric Association, 2013.

Anderson U, Eckernas SA, Harting P, et al. Striatal binding of 11C-NMSP studied with positron emission tomography in patients with persistent tardive dyskinesia: no evidence for altered dopamine D2 receptor binding. *J Neural Transm Gen Sect* 1990;79:215–26.

Andersson U, Haggstrom JE, Levin ED, et al. Reduced glutamate decarboxylase activity in the subthalamic nucleus in patients with tardive dyskinesia. *Mov Disord* 1989;4(1):37–46.

Antunez E, Estruch R, Cardenal C, et al. Usefulness of CT and MR imaging in the diagnosis of acute Wernicke's encephalopathy. *AJR Am J Roentgenol* 1998;171:1131–7.

Asch DA, Parker RM. The Libby Zion case: one step forward or two steps backward? *N Engl J Med* 1988;318:771–5.

Au-Yeung K, Lai C. Toxic leucoencephalopathy after heroin inhalation. *Australas Radiol* 2002;46:306–8.

Ayd FJ Jr. A survey of drug-induced extrapyramidal reactions. *JAMA* 1961;175:1054–60.

Aykroyd L, Welker PL. Management of serotonin syndrome: clinical considerations. *Advanced Emer Nursing J* 2008;30(4):303–9.

Bach AG, Jordan B, Wegener NA, Rusner C, Kornhuber M, Abbas J, Surov A. Heroin Spongiform Leukoencephalopathy. *Clin Neuroradiol* 2012;22:345–9.

Baker AS, Ojemann RG, Swartz MN, Richardson EP. Spinal epidural abscess. *N Engl J Med* 1975;293:463–8.

Barnes M. Botulinum toxin: mechanisms of action and clinical use in spasticity. *J Rehabil Med* 2003;41(suppl):56–9.

Barnett MH, Miller LA, Reddel SW, Davies L. Reversible delayed leukoencephalopathy following intravenous heroin overdose. *J Clin Neurosci* 2001;8:165–7.

Baumgartner GR, Rowen RC. Clonidine vs chlordiazepoxide in the management of acute alcohol withdrawal syndrome. *Arch Intern Med* 1987;147:1223–6.

Berardi D, Amore M, Keck PJ, Troia M, Dell'Atti M. Clinical and pharmacologic risk factors for neuroleptic malignant syndrome: a case-control study. *Biol Psychiatry* 1998;44:748–54.

Bhanushali MJ, Tuite PJ. The evaluation and management of patients with neuroleptic malignant syndrome. *Neurol Clin N Am* 2004;22:389–411.

Blanco G, Peters HA. Myeloneuropaty and microcytosis associated with nitrous oxide abuse. *Arch Neurol* 1983;40:416–8.

Boyer EW, Shannon M. Current concepts: the serotonin syndrome. *N Eng J Med* 2005;352:1112–20.

Brin MF. Botulinum toxin: chemistry, pharmacology, toxicity, and immunology. *Muscle Nerve Suppl* 1997;6:S146–S168.

Brook I. Botulism: the challenge of diagnosis and treatment. *Rev Neurol Dis* 2006;3(4):182–9.

Brousse G, Arnaud B, Vorspan F, et al. Alteration of glutamate/GABA balance during acute alcohol withdrawal in emergency department: a prospective analysis. *Alcohol Alcohol* 2012;47:501–8.

Burkhard PR. Acute and subacute drug-induced movement disorders. *Parkin Relat Dis* 2014;S108–S112.

Burningham MD, Walter FG, Mechem C, et al. Wound botulism. *Ann Emerg Med* 1994;24:1184–7.

Butler CC, Vidal-Alaball J, Cannings-John R, et al. Oral vitamin B12 versus intramuscular vitamin B12 for vitamin B12 deficiency: a systematic review of randomized controlled trials. *Fam Pract* 2006;23:279.

Butterworth RF, Kril JJ, Harper CG. Thiamin-dependent enzyme changes in the brains of alcoholics: relationship to the Wernicke-Korsakoff syndrome. *Alcohol Clin Exp Res* 1993;17:1084–8.

Buxton JA, Sebastian R, Clearsky L, Angus N, Shah L, Lem M, Spacey SD. Chasing the dragon – characterizing cases of leukoencephalopathy associated with heroin inhalation in British Columbia. *Harm Reduc J.* 2011;8(3).

Callaway JC, Grob CS. Ayahuasca preparations and serotonin reuptake inhibitors: a potential combination for severe adverse reactions. *J Psychoactive Drugs* 1998;30:367–9.

Caroff S, Mann SC. Neuroleptic malignant syndrome. *Med Clin North Am* 1993;77:185–202.

Caroff SN, Hurford I, Lybrand J, et al. Movement disorders induced by antipsychotic drugs: implications of the CATIE schizophrenia trial. *Neurol Clin* 2011;29(1):127–48.

Cassidy EM, O'Sullivan I, Bradshaw P, Islam T, Onovo C. Symptom-triggered benzodiazepine therapy for alch=ohol withdrawal syndrome in the emergency department: a comparison with the standard fixed dose benzodiazepine regimen. *Emerg Med J* 2012;29:802–4.

Centers for Disease Control and Prevention: Protocol #4509. IND protocol:use of botulism antitoxin heptavalent (A, B, C, D, E, G)-(Equine)(H-BAT) after exposure to Clostridium botulinum toxin or other botulinum toxin-producing clostridia species due to a naturally-occurring or isolated, unintentional incident (Investigational New Drug Application [BB-IND 6750]).

Chang GY, Ganguly G. Early antitoxin treatment in wound botulism results in better outcome. *Eur Neurol* 2003;49:151–3.

Chang W, Chang Y, Hsu S, Lin G, Chen S. Reversible delayed Leukoencephalopathy after Heroin Intoxication with Hypoxia: a Case Report. *Acta Neurol Taiwan* 2009;18:198–202.

Chao D, Nanda A. Spinal epidural abscess: a diagnostic challenge. *Am Fam Physician* 2002;65:1341–6.

Charness ME, Simon RP, Greenberg DA. (1989) Ethanol and the nervous system. *N Engl J Med* 321:442–54.

Chen C, Lee K, Lee C, Chin S, Chung H, Zimmerman RA. Heroin-Induced spongiform leukoencephalopathy: value of diffusion MR imaging. *J Comput Assist Tomogr* 2000;24(5):735–7.

Cherington M. Botulism: ten year experience. *Arch Neurol* 1974;30:432–7.

Cherington M. Botulism: update and review. *Seminars in Neurology* 2004;24(2):155–63.

Cook CC, Hallwood PM, Thomson AD. B vitamin deficiency and neuropsychiatric syndromes in alcohol misuse. *Alcohol Alcohol* 1998;33: 317–36.

Cunningham Owens DG. *A Guide to the Extrapyramidal Side-Effects of Antipsychotic Drugs.* Cambridge: Cambridge University Press, 1999, 351p.

Daeppen J-B, Gache P, Landry U, et al. Symptom-triggered vs fixed-schedule doses of benzodiazepine for alcohol withdrawal" a randomized treatment trial. *Arch Intern Med* 2002;162:1117–21.

Daniels RJ. Serotonin syndrome due to venlafaxine overdose. *J Accid Emerg Med* 1998;15:333–4.

Darouiche RO. Spinal epidural abscess. *N Eng J Med* 2006;355(19):2012–20.

Davies SB, Joshua FF, Zagame AS. Wernicke's encephalopathy in a non-alcoholic patient with a normal blood thiamine level. *Med J Aust* 2011;194:483.

Davis DP, Salazar A, Chan TC, Vilke GM. Prospective evaluation of a clinical decision guideline to diagnose spinal epidural abscess in patients who present to the emergency department with spine pain. *J Neurosurg Spine* 2011;14:765–70.

Davis DP, Wold RM, Patel RJ, et al. The clinical presentation and impact of diagnostic delays on emergency department patients with spinal epidural abscess. *J Emerg Med* 2004;26:285–91.

Day E, Bentham PW, Callaghan R, Kuruvilla T, George S. Thiamine for prevention and treatment of Wernicke-Korsakoff Syndrome in people who abuse alcohol. *Cochrane Database Syst Rev* 2013;7.

De Rosa A, Rossi F, Lieto M, Bruno R, De Renzo A, Palma V et al. Subacute combined degeneration of the spinal cord in a vegan. *Clin Neurol Neurosurg* 2012;114:1000–2.

DeSilva KE, Le Flore DB, Marston BJ, Rimland D. Serotonin syndrome in HIV infected individuals receiving antiretroviral therapy and fluoxetine. *AIDS* 2001;15:1281–5.

Devalia V. Diagnosing vitamin B-12 deficiency on the basis of serum B-12 assay. *BMJ* 2006;333:385–6.

Duchen LW, Strich SJ. The effects of botulism toxin on the pattern of innervation of skeletal muscle in the mouse. *Q J Exp Physiol Cogn Med Sci* 1968;53:84–9.

Dunkley EJ, Isbister GK, Sibbritt D, et al. The Hunter Serotonin Toxicity Criteria: simple and accurate diagnostic decision rules for serotonin toxicity. *QJM* 2003;96:635–42.

Epstein NE. Timing and prognosis of surgery for spinal epidural abscess: a review. *Surg Neurol Int* 2015;6(19):475–86.

Ericsson M, Algers G, Schliamser SE. Spinal epidural abscesses in adults: review and report of iatrogenic cases. *Scand J Infect Dis* 1990;22:249–57.

Ermens AA, Vlasveld LT, Lindemans J. Significance of elevated cobalamin (vitamin B12) levels in blood. *Clin Biochem* 2003;36:858–90.

Farde L, Nordstrom A,Weisel F, et al. Positron emission tomographic analysis of central D1 and D2 dopamine receptor occupancy in patients treated with classical neuroleptics and clozapine. *Arch Gen Psychiatry* 1992;49:539–44.

Foran PG, Davletov B, Meunier FA. Getting muscles moving again after botulinum toxin: novel therapeutic challenges. *Trends Mol Med* 2003;9:291–8.

Franques J, Chiche L, Mathis S. Sensory neuronopathy revealing severe Vitamin B12 Deficiency in a Patient with Anorexia Nervosa: an often-forgotten reversible cause. *Nutrients* 2017;9:281.

Franques J, Gazzola S. Neuropathies métaboliques et carentielles: mise au point sur le diabète, les carences en vitamine B12 et les carences en cuivre. *Rev Neurol (Paris)* 2013;169:991–6.

Gacouin A, Lavoue S, Signouret T, Person A, Dinard MD, Shpak N, Thomas R. Reversible spongiform leucoencephalopathy after inhalation of heated heroin. *Inten Care Med* 2003;29:1012–5.

Garakani A, Jaffe RJ, Savla D, Welch AK, Protin CA, Bryson EO, McDowell DM. Neurologic, psychiatric, and other medical manifestations of nitrous oxide abuse: a systematic review of the case literature. *Am J Addic* 2016;25:358–69.

Gardner MD, Lynd LD. Sumatriptan contraindications and the serotonin syndrome. *Ann Pharmacother* 1998;32:33–8.

Gardos G, Cole JO. Overview: public health issues in tardive dyskinesia. *Am J Psychiatry* 1980;137:776–81.

Giese SY, Neborsky R. Serotonin syndrome: potential consequences of Meridia combined with demerol or fentanyl. *Plast Reconstr Surg* 2001;107:293–4.

Gill M, LoVecchio F, Selden B. Serotonin syndrome in a child after a single dose of fluvoxamine. *Ann Emerg Med* 1999;33:457–9.

Gillman PK. Serotonin syndrome: history and risk. *Fundamental Clinical Pharm* 1998;12: 482–91.

Gillman PK. The serotonin syndrome and its treatment. *J Psychopharmacol* 1999;13:100–9.

Gillman PK, Whyte IM. Serotonin syndrome. In Haddad P, Dursun S, Deakin B, editors, *Adverse Syndromes and Psychiatric Drugs*. Oxford University Press, Oxford, 2004, 37–49.

Girlanda P, Vita G, Nicolosi C, et al. Botulinum toxin therapy: distant effects on neuromuscular transmission and autonomic nervous system. *J Neurol Neurosurg Psychiatry* 1992;55:844–5.

Glazer WM, Moore DC, Schooler NR, et al. Tardive dyskinesia. A discontinuation study. *Arch Gen Psychiatry* 1984;41(6):623–7.

Glazer WM, Morgenstern H, Schooler N, et al. Predictors of improvement in tardive dyskinesia following discontinuation of neuroleptic medication. *Br J Psychiatry* 1990;157:585–92.

Gold JA, Rimal B, Nolan A, Nelson LS. A strategy of escalating doses of benzodiazepines and phenobarbital administration reduces the need for mechanical ventilation in delirium tremens. *Crit Care Med* 2007;35:724–30.

Graudins A, Stearman A, Chan B. Treatment of the serotonin syndrome with cyproheptadine. *J Emerg Med* 1998;16:615–9.

Grewal S, Hocking G, Wildsmith JAW. Epidural abscesses. *Br J Anaesth* 2006;96:292–302.

Gunne LM, Haggstrom JE, Sjoquist B. Association with persistent neuroleptic induced dyskinesia of regional changes in brain GABA synthesis. *Nature* 1984;309(5966):347–9.

Gurrera RJ. Sympathoadrenal hyperactivity and the etiology of neuroleptic malignant syndrome. *Am J Psychiatry* 1999;156:169–80.

Gurrera RJ et al. An international consensus study of neuroleptic malignant syndrome diagnostic criteria using the Delphi Method. *J Clin Psychiatry* 2011;72(9):1222–8.

Gurrera RJ, Chang SS. Thermoregulatory dysfunction in neuroleptic malignant syndrome. *Biol Psychiatry* 1996;39:207–12.

Gurrera RJ, Mortillaro G, Velamoor VJ, Caroff SN. A validation study of the international consensus diagnostic criteria for neuroleptic malignant syndrome. *J Clin Psychopharmacol* 2017;37:67–71.

Hagel J, Andrews G, Vertinsky T, Heran MKS, Keogh C. "Chasing the Dragon" – Imaging of Heroin Inhalation Leukoencephalopathy. *CARJ* 2005;56(4):199–203.

Hanekamp BB, Zijlstra JG, Tuleken JE, et al. Serotonin syndrome and rhabdomyolysis in venlafaxine poisoning: a case report. *Neth J Med* 2005;63:316–8.

Harper CG, Giles M, Finlay-Jones R. Clinical signs in Wernicke Korsakoff complex: a retrospective analysis of 131 cases diagnosed at autopsy. *J Neurol Neurosurg Pschiatry* 1986;49:341–5.

Harper CG, Sheedy DL, Lara AI, Garrick TM, Hilton JM, Raisanen J. Prevalence of Wernicke-Korsakoff Syndrome in Australia: has thiamne fortification made a difference? *Med J Aust* 1998;168:542–5.

Hathout L, El-Saden S. Nitrous oxide-induced B-12 deficiency myelopathy: perspectives on the clinical biochemistry of vitamin B12. *J Neurol Sci* 2011;301:1–8.

Haugbol SR, Ebert B, Ulrichsen J. Upregulation of glutamate receptor subtypes during alcohol withdrawal in rats. *Alcohol Alcohol* 2005;40:89–95.

Hayes MT, Soto O, Ruoff KL. Case records of the Massachusetts General Hospital: case 22–1997. *N Engl J Med* 1997;337:184–90.

Healy D, Farquhar G. Immediate effects of droperidol. *Hum Psychopharmacol* 1998;13(2):113–20.

Hendey GW, Dery RA, Barnes RL, Snowden B, Mentler P. A prospective, randomized, trial of phenobarbital versus benzodiazepines for acute alcohol withdrawal. *Am J Emerg Med* 2011;29(4):382–5.

Hill MD, Cooper PW, Perry JR. Chasing the dragon – neurological toxicity associated with inhalation of heroin vapour: case report. *CMAJ* 2000;162(2):236–8.

Hitri A,Weiner W, Borison R, et al. Dopamine binding following prolonged haloperidol pretreatment. *Ann Neurol* 1978;3:134–40.

Horowitz BZ. Botulinum toxin. *Crit Care Clin* 2005;21:825–39.

Huang RC, Shapiro GS, Lim M, Sandhu HS, Lutz GE, Herzog RJ. Cervical epidural abscess after epidural steroid injection. *Spine (Phila Pa 1976)* 2004;29:E7–E9.

Hughes JM, Blumenthal JR, Merson MH, Lombard GL, Dowell VR, Gangarosa EJ. Clinical features of types A and B food-borne botulism. *Ann Intern Med* 1981;95:442–5.

Isbister GK, Bowe SJ, Dawson A, Whyte IM. Relative toxicity of selective serotonin reuptake inhibitors (SSRIs) in overdose. *J Toxicol Clin Toxicol* 2004;42:277–85.

Ivanusa Z, Hecimovic H, Demarin V. Serotonin syndrome. *Neuropsychiatry, Neuropsychol Behav Neurol* 1997;10(3):210–12.

Izzo AA, Ernst E. Interactions between herbal medicines and prescribed drugs: a systematic review. *Drugs* 2001;61:2163–75.

Jenzer G, Mumenthaler M, Ludin HP, Robert F. Autonomic dysfunction in botulism B: a clinical report. *Neurology* 1975;25:150–3.

Jevtovic-Todorovic V, Todorovic SM, Mennerick S, et al. Nitrous oxide (laughing gas) is an NMDA antagonist, neuroprotectant and neurotoxin. *Nat Med* 1998;4:460–3.

Jhala SS, Hazell AS. Modeling neurodegenerative disease pathophysiology in thiamine deficiency: consequences of impaired oxidative metabolism. *Neurochem Int* 2011;58:248–60.

Kabbara A, Rosenberg SK, Untal C. Methicillin-resistant Staphylococcus aureus epidural abscess after transforaminal epidural steroid injection. *Pain Physician* 2004;7:269–72.

Kaim S, Klett C, Rothfeld B. Threatment of the acute alcohol withdrawal state: a comparison of four drugs. *Am J Psychiatry* 1969;125:1640–6.

Kalita J, Chandra S, Bhoi SK, Agarwal R, Misra UK, Shankar SK et al. Clinical, nerve conduction and nerve biopsy study in vitamin B12 deficiency neurological syndrome with a short-term follow-up. *Nutr Neurosci* 2014;17:156–63.

Kass-Hout T, Kass-Hout O, Darkhabani MZ, Mokin M, Mehta B, Radovic V. "Chasing the Dragon"- Heroin-Associated Spongiform Leukoencephalopathy. *J Med Toxicol* 2011;7:240–2.

Kaufman DM, Kaplan JG, Litman N. Infectious agents in spinal epidural abscesses. *Neurology* 1980;30:844–50.

Keck PE Jr, Pope HG Jr, Cohen BM,McElroy SL, Nierenberg AA. Risk factors for neuroleptic malignant syndrome. A case-control study. *Arch Gen Psychiatry* 1989;46:914–8.

Keepers GA, Clappison VJ, Casey DE. Initial anticholinergic prophylaxis for neuroleptic-induced extrapyramidal syndromes. *Arch Gen Psychiatry* 1983;40(10):1113–7.

Keltner NL, Hall S. Neonatal serotonin syndrome. *Perspect Psychiatr Care* 2005;41:88–91.

Kessler R et al. Occupancy of striatal and extrastriatal Dopamine D_2 receptors by clozapine and quetiapine. *Neuropsychopharmacology* 2006;31:1991–2001.

Klee GC. Cobalamin and folate evaluation: measurement of methylmalonic acid and homocysteine vs Vitamin B12 and Folate. *Clin Chem* 2000;46:8(B).

Kono S, Miyajima H, Yoshida K, et al. Mutations in a thiamine-transporter gene and Wernicke's-like encephalopathy. *N Engl J Med* 2009;360:1792–4.

Kraus ML, Gottlieb LD, Horwitz RI, Anscher M. Randomized clinical trial of atenolol in patients with alcohol withdrawal. *N Eng J Med* 1985;313:905–9.

Kriegstein AR, Armitage BA, Kim PY. Heroin inhalation and progressive spongiform leukoencephalopathy. *N Engl J Med* 1997, 336:589–90.

Kriegstein AR, Shungu DC, Millar WS, Armitage BA, Brust JC, Chillrud S, Goldman J, Lynch T: leukoencephalopathy and raised brain lactate from heroin vapor inhalation ("chasing the dragon"). *Neurology* 1999;53:1765–73.

Kudrow DB, Henry DA, Haska DA, et al. Botulism associated with Clostridium botulinum sinusitis after intranasal cocaine abuse. *Ann Intern Med* 1988;109:984–5.

Kumar S, Porcu P, Werner DF, et al. The role of GABA(A) receptors in the acute and chronic effects of ethanol: a decade of progress. *Psychopharmacology* 2009;205:529–64.

Kumar N. Neurologic aspects of cobalamin (B12) deficiency. *Handb. Clin. Neurol* 2014;120:915–26.

Lange-Asschenfeldt C, Weigmann H, Hiemke C, Mann K. Serotonin syndrome as a result of fluoxetine in a patient with tramadol abuse: plasma level-correlated symptomatology. *J Clin Psychopharmacol* 2002;22:440–1.

Langlais PJ, McRee RC, Nalwalk JA, Hough LB. Depletion of brain histamine produces regionally selective protection against thiamine deficiency-induced lesions in the rat. *Metab Brain Dis.* 2002;17:199–210.

Lappin RI, Auchincloss EL. Treatment of the serotonin syndrome with cyproheptadine. *N Engl J Med* 1994;331:1021–22.

Latt N, Dore G. Thiamin in the treatment of Wernicke encephalopathy in patients with alcohol use disorders. *Intern Med J* 2014;44:911–15.

Layzer RB. Myeloneuropathy after prolonged exposure to nitrous oxide. *Lancet* 1978;1227–30.

Lee DO, Lee CD. Serotonin syndrome in a child associated with erythromycin and sertraline. *Pharmacotherapy* 1999;19:894–6.

Lin R, Chan H, Chang Y, Su J. Subacute combined degeneration caused by nitrous oxide intoxication: case reports. *Acta Neurol Taiwan* 2011;20:129–37.

Lishman WA. Cerebral disorder in alcoholism: syndromes of impairment. *Brain* 1981;104:1–20.

Long H, Zhou J, Zhou X, Xie Y, Xiao B. Acute hydrocephalus following heroin induced leukoencephalopathy. *Neurol Sci* 2013;34:1031–1.

Lopez-Sendon J, Mena MA, de Yebenes JG. Drug-induced parkinsonism. *Expert Opin Drug Saf* 2013;12:487–96.

Mackay FJ, Dunn NR, Mann RD. Antidepressants and the serotonin syndrome in general practice. *Br J Gen Pract* 1999;49:871–4.

Marsden CD, Jenner P. The pathophysiology of extrapyramidal side-effects of neuroleptic drugs. *Psychol Med* 1980;10:55–72.

Martin PER, Singleton CK, Hiller-Sturmhofel S. The role of thiamine deficiency in alcoholic brain disease. *Alcohol Res Health* 2003;27:134–42.

Martin RJ, Yuan HA. Neurosurgical care of spinal epidural, subdural, and intramedullary abscesses and arachnoiditis. *Orthop Clin North Am* 1996;27:125–36.

Maschke M, Fehlings T, Kastrup O, Wilhelm HW, Leonhardt G. Toxic leukoencephalopathy after intravenous consumption of heroin and cocaine with unexpected clinical recovery. *J Neurol* 1999;246:850–1.

Mason PJ, Morris VA, Balcezak TJ. Serotonin syndrome: presentation of 2 cases and review of the literature. *Med (Baltimore)* 2000;79:201–9.

May Reynolds GP, Brown JE, McCall JC, Mackay AV. Dopamine receptor abnormalities in the striatum and pallidum in tardive dyskinesia: a postmortem study. *J Neural Transm Gen Sect* 1992;87:225–30.

McMicken D, Liss JL. Alcohol-related seizures. *Emerg Med Clin North Am* 2011;29:117–24.

Mehta SH, Morgan JC, Sethi KD. Drug-induced movement disorders. *Neurol Clin* 2015;33:153–74.

Meltzer HY, Matsubara S, Lee JC. Classification of typical and atypical antipsychotic drugs on the basis of dopamine D-1, D-2 and serotonin2 pKi values. *J Pharmacol Exp Ther* 1989;251(1):238–46.

Metaxas C, Mathis D, Jeger C, Herskerger KE, Arnet I, Walter P. Early biomarker response and patient preferences to oral and intramuscular vitamin B12 substitution in primary care: a randomized parallel-group trial. *Swiss Med Wkly* 2017;147.

Metz J, Bell AH, Flicker L, Bottiglieri T, Ibrahim J, Seal E, Schultz D. The significance of subnormal serum vitamin B12, concentration in older people: a case control study. *J Am Geriatr Soc* 1996;44:1355–61.

Mills KC. Serotonin syndrome. A clinical update. *Crit Care Clin* 1997;13(4):763–83.

Munujos P, Vendrell M, Ferrer I. Proto-oncogene c-fos induction in thiamine deficient encephalopathy. Protective effects of nicardipine on pyrithiamine-induced lesions. *J Neurol Sci* 1993;118:175–80.

Mutch WJ, Dingwall-Fordyce I, Downie AW, et al. Parkinson's disease in a Scottish city. *Br Med J (Clin Res Ed)* 1986;292(6519):534–6.

Nadkarni GN, Hoskote SS, Piotrkowski J, Annapureddy N. Serotonin syndrome, disseminated intravascular coagulation, and hepatitis after a single ingestion of MDMA in an Asian woman. *Am J Therapeutics* 2012:1–3.

Nakamura M, Yasunaga H, Miyata H, et al. Mortality of neuroleptic malignant syndrome induced by typical and atypical antipsychotic drugs: a propensity-matched analysis from the Japanese diagnosis procedure combination database. *J Clin Psychiatry* 2012;73:427–30.

Nealer R, Gerhardt S, Liebman JM. Effects of dopamine agonists, catecholamine depletors, and cholinergic and GABAergic drugs on acute dyskinesia in the squirrel monkeys. *Psychopharmacology (Berl)* 1984;82:20–6.

Newman EJ, Grosset DG, Kennedy PG. The parkinsonism-hyperpyrexia syndrome. *Neurocrit Care* 2009;10:136–40.

Nisijima K, Ishiguro T. Electroconvulsive therapy for the treatment of neuroleptic malignant syndrome with psychotic symptoms: a report of five cases. *J ECT* 1999;15:158–63.

Nisijima K, Shioda K, Yoshino T, Takano K, Kato S. Memantine, an NMDA antagonist, prevents the development of hyperthermia in an animal model for serotonin syndrome. *Pharmacopsychiatry* 2004;37:57–62.

Nisijima K, Yoshino T, Yui K, Katoh S. Potent serotonin (5-HT2A) receptor antagonists completely prevent the development of hyperthermia in an animal model of the 5-HT syndrome. *Brain Res* 2001;890:23–31.

Nordstrom AL, Farde L, Halldin C. Time course of D2-dopamine receptor occupancy examined by PET after single oral doses of haloperidol. *Psychopharmacology (Berl)* 1992;106:433–8.

Nussbaum ES, Rigamonti D, Standiford H, Numaguchi Y, Wolf AL, Robinson WL. Spinal epidural abscess: a report of 40 cases and review. *Surgical Neurol* 1992;38(3):225–31.

Parrott AC. Recreational Ecstasy/MDMA, the serotonin syndrome, and serotonergic neurotoxicity. *Pharmacol Biochem Behav* 2002;71:837–44.

Parry-Strong A, Langdana F, Haeusler S, Weatherall M, Krebs J. Sublingual vitamin B12 compared to intramuscular injection in patients with type 2 diabetes treated with metformin: a randomized trial. *N Z Med J.* 2016;129(1436):67–75.

Paruchuri P, Godkar D, Anandacoomarswamy D, et al. Rare case of serotonin syndrome with therapeutic doses of paroxetine. *Am J Ther* 2006;13:550–2.

Passaro DJ, Werner SB, McGee J, et al. Wound botulism associated with black tar heroin among injecting drug users. *JAMA* 1998;279:859–63.

Patel AR, Alton TB, Bransford RJ, Lee MJ, Bellabarba CB, Chapman JR. Spinal epidural abscesses: risk factors, medical versus surgical management, a retrospective review of 128 cases. *Spine J* 2014;14:326–30.

Paul-Pletzer K, Yamamoto T, Bhat MB, et al. Identification of a dantrolene-binding sequence on the skeletal muscle ryanodine receptor. *J Biol Chem* 2002;277:34918–23.

Pennypacker LC, Allen RH, Kelly JP, Matthews LM, Grigsby J, Kaye K, et al. High prevalence of cobalamin deficiency in elderly outpatients. *J Am Geriatr Soc* 1992;40:1197–204.

Perez ER, Maeder P, Riovier L, Deonna T. Toxic leukoencephalopathy after heroin ingestion in a 2.5 year old child [letter]. *Lancet* 1992, 340:729.

Pierre JM. Extrapyramidal symptoms with atypical antipsychotics: incidence, prevention and management. *Drug Saf* 2005;28:191–208.

Pirompanich P, Chankrachang S. Intravenous heroin-associated delayed spongiform leukoencephalopathy: case report and review of the literature. *J Med Assoc Thai* 2015;98(7):703–8.

Rajapakse S, Abeynaike L, Wickramarathne T. Venlafaxine-associated serotonin syndrome causing severe rhabdomyolysis and acute renal failure in a patient with idiopathic Parkinson disease. *J Clin Psychopharmacol* 2010;30(5):620–2.

Rannelli et al. Vitamin B12 deficiency with combined hematological and neuropsychiatric derangements: a case report. *J Med Case Rep* 2014;8:277.

Rastogi R, Swarm RA, Patel TA. Case scenario: opioid association with serotonin syndrome. *Anesthesiology* 2011;115(6):1291–98.

Rayner SG, Weinert CR, Peng H, Jepse S, Broccard AF, Study Institution. Dexmedetomidine as adjunt treatment for severe alcohol withdrawal in the ICU. *Ann Intensive Care* 2012;2:12.

Reihsaus E, Waldbaur H, Seeling W. Spinal epidural abscess: a metaanalysis of 915 patients. *Neurosurg Rev* 2000;23:175–204; discussion 205.

Rigamonti D, Liem L, Sampath P, et al. Spinal epidural abscess: contemporary trends in etiology, evaluation, and management. *Surg Neurol* 1999;52:189–196; discussion 197.

Rizzuto N, Morbin M, Ferrari S, Cavallaro T, Sparaco M, Boso G, Gaetti L:Delayed spongiform leukoencephalopathy after heroin abuse. *Acta Neuropathol* 1997;94:87–90.

Rosebush PI, Stewart T, Mazurek MF. The treatment of neuroleptic malignant syndrome. Are dantrolene and bromocriptine useful adjuncts to supportive care? *Br J Psychiatry* 1991;159:709–12.

Saitz R, Mayo-Smith MF, Roberts MS. Individualized treatment for alcohol withdrawal. *JAMA* 1994;272:519–23.

Sanvisens A, Zuluago P, Fuster D, Rivas I, Tor J, Marcos M, Chamorr AJ, Muga R. Long-term mortality of patients with an alcohol-related wernicke-korsakoff syndrome. *Alcohol Alcoho* 2017;52(4):466–71.

Saper CB. Brain stem modulation of sensation, movement, and consciousness. In Kandel ER, Schwartz JH, Jessell TM (Eds.) *Principles of Neural Science.* 4th ed. New York: McGraw-Hill, 2000, 896.

Saperstein DS, Wolfe GI, Gronseth GS, Nations SP, Herbelin LL, Bryan WW, Barohn RJ. Challenges in the identification of cobalamin-deficiency polyneuropathy. *Arch Neurol* 2003;60:1296–301.

Savage K, Holtom PD, Zalavras CG. Spinal epidural abscess: early clinical outcome in patients treated medically. *Clin Orthop* 2005;439:56–60.

Savage S, Ma D. The neurotoxicity of nitrous oxide: the facts and "putative" mechanisms. *Brain Sci* 2014;4:73–90.

Schantz EJ, Johnson EA. Botulinum toxin: the story of its development for the treatment of human disease. *Perspect Biol Med* 1997;40:317–27.

Schoenfeld AJ, Wahlquist TC. Mortality, complication risk, and total charges after the treatment of epidural abscess. *Spine J* 2015;15:249–55.

Sechi GP, Serra A. Wernicke's encephalopathy – new clinical settings and recent advances in diagnosis and management. *Lancet Neurol* 2007;6:442–55.

Sendi P, Bregenzer T, Zimmerli W. Spinal epidural abscess in clinical practice. *Quart J Med* 2008;101(1):1–12.

Sesso RM, Iunes Y, Melo AC. Myeloneuropathy following nitrous oxide anesthaesia in a patient with macrocytic anaemia. *Neuroradiology* 1999;41:588–90.

Sethi KD. Movement disorders induced by dopamine blocking agents. *Semi Neurol* 2001;21(1):59–69.

Shapiro R, Hatheway CL, Swerdlow DL. Botulism in the United States: a clinical and epidemiologic review. *Ann Intern Med* 1998;129.

Sieghart W. Structure and pharmacology of gamma-aminobutyric acidA receptor subtypes. *Pharmacol Sci* 1995;47:181–234.

Smith LDS. The occurrence of *Clostridium Botulinum* and *Clostridium Tetani* in the soil of the U.S. *Health Lab Sci* 1978;15:74–80.

Sobel J. Botulism. *Clin Infect Dis* 2005;41:1167–73.

Soehle M, Wallenfang T. Spinal epidural abscesses: clinical manifestations, prognostic factors, and outcomes. *Neurosurgery* 2002;51:79–85; discussion 86–87.

Solomon LR. Functional cobalamin (vitamin B12) deficiency: role of advanced age and disorders associated with increased oxidative stress. *Eur J Clin Nutr* 2015;69(6):687–92.

Spies CD, Otter HE, Huske B, et al. Alcohol withdrawal severity is decreased by symptom-oriented adjusted bolus therapy in the ICU. *Intesive Care Med* 2003;29:2230–8.

Stabler SP. Vitamin B12 deficiency. *N Engl J Med* 2013;368:149–60.

Stacy CB, Di Rocco A, Gould RJ. Methionine in the treatment of nitrous-oxide-induced neuropathy and myeloneuropathy. *J Neurol* 1992;239:401–3.

Stephen PJ, Williamson J. Drug-induced parkinsonism in the elderly. *Lancet* 1984;2(8411):1082–3.

Sternbach H. The serotonin syndrome. *Am J Psychiatry* 1991;148:705–13.

Sun-Edelstein C, Tepper ST, Shapiro RE. Drug-induced serotonin syndrome: a review. *Expert Opin Drug Safety* 2008;7(5):587–96.

Szentesi P, Collet C, Sarkozi S, et al. Effects of dantrolene on steps of excitation-contraction coupling in mammalian skeletal muscle fibers. *J Gen Physiol* 2001;118:355–75.

Tacket CO, Shandera WX, Mann JM, Hargrett NT, Blake PA. Equine antitoxin use and other factors that predict outcome in type A foodborne botulism. *Am J Med* 1984;76:794–8.

Talvik M, Nordstrom AL, Nyberg S, Olsson H, Halldin C, Farde L. No support for regional selectivity in clozapine-treated patients: a PET study with [(11)C]raclopride and [(11)C] FLB 457. *Am J Psychiatry* 2001;158:926–30.

Tang HJ, Lin HJ, Liu YC, Li CM. Spinal epidural abscess--experience with 46 patients and evaluation of prognostic factors. *J Infect* 2002;45:76–81.

Tarsy D, Baldessarini RJ, Tarazi FI. Effects of newer antipsychotics on extrapyramidal function. *CNS Drugs* 2002;16:23–45.

Teman AJ. Spinal epidural abscess. Early detection with gadolinium magnetic resonance imaging. *Arch Neurol* 1992;49:743–6.

Thanacoody RHK. Serotonin syndrome. *Adv Drug React Bull* 2007;243:931–34.

Thanvi B, Treadwell S. Drug induced parkinsonism: a common cause of parkinsonism in older people. *Postgrad Med J* 2009;85:322–6.

Thomson AD, Cook CC, Touquet R, Henry JA. The Royal College of Physicians report on alcohol: guidelines for the managing Wernicke's encephalopathy in the accident and emergency department. *Alcohol Alcohol* 2002;37:513–21.

Thomson AD, Guerrini I, Marshall EJ. Wernicke encephalopathy: role of thiamine, nutrition issues in gastroenterology, series #75. *Pract Gastroenterol* 2009;23:21–30.

Thomson AD, Guerrini I, Marshal EJ. The evolution and treatment of Korsakoff's syndrome. *Neuropsychol Rev* 2012;22:81–92.

Tompkins MI, Panuncialman PL, Palumbo M. Spinal epidural abscess. *J Emer Med* 2010;39(3):384–90.

Torvik A. Wernicke encephalopathy:prevalence and clinical spectrum. *Alcohol* 1991;Suppl 1:381–4.

Torvik A, Lindboe CF, Rogde S. Brain lesions in alcoholics. A neuropathological study with clinical correlations. *J Neurol Sci* 1982;56:233–48.

Trollor JN, Chen X, Chitty K, Sachdev PS. Comparison of neuroleptic malignant syndrome induced by first- and second-generation antipsychotics. *Br J Psychiatry* 2012;201:52–6.

Turkel SB, Nadala JG, Wincor MZ. Possible serotonin syndrome in association with 5-HT(3) antagonist agents. *Psychosomatics* 2001;42:258–60.

Vella S, Kreis R, Lovblad KO, Steinlin M. Acute leukoencephalopathy after inhalation of a single dose of heroin. *Neuropediatrics* 2003;34:100–4.

Victor M, Adams R, Collins G. *The Wernicke–Korsakoff Syndrome and Related Neurologic Disorders due to Alcoholism and Malnutrition*. Philadelphia: F Davis, 1989.

Victor M, Adams RD. The effect of alcohol on the nervous system. *Res Publ Assoc Res Nerv Ment Dis* 1953;32:526–73.

Victor M, Adams RD, Collins GH. The Wernicke-Korsakoff syndrome: a clinical and pathological study of 245 patients, 82 with postmortem examinations. *Contemp Neurol Ser* 1971;7:1–206.

Villela C, Iorio R, Conte G, Batocchi AP, Bria P. Toxic leukoencephalopathy after intravenous heroin injection: a case with clinical and radiological reversibility. *J Neurol* 2010;257:1924–6.

Vishnubhakat SM, Beresford HR. Reversibly myeloneuropathy of nitrous oxide abuse:serial electrophysiological studies. *Muscle Nerve* 1991;14:22–6.

Waclawik AJ, Luzzio CC, Juhasz-Pocsine K, et al. Myeloneuropathy from nitrous oxide abuse: unusually high methylmalonic acid and homocysteine levels. *WMJ* 2003;102:43–5.

Waugh WH, Metts JC Jr. Severe extrapyramidal motor activity induced by prochlorperazine. Its relief by the intravenous injection of diphenhydramine. *N Engl J Med* 1960;262:353–4.

Weimann J. Toxicity of nitrous oxide. *Best Practice Res Clin Anaesthesiol* 2003;17(1):47–61.

Werner SB, Passaro DJ, McGee J, et al. Wound botulism in California, 1951–1998: a recent epidemic in heroin injectors. *Clin Infect Dis* 2000;31:1018–24.

Wolters EC, Stam FC, Lousberg RJ, Van Wijngaarden GK, Rengelink H, Schipper MEI, Verbeeten B. Leukoencephalopathy after inhaling "heroin" pyrolysate. *Lancet* 1982;II:1233–7.

Writland M, Pilbrant A, Sundwall A, Vessman J. Disposition of three benzodiazepines after single oral administration in man. *Acta Pharmacol Toxicol (Copenh)* 1977;40(suppl 1):28–39.

Xiao C, Ren C, Cheng J, Zhang Y, Li Y, Li B, Fan Y. Conventional MRI for diagnosis of subacute combined degeneration of the spinal cord due to vitamin B-12 deficiency. *Asia Pac J Clin Nutr* 2016;25(1):34–8.

Xiberas X, Martinot JL, Mallet L, Artiges E, Loc'h C, Maiere B, Paillere-Martinot ML. Extrastriatal and striatal D_2 dopamine receptor blockade with haloperidol or new antipsychotic drugs in patients with schizophrenia. *Br J Psychiatry* 2001;179:503–8.

Yin R, Lu C, Chen Q, Fan J, Lu J. Microvascular damage is involved in the pathogenesis of heroin induced spongiform leukoencephalopathy. *Int J Med Sci* 2013;10:299–306.

2 Pharmacokinetics
*Drug Absorption, Distribution, and Elimination**

Section Editors: Elisabetta Bertol and Donata Favretto[†]

CONTENTS

* Readers should note that NPS drugs are considered as a group in Chapter 8. While tramadol, methadeone, and bupranorphine are totally synthetic, as are ketamine and phencyclidine, these drugs are hardly considered either "new," "novel," nor, for that matter, are hydrocodone and oxycodone. For that reason, those drugs are discussed here, and the true undisputed NPS drugs are considered in their own chapter.

† With the collaboration of Jennifer P. Pascali and Fabio Vaiano – University of Florence.

DOI: 10.4324/9781315155159-2

INTRODUCTION

Pharmacokinetics, sometimes abbreviated as PK, is the study of how drugs are absorbed, distributed, metabolized, and excreted (ADME). The name also includes the corresponding pharmacologic, therapeutic, or toxic responses in man and animals.[1] Substances of interest include any chemical xenobiotic such as pharmaceutical drugs, pesticides, food additives, cosmetics, etc. Mathematical descriptions (pharmacokinetic models) have been developed to simplify the conceptualization of the processes that take place during the interaction between an organism and a chemical substance. Models provide estimates of certain parameters, such as the elimination half-life, which provides information about basic drug properties. They are also used to predict concentration versus time profiles for different dosing patterns.

The processes of absorption, distribution, biotransformation, and excretion or elimination, in addition to the dose, determine the concentration of drug at the effector or active site and, therefore, the intensity and duration of drug effect. The studies of pharmacokinetics are useful in clinical medicine in order to optimize the efficacy of medications administered to treat disease. In fact dose, frequency of administration and route of administration must be selected carefully to optimize the onset, intensity, and duration of therapeutic effects for a particular disease condition. In the same manner, the study of the pharmacokinetics of illicit drugs aids investigators in addiction medicine, forensic toxicology, and clinical pharmacology in understanding why particular drugs are abused, factors that affect their potential for abuse, how their use can be detected and monitored over time, and also provide a rational, scientific basis for treatment therapies.

All of these complex interactions have, to one degree or another, been completed for the more common drugs such as heroin and cocaine. Unfortunately, we are now dealing with new types of drugs – the NPS, "substances of abuse, either in a pure form or a preparation, that are not controlled by the 1961 Single Convention on Narcotic Drugs or the 1971 Convention on Psychotropic Substances, but which may pose a public health threat." The term "new" does not necessarily refer to new inventions — several NPS were first synthesized 40 years ago — but to substances that have recently become available on the market, about which virtually nothing is known except that drugs in this group may cause driving impairments and that the same drugs have been detected in victims of sudden cardiac death who die young. NPS pose a terrible problem for forensic pathologists who must determine the cause of death. Such determinations are almost impossible to make in the absence of any information about the behavior of the particular NPS in question, and the reader is referred to the separate chapter on this subject.

2.1 BASIC CONCEPTS AND MODELS

2.1.1 Transfer across Biological Membranes

The processes of absorption, distribution, biotransformation, and elimination of a xenobiotic involve its transfer or movement across biological membranes. Knowledge of how drugs penetrate membranes is fundamental to understanding the process. The membranes of the cells consist of a bilayer of phospholipids that are critical components of cell membranes. The lipid bilayer acts as a barrier to the passage of molecules and ions into and out of the cell. However, another important function of the cell membrane is to allow for the selective passage of certain substances into and out of cells. This is accomplished by the embedding of various protein molecules in and through the lipid bilayer (transmembrane proteins).

These proteins form channels through which certain specific ions and molecules can move. Many membrane proteins also contain attached carbohydrates on the outside of the lipid bilayer, allowing it to form hydrogen bonds with water. Phospholipids are amphiphilic, consisting of a hydrophilic polar head and a hydrophobic lipid tail. In membranes, polar head groups are oriented toward the outer and inner surfaces of the membrane, whereas the hydrophobic tails are oriented inward and face each other to form a continuous hydrophobic inner space. The thickness of the cell membrane is about 7–9 nm. The embedded numerous proteins function as important biological receptors or allow the formation of aqueous pores and ion channels. The fatty acids of the membrane do not have a rigid crystalline structure but are semifluid at physiologic temperatures. The fluid character of membranes is determined largely by the structure and relative abundance of unsaturated fatty acids. The more unsaturated fatty acids the membranes contain, the more fluid-like they are, facilitating more rapid active or passive transport. Toxicants cross membranes either by passive processes in which the cell expends no energy or by mechanisms in which the cell provides energy to translocate the toxicant across its membrane (active transport).[2] Between cell membranes are pores that may permit the bulk flow of substances. This is considered to be the main mechanism by which drugs cross the capillary endothelial membranes, except in the central nervous system (CNS), which possesses tight junctions that limit intercellular diffusion.[3]

2.1.1.1 Passive Diffusion and Active Transport

The physicochemical properties of the drug itself also affect its movement across cell membranes. These properties include molecular size and shape, solubility, degree of ionization, and relative lipid solubility of its ionized and nonionized forms. However, studies suggest that mass does not appear to be an important factor if it is below 400 daltons (Da). This group includes many of the drugs presently used therapeutically.[4] Another factor to consider, when evaluating a drug's effect, is the extent of protein binding to plasma and tissue components. Although such binding is reversible and usually rapid, only the free unbound form is considered capable of passing through biological membranes.

Passive movement across biological membranes is the dominant process in the absorption and distribution of drugs. A drug's lipophilicity is probably the most important determinant of permeability. A drug's lipophilicity, or fat-loving nature, is responsible for its diffusion along a concentration gradient. In this process, there is no expenditure of cellular energy. The magnitude of drug transfer in this manner is dependent on the magnitude of the concentration gradient across the membrane and the lipid:water partition coefficient (P).

Because of the very wide range of P values among therapeutic drugs, they are expressed most conveniently on a log scale (logP). Once a steady state has been reached, the concentration of free (unbound) drug will be the same on both sides of the membrane. The exception to this situation is if the drug is capable of ionization under physiological conditions. In this case, concentrations on either side of the cell membrane will be influenced by pH differences across the membrane. The degree of ionization will influence a drug's permeability because only the non-ionized form of the drug would be able to penetrate a lipophilic membrane.

A more useful measure of membrane permeability is, thus, the partition coefficient measured at a specific, biologically relevant pH (distribution coefficient [D]; logD). The movement of ionized forms is, thus, dependent on the pKa of the drug and the pH gradient. The partitioning of weak acids and bases across pH gradients may be predicted by the Henderson–Hasselbalch equation. For example, an orally ingested, weakly acidic drug may be largely un-ionized in the acidic environs of the stomach but ionized to some degree at the neutral pH of the plasma. The pH gradient and difference in the proportions of ionized/non-ionized forms of the drug promote the diffusion of the weak acid through the lipid barrier of the stomach and into the plasma. On this ground, pharmaceutical companies want to maximize the possibility of newly developed drugs that can be given orally, and much research has been conducted to try to identify critical physiochemical properties of drugs the allow absorption. Studies have emphasized the importance of a high log D value. These studies also indicate that mass and polarity are important and suggest that drugs with a molecular mass greater than 500 Da are likely to have poor membrane permeability, particularly if they also possess additional adverse physicochemical characteristics, such as polarity or poor lipophilicity.[5] In summary, transcellular permeability is highest for small lipophilic, nonpolar drugs.

Water moves across cell membranes either by the simple diffusion described above or as the result of osmotic differences across membranes. In the latter case, when water moves in bulk through aqueous pores in cellular membranes due to osmotic forces, any molecule that is small enough to pass through the pores will also be transferred. This movement of solutes is called filtration. Cell membranes throughout the body possess pores of different sizes; for example, the pores in the kidney glomerulus are typically 70 nm, but the channels in most cells are <4 nm.[2]

Another important diffusion mechanism is paracellular transport, which involves the passage of drugs through the junctions between the cells of the membrane. The process is dependent on the size of the junction and of the drug molecule. The junctions between adjacent cells of the epithelium membrane vary from one tissue to another, thus, for example, the junctions between the cells in the gastrointestinal membrane and skin are very tight and serve to hold transcellular proteins in place. This architecture presumably exists to protect the body from the penetration of foreign substances across these outside membranes. As a result, paracellular diffusion of drugs across the intestinal membrane is a very minor route of absorption[4] The movement of some compounds, usually those of high molecular weight, or very lipid soluble substances, across membranes cannot be explained by simple diffusion or filtration. Therefore, specialized processes have been postulated to account for the movement. Active processes typically involve the expenditure of cellular energy to move molecules across biological membranes. Characteristics of active transport include selectivity, competitive inhibition, saturability, and movement against an electrochemical or concentration gradient. A drug complexes with a macromolecular carrier (transporter) on one side of the membrane, traverses the membrane, and is released on the other side. The carrier then returns to the original surface. There are two broad classes of transporters: uptake transporters, which transport drugs into the cell, and efflux transporters, which extrude or transport drugs out of the cell. Active transport plays a key role in the elimination of xenobiotics.[6]

Transporters have likely evolved to protect cells against potentially harmful xenobiotics as well as to assist in the absorption and distribution of essential nutrients. Over the last 15 to 20 years, it has become apparent that drug transporters exert a profound influence on the body's exposure to drugs and on the access of drugs to the relevant site of action and/or toxicity.[4] They are involved in the movement of drugs in hepatocytes, renal tubular cells, and neuronal membranes. For example, the liver has four known active transport systems, two for organic acids, one for organic bases, and one for neutral organic compounds.[2] A different specialized transport process is termed "facilitated diffusion." This type of transport is similar to the carrier-mediated transport described above, except that no active processes are involved. The drug is not moved against an electrochemical or concentration gradient and there is no expenditure of energy. A biochemical example of this is the movement of glucose from the gastrointestinal tract through the intestinal epithelium.

2.1.1.2 Absorption

The process by which xenobiotics cross body membranes and enter the bloodstream (systemic circulation) is referred to as absorption. Drug absorption, distribution into the body, and, finally, to its site of action is fundamental for the drug to be effective. This is true except in the case of drugs that exert their effect locally or at the absorption site. The route of drug administration determines the absorption site or port of entry.

Routes of administration are either enteral or parenteral. The former term denotes all routes pertaining to the alimentary canal (sublingual, oral, and rectal). All other routes, such as intravenous, intramuscular, subcutaneous, dermal, vaginal, and intraperitoneal, are considered parenteral routes.

Absorption is characterized by the rate and extent to which a drug leaves its site of administration and enters the general circulation. Factors that, therefore, affect absorption include the physicochemical properties of the drug that determine transfer across cell membranes as described earlier; formulation or physical state of the drug; site of absorption; concentration of drug; circulation at absorption site; and area of absorbing surface.

2.1.1.2.1 Gastrointestinal

The mouth, stomach, intestine, and rectum are considered the gastrointestinal absorption sites of drugs. Absorption may occur at any point along the tract. This site of absorption is also particularly relevant to toxicologists because accidental ingestion is the most common route of unintentional exposure to a toxicant, especially for children, but also in cases of intentional overdose. The majority of drugs are absorbed by passive diffusion in the non-ionized, lipid soluble form. The absorption follows the Henderson–Hasselbalch equation, which defines the absorption of weak acids to be favored in the stomach (pH 1.5–2) and the absorption of weak bases in the alkaline/neutral environment of the small intestine. However, other factors – such as relative surface area – will influence absorption. The stomach, for example, is lined by a relatively thick mucus-covered membrane to facilitate its primary function of digestion; in comparison, the epithelium of the small intestine is thin, with villi and microvilli providing a large surface area to facilitate its primary function of absorption of nutrients. Therefore, any factor that increases gastric emptying will tend to increase the rate of drug absorption, regardless of the ionization state of the drug.[7]

The gastrointestinal (GI) tract possesses carrier-mediated transport systems for the transfer of nutrients and electrolytes across the gastric wall and these systems may additionally carry drugs and other xenobiotics into the organism, thereby leading to potential competition or interaction. For example, lead is absorbed by the calcium transporter,[8,9] 5-fluorouracil is absorbed by the pyrimidine transport system,[10] thallium utilizes the system that normally absorbs iron.[11] Drug absorption also depends on the physical characteristics of the drug, its solid form, and its particle size. For example, a highly lipid soluble drug will not dissolve in the stomach – according to the Henderson–Hasselbalch equation – while solid dosage forms will have little contact with gastric mucosa and the drug will not be absorbed until the solid is dissolved. Further, the particle size affects absorption, since the dissolution rate is proportional to particle size.[12] Compounds that increase intestinal permeability or increase the residence time in the intestine by altering intestinal motility will thereby increase the absorption of other drugs through that segment of the alimentary canal. However, the number of toxicants actively absorbed by the GI tract is low; most enter the body by simple diffusion.

Once a drug has been absorbed through the GI tract, the amount of the compound that reaches the systemic circulation depends on several factors. Firstly, the drug may be biotransformed by the GI cells or removed by the liver through which it must pass (first pass effect), thus, decreasing the total amount available. Although oral ingestion is the most common route of GI absorption, drugs may also be administered sublingually and despite the small surface area for absorption, non-ionic and highly lipid soluble drugs can be effectively absorbed by this route. The blood supply in the mouth drains into the superior vena cava and, because of this anatomic characteristic, drugs are protected from first pass metabolism by the liver. For example, the drugs nitroglycerin and buprenorphine are administered by this route.

In medical practice, when vomiting or other circumstances preclude oral administration, rectal administration can be used, although it is an uncommon route for self-administration of abused drugs. Approximately 50% of the drug that is absorbed will bypass the liver.[3] The disadvantage of this route for drug absorption is that the process is often incomplete and irregular and some drugs irritate the mucosal lining of the rectum. The same applies to the rectal or vaginal introduction of heroin and cocaine as well as other abused drugs

Food can affect drug absorption through effects on gastrointestinal physiology and the physical effects of drugs in the lumen.[7] The magnitude and direction of a food effect depends on the specific characteristics of the meal, including the composition of the meal (proteins, carbohydrates, or fats), calorie content, and the total volume of food and fluid ingested. Physiological changes brought about by food include a delay in gastric emptying; changes in gastrointestinal pH; stimulation of bile flow, and; increased liver blood flow, all of which can affect drug absorption.

2.1.1.2.2 Pulmonary

Gases, volatile liquids, and aerosols may be absorbed through the lungs by inhalation. Access to the circulation by this route is rapid due to the large surface area of the lungs and extensive capillary network at the alveoli level. In the case of gases and volatilized liquids, the ionization state and lipid solubility of the substance are less important than in GI absorption, because diffusion through cell membranes is not the rate-limiting step in the absorption process. The reasons include 1) low volatility of ionized molecules, not reaching toxic levels; 2) the short distance for diffusion among capillary network and the alveoli, and; 3) the rapid removal of absorbed substances by the blood. Furthermore, some substances may not reach the lungs because they are deposited and absorbed in the mucosal lining of the nose.[6]

Drugs may be inhaled as droplets or particulates in the air, after atomization or volatilization, and a common example is the smoking of drugs. The advantages of this route include rapid transport into the blood, avoidance of first pass hepatic metabolism, and avoidance of the medical problems associated with other routes of illicit drug administration. Disadvantages include local irritant effect on the tissues of the nasopharynx and absorption of particulate matter in the nasopharynx and bronchial tree. For a drug to be effectively absorbed and reach the circulating system it should reach the alveoli. However, absorption of particulate matter is governed by the particulate size and water solubility. Particles with diameters >5 μm are usually deposited in the nasopharyngeal region;[2] particles in between 2 μm and 5 μm in range are deposited in the tracheobronchiolar region and particles 1 μm and smaller reach the alveolar sacs.

2.1.1.2.3 Dermal

Skin is impermeable to most chemicals, however, some drugs can be absorbed by the skin in sufficient quantities to produce systemic effects (for example, insecticides by agricultural workers). For a drug to be absorbed it must pass first through the epidermal layers, or specialized tissue, such as hair follicles and sebaceous glands. Absorption through the outer layer of skin (stratum corneum), which consists of densely packed keratinized cells, is the rate-limiting step in the dermal absorption of drugs. This outer layer is commonly referred to as the "dead" layer of skin because the cells comprising this layer are without nuclei, and thus drug substances may be absorbed by simple diffusion.

The lower layers of the epidermis and the dermis consist of porous nonselective cells that pose little barrier to absorption by passive diffusion. Once a chemical reaches this level, it can rapidly reach the systemic circulation because of the extensive network of venous and lymphatic capillaries located in the dermis. Also, in this case, drug absorption through the skin depends on the characteristics of the drug and on the condition of the skin. Since the stratum corneum is the main barrier to absorption, any damage to this area, such as abrasion or burning, enhances absorption, as does any mechanism that increases cutaneous blood flow. Furthermore, skin structure is different in different body parts, resulting in different permeability throughout the body. Hydration of the stratum corneum also increases permeability and therefore enhances absorption of chemicals.[6]

Inadvertent absorption through the skin is an issue with some of the NPS drugs, particularly Fentanyl Analogues. In 2016, the DEA issued a warning to law enforcement officers and first respondents about the dangers of handling fentanyl improperly and the DEA warned that "Fentanyl can be absorbed through the skin or accidental inhalation of airborne powder can also occur. DEA is concerned about law enforcement coming in contact with fentanyl on the streets during the course of enforcement."[13]

2.1.1.2.4 Parenteral Injection

Drugs are often absorbed through the GI tract, lungs, and skin but many illicit drugs have historically been self-administered by injection. These routes typically include intravenous (IV), intramuscular, and subcutaneous administration. The intravenous route of administration introduces the drug directly into the venous bloodstream, thereby eliminating the process of absorption altogether. Locally irritating substances may be administered intravenously since the blood vessel walls are relatively insensitive. This route permits the rapid introduction of the drug to the systemic circulation and allows high concentrations to be quickly achieved. Intravenous administration may result in unfavorable physiological responses because, once introduced, the drug cannot be removed. This route of administration is dependent on maintaining patent veins and can result in extensive scar tissue formation due to chronic drug administration. Insoluble particulate matter deposited in the blood vessels is another medical problem associated with the intravenous route. Drugs usually administered intravenously are chemotherapy agents, antibiotics such as vancomycin, meropenem, and gentamicin, and pain medications such as hydromorphone and morphine.

Intramuscular and subcutaneous administration involves absorption from the injection site into the circulation by passive diffusion. For example, vaccines are administered intramuscularly. The rate of absorption is limited by the size of the capillary bed at the injection site and by the solubility of the drug in the interstitial fluid[3] If blood flow is increased at the administration site, absorption will be increased. Conversely, if blood pressure is decreased for any reason (such as cardiogenic shock) absorption will be prolonged.

After entering the circulation, drugs are distributed throughout the body, usually very rapidly. The rate of distribution to organs or tissues is determined primarily by physicochemical properties of the drug, blood flow, and the rate of diffusion out of the capillary bed into the cells of a particular organ or tissue. Drugs cross cell membranes throughout the body using two mechanisms: passive diffusion and specialized transport processes. Small water-soluble molecules and ions cross cell membranes through aqueous pores, whereas lipid soluble substances diffuse through the membrane lipid bilayer. The rate of distribution of a drug is dependent on blood flow, on the rate of diffusion across cell membranes of various tissues and organs, and, ultimately, on the affinity of a substance for certain tissues also affects the rate of distribution.

While circulating in the blood, drugs may be reversibly bound to several plasma proteins and because only unbound drug (the free fraction) is in equilibrium throughout the body, disposition is affected by binding to or dissolving in cellular constituents (i.e. basic compounds often bind to α-1-acid glycoprotein; acidic compounds bind to albumin). The extent of plasma protein binding varies among drugs: nicotine is 5% bound, whereas barbiturate and secobarbital are 50% bound, and benzodiazepine and diazepam are 96% bound.[14] The problem for forensic investigators is, with very few exceptions, that little is known about the resultant behavior once they are in the human body.

The alpha- and beta-lipoproteins are very important in the transport of lipid-soluble compounds such as vitamins, cholesterol, and steroid hormones, as well as xenobiotics. Plasma proteins bind acidic compounds such as phenylbutazone, basic compounds such as imipramine, and neutral compounds such as digitoxin.[2] The fraction of drug that is bound is governed by several factors: 1) drug concentration; 2) drug's affinity for binding sites and; 3) the number of binding sites available for binding. At low drug concentrations, the fraction bound is a function of the number of binding sites and the dissociation constant, a measure of binding affinity. When drug concentrations exceed the dissociation constant, concentration also governs the amount of protein binding. Therefore, published protein-binding fractions for drugs only apply over a certain concentration range, usually the therapeutic concentration. Plasma protein binding limits the amount of drug entering tissues and thus it affects drug toxicity. Because plasma protein binding of drugs is relatively non-selective, drugs and endogenous substances compete for binding sites, and drug displacement from binding sites by another substance can contribute to toxicity by increasing the free fraction.

2.1.1.2.5 Binding to Tissue Constituents

Plasma protein binding tends to concentrate drugs in the plasma and limit its distribution to the tissues. Tissue binding tends to concentrate a large amount of drug in a tissue of a definite region or regions. The compartment where a toxicant is concentrated is described as a storage depot. Toxicants in these depots are always in equilibrium with the free fraction in plasma, so when a xenobiotic is transformed or excreted from the body, more is released from the storage site. As a consequence, the biological half-life of stored compounds can be very long. This phenomenon explains why clinicians studying drug urinary excretion always distinguish time elapsed from the first negative urine test to the last positive test. In the case of some drugs, like THC intermittent excretion can occur for more than a month. The kidney and liver, for example, have a large capacity to act as storage depots for drugs. As a result, they concentrate more toxicants than do all the other organs combined. The mechanisms responsible for the transfer of many drugs from the blood appear to be active transport processes.[2] Ligandin, a cytoplasmic liver protein, has a high affinity for many organic acids while metallothionein binds metals in the kidney and liver. The drug concentration will vary from tissue to tissue and be greatest in those tissues where binding is most extensive.

Lipid-soluble drugs are stored in neutral fat by dissolution. Since the fat content of an obese individual may be 50% body weight, it follows that large amounts of a drug can be stored in this tissue. Once stored in fat, the concentration of a drug is lowered throughout the body, in the blood and also in target organs. Any activity, such as dieting or starvation, which serves to mobilize fat, could potentially increase blood concentrations and hence contribute to an increase in the risk of drug toxicity. This is the case for pesticides, dioxins, and polychlorinated and polybrominated biphenyls. Depending on the time interval, drug concentrations are also increased post-mortem. As fat cells undergo cell death they will release whatever drug or drugs they contain, which redistribute to the blood, yielding falsely elevated blood concentration measurements.

Storage within fat often presents a conundrum to toxicologists dealing with post-mortem material. As fat cells undergo post-mortem liquifacation they release accumulated fat into the blood. It is possible that an individual who had not used drugs in months prior to death might still test positive because of fat cell release. The same problem applies to the living that, while not having used drugs for more than a month, may still test positive because of a drug being released from fat depots.

Drugs may also be stored in bone. Drugs diffuse from the extracellular fluid through the hydration shell of the hydroxyapatite crystals of the bone mineral. Lead, fluoride, strontium, and other compounds may be deposited and stored in bone. Deposition may not necessarily be detrimental. For example, lead is not toxic to bone tissue. Chronic fluoride deposition results in the condition known as skeletal fluorosis. Generally, the storage of compounds in bone is a reversible process. Toxicants may be released from the bone by ion exchange at the crystal surface or by the dissolution of the bone during osteoclastic activity. If osteolytic activity is increased, the hydroxyapatite lattice is mobilized, increasing blood concentrations of any stored xenobiotics.[6]

2.1.1.2.6 Blood-Brain-Barrier (BBB)

The blood-brain-barrier is often viewed as an impenetrable barrier to xenobiotics. However, this is not true and a more realistic representation is simply that the BBB is less permeable to ionized substances and high-molecular-weight compounds than other membranes. Many toxicants do not enter the brain because the capillary endothelial cells are joined by tight junctions with few pores between cells; the capillaries of the CNS are surrounded by glial processes; and the interstitial fluid of the CNS has a low protein concentration. The first two anatomical features limit the entry of small- to medium-sized water-soluble molecules, whereas the entry of lipid-soluble compounds is limited by the low protein content, which restricts paracellular transport.

It is interesting to note that the permeability of the brain to toxicants varies from area to area. For example, the cortex, area postrema, and pineal body are more permeable than other regions.[2] This may be due to differences in blood supply or the nature of the barrier itself. The entry of drugs into the brain is governed by the same factors that determine transfer across membranes in other parts of the body. Only the unbound fraction is available for transfer, while lipid solubility and the degree of ionization dictate the rate of entry of drugs into the brain.

Also acting to decrease the concentration of xenobiotics in the brain are active transport processes. Four ATP-dependent transporters have been identified as part of the BBB including P-gp, Mrp2, Mrp4, and BCRP. Collectively, these transporters can efficiently efflux a wide range of anionic (Mrp2, Mrp4), cationic (P-gp, BCRP), uncharged (all four), and numerous drug conjugates (Oatp1a4, Mrp2) from the brain. In this way, some very lipophilic compounds may enter the brain but are so efficiently removed by xenobiotic transporters that they do not reach appreciable concentrations. This is particularly true for agents like cyclosporine.[2] It should be noted that the blood-brain-barrier is not fully developed at birth. In animal studies, morphine has been found to be three to ten times more toxic to newborns than adults.[15]

2.1.1.2.7 Pregnancy

Most of the vital nutrients necessary for the development of the fetus are moved by active transport systems through the placental barrier. For example, vitamins, amino acids, essential sugars, and ions such as calcium and iron are transported from mother to fetus against a concentration gradient. In contrast, most toxic chemicals pass the placenta by simple diffusion. The only exceptions are a few antimetabolites that are structurally similar to endogenous purines and pyrimidines. These act as the physiologic substrates for active transport from the maternal to the fetal circulation. The placenta may prevent some toxic substances from reaching the fetus by inactivation through biotransformation. Among the substances that cross the placenta by passive diffusion, more lipid-soluble substances rapidly attain a maternal–fetal equilibrium.[16]

2.1.2 Biotransformation

Lipophilicity, a desirable drug characteristic for absorption and distribution across biological membranes, is a hindrance to elimination. To prevent the accumulation of xenobiotics, the body chemically alters lipophilic compounds creating more water-soluble products to be excreted in urine or bile. There are exceptions, however; acetylation and methylation can actually decrease the water solubility of certain xenobiotics. The sum of all the processes that convert lipophilic substances to more hydrophilic metabolites is termed biotransformation. These biochemical processes are usually enzymatic and are commonly divided into Phase 1 and Phase 2 reactions.[17] Phase 1 reactions generally expose or introduce a polar group to the parent drug, thereby increasing its water solubility. These reactions are oxidative or hydrolytic in nature and include N- and O-dealkylation, aliphatic and aromatic hydroxylation, N- and S-oxidation, and deamination. These reactions usually result in a loss of pharmacological activity, although there are numerous examples of just the opposite occurring. Indeed, the formation of a Phase 1 product is desirable in the case of administration of prodrugs.

Phase 2 reactions are conjugation reactions and involve covalent bonding of functional groups with endogenous compounds. Highly water-soluble conjugates are formed by a combination of the drug or metabolite with glucuronic acid, sulfate, glutathione, amino acids, or acetate. Again, these products are generally pharmacologically inactive or less active than the parent compound. An exception is the metabolite morphine-6-glucuronide. In this case, glucuronidation at the *6* position increases the affinity of morphine for binding at the *mu* receptor and results in equivalent or enhanced pharmacological activity.[18]

The enzymes that catalyze the biotransformation of drugs are found mainly in the liver. This is not surprising considering the primary function of the liver is to handle compounds absorbed from the GI tract. In addition, the liver receives all the blood perfusing the splanchnic area. Therefore, this organ has developed a high capacity to remove substances from the blood, and store, transform, and/or release substances into the general circulation. In its primary role of biotransformation, the liver acts as a homogeneous unit, with all parenchymal cells or hepatocytes exhibiting enzymatic activity. In tissues involved in extrahepatic biotransformation processes, typically only one or two cell types are used. Many organs have demonstrated activity toward xenobiotics, but the major extrahepatic tissues are those involved in the absorption or excretion of chemicals. These include the kidney, lung, intestine, skin, and testes. The main cells containing biotransformation enzymes in these organs are the proximal tubular cells, Clara cells, mucosa lining cells, epithelial cells, and seminiferous tubules, respectively.

2.1.2.1 Phase 1 Enzymes

Phase 1 enzymes are located primarily in the endoplasmic reticulum of cells. These enzymes are membrane-bound within a lipoprotein matrix and are referred to as microsomal enzymes. This refers to the subcellular fraction isolated by differential centrifugation of a liver homogenate. The two most important enzyme systems involved in Phase 1 biotransformation reactions are the cytochrome P450 system and the mixed-function amine oxidase. With the advances in recombinant DNA technology, eight major mammalian gene families of hepatic and extrahepatic cytochrome P450 have been identified.[2]

A comprehensive discussion of the cytochrome P450 system is beyond the scope of this chapter and the reader is referred to a number of reviews.[18–21] Briefly, this system is comprised of two coupled enzymes: NADPH cytochrome P450 reductase and a heme-containing enzyme, cytochrome P450. Numerous oxidative pathways for xenobiotics exist, both in humans and other animals. Much drug oxidation is performed by a group of enzymes known as CYPs (from cytochrome P450, the 450 being derived from the cytochrome's maximal absorbance of light at 450 nm). The cytochrome P450s or CYPs are categorized according to amino acid sequence homology. CYPs that have less than 40% homology are placed in a different family (e.g., 1, 2, 3, and so on). CYPs that are 40% to 55% identical are assigned to different subfamilies (e.g., 1A, 1B, 1C, and so on). P450 enzymes that are more than 55% identical are classified as members of the same subfamily (e.g., 2B1, 2B2, 2B3). The P450 enzymes are expressed in numerous tissues, but prevalently in the liver.

2.1.3 Elimination

Drugs are excreted or eliminated from the body as parent compounds or metabolites. The organs involved in excretion, with the exception of the lungs, eliminate water-soluble compounds more readily than lipophilic substances. The lungs are important for the elimination of anesthetic gases and vapors. The processes of biotransformation generally produce more polar compounds for excretion. The most important excretory organ is the kidney. Substances in the feces are mainly unabsorbed drugs administered orally or compounds excreted into the bile and not reabsorbed.

Drugs may also be excreted in breast milk[22] and, even though the amounts are small, they represent an important pathway because the recipient of any drugs by this route is the nursing infant. Toxic agents are excreted into milk by simple diffusion. Because milk has an acidic pH (about 6.5), basic compounds may be concentrated in milk, whereas acidic compounds may attain lower concentrations in milk than in plasma. Despite this indisputable fact, the amounts of opiates or stimulants that actually appear in breast milk are not remotely toxic unless, of course, there is an underlying metabolic disorder (such as the ability to convert small amounts of codeine to morphine) leading to the accumulation of high concentrations.

For a comprehensive discussion of renal excretion of drugs, the reader is referred to Weiner and Mudge[23] and Masereeuw and Russel.[24] Toxic compounds are excreted in urine by the same mechanisms the kidney uses to remove the end-products of intermediary metabolism from the body. Excretion of drugs and their metabolites involves three processes, namely, glomerular filtration, passive tubular reabsorption, and active tubular secretion. As a general rule, excretion of small molecular weight (<350 Da), water-soluble compounds are favored in urine. By contrast the amount of a drug that enters the tubular lumen of the kidney is dependent on the glomerular filtration rate and the unbound (free) fraction of a drug. In the proximal renal tubule organic anions and cations are added to the filtrate by active transport processes. Glucuronide drug metabolites are secreted in this way by the carrier-mediated system for naturally occurring organic acids. In the proximal and distal tubules of the kidney, the non-ionized forms of weak acids and bases are passively reabsorbed. The necessary concentration gradient is created by the reabsorption of water with sodium. The passive reabsorption of ionized forms is pH-dependent because the tubular cells are less permeable to these moieties. Reabsorption of ionized forms is pH-dependent because the tubular cells are less permeable to these moieties.

Therefore, in the treatment of drug poisoning, the excretion of some drugs can be increased by alkalinization with sodium bicarbonate (phenobarbital or salicylate) or acidification (PCP) of the urine. Under normal physiological conditions, excretion of drugs in the sweat, saliva, and lacrimal glands is quantitatively insignificant. Elimination by these routes is dependent on pH and diffusion of the unionized lipid-soluble form of the drug through the epithelial cells of the glands. Drugs excreted in saliva enter the mouth and may be reabsorbed and swallowed. Drugs have also been detected in hair and skin. Although quantitatively unimportant, hair matrix is useful in drug detection from the forensic point of view, since it offers a retrospective time-frame window in relation to hair length.[25]

2.1.4 Pharmacokinetic Parameters

2.1.4.3 Bioavailability

The definition provided by the US Food and Drug Administration (1977) is "The rate and extent to which the active ingredient or therapeutic moiety is absorbed from a product and becomes available at the site of drug action."[26] The bioavailability of a drug refers to the fraction of the dose that reaches the systemic circulation. This parameter is dependent on the rate and extent of absorption at the site of drug administration. Obviously, it follows that drugs administered intravenously do not undergo absorption, but immediately gain access to the systemic circulation and are considered 100% bioavailable. In the case of oral administration, if the hepatic extraction ratio is known, it is possible to predict the maximum bioavailability of a drug by this route assuming first-order processes, according to the following equation:[3]

$$\text{Fmax} = 1 - E = 1 - (\text{CLhepatic}/\text{Qhepatic})$$

The bioavailability of a drug by various routes may also be determined by comparing the area under the curve (AUC) obtained from the plasma concentration versus the time curve after intravenous and other routes of administration:[2]

$$\text{Bioavailability} = \text{AUCoral}/\text{AUCIV}$$

2.1.4.4 Half-Life

The half-life is the time it takes for the plasma drug concentration to decrease by 50%. Half-life is usually determined from the log-terminal phase of the elimination curve. However, it is important to remember that this parameter is a derived term and is dependent on the clearance and volume of distribution of the drug. For example, a large clearance and a small volume of distribution will promote rapid elimination and a short half-life, but a small clearance and a large volume of distribution will promote slow elimination and a long half-life. Therefore, as CL and V change with disease, drug interactions, and age, a change in the half-life should be expected. The half-life is typically calculated from the following equation:

$$t1/2 = 0.693/k$$

where t1/2 = half-life and k = elimination rate constant. Because k = CL/V, the interrelationship between these parameters is clearly evident.

REFERENCES

1. Jambhekar, S.S., and Breen, P.J., Eds., *Basic Pharmacokinetics*, Pharmaceutical Press, Grayslake, IL, 2009.
2. Klaassen, C.D., Ed., *Casarett and Doull's Toxicology: The Basic Science of Poisons*, 7th Ed., McGraw-Hill, New York, 2008.
3. Brunton, L.L., Ed., *Goodman & Gilman's The Pharmacological Basis of Therapeutics*, 12th Ed., McGrawHill, New York, 2011.
4. Rosenbaum, S.Ed., *Basic Pharmacokinetics And Pharmacodynamics*, Wiley, Hoboken, 2011.
5. Lipinski, C.A., Lombardo, F., Dominy, B.W., and Feeney, P.J. Experimental and computational approaches to estimate solubility and permeability in drug discovery and development settings, *Adv Drug Deliv Rev*, 46, 3–26, 2001.

6. Karch, S.B., *Pharmacokinetics and Pharmacodynamics of Abused Drugs*, 1st Edition, CRC Press, 2007.
7. Doran, S., Jones, K.L., Andrews, J.M., and Horowitz, M. Effects of meal volume and posture on gastric emptying of solids and appetite, *Am J Physiol*, 275, R1712–8, 1998.
8. Sobel, A.E., Gawron, O., and Kramer, B., Influence of vitamin D in experimental lead poisoning, *Proc Soc Exp Biol Med*, 38, 433–5, 1938.
9. Fullmer, C.S., Lead-calcium interactions: involvement of 1,25-dihydroxy vitamin D, *Environ Res*, 72, 45–55, 1997.
10. Yuasa, H., Matsuhisa, E., and Watanabe, J., Intestinal brush border transport mechanism of 5-fluorocuracil in rats, *Biol Pharm Bull*, 19, 94–9, 1996.
11. Leopold, G., Furukawa, E., Forth, W., and Rummel, W., Comparative studies of absorption of heavy metals in vivo and in vitro, *Arch Pharmacol Exp Pathol*, 263, 275–6, 1969.
12. Bates, T.R., and Gibaldi, M., Gastrointestinal absorption of drugs. In Swarbuck, J., Ed., *Current Concepts in the Pharmaceutical Sciences: Biopharmaceutics*, Lea & Febiger, Philadelphia, 1970.
13. DEA: DEA Warning To Police And Public: Fentanyl Exposure Kills. DEA, https://www.dea.gov/press-releases/2016/06/10/dea-warning-police-and-public-fentanyl-exposure-kills. Last accessed December 31, 2018.
14. Baselt, R.C., and Cravey, R.H., *Disposition of Toxic Drugs and Chemicals in Man*, 11th Ed, Chemical Toxicology Institute, Foster City, CA, 2017.
15. Kupferberg, H.J., and Way, E.L., Pharmacologic basis for the increased sensitivity of the newborn rat to morphine, *J Pharmacol Exp Ther*, 141, 105–12, 1963.
16. Paxton, J.W., and Keelan, J.A., Drug transfer and metabolism by the human placenta, *Clin Pharmacokinet*, 43, 487–514, 2004.
17. Pratt, W.B., and Taylor, P., Eds., *Principles of Drug Action: The Basis of Pharmacology*, Churchill Livingstone, New York, 1990.
18. Mulder, G.J., Ed., *Sulfation of Drugs and Related Compounds*, CRC Press, Boca Raton, FL, 1981.
19. Foti, R.S., and Dalvie, D.K. Cytochrome P450 and non-cytochrome P450 oxidative metabolism: contributions to the pharmacokinetics, safety, and efficacy of xenobiotics, *Drug Metab Dispos*, 44, 1229–45, 2016.
20. McDonnell, A.M., and Dang, C.H., Basic review of the cytochrome P450 system, *J Adv Pract Oncol*, 4, 263–8, 2013.
21. Meunier, B., de Visser, S.P., and Shaik, S., Mechanism of oxidation reactions catalyzed by cytochrome p450 enzymes, *Chem Rev*, 104, 3947–80, 2004.
22. Stowe, C.M., and Plaa, G.L., Extrarenal excretion of drugs and chemicals, *Annu Rev Pharmacol*, 8, 337–56, 1968.
23. Weiner, I.M., and Mudge, G.H., Renal tubular mechanisms for excretion of organic acids and bases, *Am J Med*, 36, 743–62, 1964.
24. Masereeuw, R., and Russel, F.G., Mechanisms and clinical implications of renal drug excretion, *Drug Metab Rev*, 33, 299–351, 2001.
25. Kintz, P., Salomone, A., and Vincenti, M., *Hair Analysis in Clinical and Forensic Toxicology*, Academic Press, 2015.
26. Chen, M.L., Shah, V., Patnaik, R., Adams, W., Hussain, A., Conner, D., Mehta, M., Malinowski, H., Lazor, J., Huang, S.M., Hare, D., Lesko, L., Sporn, D., Williams, R., Bioavailability and bioequivalence: an FDA regulatory overview, *Pharm Res*, 18, 1645–50, 2001.

2.2 TOXICOKINETICS

Toxicokinetics describes the changes in the PK processes that occur as a result of a drug being administered in extremely high concentrations or "overdoses." In these conditions, the biological processes that normally underlie the drug pharmacokinetics may be altered.

When there is a delayed gastric emptying, changes in intestinal motility due to the drug PD properties, or when activated charcoal has been given as an emergency treatment, the gastrointestinal absorption may be altered. As an example, morphine and opiates delay gastric emptying and decrease intestinal motility, reducing drug passage from the stomach into the small intestine, increasing transit time through the intestine, and increasing the overall absorption.

Other mechanisms may also cause changes in drug disposition. When the metabolizing enzymes become saturated, the bioavailability of a drug may be increased and toxic concentrations can be reached; when multiple drugs are administered, competitive inhibition of metabolism also occurs. In addition, when hepatic blood flow is decreased, biotransformation of xenobiotics by hepatic enzymes may be decreased.

For those drugs that are usually plasma protein-bound, when protein binding becomes saturated the concentration of free drug increases and may result in substantial toxicity.

Drugs that have effects on the cardiovascular system may change the blood flow and result in prolonged drug distribution and higher blood concentrations, with a reduced clearance and a prolonged half-life. Alteration of renal drug clearance may be utilized to enhance drug elimination when urinary pH is adjusted. To increase the clearance of acidic drugs (e.g. salicylic acid) the urine pH may be raised above 7.5 by administration of sodium bicarbonate. Similarly, acidification of the urine may be utilized to enhance renal excretion of basic drugs such as amphetamines. However, there is some controversy about the role of urinary acidification: acidification is contraindicated with myoglobinuria and may also increase the risk of metabolic complications.

2.3 FACTORS AFFECTING PHARMACOKINETIC PARAMETERS

Other considerations that can account for changes in PK parameters include genetic factors, sex differences, age, weight, body composition, diseases and drug interactions, drug formulation, and route of administration.

2.3.1 Genetic Factors

Polymorphism in biology is the occurrence of two or more noticeably different morphs or forms, also referred to as alternative phenotypes, in the population of a species. As an example, the activity of the liver enzyme N-acetyltransferase 2 (that usually metabolizes and inactivates drugs by acetylation) differs between individuals according to their genetic pool. The general population may be divided into slow and fast acetylators; slow acetylators may exhibit severe toxicity when standard doses of drugs requiring acetylation for metabolism are administered. Some hepatic cytochrome-P450 isozymes and plasma cholinesterase have also inherited variations that produce alteration in pharmacokinetics, but the actual list of polymorphic enzymes would be much longer.

2.3.2 Sex Differences

Males and females differ in their response to drug treatment. It is, therefore, essential to understand those differences to appropriately design safe and effective treatments and to exclude unwanted and unexpected outcomes. Sex differences in drug PKs may be due to variations in body composition, hepatic metabolism, renal elimination, protein binding, or absorption.

Body fat as a percentage of total body weight is higher in women than men and increases by age in both sexes. The total body fat for an adult reference male is 13.5 kg, 16.5 kg in female (19.8 kg at 40 week's gestation). The larger proportions of body fat in women, and especially in pregnancy, may increase the body burden of lipid-soluble, slowly metabolized toxicants. Differences in body fat and organ blood flow in women have been implicated in the faster onset of action and prolonged duration of neuromuscular blockade in women (e.g., vecuronium and rocuronium).[3,4] Differences in water and body fat content are responsible for sex-related pharmacokinetic differences in the distribution of ethanol.

The main hepatic enzymes involved in drug metabolism belong to the cytochrome P450 (CYP) group, a large family of enzymes located in the smooth endoplasmic reticulum of the cell. The CYP isoenzymes are all coded for by autosomal chromosomes and it is credible that sex-related disparities in PKs arise due to variations in the expression and activity of CYP isoenzymes, most probably through endogenous hormonal influences.[5] Some of the CYP450 enzymes show clear sex-related differences (Table 2.3.1). In general, lipophilic compounds tend to pass through biological membranes and/or be stored, and are often susceptible to Phase 1 types of metabolism.

Even if there are sex differences in drug pharmacokinetics, only some drugs have shown significantly higher plasma concentrations in women. A comprehensive review of second-generation (atypical) antipsychotics (SGAs) concluded that sex differences in adverse effects have not been well studied, but some adverse effects such as weight gain, hyperprolactinemia, and cardiac effects are particularly problematic for women[6] Most studies reviewed indicate that clozapine and olanzapine are associated with greater body weight gain than other atypical antipsychotics, and that serious adverse effects such as metabolic syndrome, which includes increased visceral adiposity, hyperglycemia, hypertension, and dyslipidemia induced by SGAs, are more frequent in females. Although women are at a lower risk of sudden cardiac death, they have a higher risk of induced long QT syndrome from antiarrhythmic and, probably, antipsychotic drugs.

The effects of gender on tubular secretion and reabsorption have not been well characterized. The main binding proteins for various drugs in plasma are albumin, alpha-1 acid glycoprotein (AAG), and alpha globulins. AAG levels and AAG-glycosylations vary in association with endogenous and exogenous estrogen inducing hepatic glycosylation of these proteins, thus, decreasing plasma AAG levels, while albumin concentrations do not consistently vary by sex.[7] Estrogens also increase the levels of the serum-binding globulins (sex-hormone binding globulin, corticosteroid-binding globulin, and thyroxine-binding globulin).[5] Sex-related differences in plasma-binding of selected compounds are listed in Table 2.3.2. Variations in levels of plasma-binding can alter the free (active) fraction of drugs.

Some studies have suggested that gender influences gastric emptying rate and intestinal transit time. Women empty solids from the stomach more slowly than men and the activity of a stomach enzyme, alcohol dehydrogenase, may be much lower in women. The GI tract also contains large concentrations of the isozyme cytochrome P3A4, and gender differences in the activity of this enzyme could affect the bioavailability of certain drugs. Gender differences observed after intramuscular drug administration may be due to differences in blood flow or incorrect injection into fat in women.

Drug absorption in the lung may differ according to gender, and significantly less deposition of an aerosolized drug in women than men may be attributed to differences in breathing characteristics. It should be noted that female-specific issues may have significant effects on drug distribution and metabolism. The effects of menopause, menstruation, and hormone replacement therapy on the pharmacokinetics of drugs are largely unknown.

2.3.3 Age

Factors influencing drug absorption, such as gastric pH and gastric emptying, intestinal motility, and blood flow, largely change with age. Gastric acid secretion approaches adult levels approximately at the age of 3 and peristalsis is slow during the first months of life. Changes in the rate of drug absorption, but not the extent of drug absorption, are usually[8] seen with age. In elderly individuals, the skeletal muscle mass is limited, and muscle contractions are minimal, thus, limiting the distribution of any intramuscularly administered drug. In those subjects, higher gastric pH, delayed gastric emptying, minimal intestinal motility, and reduced blood flow are observed.

2.3.4 Drug and Disease Interactions

The pharmacokinetics of drugs is influenced by concomitant pathological processes. The clearance of many drugs decreases in people with chronic liver diseases, such as

TABLE 2.3.1
Sex Differences in Hepatic Clearance by Route of Metabolism/Elimination

METABOLIC ROUTE	Model Substrates	Drugs metabolized by route	Sex-Specific Activity
		Phase 1 enzymes	
CYP1A	Caffeine, nicotine paracetamol (acetaminophen)	Clomipramine, clozapine, olanzapine, paracetamol, tacrine, theophylline	M > F
CYP2C9	Dapsone, (S)-mephenytoin	Ibuprofen, (S)-warfarin, tolbutamide, fluvastatin, glipizide, losartan, irbesartan, piroxicam, tolbutamide, phenytoin, fluvastatin, nelfinavir	M = F
CYP2C19	(S)-Mephenytoin Diazepam	Lansoprazole, omeprazole, hexobarbital, mephobarbital, citalopram, celecoxib, irbesartan, imipramine, piroxicam, propranolol (in part)	M = F
CYP2D6	Dextromethorpha ndebrisoquine, sparteine	Codeine, encainide, flecainide, fluoxetine, hydrocodone, metoprolol, paroxetine, mexilitine, phenformin, propranolol, sertraline, timolol, haloperidol, clomipramine, desipramine, imipramine, propafenone, testosterone	M < F
CYP2E1	Chlorzoxazone	--	M > F
CYP3A	Midazolam, dapsone, cortisol, lidocaine, nifedipine, erythromycin, cortisol	Alprazolam, alfentanil, astemizole, atorvastatin, carbamazepine, cisapride, clarithromycin, cyclosporin, cyclophosphamide, diazepam, diltiazem, erythromycin, estradiol, fentanyl, indinavir, itraconazole, ketoconazole, lovastatin, quinidine, nimodipine, nisoldipine, quinidine, ritonavir, verapamil, tacrolimus, simvastatin, vincristine, vinblastine, tamoxifen, tirilazad, troglitazone	M = F; F > M
		Phase 2 enzymes	
UDP-glucuronosyl-transferases	Caffeine	Clofibric acid, diflusinal, ibuprofen, mycophenolate mofetil, paracetamol, zidovudine	M > F
Sulfo-transferases	Caffeine	--	M > F
N-Acetyl-transferases	Caffeine, dapsone	Catecholamine derivatives, mercaptopurine, isoniazid, hydralazine	M = F
Methyl-transferases	Norepinephrine, epinephrine	Ercaptopurine, azathioprine, dopamine, levodopa, 6-mercaptopurine, 6- thioguanine, tazathioprine	M > F

TABLE 2.3.2
Sex Differences in Plasma Binding

Compound	Description
Testosterone	Plasma protein binding: F > M, Estrogen increases
Chlordiazepoxide	Plasma protein binding: M > F > Foc
Diazepam	Free fraction: Foc (1.99%) > F (1.67%) > M (1.46%)
Lidocaine	Free fraction: F (34%). M (32%) < Foc (37%)
Warfarin	Free fraction: F > M
Morphine, Phenytoin Oxazepam, Lorazepam	No differences

cirrhosis. On the other hand, in reversible acute liver diseases, such as acute viral hepatitis, the clearance of some drugs is decreased or the half-life is increased, while, for others, no change is detected. The distribution volumes of some drugs remain unchanged in liver disease, while other drugs, particularly those bound to albumin[8] in people with cirrhosis, are increasing. This phenomenon is due to the decreased synthesis of albumin and other proteins. The influence of liver disease on the absorption of drugs is unclear. It is likely, however, that cirrhosis increases the oral bioavailability of drugs highly extracted from the liver. The reasons for this are a decrease in hepatic first-pass metabolism and the development of portal bypass in which blood enters the superior vena cava directly via esophageal varices. Renal diseases, such as uremia, may result in decreased renal clearance of some drugs.

Gastrointestinal diseases, such as Crohn's disease, lead to increased plasma protein binding of several drugs due to increase in binding protein levels. In addition, respiratory diseases such as cystic fibrosis increase the renal clearance of some drugs. It is common for patients to receive two or more medications simultaneously and most addicts are polydrug users. Using multiple drugs can lead to drug interactions – when the pharmacokinetics or pharmacodynamics of one drug is changed by another. The interaction may result in decreased therapeutic efficacy or increased risk of toxicity. The degree of drug interaction depends on the relative concentrations and therefore the dose and time. Changes in absorption rate, competition for plasma protein binding sites, oral bioavailability, volume of distribution, and hepatic and renal clearance have been demonstrated for therapeutic drugs, but few studies have systematically documented pharmacokinetic interactions between illicit drugs.

REFERENCES

1. *Ellenhorn's Medical Toxicology: Diagnosis and Treatment of Human Poisoning, Williams & Wilkins; Subsequent Edition*, 1997.
2. Curtis D. Klaassen, *Casarett and Doull's Toxicology: The Basic Science of Poisons*, 7th edition, McGraw-Hill, 2008.
3. L. Butera, D.A. Feinfeld, M. Bhargava, Sex differences in the subunits of glutathione-S-transferase isoenzyme from rat and human kidney. *Enzyme* 1990; 43: 175–82.
4. T.O. Eloranta, Tissue distribution of S-adenosylmethionine and S-adenosylhomocysteine in the rat. Effect of age, sex and methionine administration on the metabolism of S-adenosylmethionine, S-adenosylhomocysteine and polyamines. *Biochem J* 1977; 166: 521–9.
5. O.P. Soldin, D.R. Mattison, Sex differences in pharmacokinetics and pharmacodynamics, *Clin Pharmacokinet* 2009; 48(3): 143–57. Aichhorn W., Whitworth A.B., Weiss E.M., Hinterhuber H., Marksteiner J. Differences between men and women in side effects of second-generation antipsychotics. *Nervenarzt* 200.
6. G. Englund, F. Rorsman, A. Ronnblom, et al. Regional levels of drug transporters along the human intestinal tract: co-expression of ABC and SLC transporters and comparison with Caco-2 cells. *Eur J Pharm Sci* 2006.
7. I. Tamai, A. Saheki, R. Saitoh, Y. Sai, I. Yamada, A. Tsuji, Nonlinear intestinal absorption of 5-hydroxytryptamine receptor antagonist caused by absorptive and secretory transporters. *J Pharmacol Exp Ther* 1997; 283: 108–15.
8. M. Rowland, T.N. Tozer, *Clinical Pharmacokinetics Concepts and Applications*, Lippincott Williams & Wilkins, 2010.

2.4 PHARMACOKINETICS OF SPECIFIC DRUGS

2.4.1 Amphetamine

Amphetamines are a class of potent central nervous system (CNS) stimulants that include a wide number of structurally related compounds, such as amphetamine, methamphetamine, methylenedioxy derivatives, and synthetic amphetamine analogues. Amphetamine, with its β-phenylisopropylamine moiety, represents the prototype of all the amphetamines.

These substances occur as structural and stereo-isomers. Structural isomers have the same empirical formula, but different atomic arrangements, for example, methamphetamine and phentermine. Stereoisomers are molecules composed of the same molecules, but with a different three-dimensional orientation of atoms binding an asymmetric carbon. In the amphetamines group, the asymmetric carbon (e.g. chiral center), is the α-carbon. As a molecule with a single chiral center, amphetamine exists in two stereoisomers or enantiomers: D- (dextro-) and L- (levo-) amphetamine. Dextroamphetamine is a more potent CNS stimulant than its enantiomer. The stimulation potency is not the only difference, as D- and L-amphetamine may also differ for their pharmacokinetics characteristics. Under United States' law, dextroamphetamine is a scheduled controlled substance, but L-amphetamine is sold over the counter as an antihistamine.

Amphetamine increases alertness, wakefulness, and energy, and, at the same time, decreases the appetite. It also causes hypertension, tremors, sweating, and, at high doses, convulsions, disturbances in perception, and psychotic behavior.[1–3] These effects are mediated by increasing synaptic concentrations of norepinephrine and dopamine as a consequence of either neurotransmitter release stimulation, inhibiting of reuptake, or both.

In the past, the drug has been used to help to reduce obesity, and for the treatment of schizophrenia and obsessive-compulsive disorder. Currently, medical uses of this compound include treatment of narcolepsy in adults and attention-deficit/hyperactivity disorder (ADHA) in children.[3] In 2007, the U.S. Food and Drug Administration approved the use of an inactive prodrug of D-amphetamine, lisdexamphetamine dimesylate (LDX), to treat ADHA in patients > 6 years-old.[4] The use of LDX was then expanded to adults with moderate to severe binge eating disorders (BED) in 2015.[5] LDX is D-amphetamine coupled with L-lysine; once in the bloodstream, this bond is hydrolyzed making the active drug available. Drugs produced in this fashion have a lower Cmax, extended Tmax, and lower inter- and intra-individual variability than a corresponding D-amphetamine dose. Moreover, LDX exerts a longer therapeutic effect.[6] Recommended doses are 30 mg to 70 mg and 50 mg to 70 mg for ADHA and BED, respectively.[7] When indicated for therapeutic use, 5 mg to 60 mg or 5 mg to 20 mg of amphetamine or methamphetamine, respectively, are administered orally. An oral dose of amphetamine typically results in a peak plasma concentration of 110 ng/mL.[8]

Amphetamine is frequently used for recreational purposes. It can be self-administered orally, or via intravenous or smoking routes. In heavy abusers, where the emergence of tolerance occurs, a daily dose may rise to 2000 mg.

2.4.1.1 Adsorption

Pizarro et al.[9] administered racemic amphetamine to 17 healthy volunteers at the following doses: 20 mg, 30 mg, 35 mg, and 40 mg; mean Cmax where respectively 37.7 ng/mL, 57.6 ng/mL, 60.5 ng/mL, and 69.1 ng/mL at 2–3 h.

Comparing AUC and Cmax, they assessed that variations were linear in the range of doses; thus, plasma levels can be predicted. Asghar et al.[10] reported peak plasma levels at 41 ng/mL at 3.5 h in 25 healthy younger men consuming a single oral 25 mg dose of D-amphetamine. Rowland[11] observed a peak blood concentration of 35 ng/mL, 2 h after a 10 mg oral dose of D-amphetamine to a healthy 66 kg adult. The half-life for the D-isomer was 11 h to 13 h compared with a 39% longer half-life for the L-isomer. After a 30 mg oral dose of a preparation containing a 3:1 mixture of D- and L-amphetamine, the plasma concentration for the two stereoisomers at steady state averaged 67 ng/mL at 4.2 h and 22 ng/mL at 4.3 h, respectively; elimination half-live for the two enantiomers averaged 11 h and 14 h, respectively.[12] If the urine was acidified, excretion was enhanced, and the half-lives of both isomers were reduced to approximately 7 h. Amphetamine demonstrates a linear one-compartment open model over the dose range 20 mg to 200 mg.[13] Ermer et al.[5] published a study on LDX where 70 mg capsules were administrated to 30 healthy adult volunteers. D-amphetamine's Cmax was 61 ng/mL at 3.8 h. At the risk of repetition, it is not possible to back-extrapolate. Knowing that a 25 mg dose given to a healthy volunteer produced a peak plasma level of 41 ng/mL in no way implies that a cadaver with 61 ng/mL in its blood had concentrations anywhere near those in the living.

2.4.1.2 Distribution

The plasma protein-binding of amphetamine in humans is approximately 16% to 20% and is similar in drug-dependent and naive subjects.[14,15] Research by Rowland[11] and Franksson and Anggard[15] indicated that there was a difference in the volume of distribution between non-users (3.5 L/kg to 4.6 L/kg) and drug-dependent individuals (6.1 L/kg). It has been suggested that the larger Vd observed in drug-dependent subjects may be due to a higher tissue affinity for amphetamine in these individuals. Evidence to support this suggestion is found in studies with amphetamine-dependent animals, where higher tissue concentrations of amphetamine were found.[16] Further evidence of the tolerance phenomenon is apparently supported by a longer plasma elimination half-time in drug-dependent subjects than in non-users (21.8 ± 1.4 versus 13.9 ± h in alkaline urine) at the same 25 mg oral dose,[17] although in the postmortem setting it could also be the result of autolyzing cells liberating deep tissue stores. Concerning the two stereoisomers, it has been demonstrated that protein-binding and Vd are similar.

2.4.1.3 Metabolism and Extraction

Amphetamine is metabolized by deamination, oxidation, and hydroxylation.[18] Figure 2.4.1 illustrates the metabolic scheme for amphetamine. Deamination produces an inactive metabolite, phenylacetone, which is further oxidized to form benzoic acid that is then excreted in urine as hippuric acid and glucuronide conjugates. In addition, amphetamine is also converted to norephedrine by oxidation, before this metabolite and the parent compound are p-hydroxylated. Several metabolites, including norephedrine, its hydroxy metabolite, and hydroxyamphetamine, are pharmacologically active.[19] Amphetamine is mainly excreted by the renal route and, since it is a weak basic substance, its excretion is increased by acidic urine and decreased by urinary alkalinization. In healthy men who were administered 5 mg of isotopically labeled D,L-amphetamine, approximately 90% of the dose was excreted in the urine within three to four days.[20] Approximately 70% of the dose was excreted in the 24 h urine with 30% as unchanged drug. This increased to 74% under acidic conditions and reduced to 1% in alkaline urine. Under normal conditions, <1% is excreted as phenylacetone, 16% to 28% as hippuric acid, 4% as benzoylglucuronide, 2% as norephedrine, <0.5% as p-hydroxynorephedrine, and 2% to 4% as p-hydroxyamphetamine.[21] Mobley et al. reported an average urine

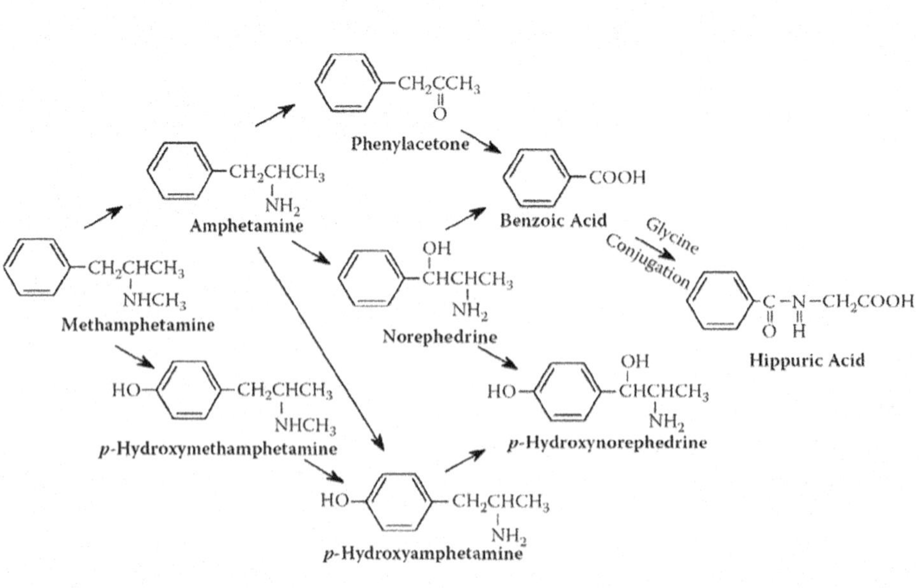

FIGURE 2.4.1 Metabolic pathway of amphetamine and methamphetamine.

amphetamine concentration of 3.3 mg/L at 12 h after a single oral 10 mg dose with a urinary elimination half-life of 12 h.[19]

L-Amphetamine is not as extensively metabolized as the D-isomer. When volunteers were orally administered 5 mg to 15 mg of D- or L-amphetamine, the mean excretion of unchanged D-amphetamine was 33% of the dose and that of the L-isomer was 49% of the dose.[8]

The metabolism of amphetamine has been studied in those presenting with amphetamine psychosis. In the presence of acidified urine, the renal elimination of amphetamine increased significantly. The intensity of the psychosis was found to correlate with the amount of basic polar metabolites excreted in the urine, such as norephedrine and p-hydroxyamphetamine, and not with the plasma amphetamine concentration. This suggests that these metabolites may play an important role in the development of paranoid psychosis in chronic amphetamine users.[16]

2.4.2 Methamphetamine

Methamphetamine, the N-methyl derivative of amphetamine, was first synthesized in 1919 and has been used since 1930 as a treatment for obesity, narcolepsy, and ADHA.[22] Like other amphetamines, this compound is a stimulant and sympathomimetic drug. Methamphetamine is available in the D-and L-forms. The D-form has reportedly greater central stimulant activity than the L-isomer, which has greater peripheral sympathomimetic activity. The D-form is the form most commonly used while the L-isomer is typically found in non-prescription inhalers as a decongestant.

Although initially available as an injectable solution for the treatment of obesity, D-methamphetamine hydrochloride now is currently available as conventional and prolonged-release tablets. Illicit methamphetamine is synthesized from the precursors phenylacetone and N-methylformamide (D,L-mixture) or, alternatively, from ephedrine or pseudoephedrine by red phosphorus/acid reduction. In the U.S., the latter is preferred because the precursors are much easier to come by.

2.4.2.1 Adsorption

Doses between 5 mg and 10 mg of methamphetamine typically result in blood concentrations between 20 ng/mL to 60 ng/mL. In one study,[21] six healthy adults were orally administered a single dose of 0.125 mg/kg methamphetamine. Peak plasma concentrations were achieved at 3.6 h with a mean concentration of 20 ng/mLng/mL. In a second study, Lebish et al.[23] observed a peak blood concentration of 30 ng/mL, 1 h after a single oral dose of 10 mg methamphetamine to one subject. In a study by Schepers et al.,[24] eight subjects were administered four oral doses of 10 mg sustained dose tablets methamphetamine over a seven-day period. Three weeks later, five subjects received four oral 20 mg doses. After the first dose, methamphetamine was detected in plasma between 0.25 h and 2 h, the Cmax was 14.5 ng/mL to 33.8 ng/mL (10 mg dose), and 26.2 ng/mL to 44.3 ng/mL (20 mg), and occurred within 2 h to 12 h. In this study, methamphetamine was first detected in oral fluid in 0.08 h to 2 h post-dose, with a Cmax of 24.7 ng/mL to 312.2 ng/mL, and 75.3 ng/mL to 321.7 ng/mL after the 10 mg and 20 mg doses, respectively. Peak methamphetamine concentrations in oral fluid occurred at 2 h to 12 h and the median oral fluid- plasma concentration ratio was 2.0 h for 24 h. In general, the detection window for drugs in oral fluid exceeded that in plasma. Mendelson et al.[25] studied peak plasma concentrations for the two methamphetamine stereoisomers. After single intravenous 0.25 mg/kg and 0.50 mg/kg doses given to 12 adult male users, average peak plasma D- and L-methamphetamine levels were 77 ng/mL and 65 ng/mL at a low dose, 132 ng/mL, and 126 ng/mL at high dose, and the half-lives for the two species averaged 10 (D-isomer) and 13.5 (L-isomer), irrespective of the dose.

2.4.2.2 Distribution

Methamphetamine distribution is not affected by the route or time of administration and it appears to be similar to that of amphetamine.[26] Concurrent alcohol consumption significantly decreases the Vd. This interaction may result from alcohol displacement of methamphetamine from peripheral binding sites.[27] In a study on [11C]D-methamphetamine distribution among human organs, it was reported that the highest uptake occurred in the lungs (22% dose) and liver (23% dose), while it was intermediate in the brain (10% dose). The heart and lungs showed the fastest clearances (7–16 min).[28]

2.4.2.3 Metabolism and Excretion

In humans, both the D- and L-forms undergo hydroxylation and N-demethylation to their respective p-hydroxymethamphetamine and amphetamine metabolites. Amphetamine is the major active metabolite of methamphetamine. Under normal conditions, up to 43% of a D-methamphetamine dose is excreted unchanged in the urine in the first 24 hours and 4% to 7% will be present as amphetamine. In acidic urine, up to 76% is present as a parent drug compared with 2% under alkaline conditions. Approximately 15% of the dose was present as p-hydroxymethamphetamine and the remaining minor metabolites were similar to those found after amphetamine administration.[29]

Urine concentrations of methamphetamine are typically 0.5 mg/L to 4 mg/L after an oral dose of 10 mg. However, methamphetamine and amphetamine urine concentrations vary widely among abusers. Lebish et al.[23] reported urine methamphetamine concentrations of 24 mg/L to 333 mg/L and amphetamine concentrations of 1 mg/L to 90 mg/L in the urine of methamphetamine abusers.

L-methamphetamine is biotransformed in a manner similar to the D-isomer, but at a slower rate. Following a 13.7 mg oral dose, the 24 h urine contained an average of 34% of the dose as L-methamphetamine and 1.7% of the dose as L-amphetamine.[30] The stereoselective nature of methamphetamine metabolism has also been reported by Li.[31] He observed a higher excretion of unchanged

L-methamphetamine than the D-isomer, possibly due to a less conversion to L-amphetamine. Oyler et al.[32] described the appearance of methamphetamine and amphetamine in urine after volunteers (n = 8) ingested 4 x 10 mg doses of methamphetamine hydrochloride daily for seven days followed by 4 x 20 mg daily several weeks later. Parent and metabolite were generally detected in the first or second void post dose in a concentration range of 82 ng/mL to 1827 ng/mL and 12 ng/mL to 180 ng/mL, respectively. Peak methamphetamine urine concentrations (1871 ng/mL to 6004 ng/mL) occurred within 1.5 h to 60 h after a single dose.

D-Methamphetamine is commonly self-administered by smoking. Both the free-base and hydrochloride salt of methamphetamine are volatile and >90% of parent drug can be recovered intact when heated to temperatures of 300°C. When cigarettes containing tobacco mixed with methamphetamine were pyrolyzed, amphetamine, phenylacetone, dimethylamphetamine, and N-cyanomethyl methamphetamine were the major resulting products.[33] Cook[34] conducted a study in which six volunteers were administered 30 mg D-methamphetamine from a pipe that was heated to approximately 300°C. Blood samples and physiological and subjective measures were collected after drug administration. Plasma methamphetamine concentrations rose rapidly after the start of smoking. However, concentrations plateaued (40 ng/mL to 44 ng/mL) after 1 h, with a slight increase in concentration over the next hour. Thereafter, concentrations in plasma declined slowly, reaching the same concentration at 8 h on the downward side of the curve as reached at 30 min on the upward side. The authors used a noncompartmental model to determine an average elimination half-life of methamphetamine 11.7 h with a range of 8 h to 17 h.

These same authors also administered methamphetamine (0.250 mg/kg) orally and the resulting plasma data were fitted to a one-compartment model with first-order elimination and a lag time. A maximum plasma concentration of 35 ng/mL to 38 ng/mL was achieved at 3.1 h with a terminal elimination half-life of 10 h. Although the plasma concentration-time curves for smoked and oral methamphetamine appeared similar, the subjective effects were markedly different, with a greater "high" being reported after smoked methamphetamine. This indicates that it may be the rate of change of plasma drug concentrations that is a significant factor in determining subjective effects. Other investigators[35] have reported the bioavailability of methamphetamine after intranasal and smoked drug to be 79% and 67% (of estimated delivered dose), respectively. Maximum blood concentrations of parent drug occurred at 2.7 h and 2.5 h after intranasal and smoked doses (n = 8).[35]

2.4.3 3,4-Methylenedioxyamphetamine

3,4-Methylenedioxyamphetamine (MDA) is a potent psychotropic amphetamine derivative first synthesized in 1910

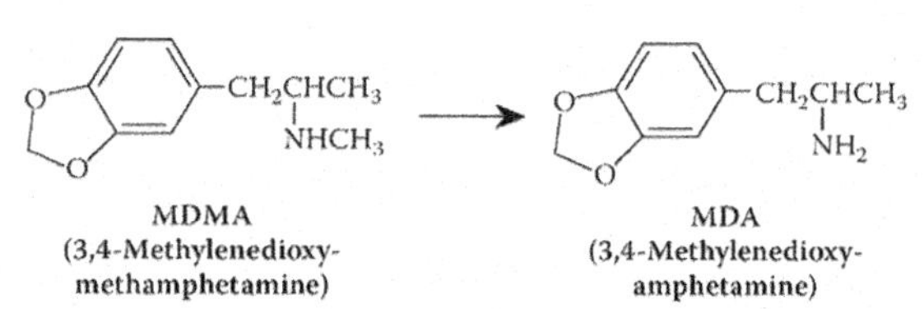

FIGURE 2.4.2 Structures of MDA and MDMA

(Figure 2.4.2). It has no accepted medical use but is self-administered orally or intravenously in doses of 50 mg to 250 mg for illicit use.[19] Blood concentrations following normal use have not been reported and, to date, there are no reported clinical studies delineating the pharmacokinetic or pharmacodynamic characteristics of this drug. Blood concentrations in humans have been reported following overdose. The average blood concentration in 12 fatal cases was 9.3 mg/L (range 1.8 to 26).[19] Post-mortem MDA concentrations in a 19-year-old male (died following overdosage) were 5.5 μg/mL in heart blood and 33 mg/L in urine.[36] The metabolism of MDA in humans has not been studied, but in other animals, MDA is metabolized by O-dealkylation, deamination, and conjugation.[37] Polymorphically expressed CYP2D6 is the major isozyme catalyzing the metabolic steps in the metabolism of MDA and MDMA.[38]

2.4.4 3,4-Methylenedioxymethamphetamine

3,4-Methylenedioxymethamphetamine (MDMA) is a ring-substituted derivative of methamphetamine (Figure 2.4.3) with widespread use as a recreational drug. This compound is able to elicit the so-called entactogenic syndrome in healthy humans, and it may be that this drug will yet find relevant therapeutic applications. The main described effects are characterized by emotional relaxation, feelings of happiness, and empathy.[39] Self-administration is typically by the oral route in doses of 100 mg to 150 mg.

2.4.4.1 Adsorption

Helmlin et al.[40] reported a mean peak plasma MDMA concentration of 300 ng/mL at 2.3 h after an oral dose of 1.5 mg/kg given to adult subjects. Kohlbrich et al.[41] measured Cmax of MDMA and its main metabolites after single oral 1 mg/kg and 1.6 mg/kg doses in a double-blind randomized study. MDMA was administered to 17 female and male healthy consumers. At low dose, mean Cmax was 162.9 ng/mL; after administration of the high dose, the Cmax increased to 291.8 ng/mL. The mean tmax was estimated in 2.4 h for both the doses; elimination half-live averaged 6.9 h. In a randomized double-blind cross-over placebo-controlled study with nine healthy male subjects, Farre et al.[42] reported greater than expected increases in plasma MDMA concentrations after a second dose of 100 mg, 24 h after the initial dose. The increase was attributed to drug accumulation. The authors suspected the reason is metabolic inhibition. Parameters such as blood pressure, heart rate, and subjective effects were also higher after the second dose than after the first.

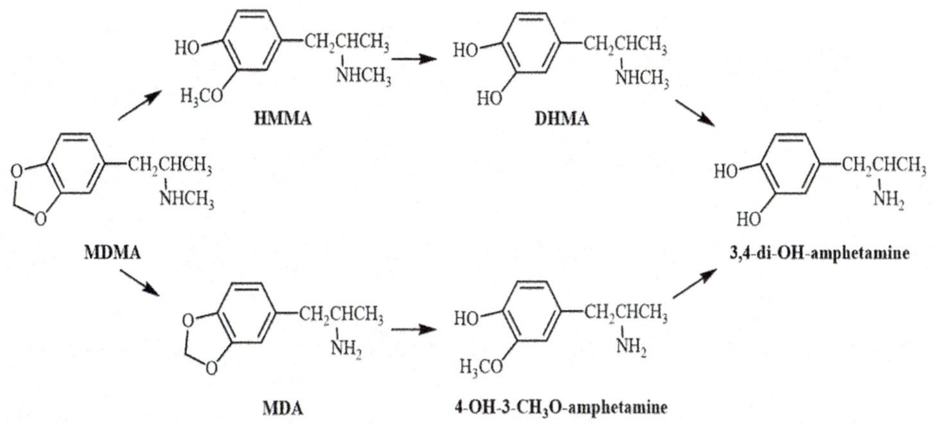

FIGURE 2.4.3 Metabolic pathway of MDMA and MDA.

2.4.4.2 Distribution

Torre et al.[43] estimated a Vd of 452 L (6.4 L/kg) after an oral 100 mg dose of MDMA. In a study on enantioselectivity disposition in humans, Fallon et al.[44] demonstrated a more extensive distribution of D-isomer.

2.4.4.3 Metabolism and Excretion

MDMA is metabolized to MDA with 65% of the dose excreted as parent drug within three days. Both MDMA and MDA are hydroxylated to mono- and di-hydroxy derivatives and subsequently conjugated before elimination. The plasma half-life has been reported to range from 5 h to 9 h.[19] In a study conducted by Schwaninger et al.[45], single oral 1.0 mg/kg and 1.6 mg/kg doses were completely excreted in five day urine as MDMA (8%–11%), MDA (0.8%–1.2%), 3,4-dihydroxymethamphetamine (DHMA, 0.2%), DHMA-3-sulgate (7.5%–8.7%), DHMA-4-sulfate (1.7%–1.9%), 4-hydroxy-3-methoxymethamphetamine (HMMA, 0.5%–0.7%), HMMA sulfate (9.7%–13%) and HMMA glucuronide (4.1%–5.2%). MDMA conversion to MDA is mainly mediated by CYP2C19, CYP2B6, and CYP1A2. Moreover, it has been demonstrated that CYP2C19 poor metabolizers show greater cardiovascular responses to MDMA compared with other CYP2C19 genotypes.[46] If MDMA is co-administered with ethanol, as 100 mg plus 0.8 g/kg ethanol, plasma concentrations of the former demonstrate a 13% increase compared with MDMA administered alone.[47] Plasma concentrations of ethanol decreased 9% to 15% after MDMA administration (n = 9).

MDMA has also been reported in alternative biological specimens. After a single oral dose of 75 mg in human volunteers, MDMA concentrations in oral fluid exceeded those in plasma with a mean peak concentration of 1215 ng/mL (n = 12) and a range of 50 ng/mL to 6982 ng/mL compared with an average peak plasma concentration of 178 ng/mL (range 21 ng/mL to 295 ng/mL).[48] In sweat the average concentration was 25 ng/wipe when measured 4 h to 5 h after ingestion of a similar dose.[43] When MDMA and MDA concentrations measured in antemortem samples have been compared, consistent and significant increases in the postmortem concentrations have been observed.[49]

REFERENCES

1. Green, A.R., Mechan, A.O., Elliot, J.M., O'Shea, E., and Cofado, M.I., The pharmacology and clinical pharmacology of 3,4-methylenedioxymethamphetamine (MDMA, "ecstasy"), *Pharmacol Rev*, 55(3), 463–508, 2003.
2. Camí, J., and Farré, M., Drug addiction, *N Engl J Med*, 349(10), 975–86, 2003.
3. Physicians Desk Reference, *Medical Economics Data, A Division of Medical Economics Company, Inc.*, Montvale, NJ, 2005, p. 1315.
4. Goodman, D.W., Lisdexamfetamine dimesylate: the first prodrug stimulant, *Psychiatry (Edgmont)*, 4(8), 39–45, 2007.
5. Ermer, J., Corcoran, M., Lasseter, K., and Martin, P.T., Relative bioavailabilities of lisdexamfetamine dimesylate and D-Amphetamine in healthy adults in an open-label, randomized, crossover study after mixing lisdexamfetamine dimesylate with food or drink, *Ther Drug Monit.*, 38(6), 769–76, 2016.
6. Ermer, J.C., Pennick, M., and Frick, G., Lisdexamfetamine dimesylate: prodrug delivery, amphetamine exposure and duration of efficacy, *Clin Drug Investig*, 36(5), 341–56, 2016.
7. Vyvanse. *Lisdexamfetamine Dimesylate.* Wayne, PA: Shire US Inc, 2015. Available at: pi.shirecontent.com/PI/PDFs/Vyvanse_USA_ENG.pdf. Accessed November 30 2018.
8. Baylor, M.R., and Crouch, D.J., Sympathomimetic amines: pharmacology, toxicology, and analysis. In-service training and continuing education AACC/TDM, *Am Assoc Clini Chem Inc, Washington, DC*, 14(5), 101–11, 1993.
9. Pizarro, N., Ortuño, J., Segura, J., Farré, M., Mas, M., Camí, J., and de la Torre, R., Quantification of amphetamine plasma concentrations by gas chromatography coupled to mass spectrometry, *J Pharm Biomed Anal*, 21(4), 739–47, 1999.
10. Asghar, S.J., Tanay, V.A., Baker, G.B., Greenshaw, A., and Silverstone, P.H., Relationship of plasma amphetamine levels to physiological, subjective, cognitive and biochemical measures in healthy volunteers, *Hum Psychopharmacol*, 18(4), 291–9, 2003.
11. Rowland, M., Amphetamine blood and urine levels in man, *J Pharm Sci*, 58, 508–9, 1969.
12. Clausen, S.B., Read, S.C., and Tulloch, S.J., Single- and multiple-dose pharmacokinetics of an oral mixed amphetamine salts extended-release formulation in adults, *CNS Spectr*, 10(12 Suppl 20), 6–15, 2005.

13. Matin, S.B., Wan, S.H., and Knight, J.B., Quantitative determination of enantiomeric compounds, biomed, *Mass Spectrosc*, 4, 118–121, 1977.
14. Quinn, D.I., Wodak, A., and Day, R.O., Pharmacokinetic and pharmacodynamic principles of illicit drug use and treatment of illicit drug users, *Clin Pharmacokinet*, 33(5), 344–400, 1997.
15. Franksson, G., and Anggard, E., The plasma protein binding of amphetamine, catecholamines and related compounds, *Acta Pharmacol Toxicol*, 28, 209–14, 1970.
16. Ellison, T., Siegel., M, Silverman, A.G., and Okun, R., Comparative metabolism of D,L H3-amphet-amine hydrochloride in tolerant and non-tolerant cats, *Proc Western Pharmacol Soc*, 11, 75–7, 1968.
17. Busto, U., Bendayan, R., and Sellers, E.M., Clinical pharmacokinetics of non-opiate abused drugs, *Clin Pharmacokinet*, 16(1), 1–26, 1989.
18. Kraemer, T., and Maurer, H.H., Toxicokinetics of amphetamines: metabolism and toxicokinetic data of designer drugs, amphetamine, methamphetamine, and their N-alkyl derivatives, *Ther Drug Monit*, 24(2), 277–89, 2002.
19. Dring, L.G., Smith, R.L., and Williams, R.T., The metabolic fate of amphetamine in man and other species, *Biochem J*, 116, 425–35, 1970.
20. Sever, P.S., Caldwell, J., Dring, L.G., and Williams, R.T., The metabolism of amphetamine in dependent subjects, *Eur J Clin Pharm*, 6, 177–80, 1973.
21. Baselt, R.C., *Disposition of Toxic Drugs and Chemicals in Man*, 10th ed., Biomedical Publications, Seal Beach, CA, 2014.
22. Puder, K.S., Kagan, D.V., and Morgan, J.P., Illicit methamphetamine: analysis, synthesis, and availability, *Am J Drug Alcohol Abuse*, 14(4), 463–73, 1989.
23. LeBish, P., Finkle, B.S., and Brackett, J.W. Jr., Determination of amphetamine, methamphetamine, and related amines in blood and urine by gas chromatography by hydrogen-flame ionization detector, *Clin Chem*, 16, 195–200, 1970.
24. Schepers, R.J.F., Oyler, J.M., Joseph, R.E., Cone, E.J., Moolchan, E.T., and Huestis, M.A., Metham- phetamine and amphetamine pharmacokinetics in oral fluid and plasma after controlled oral metham- phetamine administration to human volunteers, *Clin Chem*, 49(1), 121–32, 2003.
25. Mendelson, J., Uemura, N., Harris, D., Nath, R.P., Fernandez, E., Jacob, P. 3rd, Everhart, E.T., and Jones, R.T., Human pharmacology of the methamphetamine stereoisomers, *Clin Pharmacol Ther*, 80(4), 403–20, 2006.
26. Shappell, S.A., Kearns, G.L., Valentine, J.L., Neri, D.F., and DeJohn, C.A., Chronopharmacokinetics and chronopharmacodynamics of dextromethamphetamine in man, *J Clin Pharmacol*, 36(11), 1051–63, 1996.
27. Mendelson, J., Jones, R.T., Upton, R., and Jacob, P. 3rd, Methamphetamine and ethanol interactions in humans, *Clin Pharmacol Ther*, 57(5), 559–68, 1995.
28. Volkow, N.D., Fowler, J.S., Wang, G.J., Shumay, E., Telang, F., Thanos, P.K., and Alexoff, D., Distribution and pharmacokinetics of methamphetamine in the human body: clinical implications, *PLoS One*, 5(12), e15269, 2010.
29. Shima, N., Kamata, H.T., Katagi, M., and Tsuchihashi, H., Urinary excretion of the main metabolites of methamphetamine, including p-hydroxymethamphetamine-sulfate and p-hydroxymethamphetamine-glucuronide, in humans and rats, *Xenobiotica*, 36(2–3), 259–67, 2006.
30. Beckett, A.H., and Rowland, M., Urinary excretion kinetics of amphetamine in man, *J Pharm Pharmacol*, 17, 628–39, 1965.
31. Li, L., Everhart, T., Jacob III, P., Jones, R., and Mendelson, J., Stereoselectivity in the human metabolism of methamphetamine, *Br J Clin Pharmacol*, 69(2), 187–92, 2010.
32. Oyler, J.M., Cone, E.J., Joseph, R.E., Moolchan, E.T., and Huestis, M.A., Duration of detectable methamphetamine and amphetamine excretion in urine after controlled oral administration of meth- amphetamine to humans, *Clin. Chem*, 48(10), 1703–14, 2002.
33. Sekine, H., and Nakahara, Y., Abuse of smoking methamphetamine mixed with tobacco: I. Inhalation efficiency and pyrolysis products of methamphetamine, *J Forensic Sci*, 32(5), 1271–80, 1987.
34. Cook, C.E., Pyrolytic characteristics, pharmacokinetics, and bioavailability of smoked heroin, cocaine, phencyclidine and methamphetamine, *NIDA Research Monograph*, 99, 6–23. DHHS Pub. No. 1990.
35. Harris, D.S., Boxenbaum, H., Everhart, E.T., Sequeira, G., Mendelson, J.E., and Jones, R.T., The bioavailability of intranasal and smoked methamphetamine, *Clin Pharmacol Ther*, 74(5), 475–86, 2003.
36. Liu, R.H., Liu, H.C., and Lin, D.L., Distribution of methylenedioxymethamphetamine (MDMA) and methylenedioxyamphetamine (MDA) in postmortem and antemortem specimens, *J Anal Toxicol*, 30(8), 545–50, 2006.
37. Midha, K.K., McGilveray, I.J., Bhatnager, S.P., and Cooper, J.K., GLC identification and determi- nation of 3,4-methylenedioxyamphetamine in vivo in dog and monkey, *Drug Met Disp*, 6, 623–30, 1978.
38. Maurer, H.H., Kraemer, T., Springer, D., and Staack, R.F., Chemistry, pharmacology, toxicology, and hepatic metabolism of designer drugs of the amphetamine (ecstasy), piperazine, and pyrrolidinophe- none types: a synopsis, *Ther Drug Monit*, 26(2), 127–31, 2004.
39. Sáez-Briones, P., and Hernández, A., MDMA (3,4-Methylenedioxymethamphetamine) analogues as tools to characterize MDMA-like effects: an approach to understand entactogen pharmacology, *Curr Neuropharmacol*, 11(5), 521–34, 2013.
40. Helmlin, H.J., Bracher, K., Salamone, S.J., and Brenneisen, R., *Analysis of 3,4-Methylenedioxy- Methamphetamine (MDMA) and its Metabolites in Human Plasma and Urine*, Society of Forensic Toxicologists, Inc., Phoenix, AZ, October 1993 [Abstract].
41. Kolbrich, E.A., Goodwin, R.S., Gorelick, D.A., Hayes, R.J., Stein, E.A., and Huestis, M.A., Plasma pharmacokinetics of 3,4-methylenedioxymethamphetamine after controlled oral administration to young adults, *Ther Drug Monit*, 30(3), 320–32, 2008.
42. Farre, M., de la Torre, R., Mathuna, B.O., Roset, P.N., Peiro, A.M., Torrens, M., Ortuno, J., Pujadas, M., and Cami, J., Repeated doses administration of MDMA in humans: pharmacological effects and pharmacokinetics, *Psychopharmacology (Berlin)*, 173(3–4), 364–75, 2004.
43. De la Torre, R., Farré, M., Ortuño, J., Mas, M., Brenneisen, R., Roset, P.N., Segura, J., and Camí, J., Non-linear pharmacokinetics of MDMA ('ecstasy') in humans, *Br J Clin Pharmacol*, 49(2),104–9, 2000.
44. Fallon, J.K., Kicman, A.T., Henry, J.A., Milligan, P.J., Cowan, D.A., and Hutt, A.J., Stereospecific analysis and enantiomeric disposition of 3, 4-methylenedioxymethamphetamine (Ecstasy) in humans, *Clin Chem*, 45(7), 1058–69, 1999.
45. Schwaninger, A.E., Meyer, M.R., Barnes, A.J., Kolbrich-Spargo, E.A., Gorelick, D.A., Goodwin, R.S., Huestis, M.A., and Maurer, H.H., Urinary excretion kinetics of

3,4-methylenedioxymethamphetamine (MDMA, ecstasy) and its phase I and phase II metabolites in humans following controlled MDMA administration, *Clin Chem*, 57(12), 1748–56, 2011.
46. Vizeli, P., Schmid, Y., Prestin, K., Meyer Zu Schwabedissen, H.E., and Liechti, M.E., Pharmacogenetics of ecstasy: CYP1A2, CYP2C19, and CYP2B6 polymorphisms moderate pharmacokinetics of MDMA in healthy subjects, *Eur Neuropsychopharmacol*, 27(3), 232–8, 2017.
47. Hernandez-Lopez, C., Farre, M., Roset, P.N., Menoyo, E., Pizarro, N., Ortuno, J., Torrens, M., Cami, J., and de la Torre, R., 3,4-Methylenedioxymethamphetamine (ecstasy) and alcohol interactions in humans: psychomotor performance, subjective effects, and pharmacokinetics, *J Pharmacol Exp Ther*, 300(1), 236–44, 2002.
48. Samyn, N., De Boeck, G., Wood, M., Lamers, C.T., De Waard, D., Brookhuis, K.A., Verstraete, A.G., and Riedel, W.J., Plasma, oral fluid and sweat wipe ecstasy concentrations in controlled and real life conditions, *Forensic Sci Int*, 128(1–2), 90–7, 2002.
49. Elliott, S.P., MDMA and MDA concentrations in antemortem and postmortem specimens in fatalities following hospital admission, *J Anal Toxicol*, 29(5), 296–300, 2005.

2.4.5 Barbiturates

Barbituric acid, 2,4,6-trioxohexahydropyrimidine, was first synthesized in 1864.[1] In 1903, it was marketed for use as an anti-anxiety agent and sedative-hypnotic medication.[2] Barbituric acid is without CNS-depressant activity, but by substituting an aryl or alkyl group on C-5, anxiolytic and sedative properties may be conferred. Substitution of sulfur on C-2 produces thiobarbiturates, which have characteristically greater lipophilicity. Generally, structural changes that increase lipophilicity result in decreased duration of action, decreased latency to onset of action, increased biotransformation, and increased hypnotic potency.[3] Although the use of barbiturates as sedative-hypnotic agents has largely been replaced by the benzodiazepines, the barbiturates maintain an important role as anti-convulsant and anesthetic drugs.

2.4.5.1 Pharmacology

As a class, barbiturates exert hypnotic, sedative, anxiolytic, anticonvulsant, and anesthetic properties. The clinical use of these drugs is based on their shared properties and also the unique properties of individual drugs within this class.[1] As CNS depressants, barbiturates exert effects on excitatory and inhibitory synaptic neurotransmission. Barbiturates are known to decrease excitatory amino acid release and post-synaptic response in experimental animals by blocking the excitatory glutamate response. This may be due to a direct effect on the glutamate sensitive channel, or an indirect effect on calcium channels.[1] The ultra-short acting barbiturates used for anesthesia, such as thiopental, depress excitatory neuronal transmission to a greater extent than the anticonvulsant barbiturates.[4]

Barbiturates also exert an effect on gamma-aminobutyric acid (GABA) neurotransmission. Barbiturates, such as pentobarbital, enhance the binding of GABA to GABAA receptors. This effect occurs both in the CNS and the spinal cord. The enhanced action of GABA depresses both normal physiological processes, such as post-synaptic potential evocation, and pathophysiological processes, such as seizures.[1] Barbiturates also amplify GABA-induced chloride currents by extending the time for chloride channel opening.[5] It is important to note that some barbiturates – such as 5-(1,3-dimethylbutyl)-5-ethyl barbituric acid (DMBB) – promote convulsions by directly depolarizing the neuronal membrane and increasing transmitter release. Phenobarbital diverges from the other barbiturates because of its ability to protect against seizures at minimally sedating doses. Indeed, this compound produces only minimal sedation at therapeutic doses; in contrast, pentobarbital conce[8]ntrations inducing anticonvulsant activity overlap those causing anesthesia.[6,7]

2.4.5.2 Adsorption

When utilized as sedative-hypnotics, barbiturates are administered orally. They are rapidly and completely absorbed by this route with nearly 100% bioavailability and an onset of action ranging from 10 to 60 min.[4] Sodium salts are more rapidly absorbed than free acids. Intramuscular injections of sodium salts should be made deep into the muscle to prevent pain and tissue damage. Some barbiturates are also administered rectally; barbiturates utilized for the induction and maintenance of anesthesia (thiopental) or for treating status epilepticus (phenobarbital) are administered intravenously.

Pentobarbital is a short-acting barbiturate available for oral, intramuscular, rectal, and intravenous administration. After a single oral dose of 100 mg, peak serum concentrations of 1.2 mg/L to 3.1 mg/L were achieved at 0.5 h to 2.0 h.[8] Concentration diminished slowly to an average of 0.3 mg/L at 48 h. When administered intravenously, in a 5 min continuous infusion of 50 mg, plasma concentrations averaged 1.18 mg/L ($n = 5$) at 0.08 h, declining to 0.54 mg/L after 1 h and reaching 0.27 mg/L after 24 h.[9] Repeated intravenous doses of pentobarbital, typically 100 mg to 200 mg every 30 min to 60 min, are administered to reduce intracranial pressure and decrease cerebral oxygen demand in patients with severe head trauma or anoxic brain damage.[10] Doses are adjusted to maintain plasma concentrations between 25 mg/L to 40 mg/L.

Amobarbital is a barbituric acid derivative of an intermediate duration of action. It is administered orally in doses of 15 mg to 200 mg as a sedative-hypnotic and in ampoules of 65 mg to 500 mg for intravenous and intramuscular injection for seizure control.[10] Following a single oral dose of 120 mg, peak serum concentrations averaged 1.8 mg/L after 2 h.[11] After an oral dose of 600 mg distributed over a 3-h period, the peak blood concentration was achieved after 30 min, averaging 8.7 mg/L, with a decline to 4.1 mg/L by 18 h.[12] In two studies, half-life averaged 23 h after a single 250 mg/70 kg intravenous dose.[13,14]

Phenobarbital is utilized as a daytime sedative and anti-convulsant. It also induces several cytochrome P450 isozymes. Compared to other barbiturates, phenobarbital has a low oil/water partition coefficient, which results in slow distribution into the brain. It is available for oral, intravenous, or intramuscular administration. Doses for epileptic patients range from 60 mg to 200 mg per day. In refractory status epilepticus pediatric patients, high dose therapy (intravenous infusion of 20–70 mg/kg/day) has been successfully employed.[15] One study reported that patients' fat-free mass, postmenstrual age, serum creatinine, and age in years should be taken into account when dosing phenobarbital.[16] After a single oral dose of 30 mg, peak serum concentrations averaged 0.7 mg/L (n = 3). Repeated doses over a period of seven days resulted in an average peak concentration of 8.1 mg/L.[10] Chronic administration of 200 mg per day as anticonvulsant medication resulted in an average blood concentration of 29 mg/L (range = 16 mg/L to 48 mg/L).[17], Dalmora[18] reported an average peak plasma level of 3.1 mg/L at 1.9 h after a single oral 100 mg dose administrated to 19 healthy adults.

2.4.5.3 Distribution

Barbiturates are distributed widely throughout the body. The more highly lipophilic barbiturates, especially those used to induce anesthesia, undergo redistribution when administered intravenously. With time, barbiturates penetrate into less vascular tissues' spaces such as muscle and fat, resulting in decreased blood and brain concentrations. With drugs such as thiopental, this redistribution causes patients to wake up within 5 to 15 minutes after injection of an anesthetic dose. Pentobarbital is 65% plasma protein bound with a volume of distribution of 0.5 L/kg to 1.0 L/kg.[10] Estimates of the plasma half-life have averaged between 20 to 30 hours after intravenous administration. Amobarbital is similar to pentobarbital in the degree of plasma protein binding (59%) but with a slightly larger volume of distribution (0.9 L/kg to 1.4 L/kg). The plasma half-life, however, is dose-dependent, with a range of 15 h to 40 h.[10] Phenobarbital is approximately 50% plasma protein bound with a volume of distribution of 0.5 L/kg to 0.6 L/kg. The plasma half-life averages four days with a range of two to six days.

2.4.5.4 Metabolism and Excretion

Generally, barbiturates are metabolized by oxidation and conjugation in the liver prior to renal excretion. The oxidation of substituents at the C-5 position is the most important factor in terminating pharmacological activity.[3] Oxidation of barbiturates results in the formation of alcohols, phenols, ketones, or carboxylic acids and then conjugation with glucuronic acid. Other metabolic transformations include N-hydroxylation, desulfuration of thiobarbiturates to oxybarbiturates, the opening of the barbituric acid ring, N-dealkylation of N-alkylbarbiturates to active metabolites, e.g., mephobarbital to phenobarbital.[3]

Pentobarbital is biotransformed by oxidation of the penultimate carbon of the methyl butyl side-chain to produce a mixture of alcohols, and by N-hydroxylation. The alcoholic metabolites of pentobarbital are pharmacologically inactive. Approximately 86% of a radioactive dose is excreted in the urine in six days, about 1% as unchanged drug and up to 73% as the L- and D-diastereoisomers of 3´-hydroxypentobarbital in a 5.4:1 ratio, and up to 15% as N-hydroxypentobarbital.[19] None of these metabolites is eliminated as a conjugate. After a 600 mg oral dose, less than 0.2% of the total dose was found in urine.[12]

At therapeutic doses[20] amobarbital is extensively metabolized to polar metabolites in a process that is saturable and best described by zero-order kinetics. Two major metabolites are produced by hydroxylation and N-glycosylation. 3´-Hydroxyamobarbital possesses pharmacological activity. Approximately 92% of a single dose is excreted in the urine with 5% excreted in the feces over a six-day period.[10] Approximately 2% is excreted unchanged in the urine, 30% to 40% is excreted as free 3´-hydroxyamobarbital, 29% as N-glycosylamobarbital, and 5% as the minor metabolite, 3´-carboxyamobarbital. Only 0.4% of a single 600 mg oral dose was excreted unchanged within 21 h in 3 healthy men.[12]

Phenobarbital is primarily metabolized via N-glycosylation and by oxidation to form p-hydroxyphenobarbital followed by conjugation with glucuronic acid (Figure 2.4.4). A dihydrohydroxy metabolite has been identified in minor amounts, and is thought to arise from

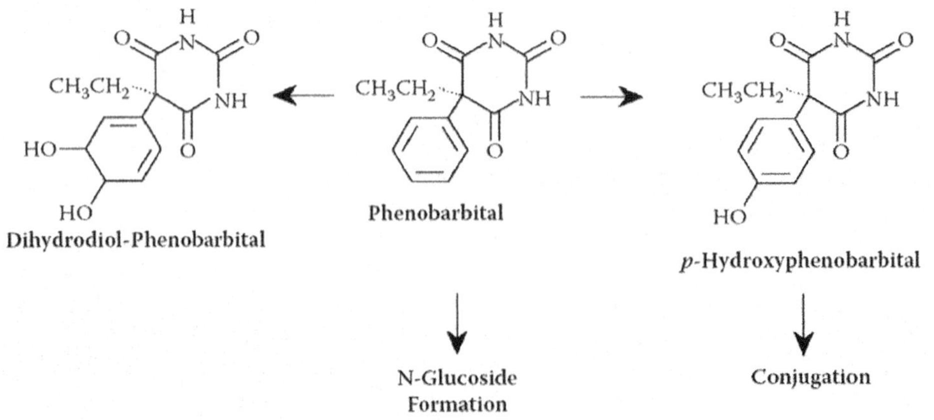

FIGURE 2.4.4 Metabolic pathway of phenobarbital

an epoxide intermediate.[21] Approximately 80% of a single labeled dose is excreted in the urine within 16 days. Unchanged drug accounts for 25% to 33% of the dose, N-glucosyl-phenobarbital for 24% to 30%, and free or conjugated p-hydroxyphenobarbital for 18% to 19%.[22] When administered chronically, approximately 25% of the dose is excreted unchanged in the 24-h urine with 8% free and 9% conjugated p-hydroxyphenobarbital. Less than 0.2% of a single 600 mg oral dose is excreted unchanged in urine during the first 21h, with urine concentrations ranging from 8 mg/L to 22 mg/L.[12]

REFERENCES

1. Smith, M.C., and Riskin, B.J., The clinical use of barbiturates in neurological disorders, *Drugs*, 42(3), 365–78, 1991.
2. Fischer, E., and von Mering, J., Ueber ein neue Klasse von Schlafmitteln, *Therapie Gegenwart*, 44, 97–101, 1903.
3. Hardman, J.G., and Limbird, L.E., Eds., *Goodman & Gilman's The Pharmacological Basis of Therapeutics*, McGraw-Hill, New York, 1996.
4. MacDonald, R.L., and Barker, J.L., Anticonvulsant and anesthetic barbiturates: different postsynaptic action in cultured mammalian neurons, *Neurology*, 29, 432–77, 1979.
5. Macdonald, R.L., and Twyman, R.E., Biophysical properties and regulation of GABAA receptor channels. *Semin Neurosci*, 3, 219–35, 1991.
6. Schober, A., Sokolova, E., and Gingrich, K.J., Pentobarbital inhibition of human recombinant a1A P/Q-type voltage-gated calcium channels involves slow, open channel block. *Br J Pharmacol*, 161, 365–83, 2010.
7. Kwan, P., and Brodie, M.J., Phenobarbital for the treatment of epilepsy in the 21st century: a critical review. *Epilepsia*, 45, 1141–9, 2004.
8. Sun, S., and Chun, A.H.C., Determination of pentobarbital in serum by electron capture GLC, *J Pharm Sci*, 66, 477–80, 1977.
9. Smith, R.B., Dittert, L.W., Griffen, W.O., Jr., and Doluisio, J.T., Pharmacokinetics of pentobarbital after intravenous and oral administration, *J Pharm Biopharm*, 1, 5–16, 1973.
10. Baselt, R.C., *Disposition of Toxic Drugs and Chemicals in Man*, 10th ed., Biomedical Publications, Seal Beach, CA, 2014.
11. Tang, B.K., Inaba, T., Endrenyi, L., and Kalow, W., Amobarbital-a probe of hepatic drug oxidation on man, *Clin Pharmacol Ther*, 20, 439–44, 1976.
12. Parker, K.D., Elliott, H.W., Wright, J.A., Nomof, N., and Hine, C.H., Blood and urine concentrations of subjects receiving barbiturates, meprobamate, glutethimide, or diphenylhydantoin, *Clin Toxicol*, 3(1), 131–45, 1970.
13. Balasubramaniam, K., Lucas, S.B., Mawer, G.E., and Simons, P.J., The kinetics of amylobarbitone metabolism in healthy men and women, *Br J Pharmacol*, 39(3), 564–72, 1970.
14. Balasubramaniam, K., Mawer, G.E., Pohl, J.E., and Simons, P.J., Impairment of cognitive function associated with hydroxyamylobarbitone accumulation in patients with renal insufficiency, *Br J Pharmacol*, 45(2), 360–7, 1972.
15. Lee, W.K., Liu, K.T., and Young, B.W., Very-high-dose phenobarbital for childhood refractory status epilepticus, *Pediatr Neurol*, 34(1), 63–5, 2006.
16. Shareef, S., and Ali, M.N., Pharmacokinetics and optimal dosing of phenobarbital, *Pediatr Neurol Briefs*, 5(32), 37, 2018.
17. Plaa, G.L. and Hine, C.H., Hydantoin and barbiturate blood levels observed in epileptics, arch. *Int Pharm Ther*, 128, 375–83, 1960.
18. Dalmora, S.L., da Silva Sangoi, M., Nogueira, D.R., Bianchini D'Avila, F., Agnaldo Moreno, R., Sverdloff, C.E., de Oliveira, R.A., and Carter Borges, N., Determination of phenobarbital in human plasma by a specific liquid chromatography method: application to a bioequivalence study, *Quim Nova*, 33(1), 124–9, 2010.
19. Tang, B.K., Inaba, T., and Kalow, W., N-Hydroxylation of pentobarbital in man, *Drug Met Disp*, 5, 71–4, 1977.
20. Garrett, E.R., Bres, J., Schnelle, K., and Rolf, L.L., Jr., Pharmacokinetics of saturably metabolized amobarbital, *J Pharm Biopharm*, 2, 43–103, 1974.
21. Harvey, D.L., Glazener, L., and Stratton, L., Detection of a 5-(3,4-dihydroxy-1,5-cyclohexadien-1-yl)- metabolite of phenobarbital and mephobarbital in rat, guinea pig and human, *Res Comm Chem Pathol Pharm*, 3, 557–65, 1972.
22. Tang, B.K., Kalow, W., and Grey, A.A., Metabolic fate of phenobarbital in man, *Drug Met Disp*, 7, 315–8, 1979.

2.4.6 Benzodiazepines

Benzodiazepines are among the most commonly encountered prescribed drugs in forensic analysis. It has been estimated that between 10% and 20% of the adult population in the Western world has ingested these drugs within any given year.[1] They are prescribed for the treatment of anxiety or panic disorders, and as a sleeping aid, anticonvulsant, or muscle relaxant. Abuse of this family of drugs is observed primarily in two forms: persistent therapeutic use – i.e., use for longer than generally recommended – and illicit use, in which the drug is self-administered without physician approval or supervision. The former type of abuse is common and typically involves use at low doses compared to the rarely encountered illicit use that may involve high doses with clear indications of acute intoxication and impairment.[2] Negative health consequences can occur when benzodiazepines are part of polydrug use patterns, typically with alcohol or illicit drugs, such as cocaine, where the benzodiazepines are taken to manage insomnia and hyperactivity. Moreover, benzodiazepine misuse contributes to increased morbidity and mortality among high-risk opioid users, though no acceptable explanation of this alleged synergy has ever been established.[3]

2.4.6.1 Pharmacology

Benzodiazepines exert central depressant effects on spinal reflexes, in part mediated by the brainstem reticular system.[4] Chlordiazepoxide, for example, depresses the duration of electrical after-discharge in the limbic system. Most benzodiazepines, such as diazepam, clonazepam, and clorazepate, elevate the seizure threshold and, therefore, may be used as anti-convulsant medications.

Benzodiazepines are positive allosteric modulators on the GABAA receptor, a ligand-gated chloride-selective ion channel highly concentrated in the cerebellum, cerebral cortex, and limbic system.[5] Benzodiazepines potentiate the inhibitory effects of GABA, the main inhibitory neurotransmitter in CNS.[6] Several benzodiazepine antagonists, such as flumazenil, and inverse agonists (compounds with opposite physiological effects to benzodiazepines), such as ethyl-b-carboline-3-carboxylate, competitively inhibit the binding of benzodiazepines. Benzodiazepines are used as hypnotics because they have the ability to increase total sleep time. They demonstrate minimal cardiovascular effects, but do have the ability to increase heart rate and decrease cardiac output. Most CNS depressants, including benzodiazepines, exhibit the ability to relax skeletal muscles. Clozapine, a dibenzodiazepine, is used in the treatment of schizophrenia because it has both sedative and antipsychotic actions. Four FDA-approved medications are approved for patients with schizophrenia. Although clozapine is by far the most widely used drug for this indication, the FDA has approved several others. However, it appears that all of the anti-schizophrenic agents can have potentially life-threatening side effects, though they have no abuse potential and, thus, will not be considered further.

2.4.6.2 Adsorption

Benzodiazepines comprise a large family of lipophilic acids (diazepam pKa = 3.4) with high octanol/water coefficients,[7] but they demonstrate a wide range of absorption rates when orally administered. Diazepam is well and rapidly adsorbed (>90%), with peak concentrations occurring in 1 h in adults and as rapidly as 15 to 30 min in children.[8] The rapid rate of absorption may be explained in part by its lipophilicity. Following a single oral dose of 10 mg, peak blood diazepam concentrations averaged 148 ng/ml at 1 h, declining to 37 ng/ml by 24 h.[7] Bioavailability is dependent on the drug formulation and route of administration, with approximately 100% bioavailability of diazepam when administered orally as tablets or in suspension, decreasing to between 50% and 60% when administered intramuscularly or as suppositories. Average peak plasma diazepam levels of 0.21 mg/L at 0.6 h and 0.31 mg/L at 0.9 h were observed after single 10 mg doses administered to 24 healthy adults by rectal and intramuscular routes, respectively.[9]

In contrast, less lipophilic benzodiazepines, such as lorazepam, exhibit slower rates of absorption, with an average time to peak blood concentration of 2 h. Greenblatt et al.[10] reported lorazepam plasma concentrations averaged 18 ng/mL at 2 h, with an apparent half-life of 12 h. Prazepam and clorazepate act as prodrugs and are decarboxylated in the stomach to nordiazepam. Consequently, absorption is slowed and a delay occurs at the onset of these drugs' action.

2.4.6.3 Distribution

The benzodiazepines exhibit a two-compartment pharmacokinetic model.[6] Central compartment distribution is rapid and a slower distribution occurs into less perfused tissues, such as fat. One-compartment pharmacokinetic models have been described for some benzodiazepines, such as lorazepam.[11] It is obvious that the more lipophilic benzodiazepines distribute more rapidly than less lipophilic drugs. Therefore, after a single dose, diazepam, a highly lipophilic drug, will have a shorter duration of action than lorazepam because it will be rapidly redistributed throughout the body. This may not be easily understood because diazepam has a longer half-life (approximately 30 h) than lorazepam (12 h to 15 h). Therefore, a long elimination half-life does not necessarily imply a long duration of action after a single dose. The majority of benzodiazepines are highly bound to plasma proteins (85% to 95%) with apparent volumes of distribution ranging from 1 L/kg to 3 L/kg[4] due to rapid removal from plasma to the brain, lungs, and adipose tissue.

2.4.6.4 Metabolism and Excretion

Benzodiazepines are extensively metabolized producing multiple metabolites, many of which share common pathways (Figure 2.4.5). Metabolic processes include hydroxylation, demethylation, and glucuronidation. Diazepam undergoes N-demethylation to an active metabolite, nordiazepam. Both of these compounds are then hydroxylated to temazepam and oxazepam, respectively.[7] These metabolites are also active, but are usually rapidly excreted and do not accumulate in the plasma. Only small amounts of diazepam and nordiazepam are detected in urine, with 33% of a dose excreted as oxazepam glucuronide and another 20% excreted as various conjugates.[11] Oxazepam, the 3-hydroxy metabolite of nordiazepam, is rapidly conjugated with glucuronic acid to form an inactive metabolite. This conjugate accounts for 61% of an oral dose that appears in the 48-h urine. Trace amounts of free drug are detected in the urine and other hydroxylation products account for less than 5% of a dose.[12]

Lorazepam is also rapidly conjugated, forming the inactive product lorazepam glucuronide. This conjugate is not rapidly excreted but may achieve plasma concentrations exceeding the parent drug, with an elimination half-life of approximately 16 h.[7] Approximately 75% of a dose is eliminated in the urine as the conjugate over five days. Minor metabolites, such as ring hydroxylation products and quinazoline derivatives, constitute another 14% of the dose. Trace amounts of free drug are found in urine. Turfus et al.[13] were able to detect lorazepam up to four days after the administration of a 2 mg dose.

Chlordiazepoxide is metabolized to four active metabolites. First, the drug is demethylated to norchlordiazepoxide, then deaminated to form demoxepam. These metabolites demonstrate pharmacological activity similar to the parent drug. Demoxepam is reduced to form nordiazepam, which accumulates in plasma with multiple dosing. Nordiazepam is then hydroxylated to produce oxazepam. Less than 1% of the dose is excreted unchanged in the urine, with approximately 6% excreted as demoxepam and the rest as glucuronide conjugates.[14] Temazepam undergoes N-demethylation to form the active metabolite oxazepam. Both parent and metabolite are subsequently conjugated. An average of 82% of a dose is excreted in urine and 12% in the feces.[7]

Alprazolam, a triazolobenzodiazepine, is also extensively metabolized by oxidation and conjugation.

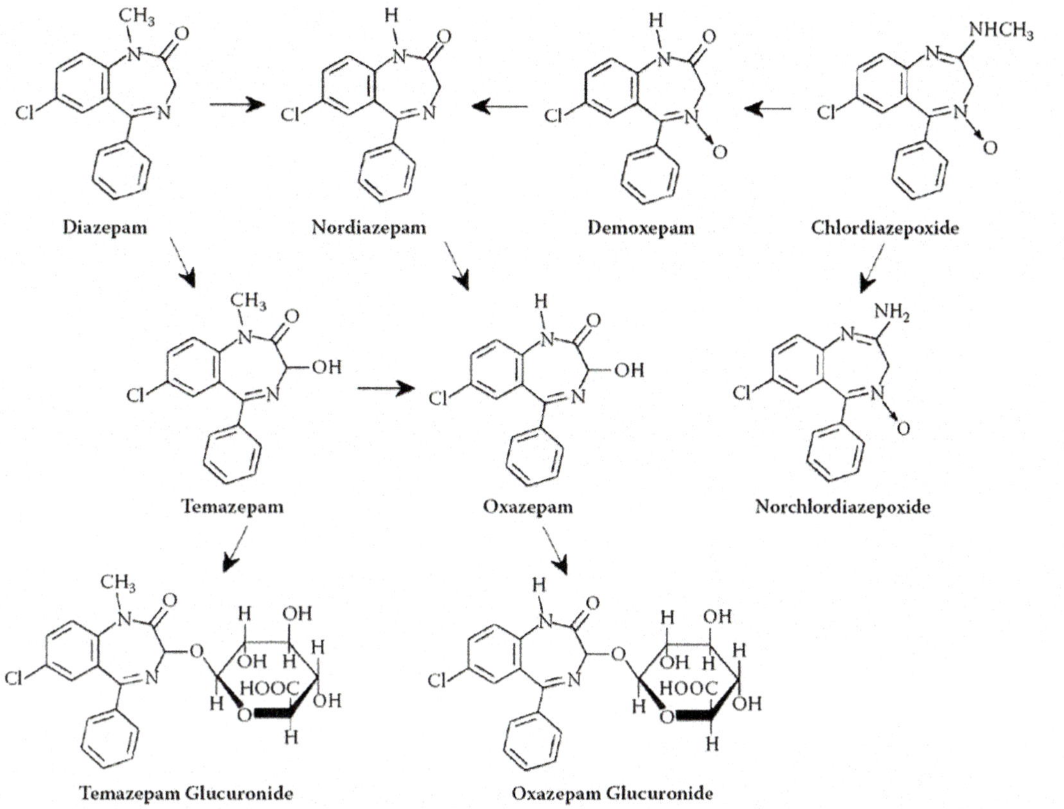

FIGURE 2.4.5 Metabolic pathway of the benzodiazepines

Metabolites include alpha-hydroxyalprazolam, 4-hydroxyalprazolam, and alpha 4-dihydroxyalprazolam. The first two metabolites possess approximately 66% and 19% of the pharmacological activity of the parent, respectively. 3-Hydroxy-5-methyltriazolyl, an analogue of chlorobenzophenone, is also formed. Approximately 94% of a dose is excreted within 72 h with 80% excreted in the urine.[15] Flunitrazepam, the N-methyl-2′-fluoro analogue of nitrazepam, undergoes biotransformation via N-demethylation, 3-hydroxylation, and glucuronidation. In addition, the nitro group is reduced to an amine and is subsequently acetylated. Approximately 84% of a labeled dose is excreted in the urine over one week, and 11% is excreted in the feces. Less than 0.5% is excreted unchanged. Norflunitrazepam and 7-aminoflunitrazepam may be detected in plasma for one day after a single dose of 2 mg. Triazolam is extensively metabolized by hydroxylation and subsequent conjugation. The major metabolite, 1-hydroxymethyltriazolam, possesses pharmacological activity. Only trace amounts of unchanged drug are excreted in the urine, with approximately 80% of a dose appearing in the urine in 72 h, mainly as glucuronide conjugates.

Since benzodiazepines are metabolized by the cytochrome P450 family of isozymes,[16] potential P450 inhibitors may produce significant increases in their blood concentrations. An example of this inhibition is the drug midazolam, administered as a pre-surgical anesthetic. Lam et al.[17] reported a mean increase in the area under the curve of midazolam caused by ketoconazole (772%) and nefazodone (444%) in a group of 40 healthy human subjects administered 200 mg ketoconazole and 400 mg nefazodone per day. The authors concluded that caution should be exercised when use of midazolam is warranted in the presence of potent CYP3A4 inhibitors.[17] In a study about the influence of ethanol on alprazolam metabolism, it was demonstrated that alcohol could change the conformation of CYP3A4 affecting the alprazolam binding. This alteration may lead to an increase in alprazolam toxicity.[18] Metabolism of benzodiazepines may be affected by polymorphism of cytochrome P450, in particular CYP2C19 for diazepam and CYP3A5 for alprazolam.[19]

REFERENCES

1. Balter, M.B., Manheimer, D.I., Mellinger, G.D., and Uhlenhuth, E.H., A cross-national comparison of anti-anxiety/sedative drug use, *Curr Med Res Opin*, 8(Suppl. 4), 5–20, 1984.
2. Busto, U., Bendayan, R., and Sellers, E.M., Clinical pharmacokinetics of non-opiate abused drugs, *Clin Pharmacokinet*, 16, 1–26, 1989.
3. EMCDDA, Perspective on drugs – the misuse of benzodiazepines among high-risk opioid users in Europe, Lisbon, June 2018. Available at: http://www.emcdda.europa.eu/publications/pods/benzodiazepines. Accessed November 30, 2018.
4. Hardman, J.G., and Limbird, L.E., Eds., *Goodman & Gilman's The Pharmacological Basis of Therapeutics*, McGraw-Hill, New York, 1996.

5. Griffin, C.E. 3rd, Kaye, A.M., Bueno, F.R., and Kaye, A.D., Benzodiazepine pharmacology and central nervous system-mediated effects, *Ochsner J*, 13(2), 214–23, 2013.
6. Fox, C., Liu, H., and Kaye, A.D., Antianxiety agents. In Manchikanti, L., Trescot, A.M., Christo, P.J., et al, Eds., *Clinical Aspects of Pain Medicine and Interventional Pain Management: A Comprehensive Review*, ASIP Publishing, Paducah, KY, 543–52, 2011.
7. Baselt, R.C., *Disposition of Toxic Drugs and Chemicals in Man*, 10th ed., Biomedical Publications, Seal Beach, CA, 2014.
8. Archer, M., Frydrych, V., and Lafleur, J., *Drug Class Review, Benzodiazepines in the Treatment of Anxiety Disorder, Final Report November 2016*, University of Utah College of Pharmacy, Salt Lake City, UT, 2016. Available at https://medicaid.utah.gov/pharmacy/ptcommittee/files/Criteria%20Review%20Documents/2016/2016.11%20Benzodiazepines%20in%20Anxiety%20Drug%20Class%20Review.pdf. Accessed November 30, 2018.
9. Garnett, W.R., Barr, W.H., Edinboro, L.E., Karnes, H.T., Mesa, M., and Wannarka, G.L., Diazepam autoinjector intramuscular delivery system versus diazepam rectal gel: a pharmacokinetic comparison, *Epilepsy Res*, 93(1), 11–6, 2011.
10. Greenblatt, D.J., Schillings, R.T., Kyriakopoulos, A.A., Shader, R.I., Sisenwine, S.F., Knowles, J.A., and Ruelius, H.W., Clinical pharmacokinetics of lorazepam. I. Absorption and disposition of oral 14C-lorazepam, *Clin Pharmacol Ther*, 20(3), 329–41, 1976.
11. Smith-Kielland, A., Skuterud, B., Olsen, K.M., and Mørland, J., Urinary excretion of diazepam metabolites in healthy volunteers and drug users, *Scand J Clin Lab Invest*, 61(3), 237–46, 2001.
12. Knowles, J.A., and Ruelius, H.W., Absorption and excretion of 7-chloro-1,3-dihydro-3-hydroxy-5- phenyl-2H-1,4-benzodiazepin-2-one (oxazepam) in humans, *Arz Forsch*, 22, 687–92, 1972.
13. Turfus, S.C., Braithwaite, R.A., Cowan, D.A., Parkin, M.C., Smith, N.W., and Kicman, A.T., Metabolites of lorazepam: relevance of past findings to present day use of LC-MS/MS in analytical toxicology, *Drug Test Anal*, 3(10), 695–704, 2011.
14. Schwartz, M.A., Pathways of metabolism of benzodiazepines. In: Garattini, S., Mussini, E., and Randall, L.O., Eds., *The Benzodiazepines*, Raven Press, New York, 1973, 53–74.
15. Dawson, G.W., Jue, S.G., and Brogden, R.N., Alprazolam: a review of its pharmacodynamic properties and efficacy in the treatment of anxiety and depression, *Drugs*, 27, 132–47, 1984.
16. Moody, D.E., Drug interactions with benzodiazepines. In Mozayani, A., and Raymon, L.P., Eds., *Handbook of Drug Interactions: A Clinical and Forensic Guide*, Humana Press, Totowa, NJ, 2004.
17. Lam, Y.W., Alfaro, C.L., Ereshefsky, L., and Miller, M., Pharmacokinetic and pharmacodynamic interactions of oral midazolam with ketoconazole, fluoxetine, fluvoxamine, and nefazodone, *J Clin Pharmacol*, 43(11), 1274–82, 2003.
18. Huang, Z., Xu. Z., Wang, H., Zhao, Z.Q., and Rao, Y., Influence of ethanol on the metabolism of alprazolam, *Expert Opin Drug Metab Toxicol*, 14(6), 551–9, 2018.
19. Fukasawa, T., Suzuki, A., and Otani, K., Effects of genetic polymorphism of cytochrome P450 enzymes on the pharmacokinetics of benzodiazepines, *J Clin Pharm Ther*, 32(4), 333–41, 2007.

2.4.7 Cocaine

Cocaine is one of the most potent CNS stimulants. The drug is a naturally occurring alkaloid obtained from the plant *Erythroxylum coca* L. This plant grows in the Andes region of South America, ideally at elevations between 1,500 and 5,000 ft.[1] A second closely related species has been identified, *Erythroxylum novogranatense* H., and each species has one variety known as *E. coca* var. ipadu Plowman and *E. coca novogranatense* var. truxillense, respectively. Each of the varieties produces different amounts of cocaine. Cocaine may also be chemically synthesized with cold aqueous succinaldehyde and cold aqueous methylamine, methylamine hydrochloride, and the potassium salt of acetone-dicarboxylic acid monomethyl ester.[2]

Cocaine was used medically by otorhinolaryngologists and plastic surgeons as an epinephrine cocaine mixture ("cocaine mud"), cocaine has the virtue of producing both anesthesia and vasoconstriction at the same time, a property allowing for fewer blood operative fields. This practice has largely been replaced by the use of other, safer, anesthetic agents. Solutions for topical application are typically less than 4% cocaine hydrochloride. In the U.S., cocaine is a scheduled drug under the federal Controlled Substances Act of 1970. Refined cocaine, in the form of the base or hydrochloride salt, is self-administered in many ways, including snorting, smoking, genital application, and injection. Cocaine hydrochloride is commonly taken by nasal insufflation or intravenous injection; the free base drug is mainly self-administered by smoking. The common dose ranges from 10 to 120 mg. When administered by smoking route, only 30–70% of the dose is available for adsorption because of pyrolysis.[3]

2.4.7.1 Pharmacology

Cocaine inhibits the presynaptic reuptake of the neurotransmitters norepinephrine, serotonin, and dopamine at synaptic junctions. This results in increased concentrations of the neurotransmitters in the synaptic cleft.[4] Since norepinephrine acts within the sympathetic nervous system, increased sympathetic stimulation is produced. Norepinephrine is the principal neurotransmitter in the heart. Physiological effects of this stimulation include tachycardia, vasoconstriction, mydriasis, and hyperthermia.[5,6] CNS stimulation results in increased alertness, diminished appetite, and increased energy. The euphoria or psychological stimulation produced by cocaine is thought to result from the inhibition of serotonin and dopamine reuptake. Cocaine also acts as a local anesthetic due to its ability to block sodium channels in neuronal cells.[7]

2.4.7.2 Absorption

Cocaine is rapidly absorbed from mucous membranes and the pulmonary vasculature and the rate at which cocaine appears in the blood is dependent on the route of administration. Studies of the oral route of administration found that chewing powdered coca leaves containing between 17 and

48 mg of cocaine produced peak plasma concentrations of 11 to 149 ng/mL (n = 6) at 0.4 to 2 h after administration.[8] In another study, healthy male volunteers were administered cocaine hydrochloride (2 mg/kg) in gelatin capsules. Peak plasma concentrations of between 104 and 424 ng/mL were achieved at 50 to 90 min. The pharmacokinetics parameters of orally administered cocaine were studied by Coe et al.[9] after the administration of two oral doses (100 and 200 mg) and one intravenous dose (40 mg) to 14 healthy participants with a current history of cocaine use. Mean Cmax was estimated at 115 ng/mL (range: 45.1–201 ng/mL), 268 ng/mL (range: 67.0–570 ng/mL) and 301 ng/mL (range: 111–925 ng/mL) respectively. Tmax was estimated at 1.3 h for oral doses and in 0.17 h for intravenous administration.

The intranasal route is commonly used. Wilkinson et al.[10] found that peak plasma concentrations of cocaine were reached 35 to 90 min after "snorting," but another study using equivalent doses found that peak plasma concentrations were achieved at between 120 and 160 min.[11] After intravenous administration of 32 mg cocaine hydrochloride the average peak plasma concentration of 308 ng/mL at five minutes.[10] Finally, in a study on nearly 40 years old, a 100 mg dose given intravenously produced concentrations of 500–1000 after only five minutes. Levels exceeded 2000 ng/mL when the dose was increased to 200 mg.[12]

Cocaine may also be self-administered by smoking it in the form of a cocaine base, commonly called "crack" or through a process known as "free-basing" in which powdered cocaine hydrochloride is converted into its base form. In a study of six subjects who each smoked 50 mg of cocaine, the average peak plasma cocaine concentration of 203 ng/mL was achieved at five minutes.[13] The bioavailability of cocaine after smoking depends on several factors, including the temperature of volatilization and drug loss in main- and side-stream smoke. Perez-Reyes et al.[14] estimated that only 32% of a dose of cocaine base placed in a pipe is actually inhaled by the smoker. Cone[15] compared the pharmacokinetics and pharmacodynamics of cocaine by the intravenous, intranasal, and smoked routes of administration in the same subjects. Venous plasma cocaine concentrations peaked within five minutes by the intravenous and smoked routes. Estimated peak cocaine concentrations ranged from 98 to 349 ng/mL and 154 to 345 ng/mL after intravenous administration of 25 mg cocaine hydrochloride and 42 mg cocaine base by the smoked route, respectively. After dosing by the intranasal route (32 mg cocaine hydrochloride), the estimated peak plasma cocaine concentrations ranged from 40 to 88 ng/mL after 0.39 to 0.85 h.[15] In this study, the average bioavailability of cocaine was 70.1% by the smoked route and 93.7% by the intranasal route. Jenkins et al.[16] described the correlation between pharmacological effects and plasma cocaine concentrations in seven volunteers after they had smoked 10 to 40 mg of cocaine. The mean plasma cocaine concentration two minutes after smoking 40 mg cocaine was 153 ± 107.5 ng/mL. Peak concentrations ranged from 160.8 ± 99.1 ng/mL. Increases in pupil diameter, systolic and diastolic blood pressure, heart rate, and subjective measures of drug effect occurred early after drug administration, with maximum effects observed at two minutes (first measure) for blood pressure and subjective measures, or after a brief delay (at five to ten minutes post-dose) for others, notably heart rate and pupil diameter. Average peak plasma levels of 1260 ng/mL at 1–2 h were found in two healthy male chronic cocaine users after administration of 2 g daily oral doses in divided portions over a 5 h period for 16 days.[17]

2.4.7.3 Distribution

After an intravenous dose of radiolabeled cocaine to rats, the highest concentrations were found in the brain, spleen, kidney, and lung after 15 min, with the lowest concentrations in the blood, heart, and muscle.[18] The disposition between human tissues is mainly determined by the high lipid solubility of cocaine.[19] Plasma protein binding in humans is approximately 91% at low concentrations.[18] Cocaine binds to the plasma protein, albumin, and also to the a1-acid glycoprotein. The steady-state volume of distribution is large (1.6 to 2.7 L/kg), reflecting extensive extravascular distribution.[3] In 1991, Ambre et al.[20] studied the pharmacokinetics of benzoylecgonine in nine human volunteers. The metabolite is much more polar than the parent and lipophobic, explaining why the measured mean Vd was only found to be 0.71. Some have spuriously attempted to estimate the time of ingestion from the Vd ratios of cocaine to its metabolite benzoylecgonine. Given the very great difference in Vd for these two compounds, their ratio has no clear meaning.

The pharmacokinetic profile of cocaine after intravenous administration fits a two-compartment open linear model.[21] The distribution phase after cocaine administration is rapid and the elimination half-life is estimated as 31 to 82 min.[22] Cone[15] fitted data to a two-compartment model after bolus input and first-order elimination for the intravenous and smoked routes. For the intranasal route, data were fitted to a two-compartment model with first-order absorption and first-order elimination. The average elimination half-life (t1/2b) was 244 min after intravenous administration, 272 min after smoked administration, and 299 min after intranasal administration. The disposition of cocaine in nontraditional testing matrices has been described. For example, Lester et al.[22] measured cocaine and benzoylecgonine (BE) concentrations in the skin, interstitial fluid (IF), sebum, and stratum corneum in five volunteers after the intravenous 1-h infusion of 1 mg/kg cocaine for five days. Peak cocaine concentrations in the skin were achieved at 1.5 h and were undetectable after 6 h. No BE was measured in the skin. Peak cocaine concentrations were achieved at 5 h after administration in the IF and were non-detectable by 24 h. BE was also found in the IF. In the sebum, peak cocaine concentrations occurred between 3 to 24 h, but in the stratum, cocaine was detected in only one subject. Antonides et al.[23] also studied cocaine distribution in the vitreous humor, where an apparent delay in distribution was observed as well as a subsequent delay in peak concentration.

It is important to remember that none of these measurements can be interpreted in isolation, particularly if the measurements are made post-mortem. As we have stated previously, there is no guarantee that a post-mortem measurement bears any relationship to what the drug concentration was during life. But, in the case of stimulant drugs, the situation is even more complicated. Chronic, long-term use of cocaine or methamphetamine can result in structural anatomic changes that favor the occurrence of sudden cardiac death. In this group of unfortunate individuals, death could be just as likely at a concentration of 100 ng/mL as 1000 ng per mil[1].

2.4.7.4 Metabolism

Cocaine's principal route of metabolism in humans is the hydrolysis of ester linkages. Pseudocholinesterase and liver esterases produce two inactive metabolites, ecgonine methyl ester (EME) (Figure 2.4.6) and benzoylecgonine (BE), which form spontaneously at physiological pHs.[24] In addition, there is evidence that BE may be formed enzymatically from cocaine by liver carboxylesterases.[25,26] N-Demethylation of BE produces benzoylnorecgonine. Further metabolism of EME and BE produces ecgonine.[27] With metabolism other minor metabolites, meta- and para-hydroxy-cocaine and are produced.[28] The proportion of each metabolite produced and the activity of the individual metabolites have yet to be completely determined.

Cocaine may be N-demethylated by the cytochrome P450 system to produce an active metabolite, norcocaine. Further breakdown produces N-hydroxynorcocaine and norcocaine nitroxide. These conversions are catalyzed by several members of the cytochrome P450 (1A, 2A, 3A, and, possibly, 3B).[29] Further metabolism produces a highly reactive free radical that is thought to be responsible for the hepatotoxicity observed in cocaine users.[1]

Pyrolysis caused by crack cocaine inhalation leads to the formation and inhalation of methyl ecgonidine which is further hydrolyzed in vivo to ecgonidine.[30] Another product is the anhydroecgonine methyl ester (AEME). Therefore, the presence of this compound indicates exposure to smoked cocaine. When cocaine is co-administered with ethanol, cocaethylene (CE) is formed in the liver via transesterification by hepatic methylesterase. CE may also be formed by fatty acid ethyl synthase.[31] This lipophilic compound crosses the blood–brain barrier and is known to contribute to the psychological effects produced by cocaine.[1] Harris et al.[32] administered deuterium-labeled cocaine (0.3 to 1.2 mg/kg) intravenously 1 h after an oral dose of ethanol (1 g/kg) to ten volunteers. When co-administered with ethanol, 17 ± 6% (mean ± S.D.) of the cocaine was converted to CE. Ethanol ingestion prior to cocaine administration decreased urine BE levels by 48%. Concomitant consumption of ethanol and cocaine has also been associated with

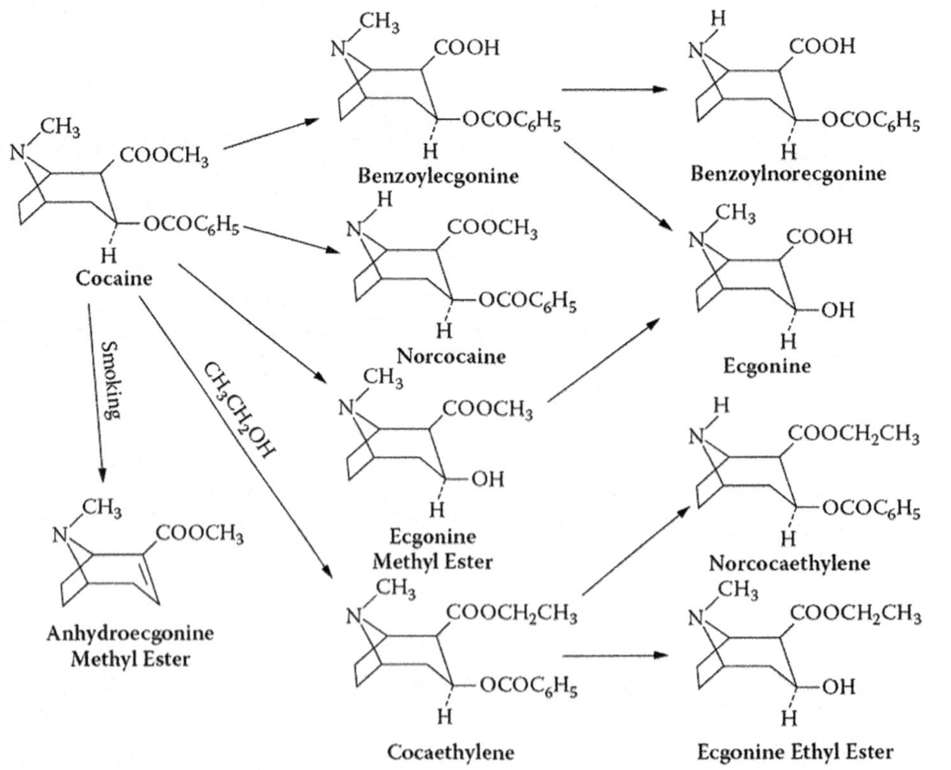

FIGURE 2.4.6 Metabolic pathway of cocaine

higher plasma concentrations of norcocaine, likely due to the increase of cocaine availability for N-demethylation.[33]

2.4.7.5 Elimination

Cocaine is rapidly eliminated at a rate of 2 L/min.[34] Based on urinary excretion, elimination half-lives of 0.8, 4.5–4.7, and 3.1 h have been reported for cocaine, BE, and EME respectively.[35] On average, the elimination half-life of COET is 1.7 hours and, in the urine, it accounts for 0.7% of a cocaine dose in the first 24 hours.[36] Approximately 85% to 90% of a dose of cocaine is recovered from the during the 24-h.[37] Unchanged drug accounts for 1% to 9% of the dose, depending on urine pH, BE for 35% to 54%, and EME, 32% to 49%. In one study, excretion data were obtained from subjects administered a bolus intravenous injection of cocaine followed by an intravenous infusion, supplying total doses of 253, 444, and 700 mg cocaine.[38]

After cocaine is administered intranasally (1.5 mg/kg), urine cocaine concentrations averaged 6.7 mg/L during the first hour, and BE concentrations peaked between four to eight hours at 35 mg/L.[18] Oral ingestion of 25 mg cocaine by a single individual resulted in a peak urine BE concentration of 7.9 mg/L in the 6- to 12-h collection period, with a decline to 0.4 mg/L by 48 h.[39] Oral consumption of Peruvian coca tea containing approximately 4 mg of cocaine resulted in a peak urine BE concentration of 3.9 mg/L after 10 h in one individual.[40] The cumulative urinary excretion of BE after approximately 48 h was 3.1 mg. Consumption of coca tea of Bolivian origin by the same individual, containing a similar amount of cocaine, resulted in a peak urine BE level of 4.9 mg/L at 3.5 h.[22] The cumulative BE excreted in urine was 2.6 mg. The minor metabolites, including the p- and m-hydroxy metabolites, and also the pyrolysis product, AEME, have been detected in urine after oral cocaine administration.[41,42]

Moolchan et al.[43] reported a prolonged plasma half-life for cocaine (3.8 h) for chronic users even following abstinence. In his study, half-lives for BE and EME were 6.6 and 5.5 h, respectively. Variability in half-life and detection period has been reported for cocaine and its metabolites.[44] This is largely due to the wide variability in phenotypes and genotypes of human esterases.[45]

REFERENCES

1. Karch, S., *The Pathology of Drug Abuse*, CRC Press, Boca Raton, FL, 1993.
2. Saferstein, R., *Forensic Science Handbook*, Vol. II, Prentice Hall, Englewood Cliffs, NJ, 1988.
3. Baselt, R.C., *Disposition of Toxic Drugs and Chemicals in Man*, 10th ed., Biomedical Publications, Seal Beach, CA, 2014.
4. Lange, R.A., and Hillis, L.D., Cardiovascular complications of cocaine use. *N Engl J Med*, 345, 351–8, 2001.
5. Warner, E.A., Cocaine abuse, *Ann Int Med*, 119(3), 226–35, 1993.
6. Casartelli, A., Dacome, L., Tessari, M., Pascali, J., Bortolotti, F., Trevisan, M.T., Bosco, O., Cristofori, P., and Tagliaro, F., Cocaine-associated increase of atrial natriuretic peptides: an early predictor of cardiac complications in cocaine users?, *Heart Asia*, 6(1), 100–7, 2014.
7. Mouhaffel, A.H., Madu, E.C., Satmary, W.A., and Fraker, T.D. Jr, Cardiovascular complications of cocaine. *Chest*, 107, 1426–34, 1995.
8. Holmstedt, B., Lindgren, J., Rivier, L., and Plowman, T., Cocaine in blood of coca chewers, *J Ethnopharm*, 1, 69–78, 1979.
9. Coe, M.A., Jufer Phipps, R.A., Cone, E.J., and Walsh, S.L., Bioavailability and pharmacokinetics of oral cocaine in humans, *J Anal Toxicol*, 42(5), 285–92, 2018.
10. Wilkinson, P., Van Dyke, C., Jatlow, P., Barash, P., and Byck, R., Intranasal and oral cocaine kinetics, *Clin Pharmacol Ther*, 27, 386–94, 1980.
11. Javaid, J.I., Musa, M.N., Fischman, M., Schuster, C.R., and Davis, J.M., Kinetics of cocaine in humans after intravenous and intranasal administration, *Biopharm Drug Disp*, 4, 9–18, 1983.
12. Barnett, G., Hawks, R., and Resnick, R., Cocaine pharmacokinetics in humans, *J Ethnopharmacol*, 3(2–3), 353–66, 1981.
13. Jeffcoat, A.R., Perez-Reyes, M., and Hill, J.M., Cocaine disposition in humans after intravenous injection, nasal insufflation (snorting), or smoking, *Drug Met Disp*, 17, 153–9, 1989.
14. Perez-Reyes, M., Di Guiseppi, S., Ondrusek, G., Jeffcoat, A.R., and Cook, C.E., Free base cocaine smoking, *Clin Pharmacol Ther*, 32, 459–65, 1982.
15. Cone, E.J., Pharmacokinetics and pharmacodynamics of cocaine, *J Anal Toxicol*, 19, 459–78, 1995.
16. Jenkins, A.J., Keenan, R.M., Henningfield, J.E., and Cone, E.J., Correlation between pharmacological effects and plasma cocaine concentrations after smoked administration, *J Anal Toxicol*, 26, 382–92, 2002.
17. Jufer, R.A., Wstadik, A., Walsh, S.L., Levine, B.S., and Cone, E.J., Elimination of cocaine and metabolites in plasma, saliva, and urine following repeated oral administration to human volunteers, *J Anal Toxicol*, 24(7), 467–77, 2000.
18. Busto, U., Bendayan, R., and Sellers, E.M., Clinical pharmacokinetics of non-opiate abused drugs, *Clin Pharmacokinet*, 16, 1–26, 1989.
19. Pélissier-Alicot, A.L., Gaulier, J.M., Champsaur, P., and Marquet, P., Mechanisms underlying postmortem redistribution of drugs: a review, *J Anal Toxicol*, 27(8), 533–44, 2003.
20. Ambre, J.J., Connelly, T.J., and Ruo, T.I., A kinetic model of benzoylecgonine disposition after cocaine administration in humans, *J Anal Toxicol*, 15(1), 17–20, 1991.
21. Chow, M.J., Ambre, J.J., Ruo, T.I., Atkinson, A.J., and Bowsher, D.J., Kinetics of cocaine distribution, elimination and chronotropic effects, *Clin Pharmacol Ther*, 38, 318–24, 1985.
22. Lester, L., Uemura, N., Ademola, J., Harkey, M.R., Nath, R.P., Kim, S.J., Jerschow, E., Henderson, G.L., Mendelson, J., and Jones, R.T., Disposition of cocaine in skin, interstitial fluid, sebum, and stratum corneum, *J Anal Toxicol*, 26, 547–53, 2002.
23. Antonides, H.M., Kiely, E.R., and Marinetti, L.J., Vitreous fluid quantification of opiates, cocaine, and benzoylecgonine: comparison of calibration curves in both blood and vitreous matrices with corresponding concentrations in blood, *J Anal Toxicol*, 31(8), 469–76, 2007.
24. Isenschmid, D.S., Levine, B.S., and Caplan, Y.H., A comprehensive study on the stability of cocaine and its metabolites. *J Anal Toxicol*, 13(5), 250–6, 1989.
25. Dean, R.A., Christian, C.D., Sample, R.H.B., and Bosron, W.F., Human liver cocaine esterases – ethanol-mediated formation of ethylcocaine, *FASEB J*, 5(12), 2735–9, 1991.

26. Bortolotti, F., Gottardo, R., Pascali, J., Tagliaro, F., Toxicokinetics of cocaine and metabolites: the forensic toxicological approach, *Curr Med Chem*, 19(33), 5658–63, 2012.
27. Skopp, G., Klingmann, A., Potsch, L., and Mattern, R., In vitro stability of cocaine in whole blood and plasma including ecgonine as a target analyte. *Ther Drug Monit*, 23(2), 174–81, 2001.
28. Karch, S.B., 2009. *Karch's Pathology of Drugs of Abuse*. 4th ed., CRC Press, Boca Raton.
29. Pellinen, P., Kulmala, L., Konttila, J., Auriola, S., Pasanen, M., and Juvonen, R., Kinetic characteristics of norcocaine N-hydroxylation in mouse and human liver microsomes: involvement of CYP enzymes. *Arch Toxicol*, 74(9), 511–20, 2000.
30. Cardona, P.S., Chaturvedi, A.K., Soper, J.W., and Canfield, D.V., Simultaneous analyses of cocaine, cocaethylene, and their possible metabolic and pyrolytic products, *Forensic Sci Int*, 157(1), 46–56, 2006.
31. Isenschmid, D.S., Cocaine. In *Principles of Forensic Toxicology*, 2nd ed., B.S. Levine, Ed., AACC Press, Washington, DC, 2003.
32. Harris, D.S., Everhart, E.T., Mendelson, J., and Jones, R.T., The pharmacology of cocaethylene in humans following cocaine and ethanol administration, *Drug Alcohol Depend*, 72(2), 169–82, 2003.
33. Farre, M., Delatorre, R., Llorente, M., Lamas, X., Ugena, B., Segura, J., and Cami, J., Alcohol and cocaine interactions in humans, *J Pharmacol Exp Ther*, 266(3), 1364–73, 1993.
34. Inaba, T., Stewart, D.J., and Kalow, W., Metabolism of cocaine in man, *Clin Pharmacol Ther*, 23(5), 547–52, 1978.
35. Ambre, J.J., Connelly, T.J., and Ruo, T.I., A kinetic-model of benzoylecgonine disposition after cocaine administration in humans, *J Anal Toxicol*, 15(1), 17–20, 1991.
36. Perez-reyes, M., Jeffcoat, A.R., Myers, M., Sihler, K., and Cook, C.E., Comparison in humans of the potency and pharmacokinetics of intravenously injected cocaethylene and cocaine, *Psychopharmacology*, 116(4), 428–32, 1994.
37. Jatlow, P., Cocaine: analysis, pharmacokinetics and disposition, *Yale J Biol Med*, 61, 105–13, 1988.
38. Ambre, J., Ruo, T.I., Nelson, J., and Belknap, S., Urinary excretion of cocaine, benzoylecgonine, and ecgonine methyl ester in humans, *J Anal Toxicol*, 12, 301–6, 1988.
39. Baselt, R., and Chang, R., Urinary excretion of cocaine and benzoylecgonine following oral ingestion in a single subject, *J Anal Toxicol*, 11, 81–2, 1987.
40. Jenkins, A.J., Llosa, T., Montoya, I., and Cone, E.J., Identification and quantitation of alkaloids in coca tea, *Forensic Sci Int*, 77, 179–89, 1996.
41. Jacob, P., III, Lewis, E.R., Elias-Baker, B.A., and Jones, R., A pyrolysis product, anhydroecgonine methyl ester (methylecgonidine) is in the urine of cocaine smokers, *J Anal Toxicol*, 14, 353–7, 1990.
42. Zhang, J.Y., and Foltz, R.L., Cocaine metabolism in man: identification of four previously unreported cocaine metabolites in human urine, *J Anal Toxicol*, 14, 201–5, 1990.
43. Moolchan, E.T., Cone, E.J., Wstadik, A., Huestis, M.A., and Preston, K.L., Cocaine and metabolite elimination patterns in chronic cocaine users during cessation: plasma and saliva analysis. *J Anal Toxicol*, 24(7), 458–66, 2000.
44. Jones, R.T., The pharmacology of cocaine. In: Grabowski, J., Ed., *Cocaine: Pharmacology, Effects and Treatment of Abuse. Research Monograph no. 50: The National Institute on Drug Abuse (NIDA) National Institute on Drug Abuse Research Monograph Series*, 1984.
45. Wu, M.H., Chen, P.X., Remo, B.F., Cook, E.H., Das, S., and Dolan, M.E., Characterisation of multiple promoters in the human carboxylesterase-2 gene, *Pharmacogenetics*, 13(7), 425–35, 2003.

2.4.8 Lysergic Acid Diethylamide

Lysergic acid diethylamide (LSD) is an indolealkylamine discovered by Albert Hoffman of Sandoz Laboratories in 1943.[1] It may be synthesized from lysergic acid and diethylamine. Lysergic acid, a naturally occurring ergot alkaloid, is present in grain parasitized by the fungus *Claviceps purpurea*. A closely related alkaloid, lysergic acid amide, is present in morning glory seeds and the Hawaiian baby wood rose.[1] In the 1950s, LSD was used as an aid in the treatment of alcoholism, opioid addiction, psychoneurosis, and sexual disorders, but currently it is classified under Schedule 1 of the federal Controlled Substances Act. There is no accepted medical use for LSD in the U.S. It is available illicitly as a powder, tablet, or gelatin capsule, or impregnated in sugar cubes, gelatin squares, blotter paper, or postage stamps.

In 2008, the FDA partially reversed its position to allow for LSD research, writing they had *successfully* "resolved all the outstanding issues in our Investigative New Drug application (#101,825) to evaluate LSD-assisted psychotherapy in our Swiss end-of-life/anxiety pilot study." The FDA is now open to the possibility of the therapeutic potential of LSD-assisted psychotherapy and will accept data from the Swiss study. Given FDA approval, one would assume that much more research will be published in the near future, however, the FDA and DEA rules must first be harmonized.

2.4.8.1 Pharmacology

LSD is a potent centrally acting drug. The D-isomer is pharmacologically active while the L-isomer is apparently inactive.[1] Neuropharmacological studies have shown that LSD exerts a selective inhibitory effect on the brain's raphe system of nuclei by halting the spontaneous firing of serotonin-containing neurons of the dorsal and median raphe nuclei. In this way, LSD acts as an indirect serotonin antagonist. However, inhibition of raphe firing is not sufficient to explain the psychotomimetic effects of LSD because the compound lisuride is an even more potent inhibitor of the raphe system, yet does not demonstrate hallucinogenic potential in humans. Therefore, other post-synaptic mechanisms such as action on glutamate or serotonin receptors may be involved.[2] One study suggests that the serotonin 2A receptor (5HT2AR) is activated by LSD leading to a hippocampal-prefrontal cortex-mediated breakdown of inhibitory processes. This may explain the formation of LSD-induced visual hallucinations.[3] LSD can induce neuroplastic modifications that can result in persistent behavioral changes.[4] There is evidence that LSD indirectly exerts effects on the neuronal cytoskeleton by reducing the amount of serotonin released from the raphe system.[5] LSD produces sympathomimetic, parasympathomimetic, and neuromuscular effects, which include mydriasis, lacrimation, tachycardia, and tremor.[6]

2.4.8.2 Absorption

LSD may be self-administered orally, nasally, or parentally, but the oral route is the most common. The normal dosage range is between 50 and 300 mg, with a minimum effective dose of 20 to 25 mg. Absorption is rapid and complete regardless of the route of administration. However, having food in the stomach does slow the absorption. Effects are observed within 5 to 10 min, with psychosis becoming evident after 15 to 20 min. Peak effects occur 30 to 90 min after dosing, with effects declining after 4 to 6 h.[7] The duration of effects may be 8 to 12 h.

Pharmacokinetic studies in humans are limited because the DEA forbade further research in the 1960s. Presumably, this situation will soon change following the FDA's ruling. Following intravenous administration of 2 mg/kg, a peak plasma LSD concentration of 5 ng/ml was observed after 1 h.[1] At 8 h, the plasma concentration had declined to 1 ng/ml. More recently studies using liquid chromatography with electrospray ionization and tandem mass spectrometric detection have been developed and validated for LSD and iso-LSD. Using this technique, the lower limit for quantitative determination is 0.02 mg/L for LSD and iso-LSD. Peak plasma levels were slightly higher than in earlier reports (case 1 plasma LSD = 0.31 mg/L, iso-LSD = 0.27 mg/L and in a second case LSD = 0.24 mg/L, iso-LSD = 0.6 mg/L in urine).[8] Dolder et al.[9] reported data from two placebo-controlled, double-blind, cross-over studies where oral 100 and 200 μg LSD doses were administrated to 24 and 16 subjects, respectively. LSD displayed dose-proportional pharmacokinetics and first-order elimination up to 12 h. Mean Cmax ranged 1.2– 19 (at low dose) and 2.6– 4.0 ng/mL (at high dose) with Tmax estimated in 1.4– 1.5 h.

2.4.8.3 Distribution

More than 80% of LSD resides in the plasma. As the drug penetrates the CNS, it is concentrated in the visual cortices of the brain as well as the limbic and reticular activating systems. This observation correlates with perceived effects. LSD is also found in the liver, spleen, and lungs.[8] The volume of distribution is reported to be low at 0.28 L/kg. Wagner et al.[10] described a two-compartment open model for LSD with an elimination half-life of 3 h. Dolder et al.[9] assessed the Vd at 46 and 37 L after the administration of oral 100 and 200 μg LSD doses, respectively.

2.4.8.4 Metabolism and Excretion

LSD metabolism was investigated using MS/MS techniques in two positive cases (case 1: LSD = 0.1 ng/mL, in plasma; case 2: LSD = 0.24 ng/mL, in plasma). The main metabolite was 2-oxo-3-hydroxy-LSD (O-H-LSD) present in urine at the concentrations of 2.5 mg/L and 6.6 mg/L, respectively, for cases 1 and 2, but it was not detected at all in plasma. Nor-LSD was also found in urine at 0.15 mg/L and 0.01 mg/L levels. Nor-iso-LSD, lysergic acid ethylamide (LAE), trioxylated-LSD, lysergic acid ethyl-2-hydroxyethylamide (LEO), and 13- and 14-hydroxy-LSD and their glucuronide conjugates were detected in urine using specific MS-MS transitions.[8]

The metabolism and elimination of LSD in humans have received limited study. Animal studies demonstrated extensive biotransformation via N-demethylation, N-deethylation, and hydroxylation to form inactive metabolites (Figure 2.4.7).[11] In humans, demethylation and aromatic hydroxylation occur to produce N-desmethyl-LSD

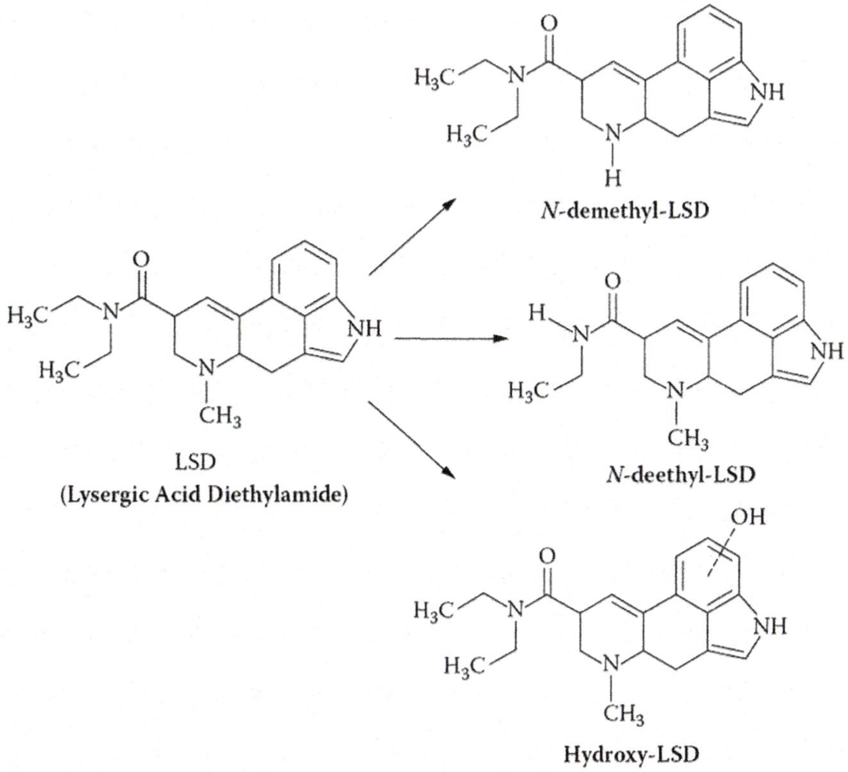

FIGURE 2.4.7 Metabolic pathway of LSD

and 13- and 14-hydroxy-LSD. Hydroxylated metabolites undergo glucuronidation to form water-soluble conjugates. Excretion into the bile accounts for approximately 80% of a dose.[8] Concentrations of unchanged drug ranged from 1 to 55 ng/ml in the 24-h urine after ingestion of 200 to 400 mg LSD in humans.[12] In a study based on analysis of 54 urine specimens from military personnel (LSD > 0.5 ng/mL) who had tested positive for, LSD and O-H-LSD urinary concentrations averaged 0.6 and 9.0 ng/mL.[13] LSD or its metabolites were detectable for 34 to 120 h following a 300-mg oral dose in seven human subjects.[14] In still another study, Dolder et al.[9] reported a half-life of 2.6 h and a clearance of 12.3 and 9.9 L/h at the oral 100 μg and 200 μg LSD doses, respectively.

REFERENCES

1. Baselt, R.C., and Cravey, R.H., *Disposition of Toxic Drugs and Chemicals in Man*, 4th ed., Chemical Toxicology Institute, Foster City, CA, 1995.
2. Goldberger, B.A., *Lysergic Acid Diethylamide. In-Service Training and Continuing Education AACC/TDM*, American Association for Clinical Chemistry, Inc., Washington, DC, 14(6), 99–100, 1993.
3. Schmidt, A., Müller, F., Lenz, C., Dolder, P.C., Schmid, Y., Zanchi, D., Lang, U.E., Liechti, M.E., and Borgwardt, S., Acute LSD effects on response inhibition neural networks, *Psychol Med,* 48(9), 1464–73, 2018.
4. Schmid, Y., and Liechti, M.E., Long-lasting subjective effects of LSD in normal subjects, *Psychopharmacology (Berl.)*, 235(2), 535–45, 2018.
5. Van Woerkom, A.E., The major hallucinogens and the central cytoskeleton: an association beyond coincidence? Towards sub-cellular mechanisms in schizophrenia, *Med Hypoth*, 31, 7–15, 1990.
6. Passie, T., Halpern, J.H., Stichtenoth, D.O., Emrich, H.M., and Hintzen, A., The pharmacology of lysergic acid diethylamide: a review, *CNS Neurosci Ther*, 14(4), 295–314, 2008.
7. Leikin, J.B., Karantz, A.J., Zell-Kanter, M., Barkin, R.L., and Hryhorczuk, D.O., Clinical features and management of intoxication due to hallucinogenic drugs, *Med Toxicol Adverse Drug Exp*, 4(5), 324–50, 1989.
8. Canezin, J., Cailleux, A., Turcant, A., Le Bouil, A., Harry, P., and Allain, P., Determination of LSD and its metabolites in human biological fluids by high-performance liquid chromatography with electrospray tandem mass spectrometry, *J Chromatogr B Biomed Sci Appl*, 765(1), 15–27, 2001.
9. Dolder, P.C., Schmid, Y., Steuer, A.E., Kraemer, T., Rentsch, K.M., Hammann, F., and Liechti, M.E., Pharmacokinetics and pharmacodynamics of lysergic acid diethylamide in healthy subjects. *Clin Pharmacokinet*, 56(10), 1219–30, 2017.
10. Wagner, J.G., Aghajanian, G.K., and Bing, O.H.L., Correlation of performance test scores with "tissue concentration" of lysergic acid diethylamide in human subjects, *Clin Pharmacol Ther*, 9, 635–8, 1968.
11. Axelrod, J., Brady, R.O., Witkop, B., and Evarts, E.V., Metabolism of lysergic acid diethylamide, *Nature*, 178, 143–4, 1956.
12. Taunton-Rigby, A., Sher, S.E., and Kelley, P.R., Lysergic acid diethylamide: radioimmunoassay, *Science*, 181, 165–6, 1973.
13. Poch, G.K., Klette, K.L., Anderson, C., The quantitation of 2-oxo-3-hydroxy lysergic acid diethylamide (O-H-LSD) in human urine specimens, a metabolite of LSD: comparative analysis using liquid chromatography-selected ion monitoring mass spectrometry and liquid chromatography-ion trap mass spectrometry, *J Anal Toxicol*, 24(3), 170–9, 2000.
14. Peel, H.W., and Boynton, A.L., Analysis of LSD in urine using radioimmunoassay — excretion and storage effects, *Can Soc For Sci J*, 13, 23–8, 1980.

2.4.9 Cannabis and Cannabinoids

Cannabis sativa L. or *Cannabis indica* plant contains the mind-altering chemical tetrahydrocannabinol (THC) and similar molecules (cannabinoids). The term marijuana refers to the dried leaves, flowers, and stems of the plant, whereas extracts can also be made from the resinous portion of the cannabis plant, yielding hashish or ash oil or honey oil or shatter – a hard, amber-colored solid. Cannabis derivatives represent the most commonly used illicit drug in the United States. Its use is widespread among young people. In 2015, more than 11 million young adults ages 18 to 25 admitted to marijuana use in the prior year.[1] According to the United States "Monitoring the Future" survey, rates of cannabis use among middle- and high-school students have dropped or leveled off in the past few years, after having increased for several years prior. These changes have occurred despite the increasing numbers of young people who believe regular marijuana use is not associated with risk.

Cannabis and its constituents, in particular cannabinoids, have been the focus of extensive chemical and biological research for almost half a century, ever since the discovery of delta-9-tetrahydrocannabinol (delta-9-THC), the principal psychoactive constituent of cannabis.[2] THC is produced by decarboxylation which occurs when cannabis leaf is heated. The main THC precursor is delta-9-tetrahydrocannabinolic acid A (THCA A)[3] and its presence contributes to the main activity of cannabis products when they are smoked, but not when they are ingested.[4] Besides delta-9-THC, more than 560 constituents have been identified in cannabis, including several non-psychoactive cannabinoids with medicinal functions, such as cannabidiol (CBD), cannabichromene (CBC), and cannabigerol (CBG), along with other non-cannabinoid constituents belonging to diverse classes of natural products.[3,4]

The onset of clinically apparent effects occurs within a few minutes after cannabis is smoked, and between 30 and 60 minutes when it is baked and eaten.[5,6] Effects last between two and six hours.[6] Short-term side effects may include decreased short-term memory, dry mouth, impaired motor skills, red eyes, and feelings of paranoia or anxiety.[5,7,8] Long-term side effects may include addiction and decreased mental ability. Behavioral problems among those who started out using THC at a young age are known, but have not been intensively studied either. Behavioral problems in children whose mothers used cannabis during pregnancy have also been reported.[5] Some studies report a relationship between cannabis use and risk for psychosis,[9] however, the cause-effect relationship is a matter of debate.[1]

2.4.9.1 Pharmacology

Marijuana can be consumed in a number of different ways. It is traditionally smoked. In the past, typical doses were 5–20 mg, however, but towards the end of the last century, the potency of cannabis began increasing,[10] though it seems to have been declining in the last decade.[11] The average THC content of cigarettes within some cannabis strains, such as "skunk," has been found in concentrations of about 50 mg in Western Europe, 61 mg in the Netherlands,[12] 42 mg in England,[13] and 63 mg in the United States. The expansion of legal cannabis markets has substantially increased the type and variety of cannabis and cannabinoid products commercially available. In addition to traditional preparations of dried cannabis plant flowers and cannabis resin ("hashish"), cannabis products available now include a large number of "edible" food and drink products, oils and tinctures, highly concentrated extracts, transdermal products, and cannabis vaporized products.[14] According to a recent survey, 29.8% of United States adults aged 18 years or over have consumed cannabis in the form of "edibles or drinks," and 9.9% had used a "vaporizer or other electronic device."[15]

The known physical and mental effects of cannabis include sedation, euphoria, feeling "high" or "stoned," altered perception, such as hallucinations and temporal distortion, along with an increase in mood and appetite. Only recently the medicinal value of metabolites such as CBD began to be appreciated. When given to experimental animals, CBD significantly reduces liver inflammation, oxidative/nitrative stress, and cell death. It also attenuates both bacterial endotoxin-triggered necrosis factor (NF)-kB activation and tumor necrosis factor (TNF)-k production in the isolated Kupfer cells. In humans (where liver changes have not been studied except in situ), adhesion molecule expression in primary human liver sinusoidal endothelial cells is stimulated by TNF-k, as is the attachment of human neutrophils to activated sinusoidal endothelium. These protective effects appear to be the result of CB1 agonism.[16]

Cannabinoid receptors are coupled to G proteins and are involved in the control of many processes, including metabolic regulation, food craving, pain, anxiety, bone growth, and immune function. Exogenous cannabinoids found in marijuana plants can also exert effects via G proteins which negatively modulate cyclic AMP levels and activate the inward rectifying K+ channels.[17] Manipulation at either receptor site may have important clinical consequences, and therapies based upon cannabinoid receptor interactions are under development. Many of these positive effects are mediated by the CB1 receptor. The highest concentrations of the CB1 receptor are found in the brain and nerve tissues. Stimulation of presynaptic CB1 receptors inhibits neurotransmitter release by stimulating K+ channels and inhibiting calcium channels.[18] The highest levels of CB2 receptors are found in the immune tissues such as the spleen, thymus, and tonsils; their stimulation seems to have immunosuppressive effects, including inhibition of proinflammatory cytokine production.[19]

In the periphery, CB receptors are expressed in the heart, kidney, spleen, small intestine, and testis or ovary, with minimal expression in the liver.[20] CB receptor stimulation leads to enhanced expression of acetyl-CoA carboxylase-1 and fatty acid synthetase, thereby increasing lipogenesis.[21] In a normal heart, both CB1 and CB2 receptors are found in roughly equal proportions, though in patients with heart failure, the concentration of CB2 receptors is greatly elevated.[22] Whether this is a cause or an effect is not known. Only CB1 receptors are found in coronary arteries and their number is increased in coronary artery disease. Blood concentrations of endocannabinoids are increased at the same time.[23]

Animal studies have shown that cannabinoid CB1 and CB2 receptors regulate Ca2+ levels and/or K+ currents in a variety of cell types, including oligodendroglial and myocardial cells. In oligodendroglial tissue cultures, cannabinoid compounds promote the Ca2+ influx elicited by transient membrane depolarization due to elevated extracellular K+. If cannabinoids exert the same effect on cardiomyocytes, this could explain the tachycardia seen in marijuana smokers.[24]

In mammals, the cannabinoid receptors for THC, particularly CB1, as well as its endogenous ligands, and the endocannabinoids anandamide and 2-arachidonoylglycerol, all have an effect on the control of energy balance. Cannabinoids are known to enhance energy storage in adipose tissue and reduce energy expenditure by influencing both lipid and glucose metabolisms. Although lipid and glucose metabolisms are normally well controlled by the complex interactions between hormones and neuropeptides, marijuana can disrupt both central and peripheral aspects of the endocannabinoid regulation of energy balance, possibly contributing to obesity and dyslipidemia.[25] All of these observations suggest that cannabinoid agonists and antagonists may have a role in the treatment of many different diseases, although their forensic utility remains an open question.

2.4.9.2 Absorption

Until the last century cannabis was almost always used as a drug of abuse and self-administered by smoking, usually in the forms of marihuana or hashish. In the last few decades many cannabis and cannabinoid products, including different types of food, beverage, vaporizing, and transdermal products, have been introduced to the market, sometimes for recreational and sometimes for therapeutic uses. The typical doses of THC, inhaled by smoking, have been reported as being between 5 mg and 20 mg.[26] However, in recent years, the average THC content per cigarette has increased to about 50–63 mg.[27] During the smoking process, pyrolysis and sidestream smoke are responsible for a significant loss of THC (more than 30%),[28] while a part of THC is deposited on the nasopharyngeal region or the upper bronchial tree, these are considered poorly absorbing surfaces, reducing the amount of drug reaching the lung alveoli where rapid transit of the drug across the lungs to the brain occurs.[29]

In controlled studies, THC bioavailability has been reported to range from 18% to 50%, with large inter and intra-subject variability.[30] The amount of drug delivered may change depending on the number, duration, and spacing of puffs, the length of time the inhalation is held, and the inhalation volume or depth of puffs affects bioavailability.[31] Obviously, in humans, there must be a great variation in intra-individual absorption. For the same reason, these variables all must be accounted for in experimental studies.

In humans THC peak plasma concentrations between 100–200 ng/mL are reached 3 min after the first puff, generally before the last puff of a cannabis cigarette is inhaled.[32] Vaporization devices for cannabis administration demonstrated delivery and blood pharmacokinetics of THC and multiple cannabinoids[33,34] comparable to previously published data after smoking[3] In controlled studies, plasma concentrations of THC have ranged from 0 to 20.0 ng/mL with a mean of 7.0 ng/mL and from 1.8 to 37.0 ng/mL with a mean of 18.1 ng/mL following the first inhalation of a low (1.75% THC) or high (3.55% THC; 35 mg THC) dose marijuana cigarette, respectively. Concentrations continued to increase and rapidly reach peak levels that ranged from 50.0 to 129.0 ng/mL, with a mean peak drug level of 84.3 ng/mL and from 76.0 to 267.0 ng/mL with a mean of 162.2 ng/mL for the 1.75% and 3.55% THC marijuana cigarettes, respectively.[35,36] In a more recent study, the THC mean maximal concentrations were reported as 135.1 ng/mL, 202.9 ng/mL, and 231.0 ng/mL after smoking 29.3, 49.1 mg, and 69.4 mg THC cigarettes, with large inter-individual variability.[37,38] Maximum THC blood concentrations are significantly higher when the drug is administered with alcohol than alone, most likely because alcohol causes blood vessel dilation, increasing ethanol absorption.[39]

THC is also absorbed into the tissues of the oral cavity. Most of the THC absorbed in this fashion comes from the inhaled smoke that can also be detected in oral fluid. The oral fluid-to-plasma (or blood) ratio is subject to large intra- and inter-subject variability and also depends on the type of collection device used. Huestis and Cone, in 2004, reported oral fluid-to-serum ratios of 0.5–2.2.[40] More recently, Toennes et al.[41] reported higher oral fluid-to-serum ratios of 0.3–425 (median 16) among volunteers who smoked a standard joint (average dose 33 mg), with maximum concentrations in chronic users (0.4–72 mg/g), higher than those in occasional users (0.4–6.4 mg/g). Oral fluid-to-serum ratios were even higher in another study of volunteers smoking low (18 mg of smoked THC) and high doses (36 mg) of marijuana – 46 and 36, respectively. While there is a relationship between oral fluid and plasma THC concentrations, it is not strong enough to allow the concentration of one to be predicted from the other.[40,42] THC concentrations in oral fluid peak very early after smoking is initiated (0.25 h) at 900 (SD 589) and 1041 (SD 652) ng/mL, respectively. In one study the 6 h the concentration was 18 (SD 12) ng/mL.[43]

The amount of THC that can be ingested from edible foods varies according to the concentration found in that product. In a position paper on the reasonable guidance values for THC in food products, the European Industrial Hemp Association (EIHA) proposed a THC concentration cut-off of 10.000 mg/kg for the identification of safe products (hemp seeds, edible oil, and processed press cake).[44]

Although the bioavailability of smoked THC is very great, that of oral THC is only 4% to 12%, and absorption is highly variable. Following oral ingestion, psychotropic effects set in with a delay of 30–90 minutes, reaching their maximum after 2–3 hours, and lasting for about 4–12 hours, depending on dose and specific effect.[43] A mean peak plasma THC concentration of 6 ng/mL is observed after oral ingestion of 20 mg.[45] Substantial amounts of the 11-hydroxy metabolite (11-OH-THC) are produced following oral administration, resulting in concentrations similar to those of THC. By comparison, intravenous administration of pure THC achieves peak plasma THC concentrations after 30 min.[29]

2.4.9.3 Distribution

THC is 95%–99% bound to plasma protein with very little present in red blood cells. After the peak, THC concentration in blood decreases rapidly and it is distributed into tissues,[46] where highly perfused organs, such as the brain, rapidly accumulate it. It distributes more slowly into, and is released more slowly from, poorly perfused tissues such as fat. Tissue distribution of THC and its metabolites is assumed to be governed only by physicochemical properties, with no specific transport processes or barriers affecting the concentration of the drug in the tissues. The distribution of THC into various tissues and organs, such as the brain, liver, heart, kidney, salivary glands, breast milk, fat, and lung is a result of THCs extremely large volume of distribution (~10 L/kg).

Hunt and Jones proposed a four-compartment model of THC distribution after intravenous injection. In their studies, they observed average half-lives of 1 min, 4 min, 1 h, and 19 h to distribute into each of the compartments.[47] They concluded that "pseudoequilibrium" is achieved between plasma and tissues 6 h after an intravenous dose. Thereafter, THC is slowly eliminated as it diffuses from tissue to the blood. The terminal elimination half-life is at least one day but has been reported to be as long as 3–13 days in frequent users, although at this point the blood THC concentration is usually well below 5 ng/mL.[48]

Over the last decade, several studies have been carried out to determine pharmacokinetic parameters of cannabinoids in blood, plasma, or serum in humans.[24,35] Other studies were performed with oral fluid only,[41] or in tandem with serum[42,43] or plasma[39] with a limited number of ten participants in each study. Two, three, or more compartment pharmacokinetic models have been applied with varying degrees of success to describe the cannabinoid time profiles.[49,50] Non-compartmental approaches have also been used, but no general consensus could be reached from any of these studies.

2.4.9.4 Metabolism

Almost all THC undergoes hepatic metabolism by cytochrome P450 (CYP) enzymes (CYP2C9, CYP2C19, and CYP3A). One of the most important metabolites of THC is 11-hydroxy-THC (11-OH-THC) which is at least as potent as THC, has a similar pharmacokinetic profile, and probably contributes significantly to the psychoactive effects observed after THC administration.[27] 11-nor-9-carboxy-THC (THCCOOH) is the main secondary metabolite of tetrahydrocannabinol (THC), formed by oxidation of 11-OH-THC by liver enzymes. It is then metabolized further by conjugation with glucuronide, yielding a water-soluble congener that can be more easily excreted by the body.

Peak concentrations of 11-OH-THC occur close to the time of smoking, while THCCOOH concentrations peak 1–4 h later.[48] THC, 11-OH-THC, and THCCOOH in chronic cannabis smokers can be detected in blood up to 30 days after cessation of the drug consumption.[51]

Multiple other compounds are produced by the actions of CYP isozymes. In addition to catalyzing the formation of significant amounts of 7-OH-THC, it has also been shown that hepatic microsomes form 6b-OH-THC at approximately the same rate. In addition, 1a, 2a-epoxyhexahydrocannabinol is also produced, but at only one-third the rate of 7-OH-THC.[52] several other minor oxidation products are also produced. Metabolism in humans involves allylic oxidation, epoxidation, aliphatic oxidation, decarboxylation, and conjugation. More than 20 different metabolites have been identified.

The two monohydroxy metabolites, 11-OH-THC and 8β-OH-THC are active, with the former exhibiting similar activity and disposition to THC, while the latter is less potent. The average plasma clearance for THC is 600–980 mL/min with a blood clearance of 1.0–1.6 L/min, which is very close to hepatic blood flow, which means that the rate of THC metabolism is dependent on hepatic blood flow. Within the first 72 h, approximately 70% of a dose of THC is excreted in the urine (30%) and feces (40%). The elimination of THC occurs slowly, partially because of the long plasma half-life but also because THC and its metabolites undergo enterohepatic circulation.

Only very small amounts of THC appear unchanged in the urine (around 2% of a given dose), but they can be found there for at least 24 h.[53] Other urinary metabolites are conjugates of THC-COOH and unidentified acidic products. After smoking 10 mg of THC, peak urinary THC-COOH concentrations of 6–129 ng/mL are detected within 16 h.[53] Huestis and Cone studied six volunteers after a single dose of marijuana (either 1.75% or 3.55%) and reported finding a mean (± SEM) urinary excretion half-life for THC- COOH of 31.5 ± 1 h, while THC-COOG and THC were at 28.6 ± 1.5 h, and 1.75% or 3.55% THC, respectively.[54]

Passive exposure to marijuana smoke may also produce detectable urinary metabolite concentrations, but the concentrations are so small they could never account for a workplace positive drug test unless persons are exposed to sidestream smoke in a small, under-ventilated room. In 2010, Dutch researchers analyzed the findings in eight healthy volunteers exposed to cannabis smoke for 3 h while sitting in a well-attended "coffee shop" (such shops contain high ambient levels of THC smoke). Blood samples were taken at baseline and again at 1.5, 3.5, 6, and 14 h after the start of the study. All the volunteers absorbed some THC, but the concentrations detected were very low. None of the urine samples produced immunoassay results above the cut-off concentration of 25 ng/mL. THC-COOH concentrations of up to 5.0 and 7.8 ng/mL before and after hydrolysis, respectively, were found in the urine. THC could be detected in trace amounts, close to the limits of detection, in the first two blood samples after initial exposure (1.5 and 3.5 h), but not after 6 h. THC-COOH could be detected after 1.5 h and was still detectable in three of the eight participants after 14 h in concentrations between 0.5 and 1.0 ng/mL.[54]

THC may be ingested orally by consuming food products containing the seeds or oil of the hemp plant. Ingestion of 0.6 mg/day (equivalent to 125 mL of hemp oil containing 5 mg/g of THC or 300 g of hulled seeds containing 2 mg/g) for ten days resulted in urine THC-COOH concentrations of < 6 ng/mL. In another study, the maximum urinary concentration of THC-COOH after ingestion of hemp oil containing 0.39–0.47 mg of THC/day for five days was 5.4–38.2 ng/mL (n = 7). In yet another study, oral administration of a higher dose (7.5 or 14.8 mg of THC/day),[55] peak urinary concentrations of THC-COOH ranged from 19.0 to 436 ng/mL.

Other controlled studies have shown that at the federally mandated U.S. and European Union cannabinoid cut-offs, it is possible, but unlikely, for a urine specimen to test positive after ingestion of manufacturer-recommended doses of low-THC hemp oils. On the other hand, a patient taking Marinol, the synthetic form of THC, approved by the U.S. Food and Drug Administration for the control of nausea and vomiting in cancer patients, will almost certainly test positive. Dronabinol or synthetic THC is present in Marinol capsules. Elsohly and Slade (2005) found that within 24 h of administering a single 15 mg dose of dronabinol to four subjects, peak urine THC-COOH concentrations were between 189 ng/mL and 362 ng/mL.[56]

Since synthetic THC (dronabinol, Marinol) and naturally occurring THC are identical, this presents difficulties in determining if the source of urinary THC metabolites is the antiemetic or whether the person being tested is a marijuana smoker. One way to make the distinction is to test for the C3 homolog of THC, known as delta-9-tetrahydrocannabivarin (THCV). THCV is a natural component of most cannabis products and is found, along with THC, in the marijuana plant. Marinol is a synthetic product and contains no THCV. THCV is metabolized by human hepatocytes to 11-nor-delta-9-THCV-9-carboxylic acid (THCV-COOH), and its presence in a urine sample should be taken as proof of marijuana smoking. This theory has been confirmed in a controlled study in human volunteers.[57]

THC is also present in hair after marijuana use, as is THC-COOH and other cannabinoids such as CBD and

CBN. Subjects using marijuana are found to have a wide range of hair concentrations. In one study, THC and THC-COOH concentrations ranged from 3.4 to >1 00 pg/mg of hair and from 0.10 to 7.3 pg/mg of hair, respectively. There was a weak correlation between THC and THC-COOH concentrations (r = 0.38). The sum total of cannabinoids had a better correlation with cumulative use of the drug, but the relationship was still weak.[58]

One of the more significant issues in hair analyses is differentiating inadvertent exposure from actual personal use. Sidestream smoke and other types of environmental contamination can cause hair samples to test positive for THC. Analysis of hair for THC-COOH is recommended to distinguish inadvertent from personal use. However, the acidic nature of this metabolite provides a much lower rate of incorporation into hair compared to THC. For example, concentrations of THC-COOH in the hair of users ranged from 0.002 to 0.39 ng/mg of hair, with an average of 0.12 ng/mg.[59] The Society of Hair Testing recommends that to confirm marijuana use, THC- COOH should be detected in concentrations of > 0. 2 pg/mg of hair (see www.soht.org). This is much lower than the cut-off used for THC (0.1 ng/mg).

REFERENCES

1. World Drug Report 2018 (United Nations publication, Sales No. E.18.XI.9). Available at https://www.unodc.org/wdr2018/prelaunch/WDR18_Booklet_1_EXSUM.pdf
2. De Zeeuw RA, Malingré TM, Merkus FW. 1-tetrahydrocannabinolic acid, an important component in the evaluation of cannabis products. *J Pharm Pharmacol* 1972;24(1):1–6.
3. Kimura M, Okamoto K. Distribution of tetrahydrocannabinolic acid in fresh wild cannabis. *Experientia* 1970;26(8):819–20.
4. Baker PB, Taylor BJ, Gough TA. The tetrahydrocannabinol and tetrahydrocannabinolic acid content of cannabis products. *J Pharm Pharmacol* 1981;33(6):369–72.
5. Schwope DM, Karschner EL, Gorelick DA, Huestis MA. Identification of recent cannabis use: whole-blood and plasma free and glucuronidated cannabinoid pharma- cokinetics following controlled smoked cannabis administration. *Clin Chem* 2011;57:1406–14.
6. Ramaekers JG, Moeller MR et al. Cognition and motor control as a function of delta9-THC concentration in serum and oral fluid: limits of impairment. *Drug Alcohol Depend* 2006;85(2):114–22.
7. Hunault CC, Mensinga TT, de Vries I, Kelholt-Dijkman HH, Hoek J, Kruidenier M, Leenders ME, Meulenbelt J. Delta-9-tetrahydrocannabinol (THC) serum concentrations and pharmacological effects in males after smoking a combination of tobacco and cannabis containing up to 69 mg THC. *Psychopharmacology (Berl)* 2008;201(2):171–81. doi: 10.1007/s00213-008-1260-2.
8. Goullé JP, Guerbet M. Tetrahydrocannabinol pharmacokinetics; new synthetic cannabinoids; road safety and cannabis. *Bull Acad Natl Med* 2014;198(3):541–56; discussion 556–7. Review.
9. Hartman, R.L. et al. Cannabis effects on lateral driving control with and without alcohol. *Drug Alcohol Depend* 2015;154:25–37.
10. Niesink RJ, Rigter S, Koeter MW, Brunt TM. Potency trends of Δ9-tetrahydrocannabinol, cannabidiol and cannabinol in cannabis in the Netherlands: 2005–15. *Addiction* 2015;110(12):1941–50.
11. Niesink RJM, Rigter S, Hoek J. *THC-Concentraties in Wiet, Nederwiet En Hash in Nederlandse Coffeshops, 2003–2004 [THC Concentrations in Cannabis, Home-Grown Cannabis and Hashish in Dutch Coffeeshops, 2003–2004].* Utrecht: Trimbos Institute, 2004.
12. Potter DJ, Clark P, Brown MB. Potency of Delta(9)-THC and other cannabinoids in cannabis in England in 2005: implications for psychoactivity and pharmacology. *J Forensic Sci* 2008;53:90–4.
13. Vandrey R, Herrmann ES, Mitchell JM, Bigelow GE, Flegel R, LoDico C, Cone EJ. Pharmacokinetic profile of oral cannabis in humans: blood and oral fluid disposition and relation to pharmacodynamic outcomes. *J Anal Toxicol* 2017;41(2):83–99. doi: 10.1093/jat/bkx012. PubMed PMID: 28158482; PubMed Central PMCID: PMC5890870.
14. Schauer GL, King BA, Bunnell RE, Promoff G, McAfee TA. Toking, vaping, and eating for health or fun: marijuana use patterns in adults, U.S., 2014. *Am J Prev Med* 2016;50:1–8.
15. Mukhopadhyay B, Cinar R, Yin S, Liu J, Tam J, Godlewski G, Harvey-White J, Mordi I, Cravatt BF, Lotersztajn S, Gao B, Yuan Q, Schuebel K, Goldman D, Kunos G. Hyperactivation of anandamide synthesis and regulation of cell-cycle progression via cannabinoid type 1 (CB1) receptors in the regenerating liver. *Proc Natl Acad Sci U S A* 2011;108(15):6323–8.
16. Mormina ME, Thakur S, Molleman A, Whelan CJ, Baydoun AR. Cannabinoid signalling in TNF-alpha induced IL-8 release. *Eur J Pharmacol* 2006;540(1–3):183–90.
17. Howlett AC. The cannabinoid receptors. *Prostaglandins Other Lipid Mediat* 2002;68–69:619–31. Review
18. Maresz K, Pryce G, Ponomarev ED, Marsicano G, Croxford JL, Shriver LP, Ledent C, Cheng X, Carrier EJ, Mann MK, Giovannoni G, Pertwee RG, Yamamura T, Buckley NE, Hillard CJ, Lutz B, Baker D, Dittel BN. Direct suppression of CNS autoimmune inflammation via the cannabinoid receptor CB1 on neurons and CB2 on autoreactive T cells. *Nat Med* 2007;13(4):492–7.
19. Pertwee RG. Pharmacology of cannabinoid CB1 and CB2 receptors. *Pharmacol Ther* 1997;74(2):129–80. Review.
20. Osei-Hyiaman D, DePetrillo M, Pacher P, Liu J, Radaeva S, Bátkai S, Harvey-White J, Mackie K, Offertáler L, Wang L, Kunos G. Endocannabinoid activation at hepatic CB1 receptors stimulates fatty acid synthesis and contributes to diet-induced obesity. *J Clin Invest* 2005;115(5): 1298–305.
21. Weis F, Beiras-Fernandez A, Hauer D, Hornuss C, Sodian R, Kreth S, Briegel J, Schelling G. Effect of anaesthesia and cardiopulmonary bypass on blood endocannabinoid concentrations during cardiac surgery. *Br J Anaesth* 2010;105(2):139–44.
22. Sugamura K, Sugiyama S, Nozaki T, Matsuzawa Y, Izumiya Y, Miyata K, Nakayama M, Kaikita K, Obata T, Takeya M, Ogawa H. Activated endocannabinoid system in coronary artery disease and antiinflammatory effects of cannabinoid 1 receptor blockade on macrophages. *Circulation* 2009;119(1):28–36.
23. Karschner EL, Darwin WD, McMahon RP, Liu F, Wright S, Goodwin RS, Huestis MA. Subjective and physiological effects after controlled sativex and oral THC administration. *Clin Pharmacol Ther* 2011;89(3):400–7.

24. Kiplinger GF, Manno JE. Dose-response relationships to cannabis in human subjects. *Pharmacol Rev* 1971;23(4):339–47. Review.
25. Di Marzo V, Piscitelli F, Mechoulam R. Cannabinoids and endocannabinoids in metabolic disorders with focus on diabetes. *Handb Exp Pharmacol* 2011;203:75–104.
26. Böcker KB, Gerritsen J, Hunault CC, Kruidenier M, Mensinga TT, Kenemans JL. Cannabis with high delta-9-THC contents affects perception and visual selective attention acutely: an event-related potential study. *Pharmacol Biochem Behav* 2010;96(1):67–74. doi: 10.1016/j.pbb.2010.04.008. Epub 2010 Apr 24. PubMed PMID: 20417659.
27. Perez-Reyes M, Timmons MC, Lipton MA, Davis KH, Wall ME. Intravenous injection in man of Δ9- tetrahydrocannabinol and 11-OH-Δ9-tetrahydrocannabinol. *Science* 1972;177:633–5.
28. McGilveray IJ. Pharmacokinetics of cannabinoids. *Pain Res Manag* 2005;10(Suppl A):15A–22A. Review.
29. Karch SB. *Pharmacokinetics and Pharmacodynamics of Abused Drugs*, 1st Edition, CRC Press, 2007.
30. Grotenhermen F. Pharmacokinetics and pharmacodynamics of cannabinoids. *Clin Pharmacokinet* 2003;42(4):327–60. Review.
31. Huestis MA et al. Blood cannabinoids. I. Absorption of THC and formation of 11-OH-THC and THCCOOH during and after smoking marijuana. *J Anal Toxicol* 1992;16:276–82.
32. Abrams DI, Vizoso HP, Shade SB, Jay C, Kelly ME, Benowitz NL. Vaporization as a smokeless cannabis deliv- ery system: a pilot study. *Clin Pharmacol Ther* 2007;82: 572–8.
33. Hartman RL, Brown TL, Milavetz G, Spurgin A, Gorelick DA, Gaffney G, Huestis MA. Controlled cannabis vaporizer administration: blood and plasma cannabinoids with and without alcohol. *Clin Chem* 2015;61:850.
34. Schwope DM, Karschner EL, Gorelick DA, Huestis MA. Identification of recent. cannabis use: whole-blood and plasma free and glucuronidated cannabinoid pharmacokinetics following controlled smoked cannabis administration. *Clin Chem* 2011;57(10):1406–14.
35. Huestis MA, Henningfield JE, Cone EJ. Blood cannabinoids. I. Absorption of THC and formation of 11-OH-THC and THCCOOH during and after smoking marijuana. *J Anal Toxicol* 1992;16(5):276–82.
36. Ramaekers JG, Moeller MR et al. Cognition and motor control as a function of delta9-THC concentration in serum and oral fluid: limits of impairment. *Drug Alcohol Depend* 2006;85(2):114–22.
37. Hunault CC, Mensinga TT, de Vries I, Kelholt-Dijkman HH, Hoek J, Kruidenier M, Leenders ME, Meulenbelt J. Delta-9-tetrahydrocannabinol (THC) serum concentrations and pharmacological effects in males after smoking a combination of tobacco and cannabis containing up to 69 mg THC. *Psychopharmacology (Berl)* 2008;201(2):171–81.
38. Goullé JP, Guerbet M. Tetrahydrocannabinol pharmacokinetics; new synthetic cannabinoids; road safety and cannabis. *Bull Acad Natl Med* 2014;198(3):541–56; discussion 556–7. Review
39. Hartman RL et al. Controlled cannabis vaporizer administration: blood and plasma cannabinoids with and without alcohol. *Clin Chem* 2015;61:850–69.
40. Huestis MA, Cone EJ. Relationship of delta9-tetrahydrocannabinol concentrations in oral fluid and plasma after controlled administration of smoked cannabis. *J Anal Toxicol* 2004;28(6):394–99.
41. Toennes SW, Ramaekers JG et al. Pharmacokinetic properties of delta9-tetrahydrocannabinol in oral fluid of occasional and chronic users. *J Anal Toxicol* 2010;34(4):216–21.
42. Ramaekers JG, Moeller MR et al. Cognition and motor control as a function of delta9-THC concentration in serum and oral fluid: limits of impairment. *Drug Alcohol Depend* 2006;85(2):114–22.
43. Kauert GF, Ramaekers JG et al. Pharmacokinetic properties of delta9-tetrahydrocannabinol in serum and oral fluid. *J Anal Toxicol* 2007;31(5):288–93.
44. http://eiha.org/media/2017/09/17-09-18-THC-Position-paper_EIHA.pdf
45. Perez-Reyes M, Timmons MC, Lipton MA, Davis KH, Wall ME. Intravenous injection in man of Δ9- tetrahydrocannabinol and 11-OH-Δ9-tetrahydrocannabinol. *Science* 1972;177:633–5.
46. Johansson E, Halldin MM. Urinary excretion half-life of delta 1-tetrahydrocannabinol-7-oic acid in heavy marijuana users after smoking. *J Anal Toxicol* 1989;13(4):218–23.
47. Hunt CA, Jones RT. Tolerance and disposition of tetrahydrocannabinol in man. *J Pharmacol Exp Ther* 1980;215(1):35–44.
48. Huestis MA, Henningfield JE, Cone EJ. Blood cannabinoids. I. Absorption of THC and formation of 11-OH-THC and THCCOOH during and after smoking marijuana. *J Anal Toxicol* 1992;16:276–82.
49. Heuberger JA, Guan Z, Oyetayo OO, Klumpers L, Morrison PD, Beumer TL, van Gerven JM, Cohen AF, Freijer J. Population pharmacokinetic model of THC integrates oral, intravenous, and pulmonary dosing and characterizes short- and long-term pharmacokinetics. *Clin Pharmacokinet* 2015;54(2):209–19.
50. Grotenhermen F. Pharmacokinetics and pharmacodynamics of cannabinoids. *Clin Pharmacokinet* 2003;42(4):327–60. Review.
51. Bergamaschi MM, Karschner EL, Goodwin RS, Scheidweiler KB, Hirvonen J, Queiroz RH, Huestis MA. Impact of prolonged cannabinoid excretion in chronic daily cannabis smokers' blood on per se drugged driving laws. 2013;59:519–26.
52. Bornheim LM, Lasker JM, Raucy JL. Human hepatic microsomal metabolism of delta 1-tetrahydrocannabinol. *Drug Metab Dispos* 1992;20(2):241–6.
53. Lowe RH, Abraham TT, Darwin WD, Herning R, Cadet JL, Huestis MA. Extended urinary Delta9-tetrahydrocannabinol excretion in chronic cannabis users precludes use as a biomarker of new drug exposure. *Drug Alcohol Depend* 2009;105(1–2):24–32.
54. Röhrich J, Schimmel I, Zörntlein S, Becker J, Drobnik S, Kaufmann T, Kuntz V, Urban R. Concentrations of delta9-tetrahydrocannabinol and 11-nor-9-carboxytetrahydrocannabinol in blood and urine after passive exposure to Cannabis smoke in a coffee shop. *J Anal Toxicol* 2010;34(4):196–203.
55. Huestis MA, Cone EJ. Differentiating new marijuana use from residual drug excretion in occasional marijuana users. *J Anal Toxicol* 1998;22(6):445–54.
56. Elsohly MA, Slade D. Chemical constituents of marijuana: the complex mixture of natural cannabinoids. *Life Sci* 2005;78(5):539–48. Epub 2005 Sep 30. Review.
57. Leson G, Pless P, Grotenhermen F, Kalant H, ElSohly MA. Evaluating the impact of hemp food consumption on workplace drug tests. *J Anal Toxicol* 2001;25(8):691–8.
58. Skopp G, Strohbeck-Kuehner P, Mann K, Hermann D. Deposition of cannabinoids in hair after long-term use of cannabis. *Forensic Sci Int* 2007;170(1):46–50.
59. Kintz P, Cirimele V, Mangin P. Testing human hair for cannabis. II. Identification of THC-COOH by GC-MS-NCI as a unique proof. *J Forensic Sci* 1995;40(4):619–22.

2.4.10 Opiates

This group includes natural compounds obtained from opium poppy usually denoted "opiates," such as morphine and codeine, and semi-synthetic or synthetic compounds such as heroin, oxycodone, buprenorphine, fentanyl, and methadone. They share many pharmacological and pharmacokinetic characteristics, the prototypic drug in this class being morphine.

When unripe seed capsules of the Papaver somniferum are incised, a milky exudate (latex) is obtained; when dried, it forms raw opium. Morphine, codeine, thebaine, papaverine, and other alkaloids are extracted from opium. Morphine represents 8% to 19% of opium by dry weight, depending on growing conditions, climate and location.[1] Morphine is the prototypic analgesic drug acting at the mu-opioid, but is different from other opioids. In the past, these differences were explained by different pharmacokinetics, but recently the concept of multiple mu receptors has emerged.

2.4.10.1 Morphine

Morphine acts as an agonist on specific receptors located in the central nervous system and the mesenteric plexus of the abdominal wall. Three types of opiate receptor μ (mu), κ (kappa), and δ (delta) are recognized; they are approximately 70% homologous, with sequence differences occurring mainly at the N and C terminal ends. The mu receptor is thought to be the most important for the opiate effects. Opiate receptors have seven loops, also called transmembrane domains.[2] when an agonist, such as morphine, or heroin, or oxycodone binds with the mu receptor, a G protein attached to the third intracellular loop is activated. The genes that determine the various receptor subtypes are located on different chromosomes. There are two mu, three kappa, and two delta subtypes, probably arising from post-translational modifications, because their genes have not been identified. A supposed fourth opiate receptor, referred to as the sigma receptor, has recently been recognized.[3] Interestingly, cocaine also binds to the same "7 domain" proteins.

Mu receptors are almost always located on the presynaptic side of the synapses. In the brain, most of them are in the periaqueductal gray region, but they are also found in the superficial dorsal horn of the spinal cord, the external plexiform layer of the olfactory bulb, the *nucleus accumbens* (implicated in the process of addiction), in some parts of the cerebral cortex, and in some of the nuclei of the amygdala. Mu receptors avidly bind enkephalins and beta-endorphin, but they have a low affinity for dynorphins (primarily a kappa receptor agonist).[4]

Morphine acts on the central nervous system to produce analgesia, respiratory depression, mood changes, mental numbness. In the gastrointestinal system, it produces nausea or vomiting, and an increase in intestinal tone with reduction of the propulsive force. Pressure is also increased in the biliary tract. The same is true in the urinary tract with increased tone of the ureter and bladder sphincters. Morphine increases the pain threshold and is particularly effective against persistent pain.

Small doses of morphine depress the respiratory rate, while large doses cause respiratory arrest (this is the accepted mechanism of death in cases of overdose). Respiratory depression occurs as a direct effect on brain stem respiratory centers, whereas mu-stimulation also depresses respiratory centers located in the pons. Tolerance to the respiratory effects develops upon constant use. Nausea and vomiting are also associated with the direct stimulus of the chemoreceptor vomiting trigger zone in the medulla. Pupillary constriction is due to its excitatory action on the parasympathetic nerves that supply the pupil. Morphine provides effective and convenient pain relief. It is also used to treat diarrhea and the cough associated with malignancy and tuberculosis.[5]

Kappa receptors are located mainly on pain neurons located in the spinal cord and to a lesser extent in the brain; they bind to an endogenously occurring ligand called dynorphin, whose exact function is unknown, and their activation also produces analgesia, but it simultaneously induces nausea and dysphoria. Blocking the actions of dynorphin helps to alleviate depression[6] and dynorphin may play an important role in determining an individual's risk for addiction.

Delta receptors normally bind to a class of endogenous ligand known as enkephalins that are produced by the pituitary gland; delta receptor activation also produces analgesia, but it can also cause seizures as well. The medicinal indications for morphine are treatment of moderate to severe pain and/or resistance to other painkillers, in particular, the pain associated with neoplasms, myocardial infarction, surgery, and acute pulmonary edema. Morphine is also indicated under general and regional anesthesia and for epidural analgesia.

2.4.10.1.1 Absorption

Morphine can be given orally, or by subcutaneous, intramuscular injection,[5] or intravenous injection. It can also be smoked or inhaled. Parenteral morphine is well absorbed, and resultant plasma levels are very similar. The oral bioavailability of morphine is quite low due to extensive first pass hepatic metabolism. A 10-mg bolus given to healthy volunteers undergoing elective surgery produced peak blood of 200 to 400 ng/mL 5 min after injection.[7] After either intramuscular or subcutaneous injection, morphine plasma levels peak in 10 to 20 min. In healthy volunteers, a dose of 10 mg/70 kg given intravenously produces a free morphine concentration of 80 ng/mL at 5 min, compared to a peak of 74 ng/mL at 15 min after the same dose was given as an intravenous bolus.[8] In stable patients with cancer receiving sufficient oral morphine to produce acceptable analgesia, the mean trough serum morphine concentration is around 18 ng/mL with roughly equal concentrations of the active metabolite M6G.[9] The half-life of morphine in blood and plasma is 2.7 hours (1.2 to 4.9 hours) and 2.95 hours (1.8 to 5 hours), respectively.[8] The mean clearance is 1.16 L/ min (0.32–1.7 L/min) in the blood and 1.09 L/min

(0.77–1.1 L/min) in the plasma. The high clearance values represent approximately 75% of the hepatic blood flow (HBF), from which it emerges that the main factor in morphine clearance is HBF and not the intrinsic capacity of liver enzymes. Being its clearance is primarily flow-dependent, drugs and environmental factors acting as metabolic inducers do not greatly alter the clearance and half-life of morphine while influencing oral bioavailability.

2.4.10.1.2 Distribution

Morphine is fairly hydrophilic and therefore has a smaller volume of distribution than most commonly used opioids. The apparent volume of distribution at steady state is 2–3 L/kg. The plasma concentration vs time curve is bi- and trixeponential.[10] In humans, in post-mortem examination, the highest concentrations were found in the blood, bile, lungs, and liver.[11] A similar distribution profile was detected in newborns of addict mothers who died 3–5 days after birth.[12]

Entry of the drug into the central nervous system is significantly impeded by the blood-brain barrier; in fact, when morphine is administered intraventricularly, it proves to be up to 900 times more powerful than when administered systemically. Furthermore, the time necessary to obtain the maximum effect is greater for morphine than for other opioids such as pethidine, fentanyl, and methadone, which have a higher lipophilicity. From investigations performed after epidural administration in the treatment of pain in patients with cancer, a linear correlation was found between the dose of morphine and its concentration in both plasma and cerebrospinal fluid (CSF); the mean value of the ratio between plasma and CSF at steady-state is 0.36 +/- 0.07.[13]

Morphine is only 25–35% bound to plasma proteins, so factors that alter this link have a negligible influence on its pharmacodynamic profile. The amount of drug that is found in breast milk is less than 1% of the dose administered to the mother.[14] The withdrawal syndrome that occurs in newborns of addicted mothers is, therefore, most likely caused by intrauterine exposure to opioids. The liver is the major site of morphine metabolism, but despite this, the hepatic excretion of the drug, its clearance, and its volume of distribution in cirrhotic patients deviate only slightly from normal values.[15]

Age is an important factor in determining the effective dose of morphine: the elderly, in fact, show a greater sensitivity to the standard dose of a drug and, although not differing in the peak of analgesic action, show a more protracted response. In the elderly, morphine has a reduced clearance and a smaller volume of distribution, and this results in a higher plasma concentration and a longer duration of action, given the same dose as a young subject.[16]

Because only a small percentage of morphine is excreted unchanged in the urine, renal failure does not modify the metabolism and the elimination of morphine as such, but the accumulation of morphine metabolites, in particular of the active 6-glucoronide metabolite, can occur in renal patients, with consequent prolongation of the opioid effects and risk of intoxication.

2.4.10.1.3 Metabolism and excretion

Morphine is extensively biotransformed both in the liver and in the intestine even before absorption: glucuronide conjugation occurs at the 3- and 6-hydroxyl group of morphine. The 3-glucuronide is the main metabolite (about 45% of the dose), while the 6-glucuronide, quantitatively less (5%) is about 40 times more active than morphine itself. The renal clearance values of 3-glucuronide and 6-glucuronide are 79 ± 32 and 103 ± 47 mL/min, respectively. Other degradation products are normorphine (1-5%), normorphine-3-glucuronide (3%), 3,6-biglucuronide morphine, and morphine-ether-sulfate, and other glucuronides of normorphine. Biliary excretion of metabolites may result in a certain degree of enterohepatic circulation. The elimination of morphine and its metabolites in feces is around 5–10%. Only a small percentage of morphine is excreted unchanged in the urine. M6G is pharmacologically active and exerts important clinical opioid effects, especially when it accumulates in the plasma of patients who have renal failure.

2.4.10.2 Heroin

Heroin, or 3,6-diacetylmorphine, was first synthesized from morphine in 1874 by C.R. Wright, and sold as an antitussive by Bayer in 1898. Under U.S. law, and the laws of many other countries, heroin has no accepted medical use and it is classified as a Schedule 1 drug under the Controlled Substances Act. However, in the UK is classified the same as morphine and is widely used. The addition of two acetyl-ester groups to the morphine molecule produces a more lipophilic compound. Experimental evidence suggests that heroin and morphine may exert their effects via different receptor mechanisms.[17,18]

Heroin is typically administered by intramuscular or intravenous injection but may also be used by nasal insufflation ("snorting") or smoking. Peak heroin concentrations in blood are achieved within 1 to 5 min after intravenous and smoked administration[19] and within 5 min after intranasal and intramuscular administration.[20] Jenkins et al.[19] reported similar pharmacokinetic profiles for the smoked and intravenous routes with mean elimination half-lives of 3.3 and 3.6 min, after smoked and intravenous administration, respectively. In the UK, it is often used in terminal care, where its high solubility allows for continuous, painless subcutaneous administration via a "syringe driver" (a small infusion pump, used to gradually administer small amounts of heroin that is simply applied to the trunk with adhesive). Clinicians have widely accepted its use, but no pharmacokinetic studies have ever been published.

Excluding the "syringe drivers," the mean residence time of heroin was less than 10 min after all doses by all other routes Cone et al.[20] reported that the pharmacokinetic profile of intranasal heroin was equivalent to that for the intramuscular route but the relative potency of intranasal heroin was estimated to be approximately one half that of intramuscular administration. Mean elimination half-lives were determined to be 0.09 ± 0.05, 0.07 ± 0.02, and 0.13 ± 0.07 (hours plus or minus SD), following

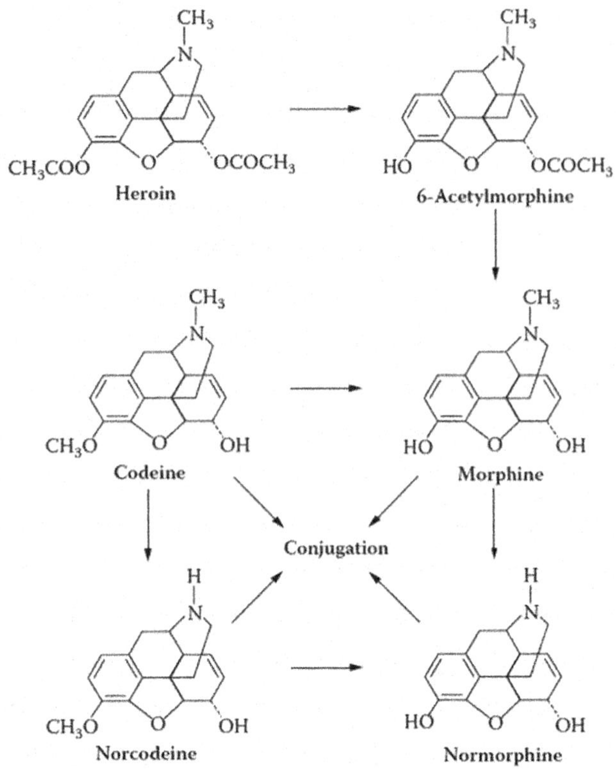

FIGURE 2.4.8 Metabolic pathway of heroin and morphine

intranasal administration of 6 mg and 12 mg, and intramuscular administration of 6 mg of heroin, respectively. Heroin may also be administered orally but hydrolysis in the gastrointestinal tract and loss due to first pass metabolism result in slow and inefficient delivery to the brain.

It is known from in vitro studies that heroin is rapidly deacetylated to an active metabolite, 6-Acetyl Morphine (6-AM), which is then hydrolyzed to morphine (see Figure 2.4.8). Spontaneous hydrolysis to 6-AM may occur under various conditions (base-catalyzed hydrolysis, presence of protic compounds such as ethanol, methanol, and aqueous media). Because cleavage of the first hydroxyl group occurs so rapidly, detection of 6-AM is, of course, solid forensic evidence of heroin use immediately prior to death.

Following low dose administration of 10 mg heroin hydrochloride, no heroin or 6-acetylmorphine was detected in blood[21] and peak morphine concentrations ranging from 2 ng/mL to 15 ng/mL (mean = 8 ng/mL, n = 6) were achieved 7.5 min to 4 h after drug administration. Girardin et al.[22] administered heroin by three different routes to eight heroin addicts. The intramuscular route demonstrated linear pharmacokinetics for heroin and the metabolites 6-acetylmorphine (6-AM) and morphine. The oral route resulted in low blood concentrations of heroin and 6-AM but linear kinetics for morphine and its glucuronides.

Following intravenous infusion of 70 mg of heroin to human volunteers, 45% of the dose was recovered in urine after 40 h. More than 38% was recovered as conjugated morphine, approximately 4% as free morphine, 1% as 6-acetylmorphine, and 0.1% as heroin. Urinary elimination half-lives of 0.6, 4.4, and 7.9 h were reported for 6-AM, morphine, and conjugated morphine, respectively, after administration of 6 mg of heroin by the intramuscular route.[22]

Heroin is often contaminated with levamisole. The U.S. FDA reported that in 2008 2009, nearly 70% of all confiscated samples of heroin were levamisole contaminated. Levamisole is metabolized to aminorex that is known to cause pulmonary hypertension,[26,27] and cases of pulmonary hypertension have been reported in known, chronic, heroin abusers. Perhaps more important is the association between levamisole and agranulocytosis, neutropenia, and vasculitis.[23–25] Just why levamisole is added remains an open question. Some have speculated that it may improve the sense of euphoria provided by heroin. There is little or no evidence to support this claim and

2.4.10.3 Methadone

Methadone is a synthetic, potent opioid agonist, with predominant actions at the μ receptor level. The analgesic activity of the racemic compound is almost entirely due to the Levorotatory isomer, which is at least ten times more powerful as an analgesic than the Dextrorotatory isomer. The D-isomer does not cause significant respiratory depression, but has antitussive effects. Methadone also has some agonist actions at κ and δ opioid receptors. These actions lead to analgesia, respiratory depression, suppression of cough, nausea and vomiting (via an effect on the chemoreceptor trigger zone), and constipation. Methadone has an effect on the oculomotor nerve nucleus, and perhaps on the opioid receptors in the pupillary muscles causing miosis. Methadone also increases the tone of smooth muscle in the lower gastrointestinal tract while decreasing the amplitude of contractions. All these effects are reversible with naloxone, with a value of PA2 similar to its anti-morphine antagonism. Like many alkaline substances, methadone enters mast cells and releases histamine via a non-immunological mechanism, which also explains why heroin users often experience intense purities with excoriations of the chest.[28] It causes a dependency syndrome similar to that of morphine, which is why it is often used in substitution therapy for the heroin-addicted. In addition, it is used clinically for the treatment of severe pain, especially in those with chronic pain syndromes.

2.4.10.4 Absorption

Methadone is one of the most liposoluble opioids and is well absorbed in the gastrointestinal tract, but undergoes a fairly extensive first-pass metabolism. Methadone is typically administered orally, with peak blood concentrations occurring after 4 h. Bioavailability is over 80%. Steady-state concentrations are reached within 5–7 days. Inturrisi and Verebely[30] reported a peak plasma concentration of 75 ng/mL at 4 h after a single 15 mg oral dose. Concentrations declined slowly, with a half-life of 15 h, reaching 30 ng/mL by 24 h. Peak plasma concentrations (mean = 830 ng/mL) after 4 h were also observed with chronic oral administration of 100 to 200 mg/day. Concentrations of methadone reach a maximum in brain tissue approximately 1 to 2 h after an oral dose.[30]

2.4.10.5 Distribution

The pharmacokinetics of methadone are unusual because there is an extensive link to tissue proteins, and a rather slow transfer between some parts of this tissue reserve and plasma. Methadone binds to albumin and other plasma proteins (87%), as well as to tissue proteins (probably lipoproteins). Methadone distributes rapidly to tissues, especially the lungs, liver, kidneys, and spleen. Pulmonary, hepatic, and renal concentrations are much higher than those in blood. The volume of distribution is 4 to 5 L/kg. Methadone is secreted in sweat and can be found in saliva, breast milk, and umbilical cord blood.

2.4.10.6 Metabolism and excretion

Methadone metabolism is primarily catalyzed by CYP3A4, but CYP2D6 and CYP2B6 are also involved to a lesser extent.[31] Metabolism occurs predominantly by N-demethylation and cyclization, which produces the main metabolites: 2-ethylidine-1,5-dimethyl-3,3-diphenylpyrrolidine (EDDP) and 2-ethyl-5-methyl-3,3-diphenyl-1-pyrrolidine (EMDP), both of which are inactive. To some extent, methanol hydroxylation also occurs through N-demethylation, with the formation of normetadol. Other metabolic reactions are also possible, and at least eight other metabolites are known.[32]

Because methadone is manufactured as a racemic mixture, users are exposed to the D form of methadone, even though it is largely inactive.[33,34] Unlike the L form, the D form binds to, and can completely blocks, the hERG potassium channel, leading to QT interval prolongation and, occasionally sudden cardiac death. This only occurs when the concentration of the D form is quite high, and that only occurs when the user is polymorphic for CYP2B6 (i.e., *slow metabolizers*).[35]

The half-life after a single oral dose is 12–18 hours (15 on average), partly reflecting the distribution in tissue deposits, as well as the metabolic and renal clearance. With regular dosing the tissue reserve is already partially filled. The result is a prolongation of the half-life to 13–47 hours (25 on average) reflecting only clearance. Methadone and related metabolites are excreted to various degrees via the fecal and urinary routes. The excretion of methadone is greatly enhanced by the acidification of urine. About 30% of the dose is eliminated in the feces, but this percentage is normally reduced with the highest doses. Approximately 75% of the total drug eliminated is in the non-conjugated form. Large individual variations in the urine excretion of methadone are observed depending on urine volume and pH, the dose, and rate of metabolism. Acidification of the urine may increase the urinary output of methadone from 5% to 22%.[37] Typically, following a 5 mg oral dose, methadone and EDDP account for 5% of the dose in the 24-h urine. In those individuals on maintenance therapy, methadone may account for 5% to 50% of the dose in the 24-h urine and EDDP may account for 3% to 25% of the dose. D- and L-methadone and EDDP have been reported in saliva and methadone in human breast milk.[38]

2.4.10.7 Oxycodone

Oxycodone is a semisynthetic opioid derived from thebaine and used for oral pain relief.[39] It is commonly formulated as an immediate-release medication or a controlled-release oxycodone formulation that provides controlled drug delivery over 12 h.[40] The oral bioavailability of this formulation is 60% to 87%. Compared to morphine, which has an absolute bioavailability of about 30%, oxycodone has an absolute high bioavailability of up to 87% after oral administration.[41] It has an elimination half-life of about 3 hours and is metabolized mainly to nor-oxycodone and oxymorphone. Oxymorphone has a certain analgesic activity, but is present in plasma at such low concentrations it is not thought to contribute to the pharmacological effect of oxycodone. The results of clinical studies of patients with postoperative and cancer pain show that oxycodone has a potency 1.5 times that of morphine.

The relative bioavailability of oxycodone prolonged-release tablets is comparable to that of rapid-release oxycodone, with maximum plasma concentrations reached approximately 3 hours after taking the prolonged-release tablets, compared to 1–1.5 hours with the immediate-release form.[42] Maximum plasma concentrations and fluctuations of oxycodone concentrations from prolonged-release and rapid-release formulations are comparable, when given at the same daily dose, at 12 and six-hour intervals, respectively.[40,42] A high-fat meal consumed prior to tablet intake does not affect the maximum concentration or extent of absorption of oxycodone. After a 10-mg oral dose of the immediate-release formulation, peak plasma concentrations ranged from 13 ng/mL to 46 ng/mL (mean = 30 ng/mL, n = 12).[41] In a study of 28 adults, the administration of 20 mg of the prolonged-release formulation, resulted in an average peak plasma concentration of 23 ng/mL.[43] The plasma half-life has been reported to be 4 to 6 h with a volume of distribution of 1.8 to 3.7 L/kg.[43]

Oxycodone is metabolized in the liver by the cytochrome P450 isozymes and the elimination half-life is prolonged in individuals with liver disease, such as cirrhosis. Metabolism by O- and N-demethylation produces the metabolites oxymorphone and noroxycodone.[44] The O-demethylated metabolite, oxymorphone, is a μ receptor agonist.[45] Both the O- and N-demethylated forms are then conjugated with glucuronic acid. CYP2D6 metabolizes oxycodone and is encoded by a polymorphic gene with three mutations (*3, *4, and *5) with a combined 95% allelic frequency and approximately 10% prevalence. Less than 65% of a single dose is excreted in the urine over a period of 24 h with 13 to 19% comprising free oxycodone.

2.4.10.8 Hydrocodone

Hydrocodone is a semisynthetic opioid derived from codeine,[46] registered in some countries as an analgesic/

antitussive and available for oral administration, often in combination with acetaminophen or ibuprofen, but most hydrocodone is prescribed predominantly within the United States. It acts as a selective agonist of the μ-opioid receptor. Hydrocodone has a low affinity for the δ-opioid receptor and the κ-opioid receptor. Studies have shown hydrocodone is stronger than codeine but only one-tenth as potent as morphine at binding to receptors and is reported to be only 59% as potent as morphine as an analgesic.[47] However, in tests conducted on rhesus monkeys, the analgesic potency of hydrocodone was actually higher than morphine. As with oxycodone, the possibility exists that some of its ability to relieve pain may actually derive from its active metabolites.[48] Oral hydrocodone has a mean equivalent daily dosage factor of 0.4, meaning that 1 mg of hydrocodone is equivalent to 0.4 mg of intravenous morphine. However, because of morphine's low oral bioavailability, there is a 1:1 correspondence between orally administered morphine and orally administered hydrocodone.

2.4.10.8.1 Absorption

Hydrocodone is legally sold only as an oral medication. It is well-absorbed, but its oral bioavailability is only approximately 25%. The onset of action of hydrocodone via this route is 10 to 20 minutes, with a peak effect (Tmax) occurring at 30 to 60 minutes, and it has a duration of four to eight hours.[49]

2.4.10.8.2 Distribution

The volume of distribution of hydrocodone is 3.3 to 4.7 L/kg. The plasma protein binding of hydrocodone is 20% to 50%.[48]

2.4.10.8.3 Metabolism and Excretion

Hydrocodone, once it has reached the liver is transformed into several metabolites including norhydrocodone, hydromorphone, 6α-hydrocodol (dihydrocodeine), and 6β-hydrocodol 6α- and 6β-hydromorphone and all of them are conjugated (via glucuronidation).[50] Hydrocodone has a terminal half-life that averages 3.8 hours (range 3.3–4.4 hours). The hepatic cytochrome P450 enzyme CYP2D6 converts hydrocodone into hydromorphone, a more potent opioid (5-fold higher binding affinity to that of MOR)[51] However, extensive and poor cytochrome 450 CYP2D6 metabolizers had similar physiological and subjective responses to hydrocodone, and CYP2D6 inhibitor quinidine did not change the responses of extensive metabolizers, suggesting that inhibition of CYP2D6 metabolism of hydrocodone has no practical importance.[52,53] Ultra-rapid CYP2D6 metabolizers (1–2% of the population) may have an increased response to hydrocodone[54]; however, hydrocodone metabolism in this population has not been studied.[53]

Norhydrocodone, the major metabolite of hydrocodone, is predominantly formed by CYP3A4-catalyzed oxidation. In contrast to hydromorphone, it is described as inactive.[53] However, norhydrocodone is actually a MOR agonist with similar potency to hydrocodone, but has been found to produce only minimal analgesia when administered peripherally to animals (likely due to poor blood-brain-barrier and, thus, central nervous system penetration). Inhibition of CYP3A4 in a child who was, in addition, a poor CYP2D6 metabolizer, resulted in a fatal overdose of hydrocodone. Approximately 40% of hydrocodone metabolism is attributed to non-cytochrome P450-catalyzed reactions. Hydrocodone is excreted in urine, mainly in the form of conjugates.[55]

2.4.10.9 Buprenorphine

Buprenorphine is a semisynthetic opiate derived from thebaine, a partial opioid agonist/antagonist that binds to the μ (mu) and κ (kappa) receptors of the brain.[67] It is a partial mu agonist with kappa antagonist activity. Buprenorphine has 25 to 50 times the potency of morphine. Effects of buprenorphine last longer because it is released more slowly from mu receptors than morphine. It is available as an injectable for intramuscular or intravenous administration for the relief of moderate to severe pain[68]. It is also available to treat opioid dependence in the formulation of a sublingual (SL) tablet, alone or in combination with naloxone, in 2 or 8 mg doses;[69,70] the recommended sublingual daily dose is 12 to 16 mg/day.

Pharmacological effects occur within 15 min of IM administration, peaking at approximately 1 h and persisting for up to 6 h; after an intravenous dose of 0.3 mg, plasma concentrations are typically less than 1 ng/mL. After SL administration, peak pharmacological effects typically occur after 100 min. Sublingual maintenance therapy of 8 mg/day resulted in plasma buprenorphine concentrations of 1 to 8 ng/mL.[69,71] Its action in the maintenance treatment against opioids is attributed to its slowly reversible binding with the μ receptors that, over a long period of time, minimizes the need for drugs in an opiate-dependent patient.[71] During clinical pharmacology studies in subjects with opioid dependence, buprenorphine demonstrated a roof effect on several parameters including positive mood, "good effect" and respiratory depression.[72,73]

2.4.10.9.1 Absorption

Taken orally, buprenorphine undergoes hepatic first pass metabolism with N-dealkylation and glucuroconjugation in the small intestine. The use of this medicine orally is therefore inappropriate. Peak plasma concentrations are reached 90 minutes after sublingual administration and the maximum dose-to-concentration ratio is linear, between 2 mg, 75 and 16 mg. Buprenorphine is approximately 96% plasma protein bound, primarily to α - and β –globulin.[74,75]

2.4.10.9.2 Distribution

Absorption of buprenorphine is followed by a rapid distribution phase and a half-life of two to five hours, with a volume of distribution of 2.5 L/kg.[75]

2.4.10.9.3 Metabolism and excretion

Buprenorphine is metabolized by an oxidative route through 14-N-dealkylation to N-desalchyl-buprenorphine (also known as norbuprenorphine) by cytochrome P450 CYP3A4, and by glucuroconjugation of the parent molecule and the dealkylated metabolite.[76] Norbuprenorphine is a μ (mu) receptor agonist with weak intrinsic activity. This metabolite and parent drug are both subject to glucuronidation[77,78] The elimination of buprenorphine is bi- or tri-exponential, with a long phase of terminal elimination ranging from 20 to 25 hours, partly explained by the reabsorption of buprenorphine after intestinal hydrolysis of the conjugated derivative, and partly with the highly lipophilic nature of the molecule. Buprenorphine is essentially eliminated in the feces by biliary excretion of the glucuroconjugate metabolites (80%), while the remainder is eliminated in the urine.[77,78]

2.4.10.10 Tramadol

Tramadol is a centrally acting opioid analgesic. It is a pure non-selective agonist of μ, δ e κ receptors.[79] Other mechanisms contributing to its analgesic effect are the inhibition of neuronal re-uptake of noradrenaline and an increase in serotonin release. It is useful for treating acute and chronic pain of medium and severe intensity, of different origins, as well as in pain induced by diagnostic and surgical interventions. Tramadol also has an antitussive effect. In contrast to morphine, tramadol has no depressive effects on respiration when administered in the range of analgesic doses. Equally, it does not affect gastrointestinal motility. The effects on the cardiovascular system tend to be mild. Tramadol's pain-relieving power is from 1/10 to 1/6 that of morphine. There are two enantiomers, and both contribute to pain relief, but via different mechanisms. (+)-Tramadol and its metabolite (+)-O-desmethyl-tramadol, which is referred to as M1, are agonists of the μ opioid receptor. (+)-Tramadol inhibits serotonin reuptake while (–)-tramadol inhibits norepinephrine reuptake.[80] This latter action enhances the inhibitory effects on pain transmission in the spinal cord. Because the actions of the two enantiomers are complementary, they are usually supplied as a racemic mixture. However, because it is a serotonin-reuptake blocker, interaction with other medications can lead to the occurrence of serotoninergic syndrome.[81] Tramadol is available as drops, capsules, and sustained-release formulations for oral use, suppositories for rectal use, and solutions for intramuscular, intravenous, and subcutaneous injection.

2.4.10.10.1 Absorption

Tramadol is readily absorbed; after single oral administration, the plasma peak is reached within one to two hours. Sustained-release tablets release the active ingredient over a period of 12 h, reach peak concentrations after 4.9 h and have a bioavailability of 87% to 95% compared with capsules. One 100 mg dose given to healthy volunteers resulted in plasma levels of 375 ng/mL at 1.5 h.[82,83]

The relationship between serum concentrations and analgesic effect is dose-dependent, however with considerable variations from case to case. A serum concentration of 100–300 ng/mL is usually effective.

2.4.10.10.2 Distribution

Tramadol has a high affinity for tissues (Vd, $\beta = 203 \pm 40$ l). Plasma protein binding is about 20%. Tramadol passes the blood-brain barrier and the placental barrier. Very small amounts of the substance and its O-desmethyl-derivative are found in breast milk[84,85] (0.1% and 0.02% depending on the dose administered).

2.4.10.10.3 Metabolism and excretion

Tramadol is metabolized in humans essentially by N- and O- demethylation and conjugation of the O-demethylated products with glucuronic acid and sulfuric acid. The O-demethylation of tramadol to M1, the main analgesic effective metabolite, is catalyzed by cytochrome P450 (CYP) 2D6, whereas N-demethylation to M2 is catalyzed by CYP2B6 and CYP3A4. Only O-desmethyltramadol is pharmacologically active.[84] From the quantitative point of view, there are significant inter-individual differences for the other metabolites. Eleven urinary metabolites have been identified so far. Animal testing has shown that O-desmethyltramadol is 2-4 times more potent than the parent substance. Its half-life (in 6 healthy volunteers) was 7.9 h (5.4 to 9.6 h) and approximately equal to that of tramadol.[83]

Inhibition of one or both of the CYP3A4 and CYP2D6 isoenzymes involved in tramadol biotransformation may alter the plasma concentration of tramadol or its active metabolite. The wide variability in the pharmacokinetic properties of tramadol can partly be ascribed to CYP polymorphism. O- and N-demethylation of tramadol as well as renal stereoselective elimination Pharmacokinetic–pharmacodynamic characterization of tramadol is difficult because of differences between tramadol concentrations in plasma and at the site of action, and because of pharmacodynamic interactions between the two enantiomers of tramadol and its active metabolites.[86]

The elimination of tramadol and its metabolites occurs almost completely by the renal route. Cumulative urinary excretion is 90% of the total radioactivity of the administered dose. The elimination half-life t ½ β is about 6 h, regardless of the route of administration. In patients over 75, it may increase by approximately 1.4x. Elimination half-lives of 13.3 ± 4.9 h (tramadol) and 18.5 ± 9.4 h (O-desmethyltramadol), with a maximum value of 22.3 h and 36 h, were determined in patients with cirrhosis of the liver. In patients with renal insufficiency (creatinine clearance < 5 ml/min), the values were 11 ± 3.2 h and 16.9 ± 3 h, with a maximum value of 19.5 and 43.2 h, respectively.[83]

2.4.10.11 Hydromorphone

Registered in the U.S. and other countries as a medicinal drug, hydromorphone is a semisynthetic opiate differing from morphine only by the presence of a 6-keto group, and the hydrogenation of the double bond at the 7–8 position.[87] It is active primarily at the mu opioid receptors, and to a lesser degree at delta receptors, sharing common pharmacologic properties with other opioid analgesics. Its effects include changes in the CNS, including increased cerebrospinal fluid pressure, increased biliary pressure, and increased parasympathetic activity. It can also produce transient hyperglycemia. Depending on the country where the drug is manufactured, a number of different time-release preparations are available.

Hydromorphone is well absorbed from the small intestine and is extensively metabolized in the liver,[88] mainly to 3-glucuronide which is devoid of analgesic effect, but can cause significant neuroexcitation. It undergoes extensive first pass metabolism (62%), accounting for its relatively low bioavailability. A single 8 mg dose of hydromorphone yields blood concentrations of approximately 2 ng/mL, while a 12 mg time-release formulation gives plasma concentrations half as high.[89,90]

REFERENCES

1. Anon., The opium alkaloids, *Bull Narcotics*, 19, 13–14, 1963.
2. Hann, V. and P. Chazot, G-proteins, *Curr Anaesth Crit Care*, 15(1), 79–81, 2004.
3. Bodnar, R.J. and G.E. Klein, Endogenous opiates and behavior: 2003, *Peptides*, 25(12), 2205–56, 2004.
4. Evans, C.J., Secrets of the opium poppy revealed, *Neuropharmacology*, 47(Suppl. 1), 293–99, 2004.
5. Skaer, T.L., Practice guidelines for transdermal opioids in malignant pain, *Drugs*, 64(23), 2629–38, 2004.
6. Morley, J.E., Anorexia of aging: physiologic and pathologic, *Am J Clin Nutr*, 66(4), 760–73, 1997.
7. Berkowitz, B.A., S.H. Ngai, J.C. Yang, J. Hempstead, et al., The disposition of morphine in surgical patients, *Clin Pharmacol Ther*, 17(6), 629–35, 1975.
8. Stuart-Harris, R., S.P. Joel, P. McDonald, D. Currow, et al., The pharmacokinetics of morphine and morphine glucuronide metabolites after subcutaneous bolus injection and subcutaneous infusion of morphine, *Br J Clin Pharmacol*, 49(3), 207–14, 2000.
9. Klepstad, P., S. Kaasa and P.C. Borchgrevink, Start of oral morphine to cancer patients: effective serum morphine concentrations and contribution from morphine-6-glucuronide to the analgesia produced by morphine, *Eur J Clin Pharmacol*, 55(10), 713–9, 2000.
10. Drost, R.H., T.I. Ionescu, J.M. van Rossum and R.A. Maes, Pharmacokinetics of morphine after epidural administration in man, *Arzneimittelforschung*, 36(7), 1096–100, 1986.
11. Drummer, O.H., Postmortem toxicology of drugs of abuse, *Forensic Sci Int*, 142(2–3), 101–13, 2004.
12. Baselt, R.C. and R.H. Cravey, *Disposition of Toxic Drugs and Chemicals in Man*, 4th ed. Chemical Toxicology Institute, Foster City, CA, 1995.
13. Wolff, T., H. Samuelsson and T. Hedner, Concentrations of morphine and morphine metabolites in CSF and plasma during continuous subcutaneous morphine administration in cancer pain patients, *Pain*, 68(2–3), 209–16, 1996.
14. D'Apolito, K., Breastfeeding and substance abuse, *Clin Obstet Gynecol*, 56(1), 202–11, 2013.
15. Hasselström, J., S. Eriksson, A. Persson, A. Rane and J.O. Svensson, Säwe the metabolism and bioavailability of morphine in patients with severe liver cirrhosis, *J Br J Clin Pharmacol*, 29(3), 289–97, 1990.
16. Villesen, H.H., A.-M. Banning, R.H. Petersen, S. Weinelt, J.B. Poulsen, S.H. Hansen and L. Lona, Christrup pharmacokinetics of morphine and oxycodone following intravenous administration in elderly patients, *Ther Clin Risk Manag*, 3(5), 961–7, 2007.
17. Rady, J.J., A.E. Takemori, P.S. Portoghese and J.M. Fujimoto, Supraspinal delta receptor subtype activity of heroin and 6-monoacetylmorphine in Swiss Webster mice, *Life Sci*, 55(8), 603–9, 1994.
18. Gilbert, A.K., S. Hosztafi, L. Mahurter and G.W. Pasternak, Pharmacological characterization of dihydromorphine, 6-acetyldihydromorphine and dihydroheroin analgesia and their differentiation from morphine, *Eur J Pharmacol*, 492(2–3), 123–30, 2004.
19. Jenkins, A.J., R.M. Keenan, J.E. Henningfield and E.J. Cone, Pharmacokinetics and pharmacodynamics of smoked heroin, *J Anal Toxicol*, 18(6), 317–30, 1994.
20. Cone, E.J., B.A. Holicky, T.M. Grant, W.D. Darwin, et al., Pharmacokinetics and pharmacodynamics of intranasal "snorted" heroin, *J Anal Toxicol*, 17(6), 327–37, 1993.
21. Jenkins, A.J., B.A. Holicky, T.M. Grant, W.D. Darwin, et al., Blood concentrations and pharmacological effects after oral heroin administration, paper presented at society of Forensic toxicologists, *The International Association of Forensic Toxicologists, Joint Conference* (October 1994), abstr. 127, 1994.
22. Girardin, F., K.M. Rentsch, M.A. Schwab, M. Maggiorini, et al., Pharmacokinetics of high doses of intramuscular and oral heroin in narcotic addicts, *Clin Pharmacol Ther*, 74(4), 341–52, 2003.
23. Karch, S.B., F. Mari, V. Bartolini and E. Bertol, Aminorex poisoning in cocaine abusers, *Int J Cardiol*, 158(3), 344–6, 2012.
24. Bertol, E., F. Mari, M.G. Milia, L. Politi, S. Furlanetto and S.B. Karch. Determination of aminorex in human urine samples by GC-MS after use of levamisole, *J Pharm Biomed Anal*, 55(5), 1186–9, 2011.
25. Srivastava, R., M. Rizwan, M. Jamil, et al., Agranulocytosis – sequelae of chronic cocaine use: case series and literature review, *Cureus*, 9(5), e1221, 2017.
26. Chang, A., J. Osterloh and J. Thomas, Levamisole: a dangerous new cocaine adulterant, *Clin Pharmacol Ther*, 88, 408–11, 2010.
27. Chai, P.R., W. Bastan, J. Machan, J.B. Hack and K.M. Babu, Levamisole exposure and hematologic indices in cocaine users, *Acad Emerg Med*, 18, 1141–7, 2011.
28. Karch, S., *The Pathology of Drug Abuse*, 5th Edition, CRC Press, 2016.
29. Toce, M.S., P.R. Chai, M.M. Burns and E.W. Boyer, Pharmacologic treatment of opioid use disorder: a review of pharmacotherapy, adjuncts, and toxicity, *J Med Toxicol*, 14(4), 306–22, 2018.
30. Chamberlain, N., Patterns of drug use in dependent opioid users in methadone treatment, *NZ Med J*, 110(1047), 258–9, 1997.
31. Inturrisi, C.E. and K. Verebely, Disposition of methadone in man after a single oral dose, *Clin Pharmacol Ther*, 13(6), 923–30, 1972.
32. Projean, D., P.E. Morin, T.M. Tu and J. Ducharme, Identification of CYP3A4 and CYP2C8 as the major cytochrome P450s responsible for morphine N-demethylation in human liver microsomes, *Xenobiotica*, 33(8), 841–54, 2003.

33. Shiran, M.R., J. Chowdry, A. Rostami-Hodjegan, S.W. Ellis, et al., A discordance between cytochrome P450 2D6 genotype and phenotype in patients undergoing methadone maintenance treatment, *Br J Clin Pharmacol*, 56(2), 220–4, 2003.
34. Rosas, M.E., K.L. Preston, D.H. Epstein, E.T. Moolchan, et al., Quantitative determination of the enantiomers of methadone and its metabolite (EDDP) in human saliva by enantioselective liquid chromatography with mass spectrometric detection, *J Chromatogr B Anal Technol Biomed LifeSci*, 796(2), 355–70, 2003.
35. Karch, S.B. and O. Drummer, Methadone toxicokinetics, in *Karch's Pathology of Drug Abuse*, 5th edition, CRC Press/Taylor and Frances, London, 2016.
36. Huh, B. and C.H. Parck, Retrospectivie analysis of low dose- methadone and QT prolongation in chronic pain partients, *Korean Journal Anesthesiology*, 58(4), 338–43, 2010.
37. Lugo, R.A., K.L. Satterfield and S.E. Kern, Pharmacokinetics of methadone, *J Pain Palliat Care Pharmacother*, 19(4), 13–24, 2005.
38. McCarthy, J.J. and B.L. Posey, Methadone levels in human milk, *J Hum Lact*, 16(2), 115–20, 2000.
39. Kalso, E., Oxycodone, *J Pain Symptom Manage.*, 29(5 Suppl.), S47–56, 2005.
40. Davis, M.P., J. Varga, D. Dickerson, D. Walsh, et al., Normal-release and controlled-release oxycodone: pharmacokinetics, pharmacodynamics, and controversy, *Support. Care Cancer*, 11(2), 84–92, 2003.
41. Beaver, W.T., S.L. Wallenstein, R.W. Houde and A. Rogers, Comparisons of the analgesic effects of oral and intramuscular oxymorphone and of intramuscular oxymorphone and morphine in patients with cancer, *J Clin Pharmacol*, 17(4), 186–98, 1977.
42. Smith, K., M. Hopp, G. Mundin, P. Leyendecker, P. Bailey, B. Grothe, R. Uhl and K. Reimer, Single- and multiple-dose pharmacokinetic evaluation of oxycodone and naloxone in an opioid agonist/antagonist prolonged-release combination in healthy adult volunteers, *Clin Ther*, 30(11), 2051–68, 2008.
43. Bass, A., J.G. Stark, G.C. Pixton, K.W. Sommerville, C.A. Zamora, M. Leibowitz and R. Rolleri, Dose proportionality and the effects of food on bioavailability of an immediate-release oxycodone hydrochloride tablet designed to discourage tampering and its relative bioavailability compared with a marketed oxycodone tablet under fed conditions: a single-dose, randomized, open-label, 5-way crossover study in healthy volunteers. *Clin Ther*, 2012, 34(7), 1601–12.
44. Chen, Z.R., R.J. Irvine, A.A. Somogyi and F. Bochner, Mu receptor binding of some commonly used opioids and their metabolites, *Life Sci*, 48(22), 2165–71, 1991.
45. Lotsch, J., Opioid metabolites, *J Pain Symptom Manage*, 29(5 Suppl.), S10–24, 2005.
46. Dhillon, S., Hydrocodone bitartrate ER (Hysingla® ER): a review in chronic pain, *Clin Drug Investig*, 2016;36(11), 969–980.
47. Davis, M.P., P. Glare and J. Hardy, *Opioids in Cancer Pain*, Oxford University Press, 2005, pp. 59–68.
48. Vallejo, R., R.L. Barkin and V.C. Wang, Pharmacology of opioids in the treatment of chronic pain syndromes, *Pain Physician*, 14(4), E343–60, 2011.
49. Abi-Aad, K.R. and A. Derian, *Hydromorphone. StatPearls* [Internet]. Treasure Island, FL: StatPearls Publishing, 2018.
50. Chen, Z.R., R.J. Irvine, A.A. Somogyi and F. Bochner, Mu receptor binding of some commonly used opioids and their metabolites. *Life Sci*, 48(22), 2165–71, 1991.
51. Zhou, S., *Cytochrome P450 2D6: Structure, Function, Regulation and Polymorphism*, CRC Press, 2016, p. 164.
52. Kaplan, H.L., U.E. Busto, G.J. Baylon, S.W. Cheung, S.V. Otton, G. Somer and E.M. Sellers, Inhibition of cytochrome P450 2D6 metabolism of hydrocodone to hydromorphone does not importantly affect abuse liability, *J Pharmacol Exp Ther*, 281(1), 103–8.
53. Dasgupta, A. and L.J. Langman, *Pharmacogenomics of Alcohol and Drugs of Abuse*, CRC Press, 2012, p. 175.
54. Monte, A.A., K.J. Heard, J. Campbell, D. Hamamura, R.M. Weinshilboum and V. Vasiliou, The effect of CYP2D6 drug-drug interactions on hydrocodone effectiveness, *Acad Emerg Med*, 21(8), 879–85, 2014.
55. Karch, S.B., *Pharmacokinetics and Pharmacodynamics of Abused Drugs*, CRC Press, 2007, p. 56.
56. NIDA, Fentanyl, 2016, June 6, Retrieved from https://www.drugabuse.gov/drugs-abuse/fentanyl Accessed December 29, 2018.
57. Darwish, M., M. Kirby, P. Robertson Jr, W. Tracewell and J.G. Jiang, Absolute and relative bioavailability of fentanyl buccal tablet and oral transmucosal fentanyl citrate, *J Clin Pharmacol*, 47(3), 343–50, 2007.
58. Mystakidou, K., E. Katsouda, E. Parpa, L. Vlahos, M.L. Tsiatas, Oral transmucosal fentanyl citrate: overview of pharmacological and clinical characteristics. *Drug Deliv*, 13(4), 269–76, 2006.
59. Park, J.H., J.H. Kim, S.C. Yun, S.W. Roh, S.C. Rhim, C.J. Kim, et al., Evaluation of efficacy and safety of fentanyl transdermal patch (Durogesic D-TRANS) in chronic pain, *Acta Neurochir (Wien)*, 153(1), 181–90, 2011.
60. Lane, M.E., The transdermal delivery of fentanyl, *Eur J Pharm Biopharm*, 84(3), 449–55, 2013.
61. FDA, Official duragesic full prescribing information, *Archived from the Original (PDF)*, https://www.accessdata.fda.gov/drugsatfda_docs/label/2018/019813s072s073lbl.pdf#page=48, Accessed December 29, 2018.
62. O'Donnell, J., R.M. Gladden, C.L. Mattson and M. Kariisa. Notes from the field: overdose deaths with carfentanil and other fentanyl analogs detected — 10 States, July 2016–June 2017, *MMWR Morb Mortal Wkly Rep*, 67, 767–8, 2018. http://dx.doi.org/10.15585/mmwr.mm6727a4.
63. Shanks, K.G. and G.S. Behonick, Detection of carfentanil by LC-MS-MS and reports of associated fatalities in the USA, *J Anal Toxicol*, 41(6), 466–72, 2017.
64. Frost, J.J., K.H. Douglass, H.S. Mayberg, R.F. Dannals, J.M. Links, A.A. Wilson, H.T. Ravert, W.C. Crozier and H.N. Wagner Jr., Multicompartmental analysis of [11C]-carfentanil binding to opiate receptors in humans measured by positron emission tomography, *J Cereb Blood Flow Metab*, 9(3), 398–409, 1989.
65. Frost, J.J., H.N. Wagner Jr, R.F. Dannals, H.T. Ravert, J.M. Links, A.A. Wilson, H.D. Burns, D.F. Wong, R.W. McPherson, A.E. Rosenbaum et al., Imaging opiate receptors in the human brain by positron tomography, *J Comput Assist Tomogr*, 9(2), 231–6, 1985.
66. Fishman, M.A. and P.S. Kim, Buprenorphine for chronic pain: a systemic review, *Curr Pain Headache Rep*, 22(12), 83, 2018.
67. Stock, C. and J.H. Shum, Buprenorphine: a new pharmacotherapy for opioid addictions treatment, *J Pain Palliat Care Pharmacother*, 18(3), 35–54, 2004.

68. Walsh, S.L., P.A. Nuzzo, S. Babalonis, V. Casselton and M.R. Lofwall, Intranasal buprenorphine alone and in combination with naloxone: abuse liability and reinforcing efficacy in physically dependent opioid abusers, *Drug Alcohol Depend*, 162, 190–8, 2016.
69. Elkader, A. and B. Sproule, Buprenorphine: clinical pharmacokinetics in the treatment of opioid dependence, *Clinical Pharmacokinetics*, 44, 661–80, 2005.
70. Wesson, D.R., Buprenorphine in the treatment of opiate dependence: its pharmacology and social context of use in the U.S., *J Psychoactive Drugs*, Suppl 2, 119–28, 2004.
71. Haasen, C. et al., Pharmacokinetics and pharmacodynamics of a buprenorphine subcutaneous depot formulation (CAM2038) for once-weekly dosing in patients with opioid use disorder, *J Subst Abuse Treat*, 78, 22–9.
72. Serafini, G., G. Adavastro, G. Canepa, D. De Berardis, A. Valchera, M. Pompili, H. Nasrallah and M. Amore, The efficacy of buprenorphine in major depression, treatment-resistant depression and suicidal behavior: a systematic review, *Int J Mol Sci*, 19(8), 2018, Epub 2018 Aug 15.
73. Perez de los Cobos, J., S. Martin, A. Etcheberrigaray, J. Trujols, et al., A controlled trial of daily versus thrice-weekly buprenorphine administration for the treatment of opioid dependence, *Drug Alcohol Depend*, 59(3), 223–33, 2000.
74. Nanovskaya, T.N., R.S. Bowen, S.L. Patrikeeva, G.D. Hankins and M.S. Ahmed, Effect of plasma proteins on buprenorphine transfer across dually perfused placental lobule. *J Mat-Fetal Neonat Med*, 22(8), 646–53, 2009.
75. Kuhlman, J.J., S. Lalani, J. Magluillo, et al., Human pharmokinetics of intravenous, sublingual, and buccal buprenorphine, *J Clin Pharmacol*, 37, 31–7, 1997.
76. Kalluri, H.V., H. Zhang, S.N. Caritis and R. Venkataramanan, A physiologically based pharmacokinetic modelling approach to predict buprenorphine pharmacokinetics following intravenous and sublingual administration, *Br J Clin Pharmacol*, 83(11), 2458–73, 2017.
77. Huang, P, G.B. Kehner, A. Cowan and L.Y. Liu-Chen, Comparison of pharmacological activities of buprenorphine and norbuprenorphine: norbuprenorphine is a potent opioid agonist, *J Pharmacol Exper Therap*, 297(2), 688–95.
78. Brown, S.M., M. Holtzman, T. Kim and E.D. Kharasch, Buprenorphine metabolites, buprenorphine-3-glucuronide and norbuprenorphine-3-glucuronide, are biologically active, *Anesthesiology*, 115(6), 1251–60, 2011.
79. Grond, S. and A. Sablotzki, Clinical pharmacology of tramadol, *Clin Pharmacokinet*, 43(13), 879–923, 2004.
80. Pedersen, R.S., P. Damkier and K. Brosen, Tramadol as a new probe for cytochrome P450 2D6phenotyping: a population study, *Clin Pharmacol Ther*, 77(6), 458–67, 2005.
81. Jones, D. and D.A. Story, Serotonin syndrome and the anaesthetist, *Anaesth. Intensive Care*, 33(2), 181–7, 2005.
82. Karhu, D., C. Fradette, M.A. Potgieter, M.M. Ferreira and J. Terblanché, Comparative pharmacokinetics of a once-daily tramadol extended-release tablet and an immediate-release reference product following single-dose and multiple-dose administration, *J Clin Pharmacol*, 50(5), 544–53, 2010.
83. Skinner-Robertson, S., C. Fradette, S. Bouchard, M.S. Mouksassi and F. Varin, Pharmacokinetics of tramadol and O-desmethyltramadol enantiomers following administration of extended-release tablets to elderly and young subjects, *Drugs Aging*, 32(12), 1029–43, 2015.
84. Palmer, G.M., B.J. Anderson and D.K. Linscott et al., Tramadol, breast feeding and safety in the newborn, *Arch Dis Child*, 103, 1110–3, 2018.
85. United States Food and Drug Administration. FDA Drug Safety Communication: FDA restricts use of prescription codeine pain and cough medicines and tramadol pain medicines in children; recommends against use in breastfeeding women. 2017, April 20. https://www.fda.gov/Drugs/DrugSafety/ucm549679.htm.
86. Miotto, K., A.K. Cho, M.A. Khalil, K. Blanco, J.D. Sasaki and R. Rawson, Trends in tramadol: pharmacology, metabolism, and misuse. *Anesth Analg*, 124(1), 44–51, 2017.
87. Murray, A. and N. Hagen, Hydromorphone, *J Pain Symptom Manage*, 29(5 Suppl. 1), 57–66, 2005.
88. Vashi, V., S. Harris, A. El-Tahtawy, D. Wu, et al., Clinical pharmacology and pharmacokinetics of once-daily hydromorphone hydrochloride extended-release capsules, *J Clin Pharmacol*, 45(5), 547–54, 2005.
89. Babul, N., A.C. Darke and N. Hagen, Hydromorphone metabolite accumulation in renal failure, *J Pain Symptom Manage*, 10(3), 184–6, 1995.
90. Murray, S. and E. Wooltorton, Alcohol-associated rapid release of a long-acting opioid, *CMAJ*, 173(7), 756, 2005.

2.4.11 Phencyclidine

Phencyclidine is a hallucinogenic drug that was used initially as an anesthetic agent in the 1950s and early 1960s, but was then withdrawn because its dissociative effects were often disturbing, severe, and prolonged. Currently, phencyclidine derivatives, such as 3-metoxy-phencyclidine, are used for recreational purposes.[1] The "out-of-body" intense psychological and behavioral effects of even low doses of phencyclidine are what led to its abuse. Phencyclidine has a complex mechanism of action since it acts at several levels of the Central Nervous System, resulting in analgesia and anesthesia.[2]

PCP caused sychomimetic states resembling schizophren in animal models of schizophrenia. PCP has a high affinity for N-methyl-D-aspartate (NMDA) receptors, which are ion channels, and also has a minor affinity for norepinephrine, serotonin, dopamine, and σ opioid receptors. Phencyclidine is a non-competitive antagonist of NMDA receptors, blocking the action of excitatory neurotransmitters such as glutamate and aspartate, by preventing the movement of sodium, potassium, and calcium ions through neuronal membranes, resulting in decreased membrane potential. However, phencyclidine cannot bind to the ion channel unless it is already open. On the other hand, it inhibits the reuptake of norepinephrine, dopamine, and serotonin and increases the production of norepinephrine and dopamine by tyrosine kinase stimulation, which results in dopaminergic and sympathomimetic effects. The psychomotor effects observed are due to the action of dopamine and the dissociative properties are associated with the antagonistic effect of glutamate at the level of NMDA receptors.[3]

Phencyclidine can be administered in different ways including oral, intravenous, subcutaneous, intranasal, or smoking.[4] The fastest effects are obtained by the intravenous route and the intranasal route (two to five minutes) and the most delayed by the oral route (30 to 60 minutes). Sedation usually occurs at doses of 0.25 mg IV, and for the same effect to occur orally, the required dose is between

1 and 5 mg.[5] It is rapidly absorbed in the respiratory and gastrointestinal tract and its oral bioavailability is greater than the amount absorbed when the compound is smoked,[6] although virtually all the amount that reaches the lungs is absorbed. It is significantly secreted into the stomach and ionized in the acidic environment; gastric concentrations may reach up to 20–50 times the levels in the bloodstream and the compound is absorbed later at the level of the duodenum in an alkaline environment.

The PKs of phencyclidine have been described by two- and three-compartment models[7] Because it is a weak base soluble in lipids, water, and alcohol, it has a high volume of distribution (6.2 L/kg) and is able to cross the placenta. The symptoms usually last four to six hours and, in cases of overdose, the effects disappear after 24 to 48 hours.[8,9] However, in chronic users, the effects may last longer because of enterohepatic recirculation or late release of the compound from lipid stores; it can accumulate in the adipose tissue and when it is remobilized it can produce the same effects weeks or months after it was originally consumed.

The metabolism of phencyclidine[10] occurs mainly at the liver level through phase I reactions, the most important being hydroxylation, which leads to the formation of 4-phenyl-4-piperidinocyclohexanol, 1-(1-phenylcyclohexyl)-4-hydroxypiperidine, and 4-(4'-hydroxypiperidine)-4-phenylcyclohexanol, metabolites excreted in the urine, which at pH below 5, increases clearance of phencyclidine.[11] Primary amines (1-phencyclohexylamine) and amino acids (5-(1-phenylcyclohexylamino) valeric acid) are also generated from phencyclidine metabolism but are secondary metabolites. It was found that the formation of hepatic metabolites leads to the inactivation of cytochrome P450 through the formation of covalent bonds with hepatic macromolecules.[12] The drug methoxitine, an analog of PCP, is usually classified as an NPS (novel psychoactive substances), and exerts many of the same effects as PCP.

REFERENCES

1. Bertol, E., Pascali, J., Palumbo, D., Catalani, V., Di Milia, M.G., Fioravanti, A., Mari, F., and Vaiano, F., 3-MeO-PCP intoxication in two young men: first in vivo detection in Italy, *Forensic Sci Int*, 274, 7–12, 2017.
2. Johnson, K.M., and Jones, S.M., Neuropharmacology of phencyclidine: basic mechanisms and therapeutic potential, *Ann Rev Pharmacol Toxicol*, 30(1), 707–50, 1990.
3. Nicholl, A.M., The non therapeutic use of psychoactive drugs, *N Engl J Med*, 308, 925–33, 1983.
4. Bey, T., and Patel, A., Phencyclidine intoxication and adverse effects: a clinical and pharmacological review of an illicit drug, *West J Emerg Med*, 8(1), 2007.
5. Cook, C.E., Brine, D.R., Jeffcoat, A.R., Hill, J.M., and Wall, M.E., Phencyclidine disposition after intravenous and oral doses, *Clin Pharmacol Ther*, 31, 625–34, 1982.
6. Cook, C.E., Brine, D.R., Quin, G.D., Perez-Reyes, M., and Di Guiseppi, S.R., Phencyclidine and. phenylcyclohexene disposition after smoking phencyclidine, *Clin Pharmacol Ther*, 31, 635–41, 1982.
7. Domino, S.E., Domino, L.E., and Domino, E.F., Comparison of two and three compartment models of phencyclidine in man, *Subst Alcohol Actions Misuse*, 2, 205–11, 1982.
8. Aronow, R., Miceli, J.N., and Done, A.K., Clinical observations during phencyclidine intoxication and treatment based on ion-trapping, National Institute on Drug Abuse, Rockville, MD, *Res Monograph Ser*, 21, 218–28, 1978.
9. Milhorn, H.T., Diagnosis and management of phencyclidine intoxication, *Am Fam Physician*, 43, 1293–301, 1991.
10. Wall, M.E., Brine, D.R., Jeffcoat, R.A., and Cook, C.E., Phencyclidine metabolism and disposition in man following a 100 µg intravenous dose, *Res Commun Subst Abuse*, 2, 161–72, 1981.
11. Perez-Reyes, M., Di Giusseppi, S., Brine, D.R., Smith, H., and Cook, C.E., Urine pH and phencyclidine excretion, *Clin Pharmacol Ther*, 32, 635–41, 1982.
12. Jushchyshyn, M.I., Wahlstrom, J.L., Hollenberg, P.F., and Wienkers, L.C., Mechanism of inactivation of human cytochrome P450 2B6 by phencyclidine, *Drug Metab Disp*, 34, 1523–9, 2006.

2.4.12 Ketamine

Ketamine (2-[2-chlorophenyl]-2-methylamino-cyclohexan-1-one) (KT), is a general anesthetic drug with dissociative properties that was first synthesized in 1962 as an alternative to its analogue, phencyclidine; ketamine has a shorter duration of action and induces fewer side effects. Ketamine produces anesthesia with depression of the thalamo-cortical system and activation of the limbic system.[1] It is also abused as a hallucinogen compound.[2] When administered by the venous route, to an experimental animal, a cataleptic state and anesthetic action, without sedative or hypnotic properties is produced. In humans, intravenous administration of 1 mg/kg causes analgesia and anesthesia in 30 seconds; the anesthetic state is maintained for three to ten minutes.[3,4] Arterial pressure and heart rate increase, and breathing is initially depressed. The blockade of painful sensitivity takes place at the integumentary and not visceral level. Thus, the osteotendinous, ciliary, corneal, photomotor, pharyngeal and laryngeal reflexes are conserved; there is pupillary dilatation and a vertical or horizontal nystagmus. Ketamine has an anticonvulsant action in both animals and humans. Ketamine is preferred over PCP for anesthetic induction. For reasons that have never been explained, ketamine causes the adrenal release of catecholamines, a very desirable feature when given as anesthetic to trauma victims.

Ketamine acts on brain neurotransmitters, interacting with muscarinic receptors, cholinergic receptors, and cerebral acetylcholinesterase. It also activates the MAO enzymatic system to produce cyclization of the catecholamine neurotransmitters; the cyclic derivatives are psychogenic and toxic These modifications are the cause of the hallucinatory phenomena that can occur upon awakening, or are sought by recreational users.[5,6] The drug causes an increase in cerebral circulation and a decrease in cerebral vascular resistance; it also increases the pressure of the cerebrospinal fluid, and the tone of skeletal muscles.

The pharmacokinetics of ketamine has been studied in rats, dogs, monkeys, and humans. Ketamine, administered orally or parenterally, is rapidly absorbed and rapidly distributed to the tissues. In humans, the intravenous injection of 2.2 mg/kg of drug produces plasma levels of 30 μg/mL 30 seconds after administration, which decreases to 1 μg/mL after ten minutes. The curve of ketamine elimination has a rapid elimination phase with a half-life of about seven minutes and a slower β phase with a half-life of about two hours.[7] Ketamine passes the placental barrier and is found with the same concentrations in maternal and fetal tissues. Ketamine does not bind in appreciable quantities to plasma proteins. Cutaneous absorption from occupational exposure to ketamine injection liquids has also been described in the veterinary setting.[8]

In both animals and humans, excretion is predominantly (85%–95%) via the urinary route, both for the parent drug and for its metabolites. The ketamine biotransformation occurs by N-demethylation of the molecule, with the formation of norketamine. This is then hydroxylated in various positions of the cyclohexanolone ring to form hydroxynorketamines which are eliminated in the urine for the most part conjugated to the glucuronic acid.[9] Analogous to many drugs of abuse with basic properties, ketamine and its metabolites easily incorporate in the hair where they can be detected mainly as the parent compound.[10]

Ketamine appears to exert little toxicity. In a review of 27 deaths occurring over a two-year period, virtually all the deaths were found to have occurred in hospitalized patients following surgical or burn treatment, and no deaths were attributed to ketamine intoxication.[11]

REFERENCES

1. Haas, D.A., and Harper, D.G., Ketamine: a review of its pharmacologic properties and use in ambulatory anesthesia, *Anesth Prog*, 39, 61–8, 1992.
2. Hirota, L.D.G., Ketamine: its mechanism of action and unusual clinical use, *Br J Anaesth*, 77, 441–4, 1996.
3. Wieber, J., Gugler, R., Hengstmann, J.H., and Dengler, H.J., Pharmacokinetics of ketamine in man, *Anaesthesia*, 24, 260–3, 1975.
4. Idvall, J., Ahlgren, I., Aronsen, K.F., and Stenberg, P., Ketamine infusions: pharmacokinetics and clinical effects, *Br J Anaesth*, 51, 1167–73, 1979.
5. Jenkins, A.J., Hallucinogens. In *Principles of Forensic Toxicology*, 2nd ed., B.S. Levine, Ed., AACC Press, Washington, DC, 2003.
6. Jansen, K.L., A review of the nonmedical use of ketamine: use, user and consequences, *J Psychoactive Drugs*, 32, 419–33, 2000.
7. Baselt, R.C., and Cravey, R.H., *Disposition of Toxic Drugs and Chemicals in Man*, 4th ed., Chemical Toxicology Institute, Foster City, CA, 1995.
8. Favretto, D., Vogliardi, S., Tucci, M., Simoncello, I., El Mazloum, R., and Snenghi, R. Occupational exposure to ketamine detected by hair analysis: a retrospective and prospective toxicological study *Forensic Sci Int*, 265, 193–9, 2016.
9. Moore, K.A., Sklerov, J., Levine, B., and Jacobs, A.J., Urine concentrations of ketamine and norketamine following illegal consumption, *J Anal Toxicol*, 25, 583–8, 2000.
10. Favretto, D., Vogliardi, S., Stocchero, G., Nalesso, A., Tucci, M, Terranova, C., and Ferrara, S.D., Determination of ketamine and norketamine in hair by micropulverized extraction and liquid chromatography–high resolution mass spectrometry, *Forensic Sci Int*, 226, 88–93, 2013.
11. Gill, J.R., and Stajic, M., Ketamine in non-hospital and hospital deaths in New York City. *J Forensic Sci*, 45, 655–8, 2000.

3 Ethanol

Section Editor: Alan W. Jones

CONTENTS

DOI: 10.4324/9781315155159-3

PREFACE

The first edition of the *Drug Abuse Handbook* (*DAH*) appeared in 1998 with a second edition published in 2007, so a third edition is indeed warranted. The "Alcohol" section of the third edition of *DAH* has been re-worked and redesigned extensively. In particular, it has been given a more appropriate title "Ethanol," which is the pharmacologically active substance contained in all alcoholic beverages. The narrative of the individual chapters has been revised and updated in numerous ways, including the preparation of many new figures and tables of data and the literature references include citations up to 2020.

Statistics from the World Health Organization in 2018 reported that the annual number of deaths attributed to excessive drinking and drunkenness reached a staggering three million worldwide. Causes of alcohol-related deaths include acute poisonings, adverse drug-alcohol interactions, and damage to body organs and tissues (especially the liver) after years of excessive drinking. Added to this are transportation fatalities resulting from road traffic crashes caused by drunken drivers, workplace accidents, and domestic violence when people are under the influence of alcohol. The over-consumption and abuse of ethanol represent a global public health problem.

The "Ethanol" section of the third edition of *DAH* deals primarily with biomedical aspects of the subject and with the main focus on forensic pharmacology and toxicology of this depressant drug. A new chapter addresses the scientific questions arising when people are prosecuted for driving under the influence in jurisdictions where statutory limits of ethanol concentration are enforced in samples of a driver's blood, breath, or urine.

Taken together, the "Ethanol" section provides a useful stand-alone text or primer for forensic practitioners, who need to take depositions, write affidavits, or testify in court as expert witnesses in drink driving cases. In brief, the various chapters in the "Ethanol" section focus on the following topics:

- 3.1 Measuring acute alcohol intoxication in the laboratory and the field
- 3.2 Analysis and disposition of ethanol in the body
- 3.3 Ethanol in post-mortem (PM) toxicology
- 3.4 Laboratory tests and biomarkers of alcohol consumption
- 3.5 The pros and cons of scientific evidence used for prosecuting traffic offenders based on measurement of ethanol in body fluids are reviewed
- 3.6 Glossary of terms on the subject of forensic toxicology of ethanol

It is common knowledge that excessive drinking leads to a state of intoxication and drunkenness. This has important consequences when skilled tasks, such as driving a motor vehicle, are performed. Epidemiological surveys from various countries show that the risk of being involved in a road traffic crash increases appreciably as the driver's blood-alcohol concentration increases. This has led to the creation of statutory limits of blood- or breath-alcohol concentration for driving a motor vehicle. In some jurisdictions, before a blood or breath-alcohol test can be administered, proof is necessary that a suspect was intoxicated. Evidence for this usually comes from making a clinical examination of suspects and testing their ability to perform various cognitive and psychomotor tests. Measuring acute alcohol intoxication is the subject of Chapter 3.1, and the various methods available for use in a laboratory environment and in apprehended drivers are reviewed.

Once absorbed into the bloodstream, most of the consumed ethanol undergoes oxidative metabolism in the liver (92%–95%) and the remainder (5%–8%) is excreted unchanged in the breath, sweat, and urine. However about 0.1%–0.2% of the dose of ethanol undergoes conjugation to form non-oxidative metabolites, ethyl glucuronide (EtG), and ethyl sulfate (EtS). Both EtG and EtS have received considerable research interest as biomarkers, because their presence in blood and urine can disclose recent drinking or relapse in people who are required to remain abstinent for various medical or security reasons. Methods for analysis of ethanol and its absorption, distribution, metabolism, and excretion in the body are the main focus of Chapter 3.2.

Ethanol tops the list of drugs encountered in post-mortem toxicology and, although the analytical methods are accurate, precise, and specific enough for forensic purposes, the interpretation of results is complicated by various PM artifacts. First and foremost, the blood specimens are not taken under sterile conditions and their quality and composition depends on the condition of the body. For example, the ethanol concentration detected in post-mortem blood might reflect both consumption of alcoholic beverages during life and mycotic fermentation of glucose after death. Methods are available to differentiate the source of ethanol, such as by complimentary analysis of various biomarkers, including the non-oxidative ethanol metabolites and other ways. Post-mortem toxicology of ethanol, with major focus on forensic medical interpretation of results, are dealt with in Chapter 3.3.

Judging whether a person drinks too much alcohol is not always easy, because a denial of the amounts consumed, and the frequency of ingestion, are very common in people suffering from an alcohol-use disorder. This makes the usual clinical interviews and questionnaires less useful to assess whether a patient has an underlying alcohol problem. To allow for early medical intervention and improve the various treatment options, much can be gained from the analysis of alcohol biomarkers. These are biochemical and laboratory tests classified as either being direct or indirect indicators of acute and/or chronic drinking and are fully discussed in Chapter 3.4.

Driving under the influence of alcohol is probably the most serious traffic violation, and millions of people are apprehended and prosecuted for this offense annually. Furthermore, drunken driving is responsible for between 20%–50% of all road traffic fatalities. Most nations now enforce statutory limits of alcohol concentration in samples of the driver's blood, breath, or urine. Indeed, these laws are increasingly interpreted as concentration per se, so there is no need for behavioral evidence that a driver was impaired for a successful prosecution. The statutory blood-alcohol limits for driving differ between countries from 0.20–0.8 g/L (0.02–0.08 g% or 20–80 mg%). This creates a razor-sharp difference in legal consequences for a person close to one of these statutory alcohol limits. The increasing sanctions imposed for people found guilty of drunken driving, including monetary fines, withdrawal of driving permits for up to two years, and various periods of incarceration have led to the analytical results being carefully scrutinized and also vigorously challenged when a case goes to trial. The pros and cons of the plethora of defense arguments raised when drunken drivers are prosecuted are the subjects of Chapter 3.5.

The "Ethanol" section in the third edition of *DAH* is supplemented by a comprehensive glossary of terms (words, acronyms, etc.) that are encountered throughout the narrative of the text and should be of general interest to forensic practitioners and others, who require a refresher course on the subject of alcohol and drug abuse.

3.1 MEASURING ACUTE ALCOHOL IMPAIRMENT/INTOXICATION IN THE LABORATORY AND IN APPREHENDED DRIVERS

Alan Wayne Jones and Christopher S. Martin

3.1.1 Introduction

Alcohol (ethanol) is probably man's oldest recreational drug and is the psychoactive substance most often encountered during forensic investigations of living and deceased persons. In this connection the old adage "the dose makes the poison" is an appropriate axiom because light to moderate drinking (1–2 units per day, corresponding to 8–16 g ethanol) is harmless, whereas chronic heavy drinking represents a public health problem of global magnitude and the cause of premature death.[1] There are some indications, derived from epidemiological studies of people's drinking habits, that the consumption of 1–2 glasses of red wine daily serves as an effective prophylactic treatment against cardiovascular diseases, such as ischemic stroke and heart failure.[2]

Despite these positive attributes of small doses of ethanol, the dangers of heavy drinking and drunkenness outweigh the benefits and some individuals are more susceptible than others to become dependent on alcohol and require medical intervention and treatment.[3,4] Furthermore, high rates of mortality and morbidity are associated with acute alcohol intoxication and the behavior of people when drunk often leads to them being admitted to hospital emergency units for treatment of injuries and trauma sustained when under the influence of alcohol.[5] Police investigations of unnatural deaths, including suicide, murder, and drowning, show a high prevalence of alcohol intoxication as major contributing factors.[6,7]

During forensic investigations of alcohol-related crimes, such as impaired driving, sexual assault, domestic violence, etc., it is often necessary to determine the degree of impairment, incapacitation, and ability to form intent.[8] A person is considered unfit to drive when his or her blood-alcohol concentration (BAC) exceeds a statutory limit, such as 0.08 g% in the USA and 0.05 g% in most other nations.[9,10] Epidemiological surveys of traffic crashes show that 20–50% of drivers killed had consumed alcohol before driving and their BAC at autopsy was above the statutory limit for driving.[11]

The classical signs and symptoms of drunkenness, including slurred speech, unsteady gait, etc. are not specific tests of alcohol influence and might not always be visible.[12] There is a definite need to develop more sophisticated tests of behavioral performance in relation to blood-alcohol concentration (BAC). The first attempts to measure the effects of alcohol intoxication on cognition and mood began in the 1940s,[13] especially in relation to the performance of skilled tasks necessary for safe driving.[14,15]

This chapter reviews the measurement of acute alcohol intoxication and impairment of body functions in relation to BAC in both a laboratory environment and in field settings, such as at the roadside when apprehended drivers are arrested.[16] In some jurisdictions, before the police are allowed to arrest a person for drunk driving, they need to generate evidence of impairment. Besides the more obvious signs and symptoms of alcohol influence, the police administer various impairment tests referred to as field sobriety tests (FSTs) because they are done at the roadside in close proximity to the traffic stop. Failing one or more of these tests gives the police officer sufficient probable cause to make an arrest and proceed with an analysis of blood or breath samples to determine the alcohol content.[17] The determination of ethanol in samples of blood or breath is a much more specific test of drunkenness and can be accomplished much more accurately than measuring a person's diminished performance after drinking alcohol.[18]

Not surprisingly, alcohol has been referred to as the Jekyll and Hyde of the drug world, because light to moderate drinking has no deleterious effects on health, whereas binge drinking and drunkenness cause premature death and disability.[19,20]

3.1.2 Measuring Alcohol-Induced Impairment

The impairment effects of alcohol are important to measure in many different situations, such as in various biomedical research projects, in clinical and emergency medicine, as well as in forensic science and legal medicine. However, measuring the performance decrement associated with excessive drinking is complex, and numerous pharmacological, motivational, and situational factors must be considered. The degree of impairment after a given dose of ethanol varies widely between different individuals even after making adjustments for differences in body weight and distribution volume.[21] The effects of ethanol are obvious at high BAC, but quantifying the degree of impairment at BAC in the range 0.02–0.08 g% is more subtle. This is the forensically important range and spans the statutory blood alcohol limits for driving in most nations. Although many impairment tasks have adequate performance characteristics in a laboratory environment, their practicality and usefulness in field settings, such as at the roadside, are limited.

This chapter is concerned with acute ethanol intoxication and the effects of this depressant drug on cognitive and psychomotor functioning in relation to BAC. Discussed are the effects of ethanol on speech and the vestibular system, including balance disturbances and spatial orientation after consumption of alcohol. Individual differences in degrees of impairment are examined in relation to temporal variations during the time alcohol is measurable in the body. It is well established that impairment effects of alcohol are more pronounced on the rising phase of the BAC curve compared with the declining phases, which commence 60–90 min post-dosing. This phenomenon is referred to as acute tolerance and was first observed in the 1920s.[22]

The bio-behavioral correlates of the hangover are also reviewed because these determine the residual effects of an evening's heavy drinking and might also cause performance decrement and accidents in the workplace.[23] The last section is concerned with the relationship between BAC and impairment of apprehended drivers who were examined by a physician within about one hour of them being arrested. The clinical signs and symptoms of drunkenness at a given BAC vary widely between different individuals depending on the sensitivity of the testing methods and development of tolerance to ethanol's impairing effects.[24]

3.1.3 Dose-Response Relationships

Like other psychoactive substances, the behavioral effects of ethanol are strongly dependent on the dose ingested and mode of administration.[25] These two factors are major determinants of the resulting BAC and more importantly the amount of ethanol reaching the central nervous system to cause impairment of body functioning. To quote from Paracelsus (1492–1541), the pioneer in toxicology,[26]

> What is there that is not poison? All things are poison and nothing is without poison. Solely the dose determines that a thing is not poison.

The response or effect of a drug treatment is usually depicted as a sigmoidal dose–effect relationship, with the response measure plotted on the y-axis against the logarithm of the dose on the x-axis as illustrated in Figure 3.1.1. The response might be any measure of drug effect, including behavioral effects and/or impairment.

The graph illustrates the response to a drug (e.g. ethanol) as the dose increases on a logarithm scale. The response variable might be some measure of impairment, such as a cognitive or psychomotor test or other signs and symptoms

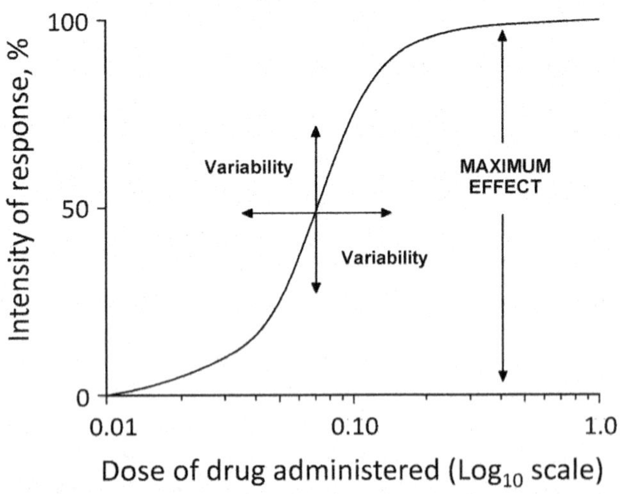

FIGURE 3.1.1 Log dose-response curve after administration of a centrally active drug such as ethanol when the response is plotted against increasing dose expressed as logarithms. This exhibits a typical sigmoidal function and the horizontal and vertical double arrows indicate changes in the position of the curve for different individuals, depending on their inherent sensitivity to drug effects. Note that the effects produced might also depend on the route of administration and the development of tolerance

of intoxication. At some point, any further increase in the dose of the drug fails to elicit any additional impairment effects, perhaps because the person is unconscious or in a comatose state. However, as illustrated by the horizontal and vertical double arrows there is appreciable variation in the response to a given dose of ethanol in different individuals leading to shifts in the dose-response curve.[27]

3.1.4 Ethanol Pharmacokinetics

Figure 3.1.2A presents some examples of the concentration-time profiles of ethanol determined in fingertip blood after healthy men (20–59 y) consumed neat whisky (40% v/v) on an empty stomach.[28] They consumed either 1.5 mL, 2.0 mL, or 2.5 mL per kg body weight, thus corresponding to ethanol doses of 0.54 g/kg, 0.68 g/kg, and 0.85 g/kg body weight. Mean curves are shown for N = 16 subjects at each ethanol dose and peak BAC ranged from 0.05 g% to 0.12 g% in most subjects. The mean BAC clearly increased with higher doses of ethanol and the areas under the curves (AUC) also increased in relation to the ethanol dose requiring longer times to eliminate ethanol from the body. As expected, the acute impairment effects of ethanol were more pronounced during the absorption phase and this was observed for all three doses of ethanol.[29]

3.1.5 Subjective Feelings of Intoxication

A simple way to judge the temporal effects of ethanol is simply to ask the subjects at various times after drinking how they are feeling according to some standardized definition of intoxication.[30] Such an experiment is referred to as "subjective intoxication" scores with the definition of "feelings of being a little high" or inebriated given a score of ten.[31,32] Each volunteer subject completes a questionnaire before starting to drink alcohol and at various times post-dosing, done in close proximity with the sampling of fingertip blood for the determination of ethanol. In this way, the changes in BAC can be directly related to temporal variations in subjective feelings of intoxication.[33]

Figure 3.1.2B plots median subjective feelings of intoxication against the time elapsed after the start of drinking for the three doses of ethanol (0.54, 0.68, and 0.85 g/kg). The median scores show that the volunteers experienced maximum intoxication at 10–15 min after the end of drinking, which agreed well with the occurrence of the peak BAC.[34] The initial subjective feelings-of-intoxication scores were not much different over the dose of ethanol administered. However, after the lowest dose of ethanol, there was a more rapid recovery in subjective feelings, which returned to pre-drinking baseline scores a lot earlier. The subjects considered themselves sober and safe to drive when BAC was still elevated in many instances.[34]

3.1.6 Behavioral Correlates of Acute Intoxication

One of the most important impairment effects of ethanol is the deterioration in coordination and cognitive functioning

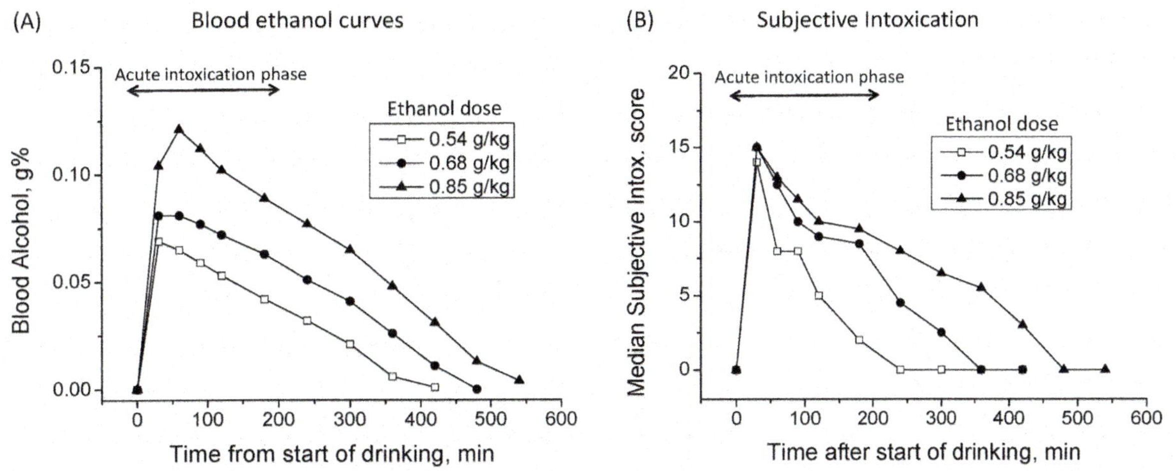

FIGURE 3.1.2 (A) Mean concentration-time profiles of ethanol in blood after healthy men (N = 16) drank three doses of ethanol, 0.54 g/kg, 0.68 g/kg, and 0.85 g/kg body weight, as neat whisky on an empty stomach, and (B) median subjective feelings of intoxication in the same subjects at times of sampling blood

it causes.[13] Most "behavioral" correlates of intoxication involve the quantitative recording and analysis of motor control and cognition.[25,35] As will be seen, the effects of alcohol are not uniform because the degree of impairment varies across different types of behavioral functions. Two areas of functioning that are particularly sensitive to impairment by alcohol and are described in detail, namely speech and vestibular functioning. In addition, this section describes individual differences in impairment in relation to the person's age, gender, and pattern of alcohol consumption.

3.1.6.1 Motor Control and Cognitive Functioning

As a pharmacological agent, ethanol is classified as a general central nervous system depressant, and this is reflected in diverse effects on body functions.[36] To the observer, one of the most obvious effects of ethanol is on motor control, particularly behaviors that require fine motor coordination. Another well-known detrimental effect of alcohol consumption is reduced cognitive control of behavioral functioning, especially the ability to perform and coordinate multiple tasks at the same time.[37,38] Research on the behavioral effects of alcohol almost always involves cognitive functions and motor control components, although the tests differ in complexity and the requirements for satisfactory performance.[39–41]

3.1.6.2 Reaction Times

Some of the most basic performance tests investigated in the literature are simple reaction time (RT) tasks, in which subjects must push a button as quickly and accurately as possible in response to a stimulus. Baylor et al.[42] found no effects of alcohol on simple RT at BACs of 0.10 g% but did find effects at very high BACs near 0.17 g%. Taberner[43] found no effect after a low dose of ethanol of 0.15 g/kg, and a small effect at a dose of 0.76 g/kg. Maylor et al.[44] found a small effect of alcohol on simple RT at a dose of 0.64 g/kg alcohol. Linnoila et al.[45] did not find any effects of alcohol on simple RT, even though other types of performance were impaired at this dose. Although the findings are somewhat variable, simple RT appears to be relatively insensitive to alcohol consumption.

Other research has examined choice RT tasks, which require people to react by making certain decisions by pressing two or more buttons in response to different stimuli. Such tasks involve motor speed as well as cognitive functions involved in categorizing a stimulus and choosing the correct response. Using a six-choice reaction time test, Fagan et al.[46] found only small effects of different BAC levels. This was confirmed by Golby[47] and other investigators, who concluded that the results of choice RT tasks were rather small or inconsistent, especially when learning effects were adjusted for.[37,48]

The scientific literature contains a number of studies examining the effects of alcohol on tracking performance, which is the ability to use a pointer to track as closely as possible a moving target.[49] Such tracking tasks are considered a sensitive indicator of fine motor control, which requires good coordination between the hands and eyes at rapid speed. Beirness and Vogel-Sprott[50] found that alcohol affected tracking performance at BACs above 0.05 g% and their results were confirmed in numerous later studies by other investigators. Wilson et al.[51] found that when BACs peaked at 0.10 g%, tracking was impaired for up to 120 mins after drinking relative to a placebo control treatment. There is consistent evidence that the acute effects of ethanol lead to deteriorated tracking performance and this has been verified numerous times.[52]

3.1.6.3 Dual-Task Performance

Alcohol impairment is found consistently during dual-task performance when subjects are required to perform multiple tasks simultaneously. When subjects were required to perform a tracking task and an RT task at the same time, Connors and Maisto[48] found that alcohol reduced tracking but not RT performance. Using a similar procedure, Maylor et al.[44] found that alcohol affected RT but not tracking.

Differences between these two studies in the task that was affected may have been due to instructions or task demands that led subjects to select one of the two tasks as primary, leading to performance deficits on the secondary task. Niaura et al.[53] combined an RT task with a task requiring the subject to circle target characters on a printed sheet and found that alcohol produced deficits on both tasks relative to placebo. Other researchers have used computerized divided-attention tasks, which require subjects to perform multiple functions simultaneously. Mills and Bisgrove[54] found that divided-attention performance (responding to numbers on central and peripheral monitors by pushing different buttons) was impaired after drinking an ethanol dose of 0.76 g/kg, but not after a lower dose of 0.37 g/kg.

The literature clearly shows that alcohol impairs various types of dual-task performance. The performance of multiple challenging tasks is thought to require the utilization of a large amount of attention, defined as limited-capacity cognitive resources that are required for effortful processing. The demonstration that alcohol produces dual-task performance deficits is consistent with the idea that alcohol produces impairment, in part, by reducing the available amount of limited-capacity attentional resources. A similar "attention allocation" model was proposed by Steele and Josephs.[55] These authors found that alcohol produced clear deficits in secondary task performance without affecting primary task performance, and suggested that alcohol serves to allocate a greater amount of attentional resources to a primary task, leading to fewer resources available for processing secondary sources of information.

Other studies of the behavioral impairment produced by alcohol have used tests designed to simulate complex real-world behaviors such as driving. Accident statistics consistently demonstrate that crash risk in the natural environment increases significantly when BACs are above 0.04 g%.[56] Automobile simulator studies generally find that the information processing and lateral guidance demands of driving are adversely affected by alcohol. Several well-designed laboratory studies have demonstrated adverse effects of alcohol on skills related to driving, beginning with BACs as low as 0.03–0.04 g%[52,57] Other research with driving simulators has examined the effects of alcohol on risk-taking, defined by levels of speed, cars overtaken, and number of accidents during automobile driving. McMillen et al.[58] observed that after drinking alcohol, the test subjects were more likely to take risks in a driving simulation. Mongrain and Standing[59] confirmed a tendency towards increased risk-taking, but only when high BACs close to 0.16 g% were reached.

The effects of alcohol on driving performance have been well studied under conditions of actual driving situations[60] as well as in driving simulators of varying degrees of sophistication.[61] Attwood et al.[62] using closed-course driving tasks found that performance variables such as speed and lane positioning together could discriminate between intoxicated and sober drivers. Huntley and Centybear[63] reported a decreased lateral guidance during a driving task when alcohol was consumed after sleep deprivation. Brewer and Sandow[64] reported that among drivers involved in traffic accidents, those with BACs above 0.05 g% were much more likely to have been engaged in a secondary activity at the time of the crash, compared to drivers with BACs below this same limit. Overall, it appears that alcohol adversely affects several types of behavioral functions involved in driving. Driving performance is complex and there are many human factors involved outside the vehicle, inside the vehicle, and in the environment, as well as situational factors and roadway conditions.

3.1.6.4 Speech

It must be a very old observation that consumption of alcohol affects speech in both sound and articulation, and bartenders are taught not to continue serving customers who are slurring their speech. Likewise, law enforcement personnel and the general public are well aware that "slurred speech" is one indication that a person might be under the influence of alcohol at the time. Because the production of speech requires fine motor control, timing, and coordination of the lips, tongue, and vocal cords, this makes it a sensitive index of impairment resulting from alcohol intoxication. Having test subjects recite the alphabet at a fast rate of speed is a well-known field sobriety test for alcohol influence. Considerable research suggests that evaluation of a person's speech can serve as a measure of alcohol consumption and intoxication.

After consuming 10 oz (~300 mL) of 86-proof alcohol (43 vol%), alcoholics were found to take longer to read a passage of text and had more word, phrase, and sound interjections, word omissions, word revisions, and broken suffixes in their speech.[65] Other research with nonalcoholic drinkers found that under intoxication, subjects made more sentence-level, word-level, and sound-level errors during spontaneous speech.[66,67] Intoxicated talkers consistently lengthen some speech sounds, particularly consonants in unstressed syllables.[68] The overall rate of speech also slows when intoxicated subjects have to read sentences and paragraphs.[69]

Pisoni and Martin[69] examined the acoustic-phonetic properties of speech for matched pairs of sentences spoken by social drinkers when sober and after they consumed alcohol to reach BACs of 0.10 g%. Sentence duration was increased after drinking, and pitch (loudness), while not consistently higher or lower, was more variable. The strongest effects of alcohol at the sound level were for speech sounds that require fine motor control and timing of articulation events in close temporal proximity. Intoxicated talkers displayed difficulty in controlling the abrupt closures and openings of the vocal tract required for stops and affricate closures. This resulted in long durations of closures before voiced stops (e.g. /d/, /b/) and the complete absence of closures before affricates (e.g. the /ch/ in "church"). These effects are consistent with what is known about the degree of precision of motor control mechanisms required for the articulation of different speech sounds. These same investigators also found that listeners can reliably discriminate speech produced while sober and when the same person is intoxicated. State Troopers showed higher discrimination levels than other listeners, suggesting that experience in detecting intoxication may increase perceptual abilities. The approach of some field sobriety tests that have persons recite the alphabet quickly may effectively capture the detrimental effects of alcohol on the articulation of speech sounds in close temporal proximity.

Despite convincing evidence that shows an effect of alcohol on speech, there are a number of limitations that make it difficult to use speech production as an index of alcohol impairment. Drinking alcohol up to a BAC of 0.10 g% has consistently shown speech deterioration, whereas the effects of lower BAC are more variable.[66,67] It is an open question whether reliable effects on speech are produced after moderate drinking up to 0.08 g% BAC.[70] Other types of impairment are likely to occur before speech is noticeably affected. It is not clear from the literature how motivation to avoid the detection of intoxication would affect speech production. Furthermore, the specificity of speech changes to alcohol intoxication (rather than fatigue, stress, etc.) needs further study. Finally, there is extreme variability between individuals as to their acoustic-phonetic properties of speech, making it difficult to estimate the degree of impairment without making a direct comparison with speech when sober.[71] Despite these limitations, the literature suggests that speech is likely to be a good *screening* test for impairment, which can then be determined using other measures.

3.1.6.5 Vestibular Functions

The vestibular system is part of the inner ear and serves to maintain spatial orientation and balance, and eye movements that support these functions. The vestibular system is comprised of two sets of interconnected canals that provide information about spatial orientation. Each canal is comprised of a membrane embedded with sensory hair cells and surrounding extracellular fluid. The *otolithic* canals provide information about the direction of gravity relative to the head and thus are sensitive to lateral (side to side) head movements. This is accomplished by the fact that the membrane has a specific gravity that is twice that of the extracellular space in otoliths. Under normal conditions, the *semicircular* canals are sensitive to rotational movements of the head and do not respond to lateral movements. Within the semicircular canals, the membrane and the extracellular fluid have the same exact specific gravity (i.e. weight by volume), such that the hair cells have neutral buoyancy and are not subject to gravitational influences.[72]

3.1.6.5.1 Positional Alcohol Nystagmus

The impairment effects of ethanol ingestion on the vestibular system are best observed when oculomotor control is evaluated, i.e. the functional effectiveness of eye movements under different conditions. During alcohol consumption many persons show significant nystagmus (jerkiness) in eye movements when the head is placed in a sideways position: this effect is known as positional alcohol nystagmus (PAN). There are two types of PAN. PAN I is characterized by nystagmus to the right when the right side of the head is down, and to the left when the left side of the head is down. PAN I normally occurs during rising and peak BACs, beginning around 0.04 g%.[73] The PAN II nystagmus usually appears between five and ten hours after the end of drinking and is characterized by eye movements in the opposite direction compared with PAN I.[74]

The mechanisms causing PAN I and II have been convincingly demonstrated.[75] Both types of PAN are produced by the effects of alcohol on the semicircular canals, making hair cells on the membrane responsive to the effects of gravity. As alcohol diffuses throughout the water compartments of the body, it first enters the membrane space (which is richly supplied with capillary blood), and gradually diffuses into the extracellular fluid. For a time, the concentration of ethanol is greater in the membrane compared with the surrounding fluid. Because alcohol is lighter than water (1 mL = 0.79 g), the specific gravity of the membrane fluid will be lower than that of the surrounding fluid before equilibration in all body fluids is complete, which makes the semicircular canals responsive to gravity and thus produces PAN I.[76] The faster the rate of drinking, the faster is the onset of PAN I.

At a certain time on the descending phase of the BAC curve, neither PAN I nor PAN II nystagmus is measurable, because the semicircular membrane and the surrounding fluid now have the same specific gravity. PAN II occurs during the alcohol elimination phase when BAC is no longer measurable, and often corresponds to the hangover phase. During PAN II, alcohol in the semicircular canals is removed from the surrounding fluid faster than from the membrane, which causes the membrane to have a greater specific gravity than the surrounding fluid, which in turn produces PAN II.[77]

The effects of alcohol on the semicircular canals appear to play a central role in many symptoms of intoxication, including feelings of dizziness, nausea, and vertigo known as the "bed spins." Both PAN I and PAN II reflect overstimulation of the semicircular canals in a similar manner to that seen in people suffering from motion sickness.[75] Laboratory studies have shown that the magnitude of PAN I is associated with higher BACs,[76] which cause greater impairment in postural control as well as subjective feelings of intoxication.[78] As described later in this chapter, it has been speculated that PAN II is associated with hangover symptoms.

3.1.6.5.2 Horizontal Gaze Nystagmus

Another type of nystagmus produced by alcohol is known as horizontal gaze nystagmus (HGN). HGN is defined by jerkiness in eye movements when following a moving target and when the gaze is directed to the side when the head is in an upright position. HGN has long been noted as a sensitive test of alcohol influence and this usually becomes apparent as BAC is rising (absorption phase) to reach concentrations of 0.06–0.08 g% and higher.[79] The presence of HGN can be ascertained in two ways. First, deficits in smooth pursuit eye movements are assessed by instructing a person to follow a moving object such as a pen when moved across their visual field, while not moving their head. Second, a subject is required to follow an object at an increasingly eccentric angle, without moving the head; the smallest angle at which nystagmus first appears is used to assess intoxication.

As with PAN, it has been demonstrated that HGN is highly associated with the effects of alcohol, as seen in studies of oculomotor control.[80] Alcohol appears to interfere with neural mechanisms of smooth pursuit. Lehti[81] reported high correlations of BACs and the angle at which nystagmus in eccentric gaze became apparent. Similar effects of alcohol have been seen when pursuit tasks are combined with active and passive head movements.[82] Tharp et al.[83] made a study to quantify the slope of a regression line predicting the angle of onset of nystagmus from BAC. They found that the angle of nystagmus onset was predicted at 45 degrees for BACs of 0.05 g%, 40 degrees for BACs of 0.10 g%, and 35 degrees for BACs of 0.15 g%. The angle of horizontal nystagmus onset has been found to have a high level of sensitivity and specificity in predicting BACs above 0.10 g% in an emergency room setting.[84] HGN appears to be much more sensitive to ethanol intoxication compared with marijuana, which has little or no effects on eye movements.[85] However, the smooth pursuit aspects of HGN are influenced significantly by other depressant drugs, such as benzodiazepines, barbiturates, and antihistamines.[86] Positive HGN test results in the absence of an elevated BAC may indicate that the person is under the influence of sedative drugs.

The widespread use of HGN testing of apprehended drivers has been under critique from some quarters, for various reasons, some more valid than others.[87,88] Nevertheless, most practitioners vouch for the continued use of HGN as a sensitive test of alcohol consumption and elevated BAC.[89,90]

Postural control tasks are some of the most widely used measures of alcohol-related impairment in the laboratory and in the field. It is likely that the functional effectiveness of the vestibular system is the primary locus of the effects of alcohol on postural control. Numerous studies, using a variety of balance platforms and similar types of apparatus, have demonstrated that body sway increases after consumption of alcohol, especially during the first 60 min post-dosing as BAC increases past 0.03–0.05 g%.[27,91,92] Other research shows that sway increases with the dose of ethanol consumed,[93,94] depending in part on the development of tolerance and family history of heavy drinking, as these individuals swayed less at the same BAC compared with moderate drinkers.[39,54] The effects of alcohol become greater as the postural control task is made more difficult, such as with eyes closed, or when the feet are in a heel-to-toe position.[93,94]

In summary, postural control appears to be a sensitive index of the impairment effects of ethanol. However, body sway shows a great deal of individual variation in a sober condition.[29] For this reason, the ability to detect impairment by measuring body sway is limited in settings in which there exists a measure of sober performance for that individual as well.

3.1.6.5.3 Individual Differences

It is common knowledge that large individual differences exist in the impairment produced by a given dose of ethanol even when adjusted for body weight and consumed under standardized conditions. Indeed, the observed peak BAC after subjects ingest the same dose of ethanol per kg body weight and after allowing for gender can differ widely.[28,95] Women tend to weigh less than men on average and they have less body water to dilute the ethanol entering the bloodstream and accordingly reach higher BACs for the same dose/kg body weight.[96,97] Even when controlling for BAC, however, there are large inter-individual differences in a person's sensitivity to alcohol impairment.[98] Perhaps the most important factor is drinking practices and habituation to alcohol. Those who drink more often and in greater amounts tend to develop a greater amount of tolerance to the impairing effects of alcohol, i.e. have an acquired decrease in the degree of impairment across multiple drinking sessions.[13,99] Greater impairment in light drinkers compared to heavier drinkers has been shown by numerous authors using a variety of performance tasks.

There are also gender differences in some aspects of alcohol pharmacokinetics. On average, women achieve higher BACs than men after they drink the same dose of ethanol because of gender differences in body composition, with more fat/kg than in males.[100] Some research studies found a lower activity of gastric alcohol dehydrogenase and therefore less first-pass metabolism of ethanol in females compared to males.[101] But whether first-pass metabolism is predominantly gastric or hepatic and whether it depends on gender is still an open question.[102] Elimination rates of ethanol from blood are slightly faster in women, owing to their larger liver weight per kg lean body mass than males.[103] In addition, there might be hormonal influences that influence hepatic enzyme activity during the mid-luteal and ovulatory phases of the menstrual cycle compared to the follicular phase.[104,105] Other research, however, has not replicated these findings.[106]

Some laboratory studies have examined whether males and females differ in their sensitivity to alcohol. Mills and Bisgrove[54] found no gender differences in a divided-attention task after a low dose of alcohol, but greater impairment in females at a higher dose. However, in this study women achieved higher BACs and reported less alcohol consumption compared to men. After controlling for gender differences, Burns and Moskowitz[107] found no significant gender differences in a series of motor and cognitive impairment tasks. In a study by Niaura et al.[53] after controlling for differences in BAC there were no longer any significant gender differences in psychomotor and cognitive responses to alcohol. Other research that controlled for gender differences in

BACs and drinking practices has found few gender differences in responses to alcohol. Overall, when controlling for BACs and drinking practices, gender differences in alcohol impairment have not been demonstrated.

Little research has examined differences in alcohol impairment that are related to age. Using volunteers with nearly equivalent drinking practices, Parker and Noble[108] found that older subjects (over 42 years old) had more deficits in abstracting and problem-solving after alcohol consumption compared to younger subjects. Linnoila et al.[45] found a trend toward increased impairment in subjects who were 25–35 years old compared to those 20–25 years old. Other studies have also found age-related increases in psychomotor impairment in humans[29] and in animals, even when BACs and drinking practices were equivalent in older and younger groups. Although there appears to be an increase in sensitivity to alcohol's effects with advancing age, there are few definite studies, and most suffer from small sample sizes. Because age effects occur even when BACs and drinking practices are controlled, some have speculated that age-related increases in alcohol impairment reflect the effects of aging on the vulnerability of the central nervous system to alcohol's effects.

3.1.7 Time of Ingestion

The effects of alcohol tend to vary dramatically over the time course of a drinking episode. An analysis of how the effects of alcohol change over time provides a clearer understanding of alcohol-related impairment. This section of the chapter reviews differences in the effects of alcohol during the rising and falling limbs of the BAC curve, the phenomenon of acute tolerance, and post-drinking hangover.

3.1.7.1 Rising vs Declining Limb of the BAC Curve

Researchers and clinicians have long described alcohol's effects as *biphasic* during a drinking episode.[109] "Biphasic" in this context refers to the fact that the stimulant effects of alcohol tend to precede the sedative effects during a single drinking episode.[110] There are substantial individual differences in the magnitude of stimulant effects of alcohol and the BACs at which they occur. Alcohol's stimulant effects are reflected in increased motor activity, talkativeness, and euphoric or positive mood at lower doses and during rising BACs. Stimulant effects of alcohol have been assessed in humans by a variety of psycho-physiological, motor activity, and self-reports, and in animals using measures such as spontaneous motor activity. Stimulant effects are present in some drinkers at BACs as low as 0.02–0.03 g% and may persist on the rising BAC limb well past 0.10 g%. Some current theories hold that stimulant effects reflect alcohol's reinforcing qualities, and that the magnitude of stimulant effects will predict future drinking and the development of alcohol dependence.

Some research suggests that the rate of change of rising BACs helps determine the degree of alcohol effects. A faster rise of ascending BACs is associated with greater euphoria and intoxication, as well as increased behavioral impairment. It is interesting to speculate that the drinking patterns shown by many heavy drinkers and alcoholics may reflect an attempt to produce a rapid rise in BACs. These patterns include gulping drinks, drinking on an empty stomach, and using progressively fewer mixers to dilute distilled spirits.

Sedative effects of alcohol usually occur at higher BACs and on the descending limb of the BAC curve. Sedation has been measured in humans using EEG patterns and self-reports of anesthetic sensations and dysphoric mood, and in animals with low motor activity and the onset of alcohol-induced sleep. Robust sedative effects tend to first appear at peak BACs near 0.06 to 0.08 g% in many drinkers, although BACs of 0.10 g% are necessary for people with higher tolerance to the sedative effects. The sedative effects of ethanol consumption are negatively correlated with drinking practices, and lower levels of sedation after drinking might characterize people at higher risk for the future development of alcohol use disorder.

Research has clearly demonstrated that alcohol-related impairment is greater on the ascending compared to the descending limb of the BAC curve.[111] This finding appears consistently across different doses and impairment tests. The most straightforward explanation for this effect is acute tolerance, described below.[112]

3.1.7.2 Acute Tolerance

In pharmacology, tolerance refers to a person's diminished response or reaction to a drug after repeated usage because the body or the brain appears to adapt to its continued presence in the bloodstream. One consequence of the development of tolerance is that more of the drug (a larger dose) is necessary to achieve the desired therapeutic effect or, in the case of recreational drugs, the same pleasurable experiences. The development of tolerance to the effects of a drug is usually illustrated by a shift in the sigmoidal dose-response curve to the right as illustrated in Figure 3.1.3. Projection of the x-axis shows that a BAC of ~0.07 g% is necessary to achieve 50% intensity of the effect

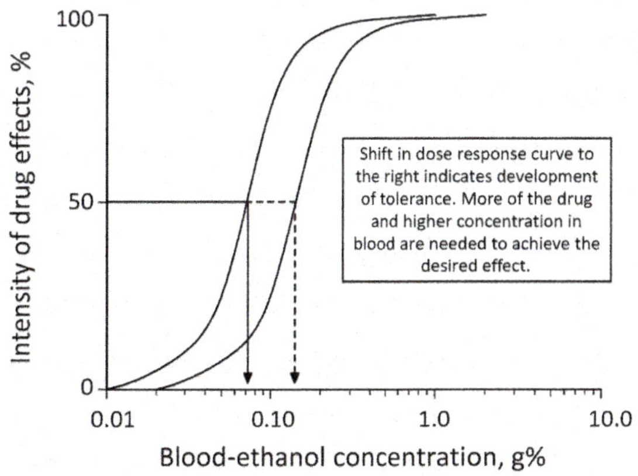

FIGURE 3.1.3 Dose-response curve showing the development of tolerance to ethanol's effects as illustrated by a shift in the sigmoidal curve to the right, so that larger doses are required to achieve the desired effect

in a non-tolerant individual, which compares with a BAC of ~0.105 g% in a person who has developed central nervous tolerance.

The concept of drug tolerance has been the subject of alcohol research since the 19th century and this manifests itself in several different ways.[99,113] Metabolic tolerance refers to an increase in the rate of ethanol metabolism after a period of continuous heavy drinking for several days or weeks. The suggested mechanism behind this observation was induction in the activity of one of the metabolizing enzymes (CYP2E1), although this increased enzymatic activity was lost after a period of abstinence.[114]

Functional tolerance is usually defined as an acquired decrease in the sensitivity to the effects of ethanol as a result of repeated exposure to the drug. The alcohol-induced impairment of body function is less pronounced in more tolerant individuals. Thus chronic tolerance refers to an acquired decrease in the effect of alcohol across multiple exposures to the drug with higher doses and BAC being necessary to produce the same desirable effects.

Acute tolerance develops rapidly and is defined as a decrease in impairment effects after administration of a moderate dose of ethanol to a previously alcohol-free subject.[115] The phenomenon of acute tolerance is one of the most robust observations and was first reported in 1919 in dogs given a single intoxicating dose of ethanol by stomach tube.[22] The animals showed greater impairment of motor co-ordination at a given BAC on the rising portion of the curve compared with the post-absorptive declining phase. This became known as the "Mellanby Effect," named after the pharmacologist, Sir Edward Mellanby (1884–1955), who first made the observation in experimental animals. He observed that the animals lost their ability to stand upright at a lower BAC on the rising limb of the blood-alcohol curve (absorption phase) compared with the BAC when they recovered on the post-absorptive phase. This finding has been verified on numerous occasions in both experimental animals and man and using a range of cognitive and psychomotor tests including standing steadiness, motor coordination, self-reported intoxication, sleep time (in mice), and body temperature.[116–118]

Some researchers suggested that the Mellanby effect, at least in part, might be accounted for by a methodological artifact, owing to the analysis of ethanol in venous blood.[119] Arterial BAC is significantly higher than venous BAC during the absorption phase of the blood-alcohol curve, and impairment effects were more pronounced early after the end of drinking compared with the post-absorptive phase several hours later. Because the brain is supplied with ethanol via the arterial blood circulation, the central nervous system is exposed to a higher concentration of ethanol during the absorption phase than is reflected by analysis of venous blood returning to the heart from the tissues.

There is a general consensus among alcohol researchers that behavioral effects of ethanol are more severe on the absorptive phase compared with the post-absorptive phase at the same BAC when the curve is rising and declining.[120] This phenomenon is robust and has been confirmed when analyzing ethanol in venous blood and when breath-alcohol analysis was used, the BrAC running closer to the arterial BAC and hence a better reflection of brain exposure.[121] Second, researchers have demonstrated the presence of acute tolerance in subjective feelings and a battery of cognitive and objective psychomotor tests of alcohol influence.[115] When BACs were maintained constant by continuous intravenous infusion, acute tolerance developed because the effects of ethanol decreased over time.[122]

The development of acute tolerance was dependent on the rate of drinking to reach a target BAC and was more pronounced after ethanol was ingested more rapidly than slowly.[123] People tend to recover from the acute effects of a dose of ethanol much earlier than BAC returns to zero through metabolism. After an ethanol dose of 1.0 g/kg, the combined impairment scores when subjects were examined by physicians had returned to baseline values when BAC was between 0.05 and 0.08 g%.[124] The morning after an evening's social drinking, people consider themselves sober despite them still having an elevated BAC (0.03–0.05 g%), yet another demonstration of acute tolerance development.[112] In a cross-over design study, investigators have demonstrated that the decreased behavioral and psychomotor impairment is not caused by practice or learning effects in the tests administered.[125–127]

In some experimental drinking models, acute tolerance occurs in a linear fashion independent of blood-ethanol concentration.[128] Others found that the development of acute tolerance was different for fast and slow drinkers and was more pronounced after a bolus dose was ingested on an empty stomach compared to reaching the same BAC over several hours.[129] These observations suggest that during the time that ethanol is being consumed and when BAC is in the post-absorptive phase, the brain adapts to some or all of the impairment effects.

Martin and Moss[112] found that with a low and high dose of ethanol the development of acute tolerance was highly correlated with time between making measurements on the ascending and descending limbs of the blood-alcohol curve. Clearly, the amount of impairment and intoxication shown during a drinking episode is not only affected by the level of BAC, but also by the amount of time alcohol has been in a person's system.

Vogel-Sprott[130] reviewed a large body of research showing that the development of acute tolerance is also influenced by the consequences of non-impaired and/or impaired performance. The prevalence of non-impaired performance increases when there is some type of financial reward or gain attached to the results.[131] These findings might be interpreted in terms of an increased motivation to appear sober and perform better in the behavioral tests administered. For example, if an intoxicated motorist is stopped for questioning and/or field sobriety tests, the driver is obviously motivated not to exhibit the effects of alcohol and to pass the impairment tests. While such attempts to appear sober will be unsuccessful when BACs are sufficiently high, it is likely that many traffic offenders escape detection when BACs are close to the statutory limit of 0.08 g%. Unfortunately, the same motorist might once again become a dangerous driver and perform worse after the immediate contingency of detection and arrest are removed. The laboratory studies reviewed in this chapter did not adequately control for or study the impact of high motivational levels on the results obtained. For this reason, it is likely that the magnitude of impairment observed in many laboratory studies is greater than would be obtained in a field setting.

An important investigation of the relationship between BAC and clinical signs and symptoms of drunkenness was undertaken in Finland and published in 1951.[124] The study was notable for several reasons, not the least of which was the number of drinking subjects involved and the fact they received increasing quantities of ethanol administered as a bolus dose on an empty stomach. Mean concentration-time profiles of ethanol in blood after subjects drank 0.75, 1.0, and 1.25 g/kg ethanol within five minutes on an empty stomach are shown in Figure 3.1.4A. The peak BAC varied between 0.075 g% and 0.15 g% and occurred 60 min after the end of drinking on average. Thereafter, BAC decreased at a constant rate per unit time in the post-absorptive phase of the ethanol profiles.

Before drinking and at various times after drinking, each subject was examined by a physician and underwent certain tests of cognitive and psychomotor functioning. Such things as counting backward, standing steady with open and closed eyes, balance disturbances, walking in a straight line, finger-to-finger test, picking up matches from the floor, and articulation of speech were scored and recorded. The overall results from these various tests were then combined into a score depicting overall symptoms of intoxication. The intensity of these symptoms increased with an increasing dose of ethanol and BAC. Figure 3.1.4B plots the median symptoms of alcohol influence at each time a blood sample was taken for determination of ethanol. For the three different doses of ethanol, the symptoms of intoxication recovered to baseline values much earlier than the BAC had decreased to zero.

Figure 3.1.5 shows the relationship between mean BAC and the median intoxication score after drinking a bolus dose of 1.0 g/kg body weight ingested on an empty stomach. Now the BAC and the impairment score are plotted on the same time axis, making it easier to see the inter-relationship between BAC and clinical effects of drunkenness. One notices that the peak "intoxication score" occurred slightly earlier than the peak BAC and returned to reach the pre-drinking baseline score by about 180–240 min post-drinking. At this time the BAC in some of the subjects was still appreciable, 0.06–0.08 g% and above the legal limit for drinking in many countries. Apart from the smell of alcohol on the breath of the subjects, the outward signs and symptoms had subsided by 3–4 h after the end of drinking. This demonstrates an adaption of the brain to the intoxication effects of ethanol and the various clinical tests were no longer sensitive enough to register a decrement in performance compared with the sober state.

3.1.7.3 Residual Effects of Alcohol: Hangover

A hangover refers to the after-effects of an evening's heavy drinking and in recent years there has been considerable research on this phenomenon and a large body of literature has accumulated.[132–135] A hangover is an unpleasant state that usually commences the morning after a night of heavy drinking, characterized by dysphoric and irritable mood, headache, nausea, dizziness, and dehydration.[136] Drinking to reach a BAC of 0.11 g% or more is considered the threshold for experiencing signs and symptoms of a hangover the next day in most drinkers.[137] Large individual differences exist in the occurrence and severity of hangovers, and this probably relates to both genetic and environmental factors including patterns of drinking, whether ingested on an empty stomach or after a meal, the type of alcoholic drink consumed, etc.[138–140]

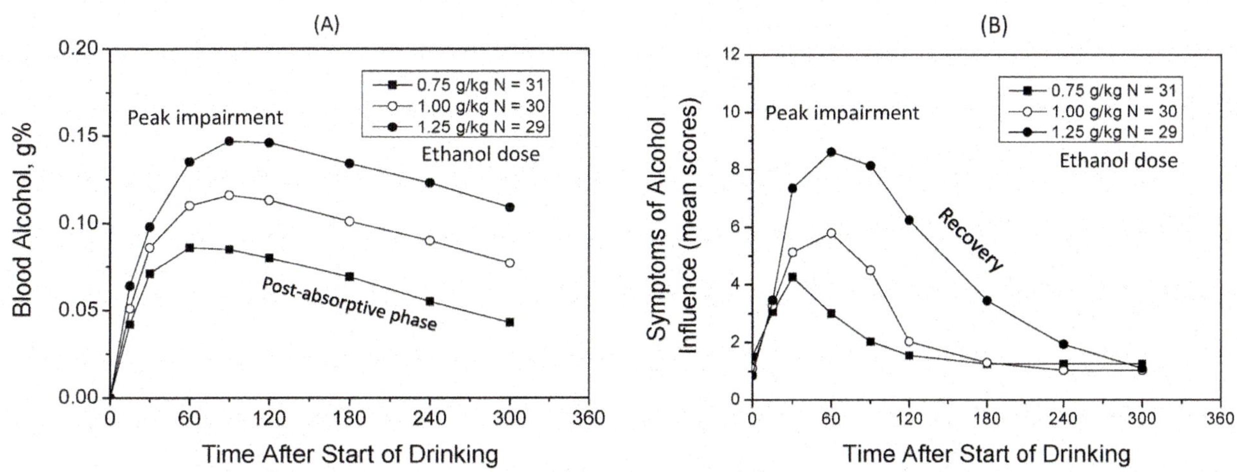

FIGURE 3.1.4 (A) Median blood-alcohol concentration-time curve in healthy men after they drank increasing doses of ethanol in the morning on an empty stomach, and (B) median intoxication score based on clinical signs and symptoms when subjects were examined by a physician

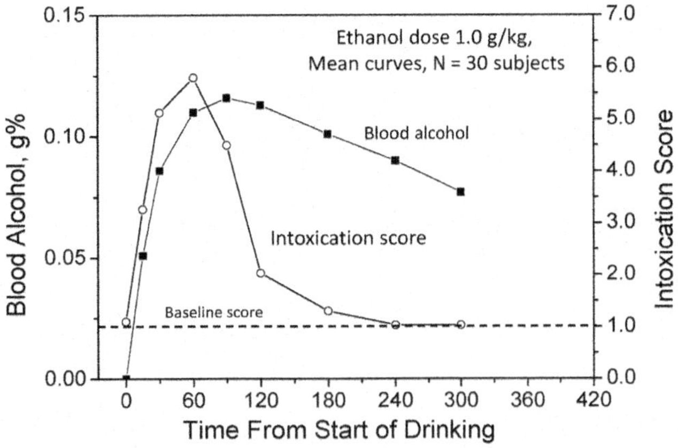

FIGURE 3.1.5 Development of acute tolerance to impairment effects of ethanol after healthy men drank a dose of 1.0 g/kg body weight in the morning after an overnight fast. Note that the median intoxication score occurred slightly earlier than the peak blood-alcohol concentration (BAC) and also returned to baseline (pre-drinking intoxication score) when BAC was still elevated, often above 0.08 g%

There is contradictory evidence whether or not people suffering from a hangover perform worse in behavioral and psychomotor performance. Several early studies failed to verify that performance decrement was much worse after BACs had returned to zero the morning after an evening of heavy drinking. Kelly et al.[31] used a variety of behavioral and psychological impairment tests 12 hours after subjects consumed a dose of ethanol sufficient to produce a mean BAC of 0.12 g%. The next morning the test subjects had very low BAC, ~0.004 g%, and were therefore close to zero. The various tests done in the morning failed to show any significant impairment, except for hand-steadiness (tremor) which was worse the morning after in the hangover arm of the study. Collins and Chiles[141] administered impairment tests before an evening drinking session, at various times after consumption, and again after subjects had slept four to five hours. Subjects were affected on the performance tests during acute intoxication, and they reported experiencing a severe hangover during the morning session. Impairment of body functioning during a hangover might be the cause of some accidents occurring in the workplace or when driving on the highway.[142]

More recent research confirms that a hangover is accompanied by impairment of both behavioral and cognitive functioning.[143] Using a simulated driving task, performance was 20% worse three hours after BAC had returned to zero after drinking to reach a peak BAC of ~0.15 g%.[144] Yesavage and Leirer[145] examined hangover effects in Navy aircraft pilots 14 hours after drinking enough alcohol to produce BACs of about 0.10 g%, using a variety of flight simulator measures. Significant detrimental effects of hangover were found for three of six measures of variance and one of six performance measures. It appears that some but not all subjects perform worse during a hangover and a lot depends on the type of impairment task the subjects are expected to perform.[146–148]

There is a suggestion that the nausea and dizziness experienced by some people during a hangover might be associated with e of PAN II, an eye movement nystagmus that occurs during the declining phase of the blood-alcohol curve when BAC is approaching low levels.[75,76] PAN II reflects the sensitivity of semicircular canal receptors to gravity, which also produces feelings similar to motion sickness.[149] More research is needed to address the role of vestibular functioning in hangovers.

Inconsistencies in the hangover literature probably reflect, to a large extent, the fact that behavioral impairment is influenced by numerous factors, including sleepiness, fatigue, mood, and motivation to behave in a non-impaired manner.[23,150,151] Moreover, there are individual differences in the frequency and duration of a hangover, even among people with similar drinking practices.[152,153] The high BACs necessary to cause a hangover in some drinkers might be impractical to reach in controlled laboratory settings, owing to ethical and safety reasons, hence studies of hangover effects are problematic.

In summary, the alcohol-induced hangover develops when BAC decreases from a fairly high concentration (> 0.11 g%) back to reach zero, which mostly occurs in the morning after heavy drinking the night before.[154] Specialists in addiction medicine consider that the hangover is a milder form of alcohol withdrawal syndrome.[155] A hangover is characterized by a general anxiety disorder lasting for up to 24 h after reaching a zero BAC. The expression "hair of the dog" refers to situations when a person drinks alcohol in the morning for the purpose of relieving the worst hangover symptoms, such as drowsiness, concentration problems, dry mouth, dizziness, gastrointestinal complaints, sweating, nausea, and hyperexcitability. Renewed interest in mechanisms and consequences of the alcohol hangover is evident in the formation of a special research interest group.[156,157] Why some people are more predisposed to experience hangovers than others is not completely understood, but it might be a genetic trait.[158,159]

3.1.8 Impairment Testing in the Field

The strengths and weaknesses of various tests of alcohol influence both in laboratory experiments and also under more real-world conditions, such as when patients are examined at hospital trauma units or when the police arrest impaired drivers, need to be carefully evaluated and fit for purpose. There are a number of concepts used to describe the characteristics of impairment tests, including scaling of results, applicability to field settings, reliability, validity, sensitivity, and specificity. These terms are defined in more detail in Boxes 3.1.1 to 3.1.4.

BOX 3.1.1 Reliability of Alcohol Impairment Tests

Reliability refers to the extent to which a test provides a result that is stable or repeatable from occasion to occasion. A reliable test is one that will yield a similar result across multiple tests in the same person (test-retest reliability), or across multiple test administrators or raters when they examine the same person (inter-rater reliability). An ideal impairment test should be consistent when applied to people who are sober, i.e. provide stable baseline scores for non-impaired performance. Furthermore, an ideal test should show consistent results when intoxicated persons are tested on different occasions. That is, multiple tests taken at the same level of impairment would show relatively little variation in the scores obtained. Reliability is a key feature of any impairment test. If scores obtained are not reliable, the results may be caused by factors other than impairment, such as variation in test administration or scoring.

BOX 3.1.2 Validity of Alcohol Impairment Tests

Validity of an impairment test refers to the extent to which the tests administered actually measure alcohol-related impairment, rather than other factors. Face validity refers to the extent to which law enforcement personnel and the test subject have confidence that the testing accurately measures alcohol impairment; many field sobriety tests have high levels of face validity. Concurrent validity refers to the extent to which an impairment test shows expected associations with other tests known to measure impairment, and with BACs. Construct validity refers to the adequacy and explanatory power of scientific concepts such as alcohol impairment. If alcohol-related impairment is highly variable across different behaviors, this will reduce the validity of any one test in measuring such a diffuse concept.

A test can be reliable but not valid. For example, a person's height can be measured in a highly reliable fashion, but the observed results would be an invalid index of alcohol impairment. In contrast, some level of reliability is needed in order for a test to show validity. If an impairment test has no reliability, it cannot be valid. The degree to which reliability is imperfect tends to place an upper limit on the degree of validity that can be shown by a test.

BOX 3.1.3 Sensitivity of Alcohol Impairment Tests

Sensitivity of an impairment test refers to the ability of a test to detect impairment, as reflected in the proportion of impaired persons (as determined by some other established measure) who are correctly classified as impaired by that particular test. Thus, an insensitive test allows persons who are impaired to escape detection (a false-negative test result). Whereas signs of intoxication are evident from test results in almost all persons when BACs become sufficiently high, many tests do not detect impairment when BACs are below 0.10 g%. Among people accustomed to heavy drinkers, many tests will be insensitive to BACs well above 0.10 g%. In some instances, there probably is little impairment to detect when a test does not reveal impairment. In other cases, however, impaired performance is likely to be present but a test is not sensitive enough to detect it.

BOX 3.1.4 Specificity of Alcohol Impairment Tests

Specificity of an impairment test refers to the extent to which the results reflect alcohol impairment and no other factors, such as fatigue, stress, and individual differences in cognitive and motor skills. A highly specific test will not be much influenced by changes in parameters other than alcohol impairment. An example of high test specificity in biological measurement is seen for BACs, where existing instrumentation allows assessment of alcohol in blood and breath that is not affected by closely related chemical compounds such as acetate, acetaldehyde, or acetone. Tests with low levels of specificity will lead to a high proportion of false-positive test identifications. That is, results for a non-specific test will often suggest that a person is impaired when they actually are not impaired (as measured by BAC or other tests). Thus, low specificity in impairment testing can lead to an inefficient expenditure of law enforcement resources.

3.1.8.1 Ideal Characteristics

Impairment tests differ in the *scaling of results*, that is, the nature of the scores or outcomes of a test. Results may be binary (impaired or not), ordinal rankings (low, medium, or high impairment), or quantitative scores. The need for precision of results depends upon the testing application. When used primarily as a screening tool for other sobriety tests or a BAC assessment, binary scores or ordinal rankings may be adequate. In other instances, continuous scores are desirable because they inform about the level of impairment.

Applicability to field settings is important when tests of impairment are applied in law enforcement practice. One requirement is that a test must have adequate reliability when administered by trained police officers under the diverse conditions encountered in field settings. A test might have acceptable reliability and validity in the laboratory, but these properties may or may not generalize to field settings. When used at the roadside there is much less control over the environment and numerous variables that can influence testing results. Reliability and validity properties in the field may be far different from the laboratory environment, in part because data from a known sober condition are not available for comparison.

There are several other important considerations in relation to field settings. Ideally, a test must be easily administered in a standard way by test administrators, and readily understood by test takers. The level of technical skill required for administering the test, collection of data, and interpretation of results should be acquired with a reasonably short duration of training. Any required instrumentation or equipment should be simple, easily available, and not require maintenance. Importantly, administration and the results from tests of alcohol intoxication must reach the high standard of acceptance as evidence in criminal prosecutions. This includes publication in scientific journals after peer review and general acceptance in the relevant scientific community.

Administration of field sobriety tests (FSTs) is necessary to generate the probable cause necessary to arrest a person suspected of driving under the influence of alcohol. The first suspicion of impairment arises from observations about the manner of driving and the general appearance and demeanor of the driver when questioned, including the smell of alcohol on the breath. Positive FSTs are then complemented by analysis of ethanol in samples of the driver's blood- or breath-alcohol at a police station. The reliability of FSTs is generally acceptable in the criminal justice system by the police authorities, prosecutors, judges, and juries. Such tests are generally discussed in relation to four criteria: (i) reliability, (ii) validity, (iii) sensitivity, and (iv) specificity (see boxes 3.1.1 to 3.1.4).

An important consideration when the sensitivity and specificity of impairment tests are evaluated is the results of the testing done in the same person when sober. Many FSTs exhibit large individual variations in results even before drinking any alcohol, owing to the person's age, gender, physical or mental health, body weight, obesity, etc. The results of laboratory research aimed at evaluating sensitivity and specificity compare a subject's performance at different BACs with their test performance when sober, usually before drinking begins. However, sensitivity and specificity are more difficult to achieve in the field, because sober baseline performance scores are not available. Therefore, tests that are known to have less variation among sober persons are preferable for field settings.

When developing cutoff scores on impairment tests, increased sensitivity almost always comes at the expense of decreased sensitivity, and vice versa. The "best" cutoff score for the definition of impairment depends upon the relative importance of sensitivity and specificity in a given application, as well as the estimated base rate of impairment in the population that will be tested. The choice of an appropriate cutoff score for an impairment test must be based on an understanding of these factors.

3.1.8.2 Reliability of Field Sobriety Tests

The field sobriety tests currently used in the United States and other nations were developed by scientists in California during the late 1970s. Careful consideration was given to the demand of them being administered by non–medically qualified personnel, such as trained police officers, under diverse environmental conditions, such as weather and lighting. SFSTs are mostly administered at the roadside in close proximity to a traffic stop when the driver is suspected of being under the influence of alcohol.

After an extensive program of research, literature review, and experimentation with subjects after drinking increasing amounts of alcohol, behavior scientists arrived at what became known as Standardized Field Sobriety Tests (SFSTs), which were endorsed by the US National Highway Traffic Safety Administration and other government agencies. The three tests of impairment that comprise the SFSTs were:

(a) *One-leg stand*—This test requires a person to stand upright on one leg with the other leg outstretched for a certain interval of time.

In the *one-leg stand test*, subjects must raise one foot at least six inches off the ground and stand on the other foot for 30 seconds, while keeping their arms at their sides. Performance is scored on a four-point scale, using items such as showing significant sway, using arms for balance, hopping, and putting down the raised foot.

(b) *Walk-and-turn*—This test requires the subject to walk a straight line with arms outstretched, turn, and then walk back along the same line.

In the *walk-and-turn test*, subjects must balance with feet positioned heel to toe and listen to test instructions. Then, subjects must walk nine steps heel to toe on a straight line, turn 180 degrees, and walk nine additional steps heel to toe, all the time counting their steps, watching their feet, and keeping their hands at their sides. Performance in the test is scored on an eight-point scale, using items such as starting before instructions are finished, stepping off the line, maintaining balance with arm movements, and taking an incorrect number of steps.

(c) *Gaze nystagmus*—A test of impairment that entails examining the suspect's eyes and looking for jerking movements of the pupils, an indication of gaze nystagmus.

The *gaze nystagmus test* focuses on horizontal gaze nystagmus. Smooth pursuit nystagmus and the angle of onset of nystagmus are assessed for each eye. Performance is scored on a six-point scale (three possible points from each eye). The cue to look for is an involuntary jerking of the eyeball when a stimulus (small pen) is moved from side to side in front of the eyes.

Both the walk-and-turn and one-leg stand tests are "divided attention" tasks requiring a person to listen and follow instructions while performing simple physical movements.

A driver might be stopped or pulled over by the police for various reasons besides involvement in a road-traffic crash. This might be a moving traffic offense, such as speeding or driving too slowly on the highway, failure to signal when turning, ignoring a stop sign, lights not working at night time, zig-zagging, or crossing lanes when not allowed to do so, etc. Important later clues of some alcohol- or drug-impairment come from the way the driver answers questions and whether they are in possession of a valid driving permit and vehicle insurance, besides other signs and symptoms of alcohol influence. The SFSTs were designed and evaluated to detect drivers with a BAC of 0.10 g% or above, which was the statutory limit for driving at the time in the USA.

When this limit was subsequently lowered to 0.08 g%, new studies were necessary to investigate the effectiveness of SFSTs at this lower threshold. Although the results in many instances were promising and gained continued support from departments of justice and the police, both false positive and false negative indications increased for those close to the 0.08 g% BAC limit. Of the three SFSTs, HGN appears to be the most sensitive test of alcohol influence. According to several studies, divided-attention tasks are sensitive enough to detect impairment associated with BAC from 0.05–0.08 g%, although this needs to be demonstrated in field settings with apprehended drivers and such studies are yet to be done.

One practical problem with the administration of SFSTs is that this might be done any time of the day under light and dark conditions and varying weather conditions and traffic intensity. Moreover, the population of licensed drivers is getting older and in most nations ranges from 18 to 95 years. Elderly individuals are more prone to have problems with their heath, especially blood pressure, and many medicate with several prescription drugs; the aged are therefore less likely to be able to perform adequately in SFSTs even when sober. Even in the younger age groups, problems arise owing to nervousness and stress when stopped by the police, obesity, and other individual characteristics. Some jurisdictions have set an upper age limit of 65 years for arrested drivers to be considered suitable to participate in SFSTs and an option to provide a roadside breath-alcohol test is a simple solution for these motorists.

In a laboratory study, Tharp et al.[83] included 297 drinking volunteers in a study of BACs from 0.0–0.18 g% who were tested by police officers trained to administer SFSTs. Inter-rater correlations ranged from 0.60 to 0.80, indicating an adequate level of reliability in the various testers. Test-retest correlation coefficients ranged from 0.40 to 0.75 between SFST scores determined on two separate drinking occasions to reach closely similar BAC. The overall SFST score was highly correlated with the person's BAC when results from all three tests were combined. Police officers correctly classified 81% of those examined as to whether their BAC was above or below 0.10 g% BAC. Similar results were obtained by Anderson et al.[160] in terms of the proportion of correct classification, although specificity and sensitivity of individual SFSTs were not evaluated.

Few studies have reported performance characteristics of individual FSTs under real-world conditions, that is, when actual traffic offenders are tested. One study found that HGN, specifically the angle of horizontal nystagmus onset, had high levels of sensitivity and specificity in predicting BACs above 0.10 g% in an emergency room setting. Perrine et al.[161] examined the reliability and validity of SFSTs in a project sponsored by the National Highway Traffic Safety Administration involving 480 subjects, and when police officers and other individuals trained in recognition of intoxication administered the tests.

Inter-rater reliability was adequate for all three FSTs and correlations with BAC were statistically significant. The correlation coefficient was lowest for walk-and-turn and one-leg stand tests. In the study by Perrine et al.[161] information was also provided about the sensitivity and specificity of various SFSTs in different BAC ranges. The HGN test had excellent sensitivity and specificity characteristics. Only 3% of subjects with a zero BAC failed the horizontal gaze nystagmus test (i.e. specificity was high when referenced to a zero BAC). Sensitivity was 100% for those with BACs over 0.15 g% and was 81% for subjects with BACs ranging from 0.10–0.149 g%.

Perrine et al.[161] determined that the ability to predict a person's BAC was much worse for the walk-and-turn and the one-leg stand tests. In particular, the specificity of the walk-and-turn test was low, and half (50%) of those with a zero BAC were classified as impaired. While sensitivity was fairly high (78%) at BACs above 0.15 g%, it dropped to less than 50% sensitivity for people with BACs between 0.08 g% and 0.10 g%. In the one-leg stand test, 30% of those with zero BAC were classified as impaired, indicating only moderate specificity. The corresponding sensitivity was only 50% for those with BACs between 0.10–0.15 g%, but this improved to 88% in subjects with BACs of 0.15 g% and higher.

The literature suggests that overall, SFSTs including walk-and-turn, one-leg stand, and horizontal gaze nystagmus are able to detect impairment under field conditions, but much depends on the BAC level of the person being examined. These tests have face validity and the results are understood by those required to take the tests. Training of those expected to administer SFSTs is crucial and results suggest that all three tests can be administered reliably and in a standardized way. The three SFSTs have validity in the sense that they do measure different aspects of alcohol impairment, such as divided attention, balance disturbances, and body sway. However, horizontal gaze nystagmus is much better at predicting BAC than the walk-and-turn and the one-leg stand tests. While they are worthwhile, the latter FSTs have significant limitations when used at the roadside, as discussed later. More research is needed to determine if improved testing procedures or different cutoff scores can improve the performance of the walk-and-turn and the one-leg stand tests.

It is important to appreciate that the reliability of SFSTs for their intended purpose depends upon the threshold BAC level of the person at the time of the test in relation to the end of drinking (acute tolerance). When SFSTs are used to judge impairment at BACs close to a statutory BAC limit their performance depends on the proportion of test subjects with BAC exceeding this limit. The SFSTs described in this article were originally designed and tested at a time when the statutory BAC limit for driving was 0.10 g%, although this is now set at 0.08 g% in all 50 states, apart from Utah, which lowered their limit to 0.05 g% in 2018. The reliability of SFSTs is expected to be worse at a BAC threshold of 0.05 g% and might not be sufficiently sensitive for the intended purpose. The handheld preliminary breath-alcohol screening tests work perfectly well at this BAC and even at 0.02 g%.

3.1.8.3 Clinical Signs and Symptoms of Alcohol Influence

Between 1941 and 1981 every person apprehended by the police in Sweden suspected of driving under the influence of alcohol was examined by a physician at a police station within 1–2 h after an arrest was made. The first suspicion of a drunk-driving offense arises from observations made about the driving, such as whether a crash occurred or a moving traffic offense was committed. Other indications included the driver's general appearance and demeanor, his or her way of answering questions, smell of alcohol on the breath, slurred speech, etc. By the 1960s, the traffic police authorities were equipped with a simple roadside breath-alcohol test device to test for alcohol influence before making an arrest and further testing including taking blood for forensic analysis.

From 1956 until 1989, the statutory BAC limit for driving in Sweden was 0.05 g% and information was gathered about the relationship between BAC and impairment. All apprehended drivers were examined by a physician (police surgeon) about 1–1.5 h after arrest and they were subjected to a series of standard tests of alcohol influence and a blood sample was taken for laboratory analysis. The physician was aware that he or she was examining a person arrested by the police on suspicion of impaired driving, but had no knowledge of the BAC when the clinical examination was made. This raises a statistical problem because ideally the examining physician should be "blinded" as to the disposition/condition of the person they were examining.

Nevertheless, the results of the clinical examination and the actual BAC provide useful diagnostic information. The physician's task was to examine the DUI suspect and ask various questions about health status, such as whether they were taking any prescribed medication, and their recent consumption of alcohol. A standardized questionnaire was administered and any clinical signs and symptoms of intoxication and drunkenness were noted including the suspect's appearance and demeanor, smell of alcohol on the breath, orientation in time and space, the color of the eyes, pupil size, etc. Furthermore, simple cognitive and psychomotor tests were administered, such as counting backward from 107, picking up small objects from the floor, Romberg's balance test, walking in a straight line, and finger-to-nose test, and the accumulated results were recorded on a special alcohol impairment protocol.[162,163] The results of these impairment tests along with the driver's BAC formed the main thrust of the prosecution's evidence when a charge of drunk driving was brought.

The physician was expected to reach a conclusion as to whether the suspect was or was not under the influence of alcohol. If the diagnosis was "under the influence" they were then expected to judge whether this was to a "mild degree," "moderate degree," or "severe degree." Finally, the physician took samples of fingertip blood, which were shipped to a forensic laboratory for determination of the ethanol content.[162]

Based on clinical tests of alcohol influence with 7,904 apprehended drivers, the percentage of suspects judged as being under the influence of alcohol is shown in Table 3.1.1 in relation to the measured BAC. One notices that as BAC increases both the number and percentage of suspects judged as not under the influence decreases and the number judged impaired by alcohol increases. For example, in the BAC range 0.05–0.099 g%, 70% were considered under the influence of alcohol compared with only 30% not under the influence.

Information in Table 3.1.2 was derived from the same drunk-driving suspects, but only considering those judged to be under the influence of alcohol. Another task of the examining physician was to categorize or grade the alcohol influence as being slight, moderate, or severe. As expected the percentage classification of "slight" decreased and the percentage deemed as being severely impaired by alcohol increased as the BAC range increased.

On the whole, the information derived from the clinical examination is insufficient to be used as the sole evidence in criminal prosecution and needs to be supported by other more objective evidence, such as the concentration of ethanol determined in blood or breath. The reliability of the behavioral evidence depends on the skill and training of the examining physician in administering these clinical tests, the sensitivity and specificity of the tests, and the ability of some people to "pull themselves together" in a critical situation. Also relevant is the age and gender of the suspect and the development of tolerance to some of the impairment effects of ethanol (tolerance).

The clinical examination of traffic offenders in Sweden was abandoned in 1981 because at the relatively low statutory BAC limit of 0.05 g%. Many of the apprehended drivers examined by physicians were considered not under the influence of alcohol, but the courts interpreted 0.05 g% as a concentration per se statute. Whenever there were discrepancies between the conclusions from the clinical examination and the laboratory analysis of blood samples, this caused confusion during the prosecution of traffic offenders. Since 1981 a clinical examination of suspects is only required when impairment is caused by drugs other than alcohol.

3.1.8.4 Degree of Impairment in Relation to BAC

The signs and symptoms of alcohol influence/intoxication are not difficult to detect when BAC is high, but more subtle tests are needed at BAC < 0.05–0.08 g%. However, this

TABLE 3.1.1

Number and Percentage of Apprehended Drivers in Sweden Judged under the Influence of Alcohol after Being Examined by a Physician in Relation to Blood-Alcohol Concentration (BAC)

Blood-alcohol concentration	N[1]	Not under the influence of alcohol N (%)	Under the influence of alcohol N (%)
0.1–0.49 g/L 0.01–0.049 g% 10–49 mg%	901	431 (48)	470 (52)
0.5–0.99 g/L 0.05–0.099 g% 50–99 mg%	1462	441 (30)	1021 (70)
1.0–1.49 g/L 0.10–0.149 g% 100–149 mg%	1914	360 (19)	1554 (81)
1.5–1.99 g/L 0.15–0.199 g% 150–199 mg%	1930	161 (8)	1769 (92)
2.0–2.49 g/L 0.20–0.249 g% 200–249 mg%	1226	51 (4)	1175 (96)
2.5–2.99 g/L 0.25–0.299 g% 250–299 mg%	389	10 (3)	379 (97)
3.0–3.49 g/L 0.30–0.349 g% 300–349 mg%	82	0	82 (100)

[1] Number of apprehended drivers within different BAC ranges.

TABLE 3.1.2

Classification of Drivers as to the Degree of Intoxication (Slight, Moderate, or Severe) According to a Clinical Examination by a Physician and Questionnaire in Relation to Blood-Alcohol Concentration (BAC)

Blood-alcohol concentration	Under the influence of alcohol, N[1]	Slight degree N (%)	Moderate degree N (%)	Severe degree N (%)
0.00–0.49 g/L 0.00–0.049 g% 0.0–49 mg%	470	411 (87)	56 (12)	3 (0.6)
0.50–0.99 g/L 0.05–0.099 g% 50–99 mg%	1021	788 (77)	218 (21)	15 (1.5)
1.00–1.49 g/L 0.10–0.149 g% 100–149 mg%	1554	998 (64)	483 (31)	73 (4.7)
1.50-1.99 g/L 0.15-0.199 g% 150–199 mg%	1769	752 (43)	774 (44)	243 (14)
2.00–2.49 g/L 0.20–0.249 g% 200–249 mg%	1175	349 (30)	544 (46)	282 (24)
2.50–2.99 g/L 0.25–0.299 g% 250–299 mg%	379	71 (19)	157 (41)	151 (40)
3.0–3.6 g/L 0.30–0.36 g% 300–360 mg%	82	4 (4.9)	28 (34)	50 (61)

[1] Number of drivers examined considered under the influence of alcohol in various BAC ranges.

level of BAC and even lower concentrations down to 0.01 g% are easy to detect by means of various handheld breath-alcohol instruments.

People experience more intense feelings of intoxication shortly after drinking before the peak BAC is reached. The degree of impairment is most pronounced after drinking neat spirits in a short time on an empty stomach because under these conditions the rate of absorption into the blood is faster. Also of importance are the person's age, body weight, and previous experience with drinking alcohol as well as the development of central nervous tolerance. Studies have shown that the signs and symptoms of drunkenness are more pronounced on the rising phase of the BAC curve (Mellanby effect) compared with the same BAC on the declining post-peak phase.[115]

Regular drinkers, matched for age and gender, exhibit fewer outward signs of drunkenness at the same BAC as occasional drinkers. More ethanol can be consumed in a shorter time in the form of spirits compared with beer or wine, which has implications for the peak BAC reached. A recent study compared peak BAC and time of reaching the peak after subjects drank the same dose of ethanol (0.50 g/kg) in the form of vodka/tonic (20% v/v), white wine (12.5% v/v), and beer (5.1% v/v).[164] The peak BACs (mean time to reach peak) were 0.077 ± 0.017 g% (3 min) after vodka/tonic, 0.062 ± 0.011 g% (54 min) after wine, and 0.05 ± 0.010 g% (62 min) after beer. Taken together, these results show that it is very difficult, in any individual case, to predict the BAC reached after drinking ethanol and then equate this BAC with impairment of body functions and observable clinical signs and symptoms of drunkenness.

Nevertheless, many tables or charts have been constructed and published over the years listing the degree of intoxication in relation to the person's BAC. Such charts are useful as a general guideline, but might not apply in any individual case. One such chart, which is widely adopted and used by the scientific community and law enforcement agencies was put together by Professor Kurt Dubowski, University of Oklahoma (USA).

The first "Dubowski chart" was entitled "stages of acute alcoholic influence/intoxication" and dates from 1956. Over the years, the information has been regularly updated and the most recent version of the "Dubowski alcohol table" appeared in 2012 and is shown in Table 3.1.3.[165] The left column of the chart shows increasing and overlapping ranges of BAC, the middle column defines the different stages of alcohol influence at these BAC levels, and the right column summarizes signs and symptoms of alcohol influence for a moderate drinker with the BACs shown. The overlapping ranges of BACs are intended to illustrate the wide variations in alcohol-induced effects in different individuals with the same BAC.

Note that seven stages of alcohol influence are defined including sub-clinical (sobriety), euphoria, excitement, confusion, stupor, coma, and death. These stages of alcohol influence are classified in relation to overlapping ranges of BAC in concentration units of g/L, g%, and mg%.

Table 3.1.3 shows that at a BAC between 0.03 g% and 0.12 g%, which covers the statutory limits for driving in most nations, some or all of the following alcohol-related effects might be evident:

- Mild euphoria, sociability, talkativeness
- Increased self-confidence, decreased inhibitions
- Diminished attention, judgment, and control
- Some sensory-motor impairment
- Slowed information processing
- Loss of efficiency in critical performance tests

3.1.9 Concluding Remarks

Overconsumption of alcohol and drunkenness are responsible for considerable morbidity and mortality as evidenced by a 2018 report from the World Health Organization. This maintained that worldwide the annual number of deaths from some alcohol-related cause reached a staggering three million.[3] Many of these deaths were directly or indirectly ascribed to acute or chronic drinking as well as alcohol-related accidents on the roads, in the workplace, and at home.[166] The degree of impairment after drinking alcohol depends on many individual factors, as well as situational and pharmacological effects, and importantly the dose of ethanol ingested and speed of drinking. Furthermore, measures of impairment are not uniform across all types of behavioral and cognitive tasks; for example, simple behaviors such as reaction times, when performed in isolation, are generally insensitive to moderate drinking and elevated BAC.[167] Furthermore, many such tests have a learning effect and well-practiced behaviors are the least sensitive to drinking alcohol unless very high BACs are reached.[168]

Impairment is consistently observed when a person performs tasks requiring simultaneous processing of multiple sources of information. The results from dual-performance and divided-attention tasks suggest that at elevated BAC a person has only a limited ability to process the information necessary to perform multiple tasks correctly. These experiments provide an important reason for the negative impact of alcohol in many types of accidents and as causative factors for injuries. For example, the intoxicated motorist may not exhibit much impairment when driving a well-known route with little other traffic on the roads. However, when a situation arises that requires the simultaneous processing of multiple sources of information, such as avoiding an unexpected obstacle in the course of driving, performance decrement is exaggerated.

Alcohol also produces deficits in activities that require fine motor control at high rates of speed. One of the most sensitive behavioral measures of impairment according to the literature is tracking performance, which requires rapid small adjustments in the muscles of the hands and eyes, and a high level of hand-eye coordination. Tracking performance is an important aspect of driving impairment, in part, because it is central to the lateral guidance of a motor vehicle. Another type of behavior sensitive to the effects of alcohol is speech, which requires fine motor control, timing, and coordination among the lips, tongue. and vocal cords at high rates of speed.

TABLE 3.1.3
Relationship between the Stage of Alcohol Influence and the Associated Clinical Signs and Symptoms of Drunkenness in Relation to the Person's Blood-Alcohol Concentration (BAC) Expressed in Different Units[1]

Blood-alcohol concentration	Stage of alcoholic influence	Typical clinical signs and/or symptoms
0.1–0.5 g/L 0.01–0.05 g% 10–50 mg%	Subclinical	Behavior nearly normal by ordinary observation. Influence/effects usually not apparent or obvious. Impairment detectable by special tests.
0.3–1.2 g/L 0.03–0.12 g% 30–120 mg%	Euphoria	Mild euphoria, sociability, talkativeness. Increased self-confidence, decreased inhibitions. Diminished attention, judgment, and control. Some sensory-motor impairment. Slowed information processing. Loss of efficiency in critical performance tests.
0.9–2.5 g/L 0.09–0.25 g% 90–250 mg%	Excitement	Emotional instability, loss of critical judgment. Impairment of perception, memory, and comprehension. Decreased sensatory response, increased reaction time. Reduced visual acuity and peripheral vision and slower glare recovery. Sensory-motor in-coordination, impaired balance, slurred speech. Vomiting, drowsiness.
1.8–3.0 g/L 0.18–0.30 g% 180–300 mg%	Confusion	Disorientation, mental confusion, vertigo, dysphoria. Exaggerated emotional states (fear, rage, grief, etc.). Disturbances of vision (diplopia, etc.) and of perception of color, form, motion, dimensions. Increased pain threshold. Increased muscular in-coordination, staggering gait, ataxia. Memory loss. Apathy with progressive lethargy.
2.5–4.0 g/L 0.25–0.40 g% 250–400 mg%	Stupor	General inertia, approaching loss of motor functions. Markedly decreased response to stimuli. Marked muscular in-coordination, inability to stand or walk. Vomiting, incontinence of urine and feces. Impaired consciousness, sleep or stupor, deep snoring.
3.5–5.0 g/L 0.35–0.50 g% 350–500 mg%	Coma	Complete unconsciousness, coma, anesthesia. Depressed or abolished reflexes. Subnormal temperature. Impairment/irregularities of circulation and respiration. Possible death.
Mean/median BAC > 3.6 g/L > 0.36 g% > 360 mg%	Death	Death from respiratory failure and/or cardiac arrest.

1 Chart prepared by Professor Kurt M Dubowski.[165]

2 Blood-alcohol concentrations (BAC) are reported in three ways; g/L as used in many EU nations, g% which is used in the USA and Australia, and mg% the unit used in the UK, Ireland, and Canada.

The characteristic eye movements and balance disturbances caused by drinking alcohol depend primarily on impairing effects of ethanol on the brain's vestibular system. Ethanol is a small water-soluble molecule that readily diffuses throughout the brain, and acts as a general depressant of the central nervous system akin to anesthetic gases. However, impairment in vestibular functioning provides an example of highly specific effects of ethanol molecules. Vestibular functioning is relatively sensitive to alcohol's impairment effects and HGN was therefore included among the SFSTs used to evaluate impairment in apprehended drivers. The mechanisms of vestibular impairment caused by ethanol are fairly well characterized and relate to the specific physiology of this brain function.

Nevertheless, individual differences in sensitivity to alcohol's effects are substantial even when the dose is adjusted for body weight and similar BACs are reached. Perhaps the most important consideration in this respect are the person's drinking habits and degree of habituation, which imparts a certain tolerance to the behavioral effects.[169] Those who drink regularly and in larger quantities tend to develop a higher degree of tolerance to the impairing effects of a given dose of ethanol.[170] However, by definition, people who consume more alcohol are also likely to reach higher BACs when they are encountered in forensic and legal settings. Advanced drinking practices are probably not predictive of a lower degree of impairment in field settings because individual differences in BACs are *not* controlled. Impairment tends to be greater in elder persons for the same dose of ethanol as consumed by younger individuals, which is likely a combination of increased neural vulnerability with aging and less body water to dilute ingested ethanol, resulting in higher BAC for the same dose/kg body weight.[171] When controlling for BACs and drinking practices, gender differences in impairment have not been demonstrated.

The impairment produced by high BAC depends upon the time course of a drinking episode. Ethanol's effects have been described as biphasic, with initial euphoria and stimulant effects during rising BACs, followed by dysphoria and sedative effects later on. Numerous measures of impairment are greater on the ascending limb compared to the descending limb of the BAC curve. This difference in impairment on the rising and declining parts of the BAC curve most likely reflects the phenomenon of acute tolerance, in which impairment effects decrease over time within a single drinking episode. When required to predict impairment, the amount of time elapsed since alcohol has been in the body can be as important a variable as BAC itself.

The time course of alcohol's effects on the individual don't always end when BACs reach zero, owing to residual or hangover effects.[172] After a single episode of heavy drinking, the next morning many people experience a hangover and generally feel anxious and tired and their ability to perform skilled tasks is likely to be impaired.[134] Earlier research failed to demonstrate consistent effects of hangovers on performance, owing to large individual differences in the severity of hangover effects and their duration.[173] However, a recent systematic review of this topic found that maintaining attention and driving skills were impaired during a hangover, whereas the results were not clear-cut for psychomotor functions, short- and long-term memory, and divided attention.[23] Hangover effects are poorly characterized compared to other effects of ethanol intoxication, although considerable research is now being done on this aspect of alcohol consumption.[174] The demonstration of significant impairment during a hangover would suggest the need for longer periods of abstinence before being allowed to perform the skilled tasks, similar to the rules often applied to airline pilots.[145]

Field sobriety tests exemplified by walk-and-turn, one-leg stand, and horizontal gaze nystagmus need to be administered in a standardized way by trained police officers because this gives the result obtained more credibility and acceptance by the courts.[17] Each of the individual tests has adequate validity, in that they assess functioning and performance known to reflect alcohol impairment. The scores obtained in the evaluation of SFSTs are reasonably well correlated with BAC and other impairment measures. Test sensitivity and specificity appear to be fairly high for the horizontal gaze nystagmus test at a critical threshold BAC of 0.08 g%. The sensitivity and specificity of walk-and-turn and one-leg stand are less adequate at this same BAC and both false positive and false negative results are appreciable.[175] These types of psychomotor and divided attention tasks are more useful to detect people with BACs of 0.10 g% or higher.

The validity of currently available SFSTs for detecting impairment at a threshold BAC below 0.08 g% has not been thoroughly evaluated and their usefulness for this purpose, e.g. at a statutory BAC limit of 0.05 g%, is doubtful. The is an urgent need to develop and evaluate more sensitive field sobriety tests for use in law enforcement because there is a trend towards lowering statutory BAC limits for driving in some states. Enforcement of lower BAC limits is not a problem when hand-held breath analyzers are used. But in some countries, the arresting police officer requires probable cause before the breath alcohol test can be administered and therefore needs to have other evidence that a driver was impaired.[176]

Scotland lowered its statutory BAC limit for driving from 0.08 g% to 0.05 g% in December 2013, although it does not appear to have been followed by a reduction in the number of road traffic accidents and driver fatalities.[177] By contrast, another study found a significant 10.4 % decrease in fatal crashes involving drunken drivers when the statutory BAC limit was lowered from 0.10 g% to 0.08 g%.[178] Whether other jurisdictions will follow the lead set by the state of Utah and also enforce a BAC of 0.05 g% for driving remains to be seen. However, statutory BAC limits for driving are even lower in other nations, such as 0.03 g% in Japan,[179] Taiwan,[180] and South Korea and 0.02 g% in China, Sweden, Norway, and Poland. The degree of alcohol impairment at these lower BACs, if any, has not been well studied, although deviation from normal performance is likely to start after the first drink.[181]

REFERENCES

1. Room R, Babor T, Rehm J. Alcohol and public health. *Lancet* 2005;365:519–30.
2. Klatsky AL. Drink to your health? *Sci Am* 2003;288:74–81.
3. WHO. *Global Status Report on Alcohol and Health, Geneva, Switzerland*. Geneva: World Health Organization, 2018.
4. Lim SS, Vos T, Flaxman AD, Danaei G, Shibuya K, Adair-Rohani H, et al. A comparative risk assessment of burden of disease and injury attributable to 67 risk factors and risk factor clusters in 21 regions, 1990–2010: a systematic analysis for the Global Burden of Disease Study 2010. *Lancet* 2012;380:2224–60.
5. Cherpitel CJ. Alcohol-related injury and the emergency department: research and policy questions for the next decade. *Addiction* 2006;101:1225–7.
6. Holmgren A, Jones AW. Demographics of suicide victims in Sweden in relation to their blood-alcohol concentration and the circumstances and manner of death. *Forensic Sci Int* 2010;198:17–22.
7. Pajunen T, Vuori E, Vincenzi FF, Lillsunde P, Smith G, Lunetta P. Unintentional drowning: role of medicinal drugs and alcohol. *BMC Public Health* 2017;17:388.
8. Tormey WP, Moore TM. Ethanol as a single toxin in non-traumatic deaths - A toxicology perspective. *Leg Med (Tokyo)* 2012.

9. Abbey A, Zawacki T, Buck PO, Testa M, Parks K, Norris J, et al. How does alcohol contribute to sexual assault? Explanations from laboratory and survey data. *Alcohol Clin Exp Res* 2002;26:575–81.
10. Felson R, Staff J. The effects of alcohol intoxication on violent versus other offending. *Crim Justice Behav* 2012;37:1343–60.
11. Ahlner J, Holmgren A, Jones AW. Prevalence of alcohol and other drugs and the concentrations in blood of drivers killed in road traffic crashes in Sweden. *Scand J Public Health* 2014;42:177–83.
12. Brick J, Erickson CK. Intoxication is not always visible: an unrecognized prevention challenge. *Alcohol Clin Exp Res* 2009;33:1489–507.
13. Goldberg L. Quantittaive studies on alcohol tolerance in man. *Acta Physiol Scand* 1943;5 Supp 16:1–128.
14. Carpenter JA. Effects of alcohol on some psychological processes. A critical review with special reference to automobile driving skill. *Q J Stud Alcohol* 1962;23:274–314.
15. Levine JM, Kramer GG, Levine EN. Effects of alcohol on human performance: an integration of research findings based on an abilities classification. *J Appl Psychol* 1975;60:285–93.
16. Brick J. *Forensic Alcohol Test Evidence (FATE)*. Springfield: Charles C. Thomas, 2017.
17. Burns M. An overview of field sobriety test research. *Percept Mot Skills* 2003;97:1187–99.
18. Zuba D. Accuracy and reliability of breath alcohol testing by handheld electrochemical analysers. *Forensic Sci Int* 2008;178:e29–33.
19. Gmel G, Rehm J. Harmful alcohol use. *Alcohol Res Health* 2003;27:52–62.
20. Bratberg GH, Wilsnack R, Havas Haugland S, Krokstad S, Sund ER, et al. Gender differences and gender convergence in alcohol use over the past three decades (1984–2008), The HUNT Study, Norway. *BMC Public Health* 2016;16:723.
21. Liangpunsakul S, Crabb DW, Qi R. Relationship among alcohol intake, body fat, and physical activity: a population-based study. *Ann Epidemiol* 2010;20:670–5.
22. Mellanby E. *Alcohol: Its Absorption Into and Disappearance from the Blood under Different Conditions*. London: Medical Research Committee, Series nr 13, HMSO, 1919.
23. Gunn C, Mackus M, Griffin C, Munafo MR, Adams S. A systematic review of the next-day effects of heavy alcohol consumption on cognitive performance. *Addiction* 2018;113:2182–93.
24. Olson KN, Smith SW, Kloss JS, Ho JD, Apple FS. Relationship between blood alcohol concentration and observable symptoms of intoxication in patients presenting to an emergency department. *Alcohol Alcohol* 2013;48:386–9.
25. Dry MJ, Burns NR, Nettelbeck T, Farquharson AL, White JM. Dose-related effects of alcohol on cognitive functioning. *PLoS One* 2012;7:e50977.
26. Deichmann WB, Henschler D, Holmstedt B, Keil G. What is there that is not poison? A study of the Third Defense by Paracelsus. *Arch Toxicol* 1986;58:207–13.
27. Modig F, Fransson PA, Magnusson M, Patel M. Blood alcohol concentration at 0.06 and 0.10% causes a complex multifaceted deterioration of body movement control. *Alcohol* 2012;46:75–88.
28. Jones AW. Pharmacokinetics of ethanol - issues of forensic importance. *Forensic Sci Rev* 2011;23:91–136.
29. Jones AW, Neri A. Age-related differences in the effects of ethanol on performance and behaviour in healthy men. *Alcohol Alcohol* 1994;29:171–9.
30. Morean ME, Corbin WR. Subjective response to alcohol: a critical review of the literature. *Alcohol Clin Exp Res* 2010;34:385–95.
31. Kelly M, Myrsten AL, Neri A, Rydberg U. Effects and after effects of alcohol on psychological and physiological functions in man - a controlle dstudy. *Blutalkohol* 1970;7:422–36.
32. Ekman G, Frankenhaeuser M, Goldberg L, Hagdahl R, Myrsten AL. Subjective and objective effects of alcohol as functions of dosage and time. *Psychopharmacologia* 1964;6:399–409.
33. Ekman G, Frankenhaeuser M, Goldberg L, Bjerver K, Jaerpe G, Myrsten AL. Effects of alcohol intake on subjective and objective variables over a five-hour period. *Psychopharmacologia* 1963;4:28–38.
34. Jones AW, Neri A. Age-related differences in blood ethanol parameters and subjective feelings of intoxication in healthy men. *Alcohol Alcohol* 1985;20:45–52.
35. Giancola PR. Executive functioning: a conceptual framework for alcohol-related aggression. *Exp Clin Psychopharmacol* 2000;8:576–97.
36. Tabakoff B, Hoffman PL. The neurobiology of alcohol consumption and alcoholism: an integrative history. *Pharmacol Biochem Behav* 2013;113:20–37.
37. Maylor EA, Rabbitt PM, James GH, Kerr SA. Effects of alcohol and extended practice on divided-attention performance. *Percept Psychophys* 1990;48:445–52.
38. Tedstone D, Coyle K. Cognitive impairments in sober alcoholics: performance on selective and divided attention tasks. *Drug Alcohol Depend* 2004;75:277–86.
39. Brumback T, Cao D, King A. Effects of alcohol on psychomotor performance and perceived impairment in heavy binge social drinkers. *Drug Alcohol Depend* 2007;91:10–7.
40. Fogarty JN, Vogel-Sprott M. Cognitive processes and motor skills differ in sensitivity to alcohol impairment. *J Stud Alcohol* 2002;63:404–11.
41. Zink N, Zhang R, Chmielewski WX, Beste C, Stock AK. Detrimental effects of a high-dose alcohol intoxication on sequential cognitive flexibility are attenuated by practice. *Prog Neuropsychopharmacol Biol Psychiatry* 2019;89:97–108.
42. Baylor AM, Layne CS, Mayfield RD, Osborne L, Spirduso WW. Effects of ethanol on human fractionated response times. *Drug Alcohol Depend* 1989;23:31–40.
43. Taberner PV. Sex differences in the effects of low doses of ethanol on human reaction time. *Psychopharmacology (Berl)* 1980;70:283–6.
44. Maylor EA, Rabbitt PM, Connolly SA. Rate of processing and judgment of response speed: comparing the effects of alcohol and practice. *Percept Psychophys* 1989;45:431–8.
45. Linnoila M, Erwin CW, Ramm D, Cleveland WP. Effects of age and alcohol on psychomotor performance of men. *J Stud Alcohol* 1980;41:488–95.
46. Fagan D, Tiplady B, Scott DB. Effects of ethanol on psychomotor performance. *Br J Anaesth* 1987;59:961–5.
47. Golby J. Use of factor analysis in the study of alcohol-induced strategy changes in skilled performance on a soccer test. *Percept Mot Skills* 1989;68:147–56.
48. Connors GJ, Maisto SA. Effects of alcohol, instructions and consumption rate and motor performance. *J Stud Alcohol* 1980;41:509–17.
49. Tiplady B, Oshinowo B, Thomson J, Drummond GB. Alcohol and cognitive function: assessment in everyday life and laboratory settings using mobile phones. *Alcohol Clin Exp Res* 2009;33:2094–102.

50. Beirness D, Vogel-Sprott M. Alcohol tolerance in social drinkers: operant and classical conditioning effects. *Psychopharmacology (Berl)* 1984;84:393–7.
51. Wilson JR, Erwin VG, McClearn GE, Plomin R, Johnson RC, Ahern FM, et al. Effects of ethanol: II. Behavioral sensitivity and acute behavioral tolerance. *Alcohol Clin Exp Res* 1984;8:366–74.
52. Moskowitz H, Burns MM, Williams AF. Skills performance at low blood alcohol levels. *J Stud Alcohol* 1985;46:482–5.
53. Niaura RS, Nathan PE, Frankenstein W, Shapiro AP, Brick J. Gender differences in acute psychomotor, cognitive, and pharmacokinetic response to alcohol. *Addict Behav* 1987;12:345–56.
54. Mills KC, Bisgrove EZ. Body sway and divided attention performance under the influence of alcohol: dose-response differences between males and females. *Alcohol Clin Exp Res* 1983;7:393–7.
55. Steele CM, Josephs RA. Drinking your troubles away. II: an attention-allocation model of alcohol's effect on psychological stress. *J Abnorm Psychol* 1988;97:196–205.
56. Zador PL. Alcohol-related relative risk of fatal driver injuries in relation to driver age and sex. *J Stud Alcohol* 1991;52:302–10.
57. Hindmarch I, Bhatti JZ, Starmer GA, Mascord DJ, Kerr JS, Sherwood N. The effects of alcohol on the cognitive function of males and females and on skills relating to car driving. *Hum Psychopharm Clin Exp* 1992;7:105–14.
58. McMillen DL, Smith SM, Wells-Parker E. The effects of alcohol, expectancy, and sensation seeking on driving risk taking. *Addict Behav* 1989;14:477–83.
59. Mongrain S, Standing L. Impairment of cognition, risk-taking, and self-perception by alcohol. *Percept Mot Skills* 1989;69:199–210.
60. O'Hanlon JF. Driving performance under the influence of drugs: rationale for, and application of, a new test. *Br J Clin Pharmacol* 1984;18 Suppl 1:121S–9S.
61. Helland A, Jenssen GD, Lervag LE, Westin AA, Moen T, Sakshaug K, et al. Comparison of driving simulator performance with real driving after alcohol intake: a randomised, single blind, placebo-controlled, cross-over trial. *Accid Anal Prev* 2013;53:9–16.
62. Attwood DA, Williams RD, Madill HD. Effects of moderate blood alcohol concentrations on closed-course driving performance. *J Stud Alcohol* 1980;41:623–34.
63. Huntley MS, Jr, Centybear TM. Alcohol, sleep deprivation, and driving speed effects upon control use during driving. *Hum Factors* 1974;16:19–28.
64. Brewer N, Sandow B. Alcohol effects on driver performance under conditions of divided attention. *Ergonomics* 1980;23:185–90.
65. Sobell LC, Sobell MB. Effects of alcohol on the speech of alcoholics. *J Speech Hear Res* 1972;15:861–8.
66. Sobell LC, Sobell MB, Coleman RF. Alcohol-induced dysfluency in nonalcoholics. *Folia Phoniatr (Basel)* 1982;34:316–23.
67. Trojan F, Kryspin-Exner K. The decay of articulation under the influence of alcohol and paraldehyde. *Folia Phoniatr (Basel)* 1968;20:217–38.
68. Chin SB, Pisoni DB. *Alcohol and Speech*. San Diego: Academic Press, 1997.
69. Pisoni DB, Martin CS. Effects of alcohol on the acoustic-phonetic properties of speech: perceptual and acoustic analyses. *Alcohol Clin Exp Res* 1989;13:577–87.
70. Tisljar-Szabo E, Rossu R, Varga V, Pleh C. The effect of alcohol on speech production. *J Psycholinguist Res* 2014;43:737–48.
71. Johnson K, Pisoni DB, Bernacki RH. Do voice recordings reveal whether a person is intoxicated? A case study. *Phonetica* 1990;47:215–37.
72. Iurato S. *Submicroscopic Structure of the Inner Ear*. London: Pergamon Press, 1967.
73. Money KE, Johnson WH, Corlett BM. Role of semicircular canals in positional alcohol nystagmus. *Am J Physiol* 1965;208:1065–70.
74. Nito Y, Johnson WH, Money KE, Ireland PE. The non-auditory labyrinth and positional alcohol nystagmus. *Acta Otolaryngol* 1964;58:65–7.
75. Money KEM, Hioffert BM. The mechanism of positional alcohol nystagmus. *Can J Otolaryngol* 1974;3:302–13.
76. Aschan G, Bergstedt M. Positional alcoholic nystagmus (PAN) in man following repeated alcohol doses. *Acta Otolaryngol Suppl* 1975;330:15–29.
77. Goldberg L. Alcohol, tranquilizers and hangover. *Q J Stud Alcohol* 1961;Suppl 1:37–56.
78. Fregly AR, Bergstedt M, Graybiel A. Relationships between blood alcohol, positional alcohol nystagmus and postural equilibrium. *Q J Stud Alcohol* 1967;28:11–21.
79. Aschan G. Different types of alcohol nystagmus. *Acta Otolaryngol Suppl* 1958;140:69–78.
80. Behrens MM. Nystagmus. *Int Ophthalmol Clin* 1978;18:57–82.
81. Lehti H. The effect of blood alcohol concentration on the onset of gaze nystagmus. *Blutalkohol* 1976;13:411–20.
82. Barnes GR, Crombie JW, Edge A. The effects of ethanol on visual-vestibular interaction during active and passive head movements. *Aviat Space Environ Med* 1985;56:695–701.
83. Tharp VK, Burns M, Moskowitz H. *Development and Field Test of Psychophysical Tests for DWI Arrest Technical Report DOT-HS-805-864 1981*. Washington, DC: Natioanl Highway Traffic Safety Administration, 1981.
84. Goding GS, Dobie RA. Gaze nystagmus and blood alcohol. *Laryngoscope* 1986;96:713–7.
85. Baloh RW, Sharma S, Moskowitz H, Griffith R. Effect of alcohol and marijuana on eye movements. *Aviat Space Environ Med* 1979;50:18–23.
86. Gentles W, Thomas EL. Commentary. Effect of benzodiazepines upon saccadic eye movements in man. *Clin Pharmacol Ther* 1971;12:563–74.
87. Booker JL. End-position nystagmus as an indicator of ethanol intoxication. *Sci Justice* 2001;41:113–6.
88. Booker JL. The Horizontal Gaze Nystagmus test: fraudulent science in the American courts. *Sci Justice* 2004;44:133–9.
89. Citek K, Ball B, Rutledge DA. Nystagmus testing in intoxicated individuals. *Optometry* 2003;74:695–710.
90. Tiffany DV. Optometric expert testimony: foundation for the horizontal gaze nystagmus test. *J Am Optom Assoc* 1986;57:705–8.
91. Modig F, Patel M, Magnusson M, Fransson PA. Study II: mechanoreceptive sensation is of increased importance for human postural control under alcohol intoxication. *Gait Posture* 2012;35:419–27.
92. Modig F, Patel M, Magnusson M, Fransson PA. Study I: effects of 0.06% and 0.10% blood alcohol concentration on human postural control. *Gait Posture* 2012;35:410–8.
93. Lipscomb TR, Nathan PE. Blood alcohol level discrimination. The effects of family history of alcoholism, drinking pattern, and tolerance. *Arch Gen Psychiatry* 1980;37:571–6.
94. O'Malley SS, Maisto SA. Factors affecting the perception of intoxication: dose, tolerance, and setting. *Addict Behav* 1984;9:111–20.

95. Coulson CE, Williams LJ, Brennan SL, Berk M, Kotowicz MA, Lubman DI, et al. Alcohol consumption and body composition in a population-based sample of elderly Australian men. *Aging Clin Exp Res* 2013;25:183–92.
96. O'Neill B, Williams AF, Dubowski KM. Variability in blood alcohol concentrations. Implications for estimating individual results. *J Stud Alcohol* 1983;44:222–30.
97. Ely M, Hardy R, Longford NT, Wadsworth ME. Gender differences in the relationship between alcohol consumption and drink problems are largely accounted for by body water. *Alcohol Alcohol* 1999;34:894–902.
98. Kalant H, LeBlanc AE, Wilson A, Homatidis S. Sensorimotor and physiological effects of various alcoholic beverages. *Can Med Assoc J* 1975;112:953–8.
99. Kalant H, LeBlanc AE, Gibbins RJ. Tolerance to, and dependence on, some non-opiate psychotropic drugs. *Pharmacol Rev* 1971;23:135–91.
100. Cole-Harding S, Wilson JR. Ethanol metabolism in men and women. *J Stud Alcohol* 1987;48:380–7.
101. Baraona E, Abittan CS, Dohmen K, Moretti M, Pozzato G, Chayes ZW, et al. Gender differences in pharmacokinetics of alcohol. *Alcohol Clin Exp Res* 2001;25:502–7.
102. Ammon E, Schafer C, Hofmann U, Klotz U. Disposition and first-pass metabolism of ethanol in humans: is it gastric or hepatic and does it depend on gender? *Clin Pharmacol Ther* 1996;59:503–13.
103. Kwo PY, Ramchandani VA, O'Connor S, Amann D, Carr LG, Sandrasegaran K, et al. Gender differences in alcohol metabolism: relationship to liver volume and effect of adjusting for body mass. *Gastroenterology* 1998;115:1552–7.
104. Mumenthaler MS, Taylor JL, O'Hara R, Fisch HU, Yesavage JA. Effects of menstrual cycle and female sex steroids on ethanol pharmacokinetics. *Alcohol Clin Exp Res* 1999;23:250–5.
105. Mumenthaler MS, Taylor JL, Yesavage JA. Ethanol pharmacokinetics in white women: nonlinear model fitting versus zero-order elimination analyses. *Alcohol Clin Exp Res* 2000;24:1353–62.
106. Correa CL, Oga S. Effects of the menstrual cycle of white women on ethanol toxicokinetics. *J Stud Alcohol* 2004;65:227–31.
107. Burns M, Moskowitz H. Gender-related differences in impairment of performance by allcohol. In: Sexias FA, editor. *Current in Alcoholism; Biological, Biochemical and Clinical Studies.* New York: Grune & Stratton, 1977.
108. Parker ES, Noble EP. Alcohol and the aging process in social drinkers. *J Stud Alcohol* 1980;41:170–8.
109. Pohorecky LA. Biphasic action of ethanol. *Biobehav Rev* 1977;1:231–40.
110. Addicott MA, Marsh-Richard DM, Mathias CW, Dougherty DM. The biphasic effects of alcohol: comparisons of subjective and objective measures of stimulation, sedation, and physical activity. *Alcohol Clin Exp Res* 2007;31:1883–90.
111. Martin CS, Earleywine M. Ascending and descending rates of change in blood alcohol concentrations and subjective intoxication ratings. *J Subst Abuse* 1990;2:345–52.
112. Martin CS, Moss HB. Measurement of acute tolerance to alcohol in human subjects. *Alcohol Clin Exp Res* 1993;17:211–6.
113. Kalant H. Research on tolerance: what can we learn from history? *Alcohol Clin Exp Res* 1998;22:67–76.
114. Keiding S, Christensen NJ, Damgaard SE, Dejgard A, Iversen HL, Jacobsen A, et al. Ethanol metabolism in heavy drinkers after massive and moderate alcohol intake. *Biochem Pharmacol* 1983;32:3097–102.
115. Holland MG, Ferner RE. A systematic review of the evidence for acute tolerance to alcohol - the "Mellanby effect." *Clin Toxicol (Phila)* 2017;55:545–56.
116. Gilliam DM. Alcohol absorption rate affects hypothermic response in mice: evidence for rapid tolerance. *Alcohol* 1989;6:357–62.
117. Martin CS, Rose RJ, Obremski KM. Estimation of blood alcohol concentrations in young male drinkers. *Alcohol Clin Exp Res* 1991;15:494–9.
118. Waller MB, McBride WJ, Lumeng L, Li TK. Initial sensitivity and acute tolerance to ethanol in the P and NP lines of rats. *Pharmacol Biochem Behav* 1983;19:683–6.
119. Forney RB, Hughes FW, Harger RN, Richards AB. Alcohol distribution in the vascular system. Concentration of orally administered alcohol in blood from various points in the vascular system, and in rebreathed air, during absorption. *Q J Stud Alcohol* 1964;25:205–17.
120. Kalant H. Current state of knowledge about the mechanisms of alcohol tolerance. *Addict Biol* 1996;1:133–41.
121. Lindberg L, Brauer S, Wollmer P, Goldberg L, Jones AW, Olsson SG. Breath alcohol concentration determined with a new analyzer using free exhalation predicts almost precisely the arterial blood alcohol concentration. *Forensic Sci Int* 2007;168:200–7.
122. Hendershot CS, Wardell JD, Strang NM, Markovich MS, Claus ED, Ramchandani VA. Application of an alcohol clamp paradigm to examine inhibitory control, subjective responses, and acute tolerance in late adolescence. *Exp Clin Psychopharmacol* 2015;23:147–58.
123. Moskowitz H, Burns M. Effects of rate of drinking on human performance. *J Stud Alcohol* 1976;37:598–605.
124. Alha A. Blood alcohol and clinical inebriation in Finnish men *Ann Acad Sci Fenn* 1951;A 26:1–136.
125. Benton RP, Banks WP, Vogler RE. Carryover of tolerance to alcohol in moderate drinkers. *J Stud Alcohol* 1982;43:1137–48.
126. Hurst PM, Bagley SK. Acute adaptation to the effects of alcohol. *Q J Stud Alcohol* 1972;33:358–78.
127. LeBlanc AE, Kalant H, Gibbins RJ. Acute tolerance to ethanol in the rat. *Psychopharmacologia* 1975;41:43–6.
128. Radlow R, Hurst PM. Temporal relations between blood alcohol concentration and alcohol effect: an experiment with human subjects. *Psychopharmacology (Berl)* 1985;85:260–6.
129. Moskowitz H, Daily J, Henderson R. The Mellanby effect in moderate and heavy drinkers. In: Johnston IR, editor. *Proceedings 7th International Conference on Alcohol, Drugsand Traffic Safety.* Canberra: Australian government publishing Company, 1979, 184–9.
130. Vogel-Sprott M. *Alcohol Tolerance and Social Drinking: Learningthe Consequences.* New York: Guilford Press, 1992.
131. Vogel-Sprott M, Kartechner W, McConnell D. Consequences of behavior influence the effect of alcohol. *J Subst Abuse* 1989;1:369–79.
132. Scholey A, Benson S, Kaufman J, Terpstra C, Ayre E, Verster JC, et al. Effects of alcohol hangover on cognitive performance: findings from a field/internet mixed methodology study. *J Clin Med* 2019;8:440.
133. Heffernan T, Samuels A, Hamilton C, McGrath-Brookes M. Alcohol hangover has detrimental impact upon both executive function and prospective memory. *Front Psychiatry* 2019;10:282.
134. Devenney LE, Coyle KB, Verster JC. Cognitive performance and mood after a normal night of drinking: a naturalistic alcohol hangover study in a non-student sample. *Addict Behav Rep* 2019;10:100197.

135. Devenney LE, Coyle KB, Verster JC. Memory and attention during an alcohol hangover. *Hum Psychopharmacol* 2019;34:e2701.
136. Verster JC, van de Loo A, Benson S, Scholey A, Stock AK. The assessment of overall hangover severity. *J Clin Med* 2020;9:786.
137. Verster JC, Kruisselbrink LD, Slot KA, Anogeianaki A, Adams S, Alford C, et al. Sensitivity to experiencing alcohol hangovers: reconsideration of the 0.11% blood alcohol concentration (BAC) threshold for having a hangover. *J Clin Med* 2020;9:179.
138. Rohsenow DJ, Howland J. The role of beverage congeners in hangover and other residual effects of alcohol intoxication: a review. *Curr Drug Abuse Rev* 2010;3:76–9.
139. Rohsenow DJ, Howland J, Alvarez L, Nelson K, Langlois B, Verster JC, et al. Effects of caffeinated vs. non-caffeinated alcoholic beverage on next-day hangover incidence and severity, perceived sleep quality, and alertness. *Addict Behav* 2014;39:329–32.
140. Rohsenow DJ, Howland J, Arnedt JT, Almeida AB, Greece J, Minsky S, et al. Intoxication with bourbon versus vodka: effects on hangover, sleep, and next-day neurocognitive performance in young adults. *Alcohol Clin Exp Res* 2010;34:509–18.
141. Collins WE, Chiles WD. Laboratory performance during acute alcohol intoxication and hangover. *Hum Factors* 1980;22:445–62.
142. Ames GM, Grube JW, Moore RS. The relationship of drinking and hangovers to workplace problems: an empirical study. *J Stud Alcohol* 1997;58:37–47.
143. Wu SH, Guo Q, Viken RJ, Reed T, Dai J. Heritability of usual alcohol intoxication and hangover in male twins: the NAS-NRC twin registry. *Alcohol Clin Exp Res* 2014;38:2307–13.
144. Laurell H, Tornros J. Investigation of alcoholic hangover effects in driving performance. *Blutalkohol* 1983;20:489–99.
145. Yesavage JA, Leirer VO. Hangover effects on aircraft pilots 14 hours after alcohol ingestion: a preliminary report. *Am J Psychiatry* 1986;143:1546–50.
146. Seppala T, Leino T, Linnoila M, Huttunen M, Ylikahri R. Effects of hangover on psychomotor skills related to driving: modification by fructose and glucose. *Acta Pharmacol Toxicol (Copenh)* 1976;38:209–18.
147. Karvinen E, Miettinen M, Ahlman K. Physical performance during hangover. *Q J Stud Alcohol* 1962;23:208–15.
148. Takala M, Siro E, Toivainen Y. Intellectual functions and dexterity during hangover; experiments after intoxication with brandy and with beer. *Q J Stud Alcohol* 1958;19:1–29.
149. Barber HO. Positional nystagmus. *Otolaryngol Head Neck Surg* 1984;92:649–55.
150. Becker J. The alcohol hangover. *Ann Intern Med* 2001;134:533–4.
151. Wolff N, Gussek P, Stock AK, Beste C. Effects of high-dose ethanol intoxication and hangover on cognitive flexibility. *Addict Biol* 2018;23:503–14.
152. Grange JA, Stephens R, Jones K, Owen L. The effect of alcohol hangover on choice response time. *J Psychopharmacol* 2016;30:654–61.
153. Stephens R, Holloway K, Grange JA, Owen L, Jones K, Kruisselbrink D. Does familial risk for alcohol use disorder predict alcohol hangover? *Psychopharmacology (Berl)* 2017;234:1795–802.
154. Swift R, Davidson D. Alcohol hangover: mechanisms and mediators. *Alcohol Health Res World* 1998;22:54–60.
155. Schuckit MA. Management of withdrawal delirium (delirium tremens). *N Engl J Med* 2015;372:580–1.
156. Verster JC, Stephens R, Penning R, Rohsenow D, McGeary J, Levy D, et al. The alcohol hangover research group consensus statement on best practice in alcohol hangover research. *Curr Drug Abuse Rev* 2010;3:116–26.
157. Merlo A, Adams S, Benson S, Devenney L, Gunn C, Iversen J, et al. Proceeding of the 9th alcohol hangover research group meeting. *Curr Drug Abuse Rev* 2017;10:68–75.
158. Slutske WS, Piasecki TM, Nathanson L, Statham DJ, Martin NG. Genetic influences on alcohol-related hangover. *Addiction* 2014;109:2027–34.
159. Schuckit MA. Subjective responses to alcohol in sons of alcoholics and control subjects. *Arch Gen Psychiatry* 1984;41:879–84.
160. Anderson TE, Schweitz RM, Snyder MB. Field evaluation of a behavioral test battery for DWI. DOT-HS-806-475 1983; National Highway Traffci Safety Administration.
161. Perrine MW, Foss RD, Meyer AR, Voas RB, Velez C. Field sobriety tests reliability and validity. In: Utelmann HD, Berghaus G, Kroj G, editors. *Alcohol, Drugs and Traffic Safety Proceedings of the 12th Intenrational Confernece.* Cologne: Verlag TUV Rheinland, 1993.
162. Bonnichsen RK, Dimberg R, Maehly A, Åqvist S. Alkohol och påverkan. *Institute för Maltdrycksforskning* 1967;17:1–27.
163. Penttila A, Tenhu M. Clinical examination as medicolegal proof of alcohol intoxication. *Med Sci Law* 1976;16:95–103.
164. Mitchell MC, Jr, Teigen EL, Ramchandani VA. Absorption and peak blood alcohol concentration after drinking beer, wine, or spirits. *Alcohol Clin Exp Res* 2014;38:1200–4.
165. Dubowski KM. The Dubowski alcohol table. *IACT Newsletter* 2012;23:7–8.
166. Cherpitel CJ, Ye Y. Alcohol and violence-related injuries among emergency room patients in an international perspective. *J Am Psychiatr Nurses Assoc* 2010;16:227–35.
167. Wardell JD, Quilty LC, Hendershot CS. Alcohol sensitivity moderates the indirect associations between impulsive traits, impaired control over drinking, and drinking outcomes. *J Stud Alcohol Drugs* 2015;76:278–86.
168. Martin TL, Solbeck PA, Mayers DJ, Langille RM, Buczek Y, Pelletier MR. A review of alcohol-impaired driving: the role of blood alcohol concentration and complexity of the driving task. *J Forensic Sci* 2013;58:1238–50.
169. Roberts JR, Dollard D. Alcohol levels do not accurately predict physical or mental impairment in ethanol-tolerant subjects: relevance to emergency medicine and dram shop laws. *J Med Toxicol* 2010;6:438–42.
170. Lapham SC. The limits of tolerance: convicted alcohol-impaired drivers share experiences driving under the influence. *Perm J* 2010;14:26–30.
171. Davies BT, Bowen CK. Total body water and peak alcohol concentration: a comparative study of young, middle-age, and older females. *Alcohol Clin Exp Res* 1999;23:969–75.
172. Verster JC. The alcohol hangover--a puzzling phenomenon. *Alcohol Alcohol* 2008;43:124–6.
173. Lemon J, Chesher G, Fox A, Greeley J, Nabke C. Investigation of the "hangover" effects of an acute dose of alcohol on psychomotor performance. *Alcohol Clin Exp Res* 1993;17:665–8.
174. Ling J, Stephens R, Heffernan TM. Cognitive and psychomotor performance during alcohol hangover. *Curr Drug Abuse Rev* 2010;3:80–7.

175. Hlastala MP, Polissar NL, Oberman S. Statistical evaluation of standardized field sobriety tests. *J Forensic Sci* 2005;50:662–9.
176. Dixon PR, Clark T, Tiplady B. Evaluation of a roadside impairment test device using alcohol. *Accid Anal Prev* 2009;41:412–8.
177. Haghpanahan H, Lewsey J, Mackay DF, McIntosh E, Pell J, Jones A, et al. An evaluation of the effects of lowering blood alcohol concentration limits for drivers on the rates of road traffic accidents and alcohol consumption: a natural experiment. *Lancet* 2019;393:321–9.
178. Scherer M, Fell JC. Effectiveness of lowering the blood alcohol concentration (BAC) limit for driving from 0.10 to 0.08 grams per deciliter in the United States. *Traffic Inj Prev* 2019;20:1–8.
179. Desapriya E, Shimizu S, Pike I, Subzwari S, Scime G. Impact of lowering the legal blood alcohol concentration limit to 0.03 on male, female and teenage drivers involved alcohol-related crashes in Japan. *Int J Inj Contr Saf Promot* 2007;14:181–7.
180. Huang CY, Chou SE, Su WT, Liu HT, Hsieh TM, Hsu SY, et al. Effect of lowering the blood alcohol concentration limit to 0.03 among hospitalized trauma patients in Southern Taiwan: a cross-sectional analysis. *Risk Manag Healthc Policy* 2020;13:571–81.
181. Friedman TW, Robinson SR, Yelland GW. Impaired perceptual judgment at low blood alcohol concentrations. *Alcohol* 2011;45:711–8.

3.2 ANALYSIS, DISPOSITION, AND FATE OF ETHANOL IN THE BODY WITH APPLICATIONS IN CLINICAL AND FORENSIC TOXICOLOGY

Alan Wayne Jones

3.2.1 Introduction

The chemical structure of ethanol (CH_3CH_2OH) is remarkably simple when one considers its wide spectrum of biochemical, behavioral, and pharmacological effects on the body.[1] Compared with other psychoactive substances, massive amounts of ethanol must be consumed to alter a person's behavior and produce signs and symptoms of drunkenness. Ethanol distributes in the total body water compartment and there is no evidence that it binds to plasma proteins or other macromolecules. When in the bloodstream, ethanol easily crosses the blood–brain barrier to reach the central nervous system and interact with various neurotransmitter systems, such as $GABA_A$ transmission, thus slowing down (dampening) brain activity.[2]

The impairment of cognitive and psychomotor functioning after drinking alcoholic beverages depends primarily on the dose of ethanol ingested, the speed of drinking, and the resulting blood-alcohol concentration (BAC).[3] On reaching a fairly low BAC (0.3–0.5 g/L), people feel less inhibited and might experience a mild euphoria. At a BAC between 0.80–1.2 g/L, there is an impairment of cognitive and psychomotor functioning. Confusion, disturbances in balance, ataxia, and slurred speech become evident at BACs between 1.0–2.0 g/L. If people manage to consume sufficient quantities of ethanol to reach a BAC of 3.0–3.5 g/L, they are often unresponsive and in a comatose state and run the risk of depression of respiratory centers in the brainstem and drug-induced asphyxiation.[4] Acute intoxication and drunkenness are tightly linked to many crimes, especially impaired driving, sexual assault, and violent behavior in general, so in law enforcement, measuring a person's BAC provides important forensic evidence.[5]

This chapter updates the one from the second edition of the *Drug Abuse Handbook* (*DAH*), although the main focus is still on analytical methods to determine ethanol in biological specimens for legal purposes and the factors influencing the disposition and fate of ethanol in the body. Knowledge about the absorption, distribution, metabolism, and excretion (ADME) of ethanol is important when various blood-alcohol concentration tests are done in forensic casework, such as in drunk-driving cases.

3.2.2 Statutory Alcohol Limits for Driving

Developments in chemistry and chemical analysis in the late 19th century led to the first attempts to determine the concentrations of ethanol in blood, breath, sweat, and urine after people had consumed alcoholic beverages.[6] Although by modern standards these procedures were rather primitive, they proved sufficiently reliable to establish that only a small amount of all the alcohol consumed was excreted unchanged.[7] Over 90% of the dose of ethanol ingested was seemingly broken down in the body in metabolic processes that provided a source of energy—actually, 7.1 kcal per gram of ethanol combusted.

By the 1920s, the methods for quantitative analysis of ethanol in samples of blood and urine were much improved and used clinically as more objective evidence that a patient's clinical condition was attributable to heavy drinking and not some medical problem, such as hypoglycemia or skull trauma.[8] It was soon recognized that the determination of ethanol concentration in samples of blood or urine provided a more specific way to diagnose intoxication compared with a clinical examination of the patient.[9] The signs and symptoms of drunkenness vary widely between different individuals depending on their age, gender, pattern of drinking, and degree of habituation, and thus the development of tolerance.

Norway introduced a statutory BAC limit of 0.50 g/L for driving in 1936 and Sweden enacted a limit of 0.80 g/L in 1941.[10] Similar legislation followed in other nations, although there was no agreement or consensus reached as to the threshold BAC that should be enforced. Still today the BAC limits for driving vary four-fold, from 0.20 g/L to 0.80 g/L, between different countries.[11] The analytical methods needed to enforce statutory BAC limits must be accurate, precise, and fit for their intended purpose. The various punishments and sanctions for this traffic crime include monetary fines, withdrawal of the driving permit, seizure of the vehicle, and even periods of imprisonment.[12] Furthermore, vehicular insurance claims become null and void if the owner of a vehicle involved in a traffic crash had a BAC exceeding the statutory limit for driving.

Table 3.2.1 reviews the statutory BAC limits for driving in selected countries shown in different units for reporting ethanol concentration. The four-fold variation in these limits is probably more a reflection of political influences rather than traffic-safety research and risk of involvement in a crash after consumption of alcohol.[13]

Alcohol use is also closely regulated in the workplace, especially for those engaged in safety-sensitive occupations (1991 Omnibus Transportation Employee Testing Act).[14] The BAC limit for operating machinery or other dangerous tasks in the USA is 0.02 g% or 0.02 g/210 L in the breath. Concentrations below these limits lead to no corrective actions, although drinking on duty or having a BAC above 0.40 g/L (0.04 g/210 L in the breath) results in instant dismissal from duty and risk of termination of the person's employment.

Fast and reliable analytical methods are needed in emergency medicine when a patient is admitted unconscious or smelling of alcohol.[15] Physicians must be able to distinguish gross intoxication from skull trauma and intracranial blood clots that need emergency surgical intervention.[16] In this connection it is important to remember that hospital clinical laboratories measure ethanol and other substances in plasma or serum, both of which contain more water than

TABLE 3.2.1
Statutory Concentration Limits of Alcohol in Blood for Driving in Various Jurisdictions Expressed in Different Concentration Units

Country	g/100 mL (g%)	g/L (mg/mL)	mg/100 mL (mg%)	mmol/L[2]
United States[1]	0.08	0.80	80	17.3
Canada	0.08	0.80	80	17.3
Australia (most states)	0.05	0.50	50	10.9
England and Wales	0.08	0.80	80	17.3
Ireland	0.05	0.50	50	10.9
Scotland	0.05	0.50	50	10.9
Germany, Poland, Sweden, and Norway[3]	0.02	0.20	20	4.3
Finland and Denmark[3]	0.05	0.50	50	10.9
Other EU countries	0.05	0.50	50	10.9
China	0.02	0.20	20	4.3
Japan, South Korea, and Taiwan	0.03	0.30	30	6.5

[1] The state of Utah lowered its BAC limit for driving to 0.05 g% in 2019.
[2] Derived as ([mg/L]/46.07), where 46.07 is the molecular weight of ethanol.
[3] In Germany and the Nordic countries the ethanol concentration unit is mass/mass (mg/g or g/kg) so 0.02 mg/g = 0.21 mg/mL because the density of whole blood is 1.055 g/mL on average.

blood and therefore higher w/v concentrations of ethanol. This must be considered whenever clinical laboratory results are later used in medicolegal investigations, such as drunken driving prosecutions (see later).[17]

The diagnosis of drunkenness has broad social-medical ramifications and great care is needed when forensic practitioners interpret a person's BAC, such as in legal depositions, affidavits, or when testifying in court as expert witnesses. The level of impairment caused by a given dose of ethanol and the resulting BAC varies widely between different individuals depending on subject demographics, drinking habits, and many other factors. Factors of importance include the person's age, gender, body weight, BMI, type of beverage consumed, rate of drinking, rising or declining phase of the BAC curve, and the development of tolerance.[18,19]

3.2.3 Properties of Ethanol and Its Metabolites

The physicochemical properties of ethanol are compared and contrasted with those of its oxidative metabolites, acetaldehyde and acetic acid, in Table 3.2.2. Acetaldehyde is much more chemically reactive than the parent drug ethanol and undergoes covalent binding with various macromolecules. The concentration of free-acetaldehyde in blood during the metabolism of ethanol is maintained at a very low level, provided the low K_m hepatic enzyme aldehyde dehydrogenase is functional.[20] The second product of ethanol metabolism, acetic acid, is a much less toxic chemical substance and undergoes extra-hepatic oxidation to the end products carbon dioxide and water.[21]

3.2.4 Biological Specimens for Alcohol Analysis

Urine was the first biological specimen used for the determination of ethanol levels because it was easy to collect and was also available in larger volumes than blood.[22] Early studies found a reasonably good correlation between the concentration of ethanol in urine and the clinical signs and symptoms associated with drunkenness.[8,23]

Ethanol has a low boiling point and is easily extracted from biological specimens by steam distillation, aeration or diffusion. One of the first analytical method sufficiently reliable for legal purposes, such as when drunken driving offences were investigated was published in 1922.[24] The ethanol contained in 100 μL of fingertip blood was removed by diffusion in specially designed micro-diffusion flasks for with a mixture of potassium dichromate and sulfuric acid. Volumetric analysis and iodometric titration was used for quantification of BAC. Results of controlled drinking studies allowed determining concentration-time profiles of ethanol in blood in relation to signs and symptoms of drunkenness.[25] By the 1960s gas chromatographic methods were introduced for the determination of ethanol in blood and other body fluids and this methodology has dominated the instrument park at toxicology laboratories ever since.[26]

In medicolegal casework ethanol is traditionally determined in specimens of whole blood or breath, whereas in hospital clinical chemistry laboratories plasma or serum are the usual specimens submitted for analysis.[27] In post-mortem toxicology, the choice of specimens, and the interpretation of the results require special considerations, which will be covered in chapter 3.3 of the *DAH*.

3.2.4.1 Concentration Units

Unfortunately, there is no generally accepted way of reporting ethanol concentrations determined in blood and other specimens, and this differs among countries and situations. Most clinical chemistry laboratories use the international system of units (SI system) established by broad agreement

TABLE 3.2.2
Chemical Structures and Main Physicochemical Properties of Ethanol and its Two Major Metabolites, Acetaldehyde and Acetic Acid

Property	Ethanol	Acetaldehyde	Acetic acid
CAS-number[1]	64-17-5	75-07-0	64-19-7
IUPAC name[2]	Ethanol	Ethanal	Ethanoic acid
Molecular weight	46.07 g/mol	44.05 g/mol	60.05 g/mol
Molecular formulae	C_2H_6O	C_2H_4O	$C_2H_5O_2$
Chemical formulae	CH_3CH_2OH	CH_3CHO	CH_3COOH
Structure	Aliphatic alcohol	Aliphatic aldehyde	Aliphatic carboxylic acid
Structural formulae	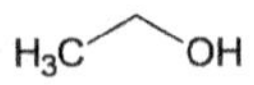	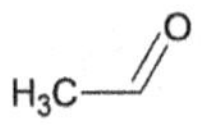	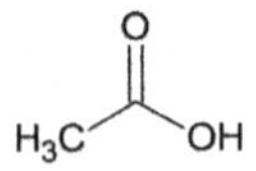
Acidity (pKa)	14.00	13.57	4.76
Boiling point	78.5° C	20.2° C	118.1° C
Melting point	−114.1° C	−123.4° C	16.7° C
Density, g/mL	0.789 at 20° C	0.784 at 20° C	1.05 at 20° C
Appearance/odor	Colorless, sweet-smelling liquid	Colorless liquid with pungent odor	Colorless liquid or crystals, irritating odor like vinegar
Water solubility	Completely miscible	Complete miscible	Completely miscible
Functional group	Hydroxyl –OH	Aldehyde –CHO highly reactive	Carboxylic acid –COOH

[1] Chemical abstract service registry number.
[2] International union of pure and applied chemistry.

using kilograms as the unit of mass, liters as the volume, and the mol as the amount of substance, hence substance concentrations are reported as mmol/L, µmol/L, or nmol/L.[28,29]

By contrast, forensic science and toxicology laboratories mostly determine ethanol and other drugs in whole blood reporting the results as mass per unit volume (mg/100 mL, g/L, or g/100 mL). If aliquots of blood had been weighed and not measured by volume then the results would be reported as mass per unit mass (g/kg or mg/g). The mass/mass unit is numerically less than the mass/volume unit by about 5.5%, owing to the specific weight of blood, which is 1.055 g/mL.[30] Accordingly, a measured BAC of 1.0 g/L (0.10 g% or 100 mg%) is the same as a BAC of 0.947 g/kg (0.0947 g/100 g or 94.7 mg/100 g). The molecular weight of ethanol is 46.07 (see Table 3.2.2) so a BAC of 1.0 g/L might also be reported as 21.7 mmol/L.

3.2.4.2 Water Content of Specimens

The water content of biological fluids and tissues is easily determined by weighing an aliquot and heating it in an oven at 110–120° C for 24 h to reach a constant weight, or alternatively by freeze-drying the sample.[31,32] The desiccation method is highly accurate and precise as demonstrated from several studies and has been applied to whole blood, plasma, and erythrocytes.[33]

Blood specimens submitted for toxicological analysis are often hemolyzed although this makes no difference for the reliability of ethanol determinations, provided the specimen is homogeneous and free from blood clots. Ethanol easily penetrates cell membranes and enters erythrocytes in proportion to their water content.[34] A knowledge of the water content of biological specimens is important when ethanol concentrations are compared and contrasted. A study from Germany involved analysis of the water content in 833 samples of serum and blood at three different laboratories by desiccation.[35] The results for the distribution of water between serum and whole blood are considered to be identical to the distribution of ethanol between the same specimens.

Table 3.2.3 summarizes the results of this study and the percentage of water is reported in mass/mass units, namely g water per 100 g specimen. To convert percent mass/mass into mass/volume units, one needs to multiply by 1.055 (the average density of whole blood is 1.055 g/ml).[30] The mean distribution ratio of water (serum/blood) was 1.157:1 with a standard deviation of 0.0163 and lowest and highest values of 1.08 and 1.25. These values can be considered representative of a healthy population of individuals and the ratio of serum to blood water was slightly lower in females, owing to a gender difference in hematocrit (normal range 41–53% males and 36–46% females). A lower haematocrit means more plasma per unit volume of blood and hence a greater water content. Dividing the plasma or serum concentration of ethanol by a factor of 1.16:1 gives the most probable BAC. No differences were found for the distribution of ethanol between serum/blood and plasma/blood.[36]

Because the water content of blood varies slightly between individuals depending on age, gender, and medical conditions influencing the proportion of red cells to plasma, this sometimes needs to be considered in forensic casework. For example, assuming a normal distribution of serum/blood ratios—mean 1.16 and standard deviation ± 0.0163—one can expect 95% of values to fall within 1.16 ± 1.96 × 0.0163. Accordingly, 2.5% of a population is likely to have a serum/

TABLE 3.2.3

Mean, Standard Deviation (SD), Coefficient of Variation (CV%), and Range of Water Contents of Serum and Whole Blood (WB) and the Serum/WB Ratios in 833 Subjects (114 Women and 719 Men

Laboratory[1]	N	Specimen	Mean g%	SD g%	CV%	Range
Kiel	230	Serum	90.49	0.86	0.95	87.2–93.3
		WB	78.35	1.44	1.83	74.8–82.9
		Serum/WB	1.156	0.0184	1.59	1.11–1.21
Köln	503	Serum	90.71	0.54	0.59	88.6–92.2
		WB	78.41	1.11	1.41	75.7–83.0
		Serum/WB	1.157	0.0145	1.25	1.10–1.20
Münster	100	Serum	90.75	0.61	0.67	89.1–92.8
		WB	78.14	1.28	1.63	74.9–83.3
		Serum/WB	1.162	0.0187	1.61	1.08–1.20
Combined	833	Serum	90.66	0.66	0.72	87.2–93.3
		WB	78.36	1.23	1.57	74.8–83.3
		Serum/WB	1.157	0.0163	1.40	1.08–1.21

Note: [1]The determination of water content was done at three different laboratories in Germany.[35]

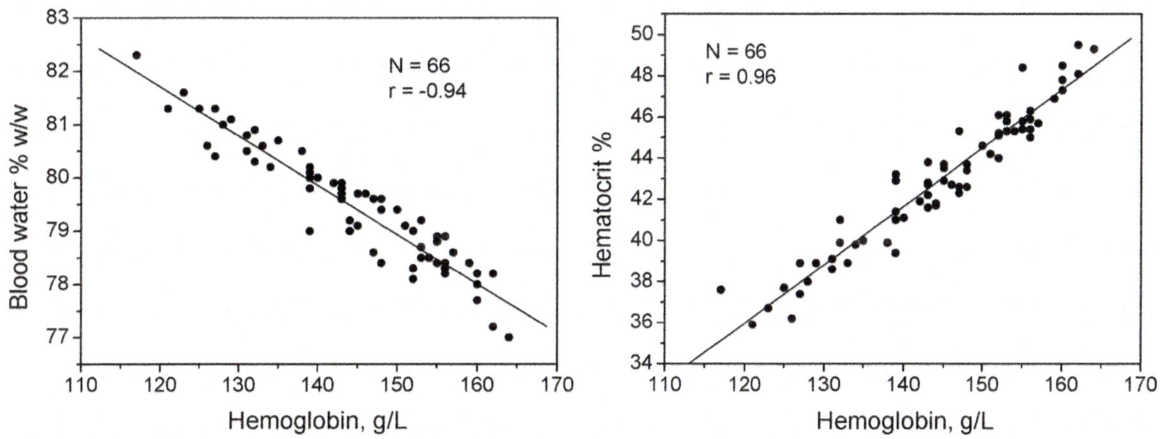

FIGURE 3.2.1 Strong negative correlation (r = –0.94) between blood water content and hemoglobin (left) and high positive correlation (r = 0.96) between hematocrit and hemoglobin content (right)

whole blood ethanol ratio higher than 1.19 and 2.5% lower than 1.12. Depending on the type of case and information about a person's state of health, more conservative estimates might need to be made. From the large German study mentioned above, minimum and maximum values of 1.08 and 1.25 were reported. In a criminal case, dividing a serum ethanol concentration by 1.20 or 1.25 would give an estimated BAC that with high probability was less than the true concentration.

3.2.4.3 Hematocrit, Hemoglobin, and Blood Water

The erythrocyte (red cell) fraction of blood expressed as a percentage is known as the hematocrit, which averages about 45% in healthy subjects. Hematocrit is easily determined by drawing a specimen of fingertip blood into a heparinized capillary tube and centrifugation. According to medical reference books mean hematocrit for men is 47 ± 5% (range 39–49%) compared with 42 ± 5% (range 35–45%) for women. The composition of serum is the same as that of plasma except for the removal of the clotting factors; hence both these biological fluids contain the same amount of water (91–92%) with no differences between males and females.

Figure 3.2.1 shows a strong positive correlation (r = 0.96) between hemoglobin content and hematocrit of the blood samples. This is expected because a higher hematocrit means more red cells per unit volume and thus greater hemoglobin content. By contrast, there was a strong negative correlation (r = –0.94) between blood-water content and hemoglobin (right pane). This follows because higher hemoglobin means a larger proportion of red cells and a smaller plasma fraction and therefore less water per unit volume of blood.

The water content of plasma and serum was the same according to one study (range 89–92% w/w, mean 91.2%) compared with whole blood water content (77–82% w/w, mean 79.7%) and erythrocytes had less water (62–70% w/w, mean 64.9%).[33] The hematocrit, hemoglobin, and water content of blood are likely to show greater variations in patients suffering from various hematological diseases, such as anemia or polycythemia. These strong associations between the hemoglobin and hematocrit of blood samples have led to the suggestion that they could serve as surrogate markers for water content.[37]

The water content of blood samples has been determined in several studies and some of the results are shown in Table 3.2.4. No differences were found for venous and arterial blood samples although women had slightly higher percentages of water than males, owing to gender differences in the hematocrit.

3.2.4.4 Distribution of Ethanol between Plasma and Whole Blood

Several studies have compared the concentrations of ethanol in whole blood with plasma/serum obtained by centrifugation of the same specimen.[38–40] The results support the conclusion that the ethanol distribution ratio depends primarily on differences in water content of blood and plasma/serum.[41] The distribution ratio of ethanol between plasma and serum was 1.0 (range 0.98–1.04) and mean ratios for serum/blood and plasma/blood ethanol distribution were not significantly different, being 1.12 ± 0.02 in one study.[36]

Figure 3.2.2 shows that concentration-time profiles of ethanol in blood and plasma were similar, but the plasma curve ran on a slightly higher level. There were nine participants in this study and each ingested 0.3 g/kg ethanol after an overnight fast. The plasma/blood ratios of ethanol were not dependent on time after drinking when samples were taken as shown by Figure 3.2.2 (upper plot). In this study, the experimentally determined plasma/whole blood ratios of alcohol ranged from 1.08 to 1.19.

TABLE 3.2.4
Water Content of Blood According to Different Studies

Subjects	N (sex)	Blood source	Water content, g% (mean ± SD)
Drunk drivers	30 (mixed)[1]	Cubital vein	77.1 ± 1.73
Healthy volunteers	9 males	Cubital vein	78.6 ± 0.89
		Radial artery	78.9 ± 0.81
Healthy volunteers	6 females	Cubital vein	80.3 ± 0.77
		Radial artery	80.2 ± 0.76
Healthy volunteers	20 males	Cubital vein	79.2 ± 1.10
Healthy volunteers	15 females	Cubital vein	81.1 ± 0.49
Healthy volunteers[2]	15 males	Cubital vein[3]	78.8 ± 0.97

[1] Mainly men. [2] Elderly male subjects. [3] Plasma from the same subjects (N = 15) contained 91.8 ± 0.775% w/w water.

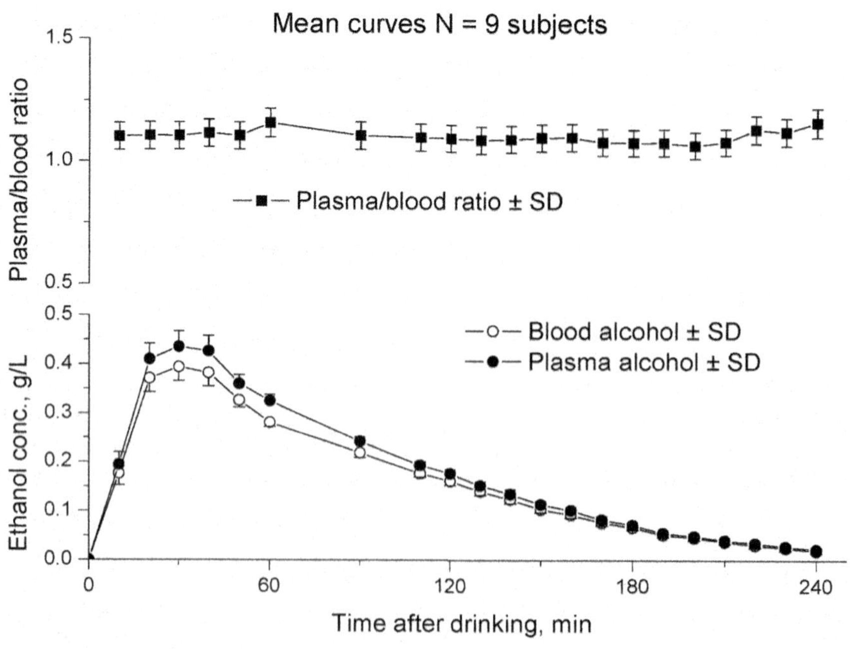

FIGURE 3.2.2 Mean concentration-time profiles of ethanol in plasma and whole blood in nine healthy men after they drank a bolus dose of ethanol (0.30 g/kg) mixed with orange juice on an empty stomach. The mean plasma/blood ratios (± SD) at each time point are plotted above the concentration-time profiles

TABLE 3.2.5
Mean Blood-Alcohol Concentrations (BAC), 95% Range, and Minimum (Min) and Maximum (Max) Values Derived from Analysis of the Ethanol Concentration in Plasma or Serum

Ethanol conc. in serum/plasma, g/L	Mean calculated blood conc., g/L	95% range of values, g/L	Min and max values, g/L
0.20	0.172	0.167–0.177	0.165, 0.185
0.50	0.431	0.419–0. 443	0.413, 0.463
0.80	0.689	0.671–0.709	0.661, 0.741
1.00	0.862	0.839–0.886	0.826, 0.926
1.50	1.293	1.258–1.329	1.239, 1.389
2.00	1.724	1.677–1.773	1.653, 1.851

[1] Mean serum/blood water ratio = 1.16:1 (Table 3.2.3), standard deviation = 0.0163, and minimum and maximum values 1.08 and 1.21 were used in the calculation of BAC.

In a study with drinking drivers, the mean distribution ratio of ethanol between plasma and whole blood was found to be 1.14:1 (standard deviation 0.041). Table 3.2.5 compares concentrations of ethanol in plasma or serum with calculated values in blood assuming a mean ratio of 1.16 and minimum and maximum values of 1.08 and 1.21. The results are shown assuming concentrations of ethanol ranging from 0.20–2.0 g/L.

As discussed by Rainey,[17] whenever the results of ethanol determination in plasma or serum are later used to calculate whole blood concentrations for law enforcement purposes, the biological variation in plasma/blood and serum/blood ratios must be considered. He recommended a rather conservative ratio of 1.22:1, which took into consideration results from several published studies and was the mean serum/blood ratio plus two standard deviations. Unfortunately, the results from the extensive German study cited above was not considered (Table 3.2.3)

The use of a conversion factor in forensic casework should be chosen to give some benefit of the doubt to a suspect because nothing is usually known about hematocrit and water content of the specimens. Thus dividing a plasma or serum ethanol concentration by 1.20 is more appropriate in criminal cases, such as drunk driving, whereas the mean of 1.16 could be used for research and clinical purposes or in civil litigation when the preponderance of evidence is the accepted practice.

3.2.5 Determination of Ethanol in Body Fluids

The first analytical methods for the determination of ethanol in blood and other body fluids appeared during the last decades of the 19th century.[6,42] Although these were rather primitive by modern standards, they were sufficiently reliable to investigate the disposition and fate of ethanol in the body.[6] In general, five analytical procedures can be identified as being used for the analysis of ethanol in biological specimens for forensic purposes:

1. Chemical oxidation after extraction of ethanol from the bio-matrix by e.g. steam distillation with reagents such as acidified potassium dichromate and/or potassium permanganate and then doing a titrimetric analysis to determine an end-point.
2. Enzymatic oxidation of ethanol with alcohol dehydrogenase (ADH) from yeast and spectrophotometric determination of the amount of reduced coenzyme (NADH) to determine the reaction end-point.
3. Gas-liquid chromatography (GLC) using a variety of stationary phases and initial dilution of the specimen with internal standard (*n*-propanol) and flame ionization detector (FID) for quantitative analysis.
4. GLC analysis after dilution of the blood specimen with internal standard (e.g. *n*-propanol) and equilibration at 50 or 60° C followed by sampling of the headspace (HS) vapor phase for chromatographic analysis with an FID detector.
5. GLC in combination with a mass spectrometric (MS) detector for identification of ethanol from its principal electron impact mass fragments.

3.2.5.1 Chemical Oxidation

The first analytical methods required the separation of ethanol from the biological matrix by distillation and chemical analysis of the distillate by oxidation with chromic acid and volumetric titration to determine the endpoint.[24] Only 100 mg of capillary blood or urine was necessary for a single determination, which meant that serial samples could be taken at various times after administration of ethanol. The following redox reaction illustrates the use of potassium dichromate and sulfuric acid as the oxidizing agent resulting in a change in color of the chromium ion from yellow to green.

$$\underset{\text{(yellow)}}{2K_2Cr_2O_7} + 8H_2SO_4 + 3C_2H_5OH$$

$$\rightarrow \underset{\text{(green)}}{2Cr_2\left(SO_4\right)_3} + 2K_2SO_4$$

$$+ 3CH_3COOH + 11H_2O$$

The amount of the oxidizing agent remaining after the oxidation reaction was complete could be determined in several ways but usually by iodometric titration. The oxidation method is not specific for ethanol, because other volatiles if present in the blood, such as acetone, methanol, ether, and/or isopropanol, were also oxidized by the chromic acid reagent to give false-positive results. Although the likelihood of these substances being present in blood samples from living subjects was low, precautions were needed when dealing with autopsy blood samples. Acetone was probably the most important volatile to consider because concentrations might be especially high in the blood of people with poorly controlled diabetes. The presence of acetone could be determined by a separate chemical test on urine using various color reactions.[43]

By the 1950s the endpoint of ethanol oxidation with chromic acid was determined by photometry instead of titrimetric analysis.[22] The history, development, and application of chemical oxidation methods of alcohol analysis have been well covered in several review articles although they are today obsolete in clinical and forensic laboratories.[22,44]

3.2.5.2 Enzymatic Oxidation

In the late 1940s, biochemists succeeded in extracting and purifying the enzyme alcohol dehydrogenase (ADH) from horse liver and yeast. This opened the possibility to develop a biochemical method for the determination of ethanol utilizing enzymatic oxidation.[45,46] This provided milder reaction conditions compared with chemical oxidation and enhanced the specificity for identification of ethanol because acetone was not oxidized by ADH.[47,48] However, other aliphatic alcohols (methanol, isopropanol, and *n*-propanol) did react with the enzyme and if present were mistakenly reported as ethanol. By optimizing the enzyme reaction conditions in terms of pH, reaction time, and temperature, methanol was not oxidized to any significant extent when yeast ADH was used to catalyze the reaction.[49,50]

$$C_2H_5OH + NAD^+ \xleftrightarrow{ADH} CH_3CHO + NADH + H^+$$

The acetaldehyde formed by the oxidation is trapped with semicarbazide to form semicarbazone. Use of the manual ADH method required first precipitating plasma proteins by adding perchloric acid, then allowing the mixture to stand in a refrigerator overnight, before centrifugation to obtain the clear supernatant containing ethanol. After being transferred to a clean dry tube, the pH was adjusted to 9.6 with a semicarbazide buffer contained the co-enzyme nicotinamide adenine dinucleotide (NAD^+) and the reaction was started by the addition of ADH (catalyst). The mixture was allowed to stand at room temperature for one hour and acetaldehyde metabolite formed from ethanol was trapped by the semicarbazide, thus driving the reaction to completion. The amount of NAD^+ that becomes converted to its reduced form (NADH) is directly proportional to the concentration of ethanol in the blood specimen. The concentration of ethanol was determined by measuring the absorbance of UV light by NADH monitored at a wavelength of 340 nm.

Multi-test clinical laboratory analyzers are available that have capabilities to determine ethanol in blood or urine by enzymatic oxidation reactions, and one of the first was the Technicon® AutoAnalyzer instrument, which allowed several hundred determinations per day on 1–10 μL of the specimen.[49] Scores of publications described a diverse array of modifications and improvements to the original ADH method and "reagent kits" became available, which were useful at the smaller hospital laboratories where throughput of samples for ethanol analysis was relatively low.[51]

Automation became the norm in clinical chemistry laboratories, with large equipment that automated sample preparation and dispensing and the mixing of reagents to increase sample throughput, and these batch analyzers or reaction rate analyzers could include the determination of ethanol, such as a micro-centrifugal analyzer using fluorescence light scattering for quantitative analysis.[52,53]

Enzymatic methods for the determination of ethanol in body fluids are still available today in some laboratories where urine drug testing is performed.[54] These procedures make use of a technique known as enzyme multiplied immunoassay (EMIT), whereby an enzyme-labeled antigen reacts with ethanol or another drug and the change in absorbance after adding a substrate is measured by spectrophotometry.[55]

Fluorescence polarization immunoassay (FPIA) and the spin-off technology of radiative energy attenuation (REA) are other examples of analytical procedures developed to meet the increasing demand for drug abuse testing in urine and therapeutic drug monitoring.[56,57] In several comparative studies, excellent agreement was found between ethanol concentrations in blood determined by REA and by gas chromatography in terms of accuracy and precision.[58] This REA technique could also be applied to specimens from living person and medical examiner cases.[58]

Figure 3.2.3 (left part) compares results of ethanol determination in urine by an automated ADH method and also by headspace gas chromatography. The results by the two methods were highly correlated ($r = 0.99$), although this does not necessarily mean a good agreement. Agreement between two methods of measurement is determined better using a Bland and Altman plot shown in Figure 3.2.3 (right part).[59] Here the individual differences (GC – ADH) are plotted on the y-axis and the average concentration ([GC + ADH]/2) plotted on the x-axis.

The mean of the individual difference is referred to as bias, which reflects the closeness of agreement, and the SD of the differences is a measure of their variability.[60] This statistical method then requires that mean difference ± 1.96 × SD is calculated and gives 95% limits of agreement between the two methods of measurement. This is indicated by the dotted horizontal lines in Figure 3.2.3 (right pane), which run in parallel with the mean difference.[61] Outlying values, which occurred at high ethanol concentration are

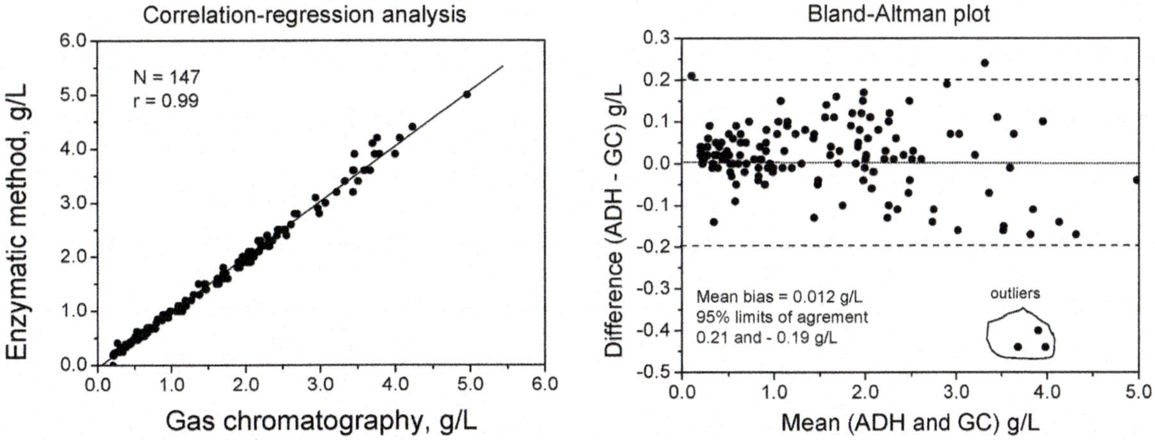

FIGURE 3.2.3 High correlation (r = 0.99) between concentrations of ethanol in urine determined by an immunoassay method (enzymatic oxidation) and by headspace gas chromatography (left plot). Statistical analysis of this method comparison study was done by constructing a Bland and Altman graph (right plot). Individual differences between the two methods of analysis are plotted on the y-axis and the mean concentration of ethanol on the x-axis. The mean difference (bias) and 95% limits of agreement are then calculated, making it easier to see the presence of three outlying values

much easier to detect using the Bland and Altman plot compared with the conventional x-y scatter plot.

Despite major developments in immunoassay technology including EMIT, FPIA, and REA, the basic analytical principle is ADH-mediated enzymatic oxidation of ethanol and measuring the formation of reduced coenzyme (NADH) by UV absorption. However, a potential problem arises when plasma samples are submitted from trauma patients, who might have elevated levels of lactate and lactate dehydrogenase (LDH) in blood because lactate is converted to pyruvate in a NAD–NADH reaction:

$$\text{Lactate} + \text{NAD}^{+} \xleftrightarrow{\text{LDH}} \text{Pyruvate} + \text{NADH}$$

In the above biochemical reaction, the coenzyme NAD^+ is reduced to NADH by endogenous substances (lactate) in the same way as exogenous substances like ethanol are oxidized to acetaldehyde. This creates the possibility of falsely elevated BAC results because the endpoint depends on the absorption of UV light by NADH. In many patients suffering from trauma, sepsis, and blood loss, there is depletion of oxygen content reaching the tissues (hypoxia) and concomitant increases in the concentration of lactate and/or LDH in the bloodstream and metabolic acidosis. Several reports suggest that when ethanol was determined in the blood of such patients by an enzymatic oxidation method there was a risk of obtaining falsely elevated results.

This raises the possibility that when the enzymatic ADH method was used to determine ethanol in blood samples with elevated lactate, this would lead to artificially high concentrations or even false-positive results because of the reaction with NAD. This was more of a problem when dealing with autopsy blood samples.[62,63]

This same source of error has been suggested when trauma patients with elevated levels of lactate and/or LDH levels were admitted to the hospital for treatment. In 37 patients with lactate levels ranging from 2.4 to 24.2 mmol/L (mean 6.54 mmoL/L) and LDH levels of 242–8,838 U/L (mean 1,695 U/L), both well above normal values, failed to find an elevation in ethanol content. Most samples were reported as negative and verified by a gas chromatographic method.[64] The interference from lactic acid leading to falsely elevated ethanol concentrations was recently reviewed in two children who later died.[65] It appears that the hospital analysis done by an EMIT method had positive ethanol results, although these could not be confirmed when re-run by a gas chromatographic method. Much seems to depend on the particular enzymatic analyzer used and the conditions for reduction of NAD^+ to NADH, and this seems to be a bigger problem with autopsy samples than with surviving trauma victims.[66,67]

3.2.5.3 Gas-Liquid Chromatography

In the early 1960s, physical-chemical methods were applied to determine ethanol and other volatile substances in body fluids, such as infrared spectrometry, electrochemical oxidation, and gas-liquid chromatography (GLC).[10] The GLC method has since become the "gold standard" procedure in forensic science and toxicology laboratories. The first GLC methods required that ethanol was extracted from the blood specimen by use of a solvent (e.g. *n*-propyl acetate) or by distillation, which was cumbersome and time consuming when many samples were dealt with.[26,68,69]

Typically, an aliquot of blood (100 μL) or other biological fluid is first diluted (1:5 or 1:10) with an aqueous solution of an internal standard (*n*-propanol or *t*-butanol).[70] This 5–10 times dilution with an aqueous internal standard removes matrix effects and allows the use of alcohol standards prepared in water to calibrate the instrument and establish a concentration-response curve from analysis with a flame ionization detector (FID).

The use of an internal standard meant that any unexpected variations in the GLC operating conditions (gas flow rates, temperature fluctuations) during an analysis influenced the ethanol and internal standard response equally so the ratio of peak heights or peak areas of the ethanol response to internal standard remained constant. The evolution of GLC methods of analysis in the field of forensic toxicology over a 50-year period was recently reviewed.[71]

About 1–5 μl of the diluted blood sample is injected into a heated chamber where vaporization and mixing with a carrier gas (helium or nitrogen) occur and volatiles are transported to the chromatographic column. The mobile gas phase flows through a thin glass or metal column having dimensions such as 2 m long by 0.3 mm inside diameter. The liquid stationary phase is spread as a thin film inside the column on an inert solid support material, thus furnishing a large adsorption surface area. The volatile components of a mixture distribute between the moving phase (carrier gas) and the liquid phase depending on their physicochemical properties, boiling points, functional groups, and relative solubility in the liquid phase. A partial or complete separation of the components of a mixture occurs during passage through the column and the components are eluted after different times, known as the retention time.

Quantitative analysis of the effluent leaving the column was achieved using a thermal conductivity (TC) detector, although this was later replaced with a flame ionization detector (FID), which was much more sensitive and gave only a small response to water vapor. The concentration in the analyzed blood sample was calculated by comparing the detector response (peak height or peak area) of ethanol/internal standard with known strength aqueous standards after constructing a calibration curve. The methodological details of many of the older GC methods of blood-alcohol analysis have been reviewed elsewhere.[72] The choice of stationary phase for the analysis of polar molecules like ethanol was polyethylene glycol (Carbowax) with high molecular weight. Other procedures described the use of porous polymer materials as column packing material, such as Poropak Q or S, which allowed complete separation of low-molecular-weight volatiles, such as aliphatic alcohols, aldehydes, and ketones.

3.2.5.4 Headspace Sampling Technique

In the 1960s, considerable interest developed in the use of headspace sampling for the analysis of volatile substances by gas chromatography.[73] An aliquot of the blood sample after dilution with internal standard was allowed to equilibrate at an elevated temperature for about 30 min before removing a sample of the headspace for analysis by GC method.[74] The manual transfer of a sample of the headspace is possible using a gas-tight syringe, but some automated sampling technique is preferred for routine applications. This gives more reproducible results and an overall higher analytical precision. Working in collaboration with the company Perkin-Elmer, Gottfried Machata (1925–2012) did a lot of the early development work adapting HC-GC for headspace analysis and medicolegal blood-ethanol determination.[75,76]

The first Perkin-Elmer instrument developed was called F40 and came on the market in 1967. Later developments included HS-42 and HS-45, which allowed 42 and 45 vials in the headspace carousel and also higher temperatures for equilibration. Next on the market was HS-100, which was mounted onto a Sigma 2000 gas chromatograph, allowing automated analysis of up to 100 specimens in the same analytical run. The most recent development, AutoSystem XL GC, is used in conjunction with TurboMatrix 110 sampler, an arrangement that allows up to 110 specimens in a single run.

Figure 3.2.4 shows a schematic diagram of the headspace gas chromatographic (HS-GC-FID) setup for the

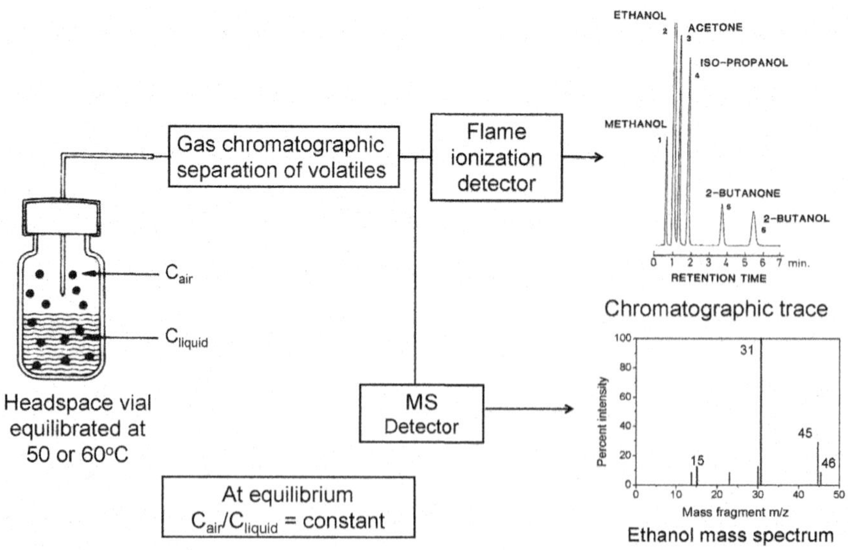

FIGURE 3.2.4 Schematic diagram of headspace gas chromatography with flame ionization detector (FID) and mass spectrometric (MS) detector. The blood sample is first diluted ten times with an aqueous solution of internal standard (*n*-propanol or *t*-butanol) and then equilibrated at 50° C or 60° C in an airtight glass vial. The GC trace shows baseline separation for six low-molecular volatile substances and retention times are used for identification. A portion of the effluent from the GC column is directed to an electron impact MS detector, giving the characteristic fragmentation pattern of ethanol; m/z 31 (base peak), m/s 45, and m/z 46 (molecular ion)

determination of ethanol in biological specimens for clinical and forensic purposes.[76] The main advantage of headspace analysis is the protection of the GC capillary column from non-volatile substances (lipids and proteins) contained in the diluted biological specimen. In a typical analysis, an aliquot of the blood sample (100 μL) is diluted with the internal standard in a ratio of 1:10 and transferred to a glass vial, which is immediately made airtight with a crimped-on Teflon coated rubber septum. The vial is then heated to a temperature of 50–60° C for about 30 min so that any volatile substances present equilibrate between the gas phase (C_G) and the liquid (C_L) phase.[77]

It is advisable not to heat the diluted blood sample above 60° C, otherwise some degradation of ethanol can occur, such as non-enzymatic oxidation to acetaldehyde by oxyhemoglobin. This effect can be minimized or avoided by the addition of sodium azide or sodium dithionite, because these substances prevent this oxidation reaction.[78] Use of higher equilibrium temperatures increase the analytical sensitivity of the method and much lower endogenous concentrations of ethanol can then be determined. The GC columns were initially made from a coiled glass or stainless steel tube and there were a lot cheaper and more robust than the wide-bore fused silica GC capillary columns, which are standard equipment in use today.

Figure 3.2.5 is an example of the gas chromatographic traces obtained by headspace analysis of four water-soluble low molecular volatiles on fused silica capillary columns specially designed for blood-ethanol analysis. These are denoted RtX-BAC1 and RtX-BAC2 and are manufactured by the Restek Corporation, USA.[79] The ethanol peak response is well resolved from potential interfering substances in this isothermal chromatographic run lasting for 2 min. Table 3.2.6 gives retention times for ethanol and other volatiles relative to the internal standard (*n*-propanol) in typical HS-GC-FID operating conditions.

Sensitivity of the headspace method can be enhanced and matrix effects eliminated in another way, namely by saturating the blood samples and aqueous ethanol standards with an inorganic salt such as NaCl, K_2CO_3, or Na_2SO_4 e.g. 0.5 ml blood + 1 g salt.[80] The salting-out technique is useful when very low concentrations of volatiles, such as endogenous ethanol and methanol, are determined in biological substances.

More recently, the headspace vapor in equilibrium with blood or other body fluid can also be removed and transferred to a GC instrument with a solid phase micro-extraction probe.[81] The needle of the probe contains a porous polymer material inserted into the headspace vapor until an equilibrium is reached with any volatiles in the headspace. The probe is then withdrawn from the vial and introduced into the heated injection port of the gas chromatograph. This sampling technique is well suited for the analysis of

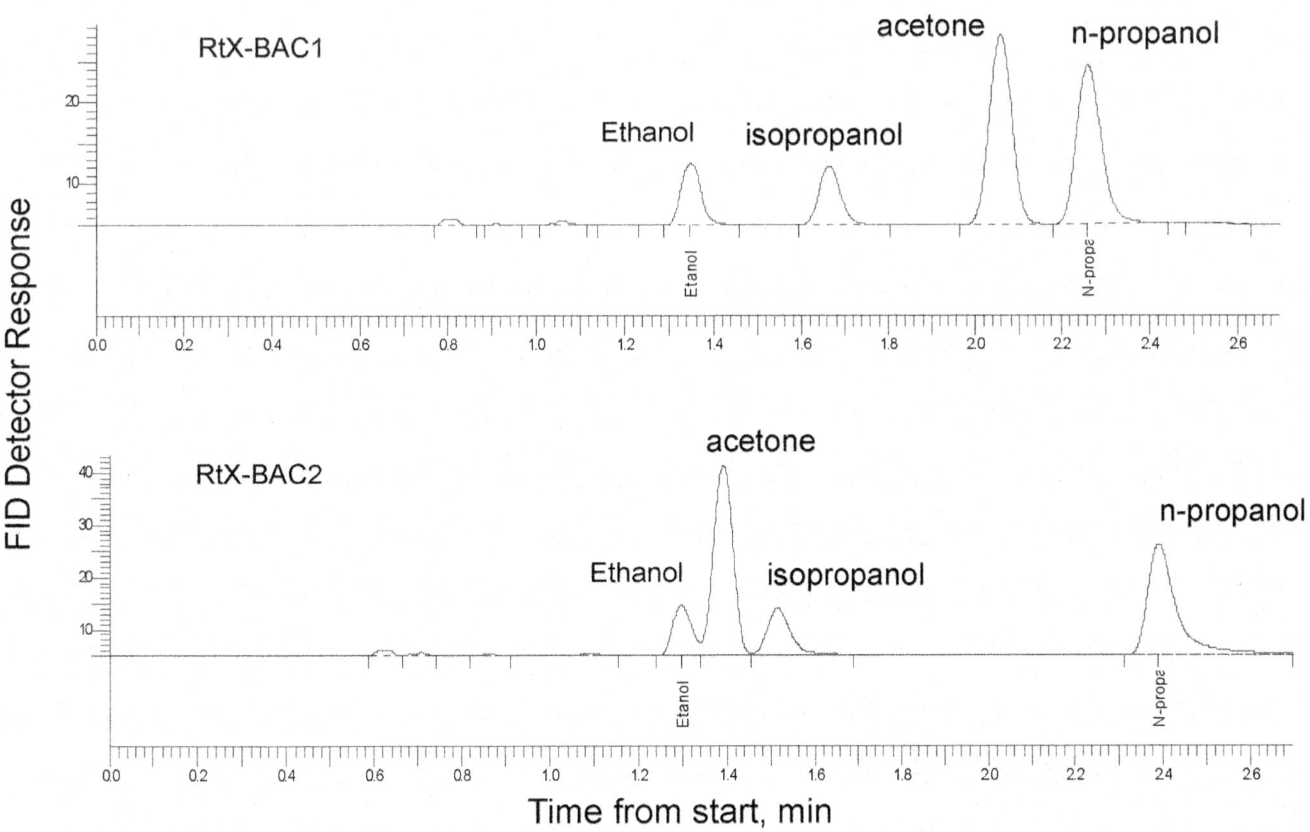

FIGURE 3.2.5 Gas chromatographic traces obtained from analysis of blood containing ethanol, isopropanol, acetone, and *n*-propanol. The sample was analyzed by an automated HS-GC-FID method in duplicate on two different chromatographic columns (RtX-BAC1 and RtX-BAC2) manufactured by Restek Cooperation USA

TABLE 3.2.6
Relative Retention Times (Min) from Gas Chromatographic Analysis of Volatile Substances on Two Types of Stationary Phase (RtX-BAC1 and RtX-BAC-2)

Substance	Stationary phase RtX-BAC1	Stationary phase RtX-BAC2
Acetaldehyde	0.53	0.34
Acetone	0.91	0.57
Acetonitrile	0.91	0.81
1-butanol	2.05	2.20
2-butanone	1.37	1.04
t-butanol	0.88	0.69
Ethanol	0.59	0.53
Isopropanol	0.74	0.62
Methanol	0.47	0.40

Note: Times are relative to *n*-propanol used as the internal standard. All determinations were made with Perkin-Elmer AutoSystem XL headspace analyzer in isothermal mode with TurboMatrix 110 headspace sampler.

a wide range of volatiles agents such as aliphatic and aromatic hydrocarbons as well as many water-soluble alcohols and ketones.[82]

A modification of the standard headspace analysis involved increasing the analytical sensitivity by use of cryofocusing with a liquid nitrogen freeze-trap technique just prior to GC separation and analysis of volatiles with FID detector.[83] This helped to concentrate the specimen prior to chromatographic analysis of volatiles with a capillary or wide-bore column and enabled endogenous concentrations of various volatile substances in blood to be determined in a quantitative way. This analytical approach was used for the determination of alcoholic beverage congeners in blood in addition to ethanol and this found forensic applications as a way to identify what type of alcoholic drink, whether a particular brand of liquor, wine, or beer, a person had consumed.[84]

GC methods have the advantage that they combine a qualitative screening analysis of substances based on their retention times after injection to the appearance of the peak with simultaneous quantitative analysis by measuring the detector response as reflected in height or area under the resulting peak response on the chromatogram. Several comprehensive reviews have dealt with forensic applications of gas chromatography including applications for blood-alcohol analysis.[26,85]

Forensic blood-alcohol analysis should always be done in at least duplicate determinations and also using two different chromatographic columns that yield different retention times for ethanol. Finding co-incident retention times increases confidence in the conclusion that ethanol was the unknown substance in the sample analyzed. The need for two different columns is important when blood or tissue becomes contaminated with bacteria, as is common in autopsy casework and when a body is decomposed.[86] Otherwise, two different methodologies such as GC and enzymatic oxidation could be used on the same sample to increase selectivity, as was the standard procedure in forensic laboratories in Germany for many years.[87]

The use of two different detectors (flame ionization and mass detector) is another way to enhance selectivity.[88] A small part of the effluent from the GC column could be directed to a mass detector, producing a characteristic electron impact fragmentation pattern of ethanol, which gives positive identification. A dual-detector system (FID and MS) was recommended in clinical toxicology to boost confidence in the identification of ethanol aid in the diagnosis of acute poisoning when a host of unknown substances might be responsible for the patient's condition.[89] The use of gas chromatography (GC) to separate the volatile components in a mixture and then mass spectrometry (MS) to identify the various substances is a standard operating procedure in many forensic toxicology laboratories.[90]

Besides identification of ethanol from its retention time, the mass spectrum furnishes unequivocal qualitative analysis if the three major mass fragments m/z 31 (base peak), m/z 45, and m/z 46 (molecular ion) are identified. The use of an isotope-labeled internal standard is also a possibility when GC-MS is utilized as the analytical method.[91] The aliquot of blood is first diluted with deuterium-labeled ethanol, such as d_5-ethanol, and besides mass fragments for ethanol, the corresponding m/z for the deuterium analog is produced. Selected ion monitoring and deuterium-labeled ethanol were also used to distinguish ethanol formed in post-mortem blood by the action of bacteria on blood glucose using an animal model.[92] In clinical pharmacokinetics, deuterium-labeled ethanol was used to study the bioavailability of ethanol and its distribution into the total body water compartment to investigate the first-pass metabolism in the gut.[93]

3.2.5.5 Other Methods

Methods of headspace sampling and analysis of ethanol have been described using both an electrochemical detector[94] and a solid-state semi-conductor sensing device.[95] However, neither of these analytical methods can match the high sensitivity, specificity, and linearity offered by analysis of samples by HS-GC-FID, which is the accepted gold-standard for the determination of volatile substances in forensic toxicology. Some investigators recommend making an initial screening analysis to detect positive ethanol cases by an enzymatic method and then re-analysis of only the positive cases by HS-GC-FID.[96] This approach has the advantage that two independent analytical techniques are used to verify the presence of ethanol in the same blood sample.

In clinical and emergency medicine, depression of the freezing point (osmometry) is often applied to screen for certain pathological conditions.[97] Diabetes mellitus and uraemia are often associated with abnormally high concentrations of plasma-glucose and plasma-urea, respectively. This difference between the osmolality expected from inorganic ions in plasma, such as Na^+ and K^+, and the results from measuring the depression of the freezing point is the osmolal gap.[98] Dedicated equipment is available at most hospital laboratories to measuring freezing point depression and only about 0.2 mL of plasma is needed for each determination. The measurement of osmometry can be done a lot faster than gas chromatography, which makes it more suitable for use in emergency hospital settings. Moreover, the method is non-destructive, which means that the same specimen of plasma can be used later for making a confirmatory toxicological analysis by HC methods.

The osmolal gap is defined as the difference between the measured serum osmolality determined by freezing point depression and the calculated serum molarity, from known osmotically active substances in the serum specimen (sodium, potassium urea, glucose, and ethanol). Indeed, in emergency medicine, ethanol is the commonest cause of increased serum osmolality.[99] Ethanol carries an appreciable osmotic effect because of its low molecular weight (46.05), high solubility in water, and the fact that large quantities must be ingested to produce a dangerous state of intoxication.

Finding a normal osmolal gap speaks against the presence of an elevated concentration of ethanol or other toxic alcohols.[100] However, an elevated osmolal gap does not necessarily prove the toxic substance was ethanol. Other toxic solvents in serum such as acetone, methanol, isopropanol, and ethylene glycol will increase the serum or plasma osmolality as revealed by the freezing point depression.[101] Perhaps the main limitation in measuring osmolal gap as a rapid test for elevated serum ethanol is its lack of selectivity because other toxic alcohols and non-electrolytes cause false-positive results. Nevertheless, papers continue to appear describing the principles and practice of freezing point osmometry in emergency toxicology.[102]

Considerable interest has developed in point-of-care or near-patient testing, where non-invasive methods are preferable. Near-infrared spectrometry is a technique in rapid development for the determination of substances like glucose and ethanol in tissue water.[103] A near-infrared (NIR) beam of light of constant wavelength is passed through a subject's fingertip or arm and absorption bands of the emitted light are processed into their specific wavelengths. Various constituents in the tissue can be identified and quantitative analysis is possible after suitable calibrations are made. However, disentangling the signals of interest from the background noise generated by other biological molecules is challenging, although results from the analysis of ethanol show a high correlation with breath-alcohol and BAC.[104]

A company from New Mexico has manufactured a device known as TruTouch technology, which incorporates NIR, and when the results were compared with direct determination of BAC there was good agreement and high correlation.[105] The same NIR spectroscopy method has already been successfully applied to the determination of blood and tissue glucose levels in a non-invasive way.[106] The future prospects of this technology for routine blood-ethanol determinations in law enforcement are hard to predict.

3.2.6 Breath-Alcohol Analysis

The smell of alcohol on a person's breath is probably one of the oldest, albeit non-specific tests for over-consumption of alcohol and drunkenness.[107] Only about 3–5% of the dose of ethanol ingested is excreted unchanged via the lungs as shown by the following example. Assume that a person's BAC was 1.0 g/L and the blood/air distribution ratio of ethanol at 37° C is known to be 1,800:1 from in-vitro studies. This person will have an ethanol concentration in the alveolar air of 0.55 mg/L. If a normal tidal volume is 500 mL per breath and when resting a person makes 16 inspirations and expirations per minute, lung ventilation corresponds to 480 L per hour. If end-exhaled breath is assumed to have the same ethanol content as alveolar air (in reality it is appreciably less), the amount of ethanol eliminated via the lungs per hour is 480 L × 0.55 mg/L or 264 mg. Because a person eliminates on average 0.10 g/kg/h through metabolism, this corresponds to 8 g for a man with a bodyweight of 80 g, so ([0.264/8] × 100) means that 3.3% of the ethanol is eliminated per hour via the lungs.

A large body of literature has accumulated on the physiological principles and practical applications of breath-alcohol analysis in law enforcement.[107,108] The sampling and analysis of a person's expired air furnishes an indirect method to monitoring volatile substances in the pulmonary blood and this approach has many interesting applications in clinical and diagnostic medicine as biomarkers of disease states.[109,110]

The use of breath-alcohol instruments to estimate BAC has been used in forensic science and law enforcement since the 1940s.[111] Significant developments over the past 20 years have been significant and many highly sophisticated microprocessor-controlled instruments are currently available. These can be subdivided into various categories depending on their intended application, whether as a roadside screening test of driver sobriety or as a way to produce evidence-quality results for later during prosecution of traffic offenders (Table 3.2.7).

TABLE 3.2.7

Classification of Currently Available Instruments for Breath-Alcohol Analysis According to the Main Area of Application (Roadside Screening Analysis) and/or Evidential Testing

Breath testing instrument	Main areas of application for the enforcement of drunk-driving laws and medical purposes	Analytical principle for the quantitative analysis of ethanol
Alcolmeter	Used by the police as a roadside screening test of driver sobriety and also for testing patients attending hospital casualty departments	Electrochemical oxidation of ethanol (fuel cell)
Alco-Sensor*	Hand-held device for roadside screening of driver sobriety, workplace alcohol testing, and medical applications	Electrochemical oxidation of ethanol (fuel cell)
Alcotest*	Roadside screening of motorists, self-testing, ignition interlock devices, workplace testing, and in emergency medicine	Electrochemical oxidation of ethanol (fuel cell)
Lifeloc	Hand-held roadside screening of motorists, also in out-patient clinics and other applications in criminal justice, such as probation	Electrochemical oxidation ethanol (fuel cell)
Alcotest 9510	Evidence quality results used for prosecution of drunk drivers	Electrochemical oxidation and infrared absorption (~9.5 μm) for analysis of ethanol
Intoxilyzer 9000	Evidence quality results used for prosecution of drunk drivers	Infrared analysis at ~3.4 μm and ~9.5 μm
Evidenzer	Evidence quality results used for prosecution of drunk drivers	Infrared analysis with five filters at wavelengths 3.37, 3.41, 3.47, 3.52, and 3.80 μm
Intox EC/IR	Evidence quality results used for prosecution of drunk drivers	Electrochemical oxidation for quantitative analysis of ethanol

*These instruments are also being used for roadside evidential testing in some jurisdictions.

3.2.6.1 Hand-Held Screening Instruments

Examples of some currently available hand-held instruments listed in Table 3.2.7 incorporate a fuel-cell detector, and ethanol in a captured sample of breath is determined by electrochemical oxidation.[112] Positive results from a roadside breath-alcohol test motivates arresting a driver and proceeding with an evidential breath-alcohol test at a police station.[113] Hand-held breath-alcohol analyzers are also widely used in hospital emergency departments as a quick and easy way to monitor whether patients are intoxicated before they are treated.[114]

Hand-held breath-alcohol screening instruments that determine ethanol content by electrochemical oxidation are highly specific and false-positive results are rare and insignificant.[115] In some nations, such as the Nordic countries, Australia, and New Zealand, millions of drivers are tested annually without any suspicion that they had consumed alcohol. A test only takes about 1–2 min for completion and the driver exhales through a plastic mouth-piece while still sitting behind the steering wheel of the vehicle. The last portion of an exhalation is sampled automatically and ethanol content is determined by electrochemical oxidation. This generates an electric current, the strength of which is proportional to the amount of ethanol in the breath sample analyzed. Acetone, which is the most abundant endogenous volatile exhaled in breath, is not oxidized at the electrode surface, so elevated concentrations of this ketone (e.g. in untreated diabetics) will not cause a false-positive response.

Other alcohols that might be consumed, such as methanol and/or isopropanol, are oxidized electrochemically and give a response on the breath-analyzer in the same way as ethanol.[116] On rare occasions, elevated concentrations of acetone in blood might be reduced to isopropanol and this can cause a false positive breath-alcohol reading.[117] The concentration of acetone in blood can reach abnormally high levels during food deprivation, prolonged fasting (dieting), or during diabetic ketoacidosis.[118]

3.2.6.2 Evidential Quality Instruments

Most breath-alcohol instruments used to produce evidence necessary for the prosecution of traffic offenders make use of infrared (IR) spectrometry as the analytical principle. Several optical filters are used to measure the absorption of IR energy at wavelengths of 3.4 or 9.5 microns, which correspond to the C-H and C-O stretching vibrations in the ethanol molecule, respectively.[107]

Some evidential breath-alcohol instruments incorporate both IR absorption at 9.5 μm as well as an electrochemical sensor that oxidizes ethanol in the breath sample, such as the Alcotest 9510 which features dual-sensor technology.[119] Another example from the latest generation of evidential breath-alcohol analyzers is the Intoxilyzer 9000, which makes use of infrared wavelengths at both 3.4 and 9.5 microns for the identification and determination of ethanol.[120] The Alcotest 9510 instrument makes use of two independent analytical methods, a single-filter 9.5 μm infrared detector and electrochemical oxidation and the two results must agree within certain narrow limits. The Intox EC-IR instruments incorporate the same two technologies, but the final quantitative analysis is obtained from the electrochemical sensor. The Evidenzer instrument determines ethanol by its absorption of infrared light at five different wavelengths close to 3.4 μm to enhance specificity and detect the presence of interfering substances.[121]

Modern evidential breath-alcohol instruments incorporate microprocessors are able to control the entire sequence of testing including the calibration control test, the analysis of room air, and the time the subject needs to wait before providing two breath samples. The breath-alcohol concentration (BrAC) is monitored during a prolonged exhalation and the trace obtained is stored in a computer for later retrieval and verification if necessary.

An example of such a BrAC profile is shown in Figure 3.2.6 after one subject made a normal inhalation and forced exhalation into a quantitative multi-filter infrared analyzer (Evidenzer). In this example, the BrAC is expressed as g/210 L and the co-existing BAC as g/100 mL, which allows a direct comparison. In the USA the statutory BAC limit is 0.08 g/100 mL and the BrAC limit is 0.08 g/210 L. One notices an initial rapid rise in BrAC as the breath-inlet tube and sampling chamber are flushed out. After about 2 s the BrAC increases more slowly but continues to rise gradually as long as the subject continues to blow into the instrument. After exhaling continuously for 6 s, which is the minimum requirement for an approved test, the BrAC is 90% of the concentration reached after a vital capacity exhalation of 11 s. The co-existing venous BAC is shown on the plot in relation to BrAC, which confirms many other studies that the breath-test gives a certain advantage to a suspect when a blood-breath ratio of 2,100:1 connects the two measurements.

The procedural requirements for administering an evidential breath-alcohol test stipulates the need for an observation period of at least 15 min after a suspect is arrested. During this time the person (suspect) is not allowed to eat, drink, or put any objects in his or her mouth. The main reason for waiting 15 min after the last drink is that the concentration of ethanol in the oral mucosa is higher than expected and this time is needed for ethanol to dissipate. Studies in which the subject has gargled with whisky or used a mouthwash preparation shows an exponential decrease in BrAC and a time of 15 min before returning to zero.

The latest generation of evidential breath-alcohol analyzers are able to monitor the shape of the BrAC exhalation profile, and slope detectors can check for any abnormalities that might indicate a so-called mouth-alcohol effect. Besides the problem with alcohol in the mouth from a recent drink, the operator of the breath instrument should also make sure that the person does not hiccup, burp, belch, or regurgitate stomach contents just before testing. This might result in a more dangerous form of mouth alcohol that is not so easily detected by monitoring the slope of the exhalation profile.

Reporting results of breath-alcohol analysis can be confusing depending on whether the testing was done for clinical or traffic law enforcement purposes. In hospitals, it is standard practice to translate the measured BrAC into the presumed concentration in venous blood, which requires the use of a calibration factor. This is referred to as the blood/breath ratio and the instrument then gives an estimate of the coexisting BAC derived as (BrAC × ratio = BAC). The value of the blood/breath ratio is generally taken to be 2,100:1 (USA and Canada) although values of 2,300:1 (UK, Ireland, and Holland) and 2,000:1 (Germany, France, and Spain) are also accepted. For legal purposes, the BrAC is not converted to BAC but instead as g/210 L breath in the USA so the 2,100:1 blood/breath ratio is affirmed by statute. However, the results from many blood-alcohol and breath-alcohol comparisons show that a factor of 2,100:1 gives a generous margin of safety to the individual.

Figure 3.2.7 compares the concentration-time profiles of ethanol in venous blood and in end-exhaled breath determined with an Intoxilyzer 5000 instrument. The results were obtained for four subjects after they drank 0.5 g/kg ethanol on an empty stomach. To allow making a direct comparison with venous BAC, the concentrations of ethanol in breath were multiplied by a factor of 2,100. On the whole, the breath-test results tended to be lower than the corresponding venous BAC except when tests were done

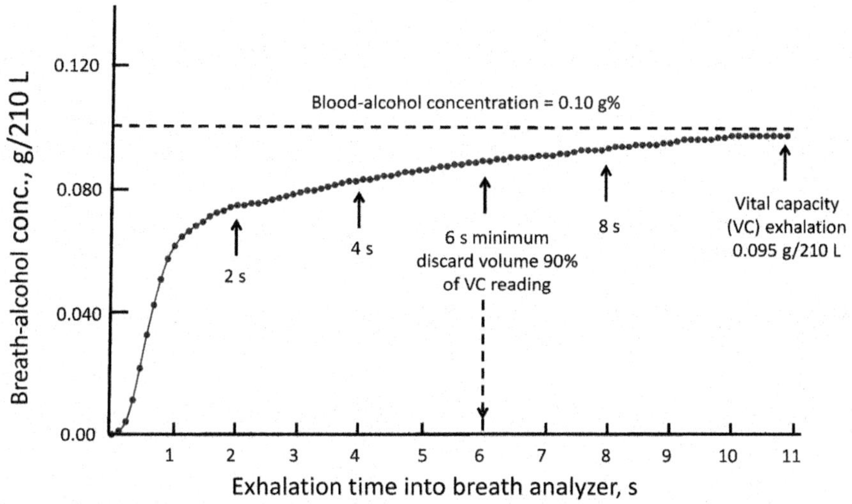

FIGURE 3.2.6 Single breath exhalation profile of ethanol determined with a quantitative infrared analyzer (Evidenzer). The blood/breath factor 2,100:1 was used to calculate the BAC (g%) from the concentration in breath (g/210 L). Despite reaching a vital capacity exhalation after blowing into the instrument for 11 s, the breath-test result was lower than the co-existing venous BAC indicated by the dashed horizontal line at BAC of 0.10 g%.

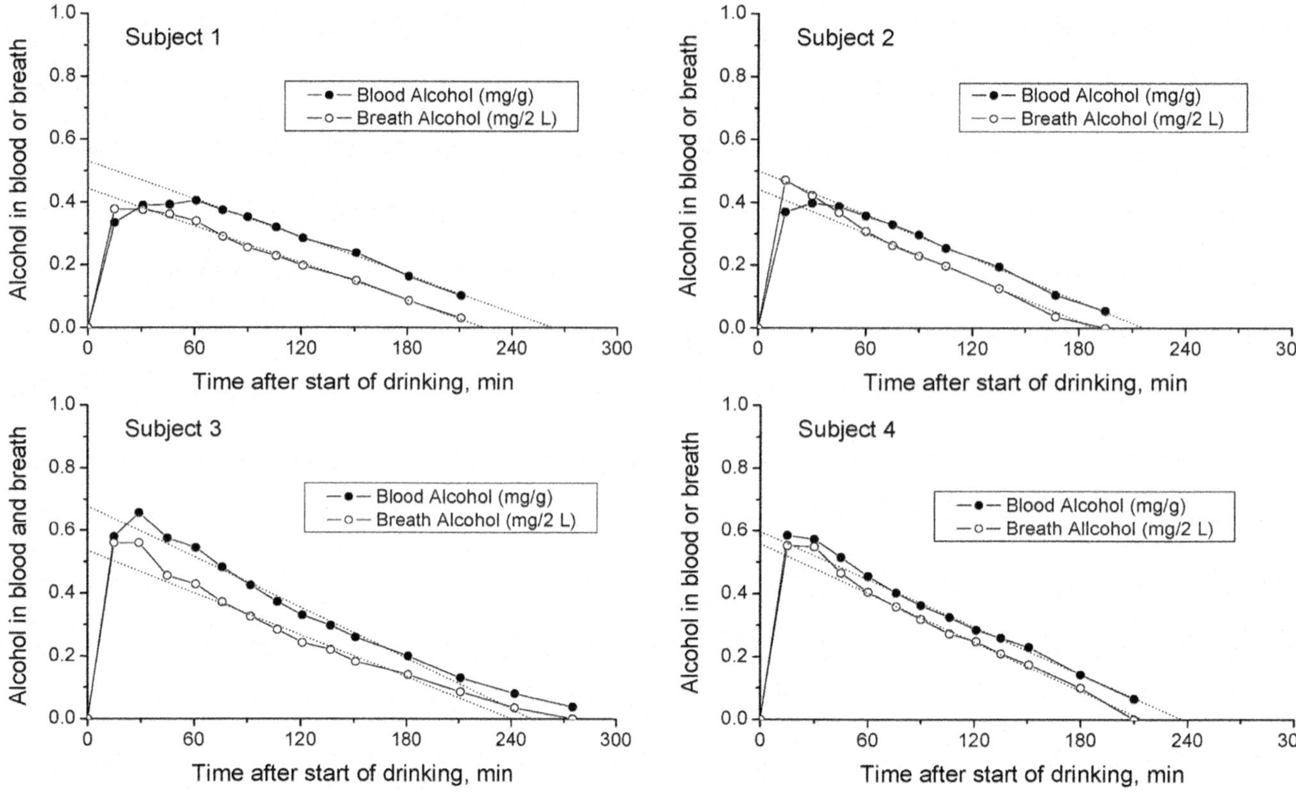

FIGURE 3.2.7 Comparison of the concentration-time profiles of ethanol in near-simultaneous samples of venous blood determined by HS-GC-FID and end-expired breath determined with a quantitative infrared analyzer (Intoxilyzer 5000). Individual traces are shown for four subjects after they drank an ethanol dose of 0.50 g/kg in 15 min on an empty stomach

during the absorption phase of the curves 15 min after the end of drinking. At this time point, BrAC × 2,100 was sometimes higher than BAC. A closer agreement in the post-absorptive phase could be achieved if a blood-breath factor of 2,300:1 had been chosen, but at the same time, this would have exaggerated the differences during the absorption phase.[122,123]

3.2.6.3 Blood/Breath Alcohol Ratios

The blood-breath ratio (BBR) of ethanol was necessary as a calibration factor so that when using the Breathalyzer® instrument the result was reported as the co-existing BAC.[124] The value of the BBR was originally taken to be 2,100:1, meaning that there was 2,100 times more alcohol in blood compared with the same volume of breath. Later studies showed that the BBR was not a constant factor but varied both between and within subjects depending on the type of instrument used and the method of sampling breath, whether end-expired, mixed-expired, or after rebreathing the initial expiration a number of times. The BrAC and therefore the BBR also depends on the subject's breathing pattern and completeness of the exhalation into the analyzer before capturing the sample.

The venous BBR also depended on time after the end of drinking when the tests were done. During the absorption phase, the BBR was less than 2,100:1, and in the post-absorptive phase greater than 2,100:1. These temporal variations were later shown to depend on arterial-venous differences in BAC and the time course of arterial BAC ran much closer to the BrAC rather than venous BAC.[125] The alcohol concentration in pulmonary blood reaching the air sacs (alveoli) of the lungs reflects ethanol concentration in arterial blood and tissue water and not the venous blood draining muscle tissue and returning to the heart.

The mean concentration-time profiles of ethanol in blood drawn a radial artery and a cubital vein on the same arm are compared in Figure 3.2.8. The subjects drank a moderate bolus dose of ethanol (0.6 g/kg body weight) in 5–15 min and arterial and venous were taken from indwelling catheters at regular intervals post-dosing.[126] The trace shows that arterial BAC is higher than venous BAC for about the first 90 min, whereas at all later times venous BAC exceeds the arterial BAC. However, the magnitude of the A–V differences during the absorption phase was larger than the V–A difference during the post-absorptive phase. The arterial and venous concentrations of ethanol were only the same at one time, which occurred about 90 min post-dosing. This time probably represents the completion of absorption and distribution of ethanol in all body fluids and tissues.

Note that for clinical applications, the breath-alcohol instruments are calibrated to estimate the alcohol concentration in whole blood and not the concentration in plasma or serum. This is often overlooked by clinicians who fail to appreciate the difference between whole blood and plasma

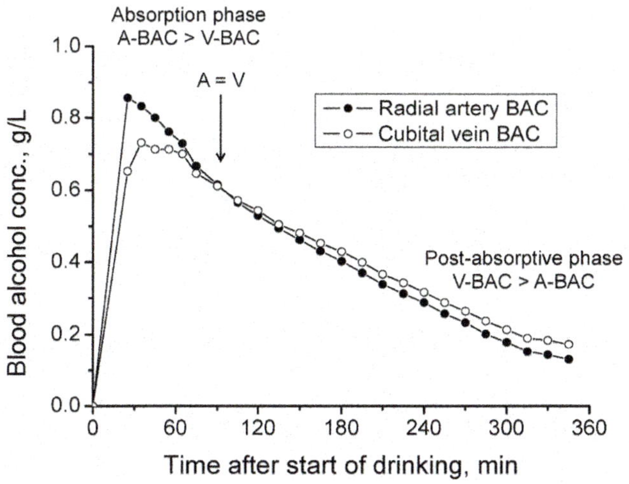

FIGURE 3.2.8 Comparison of concentration-time curves of ethanol in blood samples taken nearly simultaneously from a cubital vein and a radial artery on the same arm. Mean curves are plotted for nine healthy men after they drank 0.6 g/kg ethanol in 2–15 min. [126] Standard error bars are omitted for clarity

concentrations of alcohol. To derive the concentration of alcohol in plasma or serum indirectly by analysis of breath, the instrument would need to be calibrated with a plasma/breath factor of about 2,600:1 because whole blood contains about 15% less alcohol than the same volume of plasma or serum (Table 3.2.1).

Starting in the 1980s, drunk-driving legislation in many countries was constructed to include a statutory breath-alcohol concentration in addition to a punishable BAC. The threshold BrAC was derived from the pre-existing BAC by assuming a population average BBR. However, there was no consensus reached as to what BBR should be used when calculating the statutory BrAC limit and this varies from 2,000:1 to 2,400:1.

Breath-alcohol analysis for evidential purposes must be done using approved instruments and according to a standardized protocol with appropriate precautions and quality assurance. Every suspect needs to provide two separate breath samples between two to ten minutes apart. At the same time as the suspect is tested there needs to be a control analysis done on air from the room where the subject is tested. Also important is a calibration check on the instrument done either before, after, or before and after a suspect blows into the instrument. All results from these tests are then printed out in real-time along with the time, date, and name of the suspect and also stored online for later downloading to a central computer network.

3.2.7 Quality Assurance of Chemical Measurements

Much has been written about the quality control of clinical laboratory analysis, including the concepts of precision, accuracy, linearity, recovery, sensitivity, and limits of detection and quantitation of the methods used. When the analytical results are later used in evidence in criminal cases, other aspects of sampling, transport, and storage of specimens are important to maintain an unbroken chain of custody, which might need to be documented in every single case. The training of the phlebotomist, the names of the police officers charged with initial storage and shipment of the specimens to a laboratory for analysis, the condition of the specimens on arrival, and registration all need to be recorded by means of barcodes or other acceptable protocol for forensic specimens.

The analytical procedure used, including the chromatographic traces, proof of calibration control of the instrument with the analytical run containing a suspect's specimen might need to be documented if for some reason the integrity of the results is challenged. Today's clinical and forensic laboratories are accredited for the services they provide, as are the individual analytical methods used. This has become increasingly important to boost confidence in the results when these make the difference between punishment and acquittal in borderline cases. Evidence of satisfactory analytical work can be gleaned from results of participating in external proficiency tests. Several such programs are available for a wide range of substances and usually entail spiking the blood or plasma specimen with a known concentration of the target analyte and sending aliquots to each laboratory, along with a declared proficiency trial, and the test specimens should be included among routine samples.

The most important features of pre-analytical, analytical, and post-analytical aspects of blood-alcohol analysis are presented below.

3.2.7.1 Pre-Analytical Factors

It has often been stated that the result of an analysis is only as good as the specimen reviewed for analysis. In this connection, it is important to distinguish between samples taken under sterile conditions from living subjects and death investigations with post-mortem samples. Blood samples for analysis of ethanol in drink-driving cases are generally taken from an antecubital vein using evacuated tubes (5-ml or 10-ml Vacutainer tubes). Otherwise, blood can be drawn using a syringe and hypodermic needle, and the specimen (usually 10 mL) transferred to a glass tube labelled with the person's name and other identification before sending off to a laboratory for analysis.

In drunk-driving cases, the tubes of blood submitted for analysis should be filled as completely as possible to ensure only a small air-space above the blood. Only a few hundred microliters of blood are needed for the determination of ethanol although very often other impairing drugs are also analyzed because of drug-impaired driving legislation. After taking the blood specimen, the tubes should be gently inverted five to ten times to facilitate adequate mixing and dissolution of the chemical preservatives. The evacuated tubes contain a mixture of sodium fluoride (10 mg/mL) to inhibit the activity of various enzymes, microorganisms, and yeasts, and potassium oxalate (2–5 mg/mL) as an anticoagulant.

The evacuated tubes should be labeled with the person's name, the date, and the sampling time of the venepuncture.

The name of the phlebotomist also needs to be recorded on the tubes or accompanying paperwork. When the evacuated tubes are filled with blood they need to be sealed in such a way as to prevent unauthorized opening or tampering and adhesive paper strips or tapes are available for this purpose. The evacuated tubes with the blood samples are protected from breakage during transport and the package secured so that manipulating or adulteration is easily detected by laboratory personnel when being registered. After taking the samples, the tubes of blood should be stored in a cold room before shipment to the laboratory by express mail delivery service.

The conventional tubes used for sampling blood in drunk-driving cases are 10 mL grey stopper evacuated tubes containing 100 mg NaF (1% w/v) and potassium oxalate as an anticoagulant. Not infrequently the evacuated tubes are not filled completely with blood for various reasons and an abnormally low volume would mean a higher concentration of NaF per mL blood. When blood samples contained 1% NaF the ethanol concentration in the headspace increased by 8.2–9.6% compared with heparinized blood without any NaF.[127] This led to a suggestion that false high BAC results would be obtained if there was an abnormal concentration of NaF, which led to an acquittal in a drunk-driving trial in the UK. However, the prosecution in this case failed to call any expert testimony to evaluate the scientific basis for this claim and the suspect was acquitted.

Prior to headspace analysis, an aliquot of blood is diluted ten times with aqueous *n*-propanol as the internal standard, which also dilutes the NaF concentration ten times. Nevertheless, the effect of a deficient volume of blood in the evacuated tubes was investigated experimentally.[128] The results showed that BAC was actually lower in the blood specimens with low volume and therefore high NaF concentration.[129] With excess NaF, both ethanol and *n*-propanol are salted out into the headspace, and the peak area ratio of ethanol/propanol used for quantitative analysis should be about the same with or without excess NaF. However, actual experiments showed that the 3-carbon alcohol *n*-propanol was salted out slightly more effectively than the 2-carbon ethanol, giving a slightly lower ethanol/propanol ratio and a correspondingly lower BAC.[130]

Pre-analytical factors can be minimized by using a standardized sampling protocol for obtaining the required venous blood for analysis. After swabbing the skin with an alcohol-free disinfectant or with soap and water, two evacuated tubes should be filled in rapid succession. Obviously, the blood should not be taken from veins into which intravenous fluids are being administered.[131] Any emergency medical treatment given to a victim of a traffic crash, such as replacement fluids to counteract shock or blood transfusions, need to be documented and the effect if any on analytical results explained to the court.[132] The blood samples for forensic determination of ethanol should be taken only by trained personnel, such as a phlebotomist, registered nurse, or physician.

Pre-analytical factors include preparation of the subject and the method of taking the blood sample, whether using a syringe and needle or an evacuated tube. The sampling site on the body and the skin disinfection used, if any, are also important factors to consider. If ethanol is the target analyte then obviously it is not advisable to use an alcohol swab to clean the skin of the needle puncture site. However, studies have shown that the risk of ethanol carry-over even when swabbing the skin with alcohol is very low.[133]

There is some ongoing debate and discussion about the amount and combination of anticoagulant and preservative needed in evacuated tubes used to sample blood for determinations of ethanol.[134] No agreement has been reached about whether 5 mL or 10 mL grey-stopper evacuated tubes should be used, nor about the amount and concentration of NaF, which might vary from 0.2% w/v to 1.5% w/v for blood-ethanol analysis. The presence of NaF is to stabilize the ethanol content by acting as an enzyme inhibitor and in this way preventing the formation of ethanol in-vitro in the rare event a sample is contaminated with yeasts or bacteria. This risk is virtually non-existent when dealing with living subjects and sterile sampling conditions, although it is a major problem when blood is taken in medical examiner or coroner cases.

Documentation of the chain of custody of specimens is important in medicolegal casework, starting with the labeling of the blood tubes and how they are packaged and transported to the laboratory for analysis. Other considerations are time in transit and ambient temperature during shipment of specimens to the forensic laboratory for analysis. The packages should be carefully inspected after arrival and registration and the number of tubes of blood recorded, as well as the approximate volume of specimen in each tube and whether the blood is free-flowing or partially clotted. The blood specimens might be diluted with resuscitation fluids if taken from victims of traffic accidents, who receive life-saving treatment at the roadside and/or during emergency hospital treatment. It is important to remember that the results of a laboratory analysis are only as good as the condition of the sample as received. When the result of the analysis is close to a statutory limit for driving, the existence of analytical and pre-analytical factors could make the difference between punishment and/or acquittal in such borderline cases.

3.2.7.2 Analytical Factors

For legal purposes, blood specimens need to be analyzed in duplicate, and finding a close agreement between the two results is one indication of high analytical precision. Analyzing the specimen in duplicate is also a safeguard against any mishaps occurring during processing, such as when diluting the blood with internal standard or transferring the sample to the headspace vial and making this airtight. Ideally, the duplicate determinations should be done by different laboratory technicians, who work independently with different sets of equipment. Furthermore, the aliquots of blood should be removed from separate Vacutainer tubes if possible. This helps to minimize the risk of specimen mix-up of the samples during the analysis. To enhance analytical selectivity, the blood should be analyzed on two different chromatographic systems that yield different retention times for ethanol, which makes identification of the substance much more certain if the authentic ethanol standards have the same retention times. Alternatively, the blood specimen might be analyzed by an independent method, such as enzymatic oxidation or a mass spectrometric detector run in parallel.

Prior to analysis, the blood specimens should be carefully inspected to ensure that security tapes or seals are still intact and there has been no tampering with the specimens. If the blood seems to be unusually dilute or clotted this should also be noted. There are two ways to deal with clotted samples: (1) either centrifuge the specimen and use an aliquot of the supernatant for analysis and then report the results as a serum concentration, or (2) homogenize the clot and analyze an aliquot of the hemolyzed blood specimen. Details of any mishaps occurring during the sampling, transport, and storage of specimens, such as any leakage of blood or cracked tubes on arrival must be recorded along with the date and time of arrival in relation to the time of sampling.

Information about the patient/suspect written on the Vacutainer tubes should be compared with other documentation in the case, such as the date and time of the offense on the police reports. The same unique identification number or barcode should be added to all paperwork and biological specimens received and this number used to monitor work done on the specimens as it passes through the laboratory procedures.

Before removal of a specimen for analysis, one needs to ensure that the erythrocytes and plasma fractions are adequately mixed and homogeneous. Accurate and precise diluter-dispenser equipment is available to remove an aliquot of blood and dilute this with the internal standard. The HS-GC-FID chromatogram should ideally show one peak for the ethanol and one peak for the internal standard. Any unidentified peaks on the gas chromatograms should be noted because these might indicate the presence of other volatiles in the blood sample.

3.2.7.3 Post-Analytical Factors

Quality control charts offer a useful way to monitor the day-to-day performance of the results of analysis done at clinical and forensic laboratories. One chart should display the distribution of random errors or precision, based on differences between duplicate determinations, with another chart monitoring differences between the known concentration of standard substances and the analytical result. Accuracy is concerned with the correctness of an analytical result as reflected in the systematic error or bias inherent in a method or caused by some artifact of the analytical system.[135] Close scrutiny of both types of charts makes it easy to detect sudden deterioration in analytical performance, and unacceptable results are flagged and remedial action is taken.

Stability of the analyte during storage is a key element of post-analytical quality assurance. Long experience and many studies verify that BAC decreases during long-term storage of blood specimens in a refrigerator at a temperature of 4° C.[136] Ethanol concentrations are more stable if the blood samples are frozen.[137] The loss of ethanol from blood during storage might depend on the nature of the evacuated tubes used to collect them, whether these are made of glass or plastic, and the amount of chemical preservative (NaF) present.[138] With blood samples preserved with 1% NaF loss of ethanol was the same in glass or plastic evacuated tubes. After 12 months of storage at 4° C the BAC decreased by 0.11 g/L on average when BAC ranged from 0.1–3.0 g/L.

If the rate of degradation of ethanol during storage is well documented, corrections are possible to compare with the original analytical result. There are no published studies suggesting that ethanol concentrations in blood increase during storage, at least when the specimens are taken from living subjects under sterile conditions.[139] Most studies indicate a rate of decrease in BAC from 0.01–0.03 g/L per month of storage at 4° C.[140]

Chromatographic traces and other evidence corroborating the analytical results such as calibration plots or response factors all need to be carefully labeled and stored in fire-proof cabinets. Today it is virtually mandatory that a forensic science or toxicology laboratory is accredited for the analytical work they purport to undertake for customers. When the analytical results are later used in a criminal prosecution, such as drunk-driving offenses, information about the laboratory performance becomes relevant information of and when the result is challenged in court.

3.2.7.4 Inter-Laboratory Proficiency Tests

Regular participation in external proficiency tests has become an essential part of performance evaluation of the work done at analytical laboratories. The usual procedure is to spike blood or plasma samples with known amounts of ethanol and then distribute aliquots from the main specimen to each of the participating laboratories. Most such proficiency tests are "open" or declared because the laboratories involved know that they are being tested. The sample of blood or plasma is analyzed in exactly the same way as unknown samples and the result is reported back to the organizers. After any outlying results are removed, the mean and standard deviation of the remaining analytical results are calculated. A z-score is then calculated as follows:

$$\text{Z-score} = \frac{\begin{pmatrix}\text{mean result of all participants} \\ -\text{ individual laboratory result}\end{pmatrix}}{\text{SD}}$$

where SD is the standard deviation of results reported by all participating laboratories (after omitting outlying values). Laboratories with a z-score within ± 2 are considered to show acceptable analytical performance in the proficiency test. Regular participation in such schemes or programs is necessary when applying for laboratory accreditation.

An external proficiency trial of blood-ethanol determination by gas chromatography at clinical chemistry laboratories in Sweden were reported.[141] The between laboratory coefficient of variation (CV) ranged from 10–17%. In a similar study of laboratories in the UK, the corresponding CVs depended in part on the methodology used for the determination of ethanol, whether immunoassays or gas chromatographic methods (liquid injection and headspace technique).[142] The analytical CVs ranged from 8% to 20%, although it should be noted that analysis of ethanol in blood is not a primary task for hospital clinical chemistry laboratories. More recently, laboratories in Italy that offered customers blood-alcohol analysis were investigated, and most but not all participants showed satisfactory performance (z-score < 2.0).[143]

Better results from such external proficiency trials can be expected from laboratories that specialize in blood-alcohol analysis.[144] For example, Table 3.2.8 presents results of proficiency tests done at specialist forensic toxicology laboratories in the Nordic countries (Denmark, Finland, Iceland, Norway, and Sweden). All participants used headspace gas chromatography for ethanol determinations, and the blood samples submitted for analysis were obtained from apprehended drunk drivers. The coefficient of variation between laboratories was always less than 3% regardless of the ethanol concentration in blood, which testifies to highly reproducible analytical work. The corresponding CVs within laboratories were mostly 1% or less based on 3–6 determinations per sample. If the mean BAC in each sample is taken as the target value then all participating laboratories achieved an accuracy to within ± 5% of the attributed concentration.

3.2.7.5 Allowing for Uncertainty

All results from chemical and biochemical methods of analysis are subject to uncertainty caused by inherent variations in obtaining blood samples and the particular methodology used. The magnitude of uncertainty becomes important when a decision has to be made whether or not a certain threshold concentration, such as the statutory BAC or BrAC limits for driving had been exceeded. The sampling blood or breath, measuring the aliquot to be analyzed, and the accuracy and precision of the methods used all contribute to this uncertainty.[145] Much can be gained by following a standard operating procedure (SOP) for the particular substance to be analyzed and keeping the necessary manual operations to a minimum. Finding close agreement between the individual results from making replicate determinations indicates a high analytical precision and helps to ensure that no blunders or mishaps occurred during the sample handling and analysis.[146]

When the analytical results are intended for use in criminal cases, such as when traffic offenders are prosecuted, besides reporting the mean BAC, it is highly recommended that an allowance is made to compensate for the uncertainty (random and systematic error).[147] This is easily done by subtracting a certain amount from the mean BAC to give a value that is less than the true concentration of substance with a high level of certainty. The amount deducted is easily calculated by statistical methods using the standard deviation as a measure of precision and accuracy derived from analysis of known strength standards. However, there is no scientific consensus as to the number of replicate determinations necessary in individual cases or the best way to allow for uncertainty and the associated degree of certainty.[148,149]

The laboratory SOP used in Sweden when blood samples from apprehended drivers were analyzed required making four determinations by different laboratory assistants. Their results were then compared and if the highest minus the lowest was less than 0.25 g/L the mean BAC was calculated. Because of random variations the person's true BAC might have been somewhat higher or lower than the mean concentration according to a Gaussian distribution. This implies that 68% of individual results are within plus or minus one standard deviation (SD), 95% within two SD, and 99.7% within three SD of the mean. The analytical

TABLE 3.2.8

Excellent Agreement in the Results from a Declared Inter-Laboratory Proficiency Test of Blood-Alcohol Determinations at Five Forensic Toxicology Laboratories in the Nordic Countries[1]

Laboratory	Sample-1	Sample-2	Sample-3	Sample-4	Sample-5	Sample-6
1	0.46	1.01	2.15	1.62	0.74	1.75
2	0.47	1.01	2.27	1.70	0.78	1.83
3	0.46	1.01	2.26	1.67	0.77	1.81
4	0.47	1.00	2.17	1.66	0.78	1.81
5	0.48	1.01	2.15	1.66	0.78	1.79
Mean	0.47	1.01	2.20	1.66	0.77	1.80
SD	0.008	0.005	0.060	0.029	0.017	0.030
CV%	1.7%	0.49%	2.7%	1.7%	2.2%	1.7%

[1] The blood samples were taken from apprehended drivers by filling multiple evacuated tubes. The preservatives were sodium fluoride (1%) and potassium oxalate and tubes were shipped to each laboratory for analysis. The between laboratory coefficients of variation (CV) were less than 3% for all blood samples. The corresponding within laboratory CVs were mostly less than 1% (data not shown).

Note: All laboratories used headspace gas chromatography (HS-GC) and BAC is reported as g/kg (mg/g) in whole blood.

precision (SD) of the laboratory method is known from past experience in analyzing thousands of samples by different analysts over many years. The true ethanol concentration is expected to be within ± 3 × SD of the mean with a high degree of statistical confidence and there is only a 0.3% chance that it is outside those limits, thus a 0.15% chance the true value is below mean – 3SD and 0.15% chance that it is above mean + 3SD.

Accordingly, the prosecution BAC in a drunk driving case is obtained by subtracting 3 × SD from the mean result of analysis, which in practice amounted to an allowance of 0.14 g/L. After making this deduction, there is only a 0.15% chance (0.0015) or 1.5 in 1000 that the suspect's true BAC was lower than the result used for prosecution. In a criminal case, this makes it "beyond a reasonable doubt" that the suspect's BAC was not less than the value used for prosecution. Note that making a deduction from the mean analytical result is not customary for blood samples analyzed at clinical laboratories, where the most probable value (the mean) is reported instead. Indeed, some hospital laboratories might only make a single determination of the concentration of ethanol in the sample, because they are mainly interested in making a medical diagnosis and not in the prosecution of traffic offenders.

3.2.8 Disposition and Fate of Ethanol in the Body

Ethanol is a small polar molecule, which is completely miscible with water and easily passes through all biological membranes, including the blood–brain barrier. The ethanol contained in alcoholic beverages is rapidly absorbed from the stomach and proximal intestines (duodenum and jejunum) by passive diffusion and reaches the portal venous blood circulation. Ethanol contained in stronger drinks, such as distilled spirits (40 vol%), is absorbed into the blood slightly faster than ethanol contained in beers (~5 vol%) and table wines (~12 vol%). However, besides the alcohol content, other constituents of the drinks consumed are important considerations, such as carbohydrate content, which tends to delay gastric emptying.

The rate of ethanol absorption into the blood is faster from the duodenum and jejunum, compared with the stomach, owing to a much larger absorption surface provided by the villi and microvilli in the intestines. Factors influencing gastric emptying therefore have a major influence on the rate of ethanol absorption and time of occurrence of peak BAC after drinking. When the pyloric sphincter opens rapidly after drinking alcohol, the BAC curve often exhibits an "overshoot" peak, because the rate of absorption is faster than the blood can distribute ethanol to organs and tissues of the body.

Once absorbed into the circulating blood, alcohol diffuses rapidly across capillary walls into the various tissues, to reach equilibrium between the concentration in the water fraction of blood and the extracellular fluid. The time required to reach an ethanol equilibrium between the blood water and the total body water requires about 60–90 min after the end of drinking. This time varies between individuals depending on gastric emptying rate, the cross-sectional area of the local capillary bed, and the minute volume ratio of blood flow per gram of tissue mass. Organs and tissues with a rich supply of blood, such as the lungs, the brain, and the kidney equilibrate with the ethanol in arterial blood rapidly and one would not expect any appreciable differences between arterial and venous blood ethanol concentrations.

In Figure 3.2.9 concentration-time profiles of ethanol are compared from analyzing alternative biological specimens, namely venous blood, end-exhaled breath, bladder urine, and oral fluid (saliva). Twenty-one healthy male volunteers drank 0.68 g/kg ethanol as neat whisky in 20 min after an overnight fast.[150] Note that when constructing this graph, the breath-alcohol concentrations were multiplied by an assumed blood/breath ratio of 2,100:1 to allow making a direct comparison with ethanol concentrations in blood, saliva, and urine.

The bulk of the ethanol dose ingested (95–98%) is eliminated from the body by oxidative metabolism through enzymatic reactions occurring mainly in the liver and catalyzed by class I enzymes of alcohol dehydrogenase (ADH). Between 2–5% of the dose of ethanol is excreted unchanged in breath, urine, and sweat and a very small fraction (~0.1%) undergoes Phase II conjugation reactions to produce ethyl glucuronide and ethyl sulfate, which are excreted in the urine.[151–153] Depending on speed of gastric emptying there is also some first-pass metabolism of ethanol by enzymes located in the gastric mucosa and the liver, although the role of pre-systemic metabolism is highly variable and dependent on the dose of ethanol consumed and is not so easy to quantify.[154]

At moderate BAC (> 0.60 g/L), a microsomal enzyme (CYPE1), which has a higher K_m for oxidation of ethanol (0.60–0.80 g/L) compared with ADH (K_m = 0.02–0.05 g/L),

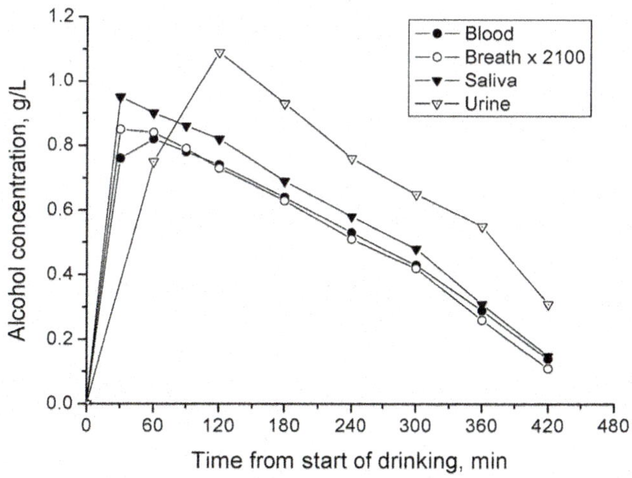

FIGURE 3.2.9 Comparison of the concentration-time profiles of ethanol in venous blood, saliva, urine, and breath. Note that breath-alcohol concentration was multiplied by 2,100 to allow a direct comparison. Mean curves are shown for N = 21 subjects who drank 0.68 g/kg ethanol as neat whisky in 20 min on an empty stomach. Standard error bars are omitted for clarity

is involved in the oxidative metabolism of ethanol.[155] P450 enzymes also metabolize many drugs and environmental chemicals, which raises the potential for drug–alcohol interactions, especially in heavy drinkers and alcoholics.[156] The activity of CYP2E1 increases after a period of continuous heavy drinking, owing to a faster *de novo* synthesis of the enzyme protein and this accounts for the development of metabolic tolerance. This is reflected in a two- to three-fold faster rate of elimination of alcohol disappearance from blood observed in alcoholics undergoing detoxification.[157]

The impairment effects of ethanol on performance and behavior are complex and involve interaction with several neurotransmitter systems, especially the inhibitory receptors glutamate and gamma-aminobutyric acid (GABA) and its chloride ion channel.[2,158] The behavioral effects of ethanol are dose-dependent and a low dose causes people to relax and become less inhibited. As drinking continues and higher BAC is reached, the impairment effects on body functioning become more obvious and pronounced, including slurred speech and unsteady gait.

Many of the pharmacological effects of ethanol are explained by its action on $GABA_A$ receptors, thus dampening brain activity. This binding also helps to explain cross-tolerance between ethanol and other depressant drugs, such as benzodiazepines and barbiturates, which also bind to the $GABA_A$ receptor complex open chloride ion-channels to alter brain functioning.[159]

Although there is a reasonably good correlation between the degree of ethanol-induced impairment and BAC, there are large individual variations in response at the same BAC. There are two main reasons for this; first, larger people tend to have more body water so ethanol is diluted with a larger volume resulting in a lower BAC compared with if lighter individuals consumed the same dose of ethanol. This phenomenon is known as consumption tolerance and stems from variations in body weight and the relative amount of adipose tissue, which is influenced by age, gender, and ethnicity. The second reason for inter-individual differences in ethanol-induced performance decrement is called concentration tolerance, which is linked to gradual habituation of brain cells to the presence of alcohol during repeated exposure to the drug.[160]

Besides the development of acute tolerance (Mellanby effect), which happens during a single exposure (see Chapter 3.1), people also develop a chronic tolerance to alcohol's effect. Among the mechanisms accounting for chronic tolerance are long-term changes in the composition of cell membranes particularly, the cholesterol content, the structure of the fatty acids and also the arrangement of proteins and phospholipids making up the lipid bilayer.[19]

In occasional drinkers, the impairment effects of ethanol are more pronounced after drinking larger quantities of ethanol and reaching higher BAC. The various clinical signs and symptoms of intoxication were classified by Dr. Emil Bogen in relation to the person's BAC ranging from being sober to being dead drunk and in a comatose state.[23] This classification scheme was further elaborated upon by Dr. Kurt Dubowski[4] and his chart has received wide circulation and use in clinical and forensic toxicology. Dubowski defined six stages of alcohol influence with overlapping ranges of BAC; subclinical (0.1–0.5 g/L), euphoria (0.3–1.2 g/L), excitement (0.9–0.25 g/L, confusion (1.8–3.0 g/L), stupor (2.5–4.0 g/L), and ending with coma and death (3.5–5.0 g/L).

The use of overlapping ranges of BAC was intended to illustrate the large individual differences in the clinical signs and symptoms of intoxication between different people, depending on the pattern of drinking and habituation to alcohol. In reality, a moderate drinker rarely consumes alcohol to reach a BAC of more than 0.8–1.0 g/L, owing to nausea and risk of vomiting. For comparison, the average BAC in apprehended drivers is between 1.5–1.8 g/L, which verifies a high proportion of binge drinkers in this population.[161] During the investigation of deaths caused by acute alcohol poisoning, the average autopsy BAC was 3.6 g/L and the 90% range was from 2.1–5.0 g/L.[162]

The impairment effects of alcohol depend to a great extent on the dose ingested and the speed of drinking and whether a person has zero BAC when drinking commences. A person's age and previous experience with alcohol consumption are also important considerations, owing to the development of central nervous system tolerance. People who are capable of functioning with a very high BAC, such as drunk drivers (e.g. 2.0–3.0 g/L is not uncommon), have probably been drinking continuously for several days or weeks so that chronic tolerance develops. Consumption of a large volume of neat spirits in a short time results in pronounced behavioral impairment and signs and symptoms of drunkenness with risk of losing consciousness and death from respiratory failure. Drinking too much too fast is dangerous and if gastric emptying is rapid, the BAC rises with such a velocity that a vomit reflex in the brain is triggered. This physiological response to acute alcohol ingestion has probably saved many lives.

Controlled studies with people who drink to reach very high BAC are difficult to accomplish because of ethical and health reasons. An exception was a study reported by Zink and Reinhardt in which male volunteers were allowed to consume massive quantities of ethanol, either as beer or spirits or both, more or less continuously for 8–10 hours.[163] The BAC profiles were established unequivocally by sampling blood from an indwelling catheter every 15–20 min for up to 10 hours. Some of the subjects reached very high BAC, several exceeding 3.0 g/kg (~3.0 g/L), and they all developed a high tolerance to impairment effects of alcohol.

Four representative graphs from the 16 participants are shown in Figure 3.2.10. BAC for legal purposes in Germany, as already mentioned (Table 3.3.1), is reported in mass/mass (g/kg) concentration units, which means that 3.0 g/kg is equivalent to 3.16 g/L. The results of this unique drinking study was re-evaluated and pharmacokinetic parameters re-calculated. It was shown that when subjects drink alcohol repeatedly over many hours there is a significant first-pass metabolism occurring because the expected BAC for the dose administered and the amount lost through

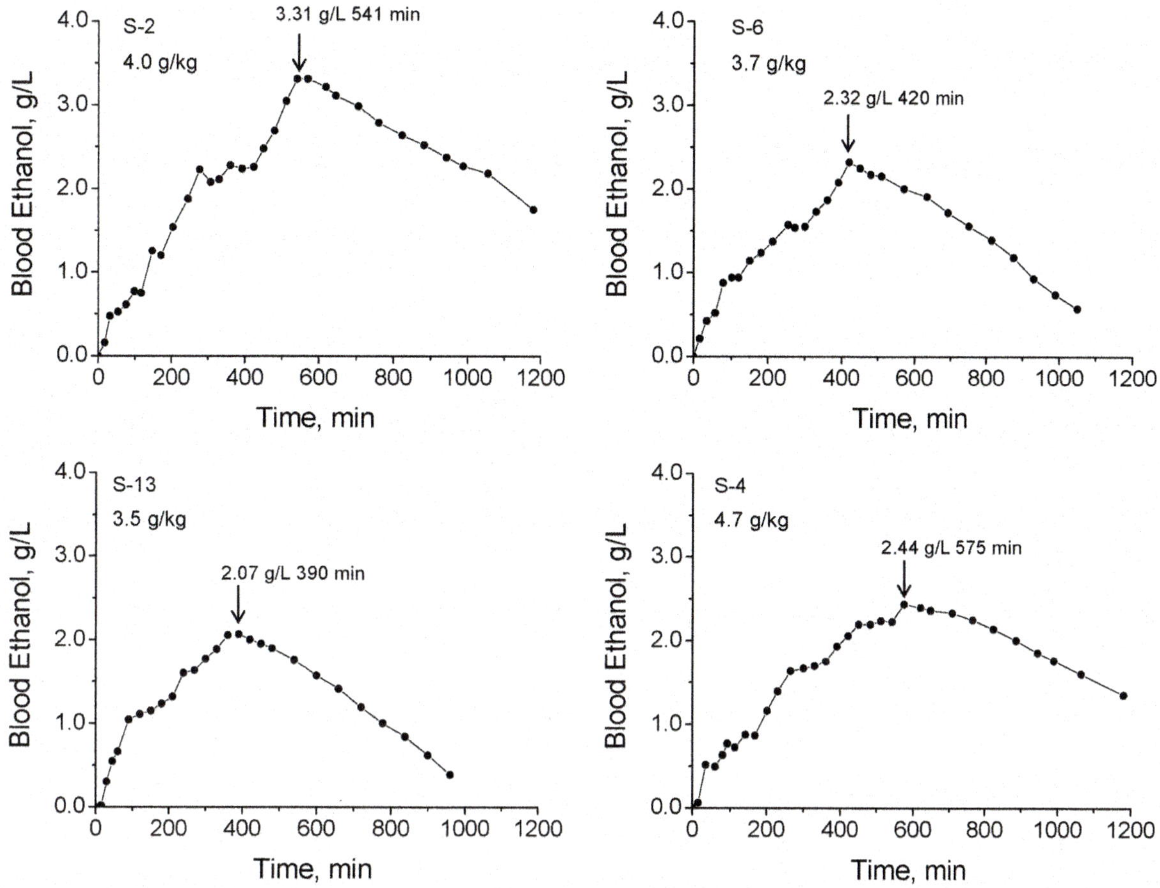

FIGURE 3.2.10 Concentration-time (C-T) profiles of ethanol in four subjects after they consumed the alcoholic beverages of their choice for up to 6–10 h to reach very high BAC. The dose of ethanol ingested, the peak BAC reached, and the time of its occurrence (from the start of drinking) are displayed on the graph. The curves were redrawn from C-T data publication by Zink and Reinhardt[163]

metabolism was a lot higher than the measured peak BAC in Figure 3.2.10.[164]

3.2.8.1 Clinical Pharmacokinetics of Ethanol

Clinical pharmacokinetics is concerned with the way that drugs and their metabolites are absorbed, distributed, metabolized, and excreted in the body and how these processes can be described in quantitative terms.[165,166] The various pharmacokinetic models used to describe the elimination rate of ethanol from blood are summarized in Box 3.2.1.

BOX 3.2.1 Definition of Three Pharmacokinetic Models Used to Describe the Elimination of Ethanol from Blood in the Post-Absorptive Phase

Zero-order kinetics: This implies that a constant amount of the drug is eliminated from the blood per unit time, such as 0.15 g/L per hour. For a drug eliminated according to zero-order kinetics, the disappearance rate is independent of the starting concentration.

First-order kinetics: This implies that a fixed proportion or fraction of the drug is eliminated per unit time, such as a percentage; 50% is eliminated after one half-life. After five half-lives ~97% of the drug is cleared from the body. In a first-order reaction, the elimination rate depends on the concentration of drug present and is therefore faster at higher concentrations according to a logarithmic function.

Michaelis-Menten kinetics: Describes the rate of enzymatic reactions where maximum velocity is denoted (V_{max}), which is approached when the enzyme system is saturated with substrate. The Michaelis constant (k_m) is a measure of the affinity of the enzyme for its substrate and the lower the value the greater is the affinity. It is sometimes referred to as non-linear or saturation kinetics. At substrate concentrations double the k_m the drug is eliminated according to zero-order kinetics and below the k_m a transition occurs towards first-order kinetics.

3.2.8.2 The Widmark Equation

The clinical pharmacokinetics of ethanol have probably been investigated more than any other drug or xenobiotic.

One reason for this is the ubiquitous use of ethanol as a recreational drug and the fact that a reliable method of analysis was available already in 1922.[24] The necessary samples of blood (100 μL) were taken from a fingertip and this permitted taking samples at 30–60 min intervals so that the concentration-time profiles of ethanol for different patterns of drinking could be identified and defined unequivocally.[167]

Figure 3.2.11 is an example of a blood-alcohol concentration-time (C-T) profile from an experiment to determine the pharmacokinetic parameters of ethanol. One male subject drank 0.68 g/kg ethanol as neat whisky in 20 min in the morning on an empty stomach.[168] All the C-T data points were first inspected to determine the start of the post-absorptive elimination phase. A straight line was drawn through the points falling on the rectilinear elimination phase and this line was extrapolated to intersect with the x- and y-axes of the graph. The y-intercept is denoted C_o and the x-intercept is denoted min_0.

The C_0 parameter represents the theoretical BAC if the entire ethanol dose was absorbed and distributed in all body fluids and tissues without any metabolism occurring. This allows calculating an important kinetic parameter referred to as rho factor by Widmark or in more modern texts as ethanol's distribution volume (V_d). This represents the ratio between the concentration of ethanol in the whole body to its concentration in the bloodstream. Dividing the dose in g/kg by the extrapolated BAC C_0 in g/L gives Vd in units of L/kg.

Because ethanol distributes into the total body water compartment its V_d can only take certain values as predicted by the water content of the body and the blood. The latter is fairly constant at 80% w/w or 84% w/v and body water in non-obese men is 60% and 50% for women. The V_d expected for normal males and females are therefore 60/84 = 0.71 L/kg and 50/84 = 0.60 L/kg, respectively. The variations in V_d between subjects depend primarily on differences in body composition, particularly the proportions of fat to lean body mass, which is dependent on the person's age, ethnicity, and gender.

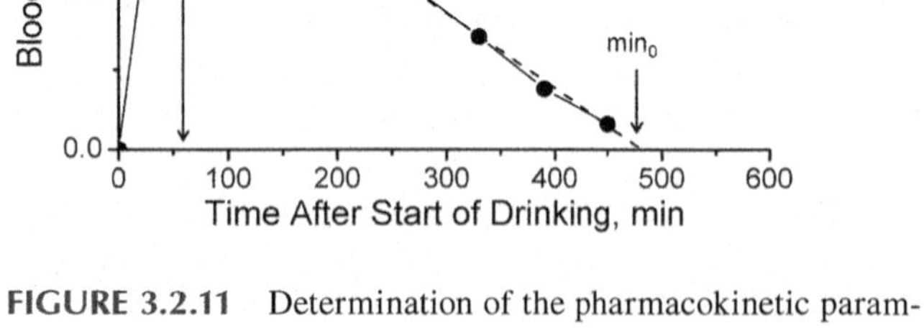

FIGURE 3.2.11 Determination of the pharmacokinetic parameters of ethanol in one male subject who drank neat whisky corresponding to 0.68 g/kg ethanol in 20 min on an empty stomach. A straight line was drawn through selected data points on the rectilinear elimination phase of the BAC curve and extrapolated back to the time of starting to drink (C_0) and time to reach zero BAC (min_0). The method of calculating both the elimination rate of ethanol from blood (β) and the volume of distribution (V_d) are shown on the graph

Alcohol is sometimes administered intravenously (IV), which is useful to avoid there being any first-pass metabolism (FPM). An example of a BAC profile after making a constant rate infusion of ethanol is shown in Figure 3.2.12. The test subject received 0.60 g/kg as a 10% w/v solution in saline at a constant rate for 40 min. The peak BAC coincided with ending the infusion and was followed by a diffusion plunge, during which time the ethanol equilibrates between the bloodstream and well-perfused tissue compartments. At about 90 min post-infusion, the BAC started to decrease at a constant rate per unit time in accordance with zero-order kinetics. The slope of the rectilinear disappearance phase is then determined in the usual way as described above.

When the BAC decreases below about 0.1–0.2 g/L or about 450 min post-dosing the linear declining phase now changes to a curvilinear function and for the remainder of the time that ethanol is measurable in the blood. The elimination of alcohol now follows first-order kinetics with elimination rate constant denoted k_1 and proportional to BAC. The transition from zero-order to first-order kinetics depends on the K_m of the ADH enzyme, which is mainly responsible for the metabolism of ethanol after moderate drinking. Enzyme kinetic studies show that K_m for class I ADH is about 0.05 g/L so at twice the K_m of 0.1–0.2 g/L the enzymes approach saturation. The elimination half-life of the terminal phase of the BAC curve is about 15–20 min.

The first person to make a comprehensive experimental study of BAC profiles and determine the pharmacokinetic parameters of ethanol was Erik MP Widmark of Sweden in the 1930s[25] and his life and work have been reviewed in detail elsewhere.[169,170] Widmark experimented with human subjects and administered moderate doses of ethanol to establish C-T profiles. In the post-absorptive elimination phase the BAC decreased at a constant rate per unit time as defined by the following equation:

$$C_t = C_o - \beta t \qquad \text{(i)}$$

where C_t is the BAC at a time "t" on the post-absorptive part of the curve, C_o is the BAC extrapolated to the time of starting to drink, β is the symbol used to denote the slope of the post-absorptive phase of the C-T profile, and "t" is the time of sampling blood. The above equation can be rearranged to give:

$$C_0 = C_t + \beta t \qquad \text{(ii)}$$

The form of the equation is useful to estimate BAC at an earlier point in time, which is often referred to as making a back-calculation or retrograde extrapolation. In this

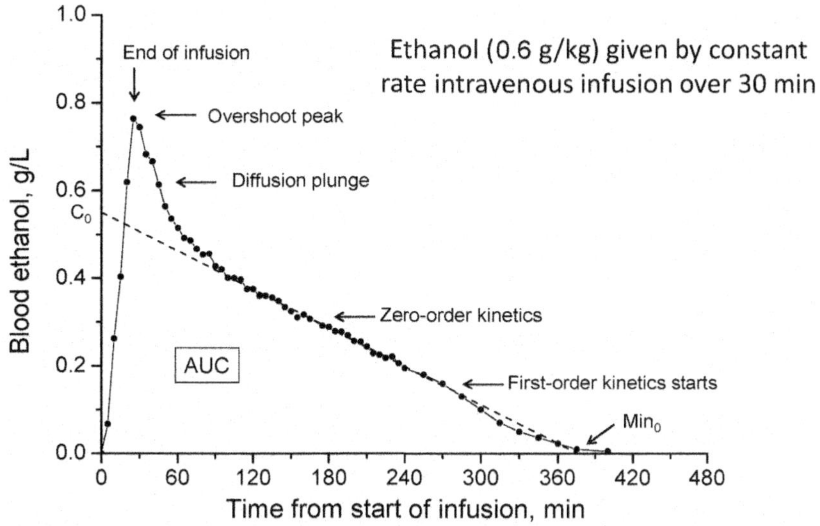

FIGURE 3.2.12 Concentration-time profile of ethanol in venous blood in one subject after an ethanol dose of 0.6 g/kg body weight was given as a constant rate intravenous infusion over 30 min. One notices an initial "overshoot" peak on ending the infusion followed by a diffusion plunge as ethanol equilibrated in all body fluids and tissues. About 60–90 min later a rectilinear elimination phase develops and this is maintained until BAC dropped to ~0.1–0.2 g/L, which marks the transition from zero-order to first-order kinetics

connection, it is important to know the elapsed time, e.g. from the time of an offense to the time of sampling blood and the elimination rate of ethanol from blood for that particular individual.

Hundreds of controlled alcohol dosing studies in men and women indicate that the rate of ethanol elimination from the blood in moderate drinkers falls within the range 10–0.25 g/L/h with a mean of 0.15 g/L/h. Higher rates were observed in drinking drivers (mean 0.19 g/L/h) and also in alcoholics undergoing detoxification (mean 0.22 g/L/h).

The faster burn-off rates observed in heavy drinkers are accounted for by the involvement of a microsomal enzyme oxidizing system denoted CYP2E1, which is inducible after periods of heavy binge drinking. The CYP2EI enzyme has a higher K_m (0.6–0.8 g/L) compared with hepatic ADH (0.02–0.05 g/L) and thus plays a more important role in ethanol metabolism when people drink larger amounts of ethanol and reach higher BAC, which is often the case in arrested drunken drivers.

In a controlled study with alcoholics undergoing detoxification, the mean β-slope was 0.22 g/L/h on average with a range from 0.13–0.36 g/L/h. Some patients suffered from liver disorders, such as alcoholic hepatitis and cirrhosis, although this did not seem to influence their ability to eliminate ethanol from the body as reflected in the β-slope. In another study, when alcoholics with higher than normal rates of ethanol elimination from blood were allowed to sober up for a few days and once again dosed with alcohol, their rates of elimination were now not far removed from values observed in moderate drinkers, namely 15 g/L/h. This shows that enzyme induction and more rapid elimination rates are transient phenomena.

The rate of elimination of alcohol from the blood was not much influenced by the time of day when 0.75 g/kg was administered at 9 am, 3 pm, 9 pm, and 3 am, according to an investigation of ethanol's chrono-pharmacokinetics. However, gastric emptying seems to occur faster in the morning as reflected in a 32% higher peak BAC and an earlier time of its occurrence when ethanol (1.1 g/kg body weight) was consumed between 7:15 and 7:45 am, compared with the same time in the evening. Smoking cigarettes slows gastric emptying and as a consequence delays the absorption of a moderate dose (0.50 g/kg) of ethanol resulting in a lower peak BAC in smokers.

By extrapolating the rectilinear elimination phase back to the time of starting to drink, one obtains the y-intercept (C_0), which corresponds to the theoretical BAC reached if the entire dose was absorbed and distributed instantaneously without any metabolism occurring (see Figure 3.2.11).

Dividing the administered dose by the person's body weight gives a ratio lower than the back-extrapolated BAC (C_0) because the water content of the blood (~78–82% w/w) is greater than the water content of the whole body (~50–60% w/w). The volume of distribution (V_d) is usually reported in units of liters/kg if the blood aliquots analyzed are measured by volume. However, in the early studies by Widmark he weighed the blood aliquots, so the dose (g/kg) divided by C_0 (g/kg) was a ratio without any dimensions. This should be considered when values of V_d found in earlier studies of the pharmacokinetics of ethanol are compared with more recent work. The density of whole blood is 1.055 g/mL, which leads to a 5.5% higher BAC expressed in mass/volume units and a correspondingly lower V_d compared with values determined by Widmark—0.68 (males) and 0.55 (females).

Values of the distribution factor "r" differ between individuals depending on their age, gender, and body composition, particularly the proportion of fat to lean body mass. Obviously, the value of "r" will also depend on whether whole blood or plasma was the specimen analyzed, because the ethanol content of plasma is about 15% higher than in whole blood. If repetitive samples of plasma or serum had been used to construct the ethanol concentration-time profile, the values of C_0 determined by back extrapolation would be higher and V_d would be lower.

According to Widmark's second equation, the relationship between alcohol in the body and alcohol in the blood at equilibrium can be represented by the following equations.

$$A/(p \times r) = C_0 \quad \text{(iii)}$$

$$A = C_0 \times (p \times r) \quad \text{(iv)}$$

A = amount of alcohol in grams absorbed and distributed in all body fluids.
p = the subject's body weight in kg.
r = Widmark's "r" factor.
C_0 = y-intercept.

These equations can be used to calculate the amount of ethanol absorbed and distributed in all body fluids and tissues from the concentration determined in a sample of blood. The value of "r" or distribution volume depends on the person's age, gender, and amount of adipose tissue per kg body weight.

After oral ingestion of ethanol, some part of the dose might not reach the systemic circulation owing to a first-pass metabolism in the gastric mucosa and the liver as the portal blood transports ethanol to the heart and lungs and on to the systemic circulation. However, 100% bioavailability of the drug administered can only be certain after the intravenous route of administration. If bioavailability is less than 100% this needs to be considered when the Widmark equation is used to estimate BAC expected from the dose ingested. The calculated BAC will be too high if some part of the dose is cleared by first-pass metabolism before absorption and distribution are completed.

Although the above equation has been much used in forensic alcohol calculations, it should not be applied to other drugs and narcotics and especially not in post-mortem toxicology, owing to problems with variation in drug concentrations in different sampling sites (see Chapter 3.2.3).

In the fasting state, the factor "r" will depend on age, gender, and body composition and Widmark reported mean values of 0.68 for 20 men (range 0.51–0.85) and 0.55 for 10 women (range 0.49–0.76). A recent evidence-based survey of ethanol distribution volumes reported average values of "r" or V_d of 0.70 L/kg for men and 0.60 L/kg for women with 95% confidence limits of about ± 15–20%.[171]

The two separate Widmark equations for β and "r" can be easily combined by eliminating C_0 to give the following equation:

$$A = pr(C_t + \beta t) \quad \text{(v)}$$

The above equation is useful to estimate the total amount of alcohol absorbed from the gastrointestinal tract since the beginning of drinking or by rearrangement, the blood alcohol concentration (C_t) expected after intake of a known amount of alcohol.

$$C_t = (A/pr) - \beta t \quad \text{(vi)}$$

When calculating BAC from the dose administered or vice versa, it is necessary to assume that systemic availability is 100% and that absorption and distribution of alcohol into total body water is complete at the time of sampling blood. Furthermore, individual variations in ß and "r" introduce uncertainty in the calculated dose (A) or BAC (C_t) when average values are applied to random subjects from the population. Various modifications or improvements have been suggested, such as by using estimates of total body water, lean body mass, or nomograms based on body mass index. The individual variation has been estimated at ± 20% for 95% confidence limits in tests involving more than 100 subjects who drank alcohol on an empty stomach. However, in the entire population of drunk drivers, these limits can be expected to be much wider.

3.2.8.3 Michaelis-Menten Kinetics

The bulk of the dose of ethanol ingested undergoes oxidative metabolism by enzymatic processes primarily in the liver. These involve the class I ADH enzymes, which have a low k_m (0.05–0.10 g/L) for ethanol as substrate and therefore saturated after 1–2 drinks (BAC > 0.20 g/L). During normal social drinking, the disappearance rate of ethanol from the bloodstream should follow zero-order kinetics (constant rate per unit time) for much of the time ethanol is in the body.

Figure 3.2.12 shows an example of a BAC profile when repetitive blood samples were taken from an indwelling catheter at short intervals of time for up to seven hours. The dose of ethanol (0.60 g/kg) was given intravenously over 40 min and the end of infusion is marked on the graph. This coincides with the peak BAC and is followed by a diffusion plunge until a linear declining BAC phase is reached after about 60 min. When BAC decreases below about 0.1–0.15 g/L (twice the K_m), the ADH enzymes are no longer saturated. This marks a gradual transition from zero- to first-order kinetics and a curvilinear disappearance phase develops. However, BACs below 0.20 g/L are not very relevant in forensic science and legal medicine so for all practical purposes it is safe to assume that the enzymatic metabolism of ethanol obeys zero-order kinetics.

The existence of capacity-limited kinetics for ethanol was first demonstrated by Lundquist and Wolthers,[172] because they had at their disposal a higher sensitive enzymatic (ADH) method for the determination of BAC. This allowed them to analyze blood samples with very low ethanol concentrations (< 0.1 g/L) below the transition from zero- to first-order kinetics. Hitherto, the chemical oxidation method of Widmark had an LOQ of about 0.05–0.10 g/L and concentrations below this could not be determined with certainty. The more sensitive enzymatic oxidation method showed that in the post-absorptive phase the BAC curve from high to low concentrations looked more like a hockey stick rather than a broom stick (straight line).[172]

The notion of Michaelis-Menten (M-M) or saturation kinetics of ethanol was also advocated by Wagner et al. and in a series of articles they derived the parameters V_{max} (g/L/h) and k_m (g/L) where V_{max} is the maximum velocity of the reaction at high substrate concentrations and K_m is the Michaelis constant, the BAC at half the maximum velocity, which is a measure of the affinity of the enzyme for its substrate.[173,174]

The M-M equation for enzymatic reactions is given below:

$$V = -dC/dt = (V_{max} \times C)/(K_m + C) \qquad \text{(vii)}$$

where V is the observed velocity of the reaction, V_{max} is the maximum velocity, K_m is the Michaelis constant for the particular enzyme, C is the substrate concentration, and t is time.

When $C >>> K_m$, the velocity of the reaction approaches V_{max} because:

$$V = -dC/dt = (V_{max} \times C)/C = V_{max}$$

Likewise, when $C <<< K_{max}$, the equation simplifies to the following:

$$V = -dC/dt = (V_{max} \times C)/K_m \text{ which further simplifies}$$

$$V = -dC/dt = k_1C \text{ where } k_1 \text{ is a first order rate constant}$$

The application of non-linear saturation kinetics of ethanol has been the subject of several review articles and V_{max} was determined to be 0.22 g/L/h and K_m close to 0.05 g/L. Although the application of M-M kinetics has found strong support among specialists in clinical pharmacokinetics, the simpler zero-order model first proposed by Widmark is still widely used in forensic science and legal medicine when BAC calculations are made.

The many variable factors and uncertainties underpinning ADME of ethanol, including the involvement of different isozymes, such as gastric and hepatic ADH and an inducible CYP2E1 enzyme, as well as racial and ethnic differences in enzyme activity, mitigate the continued use of the zero-order kinetic model. Explaining the scientific principles of non-linear PK modeling to a judge and jury is a daunting task compared with the concept of zero-order kinetics. The involvement of several different enzyme systems and polymorphisms is not strictly compatible with a single enzyme and substrate interaction, which is the basis of the M-M equation.

3.2.8.4 First-Pass Metabolism

The practical and clinical consequence of first-pass metabolism (FPM) is lowering the bioavailability of ethanol and a smaller fraction of the dose reaches the systemic circulation. After oral intake, FPM might occur in the gastrointestinal tract, the liver, and theoretically also as blood passes through the lungs. Drug metabolism enzymes are mainly located in the liver, but certain isozymes of ADH were also discovered in the gastric mucosa and shown to oxidize ethanol under in-vitro conditions, causing considerable interest in their role in-vivo and the notion of gastric FPM.

If ethanol was partly eliminated before reaching the systemic circulation, this would skew results of blood-alcohol calculations in forensic casework, such as when predicting or calculating the BAC expected for a given pattern of drinking. Inter-individual differences in gastric ADH activity and FPM might also be clinically relevant in relation to the impairment effects of a given dose of ethanol. The significance of gastric FPM tended to exhibit large intersubject variations and a lot depended on the efficacy of gastric emptying and the factors that influence this process. FPM was more pronounced after very low doses of ethanol (0.15–0.3 g/kg) when consumed about one hour after subjects had eaten a fat-rich breakfast. Drinking when there is food in the stomach is known to result in lower C_{max} for a given dose and the area under the curve is also diminished compared with drinking on an empty stomach. FPM was insignificant when moderate doses of ethanol were ingested on an empty stomach. Most of the ADH drug-metabolizing enzyme is located in the liver and not the gastric mucosa.

Distinguishing between pre-systemic oxidation of ethanol that occurred in the stomach as opposed to the liver was not very easy and much debate arose about its overall significance, e.g. gastric ADH compared with hepatic ADH. Some workers supported and others were opposed to the idea of a significant gastric FPM. The argument against rested on the fact that gastric ADH activity was only a small fraction of the total hepatic ADH activity and also the complex nature of M-M kinetics after small doses of ethanol were ingested after a meal. It was claimed that the advocates of gastric ADH and its role in FPM of ethanol had failed to consider the critical importance of gastric emptying and a more effective hepatic clearance of ethanol at low substrate concentrations. Factors that influence the rate of absorption of alcohol from (food, drugs, type of beverage, posture, time of day) also influence the ethanol concentration in the portal venous blood flowing to the liver and the degree of saturation of hepatic metabolizing enzymes.

Research on gastric FPM received a boost when several publications showed that taking certain medicinal drugs, such as aspirin and H_2-receptor antagonists (cimetidine and ranitidine), inhibited the enzyme activity. The corollary was that medicating with these substances and consuming alcohol resulted in higher than expected BAC, because gastric FPM was now considerably less likely, owing to drug action. Both C_{max} and AUC were higher in subjects taking these drugs than in placebo control groups. These drugs appeared to be effective in blocking the activity of gastric ADH under in-vitro conditions (e.g. in biopsies from the stomach), but the in-vivo effectiveness and practical importance were questioned.

Proponents of gastric ADH argued that it represented a protective barrier against some of the toxic effects of ethanol on organ and tissue damage. They showed that gastric ADH activity was lower in women and in alcoholics compared with moderate drinkers and also different in certain ethnic groups. If this barrier was weakened or removed by various over-the-counter drugs and medications, then these individuals were more likely to suffer clinical consequences of their indulgence in alcohol. Women also have less body water than men per kg body weight, which along with their lower gastric ADH activity makes them more vulnerable to the toxic effects of moderate drinking.

This conclusion proved too hasty because a flood of articles appeared challenging the notion of drug-induced effects on gastric FPM of ethanol. Indeed these newer studies incorporated an improved experimental design with many more volunteer subjects and a wider range of doses of ethanol consumed in the morning, midday, and evening both on an empty stomach and after a meal. These newer studies failed to verify the earlier reports and the significance of gastric ADH in FPM remains an interesting question, but not of any practical or forensic importance. Also, the effect of treatment with H_2-receptor antagonists (cimetidine and ranitidine) was recently reviewed and showed that effects were small and insignificant. But what did emerge was a new wave of interest in the clinical pharmacokinetics of ethanol and this demonstrated the existence of large inter- and intra-individual variations in the pharmacokinetic parameters, especially when small doses (< 0.3 g/kg) were ingested after a meal.

3.2.8.5 Inter-Individual Variations

Scores of controlled alcohol dosing studies demonstrate large inter-subject variations in peak BAC (C_{max}) and time of its occurrence (t_{max}) even when ethanol dose is adjusted for differences in the subject's body weight.[175] Much depends on individual variations in ADME of ethanol and a varying proportion of lean to fatty tissues on the person's body.

The magnitude of inter-individual variations in BAC curves is illustrated in Figure 3.2.13 using results from a controlled drinking study with 48 male subjects. Each consumed a dose of ethanol corresponding to 0.68 g/kg as neat whisky in 20 min after an overnight fast.[168]

Samples of fingertip blood samples were taken for analysis of ethanol at 30–60 min for up to 7 hours post-dosing. In these 48 volunteers, peak BAC occurred at exactly 10, 40, 70, and 100 min after the end of drinking for 23, 14, 8, and 3 of the subjects, respectively.[176] Absorptive and post-absorptive segments of the curves are indicated and times to reach C_{max} ranged from 10 to 100 min (ten-fold) despite all subjects drinking the whisky on an empty stomach. The peak BAC ranged from 0.50 to about 1.5 g/L (three-fold) even when ethanol consumed was adjusted for differences in body weight, which confirms work by other investigators.

A spike or overshoot peak in the BAC curve is clearly evident in many subjects, with C_{max} being higher than expected for the dose of ethanol consumed. The absorption is so rapid that there is insufficient time available to distribute the alcohol to tissue water compartments. Some subjects, however, showed a delayed absorption despite drinking on an empty stomach, which is probably explained by whisky causing irritation of the gastric surfaces and a pyloric spasm. A longer time to t_{max} is required because of the much smaller absorption surface area available in the stomach compared with the duodenum and jejunum, where rapid absorption is the norm.

Similar large inter-subject variations in BAC profiles have been observed for different doses of ethanol, different beverage types, and drinking by age-matched homogeneous groups of experimental subjects and standardized

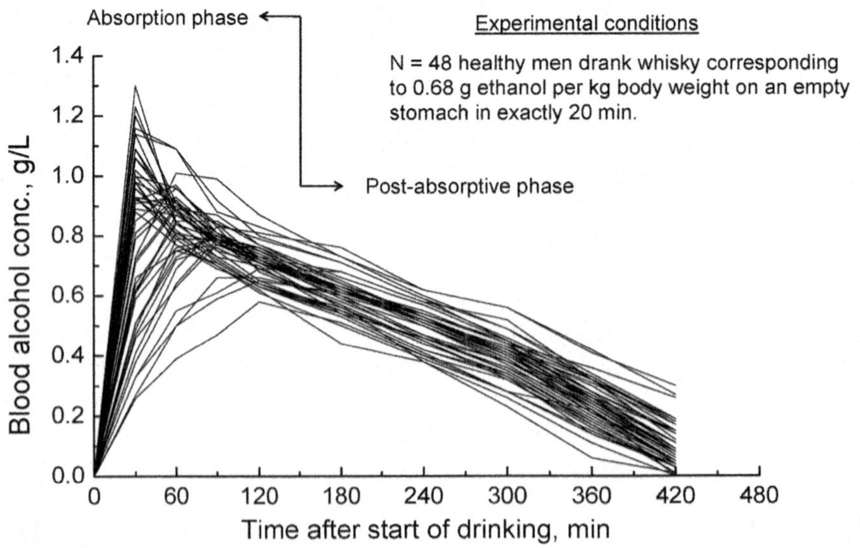

FIGURE 3.2.13 Inter-individual variations in blood-ethanol profile in 48 healthy men who ingested 0.68 g/kg ethanol as neat whisky in 20 min after an overnight fast. Between-subject variation was greatest during the first 30–120 min post-dosing, corresponding to the absorption phase of ethanol kinetics[168]

experimental conditions. The main reason and explanation for these differences is variation in gastric emptying and different distribution volumes for ethanol, resulting from different BMI and obesity. There is probably some contribution from inherent genetic differences in the activity of alcohol metabolizing enzymes, especially when different racial groups are compared in their ADME of ethanol.

3.2.8.6 Intra-Individual Variations

Compared with inter-subject variations in BAC profiles, relatively few studies have investigated variations in BAC curves within the same individual on different drinking occasions.[177] In short, little is known about the magnitude of within-subject variation in pharmacokinetic parameters of ethanol.[178] As might be expected, intra-individual variations are smaller than inter-individual variations. But as shown in Figure 3.2.14, BAC profiles on different drinking occasions are not in complete agreement. These traces are for four male subjects who drank the same dose of ethanol (0.80 g/kg body weight) on an empty stomach with roughly one week between drinking sessions.[179]

The ethanol was taken in the form of 95% v/v diluted with unsweetened orange juice to give a final concentration of 20% v/v and finished in 30 min. Repetitive samples of venous blood were taken from an indwelling catheter and ethanol concentrations were determined by gas chromatography. It seems reasonable to assume that body composition had not changed much over the time elapsed between the first and fourth drinking experiment in each subject. Accordingly, the within-subject variation in the rate of absorption and time of occurrence of the peak BAC probably reflects differences in gastric emptying on each occasion. Analysis of variance showed that there was no statistically significant difference in the rate of elimination of ethanol from blood between and within subjects.[179]

Two other studies investigated inter- and intra-subject variations in ethanol pharmacokinetics when breath-alcohol measurements were used to track the concentration-time profiles.[180,181] The variability in elimination rate and absorption rate of ethanol was investigated in 12 male volunteers on four occasions.[182] The subjects received 0.44 g/kg ethanol on the first study day, and 0.70 g/kg on subsequent study days 1, 11, and 12 weeks later. Evidence of both inter- and intra-subject variability in ethanol pharmacokinetics was observed with inter-subject variability being substantially smaller than intra-subject variability when the dose was varied.[182]

3.2.8.7 Effect of Eating a Meal on BAC Profiles

Experiments originating from the 1920s–1930s demonstrated that BAC was lowered when ethanol was ingested together with or after food compared with drinking the same on an empty stomach.[25,183] In the food arm of the study, both the C_{max} and AUC were appreciably lower and

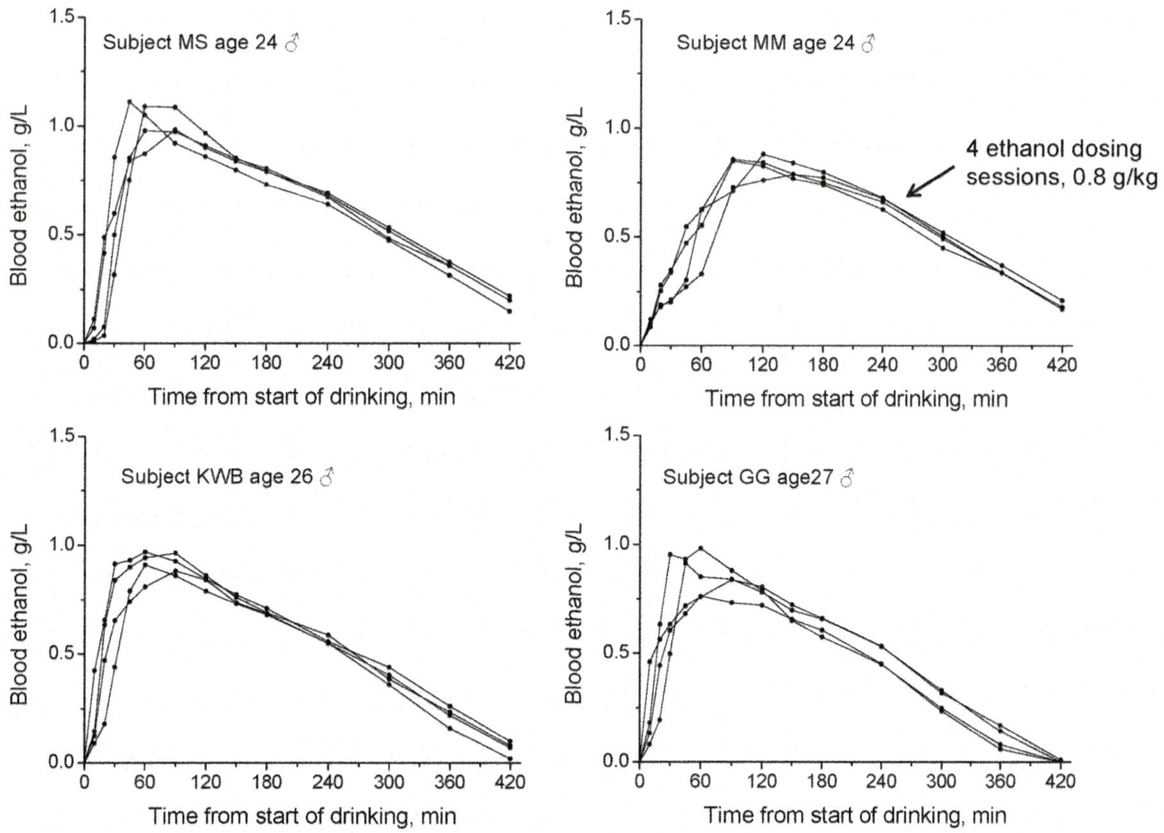

FIGURE 3.2.14 Examples of intra-individual variations in blood-alcohol curves in four healthy men who consumed doses of ethanol adjusted for body weight (0.80 g/kg) on an empty stomach on four separate occasions over a period of approximately one month[179]

gave the impression that less alcohol had been ingested in the fed-state. This was considered at the time as a "loss of alcohol" or also referred to as an "absorption deficit" and several different mechanisms were proposed to account for this finding.[184]

For example, it was speculated that ethanol might have become bound to dietary nutrients, such as amino acids, and never entered the bloodstream, but was excreted unchanged instead. Drinking alcohol with food in the stomach also delays gastric emptying and lengthens the time necessary to reach the maximum BAC, sometimes requiring up to two hours after the end of drinking. Furthermore, it has been observed in many studies that the BAC returns to zero sooner in the fed state, which implies a faster rate of metabolism in the food arm of cross-over design experiments.

Not surprisingly, the reduction in height of the peak BAC caused by food in the stomach was accompanied by a reduction in the degree of impairment produced by the same dose of ethanol as reflected in performance in cognitive and psychomotor tasks. Drinking alcohol with a meal is therefore a recommended practice to alleviate some of the detrimental effects of drinking on a person's performance and behavior. The overshoot peak, often observed when ethanol is consumed on an empty stomach, is no longer observed after postprandial ingestion. Food in the stomach appears to decrease the bioavailability of the dose of ethanol and a smaller fraction of the dose reaches the systemic circulation.[185] The magnitude of this food effect did not seem to depend on the composition of the meal in terms of its protein, fat, or carbohydrate content.

The lowered bioavailability of ethanol with food in the stomach before drinking impacts the distribution volume when this is calculated as the ratio of dose/C_0. A C_0 in the fed state means that the ratio dose/C_0 is higher than expected, sometimes reaching impossible non-physiological results (> 1.0 L/kg).[186] The food effect was recognized many years ago and was referred to as a "loss of ethanol" or an "absorption deficit." However, a more modern explanation for this food-induced lowering in the bioavailability of ethanol is an increased first-pass metabolism by gastric and/or hepatic ADH enzymes.

The impact of food and body composition on blood-alcohol concentration-time profiles for various drinking scenarios was reviewed by Kalant.[187] Ingestion of food immediately before or together with alcohol resulted in a lower C_{max} compared with drinking the same dose on an empty stomach. This lowering effect does not seem to be related to the composition of the meal in terms of macronutrients (protein, fat, or carbohydrate) but instead, the size of the meal is seemingly more important. The delayed gastric emptying causes a slower delivery of alcohol into the small intestine, the site of rapid absorption into the portal blood, and therefore a longer exposure to gastric mucosal ADH and greater possibility of gastric-first-pass metabolism of alcohol. Moreover, the role of FPM, whether gastric or hepatic, is highly variable and depends on the dose of alcohol administered. After drinking very small doses (< 0.3 g/kg), FPM appears to be more pronounced compared with normal social drinking when BACs in the forensic relevant range (0.50–0.80 g/L) are reached.

Inspection of the BAC curves shown in Figure 3.2.15 makes it strikingly obvious that when the ethanol was consumed after a meal, the peak BAC was lower and the entire curve seemed to run on a lower level compared with drinking the same dose on an empty stomach. Both C_{max} and AUC were considerably lower in the fed state, which indicates a much-reduced bioavailability of ethanol under these conditions.[188] Each subject drank 0.8 g ethanol per kg either on an empty stomach (10-h fast) or immediately after eating a standardized breakfast in a randomized cross-over design study.

Several other research groups have investigated the effect of food on the pharmacokinetics of ethanol and all agree that C_{max} is lowered and AUC is reduced in the food-arm of the experiment.[189,190] However, most studies have used oral administration of ethanol, which cannot separate the influence of food on absorption rate and gastric emptying from an influence on hepatic metabolism of ethanol.

The technique of "alcohol clamping" makes use of intravenous administration of ethanol to reach a steady-state concentration in blood and maintain this constant over several hours.[191] After eating a standardized meal, the rate of ethanol infusion had to be increased in order to maintain the same steady-state BAC.[192] This verifies a food-induced increase in rate of ethanol metabolism. The composition of the meal in terms of its fat, carbohydrate, or protein content was not so important for boosting rates of ethanol metabolism in this "alcohol-clamp" experiment.

Eating a meal when the test subjects were in the verified post-absorptive phase of the BAC curve was also effective in accelerating the rate of ethanol metabolism as indicated by comparing the zero-order decay rate before and after the meal.[188] This food-induced accelerating effect was verified even when ethanol was administered intravenously.[193] The mechanism of the food-induced acceleration of ethanol metabolism appears to depend on an enhanced activity of hepatic enzymes in a well-nourished organism.[194] Furthermore, eating a meal is known to increase liver bloodflow, which also facilitates a more rapid clearance of ethanol from the blood-stream, especially at low blood-ethanol concentrations.[195] This was demonstrated when subjects received a barium meal intravenously, which lacks calories but increases liver blood flow. Under these conditions, the rate of ethanol elimination from blood was increased by up to 27%.[196]

3.2.9 Concluding Remarks

Few if any toxic substances or drugs of abuse have been investigated as extensively and over so many years as ethanol. The gold-standard analytical method used for forensic purposes is HS-GC-FID, and this furnishes a linear response over a wide range of concentrations in blood (0.1–5.0 g/L). Some laboratories complement the HS-GC-FID

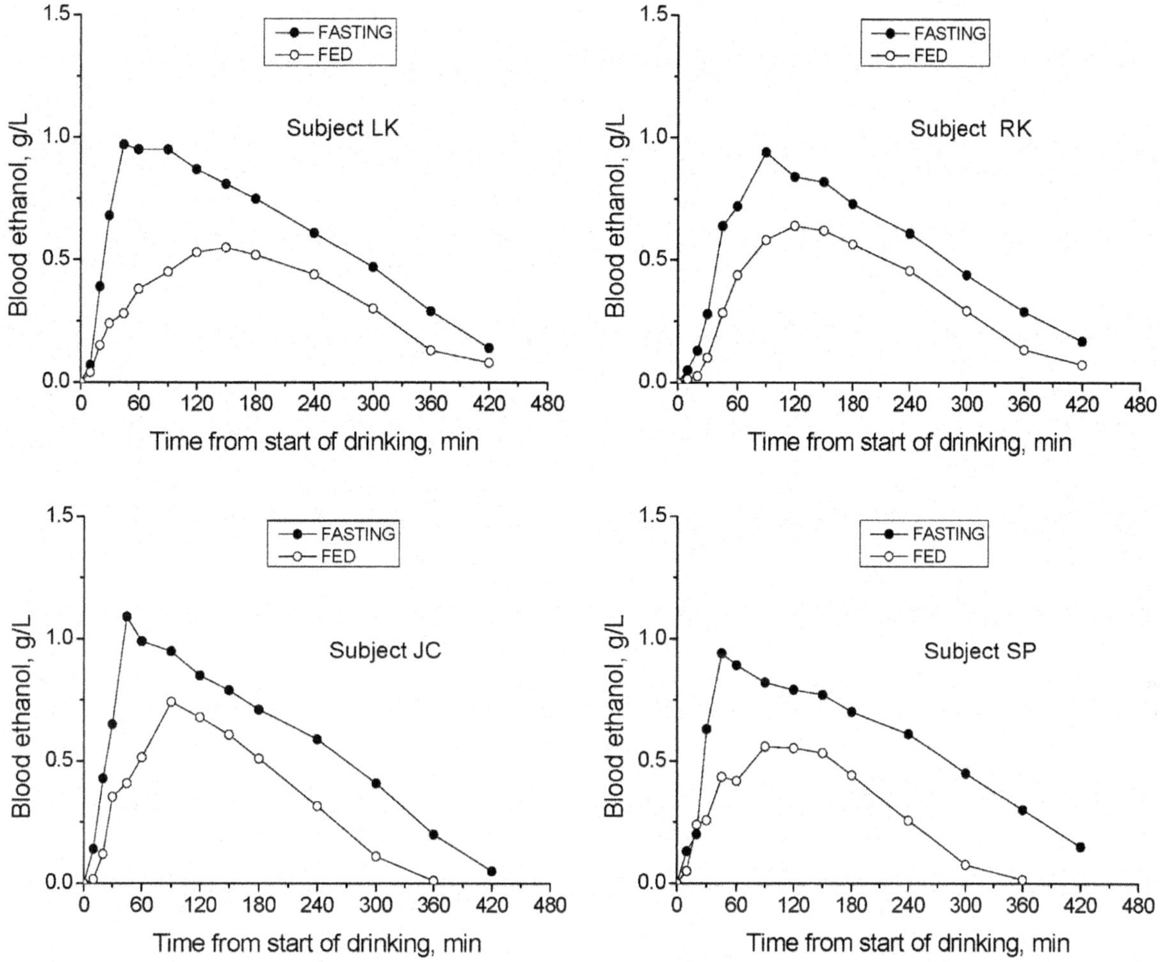

FIGURE 3.2.15 Blood-alcohol curves in four healthy men after consumption of 0.80 g/kg ethanol in 30 min on an empty stomach or after eating a standardized breakfast. This cross-over design study removes the influence of between-subject differences in BAC profiles[188]

method with a parallel determination done by mass spectrometry (MS), thus providing enhanced specificity.[197] After the separation of volatile substances by conventional GC methods, the effluent from the column is directed to both the FID and MS detector and this combination of technologies strengthens the analytical report, especially regarding positive identification of ethanol.[89]

Not all laboratories have followed this recommendation (use of both FID and MS detectors), because the BAC associated with intoxication is several thousand times higher than for other abused substances and psychoactive drugs encountered in toxicology casework. Hence the necessity to use a more specific MS detector for the identification of ethanol is not yet a standard operating procedure in most laboratories. However, the availability of small and compact GC-MS instruments might prompt more practitioners to include ethanol among the substances they determine by MS and its characteristic mass fragments (m/z 31, 46, and 45). A minimum requirement for forensic BAC determinations is making a duplicate determination by HS-GC-FID on two different GC stationary phases that yield different retention times for ethanol.[71]

One especially active area of forensic research on alcohol since the previous edition of *DAH* is the formation and analysis of non-oxidative metabolites of ethanol.[198] These include ethyl glucuronide (EtG), ethyl sulfate (EtS), and phosphatidylethanol (Peth), which are discussed in more detail in Chapter 3.4.[199] Although these metabolites represent only about 0.1–0.2% of the dose of ethanol ingested, they become excreted in urine and incorporated into hair strands and are of particular interest in forensic toxicology for several reasons.[200]

- First, the concentration of EtG in blood is about 1,000 times lower than the concentration of ethanol after a dose of 0.50 g/kg.[201]
- Second, EtG is eliminated more slowly from the body than ethanol so a positive urinary EtG test helps to disclose recent drinking even when ethanol is no longer measurable (below method LOQ, usually 0.05 or 0.10 g/L).[152]
- Third, unlike ethanol, EtG can be determined in hair strands and nails and serves as a useful biomarker that a person has relapsed to drinking when they are expected to remain sober, such as

those on probation or in detoxification and rehabilitation programs for alcohol use disorder.[202]

- Fourth, in post-mortem toxicology, the presence of EtG and EtS in body fluids verifies that ethanol has undergone metabolism in the liver and that alcoholic beverages were consumed during life. In short, EtG can differentiate the source of ethanol, whether antemortem ingestion or post-mortem synthesis.[203,204]

Forensic practitioners in the USA[205] and the UK[206] would like to see a consensus as to how various blood-alcohol calculations are done, such as Widmark calculations or back-extrapolation of BAC from time of sampling to an earlier time, such as the time of driving.[207] Several working groups are engaged in this discussion and hopefully they will reach acceptable guidelines for use in court cases when alcohol-related crimes are prosecuted.[208] However, this might be difficult under the adversarial system of justice that operates in the UK and USA, such as when expert witnesses for the defense and prosecution parties have differing opinions.

An evidence-based review found that the physiological range of ethanol elimination rates from blood in human subjects ranged from 0.10 to 0.35 g/L/h.[209] In the vast majority of moderate drinkers the range is narrower from 0.10–0.20 g/L/h (mean 0.15 g/L/h) compared with a range from 0.15–0.25 g/L/h (mean 0.20 g/L/h) in seasoned or binge drinkers, such as arrested drivers, with high BAC.[210] The elimination rate of ethanol from blood is slightly faster in females compared with males, but not so much that this should be considered important when making a back-calculation.[211] Conducting a drinking experiment with a person charged with DUI to determine his or her rate of ethanol elimination from blood is unnecessary.[178] Studies have shown that the rate of ethanol elimination varies as much between subjects as within the same subject from drinking occasion to drinking occasion.[177,179] Accordingly, working with an acceptable range of values, such as 0.10–0.20 g/L/h in actual casework is perfectly adequate for most purposes.

Gender differences in the distribution volume of ethanol are important to consider when various blood-alcohol calculations are made. Average values of 0.70 L/kg (coefficient of variation CV of 10–12%) for healthy non-obese males and 0.60 L/kg (CV 10–15%) for females are recommended values.[171] The small gender difference was statistically highly significant and depends on body composition, because women have more fat than lean tissue and thus a lower TBW per kg body weight to dilute ingested ethanol. An alternative approach is to calculate a person's TBW based on anthropometric measures, such as age, height, and body weight or BMI (kg/m^2).[212] The combination of a smaller distribution volume in females and a slightly faster rate of elimination of ethanol from blood means that the turnover rate of ethanol from the whole body is independent of gender. In this connection, a good rule of thumb is that a moderate drinker eliminates 0.10 g/kg/h on average. This equates to 6 g/h for a person weighing 60 kg or 9 g/h for a person weighing 90 kg.

Drinking a large quantity of ethanol immediately before leaving a bar or restaurant and then driving home is not a very likely scenario, but it could happen. In reality, most ethanol consumed is probably already absorbed into the blood by the time a person decides to drive home after an evening out.[164] The impact of a one-for-the-road drink was investigated in a laboratory drinking study and much depended on the amount of ethanol in the last drink.[213] Making back extrapolations of BAC should be avoided as far as possible in criminal cases, because of the many variable factors involved. When such a calculation cannot be avoided, instead of reporting the exact BAC at the time of driving, it is probably a lot better to make a statement as to whether the back-calculated BAC was above or below some threshold, such as 0.80 g/L (0.08 g%, 80 mg%) or whatever statutory alcohol limit for driving is enforced.

Another safeguard in connection with back-calculating BAC is to make an allowance for the amount of ethanol contained in the last drink before driving. The Widmark equation is suitable for this purpose assuming an average and range of distribution volumes of ethanol. Use of a relatively low rate of ethanol elimination from blood gives an additional advantage to the suspect in a back-calculation exercise. In this way, the benefit of any doubt is given to the accused, which is the norm in criminal cases. However, information about the amount of ethanol in the last drink is mostly obtained through police interviews and witness statements and is therefore unverifiable. Whatever method of calculation is adopted and used in legal depositions, signed affidavits, or testifying in court as an expert witness, all necessary assumptions and approximations need to be explained to the trier of fact.

The possibility of an adverse drug-alcohol interaction is likely if people take various over-the-counter medications and also consume alcohol deserves consideration.[214] The absorption kinetics of ethanol are highly variable and drug-induced effects on gastric emptying impacts on both peak BAC and the time of its occurrence.[215] Drinking together with or after a meal results in lower BAC compared with the same dose ingested on an empty stomach.[188] The main influence of co-ingested drugs is on the speed of absorption of ethanol and not its rate of metabolism.[185] Regardless of treatment with drugs, BAC curves exhibit large intra-individual variations as already discussed in this chapter. Cross-over design experiments are important in clinical pharmacokinetic studies when the effect of a drug is compared with placebo or no-drug treatment. Furthermore, at low BAC, small increases in C_{max} between the two treatments, such as 0.05 g/L, correspond to a percentage difference of 33% when the mean BAC after drug treatment was fairly low, such as 0.15 g/L.

Blood-ethanol concentrations encountered in most forensic cases span from 0.10–5.0 g/L, so zero-order kinetics is the appropriate PK model to use in blood-alcohol calculations.[210,216] When the BAC drops below 0.20 g/L a transition occurs from zero-order to first-order kinetics.[173] Although the operation of saturation kinetics of ethanol has theoretical interest to biochemists and alcohol researchers, it has little practical relevance in forensic cases. In many forensic laboratories, the method LOQ for blood-ethanol analysis is 0.10 g/L so concentrations below this are reported as negative or "not detected." The reasons for large biological variations in BAC profiles depend primarily on subject demographics, such as their age, gender, ethnicity, and BMI as well factors influencing gastric emptying rates, such as food in the stomach.[217,218]Age and gender differences in the pharmacokinetics of ethanol are largely accounted for by decreases in TBW during aging and the higher proportion of fat to lean body mass in the elderly.

The notion of a significant gastric first-pass metabolism of ethanol caused by taking certain medications, such as drugs to treat hyperacidity in the stomach (cimetidine and ranitidine), appears to have been much exaggerated.[219,220] Neither were there any gender or diurnal variations in FPM observed when controlled studies were performed with moderate doses of ethanol and a sufficient number of volunteer subjects.[154,221] For drugs like ethanol having Michaelis-Menten kinetics, both C_{max} and AUC do not increase in direct proportion to the dose of ethanol ingested.[165,222] FPM of ethanol was negligible when subjects consumed ethanol on an empty stomach in amounts normally associated with social drinking, corresponding to 0.35–0.75 g/kg body weight.[223]

The quantity of ethanol ingested is an important consideration because the hepatic enzymes are saturated when BAC exceeds 0.20 g/L.[224] Having food in the stomach before drinking is also an important variable and peak BAC might be lowered by 40–50% if ethanol was consumed immediately after eating a meal, such as a standardized breakfast.[188] The composition of the meal, whether high-fat, high-protein, or high-carbohydrate was less important in this respect;[225] the main variable was the dose ingested and the timing of the meal in relation to drinking alcohol.[192] When ethanol is ingested after an overnight (10 h) fast the bioavailability of the dose is close to 100% as verified by using ethanol dilution to determine TBW; the results were in good agreement with isotope dilution methods.[226,227]

This overview of the clinical and forensic toxicology of ethanol has hopefully convinced people that the BAC curves and ethanol pharmacokinetic parameters are highly variable even when the dose ingested is adjusted for the person's body weight. This deserves consideration when various alcohol calculations are required for law enforcement purposes, such as in drunk-driving cases when statutory BAC limits are enforced. Although most research on the ADME of ethanol has been done using analysis of blood samples, most jurisdictions today use instruments for breath-alcohol analysis as evidence for the prosecution of traffic offenders. This motivates doing more studies of ethanol's ADME based on repetitive determinations of ethanol in breath samples to establish the corresponding pharmacokinetic parameters.[180,181]

The concentration of ethanol in human breath can be determined just as accurately and precisely as the concentration of ethanol in blood.[228] The main advantage of breath over blood analysis is obtaining immediate results and the fact that BrAC runs closer to the concentrations of ethanol in arterial blood. Breath-alcohol testing furnishes a non-invasive way to monitor exposure of the central nervous system to ethanol's toxic effects, which is a big advantage compared with venous BAC, which reflects the concentration deoxygenated blood.[125] For forensic purposes, the analytical methods of choice for BAC determination are HS-GC-FID or HS-GC-MS or both technologies, and BrAC is determined by infrared spectrometry or electrochemical oxidation.[88]

REFERENCES

1. Goldstein A. *Addiction from Biology to Drug Policy.* New York: W.H. Freeman & Co, 1994.
2. Lobo IA, Harris RA. GABA(A) receptors and alcohol. *Pharmacol Biochem Behav* 2008;90:90–4.
3. Dry MJ, Burns NR, Nettelbeck T, Farquharson AL, White JM. Dose-related effects of alcohol on cognitive functioning. *PLoS One* 2012;7:e50977.
4. Dubowski KM. The Dubowski alcohol table. *IACT Newsletter* 2012;23:7–8.
5. Carvalho AF, Heilig M, Perez A, Probst C, Rehm J. Alcohol use disorders. *Lancet* 2019;394:781–92.
6. Anstie FE. Final experiments on the elimination of alcohol from the body. *The Practitioner* 1874;13:15–28.
7. Jones AW. Measuring alcohol in blood and breath for forensic purposes - A historical review. *Forensic Sci Rev* 1996;8:13–44.
8. Widmark EMP. Om alkoholens öfvergång i urinen samt om en enkel, kliniskt användbar metod för diagnosticering af alkoholförekomst i kroppen. *Upsala Läkareförenings Förhandlingar N F* 1914;19:241–72.
9. Brick J, Erickson CK. Intoxication is not always visible: an unrecognized prevention challenge. *Alcohol Clin Exp Res* 2009;33:1489–507.
10. Jones AW, Morland JG, Liu RH. Driving under the influence of psychoactive substances - A historical review. *Forensic Sci Rev* 2019;31:103–40.
11. Fell JC. Another major reason to lower the blood alcohol concentration limit for driving. *Am J Public Health* 2019;109:670–1.
12. Fell JC. Approaches for reducing alcohol-impaired driving: evidence-based legislation, law enforcement strategies, sanctions, and alcohol-control policies. *Forensic Sci Rev* 2019;31:161–84.
13. Blomberg RD, Peck RC, Moskowitz H, Burns M, Fiorentino D. The long beach/fort lauderdale relative risk study. *J Safety Res* 2009;40:285–92.
14. Dubowski KM, Caplan YH, Canfield DV. Alcohol testing in the workplace. In: Garriott JC, editor. *Medicolegal Aspects of Alcohol.* 5th ed. Tuscon: Lawyers & Judges Publishing Company, 2008, 437–57.
15. Afshar M, Netzer G, Salisbury-Afshar E, Murthi S, Smith GS. Injured patients with very high blood alcohol concentrations. *Injury* 2016;47:83–8.
16. Quaghebeur G, Richards P. Comatose patients smelling of alcohol. *BMJ* 1989;299:410.
17. Rainey PM. Relation between serum and whole-blood ethanol concentrations. *Clin Chem* 1993;39:2288–92.
18. Holland MG, Ferner RE. A systematic review of the evidence for acute tolerance to alcohol - the "Mellanby effect." *Clin Toxicol (Phila)* 2017;55:545–56.

19. Kalant H, LeBlanc AE, Gibbins RJ. Tolerance to, and dependence on, some non-opiate psychotropic drugs. *Pharmacol Rev* 1971;23:135–91.
20. Eriksson CJ. The role of acetaldehyde in the actions of alcohol (update 2000). *Alcohol Clin Exp Res* 2001;25 Supplement ISBRA:15S–32S.
21. Zakhari S. Overview: how is alcohol metabolized by the body? *Alcohol Res Health* 2006;29:245–54.
22. Friedemann TE, Dubowski KM. Chemical testing procedures for the determination of ethyl alcohol. *J Am Med Assoc* 1959;170:47–71.
23. Bogen E. Drunkenness - a quantittaive study of acute alcoholic intoxication. *J Am Med Assoc* 1927;89:1508–11.
24. Widmark EMP. Eine Mikromethode zur Bestimmung von Äthylalkohol im Blut. *Biochem Z* 1922;131:473–84.
25. Widmark EMP. *Die Theoretischen Grundlagen und die Praktische Verwendbarkeit der Gerichtlich-Medizinischen Alkoholbestimmung.* Berlin: Urban & Schwarzenberg, 1932.
26. Tagliaro F, Lubli G, Ghielmi S, Franchi D, Marigo M. Chromatographic methods for blood alcohol determination. *J Chromatogr* 1992;580:161–90.
27. Barnhill MT, Jr, Herbert D, Wells DJ, Jr. Comparison of hospital laboratory serum alcohol levels obtained by an enzymatic method with whole blood levels forensically determined by gas chromatography. *J Anal Toxicol* 2007;31:23–30.
28. Flanagan RJ. SI units--common sense not dogma is needed. *Br J Clin Pharmacol* 1995;39:589–94; discussion 95.
29. Flanagan RJ. Guidelines for the interpretation of analytical toxicology results and unit of measurement conversion factors. *Ann Clin Biochem* 1998;35(Pt 2):261–7.
30. Lentner C. *Geigy Scientific Tables - Units of Measurement, Body Fluids, Composition of the Body, Nutrition.* Basel: CIBA-GEIGY, 1981.
31. de Jong GM, Huizenga JR, Gips CH. Evaluation of gravimetric assays of the H2O concentration in human serum and urine. *Clin Chim Acta* 1987;163:153–64.
32. Sahin S, Karabey Y, Kaynak MS, Hincal AA. Potential use of freeze-drying technique for estimation of tissue water content. *Methods Find Exp Clin Pharmacol* 2006;28:211–5.
33. Lijnema TH, Huizenga JR, Jager J, Mackor AJ, Gips CH. Gravimetric determination of the water concentration in whole blood, plasma and erythrocytes and correlations with hematological and clinicochemical parameters. *Clin Chim Acta* 1993;214:129–38.
34. Tiscione N. The impact of hemolysis on the accuracy of ethanol determinations. *J Anal Toxicol* 2015;39:672–3.
35. Iffland R, West A, Bilzer N, Schuff A. Zur Zuverlässigkeit der Blutalkoholbestimmung. Das verkeilungsverhältnis des Wassers zwischen Serum und Vollblut. *Rechtsmedizin* 1999;9:123–30.
36. Winek CL, Carfagna M. Comparison of plasma, serum, and whole blood ethanol concentrations. *J Anal Toxicol* 1987;11:267–8.
37. Beijering RJ, Gips CH, Huizenga JR, Jager J, Mackor AJ, Salomons H, et al. Whole blood and plasma water in health and disease: longitudinal and transverse observations and correlations with several different hematological and clinicochemical parameters. *Clin Chim Acta* 1997;258:59–68.
38. Hak EA, Gerlitz BJ, Demont PM, Bowthorpe WD. Determination of serum alcohol:blood alcohol ratios. *Can Soc Forensic Sci J* 1995;28:123–6.
39. Hodgson BT, Shajani NK. Distribution of ethnaol: plasma to whole blood ratios. *Can Soc Forensic Sci J* 1985;18:73–7.
40. Payne JP, Hill DW, Wood DG. Distribution of ethanol between plasma and erythrocytes in whole blood. *Nature* 1968;217:963–4.
41. Jones AW, Hahn RG, Stalberg HP. Distribution of ethanol and water between plasma and whole blood; inter- and intra-individual variations after administration of ethanol by intravenous infusion. *Scand J Clin Lab Invest* 1990;50:775–80.
42. Atwater WO, Benedict FG. An experimental inquiry regarding the nutritive value of alcohol *Mem Natl Acad Sci* 1902;8:235–397.
43. Rabinowitch IM. A simple test for acetone in Urine. *Can Med Assoc J* 1945;52:602–5.
44. Smith HW. Methods for determining alcohol. In: Curry AS, editor. *Methods of Forensic Science.* New York: Interscience, 1965.
45. Bonnichsen RK, Theorell H. An enzymatic method for the microdetermination of ethanol. *Scand J Clin Lab Invest* 1951;3:58–62.
46. Bonnichsen RK, Wassen AM. Crystalline alcohol dehydrogenase from horse liver. *Arch Biochem* 1948;18:361–3.
47. Brink NC, Bonnichsen R, Theorell H. A modified method for the enzymatic microdetermination of ethanol. *Scand J Clin Lab Invest* 1954;10:223–36.
48. Bücher T, Redetzki H. Eine spezifische photometrische Bestimmung von Äthylalkohol auf fermentivem. *Klin Wochenschr* 1951;29:615–6.
49. Buijten JC. An automated ultramicro distillation technique for determination of ethanol in blood and urine. *Blutalkohol* 1975;14:405–16.
50. Kristoffersen L, Smith-Kielland A. An automated alcohol dehydrogenase method for ethanol quantification in urine and whole blood. *J Anal Toxicol* 2005;29:387–9.
51. Williams RH, Laikin JB. Assessment of ethanol intoxication and regulatory issues. *Lab Med* 1999;30:587–94.
52. Hadjiioannou TP, Hadjiioannou SI, Avery J, Malmstadt HV. Automated enzymic determination of ethanol in blood, serum, and urine with a miniature centrifugal analyzer. *Clin Chem* 1976;22:802–5.
53. Whitehouse LW, Paul CJ. Micro-scale enzymic determination of ethanol in plasma with a discrete analyzer, the ABA-100. *Clin Chem* 1979;25:1399–401.
54. Winek CL, Wahba WW, Windisch RM, Winek CL, Jr. Serum alcohol concentrations in trauma patients determined by immunoassay versus gas chromatography. *Forensic Sci Int* 2004;139:1–3.
55. Jortani SA, Poklis A. Emit ETS plus ethyl alcohol assay for the determination of ethanol in human serum and urine. *J Anal Toxicol* 1992;16:368–71.
56. Cary PL, Whitter PD, Johnson CA. Abbott radiative energy attenuation method for quantifying ethanol evaluated and compared with gas-liquid chromatography and the Du Pont ACA. *Clin Chem* 1984;30:1867–70.
57. Caplan YH, Levine B. The analysis of ethanol in serum, blood, and urine: a comparison of the TDx REA ethanol assay with gas chromatography. *J Anal Toxicol* 1986;10:49–52.
58. Caplan YH, Levine B. Evaluation of the Abbott TDx-radiative energy attenuation (REA) ethanol assay in a study of 1105 forensic whole blood specimens. *J Forensic Sci* 1987;32:55–61.
59. Bland JM, Altman DG. Statistical methods for assessing agreement between two methods of clinical measurement. *Lancet* 1986;1:307–10.
60. Bland JM, Altman DG. Measuring agreement in method comparison studies. *Stat Methods Med Res* 1999;8:135–60.

61. Ludbrook J. Confidence in Altman-Bland plots: a critical review of the method of differences. *Clin Exp Pharmacol Physiol* 2010;37:143–9.
62. Badcock NR, O'Reilly DA. False-positive EMIT-st ethanol screen with post-mortem infant plasma. *Clin Chem* 1992;38:434.
63. Nine JS, Moraca M, Virji MA, Rao KN. Serum-ethanol determination: comparison of lactate and lactate dehydrogenase interference in three enzymatic assays. *J Anal Toxicol* 1995;19:192–6.
64. Nacca N, Hodgman MJ, Lao K, Elkins M, Holland MG. Can elevated lactate and LDH produce a false positive enzymatic ethanol result in live patients presenting to the emergency department? *Clin Toxicol (Phila)* 2018;56:189–92.
65. Bishop-Freeman SC, Bertholf RL, Powers RH, Mayhew LC, Winecker RE. False-positive enzymatic alcohol results in perimortem specimens. *Lab Med* 2020;51:394–401.
66. Winek CL, Wahba WW. A response to "Serum-ethanol determination: comparison of lactate and lactate dehydrogenase interference in three enzymatic assays." *J Anal Toxicol* 1996;20:211–2.
67. Powers RH, Dean DE. Evaluation of potential lactate/lactate dehydrogenase interference with an enzymatic alcohol analysis. *J Anal Toxicol* 2009;33:561–3.
68. Cravey RH, Jain NC. Current status of blood alcohol methods. *J Chromatogr Sci* 1974;12:209–13.
69. Jain NC, Cravey RH. Analysis of alcohol. II. A review of gas chromatographic methods. *J Chromatogr Sci* 1972;10:263–7.
70. Curry AS, Walker GW, Simpson GS. Determination of ethanol in blood by gas chromatography. *Analyst* 1966;91:742–4.
71. Jones AW. Blood alcohol analysis by gas chromatography; Fifty years of progress. In: Verstraete A, editor. *TIAFT Our First 50 Years*. Gent: Academia Press, 2013, 145–67.
72. Dubowski KM. *Manual for Analysis of Ethanol in Biological Liquids*. Washington, DC: National Highway Traffic Safety Administration, Government Printing Office, 1977.
73. Ettre LS. The beginnings of headspace analysis. *LC-GC* 2002;20:1120–9.
74. Hachenberg H, Schmidt AP. *Gas Chromatographic Headspace Analysis*. London: Heyden & Sons, 1977.
75. Machata G. Über die gaschromatographische Blutalkoholbestimmung, Analyse der Dampfphase *Mikrochim Acta* 1964;52:262–71.
76. Machata G. The advantages of automated blood alcohol determination by head space analysis. *Z Rechtsmed* 1975;75:229–34.
77. Wang Y, McCaffrey J, Norwood DL. Recent advances in headspace gas chromatography. *J Liq Chrom & Relat Technol* 2008;31:1823–51.
78. Watts MT, McDonald OL. The effect of biologic specimen type on the gas chromatographic headspace analysis of ethanol and other volatile compounds. *Am J Clin Pathol* 1987;87:79–85.
79. O'Neal CL, Wolf CE, Levine B, Kunsman G, Poklis A. Gas chromatographic procedures for determination of ethanol in postmortem blood using t-butanol and methyl ethyl ketone as internal standards. *Forensic Sci Int* 1996;83:31–8.
80. Watts MT, McDonald OL. The effect of sodium chloride concentration, water content, and protein on the gas chromatographic headspace analysis of ethanol in plasma. *Am J Clin Pathol* 1990;93:357–62.
81. De Martinis BS, Martin CC. Automated headspace solid-phase microextraction and capillary gas chromatography analysis of ethanol in postmortem specimens. *Forensic Sci Int* 2002;128:115–9.
82. Zuba D, Parczewski A, Reichenbacher M. Optimization of solid-phase microextraction conditions for gas chromatographic determination of ethanol and other volatile compounds in blood. *J Chromatogr B Analyt Technol Biomed Life Sci* 2002;773:75–82.
83. Bonte W. *Begleitstoffe Alkoholischer Getränke Arbeitsmethoden der Medizinischen und Naturwissens chaftlichen Kriminalistik*. Lübeck: Schmidt-Römhild, 1989.
84. Barz J, Bonte W, Keultjes C, Sieland J. Concentrations of ethanol, methanol, propanol-2 and acetone in blood samples of impaired drivers. *Acta Med Leg Soc (Liege)* 1990;40:49–60.
85. Seto Y. Determination of volatile substances in biological samples by headspace gas chromatography. *J Chromatog A* 1994;674:25–62.
86. Boumba VA, Ziavrou KS, Vougiouklakis T. Biochemical pathways generating post-mortem volatile compounds co-detected during forensic ethanol analyses. *Forensic Sci Int* 2008;174:133–51.
87. Aderjan R, Daldrup T, Käferstein H, Krause D, Mußhoff F, Paul LD, et al. Richtlinien zur Bestimmung der Blutalkoholkonzentration (BAK) für forensische Zwecke. *Blutalkohol* 2011;48:137–43.
88. Tiscione NB, Alford I, Yeatman DT, Shan X. Ethanol analysis by headspace gas chromatography with simultaneous flame-ionization and mass spectrometry detection. *J Anal Toxicol* 2011;35:501–11.
89. Tiscione NB, Yeatman DT, Shan X, Kahl JH. Identification of volatiles by headspace gas chromatography with simultaneous flame ionization and mass spectrometric detection. *J Anal Toxicol* 2013;37:573–9.
90. Xiao HT, He L, Tong RS, Yu JY, Chen L, Zou J, et al. Rapid and sensitive headspace gas chromatography-mass spectrometry method for the analysis of ethanol in the whole blood. *J Clin Lab Anal* 2014;28:386–90.
91. Dean RA, Thomasson HR, Dumaual N, Amann D, Li TK. Simultaneous measurement of ethanol and ethyl-d5 alcohol by stable isotope gas chromatography-mass spectrometry. *Clin Chem* 1996;42:367–72.
92. Takayasu T, Ohshima T, Tanaka N, Maeda H, Kondo T, Nishigami J, et al. Postmortem degradation of administered ethanol-d6 and production of endogenous ethanol: experimental studies using rats and rabbits. *Forensic Sci Int* 1995;76:129–40.
93. Schellekens RC, Stellaard F, Woerdenbag HJ, Frijlink HW, Kosterink JG. Applications of stable isotopes in clinical pharmacology. *Br J Clin Pharmacol* 2011;72:879–97.
94. Jones AW. A rapid method for blood alcohol determination by headspace analysis using an electrochemical detector. *J Forensic Sci* 1978;23:283–91.
95. Dubowski KM. Method for alcohol determination in biological liquids by sensing with a solid-state detector. *Clin Chem* 1976;22:863–7.
96. Kristoffersen L, Skuterud B, Larssen BR, Skurtveit S, Smith-Kielland A. Fast quantification of ethanol in whole blood specimens by the enzymatic alcohol dehydrogenase method. Optimization by experimental design. *J Anal Toxicol* 2005;29:66–70.
97. Pickett WJ, 3rd, Hirschowitz BI, Loeb JN, Robinson AG. Measurement of plasma osmolality. *N Engl J Med* 1971;285:354–5.

98. Rasouli M, Kalantari KR. Comparison of methods for calculating serum osmolality: multivariate linear regression analysis. *Clin Chem Lab Med* 2005;43:635–40.
99. Robinson AG, Loeb JN. Ethanol ingestion--commonest cause of elevated plasma osmolality? *N Engl J Med* 1971;284:1253–5.
100. Lynd LD, Richardson KJ, Purssell RA, Abu-Laban RB, Brubacher JR, Lepik KJ, et al. An evaluation of the osmole gap as a screening test for toxic alcohol poisoning. *BMC Emerg Med* 2008;8:5.
101. Greene HR, Krasowski MD. Correlation of osmolal gap with measured concentrations of acetone, ethylene glycol, isopropanol, methanol, and propylene glycol in patients at an academic medical center. *Toxicol Rep* 2019;7:81–8.
102. Krahn J, Khajuria A. Is osmol gap an effective screen in accurate prediction of toxic volatiles? *Clin Lab* 2011;57:297–303.
103. Ridder TD, Hendee SP, Brown CD. Noninvasive alcohol testing using diffuse reflectance near-infrared spectroscopy. *Appl Spectrosc* 2005;59:181–9.
104. Ridder TD, Hull EL, Ver Steeg BJ, Laaksonen BD. Comparison of spectroscopically measured finger and forearm tissue ethanol concentration to blood and breath ethanol measurements. *J Biomed Opt* 2011;16:028003.
105. Ridder TD, Ver Steeg BJ, Laaksonen BD. Comparison of spectroscopically measured tissue alcohol concentration to blood and breath alcohol measurements. *J Biomed Opt* 2009;14:054039.
106. Pan S, Chung H, Arnold MA, Small GW. Near-infrared spectroscopic measurement of physiological glucose levels in variable matrices of protein and triglycerides. *Anal Chem* 1996;68:1124–35.
107. Jones AW. Breath analysis in law enforcement. In: Beauchamp J, Davis C, Pleil J, editors. *Breathborne Biomarkers and the Human Volatilome*. Amsterdam: Elsevier, 2020, 475–92.
108. Jones AW. Physiological aspects of breath-alcohol measurement. *Alc Drugs Driving* 1990;6:1–25.
109. Lourenco C, Turner C. Breath analysis in disease diagnosis: methodological considerations and applications. *Metabolites* 2014;4:465–98.
110. Pereira J, Porto-Figueira P, Cavaco C, Taunk K, Rapole S, Dhakne R, et al. Breath analysis as a potential and non-invasive frontier in disease diagnosis: an overview. *Metabolites* 2015;5:3–55.
111. Wigmore JG, Langille RM. Six generations of breath alcohol testing instruments: changes in the detection of breath alcohol since 1930. An historical overview. *Can Soc Forensic Sci J* 2009;42:276–83
112. Zuba D. Accuracy and reliability of breath alcohol testing by handheld electrochemical analysers. *Forensic Sci Int* 2008;178:e29–33.
113. Kriikku P, Wilhelm L, Jenckel S, Rintatalo J, Hurme J, Kramer J, et al. Comparison of breath-alcohol screening test results with venous blood alcohol concentration in suspected drunken drivers. *Forensic Sci Int* 2014;239C:57–61.
114. Kaisdotter Andersson A, Kron J, Castren M, Muntlin Athlin A, Hok B, Wiklund L. Assessment of the breath alcohol concentration in emergency care patients with different level of consciousness. *Scand J Trauma Resusc Emerg Med* 2015;23:11.
115. Poon R, Hodgson BT, Hindberg I, Rowatt C. Evaluation of three pocket-size breath alcohol analyzers. *Can Forensic Sci Soc J* 1987;20:19–27.
116. Falkensson M, Jones AW, Sorbo B. Bedside diagnosis of alcohol intoxication with a pocket-size breath-alcohol device: sampling from unconscious subjects and specificity for ethanol. *Clin Chem* 1989;35:918–21.
117. Jones AW, Rossner S. False-positive breath-alcohol test after a ketogenic diet. *Int J Obes (Lond)* 2007;31:559–61.
118. Ruzsanyi V, Peter Kalapos M. Breath acetone as a potential marker in clinical practice. *J Breath Res* 2017;11:024002.
119. Hartung B, Schwender H, Pawlik E, Ritz-Timme S, Mindiashvili N, Daldrup T. Comparison of venous blood alcohol concentrations and breath alcohol concentrations measured with Draeger Alcotest 9510 DE evidential. *Forensic Sci Int* 2016;258:64–7.
120. Martin TL. An evaluation of the Intoxilyzer® 8000C evidential breath alcohol analyzer. *Can Soc Forensic Sci J* 2011;44:22–30.
121. Jones AW, Andersson L. Determination of ethanol in breath for legal purposes using a five-filter infrared analyzer: studies on response to volatile interfering substances. *J Breath Res* 2008;2:026006.
122. Harding P, Field PH. Breathalyzer accuracy in actual law enforcement practice: a comparison of blood- and breath-alcohol results in Wisconsin drivers. *J Forensic Sci* 1987;32:1235–40.
123. Harding PM, Laessig RH, Field PH. Field performance of the Intoxilyzer 5000: a comparison of blood- and breath-alcohol results in Wisconsin drivers. *J Forensic Sci* 1990;35:1022–8.
124. Borkenstein RF, Smith HW. The Breathalyzer and its applications. *Med Sci Law* 1961;2:13–23.
125. Lindberg L, Brauer S, Wollmer P, Goldberg L, Jones AW, Olsson SG. Breath alcohol concentration determined with a new analyzer using free exhalation predicts almost precisely the arterial blood alcohol concentration. *Forensic Sci Int* 2007;168:200–7.
126. Jones AW, Lindberg L, Olsson SG. Magnitude and time-course of arterio-venous differences in blood-alcohol concentration in healthy men. *Clin Pharmacokinet* 2004;43:1157–66.
127. Jones AW. Determination of liquid/air partition coefficients for dilute solutions of ethanol in water, whole blood, and plasma. *J Anal Toxicol* 1983;7:193–7.
128. Jones AW, Fransson M. Blood analysis by headspace gas chromatography: does a deficient sample volume distort ethanol concentration? *Med Sci Law* 2003;43:241–7.
129. Jones AW. Salting-out effect of sodium fluoride and its influence on the analysis of ethanol by headspace gas chromatography. *J Anal Toxicol* 1994;18:292–3.
130. Miller BA, Day SM, Vasquez TE, Evans FM. Absence of salting out effects in forensic blood alcohol determination at various concentrations of sodium fluoride using semi-automated headspace gas chromatography. *Sci Justice* 2004;44:73–6.
131. Riley D, Wigmore JG, Yen B. Dilution of blood collected for medicolegal alcohol analysis by intravenous fluids. *J Anal Toxicol* 1996;20:330–1.
132. Kintz P. Influence of antemortem perfusion on autopsy blood ethanol concentration. *Forensic Tox* 2012;30:76–9.
133. Lippi G, Simundic AM, Musile G, Danese E, Salvagno G, Tagliaro F. The alcohol used for cleansing the venipuncture site does not jeopardize blood and plasma alcohol measurement with head-space gas chromatography and an enzymatic assay. *Biochem Med (Zagreb)* 2017;27:398–403.

134. Rodda LN, Pearring S, Harper CE, Tiscione NB, Jones AW. Inferences and legal considerations following a blood collection tube recall. *J Anal Toxicol* 2021;45:214–21.
135. Jones AW, Schuberth J. Computer-aided headspace gas chromatography applied to blood-alcohol analysis: importance of online process control. *J Forensic Sci* 1989;34:1116–27.
136. Jones AW. Are changes in blood-ethanol concentration during storage analytically significant? Importance of method imprecision. *Clin Chem Lab Med* 2007;45:1299–394.
137. Kocak FE, Isiklar OO, Kocak H, Meral A. Comparison of blood ethanol stabilities in different storage periods. *Biochem Med (Zagreb)* 2015;25:57–63.
138. Jones AW, Ericsson E. Decreases in blood ethanol concentration during storage at 4°C for 12 months were the same for specimens kept in glass and plastic tubes. *Pract Lab med* 2016;4:76–81.
139. Tiscione NB, Vacha RE, Alford I, Yeatman DT, Shan X. Long-term blood alcohol stability in forensic antemortem whole blood samples. *J Anal Toxicol* 2015;39:419–25.
140. Dubowski KM, Gadsden RH, Sr, Poklis A. The stability of ethanol in human whole blood controls: an interlaboratory evaluation. *J Anal Toxicol* 1997;21:486–91.
141. Jones AW, Edman-Falkensson M, Nilsson L. Reliability of blood alcohol determinations at clinical chemistry laboratories in Sweden. *Scand J Clin Lab Invest* 1995;55: 463–8.
142. Wilson JF, Barnett K. External quality assessment of techniques for assay of serum ethanol. *Ann Clin Biochem* 1995;32(Pt 6):540–4.
143. Zamengo L, Tedeschi G, Frison G, Griffoni C, Ponzin D, Jones AW. Inter-laboratory proficiency results of blood alcohol determinations at clinical and forensic laboratories in Italy. *Forensic Sci Int* 2019;295:213–8.
144. Devleeschouwer N, Libeer JC, Martens FK, Neels H, Van Damme M, Verstraete A, et al. Blood alcohol testing: comparison of the performance obtained with the different methods used in the Belgian external quality assessment schemes. *Clin Chem Lab Med* 2004;42:57–61.
145. Zamengo L, Frison G, Tedeschi G, Frasson S, Zancanaro F, Sciarrone R. Variability of blood alcohol content (BAC) determinations: the role of measurement uncertainty, significant figures, and decision rules for compliance assessment in the frame of a multiple BAC threshold law. *Drug Test Anal* 2014;6:1028–37.
146. Witte DL, VanNess SA, Angstadt DS, Pennell BJ. Errors, mistakes, blunders, outliers, or unacceptable results: how many? *Clin Chem* 1997;43:1352–6.
147. Searle J. Alcohol calculations and their uncertainty. *Med Sci Law* 2015;55:58–64.
148. Gullberg RG. Estimating the measurement uncertainty in forensic blood alcohol analysis. *J Anal Toxicol* 2012;36:153–61.
149. Moroni R, Blomstedt P, Wilhelm L, Reinikainen T, Sippola E, Corander J. Statistical modelling of measurement errors in gas chromatographic analyses of blood alcohol content. *Forensic Sci Int* 2010;202:71–4.
150. Jones AW. Pharmacokinetics of ethanol - issues of forensic importance. *Forensic Sci Rev* 2011;23:91–136.
151. Walsham NE, Sherwood RA. Ethyl glucuronide. *Ann Clin Biochem* 2012;49:110–7.
152. Hoiseth G, Morini L, Polettini A, Christophersen A, Morland J. Blood kinetics of ethyl glucuronide and ethyl sulphate in heavy drinkers during alcohol detoxification. *Forensic Sci Int* 2009;188:52–6.
153. Helander A, Bottcher M, Fehr C, Dahmen N, Beck O. Detection times for urinary ethyl glucuronide and ethyl sulfate in heavy drinkers during alcohol detoxification. *Alcohol Alcohol* 2009;44:55–61.
154. Ammon E, Schafer C, Hofmann U, Klotz U. Disposition and first-pass metabolism of ethanol in humans: is it gastric or hepatic and does it depend on gender? *Clin Pharmacol Ther* 1996;59:503–13.
155. Oneta CM, Lieber CS, Li J, Ruttimann S, Schmid B, Lattmann J, et al. Dynamics of cytochrome P4502E1 activity in man: induction by ethanol and disappearance during withdrawal phase. *J Hepatol* 2002;36:47–52.
156. Tanaka E, Terada M, Misawa S. Cytochrome P450 2E1: its clinical and toxicological role. *J Clin Pharm Ther* 2000;25:165–75.
157. Lieber CS. Mechanisms of ethanol-drug-nutrition interactions. *J Toxicol Clin Toxicol* 1994;32:631–81.
158. Davies M. The role of GABAA receptors in mediating the effects of alcohol in the central nervous system. *J Psychiatry Neurosci* 2003;28:263–74.
159. Hanchar HJ, Dodson PD, Olsen RW, Otis TS, Wallner M. Alcohol-induced motor impairment caused by increased extrasynaptic GABA(A) receptor activity. *Nat Neurosci* 2005;8:339–45.
160. Kalant H. Current state of knowledge about the mechanisms of alcohol tolerance. *Addict Biol* 1996;1:133–41.
161. Jones AW, Holmgren A. Age and gender differences in blood-alcohol concentration in apprehended drivers in relation to the amounts of alcohol consumed. *Forensic Sci Int* 2009;188:40–5.
162. Jones AW, Holmgren P. Comparison of blood-ethanol concentration in deaths attributed to acute alcohol poisoning and chronic alcoholism. *J Forensic Sci* 2003;48:874–9.
163. Zink P, Reinhardt G. Der Verlauf der Blutalkoholkurve bei großem Trinkmengen. *Blutalkohol* 1984;21:422–42.
164. Jones AW, Wigmore JG, House CJ. The course of the blood-alcohol curve after consumption of large amounts of alcohol under realistic conditions. *Can Soc Forensic Sci J* 2006;39:125–40.
165. Holford NH. Clinical pharmacokinetics of ethanol. *Clin Pharmacokinet* 1987;13:273–92.
166. Norberg A, Jones AW, Hahn RG, Gabrielsson JL. Role of variability in explaining ethanol pharmacokinetics: research and forensic applications. *Clin Pharmacokinet* 2003;42:1–31.
167. Widmark EMP. *Principles and Applications of Medicolegal Alcohol Determinations.* Davis: Biomedical Publications, 1981.
168. Jones AW. Interindividual variations in the disposition and metabolism of ethanol in healthy men. *Alcohol* 1984;1:385–91.
169. Andreasson R, Jones AW. The life and work of Erik M. P. Widmark. *Am J Forensic Med Pathol* 1996;17:177–90.
170. Jones AW, Erik MP. Widmark - bridged the gap between forensic toxicology and alcohol and traffic safety research. *Blutalkohol* 2009;46:15–23.
171. Maskell PD, Jones AW, Savage A, Scott-Ham M. Evidence based survey of the distribution volume of ethanol: comparison of empirically determined values with anthropometric measures. *Forensic Sci Int* 2019;294:124–31.
172. Lundquist F, Wolthers H. The kinetics of alcohol elimination in man. *Acta Pharmacol Toxicol (Copenh)* 1958;14:265–89.
173. Rangno RE, Kreeft JH, Sitar DS. Ethanol 'dose-dependent' elimination: Michaelis-Menten v classical kinetic analysis. *Br J Clin Pharmacol* 1981;12:667–73.

174. Wilkinson PK. Pharmacokinetics of ethanol: a review. *Alcohol Clin Exp Res* 1980;4:6–21.
175. O'Neill B, Williams AF, Dubowski KM. Variability in blood alcohol concentrations. Implications for estimating individual results. *J Stud Alcohol* 1983;44:222–30.
176. Jones AW, Jonsson KA, Neri A. Peak blood-ethanol concentration and the time of its occurrence after rapid drinking on an empty stomach. *J Forensic Sci* 1991;36:376–85.
177. Fraser AG, Rosalki SB, Gamble GD, Pounder RE. Inter-individual and intra-individual variability of ethanol concentration-time profiles: comparison of ethanol ingestion before or after an evening meal. *Br J Clin Pharmacol* 1995;40:387–92.
178. Piekoszewski W, Gubala W. Inter- and intra-individual variability of ethanol pharmacokinetics over a long period of time. *Pol J Pharmacol* 2000;52:389–95.
179. Jones AW, Jonsson KA. Between-subject and within-subject variations in the pharmacokinetics of ethanol. *Br J Clin Pharmacol* 1994;37:427–31.
180. Sadler DW, Fox J. Intra-individual and inter-individual variation in breath alcohol pharmacokinetics: the effect of food on absorption. *Sci Justice* 2011;51:3–9.
181. Sadler DW, Lennox S. Intra-individual and inter-individual variation in breath alcohol pharmacokinetics: variation over three visits. *J Forensic Leg Med* 2015;34:88–98.
182. Yelland LN, Burns JP, Sims DN, Salter AB, White JM. Inter- and intra-subject variability in ethanol pharmacokinetic parameters: effects of testing interval and dose. *Forensic Sci Int* 2008;175:65–72.
183. Mellanby E. *Alcohol: Its Absorption into and Disappearance from the Blood under Different Conditions*. London: Medical Research Committee, Series nr 13, HMSO, 1919.
184. Thierauf A, Kempf J, Eschbach J, Auwarter V, Weinmann W, Gnann H. A case of a distinct difference between the measured blood ethanol concentration and the concentration estimated by Widmark's equation. *Med Sci Law* 2013;53:96–9.
185. Kalant H. Effects of food and body composition on blood alcohol curves. *Alcohol Clin Exp Res* 2000;24:413–4.
186. Jones AW, Neri A. Evaluation of blood-alcohol profiles after consumption of alcohol together with a large meal. *Can Soc Forensic Sci J* 1991;24:165–73.
187. Kalant H. Effects of food and body composition on blood alcohol levels. In: Preedy V, Watson R, editors. *Comprehensive Handbook of Alcohol Related Pathology*, 2004, 87–101.
188. Jones AW, Jonsson KA. Food-induced lowering of blood-ethanol profiles and increased rate of elimination immediately after a meal. *J Forensic Sci* 1994;39:1084–93.
189. Sedman AJ, Wilkinson PK, Sakmar E, Weidler DJ, Wagner JG. Food effects on absorption and metabolism of alcohol. *J Stud Alcohol* 1976;37:1197–214.
190. Watkins RL, Adler EV. The effect of food on alcohol absorption and elimination patterns. *J Forensic Sci* 1993;38:285–91.
191. Ramchandani VA, O'Connor S. Studying alcohol elimination using the alcohol clamp method. *Alcohol Res Health* 2006;29:286–90.
192. Ramchandani VA, Kwo PY, Li TK. Effect of food and food composition on alcohol elimination rates in healthy men and women. *J Clin Pharmacol* 2001;41:1345–50.
193. Hahn RG, Norberg A, Gabrielsson J, Danielsson A, Jones AW. Eating a meal increases the clearance of ethanol given by intravenous infusion. *Alcohol Alcohol* 1994;29:673–7.
194. Lisander B, Lundvall O, Tomner J, Jones AW. Enhanced rate of ethanol elimination from blood after intravenous administration of amino acids compared with equicaloric glucose. *Alcohol Alcohol* 2006;41:39–43.
195. Rheingold JL, Lindstrom RE, Wilkinson PK. A new blood-flow pharmacokinetic model for ethanol. *J Pharmacokinet Biopharm* 1981;9:261–78.
196. Schmidt V, Oehmichen M, Pedal I. [Increased ethanol elimination after barium meal--human experimental study with parenteral alcohol administration]. *Blutalkohol* 1992;29:119–29.
197. Bonnichsen R, Hedfjall B, Ryhage R. Determination of ethyl alcohol by computerized mass chromatography. *Z Rechtsmed* 1972;71:134–8.
198. Heier C, Xie H, Zimmermann R. Nonoxidative ethanol metabolism in humans-from biomarkers to bioactive lipids. *IUBMB Life* 2016;68:916–23.
199. Bortolotti F, Tagliaro F. Biomarkers for the identification of alcohol use/abuse: a critical review. *Forensic Sci Rev* 2011;23:55–72.
200. Dahl H, Hammarberg A, Franck J, Helander A. Urinary ethyl glucuronide and ethyl sulfate testing for recent drinking in alcohol-dependent outpatients treated with acamprosate or placebo. *Alcohol Alcohol* 2011;46:553–7.
201. Hoiseth G, Bernard JP, Karinen R, Johnsen L, Helander A, Christophersen AS, et al. A pharmacokinetic study of ethyl glucuronide in blood and urine: applications to forensic toxicology. *Forensic Sci Int* 2007;172:119–24.
202. Biondi A, Freni F, Carelli C, Moretti M, Morini L. Ethyl glucuronide hair testing: a review. *Forensic Sci Int* 2019;300:106–19.
203. Krabseth H, Morland J, Hoiseth G. Assistance of ethyl glucuronide and ethyl sulfate in the interpretation of postmortem ethanol findings. *Int J Legal Med* 2014;128:765–70.
204. Sundstrom M, Jones AW, Ojanpera I. Utility of urinary ethyl glucuronide analysis in post-mortem toxicology when investigating alcohol-related deaths. *Forensic Sci Int* 2014;241:178–82.
205. Labay L, Logan B. Letter to the editor - call for a scientific consensus regarding the application of retrograde extrapolation to determine blood alcohol content in DUI cases. *J Forensic Sci* 2018;63:1602–3.
206. Maskell PD, Scott-Ham M. Letter to the editor-consensus on retrograde extrapolations. *J Forensic Sci* 2018;63:1933.
207. Al-Lanqawi Y, Moreland TA, McEwen J, Halliday F, Durnin CJ, Stevenson IH. Ethanol kinetics: extent of error in back extrapolation procedures. *Br J Clin Pharmacol* 1992;34:316–21.
208. LeBeau MA, Limoges JF. Call for a scientific consensus regarding the application of retrograde extrapolation to determine blood alcohol content in DUI cases. *J Forensic Sci* 2019;64:322.
209. Jones AW. Evidence-based survey of the elimination rates of ethanol from blood with applications in forensic casework. *Forensic Sci Int* 2010;200:1–20.
210. Simic M, Tasic M. The relationship between alcohol elimination rate and increasing blood alcohol concentration--calculated from two consecutive blood specimens. *Forensic Sci Int* 2007;172:28–32.
211. Dettling A, Fischer F, Bohler S, Ulrichs F, Skopp G, Graw M, et al. Ethanol elimination rates in men and women in consideration of the calculated liver weight. *Alcohol* 2007;41:415–20.

212. Maudens KE, Patteet L, van Nuijs AL, Van Broekhoven C, Covaci A, Neels H. The influence of the body mass index (BMI) on the volume of distribution of ethanol. *Forensic Sci Int* 2014;243:74–8.
213. Breen MH, Dang QT, Jaing JT, Boyd GN. The effect of a 'one for the road' drink of hard liquor, beer or wine on peak breath alcohol concentration in a social drinking environment with food consumption. *Med Sci Law* 1998;38:62–9.
214. Langford NJ, Ferner RE. The medico-legal significance of pharmacokinetic interactions with ethanol. *Med Sci Law* 2013;53:1–5.
215. Weathermon R, Crabb DW. Alcohol and medication interactions. *Alcohol Res Health* 1999;23:40–54.
216. Hoiseth G, Wiik E, Kristoffersen L, Morland J. Ethanol elimination rates at low concentrations based on two consecutive blood samples. *Forensic Sci Int* 2016;266:191–6.
217. Furne J, Levitt MD. Speed of gastric emptying and metabolism of ethanol. *Gut* 1999;45:916.
218. Oneta CM, Simanowski UA, Martinez M, Allali-Hassani A, Pares X, Homann N, et al. First pass metabolism of ethanol is strikingly influenced by the speed of gastric emptying. *Gut* 1998;43:612–9.
219. Moody DE. The inhibition of first-pass metabolism of ethanol by H2-receptor antagonists: a tabulated review. *Expert Opin Drug Saf* 2018;17:917–34.
220. Fraser AG. Is there an interaction between H2-antagonists and alcohol? *Drug Metabol Drug Interact* 1998;14:123–45.
221. Toon S, Khan AZ, Holt BI, Mullins FG, Langley SJ, Rowland MM. Absence of effect of ranitidine on blood alcohol concentrations when taken morning, midday, or evening with or without food. *Clin Pharmacol Ther* 1994;55:385–91.
222. Rowland M, Tozer TN. *Clinical Pharmacokinetics - Concepts and Applications.* third ed. Baltimore: Williams & Wilkins, 1995.
223. Wagner JG. Lack of first-pass metabolism of ethanol at blood concentrations in the social drinking range. *Life Sci* 1986;39:407–14.
224. Holford NH. Complex PK/PD models--an alcoholic experience. *Int J Clin Pharmacol Ther* 1997;35:465–8.
225. Jones AW, Jonsson KA, Kechagias S. Effect of high-fat, high-protein, and high-carbohydrate meals on the pharmacokinetics of a small dose of ethanol. *Br J Clin Pharmacol* 1997;44:521–6.
226. Norberg A, Sandhagen B, Bratteby LE, Gabrielsson J, Jones AW, Fan H, et al. Do ethanol and deuterium oxide distribute into the same water space in healthy volunteers? *Alcohol Clin Exp Res* 2001;25:1423–30.
227. Jones AW, Hahn RG, Stalberg HP. Pharmacokinetics of ethanol in plasma and whole blood: estimation of total body water by the dilution principle. *Eur J Clin Pharmacol* 1992;42:445–8.
228. Grubb D, Rasmussen B, Linnet K, Olsson SG, Lindberg L. Breath alcohol analysis incorporating standardization to water vapour is as precise as blood alcohol analysis. *Forensic Sci Int* 2012;216:88–91.
229. Jones AW, Cowan MJ. Reflections on variability in the blood-breath ratio of ethanol and its importance when evidential breath-alcohol instruments are used in law enforcement. *Forensic Sci Res* 2021;5:300–308.

3.3 DETERMINATION OF ETHANOL IN POST-MORTEM SPECIMENS: IMPORTANT CONSIDERATIONS FOR INTERPRETING RESULTS

Alan Wayne Jones and Derrick J. Pounder

3.3.1 Introduction

Whenever a sudden, unexpected, and/or suspicious death occurs, the resulting police investigation almost always includes a medicolegal autopsy of the deceased, the aim of which is to discover the cause and manner of death.[1,2] If the autopsy results are negative, unremarkable, or inconclusive, this shifts attention toward the possibility of a fatal poisoning or a drug overdose death. Evidence needed to support this conclusion comes from a toxicological analysis of ethanol, drugs, and xenobiotics in blood and other biological materials procured during the post-mortem examination.[3,4]

The most important specimens for toxicological analysis are peripheral blood, bladder urine, and vitreous humor (VH), although bile, cerebrospinal fluid, hair strands, and nails might also be available for analysis.[5] Polypharmacy is common in today's society, especially in the elderly, which increases the risk of death from adverse drug–drug interactions.[6] Depending on the results of toxicological analysis and the concentrations of chemical substances in autopsy blood, tentative conclusions can be drawn whether or not drug intoxication was a probable cause of death.[7]

Among a plethora of toxic substances encountered in post-mortem (PM) blood, topping the list is the legal drug ethanol (CH_3CH_2OH), which is the pharmacologically active substance contained in alcoholic beverages.[8,9] Several studies indicate that blood-alcohol concentration (BAC) is elevated (> 0.2 g/L) in 40–50% of all unnatural deaths.[10] The analytical methods available for the determination of ethanol in blood and other specimens are accurate, precise, and fit for their intended purpose. Since the mid-1960s the method of choice is headspace gas chromatography (HS-GC) with a flame-ionization detector (FID).[11] This method works well with specimens from living and deceased persons, but depending on the complexity of the case, such as the condition of the body, the results are strengthened if separate determinations are made by an alternative method, such as HS-GC coupled with a mass spectrometric (MS) detector.[12]

During an autopsy, the blood and other biological specimens for toxicology should be taken before the body is eviscerated. The preferred source of blood is a peripheral vein, such as a femoral vein in the thigh (femoral venous blood) or an iliac vein, which drains blood from the pelvis and lower limbs.[13] However, in most death investigations pathologists also submit cardiac blood, which is easier to collect and is available in larger volumes.[5] The concentrations of various drugs are not necessarily the same in cardiac and peripheral blood, depending on properties of the drug, such as its volume of distribution, the condition of the body, and the PM interval.[14]

Differences in the concentration of ethanol in autopsy blood depending on central or peripheral sampling sites have been much discussed already in the 1950s.[15,16] In a case series of 75 autopsies, blood was obtained from the chambers of the heart and a femoral vein and ethanol content was determined by chemical oxidation methods. In 35 cases the concentration of ethanol in cardiac blood was higher than in femoral blood and the difference was too large to be explained by analytics or sampling variations.[17] The article contained the following statement;

> Alcohol has been shown to diffuse through the stomach wall after death if it is present there as a beverage taken before death. It can diffuse into neighboring structures including the heart. Since this can lead to serious error in medicolegal situations, it is recommended that postmortem samples of blood to be analyzed for alcohol be taken from the femoral veins. This is done at autopsy immediately after opening the abdomen.

The risk of diffusion of ethanol from the stomach contents after death to reach other parts of the body is well-recognized, and this problem is more of a concern for pericardial tissues. Hence the strong recommendation to sample peripheral blood (femoral vein) for toxicological analysis.[18] The question of post-mortem diffusion of drugs and the unexplained discrepancies between concentrations in different sampling sites has been demonstrated consistently by many investigators.[19] This represents a much bigger problem for drugs that are inclined to distribute into adipose tissue compartments than for ethanol, which distributes into the body water compartment and is not concentrated in fatty tissue.[20,21]

The analytical details and the technical equipment needed for the determination of ethanol in biological specimens are essentially the same regardless of whether these are from a corpse or from a living person (e.g. drunk drivers).[22] However, interpreting the results is more challenging in death investigations, owing to various artifacts and confounding factors, such as the degree of trauma to the body, PM interval, exsanguination, decomposition, and putrefaction processes.

The existence of various microbial processes and availability of fermentable carbohydrates can lead to the production of ethanol in the body after death. This, in a nutshell, is the biggest problem for making a correct interpretation of the results of ethanol determination in PM specimens, namely being able to distinguish PM synthesis from antemortem ingestion.[23] Drawing the wrong conclusions is often referred to as a PM artifact, meaning that it was caused by something occurring after death.[24] PM artifacts are defined as changes that occur in the body after death that are incorrectly interpreted as reflecting a situation that prevailed prior to death.[25]

The appearance and composition of autopsy blood are often unlike blood taken from living subjects under sterile and aseptic conditions, usually from a cubital vein at the elbow.[26,27] Autopsy specimens tend to be darker in color, some have a foul smell, they have less homogeneity, are sometimes clotted, and have more variable water content. The sampling site for obtaining PM might include arteries, veins, or even directly from the chest cavity, although the latter is not recommended because of the risk of dilution with other body fluids.[28] The diffusion of ethanol and drug molecules from tissue compartments into the vascular system after death is another complicating factor to consider when PM drug concentrations are interpreted.[29]

If a person dies shortly after consumption of an alcoholic beverage, some of the ethanol probably remains unabsorbed in the stomach, which heightens the possibility for diffusion from gastric residue into the vascular system after death.[30] Agonal events, such as vomiting, can cause some contamination of the airways with stomach contents and promote the diffusion of ethanol to organs in close proximity with the lungs.[31] Information from the death scene, such as positioning and condition of the body and whether the deceased had vomited, is important for further forensic investigation.

The present review updates chapter 5.3 from the second edition of the *Drug Abuse Handbook* (*DAH*)[32] and includes considerable new material as well as an updated list of literature references. However, the main focus of this chapter is problems and pitfalls associated with making a correct interpretation of BAC in medicolegal casework. Considering the ubiquitous use and abuse of alcohol in society, the risk of ethanol being produced in the body after death can lead to wrong conclusions.[33]

3.3.2 Importance of Blood-Ethanol Determinations

It is generally accepted that there is a pharmacological relationship between the amount of ethanol consumed, the resulting BAC, the impairment of performance and behavior, and the risk of an ethanol poisoning death. A person is often considered legally drunk when his or her BAC exceeds the statutory blood alcohol limit for driving, which is 80 mg% (0.80 g/L) in the USA, England, and Wales. However, this is an unfortunate definition, because statutory alcohol limits for driving differ between countries and most EU nations enforce a limit of 50 mg% (0.5 g/L). In connection with unnatural death investigations, the concentrations of ethanol and other drugs in autopsy blood become crucial information when the cause of death is determined.

Whether the deceased was intoxicated at the time of death is important when fatal accidents are investigated in the home, the workplace, and on the roads. Statistics show that between 20–50% of drivers killed in road-traffic crashes had been drinking and that their autopsy BAC exceeded the statutory limits for driving.[34] Furthermore, people engaged in dangerous occupations are not allowed to consume alcohol, and when a workplace fatality occurs the deceased's BAC becomes important evidence when culpability is assessed and when insurance claims are made. In this connection, it is obviously important to rule out that any ethanol detected in PM blood was produced in the body after death. This possibility made headline news when positive ethanol concentrations where reported in the blood from the driver of an underground train crash in London in 1975 (Moorgate station) in which there were 43 fatalities. The badly traumatized body of the driver was trapped in the wreckage for several days before being recovered and during this time ethanol could easily have been produced by PM synthesis.

A major difficulty with the interpretation of PM ethanol concentrations is the variable condition of the corpse and the quality of the blood specimens collected for toxicology. Much depends on the manner of death, including trauma and blood loss, the stage of decomposition and putrefaction, and the activity of viable microbes. Ethanol is one of the few toxic substances that can be produced in the body after death by mycotic fermentation of glucose and other substrates.[35] A positive autopsy BAC might therefore represent drinking alcohol during life or the synthesis of ethanol after death or both. The possibility that ethanol might have been produced in the body after death is a constant dilemma in PM toxicology.[36] It is recommended that the analytical cut-off concentration for reporting positive BAC is appropriate so that false positives are avoided. In routine casework, BAC of 0.10 g/L or 0.20 g/L or less should be reported as ethanol "not detected," not as < 0.10 g/L or < 0.20 g/L, which gives the false impression that some low ethanol concentration was present before death, although this is not necessarily the case.

The difficulties in interpreting BAC in autopsy blood are partially compensated for by the fact that there are alternative specimens available for toxicological analysis.[37] Besides anatomical and histological findings from the autopsy, photographing of the death scene, anamnestic data about the deceased, police reports, and interviews with witnesses all need to be considered. An autopsy BAC might be uninterpretable without this additional information, hence the need to submit samples of VH and urine for analysis to compare with ethanol concentrations in blood.[38,39] The importance of considering the totality of information in each death investigation when the toxicology results are interpreted hardly needs repeating in unnatural death investigations.[40]

3.3.2.1 Body Water Distribution

After drinking alcoholic beverages, the ethanol they contain is rapidly absorbed from the stomach and intestines into the portal venous blood, which passes first to the liver, then via the hepatic vein and inferior vena cava to the heart and lungs before ethanol is distributed throughout the total body water (TBW) compartment.[41] Body water makes up about 55–60% of body weight in healthy non-obese males and 50–55% in females.[42] Neonates have a higher TBW in relation to their body weight (75–80%) and TBW is lower in geriatric patients. A young man with a body weight of 70–80 kg has 42–48 liters of water (0.6×70 or 0.6×80) in the entire body, which dilutes water-soluble drugs like alcohol.[43] The volume of blood in humans corresponds to

7–8% of body weight or ~5 L in a person weighing 70 kg and ~6.3 L if body weight is 90 kg. TBW decreases during aging, especially in men.

Roughly 60% of body water is located within the cells (intracellular fluid) and the remainder (40%) is extracellular. The latter is comprised of intravascular fluid (plasma fraction ~3–4 L) and extravascular water (11 L). The extravascular water comprises interstitial fluid (~11 L) and transcellular fluids (~0.5 L), e.g. spinal fluid and ocular fluids, etc.

The speed with which various organs and tissues reach equilibrium with ethanol depends on the ratio of blood flow rate to the mass of the tissues, and the brain, lungs, and kidney equilibrate much faster than the bulky skeletal muscle tissue. What this means is that before absorption and distribution of ethanol are complete, the arterial blood concentration (e.g. radial artery) is higher than the venous blood concentration (e.g. cubital vein).

When ethanol equilibrates between the bloodstream and the rest of the body, which usually takes between 1–2 h after the end of drinking, the concentrations in various body fluids and tissues are in direct proportion to water content of the specimens analyzed. Accordingly, urine, vitreous humor, and cerebrospinal fluid (CSF), which contain 95–99% w/w water, are expected to contain higher concentrations of ethanol than whole blood, which is about 80% w/w water.[44] Most of the organs and tissues of the body contain about 70% w/w water; kidneys contain 83% water, and muscles 76% water (Table 3.3.1). The water content of brain tissue is more variable depending on the amount of edema in relation to the cause of death.

3.3.2.2 Water Content of Post-Mortem (PM) Blood

The water content of blood and other biological specimens is easy to determine by desiccation, that is, by accurately weighing an aliquot and then heating in an oven at 105–110° C to reach a constant weight.[45] Reference books, such as the GEIGY scientific tables, quote the density of blood as being 1.06 g/mL (kg/L) with a water content of 850 g/L (85% w/v).[46] This means that the percentage of water in blood depends on whether mass/volume or mass/mass units are chosen. Thus 85% w/v is the same as 80% w/w (85/1.06). The water content of whole blood will also depend on hematocrit, which on average is lower in women than in men, and a higher plasma fraction in female blood means slightly more water per unit volume. GEIGY tables report that the water contents of plasma and serum are almost identical, 945 g/L (94.5% w/v) with no gender differences, and a density of 1.027 g/mL gives a water content of 92% w/w.

The water content of PM blood decreases as the PM interval increases and dehydration of the corpse progresses, depending on environmental temperature and humidity. Table 3.3.2 reports the water content of PM blood determined by different investigators in relation to PM intervals.[46–48]

In a study of 71 cadavers with a blood sample taken within 10 hours after death (mean 2.1 hours, range 0–9.6 hours) the water content ranged between 72% and 89%, mean 80.4%, which is closely similar to the water content of blood from living persons (79–82% w/w for women and 76–81% for men). Second samples taken from the same cadavers from 8–229 hours post-mortem had a lower water content ranging between 64.4% and 88.0%, mean 74.0%. However, differences in blood-ethanol concentration between the two sampling times were more strongly influenced by other post-mortem factors, such as putrefaction, rather than by water content changes, so that correcting a post-mortem blood alcohol for water content is not generally recommended. Note that water content expressed as percent w/w is not the same as percent w/v because the density of blood is 1.055 on average. Accordingly, an average blood water of 80% w/w would correspond to 84.4% w/v ($80 \times 1.055 = 84.4$).

Forensic pathologists in Germany advocated that when autopsy blood ethanol was determined, the analytical results should be corrected for variable amounts of water present. Accordingly, a method was described for the analysis of both ethanol and water content of autopsy blood specimen. The concentration of ethanol was then correct to a blood water content of 80% w/w without considering any gender differences. The following equation

TABLE 3.3.1
Water Content of Body Fluids, Organs, and Tissues Taken at Autopsy (N = 24)[44]

Specimen	Water content, mean ± SD w/w	Specimen	Water content, mean ± SD, w/w
Synovial fluid	94.0 ± 5.6%	Pancreas	76.1 ± 3.6 %
Bladder urine	96.7 (91–98)%[1]	Diaphragm	75.3 ± 5.8 %
Bile	87.8 ± 3.7%	Lung	80.4 ± 3.2 %
Vitreous humor	98.4 ± 0.8%	Heart muscle	78.3 ± 5.7 %
Cerebrospinal fluid	95.0 ± 2.8%	Spleen	76.6 ± 1.7 %
Muscle	74.0 ± 4.4%	Liver	70.5 ± 4.8 %
Kidney	80.0 ± 4.4%	Testicle	85.6 ± 2.1 %
Brain	70–80%[1]	Thyroid	74.2 ± 6.1 %

[1] A range is given because of large variations in some of the cases studied.

TABLE 3.3.2

Water Contents (% w/w) of Autopsy Blood Samples (Femoral Vein) in Relation to the Post-Mortem (PM) Interval in Hours

Investigators	N (cases)	PM interval, h Mean (range)	Water content % w/w mean ± SD	Mean BAC g/L	Sampling site
Brettel[47]	34	13.9 (2–24)	79.3 ± 4.9	0.594	Femoral vein (left leg)
	34	58.5 (49–74)	75.4 ±4.3	0.556	Femoral vein (right leg)
	31	61.7 (27–106)	74.9 ± 4.2	0.610	Femoral vein (left leg)
	31	88.7 (42–171)	73.6 ± 3.5	0.575	Femoral vein (right leg)
Felby and Nielson[48,332]	71	2.1 (0–10)	80.4 (range 72–89)	0.1–3.9 (range)	Femoral vein
	71	98.7 (8–229)	74.0 (range 64–88)	0.1–3.6 (range)	Femoral vein
Jones (unpublished)	30[1]	Routine forensic autopsies[2]	73.0 ± 5.5 (range 64–91)	0.1–3.8 (range)	Femoral vein

[1] Blood samples were from predominantly male deaths.
[2] Time of death to autopsy not known, but was at least several days.

can be used to correct the ethanol concentration in blood taken at autopsy to a result more compatible with BAC at the time of death:

$$\frac{\text{Ethanol concentration in PM blood sample} \times 80\%\ \text{w/w}}{\text{Water content of PM blood sample \% w/w}}$$

3.3.2.3 Variable Composition of Blood Specimens

Within a few hours after death, the blood within the vascular system starts to coagulate and more or less simultaneously there is lysis of the red cells. The effectiveness of the clot lysis will determine whether a blood sample obtained at autopsy is clotted, completely fluid, or, as is often the case, partly clotted and partly fluid. The fibrin clots invariably entrap large numbers of red blood cells so that the resulting clot is relatively rich in erythrocytes and deficient in serum. Occasionally the heart and great vessels may contain a large two-layered clot, the lower part typically red-colored, and the upper part a pale yellow rubbery clot devoid of red cells (so-called "chicken fat").

Consequently, "blood samples" obtained at autopsy have variable proportions of red cells, fats, proteins, and water content, which impacts the concentration of ethanol and other drugs depending on their physicochemical properties and relative fat to water solubility. Blood samples taken from limb vessels are more likely to be fluid and largely devoid of clots and therefore more homogeneous, and thus provide a good specimen for toxicological analysis. The presence of clots in the blood will not necessarily have a negative influence on the reliability of ethanol determinations provided that the necessary aliquot for analysis can be accurately measured, either by weight or by volume.[49]

3.3.2.4 Plasma and Serum vs Whole Blood

Serum and plasma contain approximately 10–15% more water than the same volume of whole blood and will therefore also have higher ethanol concentrations.[50] This should be borne in mind whenever the results from analysis of ethanol in serum or plasma are interpreted in a legal context. In trauma victims admitted to the hospital for treatment of life-threatening injuries, a blood sample for toxicological analysis might already have been taken before the patient dies. The hospital analysis for ethanol and drugs was probably done on plasma or serum and not with whole blood, whereas at medicolegal autopsy of the deceased person involved sampling blood for analysis.[51]

Provided circulation through the liver is not interrupted by the patient's trauma injuries, ethanol is continuously being metabolized and the BAC decreasing at a rate of about 0.15 g/L/h (0.10 g/L/h to 0.25 g/L/h). Decreases in BAC through metabolism should always be considered when an autopsy BAC is compared with results of ethanol analysis on blood samples taken when the patient is still alive in the hospital intensive care unit. The distribution ratio of ethanol between plasma/serum and whole blood has been the subject of numerous investigations.

In a controlled drinking study with 134 subjects, two blood samples were drawn nearly simultaneously in two types of evacuated tubes.[52] One specimen was taken into a fluoride-oxalate gray stoppered tube and the other in a serum separator tube. Ethanol concentrations in serum and whole blood were determined by gas chromatography after dilution with *n*-propanol as the internal standard. The mean BAC was 1.05 g/L (range 0.22–1.55) and the mean serum alcohol concentration was 1.21 g/L (range 0.25–1.83), giving a mean serum/blood ethanol ratio of 1.15 (range 1.10–1.25, SD 0.02). None of the serum/blood ratios were below 1.10:1 and three were between 1.21 and 1.25.

A larger study involving 235 subjects found a mean serum/blood ratio of 1.14 with a range from 1.04 to 1.26 and a normal distribution of values with SD 0.041.[53] The same investigators determined the ethanol concentration in red blood cells from 167 of the volunteer subjects. The ethanol distribution ratio between erythrocytes/whole blood ranged from 0.66–1.00 with a mean of 0.865. The frequency distribution of the ratios was skewed and the standard deviation (SD) was 0.065.

A multi-center study was done in Germany that involved the analysis of 833 samples of blood and serum, and water content was determined by desiccation. The mean serum/blood ratio of water was 1.16 ± 0.0187 (SD) with minimum and maximum values of 1.08 and 1.20.[50] Considering the similarity in the distribution of ethanol and water between plasma, red-cells, and whole blood, it is safe to assume that the distribution ratio of ethanol is the same as for water.[54] Dividing a plasma or serum ethanol concentration by 1.16 gives the most probable concentration in whole blood. The 95% limits are given by 1.96 times the standard deviation, thus ± 0.0366 giving a range from 1.12 to 1.20 and these are the values recommended for use in medicolegal casework.

If an autopsy blood sample appears to be unusually dilute, this can be determined by the analysis of hemoglobin content and comparing results with normal values for living patients. Otherwise, the water content of the specimen is also easy to determine by desiccation.[55] As already mentioned, autopsy blood samples tend to be plasma-rich rather than erythrocyte-rich, in part because when a pathologist or mortuary assistant takes the specimens they tend to avoid sampling clots. This suggests that autopsy blood samples submitted for toxicological analysis have a slightly higher water (and ethanol) content compared with samples having normal hematocrit values. In practice, this difference is probably unimportant considering the many other sources of variation and variable quality of post-mortem blood specimens.

3.3.3 Blood-Ethanol Concentration in Unnatural Deaths

Elevated BAC is the most common toxicological finding in routine PM casework in most nations where alcoholic beverages are consumed and are available for purchase without any restrictions. However, a high BAC alone is not so easy to interpret without further information on a particular case. Whether ethanol alone was sufficient to cause incapacitation, coma or manifest drunkenness, or even an acute alcohol poisoning death is often dependent on many other factors. Variable BAC in acute poisoning deaths might depend on a person's age, pattern of drinking, state of health, development of tolerance, positional asphyxia, aspiration of vomitus, and any emergency life-saving treatment administered.

3.3.3.1 All Causes of Death

Table 3.3.3 compares age, gender, and BAC in a large number of medicolegal autopsies done in Finland and Sweden, countries where similar quality assurance routines are in use for unnatural death investigations. Both countries determined ethanol in femoral blood by similar analytical methodology (HS-GC-FID).[8,9] The analytical cut-off used with cases from Sweden was 0.10 g/L, whereas in Finland the cut-off for reporting ethanol positive cases was higher (0.20 g/L). The results show that in both countries BAC was positive in ~35% of all medicolegal autopsies, which increased to 55% when only drug intoxication deaths were selected for evaluation.[56]

Subject demographics were remarkably similar in these two Nordic countries, with the proportion of males (80%) dominating female (20%) victims, although the males were a few years older (mean 55 y) compared to females (mean 50 y). Furthermore, the mean autopsy BAC was slightly higher in Finland (1.55 g/L) compared with Sweden (1.25 g/L).

3.3.3.2 Acute Intoxication Deaths

Most forensic practitioners agree that it is unwise in any individual case to state categorically the BAC associated with an acute poisoning death. Many factors warrant considered not the least of which are the person's age, gender, body weight, health status (respiratory function), drinking experience (tolerance), concomitant drug intake, aspiration of vomit, ambient temperature (hypothermia aggravates ethanol toxicity), positional asphyxia, etc. Information about the toxicity of ethanol can be gleaned from a review

TABLE 3.3.3
Concentrations of Ethanol in Femoral Blood in Routine Forensic Autopsies from Sweden and Finland Representing All Causes of Death

Country	Gender	N (%)	Mean BAC g/L[1]	Median BAC g/L	Highest BAC g/L
Finland[9]	Male	35,889 (81%)	1.80	1.69	8.1
	Female	8,243 (19%)	1.73	1.58	8.9
	Both sexes	44,132 (100%)	1.79	1.69	8.9
Sweden[8]	Male	6,389 (79%)	1.45	1.30	7.4
	Female	1,719 (21%)	1.34	1.10	8.0
	Both sexes	8,108 (100%)	1.42	1.20	8.0

[1] BAC < 0.2 g/L reported as negative and results are not included.

of human fatalities and case series of alcohol-related deaths as well as experimental studies in rats, mice, and guinea-pigs to determine median lethal dose (LD_{50}). The case-series of alcohol-related deaths suggest that a BAC of 3.0 to 4.0 g/L is consistent with an alcohol poisoning death, whereas LD_{50} studies put BACs in the range 5.0–5.5 g/L, depending on the age and maturity of the particular animal species tested.[57–59]

The autopsy BAC in alcohol-related deaths depends if this was attributed to acute alcohol poisoning or a result of chronic heavy drinking and alcoholism.[60] However, a review of actual coroner cases suggests that a BAC of 2.50 g/L might be potentially lethal, rather than the concentration range 3.5 to 4.0 g/L commonly quoted in textbooks of forensic medicine.[61] A fairly recent study of 1,545 forensic autopsies when acute ethanol intoxication was considered the primary cause of death found an association between the degree of obesity and the autopsy BAC.[62] Fatalities with body mass index (BMI) over 30 had a lower concentration of ethanol in femoral blood (3.2 g/L) compared with people of normal weight or those not judged as being clinically obese at time of death (3.5 g/L).

In a retrospective review of 693 deaths attributed to acute alcohol poisoning, the mean femoral venous blood concentration of ethanol was 3.6 g/L and the 5th and 95th percentiles were 2.2 g/L and 5.0 g/L.[60] The oft-quoted lethal range of BAC of 3.5–4.0 g/L for an uncomplicated alcohol poisoning death is supported by published studies appearing in peer-reviewed journals (see Table 3.3.4). Much might depend on the deceased person's drinking habits with moderate drinkers succumbing at lower BAC than people habituated to alcohol and having a history of alcohol abuse.[63]

The concentrations of ethanol in blood in acute poisoning deaths are lower when an element of asphyxiation and/or vomit in the airways is discovered at autopsy.[64] Table 3.3.4 presents a summary of mean, median, and highest BACs measured in medicolegal autopsies done in Sweden, Finland, Northern Ireland, and the USA. The results are remarkably consistent, regardless of the country, showing a mean blood-ethanol concentration in the range 3.4–3.6 g/L with the vast majority of cases between 2.5 and 5.0 g/L, although there are some notable exceptions. Autopsy BACs in fatal poisonings tend to be higher when ethanol is the only centrally active drug identified in the victim's blood. Ethanol toxicity is enhanced if a person drinks alcohol and medicates with sedative-hypnotic drugs and autopsy BAC is lower in such cases.[64,65]

The complexity of interpreting BAC in coroner cases is illustrated by a review of all fatalities with an autopsy BAC above 3.0 g/L.[66] There were 502 cases attributable to acute ethanol poisoning alone and 24 resulting from well-documented natural causes, 260 were obviously victims of trauma and violence, and the remaining 28 were a combination of high BAC and co-ingested additional drugs.

In a series of 115 alcohol-related deaths, 59% showed some asphyxia element, either postural asphyxia (positional asphyxia) or inhalation of vomit.[61] The PM BAC in alcohol-related deaths with a positional asphyxia element is generally lower than that observed in uncomplicated acute poisoning deaths (mean 3.6 g/L). This makes it important to photograph and document the position of the body at the scene of death and those who discover the body and notify the police authorities. Such things as whether there was evidence of vomiting by the deceased are pertinent because passive regurgitation of gastric contents leads to contamination of the airways and aspiration deaths.

In many alcohol-related deaths, asphyxia is a contributing factor, and the urinary ethanol concentration is usually higher by a factor of 1.3 or 1.4 than the BAC, suggesting death occurred several hours after the last drink during the post-absorptive phase. The victim probably entered a comatose state from a bout of heavy drinking but continued to breathe with blood still circulating through the body organs and tissues.[67] Ethanol continues to be metabolized

TABLE 3.3.4

Subject Demographics and Mean and Median Blood-Alcohol Concentrations (BAC) When the Cause of Death Was Reported as Acute Alcohol Poisoning

Reference	Country	Gender	N cases	Mean age at death	BAC, g/L mean, median, or range
Heatley and Crane[172]	Northern Ireland	Male	144	48 y	3.62
		Female	29	55 y	3.19
Jones and Holmgren[60]	Sweden	Male	529	54 y	3.46
		Female	164	53 y	3.73
Jones et al.[56]	Sweden	Both sexes[1]	976	56 y	3.10
Jones et al.[333]	Sweden	Both sexes[1]	1,585	55 y	3.20
Kriikku and Ojanpera[334]	Finland	Male	9,711	50 y	3.48
		Female	2,415	53 y	3.38
Koski et al.[65]	Finland	Both sexes[2]	615	53 y	3.48
Kaye[335]	USA	Both sexes[1]	94	25–50 y (range)	1.8–6.0 (range)

[1] 88% males. [2] Predominantly males.

until circulation of the blood and breathing ceases, whereas there is no metabolism occurring in the urinary bladder. The autopsy UAC is a reflection of the BAC prevailing during the time that urine was produced in the kidney and secreted into the bladder. This makes it clear that the BAC determined in autopsy blood is not necessarily the highest BAC that the central nervous system was exposed to during life.

The main feature of accidental postural asphyxia is finding the body in a compromising position, such as abnormal neck flexion or limitation of chest movement. A body found slumped in a chair with the head pointing downwards toward the chest, after falling asleep in a state of alcohol intoxication, is typical and in the absence of another explanation, positional asphyxia is a reasonable conclusion as the cause of death.[68] Acute alcohol intoxication is a significant risk factor for this mode of death and 22 of 30 alcohol-related deaths in one study were attributed to positional asphyxia.[69] There is also a high prevalence of alcohol intoxication (30–50%) in sauna-related deaths, hence a hyperthermia state.[70,71]

Finding a high BAC at autopsy verifies excessive drinking and intoxication before death, although it does not necessarily allow drawing conclusions that there were manifest signs and symptoms of clinical drunkenness, especially in habituated individuals and alcoholics.[72–74] The degree of tolerance cannot be diagnosed at autopsy although heavy drinkers learn to cope and function despite high BAC, sometimes at concentrations in the lethal range.[75]

In this connection, it is useful to remember that the autopsy BAC is what you die with, not the level of ethanol that the person's brain was exposed to during a drinking binge.[76,77] Incapacitation caused by binge drinking and near comatose state leads to hampered breathing, although as long as the blood continues to circulate through the liver, BAC decreases through metabolism at a mean rate of 0.15 g/L/h (range 0.10–0.25 g/L/h). Accordingly, if a person survives a drinking binge for eight hours in a comatose state before death, the body eliminates (8 × 0.15) or 1.2 g/L, which should be added to the autopsy BAC to get a better indication about the consumption of ethanol during life.

On balance, a lot of credible evidence leads to the conclusion that an evening's drinking to reach BAC between 3.0–5.0 g/L can lead to a comatose state with shallow breathing, paralysis of the respiratory centers in the brainstem, and a drug-induced asphyxiation death.[78] However, there are exceptions and some people survive high BAC (> 4.0 g/L) with no apparent consequence for their health—as always, lady luck plays a major role in such cases.

3.3.3.3 Surviving Very High Blood-Ethanol Levels

There are anecdotal descriptions of heavy drinkers and alcoholics surviving very high blood-ethanol concentrations, occasionally in excess of 10 g/L.[79] In an Australian study BAC was determined in chronic alcoholics presenting to a detoxification service.[80] Of the 32 subjects, all appeared affected by alcohol to a varying extent; 23 showed altered mood or behavior, six appeared confused, and three were drowsy, but none were in a stupor or comatose. All displayed ataxia and dysarthria of varying degrees. The blood-ethanol concentration ranged from 1.8 to 4.5 g/L with a mean of 3.1 g/L and 26 of the 32 were above 2.5 g/L.

A similar study from Sweden identified 24 patients who attended a hospital casualty department and were found to have blood-ethanol concentrations above 5.0 g/L.[81] Of the 16 patients for whom there was complete data available, eight were either awake or could be aroused by non-painful stimuli. All left the hospital alive within 24 hours. It is suggested that this tolerance to high blood-ethanol levels in chronic alcoholics is primarily the result of neuronal adaptation. Physical dependence on ethanol, as demonstrated by the development of withdrawal signs and symptoms upon stopping drinking, similarly indicates the existence of an adaptation process.

The highest recorded serum ethanol concentration in a living person, albeit after emergency life-saving treatment, was 15.1 g/L.[82] This occurred in a 24-year-old woman with alcohol use disorder who presented to the hospital with abdominal pains. She was agitated and slightly confused but alert, responsive to questioning, and oriented to person and place, though unclear as to time. The serum ethanol concentration of 15.1 g/L corresponds to a calculated BAC of 13.1 g/L (15.1/1.15 = 13.1) assuming a 1.15:1 serum/blood distribution ratio. After intensive care monitoring for 12 h, including intravenous fluids to counteract dehydration and electrolyte replacement as well as anxiolytic drugs, the patient survived and could be discharged from the hospital two days later. In another case report a 52-year-old man (body weight 66 kg) was found unconscious in a bar and a blood sample taken on admission to the hospital had an ethanol concentration of 6.5 g/L.[83] The patient was kept under observation to protect against aspiration of vomit, kept warm, and given occasional oxygen therapy, and made a full recovery.

A 23-year-old female chronic alcoholic weighing 57 kg was admitted to the hospital in a comatose state and her BAC was reported as 7.8 g/L.[84] She had apparently consumed 390 ml of bourbon whisky and was discharged from hospital 11 h later with a blood-ethanol level of 1.9 g/L. Blood samples were taken on several occasions during the treatment and it appears that the decrease in BAC followed a logarithmic function (first-order kinetics). Two additional case reports of abnormally high BAC described more stormy clinical courses but survival after emergency treatment. One of the patients had a serum ethanol concentration of 11.2 g/L,[85] and the other a blood-ethanol level of 15.0 g/L.[86] The elimination of ethanol from blood in this latter case also seemed to follow first-order rather than zero-order kinetics, but the number of blood samples post-absorption phase of the BAC curve was rather limited. A publication from 2016 reported finding a BAC of 8.68 g/L in a non-tolerant female patient, who attempted suicide by drinking massive amounts of alcohol.[87] The patient survived after tracheal intubation, ventilation, and supportive care ensuring the airways were kept clear of vomit. Four blood samples were taken from the patient during intensive care treatment over 22 h and the rate of ethanol elimination from blood was 0.344 g/L/h (zero-order kinetics).

Surviving such unusually high ethanol concentrations in blood or serum is rare and these single cases should not be taken as representative of the BAC causing death by acute alcohol poisoning, which is closer to 3.6 g/L (see earlier sections). Furthermore, it is important to exclude pre-analytical artifacts, such as the use of an ethanol swab to clean the skin before sampling blood, or the use of a clinical laboratory enzymatic methods of analysis, as these are less specific than gas chromatographic methods. There is also a need to distinguish ethanol intoxication from consumption of other toxic alcohols, such as methanol and isopropanol.[88] Cross-reactivity with lactic acid and lactate dehydrogenase has been reported with some enzymatic methods of ethanol analysis.[89,90] Also, the results from analysis of plasma or serum, which are more common in hospital environments, should not be interpreted as blood-ethanol concentrations without the use of a correction factor.[91]

Many drunken drivers are arrested with BAC exceeding 3.6 g/L even though this has already been suggested as sufficient to cause an acute alcohol poisoning death. A retrospective study of traffic offenders arrested in Sweden and the state of Wisconsin (USA) showed that BACs of 4.0 g/L were encountered in some apprehended drivers. Over a 20–30-year period, several hundred such cases were identified and the highest BAC in a person attempting to drive was 5.45 g/L.[92]

Although many of those individuals were unable to walk, speak coherently, or stand unaided, they were not considered sufficiently incapacitated to require life-saving treatment and all survived this drinking binge. After they were allowed to "sleep it off" in police custody for a few hours, many of these drunk-driving suspects were coherent and could be interviewed and were later released from custody, albeit without the keys to their vehicle. People develop an appreciable tolerance to the impairment effects of ethanol, which makes it difficult to interpret the significance of BAC alone when investigating alcohol poisoning deaths.[93]

If an autopsy BAC of 5.0 g/L is taken as a threshold limit necessary for causing a poisoning death it is easy to calculate the quantity of ethanol absorbed and distributed in the body at the time of death. This information is shown in Table 3.3.5 for males and females of different body weights. The results show that a man with a body weight of 70–90 kg would need to drink at least a whole bottle (750 mL) of spirits (40% v/v) to achieve this BAC of 5.0 g/L. These amounts of ethanol should be considered minimum values, because of metabolism occurring in the liver up to the moment of death.

The autopsy BAC is just one element of an alcohol-related death investigation. Another important consideration is the ambient temperature and thermal regulation at the time of death. Deaths occurring outdoors in winter climates are often associated with hypothermia (core body temperature < 35° C) exacerbated by heavy drinking and drunkenness. There is a large body of experimental and clinical evidence in animals and humans, which supports the contention that high BAC and low body temperature exaggerate ethanol toxicity.[94] If a person falls asleep outdoors after an evening of heavy drinking, during winter months, without proper clothing, this increases the risk of a hypothermia-related death. The overall effect of alcohol and high BAC is to lower core body temperature, making it more difficult to generate body heat in response to exposure to very cold environments. Enzyme activity decreases during hypothermia and blood circulation alters to conserve heat, and autopsy BACs in hyperthermia-related deaths are lower than expected.[95]

TABLE 3.3.5

Estimated Amounts of Ethanol (Grams) Absorbed and Distributed in All Body Fluids and Tissues in Relation to Body Weight in Male and Female Deaths with Autopsy Blood-Alcohol Concentration of 5.0 g/L (0.5 g% or 500 mg%)

Body weight, kg	Grams ethanol in body for males, mean (95% range)[1]	Grams ethanol in body for females, mean (95% range)[2]
10	35 (28–41)	30 (24–36)
20	70 (56–84)	60 (48–72)
30	105 (84–126)	90 (72–108)
40	140 (112–168)	120 (96–144)
50	175 (134–216)	150 (120–180)
60	210 (168–252)	180 (144–216)
70	245 (196–294)[3]	210 (168–252)
80	280 (224–336)	240 (192–288)[3]
90	315 (252–378)	270 (216–324)
100	350 (280–420)	300 (240–360)

[1] Average distribution volume of ethanol for males was 0.70 L/kg with a 95% range of ± 20%.

[2] Average distribution volume of ethanol for females was 0.60 L/kg with a 95% range ± 20%.

[3] One bottle of spirits (750 mL 40% v/v ethanol) contains about 240 g ethanol.

The mean BAC in a case series of hypothermia-associated deaths was 1.7 g/L compared with a mean of 3.6 g/L in deaths without any associated hypothermia.[96] Alcohol consumption accelerates the body's heat losses by inducing dilatation of peripheral blood vessels and relaxing smooth muscles, thereby inhibiting shivering thermogenesis. Heat loss is further facilitated by behavioral effects consequent to a feeling of warmth and comfort, and the central nervous system depression effects. At a biochemical level, alcohol ingestion might ameliorate the protective effect of hypothermia-induced ketogenesis, thus shortening the survival time.[97]

Deaths from hypothermia associated with sobriety or a BAC of less than 1.0 g/L have a higher frequency of macroscopic autopsy signs of hypothermia—bright red lividity, violet patches over the knees and elbows, acute gastric mucosa erosions, pancreatitis, and paradoxical undressing. By contrast, cases with a BAC greater than 1.0 g/L, suggesting that intoxication is associated with more rapid death before visible pathological signs develop.

The role of ethanol intoxication in hyperthermia deaths is well illustrated by Finnish sauna fatalities. In a series of 228 hyperthermia deaths (221 sauna-related), alcohol had been consumed in 192 cases and the consumption was categorized as "heavy" in 61 of these fatalities.[71] This high prevalence of alcohol intoxication in sauna deaths (exposure to heat and hyperthermia) has also been verified by more recent studies from Sweden[98] and Korea.[99]

Similarly, complex cerebral dysfunctions induced by alcohol are thought to be significant in the syndrome of sudden, alcohol-associated, craniofacial traumatic death. In this syndrome, people who collapse and die at the scene of an assault are found at autopsy to have facial trauma insufficient to account for the death together with a high but nonlethal BAC.

3.3.4 Disposition and Fate of Ethanol in the Body

After drinking alcoholic beverages, the ethanol they contain is rapidly absorbed from the stomach and intestine to reach the portal venous blood and thereafter distributed to all body fluids and tissues at rates that depend on blood flow rate to tissue mass.[100] Ethanol is a small uncharged molecule at physiological pH, and it does not bind to plasma proteins so easily passes through the blood–brain barrier to interact with various receptor systems and cause impairment of body functions. When absorption is complete ethanol distributes itself in the total body water compartment and the concentrations reached in various fluids and tissues at equilibrium are dependent on their water content.[101] Ethanol is classified as a depressant of the central nervous system and it interacts with various neurotransmitter systems, especially by binding to $GABA_A$ inhibitory receptors, opening its chloride ion channel, and slowing down brain activity.

Deaths from acute ethanol poisoning are attributed to the inhibition of areas of the brain that control breathing, heart rate, and circulation, especially the medulla oblongata (brainstem function). As will be seen later, most acute intoxication deaths occur when BAC is 3.6 g/L or higher. Furthermore, drinking to reach very high BAC depresses the gag reflex such that many people die by choking on vomit (asphyxiation) when they are in a semi-conscious state (aspiration deaths). The autopsy BAC might be a lot lower than 3.6 g/L when aspiration of vomit and suffocation occurs.[64]

The pathways of ethanol metabolism were elucidated during the first half of the 20th century. In 1948 the hepatic enzyme mainly responsible for the oxidative metabolism of ethanol, cytosolic alcohol dehydrogenase (ADH), was isolated and purified from horse liver.[102] Shortly afterwards, human liver ADH was extracted and its kinetic properties and substrate specificity were evaluated. Another important liver enzyme involved in the oxidative metabolism of ethanol is low K_m aldehyde dehydrogenase (ALDH), which is mainly located in the mitochondria.[103] Acetaldehyde is much more toxic and chemically reactive than ethanol and needs to be effectively cleared from the bloodstream by further oxidation to acetic acid. The acetate produced during ethanol oxidation is mainly metabolized in extra-hepatic tissues into carbon dioxide and water.[104]

Figure 3.3.1 shows the pathways of ethanol metabolism in the body indicating that 90–95% of the dose ingested undergoes oxidation first to acetaldehyde and then to acetic acid. Only 2–10% of the amount reaching the bloodstream is excreted unchanged in breath, urine, and sweat. Also shown in the graph are the two non-oxidative metabolites of ethanol, namely ethyl glucuronide (EtG) and ethyl sulfate (EtS), which together account for only 0.1–0.2 % of the amount of ethanol consumed.[105]

Analysis of these phase II metabolites of ethanol has attracted considerable research interest because they exhibit a different pharmacokinetic profile compared with parent drug ethanol.[106]After drinking ethanol (0.50 g/kg body weight), the concentrations of EtG and EtS in blood were about 1,000 times lower than the ethanol concentrations.[107] Both EtG and EtS reach peak concentrations about 1–2 hours later than the ethanol C_{max} and the phase II metabolites are eliminated from the body more slowly.[105] This slower rate of elimination has led to the utilization of EtG and EtS as biomarkers of recent drinking after ethanol has already been cleared from the bloodstream.[108]

The alcohol metabolizing enzymes (ADH and ALDH) show both racial and ethnic differences in their kinetic properties and they are both polymorphic.[103] This is best illustrated by the ALDH enzyme, which is responsible for maintaining very low levels of acetaldehyde from the bloodstream during the oxidation of ethanol. There are two forms of this enzyme denoted ALDH1 and ALDH2, the most important of which is the low Km variant (ALDH2) located in mitochondria.[109] A high proportion of people of East Indian heritage (Japan, China, Korea, and Vietnam) are born with a deficient form of ALDH2, and their ability to oxidize acetaldehyde to acetate is diminished considerably.[110] When these individuals drink excessive amounts of alcohol, they

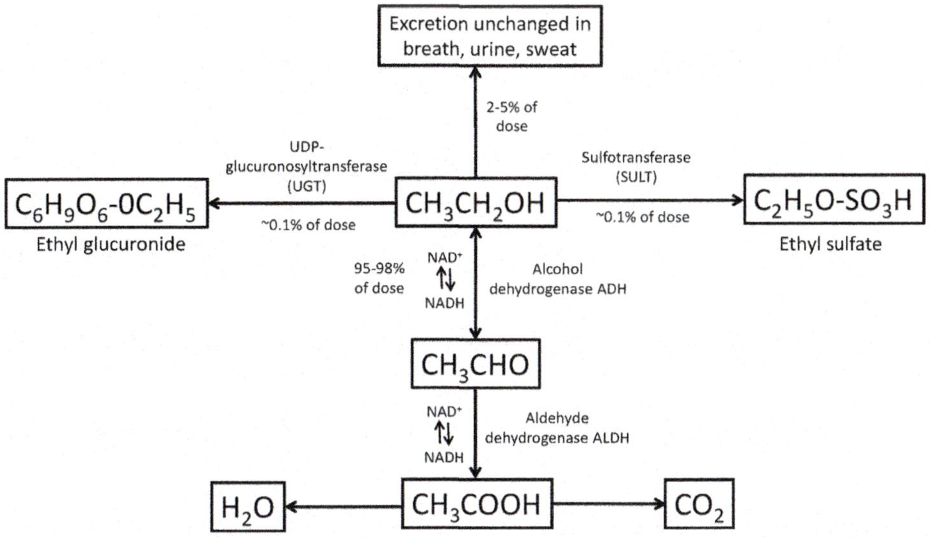

FIGURE 3.3.1 Scheme showing the hepatic metabolism of ethanol, its oxidative metabolites (acetaldehyde and acetic acid), and non-oxidative metabolites (ethyl glucuronide, EtG, and ethyl sulfate, EtS) as well as the percentage of the ethanol dose excreted unchanged in breath, urine, and sweat. Figure from Lin et al.[237] with permission

start to flush in the face and experience a number of unpleasant physiological responses.[111] The prevalence and intensity of the alcohol-flush reaction vary widely within these countries, but an estimated 30–40% of Japanese, Chinese, and other Asian populations have this inherited trait.[112]

Acetaldehyde reacts with β-adrenergic receptors of the autonomic nervous system leading to violent and unpleasant vasomotor responses. Many of those who inherit a defective form of the ALDH enzyme are allergic to ethanol, because of the unpleasant effects caused by the metabolite acetaldehyde, which cannot be converted effectively to acetate. Accordingly, many Asians are genetically prone to react strongly after drinking even very small amounts of ethanol, and are thus equipped with a natural aversion and rarely develop problems with alcohol abuse and alcoholism.[113] An autopsy report describes a fatality in a Japanese subject, who was ALDH2 heterozygote, and this genetic trait meant that abnormally high acetaldehyde concentrations were generated after drinking alcoholic beverages.[114]

3.3.4.1 Adverse Drug-Alcohol Interactions

People taking prescription medication, especially centrally acting drugs like opioids and sedative-hypnotics, should be careful with their consumption of alcohol, owing to the risk of experiencing more pronounced and unexpected pharmacological effects.[115] The ubiquitous use of ethanol in today's society and the increasing poly-pharmacy heighten the risk of people experiencing an adverse drug-alcohol interaction.[116] Some medications are more dangerous than others in this respect, especially sedative-hypnotics such as barbiturates and benzodiazepines when combined with ethanol, and this has resulted in many fatalities.[117] Drug–alcohol interactions need to be considered when autopsy BAC results are interpreted and depending on the types of other drugs identified in the each case.[118] As a general rule, any drug or chemical substance with psychoactive properties, that is, with its site of action in the central nervous system, has the potential for potentiating the effects of ethanol and causing an unexpected death.

There is a well-known pharmacokinetic interaction between ethanol and disulfiram (Antabuse®), an orally active drug widely used in the medical treatment of alcoholics as aversion therapy since the late 1940s.[119] Disulfiram works as an inhibitor of the hepatic enzyme low K_m aldehyde dehydrogenase (ALDH), which converts acetaldehyde into non-toxic acetate.[120] If patients treated with Antabuse also drink alcohol, the ethanol is oxidized in the liver into acetaldehyde by alcohol dehydrogenase (ADH), but because ALDH is blocked by disulfiram, concentrations of the more toxic metabolite acetaldehyde increase in blood and tissues. This triggers a constellation of unpleasant effects including pronounced flushing in the face and neck, hypotension, difficulties in breathing, and feelings of nausea and vomiting, all of which are intended to scare the drinker from continuing to consume alcohol.[121,122]

Treatment with Antabuse® has become known as aversion therapy because the aim was to scare the patient from continuing to drink alcohol when the first adverse effects appear. One problem with this type of pharmacotherapy for alcohol-use disorder is compliance because patients need to take the drug once daily.[123] An alternative approach involved implanting the drug under the skin to improve clinical effectiveness, although this route of administration resulting in highly variable blood concentrations and the desired effect was not achieved.[124] Furthermore, it has been alleged that some alcoholics develop tolerance to the physiological response of the Antabuse–ethanol interaction and therefore continue to drink despite the unpleasant effects. A number of fatalities have been reported after drinking ethanol and taking Antabuse® medication, the first of which was reported in 1952.[125] Another exceptional case reported a low autopsy blood-ethanol concentrations with an acetaldehyde concentrations between 12–41 mg/L.[126]

After eating the edible Inky Cap wild mushroom (*Coprinus atramentarius*) people experienced an Antabuse-like reaction if they drank alcohol with the meal.[127] This fungus contains the chemical substance coprine (N5-1-hydroxycyclopropyl-L-glutamine), which is an amino-acid derivative converted in the body to 1-aminocyclopropanol, which acts as an inhibitor of hepatic ALDH.[128] The inhibition of ALDH generally lasts for about 72 hours but may continue for up to five days, so consumption of ethanol during this period is likely to exert unpleasant effects.

Metronidazole, an antibiotic medication, when used together with ethanol was reputed to cause a dangerous Antabuse-like reaction.[129] Package inserts had warnings on several types of antibiotic medications, advising patients to refrain from drinking alcohol, although the scientific basis for this caution has been questioned.[130] Instead, there might have been an allergic reaction to the drug modified by the presence of elevated blood-ethanol.[131] Other medications reported to interact with ethanol, causing an Antabuse-like reaction, are chlorpropamide and tolbutamide, both of which are prescribed as oral hypoglycemic agents for type II diabetes.

The simultaneous presence of one or more other drugs in autopsy blood in addition to ethanol further complicates making a correct interpretation of whether the BAC was in a toxic range. Investigations into drug–alcohol interactions are complex because they are influenced by the timing of administration of the ethanol relative to the drug and the specific dosages and metabolic pathways involved.[132]

3.3.4.2 Induction of CYP2E1 Enzymes

As well as being oxidized by alcohol dehydrogenase (ADH), ethanol is metabolized to acetaldehyde by a microsomal enzyme, denoted cytochrome P4502E1 (CYP2E1). After chronic heavy drinking, an induction of enzyme protein occurs and the CYP2E1 enzyme has increased activity in reacting with substrates. This has serious clinical consequences because CYP2E1 is involved in the oxidative metabolism of certain organic solvents and therapeutic drugs, which opens the possibility for an adverse drug–alcohol interaction. Alcoholics are more prone to suffer from hepatotoxicity from taking acetaminophen (paracetamol), owing to their more active CYP2E1 detoxification enzymes, which convert acetaminophen into a chemically reactive and toxic intermediate compound, N-acetyl-*p*-benzoquinone imine (NAPQI).[133,134]

The toxicity of the painkiller propoxyphene is enhanced in alcohol abusers and many barbiturates are more dangerous in people who also drink alcohol.[118] Although the mechanism of the interaction with ethanol is not completely understood, it appears to be related to synaptic activity at the $GABA_A$ and opiate receptors with additive effects on the depression of respiration. Sedative-hypnotic drugs, which are widely prescribed, are obvious candidates for interaction with ethanol, owing to the similar mechanism and sites of action in the brain, namely the GABA receptor complex.

Examples of sedative-hypnotic drugs associated with fatalities when combined with ethanol are promazine, doxepin, zopiclone, zolpidem, as well as several benzodiazepines.[117] However, in single case fatalities it has proven difficult to establish an added toxic effect from concurrent use of diazepam with ethanol, and autopsy BAC was about the same with or without the presence of diazepam in blood.[135] Fatalities resulting from co-ingestion of ethanol and barbiturate-like drugs are well recognized and co-ingestion is not an uncommon way to commit suicide.[136]

An interesting interaction occurs when cocaine and ethanol are co-ingested, which leads to the formation of cocaethylene (CE), an equipotent pharmacologically active substance to cocaine.[132] Cocaine has a relatively short plasma elimination half-life of about 1–1.5 so after an acute dose of the concentration of the stimulant is no longer measurable after 5–7.5 h. The main metabolite of cocaine excreted in urine is the inactive substance benzoylecgonine.

However, if a person first consumes alcohol to reach elevated BAC and afterward starts to snort or abuse cocaine, CE is synthesized in the liver by a transesterification metabolic pathway.[137] Like cocaine, CE passes easily across the blood–brain barrier to exert its pharmacological effects via the dopamine receptor, producing more intense and prolonged feelings of euphoria, which might explain why some cocaine users intentionally consume ethanol. Since the elimination half-life of cocaethylene (~2–3 h) is longer than for cocaine (~1 h), the pharmacological effects and "feelings of high" last for longer when people drink ethanol before snorting cocaine.[138]

Both cocaine and CE are powerful stimulants of the central nervous system acting via dopaminergic neurons, leading to hypertension, increased heartbeat, and rising body temperature (hyperthermia), which probably exaggerates the risk for cardiotoxicity. Anecdotal evidence suggests that chronic cocaine users can suffer from excited delirium and drug-induced convulsions. Also, CE is claimed to have greater cardiovascular toxicity compared with cocaine.[132]

3.3.5 Post-Mortem Specimens for Ethanol Analysis

Although the most important biological specimen in PM toxicology is blood, many alternative specimens are available as exemplified by Figure 3.3.2. The preferred specimens for analytical toxicology, especially ethanol determinations, are femoral blood, bladder urine, and vitreous humor.[139] The blood samples should be taken from a vein in the thigh or an iliac vein, before the body is dissected. A chemical preservative such as sodium fluoride (1–2% w/v) is then added and the samples are kept in a refrigerator until analyzed. Depending on the circumstances surrounding the death and the condition of the body, e.g. extent of decomposition, other types of biological specimens should be considered for toxicological analysis, such as hair strands and nails.[140]

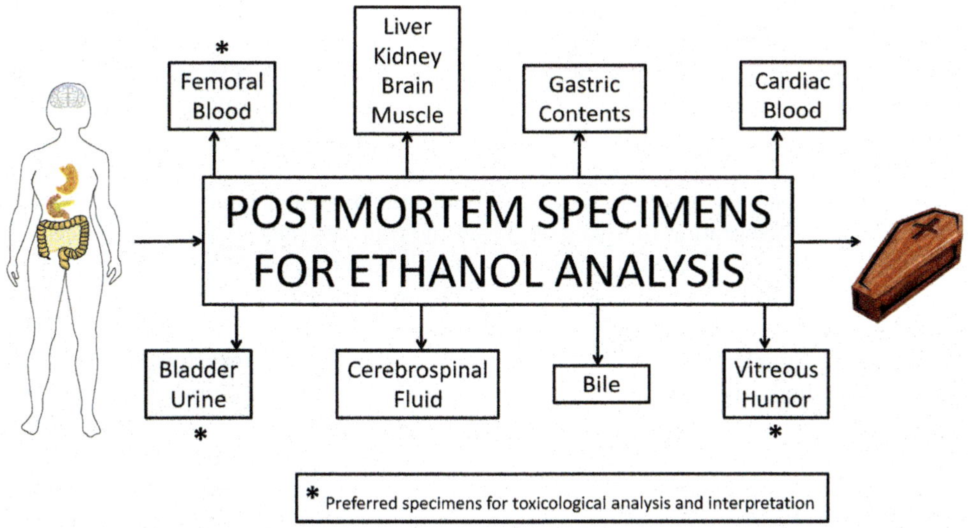

FIGURE 3.3.2 Examples of biological specimens procured for analysis of ethanol in connection with forensic autopsies (medical examiner cases). As indicated, the preferred specimens for the best possible interpretation of ethanol concentrations are femoral blood, bladder urine, and vitreous humor (VH)

3.3.5.1 Vitreous Humor

Vitreous means glassy and humor means fluid, hence VH is the glassy fluid within the globus of the eye, located between the retina and the lens.[141] Specimens of VH can be collected at autopsy using a syringe and 20-gauge needle by insertion into the eye for ~2 cm and the fluid can be gradually withdrawn. Analysis of VH has been widely used in death investigations as a way to determine PM interval (potassium analysis)[142] and whether the deceased suffered from hyperglycemia (glucose analysis) before death.[143,144]

The volume of VH available from each eye is about 4–5 mL and this can be pooled together to increase the volume of specimen for toxicological analysis. A fluoride preservative should be added to VH specimens intended for the determination of ethanol and then stored in a refrigerator pending analysis.

VH is a clear non-cellular liquid composed predominantly of water (97–99%) and also contains small amounts of glucose, lactate, hyaluronic acid, inorganic salts, as well as ascorbic acid.[145,146] VH is an important specimen in postmortem toxicology because of its anatomical remoteness from the gut, where autolysis and the spread of bacteria start.[147] This makes the VH less susceptible to putrefaction changes, which is an important consideration in the case of ethanol determinations. Sampling and analysis of VH are often feasible even in embalmed bodies.[148] Care is needed to ensure that the eyes of a corpse are not contaminated with extraneous liquids, such as alcoholic beverages, or vomiting as part of an agonal event. Care is also needed when vitreous is analyzed from bodies recovered from water (emersion deaths).[149,150]

The concentration of ethanol determined in VH can be used to corroborate or challenge the results of ethanol in PM blood and also help to distinguish microbial synthesis of ethanol from antemortem ingestion.[151] VH can also serve as an alternative specimen when, for some reason, the blood was contaminated, e.g. after embalming. In most cases, the specimen of eye fluid is easily obtained and can be drawn with a syringe and needle without performing a full autopsy. Vitreous humor is a clear, serous fluid that is easy to work with analytically. Its anatomically isolated position protects it from bacterial putrefaction. In microbiological studies of vitreous obtained from 51 cadavers between one and five days post-mortem, it was found that none of the samples contained large numbers of bacteria and only one contained fungi.[152]

The high correlation between ethanol determined in VH and femoral blood is seen from the scatter plot shown in Figure 3.3.3 which represents 134 routine forensic necropsies.[37] The Pearson correlation coefficient was statistically highly significant (r = 0.97), although the residual standard

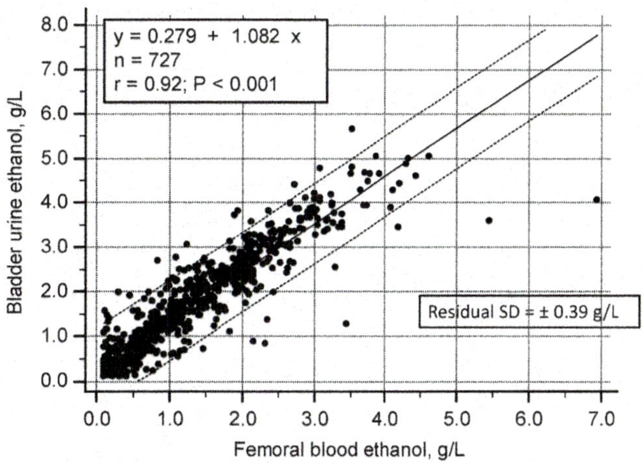

FIGURE 3.3.3 High correlation between concentrations of ethanol determined in femoral blood and in vitreous humor from medicolegal autopsies performed in Sweden

deviation was appreciable (± 0.216 g/L). This large scatter of data points around the regression line would lead to large uncertainty in individual cases if autopsy BAC was estimated indirectly from the concentration determined in VH.

The predictive value of analyzing VH to estimate BAC in a single case remains contentious, despite many studies of this relationship in large case series. As a rough guideline, dividing the VH ethanol concentration by two would be very unlikely to overestimate the coexisting autopsy BAC. The need to estimate BAC sometimes arises in special cases, such as road-traffic deaths or workplace accidents, when a suitable blood sample is not available for analysis.[153] A number of methods have been suggested, including the use of a simple mean conversion factor (VH/BAC ratio) to calculate BAC from VH, but this fails to consider the uncertainty in such a prediction an individual cases, so least squares regression analysis is the preferred statistical method.

In one case series simple linear regression was applied with BAC as outcome y-variable and VH as predictor x-variable (range 0.01–7.05 g/L).[154] The regression equation was BAC = 0.03 + 0.852 VHAC with a residual standard deviation of 0.26 g/L The formula below allows calculating the 95% prediction interval of BAC as derived from a given VH concentration.

$$\pm 0.00019\sqrt{\left[7157272+\left(\text{VH}-1.897\right)^2\right]}.$$

The results of BAC calculations using the regression equation and assuming certain VH concentrations of ethanol are shown in Table 3.36. The mean values and 95% or 99% prediction intervals are also displayed in the table, which suggests that the prediction interval is probably too wide to be of much practical use in forensic cases in reference to a statutory BAC.

From the viewpoint of medicolegal casework, it seems unreasonable to estimate BAC from the concentration determined in VH without also providing a 95% prediction interval. Data from another large study comparing BAC with vitreous ethanol was used to construct a Bland and Altman plot, which allowed calculating the mean difference (bias) between results along with a 95% prediction interval and confidence limits on the upper and lower level.[155]

Compared with VH, which is 98–99% water, fresh autopsy blood contains between 75–80% water, so the mean VH/blood ratio is expected to be greater than unity (1.0). In cases when the HH/BAC ratio is 1.1 to 1.2, this indicates diffusion equilibration of ethanol had occurred at the time of death.[156] Animal models have indicated that after intraperitoneal or intravenous injection of ethanol, the BAC/VH ratios may be greater than 0.95 for 30 minutes or longer.[157,158]

In 43 fatalities, investigators found a bimodal distribution of blood/VH ratios of ethanol: the first mode was between 0.72–0.90 and a positively skewed distribution from 0.94–1.37.[159] It seems that the first mode represents the post-absorptive elimination phase of the blood alcohol curve and the second mode the absorption phase prior to equilibrium in all body fluids and tissues.

This bimodal distribution was confirmed in a second study of 86 autopsies and blood/VH ratios greater than 0.95 were considered indicative of deaths occurring prior to complete equilibration of ethanol and therefore death not long after the last drink was finished.[160] The mean blood/VH vitreous ratio in this early phase was 1.09 (SD = 0.38) compared to a mean of 0.80 (SD = 0.09) in late absorptive and elimination phases. Not all investigators have confirmed the existence of a bimodal distribution, perhaps depending on how many deaths occurred in the absorption phase of the BAC curve.[161]

Other evidence, such as by comparison of UAC and BAC ratios, give strong support for alcohol-related deaths happening when people are already in the post-absorptive phase. Very likely, the proportion of absorptive phase deaths in published studies has varied considerably, which explains why not all investigators have identified a bimodal distribution.

It seems reasonable to expect ethanol to diffuse into or out of the vitreous fluid post-mortem. The chemical constituents of embalming fluid may diffuse into the vitreous humor after a body has been embalmed. Fortunately, almost all commercial embalming fluids are free of ethyl alcohol, although they commonly contain methanol. A comparison

TABLE 3.3.6

Estimation of the Blood-Alcohol Concentration (BAC) from Analysis of Vitreous Humor Showing Mean Concentration as Well as 95% and 99% Prediction Intervals

Vitreous humor ethanol, g/L	Estimated mean BAC, g/L	95% prediction interval, g/L	99% prediction interval, g/L
0.90	0.80	0.29–1.31	0.13–1.47
1.50	1.31	0.80–1.82	0.64–1.98
1.69	1.47	0.96–1.98	0.80–2.14
1.73	1.50	1.00–2.01	0.83–2.17
2.32	2.01	1.50–2.51	1.34–2.68
2.51	2.17	1.66–2.68	1.50–2.84

Note: BAC was derived from a linear regression equation; BAC = 0.03 + 0.852 VH and residual standard deviation was 0.026 g/L.[154]

of ethanol concentrations in 38 corpses both pre- and post-embalming suggested that there was no significant change in the vitreous humor ethanol concentration in the immediate aftermath of embalming.[162] However, in one case the embalmer cleaned the globus of the eye with ethanol on a cotton swab prior to placing an eye cap into position and this caused an elevation of vitreous ethanol from 0 to 3.4 g/L. In another fatality, an unusually high VH ethanol was attributed to prolonged post-mortem exposure of the eye surface to alcohol-containing vomit.[163]

Bodies recovered from water complicate the interpretation of autopsy BAC results, owing to the risk of dilution of the specimens and losses of ethanol by diffusion. Conversely, prolonged submersion of a body in water may result in the diffusion of alcohol out of the vitreous.[149] This was the proposed explanation for finding a zero ethanol concentration in vitreous but concentrations of 3.70 g/L in urine and 2.23 g/L in blood (blood acetone 0.46 g/L) in a man submerged in cold fresh water for about six weeks. In a rabbit model which duplicated these circumstances, the vitreous ethanol level fell from a mean of 1.96 g/L to 0.30 g/L over the six-week period.[164]

Several comprehensive reviews have dealt with the advantages and limitations of VH as a biological specimen for the analysis of drugs in PM toxicology.[165,166] VH can be used for both screening analysis[167] and a wide range of xenobiotics.[168] In summary VH is an ideal biological specimen for the determination of ethanol, and has been in use since 1966.[169] Thanks to its remote anatomical location it is less prone to be infiltrated with bacteria spreading from the abdomen when a body decomposes and hence carries less risk of PM synthesis of ethanol.

3.3.5.2 Bladder Urine

Urine can be considered an ultra-filtrate of the plasma and is a watery fluid (~95–99% water) secreted by the kidneys and stored in the bladder before there is an urge to void, which usually occurs after a volume of ~300 mL has accumulated. The normal production rate of urine varies widely, but on average is about 1.0 ml/min, although during periods of diuresis this rate could increase to ~10 mL/min or more. Most drugs and/or their metabolites are secreted into the urine, including ethanol and ethyl glucuronide. Because the urine secreted by healthy individuals contains only trace amounts of glucose, this makes bladder urine a useful specimen for the determination of ethanol and helps to distinguish PM synthesis by fermentation processes from antemortem alcohol ingestion.[170]

The ureteral urine, which is the urine before it enters the bladder, is expected to have a roughly 20% higher ethanol concentration than the blood (UAC/BAC = 1.2), owing to its greater water content. In most investigations, the urine sample obtained is pooled bladder urine, which has accumulated over an unknown time interval between last urination and death. Consequently, the bladder urine alcohol concentration does not necessarily reflect the blood-alcohol concentration existing at the time of death. Instead, it reflects the average BAC prevailing during the period that urine accumulates in the bladder since it was last emptied.

Nevertheless, the bladder urine and femoral blood concentrations of ethanol are highly correlated as shown by the scatter plot in Figure 3.3.4 representing 727 autopsy cases.[37] The Pearson correlation coefficient was high ($r = 0.92$, $p < 0.001$), although the residual standard deviation, a measure of the scatter of the data points around the regression line, was ± 0.39 g/L, making predictions in individual cases prone to large errors.

Several studies have examined the range of ratios between BAC and pooled bladder UAC at autopsy. One study reported an average UAC/BAC ratio of 1.28:1 with a wide range of 0.21 to 2.66.[171] In another study the mean UAC:BAC ratio was 1.21:1 with a range from 0.22 to 2.07 when a direct-injection GC analytical method was used compared with a mean ratio of 1.16:1 with a range of 0.20 to 2.10 with the more widely used headspace GC technique.[172]

In a large case series, simple linear regression analysis with BAC as the outcome variable and UAC as the predictor variable (n = 435, range 0.03 to 5.87 g/L) gave the regression equation BAC = −0.056 + 0.811 UAC.[173] The 95% prediction interval around the regression line can be calculated from the following equation;

$$\pm 0.00026\sqrt{\left[9465804 + (\text{UAC} - 2.132)^2\right]}.$$

This equation also indicates that a UAC of 2.04 g/L is necessary to predict a BAC of 0.8 g/L with 95% confidence. Similarly, a BAC of 1.50 g/L is predicted by a UAC of 2.91 g/L. Because the prediction intervals are so wide, the calculations have limited utility in predicting the unknown BAC in individual cases, such as in connection with driving under the influence of alcohol.

Although it would not be advisable to convert the autopsy UAC into the coexisting antemortem BAC, the UAC gives a good reflection of the BAC existing during the time the

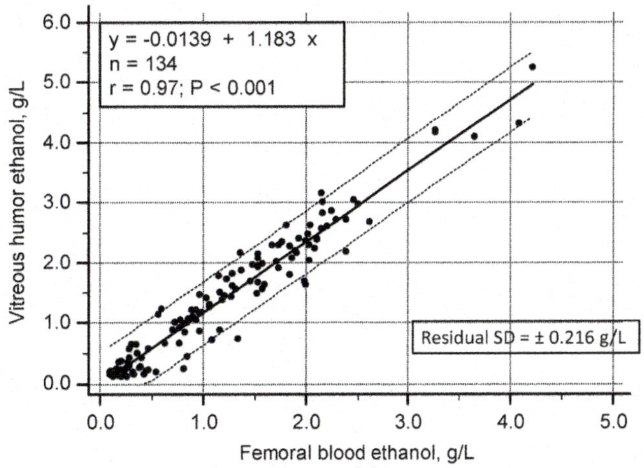

FIGURE 3.3.4 High correlation between concentrations of ethanol determined in femoral blood and in bladder urine from medicolegal autopsies performed in Sweden

urine was being produced in the kidney and stored in the bladder. By dividing the measured autopsy UAC by 1.35 (or multiplying by 0.74) gives an estimate of the expected BAC. However, if the BAC curve was rising, which might be the case if death occurred soon after drinking ended, the calculation UAC/1.35 underestimates the co-existing BAC.

When both urine and blood specimens are available at autopsy, calculating the UAC/BAC ratio provides a useful way to judge the state of alcohol absorption and elimination in the body at the time of death.[174,175] Finding a ratio less than unity or not more about 1.1–1.2 suggests, but does not prove, recent drinking before death and the existence of a rising BAC. If the UAC/BAC ratio exceeds 1.3 this is strongly indicative of the existence of the post-absorptive stage of the BAC curve at the time of death. UAC/BAC ratios higher than 1.4–1.5:1 at autopsy mean that the drinking ended several hours before death, such as if a person was asleep, unconscious, or comatose before circulatory and respiratory functions terminated. In many PM investigations, ethanol is elevated in the urine but reported as being not detected in blood (below method LOQ of 0.1–0.2 g/L).[67] In delayed traumatic deaths, post-mortem urine ethanol concentrations may help establish or exclude the role played by alcohol consumption. A urine ethanol content of 2.0 g/L seems possible with no alcohol present in the blood.

The UAC:BAC ratio in 628 deaths from acute ethanol poisoning was 1.18 (SD = 0.182) and in 647 chronic alcoholic deaths the UAC/BAC ratio was 1.30 (SD = 0.29), suggesting that the former group died typically before complete absorption and distribution of alcohol in the body, while the latter group died typically after complete absorption and distribution.[176]

However, evidence that a person had been drinking alcohol immediately prior to death is more easily achieved by obtaining a sample of stomach contents at autopsy and measuring the ethanol concentration. A gastric contents concentration < 5.0 g/L has been taken to indicate a post-absorptive state. Autopsy cases with abnormally high UAC/BAC ratios indicate that longer periods of time have elapsed before death and urine volumes accumulated in the bladder are likely to be higher than normal in such cases. In delayed deaths from acute alcohol poisoning, it is useful to measure and report the total volume of urine contained in the bladder.[177]

The practical usefulness of UAC in PM toxicology is not so much as a way to estimate BAC, but as an alternative specimen to compare with BAC when there were long PM intervals and decomposition had occurred. Normal urine secreted by healthy individuals does not contain any glucose so there is no available substrate for PM synthesis of ethanol.[178] However, the urine from people with diabetes mellitus might be loaded with sugar and urinary tract infections or candidiasis, means that there is a definite risk of PM synthesis of ethanol by fermentation.[179,180]

3.3.5.3 Alternative Biological Samples

All biological specimens containing water will also contain ethanol if a person has consumed alcoholic beverages before their demise. Many studies have correlated ethanol concentrations in blood with concentrations in alternative specimen types in addition to urine and VH already discussed. Examples of alternative specimens include bile, cerebrospinal fluid, brain, liver, kidney, bone marrow, and skeletal muscle. The mean concentration of ethanol in blood derived from analysis of one of these other specimens can be predicted, and the limits of uncertainty on the results obtained calculated by statistical methods. However, verification of ethanol in several different specimen types strengthens the conclusion that the deceased had consumed alcohol before death and whether the concentration was sufficient to have caused death.

Since ethanol distribution in the body follows the distribution of water, the relative ethanol content of these unconventional specimens is predictable from a knowledge of body water distribution. Whenever necessary, water content is easy to determine by desiccation. Cerebrospinal fluid is 98–99% water w/w and therefore generally will have a higher ethanol content than blood, whereas muscle, brain, liver, and kidney, with a water content of 75–78% w/w, will have lower concentrations of alcohol than blood. Moreover, the continuing post-mortem enzymatic activity within the liver and kidneys may reduce their ethanol content.

For blood alcohol levels greater than 0.40 g/L the average liver/heart BAC ratio in 103 cases was 0.56, SD 0.30, with a range of 0–1.40.[181] However, the liver is not recommended as a suitable sample for post-mortem ethanol analysis because it is rapidly invaded by gut micro-organisms and provides abundant glycogen as a substrate for ethanol production by fermentation, as well as being subject to post-mortem diffusion from gastric residue.

3.3.5.3.1 Brain Tissue

The human brain is located and protected within the skull and weighs about 1.3–1.4 kg in adults. Because the impairment effects of ethanol on body functioning depend on drug concentrations reaching the brain and interfering with neurotransmission and binding to receptors, it would seem logical to take sections of the brain tissue at autopsy for toxicological analysis. However, this is not standard practice for two reasons. First, the analysis of post-mortem blood is more helpful since it allows comparison with data available from living persons. Second, the brain is extremely heterogeneous and ethanol is not distributed evenly within different brain regions and can vary two- to three-fold. The highest concentrations are found in the cerebellum and pituitary and the lowest concentrations in the medulla and pons.

GC methods of analysis have been described for ethanol determinations in brain tissue.[182] Specimens obtained from the frontal lobe (n = 33 showed a range of BAC from 0.72–3.88 g/L) with an average brain/blood ratio of 0.86 and 95% range from 0.64–1.20.[140] Part of this large variation might be relayed to cerebral edema, an accumulation of excessive fluid and hence variable water contents, also known as swelling of the brain or wet-brain.

The analysis of drugs in brain tissue is undergoing a renaissance judging by a series of articles from forensic toxicologists in Copenhagen.[183,184] In a long series of articles they have compared blood and brain concentrations of many different drugs both medicinal substances[185] and recreational drugs of abuse.[186] However, they have not yet investigated the brain/blood distribution ratio of ethanol.

3.3.5.3.2 Sequestered Hematomas

That ethanol might be measured in sequestered hematomas was first suggested by Hirsch and Adelson,[187] although they claimed no originality, explaining that it is one of the "tricks of the trade." This type of specimen is most commonly applied in cases of death from head trauma with subdural or epidural hematomas, but also to intracerebral clots.[188–192] Although primarily used for ethanol analysis, any toxicant might be measured in the hematoma. From the accumulated PM case data, it becomes evident that the concentrations of ethanol in subdural hematomas may be markedly different from autopsy peripheral blood.

In interpreting the significance of the results, several possibilities should be considered. The hematoma may have developed rapidly at the time of injury; alternatively, it may have been delayed and not developed for some hours, or it may have evolved over a period of time as the result of continuous or intermittent bleeding. If the hematoma accumulates over a period of hours then its ethanol content will reflect a changing blood-ethanol concentration during that time. Furthermore, the hematoma might not be perfectly sequestered and ethanol is then diffused both out of it and into it. The possibility of ethanol being produced in the blood clot after death also needs consideration.[188]

In cases of head trauma associated with subdural or extradural hematomas and with a prolonged survival time, the autopsy blood-ethanol concentration may be very low or even zero (< 0.1 g/L) whereas the concentration in the hematoma blood is appreciably higher. This is an indication that the deceased may have been intoxicated at the time of injury. In a study of 75 cases in which ethanol was measured in subdural hematomas and cardiac blood, the analysis provided useful new information only in those cases with survival times greater than nine hours, since it was these cases in which the blood ethanol had diminished markedly or was metabolized completely.[188]

In another case series consisting of 15 fatalities from penetrating and non-penetrating head injuries, there was an antemortem blood-ethanol measurement available.[190] Findings in non-penetrating injuries (Table 3.3.7) and penetrating injuries were similar in that the concentrations of ethanol in intracranial hematomas did not accurately reflect circulating blood concentrations at the time of injury. Therefore, caution is needed when making quantitative interpretations from ethanol levels in hematomas.

After suffering trauma, the development of an intracranial hemorrhage, either subdural or intracerebral, may be delayed. If the victim was intoxicated at the time of injury then this delay may be sufficient to allow clearance of ethanol from the bloodstream through metabolism. The intracranial hematoma will then contain no ethanol despite the history of injury when intoxicated. This apparent conflict between the history of the circumstances of the injury and the absence of ethanol in the hematoma has been used to provide corroboration that the development of the hematoma was a delayed event.[189] Animal models, using rabbits, support the use of subdural hematomas for analysis of ethanol in PM toxicology.[193]

3.3.5.3.3 Bile

Bile is the greenish-yellow fluid produced in the liver and stored in the gall bladder, a pear-shaped organ lying just underneath the liver. Bile is released into the duodenum to aid in the digestion of lipids (fats) and to facilitate the absorption of nutrients from the small intestine into the portal venous blood. A suitable specimen can be aspirated directly from the gall bladder and transferred to a suitable container, fluoride preservative added, and submitted for toxicological analysis.

Several recent review articles have dealt with the use of bile as an alternative specimen in PM toxicology for analysis of a wide range of xenobiotics.[166,194,195] This seems to

TABLE 3.3.7
Blood-Alcohol Concentration (BAC) in Victims of Skull Trauma on Admission to Hospital (Antemortem Sample), and at Post-Mortem as Determined in Subdural Hematoma (SDH)[190]

Time (trauma to sampling blood), h	Time (sampling blood to death), h	BAC, g/L before death	BAC, g/L after death	Ethanol in SDH, g/L
1	21	5.35	< 0.1 (negative)	1.7
3	7	4.86	1.3	1.9
5	8.5	1.83	< 0.1 (negative)	0.9
3	41	1.61	< 0.1 (negative)	0.4
1.5	4.5	1.64	0.70 (negative)	1.1
2	18	0.93	< 0.1 (negative)	1.2
1	25.5	2.40	< 0.1 (negative)	1.1
1	58	1.02	< 0.1 (negative)	0.4

BAC under 0.10 g/L reported as negative.
SDH = subdural hematoma

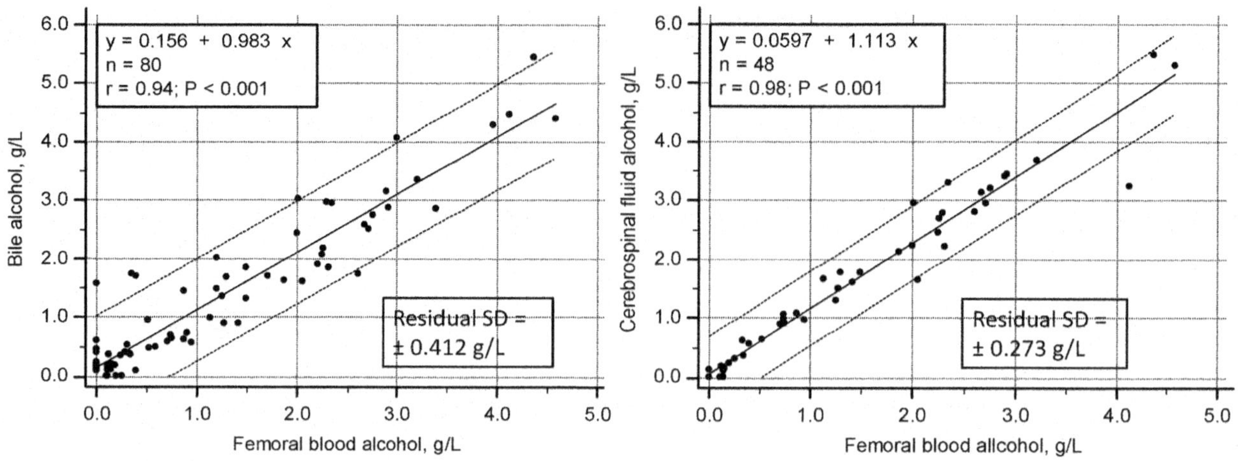

FIGURE 3.3.5 High correlations between the concentrations of ethanol determined in femoral blood and bile (left graph) and femoral blood and cerebrospinal fluid (right graph) from medicolegal autopsies in Sweden

extend the window of detection compared with blood and urine specimens because drugs and metabolites are detectable in bile while the levels in blood and urine are below LOQ of the analytical methods. Figure 3.3.5 shows scatter plots depicting the high correlations between ethanol content of bile and CSF compared with femoral venous blood.

For bile, in 89 cases with blood ethanol ranging from 0.46–6.97 g/L the bile/blood ratio averaged 0.99, range 0.48–2.04.[196] Bile was suggested as being superior to vitreous humor as an alternative specimen to corroboration BAC in PM toxicology but, unfortunately, bile is more vulnerable to post-mortem diffusion of unabsorbed alcohol from the stomach.[30]

3.3.5.3.4 Cerebrospinal Fluid

Another biological specimen sometimes taken at necropsy for toxicological analysis is cerebrospinal fluid (CSF), the clear watery liquid that surrounds the brain and spinal cord. In adults the volume of CSF is between 60–300 mL and is often required for analysis in various neurological disorders. The clean nature of CSF and its protection from the spread of bacteria after death makes it a useful fluid for the analysis of ethanol and other drugs in forensic toxicology.[197,198]

In living subjects, lumbar CSF is the specimen taken, whereas at post-mortem the CSF is drawn from the cisterna magnum while the deceased is placed in a prone position with a block under the chest. The pharmacokinetics of ethanol in lumbar fluid has been studied in men and the concentrations show a time-lag compared with BAC.[199] The maximum concentration in CSF appears later and is likely to be higher than the simultaneous BAC, owing to its higher water content.

For cerebrospinal fluid (n = 54, blood-ethanol range 0.46–6.97 g/L) the average ratio was 1.14 and range 0.79–1.64.[140]

3.3.5.3.5 Stomach Contents

Opinions differ as to the concentrations of ethanol that are measurable in the stomach contents at various times post-mortem in typical cases. In one series, the highest ethanol concentration reported was 29.5 g/L (2.95%) and the author quoted a similar high of 50 g/L (5%) in a previous study.[200] In another series of alcohol-related deaths only one of 60 cases had a concentration as high as 51 g/L (5.1%).[201] In a small study the highest concentration observed was 87 g/L (8.7%) and this was in a suicidal hanging.[18] Because alcohol is also rapidly absorbed from the stomach, in cases with high ethanol concentrations in gastric contents this must indicate that death occurred within about an hour or less after substantial amounts of alcohol were consumed.

Researchers in the 1940s and 1950s debated the suitability of using heart blood for ethanol analysis on the grounds of possible artifactual elevation resulting from post-mortem diffusion of alcohol that might have been present in the stomach at the time of death.[15–17,202,203] Later investigations, done mainly by pathologists in Australia, verified the possibility for ethanol to diffuse from the stomach into the pericardial sac and left pleural cavity after death, although the cardiac chambers were less susceptible to this PM artifact.[200, 204–207] More recent case studies, including a human cadaver model, showed that even blood from cardiac chambers, aorta, and other torso blood samples may be significantly affected by gastric diffusion artifact.[18]

In 307 cadavers without significant decomposition, BAC was determined in samples from the right atrium, ascending aorta, and the inferior vena cava in cases when BAC was always greater than 0.5 g/L.[208] In 104 cases (33.9%), there was one blood sample with a concentration 20% lower than the highest concentration. The most striking differences were seen when gastric ethanol concentrations were above 8.0 g/L and with associated evidence of aspiration.

In a second cadaver study blood was obtained from the femoral vein, the aortic root, and the right atrium in 60 cases with blood-ethanol concentrations of 0.5 g/L or greater and no gross trauma or significant decomposition.[201] Although the mean alcohol concentrations for the different blood sampling sites were not significantly different, there were wide variations in ethanol concentration among the blood sample sites in the individual cases. Twenty of the cases (33.3%) had within-case BAC differences greater than 25%; four had differences greater than 50%, and one case it exceeded 400%. Indeed, three of the four latter cases had gastric alcohol concentrations between 10 and 51 g/L and the fourth had a concentration between 5 and 10 g/L, whereas, for the 60 cases as a whole, 22 were between 5 and 10 g/L and 11 were above 10 g/L.

In a third study of nine fatalities with known alcohol consumption shortly before death, two showed marked variations in BAC in samples from ten sites, ranging from 0.97 to 2.38 g/L and 2.78 to 13.95 g/L; pericardial fluid 10.6 g/L and 6.86 g/L; vitreous humor 0.34 and 2.25 g/L; and stomach contents 300 ml at 55 g/L and 85 ml at 19 g/L respectively.[18] These studies suggest that post-mortem diffusion of alcohol from the stomach into the blood may be a significant factor under some circumstances, although an uncommon problem when femoral blood is used for analysis.

The above findings were corroborated by a human cadaver model involving multiple site sampling of blood after introducing 400 ml of an alcohol solution (5%, 10%, 20%, or 40% weight/volume in water) into the stomach by esophageal tube.[18] The pattern of ethanol diffusion showed marked between-case variability but typically the concentrations were highest in pericardial fluid and, in decreasing order, in the left pulmonary vein, aorta, left heart, pulmonary artery, superior vena cava, inferior vena cava, right heart, right pulmonary vein, and femoral vein. Diffusional flux was broadly proportional to the concentration of ethanol administered and was time-dependent (as determined by 24-hour and 48-hour sampling), and was markedly inhibited by refrigeration of the corpse at 4° C.

After gastric instillation of 400 ml of 5% ethanol for 48 hours at room temperature in paired cadavers, the concentrations (g/L) were as follows; pericardial fluid 1.35, 2.22, aorta 0.50, 0.68; left heart 0.77, 0.26, right heart 0.41, 0.28, femoral vein 0.0, 0.0. With a 10% solution of ethanol in the stomach, concentrations (g/L) were: pericardial fluid 4.01, 2.55; aorta 1.29, 1.34; left heart 0.61, 0.93; right heart 0.31, 0.41; femoral vein 0.05, 0.07. The much higher concentrations of alcohol determined in the pericardial fluid emphasize the potential for serious contamination of any blood sample allowed to pool in the pericardial sac. Introducing 50 ml of 10% w/v ethanol solution into the esophagus after ligation of the esophageal gastric junction produced similar aortic blood-ethanol concentrations to those seen after gastric instillation. This suggests that post-mortem gastroesophageal reflux and diffusion from the esophagus is one mechanism for artifactual elevation of aortic blood-ethanol levels.

Post-mortem relaxation of the gastro-esophageal sphincter permits passive regurgitation of gastric contents into the esophagus, if position of the body and the volume of gastric contents permit this to happen. Furthermore, manipulation of the body during removal and transport might easily lead to contamination of the airways by gastric material, simulating agonal aspiration of vomitus. Alcohol in this gastric material could then diffuse from the airways into the blood. An experimental study demonstrated that a relatively small amount of ethanol introduced into the trachea of cadavers was readily absorbed into cardiac blood and also that there was direct diffusion from the trachea into both the aorta and superior vena cava.[31]

3.3.6 Stability of Ethanol in PM Blood

Alcohol loss from body tissues and fluids may occur post-mortem as a result of evaporation, shifts in the water content of tissues, enzymatic breakdown, and bacterial degradation. Following the death of an individual, many of the cells of the body survive for a variable time, providing the window of opportunity for tissue and organ transplantation from non-beating-heart donors. During this period of cellular life following somatic death, cellular enzymatic activity continues, ethanol is metabolized, and ethanol concentrations may fall slightly. Later bacterial invasion of tissues may result in further ethanol loss from bacterial degradation of ethanol. Ethanol is both utilized and produced by microorganisms, so that bodies with high initial levels may show a decrease, and bodies with low initial levels may show an increase.[35] However, in practice it is the ethanol produced by bacteria that represents the principal effect, as demonstrated in an animal (rat) model and the administration of deuterium-labeled ethanol.[209,210]

The information in Table 3.3.8 gives an example of the short-term stability of ethanol in PM blood samples that were analyzed on arrival at the laboratory and again after 8–10 days of storage in a refrigerator at 4° C. On each occasion, duplicate determinations were made by HS-GC-FID and excellent agreement was obtained indicating high analytical precision. The mean BAC at the time of the first analysis was 1.70 g/L, which decreased to a mean of 1.66 g/L on re-analysis 8–10 days later.

Stability of ethanol was also investigated in blood and VH specimens stored frozen for 12 months.[211] Femoral blood was taken at autopsy (N = 16), treated with potassium fluoride (1–2%) and BAC determined on arrival at the laboratory and initial storage at +4° C pending analysis a few days later. The mean and range of BAC by HS-GC-FID analysis was 1.75 g/L (range 0.4–3.6 g/L). After 12 months of storage at –20° C, the specimens were allowed to thaw, and then re-analyzed by HS-GC-FID. The mean and range of concentration were now 1.61 g/L and 0.2–3.4 g/L, showing a significant loss during storage when tested statistically by Student's t-test.

The storage stability of ethanol in 79 post-mortem blood specimens with fluoride preservative was investigated by an HS-GC-FID method 1–4 days after sampling. The same blood specimens were then re-analyzed after storage at –20° C for between 191 to 468 days. The results before and after storage were highly correlated and the mean decrease in BAC was –10%, hence if the starting concentration was 1.0 g/L the result after storage was 0.90 g/L (0.1 g/L ethanol loss).[212]

TABLE 3.3.8
Short-Term Stability of the Concentration of Ethanol in Femoral Blood Determined By HS-GC-FID before and after Storage for 8–10 Days at 4° C (Jones, Unpublished Work)

Post-mortem case number	BAC on arrival, g/L[1]	Days of storage at 4° C	BAC after re-analysis, g/L[1]
A-957	0.86	10	0.85
	0.86		0.88
A-958	1.74	10	1.72
	1.69		1.73
A-961	1.10	10	1.12
	1.10		1.14
A-945	3.30	10	3.30
	3.34		3.54
A-996	2.85	10	2.91
	2.81		2.93
A-1021	1.88	9	1.89
	1.89		1.88
A-1037	0.22	8	0.21
	0.22		0.21
A-1046	0.70	8	0.65
	0.70		0.65
A-1059	0.26	8	0.26
	0.24		0.25
A-1056	2.63	8	2.51
	2.62		2.54
A-1074	2.68	8	2.41
	2.69		2.43
A-1075	0.92	8	0.82
	0.93		0.86
A-1076	2.95	8	2.84
	2.99		2.80
A-1086	1.69	8	1.57
	1.69		1.60
Mean (median)	1.70 (1.69)	14 cases	1.66 (1.66)

[1] Duplicate determinations on aliquots of femoral blood containing 1–2% potassium fluoride as a chemical preservative and stored in a refrigerator at 4° C.

Overall, the available experimental evidence indicates that ethanol is fairly stable in PM blood for at least 7–10 days after sampling, provided a fluoride preservative is included. For longer storage periods the blood samples should be frozen at –20° C and then the loss of ethanol is likely to be 10–15% after 12 months of storage.

3.3.7 Microbial Synthesis of Ethanol

Judging whether the ethanol determined in PM blood reflects ingestion of alcoholic beverages before death or was produced in the body after death by fermentation processes is a common problem. Ethanol formation may occur in blood putrefying in a cadaver or in blood putrefying in-vitro in the collection tubes sent for toxicological analysis.[213] It appears that ethanol is not formed post-mortem except by microbial action, because post-mortem autolysis of germ-free mice produces low levels of acetone and acetaldehyde but not ethanol.[214] By contrast, putrefying conventional mice produced significant amounts of ethanol, propionic acid, isopropyl alcohol, and *n*-propyl alcohol.

Ethanol production in corpses takes place by a pathway opposite to that of ethanol catabolism in the living body.[215] The necessary alcohol dehydrogenase (ADH) and acetaldehyde dehydrogenase (ALDH) enzymes are provided by the micro-organisms associated with putrefaction, whereas the carbohydrate substrates (e.g. glucose) are present in blood and tissues. The level of tissue glycogen available for post-mortem glycolysis and subsequent microbial ethanol production varies considerably between tissues. A human liver contains about 1–8 g glycogen/100 g wet tissue; skeletal muscle 1–4 g/100 g; brains from a variety of animals 70–130 mg/100 g; and retina (ox) 90 mg/100 g (all figures calculated from dry weight assuming 75% water).[216] Anaerobic glycolysis produces pyruvate, the main substrate for ethanol production.

Besides glucose, lactate is also a source of pyruvate through the action of lactate dehydrogenase. Since lactate is found in relatively high concentrations in all post-mortem tissues (about 1.5–6.5 g/kg), it may well be an important source of ethanol.[209] A study in-vitro with putrefying post-mortem blood under anaerobic conditions at room temperature demonstrated that ethanol formation occurred not only by way of glycolysis but also from lactate via conversion into pyruvate. There is also evidence that ethanol might be produced by bacterial catabolism of amino acids and fatty acids.[217]

Large numbers of bacteria escape from the gut during autolysis, in the first instance via the lymphatics and portal venous system, within a few hours after death. At room temperature, bacterial contamination of the systemic circulation occurs after about six hours, and after 24 hours there is direct bacterial penetration of the intestinal wall. Generally, the tissues remain relatively free of viable bacteria during the first 24 hours. Trauma immediately prior to death, intestinal lesions and neoplastic disease, generalized infection, and gangrene are all conditions associated with the early spread of bacteria post-mortem.

In a living person, ethanol was produced by gut bacteria present in the infected intra-peritoneal fluid associated with peritonitis after a fatal stabbing.[218] A wide variety of bacteria normally present in the gut and responsible for putrefaction can generate ethanol in blood, brain, liver, and other tissues.[219] Yeasts such as *Candida albicans* can also ferment glucose into ethanol, hence the need to add sodium or potassium fluoride to the blood and urine specimens as enzyme inhibitors.[220]

Candida overgrowth in the gut in the living may cause intra-gastrointestinal alcohol fermentation syndrome, a rare condition originally described in Japan where a high proportion of the population lacks an effective enzyme for the metabolism of acetaldehyde.[221] Candida colonization of the gut, stagnation of food, and a high-carbohydrate (rice) diet allows fermentation to produce sufficient alcohol to cause intoxication to the point of illness, with a BAC of 2.54 g/L reported in one case.[222]

There is increasing evidence that in rare circumstances intoxicating concentrations of ethanol are generated within the body without consumption of alcohol and this is referred to as "auto-brewery syndrome."[222] Several recent examples of patients becoming drunk by endogenous ethanol production and single cases are described in the literature, although its prevalence in different societies is unknown.[223–225]

3.3.7.1 Extent of the Problem

If blood glucose is accepted as the primary source of fermentable carbohydrate, then a normal blood glucose level of 1.0 g/L could theoretically produce ~0.50 g/L ethanol and the liberation of carbon dioxide in the process. However, in death investigations, blood-glucose levels might be appreciably higher, such as in patients with poorly controlled diabetes that suffer from hyperglycemia at the time of death.[226] Taken together, there is plenty of fermentable substrate available for the biosynthesis of ethanol by micro-organisms, bacteria, and yeasts.

Several reports suggest that ethanol concentrations in blood of 0.5–0.6 g/L can be determined in decomposed bodies when there is no evidence to suggest exposure to alcohol before death. In individual cases, the PM concentration might reach 1.50 g/L when putrefaction is in advanced stages, such as when the body is kept at elevated temperatures for a few days.[227] In a study of 130 decomposing bodies, there were 23 with presumed post-mortem ethanol production. Of these, 19 had ethanol concentrations of 0.7 g/L or less and the other four had levels of 1.1, 1.2, 1.3, and 2.2 g/L. Since both bacterial growth and enzyme activity are temperature-dependent, it is reasonable to assume that post-mortem production of ethanol is inhibited during refrigeration.

For example, a series of 26 in-hospital deaths refrigerated within one hour of death and stored at 6° C for three to 27 hours before autopsy showed no evidence of any post-mortem ethanol production despite positive blood cultures in 13 cases, and seven cases had elevated blood glucose levels. The use of a chemical inhibitor of bacterial growth, such as sodium fluoride (1–2%), prevents the production of ethanol in post-mortem specimens. Storage of the specimens in a refrigerator at 4° C or deep-frozen also prevents PM synthesis of ethanol.

Table 3.3.9 summarizes the results of a study by Hanzlick[228] who classified autopsy BAC levels in relation to the stage of decomposition of the body. The results indicated

TABLE 3.3.9

Prevalence of Ethanol-Positive Cases and Median Blood-Alcohol Concentration (BAC) in Relation to the Condition of the Corpse in Terms of the Stage of Decomposition[228,229]

Condition of the body	Number of cases	Ethanol-positive cases, N (%)	Median BAC, g/L	Cases (N) and % with BAC > 2.0 g/L
No obvious PM changes	3042	553 (18%)	1.25	150 (27%)
Early changes in color of the body	150	63 (42%)	0.68	8 (13%)
Evidence of bloating and blisters	88	69 (78%)	0.76	14 (20%)
Advanced PM changes, putrefaction	28	24 (86%)	0.71	2 (8%)
All cases with some PM change	266	156 (59%)	0.70	24 (15%)

that the percentage of ethanol-positive cases increased (42–86%) as decomposition and putrefaction became more advanced. However, the median BAC remained fairly constant (0.68–0.71 g/L). Note that some of these ethanol-positive cases probably reflect antemortem ingestion of ethanol, because many of the deceased had a history of alcohol abuse and bottles of liquor were discovered at the death scene. The article concluded that PM synthesis was a valid consideration, but that it was rare to encounter BAC greater than 0.70 g/L from microbial activity.[229]

Another fairly recent study of the BAC produced in decomposed bodies originated from Germany and the investigators concluded it was rare to find concentrations about 0.60 g/L as a PM artifact.[230] Ethanol was determined in blood from a femoral vein in 290 forensic cases when the PM interval varied from a few days to several weeks. As a control group, there were 197 corpses without any signs of putrefaction. The number of cases with BAC between 0.1 and 1.0 g/L increased with the degree of putrefaction. The mean BAC-associated putrefaction was 0.62 g/L, but in isolated cases as much as 3.0 g/L was observed. Other alcohols, such as 1-butanol and 1-propanol, were sometimes detected in the blood samples, at concentration > 0.02 g/L, which was suggested as a cut-off level for ethanol production after death.

Circumstances that might promote post-mortem synthesis of ethanol include prolonged exposure to a high environmental temperature, terminal hyperglycemia, death from infectious disease with septicemia, and death from natural diseases such as ischemia affecting the large bowel, abdominal trauma, and severe trauma with wound contamination. Disruption of the body to an extent commonly seen in aviation disasters helps to promote microbial contamination of body organs and tissues, thus making it more likely that ethanol is produced in the body after death.

In a series of 975 victims of fatal aircraft accidents, the blood-alcohol concentration exceeded 0.4 g/L in 79 cases, and of these, it was considered based on ethanol distribution in urine, vitreous humor, and blood that 27% represented post-mortem production and 28% ingestion but 45% were unresolved.[231] In such traumatic deaths, blood concentrations as high as 3.0 g/L might be synthesized post-mortem. When an explosion occurred in a gun turret on the ship USS *Iowa* there were 47 sailors killed and no evidence that they had consumed alcohol. The highest ethanol concentration in blood attributed to post-mortem fermentation was 1.9 g/L, although whether a fluoride preservative was present or not was not clearly established.[232]

3.3.7.2 Biomarkers of PM Synthesis of Ethanol

In determining whether an elevated BAC at autopsy represents post-mortem synthesis of ethanol or consumption of ethanol before death, considerable assistance is obtained from corroborative analyses of ethanol in vitreous humor and urine.[37] Although vitreous contains glucose and lactate, both substrates for bacterial production of ethanol, the eye socket is remote from the gut and thus less susceptible to the spread of bacteria during putrefactive processes. Urine is also useful as a specimen for analysis because in healthy individuals it does not contain sugar, the main substrate for bacterial conversion to ethanol.[178] An exception occurs if the urine is collected from diabetics, who might not have been medicating properly before death because under these circumstances the urine might be loaded with sugar (glucose), which is readily fermented to ethanol and carbon dioxide.[233]

The problem of bacterial formation of ethanol was the subject of a comprehensive review and the information the article contained remains valid still today.[35] If an autopsy is performed within about 24 hours after death and especially if the body is refrigerated, then there is little risk or opportunity for PM synthesis of ethanol. Starting at about 2–3 days after death, the putrefactive phase starts although this time varies considerably depending on environmental conditions, primarily temperature and humidity. During the putrefaction period, when a sample of vitreous humor is still obtainable, the presence of ethanol in VH is the best evidence of ethanol ingestion antemortem. The presence of ethanol in the urine is also a good indicator of ethanol ingestion before death, provided the deceased did not suffer from diabetes (type I and II) or another metabolic disorder than leads to urinary secretion of glucose and glycosuria.[233]

Once decomposition has progressed so that the vitreous is no longer available, due to collapse of the eyeballs, and blood cannot be obtained because the blood vessels are filled with putrefactive gases, then no reliance can be placed upon any sample and interpretation of analytical results is hazardous if not impossible. In these cases, anamnestic data may be more reliable than analytical data. In around 20% of decomposed bodies, the presence of ethanol is probably derived from endogenous sources as judged by its absence from vitreous humor and/or urine. But in many cases with low concentrations, the endogenous production cannot be distinguished from antemortem ingestion. Post-mortem synthesis of ethanol in over 95% of cases did not exceed 1.5 g/L, but this general observation does not assist in evaluating higher levels in an individual case under special circumstances. PM synthesis of ethanol is not unique to blood samples and might occur in the bile, and this is especially marked in the sanguineous putrefactive fluid which accumulates in the pleural cavities.

The importance of measuring ethanol concurrently in vitreous, urine, and blood samples was demonstrated in the assessment of low post-mortem blood alcohol concentrations. A series of 381 cases with autopsy BAC less than 0.5 g/L were evaluated using the presence of ethanol in the vitreous and/or urine as indicators of antemortem ingestion rather than post-mortem production.[105] When the BAC was 0.1–0.19 g/L the investigators found that 54% of cases had positive vitreous or urine ethanol concentrations (greater than 0.1 g/L); when the BAC was 0.2–0.29 g/L this percentage increased to 63%; when the BAC was 0.3–0.39 g/L the percentage was 73% and when the BAC was 0.4–0.49 g/L, 92% of the cases had an alternative specimen positive for ethanol. Of the 165 cases where both vitreous and urine were available, over 90% demonstrated consistent results, however, in 14 cases there was inconsistency with one specimen positive and the other negative.

Bacterial production of ethanol by fermentation is also associated with generating small amounts of other organic volatiles, such as methyl alcohol, isoamyl alcohol, formaldehyde, *n*-propyl alcohol, isopropyl alcohol, propionic acid, acetone, acetic acid, acetaldehyde, *n*-butanol, sec-butanol, t-butanol, n-butyric acid, and isobutyric acid.[234] Of these the butyric acids considered most prevalent as indicators of PM synthesis of ethanol. Others have advocated the notion of measuring *n*-propanol and *n*-butanol in blood as biomarkers of microbial fermentation.[235,236] However, variability in metabolic pathways between micro-organisms leads to variability in the final products of glucose fermentation.[25] Furthermore, the concentrations of *n*-propanol produced are appreciably lower than the concentrations of ethanol, and quantitative relationships such as the ethanol/*n*-propanol ratio are not easy to determine. This limits the potential usefulness of measuring and analyzing these other low-molecular alcohols to distinguish between antemortem ingestion and post-mortem production.

A variety of approaches are available to assist practitioners in evaluating the source of ethanol in PM blood and this was the subject of a recent review.[237] The major enzymatic pathway for disposal of ethanol is oxidative metabolism with Class I isozymes of alcohol dehydrogenase (ADH) to produce acetaldehyde and this toxic metabolite is oxidized further by aldehyde dehydrogenase (ALDH) to acetic acid (see Figure 3.3.1). But a small amount of ingested ethanol (< 1%) undergoes non-oxidative metabolism by three different reaction mechanisms.[238] Like many drug molecules with hydroxyl groups, ethanol is conjugated by liver enzymes to produce glucuronide (EtG) and sulfate (EtS) metabolites.[239] These are specific metabolites of ethanol, they are not generated by microbial activity and are therefore useful in clinical and forensic toxicology as biomarkers of ethanol consumption. Moreover, EtG and EtS can be determined in many types of biological specimens, including hair and nails[240] by accurate, precision, and specific analytical methods utilizing liquid chromatography-mass spectrometry methods.[241]

Two other biomarkers of ethanol consumption are phosphatidyl ethanol (PEth)[242] and fatty acid ethyl esters, both of which are produced after a period of continuous heavy drinking.[243] These non-oxidative metabolites are measurable in blood and tissues and are excreted in urine with half-lives longer than ethanol itself. Finding these non-oxidative metabolites, e.g. in urine taken at autopsy, is a strong indication that the deceased had consumed alcohol sometime before death. The utility of these markers and their advantages and disadvantages in PM toxicology compared with EtG remains to be established.[244,245]

Another biochemical approach to identify the source of ethanol is the metabolic interaction between ethanol and serotonin (see Figure 3.3.6).[246] Under normal circumstances, serotonin (5-hydroxytryptamine) undergoes oxidative deamination to produce 5-hydroxyindolealdehyde (5-HIALD). This short-lived intermediate is mainly oxidized to 5-hydroxyindoleacetic acid (5-HIAA) and at the same time, a very small fraction (~1%) is reduced to

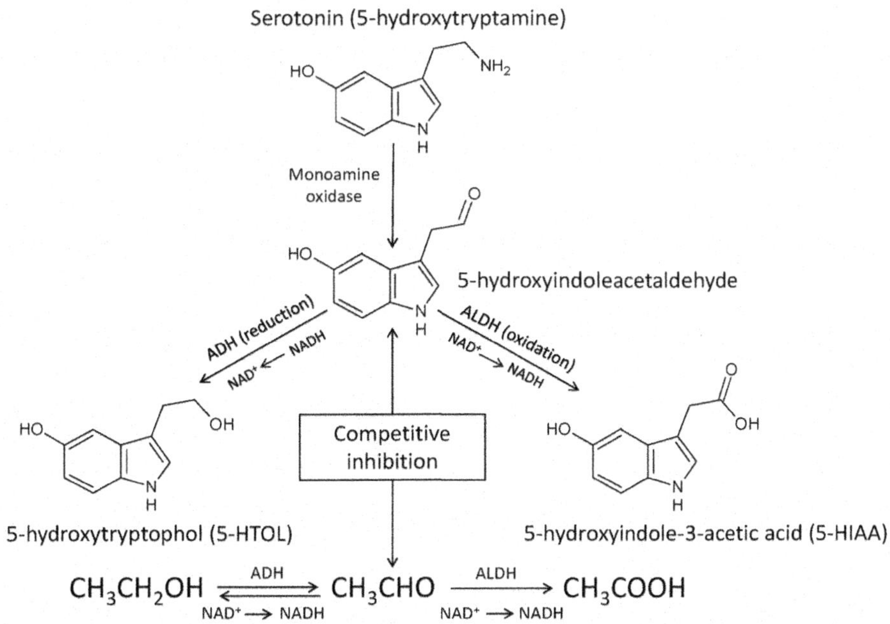

FIGURE 3.3.6 Metabolism of 5-hydroxytryptamine (5-HT, serotonin) to an intermediate aldehyde by monoamine oxidase, and further conversion of the aldehyde to a predominant oxidative metabolite 5-hydroxyindoleacetic acid (5-HIAA) and reduction to a minor alcohol metabolite 5-hydroxytryptophol (5-HTOL). After consumption of ethanol, there is a shift in the metabolism of 5-HT towards the alcohol metabolite (5-HTOL), and the urinary concentration ratio 5-HTOL/5-HIAA increases appreciably. Figure taken from Lin et al.[237] with permission

5-hydroxytryptophol (5-HTOL). Accordingly, carboxylic acid (5-HIAA) is the predominant metabolite and the 5HTOL/5-HIAA ratio in urine is normally very low (< 15 nmol/μmol). However, after a person drinks ethanol, which is oxidized to acetaldehyde, the 5-HTOL/5-HIAA ratio increases appreciably, owing to competitive inhibition for ALDH, which is now engaged in the metabolism of acetaldehyde to acetic acid. Measuring the 5-HTOL/5-HIAA ratio in urine has therefore found applications in clinical medicine to disclose consumption of alcohol e.g. in alcohol and drug abusers who must refrain from drinking as part of their treatment. The ratio of serotonin metabolites can also be used to differentiate between antemortem ingestion of ethanol and post-mortem microbial synthesis.

Finding an elevated concentration of ethanol in urine when the 5-HTOL/5-HIAA ratio was less than 15 nmol/μmol strongly suggests that ethanol was produced by microbial synthesis after death.[247] However, the question of whether ethanol was partly produced by microbial synthesis and partly by antemortem ingestion cannot be resolved by these laboratory biochemical methods.[248]

During alcoholic fermentation processes, besides the production of ethanol and carbon dioxide other low-molecular-weight alcohols are also produced, such as *n*-propanol and *n*-butanol.[249] Accordingly, if there is a measurable response on the HC-GC-FID chromatogram at the retention times of *n*-propanol and/or *n*-butanol, this is an indication that some of the ethanol was produced post-mortem. The concentrations of these other alcohols are about 20 times less than for ethanol produced by the fermentation of glucose.[236] Attempts have been made to define a threshold concentration of *n*-propanol for use as a biomarker of PM ethanol synthesis.[235]

3.3.7.3 Differentiating the Source of Ethanol in PM Blood

The prevalence of alcohol abuse and alcoholism in the forensic autopsy population varies between jurisdictions but might be as much as 10% or more, especially in male decedents. Clues from poor hygiene to multiple bruises of different ages are more common in chronic alcoholics than in the general forensic autopsy population and should raise a suspicion of alcohol involvement in the death. The traditional method of diagnosing chronic alcoholism post-mortem is from BAC and liver histology in the light of the available medical history of the deceased. Finding measurable amounts of ethanol in PM blood merely indicates that the deceased had been drinking prior to death and almost half of all alcoholics die with a zero BAC. Furthermore, the pathological features of alcoholic liver disease are relatively non-specific and liver pathology in many alcoholics is no worse than in the general forensic autopsy population. Furthermore, NAFLD is a growing problem in society along with obesity.[250,251]

The spectrum of alcoholic liver disease includes a combination of hepatomegaly, steatosis with or without lipogranulomas, alcoholic hepatitis, and cirrhosis.[252] This complete spectrum, including alcoholic-type hepatitis, can be perfectly mimicked by a few non-alcohol-related conditions, such as obesity with or without dieting, undergoing a jejuno-ileal bypass for obesity, diabetes mellitus, and drug toxicity. Hepatic steatosis is the most common form of alcoholic liver disease observed at necropsy, and fatty liver is not unusual after the amounts of alcohol consumed by many social drinkers.

Following the withdrawal of alcohol, the mobilization of this accumulated fat begins after a few days and is complete in four to six weeks even in severe cases. While hepatic steatosis is potentially reversible, alcoholic hepatitis is considered to represent the point of no return, because once this stage is reached the disorder tends to progress to liver cirrhosis. Even so, a person with alcoholic hepatitis may be symptom-free and able to function normally. In general, there is not always a good correlation between symptoms and morphological findings in alcoholic hepatitis.

Histologically, alcoholic hepatitis is characterized by liver cell necrosis with a predominantly neutrophil polymorph reaction and peri-cellular fibrosis. The hepatitis is mainly centrilobular in distribution and classically associated with the presence of Mallory's hyaline. More than half of all cases of cirrhosis coming to autopsy are the result of alcohol abuse, which implicates ethanol and excessive drinking as a predominant risk factor. The classical alcoholic cirrhosis is micronodular and fatty, but this is not necessarily the case and still evolves into macronodular cirrhosis. Heavy drinkers who also ingest other drugs are at risk of developing drug-related hepatotoxicity, in particular, late acetaminophen (paracetamol) toxicity from excessive, but not suicidal, doses of this antipyretic drug.

The search for a corroborative post-mortem biochemical marker for chronic alcoholism has taken as a starting point those clinical studies on the value of biochemical markers of alcoholism in the living. The serum enzyme γ-glutamyltransferase (GGT) is one of the most frequently used clinical markers and has a reported sensitivity of 39–87% but a specificity of only 11–50%.[253] This low specificity is accounted for by interferences from various hepatic and other diseases, as well as drug therapy. At autopsy, the difficulties are magnified because GGT is subject to significant post-mortem changes. GGT levels in right heart blood may be 2–8 times greater than in femoral venous blood owing to post-mortem diffusion of GGT from the liver. Furthermore, post-mortem hemolysis interferes with some quantitative enzymatic GGT methods.

A more widely used biomarker of alcohol use and abuse is carbohydrate-deficient transferrin (CDT), which in clinical studies has shown to have a sensitivity of 83–90% and specificity of 99%.[254] Abnormal CDT occurs after daily excessive drinking in amounts corresponding to about one bottle of wine (50–80 g ethanol), perhaps somewhat smaller amounts of females compared to male drinkers.[255] The utility of CDT to diagnose problem drinking was assessed in an autopsy study where the sensitivity was 70% and the specificity was 85%, although it was necessary to use a higher analytical cut-off level compared with that accepted and used in clinical practice.[256] This suggests that both CDT and GGT are likely to be subject to post-mortem changes and more studies are needed to evaluate the stability of alcohol biomarkers after death.[257]

Since the last edition of the *DAH*, a range of newer alcohol biomarkers have been developed and these are reviewed elsewhere.[258] One PM study compared the analysis of ethyl glucuronide (EtG) in hair strands with phosphatidyl ethanol (PEth) in a case series of alcohol-related deaths.[259] Another PM study compared analysis of CDT and EtG in blood, VH, and CSF in the deceased having a history of alcohol abuse, as indicated by a review of their medical and police records.[260] The results indicated that the analysis of EtG in urine or vitreous humor gives the best diagnostic accuracy in predicting excessive drinking.

3.3.8 Alcoholic Ketoacidosis Deaths

Ketoacidosis is the term used to describe metabolic acidosis associated with excess ketone bodies in the blood.[261] The commonest cause of this condition is untreated type I diabetes, although elevated levels of ketones are also produced during starvation (starvation ketosis) and in connection with binge-drinking and negligible food intake during the withdrawal period (alcoholic ketoacidosis).[262–264]

Sudden death in a chronic alcoholic with subsequent negative autopsy is not an unusual observation in routine medicolegal examinations. The autopsy results have only the stigmata of alcoholism, such as a fatty liver, and the BAC is inconsequential, often low (< 0.2 g/L) or negative. The exact mechanism of such deaths remains obscure, and recently the syndrome of alcoholic ketoacidosis was proposed as a possible cause of death.[265–268] Clinical case reports pertaining to alcoholic ketoacidosis (AKA) are scant, and probably belie the true frequency of the syndrome, but typically AKA is a relatively benign condition and only fatal when associated with some other disease process.

Fatty liver is a common finding in clinical practice and at autopsy.[269] It is most commonly seen associated with alcohol abuse and in non-alcoholic fatty liver disease (NAFLD). Fatty liver has been associated with sudden death and this topic and its medicolegal significance were recently reviewed.[270]

Figure 3.3.7 shows a flow chart depicting the combination of food deprivation during a drinking binge and inhibition of gluconeogenesis, which are key elements in precipitating the AKA syndrome. During a drinking binge, the person often neglects to eat properly, because they obtain calories from the metabolism of ethanol. During hepatic metabolism of ethanol to acetaldehyde and acetic acid, the $NADH/NAD^+$ ratio is elevated, which results in inhibition of gluconeogenesis, and glycogen stores are depleted. When the consumption of alcohol ends, ethanol continues to be metabolized, although by about 12–24 hours post-drinking BAC eventually reaches zero, depending on individual rates of metabolism. During this initial withdrawal period, the person is anxious, stressed, and dehydrated and might be experiencing nausea and vomiting. These combined physiological influences trigger the catabolism of fatty acids (lipolysis) as a source of energy, and the production of ketone bodies, acetone, acetoacetate (AcAc), and β-hydroxybutyric acid (BHB) in excess. An abnormally high concentration of BHB in blood is the main cause of metabolic acidosis and a lowering of the pH.

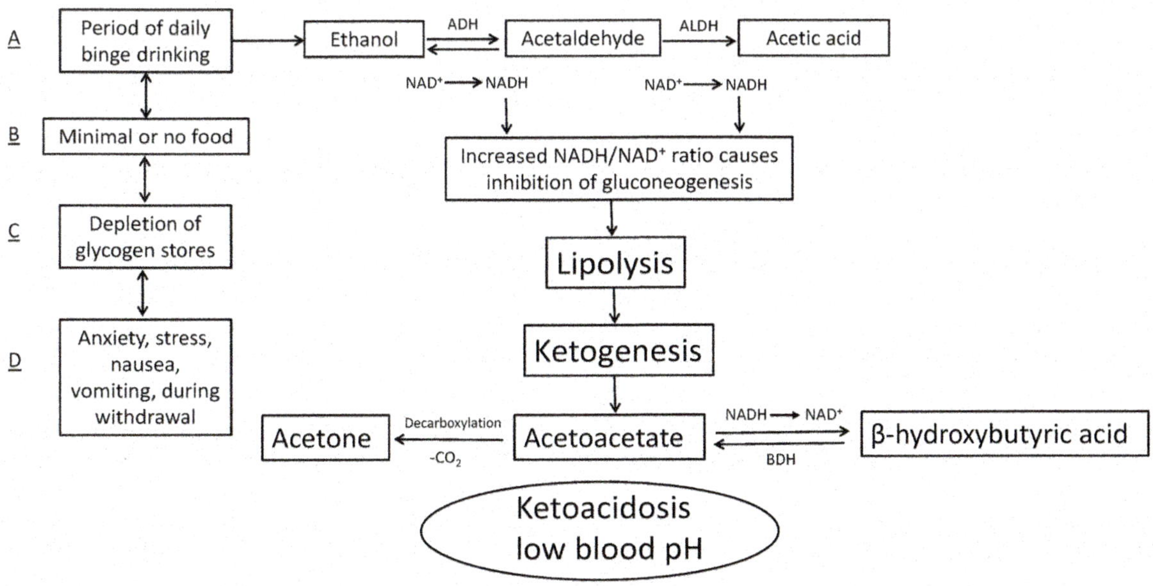

FIGURE 3.3.7 Factors influencing the development of a state of alcoholic ketoacidosis (AKA) after a period of continuous heavy drinking, food deprivation, anxiety, stress, nausea, and vomiting. Depletion of glycogen stores and the inhibition of gluconeogenesis by elevated NADH triggers lipolysis and production of ketone bodies in excess (acetone, acetoacetate, and β-hydroxybutyrate [BHB]) and a dangerous state of metabolic acidosis

The typical clinical picture in AKA is the combined influences of an alcohol debauch terminated by anorexia, cessation of food and alcohol intake, and finally, a variable period of hyperemesis. In most cases, at the time of a dangerous AKA there is no measurable BAC, but elevated concentrations of acetone and BHB in specimens of blood and urine. The common symptoms of nausea, vomiting, and abdominal pains are accompanied by few objective physical findings and the person's mental status is usually normal or only slightly impaired, but with an altered level of consciousness and occasionally a comatose state until death ensues.

Although the pathophysiology of AKA is complex, it seems that the most important variable is insulin deficiency, owing to starvation with consequent hepatic glycogen depletion and ethanol-induced inhibition of gluconeogenesis, and there is depletion of extra-cellular fluid volume via α-adrenergic inhibition of insulin secretion. Individuals with higher insulin levels would likely present with the syndrome of alcohol-induced hypoglycemia without ketoacidosis.

Extremely high free fatty acid levels in blood, ranging from 1,800 to 3,800 μEq/L have been a consistent finding in clinical cases of alcoholic ketoacidosis. Beta-oxidation of these fatty acids generates acetyl-CoA, which is the precursor of the two other ketone bodies. Two critical enzymes in the ketogenesis pathway are located in liver mitochondria only, so the liver is the anatomical site for biosynthesis of ketone bodies. Acetone is produced by decarboxylation of AcAc in a non-enzymatic reaction. The AcAc is also converted to BHB in a reaction catalyzed by β-hydroxybutyrate dehydrogenase and the two are in equilibrium.

Extrahepatic tissues can convert BHB back into AcAc and utilize both ketone bodies as respiratory substrates to provide energy to the brain when blood-glucose is low and insufficient. For convenience, the term "ketone bodies" refers to acetone, acetoacetate, and BHB. While this terminology is convenient considering the three are metabolically related, it is inaccurate because it excludes other biologically important ketones, e.g. pyruvate. BHB does not have a ketone structure, although is a component of ketone metabolism and in equilibrium with AcAc., However, the risk of post-mortem conversion of AcAc to acetone is not known so it is advisable to measure all three ketone bodies and add the concentrations together to give the total ketone body level. The analysis of acetone in blood was suggested as a biomarker before attention was directed to BHB, because this requires a separate analysis and acetone is determined along with ethanol by gas chromatography; the two ketone bodies are correlated.[271]

The biochemical hallmark of AKA is ketoacidosis without marked hyperglycemia, while by contrast diabetic ketoacidosis is defined by the triad of hyperglycemia, acidosis, and ketosis.[272] In AKA the ratio of serum BHB to acetoacetate, which is normally 1:1, increases to between 2:1 and 9:1, a ratio higher than that generally found in diabetic ketoacidosis.[273] The clinical diagnosis of AKA is hampered because the nitroprusside test (Acetest) for ketones in the urine is sensitive to acetoacetate but not to BHB.[274]

In fasting subjects, the concentration of acetoacetate in plasma might range up to 0.23 mmol/L, and that of BHB up to 0.65 mmol/L. In comparison, in AKA the corresponding concentrations of acetoacetate were as much as 7.5 mmol/L and BHB up to 20.5 mmol/L.[275] In one autopsy study of ketoacidosis deaths, total ketones in 71 non-alcoholics were: vitreous 0.19–3.35 mmol/L (median 0.49); pericardial fluid 0.02–1.54 mmol/L (median 0.35); and femoral blood 0.23–8.08 mmol/L (median 1.00).[267] The higher levels of ketone bodies found in this autopsy case series probably reflect deaths from chronic disease or prolonged agonal periods. Among 22 alcoholics, 18 had ketone levels not statistically different from non-alcoholics, but there were four cases with femoral blood total ketone levels of 129.9 mmol/L (also diabetic), 39.4 mmol/L (no anatomical cause of death), 38.5 mmol/L (suicidal hanging), and 18.6 mmol/L (hypothermia), suggesting that while alcoholic ketoacidosis may be a previously overlooked potential cause of death, interpretation requires cautious and made within the total case context. This is in keeping with the clinical consensus that AKA is fatal only when associated with some other illness.

Research on AKA-related deaths still continues, although it remains uncertain whether this condition alone is sufficient to account for the fatality. But elevated concentrations of ketones (> 10 mmol/L in femoral blood and > 5 mmol/L in vitreous) are indicative of profound AKA and might be expected in ~10% of alcoholics who are subjected to a forensic autopsy.[276] Both vitreous and pericardial fluid levels of acetone and other ketones are lower than concentrations in post-mortem blood, possibly because they are less influenced by agonal events or post-mortem changes.

A paper from 2020 reported 496 autopsy cases positive for BHB and these fatalities were subdivided into different causes of death.[277] The quantitative analysis of BHB was considered crucial for making a correct diagnosis of ketoacidosis death and the following results were reported:

- Cases of death due to diabetic ketoacidosis (DKA, n = 54) had the highest levels of BHB (median 1,085 mg/L) and acetone (median 330 mg/L).
- Cases of death due to alcoholic ketoacidosis (AKA, n = 57) had high levels of BHB (median 500 mg/L) and acetone (median 110 mg/L).
- Cases of death due to hypothermia (n = 12) had similar BHB and acetone levels as the AKA group (median BHB 520 mg/L and acetone 80 mg/L).
- Cases of death due to isopropanol intoxication (n = 17) had high levels of isopropanol (median 430 mg/L) and acetone (330 mg/L), but undetected or low levels of BHB.
- Cases used as controls with other causes of death than the above (n = 349) had a median BHB of 100 mg/L and median acetone of 20 mg/L.

VH is a very useful biological specimen in PM toxicology not only for analysis of ethanol and other drugs but also endogenous substances including ketone bodies, especially acetone and BHB[278] as well as other metabolites.[279]

Large case series have been reported comparing BHB in VH and in blood in 453 cadavers classified as diabetic and non-diabetic.[280] Higher BHB concentrations were observed in VH from the deaths in people clinically diagnosed as being diabetic. In another retrospective study of 1,785 forensic cases, further support for analysis of BHB in VH was obtained. Concentrations of BHB < 0.4 mmol/L were normal; 0.41–1.2 mmol/L considered slightly elevated, 1.21–2.0 mmol/L moderately elevated, and 2.01–6.0 mmol/L significantly elevated. Analysis of VH BHB was helpful in evaluating cases with ketogenic conditions, especially in diabetes and alcohol abusers.[281] A 2020 study took another look at BHB levels in VH in forensic cases (N = 967) in deaths associated with metabolic acidosis, either DKA or AKA. The authors suggested a BHB concentration of 3.43 mmol/L being used as a cut-off for diagnostic purposes giving a reasonable sensitivity (96.2%) and specificity (98.3%).[276]

The diagnosis of alcoholic ketoacidosis at autopsy requires the analysis of total ketone bodies (acetone, acetoacetate, and BHB) in vitreous humor, pericardial fluid, and/or peripheral blood samples. Finding significantly elevated levels, especially in the case of BHB, in association with a typical history of heavy drinking, clinical diagnosis of alcohol abuse, a recent alcoholic binge followed by a day or more of withdrawal, anorexia, and consequently an insignificant BAC. When the post-mortem results are negative apart from a fatty liver and knowledge that the deceased was alcoholic, in these cases AKA might have accounted for the sudden death owing to profound metabolic acidosis, with a critical fall in blood pH to around 7.0, precipitating vascular collapse.

Another recent study determined ketone bodies in deaths related to alcohol abuse and/or diabetes or both conditions, hence potential AKA or DKA fatalities.[282] The investigators concluded that BAC in such deaths is not always low or zero, as was earlier proposed. They also found that using a BHB concentration in blood > 250 mg/L to indicate a ketoacidosis-related death, all cases also tested positive for acetone (> 2 mg/L). By contrast, at BHB concentrations < 250 mg/L acetone was not always measurable in the blood samples above the analytical cut-off level. This led to the suggestion that acetone above the cut-off of 2 mg/L might serve as a biomarker for pathologically significant ketoacidosis, and only in these cases was it motivated to perform a separate quantitative analysis of BHB.

Acetone is a lot easier to determine in forensic blood samples than BHB, and the traditional HS-GC-FID method used for ethanol analysis can be separately calibrated to quantitate acetone. This prompted investigators from Belgium to question the need for a separate analysis of BHB in routine PM casework.[271] They made a retrospective analysis of BHB in 599 cases, comprising 553 blood, 232 urine, and 62 VH samples. Cases with BHB concentrations above 100 mg/L (in blood, urine, and/or VH) were invariably associated with elevated levels of acetone. There were no positive BHB cases (> 100 mg/L) without there also being an elevated concentration of acetone. The results of this study also support the use of acetone as an initial biomarker for potential AAK- or DKA-related deaths.

3.3.9 Methanol Toxicity

Methanol (wood alcohol) is a common organic solvent in industry, an antifreeze, a laboratory reagent, a photocopier developer, a paint remover, a solvent in varnishes, and is also used to denature ethanol in methylated spirit for use as a clean fuel. The distribution of methanol in body fluids (including vitreous humor) and tissues is similar to that of ethanol because of the high solubility in water and lack of protein binding.[283] Pure methanol solvent is very dangerous to consume, although the lethal dose shows marked species variations.[284] Between 30 ml and 120 mL of pure methanol is sufficient to cause death in men, although the exact amount depends a lot on whether the victim had also consumed ethanol, which is customary when alcoholic beverages are manufactured illegally. Clusters of poisonings and mass deaths are seen secondary to consumption of adulterated alcoholic beverages in some nations (Bangladesh, Estonia, Kenya, Libya, Kenya, Malaysia, Mexico, and Siberia), when conventional alcoholic drinks are forbidden, expensive, or not available.[285–287]

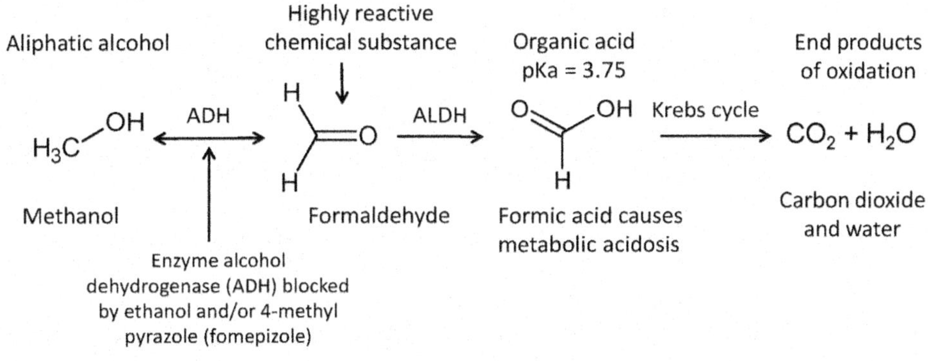

FIGURE 3.3.8 Oxidative metabolism of the primary alcohol methanol (wood alcohol) into its more toxic metabolites, formaldehyde, and formic acid. This enzymatic oxidation reaction is blocked by the administration of ethanol and/or fomepizole (4-methyl pyrazole)

Methanol itself is about as toxic as ethanol in terms of its narcotic action, but the consumption of methanol is much more dangerous, owing to its toxic metabolites, namely formaldehyde and formic acid (Figure 3.3.8).[288] Trace amounts of methanol (less than 1.0 mg/L) are measurable in the blood of abstainers and is derived from various biochemical pathways of intermediary metabolism.[289] Methanol also occurs as a congener in alcoholic beverages, especially in fruit brandies, and blood concentrations in heavy drinking might reach 10 mg/L or more.[290] The methanol determined in forensic blood samples probably represents a combination of endogenous synthesis when hepatic ADH is blocked by oxidation of ethanol, and congener present in the alcoholic beverage consumed. Methanol is a ubiquitous congener, with the lowest amounts in vodka and highest concentrations in fruity brandies.[291] Dietary sources of methanol, such as pectin, also exist, and methyl esters are present in fresh fruits and fruit juices, and the artificial sweetener aspartate is a methyl ester, becoming hydrolyzed in the gut to methanol.[292]

During a period of heavy drinking lasting days or weeks to reach a high BAC of 1.5–4.50 g/L the concentration of methanol in blood and urine progressively increases to levels of 10–40 mg/L.[293] After the end of drinking, the elimination of methanol lags behind that of ethanol by 12 to 24 hours and seems to follow the approximate same time course as ethanol withdrawal symptoms leading to speculation on the role of methanol and/or its metabolites in alcohol withdrawal and hangover.[294] Below a blood-ethanol concentration of about 0.1–0.2 g/L, hepatic ADH is no longer saturated with its preferred substrate and the metabolism of methanol occurs to its toxic metabolites.[295] The half-life of methanol is about ten times longer than ethanol, which means that elevated concentrations of methanol persist in the blood for longer and this was suggested as a biomarker of recent drinking.

Blood-methanol levels in 24 teetotalers ranged from 0.1–0.8 mg/L with a mean of 0.44 mg/L so that these levels can be regarded as physiological. By contrast, blood-methanol concentrations in samples taken upon admission of 20 chronic alcoholics to the hospital ranged from 0.22 to 20.1 mg/L. The general extent to which methanol may accumulate in the blood of heavy drinkers and alcoholics can be gauged from a study of ethanol and methanol concentrations in blood samples from 519 drunk driving suspects.[296] The mean concentration of ethanol in blood was 1.83 g/L (range 0.1–3.52 g/L), whereas the same blood samples contained a mean methanol concentration of 7.3 mg/L (range 1–23 mg/L). Higher blood-methanol was associated with higher methanol levels because the concentrations were positively correlated ($r = 0.47$, $p < 0.001$). By contrast, in 15 fatalities following hospital admission for methanol poisoning, the concentrations of methanol in post-mortem blood from the heart ranged from 0.23–2.68 g/L.[297]

Acute methanol poisoning produces a distinct clinical picture with a latent period lasting several hours to days between consumption and the appearance of first symptoms.[298] A combination of blurred vision with abdominal pain and vomiting is found in the majority of victims within the first 24 hours after presentation to the hospital. Visual disturbances, pancreatitis, metabolic acidosis, and diffuse encephalopathy may be seen in severe cases.[299] The characteristic delay between ingestion and onset of symptoms is thought to reflect the delayed appearance of metabolites (formaldehyde and formic acid), which are more toxic than methanol itself.

Methanol poisoning is characterized by metabolic acidosis with an elevated anion gap. The serum anion gap is defined as (sodium + potassium) – (bicarbonate + chlorid e) and represents the difference in unmeasured cations and unmeasured anions, which includes organic acids. Both formic acid, produced by methanol catabolism, and lactic acid, resulting from disturbed cellular metabolism, are responsible for metabolic acidosis.[300] The severity of the poisoning correlates with the degree of metabolic acidosis more closely than with the blood concentration of methanol.[301] Measuring formic acid concentrations may be of some value in assessing methanol poisoning and the concentrations in blood in two fatalities were 0.32 g/L and 0.23 g/L compared with 2.27 g/L and 0.47 g/L in urine.[302] The value of analyzing formic acid as the toxic metabolite of methanol was supported by a more recent PM study of methanol-related deaths.[303]

An outbreak of methanol poisoning occurred in Norway between 2002 and 2004 and the background and clinical outcome of these cases were well documented.[304] A total of 51 patients were hospitalized after drinking alcoholic beverages spiked with high concentrations of methanol. Eight died before being admitted to hospital, some were comatose and nine other fatalities occurred despite emergency life-saving treatment. The median serum concentration of methanol was 0.8 g/L (range 0.1–4.70 g/L), the median blood pH was 7.20 (range 6.50–7.50), and the median base deficit was 22 mmol/L (range 0–31 mmol/L). The most common clinical features were visual disturbances (55%), dyspnea (41%), and gastrointestinal symptoms (43%). The physicians concluded that methanol poisoning has high morbidity and mortality mainly because of a late diagnosis and admission for invasive treatment including hemodialysis.[305] The strongest predictors of a fatal outcome were coma on admission, metabolic acidosis ($pH < 6.90$), and base deficit > 28 mmol/L.

Treatment recommendations for methanol poisoning have been promulgated by an international body of experts.[304] This included admission to hospital as soon as possible after poisoning was suspected, administration of inhibitors of hepatic alcohol dehydrogenase (ADH), bicarbonate to alleviate metabolic acidosis, and hemodialysis to remove non-metabolized methanol and formic acid from the blood circulation.[306] Both methanol and ethanol are substrates for ADH, although the affinity of the enzyme is much higher for ethanol than for methanol by about 10:1.[307] Consequently, the biotransformation of methanol into its metabolites can be blocked by administration of ethanol and maintaining a steady-state concentration of the antidote in blood of about 1.1–2 g/L for several hours.

A more modern antidote for the treatment of methanol poisoning, although more costly than ethanol, is fomepizole (4-methyl pyrazole or Antizol®), which is also a competitive inhibitor of liver ADH.[308] This therapeutic drug is preferred to ethanol when pediatric patients are admitted for treatment or in adults who might suffer from liver dysfunction, such as cirrhosis.[309] Sterile solutions are available in the emergency departments as in infusion flasks for treatment of poisonings from toxic alcohols, although this treatment also depresses the central nervous system, which is an undesirable effect of using this antidote. Analyzing the concentration of formate and formic acid in blood, which is mainly responsible for metabolic acidosis, is recommended to monitor a patient's condition and prognosis for a fatal outcome.[310]

3.3.10 Isopropanol Poisoning

Isopropyl alcohol (isopropanol or 2-propanol) might be consumed by some people as a cheap substitute for ethanol, such as by skid-row alcoholics.[311] However, the secondary alcohol is also used as an antiseptic to clean the skin before venipuncture and is available in many home-cleaning products, such as antifreeze and skin lotions. Years ago a 70% solution of isopropanol was sold as "rubbing alcohol" being applied to the skin, allowed to evaporate, and bringing about a cooling effect lowering body temperature in people with a fever.[312,313]

Isopropanol is a three-carbon secondary alcohol and has a characteristic odor and a slightly bitter taste and should not be confused with its structural isomer (*n*-propanol), which is sometimes used as an internal standard for HS-GC-FID analysis of blood-ethanol. Although much less toxic than methanol, over the years many fatal poisonings have been reported from drinking isopropanol.[314,315] The review article from 2014 dealt with isopropanol poisoning and included information about its disposition and fate in the body, the clinical manifestation of poisoning, and treatment strategies available.[316] Fatalities may occur rapidly as a result of central nervous system depression or may be delayed when the presence or absence of shock with hypotension is the most important single prognostic factor.[317]

Isopropanol is a secondary alcohol and is metabolized via alcohol dehydrogenase to acetone, which imparts a fruity smell on the breath of someone intoxicated from drinking isopropanol. Acetone is metabolized at a much slower rate than its precursor isopropanol, and CYP2EI seems to be the hydroxylating enzyme given acetol (hydroxyacetone) as its first metabolite, the latter being further metabolized to 1,2-propanediol as depicted in Figure 3.3.9.[318] In many deaths associated with isopropanol poisoning, it is not unusual to see elevated blood-acetone concentrations at autopsy, but the isopropanol concentration reported as not-detected or negative, which is verifies the longer elimination half-life of acetone.[317]

After absorption into the blood, isopropanol distributes in the total body water and its apparent volume of distribution is similar to that of ethanol, namely 0.6–0.7 L/kg. After about 1–2 h post-dosing a peak blood concentration of isopropanol is reached and its elimination from blood approximates to first-order kinetics and the half-life (t½) is about 4–6 h.[319,320] Likewise, the primary metabolite acetone is also eliminated by first-order kinetics, but its half-life is much longer than for the parent drug, being about 16–22 h from different studies. In a case report of a non-alcoholic female (46 y) the plasma elimination half-lives of isopropanol and acetone were found to be 6.4 h and 22.4 h, respectively.[320]

In a review of isopropanol deaths, 31 cases were attributed to isopropanol poisoning alone, and the blood isopropanol concentrations ranged from 0.10–2.50 g/L, mean 1.40 g/L, and acetone ranged from 0.40–3.0 g/L, mean 1.7 g/L.[311] In four cases with low blood isopropanol levels (0.1–0.3 g/L) there were also high concentrations of acetone (1.10–2.00 g/L). For this reason, both acetone and isopropanol should be measured in suspected cases of isopropanol poisoning.[321]

Elevated concentrations of acetone in blood (> 0.1 g/L) are mostly observed when the deceased person suffered from diabetes mellitus or starvation ketosis. Under these circumstances, there is a possibility that acetone might be reduced to isopropanol via hepatic alcohol dehydrogenase during life.[322,323] This was the explanation suggested to account for low concentrations of isopropanol in blood in forensic cases when there was no evidence to suggest exposure to isopropanol.[324] In 27 such fatalities blood isopropanol concentrations ranged from less than 0.10 to 0.44 g/L with a mean of 0.14 g/L and exceeded 0.20 g/L in only three PM cases. The highest concentration of acetone was 0.56 g/L and the combined concentration of isopropanol and acetone were much lower than those seen in isopropanol poisoning deaths.[325] The reduction of acetone to

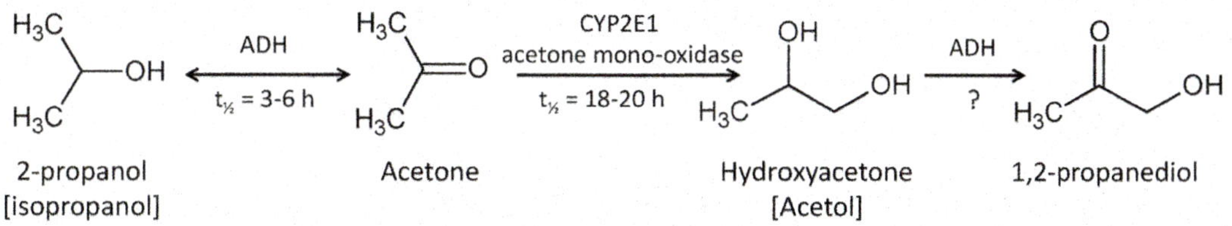

FIGURE 3.3.9 Oxidative metabolism of the secondary alcohol isopropanol (2-propanol) into acetone and much slower oxidation of the latter first into acetol (hydroxyacetone) and then 1,2-propanediol

isopropanol was reported in a case of a 40-year-old alcoholic patient with AKA, elevated anion gap, and a blood pH of 6.96, and the toxicology screening showed blood-acetone of 0.50 g/L and blood-isopropanol of 0.06 g/L.[322]

In another recent study, the inter-relationship between isopropanol, ethanol, and acetone were evaluated in 1,366 PM cases, which were selected if blood-acetone exceeded 0.10 g/L, the analytical cut-off used at the time.[326] The mean (median) and highest acetone concentrations in these cases were 0.26 g/L (0.19 g/L) and 2.4 g/L, respectively. Isopropanol was detected in 256 cases (19%) at mean (median) and highest concentrations of 0.30 g/L (0.15 g/L) and 3.1 g/L, respectively. Blood-ethanol was positive (> 0.1 g/L) in 500 of these same cases (37%) at mean (median) and highest concentrations of 1.1 g/L (0.68 g/L) and 6.2 g/L, respectively.

3.3.11 Concluding Remarks

Accurate and precise determinations of the concentrations of ethanol in autopsy blood and other biological specimens are important in medicolegal cases. Depending on the autopsy BAC, coroner courts often seek information about the deceased's degree of intoxication and whether body functioning was impaired at the time of death. Knowledge of the BAC in both victims and perpetrators of crimes are needed to make decisions of culpability, ability to form intent, pathological intoxication, and alcohol-induced automatism.[327]

The autopsy BAC is of particular interest in transportation fatalities, such as on the roads, at sea, and in the air, owing to the existence of statutory BAC limits for driving and rules and regulations about alcohol use in the workplace. When these limits were enacted, they were intended to apply to the analysis of blood samples from living subjects taken under sterile conditions and not at autopsy when the body might be damaged and decomposed. In traumatic deaths, such as in aviation disasters or explosions, microbial production of ethanol after death is a distinct possibility.[232,328,329] The origin of any ethanol determined in blood samples from transportation fatalities, whether this reflects antemortem drinking or PM synthesis remains a challenging problem for forensic investigators.[247]

Statistics show that a staggering three million people died in 2018 because of their harmful use of alcohol, which amounted to 5.3% of all deaths.[330] In addition to deaths from acute alcohol ingestion and chronic alcoholism, excessive drinking and drunkenness are tightly linked to accidents occurring in the home, in the workplace, and on the roads and trauma patients are often under the influence of alcohol when treated.[331] When the death is from natural causes, a comprehensive toxicological analysis for ethanol and drugs is probably not motivated, unless the deceased had a history of substance abuse.

Guidelines are available for sampling blood and other specimens for analytical toxicology and it is generally agreed that blood should *not* be taken from the heart, aorta, or other large vessels in the chest or abdomen or the liquid that pools after death in the pericardial sac, pleural cavities, or abdominal spaces. In the worst-case scenario, if specimens of blood are from these anatomical sites, then their provenance should be carefully considered and declared when the analytical results are interpreted. Furthermore, prior to shipment for analysis, the specimens must be transferred into clean and dry containers containing enough sodium or potassium fluoride to give a final concentration of 1–2% w/v. Whenever possible, the biological specimens should be sent by special delivery in refrigerated containers and stored at 4° C pending analysis of ethanol and other drugs.

A blind needle puncture of the chest to obtain a "cardiac" blood sample, or a so-called "subclavian stab," is not recommended because at best it produces a chest cavity blood sample of unknown origin and at worst a sample contaminated with stomach contents. The recommended autopsy blood samples for determination of ethanol as well as other drugs is one obtained from either the femoral vein or the external iliac vein using a needle and syringe after clamping or tying off the vessel proximally. Samples of VH and urine are sometimes crucial for the determination of ethanol to aid in interpretation and these should be stored and sent for analysis in tubes containing a fluoride preservative. The interpretation of positive ethanol concentrations must, of necessity, take into account the PM interval, the condition of the body, the anatomical findings after an autopsy, circumstances surrounding the death, discoveries at the scene, as well as any information about the drinking and drug habits of the deceased.

The medicolegal significance of a high BAC in PM blood is questionable, without supporting information about the concentrations present in alternative specimens (VH and urine) and the condition of the body (stage of decomposition), such as whether the body was incinerated or submersion in water, etc. The positioning of the dead body when discovered, whether there was any vomit evident, the presence of drug paraphernalia, empty pill or liquor bottles, etc. all help in reaching a final decision. Without all these considerations, a single BAC might be uninterpretable in relation to whether alcohol intoxication was a contributor or cause of the person's death.

REFERENCES

1. Eriksson A. Forensic pathology. In: Freeman MD, Zeegers MP, editors. *Forensic Epidemiology: Principles and Practice.* Amsterdam: Elsevier, 2016, 151–77.
2. Saukko P, Knight B. *Knight's Forensic Pathology.* 4th ed. Boca Raton: CRC Press, 2015.
3. Meilia PDI, Freeman MD, Herkutanto, ZMP. A review of causal inference in forensic medicine. *Forensic Sci Med Pathol* 2020;16:313–20.
4. Jones AW. Alcohol, acute and chronic use and postmortem findings In: Payne-James J, Byard RW, editors. *Encyclopedia of Forensic and Legal Medicine* Second ed. Oxford: Elsevier, 2016, 84–107.
5. Dinis-Oliveira RJ, Carvalho F, Duarte JA, Remiao F, Marques A, Santos A, et al. Collection of biological samples in forensic toxicology. *Toxicol Mech Methods* 2010;20:363–414.

6. Wastesson JW, Morin L, Tan ECK, Johnell K. An update on the clinical consequences of polypharmacy in older adults: a narrative review. *Expert Opin Drug Saf* 2018;17:1185–96.
7. Drummer OH, Kennedy B, Bugeja L, Ibrahim JE, Ozanne-Smith J. Interpretation of postmortem forensic toxicology results for injury prevention research. *Inj Prev* 2013;19:284–9.
8. Jones AW, Holmgren A. Concentration distributions of the drugs most frequently identified in post-mortem femoral blood representing all causes of death. *Med Sci Law* 2009;49:257–73.
9. Ketola RA, Ojanpera I. Summary statistics for drug concentrations in post-mortem femoral blood representing all causes of death. *Drug Test Anal* 2019;11:1326–37.
10. Rutty GN, Carter N, Forrest ARW. Alcohol estimation at necroscopy: epidemiology, economics and the elderly. *J Clin Pathol* 1997;50:796–7.
11. Tagliaro F, Lubli G, Ghielmi S, Franchi D, Marigo M. Chromatographic methods for blood alcohol determination. *J Chromatogr* 1992;580:161–90.
12. Tiscione NB, Alford I, Yeatman DT, Shan X. Ethanol analysis by headspace gas chromatography with simultaneous flame-ionization and mass spectrometry detection. *J Anal Toxicol* 2011;35:501–11.
13. Dinis-Oliveira RJ, Vieira DN, Magalhaes T. Guidelines for collection of biological samples for clinical and forensic toxicological analysis. *Forensic Sci Res* 2016;1:42–51.
14. Zilg B, Thelander G, Giebe B, Druid H. Postmortem blood sampling-Comparison of drug concentrations at different sample sites. *Forensic Sci Int* 2017;278:296–303.
15. Gifford H, Turkel HW. Diffusion of alcohol through stomach wall after death. *J Am Med Assoc* 1956;161:866–8.
16. Harger RN. Heart blood vs. femoral vein blood for postmortem alcohol determination (letter to the editor). *JAMA* 1957;165:725.
17. Turkel HW, Gifford H. Erroneous blood alcohol findings at autopsy; avoidance by proper sampling technique. *J Am Med Assoc* 1957;164:1077–9.
18. Pounder DJ, Smith DR. Postmortem diffusion of alcohol from the stomach. *Am J Forensic Med Pathol* 1995;16:89–96.
19. Prouty RW, Anderson WH. A comparison of postmortem heart blood and femoral blood ethyl alcohol concentrations. *J Anal Toxicol* 1987;11:191–7.
20. Cook DS, Braithwaite RA, Hale KA. Estimating antemortem drug concentrations from postmortem blood samples: the influence of postmortem redistribution. *J Clin Pathol* 2000;53:282–5.
21. Pounder DJ, Jones GR. Post-mortem drug redistribution - a toxicological nightmare. *Forensic Sci Int* 1990;45:253–63.
22. Jones AW. Blood-alcohol analysis by gas chromatography: fifty years of progress. In: Verstraete A, editor. *TIAFT our First 50 Years*. Gent: Aademia Press, 2013, 145–68.
23. Morris JA, Harrison LM, Partridge SM. Postmortem bacteriology: a re-evaluation. *J Clin Pathol* 2006;59:1–9.
24. Skopp G. Preanalytic aspects in postmortem toxicology. *Forensic Sci Int* 2004;142:75–100.
25. Boumba VA, Ziavrou KS, Vougiouklakis T. Biochemical pathways generating post-mortem volatile compounds co-detected during forensic ethanol analyses. *Forensic Sci Int* 2008;174:133–51.
26. Drummer OH. Requirements for bioanalytical procedures in postmortem toxicology. *Anal Bioanal Chem* 2007;388:1495–503.
27. Ferner RE. Post-mortem clinical pharmacology. *Br J Clin Pharmacol* 2008;66:430–43.
28. Flanagan RJ, Connally G, Evans JM. Analytical toxicology. Guidelines for sample collection post-mortem. *Toxicol Rev* 2005;24:63–71.
29. Pelissier-Alicot AL, Gaulier JM, Champsaur P, Marquet P. Mechanisms underlying postmortem redistribution of drugs: a review. *J Anal Toxicol* 2003;27:533–44.
30. Pounder DJ, Fuke C, Cox DE, Smith D, Kuroda N. Postmortem diffusion of drugs from gastric residue: an experimental study. *Am J Forensic Med Pathol* 1996;17:1–7.
31. Pounder DJ, Yonemitsu K. Postmortem absorption of drugs and ethanol from aspirated vomitus - an experimental model. *Forensic Sci Int* 1991;51:189–95.
32. Pounder DJ, Jones AW. Postmortem alcohol - aspects of interpretation. In: Karch SB, editor. *Drug Abuse Handbook*. Second ed. Boca Raton: Taylor and Francis CRC Press, 2007, 376–401.
33. Leikin JB, Watson WA. Post-mortem toxicology: what the dead can and cannot tell us. *J Toxicol Clin Toxicol* 2003;41:47–56.
34. Jones AW, Kugelberg FC, Holmgren A, Ahlner J. Five-year update on the occurrence of alcohol and other drugs in blood samples from drivers killed in road-traffic crashes in Sweden. *Forensic Sci Int* 2009;186:56–62.
35. Corry JE. A review. Possible sources of ethanol ante- and post-mortem: its relationship to the biochemistry and microbiology of decomposition. *J Appl Bacteriol* 1978;44:1–56.
36. Levine B, Smith ML, Smialek JE, Caplan YH. Interpretation of low postmortem concentrations of ethanol. *J Forensic Sci* 1993;38:663–7.
37. Thelander G, Kugelberg FC, Jones AW. High correlation between ethanol concentrations in post-mortem femoral blood and in alternative biological specimens, but large uncertainty when the linear regression model was used for prediction in individual cases. *J Anal Toxicol* 2020;44:415–21.
38. Gill JR. From death to death certificate: what do the dead say? *J Med Toxicol* 2017;13:111–6.
39. Clark JC. Sudden death in the chronic alcoholic. *Forensic Sci Int* 1988;36:105–11.
40. Cowan DM, Maskrey JR, Fung ES, Woods TA, Stabryla LM, Scott PK, et al. Best-practices approach to determination of blood alcohol concentration (BAC) at specific time points: combination of ante-mortem alcohol pharmacokinetic modeling and post-mortem alcohol generation and transport considerations. *Regul Toxicol Pharmacol* 2016;78:24–36.
41. Jones AW. Alcohol; acute and chronic use, postmortem findings. In: Payne-James J, Byard RW, Corey TS, Henderson C, editors. *Encyclopedia of Forensic and Legal Medicine*. London: Elsevier Academic Press, 2005, 39–58.
42. Steen B. Body water in the elderly--a review. *J Nutr Health Aging* 1997;1:142–5.
43. Chumlea WC, Guo SS, Zeller CM, Reo NV, Siervogel RM. Total body water data for white adults 18 to 64 years of age: the Fels Longitudinal Study. *Kidney Int* 1999;56:244–52.
44. Bilzer N, Kühnholz B. Methodik zur Bestimmung des Wasser- und Äthanolgehaltes in Organproben. *Blutalkohol* 1979;16:467–73.
45. de Jong GM, Huizenga JR, Gips CH. Evaluation of gravimetric assays of the H2O concentration in human serum and urine. *Clin Chim Acta* 1987;163:153–64.
46. Lentner C. *Units of Measurement, Body Fluids, Composition of the Body, Nutrition*. Basel: CIBA-GEIGY Ltd, 1981.
47. Brettel HF. über Beziehungen zwischen dem Abfall der Blutalkoholkonzentrtion und dem Waserverlust des Blutes nach dem Tode. *Blutalkohol* 1970;7:54–64.

48. Felby S, Nielsen E. The postmortem blood alcohol concentration and the water content. *Blutalkohol* 1994;31:24–32.
49. Senkowski CM, Thompson KA. The accuracy of blood alcohol analysis using headspace gas chromatography when performed on clotted samples. *J Forensic Sci* 1990;35:176–80.
50. Iffland R, West A, Bilzer N, Schuff A. Zur Zuverlässigkeit der Blutalkoholbestimmung. Das Verteilungsverhältnis des Wassers zwischen Serum und Vollblut. *Rechtsmedizin* 1999;9:123–30.
51. Barnhill MT, Jr, Herbert D, Wells DJ, Jr. Comparison of hospital laboratory serum alcohol levels obtained by an enzymatic method with whole blood levels forensically determined by gas chromatography. *J Anal Toxicol* 2007;31:23–30.
52. Hak EA, Gerlitz BJ, Demont PM, Bowthorpe WD. Determination of serum alcohol:blood alcohol ratios. *Can Soc Forensic Sci J* 1995;28:123–6.
53. Charlebois RC, Corbett MR, Wigmore JG. Comparison of ethanol concentrations in blood, serum, and blood cells for forensic application. *J Anal Toxicol* 1996;20:171–8.
54. Jones AW, Hahn RG, Stalberg HP. Distribution of ethanol and water between plasma and whole blood; inter- and intra-individual variations after administration of ethanol by intravenous infusion. *Scand J Clin Lab Invest* 1990;50:775–80.
55. Riley D, Wigmore JG, Yen B. Dilution of blood collected for medicolegal alcohol analysis by intravenous fluids. *J Anal Toxicol* 1996;20:330–1.
56. Jones AW, Kugelberg FC, Holmgren A, Ahlner J. Drug poisoning deaths in Sweden show a predominance of ethanol in mono-intoxications, adverse drug-alcohol interactions and poly-drug use. *Forensic Sci Int* 2011;206:43–51.
57. Hollstedt C, Neri A, Rydberg U. Ethanol-induced lethality in the developing rat. *Blutalkohol* 1981;18:245–52.
58. Tsibulsky VL, Amit Z. Tolerance to effects of high doses of ethanol: 1. Lethal effects in mice. *Pharmacol Biochem Behav* 1993;45:465–72.
59. Wiberg GS, Trenholm HL, Coldwell BB. Increased ethanol toxicity in old rats: changes in LD50, in vivo and in vitro metabolism, and liver alcohol dehydrogenase activity. *Toxicol Appl Pharmacol* 1970;16:718–27.
60. Jones AW, Holmgren P. Comparison of blood-ethanol concentration in deaths attributed to acute alcohol poisoning and chronic alcoholism. *J Forensic Sci* 2003;48:874–9.
61. Johnson HR. At what blood levels does alcohol kill? *Med Sci Law* 1985;25:127–30.
62. Wingren CJ, Ottosson A. The association between obesity and lethal blood alcohol concentrations: a nationwide register-based study of medicolegal autopsy cases in Sweden. *Forensic Sci Int* 2014;244:285–8.
63. Jones AW, Holmgren A. Age and gender differences in blood-alcohol concentration in apprehended drivers in relation to the amounts of alcohol consumed. *Forensic Sci Int* 2009;188:40–5.
64. Poikolainen K. Estimated lethal ethanol concentrations in relation to age, aspiration, and drugs. *Alcohol Clin Exp Res* 1984;8:223–5.
65. Koski A, Ojanpera I, Vuori E. Interaction of alcohol and drugs in fatal poisonings. *Hum Exp Toxicol* 2003;22:281–7.
66. Taylor HL, Hudson RP, Jr. Acute ethanol poisoning: a two-year study of deaths in North Carolina. *J Forensic Sci* 1977;22:639–53.
67. Alha AR, Tamminen V. Fatal cases with an elevated urine alcohol but without alcohol in the blood. *J Forensic Med* 1964;11:3–5.
68. Padosch SA, Schmidt PH, Kroner LU, Madea B. Death due to positional asphyxia under severe alcoholisation: pathophysiologic and forensic considerations. *Forensic Sci Int* 2005;149:67–73.
69. Bell MD, Rao VJ, Wetli CV, Rodriguez RN. Positional asphyxiation in adults. A series of 30 cases from the Dade and Broward County Florida Medical Examiner Offices from 1982 to 1990. *Am J Forensic Med Pathol* 1992;13:101–7.
70. Kenttamies A, Karkola K. Death in sauna. *J Forensic Sci* 2008;53:724–9.
71. Kortelainen ML. Drugs and alcohol in hypothermia and hyperthermia related deaths: a retrospective study. *J Forensic Sci* 1987;32:1704–12.
72. Perper JA, Twerski A, Wienand JW. Tolerance at high blood alcohol concentrations: a study of 110 cases and review of the literature. *J Forensic Sci* 1986;31:212–21.
73. Roberts JR, Dollard D. Alcohol levels do not accurately predict physical or mental impairment in ethanol-tolerant subjects: relevance to emergency medicine and dram shop laws. *J Med Toxicol* 2010;6:438–42.
74. Urso T, Gavaler JS, Van Thiel DH. Blood ethanol levels in sober alcohol users seen in an emergency room. *Life Sci* 1981;28:1053–6.
75. Pletcher MJ, Maselli J, Gonzales R. Uncomplicated alcohol intoxication in the emergency department: an analysis of the National Hospital Ambulatory Medical Care Survey. *Am J Med* 2004;117:863–7.
76. Darke S, Duflou J, Torok M, Prolov T. Toxicology, circumstances and pathology of deaths from acute alcohol toxicity. *J Forensic Leg Med* 2013;20:1122–5.
77. Darke S, Duflou J, Torok M, Prolov T. Characteristics, circumstances and toxicology of sudden or unnatural deaths involving very high-range alcohol concentrations. *Addiction* 2013;108:1411–7.
78. Morley SR, Smith P, Johnson C. Acute alcohol toxicity. *Acad Forensic Pathol* 2014;4:161–7.
79. Jones AW. The drunkest drinking driver in Sweden: blood alcohol concentration 0.545% w/v. *J Stud Alcohol* 1999;60:400–6.
80. Davis AR, Lipson AH. Central nervous system tolerance to high blood alcohol levels. *Med J Aust* 1986;144:9–12.
81. Lindblad B, Olsson R. Unusually high levels of blood alcohol? *JAMA* 1976;236:1600–2.
82. Johnson RA, Noll EC, Rodney WM. Survival after a serum ethanol concentration of 1 1/2%. *Lancet* 1982;2:1394.
83. Poklis A, Pearson MA. An unusually high blood ethanol level in a living patient. *Clin Toxicol* 1977;10:429–31.
84. Hammond KB, Rumack BH, Rodgerson DO. Blood ethanol. A report of unusually high levels in a living patient. *JAMA* 1973;226:63–4.
85. Berild D, Hasselbalch H. Survival after a blood alcohol of 1127 mg/dl. *Lancet* 1981;2:363.
86. O'Neill S, Tipton KF, Prichard JS, Quinlan A. Survival after high blood alcohol levels. Association with first-order elimination kinetics. *Arch Intern Med* 1984;144:641–2.
87. Malejko K, Graf H, Gahr M. Survival of very high blood alcohol concentration without consequential damage in a patient without a previous substance use disorder. *J Forensic Sci* 2016;61:1155–7.
88. Kraut JA. Diagnosis of toxic alcohols: limitations of present methods. *Clin Toxicol (Phila)* 2015;53:589–95.
89. Bishop-Freeman SC, Bertholf RL, Powers RH, Mayhew LC, Winecker RE. False-positive enzymatic alcohol results in perimortem specimens. *Lab Med* 2020;51:394–401.

90. Nacca N, Hodgman MJ, Lao K, Elkins M, Holland MG. Can elevated lactate and LDH produce a false positive enzymatic ethanol result in live patients presenting to the emergency department? *Clin Toxicol (Phila)* 2018;56: 189–92.
91. Rainey PM. Relation between serum and whole-blood ethanol concentrations. *Clin Chem* 1993;39:2288–92.
92. Jones AW, Harding P. Driving under the influence with blood alcohol concentrations over 0.4 g%. *Forensic Sci Int* 2013;231:349–53.
93. Kalant H. Current state of knowledge about the mechanisms of alcohol tolerance. *Addict Biol* 1996;1:133–41.
94. Kalant H, Le AD. Effects of ethanol on thermoregulation. *Pharmacol Ther* 1983;23:313–64.
95. Meiman J, Anderson H, Tomasallo C, Centers for Disease C, Prevention. Hypothermia-related deaths--Wisconsin, 2014, and United States, 2003–2013. *MMWR Morb Mortal Wkly Rep* 2015;64:141–3.
96. Teige B, Fleischer E. [Blood concentrations in acute fatal poisoning. Experiences with forensic cases]. *Tidsskr Nor Laegeforen* 1983;103:679–85.
97. Teresinski G, Buszewicz G, Madro R. Biochemical background of ethanol-induced cold susceptibility. *Leg Med (Tokyo)* 2005;7:15–23.
98. Rodhe A, Eriksson A. Sauna deaths in Sweden, 1992–2003. *Am J Forensic Med Pathol* 2008;29:27–31.
99. Yang KM, Lee BW, Oh J, Yoo SH. Characteristics of sauna deaths in Korea in relation to different blood alcohol concentrations. *Forensic Sci Med Pathol* 2018;14:307–13.
100. Cederbaum AI. Alcohol metabolism. *Clin Liver Dis* 2012;16:667–85.
101. Zakhari S. Overview: how is alcohol metabolized by the body? *Alcohol Res Health* 2006;29:245–54.
102. Bonnichsen RK, Wassen AM. Crystalline alcohol dehydrogenase from horse liver. *Arch Biochem* 1948;18:361–3.
103. Edenberg HJ. The genetics of alcohol metabolism: role of alcohol dehydrogenase and aldehyde dehydrogenase variants. *Alcohol Res Health* 2007;30:5–13.
104. Nuutinen H, Lindros K, Hekali P, Salaspuro M. Elevated blood acetate as indicator of fast ethanol elimination in chronic alcoholics. *Alcohol* 1985;2:623–6.
105. Helander A, Bottcher M, Fehr C, Dahmen N, Beck O. Detection times for urinary ethyl glucuronide and ethyl sulfate in heavy drinkers during alcohol detoxification. *Alcohol Alcohol* 2009;44:55–61.
106. Hoiseth G, Morini L, Polettini A, Christophersen A, Morland J. Blood kinetics of ethyl glucuronide and ethyl sulphate in heavy drinkers during alcohol detoxification. *Forensic Sci Int* 2009;188:52–6.
107. Hoiseth G, Bernard JP, Karinen R, Johnsen L, Helander A, Christophersen AS, et al. A pharmacokinetic study of ethyl glucuronide in blood and urine: applications to forensic toxicology. *Forensic Sci Int* 2007;172:119–24.
108. Neumann T, Helander A, Dahl H, Holzmann T, Neuner B, Weiss-Gerlach E, et al. Value of ethyl glucuronide in plasma as a biomarker for recent alcohol consumption in the emergency room. *Alcohol Alcohol* 2008;43:431–5.
109. Crabb DW, Edenberg HJ, Bosron WF, Li TK. Genotypes for aldehyde dehydrogenase deficiency and alcohol sensitivity. The inactive ALDH2(2) allele is dominant. *J Clin Invest* 1989;83:314–6.
110. Chen CH, Cruz LA, Mochly-Rosen D. Pharmacological recruitment of aldehyde dehydrogenase 3A1 (ALDH3A1) to assist ALDH2 in acetaldehyde and ethanol metabolism in vivo. *Proc Natl Acad Sci U S A* 2015;112:3074–9.
111. Koppaka V, Thompson DC, Chen Y, Ellermann M, Nicolaou KC, Juvonen RO, et al. Aldehyde dehydrogenase inhibitors: a comprehensive review of the pharmacology, mechanism of action, substrate specificity, and clinical application. *Pharmacol Rev* 2012;64:520–39.
112. Goldman D. Aldehyde dehydrogenase deficiency as cause of facial flushing reaction to alcohol in Japanese. *Alcohol Health Res World* 1995;19:48–9.
113. Thomasson HR, Crabb DW, Edenberg HJ, Li TK. Alcohol and aldehyde dehydrogenase polymorphisms and alcoholism. *Behav Genet* 1993;23:131–6.
114. Yamamoto H, Tanegashima A, Hosoe H, Fukunaga T. Fatal acute alcohol intoxication in an ALDH2 heterozygote: a case report. *Forensic Sci Int* 2000;112:201–7.
115. Langford NJ, Ferner RE. The medico-legal significance of pharmacokinetic interactions with ethanol. *Med Sci Law* 2013;53:1–5.
116. Leelakanok N, Holcombe AL, Lund BC, Gu X, Schweizer ML. Association between polypharmacy and death: a systematic review and meta-analysis. *J Am Pharm Assoc (2003)* 2017;57:729–38, e10.
117. Launiainen T, Vuori E, Ojanpera I. Prevalence of adverse drug combinations in a large post-mortem toxicology database. *Int J Legal Med* 2009;123:109–15.
118. Koski A, Vuori E, Ojanpera I. Relation of postmortem blood alcohol and drug concentrations in fatal poisonings involving amitriptyline, propoxyphene and promazine. *Hum Exp Toxicol* 2005;24:389–96.
119. Skinner MD, Lahmek P, Pham H, Aubin HJ. Disulfiram efficacy in the treatment of alcohol dependence: a meta-analysis. *PLoS One* 2014;9:e87366.
120. Hald J, Jacobsen E, Larsen V. The antabuse effect of some compounds related to antabuse and cyanamide. *Acta Pharmacol Toxicol (Copenh)* 1952;8:329–37.
121. Hald J, Jacobsen E, Larsen V. Formation of acetaldehyde in the organism in relation to dosage of antabuse (tetraethylthiuramdisulphide) and to alcohol-concentration in blood. *Acta Pharmacol Toxicol (Copenh)* 1949;5:179–88.
122. Elkins RL, Richards TL, Nielsen R, Repass R, Stahlbrandt H, Hoffman HG. The neurobiological mechanism of chemical aversion (Emetic) therapy for alcohol use disorder: an fMRI study. *Front Behav Neurosci* 2017;11:182.
123. Neto D, Lambaz R, Tavares JE. Compliance with aftercare treatment, including disulfiram, and effect on outcome in alcohol-dependent patients. *Alcohol Alcohol* 2007;42:604–9.
124. Sezgin B, Sibar S, Bulam H, Findikcioglu K, Tuncer S, Dogan B. Disulfiram implantation for the treatment of alcoholism: clinical experiences from the plastic surgeon's point of view. *Arch Plast Surg* 2014;41:571–5.
125. Becker MC, Sugarman G. Death following "test drink" of alcohol in patients receiving Antabuse®. *JAMA* 1952;149:568–71.
126. Heath MJ, Pachar JV, Perez Martinez AL, Toseland PA. An exceptional case of lethal disulfiram-alcohol reaction. *Forensic Sci Int* 1992;56:45–50.
127. Michelot D. Poisoning by Coprinus atramentarius. *Nat Toxins* 1992;1:73–80.
128. Wiseman JS, Abeles RH. Mechanism of inhibition of aldehyde dehydrogenase by cyclopropranone hydrate and the mushroom toxin coprine. *Biochemistry* 1979;18: 427–35.
129. Williams CS, Woodcock KR. Do ethanol and metronidazole interact to produce a disulfiram-like reaction? *Ann Pharmacother* 2000;34:255–7.

130. Mergenhagen KA, Wattengel BA, Skelly MK, Clark CM, Russo TA. Fact versus fiction: a review of the evidence behind alcohol and antibiotic interactions. *Antimicrob Agents Chemother* 2020;64:e02167–19.
131. Visapaa JP, Tillonen JS, Kaihovaara PS, Salaspuro MP. Lack of disulfiram-like reaction with metronidazole and ethanol. *Ann Pharmacother* 2002;36:971–4.
132. Jones AW. Forensic drug profile: cocaethylene. *J Anal Toxicol* 2019;43:155–60.
133. Prescott LF. Paracetamol: past, present, and future. *Am J Ther* 2000;7:143–7.
134. Prescott LF. Paracetamol, alcohol and the liver. *Br J Clin Pharmacol* 2000;49:291–301.
135. Holmgren P, Jones AW. Coexistence and concentrations of ethanol and diazepam in postmortem blood specimens: risk for enhanced toxicity? *J Forensic Sci* 2003;48:1416–21.
136. Brooke EM, Glatt MM. More and more barbiturates. *Med Sci Law* 1964;4:277–82.
137. Jatlow P. Cocaethylene: pharmacologic activity and clinical significance. *Ther Drug Monit* 1993;15:533–6.
138. McCance-Katz EF, Price LH, McDougle CJ, Kosten TR, Black JE, Jatlow PI. Concurrent cocaine-ethanol ingestion in humans: pharmacology, physiology, behavior, and the role of cocaethylene. *Psychopharmacology (Berl)* 1993;111:39–46.
139. Kugelberg FC, Jones AW. Interpreting results of ethanol analysis in postmortem specimens: a review of the literature. *Forensic Sci Int* 2007;165:10–29.
140. Backer RC, Pisano RV, Sopher IM. The comparison of alcohol concentrations in postmortem fluids and tissues. *J Forensic Sci* 1980;25:327–31.
141. Sebag J. *The Vitreous in Health and Disease* Berlin: Springer, 2014.
142. Ortmann J, Markwerth P, Madea B. Precision of estimating the time since death by vitreous potassium-Comparison of 5 different equations. *Forensic Sci Int* 2016;269:1–7.
143. Musshoff F, Hess C, Madea B. Disorders of glucose metabolism: post mortem analyses in forensic cases--part II. *Int J Legal Med* 2011;125:171–80.
144. Zilg B, Alkass K, Berg S, Druid H. Postmortem identification of hyperglycemia. *Forensic Sci Int* 2009;185:89–95.
145. Kokavec J, Min SH, Tan MH, Gilhotra JS, Newland HS, Durkin SR, et al. Antemortem vitreous potassium may strengthen postmortem interval estimates. *Forensic Sci Int* 2016;263:e18.
146. Reddy DV, Kinsey VE. Composition of the vitreous humor in relation to that of plasma and aqueous humors. *Arch Ophthalmol* 1960;63:715–20.
147. Forrest ARW. Obtaining samples at post mortem examination for toxicological and biochemical analyses. *J Clin Pathol* 1993;46:292–6.
148. Coe JI. Comparative postmortem chemistries of vitreous humor before and after embalming. *J Forensic Sci* 1976;21:583–6.
149. Singer PP, Jones GR, Lewis R, Johnson R. Loss of ethanol from vitreous humor in drowning death. *J Anal Toxicol* 2007;31:522–5.
150. Hadley JA, Smith GS. Evidence for an early onset of endogenous alcohol production in bodies recovered from the water: implications for studying alcohol and drowning. *Accid Anal Prev* 2003;35:763–9.
151. O'Neal CL, Poklis A. Postmortem production of ethanol and factors that influence interpretation: a critical review. *Am J Forensic Med Pathol* 1996;17:8–20.
152. Harper DR. A comparative study of the microbiological contamination of postmortem blood and vitreous humour samples taken for ethanol determination. *Forensic Sci Int* 1989;43:37–44.
153. Sturner WQ, Herrmann MA, Boden C, Scarritt TP, Jr, Sherman RE, Harmon TS, et al. The Frye hearing in Florida: an attempt to exclude scientific evidence. *J Forensic Sci* 2000;45:908–10.
154. Pounder DJ, Kuroda N. Vitreous alcohol is of limited value in predicting blood alcohol. *Forensic Sci Int* 1994;65:73–80.
155. Jones AW, Holmgren P. Uncertainty in estimating blood ethanol concentrations by analysis of vitreous humour. *J Clin Pathol* 2001;54:699–702.
156. Felby S, Olsen J. Comparative studies of postmortem ethyl alcohol in vitreous humor, blood, and muscle. *J Forensic Sci* 1969;14:93–101.
157. Fernandez P, Lopez-Rivadulla M, Linares JM, Tato F, Bermejo AM. A comparative pharmacokinetic study of ethanol in the blood, vitreous humour and aqueous humour of rabbits. *Forensic Sci Int* 1989;41:61–5.
158. Olsen JE. Penetration rate of alcohol into the vitreous humor studied with a new in vivo technique. *Acta Ophthalmol (Copenh)* 1971;49:585–8.
159. Caughlin JD. Correlation of postmortem blood and vitreous humor alcohol concentration. *Can Soc Forensic Sci J* 1983;16:61–8.
160. Yip DCP, Shum BSF. A study on the correlation of blood and vitreous humour alcohol levels in the late absorption and elimination phases. *Med Sci Law* 1990;30:29–33.
161. Jollymore BD, Fraser AD, Moss MA, Perry RA. Comparative study of ethyl alcohol in blood and vitreous humor. *Can Soc Forensic Sci J* 1984;17:50–4.
162. Scott W, Root I, Sanborn B. The use of vitreous humor for determination of ethyl alcohol in previously embalmed bodies. *J Forensic Sci* 1974;19:913–6.
163. Singer PP, Jones GR. Very unusual ethanol distribution in a fatality. *J Anal Toxicol* 1997;21:506–8.
164. Basu PK, Avaria M, Jankie R, Kapur BM, Lucas DM. Effect of prolonged immersion on the ethanol concentration of vitreous humor. *Can Soc Forensic Sci J* 1983;16:78–82.
165. Bevalot F, Cartiser N, Bottinelli C, Fanton L, Guitton J. Vitreous humor analysis for the detection of xenobiotics in forensic toxicology: a review. *Forensic Toxicol* 2016;34:12–40.
166. Bevalot F, Cartiser N, Bottinelli C, Guitton J, Fanton L. State of the art in bile analysis in forensic toxicology. *Forensic Sci Int* 2016;259:133–54.
167. Pelander A, Ristimaa J, Ojanpera I. Vitreous humor as an alternative matrix for comprehensive drug screening in postmortem toxicology by liquid chromatography-time-of-flight mass spectrometry. *J Anal Toxicol* 2010;34:312–8.
168. Metushi IG, Fitzgerald RL, McIntyre IM. Assessment and comparison of vitreous humor as an alternative matrix for forensic toxicology screening by GC-MS. *J Anal Toxicol* 2016;40:243–7.
169. Sturner WQ, Coumbis RJ. The quantitation of ethyl alcohol in vitreous humor and blood by gas chromatography. *Am J Clin Pathol* 1966;46:349–51.
170. Jones AW. Urine as a biological specimen for forensic analysis of alcohol and variability in the urine-to-blood relationship. *Toxicol Rev* 2006;25:15–35.
171. Kaye S, Cardona E. Errors of converting a urine alcohol value into a blood alcohol level. *Am J Clin Pathol* 1969;52:577–84.

172. Heatley MK, Crane J. The relationship between blood and urine alcohol concentrations at autopsy. *Med Sci Law* 1989;29:209–17.
173. Kuroda N, Williams K, Pounder DJ. Estimating blood alcohol from urinary alcohol at autopsy. *Am J Forensic Med Pathol* 1995;16:219–22.
174. Levine B, Smialek JE. Status of alcohol absorption in drinking drivers killed in traffic accidents. *J Forensic Sci* 2000;45:3–6.
175. Lahti RA, Pitkaniemi J, Jones AW, Sajantila A, Poikolainen K, Vuori E. Cause and manner of death and phase of the blood alcohol curve. *Forensic Sci Int* 2014;244C:306–12.
176. Jones AW, Holmgren P. Urine/blood ratios of ethanol in deaths attributed to acute alcohol poisoning and chronic alcoholism. *Forensic Sci Int* 2003;135:206–12.
177. Mittmeyer HJ, Blattert AK. UAK/BAK-Quotient unter Berücksichtigung der Harnblasenfüllung. *Beitr Gerichtl Med* 1991;49:263–7.
178. Fine J. Glucose content of normal urine. *Br Med J* 1965;1:1209–14.
179. Alexander WD, Wills PD, Eldred N, Gower R. Urinary ethanol levels and diabetes. *Lancet* 1981;1:789.
180. Antonides H, Marinetti L. Ethanol production in a postmortem urine sample. *J Anal Toxicol* 2011;35:516–8.
181. Jenkins AJ, Levine BS, Smialek JE. Distribution of ethanol in postmortem liver. *J Forensic Sci* 1995;40:611–3.
182. Chun HJ, Poklis JL, Poklis A, Wolf CE. Development and validation of a method for alcohol analysis in brain tissue by headspace gas chromatography with flame ionization detector. *J Anal Toxicol* 2016.
183. Nedahl M, Johansen SS, Linnet K. Brain-blood ratio of morphine in heroin and morphine autopsy cases. *Forensic Sci Int* 2019;301:388–93.
184. Nedahl M, Johansen SS, Linnet K. Postmortem brain-blood ratios of amphetamine, cocaine, ephedrine, MDMA and methylphenidate. *J Anal Toxicol* 2019;43:378–84.
185. Skov L, Holm KM, Johansen SS, Linnet K. Postmortem brain and blood reference concentrations of alprazolam, bromazepam, chlordiazepoxide, diazepam, and their metabolites and a review of the literature. *J Anal Toxicol* 2016;40:529–36.
186. Thomsen R, Rasmussen BS, Johansen SS, Linnet K. Postmortem concentrations of gamma-hydroxybutyrate (GHB) in peripheral blood and brain tissue - differentiating between postmortem formation and antemortem intake. *Forensic Sci Int* 2017;272:154–8.
187. Hirsch CS, Adelson L. Ethanol in sequestered hematomas. *Am J Clin Pathol* 1973;59:429–33.
188. Buchsbaum RM, Adelson L, Sunshine I. A comparison of post-mortem ethanol levels obtained from blood and subdural specimens. *Forensic Sci Int* 1989;41:237–43.
189. Cassin BJ, Spitz WU. Concentration of alcohol in delayed subdural hematoma. *J Forensic Sci* 1983;28:1013–5.
190. Eisele JW, Reay DT, Bonnell HJ. Ethanol in sequestered hematomas: quantitative evaluation. *Am J Clin Pathol* 1984;81:352–5.
191. Freireich AW, Bidanset JH, Lukash L. Alcohol levels in intracranial blood clots. *J Forensic Sci* 1975;20:83–5.
192. Smialek JE, Spitz WU, Wolfe JA. Ethanol in intracerebral clot. Report of two homicidal cases with prolonged survival after injury. *Am J Forensic Med Pathol* 1980;1:149–50.
193. Takahashi K, Ikeda N, Kudo K, Funayama M. Forensic significance of concentrations of ethanol in brain tissues following induced acute subdural hemorrhage. *Int J Legal Med* 2001;115:1–5.
194. Ferner RE, Aronson JK. The toxicological significance of post-mortem drug concentrations in bile. *Clin Toxicol (Phila)* 2018;56:7–14.
195. Bierly J, Labay LM. The utility of bile in postmortem forensic toxicology. *Acad Forensic Pathol* 2018;8:324–7.
196. Stone BE, Rooney PA. A study using body fluids to determine blood alcohol. *J Anal Toxicol* 1984;8:95–6.
197. Tominaga M, Michiue T, Ishikawa T, Inamori-Kawamoto O, Oritani S, Maeda H. Evaluation of postmortem drug concentrations in cerebrospinal fluid compared with blood and pericardial fluid. *Forensic Sci Int* 2015;254:118–25.
198. Engelhart DA, Jenkins AJ. Comparison of drug concentrations in postmortem cerebrospinal fluid and blood specimens. *J Anal Toxicol* 2007;31:581–7.
199. Fleming R, Stotz E. Experimental studies in alcoholism; The alcohol content of the blood and cerebrospinal fluid following oral administration in chronic alcoholism and the psychoses. *Arch NeurPsych* 1935;33:492–506.
200. Plueckhahn VD. Alcohol levels in autopsy heart blood. *J Forensic Med* 1968;15:12–21.
201. Briglia EJ, Bidanset JH, Dal Cortivo LA. The distribution of ethanol in postmortem blood specimens. *J Forensic Sci* 1992;37:991–8.
202. Bowden KM, McCallum NEW. Blood alcohol content - some aspects of its postmortem uses. *Med J Aust* 1949;2:78–81.
203. Heise HA. Erroneous postmortem blood alcohol levels (letter to the editor). *JAMA* 1957;165:1739.
204. Plueckhahn VD. The significance of blood alcohol levels at autopsy *Med J Aust* 1967;2:118–24.
205. Plueckhahn VD. The evaluation of autopsy blood alcohol levels. *Med Sci Law* 1968;8:168–76.
206. Plueckhahn VD, Ballard B. Diffusion of stomach alcohol and heart blood alcohol concentrations at autopsy. *J Forensic Sci* 1967;12:463–70.
207. Plueckhahn VD, Ballard B. Factors influencing the significance of alcohol concentrations in autopsy blood samples. *Med J Aust* 1968;1:939–43.
208. Marraccini JV, Carroll T, Grant S, Halleran S, Benz JA. Differences between multisite postmortem ethanol concentrations as related to agonal events. *J Forensic Sci* 1990;35:1360–6.
209. Takayasu T, Ohshima T, Tanaka N, Maeda H, Kondo T, Nishigami J, et al. Postmortem degradation of administered ethanol-d6 and production of endogenous ethanol: experimental studies using rats and rabbits. *Forensic Sci Int* 1995;76:129–40.
210. Takayasu T, Ohshima T, Tanaka N, Maeda H, Kondo T, Nishigami J, et al. Experimental studies on postmortem diffusion of ethanol-d6 using rats. *Forensic Sci Int* 1995;76:179–88.
211. Holmgren P, Druid H, Holmgren A, Ahlner J. Stability of drugs in stored postmortem femoral blood and vitreous humor. *J Forensic Sci* 2004;49:820–5.
212. Sutlovic D, Versic-Bratincevic M, Definis-Gojanovic M. Blood alcohol stability in postmortem blood samples. *Am J Forensic Med Pathol* 2014;35:55–8.
213. Quintas MJ, Costa P, Melo P, Castro A, Franco JM, Teixeira HM. Postmortem in vitro ethanol production-It could be more common than we think! *Forensic Sci Int* 2017;274:113–6.
214. Davis GL, Leffert RL, Rantanen NW. Putrefactive ethanol sources in postmortem tissues of conventional and germ-free mice. *Arch Pathol* 1972;94:71–4.

215. Nanikawa R, Moriya F, Hashimoto Y. Experimental studies on the mechanism of ethanol formation in corpses. *Z Rechtsmed* 1988;101:21–6.
216. Bogusz M, Guminska M, Markiewicz J. Studies on the formation of endogenous ethanol in blood putrefying in vitro. *J Forensic Med* 1970;17:156–68.
217. de Lima IV, Midio AF. Origin of blood ethanol in decomposed bodies. *Forensic Sci Int* 1999;106:157–62.
218. Moriya F, Ishizu H. Can microorganisms produce alcohol in body cavities of a living person?: a case report. *J Forensic Sci* 1994;39:883–8.
219. Blackmore DJ. The bacterial production of ethyl alcohol. *J Forensic Sci Soc* 1968;8:73–8.
220. Gormsen H. Yeasts and the production of alcohol post mortem. *J Forensic Med* 1954;1:170–1.
221. Logan BK, Jones AW. Endogenous ethanol 'auto-brewery syndrome' as a drunk-driving defence challenge. *Med Sci Law* 2000;40:206–15.
222. Kaji H, Asanuma Y, Yaahara O, Shibue H, Hisamura M, Saito N, et al. Intragastrointestinal alcohol fermentation syndrome: report of two cases and review of the literature. *J Forensic Sci Soc* 1983;24:461–71.
223. Akbaba M. A medicolegal approach to the very rare Auto-Brewery (endogenous alcohol fermentation) syndrome. *Traffic Inj Prev* 2020;21:295–7.
224. Malik F, Wickremesinghe P, Saverimuttu J. Case report and literature review of auto-brewery syndrome: probably an underdiagnosed medical condition. *BMJ Open Gastroenterol* 2019;6:e000325.
225. Cordell BJ, Kanodia A, Miller GK. Case-control research study of auto-brewery syndrome. *Glob Adv Health Med* 2019;8:2164956119837566.
226. Gill JR. The certification of fatalities related to diabetes mellitus: a shot in the dark? *Acad Forensic Pathol* 2016;6:184–90.
227. Zumwalt RE, Bost RO, Sunshine I. Evaluation of ethanol concentrations in decomposed bodies. *J Forensic Sci* 1982;27:549–54.
228. Hanzlick RL. Ethanol concentration in decomposing bodies: another look, less concern. *Am J Forenisc Med Pathol* 2009;30:88.
229. Hanzlick RL. Postmortem ethanol concentration and postmortem ethanol production. *Acad Forensic Pathol* 2014;4:156–60.
230. Ehrlich E, Kästner J, Hegewald C, Rießelmann B. Alkoholbefunde bei fäulnisveränderten Leichen *Rechtsmedizin* 2010;20:258–61.
231. Canfield DV, Kupiec T, Huffine E. Postmortem alcohol production in fatal aircraft accidents. *J Forensic Sci* 1993;38:914–7.
232. Mayes R, Levine B, Smith ML, Wagner GN, Froede R. Toxicologic findings in the USS Iowa disaster. *J Forensic Sci* 1992;37:1352–7.
233. Alexander WD, Wills PD, Eldred N. Urinary ethanol and diabetes mellitus. *Diabet Med* 1988;5:463–4.
234. Boumba VA, Kourkoumelis N, Gousia P, Economou V, Papadopoulou C, Vougiouklakis T. Modeling microbial ethanol production by E. coli under aerobic/anaerobic conditions: applicability to real postmortem cases and to postmortem blood derived microbial cultures. *Forensic Sci Int* 2013;232:191–8.
235. Boumba VA, Kourkoumelis N, Ziavrou K, Vougiouklakis T. Estimating a reliable cutoff point of 1 propanol in postmortem blood as marker of microbial ethanol production. *J Forensic Sci Med* 2019;5:141–6.
236. Liang H, Kuang S, Guo L, Yu T, Rao Y. Assessment of the role played by n-propanol found in postmortem blood in the discrimination between antemortem consumption and postmortem formation of ethanol using rats. *J Forensic Sci* 2016;61:122–6.
237. Lin Z, Wang H, Jones AW, Wang F, Zhang Y, Yulan R. Evaluation and review of ways to differentiate sources of ethanol in postmortem blood *Int J Legal Med* 2020;134:2081–93.
238. Schmitt G, Aderjan R, Keller T, Wu M. Ethyl glucuronide: an unusual ethanol metabolite in humans. Synthesis, analytical data, and determination in serum and urine. *J Anal Toxicol* 1995;19:91–4.
239. Palmer RB. A review of the use of ethyl glucuronide as a marker for ethanol consumption in forensic and clinical medicine. *Semin Diagn Pathol* 2009;26:18–27.
240. Berger L, Fendrich M, Jones J, Fuhrmann D, Plate C, Lewis D. Ethyl glucuronide in hair and fingernails as a long-term alcohol biomarker. *Addiction* 2014;109:425–31.
241. Stephanson N, Dahl H, Helander A, Beck O. Direct quantification of ethyl glucuronide in clinical urine samples by liquid chromatography-mass spectrometry. *Ther Drug Monit* 2002;24:645–51.
242. Hansson P, Varga A, Krantz P, Alling C. Phosphatidylethanol in post-mortem blood as a marker of previous heavy drinking. *Int J Legal Med* 2001;115:158–61.
243. Soderberg BL, Salem RO, Best CA, Cluette-Brown JE, Laposata M. Fatty acid ethyl esters. Ethanol metabolites that reflect ethanol intake. *Am J Clin Pathol* 2003;119 Suppl:S94–9.
244. Refaai MA, Nguyen PN, Steffensen TS, Evans RJ, Cluette-Brown JE, Laposata M. Liver and adipose tissue fatty acid ethyl esters obtained at autopsy are postmortem markers for premortem ethanol intake. *Clin Chem* 2002;48: 77–83.
245. Sundstrom M, Jones AW, Ojanpera I. Utility of urinary ethyl glucuronide analysis in post-mortem toxicology when investigating alcohol-related deaths. *Forensic Sci Int* 2014;241:178–82.
246. Helander A, Beck O, Jones AW. Distinguishing ingested ethanol from microbial formation by analysis of urinary 5-hydroxytryptophol and 5-hydroxyindoleacetic acid. *J Forensic Sci* 1995;40:95–8.
247. Canfield D, Brink J, Johnson R, Lewis R, Dubowski K. Clarification of ethanol-positive case using urine serotonin metabolite ratio. *J Anal Toxicol* 2007;31:592–5.
248. Kapur BM, Aleksa K. What the lab can and cannot do: clinical interpretation of drug testing results. *Crit Rev Clin Lab Sci* 2020;57:548–85.
249. Boumba VA, Economou V, Kourkoumelis N, Gousia P, Papadopoulou C, Vougiouklakis T. Microbial ethanol production: experimental study and multivariate evaluation. *Forensic Sci Int* 2012;215:189–98.
250. Koppe SW. Obesity and the liver: nonalcoholic fatty liver disease. *Transl Res* 2014;164:312–22.
251. Sarwar R, Pierce N, Koppe S. Obesity and nonalcoholic fatty liver disease: current perspectives. *Diabetes Metab Syndr Obes* 2018;11:533–42.
252. Pounder DJ. Problems in the necropsy diagnosis of alcoholic liver disease. *Am J Forensic Med Pathol* 1984;5:103–9.
253. Mihas AA, Tavassoli M. Laboratory markers of ethanol intake and abuse: a critical appraisal. *Am J Med Sci* 1992;303:415–28.
254. Bortolotti F, Tagliaro F. Biomarkers for the identification of alcohol use/abuse: a critical review. *Forensic Sci Rev* 2011;23:55–72.

255. Peterson K. Biomarkers for alcohol use and abuse--a summary. *Alcohol Res Health* 2004;28:30–7.
256. Sadler DW, Girela E, Pounder DJ. Post mortem markers of chronic alcoholism. *Forensic Sci Int* 1996;82:153–63.
257. Rainio J, De Giorgio F, Bortolotti F, Tagliaro F. Objective post-mortem diagnosis of chronic alcohol abuse--a review of studies on new markers. *Leg Med (Tokyo)* 2008;10:229–35.
258. Nanau RM, Neuman MG. Biomolecules and biomarkers used in diagnosis of alcohol drinking and in monitoring therapeutic interventions. *Biomolecules* 2015;5:1339–85.
259. Bendroth P, Kronstrand R, Helander A, Greby J, Stephanson N, Krantz P. Comparison of ethyl glucuronide in hair with phosphatidylethanol in whole blood as post-mortem markers of alcohol abuse. *Forensic Sci Int* 2008;176:76–81.
260. Rainio J, Ahola S, Kangastupa P, Kultti J, Tuomi H, Karhunen PJ, et al. Comparison of ethyl glucuronide and carbohydrate-deficient transferrin in different body fluids for post-mortem identification of alcohol use. *Alcohol Alcohol* 2014;49:55–9.
261. Cahill GF, Jr. Ketosis. *Kidney Int* 1981;20:416–25.
262. Irwin J, Cohle SD. Sudden death due to diabetic ketoacidosis. *Am J Forensic Med Pathol* 1988;9:119–21.
263. Kadis P, Balazic J, Ferlan-Marolt V. Alcoholic ketoacidosis: a cause of sudden death of chronic alcoholics. *Forensic Sci Int* 1999;103:S53–S9.
264. Kamel KS, Halperin ML. Acid-base problems in diabetic ketoacidosis. *N Engl J Med* 2015;372:1969–70.
265. Brinkmann B, Fechner G, Karger B, DuChesne A. Ketoacidosis and lactic acidosis - frequent causes of death in chronic alcoholics? *Int J Legal Med* 1998;111:115–9.
266. Denmark LN. The investigation of beta-hydroxybutyrate as a marker for sudden death due to hypoglycemia in alcoholics. *Forensic Sci Int* 1993;62:225–32.
267. Pounder DJ, Stevenson RJ, Taylor KK. Alcoholic ketoacidosis at autopsy. *J Forensic Sci* 1998;43:812–6.
268. Thomsen JL, Felby S, Theilade P, Nielsen E. Alcoholic ketoacidosis as a cause of death in forensic cases. *Forensic Sci Int* 1995;75:163–71.
269. Randall B. Fatty liver and sudden death. *Human Pathol* 1980;11:147–53.
270. Milroy CM. Fatty liver and the forensic pathologist. *Acad Forensic Pathol* 2018;8:296–310.
271. Sadones N, Lambert WE, Stove CP. The (non)sense of routinely analysing beta-hydroxybutyric acid in forensic toxicology casework. *Forensic Sci Int* 2017;274:38–43.
272. Palmer JP. Alcoholic ketoacidosis: clinical and laboratory presentation, pathophysiology and treatment. *Clin Endocrinol Metab* 1983;12:381–9.
273. Isselbacher KJ. Metabolic and hepatic effects of alcohol. *N Eng J Med* 1977;290:612–6.
274. Levy LJ, Duga J, Girgis M, Gordon EE. Ketoacidosis associated with alcoholism in nondiabetic subjects. *Ann Intern Med* 1973;78:213–9.
275. Kanetake J, Kanawaku Y, Mimasaka S, Sakai J, Hashiyada M, Nata M, et al. The relationship of a high level of serum beta-hydroxybutyrate to cause of death. *Leg Med* 2005;7:169–74.
276. Klaric KA, Milroy CM, Parai JL. Utility of postmortem vitreous beta-hydroxybutyrate testing for distinguishing sudden from prolonged deaths and for diagnosing ketoacidosis. *J Forensic Sci* 2020;61:1588–93.
277. Eriksson Hydara Y, Zilg B. Postmortem diagnosis of ketoacidosis: levels of beta-hydroxybutyrate, acetone and isopropanol in different causes of death. *Forensic Sci Int* 2020;314:110418.
278. Gagajewski A, Murakami MM, Kloss J, Edstrom M, Hillyer M, Peterson GF, et al. Measurement of chemical analytes in vitreous humor: stability and precision studies. *J Forensic Sci* 2004;49:371–4.
279. Pigaiani N, Bertaso A, De Palo EF, Bortolotti F, Tagliaro F. Vitreous humor endogenous compounds analysis for post-mortem forensic investigation. *Forensic Sci Int* 2020;310:110235.
280. Osuna E, Vivero G, Conejero J, Abenza JM, Martinez P, Luna A, et al. Postmortem vitreous humor beta-hydroxybutyrate: its utility for the postmortem interpretation of diabetes mellitus. *Forensic Sci Int* 2005;153:189–95.
281. Heninger M. Postmortem vitreous beta-hydroxybutyrate: interpretation in a forensic setting. *J Forensic Sci* 2012;57:1234–40.
282. Elliott S, Smith C, Cassidy D. The post-mortem relationship between beta-hydroxybutyrate (BHB), acetone and ethanol in ketoacidosis. *Forensic Sci Int* 2010;198:53–7.
283. Pla A, Hernandez AF, Gil F, Garcia-Alonso M, Villanueva E. A fatal case of oral ingestion of methanol. Distribution in postmortem tissues and fluids including pericardial fluid and vitreous humor. *Forensic Sci Int* 1991;49:193–6.
284. Roe O. Species differences in methanol poisoning. *Crit Rev Toxicol* 1982;10:275–86.
285. Aghababaeian H, Araghi Ahvazi L, Ostadtaghizadeh A. The methanol poisoning outbreaks in Iran 2018. *Alcohol Alcohol* 2019;54:128–30.
286. Gulen M, Satar S, Avci A, Acehan S, Orhan U, Nazik H. Methanol poisoning in Turkey: two outbreaks, a single center experience. *Alcohol* 2020;88:83–90.
287. Rostrup M, Edwards JK, Abukalish M, Ezzabi M, Some D, Ritter H, et al. The methanol poisoning outbreaks in Libya 2013 and Kenya 2014. *PLoS One* 2016;11:e0152676.
288. Kraut JA, Mullins ME. Toxic alcohols. *N Engl J Med* 2018;378:270–80.
289. Gilg T. Methanol and congeners as markers of alcohol use and abuse. In: Wurst FW, editor. *New and Upcoming Markers of Alcohol Consumption*. Darmstadt: Steinkopff Verlag, 2001, 35–52.
290. Haffner HT, Graw M, Besserer K, Blickle U, Henssge C. Endogenous methanol: variability in concentration and rate of production. Evidence of a deep compartment? *Forensic Sci Int* 1996;79:145–54.
291. Ohimain EI. Methanol contamination in traditionally fermented alcoholic beverages: the microbial dimension. *Springerplus* 2016;5:1607.
292. Butchko HH, Stargel WW, Comer CP, Mayhew DA, Benninger C, Blackburn GL, et al. Aspartame: review of safety. *Regul Toxicol Pharmacol* 2002;35:S1–93.
293. Majchrowicz E, Mendelson JH. Blood methanol concentrations during experimentally induced ethanol intoxication in alcoholics. *J Pharmacol Exp Ther* 1971;179:293–300.
294. Jones AW. Elimination half-life of methanol during hangover. *Pharmacol Toxicol* 1987;60:217–20.
295. Haffner HT, Besserer K, Graw M, Voges S. Methanol elimination in non-alcoholics: inter- and intraindividual variation. *Forensic Sci Int* 1997;86:69–76.
296. Jones AW, Lowinger H. Relationship between the concentration of ethanol and methanol in blood samples from Swedish drinking drivers. *Forensic Sci Int* 1988;37:277–85.
297. Hashemy Tonkabony SE. Post-mortem blood concentration of methanol in 17 cases of fatal poisoning from contraband vodka. *Forensic Sci* 1975;6:1–3.
298. Paasma R, Hovda KE, Tikkerberi A, Jacobsen D. Methanol mass poisoning in Estonia: outbreak in 154 patients. *Clin Toxicol (Phila)* 2007;45:152–7.

299. Paasma R, Hovda KE, Jacobsen D. Methanol poisoning and long term sequelae - a six years follow-up after a large methanol outbreak. *BMC Clin Pharmacol* 2009;9:5.
300. Shahangian S, Ash KO. Formic and lactic acidosis in a fatal case of methanol intoxication. *Clin Chem* 1986;32:395–7.
301. Jacobsen D, Jansen H, Wiik-Larsen E, Bredesen JE, Halvorsen S. Studies on methanol poisoning. *Acta Med Scand* 1982;212:5–10.
302. Tanaka E, Honda K, Horiguchi H, Misawa S. Postmortem determination of the biological distribution of formic acid in methanol intoxication. *J Forensic Sci* 1991;36:936–8.
303. Jones GR, Singer PP, Rittenbach K. The relationship of methanol and formate concentrations in fatalities where methanol is detected. *J Forensic Sci* 2007;52:1376–82.
304. Hovda KE, Hunderi OH, Tafjord AB, Dunlop O, Rudberg N, Jacobsen D. Methanol outbreak in Norway 2002–2004: epidemiology, clinical features and prognostic signs. *J Intern Med* 2005;258:181–90.
305. Zakharov S, Pelclova D, Navratil T, Belacek J, Komarc M, Eddleston M, et al. Fomepizole versus ethanol in the treatment of acute methanol poisoning: comparison of clinical effectiveness in a mass poisoning outbreak. *Clin Toxicol (Phila)* 2015;53:797–806.
306. McMartin K, Jacobsen D, Hovda KE. Antidotes for poisoning by alcohols that form toxic metabolites. *Br J Clin Pharmacol* 2016;81:505–15.
307. Mani JC, Pietruszko R, Theorell H. Methanol activity o alcohol dehydrogenases from human liver, horse liver, and yeast. *Arch Biochem Biophys* 1970;140:52–9.
308. Brent J, McMartin K, Phillips S, Aaron C, Kulig K, Methylpyrazole for toxic alcohols study G. Fomepizole for the treatment of methanol poisoning. *N Engl J Med* 2001;344:424–9.
309. Brent J. Fomepizole for the treatment of pediatric ethylene and diethylene glycol, butoxyethanol, and methanol poisonings. *Clin Toxicol (Phila)* 2010;48:401–6.
310. Hassanian-Moghaddam H, Zamani N, Roberts DM, Brent J, McMartin K, Aaron C, et al. Consensus statements on the approach to patients in a methanol poisoning outbreak. *Clin Toxicol (Phila)* 2019;57:1129–36.
311. Alexander CB, McBay AJ, Hudson RP. Isopropanol and isopropanol deaths-ten years' experience. *J Forensic Sci* 1982;27:541–8.
312. McFadden SW, Haddow JE. Coma produced by topical application of isopropanol. *Pediatrics* 1969;43:622–3.
313. Wise JR, Jr. Alcohol sponge baths. *N Engl J Med* 1969;280:840.
314. Adelson L. Fatal intoxication with isopropyl alcohol (rubbing alcohol). *Am J Clin Pathol* 1962;38:144–51.
315. Lehman AJ, Chase HF. The acute and chronic toxicity of isopropyl alcohol. *J Lab Clin Med* 1944;29:561–7.
316. Slaughter RJ, Mason RW, Beasley DM, Vale JA, Schep LJ. Isopropanol poisoning. *Clin Toxicol (Phila)* 2014;52:470–8.
317. Molina DK. A characterization of sources of isopropanol detected on postmortem toxicologic analysis. *J Forensic Sci* 2010;55:998–1002.
318. Jones AW. Elimination half-life of acetone in humans: case reports and review of the literature. *J Anal Toxicol* 2000;24:8–10.
319. Natowicz M, Donahue J, Gorman L, Kane M, McKissick J, Shaw L. Pharmacokinetic analysis of a case of isopropanol intoxication. *Clin Chem* 1985;31:326–8.
320. Monaghan MS, Olsen KM, Ackerman BH, Fuller GL, Porter WH, Pappas AA. Measurement of serum isopropanol and the acetone metabolite by proton nuclear magnetic resonance: application to pharmacokinetic evaluation in a simulated overdose model. *J Toxicol Clin Toxicol* 1995;33:141–9.
321. Palmiere C, Sporkert F, Werner D, Bardy D, Augsburger M, Mangin P. Blood, urine and vitreous isopropyl alcohol as biochemical markers in forensic investigations. *Leg Med (Tokyo)* 2012;14:17–20.
322. Dwyer JB, Tamama K. Ketoacidosis and trace amounts of isopropanol in a chronic alcoholic patient. *Clin Chim Acta* 2013;415:245–9.
323. Petersen TH, Williams T, Nuwayhid N, Harruff R. Postmortem detection of isopropanol in ketoacidosis. *J Forensic Sci* 2012;57:674–8.
324. Jones AW, Andersson L. Biotransformation of acetone to isopropanol observed in a motorist involved in a sobriety check. *J Forensic Sci* 1995;40:686–7.
325. Lewis GD, Laufman AK, McAnalley BH, Garriott JC. Metabolism of acetone to isopropyl alcohol in rats and humans. *J Forensic Sci* 1984;29:541–9.
326. Jones AW, Holmgren A. Occurrence of acetone concentrations >0.10 g/L in post-mortem femoral blood and association with ethanol and isopropanol concentrations. *Toxic Anal Clin* 2015;27:226–32.
327. Kalant H. Intoxicated automatism: legal concept vs. scientific evidence. *Contempt Drug Prob* 1996;23:631–48.
328. Lewis RJ, Johnson RD, Angier MK, Vu NT. Ethanol formation in unadulterated postmortem tissues. *Forensic Sci Int* 2004;146:17–24.
329. Canfield DV, Dubowski KM, Chaturvedi AK, Whinnery JE. Drugs and alcohol found in civil aviation accident pilot fatalities from 2004–2008. *Aviat Space Environ Med* 2012;83:764–70.
330. WHO. *Global Status Report on Alcohol and Health, Geneva, Switzerland.* Geneva: World Health Organization, 2018.
331. White AM, Slater ME, Ng G, Hingson R, Breslow R. Trends in alcohol-related emergency department visits in the United States: results from the nationwide emergency dpartment sample, 2006 to 2014. *Alcohol Clin Exp Res* 2018;42:352–9.
332. Felby S, Nielsen E. Postmortem blood alcohol concentration. *Blutalkohol* 1993;30:244–50.
333. Jones AW, Holmgren A, Ahlner J. Post-mortem concentrations of drugs determined in femoral blood in single-drug fatalities compared with multi-drug poisoning deaths. *Forensic Sci Int* 2016;267:96–103.
334. Kriikku P, Ojanpera I. Significant decrease in the rate of fatal alcohol poisonings in Finland validated by blood alcohol concentration statistics. *Drug Alcohol Depend* 2020;206:107722.
335. Kaye S, Haag HB. Terminal blood alcohol concentrations in ninety-four fatal cases of acute alcoholism. *J Am Med Assoc* 1957;165:451–2.

3.4 LABORATORY TESTS AND BIOMARKERS OF ACUTE AND CHRONIC ETHANOL CONSUMPTION

Alan Wayne Jones and Anders Helander

3.4.1 Introduction

Ethanol is a legal drug and light-to-moderate drinking of alcoholic beverages should not represent a danger to a person's health or longevity.[1] However, depending on genetic predisposition and other factors – such as mental illness, personality disorders, and peer-group influences – maintaining abstinence is the safest policy.[2,3] Furthermore, for about 10%–15% of the population, especially among men, initial moderate drinking may eventually lead to chronic heavy drinking and abuse of alcohol, and the development of a serious alcohol-use disorder.[4,5] Excessive drinking and drunkenness are global problems for public health, with enormous costs to society for the treatment and rehabilitation of alcohol dependence and often resulting in early death and morbidity.[2,6,7] Binge drinking, which is usually defined as the consumption of five or more drinks within two hours resulting in a blood-alcohol concentration (BAC) of 0.80 g/L (0.08%) or more, triggers a range of deviant behaviors, including hooliganism, sexual assaults, and drunken driving.[8,9]

The epidemiology of alcohol consumption and drinking habits differs between countries although per capita consumption (people > 15 y) is relatively high throughout all age groups with an increasing prevalence in women. Early intervention and treatment require ways to identify those at greatest risk of developing an alcohol-use disorder.[10–12] However, making a correct diagnosis of alcohol addiction or dependence is not easy, because most people are not truthful about the quantities and frequency of their drinking. This has created an urgent need for sensitive and specific biochemical laboratory testing of excessive and problematic drinking.[13] According to the American Medical Association, the difference between moderate use, abuse, and alcohol dependence ("alcoholism") can be considered as follows.

- **Moderate use** is the consumption of alcohol in amounts considered harmless to health, at the most one to two drinks per day (~10 g–20 g ethanol), and never first thing in the morning or on an empty stomach. The person's BAC should not exceed 0.2 g/L on any drinking occasion.
- **Abuse of alcohol** is a pattern of drinking that is accompanied by one or more of the following elements: (a) failure to fulfill major work, school, or home responsibilities because of drinking; (b) drinking in situations that are physically dangerous, such as while driving or operating machinery; (c) recurring problems with law enforcement, such as being arrested for driving under the influence of alcohol or for physically hurting someone while drunk (e.g. domestic violence), and; (d) having social or relationship problems that are caused by, or worsened by, the effects of alcohol.
- **Alcohol dependence** is a more chronic and dangerous drinking behvior that includes persistent drinking in spite of obvious physical, mental, and social problems caused by the alcohol abuse. Also typical for people with this disorder are (a) loss of control and inability to stop drinking once started; (b) experiencing withdrawal symptoms when drinking ends, such as nausea, sweating, shakiness, and anxiety, and; (c) increasing tolerance to alcohol's effects, and the need to increase the amounts consumed in order to feel drunk.

The denial of problem drinking represents a major stumbling block in addiction medicine for initiating suitable treatment and rehabilitation programs.[14] Drinking histories are notoriously unreliable, which means that the results of clinical interviews and questionnaires often fail to identify those likely to become dependent on alcohol.[15,16] Much research has, therefore, focused on developing more objective ways to disclose excessive drinking using biochemical and laboratory analysis of body fluids.[17] The use of various clinical laboratory tests or biomarkers provide a useful complement to self-report drinking questionnaires, such as the AUDIT, MAST and CAGE.[18,19] The latter are intended to divulge quantity and frequency of drinking and various social-medical consequences when under the influence of alcohol.

Research on alcohol biomarkers is extensive and has resulted in the development of sensitive tests to divulge over-consumption of alcohol and damage to body organs and tissues from years of chronic drinking.[20–23] Ethanol is mainly metabolized in the liver to acetaldehyde and acetic acid. The liver is, therefore, susceptible to damage caused by regular excessive drinking, which causes a leakage of various hepatic enzymes, such as γ-glutamyl transferase (GGT) and alanine aminotransferase (ALT), into the bloodstream.[24,25] However, it appears that some people can drink excessively for years without displaying elevated levels of these enzymes, which implies a low *sensitivity* as a biomarker for detecting hazardous drinking. In contrast, some biological markers yield positive results even after moderate daily drinking, and in patients suffering from a non-alcohol-related liver problem, or as a result of taking certain medications, which implies these biomarkers have a low *specificity* for detecting alcohol abuse.

Nevertheless, biochemical tests or biomarkers are valuable tools for use in addiction medicine to complement clinical and psychological tests of a person's drinking habits and as a screening instrument to detect patients at greatest risk of developing an alcohol-use disorder.[23,26,27] Besides applications in clinical medicine, the rehabilitation of alcoholics, and drug-abuse treatment programs,[28] there are applications of these same biochemical markers in occupational medicine,[29,30] forensic science,[31–34] and biomedical alcohol research.[35,36] In general, three major classes of tests or biochemical markers have been distinguished (examples are given in Table 3.4.1).

TABLE 3.4.1

Examples of Direct and Indirect Biochemical Markers of Alcohol Use and Abuse, and of Possible Predisposition to Develop Alcohol Dependence

Classification of the biomarker	Direct/indirect marker[1]	Examples of the laboratory test or analysis of acute or chronic drinking	Bio-specimen analyzed
Acute Markers	Direct	Ethanol (EtOH)	Breath, blood, urine
	Indirect	Methanol (MeOH)	Blood, urine
	Indirect	Serotonin metabolites 5-hydroxytryptophol (5HTOL) to 5-hydroxyindoleactic acid (5HIAA) ratio	Urine
	Direct	Ethyl glucuronide (EtG)	Urine, blood, hair
	Direct	Ethyl sulfate (EtS)	Urine, blood
	Direct	Fatty acid ethyl esters (FAEE)	Hair, blood
State Markers	Indirect	γ-glutamyl transferase (GGT)	Plasma, serum
	Indirect	Alanine aminotransferase (ALT) and aspartate aminotransferase (AST)	Plasma, serum
	Indirect	Erythrocyte mean corpuscular volume (MCV)	Whole blood
	Indirect	Carbohydrate-deficient transferrin (CDT)	Serum
	Direct	Phosphatidylethanol (PEth)	Whole blood
Trait Markers		Monoamine oxidase (MAO)	Platelets
		Adenylyl cyclase (AC)	Whole blood
		Neuropeptide Y (NPY)	Whole blood

[1] Direct alcohol biomarkers originate directly from the analysis of ethanol, or typically one of its non-oxidative metabolites or adducts, whereas an indirect marker is a secondary effect, such as an altered biochemical or hematologic profile in body fluids or body organ function, appearing after acute or chronic drinking.

1. Tests sufficiently sensitive to detect even a single intake of alcohol are known as *acute markers* or *relapse markers*. The latter might involve the identification of certain ethanol metabolites in blood, urine, or other bio-fluid.
2. Tests that indicate disturbed metabolic processes, or malfunction of body organs and/or tissue caused by long-term exposure to ethanol. This is reflected in, among other things, altered biochemical and/or hematological parameters or activity of certain liver enzymes. Such tests are referred to as *state markers* of hazardous consumption of alcohol.
3. Tests that indicate whether a person carries a genetic predisposition for heavy drinking, abuse of alcohol, and development of alcohol dependence. Such tests are known as *trait markers* and often rely on identifying an abnormal enzyme or receptor protein at the molecular level. Like many diseases, substance abuse is, in part, hereditary and many heavy drinkers and drug addicts suffer from a personality disorder. This dual diagnosis is a major goal for medical intervention. Many people exhibit early on-set abuse of ethanol and other drugs. They often exhibit sensation-seeking behavior and criminality at an early age. This is predominantly seen in the male gender.

The scientific literature dealing with alcohol biomarkers of acute and chronic drinking is extensive and the different approaches available tend to be classified as direct or indirect markers. Direct markers entail the analysis and identification of ethanol itself in body fluids, or one of its non-oxidative metabolites, whereas indirect markers focus on ethanol-induced changes in metabolic and/or biochemical reactions as a result of chronic heavy drinking.

The present chapter is an update on our article published in the second edition of *The Drug Abuse Handbook* and includes updated literature references. The advantages, limitations, and practical utility of the plethora of markers currently available are discussed along with their clinical and/or forensic applications. Table 3.4.1 lists the various alcohol biomarkers, along with whether these are classified as direct or indirect markers, and offers the types of biological specimens most suitable for laboratory analysis.

3.4.2 Diagnostic Sensitivity and Specificity

Biochemical markers are usually evaluated in terms of diagnostic sensitivity and specificity. *Sensitivity* refers to the ability of a test to detect the presence of the clinical condition in question, whereas *specificity* refers to its ability to exclude individuals without this trait. Consequently, a marker with high sensitivity yields relatively few false-negative results, and one with high specificity gives few false positives. The ideal marker should, of course, be both 100% sensitive and specific, but this is hardly ever achieved because reference ranges for "normal" and "abnormal" values always tend to overlap. Instead, a cut-off, or threshold limit, is established for what is considered normal. These limits are usually determined empirically and calculated as the mean plus or minus two standard deviations (SD) of the test results for a healthy control population. Assuming a Gaussian distribution of values, ~2.5% of individuals will be above the upper limit and ~2.5% below the lower limit and the test specificity will always be less than 100%.

To obtain a sufficiently high specificity for routine purposes, the sensitivity of the marker has to be gradually reduced. On the other hand, most tests aimed at indicating liver damage caused by prolonged alcohol abuse tend to suffer from low specificity, because many liver diseases have a non-alcoholic origin. So-called receiver-operating characteristic (ROC) curves have been widely used for evaluating the utility of biochemical markers, identifying optimal cut-offs, and for comparing different analytical methods.[37] ROC curves are graphic illustrations created by plotting the relation between sensitivity (i.e., the percentage of true positives) against 1-specificity (i.e., the percentage of false positives) at different cut-off limits between normal and abnormal values.[38]

Most studies aimed at evaluating the sensitivity and specificity of alcohol biomarkers rely heavily on patient self-reports about drinking as the reference or gold standard. However, considering that many patients fail to provide an accurate history of their true alcohol consumption, this creates a validity problem. Hence, besides the use of sensitive and specific markers of excessive alcohol consumption, there is also a need to develop and evaluate laboratory tests to monitor recent alcohol consumption in a more objective way.

3.4.3 Tests for Acute Alcohol Ingestion

3.4.3.1 Determination of Ethanol in Body Fluids

Ethanol and water mix in all proportions and, after drinking alcoholic beverages, the ethanol distributes into all body fluids and tissues in proportion to the amount of water in these fluids and tissues. The body water in men makes up ~60% of their body weight and the corresponding figure for women is ~50%, although there are large inter-individual differences in these average figures, depending on age and, especially, the amount of adipose tissue. Accordingly, the most specific and direct way to demonstrate that a person has been drinking alcohol is to analyze a sample of blood, breath, urine, or saliva for ethanol. However, because concentrations of ethanol in these body fluids decrease over time, owing to metabolism and excretion processes, the time frame for a positive identification is rather limited.[39,40]

The smell of alcohol on the breath is perhaps the oldest and most obvious indication that a person has been drinking. But many alcoholics use breath fresheners or can regulate their intake so that BAC remains low or zero when they are examined by a nurse or physician.[41] A more objective way to disclose recent alcohol consumption is to measure the concentration of ethanol in the exhaled air. Several kinds of hand-held breath-alcohol analyzers are available for this purpose. The ethanol in a sample of breath is oxidized with an electrochemical sensor and the magnitude of the response is directly proportional to the concentration of ethanol.[42] Studies have shown that many such breath analyzers are accurate, precise, and selective for their intended purpose. Endogenous breath volatiles, such as acetone, are not oxidized under the same conditions and therefore do not interfere with the selectivity of the test for ethanol.

An early morning appointment with a nurse or primary care physician along with a breath-alcohol test should be a mandatory requirement if patients or employees are required to refrain from drinking for various reasons.[43] However, a positive breath-alcohol test needs to be repeated not less than 15 min later as a safeguard that the patient had not used a mouth freshener or other liquid containing alcohol. Most hand-held breath-alcohol analyzers have an analytical sensitivity of ~0.05 mg/L, which corresponds to a blood-ethanol equivalent of 0.1 g/L (~2.2 mmol/L). Breath test results are available about 30 s after capturing a sample for analysis, although there is no consensus about the most appropriate concentration unit to use. In the U.S., breath alcohol for legal purposes is reported in units of g/210 L, the UK uses µg/100 mL, and Sweden – along with many other countries – uses mg/L. In many hospitals and clinics, the breath-alcohol test results are translated into the presumed coexisting BAC. The instruments need to be pre-calibrated for this purpose, assuming a population average blood/breath ratio of 2100:1 or 2300:1. Careful control of the calibration stability and instrument maintenance is essential if clinical or legal decisions are made depending on the breath-test result.

Measuring the concentration of ethanol in whole blood or plasma/serum will also provide reliable information about recent drinking. However, obtaining a sample of blood is an invasive procedure, and the concentration of ethanol, if any, is not obtained immediately after sampling. The analysis of ethanol in blood or plasma is, therefore, less practical than breath-testing, for clinical purposes as a rapid screening test for recent drinking. The sensitivity of the currently available methods of blood-alcohol analysis (e.g., by headspace gas chromatography) allows for the determination of endogenous concentrations of ethanol (~1.0 mg/L). However, for clinical applications, the usually recommended analytical cut-off is 0.05 g/L or sometimes even 0.10 g/L for reporting positive results. This helps to avoid discussions about the source of the ethanol, whether from alcoholic beverages or the use of a cough medication, a pick-me-up tonic, or even hand sanitizers that contain ethanol.

After the absorption and distribution of ethanol in body fluids and tissues are complete, there is a close correlation between the concentrations in saliva, blood, and urine. The equilibration of ethanol between blood and saliva is fairly rapid, which makes saliva sampling more suitable than urine for clinical purposes.[44,45] A number of devices have been developed for measuring ethanol in saliva and these have proven useful for screening purposes in clinical settings. A saliva-test device called QED has been extensively evaluated and gives on-the-spot results whether a person has consumed alcohol. The QED test incorporates alcohol dehydrogenase (ADH) to oxidize ethanol with the coenzyme NAD^+. Ethanol is converted into acetaldehyde and NADH is formed in direct proportion to the concentration of ethanol present. The acetaldehyde is trapped with semicarbazide, to drive the reaction to completion. The NADH is then re-oxidized to produce a colored end-product by reaction with the enzyme diaphorase and a tetrazolium salt incorporated on a solid phase support. The length of the resulting blue-colored bar is directly proportional to the concentration of ethanol in the saliva sample and permits a direct readout of the concentration within about 1 min later. Saliva-alcohol concentrations determined with QED device agreed well with the BAC and breath-alcohol concentration (BrAC) in a controlled drinking experiment.[46,47]

Numerous studies have compared concentrations of ethanol in blood and urine sampled at various times after end of drinking.[48,49] and some have tried to estimate the BAC indirectly from the UAC, assuming a population average UAC/BAC ratio. However, there are large inter- and intra-individual variations in this relationship, which means that the estimated BAC will have considerable uncertainty in any individual case. Because of the difference in water content of these body fluids, namely 100% for urine vs ~80% for whole blood, one expects to find a higher ethanol concentration in urine compared with blood (UAC/BAC ratio ~1.25:1). In reality, this ratio also depends on the time after drinking, when the bladder was last voided, and how frequently the person urinates. Urine is stored but not metabolized in the bladder, whereas the BAC changes continuously, depending on the stage of metabolism and the rate of hepatic oxidation. Shortly after drinking during the absorption phase, the UAC and BAC are not well correlated, whereas in the post-absorptive phase, when BAC is decreasing at a constant rate of about 0.15 g/L/h, a good correlation exists between BAC and UAC ($r > 0.95$).

The average venous blood and urine concentration-time profiles of ethanol are compared in Figure 3.4.1 obtained after subjects drank 0.85 g/kg ethanol on an empty stomach.

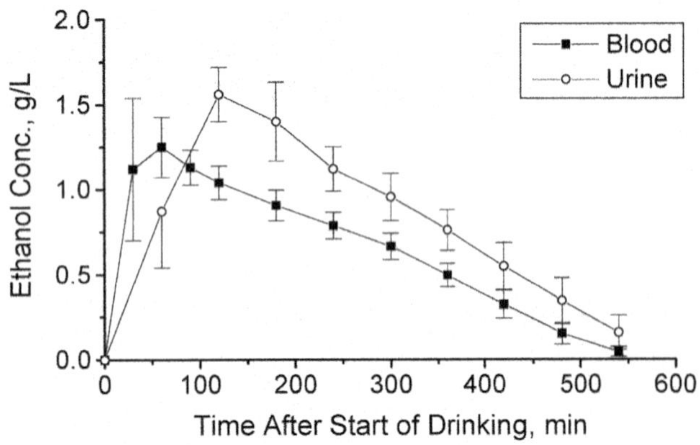

FIGURE 3.4.1 Mean concentration-time profiles of ethanol in blood and urine in 30 healthy men after they drank 0.68 g/kg body weight as neat whisky after an overnight fast. The bladder was emptied before the start of drinking and urinary voids collected every 60 min afterwards for up to 9 h

One notes that UAC and BAC curves are shifted in time, as a consequence of the time-lag between ethanol being absorbed into the bloodstream, secreted through the kidney with the glomerular filtrate, and then stored in the bladder for various periods before voiding. There is no metabolism of ethanol occurring in the urinary bladder, and the back diffusion of ethanol into the bloodstream is negligible, owing to the limited blood circulation.

Figure 3.4.1 shows that shortly after the end of drinking, the UAC is less than the BAC (UAC/BAC < 1.0). After the peak BAC is reached, the two curves cross and the UAC is now higher compared with the BAC during the entire post-absorptive phase of ethanol metabolism. The UAC to BAC ratio in the post-peak phase is about 1.3 to 1.4. The UAC reflects the average BAC prevailing during the time that urine was produced and stored in the bladder since the previous void. The UAC in a random void, therefore, does not reflect the BAC at the time of emptying the bladder and, in this respect, is less useful than blood, saliva, or breath as a test of alcohol influence. Instead, the UAC reflects the BAC during the production and storage of urine in the bladder. The UAC remains elevated for ~1–2 h after the BAC has reached zero. Accordingly, the first morning void after an evening's heavy drinking might be positive for ethanol, although the concentrations in blood or breath in the morning were already zero.[50] This relationship suggests that the BAC reaches zero sometime during the night and ethanol in the urine is then diluted with ethanol-free urine produced after metabolism of ethanol is completed.

Small quantities of ethanol are excreted through the skin by passive diffusion and also secreted through the sweat glands. Although the transdermal elimination of ethanol corresponds to only ~0.5 to 1% of the dose ingested,[51] this route of excretion has found applications in clinical medicine, as a way to monitor alcohol consumption over periods of several weeks or months. This approach might be useful as a way to control if alcohol-dependent subjects manage to remain abstinent, and has led to development of a procedure known as transdermal dosimeter or more simply called the sweat-patch test.[52,53] Similar procedures can be used to analyze other drugs of abuse as well.[54,55] The test person wears a tamper-proof and water-proof pad, positioned on an arm or leg, and the low-molecular substances that pass through the skin are collected during the time the patch remains intact. Ethanol and other volatiles are extracted with water and the concentration determined provides a cumulative index of alcohol exposure. The analysis of ethanol collected in the cotton pad can be done in a number of ways, such as by extraction with water and GC analysis or by headspace vapor analysis with a hand-held electrochemical sensor, which was originally designed for breath-alcohol testing.[56] A miniaturized electronic device for continuous sampling and monitoring of transcutaneous ethanol has been introduced.[57,58]

3.4.3.2 Oxidative Metabolism of Ethanol

The disposition and fate of ethanol in the body have been studied extensively since the 1930s and knowledge about this legal drug in terms of its pharmacokinetics far exceeds that of other psychoactive substances. Ethanol is mainly cleared from the bloodstream by oxidation, but there are also minor synthetic pathways involving the formation of ethanol conjugates (Figure 3.4.2). The non-oxidative pathways have received considerable interest for use as biomarkers in clinical and forensic medicine, since the second edition of the *Drug Abuse Handbook* appeared in 2007.

The main ethanol metabolizing enzymes are located in the liver, the kidney, and the gastric mucosa. The bulk of the dose of ethanol consumed undergoes hepatic metabolism by the action of Class I alcohol dehydrogenase (ADH), which exists in various molecular forms (isozymes). Ethanol is metabolized in a two-stage process, first to acetaldehyde and this primary metabolite is then rapidly converted to acetate (acetic acid) by the action of low K_m aldehyde dehydrogenase (ALDH2) located in the mitochondria. The end products of the oxidation of ethanol are carbon dioxide and water (see Figure 3.4.2).

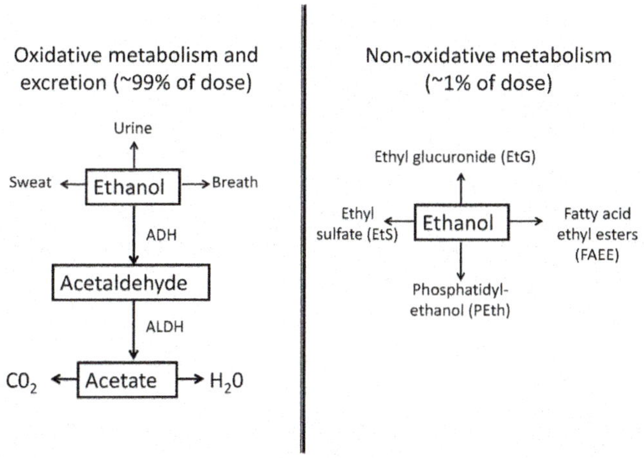

FIGURE 3.4.2 Fate of alcohol in the body illustrating both the oxidative and non-oxidative pathways of ethanol metabolism

The hepatic enzyme ADH is not specific for the oxidation of ethanol, because other aliphatic alcohols (e.g. methanol, isopropanol), if present in the blood, as well as some endogenous substances (e.g., prostaglandins and some hydroxysteroids), also serve as substrates. The substrate specificity of ADH is about ten times higher for ethanol than methanol.[59] The biotransformation of ethanol and methanol, their more toxic metabolites, and the names of two drugs that block the action of the metabolizing enzymes, fomepizole (inhibitor of ADH) and disulfiram (inhibitor of ALDH) are illustrated in Figure 3.4.3.

Higher than normal concentrations of acetaldehyde in blood during the hepatic oxidation of ethanol were proposed as a marker of metabolic tolerance that develops during chronic heavy drinking.[58] However, the quantitative analysis of acetaldehyde in blood is not easy and there is a risk of artifact formation in erythrocytes in the presence of ethanol, so the analytical procedures are much more challenging.[60] Moreover, acetaldehyde is rapidly converted to acetate by low K_m ALDH in mitochondria and this chemically reactive substance binds to various endogenous molecules, such as proteins and amino acids. Corrections to analytical results need to be made if the blood samples also contain ethanol, because acetaldehyde is formed in-vitro after sampling resulting in falsely high concentrations.[60,61] Measuring acetaldehyde in the breath instead of blood has been suggested as an alternative approach, although even breath testing is not without its difficulties.[62]

The concentration of acetate in the blood depends on the rate of ethanol oxidation and utilization of the acetate formed by peripheral tissues. The blood acetate concentration appears to be independent of the blood-ethanol concentration, and tends to be higher after the development of metabolic tolerance to alcohol (i.e., rate of ethanol elimination).[63,64] Measuring blood acetate has been suggested as a marker of chronic abuse of alcohol,[65,66] and the sensitivity and specificity of this test was significantly higher than, for example, γ-glutamyl transferrase.[65] It should be emphasized, however, that blood-acetate remains elevated only as long as ethanol is being metabolized and, moreover, the

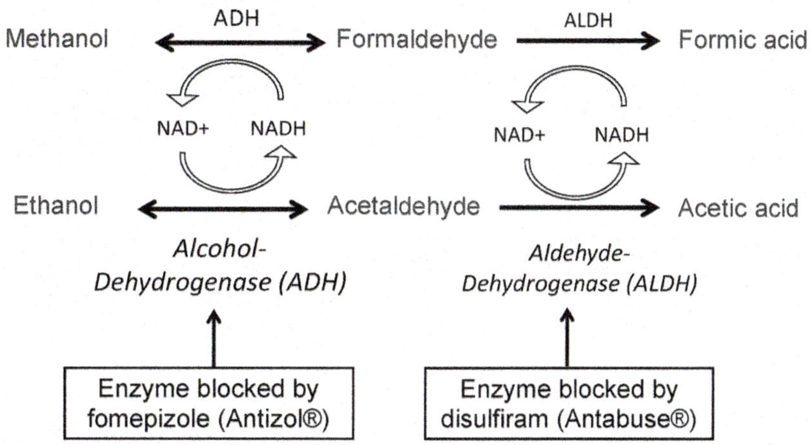

FIGURE 3.4.3 Schematic diagram comparing the metabolism of ethanol and methanol via the alcohol dehydrogenase pathway: NAD^+ = oxidized form of the coenzyme nicotinamide adenine dinucleotide; NADH = reduced form of the coenzyme. The various isozymes of alcohol dehydrogenase (ADH) and aldehyde dehydrogenase (ALDH) are indicated

rates of ethanol metabolism exhibit large inter-individual variations even in moderate drinkers.

3.4.3.3 Determination of Methanol in Body Fluids

Ethanol and methanol are endogenous alcohols and are always present in biological specimens, albeit at extremely low concentrations (< 1 mg/L). Moreover, trace quantities of the free alcohols or their esters might be ingested with common foodstuffs or might be contained in soft drinks such as fruit juices and sodas, or they could be formed by fermentation of dietary carbohydrates through the action of micro-organisms inhabiting the gut.[67–70]

During the end-stages of carbohydrate metabolism, trace amounts of acetaldehyde are produced from pyruvate and, after reduction via the ADH/NAD^+ pathway, also leads to small amounts of ethanol being present in body fluids.[71] The trace amounts of endogenous alcohols produced in the gut are rapidly cleared from the portal venous blood, as it passes through the liver for the first time. The existence of an effective first-pass metabolism ensures that only vanishingly small concentrations of endogenous ethanol and methanol reach the peripheral circulation (~0.05 to 1.5 mg/L).[72,73]

Ethanol and methanol compete for binding sites on the class I isozymes of ADH, which shows a stronger preference for the oxidation of ethanol.[59] As a consequence, during the metabolism of ethanol, the concentration of methanol in blood increases and remains on a more or less constant level, until the BAC decreases below 0.20 g/L (Figure 3.4.4). Thereafter, methanol is cleared with a half-life of ~2 to 3 h, which means that methanol can be detected in body fluids long after the concentration of ethanol has returned to zero or endogenous levels.[39,74–76] This protracted wash-out of methanol opens the possibility of verifying recent drinking for several hours after ethanol has been cleared from the body.

The analysis of methanol in blood and urine is included in some forensic investigations, when accountability for road-traffic and workplace accidents is investigated.[40] Besides the acute effects of alcohol on performance and behavior, many people are impaired the morning after an evening's heavy drinking; these post-intoxication effects of heavy drinking are known as the hangover phase.

The higher affinity of ADH for oxidation of ethanol compared with methanol also explains the mechanism behind the therapeutic usefulness of ethanol in treating methanol (wood alcohol) poisoning. Ethanol is given to the poisoned patient by an intravenous infusion to reach and maintain a BAC of ~1.0–1.2 g/L, which competes for enzyme binding to ADH and effectively blocks the on-going metabolism of methanol.[77] Thereafter, the more toxic metabolites of methanol, formaldehyde and formic acid are removed from the blood by dialysis and bicarbonate is administered to counteract a metabolic acidosis.[78] However, there are some reservations against the continued use of ethanol as an antidote, because of the effects it exerts on the central nervous system, such as when children might inadvertently have ingested a solvent containing methanol.[79] The antidote currently in vogue for treatment of people poisoned with methanol is 4-methyl pyrazole (fomepizole), a competitive inhibitor of ADH, registered as Antizol.®[80,81]

Although alcoholic beverages are primarily mixtures of ethanol and water, they also contain a multitude of other chemical compounds, albeit at extremely low concentrations. These other low-molecular substances are produced as by-products of the fermentation process and are known collectively as the congeners, which impart the smell and flavor to the alcoholic beverage.[82] Methanol concentrations in beers range from 5–10 mg/L, red and white wines contain 30–120 mg/L, distilled spirits (gin and whisky contain 100–200 mg/L, and brandies and cognac 200–400 mg/L.[83] An elevated concentration of methanol in the blood or other body fluids after drinking alcoholic beverages can partly be explained by the congener profile in the different types of drinks consumed. When blood-ethanol concentrations are elevated, the endogenous production of methanol still continues and its metabolism is blocked, because hepatic ADH is engaged in the catabolism of ethanol.[84] If the analysis of a blood sample shows a concentration of methanol above 0.01 g/L (10 mg/L) this indicates long periods of continuous heavy drinking and this can serve as a biomarker for alcohol use disorder.[85–87] Methanol is an ubiquitous congener in

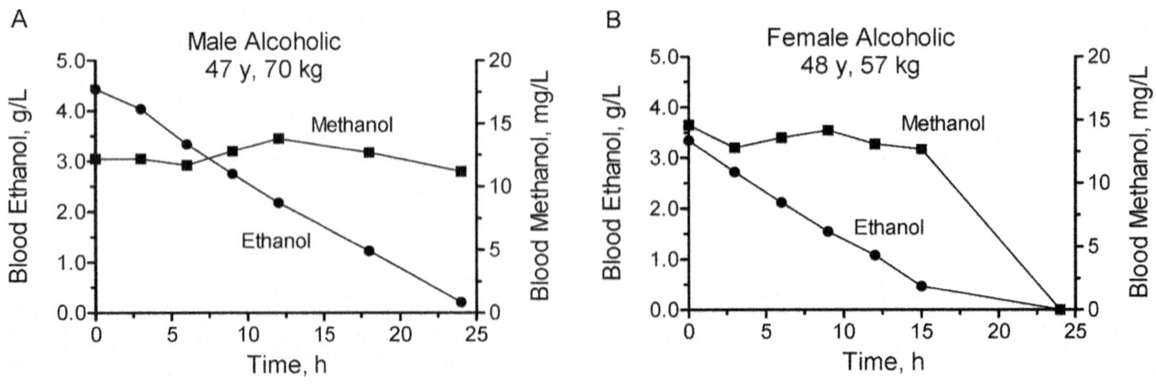

FIGURE 3.4.4 Elimination kinetics of ethanol and methanol in two alcoholics during detoxification. Note that the concentration of methanol in blood remains fairly constant at about 10 mg/L until the concentration of ethanol decreases to low or zero levels

alcoholic beverages with the lowest concentrations found in vodka and highest concentrations (1500–3000 mg/L) contained in various fruit brandies.[83,88,89]

3.4.3.4 Non-Oxidative Metabolites of Ethanol

A small fraction of the dose of ethanol ingested (~0.1–0.2%) undergoes non-oxidative metabolism to produce ethyl glucuronide (EtG) and ethyl sulfate (EtS). This glucuronidation pathway of drug metabolism was discovered at the end of the nineteenth century and substances with hydroxyl and carboxylic acid groups are prone to conjugation.[90] By the 1950s, it was discovered that aliphatic alcohols, such as ethanol, was also converted into EtG, and this minor metabolite was identified in urine.[91] However, research about this non-oxidative pathway of ethanol metabolism was hampered, owing to complexity of the analytical methods needed to determine the low EtG concentrations in body fluids.[92,93] However, the advent of modern analytical techniques, such as highly sensitive and specific gas and liquid chromatography combined with mass spectrometry (GC-MS and LC-MS),[94] radically changed the situation and spawned in a new area of alcohol biomarker research. Careful studies showed that only a very small fraction of the ingested ethanol (< 0.1%) undergoes conjugation reactions with glucuronic or sulfuric acid to produce EtG and EtS, respectively (Figure 3.4.5).[95,96] These water soluble non-oxidative metabolites of ethanol are excreted with the urine, for several hours after ethanol is no longer detectable.[95, 97–99]

Determination of EtG in urine provides a test to verify sobriety or whether a person has recently consumed alcohol, even after ethanol is no longer detectable in body fluids. The EtG detection time depends on the amount of alcohol consumed. The resulting higher sensitivity of the EtG test, compared with the analysis of ethanol itself, has obvious practical advantages as an acute marker of alcohol consumption. Furthermore, there is no accumulation of EtG in body fluids,[100] but EtG may be retained in the hair strands.[101] An advantage of hair over other body specimens for drug analysis is the extended window of detection offered, and, based on segmental analysis and an average hair growth rate, some idea can be obtained about when the drug was last being used.[102]

The availability of sensitive analytical methods for EtG, based on GC-MS and LC-MS,[97,103,104] has prompted several research groups to make detailed studies of this unique metabolite of ethanol as a sensitive and specific biomarker of acute alcohol consumption.[23,105] As expected from earlier knowledge of drug glucuronides, EtG is sensitive to urine dilution. Accordingly, the EtG concentration in urine can be lowered markedly by drinking large amounts of fluid prior to voiding, whereas this does not influence the EtG/creatinine ratio.[95] Furthermore, EtG is sensitive to enzymatic hydrolysis so, if biological samples are contaminated with certain bacteria (e.g., *E. coli* which is common in urinary tract infections), this represents another reason for obtaining falsely low or false-negative results.[106]

Another phase II metabolic pathway, namely sulfate conjugation or sulfation, is also active with ethanol. EtS is a minor ethanol metabolite (< 0.1%) and can be detected in blood and urine.[96,99] EtS shows similar excretion kinetics to EtG[96,99,107,108] but, in contrast to EtG, it is less sensitive to bacterial hydrolysis.[106] Other minor metabolites of ethanol with potential use as alcohol biomarkers include ethyl nitrite and ethyl phosphate, although their clinical utility is unknown.[109]

3.4.3.5 Fatty-Acid Ethyl Esters (FAEE)

Fatty-acid ethyl esters (FAEE), such as ethyl palmitate and ethyl oleate, are esterification products of fatty acids and ethanol synthesized through the action of the enzyme

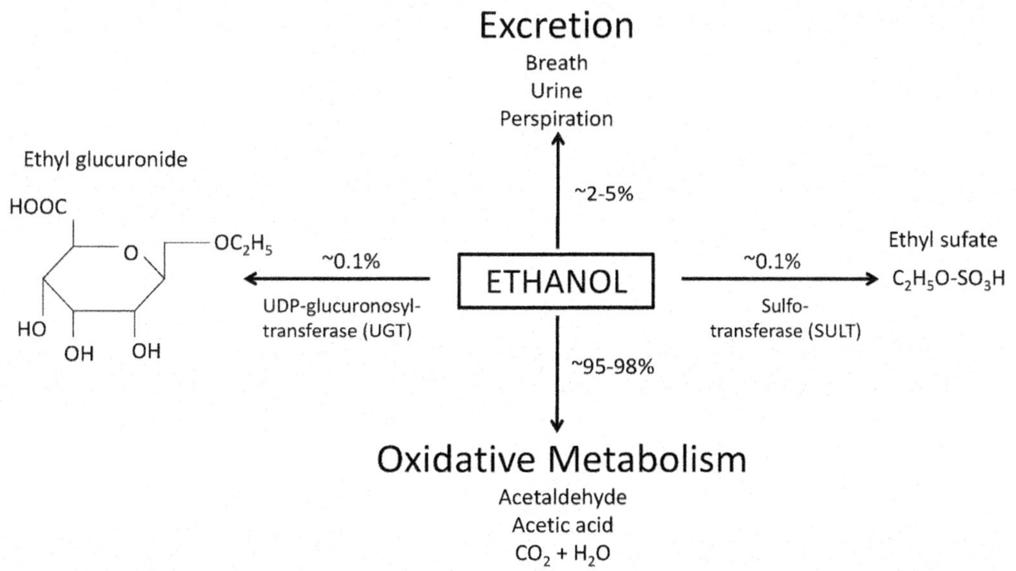

FIGURE 3.4.5 Schematic diagram illustrating the relative importance of the oxidative (phase 1) and non-oxidative conjugation (phase 2) elimination pathways for ethanol in the human body

FAEE synthase. The presence of these short-chain esters in samples of blood, tissue, or hair, has been proposed as useful biomarker of alcohol intake with clinical and forensic applications.[102,110–112] After ethanol consumption, the serum concentration of FAEE initially closely parallels that of ethanol (e.g., similar time for peak concentrations) but, because of a very slow terminal elimination phase, FAEE persists in the blood for some time after ethanol is no longer detectable.[113,114] The elimination rate of FAEE is faster than for some of the other acute alcohol biomarkers, implying a lower sensitivity for recent drinking.[114,115] There is increasing evidence suggesting that FAEE might be toxic metabolites and, as such, possible mediators of ethanol-induced organ and tissue damage.[116]

3.4.3.6 Metabolites of Serotonin

The biogenic amine serotonin (5-hydroxytryptamine, 5-HT) has been extensively studied in terms of its biochemistry and neurochemistry. The normally dominant urinary metabolite of 5-HT is 5-hydroxyindole-3-acetic acid (5HIAA) and a much smaller amount of 5-hydroxytryptophol (5HTOL) is excreted. Studies have shown that the metabolic interaction between ethanol and serotonin can help to detect recent consumption of alcohol after ethanol is no longer measurable.[117,118] After drinking ethanol, the urinary ratio of 5-HTOL to 5-HIAA increases appreciably because the intermediate aldehyde metabolite of 5-HT is preferentially reduced to give 5HTOL instead of being oxidized to an acid metabolite. This occurs owing to competitive inhibition of 5-HT aldehyde oxidation by acetaldehyde derived from ethanol oxidation.[119] Furthermore, during the metabolism of ethanol and acetaldehyde, the redox state of the liver is shifted towards a more reduced potential with elevated levels of NADH in the cytosol and mitochondria compartments. This alters the equilibrium between several endogenous NAD-dependent reactions, such as lactate/pyruvate and β-hydroxybutyrate/acetoacetate ratios. The combined influences of the competitive inhibition of ALDH and altered redox state of the liver promote the formation of 5HTOL at the expense of 5HIAA.[120,121] Most importantly, however, the urinary excretion of 5HTOL will not normalize for several hours after blood and urinary ethanol reach zero (Figure 3.4.6).[118] On the basis of this time lag, an increased urinary concentration of 5HTOL provides a sensitive biochemical marker of recent drinking.[122–124]

Expressing 5HTOL as a ratio to 5HIAA, rather than 5HTOL/creatinine, improves test accuracy because dietary serotonin (high amounts in banana, pineapple, kiwi fruit, and walnuts) might otherwise cause false-positive results, owing to a general increase in the urinary output of serotonin metabolites.[125] This analytical strategy also compensates for variations in the 5HTOL concentration caused by urine dilution after drinking fluids. To discriminate between a normal and elevated urinary 5HTOL/5HIAA ratio, a cut-off limit of 15 pmol/nmol (i.e., 1.5%) was recommended for use in clinical practice,[124] based on studies of alcohol-free subjects of both Caucasian and Oriental origin.[126] The 5HTOL/5HIAA ratio is stable both within- and between-days during

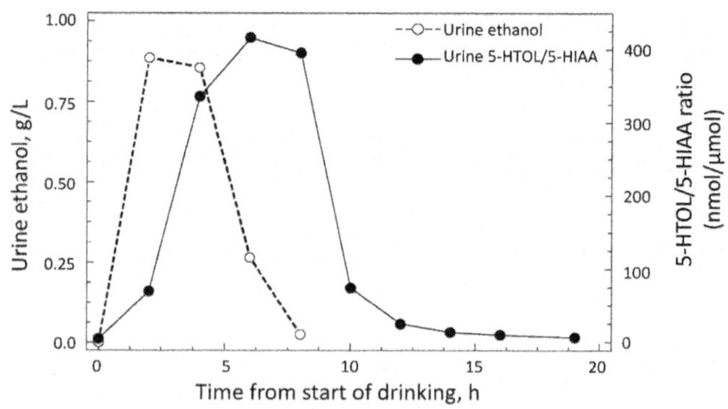

FIGURE 3.4.6 Time course of ethanol concentration and ratio of 5-hydroxytryptophol (5HTOL) to 5-hydroxyindole-3-acetic acid (5HIAA) in urine after a person drank a single moderate dose of ethanol. The elevated urinary 5HTOL/5HIAA ratio extends the time of detecting recent consumption of alcohol

abstinence, and during transport, handling, and long-term storage of urine specimens. Neither gender nor genetic variations in ADH and ALDH isozyme patterns seem to influence the baseline ratio of 5HTOL/5HIAA.[39,126]

An increased urinary 5HTOL/5HIAA ratio furnishes a specific and more sensitive laboratory test of recent drinking compared with measuring the concentration of ethanol or methanol in body fluids.[39,76] Analysis of urinary EtG and EtS, has an advantage over 5HTOL/5HIAA ratio in that the phase II metabolites remain elevated for several hours longer, thereby improving the ability to detect covert drinking. Furthermore, the baseline ratio of 5HTOL/5HIAA is not elevated after prolonged intermittent alcohol intake and can therefore identify recent drinking in both moderate and chronic drinkers.[100] Apart from alcohol ingestion, the only factor known to increase the 5HTOL/5HIAA ratio is treatment with ALDH inhibitors such as disulfiram (Antabuse) and/or cyanamide.[31] Urinary 5HTOL testing utilizes methods based on GC-MS or LC-MS.[124,127,128]

Analysis of urinary 5HTOL has been used in clinical practice, to detect relapses during outpatient treatment of alcohol-dependent subjects,[129,130] in heroin addicts on methadone maintenance,[41] and in surgical patients with chronic alcohol abuse.[131] Furthermore, the test has found applications in forensic medicine, to distinguish antemortem ingestion of ethanol from microbial synthesis post-mortem. Ethanol can be produced by fermentation of glucose when the body becomes decomposed or in urine from diabetics or others with urinary tract infections.[31,32,34,132] The 5HTOL/5HIAA ratio has also been used during forensic investigations of aviation crashes,[133] where the risk for post-mortem synthesis of ethanol is exaggerated.[127,134]

3.4.4 Laboratory Testing for Excessive Drinking

3.4.4.1 γ-Glutamyl Transferase (GGT)

Ever since the early 1970s, measuring the activity of the liver enzyme GGT in plasma/serum has been the most widely used biochemical test for heavy drinking and abuse of alcohol.[135] GGT is a membrane-bound glycoprotein distributed in various body organs, and plays an important role in glutathione synthesis, amino acid transport, and peptide nitrogen storage. Only trace amounts are normally present in the blood. However, in liver damage, for example, resulting from continuous heavy drinking, a significant elevation of GGT in blood occurs.[136,137] Although the mechanisms responsible are not known exactly, damage to hepatocytes and/or induction of hepatic GGT may allow the enzyme to leak into the blood.[138,139] After withdrawal from ethanol, the GGT activity returns to baseline levels within ~4 to 5 weeks.

Determination of GGT is routinely included as part of blood-chemistry profiles on admission to hospital. The major disadvantage of GGT as an alcohol biomarker is that the test is influenced by a variety of other conditions, thereby reducing its diagnostic specificity.[135,140,141] Examples include several common medications, such as barbiturates and antiepileptic drugs, and various liver disorders of non-alcohol origin also elevate serum GGT. Moreover, accepted normal ranges depend on nutritional status, body weight, age, and gender, and different threshold limits depicting abnormal values need to be applied for women and men separately. Although GGT has limited utility as a single screening test for hazardous alcohol consumption in non-selected populations,[142] many of the confounding factors are well-known and can often be excluded or controlled for in clinical situations. An advantage of GGT as a biomarker of alcohol abuse is its ready availability at a low cost from most clinical laboratories, but a positive test should be considered preliminary until confirmed by a more specific alcohol biomarker.

3.4.4.2 Alanine and Aspartate Aminotransferase (ALT and AST)

Other standard tests of liver dysfunction caused by hazardous drinking include raised plasma/serum levels of the transaminases ALT and AST, which are enzymes involved in amino acid metabolism. Like GGT, certain medical conditions other than alcohol abuse can cause abnormal results, and both markers are typically less sensitive, but possibly somewhat more specific, than GGT.[143,144] The ALT/AST ratio[140] and the proportion of mitochondrial to total AST[145,146] have been suggested as ways to discriminate alcohol-induced elevations from non-alcoholic liver disease, but this notion was not confirmed in studies of unselected populations.[147,148] The transaminases may be useful in combination with other biochemical tests,[149] and for the follow-up of patients with already established alcoholic liver disease[150] but not as stand-alone indicators of heavy drinking.

3.4.4.3 Erythrocyte Mean Corpuscular Volume (MCV)

MCV is included as part of a routine blood count and indicates the average size of red blood cells (erythrocytes). An elevated MCV is often observed in alcoholic patients,[151] and has been widely used as a marker of excessive alcohol consumption.[152] The underlying cause of the alcohol-induced swelling of red cells is unknown but may be a direct toxic effect of ethanol, or the alcohol-mediated deficiency of folic acid. The sensitivity of MCV as a biochemical marker of heavy drinking is much too low to motivate its use as a sole indicator.[153] Besides, there might be other explanations for an elevated MCV in addition to heavy drinking – for example, smoking which is very common in this population.[154,155] MCV shows higher specificity than GGT,[149,152,156,157] and it has often been used in combination with other standard laboratory parameters and has the added advantage that it takes longer (months) for MCV to recover to normal values after cessation of heavy drinking. However, besides the low-to-moderate sensitivity and specificity, another disadvantage of MCV is the need for fresh blood samples.

3.4.4.4 Carbohydrate-Deficient Transferrin (CDT)

The presence of an abnormal glycoform pattern of the iron transport glycoprotein transferrin in serum, named carbohydrate-deficient transferrin or CDT, emerged as a reliable method for detection of continuous high alcohol consumption for ~2 or more weeks.[158] The discovery of CDT as an alcohol biomarker dates back more than 30 years.[159] The finding of an abnormal transferrin pattern in blood-serum is fairly specific for over-consumption of alcohol and CDT recovers to normal during abstinence with a half-life of ~1.5 to 2 weeks.[159,160]

Normal variations in transferrin glycoform patterns could stem from genetic polymorphism, the degree of iron saturation, or the number of terminal sialic acid residues in the two *N*-linked oligosaccharide chains (*N*-glycans).[161–163] Normally, the most abundant glycoform in serum is tetrasialotransferrin, containing two biantennary carbohydrate chains with a total of four terminal sialic acid residues.[164,165] After prolonged heavy drinking, the abundance of transferrin molecules lacking one or both of the entire *N*-glycans (called disialo- and asialotransferrin, respectively) increases appreciably (Figure 3.4.7).[166–168] The underlying mechanism causing this elevation of CDT may involve acetaldehyde-mediated inhibition of the enzymes responsible for glycosyl transfer.[169–171]

CDT is a more specific indicator of excessive drinking than any of the traditional laboratory tests (i.e., liver enzymes and MCV), and it was also reported to have better sensitivity for early detection of alcohol abuse than GGT.[159,172,173] However, most people need to drink considerable amounts of alcohol, ~50 to 80 g ethanol or more daily, for 1–2 weeks before abnormal CDT values develop.[159,174,175] Falsely high CDT results are possible in patients with an extremely rare congenital disorders of glycosylation (CDG),[176,177] and the CDT test is useful as a screening test for CDG in newborns. The CDT prevalence increases moderately during the late stages of pregnancy (third trimester), whereas liver disorders do not cause false-high values. The CDT content should be expressed in relation to total transferrin (i.e., % CDT), instead of as an absolute amount (e.g., mg/L). This strategy has an analytical advantage, because abnormally high or low serum transferrin concentrations could otherwise render falsely high or low CDT results.[178–180]

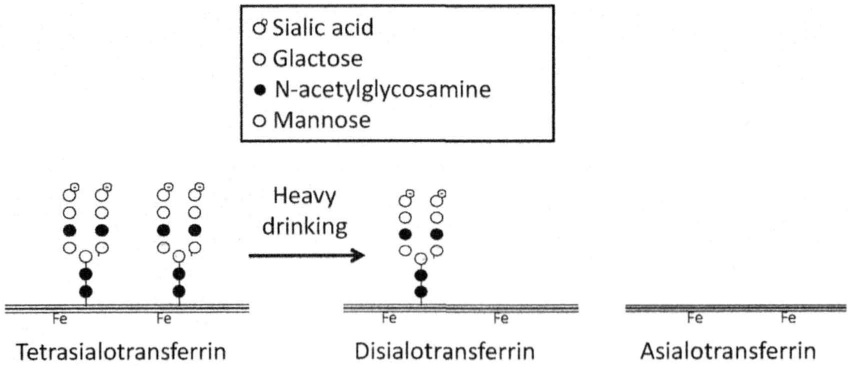

FIGURE 3.4.7 Schematic illustration of alcohol-induced changes in the glycosylation pattern of transferrin molecules. Tetrasialotransferrin is normally the major glycoform (~75–80%). After prolonged heavy drinking (~50–60 g or more/day), the relative amounts increase of transferrin molecules that lack one or both of the *N*-glycan side-chains (disialo- and asialotransferrin, respectively), called carbohydrate-deficient transferrin (CDT). When CDT is used as an alcohol marker, the relative amount of disialotransferrin to total transferrin (% CDT) is measured

Because disialo- and asialotransferrin, lacking 2 and 4 terminal sialic acid residues, respectively, are less negatively charged than tetrasialotransferrin, they are readily separated using bioanalytical techniques such as capillary electrophoresis (CE) and ion-exchange chromatography (HPLC).[124,160,162,181,182] An advantage of these analytical methods is the visible documentation of the transferrin glycoform pattern, reducing the risk of obtaining false-positive results caused by genetic variants or chromatographic interferences.[163] A direct immunoassay for determination of %CDT is also available, which appears to be insensitive to interference by genetic transferrin variants.[183,184]

Under the auspices of the International Federation of Clinical Chemistry and Laboratory Medicine (IFCC), an international standardization of the measurement of CDT has been achieved, such that all current CDT methods can be calibrated to match the HPLC reference method.[185] The normalized CDT results are denoted CDT_{IFCC} and the values obtained are directly comparable, irrespective of the analytical method used, and a common cut-off is able to distinguish abnormal values.[186]

3.4.4.5 Phosphatidylethanol (PEth)

Considerable clinical interest has developed in another non-oxidative pathway of ethanol elimination, namely the formation of an abnormal phospholipid denoted phosphatidylethanol (PEth). Without the consumption of alcohol, the endogenous phospholipid phosphatidylcholine is hydrolyzed to produce phosphatidic acid by the action of the enzyme phospholipase D. However, it was discovered in the early 1980s that when rats received daily injections of a high dose of ethanol, phosphatidylcholine was preferentially converted to PEth, as illustrated in Figure 3.4.8.[187] However, PEth is not a single molecular species, but is comprised of a family of structural variants containing a common phospho-ethanol head group to which two fatty acids are attached, although the later might have a different number of carbon atoms and saturation.

Accordingly, PEth is unique in that it is formed in cell membranes only in the presence of ethanol.[187,188] Of the several molecular species of PEth identified in blood after periods of alcohol consumption, PEth 16:0/18:1, which contains one palmitic acid and one oleic acid, is the most abundant homolog and the main analytical target for PEth testing in the clinic.[189,190] Sensitive and specific methods for determination of PEth based on LC-MS are available. The elimination half-life for PEth in whole blood (i.e., mainly red blood cells) is usually ~4–7 days and the window of detection ranges from several weeks to about one month, largely depending on the pattern of drinking and the starting concentration of PEth.[191]

The value of PEth as a biomarker of excessive driving is that it is a direct metabolite of ethanol and as such a highly specific clinical indication of recent heavy drinking over the past weeks. After alcohol-dependent patients, with a self-reported high daily ethanol intake lasting at least one week, were admitted to a detoxification clinic, PEth was detectable in their blood for another two weeks.[192,193] The results also showed a high sensitivity and positive predictive value and this observation has since been confirmed in several other studies. There is some debate about the daily consumption pattern necessary to generate an elevated PEth, although it appears to be similar to CDT in this respect (~50–60 g/day for several weeks). However, recent drinking studies have also demonstrated a considerable inter-individual variation in ethanol dose versus PEth response.[194] Furthermore, with the aid of highly sensitive LC-MS methodology, PEth can be identified in blood shortly after drinking a single moderate amount of ethanol,[195,196] meaning that different cutoffs are available to differentiate between abstinence and moderate drinking, or prolonged high intake, respectively.[197,198]

The practical use of PEth in comparison with EtG is illustrated in Figure 3.4.9 which shows the results of analyzing these two biomarkers in consecutive blood and urine samples from one patient enrolled in a clinical for alcohol-use disorder.[191] For obvious reasons, strict rules of remaining abstinent are required during treatment and rehabilitation.

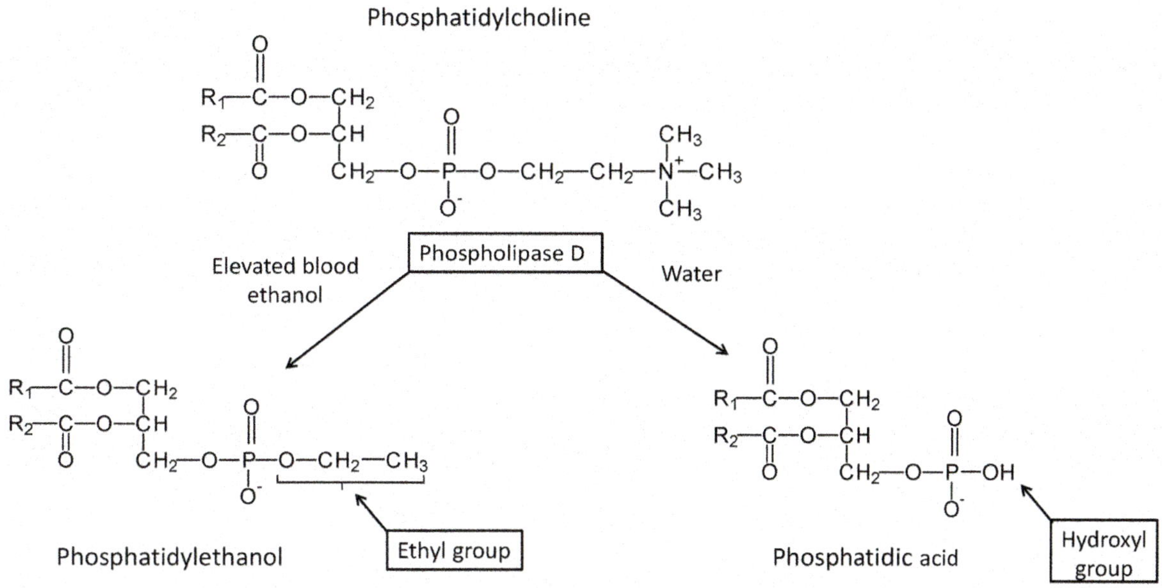

FIGURE 3.4.8 Biosynthesis of phosphatidylethanol (PEth) from phosphatidylcholine in preference to phosphatidic acid, when elevated concentrations of ethanol exist in blood and tissue. R_1 and R_2 denote fatty acid side chains, e.g. 16:0/18:1 (palmitic acid/oleic acid) and 16:0/18:2 (palmitic acid/linoleic acid)

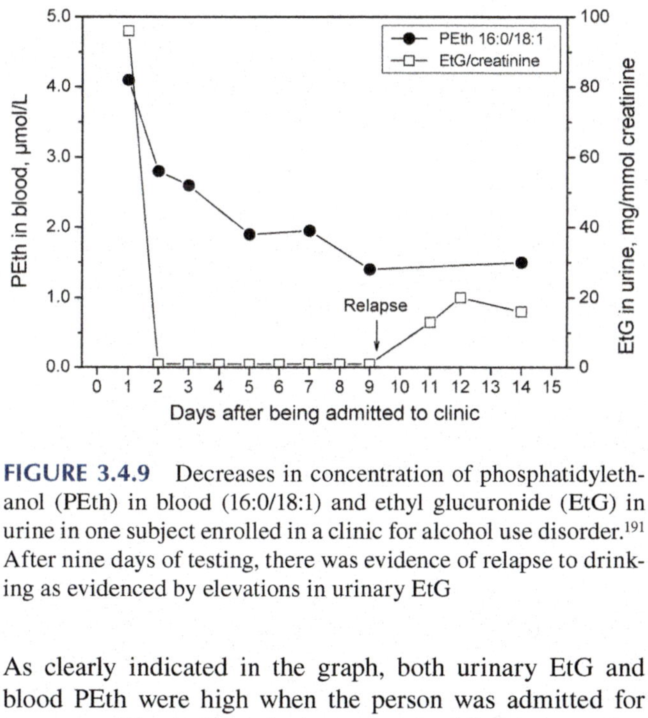

FIGURE 3.4.9 Decreases in concentration of phosphatidylethanol (PEth) in blood (16:0/18:1) and ethyl glucuronide (EtG) in urine in one subject enrolled in a clinic for alcohol use disorder.[191] After nine days of testing, there was evidence of relapse to drinking as evidenced by elevations in urinary EtG

As clearly indicated in the graph, both urinary EtG and blood PEth were high when the person was admitted for treatment. The EtG level returned to baseline values after two days of abstinence (short-term biomarker). EtG was thereafter below the analytical cut-off for about nine days when subsequent testing showed an increase in urinary EtG, which is evidence of relapsing and exposure to beverages containing alcohol. Levels of PEth in blood also decreased during abstinence, but much more slowly than EtG indicating an advantage of this phospholipid as a longer-term biomarker. After nine days of abstinence the PEth leveled out, which might also be interpreted as relapse to drinking. However, the analysis of EtG in urine is more sensitive and useful as a rapid response relapse marker than PEth.

One remaining problem with PEth analysis and its specificity as an alcohol biomarker, is the risk of artifact formation after sampling and long-term storage of specimens that also contain high concentrations of ethanol. This artifact formation even occurs when the blood and tissue specimens are stored frozen at –20°C but it can be prevented by adding phospholipase D inhibitors.[190,199]

3.4.4.6 Acetaldehyde Adducts

Acetaldehyde, the proximate metabolite of ethanol oxidation, is a highly reactive chemical species and forms adducts with various biomolecules, including DNA, phospholipids, and proteins.[200–202] The binding of acetaldehyde to hepatocellular macromolecules has been suggested as the underlying cause of alcoholic liver injury.[203–205] Measurement of "whole blood-associated" acetaldehyde, acetaldehyde-hemoglobin adducts, or antibodies that recognize acetaldehyde-modified structures, have been proposed as possible biochemical markers of excessive drinking.[206–209] However, some of these positive results were only obtained in-vitro after non-physiological concentrations of acetaldehyde were administered, and the relevance of these findings in-vivo has been a matter of debate. The analysis of various forms of bound acetaldehyde has shown promising results, and, indeed, were reported to be more sensitive for the detection of chronic excessive drinking than GGT and MCV.[210,211] However, more work is needed to determine the reliability and diagnostic potential for identification of heavy drinking in unselected populations.

3.4.4.7 Other Potential Tests or Markers of Chronic Drinking

Numerous candidate biochemical tests of alcohol use and abuse have been evaluated over the years, but only a few have gained general acceptance.[20,21] The major deficiencies are either their poor sensitivity or specificity for detecting heavy drinking or requiring laborious assay procedures unsuitable for routine use. Some markers have not been tested in sufficiently large enough cohorts of subjects with the most appropriate control groups.

Several studies have reported that alcoholics after a recent or ongoing chronic drinking binge develop a lower ALDH activity in blood compared to healthy controls.[61] However, there is a considerable inter-individual overlap between heavy and moderate consumers of alcohol in this respect, and even between heavy drinkers and teetotalers.[212,213] Consequently, to obtain sufficient sensitivity, the specificity of this ALDH enzyme marker must be very limited. In addition, several drugs, including the alcohol-sensitizing agents' disulfiram (Antabuse) and calcium carbimide, as well as environmental factors like smoking, may cause long-lasting depression of the ALDH activity in blood.[61]

An increased level of the lysosomal enzyme β-hexosaminidase was observed in serum from alcoholics, and this was proposed as a more sensitive marker of heavy drinking than GGT.[214,215] In a study on patients undergoing detoxification, the B-isoforms of the enzyme compared well with CDT in terms of sensitivity and disappearance rate from the circulation during the alcohol withdrawal phase.[216] However, the diagnostic sensitivity was much lower when unselected populations were examined,[217] and it should be noted that serum β-hexosaminidase is elevated not only after chronic heavy drinking but also in non-alcoholic liver disease, diabetes, hypertension, and pregnancy,[218] implying a low specificity as an alcohol biomarker.

As mentioned earlier in this chapter, trace amounts of both methanol and ethanol (0.5–1.5 mg/L) are produced naturally in the body during the course of intermediary metabolism or via bacteria in the colon acting on dietary carbohydrates. When the BAC exceeds 0.2 g/L, the hepatic class 1 isozymes of ADH are saturated with substrate and fully engaged in the oxidative metabolism of ethanol. When the liver is metabolizing ethanol at full capacity, it cannot also metabolize methanol, which is produced endogenously at a very low rates. Methanol concentrations in the blood also increase, because it exists as a congener in the alcoholic beverages the person consumes. Recent studies have shown that this metabolic interaction between methanol and ethanol can help to distinguish between acute and chronic drinking practices.[219] After a single intoxicating dose of ethanol, the BAC rarely exceeds 1.5 g/L and the corresponding concentration of methanol in blood is generally only 2–5 mg/L. However, if a person drinks daily to reach high BAC (2.5 g/L), this circumstance would cause an accumulation of methanol, and concentrations of 10 mg/L of higher might be achieved in body fluids.[220]

Depending on the intensity and duration of the drinking spree, as well as the methanol content of the drinks consumed, methanol concentration in blood can increase appreciably and 10 mg/L was suggested as a biomarker of chronic heavy drinking and alcohol dependence.[219] Because the metabolism of methanol is blocked when the BAC exceeds 0.2 g/L (see Figure 3.4.4), this allows methanol to accumulate in the bloodstream. The ongoing endogenous synthesis of methanol continues along with the contributions from the congeners in the drinks consumed. A lot of research on endogenous concentrations of methanol and its use as a biochemical marker of alcohol dependence has been done in Germany, and is used in traffic medicine when convicted drunk drivers re-apply for a new driving license or when the options of monetary fines, imprisonment, or treatment for alcohol-use disorder are discussed during sentencing.[219]

3.4.5 Clinical Applications of Alcohol Biomarkers

3.4.5.1 Single Tests Versus Test Combinations

As already indicated, some of the classical laboratory tests for alcohol abuse lack sufficient sensitivity and/or specificity to warrant their use as sole evidence of heavy drinking. To increase diagnostic sensitivity, various combinations of markers have therefore been evaluated, such as GGT, MCV, AST, ALT, CDT, and/or PEth.[221–225] Even though combinations of markers tend to increase the diagnostic sensitivity of the traditional markers, at the same time this approach might reduce diagnostic specificity.[226–228] Furthermore, using multiple markers tends to complicate the interpretation of results and of course also increases the overall costs.

Nevertheless, a useful approach is to use two or more markers that are independently associated with heavy drinking.[28] Whereas a strong association is usually obtained between liver function tests like GGT, ALT, and AST, this is not the case for GGT and CDT.[229–231] Rather, in one study, several of the highest CDT levels were observed in alcoholic subjects possessing normal or only moderately elevated GGT results and vice versa.[230] This was further confirmed by another study in which a negative correlation between CDT and the severity of liver disease was reported.[232] It seems that the combined use of GGT and CDT improves identification of heavy drinkers and thereby those at most risk of becoming dependent on alcohol.[227,230,231]

A combination of short-term and long-term markers of alcohol consumption was used successfully during outpatient treatment of alcohol-dependent subjects.[129,130] Finding an increased CDT or PEth suggests the person has returned to their habit of continuous heavy drinking after a period of abstinence, whereas normal/negative CDT and PEth results but instead a positive morning breath alcohol test or other more sensitive biomarker, such as urinary EtG and EtS, will identify single lapses.[224,225]

3.4.5.2 Screening for Excessive Drinking in Unselected Populations

Many biochemical screening tests used for the early detection of harmful consumption of alcohol give excellent results (i.e., high sensitivity and specificity), when studies are done on selected populations, e.g., alcoholics undergoing detoxification as opposed to moderate drinkers or teetotallers. By contrast, in studies on single individuals, and when screening people from the general population, many biochemical tests are less satisfactory, mainly because of a considerable overlap between results for heavy and moderate drinkers. Furthermore, because certain medical and environmental conditions might also influence the test results, false positives are not uncommon. An example illustrates this point. Assuming that the prevalence of excessive drinking was 10%, a marker with 90% sensitivity and specificity will correctly identify 9 of 10 heavy drinkers in a study population of 100, but, at the same time, it will incorrectly identify 9 of 90 healthy individuals as having drinking problems. What this means is that the chance of a correct classification under these conditions is only 50% (the positive predictive value). For some of the conventional laboratory markers of alcohol abuse (i.e., liver markers), a single abnormal test result might be difficult or impossible to interpret in an unequivocal way unless confirmed by complementary testing using a specific alcohol biomarker such as CDT or PEth to exclude other potential causes.

Another important factor to consider is the time delay between drinking and sampling. Because different alcohol biomarkers have different life spans, the time since the subject's last drink should always be considered when evaluating the sensitivity of a biochemical test. The widely used GGT and CDT, for example, have biological half-lives of ~2 to 3 weeks, so the specimen should preferably be collected no later than one week after admission to hospital or during alcohol withdrawal, otherwise, the sensitivity of the test will be reduced considerably.

3.4.5.3 Follow-up Treatment of Alcohol-Dependent Patients

It is not uncommon for patients undergoing treatment for alcohol-use disorder and/or alcohol dependence to relapse and continue to drink heavily. The progress and success of a treatment regime necessitates repeated analysis of CDT, PEth, and EtG, during the withdrawal period lasting 2–4 weeks (e.g., during hospitalization or other inpatient treatment, or medication with disulfiram).[230,233] Decreasing concentrations of the various biomarkers towards "normal values" confirms that alcohol abuse was the most likely cause of elevated biomarker results.

After discharge from the hospital, continued use of biomarkers should be done on a routine basis in connection with return visits to the clinic. This facilitates early identification of relapse,[234] when combined with an early morning breath-alcohol test or a more sensitive biomarker of acute drinking, such as urinary EtG and EtS.[28] The optimal testing frequency depends in part on the life-span of the marker in question.[235] Providing feedback to patients about the results of the tests, for example by presenting these graphically, can be very informative and might also improve self-report and treatment outcome.[236,237] However, if this strategy is used, it is imperative that the results are reliable (i.e., only using alcohol-specific tests), otherwise the patient may become demoralized and lose faith in the usefulness of laboratory markers.

Repeated analysis of biomarkers makes it possible to use individualized, instead of population-based, reference limits, thereby improving considerably the reliability of clinical diagnosis.[130,150] Normal values are usually distinguished from elevated test results on the assumption of a Gaussian distribution in healthy control subjects; 67%, 95%, and 99.7%, that is within ± one, two, or three standard deviations, respectively. However, because of inter-individual variations in response and differences in enzymatic activity, age, gender body size, adiposity, and volume distribution of ethanol, some people need to drink a lot more than others to achieve the same BAC. Biological variations in baseline response are appreciable for certain biomarkers, so the use of individualized cut-off levels as indicative of further drinking or continuous heavy drinking is significantly improved.[130,238]

3.4.6 Genetic and Trait Markers of Alcohol Dependence

Eugenic studies from the 1800s demonstrated that excessive drinking and alcohol dependence ran in families, especially from father to son. Unequivocal evidence of a genetic component in the propensity for certain people to become dependent on alcohol arose from adoption studies involving monozygotic and dizygotic twins.[239,240] This led to a definition of inheritance of risk for alcohol dependence consisting of type 1 and type 2 subtypes, and this nomenclature has become widely accepted in the field of clinical and biological alcohol research.[241] It seems that some people have a greater predisposition for alcohol addiction when they start to drink regularly, and for this reason, efforts have been made to develop trait markers of dependence.[242–244]

Examples of such genetic or trait markers of a vulnerability to develop alcohol dependence include various neurotransmitter systems, such as the dopamine D2 receptor gene, the activity of monoamine oxidase (MAO) and adenylyl cyclase (AC) enzymes, and the serotonin transporter (5HTT), as well as some neuropeptides (e.g., NPY), which are implicated in various aspects of compulsive, impulsive, and addictive behavior, including pleasure-seeking and reward areas of the brain.[244,245] A significantly lower activity of MAO in blood platelets of alcoholics compared to controls was reported,[246] although concerns were raised about the exact mechanism behind this difference.[247] Tobacco use, for example, which is common in alcoholics, can also lower MAO activity.[248] Another important issue, in this respect, is better standardization of the assay methods and having control of the magnitude of pre-analytical and inter-laboratory variations.

Hitherto, the only clear-cut evidence linking alcohol use and abuse to genetics is the polymorphism observed for ADH and ALDH enzymes in Japanese and some other Oriental populations, such as Chinese, Korean, and Vietnamese.[249,250] They inherit an inactive mitochondrial

ALDH2 isozyme making them hypersensitive to acetaldehyde, and abnormally high concentrations in blood occur after drinking small amounts of ethanol. This triggers a range of unpleasant clinical effects including facial flushing, nausea, tachycardia, breathing impairment, etc., which helps to stop these people from continuing to drink. This Antabuse-like reaction creates an aversion to drinking alcohol, which decreases the risk of these individuals from becoming problem drinkers.[251]

3.4.7 Concluding Remarks

Throughout the Western world, alcohol is the first choice as a recreational drug for most individuals, and ingestion of 10–20 g per day has no detrimental effects on a person's health and life expectancy. Indeed, several epidemiological studies indicate that drinking small amounts of ethanol daily, especially in the form of red wine, has beneficial effects on health by lowering the risk of cardiovascular diseases, such as ischemic stroke, and type II diabetes.[2,252] By contrast, the irresponsible use and abuse of alcohol are major risk factors for sudden and unnatural deaths, including acute poisonings, various cancers, alcohol-related accidents in the workplace, the home, and on the roads.[253]

Early recognition of patients suffering from an alcohol-use disorder improves the choice of treatment, such as whether some type of pharmacotherapy or psychotherapy is more appropriate, or group therapy and participation in rehabilitation programs, etc. There is an increasing need to monitor a person's drinking habits such as when working in security environments,[198] child-custody cases,[254] occupational medicine,[255] transplant surgery,[256] and the re-granting of driving licenses,[257] as well as in out-patient clinics for psychiatric disorders.[224] Reliable information about a person's drinking habits is difficult to obtain using self-reports, clinical interviews, and questionnaires about the frequency of drinking, the amounts consumed on each occasion. This has led to an underreporting of the amounts of alcohol consumed, at least in the early stages of a treatment program, and the erroneous classification of many patients as problematic drinkers is not uncommon.[147,258,259]

The traditional alcohol biomarkers focused on biochemical and pathological changes related to ethanol toxicity as reflected in certain abnormalities in blood chemistry and liver function tests. The perfect biomarker should exhibit both a high sensitivity and specificity for its intended purpose, whether as a relapse marker, identifying irresponsible and dangerous drinking practices or pathological changes in body organs and tissues. Some tests might perform well in selected high-risk populations, such as alcohol-dependent or psychiatric out-patients but are less satisfactory in randomly selected individuals. Furthermore, laboratory tests should be inexpensive to administer, the results should be easy to understand and interpret by primary care physicians and by the patients themselves.[260]

The biomarkers of choice as indicative of organ and tissue damage are the liver enzymes ALT, AST, and GGT, and these give a first hint of chronic problematic drinking. However, these markers have limited clinical utility, owing to their low diagnostic sensitivity; some people can drink copious amounts of ethanol without being detected. These same markers also show many false-positive indications (low specificity), because of certain prescription medications, heavy smoking, and dietary factors (high-fat diets), and in pregnancy, obesity, and non-alcohol fatty liver disease.[261] The best indirect biomarker of problematic drinking with acceptable specificity and sensitivity is the analysis of CDT in serum samples as discussed in more detail earlier in this chapter.

The most obvious direct alcohol biomarker is ethanol determined in the breath or other body fluids (i.e., blood, saliva, or urine). But because of ongoing metabolism of ethanol in the body, the timing of the sampling in relation to the end of drinking is crucial. Most people eliminate ethanol from the bloodstream at a rate of 0.1–0.2 g/L/h, so after a night of heavy drinking the concentration in blood will be below an analytical cut-off (~0.05–0.1 g/L) when a test is done the next morning (12–24 h later). The window of detection for disclosing recent drinking is widened by ~12 h, or longer, depending on the ethanol dose, if the non-oxidative metabolites EtG and EtS are analyzed in the urine samples.[99,262]

Considerable research has been devoted to the determination of EtG in hair strands as a way to investigate a person's drinking habits. Hair, as the biological matrix, offers a much longer window of detection compared to other biological specimens.[263] Indeed, the segmental analysis of hair strands for EtG is a way to establish a time-line of ethanol consumption over several months or years.[264] Guidelines have been promulgated for obtaining suitable hair strands for analysis, the most effective decontamination procedures, to use as well as the analytical methods and cut-off values that indicate positive results. Concentrations of EtG in hair depend, in part, on sample preparation, such as length of the hair strand taken, method of grinding, and solvent extraction procedures, which often differ between different laboratories.[265,266] A number of analytical artifacts have also been identified when EtG is determined in hair strands, such as the need to avoid external contamination from, for example, shampoos, bleaching agents, hair lotions, and/or conditioners.[263]

Choosing the most appropriate analytical cut-off concentration for reporting positive EtG findings in hair strands – whether this should be 7 pg/mg as indicative of abstinence or 30 pg/mg as verifying continuous heavy drinking – has been an ongoing debate for many years.[263] Nevertheless, there is medicolegal interest in the analysis of EtG in hair strands and other keratinous matrixes, such as nails, because the results furnish a much longer window of detection.[267] Requests for analysis of EtG in hair are common in social-medical contexts when abstinence is a requirement, such as when people are being rehabilitated for an alcohol- or drug-related problem, or might be incarcerated, or on probation as well as in decisions about suitability for child custody – for example, such as when one or both parents suffer from some form of addiction.

For clinical purposes, it is a recommended practice to combine the results derived from several different biomarkers as a way to improve overall sensitivity and specificity, such as the indirect biomarker CDT and direct biomarker PEth and/or EtG. It is generally accepted that there are hereditary influences that predispose some people to become heavy drinkers, such as the sons of alcoholics. Besides early-onset heavy drinking, many of these individuals also exhibit sensation-seeking behaviors, some suffer from a personality disorder, and abuse various non-alcohol recreational drugs, such as cannabis.[268]

The per capita consumption of alcohol in people aged 15 y or older is highest in "wine-drinking nations," as is the prevalence of alcohol-related liver diseases, such as cirrhosis, which is highly correlated with a country's total alcohol consumption.[269,270] A drinking pattern considered harmless to one person might be dangerous to another, owing to various genetic and environmental factors. The diverse laboratory tests and biomarkers described in this review constitute an essential part of the treatment and rehabilitation of people diagnosed with an alcohol-use disorder to complement clinical interviews and screening questionnaires, about the person's drinking habits.

All-in-all, the need for laboratory tests and biomarkers of acute and chronic drinking is expanding worldwide, not only in addiction medicine, but also in social medicine and forensic science. Reliable information about whether a person has remained abstinent is often required in child custody cases, as a condition of employment in certain occupations, and in the criminal justice system when decisions about day-release or probation are made.

Research articles and reviews devoted to the subject of clinical and forensic applications of alcohol biomarkers continue to appear,[271–273] including a recent book.[274] The laboratory methodology available continues to improve, including the use of sophisticated techniques, such as LC-tandem-MS, which offer an unsurpassed analytical sensitivity and specificity. However, more effort should be made to harmonize the analytical methodology in relation to the most appropriate cut-off values as indicative of a positive result and how this should be interpreted in clinical and forensic contexts. Much could be gained by more standardization and consensus when results are interpreted, such as by comparisons between different biological specimens with different cut-off concentrations and shorter or longer windows of detection.

The best strategy is to err on the side of the patient when deciding whether he or she has relapsed and continues to drink alcohol in different situations. People might be exposed to alcohol in other ways than drinking alcoholic beverages, such as COVID-19 use of hand sanitizers or other products containing ethanol including mouthwash, certain cough medicines, and over-the-counter medications like Nyquil. When laboratory reports are interpreted, the entire case scenario must be considered when reaching a conclusion that a person has consumed alcohol. In conclusion, a combination of the current panel of direct and indirect biomarkers of alcohol use and abuse can help to identify people who are at greatest risk of developing an alcohol-related problem and for the follow-up of drinking practices to ensure they remain abstinent.

REFERENCES

1. Doll R. The benefit of alcohol in moderation. *Drug Alcohol Rev* 1998;17:353–63.
2. Collaborators GA. Alcohol use and burden for 195 countries and territories, 1990–2016: a systematic analysis for the Global Burden of Disease Study 2016. *Lancet* 2018;392:1015–35.
3. Mellinger JL. Epidemiology of alcohol use and alcoholic liver disease. *Clin Liver Dis (Hoboken)* 2019;13:136–9.
4. Hanson GR, Li TK. Public health implications of excessive alcohol consumption. *Jama* 2003;289:1031–2.
5. Room R, Babor T, Rehm J. Alcohol and public health. *Lancet* 2005;365:519–30.
6. Cherpitel CJ. Drinking patterns and problems and drinking in the injury event: an analysis of emergency room patients by ethnicity. *Drug Alcohol Rev* 1998;17:423–31.
7. Connor J, Norton R, Ameratunga S, Jackson R. The contribution of alcohol to serious car crash injuries. *Epidemiology* 2004;15:337–44.
8. Richardson A, Budd T. Young adults, alcohol, crime and disorder. *Crim Behav Ment Health* 2003;13:5–16.
9. Brewer RD, Swahn MH. Binge drinking and violence. *Jama* 2005;294:616–8.
10. Serdula MK, Brewer RD, Gillespie C, Denny CH, Mokdad A. Trends in alcohol use and binge drinking, 1985–1999: results of a multi-state survey. *Am J Prev Med* 2004;26:294–8.
11. Borges G, Cherpitel C, Mittleman M. Risk of injury after alcohol consumption: a case-crossover study in the emergency department. *Soc Sci Med* 2004;58:1191–200.
12. Hall W. British drinking: a suitable case for treatment? *BMJ* 2005;331:527–8.
13. Meyerhoff DJ, Bode C, Nixon SJ, de Bruin EA, Bode JC, Seitz HK. Health risks of chronic moderate and heavy alcohol consumption: how much is too much? *Alcohol Clin Exp Res* 2005;29:1334–40.
14. Jellinek EM. *The Disease Concept of Alcoholism*. New Haven: Hillhouse Press, 1960.
15. Fuller RK, Lee KK, Gordis E. Validity of self-report in alcoholism research: results of a veterans administration cooperative study. *Alcohol Clin Exp Res* 1988;12:201–5.
16. Ness DE, Ende J. Denial in the medical interview: recognition and management. *J Am Med Assoc* 1994;272:1777–81.
17. Wilson RS. *Diagnosis of Alcohol Abuse*. Boca Raton: CRC Press, 1989.
18. Mayfield D, McLeod G, Hall P. The CAGE questionnaire: validation of a new alcoholism screening instrument. *Am J Psychiat* 1974;131:1121–3.
19. Selzer ML. The Michigan Alcoholism Screening Test: the quest for a new diagnostic instrument. *Am J Psychiat* 1981;127:89–94.
20. Mihas AA, Tavassoli M. Laboratory markers of ethanol intake and abuse: a critical appraisal. *Am J Med Sci* 1992;303:415–28.

21. Goldberg DM, Kapur BM. Enzymes and circulating proteins as markers of alcohol abuse. *Clin Chim Acta* 1994;226:191–209.
22. Conigrave KM, Saunders JB, Whitfield JB. Diagnostic tests for alcohol consumption. *Alcohol Alcohol* 1995;30:13–26.
23. Helander A. Biological markers in alcoholism. *J Neural Transm Suppl* 2003:15–32.
24. Salaspuro M. Characteristics of laboratory markers in alcohol-related organ damage. *Scand J Gastroenterol* 1989;24:769–80.
25. Rosman AS, Lieber CS. Diagnostic utility of laboratory tests in alcoholic liver disease. *Clin Chem* 1994;40:1641–51.
26. Wilson RS, Mohs ME, Eskelson C, Sampliner RE, Hartmann B. Identification of alcohol abuse and alcoholism with biological parameters. *Alcohol Clin Exp Res* 1986;10:364–85.
27. Sharpe PC. Biochemical detection and monitoring of alcohol abuse and abstinence. *Ann Clin Biochem* 2001;38:652–64.
28. Helander A. Biological markers of alcohol use and abuse in theory and practice. In: Agarwal DP, Seitz HK, editors. *Alcohol in Health and Disease*. New York: Marcel Dekker, Inc., 2001, 177–205.
29. Bergström G, Bjorklund C, Fried I, Lisspers J, Nathell L, Hermansson U, et al. A comprehensive workplace intervention and its outcome with regard to lifestyle, health and sick leave: the AHA study. *Work* 2008;31:167–80.
30. Hermansson U, Knutsson A, Brandt L, Huss A, Rönnberg S, Helander A. Screening for high-risk and elevated alcohol consumption in day and shift workers by use of the AUDIT and CDT. *Occup Med (Lond)* 2003;53:518–26.
31. Beck O, Helander A, Carlsson S, Borg S. Changes in serotonin metabolism during treatment with the aldehyde dehydrogenase inhibitors disulfiram and cyanamide. *Pharmacol Toxicol* 1995;77:323–6.
32. Helander A, Jones AW. [5-HTOL--a new biochemical alcohol marker with forensic applications]. *Lakartidningen* 2002;99:3950–4.
33. Bergström J, Helander A, Jones AW. Ethyl glucuronide concentrations in two successive urinary voids from drinking drivers: relationship to creatinine content and blood and urine ethanol concentrations. *Forensic Sci Int* 2003;133:86–94.
34. Jones AW, Eklund A, Helander A. Misleading results of ethanol analysis in urine specimens from rape victims suffering from diabetes. *J Clin Forensic Med* 2000;7:144–6.
35. Balldin J, Berglund M, Borg S, Mansson M, Bendtsen P, Franck J, et al. A 6-month controlled naltrexone study: combined effect with cognitive behavioral therapy in outpatient treatment of alcohol dependence. *Alcohol Clin Exp Res* 2003;27:1142–9.
36. Anton RF, Moak DH, Latham P, Waid LR, Myrick H, Voronin K, et al. Naltrexone combined with either cognitive behavioral or motivational enhancement therapy for alcohol dependence. *J Clin Psychopharmacol* 2005;25:349–57.
37. Zweig MH, Campbell G. Receiver-operating characteristic (ROC) plots: a fundamental evaluation tool in clinical medicine. *Clin Chem* 1993;39:561–77.
38. Henderson AR. Assessing test accuracy and its clinical consequences: a primer for receiver operating characteristic curve analysis. *Ann Clin Biochem* 1993;30:521–39.
39. Helander A, Beck O, Jones AW. Laboratory testing for recent alcohol consumption: comparison of ethanol, methanol, and 5-hydroxytryptophol. *Clin Chem* 1996;42:618–24.
40. Jones AW, Helander A. Disclosing recent drinking after alcohol has been cleared from the body. *J Anal Toxicol* 1996;20:141–2.
41. Helander A, von Wachenfeldt J, Hiltunen A, Beck O, Liljeberg P, Borg S. Comparison of urinary 5-hydroxytryptophol, breath ethanol, and self-report for detection of recent alcohol use during outpatient treatment: a study on methadone patients. *Drug Alcohol Depend* 1999;56:33–8.
42. Jones AW. Measuring alcohol in blood and breath for forensic purposes: a historical review. *Forens Sci Rev* 1996;8:13–44.
43. Dubowski KM, Caplan YH. Alcohol testing in the workplace. In: Garriott JC, editor. *Medicolehal Aspects of Alcohol*. Tucson: Laywers & Judges Publ. Co., 1996, 439–75.
44. Haeckel R, Hanecke P. Application of saliva for drug monitoring. An in vivo model for transmembrane transport. *Eur J Clin Chem Clin Biochem* 1996;34:171–91.
45. Toennes SW, Kauert GF, Steinmeyer S, Moeller MR. Driving under the influence of drugs -- evaluation of analytical data of drugs in oral fluid, serum and urine, and correlation with impairment symptoms. *Forensic Sci Int* 2005;152:149–55.
46. Jones AW. Measuring ethanol in saliva with the QED enzymatic test device: comparison of results with blood and breath-alcohol concentration. *J Anal Toxicol* 1995;19:169–73.
47. Degutis LC, Rabinovici R, Sabbaj A, Mascia R, D'Onofrio G. The saliva strip test is an accurate method to determine blood alcohol concentration in trauma patients. *Acad Emerg Med* 2004;11:885–7.
48. Jones AW, Norberg A, Hahn RG. Concentration-time profiles of ethanol in arterial and venous blood and end-expired breath during and after intravenous infusion. *J Forensic Sci* 1997;42:1088–94.
49. Jones AW. Reference limits for urine/blood ratios of ethanol in two successive voids from drinking drivers. *J Anal Toxicol* 2002;26:333–9.
50. Bendtsen P, Jones AW, Helander A. Urinary excretion of methanol and 5-hydroxytryptophol as biochemical markers of recent drinking in the hangover state. *Alcohol Alcohol* 1998;33:431–8.
51. Pawan GLS, Grice K. Distribution of alcohol in urine and sweat after drinking. *Lancet* 1968;ii:1016.
52. Swift RM, Martin CS, Swette L, LaConti A, Kackley N. Studies on a wearable, electronic, transdermal alcohol sensor. *Alcohol Clin Exp Res* 1992;16:721–5.
53. Phillips M, Greenberg J, Andrzejewski J. Evaluation of the alcopatch, a transdermal dosimeter for monitoring alcohol consumption. *Alcohol Clin Exp Res* 1995;19:1547–9.
54. Cone EJ, Hillsgrove MJ, Jenkins AJ, Keenan RM, Darwin WD. Sweat testing for heroin, cocaine, and metabolites. *J Anal Toxicol* 1994;18:298.
55. Huestis MA, Cone EJ, Wong CJ, Umbricht A, Preston KL. Monitoring opiate use in substance abuse treatment patients with sweat and urine drug testing. *J Anal Toxicol* 2000;24:509–21.
56. Phillips M. Sweat patch test for alcohol consumption: rapid assay with an electrochemical detector. *Alcohol Clin Exp Res* 1982;6:532–4.
57. Swift R, Davidson D, Fitz E. Transdermal alcohol detection with a new miniaturized sensor, the miniTAS. *Alcohol Clin Exp Res* 1996;20:45A.

58. Swift R. Direct measurement of alcohol and its metabolites. *Addiction* 2003;98 Suppl 2:73–80.
59. Mani JC, Pietruszko R, Theorell H. Methanol activity of alcohol dehydrogenase from human liver, horse liver, and yeast. *Arch Biochem Biophys* 1970;140:52.
60. Eriksson CJP, Fukunaga T. Human blood acetaldehyde (update 1992). *Alcohol Alcohol Suppl* 1993;2:9–25.
61. Helander A. Aldehyde dehydrogenase in blood: distribution, characteristics and possible use as marker of alcohol misuse. *Alcohol Alcohol* 1993;28:135–45.
62. Jones AW. Measuring and reporting the concentration of acetaldehyde in human breath. *Alcohol Alcohol* 1995;30:271–85.
63. Lundquist F. Production and utilization of free acetate in man. *Nature* 1962;193:579–80.
64. Nuutinen H, Lindros K, Hekali P, Salaspuro M. Elevated blood acetate as indicator of fast ethanol elimination in chronic alcoholics. *Alcohol* 1985;2:623–6.
65. Korri U-M, Nuutinen H, Salaspuro M. Increased blood acetate: a new laboratory marker of alcoholism and heavy drinking. *Alcohol Clin Exp Res* 1985;9:468–71.
66. Roine RP, Korri U-M, Ylikahri R, Pentillä A, Pikkarainen J, Salapuro M. Increased serum acetate as a marker of problem drinking among drunken drivers. *Alcohol Alcohol* 1988;23:123–6.
67. Goldberger BA, Cone EJ, Kadehjian L. Unsuspected ethanol ingestion through soft drinks and flavored beverages. *J Anal Toxicol* 1996;20:332–3.
68. Logan BK, Distefano S. Ethanol content of various foods and soft drinks and their potential for interference with a breath-alcohol test. *J Anal Toxicol* 1998;22:181–3.
69. Logan BK, Jones AW. Endogenous ethanol 'auto-brewery syndrome' as a drunk-driving defence challenge. *Med Sci Law* 2000;40:206–15.
70. Ostrovsky YM. Endogenous ethanol - its metabolic, behavioral and biomedical significance. *Alcohol* 1986;3:239–47.
71. Krebs HA, Perkins JR. The physiological role of liver alcohol dehydrogenase. *Biochem J* 1970;118:635–44.
72. Sprung R, Bonte W, Rüdell E, Domke M, Frauenrath C. Zum Problem des endogenen Alkohols. *Blutalkohol* 1981;18:65–70.
73. Haffner H-T, Graw M, Besserer K, Blicke U, Henssge C. Endogenous methanol: variability in concentration and rate of production. Evidence of a deep compartment? *Forens Sci Int* 1996;79:145–54.
74. Jones AW. Elimination half-life of methanol during hangover. *Pharmacol Toxicol* 1987;60:217–20.
75. Haffner H-T, Wehner HD, Scheytt KD, Besserer K. The elimination kinetics of methanol and the influence of ethanol. *Int J Leg Med* 1992;105:111–4.
76. Helander A, Eriksson CJ. Laboratory tests for acute alcohol consumption: results of the WHO/ISBRA study on state and trait markers of alcohol use and dependence. *Alcohol Clin Exp Res* 2002;26:1070–7.
77. Jacobsen D, Jansen H, Wiik-Larsen E, Bredesen J-E, Halvorsen S. Studies on methanol poisoning. *Acta Med Scand* 1982;212:5.
78. Prabhakaran V, Ettler H, Mills A. Methanol poisoning: two cases with similar plasma methanol concentrations but different outcomes. *Can Med Assoc J* 1993;148:981.
79. Hantson P, Wittebole X, Haufroid V. Ethanol therapy for methanol poisoning: duration and problems. *Eur J Emerg Med* 2002;9:278–9.
80. Jacobsen D, McMartin KE. Antidotes for methanol and ethylene glycol poisoning. *J Toxicol Clin Toxicol* 1997;35:127–43.
81. Brent J, McMartin K, Phillips S, Aaron C, Kulig K. Fomepizole for the treatment of methanol poisoning. *N Engl J Med* 2001;344:424–9.
82. McAnalley BH. Chemistry of alcoholic beverages. In: Garriott JC, editor. *Medicolehal Aspects of Alcohol.* Tucson: Lawyers & Judges Publ. Co., 1996, 1–33.
83. Gilg T. Alkoholbedingte Fahruntuchtigkeit. *Rechtsmedizin* 2005;15:97–112.
84. Majchrowicz E, Mendelson JH. Blood methanol concentrations during experimentally induced ethanol intoxication in alcoholics. *J Pharmacol Exp Ther* 1971;179:293–300.
85. Iffland R. New ways to use biochemical indicators of alcohol abuse to regrant licences in a fairer manner after drunken driving in Germany. *Alcohol Alcohol* 1996;31:619–20.
86. Haffner HT, Banger M, Graw M, Besserer K, Brink T. The kinetics of methanol elimination in alcoholics and the influence of ethanol. *Forensic Sci Int* 1997;89:129–36.
87. Graw M, Haffner HT, Althaus L, Besserer K, Voges S. Invasion and distribution of methanol. *Arch Toxicol* 2000;74:313–21.
88. Taucher J, Lagg A, Hansel A, Vogel W, Lindinger W. Methanol in human breath. *Alcohol Clin Exp Res* 1995;19:1147–50.
89. Lindinger W, Taucher J, Jordan A, Hansel A, Vogel W. Endogenous production of methanol after the consumption of fruit. *Alcohol Clin Exp Res* 1997;21:939–43.
90. Bachmann C, Bickel MH. History of drug metabolism: the first half of the 20th century. *Drug Metab Rev* 1985;16:185–253.
91. Neubauer O. Uber Glukuronsaure paarung bei Stoffen der Fettreihe. *Arch Exp Pathol Pharmacol* 1901;46:133.
92. Kamil IA, Smith JN, Williams RT. A new aspect of ethanol metabolism: isolation of ethyl glucuronide. *Biochem J* 1952;51:32–3.
93. Jaakonmaki PI, Knox KL, Horning EC, Horning MG. The characterization by gas-liquid chromatography of ethyl b-D-glucosiduronic acid as a metabolite of ethanol in rat and man. *Eur J Pharmacol* 1967;1:63–70.
94. Hanai T. Chromatography and computational chemical analysis for drug discovery. *Curr Med Chem* 2005;12:501–25.
95. Dahl H, Stephanson N, Beck O, Helander A. Comparison of urinary excretion characteristics of ethanol and ethyl glucuronide. *J Anal Toxicol* 2002;26:201–4.
96. Helander A, Beck O. Mass spectrometric identification of ethyl sulfate as an ethanol metabolite in humans. *Clin Chem* 2004;50:936–7.
97. Schmitt G, Aderjan R, Keller T, Wu M. Ethyl glucuronide: an unusual ethanol metabolite in humans. Synthesis, analytical data, and determination in serum and urine. *J Anal Toxicol* 1995;19:91–4.
98. Schmitt G, Droenner P, Skopp G, Aderjan R. Ethyl glucuronide concentration in serum of human volunteers, teetotalers, and suspected drinking drivers. *J Forens Sci* 1997;42:1099–102.
99. Helander A, Beck O. Ethyl sulfate: a metabolite of ethanol in humans and a potential biomarker of acute alcohol intake. *J Anal Toxicol* 2005;29:270–4.

100. Sarkola T, Dahl H, Eriksson CJ, Helander A. Urinary ethyl glucuronide and 5-hydroxytryptophol levels during repeated ethanol ingestion in healthy human subjects. *Alcohol Alcohol* 2003;38:347–51.
101. Skopp G, Schmitt G, Potsch L, Dronner P, Aderjan R, Mattern R. Ethyl glucuronide in human hair. *Alcohol Alcohol* 2000;35:283–5.
102. Yegles M, Labarthe A, Auwarter V, Hartwig S, Vater H, Wennig R, et al. Comparison of ethyl glucuronide and fatty acid ethyl ester concentrations in hair of alcoholics, social drinkers and teetotallers. *Forensic Sci Int* 2004;145:167–73.
103. Stephanson N, Dahl H, Helander A, Beck O. Direct quantification of ethyl glucuronide in clinical urine samples by liquid chromatography-mass spectrometry. *Ther Drug Monit* 2002;24:645–51.
104. Nishikawa M, Tsuchihashi H, Miki A, Katagi M, Schmitt G, Zimmer H, et al. Determination of ethyl glucuronide, a minor metabolite of ethanol, in human serum by liquid chromatography-electrospray ionization mass spectrometry. *J Chromatogr B Biomed Sci Appl* 1999;726:105–10.
105. Seidl S, Wurst FM, Alt A. Ethyl glucuronide-a biological marker for recent alcohol consumption. *Addict Biol* 2001;6:205–12.
106. Helander A, Dahl H. Urinary tract infection: a risk factor for false-negative urinary ethyl glucuronide but not ethyl sulfate in the detection of recent alcohol consumption. *Clin Chem* 2005;51:1728–30.
107. Schneider H, Glatt H. Sulpho-conjugation of ethanol in humans in vivo and by individual sulphotransferase forms in vitro. *Biochem J* 2004;383:543–9.
108. Dresen S, Weinmann W, Wurst FM. Forensic confirmatory analysis of ethyl sulfate--a new marker for alcohol consumption--by liquid-chromatography/electrospray ionization/tandem mass spectrometry. *J Am Soc Mass Spectrom* 2004;15:1644–8.
109. Deng XS, Bludeau P, Deitrich RA. Formation of ethyl nitrite in vivo after ethanol administration. *Alcohol* 2004;34:217–23.
110. Lange LG, Sobel BE. Myocardial metabolites of ethanol. *Circ Res* 1983;52:479–82.
111. Laposata M, Hasaba A, Best CA, Yoerger DM, McQuillan BM, Salem RO, et al. Fatty acid ethyl esters: recent observations. *Prostaglandins Leukot Essent Fatty Acids* 2002;67:193–6.
112. Kaphalia BS, Cai P, Khan MF, Okorodudu AO, Ansari GA. Fatty acid ethyl esters: markers of alcohol abuse and alcoholism. *Alcohol* 2004;34:151–8.
113. Soderberg BL, Salem RO, Best CA, Cluette-Brown JE, Laposata M. Fatty acid ethyl esters. Ethanol metabolites that reflect ethanol intake. *Am J Clin Pathol* 2003;119 Suppl:S94–9.
114. Bisaga A, Laposata M, Xie S, Evans SM. Comparison of serum fatty acid ethyl esters and urinary 5-hydroxytryptophol as biochemical markers of recent ethanol consumption. *Alcohol Alcohol* 2005;40:214–8.
115. Borucki K, Schreiner R, Dierkes J, Jachau K, Krause D, Westphal S, et al. Detection of recent ethanol intake with new markers: comparison of fatty acid ethyl esters in serum and of ethyl glucuronide and the ratio of 5-hydroxytryptophol to 5-hydroxyindole acetic acid in urine. *Alcohol Clin Exp Res* 2005;29:781–7.
116. Nanji AA, Su GL, Laposata M, French SW. Pathogenesis of alcoholic liver disease--recent advances. *Alcohol Clin Exp Res* 2002;26:731–6.
117. Davis VE, Brown H, Huff JA, Cashaw JL. The alteration of serotonin metabolism to 5-hydroxytryptophol by ethanol ingestion in man. *J Lab Clin Med* 1967;69:132–40.
118. Helander A, Beck O, Jacobsson G, Löwenmo C, Wikström T. Time course of ethanol-induced changes in serotonin metabolism. *Life Sci* 1993;53:847–55.
119. Lahti RA, Majchrowicz E. Ethanol and acetaldehyde effects on metabolism and binding of biogenic amines. *Quart J Stud Alc* 1974;35:1–14.
120. Feldstein A, Williamson O. 5-Hydroxytryptamine metabolism in rat brain and liver homogenates. *Brit J Pharmacol* 1968;34:38–42.
121. Svensson S, Some M, Lundsjo A, Helander A, Cronholm T, Hoog JO. Activities of human alcohol dehydrogenases in the metabolic pathways of ethanol and serotonin. *Eur J Biochem* 1999;262:324–9.
122. Voltaire A, Beck O, Borg S. Urinary 5-hydroxytryptophol: a possible marker of recent alcohol consumption. *Alcohol Clin Exp Res* 1992;16:281–5.
123. Helander A, Beck O, Borg S. The use of 5-hydroxytryptophol as an alcohol intake marker. *Alcohol Alcohol* 1994;Suppl 2:497–502.
124. Beck O, Helander A. 5-hydroxytryptophol as a marker for recent alcohol intake. *Addiction* 2003;98 Suppl 2:63–72.
125. Helander A, Wikstrom T, Lowenmo C, Jacobsson G, Beck O. Urinary excretion of 5-hydroxyindole-3-acetic acid and 5- hydroxytryptophol after oral loading with serotonin. *Life Sci* 1992;50:1207–13.
126. Borg S, Carlsson AV, Helander A, Brandt AM, Beck O, Stibler H. Detection of relapses in alcohol dependent patients using serum carbohydrate deficient transferrin: improvement with individualized reference levels. *Alcohol Alcohol Suppl* 1994;2:493–6.
127. Johnson RD, Lewis RJ, Canfield DV, Blank CL. Accurate assignment of ethanol origin in postmortem urine: liquid chromatographic-mass spectrometric determination of serotonin metabolites. *J Chromatogr B Analyt Technol Biomed Life Sci* 2004;805:223–34.
128. Stephanson N, Dahl H, Helander A, Beck O. Determination of urinary 5-hydroxytryptophol glucuronide by liquid chromatography-mass spectrometry. *J Chromatogr B Analyt Technol Biomed Life Sci* 2005;816:107–12.
129. Voltaire Carlsson A, Hiltunen AJ, Beck O, Stibler H, Borg S. Detection of relapses in alcohol-dependent patients: comparison of carbohydrate-deficient transferrin in serum, 5-hydroxytryptophol in urine, and self-reports. *Alcohol Clin Exp Res* 1993;17:703–8.
130. Borg S, Helander A, Voltaire Carlsson A, Hogstrom Brandt AM. Detection of relapses in alcohol-dependent patients using carbohydrate- deficient transferrin: improvement with individualized reference levels during long-term monitoring. *Alcohol Clin Exp Res* 1995;19:961–3.
131. Spies CD, Herpell J, Beck O, Muller C, Pragst F, Borg S, et al. The urinary ratio of 5-hydroxytryptophol to 5-hydroxyindole-3-acetic acid in surgical patients with chronic alcohol misuse. *Alcohol* 1999;17:19–27.
132. Helander A, Beck O, Borg S. Determination of urinary 5-hydroxytryptophol by high-performance liquid chromatography with electrochemical detection. *J Chromat Biomed Appl* 1992;579:340–5.
133. Hagan RL, Helander A. Urinary 5-hydroxytryptophol following acute ethanol consumption: clinical evaluation and potential aviation applications. *Aviat Space Environ Med* 1997;68:30–4.

134. Johnson RD, Lewis RJ, Canfield DV, Dubowski KM, Blank CL. Utilizing the urinary 5-HTOL/5-HIAA ratio to determine ethanol origin in civil aviation accident victims. *J Forensic Sci* 2005;50:670–5.
135. Rosalki SB, Rau D. Serum gamma-glutamyl transpeptidase activity in alcoholism. *Clin Chim Acta* 1972;39:41–7.
136. Rosalki SB. Gamma-glutamyl transpeptidase. *Adv Clin Chem* 1975;17:53–101.
137. Nemesánszky E, Lott JA. Gamma-glutamyl transferase and its isoenzymes: progress and problems. *Clin Chem* 1985;31:797–803.
138. Shaw S, Lieber CS. Mechanism of increased gamma glutamyl transpeptidase after chronic alcohol consumption: hepatic microsomal induction rather than dietary imbalance. *Substance Alcohol Actions/Misuse* 1980;1:423–8.
139. Wu A, Slavin G, Levi AJ. Elevated serum gamma-glutamyl-transferase (transpeptidase) and histological liver damage in alcoholism. *Am J Gastroenterol* 1976;65:318–23.
140. Salaspuro M. Use of enzymes for the diagnosis of alcohol related organ damage. *Enzyme* 1987;37:87–107.
141. Nilssen O, Førde OH. Seven-year longitudinal population study of change in gamma-glutamyl transferase: the Tromsø study. *Am J Epidemiol* 1994;139:787–92.
142. Penn R, Worthington LJ. Is serum gamma-glutamyl transferase a misleading test? *Br Med J* 1983;286:531–5.
143. Nalpas R, Vassault A, Charpin S, Lacour B, Berthelot P. Serum mitochondrial aspartate aminotransferase as a marker of chronic alcoholism: diagnostic value and interpretation in a liver unit. *Hepatology* 1986;6:608–14.
144. Gluud C, Andersen I, Dietrichson O, Gluud B, Jacobsen A, Juhl E. Gamma-glutamyl transferase, aspartate aminotransferase and alkaline phosphatase as marker of alcohol consumption in outpatient alcoholics. *Eur J Clin Invest* 1981;11:171–6.
145. Nalpas B, Vassault A, Le Guillou A, Lesgourgues B, Ferry N, Lacour B, et al. Serum activity of mitochondrial asparate aminotransferase: a sensitive marker of alcoholism with or without alcoholic hepatitis. *Hepatology* 1984;5:893–6.
146. Nalpas R, Poupon RE, Vassault A, Hauzanneau P, Sage Y, Schellenberg F, et al. Evaluations of mAST/tAST ratio as a marker of alcohol misuse in a non-selected population. *Alcohol Alcohol* 1989;24:415–9.
147. Nilssen O, Huseby NE, Hoyer G, Brenn T, Schirmer H, Forde OH. New alcohol markers--how useful are they in population studies: the Svalbard Study 1988-89. *Alcohol Clin Exp Res* 1992;16:82–6.
148. Schiele F, Artur Y, Varasteh A, Wellman M, Siest G. Serum mitochondrial aspartate aminotransferase activity: not useful as marker of excessive alcohol consumption in an unselected population. *Clin Chem* 1989;35:926–30.
149. Sillanaukee P, Seppa K, Lof K, Koivula T. CDT by anion-exchange chromatography followed by RIA as a marker of heavy drinking among men. *Alcohol Clin Exp Res* 1993;17:230–3.
150. Irwin M, Baird S, Smith TL, Schuckit M. Use of laboratory tests to monitor heavy drinking by alcoholic men discharged from a treatment program. *Am J Psychiatry* 1988;145:595–9.
151. Wu A, Chanarin I, Levi AJ. Macrocytosis in chronic alcoholism. *Lancet* 1974;i:829–30.
152. Chick J, Kreitman N, Plant M. Mean cell volume and gamma-glutamyltranspeptidase as markers of drinking in working men. *Lancet* 1981;i:1249–51.
153. Stimmel B, Kurtz D, Jackson G, Gilbert HS. Failure of mean red cell volume to serve as a biologic marker for alcoholism in narcotic dependence. *Am J Med* 1983;74:369–73.
154. Whitehead TP, Robinson D, Allaway SL, Hale AC. The effects of cigarette smoking and alcohol consumption on blood haemoglobin, erythrocytes and leucocytes: a dose related study on male subjects. *Clin Lab Haematol* 1995;17:131–8.
155. DiFranza JR, Guerrera MP. Alcoholism and smoking. *J Stud Alcohol* 1990;51:130–5.
156. Behrens UJ, Worner TM, Braly LF, Schaffner F, Lieber CS. Carbohydrate-deficient transferrin, a marker for chronic alcohol consumption in different ethnic populations. *Alcohol Clin Exp Res* 1988;12:427–32.
157. Bell H, Tallaksen CM, Try K, Haug E. Carbohydrate-deficient transferrin and other markers of high alcohol consumption: a study of 502 patients admitted consecutively to a medical department. *Alcohol Clin Exp Res* 1994;18:1103–8.
158. Salaspuro M. Carbohydrate-deficient transferrin as compared to other markers of alcoholism: a systematic review. *Alcohol* 1999;19:261–71.
159. Stibler H. Carbohydrate-deficient transferrin in serum: a new marker of potentially harmful alcohol consumption reviewed. *Clin Chem* 1991;37:2029–37.
160. Jeppsson JO, Kristensson H, Fimiani C. Carbohydrate-deficient transferrin quantified by HPLC to determine heavy consumption of alcohol. *Clin Chem* 1993;39:2115–20.
161. de Jong G, van Dijk JP, van Eijk HG. The biology of transferrin. *Clin Chim Acta* 1990;190:1–46.
162. Arndt T. Carbohydrate-deficient transferrin as a marker of chronic alcohol abuse: a critical review of preanalysis, analysis, and interpretation. *Clin Chem* 2001;47:13–27.
163. Helander A, Eriksson G, Stibler H, Jeppsson J-O. Interference of transferrin isoform types with carbohydrate-deficient transferrin quantification in the identification of alcohol abuse. *Clin Chem* 2001;47:1225–33.
164. Helander A, Husa A, Jeppsson J-O. Improved HPLC method for carbohydrate-deficient transferrin in serum. *Clin Chem* 2003;49:1881–90.
165. Oberrauch W, Bergman AC, Helander A. HPLC and mass spectrometric characterization of a candidate reference material for the alcohol biomarker carbohydrate-deficient transferrin (CDT). *Clin Chim Acta* 2008;395:142–5.
166. Landberg E, Påhlsson P, Lundblad A, Arnetorp A, Jeppsson JO. Carbohydrate composition of serum transferrin isoforms from patients with high alcohol consumption. *Biochem Biophys Res Commun* 1995;210:267–74.
167. Flahaut C, Michalski JC, Danel T, Humbert MH, Klein A. The effects of ethanol on the glycosylation of human transferrin. *Glycobiology* 2003;13:191–8.
168. Peter J, Unverzagt C, Engel WD, Renauer D, Seidel C, Hösel W. Identification of carbohydrate deficient transferrin forms by MALDI-TOF mass spectrometry and lectin ELISA. *Biochim Biophys Acta* 1998;1380:93–101.
169. Stibler H, Borg S. Glycoprotein glycosyltransferase activities in serum in alcohol-abusing patients and healthy controls. *Scand J Clin Lab Invest* 1991;51:43–51.
170. Lieber CS. Carbohydrate deficient transferrin in alcoholic liver disease: mechanisms and clinical implications. *Alcohol* 1999;19:249–54.
171. Sillanaukee P, Strid N, Allen JP, Litten RZ. Possible reasons why heavy drinking increases carbohydrate-deficient transferrin. *Alcohol Clin Exp Res* 2001;25:34–40.

172. Allen JP, Litten RZ, Anton RF, Cross GM. Carbohydrate-deficient transferrin as a measure of immoderate drinking: remaining issues. *Alcohol Clin Exp Res* 1994;18:799–812.
173. Conigrave KM, Degenhardt LJ, Whitfield JB, Saunders JB, Helander A, Tabakoff B. CDT, GGT, and AST as markers of alcohol use: the WHO/ISBRA collaborative project. *Alcohol Clin Exp Res* 2002;26:332–9.
174. Salmela KS, Laitinen K, Nystrom M, Salaspuro M. Carbohydrate-deficient transferrin during 3 weeks' heavy alcohol consumption. *Alcohol Clin Exp Res* 1994;18:228–30.
175. Lesch OM, Walter H, Antal J, Heggli DE, Kovacz A, Leitner A, et al. Carbohydrate-deficient transferrin as a marker of alcohol intake: a study with healthy subjects. *Alcohol Alcohol* 1996;31:265–71.
176. Marquardt T, Denecke J. Congenital disorders of glycosylation: review of their molecular bases, clinical presentations and specific therapies. *Eur J Pediatr* 2003;162:359–79.
177. Jaeken J. Komrower Lecture. Congenital disorders of glycosylation (CDG): it's all in it! *J Inherit Metab Dis* 2003;26:99–118.
178. Sorvajärvi K, Blake JE, Israel Y, Niemelä O. Sensitivity and specificity of carbohydrate-deficient transferrin as a marker of alcohol abuse are significantly influenced by alterations in serum transferrin: comparison of two methods. *Alcohol Clin Exp Res* 1996;20:449–54.
179. Helander A. Absolute or relative measurement of carbohydrate-deficient transferrin in serum? Experiences with three immunological assays. *Clin Chem* 1999;45:131–5.
180. Keating J, Cheung C, Peters TJ, Sherwood RA. Carbohydrate deficient transferrin in the assessment of alcohol misuse: absolute or relative measurements? A comparison of two methods with regard to total transferrin concentration. *Clin Chim Acta* 1998;272:159–69.
181. Stibler H, Borg S, Joustra M. A modified method for the assay of carbohydrate-deficient transferrin (CDT) in serum. *Alcohol Alcohol* 1991;Suppl 1:451–4.
182. Helander A, Wielders JP, Te Stroet R, Bergstrom JP. Comparison of HPLC and capillary electrophoresis for confirmatory testing of the alcohol misuse marker carbohydrate-deficient transferrin. *Clin Chem* 2005;51:1528–31.
183. Helander A, Dahl H, Swanson I, Bergström J. Evaluation of Dade Behring N Latex CDT: a novel homogenous immunoassay for carbohydrate-deficient transferrin. *Alcohol Clin Exp Res* 2004;28 (Suppl):33A.
184. Kraul D, Hackler R, Althaus H. A novel particle-enhanced assay for the immuno-nephelometric determination of carbohydrate-deficient transferrin. *Alcohol Clin Exp Res* 2004;28 (Suppl):34A.
185. Helander A, Wielders J, Anton R, Arndt T, Bianchi V, Deenmamode J, et al. Standardisation and use of the alcohol biomarker carbohydrate-deficient transferrin (CDT). *Clin Chim Acta* 2016;459:19–24.
186. Schellenberg F, Wielders J, Anton R, Bianchi V, Deenmamode J, Weykamp C, et al. IFCC approved HPLC reference measurement procedure for the alcohol consumption biomarker carbohydrate-deficient transferrin (CDT): its validation and use. *Clin Chim Acta* 2017;465:91–100.
187. Alling C, Gustavsson L, Änggård E. An abnormal phospholipid in rat organs after ethanol treatment. *FEBS Lett* 1983;152:24–8.
188. Mueller GC, Fleming MF, LeMahieu MA, Lybrand GS, Barry KJ. Synthesis of phosphatidylethanol--a potential marker for adult males at risk for alcoholism. *Proc Natl Acad Sci U S A* 1988;85:9778–82.
189. Zheng Y, Beck O, Helander A. Method development for routine liquid chromatography-mass spectrometry measurement of the alcohol biomarker phosphatidylethanol (PEth) in blood. *Clin Chim Acta* 2011;412:1428–35.
190. Helander A, Zheng Y. Molecular species of the alcohol biomarker phosphatidylethanol in human blood measured by LC-MS. *Clin Chem* 2009;55:1395–405.
191. Helander A, Böttcher M, Dahmen N, Beck O. Elimination characteristics of the alcohol biomarker phosphatidylethanol (PEth) in blood during alcohol detoxification. *Alcohol Alcohol* 2019;54:251–7.
192. Hansson P, Caron M, Johnson G, Gustavsson L, Alling C. Blood phosphatidylethanol as a marker of alcohol abuse: levels in alcoholic males during withdrawal. *Alcohol Clin Exp Res* 1997;21:108–10.
193. Varga A, Alling C. Formation of phosphatidylethanol in vitro in red blood cells from healthy volunteers and chronic alcoholics. *J Lab Clin Med* 2002;140:79–83.
194. Helander A, Hermansson U, Beck O. Dose-response characteristics of the alcohol biomarker phosphatidylethanol (PEth)-a study of outpatients in treatment for reduced drinking. *Alcohol Alcohol* 2019;54:567–73.
195. Schrock A, Thierauf-Emberger A, Schurch S, Weinmann W. Phosphatidylethanol (PEth) detected in blood for 3 to 12 days after single consumption of alcohol-a drinking study with 16 volunteers. *Int J Legal Med* 2017;131:153–60.
196. Javors MA, Hill-Kapturczak N, Roache JD, Karns-Wright TE, Dougherty DM. Characterization of the pharmacokinetics of phosphatidylethanol 16:0/18:1 and 16:0/18:2 in human whole blood after alcohol consumption in a clinical laboratory study. *Alcohol Clin Exp Res* 2016;40:1228–34.
197. Helander A, Hansson T. [National harmonization of the alcohol biomarker PEth]. *Lakartidningen* 2013;110:1747–8.
198. Ulwelling W, Smith K. The PEth blood test in the security environment: what it is; why it is important; and interpretative guidelines. *J Forensic Sci* 2018;63:1634–40.
199. Aradottir S, Seidl S, Wurst FM, Jönsson BA, Alling C. Phosphatidylethanol in human organs and blood: a study on autopsy material and influences by storage conditions. *Alcohol Clin Exp Res* 2004;28:1718–23.
200. Stevens VJ, Fantl WJ, Newman CB, Sims RV, Cerami A, Peterson CM. Acetaldehyde adducts with hemoglobin. *J Clin Invest* 1981;67:361–9.
201. Tuma DJ, Casey CA. Dangerous byproducts of alcohol breakdown--focus on adducts. *Alcohol Res Health* 2003;27:285–90.
202. Niemelä O, Parkkila S. Alcoholic macrocytosis--is there a role for acetaldehyde and adducts? *Addict Biol* 2004;9:3–10.
203. Sorrell MF, Tuma DJ. Hypothesis: alcoholic liver injury and the covalent binding of acetaldehyde. *Alcohol Clin Exp Res* 1985;9:306–9.
204. Niemelä O. Distribution of ethanol-induced protein adducts in vivo: relationship to tissue injury. *Free Radic Biol Med* 2001;31:1533–8.
205. Lieber CS. Alcoholic fatty liver: its pathogenesis and mechanism of progression to inflammation and fibrosis. *Alcohol* 2004;34:9–19.
206. Hoerner M, Behrens UJ, Worner T, Lieber CS. Humoral immune response to acetaldehyde adducts in alcoholic patients. *Res Commun Chem Pathol Pharmacol* 1986;54:3–12.
207. Peterson KP, Bowers C, Peterson CM. Prevalence of ethanol consumption may be higher in women than men in a university health service population as determined by a

biochemical marker: whole blood-associated acetaldehyde above the 99th percentile for teetotalers. *J Addict Dis* 1998;17:13–23.
208. Itälä L, Seppä K, Turpeinen U, Sillanaukee P. Separation of hemoglobin acetaldehyde adducts by high-performance liquid chromatography-cation-exchange chromatography. *Anal Biochem* 1995;224:323–9.
209. Viitala K, Israel Y, Blake JE, Niemela O. Serum IgA, IgG, and IgM antibodies directed against acetaldehyde-derived epitopes: relationship to liver disease severity and alcohol consumption. *Hepatology* 1997;25:1418–24.
210. Sillanaukee P, Seppä K, Koivula T, Israel Y, Niemelä O. Acetaldehyde-modified hemoglobin as a marker of alcohol consumption: comparison of two new methods. *J Lab Clin Med* 1992;120:42–7.
211. Halvorsen MR, Campbell JL, Sprague G, Slater K, Noffsinger JK, Peterson CM. Comparative evaluation of the clinical utility of three markers of ethanol intake: the effect of gender. *Alcohol Clin Exp Res* 1993;17:225–9.
212. Johnson RD, Bahnisch J, Stewart B, Shearman DJC, Edwards JB. Optimized spectrophotometric determination of aldehyde dehydrogenase activity in erythrocytes. *Clin Chem* 1992;38:584–8.
213. Hansell NK, Pang D, Heath AC, Martin NG, Whitfield JB. Erythrocyte aldehyde dehydrogenase activity: lack of association with alcohol use and dependence or alcohol reactions in Australian twins. *Alcohol Alcohol* 2005;40:343–8.
214. Kärkkäinen P, Poikolainen K, Salaspuro M. Serum b-hexosaminidase as a marker of heavy drinking. *Alcohol Clin Exp Res* 1990;14:187–90.
215. Hultberg B, Isaksson A, Berglund M, Moberg A-L. Serum b-hexosaminidase isoenzyme: a sensitive marker for alcohol abuse. *Alcohol Clin Exp Res* 1991;15:549–52.
216. Hultberg B, Isaksson A, Berglund M, Alling C. Increases and time-course variations in beta-hexosaminidase isoenzyme B and carbohydrate-deficient transferrin in serum from alcoholics are similar. *Alcohol Clin Exp Res* 1995;19:452–6.
217. Nyström M, Peräsalo J, Salaspuro M. Serum b-hexosaminidase in young university students. *Alcohol Clin Exp Res* 1991;15:877–80.
218. Hultberg B, Isaksson A. Isoenzyme pattern of serum b-hexosaminidase in liver disease, alcohol intoxication and pregnancy. *Enzyme* 1983;30:166–71.
219. Iffland R, Grassnack F. Untersuchung zum CDT und anderen Indikatoren für Alkoholprobleme im Blut alkoholauffälliger Pkw-Fahrer. *Blutalkohol* 1995;32:26–41.
220. Haffner H-T, Batra A, Wehner HD, Besserer K, Mann K. Methanolspiegel und Methanolelimination bei Alkoholikern. *Blutalkohol* 1993;30:52–62.
221. Hollstedt C, Dahlgren L. Peripheral markers in the female "hidden alcoholic." *Acta Psychiatr Scand* 1987;75:591–6.
222. Harasymiw J, Bean P. The combined use of the early detection of alcohol consumption (EDAC) test and carbohydrate-deficient transferrin to identify heavy drinking behaviour in males. *Alcohol Alcohol* 2001;36:349–53.
223. Javors MA, Johnson BA. Current status of carbohydrate deficient transferrin, total serum sialic acid, sialic acid index of apolipoprotein J and serum beta-hexosaminidase as markers for alcohol consumption. *Addiction* 2003;98 Suppl 2:45–50.
224. Helander A, Peter O, Zheng Y. Monitoring of the alcohol biomarkers PEth, CDT and EtG/EtS in an outpatient treatment setting. *Alcohol Alcohol* 2012;47:552–7.
225. Neumann J, Beck O, Helander A, Böttcher M. Performance of PEth compared with other alcohol biomarkers in subjects pfesenting for occupational and pre-employment medical examination. *Alcohol Alcohol* 2020;55:401–8.
226. Sillanaukee P, Aalto M, Seppa K. Carbohydrate-deficient transferrin and conventional alcohol markers as indicators for brief intervention among heavy drinkers in primary health care. *Alcohol Clin Exp Res* 1998;22:892–6.
227. Sillanaukee P, Olsson U. Improved diagnostic classification of alcohol abusers by combining carbohydrate-deficient transferrin and gamma-glutamyl transferase. *Clin Chem* 2001;47:681–5.
228. Bell H, Tallaksen C, Sjaheim T, Weberg R, Raknerud N, Orjasaeter H, et al. Serum carbohydrate-deficient transferrin as a marker of alcohol consumption in patients with chronic liver diseases. *Alcohol Clin Exp Res* 1993;17:246–52.
229. Gjerde H, Johnsen J, Bjorneboe A, Bjorneboe GE, Morland J. A comparison of serum carbohydrate-deficient transferrin with other biological markers of excessive drinking. *Scand J Clin Lab Invest* 1988;48:1–6.
230. Helander A, Carlsson AV, Borg S. Longitudinal comparison of carbohydrate-deficient transferrin and gamma- glutamyl transferase: complementary markers of excessive alcohol consumption. *Alcohol Alcohol* 1996;31:101–7.
231. Randell E, Diamandis EP, Goldberg DM. Changes in serum carbohydrate-deficient transferrin and gammaglutamyl transferase after moderate wine consumption in healthy males. *J Clin Lab Anal* 1998;12:92–7.
232. Niemelä O, Sorvajärvi K, Blake JE, Israel Y. Carbohydrate-deficient transferrin as a marker of alcohol abuse: relationship to alcohol consumption, severity of liver disease, and fibrogenesis. *Alcohol Clin Exp Res* 1995;19:1203–8.
233. Helander A, Carlsson S. Carbohydrate-deficient transferrin and gamma-glutamyl transferase levels during disulfiram therapy. *Alcohol Clin Exp Res* 1996;20:1202–5.
234. Rosman AS, Basu P, Galvin K, Lieber CS. Utility of carbohydrate-deficient transferrin as a marker of relapse in alcoholic patients. *Alcohol Clin Exp Res* 1995;19:611–6.
235. Keso L, Salaspuro M. Laboratory tests in the follow-up of treated alcoholics: how often should testing be repeated? *Alcohol Alcohol* 1990;25:359–63.
236. Kristenson H, Öhlin H, Hulten-Nosslin MB, Trell E, Hood B. Identification and intervention of heavy drinking in middle-aged men: results and follow-up of 24–60 months of long-term study with randomized controls. *Alcohol Clin Exp Res* 1983;7:203–9.
237. Kristenson H, Jeppsson JO. Drunken driver examinations. CD-transferrin is a valuable marker of alcohol consumption. *Lakartidningen* 1998;95:1429–30.
238. Anton RF, Lieber C, Tabakoff B. Carbohydrate-deficient transferrin and gamma-glutamyl transferase for the detection and monitoring of alcohol use: results from a multisite study. *Alcohol Clin Exp Res* 2002;26:1215–22.
239. Goodwin DW, Schulsinger F, Hermanssen L, Guze SH, Windkure G. Alcohol problems in adoptees raised apart from alcoholic biological parents. *Arch Gen Psychiat* 1973;28:238.
240. Cloninger CR, Bohman M, Sigvardsson S. Inheritance of alcohol abuse: cross fostering analysis of adopted men. *Arch Gen Psychiat* 1981;38:861.
241. Cloninger CR. Neurogenetic adaptive mechanisms in alcoholism. *Science* 1987;236:410–6.
242. Devor EJ, Cloninger CR. Genetics of alcoholism. *Ann Rev Genet* 1989;23:19–36.

243. Ball DM, Murray RM. Genetics of alcohol misuse. *Br Med Bull* 1994;50:18–35.
244. Ratsma JE, Van Der Stelt O, Gunning WB. Neurochemical markers of alcoholism vulnerability in humans. *Alcohol Alcohol* 2002;37:522–33.
245. Cowen MS, Chen F, Lawrence AJ. Neuropeptides: implications for alcoholism. *J Neurochem* 2004;89:273–85.
246. von Knorring AL, Bohman M, von Knorring L, Oreland L. Platelet MAO activity as a biological marker in subgroups of alcoholism. *Acta Psychiat Scand* 1985;72:51–8.
247. Begleiter H. The collaborative study on the genetics of alcoholism. *Alcohol Health Res World* 1995;19:228–9.
248. Fowler JS, Volkow ND, Wang G-J, Pappas N, Logan J, MacGregor R, et al. Inhibition of monoamine oxidase B in the brains of smokers. *Nature* 1996;379:733–6.
249. Agarwal DP. Molecular genetic aspects of alcohol metabolism and alcoholism. *Pharmacopsychiatry* 1997;30:79–84.
250. Edenberg HJ, McClintick JN. Alcohol dehydrogenases, aldehyde dehydrogenases, and alcohol use disorders: a critical review. *Alcohol Clin Exp Res* 2018;42:2281–97.
251. Chen CC, Lu RB, Chen YC, Wang MF, Chang YC, Li TK, et al. Interaction between the functional polymorphisms of the alcohol-metabolism genes in protection against alcoholism. *Am J Hum Genet* 1999;65:795–807.
252. O'Keefe EL, DiNicolantonio JJ, O'Keefe JH, Lavie CJ. Alcohol and CV health: Jekyll and Hyde J-curves. *Prog Cardiovasc Dis* 2018;61:68–75.
253. Glucksman E. Alcohol and accidents. *Brit Med Bull* 1994;50:76–84.
254. Westreich LM. Evaluating and monitoring drug and alcohol use during child custody disputes. *Curr Psychiatry* 2017;16:30–42.
255. Hermansson U, Helander A, Brandt L, Huss A, Ronnberg S. Screening and brief intervention for risky alcohol consumption in the workplace: results of a 1-year randomized controlled study. *Alcohol Alcohol* 2010;45:252–7.
256. Erim Y, Böttcher M, Schieber K, Lindner M, Klein C, Paul A, et al. Feasibility and acceptability of an alcohol addiction therapy integrated in a transplant center for patients awaiting liver transplantation. *Alcohol Alcohol* 2016;51:40–6.
257. Kummer N, Wille SM, Poll A, Lambert WE, Samyn N, Stove CP. Quantification of EtG in hair, EtG and EtS in urine and PEth species in capillary dried blood spots to assess the alcohol consumption in driver's licence regranting cases. *Drug Alcohol Depend* 2016;165:191–7.
258. Midanik L. The validity of self-reported alcohol consumption and alcohol problems: a literature review. *Br J Addic* 1982;77:357–82.
259. Del Boca FK, Darkes J. The validity of self-reports of alcohol consumption: state of the science and challenges for research. *Addiction* 2003;98 Suppl 2:1–12.
260. Nanau RM, Neuman MG. Biomolecules and biomarkers used in diagnosis of alcohol drinking and in monitoring therapeutic interventions. *Biomolecules* 2015;5:1339–85.
261. Kechagias S, Dernroth DN, Blomgren A, Hansson T, Isaksson A, Walther L, et al. Phosphatidylethanol compared with other blood tests as a biomarker of moderate alcohol consumption in healthy volunteers: a prospective randomized study. *Alcohol Alcohol* 2015;50:399–406.
262. Helander A, Böttcher M, Fehr C, Dahmen N, Beck O. Detection times for urinary ethyl glucuronide and ethyl sulfate in heavy drinkers during alcohol detoxification. *Alcohol Alcohol* 2009;44:55–61.
263. Biondi A, Freni F, Carelli C, Moretti M, Morini L. Ethyl glucuronide hair testing: a review. *Forensic Sci Int* 2019;300:106–19.
264. Hoiseth G, Morini L, Polettini A, Christophersen A, Morland J. Ethyl glucuronide in hair compared with traditional alcohol biomarkers--a pilot study of heavy drinkers referred to an alcohol detoxification unit. *Alcohol Clin Exp Res* 2009;33:812–6.
265. Kintz P. Consensus of the society of hair testing on hair testing for chronic excessive alcohol consumption 2009. *Forensic Sci Int* 2010;196:2.
266. Paul R. Alcohol markers in hair: an issue of interpretation. *Forensic Sci Med Pathol* 2019;15:281–3.
267. Fosen JT, Hoiseth G, Sempio C, Giarratana N, Enger A, Morland J, et al. Hair EtG: alterations in segment levels accompanying hair growth. *Drug Test Anal* 2019;11:112–8.
268. Hagström H, Hemmingsson T, Discacciati A, Andreasson A. Risk behaviors associated with alcohol consumption predict future severe liver disease. *Dig Dis Sci* 2019;64: 2014–23.
269. Mann RE, Smart RG, Govoni R. The epidemiology of alcoholic liver disease. *Alcohol Res Health* 2003;27:209–19.
270. Simpson RF, Hermon C, Liu B, Green J, Reeves GK, Beral V, et al. Alcohol drinking patterns and liver cirrhosis risk: analysis of the prospective UK Million Women Study. *Lancet Public Health* 2019;4:e41–e8.
271. Andresen-Streichert H, Muller A, Glahn A, Skopp G, Sterneck M. Alcohol biomarkers in clinical and forensic contexts. *Dtsch Arztebl Int* 2018;115:309–15.
272. Bortolotti F, Tagliaro F. Biomarkers for identification of alcohol use/misuse. In: Jones AW, Morland JG, Liu RH, editors. *Alcohol, Drugs and Impaired Driving – Forensic Science and Law Enforcement Issues.* Boca Raton: CRC Press, 2020, 347–80.
273. De Vos A, De Troyer R, Stove C. Biomarkers of alcohol misuse. In: Preedy V, editor. *Neuroscience of Alcohol: Mechanisms and Treatment.* Amsterdam: Elsevier, 2019, 557–65.
274. Dasgupta A. *Alcohol and its Biomarkers: Clinical Aspects and Laboratory Determination.* San Diego: Elsevier, 2015.

3.5 FORENSIC ISSUES RELATED TO ETHANOL DETERMINATION IN BIOLOGICAL SPECIMENS AS EVIDENCE FOR PROSECUTION OF TRAFFIC OFFENDERS WHEN STATUTORY CONCENTRATION LIMITS ARE ENFORCED

Alan Wayne Jones

3.5.1 Introduction

The history of driving under the influence (DUI) of alcohol and other psychoactive substances was recently reviewed by Jones et al.[1] and they traced the first drunk-driving prosecution to London, the U.K., in 1897. According to *The Morning Post* (Saturday, 11 September 1897), Mr. George Smith lost control of the vehicle he was driving, was seen swerving from one side of the road to the other, drove across a footpath, and crashed into a wall, although nobody was injured. Some passers-by helped Mr. Smith from the vehicle and reported smelling alcohol on his breath. He was subsequently arrested by the police and charged with DUI. When brought before a magistrate, Mr. Smith admitted to drinking two or three glasses of beer before driving, but claimed that he did not feel drunk. Nevertheless, he was found guilty and fined 20 shillings (= £1 or about £125 today) and warned not to drink alcohol before driving in the future.

An editorial published in the July 1904 issue of *Quarterly Journal of Inebriety* drew attention to the dangers associated with driving a "motor wagon" after consuming alcohol.[2] The editorial mentioned 25 fatal accidents in which 15 persons occupying these wagons were killed outright, five more died two days later, and three others a few weeks after the respective accidents, making a total of 23 fatalities. Investigations revealed that in 19 instances the driver had used spirits within an hour or more before the disaster.

The first U.S. jurisdiction to criminalize DUI was New York in 1910, quickly followed by New Jersey.[3] After prohibition was abolished in 1933, the consumption of alcohol escalated, as did many alcohol-related crimes, including drunken driving. State legislators were concerned about what easy access to alcoholic drinks would mean for motor transportation, traffic safety, and public health. Enacting laws prohibiting drunken driving was one thing, but could these be effectively enforced? What evidence would be necessary to prove, beyond a reasonable doubt, that a person was in breach of the law? Opinions were divided about how much alcohol a person could consume before they were a danger for traffic safety and unfit to drive safely and could therefore be charged with DUI.

The well-known signs and symptoms of drunkenness, such as the smell of alcohol on a person's breath, inability to walk a chalk line, slurred speech, etc., were not very reliable and more specific ways to prove a person was under the influence of alcohol were needed.[4] Evidence of intoxication was strengthened when arrested drivers were examined by a physician or police surgeon. The suspect's general appearance and behavior were noted and a number of cognitive and psychomotor tests of impairment were administered.[5] The physician's report, along with testimony from the arresting police officer or any eyewitnesses, formed the nucleus of the prosecution case.

In Norway (1936) and Sweden (1941) evidence for the over-consumption of alcohol and unfitness to drive was derived from the chemical analysis of a sample of the driver's blood.[6] The first statutory blood-alcohol concentration (BAC) limits for driving in the U.S. were enacted in Indiana and Maine in 1939 and *prima facie* evidence of intoxication was equated with a BAC of 0.15 g% (150 mg%).[7] This compared with punishable limits for driving of 0.05 g% and 0.08 g% in Norway and Sweden, respectively. A suspected driver would need to consume considerable amounts of alcohol, within a relatively short time, to reach a BAC of 0.15 g%, which would be difficult for normal social drinkers. This limit was later lowered, first to 0.10 g% (100 mg%) and then 0.08 g% (80 mg%), where it stands today in 49 of 50 states.[8] Utah lowered its BAC limit for driving in 2019 to 0.05 g%, and with the passage of time more states will follow this lead.[9]

The BAC enforced for novice drivers (aged under 21 y) is 0.02 g% in most U.S. jurisdictions and 0.04 g% for drivers of commercial vehicles.[10] Most European nations as well as Australia enforce limits of 0.05 g%, whereas Sweden lowered its limit to 0.02 g% in 1990 followed by Norway in 2001. The British Road-Traffic Act of 1967 introduced a statutory BAC limit for driving of 80 mg% (0.08 g%), whereas Scotland lowered its limit to 50 mg% (0.05 g%) in December 2014. A recent study of alcohol-related road-traffic crashes and fatalities in Scotland failed to confirm any improvement after the limit was lowered.[11]

Table 3.5.1 contains information about the statutory BAC and breath-alcohol concentration (BrAC) limits for driving in different parts of the world. One notes a four-fold difference, which is probably more a reflection of public attitudes and political forces rather than results of traffic safety research and crash risk in relation to BAC.[12]

Punishments and sanctions for a drunk-driving offense differ between jurisdictions and depend on circumstances, such as whether in addition to a punishable BAC the driver was involved in a crash and if other road users were injured or killed. Among the various penalties for a DUI are monetary fines, withdrawal of the driving permit, confiscation of the vehicle, incarceration, and/or mandatory treatment for an alcohol use disorder.[13] Stiffer penalties are imposed for repeat offenders, because recidivism rates are high in drunk and drugged-driving cases [14] and these hard-core offenders are a major problem for traffic safety. It has been shown that people who repeatedly drive impaired by alcohol and/or drugs often suffer from a personality disorder or some other mental health problem.[15] Most nations impose stiffer penalties for repeat offenders and those with high BAC, such as 0.15 g%, 0.18 g%, or 0.20 g% BAC when apprehended.[16]

TABLE 3.5.1
Statutory Blood-Alcohol Concentration (BAC) and Breath-Alcohol Concentration (BrAC) Limits in Various Countries throughout the World and the Blood/Breath Ratios (BBR) Adopted When Estimating BAC or Setting the Statutory BrAC Limit from the Existing BAC

Country/Nation[1,2]	Statutory BAC[3]	Statutory BrAC[3]	Assumed BBR
Most European Nations	0.50 mg/mL (g/L)	0.25 mg/L	2000:1
The Netherlands	0.50 mg/mL (g/L)	220 μg/L	2300:1
Norway, Sweden, Poland	0.20 mg/g (g/kg)[4]	0.10 mg/L	2100:1[4]
Finland	0.50 mg/g (g/kg)[4]	0.22 mg/L	2400:1
United States of America[5]	0.08 g/100 mL	0.08 g/210 L	2100:1
England, Wales	80 mg/100 mL	35 μg/100 mL	2300:1
Ireland, Scotland	50 mg/100 mL	22 μg/100 mL	2300:1
Japan, Taiwan, S. Korea	0.30 mg/mL	0.15 mg/L	2000:1
India	30 mg/100 mL	Screening test only	2100:1
China[6]	0.20 mg/mL	0.20 mg/L	2100:1
Canada	0.08 g/100 mL	0.08 g/210 L	2100:1
Australia	0.05 g/100 mL	0.05 g/210 L	2100:1
South Africa	0.05 g/100 mL	0.22 mg/L	2300:1
New Zealand	50 mg/100 mL	250 μg/L	2000:1

[1] Some countries also enforce a lower limit for novice or provisional drivers, for those under 21 y in the U.S. the limit is 0.02 g%, and 0.04 g% for operators of commercial vehicles.
[2] Most countries also enforce a higher statutory limit corresponding to a more serious offense of aggravated drunken driving with stricter penalties, including incarceration.
[3] The units of concentration used to report BAC and BrAC are those used in the respective countries.
[4] Because density of whole blood is 1.055 g/mL on average, 0.20 g/kg is the same as 0.21 g/L, which means that the blood/breath ratio of ethanol in Norway and Sweden is 2100:1.
[5] The state of Utah lowered its statutory BAC limit for driving to 0.05 g% in December 2018.
[6] Breath analysis is used to estimate BAC.

When BAC or BrAC limits *per se* are enforced, there should be no need to prove that a driver was impaired by alcohol at the time of driving, simply that the concentration in a sample of blood or breath exceeded the statutory limits for driving. Indeed, in countries with low BAC limits of 0.02 g% or 0.05 g%, signs and symptoms of alcohol intoxication are not obvious, especially in borderline cases.[17] Epidemiological surveys show that the BAC of most traffic offenders when apprehended is several times higher than the statutory limits, with average concentrations of 0.15–0.18 g%.[18]

There is a large body of literature, as well as many textbooks, about the science and law of DUI for use by lawyers. These present relevant case law and review the strengths and weaknesses of scientific evidence in such cases.[19] Some material is written as a collaboration between a scientist and a lawyer, such as the article by Hume and Fitzgerald that appeared in *Analytical Chemistry* in 1985.[20] This article refers to many relevant forensic questions that arise in DUI cases, including the use of accurate and precise analytical methods, aspects of the disposition and fate of ethanol in the body, and biological variations between subjects.[21]

Admittedly, some defense lawyers are inclined to use "smoke and mirror tactics" or a "shot-gun" approach to create a reasonable doubt in the eyes of a judge and/or jury and, therefore, win an acquittal.[22] Many common defense arguments in DUI cases in the U.S. were critically reviewed in a document published by the National Traffic Law Center and the National District Attorneys Association. This was entitled "claims and responses to common challenges and defenses in driving while impaired cases" and gives useful information to counteract or rebut certain arguments raised during the prosecution of traffic offenders.[23]

3.5.2 Chemical Tests for Alcohol Intoxication

At the start of the 20th century, analytical chemistry was developing rapidly and methods were described for the determination of ethanol in biological specimens.[24] A reasonably good correlation was found between clinical signs and symptoms of drunkenness and the concentration of ethanol in a patient's blood or urine.[25] However, it was not until the 1920–1930s that the first determinations of ethanol in blood were considered reliable enough for legal purposes as supporting evidence in drunk-driving cases, as reviewed by Ladd and Gibson.[26] Various constitutional law issues related to the use of chemical testing evidence for intoxication and appeal court decisions appeared in a 1950 monograph by Donigan.[27]

The analytical methods for determination of ethanol in blood, breath, or urine were much improved in the 1950s, and the results of analysis were given more weight as evidence of intoxication in criminal cases.[28–30] The gold-standard method today for medicolegal determination of BAC is headspace (HS) gas chromatography (GC) with a flame ionization detector (FID).[31] The Breathalyzer instrument was introduced in 1954, and this device simplified and strengthened the gathering of evidence necessary for the prosecution of traffic offenders, although this instrument is now obsolete. Modern evidential breath-alcohol analyzers incorporate infrared spectrometry and/or electrochemical oxidation for determination of ethanol.[32]

The first GC methods of analysis appeared in the 1960s and, besides ethanol, other volatile substances in the blood could also be determined and identified from their retention times (RT) – that is, the time elapsed after injection of the sample until the appearance of a peak response on the chromatogram.[33] Analytical specificity was improved when duplicate determinations – under slightly different chromatographic conditions – yielded different RTs for ethanol and coincided with RTs from analysis of authentic ethanol standards. Some laboratories have started to perform a parallel determination by mass spectrometry (MS), which provides even higher selectivity by obtaining a characteristic mass-fragmentation pattern of the ethanol molecule.[34] However, the need for this more elaborate GC-MS method of analysis for a simple drug like ethanol, which is present at such high concentrations in blood of traffic offenders, remains an open question.

Defending drunk drivers has become a specialty area of litigation for many lawyers and law firms, especially in countries where the adversarial system of justice operates, such as Australia, New Zealand, the U.K., and the U.S.[35,36] These firms advertise their services via websites, blogs, and video recordings reviewing various defense arguments and their experiences in court when defending their clients. There are also a number of organizations in the U.S., such as the National College for Defending Drinking Drivers, who regularly hold seminars with invited guest speakers lecturing about the pros and cons of scientific evidence in DUI cases. One can find a library of textbooks dealing with the science and law of drunk-driving litigation including information about the basic physiology and pharmacology of ethanol intoxication, pitfalls in the methods used to determine ethanol in body fluids, etc.[19,21] These books are often written by lawyers who specialize in defending people suspected of serious traffic crimes, such as alcohol and/or drug-impaired driving.[37]

Another U.S. organization active in DUI defense is the National Association of Criminal Defense Lawyers (NACDL), which publishes a newsletter entitled *The Champion* – a useful resource for lawyers specializing in the defense of DUI cases.[38,39] A newer publication in this field, with a lot of useful information about scientific issues arising in drunk-driving cases, is called *Counterpoint: the journal of science and the law*, edited by and mostly written by Jan Semenoff from Canada (Counterpoint-journal.com).

Procedural issues related to impaired driving, such as whether the traffic police officer had probable cause to make an arrest, is another key element in such cases, because of potential breaches of a person's fourth amendment rights. The necessary evidence to arrest a driver is obtained by administering so-called standardized field sobriety tests and these are done at the roadside under widely variable environmental conditions, close to where a vehicle was stopped. In most countries, including Canada, field sobriety tests are unnecessary, because the police instead administer a roadside breath-alcohol screening test for alcohol influence. If the result is a "fail" then this motivates arresting a suspect and proceeding with a more reliable evidential test done at a police station. The use of preliminary breath testing is rapid and effective and can be administered with the driver still sitting behind the steering wheel. In some nations, drivers can be selected at random from the traffic flow and requested to provide a breath-alcohol test. Tens of millions of drivers are tested annually without any prior suspicion that they were impaired or had consumed alcohol.

This chapter deals with various forensic questions that often arise in connection with the arrest and prosecution of traffic offenders suspected of driving under the influence of alcohol. The increasing adoption of alcohol concentration *per se* statutes focuses the spotlight on the reliability of the analytical methods used for legal purposes. This has given rise to a plethora of defense arguments that are intended to cast doubt on the veracity of the BAC or BrAC evidence thus leading to an acquittal.[22] Examples include alleged consumption of alcohol after driving (hip-flask defense), contamination of the blood or breath samples with extraneous alcohol, medical health issues that might impact on absorption, distribution, metabolism, and excretion (ADME) of ethanol in the body, etc.

3.5.3 General Challenges

3.5.3.1 Drinking After the Offense

A common defense argument in some countries is alleged consumption of alcohol after being involved in a road traffic crash, supposedly to calm down and relieve anxiety. This defense tactic has been aptly referred to as post-offense drinking or the "hip-flask defense," thus, referring to a small silver flask, usually containing spirits, kept in a jacket pocket or the glove compartment of the vehicle.[40] For this defense to succeed, lawyers for the accused need to convince the court that their client's BAC or BrAC would have been below a statutory limit if not for the additional drink consumed after driving. Normally, the burden of proof in criminal cases is on the prosecution, but according to legal practice in the U.K. and other jurisdictions, this shifts to the defendant in "after-drink" cases. However, in those countries where an inquisitorial system (such as continental Europe) of justice operates, the prosecution has to rebut claims of drinking alcohol after driving, which is not at all easy and many acquittals can be documented.

In typical drunk-driving cases, samples of blood or breath are obtained for analysis between 30–120 min after the time of driving or arrest. In real-world situations, such as after a road-traffic crash, the driver sometimes manages to drive home or to a friend's house and, when eventually interviewed by the police, claims that alcohol consumption had occurred after driving ended. A prosecution for leaving the scene of a crash is appropriate, but the much more serious offense of drunken-driving or causing property damage or injuries might have to be dropped, because of the alleged drinking of alcohol after driving.

Long experience from investigating after-drink cases in Sweden shows that many suspects persist with this defense even when there is no supporting evidence, such as empty or opened bottles of liquor in proximity to the vehicle. Some of the more experienced DUI offenders, especially repeat offenders, keep alcohol in their vehicle for this express purpose, hence the term "hip-flask defense." Forensic investigations require detailed information about the quantity of ethanol consumed after driving to enable calculating what this means for the prosecution BAC. With the help of an expert witness, the BAC expected from the amount of ethanol in the after drink can be calculated and compared with the result on the analytical report. In this way, it can often be shown that despite the "after-drink," the driver's BAC exceeded the statutory limit at the time of driving.

It is important to consider all the observations made by the arresting police officers and the testimony of witnesses in such after-drink cases, such as to whether they saw the suspect drinking alcohol. Was there an opportunity to consume alcohol while sitting behind the steering wheel? The driver might be trapped in the vehicle after a crash with no opportunity to reach for a bottle of liquor until rescued. The suspect's general appearance, behavior, and state of inebriation are important to document, such as whether intoxication was increasing or decreasing after arrest. If a person consumes a large quantity of ethanol in a relatively short time, the impairment effects produced are more pronounced shortly after drinking worsening as more time passes. By contrast, if the drinking ended several hours earlier despite a high BAC, people tend to sober up during the post-absorptive phase of the blood-alcohol curve and signs and symptoms of drunkenness are less obvious.[22]

Most BAC calculations are done using the Widmark equation, or some modification thereof, and these make use of a person's age, body weight, and gender. Both parties in a DUI case need to agree on the amount of ethanol, if any, that was consumed after driving. In criminal cases giving a suspect the "benefit of the doubt" is standard practice, and so it should be in any blood-alcohol calculation. If several hours have elapsed since drinking the alcohol and sampling blood, then under these circumstances, it seems appropriate to adjust the Widmark calculation for the metabolism of ethanol over this time period.

Expert witnesses should be asked to calculate the most probable BAC, along with an upper and lower 95% prediction interval, based on the amount of ethanol contained in the after-drink. The results obtained should then be compared with the analytical report produced by the forensic laboratory and a positive difference reflects the driver's BAC before the after-drink. Grossly exaggerated claims of the amounts of ethanol consumed after driving, such as an entire bottle of wine or liquor, should be considered unrealistic and dealt with accordingly.

The average BAC in apprehended DUI suspects in most nations is usually between 0.15–0.18 g%, and many exceed 0.3 g%. In reality, people don't have much idea what their BAC is when they are arrested for DUI and before they later claim consumption of alcohol after driving.[41,42] For example, consumption of a few normal strength beers (4–6 vol%) after driving for an 80 kg male subject cannot account for a BAC of 0.15–0.18 g%. So, even after deducting the BAC resulting from the after-drink, the person still exceeded the statutory limit and a DUI prosecution should proceed. Defendants should not be allowed to change their statement as to how much they drank afterwards, if the calculation does not help their case.

If both urine and blood samples are available for analysis, the UAC/BAC relationship provides useful information to judge the truthfulness of after-drink claims.[43] If the UAC/BAC ratio is less than unity (1.0) or below 1.1, then absorption and distribution of ethanol in the body is not complete, which supports the contention of recent drinking. By contrast, if the UAC/BAC ratio is 1.3 or more, this indicates that the blood-alcohol curve is in the post-absorptive phase at the time of sampling, so drinking probably ended several hours earlier.

Iffland and Jones[44] investigated double blood samples taken about 1 h apart and evaluated whether the UAC/BAC ratios could be useful when investigating claimed drinking alcohol after driving. They found that UAC/BAC ratios were more useful to evaluate the truthfulness in such defense arguments. The problem with double blood samples is that when ethanol is consumed on an empty stomach, the rate of absorption into the blood is very rapid. This means that the second BAC will be lower than the first BAC even if alcohol was consumed after driving. However, during the absorption phase of the blood-alcohol curve before ethanol is fully equilibrated in all body fluids, the ethanol concentration in bladder urine is lower than in the peripheral blood. This contrasts with urine voids made during the post-absorptive phase of ethanol metabolism when the UAC is always higher than the BAC and UAC/BAC ratios might be between 1.3–1.5 or higher.[45]

The ethanol concentration in bladder urine reflects the BAC during the time that urine was being produced in the kidneys and stored in the bladder. Because the water content of urine is about 20% greater than an equal volume of whole blood, the ethanol concentration in newly secreted urine should be 20% higher, giving a urine/blood ratio of 1.2:1. By dividing the measured UAC by 1.2, an estimate is obtained as to the lowest BAC at the time of voiding or since the bladder was last emptied. Drinking a 500 mL of water and diuresis did not alter the UAC/BAC ratios.[46]

If a driver is not sitting behind the steering wheel when arrested by the police, this gives an opportunity to claim consumption of alcohol after driving. Whenever this happens, efforts should be made to obtain a sample of blood as well as two urinary voids 30–60 min apart. If the UAC of the second void is higher than the first void, this would support recent drinking and that absorption and distribution of ingested ethanol were incomplete at the times of sampling.[47] On the other hand, if the UAC decreases between the first and second void, this is evidence of a post-absorptive phase and the main part of the alcohol was probably imbibed at least 1–2 hours earlier.

If the UAC/BAC ratios are less than or close to unity this also indicates recent drinking and that the BAC was still rising towards its peak level. When interpreting UAC/BAC ratios a lot depends on the frequency of emptying the bladder and the possibility of urine retention (incomplete voiding). Furthermore, if there was an alcohol-free pool of urine in the bladder before the drinking started, this would dilute the ethanol concentration in newly secreted urine giving abnormally low UAC/BAC ratios in the first void of the bladder afterwards. In apprehended drivers, even a random urinary void is a good reflection of the BAC some time earlier. This follows because during a drinking binge necessary to reach such a high BAC observed in apprehended drivers (mean 0.15–0.18 g%), the person has probably voided the bladder several times, owing to the diuretic action of alcohol consumption.[48]

Evaluating the change in BAC between the times of taking two blood samples 30–60 min apart can sometimes indicate whether the BAC was rising or falling sometime earlier. With a rapid gastric emptying, this can mean that BAC might start to decline within about 10–15 min post-drinking. The first sample of blood in typical drunk-driving cases is not usually obtained until 30–90 min after an arrest. Accordingly, a declining BAC between the two successive blood samples is not sufficient evidence to determine when the last drink was taken and therefore whether alcohol had been consumed after driving.[44]

Forensic toxicologists in Germany have developed a method known as congener analysis to investigate claims of drinking alcohol after driving.[49] Congeners are other low-molecular substances produced during fermentation processes besides ethanol and some are imparted during the aging process in oak casks etc. The congeners impart the smell, flavor, and taste to the beverage. In brief, use of a congener analysis requires the availability of highly sensitive methods of analysis by HS-GC-FID and a salting-out procedure to enhance the concentrations of volatiles in the headspace vapor.[50] By matching the known congeners in the types of alcoholic beverage allegedly consumed after driving with the congener profile in the driver's blood and urine samples can furnish useful forensic information.

The typical profile of volatile congeners include methanol, 1-propanol, 2-butanol, 1-butanol, and 2-methyl-1-propanol and all can be determined, along with ethanol, by HS-GC-FID methods.[51] The quantitative analysis of congeners requires some refinements, such as saturation of the sample with inorganic salts, such as sodium sulfate, and the use of cryogenic trapping prior to GC analysis.[52] Considerable research has been done in Germany on the quantitative analysis of congeners and their non-oxidative urinary metabolites in forensic science and legal medicine to help identify the source of ethanol in blood and urine.[53,54]

The results of congener analysis, together with other information, have been accepted by the high court in many German provinces after hit-and-run crashes, and when a suspect claims they also consumed alcohol after driving. The usefulness of this approach is limited by the fact that a driver might have consumed the same type of alcoholic beverage both before and after driving. Methanol is a prominent alcoholic beverage congener, and the lowest concentrations found in vodka and highest in fruit brandies. Methanol is also produced endogenously and the concentrations in blood are usually between 0.5–1.5 mg/L.[55] This concentration begins to increase when people drink ethanol because of competition inhibition for oxidative enzyme liver alcohol dehydrogenase.[56] Nevertheless, elevated concentration of methanol in body fluids can be used as a biomarker of recent drinking and the diagnosis of binge drinking in clinical medicine. If the concentrations of methanol in blood of arrested drivers exceeds 10 mg/L, this serves as one indication of chronic heavy drinking and the possibility of an alcohol use disorder and dependence.[57]

The defense argument of drinking alcohol after driving can be minimized by appropriate legislation, such as that in Norway, which stipulates that it is illegal to consume alcohol within 6 h after driving if there is reason to believe that the police will want to investigate some event or occurrence during the driving. The punishment for consumption of alcohol within 6 h after driving, if the BAC exceeds the statutory alcohol limit is the same as for drunken driving (Norwegian traffic law, paragraph 22). This type of legislation does not exist in other Nordic countries so a common defense argument in both Finland and Sweden is consumption of alcohol after driving or after involvement in a traffic crash.[40]

The preferred method in Sweden to investigate claims of drinking after driving is to look at the UAC/BAC ratio and the change in UAC between two successive voids.[43] Finding low UAC/BAC ratios, such as under 1.1 indicates recent drinking, whereas ratios greater than 1.3 or more are indicative of the post-absorptive phase of ethanol metabolism. Arrested drivers in Sweden often maintain that they drank alcohol after driving even when there is no supporting evidence, such as witnesses or empty bottles found in close proximity to the vehicle.[43] It sometimes happens that a suspect might admit to a drunk-driving offense initially, but when interviewed by the police a few weeks later, after consultation with a defense lawyer, recalls drinking afterwards.

The ethanol concentration in the first urine specimen, voided after the end of drinking, can be used to give a good indication of the BAC at the time of driving, provided the bladder was not emptied between the time of driving and collection of the urine void used for forensic analysis. Dividing the UAC by a factor of 2.0 gives a conservative estimate of the person's BAC at the time of driving, provided there was no drinking after the offense.[47]

Knowledge of the stage of ethanol absorption, distribution, and elimination in the body is important in hip-flask cases, as well as other forensic cases, such as retrograde extrapolation. The usefulness of evaluating UAC/BAC ratios in alleged after-drink cases was recently tested experimentally.[58] The volunteer subjects first received a priming dose of ethanol to reach a certain BAC and then drank a second bolus dose of ethanol to mimic a real-world after-drink scenario. The authors concluded that UAC/BAC ratios provide useful information to determine the veracity of such statements made by people accused of a drunk-driving offense.

A small fraction of ingested ethanol (~0.1%) undergoes a non-oxidative metabolism to produce ethyl glucuronide (EtG) conjugate, which is measurable in samples of blood and urine.[59] The pharmacokinetics of ethanol and EtG are different in that the concentration-time curves are shifted in time by 1–2 h, similar to the UAC and BAC curves.[60] This led to the suggestion that evaluating the changes in EtG concentration between two consecutive blood samples 30–60 min apart might provide useful information to evaluate claims of drinking alcohol after driving.[61]

3.5.3.2 Laced or Spiked Drinks

Another defense argument sometimes encountered is "laced or spiked drinks" whereby a person arrested for DUI claims that the beer he was drinking had been fortified with additional ethanol without his knowledge. After being arrested for DUI with a BAC above the statutory limit the defendant maintains that he only consumed 2–3 beers, so something must be wrong. Evidence then surfaces that a friend or colleague admits that they added a double vodka to the defendant's beer while he was at the restrooms on the dance floor. Accordingly, the defendant would not have been above the statutory alcohol limit for driving had it not been for the vodka added to his beer.

Whether people can taste whether their drink was spiked with additional alcohol was actually evaluated experimentally in a double-blind study. Those participating in the study were not very good at discriminating between laced and non-laced drinks even when 75–100 mL of vodka had been added to a pint of beer.[62]

A different spin on this same defense tactic visiting friends' homes and being invited to drink from their homemade punch bowl, a fruity drink without knowing it also contained alcohol. Either the punch had been spiked with additional alcohol or fungi in the fruit had fermented the carbohydrate content during preparation and storage. Only when driving home and after being arrested for DUI did the suspect realize that this was indeed a possibility. Most people have great difficulty in estimating their own BAC, especially when this is close to a legal limit, such as 0.02 g%, 0.05 g%, or 0.08 g%.[63,64] The subjective feelings of inebriation at these low-to-moderate BACs vary widely between different individuals, and apprehended drivers might argue that they were in breach of the law limit, but without intent.

Forensic blood-alcohol calculations can be done based on information about how much additional alcohol was added to the beer. However, the results of these calculations show large discrepancies, because people arrested for DUI are not always truthful about the amounts of ethanol they had actually consumed. Drawing firm and unequivocal conclusions about the expected signs and symptoms of drunkenness in relation to a certain BAC is not easy, owing to variations in patterns of drinking and the development of tolerance.[65]

In the U.S., dram-shop laws are common litigation whereby the owner of a bar or pub is charged with selling or serving alcohol to a drunken person, who is later involved in a traffic crash or some other disturbance with property damage or injury. Your host at a party might also be held responsibility if one of the guests was involved in a road-traffic crash when driving home, hence the need for a designated driver.[66] Some law firms and forensic investigators specialize in dram-shop cases, but judging another person's level of intoxication is a tricky and much depends on body weight, pattern of drinking, empty versus full stomach, habituation, and ability to disguise the outward effects and appear sober. The signs and symptoms of alcohol intoxication are not always visible and the smell of alcohol on the breath is fairly easy to mask with mints and mouth fresheners.[17]

In Sweden, a woman was arrested and charged with aggravated DUI, because she had a BAC of 0.17 g% when stopped by the police on a routine control. When the case went to trial, the defendant admitted moderate drinking at a friend's house, but would not accept that the amounts consumed could account for the measured BAC. The witness testimony at the trial revealed that the woman had been offered drinks from a "punch bowl" and, unbeknown to her, this drink had been fortified with 96% v/v ethanol. The medicolegal experts in the case refused to state with certainty that the suspect must have felt she was unfit to drive with a BAC of 0.17 g%. This lower court decision was later ratified in the appeals court and the Supreme Court refused to hear the case.

The trend toward lower statutory alcohol limits for driving, and zero tolerance laws for novice drivers, makes the laced drinks defense hard to disprove. In general, people have difficulty judging their own BAC, especially when close to threshold limits such as 0.02 g/% or 0.05 g%. The rates of ethanol metabolism differ between different individuals and, after an evening of alcohol consumption, it is feasible that a person still has alcohol in the body when driving to work the next morning. Much will depend on BAC at bedtime, the rate of ethanol metabolism, and time of arising early the next morning. The question of how long a person needs to wait after a drinking spree before driving is a difficult one and some advocate for the use of ignition interlock devises.[67] These devices are often fitted to vehicles owned by repeat offenders as a condition for re-licensing and a negative breath-alcohol test is required before the vehicle will start. The average rate of ethanol elimination from blood is 0.015 g% per h (range 0.0–0.025 g% per h), so if a person had consumed sufficient alcohol to reach a peak BAC of 0.15 g% it would require about 10 h to become alcohol-free (0.15/0.015 = 10), varying from 6–15 h depending on the actual rate of ethanol metabolism in individual cases.[68]

3.5.3.3 Rising Blood-Alcohol Curve

In some jurisdictions, the punishable BAC in a drunk-driving case is that existing at the time of driving or when a traffic offense was committed. This has led to some traffic offenders claiming that they had recently finished drinking and that their BAC was below the statutory limit of 0.08 g% at the time of driving, but had risen to a level over the limit by the time a blood sample was taken.[40] This defense argument is less relevant when lower statutory limits of 0.02 g% or 0.05 g% are enforced, because these levels are reached after the first few drinks.

An important question to consider when this defense argument is considered is the absorption kinetics of ethanol and the time necessary to reach peak BAC after the end of drinking. Controlled alcohol dosing studies show that the rate of absorption of ethanol from the stomach is highly depending on the contents of the stomach before drinking, etc. The peak BAC might occur between 5–120 min after the last drink. Information about the actual increase in a person's BAC or BrAC after end of drinking is hard to find in the scientific literature.

The drunk-driving laws in some countries refer to the BAC existing during or after driving, which means there is no need to know the BAC at the time of driving. The prosecution BAC or BrAC is determined at the time of sampling. After starting to drink an alcoholic beverage, the ethanol it contains first enters the stomach, before absorption occurs through the gastric lumen to reach the portal venous blood. Low statutory BAC such as 0.02 g% or 0.05 g% should be attained fairly rapidly after the end of drinking. Ethanol does not remain unabsorbed in the stomach during a drinking spree and only begin when a person starts to drive home.

The absorption kinetics of ethanol shows that large inter-individual variations and depends on factors influencing gastric emptying, because the surface area available for absorption is much greater in the duodenum and jejunum. Table 3.5.2 gives examples of times necessary to reach peak BAC after the end of drinking when subjects drank a bolus dose of ethanol ranging from 0.35 to 1.05 g/kg as neat whisky on an empty stomach.[69] The times necessary to reach peak BAC after the end of drinking, and the magnitude of the rise in BAC before reaching a peak, are shown in the table.[70]

Ethanol starts to be absorbed from the stomach and intestine immediately after drinking starts and regardless of whether the person has an empty or full stomach.[71] It is not correct to assume that ethanol remains unabsorbed in the stomach for several hours during the time the person spends at a bar or restaurant. It might be likely that some amount of the ethanol contained in the last drink might be unabsorbed in the stomach when a driver is pulled over and gets apprehended by the police. Absorption of ethanol occurs continuously, albeit at widely varying rates, and the last part of the amount ingested might take several hours for complete absorption in the total body water to be completed.

TABLE 3.5.2
Relationship between the Dose of Ethanol Ingested (g/kg) on an Empty Stomach and Mean and Range of Blood-Alcohol Concentrations (BACs) Reached

				Number of subjects reaching peak BAC within			
Ethanol[1] g/kg	N[2]	BAC[3] g%	Range[4] g%	5–15 min[5]	35–45 min	65–75 min	95–105 min
0.34	6	0.056	0.043–0.067	5	1	0	0
0.51	16	0.074	0.054–0.091	11	3	1	1
0.68	83	0.092	0.052–0.136	33	26	21	3
0.85	44	0.120	0.083–0.178	13	24	7	0
1.02	3[6]	0.134	0.116–0.149	0	1	1	1
All doses	152	0.094	0.043–0.149	62 (41%)	55 (36%)	30 (20%)	5 (3%)

[1] Ethanol dose grams per kg body weight.
[2] Number of drinking subjects at each dose.
[3] Average peak BAC.
[4] Lowest and highest BAC in individual subjects.
[5] Measured from end of drinking, which lasted 15 min (doses 0.34 and 0.51 g/kg), 20 min (0.68 g/kg) and 25 min (0.85 and 1.02 g/kg).
[6] One subject vomited when BAC passed 0.15 g% at 35 min after the end of drinking.

Note: Number and percentage of volunteer subjects reaching peak BAC at different time intervals after the end of drinking are also shown.

But unlike most other drugs, ethanol is a tiny uncharged molecule and is totally miscible with water. It easily penetrates the gastric mucosa and so it is not necessary for it to reach the small intestines before absorption occurs. However, the rate of uptake into the portal blood is a lot faster from the intestines than from the intestine, owing to large differences in absorption surface areas. Depending on the amount of food in the stomach before drinking, the time for complete absorption can take several hours, although the bulk of the dose ingested is absorbed fairly rapidly into the bloodstream.[72] Another thing to remember is that most people indulge in drinking alcoholic beverages for the pleasant effects produced, such as for relaxation, relief of anxiety, or mild euphoria, and ethanol needs to become absorbed and pass the blood-brain-barrier to experience these pharmacological effects.

The intoxicating effects of a given dose of ethanol are more pronounced during the rising limb of the BAC profile. People would surely be surprised if they had been buying drinks for several hours without experiencing any of the feelings associated with mild inebriation.[73] Unfortunately, there are only limited studies of the pharmacokinetic profiles of ethanol in real-world drinking scenarios and with few participants.[74]

The number of drinking subjects participating in research studies on the forensic aspects of ethanol is, of course, limited compared to real-world consumption of alcoholic beverages. The more people involved – in terms of their age and gender – allows much firmer conclusions to be drawn about the times necessary to reach peak BAC after the end of drinking. The type of beverage consumed impacts the maximum BAC reached, as well as the time of its occurrence, as demonstrated in a fairly recent cross-over designed study.[75] In this study, the same dose of ethanol (0.50 g/kg) was consumed in the form of beer (5.1 vol%), wine (12.5 vol%), or vodka/tonic (20 vol%) over 20 min after an overnight fast. The lowest mean BAC was observed after the subjects drank beer (0.050 ± 0.01 g%) and occurred 62 min after the end of drinking. This compared with a mean peak BAC of 0.077 ± 0.017 g% after vodka/tonic (mean time to peak 36 min), and 0.062 ± 0.011 g% after white wine (mean time to peak 54 min).

Gullberg[76] reported results of a drinking study in 39 subjects who had consumed various amounts of alcohol, either with or without eating food, to mimic real-world conditions. He reported that the time required to reach peak BAC after the end of drinking averaged 19 min (span 0–80 min), and 81% of subjects had reached their peak BAC within 30 min after the end of drinking.

Shajani and Dinn[77] investigated the time needed to reach peak BAC under social drinking conditions in eight men and eight women, who drank alcoholic beverages of their choice. The maximum BAC was reached in 35 min (span 17–68 min) after the end of intake. Taken together, these studies and a few others suggest the low probability that the result of a blood- or breath-alcohol test made some time after driving will be higher than at the time of driving, which is often 1–2 hours earlier.

Zink and Reinhardt[78] made an important contribution to drinking studies when they allowed heavy drinkers to consume as much alcohol as they wanted over periods of 6–10 hours. During and after drinking, samples of blood were taken from an indwelling catheter at ~15 min intervals and the BAC was measured by forensic methods used in Germany. In this way, a detailed picture of the BAC profile was obtained, including the rates of absorption, time to peak, and elimination rate from blood. The results from this study showed that some individuals reached their peak BAC even before the last drink was taken. The longest time to reach a peak BAC was 50 min after the end of drinking. This study is considered important because of the huge amounts of ethanol consumed and reaching very high BAC in this range is often encountered in drunken drivers. The results from this unique drinking study, which original was written in the German language, was later re-assessed and republished in English.[79]

The effect of drinking alcohol while eating a meal was investigated by Jones and Neri[71] in a study design that attempted to mimic a typical Swedish dinner party. Despite consumption of ethanol together with food, ethanol was initially absorbed into the blood rapidly and on average 70–80% of the peak BAC was reached 15 minutes after end of drinking. However, the remainder of the ethanol consumed took a lot longer to become absorbed and a BAC plateau developed. This was interpreted to mean that the rate of absorption of ethanol from the stomach was occurring at the same rate as it was metabolized in the liver, hence no changes in peripheral blood concentrations. More controlled studies of rates of ethanol absorption would be welcomed when consumption of alcoholic beverages occur together with, or after, a meal.[80]

3.5.3.4 Retrograde Extrapolation

The pharmacokinetics of ethanol has probably been studied for a longer time and more extensively than any other drugs. This follows from the early availability of a reliable analytical method (since at least 1922), the popularity of ethanol as a recreational drug, and the fact that blood-ethanol concentrations after a moderate dose are much higher than for other recreational drugs. The creation of statutory blood-alcohol limits for driving has also necessitated making extensive pharmacokinetic studies to establish a relationship between dose administered and peak BAC. Nevertheless, the bulk of the experimental studies show considerable inter-subject variation in shapes of the BAC profiles even when drinking occurs under standardized conditions and adjustments are made for different body weights.

Figure 3.5.1 shows concentration-time profiles of ethanol in nine male subjects who drank 0.68 g/kg ethanol as neat whisky on an empty stomach in a time of exactly 20 min. Inspection of these traces shows wide variation in maximum BAC reached and also the time of its occurrence. Based on hundreds of similar controlled alcohol dosing studies involving consumption on an empty stomach or after a meal, it can be concluded that in the vast majority

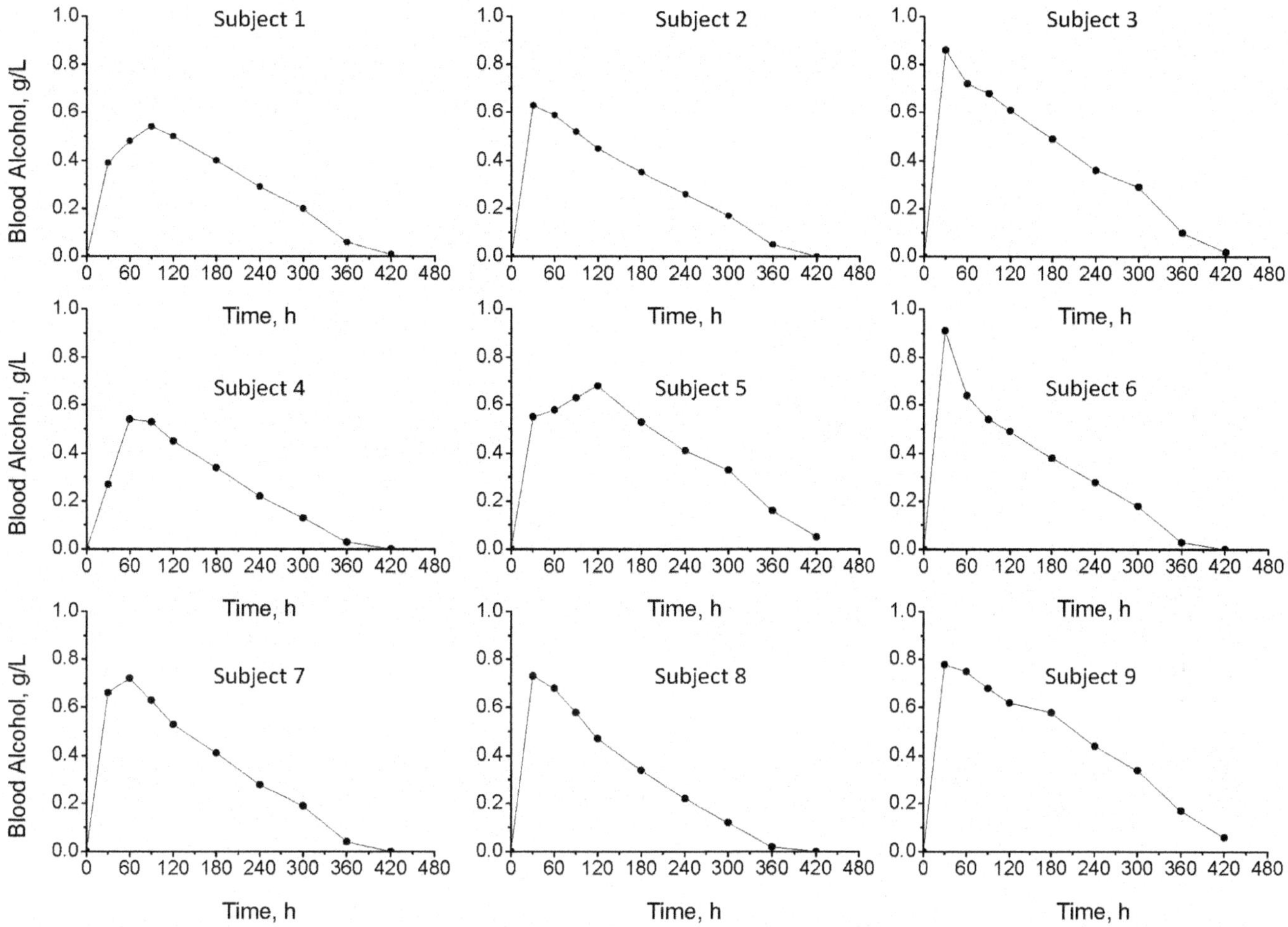

FIGURE 3.5.1 Blood-alcohol concentration (BAC) time profiles in nine subjects who consumed 0.68 g ethanol/kg body eight as neat whisky on an empty stomach in 20 min. Note the wide variation in rate of ethanol absorption during first 120 min post-dosing

of people, the peak BAC is reached between 5 and 120 min after the end of drinking. For the same dose of ethanol after adjustment for body weight, the peak BAC might vary about three fold. Lowest concentrations in blood are associated with slow absorption and later occurring peak BAC (100–120 min) and highest BAC with rapid absorption (5–30 min).

Once the absorption of ethanol is complete, the person's BAC reaches a peak or maximum level and the concentration then starts to decline at a constant rate per unit time, in accordance with zero-order kinetics. The time of reaching peak BAC is very much dependent on factors influencing gastric emptying rate. In any individual DUI cases it is not possible to state categorically the position of the BAC curve at the time of driving, although in the vast majority of cases it is a reasonable assumption that this is close to the peak BAC or in the post-absorptive phase.

Figure 3.5.1 also shows that by 120 min post-drinking all BAC curves showed a rectilinear declining phase, which indicates that ethanol is being cleared from the bloodstream at a constant rate per unit time. The slope of this declining phase is an important pharmacokinetic parameter in legal medicine, such as when a back extrapolation is made or other blood-alcohol calculation. Studies have shown that the elimination rate of ethanol from blood can vary by a factor of three between individuals (0.01–0.03 g% per h). Lowest rates are found in fasting or malnourished subjects, and the highest rates are seen in alcoholics during detoxification. The vast majority of moderate drinkers are expected to have elimination rates of ethanol from blood varying form 0.01–0.25 g% per h.

In some jurisdictions, the relevant BAC or BrAC in a DUI for prosecution is that existing at the time of driving. However, in actual casework, samples of a driver's blood or breath are not obtained until a few hours afterwards. Some jurisdictions accept the BAC or BrAC within two hours of the driving as being not less than the concentration at the time of driving, which sidesteps the need to do a back extrapolation. If the time between driving and sampling body fluids is longer than two hours, the prosecution will need to call an expert witness to perform a back calculation of the BAC to the time of driving.

This procedure is fairly straightforward, provided the suspect was in the post-absorptive phase of the blood-alcohol curve at the time of driving and at the time of sampling blood or breath. From the results of hundreds of controlled alcohol dosing studies, there is convincing evidence that the mean rate of ethanol elimination

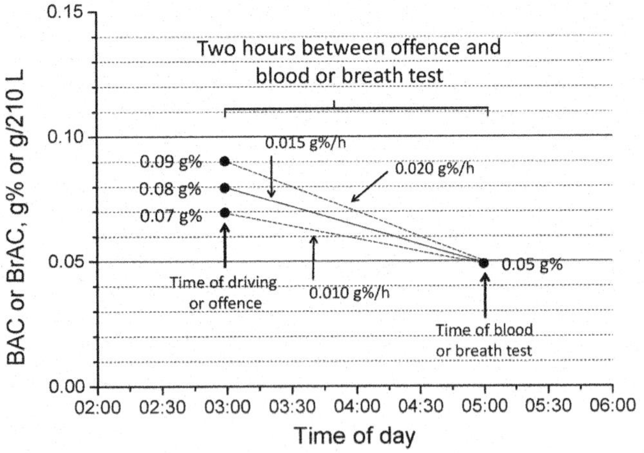

FIGURE 3.5.2 Graphical illustration of back calculation of a driver's blood-alcohol concentration (BAC) from time of sampling blood to the time of a traffic offense, two hours earlier. The calculation is done assuming three different elimination rates of ethanol from blood (0.010, 0.015, and 0.020 g% per h) to obtain an estimate of the BAC at time of driving

from blood in moderate drinkers is 0.015 g% per hour or 0.015 g/210 L per hour from breath. Because the rate of elimination varies between different subjects, a useful strategy is to use a range of values in the back-calculation, such as 0.01–0.02 g% per h, and provide the court with a low, average, or high estimated BAC as illustrated in Figure 3.5.2. This shows the post-absorptive part of the BAC curve, and a back-calculation should be conducted assuming a mean elimination rate of 0.015 g% per h and minimum and maximum values of 0.01–0.02 g% per h. Obviously, the use of a lowest value of 0.01 g% per h gives a certain advantage to the suspect.

From an evaluation of double blood samples taken from over 1,000 DUI suspects, the mean rate of ethanol elimination from blood was 0.019 g% per hour with a 95% range spanning from 0.009–0.029 g% per h. In this population of heavy drinkers (mean BAC 0.16–0.18 g%), the assumption of a mean elimination rate of 0.020 g% per hour and a range from 0.015 to 0.025 g% per h seems justifiable. Two other large studies of double blood samples from apprehended drivers reported similar mean and ranges of ethanol elimination rates from blood.[81,82]

Furthermore, the assumption that most traffic offenders are in the post-absorptive phase of the blood-alcohol curve when apprehended is supported by results from hundreds of controlled drinking experiments,[45] and double blood samples from apprehended drivers in different countries.[83] The proportion of DUI cases in which UAC/BAC ratios were less than or close to unity, which is one indication of pre-peak phase of the blood-alcohol curve, was very low.[47] In the vast majority of cases, the UAC/BAC ratios were 1.3–1.4 or greater for a first void which indicates complete absorption and distribution of ethanol in total body water compartment. Post-mortem studies of alcohol-related deaths also show a predominance of people with high UAC/BAC ratios and the existence of the post-absorptive phase of the blood-alcohol curve.[84]

Making a retrograde extrapolation (back calculation) of BAC or BrAC becomes a contentious issue if the concentration at time of sampling was under a statutory limit at time of sampling, but above the limit after performing a back extrapolation. A real-life scenario might involve investigation of a road-traffic crash in which the driver was injured and/or trapped in the vehicle for a few hours before being rescued. On being transported to a hospital for emergency treatment several hours might have elapsed and the driver's BAC involved had decreased to below the punishable limit for driving. During the police investigation and culpability for the crash the prosecution will probable request making a back-calculation to add on the BAC lost through metabolism.[85] This makes it necessary to assume that the person's BAC was in the declining phase at the time of the traffic incident and at the time of obtaining a blood sample for determination of ethanol.

The BAC at the time of the crash is not known with certainty, because there was no specimen taken for analysis. Reporting a quantitative result of the presumed BAC at time of traffic crash should probably be avoided and instead a range of probable values reported. Otherwise reaching a conclusion as to whether or not the driver's BAC was at the time of driving was above or below a statutory alcohol limit, such as 0.02, 0.05, or 0.08 g% is probably sufficient for the prosecution case. If credible information is obtained about the person's pattern of drinking prior to driving, such as via witness statements, CCTV capture, or credit card receipts, the amount of ethanol in the last drink could be deducted from the back-extrapolated BAC to give some benefit of doubt to the suspect.

Making a back-calculation is unnecessary in those jurisdictions that accept the presumption that BAC in a specimen taken within 2 h after driving is not less than the concentration at the time of driving. However, if a longer time than 2 h elapses, as might happen in road traffic crash when people are trapped and needed to be rescued and transported to hospital back-calculation is required. But whether this necessitates calculating back to time of driving or to within the 2 h time window differs between jurisdictions. Accordingly, if a blood sample was taken from a driver 5 h after a road-traffic crash, the back-calculation might either be done for 5 h, thus adding on a BAC of 0.075 g% (5 × 0.015) or 0.045 g% (3 × 0.015) to within the stipulated 2 h time window. The latter approach is preferable, because it is more likely that the post-absorptive phase existed 2 h after driving rather than at the time of driving.

The metabolism of ethanol commences immediately after the start of drinking, although initially, the rate of absorption from the gut is a lot faster than the rate of metabolism and excretion. This means that BAC increases during absorption and for some time after finishing the last drink. Thus, by the time the drinking ends, most of the ethanol ingested is already absorbed into the bloodstream. Some of the ethanol in the last drink is absorbed more slowly until rate of absorption becomes equal to or less than the rate of metabolism of ethanol in the liver. When this occurs, the BAC reaches its peak level and then starts to decline at a constant rate per unit of time, referred to as the post-absorptive phase.

Under some circumstances, such as when eating a meal and drinking alcohol at the same time or consumption of ethanol immediately after a meal, it appears that most of the alcohol still gets absorbed into the blood, but part of the dose is also bound together with the constituents of the food and this part of the total amount ingested is absorbed much more slowly. This can result in the BAC taking the form of a plateau rather than abrupt transition from rising to declining phase when drinking occurs on an empty stomach. The duration of the plateau is variable depending on the amount of ethanol retained in the stomach with the food, but it might last for 2–3 hours before eventually turning into a rectilinear declining phase.

Ethanol is a good example of a drug that is absorbed from both the stomach and the intestines, albeit more rapidly from the latter owing to the larger absorption surface area available in the duodenum and jejunum. Absorbed ethanol reaches the portal venous blood and is carried to the liver, then to the heart, lungs, and later the entire systemic circulation. How long it takes to reach peak BAC after drinking depends on many factors, including the subject's pattern of drinking, the type of beverage consumed, and other factors that influence gastric emptying rate. In particular, the time of last meal, size and composition of the meal, whether a sandwich or steak and massed potatoes, and smoking cigarettes delays gastric emptying. Certain medications might also delay or accelerate the opening of the pyloric sphincter.

From the results of hundreds of controlled dosing studies, the time required to reach peak BAC after the end of drinking ranges from 0–120 min. When ethanol is given by intravenous infusion, the highest BAC coincides with ending the infusion. Thereafter, there occurs a diffusion plunge when ethanol in the bloodstream diffuse into all other body fluids and tissues over the next 90 min. The shape of the BAC curve when neat spirits are consumed on an empty stomach, provided a pyloric spasm does not occur, resembles those seen after the administration of ethanol intravenously. The other extreme is when neat spirits (40% v/v) are consumed as a bolus dose on an empty stomach. In some individuals, this triggers a pyloric spasm, causing a delay in gastric emptying, and the absorption of ethanol occurs primarily through the stomach surfaces. Under these circumstances, the time need to reach peak BAC might be delayed up to 120 min after drinking.

3.5.3.5 Pathological States

The pharmacokinetics of many prescription drugs have been carefully investigated in patients with various medical conditions and disease states. Much less work has been done concerning the influence of disease states on absorption, distribution, and metabolism of the social drug ethanol. However, DUI suspects sometimes claim they suffer from certain medical conditions or pathological states which they hope might explain their BAC being above the legal limit for driving. Many claims of this kind have been documented such as liver cirrhosis, kidney failure, or the absence of a kidney or one lobe of the lung. Because only 2–5% of the total quantity of alcohol consumed is excreted in urine and breath, reducing the efficiency of the lungs or kidney has marginal effects on the total amount of alcohol eliminated from the body. The rate of alcohol elimination from blood in patients with kidney failure scheduled for hemodialysis was no different from the burn-off rate in healthy control subjects.

Major surgery to the gastrointestinal canal, such as gastrectomy, is known to cause a more rapid absorption of alcohol leading to an "overshoot" peak which tends to be somewhat higher than the maximum BAC expected. A similar phenomenon is often observed when drinking neat liquor on an empty stomach. However, 1–2 hours after drinking ends, the BAC should approach the value expected for the dose of alcohol ingested and the person's gender and body weight because alcohol has now had sufficient time to equilibrate in the total body water. The rate of absorption of alcohol shows wide inter-individual variations even in apparently healthy individuals and estimating the peak BAC from amount consumed is subject to considerable uncertainty.[41] Jokipii[58] devoted his thesis work to compare blood-alcohol profiles under controlled conditions in healthy subjects and in those with various diseases (liver cirrhosis, acute hepatitis, hyperthyrosis, diabetes mellitus, and neurocirculatory asthenia or dystonia). This publication is, unfortunately, not widely available, although its salient features were reviewed with the conclusion that these particular pathological states did not cause distorted alcohol burn-off rates or abnormal distribution volumes of ethanol compared with healthy control subjects.

Drunk drivers with *de facto* diseased liver, such as alcohol hepatitis or cirrhosis, may insist that this renders them slow metabolizers of ethanol compared to individuals with normal liver function. Controlled studies of the effect of various liver diseases on the rate of disappearance of alcohol from blood are rather sparse because ethical issues preclude embarking on detailed investigations of this topic. Those few studies available do not support the notion of a slower rate of metabolism outside the limits of 0.009–0.025 g% per h seen in healthy individuals. Moreover, results of alcohol drinking experiments in patients with cirrhosis are often confounded by the problem of malnutrition in these test subjects, which also leads to a slower elimination rate of alcohol from blood. In patients with cirrhosis and severe portal hypertension (in which portions of the blood are forced to bypass the liver) there is some evidence to suggest a slower rate of ethanol disappearance (0.007 g/%/h). The reason for this finding is probably the diminished flow of blood to the alcohol metabolizing enzymes and not so much the necrosis of the liver tissue.

People suffering from chronic cirrhosis suffer from ascites, which is an accumulation of fluid in the peritoneal cavity, sometimes amounting to several liters in volume. Because the ascites fluid is mainly water, this furnishes a body fluid or reservoir for dilution of ingested ethanol thus increasing the person's volume of distribution. The volume of ascites fluid can vary widely between different individuals and up to five liters is not uncommon. An increased total body water in patients with ascites raises the volume of distribution for other hydrophilic drugs besides ethanol. The concentration of alcohol in ascites will be closer to the concentration in plasma and serum than in whole blood. When alcohol has been cleared from the blood circulation the pool of alcohol in the ascites fluid can redistribute back into the bloodstream. However, alcohol cannot concentrate in this fluid space and ascites fluid should therefore contain approximately 10–20% more alcohol than an equal volume of whole blood. Similar to the situation with urine (see Chapter 3.4), there should also be a time-lag in the clearance of the alcohol from ascites fluid compared with blood.

Most of the scientific evidence indicates that alcoholics generally tend to metabolize alcohol faster than moderate drinkers owing to induction of the microsomal enzyme denoted P4502E1, one of the consequences of long-term heavy drinking. In a recent study in alcoholics undergoing detoxification, with initial BACs of 0.20–0.45 g/%, the burn-off rate (β-slopes) ranged from 0.013–0.036 g/%/h with an average of 0.022 g/%/h. A similar mean value was reported when the work of several research groups based in Germany were compiled together; average elimination rate 0.022 ± 0.005 g/%/h (mean ± SD). Many DUI suspects are clearly alcoholics and in a study of 1090 apprehended drunk drivers from whom two blood samples were taken 60 min apart, the mean ß-slope was 0.019 g/%/h with 95% limits of agreement of 0.009 to 0.029 g/%/h, being in close agreement with values for alcoholics during detoxification.

Individuals suffering from diabetes mellitus with impaired glucose metabolism might have elevated concentrations of ketone bodies, including acetone, circulating in their blood. It is worth noting that the acetone produced can also become reduced to isopropanol in the liver through the alcohol dehydrogenase pathway. However, when modern gas chromatographic (GC) methods are used for blood alcohol analysis, acetone, and isopropanol are easily distinguished so that defense challenges directed at the lack of specificity of GC methods of alcohol analysis are, therefore, pointless if two or more different stationary phases are used for the chromatography. There is no evidence to suggest that the rate of ethanol metabolism should be any different in people with diabetes than in healthy control subjects. The metabolic disturbances associated with insulin-dependent diabetes are not related to the enzymes involved in the disposal of ethanol. Total body water and activity of alcohol dehydrogenase enzymes decreases in states of malnutrition and protein deficiency and this is reflected in slower burn-off rates of alcohol. However, moderate losses of body water after prolonged sauna bathing did not results in any marked differences in the shape of blood-alcohol profiles. A low relative TBW/kg body weight is associated with a smaller volume of distribution for ethanol and this explains observed male-female difference in peak BAC and area under the curve for the same dose of alcohol per kg body weight. The distribution volume of ethanol was shown to decrease in male subjects between the ages of 20–60 y along with a decrease in total body water in the elderly.

People involved in traffic accidents might be badly injured and suffer from shock and hemorrhage, owing to massive losses of blood. This raises the question about the influence of trauma and shock on the hepatic metabolism of alcohol and the resulting blood-alcohol profiles. In a recent study of ten subjects involved in accidents while under the influence of alcohol, and suffering from poly-traumatic shock, a series of venous and arterial blood samples were obtained for determination of ethanol. The rate of alcohol disappearance from blood ranged from 0.017–0.021 g/%/h (mean 0.018 g/%/h), and these values were the same regardless of whether arterial or venous blood sampling sites were used. The results of this study confirm many other anecdotes and case reports regarding alcohol pharmacokinetics in people injured while drunk.

Hypovolemic shock following massive loss of blood will result in a redistribution of body fluids, and higher proportions of plasma will enter the intravascular space to maintain an effective circulation and tissue perfusion. This might alter the relative distribution of some protein-bound drugs and endogenous substances between body compartments but the concentration of alcohol in the blood is not markedly influenced. Nevertheless, some people continue to speculate about the impact of trauma on blood-alcohol concentrations and alcohol burn-off rates even though a careful review of the literature shows that there is no substance to these opinions.

3.5.3.6 Drug–Alcohol Interactions

It is not only alcoholic beverages that contain ethanol. Some cough medicines, vitamin mixtures, pick-me-ups, and other healthstore products may contain considerable quantities of alcohol (> 10% v/v). Thus, ingesting these products will obviously elevate a person's BAC.[86] Much will depend on the quantities consumed and the concentration of ethanol in the blood in relation to the time of driving. Medications in tablet form or applied externally to the skin are not expected to lead to an elevated content in the blood. However, combining ethanol with other psychoactive substances can cause a more pronounced impairment, without any change in the BAC.[87]

Ethanol acts on the brain as a depressant drug, so the co-ingestion with sedative-hypnotic medications has detrimental effects on a person's performance and behavior, which is especially important in older adults.[88] Barbiturates and benzodiazepine derivatives are typical examples of medications that can interact and worsen the behavioral effects of a given dose of ethanol.[89] Apart from an influence on gastric emptying, there is no evidence that concurrent use of drugs increases a person's BAC above the level expected from the dose/kg ingested on an empty stomach.

In countries where cannabis is legalized, such as Canada, the statutory BAC for driving is normally 0.08 g%, but if a motorist also uses cannabis and the concentration of its active metabolite THC in blood is exceeds 2.5 ng/mL, the statutory BAC for driving enforced is lowered to 0.05 g%. This emphasizes the fact that the combined psychotropic effects of alcohol and cannabis cause greater impairment than either drug alone.

The intake of alcohol can modify the pharmacokinetics and behavioral effects of drugs that are oxidized by P4502E1 enzymes or which interact with the GABA receptor to elicit their effects on the central nervous system. However, these change are seemingly not reciprocated in an altered pharmacokinetic profile of ethanol or a raised BAC above that obtained in control experiments when the same dose of alcohol was consumed on an empty stomach.[90] The alleged increase in BAC, caused by drinking alcohol after medicating with histamine-2-antagonists, could not be confirmed in most experimental studies of this drug-alcohol interaction.[91,92]

A therapeutic agent that blocks hepatic metabolism of ethanol by competitive inhibition of alcohol dehydrogenase is 4-methyl pyrazole (fomepizole or Antizol®).[93] This medication is currently available to treat patients poisoned by methanol or ethylene glycol and works by preventing their conversion to more toxic metabolites. However, it needs to be administered intravenously and would also be effective in slowing down the rate of ethanol metabolism.[94]

3.5.3.7 Auto-Brewery Syndrome

Auto-brewery syndrome (ABS), also known as "gut-fermentation syndrome" is a rare medical condition that results in ethanol being produced in the body naturally. In this syndrome, a person's gut is infected with various strains of yeast or a bacterial overgrowth, and depending on the dietary carbohydrates consumed, ethanol is produced by fermentation.[95] Alleged ABS has increasingly been used as a defense argument in DUI cases, supported by several clinical reports showing the biosynthesis of ethanol to be a real possibility.[96]

This syndrome was first reported in people from Japan, who are particularly vulnerable because of a genetic defect. The hepatic enzyme responsible for oxidation of acetaldehyde, which is formed during fermentation is inactive, owing to a polymorphism. When these people ate a carbohydrate-rich type of rice they became intoxicated and their breath smelt of alcohol as confirmed by determination of ethanol in blood samples.[97] The prevalence of this endogenous synthesis of ethanol in different populations has been discussed and debated for many years. Several reports of this syndrome have appeared in articles published in well-respected scientific journals.[98] ABS is considered a reality, but a rare medical condition, although clinical cases continue to appear in the literature including a 2020 article in Annals of Internal Medicine.[99] Others are more skeptical, owing to the fact that fermentation is not an instantaneous process and large volumes of carbon dioxide are produced and this needs to be expelled from the body. Furthermore, a normal blood-glucose is 0.01 g% when if this is converted to ethanol by fermentation the resulting BAC would be 0.05 g%, so abundant amounts of extra carbohydrates are needed to generate higher BAC.

With the help of sensitive and specific methods of analysis, low concentrations of ethanol (0.5–1.5 mg/L) can be determined in body fluids from people, who have not consumed any alcoholic beverages.[100] It seems that endogenous ethanol (EE) is produced in the gut by microbes, bacteria, and/or yeasts acting on dietary carbohydrates, but other biochemical pathways also exist according to a comprehensive review of this subject.[101] Indeed, the existence of other metabolic precursors of ethanol was confirmed in experiments with germ-free rats, because these animals lack the microflora to allow fermentation.[102] Because the portal blood draining the stomach and intestine must pass through the liver before reaching the heart, lungs, and circulatory system, low ethanol concentrations produced in the gut are removed during the first-pass of blood through the liver. Any defects in enzymatic activity of ADH and ALDH might work to prevent this first-pass metabolism from occurring.

Abnormally high concentrations of ethanol were determined in samples of blood and cerebrospinal fluid in hospitalized patients, who apparently had abstained from alcohol. But the analytical method used in this work was not "gas chromatography" and dietary and medicinal sources of ethanol could not be ruled out.[103] Some of the reports of finding high concentrations of EE in the blood of children with various medical conditions, such a short-gut syndrome, have not included sufficient details about the analytical methods used and a cross reactivity with other substances cannot be excluded.[104,105]

Small amounts of ethanol normally synthesized in the gastrointestinal system are usually cleared from the portal venous blood during its first passage through the liver. If massive amounts of ethanol are produced in the gut overwhelming the capacity of the liver enzymes then this ethanol will reach the peripheral blood circulation. Japanese subjects suffering from various metabolic disorders and who were infected with Candida in the gut complained of experiencing feelings of drunkenness after eating their usual carbohydrate-rich rice meals.[106] This report was convincing, because gas chromatography was used determine ethanol concentrations in body fluids. The patients were apparently kept under strict observation for the duration of the study and the elevated BAC was attributed to endogenous synthesis in this racial group of subjects.[97]

This phenomenon of ABS has been investigated and reported in a number of case reports in other racial groups, including Caucasians.[95,98,107,108] However, as already mentioned, East Asians are probably more susceptible to suffer ABS, because of the inactive form of the low Km enzyme aldehyde dehydrogenase in about 50% of the population.[109] This enzyme defect does not influence their ability to oxidize ethanol, but conversion of acetaldehyde to acetic acid is hindered. During the fermentation of glucose to produce acetaldehyde, its further oxidation is blocked and instead might then be reduced via alcohol dehydrogenase to ethanol. Most of the individuals with this syndrome also have a past history of suffering from gastrointestinal ailments and complain to their physicians about experiencing fatigue and feelings of drunkenness after eating carbohydrate-rich meals.

The occurrence of EE has also attracted interest in clinical and diagnostic medicine as an indirect way to furnish evidence of yeast infections in the gut.[110] After obtaining a control pre-treatment blood sample, fasted ingests ~5 g of glucose and another blood sample is taken about 1–2 hours later and its ethanol content determined. If the concentration in the second sample is significantly higher than the first, this is taken as evidence for yeast overgrowth in the stomach or small intestine and a gut-fermentation reaction.[111]

Endogenous ethanol concentrations are normally very low (median ~1.0 mg/L) and barely measurable by the gas chromatographic methods used for forensic blood-ethanol analysis, which often have limits of detection of 10–50 mg/L.[100] Such vanishingly small concentrations lack any forensic significance, except in exceptional circumstances, such as already described in Japanese subjects with gastrointestinal disorder (auto-brewery syndrome). Concentrations of EE in blood samples from people with diabetes mellitus, as well as other metabolic disorders, were not much different to the values observed in healthy control subjects.[112,113]

3.5.3.8 Margin of Error – Analytical Uncertainty

The legal importance attached to the results of ethanol analysis in a suspect's blood or breath in drunk-driving cases, especially when an alcohol concentration per se statute is enforced, makes it obvious that the methods used must be fit for their intended purpose. The properties of analytical methods used for forensic purposes including accuracy, precision, specificity of analysis needs to be documented continuously for routine purposes. Other aspects of quantitative chemical analysis includes determining the sensitivity, linearity, limits of detection and limits of quantitation, etc. Guidelines exist for method validation in forensic toxicology[114] and similar principles can be applied to determination of ethanol in blood and breath, including participating in external proficiency testing.[115]

All analytical methods have some degree of uncertainty in the measurements and deciding whether the results exceeds some critical threshold, such as the statutory alcohol limit for driving, needs to consider the magnitude of uncertainty.[116] This will allow the trier of fact can make well-founded decisions as to whether the threshold value was exceeded or not with sufficient degree of certainty.[117] If an analytical chemist makes repeated determinations of ethanol in the same blood specimen, the results are going to differ slightly from occasion to occasion, because it is not possible to repeat exactly each step in the analytical process. The deviations between repeated measurements are expected to be greater if different analysts were involved or when the same blood specimen was sent to different laboratories for analysis.[118,119]

In plain English, uncertainty means not being certain about something and, in DUI cases, this refers to whether the ethanol concentration exceeded the statutory limits for driving. A more formal definition of uncertainty is "a parameter associated with the result of a measurement that characterizes the dispersion of values that could reasonably be attributed to the measurand."

Analytical errors might be systematic or random in nature. Systematic errors are related to the care taken in calibrating the analytical equipment and the source of the known strength ethanol standard solutions used. If there is a known systemic error between the known result and the reported value, either positive or negative, this is easy to adjust for by adding or subtracting a certain amount to give an unbiased final result. The other source of error is random in nature and reflects the dispersion of results after an infinite number of repeated determinations are made. In mathematical terms this is reflected in the size of the standard deviation (SD) of the repeated measurements. There is a basic assumption made that these deviations follow a normal of Gaussian distribution such that 68% of the data are within $\pm$ 1 × SD, 95% are within $\pm$ 2 × SD and 99.7% are within 3 × SD of the mean.

In the field of laboratory medicine, a probability of 0.95 (95%) is taken as the norm used when clinical results are interpreted, such as when deciding whether a person's blood glucose is within the accepted normal range. In statistical terms this corresponds to reporting a mean result $\pm$ 2 × SD, which implies that 95% of the results are within this interval and 5% (P = 0.05) are outside, with 2½% (P = 0.025) being too high and 2½% (P = 0.025) too low, suggesting risk of hyper- or hypo-glycemia, respectively.

When the results of a chemical or biochemical analysis are used in criminal cases, not unexpectedly, a higher statistical probability is necessary to ensure that the final result is not incorrectly claimed to have exceeded the statutory alcohol limit for driving. With reference to the Gaussian distribution of errors, it can be shown that 99% (P = 0.99) of values are within $\pm$ 2.57 × SD and 1% (P = 0.01) outside these limits, P = 0.005 above and P = 0.005 below. The magnitude of the uncertainty in BAC or BrAC determinations are critically important when close to a threshold limit (e.g. statutory BAC or BrAC limit for driving) as exemplified by Figure 3.5.3.

The graph shows that the mean BrAC using both instruments was 0.087 g/210 L, but one of the instruments had a standard deviation (SD) of 0.002 g/210 L and the other 0.003 g/210 L. Assuming a normal distribution of errors, the statistical range for 99% (2.57 × SD) of repeated measurements are ±0.005 g/210 L and ±0.008 g/210 L, respectively. Accordingly, when analysis is done by the more precise method, 99% of results are expected to fall within the range 0.082–0.092 g/210 L (0.087 $\pm$ 2.57 × 0.002) whereas they are in the range 0.079–0.095 g/210 L (0.087 $\pm$ 2.57 × 0.003) with the less precise method.

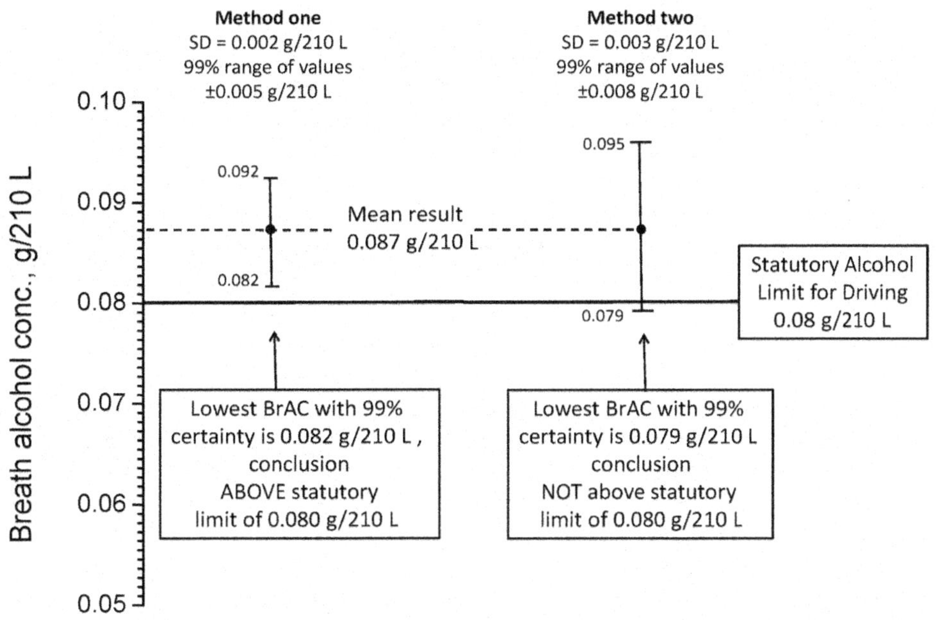

FIGURE 3.5.3 The impact of margin of error when two methods of breath-alcohol analysis were used to test an apprehended driver. Both instruments reported the same mean breath-alcohol concentration of 0.087 g/210 L. But whether the suspect was above the statutory alcohol limit of 0.08 g/210 L with a probability of 99% depends on analytical uncertainty as reflected in the standard deviation

The statistical conclusion drawn from this calculation is that the result of 0.087 g/210 L, given by the least precise method of analysis (SD ± 0.003 g/210 L), is not above the statutory BrAC limit for driving of 0.08 g/L with sufficient statistical certainty, which here is assumed to be at least 99%.[120] This calculation underscores the need to establish SD of the method of forensic breath-alcohol analysis, and this tends to increase with increasing ethanol concentration in the breath, indicating a lower analytical precision and greater uncertainty.[121]

In jurisdictions where an alcohol concentration *per se* statute is enforced, it is obviously important to consider the margin of error or uncertainty in the analytical method used to determine the suspect's BAC or BrAC. This becomes especially important when a suspect is close to a threshold limit for driving and when a "beyond a reasonable doubt" conclusion is necessary, as is the case in criminal prosecution. Many factors need to be considered when the strengths and weaknesses of scientific evidence are evaluated, as illustrated here, for analytical uncertainty. Indeed, in drunk-driving cases with a concentration *per se* law the single most important evidence that a crime was committed is the driver's BAC or BrAC at the time of sampling or at the time of driving, depending on the way the law is written.

There are several ways used to make an allowance for analytical variations when the blood or breath ethanol concentrations are used for forensic purposes. Although the mean concentration gives the best estimate of the true concentration, there is a 0.5 (50%) probability the true result is higher or lower than the mean. Some jurisdictions report the lower of the two independent test results, but this is not very helpful if both numbers are the same, as is often the case. Neither is truncating the third decimal beneficial, because this could be a nine or a zero. A better approach to allow for uncertainty is to make a deduction from the mean concentration so that the prosecution BAC or BrAC can then be stated as being not less than the true value with a statistical probability of 99%. The odds of the result used for prosecution being too high is then 1 in 99, as explained above. Depending on the accuracy and precision of the evidential breath-alcohol analyzer, this might require deducting 0.015 g/210 L from the mean result of an analysis.

Some jurisdictions make an allowance for uncertainty with a "guard band" approach. For example, if the statutory limit for driving is 0.08 g/210 L a prosecution is not initiated until the BrAC reaches 0.09 g/210 L or 0.10 g/210 L, thus allowing 0.01 and 0.02 g/210, respectively as a safety margin. In England and Wales, the statutory breath-alcohol limit for driving is 35 μg% but there is no prosecution of a suspect until the lowest of two breath-alcohol tests reaches 40 μg%, which is 14% above the threshold BrAC limit for driving.

3.5.4 Urine Alcohol Concentration

From a historical perspective, the first determinations of ethanol for clinical and forensic purposes to diagnose intoxication were done on urine samples, because this biological specimen was easier to collect and was available in large volumes.[122] Urine mainly consists of water (95–98%), so it is easier to analyze than blood, because the laboratory does not need to conduct any chemical extractions or distillations prior to analysis. About 2–3% of the total amount of ethanol ingested is recoverable in the urine and is stored in the bladder until voiding.[48] However, urine is rarely used as a biological specimen for analysis of ethanol, because the concentrations present do not reflect the state of intoxication at the time of voiding.

The concentration of ethanol in bladder urine reflects the concentration in renal artery blood during the time that the urine was produced in the kidney and collected in the bladder. The UAC in a random void gives an indication of the average BAC during the time elapsed since the previous void.[123] During this time, the BAC will have changed, sometimes appreciably, such as during the absorption phase when BAC increases rapidly.[47] Furthermore, ethanol might be detectable in the urine after BAC reaches zero. For example, after an evening's drinking, the first morning void might contain measurable amounts of ethanol, although a morning blood or breath-alcohol test is negative. The UAC reflects the person's BAC during the night, while asleep, after voiding the bladder before bedtime.

Because urine contains about 20% more water than an equal volume of whole blood, the concentration of alcohol in freshly produced urine entering the ureter will always be higher than the BAC. The urine–blood relationship has been studied extensively in laboratory experiments,[45] and in drunk drivers.[83] After ingestion of ethanol, a short time exists between absorption into the bloodstream and production of urine so the pharmacokinetic profiles of ethanol in blood and ureteral urine are separated in time. This time lag is extended when comparisons are made between BAC and bladder urine, depending on the frequency of emptying the bladder to collect samples after the end of drinking. There are large inter- and intra-individual variations in UAC/BAC ratios exist, the urine/blood ratio in the post-peak phase of alcohol metabolism is about 1.33:1 on the average.

With the introduction of the British Road Traffic Act of 1967 came a statutory BAC limit of 80 mg% was introduced along with a statutory UAC of 107 mg%. A provision for collecting urine specimens was made available for those people with needle phobia or for other reasons were not inclined to provide a blood sample for analysis of ethanol in drunk-driving cases.[124] In practice, two samples of urine were collected 30–60 min apart and it was the concentration in the second void that was compared with the statutory 107 mg% limit. The first void was intended to empty the bladder of old urine that might reflect the blood-concentration several hours earlier, long before the time of an arrest for a traffic offense.

The urine/blood ratio of alcohol, as well as its variability, increases as the blood-alcohol concentration decreases. The mean ratio of 1.33:1 is higher than expected on the basis of water content differences (1.2:1), in part because of the time-lag between formation of urine in the ureter and storage in the bladder before voiding (see Chapter 3.3). With frequent voiding and thus short storage times in the bladder, the UAC/BAC ratio might be close to the value expected based on differences in water content, namely 100/80 = 1.2:1. Note that in U.K. traffic-law enforcement, the DUI suspect's BAC is not estimated indirectly from the measured UAC. Instead, the legislature has adopted an alcohol concentration of 107 mg% in urine as being equivalent to 80 mg% blood (107/80 = 1.33). This approach is similar to the way that the threshold limits of BrAC have been derived from the existing BAC and the blood/breath conversion factor is adopted by the legislature in the respective countries (see Table 3.5.1). Indeed, because of individual variations in the urine/blood and breath/blood ratios of alcohol, it is strongly recommended not to convert a measured UAC or BrAC into a presumed BAC as a measure of guilt in DUI prosecution. Instead, the threshold concentration of alcohol should be defined in terms of the body fluid analyzed, whether this is breath or urine.

The use of ethanol concentrations in urine as evidence for the prosecution in DUI cases, when a concentration *per se* law operates, is not advisable if the aim is to convert UAC into the presumed BAC. This follows because of large variations in the UAC/BAC ratio in individual cases. The situation is improved of the urine sample analyzed is the second of two voids, hence a relatively freshly produced specimen.

The UAC/BAC ratio is not influenced by diuresis, because alcohol is handled by the kidneys exactly like water in a passive diffusion process.[125] Increasing the volume of urine excreted by drinking large volumes of water may dilute the urine as reflected by its creatinine content but the concentration of alcohol in the specimen will remain unchanged.[46] One objection often raised against the use of urine-alcohol evidence in the prosecution of DUI suspects is that some people cannot completely empty their bladders on demand. The retention of "old urine" with a higher content of alcohol than expected for the prevailing BAC at the time of voiding introduces uncertainty. The prevalence of urine retention in the population at large is hard to estimate although this problem is seemingly more common in elder men and some studies have detected 25 ml of residual urine. However, the impact of urine retention on the concentration of alcohol determined in successive voids and the magnitude of error incurred if the UAC is converted into presumed BAC has not been demonstrated experimentally.

Because some people might excrete glucose in their urine, especially those suffering from diabetes mellitus, there is always a risk that ethanol can be produced in-vitro through the fermentation of sugar by micro-organisms or yeasts infecting the bladder or urinary tract. Some reports claim that ethanol can be produced in the bladder itself, as so-called "bladder beer."[126] This makes it important to ensure that the sampling tubes contain 1% sodium or potassium fluoride, which serves as an enzyme inhibitor and blocks the microbial synthesis of ethanol.[127] Storage of urine specimens in a refrigerator immediately after collection is also effective in preventing the fermentation of glucose by *Candida albicans*.

The phenomenon of "bladder ethanol" was recently reported in a female patient with cirrhosis and poorly treated diabetes.[99] She was rejected for a liver transplant, because her urine repeatedly tested positive for ethanol, with concentrations reaching 0.18 g%, but no obvious symptoms of intoxication. Moreover, the patient denied drinking alcoholic beverages, here BAC was negative and urinary ethyl glucuronide, a non-oxidative metabolite of ethanol, was not detectable. Subsequent testing showed the woman's bladder was infected with a species of yeast called *Candida glabrata*, which together with glycosuria produced ethanol by fermentation. This case report confirmed an earlier study detecting ethanol being produced in the urinary bladder. These two cases need to be distinguished from the phenomenon of "gut fermentation syndrome" discussed earlier, because the latter condition leads to elevated levels of ethanol in blood and clinical intoxication.[126]

Production of ethanol in urine in-vitro after taking a sample is not uncommon if the collecting tubes lack sodium fluoride.[127]Although urine from healthy individuals has only trace amounts of sugar and, therefore, is insufficient substrate for fermentation,[128] many people do secrete sugar in their urine, especially poorly treated diabetics and those in a pre-diabetic condition. This has had negative consequences in forensic cases, raising a false alarm that people were intoxicated, when the source of ethanol in urine was in-vitro fermentation during transport and storage prior to analysis.[129]

3.5.5 Blood-Alcohol Analysis

3.5.5.1 Use of Alcohol Swabs for Skin Disinfection

Blood specimens collected for the analysis of ethanol in road-traffic cases are generally taken from an antecubital vein with the aid of sterile equipment, such as evacuated tubes (Vacutainer) or a disposable plastic syringe and needle. The swabbing of the skin at the site of blood sampling with disinfectants such as ethanol (70% v/v) or isopropanol (70% v/v) should be avoided if ethanol is the substance to be analyzed, simply to avoid later questions about contamination of the blood by carry-over from the swabbing.

Because sterile equipment is used to take the blood, disinfection of the skin at the site of sampling is not really necessary and cleaning with saline or soap and water should be sufficient. Nevertheless, alleged contamination with ethanol or isopropanol contained in the swabs used to disinfect the skin arises from time-to-time in drunk-driving prosecution and defenses. Hence, there was motivation to investigate the question of contamination of blood samples with alcohol swabs by several groups of investigators in the 1960s.[130,131]

Several later investigations were also done using different methods of sampling blood, different ethanol concentrations in the swab, and other variable factors were considered. Tests were done with healthy volunteers who had consumed alcohol drawing blood from different arms,[132] and in hospital patients.[133] Some studies were conducted without the use of ethanol swabs[134] and isopropanol swabs.[135] Another experimental study made use of a "dummy" venipuncture training arm and varied the way the needle was withdrawn, with or without a cotton swab impregnated with alcohol and with or without vacuum still in the tube.[136] The authors recommended that alcohol containing skin disinfectants should be avoided and, if evacuated tubes are used to draw blood, it is advisable to "remove the tube from the collection needle and holder before withdrawing the needle from the puncture site."

If evacuated tubes are used for sampling blood, it is also advisable to fill two tubes in rapid succession and these need to be gently inverted 8–10 times to allow an adequate mixing with the chemical preservatives. The evacuated tubes for blood-ethanol analysis are ray stopper 5 Ml or 10 Ml volume tubes containing a mixture of sodium fluoride as an inhibitor of glycolysis and micro-organisms and potassium oxalate serves as an anticoagulant. These chemicals, in powder form, are already in the tubes as supplied by the manufacturer, although the actual amount of fluoride preservative when samples are taken from living subjects under sterile conditions is an open question.

Unless a person suffers from systemic candidiasis, which is a life threatening condition, the only time the blood sample might be contaminated with yeasts is at the point of inserting the needle from the skin and into a vein. Swabbing and/or cleaning the skin prior to sampling removes this possibility. Traditionally, the 10 mL gray stopper tubes used in drunk-driving cases contain 100 mg NaF and 12.5 mg potassium oxalate as preservatives. But also available for purchase are gray stopper evacuated tubes with smaller nominal volume, such as 3 mL and 5 mL. These tubes are often used for blood-glucose assays and contain smaller amounts of NaF and heparin or EDTA as the anticoagulant. There does not appear a consensus among forensic practitioners about the minimum amount of NaF necessary for blood samples intended for determination of ethanol in apprehended drivers.[137]

If the concentration of NaF in the blood is challenged after sampling, then there are procedures to determine the concentration of fluoride ions, for example by use of ion-sensitive electrodes.[138] Removing the aliquots of blood analyzed from two separate tubes of blood and finding a close agreement in the results is a useful strategy, because large differences in ethanol concentration might mean one of the blood samples was contaminated with extraneous ethanol.

The concentration of ethanol in blood samples decreases during storage at 4°C despite there being 1% w/v NaF included as a preservative. However, the rate of loss is less than 0.003 g% per month and the mechanism of loss seems to be non-enzymatic oxidation involving oxyhemoglobin. If blood specimens become contaminated with micro-organisms when the Vacutainer tubes are opened to remove aliquots for analysis, this can lead to a much more rapid disappearance of alcohol during storage compared with unopened tubes. It seems that various species of micro-organism utilize alcohol as a food.

The risk of ethanol being absorbed through the skin after liberal and frequent use of ethanol-based hand disinfections was considered if people might drive a motor vehicle directly afterwards.[139,140] This has been subjected to experimental testing and there was neither an elevated BAC not positive breath-alcohol tests obtained. However, drinking these hand sanitizers will of course produce elevated BAC and positive breath-test results.[141] Liberal use of ethanol-containing hand sanitizers in the same room where a person was being breath-tested is inadvisable, because of the risk of obtaining false positive results is exaggerated.[139] Hand-held breath analyzers aspirate samples of room air into the detector as a blank test and this could lead to transient false-high readings if there is vapor from the sanitizer in the room air.[142]

The possibility of ethanol absorption through the skin was investigated many years ago by Bowers et al.[143] They reported controlled experiments with several children and one adult with their legs wrapped in cotton soaked in 200 ml of 95% ethanol and secured with rubber sheeting and sealed with adhesive tapes. Blood samples were taken before and at various times after this extreme skin treatment, although neither clinical signs of inebriation nor raised BAC were reported.

The available evidence does not support the contention that significant amounts of ethanol can be absorbed into the blood through the intact skin or via inhalation.[144] However, small amounts of ethanol might be absorbed if there are open blood vessels or abrasions on the skin, but more than about 7–9 g ethanol per hour would need to be absorbed to result in accumulation, because this is the amount metabolized per hour in healthy men. The uptake of ethanol through the intact skin is not a valid excuse in drunk-driving cases, because there is no experimental support that this could indeed be the case.[145] A review article investigated this question and concluded "that there was no significant absorption of alcohol through the skin of adults by the use of hand sanitizers and hence would not produce forensically significant elevated breath or blood alcohol concentrations."

The question of a blood sample being contaminated with extraneous ethanol, if the skin at the venipuncture was swabbed with alcohol, has been a recurring issue in DUI cases and was investigated experimentally in a 2017 article.[146] The results confirmed earlier studies that the carry-over of ethanol from the skin or the swab was not at all likely, even when a sloppy sampling technique was practiced. So this source of ethanol will not result in spurious or false positive results of ethanol determination. Having said that, it would not be wise to use an alcohol swab for skin disinfection if ethanol was to be the substance analyzed, thus avoiding that this loophole arises in criminal cases and DUI prosecutions.

3.5.5.2 Trauma, Massive Blood Loss, and Intravenous Fluids

Drunk and drugged drivers are over-represented in road-traffic crashes that often require emergency hospital treatment for any injuries sustained. This might entail administering of life-saving medicines, including intravenous resuscitation fluids to counteract shock to replace depleted body fluids.[147] Massive blood loss is a life threatening condition, which precipitates hypovolemic shock and this requires giving various fluids to maintain blood circulation and supply of oxygen to the brain.

Blood samples taken from victims of traffic crashes are often acquired during treatment at hospital, and the integrity of the specimen such as correct sampling tube, sampling site and other factors need consideration. The differences between ethanol determinations in plasma/serum and whole blood have already been discussed. Errors incurred in sampling blood from victims of trauma and receiving intravenous fluids have already been highlighted.[148] The blood sample obviously should not be taken from a cubital vein at the elbow when an intravenous (IV) line is administered into a vein on the hand. This would lead to dilution of the blood sample with the IV fluid. If blood samples submitted for toxicological analysis appear to be unusually dilute, this might be verified by analysis of the hemoglobin content and corrections made to the concentration of ethanol.

Routinely analyzing aliquots of blood from two separate Vacutainer tubes helps to identify any discrepant results and problems with the sampling. If the tube-to-tube difference in BAC exceeds that expected from knowledge of random analytical errors in the methodology used, this points to other influences such as pre-analytical errors associated with the sampling. Abnormally large differences in BAC between the two tubes can often be traced to dilution or coagulation of one or both because of inadequate mixing after collection. After massive blood loss there is a re-distribution of body fluids and a change in the composition of the blood specimen, which becomes more like plasma and more watery.

The question of trauma, massive blood loss, and the administration of intravenous fluids was the subject of a recent review.[149] This article considered the theoretical and physiological aspects of trauma and blood loss, and how this impacts on the results of ethanol analysis based on both animal experiments and human victims of trauma undergoing life-saving emergency treatment. The conclusion reached was that the rate of ethanol metabolism was not significantly influenced by trauma and blood loss, unless the flow of blood to the liver was prevented or interrupted by the nature of the trauma. However, the rate of absorption of ethanol in the stomach before suffering trauma and blood loss is likely to be absorbed into the bloodstream much more slowly. Furthermore, the blood specimen after trauma is expected to be closer to plasma and therefore contain more water and a higher concentration of ethanol. This could be checked by the analysis of hemoglobin content.

In patients suffering from burn trauma, the rate of ethanol metabolism was slightly faster than in control subjects.[150] Massive burns leads to an accumulation of body water and a hypermetabolic state with increased oxygen consumption and higher basal metabolic rates.[151]

3.5.5.3 Hospital Versus Forensic Laboratory Results

The analytical results of ethanol determinations at hospital clinical laboratories are sometimes used in criminal cases for various reasons.[152] This makes it important to ensure whether the hospital specimen analyzed was plasma, serum, or whole blood.[153] As discussed below, ethanol is not evenly distributed between the plasma and red-cell fraction of blood, because the water content of these fluids are different. The hematocrit of blood is influenced to some extent by the person's age, gender, and certain diseases that impact the erythrocyte volume, such as anemia or other hematology. If ethanol is determined at a hospital clinical laboratory on a specimen of plasma or serum the result is expected to be higher than the concentration in whole blood.[154]

The water content of biological specimens is easily determine by weighing an aliquot and heating to dryness in an oven at 105–110°C to reach a constant weight. The water content is then calculated from change in weight after before and after desiccation. According to scientific tables whole blood contains 85 g water per 100 ml (95% range 83.0–86.5 g/100 ml).[155] And the same tables report specific gravity of whole blood is 1.059, so the water content is ~6% less when expressed in mass/mass units; 85.0% w/v corresponds to 80.2% w/w. Women tend to have approximately 1–2% more water in their blood than men owing to their lower hematocrit during periods of menstruation.

Blood hematocrit is defined as the volume of red blood cells per 100 ml of whole blood and in normal healthy individuals values of 42–50% for men and 37–47% for women are usually quoted.[147] After ethanol is absorbed into the blood stream, it distributes into the various components of the blood in relation to their water content. Hence plasma, which is 92% w/w water contains a higher concentration than whole blood, which is 80% w/w water and lowest concentration is in the red-cells (~64% w/w water).

Based on these differences in water content, one can expect a plasma/blood distribution ratio of ethanol of 92/80 = .15 and a ratio of 92/64 = 1.43 for the plasma/red cells distribution. These theoretical values align very well with the results of measuring ethanol in plasma, blood, and erythrocytes in experimental studies.[156] The main difference between plasma and serum is the clotting factors (fibrinogen), which are absent from serum, although water content is the same, hence ~92% w/w and plasma/blood and serum/blood distribution ratios of ethanol are the same, being 1.12 on average according to one study.[157] Besides gender difference in hematocrit, medical conditions, such as anemia is associated with too few red blood cells. People might suffer fatigue and breathlessness, although anemia often causes no noticeable symptoms. And polycythemia, which is an abnormally high proportion of red blood cells, can result from living at high altitudes when there are low blood oxygen levels. The water content of blood is not routinely determined in drunk-driving cases, so if BAC is determined from the results of analysis of ethanol in plasma or serum, the conversion factor used should be chosen to give a suspect the benefit of the doubt. The 95% range of serum/blood and water/blood ratios are from 1.1–1.2 so dividing the plasma or serum concentration of ethanol by 1.2 gives a conservative estimate of the concentration in whole blood.[158]

3.5.5.4 Low Volume of Blood in Sampling Tubes

Most jurisdictions make use of evacuated tubes for sampling blood for forensic analysis of ethanol and other drugs. This helps to standardize the sampling procedure and makes it easy to fill several tubes with blood if necessary. This avoids the need to transfer aliquots of blood to a secondary container, such as the specimens made available to a suspect to arrange for an independent analysis.[159] Evacuated tubes are marked with an expiry date, although it is important to appreciate that this refers to the manufacture's guarantee on integrity of the vacuum and not the stability or correctness of the blood-ethanol concentration. A direct comparison was made between BAC determined in samples taken in expired and un-expired tubes and no statistically significant differences were noted.[160]

The 10 mL grey-stopper evacuated tubes for blood-alcohol analysis contain a mixture of sodium fluoride (~100 mg) as preservative and potassium oxalate (~22.5 mg) as an anticoagulant. The exact volume of blood drawn into the tubes during sampling need not be known exactly, because an aliquot of blood, such as 100 μL, is removed for analysis. The volume of blood in a 10 mL tube might vary widely from < 1.0 to 9.0 mL depending on difficulties experienced by phlebotomist and condition of the superficial veins, which sometimes collapse. After drawing the blood specimen, the tubes should be gently inverted 8-10 times to ensure thorough mixing of with the chemical preservatives so that the specimen does not coagulate during transport to the laboratory.

If the volume of blood in a 10 mL evacuated tube is unusually low this means that it contains an unusually high concentration of inorganic salt (NaF). This has some significance when headspace analysis is used, because of a "salting out" of non-electrolytes during the equilibration process. However, prior to headspace analysis, an aliquot of the blood specimen is diluted with an aqueous solution of internal standard (e.g. n-propanol), usually in the ratio 1 + 10. This means that the concentration of inorganic salt in the blood aliquot in the headspace vial is ~10 time lower than in the original blood specimen. Nevertheless, in forensic casework, questions have arisen about false high results caused by salting out when the evacuated tubes received for analysis contained an abnormally low blood volume.

This notion was tested experimentally when 10 mL evacuated tubes contained between 0.5 and 9 mL of blood.[161] The BAC determined by HS-GC was not significantly different over this 18 fold difference in salt concentration. In fact, the BAC in the tubes with the smallest volume (0.5 mL) decreased by 2–3% compared with 9 mL volume of blood. The investigators explained this by a more effective salting-out of the 3-carbon n-propanol (internal standard) compared with 2-carbon ethanol. Since the GC response ratio peak-area ethanol/n-propanol is used for quantitative analysis, this gave slightly lower final results when calibration curves were used based on analysis of aqueous ethanol standards. Other investigators arrived at similar results and conclusions using a different experimental approach to the same question.[162] The results from both studies leads to the conclusion that an abnormally low blood volume is not any disadvantage to a person charged with a DUI and when HS-GC is the analytical method used.

3.5.5.5 Type of Evacuated Tubes and Chemical Preservatives

The traditional evacuated tubes used to collect blood for forensic analysis of ethanol were made from soda glass with had a nominal volume of 10 mL. These tubes are fitted with a grey rubber stopper and contain 100 mg sodium fluoride as an enzyme inhibitor and 12–25 mg potassium oxalate as an anticoagulant. Over the years the acquisition and purchase of such tubes has become increasingly difficult, owing to changes in the manufacturing process and other commercial issues that are beyond the control of the end-user.

For example, most manufacturers have opted to produce plastic instead of glass tubes for various reasons. This necessitated a study of the stability of ethanol during storage when specimens were collected in plastic vs glass evacuated tubes with the same preservatives.[163] The blood-ethanol concentration was found to during storage for up to 12 months at 4oC at the same rate regardless of the material (glass or plastic) used to construct the evacuated tubes. The ethanol content decreased by about 0.11 g/L after 12 months of storage.

Gray stopper evacuated tubes, mainly intended for blood-glucose analysis, are also being increasingly used for determinations of ethanol in forensic cases. These tubes have a lower nominal volume (usually 5 mL) and contain less sodium fluoride as enzyme inhibitor, often appreciably less, compared with ~1% w/v in the original 10 mL gray stoppered tubes. The amount of NaF necessary to stabilize ethanol concentrations in blood samples when these are taken under sterile conditions from living subjects has not been adequately investigated or discussed.[164] On the other hand, the use of 1–2% NaF is essential as a preservative for blood and urine specimens taken at post-mortem for the determination of ethanol content.[127,165]

A manufacturing problem with a commonly used grey stopper evacuated tubes in drunk-driving cases led to a batch of tubes being shipped to end-users without the required chemical preservatives, neither NaF nor anticoagulant. This prompted the manufacturer to issue a re-call notice for the entire production batch, but unfortunately the tubes had already been received by end-users and used in some forensic cases.[137] Without an anticoagulant, freshly drawn blood will start to clot in about 30 min and this becomes strikingly obvious on arrival and registration at the laboratory for analysis. Specially modified analytical procedures are necessary if a blood sample is clotted and the aim is to report the ethanol concentration in whole blood. With these precautions, the results are not expected to be much different from blood samples taken in the required grey stoppered tubes with preservatives.[166]

3.5.6 Breath-Alcohol Analysis

The first methods for the analysis of ethanol in breath, to serve as an indirect way to determine co-existing BAC, appeared in the U.S. in the 1930s–1940s. However, a major breakthrough in this technology came with the development of the Breathalyzer® instrument in 1954. This gained wide acceptance not only in the United States but also in Australia and Canada and was in widespread use until the 1970s.[32] In European nations, breath-alcohol analysis was used as a preliminary roadside screening test for alcohol influence until the 1980s. The advances being made with new technology for breath-alcohol analysis and of microprocessor control of the testing procedures prompted many countries to evaluate the performance of breath-alcohol analyzers. Instead of the chemical oxidation of ethanol in the breath as was done with the Breathalyzer, analytical techniques such as infrared absorption spectrometry and electrochemical oxidation were used.[167] Furthermore, instead the BrAC was not translated into the coexisting BAC, but instead European countries enacted statutory BrAC limits above which a driver was in breach of the law.

The new statutory BrAC limits were derived from the pre-existing BAC limits by assuming a population average blood-breath ratio (BBR) of alcohol (BrAC = BAC/BBR). However, there was no consensus reached when this BBR was adopted and values ranged from 2000:1 to 2400:1 in different jurisdictions.[168] With the Breathalyzer® instrument, the ethanol content in breath was determined by chemical oxidation and the co-existing BAC was obtained by calibrating the instrument with an assumed BBR of 2100:1.[169]

For law enforcement purposes, two main types of breath-alcohol analyzers are currently used by police authorities to apprehend and prosecute traffic offenders. These are the handheld devices intended and used as roadside screening tests of driver sobriety,[170] and desktop instruments located at police stations that produce evidence-quality results used for prosecution.[171]

Examples of commonly used hand-held instruments for breath-alcohol analysis as roadside screening tests are listed in Table 3.5.3. All the devices listed incorporate electrochemical oxidation methods for the determination of ethanol, which is an accurate, precise, and specific method of analysis.[172] Although originally designed as preliminary breath-alcohol tests, some of the hand-held instruments with electrochemical detectors were later equipped with a printer and deemed sufficiently reliable for evidential testing.[173] The greater portability meant that the evidential test could also be done at the roadside in closer proximity to the time of driving, which obviated the need back calculated analytical results to time of driving.[174] The latest generation of evidential breath-alcohol analyzers are smaller, weigh less, and are generally more robust and driven by microprocessors incorporating various quality assurance features. This gives more confidence in the evidential quality of the results when used in criminal prosecutions, including

TABLE 3.5.3
Examples of Hand-Held Breath-Alcohol Instruments Used in Various Countries as Preliminary Roadside Screening Tests for Driver Sobriety

Hand-held screening instrument	Method for ethanol determination in breath	Examples of where the instruments are used by police authorities
Alcolmeter[1]	Electrochemical (fuel-cell) oxidation	Police forces in the U.K. and many other countries
Alcotest[1]	Electrochemical (fuel-cell) oxidation	Used in German, the Nordic countries and worldwide
AlcoSensor[1]	Electrochemical (fuel-cell) oxidation	Used throughout USA, Canada and other some other nations
Alcodoose[1]	Infrared absorption 9.5 μm	Used mainly in France
SAF'IR	Infrared absorption 9.45 μm	Used by the police in Spain
LifeLock[1]	Electrochemical (fuel-cell) oxidation	Used in several states of America
Alcolizer[1]	Electrochemical (fuel-cell) oxidation	Alcolizer technology, used in Australia and New Zealand

[1] Many different models are available with options for displaying the results, digitally or with colored light diodes, and some can include a print-out in real-time for later use in a prosecution. With most instruments, a plastic mouthpiece tube is necessary for each test, but there are also options for sampling breath passively, such as with use of Alcolizer technology.

a printed record generated in real-time as well as online storage for later evaluation by independent experts and the court.[175]

Random roadside breath testing of motorists is permitted in many countries and a driver can be tested while sitting behind the steering wheel with sobriety confirmed in as little as 15–30 s. The results of roadside tests might be displayed as a pass, warn, or fail in colored light diodes or a digital readout of the ethanol concentration in breath. When roadside breath tests are administered there is no formal 15 min waiting period, so a false high reading caused by mouth alcohol from a recent drink cannot be excluded. After a positive test, the protocol requires a confirmation analysis done 10–15 min afterward, before making an arrest. The specificity of analysis and identification of ethanol is when electrochemical oxidation methods of analysis – and in some countries millions of random tests – are performed annually.[176] The random testing of such larger numbers of motorist without prior suspicion of any alcohol consumption one would expect a high prevalence of false-positive results there was some interfering substance in human breath, but this is not the case.

Electrochemical oxidation methods do not react to acetone in breath, which under some circumstances might be at elevated concentrations in people with poorly treated or non-diagnosed diabetes.[177] However, under some rare metabolic conditions, acetone might be reduced in the body to isopropanol, and this secondary alcohol is oxidized at the fuel cell sensor and cannot be distinguished from ethanol.[178] Methanol, which is much more toxic than ethanol, is also oxidized and cannot be differentiated from ethanol as reported in people attending hospital emergency departments after drinking wood alcohol.[179] Obtaining a positive roadside breath-alcohol test result gives the police sufficient cause to arrest a driver for further testing to ascertain whether a statutory alcohol limit is exceeded. This entails an evidential breath-alcohol test or sampling of venous blood for determination of ethanol by gas chromatography.

The passage of time between taking a roadside breath-alcohol test and the evidential test, depending on geographic location of the road-traffic incident and driving a suspect to a police station, questioning of the driver, and a mandatory 15 min observation period. Most breath-testing protocols require making a duplicate test, and the lower of the two results is the one used in an eventual prosecution. What all this means is that a driver might be above the statutory limit for driving when the breath-test was done at the roadside, but below the limit when the evidential test is administered. Not surprisingly, many of the positive roadside screening test results turn out to be negative (below the limit) when an evidential breath test is made, owing to the ongoing metabolism of ethanol.

Evidential breath-alcohol instruments are considerably more sophisticated in their construction and scientific safeguards compared with hand-held breath-analyzers used for roadside screening purposes. For example, modern evidential instruments are equipped with various algorithms to verify that an end-exhaled sample of breath is obtained, and that this is not contaminated with mouth alcohol. An approved breath-alcohol test requires that a subject makes a continuous exhalation for at least 5–6 s and at the same time maintain a minimum breath flow rate and a discard volume of 1.5 L of top-lung breath. The instruments are fitted with slope detectors capable of monitoring the increase in breath-ethanol concentration during a prolonged exhalation. By looking at instantaneous changes in the slope of the alcohol curve, it is possible to decide if the person has recently consumed alcohol or has had some alcohol solution in the mouth before sampling. However, slope detectors on some instruments are better than others for their intended purpose and are not a substitute for a mandatory 15 min observation/deprivation time prior to testing.[180] There is overwhelming evidence that 15 min is an adequate waiting period for dissipation of any excess alcohol from the oral cavity prior to the evidential breath-alcohol test.[181]

TABLE 3.5.4
Examples of Some Currently Available Instruments for Evidential Breath-Alcohol Analysis and the Analytical Principles They Incorporate for Identification and Quantitative Analysis of Ethanol

Evidential breath analyzer	Analytical principles for detection and quantification of ethanol
Intoxilyzer 9000	Absorption of infrared (IR) light at two different wavelengths ~3.4 and ~9.5 microns to identify the C-H bond stretching and C-O bond in ethanol molecules for enhanced selectivity
Intox EC/IR	Measurement of carbon dioxide and ethanol in breath by infrared absorption to ensure that the sample captured for analysis is not contamination with mouth alcohol. The ethanol content of the breath sample is determined by electrochemical oxidation.
Alcotest 9510	Absorption of infrared radiation at wavelength around ~9.5 microns and electrochemical oxidation of ethanol. The response from both detectors is reported and compared and contrasted, with large differences suggesting an interfering substance. Use of dual detector technology improves the selectivity for identification of ethanol. There is also an option to measure the temperature of end-exhaled breath and correct ethanol results to 34°C.
Intox DMT	Multi-filter infrared spectrometry (3.4 and 9.5 μm) or a dual detector option of infrared and electrochemical oxidation (fuel-cell). Originally known as the DataMaster, this instrument is now produced by the same manufacturer as the Intox EC/IR.
Evidenzer	Infrared absorption of light measuring C-H stretching vibrations in ethanol molecules using multiple (5) wavelength filters in the range 3.3 to 3.8 μm. A robust instrument design allows the use of the Evidenzer in the field for roadside evidential testing.

The breath-alcohol analyzers listed in Table 3.5.4 are currently available and used by the police in different countries. Different models have appeared over the years with various design features, such as the size of the units, portability, key-board versus touch screen, various computer graphics options, and the recording of all test results in real-time. Because the entire sequence of sampling is done by microprocessors, the main task of the instrument operator is to initiate the test and encourage the suspect to make a forced exhalation into the instrument on two separate occasions.

The time interval between taking the last drink of alcohol and submitting to an evidential breath-alcohol test depends on many factors, such as how long after leaving a pub or bar was the driver stopped by the police, whether there was any drinking alcohol during or after driving, etc. The observation/deprivation period of 15 min should start after the suspect is brought to a police station, so that considerably more time must have passed since the last drink. Because of a continuous absorption of ethanol from the stomach and intestine into the blood after the last drink, the concentration of ethanol in the gastric contents is probably very low at the time an evidential breath-alcohol test is done. Indeed, this concentration is probably not much more than that prevailing in the oral mucosa, so regurgitation prior to the breath-test is not a significant problem for validity of the results.

During the 15 min observation period, the suspect is not allowed to drink, eat, smoke, or place anything in the mouth before submitting to the breath-alcohol test. Moreover, most protocols require taking two samples of breath between 2–10 min apart. Good agreement between the two tests or when the second test result is lower than the first speaks against any contamination from any regurgitated stomach contents. The inclusion of a check on the correct calibration of the breath-alcohol instrument in conjunction with a suspect being tested is an important quality assurance measure.[182] Traditionally, control of the calibration was done using a wet-bath simulator device fitted to the instrument that generated a known ethanol vapor concentration, close to the statutory BrAC limit for driving.[183] But more commonly today, a calibration control is done with drug-gas ethanol standards contained in pressurized tanks mixed with an inert gas, such as nitrogen.[184] The analysis of ambient air from the room where the breath-test was administered is necessary to verify the absence of any ethanol that might have given spurious results. The need to make two consecutive breath-alcohol tests with each subject is virtually written in stone.

The necessary quality assurance requirements, in conjunction with evidential breath-alcohol testing, vary somewhat between countries and jurisdictions. These need to be standardized and accepted by the courts in order to support the integrity of the evidence for prosecution in criminal cases.[29] The key elements in such a quality assurance program are summarized below:

- At least a 15 min deprivation/observation period after arrest and before the breath-alcohol test.
  - Whether the focus is on alcohol deprivation or observation or both is uncertain.
- At least one calibration control test done before or after a suspect is tested.
  - Wet-bath simulator or dry-gas standard can be used to control instrument calibration.
  - Wet-bath simulator is more difficult to control but is more like human breath in its composition, being saturated with water vapor at breath temperature.
  - Wet-bath simulator is not influenced by variations in atmospheric pressure.
  - Corrections needed to the results generated from pressurized gas tanks used at high altitudes.
- Analyze two separate breath tests from each suspect.

- The between the two breath tests should be between 2 and 10 min.
- Analysis of room-air as a blank test between the subject and the known alcohol standard.

Despite the many scientific safeguards, the results generated by evidential breath-alcohol instruments continue to be challenged for various reasons. Some defense arguments are valid but most appear to be speculative. The breath-alcohol test is usually administered by a trained police officer, whereas the determination of ethanol in blood samples is done by scientists working at government-controlled forensic laboratories.

3.5.6.1 Residual Mouth Alcohol

Alcoholic beverages vary in their ethanol concentration from 5–40 vol%, which is considerably higher than the concentrations contained in a person's blood or expired breath after drinking. The oral mucosa therefore becomes contaminated with this higher ethanol content for some time after the last drink. Studies have shown that it takes at least 15 min for the higher ethanol content in the mouth to become absorbed through the oral mucosa. A breath-alcohol test done immediately after finishing drinking can produce gross errors in instrument reading compared with the co-existing BAC.[185] When referring to his experience with breath-alcohol testing Dr. Francis Anstie wrote.[186]

> It must not be tried during at least the first quarter of an hour after a dose had been taken for the mouth retains the characteristic smell even if the most moderate dose of any of the stronger smelling drinks for fully this time.

Contamination of the breath with alcohol from a recent drink was also noted by an American scientist Dr. Emil Bogen[187] in his 1927 publication in the *Journal of the American Medical Association* when he wrote:

> As soon as the disturbing factor of alcoholic liquor still in the mouth is removed, which occurs usually within fifteen minutes after imbibition, in the absence of hiccuping or belching, the alcoholic content of 2 liters of expired air was a little greater than 1 cc of urine.

A mouth-alcohol effect has been confirmed many times since and is the reason for the mandatory 15 min observation period prior to an evidential breath-alcohol test.[188] During the 15 min observation period, a suspect is not allowed to eat, drink, or place any materials in the mouth, such as tobacco, etc. Some smokeless tobacco contains an alcohol flavoring, although this does not seem to prolong the need to wait a longer time than 15 min before a breath test is administered.[189,190]

The experimental investigations of the mouth-alcohol effect have allowed alcohol-free subjects to rinse their mouths with ethanol solutions or alcoholic beverages for up to 30 seconds without swallowing the liquids.[191–193]After spitting out the solution, breath-alcohol tests are usually made at 2–5 min intervals for up to 30 min. As expected the first test results are abnormally high sometimes > 0.3 g/210 L because of alcohol dissolved in the oral cavity contaminating the exhaled breath sample. The breath test readings then dropped exponential over time so that by 10–15 min later the instrument response was zero or below the analytical cut-off concentration e.g. 0.01 g/210 L.

Other experimental designs to investigate the mouth alcohol effect require the subject to first drink alcohol to reach a certain BAC and then swirl alcohol around in the mouth prior to sampling breath for analysis.[194,195] Under these conditions, the time necessary to return the BrAC result to a level measured before contaminating the mouth with alcohol tends to be shorter.[180,196]

In conclusion, erroneous results of evidential breath-alcohol testing attributed to the so-called mouth-alcohol effect are much exaggerated. Provided a 15 min observation/deprivation period is strictly enforced in the testing protocol, the only source of mouth alcohol is through regurgitating or reflux of stomach. Waiting 15 min before testing is not a part of most roadside breath-alcohol testing protocols, although if a driver had not been drinking while driving this should not present a problem. In the vast majority of instances a considerably longer time than 15 min would have elapsed after finishing the last drink and commencing to drive home.

Many mouthwash preparations and cough medicines contain high concentrations of ethanol and they should not be used prior to an evidential breath-alcohol test, so as to avoid any false-positive results.[197] However, if a person drinks these preparations, intentionally or unintentionally, like any alcoholic drink and – depending on the dose – can lead to elevated ethanol concentrations in the blood and breath.

The effect of mouthwash preparations such as Listerine (29.6% ethanol), Scope (18.9% ethanol), and Lavoris (6.0% ethanol) was carefully investigated and reported in the *Journal of the American Medical Association*.[197] The Breathalyzer 900 was the instrument used and this device cannot identify the presence of mouth alcohol. Volunteers used the various mouthwash preparations in accordance with manufacturer's instructions, spat out the solution, and then provided samples of breath at 2 min intervals for up 20 min. As expected, the first readings were abnormally high, equivalent to a BAC of 0.24 g% when the true BAC was zero. The instrument response dropped precipitously as time passed, so that by 10 min post-mouth washing all results were less than 0.08–0.10 g%, and by 15 min the instrument readings were all under 0.01 g%.

Results of tests made with an ALCOMAT infrared breath analyzer were negative 10–15 min after subjects used various mouthwashes, aftershave lotions, and perfumes available in Germany.[198] The question of mouthwash preparations and their influence on breath-alcohol test results was re-investigated in a study done in 2015 involving 40 subjects aged 21–30 y.[199] The subjects were required to rinse their mouths for 30–60 s with four commercially available mouth fresheners that contained between 10 and 22 vol% ethanol. All test results were negative at the start, although after the mouth fresheners were used abnormally high BrAC results were obtained. However, by 10 min post-rinsing the ethanol concentrations had decreased appreciably and by 20 min all results were insignificant. The authors concluded that the use of these mouth fresheners containing alcohol was not a problem for forensic breath-alcohol testing provided there was a 15 min deprivation period.

Injuries to the face, such as after involvement in a motor-vehicle crash, could produce blood in the mouth, which makes it less practical to conduct an evidential breath-alcohol test with a suspect. The inlet tube and spit-trap of the instrument is likely to be contaminated with the subject's blood, but the question is whether this impacts on the measured breath-ethanol concentration. A person's BAC is similar to that of the oral mucosa, which is much less than after having an alcoholic beverage in the mouth. Two studies were done to determine the effect of blood in the mouth, one used aqueous ethanol solutions[200] and in the another the test person's own blood was place in the mouth after they had consumed alcohol to reach a moderate BAC.[201] The results from both studies failed to identify any elevation in BrAC if there was blood in the subject's mouth.

3.5.6.2 Gastro Esophageal Reflux Disease (GERD)

As early as 1927, Bogen warned about the problem of hiccupping, burping, and belching prior to sampling breath in a football bladder for analysis. Many people suffer from acid-reflux disorders, known as gastro-esophageal reflux disease (GERD or GORD), which is caused by a dysfunctional lower esophageal sphincter (LES), allowing stomach contents to rise into the esophagus and even into the throat and mouth. A common cause of acid reflux disease is a stomach abnormality called a hiatal hernia. This occurs when the upper part of the stomach and LES move above the diaphragm, a muscle that separates your stomach from your chest. Indeed, GERD is aggravated after drinking certain alcoholic beverages and eating spicy foods.

The impact of GERD on results of evidential breath-alcohol testing has not yet been very much investigated in any controlled drinking studies. Nevertheless, this medical condition has been raised as a defense challenge from DUI suspects who maintain they experienced a reflux from the stomach into the mouth immediately prior to providing a breath-alcohol sample. The higher the concentration of alcohol prevailing in the stomach during a reflux, the greater the risk of contaminating the breath-sample in a similar way to the mouth-alcohol effect. The allegation is that GERD was the cause of a person's BrAC being above the legal limit for driving and medical experts have testified to this effect leading to an acquittal of the DUI suspect. However, the validity of this defense argument was strongly questioned by another expert witness, who noted that the expert appearing for the defense "ignored one of the basic maxims in the business" namely "what the subject says he has drunk is not evidence."

The practice of always making duplicate analysis of breath-alcohol concentration, that is, two separate exhalations is a good approach to counter the GERD defense challenge. Obtaining close agreement between the two independent results speaks against any influence of regurgitation of stomach contents containing alcohol just prior to making the first breath-test or between the first and the second test. Furthermore, the risk of GERD negatively influencing results of evidential breath tests decreases as the time after drinking alcohol increases because of the ongoing absorption of alcohol from the stomach and the emptying of the stomach contents into the duodenum. Evidential breath-alcohol programs that require making only a single breath-alcohol test are dubious and should be abandoned especially if GERD is a recurring defense argument. The single chemical test for alcohol influence has no place in jurisdictions where per se statutes operate regardless of whether blood or breath sampling is used for forensic purposes.

A controlled study of the GERD effect on results of breath-alcohol analysis was published in Journal of Forensic Sciences in 1999.[202] Twelve chronic suffers of GERD were recruited from patients at a university hospital, who were scheduled for corrective surgery. The clinical condition of GERD was well documented by pH measurements in the esophagus etc and none of the patients were taking anti-GERD medication at the time. At about 9 am in the morning, they drank 0.30 g/kg ethanol as either two bottles of beer, two glasses of white wine, or the equivalent amount of vodka diluted with orange juice. The drinking was done on an empty stomach and repetitive samples of breath were analyzed with a DataMaster infrared analyzer and blood samples were taken at 15 min intervals for analysis by gas chromatography.

The BAC and BrAC curves in GERD patients was not much different from the BAC-BrAC relationship seen in patients who did not have problems with GERD; BrAC was higher than venous BAC during the absorption phase and vice versa in the post-absorptive declining phase. The GERD defense is related to a mouth-alcohol effect, but the source of the ethanol is the stomach and the recent drink, rather than swirling alcohol in the mouth. Much depends on time elapsed after the end of drinking when a GERD attach occurs. The authors of the article reached the following conclusions:

> We conclude that the risk of a person experiencing gastric reflux during the time he or she participates in a breath-alcohol test procedure is very low. Even if reflux does occur, our study shows that it is not very likely that an abnormally high BrAC reading will be obtained. However, the mandatory 15 min observation period still remains an important element of the evidential breath-alcohol test protocol because this can help to rebut allegations that gastric reflux occurred. Likewise the routine practice of analyzing duplicate breath samples is an additional safeguard in this respect.

The medical condition of GERD is highly prevalent in society and depends on a patient's age and gender and is exaggerated in people suffering from heart-burn and after drinking alcoholic beverages, smoking cigarettes and eating spicy foods.[203,204] Not surprisingly, this defense tactic has been tested many times in drunk-driving cases with limited success. In an actual DUI case in Washington State, the defense alleged that the test result was falsely high, owing to problems with GERD. The suspect volunteered to participate in an experiment to verify this argument and was given a measured amount of alcohol to drink.[205] However, the results failed to confirm that GERD was a problem, because the breath-alcohol tests were as expected for the dose of alcohol administered.

One other drinking study was done with 15 subjects allegedly suffering from GERD, but this diagnosis was not verified clinically by measurement of esophageal pH. Rather, it seemed to depend more on other factors.[206] The subjects were allowed to consume large doses of ethanol and a good agreement was observed between BAC and BrAC in the post-absorptive phase of ethanol kinetics. However, the relationship between BAC and BrAC was highly variable in the absorption phase and the authors warned about inter-subject variations in gastroparesis, because food and drink might remain in the stomach for unexpectedly long times.

3.5.6.3 Dentures and Denture Adhesives

The question of whether people with dentures or individuals who might be fitted with special dental repair work can trap high concentrations of alcohol from a recent drink in the mouth has received some attention. An early drinking study form 1964 in the U.K. investigated various aspects of breath-alcohol testing as a tool in law enforcement and some of the volunteer subjects were fitted with dentures. The authors concluded that the results of the breath-alcohol test are not invalidated by the mouth-alcohol effect if done at least 15 minutes after the last drink. The presence or absence of dentures had no significant influence on the magnitude or duration of the mouth-alcohol retention, and rinsing the mouth with water did not make much difference.[207]

The effect of having dentures in the mouth in conjunction with a breath-alcohol test was investigated in a controlled study using the Intoxilyzer 5000 breath-analyzer.[208] In a relevant study of 24 subjects, each wore various types of dentures some held in the mouth more loosely than others with and without denture adhesives. All volunteers held 30 ml of 80 proof brandy in their mouths for two minutes without swallowing. After spitting out the alcohol, samples of breath were taken for analysis at regular intervals and the rate of decline in mouth alcohol was monitored. By 20 min after rinsing, no result was higher than 0.01 g/210 L. This speaks against the notion that those wearing dentures are at a disadvantage if and when they are required to provide an evidential breath-alcohol test. The authors concluded "Denture use, both with and without the concurrent use of adhesives does not significantly affect BrAC as long as a pretest alcohol deprivation period of 20 min is observed."

Another report described an experiment in a person wearing dentures who was apprehended for DUI. The defense claimed that the denture adhesive had retained alcohol and because of that the breath instrument reading was falsely elevated and above the statutory limit for driving.[209] After the subject held 86 proof whisky in the mouth Breathalyzer test results were said to be elevated for several hours afterward. The authors suggested that some brands of denture adhesives might retain alcohol for longer than others thus prolonging the mouth alcohol effect. However, the tests were done with a Breathalyzer model 900 instrument and no simultaneous blood samples were taken for the identifcation of ethanol as a control.

Many of the latest generation of breath-alcohol analyzers approved for evidential purposes are equipped with slope-detectors, which are designed to monitor the shape of the exhalation profile of BrAC during a test. Depending on the rate of increase in BrAC during exhalation, the result at the start of the exhalation is compared with end exhalation, and this change in slope indicates the likelihood of a mouth-alcohol effect or perhaps regurgitation of stomach contents or GERD. More research is required to evaluate the effectiveness of the slope detectors fitted to evidential breath-alcohol analyzers.

Other studies of the mouth-alcohol effect have been done using more modern breath-alcohol technology in alcohol-free subjects who rinse their mouth with alcohol and in people who have consumed alcohol before mouth rinsing.[210,211]

3.5.6.4 Interfering Substances in Breath

An important property of an analytical method is its specificity for the particular substance it purports to analyze. Over the years, many challenges have arisen in DUI trials claiming that the breath-alcohol analyzer gave a response to some interfering substance in a person's breath thus causing a false-high ethanol concentration. In short, the particular breath-analyzer used had failed to distinguish ethanol from some other volatile substance exhaled in breath. Obviously, much will depend on the inherent selectivity of the method of ethanol analysis used and this has changed very much over the years. The U.S. National Safety Council on Alcohol and Other Drugs have produced the following criteria that should be fulfilled for a non-alcohol volatile substance to be considered a practical problem;

- It must be a gas or volatile substance under normal physiological conditions of temperature and pressure.
- If the alleged interfering substance is of exogenous origin, then it has to enter the body via the mouth, skin, or lungs, dissolve in the blood and reach a sufficiently high concentration to be detected with the breath-alcohol instrument.

- It must be exhaled in human breath of living, conscious subjects and the analytical principle incorporated into the breath-instrument fails to distinguish it from ethanol.
- It should not be toxic to the organism or metabolized into a toxic substance.
- If the evidential breath-alcohol instrument incorporates infrared spectrometry, the interfering substance must absorb infrared energy at the relevant "ethanol" wavelengths (3.4 or 9.5 microns).
- If the evidential breath-alcohol instrument incorporates a fuel-cell (electrochemical) sensor, the interfering substance must undergo oxidation at the same electrode potential as ethanol and show a similar time-response profile to reach peak response and area under curve.

Based on the above criteria, it is important to consider volatiles produced endogenously and volatile organic compounds (VOCs) that enter the body by inhalation with the ambient air breathed, such as in connection with occupational exposure. Organic solvent abuse (sniffing or huffing) is a way to increase uptake into the blood through the lungs and this results in higher concentrations of various substances in blood and exhaled breath, and might increase the risk of a false "apparent ethanol" response on some breath analyzers.[212,213]

The classic Breathalyzer 900 instrument determined ethanol in the breath by a non-specific chemical oxidation reaction (dichromate-sulfuric acid). If the breath sample contains other oxidizable substances this could result in falsely high readings. By measuring the absorbance of light after exactly 90 seconds minimized the problem of interfering substances when using the Breathalyzer. The rates of chemical oxidation were different for different volatile substances. For example, inhalation of toluene and gasoline fumes were shown to have only minor cross-reactivity with the Breathalyzer reagent.[214–216]

With the advent of multi-wavelength infrared breath analyzers, the ability to detect interfering substances was much improved. Some instruments incorporate five different wavelength filters around the C-H bond stretching region of the spectrum 3.3–3.5 μm. Other modern infrared breath-alcohol analyzers measure infrared absorption at wavelengths of 3.4 microns (C-H stretching) and 9.5 microns (C-O) stretching in ethanol molecules, which is another way to enhance analytical specificity and detection of ethanol.[217–219]

A study of the prevalence of interfering substances in breath of apprehended drivers was done in Sweden where the approved instrument is a multi-filter infrared analyzer (Evidenzer) that looks at C-H bond stretching frequencies at wavelengths of 3.37, 3.41, 3.47, and 3.52 μm.[220] During the calibration of the instrument the absorbance at the four filters is adjusted to be the same when ethanol is the only absorbing volatile in the breath. If some other interfering substance was present and this absorbed IR radiation at one of these wavelengths, this unbalances the response expected for ethanol and the evidential breath test is aborted. Whenever this occurred a sample of venous was taken from the DUI suspects for determination of ethanol and other volatiles by HS-GC-FID.

From a total of 24,072 evidential breath-alcohol tests in apprehended drivers, there were N = 27 instances of an interfering substance being detected (0.11%). The results of HS-GC analysis of blood showed that the principal volatile organic compound in breath (besides ethanol) was acetone, isopropanol, and/or methyl ethyl ketone or all three substances.[220] This real-world experiment confirms the very low prevalence of non-ethanol volatile substances in the breath of drivers apprehended for DUI in Sweden. In most the aborted breath-alcohol test the concentration of ethanol present was well above the statutory limit for driving. The source of the non-ethanol volatiles was attributed to consumption of denatured alcohol preparations before driving.[221]

3.5.6.4.1 Endogenous Breath Volatiles

Human breath contains a mixture of gases, being mainly oxygen, nitrogen, carbon dioxide, water vapor, and very low concentrations of many volatile organic compounds (VOCs). The latter are either produced endogenously as a result of different metabolic processes or they are inhaled from the ambient air during breathing.[222,223] The principal constituents of human breath are not a problem in connection with analytical specificity, because they don't absorb infrared radiation at the same wavelengths as ethanol using the approved instruments intended for breath-alcohol analysis.[169]

The trace concentrations of VOCs in the breath of healthy individuals are so low that they do not pose a problem for evidential breath-alcohol testing even when non-specific analytical methods are used.[224,225] Experiments to determine whether breath-alcohol analyzers respond to VOCs other than ethanol are usually done under in-vitro conditions by producing known concentrations of the gas or vapor mixed with air, such as acetone, isopropanol, methanol, and toluene, etc.[226]

The analysis of human breath by highly sensitive GC-FID or MS methods shows that the most abundant endogenous VOCs are acetone, methane, and the unsaturated hydrocarbon isoprene (2-methyl-1,3-butadiene).[227,228] In healthy individuals, the concentration of acetone expelled in breath are relatively low and are within the range 0.5–5 μg/L, but concentrations can increase appreciably after food deprivation for 36 h or after eating low carbohydrate diets or in people with type 1 diabetes.[229,230]

The boiling point of acetone is 56°C and its blood/air partition ratio at body temperature is ~300:1, so elevated blood concentrations are exhaled in the breath making acetone a potential interfering substance.[218] However, this problem is eliminated when absorption of IR radiation is monitored at several different wavelengths in the 3.3–3.5 μm range corresponding to C-H bond vibrations. Moreover, acetone does not absorb IR radiation at 9.4–9.5 μm, which corresponds to stretching vibrations of the C-O bond in ethanol molecules.

Breath-testing instruments incorporating electrochemical detectors don't respond to acetone, which is not oxidized at the same electrode potential as used for ethanol.[231–233]

The notion that VOCs other than ethanol might represent a problem in law enforcement when testing apprehending drivers arose in the 1970s when the first infrared analyzer was introduced.[234] This instrument measured ethanol in breath by its absorption of infrared radiation at a single wavelength of 3.39 μm and, therefore, also gave a signal for any acetone if present in the breath at a high enough concentration. This problem was quickly resolved by designing instruments that monitored the absorption of infrared radiation at two wavelengths, such as 3.39 and 3.48 μm as was the case with the Intoxilyzer 5000.[218,226] Another approach to enhance selectivity is by the use of two independent methods of analysis, such as by infrared absorption and electrochemical oxidation exemplified by the Alcotest 7110 and Alcotest 9510 instruments.[235]

When properly adjusted, the Intoxilyzer 5000 and later models corrected the ethanol response for the presence of low concentrations of acetone in breath or otherwise the test was aborted and the instrument readout indicated an interfering substances was present. This happened when the was an imbalance between the two IR filters above a preset threshold set to occur when acetone in breath exceeded 300–600 μg/L, which corresponds to a blood acetone concentrations of 0.009–0.018 g%.[217]

Under some rare circumstances, when there are high concentrations of acetone in a person's blood, this ketone can be reduced in the liver by alcohol dehydrogenase to give isopropanol.[151] Isopropanol is a volatile substance and is expelled in the breath and represents a potential interfering substance when both IR and EC detectors are used. The prevalence of cases with elevated isopropanol in blood and breath, resulting from the reduction of acetone, is not known with any certainty in forensic casework, but represents a theoretical possibility.[236] In clinical medicine, isopropanol has been detected in the blood of poorly treated diabetics and the source was attributed to acetone reduction.[237] Several other clinical cases have reported finding low concentrations of isopropanol in blood of living subjects who had problems with ketosis.[238,239] Measuring exhaled isopropanol concentrations was suggested as a biomarker in diabetics and its metabolic correlations with breath acetone were investigated.[240] The concentrations of exhaled isopropanol in the diabetic group (mean 0.085 mg/L) were significantly higher than in controls (0.018 mg/L), but these are both too low to cause a concern as an interfering substance in forensic breath-alcohol testing.

Methanol, a much more toxic alcohol than ethanol, but differing by only a single carbon atom, it is hard to distinguish by infrared and EC breath-test instruments. With high levels of methanol in the breath, it cannot be distinguished from ethanol.[179,226] However, a person who drinks methanol for intoxication purposes would require emergency life-saving treatment to survive and is hardly likely to be driving a motor vehicle on the highway.[94]

Isoprene is another endogenous VOC expelled in the breath. In relevant experiments with 16 healthy subjects, the concentration ranged from 0.11 to 0.70 μg/L, as determined by thermal desorption gas chromatography and UV detection.[241] Accordingly, the concentrations of this volatile hydrocarbon are much too low to interfere with the measurement of breath-alcohol by infrared technology.[242,243] Methane is produced in the gut by the action of colonic bacteria on disaccharides and this VOC can be detected in human expired air. It seems that some individuals are more prone than others to generate methane in the large intestine and the concentration of this hydrocarbon expelled in breath under different conditions requires more documentation.[192] Methane should perhaps be considered as a potential interfering substance in connection with forensic breath-alcohol testing by infrared detectors, although more research is necessary on this topic before raising an alarm.[244] However, in healthy individuals methane concentrations in breath are much too low to warrant consideration as an interference problem in connection with evidential breath-alcohol analysis with Intox EC-IR.[245]

Acetaldehyde is a VOC produced in the body during the metabolism of ethanol in the liver and it is also a major constituent of cigarette smoke.[246,247] Acetaldehyde has a low boiling point and low blood/air partition coefficient of 190:1, which means that this substance crosses the alveolar-capillary membrane of the lungs and enters the breath.[248] Because acetaldehyde also contains C-H bonds it will absorb IR radiation at wavelengths in the same range as ethanol (3.4–3.5 μm), which makes it a potential interfering substance in connection with evidential breath-alcohol testing. An experiment was done with human subjects who were treated with a drug (calcium carbimide) that blocks the enzyme aldehyde dehydrogenase before they drank a small dose of ethanol (0.25 g/kg).[249] This treatment led to much higher concentrations of acetaldehyde being expelled in their breath, which were analyzed using a single wavelength (3.39 μm) infrared analyzer. The breath acetaldehyde concentration increased 50 fold after treatment with the alcohol-sensitizing drug compared to a control group of subjects who consumed the same dose of ethanol after a placebo treatment. Both ethanol and acetaldehyde in breath were determined by gas chromatography. Even under these extreme conditions, there were no false-high ethanol results using the single wavelength infrared analyzer when compared with results of analyzing ethanol and acetaldehyde in breath by gas chromatography.

In a comprehensive review of the concentrations of acetaldehyde in blood and breath of human subjects during oxidation of ethanol 88 μg/L or less in blood were considered possible, which corresponds to 0.46 μg/L in breath.[250,251]Accordingly, this metabolite of ethanol oxidation cannot seriously be considered an interfering VOC when testing drunk drivers with the aid of infrared breath-analyzers.[252]

3.5.6.4.2 Occupational Exposure to Organic Solvents

People might be exposed to a wide range of organic solvents in the working environment, although there are rules and regulations about permissible limits in the atmosphere and mandatory use of protective clothing, such as eye-shields and face masks. Nevertheless, many challenges have arisen in DUI cases about organic solvents being responsible for the "apparent ethanol" response when infra-red based analytical technology was used. These allegations have sometimes been investigated experimentally after the fact, although the results have failed to support the notion that an organic solvent other than ethanol was responsible. Occupational exposure to paint thinner was tested on an Intoxilyzer 5000 infrared instrument without obtaining false positive results.[253]

In an effort to investigate claims made by two drunk drivers that they were wrongly convicted and that the "apparent ethanol" content in their breath was caused by organic solvents, both men volunteered to participate in an experiment.[254] Without the use of face masks or other protection, they sprayed cars with a toluene/xylene/methanol-based paint thinner under rather extreme exposure conditions. The spraying work continued for several hours in a small and poorly ventilated room, and 5–7 liters of paint were used up. The men's eyes became watery and irritated, and they were often coughing and regularly complained of sore mouths and throats. Tests with a single wavelength infrared analyzer (Intoximeter 3000) conducted immediately after exposure to paint thinner produced a positive ethanol reading. Near simultaneous tests with an instrument using an electrochemical sensor (Alcolmeter S-D2) were always lower than the IR analyzer. Breath tests done at 0 min, 15 min, and 30 min post-exposure, gave "apparent ethanol" results of 0.019, 0.010, and 0.002 g/210 L, respectively, on the IR instrument. Tests done with the other volunteer did not show any response on the IR analyzer, which was explained by a lower environmental temperature on the day of the testing.

The inhalation of gasoline fumes, such as if a person syphons gasoline between vehicles, might be expected to cause false-high ethanol readings with IR instruments. In an actual DUI case, the Intoxilyzer 5000 reacted by aborting the test because an interfering substance was detected. Gasoline contains, among other things, a complex mixture of aliphatic and aromatic hydrocarbons and these were also qualitatively identified in a blood sample taken from the suspect whose blood-alcohol concentration was zero.[215,255]Abuse of organic solvents such as paint thinner or glue is another source of interfering substances in connection with evidential breath-alcohol. People who abuse these materials often have a special appearance and tend to smell of the solvents they have been sniffing; if there is a strong suspicion of solvent abuse, arrangements can be made for obtaining blood samples instead.

Diethyl ether is a highly volatile chemical substance with C-H bonds (two ethyl groups) and is therefore a potential interfering substance with infrared breath-alcohol instruments and might mistakenly be identified as ethanol.[256,257] However, ether is no longer widely used in industry or hospitals, so the risk of human exposure to this solvent in everyday life is minimal. Several other case reports have appeared suggesting that inhalation of toluene and/or lacquer fumes in conjunction with normal occupational exposure causes "apparent ethanol" readings on IR breath analyzers even exceeding a concentration of 0.10 g/210 L.[258] However the person who was apprehended for DUI exhibited behavioral manifestations of solvent inhalation or abuse and was chronically exposed to these agents over long periods, so accumulation of toluene in body fat depots cannot be excluded.

Some people apprehended for DUI drink technical alcohol for intoxication purposes and besides high concentrations of ethanol, these solvents contain several other volatile substances, such as methanol, methyl ethyl ketone, ethyl acetate, isopropanol, etc.[259] These are also absorbed into the blood stream and expelled in the breath, and are potential interfering substances when single wavelength IR breath-instrument are used for analysis. Information about the presence of interfering substances can be obtained by comparing the results from the roadside breath-alcohol test, which incorporates an electrochemical sensor, with the evidential test using a single wavelength IR detector. The two detector systems (IR absorption and electrochemical oxidation) respond differently to different VOCs in the breath. For example, electrochemical sensors don't respond to acetone or hydrocarbons. The response of various evidential breath alcohol instruments to organic solvents was investigated in the U.K. when evidential breath testing was introduced in 1983. Two single wavelength infrared analyzers; Intoximeter 3000 and Camic breath-alcohol analyzer were approved for legal purposes.[260]

The response of these instruments was tested after human volunteers were exposed on different occasions to toluene, 1,1,1-trichlorethane, butane, white spirit, and nonane. This laboratory experiment was done under controlled conditions and exposure to the organic solvents was achieved using an exposure chamber. The volunteers were at rest, talking and playing cards, during a four-hour exposure period and breathing the solvent vapor at concentrations close to the upper limits prescribed for the workplaces in U.K.[261] After inhalation of butane vapor, a transient response was obtained on the Intoximeter 3000 instrument that persisted for between 1–5 min after exposure, before rapidly declining to zero.[262] Exposure to toluene and 1,1,1-trichloroethane failed to produce an "apparent ethanol" response on the IR breath analyzers, although these substances were identified at low concentrations in blood samples for up to eight hours after exposure ended.

The volatile substances in blood and breath decreased rapidly when the subjects left the exposure chamber environment. This supports the conclusion that exposure to solvents in a work environment is unlikely to pose a problem with evidential breath-alcohol testing done with a single wavelength infrared analyzer some time afterward. Similar negative results were obtained when subjects were exposed to and inhaled nonane and white spirit during domestic painting.[263] The theoretical basis for inhalation of various gases and vapors, their potential for uptake into the blood in relation to the concentration measured in exhaled breath were reviewed for a number of volatile substances.[264]

Inhalation of ethanol vapors, by people working in the brewing or liquor industries, might be considered a way to elevate BAC provided sufficiently high atmospheric concentrations existed and when people are engaged in strenuous work with excessive lung ventilation.[265] One of the first studies to investigate inhalation of ethanol vapors and whether this might lead to an elevated BAC was published in 1951.[266] The volunteer subjects breathed ethanol-air mixtures, sometimes at very high concentrations, more or less continuously for up to 6 h. The BAC reached was directly proportional to the concentration of ethanol in the inhaled air and the degree of lung ventilation during the exposure. However, extreme conditions were necessary to reach a BAC of 0.01 g%. This is explained, at least in part, by the fact a person can eliminate 6-8 grams of ethanol per hour from the body by metabolism in the liver.[267] Accordingly, more than 6–8 g of ethanol per hour must get absorbed via the lungs into the blood before an accumulation is possible.[267] Because of the high solubility of ethanol in water, during inhalation it dissolves in the mucus surfaces of the upper airways where absorption into the blood takes place and is unlikely to ever reach the alveolar air sacs and large surface area available deep in the lungs.[268] When subjects inhaled air contained 10–20 mg/L ethanol they tended to cough and complained of irritation of their eyes and throat. Untoward effects became almost unbearable when the inhaled concentrations reached 30–40 mg/L making it impossible to remain in this atmosphere for lengthy periods of time.

Several more recent studies have considered inhalation of ethanol vapor from the atmosphere or via a breathing chamber.[210] The conclusion reached was that BACs of 0.003–0.005 g% might be achieved by normal occupational exposure, which from a medicolegal perspective are insignificant. However, if a person was exposed to ethanol vapors by inhalation when they already had an elevated BAC, the clearance rate of ethanol from blood slowed down, as reflected in a change in the slope of the declining phase.[269] The question of alcohol inhalation and its consequences, such as the risk of generating an elevated BAC and other alcohol effects were the subject of a recent review article.[270]

3.5.6.5 Blood/Breath Alcohol Ratios

The Breathalyzer® instrument, which was once widely used for law enforcement in the U.S., Canada, and Australia captures a known volume of a subject's breath, determines the amount of ethanol present, and translates this into the presumed venous BAC.[271] The non-invasive nature of sampling breath compared with sticking a needle into a vein to draw 10–20 mL of blood, means that breath-testing was considered more practical for legal purposes. Furthermore, the results of a breath-alcohol test are obtained immediately, providing information about a person's state of intoxication and whether the statutory alcohol limit was exceeded. If a driver was in breach of the law, immediate sanctions can be imposed such as confiscation of the vehicle or the driving permit, arrest, and incarceration of the driver until sober, etc.

The calibration factor used to convert a measured BrAC into the presumed BAC with the Breathalyzer instrument became known as the blood-breath ratio (BBR) of alcohol and was assumed to be 2100:1. The results from many blood-breath correlation studies indicated that a 2100 BBR produces estimates of the venous BAC that were ~10–15% too low.[207,272] A closer agreement between BAC and BrAC was obtained when a BBR of 2300:1 was used as the calibration factor. Furthermore, the BBR tended to be lower during the absorption phase and higher late in the elimination phase of the blood-alcohol curve.[273] These between subject variations in the BBR of alcohol became a topic of much debate and discussion in drunk-driving litigation. Breath-tests done when subjects reached the post-absorptive phase of the blood-alcohol curve showed closer agreement with BAC using a BBR of 2300:1 rather than 2100:1.[274]

The blood/breath ratio of ethanol in-vivo should not be confused with the blood/air partition ratio in-vitro; the latter is usually referred to as the Ostwald solubility coefficient. The in-vitro partition ratio of ethanol is easy to determine by spiking blood with known amounts of ethanol, and then allowing the blood to equilibrate in an air-tight glass flask at constant temperature.[275] Analysis of the concentrations of ethanol in the air-phase and liquid phase at equilibrium allows calculating the blood/air partition coefficient.[276] The results of an in-vitro study to determine the equilibrium distribution of ethanol between air and blood are shown in Table 3.5.5.

Blood samples from 20 healthy men and 15 healthy women, all of whom were volunteer blood donors, were spiked with known amounts of ethanol. Aliquots of the blood were allowed to equilibrate at exactly controlled temperatures of 34°C and 37°C. The results showed that the temperature coefficient of ethanol solubility in blood, water and plasma was 6.5% per 1°C change in temperature. The ethanol distribution ratio depended on water content of the blood and the amount of inorganic salt present. The data in Table 3.5.5 were obtained with heparin as the anticoagulant, and the vapor phase concentration of ethanol at equilibrium was uninfluenced.

The small gender difference in partition ratio is explained by a lower hematocrit of female blood and accordingly a higher water content. Table 3.5.5 also shows that under in-vitro conditions, the blood/air partition ratio of ethanol could be determined with high precision and accuracy. The between subject variations are about 2% as shown by experimental SD and coefficient of variation. The small biological variation of the in-vitro blood/air ratios of ethanol should not be confused with large variations in the blood/breath ratio in-vivo.

If it had been possible to sample breath close to the alveolar-capillary membrane of the lungs, it is very likely that a blood/breath ratio would be close to the in-vitro partition coefficient at 37°C. However, during exhalation, the alveolar air cools as it passes through the trachea and upper

TABLE 3.5.5
Blood/Air Partition Ratios (Oswald Solubility Coefficients) of Ethanol Determined In-Vitro at Equilibrium Temperatures of 34°C and 37°C

Source of blood	N	Blood-water g/100 g	Hematocrit %	Equilibrium temperature	Blood/air partition ratio mean ± SD (CV%)
Healthy males	20	79.3 ± 1.1[1]	44.3 ± 3.2[1]	34°C	2157 ± 43 (2.0)[1]
				37°C	1783 ± 36 (2.0)[1]
Healthy females	15	81.1 ± 0.5	40.0 ± 3.0	34°C	2195 ± 42 (1.9)
				37°C	1830 ± 30 (1.9)

[1] Statistically significant gender differences in blood water content, hematocrit, and blood/air partition coefficient.

Note: The blood samples were from healthy male and female blood donors after adding known amounts of ethanol and equilibration in air-tight glass flasks. Results show mean ± standard deviation (SD) and coefficient of variation (CV%) for blood/air ratios.

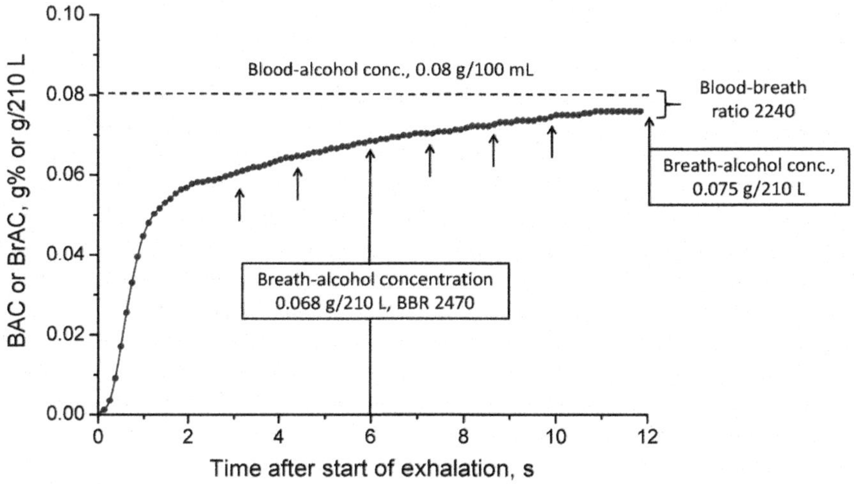

FIGURE 3.5.4 The changes in breath-alcohol concentration during a prolonged exhalation into an evidential breath-alcohol analyzer (Evidenzer) that uses infra-red absorption technology for analysis of ethanol. The instrument requires making a continuous exhalation for a minimum time of 6 s for an approved test. The trace illustrates that the operational blood-breath ratio (BBR) of alcohol is strongly influenced by the exhalation time into the instrument. After 6 s the blood-breath ratio was 2470:1 and after 12 s 2240:1

airways and by the time it leaves the mouth its temperature has dropped to about 34.5°C. Accordingly, the in-vivo blood/blood ratio of alcohol is expected to be closer to the in-vitro blood/air partition ratio at 34°C.

Exhaled breath ethanol concentrations are highly correlated with the concentration determined in samples of venous blood for different patterns of drinking. However, obtaining a representative sample of breath that gives a true reflection of the alveolar air concentration is problematic for highly water soluble gases like ethanol.[277] During the process of inhalation and exhalation ethanol evaporates and re-equilibrates with the watery mucus surfaces covering the upper airways. Breath ethanol concentrations are different for mixed-expired breath, end-expired breath and when an initial exhalation is rebreathed a number of times before sampling.[278,279] Likewise, the subject's pattern of breathing before exhalation, such as whether any hyper- or hypoventilation or breath holding occurred, impacts the exhaled ethanol concentration.[280,281] For these, and other reasons, the blood/breath distribution ratios in-vivo will vary much more than the blood/air partition ratio determined in-vitro at the same temperature. The volume of top-lung air discarded prior to sampling breath for analysis of ethanol in an important variable as illustrated in Figure 3.5.4.[282]

Figure 3.5.4 shows the increase in BrAC in one subject during a prolonged exhalation into a quantitative infrared breath-alcohol analyzer, the Evidenzer.[283] The trace first shows a rapid rise in BrAC as the ambient air inside the IR chamber gets flushed out. After about 2 s into the exhalation, the BrAC rises more slowly as the test subject reaches a vital capacity exhalation after about 12 s. The trace also illustrates how the operational BBR of alcohol depends on sampling time during the prolonged exhalation before a sample is captured for analysis. In this example, the coexisting venous BAC was 0.08 g/100 mL and the instrument reading at end exhalation was 0.075 g/210 L, which gives a BBR of 2240:1. If the breath samples had been analyzed after blowing for less than the 6 s minimum for an approved test, this would have a lower ethanol content and lead to a higher BBR.

The blood/air partition ratio of ethanol determined in-vitro is expected to be the same for arterial and venous blood samples, because the main difference between the two samples is the oxygen content. The water and salt concentrations of arterial and venous samples are expected to be the same. However, studies have shown that ethanol concentrations in arterial and venous blood are not the same after people consume alcoholic beverages. The A-BAC is higher than the V-BAC during the absorption phase of the blood-alcohol curve and lower during the post-absorptive phase. This distribution artifact has implications for the calculated BBRs of ethanol, because BrAC runs closer to the A-BAC rather than the V-BAC.[273,284]

According to the results of controlled drinking experiments and apprehended drivers, the mean and median BBRs of alcohol are closer to 2300:1 or 2400:1 rather than the 2100:1 ratio adopted in the U.S. to set their statutory limit of 0.08 g/210 L. This means that (BrAC × 2100) gives a result lower than the actual co-existing venous BAC, which is beneficial to the suspect, and thus tolerable in criminal cases. After drinking a bolus dose of ethanol, the venous BBR depends to some extent on the time after the end of drinking when samples are taken. Venous BBRs are lower if determined early after the end of drinking during the absorption phase of the blood-alcohol curve. This is attributed to the existence of slightly different ethanol concentrations in arterial (A) and venous (V) blood circulation. The A-BAC exceeds V-BAC during absorptive and V-BAC exceeds A-BAC in the post-absorptive phase of ethanol metabolism.[284] However, the magnitude of A-V differences in concentration of ethanol during social drinking, that is when people consume alcoholic beverages more slowly over several hours has never been investigated.

Variations in BBRs of ethanol have been determined in many controlled laboratory drinking studies and in actual drinking drivers. The mean values reported range from about 1600:1 to over 3000:1. Lower BBRs are encountered more often when the testing is done early after the end of drinking and before reaching a peak BAC, owing to the aforementioned differences between A-BAC and V-BAC. The complete equilibration of ethanol in all body fluids and tissues takes between 60–90 min after the end of drinking for completion.

The biological variations in BBR led to many challenges in court with claims that the defendant did not have a ratio of 2100:1, which is an underlying assumption that when the Breathalyzer was used to test apprehended drivers. In the 1980s, two U.S. scientists, Morton Mason (1902–1985) and Kurt M. Dubowski (1921–2016), suggested that much might be gained by drafting legislation that defined a punishable BrAC and not make the conversion to BAC in every single case.[285] The statutory BAC limit from driving in all 50 states was 0.08 g/100 mL at the time, so the suggested statutory BrAC was set at 0.08 g/210 L breath. The inclusion of 210 L in the denominator meant that the numerator 0.08 g ethanol was the same regardless of whether blood- or breath-specimens were taken for analysis of ethanol. This made arguments, such as that "my client does not have a 2100 BBR" redundant, because the relation between ethanol in blood and breath (2100:1) was written into the law. In a seminal review article, Mason and Dubowski stated;

> We believe that the conversion of a breath quantity to a blood concentration of ethanol, for forensic purposes, should be abandoned and that the offense of driving while under the influence of alcohol should be statutorily defined in terms of the concentration of ethanol found in the breath in jurisdictions employing breath analysis. The breath sample should be obtained and analyzed only with instruments having capabilities which would require some extension of present federal standards for evidential breath-testing devices.

Most nations have adopted separate BAC and BrAC limits for driving, although the threshold BrAC was derived from the pre-existing BAC assuming different BBRs of alcohol. The British Road-Traffic Act of 1967 specified a statutory BAC limit for driving of 80 mg% (0.08 g%) and the police were allowed to administer roadside breath-tests to determine driver sobriety.[286] In the 1980s, evidential breath-alcohol instruments were accepted by the British government to generate the evidence necessary to prosecute traffic offenders.[167] The statutory BrAC limit was derived from the existing BAC of 80 mg% and assuming a 2300:1 BBR as follows:

$$\mathrm{BAC/BrAC} = 2300$$

$$\mathrm{BrAC} = \mathrm{BAC}/2300 = 80/2300 = 0.03478\ \mathrm{mg/100\ mL}$$

This is equivalent to 34.78 μg/100 mL and rounded up to 35 μg/100 mL.

Scotland lowered its statutory BAC limit for driving to 50 mg/100 mL in 2016, which necessitated also re-calculating the statutory BrAC limit as follows:

$$\mathrm{BAC/BrAC} = 2300$$

$$\mathrm{BrAC} = \mathrm{BAC}/2300 = 50/2300 = 0.0217\ \mathrm{mg/100\ mL}$$

This is equivalent to 21.7 μg/100 mL of breath and rounded up to 22 μg/100 mL

The existence of different statutory limits in the same country means that, in reality, a person might be driving illegally in one country, such as Scotland, whereas upon crossing the border into England would be below the statutory limit of 0.08 g%. It is hard to fathom why different countries should enforce different statutory alcohol limits for driving, apart from the obvious political and lobbying reasons.

In the U.S., the statutory BAC limit of 0.08 g% and a population average BBR of 2100:1 were assumed when the Breathalyzer instrument was used to test traffic offenders. In the 1980s, a decision was made to stop converting BrAC into BAC and instead enforce a statutory BrAC limit of 0.08 g/210 L, hence the 2100:1 ratio was defined by statute. This change in legislation helped to avoid unnecessary discussions about biological variations in the BBR. Other nations assumed other BBRs when their statutory BrAC limits were set, such as 2000:1 or 2300:1.

The results of large-scale investigations of BBRs in apprehended drivers gave results showing that in reality the value was closer to 2400:1 rather than 2100:1.[260,287] However, in some jurisdictions BrAC results are still converted into BAC (e.g. China) and in the states of New Jersey and New York assuming a 2100:1 BBR. If the person's BBR was higher than 2100 at time of testing this would give a certain advantage compared with results from determining ethanol in venous blood.

The legal consequences for a person having a BBR varying from 1,800 to 2,500 in a jurisdiction where the assumed ratio was 2,100 is illustrated in Table 3.5.6.[288] The calculations were done assuming statutory alcohol limits of either 0.02 g%, 0.05 g%, or 0.08 g%. The results show that if the person tested happened to have a BBR of exactly 2100:1 then the venous BAC and the result of the breath-alcohol test would be the same. The table also shows that people with a BBR of less than 2100 are at a slight disadvantage, because their BAC derived from the analysis of breath would be slightly higher. The largest difference between BAC and BrAC were found when higher statutory alcohol limits were enforced, such as 0.08 g% and was insignificant when a limit of 0.02 g% operated.

Many jurisdictions in the U.S. operate a policy of using the lower of two breath-test results and also truncating the third decimal before a decision is made whether to charge a person with DUI. This gives benefit of the doubt to a suspect and compensates to some extent for variations in the BBR within the range 1800-2500 (Table 3.5.6). At a statutory BAC of 0.05 g%, the truncated BrAC would be 0.05 g/210 L for people with BBRs between 1,800 and 2,100. The result would be 0.04 g/210 L when the person's BBR was between 2,200 and 2,500. To the best of my knowledge, the prevalence of apprehended drivers with BBRs lower than 1,800:1 has never been determined.

The statutory BrAC limits in EU nations were derived from the pre-existing BAC limits by dividing by an assumed

TABLE 3.5.6

Results of Evidential Breath-Alcohol Testing in Subjects with Blood-Breath Ratios (BBR) of Alcohol Varying between 1,800 and 2,500 When the Population Average Ratio for Legal Purposes Was Assumed to Be 2,100

Blood-breath ratio (BBR)	Statutory breath alcohol limit g/210 L	Result of breath-alcohol test: 3-decimals[1]	Result of breath-alcohol test: 2-decimals[2]
1800	0.02	0.023	0.02
	0.05	0.058	0.05
	0.08	0.093	0.09
1900	0.02	0.022	0.02
	0.05	0.055	0.05
	0.08	0.088	0.08
2000	0.02	0.021	0.02
	0.05	0.052	0.05
	0.08	0.084	0.08
2100	0.02	0.020	0.02
	0.05	0.050	0.05
	0.08	0.080	0.08
2200	0.02	0.019	0.01
	0.05	0.047	0.04
	0.08	0.076	0.07
2300	0.02	0.018	0.01
	0.05	0.045	0.04
	0.08	0.073	0.07
2400	0.02	0.017	0.01
	0.05	0.043	0.04
	0.08	0.070	0.07
2500	0.02	0.016	0.01
	0.05	0.042	0.04
	0.08	0.067	0.06

[1] Derived as statutory BrAC × 2100/BBR.

[2] Third decimal truncated.

Note: Calculations are shown at statutory alcohol limits of 0.02, 0.05, and 0.08 g/210 L with and without truncation of the third decimal.

population average BBR. However, there was no consensus reached about the most appropriate BBR to use and values ranged from 2000:1 to 2400:1. In the Netherlands, the BAC limit for driving of 0.50 mg/ml in blood, converted to 220 μg/L in breath, assuming a 2300:1 ratio, hence 0.50/2300 = 0.000217 and this was rounded to 0.00022 and shifting the decimal point to give units of μg/L. In France, Spain and some other countries their statutory BAC limit of 0.50 g/L was divided by an assumed BBR of 2,000 to give the statutory BrAC limit of 0.25 mg/L.

3.5.6.6 Respiratory Function and Failure to Provide a Specimen

The requirement for an approved evidential breath-alcohol test is usually to provide a continuous forced exhalation at a minimum flow rate for at least five to six seconds into the inlet tube of the instrument. This should ensure that at least 1.5 L of top-lung breath has been discarded and the infrared sample chamber then contains a representative sample of deep-lung breath for determination of ethanol. Depending on the resistance to exhalation and other design features of the instrument, some people, such as those with small stature or suffering from pulmonary dysfunction, such as heavy smokers or people with asthma or COPD, are unable to provide the required end-exhaled breath sample.

This problem is well-illustrated in Figure 3.5.5, derived from the large scale testing of apprehended drivers in Sweden (35,000 men and 4,000 women) with an Intoxilyzer 5000 infrared analyzer.[287] Plotted on the graph is the prevalence of failures to provide two consecutive end-exhaled samples of breaths and shows that women had greater difficulty than the males in exhaling for at least 6 s at the minimum pressure and flow rate. The failure to provide a sample increased with increasing age in both males and females, but was especially marked in females aged 55–64 y. Some of the failures to provide might be explained by the suspects

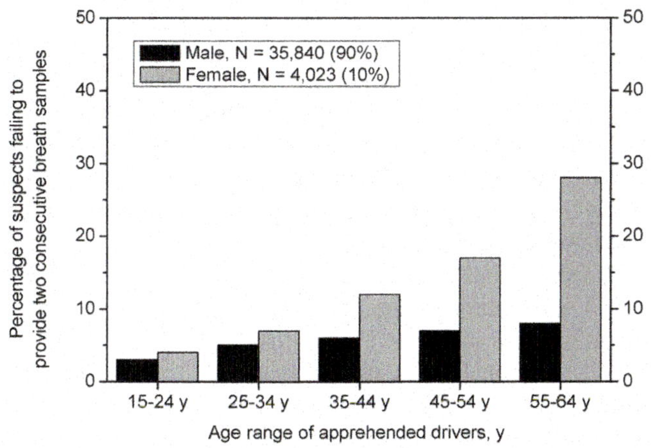

FIGURE 3.5.5 Percentages of male and female drivers who failed to provide two consecutive end-exhaled breath samples into an Intoxilyzer 5000 infrared breath analyzer used in Sweden for legal purposes from 1989–2000. The prevalence of failing to provide increased with age of subjects for both males and females and especially in females in the oldest age group of 55–64 y

being too intoxicated or being able to understand and/or comply with instructions. Whenever a person failed to provide two consecutive samples of breath, the police arranged to analyze ethanol in a sample of venous blood. Starting in 2001, when the approved evidential breath-alcohol analyzer was changed from Intoxilyzer 5000 to Evidenzer, the number of failures to provide two acceptable samples of breath dropped appreciably.

The physiological principles of breath-alcohol testing as a surrogate for analyzing ethanol in blood depends on the assumption of complete equilibrium of ethanol between pulmonary capillary blood in the lungs and the alveolar air sacks at normal body temperature. The large surface area in the alveoli region of the lungs and the thin alveolar-capillary membrane makes it easy for gases and vapors to diffuse from the blood into the breath. However, the concentration of ethanol in alveolar air is significantly higher than in the end-exhaled air for several reasons. First, the breath cools from a temperature of 37°C in the alveoli to 34.5°C as breath leaves the mouth. As already discussed, the temperature coefficient of ethanol solubility is 6.5% per 1°C. This suggests that the end-exhaled breath ethanol content will be (2.5°C × 6.5%) or 16.3% lower than the concentration in alveolar air according to the temperature differential alone. Unlike the respiratory gases (N_2, O_2, and CO_2) ethanol is a much more soluble gas and therefore dissolves in the watery mucosa of the upper respiratory tract during inhalation and exhalation.[277] The pattern of breathing prior to exhalation, therefore determines to some extent the resulting breath-alcohol concentration.

Rules and regulations pertaining to evidential breath-alcohol testing are different in different jurisdictions. For example in the U.K. "failure to provide a specimen" is a separate offense that carries the same penalty as if the ethanol content was above the statutory limit.[289] The operator of the evidential breath-alcohol instrument makes the decision whether a suspect is purposely trying not to provide the required sample. When this has happened, some of the those charged for failing to provide a proper breath sample have undergone pulmonary function tests and produced evidence that asthma or COPD were indeed the reasons they failed to provide the required sample of breath.[290,291] A lot depends on the type of breath-alcohol analyzer used, such as its resistance to exhalation and requirements for a minimum discard volume.[292]

This prompted British Home Office scientists to embark on a series of studies into the ability of people with small stature and impaired lung function to satisfy the sampling requirements of various breath-alcohol testing instruments.[293,294] The results showed that if the forced expiratory volume in one second ($FEV_{1.0}$) was less than 2.0 liters and forced vital capacity (FVC) was less than 2.6 liters they might legitimately not be able to provide a specimen with some evidential breath-alcohol analyzers. Those shorter than five foot five inches (165 m) were more likely to fail to provide the required sample of breath for analysis. This report did not specify how old the test subjects were or whether they were smokers or under the influence of alcohol at the time.

Asthma is an inflammatory disease of the airways causing obstruction to breathing and a reduction in air flow. Respiratory inhalers used by asthmatics contain salbutamol (β_2-adrenergic bronchodilator) as the active ingredient, which is the mainstay treatment for acute attacks of asthma. The effect of using this medication just prior to a breath-alcohol test with Intoximeter 3000 (infrared) and Alcolmeter S-D2 (electrochemistry) was tested by experiment.[295–297] A small positive response "apparent ethanol" was obtaining immediately after using such nasal sprays for impaired lung function, but the response was very transient. Some asthma inhalers contain trace amounts of ethanol and, thus, a mouth-alcohol effect is possible immediately after usage.[298] However by 2–9 min after subjects had inhaled various medications and nasal sprays, the breath-analyzers gave zero readings again.[299]

The effect of chronic obstructive pulmonary disease (COPD) was investigated in elderly men after they consumed 60–70 g of ethanol. Their BrAC was determined with a Breathalyzer model 900 instrument.[300] The blood/breath ratios of ethanol in COPD patients were consistently higher than the generally accepted 2100:1 factor used to calibrate the instrument. A more recent study involved 12 COPD patients as well as an age-matched control group of subjects with normal lung function. They received ethanol (0.60 g/kg) by intravenous infusion and BrAC and venous BAC were determined for up to four hours.[301] The BBRs varied with time after administration of ethanol, and in the post-absorptive phase of the blood-alcohol curve values were 2400:1 on average in COPD patients and controls. It is certainly possible that people with impaired lung functioning (asthma, COPD, emphysema) might not be able to provide sample of breath with some types of evidential breath-testing instruments. However, if they do manage to provide a sample, there is no evidence that they are disadvantaged compared to age-matched control subjects with normal lung function.[290,302]

The blood-breath ratios vary both between and within subjects depending on the duration of the exhalation before capturing a breath sample for analysis of ethanol. Other factors that influence BrAC and the venous BBR are the amount of time elapsed after drinking when samples are taken, and the subject's pattern of breathing prior to exhalation.[303] There is overwhelming evidence that in subjects with healthy lungs and respiratory dysfunction the BrAC is lower than the co-existing venous BAC by about 10–15% when samples are taken in the post-absorptive phase of the blood-alcohol curve.[288]

3.5.6.7 Breathing Pattern

An important variable in connection with any evidential breath-alcohol testing is the pattern of breathing prior to exhaling into the breath analyzer.[280] Evidence from physiology of respiration verifies that gases and volatile substances in the pulmonary capillary blood equilibrate with alveolar air at body temperature (~37°C). However, during an exhalation as the breath passes the bifurcation of the trachea, temperature is lowered and when it leaves the mouth measurements show a temperature of 34.5°C.[304,305]During an exhalation ethanol from the alveolar regions of the lung condense on the cooler watery mucus surfaces of the upper-airways and mouth and this equilibration depends on the person's pattern of breathing prior to exhalation.

Some of the factors to consider are whether a person holds their breath for some time, as well as extent of hyper- and hypo-ventilation, all of which impacts on the exhaled concentrations of ethanol. Studies have shown that ethanol concentration in the exhaled breath are higher after the initial exhalation has been re-breathed a number of times.[279,306] During the process of re-breathing, there is less depletion of the ethanol contained in the mucus membranes and, hence, a breath-sample is eventually obtained closer in composition to the alveolar air. It is not possible to obtain a sample of exhaled breath with the same ethanol content as the alveolar air by making a single prolonged exhalation.[307]

Nevertheless, the concentration of ethanol in end-exhaled breath and both the venous and arterial blood circulation are very highly correlated for different patterns of drinking, and BAC reached in forensic casework from 0.02–0.40 g%. This means that BAC and BrAC are both equally valid and objective ways to prove over-consumption of alcohol and that a person was in breach of the drunk-driving law.

The influence of a person's breathing pattern prior to exhalation has been evaluated including effects of breath-holding, hyper- and hypo-ventilation, as well as slow and shallow pattern of breathing.[280] Most changes in the pattern of breath resulted in a decrease in the ethanol content of end-exhaled breath.[281] The exception was after holding the breath for about 30 s or hypo-ventilation just before delivering a prolonged exhalation, which increased ethanol concentration by about 10–20%.

3.5.6.8 Body and Breath-Temperature – Fever

In-vitro studies of the equilibration of ethanol between blood and air at various temperatures has shown that the temperature coefficient of ethanol solubility is about 6.5% per 1°C change in temperature.[276] This means that for every 1°C increase or decrease in temperature the ethanol concentration in the vapor (breath) will change by ± 6.5%. The temperature of end-exhaled breath is assumed to be 34°C, which is the temperature of equilibrium when a wet-batch simulator device is used to calibration evidential breath analyzers, actually 34.0 ± 0.05°C.[308] More recent studies have found that the average temperature of end-exhaled breath is closer to 34.5°C rather than 34°C.[309]

It is a reasonable assumption that body-temperature and breath-temperature are positively correlated. One manufacturer of evidential breath-alcohol analyzers (Draeger) equipped their Alcotest 7110 and 9510 instruments with thermistor probes. These were located at the entrance of the breath-inlet tube just after the spit trap and could measure the temperature at the end of an exhalation. The temperature was then compared with the assumed normal breath temperature of 34°C. If the result was higher than 34°C, the BrAC result was adjusted downwards by 6.5% per 1°C of temperature increase. However, if the temperature was lower than 34°C, the BrAC was not increased. Other manufacturers of evidential breath-alcohol analyzers have not considered it necessary to measure temperature of exhaled breath. Indeed, it remains an open question whether breath temperature is relevant at all and there is no consensus about this within the scientific community. Questions, such as fragility and calibration of the thermistor probes become an issue and it is worth remembering that evidential breath-alcohol test is not being done to estimate the co-existing BAC. Such a test is intended to determine a suspect's BrAC and whether this exceeds the statutory limit – not whether the person tested was suffering from a fever.

The subject's breathing pattern just before making a prolonged exhalation into a breath-analyzer can influence the temperature of the breath sample and the BrAC. Likewise, the temperature and humidity of the ambient air breathed impacts the breath temperature and BrAC. Cooling of the mouth and upper-airway by rapidly inhaling and exhaling very cold air lowers the temperature of the end exhalation.[310] Rinsing the mouth with water at different temperatures causes small deviations in BrAC; ice-water lowering the concentration, in part by lowering the temperature in the mouth and dissolving ethanol in the deposits of water in the mouth during exhalation.[311]

Fox and Hayward[312,313] did an investigation of the effects of deep-core body temperature on BrAC, measured with a Breathalyzer instrument model 900, by immersing volunteer subjects up to their necks in hot or cold water. They induced hyperthermia, by having the subjects stand in water kept at 42°C for 45 minutes.[313] This caused a mean increase in rectal temperature by 2.5°C and the resulting BrAC was increased by, on average, 23%. They induced hypothermia by having the volunteer subjects standing up to their necks in cold water at 10°C for 45 minutes.[312] As expected, the BrAC was now lowered by 22% when tests were done with the Breathalyzer instrument compared with normothermic conditions.

In the above experiments, after the subjects had been returned to their normal body temperature, the BrAC results recovered to the values expected assuming a 2100:1 BBR. The Breathalyzer instrument is now extinct, so it would be useful to repeat these experiments on body temperature with more modern analytical technology, such as electrochemical oxidation or infrared absorption methods of analysis. Nevertheless, hyperthermia increases and hypothermia decreases a person's BrAC determined with the Breathalyzer.[314]

Normal body temperature in healthy individuals is close to 37°C, but there are small variations around this average measurement. Without measuring body temperature it is not possible to know whether a person was suffering from a fever when an evidential breath-alcohol test was administered. Measuring the end-exhaled breath temperature is an indirect way, because this value should be correlated with body-temperature. There does not appear to be experimental studies published comparing BAC and BrAC in people suffering from a fever, although ethanol's solubility coefficient can be used to make theoretical calculations. A person with 39°C fever (two degrees above normal) is expected to have a higher BrAC by 13% (2 × 6.5% per 1°C). In borderline cases this could certainly make the difference between whether a statutory alcohol limit was exceeded or not, but driving on the highway after consumption of alcohol when suffering from a 39°C fever is questionable.

3.5.7 Concluding Remarks

The relevant literature dealing with forensic aspects of ethanol analysis in biological specimens (blood, breath, and urine) and ethanol pharmacokinetics is spread throughout many different scientific journals. Besides the forensic science and legal medicine journals, important articles can also be found in biochemical and general medical, as well as respiratory physiology, journals. A number of newsletters devoted to the defense and prosecution of traffic offenders have appeared over the years, such as *DWI Journal, Law and Science*, *Drinking-Driving Law Letter*, and *The Champion*. The information they contain are of principal interest to lawyers and law firms that specialize in road traffic crimes.

Other relevant sources of information are contained in a diverse range of forensic science legal medicine and toxicology peer-reviewed journals. James Wigmore (Toronto) collected together the results from hundreds of published studies relevant to forensic aspects of alcohol analysis and the many questions arising during prosecution and defense of drunken drivers.[315] His book summarizes the results and conclusions reached by the authors of the article and Wigmore also makes his own interpretation of the conclusions for DUI prosecutions under a concentration *per se* statute.

Expert testimony is often required in connection with drunk- and drugged-driving cases when reliability of the determined ethanol concentrations in samples of blood or breath are challenged. If the defense calls an expert witness, then the prosecution will almost certainly need a rebuttal witness, usually the person who performed the analysis or other suitably qualified scientist. The use of expert witnesses and admissibility of scientific evidence has a long history in criminal and civil trials.[316] The principal difference between a lay witness and an expert witness is that the latter is allowed to give opinionated evidence about the scientific facts in a case, derived from their special training, skill, and acquired knowledge.

Those called to testify as expert witnesses must possess specialist knowledge and expertise beyond the ken of the judge and jury. The presiding judge determines whether a proposed expert witness meets the threshold of admissibility. This requires a close scrutiny of their academic education, work experience, and research on the subject being litigated. Unlike an ordinary witness, who testifies about what they saw when a particular crime was committed, an expert witness renders personal opinions and reviews the current state of knowledge on a scientific topic or discipline. In my experience, the threshold for being admitted as an expert witness differs between different countries and it sometimes suffices to have a BS or BSc degree, or being employed by a government laboratory and familiarity with the analytical methods. Not enough attention is given to participation in research projects and authoring publications in academic journals on topics closely related to what is being discussed and litigated in the case. This sometimes results in spurious evidence and, at worst, miscarriages of justice; shaken baby syndrome is a typical example.[317,318]

It is problematic for a judge and jury when experts hired by the opposing sides in a case render quite different opinions based on the same scientific facts. This problem is not new and was aptly summed up in a judgment made by Learned Hand a New York superior court judge in a case from 1901[319] when he wrote:

> The whole object of the expert is to tell the jury, not facts… but general truths derived from his specialized experience. But how can the jury judge between two statements each founded upon an experience confessedly foreign in kind to their own? It is just because they are incompetent for such a task that the expert is necessary at all.

The enforcement of alcohol concentration *per se* laws puts considerable emphasis on the way the methods used to determine BAC or BrAC. This makes behavioral impairment and clinical tests of drunkenness less relevant for a successful prosecution. Those defending apprehended drivers focus a lot of attention on finding faults with the way samples were taken and the accuracy, precision and selectivity of the determination of ethanol. Forensic methods of analysis are not foolproof and results will always have some uncertainty. When a different technician repeats the analysis using the same measurement procedure slightly different results are usually obtained. The variance (spread) of the measurements is likely to be greater if the work is done by different methods in the same laboratory and greater still if the samples are sent to different laboratories for analysis.[118] These aspects of clinical laboratory analysis should not prejudice the outcome of a criminal prosecution when a concentration per se statute is enforced as in drunk-driving cases.[320]

The magnitude of variance in most analytical methods tends to increase with the concentration of the substance in the samples, which means more uncertainty in the mean result.[321] This deserves consideration in those jurisdictions where there are graded penalties if the BAC or BrAC exceeds some upper limit, such as double or triple the statutory levels. This makes it important to consider the analytical errors as a function of the ethanol concentration as was discussed for HS-GC-FID methods of blood analysis.[322] In borderline cases, when the analytical result is close to a threshold limit, the margin of error in the method can make the difference between punishment or acquittal. A book devoted to metrology in forensic science is a useful resource for lawyers and expert witnesses, who might require more general information about analytical measurements, their accuracy and precision, and the statistical aspects of measurement uncertainty in particular.[323]

The results obtained from evidential breath-alcohol instruments tend to be challenged more often than the determinations of blood-ethanol concentration. There are probably several reasons for this, but blood samples are shipped to a forensic laboratory and analyzed by university-trained chemists, whereas evidential breath-alcohol instruments are operated by trained police officers. Furthermore, there are more sources of biological variation in obtaining the required specimen of end-expired breath and lung physiological parameters to consider compared with drawing a blood sample for analysis.[278,324]

Modern evidential breath-alcohol analyzers are controlled by microprocessors, which simplifies the entire sampling and analytical procedure. The police operator only needs to encourage the suspect to exhale into the instrument at the appropriate time and to maintain a forced exhalation lasting for at least 6 s. Control of the instrument calibration and the analysis of ambient room air are done automatically before and/or after a suspect is tested. All results of the evidential breath-alcohol test are then printed out in real-time and are also stored in a computer for later scrutiny and quality assurance. However, police authorities are sometimes accused of having a vested interest in obtaining a drunk-driving conviction and that they lack enough formal training in clinical laboratory methods.

The notion of using a checklist to document certain key aspects of obtaining the requisite sample, such as use of a tourniquet, left or right arm cubital vein, number of tubes of blood collected, type of evacuated tube, and amount of chemical preservatives, the type of antiseptic to clean the skin etc., is much recommended for use in forensic practice. A video recording of the suspect when the samples of blood or breath are being collected is another measure that might strengthen the prosecution evidence in DUI cases. It is simple to take a digital photograph of the evacuated tubes before and after collection of blood, thus, documenting they have the proper expiry date, the date and time of the blood draw, and the correct name and date of birth of the suspect.

The analysis of blood ethanol should, of course, be done at an accredited laboratory following a standard operating procedure, because this helps to boost confidence in the analytical results when used for legal purposes. The enforcement of a concentration *per se* statute makes it essential that the analytical methods used are fit for forensic purposes.[28] This includes establishing the magnitude of analytical uncertainty and in some way making an allowance for this, such as by subtracting 10–15% from the mean ethanol concentration to safeguard that the prosecution BAC is not less than the true concentration with a high degree of statistical certainty.[120]

To launch a successful attack on the reliability of the forensic evidence in criminal and civil cases, the lawyers working these cases need the services of an expert witness with appropriate academic qualifications, expertise, and training on the issues being litigated. Government-employed scientists almost always testify for the prosecution side in a DUI case, although there are many university professors and retired forensic scientists who are also willing to testify for either side in a case, provided their fees are paid.

Much has been written about the pros and cons of expert evidence in civil and criminal cases, and dubious expert witnesses are sometimes called to testify and present scientific evidence. An editorial in the British journal *Nature* made the following statement about expert witnesses.

> The so-called expert witness in court may be a hired-gun, willing to testify to anything for a fee, or a crackpot whose insupportable ideas are masked by an advanced degree (Ph.D.) often from a respectable university.

William S. Lovell (chemist and district attorney) made the following remarks about expert testimony in DUI litigation as long ago as 1972.

> Courts are indeed plagued by the instant expert, who whether out of a misguided eagerness to earn his fee or an overreaction to his own self-described credentials, may expound far reaching opinions.

The courtroom is unlike the classroom, and many academics who might volunteer their services as expert witness are ill-prepared for vigorous cross examination of their expertise by a skilled attorney. Moreover, the adversarial system of justice tends to create a polarized atmosphere and partisan environment depending on which of the two parties you are representing.[325] The inquisitorial system of justice, which operates in continental Europe and Scandinavia involves a panel of judges who probe the strengths and weakness of the scientific evidence.[326] This gives less opportunity for conflicting opinions by opposing experts and it is more likely that a compromise is reached or a joint statement prepared for review by the court. This might take the form of written opinion, similar to a deposition given under oath. In Nordic countries, an acquittal in a DUI case in the lower court can be appealed by the prosecution to an upper court.

Whenever possible, expert testimony should be based on research studies and articles published in peer-reviewed journals. But even peer-reviewers sometimes make mistakes and publication per se does not make the results and conclusions gospel. Scientists are not infallible, and unsubstantiated opinions or arguments are common in DUI litigation.[327] Much might be gained by more reliance on a court appointed expert, instead of using expert witnesses instructed by the two sides in the case. Today there are accepted codes of conduct for forensic practitioners, when they appear in court and testify as expert witnesses, and a disclosure form has to be completed and signed.[328] In the U.K., the crown prosecution service has produced a guidance booklet for use by expert witnesses, and this is available online for future reference.

Difficulties often arise in the adversarial system of justice, because juries might be swayed by the charisma, demeanor, and personality of the expert witness rather than the correctness of the science they are explaining to a jury. To quote from the famous geneticist and pioneer in use of DNA fingerprinting in forensic science, Sir Alec Jeffreys:

> I lost my faith in the adversarial system the first time I stood up in court as an expert witness, due to the realization that it all depends on the chemistry between the witness and the jury.

Scientific evidence is often controversial and not easy to discuss and debate in the courtroom before a judge and jury, especially when the expert witness is being cross-examined and is asked to provide a simple "yes" or "no" answer to a complex question. Under these circumstances, the judge needs to intervene and allow the expert to expand on his answer explaining any assumptions made and other caveats. Statements like "this is my opinion with reasonable scientific certainty" or this opinion is shared by the relevant scientific community are typically seen when reading trial transcripts.

There is a lot to recommend having pre-trial hearings between the experts hired by each side in a case when the scientific evidence is pivotal for the outcome. In this way, it might become possible to reach a compromise or highlight points of agreement or disagreement. Alternatively, a court-appointed expert has the task of advising the preceding judge with regard to the present status of research on certain thorny questions and how best to interpret scientific evidence in the case. A golden rule for those who frequently testify in court as expert witnesses is never to give opinions beyond your level of expertise, such as on statistical matters like probability and likelihood ratios if statistics is not your speciality discipline. The U.K. Government has started to produce primers dealing with the best way to interpret scientific evidence often encountered in criminal cases.[329] These documents contain up-to-date information on certain topics, such as forensic DNA evidence and gait analysis, and are written so as to be understandable by non-scientists, such as people within the legal profession and members of a jury. Hopefully, these primers will be extended to cover other topics, such as back extrapolation of ethanol and interpretation of drug concentrations in blood, which are more relevant to the crimes of drunk or drugged driving.

REFERENCES

1. Jones AW, Morland JG, Liu RH. Driving under the influence of psychoactive substances – A historical review. *Forensic Sci Rev* 2019;31:103–40.
2. Crothers TD. Editorial. *Q J Inebriety* 1904;XXV1:308.

3. Lerner BH. *One for the Road*. Baltimore: The Johns Hopkins University Press, 2011.
4. BMA. Test for drunkenness. *Br Med J* 1927:53–8.
5. Penttila A, Tenhu M. Clinical examination as medicolegal proof of alcohol intoxication. *Med Sci Law* 1976;16: 95–103.
6. Jones AW. Enforcement of drink-driving laws by use of "per se" legal alcohol limits: blood and/or breath concentration as evidence of impairment. *Alcohol, Drugs & Driving* 1988;4:99–112.
7. Borkenstein RF. Historical perspective: North American traditional and experimental response. *J Stud Alcohol* 1985;10 Suppl:3–12.
8. Fell JC, Voas RB. The effectiveness of reducing illegal blood alcohol concentration (BAC) limits for driving: evidence for lowering the limit to .05 BAC. *J Safety Res* 2006;37:233–43.
9. Fell JC. Another major reason to lower the blood alcohol concentration limit for driving. *Am J Public Health* 2019;109:670–1.
10. Wagenaar AC, O'Malley PM, LaFond C. Lowered legal blood alcohol limits for young drivers: effects on drinking, driving, and driving-after-drinking behaviors in 30 states. *Am J Public Health* 2001;91:801–4.
11. Haghpanahan H, Lewsey J, Mackay DF, McIntosh E, Pell J, Jones A, et al. An evaluation of the effects of lowering blood alcohol concentration limits for drivers on the rates of road traffic accidents and alcohol consumption: a natural experiment. *Lancet* 2019;393:321–9.
12. Blomberg RD, Peck RC, Moskowitz H, Burns M, Florentino D. The long beach/fort lauderdale relative risk study. *J Safety Res* 2009;40:285–92.
13. Fell J. Approaches for reducing alcohol-impaired driving: evidence-based legislation, law enforcement strategies. sanctions, and alcohol-control policies. In: Jones AW, Morland JG, Liu RH, editors. *Alcohol, Drugs and Impaired Driving: Forensic Science and Law Ennforcement Issues*. Boca Raton: CRC Press, 2020, 653–90.
14. Simpson HM, Beirness DJ, Robertson RD, Mayhew DR, Hedlund JH. Hard core drinking drivers. *Traffic Inj Prev* 2004;5:261–9.
15. Karjalainen K, Lintonen T, Impinen A, Makela P, Rahkonen O, Lillsunde P, et al. Mortality and causes of death among drugged drivers. *J Epidemiol Community Health* 2010;64:506–12.
16. Williams AF, McCartt AT, Ferguson SA. Hardcore drinking drivers and other contributors to the alcohol-impaired driving problem: need for a comprehensive approach. *Traffic Inj Prev* 2007;8:1–10.
17. Brick J, Erickson CK. Intoxication is not always visible: an unrecognized prevention challenge. *Alcohol Clin Exp Res* 2009;33:1489–507.
18. Jones AW, Holmgren A. Age and gender differences in blood-alcohol concentration in apprehended drivers in relation to the amounts of alcohol consumed. *Forensic Sci Int* 2009;188:40–5.
19. Cohen HM, Green JB. *Apprehending and Prosecuting the Drunk Driver*. New York: Matthew Bender, 1995.
20. Hume DN, Fitzgerald EF. Chemical tests for intoxication: what do the numbers really mean? *Anal Chem* 1985;57:876A–84A.
21. Fitzgerald EF. *Intoxication Test Evidence*. Eagen: Thompson Reuters, 2001.
22. Williams PM. Current defence strategies in some contested drunkdrive prosecutions: is it now time for some additional statutory assumptions? *Forensic Sci Int* 2018;293:e5–e9.
23. Annon. Challenges and defenses: Claims and responses to common challenges and defenses in driving while impaired cases: NHTSA Department of Transportation, Arlington DOT HS 811 707 2013.
24. Atwater WO, Benedict FG. An experimental inquiry regarding the nutritive value of alcohol *Mem Natl Acad Sci* 1902;8:235–397.
25. Widmark EMP. Om alkoholens öfvergång i urinen samt om en enkel, kliniskt användbar metod för diagnosticering af alkoholförekomst i kroppen. *Upsala Läkareförenings Förhandlingar N F* 1914;19:241–72.
26. Ladd M, Gibson RB. The medico-legal aspects of the blood test to determine intoxication. *Iowa Law Rev* 1939;24:1–77.
27. Donigan RL. *Chemical Test Case Law; Legal Aspects of Constitutional Issues Involved in Chemical Tests to Determine Intoxication*. Evenston: The Traffic Institute, Northwestern University, 1950.
28. Gullberg RG. Quality assurance in forensic breath alcohol analysis. In: Jones AW, Morland JG, Liu RH, editors. *Alcohol, Drugs and Impaired Driving: Forensic Science and Law Ennforcement Issues*. Boca Raton: CRC Press, 2020, 245–74.
29. Dubowski KM. Quality assurance in breath-alcohol analysis. *J Anal Toxicol* 1994;18:306–11.
30. AMA. *Chemical Tests for the Determination of Ethyl Alcohol. Alcohol and the Impaired Driver*. Chicago: American Medical Association, 1970, 61–123.
31. Jones AW. Alcohol, its analysis in blood and breath for forensic purposes, impairment effects, and acute toxicity. *WIRE Forensic Sci* 2019;1.
32. Jones AW. The analysis of ethanol in blood and breath for legal purposes: a historical review. In: Jones AW, Morland JG, Liu RH, editors. *Alcohol, Drugs and Impaired Driving: Forensic Science and Law Ennforcement Issues*. Boca Raton: CRC Press, 2020, 105–53.
33. Tagliaro F, Lubli G, Ghielmi S, Franchi D, Marigo M. Chromatographic methods for blood alcohol determination. *J Chromatogr* 1992;580:161–90.
34. Tiscione NB, Alford I, Yeatman DT, Shan X. Ethanol analysis by headspace gas chromatography with simultaneous flame-ionization and mass spectrometry detection. *J Anal Toxicol* 2011;35:501–11.
35. Callow PM. *The Drink- and Drug-Drive Offences*. second ed. London: Wildy, Simmonds & Hill, 2018.
36. Ley NJ. *Drink Driivng Law and Practice*. second ed. London: Sweet & Maxwell, 1997.
37. Nesci J. *How to Beat a DUI*. Tuscon: Lawyers & Judges, 2008.
38. Stamm MR. The top 20 myths of blood, breath and urine tests: part II. *The Champion* 2005:44–50.
39. Stamm MR. The top 20 myths of blood, breath and urine tests: part I. *The Champion* 2005:20–6.
40. Jones AW. Top ten defence challenges among drinking drivers in Sweden. *Med Sci Law* 1991;31:229–38.
41. Grant S, LaBrie JW, Hummer JF, Lac A. How drunk am I? Misperceiving one's level of intoxication in the college drinking environment. *Psychol Addict Behav* 2012;26:51–8.
42. Sharman JR, Lindley TN, Abernethy MH. Blood alcohol levels. How accurately can they be guessed? *N Z Med J* 1978;87:438–40.

43. Jones AW, Kugelberg FC. Relationship between blood and urine alcohol concentrations in apprehended drivers who claimed consumption of alcohol after driving with and without supporting evidence. *Forensic Sci Int* 2010;194:97–102.
44. Iffland R, Jones AW. Evaluating alleged drinking after driving--the hip-flask defence. Part 1. Double blood samples and urine-to-blood alcohol relationship. *Med Sci Law* 2002;42:207–24.
45. Jones AW. Ethanol distribution ratios between urine and capillary blood in controlled experiments and in apprehended drinking drivers. *J Forensic Sci* 1992;37:21–34.
46. Jones AW. Lack of association between urinary creatinine and ethanol concentrations and urine/blood ratio of ethanol in two successive voids from drinking drivers. *J Anal Toxicol* 1998;22:184–90.
47. Jones AW. Urine as a biological specimen for forensic analysis of alcohol and variability in the urine-to-blood relationship. *Toxicol Rev* 2006;25:15–35.
48. Jones AW. Excretion of alcohol in urine and diuresis in healthy men in relation to their age, the dose administered and the time after drinking. *Forensic Sci Int* 1990;45:217–24.
49. Iffland R, Jones AW. Evaluating alleged drinking after driving--the hip-flask defence. Part 2. Congener analysis. *Med Sci Law* 2003;43:39–68.
50. Jung A, Jung H, Auwärter V, Pollak S, Farr AM, Schiopu A. Volatile congeners in alcoholic beverages: analysis and forensic significance. *Rom J Leg Med* 2010;18:265–70.
51. Bonte W. *Begleitstoffe Alkoholischer Getränke Arbeitsmethoden der Medizinischen und Naturwissenschaftlichen Kriminalistik*. Lübeck: Schmidt-Römhild, 1989.
52. Felby S, Nielsen E. Congener production in blood samples during preparation and storage. *Blutalkohol* 1995;32:50–8.
53. Bonte W. Alcohol - congener analysis. In: Siegel JA, Saakko PJ, editors. *Encyclopedia of Forensic Sciences*. London: Academic Press, 1990, 93–102.
54. Rodda LN, Beyer J, Gerostamoulos D, Drummer OH. Alcohol congener analysis and the source of alcohol: a review. *Forensic Sci Med Pathol* 2013;9:194–207.
55. Haffner HT, Graw M, Besserer K, Blickle U, Henssge C. Endogenous methanol: variability in concentration and rate of production. Evidence of a deep compartment? *Forensic Sci Int* 1996;79:145–54.
56. Gilg T. Alkoholbedingte Fahruntüchtigkeit. *Rechtsmedizin* 2005;15:97–112.
57. Gilg T. Methanol and congeners as markers of alcohol use and abuse. In: Wurst FM, editor. *New and Upcoming Markers of Alcohol Consumption*. Darmstadt: Steinkopff-Verlag, 2001, 35–52.
58. Kronstrand C, Nilsson G, Cherma MD, Ahlner J, Kugelberg FC, Kronstrand R. Evaluating the hip-flask defence in subjects with alcohol on board: an experimental study. *Forensic Sci Int* 2019;294:189–95.
59. Walsham NE, Sherwood RA. Ethyl glucuronide. *Ann Clin Biochem* 2012;49:110–7.
60. Hoiseth G, Bernard JP, Karinen R, Johnsen L, Helander A, Christophersen AS, et al. A pharmacokinetic study of ethyl glucuronide in blood and urine: applications to forensic toxicology. *Forensic Sci Int* 2007;172:119–24.
61. Hoiseth G, Berg-Hansen GO, Morland J. Evaluation of the hip-flask defence by determination of ethyl glucuronide and ethyl sulphate concentrations in blood. *Forensic Sci Int* 2015;257:398–402.
62. Langford NJ, Marshall T, Ferner RE. The lacing defence: double blind study of thresholds for detecting addition of ethanol to drinks. *BMJ* 1999;319:1610.
63. Aston ER, Liguori A. Self-estimation of blood alcohol concentration: a review. *Addict Behav* 2013;38:1944–51.
64. Wicki J, Gache P, Rutschmann OT. Self-estimates of blood-alcohol concentration and ability to drive in a population of soldiers. *Alcohol Alcohol* 2000;35:104–5.
65. Brick J, Carpenter JA. The identification of alcohol intoxication by police. *Alcohol Clin Exp Res* 2001;25:850–5.
66. Rivara FP, Relyea-Chew A, Wang J, Riley S, Boisvert D, Gomez T. Drinking behaviors in young adults: the potential role of designated driver and safe ride home programs. *Inj Prev* 2007;13:168–72.
67. Elder RW, Voas R, Beirness D, Shults RA, Sleet DA, Nichols JL, et al. Effectiveness of ignition interlocks for preventing alcohol-impaired driving and alcohol-related crashes: a community guide systematic review. *Am J Prev Med* 2011;40:362–76.
68. Jones AW. Evidence-based survey of the elimination rates of ethanol from blood with applications in forensic casework. *Forensic Sci Int* 2010;200:1–20.
69. Jones AW, Jonsson KA, Neri A. Peak blood-ethanol concentration and the time of its occurrence after rapid drinking on an empty stomach. *J Forensic Sci* 1991;36: 376–85.
70. Jones AW, Jonsson KA. Food-induced lowering of blood-ethanol profiles and increased rate of elimination immediately after a meal. *J Forensic Sci* 1994;39:1084–93.
71. Jones AW, Neri A. Evaluation of blood-alcohol profiles after consumption of alcohol together with a large meal. *Can Soc Forensic Sci J* 1991;24:165–73.
72. Cortot A, Jobin G, Ducrot F, Aymes C, Giraudeaux V, Modigliani R. Gastric emptying and gastrointestinal absorption of alcohol ingested with a meal. *Dig Dis Sci* 1986;31:343–8.
73. Holland MG, Ferner RE. A systematic review of the evidence for acute tolerance to alcohol - the "Mellanby effect." *Clin Toxicol (Phila)* 2017;55:545–56.
74. Watkins RL, Adler EV. The effect of food on alcohol absorption and elimination patterns. *J Forensic Sci* 1993;38:285–91.
75. Mitchell MC, Jr, Teigen EL, Ramchandani VA. Absorption and peak blood alcohol concentration after drinking beer, wine, or spirits. *Alcohol Clin Exp Res* 2014;38:1200–4.
76. Gullberg RG. Variation in blood-alcohol concentration following the last drink. *J Police Sci Adm* 1982;10:289–96.
77. Shajani NK, Dinn HM. Blood alcohol concentrations reached in human subjects after consumption of alcoholic beverages in a social etting. *Can Soc Forensic Sci J* 1985;18:38–48.
78. Zink P, Reinhardt G. Der Verlauf der Blutalkoholkurve bei großem Trinkmengen. *Blutalkohol* 1984;21:422–42.
79. Jones AW, Wigmore JG, House CJ. The course of the blood-alcohol curve after consumption of large amounts of alcohol under realistic conditions. *Can Soc Forensic Sci J* 2006;39:125–40.
80. Kalant H. Effects of food and body composition on blood alcohol levels. In: Preedy V, Watson R, editors. *Comprehensive Handbook of Alcohol Related Pathology*, 2004, 87–101.
81. Hoiseth G, Wiik E, Kristoffersen L, Morland J. Ethanol elimination rates at low concentrations based on two consecutive blood samples. *Forensic Sci Int* 2016;266:191–6.

82. Pavlic M, Grubwieser P, Libiseller K, Rabl W. Elimination rates of breath alcohol. *Forensic Sci Int* 2007;171:16–21.
83. Jones AW. Reference limits for urine/blood ratios of ethanol in two successive voids from drinking drivers. *J Anal Toxicol* 2002;26:333–9.
84. Jones AW, Holmgren P. Urine/blood ratios of ethanol in deaths attributed to acute alcohol poisoning and chronic alcoholism. *Forensic Sci Int* 2003;135:206–12.
85. Stowell AR, Stowell LI. Estimation of blood alcohol concentrations after social drinking. *J Forensic Sci* 1998;43:14–21.
86. Weathermon R, Crabb DW. Alcohol and medication interactions. *Alcohol Res Health* 1999;23:40–54.
87. Langford NJ, Ferner RE. The medico-legal significance of pharmacokinetic interactions with ethanol. *Med Sci Law* 2013;53:1–5.
88. Immonen S, Valvanne J, Pitkala KH. The prevalence of potential alcohol-drug interactions in older adults. *Scand J Prim Health Care* 2013;31:73–8.
89. Holton AE, Gallagher P, Fahey T, Cousins G. Concurrent use of alcohol interactive medications and alcohol in older adults: a systematic review of prevalence and associated adverse outcomes. *BMC Geriatr* 2017;17:148.
90. Fraser AG. Pharmacokinetic interactions between alcohol and other drugs. *Clin Pharmacokinet* 1997;33:79–90.
91. Fraser AG, Prewett EJ, Hudson M, Sawyerr AM, Rosalki SB, Pounder RE. The effect of ranitidine, cimetidine or famotidine on low-dose post-prandial alcohol absorption. *Aliment Pharmacol Ther* 1991;5:263–72.
92. Moody DE. The inhibition of first-pass metabolism of ethanol by H2-receptor antagonists: a tabulated review. *Expert Opin Drug Saf* 2018;17:917–34.
93. Brent J. Fomepizole for ethylene glycol and methanol poisoning. *N Engl J Med* 2009;360:2216–23.
94. Kraut JA. Approach to the treatment of methanol intoxication. *Am J Kidney Dis* 2016;68:161–7.
95. Malik F, Wickremesinghe P, Saverimuttu J. Case report and literature review of auto-brewery syndrome: probably an underdiagnosed medical condition. *BMJ Open Gastroenterol* 2019;6:e000325.
96. Cordell B, Kanodia A. Auto-brewery as an emerging syndrome: three representative case studies. *J Clin Med Case Report* 2015;2:1–5.
97. Kaji H, Asanuma Y, Yaahara O, Shibue H, Hisamura M, Saito N, et al. Intragastrointestinal alcohol fermentation syndrome: report of two cases and review of the literature. *J Forensic Sci Soc* 1983;24:461–71.
98. Akbaba M. A medicolegal approach to the very rare Auto-Brewery (endogenous alcohol fermentation) syndrome. *Traffic Inj Prev* 2020;21:295–7.
99. Kruckenberg KM, DiMartini AF, Rymer JA, Pasculle AW, Tamama K. Urinary auto-brewery syndrome: a case report. *Ann Intern Med* 2020;172:702–4.
100. Sprung R, Bonte W, Rudell E, Domke M, Frauenrath C. Zum Problem des endogenen Alkohols. *Blutalkohol* 1981;18:65–70.
101. Ostrovsky Yu M. Endogenous ethanol--its metabolic, behavioral and biomedical significance. *Alcohol* 1986;3:239–47.
102. Jones AW, Ostrovsky Yu M, Wallin A, Midtvedt T. Lack of differences in blood and tissue concentrations of endogenous ethanol in conventional and germfree rats. *Alcohol* 1984;1:393–6.
103. Jones AW. Concentration of endogenous ethanol in blood and CSF. *Acta Neurol Scand* 1994;89:149–50.
104. Dahshan A, Donovan K. Auto-brewery syndrome in a child with short gut syndrome: case report and review of the literature. *J Pediatr Gastroenterol Nutr* 2001;33:214–5.
105. Logan BK, Jones AW. Endogenous ethanol production in a child with short gut syndrome. *J Pediatr Gastroenterol Nutr* 2003;36:419–20; author's reply 20-1.
106. Kaji H, Asanuma Y, Ide H, Saito N, Hisamura M, Murao M, et al. The auto-brewery syndrome--the repeated attacks of alcoholic intoxication due to the overgrowth of Candida (albicans) in the gastrointestinal tract. *Mater Med Pol* 1976;8:429–35.
107. Cordell BJ, Kanodia A, Miller GK. Case-control research study of auto-brewery syndrome. *Glob Adv Health Med* 2019;8:2164956119837566.
108. Akhavan BJ, Ostrosky-Zeichner L, Thomas EJ. Drunk without drinking: a case of auto-brewery syndrome. *ACG Case Rep J* 2019;6:e00208.
109. Mizoi Y, Fukunaga T, Ueno Y, Adachi J, Fujiwara S, Nishimura A. The flushing syndrome after ethanol intake caused by aldehyde dehydrogenase deficiency in orientals. *Acta Med Leg Soc (Liege)* 1989;39:481–7.
110. Hunnisett A, Howard J, Davis S. Gut fermentation (or the 'Auto-brewery') syndrome: a new clinical test with initial observations and discussion of clinical and biochemical implications. *J Nutr Med* 1990;1:33–8.
111. Jansson-Nettelbladt E, Meurling S, Petrini B, Sjolin J. Endogenous ethanol fermentation in a child with short bowel syndrome. *Acta Paediatr* 2006;95:502–4.
112. Hafez EM, Hamad MA, Fouad M, Abdel-Lateff A. Auto-brewery syndrome: Ethanol pseudo-toxicity in diabetic and hepatic patients. *Hum Exp Toxicol* 2017;36:445–50.
113. Simic M, Ajdukovic N, Veselinovic I, Mitrovic M, Djurendic-Brenesel M. Endogenous ethanol production in patients with diabetes mellitus as a medicolegal problem. *Forensic Sci Int* 2012;216:97–100.
114. Peters FT, Drummer OH, Musshoff F. Validation of new methods. *Forensic Sci Int* 2007;165:216–24.
115. Gullberg RG, Logan BK. Results of a proposed breath alcohol proficiency test program. *J Forensic Sci* 2006;51: 168–72.
116. Searle J. Alcohol calculations and their uncertainty. *Med Sci Law* 2015;55:58–64.
117. Gullberg RG. Estimating the measurement uncertainty in forensic blood alcohol analysis. *J Anal Toxicol* 2012;36:153–61.
118. Zamengo L, Tedeschi G, Frison G, Griffoni C, Ponzin D, Jones AW. Inter-laboratory proficiency results of blood alcohol determinations at clinical and forensic laboratories in Italy. *Forensic Sci Int* 2019;295:213–8.
119. Zamengo L, Frison G, Tedeschi G, Frasson S, Zancanaro F, Sciarrone R. Variability of blood alcohol content (BAC) determinations: the role of measurement uncertainty, significant figures, and decision rules for compliance assessment in the frame of a multiple BAC threshold law. *Drug Test Anal* 2014;6:1028–37.
120. Gullberg RG. Estimating the measurement uncertainty in forensic breath-alcohol analysis. *Accred Qual Assur* 2006;11:562–8.
121. Gullberg RG. Breath alcohol measurement variability associated with different instrumentation and protocols. *Forensic Sci Int* 2003;131:30–5.
122. Southgate HW, Carter G. Excretion of alcohol in the urine as a guide to alcoholic intoxication. *Br Med J* 1926;1:463–9.

123. Biasotti AA, Valentine TE. Blood alcohol concentration determined from urine samples as a practical equivalent or alternative to blood and breath alcohol tests. *J Forensic Sci* 1985;30:194–207.
124. Rik KJ. Blood or needle phobia as a defence under the Road Traffic Act 1988. *J Clin Forensic Med* 1996;3:173–7.
125. Bendtsen P, Jones AW. Impact of water-induced diuresis on excretion profiles of ethanol, urinary creatinine, and urinary osmolality. *J Anal Toxicol* 1999;23:565–9.
126. Mulholland JH, Townsend FJ. Bladder beer--a new clinical observation. *Trans Am Clin Climatol Assoc* 1984;95:34–9.
127. Jones AW, Hylen L, Svensson E, Helander A. Storage of specimens at 4 degrees C or addition of sodium fluoride (1%) prevents formation of ethanol in urine inoculated with Candida albicans. *J Anal Toxicol* 1999;23:333–6.
128. Fine J. Glucose content of normal urine. *Br Med J* 1965;1:1209–14.
129. Jones AW, Eklund A, Helander A. Misleading results of ethanol analysis in urine specimens from rape victims suffering from diabetes. *J Clin Forensic Med* 2000;7: 144–6.
130. Heise HA. How extraneous alcohol affects the blood test for alcohol; pitfalls to be avoided when withdrawing blood for medicolegal purposes. *Am J Clin Pathol* 1959;32:169–70.
131. Heise HA. Extraneous alcohol and blood alcohol test; further measurements obtained by a robot method. *Q J Stud Alcohol* 1966;27:102–6.
132. Peek GJ, Marsh A, Keating J, Ward RJ, Peters TJ. The effects of swabbing the skin on apparent blood ethanol concentration. *Alcohol Alcohol* 1990;25:639–40.
133. Malingre M, Ververs T, Bos S, van Kesteren C, van Rijn H. Alcohol swabs and venipuncture in a routine hospital setting: no effect on blood ethanol measurement. *Ther Drug Monit* 2005;27:403–4.
134. McIvor RA, Cosbey SH. Effect of using alcoholic and non-alcoholic skin cleansing swabs when sampling blood for alcohol estimation using gas chromatography. *Br J Clin Pract* 1990;44:235–6.
135. Goldfinger TM, Schaber D. A comparison of blood alcohol concentration using non-alcohol- and alcohol-containing skin antiseptics. *Ann Emerg Med* 1982;11:665–7.
136. Dubowski KM, Essary NA. Contamination of blood specimens for alcohol analysis during collection. *Abs Rev Alc Drug Driving* 1983;4:3–7.
137. Rodda LN, Pearring S, Harper CE, Tiscione NB, Jones AW. Inferences and legal considerations following a blood collection tube recall. *J Anal Toxicol* 2021;45:211–14.
138. Shajani NK. Determination of fluoride in blood samples for analysis of ethnaol. *Can Soc Forensic Sci J* 1985;18:49–52.
139. Ali SS, Wilson MP, Castillo EM, Witucki P, Simmons TT, Vilke GM. Common hand sanitizer may distort readings of breathalyzer tests in the absence of acute intoxication. *Acad Emerg Med* 2013;20:212–5.
140. Brown TL, Gamon S, Tester P, Martin R, Hosking K, Bowkett GC, et al. Can alcohol-based hand-rub solutions cause you to lose your driver's license? Comparative cutaneous absorption of various alcohols. *Antimicrob Agents Chemother* 2007;51:1107–8.
141. Gormley NJ, Bronstein AC, Rasimas JJ, Pao M, Wratney AT, Sun J, et al. The rising incidence of intentional ingestion of ethanol-containing hand sanitizers. *Crit Care Med* 2012;40:290–4.
142. Strawsine E, Lutmer B. The effect of alcohol-based hand sanitizer Vapors on evidential breath alcohol test results. *J Forensic Sci* 2018;63:1284–90.
143. Bowers RV, Burleson WD, Blades JF. Alcohol absorption from the skin in man. *Quat J Stud Alcohol* 1942;3:31–3.
144. Lachenmeier DW. Safety evaluation of topical applications of ethanol on the skin and inside the oral cavity. *J Occup Med Toxicol* 2008;3:26–32.
145. Pendlington RU, Whittle E, Robinson JA, Howes D. Fate of ethanol topically applied to skin. *Food Chem Toxicol* 2001;39:169–74.
146. Lippi G, Simundic AM, Musile G, Danese E, Salvagno G, Tagliaro F. The alcohol used for cleansing the venipuncture site does not jeopardize blood and plasma alcohol measurement with head-space gas chromatography and an enzymatic assay. *Biochem Med (Zagreb)* 2017;27:398–403.
147. Kintz P. Influence of antemortem perfusion on autopsy blood ethanol concentration. *Forensic Tox* 2012;30:76–9.
148. Riley D, Wigmore JG, Yen B. Dilution of blood collected for medicolegal alcohol analysis by intravenous fluids. *J Anal Toxicol* 1996;20:330–1.
149. Jones AW. Impact of trauma, massive blood loss and administration of resucitation fluids on a person's blood-alcohol concentration and rate of ethanol metabolism. *Acad Forensic Pathol* 2016;6:77–88.
150. Jones AW, Zdolsek HJ, Sjoberg F, Lisander B. Accelerated metabolism of ethanol in patients with burn injury. *Alcohol Alcohol* 1997;32:628–30.
151. Porter C, Tompkins RG, Finnerty CC, Sidossis LS, Suman OE, Herndon DN. The metabolic stress response to burn trauma: current understanding and therapies. *Lancet* 2016;388:1417–26.
152. Barnhill MT, Jr, Herbert D, Wells DJ, Jr. Comparison of hospital laboratory serum alcohol levels obtained by an enzymatic method with whole blood levels forensically determined by gas chromatography. *J Anal Toxicol* 2007;31:23–30.
153. Rainey PM. Relation between serum and whole-blood ethanol concentrations. *Clin Chem* 1993;39:2288–92.
154. Frajola WJ. Blood alcohol testing in the clinical laboratory: problems and suggested remedies. *Clin Chem* 1993;39:377–9.
155. Lentner C. *Geigy Scientific Tables - Units of Measurement, Body Fluids, Composition of the Body, Nutrition*. Basel: CIBA-GEIGY, 1981.
156. Charlebois RC, Corbett MR, Wigmore JG. Comparison of ethanol concentrations in blood, serum, and blood cells for forensic application. *J Anal Toxicol* 1996;20:171–8.
157. Winek CL, Carfagna M. Comparison of plasma, serum, and whole blood ethanol concentrations. *J Anal Toxicol* 1987;11:267–8.
158. Iffland R, West A, Bilzer N, Schuff A. Zur Zuverlässigkeit der Blutalkoholbestimmung Das Verteilungsverhältnis des Wassers zwischen Serum und Vollblut. *Rechtsmedizin* 1999;9:123–30.
159. Oliver JS, Sloan E, Smith H, Roger WJ. Alcohol and driving: a survey of prosecution and defence alcohol estimations. *Med Sci Law* 1975;15:211–7.
160. Zittel DB, Hardin GG. Comparison of blood ethanol concentrations in samples simultaneously collected into expired and unexpired venipuncture tubes. *J Anal Toxicol* 2006;30:317–8.
161. Jones AW, Fransson M. Blood analysis by headspace gas chromatography: does a deficient sample volume distort ethanol concentration? *Med Sci Law* 2003;43:241–7.
162. Miller BA, Day SM, Vasquez TE, Evans FM. Absence of salting out effects in forensic blood alcohol determination at various concentrations of sodium fluoride using semi-automated headspace gas chromatography. *Sci Justice* 2004;44:73–6.

163. Jones AW, Ericsson E. Decreases in blood ethanol concentration during storage at 4°C for 12 months were the same for specimens kept in glass and plastic tubes. *Pract Lab Med* 2016;4:76–81.
164. Penetar DM, McNeil JF, Ryan ET, Lukas SE. Comparison among plasma, serum, and whole blood ethanol concentrations: impact of storage conditions and collection tubes. *J Anal Toxicol* 2008;32:505–10.
165. Yajima D, Motani H, Kamei K, Sato Y, Hayakawa M, Iwase H. Ethanol production by Candida albicans in postmortem human blood samples: effects of blood glucose level and dilution. *Forensic Sci Int* 2006;164:116–21.
166. Senkowski CM, Thompson KA. The accuracy of blood alcohol analysis using headspace gas chromatography when performed on clotted samples. *J Forensic Sci* 1990;35:176–80.
167. Emerson VJ, Holleyhead R, Isaacs MD, Fuller NA, Hunt DJ. The measurement of breath alcohol. The laboratory evaluation of substantive breath test equipment and the report of an operational police trial. *J Forensic Sci Soc* 1980;20:3–70.
168. Mulder JA, Neuteboom W, Wessel RM. Breath alcohol legislation in the Netherlands. *Blutalkohol* 1991;28:94–107.
169. Dubowski KM. *The Technology of Breath Alcohol Analysis. US Department of Health and Human Services.* Rockville, MA: NIAAA, 1991, 38.
170. Polissar NL, Suwanvijit W, Gullberg RG. The accuracy of handheld pre-arrest breath test instruments as a predictor of the evidential breath alcohol test results. *J Forensic Sci* 2015;60:482–7.
171. Korkosh SL, Hackett JA, Mastpetit JC. Blood alcohol and breath comparisons using Intox EC/IR II. *Can Soc Forensic Sci J* 2012;45:195–200.
172. Zuba D. Accuracy and reliability of breath alcohol testing by handheld electrochemical analysers. *Forensic Sci Int* 2008;178:e29–33.
173. Razatos G, Luthi R, Kerrigan S. Evaluation of a portable evidential breath alcohol analyzer. *Forensic Sci Int* 2005;153:17–21.
174. Frankvoort W, Mulder JA, Neuteboom W. The laboratory testing of evidential breath-testing (EBT) machines. *Forensic Sci Int* 1987;35:27–43.
175. Schechtman E, Shinar D. An analysis of alcohol breath tests results with portable and desktop breath testers as surrogates of blood alcohol levels. *Accid Anal Prev* 2011;43:2188–94.
176. Kriikku P, Wilhelm L, Jenckel S, Rintatalo J, Hurme J, Kramer J, et al. Comparison of breath-alcohol screening test results with venous blood alcohol concentration in suspected drunken drivers. *Forensic Sci Int* 2014;239:57–61.
177. Ruzsanyi V, Peter Kalapos M. Breath acetone as a potential marker in clinical practice. *J Breath Res* 2017;11:024002.
178. Jones AW, Andersson L. Biotransformation of acetone to isopropanol observed in a motorist involved in a sobriety check. *J Forensic Sci* 1995;40:686–7.
179. Caravati EM, Anderson KT. Breath alcohol analyzer mistakes methanol poisoning for alcohol intoxication. *Ann Emerg Med* 2010;55:198–200.
180. Wigmore JG, Leslie GM. The effect of swallowing or rinsing alcohol solution on the mouth alcohol effect and slope detection of the intoxilyzer 5000. *J Anal Toxicol* 2001;25:112–4.
181. Labianca DA. Non-foolproof nature of the slope detection technology in the Dräger Alcotest 9510. *Forensic Tox* 2018;36:222–4.
182. Anghel MA. Quality assurance in breath-alcohol analysis. *UPB Sci Bull Series A* 2006;68:61–70.
183. Dubowski KM. Breath-alcohol simulators: scientific basis and actual performance. *J Anal Toxicol* 1979;3:177–82.
184. Dubowski KM, Essary NA. Vapor-alcohol control tests with compressed ethanol-gas mixtures: scientific basis and actual performance. *J Anal Toxicol* 1996;20:484–91.
185. Spector NH. Alcohol breath tests: gross errors in current methods of measuring alveolar gas concentrations. *Science* 1971;172:57–9.
186. Anstie FE. Prognosis and treatment of certain acute diseases. *Lancet* 1867:385–7.
187. Bogen E. Drunkennes: A quantitative study of acute alcoholic intoxication. *JAMA* 1927;89:1508–11.
188. Caddy GR, Sobell MB, Sobell LC. Alcohol breath tests: criterion times for avoiding contaminaion by "mouth alcohol." *Beh Res Meth Instrument* 1978;10:814–8.
189. DeChano WD. The effects of dosed tobacco in evidentiary breath testing using non-drinking subjects. *Sci Justice* 2012;52:142–4.
190. Glinn M, Curtis P. Effects of smokeless tobacco and belching on DMT bretah alcohol results. *IACT Newsletter* 2011;22:4–6.
191. Dubowski KM. Studies in breath-alcohol analysis: biological factors. *Z Rechtsmed* 1975;76:93–117.
192. Fessler CC, Tulleners FA, Howitt DG, Richards JR. Determination of mouth alcohol using the drager evidential portable alcohol system. *Sci Justice* 2008;48:16–23.
193. Gullberg RG. The elimination rate of mouth alcohol: mathematical modeling and implications in breath alcohol analysis. *J Forensic Sci* 1992;37:1363–72.
194. Sterling K. The rate of dissipation of mouth alcohol in alcohol positive subjects. *J Forensic Sci* 2012;57:802–5.
195. Buczek Y, Wigmore JG. The significance of breath sampling frequency on the mouth alcohol effect. *Can Soc Forensic Sci J* 2002;35:185–93.
196. Wigmore JG, Bugyra IM. Decreasing the mouth alcohol effect by increasing the salivary flow rate. *Can Soc Forensic Sci J* 2003;36:211–6.
197. Modell JG, Taylor JP, Lee JY. Breath alcohol values following mouthwash use. *J Am Med Assoc* 1993;270:2955–6.
198. Gruner O, Bilzer N. [Modification of Alcomat breath alcohol measurements by various substances of routine use (mouthwash, perfume, after-shave lotion etc]. *Blutalkohol* 1990;27:119–30.
199. Foglio-Bonda PL, Poggia F, Foglio-Bonda A, Mantovani C, Pattarino F, Giglietta A. Determination of breath alcohol value after using mouthwashes containing ethanol in healthy young adults. *Eur Rev Med Pharmacol Sci* 2015;19:2562–6.
200. Chu M, Wells DL, King RG, Farrar J, Drummer OH. The effect of blood in the oral cavity on breath alcohol analysis. *J Clin Forensic Med* 1998;5:114–8.
201. Wigmore JG, Wilke MP. A simulation of the effect of blood in the mouth on breath alcohol concentrations of drinking subjects. *Can Soc Forensic Sci J* 2002;35:9–16.
202. Kechagias S, Jonsson KA, Franzen T, Andersson L, Jones AW. Reliability of breath-alcohol analysis in individuals with gastroesophageal reflux disease. *J Forensic Sci* 1999;44:814–8.
203. Nirwan JS, Hasan SS, Babar ZU, Conway BR, Ghori MU. Global prevalence and risk factors of Gastro-oesophageal Reflux Disease (GORD): systematic review with meta-analysis. *Sci Rep* 2020;10:5814.

204. Manterola C, Grande L, Bustos L, Otzen T. Prevalence of gastroesophageal reflux disease: a population-based cross-sectional study in southern Chile. *Gastroenterol Rep (Oxf)* 2020;8:286–92.
205. Gullberg RG. Breath alcohol analysis in one subject with gastroesophageal reflux disease. *J Forensic Sci* 2001;46:1498–503.
206. Booker JL, Renfroe K. The effects of gastroesophageal reflux disease on forensic breath alcohol testing. *J Forensic Sci* 2015;60:1516–22.
207. Begg TB, Hill ID, Nickolls LC. Breathalyzer and Kitagawa-Wright methods of measuring breath alcohol. *Br Med J* 1964;1:9–15.
208. Harding PM, McMurray MC, Laessig RH, Simley DO, 2nd, Correll PJ, Tsunehiro JK. The effect of dentures and denture adhesives on mouth alcohol retention. *J Forensic Sci* 1992;37:999–1007.
209. Cohen HM, Saferstein R. Mouth alcohol, denture adhesives and bretah-alcohol testing. *Drunk Driving Liquor Liability Reporter* 1992;6:24–30.
210. Ernstgard L, Pexaras A, Johanson G. Washout kinetics of ethanol from the airways following inhalation of ethanol vapors and use of mouthwash. *Clin Toxicol (Phila)* 2020;58:171–7.
211. Lindberg L, Grubb D, Dencker D, Finnhult M, Olsson SG. Detection of mouth alcohol during breath alcohol analysis. *Forensic Sci Int* 2015;249:66–72.
212. Edwards MA, Giguiere W, Lewis D, Baselt RC. Intoxilyzer interference by solvents. *J Anal Toxicol* 1986;10:125.
213. Aderjan R, Schmitt G, Wu M. [Glue solvent as the cause of a "breath alcohol value" of "1.96 promille"]. *Blutalkohol* 1992;29:360–4.
214. Oliver RD, Garriott JC. The effects of acetone and toluene on Breathalyzer® results. *J Anal Toxicol* 1979;3:99–101.
215. Cooper S. Infrared breath alcohol analysis following inhalation of gasoline fumes. *J Anal Toxicol* 1981;5:198–9.
216. Ran R, Mullins ME. Can handling E85 motor fuel cause positive breath alcohol test results? *J Anal Toxicol* 2013;37:430–2.
217. Woodall KL, Palmentier JP. Intoxilyzer® 8000C breath results obtained from a suspected impaired driver following reported occupational solvent exposure. *Can Soc Forensic Sci J* 2017;50:84–9.
218. Wallage HR, Bugyra IM. Interferent detect on the Intoxilyzer® 8000C in an individual with an elevated blood acetone concentration due to ketoacidosis. *Can Soc Forensic Sci J* 2017;50.
219. Martin TL. An evaluation of the Intoxilyzer® 8000C evidential breath alcohol analyzer. *Can Soc Forensic Sci J* 2011;44:22–30.
220. Jones AW, Andersson L. Determination of ethanol in breath for legal purposes using a five-filter infrared analyzer: studies on response to volatile interfering substances. *J Breath Res* 2008;2:026006.
221. Jones AW, Andersson L, berglund K. Interfering substances identified in the breath of drinking drivers with Intoxilyzer 5000S. *J Anal Toxicol* 1996;20:522–7.
222. Mazzone PJ. Analysis of volatile organic compounds in the exhaled breath for the diagnosis of lung cancer. *J Thorac Oncol* 2008;3:774–80.
223. Filipiak W, Ruzsanyi V, Mochalski P, Filipiak A, Bajtarevic A, Ager C, et al. Dependence of exhaled breath composition on exogenous factors, smoking habits and exposure to air pollutants. *J Breath Res* 2012;6:036008.
224. O'Hara ME, Clutton-Brock TH, Green S, Mayhew CA. Endogenous volatile organic compounds in breath and blood of healthy volunteers: examining breath analysis as a surrogate for blood measurements. *J Breath Res* 2009;3:027005.
225. Blanchet L, Smolinska A, Baranska A, Tigchelaar E, Swertz M, Zhernakova A, et al. Factors that influence the volatile organic compound content in human breath. *J Breath Res* 2017;11:016013.
226. Watterson JH. Assessment of response of the Intoxilyzer 8000C to volatiles of forensic relevance in vitro, part I: acetone, isopropanol, and methanol. *J Anal Toxicol* 2009;33:109–17.
227. Jones AW. Excretion of low-molecular weight volatile substances in human breath: focus on endogenous ethanol. *J Anal Toxicol* 1985;9:246–50.
228. Dallinga JW, Smolinska A, van Schooten FJ. Analysis of volatile organic compounds in exhaled breath by gas chromatography-mass spectrometry combined with chemometric analysis. *Methods Mol Biol* 2014;1198:251–63.
229. Jones AW. Breath-acetone concentrations in fasting healthy men: response of infrared breath-alcohol analyzers. *J Anal Toxicol* 1987;11:67–9.
230. Dubowski KM, Essary NA. Response of breath-alcohol analyzers to acetone. *J Anal Toxicol* 1983;7:231–4.
231. Dubowski KM, Essary NA. Response of breath-alcohol analyzers to acetone: further studies. *J Anal Toxicol* 1984;8:205–8.
232. Krishan S, Lui SM. A study of acetone interference in Intoxilyzer® 5000C. *Can Soc Forensic Sci J* 2002;35:159–64.
233. Smith DJ, Laslett R. Evaluation of the Drager Alcotest model 7110 infrared breath alcohol analysing instrument. *J Forensic Sci Soc* 1990;30:349–56.
234. Harte RA. An instrument for the determination of ethanol in breath in law-enforcement practice. *J Forensic Sci* 1971;16:493–510.
235. Hodgson BT, Taylor MD. Evaluation of the Dräger Alcotest 7110 MKIII Dual C Evidential Breath Alcohol Analyzer. *Can Soc Forensic Sci J* 2001;34:95–101.
236. Jones AW, Rossner S. False-positive breath-alcohol test after a ketogenic diet. *Int J Obes (Lond)* 2007;31:559–61.
237. Bailey DN. Detection of isopropanol in acetonemic patients not exposed to isopropanol. *J Toxicol Clin Toxicol* 1990;28:459–66.
238. Dwyer JB, Tamama K. Ketoacidosis and trace amounts of isopropanol in a chronic alcoholic patient. *Clin Chim Acta* 2013;415:245–9.
239. Jones AE, Summers RL. Detection of isopropyl alcohol in a patient with diabetic ketoacidosis. *J Emerg Med* 2000;19:165–8.
240. Li W, Liu Y, Cheng S, Duan Y. Exhaled isopropanol: new potential biomarker in diabetic breathomics and its metabolic correlations with acetone *RCS Adv* 2017;7:17480–88.
241. Jones AW, Lagesson V, Tagesson C. Determination of isoprene in human breath by thermal desorption gas chromatography with ultraviolet detection. *J Chromatogr B Biomed Appl* 1995;672:1–6.
242. Miekisch W, Schubert JK, Noeldge-Schomburg GF. Diagnostic potential of breath analysis--focus on volatile organic compounds. *Clin Chim Acta* 2004;347:25–39.
243. Hornuss C, Zagler A, Dolch ME, Wiepcke D, Praun S, Boulesteix AL, et al. Breath isoprene concentrations in persons undergoing general anesthesia and in healthy volunteers. *J Breath Res* 2012;6:046004.

244. de Lacy Costello BP, Ledochowski M, Ratcliffe NM. The importance of methane breath testing: a review. *J Breath Res* 2013;7:024001.
245. Kramer-Sarrett M, Lin E, Shari Chua K, Pichetshote N, Rezaie A, Pimentel M. Examination of the effects of breath hydrogen and methane levels on the EC/IR II. *Can Soc Forensic Sci J* 2017;50:125–30.
246. Cao J, Belluzzi JD, Loughlin SE, Keyler DE, Pentel PR, Leslie FM. Acetaldehyde, a major constituent of tobacco smoke, enhances behavioral, endocrine, and neuronal responses to nicotine in adolescent and adult rats. *Neuropsychopharmacology* 2007;32:2025–35.
247. Talhout R, Opperhuizen A, van Amsterdam JG. Role of acetaldehyde in tobacco smoke addiction. *Eur Neuropsychopharmacol* 2007;17:627–36.
248. Jones AW, Sato A, Forsander OA. Liquid/air partition coefficients of acetaldehyde: values and limitations in estimating blood concentrations from analysis of breath. *Alcohol Clin Exp Res* 1985;9:461–4.
249. Jones AW. Drug-alcohol flush reaction and breath acetaldehyde concentration: no interference with an infrared breath alcohol analyzer. *J Anal Toxicol* 1986;10:98–101.
250. Freund G, O'Hollaren P. Acetaldehyde concentrations in alveolar air following a standard dose of ethanol in man. *J Lipid Res* 1965;6:471–7.
251. Jones AW. Measuring and reporting the concentration of acetaldehyde in human breath. *Alcohol Alcohol* 1995;30:271–85.
252. Cowan JM, Jr, Oliver RD. An in vitro study of the effects of acetaldehyde on Intoxilyzer 4011AS-A results. *J Anal Toxicol* 1989;13:208–10.
253. ImObersteg AD, King A, Cardema M, Mulrine E. The effects of occupational exposure to paint solvents on the Intoxilyzer 5000: a field study. *J Anal Toxicol* 1993;17:254–5.
254. Denney RC. Solvent inhalation and 'apparent' alcohol studies on the Lion Intoximeter 3000. *J Forensic Sci Soc* 1990;30:357–61.
255. Dalley R. DUI and petrol consumption. *J Forensic Sci Soc* 1985;25:53–4.
256. Laakso O, Pennanen T, Himberg K, Kuitunen T, Himberg JJ. Effect of eight solvents on ethanol analysis by Drager 7110 Evidential breath analyzer. *J Forensic Sci* 2004;49:1113–6.
257. Bell CM, Gutowski SJ, Young S, Wells D. Diethyl ether interference with infrared breath analysis. *J Anal Toxicol* 1992;16:166–8.
258. Garriott JC, Foerster E, Juarez L, de la Garza F, Mendiola I, Curoe J. Measurement of toluene in blood and breath in cases of solvent abuse. *Clin Toxicol* 1981;18:471–9.
259. Jones AW, Lund M, Andersson E. Drinking drivers in Sweden who consume denatured alcohol preparations: an analytical-toxicological study. *J Anal Toxicol* 1989;13:199–203.
260. Cobb PGW, Dabbs MDG. *Report on the Performance of the Intoximeter 3000 and Camic Breath Evidential Instruments During the Period 16 April 1984 to 15 October 1984*. London: HMSO, 1985.
261. Gill R, Hatchett SE, Broster CG, Osselton MD, Ramsey JD, Wilson HK, et al. The response of evidential breath alcohol testing instruments with subjects exposed to organic solvents and gases. I. Toluene, 1,1,1-trichloroethane and butane. *Med Sci Law* 1991;31:187–200.
262. Gill R, Warner HE, Broster CG, Osselton MD, Ramsey JD, Wilson HK, et al. The response of evidential breath alcohol testing instruments with subjects exposed to organic solvents and gases. II. White spirit and nonane. *Med Sci Law* 1991;31:201–13.
263. Gill R, Osselton MD, Broad JE, Ramsey JD. The response of evidential breath alcohol testing instruments with subjects exposed to organic solvents and gases. III. White spirit exposure during domestic painting. *Med Sci Law* 1991;31:214–20.
264. Spanel P, Dryahina K, Smith D. A quantitative study of the influence of inhaled compounds on their concentrations in exhaled breath. *J Breath Res* 2013;7:017106.
265. Truchon G, Brochu M, Tardif R. Effect of physical exertion on the biological monitoring of exposure to various solvents following exposure by inhalation in human volunteers: III. Styrene. *J Occup Environ Hyg* 2009;6:460–7.
266. Lester D, Greenberg LA. The inhalation of ethyl alcohol by man. I. Industrial hygiene and medicolegal aspects. II. Individuals treated with tetraethylthiuram disulfide. *Q J Stud Alcohol* 1951;12:168–78.
267. Lewis MJ. A theoretical treatment for the estimation of blood alcohol concentration arising from inhalation of ethanol vapour. *J Forensic Sci Soc* 1985;25:11–22.
268. Mason JK, Blackmore DJ. Experimental inhalation of ethanol vapour. *Med Sci Law* 1972;12:205–8.
269. Kruhoffer PW. Handling of inspired vaporized ethanol in the airways and lungs (with comments on forensic aspects). *Forensic Sci Int* 1983;21:1–17.
270. MacLean RR, Valentine GW, Jatlow PI, Sofuoglu M. Inhalation of alcohol vapor: measurement and implications. *Alcohol Clin Exp Res* 2017;41:238–50.
271. Borkenstein RF. The evolution of modern instruments for breath alcohol analysis. *J Forensic Sci* 1960;5:395–407.
272. Harding P, Field PH. Breathalyzer accuracy in actual law enforcement practice: a comparison of blood- and breath-alcohol results in Wisconsin drivers. *J Forensic Sci* 1987;32:1235–40.
273. Martin E, Moll W, Schmid P, Dettli L. The pharmacokinetics of alcohol in human breath, venous and arterial blood after oral ingestion. *Eur J Clin Pharmacol* 1984;26:619–26.
274. Jones AW, Andersson L. Comparison of ethanol concentrations in venous blood and end-expired breath during a controlled drinking study. *Forensic Sci Int* 2003;132:18–25.
275. Harger RN, Raney BB, Bridwell EG, Kitchel MF. The partition ratio of alcohol between air and water, urine and blood: estimation and identification of alcohol in these liquids from analysis of air equilbrated with them. *J Biol Chem* 1950;183:197–213.
276. Jones AW. Determination of liquid/air partition coefficients for dilute solutions of ethanol in water, whole blood, and plasma. *J Anal Toxicol* 1983;7:193–7.
277. Hlastala MP, Anderson JC. Alcohol breath test: gas exchange issues. *J Appl Physiol* 2016;121:367–75.
278. Hlastala MP, Anderson JC. The impact of breathing pattern and lung size on the alcohol breath test. *Ann Biomed Eng* 2007;35:264–72.
279. Jones AW. Role of rebreathing in determination of the blood-breath ratio of expired ethanol. *J Appl Physiol Respir Environ Exerc Physiol* 1983;55:1237–41.
280. Jones AW. How breathing technique can influence the results of breath-alcohol analysis. *Med Sci Law* 1982;22:275–80.
281. Mulder JA, Neuteboom W. The effects of hypo- and hyperventilation on breath alcohol measurements. *Blutalkohol* 1987;24:341–7.
282. Anderson JC, Hlastala MP. The alcohol breath test in practice: effects of exhaled volume. *J Appl Physiol* 2019;126:1630–5.
283. Fransson M, Jones AW, Andersson L. Laboratory evaluation of a new evidential breath-alcohol analyser designed for mobile testing--the evidenzer. *Med Sci Law* 2005;45:61–70.

284. Lindberg L, Brauer S, Wollmer P, Goldberg L, Jones AW, Olsson SG. Breath alcohol concentration determined with a new analyzer using free exhalation predicts almost precisely the arterial blood alcohol concentration. *Forensic Sci Int* 2007;168:200–7.
285. Mason MF, Dubowski KM. Breath-alcohol analysis: uses, methods, and some forensic problems--review and opinion. *J Forensic Sci* 1976;21:9–41.
286. Turnbridge R. *Fifty Years of the Breathalyser - Where Now for Drink Driving?* London: Parliamentary Advisory Council for Transport, 2017.
287. Jones AW, Andersson L. Variability of the blood/breath alcohol ratio in drinking drivers. *J Forensic Sci* 1996;41:916–21.
288. jones AW, Cowan DM. Reflections on variability in the blood–breath ratio of ethanol and its importance when evidential breath-alcohol instruments are used in law enforcement. *Forensic Sci Res* 2021;6:1–6.
289. Morris MJ. Alcohol breath testing in patients with respiratory disease. *Thorax* 1990;45:717–21.
290. Seccombe LM, Rogers PG, Buddle L, Karet B, Cossa G, Peters MJ, et al. The impact of severe lung disease on evidential breath analysis collection. *Sci Justice* 2016;56:256–9.
291. Stephens A, Franklin SD. Level of lung function required to use the Camic Datamaster breath alcohol testing device. *Sci Justice* 2001;41:49–52.
292. Crockett AJ, Rozee M, Laslett R, Alpers JH. Minimum lung function for breath alcohol testing using the Lion Alcolmeter SD-400. *Sci Justice* 1999;39:173–7.
293. Gomm PJ, Broster CG, Johnson NM, Hammond K. Study into the ability of healthy people of small stature to satisfy the sampling requirements of breath alcohol testing instruments. *Med Sci Law* 1993;33:311–4.
294. Gomm PJ, Osselton MD, Broster CG, Johnson NM, Upton K. Study into the ability of patients with impaired lung function to use breath alcohol testing devices. *Med Sci Law* 1991;31:221–5.
295. Logan BK, Distefano S, Case GA. Evaluation of the effect of asthma inhalers and nasal decongestant sprays on a breath alcohol test. *J Forensic Sci* 1998;43:197–9.
296. Gomm PJ, Weston SI, Osselton MD. The effect of respiratory aerosol inhalers and nasal sprays on breath alcohol testing devices used in Great Britain. *Med Sci Law* 1990;30:203–6.
297. Gomm PJ, Osselton MD, Broster CG, Johnson NM, Upton K. The effect of salbutamol on breath alcohol testing in asthmatics. *Med Sci Law* 1991;31:226–8.
298. Ignacio-Garcia JM, Ignacio-Garcia JM, Almenara-Barrios J, Chocron-Giraldez MJ, Hita-Iglesias C. A comparison of standard inhalers for asthma with and without alcohol as the propellant on the measurement of alcohol in breath. *J Aerosol Med* 2005;18:193–7.
299. Westenbrink W, Sauve L. The effect of asthma inhalers on the A.L.E.R.T. J3A, Breathalyzer 900A and Mk IV GC Intoximeter. *Can Soc Forensic Sci J* 1991;24:23–35.
300. Haas H, Morris JF. Breath-alcohol analysis in chronic bronchopulmonary disease. *Arch Environ Health* 1972;25:114–8.
301. Hahn RG, Jones AW, Billing B, Stalberg HP. Expired-breath ethanol measurement in chronic obstructive pulmonary disease: implications for transurethral surgery. *Acta Anaesthesiol Scand* 1991;35:393–7.
302. Briggs JE, Patel H, Butterfield K, Honeybourne D. The effects of chronic obstructive airways disease on the ability to drive and to use a roadside alcolmeter. *Respir Med* 1990;84:43–6.
303. Lindberg L. A review of basic physical properties and physiological mechanisms involved in alcohol airway exchange proccesses and the alcohol breath test. *Blutalkohol* 2018;55:395–415.
304. Cowan JM, Burris JM, Hughes JR, Cunningham MP. The relationship of normal body temperature, end-expired breath temperature, and BAC/BrAC ratio in 98 physically fit human test subjects. *J Anal Toxicol* 2010;34:238–42.
305. Jones AW. Quantitative measurements of the alcohol concentration and the temperature of breath during a prolonged exhalation. *Acta Physiol Scand* 1982;114:407–12.
306. Ohlsson J, Ralph DD, Mandelkorn MA, Babb AL, Hlastala MP. Accurate measurement of blood alcohol concentration with isothermal rebreathing. *J Stud Alcohol* 1990;51:6–13.
307. Hlastala MP. Paradigm shift for the alcohol breath test. *J Forensic Sci* 2010;55:451–6.
308. Dubowski KM, Essary NA. Evaluation of commercial breath-alcohol simulators: further studies. *J Anal Toxicol* 1991;15:272–5.
309. Cowan M, Burns J, Hughes J, Cunningham M. The relationship of normal body temperature, end-expired bretah temperature and BAC/BrAC ratio in 98 physically fit human test subjects. *J Anal Toxicol* 2010;34.
310. Jones AW. Effects of temperature and humidity of inhaled air on the concentration of ethanol in a man's exhaled breath. *Clin Sci (Lond)* 1982;63:441–5.
311. Gaylarde PM, Stambuk D, Morgan MY. Reductions in breath ethanol readings in normal male volunteers following mouth rinsing with water at differing temperatures. *Alcohol Alcohol* 1987;22:113–6.
312. Fox GR, Hayward JS. Effect of hypothermia on breath-alcohol analysis. *J Forensic Sci* 1987;32:320–5.
313. Fox GR, Hayward JS. Effect of hyperthermia on breath-alcohol analysis. *J Forensic Sci* 1989;34:836–41.
314. Wigmore JG. Up to their necks in hot water: body temperature and the BAC/BrAC ratio. *J Anal Toxicol* 2010;34:605–6.
315. Wigmore JG. *Wigmore on Alcohol: Courtroom Alcohol Toxicology for the Medicolegal Professional.* Toronto: Irwin Law Inc, 2011.
316. Milroy CM. A brief history of the expert witness. *Acad Forensic Pathol* 2017;7:516–26.
317. Lynoe N, Elinder G, Hallberg B, Rosen M, Sundgren P, Eriksson A. Insufficient evidence for "shaken baby syndrome" – a systematic review. *Acta Paediatr* 2017;106:1021–7.
318. Lynoe N, Rosen M, Elinder G, Hallberg B, Sundgren P, Eriksson A. Pouring out the dirty bathwater without throwing away either the baby or its parents: commentary to Saunders et al. *Pediatr Radiol* 2018;48:284–6.
319. Hand L. Historical and practical considerations regarding expert testimony. *Hav L Rev* 1901;40:53–65.
320. Jones AW. Dealing with uncertanty in chemical measurements. *IACT Newsletter* 2003;14:6–11.
321. Gullberg RG. The relationship between duplicate reproducibility and concentration in breath alcohol testing programs. *J Anal Toxicol* 1992;16:272–3.
322. Jones AW, Schuberth J. Computer-aided headspace gas chromatography applied to blood-alcohol analysis: importance of online process control. *J Forensic Sci* 1989;34:1116–27.
323. Vosk T, Emery AF. *Forensic Metrology: Scientific Measurement and Inference for Lawyers, Judges, and Criminalists.* Boca Raton: Taylor & Francis, 2015.
324. Hlastala MP. The alcohol breath test--a review. *J Appl Physiol (1985)* 1998;84:401–8.

325. Beran RG. The role of the expert witness in the adversarial legal system. *J Law Med* 2009;17:133–7.
326. Margot P. The role of the forensic scientist in an inquisitorial system of justice. *Sci Justice* 1998;38:71–3.
327. Dror IE. Biases in forensic experts. *Science* 2018;360: 243.
328. Chin JM, McFadden R. Expert witness codes of conduct for forensic practitioners: a review and proposal for reform. *Can J Law & Justice* 2020;23:23–50.
329. O'Brien E, Nic Daeid N, Black S. Science in the court: pitfalls, challenges and solutions. *Philos Trans R Soc Lond B Biol Sci* 2015;370.

3.6 GLOSSARY OF TERMS

3.6.1 Forensic Aspects of Ethanol

Alan Wayne Jones

Forensic science and legal medicine are multidisciplinary topics and toxicology is one of the key sub-disciplines. In this connection, the toxic substance most often encountered during investigations of living subjects as well as medical examiner (post-mortem) cases is ethanol or ethyl alcohol. This A-Z glossary is intended to serve as a complement to the various chapters including in the ETHANOL section of Drug Abuse Handbook (3rd edition). Indeed, many items in the glossary might also be relevant for the chapters dealing with use and abuse of other psychoactive substances. Some entries in the glossary (acronyms, words, phrases) are explained in more detail than others, although this was done intentionally to enhance the learning process.

A

Absorption: This refers to the uptake of a drug or poison (e.g., alcohol) from outside of the body into the bloodstream.

Abstinence: The state or condition of remaining free of alcohol or other drugs (see also, "abstainers").

Accreditation: A formal process by which a laboratory is evaluated, with respect to established criteria, for its competence to perform a specified type of work.

Accuracy: A statistical measure of the closeness of agreement between the analytical result and the true (known or assigned) value of the quantity.

Acidosis: Too much acid (low pH) in the blood and body fluids (opposite = alkalosis).

Acute: Something that happens suddenly, usually severe, often dangerous, such as acute on-set of an illness, or rapid administration of a drug.

Acute tolerance: The development of tolerance within the course of a single exposure to a drug.

Addictive drug: This usually refers to a psychoactive substance, which is self-administered without a medical prescription, repeatedly and compulsively.

ADME: Acronym for absorption, distribution, metabolism, and excretion – often used in connection with the disposition and fate of drugs in the body.

Agonal event: A final event occurring when a person dies – whether or not it actually contributes to the death – e.g., terminal bronchopneumonia or inhalation of stomach contents (see below, under aspiration).

Agonist: An agonist drug is a chemical substance that binds to a receptor to produce an effect or start a sequence of events leading to a physiological response.

Alcoholic ketoacidosis (AKA): An excess of ketone bodies in the blood that might result after a period of continuous heavy drinking. During a drinking binge, alcoholics might neglect to eat properly and many are malnourished, because their caloric needs (energy) come from the combustion of ethanol (7.1 kcal per gram).

Alcoholic strength: This is the term used to denote the amount of ethanol in a solution, such as an alcoholic beverage (beer, wines, and neat spirits), and is usually reported as a percentage by volume (% v/v) or (% ABV) alcohol by volume.

Alcohols: A collective name for a class of organic compounds containing carbon, hydrogen and oxygen, and one or more hydroxyl (-OH) groups. Alcohols are often classified as mono-hydroxy (e.g., methanol), di-hydroxy (e.g., ethylene glycol), tri-hydroxy alcohols (e.g., glycerol), and poly-hydroxy (e.g., mannitol).

Alcohol dehydrogenase (ADH): An enzyme located in the cytosol fraction of hepatocytes that catalyzes the conversion of primary alcohols into aldehydes and secondary alcohols into ketones. Thus, ethanol is oxidized into acetaldehyde and isopropanol is converted to acetone.

Alcohol-withdrawal: Alcohol-withdrawal refers to a spectrum of unpleasant symptoms that occur when an alcoholic suddenly stops drinking. These symptoms can develop into life-threatening physiological and psychological disturbances of body functions if a long period of heavy drinking ends abruptly.

Aldehyde dehydrogenase (ALDH): An oxidative enzyme mainly located in liver mitochondria that converts the toxic metabolite of ethanol (acetaldehyde) into less toxic acetic acid.

Algor Mortis: From the Latin words for cooling and death (Mortis), hence, a drop in body temperature after death is also known as "the chill of death."

Aliquot: A portion of the biological sample removed by weight or volume and subjected to analysis.

Alveolar air: This is deep-lung air in equilibrium with the pulmonary-arterial blood. Obtaining unadulterated alveolar air for analysis of ethanol and other volatiles is not possible, but, instead, a specimen of end-exhaled breath is captured for analysis.

Analyte: The specific component measured in a chemical analysis.

Analytical run: A set or series of measurements carried out successively by one analyst using the same measuring system, at the same location, under the same conditions, and during the same period of time, usually the same day.

Analytical sensitivity: The ability of a method or instrument to discriminate between samples having different concentrations of the analyte. The slope of the analytical calibration function (plot) is one index of a method's sensitivity; the steeper the slope the more sensitive is the method.

Analytical specificity: The ability of a method of analysis to determine solely the compound it purports to measure, and to discriminate between other substances that might also be present in the specimen received for analysis.

Analytical toxicology: This entails extraction, detection, identification, and quantitative analysis of drugs and poisons (xenobiotics) and their metabolites in biological fluids and tissues.

Analytical wavelength: Any wavelength at which an absorbance measurement is made for the purpose of the determination of a constituent of a sample.

Antagonist: A chemical substance (drug) that binds to a receptor to block or reverse the action of another drug or chemical substance; Naloxone is an opiate antagonist that reverses the action of morphine at its receptor.

Antemortem: Refers to conditions or events before death.

Anterograde amnesia: Loss of memory for events occurring subsequent to an event that caused the amnesia, such as the administration of a drug. Long-term memories from before the event remain intact. This contrasts with retrograde amnesia where memories created prior to the event are lost.

Anthropometric data: Measurements of body height, weight, age, and skin-fold thickness can provide an indirect assessment of body composition, body size, and development.

Antiseptic: An agent that inhibits or destroys microorganisms on living tissue including skin, oral cavities, and open wounds.

Apnea: Apnea is the cessation of breathing (see asphyxia), often temporarily, such as might occur during sleep, hence, "obstructive sleep apnea." Holding the breath is an example of voluntary apnea.

Area under the Curve: Abbreviated as AUC, this refers to the area under the concentration-time profile of ethanol – or another drug – in blood, plasma, or some other body fluid obtained by repetitive sampling.

Artefact: An artificial product or result in relation to an autopsy, owing to post-mortem changes.

Asphyxia: A term derived from Greek, literally meaning "pulseless." This might result from a lack of oxygen as occurs after mechanical restriction of breathing, owing to choking, drowning, suffocation, or compression of the neck (strangulation or hanging).

Asphyxiation: Synonymous with asphyxia and refers to loss of consciousness occurring when the blood supply to the brain fails to deliver sufficient oxygen. Asphyxiation can occur after smothering, strangling, choking, drowning, exposure to noxious gases, or overdosing with drugs.

Aspiration: Refers to pulmonary aspiration of stomach contents into the airways and lungs, which prevents the flow of oxygen. Often a common finding during post-mortem examination, although its significance needs careful investigation, because it might be caused by an agonal event or after death. In a limited number of cases, it is probably significant in precipitating death in severely intoxicated individuals or those comatose or unconscious after overdosing with alcohol or other sedative drugs.

Assignable cause: A cause believed to be responsible for an identifiable change in precision or accuracy of a measurement process.

Ataxia: This is the inability to coordinate voluntary muscle movements, owing to various external influences (drugs or diseases) acting on the cerebellum.

Auto-brewery syndrome: Also known as gut fermentation syndrome, this refers to the endogenous synthesis of ethanol in the gut by fermentation of dietary carbohydrates.

Autolysis: Self-digestion of the tissues after death owing to chemical and/or enzyme activity. This enzymatic self-digestion occurs at an early stage, before the much more destructive changes caused by the action of bacteria (putrefaction).

Autopsy: The word autopsy comes from the Greek word *autopsia*, meaning "to see for oneself" (*autos* = oneself and *opsis* = eye). In the U.K., the term "necropsy" is used as an alternative word to autopsy, which comes from the Greek word for "seeing a dead body." In the USA "autopsy" is synonymous with the post-mortem examination done by a medical examiner.

B

Back-calculation: Back-calculation (back-tracking or retrograde extrapolation) refers to calculating the BAC or BrAC at the time of driving from the analytical results at the time of sampling, often several hours after a traffic offense.

Baseline measure: An observation made or a quantitative measurement before administration of any experimental treatment or procedure, such as alcohol or a drug. When the results of an experiment are evaluated, the post-treatment measures are compared with the baseline measures.

BBB: Short for blood-brain-barrier, a dynamic interface between the circulatory system and the central nervous system (the brain). The BBB consists of specialized endothelial cells with main function of protecting the brain from potentially harmful substances in the food eaten or toxins in the environment.

Beer's law: This concerns the absorbance of light by a homogeneous sample containing an absorbing substance in direct proportion to the concentration of that substance.

Bias: Refers to a tendency of an analytical method or procedure to give results distant from the true or known value (systematic error).

Bile: This is a greenish-yellow fluid produced in the liver and stored in the gall bladder, a pear-shaped organ lying just underneath the liver. Bile is released into the duodenum to aid in the digestion of lipids and facilitate absorption of nutrients from the small intestine into the portal venous blood.

Binge drinking: Two definitions of binge drinking are in current use. (1) Consumption of sufficient ethanol within two hours to reach a blood alcohol concentration of 0.08 g% or higher. (2) A period of continuous heavy drinking over several days, hence, "a binge," during which time other duties are neglected.

Bioavailability: Often denoted as "F" describes the fractional extent to which an administered dose of a drug reaches the systemic circulation after a particular route of administration, usually oral intake. By definition $F = 1$ after intravenous administration.

Biological matrix: The composition of the biological material that is being processed for analysis and might consist of differing amounts of proteins, fats, water, and other biomolecules.

Biomarkers: These are endogenous substances analyzed in blood or other biological specimen to assess the prognosis of developing a disease, exposure to chemicals, or efficacy of a certain treatment.

Biotransformation: The chemical conversion of a drug into its metabolites, involving some chemical conversion; oxidation, reduction, hydrolysis (phase 1 reactions) or acetylation, sulfation, or glucuronidation (phase 2 reactions).

Blank: A blank sample has a composition similar to the material submitted for analysis but the target analyte is lacking. A blood sample with no detectable drugs present is analyzed along with the actual routine cases to ensure that no false-positive results are obtained.

Blind (masked) sample: A test of proficiency in which the analyst or participating laboratory is unaware of the origin of the test sample at the time of the analysis. An undeclared proficiency trial entails submitting samples for analysis blinded or masked.

Blinding: A term often used in connection with clinical trials of drug treatments in which knowledge of the intervention or treatment is hidden from participants and/or investigators (single-blind), or both (double-blind).

Blind-stick: Referring to a method of obtaining biological fluid samples from a corpse, either before or without the need for dissection of the body.

Bloating: A feature of decomposition and the result of anaerobic bacteria digesting the tissues and producing various malodorous gases (ammonia, hydrogen sulfide, aliphatic amines)

Blood: Fluid circulating through the heart and blood vessels the volume of which in an adult corresponds to about 7–8% of the bodyweight (~5.5 liter). Whole blood contains ~80% w/w water and cellular elements comprised of red cells (erythrocytes), white cells (leukocytes), and platelets suspended in the plasma fraction (a pale yellow liquid).

Blood-brain barrier: A permeable barrier consisting of cells and small blood vessels having the important task of controlling the passage of endogenous and exogenous substances from the bloodstream into the brain and cerebrospinal fluid.

BMI: An acronym for body mass index serving as a useful measure of the degree of obesity. BMI is derived by dividing the person's weight in kg by their height in meters squared, hence the units (kg/m^2). Normal BMI is 18.5 to 24.9, overweight spans from 25–29.9 kg/m^2.

Bolus: A bolus dose refers to the amount of drug swallowed at one time.

Bone marrow: A semi-solid material in the interior of many bones (mainly long bones) where blood cells are manufactured.

Brainstem: The stem-like part of the brain that connects the cerebral hemispheres with the spinal cord.

C

Calibrant: A chemical substance obtained from a reliable and traceable source commonly used to calibrate an instrument to establish its analytical response as a function of concentration.

Calibration: A process or sequence of steps in which an analytical instrument or method is standardized to permit making quantitative or semi-quantitative measurements. This might entail the purchase or preparation of know authentic standard substances. The instrument response can then be adjusted to conform to this known standard quantity or concentration.

Case-controlled study: A type of epidemiological study design often utilized to identify factors that contribute to a certain medical condition, for example by comparing a group of patients suffering from the ailment (e.g., alcoholism or drug dependence) with a group of patients not previously diagnosed with this condition.

Candida Albicans: A type of yeast or fungus sometimes present in living human subjects (on skin, mouth, gut, or vagina), that can utilize glucose to produce ethanol. Systemic candidiasis is a much rarer and potentially fatal condition.

Cardiac: Pertaining to the heart.

Cause of death: The physical or medical condition that directly caused the victims death. This contrasts with *manner* of death, i.e., accident, suicide, or homicide. Cause of death can only be determined after a consideration of the deceased's medical history, the circumstances of the death and the findings from a post mortem examination (with or without further laboratory investigations), and toxicological analysis. In the case of unnatural deaths, the cause is usually established after an inquest and then recorded on a death certificate.

CEDIA: This is an acronym for **C**loned **E**nzyme **D**onor **I**mmuno**A**ssay, which has become a widely used analytical technique in clinical and forensic laboratories.

Central nervous system (CNS): The part of the nervous system consisting of the brain and spinal cord.

Cerebellum: The structure at the base of the brain involved in the control of skeletal muscles, balance, and sensorimotor coordination of movements.

Cerebral cortex: This is the outer layer of gray matter covering the cerebellum. The cerebral cortex processes sensory information needed for the control of motor functions, speech, higher cognitive functions, emotions, behavior, and memory.

Cerebrospinal fluid: The clear fluid that fills the cavities (ventricles) that surround the brain and spinal cord.

Certification: A written declaration that a particular product or service complies with stated criteria.

Certified value: A value printed on a certificate that states the amount of substance or some other property of a certified reference material along with its inherent uncertainty.

Chain-of-custody: Abbreviated COC is the procedure used to document the way that laboratories receive and handle the specimens starting at time of collection, during transport, arrival at the laboratory, registration, and throughout the testing process. Maintaining COC is important to document in legal testimony integrity of the analytical result.

Chromatography: A widely used method of analysis that is able to separate compounds in a mixture based on their differential rates of movement through a two-phase system (e.g., gas-liquid, liquid-liquid, solid-liquid). The rate of movement of the molecules is determined by various physicochemical properties, such as size, solubility, boiling point, electric charge, and functional groups present in the molecules.

Chronic: Persistent, prolonged, repeated.

Chronic tolerance: The gradual decrease in pharmacological effect of a drug, e.g., intoxication by alcohol that builds up gradually in the course of repeated exposures.

Cirrhosis: A word derived from the Greek *kirrhos* (meaning a tawny color), referring to the yellowish-orange color of a diseased (cirrhotic) liver. This contrasts with the normal healthy liver, which is dark brown and smooth. A type of chronic progressive liver disease in which the liver cells are replaced by scar tissue.

Clinical Pharmacology: The word pharmacology derives from a Greek word for drug (*pharmakon*) and discourse or reasoning (logos). Clinical pharmacology is concerned with the safe and effective therapeutic management of a patient with medicines. This is tightly linked to the concentrations of drugs determined in blood or plasma in relation to their therapeutic efficacy – hence, the emergence of therapeutic drug monitoring (TDM) programs.

Coefficient of variation: The standard deviation divided by the mean value of the parameter, usually expressed as a percentage.

Cognition: The term cognition involves all the mental functions through which information and knowledge are processed. It includes global functions such as consciousness, drive, and attention as well as specific functions like memory, language, and calculations.

Coma: A state of profound unresponsiveness, usually the result of a blow or injury to the skull and brain. However, a person might become unconscious for other reasons, such as from overconsumption of alcohol or taking other psychoactive drugs. A comatose patient typically has closed eyes, cannot be roused, and fails to respond to active "painful" stimuli, such as a pin-prick (see Glasgow Coma Scale).

Comparative method: An independent analytical method used to analyze an aliquot of the same specimen to verify the correctness of a result.

Concentration: The quantity of a substance contained in a unit quantity of sample. When working with solutions, the recommended unit of concentration is grams of solute per liter of solution.

Confidence interval: The range of values calculated from an estimate of the mean and the standard deviation, which is expected to include the population mean with a stated level of confidence.

Confirmation: Synonymous with verification and refers to a second test done using an alternate method of analysis to identify with certainty the presence of a drug or metabolite.

Control chart: A graphical plot of the results of an analysis with respect to time or sequence of measurement. The chart usually has upper and lower control limits within which the results are expected to fall when the method is working under statistical control.

Control sample: A material of known composition that is analyzed concurrently with test samples to evaluate the measurement process.

Controls: These are known strength solutions analyzed in parallel with experimental (unknown) samples designed to demonstrate the method is working correctly.

Confirmatory tests: An independent test used to verify (confirm) the presence of a particular compound in a biological specimen and usually requires some type of chromatography to separate closely relation substances followed by detection and quantitation of a target analyte by mass spectrometry or other highly sensitive and selective conclusive method.

Confounding: Extraneous variables causing effects that obscure or exaggerate the "true" effect of an intervention or treatment.

Congener: A substance or thing of the same kind or form, e.g., the other constituents of alcoholic beverages besides ethanol and water, such as other alcohols, aldehydes, and esters.

Correlation coefficient: This is a statistic that measures the strength of the relationship between two variables, such as that between the analytical results obtained by two different methods on the same sample or the strength of association between any two variables.

COPD: Is an acronym for **C**hronic **O**bstructive **P**ulmonary **D**isease, which is a common lung disorder in adults.

Coroner: An elected official, usually a physician or lawyer, charged with investigating sudden, violent or unnatural deaths and producing a death certificate where cause and manner of death are reported. A medical examiner does this same work in many jurisdictions of the USA.

Craving: This refers to an intense desire to re-experience the effects of a psychoactive substance and represents the principal reason that people relapse to abuse of drugs after a period of abstinence.

Cross-over design: This refers to a repeated measurement experimental design whereby the same subject or patient serves as his or her own control.

Cross-reactivity: This refers to the response caused by the presence of a substance other than the target drug intended to be analyzed. Usually, an antibody for an immunoassay recognizes only a part of the target drug by binding to a specific functional group or structure in the molecule.

Cross tolerance: A physiological **c**ondition in which tolerance to the effects of one drug results in a diminished response to the effects of another substance.

Cutaneous: Associated with the skin – subcutaneous = beneath the skin.

Cut-off level: This is some threshold value serving as an administrative decision limit to differentiate drug-positive from drug-negative samples.

Cyanosis: A bluish coloration of the skin of the face and extremities caused by a reduced oxygen content of the blood (low level of oxyhemoglobin) near the skin surface. The word derives from Greek for the color blue (cyan).

Cytochrome P450: A family of enzymes found in animals, plants, and bacteria that play an important role in drug metabolism.

D

Decomposition: In pathology this refers to the continuous process of decay of a body after death by a combination of chemical and enzymatic digestion (autolysis) and the action of bacteria and other micro-organisms, most of which are derived from the normal intestinal flora. The first evidence of putrefaction is a greenish discoloration of the skin over the lower abdomen (the part nearest the bowel).

Delirium: This describes a shifting mental state as reflected in altered cognition and perception and behavior, sometimes with hallucinations and an abnormal speech pattern.

Depressant drug: A class of psychoactive drugs, both licit and illicit, that relieve anxiety by depressing the central nervous system (CNS).

Detoxification: The process by which the body rids itself of a drug (or its metabolites). During this withdrawal period, unpleasant and sometimes life-threatening symptoms can emerge that may require medical treatment.

Diabetic ketoacidosis (DKA): This is a life-threatening condition caused by an accumulation of ketone bodies (acetone, acetoacetate, and β-hydroxybutyric acid) in the blood. People suffering from DKA are unable to utilize glucose and glycogen as energy sources, owing to an insulin deficiency caused by conditions, such as diabetes.

Digestive system: The organs responsible for getting food into and out of the body comprising the esophagus, stomach, liver, gallbladder, pancreas, small intestine, colon, and rectum.

Disinfectant: A chemical or physical agent that destroys or removes vegetative forms of harmful microorganisms when applied to a surface.

Disposition: This refers to the sum of all pharmacokinetics processes after a drug reaches the blood circulation, including distribution and elimination (metabolism and excretion) but excluding absorption and other pre-systemic processes.

Distribution: The transport of absorbed drug or alcohol by the bloodstream to all parts of the body. The distribution of alcohol follows the distribution of body water and the rate of distribution depends on the flow rate of blood to various organs and tissue.

Dosage form: The dosage form of a drug refers to the actual physical form in which the drug is given to the patient, liquid, solid, spray, cream.

Dose-response relationship: The quantitative relationship between the quantity (dose) of a drug administered and the effect or response it produces on the individual. The study of dose-response relationships is a fundamental part of pharmacology and testing of drug toxicity, LD_{50}.

Drug Addiction: A chronic relapsing disorder in which compulsive drug-seeking and drug-taking behaviors persist despite serious negative consequences for the individual and his or her family and friends.

Drug-related death: Any death in which the underlying cause was intoxication by intake of alcohol or some other drug or even an idiosyncratic reaction to drugs. Many of the victims are users of recreational drugs or they engage in inappropriate polypharmacy with medicinal drugs.

DSM-V codes: Diagnostic and statistical manual of mental disorders, 5th edition is a reference book published by the American Psychiatric Association with detailed information about all currently recognized mental health disorders.

Dubowski chart: A table, originally designed by Professor Kurt M Dubowski (Oklahoma City, U.S.) showing signs and symptoms of alcohol influence in relation to a person's blood-alcohol concentration (BAC).

DUI: Acronym for driving under the influence (usually under the influence of alcohol).

DUID: Acronym for driving under the influence of drugs.

Duodenum: The first part (~12 inches) of the small intestine extending from the pylorus to the jejunum.

Duplicate determination: A second measurement made on an aliquot of the same specimen thus allowing a direct comparison between the two analytical results. Close agreement between the duplicates indicates a high precision.

DWI: Acronym for driving while impaired or intoxicated (usually taken to mean impairment caused by alcohol).

E

Elimination: The term used to denote removal of a drug (e.g., alcohol) from the body. The process of elimination involves both metabolic breakdown (biotransformation) and removal in an unchanged form, such as in breath, urine, and sweat (excretion).

ELISA: Is an acronym for **E**nzyme **L**inked **I**mmuno**S**orbent **A**ssay a method mainly developed as a preliminary screening analysis of a range of abused drugs in urine or other body fluids.

EMIT: Is an acronym for **E**nzyme **M**ultiplied **I**mmunoassay **T**echnique, which is widely used in analytical toxicology as a preliminary screening test, such as during urine drug testing programs. EMIT is a homogenous assay and a major advantage is that a prior clean-up or extraction of the target analyte from the biological matrix prior to analysis is not necessary.

Emaciated: Abnormally thin or weak, especially because of illness or a lack of food.

Embalming: Treatment of a corpse with chemical preservatives in an effort to prevent further decay and help maintain as normal an appearance as possible. Typical embalming fluids might contain solvents, such as formaldehyde (10 vol%), glutaraldehyde, ethanol, and/or methanol.

Endogenous: Produced or originating within the body by natural processes such as intermediary metabolism, opposite to exogenous.

Enzymes: Proteins that act as biological catalysts to enable certain chemical reactions to proceed at a body temperature of 37°C.

Error: The word error comes from a Latin root for wander or stray, although in the field of metrology a measurement "error" does not necessarily mean a mistake was made.

Erythrocytes: The name given to the red blood cells.

Esophagus: A tube-like structure connecting the pharynx with the stomach.

Etiology: Relating to the cause of disease or the study of such causes.

Ethyl glucuronide: Abbreviated as EtG, this is a non-oxidative metabolite of ethanol formed in the liver by a phase 2 enzyme-catalyzed reaction involving glucuronic acid (glucuronidase). EtG is eliminated from the body more slowly than ethanol itself, which makes it useful to analyze as a biomarker of recent drinking.

Ethyl sulfate: Often abbreviated EtS is a non-oxidative metabolite of ethanol formed in the liver by a phase 2 enzyme-catalyzed reaction involving sulfatase and ethanol.

Evisceration: Deprive someone of their essential contents (gutted) hence removal of the internal organs during an autopsy examination, for inspection and dissection. Samples of blood for forensic toxicology (preferably from a femoral vein), are normally taken after starting an autopsy but before evisceration.

Excretion: This refers to the removal of alcohol or other drug from the body in an unchanged form, usually in excreta – urine, breath, sweat, stools, and saliva (if the latter is ejected as oral fluid).

Exsanguination: From the Latin for "out of" ("ex") and "sanguine" (blood). Hence, an appreciable loss of blood, owing to internal or external hemorrhage – a common cause of death after trauma.

External proficiency tests: These are designed to test the proficiency of work done at analytical laboratories. A good track record in such tests has become an important element in laboratory accreditation.

Extravascular: Outside of the bloodstream.

Extracellular fluid: Denotes all body fluids outside the cells (interstitial fluid, plasma volume, and transcellular fluid) amounting to about 20% of bodyweight or about 14 liters.

F

False-negative result: An erroneous result of an analysis assay that indicates the absence of a drug when it is actually present.

False-positive result: An erroneous result of an analysis that indicates a substance is present, when in reality it is not.

Fatal toxicity index (FTI): For a certain prescription drug is commonly defined as the absolute number of fatal poisonings in a region or a country linked to use of that particular medication expressed as a ratio to the sales (prescriptions) of the medication over the same time period.

Fatty acid ethyl esters (FAEE): These are compounds formed in the body by enzyme-catalyzed reactions between ethanol and various short-chain fatty acids, such as ethyl palmitate, ethyl stearate, ethyl oleate, and ethyl linoleate.

Femoral blood: Peripheral venous blood taken at the groin (i.e., femoral vein), which is the preferred specimen for the toxicological analysis of alcohol and other drugs as evidence of drug use by a deceased person.

Fermentation: An enzymatically controlled anaerobic decomposition of carbohydrates to produce ethanol with concomitant liberation of carbon dioxide.

First-order kinetics: The change in drug concentration at any time (-dC/dt) is proportional to the concentration in blood or plasma at that time. Proportionally more of the drug is eliminated at high concentrations in blood than at low concentrations.

First-pass metabolism: This refers to the metabolism (removal) of part of the dose of a drug such as alcohol when administered orally and before it reaches the systemic circulation. First-pass metabolism can occur either in the stomach or in the liver and for some substances also in the lung.

Forensic: From the Latin word *forensis* meaning of the forum. In ancient Rome the forum was where debates took place and as such served as the courtroom.

Forensic toxicology: A scientific discipline closely related to analytical chemistry that deals with the isolation, identification, and quantitative analysis of drugs, poisons, and their metabolites in biological specimens and the interpretation of the analytical results in a legal or medico-legal context.

Frontal cortex: The front part of the brain involved with reasoning, planning, problem-solving, and other higher cognitive functions

Fuel cell: A fuel cell is a device that converts energy from a chemical reaction into electricity through a chemical reaction with oxygen. Such electrochemical detectors are widely used in instruments for breath-alcohol analysis.

G

GABA: This is an acronym for gamma-aminobutyric acid. GABA, which is the major inhibitory neurotransmitter in the brain and activation of GABA receptors lowers activity of nerve cells and applies brakes on the brain.

Gag reflex: A reflex contraction at the back of the throat evoked by touching the pharynx. In individuals comatose through intoxication or injury, this reflex is absent, putting them at risk of inhaling vomit into the airways and lungs.

Gas Chromatography: An analytical technique widely used for separating volatile substances on the basis of their solubility and partition between a gas and a liquid phase (GLC) or a gas and solid phase (GSC).

Gastric bypass: A surgical procedure used in the treatment of morbid obesity that involves bypassing the duodenum and other segments of the small intestine.

Gastric contents: The material contained in the stomach which in the investigation of a death may provide some information about the post mortem interval and the composition of the last meal eaten.

Gastrointestinal tract: A hollow tube of variable diameter extending from the mouth to the anus with the function of taking in, digesting, and absorbing foodstuffs and fluids into the body. The tract comprises the esophagus, stomach, small intestine, large intestine, rectum, and anus, some sections controlled by sphincters which open and close as foodstuffs pass along.

Gastroparesis: Gastro pertains to the stomach and *paresis* means paralysis, hence, paralysis of the stomach a condition in which gastric emptying is delayed.

GERD: Abbreviation for gastroesophageal reflux disease, which is a clinical syndrome that manifests as heartburn and regurgitation, owing to reflux of gastric contents into the esophagus.

Glasgow Coma Scale (GCS): A clinically useful neurological scale originally developed by neurosurgeons working in Glasgow, Scotland to judge the state of consciousness in trauma patients. Individual elements of the scale include assessment of eyes, verbal communication and motor responses, and perception of pain (pin-prick). The three elements separately and their sum are used in a final diagnosis. The lowest possible GCS score is three (deep coma or death), while the highest is 15 (fully awake).

GLP: Is short for **G**ood **L**aboratory **P**ractice and refers to the quality of work being done at analytical and clinical laboratories.

H

Habituation: Is the process of becoming accustomed to any behavior or condition, including the use of psychoactive substances. Habituation is often taken to mean dependence. In 1957, a WHO Expert Committee distinguished habituation from drug addiction on the basis of the absence of physical dependence, desire rather than compulsion to take the drug, and little or no tendency to increase the dose (see tolerance). In 1964, another WHO Expert Committee replaced both terms with drug dependence.

Half-life: The elimination half-life ($t_{½}$) of a drug is an important concept in clinical pharmacology because it expresses the rate of change in concentration in blood or plasma in units of time. For drugs metabolized by first-order kinetics, the half-life is the time required for the concentration in blood or plasma and/or the amount of drug in the body to decrease by half or 50%.

Hallucinogens: These are drugs or naturally occurring substances that after ingestion can bring about a state of dreaming or wandering of the mind characterized by an altered perception of sights and sound.

Hangover: A post-intoxication state comprising the immediate after-effects of excessive drinking of alcoholic beverages. Some believe that the non-ethanol components of alcoholic beverages (so-called congeners) might be involved in the etiology of hangover. Subjective feelings of hangover include fatigue, headache, thirst, vertigo, gastric disorder, nausea, vomiting, insomnia, fine tremors of the hands, and raised or lowered blood pressure. Psychological symptoms include acute anxiety, guilt, depression, irritability, and extreme sensitivity.

Headspace sampling: Headspace is the gaseous phase above a sample (e.g., blood or urine) of a liquid or solid material that contains volatile or semi-volatile compounds that are released from the liquid or solid material.

Hyperglycemia: An excessive amount of glucose in the blood.

Hematocrit: The percentage of blood volume occupied by erythrocytes; normal values often usually cited as being between 44–54% for men and 38–48% for women. Blood with lower hematocrit (e.g., from a person with anemia) will have more plasma relative to red-cells and therefore a higher percentage of water.

Hemolysis: This term is used to describe the bursting or breakage of red blood cell (RBC) membranes, causing the release of hemoglobin and other constituents into the surrounding fluid. A reddish coloration of the serum or plasma fraction gives evidence that a blood specimen has undergone hemolysis.

Hemorrhage: The loss of blood from a ruptured blood vessel.

Henry's law: This refers to a scientific principle discovered by William Henry (1774–1836) that teaches us about the solubility of gases. The concentration of a volatile substance dissolved in a liquid in a closed container and kept at a constant temperature and pressure is directly proportional to the concentration of that substance in the air phase in equilibrium with the liquid.

Hepatic vein: This is the vein that receives blood after it passes through the central veins of the liver transporting blood into the inferior vena cava of the heart.

Hepatitis: Generalized inflammation of the liver and characterized by jaundice, fever, liver enlargement, and abdominal pains.

Hepatocyte: The name of the principal cells within the liver responsible for most of the metabolic activity.

Histogram: A histogram is a graphical method used to display the frequency of continuous date, such as a person's height, age, or concentration of a substance in blood.

Homeostasis: The maintenance of a relatively constant internal body condition; a state of equilibrium within the body with respect to functions and chemical composition of body fluids and tissues.

HPLC: This is an acronym for High-Performance Liquid Chromatography a widely used analytical technique in forensic and other laboratories for separation and quantification of chemical substances such as drugs of abuse in bio-fluids.

Hyperglycemia: High blood glucose, which is a medical condition characterized by an excessive amount of glucose circulating in the bloodstream.

Hippocampus: A seahorse-shaped structure located within the brain that constitutes an important part of the limbic system. One of the most studied areas of the brain, the hippocampus plays key roles in learning, memory, and emotion.

Hypoglycemia: An abnormally low concentration of glucose in the blood, which is a potentially life threatening medical condition requiring emergency treatment.

Hypostasis: One of the early post mortem changes, sometimes known as lividity (and occasionally as livor mortis) caused by the settling of blood in the tissues after death. This process develops within a matter of hours after death and is complete after 12–18 h. When the heart stops pumping the blood coagulates in veins and arteries as reflected in the appearance of dark bluish-gray patches on the skin.

Hypoventilation: The term hypoventilation defines a condition in which alveolar ventilation is insufficient to meet the metabolic demands of the individual and carbon dioxide content in blood is too high.

Hypothermia: This is a reduced or lowered body temperature, such as when the body dissipates more heat than it absorbs. In humans hypothermia is defined as a core body temperature lower than 35°C, that is, 2 degrees below normal (37°C). The signs and symptoms of mild hypothermia are shivering and mental confusion, whereas in severe hypothermia there are reports of paradoxical undressing.

Hypovolemia: A state of decreased blood volume, usually associated with hemorrhage as a result of trauma or from internal or external bleeding. Normal blood volume in adults is ~7% of bodyweight or 4.9–5.6 L in a person weighing 70–80 kg. Loss of ~20% of blood volume causes a hypovolemic shock, which requires emergency treatment and administration of replacement fluids.

Hypovolemic shock: The shock associated with massive loss of blood leading to an inadequate supply of oxygen to the brain. This precipitates a range of physiological responses and requires swift emergency measures to maintain circulation, blood pressure, and an adequate supply of oxygen to the brain, such as by administration of intravenous replacement fluids.

Hypoxia: A diminished or inadequate supply of oxygen, or utilization of oxygen in the blood supplied to various body tissues.

I

ICD-10 codes: Short for International Classification of Disease, Version 10, is a document that provides a means of coding various diseases and causes of death in a systematic way. The codes were developed and agreed upon by the World Health Organization (WHO) in an effort to standardize mortality statistics, both nationally and internationally.

Idiosyncratic reaction: A rare and unexpected reaction to a drug treatment, which is often an adverse effect of taking certain medication or dietary factors, probably with an immune-related mechanism of toxicity.

Iliac veins: The veins draining blood from the pelvis and lower limbs and into which the femoral veins flow. They represent a source of peripheral blood, which is a useful sampling site for toxicological analysis.

Impairment: A state of diminished performance in physical or mental ability as a result of a medical condition or after the consumption of alcohol or intake of other psychoactive drugs. Impairment is reflected in a person's decreased ability to perform skilled tasks, such as driving.

Infrared: Pertaining to the region of the electromagnetic spectrum from approximately 0.78 to 300 microns.

Interfering substance: A chemical substance other than the target analyte that the method of analysis responds to falsely elevate the analytical result.

Inter-individual variation: The amount of variation in a set of measurements between different individuals, between-subject variability.

Intoxication: The intoxicated state, when this is caused by excessive drinking is referred to as drunkenness, or inebriation. A person's physical or mental control and capacity are diminished, owing to the effects of psychoactive drugs on the brain.

Intra-cranial: Within or introduced into the skull.

Intra-individual variation: The amount of variation in a set of measurements when repeated within the same individual (within-subject variability).

Intravascular: Within the blood vessels.

In-vitro: From the Latin meaning *in glass* a term commonly used to signify experiments done in a test tube or flask as opposed to in the living organism.

In-vivo: From the Latin meaning *in the living body* a term commonly used to signify tests made with living subjects (humans or animals).

J

Jejunum: Pertaining to the second part of the small intestine from the duodenum to the ileum.

K

Ketogenic diet: This refers to eating meals with high fat and low carbohydrate content that mimics prolonged starvation. The use of fat as an energy source results in the accumulation of ketone bodies in the blood (acetone, β-hydroxybutyrate, and acetoacetate). High fat and low carbohydrate diets (Atkins) are often used by dieters or people suffering from obesity.

Ketoacidosis: A metabolic condition associated with abnormally high concentrations of ketone bodies in the blood and tissues, mainly β-hydroxybutyrate, but also acetoacetate (AcAc) and acetone. The excess of keto-acids lowers pH of the blood (more acidic), sometimes reaching dangerously low levels resulting in coma and/or death. Such a diagnosis is common in patients with untreated diabetes mellitus, because the body derives its calories from the metabolism of lipids and fatty acids, whereby ketone bodies are produced and these accumulate in blood and tissues.

Ketone bodies: These are the end-products of lipid (fat) metabolism whereby triglycerides are transformed into free fatty acids and then acetylCoA, which functions as a precursor of acetoacetate. This latter compound either undergoes non-enzymatic decarboxylation to give acetone or is reduced enzymatically in a NAD-NADH reaction to give β-hydroxybutyrate.

Ketonemia: Excess ketone bodies (acetone, acetoacetate, and β-hydroxybutyrate) in the blood.

Ketonuria: Excess ketone bodies in the urine.

L

LD_{50}: Abbreviation for lethal dose 50 or "median lethal dose," corresponding to the amount of a substance (the dose) necessary to kill 50% of a test population of animals, usually mice or rats.

Licit: Means lawful or permitted and describes pharmaceutical preparations obtainable on prescription or over-the-counter as opposed to illicit or unlawful drugs classified as controlled (scheduled) substances, such as heroin, methamphetamine, and cannabis.

Limbic system: This complex brain system comprises several structures associated with memory and emotion. Damage to this area of the brain impairs each of these functions.

Limit of detection (LOD): The lowest concentration of a drug that can reliably distinguished from a blank.

The smallest result of a measurement that can be reported with a desired level of confidence as being present. Usually defined as 3 x standard deviation of measuring blank samples.

Limit of quantification (LOQ): The lower limit of concentration or amount of substance that must be present before a method is considered to provide quantitative results. By convention, LOQ = 10 times standard deviation of the blank.

Linearity: This reflects the ability of a method to give results that are directly proportional to the concentration of the target analyte or can be expressed by a well-defined mathematical transformation of the response as a function of concentration over a certain range.

Linear regression: A mathematically method to describe the relationship between two or more variables and which entails calculating a best-fitting straight line to a set of data points, the x-variable is denoted as the independent and the y-variable the dependent.

Liver: The largest internal body organ and the most important organ for drugs detoxification. In a healthy adult the liver weights ~1.5 kg and its blood supply comes from the portal vein and the hepatic artery; average flow rate is ~1.5 L per minute.

Livor-mortis: Also known as lividity or hypostasis is a pooling of the blood after death. Manifesting in a dark blue staining of the skin surface on a cadaver, resulting from pooling and congestion of blood.

Lumen: In biology, a lumen is the inside space of a tubular structure, such as an artery or vein or the stomach or intestine. The gastric lumen is the inside space of the stomach.

M

Macronutrients: Refers to dietary nutrients as sources of energy and are required in large quantities, namely protein (4 kcal per g), fat (9 kcal per g) and carbohydrate (4 kcal per g).

Malnutrition: Undernourishment, a condition that develops when the body does not receive sufficient nutrients

Manner of death: The circumstances under which death occurs – hence, *how* a death came about, as opposed to the actual physical cause of death, thus reflecting its general nature. Typically, a death would be classified as natural, accidental, suicidal, homicidal, or undetermined.

Matrix: The material that contains the analyte of interest, e.g., blood, urine, or tissue.

Matrix effects: Influence of a normal component in the analytical sample, other than the substance being investigated, on reliability of the measurement being made.

Median: The middle value of a ranked set of measurement data. For skewed data, the median is a better measure of central tendency than the arithmetic mean and is always lower than the mean. In a normal distribution, the mean and median are the same.

Medulla oblongata: This is the lower portion of the brainstem, where the centers for the control of autonomic functions (such as breathing and heartbeat) are located.

Mellanby effect: Named after Sir Edward Mellanby (1884–1955) a British pharmacologist who noted that the effects of a given dose of ethanol were more pronounced on the ascending limb of the blood alcohol curve (absorption phase) compared with the descending limb (post-absorptive phase). Another term for this phenomenon is acute tolerance.

MEOS: Acronym for microsomal ethanol oxidizing system, an enzyme system located in the smooth endoplasmic reticulum of liver cells that converts ethanol to acetaldehyde.

Metabolism: The name given to various chemical reactions occurring in a cell, an organ, or the body as a whole. The term is sometimes applied more narrowly to the breakdown of a particular substance – e.g., the degradation of ethanol or some other drug by specific enzymes.

Metabolite: A compound produced by a chemical (enzymatic) reaction taking place in the body, such as the metabolism of a drug or other substance; acetaldehyde is the proximate metabolite of ethanol.

Metrology: The science of measurement.

Micronutrients: Refers to the vitamin and mineral constituents of the diet.

Microsomal enzymes: Detoxifying enzymes associated with certain membranes and abundant in smooth endoplasmic reticulum within hepatocytes.

Microsomes: Subcellular particles of liver cells obtained by differential centrifugation after specimens of this body organ are homogenized and are contained in the smooth endoplasmic reticulum. Various drug-metabolizing enzymes in the microsomal fraction include CYP2E1, CYP2D6, and CYP2C19, where CYP stands for cytochrome.

Microvilli: Plural of villus, referring to small vascular protrusions growing on a mucous surface. The intestinal villi are the microscopic thread-like or finger-like projections covering the mucosa of the small intestine, with main function of increasing the absorption surface area.

Michaelis-Menten (M-M): Leonor Michaelis (1875–1949) and Maud Menten (1879–1960) collaborated to develop an equation to describe the kinetics of biochemical reactions in terms of a capacity limited process (saturation kinetics), often associated with enzymatic reactions.

Mode: The most frequently occurring value in a set of numbers.

Motor function: This is a general term and refers to movement, mobility and behavior.

MS: Short for mass spectrometry a powerful analytical technique used to identify compounds based on their mass to charge ratios.

N

NAD: Acronym for nicotinamide adenine dinucleotide (NAD), which is an important cellular coenzyme that accepts a hydrogen atom during biochemical reactions.

Necropsy: A synonym for autopsy or post-mortem examination often used in Great Britain.

Neoformation: Means new formation or generation and is used in forensic medicine and toxicology to signify formation of ethanol in bodies after death.

Neuron: A nerve cell – the functional unit of the nervous system consisting of the nerve cell body, the dendrites, and the axon.

Neurotransmitters: These are brain chemicals that transmit messages from one nerve cell (neuron) to another. They are located and released in the brain and an impulse travels through the axon that can activate or inhibit an adjacent neuron.

Nystagmus.: An involuntary movement of the eye ball, usually involving quick and jittery movements of both eyes and can occur both horizontally and vertically – bouncing or jerking movement. Gaze nystagmus occurs when the eyes gaze or move to the side along a horizontal plane.

O

Obesity: The word obesity is derived from the Latin word meaning "to overeat." A person is considered obese if they have a body mass index (BMI) over 30 kg/m^2.

Obtundation: This refers to less than full alertness or an altered level of consciousness typically as a result of a medical condition, trauma, or the effects of an impairing drug, close to a comatose state.

Ordinal scale: Ordered set of measurements consisting of words and/or numbers indicating the magnitude of the possible values that a type of quantity can take.

Osmolality: Is used in clinical chemistry as an expression of the concentration of a biological fluid, e.g., serum or urine. It is expressed in terms of the total number of solute particles present per kilogram solvent (water). A random urine void might have an osmolality ranging from 50 to 1400 mOsmol/kg

OUI: Acronym for operating a motor vehicle under the influence of alcohol, which is an alternative term used in some jurisdictions for driving a motor vehicle when under the influence of alcohol (DUI) or driving while intoxicated (DWI).

Outlier: One value in a series of measurements so distant from the other data points as to suggest that it may come have some unusually large error of measurement or mistake.

Overdose deaths: This refers to deaths caused directly by the consumption of one or more drugs commonly referred to as poisonings or drug-induced deaths.

P

Palcohol: Brand name for powdered alcohol (ethanol) that has been absorbed into a carbohydrate, such as dextrin to produce a dry state instead of a liquid.

Parallel group design: In a parallel group design experiment, the patients or test subjects are randomized into two separate groups and each group receives one particular treatment throughout the study.

Parenteral: Parenteral is defined as something that is put inside the body, but not by swallowing. An example of something parenteral is an injection given into a muscle, beneath the skin (subcutaneous) or by injection into a vein (intravenous).

Pathogenesis: The physiological and biochemical mechanisms, by which diseases start, develop and progress.

Pathology: The word pathology comes from the Greek word *pathos*, suffering, distressed state, or the disturbance of vital processes.

PBT: Acronym for **P**reliminary **B**reath **T**est and alludes to testing the sobriety of drivers, usually with a hand-held breath analyzer at the roadside in close proximity to driving.

Perimortem: At or near the time of death.

Peer review: The judgment of something, usually a scientific article or study (manuscript), by referees "peers" with documented expertise and experience in the same or a closely related area of research.

Per se: This is a Latin expression for "in or by itself" and in forensics is used in connection with statutory concentration limits of alcohol in blood, breath, or urine above when a motorist is in violation of the law, hence a per se statute.

Pharmacodynamics: The study of the relationship of drug concentration to its effects on the individual — what the drug does to the body.

Pharmacogenetics: Is from the Greek words *pharmacon* (drug or poison) and genetics and is the study of the role of inheritance on inter-individual variation in drug response. Pharmacogenetics entails studies of racial, ethnic, and genetic factors that alter kinetics and dynamics of drugs and related substances that could explain the observed variability in pharmacokinetic parameters.

Pharmacokinetics: The study of the time course of drugs in the body (absorption, distribution, metabolism, and excretion ADME) – what the body does to the drug.

Phenotype: The observable properties, traits, or physical appearance of an organism resulting from the interaction of the genotype with environmental factors.

Phlebotomy: This pertains to the process of making an incision in a vein with a needle, also known as venipuncture.

Phosphatidylethanol: Abbreviated PEth is an abnormal phospholipid formed in cell membranes in the presence of ethanol in a reaction catalyzed by the enzyme phospholipase D.

Physical dependence: A state that develops after chronic long-term exposure to a psychoactive drug. The individual develops tolerance and in parallel with this a condition of physical dependence. This is reflected in the emergence of physiological disturbances (abstinence) when intake of the drug is terminated.

Placebo: Derived from the Latin "I shall be acceptable or pleasing" and is a treatment that lacks any known pharmacological effect.

Plasma: The yellowish clear liquid component of an anticoagulated blood specimen. The blood specimen is spun-down and the supernatant plasma is removed for analysis. Plasma contains fibrinogen. The plasma volume in an adult is approximately 4 liters.

Pleural fluid: Fluid that accumulates in the pleural or chest cavity, the normally empty space surrounding each lung. It may be produced in heart failure, pneumonia, or during decomposition and while not recommended as a specimen for toxicological analysis, owing to the risk of contamination from nearby stomach contents, in decomposed bodies it may be the only fluid available.

Poison: A chemical substance or natural product, which after absorption into the body by various routes of administration (ingestion, inhalation, injection, or through the skin) disturbs normal body functioning, damages organs and/or tissues, and sometimes results in death.

Polypharmacy: This is defined as the chronic co-prescribing of several drugs and which can result in adverse drug-drug interactions and sometimes death.

Polyuria: The excretion of large volumes of urine, greater than 3 L per day, and one of the cardinal signs of diabetes.

Popliteal vein: A peripheral vein in the leg, lying behind the knee and leading into the femoral vein, and a potential source of blood for use in toxicological analysis as an alternative specimen.

Portal vein: The name of a large blood vessel that collects blood from the stomach and intestine and transports absorbed nutrients, drugs, and other orally ingested substances to the liver.

Positional asphyxia: A form of mechanical asphyxia caused by inappropriate positioning of the body of a person, which adversely affects their breathing. People might be unconscious or comatose, owing to excessive drinking or a drug overdose, and then lay in a contorted position so that their breathing is severely compromised. This leads to a combination of respiratory depression, asphyxia and subsequent death.

Postprandial: The physiological condition or state after eating a meal.

Post-mortem: After death pertaining to a post-mortem examination or autopsy.

Post-mortem changes: Physical changes which occur in the body after death, starting at the moment of death and continuing for weeks and months thereafter. The initial changes are temperature drop, hypostasis and rigor mortis, followed by decomposition as the body tissues degenerate and disappear. While many variables can affect the speed and nature of the changes, particularly temperature, they can nevertheless be of some use in estimating time since death, at least in the early period.

Post-mortem diffusion: The passive diffusion of alcohol and/or other drugs from higher concentrations in the stomach contents into the surrounding blood and tissue compartments, which occurs after death. This diffusion process can falsely raise the concentrations of drugs in post-mortem blood in relation to the antemortem concentrations.

Post-mortem examination: Also known as necropsy or autopsy.

Post-mortem interval (PMI): The time that elapses between death and discovery of the body i.e., time since death. Estimation of the PMI provides important information in many investigations of unnatural deaths. Much depends on past experience and knowledge of the normal physical changes that occur in the body after death and to what extent these are predictable (see above under post mortem changes and related entries).

Post-mortem redistribution (PMR): Time-dependent change in concentration of drugs in blood after death depending on properties of the drug itself and the sampling site. PMR is one of the factors that complicate interpreting post-mortem drug concentrations and relating these to antemortem concentrations. Drug concentrations in central or cardiac blood (C) tend to be higher than in peripheral blood (P) and a high C/P concentration ratio is taken as one indication that post-mortem drug redistribution has occurred. Diffusion of drugs from the stomach into surrounding tissues and blood vessels after death is another aspect of PMR. In general, drugs with large volumes of distribution (e.g., tricyclic antidepressants) are especially prone to re-distribute after death, and for this class of drugs and probably for many others the post-mortem concentrations should not be equated with antemortem concentrations.

Potentiation: The action of two drugs for which the combined effects are greater than the sum of the individual effects.

Precision: Closeness of agreement between independent results of repeated measurement of the same quantity under prescribed conditions (standard deviation).

Presumptive tests: These are preliminary analytical tests, mostly qualitative tests, often involving a color change of a chemical reagent after mixing with a test specimen. The main application of such tests is for broad screening purposes to identify a class of compounds, such as certain types of drugs and poisons.

Prevalence: The frequency with which a variable (condition, symptom, disease, or trait) occurs in the population at a certain point in time. Prevalence is the measure of the number of cases at a single point in time and has no units.

Proficiency-testing: A scheme to evaluate the performance of an analytical method used in different laboratories. Specimens are usually shipped to the various participants as a declared proficiency trial.

Psychoactive substances: Drugs (licit or illicit) which, after administration reach the bloodstream and cross the blood-brain barrier to interact in regions of the brain that are important for behavior. This manifests in altered perception, changes in mood, impaired cognition and/or motor functioning, etc. Psychoactive substances are either legitimate medicines or recreational drugs of abuse and include opioid and opiate analgesics, sedative-hypnotics, central nervous stimulants, and/or hallucinogens.

Psychomotor: Pertaining to muscular activity associated with the mental process.

Psychomotor functioning: Motor functions as a consequence of mental activity.

Psychosis: Severe mental disorder, with or without organic damage, characterized by deterioration of normal intellectual functioning. Partial or complete withdrawal from reality and seeing hallucinations.

Psychotropic: Having a mind-altering effect, e.g., psychotropic drugs.

Psychotropic drug: A drug with its main site of action in the central nervous system (brain) often associated with altered mood, disturbed thought processes and behavior.

Pulmonary: Pertaining to or associated with the lungs.

Pulmonary edema: The build-up of fluid in the air sacs of the lungs. This condition commonly occurs in natural diseases, such as heart failure, but may also be one feature in other terminal events, such as drug overdose, particularly with heroin or other opiates.

Purge fluid: Otherwise known as decomposition fluid, this is a reddish-brown liquid that emerges from the nose and mouth and other body orifices during decomposition. This process results in the build-up of gas within the body cavities and tissues. Purge fluid is occasionally submitted for toxicological analysis when no other fluids are available, although great care is needed when drug concentrations in "purge" are interpreted.

Putrefaction: The main process in decomposition, the word being derived from putrid (foul-smelling or rotten). It is the last of the post-mortem changes to occur and under normal circumstances starts two to three days after death. In putrefaction, the body decays as anaerobic bacteria split proteins into simpler malodorous molecules. Putrefactive processes can interfere with the toxicological analysis of some drugs, such as ethanol and GHB, the concentrations of which increase after death.

Pylorus: The sphincter muscle separating the stomach from the small intestine, also called *pyloric sphincter.*

Q

Qualitative test: Chemical analysis to identify one or more components of a mixture.

Quality assurance: Abbreviated as QA, this pertains to the overall practices and procedures designed to assure that laboratory results are accurate and precise for the intended purpose.

Quality control: Abbreviated as QC, this pertains to various techniques and procedures applied to monitor the performance of a laboratory and the results of the analyses they undertake.

Quantitative test: Chemical analysis to determine the amounts or concentrations of one or more components of a mixture.

R

Range: The difference between the largest and smallest values in a collection of measurements.

RBT: Acronym for random breath test (RBT), alluding to testing drivers for alcohol influence without any prior suspicion of alcohol consumption.

Reaction time: The time interval between presentation of a stimulus and initiation of a response.

Receptor: A protein embedded in the wall of a neuron or other cell that recognizes and binds a neurotransmitter or other chemical messenger.

Recovery: A characteristic of an analytical method – normally expressed as a percentage – and referring to the amount of drug removed from the original sample, that reaches the end of the analytical procedure. Poor recovery can be compensated for by adding an internal standard to the bio-fluid before starting the analysis.

Reference standard: A sample prepared or purchased that has known properties in terms of identity, purity, chemical composition, and concentration. Reference standards are used for the purpose of calibrating analytical equipment and for use as a control of the accuracy of the method.

Relapse: This refers to the resumption of drug-seeking or drug-taking behavior after a period of abstinence.

Repeatability: Closeness of agreement between the results of successive measurements during a short time (the within-run standard deviation).

Reproducibility: Closeness of agreement between the results of repeated measurements over longer time periods and obtained by different observers, using different calibrations (between-run standard deviation).

Resuscitation fluid: Sterile fluids administered intravenously to critically ill or trauma patients, such as after massive blood loss. Examples include physiological saline, albumin, Ringers lactate, and various blood substitutes. In a patient who subsequently dies, giving a large volume of resuscitation fluid can alter the concentrations of alcohol and/or other drugs in biological samples taken at autopsy.

Retrograde extrapolation: The practice of estimating a person's blood or breath alcohol concentration at some time prior to the time of obtaining a specimen for analysis - back extrapolation, back-tracking.

RIA: Acronym for radioimmunoassay, a highly sensitive in-vitro analytical technique involving radio-labeled molecules.

Rigor-mortis: The stiffening of muscles after death (rigidity), owing to depletion of adenosine triphosphate (ATP), the normal energy source within muscle fibers allowing them to contract and relax. Rigor mortis is one of the early post-mortem changes, beginning within the first few hours and up to 18 h until it is fully developed. It diminishes by 24–48 h with the onset of decomposition. Hence, the slang American word "stiff" referring to a dead body. Rigor is delayed in cold and hypothermic conditions, and accelerated in warm conditions.

Route of administration: Defines the way a drug gets into the bloodstream. Although oral ingestion is the most convenient route, under some circumstances this might not be practical. For example, after swallowing a drug it has to pass the gastrointestinal canal and liver where metabolism can occur. The usual route of administration is by swallowing or drinking (oral), but some drugs are administered via the lungs by inhalation (smoking), or injected directly into an artery, muscle, or vein, or even under the skin (subcutaneously).

S

Saccadic eye movements: Rapid conjugate movements of the eyes when a person is instructed to follow a target object.

Scatter plot: A scatter plot usually displays the relation between two continuous variables plotted on the x- and y-axes. A one-way or one-dimensional scatter plot may be used to display a single continuous variable.

SCRAM: Acronym for Secure, Continuous, Remote, Alcohol, Monitoring a device that measures alcohol in perspiration. A SCRAM device is often worn as an ankle bracelet by people who, for various reasons, are not permitted to consume alcohol.

Screening analysis: A series of initial tests designed to differentiate drug positive from negative samples or whether the concentrations present are above or below some threshold value.

Screening device: In connection with traffic law enforcement, a screening device refers to a small handheld breath analyzer used by police officers to test for alcohol influence. Such testing is usually done at the roadside close to the time of driving and positive results give an indication of whether a more elaborate test should be done.

Screening test: Screening refers to early detection of a disease or condition. Early detection allows for medical intervention at an earlier stage in the development of the disease. In addiction medicine, individuals are screened for damage to body organs and tissue caused by excessive consumption of alcohol.

Seizure: The clinical consequence of abnormal electrical activity in the brain reflected in altered behavior patterns and movement. Seizures are a common cause of drug toxicity and intoxication in overdose deaths. Seizures might also result from abrupt withdrawal of drugs after a period of continuous chronic usage (e.g., alcohol withdrawal).

Sensitivity: The detection limit, expressed as a concentration of the analyte in the specimen.

Sensorimotor functions: Functions involving perception of information from the senses and the resulting physical reactions of muscles.

Serum: The clear fluid portion of blood remaining after coagulation (removal of fibrin and blood cells). If a chemical test requires serum then the blood sample must be drawn into a tube that will allow the sample to clot (red top evacuated tubes).

SFST: Acronym for **S**tandardized **F**ield **S**obriety **T**ests and refers to a set of tests done with people suspected of driving under the influence of alcohol (or drugs). Such tests are conducted by a trained police officer, usually at the roadside, with the aim of gathering probable cause to make an arrest for further more elaborate evidential testing. SFSTs comprise a battery of three tests including one-leg-stand, walk-and-turn, and gaze nystagmus.

Side effects: The effects of a drug other than the desired or intended ones. These undesirable or adverse effects sometimes have dangerous consequences for the patient and might prove fatal.

Signs and symptoms: In medicine, a symptom is generally a subjective observation, whereas a sign is objective. The flushing in the face, heavy breathing, high blood pressure, hypoglycemia are signs commonly observed by a physician. By contrast, stomach aches, other types of pain, and fatigue are symptoms reported by the patient.

Skin slippage: One of the signs of putrefaction (along with discoloration, bloating, and marbling), as the outer layers of the skin peel off and hair and nails begin to detach.

Slurred speech: A typical clinical sign of intoxication e.g., after drinking alcohol or taking certain drugs resulting in imprecise speech articulation including deviation in rate, pitch and intensity and often an incorrect production of consonants and vowels.

Small intestine: The small intestine (small bowel) consists of a long coiled tube about 5 m in length into which digested foodstuffs from the stomach empty and from which the bulk of the body's nutrients and other substances are absorbed. Although a continuous structure, it has three parts – the duodenum which is relatively short, the jejunum which is much longer, and the ileum which ultimately leads into the large intestine.

SOP: This is an acronym for **S**tandard **O**perating **P**rocedure and refers to written instructions used by people working at a laboratory when they perform a test or conduct an analysis of a sample sent to the laboratory.

Specificity: The quality of an analytical technique that tends to exclude all substances apart from the analyte of interest.

Specificity of a diagnostic test: This is defined as the proportion of healthy subjects in whom the test results were negative.

Splanchnic: A term occasionally used to describe organs in the abdominal cavity. The term splanchnic circulation describes the blood flow to the abdominal gastrointestinal organs including the stomach, liver, spleen, pancreas, small intestine, and large intestine.

Split samples: Laboratory specimen that is divided into two portions and submitted to the analyst, unknown to him or her, as two different specimens with different identifications.

Standard drink: In the U.S., one standard drink contains 14 gram ethanol, and this corresponds to consumption of 5 oz (150 ml) table wine (12 vol%), 1½ oz (45 mL) spirits (40 vol%), 12 oz (360 mL) beer (5 vol%).

Steatosis: Accumulation of fat in the liver, often caused by heavy consumption of alcohol, a condition more commonly referred to as fatty liver.

Sterile: Sterile conditions implies the complete absence of micro-organisms including bacteria, fungi and other micro-organisms.

Stimulants: Represent a class of drugs that stimulate the central nervous system (CNS) by interfering with the brain's neurotransmitters.

Stupor: A state in which a person is almost unconscious and non-responsive.

Substrate: The substance (molecule) acted upon by an enzyme.

Subdural hematoma: This is an accumulation of blood between the dura (the outer layer of the meninges covering the brain) and the brain itself. By far the most common cause of a hematoma is from a head injury or trauma, such as falling or striking the head. Such injuries often occur when people are under the influence of alcohol. Onset of symptoms might take up to 24 h after the traumatic event, when the bleeding gradually compresses the brain. This leads to progressive drowsiness, disorientation, nausea, vomiting, and without emergency surgical intervention, subdural hematomas are a common cause of death.

Symptom: Any subjective evidence of a disease or of a patient's condition.

Synapse: Region of a nerve cell (neuron), from which nerve signals are transmitted to neighboring neurons. The synapse is a microscopic gap (or cleft) separating pre-synaptic and post-synaptic neurons.

Synovial fluid: Straw-colored viscous fluid within the joints where it serves as a lubricant, with the largest volumes being found in the knee joints. It has been used as an alternative specimen for toxicological analysis in certain circumstances.

T

TBW: Acronym for total body water, which depends on a person's age, gender, and degree of adiposity. TBW is often reported as a percentage of a person's bodyweight and for healthy non-obese adults TBW is about 50% of bodyweight for women (35 L if 70 kg) and 60% (42 L if 70 kg) for men.

TDM: An acronym for Therapeutic Drug Monitoring, which refers to the analysis of biological samples, usually blood, plasma or serum, to determine the concentration of medicinal drugs at specified times after dosing as a way to control that the expected concentrations of the active substance are reached.

Thantology: The study of death and dying and the underlying circumstances. From Greek "thanatos" meaning death and "ology" meaning study of or learning.

Therapeutic index (ratio): This is a way to express a drug's relative safety margin commonly defined as the ratio between the dose producing toxicity in 50% of patients to the dose that produces the desired therapeutic response in 50% of patients ($TI = TD_{50}/ED_{50}$). If a drug has a TI of 100, this means that the toxic dose is about 100 times larger than the effective dose and this particular drug has a wide safety margin.

Therapeutic interval: Also referred to as therapeutic range, defines the concentration range of a drug in serum or plasma that produces the desired therapeutic effect for the patient. If the plasma concentration of a drug exceeds the therapeutic range, there is a risk of experiencing adverse effects. If the plasma concentration is lower than the lower limit of the therapeutic range, then the drug is ineffective for its intended purpose.

Tidal volume: The volume of air inspired and expired in a single breath and this volume corresponds to approximately 500 ml in healthy adults.

Time since death: Estimating the time since death, also referred to as post-mortem interval (PMI), provides important information in forensic medical investigations. However, many variables must be considered when PMI is determined. These include the environmental temperature, whether the body was found indoors or outdoors, the amount and type of clothing, bodyweight and adiposity, burial, and whether submerged in water, etc. For the early post-mortem period, nomograms are available that consider the rate of decrease in core body temperature and a consideration of some of the variables. As a rough guide, pathologists consider that a body may be warm and flaccid (< 3 hours after death), warm and stiff (3–8 hours), and cool and flaccid (> 36 hours after death). Flaccidity refers to the presence or absence of rigor mortis.

Tolerance: A state that develops after long-term exposure to a drug. Metabolic tolerance infers a faster removal, such as enhanced oxidation by the liver. Functional tolerance infers a change in sensitivity of the organism to the effects of the drug.

Tolerance Interval: The range within which a specified percentage of individual values of a population are expected to fall with a stated level of confidence.

Toxicity: The ability of a substance to harm living organisms – all substances are toxic, even water, if ingested in large enough amounts.

Toxicokinetics: Refers to the clinical pharmacokinetics of drug overdose. It concerns the elimination of drugs and the processes involved in their clearance from the body in poisoned patients.

Toxicology: The word toxicology derives from the Greek term "toxikon" which means a bow for shooting arrows. During antiquity poisons were often placed on the tips of arrows making them more deadly, giving rise to the word *toxicos* and *intoxicated*, which means made sick by poison. Hence, "toxicology" is the study of how poisonous substances interact with living organisms.

Traceability: Traceability means that a result of measurement can be traced back, through an unbroken chain of comparisons, to a national or international standard value. The traceability of the ethanol standards used to calibrate the gas chromatography needs to be well documented.

Tracking: The name given to a laboratory test used to measure effects of alcohol on an individual and might involves adjusting an instrument to maintain a desired value (compensatory tracking) or to follow a moving reference marker or object (pursuit tracking).

Trauma: An injury caused by an external force that potentially causes death or permanent disability. Blunt force and sharp force trauma are terms often encountered in forensic pathology when describing particular injuries or patterns of injury. The term trauma might also be used to describe emotional or psychological shock or distress.

U

U-Creatinine: The creatinine content of urine can span over a wide range depending on the relative concentration of water in the specimen. U-creatinine below 0.2 g/L (20 mg%) indicates a highly dilute specimen, which might result from manipulation of the specimen by adding water in-vitro or by drinking large volumes of water or an alcoholic beverages before voiding.

Ultraviolet: Pertaining to the region of the electromagnetic spectrum from approximately 10 to 380 nm.

Uncertainty: The word uncertainty means doubt in something, such as the result of analysis. Analytical uncertainty is defined as a parameter associated with the result of a measurement, which characterizes the spread or dispersion of the results that could reasonably be attributed to the quantity being measured.

Under the influence: Usually refers to being under the influence or intoxicated by alcohol.

Unit of alcohol: In the United Kingdom, one unit of alcohol equals 10 mL ethanol (1 mL = 0.79 g) so ~8 gram ethanol. In Australia, one unit equals 10 g ethanol.

Unnatural deaths: Deaths resulting from some non-natural cause or causes i.e., road-traffic fatality, accidental fall from height, abuse of alcohol and/or other drugs, suicidal hanging, drowning, stabbing etc., might all be classified as unnatural deaths.

Upper respiratory tract: Abbreviated as URT, and this part of the lungs comprises the nasal cavity, pharynx and its associated structures. The URT is covered with a watery mucous membrane.

Urine: The aqueous fluid secreted by the kidneys and stored in the bladder before being voided. Although urine is mainly water, its chemical composition varies widely in health and disease and is also dependent on the quantity and type of food and drink consumed.

V

Vertigo: The sensation of dizziness.

Viscera: Pertaining to the internal organs – the soft parts – the internal organs of the chest and abdominal cavity.

Visible light: Pertaining to radiant energy in the electromagnetic spectral range that is visible to the human eye. This corresponds to light of wavelengths from approximately 380 to 780 nm.

Vital capacity (VC): This is defined as the total volume of air that can be expelled from the lungs after a maximum inspiration to maximum expiration. A healthy adult person might have a vital capacity of approximately 4600 ml, being less in women compared with men and markedly diminished in heavy smokers and those with lung disease.

Vitreous humor (VH): Means, literally, glassy fluid and refers to a transparent jelly-like substance that fills the space between the lens and the retina of the eye, and is a fluid commonly sampled for forensic analysis of ethanol in post-mortem toxicology. The major advantage of VH is that there is less risk for contamination by bacteria spreading from the gut.

Volume of distribution: The volume of distribution (V_d) of a drug expresses a relationship between amount of drug in the entire body to the concentration determined in a reference compartment, usually blood or plasma. Note that V_d is an "apparent" volume and does not represent any particular physiological or anatomical compartment or space within the body. V_d is a body volume in liters necessary to contain the same quantity of the drug as determined in a sample of blood or plasma.

W

Wavelength: A property of radiant energy, such as IR, visible, or UV. The distance measured along the line of propagation, between two points that are in phase on adjacent waves.

Whole blood: This is an anticoagulated specimen of blood where the cellular elements remain mixed with the plasma and this is the body fluid commonly used for forensic purposes. Prior to removing an aliquot for analysis the tube of blood should be inverted several times to ensure that the plasma and red cells are thoroughly mixed together.

Widmark: Erik MP Widmark (1889–1945), was a pioneer in forensic research on alcohol, and is perhaps best known for his seminal work on ethanol pharmacokinetics as reported in his 1932 monograph.

Widmark's β-factor: This denotes the slope of the post-absorptive elimination phase assuming zero-order kinetics. Hence the rate at which ethanol is eliminated from the bloodstream per unit time, usually reported as g% per h or g/L per h. A slang term often used is the alcohol burn-off rate.

Widmark's equation: A simple mathematical equation derived by Widmark in the 1930s expressing the relationship between amount of ethanol absorbed and distributed in all body fluids and tissues to the concentration determined in a sample of blood.

Widmark's rho-factor: This pharmacokinetic parameter describes the relationship between the distribution of ethanol between the entire body (g/kg) and the concentration in a sample of the blood (mg/g). Synonymous with volume of distribution (V_d).

Window of detection: This refers to the time after administration of a drug during which the substance or one of its metabolites can still be detected in blood or another body fluid. The window of detection is longer for drugs determined in urine compared with blood or plasma.

Withdrawal syndrome: A constellation of unpleasant signs and symptoms following abrupt discontinuation or intake of a drug after its repeated usage. Withdrawal symptoms can also be precipitated by administering a drug that counteracts (antagonizes) the action of the psychoactive substance (e.g., naloxone in heroin addiction). The severity of withdrawal symptoms varies depending on the drug, but often include sweating and shaking. A fear of experiencing withdrawal symptoms is one reason that an addict continues to take the drug despite the negative consequences.

X

Xenobiotic: From the Greek *xeno* (foreign), and usually refers to chemical substances (drugs or toxins) that enter the body from the environment or by ingestion.

Y

Yeast infection: Fungal infection, such as genital candidiasis, caused by proliferation of the yeast *Candida albicans.* This clinical condition is common in women suffering from type 1 diabetes.

Z

Zero-order: A term used to describe rates of chemical and biochemical reactions, such as zero-order kinetics, which means that the rate of elimination from blood or plasma is independent of the dose and starting concentration.

Zero-tolerance law: Refers to a type of traffic safety legislation whereby the presence of any amount of a controlled substance in the driver's blood is deemed a punishable offence. Zero-tolerance laws simplify the prosecution of drug-impaired drivers, because they avoid the need to produce clinical or other evidence of impairment by drugs.

Z-score: The Z-score is a mathematical device used to compare results of external proficiency tests and is calculated as the difference (laboratory result – assigned or target value) divided by the standard deviation (SD) of the results from all participants.

4 Sports Drug Testing

Section Editor: Mario Thevis

CONTENTS

DOI: 10.4324/9781315155159-4

4.1 A BRIEF INTRODUCTION TO SPORTS DRUG TESTING

M. Thevis

The relevance of (anti-doping) regulations in sport and consequently, the means to ensure athletes' compliance with the rules of sportsmanship have reportedly been recognized and enforced since the era of the ancient Olympic Games. Supervised by the so-called *Helenedonakai* (the judges), athletes who passed the initial selection criteria (including the individuals' law-abiding integrity and the completion of a mandatory 10-month training period for the Games) had to exercise for 4 weeks on-site at Olympia, as also in ancient times, athletes did not compete for sport's sake only. The successful athletes were rewarded generously, which already at that time fueled the desire for a competitive advantage over rivals, and some approaches towards that goal would nowadays be subsumed under the term "doping," such as, e.g., attempts at bribery, manipulation of the opponent's weapon, and the use of plant-derived alkaloids. Doping practices have not been limited to humans; quite the opposite has been reported, and racing animals (mainly horses and dogs) have been subject to manipulation, which resulted, *inter alia*, in regulations prohibiting the administration of substances with the purpose of performance manipulation in England as early as 1666.[1] Violation of the decree was severely punished; one of the most prominent verdicts, in 1812, was issued concerning Daniel Dawson, who was found guilty of poisoning the odds-on favorites by fortifying the animals' trough with white arsenic and who was eventually sentenced to death.[2] The motivation to provide scientific means to detect the use of illicit substances in sport was therefore found in the racing industry in the late 19th century, long before modern anti-doping rules were established in human sports. A brief historical overview of (bio)chemical analytical methods concerning today's doping agents and the evolution of anti-doping test methods can be found elsewhere.[3]

Since 2004, international efforts concerning doping controls are governed by the World Anti-Doping Agency (WADA), which on an annual basis, issues the Prohibited List, i.e., the document that defines prohibited substances and methods of doping. The Prohibited List is referred to as "a living document subject to continual review and modifications,"[4] and its foundations were laid as early as 1928 by the International Amateur Athletic Federation (IAAF), who decided to ban stimulants in sport.[5] A substantial number of additions have been made since, resulting in a globally enforced compilation of compounds and methods prohibited either at all times or in competition only.[6] A considerable variety of drugs and drug candidates from the categories of, e.g., anabolic agents, erythropoiesis-stimulating agents, agents modifying activin and myostatin activities, etc. has been outlawed, and consequently, demands concerning testing approaches have been continuously growing as laboratories have been urged to determine the presence and/or absence of banned substances. These substances range from low–molecular mass gaseous and inorganic compounds to higher–molecular mass proteinaceous organic molecules, necessitating a considerable array of sampling and testing strategies as well as analytical instrumentation. Moreover, in the case of the misuse of substances that are synthetically derived but for which endogenously produced analogs also exist, differentiation between the organism's genuine hormone (e.g., testosterone, erythropoietin, or growth hormone) and the corresponding pharmaceutical product is required. Finally, the utmost sensitivity of test methods is crucial in order to ensure adequate retrospectivity, i.e., the capability to detect the misuse of a substance (or the use of a prohibited method) for an appropriate period of time in an athlete's doping control sample.

Worldwide, doping control laboratories have devoted themselves to improving the available analytical portfolio over the past four decades. Gas chromatography–mass spectrometry (GC-MS) was the cornerstone for the detection of most prohibited substances until the late 20th century, and the typical approach to a comprehensive analytical spectrum was based on preparing and analyzing sports drug testing samples by means of dedicated and drug class–dictated testing procedures.[7] The continuously improving performance characteristics of liquid chromatography–(tandem) mass spectrometry (LC-MS/MS) instruments proved groundbreaking for anti-doping test methods, and a paradigm shift towards technique-driven analytical approaches was observed in early 2000. This analytical strategy resulted in increased effort to develop and apply multi-analyte test methods in doping controls, especially using high-resolution accurate-mass (HRAM) MS.[8–10] Here, comprehensive datasets are generated, and analytes of interest are visualized by diagnostic (protonated or deprotonated) intact molecules and/or fragment and product ions. A substantial number of prohibited substances are readily covered by this approach, and flanked by dedicated methods for, e.g. peptidic drugs[11] or steroid profiling,[12] it represents state-of-the-art initial testing in doping control.

The enhanced sensitivity and retrospectivity of sports drug testing methods have been found to represent two sides of the same coin. On the one hand, it is of the utmost importance to ensure the detection windows necessary for effective anti-doping analyses. The identification of so-called long-term metabolites (LTMs) of banned substances combined with the continuously improving instrumental quality has enabled detection windows to be considerably prolonged, especially for anabolic agents, which has led to a series of adverse analytical findings (AAFs), particularly in re-testing programs. On the other hand, the accomplishment of ultra-low detection limits also resulted in a series of findings whereby inadvertent drug administration via food/drug contamination was eventually identified as the source of the doping agent.[13–16] In such situations, innocent athletes are confronted with doping allegations due to the presence of a prohibited substance in their doping control specimen, and in-depth investigations are required to demonstrate that the athletes did not intentionally administer the banned substance and/or that no pharmacologically relevant amount was present in the athlete's body.[17]

In this context in particular, the utility of matrices complementary to conventional urine and blood testing has been illustrated.[18] By means of these so-called alternative matrices, which commonly include dried blood spots (DBS), dried plasma spots (DPS), oral fluid (OF), hair, and more recently, also exhaled breath (EB), additional information can be obtained, contributing to the elucidation of situations where unclarified aspects prevail.[19]

The 2019 Prohibited List encompasses 11 classes of prohibited substances and 3 classes of prohibited methods of doping. The great majority of substances banned in sports are of organic nature and low molecular mass, with stimulants in particular representing those drugs that have been outlawed since the first anti-doping regulations were formulated. Other drugs followed, including narcotics, anabolic-androgenic steroids (AAS), diuretics, etc., and more recently, a growing number of other relevant analytes, including noble gases such as xenon, the transition metal cobalt, new drug entities such as selective androgen receptor modulators (SARMs) or peroxisome proliferator-activated receptor (PPAR)δ agonists, and RNA-derived and antibody- or receptor-based drug candidates, have been added. The coverage of the enormous breadth of substances that necessitate consideration in doping controls plus the theoretically infinite number of designer derivatives has been a major challenge not only in the daily routine work of doping control laboratories but also in the preparation of a book chapter on sports drug testing. Fortunately, various aspects were dealt with in excellent chapters in earlier editions of this book, which the interested reader is highly recommended to refer to.[20–21] Complementary to these, the authors of this chapter focused on topics that have undergone substantial modifications in the past or are more recent additions to the arena of doping control.

REFERENCES

1. Clarke EG. The doping of racehorses. *Med Leg J* 1962;30:180–95.
2. Kent G. *The Second Trial and Capital Conviction of Daniel Dawson for Poisoning Horses*. Glindon: Haymarket, 1812.
3. Thevis M. *Mass Spectrometry in Sports Drug Testing - Characterization of Prohibited Substances and Doping Control Analytical Assays*. Wiley: Hoboken, 2010, 360.
4. Vernec A, Pipe A, Slack A. A painful dilemma? Analgesic use in sport and the role of anti-doping. *Br J Sports Med* 2017;51(17):1243–4.
5. IAAF. *Handbook of the International Amateur Athletic Federation*. International Amateur Athletic Federation: Sweden, 1928.
6. World Anti-Doping Agency. *The 2018 Prohibited List*. https://www.wada-ama.org/sites/default/files/prohibited_list_2018_en.pdf (accessed 26.10.2017).
7. Schänzer W, Thevis M. Human sports drug testing by mass spectrometry. *Mass Spectrom Rev* 2017;36:16–46.
8. Vonaparti A, Lyris E, Angelis YS, Panderi I, Koupparis M, Tsantili-Kakoulidou A, Peters RJ, Nielen MW, Georgakopoulos C. Preventive doping control screening analysis of prohibited substances in human urine using rapid-resolution liquid chromatography/high-resolution time-of-flight mass spectrometry. *Rapid Commun Mass Spectrom* 2010;24(11):1595–609.
9. Musenga A, Cowan DA. Use of ultra-high pressure liquid chromatography coupled to high resolution mass spectrometry for fast screening in high throughput doping control. *J Chromatogr A* 2013;1288:82–95.
10. Görgens C, Guddat S, Thomas A, Wachsmuth P, Orlovius AK, Sigmund G, Thevis M, Schänzer W. Simplifying and expanding analytical capabilities for various classes

of doping agents by means of direct urine injection high performance liquid chromatography high resolution/high accuracy mass spectrometry. *J Pharm Biomed Anal* 2016;131:482–96.
11. Thomas A, Schänzer W, Delahaut P, Thevis M. Immunoaffinity purification of peptide hormones prior to liquid chromatography-mass spectrometry in doping controls. *Methods* 2012;56(2):230–5.
12. Mareck U, Geyer H, Opfermann G, Thevis M, Schänzer W. Factors influencing the steroid profile in doping control analysis. *J Mass Spectrom* 2008;43(7):877–91.
13. Guddat S, Fusshöller G, Geyer H, Thomas A, Braun H, Haenelt N, Schwenke A, Klose C, Thevis M, Schänzer W. Clenbuterol - regional food contamination a possible source for inadvertent doping in sports. *Drug Test Anal* 2012;4(6):534–8.
14. Geyer H, Schänzer W, Thevis M. Anabolic agents: recent strategies for their detection and protection from inadvertent doping. *Br J Sports Med* 2014;48(10):820–6.
15. Thevis M, Geyer H, Thomas A, Tretzel L, Bailloux I, Buisson C, Lasne F, Schaefer MS, Kienbaum P, Mueller-Stoever I, Schänzer W. Formation of the diuretic chlorazanil from the antimalarial drug proguanil-Implications for sports drug testing. *J Pharm Biomed Anal* 2015;115:208–13.
16. Helmlin H-J, Mürner A, Steiner S, Kamber M, Weber C, Geyer H, Guddat S, Schänzer W, Thevis M. Detection of the diuretic hydrochlorothiazide in a doping control urine sample as the result of a non-steroidal anti-inflammatory drug (NSAID) tablet contamination. *Forensic Sci Int* 2016;267:166–72.
17. Krumbholz A, Anielski P, Gfrerer L, Graw M, Geyer H, Schänzer W, Dvorak J, Thieme D. Statistical significance of hair analysis of clenbuterol to discriminate therapeutic use from contamination. *Drug Test Anal* 2014;6(11–12):1108–16.
18. Thieme D. Potential and limitations of alternative specimens in doping control. *Bioanalysis* 2012;4(13):1613–22.
19. Segura J. Is anti-doping analysis so far from clinical, legal or forensic targets?: the added value of close relationships between related disciplines. *Drug Test Anal* 2009;1:479–84.
20. Karch SB. *Drug Abuse Handbook*. 1st ed. CRC Press: Boca Raton, 1998.
21. Karch SB. *Drug Abuse Handbook*. 2nd ed. CRC Press: Boca Raton, 2007.

4.2 ANABOLIC AGENTS

T. Piper and M. Thevis

For many years, anabolic agents (AAs) have been the most frequently detected class of prohibited substances according to the statistics of the World Anti-Doping Agency (WADA). Their easy worldwide availability via Internet-based providers and the numerous (assumed) beneficial effects for athletes are potential reasons for this phenomenon. Besides enhancing power and strength, AAs can also accelerate the athlete's recovery or increase endurance performance. In addition, the analytical capabilities to detect AA misuse are constantly improving, which also contributes to the numerous adverse analytical findings (AAFs) concerning this class of doping agents. Recent developments in analytical methods are described separately for both endogenous and exogenous steroids, as the strategies to detect their misuse differ significantly.

4.2.1 Endogenous Anabolic-Androgenic Steroids (AAS)

4.2.1.1 Introduction

Starting from *de novo* synthesized cholesterol, every human being metabolizes a defined subset of corticoid and anabolic-androgenic steroids. The most prominent one regarding doping controls is testosterone (T). As T and its metabolites are ubiquitous in human urine, the presence of these molecules alone cannot be employed as a marker for illicit administration. Therefore, starting in the early 1980s, urinary concentrations of T and its metabolites together with concentration ratios were determined and evaluated in order to detect the misuse of natural (pseudo-)endogenous steroidal substances. This strategy was based on methods derived from clinical endocrinology and adapted for sports drug testing.[1,2]

As endogenous steroids show a wide range of urinary concentrations – including at the intra-individual level depending on diurnal excretion, hydration status, or physical workload – concentration ratios such as T/epitestosterone (E) were established. While these ratios exhibit considerable inter-individual variations, they are known to be stable within an individual athlete over years. Consequently, the T/E ratio was implemented in the 1980s to detect T or T-prohormone misuse by applying a threshold of 6. Emanating from this basis and including numerous scientific research over the years, the steroid profile as established today was developed.[3,4]

4.2.1.2 Individualized Steroid Profiles

In 2004, a technical document issued by WADA was published, aiming for harmonization of the steroid profile measured in all WADA-accredited laboratories worldwide. At that time, only reference population-based thresholds had been established for T/E ratios together with concentration limits. Ten years later, the currently applied steroid profile was introduced, consisting of six steroids and the well-known T/E. The steroids under consideration were T, E, 5α-androstane-3α,17β-diol (5a), 5β-androstane-3α,17β-diol (5b), androsterone (A), and etiocholanolone (ETIO), all depicted in Figure 4.2.1. Besides T/E, other potential ratios like A/T, A/ETIO, or 5a/5b and 5a/E were considered for steroid profile evaluations together with concentration thresholds. The main breakthrough at that time was the introduction of the so-called "Steroidal Module" as part of the Athlete Biological Passport (ABP). The principle of the ABP was introduced 5 years earlier and successfully applied by monitoring hematological parameters of individual athletes in order to detect the misuse of doping agents or methods altering blood parameters. This allowed, for the first time, individual reference ranges to be established for diagnostic steroid ratios, tailoring the reference population-based criteria to the individual athlete's urinary steroid profile. The idea of longitudinally monitoring a profile of an athlete had already been described 20 years earlier, but this approach was routinely applied only from 2014 onwards.[4,5]

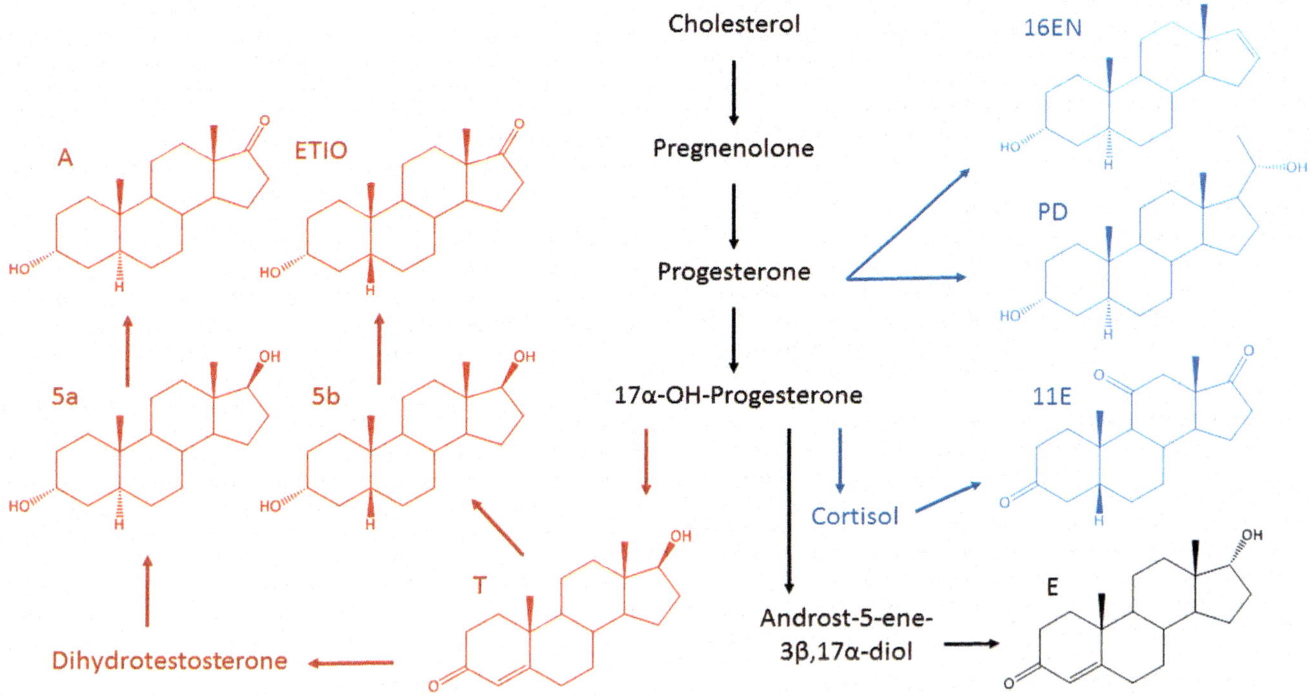

FIGURE 4.2.1 Simplified human steroid metabolism. Target analytes are shown on the left side (red), endogenous reference compounds (ERCs) on the right (blue).

While at the beginning, only the T/E ratio was considered for identifying suspicious doping control samples, the use of all diagnostic steroid profile parameters became mandatory and was implemented into the fully automated evaluation of the longitudinal profiles in 2018.[6]

As mentioned earlier, worldwide harmonization of the analytical approach to determine the steroid profile was inevitable. Nowadays, the use of gas chromatography coupled to mass spectrometry (GC-MS) or triple quadrupole mass spectrometry (GC-QqQ-MS) is mandatory, necessitating the use of a defined derivatization technique (trimethylsilylation). The steroid profile must rely only on steroids excreted in either unconjugated or glucuronidated form, and the use of isotopically labeled internal standards is required. All these stipulations were necessary because analytical parameters can strongly influence the steroid profile determinations.[3]

4.2.1.2.1 Benefits of Individualization

The main advantage of longitudinal monitoring is the enhanced sensitivity of the approach to detect steroid administration. As the inter-individual variation even for diagnostic ratios is relatively high, the derived reference population-based thresholds are conservatively computed. In accordance with approaches in clinical chemistry, thresholds are calculated by combining the variation of the data with the mean or median value. As soon as individual data is under consideration, the thresholds can be adapted, and after two or three samples have been investigated and implemented into the passport, thresholds become sensitive and effective.

The individualized limits allow detection even if only low amounts of T or T-prohormones are administered, specific routes of administration are applied (e.g., transdermal T-formulations), or steroids have been used that in general are difficult to detect, like dihydrotestosterone (DHT). Additionally, the detection times for an application are prolonged by individualized steroid profile–derived thresholds.

4.2.1.2.2 Limitations of the Steroid Profile

As well as all the aforementioned benefits of applying steroid profiles to detect the misuse of endogenously occurring steroids, one insurmountable drawback exists: not only the administration of AAs, but also a variety of confounding factors, can alter the diagnostic ratios and urinary concentrations of endogenous steroids.[3,4] While this might not be too problematic in cases where other exogenous AAs or aromatase or 5α-reductase inhibitors have been misused (as these are commonly detected in comprehensive initial testing procedures and used to explain the aberrations of the steroid profile), other confounding factors are more difficult to cope with. The most common factor is the ingestion of ethanol. Especially concerning the T/E, ethanol consumption can have a strong impact, which can mimic the urinary picture of a T administration. In order to implement analytical methods indicating an athlete's ingestion of ethanol, the measurement of urinary concentrations of ethanol phase-II-metabolites (ethanol glucuronide and sulfate) was incorporated into routine doping control methods, and elevated levels are reported together with the steroid profile data. Unfortunately, all these confounding factors may impede using steroid profile data alone to prove an administration of endogenously occurring steroids. Therefore, suspicious samples showing elevated ratios or concentrations are forwarded to isotope ratio mass spectrometry (IRMS) to distinguish between steroid administration and other factors responsible for the aberrations found in the steroid profile.

4.2.2 Isotope Ratio Mass Spectrometry (IRMS)

4.2.2.1 Carbon Isotope Ratios (CIRs)

Currently, carbon isotope ratio (CIR) prevails in sports drug testing and will therefore be introduced in more detail. The element carbon (C) exists in the form of two stable isotopes, ^{12}C and ^{13}C. While both isotopes exhibit similar chemical properties, their masses differ by 1 Da, as ^{13}C consists of six protons and seven neutrons, while ^{12}C contains only six neutrons. Their distribution on earth is ca. 1.1% ^{13}C and 98.9% ^{12}C, resulting in a stable $^{13}C/^{12}C$ isotope ratio.

As soon as carbon bonds are involved in chemical reactions, i.e., a bond is broken or formed, the two stable isotopes behave slightly differently. Generally, the reactivity of a functional group and bond cleavage kinetics are reduced if ^{13}C is involved. This effect is known as isotopic fractionation and may result in slightly different CIRs of the starting material and the product of a chemical reaction or enzymatic conversion.

The CIR of human beings is mainly driven by the composition of the diet, as C3-, C4-, and CAM-plants show significantly different CIRs due to the different processes involved in carbon fixation being strongly affected by isotopic fractionation. C3-plants show the lowest ^{13}C content, while C4-plants are comparatively enriched in ^{13}C, and CAM-plants are found in between. Depending on the individual´s dietary habits and resulting mixtures of C3- and C4-products (consumed either directly as plants or indirectly as meat derived from animals fed with specific C3- or C4-plant pasture), the personal CIR of the body (and the endogenous steroids) is determined and is usually stable over a long period as long as the eating habits do not change significantly.

Exogenous steroids are usually solely synthesized from C3-based plant material and therefore depleted in ^{13}C, i.e., they have a low content of the heavy ^{13}C isotope. This difference enables the use of CIR in sports drug testing.

4.2.2.2 How to Distinguish Endogenous from Exogenous Steroids

As mentioned before, cholesterol is a central structure of human endogenous steroid biosynthesis. Via different branching points, cholesterol is converted to either androgens such as T or to other steroids like pregnane-based compounds (mainly pregnanediol [PD]) or corticoids (Figure 4.2.1).[7] Within these biosynthetic pathways, carbon bonds are cleaved and formed, i.e., isotopic fractionation can occur. However, the CIRs of different urinary steroids exhibit only slightly different isotopic signatures.

By the administration of exogenous (and therefore commonly ^{13}C-depleted) T, only the CIRs of T itself and of all T-metabolites are affected. Steroids derived from other branches of metabolism, such as PD, are not influenced and can serve as so-called endogenous reference compounds (ERCs). By comparison of the CIRs of the ERCs and the target compounds (TCs), it is possible to identify unphysiological differences attributable to illicit steroid administrations. As TCs, usually T together with 5a, 5b, A, and ETIO is employed, while most commonly employed ERCs are PD, 16-androstenol (16EN), and 11-oxo-etiocholanolone (11E) (Figure 4.2.1). Hence, individual CIRs of ERCs are available for each athlete, which results in a particular sensitivity and reliability of the methodology.

4.2.2.3 Instrumentation and δ-Values

The determination of isotope ratios is complicated as the utmost analytical accuracy is required. In order to obtain CIRs, analytes are completely combusted to yield carbon dioxide (CO_2) and water. Then, the CO_2 is dried and forwarded to the IRMS, where ion beams at m/z 44 ($^{12}CO_2$) and m/z 45 ($^{13}CO_2$) are continuously monitored together with m/z 46 (as a correction for the occurrence of ^{17}O and ^{18}O).[8] Software-based integration and comparison of the different areas under the peaks of the different masses enable the calculation of CIR.

While in the early days of IRMS, only offline combustion was feasible, continuous flow applications were invented 40 years ago and have become routine applications over the years.[8] To determine the CIR of steroids, GC coupled via a combustion unit (C) to the IRMS is the method of choice. The GC combines the advantage of powerful steroid separation to achieve clean peaks with very good sensitivity, which is especially necessary for those steroids found at low endogenous urinary concentrations. As the GC alone is not sufficient to separate all analytes from the complex biological matrix urine, several clean-up steps comprising solid-phase-extraction (SPE) and high performance liquid chromatography (HPLC) fractionation are involved in sample preparation methods.[7,9]

As the fluctuations in CIR are small, and absolute $^{13}C/^{12}C$ ratios are complex to determine, analyses rely on the differences between the analyte of interest and an internationally accepted reference material. Applying this, CIR can be calculated and indicated in the δ-notation following Equation 4.2.1:

$$\delta^{13}C_{VPDB} = \frac{\left(^{13}C/^{12}C\right)_{SAMPLE}}{\left(^{13}C/^{12}C\right)_{VPDB}} - 1 \qquad (4.2.1)$$

The reference material referred to is Vienna Pee Dee Belemnite (VPDB), and δ-values are given in [‰] or, equivalently and recently introduced, in [mUr].

Using the δ-notation, C4-, C3-, and CAM-plants cover a range from −33 to −12 mUr.[8] Endogenous steroids are found between −25 and −16 mUr, while exogenous steroids mostly fall below −27 mUr.[10,11] In order to detect steroid misuse, it is not the δ-values that are considered but differences between

TCs and ERCs called Δ-values and calculated according to Equation 4.2.2:

$$\Delta[\text{‰}] = \delta^{13}C_{ERC} - \delta^{13}C_{TC} \quad (4.2.2)$$

4.2.2.4 Current Applications of CIR in Doping Controls

4.2.2.4.1 Harmonization

In parallel to the developments and approaches on harmonization described for the steroid profile, both methods for sample preparation and prerequisites for measurements of CIR have been harmonized by WADA in the last 15 years.

Due to the fact that all analytes are combusted to CO_2 prior to the determination of CIR, all structural information is lost, and overlapping peaks become indistinguishable. So, any co-elution of analytes of interest or of analytes and matrix components has to be avoided. Especially, HPLC clean-up was found to be indispensable and is therefore strongly recommended by WADA.[9,12]

Calibration of the instrument in order to make the measured values traceable to VPDB is always an issue in IRMS. Regarding steroids, appropriate reference material was not available for quite some time, but in 2009, steroids with defined CIR became available.[13] Nowadays, their use is mandatory.

Besides this, several requirements regarding instrument performance and method validation became obligatory. These requirements encompass, amongst others, the linear range of the instrument together with a defined limit of detection (LOD), stability over time, and measurement uncertainty.[9,12] The ability to perform in accordance with all requirements has to be demonstrated by each laboratory by the determination of a population of negative samples of 40 individuals.

All these steps in harmonization were inevitable as by the technical document defined thresholds are given for each pair of ERC and TC.[12] As soon as the Δ-values in a suspicious sample are found to be elevated beyond the thresholds, the sample is declared as an AAF.

4.2.2.4.2 From δ- to Δ-Values to Thresholds

Similarly to the approach in steroid profiling, the determination of CIR thresholds is based on procedures usually applied in clinical chemistry. The first step was to identify normal or physiologically plausible δ- and Δ-values. This was done by the investigation of reference populations and subsequent downstream analysis of a large subset of athlete samples forwarded to IRMS.[7,11,14] In Figure 4.2.2, an example distribution of δ- and Δ-values is shown, derived from a reference population of $n = 69$ individuals investigated in 2011.[15] As all the volunteers were recruited from Switzerland and Germany, the δ-values covered only a range from −20 to −24 mUr and not the complete worldwide possible range as mentioned earlier. But even for this subset of individuals, all living under comparable conditions, the influence of different dietary habits resulted in a standard deviation (SD) around 0.7 mUr. Theoretically, the differences in δ-values should be eliminated as soon as Δ-values are calculated. And taking a look at the Δ-values in Figure 4.2.2c, this obviously is the case. For this particular pair of ERC and TC, the mean value is close to zero and the SD of 0.42 mUr much smaller than that found for the absolute CIR. Based on such reference population-derived values, thresholds can be calculated. As all Δ-values so far have been found to be Gaussian-distributed, the calculation of reference limits is straightforwardly done by adding three or four times the SD to the mean value according to the desired statistical significance.

In the long run, these initial thresholds can be verified by summarizing data from more than 1,000 samples gathered over years.[11,14] So far, no statistically significant difference between an initially fixed reference limit and subsequently analyzed data could be substantiated. This strongly supports the approach of reference population-based thresholds to be used in sports drug testing to identify those ranges for any pair of ERC–TC that can be assumed to occur naturally.

4.2.2.4.3 Application of the Technical Document

Taking the described results obtained from reference population studies as the basis, the technical document defines a subset of ERCs and TCs to be analyzed if a sample exhibits a suspicious steroid profile. Besides those shown in Figure 4.2.1, 11-OH-androsterone can be used as ERC, and E can become a TC in those cases where administration of E as a masking agent is assumed.

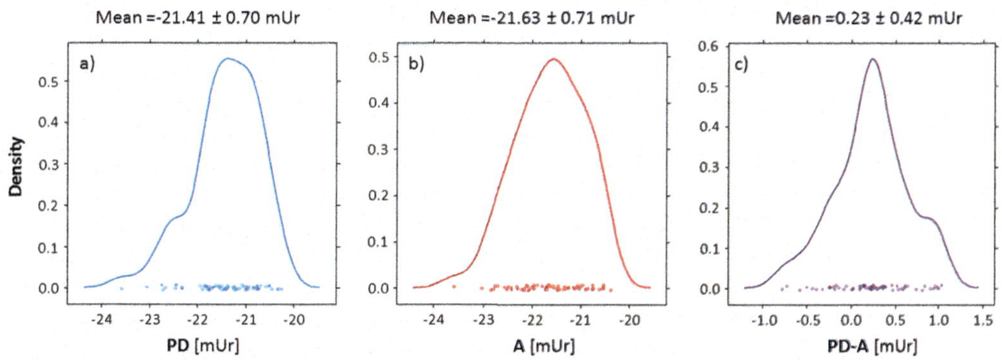

FIGURE 4.2.2 Results (mean and SD) obtained in a reference population of $n = 69$ males and females. The density plots show the distribution of δ-values of (a) PD and (b) A and (c) the calculated Δ-values of PD-A.

PD was chosen as the primary ERC because most scientific data was available for this steroid, and it is commonly found at sufficient urinary concentrations to enable a straightforward IRMS determination. Only in those cases where PD is affected by co-elutions or shows a depleted CIR due to the administration of progesterone or pregnenolone should other ERCs be considered.

Regarding the TCs, those that triggered the IRMS should be preferentially considered, i.e., for an elevated T/E, T and 5a and 5b are expected to be influenced; if ETIO or A were found above their concentration limit, these should show depleted values. Especially for T or 5a, the urinary concentrations found are occasionally too low for a valid IRMS measurement; further, the steroid metabolism can show strong inter-individual variations. Therefore, it is only recommended to prioritize those steroids triggering the IRMS; it is not mandatory to utilize these analytes exclusively. As soon as the thresholds implemented by WADA are exceeded, the sample is no longer considered not suspicious.

Additionally, the isotopic fingerprint visible in different metabolites depends not only on the individual´s metabolism but also on the pharmaceutical formulation of administration and, of course, on the steroid administered, as shown in the next paragraph.

4.2.2.4.4 Post-Administration Samples

The first example deals with different routes of administration of T. In Figure 4.2.3, a comparison of δ-values obtained after the topical application of T-gel and the oral administration of T is shown. The results were obtained from the same volunteer participating in two different studies. The T-gel was administered over seven consecutive days; each day, 2.5 g of gel containing 25 mg T was applied in the evening, starting on day 2. The CIRs were determined in the morning urine specimens. Due to the relatively low amount of T and this special form of application, the CIR of T became slowly but consistently more and more depleted over the week of administration. While 5b followed the δ-values of T, 5a showed exceptional CIRs that were more depleted than T itself throughout the study. This phenomenon has been described in the literature and is most probably due to 5α-reductase activity present in the human skin.[16]

After the oral administration of 100 mg of T, the picture of CIR was substantially different. Directly after the administration, the CIR of T exhibited the strongest impact and started to rapidly return to endogenous CIR values after 15 h. Further, the CIR of 5b and not 5a remained depleted for the longest time. Depending on the time point of urine collection, the different pharmaceutical formulations of T may give different results in both urinary concentrations and CIR. Consequently, it is impossible to elucidate either the time point or the form of an administration from just one urine sample collected in the context of doping controls.

Additional factors potentially complicating the evaluation of AAFs are so-called prohormones. As shown in Figure 4.2.4, even closely related steroids differ significantly in human metabolism excretion patterns. Dehydroepiandrosterone (DHEA) is a steroid hormone precursor in humans that is sequestered in considerable amounts as a sulfoconjugate in the human body and is tissue-selectively converted to a variety of androgens. The main intermediate between DHEA and T (as well as its metabolites) is 4-androstene-3,17-dione (ADION). Consequently, similar excretion patterns after misuse of either steroid are expected. However, as shown in Figure 4.2.4, this is not the case. The same individual underwent administration studies with one steroid at a time, i.e., 100 mg of DHEA or 80 mg of ADION being orally ingested. After DHEA intake, especially the CIR of 5a showed a short but pronounced depletion, while the CIR of T was only briefly and moderately depleted. Hence, both 5a and 5b appeared to be the most promising candidates to detect DHEA administration.

After ADION ingestion, all three metabolites yielded significantly depleted CIRs, and values returned to starting conditions more or less simultaneously. The difference found for both steroids (DHEA and ADION) can be attributed to a strong first pass effect in the liver, not reflecting the usual metabolic pathways of steroids, and demonstrate that urinary steroid concentrations or CIRs may not be the best targets to investigate endogenous steroid metabolism. Regarding doping controls, both examples show that it cannot be expected that all TCs will be influenced in the same way, and therefore, the careful interpretation of steroid profiles and CIRs is advisable.

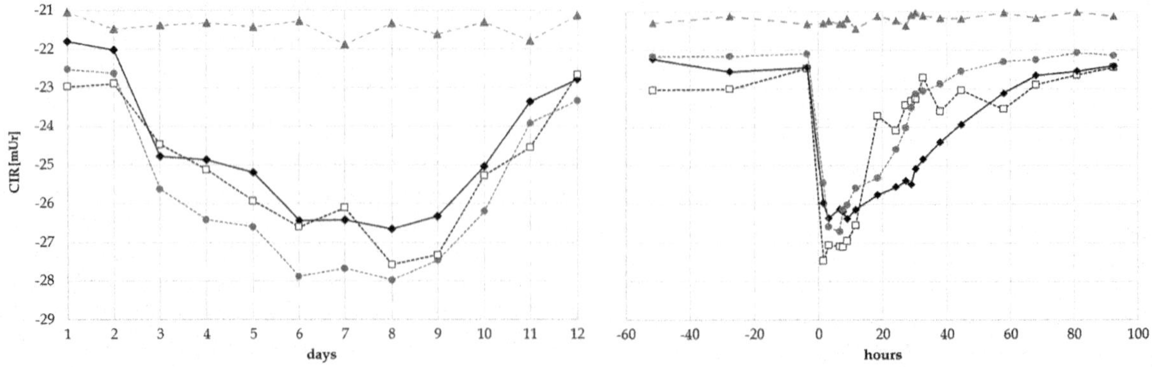

FIGURE 4.2.3 CIR after the topical administration of T-gel (a) and oral administration of T (b). Grey triangles represent PD, open squares T, grey circles 5a, and black diamonds 5b. Further information in the text.

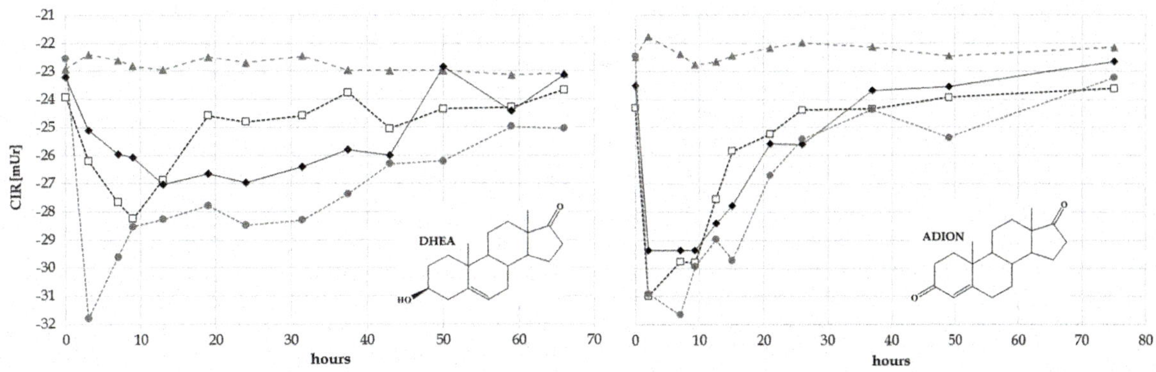

FIGURE 4.2.4 CIR after oral administration of two different T-prohormones: DHEA (a) and 4-androstenedione (b). Grey triangles represent PD, open squares T, grey circles 5a, and black diamonds 5b.

4.2.2.4.5 *Limitations of the Current Approach*

In many cases, it is possible to identify the source of urinary steroids by IRMS, i.e., endogenous and exogenous steroids are distinguishable. In rare cases, however, steroid preparations with an endogenous-like δ-value have been reported. If the CIR of the doping agent falls between −25 and −20 mUr, it might be too similar to the endogenous CIR signature of the athlete's naturally biosynthesized steroids. Here, hydrogen isotope ratios (HIRs) might offer a solution, as explored in recent years.[7,15]

As illustrated in Figures 4.2.3 and 4.2.4, the CIRs of TCs quickly return to their starting values after cessation of single oral dose administrations. Usually, steroid applications can be visualized by means of IRMS for a longer time period than through the steroid profile, but due to the continuous production of endogenous metabolites, detection windows remain short. Hence, various scientific investigations have been focused on either new long-term metabolites of steroid administrations or further attempts to individualize reference limits.[17,18]

4.2.2.5 Recent Developments in IRMS in Doping Controls

4.2.2.5.1 *Hydrogen Isotope Ratios (HIRs)*

Several available steroid preparations were found to comprise CIRs in the range of endogenous δ-values (−25 or even −26 mUr) prevailing especially in individuals from northern Europe. Therefore, HIRs have been investigated regarding their potential to substitute or complement CIR determinations in sports drug testing. The first investigations were conducted in 2004 and 2009, and the first comprehensive, fully validated methods including reference population-based studies were published in 2012.[19] As with CIRs, the calculation of reference population-based thresholds was feasible, and HIRs were found to be significantly influenced by the administration of exogenous T. The limits of detection were inferior to those obtained for CIR-based analyses, as the IRMS of HIR requires more analyte to be converted to hydrogen gas for sufficient peak heights. This could be partly compensated by using larger urine volumes during sample preparation but will be a limitation for TCs of low urinary concentration.

The main drawback found for HIR was the distinctive overlap of endogenous steroids and pharmaceutical preparations. Within the reference population of n = 67 (males and females), the HIR ranged from −320 to −240 mUr (the values are substantially different than those of CIR, as for HIR, a different reference material is employed, so-called Vienna Standard Mean Ocean Water).[19] For a subset of n = 173 different T preparations, HIRs ranging from −270 to −180 mUr have been reported.[10] Hence, T preparations tend to be more enriched in HIR, i.e., they show less negative values, but with a mean value of −230 mUr, they are close to the range found for endogenous urinary steroids. Nevertheless, as long as the δ-value of the administered T is significantly different from the individual's endogenous values, HIR can prove illicit androgen administration similarly to CIR.

Due to the overlap found, a combination of CIR and HIR was considered to be more useful in sports drug testing.[15] If the same sample has been analyzed for both HIR and CIR, the data can be evaluated as a combined dataset, allowing the thresholds for both isotopic systems to be reduced by improving the statistical confidence of each value. For example, instead of calculating a threshold by adding the threefold SD to a mean value, it would be sufficient to add the twofold SD if this is applied to both HIR and CIR simultaneously. As this procedure is time-consuming and expensive, it can only be applied to selected suspicious doping control samples. Usually, samples showing a strong deviation in their steroid profile but CIR values that are only slightly influenced, if at all, are forwarded to HIR determinations.

4.2.2.5.2 *Long-Term Metabolite Epiandrosterone*

After a single oral dose of T and even after prolonged misuse of T or T-prohormones, the detection windows are usually as short as only 24 to 48 h. As all the steroids under investigation are constantly produced endogenously, combined with a fast and constant metabolic clearance, both the concentrations and the CIR return to natural endogenous values relatively quickly. Recently, one steroid was detected and carefully investigated regarding its potential to prolong these detection times: epiandrosterone (EpiA). Compared with the currently applied TCs, EpiA more than doubles the detection time.[18] In Figure 4.2.5, the already discussed ADION excretion study (Figure 4.2.4) is shown after addition of the CIR data obtained for EpiA. Using the regular TCs T, 5a, and 5b, the individual is found to produce an adverse analytical test result for less than 30 h. Employing EpiA prolongs the detection time to more than 130 h.

Naturally, the prolongation of the detection time depends on the individual and on the steroid applied, but in all studies available today, EpiA outperforms other commonly monitored TCs. The explanation for these findings cannot be reduced to the fact that EpiA is excreted as a sulfoconjugate. While sulfates are known to exhibit slower excretion rates than the respective glucuronides, this effect is also observed for ETIO or A but usually does not result in prolonged detection windows. EpiA appears to generate its own metabolic pool, which has a relatively slow turnover. Once the steroidal content of this pool is predominantly composed of exogenous ^{13}C-depleted compounds, its renewal by endogenously produced EpiA is delayed, resulting in a depleted CIR for a prolonged time period.

The aforementioned elimination of EpiA as a sulfoconjugate is, however, also a major drawback. All other ERCs and TCs considered in sports drug testing are excreted in glucuronidated form. Therefore, an additional step in the sample preparation is necessary, which hampers a straightforward implementation of this new long-term metabolite into routine doping control protocols. Consequently, it is currently used as a complement in cases where the measured CIRs show depleted values but are not exceeding the defined thresholds. Very recently, the first investigations started to use EpiA and other sulfoconjugated steroids as markers in the steroid profile. yielding promising results.[20]

4.2.2.5.3 Individualized Thresholds for Δ-Values

In parallel to the approach described for the steroid profile, the hypothesis was investigated that individualized δ- and Δ-values may improve the detection capability of IRMS.[17] Taking into account that the individual CIR will remain constant over time as long as no change in dietary habits occurs, this idea sounds promising. For both the absolute CIR and Δ-values, individual thresholds could be defined, improving the detection of steroid administrations. The main drawback of this approach is the large number of samples that would have to be investigated by IRMS approaches in order to implement individual reference limits. At least three different urine specimens from an individual are necessary to establish corresponding thresholds. As IRMS sample preparation methods are complicated and time-consuming, it is hardly possible to do this for each athlete today.

4.2.2.5.4 Shortening Sample Preparation and Analysis Times

Not necessarily in order to enable longitudinal individual profiling but to accelerate IRMS measurements in general, new methods for sample clean-up were recently investigated. A promising approach was to circumvent the HPLC by introducing a second GC for sample fractionation. The resulting concept is a multi-dimensional gas chromatograph (MDGC), known to enhance the separation power for complex biological matrices and now adapted for IRMS and sports drug testing.[18,21] After improved sample clean-up using solid phase extraction (SPE) cartridges, the samples can be injected directly into the MDGC, resulting in peaks comparably pure to those obtained by HPLC clean-up. This modification reduced sample preparation times by ca. 50% and offers an alternative that supports speeding up IRMS analyses in the future.

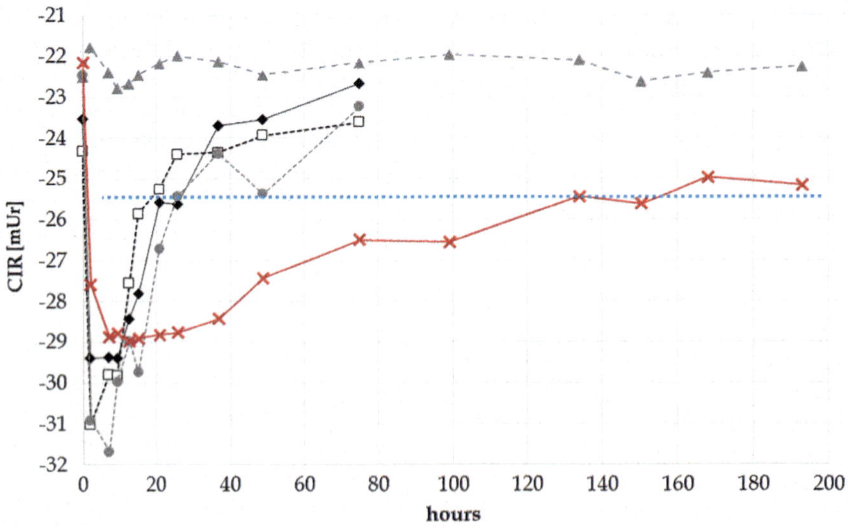

FIGURE 4.2.5 CIR after oral administration of 80 mg of ADION. Grey triangles represent PD, open squares T, grey circles 5a, and black diamonds 5b. Red crosses stand for EpiA, the recently detected long-term metabolite of T and T-prohormones. The dotted blue line represents the threshold.

Especially if a twofold HPLC clean-up is applied, the peak purity of all analytes still supersedes the purity of the MDGC approach. Therefore, the MDGC is mainly used as an initial testing procedure for samples subjected to IRMS, which enables the 95% of clearly negative specimens to be separated from suspicious ones that justify enhanced sample preparation protocols employing HPLC.

Another option that has been tested to accelerate sample preparation was the shortening of the HPLC run time in connection with a combination of different fractions before injecting samples onto the IRMS.[22] In parallel to the MDGC approach, this worked fine as a screening tool and had to be complemented by the regular HPLC method for suspicious samples.

4.2.3 Exogenous AAS

4.2.3.1 Introduction

The detection of exogenous AAS compared with those naturally occurring in humans appears to be less complicated, as here, the presence of the administered compound or its metabolite(s) in urine is sufficient to identify the misuse of the substance. Nevertheless, a lot of scientific effort is constantly spent on improving the detection of exogenous AAS in order to prolong detection times. As most AAS are expected to be misused out of competition, adequate retrospectivity is a prerequisite for successful doping controls. This requirement can be met by either improving the sensitivity of a method to enable the detection of a relevant metabolite at the lowest concentration or by identifying those metabolites that are excreted for the longest time period after drug administration. These metabolites are of the utmost importance in sports drug testing and are referred to as LTMs.

Within this chapter, the focus will be on the recent developments in the detection of LTMs and their impact on sports drug testing. Additionally, different possible strategies to detect LTMs will be presented.

4.2.3.2 Instrumental Methods Applied

As early as the 1970s, the first initial testing procedures for AAS were applied, relying mainly on radioimmunoassays (RIAs). Due to a lack of specificity, these assays were soon complemented or replaced by GC-MS-based methods. These have characterized steroid analyses for more than 30 years and are still employed in all doping control laboratories, while in the last decade, more and more investigations and applications have shifted to liquid chromatography-mass spectrometry (LC-MS)-based methods.

The majority of exogenous steroids are structurally closely related to T and therefore prone to be chromatographically separated on a GC system due to their non-polar properties, especially after derivatization. But this only holds true for the steroid itself or its phase-I metabolite. During this first step in metabolism, the polarity of exogenous compounds is increased in order to enhance renal clearance. Regarding steroids, this first step usually comprises the addition of one or more oxygen atoms. These are then the preferred binding sites for phase-II metabolism. As the polarity is commonly not sufficient after hydroxylation, polar moieties are conjugated, such as glucuronic acid or a sulfate group. These phase-II metabolites are then predominantly excreted into urine and are the main targets for doping controls: either by GC-MS, after cleavage of the glucuronic or sulfate moiety during sample preparation, or by LC-MS-based methods directly addressing the intact metabolites.

In the early 1990s, extensive studies on the metabolism of steroids were conducted using solely GC-MS techniques.[23] Besides expected transformations ascribed to well-known enzyme systems like 5α- and 5β-reductase or cytochrome P450 mono-oxygenase, other unexpected modifications were discovered, such as 17-epimerization of 17β-hydroxy-17α-methyl steroids. This interesting change in isomerism occurs after sulfoconjugation of the 17β-hydroxyl-group and subsequent cleavage of the sulfate moiety, breaking the oxygen–carbon bond at C17. Revealing this mechanism enabled the first detection of an LTM of metandienone (MD).[24] Besides MD, several other steroids were under investigation in the early 1990s, for instance stanozolol (ST), trenbolone (TREN), oxandrolone (OX), and dehydrochloromethyltestosterone (DHCMT).[23–25] All these steroids have been subjected to detailed investigations several times over the subsequent years. The milestones of these efforts will be presented chronologically.

4.2.3.2.1 *Metandienone (MD)*

Marketed by CIBA (Basel, Switzerland) under the brand name Dianabol, MD was approved for the treatment of hypogonadism but has been withdrawn from the market in most countries, although it remains available on the black market.

One of the first LTMs of MD implemented in routine doping controls was a product of the described epimerization of the 17β-hydroxy-17α-methyl groups, as depicted in Figure 4.2.6 (MD1). After elimination of the sulfate moiety,

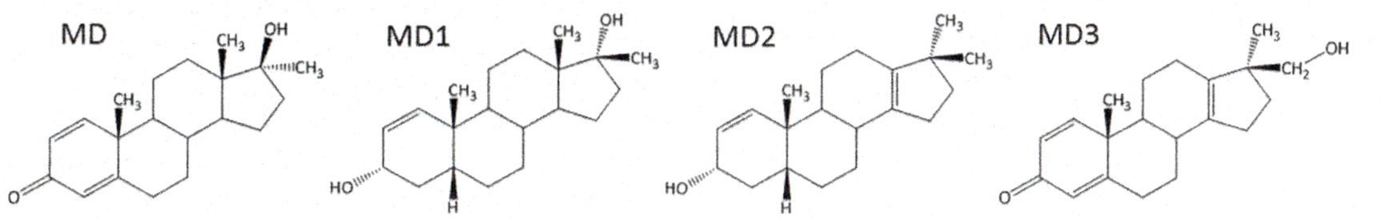

FIGURE 4.2.6 Metandienone and its most important urinary metabolites for sports drug testing: MD1 (17β-methyl-5β-androst-1-ene-3α,17α-diol), MD2 (18-nor-17,17-dimethyl-5β-androst-1,13-dien-3α-ol), and MD3 (18-nor-17β-hydroxymethyl,17α-methylandrost-1,4,13-trien-3-one).

an intramolecular rearrangement of the methyl group (C18) occurs, accompanied by the loss of water, resulting in MD2. Both these metabolites were employed in doping controls for many years and enabled retrospective detection for up to 6 days after a single oral administration.

In 2006, a novel LTM of MD was introduced to sports drug testing that prolonged the detection capabilities for up to 20 days.[26] In comparison to the structure of MD2, the new metabolite was additionally hydroxylated at the 17β-methyl group. Against all expectations, the more polar compound MD3 (compared with MD2) is cleared significantly more slowly from the circulation. This might be due to a distinct compartmentalization of MD3, but this is still not unambiguously clarified. Several years later, it was demonstrated that MD3 is excreted not only in its glucuronidated form, as described during the initial investigations, but also as a sulfoconjugate, supporting the hypothesis of a slow turnover compartment for MD3.[27]

While MD1 and MD2 were accessible by GC-MS, LC-MS was employed for MD3 during metabolite detection and method development. Later on, MD3 was also added to the initial testing procedure for AAs, and by using GC-QqQ-MS, adequate sensitivity was achieved.

The importance of this new LTM can be derived from the number of AAFs attributed to MD over the years 2003 to 2006. While the worldwide findings for MD in the years 2003, 2004, and 2005 were around 60/year, this number doubled to more than 120 in the year 2006 after MD3 was implemented into the screening procedure for AAS. Especially in the laboratory in Cologne, which first described and implemented this metabolite, the number of positive cases for MD increased from 15/year between 2003 and 2005 to more than 60 in 2006. Interestingly, during the years 2007 and 2008, the number of AAFs decreased substantially for MD in the Cologne laboratory, suggesting that athletes or their medical support are well aware of current detection windows for the different steroids. By more than doubling the time for retrospective detection of a substance, obviously several athletes were caught cheating by surprise, and either an adaptation to the new detection windows occurred in the following years, other substances were used instead, or more athletes did indeed stop considering the use of AAS. Taking a look at the worldwide findings (Figure 4.2.7) results in a slightly different picture. The strong increase of AAFs after the year 2006 is obvious, but the decrease in numbers is not visible. This may be due to the fact that bit by bit, all laboratories implemented the novel LTM and increased their detection capability, which resulted in more positive findings over several years. And indeed, the urinary concentrations detected by doping control laboratories decreased constantly over time from the ng/mL range to tens or hundreds of pg/mL. In any case, LTMs have considerably enhanced the detection capabilities of doping control laboratories and support the reduction in misuse of AAS.

4.2.3.2.2 *Dehydrochloromethyltestosterone (DHCMT)*

Structurally closely related to MD (Figure 4.2.8), DHCMT was developed and marketed by Jenapharm (Jena, Germany) in the 1960s under the brand name Oral-Turinabol. It gained notoriety as one of the main AAs misused in East Germany's governmental doping program over the years. It also possesses high oral bioavailability and even more pronounced anabolic activity than MD.

Investigations on the detection capability employing GC-MS in the early 1990s pointed toward DHCMT_1 (Figure 4.2.8) as a promising candidate for retrospective detection of DHCMT administrations.[25] In the following two decades, test methods were constantly improved, and the gain in sensitivity was mainly due to the use of

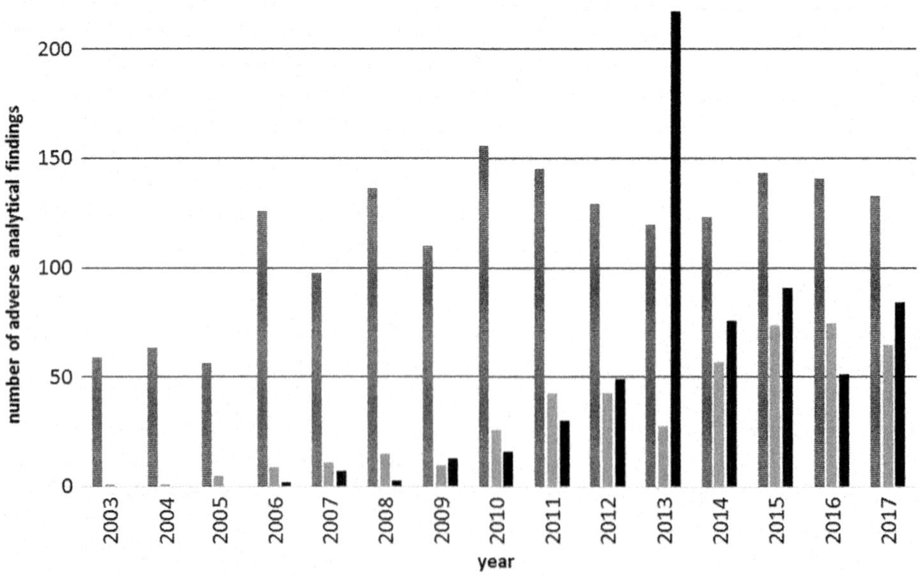

FIGURE 4.2.7 Number of AAFs over the years for MD (black striped), DHCMT (black), and TREN (grey). Numbers taken from the WADA testing figures reports.

GC-MS/MS instruments until 2012. In 2012, the Moscow anti-doping laboratory published an in-depth investigation on DHCMT metabolism, demonstrating the presence of a new and formerly undetected LTM.[28] The chemical structure of metabolite DHCMT_2 (Figure 4.2.8) was tentatively assigned, and a remarkable impact on the frequency of AAFs was observed (Figure 4.2.7). The global number of anti-doping rule violations based on DHCMT increased dramatically in 2013, returning to significantly lower frequencies as early as 2014, demonstrating again the adaptation of cheating athletes to laboratory detection capabilities. Increasing the detection time from fewer than 20 to more than 200 days resulted in DHCMT being a very unattractive option for misuse in sport. The complete and accurate chemical structure of DHCMT_2 was published in 2018, closing this chapter of LTM detection.[29] In 2012, it was already possible to derive the conformation at the carbon atom C17 from the mass spectra, showing that the new metabolite had a similar structure to the LTM of MD, but the A-ring configuration remained tentative until 2018.

4.2.3.2.3 Oxandrolone (OX)

Under the brand names Oxandrin and Anavar, OX was marketed in the early 1960s. It was approved for human use by the Food and Drug Administration (FDA) and is still available as a human prescription drug. Besides this, OX is constantly offered on the black market.

Due to the structural concordance between the LTMs of MD and DHCMT, it was hypothesized that other steroids containing a 17β-hydroxy-17α-methyl group could also show the presence of a 18-nor-17β-hydroxymethyl,17α-methyl metabolite. For OX, this hypothesis was found to be true, and the two detected epimeric LTMs tripled the detection window for OX misuse.[30] For both metabolites, LC-MS- as well as GC-MS-based methods were found suitable for analysis.

4.2.3.2.4 Stanozolol (ST)

ST was first marketed in the 1960s by Winthrop Laboratories (New York). It was approved for both human and animal use and also showed good oral bioavailability. In sports drug testing, it played an infamous role during the Summer Olympics in Seoul 1988, when the Canadian sprint star Ben Johnson tested positive for ST after winning the gold medal.

Surprisingly, the hypothesized LTM for ST could not be confirmed. However, during the in-depth investigations on novel LTMs of ST, two unexpected phase-II metabolites were identified that enabled prolonged detection windows (Figure 4.2.9).[31,32] First, the 3′-hydroxystanozolol-glucuronide (Figure 4.2.9) was established as a valuable alternative for ST detection using LC-MS systems.[31] Using this metabolite enabled the detection of a single ST administration for up to 240 h, which was an increase in detectability of a factor of five compared with GC-MS-based approaches. Employing the *N*-glucuronide further doubled the detection time, resulting in approx. 600 h of detectability after administration of a single oral dose of ST.[32] This outstanding retrospectivity was accomplished by employing liquid chromatography–high-resolution accurate-mass mass spectrometry (LC-HRAM-MS). Here, the nitrogens in ST and the corresponding mass defect, which differs slightly but significantly from other steroids composed of carbon, hydrogen, and oxygen, only enabled the specific detection of the *N*-glucuronide even in complex biological matrices such as urine.

Moreover, a substantial increase in AAFs for ST was seen in 2013 in the Cologne laboratory, the first year the new LTMs of ST were applied. But as soon as 2014, the frequency of AAFs returned to levels observed in the pre-LTM era, demonstrating the speed at which athletes adapt to improved detection capabilities. Nevertheless, the worldwide findings for ST were always numerous, but even at this

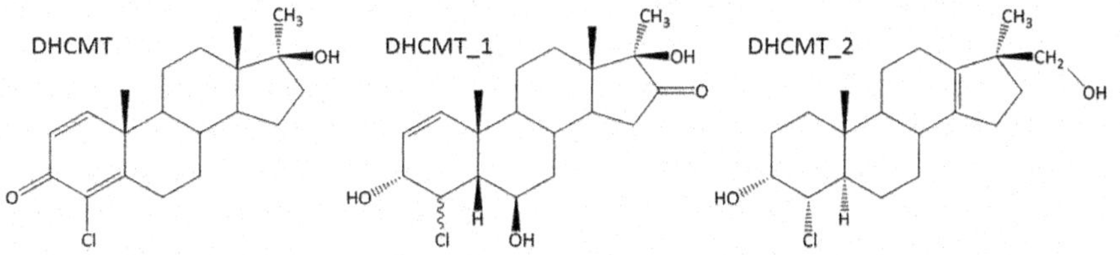

FIGURE 4.2.8 DHCMT and two important urinary metabolites, DHCMT_1 (4-chloro-3α,6β,17β-trihydroxy-17α-methyl-5β-andro st-1-en-16-one) and DHCMT_2 (4α-chloro-18-nor-17β-hydroxymethyl-17α-methyl-5α-androst-13-en-3α-ol).

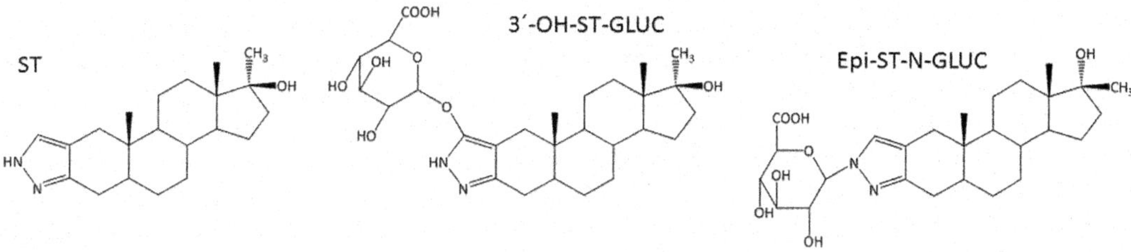

FIGURE 4.2.9 ST (a) and phase-II metabolites employed as LTMs in sports drug testing: 3′-hydroxystanozolol-glucuronide (b) and 17-epistanozolol-*N*-glucuronide (c).

high level, the increase from 240 to 329 in the years 2012 and 2013 was remarkable. Also, the detection capabilities improved from the ng/mL to the pg/mL range, enabling the detection of up to 300 cheating athletes per year over the last 3 years.

4.2.3.2.5 Trenbolone (TREN)

While approved for veterinary use, TREN was never marketed as a human drug. Nevertheless, it has been detected in athletes' urine regularly and was one of the compounds (together with OX and others) that were allegedly administered as a cocktail to Russian athletes prior to the Winter Olympics in Sochi, 2014.

As TREN lacks a 17α-methyl group, the search for LTMs focused directly on phase-II metabolites (Figure 4.2.10). TREN glucuronide was detected as a promising target for doping controls, as TREN was known to be excreted mainly in glucuronidated and sulfated forms, similarly to most other steroids.[33] A less well-known possible phase-II conjugate, the cysteinyl conjugate, was found to work even better for doping controls, prolonging the detection window up to 30 days.[33] Again, as for the other phase-II metabolites, LC-MS techniques have to be employed for suitable detection, and especially for the cysteinyl metabolite, which contains a sulfur and a nitrogen atom, HRAM-MS further improves the detection capabilities. For TREN, a more or less constant increase in AAFs is shown in Figure 4.2.7, reflecting mainly the constant improvements in analytical techniques and only partly the implementation of the novel LTMs.

4.2.3.3 Detection of Long-Term Metabolites (LTMs)

LTMS are a powerful tool in the fight against doping. On the one hand, they enable improved detection of athletes misusing a specific substance, and on the other hand, they constitute a significant deterrent. Consequently, considerable investment has been made in the identification of new potential LTMs, employing three different analytical and methodical strategies.

4.2.3.3.1 The Classical Approach

This technique has been applied since the early days of GC-MS, relying on a comparison of one or more samples collected before with several samples collected after administration of the drug under investigation. In a first step, after sample preparation and measurement, the total ion chromatograms (TICs) of different pre- and post-administration samples are overlaid, and peaks emerging only in the post-administration samples are further investigated as possible unknown drug metabolites. The mass spectra obtained are a valuable source of information, as they can provide a nominal mass and characteristic fragments that support the structure elucidation of the peak of interest. If everything fits with the administered compound, taking into account human metabolism, the likelihood of facing a new metabolite of this drug is very high. This can then be further substantiated by implementing this metabolite into current screening procedures and by re-investigating several known positive cases. In a final step, this metabolite has to be characterized as well as possible, which usually necessitates chemical synthesis of this compound to provide appropriate reference material. Examples for this classical procedure can be found, for instance, in Schänzer et al.[24,25] This approach works nicely for those metabolites excreted at elevated levels after administration. Metabolites of lower concentration might go undetected, as they cannot be identified in the complex urinary matrix.

4.2.3.3.2 The Targeted Approach

The targeted approach has mainly been optimized for LC-MS/MS-based systems but in general also works when applying GC-MS/MS instruments. Two basic assumptions are combined here. First, the fragmentation pattern of steroids (and other compounds of interest) is well known and does not change significantly even if the molecule undergoes some minor metabolic modifications. Further, most of the metabolic reactions can be anticipated and modeled, as the most relevant enzymes active during the metabolism of steroidal agents for drug clearance are well established. Combining both pieces of knowledge allows the prediction of metabolites and corresponding mass spectrometric fragment ions. Extracting the information on diagnostic fragment ions and dissociation patterns significantly facilitates the detection of metabolite(s) in urine as soon as a post-administration sample is available.

In 2005, this method was applied to enable doping control laboratories to screen for so-called designer steroids, i.e., steroids that were chemically modified to hinder routine detection.[34] Later, the scope was broadened to steroid metabolites, and nowadays, even phase-II metabolites are under investigation.[35] The benefits of these approaches are that even analytes at low concentration can be detected due to the MS/MS set-up, and also intact phase-II metabolites can be investigated, which might be of particular

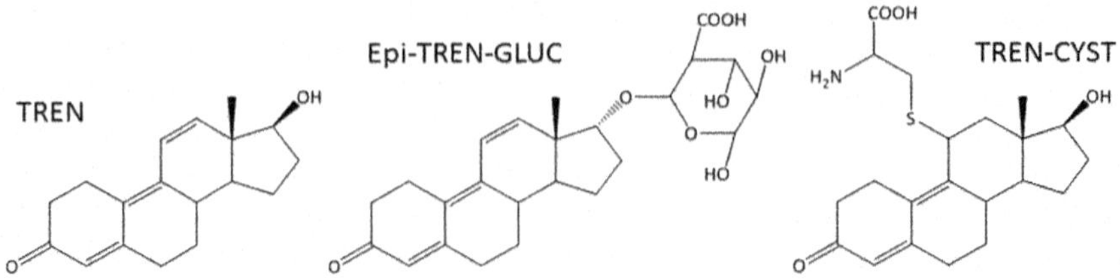

FIGURE 4.2.10 TREN (a) and its phase-II metabolites suitable to prolong the detection of its illicit administration: epi-TREN-17-*O*-glucuronide (b) and the cysteinyl conjugate of TREN (c).

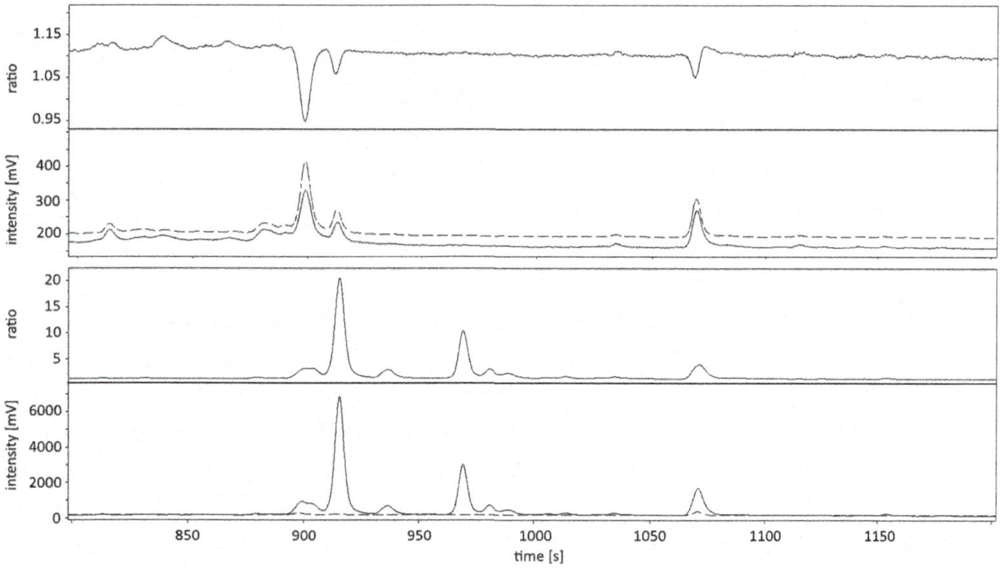

FIGURE 4.2.11 HIR chromatogram before (a) and after (b) the administration of a deuterated compound. Regarding the intensities, the dashed line represents *m*/*z* = 2 and the solid line *m*/*z* = 3; the ratio trace is built by dividing *m*/*z* = 3 over *m*/*z* = 2.

importance in those cases where these metabolites are not hydrolyzed under routinely applied conditions. The main drawback here is that due to the experimental design, unexpected metabolites will remain undetected even if they are present at higher concentrations. As a logical consequence, a combination of the classical and the untargeted approach is often applied.

4.2.3.3.3 *The Hydrogen Isotope Ratio (HIR) Approach*

Using HIR in a different way than reported earlier allows an untargeted detection approach, indicating the presence of the vast majority of steroid metabolites. The basic idea is to administer stable isotope-labeled steroids (or other compounds of interest) and to utilize IRMS to flag metabolites containing deuterium. Adding three deuterium atoms to the steroidal backbone of MD enabled the detection of all known metabolites, including the LTM and several metabolites not formerly described, such as the excreted sulfoconjugate.[27] The detection limit of this approach was estimated to be below 0.5 ng/mL, which readily allows the identification of urinary metabolites exhibiting low urinary concentrations.

This outstanding sensitivity is the result of applying IRMS to an artificially enriched molecule. When operating IRMS for hydrogen at natural abundance, usually 1 out of 6,500 atoms represents deuterium. After stable isotope labeling, approximately 3 out of 30 hydrogen atoms represent deuterium. This results in a very strong increase of the mass trace 3 as soon as a labeled compound elutes from the GC column (Figure 4.2.11). The example shows a blank urine sample and a urine specimen collected 9 h after administration of sixfold deuterated YK11, a novel selective androgen receptor modulator (SARM). In this case, as the metabolism of this compound was completely unknown, only the application of the HIR approach enabled the detection of useful metabolites, whereas the other described approaches were largely unsuccessful. Besides other steroids, T was also investigated with this technique and enabled the identification of EpiA as a LTM for CIR, as described in Section 4.2.2.5.2.[18,36]

The main limitation of this approach is that only compounds that are suitable for separation by GC can be investigated. Working with different derivatization techniques can help to circumvent this limitation, but due to the unknown character of the metabolites, it cannot be excluded that some relevant analytes might remain undetected. The same holds true for phase-II metabolites that might not be cleaved by the applied chemical or enzymatic methods. Again, variations in the applied chemical hydrolysis can minimize this problem but never completely eliminate it.

4.2.4 Conclusion

This short chapter on AAs can, of course, provide only a very condensed insight into the current status of doping control analysis and is naturally far from being complete. An overview of recent developments in research and routine doping controls was provided, focusing on both endogenous and exogenous steroidal agents. For endogenous steroids, the main challenge was and still is to improve the predictive power of initial testing procedures in identifying suspicious samples; for exogenous steroids, a considerable amount of work concerning the discovery and characterization of LTMs still needs to be done.

References

1. Shackleton CHL, Review: profiling steroid hormones and urinary steroids. *J Chrom B* 1986;379:91–156.

2. Donike M, Bärwald KR, Klostermann K, Schänzer W, Zimmermann J. Nachweis von exogenem testosteron (The detection of exogenous testosterone). In: *Sport: Leistung und Gesundheit*, Heck H, Hollmann W, Liesen H, Rost R. (eds.) Deutscher Ärzte Verlag: Köln, 1983, 293–298.
3. Mareck U, Geyer H, Opfermann G, Thevis M, Schänzer W. Factors influencing the steroid profile in doping control analysis. *J Mass Spectrom* 2008;43:877–91.
4. Kuuranne T, Saugy M, Baume N. Confounding factors and genetic polymorphism in the evaluation of individual steroid profiling. *Br J Sports Med* 2014;48:848–55.
5. Donike M, Rauth S, Mareck-Engelke U, Geyer H, Nitschke R. Evaluation of longitudinal studies, the determination of subject based reference ranges of the testosterone/ epitestosterone ratio. In: *Recent Advances in Doping Analysis*, Donike M, Geyer H, Gotzmann A, Mareck-Engelke U, Rauth S (eds.) Sport und Buch Strauß: Köln, 1994, 33–40.
6. World Anti-Doping Agency. WADA Technical Document – TD2018EAAS. Available at: https://www.wada-ama.org/sites/default/files/resources/files/td2018eaas_final_eng.pdf (accessed 14.08.2018).
7. Piper T, Emery C, Saugy M. Recent developments in the use of isotope ratio mass spectrometry in sports drug testing. *Anal Bioanal Chem* 2011;401:433–47.
8. Brand WA. High precision isotope ratio monitoring techniques in mass spectrometry. *J Mass Spectrom* 1996;31:225–35.
9. Piper T, Thevis M. Applications of isotope ratio mass spectrometry in sports drug testing accounting for isotope fractionation in analysis of biological samples. *Methods Enzymol* 2017;596:403–29.
10. Cawley A, Collins M, Kazlauskas R, Handelsman DJ, Heywood R, Longworth M, Arenas-Queralt A. Stable isotope ratio profiling of testosterone preparations. *Drug Test Anal* 2010;2:557–67.
11. Piper T, Flenker U, Mareck U, Schänzer W. $^{13}C/^{12}C$ Ratios of endogenous urinary steroids investigated for doping control purposes. *Drug Test Anal* 2009;1:65–72.
12. World Anti-Doping Agency. WADA Technical Document – TD2016IRMS. Available at: https://www.wada-ama.org/sites/default/files/resources/files/wada-td2016irms-detection_synthetic_forms_eaas_by_irms-en.pdf (accessed 14.08.2018).
13. Zhang Y, Tobias HJ, Brenna JT. Steroid isotopic standards for gas chromatography-combustion isotope ratio mass spectrometry (GCC-IRMS). *Steroids* 2009;74:369–78.
14. Cawley AT, Trout GJ, Kazlauskas R, Howe CJ, George AV. Carbon isotope ratio ($\delta\ ^{13}C$) values of urinary steroids for doping control in sport. *Steroids* 2009;74,379–392.
15. Piper T, Emery C, Thomas A, Saugy M, Thevis M. Combination of carbon isotope ratio with hydrogen isotope ratio determinations in sports drug testing. *Anal Bioanal Chem* 2013;405:5455–66.
16. Piper T, Mareck U, Geyer H, Flenker U, Thevis M, Platen P, Schänzer W. Determination of $^{13}C/^{12}C$ ratios of endogenous urinary steroids: method validation, reference population and application to doping control purposes. *Rapid Commun Mass Spectrom* 2008;22:2161–75.
17. Jardines D, Botrè F, Colamonici C, Curcio D, Procida G, de la Torre X. Longitudinal evaluation of the isotope ratio mass spectrometric data: towards the "isotopic module" of the athletic biological passport. *Drug Test Anal* 2016;8:1212–21.
18. Piper T, Putz M, Schänzer W, Pop V, McLeod MD, Uduwela DR, Stevenson BJ, Thevis M. Epiandrosterone sulfate prolongs the detectability of testosterone, 4-androstenedione, and dihydrotestosterone misuse by means of carbon isotope ratio mass spectrometry. *Drug Test Anal* 2017;9:1695–703.
19. Piper T, Thomas A, Thevis M, Saugy M. Investigations on hydrogen isotope ratios of endogenous urinary steroids: reference population-based thresholds and proof-of-concept. *Drug Test Anal* 2012;4:717–27.
20. Esquivel A, Alechaga E, Monfort N, Ventura R. Sulfate metabolites improve retrospectivity after oral testosterone administration. *Drug Test Anal* 2018;doi:10.1002/dta.2529.
21. Putz M, Piper T, Casilli A, Radler de Aquino Neto F, Pigozzo F, Thevis M. Development and validation of a multidimensional gas chromatography/combustion/isotope ratio mass spectrometry-based test method for analyzing urinary steroids in doping controls. *Anal Chim Acta* 2018;1030:105–14.
22. de la Torre X, Colamonici C, Curcio D, Botrè F. Fast IRMS screening of pseudoendogenous steroids in doping analyses. *Drug Test Anal* 2017;9:1804–12.
23. Schänzer W. Metabolism of anabolic androgenic steroids. *Clin Chem* 1996;42:1001–20.
24. Schänzer W, Delahaut P, Geyer H, Machnik M, Horning S. Long term detection and identification of metandienone and stanozolol abuse in athletes by gas chromatography-high-resolution mass spectrometry. *J Chrom B* 1996;687:93–108.
25. Schänzer W, Horning S, Opfermann G, Donike M. Gas chromatography/mass spectrometry identification of long-term excreted metabolites of the anabolic steroid 4-Chloro-1,2-dehydro-17a-methyltestosterone in humans. *J. Steroid Biochem Molec Biol* 1996;57:363–76.
26. Schänzer W, Geyer H, Fusshöller G, Halatcheva N, Kohler M, Parr MK, Guddat S, Thomas A, Thevis M. Mass spectrometric identification and characterization of a new long-term metabolite of metandienone in human urine. *Rapid Commun Mass Spectrom* 2006;20:2252–8.
27. Thevis M, Piper T, Horning S, Juchelka D, Schänzer W. Hydrogen isotope ratio mass spectrometry and high-resolution/high-accuracy mass spectrometry in metabolite identification studies: detecting target compounds for sport drug testing. *Rapid Commun Mass Spectrom* 2013;27:1904–12.
28. Sobolevsky T., Rodchenkow G. Detection and mass spectrometric characterization of novel long-term dehydrochloromethyltestosterone metabolites in human urine. *J Steroid Biochem & Mol Biol* 2012;128:121–7.
29. Forsdahl G, Geisendorfer T, Göschl L, Pfeffer S, Gärtner P, Thevis M, Gmeiner G. Unambiguous identification and characterization of a long-term human metabolite of dehydrochloromethyltestosterone. *Drug Test Anal* 2018;10:1244–50.
30. Guddat S, Fußhöller G, Beuck S, Thomas A, Geyer H, Rydevik A, Bondesson U, Hedeland M, Lagojda A, Schänzer W, Thevis M. Synthesis, characterization, and detection of new oxandrolone metabolites as long-term markers in sports drug testing. *Anal Bioanal Chem* 2013;405:8285–94.
31. Tudela E., Deventer K, Van Eenoo P. Sensitive detection of 3′-hydroxy-stanozolol glucuronide by liquid chromatography–tandem mass spectrometry. *J Chrom A* 2013;1292:195–200.
32. Schänzer W, Guddat S, Thomas A, Opfermann G, Geyer H, Thevis M. Expanding analytical possibilities concerning the detection of stanozolol misuse by means of high resolution/high accuracy mass spectrometric detection of stanozolol glucuronides in human sports drug testing. *Drug Test Anal* 2013;5:810–8.
33. Sobolevsky T, Rodchenkov G. Detection of epitrenbolone glucuronide and cysteinyl conjugate of trenbolone may provide better retrospectivity of trenbolone abuse. In: *Recent Advances in Doping Analysis (23)*, Schänzer W, Thevis M, Geyer H, Mareck U (eds.) Sportverlag Strauß: Köln, 2015, 26–32.

34. Thevis M, Geyer H, Mareck U, Schänzer W. Screening for unknown synthetic steroids in human urine by liquid chromatography-tandem mass spectrometry. *J Mass Spectrom* 2005;40:955–62.
35. Gomez C, Fabregat A, Pozo OJ, Marcos J, Segura J, Ventura R. Analytical strategies based on mass spectrometric techniques for the study of steroid metabolism. *Trends Anal Chem* 2014;53:106–16.
36. Piper T, Schänzer W, Thevis M. Genotype-dependent metabolism of exogenous testosterone – new biomarkers result in prolonged detectability. *Drug Test Anal* 2016;8:1163–73.

4.3 ERYTHROPOIESIS-STIMULATING AGENTS (ESAS) – FROM INORGANIC AGENTS TO BIOMOLECULES

P. Reihlen, A. Thomas, T. Piper, O. Krug, K. Walpurgis and M. Thevis

Endurance performance is limited by the supply of oxygen to the exercising muscles.[1] Erythropoiesis-stimulating agents (ESAs) represent a large and very heterogeneous class of doping agents, which artificially increase the number of circulating red blood cells (RBCs) and thus improve the oxygen delivering capacity of the blood. They comprise recombinant human erythropoietin (rEPO) and its biosimilars as well as EPO mimetic peptides, small molecule hypoxia inducible factor (HIF) stabilizers and activators, and recombinant proteins acting independently of the EPO receptor, such as TGF-β inhibitors.[2] While EPO and its biosimilars are approved pharmaceuticals for anemia therapy, most of the other ESAs are still under clinical investigation. Nevertheless, they are included in the Prohibited List of the World Anti-Doping Agency (WADA) (S2: Peptide hormones, growth factors, related substances, and mimetics),[3] and immunological and/or mass spectrometric assays were proactively developed to enable their detection in doping control samples.

4.3.1 Erythropoietins and Their Detection

EPO is a glycoprotein regulating erythropoiesis by promoting erythroid proliferation and maturation in the bone marrow. The ability to boost RBC mass has made EPO a valuable product for the pharmaceutical industry, with annual sales of over US$10 billion in 2007. Anemia caused by, e.g., chronic kidney disease, massive blood loss, or chemotherapy can be treated with recombinantly produced EPO. While being a life-saving treatment for patients with severe anemia, EPO may be misused by healthy athletes to enhance the oxygen transport capacity beyond the individual´s physiological boundaries. Cheating athletes and their medical entourage follow pharmaceutical developments closely, and rumors existed about rEPO misuse during the 1988 Winter Games in Calgary. The International Olympic Committee (IOC) added EPO to its list of prohibited substances in 1990, and it has also been banned under WADA´s governance and is included in WADA´s Prohibited List. For the first time, proof of EPO abuse was documented in 1998. During the Tour de France of 1998, EPO was confiscated from the trunk of an automobile escorting a team of riders.[4] While EPO abuse was especially noted in cycling in the 1990s and 2000s, its misuse is not limited to this sport discipline, nor has it become less attractive to doping athletes. The 2017 Anti-Doping Testing Figures document 85 cases of rEPO and rEPO analog abuse reported by the WADA laboratories.[5] Endurance sport athletes in particular would benefit from an increase of erythrocytes (RBC mass) and its effect on the oxygen transport capacity, although the efficiency of EPO doping has been the subject of controversies lately. Ekblom et al. demonstrated that low-dose subcutaneous injections of rEPO (20–40 IU/kg bodyweight administered to healthy volunteers) over a period of 6 weeks increased hemoglobin by 10%. Subsequently, VO_{2max} increased, as did physical performance measured during a standard running test.[6] In a recent study, the increase of red cell volume monitored over 4 weeks after rEPO application was found to be linear and dose dependent. During the same time, submaximal VO_2 did not increase, and VO_{2max} was only elevated by 6%. Yet, the time to exhaustion in a standard submaximal cycling test was increased by up to 70%, leading the authors to believe that the increase in performance could not be attributed to higher oxygen transport capacity alone. A possible reduction of central fatigue and a direct effect on skeletal muscles have been hypothesized as possible non-hematopoietic effects of rEPO explaining the enhancement in performance.[7] Performance-enhancing effects were also reported by Haile et al. In a comparative study, two groups, 20 Kenyan and 19 Caucasian endurance athletes, were injected with 50 IU/kg Neorecormon every second day over a course of 4 weeks. While the hematological changes after rHuEpo were not as pronounced in Kenyans as in Caucasians, reflected by an increase in hemoglobin and hematocrit of ~10% in Kenyans compared with ~17% in Caucasians, the relative improvements in running performance and VO_{2max} were comparable (~5 vs. ~7%).[8]

Another rEPO application study, conducted by Heuberger et al., investigated the effects of rEPO in well-trained cyclists during maximal and submaximal exercise as well as during a road race performance. While an ergogenic effect was detectable in a maximal exercise test leading to exhaustion, the authors concluded that this was not the case under submaximal conditions or during the road race performance.[9] Nevertheless, EPO misuse has been revealed in, e.g., cycling, long distance running, race walking, biathlon, and triathlon.[5,10,11]

4.3.1.1 Erythropoiesis

The peritubular interstitial cells of the kidneys are the main sites of EPO production in adult humans. Yet, EPO is also produced and released into the surrounding environment by virtually every tissue studied under conditions of hypoxia or metabolic stress, e.g., glucopenia, intense cellular metabolic work, infection, or trauma. Here, EPO is a primary component of the innate immune response to injury opposing apoptosis and actions of pro-inflammatory cytokines in tissues.[12] In contradistinction, synthesis of the endocrine EPO is dependent on kidney tissue oxygenation. The peritubular interstitial cells of the kidneys are the main sites of EPO production in adult humans.[13] While brain and liver tissue are also able to synthesize EPO, the amount produced there is insufficient to maintain erythropoiesis.[14] EPO expression is regulated by blood oxygen abundance detected through an oxygen sensor within the renal cells. Hypoxic conditions lead to stabilization of the otherwise rapidly degraded constitutively expressed alpha subunit of HIF. HIF-α together with the second subunit HIF-β forms a heterodimeric transcription factor regulating the release of EPO into the blood (see also Section 4.3.2). The released EPO stimulates erythrocyte progenitor proliferation and maturation, thereby increasing renal tissue oxygenation. The complex process of erythropoiesis is described briefly as follows. Erythrocytes primarily originate from CD34+ pluripotent hematopoietic stem cells of the bone marrow. These stem cells respond to the stem cell factor (SCF), a cytokine initiating an intracellular signaling pathway upon autophosphorylation of the cytoplasmic region of its associated receptor (SCFR). This SCFR pathway is amplified by early acting cytokines, e.g., interleukins (IL-3, IL-6, IL-9), granulocyte colony-stimulating factor (G-CSF), and granulocyte-macrophage colony-stimulating factor (GM-CSF) secreted by the local macrophages, monocytes, and lymphocytes.[15] This leads to the development of colony-forming units (CFU). Now, the erythroid-committed cells originating from a shared precursor CFU-GEMM (granulocyte erythrocyte macrophage megakaryocyte) develop from erythroid burst-forming units (BFU-E) to erythroid colony-forming units (CFU-E) under the stimulation of interleukins, GM-CSF, and insulin-like growth factor I (IGF-I). The early BFU-E only show weak responsiveness to EPO due to the lack of EPO receptor (EPOR) in the membranes of the cell. Late BFU-E and CFU-E show an increased expression of EPOR and are responsive to EPO, which inhibits apoptosis and further stimulates cell growth. Further maturation stages from the pro-normoblast to the orthochromatic normoblast involve the decrease and finally, the cessation of cell division. After the following extrusion of the cell nucleus, the anuclear cells are referred to as reticulocytes. Residual strands of RNA (reticulin) still remain in these cells. Subsequently, adhesion molecules, which had retained the cells in the bone marrow during proliferation, are removed, resulting in the release of reticulocytes and matured erythrocytes into the blood.[16]

EPO was isolated from human urine for the first time in 1977 by Miyake et al. This had been quite an elusive task due to the extremely low abundance of EPO in human urine and serum (typically in the low ng/L range).[17,18] In 1985, Jacobs and colleagues successfully cloned the human EPO gene using transfected Chinese hamster ovary (CHO) cells.[19] EPO is part of the cytokine hormone family. It is composed of a 165–amino acid backbone with three N-linked (asparagines 24, 38, and 83) and one O-linked (serine 126) glycan chains, which contribute approximately 40% to its molecular weight (MW) of 30 kDa.[20] Carbohydrate composition and post-translational modifications lead to a microheterogeneity of the EPO molecule. It displays numerous isoforms after isoelectric separation.[21] The glycan chains are vital for the *in vivo* activity of EPO. Particularly, sialylation of the galactose residues is crucial. Asialo-EPO has a plasma half-life of only a few minutes and is rapidly cleared before it can exhibit erythropoietic activity.[22]

4.3.1.2 Epoetins

The first commercially available rEPO approved by the US Food and Drug Administration (FDA) in 1989, epoetin alfa, was produced from a CHO cell line. It has been marketed under different names, e.g., Epogen, Procrit, Eprex, Erypo, or Espo.[23] It is composed of the same 165 amino acids as the endogenous EPO, but the expression in a CHO cell line leads to differences in the molecule´s glycan moieties and post-translational modifications. These differences compared with human urinary EPO can be visualized by deviating isoform patterns after isoelectric separation and by a slightly higher apparent MW (ca. 2–4 kDa) when separation is performed with sodium dodecyl sulfate polyacrylamide gel electrophoresis (SDS-PAGE).

Since 1989, several clinically approved rEPO preparations, such as epoetin beta (cell line: CHO), epoetin delta (cell line: human fibrosarcoma cell), and epoetin omega (cell line: baby hamster kidney cell [BHK]), have become commercially available. In addition, a number of new EPO-biosimilar products have been launched since the recent expiration of patents. Most of these drugs are produced in CHO cell lines. Due to the complex production process, numerous factors will influence the composition of recombinant medicines, such as:

(1) plasmid (promoter, marker genes)
(2) host cell (origin, species, clone)
(3) culturing process (fermenter, culture media)
(4) purification steps
(5) post-translational modifications (oxidation, deamidation; addition of polymers)
(6) formulation[24]

A comparative biochemical assessment of follow-up products from Asia (China, India, and Korea) illustrated differences in comparison to the original Eprex product, resulting from factors such as the ones listed. These biosimilars were found to contain additional glycoforms and other impurities even up to covalent aggregates. The study underscored the variability existing among biopharmaceuticals.[25] These variations may also lead to differences in MW and isoform pattern between different epoetins, affecting detectability and identification (see Figure 4.3.1).

4.3.1.3 Novel Erythropoiesis-Stimulating Protein (NESP)

In addition to rEPO, genetically modified pharmaceuticals have been developed as a second generation of epoetins, which result in substantial differences in isoform pattern and

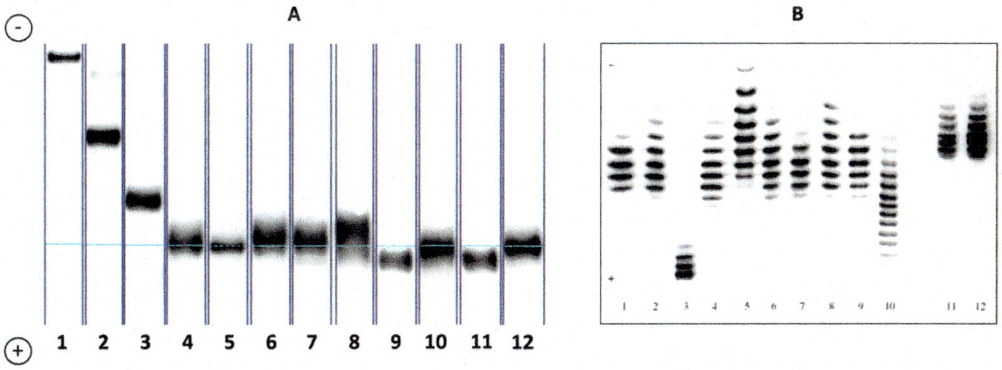

FIGURE 4.3.1 **A**: Chemiluminescent immuno-detection of different EPO pharmaceuticals after SAR-PAGE. Mircera (1), EPO-Fc (2), Aranesp (3), Neorecormon (4), Dynepo (5), Silapo (6), Biopoin (7), Wepox (8), endogenous EPO (9), Shanpoietin (10), Repotin (11), and Beijing4rings (12). Blue line marks MW cut-off for rEPO defined by epoetin delta. **B**: IEF-PAGE of various original and biosimilar erythropoietins. 1. Erypo, 2. NeoRecormon, 3. NESP, 4. Dynepo, 5. Repotin (South Africa), 6. Hemax (Brazil), 7. Alfaepoetina (Brazil), 8. Epocrin (Ukraine), 9. Erythrostim (Russia), 10. uhEPO (NIBSC) (0.2 ng each), 11. and 12. MIRCERA (0.5 and 1.0 ng, respectively). (From Reichel *et al.* 2009. Copyright Wiley-VCH Verlag GmbH & Co. KGaA. Reproduced with permission.)

MW when compared with the original epoetin due to the altered composition of glycans. Second-generation epoetins differ in serum half-life and affinity to the EPOR. In 2001, Amgen (Thousand Oaks, CA) produced the NESP darbepoetin alfa using a CHO cell line but with a modified human EPO gene. Five amino acids were replaced with arginine. Thus, NESP exhibits two additional N-linked carbohydrate chains with terminal sialic acids, leading to a prolonged half-life of 26.3 hours after intravenous injection.[26] This is due to a decreased affinity to the EPOR, also facilitating EPO degradation. The consequence is that more NESP than EPO is required for equivalent EPOR signaling in acute cell stimulation.[27] Yet, it can be administered less frequently to obtain a similar biological response. The additional carbohydrate chains with terminal sialic acids lead to a greater negative charge and MW, resulting in a more "acidic" isoform pattern after isoelectric focusing polyacrylamide gel electrophoresis (isoelectric focusing [IEF]-PAGE) and a typical band at an apparent MW of about 55 kDa after SDS-PAGE. Both isoform pattern and apparent MW are easily distinguishable from endogenous EPO (see Figure 4.3.1).

4.3.1.4 Continuous Erythropoietin Receptor Activator (CERA)

In addition, epoetins have been chemically modified to prolong serum half-life. CERA (methoxy-polyethylene glycol epoetin beta) is an epoetin beta linked via amide bonds to an approximately 30 kDa methoxy-polyethylene polymer (mPEG), thereby doubling its MW to ca. 60 kDa. CERA shows a further decreased affinity for the EPOR than NESP, which further reduces degradation kinetics and allows a serum half-life of up to 6 days.[23,28] A recent study documenting a single-dose application of CERA to eight subjects (50 μg to females, 75 μg to males) demonstrated that successful detection (PAGE, blotting, and immunodetection) was more probable in serum than in urine.[29] This may be attributed to CERA's size and limited renal clearance. The conjugation of epoetin beta to mPEG simplifies the differentiation of this drug from other epoetins and endogenous EPO when separated by MW or isoform pattern (e.g., SDS-PAGE or IEF-PAGE) (see Figure 4.3.1).

4.3.1.5 EPO-Fc

Another, more recent approach to prolong EPO serum half-life is fusion proteins consisting of EPO and the Fc-part of human IgG. EPO-Fc can use the classical application routes of intravenous or subcutaneous injection. It is also possible to use a pulmonary administration route via the neonatal Fc receptor, which is expressed on human lung epithelial cells.[30] So far, two prototypes of the EPO-Fc fusion protein have been developed: two EPO molecules linked to an Fc dimer and one EPO linked to an Fc monomer. Reduced steric hindrance of the monomeric prototype resulted in greater pharmacological activity compared with the dimer. To date, EPO-Fc has not been approved for clinical application. Several non-pharmaceutical companies market the dimeric form of EPO-Fc for research purposes. A recent publication showed that EPO-Fc was detectable in spiked serum samples. Furthermore, it could be differentiated from endogenous EPO and other epoetins using immunoaffinity purification followed by electrophoretic MW separation coupled with immunodetection of the EPO part of the molecule. SDS-PAGE analysis of EPO-Fc showed two bands with an apparent MW of ca. 60 kDa and one above 116 kDa (see Figure 4.3.1).[31] Currently, there is no data available illustrating the excretion of EPO-Fc in urine. Yet, the size of EPO-Fc suggests a decreased renal clearance and better chance of detection in blood. All the above-mentioned variants and constructs of EPO are prohibited in sports and currently summarized in the WADA Prohibited List 2019 under section S2-1 "Erythropoietins (EPO) and agents affecting erythropoiesis".[3]

4.3.1.6 Detection of EPO Abuse in Sports Drug Testing

In the following, a summary of currently available detection procedures for different EPO analogs in sports drug testing is presented. The low abundance of EPO in blood and urine and its closeness in nature to its endogenous counterparts have forced anti-doping laboratories to employ other strategies than those commonly employed for lower–molecular mass analytes. Lasne et al. installed the first viable direct detection method for EPO abuse, using IEF-PAGE coupled with Western blotting and an antibody-based chemiluminescent detection.[32]

4.3.1.6.1 IEF-PAGE

The concentration of urine samples via ultrafiltration is a pre-requisite for IEF-PAGE analysis to obtain detectable quantities of EPO. IEF gels have the loading capacity to separate urine samples after ultrafiltration. However, reducing the complexity of the matrix by employing selective protein precipitation[33] or immunoaffinity purification utilizing an enzyme-linked immunosorbent assay (ELISA),[34] magnetic beads,[35] immunoaffinity columns,[36,37] or microtiter plates[38] has been shown to improve isoelectric separation during electrophoresis. While this is optional for urine samples, it is mandatory for blood samples due to the higher protein content potentially interfering with the analysis. During electrophoresis, the samples' proteins are typically separated in a pH gradient between 2 and 6. The separated isoforms of EPO and its analogs (later detected as discrete bands) constitute a characteristic isoform profile. Once transferred to a membrane via double blotting, these profiles can be visualized by employing a monoclonal primary antibody against the N-terminal region of EPO.[32] Briefly, the identification of EPO abuse is reliant on densitometric quantification of the isoforms detected after IEF-PAGE. WADA classified the detectable isoforms into three areas ("basic", endogenous, and "acidic") defined by the applied rEPO ("basic") and NESP ("acidic") standards. The positivity criteria are met at certain ratios when comparing isoforms of the "basic" or "acidic" area with those observed in the endogenous region (see Figure 4.3.2) While, e.g., Eprex (epoetin alfa) shows a maximum of 6 rather "basic" isoforms (focusing above pH 4), the profile of endogenous EPO consists of up to 15 isoforms (distributed over the entire pH 2–6 range), with many of them being more "acidic" than those present in rEPO. Consequently, samples containing both endogenous EPO and rEPO exhibit an isoform shift towards higher or lower pI. These positivity criteria for various rEPOs and analogs have been defined by WADA in frequently updated technical documents.[39] Blood (serum/plasma) will exhibit more "basic" isoform profiles compared with urine samples of the same individual. The mechanism of this acidification of urinary EPO is still unknown.[40] WADA has taken this into account by having separate positivity criteria ratios for blood and urine.[39]

Isoform profiles may also be influenced by proteinuria induced through extensive exercise, shifting them towards the "basic" area. These so-called "effort urines" necessitated conservative positivity criteria to avoid falsely identified suspicious test results while accepting a reduced test sensitivity.[41,42] Also, the existence of specimens referred to

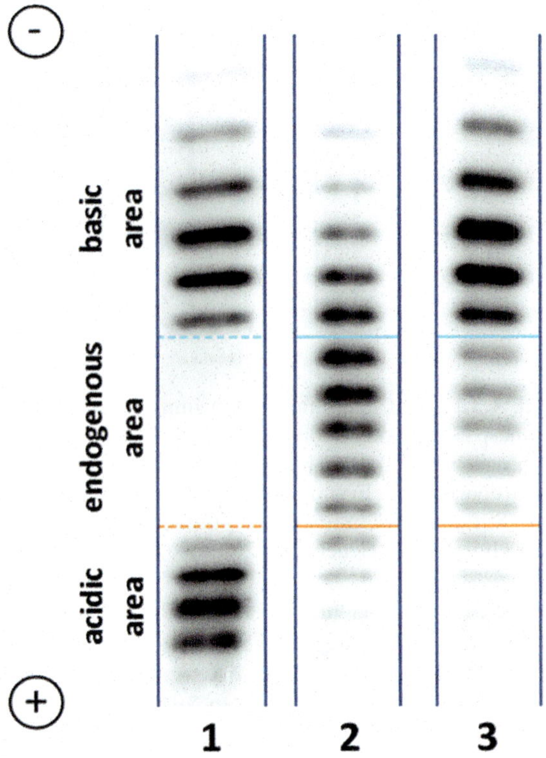

FIGURE 4.3.2 Chemiluminescent immuno-detection of urinary EPO isoform patterns after IEF-PAGE. Identification areas are defined by NESP (acidic area) and rEPO (basic area) standards (1); urine sample containing endogenous EPO (2), and urine sample containing endogenous EPO and rEPO (3).

as "active urines" can affect IEF-PAGE analysis and profile interpretation. Such urine samples exhibit enzymatic activity, which has to date not been elucidated in detail. Yet, the loss of carbohydrate moieties and accordingly, acidity results in a shift of isoform pattern towards the more "basic" (rEPO) area.[43]

4.3.1.6.2 SDS-PAGE

SDS-PAGE is an established approach in biochemistry, frequently employed to separate proteins in a polyacrylamide matrix by MW.[44] It was successfully introduced for EPO analysis in 2008, exploiting the higher MW of rEPO and its analogs compared with endogenous EPO found in urine/blood.[45,46] For EPO detection, it is combined with a Western blot and downstream antibody-based detection, similarly to the IEF-PAGE analysis described before. Both blood and urine samples can be analyzed following immunoaffinity purification by, e.g., antibody-coated well plates, magnetic beads, columns, or microtiter plates to ensure proper band separation.[35–38,47] Both urinary and blood EPO show the same apparent MW (ca. 34 kDa) in SDS-PAGE analysis. Using this method, ESAs of higher molecular mass such as CERA, NESP, and EPO-Fc are readily distinguished from endogenous EPO. rEPO derived from CHO (e.g., epoetin alfa, beta, zeta, and theta) and human fibrosarcoma (epoetin delta) cell lines deviates from endogenous EPO only by a few kDa. Additionally, glycosylated proteins such as

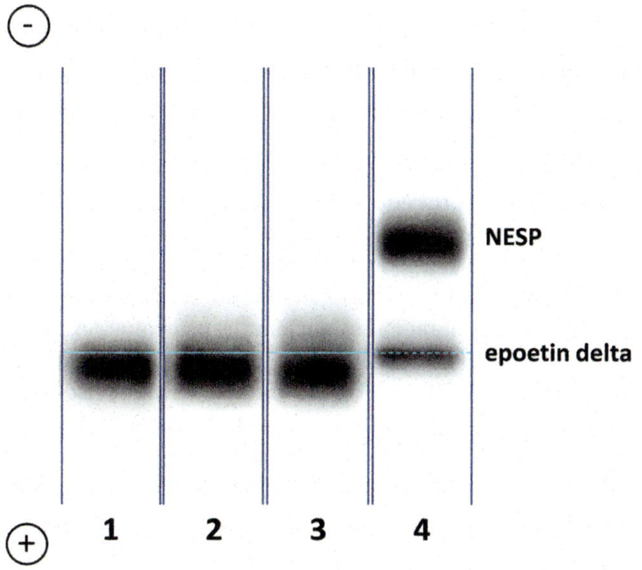

FIGURE 4.3.3 Chemiluminescent immuno-detection of EPO after SAR-PAGE. Epoetin delta reference (4) defining MW cut-off for rEPO; urine sample containing endogenous EPO (1), and urine samples containing endogenous EPO and rEPO (2, 3).

EPO exhibit a glycoform mass distribution leading to a broader band when analyzed by SDS-PAGE. Therefore, the electrophoretic separation of endogenous and recombinant EPO both present in one sample is incomplete, resulting in one broad band with part of the signal at the higher apparent MW of rEPO (see Figure 4.3.3). Such pictures are referred to by WADA's technical document as a mixed profile due to the presence of both endogenous EPO and rEPO. In contrast to the intricate densitometric calculations needed to determine a suspicious isoform profile, a sample is considered an adverse analytical finding (AAF) as determined by SDS-PAGE analysis when a signal at the MW of a recombinant reference is observed. Recently, Okano et al. have shown SDS-PAGE data of an intravenous application of epoetin kappa.[48] Though derived from a CHO cell line, epoetin kappa showed separated rEPO and endogenous EPO bands in urine samples 24–48 h after application. SDS-PAGE analysis of EPO derived from BHK cell lines (epoetin omega) may be more challenging, since its mass is comparable to endogenous EPO.[49] Interestingly, its isoform profile is different.[40] A comparative study of effort urine and active urine illustrated some benefits of the SDS-PAGE. Using IEF-PAGE, enzyme activity in the sample shifted the isoform profile to produce a suspicious result. Analysis of the same sample with SDS-PAGE showed a loss in MW, avoiding an erroneous suspicious result. Additionally, so-called effort urines also did not produce suspicious results with SDS-PAGE, as the MW remained unaltered.[45]

4.3.1.6.3 SAR-PAGE

In 2013, WADA introduced sodium N-lauroylsarcosinate (SAR, SARCOSYL)-PAGE to the technical document to ameliorate previously perceived shortcomings regarding the assay's sensitivity for CERA. While the sensitivity of most epoetins is similar on SDS-PAGE, a considerably inferior detection limit existed for CERA. SDS does not adequately solubilize PEGs under PAGE conditions, leading to reduced primary antibody binding.[50] Substitution of SDS by SAR as a detergent in running and loading buffer corrected this limitation. Over the last years, requests for EPO testing by federations and anti-doping authorities have drastically increased (EPO tests performed in urine 2014: 28,811; 2017: 44,322).[5,51] Therefore, the procedure has been optimized to keep up with increasing sample numbers.[47]

4.3.1.6.4 MAIIA SeLect

MAIIA SeLect was designed as a fast screening test for EPO detection in blood and urine. Briefly, the test consists of two dipsticks, each of which is immersed into the concentrated and if needed, immunopurified urine/blood sample. One dipstick, the so-called EPO total strip, allows EPO by lateral flow to reach a binding zone at its end. There, EPO is bound by an antibody coated to this zone. All EPO and possible EPO analogs will be found in this binding zone. The second dipstick exhibits the same binding zone but with a preceding wheat germ agglutinin (WGA) zone. EPO and EPO analogs from the sample will bind with different affinity to WGA in this so-called isoform strip. Elution with N-acetyl glucosamine (GlcNAc) will partly release WGA-bound EPO, which will then bind to the antibody-coated binding zone of the strip. Bound EPO is detected by a second EPO-antibody labeled with carbon black nano-strings. Quantification of the obtained blackness in both strips is proportional to the EPO concentration. The calculated PMI (percentage of migrated isoforms) is a ratio of the EPO concentrations (isoform/total strip × 100).[52] The binding affinity of rEPO and EPO analogs to WGA is higher than that of endogenous EPO, resulting in a low PMI. The more rEPO a sample contains, the lower the PMI will be. The method was able to detect microdosing (application of 7.5 IU/kg epoetin beta) of EPO in blood and urine with a sensitivity comparable to SAR-PAGE.[53] While Mørkeberg et al. did not compare the MAIIA test with electrophoretic methods, they came to the conclusion that microdosing (10 IU/kg) was detectable for up to 72 hours using MAIIA.[54] So far, MAIIA SeLect has not been approved by WADA as a routine method for EPO testing in sport.

4.3.1.6.5 Mass Spectrometry (MS)

MS has widely been used to characterize rEPO molecules and their glycoforms.[55–57] Yet, the development of an MS-based doping test has not been accomplished so far. The encountered limitations largely concern (1) the lack of highly purified endogenous EPO reference material, (2) the low abundance of EPO in urine/blood, (3) the minute differences between recombinant and natural EPO glycan structures, and (4) considerable analyte losses during sample purification.[58] The sensitivity of the electrophoretic methods (SDS-, SAR-, and IEF-PAGE) routinely used in sports drug testing for EPO analysis has so far not been reached.

NESP is an exception due to its modified amino acid sequence. Okano et al. developed a method for the detection of NESP in human urine. In short, the method consists of an immunoaffinity purification step, a V8 digest, and ultra-performance liquid chromatography-tandem mass spectrometry (UPLC-MS/MS) detection of the digested peptide V9. NESP was detected in samples of an administration study as proof of concept.[59] In a similar approach, Guan et al. immunopurified endogenous EPO and NESP from human plasma, performed a dual digestion with trypsin and PNGase F, and detected the unique T9 peptide utilizing LC-MS/MS for unequivocal identification of NESP.[60] Vogel et al. developed a more generic purification approach with the potential to isolate erythropoietins such as epoetin zeta, NESP, and CERA as well as structurally unrelated erythropoietin-mimetic agents such as, for example, Peginesatide by using magnetic beads crosslinked to EPOR-Fc.[61,62] The EPOR-based purification was successfully combined with LC-MS/MS analysis and SAR-PAGE. In 2013, Reichel et al. demonstrated a difference in O-acetylation of sialic acids between urinary EPO and rEPO. Endogenous urinary EPO and 40 different recombinant EPO pharmaceuticals were purified and digested with trypsin. The use of HPLC separation and high-resolution/high-accuracy mass spectrometry (on an LTQ-Orbitrap) allowed a detailed comparison of the degree of O-acetylation present in the purified samples. The study demonstrated that O-glycans of urinary EPO significantly differed in sialic acid O-acetylation (at S126) compared with 40 rEPO pharmaceuticals: While all rEPOs contained a variable but relatively high degree of O-acetylation, only traces of O-acetylation were observed on two glycans of the urinary EPO.[63] The amounts of purified EPO utilized in this study far exceeded the abundance in doping control samples (8 ng/L in urine; 800 ng used for characterization).

4.3.2 Hypoxia Inducible Factor (HIF) Stabilizers and Activators

HIF stabilizers and activators represent a class of compounds that potentially increase the number of RBCs in the organism due to an indirect stimulation of erythropoiesis and regulation of iron homeostasis.[64] The oxygen transport capacity of the blood is consequently significantly increased, and the resulting performance-enhancing effects would undoubtedly be advantageous in endurance sports. Especially, the misuse of organic HIF stabilizers – which are currently in clinical development for the oral treatment of anemia in patients – by healthy athletes in professional sport represents an obvious issue. Therefore, the WADA banned the use of HIF stabilizers and activators in 2011 and added the compounds to the annually renewed list of prohibited substances.

4.3.2.1 Regulation of Erythropoiesis through HIF

HIFs are transcription factors that act as oxygen sensors in the body. If the oxygen supply is restricted, EPO gene expression and thus, RBC production are upregulated.[65] The biological processes, proteins, and protein aggregates involved in this are more complex. Briefly, HIF, a heterodimeric protein complex composed of an α- and a β-subunit (generating a heterodimeric molecule of ca. 120 kDa), plays an important role due to DNA-binding to the hypoxia-responsive element (HRE) in the nucleus, which promotes the expression of the EPO gene.[64–66] While the β-subunit is permanently translated and stable, HIF-α is the limiting unit for generating the functional heterodimer. Notably, uniisoformic HIF-β is sometimes also named the aryl hydrocarbon receptor nuclear translocator (ARNT), which unfortunately conceals its identity as the dimerization partner of HIF-α. For the α-subunit, three isoforms are known: HIF-1α, HIF-2α, and HIF-3α, all of which represent potential dimerization partners. Under normoxic conditions, HIF-α is hydroxylated at specific proline residues (Pro402 and Pro564 for HIF-1α, Pro405 and Pro531 for HIF-2α) by HIF-prolyl hydroxylases (HIF-PH) that are commonly known as prolyl hydroxylases domain (PHD) enzymes.[67] This hydroxylation represents the key process of HIF destabilization under conditions with sufficient oxygen supply (normoxia). To date, three variants of PHD enzymes are known (PHD-1, PHD-2, and PHD-3), of which PHD-2 is described as the main regulator of HIF activity in the normoxic state, and PHD-1 shows more affinity towards HIF-2α than HIF-1α. Hydroxylated HIF-α undergoes proteasomal degradation complexed by E3 ubiquitin ligase after being recognized by the von Hippel-Lindau tumor suppressor protein (pVHL).[66] Another hydroxylation site of HIF-α was found at the C-terminal Asp residue induced by factor inhibiting HIF (FIH) enzymes, which also influence (limit) the activity of HIF. *In vivo* knockout experiments have shown that HIF-2α is the primary regulator of renal and liver EPO production under hypoxia.[65] HIF-2α is expressed in the peritubular fibroblasts, while HIF-1α is expressed ubiquitously in several types of cells. Accordingly, HIF-1α is involved in a plethora of metabolic processes (e.g., glucose metabolism), whereas HIF-2α is more restricted to EPO production in the kidney.[68] Under restriction of oxygen, the HIF-α subunits translocate into the cell nucleus, followed by dimerization with HIF-β and triggering of erythropoiesis. Recently, it was also recognized that the HIF pathway impacts iron homeostasis via direct and indirect mechanisms.[64] This is of the utmost importance due to the elevated iron demands during erythropoiesis for effective RBC maturation. Direct mechanisms are represented by translation of duodenal cytochrome b (DCYTB) and divalent metal transporter-1 (DMT1) due to HIF-2. Dietary ferric (Fe^{3+}) iron is reduced to ferrous (Fe^{2+}) iron accordingly, before the transport into the enterocyte is enabled. Ferroportin, another important iron modulating protein, is upregulated by HIF-2 also. Additionally, transferrin (including its receptor genes) and ceruloplasmin are upregulated by HIF-1 directly. Elevated iron transport, modulation, and utilization are triggered accordingly. On the other hand, the primary mechanism of iron metabolism is most likely represented by indirect processes. Here, hepcidin owns a key switch position, and its levels strongly correlate with EPO production. The suppression of hepcidin is induced by the production of erythroferrone (ERFE) in the erythroblasts during erythropoiesis. Downregulation of hepcidin in the liver is the consequence and elevates the level of available iron for RBC maturation accordingly.

4.3.2.2 HIF Stabilizers and Activators – Overview

Under normoxia, the destabilization of the EPO transcription factor HIF is mediated by enzymes of the PHD family by hydroxylation of the HIF-α subunit (see Section 4.3.2.1).[67] Therefore, agents affecting PHD activity can be employed as HIF stabilizers. The oldest HIF stabilizer is the transition metal cobalt (Co; see Section 4.3.2.2.2), which is currently still employed to normalize the activity of rEPO preparations (5 μmol of Co^{2+} corresponds to 1 IU of rEPO).[68] PHD activity requires metal ions (Fe^{2+}) and 2-oxoglutarate (2-OG) as co-substrates. Co^{2+} (as well as Cu^{2+} and Ni^{2+}) ions bind competitively to the PHD iron binding site and thus prevent the hydroxylation of HIF-α and subsequent degradation by the pVHL protein and the E3 ubiquitin ligase. For effective erythropoiesis stimulation, daily doses of 10 to 300 mg of cobalt chloride are required; however, considerable toxic and potential carcinogenic effects can appear in the case of chronic use.[68,69] By contrast, several promising organic compounds acting as PHD inhibitors (see Section 4.3.2.2.1) are currently in clinical development. Moreover, the noble gas xenon (Xe) has been found to act as an HIF activator (see Section 4.3.2.2.2). Therefore, its use (misuse) in sports was banned by the WADA in 2014 (after the Olympic Winter Games in Sochi).[70]

4.3.2.2.1 Organic HIF Stabilizers

The first organic compounds evaluated for PHD inhibition were deferoxamine, 3,4-dihydroxybenzoic acid, 1,10-phenanthrolines, and quercetin, which are all characterized by iron chelating properties. But due to toxicity issues and lack of specificity, these candidates were discontinued in early stages of clinical development.[67] In more sophisticated investigations, 2-OG derivatives were designed, which were known to establish salt bridges between the carboxylate and Arg383 of PHD. On the opposite, the essential iron is chelated by the C1 and C2-atoms (with sp2-hybridized orbitals) of the 2-OG molecule. Selective targeted modifications (derivatizations) of 2-OG (e.g., oxalylglycine and NOG) have led to a plethora of potential HIF stabilizers, from which finally, the first drug candidate, FG-2216, emerged (see Figure 4.3.4).[67] Further important HIF stabilizers following FG-2216 in clinical trials are Roxadustat (FG-4592, ASP1517), Vadadustat (AKB-6548), Daprodustat (GSK1278863), Molidustat (BAY 85-3934), and Desidustat (ZYAN1).[67] Figure 4.3.4 shows the chemical structures of these HIF stabilizing candidates. They all represent orally active, erythropoiesis-stimulating drugs (by PHD inhibition) for the treatment of diseases with malfunctioning hemoglobin regulation (e.g., anemia due to chronic kidney disease). Chemically, these candidates are categorized into carboxylic (FG-2216, Roxadustat, Vadadustat, Daprodustat, and Desidustat) and non-carboxylic PHD inhibitors (Molidustat), whereby the carboxyl function is responsible for the coordinative attachment to the Arg383 of PHD. In the case of Molidustat, (non-carboxylic) docking of the pyrazolol tautomer to the active region of PDH2 and iron chelation via the nitrogen in the pyrazolol ring is discussed. Binding as electrostatic interaction with Arg383 of PHD is proposed due to the triazole residue. Additionally, manifold structurally related substances (with partly unknown detailed structure) are also under development and emphasize the importance of smart, preventive, and non-targeted testing protocols (SPNT-control) in the future of doping controls in order to identify also all these analogs, including their metabolites. Beuck et al. listed 30 HIF candidates in 2012, and Joharapurkat et al. compiled 58 different substances with PHD inhibiting properties in 2018.[66,67] And, despite missing clinical approval, AAFs have already been reported from the doping control laboratories in recent years, starting with Roxadustat in 2015 and later Molidustat in 2017.[71] The availability for athletes (professional or not) is facilitated by the worldwide access via black market providers. Generally, liquid chromatography coupled to (high-resolution) mass spectrometry (LC-[HR]MS) is the method of choice for efficient analysis of the aforementioned candidates in urine

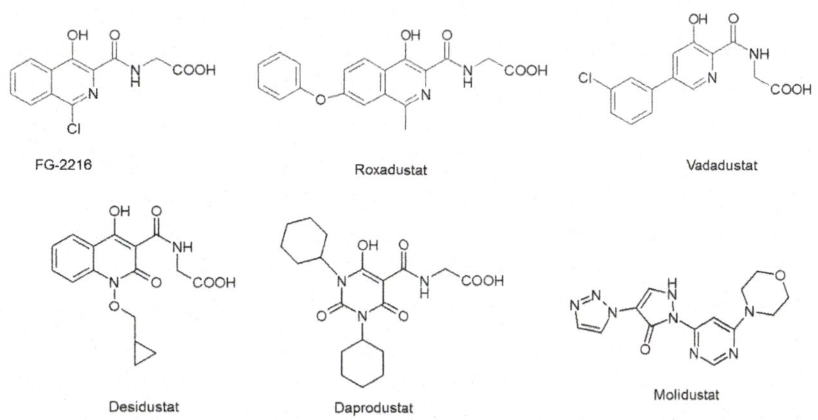

FIGURE 4.3.4 Chemical structures of the most important HIF stabilizers from clinical trials.

samples, and several assays were published recently.[72–75] One of the most recent candidates is the N-alkoxyquinolone derivate Desidustat, which is currently undergoing phase 2 clinical trials. Figure 4.3.5 shows the high-resolution mass spectrum of the protonated $[M+H]^+$ compared with the deprotonated $[M-H]^-$ precursor of Desidustat at m/z = 333 and 331, respectively, with a series of product ions derived after higher collisional dissociation. Interestingly, the product ion mass spectrum in positive mode shows the already reported unusual dissociation behavior with the characteristic elimination of −11 Da. For Desidustat, this was shown in a pseudo-MS^3 experiment, when the first precursor at m/z = 333 was dissociated by forced collision with atmospheric gas in the ion source to generate the second precursor at m/z = 233 ("in-source fragmentation") before entering the mass spectrometer (see small inset at Figure 4.3.5a)*). In addition, the characteristic product ion at m/z = 100.004 occurs in negative ionization mode, just as the elimination of 2,5-oxazolidione ($C_3H_3NO_3$) yields the abundant product ion at m/z = 230.082.[66,76] Besides the mass spectrometric characterization of the HIF stabilizers, knowledge of their metabolic fate after administration and the identification of relevant metabolites is essential. Mostly hydroxylated metabolites and their conjugates with glucuronic acid and sulfates, but also N-glucuronidation in case of Molidustat, were described recently and represent the target analytes for successful initial testing procedures in doping controls.[72–75]

4.3.2.2.2 Inorganic HIF Stabilizers and Activators

In the context of doping controls, two purely inorganic compounds mainly came into focus as agents stimulating erythropoiesis: the noble gas Xe and the transition metal Co. Both can have an impact on the hematological parameters of athletes and are therefore banned by the WADA. For both elements, different analytical approaches to detect their misuse in sports are applied, as detailed in the following subsections.

4.3.2.2.2.1 Xenon (Xe) Since the 1950s, Xe has been used as an anesthetic agent. Despite its remarkable safety profile, it was only used in selected cases due to its high manufacturing costs. Especially regarding its preconditioning effects, i.e., its ability to aid in the protection of an organ from ischemic injury, the underlying metabolic effects were not traceable for many years. In 2007, the impact of Xe on HIF-1α and its downstream effectors, including EPO, was demonstrated and offered an explanation for the benefits of Xe anesthesia.[70,77]

In the context of doping controls, Xe came into focus in 2014, when Russian athletes were reported to use Xe in their preparation for major sporting events, including the Winter Olympic Games.[78] A "guideline" published by the Russian Research Institute of the Ministry of Defense outlined how Xe should be used regularly to enhance athletic performance. The recommended dose consisted of a mixture of 50/50 oxygen/Xe and was therefore below common dosages applied for anesthesia. At the time of the Winter Olympic Games in 2014, Xe was not explicitly listed on WADA's Prohibited List but was added soon after, resulting in a revised version of the list, which came into effect in September 2014. This necessitated the availability of test methods for the detection of Xe in blood and/or urine.

One of the advantages of Xe over other anesthetics is its rapid elimination via the lung, which enables an almost immediate awakening of patients directly after cessation of the Xe supply. However, this feature raised concerns in doping controls regarding whether/how long Xe would be detectable in sports drug testing samples. The methods

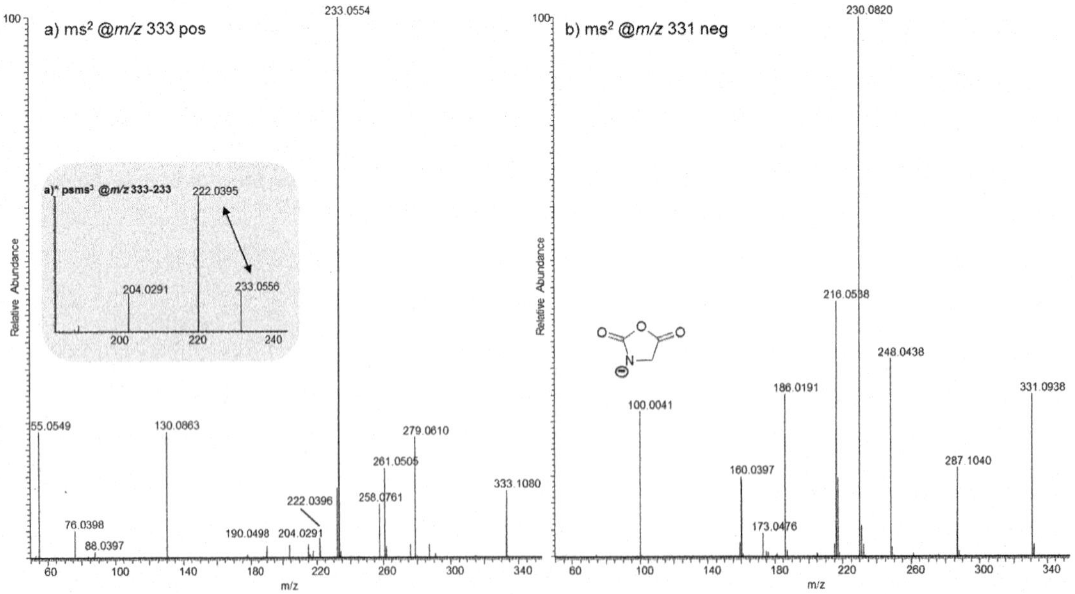

FIGURE 4.3.5 High-resolution product ion mass spectra of Desidustat: a) in positive ionization mode as $[M+H]^+$ at m/z 333 and b) in negative ionization mode as $[M-H]^-$ at m/z 331. The small inset a)* shows the characteristic elimination of −11 Da according to Beuck et al. triggered by pseudoMS^3 ($psms^3$) experiments.[63]

developed for Xe detection rely on so-called headspace injections into a gas chromatograph coupled to a triple quadrupole (qQq) or a time-of-flight (TOF) mass spectrometer.[79,80] The underlying principle takes advantage of the physical properties of Xe, i.e., its temperature-dependent solubility in water. Doping control specimens such as urine and blood are transported and stored refrigerated. In the cooled matrices, Xe is retained in the liquid phase at stable concentrations for more than 2 weeks.[80] As soon as an aliquot of the liquid phase is heated, Xe partitions into the gaseous phase above the liquid layer for headspace injections. Removing a defined amount from the gas in the headspace using a gastight syringe and injecting this into the gas chromatograph enables the amount of Xe present in the doping control sample to be detected and quantified.

Using authentic samples collected from patients scheduled for surgery under Xe-based anesthesia allowed the detection of Xe for up to 2 days after cessation of Xe. The oxygen/Xe ratio was 40/60 and therefore close to the formerly suggested dosing allegedly used by athletes.[80] Subsequently, the developed method was applied to routine doping control samples, but no AAFs have been detected.

4.3.2.2.2.2 Cobalt (Co) Co is one of the essential trace elements in the human body. It occurs naturally in organic and inorganic forms. Organic versions are ubiquitously present in green plants, fish, cereals, and water, while the inorganic form is essential for humans. As for all essential elements, both surplus and deficit amounts have unfavorable effects on the organism. Co is present in the human body with a total amount of 1 to 2 mg, and the daily uptake is estimated to be in the low μg range (based on cobalamin). The most prominent coenzyme of which Co is part is Vitamin B12.

As early as the 1930s, the beneficial effects of Co on erythropoiesis were described and carefully investigated.[81] In 2005, the possible impact of Co on blood doping was discussed as Co was suspected to influence, similarly to Xe, the HIF-α cascade.[82] The biologically active form of Co acting on the HIF-α cascade is Co^{2+}. Preferred preparations to elevate EPO levels usually contain cobalt(II) chloride and are readily available as nutritional supplements. Besides serious side effects including heart failure or hypothyroidism, chronic exposure may cause accompanying ill effects such as nausea and vomiting.

Despite the fact that a potential misuse of Co in sports was recognized many years ago, doping control efforts did not begin to investigate this phenomenon until 2014, when the first pilot studies on urinary Co concentrations were published for humans and horses.[83,84] As Co is ubiquitously present, the study investigated naturally occurring Co concentrations in athlete samples and compared those with a reference population of sportive men and women not included in anti-doping test pools. Available samples of Co elimination studies were also investigated. While Co concentrations in athletes were found to be slightly but significantly elevated, they still fell into the expected normal range of concentrations between 0.1 and 2.2 ng/mL. After single-dose administrations of cobalt(II) chloride, human urinary Co concentrations peaked at concentrations up to 300 ng/mL and were elevated for more than 1 day. The detectability of Co administrations could be further enhanced by applying a diagnostic ratio, e.g., Co/cadmium. The pilot study demonstrated the ability to test for acute Co misuse if threshold levels existed, derived from an adequate reference population and consideration of potential confounding factors. To date, analyses for Co administrations in sport have not been extensive, arguably due to the fact that analytical instruments are required that are not frequently employed in sports drug testing. The method of choice for sensitive Co measurements relies on inductively coupled plasma–mass spectrometry (ICP-MS). In order to ionize metals like Co, argon is energized using high-frequency currents before applying it to the sample, which is heated to thousands of degrees Celsius. The metal atoms are not only ionized but also vaporized and can then enter the mass spectrometer for detection and quantification. ICP-MS is widely used in forensics and toxicology but as yet, has no other applications in sports drug testing besides Co determination.

4.3.3 TGF-β Inhibitors

4.3.3.1 TGF-β Cytokines and Their Role during Erythropoiesis

A variety of diseases is associated with anemia, and classical treatment strategies comprise blood transfusions as well as the use of ESAs.[85,86] EPO and its derivatives are most commonly used for ESA therapy but were found to be insufficient in certain types of anemia caused by ineffective erythropoiesis, such as β-thalassemia and myelodysplastic syndromes.[85–89] This can be attributed to the differential pathogenesis of erythropoietic disorders and the distinct regulation of early- and late-stage erythropoiesis: while EPO stimulates the differentiation of committed progenitor cells into proerythroblasts/pronormoblasts, the further maturation through several normoblast stages into enucleated reticulocytes and finally, RBCs becomes more and more independent of EPO and is negatively regulated by TGF-β cytokines such as GDF-11, GDF-8 (myostatin), and activin A.[86–88,90,91] These growth factors are produced by the microenvironment of the bone marrow[88,92] and exert their biological functions via the activin receptors type II A and B (ActRIIA and ActRIIB). The activation of these serine/threonine kinase receptors results in the association with activin like kinase-4 or -5 and the induction of complex intracellular SMAD 2/3 signaling pathways, which finally lead to changes in erythroid-specific gene expression.[86,93]

Agents modifying TGF-β signaling could be a promising treatment strategy for rare blood diseases originating from EPO-independent defects in RBC production, and two closely related Fc fusion proteins derived from ActRIIA and ActRIIB are currently in clinical development.[89]

4.3.3.2 ActRII-Fc Fusion Proteins: Sotatercept and Luspatercept

Many therapeutic proteins or peptides are recombinantly fused to an immunoglobulin (Ig) Fc domain in order to improve both their biological and pharmacological properties.[94] The slowed renal clearance due to the higher molecular mass and interaction with the neonatal Fc receptor result in an increased plasma half-life and prolonged therapeutic activity of the drug. Moreover, the molecules are characterized by improved solubility and stability and can easily be purified during the production process by using protein A or G. Compared with therapeutic antibodies, many Fc fusion proteins have a significantly shorter half-life (1–2 weeks instead of 3–4 weeks), which can be attributed, among other reasons, to a lower affinity for the neonatal Fc receptor and receptor-mediated clearance by the fusion partner.[94,95]

Sotatercept (ACE-011; Acceleron Pharma, Cambridge, MA) is a glycosylated, dimeric Fc fusion protein composed of the extracellular domain of ActRIIA and the Fc fragment of human IgG1.[88,96] The protein drug acts as a decoy receptor and ligand trap, which prevents activin A, GDF-11, and other TGF-β cytokines from interacting with their endogenous receptors (Figure 4.3.6).[88]

One of activin A's functions is the role of a negative regulator of bone formation, and Sotatercept was originally developed for the therapy of osteoporosis and other diseases involving bone loss.[85,96] During a phase 1 clinical trial in healthy postmenopausal women, the protein drug was administered as a single dose of 0.01–3 mg/kg intravenously or 0.03–0.1 mg/kg subcutaneously and found to significantly increase markers of bone formation while simultaneously decreasing markers of bone resorption.[96] The mean biological half-life ranged between 24 and 32 days and only mild and transient side effects, such as infusion site reactions, were observed. Surprisingly, Sotatercept also induced rapid and sustained dose-dependent elevations of the RBC count (+3–19%), hematocrit (+3–18%), hemoglobin concentration (+2–18%), and reticulocyte percentage (+128–177%) between days 15 and 85 following administration.

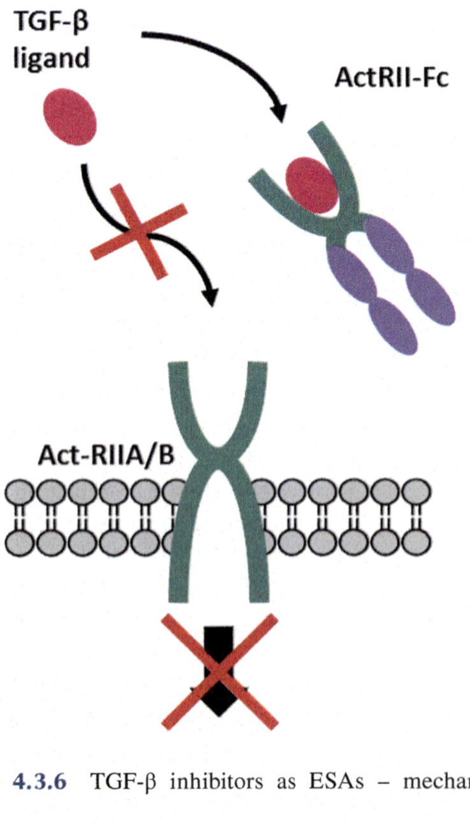

FIGURE 4.3.6 TGF-β inhibitors as ESAs – mechanism of action.

To elucidate potential erythropoiesis-stimulating effects of the drug, an additional animal study was conducted with wild-type mice, which received a single intraperitoneal injection of a murine analog of Sotatercept (RAP-011, ActRIIA-mIgG2aFc, 30 mg/kg).[88] Within 24 hours of administration, significant increases in RBC count, hemoglobin concentration, and hematocrit were observed. Further investigations and experiments demonstrated that the fusion protein affects late-stage erythropoiesis by inhibition of activin A and GDF-11 and could be a promising therapeutic agent for the treatment of anemia due to ineffective erythropoiesis. In a mouse model of β-thalassemia,[97] the neutralization of GDF-11 through RAP-011 could correct ineffective erythropoiesis and reduce the symptoms of anemia by improving hematological parameters. In a novel phase 1 clinical study, up to four doses of Sotatercept ranging from 0.1 to 1 mg/kg were administered to healthy volunteers by subcutaneous injection every 4 weeks.[85] Again, the fusion protein was well tolerated by most of the participants, and significant long-lasting effects on erythropoiesis (hemoglobin concentration, RBC count, and hematocrit), bone formation, and bone mineral density could be observed. Maximum plasma concentrations of 746–7,394 ng/mL were reached 7 days following administration, and the biological half-life varied between 21 and 23 days. Phase 2 clinical trials were conducted in patients with myelodysplastic syndromes, multiple myeloma, end-stage kidney disease, β-thalassemia, and chemotherapy-induced anemia.[98–102] Multiple subcutaneous Sotatercept injections (0.1–2 mg/kg) induced a significant dose-dependent increase in the hemoglobin concentration of many subjects. Further phase 2 studies evaluating Sotatercept in Diamond Blackfan anemia, myeloproliferative neoplasm (MPN)-associated myelofibrosis, β-thalassemia, and multiple myeloma are currently ongoing.[103] Additionally, the protein drug is in phase 2 clinical trials for the therapy of pulmonary arterial hypertension, a rare blood vessel disorder.[103–105]

The current lead product candidate of Acceleron Pharma for the therapy of chronic anemia in a variety of blood diseases is Luspatercept (ACE-536), a recombinant fusion protein derived from the extracellular domain of ActRIIB and the Fc domain of human IgG1.[86,87,105] In contrast to endogenous ActRIIB, an amino acid exchange (L79D) was introduced to reduce activin binding, and both the N- and the C-terminus of the extracellular receptor domain are truncated. Similarly to Sotatercept, Luspatercept acts as a ligand trap, which neutralizes circulating GDF-11 and

GDF-8, thus preventing receptor binding and activation (Figure 4.3.6).[86,87]

In preclinical studies, Luspatercept and its murine analog RAP-536 were administered to mice, rats, and cynomolgus monkeys and found to induce sustained dose-dependent increases in RBC count, hemoglobin concentration, and hematocrit.[86] In different rodent models of acute and chronic anemia due to blood loss, chemotherapy, chronic kidney disease, myelodysplastic syndromes, and β-thalassemia, the protein drug was able to significantly improve RBC parameters.[86,106] A phase 1 clinical trial was conducted in healthy volunteers, who received up to two subcutaneous Luspatercept doses of 0.0625–0.25 mg/kg.[87] Maximum serum concentrations up to 1.9 µg/mL were observed 7–10 days after the first dose, and the biological half-life varied between 15 and 16 days. No serious side effects were reported, and significant, long-lasting increases in hematological parameters (RBC number, hematocrit, and hemoglobin concentration) maintained for several weeks were observed. The erythropoiesis-stimulating effects were confirmed in different phase 2 studies in patients with myelodysplastic syndromes and β-thalassemia, in whom anemia could be effectively treated with multiple subcutaneous Luspatercept injections at doses from 0.125–1.75 mg/kg.[107,108] Currently, the protein drug is undergoing multiple phase 2 and 3 clinical trials for the treatment of anemia associated with different hematological disorders such as myelodysplastic syndromes, β-thalassemia, and myelofibrosis.[103]

4.3.3.3 TGF-β Inhibitors in Sports Drug Testing

Due to their presumed effects on RBC production, TGF-β inhibitors such as Sotatercept and Luspatercept are also discussed as potential performance-enhancing agents in sports. In 2016, they were added to the WADA Prohibited List and are now listed among the ESAs in section S2 – "Peptide hormones, growth factors, related substances and mimetics."[109] Although neither of these drug candidates has obtained clinical approval yet, different immunological and MS-based detection methods suitable for doping control serum/plasma samples as well as dried blood spots (DBS; see also Section 7.1) have been proactively developed (Table 4.3.1).

In 2016, a doping control detection assay for Sotatercept employing ammonium sulfate precipitation, affinity purification, tryptic digestion, and LC in combination with ion mobility (IM) separation and HRMS (LC-IM-HRMS) was published. It was shown to be highly specific for proteolytic signature peptides originating from both the receptor and the Fc domain of the fusion protein, and offers an adequate limit of detection (LOD) of 10 ng/mL.[110] The MS-based analytical method is complemented by a non-targeted immunological assay, which can detect different IgG-based TGF-β inhibitors irrespective of their amino acid sequence: by immobilizing dimeric activin A on a Western blotting membrane, all proteins specifically binding to the TGF-β cytokine can be enriched and subsequently detected with an enzyme-linked secondary antibody directed against the Fc domain of human IgG1. The estimated LOD of the approach was 200 ng/mL. A multiplexed assay for the combined mass spectrometric detection of Sotatercept and Luspatercept was just recently developed.[111] Ammonium sulfate precipitation and immunoaffinity purification with antibodies directed against the extracellular domains of ActRIIA and ActRIIB are used for the isolation of the target proteins

TABLE 4.3.1
Doping Control Detection Methods for TGF-β Inhibitors

Target analyte	Isolation strategy	Detection strategy	Sample matrix	Sample volume (µL)	LOD (ng/mL)	Reference
Sotatercept	Affinity purification (activin A)	LC-IM-HRMS	Serum	200	~10	[110]
	Affinity purification (activin A)	SDS-PAGE & Western blotting (activin A, anti-human IgG1)	Serum	200	~200	[110]
	Immunoaffinity purification (anti-ActRIIA)	SAR-PAGE & Western blotting (anti-ActRIIA)	Serum	50	~0.1	[113, 115]
	Affinity purification (Protein G)	LC-MS/MS	DBS	20	~250	[117]
	Affinity purification (activin A)	LC-MS/MS	DBS	20	~250	
Luspatercept	Immunoaffinity purification (anti-ActRIIB)	SAR-PAGE & Western blotting (anti-ActRIIB)	Serum	50	~1	[112, 115]
	Commercial ActRIIB ELISA		Serum	100	~16	[112]
Sotatercept, Luspatercept	Immunoaffinity purification (anti-ActRIIA, anti-ActRIIB)	LC-MS/MS	Serum	200	~50	[111]
	Immunoaffinity purification (anti-ActRIIA, anti-ActRIIB)	SDS-PAGE and western blotting (anti-ActRIIA, anti-ActRIIB)	Serum/Plasma	300	~0.1–3.3	[114]
	Immunoaffinity purification (anti-ActRIIA, anti-ActRIIB)	IEF and western blotting (anti-ActRIIA, anti-ActRIIB)	Serum/Plasma	300–1,000	<5	[116]

from the biological matrix, and characteristic tryptic peptides are detected by means of LC-MS/MS. The assay's LOD was approximately 50 ng/mL. A significantly higher sensitivity with LODs as low as 0.1 ng/mL was achieved by combining immunoaffinity purification with SAR- or SDS-PAGE and Western blotting.[112–115] Thereby, different antibodies directed against the extracellular receptor domains of Sotatercept and Luspatercept were used for immunoprecipitation and Western blot detection. Additionally, the IEF-based doping control detection method for EPO and its derivatives (see Section 4.3.1.6.1) was modified to enable a combined immunoaffinity purification, isoform separation, and detection of different ESAs.[116] The resulting LODs were below 5 ng/mL for Sotatercept and Luspatercept, 15 pg/mL for epoetin alpha and beta, 35 pg/mL for NESP, 25 pg/mL for CERA, and 100 pg/mL for EPO-Fc. Moreover, a commercial anti-ActRIIB ELISA was investigated for sports drug testing and found to be suitable as a fast screening tool for Luspatercept with an LOD of approximately 16 ng/mL.[112]

Furthermore, two complementary assays for the detection of Sotatercept from DBS were developed by using ultrasonication-assisted extraction in combination with affinity purification (Protein G- or activin A-conjugated magnetic beads) and LC-HRMS.[117] For DBS with a sample volume of approximately 20 µL, the LOD was estimated as 250 ng/mL.

Within clinical trials, Sotatercept serum concentrations were determined by using a validated competitive ELISA test based on anti-human ActRIIA antibodies, which has a working range of 8–400 ng/mL.[85] Similarly, Luspatercept concentrations in clinical post-administration samples were measured using a sandwich ELISA employing an anti-Luspatercept antibody for the isolation of the fusion protein and an anti-human IgG1 antibody for detection purposes. The assay had an analytical range from 50 to 600 ng/mL.[87]

As mentioned earlier, both Sotatercept and Luspatercept are still undergoing clinical investigation. Therefore, reference proteins intended for research purposes had to be used for the development, optimization, and validation of the different doping control assays. The results of a recent study indicate that the use of such reference material necessitates particular caution, as there can be significant differences to the pharmaceutical products and the results from earlier preclinical and clinical studies.[111] Therefore, all the presented detection methods need to be tested with the authentic pharmaceutical products and post-administration samples as soon as both become available through clinical approval or industry partners.

REFERENCES

1. Jelkmann W, Lundby C. Blood doping and its detection. *Blood* 2011;118(9):2395–404.
2. Jelkmann W. The ESA scenario gets complex: from biosimilar epoetins to activin traps. *Nephrol Dial Transplant* 2015;30(4):553–9.
3. World Anti-Doping Agency (WADA). Prohibited list 2019. https://www.wada-ama.org/sites/default/files/wada_2019_english_prohibited_list.pdf (accessed 24.10.2018).
4. Catlin DH, Hatton CK, Lasne F. Abuse of recombinant erythropoietins by athletes. In: *Erythropoietins and Erythropoiesis: Molecular, Cellular, Preclinical, and Clinical Biology*, Molineux G, Foote MA, Elliott SG (eds.) Birkhäuser Basel: Basel, 2006, 205–227.
5. World Anti-Doping Agency (WADA). 2017 Anti-doping testing figures. https://www.wada-ama.org/sites/default/files/resources/files/2017_anti-doping_testing_figures_en_0.pdf (accessed 24.10.2018).
6. Ekblom B, Berglund B. Effect of erythropoietin administration on mammal aerobic power. *Scand J Med Sci* 1991;1(2):88–93.
7. Annaheim S, Jacob M, Krafft A, Breymann C, Rehm M, Boutellier U. RhEPO improves time to exhaustion by non-hematopoietic factors in humans. *Eur J Appl Physiol* 2016;116(3):623–33.
8. Haile DW, Durussel J, Mekonen W, Ongaro N, Anjila E, Mooses M, Daskalaki E, Mooses K, McClure JD, Sutehall S, Pitsiladis YP. Effects of EPO on blood parameters and running performance in Kenyan athletes. *Med Sci Sports Exerc* 2019;51(2):299–307.
9. Heuberger JAAC, Rotmans JI, Gal P, Stuurman FE, van 't Westende J, Post TE, Daniels JMA, Moerland M, van Veldhoven PLJ, de Kam ML, Ram H, de Hon O, Posthuma JJ, Burggraaf J, Cohen AF. Effects of erythropoietin on cycling performance of well trained cyclists: a double-blind, randomised, placebo-controlled trial. *Lancet Haematol* 2017;4(8):e374–e386.
10. World Anti-Doping Agency (WADA). 2015 Anti-doping testing figures. https://www.wada-ama.org/sites/default/files/resources/files/2015_wada_anti-doping_testing_figures_report_0.pdf (accessed 25.10.2018).
11. World Anti-Doping Agency (WADA). 2014 Anti-doping testing figures. https://www.wada-ama.org/sites/default/files/wada_2014_anti-doping-testing-figures_full-report_en.pdf (accessed 25.10.2018).
12. Brines M, Cerami A. Erythropoietin-mediated tissue protection: reducing collateral damage from the primary injury response. *J Intern Med* 2008;264(5):405–32.
13. Congote LF. Regulation of fetal liver erythropoiesis. *J Steroid Biochem* 1977;8(5):423–8.
14. Foote M. Studies of erythropoiesis and the discovery and cloning of recombinant human erythropoietin. In: *Erythropoietins and Erythropoiesis: Molecular, Cellular, Preclinical, and Clinical Biology*, Molineux G, Foote MA, Elliott SG (eds.) Birkhäuser Basel: Basel, 2006, 15–23.
15. Whetton AD, Graham GJ. Homing and mobilization in the stem cell niche. *Trends Cell Biol* 1999;9(6):233–8.
16. Israels LG, Israels ED. Erythropoiesis: an overview. In: *Erythropoietins and Erythropoiesis: Molecular, Cellular, Preclinical, and Clinical Biology*, Molineux G, Foote MA, Elliott SG (eds.) Birkhäuser Basel: Basel, 2006, 3–14.
17. Miyake T, Kung CK, Goldwasser E. Purification of human erythropoietin. *J Biol Chem* 1977;252(15):5558–64.
18. Reichel C. The overlooked difference between human endogenous and recombinant erythropoietins and its implication for sports drug testing and pharmaceutical drug design. *Drug Test Anal* 2011;3(11–12):883–91.
19. Jacobs K, Shoemaker C, Rudersdorf R, Neill SD, Kaufman RJ, Mufson A, Seehra J, Jones SS, Hewick R, Fritsch EF, et al. Isolation and characterization of genomic and cDNA clones of human erythropoietin. *Nature* 1985;313(6005):806–10.

20. Molineux G. Biology of erythropoietin. In: *Erythropoietins and Erythropoiesis: Molecular, Cellular, Preclinical, and Clinical Biology*, Molineux G, Foote MA, Elliott SG (eds.) Birkhäuser Basel: Basel, 2006, 113–132.
21. Lasne F. Double-blotting: a solution to the problem of non-specific binding of secondary antibodies in immunoblotting procedures. *J Immunol Methods* 2001;253(1–2):125–31.
22. Fukuda MN, Sasaki H, Lopez L, Fukuda M. Survival of recombinant erythropoietin in the circulation: the role of carbohydrates. *Blood* 1989;73(1):84–9.
23. Jelkmann W. Developments in the therapeutic use of erythropoiesis stimulating agents. *Br J Haematol* 2008;141(3):287–97.
24. Jelkmann W. Recombinant EPO production-points the nephrologist should know. *Nephrol Dial Transplant* 2007;22(10):2749–53.
25. Park SS, Park J, Ko J, Chen L, Meriage D, Crouse-Zeineddini J, Wong W, Kerwin BA. Biochemical assessment of erythropoietin products from Asia versus US Epoetin alfa manufactured by Amgen. *J Pharm Sci* 2009;98(5):1688–99.
26. Egrie JC, Browne JK. Development and characterization of novel erythropoiesis stimulating protein (NESP). *Nephrol Dial Transplant* 2001;16 Suppl 3:3–13.
27. Gross AW, Lodish HF. Cellular trafficking and degradation of erythropoietin and novel erythropoiesis stimulating protein (NESP). *J Biol Chem* 2006;281(4):2024–32.
28. Macdougall IC. Novel erythropoiesis-stimulating agents: a new era in anemia management. *Clin J Am Soc Nephrol* 2008;3(1):200–7.
29. Dehnes Y, Hemmersbach P. Effect of single doses of methoxypolyethylene glycol-epoetin beta (CERA, Mircera) and epoetin delta (Dynepo) on isoelectric erythropoietin profiles and haematological parameters. *Drug Test Anal* 2011;3(5):291–9.
30. Bitonti AJ, Dumont JA. Pulmonary administration of therapeutic proteins using an immunoglobulin transport pathway. *Adv Drug Deliv Rev* 2006;58(9–10):1106–18.
31. Reichel C, Thevis M. Detection of EPO-Fc fusion protein in human blood: screening and confirmation protocols for sports drug testing. *Drug Test Anal* 2012;4(11):818–29.
32. Lasne F, Martin L, Crepin N, de Ceaurriz J. Detection of isoelectric profiles of erythropoietin in urine: differentiation of natural and administered recombinant hormones. *Anal Biochem* 2002;311(2):119–26.
33. Lasne F, Martin L, Martin JA. A fast preparative method for detection of recombinant erythropoietin in blood samples. *Drug Test Anal* 2010;2(10):494–5.
34. Reihlen P, Volker-Schänzer E, Majer B, Schänzer W. Easy-to-use IEF compatible immunoaffinity purification of Erythropoietin from urine retentates. *Drug Test Anal* 2012;4(11):813–7.
35. Desharnais P, Naud JF, Ayotte C. Immunomagnetic beads-based isolation of erythropoietins from urine and blood for sports anti-doping control. *Drug Test Anal* 2017;9(11–12):1744–52.
36. Dehnes Y, Lamon S, Lönnberg M. Erythropoietin (EPO) immunoaffinity columns--a powerful tool for purifying EPO and its recombinant analogues. *J Pharm Biomed Anal* 2010;53(4):1028–32.
37. Lönnberg M, Dehnes Y, Drevin M, Garle M, Lamon S, Leuenberger N, Quach T, Carlsson J. Rapid affinity purification of erythropoietin from biological samples using disposable monoliths. *J Chromatogr A* 2010;1217(45):7031–7.
38. Mallorqui J, Llop E, de Bolos C, Gutierrez-Gallego R, Segura J, Pascual JA. Purification of erythropoietin from human plasma samples using an immunoaffinity well plate. *J Chromatogr B Analyt Technol Biomed Life Sci* 2010;878(23):2117–22.
39. WADA EPO Working Group. TD2014EPO – Harmonization of analysis and reporting of erythropoiesis stimulating agents (ESAs) by electrophoretic techniques. https://www.wada-ama.org/sites/default/files/resources/files/WADA-TD2014EPO-v1-Harmonization-of-Analysis-and-Reporting-of-ESAs-by-Electrophoretic-Techniques-EN.pdf (accessed 24.10.2018).
40. Lasne F, Martin L, Martin JA, de Ceaurriz J. Isoelectric profiles of human erythropoietin are different in serum and urine. *Int J Biol Macromol* 2007;41(3):354–7.
41. Lamon S, Martin L, Robinson N, Saugy M, Ceaurriz J, Lasne F. Effects of exercise on the isoelectric patterns of erythropoietin. *Clin J Sport Med* 2009;19(4):311–5.
42. Catlin D, Howe C, Lasne F, Nissen-Lie G, Pascual JA, Saugy M. TD2007EPO – Harmonization of the method for the identification of epoetin alfa and beta (rEPO) and darbepoetin alfa (NESP) by IEF-dounle blotting and chemiluminescent detection. https://www.wada-ama.org/sites/default/files/resources/files/WADA_TD2007EPO_%20Harmonization_Method_Identification_Recombinant_Erythropoietins_Analogues_EN.pdf (accessed 24.10.2018).
43. Belalcazar V, Gutierrez Gallego R, Llop E, Segura J, Pascual JA. Assessing the instability of the isoelectric focusing patterns of erythropoietin in urine. *Electrophoresis* 2006;27(22):4387–95.
44. Laemmli UK. Cleavage of structural proteins during the assembly of the head of bacteriophage T4. *Nature* 1970;227:680.
45. Reichel C, Kulovics R, Jordan V, Watzinger M, Geisendorfer T. SDS-PAGE of recombinant and endogenous erythropoietins: benefits and limitations of the method for application in doping control. *Drug Test Anal* 2009;1(1):43–50.
46. Kohler M, Ayotte C, Desharnais P, Flenker U, Ludke S, Thevis M, Volker-Schänzer E, Schänzer W. Discrimination of recombinant and endogenous urinary erythropoietin by calculating relative mobility values from SDS gels. *Int J Sports Med* 2008;29(1):1–6.
47. Reihlen P, Blobel M, Kempkes R, Reichel C, Volker Schänzer E, Majer B, Schänzer W. Optimizing SAR-PAGE. *Drug Test Anal* 2015;7(11–12):1014–6.
48. Okano M, Sato M, Kaneko E, Kageyama S. Doping control of biosimilar epoetin kappa and other recombinant erythropoietins after intravenous application. *Drug Test Anal* 2011;3(11–12):798–805.
49. Skibeli V, Nissen-Lie G, Torjesen P. Sugar profiling proves that human serum erythropoietin differs from recombinant human erythropoietin. *Blood* 2001;98(13):3626–34.
50. Reichel C, Abzieher F, Geisendorfer T. SARCOSYL-PAGE: a new method for the detection of MIRCERA- and EPO-doping in blood. *Drug Test Anal* 2009;1(11–12):494–504.
51. World Anti-Doping Agency (WADA). 2014 Anti-doping testing figures report. https://www.wada-ama.org/sites/default/files/wada_2014_anti-doping-testing-figures_full-report_en.pdf (accessed 24.10.2018).
52. Dehnes Y, Myrvold L, Strom H, Ericsson M, Hemmersbach P. MAIIA EPO SeLect-a rapid screening kit for the detection of recombinant EPO analogues in doping control: inter-laboratory prevalidation and normative study of athlete urine and plasma samples. *Drug Test Anal* 2014;6(11–12):1144–50.

53. Dehnes Y, Shalina A, Myrvold L. Detection of recombinant EPO in blood and urine samples with EPO WGA MAIIA, IEF and SAR-PAGE after microdose injections. *Drug Test Anal* 2013;5(11–12):861–9.
54. Mørkeberg J, Sharpe K, Karstoft K, Ashenden MJ. Detection of microdoses of rhEPO with the MAIIA test. *Scand J Med Sci Sports* 2014;24(4):634–41.
55. Balaguer E, Demelbauer U, Pelzing M, Sanz-Nebot V, Barbosa J, Neususs C. Glycoform characterization of erythropoietin combining glycan and intact protein analysis by capillary electrophoresis-electrosp ray-time-of-flight mass spectrometry. *Electrophoresis* 2006;27(13):2638–50.
56. Neususs C, Demelbauer U, Pelzing M. Glycoform characterization of intact erythropoietin by capillary electrophoresis-electrospray-time of flight-mass spectrometry. *Electrophoresis* 2005;26(7–8):1442–50.
57. Yu B, Cong H, Liu H, Li Y, Liu F. Ionene-dynamically coated capillary for analysis of urinary and recombinant human erythropoietin by capillary electrophoresis and online electrospray ionization mass spectrometry. *J Sep Sci* 2005;28(17):2390–400.
58. Reichel C. Detection of peptidic erythropoiesis-stimulating agents in sport. *Br J Sports Med* 2014;48(10):842–7.
59. Okano M, Sato M, Kageyama S. Identification of the long-acting erythropoiesis-stimulating agent darbepoetin alfa in human urine by liquid chromatography-tandem mass spectrometry. *Anal Bioanal Chem* 2014;406(5):1317–29.
60. Guan F, Uboh CE, Soma LR, Birksz E, Chen J. Identification of darbepoetin alfa in human plasma by liquid chromatography coupled to mass spectrometry for doping control. *Int J Sports Med* 2009;30(2):80–6.
61. Vogel M, Blobel M, Thomas A, Walpurgis K, Schänzer W, Reichel C, Thevis M. Isolation, enrichment, and analysis of erythropoietins in anti-doping analysis by receptor-coated magnetic beads and liquid chromatography-mass spectrometry. *Anal Chem* 2014;86(24):12014–21.
62. Vogel M, Thomas A, Schänzer W, Thevis M. EPOR-based purification and analysis of erythropoietin mimetic peptides from human urine by Cys-specific cleavage and LC/MS/MS. *J Am Soc Mass Spectrom* 2015;26(9): 1617–25.
63. Reichel C. Differences in sialic acid O-acetylation between human urinary and recombinant erythropoietins: a possible mass spectrometric marker for doping control. *Drug Test Anal* 2013;5(11–12):877–89.
64. Kular D, Macdougall IC. HIF stabilizers in the management of renal anemia: from bench to bedside to pediatrics. *Pediatr Nephrol* 2018.
65. Gupta N, Wish JB. Hypoxia-inducible factor prolyl hydroxylase inhibitors: a potential new treatment for anemia in patients with CKD. *Am J Kidney Dis* 2017;69(6):815–26.
66. Beuck S, Schänzer W, Thevis M. Hypoxia-inducible factor stabilizers and other small-molecule erythropoiesis-stimulating agents in current and preventive doping analysis. *Drug Test Anal* 2012;4(11):830–45.
67. Joharapurkar AA, Pandya VB, Patel VJ, Desai RC, Jain MR. Prolyl hydroxylase inhibitors: a breakthrough in the therapy of anemia associated with chronic diseases. *J Med Chem* 2018;61(16):6964–82.
68. Jelkmann W. Erythropoietin. *Front Horm Res* 2016;47:115–27.
69. Hoffmeister T, Schwenke D, Wachsmuth N, Krug O, Thevis M, Byrnes WC, Schmidt WFJ. Erythropoietic effects of low-dose cobalt application. *Drug Test Anal* 2018.
70. Stoppe C, Ney J, Brenke M, Goetzenich A, Emontzpohl C, Schalte G, Grottke O, Moeller M, Rossaint R, Coburn M. Sub-anesthetic xenon increases erythropoietin levels in humans: a randomized controlled trial. *Sports Med* 2016;46(11):1753–66.
71. Buisson C, Marchand A, Bailloux I, Lahaussois A, Martin L, Molina A. Detection by LC-MS/MS of HIF stabilizer FG-4592 used as a new doping agent: investigation on a positive case. *J Pharm Biomed Anal* 2016;121:181–7.
72. Dib J, Mongongu C, Buisson C, Molina A, Schänzer W, Thuss U, Thevis M. Mass spectrometric characterization of the hypoxia-inducible factor (HIF) stabilizer drug candidate BAY 85–3934 (molidustat) and its glucuronidated metabolite BAY-348, and their implementation into routine doping controls. *Drug Test Anal* 2017;9(1):61–7.
73. Eichner D, Van Wagoner RM, Brenner M, Chou J, Leigh S, Wright LR, Flippin LA, Martinelli M, Krug O, Schänzer W, Thevis M. Implementation of the prolyl hydroxylase inhibitor Roxadustat (FG-4592) and its main metabolites into routine doping controls. *Drug Test Anal* 2017;9(11–12):1768–78.
74. Hansson A, Thevis M, Cox H, Miller G, Eichner D, Bondesson U, Hedeland M. Investigation of the metabolites of the HIF stabilizer FG-4592 (roxadustat) in five different *in vitro* models and in a human doping control sample using high resolution mass spectrometry. *J Pharm Biomed Anal* 2017;134:228–36.
75. Saigusa D, Suzuki N, Matsumoto Y, Umeda K, Tomioka Y, Koshiba S, Yamamoto M. Detection of novel metabolite for roxadustat doping by global metabolomics. *J Biochem* 2018;163(6):e1.
76. Beuck S, Schwabe T, Grimme S, Schlörer N, Kamber M, Schänzer W, Thevis M. Unusual mass spectrometric dissociation pathway of protonated isoquinoline-3-carboxamides due to multiple reversible water adduct formation in the gas phase. *J Am Soc Mass Spectrom* 2009;20(11):2034–48.
77. Ma D, Lim T, Xu J, Tang H, Wan Y, Zhao H, Hossain M, Maxwell PH, Maze M. Xenon preconditioning protects against renal ischemic-reperfusion injury via HIF-1alpha activation. *J Am Soc Nephrol* 2009;20(4):713–20.
78. Breathe It In. *The Economist*, 2014.
79. Thevis M, Piper T, Geyer H, Thomas A, Schaefer MS, Kienbaum P, Schänzer W. Measuring xenon in human plasma and blood by gas chromatography/mass spectrometry. *Rapid Commun Mass Spectrom* 2014;28(13):1501–6.
80. Thevis M, Piper T, Geyer H, Schaefer MS, Schneemann J, Kienbaum P, Schänzer W. Urine analysis concerning xenon for doping control purposes. *Rapid Commun Mass Spectrom* 2015;29(1):61–6.
81. Orten J. On the mechanism of the ematopoietic action of cobalt. *Am J Physiol* 1935;114:414–22.
82. Lippi G, Franchini M, Guidi GC. Cobalt chloride administration in athletes: a new perspective in blood doping? *Br J Sports Med* 2005;39(11):872–3.
83. Krug O, Kutscher D, Piper T, Geyer H, Schänzer W, Thevis M. Quantifying cobalt in doping control urine samples-a pilot study. *Drug Test Anal* 2014;6(11–12):1186–90.
84. Ho EN, Chan GH, Wan TS, Curl P, Riggs CM, Hurley MJ, Sykes D. Controlling the misuse of cobalt in horses. *Drug Test Anal* 2015;7(1):21–30.
85. Sherman ML, Borgstein NG, Mook L, Wilson D, Yang Y, Chen N, Kumar R, Kim K, Laadem A. Multiple-dose, safety, pharmacokinetic, and pharmacodynamic study of Sotatercept (ActRIIA-IgG1), a novel erythropoietic agent, in healthy postmenopausal women. *J Clin Pharmacol* 2013;53(11):1121–30.

86. Suragani RN, Cadena SM, Cawley SM, Sako D, Mitchell D, Li R, Davies MV, Alexander MJ, Devine M, Loveday KS, Underwood KW, Grinberg AV, Quisel JD, Chopra R, Pearsall RS, Seehra J, Kumar R. Transforming growth factor-beta superfamily ligand trap ACE-536 corrects anemia by promoting late-stage erythropoiesis. *Nat Med* 2014;20(4):408–14.
87. Attie KM, Allison MJ, McClure T, Boyd IE, Wilson DM, Pearsall AE, Sherman ML. A phase 1 study of ACE-536, a regulator of erythroid differentiation, in healthy volunteers. *Am J Hematol* 2014;89(7):766–70.
88. Carrancio S, Markovics J, Wong P, Leisten J, Castiglioni P, Groza MC, Raymon HK, Heise C, Daniel T, Chopra R, Sung V. An activin receptor IIA ligand trap promotes erythropoiesis resulting in a rapid induction of red blood cells and haemoglobin. *Br J Haematol* 2014;165(6):870–82.
89. Mies A, Platzbecker U. Increasing the effectiveness of hematopoiesis in myelodysplastic syndromes: erythropoiesis-stimulating agents and transforming growth factor-beta superfamily inhibitors. *Semin Hematol* 2017;54(3):141–6.
90. Hattangadi SM, Wong P, Zhang L, Flygare J, Lodish HF. From stem cell to red cell: regulation of erythropoiesis at multiple levels by multiple proteins, RNAs, and chromatin modifications. *Blood* 2011;118(24):6258–68.
91. Doshi S, Krzyzanski W, Yue S, Elliott S, Chow A, Perez-Ruixo JJ. Clinical pharmacokinetics and pharmacodynamics of erythropoiesis-stimulating agents. *Clin Pharmacokinet* 2013;52(12):1063–83.
92. Iancu-Rubin C, Mosoyan G, Wang J, Kraus T, Sung V, Hoffman R. Stromal cell-mediated inhibition of erythropoiesis can be attenuated by Sotatercept (ACE-011), an activin receptor type II ligand trap. *Exp Hematol* 2013;41(2):155–166 e17.
93. Larsson J, Karlsson S. The role of smad signaling in hematopoiesis. *Oncogene* 2005;24(37):5676–92.
94. Czajkowsky DM, Hu J, Shao Z, Pleass RJ. Fc-fusion proteins: new developments and future perspectives. *EMBO Mol Med* 2012;4(10):1015–28.
95. Liu L. Antibody glycosylation and its impact on the pharmacokinetics and pharmacodynamics of monoclonal antibodies and Fc-fusion proteins. *J Pharm Sci* 2015;104(6):1866–84.
96. Ruckle J, Jacobs M, Kramer W, Pearsall AE, Kumar R, Underwood KW, Seehra J, Yang Y, Condon CH, Sherman ML. Single-dose, randomized, double-blind, placebo-controlled study of ACE-011 (ActRIIA-IgG1) in postmenopausal women. *J Bone Miner Res* 2009;24(4):744–52.
97. Dussiot M, Maciel TT, Fricot A, Chartier C, Negre O, Veiga J, Grapton D, Paubelle E, Payen E, Beuzard Y, Leboulch P, Ribeil JA, Arlet JB, Cote F, Courtois G, Ginzburg YZ, Daniel TO, Chopra R, Sung V, Hermine O, Moura IC. An activin receptor IIA ligand trap corrects ineffective erythropoiesis in beta-thalassemia. *Nat Med* 2014;20(4):398–407.
98. Raftopoulos H, Laadem A, Hesketh PJ, Goldschmidt J, Gabrail N, Osborne C, Ali M, Sherman ML, Wang D, Glaspy JA, Puccio-Pick M, Zou J, Crawford J. Sotatercept (ACE-011) for the treatment of chemotherapy-induced anemia in patients with metastatic breast cancer or advanced or metastatic solid tumors treated with platinum-based chemotherapeutic regimens: results from two phase 2 studies. *Support Care Cancer* 2016;24(4):1517–25.
99. Abdulkadyrov KM, Salogub GN, Khuazheva NK, Sherman ML, Laadem A, Barger R, Knight R, Srinivasan S, Terpos E. Sotatercept in patients with osteolytic lesions of multiple myeloma. *Br J Haematol* 2014;165(6):814–23.
100. Komrokji R, Garcia-Manero G, Ades L, Prebet T, Steensma DP, Jurcic JG, Sekeres MA, Berdeja J, Savona MR, Beyne-Rauzy O, Stamatoullas A, DeZern AE, Delaunay J, Borthakur G, Rifkin R, Boyd TE, Laadem A, Vo B, Zhang J, Puccio-Pick M, Attie KM, Fenaux P, List AF. Sotatercept with long-term extension for the treatment of anaemia in patients with lower-risk myelodysplastic syndromes: a phase 2, dose-ranging trial. *Lancet Haematol* 2018;5(2):e63–e72.
101. Cappellini MD, Porter J, Origa R, Forni GL, Laadem A, Galacteros F, Miteva D, Sung V, Chopra R, Arlet J-B, Ribeil J-A, Klesczewski K, Attie KM, Garbowski M, Hermine O. A phase 2A, open-label, dose-finding study to determine the safety and tolerability of Sotatercept (ACE-011) in adults with beta (β)-thalassemia: intermin results. *55Th Annual Meeting of the American Society of Hematology (ASH)*, New Orleans, 2013.
102. Havill J, Kopyt N, Coyne D, Weiswasser M, Smith WT. Sotatercept improves anemia, vascular calcification, and bone loss in patients with end-stage kidney disease on hemodialysis. *The American Society of Nephrology (ASN) Kidney Week 2015 Annual Meeting*, San Diego, CA, 2015.
103. U.S. National Library of Medicine. ClinicalTrials.gov. https://clinicaltrials.gov/ (accessed 25/07/18).
104. Acceleron Pharma. Product candidates: Sotatercept. http://acceleronpharma.com/product-candidates/sotatercept/ (accessed 14/08/18).
105. Acceleron Pharma. Product Candidates: luspatercept. http://acceleronpharma.com/product-candidates/luspatercept/ (accessed 14/08/18).
106. Suragani RN, Cawley SM, Li R, Wallner S, Alexander MJ, Mulivor AW, Gardenghi S, Rivella S, Grinberg AV, Pearsall RS, Kumar R. Modified activin receptor IIB ligand trap mitigates ineffective erythropoiesis and disease complications in murine β-thalassemia. *Blood* 2014;123(25).
107. Platzbecker U, Germing U, Gotze KS, Kiewe P, Mayer K, Chromik J, Radsak M, Wolff T, Zhang X, Laadem A, Sherman ML, Attie KM, Giagounidis A. Luspatercept for the treatment of anaemia in patients with lower-risk myelodysplastic syndromes (PACE-MDS): a multicentre, open-label phase 2 dose-finding study with long-term extension study. *Lancet Oncol* 2017;18(10):1338–47.
108. Piga AG, Perrotta S, Melpignano A, Borgna-Pignatti C, Gamberini MR, Voskaridou E, Caruso V, Ricchi P, Pietrangelo A, Zhang X, Wilson DM, Bellevue A, Laadem A, Sherman ML, Attie KM. Luspatercept increases hemoglobin, reduces liver iron concentration and improves quality of life in non-transfusion dependent adults with beta-thalassemia. *21st Congress of the European Hematology Association*, Copenhagen, Denmark, 2016.
109. World Anti-Doping Agency. The world anti-doping code - international standard: prohibited list (January 2017). 2016. www.wada-ama.org (accessed 14/08/18).
110. Walpurgis K, Thomas A, Vogel M, Reichel C, Geyer H, Schänzer W, Thevis M. Testing for the erythropoiesis-stimulating agent Sotatercept/ACE-011 (ActRIIA-Fc) in serum by means of Western blotting and LC-HRMS. *Drug Test Anal* 2016;8(11–12):1152–61.
111. Walpurgis K, Thomas A, Lange T, Reichel C, Geyer H, Thevis M. Combined detection of the ActRII-Fc fusion proteins Sotatercept (ActRIIA-Fc) and Luspatercept (modified ActRIIB-Fc) in serum by means of immunoaffinity purification, tryptic digestion, and LC-MS/MS. *Drug Test Anal* 2018.
112. Reichel C, Gmeiner G, Thevis M. Antibody-based strategies for the detection of Luspatercept (ACE-536) in human serum. *Drug Test Anal* 2017;9(11–12):1721–30.

113. Reichel C, Farmer L, Gmeiner G, Walpurgis K, Thevis M. Detection of Sotatercept (ACE-011) in human serum by SAR-PAGE and western single blotting. *Drug Test Anal* 2018;10(6):927–37.
114. Martin L, Zouhiri N, Audran M, Marchand A. A validated, sensitive electrophoretic method for the detection of activin receptor type II-Fc fusion proteins in human blood. *Drug Test Anal* 2018.
115. Reichel C, Gmeiner G, Walpurgis K, Thevis M. Updated protocols for the detection of Sotatercept and Luspatercept in human serum. *Drug Test Anal* 2019;10:1708–13.
116. Martin L, Audran M, Marchand A. Combined immunopurification and detection of recombinant EPOs and ActRII-Fc proteins by isoelectric focusing (IEF) for application in doping control. *Drug Test Anal* 2019;11(1):168–72.
117. Lange T, Walpurgis K, Thomas A, Geyer H, Thevis M. Development of two complementary LC–HRMS methods for analyzing Sotatercept in dried blood spots for doping controls. *Bioanalysis* 2019;11(10):923–40.

4.4 PEPTIDE HORMONES

A. Thomas and M. Thevis

4.4.1 Introduction

Historically, peptide hormones were isolated from natural sources such as animal pancreas or pituitary gland for insulin or adrenocorticotropic hormone (ACTH) identification, characterization, and preparation of therapeutic agents.[1,2] These early stage peptidic drugs represented revolutionary new live-saving medicines in the early 20th century. Such peptides were used for therapeutic interventions to mimic the intrinsic activity of the hormone of interest if the endogenous production is inadequate or missing. The treatment of *diabetes mellitus* with insulin extracted from bovine pancreas is an excellent example.[1] During the last decades, the usage of peptides as therapeutics has become more and more sophisticated because the progress in human genomics and proteomics has enabled the detailed molecular characterization of receptors for many endogenous peptide hormones.[3,4] In addition, the production processes for peptidic drugs (e.g., solid-phase synthesis) have significantly improved in terms of quality, quantity, and costs, and thus, the availability of highly specific biopharmaceuticals of good quality has been guaranteed.[5] However, limitations and shortcomings have also become obvious. Generally, peptide hormones show a short plasma half-life after parenteral administration and possess (if any) limited oral bioavailability. Classical and convenient oral replacement therapies are tempered accordingly. The following development of "bio-similar" or "bio-better" peptide analogues sometimes overcomes these issues, but not in all cases. Particularly, the introduction of non-natural (non-proteinogenic) amino acids into the peptide's backbone, cyclization, or conjugation (to polyethylene glycol [PEG], lipids, sugars, etc.) drastically alters the pharmacokinetic properties of the peptide hormone and opens new fields of therapy.[6] Nowadays, the worldwide availability of biopharmaceuticals represents a several billion-dollar business for various therapeutic areas, such as cancer, inflammation, autoimmune diseases, obesity, and growth disorders.[4]

Peptide hormones in sports drug testing share a comparably short history due to the aforementioned increasing relevance of peptide-based drugs in modern pharmacology. Together with the expanding knowledge about the structure, function, and production of macromolecules such as peptides and proteins (proteomics), the importance of this class of bioactive substances for doping control authorities is growing accordingly. In principle, several performance-enhancing or modulating pathways in the human organism represent reasonable target processes, which share the potential for manipulation with peptide-based drugs. Among others, growth promoting, erythropoiesis-stimulating, or metabolism-modulating processes provide considerable opportunities for efficient manipulation of an athlete`s performance.[7,8] Accordingly, the annually renewed Prohibited List[9] of the World Anti-Doping Agency (WADA) is categorized in section S2:

S2 – "Peptide hormones, growth factors, related substances, and mimetics":

1. Erythropoietins (EPO) and agents affecting erythropoiesis
2. Peptide Hormones and their releasing factors
   - 2.1 Chorionic Gonadotrophin (CG) and Luteinizing Hormone (LH) and their releasing factors (in males)
   - 2.2 Corticotrophins and their releasing factors
   - 2.3 Growth Hormone (GH), its fragments and releasing factors
3. Growth Factors and Growth Factor Modulators (e.g. Fibroblast Growth Factors, Hepatocyte Growth Factor, Insulin-like Growth Factor-1 and its analogues)

Additionally, several peptide hormones were found in other categories of the list, such as insulins in section S4 – "Hormone and metabolic modulators" and desmopressin in section S5 – "Diuretics and masking agents."

Doping control laboratories commonly follow two principal strategies for the detection of prohibited peptide hormones. The first one is based on immunological assays (including Western blotting, enzyme-linked immunosorbent assays [ELISAs], etc.) and represents the classical approach for the determination of macromolecules in biological fluids. Recently, more and more mass spectrometry (MS)-based methods have been developed for these substances, with higher–molecular mass proteins being hydrolyzed prior to liquid chromatography–mass spectrometry (LC-MS) analysis (bottom-up) and lower–molecular mass proteins or peptides (<10 kDa) being analyzed as intact molecules (top-down). The combination of immunoaffinity purification with MS has also become an established technique in doping controls as well as in other analytical disciplines.[10]

4.4.2 Growth Hormone Releasing Factors (GHRFs): Metabolism and Detection

The term *growth hormone releasing factors* (GHRFs) subsumes several classes of bioactive compounds, all of which share the potential to increase the endogenous secretion of GH from the pituitary gland.[11–13] Two target receptors, the growth hormone releasing hormone (GH-RH) receptor and the ghrelin receptor, are essential to well-characterized biological pathways, where agonistic mediation increases the GH secretion from the pituitary gland. Thus, compounds mimicking GH-RH and ghrelin were developed in the last decades, enabling the treatment of GH deficiency, on the one hand, and having the potential for misuse in sport, on the other hand. GH-RH (Somatoliberin) is a single-chain 40–amino acid peptide with a molecular mass of 5,037 Da, and ghrelin (obestatin) consists of 28 amino acids (including a caprylic acid at Ser3), resulting in a molecular mass of 3,369 Da. The group of mimetic agents for both axes is very heterogeneous and ranges from small molecule candidates (<500 Da) to larger peptides (>5 kDa).[14] The respective forms of application, metabolism, and detection strategies are accordingly multifaceted. Ibutamoren (MK-667), Anamorelin, and Capromorelin represent the most important candidates for the non-peptidic agonists. In Figure 4.4.1, their chemical structures are shown, illustrating the non-peptidic but still peptide-related backbone of these drugs. The metabolism of peptides manipulating the GH axis follows generally the same rules as all peptide hormones. In contrast to small molecule drugs, which are mainly metabolized in the liver by phase I (functionalization) and phase II (conjugation) reactions, essentially enzymatic degradation processes are responsible for the inactivation of peptides in the human organism. This degradation is regulated by proteolytic enzymes such as endo- or exoproteases, which act according to their specificity at the N-/C-terminus (exoproteases) or at distinct motifs within the peptide chain (endoproteases).[15] Due to the ubiquitous distribution of these proteases, proteolytic processes occur very rapidly and effectively in nearly all tissues and compartments in the organism and thus, trigger the inactivation of therapeutic peptides immediately after administration. The resulting pharmacokinetic properties are often very poor and represent the major shortcomings of first-generation peptide therapeutics, which were isolated mostly from natural sources and should resemble the endogenous paradigm. Nevertheless, chemical stabilization of natural amino acids led eventually to more convenient drug candidates, which are still predominantly applied via parenteral routes, but in some cases, oral bioavailability has also been recorded for peptide-derived therapeutics.

Growth hormone releasing peptides (GHRPs) are short, potentially performance enhancing peptides with four to six amino acid residues.[16] They all act on the ghrelin receptor and boost the endogenous GH secretion from the pituitary gland. Table 4.4.1 illustrates the main characteristics of these peptides. All of them contain at least one non-natural amino acid, which enhances the resistance against proteolytic degradation and allows for some of them a low but considerable oral bioavailability.[17] In terms of doping controls, these synthetic amino acids act as proteolytic barriers and remain as markers in the excreted metabolites.[18] Serendipitously, the unambiguous identification and discrimination from endogenous hormones by MS is facilitated by these residue modifications. Recently, several *in vitro* and *in vivo* metabolism studies were conducted in order to identify and characterize diagnostic metabolites for sports drug testing.[18–23] LC-MS is the most established detection method for these lower–molecular mass peptides and their metabolites in urine or blood samples.[22,24–27] While the first-generation methods require a sample clean-up and pre-concentration step (e.g., solid-phase extraction [SPE]), recent methods focus on direct urine injection for increased effectiveness.[19,22,25–29] The minimum required performance levels for GHRPs in urine samples are set at 2 ng/mL, but ultimate sensitivity is desirable per se in sports drug testing.[30] The recent technical developments for high resolution mass spectrometry (HRMS) (also in combination with orthogonal separation techniques such as ion mobility [IM]) enable today the reliable measurement

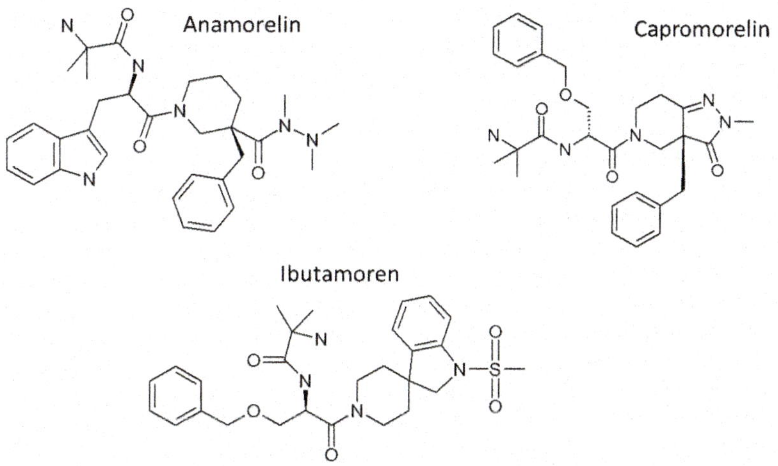

FIGURE 4.4.1 Chemical structure of the non-peptidic GHRFs Anamorelin, Capromorelin, and Ibutamoren.

TABLE 4.4.1
Characteristics of GHRPs

Peptide	Amino acid sequence	Monoisotopic mass	WADA list
GHRP1	Ala-His-(*D*-β-Nal)-Ala-Trp-(*D*-Phe)-Lys-NH_2	954.49	S2.5
GHRP2	(D-Ala)-(*D*-β-Nal)-Ala-Trp-(*D*-Phe)-Lys-NH_2	817.43	S2.5
GHRP3	Aib-(D-Trp)-(D-Pro)-(D-Ile)-Arg-NH_2	654.40	S2.5
GHRP4	(D-Trp)-Ala-Trp-(D-Phe)-NH_2	607.29	S2.5
GHRP5	Tyr-(D-Trp)-Ala-Trp-(D-Phe)-NH_2	770.35	S2.5
GHRP6	His-(*D*-Trp)-Ala-Trp-(*D*-Phe)-Lys-NH_2	872.44	S2.5
Alexamorelin	Ala-His-(D-Mrp)-Ala-Trp-(D-Phe)-Lys-NH_2	957.50	S2.5
Ipamorelin	Aib-His-(*D*-2-Nal)-(*D*-Phe)-Lys-NH_2	711.39	S2.5
Hexarelin	His-(D-Mrp)-Ala-Trp-(D-Phe)-Lys-NH2	886.46	S2.5

Nal: Naphthylalanine.
Aib: Aminoisobutyric acid.
Mrp: 2-methyltryptophan.

TABLE 4.4.2
Characteristics of GH-RH analogues

Peptide	Amino acid sequence
Geref	YADAIFTNSYRKVLGQLSARKLLQDIMSR-NH_2
CJC-1293	Y**dA**DAIFTNSYRKVLGQLSARKLLQDIMSR-NH_2
CJC-1295	YANAIFTQSYRKVLAQLSARKLLQDILSR-NH_2
Tesamorelin	***Hex***-YADAIFTNSYRKVLGQLSARKLLQDIMSRQQGESNQERGARARL-NH_2
Geref Met	DAIFTNSYRKVLGQLSARKLLQDIMSR-NH_2
CJC-1293 met	**dA**DAIFTNSYRKVLGQLSARKLLQDIMSR-NH_2

Hex: hexenoic acid

of GHRPs in urine after direct injection in sub-ng/mL concentrations.[26]

The determination of GH-RH analogues (>3 kDa) is considerably more complex due to the need for sophisticated and laborious sample extraction procedures. Mainly immunoaffinity purification–based approaches (e.g., by means of coated magnetic nanoparticles) but also hyphenated SPE protocols have recently been developed for the efficient extraction of GH-RH and its analogues from urine or blood samples.[10,31–34] These assays mainly focus on the MS of the intact peptides or their slightly metabolized truncated forms due to the required intact epitope in the target peptides for immunoaffinity purification. Table 4.4.2 summarizes the characteristics of the main GH-RH analogues and their established metabolites. Obviously, all these analogues share a considerable sequence homology among each other and also with their endogenous counterpart GH-RH. Thus, reliable, unambiguous identification is of the utmost importance, and this is especially challenging for the two analogues Geref and CJC-1293, which differ by one D-Ala (instead of L-Ala) at position 3 only. The intact drugs are scarcely distinguished by established separation techniques (LC, IM, etc.); thus, only the occurrence and detection of different metabolites allows reliable differentiation.[31,35] All GH-RH analogues contain an amidated C-terminus, which prevents the peptide's exoproteolytic degradation; thus, proteolysis is expected to be initiated preferably from the N-terminus. Generally, after sophisticated sample preparation, LC-MS is the method of choice to detect GH-RH analogues in sports drug testing, and urine or blood (plasma or serum) specimens are appropriate matrices.[10,31,34] Major challenges are the low concentrations (low ng/mL in blood) and the fast clearance from the organism. Whether and to what extent the GH-RH analogues and their metabolites occur in urine after administration has not been investigated yet, while expected blood concentrations were described recently.[31]

4.4.3 Insulins: Metabolism and Detection

In contrast to the heterogeneous class of GHRFs, insulin and its synthetic or animal analogues represent a family of peptides exhibiting largely conserved structural features with only minor deviations from their endogenous counterpart. The approximately 6-kDa peptide (sometimes also classified as a small protein) consists of two amino acid chains (α+β), which are linked by two disulfide bridges and an additional intra-α-chain disulfide bond.[1] Insulin is produced in the islets of Langerhans in the pancreas as a single-chain peptide (referred to as proinsulin) consisting of insulin that is connected to the biologically inactive C-peptide. After endoproteolytic cleavage, equimolar amounts of insulin and C-peptide are secreted into the blood stream. Figure 4.4.2 shows the structure of human insulin and C-peptide as well as their two connecting dipeptides. Unquestionably, insulin plays an important role as a pioneer candidate for peptide and protein science. Discovered in the early 20th century, insulin was rapidly established as a therapeutic drug to treat *diabetes mellitus*, a metabolic disease with increasing impact in modern, mis-nourished society (*diabetes mellitus* type II) or due an autoimmune reaction of the pancreas (diabetes mellitus Type I). In the early 1980s, insulin was the first recombinantly produced peptide hormone, and later in this century, the first synthetic analogues were developed. These new products overcome the inconvenience of using insulin from natural sources and allow further improvement of the pharmacokinetic properties (e.g., by addition of protamine or zinc ions). The following rapid- or long-acting insulin analogues are nowadays commercially available: Insulin Lispro (Humalog), Insulin Aspart (Novolog), Insulin Glulisine (Apidra), Insulin Degludec (Tresiba), and Insulin Glargine (Lantus). The amino acid sequences are shown in Table 4.4.3. Recently, sophisticated insulin-pumps have been developed, enabling the automated and smart supply of the hormone to ideally simulate the endogenous profile. In the presence of zinc ions, insulin tends to form hexamers, and after subcutaneous administration, the hexamers dissociate prior to entering the blood stream. The time period from injection to the blood glucose-lowering activity is called the "lag-phase" and strongly depends on whether it is a rapid- or long-acting insulin. Various tissues are known to be involved in the metabolism of insulin. Starting directly after injection, subcutaneous degradation starts by exoproteolytic processes, which has recently been shown.[36] The resulting truncated product, DesB30 human insulin, may serve as a diagnostic marker to uncover the illicit use of recombinant human insulin. In the blood circulation, insulin is quite stable, although the plasma half-life is very short (several minutes) due to fast renal clearance or binding to insulin sensitive receptors.[37–39] Furthermore, the degradation of insulin is also described to occur in liver and kidney by specific enzymes such as the insulin degrading enzyme (IDE) and the endosomal acidic insulinase (EAI).[39] All metabolites and the intact peptides are renally cleared, and thus, the urinary analysis shows the intact drug as well as the truncated metabolites.[40] Notably, this is valid for human insulin as well as for all synthetic insulin analogues.[41] In professional sport, insulin (and its analogues) has been prohibited for non-diabetics since 1999, mainly due to its anabolic (inhibition of protein breakdown) effects and its ability to increase the glycogen content of the muscle tissue.[8] In contrast to other doping agents, the administration of insulin to healthy humans may cause spontaneous physiological hazards (hypoglycemia), which makes misuse dangerous. Notably, oral anti-diabetic drugs (e.g., sulfonylureas), which act as insulin releasing factors, are not

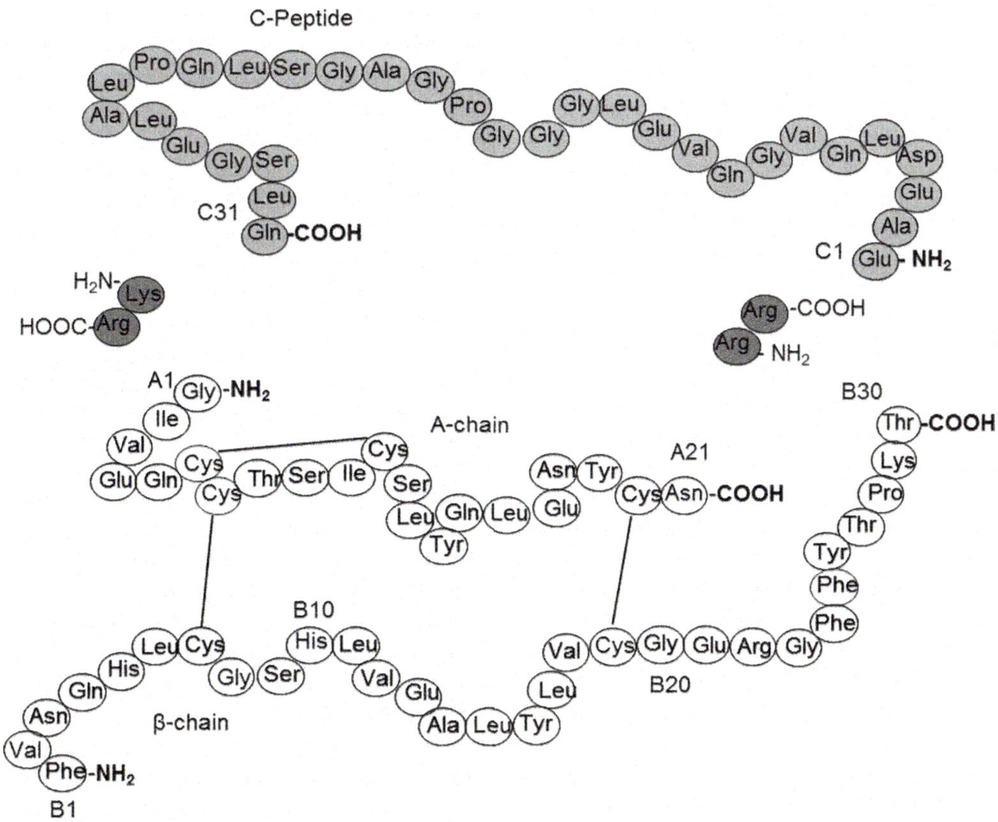

FIGURE 4.4.2 Structure of human insulin and C-peptide with the enzymatic cleavage sites.

TABLE 4.4.3
Amino Acid Sequences of All Available Insulin Analogues and Metabolites

Peptide	Amino acid sequence
Human insulin	GIVEQCCTSICSLYQLENYCN – FVNQHLCGSHLVEALYLVCGERGFFYTPKT
Bovine insulin	GIVEQCC**ASV**CSLYQLENYCN - FVNQHLCGSHLVEALYLVCGERGFFYTPK**A**
Lispro	GIVEQCCTSICSLYQLENYCN – FVNQHLCGSHLVEALYLVCGERGFFYT***KP***T
Aspart	GIVEQCCTSICSLYQLENYCN – FVNQHLCGSHLVEALYLVCGERGFFYT**D**KT
Glulisine	GIVEQCCTSICSLYQLENYCN – FV**K**QHLCGSHLVEALYLVCGERGFFYTP**E**T
Glargine Met 1	GIVEQCCTSICSLYQLENYC**G** – FVNQHLCGSHLVEALYLVCGERGFFYTPK
Glargine Met 2	GIVEQCCTSICSLYQLENYC**G** – FVNQHLCGSHLVEALYLVCGERGFFYTPKT
Porcine insulin	GIVEQCCTSICSLYQLENYCN – FVNQHLCGSHLVEALYLVCGERGFFYTPK**A**
Detemir	GIVEQCCTSICSLYQLENYCN-FVNQHLCGSHLVEALYLVCGERGFFYTP**K-*Myr***
Degludec	GIVEQCCTSICSLYQLENYCN – FVNQHLCGSHLVEALYLVCGERGFFYTPK-***γ-L-Glu-Pal***

Note: Differences from human insulin are indicated in bold letters.
Myr: Myristic acid.
Pal: Palmitic acid.

prohibited. A closer look at the methods for the analysis of insulin shows that besides immunoassay-based approaches (e.g., ELISA, etc.), which barely enable differentiation between the endogenous hormone and its synthetic or animal analogues, mainly LC-MS-based methods are used to detect insulin from urine or blood.[10,29,34,36,42,43] Here, because of the low urinary (low pg/mL) or blood (low ng/mL) concentrations, mainly high sensitivity rather than high throughput LC-MS assays have been developed for doping control purposes. All these methods share extraction by sophisticated sample preparation (e.g., immunoaffinity purification), separation by reversed-phase liquid chromatography (RPLC), ionization by electrospray, and detection of the intact four-, five- or sixfold protonated precursor ions by MS (using either high or low resolution instruments).[44–47] Unambiguous identification of the different insulins by means of MS is enabled due to their altered amino acid sequences (see Table 4.4.3). Either accurate mass measurements of the intact molecule and/or tandem mass spectrometric (MS/MS) data are commonly employed in doping controls.[29,34,41,43] Subsequent analysis of the isolated insulin β-chain after reduction of the disulfide bonds can provide additional information due to the amino acid residue alterations of the analogues located mainly in the β-chain of the peptide. Although immense progress in the analysis of insulin has been achieved in the last decade, uncovering the illicit use of recombinant human insulin is still a challenge and represents to date an unsolved problem in doping controls. Notably, a promising but not yet established approach to this is based on altered metabolism of insulin after subcutaneous injection and the additional comparison with C-peptide in blood samples, as published recently.[36,42]

4.4.4 Other Peptides

Several other peptides with potential performance enhancing properties are included in the WADA Prohibited List.[9] For example, the usage of gonadotropins (such as Gonadorelin or its analogues) is prohibited due to manipulation of the gonadal axis caused by the upregulation of the endogenous LH secretion and testosterone production from the interstitial cells of Leydig. Recent studies have shown that with the parenteral administration of leuprolide (a Gonadorelin analogue), the concentrations of LH and testosterone in serum and urine increase slightly but significantly.[48] The *in vitro* and *in vivo* metabolism of these bioactive peptides under consideration for their doping control aspects was investigated accordingly.[20,48–51] Another example is provided by the anti-diuretic peptide desmopressin, which is classified as a masking agent due to its impact on hematological parameters. Interestingly, this small (<2 kDa) peptide possesses considerable oral bioavailability and is excreted intact into urine.[52] The quantification of insulin-like growth factor I (IGF-I) in blood samples represents another important strategy in doping controls, because IGF-I levels significantly increase after administration of GH. IGF-I is a single-chain 7-kDa peptide with three intramolecular disulfide bonds. Elevated IGF-I levels are measurable for much longer than the direct identification of the administered recombinant GH itself, and the detection window is prolonged accordingly.[53] Also, the administration of the aforementioned GHRFs (GHRPs, GHRHs, etc.) will finally result in an elevated IGF-I level, and monitoring of the IGF-I concentrations in athletes is capable of detecting manipulation of the complete GH axis. Notably, all these determinations are enabled by LC-MS-based methods, which represent the state of the art technique for these purposes.[18–20,27,28,53,54]

REFERENCES

1. Rosenfeld L. Insulin: discovery and controversy. *Clin Chem* 2002;48(12):2270–88.
2. Li CH, Geschwind, II, Dixon JS, Levy AL, Harris JI. Corticotropins (ACTH). I. Isolation of alpha-corticotropin from sheep pituitary glands. *J Biol Chem* 1955;213(1):171–85.

3. Fosgerau K, Hoffmann T. Peptide therapeutics: current status and future directions. *Drug Discov Today* 2015;20(1):122–8.
4. Lau JL, Dunn MK. Therapeutic peptides: historical perspectives, current development trends, and future directions. *Bioorg Med Chem* 2018;26(10):2700–7.
5. Merrifield RB. Solid phase peptide synthesis. I. The synthesis of atetrapeptide. *J Am Chem Soc* 1963;85:2149–54.
6. Werle M, Bernkop-Schnürch A. Strategies to improve plasma half life time of peptide and protein drugs. *Amino Acids* 2006;30(4):351–67.
7. Widdowson WM, Healy ML, Sonksen PH, Gibney J. The physiology of growth hormone and sport. *Growth Horm IGF Res* 2009;19(4):308–19.
8. Sonksen PH. Insulin, growth hormone and sport. *J Endocrinol* 2001;170(1):13–25.
9. World Anti-Doping Agency. The prohibited list 2019. https://www.wada-ama.org/sites/default/files/wada_2019_english_prohibited_list.pdf (accessed 02.10.2018).
10. Thomas A, Schänzer W, Delahaut P, Thevis M. Immunoaffinity purification of peptide hormones prior to liquid chromatography-mass spectrometry in doping controls. *Methods* 2012;56(2):230–5.
11. Ghigo E, Arvat E, Muccioli G, Camanni F. Growth hormone-releasing peptides. *Eur J Endocrinol* 1997;136(5):445–60.
12. Garin MC, Burns CM, Kaul S, Cappola AR. Clinical review: the human experience with ghrelin administration. *J Clin Endocrinol Metab* 2013;98(5):1826–37.
13. Bowers CY, Alster DK, Frentz JM. The growth hormone-releasing activity of a synthetic hexapeptide in normal men and short statured children after oral administration. *J Clin Endocrinol Metab* 1992;74(2):292–8.
14. Thevis M, Wilkens F, Geyer H, Schänzer W. Determination of therapeutics with growth-hormone secretagogue activity in human urine for doping control purposes. *Rapid Commun Mass Spectrom* 2006;20(22):3393–402.
15. Katsila T, Siskos AP, Tamvakopoulos C. Peptide and protein drugs: the study of their metabolism and catabolism by mass spectrometry. *Mass Spectrom Rev* 2011;31(1):110–33.
16. Camanni F, Ghigo E, Arvat E. Growth hormone-releasing peptides and their analogs. *Front Neuroendocrinol* 1998;19(1):47–72.
17. Hashizume T, Tanabe Y, Ohtsuki K, Mori A, Matsumoto N, Hara S. Plasma growth hormone (GH) responses after administration of the peptidergic GH secretagogue KP102 into the oral cavity, rumen, abomasum and duodenum in adult goats. *Domest Anim Endocrinol* 2001;20(1), 37–46.
18. Thomas A, Delahaut P, Krug O, Schänzer W, Thevis M. Metabolism of growth hormone releasing peptides. *Anal Chem* 2012;84(23):10252–9.
19. Cox HD, Hughes CM, Eichner D. Detection of GHRP-2 and GHRP-6 in urine samples from athletes. *Drug Test Anal* 2015;7(5):439–44.
20. Esposito S, Deventer K, Geldof L, Van Eenoo P. *In vitro* models for metabolic studies of small peptide hormones in sport drug testing. *J Pept Sci* 2015;21(1):1–9.
21. Esposito S, Deventer K, Goeman J, Van der Eycken J, Van Eenoo P. Synthesis and characterization of the N-terminal acetylated 17–23 fragment of thymosin beta 4 identified in TB-500, a product suspected to possess doping potential. *Drug Test Anal* 2012;4(9):733–8.
22. Semenistaya E, Zvereva I, Thomas A, Thevis M, Krotov G, Rodchenkov G. Determination of growth hormone releasing peptides metabolites in human urine after nasal administration of GHRP-1, GHRP-2, GHRP-6, Hexarelin, and Ipamorelin. *Drug Test Anal* 2015;7(10):919–25.
23. Thomas A, Knoop A, Schänzer W, Thevis M. Characterization of in vitro generated metabolites of selected peptides <2 kDa prohibited in sports. *Drug Test Anal* 2017;9(11–12):1799–803.
24. Gil J, Cabrales A, Reyes O, Morera V, Betancourt L, Sanchez A, Garcia G, Moya G, Padron G, Besada V, Gonzalez LJ. Development and validation of a bioanalytical LC-MS method for the quantification of GHRP-6 in human plasma. *J Pharm Biomed Anal* 2012;60:19–25.
25. Okano M, Sato M, Ikekita A, Kageyama S. Determination of growth hormone secretagogue pralmorelin (GHRP-2) and its metabolite in human urine by liquid chromatography/electrospray ionization tandem mass spectrometry. *Rapid Commun Mass Spectrom* 2011;24(14):2046–56.
26. Thomas A, Görgens C, Guddat S, Thieme D, Dellanna F, Schänzer W, Thevis M. Simplifying and expanding the screening for peptides <2 kDa by direct urine injection, liquid chromatography, and ion mobility mass spectrometry. *J Sep Sci* 2016;39(2):333–41.
27. Möller I, Wintermeyer A, Bender K, Jubner M, Thomas A, Krug O, Schänzer W, Thevis M. Screening for the synthetic cannabinoid JWH-018 and its major metabolites in human doping controls. *Drug Test Anal* 2011;3(9):609–20.
28. Gorgens C, Guddat S, Thomas A, Wachsmuth P, Orlovius AK, Sigmund G, Thevis M, Schänzer W. Simplifying and expanding analytical capabilities for various classes of doping agents by means of direct urine injection high performance liquid chromatography high resolution/high accuracy mass spectrometry. *J Pharm Biomed Anal* 2016;131:482–96.
29. Judak P, Grainger J, Goebel C, Van Eenoo P, Deventer K. DMSO assisted electrospray ionization for the detection of small peptide hormones in urine by dilute-and-shoot-liquid-chromatography-high resolution mass spectrometry. *J Am Soc Mass Spectrom* 2017;28(8):1657–65.
30. World Anti-Doping Agency. TD2018MRPL. 2018. https://www.wada-ama.org/en/resources/science-medicine/td2018mrpl-0 (accessed 02.10.2018).
31. Knoop A, Thomas A, Fichant E, Delahaut P, Schänzer W, Thevis M. Qualitative identification of growth hormone-releasing hormones in human plasma by means of immunoaffinity purification and LC-HRMS/MS. *Anal Bioanal Chem* 2016;408(12):3145–53.
32. Kwok WH, Ho EN, Lau MY, Leung GN, Wong AS, Wan TS. Doping control analysis of seven bioactive peptides in horse plasma by liquid chromatography-mass spectrometry. *Anal Bioanal Chem* 2013;405(8):2595–606.
33. Thomas A, Schänzer W, Thevis M. Immunoaffinity techniques coupled to mass spectrometry for the analysis of human peptide hormones: advances and applications. *Expert Rev Proteomics* 2017;14(9):799–807.
34. Thomas A, Walpurgis K, Tretzel L, Brinkkötter P, Fichant E, Delahaut P, Schänzer W, Thevis M. Expanded test method for peptides >2 kDa employing immunoaffinity purification and LC-HRMS/MS. *Drug Test Anal* 2015;7(11–12):990–8.
35. Jette L, Leger R, Thibaudeau K, Benquet C, Robitaille M, Pellerin I, Paradis V, van Wyk P, Pham K, Bridon DP. Human growth hormone-releasing factor (hGRF)1–29-albumin bioconjugates activate the GRF receptor on the anterior pituitary in rats: identification of CJC-1295 as a long-lasting GRF analog. *Endocrinology* 2005;146(7):3052–8.
36. Thomas A, Brinkkötter P, Schänzer W, Thevis M. Metabolism of human insulin after subcutaneous administration: a possible means to uncover insulin misuse. *Anal Chim Acta* 2015;897:53–61.

37. Berger M, Halban PA, Girardier L, Seydoux J, Offord RE, Renold AE. Absorption kinetics of subcutaneously injected insulin. Evidence for degradation at the injection site. *Diabetologia* 1979;17(2):97–9.
38. Seabright PJ, Smith GD. The characterization of endosomal insulin degradation intermediates and their sequence of production. *Biochem J* 1996;320:947–56.
39. Duckworth WC, Bennett RG, Hamel FG. Insulin degradation: progress and potential. *Endocr Rev* 1998;19(5):608–24.
40. Rabkin R, Ryan MP, Duckworth WC. The renal metabolism of insulin. *Diabetologia* 1984;27(3):351–7.
41. Thomas A, Thevis M, Delahaut P, Bosseloir A, Schänzer W. Mass spectrometric identification of degradation products of insulin and its long-acting analogues in human urine for doping control purposes. *Anal Chem* 2007;79(6):2518–24.
42. Thomas A, Brinkkötter P, Schänzer W, Thevis M. Simultaneous determination of insulin, DesB30 insulin, proinsulin, and C-peptide in human plasma samples by liquid chromatography coupled to high resolution mass spectrometry. *Forensic Toxicol* 2016;35(1):106–13.
43. Thomas A, Schänzer W, Thevis M. Determination of human insulin and its analogues in human blood using liquid chromatography coupled to ion mobility mass spectrometry (LC-IM-MS). *Drug Test Anal* 2014;6(11–12):1125–32.
44. Blackburn M. Advances in the quantitation of therapeutic insulin analogues by LC–MS/MS. *Bioanalysis* 2013;5(23):2933–46.
45. Hess C, Thomas A, Thevis M, Stratmann B, Quester W, Tschoepe D, Madea B, Musshoff F. Simultaneous determination and validated quantification of human insulin and its synthetic analogues in human blood serum by immunoaffinity purification and liquid chromatography-mass spectrometry. *Anal Bioanal Chem* 2012;404(6–7):1813–22.
46. Kippen AD, Cerini F, Vadas L, Stöcklin R, Vu L, Offord RE, Rose K. Development of an isotope dilution assay for precise determination of insulin, C-peptide, and proinsulin levels in non-diabetic and type II diabetic individuals with comparison to immunoassay. *J Biol Chem* 1997;272(19):12513–22.
47. Stöcklin R, Vu L, Vadas L, Cerini F, Kippen AD, Offord RE, Rose K. A stable isotope dilution assay for the in vivo determination of insulin levels in humans by mass spectrometry. *Diabetes* 1997;46(1):44–50.
48. Handelsman DJ, Idan A, Grainger J, Goebel C, Turner L, Conway AJ. Detection and effects on serum and urine steroid and LH of repeated GnRH analog (leuprolide) stimulation. *J Steroid Biochem Mol Biol* 2014;141:113–20.
49. Palmer D, Rademaker K, Martin I, Hessell J, Howitt R. Identification of gonadotropin-releasing hormone metabolites in greyhound urine. *Drug Testing and Analysis* 2017;9(10), 1499–1505.
50. Thomas A, Knoop A, Schänzer W, Thevis M. Characterization of *in-vitro* generated metabolites of selected peptides <2 kDa prohibited in sports. *Drug Test Anal* 2017;9(11–12):1799–803.
51. Zvereva I, Dudko G, Dikunets M. Determination of GnRH and its synthetic analogues' abuse in doping control: small bioactive peptide UPLC-MS/MS method extension by addition of in vitro and in vivo metabolism data; evaluation of LH and steroid profile parameter fluctuations as suitable biomarkers. *Drug Test Anal* 2018;10(4):711–22.
52. Thomas A, Solymos E, Schänzer W, Baume N, Saugy M, Dellanna F, Thevis M. Determination of Vasopressin and Desmopressin in urine by means of liquid chromatography coupled to quadrupole time-of-flight mass spectrometry for doping control purposes. *Anal Chim Acta* 2011;707(1–2):107–13.
53. Cox HD, Lopes F, Woldemariam GA, Becker JO, Parkin MC, Thomas A, Butch AW, Cowan DA, Thevis M, Bowers LD, Hoofnagle AN. Interlaboratory agreement of insulin-like growth factor 1 concentrations measured by mass spectrometry. *Clin Chem* 2014;60(3):541–8.
54. Thomas A, Walpurgis K, Delahaut P, Fichant E, Schänzer W, Thevis M. Determination of LongR3-IGF-I, R3-IGF-I, Des1-3 IGF-I and their metabolites in human plasma samples by means of LC-MS. *Growth Horm IGF Res* 2017;35:33–9.

4.5 AGENTS MODIFYING MYOSTATIN FUNCTIONS: CLASSIFICATION AND DETECTION

K. Walpurgis, A. Thomas and M. Thevis

Drugs and drug candidates positively influencing athletes' muscle mass have been of particular relevance to anti-doping organizations and consequently, to sports drug testing laboratories. Besides typical anabolic agents (AAs; see Section 4.2), a new class of compounds has received increasing attention, namely, agents modifying myostatin functions. While these substances have been undergoing extensive clinical trials aiming at the treatment of a variety of conditions, their potential for misuse in sports is considered to be particularly high. Consequently, proactive measures have been initiated to allow anti-doping testing strategies for these emerging drugs to be implemented prior to their launch.

4.5.1 Myostatin Signaling

Skeletal muscle mass is negatively regulated by myostatin (growth differentiation factor-8 [GDF-8]) and other members of the transforming growth factor-β (TGF-β) superfamily.[1–3] The cytokine is highly conserved between species and predominantly expressed in developing embryonic and adult skeletal muscle. However, it can also be found in a few other tissues, such as cardiac muscle and adipose tissue.[1,4] Homozygotic myostatin knockout mice ($Mstn^{-/-}$) were found to be significantly larger than heterozygotic and wild-type animals and characterized by increased skeletal muscle mass, which can be attributed to both muscle fiber hypertrophy and hyperplasia.[1] Several livestock and dog breeds with extreme muscularity have naturally occurring mutations in the myostatin gene.[5–8] A similar mutation was also identified in a child with muscle hypertrophy.[9] Similarly to other TGF-β cytokines, myostatin is synthesized as a precursor polypeptide comprising an N-terminal signal sequence for secretion, a regulatory propeptide, and a C-terminal bioactive domain.[1,10] Following proteolytic cleavage at two different positions, the mature C-terminal peptide forms a disulfide-linked homodimer, which exerts its main biological functions through binding to activin type II receptors (ActRII).[1,10,11] After receptor activation and recruitment of activin like kinase-4 or -5, intracellular signaling pathways involving SMADs and mitogen-activated protein kinases (MAPKs) are induced, finally resulting in altered cellular gene expression and protein synthesis.[12,13] Molecular targets comprise, among others, transcription factors of the MyoD family of muscle regulatory factors.[12]

4.5.2 Myostatin Inhibitors

Due to its central role in the regulation of skeletal muscle mass, myostatin represents a promising therapeutic target for the treatment of muscular diseases comprising muscle degeneration (e.g., Duchenne Muscular Dystrophy [DMD]) and/or muscle wasting (e.g., sarcopenia; cachexia due to cancer, AIDS, or sepsis) as well as metabolic disorders such as obesity and *diabetes mellitus* type II.[10,14] Different types of myostatin inhibitors are currently in preclinical and clinical investigation (Table 4.5.1 and Figure 4.5.1). They comprise drug candidates specifically targeting myostatin, such as anti-myostatin antibodies and myostatin-binding proteins, as well as multi-targeting approaches such as, for example, receptor competitors and anti-ActRII antibodies.[14] While multi-targeting approaches were found to be more effective than myostatin-specific agents,[2,15] their broader activity can also be associated with an increased risk for undesired side effects, as was shown for Ramatercept (ACE-031).[14,16]

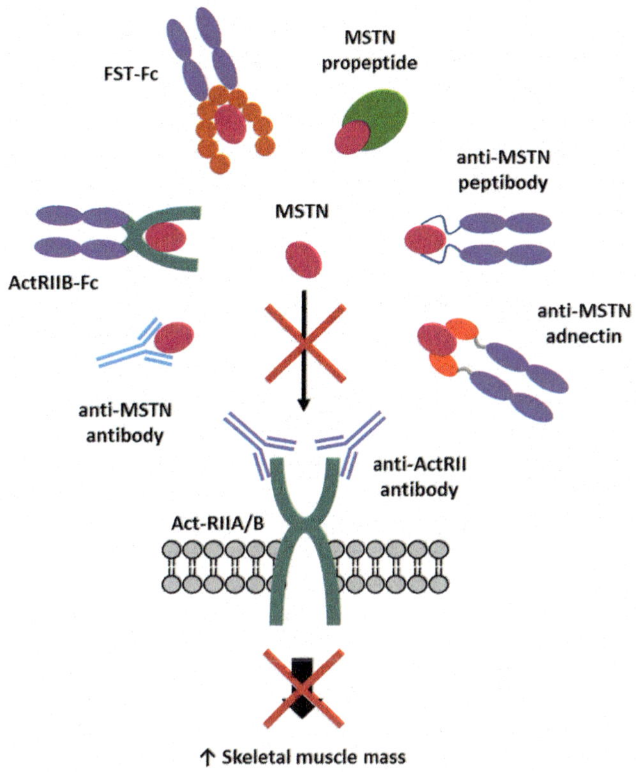

FIGURE 4.5.1 Strategies for myostatin inhibition.

4.5.2.1 Therapeutic Antibodies

4.5.2.1.1 Anti-Myostatin Antibodies: Stamulumab, Domagrozumab, Landogrozumab, Trevogrumab

Specific inhibition of myostatin can be achieved by using therapeutic antibodies that neutralize the circulating cytokine and prevent receptor activation.[17,18] Therapeutic antibodies are an emerging class of pharmaceuticals, which are characterized by high antigen-binding specificity and affinity, good tolerability, and long biological half-lives up to several weeks.[19] But as their therapeutic efficacy can be compromised by their immunogenicity and poor tissue penetration, high doses of several milligrams per kilogram are usually administered via parenteral routes. The immunogenicity of a therapeutic antibody depends on the degree of humanization:[19–21] While chimeric antibodies are 70% human and comprise human constant and murine variable domains, humanized antibodies are 85–90% human, as only the antigen-binding regions are of murine origin. Fully human antibodies are entirely derived from a human source and have the lowest immunogenicity.

The first anti-myostatin antibody in clinical trials was Stamulumab (MYO-029), a recombinant human IgG1(λ) developed by Wyeth Pharmaceuticals.[17] In preclinical animal studies, a murine analog of the antibody was administered to wild-type mice and found to induce significant increases in body weight (+10%), muscle mass (+11–30%),

TABLE 4.5.1
Overview of Protein-Based Myostatin Inhibitors

Drug class	Drug candidates	Manufacturer	Clinical development
Anti-myostatin antibodies	Stamulumab (MYO-029)	Wyeth	Discontinued after Phase 1 and 2 testing
	Domagrozumab (PF-06252616)	Pfizer	Discontinued after Phase 1 and 2 testing
	Landogrozumab (LY2495655)	Eli Lilly	Phase 1 and 2 testing completed
	Trevogrumab (REGN1033)	Regeneron	Phase 1 and 2 testing completed
Anti-ActRII antibodies	Bimagrumab	Novartis	Phase 2 and 3 testing completed
ActRIIB-Fc fusion proteins	Ramatercept (ACE-031)	Acceleron	Discontinued after Phase 1 and 2 testing
	ACE-2494	Acceleron	Discontinued after Phase 1 testing
FST-Fc fusion proteins	ACE-083	Acceleron	Phase 2 testing ongoing
Agents derived from the myostatin propeptide			Preclinical development
Anti-myostatin peptibodies	PINTA-745 (AMG-745)	Amgen/Atara Biotherapeutics	Discontinued after Phase 1 and 2 testing
Anti-myostatin adnectins	Talditercept alpha/RG6206	Bristol-Myers Squibb/Hoffmann-La Roche	Phase 2/3 testing ongoing

and muscle strength (+10%) due to muscle fiber hypertrophy.[22] Similar results were obtained in a mouse model of DMD, indicating that Stamulumab could be a promising therapeutic agent for the treatment of different muscle wasting disorders.[23] Therefore, a Phase 1/2 clinical trial was conducted in adult subjects with different forms of muscular dystrophy.[24] The participants received fortnightly intravenous (IV) Stamulumab injections at doses of 1–30 mg/kg for a total of 6 months. In general, the antibody was found to be well tolerated with only mild drug-induced side effects such as cutaneous hypersensitivity reactions. Unfortunately, no significant improvements in muscle strength, lean body mass, and muscle function were observed, and only a limited number of subjects was characterized by an increased muscle fiber size. These findings were confirmed in a series of individual case studies where five patients with different muscular disorders were treated with Stamulumab infusions (1 or 10 mg/kg every 2 weeks) over a period of 6 months.[25] In most of the subjects, antibody treatment resulted in increased single muscle fiber contractile properties; however, no improvements with regard to overall muscle strength could be observed. As the first clinical studies with Stamulumab could not demonstrate any significant beneficial effects on muscle mass and function, the development of the protein drug was eventually discontinued.[17]

Domagrozuman (PF-06252616) is a humanized IgG1(κ) developed by Pfizer (New York City, NY).[18,26] In different animal studies comprising wild-type mice, a mouse model of DMD, and non-human primates, the antibody was found to significantly increase body weight, lean mass, muscle weight, and muscle strength.[27] Due to the promising results, a Phase 1 clinical trial was conducted in healthy human subjects, who received a single dose of 1–40 mg/kg IV, a single dose of 3 mg/kg subcutaneously (SC), or three injections of 10 mg/kg IV every 2 weeks.[18] Following IV administration, maximum serum concentrations of 25–919 μg/mL were reached within 4 hours, and the biological half-life varied dose-dependently between 12 and 19 days. After SC injection, maximum serum concentrations of 22 μg/mL were observed 168 hours following administration, and the biological half-life was 13 days. In all subjects, Domagrozumab was found to be safe and well tolerated. However, significant changes in lean body mass (+5.4% at day 29 post-administration) or muscle volume (+4.5% at day 113 post-administration) were only observed in two out of seven Domagrozumab-treated cohorts (10 mg single-dose and 10 mg repeat-dose). The drug was also tested in several Phase 2 clinical trials for the treatment of DMD, which were terminated in 2018 as the primary efficacy endpoint was not met.[18,28]

Another humanized antibody that neutralizes circulating myostatin is Landogrozumab (LY2495655; Eli Lilly, Indianapolis, IN).[29] In two Phase 1 clinical studies, the antibody of the type IgG4(κ) was administered to healthy subjects and cancer patients as single doses of 0.7–700 mg (SC and IV).[29,30] All dose levels of the protein drug were found to be well tolerated. In healthy subjects, dose-dependent increases in thigh muscle volume were observed. By contrast, only two cohorts of the cancer patients (21 and 70 mg) were characterized by an elevated muscle mass. But treatment with doses higher than 21 mg resulted in improved muscle strength and function. The effects of the antibody on elderly subjects with age-related muscle weakness,[31] patients with a total hip arthroplasty,[32] and patients with pancreatic cancer[33] were investigated in several Phase 2 clinical trials. In the sarcopenic participants, six SC injections of 315 mg every 4 weeks led to moderate changes in appendicular lean body mass (+2.5%) and improvements in muscle function. Similar results were obtained in patients with osteoarthritis undergoing a total hip replacement, which can potentially lead to post-operative muscle atrophy. A total of four SC injections with 35–315 mg of the drug both before and after the surgery (dosing intervals of 4 weeks) was found to induce significant dose-dependent increases in appendicular lean body mass; however, the threshold of the study's primary objective (+2.5% at week 12) was not exceeded. In the third Phase 2 study,[33] chemotherapy patients with pancreatic cancer received IV Landogrozumab injections at doses of 100 or 300 mg every 2 weeks. Unfortunately, Landogrozumab did not improve overall survival in the different treatment groups. In all studies, the antibody was well tolerated, and only mild drug-associated side effects such as injection site reactions were observed. Currently, no further clinical trials are ongoing.[34]

Regeneron (Tarrytown, NY) has developed a fully human myostatin-blocking antibody named Trevogrumab (REGN1033).[29,35] In mice, the IgG4(κ) antibody was able to significantly increase the body weight (+3–7%), muscle mass (+19–25%), and muscle force (+17%) and reduce muscular atrophy due to casting immobilization, dexamethasone-treatment, and hindlimb suspension.[35] Moreover, Trevogrumab successfully alleviated the symptoms of age-related sarcopenia, as the muscle mass, muscle force, and running endurance during a treadmill test were elevated. Trevogrumab has already been evaluated in different Phase 1 and 2 clinical tests, but no further studies are currently planned.[34]

4.5.2.1.2 Anti-ActRII Antibodies: Bimagrumab

In contrast to the abovementioned myostatin-specific approaches, Bimagrumab (BYM338, Novartis, Basel, Switzerland) is a human IgG1(λ2) antibody targeting multiple ligands of the TGF-β superfamily, which signal through ActRIIA and ActRIIB.[2,15,36] The antibody binds highly specifically to the extracellular domains of both ActRIIs (ActRIIB > ActRIIA), thus preventing ligand interaction and receptor activation.[2,15]

In preclinical animal studies, it could be demonstrated that Bimagrumab not only induces significant dose-dependent increases in body weight and skeletal muscle mass (+18–50%) but is also more effective than other myostatin inhibitors, such as a stabilized myostatin propeptide (D76A) and antibodies directed against either ActRIIA or ActRIIB.[2,15] In hypermuscular myostatin-deficient mice,

Bimagrumab treatment was able to further increase the body weight, lean mass, and muscle weight, indicating that the anti-ActRII antibody induces muscle hypertrophy through inhibition of TGF-β ligands beyond myostatin.[2] Moreover, a murinized version of Bimagrumab (CDD866) was found to successfully protect mice from glucocorticoid-induced muscle atrophy, cancer cachexia, and chemotherapy-induced muscle wasting.[2,37] Due to the promising results in the different mouse models, Bimagrumab was further investigated in human subjects. In a proof-of-concept study, patients with sporadic inclusion body myositis, a neuromuscular disease, were treated with a single antibody dose of 30 mg/kg (IV).[38] Eight weeks following injection, significant increases in thigh muscle volume (+6.5/7.6%), lean body mass (+5.7%), and muscle function (+14.6%) were observed. Moreover, non-significant improvements in muscle strength could be detected, and the drug was well tolerated with only mild side effects such as muscle spasms, diarrhea, and acne. Similar results were obtained in a Phase 2 clinical study where patients with sarcopenia received up to two IV Bimagrumab infusions at a dosage of 30 mg/kg.[39] Up to 24 weeks following administration, the participants were characterized by a significantly increased thigh muscle volume (+5–8%), lean body mass (+3–6%), muscle strength (+14–27%), and mobility. Moreover, a single dose of Bimagrumab (30 mg/kg IV) was found to successfully accelerate the recovery of the thigh muscle volume in healthy subjects with casting-induced muscle atrophy[40] and improve the body composition (increased lean muscle mass and reduced fat mass) and insulin sensitivity in healthy volunteers with insulin resistance.[41] A multicenter Phase 2b trial was conducted to further investigate the effects of Bimagrumab on inclusion body myositis.[42] The study participants received IV Bimagrumab infusions at a dosage of 1, 3, or 10 mg/kg every 4 weeks for a period of at least 48 weeks. The antibody showed a good safety profile but had no positive effects on a 6-min walking distance. In a Phase 2a study, patients with chronic obstructive pulmonary disease (COPD) were treated with two doses of Bimagrumab (30 mg/kg, study days 1 and 57).[43] Again, no positive effects on muscle function could be observed, but thigh muscle volume was found to be significantly increased (+5–8%) starting 4 weeks after the first dose of the antibody. Bimagrumab has already proceeded into Phase 2 and 3 clinical testing and has been evaluated for the treatment of muscular and metabolic diseases such as sporadic inclusion body myositis and diabetes mellitus type II.[34] Currently, no clinical trials are ongoing.

4.5.2.2 ActRII-Fc Fusion Proteins: Ramatercept (ACE-031) and ACE-2494

As mentioned earlier, myostatin and several other TGF-β cytokines involved in the negative regulation of muscle mass predominantly signal through ActRIIB.[11] Analogous to Sotatercept (ACE-011, ActRIIA-Fc; see 3.3), Ramatercept (ACE-031, Acceleron Pharma) is a soluble fusion protein composed of the extracellular domain of ActRIIB and the Fc fragment of human IgG1.[3,17,44] The disulfide-linked dimer acts as a ligand trap/decoy receptor, which binds to the circulating TGF-β cytokines and disrupts ActRIIB signaling. When administered to wild-type mice, the protein drug dramatically increased the muscle mass by up to 61% within 2 weeks.[3] The observed effects on muscle growth were considerably larger than those obtained for other experimental drugs directed solely against myostatin (e.g., an anti-myostatin antibody). This can probably be attributed to the broader specificity of the drug, which targets not only myostatin but also other ligands of ActRIIB: The administration of the fusion protein to hypermuscular myostatin knockout mice resulted in further increases in muscle weight of 15–26%. A murinized version of Ramatercept was successfully tested in different murine disease models, where it was found to significantly increase the body weight, muscle mass, and muscle strength.[45,46] Ramatercept was also evaluated in humans in Phase 1 and 2 clinical trials.[16,44] In healthy volunteers, single doses of 0.02–3 mg/kg SC yielded significant increases in total lean mass (+3.3%) and muscle volume (+5.1%) with only moderate side effects, such as injection site erythema.[44] Serum levels of Ramatercept were only detectable in the samples collected from volunteers treated with at least 0.3 mg/kg of the drug. The biological half-life varied between 11 and 15 days, and maximum serum concentrations of 3–33 μg/mL were reached within 5–7 days. In a subsequent Phase 2 study, young patients with DMD received multiple doses of 0.5 and 1 mg/kg SC over a period of 14–16 weeks.[16] Unfortunately, only moderate effects on lean body mass could be observed, and with increasing doses, additional adverse events comprising nose bleeding and skin telangiectasia occurred. The observed effects on the vascular system can probably be attributed to the Ramatercept-mediated inhibition of the bone morphogenic proteins BMP9 and BMP10, which play pivotal roles during angiogenesis.[16,47] Eventually, clinical development of Ramatercept was terminated and research focused on alternative myostatin inhibitors such as ACE-2494.[17,47,48] This fusion protein is derived from ActRIIB and IgG1-Fc and has a reduced affinity for BMP9 and BMP10. In a preclinical study, systemic administration of ACE-2494 to mice led to significant dose-dependent increases in muscle mass of 25–87%[47]. After completion of a Phase 1 clinical trial with healthy volunteers, the development of ACE-2494 was discontinued due to the formation of anti-drug antibodies.[49]

4.5.2.3 Follistatin-Fc (FST-Fc) Fusion Proteins: ACE-083

Follistatin (FST) is an autocrine, monomeric glycoprotein, which comprises 344 amino acids and is characterized by a complex structure with several functional domains, disulfide bonds, and glycosylation sites.[50–53] In humans, two major isoforms are generated by alternative mRNA splicing: FST315 and FST288. They differ in the presence of an acidic C-terminal amino acid tail, which reduces the affinity of FST315 for heparin through association with a heparin-binding sequence (HBS) located in the first FST domain FSD1.[51–55] Consequently, FST-315 is thought to be the major circulating form, while FST-288 is considered to have a local activity.[56,57] An additional isoform named FST303 is derived from FST315 by proteolysis. All three isoforms have distinct ligand affinities and localizations, resulting in diverse biological functions.[52,53,55] Most importantly, FST is involved in the regulation of TGF-β cytokines such as activin and myostatin.[50,51,53,55] The interaction between FST and the circulating growth factors prevents receptor binding and activation, which leads to changes in various downstream processes such as, for example, muscle growth, bone homeostasis, and inflammation.[52]

Especially due to that regulatory function, FST is a promising candidate as a protein therapeutic. However, the high complexity of the glycoprotein as well as its strong affinity towards heparin results in rather poor pharmacokinetic and pharmacodynamic properties. Therefore, different dimeric FST-Fc fusion proteins were constructed in order to improve tissue distribution and slow down systemic clearance.[50,54] They comprise the natural FST variants FST288 and FST315 as well as FST291, a truncated version of FST315. In general, both the ligand-binding activity and biological half-life of FST were significantly improved through the dimerization of the molecule and the addition of an Fc-tag, which increases the molecular mass from circa 38 kDa to approximately 120 kDa.[50] In a preclinical animal study,[56] wild-type mice received unilateral intramuscular injections with 10–100 μg of a recombinant FST288-IgG1 Fc fusion protein twice weekly for a period of 4 weeks. Compared with vehicle controls, the weight of the injected muscle was found to be increased by 19–42%, and no systemic activity could be observed. Moreover, the effects of a systemic administration of the fusion protein (2 x 10 mg/kg/week over a period of 4 weeks) were investigated. Both the body composition and muscle mass were found to be unaffected, which could be attributed to a rapid proteolytic degradation of systemically administered FST288-Fc. So far, all Fc fusion proteins with clinical approval have an Fc domain originating from IgG1.[58] But for FST constructs retaining strong heparin affinity, the presence of an IgG1 portion can be disadvantageous, as the adhesion of such a fusion protein to its target cells can cause antibody-dependent cell-mediated cytotoxicity (ADCC) or complement dependent cytotoxicity (CDC), resulting in cytolysis.[51,58] Therefore, constructs with an IgG2-Fc domain were additionally tested, as it is known to have lower ADCC and CDC activities.[58]

ACE-083 (Acceleron Pharma) is a recombinant fusion protein composed of human FST291 and the Fc domain of human IgG2.[57,59–61] The protein drug acts locally in the injected muscle through inhibition of myostatin and other TGF-β cytokines involved in the negative regulation of muscle mass. After entering the circulation, the fusion protein is rapidly inactivated, resulting in a localized therapeutic effect and reduced potential for systemic side effects. In several preclinical studies with healthy wild-type mice, local ACE-083 treatment with multiple doses ranging from 3 to 300 μg resulted in dose-dependent muscle hypertrophy (+16–96%) and substantial improvements in muscle force.[57,62,63] No systemic effects were observed. Moreover, the protein drug was tested in mouse models of Charcot–Marie–Tooth (CMT) disease and DMD.[57] In both studies, repeated intramuscular injections of ACE-083 (dose: 2 x 100 μg/week for a period of 4 weeks) led to a local increase of muscle mass and force. A Phase 1 clinical study was conducted with healthy volunteers who received one or two intramuscular doses of 50–200 mg.[60,61] Local administration of the protein drug was found to be safe and well tolerated, and the collected pharmacokinetic data demonstrate that systemic exposure is limited to the first 24 hours following injection. Significant dose-dependent increases in muscle mass up to 15% without concomitant improvements in strength were observed. According to the authors, a prolonged treatment period might be required to induce measurable changes in muscle strength. Currently, ACE-083 is in Phase 2 clinical trials for the treatment of different neuromuscular disorders.[34]

4.5.2.4 Agents Derived from the Myostatin Propeptide

In vivo, the activity of myostatin is regulated by different binding proteins, which form biologically inactive complexes with the circulating protein, thus preventing receptor binding and activation.[11,64,65] One of these regulators is the myostatin propeptide, which is generated by proteolytic cleavage of the myostatin precursor. In order to release active myostatin, the propeptide has to be cleaved by metalloproteases of the bone morphogenetic protein 1/tolloid family (BMP-1/TLD).[64,65] Due to the inhibiting effect on myostatin, the myostatin propeptide is a promising drug candidate for the treatment of different muscular and metabolic diseases.[65]

Unmodified propeptide was successfully administered to mice with musculoskeletal injuries, where it had positive effects on both muscle regeneration (+18%) and fracture healing.[66] In order to increase the biological half-life, different propeptide-Fc fusion proteins were generated and tested in different mouse models. In aged wild-type mice, repeated injections with propeptide-Fc yielded significant increases in muscle mass (+7%) and muscle fiber size (+6–16%).[67] A propeptide-Fc construct comprising an amino acid exchange at the proteolytic cleavage site for BMP-1/TLD (Asp76 → Ala) was even able to induce changes in muscle weight of 18–27% when administered to adult wild-type mice.[65] In a mouse model of DMD, multiple injections with propeptide-Fc resulted in significant increases in muscle mass and strength.[68] These findings demonstrate that a propeptide-based myostatin inhibitor could be a promising protein therapeutic for the treatment of muscle wasting disorders, especially as anti-idiotypic responses – which are characteristic for therapeutic antibodies and limit the effectiveness of the drug – would not be expected. So far, there are no published studies in which a therapeutic protein derived from the myostatin propeptide was tested in human subjects.

4.5.2.5 Anti-Myostatin Peptibodies: PINTA-745

A promising alternative to therapeutic antibodies are peptibodies – homodimeric fusion proteins composed of a biologically active peptide and the Fc domain of human IgG1.[69] Due to the increased molecular weight and recycling mediated by the neonatal Fc-receptor, the attachment of a peptide to an Fc moiety results in a prolonged biological half-life of 3 to 8 days and improved pharmacokinetic properties.

PINTA-745 (formerly AMG-745) is an anti-myostatin peptibody developed by Amgen (Thousand Oaks, CA) and Atara Biotherapeutics (South San Francisco, CA).[70] In a mouse model with transient cerebral ischemia,[71] the drug was found to significantly reduce body weight losses and increase muscle weight, strength, and function, indicating that peptibody-mediated myostatin inhibition can successfully reduce the deleterious effects of stroke on the muscular system. Moreover, a murine analog of PINTA-745 was able to improve muscle growth and insulin resistance in mice fed with a high fat diet[72] and prevent the development of muscle atrophy in mice with chronic kidney disease.[73] According to the manufacturer, PINTA-745 was also successfully tested in clinical studies with healthy subjects as well as patients with prostate cancer.[70] However, clinical development was discontinued, as the primary efficacy endpoint of a Phase 2 proof-of-concept study in patients with end stage renal disease could not be met.[74]

4.5.2.6 Anti-Myostatin Adnectins: Taldicercept Alpha/RG6206

Adnectins represent a novel class of therapeutic proteins, which are derived from the tenth type III domain of human fibronectin.[75] The structure of these target-binding proteins is very similar to the antibody variable domains, resulting in high affinity and specificity for their molecular targets. But at the same time, they have a much simpler structure, with only one functional domain and without disulfide bonds.

Talditercept alpha/RG6206 (formerly BMS-986089, Bristol-Myers Squibb, New York City, NY and Hoffmann-La Roche, Basel, Switzerland) is an anti-myostatin adnectin linked to the C-terminus of a human IgG1 Fc domain.[76,77] In preclinical trials, Talditercept alpha was administered to immunodeficient SCID mice, rats, and cynomolgus monkeys, and dose- and time-dependent increases in muscle mass of 5–30% could be observed.[78] The results of a Phase 1 clinical trial with healthy volunteers were published in 2016,[79] reporting dose-dependent increases in thigh muscle volume and lean body mass after five weekly subcutaneous injections of 45–180 mg. Maximum serum concentrations were reached 3–5 days post-administration, and the serum half-life varied between 7 and 10 days. The protein drug was found to be safe and well tolerated with only mild side effects, such as injection site erythema. In a Phase 1b/2 study, ambulatory boys with DMD received weekly subcutaneous injections of 4–50 mg of Talditercept alpha/RG6206 for a period of 24 weeks.[80] The protein drug was found to be well tolerated and caused a dose-dependent reduction in free myostatin (77–97%). Moreover, increases in muscle volume and lean body mass were observed. A Phase 2/3 clinical study in patients with DMD is currently ongoing.[34,77,79]

4.5.3 Myostatin Inhibitors in Sports Drug Testing

The misuse of agents modifying myostatin function in sports is prohibited both in and out of competition, and myostatin inhibitors are listed in the section S4 – "Hormone and Metabolic Modulators" of the WADA Prohibited List.[81] Although no drug candidates have obtained clinical approval yet, the proactive development of specific and sensitive detection methods is of the utmost importance, in particular as several related substances are sold online for research purposes and on the black market. Possible detection strategies suitable for sports drug testing are illustrated in Figure 4.5.2.

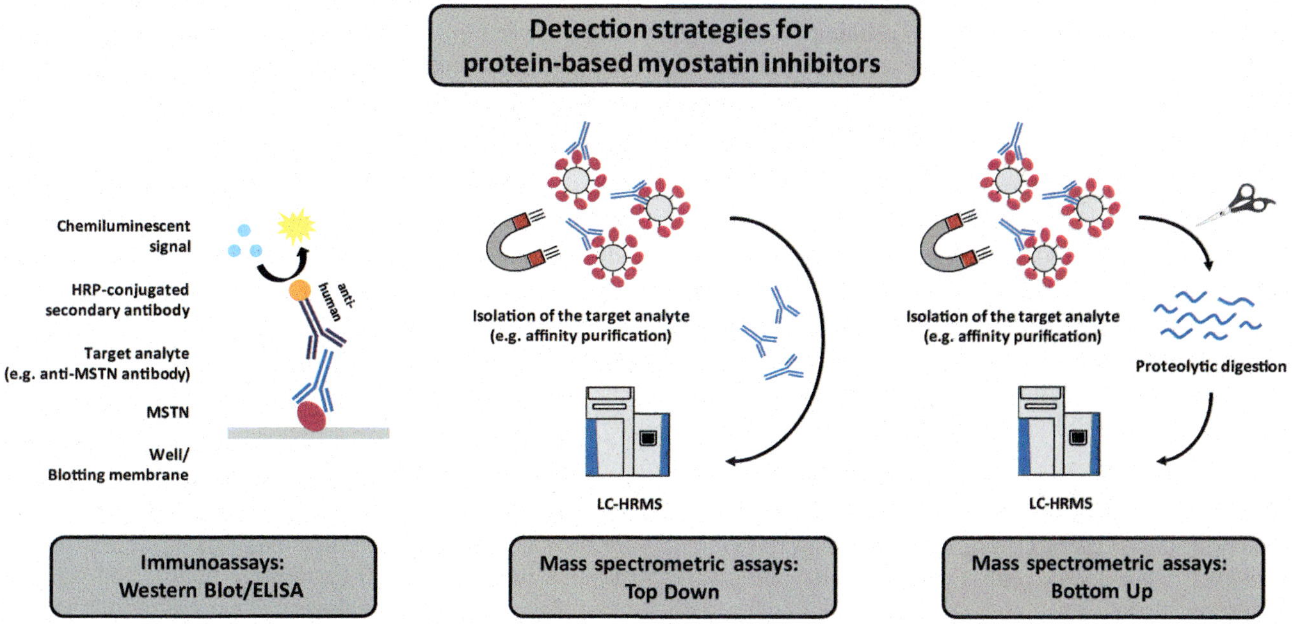

FIGURE 4.5.2 Detection strategies for protein-based myostatin inhibitors.

4.5.3.1 Therapeutic Antibodies

Although therapeutic antibodies are characterized by relatively high serum concentrations and biological half-lives,[19] their detection in biological matrices can be challenging, as the protein drugs need to be clearly distinguished from circulating endogenous IgGs. Mass spectrometric approaches enable unambiguous identification of the target analytes; however, this requires information about the amino acid sequence of the compound, which is commonly not available prior to market launch.

In both preclinical and clinical studies, enzyme-linked immunosorbent assays (ELISAs) were employed for the quantitative determination of the anti-myostatin antibodies Stamulumab and Domagrozumab in serum.[18,82] In these assays, biotinylated myostatin was immobilized on a streptavidin-coated microtiter plate and used to isolate Stamulumab/Domagrozumab from the biological matrix. Then, the bound target proteins were detected with a mouse anti-human IgG conjugated with horseradish peroxidase (HRP). In human serum, the ranges of quantitation were 63.2–720 ng/mL for Stamulumab[82] and 30–1,600 ng/mL for Domagrozumab.[18] A similar immunological assay based on Western blotting was developed for sports drug testing and published in 2016.[83] Following affinity purification with Protein A–conjugated magnetic beads, the antibody extracts are subjected to Western blotting, where myostatin is used as bait protein to isolate all molecules specifically binding to the cytokine from the biological matrix. Bound proteins with a human Fc domain are then detected using an enzyme-linked secondary antibody specific for the Fc fragment of human IgG. The assay was comprehensively characterized and has a limit of detection (LOD) of 100 ng/mL. Similarly to the abovementioned ELISAs, this assay can detect different types of proteins specifically binding to myostatin. However, it cannot distinguish between anti-myostatin antibodies and Fc fusion proteins directed against the cytokine. Therefore, additional mass spectrometric assays are necessary to enable an unambiguous identification of the target analyte, which is of the utmost importance, especially for sports drug testing. For Domagrozumab, such a mass spectrometric detection assay was just recently developed.[84] By using ammonium sulfate precipitation in combination with tryptic digestion and LC-HRMS, diagnostic peptides originating from both the heavy and light chains of the antibody could be detected in 200 μL of serum down to a concentration of 50 ng/mL. In the case of positive LC-MS findings, complementary information can be obtained by using an additional immunological assay based on immunoaffinity purification and Western blotting, which generally demonstrates the presence of a myostatin-binding protein with a human Fc domain.

In clinical studies, serum concentrations of the anti-ActRII antibody Bimagrumab were determined by using a validated bridging ELISA with a limit of quantitation (LOQ) of 176 ng/mL.[41] For doping control purposes, a detection assay highly specific for proteolytic signature peptides of the antibody was developed using ammonium sulfate precipitation, immunoaffinity purification with ActRIIB-Fc conjugated magnetic beads, tryptic digestion, and liquid chromatography coupled to ion mobility high-resolution mass spectrometry (LC-IM-HRMS).[85] The assay was found to be highly specific and sensitive with an LOD of 20 ng/mL. Its applicability to authentic serum specimens was demonstrated by successfully analyzing a set of clinical samples.

4.5.3.2 Fc Fusion Proteins

In general, Fc fusion proteins are artificial protein constructs, which do not occur naturally in the human body. Therefore, they can be easily distinguished from endogenous serum proteins by using either immunological approaches or LC-MS/MS.

During clinical testing, a competitive ELISA with an analytical range from 250 to 20,000 ng/mL was employed for the detection of the ActRIIB-Fc fusion protein Ramatercept (ACE-031) in serum.[44] The assay uses a goat-anti-ActRIIB antibody for the isolation of the target analyte, biotinylated Ramatercept as tracer, and HRP-avidin in combination with 3,3′,5,5′-tetramethylbenzidine (TMB) for detection. For doping control purposes, the existing LC-HRMS detection method for the ActRIIA-Fc fusion protein Sotatercept[86] was modified to include a commercially available ActRIIB-Fc fusion protein related to Ramatercept.[87] As the Fc domain of the ActRIIB-Fc reference protein is identical to endogenous IgG1, which is abundantly present in serum, only peptides located in the receptor domain can be used for identification purposes. Consequently, an additional analysis such as Western blotting needs to be conducted in order to demonstrate that an Fc fusion protein is present in the sample. The MS method was comprehensively characterized and has an estimated LOD of 10 ng/mL. The ActRIIB-derived Fc fusion protein ACE-2494 can be implemented into the assay as soon as authentic reference material is available.

So far, there are no validated doping detection methods for the FST-Fc fusion protein ACE-083, but both an ELISA with a lower limit of quantification (LLOQ) of 100 ng/mL and a slightly more sensitive LC-MS/MS method measuring the intact protein (LLOQ: 10 ng/mL) have been used for quantification purposes within clinical trials.[60] However, pharmacokinetic data suggest that the detection of ACE-083 in doping control serum samples might be challenging, as the drug was only detectable during the first 24 hours following administration in some of the participants, with maximum serum concentrations slightly above the LLOQ of 10 ng/mL.

For the quantitative determination of the anti-myostatin Adnectin Talditercept alpha/RG6206 in preclinical and clinical serum samples, a detection assay employing methanol-based protein precipitation, tryptic digestion, and LC-MS/MS was developed and comprehensively characterized.[76] Characteristic peptides originating from the Fc and Adnectin domains of Talditercept alpha/RG6206 are used for the unambiguous identification of the protein drug. The assay is linear from 390 to 100,000 ng/mL and was successfully employed to analyze murine post-administration samples.

Similar detection assays for Fc fusion proteins derived from the myostatin propeptide and anti-myostatin peptibodies in doping control serum samples can be established as soon as authentic reference material is available.

REFERENCES

1. McPherron AC, Lawler AM, Lee SJ. Regulation of skeletal muscle mass in mice by a new TGF-beta superfamily member. *Nature* 1997;387(6628):83–90.
2. Lach-Trifilieff E, Minetti GC, Sheppard K, Ibebunjo C, Feige JN, Hartmann S, Brachat S, Rivet H, Koelbing C, Morvan F, Hatakeyama S, Glass DJ. An antibody blocking activin type II receptors induces strong skeletal muscle hypertrophy and protects from atrophy. *Mol Cell Biol* 2014;34(4):606–18.
3. Lee SJ, Reed LA, Davies MV, Girgenrath S, Goad ME, Tomkinson KN, Wright JF, Barker C, Ehrmantraut G, Holmstrom J, Trowell B, Gertz B, Jiang MS, Sebald SM, Matzuk M, Li E, Liang LF, Quattlebaum E, Stotish RL, Wolfman NM. Regulation of muscle growth by multiple ligands signaling through activin type II receptors. *Proc Natl Acad Sci USA* 2005;102(50):18117–22.
4. Sharma M, Kambadur R, Matthews KG, Somers WG, Devlin GP, Conaglen JV, Fowke PJ, Bass JJ. Myostatin, a transforming growth factor-beta superfamily member, is expressed in heart muscle and is upregulated in cardiomyocytes after infarct. *J Cell Physiol* 1999;180(1):1–9.
5. Kambadur R, Sharma M, Smith TP, Bass JJ. Mutations in myostatin (GDF8) in double-muscled Belgian Blue and Piedmontese cattle. *Genome Res* 1997;7(9):910–6.
6. Mosher DS, Quignon P, Bustamante CD, Sutter NB, Mellersh CS, Parker HG, Ostrander EA. A mutation in the myostatin gene increases muscle mass and enhances racing performance in heterozygote dogs. *PLoS Genet* 2007;3(5):e79.
7. Shelton GD, Engvall E. Gross muscle hypertrophy in whippet dogs is caused by a mutation in the myostatin gene. *Neuromuscul Disord* 2007;17(9–10):721–2.
8. Clop A, Marcq F, Takeda H, Pirottin D, Tordoir X, Bibe B, Bouix J, Caiment F, Elsen JM, Eychenne F, Larzul C, Laville E, Meish F, Milenkovic D, Tobin J, Charlier C, Georges M. A mutation creating a potential illegitimate microRNA target site in the myostatin gene affects muscularity in sheep. *Nat Genet* 2006;38(7):813–8.
9. Schuelke M, Wagner KR, Stolz LE, Hubner C, Riebel T, Komen W, Braun T, Tobin JF, Lee SJ. Myostatin mutation associated with gross muscle hypertrophy in a child. *N Engl J Med* 2004;350(26):2682–8.
10. Lee SJ. Regulation of muscle mass by myostatin. *Annu Rev Cell Dev Biol* 2004;20:61–86.
11. Lee SJ, McPherron AC. Regulation of myostatin activity and muscle growth. *Proc Natl Acad Sci USA* 2001;98(16):9306–11.
12. Langley B, Thomas M, Bishop A, Sharma M, Gilmour S, Kambadur R. Myostatin inhibits myoblast differentiation by down-regulating MyoD expression. *J Biol Chem* 2002;277(51):49831–40.
13. Elkina Y, von Haehling S, Anker SD, Springer J. The role of myostatin in muscle wasting: an overview. *J Cachexia Sarcopenia Muscle* 2011;2(3):143–51.
14. Smith RC, Lin BK. Myostatin inhibitors as therapies for muscle wasting associated with cancer and other disorders. *Curr Opin Support Palliat Care* 2013;7(4):352–60.
15. Morvan F, Rondeau JM, Zou C, Minetti G, Scheufler C, Scharenberg M, Jacobi C, Brebbia P, Ritter V, Toussaint G, Koelbing C, Leber X, Schilb A, Witte F, Lehmann S, Koch E, Geisse S, Glass DJ, Lach-Trifilieff E. Blockade of activin type II receptors with a dual anti-ActRIIA/IIB antibody is critical to promote maximal skeletal muscle hypertrophy. *Proc Natl Acad Sci USA* 2017;114(47):12448–53.
16. Campbell C, McMillan HJ, Mah JK, Tarnopolsky M, Selby K, McClure T, Wilson DM, Sherman ML, Escolar D, Attie KM. Myostatin inhibitor ACE-031 treatment of ambulatory boys with Duchenne muscular dystrophy: results of a randomized, placebo-controlled clinical trial. *Muscle Nerve* 2017;55(4):458–64.
17. Saitoh M, Ishida J, Ebner N, Anker SD, Springer J, von Haehling S. Myostatin inhibitors as pharmacological treatment for muscle wasting and muscular dystrophy. *J Cachexia Sarcopenia Muscle* 2017;2(1).
18. Bhattacharya I, Pawlak S, Marraffino S, Christensen J, Sherlock SP, Alvey C, Morris C, Arkin S, Binks M. Safety, tolerability, pharmacokinetics, and pharmacodynamics of domagrozumab (PF-06252616), an antimyostatin monoclonal antibody, in healthy subjects. *Clin Pharmacol Drug Dev* 2018;7(5):484–97.
19. Chames P, Van Regenmortel M, Weiss E, Baty D. Therapeutic antibodies: successes, limitations and hopes for the future. *Br J Pharmacol* 2009;157(2):220–33.
20. Apgar JR, Mader M, Agostinelli R, Benard S, Bialek P, Johnson M, Gao Y, Krebs M, Owens J, Parris K, St Andre M, Svenson K, Morris C, Tchistiakova L. Beyond CDR-grafting: structure-guided humanization of framework and CDR regions of an anti-myostatin antibody. *MAbs* 2016;8(7):1302–18.
21. Reichert JM, Rosensweig CJ, Faden LB, Dewitz MC. Monoclonal antibody successes in the clinic. *Nat Biotechnol* 2005;23(9):1073–8.
22. Whittemore LA, Song K, Li X, Aghajanian J, Davies M, Girgenrath S, Hill JJ, Jalenak M, Kelley P, Knight A, Maylor R, O'Hara D, Pearson A, Quazi A, Ryerson S, Tan XY, Tomkinson KN, Veldman GM, Widom A, Wright JF, Wudyka S, Zhao L, Wolfman NM. Inhibition of myostatin in adult mice increases skeletal muscle mass and strength. *Biochem Biophys Res Commun* 2003;300(4):965–71.
23. Bogdanovich S, Krag TO, Barton ER, Morris LD, Whittemore LA, Ahima RS, Khurana TS. Functional improvement of dystrophic muscle by myostatin blockade. *Nature* 2002;420(6914):418–21.
24. Wagner KR, Fleckenstein JL, Amato AA, Barohn RJ, Bushby K, Escolar DM, Flanigan KM, Pestronk A, Tawil R, Wolfe GI, Eagle M, Florence JM, King WM, Pandya S, Straub V, Juneau P, Meyers K, Csimma C, Araujo T, Allen R, Parsons SA, Wozney JM, Lavallie ER, Mendell JR. A phase I/IItrial of MYO-029 in adult subjects with muscular dystrophy. *Ann Neurol* 2008;63(5):561–71.
25. Krivickas LS, Walsh R, Amato AA. Single muscle fiber contractile properties in adults with muscular dystrophy treated with MYO-029. *Muscle Nerve* 2009;39(1):3–9.
26. World Health Organization. WHO drug information, international nonproprietary names for pharmaceutical substances (INN). 2015;29(4).
27. St Andre M, Johnson M, Bansal PN, Wellen J, Robertson A, Opsahl A, Burch PM, Bialek P, Morris C, Owens J. A mouse anti-myostatin antibody increases muscle mass and improves muscle strength and contractility in the mdx mouse model of Duchenne muscular dystrophy and its humanized equivalent, domagrozumab (PF-06252616), increases muscle volume in cynomolgus monkeys. *Skelet Muscle* 2017;7(1):25.

28. Pfizer. Pfizer terminates Domagrozuman (PF-06252616) clinical studies for the treatment of Duchenne muscular dystrophy. https://www.pfizer.com/news/press-release/press-release-detail/pfizer_terminates_domagrozumab_pf_06252616_clinical_studies_for_the_treatment_of_duchenne_muscular_dystrophy (accessed 23709719).
29. World Health Organization. WHO drug information, international nonproprietary names for pharmaceutical substances (INN). 2015;29(2).
30. Jameson GS, Von Hoff DD, Weiss GJ, Richards DA, Smith DA, Becerra C, Benson MC, Yuan Z, Robins DA, Turik M, Wagner M, Hu L, Lin BK. Safety of the antimyostatin monoclonal antibody LY2495655 in healthy subjects and patients with advanced cancer. *J Clin Oncol* 2012.
31. Becker C, Lord SR, Studenski SA, Warden SJ, Fielding RA, Recknor CP, Hochberg MC, Ferrari SL, Blain H, Binder EF, Rolland Y, Poiraudeau S, Benson CT, Myers SL, Hu L, Ahmad QI, Pacuch KR, Gomez EV, Benichou O, Group S. Myostatin antibody (LY2495655) in older weak fallers: a proof-of-concept, randomised, phase 2 trial. *Lancet Diabetes Endocrinol* 2015;3(12):948–57.
32. Woodhouse L, Gandhi R, Warden SJ, Poiraudeau S, Myers SL, Benson CT, Hu L, Ahmad QI, Linnemeier P, Gomez EV, Benichou O, Study I. A phase 2 randomized study investigating the efficacy and safety of myostatin antibody LY2495655 versus Placebo in patients undergoing elective total hip arthroplasty. *J Frailty Aging* 2016;5(1):62–70.
33. Golan T, Geva R, Richards D, Madhusudan S, Kin Lin B, Wang HF, Walgren RA, Stemmer SM. LY2495655, an anti-myostatin antibody, in pancreatic cancer: a randomized, phase 2 trial. *J Cachexia Sarcopenia Muscle* 2018;9:871–9.
34. U.S. National Library of Medicine. ClinicalTrials.gov. https://clinicaltrials.gov/ (accessed 25.07.18).
35. Latres E, Pangilinan J, Miloscio L, Bauerlein R, Na E, Potocky TB, Huang Y, Eckersdorff M, Rafique A, Mastaitis J, Lin C, Murphy AJ, Yancopoulos GD, Gromada J, Stitt T. Myostatin blockade with a fully human monoclonal antibody induces muscle hypertrophy and reverses muscle atrophy in young and aged mice. *Skelet Muscle* 2015;5:34.
36. World Health Organization. *WHO Drug Information, International Nonproprietary Names for Pharmaceutical Substances (INN).* 2012;26(4).
37. Hatakeyama S, Summermatter S, Jourdain M, Melly S, Minetti GC, Lach-Trifilieff E. ActRII blockade protects mice from cancer cachexia and prolongs survival in the presence of anti-cancer treatments. *Skelet Muscle* 2016;6:26.
38. Amato AA, Sivakumar K, Goyal N, David WS, Salajegheh M, Praestgaard J, Lach-Trifilieff E, Trendelenburg AU, Laurent D, Glass DJ, Roubenoff R, Tseng BS, Greenberg SA. Treatment of sporadic inclusion body myositis with bimagrumab. *Neurology* 2014;83(24):2239–46.
39. Rooks D, Praestgaard J, Hariry S, Laurent D, Petricoul O, Perry RG, Lach-Trifilieff E, Roubenoff R. Treatment of sarcopenia with bimagrumab: results from a phase II, randomized, controlled, proof-of-concept study. *J Am Geriatr Soc* 2017;65(9):1988–95.
40. Rooks DS, Laurent D, Praestgaard J, Rasmussen S, Bartlett M, Tanko LB. Effect of bimagrumab on thigh muscle volume and composition in men with casting-induced atrophy. *J Cachexia Sarcopenia Muscle* 2017;8(5):727–34.
41. Garito T, Roubenoff R, Hompesch M, Morrow L, Gomez K, Rooks D, Meyers C, Buchsbaum MS, Neelakantham S, Swan T, Filosa LA, Laurent D, Petricoul O, Zakaria M. Bimagrumab improves body composition and insulin sensitivity in insulin-resistant individuals. *Diabetes Obes Metab* 2018;20(1):94–102.
42. Hanna MG, Badrising UA, Benveniste O, Lloyd TE, Needham M, Chinoy H, Aoki M, Machado PM, Liang C, Reardon KA, de Visser M, Ascherman DP, Barohn RJ, Dimachkie MM, Miller JAL, Kissel JT, Oskarsson B, Joyce NC, Van den Bergh P, Baets J, De Bleecker JL, Karam C, David WS, Mirabella M, Nations SP, Jung HH, Pegoraro E, Maggi L, Rodolico C, Filosto M, Shaibani AI, Sivakumar K, Goyal NA, Mori-Yoshimura M, Yamashita S, Suzuki N, Katsuno M, Murata K, Nodera H, Nishino I, Romano CD, Williams VSL, Vissing J, Auberson LZ, Wu M, de Vera A, Papanicolaou DA, Amato AA. Safety and efficacy of intravenous bimagrumab in inclusion body myositis (RESILIENT): a randomised, double-blind, placebo-controlled phase 2b trial. *Lancet Neurol* 2019;18(9):834–44.
43. Polkey MI, Praestgaard J, Berwick A, Franssen FME, Singh D, Steiner MC, Casaburi R, Tillmann HC, Lach-Trifilieff E, Roubenoff R, Rooks DS. Activin type II receptor blockade for treatment of muscle depletion in chronic obstructive pulmonary disease. A randomized trial. *Am J Respir Crit Care Med* 2019;199(3):313–20.
44. Attie KM, Borgstein NG, Yang Y, Condon CH, Wilson DM, Pearsall AE, Kumar R, Willins DA, Seehra JS, Sherman ML. A single ascending-dose study of muscle regulator ACE-031 in healthy volunteers. *Muscle Nerve* 2013;47(3):416–23.
45. Pistilli EE, Bogdanovich S, Goncalves MD, Ahima RS, Lachey J, Seehra J, Khurana T. Targeting the activin type IIB receptor to improve muscle mass and function in the mdx mouse model of Duchenne muscular dystrophy. *Am J Pathol* 2011;178(3):1287–97.
46. Morrison BM, Lachey JL, Warsing LC, Ting BL, Pullen AE, Underwood KW, Kumar R, Sako D, Grinberg A, Wong V, Colantuoni E, Seehra JS, Wagner KR. A soluble activin type IIB receptor improves function in a mouse model of amyotrophic lateral sclerosis. *Exp Neurol* 2009;217(2):258–68.
47. Pearsall AE, Sako D, Liu J, Davies M, Heveron K, Castonguay R, Krishnan L, Troy M, Liharska K, Steeves R, Cannell M, Alimzhanov M, Grinberg A, Kumar R. ACE-2494, a novel GDF ligand trap, increases muscle mass upon systemic administration in mice. *20th International Congress of the World Muscle Society*, Brighton, 2015.
48. Pearsall RS, Sako D, Liu J, Davies M, Heveron K, Castonguay R, Krishnan L, Troy M, Liharska K, Steeves R, Cannell M, Alimzhanov M, Grinberg A, Kumar R In ACE-2494, a novel GDF ligand trap, increases muscle and bone mass upon systemic administration in mice. *20th International Congress of The World Muscle Society*, Brighton, 2015.
49. Acceleron Pharma. Acceleron discontinues development of phase 1 molecule ACE-2494. http://investor.acceleronpharma.com/news-releases/news-release-details/acceleron-discontinues-development-phase-1-molecule-ace-2494 (accessed 23.09.2019).
50. Datta-Mannan A, Yaden B, Krishnan V, Jones BE, Croy JE. An engineered human follistatin variant: insights into the pharmacokinetic and pharmocodynamic relationships of a novel molecule with broad therapeutic potential. *J Pharmacol Exp Ther* 2013;344(3):616–23.
51. Kumar R, Grinberg A. Methods and compositions for treatment of disorders with follistatin polypeptides. 2014. WO application WO2015187977A1.
52. Shen C, Iskenderian A, Lundberg D, He T, Palmieri K, Crooker R, Deng Q, Traylor M, Gu S, Rong H, Ehmann D, Pescatore B, Strack-Logue B, Romashko A, Baviello G, Gill J, Zhang B, Meiyappan M, Pan C, Norton AW. Protein

engineering on human recombinant follistatin: enhancing pharmacokinetic characteristics for therapeutic application. *J Pharmacol Exp Ther* 2018;366(2):291–302.
53. Lerch TF, Shimasaki S, Woodruff TK, Jardetzky TS. Structural and biophysical coupling of heparin and activin binding to follistatin isoform functions. *J Biol Chem* 2007;282(21):15930–9.
54. Yaden BC, Croy JE, Wang Y, Wilson JM, Datta-Mannan A, Shetler P, Milner A, Bryant HU, Andrews J, Dai G, Krishnan V. Follistatin: a novel therapeutic for the improvement of muscle regeneration. *J Pharmacol Exp Ther* 2014;349(2):355–71.
55. Sugino K, Kurosawa N, Nakamura T, Takio K, Shimasaki S, Ling N, Titani K, Sugino H. Molecular heterogeneity of follistatin, an activin-binding protein. Higher affinity of the carboxyl-terminal truncated forms for heparan sulfate proteoglycans on the ovarian granulosa cell. *J Biol Chem* 1993;268(21):15579–87.
56. Castonguay R, Lachey J, Wallner S, Strand J, Liharska K, Watanabe AE, Cannell M, Davies MV, Sako D, Troy ME, Krishnan L, Mulivor AW, Li H, Keates S, Alexander MJ, Pearsall RS, Kumar R. Follistatin-288-Fc fusion protein promotes localized growth of skeletal muscle. *J Pharmacol Exp Ther* 2019;368(3):435–45.
57. Pearsall RS, Davies MV, Cannell M, Li J, Widrick J, Mulivor AW2, Wallner S, Troy ME, Spaits M, Liharska K, Sako D, Castonguay R, Keates S, Grinberg AV, Suragani RNVS, Kumar R. Follistatin-based ligand trap ACE-083 induces localized hypertrophy of skeletal muscle with functional improvement in models of neuromuscular disease. *Sci Rep* 2019;9(1):11392.
58. Czajkowsky DM, Hu J, Shao Z, Pleass RJ. Fc-fusion proteins: new developments and future perspectives. *EMBO Mol Med* 2012;4(10):1015–28.
59. Acceleron Pharma. Product candidates: ACE-083. http://acceleronpharma.com/product-candidates/ace-083/ (accessed 07.06.2018).
60. Glasser CE, Gartner MR, Wilson D, Miller B, Sherman ML, Attie KM. Locally acting ACE-083 increases muscle volume in healthy volunteers. *Muscle Nerve* 2018;57(6):921–6.
61. Attie KM, Glasser CE, Gartner MR, Boes BL, Pearsall RS, Zhang X, Sun J, Wilson DM, Bellevue A, Hankin M, Sherman ML. ACE-083, a locally acting TGF-Beta superfamily ligand trap, increases muscle volume of targeted muscle: preliminary results from a phase 1 dose escalation study in healthy volunteers. *The Endocrine Society Annual Meeting (ENDO)*, Boston, MA, 2016.
62. Mulivor A, Cannell M, Davies M, Sako D, Liu J, Bresnahan D, Hevron K, Steeves R, Castonguay R, Wallner S, Grinberg A, Pearsall RS, Kumar R. A modified cysteine knot ligand trap of the TGF-β superfamily, ACE-083, increases muscle mass locally in mice. *13th International Congress on Neuromuscular Diseases, Nice*, France, 2014.
63. Pearsall RS, Widrick J, Cotton E, Sako D, Liu J, Davies M, Heveron K, Maguire M, Castonguay R, Krishnan L, Troy M, Liharska K, Steeves R, Cannell M, Alimzhanov M, Grinberg A, Kumar R. ACE-083 increases muscle hypertrophy and strength in C57BL/6 mice. *20th International Congress of the World Muscle Society*, Brighton, 2015.
64. Hill JJ, Davies MV, Pearson AA, Wang JH, Hewick RM, Wolfman NM, Qiu Y. The myostatin propeptide and the follistatin-related gene are inhibitory binding proteins of myostatin in normal serum. *J Biol Chem* 2002;277(43):40735–41.
65. Wolfman NM, McPherron AC, Pappano WN, Davies MV, Song K, Tomkinson KN, Wright JF, Zhao L, Sebald SM, Greenspan DS, Lee SJ. Activation of latent myostatin by the BMP-1/tolloid family of metalloproteinases. *Proc Natl Acad Sci USA* 2003;100(26):15842–6.
66. Hamrick MW, Arounleut P, Kellum E, Cain M, Immel D, Liang LF. Recombinant myostatin (GDF-8) propeptide enhances the repair and regeneration of both muscle and bone in a model of deep penetrant musculoskeletal injury. *J Trauma* 2010;69(3):579–83.
67. Arounleut P, Bialek P, Liang LF, Upadhyay S, Fulzele S, Johnson M, Elsalanty M, Isales CM, Hamrick MW. A myostatin inhibitor (propeptide-Fc) increases muscle mass and muscle fiber size in aged mice but does not increase bone density or bone strength. *Exp Gerontol* 2013;48(9):898–904.
68. Bogdanovich S, Perkins KJ, Krag TO, Whittemore LA, Khurana TS. Myostatin propeptide-mediated amelioration of dystrophic pathophysiology. *FASEB J* 2005;19(6):543–9.
69. Shimamoto G, Gegg C, Boone T, Queva C. Peptibodies: a flexible alternative format to antibodies. *MAbs* 2012;4(5):586–91.
70. Atara Biotherapeutics. Form S-1 registration statement under the securities Act of 1933. United States securities and exchange commission 2014. https://www.sec.gov (accessed 11.07.18).
71. Desgeorges MM, Devillard X, Toutain J, Castells J, Divoux D, Arnould DF, Haqq C, Bernaudin M, Durieux AC, Touzani O, Freyssenet DG. Pharmacological inhibition of myostatin improves skeletal muscle mass and function in a mouse model of stroke. *Sci Rep* 2017;7(1):14000.
72. Dong J, Dong Y, Dong Y, Chen F, Mitch WE, Zhang L. Inhibition of myostatin in mice improves insulin sensitivity via irisin-mediated cross talk between muscle and adipose tissues. *Int J Obes (Lond)* 2016;40(3):434–42.
73. Zhang L, Rajan V, Lin E, Hu Z, Han HQ, Zhou X, Song Y, Min H, Wang X, Du J, Mitch WE. Pharmacological inhibition of myostatin suppresses systemic inflammation and muscle atrophy in mice with chronic kidney disease. *FASEB J* 2011;25(5):1653–63.
74. Atara Biotherapeutics. Atara Bio announces results from the Phase 2 proof-of-concept PINTA 745 clinical trial for protein energy wasting in patients with end stage renal disease. 2015. http://investors.atarabio.com/news-releases/news-release-details/atara-bio-announces-results-phase-2-proof-concept-pinta-745 (accessed 11.07.18).
75. Lipovsek D. Adnectins: engineered target-binding protein therapeutics. *Protein Eng Des Sel* 2011;24(1–2):3–9.
76. Zhu Y, D'Arienzo C, Lou Z, Kozhich A, Madireddi M, Chimalakonda A, Tymiak A, Olah TV. LC-MS/MS multiplexed assay for the quantitation of a therapeutic protein BMS-986089 and the target protein Myostatin. *Bioanalysis* 2016;8(3):193–204.
77. Verissimo M. RG6206 (Formerly BMS-986089) for DMD. *Muscular Dystrophy News Today*. https://musculardystrophynews.com/bms-98609-for-dmd/ (accessed 23.09.19).
78. Madireddi M, Malone H, Kukral D, Chimalakonda A, Kozhich A, Xiling Y, Swain J, Yamniuk A, Ahlijanian M. BMS-986089 is a high affinity anti-myostatin adnectin that increases muscle volume in three preclinical studies. *21st International Congress of the World Muscle Society*, Granada, 2016.
79. Jacobsen L, Bechthold C, Tirucherai G, Ahlijanian M, Luo F. BMS-986089: a novel adnectin protein that dose dependently lowers free myostatin and increases musle volume and lean body mass. *In 21st International Congress of the World Muscle Society*, Granada, 2016.
80. Wagner K, Wong B, Byrne B, Sweeney L, Jacobsen L, Tirucherai G, Rabbia M, Buchbjerg J, Krishnan M, Bechtold C. A randomized, placebo-controlled, double-blind, Phase 1b/2 study of the novel antimyostatin adnectin RG6206 (BMS-986089) in ambulatory boys with Duchenne

muscular dystrophy (P5.431). *Neurology* 2018;https://n.neurology.org/content/90/15_Supplement/P5.431 (accessed 23.09.19).
81. World Anti-Doping Agency. The world anti-doping code - international standard: prohibited list (January 2019). 2018. www.wada-ama.org (accessed 26.09.19).
82. Singh P, Rong H, Gordi T, Bosley J, Bhattacharya I. Translational pharmacokinetic/pharmacodynamic analysis of MYO-029 antibody for muscular dystrophy. *Clin Transl Sci* 2016;9(6):302–10.
83. Walpurgis K, Thomas A, Schänzer W, Thevis M. Myostatin inhibitors in sports drug testing: detection of myostatin-neutralizing antibodies in plasma/serum by affinity purification and Western blotting. *Proteomics Clin Appl* 2016;10(2):195–205.
84. Walpurgis K, Thomas A, Thevis M. Detection of the myostatin-neutralizing antibody Domagrozumab in serum by means of Western blotting and LC-HRMS. *Drug Test Anal* 2019;submitted for publication.
85. Walpurgis K, Thomas A, Dellanna F, Schänzer W, Thevis M. Detection of the human anti-ActRII antibody bimagrumab in serum by means of affinity purification, tryptic digestion, and LC-HRMS. *Proteomics Clin Appl* 2018;12(3):e1700120.
86. Walpurgis K, Thomas A, Vogel M, Reichel C, Geyer H, Schänzer W, Thevis M. Testing for the erythropoiesis-stimulating agent Sotatercept/ACE-011 (ActRIIA-Fc) in serum by means of Western blotting and LC-HRMS. *Drug Test Anal* 2016;8(11–12):1152–61.
87. Walpurgis K, Thomas A, Dellanna F, Geyer H, Schänzer W, Thevis M. In multiplexed detection of ActRII-Fc fusion proteins in serum by means of Western blotting and LC-HRMS. *The 35th Manfred Donike Workshop on Doping Analysis*, Cologne, Germany, 2017.

4.6 MULTI-ANALYTE TEST METHODS IN SPORTS DRUG TESTING: CHALLENGES AND SOLUTIONS

C. Görgens, S. Guddat and M. Thevis

Since its introduction into the area of sports drug testing in the late 1990s, the use of liquid chromatography-mass spectrometry (LC-MS) has received continuously growing attention. The rapid instrumental progress in the field of LC-MS provided new opportunities for doping control laboratories to follow up on new strategies and to move from drug class–dictated testing procedures to more technique-driven analytical approaches for the initial testing of urine specimens. In early 2000, prohibited classes of substances such as diuretics, β2-agonists, stimulants, and narcotics were commonly covered using drug class–specific screening assays.[1–3] Since on the one hand, laboratories are faced with a constantly increasing number of samples and mandatory target analytes, and on the other hand, they need to comply with required detection limits and additional technical regulations, a change in the analytical strategy was inevitable.[4,5] Fortunately, the ongoing refinement in instrumentation allowed the combination of different classes of prohibited substances with diverse chemical structures in straightforward multi-target analytical approaches. On the basis of modern and powerful analytical instruments, using sophisticated liquid chromatographs equipped with state-of-the-art, multi-functional columns coupled to sensitive mass spectrometers, e.g., triple-quadrupole (QqQ), time-of-flight (TOF), or Fourier transform (Orbitrap) instruments, many new multi-target assays have been developed. Most of the initial testing approaches are based on “dilute-and-inject” of native urine specimens or pre-concentration via online solid-phase extraction (SPE) prior to liquid chromatography-tandem mass spectrometry (LC-MS/MS) analysis, providing a wide applicability to screen for many different compounds and their metabolites at the required performance levels in human urine without time-consuming sample preparation steps.

In 2009, the first multi-target approaches were introduced for sports drug testing purposes, using liquid chromatography interfaced with high-resolution time-of-flight mass spectrometry (LC-HR-TOF-MS) after liquid/liquid extraction or SPE, covering approx. 200 target analytes.[6,7] Here, the possibility of retrospective data evaluation was provided using full-scan analyses, while a main limitation originated from the missing polarity switching opportunity of the TOF instrument. A first “dilute-and-shoot” multi-target assay based on liquid chromatography-electrospray ionization-tandem mass spectrometry (LC-ESI-MS/MS) was presented in 2011. With a highly sensitive QqQ instrument applying scan-to-scan polarity switching, numerous classes of substances with different physico-chemical properties, such as diuretics, β2-agonists, stimulants, narcotics, plasma volume expanders, selective androgen receptor modulators (SARMs), and the growth hormone releasing peptide GHRP-2 were successfully detected far below the minimum required performance levels (MRPLs).[5] The robust approach proved to be time- and cost-saving (run time: 11 min) as well as particularly flexible.[8]

In the last years, most of the developed multi-analyte test methods were based on high-performance liquid chromatography high-resolution accurate-mass mass spectrometry (HPLC-HRAM-MS) (TOF or Orbitrap). Comparably to TOF, Orbitrap MS provides the opportunity of retrospective data evaluation using HR full-scan data acquisition, but in contrast, it benefits from scan-to-scan polarity switching possibilities, achieving optimal ionization conditions regarding differences in the acidic or basic character of the analytes. Especially for major events such as the Olympic Games, laboratories have to analyze a large number of samples in a very short time (>100/day). In 2013, Musenga and Cowan presented a comprehensive assay using LC-Orbitrap MS developed for the analysis of approx. 5,000 doping control samples during the London 2012 Olympic and Paralympic Games. Doping control urine samples were prepared based on enzymatic hydrolysis and pre-concentration, applying mixed-mode ion-exchange extraction. Within a relatively short chromatographic run time (10 min), target analytes (anabolic agents [AAs], β2-agonists, hormone antagonists and modulators, diuretics, stimulants, narcotics, glucocorticoids, and β-blockers) were detected in both positive and negative ionization full-scan mode at a resolution of 25,000 full width at half maximum (FWHM). To increase specificity and to reduce the number of false suspects in the initial screening, an all ion fragmentation (AIF) experiment (without precursor selection) was also applied.[9]

However, with the ongoing evolution of instrumentation, using a next-generation quadrupole Orbitrap mass spectrometer that provides increased resolution, faster scan rates, and improved sensitivity, a fast and comprehensive LC-qOrbitrap-MS multi-target approach was developed based on direct injection of native urine specimens using a two-dimensional online trapping strategy. The online clean-up and pre-concentration of the urine has proved to protect the analytical column as well as the mass spectrometer from interfering matrix contaminants. Here, the combination of non-targeted (Full-MS, AIF) and targeted mass spectrometric acquisition modes (t-HCD) with scan-to-scan polarity switching provides high selectivity and sensitivity. With the assay, more than 200 analytes covering classic categories of doping agents, such as diuretics, stimulants, β2-agonists, narcotics, and anabolic androgenic steroids (AAS), as well as various newer target compounds, for example hypoxia-inducible factor (HIF) activating/stimulating agents, SARMs, selective estrogen receptor modulators (SERMs), plasma volume expanders, and other doping-related compounds, were detected far below the corresponding MRPLs. Notably, for the first time, GHRPs (<2 kDa), which are commonly determined by laborious and time-consuming stand-alone procedures, were implemented into a multi-target assay. Additionally, the implementation of phase-II metabolites of AAS proved to be very powerful. Here, the sensitive detection of 3′-hydroxy-stanozolol glucuronide in the lower pg/mL range has led to several hundreds of adverse analytical findings (AAFs) concerning the use of stanozolol in doping controls.[10]

Within the last years, several assays were presented using LC-qOrbitrap-MS. For the 2016 Summer Olympic and Paralympic Games in Rio, a comprehensive assay was developed by Sardela et al. Here, the combination of a mixed-mode ion-exchange SPE extract after enzymatic hydrolysis with diluted native urine was utilized to screen for a wide range of substances and to ensure wide applicability and flexibility of the method. With the initial testing method, approx. 450 target analytes were successfully screened, covering different classes of prohibited substances and metabolites.[11] Abushareeda et al. presented a similar method based on LC-qOrbitrap-MS for screening of various classes of prohibited substances for sports drug testing. The validated method was established in particular for the quantitation of endogenous sulfoconjugated steroids, e.g., testosterone and epitestosterone.[12]

4.6.1 Analysis of Highly Polar Prohibited Compounds in Sports Drug Testing

As described in the previous subsection, assays based on LC-HRMS are ideally suited for large multi-target approaches covering various classes of doping agents from the World Anti-Doping Agency's (WADA's) list of prohibited substances. Due to their chemical structures, most of the compounds concerned demonstrate nonpolar to moderately polar properties, ensuring adequate retention on typical reversed phase (RP) columns. However, there are some prohibited compounds that show distinct hydrophilic characteristics, which lead to poor retention on hydrophobic RP materials. Even polar endcapped stationary phases, containing embedded amide, amino, cyano, or hydroxyl moieties, do not provide satisfactory retention for these kinds of analytes. Furthermore, conventional normal phase liquid chromatography (NPLC) or ion chromatographic techniques (IC) do not represent suitable analytical alternatives due to reduced compatibility with a mass spectrometer, which is still the state-of-the-art analyzer in sports drug testing.

In order to achieve adequate chromatographic separation of highly polar compounds while maintaining full compatibility with MS, hydrophilic interaction liquid chromatography (HILIC) has become established in sports drug testing over the last years. As an RPLC complementary technique, HILIC enables the use of polar stationary phases, as used in NPLC, in combination with MS-compatible eluents. Here, the application of polar modified silica gels or polymers with diol, amino, or zwitterionic residues as stationary phases and aqueous buffer systems with a high content (>60%) of an organic modifier such as acetonitrile or methanol leads to the formation of an immobilized water-rich layer on the surface of the stationary phase. Although the HILIC retention mechanism involves more than one interaction, its main mechanism is based on a hydrophilic partitioning process between the aforementioned immobilized water-rich layer and the hydrophobic environment created by the highly organic mobile phase. The resulting equilibrium between these two layers can be envisioned as continuing liquid/liquid extractions along the stationary phase. In addition to the partitioning process, weak electrostatic interactions with chemically bonded polar ligands of the stationary phase contribute to chromatographic separation of highly polar or permanently charged analytes in HILIC columns.

While the first HILIC methods in the field of sports drug testing were developed to solve chromatographic issues of certain hydrophilic target analytes such as ephedrines,[13,14] morphine, codeine, and their phase-II conjugates,[15] more recent publications demonstrate multi-target approaches covering hydrophilic analytes of various classes of prohibited compounds. Mazzarino et al. demonstrated a HILIC-QqQ approach for initial testing and confirmatory analysis of polar stimulants, narcotics, and beta-adrenergic agents in human urine. After alkalization and liquid/liquid extraction with tert-butyl methyl ether (TBME), the organic layer was separated, acidified, and evaporated under nitrogen. Prior to the injection into the instrument, the residue was reconstituted in 50 μL of mobile phase.[16]

As already demonstrated for multi-target LC-MS assays covering nonpolar to moderately polar compounds, HILIC assays have also been optimized continuously to reduce sample preparation efforts to a minimum while preserving highest possible sensitivity and specificity. Therefore, in a more recent study, it was further demonstrated that "dilute-and-inject" approaches are also possible using an appropriate urine dilution with organic solvent and applying zwitterionic HILIC phases as well as Orbitrap MS.[17] Due to the use of an online sample clean-up system, accomplished by a dual pump setup, equipped with a HILIC trapping column and a HILIC analytical column, laborious purification steps have been omitted. After injection into the instrument, the diluted urine sample was loaded onto the HILIC trapping column, where hydrophilic compounds accumulated and therefore were separated from hydrophobic matrix components. In a second step, the trapped hydrophilic compounds were backflushed from the trapping column to the analytical column in order to chromatographically separate the target analytes.

During the last years, one of the most prominent representatives of highly polar substances prohibited in sport was meldonium (3-(2,2,2-trimethylhydrazinium)propionate). Due to its pharmacological effect of shifting energy metabolism from fatty acid oxidation to enhanced glucose consumption and increasing the adenosine triphosphate (ATP) balance under hypoxia, beneficial effects of meldonium in terms of improved physical working capacity, enhanced endurance performance, and accelerated recovery after physical activity were discussed.[18] In fact, applications of the hitherto non-prohibited substance meldonium were frequently observed on the declaration of medications on official doping control forms. Therefore, in 2015, the WADA initiated a 1-year monitoring program to investigate the prevalence of meldonium in sports, which provided clear analytical evidence of massive meldonium use by athletes.[19–21] Therefore, the WADA Prohibited List, which became effective in January 2016, classified meldonium as a banned substance under S4 – "Hormone and Metabolic Modulators."[4]

In the first months of 2016, an extraordinarily high number of AAFs,[22] among them several elite athletes of various disciplines coming from Eastern European countries, triggered an active discussion on the pharmacokinetics and pharmacodynamics of the drug and especially on its classification as a doping substance. Most of the athletes who tested positive stated that their last meldonium intake was before the ban of the drug came into effect in January 2016. At that time, information on the pharmacokinetic properties of meldonium was limited to few single- and multiple-dose administration studies, where the drug's concentration and excretion were monitored in plasma and urine over 24–50 h post-administration without any evidence of extensively prolonged urinary elimination times of the drug.[18] However, the high number of AAFs raised the question of whether the pharmacokinetic properties of meldonium needed further investigation.

As a result, several elimination studies investigating different matrices, application forms, and dose regimens were performed, aiming to generate the data required to address this issue. Indeed, these studies indicated a dose-dependent elimination of the drug resulting in extraordinarily prolonged half-lives and detection windows spanning several months in blood and urine samples, especially after multiple oral or parenteral administrations.[23–26] As a consequence, in 2016, WADA established urinary threshold concentrations under which AAFs shall not be reported, as these concentrations most likely correspond to a meldonium intake before the ban of the drug in January 2016. With 515 cases, meldonium was by far the most common substance reported as an AAF during 2016. However, most of the athletes who returned an AAF for meldonium were not penalized.[22] According to the recommended dose regimen of several grams per day, actual meldonium cases are only to be reported above a urinary level of 100 ng/mL.[5]

Another example of a highly polar substance with sophisticated analytical behavior is myo-inositol trispyrophosphate (ITPP), which is prohibited in sports under section M1.2 – "Manipulation of blood and blood components."[4] Pharmacologically, the non-approved substance ITPP is a representative of the therapeutic class of allosteric hemoglobin effectors, regulating oxygen uptake and release from erythrocytes, and therefore exhibits significant abuse potential in sports, since increased oxygenation of tissues can improve athletic performance. Under the designation OXY111A, ITPP is currently undergoing Phase Ib/IIa clinical trials as a potential anti-tumor agent because of its hypoxia-counteracting effects.[27] Due to its chemical structure, ITPP is an ideal candidate for HILIC applications. For doping control purposes, the non-approved drug is generally determined using "dilute-and-inject" approaches or following SPE using weak-anion-exchange cartridges.[17,28] Moreover, for an adequate chromatographic separation, sensitive detection in the low ng/mL range, and reliable identification of the substance in human urine, HILIC-HRMS/MS approaches are mandatory. Here, the doubly charged and twofold deprotonated precursor ion $[M-2H]^{2-}$ at *m/z* 301.9065 is analyzed using full scan and parallel reaction monitoring (PRM) acquisition mode of the mass spectrometer. In Figure 4.6.1, the extracted ion chromatograms of an ITPP-containing urine sample as well as the corresponding product ion spectrum are depicted. Although ITPP is the subject of active discussions on various Internet platforms, black market products are commercially available, and analytical assays for the detection of the drug have been used for years in sports drug testing, AAFs are still missing worldwide. Therefore, the assumed elimination behavior of ITPP, which was expected to be an unchanged urinary excretion of the drug (according to the molecule's hydrophilic nature and results from published administration studies in horses), needed to be investigated.[29] In the context of a pilot study to verify the aforementioned hypothesis, Görgens et al. initiated an excretion study of orally administered ITPP in one healthy male volunteer.[30] After the application of a 10-mg capsule of ITPP, which represents only 0.1–1% of the clinically relevant dose, the unmetabolized drug was detected in all post-administration urine samples until termination

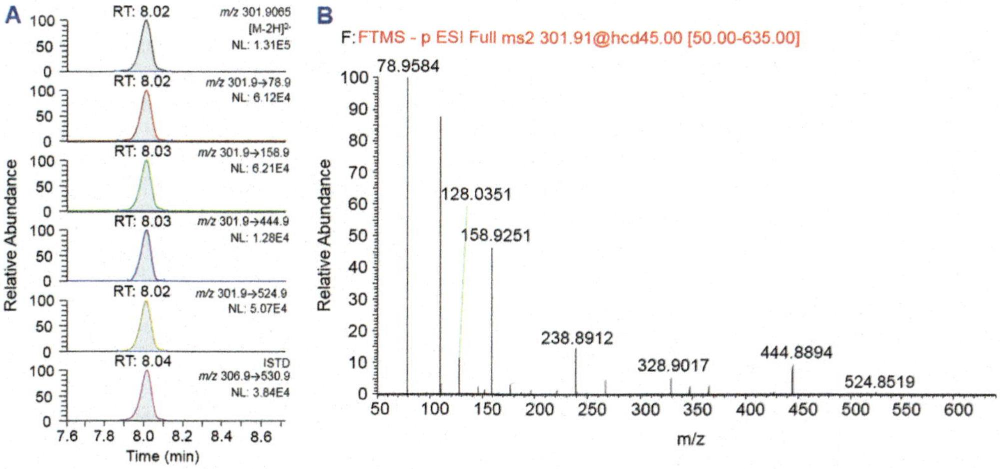

FIGURE 4.6.1 Extracted ion chromatograms (full scan and PRM mode) of an ITPP-containing urine sample (a) and corresponding product ion spectrum (b) of the doubly charged, twofold deprotonated precursor ion [M-2H]$^{2-}$ of ITPP (NCE: 45).

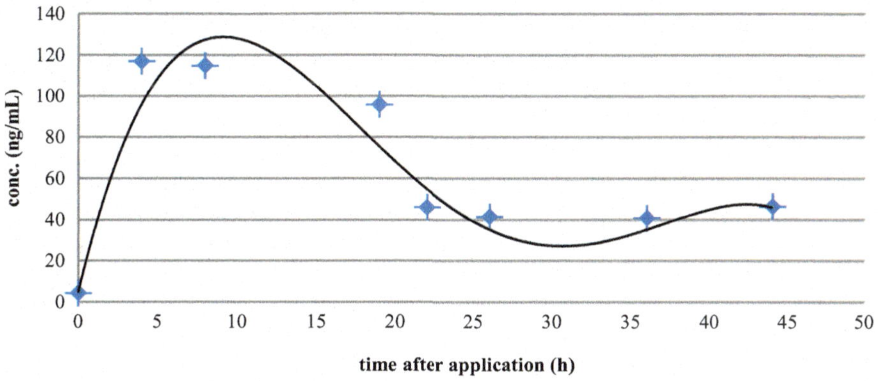

FIGURE 4.6.2 Urinary excretion profile of ITPP after single oral administration of a 10-mg capsule (concentration specific gravity adjusted to 1.020).

of the study after 44 h. ITPP demonstrated an undulating urinary excretion pattern (Figure 4.6.2), and the peak concentration of 140 ng/mL was detected at 4 h post-administration. In a subsequent urine sample collected 14 days post-administration, the drug was not detectable. However, taking into consideration the recommended dose regimen of 5,598 –43,500 mg/m^2 weekly dosing during preclinical and Phase I clinical trials, indicating a dose-dependent pharmacokinetic profile of the substance, ITPP is probably detectable multiple days after oral or parenteral administration of the drug. Hence, the administration of higher dosages may result in significantly longer urinary detection windows than estimated in this pilot study.

However, in the field of sports drug testing, the popularity of HRMS is still increasing. Multi-analyte HRMS assays proved to be very time- and cost-efficient and to reduce the sample turn-around time. Principally, the use of a non-targeted acquisition mode transfers the biological into a digital matrix that provides the full raw data and enables re-processing of data to investigate samples for new substances. Additionally, the re-processing of data allows monitoring of substances that are not on the prohibited list in order to detect their misuse in sport. In 2018, as a recent example, the actoprotector bemitil was implemented into the WADA monitoring program. Here, retrospective HRMS data evaluation provided the first bemitil findings in official doping control samples. In the past years, there is an obvious trend towards LC-qOrbitrap-MS based approaches. Compared with TOF-based approaches, the overall instrumental performance regarding resolution and scan-to-scan polarity switching possibilities provides a clear advantage for initial testing procedures and delivers the required flexibility of the assays. This is of the utmost importance for doping control laboratories to allow simple and fast implementation of new target analytes.

REFERENCES

1. Deventer K, Pozo OJ, Van Eenoo P, Delbeke FT. Development of a qualitative liquid chromatography/tandem mass spectrometric method for the detection of narcotics in urine relevant to doping analysis. *Rapid Commun Mass Spectrom* 2007;21(18):3015–23.
2. Thevis M, Opfermann G, Schänzer W. Liquid chromatography/electrospray ionization tandem mass spectrometric screening and confirmation methods for beta2-agonists in human or equine urine. *J Mass Spectrom* 2003;38(11):1197–206.

3. Thieme D, Grosse J, Lang R, Mueller RK, Wahl A. Screening, confirmation and quantification of diuretics in urine for doping control analysis by high-performance liquid chromatography-atmospheric pressure ionisation tandem mass spectrometry. *J Chromatogr B Biomed Sci Appl* 2001;757(1):49–57.
4. World Anti-Doping Agency. World anti-doping code. Prohibited list 2018. https://www.wada-ama.org/sites/default/files/prohibited_list_2018_en.pdf (accessed 22.10.2018).
5. World Anti-Doping Agency. Technical Document - TD2018MRPL. Minimum required performance levels for detection and identification of non-threshold substances. https://www.wada-ama.org/sites/default/files/resources/files/td2018mrpl_v1_finaleng.pdf (accessed 22.10.2018).
6. Kolmonen M, Leinonen A, Kuuranne T, Pelander A, Ojanpera I. Generic sample preparation and dual polarity liquid chromatography-time-of-flight mass spectrometry for high-throughput screening in doping analysis. *Drug Test Anal* 2009;1(6):250–66.
7. Vonaparti A, Lyris E, Angelis YS, Panderi I, Koupparis M, Tsantili-Kakoulidou A, Peters RJ, Nielen MW, Georgakopoulos C. Preventive doping control screening analysis of prohibited substances in human urine using rapid-resolution liquid chromatography/high-resolution time-of-flight mass spectrometry. *Rapid Commun Mass Spectrom* 2010;24(11):1595–609.
8. Guddat S, Solymos E, Orlovius A, Thomas A, Sigmund G, Geyer H, Thevis M, Schänzer W. High-throughput screening for various classes of doping agents using a new 'dilute-and-shoot' liquid chromatography-tandem mass spectrometry multi-target approach. *Drug Test Anal* 2011;3(11–12):836–50.
9. Musenga A, Cowan DA. Use of ultra-high pressure liquid chromatography coupled to high resolution mass spectrometry for fast screening in high throughput doping control. *J Chrom A* 2013;1288:82–95.
10. Görgens C, Guddat S, Thomas A, Wachsmuth P, Orlovius AK, Sigmund G, Thevis M, Schänzer W. Simplifying and expanding analytical capabilities for various classes of doping agents by means of direct urine injection high performance liquid chromatography high resolution/high accuracy mass spectrometry. *J Pharm Biomed Anal* 2016;131:482–96.
11. Sardela VF, Martucci MEP, de Araujo ALD, Leal EC, Oliveira DS, Carneiro GRA, Deventer K, Van Eenoo P, Pereira HMG, Aquino Neto FR. Comprehensive analysis by liquid chromatography Q-Orbitrap mass spectrometry: fast screening of peptides and organic molecules. *J Mass Spectrom* 2018;53(6):476–503.
12. Abushareeda W, Vonaparti A, Saad KA, Almansoori M, Meloug M, Saleh A, Aguilera R, Angelis Y, Horvatovich PL, Lommen A, Alsayrafi M, Georgakopoulos C. High resolution full scan liquid chromatography mass spectrometry comprehensive screening in sports antidoping urine analysis. *J Pharm Biomed Anal* 2018;151:10–24.
13. Heaton J, Gray N, Cowan DA, Plumb RS, Legido-Quigley C, Smith NW. Comparison of reversed-phase and hydrophilic interaction liquid chromatography for the separation of ephedrines. *J Chrom A* 2012;1228:329–37.
14. Gray N, Heaton J, Musenga A, Cowan DA, Plumb RS, Smith NW. Comparison of reversed-phase and hydrophilic interaction liquid chromatography for the quantification of ephedrines using medium-resolution accurate mass spectrometry. *J Chrom A* 2013;1289:37–46.
15. Kolmonen M, Leinonen A, Kuuranne T, Pelander A, Ojanpera I. Hydrophilic interaction liquid chromatography and accurate mass measurement for quantification and confirmation of morphine, codeine and their glucuronide conjugates in human urine. *J Chromatogr B Analyt Technol Biomed Life Sci* 2010;878(29):2959–66.
16. Mazzarino M, Fiacco I, de la Torre X, Botre F. Screening and confirmation analysis of stimulants, narcotics and beta-adrenergic agents in human urine by hydrophilic interaction liquid chromatography coupled to mass spectrometry. *J Chrom A* 2011;1218(45):8156–67.
17. Görgens C, Guddat S, Orlovius AK, Sigmund G, Thomas A, Thevis M, Schänzer W. "Dilute-and-inject" multi-target screening assay for highly polar doping agents using hydrophilic interaction liquid chromatography high resolution/high accuracy mass spectrometry for sports drug testing. *Anal Bioanal Chem* 2015;407(18):5365–79.
18. Schobersberger W, Dunnwald T, Gmeiner G, Blank C. Story behind meldonium-from pharmacology to performance enhancement: a narrative review. *Br J Sports Med* 2017;51(1):22–5.
19. Sobolevsky M. Use of meldonium and emoxypine by Russian athletes: a prevalence study. *Poster Presented at the Manfred Donike Workshop, 33rd Cologne Workshop on Dope Analysis*, Cologne, Germany, 2015.
20. Görgens C, Guddat S, Dib J, Geyer H, Schänzer W, Thevis M. Mildronate (Meldonium) in professional sports – monitoring doping control urine samples using hydrophilic interaction liquid chromatography – high resolution/high accuracy mass spectrometry. *Drug Test Anal* 2015;7(11–12):973–9.
21. Stuart M, Schneider C, Steinbach K. Meldonium use by athletes at the Baku 2015 European Games. *Br J Sports Med* 2016;50(11):694–8.
22. World Anti-Doping Agency. 2016 Anti-doping testing figures report. https://www.wada-ama.org/sites/default/files/resources/files/2016_anti-doping_testing_figures.pdf (accessed 01.10.2018).
23. Tretzel L, Görgens C, Geyer H, Thomas A, Dib J, Guddat S, Pop V, Schänzer W, Thevis M. Analyses of meldonium (Mildronate) from blood, Dried Blood Spots (DBS), and urine suggest drug incorporation into erythrocytes. *Int J Sports Med* 2016;37(06):500–2.
24. Liepinsh E, Dambrova M. The unusual pharmacokinetics of meldonium: implications for doping. *Pharmacol Res* 2016;111:100.
25. Görgens C, Guddat S, Bosse C, Geyer H, Pop V, Schänzer W, Thevis M. The atypical excretion profile of meldonium: comparison of urinary detection windows after single- and multiple-dose application in healthy volunteers. *J Pharmac Biomed Anal* 2017;138:175–9.
26. Forsdahl G, Jancic-Stojanovic B, Andelkovic M, Dikic N, Geisendorfer T, Jeitler V, Gmeiner G. Urinary excretion studies of meldonium after multidose parenteral application. *J Pharm Biomed Anal* 2018;161:289–95.
27. Limani P, Linecker M, Kron P, Samaras P, Pestalozzi B, Stupp R, Jetter A, Dutkowski P, Mullhaupt B, Schlegel A, Nicolau C, Lehn JM, Petrowsky H, Humar B, Graf R, Clavien PA. Development of OXY111A, a novel hypoxia-modifier as a potential antitumor agent in patients with hepato-pancreato-biliary neoplasms - Protocol of a first Ib/IIa clinical trial. *BMC Cancer* 2016;16(1):812.
28. Görgens C, Guddat S, Schänzer W, Thevis M. Screening and confirmation of myo-inositol trispyrophosphate (ITPP) in human urine by hydrophilic interaction liquid

chromatography high resolution / high accuracy mass spectrometry for doping control purposes. *Drug Test Anal* 2014;6(11–12):1102–7.
29. Lam G, Zhao S, Sandhu J, Yi R, Loganathan D, Morrissey B. Detection of myo-inositol tris pyrophosphate (ITPP) in equine following an administration of ITPP. *Drug Test Anal* 2013;6(3):268–76.
30. Görgens C, Guddat S, Södje D, Geyer H, Thevis M. Detection of myo-inositol trispyrophosphate (ITP) in human urine following an oral administration of ITPP – a pilot study. *Poster Presented at the Manfred Donike Workshop, 36th Cologne Workshop on Dope Analysis*, Cologne, Germany, 2018.

4.7 ALTERNATIVE MATRICES: ADVANTAGES AND LIMITATIONS

K. Walpurgis, A. Thomas, J. Dib, O. Krug and M. Thevis

In sports drug testing, the most commonly collected specimens are currently urine, serum, and whole blood.[1] These matrices allow the reliable and sensitive detection of a variety of doping agents and are suitable for standardized sample collection and transport.

Urine can be collected easily and non-invasively, and the sample volumes are usually sufficient for multiple analyses.[1–3] As the risk for sample manipulation (e.g., by dilution, substitution, or the addition of proteases) is relatively high, the sampling process has to be conducted under constant supervision by the doping control officer, resulting in a considerable intrusiveness for the tested athletes.[1,3] Due to both psychological and physiological reasons, such as post-exercise dehydration, urine collection can necessitate several hours of sampling time.[1,3,4] Urinary drug concentrations represent the integral of circulating blood levels, they depend on the athlete's fluid balance, and specific gravity adjustment can be necessary to eliminate dilution effects.[2,5] Many lower–molecular mass drugs are predominantly excreted into urine as their metabolites, resulting in prolonged detection windows (up to several weeks) and consequently, in significant retrospectivity.[1,2,6] While such long detection times are of great importance for the analysis of compounds prohibited at all times, data interpretation can be considerably complicated for substances that are banned only in competition or by defined routes of administration.[3] As the renal excretion of large proteins is limited by the MW cut-off for glomerular filtration, some protein therapeutics, such as human growth hormone (hGH) and Continuous Erythropoiesis Receptor Activator (CERA), are barely detectable in urine.[1,3,6]

By contrast, blood and serum specimens have a moderate volume of 2–3 mL and are invasively obtained by venipuncture, which necessitates trained medical staff for sample collection.[1–3] The sampling procedure itself has a short duration and does not invade the athlete's privacy.[1,3] To ensure sample and analyte stability, blood and serum specimens need to be refrigerated during transportation to the doping control laboratory, resulting in high overall costs.[1] While whole blood samples are required to evaluate hematological and hormonal profiles for the Athlete Biological Passport (ABP), serum is employed to test athletes for compounds with a higher molecular mass, which are not excreted into urine in large amounts (e.g., hGH and CERA).[1–3,6] In principle, a broad range of both high– and low–molecular mass analytes can be detected in blood/serum, but the detection windows – especially for small molecules – are usually significantly shorter than in urine (exceptions: AICAR and meldonium).[1] But as the concentrations of circulating drugs in blood/serum correlate closely with their bioavailability and biological effects – independently of application routes, resorption processes, and biotransformation reactions – blood/serum analysis can be employed to demonstrate the presence of pharmacologically relevant drug concentrations during competition.[1,3,6]

Alternative matrices such as dried blood spots (DBS), dried plasma spots (DPS), hair, oral fluid (OF), exhaled breath (EB), and sweat can potentially be advantageous with regard to the invasiveness, intrusiveness, and duration of the sampling procedure, the risk for sample manipulation, the stability of the analytes, the retrospectivity, and the effort and costs for sample transportation and storage (Table 4.7.1). Their usage is allowed in principle by the World Anti-Doping Agency (WADA); however, the results cannot be used to counter adverse analytical findings (AAFs) or atypical findings from blood or urine.[1,6,7] The most relevant alternative matrices and their potential for sports drug testing will be presented in the following sections.

4.7.1 Dried Blood Spots (DBS)

DBS are small amounts of capillary whole blood, which are blotted and dried on filter paper.[8] The first application for DBS was developed in 1963 by Guthrie and Susi, enabling the fast screening of a large number of newborns for the metabolic disease phenylketonuria.[9] Nowadays, DBS-based neonatal screening is one of the most important health initiatives for the early diagnosis of metabolic, endocrine, hematologic, and immune disorders.[10]

The use of DBS as an alternative matrix for sports drug testing has several benefits, some of which are associated with the simple, fast, and non-intrusive sample collection procedure, which is additionally very robust against manipulation. Compared with venous blood sampling, only 10–20 µL of capillary whole blood is needed, which can be obtained with minimal invasiveness by a finger, ear, or heel prick. The low space requirement of DBS cards results in easy shipping and storage conditions and therefore, low overall costs. Also, the stability of analytes is generally significantly higher in DBS than in urine, whole blood, plasma, and serum, as enzymatic degradation processes are inactivated during the drying process and by modified collection card surfaces. During in-competition testing, DBS can be employed to determine the current blood concentrations of circulating drugs, which is of the utmost importance for compounds such as stimulants and glucocorticoids, whose

TABLE 4.7.1
Routine and Alternative Matrices in Sports Drug Testing – Overview

Aspect	Sample matrix					
	Urine	Serum/Plasma	Dried blood spots (DBS)	Hair	Oral fluid (OF)	Exhaled breath (EB)
		Sample collection procedure				
Duration	short-long	short	short	short	short	short
Intrusiveness	high	moderate	low	low	low	low
Invasiveness	low	high	low	low	low	low
Risk for sample manipulation	low[a]	low	low	low	low	low
Available sample volume	high	moderate	low	low	low-moderate	low-moderate
		Sample logistics				
Efforts and costs for transportation	moderate	high	low	moderate	moderate	moderate
Efforts and costs for storage	moderate	moderate	low	moderate	moderate	moderate
		Sample analysis				
Analyte stability at room temperature	moderate	low	high	high	moderate	n.a.
Retrospectivity (analytes with a low MW)	high	moderate	moderate	high[b]	moderate	low
Retrospectivity (analytes with a high MW)	low	high	moderate	n.a.	n.a.	n.a.
Achievable analytical spectrum	high	high	high	moderate	moderate	moderate

[a] When performed under constant supervision.
[b] For selected analytes.
n.a., not applicable.

use during training periods is not regulated by anti-doping authorities. The main disadvantage of DBS is the limited sample volume. As the blood levels of many performance-enhancing drugs are very low, the utmost sensitivity is required to achieve adequate limits of detection (LODs). Moreover, the hematocrit can have a significant influence on DBS, as the spot area decreases with increasing hematocrit levels. Therefore, the potential effect of the hematocrit on a quantitative analysis needs to be monitored during method development.[1,11–13]

Although DBS specimens are not considered as replacements for conventional urine and blood samples in sports drug testing, they can be employed to enable a fast, straightforward, and minimally invasive sample collection in mass sport events or adolescent athletes. The first successful application of DBS to doping control analysis was published in 2000.[14] DBS were prepared from venous blood collected after oral administration of 120 mg of testosterone undecanoate. The dried spots were cut into small pieces, covered with sodium phosphate buffer and potassium hydroxide, and the non-conjugated steroids were isolated by liquid–liquid extraction with a mixture of *n*-hexane and ethyl acetate. The remaining potassium hydroxide-water phase was neutralized and subjected to hydrolysis with β-glucuronidase. Then, the pH was adjusted to 10 with potassium carbonate, and conjugated steroids were extracted with t-butyl methyl ether. Following evaporation and derivatization, steroids were analyzed by gas chromatography-mass spectrometry (GC-MS). While the testosterone level increased from 17.8 nmol/L to a maximum of 21 nmol/L within 1 hour following administration, glucuronidated metabolites could be detected at maximum concentrations of 310 nmol/L (testosterone glucuronide), 2,576 nmol/L (androsterone glucuronide), and 1,814 nmol/L (etiocholanolone glucuronide). These concentrations were found to correlate well with the simultaneously analyzed plasma samples, which demonstrates that DBS can be a suitable alternative for sports drug testing. In the following years, further studies were conducted to investigate the applicability of DBS to doping control analysis, and several methods for the detection of substances representing the different drug classes of the WADA Prohibited List were developed and validated. An overview of the compounds and corresponding detection limits can be found in Table 4.7.2. Anabolic agents (AAs) represent the most frequently detected class of doping agents,[15] and a sensitive DBS detection method for eight different steroid esters with detection limits between 0.1 and 0.5 ng/mL was published in 2014.[16] Here, a mixture of tert-butyl methyl ether (TBME), 2-propanol, and methanol was used for the extraction of the spots, and following derivatization, steroids were analyzed by means of liquid chromatography–tandem mass spectrometry (LC-MS/MS). Stanozolol, metandienone, clenbuterol, and the SARMs S1 and S4 (Andarine) were included in a multi-analyte detection method comprising more than 25 compounds from different drug classes such as AAs, β2-agonists, metabolic modulators, diuretics, stimulants, glucocorticoids, and beta-blockers with

TABLE 4.7.2
Detection Methods for Doping Agents in DBS

Prohibited List Group	Substances/Methods	Reference	LOD (ng/mL)
Non-approved substances	SIRT1 activating compounds (STACs)	[28]	10–50
	AdipoR-agonists	[29]	5–10
Anabolic agents	Several testosterone esters	[16]	all at 0.1
	Trenbolone enanthate		0.1
	Nandrolone/Nandrolone phenylpropionate		0.1/0.5
	Testosterone	[14]	n.d.
	Testosterone/Androsterone/Etiocholanolone glucuronide		
	Stanozolol	[17]	0.125
	Clenbuterol		0.05
	Andarine (S4)		0.05
	S1		0.05
	Metandienone		0.5
Peptide hormones, growth factors, related substances, and mimetics	Synacthen	[11]	0.05
	Peginesatide	[21]	10
	rEPO	[24]	0.06
	NESP		0.06
	CERA		1.2
	Fibronectin 1 (rhGH biomarker)	[23]	n.d.
	Human IGF-1	[22]	50 (LLOQ)
	Human growth hormone (hGH)	[25]	0.02/0.2
	Sotatercept	[27]	250
β_2-Agonists	Salbutamol	[17]	0.5
	Formoterol		0.5
Hormone and metabolic modulators	Anastrazole	[17]	0.05
	Clomiphene		0.05
	Exemestane		0.125
	Meldonium	[34]	20
	Insulins	[26]	0.5–1.5
Diuretics and masking agents	Hydrochlorothiazide	[17]	0.25
Stimulants	Amphetamine	[13]	10
	Pseudoephedrine		5
	Ephedrine	[18]	5
	Methylephedrine		5
	Methylhexanamine	[17]	0.25
	Methylphenidate		0.05
	Cocaine		0.05
	MDA		0.5
	MDMA		0.25
	Nikethamide		0.05
	Strychnine		0.125
	Mesocarb		0.05
Narcotics	Oxycodone (and two metabolites)	[20]	0.15
	Fentanyl	[33]	0.1 (LLOQ)
	Morphine		1 (LLOQ)
	Codeine		1 (LLOQ)
	Hydrocodone		1 (LLOQ)
Cannabinoids	THC (and metabolites)	[19]	0.03–0.05
	JWH-018		0.05
	JWH-073		0.03
	JWH-250		0.05
	JWH-200		0.03
	JWH-019		0.03

(Continued)

TABLE 4.7.2 (CONTINUED)
Detection Methods for Doping Agents in DBS

Prohibited List Group	Substances/Methods	Reference	LOD (ng/mL)
	JWH-122		0.03
	JWH-081		0.03
	HU-211		0.1
	CP47,497		0.1
	AM2201		0.03
Glucocoticoids	Dexamethasone	[17]	0.125
	Budesonide		0.25
Beta-blocker	Metoprolol	[17]	0.05
	Bisoprolol		0.125
	Propranolol		0.05
Manipulation of blood and blood components	Autologous blood transfusion/Blood doping	[30]/[31]	n.d.

n.d., not detected.

LODs between 0.05 and 0.5 ng/mL.[17] Spots were extracted twice – first with a mixture of methanol and TBME, then with acetone. The combined extracts were evaporated and subjected to LC-MS/MS analysis. Further assays for stimulants (e.g., amphetamine, benzoylecgonine, cocaine, [pseudo-]ephedrine, and methylephedrine), β2-agonists (e.g., salbutamol), and cannabinoids (e.g., JWH-018) were developed. These used either a mixture of methanol, acetonitrile, and aqueous acetic acid (2%) for spot extraction[13] or both TBME and acetone.[18] The detection limits varied between 2 and 10 ng/mL.[13,18] Protti et al. developed both DBS and volumetric absorptive microsampling (VAMS™) approaches for the detection of natural and synthetic cannabinoids, which included THC and two metabolites, seven different JWHs, and three other synthetic cannabinoids.[19] Both the DBS and VAMS samples were extracted with methanol and analyzed by means of LC-MS/MS, resulting in LODs of 0.03 and 0.1 ng/mL. Recently, the same group established a similar assay for the detection of the narcotic oxycodone and two metabolites with a detection limit of 0.15 ng/mL.[20]

While the first assays developed for the detection of doping-relevant substances in DBS were mainly focused on low–molecular mass substances, a method for the mass spectrometric detection of Peginesatide in DBS was published in 2012.[21] Peginesatide is a PEGylated erythropoietin-mimetic peptide with a MW of approximately 45 kDa. Following extraction (water/acetonitrile), proteolytic digestion, and cation-exchange purification, it could be detected by liquid chromatography–mass spectrometry (LC-MS) with an LOD of 10 ng/mL. In the following years, several other DBS detection methods for doping-relevant high–molecular mass analytes were developed.[11,22–25] Recombinant erythropoietin (rEPO) and the analogues Darbepoetin (NESP) and CERA were analyzed from DBS by using immunoaffinity purification and Western blotting with LODs between 0.06 and 1.2 ng/mL.[24] hGH is an endogenously produced peptide hormone with presumed performance-enhancing effects. To differentiate endogenous hGH levels from an exogenous administration, two separate immunoassays are currently employed, which quantify the different hGH variants in serum by using highly specific monoclonal antibodies. These assays were also successfully employed for the analysis of DBS, which thus represent a promising alternative matrix for testing recent growth hormone abuse.[25] The main biological effects of hGH are mediated by the endogenous peptide IGF-I, which therefore serves as a biomarker for an exogenous application of this peptide hormone. To enable a quantitative determination of intact IGF-1 in DBS, an assay combining acid-acetonitrile extraction and LC-MS/MS analysis was set up. The limit of quantification (LOQ) was estimated as 50 ng/mL.[22] Fibronectin 1 is another potential biomarker for the detection of hGH misuse and was successfully identified in DBS post-administration samples by using a commercially available fibronectin enzyme-linked immunosorbent assay (ELISA) kit.[23] The synthetic peptide Synacthen could be detected at concentrations as low as 0.05 ng/mL by using a mixture of aqueous acetic acid, acetonitrile, and urea for extraction, ultrafiltration and immunoaffinity-assisted isolation for analyte purification, and LC-MS for detection purposes.[11] In 2018, a detection method for the peptide hormone insulin and its synthetic/animal analogues from DBS was developed, which employs an ultrasonication-assisted extraction, immunoaffinity purification, and liquid chromatography coupled to ion mobility high-resolution mass spectrometry (LC-IM-HRMS).[26] The LOD varied between 0.5 and 1.5 ng/mL, and authentic DBS specimens from healthy subjects in the non-fasting state and a diabetic volunteer treated with insulin aspart were analyzed as proof-of-concept. Sotatercept is a recombinant fusion protein derived from the extracellular domain of the human activin receptor type IIA (ActRIIA) and the Fc fragment of human immunoglobulin G1 (IgG1), which acts as an erythropoiesis-stimulating agent through specific inhibition of activin A and other cytokines of the transforming growth factor-β (TGF-β) superfamily.[27] By using an ultrasonication-assisted extraction in combination with affinity purification (Protein G– or activin A–conjugated magnetic beads) and LC-HRMS, the protein drug could be detected in DBS at concentrations down to 250 ng/mL. Moreover, it was successfully demonstrated that the use of Protein G beads for analyte extraction allows the simultaneous detection of different IgG-based protein therapeutics (e.g., the ActRIIB-Fc fusion protein Luspatercept and the anti-myostatin antibody Bimagrumab) in a multiplexed approach.

Overall, it has been proved that it is possible in principle to detect a wide range of prohibited doping agents at very low concentrations in DBS but that parameters such as extraction solvents and subsequent purification strategies necessitate thorough optimization. Several other assays were developed for non-approved substances with potential performance-enhancing effects, such as SIRT1 activating drugs (detection limit: 10–50 ng/mL) and adiponectin receptor agonists (detection limit: 5–10 ng/mL).[28,29] Moreover, DBS were successfully analyzed to provide evidence for blood doping practices by measuring cell-specific membrane proteins.[30,31]

So far, all DBS approaches have been based on manual cutting and extraction of the spots (Figure 4.7.1), which was followed by different purification steps such as solid phase extraction (SPE), protein precipitation, or ultrafiltration. However, a time-saving automated sample preparation and subsequent analysis are necessary to qualify DBS as an alternative matrix for high-throughput routine analysis. Further benefits of automation are improved extraction efficiency, a significantly reduced risk for analyte losses and therefore, enhanced assay sensitivity, a lower risk for sample contamination, and equivalent or superior reproducibility and precision.[32] The first fully automated DBS-SPE-LC-(HR)MS/MS method was published in 2015 and comprised five opioids, which could be detected with lower limits of quantification (LLOQs) of 0.1 (fentanyl) and 1 ng/mL (morphine, codeine, oxycodone, and hydrocodone).[33] Shortly afterwards, a similar approach was employed for the detection of the anti-ischemic and cardioprotective drug meldonium from DBS, which had a detection limit of 20 ng/mL.[34] In another recent project, a multi-target initial testing approach for various prohibited substances after fully automated DBS extraction was established. The method covers a wide range of 32 different model compounds from nearly all classes (AAs, β2-agonists, metabolic modulators, diuretics, stimulants, glucocorticoids, and non-approved compounds). The assay's validation outlined that the method provides reliable and robust results with the required sensitivity for effective doping controls (Table 4.7.3). Additionally, high-resolution full scan mass spectrometry enables the simultaneous acquisition of a complete data set, which can potentially also be used to evaluate the results in a retrospective manner. The proof-of-principle for this

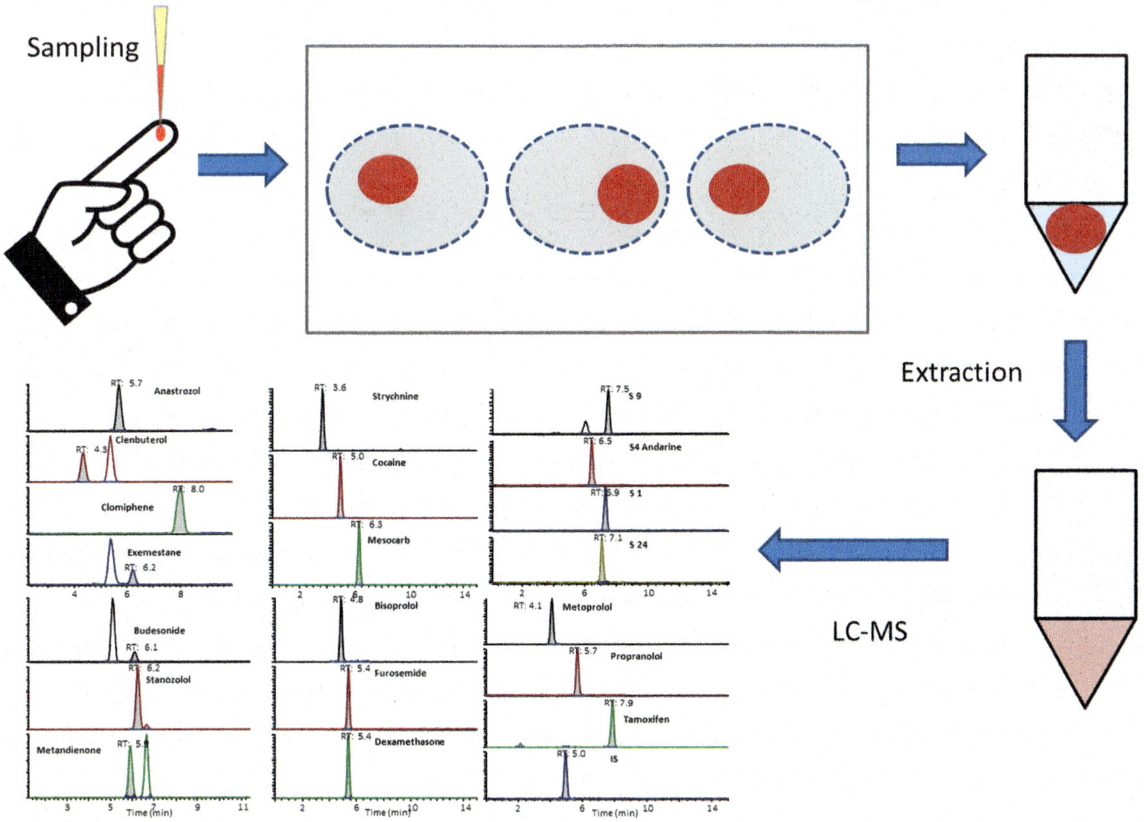

FIGURE 4.7.1 Principle of DBS analysis.

TABLE 4.7.3
Validation Parameters of Multi-Target Initial Testing Approach Using Automated Sample Preparation

Classes Prohibited List	Name	Recovery in %	LOD (ng/mL)	Intraday imprecision (CV in %)		Interday imprecision (CV in %)		Accuracy in %		Linearity	Specificity
		50 ng/mL		50 ng/mL	200 ng/mL	50 ng/mL	200 ng/mL	50 ng/mL	200 ng/mL	R^2	
S1	Stanozolol	39–69	1	6–8	8–9	7	8	84	96	0.996	✓
	Clenbuterol	56–71	1	2–6	3–5	5	4	99	102	0.991	✓
	Metandienone	47–87	1	3–17	6–9	18	12	94	95	0.994	✓
	CDMT	46–82	5	6–19	6–9	16	13	98	109	0.991	✓
	Trenbolone	38–64	1	7–18	7–11	18	12	85	82	0.991	✓
	Methyltestosterone	41–80	5	6–7	9–10	10	13	79	93	0.991	✓
S3	Formoterol	31–58	10	11–18	8–10	17	11	99	104	0.991	✓
S4	Meldonium	72–95	10	8–19	6–13	25	11	101	90	0.964	✓
	Clomifene	46–83	5	9–10	3–4	10	4	108	120	0.979	✓
	Trimetazidine	42–62	1	3–7	2–4	14	12	111	110	0.996	✓
	Anastrozole	49–86	1	6–20	5–10	15	9	111	113	0.994	✓
S5	Hydrochlorothiazide	54–73	10	7–9	4–7	9	7	97	96	0.992	✓
	Bumetanide	43–70	5	6–14	9–12	15	14	93	112	0.994	✓
S6	Methylhexanamine	62–73	5	5–8	4–8	8	7	94	94	0.990	✓
	Methylphenidate	69–81	1	4–6	3–6	12	10	105	110	0.995	✓
	Amphetamine	64–71	10	2–7	2–5	5	5	99	102	0.990	✓
	Cocaine	61–81	1	10–11	8–10	13	10	90	110	0.984	✓
	Desmethyl-Sibutramine	49–86	5	4–8	4–8	7	7	101	105	0.991	✓
	Ephedrine	66–75	1	2–6	3–5	7	6	101	103	0.995	✓
	Benzoylecgonine	59–82	5	6–9	4–5	7	5	102	118	0.996	✓

approach was obtained by analyzing several hundreds of doping control DBS samples from which AAFs (e.g., for stanozolol and trenbolone) were obtained. Recently, a multi-analyte approach including 46 peptidic compounds such as Ghrelin- and GnRH-receptor agonists was developed, which combines a robotic-assisted DBS sample preparation via a DBS autosampler with online SPE (strong cation exchange) and evaporation with LC-HRMS.[35] The estimated LODs vary from 0.5 to 10 ng/mL.

Taken together, DBS are an effective and advantageous way to probe large groups of athletes and thus are of great value for sports drug testing. However, modern mass spectrometers with high sensitivity and accuracy are required for the implementation of DBS into doping control analysis, since very low analyte concentrations prevail in the samples. Several assays for a wide range of doping agents are already available, and further research is currently ongoing to develop more sensitive and simpler detection methods.

4.7.2 Hair

Hair represents one of the first complementary matrices that have been used for a variety of forensic, pharmacological, and doping control applications.[36] Hair is particularly robust and stable, consisting of proteins (65–95%), water (15–35%), lipids (1–9%), and minerals (≤1%).[36–38] The most abundant protein in hair is keratin, which forms long fibers chemically crosslinked via disulfide bonds. Hair strands originate in epidermal hair follicles, where new hair cells are produced and undergo keratinization. The follicle is tightly associated with sebaceous, sweat, and apocrine glands as well as dense capillary networks delivering nutrients to the cells. Each hair strand is composed of three different layers. The cuticle is an outer layer of dead, overlapping, keratinized cells, which anchors the hair shaft in the follicle and protects the inner parts of the hair strand. The cortex is the main component of the hair shaft, formed by tightly compacted, keratinized cells arranged as long, stable fibers. The central medulla – which is not present in all types of hair – consists of loosely packed cells, which shrink continuously due to dehydration, resulting in a series of vacuoles along the axis of the hair strand. Different mechanisms have been discussed to explain the incorporation of circulating drugs and metabolites into hair:[6,36,39] passive diffusion from the blood into the hair follicle, active secretion from the associated glands, transfer from surrounding skin tissue, and passive external contamination from the environment. During hair growth, the cells undergo apoptosis, then keratinization, and are finally fused into highly stable fibers, while the incorporated drugs and metabolites are immobilized through binding to lipids and proteins (e.g., to the hair pigment melanin) and entrapped for up to several months. Drug incorporation into hair depends on different physicochemical factors such as the compound's lipophilicity, alkalinity, membrane permeability, chemical structure, molecular mass, and protein affinity.[6,36,40,41] Further influencing factors are the administered drug dose and its bioavailability as well as inter-individual differences such as age, gender, hair pigmentation, and cosmetic hair treatments.

The use of hair as an alternative/complementary matrix offers several advantages.[1,6,36,38,40–44] Hair samples can be collected non-invasively without privacy invasion and are easily stored for extended time periods. Due to the complex structure of hair, sample adulteration is rather difficult, but nevertheless, many types of pharmaceuticals can be extracted and subsequently analyzed by using immunoassays or mass spectrometry. However, the greatest benefit of hair as a biological matrix is the long drug detection window up to several months (depending on the hair length; growth rate: circa 1 cm/month), which provides retrospective information about drug exposure and enables distinction between single dose administration and chronic/repeated drug use. However, hair analysis is limited by its susceptibility to external contamination, potential migration of drugs, low concentrations of incorporated drugs, poor retrospective accuracy, and the dependence on inter-individual factors such as, for example, ethnicity and cosmetic hair treatments (hair cutting, coloring, bleaching, etc.). Moreover, recent drug abuse cannot be detected, as it takes several days until growing hair reaches the surface of the scalp.

Several sample preparation steps are necessary in order to detect drugs from hair specimens.[36,38] During an initial washing step, potential external contaminations are removed, and the dried hair is then pulverized or cut into small pieces. Depending on the chemical properties of the target analytes, different strategies comprising an enzymatic/organic/alkaline/acidic hydrolysis, heating, ultrasonication, and incubation in appropriate buffers/solvents can be employed for the subsequent extraction of the drugs.[36] As hair is a highly complex matrix in which most analytes are present in rather low concentrations, hair extracts are commonly subjected to additional purification and concentration steps employing, for example, liquid–liquid extraction, SPE, or chromatography. For the detection and quantification of the drugs, both immunoassays such as ELISAs and radioimmunoassays (RIAs) and mass spectrometry in combination with liquid or gas chromatography can be used. An important aspect for method characterization is the difficulty of determining the exact recovery of an analyte from hair. Therefore, all validation parameters (e.g., LOD and LOQ) need to be estimated, and no reliable quantifications can be conducted.

In sports drug testing, hair analysis is only applicable to doping agents whose physicochemical properties allow both incorporation into and extraction from hair. While the transfer of most diuretics to hair is limited by their acidity, many peptide hormones cannot be incorporated into the hair follicle due to their high molecular mass.[1,6] But a proteomics study published in 2006 demonstrated that it is principally possible to extract proteins from hair and analyze them by means of LC-MS/MS.[45] By contrast, basic and/or lipophilic drugs with a low molecular mass are easily detectable from hair; however, data interpretation can be difficult for threshold substances such as β2-agonists as well as compounds whose misuse in sports is only prohibited in competition (stimulants, narcotics, cannabinoids, and glucocorticoids).[1,6,46,47]

In the past, hair analysis was successfully employed for the detection of various anabolic steroids, and especially their precursors (e.g., steroid esters) were identified as very promising analytical targets.[6,40–42,46,48–51] As these prodrugs were found to be incorporated into hair, their extraction and subsequent detection can provide evidence for the exogenous application of endogenous steroids such as testosterone and nandrolone.[41,43,46] Additionally, several studies have demonstrated that parent compounds of both exogenous and endogenous AAs, rather than their metabolites, are incorporated into hair, which enables an unambiguous identification of the administered drugs.[40,43,46] For example, hair analysis was successfully employed to distinguish nandrolone from other 19-norsteroids (e.g., norandrostenedione) that have the same urinary metabolites.[44,48] For several synthetic anabolic steroids, quantitative assays with detection limits of 0.05 pg/mg for stanozolol,[42] 2 pg/mg for metandienone[49] and bolasterone,[51] and 5 pg/mg for trenbolone, mesterolone, and methytestosterone[51] were developed. Unfortunately, such steroid concentrations in hair usually result only from repeated or long-term misuse, which would also be associated with continual positive results in urine testing.[1,6] In order to provide additional information in doping cases involving the synthetic anabolic-androgenic steroid clostebol, a sensitive detection method employing ultra-high performance liquid chromatography–tandem mass spectrometry (UHPLC-MS/MS) was developed, which was successfully applied to authentic athlete head- and body-hair samples and allowed the detection of clostebol acetate in the low pg/mg range.[52]

With regard to non-steroidal AAs, hair analysis was found to be very advantageous for the detection of the β2-agonist clenbuterol.[1,6,53] Due to its beneficial effects on muscle and body fat mass, clenbuterol is misused not only as a performance-enhancing agent in sports but also as a growth-promoting agent in the livestock industry.[53–56] The consumption of meat from clenbuterol-treated animals can result in severe side-effects and cause AAFs in sports drug testing. But although administration to meat-producing animals is strictly regulated, illegal misuse has been reported for several countries, such as China and Mexico.[54–56] Clenbuterol is a basic, lipophilic molecule with a low molecular mass and high affinity for the hair pigment melanin and is therefore strongly incorporated, especially into pigmented hair.[53] By using LC-MS/MS, amounts as low as 0.02 pg per mg of hair could be detected. In an application study, it was demonstrated that both sub-therapeutic clenbuterol doses (30 μg in total) and food contamination result in positive hair samples with concentrations of 0.4–4.8 and 0.02–1.9 pg/mg, respectively.[53] But as the detected concentrations were significantly lower than after therapeutic use (>15 pg/mg),[57,58] the introduction of a threshold was suggested to distinguish clenbuterol contamination from misuse. In comparison, the interpretation of urinary clenbuterol concentrations can be difficult, as they are subject to individual variations and provide no retrospective information (e.g., whether a low concentration was caused by food contamination or preceding clenbuterol misuse).[1,53] Another example is the non-steroidal estrogen zeranol, which is not only an anabolic agent but also a metabolite of the *Fusarium* mycotoxin and food contaminant zearalenone.[59] Here, hair analysis was successfully utilized to differentiate between mycotoxin exposure and zeranol misuse.

Recently, hair analysis was also employed for the detection of a few other doping agents. Hydrochlorothiazide is a diuretic of the benzothiadiazine family, which can be misused by athletes as a masking agent or to lose weight in weight class sports such as boxing.[60] By using a specific UPLC-MS/MS method with an LOQ of 5 pg/mg, hydrochlorothiazide could be detected in authentic post-administration samples. While a single exposure to the drug was not detectable in hair, repeated administration yielded concentrations of 12–1,845 pg/mg.

In summary, hair analysis currently does not have the potential to replace urine and blood as matrices in sports drug testing, but it can certainly provide valuable additional retrospective information to distinguish single from repetitive drug misuse and enable the detection of steroid esters.[40,41,43,44,52,61]

4.7.3 Oral Fluid (OF)

OF is a complex matrix composed of saliva, mucosal transudate, crevicular fluid from the gingiva, oro-nasopharyngeal secretions, food debris, and different types of cells, including bacteria.[44,62–65] Both its volume and its exact composition are subject to high intra- and inter-individual variation. Saliva fulfills several important functions in the human body. It plays a pivotal role in the maintenance of oral health, as it protects the oral and perioral tissues and facilitates both eating and speaking.[64–66] Saliva is primarily produced by three pairs of major glands:[62–66] The parotid glands release a serous watery secretion, the submandibular glands a sero-mucous fluid, and the sublingual glands more viscous-mucous saliva. Several hundred minor accessory salivary glands are additionally located on the buccal mucosae, the tongue, and the palate and produce a viscous fluid. Salivation is a reflex response, which follows a circadian rhythm and is controlled by both sympathetic and parasympathetic innervation.[64,67] Depending on water balance and stimulation, healthy adults produce between 500 and 1500 mL of saliva per day, and the secretion rate varies from 0.1 mL/min during rest to 6 mL/min during food intake.[62–66] The production and release of saliva depend on many different parameters, such as stress, aggression, pain, gustatory/olfactory stimuli, mechanical stimulation through chewing, physical exercise, and hormonal changes.[62,64–65] Furthermore, several systemic diseases (e.g., cystic fibrosis) and drugs targeting the central and peripheral nervous system (e.g., analgesics and sympathomimetics) were found to affect both the composition and the flow rate of saliva.[6,62,64]

Primary saliva is isotonic to plasma and produced in the acini of the salivary glands.[62–65] It is stored in secretion granules and transported to the oral cavity following sympathetic and parasympathetic stimulation. During transportation, salivary electrolyte concentrations change through active secretion and resorption processes, finally resulting in a slightly acidic, hypotonic fluid (pH 6–7) consisting of water, electrolytes, mucus, proteins, leukocytes, and epithelial cells. Most of the salivary proteins are synthesized by secretory acinar cells and comprise antibacterial and antifungal compounds such as lysozyme and cystatins as well as digestive enzymes such as, for example, alpha-amylase, lipase, and proteinase. The acini of the salivary glands are tightly associated with blood capillaries, and the transfer of circulating endogenous compounds and drugs into saliva is mediated by three different mechanisms.[2,6,62,63,65] While small, lipophilic, unconjugated molecules (<500 Da) can passively diffuse from the blood through the capillary wall, the basement membrane, and the membrane of the glandular epithelial cells into the salivary duct, electrolytes, serum proteins/peptides (e.g., IgA and insulin), and certain drugs have to be actively transported. By contrast, small polar molecules (<1,900 Da) can enter saliva by ultrafiltration through membrane pores. Therefore, favorable physicochemical properties for drug transfer into saliva are low molecular mass and protein affinity as well as high lipophilicity and basicity.[2,6]

The main reasons for using OF as an alternative matrix are the simplicity and non-invasiveness of the sample collection procedure, which can be conducted under direct supervision by non-medical staff.[2,6,62,63,65,68] Moreover, the athletes' privacy is not compromised, and the potential for sample adulteration/substitution is very low. Limitations are the high intra- and inter-individual variability with regard to the composition of OF, the small sample volume, and the potential for contamination following oral, intranasal, and smoked drug administration.[2,44,65,68]

For OF sampling, different sample collection devices are commercially available; however, they differ with regard to the drug recovery, and some were found to interfere with sample analysis.[44,63,68] The extraction of OF is similar to other biological fluids such as blood and urine, and both immunological assays such as ELISAs and mass spectrometry can be employed for the detection and identification of the target analytes.[44,63,68]

So far, the applicability of OF as an alternative matrix for in- and out-of-competition sports drug testing has only been evaluated for a few model compounds representing different classes of prohibited substances. Most of the studies demonstrated that OF cannot replace blood or urine analysis but can provide complementary qualitative and quantitative information, especially for compounds that are only prohibited in competition and in particular sport disciplines.[1,2,6,68,69]

For small, basic or neutral, lipophilic drugs, the concentrations in OF correlate well with blood and thus, the bioavailability and biological effects of a drug.[6,70] Consequently, the parent compounds of many stimulants, narcotics, cannabinoids, corticosteroids, and β-blockers are suitable for detection from OF.[1,6,68] The concentrations of the corresponding metabolites are usually several orders of magnitude lower than in plasma, which can be attributed to the higher polarity of biotransformation products.[2,6,69] For most of these compounds, the detection times in OF were found to be significantly shorter than in urine (a few hours/days vs. several hours/days), which can be employed to define thresholds to distinguish between recent and earlier drug use.[2,69] In 2008, a comprehensive study was published in which different stimulants such as modafinil (100 mg) and selegiline (10 mg) were orally administered to healthy volunteers.[69] Both urine and OF samples were collected, and a GC-MS method for the detection of 14 different stimulants at concentrations down to 2–10 ng/mL was employed for OF analysis. Modafinil was detectable for 24 hours in OF and at least 72 hours in urine. Selegiline and its main metabolites metamphetamine, amphetamine, and nor-selegiline could be detected in OF for 3–15 hours and in urine for 36–48 hours. Therefore, the analysis of OF can be of considerable value in cases where only a small amount of a metabolite without the corresponding parent compound is present in urine, making it very difficult to differentiate a recent ingestion of a low drug dose from an earlier administration of a high dose.[69] Here, a combined evaluation of urinary and salivary drug concentrations could be beneficial. The applicability of OF as an alternative matrix for in-competition sports drug testing was recently investigated by analyzing a set of 521 matched OF, EB, and urine samples collected from athletes.[71] For OF collection, Quantisal devices were used, and samples were extracted employing a weak cation mixed mode SPE. Following evaporation, eluates were analyzed by means of LC-MS/MS and tested for the presence of different doping agents such as stimulants, narcotics, cannabinoids, and glucocorticoids. Overall, 89/521 urine samples tested positive, and 35 of these findings could be corroborated by OF analysis. They comprised narcotics, cannabinoids, stimulants, beta-blockers, and diuretics. While 46 of the total findings could only be detected in urine, 4 were only detectable in OF (1 in OF and EB). Compared with urine, the detection of cannabinoids, diuretics, and glucocorticoids especially was found to be less sensitive in OF. But due to the quick, easy, and non-invasive sample collection procedure, this matrix was preferred by the participants to conventional urine samples.

For stimulants, narcotics, and cannabinoids, special devices for on-site drug detection in OF have been developed,[6,68] which might also be applicable for in-competition sports drug testing. However, sample contamination following inhalative cannabis consumption and environmental cannabis smoke represents a pitfall, which should be taken into consideration when using OF as an alternative biological matrix for the detection of THC.[1,2,44]

For most of the drug classes prohibited at all times, the use of OF as a biological matrix was found to be inferior compared with blood and urine. While the parent compounds of endogenous anabolic-androgenic steroids (AAS) can passively diffuse from the blood into saliva, phase II metabolites only enter via ultrafiltration, resulting in concentrations that are 300 to 3,000 times lower than in plasma.[2,6,65,70] However, an additional isotope-ratio mass spectrometry (IRMS) analysis is required to distinguish endogenous steroid levels from an exogenous administration. Unfortunately, OF appears to be inappropriate for IRMS analysis, as the sample volumes are small and the concentrations of steroids significantly lower than in urine (pg/mL vs. ng/mL).[2,72] Surprisingly, a testosterone administration study published in 2013 has demonstrated that the concentration of free testosterone in OF could be a valuable diagnostic marker for a transdermal application of the drug.[70] Following administration of Testogel® (5 g of gel containing 50 mg of testosterone) and two Testopatches® (releasing 2.4 mg of testosterone in 24 h), salivary testosterone concentrations increased from base levels (30–92 pg/mL) to a maximum of 1,150 pg/mL. By contrast, urinary thresholds for the testosterone/epitestosterone ratio and different endogenous steroids were not exceeded in the corresponding urine samples. This phenomenon can probably be attributed to a temporarily elevated amount of unbound circulating testosterone, which diffuses freely into saliva but undergoes biotransformation before urinary excretion. Therefore, the determination of salivary testosterone values might be employed to screen for a transdermal application of the drug. Recently, a method for the quantitative determination of five endogenous steroids in OF was published, and a total of 826 samples were analyzed to establish reference population thresholds and steroid ratios in order to distinguish between physiological steroid concentrations and elevated levels due to an exogenous administration.[72] Additionally, the intra-individual stability of the steroid concentrations and ratios was investigated, and an administration study with testosterone gel (3 × 50 mg/5 g, every 24 hours) was conducted to serve as proof-of-concept. While the urinary inter- and intra-individual thresholds were exceeded for 24 and 60 h following administration, salivary parameters changed for a period of 76 h, with a maximum testosterone concentration of 7,300 pg/mL (intra-individual reference limit: 130 pg/mL). These findings demonstrate that OF is superior to urine analysis to uncover transdermal testosterone application.

So far, only a few studies have been carried out to investigate the detection of synthetic anabolic steroids in OF.[1,2] But as both oxymetholone and tibolone were found to have very short detection times (≤1 hour) in OF following oral administration, it can be assumed that it is not a suitable matrix for the analysis of exogenous steroids.

As active transport mechanisms are required to transfer circulating proteins and peptides (>1,900 Da) into saliva, their concentrations in OF are significantly lower than in blood.[1,2,6] Consequently, it appears rather unlikely that current detection methods for EPO and hGH can be employed for OF analysis. By contrast, a good correlation between OF and blood concentrations was observed for insulin, indicating that this matrix can potentially be used for insulin detection by means of LC-MS/MS.[2]

β2-agonists are therapeutics for the treatment of pulmonary diseases such as asthma, and thresholds were defined to distinguish inhalative therapeutic dosages from systemic administration for doping purposes.[47] Although β2-agonists are detectable in OF, the high risk for sample contamination following inhalation makes this matrix rather inappropriate for sports drug testing.[1,2]

4.7.4 Exhaled Breath (EB)

During the last years, EB has gained increasing importance as an alternative matrix for clinical, toxicological, and forensic applications as well as sports drug testing.[73,74] This can be particularly attributed to the easy, short, and non-invasive sample collection procedure, which respects the privacy of the patients/athletes and has proved robust against manipulation.[1,74] However, the available sample volume is relatively low, which necessitates highly sensitive detection methods. Moreover, the achievable analytical spectrum is limited, as predominantly lower–molecular mass analytes are eliminated into EB.

Since the early 1970s, the composition of EB has been systematically investigated in order to identify and quantitate potential biomarkers for medical approaches.[75] In 1971, Linus Pauling quantified about 250 volatile organic compounds from breath by using gas-liquid partition chromatography.[76] By now, EB and its condensate have been found to contain more than 3,500 different compounds, comprising different gases such as nitrogen, oxygen, carbon dioxide, and water as well as water-soluble volatile and non-volatile components.[74,77–79] The volatile organic compounds (VOCs) present in EB are of either exogenous or endogenous origin.[77,80] While exogenous VOCs include substances produced during the oral ingestion of food as well as volatiles inhaled from the environment, endogenous VOCs are either released from the blood into the lungs or synthesized by bacteria. By contrast, non-volatile components of EB are part of an aerosol formed from bursting fluid blockages of the lower bronchioles during the inhalation phase of breathing.[74,81] The alveoli and lower bronchioles are covered by a fluid, which is generated and secreted by epithelial cells and contains a surface active agent (surfactant) consisting primarily of neutral lipids, phospholipids, and proteins.[74,82–84] It functions as a solvent for both hydrophobic and water-soluble analytes and fulfills important mechanical and protective functions. Several barriers, including the alveolar epithelium, its basement membranes, and the capillary endothelium, separate the alveolar lining fluid from the blood stream. and different mechanisms for the transport of drugs into the lung tissue have been discussed.[73,85] They depend on the physico-chemical properties of the compounds (e.g., molecular mass, protein binding, and lipophilicity) and comprise passive diffusion, permeation, active transport, and bulk flow. During the inhalation phase of breathing, fluid closures in the bronchioles are reopened, resulting in bursting of the fluid film and the formation of an aerosol.[81,86] The exhaled particles have diameters between 0.3 and 2.5 μm,[87] and their number in the aerosol varies – depending on the breathing modalities – from 0.1 to 4 particles per cm^3.[88]

Originally, EB was collected as condensate containing the aerosol particles, condensed water, and water-soluble volatile compounds by using stationary or portable devices with cold traps.[74,76,89–92] The sampled individuals have to apply a nose-clip and subsequently breathe for several minutes into a mouthpiece equipped with a salivary trap.[74,78] The EB is directly condensed by cooling and collected as a liquid sample, which is then subjected to further extraction and concentration steps employing techniques such as immunoaffinity purification and SPE.[92] For the analysis of the extracted compounds, a variety of techniques including immunological, chromatographic, and mass spectrometric approaches can be utilized. However, this sampling technique is limited by the lack of standardization and the considerable dilution of the analytes in the condensed water, resulting in extremely low concentrations, especially of non-volatiles.

The first successful attempt to collect and quantitate the EB particles containing the non-volatile analytes was published in 2009.[93] Here, a cascade impactor was used to concentrate the particles of the bioaerosol onto silicon wafers with a highly hydrophilic surface. Later, silica-based SPE cartridges (e.g., SPEC DAS cartridge) and Empore C18 extraction disks were successfully employed for EB sampling.[94,95] The first commercial devices for the collection of non-volatile EB components were developed by SensAbues (Huddinge, Sweden). As shown in Figure 4.7.2, they consist of a cartridge with an embedded electret (electrostatic-based) filter, which captures the exhaled bioaerosol particles.[73,96–100] The design of the mouthpiece allows only micro-particles to pass through to the filter, while saliva and larger particles are retained. The efficacy of the trapping baffles integrated in the mouthpiece was recently investigated by Garzinsky et al.[101] Both EB and OF were collected under varying conditions from a total of 14 healthy volunteers, and bottom-up proteomics approaches such as gel electrophoresis, tryptic digestion, and LC-MS were employed to test the samples for the presence of abundant salivary proteins such as α-amylase. Since no saliva breakthrough was detectable, it was concluded that the OF introduced into the mouthpiece is effectively retained by the trapping baffles. The salivary enzyme α-amylase was additionally found to be unaffected by storage, food intake, smoking, and exercise. Consequently, it appears to be a useful marker to uncover OF contaminations of EB collection devices.

Following sample collection, the mouthpiece is discarded, and the cartridge with the filter is sealed and subjected to sample extraction and analysis. For the detection of non-volatile drugs in EB, the filter/cartridges/membranes employed for aerosol particle collection are usually extracted with a suitable solvent such as methanol. The resulting extracts are either purified by using techniques

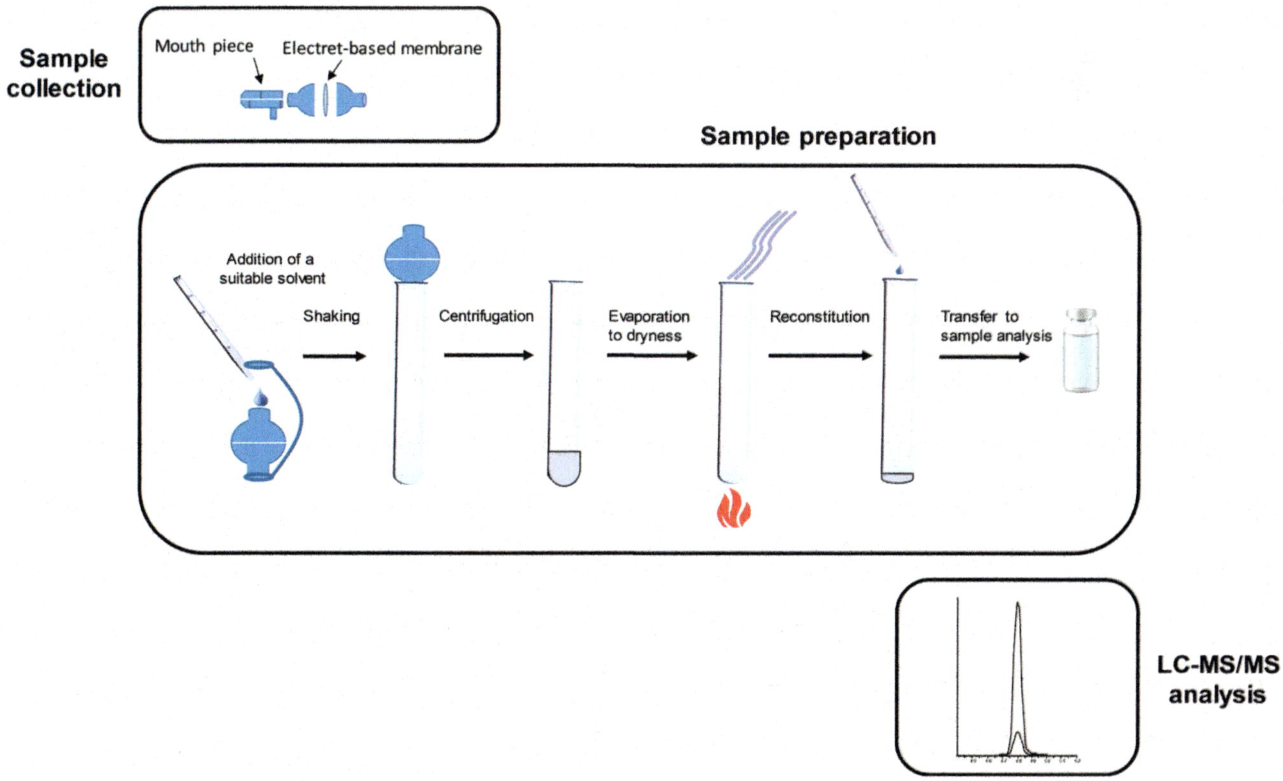

FIGURE 4.7.2 Principle of EB analysis employing SensAbues collection devices.

such as SPE[102,103] or directly evaporated to dryness, reconstituted with a smaller volume of solvent, and analyzed by means of LC-MS.[73,94,95,98,104–108]

The idea of analyzing EB emerged a long time ago, when the olfactory senses of both humans and animals (e.g., dogs and rats) were employed for the diagnosis of various diseases.[75,109–111] In ancient times (2000 BC), the Chinese and Greeks diagnosed infectious diseases, for example tuberculosis, on the basis of the patient's scent.[109] About 400 BC, Hippocrates suggested using the odor of breath for the identification of patients with diabetes, liver disease, and kidney failure.[112,113] While ketoacidosis induced by diabetes results in a sweet acetone scent,[80,110] liver failure (e.g., due to liver cirrhosis) is accompanied by a sweet, musty smell, which is called *fetor hepaticus* and is caused by the presence of sulfur-containing compounds such as dimethyl sulfide and ketones.[110,114] By contrast, patients with chronic kidney disease were found to be characterized by increased breath levels of nitrogen-containing compounds, for example ammonia.[80,115] In the late 1980s, patients with different types of cancer could be successfully identified by dogs, whose extraordinary olfactory sense is capable of detecting changes in VOCs such as alkanes and aromatic compounds in EB.[80,111] During anesthesia, patients are routinely monitored by measuring the concentrations of both volatile anesthetics (e.g., N_2O) and breathing gases (O_2 and CO_2) in EB.[116]

Due to technical and scientific progress, especially during the second half of the 20th century, technologies such as Raman and infrared spectroscopy, gas and liquid chromatography, ion-mobility spectrometry, and (HR)MS can now be employed for the sensitive detection of a broad spectrum of endogenous and exogenous compounds in EB.[74,80,110,116] Consequently, the field of application is also continuously growing, and in addition to medical investigations, EB testing is now being extensively used for forensic and toxicological applications.[74] Meanwhile, the analysis of EB for the presence of alcohol has quite a long tradition in both roadside sobriety and workplace drug testing.[117] Moreover, it has been demonstrated that excessive drinking can be uncovered by the detection of phosphatidylethanols in EB. In 2010, the first study was published in which stimulants such as amphetamine and methamphetamine could be successfully identified in EB from drug addicts by using silica-based SPEC DAS cartridges for sample collection and LC-MS/MS for subsequent analysis.[94] Further studies included methadone,[89,100,104,105] Δ9-tetrahydrocannabinol (THC),[95,103] and methylphenidate.[106] A comprehensive LC-MS screening method comprising 12 different stimulants, narcotics, cannabinoids, and benzodiazepines was published in 2013.[98] For EB sampling, the abovementioned SensAbues cartridges were employed. Following method validation, the approach was tested by analyzing EB samples collected from 47 patients. The detection limits of the model compounds ranged from 0.5 to 3 pg/filter, and in most of the authentic EB specimens, the drug concentrations were found to be significantly higher, in the ng per filter scale. Remarkably, the cocaine metabolite benzoylecgonine could also be identified in a few samples, which was confirmed in another study published in 2014, where both benzoylecgonine and ecgonine methyl ester were detected in post-administration EB samples.[102] O-desmethyltramadol is an active metabolite of the opioid tramadol and could be identified in EB specimens from subjects who received a single oral dose of 50 mg;[107] however, the ratio of the metabolite to the parent compound was found to be significantly lower than in plasma. These findings demonstrate that further studies should be conducted in order to investigate the pharmacokinetics of drugs and their metabolites in EB. Recently, a similar LC-MS method comprising 28 different drugs of abuse such as stimulants, narcotics, and benzodiazepines was published.[108] The LODs varied between 0.3 and 50 pg/filter, and again, a set of authentic EB specimens served as proof-of-concept.

The potential of EB as an alternative test matrix for sports drug testing was investigated in a pilot study published in 2017.[73] Following ventilation, the filters of the SensAbues collection devices were extracted with methanol, which was then evaporated under a stream of nitrogen. The reconstituted samples were finally subjected to LC-MS/MS using UniSpray™ ionization. The multi-analyte approach was successfully validated for a total of 12 model compounds representing different classes of doping agents (S1 – AAs, S4 – hormone and metabolic modulators, S6 – stimulants, and P2 – beta-blockers) and yielded detection limits between 5 and 100 pg/filter. The analysis of authentic EB samples collected from patients and participants of administration studies demonstrated that doping-relevant compounds such as the stimulants methylhexanamine and pseudoephedrine, the anabolic-androgenic steroid dehydrochloromethyltestosterone (DHCMT), the beta-blocker bisoprolol, and the metabolic modulator meldonium are actually eliminated via EB, indicating that it could be a promising alternative matrix for sports drug testing. Recently, the abovementioned method was further optimized and expanded, now comprising a total of 38 doping agents (Table 4.7.4), which can be detected at concentrations of 5–500 pg per filter. Again, authentic post-administration EB specimens served as proof-of-concept for the applicability of the presented approach, and the selective androgen-receptor modulator (SARM) Ostarine was successfully detected from EB. For selected drugs, the detectability of the parent compounds in EB was additionally compared with DBS and urine. While the glucocorticoid dexamethasone could be detected for 2 h in EB, 24 h in DBS, and more than 48 h in urine, methylprednisolone had a detection window of 7 h in all three matrices.

Recently, a total of 521 sample sets comprising matched EB, OF, and urine specimens were analyzed by means of GC-MS/MS and LC-MS/MS in order to evaluate the applicability of EB and OF to sports drug testing.[71] Overall, 89/521 urine samples tested positive, and while the drug findings in OF were found to correlate reasonably well with the results obtained from urine analysis, only 8 of the urine

TABLE 4.7.4
Doping Agents Included in the Validated LC-MS Method for the Extraction and Analysis of EB Specimens

WADA drug class	S1 Anabolic agents	S3 Beta-2-agonists	S4 Hormone and metabolic modulators	S5 Diuretics	S6 Stimulants	S7 Narcotics	S8 Cannabinoids	S9 Glucocorticoids	P1 Beta-blockers
Model analyte	DHCMT	Anastrozole	Anastrozole	Triamterene	Methylhexanamine	Pethidine	JWH-073	Dexamethasone	Carvedilol
	Stanozolol	Letrozole	Letrozole		Amphetamine	Morphine	JWH-122	Prednisolone	Propranolol
	Ostarine		Meldonium		Pseudoephedrine	Methadone	AM-1220	Budesonide	Metoprolol
	Trenbolone				Methylphenidate	Oxycodone	UR-144		Bisoprolol
	YK-11				Modafinil		JWH-019		Acebutolol
					Sibutramine				
					25-I-NBOMe				
					Pentylone				
					Methiopropanamine				
					X-Ethyl methcathinone				

and 1 of the OF findings could be confirmed in EB. The small sample volume of EB was considered as one of the limiting factors for sensitivity.

The findings obtained in these pilot studies demonstrate that the analysis of EB could be particularly advantageous for the detection of pharmacologically relevant drug concentrations during in-competition sports drug testing. However, such short detection windows are disadvantageous for the analysis of compounds prohibited at all times. In order to assess the full potential of EB for sports drug testing, further studies evaluating parameters such as the sample stability and inter-individual variations need to be conducted.

REFERENCES

1. Thevis M, Geyer H, Tretzel L, Schänzer W. Sports drug testing using complementary matrices: advantages and limitations. *J Pharm Biomed Anal* 2016;130:220–30.
2. Anizan S, Huestis MA. The potential role of oral fluid in antidoping testing. *Clin Chem* 2014;60(2):307–22.
3. Saugy M, Robinson N, Saudan C. The fight against doping: back on track with blood. *Drug Test Anal* 2009;1(11–12):474–8.
4. Elbe AM, Jensen SN, Elsborg P, Wetzke M, Woldemariam GA, Huppertz B, Keller R, Butch AW. The urine marker test: an alternative approach to supervised urine collection for doping control. *Sports Med* 2016;46(1):15–22.
5. Athanasiadou I, Kraiem S, Al-Sowaidi S, Al-Mohammed H, Dbes N, Al-Yazedi S, Samsam W, Mohamed-Ali V, Dokoumetzidis A, Alsayrafi M, Valsami G, Georgakopoulos C. The effect of athletes` hyperhydration on the urinary 'steroid profile' markers in doping control analysis. *Drug Test Anal* 2018.
6. Thieme D. Potential and limitations of alternative specimens in doping control. *Bioanalysis* 2012;4(13):1613–22.
7. World Anti-Doping Agency. International standard for laboratories. 2016. www.wada-ama.org (accessed 04.10.2018).
8. Parker SP, Cubitt WD. The use of the dried blood spot sample in epidemiological studies. *J Clin Pathol* 1999;52(9):633–9.
9. Guthrie R, Susi A. A simple phenylalanine method for detecting phenylketonuria in large populations of newborn infants. *Pediatrics* 1963;32:338–43.
10. Rajabi F. Updates in newborn screening. *Pediatr Ann* 2018;47:e187–e190.
11. Tretzel L, Thomas A, Geyer H, Delahaut P, Schänzer W, Thevis M. Determination of Synacthen in dried blood spots for doping control analysis using liquid chromatography tandem mass spectrometry. *Anal Bioanal Chem* 2015;407(16):4709–20.
12. Denniff P, Spooner N. The effect of hematocrit on assay bias when using DBS samples for the quantitative bioanalysis of drugs. *Bioanalysis* 2010;2(8):1385–95.
13. Thomas A, Geyer H, Guddat S, Schänzer W, Thevis M. Dried blood spots (DBS) for doping control analysis. *Drug Test Anal* 2011;3(3):806–13.
14. Peng SH, Segura J, Farre M, de la Torre X. Oral testosterone administration detected by testosterone glucuronidation measured in blood spots dried on filter paper. *Clin Chem* 2000;46(4):515–22.
15. World Anti-Doping Agency. Anti-doping testing figures report 2017. 2018. www.wada-ama.org (accessed 04.10.2018).
16. Tretzel L, Thomas A, Geyer H, Gmeiner G, Forsdahl G, Pop V, Schänzer W, Thevis M. Use of dried blood spots in doping control analysis of anabolic steroid esters. *J Pharm Biomed Anal* 2014;96:21–30.
17. Thomas A, Geyer H, Schänzer W, Crone C, Kellmann M, Moehring T, Thevis M. Sensitive determination of prohibited drugs in dried blood spots (DBS) for doping controls by means of a benchtop quadrupole/Orbitrap mass spectrometer. *Anal Bioanal Chem* 2012;403(5):1279–89.
18. Kojima A, Nishitani Y, Sato M, Kageyama S, Dohi M, Okano M. Comparison of urine analysis and dried blood spot analysis for the detection of ephedrine and methylephedrine in doping control. *Drug Test Anal* 2016;8(2):189–98.
19. Protti M, Rudge J, Sberna AE, Gerra G, Mercolini L. Dried haematic microsamples and LC–MS/MS for the analysis of natural and synthetic cannabinoids. *J Chromatogr B* 2017;1044–1045:77–86.
20. Protti M, Catapano MC, Samolsky Dekel BG, Rudge J, Gerra G, Somaini L, Mandrioli R, Mercolini L. Determination of oxycodone and its major metabolites in haematic and urinary matrices: comparison of traditional and miniaturised sampling approaches. *J Pharm Biomed Anal* 2018;152:204–14.
21. Möller I, Thomas A, Geyer H, Schänzer W, Thevis M. Development and validation of a mass spectrometric detection method of peginesatide in dried blood spots for sports drug testing. *Anal Bioanal Chem* 2012.
22. Cox HD, Rampton J, Eichner D. Quantification of insulin-like growth factor-1 in dried blood spots for detection of growth hormone abuse in sport. *Anal Bioanal Chem* 2013;405(6):1949–58.
23. Ferro P, Ventura R, Perez-Mana C, Farre M, Segura J. Evaluation of fibronectin 1 in one dried blood spot and in urine after rhGH treatment. *Drug Test Anal* 2017;9(7):1011–6.
24. Reverter-Branchat G, Ventura R, Ezzel Din M, Mateus J, Pedro C, Segura J. Detection of erythropoiesis-stimulating agents in a single dried blood spot. *Drug Test Anal* 2018;10(10):1496–507.
25. Reverter-Branchat G, Bosch J, Vall J, Farre M, Papaseit E, Pichini S, Segura J. Determination of recent growth hormone abuse using a single dried blood spot. *Clin Chem* 2016;62(10):1353–60.
26. Thomas A, Thevis M. Analysis of insulin and insulin analogues from dried blood spots by means of LC-HRMS. *Drug Test Anal* 2018;10(11–12):1761–8.
27. Lange T, Walpurgis K, Thomas A, Geyer H, Thevis M. Development of two complementary LC–HRMS methods for analyzing Sotatercept in dried blood spots for doping controls. *Bioanalysis* 2019;11(10):923–40.
28. Höppner S, Delahaut P, Schänzer W, Thevis M. Mass spectrometric studies on the *in vivo* metabolism and excretion of SIRT1 activating drugs in rat urine, dried blood spots, and plasma samples for doping control purposes. *J Pharm Biomed Anal* 2014;88:649–59.
29. Dib J, Tretzel L, Piper T, Lagojda A, Kuehne D, Schänzer W, Thevis M. Screening for adiponectin receptor agonists and their metabolites in urine and dried blood spots. *Clin Mass Spec* 2017;6:13–20.
30. Cox HD, Miller GD, Lai A, Cushman D, Eichner D. Detection of autologous blood transfusions using a novel dried blood spot method. *Drug Test Anal* 2017;9(11–12):1713–20.

31. Cox HD, Eichner D. Mass spectrometry method to measure membrane proteins in dried blood spots for the detection of blood doping practices in sport. *Anal Chem* 2017;89(18):10029–10036.
32. Tretzel L, Thomas A, Piper T, Hedeland M, Geyer H, Schänzer W, Thevis M. Fully automated determination of nicotine and its major metabolites in whole blood by means of a DBS online-SPE LC-HR-MS/MS approach for sports drug testing. *J Pharm Biomed Anal* 2016;123:132–40.
33. Verplaetse R, Henion J. Quantitative determination of opioids in whole blood using fully automated dried blood spot desorption coupled to on-line SPE-LC-MS/MS. *Drug Test Anal* 2016;8(1):30–8.
34. Tretzel L, Görgens C, Geyer H, Thomas A, Dib J, Guddat S, Pop V, Schänzer W, Thevis M. Analyses of meldonium (Mildronate) from blood, Dried Blood Spots (DBS), and urine suggest drug incorporation into erythrocytes. *Int J Sports Med* 2016;37(06):500–2.
35. Lange T, Thomas A, Thevis M. Fully automated DBS sample preparation and hematocrit determination enable peptide detection in sports drug testing by means of LC-HRMS. Manuscript in preparation.
36. Barbosa J, Faria J, Carvalho F, Pedro M, Queiros O, Moreira R, Dinis-Oliveira RJ. Hair as an alternative matrix in bioanalysis. *Bioanalysis* 2013;5(8):895–914.
37. Harkey MR. Anatomy and physiology of hair. *Forensic Sci Int* 1993;63(1–3):9–18.
38. Kintz P, Villain M, Cirimele V. Hair analysis for drug detection. *Ther Drug Monit* 2006;28(3):442–6.
39. Henderson GL. Mechanisms of drug incorporation into hair. *Forensic Sci Int* 1993;63(1–3):19–29.
40. Deshmukh N, Hussain I, Barker J, Petroczi A, Naughton DP. Analysis of anabolic steroids in human hair using LC-MS/MS. *Steroids* 2010;75(10):710–4.
41. Gosetti F, Mazzucco E, Gennaro MC, Marengo E. Ultra high performance liquid chromatography tandem mass spectrometry determination and profiling of prohibited steroids in human biological matrices. A review. *J Chromatogr B Analyt Technol Biomed Life Sci* 2013;927: 22–36.
42. Shah I, Petroczi A, Uvacsek M, Ranky M, Naughton DP. Hair-based rapid analyses for multiple drugs in forensics and doping: application of dynamic multiple reaction monitoring with LC-MS/MS. *Chem Cent J* 2014;8(1):73.
43. Strano-Rossi S, Fiore C, Chiarotti M, Centini F. Analytical techniques in androgen anabolic steroids (AASs) analysis for antidoping and forensic purposes. *Mini Rev Med Chem* 2011;11(5):451–8.
44. Kintz P, Samyn N. Use of alternative specimens: drugs of abuse in saliva and doping agents in hair. *Ther Drug Monit* 2002;24(2):239–46.
45. Lee YJ, Rice RH, Lee YM. Proteome analysis of human hair shaft: from protein identification to posttranslational modification. *Mol Cell Proteomics* 2006;5(5):789–800.
46. Thieme D, Grosse J, Sachs H, Mueller RK. Analytical strategy for detecting doping agents in hair. *Forensic Sci Int* 2000;107(1–3):335–45.
47. World Anti-Doping Agency. The world anti-doping code - international standard: prohibited list (January 2019). 2018. www.wada-ama.org (accessed 27.09.2019).
48. Kintz P, Cirimele V, Ludes B. Discrimination of the nature of doping with 19-norsteroids through hair analysis. *Clin Chem* 2000;46(12):2020–2.
49. Bresson M, Cirimele V, Villain M, Kintz P. Doping control for metandienone using hair analyzed by gas chromatography-tandem mass spectrometry. *J Chromatogr B Analyt Technol Biomed Life Sci* 2006;836(1–2):124–8.
50. Cirimele V, Kintz P, Ludes B. Testing of the anabolic stanozolol in human hair by gas chromatography-negative ion chemical ionization mass spectrometry. *J Chromatogr B Biomed Sci Appl* 2000;740(2):265–71.
51. Deng XS, Kurosu A, Pounder DJ. Detection of anabolic steroids in head hair. *J Forensic Sci* 1999;44(2):343–6.
52. Salomone A, Gerace E, Di Corcia D, Alladio E, Vincenti M, Kintz P. Hair analysis can provide additional information in doping and forensic cases involving clostebol. *Drug Test Anal* 2019;11(1):95–101.
53. Krumbholz A, Anielski P, Gfrerer L, Graw M, Geyer H, Schänzer W, Dvorak J, Thieme D. Statistical significance of hair analysis of clenbuterol to discriminate therapeutic use from contamination. *Drug Test Anal* 2014;6(11–12):1108–16.
54. Guddat S, Fussholler G, Geyer H, Thomas A, Braun H, Haenelt N, Schwenke A, Klose C, Thevis M, Schänzer W. Clenbuterol - regional food contamination a possible source for inadvertent doping in sports. *Drug Test Anal* 2012;4(6):534–8.
55. Thevis M, Geyer L, Geyer H, Guddat S, Dvorak J, Butch A, Sterk SS, Schänzer W. Adverse analytical findings with clenbuterol among U-17 soccer players attributed to food contamination issues. *Drug Test Anal* 2013;5(5):372–6.
56. Jia JY, Zhang LN, Lu YL, Zhang MQ, Liu GY, Liu YM, Lu C, Li SJ, Lu Y, Zhang RW, Yu C. Hair analysis, a reliable and non-invasive method to evaluate the contamination by clenbuterol. *Ecotoxicol Environ Saf* 2013;93:186–90.
57. Dumestre-Toulet V, Cirimele V, Ludes B, Gromb S, Kintz P. Hair analysis of seven bodybuilders for anabolic steroids, ephedrine, and clenbuterol. *J Forensic Sci* 2002;47(1):211–4.
58. Gleixner A, Sauerwein H, Meyer HH. Detection of the anabolic beta 2-adrenoceptor agonist clenbuterol in human scalp hair by HPLC/EIA. *Clin Chem* 1996;42(11):1869–71.
59. Kintz P, Ameline A, Raul JS. Discrimination between zeranol and zearalenone exposure using hair analysis. Application to an adverse analytical finding case. *Drug Test Anal* 2018;10(5):906–9.
60. Gheddar L, Raul JS, Kintz P. First identification of a diuretic, hydrochlorothiazide, in hair: application to a doping case and interpretation of the results. *Drug Test Anal* 2019;11(1):157–61.
61. Gaillard Y, Vayssette F, Pepin G. Compared interest between hair analysis and urinalysis in doping controls. Results for amphetamines, corticosteroids and anabolic steroids in racing cyclists. *Forensic Sci Int* 2000;107(1–3):361–79.
62. Aps JK, Martens LC. Review: the physiology of saliva and transfer of drugs into saliva. *Forensic Sci Int* 2005;150(2–3):119–31.
63. Groschl M. Saliva: a reliable sample matrix in bioanalytics. *Bioanalysis* 2017;9(8):655–68.
64. Humphrey SP, Williamson RT. A review of saliva: normal composition, flow, and function. *J Prosthet Dent* 2001;85(2):162–9.
65. Pfaffe T, Cooper-White J, Beyerlein P, Kostner K, Punyadeera C. Diagnostic potential of saliva: current state and future applications. *Clin Chem* 2011;57(5):675–87.
66. Dodds M, Roland S, Edgar M, Thornhill M. Saliva A review of its role in maintaining oral health and preventing dental disease. *Bdj Team* 2015;2:15123.

67. Abdulkadyrov KM, Salogub GN, Khuazheva NK, Sherman ML, Laadem A, Barger R, Knight R, Srinivasan S, Terpos E. Sotatercept in patients with osteolytic lesions of multiple myeloma. *Br J Haematol* 2014;165(6):814–23.
68. Drummer OH. Drug testing in oral fluid. *Clin Biochem Rev* 2006;27(3):147–59.
69. Strano-Rossi S, Colamonici C, Botre F. Parallel analysis of stimulants in saliva and urine by gas chromatography/mass spectrometry: perspectives for "in competition" anti-doping analysis. *Anal Chim Acta* 2008;606(2):217–22.
70. Thieme D, Rautenberg C, Grosse J, Schoenfelder M. Significant increase of salivary testosterone levels after single therapeutic transdermal administration of testosterone: suitability as a potential screening parameter in doping control. *Drug Test Anal* 2013;5(11–12):819–25.
71. Miller GD, Van Wagoner RM, Bruno BJ, Husk JD, Fedoruk MN, Eichner D. Investigating oral fluid and exhaled breath as alternative matrices for anti-doping testing: analysis of 521 matched samples. *J Pharm Biomed Anal* 2019;176:112810.
72. Polet M, De Wilde L, Van Renterghem P, Van Gansbeke W, Van Eenoo P. Potential of saliva steroid profiling for the detection of endogenous steroid abuse: reference thresholds for oral fluid steroid concentrations and ratios. *Anal Chim Acta* 2018;999:1–12.
73. Thevis M, Krug O, Geyer H, Schänzer W. Expanding analytical options in sports drug testing: mass spectrometric detection of prohibited substances in exhaled breath. *Rapid Commun Mass Spectrom* 2017;31(15):1290–6.
74. Beck O, Olin AC, Mirgorodskaya E. Potential of mass spectrometry in developing clinical laboratory biomarkers of nonvolatiles in exhaled breath. *Clinical Chemistry* 2016;62(1):84–91.
75. Dweik RA, Amann A. Exhaled breath analysis: the new frontier in medical testing. *J Breath Res* 2008;2(3).
76. Pauling L, Robinson AB, Teranishi R, Cary P. Quantitative analysis of urine vapor and breath by gas-liquid partition chromatography. *Proc Natl Acad Sci USA* 1971;68(10):2374–6.
77. Popov TA. Human exhaled breath analysis. *Ann Allergy Asthma Immunol* 2011;106(6):451–6; quiz 457.
78. Hunt J. Exhaled breath condensate: an overview. *Immunol Allergy Clin North Am* 2007;27(4):587–96.
79. Ahmed WM, Lawal O, Nijsen TM, Goodacre R, Fowler SJ. Exhaled volatile organic compounds of infection: a systematic review. *ACS Infect Dis* 2017;3(10):695–710.
80. Shirasu M, Touhara K. The scent of disease: volatile organic compounds of the human body related to disease and disorder. *J Biochem* 2011;150(3):257–66.
81. Johnson GR, Morawska L. The mechanism of breath aerosol formation. *J Aerosol Med Pulm Drug Deliv* 2009;22(3):229–37.
82. Moliva JI, Rajaram MV, Sidiki S, Sasindran SJ, Guirado E, Pan XJ, Wang SH, Ross P, Jr., Lafuse WP, Schlesinger LS, Turner J, Torrelles JB. Molecular composition of the alveolar lining fluid in the aging lung. *Age (Dordr)* 2014;36(3):9633.
83. Nkadi PO, Merritt TA, Pillers DA. An overview of pulmonary surfactant in the neonate: genetics, metabolism, and the role of surfactant in health and disease. *Mol Genet Metab* 2009;97(2):95–101.
84. Shelley SA, Balis JU, Paciga JE, Espinoza CG, Richman AV. Biochemical composition of adult human lung surfactant. *Lung* 1982;160(4):195–206.
85. Honeybourne D. Antibiotic penetration into lung tissues. *Thorax* 1994;49(2):104–6.
86. Almstrand AC, Bake B, Ljungstrom E, Larsson P, Bredberg A, Mirgorodskaya E, Olin AC. Effect of airway opening on production of exhaled particles. *J Appl Physiol (1985)* 2010;108(3):584–8.
87. Papineni RS, Rosenthal FS. The size distribution of droplets in the exhaled breath of healthy human subjects. *J Aerosol Med* 1997;10(2):105–16.
88. Fairchild CI, Stampfer JF. Particle concentration in exhaled breath. *Am Ind Hyg Assoc J* 1987;48(11):948–9.
89. Beck O, Sandqvist S, Eriksen P, Franck J, Palmskog G. Determination of methadone in exhaled breath condensate by liquid chromatography-tandem mass spectrometry. *J Anal Toxicol* 2011;35(3):129–33.
90. Kietzmann D, Kahl R, Muller M, Burchardi H, Kettler D. Hydrogen peroxide in expired breath condensate of patients with acute respiratory failure and with ARDS. *Intensive Care Med* 1993;19(2):78–81.
91. Effros RM, Hoagland KW, Bosbous M, Castillo D, Foss B, Dunning M, Gare M, Lin W, Sun F. Dilution of respiratory solutes in exhaled condensates. *Am J Respir Crit Care Med* 2002;165(5):663–9.
92. Konstantinidi EM, Lappas AS, Tzortzi AS, Behrakis PK. Exhaled breath condensate: technical and diagnostic aspects. *ScientificWorldJournal* 2015;2015:435160.
93. Almstrand AC, Ljungstrom E, Lausmaa J, Bake B, Sjovall P, Olin AC. Airway monitoring by collection and mass spectrometric analysis of exhaled particles. *Anal Chem* 2009;81(2):662–8.
94. Beck O, Leine K, Palmskog G, Franck J. Amphetamines detected in exhaled breath from drug addicts: a new possible method for drugs-of-abuse testing. *J Anal Toxicol* 2010;34(5):233–7.
95. Beck O, Sandqvist S, Dubbelboer I, Franck J. Detection of Delta9-tetrahydrocannabinol in exhaled breath collected from cannabis users. *J Anal Toxicol* 2011;35(8):541–4.
96. Beck O. Exhaled breath for drugs of abuse testing - evaluation in criminal justice settings. *Sci Justice* 2014;54(1):57–60.
97. Sensabues AB. SensAbues® - Next generation drug detection and health monitoring. http://sensabues.com (accessed 03.09.2018).
98. Beck O, Stephanson N, Sandqvist S, Franck J. Detection of drugs of abuse in exhaled breath using a device for rapid collection: comparison with plasma, urine and self-reporting in 47 drug users. *J Breath Res* 2013;7(2):026006.
99. Seferaj S, Ullah S, Tinglev A, Carlsson S, Winberg J, Stambeck P, Beck O. Evaluation of a new simple collection device for sampling of microparticles in exhaled breath. *J Breath Res* 2018;12(3):036005.
100. Ljungkvist G, Ullah S, Tinglev A, Stein K, Bake B, Larsson P, Almstrand AC, Viklund E, Hammar O, Sandqvist S, Beck O, Olin AC. Two techniques to sample non-volatiles in breath-exemplified by methadone. *J Breath Res* 2017;12(1):016011.
101. Garzinsky A, Walpurgis K, Krug O, Thevis M. Does oral fluid contribute to exhaled breath samples collected by means of an electret membrane? *Drug Test Anal* 2019.
102. Ellefsen KN, Concheiro M, Beck O, Gorelick DA, Pirard S, Huestis MA. Quantification of cocaine and metabolites in exhaled breath by liquid chromatography-high-resolution mass spectrometry following controlled administration of intravenous cocaine. *Anal Bioanal Chem* 2014;406(25):6213–23.

103. Himes SK, Scheidweiler KB, Beck O, Gorelick DA, Desrosiers NA, Huestis MA. Cannabinoids in exhaled breath following controlled administration of smoked cannabis. *Clin Chem* 2013;59(12):1780–9.
104. Beck O, Sandqvist S, Bottcher M, Eriksen P, Franck J, Palmskog G. Study on the sampling of methadone from exhaled breath. *J Anal Toxicol* 2011;35(5):257–63.
105. Beck O, Sandqvist S, Eriksen P, Franck J, Palmskog G. Method for determination of methadone in exhaled breath collected from subjects undergoing methadone maintenance treatment. *J Chromatogr B Analyt Technol Biomed Life Sci* 2010;878(24):2255–9.
106. Beck O, Stephanson N, Sandqvist S, Franck J. Determination of amphetamine and methylphenidate in exhaled breath of patients undergoing attention-deficit/hyperactivity disorder treatment. *Ther Drug Monit* 2014;36(4):528–34.
107. Meyer MR, Rosenborg S, Stenberg M, Beck O. First report on the pharmacokinetics of tramadol and O-desmethyltramadol in exhaled breath compared to plasma and oral fluid after a single oral dose. *Biochem Pharmacol* 2015;98(3):502–10.
108. Ullah S, Sandqvist S, Beck O. A liquid chromatography and tandem mass spectrometry method to determine 28 non-volatile drugs of abuse in exhaled breath. *J Pharm Biomed Anal* 2018;148:251–8.
109. Bijland LR, Bomers MK, Smulders YM. Smelling the diagnosis: a review on the use of scent in diagnosing disease. *Neth J Med* 2013;71(6):300–7.
110. Buszewski B, Kesy M, Ligor T, Amann A. Human exhaled air analytics: biomarkers of diseases. *Biomed Chromatogr* 2007;21(6):553–66.
111. McCulloch M, Jezierski T, Broffman M, Hubbard A, Turner K, Janecki T. Diagnostic accuracy of canine scent detection in early- and late-stage lung and breast cancers. *Integr Cancer Ther* 2006;5(1):30–9.
112. Wallace MAG, Pleil JD. Evolution of clinical and environmental health applications of exhaled breath research: review of methods and instrumentation for gas-phase, condensate, and aerosols. *Anal Chim Acta* 2018;1024:18–38.
113. Horowitz S. The olfactory sense and its clinical applications. *Altern Complement Ther* 2014;20(3):130–5.
114. Van den Velde S, Nevens F, Van Hee P, van Steenberghe D, Quirynen M. GC-MS analysis of breath odor compounds in liver patients. *J Chromatogr B Analyt Technol Biomed Life Sci* 2008;875(2):344–8.
115. Bevc S, Mohorko E, Kolar M, Brglez P, Holobar A, Kniepeiss D, Podbregar M, Piko N, Hojs N, Knehtl M, Ekart R, Hojs R. Measurement of breath ammonia for detection of patients with chronic kidney disease. *Clin Nephrol* 2017;88(13):14–7.
116. Gilly H. Anasthesiegase: N2O und volatile Anasthetika. In: *Monitoring in Anästhesie und Intensivmedizin*, Metzler H, Pasch T, List WF (eds.) Berlin Heidelberg, 1998.
117. Helander A, Ullah S, Beck O. Phosphatidylethanols in breath: a possible noninvasive screening test for heavy alcohol consumption. *Clin Chem* 2015;61(7):991–3.

5 Genetics in Death Investigations

Section Editors: Loralie J. Langman and Peter T. Lin

CONTENTS

5.1 INTRODUCTION

Genetic testing can be a valuable ancillary tool in the investigation of deaths if ordered under appropriate circumstances and interpreted within the context of what is actually known about the genetic variants found. When used appropriately, genetic testing may reveal the presence of disease that was otherwise undetected by autopsy, scene investigation, and other post-mortem studies. An example of this is the use of genetic testing for the diagnosis of inherited arrhythmia syndromes ("cardiac channelopathies") in sudden unexplained infant and child deaths in which autopsy, scene investigation, and other relevant ancillary studies failed to identify an underlying cause of death. In addition, when the presence of an underlying disease is suspected but not confirmed, genetic testing may be helpful for confirming the diagnosis. For example, genetic testing may be helpful for confirming a diagnosis of arrhythmogenic cardiomyopathy (previously known as arrhythmogenic right ventricular cardiomyopathy) when cardiac morphologic findings overlap between idiopathic dilated cardiomyopathy and arrhythmogenic cardiomyopathy patterns. Even in cases where the cause of death is known, genetic testing may be helpful for identifying risk factors that contributed to death. For example, pharmacogenetic testing may help to explain why an accidental overdose of a prescription medication occurred even though an appropriate dose was administered. Most importantly, in all these applications of genetic testing, there is the possibility that the post-mortem diagnosis of a genetic disease may ultimately help to identify when family members may be at risk and who can be treated to prevent them from suffering the same outcome, thereby achieving the ultimate goal of death investigation – to help the living.

DOI: 10.4324/9781315155159-5

In this chapter, we discuss the general background of post-mortem genetic and genomic testing and provide a detailed discussion of the application of these methods in the investigation of toxicology and cardiovascular disease–related deaths. We also discuss the limitations of genetic testing and caution against attributing too much significance to the results of genetic testing. It is important to recognize that the presence of disease does not necessarily imply that it is the cause of death. Cause of death should be determined only after careful consideration of all available, relevant information from the history, scene investigation, autopsy, toxicology testing, and other relevant ancillary studies, which may include genetic testing. Furthermore, interpretation of genetic test results is particularly challenging due to the continual change in our understanding of the significance of genetic variants, which has led to the reclassification of a number of variants from pathogenic to uncertain to benign, or vice versa. One must also be careful not to blindly accept a laboratory report's interpretation of the significance of a genetic variant, as that interpretation may rely upon flawed or incomplete evidence. Finally, we discuss the role of contemporary genomic approaches to genetic testing, which attempt to apply a more holistic approach to genetic testing by cataloguing all genetic variants present within the genome. By applying these genomic studies on a large scale, there is hope that we may obtain a more precise understanding of the significance of the myriad genetic variants and their interactions with one another.

5.1.1 Genetics, Genomics, and Personalized Medicine

The classical view of the Central Dogma[1–3] postulates that genetic mutations result in phenotypic disease because altered genetic code impairs normal transcription to mRNA and normal translation to protein, such that the normal physiologic processes performed by that protein are disrupted. However, we now recognize that a one-to-one correspondence between a specific genetic mutation and manifestation of disease is too simplistic a paradigm for human disease and does not apply to the most common diseases that afflict humans, such as cancer, hypertension, atherosclerosis, and dementia.[4] Interestingly, a closer correspondence between genetic mutation and disease tends to be observed for relatively rare diseases. The explanation for this apparent inverse relationship between variant pathogenicity and disease frequency is the subject of ongoing debate and has significant implications for devising large-scale strategies to identify pathogenic variants and quantify their effects.[5,6] Another consequence of this inverse relationship is that our most detailed understanding of the role of genetics in human disease concerns relatively rare diseases, such as inherited arrhythmia syndromes ("cardiac channelopathies") and cardiomyopathies.

Even diseases that exhibit classical Mendelian inheritance patterns, such as sickle cell disease[7] and cystic fibrosis,[8] are subject to modifications at the DNA, RNA, and protein levels, recapitulating the well-recognized clinical observation that inheritance of the same mutations in different individuals results in variable expression of disease. Common human diseases are rarely monogenetic in causation but instead typically involve multiple genes and multiple variants within those genes, interacting in concert to produce a wide spectrum of phenotypic disease. Among these genetic variations are so-called single nucleotide polymorphisms (SNPs), which are single nucleotide genetic variations that may not cause disease in themselves but instead, modulate susceptibility to disease by a number of means, such as inhibiting or enhancing transcription, inducing splicing variants, changing translation patterns, protein folding, or acting as a target for other modulating factors. Because these SNPs may potentially affect not only risk of disease onset but also disease course and response to treatment, a genome-wide catalogue of SNPs within an individual offers the promise of a truly personalized form of medicine, whereby a comprehensive assessment of all genetic variations within an individual might provide a detailed risk assessment for disease onset, a roadmap for expected disease course, and a detailed prescription for tailored therapy (i.e., "precision medicine"). However, our current limited state of understanding of the significance of the vast number of SNPs, and how those variations may or may not have downstream consequences for the expression of disease, is a major obstacle to achieving a truly personalized practice of medicine. To date, numerous genome-wide association studies that attempt to correlate SNPs with common diseases have identified a small number of variations that can account for only an estimated 5–10% of the heritable component of common diseases.[5]

Further complicating simplistic genotype–phenotype correlations are so-called epigenetic mechanisms, which are heritable modifications of genetic expression that do not involve modification of the genetic code itself. Epigenetic modifications are especially fascinating because they can be modified in response to environmental factors *and* they have been shown to be inheritable across multiple generations, though the strength of the evidence for transgenerational inheritability in mammals is still somewhat controversial.[9] This combination of environmental adaptability and transgenerational inheritability represents a fundamental paradigm shift from the classical view of the Central Dogma, which holds that inheritable information only travels in one direction, from gene to protein. An example of such an epigenetic modification is DNA methylation, whereby a methyl group is bonded to cytosine residues within certain segments of DNA. Generally, the presence of a methyl group on certain segments of DNA results in reduced transcription of nearby genes, though the mechanism for transcriptional repression remains uncertain.[10] Another mechanism of epigenetic modification involves acetylation of histones, which are proteins around which DNA is normally wrapped in a tight complex that inhibits transcription. Acetylation of histones decreases histone affinity for DNA, thereby loosening the complex and increasing availability for DNA binding by transcription factors.[11] Conversely, de-acetylation of histones inhibits transcription activity. Inhibitors of DNA methyltransferases[12] and histone deacetylases[13] are currently active epigenetic pharmacotherapeutic agents for cancer and may potentially play a role in epigenetically modified cardiovascular disease as well.[14,15] Epigenetic modifications have also been observed in the setting of substance abuse, such as in the hyper-methylation of lymphocyte DNA in chronic alcoholics compared with normal controls, though it is unclear whether these changes are secondary to substance abuse or reflect an epigenetically modified susceptibility to substance abuse.[16]

Another mechanism of genetic regulation that results in the wide spectrum of phenotypic variability is genetic regulation via non-coding RNAs. Within the framework of the traditional Central Dogma, messenger RNA provides the working template (itself derived from the DNA code) to produce multiple copies of proteins, and another form of RNA known as transfer RNA (tRNA) facilitates the translation of the mRNA into protein. However, yet another class of RNA has been discovered, which serves primarily to regulate gene expression rather than to act as a template for protein synthesis or to facilitate translation. This large and growing class of RNA is now known as non-coding RNAs and includes micro RNAs, small interfering RNAs, and long non-coding RNAs. The known mechanisms of action of these non-coding RNAs are numerous, involving binding to complementary sequences on messenger RNA to target for degradation,[17] enhancement or repression of translation, or in the case of very large non-coding RNAs, changing the conformational structure of chromatin.[18] Numerous studies have demonstrated that these non-coding RNAs play an important role in managing normal and pathophysiologic processes, including regulating the response to environmental stressors such as substance abuse, and likely play an important role in the development of addiction.[19] Because of their continual up-regulation and down-regulation in different physiologic states, circulating microRNAs may be useful as biomarkers for diseases such as cancer and cardiovascular diseases.[20] Technology that allows the synthesis of large quantities of nucleic acid strands that can inhibit or enhance the activity of non-coding RNAs has created a new area of pharmacotherapy that targets the activity of non-coding RNAs.[21]

Given the numerous mechanisms for modification of gene expression described here, including but not limited to SNPs, epigenetic modifications, and non-coding RNAs, and the inherent difficulty in quantifying the effects of environmental factors, it should not be a surprise that genetic variations do not manifest as uniform disease with a one-to-one concordance, and by implication, a catalogue of only genetic variations is unlikely to fully explain the phenotypic spectrum of disease. Rather, a complete catalogue of the human genome, epigenome, transcriptome, proteome, microbiome, and numerous other "-omes" will be required. And perhaps even more challenging will be the systematic collection of the human phenome – that is, a complete catalogue of human phenotypic data. However, as discussed later, now is an opportune time to begin this enterprise, which will likely require the course of several generations.

5.1.2 Phenotypic Data

Technological advances in our ability to examine genetic material more efficiently and rapidly, such as next-generation sequencing, have dramatically reduced the cost of producing a high-quality draft human genome from approximately $14 million dollars in 2006 to under $1,500 in 2016.[22] It seems inevitable that the ability to sequence one's genome at an affordable price will become reality within the next decade. This incredible technological feat has brought the promise of great advances in our understanding of disease and our ability to treat and prevent it. However, a number of significant obstacles have yet to be overcome before that vision can be realized. Perhaps the most significant obstacle is that our ability to sequence the genome has progressed at a much faster rate than our ability to understand the significance of the many genetic variants discovered. Significant uncertainty often arises when attempting to distinguish between pathogenic and benign genetic variants, resulting in a nebulous categorization as variants of uncertain significance.[23] The uncertainty is particularly problematic in scenarios where the clinical phenotype in question is without widely accepted diagnostic criteria or represents a variety of etiologically non-specific disease states. Furthermore, the role of environmental factors as a modifier of genetic susceptibility to disease is difficult to quantify without large-scale epidemiological studies.

The process of phenotyping genetic variants is slow and laborious, involving comparison with various population databases, application of multiple computer prediction models to assess predicted conformational changes (in which each model may produce differing results), *in vivo* and *ex vivo* functional studies of the altered protein, examination of disease and variant segregation patterns within large family trees, and a detailed literature search for relevant studies and case reports.[23] Determining the pathogenicity of previously unreported rare variants is especially challenging and requires consideration of conservation across different species, nearby variants, and application of advanced statistical genetics.[24] And even then, the final determination of pathogenicity is often of questionable significance without additional clinical data. But of course, clinical data itself is quite often vague, misleading, or inaccurate, which may lead to a mistaken interpretation of the pathogenicity of a variant. Ultimately, no single method is dispositive as to the pathogenicity of a genetic variant, and the categorization based on the totality of available information is in the end, an opinion rather than a fact – an opinion that may vary between individuals, groups, and laboratories, and is subject to change as additional information comes to light (not unlike the determination of the cause and manner of death by medical examiners). While significant progress has been achieved in the interpretation of many genetic variants, many more are being discovered at a faster rate than can be processed by the community of medical geneticists, molecular pathologists, basic scientists, and others involved with the classification of genetic variants.

Even if all genetic variants could be systematically and accurately assessed at a molecular and cellular level, that data must still be correlated with observed clinical data. This correlation cannot occur without a systematic method for characterizing the so-called human phenome – the set of all phenotypic manifestations for a single individual throughout a lifetime, including significant temporal and causal relationships between diseases, treatments, and complications. Without a large database of well-characterized phenomes to provide correlation, genomic data is largely uninterpretable as a whole. The recently announced National Institutes of Health (NIH)–sponsored Precision Medicine Initiative[25] represents such an attempt to match our rapidly increasing knowledge of the molecular and cellular basis of disease with our existing and evolving body of clinical knowledge of health and disease by systematically collecting genetic, transcriptomic, proteomic, and clinical data on at least one million volunteers. Private–public partnerships are also essential for this initiative[26] in consideration of the growing number of commercial companies now performing genetic testing and the economic incentives for commercial testing companies to keep their private databases of genetic variants secret.[27]

Despite these daunting challenges, now is an opportune time to start such a systematic collection of clinical data due to the increasingly wide-spread use of electronic medical records and the burgeoning field of clinical informatics and artificial intelligence. The government-incentivized use of electronic medical records within hospitals and clinics offers the possibility of large-scale, systematic collection of clinical data, including but not limited to clinical course, laboratory, imaging, and clinical genetic tests. An NIH-sponsored initiative known as eMERGE has already begun systematically collecting such electronic medical record data from a consortium of clinical institutions while addressing the necessary ethical and regulatory issues, such as the need to maintain patient confidentiality and provide a mechanism for informing patients of genetic findings that may have clinical impact.[28] But the collection of all of this data is only a prelude to the more challenging task of interpreting it, especially in consideration of the fact that much of the data may be incorrect, incomplete, or misleading. The analysis of this data may require the use of machine learning methods that are more adept than the human mind at drawing associations in very large amounts of imperfect data.

Clearly, if progress is to be made in this endeavor, it is imperative that the data that is collected is verified to be true to the greatest extent possible. To this end, an extremely valuable tool for collecting and verifying phenotypic data is unfortunately largely neglected as a component of the Precision Medicine Initiative, namely, the autopsy. While the medical record is a rich resource for clinical data, much of that data may be uncertain or incorrect. Death certificate data is also notoriously filled with errors due to improper training of providers on how to fill out death certificates and is not a proxy for the actual cause of death and the presence of other significant diseases and injuries detected at autopsy. The autopsy, including a comprehensive review of medical history, is the most complete diagnostic procedure available and an invaluable tool for confirming or refuting what is in the medical record and determining the presence or absence of disease as well as the actual cause of death. When death certificates are supported by autopsy data and filled out by pathologists who have also reviewed the medical record, the cause of death is much more accurate.[29–31] In order to have the most precise phenotypic data to correlate with genomic data, it would seem prudent to also perform autopsies on patients who have been genotyped and reconsider a better strategy for systematically obtaining quality cause of death data. Ultimately, the most useful information will be gained through very long-term longitudinal studies over the course of lifetimes across multiple generations. In view of the very long-term nature of such a project, the time of death would be an opportune time to collect phenotypic data as well as to collect tissue for additional "-omic" studies. Unfortunately, largely due to lack of reimbursement for autopsies, inadequate training of pathologists in autopsy performance, and general over-confidence in the reliability of clinical diagnosis, the non-forensic hospital autopsy is rapidly becoming a lost art.[32,33]

5.1.3 Determining the Cause of Death

Before embarking on a discussion of the role of postmortem genetic testing in death investigation, it would be helpful to briefly review the organization of the death investigation system in the United States and how cause of death is determined.

Medical examiners and coroners in the United States are responsible for investigating and certifying the cause and manner of sudden, unexpected, unusual, and unnatural deaths. Medical examiners are trained physicians (M.D. or D.O.) who have received specialty training in anatomic pathology and forensic pathology, which is a medical field concerned with the investigation of deaths, both natural and unnatural. Most deaths investigated by medical examiner offices are natural deaths, representing slightly over 50% of cases in many large offices.[34] In the United States, coroners are usually appointed or elected officials who may have no training in medicine and yet are responsible for certifying the cause of death, even though the process of determining the cause of death is very similar to arriving at clinical diagnosis, which would be considered the practice of medicine in a living person. Government-sponsored systematic reviews of the death investigation system in the United States have repeatedly recommended the conversion of coroner systems to medical examiner systems,[35] but the lack of sufficient funding and a shortage of board-certified forensic pathologists remain lasting obstacles.[36]

The cause of death is defined as the etiologically specific disease or injury that initiates the chain of events leading to death. An unfortunate and common misconception among clinicians is that the cause of death is the final pathophysiological state preceding death, such as multi-organ failure, cardiac arrhythmia, sepsis, or respiratory failure. This final physiological state is the *mechanism of death*, not the *cause* of death, and is usually non-specific and not very informative as to the true underlying cause of death. The pathophysiological state that immediately precedes the mechanism of death, such as bronchopneumonia, urinary tract infection, or pulmonary embolism, while informative, is also not etiologically specific and requires a continued search for an underlying cause. When one seeks to determine the cause of death, one should seek to determine the *initial* disease or injury that started the chain of events leading to death. Therefore, the thought process generally proceeds backwards until an etiologically specific cause is found.[37] Each successive condition between the initial disease and death represents a complication of the initial disease. While there is significant value in describing the sequence of events leading to death, the ultimate purpose of the death certificate is to cite the underlying cause of death. To list multiple complications, while omitting the underlying cause, defeats the purpose and validity of the death certificate. In the case of natural deaths, when an etiologically specific cause of death is sought in such a manner, the underlying cause is quite frequently related to hypertensive and atherosclerotic cardiovascular disease, cancer, or dementia.

The cause of death is an opinion based on all available information. However, the amount of information available is directly proportional to the amount of effort expended in collecting information. Therefore, a cause of death is more likely to be undetermined when only cursory effort has been expended in performing the autopsy, scene investigation, ancillary studies, and obtaining specialty consultations. Unfortunately, within the United States, the death investigation system remains a patchwork of local and state jurisdictions with markedly differing standards, practices, and administrative structures. A death that is considered unexplained in one jurisdiction may be considered explained in an adjacent jurisdiction due to differing thresholds for death certification and differing levels of effort expended to search for elusive causes of death. However, even when all appropriate studies and consultations have been performed, the cause of death may still remain elusive and may be subject to differing opinions. Post-mortem genetic testing may be a valuable ancillary test in the investigation of this category of unexplained deaths.

5.1.4 Post-Mortem Genetic Testing

DNA technology has long played an important role in death investigation and forensic science. One of the first real-world applications of DNA technology was in identifying a suspect in a murder-rape investigation in Leicestershire, United Kingdom in the 1980s.[38] DNA also plays a critical role in exonerating suspects and convicts. The application of highly sensitive, low–copy number DNA technology has expanded the potential usage of DNA technology in criminal investigation beyond homicides and sexual crimes to encompass property crimes and other lesser crimes where usable DNA profiles may be obtained from scant traces of DNA left by perpetrators through simple touching of objects at the scene, though there is a higher risk for contamination and other artifacts.[39,40] Genetic testing also plays an important role as a method of identification for bodies that are not otherwise identifiable due to extensive trauma or decomposition. More recently, DNA technology is becoming increasingly important as a tool for assisting in the determination of the cause of death.

Overall, approximately 1–10% of forensic autopsies do not reveal a cause of death even after appropriate ancillary studies have been performed.[41] This percentage is higher in infants, children, young adults, and those with seizure disorders. A prospective study of sudden cardiac death in children and young adults up to age 35 in Australia and New Zealand reported that 40% of deaths remained unexplained after complete autopsy, histologic, and toxicologic studies. In this study, genetic testing was performed, and a clinically relevant gene mutation was identified in 31 of 113 cases (27%) of unexplained sudden cardiac death.[42] However, differing mutation yield rates are likely to be seen depending on the case selection process for genetic testing and the process used for variant interpretation.[43]

5.1.5 Specimen Retention for Post-Mortem Genetic Testing

Retention of blood and/or tissue at the time of autopsy for potential genetic testing is highly recommended. If it is not practical to retain specimens on all cases, at least selected cases of sudden unexpected death in infants, children, and young adults up to approximately age 40 should be retained. Specimens from decedents with suspected genetic diseases such as inherited cardiomyopathies, aortopathies, and arrhythmia syndromes should also be retained. Unexplained drowning deaths and sudden deaths in athletes are additional categories where genetic testing may eventually be sought.

An ideal specimen would be 5–10 mL of whole blood in a preservative tube (EDTA, purple-top tube), refrigerated (short term) or frozen at −70 °C (long term). The storage times for blood should be significant (at least 1 year, preferably several years or indefinitely) but will be dictated by local storage capacities and policies.[44] A blood spot card may be an adequate alternative or supplement to retained blood. Whole-exome or genome sequencing will likely be possible on blood spot cards in the near future.[45] Formalin-fixed, paraffin-embedded tissue may also soon be amenable to whole-exome or whole-genome sequencing, although blood or fresh frozen tissue is still preferable.[46]

5.2 PHARMACOGENOMICS IN POST-MORTEM TOXICOLOGY

5.2.1 Background

Toxicology is a broad, multidisciplinary science whose goal is to determine the effects of chemical agents on living systems. Innumerable potential toxins can inflict harm, including pharmaceuticals, herbals, household products, environmental agents, occupational chemicals, drugs of abuse (DOAs), and chemical terrorism threats. The Centers for Disease Control has reported that poisoning (both intentional and unintentional) is one of the top ten causes of injury-related death in the United States in all adult age groups. From the beginnings of written history, poisons and their effects have been well described. Paracelsus (1493–1541) correctly noted that "Alle Dinge sind Gift, und nichts ist ohne Gift; allein die Dosis macht, daß ein Ding kein Gift sei," which means "Everything is a poison; there is nothing which is not. Only the dose differentiates a poison."[47]

An expansion of Paracelsus's statement might be that the "right dose" for one individual may not be the "right dose" or even the right drug for another due to differences in each individual's genetic makeup. The determination of what is the "right dose" and in some cases, what is even the right drug for a given individual constitutes the reason for the development of the sciences of pharmacogenetics (PGx) and pharmacogenomics.

The beginning of pharmacogenetics can be traced to early observations in the 1950s, when it was realized that the antimalarial drug primaquine caused intravascular hemolysis in about 10% of African Americans but rarely among Caucasians. A deficiency of glucose-6-phosphate dehydrogenase was identified as the cause of this disparate response.[48] In addition, some patients experienced prolonged neuromuscular paralysis following succinylcholine anesthesia due to deficiencies in human butyrylcholinesterase (BChE), also called serum cholinesterase or pseudocholinesterase.[49,50] Individual differences in the metabolism of the tuberculosis drug isoniazid could be classified as rapid or slow acetylators.[51,52] Recent years have seen a great deal of interest and research dedicated towards pharmacogenetics and pharmacogenomics.

Although the terms are often used interchangeably,[53] there are subtle differences between pharmacogenetics and pharmacogenomics. In general, pharmacogenomics refers to the study of many different genes that determine drug behavior, and pharmacogenetics refers to the study of inherited variations in drug metabolism and response (www.mlo-online.com/pharmacogenomics-pharmacogenetics-and-scientific-research.php accessed August 13, 2016). Interestingly, the differentiation of these two terms is linked to the technology employed. Commercially available kits for common clinical laboratory testing of specific genetic variations in drug enzymes or receptors are an example of pharmacogenetic tests. Alternatively, microarray technologies that evaluate many genes are considered pharmacogenomic tests. As the technology of molecular testing improves, the availability of testing is bolstered, the cost burden is eased, and certified clinical laboratories have the ability to perform more pharmacogenomic testing. Regardless, both terms are used to refer to heritable variability in the processes of pharmacokinetics (PK) – what the body does to the drug – and pharmacodynamics (PD) – what the drug does to the body. Pharmacogenetic studies have addressed the importance of genetic variation in areas such as individual susceptibility to addiction, preference for a given DOA, or ability to cease drug use.[54]

A full description of the practice of pharmacogenetics in clinical medicine is beyond the scope of this chapter. Please refer to the many textbooks and textbook chapters that have been devoted to this topic.

This section will briefly discuss pharmacogenetic knowledge relevant to some of the major PK and PD pathways and to the debate surrounding the so-called "genetic gap" between heritability predictions and identified associations.

5.2.1.1 Importance of Pharmacogenetics to Variability in Drug Response

It is widely recognized that a genotype refers to one's unique inherited structural makeup (genetic code), and a phenotype refers to the observable physical manifestation of one's genotype through a composite of biological influences. Clearly, many factors influence a phenotype, and indeed, individuals with differing genotypes can be phenotypically similar. Therefore, the manifestation of a biological phenotype defining a drug response is dynamic and considered to be multifactorial. That is, an individual's response to a drug depends on a combination of environmental factors and genetic factors.[55] Environmental factors are inextricably intertwined with pharmacogenetics – individuals who are never exposed to a DOA cannot become dependent upon it, regardless of the strength of their genetic predisposition toward addiction,[54] which creates a great deal of complexity for clinicians attempting to address individual differences in drug response or treatment. Not surprisingly, many clinicians feel unprepared to interpret genetic information.[56]

In addition to the difficulty presented by the complex gene–environment relationship, the typical concerns related to genetic studies must be considered, including differences in experimental strategies, study populations, and gene variants. The prevalence of any given variant can be vastly different between ethnic groups; there are numerous instances of alleles that are rare in one population being quite common in a different group.[57,58]

5.2.2 Pharmacokinetics and Pharmacodynamics

In order to understand and control the therapeutic action of drugs in the human body, one must know how much drug will reach the site(s) of drug action and when this will occur. The absorption, distribution, metabolism (biotransformation), and elimination of drugs (often referred to collectively as ADME) are the processes of pharmacokinetics.[59]

Together, these steps describe what the body does to a drug from initial entry of the compound until it is removed in waste. In contrast, pharmacodynamics is the study of the biochemical and physiological effects of drugs and their mechanisms of action.[60]

5.2.2.1 Pharmacokinetics

Although genetic variation can have an effect on both PK and PD, the most studied variations are those involved in the processes of pharmacokinetics. Within PK, the greatest pharmacogenetic knowledge exists regarding polymorphisms in metabolic enzymes and drug transporters. The most commonly studied metabolic enzymes are the CYPs, but clinically important genetic variations have also been characterized in uridine diphosphate glucuronyltransferases (UGTs), esterases, and other enzyme families.[61] By comparison, drug transporters are less well-characterized, but there is great interest in the role of P-glycoprotein (P-gp, encoded by *ABCBI/MDR1*) and related proteins, which mediate drug entry into and exit from target sites. Metabolic enzymes and drug transporters affect virtually all aspects of PK.

Common features of these PGx targets include:

- The enzyme of interest is the primary pathway for metabolism of the drug.
- Changes in enzyme activity resulting from the polymorphism have a significant effect on the relationship between dose and plasma concentration.
- The efficacy and/or toxicity of the drug correlate with changes in plasma concentration.
- The drugs affected have a narrow therapeutic index.

Each process in PK is subject to both environmental and genetic variability.

5.2.2.1.1 Cytochrome P450 Enzymes

Probably among the best studied are the cytochrome P450 (CYPs) enzymes (the 450 being derived from the cytochrome's maximal absorbance of light at 450 nm). These are a superfamily of enzymes, all of which contain a molecule of heme that is non-covalently bound to the polypeptide chain. The enzymes require reduced nicotinamide adenine dinucleotide phosphate (NADPH) as a cofactor to carry out the oxidation of substrates. The H^+ is supplied through the enzyme NADPH-cytochrome P450 oxidoreductase (POR).[62] The CYPs are categorized according to amino acid sequence homology.

More than 50 individual CYPs have been identified in humans,[62] but only a few are known to be important for the metabolism of drugs. The liver expresses the greatest abundance of these proteins, thus contributing to first-pass metabolism. CYPs are also expressed throughout the gastrointestinal (GI) tract and in lower amounts in lung, in kidney, and even in the central nervous system (CNS).[62] The expression of the different CYPs can differ markedly as a result of dietary and environmental exposure to inducers or through inter-individual changes resulting from heritable polymorphic differences in gene structure; tissue-specific expression patterns can affect overall drug metabolism and clearance.[62] Their complete description is beyond the scope of this section; however, the CYPs that are important to human drug metabolism are discussed in the following subsections.

5.2.2.1.1.1 CYP2D6 *CYP2D6* is one of the most polymorphic genes of pharmacogenetic relevance, with over 100 different alleles described (www.cypalleles.ki.se/cyp2d6.htm, accessed September 10, 2016). The enzyme is involved in the metabolism of roughly 25% of drugs, including nicotine and some opioids; various genotypes result in an extremely wide range of phenotypes ranging from null alleles (no enzyme activity) to expression many-fold higher than average.[57,63,64]

There are significant ethnic differences in the frequency of *CYP2D6* variants; one of the most important PM alleles, *CYP2D6*4*, is present in 12–21% of individuals of Northern European descent but is found in only 1–2% of Asians and Black Africans.[65] Some variants can be quite common, as seen with *CYP2D6*10*, which confers an intermediate metabolizer (IM) phenotype and is present in 57% of Han Chinese.[66,67]

Individuals designated as wild type are called CYP2D6*1, meaning that no polymorphisms, deletions, or duplications are identified, and are given the phenotype of an extensive drug metabolizer (normal). The major CYP2D6 alleles included are outlined in Table 5.1.

Depending on the combination of genotypes, the predicted phenotype, enzymatic activity, of CYP2D6 varies

TABLE 5.1
Enzyme Activity of Individual Star Alleles

Enzyme activity	Examples of CYP2D6 star alleles
Extensive metabolism (normal)	*1, *35
Increased activity	*2A
Decreased activity	*2, *9, *10, *14B, *17, *29, *41
Negligible activity	*36
No or null activity	*3, *4, * *5, *6, *7, *8, *11, *12, *13, *14A, *15, *68

TABLE 5.2
Phenotype Assignment of CYP2D6

Predicted Drug Metabolizer Phenotype[a]	Without Gene Duplication
UM	Two increased activity alleles Gene duplication of functional alleles
EM	Two normal activity alleles; a combination of one increased activity allele with one decreased allele
IM	One normal activity allele with one null activity allele; two decreased activity alleles
PM	Only null alleles detected

[a] Ultra-rapid metabolizer, UM; extensive metabolizer, EM; intermediate metabolizer, IM; poor metabolizer, PM.

greatly between individuals. CYP2D6 phenotype may be predicted based upon the number of functional, partially functional, and non-functional alleles present in a sample; a simplified version is outlined in Table 5.2. The resulting enzymatic activity allows individuals to be categorized into poor (PM), intermediate (IM), extensive (EM), and ultra-rapid (UM) metabolizers.[68]

However, it is critical to remember that individuals without a detectable gene alteration will have the predicted phenotype of an extensive drug metabolizer and are designated as CYP2D6 *1/*1, in other words, a designation by exclusion. This means that the assigned genotype can vary depending on the technology used and the SNPs looked for. For example, if the method used does not identify *41 (decreased activity), then an individual would be called *1.

Important drugs impacted by CYP2D6 metabolism include codeine, tramadol, oxycodone, and hydrocodone.[69–72] Codeine has only about one-tenth the analgesic potency of morphine and shows poor affinity for mu receptor (MOR), with only a fraction of the pain-relieving capacity of morphine; therefore, it is generally considered a prodrug.[73] Analgesia is attributed to the small fraction (<10%) of codeine converted to morphine by CYP2D6 via O-demethylation by CYP2D6.[74] Individuals who are CYP2D6 poor metabolizers are less able to convert codeine to morphine by CYP2D6-mediated demethylation, and as a result, these individuals do not experience morphine's analgesic effects but are likely to experience parent drug side effects.[69,70] Conversely, individuals who are CYP2D6 ultra-rapid metabolizers rapidly and effectively convert codeine to morphine, and as a result, these individuals are more likely to experience excessive morphine effects and toxicities from the effects of the metabolite.[69,70]

The most difficult group in which to predict enzyme activity is the IM phenotype, a distinct population subgroup comprising those with impaired but detectable residual enzyme activity. The cause of this phenotype cannot be explained solely by a reduced gene dose, because most individuals carrying only one functional allele appear to be metabolically normal.[64,75] Traditionally, individuals were classified as EM or IM based on the metabolic activity of a few "probe drugs," often bufuralol, dextromethorphan, codeine, or metoprolol. In a study by Yu et al., it was found that individuals with the **2*,**10*, and **17* alleles had impaired metabolism of: dextromethorphan *O*-demethylation, codeine *O*-demethylation, and fluoxetine *N*-demethylation. However, for the *N*-demethylation of dextromethorphan, the kinetics mediated by *2 were similar to **1*, and for **10* and **17*, the kinetics were less impaired compared with the *O*-demethylation reactions. This suggests that changes in kinetics caused by allelic variation may be reaction type and substrate dependent.[76] To make it more complex, studies by Bogni et al.[77] suggest that "generalizations" regarding the activity profile of the *CYP2D6* alleles based on a small number of probe drugs may be inaccurate. Needless to say, this has not been studied for the majority of drugs. This brings into question the non-selective genotyping of individual or cases.

5.2.2.1.1.2 Other CYPs

5.2.2.1.1.2.1 CYP3A On the protein level, as well as because of its involvement in the metabolism of 35–50% of all drugs, the CYP3A subfamily is of major importance. The human P-450 3A subfamily contains three members: P-450s 3A4, 3A5, and 3A7.[78] P-450 3A4 probably has the broadest catalytic selectivity and is the most abundant P-450 expressed in human liver and small intestine. P-450 contributes to the metabolism of approximately half of the therapeutic and abused drugs in use today.[79] There are fewer relevant polymorphisms in these genes, although a substantial fraction of the population (up to 90% in Caucasians) carries the *CYP3A5*3* null allele and therefore does not express CYP3A5.[58] However, environmental regulation of this system appears to trump genetic variation, and a wide array of enzyme inducers and inhibitors have been identified for CYP3A4/5.[80]

5.2.2.1.1.2.2 CYP2C The CYP2C family includes the clinically relevant 2C9 and 2C19. More than 100 currently used drugs have been identified as substrates of CYP2C9 by biochemical analysis, corresponding to about 10% to 20% of commonly prescribed drugs. More than 50 SNPs have been described in the regulatory and coding regions of the *CYP2C9* gene, but only 2 coding variants, termed *CYP2C9*2* and *CYP2C9*3*, with functional consequence are common, having allele frequencies of around 11% (*2) and 7% (**3*).[81] However, the clinical consequences of *CYP2C9* polymorphisms have been investigated for only some drugs,[82] the most studied of which is warfarin. Ultimately, both pharmacokinetic and pharmacodynamic polymorphisms affect warfarin dosing. The anticoagulant activity of warfarin is mediated by polymorphism in the metabolic enzyme (*CYP2C9*) and a drug target (*VKORC1*).[83,84]

CYP2C19 participates in the metabolism of a wide variety of drugs, including the activation of the anticoagulant clopidogrel and the inactivation of citalopram.[85] The frequency of poor metabolizer *CYP2C19* polymorphisms depends on ethnicity. Interestingly, *17 is associated with increased enzyme activity and enhanced metabolism of drugs.[86]

Other CYP enzymes are important in the metabolism of individual DOAs, including CYP2A6, which metabolizes nicotine, and CYP2B6, which metabolizes methadone.[63,80] Most CYP genes have polymorphisms described in the literature, although the clinical significance varies greatly depending on the prevalence of alleles with altered function as well as the contribution of that particular enzyme to the drug in question. An example of this is *CYP2B6* polymorphism in relation to methadone metabolism: mutant alleles are relatively common and typically decrease enzyme activity.[57] However, although CYP2B6 is generally the dominant enzyme in methadone metabolism, there are alternate biotransformation pathways that may mask any effect of *CYP2B6* reduced-function alleles.[87]

5.2.2.1.2 ABCB1

The distribution phase of pharmacokinetics can be dependent on drug transporters, particularly as concerns the blood–brain barrier (BBB). ABCB1 (adenosine triphosphate–binding cassette subfamily B member 1), also known as P-glycoprotein or multidrug resistance protein 1 (MDR1) or cluster of differentiation 243 (CD243), acts as a transmembrane efflux pump involved in energy-dependent export of xenobiotics from inside the cell.[88,89] The specific tissue expression of ABCB1 suggests that it functions as a protective barrier, which ultimately affects drug absorption from the gut and distribution among body compartments as well as metabolism and excretion.[89–91] ACBC1 is extensively distributed and expressed in the intestinal epithelium, where it pumps xenobiotics (such as toxins or drugs) back into the intestinal lumen; in liver cells, where it pumps them into bile ducts; in the cells of the proximal tubule of the kidney, where it pumps them into urine-conducting ducts; and in the capillary endothelial cells comprising the blood–brain barrier and blood–testis barrier, where it pumps them back into the capillaries.[92]

ACBC1 and related proteins serve to enforce the distribution barrier between the CNS and the systemic circulation; thus, altered function of these drug transporters can easily result in unexpected consequences due to atypical drug distribution. An excellent example of this is seen with loperamide, an opioid anti-diarrheal agent which normally does not efficiently pass the BBB and therefore does not have the CNS effects (e.g., respiratory depression) associated with opioids. Lack of ACBC1 function during the administration of loperamide can induce respiratory depression due to the inability to exclude the drug from the CNS.[93] As with *CYP*s, environmental effects that can have an effect on gene transcription and enzyme activity (inhibition or inhibition) typically predominate over the influence of SNPs.[94]

5.2.2.1.3 Alcohol Dehydrogenase and Aldehyde Dehydrogenase

Two of the earliest and best-characterized examples of metabolic enzymes affecting drug abuse are the genes encoding alcohol dehydrogenase (ADH) and aldehyde dehydrogenase (ALDH), both essential in the conversion of ethanol to ultimately, acetic acid.[95,96]

5.2.2.1.3.1 Alcohol Dehydrogenase ADH is part a group of dehydrogenase enzymes that occur in many organisms and facilitate the biotransformation of alcohols with the reduction of nicotinamide adenine dinucleotide (NAD^+ to NADH). Specifically, this enzyme promotes the metabolism of ethanol to acetaldehyde. In humans, ADH is divided into five classes (I–V), where Class I enzymes are the class mainly involved in the metabolism of ethanol. Class I consists of α, β, and γ subunits that are encoded by the genes ADH-1A, ADH-1B, and ADH-1C.[97]

Clinically significant polymorphisms with altered affinity for ethanol and altered metabolic activity are described, the best studied of which include *ADH-1B*2* (His47Arg) and the *ADH-1B*3* (Arg369Cys). These alleles are associated with high activity (>30-fold higher than normal) and therefore, a rapid conversion of ethanol to acetaldehyde. ADH-1B*2 is present in 85% of Asians and is expressed to a lesser degree in Caucasians, Native Americans, and Asian Indians.[98] The ADH1B*3 allele is most common in Native American and African populations.[99]

5.2.2.1.3.2 Aldehyde Dehydrogenase At least 19 putative genes and several pseudogenes are included in the ALDH gene superfamily, yet just ALDH-I (chromosome 9, cytosolic) and ALDH-2 (chromosome 12, mitochondrial) are associated specifically with acetaldehyde oxidation and ethanol metabolism. *ALDH-2*2* (Glu487Lys), common to several ethnic populations, leads to reduced activity and like *ADH-IB*2*, is associated with accumulation of acetaldehyde following alcohol intake. Promoter variants in ALDH-I (*ALDH-IAl*2*, a 17-bp deletion, and *ALDH-IAl*3*, a 3-bp insertion) are associated with reduced expression of ALDH. All these ALDH alleles are associated with accumulation of acetaldehyde.

The ADH-1B*2 and ALDH-2*2 alleles are common, and individuals who inherit the combination of a rapid-metabolizing ADH allele and the impaired-metabolizing ALDH alleles have a particularly reduced risk for alcoholism due to the accumulation of acetaldehyde, which is aversive for alcohol intake. Interestingly, the phenotype mimics the pharmacological effect of the drug disulfiram, which is used in the treatment of alcohol addiction.[99]

5.2.2.1.4 Other Pharmacogenetic Targets

There are a number of other target enzymes, both confirmed and theoretical, whose genetic variability could play a role in metabolism of various DOAs. For example, butyrylcholinesterase (also called pseudocholinesterase) is present in the metabolic cascades of both cocaine (to benzoylecgonine) and heroin (to 6-acetylmorphine).[100] Partial or complete deficiency of this enzyme could prolong the CNS effects of both these drugs, potentially affecting an individual's risk of addiction or negative response. Although just a few genes encoding metabolic enzymes have been conclusively associated with effects, given the rich complexity of drug metabolism, it is likely that current studies have only begun to address the contributions of this area to DOA pharmacogenetics.

5.2.2.2 Pharmacodynamics

The flip side to PK is PD – the effects a drug has on the body. This includes not only the receptor responsible for binding a given drug but also the downstream signaling, regulatory processes, gene transcription, and interacting signaling pathways. Most DOAs affect one or more of the neural pathways involved in mediating reward, particularly those relating to monoamine neurotransmitter and opioid receptor signaling.[101] PD responses to different DOAs display a great deal of overlap and crosstalk.

5.2.2.2.1 Monoamine Neurotransmitter System

Some of the most important neurological pathways implicated in substance abuse are those regulated by monoamine neurotransmitters such as dopamine and serotonin.[96,101]

The monoaminergic neurotransmitters act as messengers throughout various regions of the nervous system and function in aspects pertinent to addiction, including impulse control, behavior modulation, reward response, and positive motivation.

Many DOAs affect the release and/or regulation of monoamines at the synapse; most commonly abused stimulants exert a great deal of their pharmacological activity through this mechanism. Dopamine in particular has been associated strongly with the reinforcing properties of cocaine, amphetamines, and other stimulants, with lesser (though still significant) roles ascribed to other monoamines.[101–104] Monoaminergic signaling is thus essential in the development of addiction to cocaine and other stimulants that directly affect one or more components of the system, but intriguingly, monoamines also play an indirect role in addiction to non-stimulant DOAs, including alcohol.

The regulation of monoaminergic signaling is quite complex and can be altered at a variety of levels by genetic or environmental influences. Neuronal transporter proteins are responsible for controlling release and reuptake and are therefore essential in modulating synaptic neurotransmitter levels. The presynaptic neuron synthesizes and stores monoamine neurotransmitters until it is stimulated to release them into the synaptic cleft; from there, they may be reclaimed by reuptake transporters on the presynaptic neuron or bound by receptors on the postsynaptic neuron.[105] Because of this, both monoamine receptors and transporters have been the targets of human genetic analyses in the study of addiction. Studies have tentatively linked aspects of substance abuse and potentially, response to gene variants in all stages from beginning to end of this process. Examples include enzymes involved in monoamine synthesis (tryptophan hydroxylase, *TPH1/2*) and catalysis (dopamine hydroxylase, *DβH*, and catechol-*o*-methyl transferase, *COMT*); monoamine transporters (dopamine and serotonin transporters, *SLC6A3* and *SLC6A4*, respectively); and receptors (dopamine receptors, *DRD2*, *DRD3*, and *DRD4*), among others.[96,105]

5.2.2.2.2 Opioid Receptors

Another important neurological network in the pharmacodynamics of DOA is that related to opioid receptors. The mu (μ), delta (δ), and kappa (κ) opioid receptors interact with endogenous opioid peptides (e.g., endorphins and enkephalins) as well as exogenous opioid drugs to regulate pain sensation, stress response, respiration, GI motility, and numerous other activities.[101,106] Much of the analgesic capacity of endogenous and exogenous opioids is thought to be mediated by the MOR, encoded by *OPRM1*. The delta (DOR) and kappa receptors (KOR), encoded by *OPRD1* and *OPRK1*, respectively, also function to regulate nociception, although their contributions are less well understood as compared with the MOR.[106]

Opioid receptors are also important in modulating responses to other drugs, including cocaine, other psychostimulants, and alcohol.[101] There appears to be extensive interactions between the dopaminergic, serotonergic, and opioidergic systems in modulating reward, substance dependence, and drug withdrawal.[53,101,107] The kappa opioid receptor in particular is capable of modulating the effects of dopamine surges, such as those that occur during repeated administration of cocaine.[101] Further support for an integral role of opioid receptor signaling in non-opioid addiction is the utility of naloxone and other opioid receptor antagonists in the treatment of alcoholism.[96,101]

5.2.2.2.3 Other Targets

Although less well characterized to date, several additional PD targets show promise as being relevant to DOA pharmacogenetics. Examples include the hypothalamic stress-response axis, cannabinoid receptors, nicotinic acetylcholine receptors, and gamma-aminobutyric acid (GABA)-responsive signaling.[63,95,101] Understanding of the genes related to these pathways and their specific influences lags behind the depth of knowledge of monoaminergic and opioidergic pathways.

5.2.3 Genotype/Phenotype Relationship

The fundamental assumption for pharmacogenetics is that genotype equals phenotype, and therefore, the pharmacogenetic constitution of an individual is predicted to have an effect on the pharmacokinetics and pharmacodynamics of the administered drug.[52] Traditionally, information on an individual's metabolic capacity, their phenotype, is obtained by measuring the concentrations of the parental drug and its metabolite. The goal of pharmacogenetic analysis is to link an individual's genotype to a phenotype and ultimately, drug metabolism, response, or toxicity.[108] This would allow the use of pharmacogenetic information to provide a phenotypic prediction based on a person's genotype.

The correlation between genotype and phenotype is not straightforward; there is substantial overlap in activity within and between the other phenotypic classificaitons.[109] Subjects with identical genotypes may also exhibit different phenotypic activities for the same drug, and the functional consequences of the genetic variation may be substrate (e.g., the drug or its metabolite) specific,[110] as discussed in the Cyp2D6 section earlier. It should be recognized that an individual's phenotype is also affected by much more than the genotype. In general, drug response depends on pharmacogenetics and external factors, including patient compliance, age of the patient, disease state, drug–drug interactions, food–drug interactions, formulation, gender, environmental factors (pollutants, smoking, etc.), pregnancy, and route of administration. Additionally, although the metabolism of a drug may be impaired, the elimination by other routes may not: there may be adequate renal excretion or up-regulation of transporters[111] that ultimately make the effect of the altered metabolism mute.

Adverse drug reaction (ADR, or adverse drug effect) is a broad term referring to any unwanted, uncomfortable, or dangerous effect that a drug may have.[11] ADRs, including drug–drug interactions, are the fourth leading cause of death in the United States; ADRs are the cause of 3% to 7% of all hospitalizations and occur during 10% to 20% of hospitalizations due to other causes. The incidence of death due to ADRs is unknown; suggested rates of 0.5% to 0.9% may be falsely high because many of the patients included had serious and complex disorders.[11]

In PK-based drug interactions, one drug alters the absorption, distribution, protein binding, metabolism, or excretion of another drug, and therefore, the amount and duration of available drug at receptor sites are affected.[112,113] PK interactions alter the magnitude and duration of a drug's effect, not its type.[11] On the other hand, PD interactions, the sensitivity or responsiveness of the body to of pne drug to another drug by having the same (agonistic) or a blocking (antagonistic) effect at the site of action. These effects usually occur at the receptor level but may occur intracellularly.[11,112,113]

The enormous amount of information available regarding drug–drug interactions, genetic alterations, and other sources of PK variability has only recently begun to be summarized into readily accessible formats, such as online tools for predicting interactions between therapeutic drugs or for determining genetic influences on initial drug dosing. However, whereas these resources are now emerging for therapeutic agents, there are notable deficiencies related to DOAs. One issue of particular concern is that these tools – and the clinicians who employ them – often neglect the influences of DOAs. Just as certain therapeutic agents can alter PK parameters of other drugs, there are DOAs with similar capabilities. Yet, online tools and scientific publications rarely explore this clinically relevant area of abused drugs.

For example, many drugs have been reported to inhibit the CYP2D6 enzyme system (http://medicine.iupui.edu/clinpharm/ddis/table.asp). The vast majority of these drugs are prescription drugs, but at least two CYP2D6 inhibitors are also known for their potential as DOAs, namely, methadone and cocaine. Indeed, cocaine is a potent inhibitor and appears to have a lower inhibition constant[114,115] than do paroxetine and fluoxetine,[116,117] suggesting that it is a more potent inhibitor of CYP2D6. It has also been suggested that 3,4-methylenedioxymethamphetamine (MDMA, Ecstasy) has a similar inhibition constant to fluoxetine.[118] The use of DOAs, prescription and non-prescribed medications, herbal supplements, and some foods can inhibit or induce enzymatic activity manyfold, to the extent that a PM phenotype, a phenocopy, may be induced regardless of genotype. And some drugs may have this influence long after the drug is metabolized from the body. The inhibition of CYP2D6 after discontinuation of fluoxetine treatment may require 5 weeks to be completely reversed; at that time, fluoxetine and norfluoxetine may not be detectable.[119]

5.2.4 Post-Mortem Toxicology Case

Koren et al.[120] reported a case where a full-term healthy male infant showed intermittent periods of difficulty in breastfeeding and lethargy starting on day 7 and was found dead on day 13. Post-mortem analysis of the infant showed no anatomical anomalies, but the blood concentration of morphine was 70 ng/mL. Neonates breastfed by mothers receiving codeine typically have morphine serum concentrations of 0–2.2 ng/mL.[121] The clinical and laboratory picture was consistent with opioid toxicity leading to neonatal death.

The mother was prescribed two tablets of a combination preparation of codeine 30 mg and acetaminophen 500 mg for episiotomy pain every 12 h. However, she reduced to one tablet starting on day 2 because she experienced somnolence and constipation, both of which are side effects of excess morphine. During the investigation of the cause of the infant's elevated morphine, the mother's stored milk from day 10 was assayed for morphine, and the concentration was determined to be 87 ng/mL. The typical range of breast milk concentrations after repeated maternal codeine administration of 60 mg every 6 h is 1.9–20.5 ng/mL.[120] In this case, when the milk was collected, the mother's dose was 30 mg every 12 hours.

CYP2D6 is the enzyme responsible for the O-demethylation of codeine to morphine.[122] Both the maternal symptomatology and the elevated breast milk morphine strongly suggest that the mother was producing excessive levels of morphine from the codeine, consistently with an ultra-rapid CYP2D6 phenotype. Unfortunately, no codeine results were reported in the breast milk or the neonate. Genotyping for CYP2D6 performed on the mother revealed that she was a CYP2D6 *2A/*2XN, confirming the ultra-rapid metabolizer phenotype.

Given the elevated morphine dose the neonate was receiving from the mother's milk, and that neonates typically have impaired capacity to metabolize and eliminate morphine, it is not surprising that the infant accumulated high levels of morphine, ultimately leading to death. While the cause of death was morphine poisoning, the mechanism of death was demonstrably accidental, and the pharmacogenetic findings support this conclusion.

5.2.5 Inappropriate Uses of Pharmacogenetic Tests

As with any laboratory analysis, before requesting expensive pharmacogenetic testing, it is critically important to consider the indication and whether it will provide interpretable data. Genotyping will only be of significant value when there is a well-established relationship between the genotype and the phenotype. It would seem obvious that in death investigations, for PGx to be useful, the cause of death must be drug related. Additionally, the results of pharmacogenetic testing must also meet criteria for clinical utility. As we have seen, for the vast majority of drugs, we simply don't have enough data to be able to establish these criteria. And to complicate matters, most drug deaths involve the ingestion of multiple drugs; drug–drug interactions are likely to contribute more to the toxicity than genetic influences.

PGx has been shown to be useful to support the hypothesis of an altered metabolizer status based on the toxicology finding, and few cases to demonstrate cases where PGx testing was the sole piece of information crucial to the outcome of the death investigation. Studies suggest that genetic factors account for between 20% and 95% of variability in drug disposition and drug effects, depending on the individual drug.[123] However, the lack of understanding of the effect of genetic factors on the vast majority of drugs and the high population prevalence for some atypical polymorphisms means that there is a significant probability that an abnormal genotype will be identified even in cases where drugs were not the cause of death or where the genotype was not actually contributory. Therefore, genotyping all cases can easily lead to misinterpretations. However, it is recommended to consult an expert in PGx prior to and following testing for correct test requesting and interpretation of the results.

Lastly, it is tempting to order the testing when the family are concerned about their own risk for PGx-related adverse reactions. However, genotyping the decedent will not be able to determine the real risk of another family member. That can only be done by genotyping the family member themselves.

5.3 CARDIOVASCULAR GENETICS AND SUBSTANCE ABUSE

5.3.1 Epidemiology and Genetics of Substance Abuse

Abuse of alcohol, prescription drugs, and illicit drugs is a major cause of morbidity and mortality in the United States and throughout the world.[124–126] An epidemiologic survey of U.S. adults in 2007 revealed a lifetime prevalence rate of 17.8% for alcohol abuse and 7.7% for prescription or illicit drug abuse.[124] There is strong evidence to support the contributory role of genetics in the development of substance abuse disorders. Numerous studies have found familial aggregation patterns in substance abuse.[125,127,128] Twin studies have demonstrated a roughly doubled risk of substance abuse disorders among monozygotic twins compared with dizygotic twins.[129] Genetics also plays a role in susceptibility to downstream complications of substance abuse (overdose, endocarditis, cardiac arrhythmias, sudden death, etc.) through either genetic variations in metabolic capacity (toxicogenetics), exacerbation of pre-existing cardiovascular disease, or increased susceptibility to direct toxic injury.

5.3.1.1 Cardiovascular Complications of Cocaine and Methamphetamine

The acute cardiovascular effects of cocaine and methamphetamine are mediated predominantly by a physiological state of catecholamine excess resulting in increased adrenergic receptor stimulation. Stimulation of adrenergic receptors results in increased heart rate (tachycardia) and increased systemic blood pressure (hypertension), both of which increase myocardial oxygen demand.[130] Cocaine also induces vasoconstriction of coronary arteries.[131] Therefore, cocaine paradoxically increases myocardial oxygen demand while simultaneously reducing oxygen supply.[132–134] Cocaine may also induce prolonged coronary artery vasospasm, leading to acute myocardial infarction, cardiac arrhythmias, and sudden death, even in the absence of pre-existing coronary atherosclerosis.[135]

Cocaine- and methamphetamine-induced catecholamine excess may also induce acute left ventricular systolic dysfunction via a syndrome known as takotsubo cardiomyopathy or takotsubo syndrome.[136,137] Other names for the same entity include stress-related cardiomyopathy and apical-ballooning syndrome. Takotsubo syndrome was first described in 1990 among young Japanese women presenting with transient acute systolic heart failure following episodes of extreme emotional distress.[138] The characteristic echocardiographic appearance of left ventricular apical hypokinesis results in the appearance of a ballooning left ventricular apex with a narrow mid-basal neck, similar in appearance to a Japanese octopus trap called a takotsubo. A related entity of fatal human stress cardiomyopathy caused by extreme stress-induced catecholamine excess was previously described in 1980 among homicide victims.[139] Fatal acute stress cardiomyopathy may represent a severe form of takotsubo cardiomyopathy. Though catecholamine excess likely plays an important role in takotsubo cardiomyopathy, the precise pathophysiologic mechanism and the higher prevalence among women remain unexplained.[137,140] Stimulants such as cocaine and methamphetamine may induce a secondary form of takotsubo cardiomyopathy.[141] Histopathologic findings in takotsubo cardiomyopathy remain poorly characterized. Rare case reports indicate the presence of non-specific histopathologic changes indicative of acute and chronic ischemia in the setting of catecholamine excess, such as interstitial edema, contraction bands, myofibrillar degeneration, and interstitial fibrosis.[142,143] Takotsubo cardiomyopathy is not considered a true genetic cardiomyopathy, and some have recommended it be renamed takotsubo syndrome to avoid confusion.[137]

In addition to the acute pathophysiologic effects mediated by adrenergic stimulation, cocaine may also directly induce cardiac arrhythmias via inhibition of cardiac sodium and potassium channels.[132,133] Cocaine inhibits the activity of sodium and potassium channels, including the SCN5A sodium[144] and HERG potassium[145,146] channels expressed in the heart, which results in reduced current,[147] prolongation of the QRS interval, and slowed cardiac conduction.[148] Interestingly, recreational use of cocaine has also been reported to induce transient electrocardiographic abnormalities similar to Brugada syndrome, a cardiac channelopathy associated with mutations in the SCN5A gene.[149,150] Cocaine may also induce prolongation of the QT interval, presumably through inhibitory activity on the HERG potassium channel.[151,152]

Despite the similarities with cocaine in terms of adrenergic stimulation, relatively little is known about the direct toxic effects of methamphetamine upon the heart.[153] In vitro studies indicate that methamphetamine has a detrimental effect upon cardiac myocyte contractility. Methamphetamine has a direct effect upon myocytes by increasing the activity of L-type calcium channels[154] and potassium channels,[154,155] but additional investigations to elucidate specific pathophysiological mechanisms are necessary. Nonetheless, it is clear from clinical observations that methamphetamine abuse has a deleterious effect upon the heart and may result in end-stage cardiomyopathy, either through direct cardiotoxicity or secondarily through hypertensive and ischemic changes.[156]

The chronic effects of cocaine and methamphetamine abuse are primarily related to myocardial ischemic injury, chronic systemic hypertension, and direct cardiomyocyte toxicity. There are likely multiple mechanisms by which cocaine and methamphetamine induce myocardial ischemic injury, including acute coronary artery vasoconstriction, increased myocardial demand mediated by chronic systemic hypertension and episodes of tachycardia, accelerated coronary artery atherosclerosis, increased risk for coronary artery thrombus formation, and development of non-atherosclerotic coronary artery intimal fibrosis.[157] Chronic cocaine abuse has long been recognized as a cause of early development of coronary artery atherosclerosis in the young.[158] Coronary artery disease is seen more commonly among abusers of methamphetamine relative to drug-free controls.[159]

The typical gross and microscopic correlates at autopsy in the setting of chronic cocaine and methamphetamine abuse are cardiac hypertrophy associated with microscopic myocyte hypertrophy and interstitial fibrosis, and coronary artery atherosclerosis, often more severe than would be expected for the given age and other risk factors. The autopsy findings are identical to those of an individual with ischemic heart disease due to conventional risk factors such as hypertension, hyperlipidemia, obesity and diabetes mellitus. The distinction is largely based on a history of substance abuse, relatively younger age at presentation, and the lack of conventional risk factors. One distinguishing feature may be the appearance of the coronary artery lesions. The pattern of coronary artery atherosclerosis in chronic cocaine abuse has been reported to be somewhat distinct, with lesions consisting of concentric intimal fibrosis, similar to what is seen in the setting of chronic graft vasculopathy in heart transplant patients, as opposed to more typical eccentric calcific lesions seen in conventional coronary atherosclerosis.[160] Chronic cocaine or methamphetamine abuse may also present in later stages with a dilated cardiomyopathy phenotype, presumably secondary to either direct toxic injury to cardiac myocytes or chronic myocardial ischemic injury through the mechanisms described earlier.

5.3.1.2 Cardiovascular Complications of Heroin and Intravenous Drug Abuse

Heroin toxicity arises primarily from respiratory depression secondary to opiate receptor binding within the CNS.[161] Respiratory failure may be accompanied by cardiac arrest due to myocardial hypoxemia, with secondary hypoxic-ischemic changes in the heart seen at the time of autopsy, especially if there was a survival interval between the hypoxemic-ischemic injury and death. The direct pathologic effects of heroin, morphine, and other opiates upon the heart are not well known. There is some suggestion that morphine may actually be cardio-protective in the setting of cocaine toxicity.[162] Myocyte hypertrophy and interstitial fibrosis are frequently observed at autopsy in abusers of heroin, but these changes may be secondary to concurrent stimulant abuse.[130]

Nonetheless, heroin abuse is associated with significant cardiovascular morbidity and mortality, largely through complications of intravenous drug abuse. It is important to note that intravenous injection of substances is not limited to heroin. Any substance, including cocaine, methamphetamine, and prescription pain medications, may be injected intravenously. All are associated with significant downstream cardiovascular complications, many of which are infectious in causation. The injection of pulverized prescription pain medications is especially important, because the filler material that is used as a binding agent in many prescription pills, such as talc and cellulose, may become entrapped within the pulmonary capillary vasculature, resulting in the formation of foreign-body granulomas, which can lead to pulmonary hypertension and secondary right heart failure (cor pulmonale).[163,164]

The most significant cardiovascular complication of intravenous drug abuse is infective endocarditis, which refers to an infection of the heart valves. Typically, the infection is bacterial, though fungal endocarditis may also occur, especially in the setting of an immunocompromised host due to HIV infection. Infective endocarditis associated with intravenous drug abuse typically afflicts the right-sided heart valves,[165] presumably due to repeated valve injury from particulate matter injected into the venous system.[166] Though right-sided endocarditis is characteristic, left-sided endocarditis also commonly occurs in intravenous drug abuse. The most common organisms implicated in infective endocarditis are Staphylococcus and Streptococcus species.[167] The clinical diagnosis may be difficult to establish and is frequently made after an insidious course of fever, weight loss, and lethargy over weeks and months.[168]

Endocarditis is manifest on heart valves by the presence of a friable mass lesion (vegetation) adherent to the surface of the valve, composed of bacterial colonies, inflammatory cells, fibrin, and platelets. Complications are potentially catastrophic and include septic embolization to other organs of the body causing stroke, myocardial infarct, or other catastrophic end-organ ischemic injury. If the vegetation erodes through the valve, acute systolic heart failure may occur secondary to acute regurgitation. If the vegetation involves the aortic valve, the infection may extend to the root of the aorta, where it can form an abscess that may erode into the major vessels and chambers of the heart, resulting in fistulas and fatal hemorrhage. The treatment for infective endocarditis typically involves a long course of antibiotics, sometimes followed by open heart surgery to replace irreparably damaged valves.[169]

5.3.2 Post-Mortem Genetic Testing for Cardiac Channelopathies

Commonly suspected inherited arrhythmic diseases in sudden unexpected, unexplained deaths include Long QT syndrome, Brugada syndrome, and catecholaminergic polymorphic ventricular tachycardia (CPVT). Although there are numerous other inherited arrhythmia syndromes, we will limit our discussion to these entities.

5.3.2.1 Long QT Syndrome

Congenital long QT syndrome is an inheritable arrhythmic heart disease characterized by prolongation of the QT segment interval on electrocardiogram, usually to greater than 500 milliseconds in length. It is associated with syncopal episodes and an increased risk for potentially fatal cardiac arrhythmias, such as Torsades de Pointes. The prevalence of long QT syndrome is estimated to be as high as 1 in 2,000.[170] Most cases of long QT syndrome exhibit an autosomal dominant inheritance pattern, though autosomal recessive patterns also exist. Long QT syndrome is caused by mutations in genes that code for various cardiac channels that regulate the flow of ions across the cardiac myocyte membrane.[171] The major genes that are implicated in congenital long QT syndrome are the potassium channels KCNQ1 and KCNH2 and the sodium channel SCN5A. Other genes that are associated with long QT syndrome include KCNE1 and KCNE2, along with numerous other genes. The particular gene that is involved influences the phenotypic expression of disease, as does the particular site and type of mutation that is present. Different mutations within the same genes may also cause short QT syndrome, an inheritable arrhythmic disease characterized by a shortened QT interval, which is also associated with malignant arrhythmias.[172] QT interval prolongation, in itself, is not diagnostic for inheritable arrhythmic disease, because a prolonged interval may be induced by a wide variety of medications, including macrolide antibiotics, antiarrhythmic medications, and psychotropic medications.[173] However, acquired QT prolongation is also associated with malignant arrhythmias such as Torsades de Pointes. Treatment of congenital long QT syndrome includes avoidance of drugs associated with QT prolongation, avoidance of strenuous exercise, beta-blockers, and consideration of an implantable cardioverter-defibrillator (ICD).[174]

5.3.2.2 Brugada Syndrome

Brugada syndrome is an inherited arrhythmic heart disease characterized by electrocardiographic abnormalities, specifically a coved pattern of ST segment elevation and negative T waves in the right precordial leads, and associated with an increased risk for development of fatal cardiac arrhythmias.[171] The diagnostic electrocardiographic findings can be induced by administration of a sodium channel blocking agent.[174] A Brugada-type pattern on electrocardiogram may be induced by other causes. Notably, cocaine use may result in a Brugada-like pattern due to the inhibitory effects of cocaine on sodium channels. Though precise data is lacking, recent data suggests a prevalence of approximately 1 in 2,000, with the highest areas of prevalence in Southeast Asia, where it may be the cause of sudden unexpected nocturnal death syndrome (SUNDS).[175] There is a male predominance, and the inheritance pattern is typically autosomal dominant. Brugada syndrome may be caused by mutations in numerous sodium, potassium, and calcium channel genes, though the most commonly implicated gene is the SCN5A sodium channel. As with long QT syndrome, the type and location of the mutation associated with SCN5A may affect the phenotypic disease expression, demonstrating a correlation between genotype and phenotype. However, as with long QT syndrome, disease expression associated with the same mutation may be modified by other polymorphisms.[176] The same mutation in the SCN5A gene may result in a clinical phenotype with overlapping clinical features within the same individual, or with differing phenotypes amongst family members with the same mutation, presumably due to other disease modifying factors.[177] Treatment options include antiarrhythmic pharmacotherapy, implantation of an ICD, and possible radiofrequency catheter ablation along the right ventricular outflow tract.[174]

5.3.2.3 Catecholaminergic Polymorphic Ventricular Tachycardia (CPVT)

Catecholaminergic polymorphic ventricular tachycardia (CPVT) is an inherited arrhythmic heart disease characterized by exercise-induced syncopal episodes and a polymorphic form of ventricular tachycardia on electrocardiogram. At rest, the electrocardiographic findings are unremarkable, but with exercise, characteristic electrocardiographic findings include increasing frequency of premature ventricular complexes progressing to a characteristic bidirectional or polymorphic ventricular tachycardia.[178] The prevalence of CPVT is unknown, with recent estimates of approximately 1 in 10,000.[174] The true prevalence is likely higher, and CPVT may be a significant undiagnosed cause of drowning in young individuals.[179] Despite the lower estimated prevalence compared with long QT and Brugada syndrome, CPVT is thought to have a much higher mortality, with rates as high as 30% to 50%.[171] CPVT is caused by mutations in the RYR2 calcium channel, which is one of the largest genes in the human genome with 105 exons. CPVT typically exhibits an autosomal dominant inheritance pattern.[171] Another gene associated with CPVT is the cardiac calsequestrin gene (CASQ2), which has an autosomal recessive inheritance pattern. Treatment includes beta blockers, exercise restriction, ICD implantation, and possible ablation therapy.

5.3.2.4 Post-Mortem Diagnosis of Inherited Arrhythmia Syndromes

The diagnostic yield of post-mortem genetic testing in the setting of a negative autopsy has been variably reported, with a wide range between approximately 4% and 45%. One study from the Harris County Medical Examiner Office of 351 sudden deaths in infants and young adults, utilizing targeted sequencing of full exon sequences of 64 genes, found pathogenic mutations in 13 individuals, for a discovery rate of 3.7%.[180] At the other higher of the spectrum was a recent study utilizing a whole-exome sequencing approach among 32 cases of exercise-related sudden unexplained death referred by medical examiners for post-mortem genetic testing, which revealed a mutation detection rate of 44%.[181] Of note, these two studies varied significantly in terms of the population studied (cases referred from a single medical examiner office vs. a referred population without geographic restriction) and methodology (targeted sequencing vs. whole-exome sequencing) and may have differed in their approach to the interpretation of variants as pathogenic.

There is an expectation that as genome sequencing technology becomes more accessible, the discovery rate of mutations that can explain an otherwise unexplained death will increase. However, there is reason to be cautious with our expectations. The rate at which sequencing technology is advancing outpaces that of our ability to categorize variants as pathogenic or benign. Existing methodologies for classifying variants, including computerized prediction models, reliance upon prior reports of pathogenicity in the literature, and scarce in vivo and ex vivo experiments, often provide conflicting and confusing data, which if acted upon, may potentially harm surviving family members.[182]

Interpretation of genetic variants is especially problematic when proper interpretation requires correlation with a condition such as sudden unexplained death, in which the studied group is defined by the absence of findings as opposed to the presence of positive findings. Due to the lack of standardization and the general lack of funding for death investigation systems, it can be extremely difficult, if not impossible, to distinguish between a death that is truly unexplained after a thorough death investigation and one in which a cause of death would have been revealed if a thorough investigation had been performed. Furthermore, even if a thorough death investigation is performed, there are still a number of causes of death, such as asphyxial deaths, that are so-called "diagnoses of exclusion," meaning that the diagnosis can be made only after ruling out other reasonable causes of death. As a side note, most diagnoses of exclusion are in fact not strictly diagnoses of exclusion, because it is simply impossible to rule out some causes of death with certainty. Rather, the term is used to refer to diagnoses that are based on subtle, but non-specific, findings from the autopsy, scene investigation, ancillary studies, or history. Nonetheless, the presence of multiple "diagnoses of exclusion" within the differential diagnosis is a very challenging and not uncommon problem, especially among sudden deaths of infants and young children who are found in unsafe sleep environments that are suggestive of, but not sufficient for, a diagnosis for asphyxia. In such a setting, even if a genetic mutation is discovered, "undetermined" may still be the most appropriate cause and manner of death, but this determination should include consideration of a number of factors, such as the reliability of the variant classification and the degree of suspicion for asphyxia or other alternative cause of death. Ultimately, as with the classification of the pathogenicity of a genetic variant, the final determination of the cause and manner of death is an opinion, and as such, it is subject to differing interpretations.

5.3.3 Post-Mortem Genetic Testing for Cardiomyopathies

Cardiomyopathy generally refers to a heterogeneous group of cardiac diseases associated with an intrinsic defect of the myocardium, often due to an underlying genetic abnormality that affects the sarcomeric or desmosomal apparatus of the cardiac myocyte, and characterized clinically by mechanical and/or electrical ventricular dysfunction and structurally by ventricular hypertrophy and/or dilatation. Strictly speaking, cardiomyopathic processes do not encompass myocardial dysfunction due to ischemia, valvular dysfunction, hypertension, or congenital heart disease.[171] The classification of cardiomyopathies has traditionally been based on phenotypic features such as ventricular hypertrophy or dilatation. A recently proposed classification called the MOGE(S) system incorporates genetic information but is somewhat complex and not widely used in the United States.[183] The most common types of cardiomyopathies that are encountered in the setting of sudden unexplained death in the young are hypertrophic cardiomyopathy, dilated cardiomyopathy, and arrhythmogenic cardiomyopathy (also known as arrhythmogenic right ventricular dysplasia/cardiomyopathy). Each of these cardiomyopathies, while distinct in their classical manifestations, also reflects a spectrum of phenotypic disease with significant overlap. Therefore, when considering post-mortem genetic testing for cardiomyopathies, a panel approach that includes genes implicated in hypertrophic, dilated, and arrhythmogenic forms of cardiomyopathy may be of greatest utility.

5.3.3.1 Hypertrophic Cardiomyopathy

Hypertrophic cardiomyopathy is typically characterized by asymmetric ventricular septal hypertrophy, although concentric forms of hypertrophy may also occur. The septal hypertrophy may be most apparent at the basal, mid, or apical levels. The classic pathophysiological correlate is dynamic left ventricular outflow tract obstruction, due to contact of the bulging left ventricular septum with the anterior leaflet of the mitral valve during ventricular systole ("systolic anterior motion"), but non-obstructive forms of hypertrophic cardiomyopathy may also occur. Anatomically, a region of endocardial fibrosis may be observed in the left ventricular outflow tract corresponding to the shape of the anterior leaflet of the mitral valve. The heart weight usually significantly exceeds the expected normal weight at autopsy. On microscopic examination, myocyte disarray is often observed, referring to a disorganized or herringbone pattern of myofiber orientation. Of note, focal myocyte disarray is a normal finding in the right ventricle, particularly at the junction of the right ventricle and the interventricular septum, and should not be misinterpreted as diagnostic of hypertrophic cardiomyopathy in the absence of other corroborative gross findings. The prevalence of hypertrophic cardiomyopathy is estimated to be approximately 1 in 500.[184] In addition to the hemodynamic abnormalities, hypertrophic cardiomyopathy is also associated with an increased risk for fatal tachyarrhythmias, and it is a significant cause of sudden death in young adults, especially athletes. Along with dilated cardiomyopathy, hypertrophic cardiomyopathy is a common cardiomyopathy detected at autopsy in sudden unexplained death in the young, especially athletes.[185,186] Overall, however, the most common finding in sudden death among athletes is a structurally normal heart.[185,186] Most commonly, hypertrophic cardiomyopathy is inherited in an autosomal dominant pattern. Treatment options for hypertrophic cardiomyopathy include implantation of an ICD, surgical septal myectomy, or alcohol septal ablation.

The pathogenesis of hypertrophic cardiomyopathy is related to mutations that occur in multiple genes that encode proteins for the sarcomeric contractile apparatus. The most commonly implicated genes are those encoding for beta myosin heavy chain (MYH7) and myosin binding protein C (MYBPC3), accounting for 75% of detected mutations.[187] If a known causative mutation is identified, genetic testing can assist with risk stratification for surviving family members, but variants of uncertain significance are increasingly being discovered, which may not provide useful information for risk stratification.[188] Despite earlier optimism, genotype has not proven to be as predictive of outcome as anticipated, with some individuals with positive genotypes and negative phenotypes posing diagnostic and therapeutic dilemmas.[189] The post-mortem detection of previously undiagnosed hypertrophic cardiomyopathy, even without genetic testing, is of tremendous value to family members, because it will prompt clinical screening of surviving family members, which may result in clinical intervention. Genetic testing can potentially be of assistance if the phenotype of hypertrophic cardiomyopathy is uncertain. The classical gross features of hypertrophic cardiomyopathy may be subtle or masked in the early and late stages of hypertrophic cardiomyopathy. For example, genotype positive individuals may only have subtle ventricular hypertrophy or no hypertrophy at all, particularly in pre-adolescence.[190] Myocardial fibrosis may precede left ventricular hypertrophy in some cases.[191] In the late stages of hypertrophic cardiomyopathy, sometimes referred to as the "burnt out" or "end-stage" phase of hypertrophic cardiomyopathy, the heart may be essentially indistinguishable from dilated cardiomyopathy with a symmetrically dilated left ventricle.[192,193]

5.3.3.2 Dilated Cardiomyopathy

Dilated cardiomyopathy, strictly used, corresponds to a cardiomyopathy characterized by left ventricular dilatation and systolic dysfunction due to an intrinsic defect of the myocardium that impairs myocardial contractility rather than secondary to other causes that may also result in a dilated, dysfunctional left ventricle, such as ischemic heart disease, hypertension, valvular heart disease, and various toxic injuries.[171] However, the term *dilated cardiomyopathy* is also sometimes used to refer to the phenotypic manifestation of left ventricular dilatation and systolic dysfunction, regardless of causation, resulting in significant confusion within the medical literature. Of note, many forms of dilated cardiomyopathy that are secondary to toxic injury, such as alcohol-related cardiomyopathy, are indistinguishable on morphologic and microscopic grounds from idiopathic dilated cardiomyopathy. Therefore, the distinction is often based on personal and family history and other clinical and autopsy findings. The prevalence of dilated cardiomyopathy is unknown and varies by definition but has been estimated at approximately 1 in 250.[194]

Causative mutations for familial forms of dilated cardiomyopathy have been identified in multiple genes that code for contractile proteins, desmosomal proteins, and membrane channels. Compared with hypertrophic cardiomyopathy, where approximately 75% of mutations are identified within two genes (MYH7 and MYBPC3) involved with sarcomeric contractility, familial dilated cardiomyopathy may be associated with mutations in a much wider array of genes involved with sarcomere contractility, membrane channels, and structural membrane proteins.[187] Currently, genetic testing for dilated cardiomyopathy yields a detection rate of approximately 40%.[195] Some of the same genes implicated in dilated cardiomyopathy have also been associated with hypertrophic cardiomyopathy, arrhythmogenic cardiomyopathy, and cardiac channelopathies, suggesting significant diagnostic overlap and heterogeneity of causation within this group of diseases.[194] Given this genotypic and phenotypic heterogeneity and overlap, genotype–phenotype correlations remain a challenge. Some genotypes are associated with characteristic phenotypic profiles, such as the combination of conduction system disease with dilated cardiomyopathy due to lamin A/C mutations (LMNA).[196] Nonetheless, if a well-characterized causative mutation is discovered, surviving family members can benefit from targeted screening, and clinical treatment may still be guided by the results of genetic testing.[195]

The post-mortem diagnosis of dilated cardiomyopathy may be challenging in some cases. The morphologic appearance of the heart is characteristically dilated, often biventricular, and the weight is typically significantly above the expected weight. Distinction from artifactual dilation due to body decomposition can be difficult in the early stages of decomposition. The etiologic distinction from ischemic, hypertensive, and valvular heart disease is based upon the presence of coronary atherosclerosis, valvular disease, or changes indicative of systemic hypertension, such as arteriolar nephrosclerosis. However, the mere presence of coronary atherosclerosis, valvular heart disease, or hypertensive changes does not rule out the possibility of an underlying familial dilated cardiomyopathy. Consideration should be given to whether the extent of hypertrophy and dilatation is out of proportion to the severity of ischemic, valvular, or hypertensive heart disease. The etiologic distinction from toxic injury due to substance abuse is based almost entirely on history and correlation with other historical and autopsy findings indicative of substance abuse. Electron microscopy may be helpful for identifying ultrastructural features of some medication-induced cardiomyopathies, such as those due to anthracyclines or hydroxychloroquine.

5.3.3.3 Arrhythmogenic Cardiomyopathy

Arrhythmogenic right ventricular cardiomyopathy (ARVC) is also known as arrhythmogenic right ventricular dysplasia or arrhythmogenic cardiomyopathy. ARVC was first described as a cardiomyopathy involving the right ventricle and clinically associated with arrhythmias arising from the right side of the heart.[197] However, ARVC is now recognized as a cardiomyopathy that may involve both ventricles, though right ventricle involvement is still more common. The characteristic gross and microscopic finding in ARVC is fibrofatty infiltration of the right ventricle, often most apparent in the "triangle of dysplasia" involving the anterior basal third of the right ventricle. When the left ventricle is involved, there is subepicardial infiltration of adipose and fibrous tissue. On gross examination of the heart, the right ventricle wall is markedly thinned and can be transilluminated such that a light source can be easily seen through the wall. On short-axis sections of the heart, the right ventricular wall is markedly thinned and may appear to be completely replaced by adipose tissue. On microscopic examination, there is transmural replacement of the right ventricular myocardium by fibrofatty infiltration, or subepicardial infiltration of the left ventricle by fibrous and adipose tissue. Foci of myocarditis may also be present, which are of uncertain cause.[198,199] The overall prevalence of ARVC in the general population is estimated to be between 1 in 1,000 and 1 in 5,000,[200] while some regions may have much higher local prevalence.[201] ARVC is typically inherited in an autosomal dominant pattern. The pathogenetic cause of ARVC has been identified as mutations occurring in a set of genes encoding for desmosomal proteins, such as plakoglobin (JUP), desmoplakin (DSP), plakophilin-2 (PKP2), desmoglein-2 (DSG2), desmocollin-2 (DSC2), transforming growth factor beta-3 (TGFB3), and TMEM43.[199] Mutations in RYR2, which is associated with CPVT, have also been reported in the setting of ARVC.[199]

If the diagnosis is already established by clinical, gross, and microscopic morphologic features, post-mortem genetic testing may be beneficial for identifying a causative mutation that can be screened for in relatives. If the diagnosis is suspected but not confirmed, genetic testing may be dispositive if a well-characterized mutation is identified within a desmosomal protein. Situations that may prove to be challenging for a post-mortem diagnosis include distinguishing obesity-related fatty infiltration from pathologic fibro-fatty infiltration. Obesity-related adipose infiltration is typically not associated with fibrous replacement. However, some forms of ARVC present with predominantly adipose tissue infiltration with minimal fibrous tissue. Again, consultation with a cardiovascular pathologist and correlation with ante-mortem findings, especially if there is a personal or family history of syncopal episodes or arrhythmias, may be helpful.

5.4 SUMMARY

Genetic testing can be a very useful tool in death investigations when ordered under appropriate circumstances, and its utility will likely increase in the future as we improve our ability to assess the significance of genetic variants. In current practice, genetic testing may be a helpful adjunct in the investigation of some categories of cardiovascular disease and toxicology-related deaths. However, caution must be exercised in attributing too much significance to the results of isolated genetic tests, as much remains to be learned regarding the myriad genetic variants present within the genome and the complex processes that modulate the expression of these genetic variants, resulting in an even wider spectrum of phenotypic diversity.

REFERENCES

1. Bustamante C, Cheng W, Mejia YX. Revisiting the central dogma one molecule at a time. *Cell.* 2011;144(4):480–497.
2. Calabrese RL. Channeling the central dogma. *Neuron.* 2014;82(4):725–727.
3. Cooper S. The central dogma of cell biology. *Cell Biol Int Rep.* 1981;5(6):539–549.
4. Shah SH, Arnett D, Houser SR, et al. Opportunities for the cardiovascular community in the precision medicine initiative. *Circulation.* 2016;133(2):226–231.
5. Schork NJ, Murray SS, Frazer KA, Topol EJ. Common vs. rare allele hypotheses for complex diseases. *Curr Opin Genet Dev.* 2009;19(3):212–219.
6. Bodmer W, Bonilla C. Common and rare variants in multifactorial susceptibility to common diseases. *Nat Genet.* 2008;40(6):695–701.
7. Steinberg MH, Sebastiani P. Genetic modifiers of sickle cell disease. *Am J Hematol.* 2012;87(8):795–803.
8. Gallati S. Disease-modifying genes and monogenic disorders: experience in cystic fibrosis. *Appl Clin Genet.* 2014;7:133–146.
9. van Otterdijk SD, Michels KB. Transgenerational epigenetic inheritance in mammals: how good is the evidence? *Faseb J.* 2016.
10. Maurano MT, Wang H, John S, et al. Role of DNA methylation in modulating transcription factor occupancy. *Cell Rep.* 2015;12(7):1184–1195.
11. Grunstein M. Histone acetylation in chromatin structure and transcription. *Nature.* 1997;389(6649):349–352.
12. Gnyszka A, Jastrzebski Z, Flis S. DNA methyltransferase inhibitors and their emerging role in epigenetic therapy of cancer. *Anticancer Res.* 2013;33(8):2989–2996.
13. Xu WS, Parmigiani RB, Marks PA. Histone deacetylase inhibitors: molecular mechanisms of action. *Oncogene.* 2007;26(37):5541–5552.
14. Handy DE, Castro R, Loscalzo J. Epigenetic modifications: basic mechanisms and role in cardiovascular disease. *Circulation.* 2011;123(19):2145–2156.
15. Ordovas JM, Smith CE. Epigenetics and cardiovascular disease. *Nat Rev Cardiol.* 2010;7(9):510–519.
16. Nielsen DA, Utrankar A, Reyes JA, Simons DD, Kosten TR. Epigenetics of drug abuse: predisposition or response. *Pharmacogenomics.* 2012;13(10):1149–1160.
17. Ling H, Fabbri M, Calin GA. MicroRNAs and other noncoding RNAs as targets for anticancer drug development. *Nat Rev Drug Discov.* 2013;12(11):847–865.
18. Wang KC, Chang HY. Molecular mechanisms of long noncoding RNAs. *Mol Cell.* 2011;43(6):904–914.
19. Kenny PJ. Epigenetics, microRNA, and addiction. *Dialogues Clin Neurosci.* 2014;16(3):335–344.
20. Etheridge A, Lee I, Hood L, Galas D, Wang K. Extracellular microRNA: a new source of biomarkers. *Mutat Res.* 2011;717(1–2):85–90.
21. van Rooij E, Purcell AL, Levin AA. Developing microRNA therapeutics. *Circ Res.* 2012;110(3):496–507.
22. Wetterstrand K. DNA sequencing costs: data from the NHGRI Genome Sequencing Program (GSP). Available at www.genome.gov/sequencingcosts. 2016. Accessed April 25, 2016.
23. Richards S, Aziz N, Bale S, et al. Standards and guidelines for the interpretation of sequence variants: a joint consensus recommendation of the American College of Medical Genetics and Genomics and the Association for Molecular Pathology. *Genet Med.* 2015;17(5):405–424.
24. Capanu M, Seshan VE. False discovery rates for rare variants from sequenced data. *Genet Epidemiol.* 2015;39(2):65–76.
25. Collins FS, Varmus H. A new initiative on precision medicine. *N Engl J Med.* 2015;372(9):793–795.
26. Chakradhar S. Disease drivers: global consortia aim to unpack genetics of diabetes and obesity. *Nat Med.* 2016;22(8):828–830.
27. Cook-Deegan R, Conley JM, Evans JP, Vorhaus D. The next controversy in genetic testing: clinical data as trade secrets? *Eur J Hum Genet.* 2013;21(6):585–588.
28. Gottesman O, Kuivaniemi H, Tromp G, et al. The electronic medical records and genomics (eMERGE) network: past, present, and future. *Genet Med.* 2013;15(10):761–771.
29. Pritt BS, Hardin NJ, Richmond JA, Shapiro SL. Death certification errors at an academic institution. *Arch Pathol Lab Med.* 2005;129(11):1476–1479.
30. McCaw-Binns A, Holder Y, Mullings J. Certification of coroners cases by pathologists would improve the completeness of death registration in Jamaica. *J Clin Epidemiol.* 2015;68(9):979–987.
31. Roulson J, Benbow EW, Hasleton PS. Discrepancies between clinical and autopsy diagnosis and the value of post mortem histology; a meta-analysis and review. *Histopathology.* 2005;47(6):551–559.
32. Turnbull A, Osborn M, Nicholas N. Hospital autopsy: endangered or extinct? *J Clin Pathol.* 2015;68(8):601–604.
33. Shojania KG, Burton EC. The vanishing nonforensic autopsy. *N Engl J Med.* 2008;358(9):873–875.
34. Christiansen LR, Collins KA. Natural death in the forensic setting: a study and approach to the autopsy. *Am J Forensic Med Pathol.* 2007;28(1):20–23.
35. Committee on Identifying the Needs of the Forensic Sciences Community NRC. *Strengthening Forensic Science in the United States: A Path Forward.* The National Academies Press; 2009.
36. *Increasing the Number, Retention and Quality of Board Certified Forensic Pathologists.* National Commission of Forensic Science; 2013.
37. Centers for Disease Control and Prevention NCfHS. *Physicians' Handbook on Medical Certification of Death.* Hyattsville, MD; 2003.
38. Lynch M. God's signature: DNA profiling, the new gold standard in forensic science. *Endeavour.* 2003;27(2):93–97.
39. Smith PJ, Ballantyne J. Simplified low-copy-number DNA analysis by post-PCR purification. *J Forensic Sci.* 2007;52(4):820–829.
40. Gill P. Application of low copy number DNA profiling. *Croat Med J.* 2001;42(3):229–232.
41. Cohle SD, Sampson BA. The negative autopsy: sudden cardiac death or other? *Cardiovasc Pathol.* 2001;10(5):219–222.
42. Bagnall RD, Weintraub RG, Ingles J, et al. A prospective study of sudden cardiac death among children and young adults. *N Engl J Med.* 2016;374(25):2441–2452.
43. Erdmann J. Telltale hearts. *Nat Med.* 2013;19(11):1361–1364.
44. Middleton O, Baxter S, Demo E, et al. National assocation of medical examiners position paper: retaining postmortem samples for genetic testing. *Acad Forensic Pathol.* 2013;3(2):191–194.
45. Poulsen JB, Lescai F, Grove J, et al. High-quality exome sequencing of whole-genome amplified neonatal dried blood spot DNA. *PLoS One.* 2016;11(4):e0153253.
46. Oh E, Choi YL, Kwon MJ, et al. Comparison of accuracy of whole-exome sequencing with formalin-fixed paraffin-embedded and fresh frozen tissue samples. *PLoS One.* 2015;10(12):e0144162.

47. Langman LJ, Bechtel L, Holstege CP. Clinical toxicology. In: Burtis CA, Ashwood ER, Bruns DE, eds. *Tietz Textbook of Clinical Chemistry and Molecular Diagnostics*. 5th ed. St. Louis, MO: Elsevier Saunders; 2012:1109–1188.
48. Alving AS, Carson PE, Flanagan CL, Ickes CE. Enzymatic deficiency in primaquine-sensitive erythrocytes. *Science*. 1956;124(3220):484–485.
49. Weber WW. Human drug-metabolizing enzyme variants. In: Weber WW, ed. *Pharmacogenetics*. New York: Oxford University Press; 1997:181–186.
50. Kalow W, Genest K. A method for the detection of atypical forms of human serum cholinesterase; determination of dibucaine numbers. *Can J Biochem Physiol*. 1957;35(6):339–346.
51. Evans DA, Manley KA, Mc KV. Genetic control of isoniazid metabolism in man. *Br Med J*. 1960;2(5197):485–491.
52. Sajantila A, Palo JU, Ojanpera I, Davis C, Budowle B. Pharmacogenetics in medico-legal context. *Forensic Sci Int*. 2010;203(1–3):44–52.
53. Herz A. Bidirectional effects of opioids in motivational processes and the involvement of D1 dopamine receptors. *NIDA Res Monogr*. 1988;90:17–26.
54. Snozek CLH, Langman LJ. Chapter 1 Pharmacogenomics principles of alcohol and DOA. In: Dasgupta A, Langman LJ, eds. *Pharmacogenomics of Alcohol and Drugs of Abuse*. Boca Raton, FL: CRC Press; 2012:1–10.
55. Relling MV, Giacomini KM. Pharmacogenetics. In: Brunton LL, Chabner BA, Knollmann BC, eds. *Goodman & Gilman's: The Pharmacological Basis of Therapeutics, 12e*. New York: McGraw-Hill Education; 2011.
56. Shields AE, Lerman C. Anticipating clinical integration of pharmacogenetic treatment strategies for addiction: are primary care physicians ready? *Clin Pharmacol Ther*. 2008;83(4):635–639.
57. Johansson I, Ingelman-Sundberg M. Genetic polymorphism and toxicology--with emphasis on cytochrome p450. *Toxicol Sci*. 2011;120(1):1–13.
58. Lamba JK, Lin YS, Schuetz EG, Thummel KE. Genetic contribution to variable human CYP3A-mediated metabolism. *Adv Drug Deliv Rev*. 2002;54(10):1271–1294.
59. Buxton ILO, Benet LZ. Pharmacokinetics: the dynamics of drug absorption, distribution, metabolism, and elimination. In: Brunton LL, Chabner BA, Knollmann BC, eds. *Goodman & Gilman's: The Pharmacological Basis of Therapeutics, 12e*. New York: McGraw-Hill Education; 2011.
60. Blumenthal DK, Garrison JC. Pharmacodynamics: molecular mechanisms of drug action. In: Brunton LL, Chabner BA, Knollmann BC, eds. *Goodman & Gilman's: The Pharmacological Basis of Therapeutics, 12e*. New York: McGraw-Hill Education; 2011.
61. Meyer MR, Maurer HH. Absorption, distribution, metabolism and excretion pharmacogenomics of drugs of abuse. *Pharmacogenomics*. 2011;12(2):215–233.
62. Gonzalez FJ, Coughtrie M, Tukey RH. Chapter 6. Drug metabolism. In: Brunton L, Chabner B, Knollmann B, eds. *Goodman & Gilman's The Pharmacological Basis of Therapeutics*. 12th ed. New York: McGraw-Hill; 2011. http://accessmedicine.mhmedical.com/content.aspx?bookid=374&Sectionid=41266211. Accessed November 41266225, 41262014.
63. Rutter JL. Symbiotic relationship of pharmacogenetics and drugs of abuse. *Aaps J*. 2006;8(1):E174–184.
64. Shimada T, Yamazaki H, Mimura M, Inui Y, Guengerich FP. Interindividual variations in human liver cytochrome P-450 enzymes involved in the oxidation of drugs, carcinogens and toxic chemicals: studies with liver microsomes of 30 Japanese and 30 Caucasians. *J Pharmacol Exp Ther*. 1994;270(1):414–423.
65. Ingelman-Sundberg M, Sim SC, Gomez A, Rodriguez-Antona C. Influence of cytochrome P450 polymorphisms on drug therapies: pharmacogenetic, pharmacoepigenetic and clinical aspects. *Pharmacol Ther*. 2007;116(3):496–526.
66. Bradford LD. CYP2D6 allele frequency in European Caucasians, Asians, Africans and their descendants. *Pharmacogenomics*. 2002;3(2):229–243.
67. Garcia-Barcelo M, Chow LY, Chiu HF, et al. Genetic analysis of the CYP2D6 locus in a Hong Kong Chinese population. *Clin Chem*. 2000;46(1):18–23.
68. Ingelman-Sundberg M. Pharmacogenetics of cytochrome P450 and its applications in drug therapy: the past, present and future. *Trends Pharmacol Sci*. 2004;25(4):193–200.
69. Iohom G, Fitzgerald D, Cunningham AJ. Principles of pharmacogenetics--implications for the anaesthetist. *Br J Anaesth*. 2004;93(3):440–450.
70. Galley HF, Mahdy A, Lowes DA. Pharmacogenetics and anesthesiologists. *Pharmacogenomics*. 2005;6(8):849–856.
71. Searle R, Hopkins PM. Pharmacogenomic variability and anaesthesia. *Br J Anaesth*. 2009;103(1):14–25.
72. Frye RF. Probing the world of cytochrome P450 enzymes. *Mol Interv*. 2004;4(3):157–162.
73. Baselt RC. In: Baselt RC, ed. *Dispositition of Toxic Drugs and Chemical in Man*. 10th ed. Seal Beach, CA: Biomedical Publications; 2014.
74. Lotsch J. Opioid metabolites. *J Pain Symptom Manag*. 2005;29(5 Suppl):S10–24.
75. Zanger UM, Raimundo S, Eichelbaum M. Cytochrome P450 2D6: overview and update on pharmacology, genetics, biochemistry. *Naunyn-Schmiedeberg's Arch Pharmacol*. 2004;369(1):23–37.
76. Yu A, Kneller BM, Rettie AE, Haining RL. Expression, purification, biochemical characterization, and comparative function of human cytochrome P450 2D6.1, 2D6.2, 2D6.10, and 2D6.17 allelic isoforms. *J Pharmacol Exp Ther*. 2002;303(3):1291–1300.
77. Bogni A, Monshouwer M, Moscone A, et al. Substrate specific metabolism by polymorphic cytochrome P450 2D6 alleles. *Toxicol In Vitro*. 2005;19(5):621–629.
78. Nelson DR, Koymans L, Kamataki T, et al. P450 superfamily: update on new sequences, gene mapping, accession numbers and nomenclature. *Pharmacogenetics*. 1996;6(1):1–42.
79. Guengerich FP. Cytochrome P-450 3A4: regulation and role in drug metabolism. *Annu Rev Pharmacol Toxicol*. 1999;39:1–17.
80. Musshoff F, Stamer UM, Madea B. Pharmacogenetics and forensic toxicology. *Forensic Sci Int*. 2010;203(1–3):53–62.
81. Kirchheiner J, Brockmoller J. Clinical consequences of cytochrome P450 2C9 polymorphisms. *Clin Pharmacol Ther*. 2005;77(1):1–16.
82. Kirchheiner J. CYP2D6 and CYP2C19 genotype-based dose recommendations for antidepressants: a first step towards subpopulation dosages (vol 104, pg 173, 2001). *Acta Psychiatr Scand*. 2001;104(6):475–475.
83. Gage BF, Eby C, Johnson JA, et al. Use of pharmacogenetic and clinical factors to predict the therapeutic dose of warfarin. *Clin Pharmacol Ther*. 2008;84(3):326–331.
84. Gage BF, Lesko LJ. Pharmacogenetics of warfarin: regulatory, scientific, and clinical issues. *J Thromb Thrombolysis*. 2008;25(1):45–51.

85. Blaisdell J, Mohrenweiser H, Jackson J, et al. Identification and functional characterization of new potentially defective alleles of human CYP2C19. *Pharmacogenetics.* 2002;12(9):703–711.
86. Mega JL, Close SL, Wiviott SD, et al. Cytochrome p-450 polymorphisms and response to clopidogrel. *N Engl J Med.* 2009;360(4):354–362.
87. Somogyi AA, Barratt DT, Coller JK. Pharmacogenetics of opioids. *Clin Pharmacol Ther.* 2007;81(3):429–444.
88. Ueda K, Clark DP, Chen CJ, Roninson IB, Gottesman MM, Pastan I. The human multidrug resistance (mdrl) gene. cDNA cloning and transcription initiation. *J Biol Chem.* 1987;262(2):505–508.
89. Vafadari R, Bouamar R, Hesselink DA, et al. Genetic polymorphisms in ABCB1 influence the pharmacodynamics of tacrolimus. *Ther Drug Monit.* 2013;35(4):459–465.
90. Ayrton A, Morgan P. Role of transport proteins in drug absorption, distribution and excretion. *Xenobiotica.* 2001;31(8–9):469–497.
91. Rong G, Jing L, Deng-Qing L, Hong-Shan Z, Shai-Hong Z, Xin-Min N. Influence of CYP3A5 and MDR1(ABCB1) polymorphisms on the pharmacokinetics of tacrolimus in Chinese renal transplant recipients. *Transpl Proc.* 2010;42(9):3455–3458.
92. Thiebaut F, Tsuruo T, Hamada H, Gottesman MM, Pastan I, Willingham MC. Cellular localization of the multidrug-resistance gene product P-glycoprotein in normal human tissues. *Proc Natl Acad Sci U S A.* 1987;84(21):7735–7738.
93. Linnet K, Ejsing TB. A review on the impact of P-glycoprotein on the penetration of drugs into the brain. Focus on psychotropic drugs. *Eur Neuropsychopharmacol.* 2008;18(3):157–169.
94. Yuferov V, Levran O, Proudnikov D, Nielsen DA, Kreek MJ. Search for genetic markers and functional variants involved in the development of opiate and cocaine addiction and treatment. *Ann N Y Acad Sci.* 2010;1187:184–207.
95. Bierut LJ. Genetic vulnerability and susceptibility to substance dependence. *Neuron.* 2011;69(4):618–627.
96. Khokhar JY, Ferguson CS, Zhu AZ, Tyndale RF. Pharmacogenetics of drug dependence: role of gene variations in susceptibility and treatment. *Annu Rev Pharmacol Toxicol.* 2010;50:39–61.
97. Sultatos LG, Pastino GM, Rosenfeld CA, Flynn EJ. Incorporation of the genetic control of alcohol dehydrogenase into a physiologically based pharmacokinetic model for ethanol in humans. *Toxicol Sci.* 2004;78(1):20–31.
98. Forney RB. Disposition and fate of ethanol in the body. In: Caplan YH, Goldberger BA, eds. *Garriott's Medical-Legal Aspects of Alcohol.* 6th ed. Tucson, AZ: Lawyers & Judges Publishing Company; 2015:49–158.
99. Radel M, Goldman D. Pharmacogenetics of alcohol response and alcoholism: the interplay of genes and environmental factors in thresholds for alcoholism. *Drug Metab Dispos.* 2001;29(4 Pt 2):489–494.
100. Kamendulis LM, Brzezinski MR, Pindel EV, Bosron WF, Dean RA. Metabolism of cocaine and heroin is catalyzed by the same human liver carboxylesterases. *J Pharmacol Exp Ther.* 1996;279(2):713–717.
101. Kreek MJ, LaForge KS, Butelman E. Pharmacotherapy of addictions. *Nat Rev.* 2002;1(9):710–726.
102. Molinoff PB, Axelrod J. Biochemistry of catecholamines. *Annu Rev Biochem.* 1971;40:465–500.
103. Axelrod J. Biochemical pharmacology of catecholamines and its clinical implications. *Trans Am Neurol Assoc.* 1971;96:179–186.
104. *Goodman & Gilman's: The Pharmacological Basis of Therapeutics.* 10th ed. McGraw-Hill; 2001.
105. Kreek MJ, Bart G, Lilly C, LaForge KS, Nielsen DA. Pharmacogenetics and human molecular genetics of opiate and cocaine addictions and their treatments. *Pharmacol Rev.* 2005;57(1):1–26.
106. Vanderah TW. Delta and kappa opioid receptors as suitable drug targets for pain. *Clin J Pain.* 2010;26 Suppl 10:S10–15.
107. Di Chiara G, Imperato A. Opposite effects of mu and kappa opiate agonists on dopamine release in the nucleus accumbens and in the dorsal caudate of freely moving rats. *J Pharmacol Exp Ther.* 1988;244(3):1067–1080.
108. Langman LJ, Snozek CL. The challenges of personalized medicine. *Clin Biochem.* 2012;45(6):382–383.
109. Gaedigk A, Simon SD, Pearce RE, Bradford LD, Kennedy MJ, Leeder JS. The CYP2D6 activity score: translating genotype information into a qualitative measure of phenotype. *Clin Pharmacol Ther.* 2008;83(2):234–242.
110. Koski A, Sistonen J, Ojanpera I, Gergov M, Vuori E, Sajantila A. CYP2D6 and CYP2C19 genotypes and amitriptyline metabolite ratios in a series of medicolegal autopsies. *Forensic Sci Int.* 2006;158(2–3):177–183.
111. Barnes SN, Aleksunes LM, Augustine L, et al. Induction of hepatobiliary efflux transporters in acetaminophen-induced acute liver failure cases. *Drug Metab Dispos.* 2007;35(10):1963–1969.
112. Eaton DL, Gilbert SG. Chapter 2. Principles of toxicology. In: Watkins JBI, Klaassen C, eds. *Essentials of Toxicology.* 2nd ed. McGraw-Hill Companies, Inc.; 2010.
113. Eaton DL, Gilbert SG. Chapter 2. Principles of toxicology. In: Klaassen C, ed. *Toxicology: The Basic Science of Poisons.* 7th ed. McGraw-Hill Companies, Inc.; 2007.
114. Shen H, He MM, Liu H, et al. Comparative metabolic capabilities and inhibitory profiles of CYP2D6.1, CYP2D6.10, and CYP2D6.17. *Drug Metab Dispos.* 2007;35(8):1292–1300.
115. Tyndale RF, Sunahara R, Inaba T, Kalow W, Gonzalez FJ, Niznik HB. Neuronal cytochrome P450IID1 (debrisoquine/sparteine-type): potent inhibition of activity by (-)-cocaine and nucleotide sequence identity to human hepatic P450 gene CYP2D6. *Mol Pharmacol.* 1991;40(1):63–68.
116. Otton SV, Ball SE, Cheung SW, Inaba T, Rudolph RL, Sellers EM. Venlafaxine oxidation in vitro is catalysed by CYP2D6. *Br J Clin Pharmacol.* 1996;41(2):149–156.
117. Owen JR, Nemeroff CB. New antidepressants and the cytochrome P450 system: focus on venlafaxine, nefazodone, and mirtazapine. *Depression and Anxiety.* 1998;7 Suppl 1:24–32.
118. Ramamoorthy Y, Tyndale RF, Sellers EM. Cytochrome P450 2D6.1 and cytochrome P450 2D6.10 differ in catalytic activity for multiple substrates. *Pharmacogenetics.* 2001;11(6):477–487.
119. Druid H, Holmgren P, Carlsson B, Ahlner J. Cytochrome P450 2D6 (CYP2D6) genotyping on postmortem blood as a supplementary tool for interpretation of forensic toxicological results. *Forensic Sci Int.* 1999;99(1):25–34.
120. Koren G, Cairns J, Chitayat D, Gaedigk A, Leeder SJ. Pharmacogenetics of morphine poisoning in a breastfed neonate of a codeine-prescribed mother. *Lancet.* 2006;368(9536):704.
121. Meny RG, Naumburg EG, Alger LS, Brill-Miller JL, Brown S. Codeine and the breastfed neonate. *J Hum Lact.* 1993;9(4):237–240.
122. Meyer UA. Pharmacogenetics and adverse drug reactions. *Lancet.* 2000;356(9242):1667–1671.

123. Hilmer SN, Ford GA. Chapter 8. General principles of pharmacology. In: Halter JB, Ouslander JG, Tinetti ME, Studenski S, High KP, Asthana S, eds. *Hazzard's Geriatric Medicine and Gerontology, 6ème*. New York: The McGraw-Hill Companies; 2009.
124. Compton WM, Thomas YF, Stinson FS, Grant BF. Prevalence, correlates, disability, and comorbidity of DSM-IV drug abuse and dependence in the United States: results from the national epidemiologic survey on alcohol and related conditions. *Arch Gen Psychiatry*. 2007;64(5):566–576.
125. Merikangas KR, McClair VL. Epidemiology of substance use disorders. *Hum Genet*. 2012;131(6):779–789.
126. Martins SS, Sampson L, Cerda M, Galea S. Worldwide prevalence and trends in unintentional drug overdose: a systematic review of the literature. *Am J Public Health*. 2015;105(11):e29–49.
127. Verhulst B, Neale MC, Kendler KS. The heritability of alcohol use disorders: a meta-analysis of twin and adoption studies. *Psychol Med*. 2015;45(5):1061–1072.
128. Agrawal A, Lynskey MT. Are there genetic influences on addiction: evidence from family, adoption and twin studies. *Addiction*. 2008;103(7):1069–1081.
129. Swendsen J, Le Moal M. Individual vulnerability to addiction. *Ann N Y Acad Sci*. 2011;1216:73–85.
130. Karch S. *Karch's Pathology of Drug Abuse*. Boca Raton, FL: CRC Press; 2002.
131. Kloner RA, Hale S, Alker K, Rezkalla S. The effects of acute and chronic cocaine use on the heart. *Circulation*. 1992;85(2):407–419.
132. Schwartz BG, Rezkalla S, Kloner RA. Cardiovascular effects of cocaine. *Circulation*. 2010;122(24):2558–2569.
133. Stankowski RV, Kloner RA, Rezkalla SH. Cardiovascular consequences of cocaine use. *Trends Cardiovasc Med*. 2015;25(6):517–526.
134. Flores ED, Lange RA, Cigarroa RG, Hillis LD. Effect of cocaine on coronary artery dimensions in atherosclerotic coronary artery disease: enhanced vasoconstriction at sites of significant stenoses. *J Am Coll Cardiol*. 1990;16(1):74–79.
135. Almaddah N, Ajayi TO. IMAGES IN CLINICAL MEDICINE. Cocaine-induced coronary-artery vasospasm. *N Engl J Med*. 2016;374(5):e5.
136. Templin C, Ghadri JR, Diekmann J, et al. Clinical features and outcomes of Takotsubo (stress) cardiomyopathy. *N Engl J Med*. 2015;373(10):929–938.
137. Lyon AR, Bossone E, Schneider B, et al. Current state of knowledge on Takotsubo syndrome: a position statement from the taskforce on Takotsubo syndrome of the heart failure association of the European society of cardiology. *Eur J Heart Fail*. 2016;18(1):8–27.
138. Templin C, Ghadri JR, Napp LC. Takotsubo (stress) cardiomyopathy. *N Engl J Med*. 2015;373(27):2689–2691.
139. Cebelin MS, Hirsch CS. Human stress cardiomyopathy. Myocardial lesions in victims of homicidal assaults without internal injuries. *Hum Pathol*. 1980;11(2):123–132.
140. Deshmukh A, Kumar G, Pant S, Rihal C, Murugiah K, Mehta JL. Prevalence of Takotsubo cardiomyopathy in the United States. *Am Heart J*. 2012;164(1):66–71.
141. Butterfield M, Riguzzi C, Frenkel O, Nagdev A. Stimulant-related Takotsubo cardiomyopathy. *Am J Emerg Med*. 2015;33(3):476 e471–473.
142. Aoki Y, Kodera S, Watanabe T, Miyauchi Y, Kanda J, Ooe K. Autopsy findings in takotsubo cardiomyopathy with special reference to the autonomic nervous system. *Int J Cardiol*. 2016;203:236–237.
143. Tran K, Milne N, Duhig E, Altman M. Inverted Takotsubo cardiomyopathy--clinicopathologic correlation. *Am J Forensic Med Pathol*. 2013;34(3):217–221.
144. Veerman CC, Wilde AA, Lodder EM. The cardiac sodium channel gene SCN5A and its gene product NaV1.5: role in physiology and pathophysiology. *Gene*. 2015;573(2):177–187.
145. Zhang S, Rajamani S, Chen Y, et al. Cocaine blocks HERG, but not KvLQT1+minK, potassium channels. *Mol Pharmacol*. 2001;59(5):1069–1076.
146. Sanguinetti MC, Tristani-Firouzi M. hERG potassium channels and cardiac arrhythmia. *Nature*. 2006;440(7083):463–469.
147. Crumb WJ, Jr., Clarkson CW. Characterization of cocaine-induced block of cardiac sodium channels. *Biophys J*. 1990;57(3):589–599.
148. O'Leary ME, Hancox JC. Role of voltage-gated sodium, potassium and calcium channels in the development of cocaine-associated cardiac arrhythmias. *Br J Clin Pharmacol*. 2010;69(5):427–442.
149. Littmann L, Monroe MH, Svenson RH. Brugada-type electrocardiographic pattern induced by cocaine. *Mayo Clin Proc*. 2000;75(8):845–849.
150. Ortega-Carnicer J, Bertos-Polo J, Gutierrez-Tirado C. Aborted sudden death, transient Brugada pattern, and wide QRS dysrrhythmias after massive cocaine ingestion. *J Electrocardiol*. 2001;34(4):345–349.
151. Perera R, Kraebber A, Schwartz MJ. Prolonged QT interval and cocaine use. *J Electrocardiol*. 1997;30(4):337–339.
152. Taylor D, Parish D, Thompson L, Cavaliere M. Cocaine induced prolongation of the QT interval. *Emerg Med J*. 2004;21(2):252–253.
153. Hawley LA, Auten JD, Matteucci MJ, et al. Cardiac complications of adult methamphetamine exposures. *J Emerg Med*. 2013;45(6):821–827.
154. Liang R, Zhou Y, Wu F, et al. Effect of methamphetamine on potassium and L-type calcium currents in rat ventricular myocytes. *Toxicol Mech Methods*. 2010;20(8):458–465.
155. Wang YJ, Chan MH, Chen HH. Methamphetamine inhibits voltage-gated potassium currents in NG108-15 cells: possible contribution of large-conductance calcium-activated potassium channels. *Toxicol Lett*. 2013;223(2):139–145.
156. Won S, Hong RA, Shohet RV, Seto TB, Parikh NI. Methamphetamine-associated cardiomyopathy. *Clin Cardiol*. 2013;36(12):737–742.
157. Benzaquen BS, Cohen V, Eisenberg MJ. Effects of cocaine on the coronary arteries. *Am Heart J*. 2001;142(3):402–410.
158. Patrizi R, Pasceri V, Sciahbasi A, Summaria F, Rosano GM, Lioy E. Evidence of cocaine-related coronary atherosclerosis in young patients with myocardial infarction. *J Am Coll Cardiol*. 2006;47(10):2120–2122.
159. Karch SB, Stephens BG, Ho CH. Methamphetamine-related deaths in San Francisco: demographic, pathologic, and toxicologic profiles. *J Forensic Sci*. 1999;44(2):359–368.
160. Simpson RW, Edwards WD. Pathogenesis of cocaine-induced ischemic heart disease. Autopsy findings in a 21-year-old man. *Arch Pathol Lab Med*. 1986;110(6):479–484.
161. Pattinson KT. Opioids and the control of respiration. *Br J Anaesth*. 2008;100(6):747–758.
162. Plunkett LM, Seifen E, Kennedy RH. Effects of morphine pretreatment on cocaine cardiotoxicity in anesthetized guinea-pigs. *Arch Int Pharmacodyn Ther*. 1989;297:60–67.
163. Tomashefski JF, Jr., Hirsch CS. The pulmonary vascular lesions of intravenous drug abuse. *Hum Pathol*. 1980;11(2):133–145.
164. Hind CR. Pulmonary complications of intravenous drug misuse. 1. Epidemiology and non-infective complications. *Thorax*. 1990;45(11):891–898.

165. Frontera JA, Gradon JD. Right-side endocarditis in injection drug users: review of proposed mechanisms of pathogenesis. *Clin Infect Dis.* 2000;30(2):374–379.
166. Moss R, Munt B. Injection drug use and right sided endocarditis. *Heart.* 2003;89(5):577–581.
167. Mathew J, Addai T, Anand A, Morrobel A, Maheshwari P, Freels S. Clinical features, site of involvement, bacteriologic findings, and outcome of infective endocarditis in intravenous drug users. *Arch Intern Med.* 1995;155(15):1641–1648.
168. Baddour LM, Wilson WR, Bayer AS, et al. Infective endocarditis: diagnosis, antimicrobial therapy, and management of complications: a statement for healthcare professionals from the Committee on Rheumatic Fever, Endocarditis, and Kawasaki Disease, Council on Cardiovascular Disease in the Young, and the Councils on Clinical Cardiology, Stroke, and Cardiovascular Surgery and Anesthesia, American Heart Association: endorsed by the Infectious Diseases Society of America. *Circulation.* 2005;111(23):e394–434.
169. Castonguay MC, Burner KD, Edwards WD, Baddour LM, Maleszewski JJ. Surgical pathology of native valve endocarditis in 310 specimens from 287 patients (1985–2004). *Cardiovasc Pathol.* 2013;22(1):19–27.
170. Schwartz PJ, Stramba-Badiale M, Crotti L, et al. Prevalence of the congenital long-QT syndrome. *Circulation.* 2009;120(18):1761–1767.
171. Mann D, Zipes D, Libby P, Bonow R, Braunwald E, eds. *Braunwald's Heart Disease: A Textbook of Cardiovascular Medicine.* Philadelphia, PA: Elsevier Saunders; 2015.
172. Khera S, Jacobson JT. Short QT syndrome in current clinical practice. *Cardiol Rev.* 2016;24(4):190–193.
173. Schwartz PJ, Woosley RL. Predicting the unpredictable: drug-induced QT prolongation and Torsades de Pointes. *J Am Coll Cardiol.* 2016;67(13):1639–1650.
174. Priori SG, Wilde AA, Horie M, et al. Executive summary: HRS/EHRA/APHRS expert consensus statement on the diagnosis and management of patients with inherited primary arrhythmia syndromes. *Heart Rhythm.* 2013;10(12):e85–108.
175. Postema PG. About Brugada syndrome and its prevalence. *Europace.* 2012;14(7):925–928.
176. Mizusawa Y, Wilde AA. Brugada syndrome. *Circ Arrhythm Electrophysiol.* 2012;5(3):606–616.
177. Veltmann C, Barajas-Martinez H, Wolpert C, et al. Further insights in the most common SCN5A mutation causing overlapping phenotype of long QT syndrome, Brugada syndrome, and conduction defect. *J Am Heart Assoc.* 2016;5(7).
178. Leenhardt A, Lucet V, Denjoy I, Grau F, Ngoc DD, Coumel P. Catecholaminergic polymorphic ventricular tachycardia in children. A 7-year follow-up of 21 patients. *Circulation.* 1995;91(5):1512–1519.
179. Tester DJ, Medeiros-Domingo A, Will ML, Ackerman MJ. Unexplained drownings and the cardiac channelopathies: a molecular autopsy series. *Mayo Clin Proc.* 2011;86(10):941–947.
180. Methner DN, Scherer SE, Welch K, et al. Postmortem genetic screening for the identification, verification, and reporting of genetic variants contributing to the sudden death of the young. *Genome Res.* 2016.
181. Anderson JH, Tester DJ, Will ML, Ackerman MJ. Whole-exome molecular autopsy after exertion-related sudden unexplained death in the young. *Circ Cardiovasc Genet.* 2016;9(3):259–265.
182. Ackerman MJ. Genetic purgatory and the cardiac channelopathies: exposing the variants of uncertain/unknown significance issue. *Heart Rhythm.* 2015;12(11):2325–2331.
183. Arbustini E, Narula N, Tavazzi L, et al. The MOGE(S) classification of cardiomyopathy for clinicians. *J Am Coll Cardiol.* 2014;64(3):304–318.
184. Maron BJ, Gardin JM, Flack JM, Gidding SS, Kurosaki TT, Bild DE. Prevalence of hypertrophic cardiomyopathy in a general population of young adults. Echocardiographic analysis of 4111 subjects in the CARDIA Study. Coronary Artery Risk Development in (Young) Adults. *Circulation.* 1995;92(4):785–789.
185. Harmon KG, Asif IM, Maleszewski JJ, et al. Incidence, cause, and comparative frequency of sudden cardiac death in National Collegiate Athletic Association Athletes: a decade in review. *Circulation.* 2015;132(1):10–19.
186. Harmon KG, Drezner JA, Maleszewski JJ, et al. Pathogeneses of sudden cardiac death in national collegiate athletic association athletes. *Circ Arrhythm Electrophysiol.* 2014;7(2):198–204.
187. McNally EM, Golbus JR, Puckelwartz MJ. Genetic mutations and mechanisms in dilated cardiomyopathy. *J Clin Invest.* 2013;123(1):19–26.
188. Maron BJ, Maron MS, Semsarian C. Genetics of hypertrophic cardiomyopathy after 20 years: clinical perspectives. *J Am Coll Cardiol.* 2012;60(8):705–715.
189. Sylvester J, Seidenberg P, Silvis M. The dilemma of genotype positive-phenotype negative hypertrophic cardiomyopathy. *Curr Sports Med Rep.* 2014;13(2):94–99.
190. Maron BJ, Ho CY. Hypertrophic cardiomyopathy without hypertrophy: an emerging pre-clinical subgroup composed of genetically affected family members. *JACC Cardiovasc Imaging.* 2009;2(1):65–68.
191. Ho CY, Lopez B, Coelho-Filho OR, et al. Myocardial fibrosis as an early manifestation of hypertrophic cardiomyopathy. *N Engl J Med.* 2010;363(6):552–563.
192. Maron BJ, Spirito P. Implications of left ventricular remodeling in hypertrophic cardiomyopathy. *Am J Cardiol.* 1998;81(11):1339–1344.
193. Olivotto I, Cecchi F, Poggesi C, Yacoub MH. Patterns of disease progression in hypertrophic cardiomyopathy: an individualized approach to clinical staging. *Circ Heart Fail.* 2012;5(4):535–546.
194. Hershberger RE, Hedges DJ, Morales A. Dilated cardiomyopathy: the complexity of a diverse genetic architecture. *Nat Rev Cardiol.* 2013;10(9):531–547.
195. Morales A, Hershberger RE. Genetic evaluation of dilated cardiomyopathy. *Curr Cardiol Rep.* 2013;15(7):375.
196. MacLeod HM, Culley MR, Huber JM, McNally EM. Lamin A/C truncation in dilated cardiomyopathy with conduction disease. *BMC Med Genet.* 2003;4:4.
197. Marcus FI, McKenna WJ, Sherrill D, et al. Diagnosis of arrhythmogenic right ventricular cardiomyopathy/dysplasia: proposed modification of the task force criteria. *Circulation.* 2010;121(13):1533–1541.
198. Basso C, Thiene G, Corrado D, Angelini A, Nava A, Valente M. Arrhythmogenic right ventricular cardiomyopathy. Dysplasia, dystrophy, or myocarditis? *Circulation.* 1996;94(5):983–991.
199. Marcus FI, McKenna WJ, Sherrill D, et al. Diagnosis of arrhythmogenic right ventricular cardiomyopathy/dysplasia: proposed modification of the task force criteria. *Eur Heart J.* 2010;31(7):806–814.
200. Corrado D, Thiene G. Arrhythmogenic right ventricular cardiomyopathy/dysplasia: clinical impact of molecular genetic studies. *Circulation.* 2006;113(13):1634–1637.
201. Thiene G, Nava A, Corrado D, Rossi L, Pennelli N. Right ventricular cardiomyopathy and sudden death in young people. *N Engl J Med.* 1988;318(3):129–133.

6 Point of Collection Drug Testing

Section Editor: Dennis J. Crouch

CONTENTS

DOI: 10.4324/9781315155159-6

6.1 POC TESTING OF ALTERNATE SPECIMENS (OTHER THAN URINE)

J. Michael Walsh

This chapter was originally written between 2002 and 2004 with co-author Alain Verstraete. The following is an attempt to update the subject matter to include scientific and technical developments that have occurred over the last 15 years. As you will come to understand, during this time period there have been many acquisitions and mergers of the diagnostic companies involved in the development and manufacturing of the subject devices, some companies no longer exist, and some devices have reappeared with new names. An extensive internet search revealed that there are only a relative few devices developed by major diagnostic companies and a plethora of private label devices made by OEM manufacturers. In the marketing and advertising materials for many of the less expensive bulk purchased devices, there is no information regarding the actual manufacturer of the device and it is difficult to determine whether these devices offer varying technical advantages or whether they are essentially all the same.

In 1984, Rodgers et al.[1] developed an enzyme-channeling test strip immunoassay for the detection of cannabinoids in saliva. The limit of detection was 10 ng/ml of THCCOOH. The antibody had high cross-reactivity for THC, and the test was positive for 2 to 2.5 h after smoking. Since the mid-1990s, there has been a growing interest in POCT testing of alternative specimens for drugs.

Some researchers and device manufacturers have attempted to use POCT tests (designed for urine) to test alternative matrices, but with mixed results. Indeed, in alternative matrices, the drug concentrations are often lower than in urine and the parent molecules are excreted, more than the metabolites. Therefore, antibodies with other target molecules must be used. Iwersen and Schmoldt[2] tried to adapt the Boehringer Frontline urine assay (which was subsequently used in the Drugwipe) for analysis of saliva. By increasing the contact time of the saliva specimen to the collection pad they could perform the analysis; however, up to 8 min was needed in some cases to obtain sufficient moistening of the pad. They observed no false-positive, but many false-negative cases. The sensitivity of the modified procedure was 73%, 53%, and 75% for cocaine, cannabis, and opiates, respectively.

The first on-site or Point-of-Collection testing (POCT) devices that were commercially available for oral fluid analyses were the Securetec Drugwipe® (that could be used for sweat, as well), Avitar Oralscreen,™ and Cozart Rapiscan. The European project ROSITA[3] (Roadside Testing Assessment) was the first large-scale evaluation of POCT oral fluid- and sweat-testing devices, and it provided a strong impetus for further development of POCT products for saliva/oral fluid and sweat.

TABLE 6.1.1
Possible Applications of Point-of-Collection Drug Testing Devices

1. Workplace drug testing
2. Roadside drug testing/Traffic Enforcement
3. Treatment centers/Rehabilitation programs
4. Correctional [Prisons/Probation & Parole programs]
5. Insurance physicals
6. Emergency departments
7. Autopsy rooms
8. Security

Most POCT research and development efforts in the last 20 years, for specimens other than urine, have been directed primarily toward testing of saliva/oral fluid. Although some testing of perspiration/sweat has been carried out, this has been done on a much more limited scale. To the author's knowledge, no Point-of-Collection tests currently exist for hair or nails.

Table 6.1.1 lists possible applications of oral fluid POCT devices. The most likely applications are workplace, correctional programs, and roadside drug-testing in traffic enforcement. As of 2004, POCT oral fluid tests were beginning to be used in prisons and some workplaces (mining, printing, transportation, and manufacturing). Over the last 15 years, while laboratory-based oral fluid testing has become quite widespread in workplace testing (e.g., Quest Diagnostics reported testing roughly one million oral fluid workplace specimens in 2015),[4] however, the use of POCT devices in the workplace remains somewhat limited and typically are limited to pre-employment tests. At the time of this writing, the U.S. Department of Health and Human Services has approved oral fluid as an authorized specimen for federally regulated drug-testing programs, but not sweat nor any POCT device.

POCT roadside controls by police using alternative matrices such as oral fluid have generally only been performed on an experimental basis, although legislation enacted in Australia authorizes police to perform roadside oral fluid tests for cannabis, methamphetamine, and methylenedioxymethamphetamine (MDMA) using POCT devices.[5] Australian police have used a two-test procedure where they screen using the Drugwipe II device and confirm presumptive positives using the Cozart Rapiscan (now the Alere DDS2). Research reports indicate that a problem they have encountered has been the dissonance in the sensitivity of the two devices and a failure to confirm screened positives because the confirmation test was less sensitive than the screening assay. Recent legislative changes in some European countries (e.g. Belgium) have also permitted the use of oral fluid POCT devices as a screening test for police traffic enforcement.

In the U.K., the Cozart Rapiscan has been in use since 2001 by the Home Office to test for drugs of abuse (cocaine and heroin) in arrestees detained in police custody.[5]

A few of the rapid POCT devices currently available on the market today are instrumented and automated. Automated devices include the Draeger 5000, the Alere DDS2 device (an improved version of the former Cozart Rapiscan), and the BIOSENS®300 and 600 versions. The Draeger and BIOSENS devices are desktop models, whereas the DDS2 is a handheld device. The majority of the rest of available POCT assays on the market are visually interpreted devices that rely primarily on lateral flow immunoassay technology.

There are many variables to consider when using any of these devices including:

- Time necessary to conduct the test
- Whether there is a sample adequacy indicator to assure adequate sample has been collected
- The number and type of drugs tested per test sample
- The cut-off values of each drug being tested
- Specificity and sensitivity of each of the assays
- False-positives/false-negatives
- The population being tested
- Cost per test
- Failure rates of the device being able to run to completion

Table 6.1.2 is an overview of commercially available devices currently being marketed by direct marketing and on the Internet. The web sites cited provide marketing information, and some manufacturers offer detailed product information, but generally only limited technical information is available especially for the OEM products.

6.1.1 Testing Devices/Techniques

6.1.1.1 Examples of Devices

During the 1999–2000 ROSITA project,[3] three POCT devices for saliva and one device for sweat were identified. By the end of 2003, ten different devices were commercially available. Over the years, some devices have disappeared or have been withdrawn from the market, some have been significantly redesigned, and a plethora of new devices have appeared. In 2015, the DRUID project reported the results of an evaluation on 13 devices, and in our 2017 assessment we have identified 18 devices that are currently being marketed.

6.1.1.2 Principle of POC Testing Methods

Most rapid oral fluid and sweat tests use lateral flow immunoassay technology, based on the principle of competitive binding where drugs in the specimen compete against their respective drug conjugate for binding sites on their specific antibody. Typically the results are interpreted by visual evaluation, however, some of the devices can be coupled to electronic readers and the results read automatically.

TABLE 6.1.2
Overview of POCT Oral Fluid Drug Tests

Manufacturer	Device	Auto	Visual	# Drugs Tested	Website
Alere Toxicology, USA	DDS®2	X	X	7 drug options	http://www.alere.com/en/home/product-details/dds2-mobile-test-system.html
	Oratect®		X	6 drugs	
	DDS®V			Up to 6 drugs	
	IScreen OFD			Up to 6 drugs	
Biosensor AB, Sweden	Biosens 600	X			Biosensor.se/products/biosens-600/
Draeger Safety, Germany	DrugTest 5000	X	X		https://www.draeger.com/Products/Content/drugtest%205000%20analyzer_06_14_2013_drug%20test%205000 %20analyzer%20low%20res-1.pdf
	DrugCheck 3000				
Securetec AG, Germany	DrugWipe®S		X	7 Drugs	https://www.securetec.net/en/saliva-drug-test-drugwipe
Marvand GmbH, Germany	Rapid Stat		X	2 to 7 drugs	mavand.de/en/products/drug-tests/rapid-statr.html
ABMC, USA	Oralstat		X	6 or 10 drugs	abmc.com
Envitec GmbH, Germany	Smartclip			2 or 4 drugs	
Ulti Med, Germany	SalivaScreen		X	Up to 11 drugs	Ultimed.org
Confirm Biosciences	SalivaConfirm		X	5, 6, and 10 panels	Confirmbiosciences.com
	Swab Cube		X	10 drug test + alcohol	http://www.swab-cube.com/
Innovacon*, USA	Oralert		X	6 drugs	http://oralert.com/ or Innovaconinc.com
	MD Saliva Screen		X	10 drug panel	https://www.medicaldisposables.us/10-panel-saliva-drug-test-p/md-s6101.htm
	Oral Cube		X	11 drugs + alcohol	Amazon.com, Rapidexams.com, and others
Alfa Scientific Designs	Driven Flow		X		alfascientific.com/products/saliva-cards/

*Innovacon Inc. is a subsidiary of Alere Toxicology specializing in OEM production.

Another technology, used by the BIOSENS system, is based on immunoassay principles combined with Surface Acoustic Wave (SAW) technology. This technology currently enables detection of trace amounts of up to 12 substance groups simultaneously.

6.1.1.3 Operation (General)

One can sort out the available POCT devices in various ways, such as by cost, number of drugs tested, time to complete the test, cut-offs, setting where the testing will occur, complexity of the device operation, etc. A comprehensive discussion on all available devices is beyond the scope of this chapter so six examples are briefly presented to provide some level of comparison across the continuum of different types of devices available ranging from the least expensive simple tests to the more expensive automated devices (Figures 6.1.1 to 6.1.5).

The Oratect saliva drug test kit is an on-site saliva test used to detect the presence of six commonly abused drugs. Formerly called Oratect III, the new HM15 Oratect drug test kit is made in the U.S. and the manufacturer claims it is the only FDA-cleared saliva drug test kit. The Oratect saliva test kit detects the presence of amphetamines (AMP), cocaine (COC), marijuana (THC), methamphetamines including MDMA (Ecstasy), opiates (OPI), and phencyclidine (PCP), using a single saliva sample.

The Dräger DrugTest®5000 system comprises two main components, the DrugTest 5000 Test Kits and the DrugTest 5000 Analyzer. The manufacturer claims the system is a fast, accurate means of testing oral fluid samples for drugs of abuse, such as amphetamines, designer amphetamines, opiates, cocaine and metabolites, benzodiazepine, cannabinoids, or methadone. Draeger offers a very low cut-off for THC at 5 ng/ml.

Draeger DrugTest 5000 – operation requires three steps (Figure 6.1.6):

1) **Specimen collection**: the oral fluid donor moves the top part of the collector briefly back and forth between his/her cheek and gum until the integrated specimen volume indicator signals that an adequate sample has been collected.
2) **Analysis**: the operator inserts the test cassette and cartridge directly into the Dräger DrugTest 5000 Analyzer for evaluation, and
3) **Read results**: once the device is put into operation, the analysis will run automatically and results displayed and printed out.

6.1.1.4 Evaluations of Devices

Over the last 15 years a few major research projects (ROSITA, ROSITA II, and the DRUID projects) have been conducted. Within the framework of these projects were a number of studies evaluating many of the devices that are currently available on the market. During the first ROSITA study[3] [1999–2000] the three devices available at the time were evaluated for possible use in police traffic enforcement. The results (Table 6.1.3) indicated that their sensitivity, specificity, and accuracy were not sufficient to recommend for police or workplace, but differences in confirmation techniques and prevalence of positive samples made comparisons difficult. Over the last 15 years many of these devices were modified to improve their sensitivity and reliability.

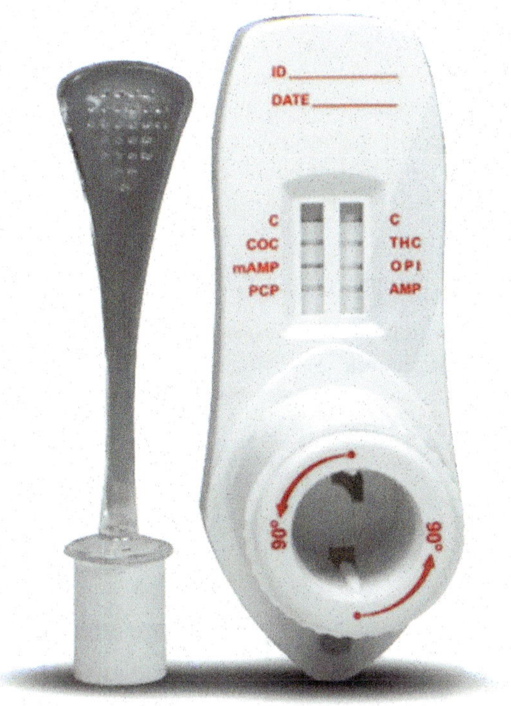

FIGURE 6.1.1 Oralert 6 Panel Oral Fluids Device (COC/AMP/mAMP/THC/OPI/BZO). For forensic and research use only. Not intended for home use. This Instant 6 Panel Multi-Drug Test can detect 6 different drugs using oral human fluid (saliva). The manufacturer claims this test is easy to use, accurate and easy to read. Collection time is about three minutes to completely saturate the collector sponge and results are ready to read in about nine minutes. However, the operational instructions include roughly five steps as follows: (1). Place sponge in donor's mouth. Actively swab the inside of the mouth and tongue with sponge. As soon as the sponge softens slightly, gently press the sponge between the tongue and teeth to ensure complete saturation. The sponge is saturated when no hard spots can be detected. Collect for a total of three minutes before removing sponge. (2). Insert the sponge collector into device, push collector down into chamber, turn collector clockwise to lock into chamber and wait one minute. (3). Rotate collection chamber 90° counterclockwise. 4(). Wait nine minutes and read results. (5). If results are positive, remove collector form device and secure the reservoir with tamper evident tape. Secure cap onto collection chamber. Send device to laboratory for confirmation. Laboratory can access reservoir through stopper.

The ROSITA II project was carried out in 2003–2006 to evaluate the usability and analytical reliability of the onsite oral fluid (saliva) drug-testing devices. The project, a joint E.U.-U.S. collaboration, included research teams in six European countries (Belgium, Finland, France, Germany, Norway, and Spain), and four U.S. states (Florida, Utah,

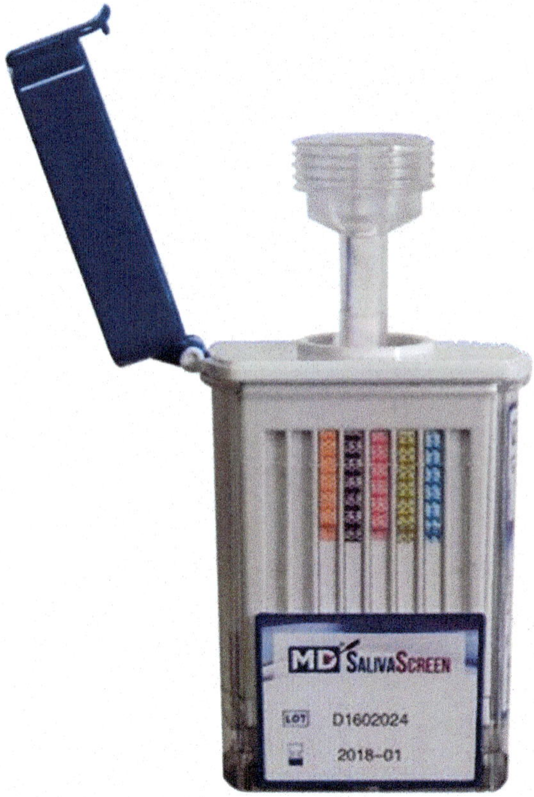

FIGURE 6.1.2 Saliva Screen – MD SalivaScreen - Oral Fluids Drug Test-10 Panel. For Forensic Use Only – The MD Saliva Screen 10 panel Oral Fluids Drug Test can simultaneously screen for 10 drugs of abuse. The manufacturer claims the drug test provides results in minutes. Sold in bulk as low as $8.45/device (see https://www.medicaldisposables.us/10-panel-saliva-drug-test-p/md-s6101.htm). Operationally, there are roughly four steps in running this device. (1). Specimen collection – the oral fluid specimen should be collected using the collector provided with the kit. No other collection devices should be used with this assay. Instruct the donor to not place anything in the mouth including food, drink, gum, or tobacco products for at least ten minutes prior to collection. Using the provided collection swab, have donor sweep inside of mouth (cheek, gums, tongue) several times, then hold swab in mouth until color on the saturation indicator strip appears in the indicator window of collection swab. Important: Do not bite, suck, or chew on the sponge. NOTE: If after seven minutes, color on the saturation indicator has not appeared in the indicator window, proceed with the test. (2). Remove collection swab from mouth and insert it sponge first into the screening device, pushing until the locking flange locks in place in the bottom of the device. (3). Keep test device upright on flat surface and keep upright while test is running. Wait for the colored bands to appear in test results area. (4). Read results at ten minutes. NOTE: Once the collection swab locks in place, the device is airtight, tamper evident, and ready to be disposed or sent to lab for confirmation (on presumptive positive result).

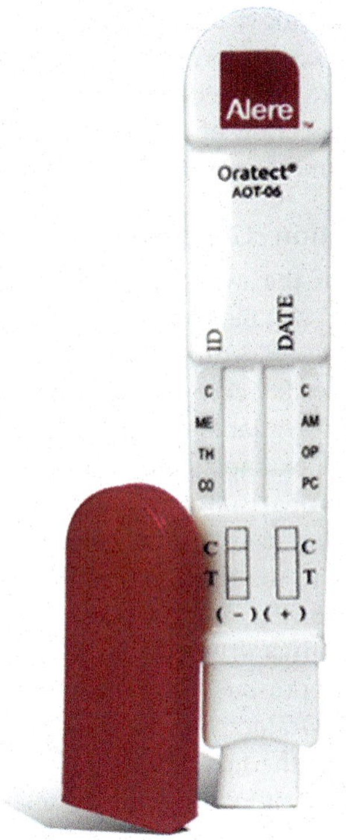

FIGURE 6.1.3 ORATECT Saliva Drug Test. Operationally this device requires a four step procedure: 1) Remove cap over collection pad, 2) Gently swab the collection pad on the inside of mouth and tongue. 3) Replace cover over collection pad, and lay the device flat. 4) Read results in five minutes.

Washington, and Wisconsin), with 9 devices evaluated: American Biomedica Oralstat, Branan Medical Oratect, Cozart Bioscience RapiScan (only in the U.S.), Dräger/Orasure DrugTest/Uplink, Lifepoint Impact, Securetec Drugwipe, Sun Biomedical Oraline, Ultimed Salivascreen, and Varian OraLab. The devices were tested for the following drugs: amphetamines, methamphetamine, cannabis, cocaine and opiates. Three devices also had a test for benzodiazepines. During the study, two devices were withdrawn from the market (Dräger/OrasureDrugTest/Uplink and Lifepoint Impact). Some 2,046 subjects were included in the study and 2,605 device evaluations were performed.

ROSITA II results indicated that, for some devices, a very high percentage of "failure to run to completion" was observed. Depending on the type of device, this was apparently due to too little or too viscous saliva (the fluid didn't migrate sufficiently to reach the control line, or it caused smears), or a malfunctioning of the instrument that read the results. For six devices (Varian Oralab, Lifepoint Impact, Branan Oratect 2nd generation, Sun Oraline, Ultimed Salivascreen, and Branan Oratect 1st generation), more than 25% of the devices failed to run. For the other devices, failures accounted for less than 10% (American Biomedica Oralstat, and Dräger DrugTest/Orasure Uplink) or less than 5% (Cozart Rapiscan and Securetec Drugwipe). The ROSITA II evaluators considered that a failure rate of maximum 5–10% was acceptable.

The number of evaluations per device varied widely, with two devices evaluated more than 500 times, one 190 times and six less than 50 times. The explanation lies in the large number of failures for Branan Medical Oratect, Ultimed Salivascreen and Varian OraLab, which led to their exclusion from the study and the late start of the evaluation of the

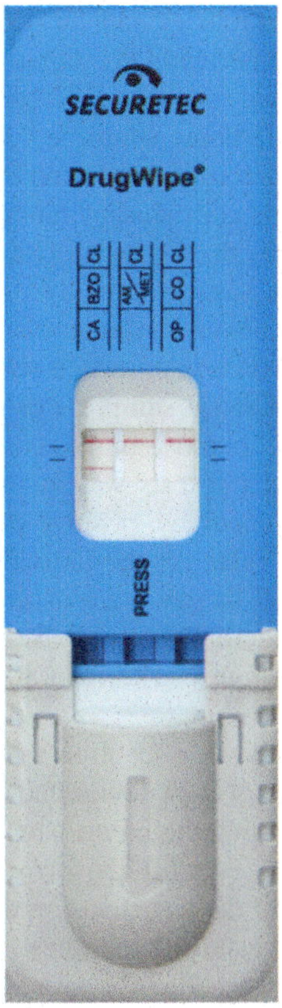

FIGURE 6.1.4 DrugWipe™ S – Saliva/Sweat Drug Screener. DrugWipe™ S is the latest version of a drug screener that tests for controlled substance in saliva/sweat. The DrugWipe™ S can test for different drug groups, including: cannabis, opiates, cocaine, amphetamine, methamphetamines (MDMA, ecstasy) and benzodiazepines. The DrugWipe™ S allows you to test for one substance or a few substances at the same time. It is convenient, hygienic and provides reliable results in less than 10 minutes (see operation video at https://youtu.be/M1DHJZyEIzU). Operationally the device requires six steps to complete the test: 1) Open safety cap, 2) Remove blue sample cover, 3) Collect sample on sample collector pads, 4) Replace cover and lock in, 5) Hold kit vertical and break ampule, 6) Read results in 8 mins.

American Biomedica Oralstat, Lifepoint Impact and Sun Biomedical Oraline.

More recently, Walsh et al.[7] evaluated the performance of six devices with drug-fortified oral fluid samples. A summary of the detection limits for the different drugs is given in Table 6.1.4. For amphetamine, methamphetamine, and opiates testing, several devices were able to successfully detect concentrations lower than the oral fluid cut-offs mentioned in "draft #4" of the SAMHSA guidelines for workplace drug testing.[8] However, there were some problems in testing cocaine (most devices target benzoylecgonine) and no device could detect THC at the 4 ng/ml recommended cut-off.

In subsequent laboratory evaluations[9,10] additional devices (Oralstat [ABMC], SmartClip [Envitec], Impact (Lifepoint], and OraLine [Sun Biomedical]) were evaluated for the ability to meet the claimed cut-off concentrations set

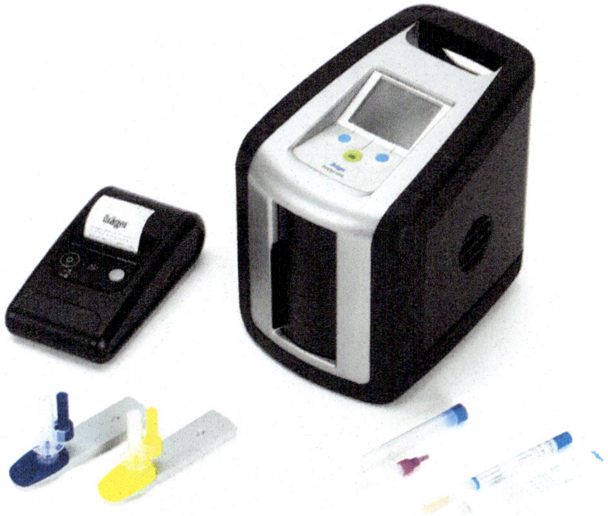

FIGURE 6.1.5 The Dräger DrugTest with optional keyboard. Operationally the device requires six steps to complete the test: 1) Open safety cap, 2) Remove blue sample cover, 3) Collect sample on sample collector pads, 4) Replace cover and lock in, 5) Hold kit vertical and break ampule, 6) Read results in 8 mins.

by the manufacturers for the detection of amphetamines(s), cocaine, opiates, and cannabinoids. Most devices performed well for the detection of opiates, and amphetamines, but approximately half of the devices had cut-off concentrations greater than that proposed by the SAMHSA. Only three devices had cocaine cut-offs less than or equal to 20 ng/ml (SAMHSA recommended), and a number of false negative results were recorded. False positive results were only observed with the Sun Biomedical OraLine device. None of the devices were capable of detecting delta 9 – THC at the 4 ng cut-off recommended by SAMHSA. Overall, results of these evaluations indicated that the sensitivity, and performance of the commercially available devices was improving but remained problematical for the reliable detection of cannabinoid use.

The DRUID Project (Driving Under the Influence of Drugs, Alcohol and Medicines) was a five-year multi-phase undertaking funded by the European Commission (2006–2010). The omnibus project looked at experimental studies, epidemiological studies, enforcement, classification of medicines, driver rehabilitation, withdrawal of driving license, driver drug testing, and dissemination and guidelines. As a result of more than five years of work by researchers across 18 countries, the project has produced some 50 reports, each one contributing key evidence to road safety policy. One of the key research projects within the framework was the "Evaluation of oral fluid Screening devices by TISPOL to Harmonize European police Requirements "(Project ESTHER). In ESTHER police officers conducted operational evaluations on 13 screening devices proposed for use in police practice. Eleven teams of police forces in six EU member states; Germany (3x), Belgium (2x), Ireland, Finland, Spain, and the Netherlands (3 x) conducted the

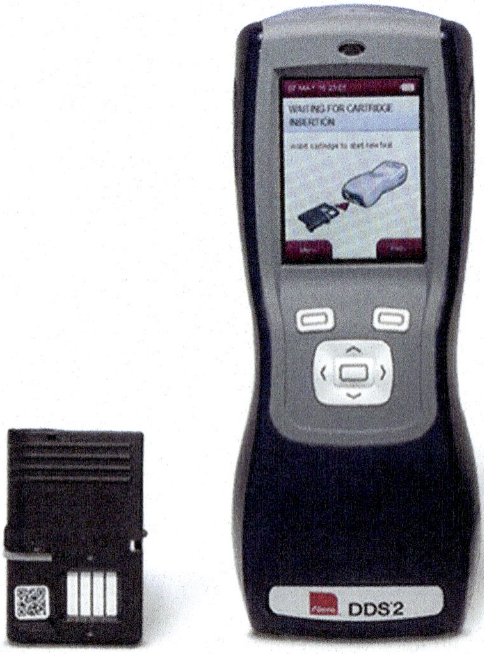

FIGURE 6.1.6 Alere DDS 2 – Alere DDS®2 Mobile Test System - Rapid Drug Screening in Oral Fluid. The Alere DDS®2 Mobile Test System is a portable system designed for rapid screening and detection for drugs of abuse in oral fluid. With actionable screening results for as many as 6 drugs in 5 minutes, the battery-operated device is portable, lightweight, and easy to use, making it ideal for roadside drug screening. Operation requires three steps: 1) insert test cartridge into analyzer, 2) collect oral fluid sample, and 3) insert oral fluid collector into the test cartridge.

evaluations. These evaluations focused on police operational issues regarding whether the device was suitable in law enforcement, for example: Simplicity of device operation, Ease of use at the roadside in all light and weather conditions, Time to get adequate specimen, Time to complete the test, Number of failure rates etc. The analytical testing of sensitivity, and specificity of the device was not a focus of these operational evaluations, but was evaluated in another DRUID project discussed below. Results of the police operational evaluations are shown in Table 6.1.5. The evaluations were conducted in two phases, and some device manufacturers made improvements to the devices which were evaluated in phase II. Data in the table showing two results indicate data collected in Phase I and Phase II.

As mentioned, another key project within the DRUID framework was the "Analytical evaluation of oral fluid screening devices and preceding selection procedures" (DRUID deliverable 3.2.2. March 2010). The analytical study was carried out by research teams in Belgium, Finland, and the Netherlands. Eight on-site tests were evaluated: BIOSENS Dynamic (Biosensor Applications Sweden AB), Cozart DDS (Cozart Bioscience Ltd.), DrugWipe 5+ (Securetec Detections-Systeme AG), Dräger DrugTest 5000 (Dräger Safety), OraLab6 (Varian), OrAlert (Innovacon), Oratect III (Branan Medical Corporation) and Rapid STAT (Mavand Solutions GmBH). The Rapid STAT device was tested in all three countries and DrugTest 5000 device in Belgium and the Netherlands. All other devices were tested in only one country. The tested substance classes were amphetamine(s), methamphetamine, MDMA, cannabis, cocaine, opiates, benzodiazepines and PCP.

Study populations consisted of randomly selected drivers from the roadside survey for DRUID (Work package 2, Task 2.2a1), drivers suspected of driving under the influence of drugs, patients of treatment centers and rehabilitation clinics and customers of coffee-shops. Oral fluid was collected as the reference sample. For some cases, in the Netherlands, whole blood samples were also collected. The performance of the tests was assessed based on sensitivity, specificity, accuracy, positive predictive value and negative predictive value for the individual substance tests of the device. These factors were assessed based on both DRUID and manufacturer cut-offs. Sensitivity, specificity and accuracy performance criteria of 80% or more were set as a desirable target value.

The DRUID researchers caution that the results of the analytical evaluation of each device need to be viewed in the context of the study population on which they were tested. For some of the devices, a full performance evaluation was not possible for all of the test strips on the panel due to low prevalence of the substance(s) in question. That said, none of the devices tested reached the target criteria of 80% for sensitivity, specificity, and accuracy for all the tested drugs on the device. However, there were tests that performed on a very promising level for one or more substance classes. The DrugTest 5000 had the best overall results. The next best device was Rapid STAT, which performed at a similar level, except for the cocaine test that was somewhat less sensitive. Clearly the best device in terms of sensitivity for amphetamines was the DrugWipe 5+.

More recently, a Belgian team[11] reported additional evaluations including four On-Site Oral Fluid devices [Draeger DrugTest5000, Cozart/Alere DDS2, Mavand Rapid STAT, and the Innovacon Oralert] with generally similar results. Overall specificity was good, however sensitivity remained less than the desired target criteria for most drugs. The researchers found that among the four devices tested, the DrugTest5000 was the easiest to use, and it demonstrated a sensitivity of > 50% for al drug classes, and 81% for cannabis the most prevalent drug in DUID enforcement. The Belgian team concluded that compared to previous evaluations they noted progress in improving sensitivity and specificity although "more improvement is required."

Strano-Rossi et al.[12] in Italy also reported evaluating four oral fluid devices (Cozart/Alere DDS2, DrugTest5000, DrugWipe 5+, and the Rapid Stat). Generally the results supported the Belgian findings and the findings of the DRUID project. The Italian team concluded that "To ensure adequate reliability, MS confirmation of on-site oral fluid screening tests is always necessary, due to the presence of a significant number of false positive results even when using the commercial kit with the best performance.

TABLE 6.1.3

Summary of the Results Obtained with POCT Oral Fluid and Sweat Tests during the First ROSITA Study[3]

	RapiScan					Drugwipe					Oralscreen				
Oral Fluid	**n**	**Prev.**	**Sens.**	**Spec.**	**Acc.**	**n**	**Prev.**	**Sens.**	**Spec.**	**Acc.**	**n**	**Prev.**	**Sens.**	**Spec.**	**Acc.**
Amphetamines	80	73%	83%	68%	79%	120	74%	87%	55%	78%					
Benzodiazepines	133	47%	17%	90%	56%										
Cannabinoids	9										190	2%	25%	84%	83%
Cocaine	33	0%	—	100%	100%	118	25%	59%	92%	84%	180	0%	—	99%	99%
Opiates	37	49%	61%	26%	43%	46	48%	41%	79%	61%	183	4%	57%	93%	91%
Sweat															
Amphetamines						63	92%	94%	67%	92%					
Cocaine						22	100%	77%	—	77%					
Opiates						9	100%	89%	—	89%					

Note: All POCT results were compared to GC-MS in oral fluid/sweat, except for benzodiazepines, where they were compared to blood.

Abbreviations: n: number of comparisons, Prev: prevalence of positive samples, Sens: sensitivity of the test, Spec: specificity of the test, Acc: accuracy of the test, = number of true positives and true negatives divided by the number of tests.

TABLE 6.1.4
Detection Limits (ng/ml) of Six POCT Tests in Spiked Oral Fluid Samples[6,7]

	Amphetamine	THC	Morphine	Cocaine	Methamphetamine
Drugwipe	500	50	20	200	100
Oratect	25	ND	20	40	25
Rapiscan	25	50	80	200	100
OraLab	500	100	80	10	500
Saliva screen	NT	ND	20	40	25
Uplink	25	20	20	200	25

NT: not tested; ND: no THC could be detected, even at 100 ng/ml.

TABLE 6.1.5
DRUID TISPOL Evaluation Relevant Operational Findings of Tested Devices

	Average Time to Collect Sample in Minutes	Average Analysis Time in mins.	% Analysis Successful	Recommend as a Promising Device
Mavand RapidSTAT	2.3 /2.0	11.00/7.00	77/93	YES
Avitar Drugometer	3.00	3.00	62	NO
Brannan Oratect III	4.3/3.0	5.3/6.0	67/89	YES
EnviteC SmartClip	1.45	3.15	97	NO
Innovacon OraAlert	3.00	7.00	90	YES*
Securetec Drugwipe 5+	1.0/1.3	5.10/4.30	98/98	YES
Sun OraLine	2.3 /2.0	8.30	73	N0
Surescreen	2.3/1.3	7.3/4.3	75/96	YES*
Ultimed Salivascreen VI	5.00	8.00	57	NO
Varian OraLab	3.50	7.20	80	YES
Cozart DDS	2.00	6.00	99	YES
Draeger DrugTest 5000	3.00	11.00	97	YES
Biosenson BIOSENS	0.50	2.15	100	YES

*Innovacon Oralert and Surescreen are similar devices

6.1.2 Developing Technologies

In addition to lateral flow immunoassays and up-converting phosphor technology, some other technologies have been proposed for POCT drug testing in oral fluid. In the earlier version of this chapter we discussed surface-enhanced Raman spectroscopy, which had been applied to analysis of amphetamines in oral fluid,[13] and ion mobility spectroscopy, which has been tried for the detection of drugs in oral fluid but to date this has not been successful. None of these early "promising" technologies have advanced very far over the last 15 years. One new development that does show promise is the SensAbues test which offers a new format biomatrix based upon a non-intrusive specimen sampling technique. The manufacturer claims "This is a recently discovered, novel and proprietary procedure for the indirect collection, detection and identification of non-volatile substances in blood using exhaled breath. The breath sample can be used to test for exogenous substances, such as performance enhancing drugs (stimulants) in sports, drugs of abuse (narcotics/cannabinoids) and therapeutic drugs (antibiotics). Also, these can be a wide range of endogenous substances associated with the study of metabolomics and determination of biomarkers." (http://sensabues.com/). Several research evaluations have been conducted on this device recently[14] that have shown good promise. However, at this point in time the analysis must be done using very sophisticated, sensitive and expensive laboratory equipment [LCMSMS], but it does allow non-invasive rapid collection at the roadside. The key to success of this technology will be to find instrumentation that can be used at the roadside.

The very latest technology to appear is "Intelligent Fingerprinting" a rapid non-invasive drug screening "at the touch of a finger." (see www.intelligentfingerprinting.com). The system screens for drug use by analyzing metabolites contained in the minute traces of eccrine sweat found in a fingerprint. The manufacturer claims that the presence of drug metabolites in someone's fingerprint sweat indicates drug use by that individual. Drug metabolites are produced by the body as a result of normal metabolic processes and can be analyzed to identify the drug substances a person may have ingested, inhaled or injected. The fingerprint sample is collected onto the Intelligent Fingerprinting Cartridge. The Cartridge is analyzed using the portable Intelligent Fingerprinting Reader 1000 (which is battery-powered or can be plugged into the mains), touchscreen-operated and fully automated. Within ten minutes the screen displays a simple negative or positive result against pre-determined thresholds for each drug in the test used. This device is still in end stage evaluation and is not yet available. No data is as yet available to determine accuracy, reliability, sensitivity or specificity.

6.1.3 Conclusions

There is a strong need for POC testing of alternative matrices to urine, particularly for roadside testing. The use of oral fluid has the advantage that the parent drug will be detected and that the presence of a drug in oral fluid may correlate better with impairment than the presence of drug metabolites in urine. Obtaining an oral fluid sample can be done under supervision and without embarrassment. However, individuals who have recently consumed drugs often have very little and viscous oral fluid. Therefore, obtaining a suitable sample can at times take 15 to 20 min or may be impossible. There has been tremendous progress in the performance of POC drug tests for alternative matrices and specificity, sensitivity, and accuracy continues to improve. However, the selection of a particular device over another still often depends on the population being tested (e.g., Workplace testing, Roadside, Methadone Clinics etc.), and the prevalence of expected drugs. Some devices are excellent for detecting amphetamines, and others for THC. No single device has been found to be excellent for all commonly abuse drugs.

Recently Verstraete commented in an editorial in Clinical Chemistry[15] "it seems that the long quest for a sensitive on-site test for detecting cannabinoids in OF is finally over" referring to the consistent research findings that the Draeger DrugTest5000 can accurately and reliably detect THC at 5 ng/ml. However, it is clear that more research is needed on the influence of collection, adulterants, and other parameters that could violate the integrity of the specimen, the concentrations seen after passive exposure, and most importantly continued further research is needed to improve the sensitivity for detection of THC and benzodiazepines.

REFERENCES

1. Rodgers, R., Lee, R.H., Allen, M.P. et al., Detection of cannabis in saliva using a test strip immunoassay, in *TIAFT Proceedings*, Dunnett, N. and Kimber, K.J., Eds., TIAFT, Brighton, 1984, 215.
2. Iwersen, S. and Schmoldt, A., Frontline test sticks for drug testing in saliva? in *TIAFT Proceedings*, Sachs, H., Bernhard, W., and Jeger, A., Eds., TIAFT, Munich, 1996.
3. Verstraete, A.G. and Puddu, M., Evaluation of different roadside drug tests, in *Rosita*, in *Roadside Testing Assessment*, A.G. Verstraete, Ed., Rosita Consortium, Gent, 2001, 167–232.
4. http://www.questdiagnostics.com/home/physicians/health-trends/drug-testing
5. Parliament of Victoria. Road Safety (drug driving) Act 2003. 111/2003. 9-12-2003.
6. Skopp, G. and Potsch, L., Perspiration versus saliva — basic aspects concerning their use in roadside drug testing. *Int. J. Legal Med.* 112, 213–221, 1999.
7. Niedbala, R.S., Feindt, H., Kardos, K. et al., Detection of analytes by immunoassay using up-converting phosphor technology. *Anal. Biochem.* 293, 22–30, 2001.
8. Walsh, J.M., Flegel, R., Crouch, D.J. et al., An evaluation of rapid point-of-collection oral fluid drug-testing devices. *J. Anal. Toxicol.* 27, 429–439, 2003.
9. Walsh, J.M., Crouch, D.J., Danaceau, J.P., Cangianelli, L., Liddicoat, L. and Adkins, R., Evaluation of ten oral fluid point-of-collection drug-testing devices. *J. Anal. Toxicol.* 31, 44–54, 2007.
10. Crouch, D.J., Walsh, J.M., Cangianelli, L. and Quintela, O., Laboratory evaluation and field application of roadside oral fluid collectors and drug testing devices. *Therap. Drug Monit.* 30(2), 188–195, 2008.
11. Vanstechelman, S., Isalberti, C., Van der Linden, T., Pil, K., Legrand, S.A., and Verstraete, A.G. Analytical evaluation of four on-site oral fluid drug testing devices. *J. Anal. Toxicol.* 36, 136–140, 2012.
12. Strano-Rossi, S., Castrignano, E., Anzillotti, L., Serpolloni, G., Mollica, R., Tagliaro, F., Pascalli, J., Stefano, D., Sgalla, R., Evaluation of four oral fluid devices [DDS®2, DrugTest5000, DrugWipe 5+, and RapidSTAT] for on-site monitoring drugged driving in comparison with UHPLC-MSMS analysis. *Forensic Sci. Int.* 221(1–3), 70–76, 2012.
13. George, S. and Braithwaite, R.A., Use of on-site testing for drugs of abuse. *Clin. Chem.* 48, 1639–1646, 2002.
14. Himes, S.K., Scheidweiler, K.B., Beck, O., Gorelick, D.A., Desrosiers, N.A. and Huestis, M.A. Cannabinoids in exhaled breath following controlled administration of smoked cannabis. *Clin. Chem.* 59(12), 1780–1789, 2013.
15. Verstraete, A.G., More reliable on-site detection of cannabis in oral fluid, *Clin. Chem.* 58(10), 1389–1391, 2012.

6.2 POINT OF COLLECTION TESTING IN CRIMINAL JUSTICE

Leo Kadehjian

6.2.1 Introduction

With the well-established association between drug use and crime, the criminal justice system is presented with a population that includes a high prevalence of drug users. Current (2013) data from the Arrestee Drug Abuse Monitoring program (ADAM II) surveying arrestees in five counties across the U.S. indicate that 63% to 83% of adult male arrestees tested positive by urinalysis for at least one of the ten drugs tested, with between 12% and 50% testing positive for multiple drugs.[1]

It is critical that the criminal justice system monitors those under its supervision to ensure that ongoing drug use is both detected and deterred. This is most effectively done through urine drug-testing, which has been demonstrated to be an objective and effective tool.[2–54] Such drug testing is often specifically mandated by law.

Accordingly, there has been a great demand for effective urine drug-testing programs within criminal justice contexts. These urine drug-testing programs have been implemented in a variety of criminal justice contexts including testing of arrestees before their initial appearance in court, testing imposed by the court as a condition of release pending trial,[18–41] pre-sentence testing, testing while on probation or parole,[42–47] and testing within jails and prisons.[48–54] Furthermore, drug testing is a cornerstone of effective specialized drug courts,[3–5] community corrections programs, and court-mandated treatment programs.

6.2.2 Point of Collection Drug Testing

By far, the drug-testing technology most used in point of collection (POC) testing programs within the criminal justice setting is urine testing. This specimen has the benefit of gathering a large specimen volume allowing for multiple tests and retests, including the possibility to split the original specimen at the time of collection ensuring that a second untouched specimen is available in the event of challenges. Furthermore, there are well-established testing methodologies for both laboratory and POC use, and recognized testing procedures and laboratory standards. There is also a large body of clinical and scientific literature addressing the detection of drugs in urine. In addition, urine benefits from having drug and/or metabolite concentrations generally 100 times those found in many other body specimens (e.g., blood, oral fluid, sweat, hair). However, urine does suffer from awkward specimen collection procedures and the possibility of specimen adulteration, substitution, and dilution. Nonetheless, urine remains the specimen of choice for drug testing within criminal justice contexts.

Criminal justice drug-testing programs have historically utilized commercial laboratories, with trained and experienced scientists, providing assurance of quality results, but with often frustrating delays between specimen collection, transport to the laboratory, testing, reporting of the result, and ultimately responding to the substance user. With the availability of simple, robust, and accurate automated bench-top immunoassay analyzers, many testing programs established their own POC drug testing facilities. Since the first court-based testing laboratory was established in 1971, in the Superior Court of the District of Columbia, a wide variety of POC testing programs have been implemented nationwide. These programs have recognized the value of rapid drug test results with the benefit of immediate responses to ongoing drug use, as well as immediate positive reinforcement for not using drugs. For many of these criminal justice applications, POC bench-top automated immunoassay analyzers have been used successfully for many years. For example, within the U.S. federal courts, numerous pre-trial and probation drug testing programs use automated immunoassay analyzers, with a few even using sophisticated high-volume analyzers as found in clinical and commercial laboratories. Many of these POC testing programs using simple bench-top automated immunoassay analyzers have their testing competently performed by officers who have been trained and certified by the test system manufacturer, although they may have had no other formal laboratory training. In addition, these POC testing programs within the federal courts are subjected to rigorous on-site inspections, and participate in periodic blind proficiency testing, demonstrating excellent performance. Test results from these POC testing programs have been repeatedly upheld in numerous legal challenges. As early as 1991, a National Institute of Justice study of drug testing technologies recognized that on-site automated immunoassay analyzers demonstrated performance equal to commercial laboratory-based testing.[12]

Although POC bench-top automated analyzers offer the benefits of rapid turnaround time, objective hard copy results, reduced test costs (dependent on volume), and a proven track record of performance and admissibility in a variety of legal and administrative proceedings, not all criminal justice testing programs have either the budget or a sufficient number of specimens to justify having an automated analyzer at the point of collection. Furthermore, there may not be the availability of a dedicated and properly trained staff member to operate the analyzer.

However, as a result of impressive advancements in immunoassay technology, urine drug tests as performed on automated analyzers have now been made available in simple, economical, rapid, easy-to-use, visually read test strips. Such non-instrumented test strips allow for rapid, accurate, and reliable testing in those sites that cannot justify an automated analyzer as well as in numerous field situations.

Some of the key comparative issues between on-site automated analyzers and non-instrumented drug testing devices within a criminal justice setting are shown in Table 6.2.1.

6.2.3 Non-Instrumented POC Drug Tests

There are a wide variety of non-instrumented drug test devices available, from simple dipsticks, which are briefly inserted into a specimen and then allowed to develop over a few minutes, to cassettes where a few drops of the specimen are added to wells in the cassette with a plastic pipette or calibrated syringe, and even specimen collections cups with the test strips incorporated directly into their walls or cap, which obviate any handling or pipetting of the specimen. Furthermore, many of the non-instrumented test devices are available in single drug assay or multidrug assay formats. As discussed below, some of these devices also have specimen validity test strips incorporated into the device. For all of these devices, the test results are available anywhere from 3 to 15 min. These devices utilize well-established immunoassay technologies (described in detail in other chapters of this section), with antigen–antibody reactions similar to the automated instrument homogeneous immunoassay technologies. However, for these test strips, the antigen–antibody reaction occurs on chromatographic test strips and so they

TABLE 6.2.1
Comparison between Instrumented and Non-Instrumented Drug Test Devices

Automated Bench-Top Analyzer	Non-Instrumented Devices
Objective read	Subjective read
Suitable for moderate to high volume	Suitable for low volume
Rapid turnaround time	Immediate turnaround time
Variable cost per test by volume	Low cost per test
Daily calibration/controls	No calibration, use internal control(s)
Established QC practices	No established QC requirements
Established proficiency testing programs	Proficiency testing programs available
Hardcopy print-out	No hardcopy print-out
Established case law	Little case law
Repeat testing often meets due process	Due process requirements uncertain

are considered solid-phase immunoassays. Because the specimen wicks along the chromatographic test strips, they are also called lateral-flow immunoassays. The immunoassay strips are labeled with antibodies directed to the specific drug and/or drug metabolites to be detected. The test results are read visually within a few minutes as the presence or absence of a colored line at a specified position on the strip pertaining to each drug in question. The test strips also have control lines, so each test is in part internally controlled. The great interest in these devices is evidenced by the rapid proliferation of the wide variety of these devices, with numerous manufacturers and even more distributors.

However, there has been ongoing concern that these simple, visually read devices may not provide sufficient scientific or forensic accuracy for use in some of the above-mentioned criminal justice applications. The concerns of the accuracy of these devices are based mainly on the subjective nature of visually reading the test results as the presence or absence of a colored line. There has been a concern that specimens with drug concentrations at or near the specified test cutoff concentration may yield indeterminate lines challenging the reader to determine if the result should be called positive or negative. The device package inserts which provide instructions for use and performance characteristics indicate that any such equivocal or borderline results should be reported as negative, taking a conservative approach. There even are a few POC testing devices that utilize a small electronic reader to provide an objective readout of the result and may even include a print-out of the test result.[55,56] Such electronic readers are available not only for POC urine test devices but also for POC oral fluid testing.[57]

Since the introduction of POC non-instrumented urine drug testing strips in the 1980s, there have been numerous technological advancements and performance improvements such that many of these devices perform quite well, even comparable to a bench-top analyzer. There have been numerous performance evaluations of these devices presented at scientific meetings and in peer-reviewed scientific publications. Although not intended to be a comprehensive review of these studies, nor to imply any specific recommendation of any particular device, some representative examples are provided in the references below.[58–71]

In 1996, the Administrative Office of the U.S. Courts commissioned a comprehensive study of the available non-instrumented urine drug testing devices. That study of 15 non-instrumented devices performed in a laboratory setting found that many of these devices performed amazingly well, especially considering a challenging specimen set, artificially weighted around the immunoassay cutoffs, with accuracies (against the gold standard of GC/MS confirmation) comparable to a commonly used automated bench-top analyzer. The non-instrumented devices demonstrated an overall accuracy of 71% (52% to 79%) vs. the automated analyzer's average of 80% (78% to 82%).[61] A second similar comprehensive study was commissioned in 1998 by the Substance Abuse and Mental Health Services Administration (SAMHSA) with similarly impressive results, with the 15 devices demonstrating an overall accuracy of 70% (61% to 78%) versus automated analyzer 76%.[61] It is important to remember that these studies used artificially weighted specimen sets with drug concentrations around the cutoffs to challenge the devices. With specimens that were drug-free or had much higher concentrations of drugs, the accuracies of the devices were much higher. These devices are expected to demonstrate even higher accuracies with specimen populations actually encountered in routine criminal justice settings.

Another large criminal justice study compared confirmation rates for proficiency test specimens tested by numerous sites in the field using either a variety of non-instrumented devices or a standard automated analyzer.[65] The sites using the various non-instrumented devices had highly variable performance and in general not as good as the automated analyzers. However, some sites using the non-instrumented devices had performance comparable to that for the analyzer sites (Figure 6.2.1).

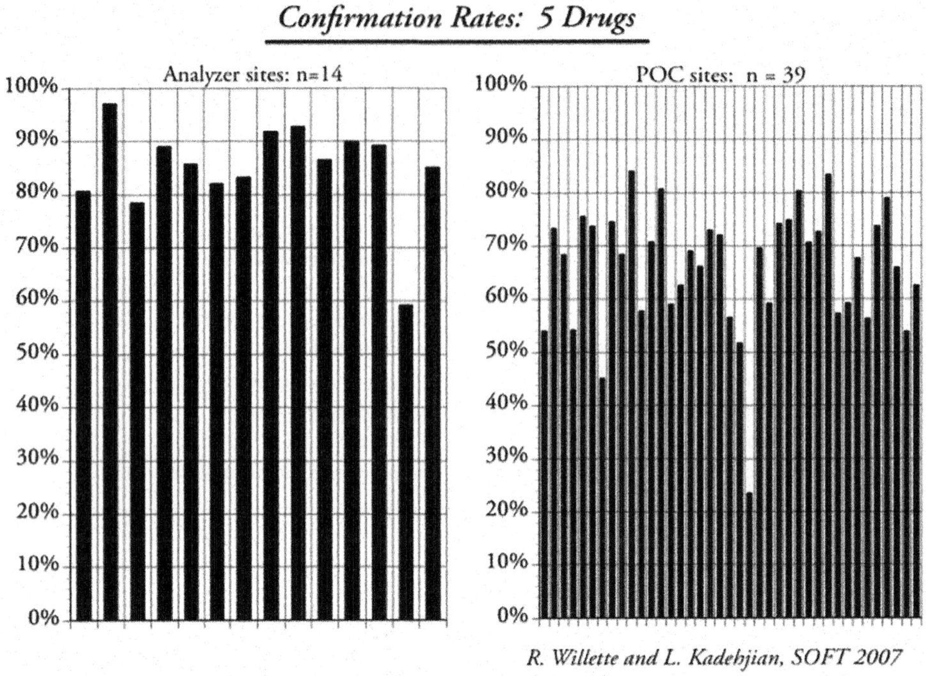

FIGURE 6.2.1 Comparison of confirmation rates using numerous sites

There are also concerns about accuracy since in a criminal justice setting the tests may likely be performed by nontechnical staff without formal laboratory experience. To address the use of these devices by nonscientists another study also utilizing challenging near cut-off specimens, had results independently read by both a scientist and a nonscientist with almost identical performance.[62]

It should be noted that some devices prove to be relatively "aggressive"; that is, they give positive results for specimens with amounts of drug just below the specified cutoff. It is important to note that these positive results should not be considered false positives when they have in fact correctly identified drug use. The device in fact may be correct in accurately identifying drug presence but simply at a concentration that may not always confirm when subjected to laboratory-based testing, e.g., using SAMHSA's federal workplace GC/MS confirmation criteria. Consideration should be given to confirmation testing at lower cutoffs than specified within the federal workplace drug testing programs. It should also be noted that some devices proved to be relatively "conservative," missing some specimens with drug concentrations at or slightly above the specified cutoff and reporting those as negative.[61]

Furthermore, the performance of these and other unit test devices have undergone regulatory review by numerous agencies: by the U.S. Food and Drug Administration (FDA) establishing regulatory criteria for clearance for marketing; by SAMHSA for potential application in federally-regulated workplace drug testing programs;[72] by a wide variety of criminal justice agencies; and by laboratory accreditation and standards organizations such as the College of American Pathologists (CAP), the Centers for Medicare and Medicaid Services (CLIA regulations), and the National Committee for Clinical Laboratory Standards (NCCLS). Because there has been ongoing development and improvement in these devices, the most recent data available on any given device should be reviewed before deciding upon incorporating its use into a drug testing program, e.g., if the device's performance has been published in the peer-reviewed scientific literature.

In spite of the impressive performance of such simple, rapid, and easy-to-use devices, there appears to be a consensus within the laboratory community that the results of these devices alone should not be used to impose significant sanctions without some form of further confirmation testing. It is interesting to note that, although these devices are now being widely used in numerous settings, there is little significant case law where there has been detailed judicial scrutiny of their accuracy and whether use of these devices fulfills the due process requirements in each of the variety of criminal justice settings.

6.2.4 Detection of Adulteration/Dilution

One limitation to the use of urine as a specimen for drug testing is the potential for specimen adulteration, substitution, and dilution. Given that urine specimen collections in the criminal justice context are generally performed under direct observation, the possibility of adulteration or substitution is minimized. In fact, by performing the drug test immediately upon specimen collection, the opportunity for an adulterant to be effective may be minimized because often some time is required for the adulterant to perform its disruptive chemistry. However, specimen dilution through excess fluid ingestion prior to specimen collection is an issue that merits careful attention. To address these challenges to effective urine drug testing there are a variety of POC devices to assess specimen integrity. These include handheld refractometers to measure specific gravity, as well as simple dipsticks, which can assess a variety of adulterants, oxidants, pH, and creatinine. Some of the non-instrumented drug test devices actually incorporate such specimen validity tests in the test device. Non-instrumented devices may also offer indications of inappropriate specimens or failure of the test to perform properly through the use of built-in control lines.

6.2.5 Other Issues

There are some additional issues to consider when an officer is asked to perform drug testing in the presence of a defendant or offender. Officers may be resistant to taking on testing responsibilities as they may feel it is not part of their job function. The officers may also fear increased risk of exposure to infectious disease in handling urine specimens (although the 1991 OSHA Bloodborne Pathogen Regulations, 56 FR 64004, recognized the extremely low risk from casual exposure to urine specimens when not visibly contaminated with blood). There is also the potential for physical harm when confronting a potentially violent offender with a positive drug test result. It may be easier for the officer to deal with a confirmed positive report from a formal laboratory than with a presumptive positive test result from a non-instrumented device. Despite these concerns, there are clear benefits in the use of these non-instrumented drug test devices near the donor. Many offenders, when told of the accuracy of the device, will admit to drug use even as the test is being run. Furthermore, when faced with a positive test result many will admit to drug use. In contrast, it is rare for an offender to admit to drug use when the specimen is collected for shipment to an off-site laboratory. Also, when on-site test results are negative, the officer can provide immediate positive reinforcement for maintaining abstinence. When on-site test results are positive, the officer can confront the issue directly and immediately, rather than later dealing with "prior" drug use. One issue is whether the donor should be allowed or asked to view the actual test result on the device and acknowledge the result. This author does not recommend this practice as the donor has not been trained to read or interpret the test result.

Another emerging challenge for all types of drug testing is the growing and ever-changing variety of "Designer Drugs" or "Novel Psychoactive Substances." These new illicit drugs are found in several different classes including synthetic cannabinoids, amphetamine-like cathinone derivatives, and a number of others. These new drugs are sufficiently different in molecular structure from the classic drugs historically tested for in urine drug testing programs, such that they are not detected by the conventional immunoassays, whether performed on an analyzer or using a POC device. Because these new drugs are rapidly and ever-changing, it has been difficult for immunoassay manufacturers to keep up. Furthermore, for many of these new drugs little is known about which metabolites of these drugs are found in urine specimens. Thus, detecting the use of these new drugs is especially challenging, even for laboratory-based testing.

6.2.6 Other Technologies

There are several other specimens and technologies used within the criminal justice system to detect drug use. These include oral fluid testing, sweat patch testing, hair testing, and trace drug residue analysis. Hair testing and sweat patch testing are not considered POC testing technologies as these specimens must currently be sent to a laboratory for analysis.

Oral fluid testing is certainly receiving attention as a specimen suitable for a variety of POC testing contexts, especially roadside testing,[73–79] but also in criminal justice settings.[80] There are both laboratory-based methods as well as POC testing devices available, similar to the POC urine testing devices. The main benefit of oral fluid is the ease and gender-neutrality of specimen collection. That oral fluid as a specimen for drug testing has reached a level of scientific acceptance is manifested in the fact that SAMHSA had proposed the use of oral fluid for use in federally regulated workplace testing programs as long ago as 2004,[72] and finalized the rules for its use in 2019.[81] It is also of note that saliva has been well-recognized as a suitable specimen for alcohol testing and is allowed under the Department of Transportation's non-evidential on-site alcohol testing procedures (49 CFR Part 40) with a few saliva test devices included in NHTSA's Conforming Products List.[82]

Another technology occasionally found within corrections settings is a device designed to detect trace amounts of drugs on persons, not only inmates, but also those visiting prisons and even prison staff.[83]

6.2.7 Regulatory Issues

There are few formal regulations specifically regarding drug-testing technologies in criminal justice contexts. Although there are several statutory requirements regarding drug testing within corrections settings, these statutes are generally broadly worded leaving specifics about technologies up to those implementing the testing requirements. Generally, the major issues involve whether there must be confirmation testing (generally specified as GC/MS) before certain sanctions may occur.

The Federal Bureau of Prisons has a statutory requirement that, for those serving their sentence in a contract community treatment center, all positive test results must be validated to substantiate the positive result (28 CFR §550.42[c]). The current federal probation regulations also require that if a probationer is to be returned to prison based on a drug test, it must be confirmed by GC/MS or equivalent (18 U.S.C. 3583[d]). Otherwise, corrections-based urine drug testing programs are generally not strictly regulated. However, in order to withstand legal scrutiny, such on-site testing programs should conform to established standards of good laboratory practice, including quality control practices and participation in proficiency testing. The on-site testing programs of the U.S. federal courts utilizing automated analyzers have been following such practices for many years, including on-site inspections and participation in external proficiency testing. More recently similar quality control practices, external proficiency testing, and appropriate inspection criteria have been developed for the federal courts' programs utilizing non-instrumented POC drug testing devices.

Any criminal justice drug testing program should take into account any state or federal regulations regarding drug testing in other contexts, such as workplace testing, as these standards may be brought up in any challenge to the criminal justice testing program. However, due process issues are generally diminished within a criminal justice context and, accordingly, drug testing programs and technologies may be held to a lower standard than in workplace testing. Another concern should be state and federal regulations addressing laboratories testing human specimens in general. These regulations typically apply to clinical laboratories (e.g., under CLIA regulations), while corrections-based testing programs are generally not considered to be "clinical" when test results are strictly used for compliance purposes rather than health care purposes. However, drug testing utilized in corrections-based treatment programs may be considered "clinical" and thereby subject to stricter regulation through CLIA.

6.2.8 Legal Issues

There has been a long history of drug testing within corrections settings and, accordingly, ample case law regarding many aspects of such corrections-based testing programs. There are numerous case law precedents in many criminal justice contexts for the admissibility of instrumented immunoassay urine drug testing, both when performed in a laboratory and when performed at the point of collection. Most of these cases have upheld the use of repeat instrumented immunoassay testing as meeting the due process requirements for use in prison disciplinary hearings and even in probation revocations, even without additional confirmation testing.

In contrast, there have been few significant cases specifically addressing non-instrumented drug testing technologies, at least at the appellate court level. This may be, in part, because these visually read tests are not generally being used alone for imposing sanctions without some form of confirmation testing or admission of use. One area where legal challenges could occur would be the admissibility of the test results themselves, arguing that the testing technology is new and of either unproven or insufficient scientific validity. The aforementioned performance studies should be persuasive in demonstrating the scientific reliability and acceptance of these devices. A question that requires resolution is whether these non-instrumented devices are accurate enough to be used alone or with repeat testing, but without further confirmation testing by an alternative technique, such as GC/MS.

In order for non-instrumented drug test results to be used in these various corrections contexts, not only must the inherent performance of the devices be demonstrated, but it must also be made clear if the devices were properly used. Issues such as operator training, proper chain of custody, specimen handling, device and ancillary storage conditions, and record-keeping procedures must be documented. On-site inspection of these non-instrumented testing programs, as well as participation in external proficiency testing programs, will also be important components in assessing the admissibility and evidentiary weight the results of such non-instrumented drug testing evidence should receive. Within the federal courts' pre-trial and probation on-site testing programs, appropriate inspection checklists and proficiency testing programs have been developed and implemented for use of these non-instrumented drug test devices.

It must be recognized that due process requirements will vary depending on the corrections context, from a fairly low "some evidence" standard in prison disciplinary hearings, to a "beyond a reasonable doubt" standard in criminal cases. Given that studies have demonstrated that several of these non-instrumented drug test devices have overall accuracies on the order of 70%, they would generally meet the preponderance of the evidence standard (> 50%), and possibly even the higher "clear and convincing" evidence standard. Certainly, this would be the case for assays for cannabis or cocaine metabolite, where the potential for any cross-reacting substances is minimal and accordingly interpretation of test results is relatively straightforward. However, it is unlikely that these devices alone would be held to meet the "beyond a reasonable doubt" criminal standard (e.g., 95% or higher). It is important to note that these devices would be expected to demonstrate accuracies well beyond the 70% accuracy which was observed when challenged with near-cutoff specimens, when testing specimens within the criminal justice context with a less-challenging concentration distribution. Furthermore, when examining the performance of these devices against the criteria of drug presence or absence (rather than GC/MS confirmation cutoff criteria) these devices have demonstrated positive predictive values of virtually one. That is, a positive on-site non-instrumented drug test result, at least for cocaine or cannabinoids, can be relied on to indicate the presence of a drug in the specimen, even though there may be insufficient amounts to be confirmed positive when using standard confirmation cutoffs.

6.2.9 Conclusions

There is no question that several of the non-instrumented drug testing devices are not only rapid and easy to use, but are also sufficiently accurate and reliable for use within a variety of criminal justice programs. There is ample peer-reviewed scientific literature supporting the accuracy of these devices as well as many studies demonstrating their utility within a wide variety of criminal justice settings. That they have been proposed for use within the federally regulated workplace testing programs is also a testament to their level of scientific and regulatory acceptance. Furthermore, there is a small but growing body of case law addressing these devices' levels of accuracy and reliability and how they comport with various due process requirements. However, at the moment, positive results from these devices will still likely need to be used with some form of confirmation testing if significant sanctions are to be imposed.

REFERENCES

1. ADAM II 2013 Annual Report, Arrestee Drug Abuse Monitoring Program, Office of National Drug Control Policy, Executive Office of the President, Washington, DC, January 2014.
2. Kadehjian, L. and Baer, J., *On-Site Testing Devices in the Criminal Justice System, On-Site Drug Testing*, Jenkins, A.J. and Goldberger, B.A., Eds., Humana Press, Totowa, NJ, 2002, chap. 5.
3. Robinson, J. and Jones, J., *Drug Testing in a Drug Court Environment: Common Issues to Address*, NCJ 18603, May 2000.
4. *Adult Drug Court Best Practice Standards*, Volume II, National Association of Drug Court Professionals, Alexandria, VA. 2015.
5. Marlowe, D.B., Festinger, D., Dugosh, K., Benascutti, K., Fox, G., and Harron, A., An experimental trial of adaptive programming in drug court: Outcomes at 6, 12 and 18 months, *J. Exp. Criminol.*, 10(2), 129, 2014.
6. Crowe, A. and Sydney, L., *Ten Steps for Implementing a Program of Controlled Substance Testing of Juveniles*, NCJ 178897, 2000.
7. Crowe, A. and Sydney, L., *Developing a Policy for Controlled Substance Testing of Juveniles*. June, NCJ 178896, 2000.
8. Torres, S., The use of a credible drug testing program for accountability and intervention, *Fed. Prob.*, 60(4), 18, 1996.
9. Carver, J.A., Using drug testing to reduce detention, *Fed. Prob.*, 57(1), 42, 1993.
10. *The Impact of Systemwide Drug Testing in Multnomah County, Oregon*, National Institute of Justice, NCJ 184409, April 1995.
11. Stephens, R. and Feucht, T., Reliability of self-reported drug use and urinalysis in the drug use forecasting system, *Prison J.*, 73(3–4), 279, 1993.
12. Visher, C. and McFadden, K., *A Comparison of Urinalysis Technologies for Drug Testing in Criminal Justice*, National Institute of Justice, 1991.
13. Wish, E. and Gropper, B., Drug testing by the criminal justice system: method, research, and application, in *Crime and Justice, Vol. 13: Drugs and Crime*. University of Chicago Press, Chicago, 1990.
14. BJA Monograph, *Urinalysis as a Part of a Treatment Alternative to Street Crime Program*, Bureau of Justice Assistance, NCJ 115416, 1988.
15. Wish, E., Toborg, M., and Bellassai, J.P., *Identifying Drug Users and Monitoring Them during Conditional Release*, National Institute of Justice, NCJ 108560, 1988.
16. Carver, J., *Drugs and Crime: Controlling Use and Reducing Risk through Testing*, National Institute of Justice, 1986.
17. Wish, E., *Drug Testing*, National Institute of Justice, NCJ 104556, 1988.
18. *Integrating Drug Testing into a Pretrial Services System: 1999 Update*, NCJ 176340, 1999.
19. Henry, D. and Clark, J., *Pretrial Drug Testing: An Overview of Issues and Practices*, NCJ 176341, 1999.
20. Rhodes, W., Hyatt, R., and Scheiman, P., *Predicting Pretrial Misconduct with Drug Tests of Arrestees. Evidence from Six Sites*, National Institute of Justice, Research in Brief, NCJ 157108, 1996.
21. Rhodes, W., Hyatt, R., and Scheiman, P., Predicting pretrial misconduct with drug tests of arrestees: evidence from eight settings, *J. Quant. Criminol.*, 12(3), 315, 1996.
22. *Drug Testing. Guidelines for Pretrial Release and Diversion*, National Association of Pretrial Services Agencies, 1995.
23. BJA Monograph, *Integrating Drug Testing into a Pretrial Services System*, Bureau of Justice Assistance, NCJ 142414, 1993.
24. Jones, P.R. and Goldkamp, J.S., Implementing pretrial drug testing programs in two experimental sites: some deterrence and jail bed implications, *Prison J.*, 73(2), 199–219, 1993.
25. Britt, C., Gottfredson, M., and Goldkamp, J., Drug testing and pretrial misconduct: an experiment on the specific deterrent effects of drug monitoring defendants on pretrial release, *J. Res. Crime Delinquency*, 29(1), 62, 1992.
26. Goldkamp, J.S. and Jones, P.R., Pretrial drug testing experiments in Milwaukee and Prince George's County: the context of implementation, *J. Res. Crime Delinquency*, 29(4), 430–465, 1992.
27. Smith, D. and Polsenberg, C., Specifying the relationship between arrestee drug use test results and recidivism, *J. Crim. Law Criminol.*, 83(2), 364, 1992.
28. Visher, C., Pretrial drug testing: panacea or Pandora's box? *Ann. Am. Acad.*, 521, 112, 1992.
29. Visher, C., *Pretrial Drug Testing*, National Institute of Justice, 1992.
30. Carver, J., Pretrial drug testing: an essential step in bail reform, *B.Y.U. J. Pub. Law*, 5(2), 371, 1991.
31. Nielson, D., Consenting to searches after being arrested: pretrial drug testing, *B.Y.U. J. Pub. Law*, 5(2), 439, 1991.
32. Meyers, P. Pretrial drug testing: is it vulnerable to due process challenges? *B.Y.U. J. Pub. Law*, 5(2), 285, 1991.
33. Walton R., Peters, G., and Towns, J., Pretrial drug testing – an essential component of the national drug control strategy, *B.Y.U. J. Pub. Law*, 5(2), 341, 1991.
34. Jensen, C., Survey of current and prior pretrial drug testing sites, *B.Y.U. J. Pub. Law*, 5(2), 451, 1991.
35. Skousen, R., A special needs exception to the warrant and probable cause requirements for mandatory and uniform pre-arraignment drug testing in the wake of *Skinner v. Railway Labor Executives' Association and National Treasury Employees' Union v. Von Raab*, *B.Y.U. J. Pub. Law*, 5(2), 409, 1991.
36. Goldkamp, J., Gottfredson, M., and Weiland, D., Pretrial drug testing and defendant risk, *J. Crim. Law Criminol.*, 81(3), 585, 1990.
37. Visher, C., Using drug testing to identify high-risk defendants on release: a study in the District of Columbia, *J. Crim. Justice*, 18, 321, 1990.
38. Toborg, M., Bellassai, J., Yezer, A., and Trost, R., *Assessment of Pretrial Urine Testing in the District of Columbia*, National Institute of Justice, 1989.

39. BJA Monograph, *Estimating the Cost of Drug Testing for a Pretrial Services Program*, Bureau of Justice Assistance, 1989.
40. Rosen, C. and Goldkamp, J., The constitutionality of drug testing at the bail stage, *J. Crim. Law Criminol.*, 80(1), 114, 1989.
41. Abell, R., Pretrial drug testing: expanding rights and protecting public safety, *Geo. Wash. Law Rev.*, 57(4), 943, 1989.
42. BJA Monograph, *Drug Testing Guidelines and Practices for Adult Probation and Parole Agencies*, Bureau of Justice Assistance, NCJ 129199, 1991.
43. Rosen, C., The Fourth Amendment implications of urine testing for evidence of drug use in probation, *Brooklyn Law Rev.*, 55, 1159, 1990.
44. delCarmen, R. and Sorensen, J., *Legal Issues in Drug Testing Probation and Parole Clients and Employees*, Department of Justice, National Institute of Corrections, 1989.
45. delCarmen, R. and Sorensen, J., Legal issues in drug testing probationers and parolees, *Fed. Prob.*, 19, 1988.
46. Grommon, E., Cox, S., Davidson, W., and Bynum, T., Alternative models of instant drug testing: evidence from an experimental trial, *J. Exp. Criminol.*, 9(2), 145, 2013.
47. Hawken, A., Kulick, J., Smith, K., Mei, J., Zhang, Y., Jarman, S., Yu, T., Carson, C., and Vial, T., HOPE II: A Follow-Up to Hawai'i's HOPE Evaluation, NCJRS 249912, May 17, 2016.
48. Wilson, D., *Drug Use, Testing, and Treatment in Jails*, NCJ 179999, May 2000.
49. Bird, A., Gore, S., Hutchinson, S., Lewis, S., Cameron, S., and Burns, S., Harm reduction measures and injecting inside prison versus mandatory drug testing: results of a cross sectional anonymous questionnaire survey, *Br. Med. J.*, 315, 21, 1997.
50. Gore, S. and Bird, A., Cost implications of random mandatory drug tests in prisons, *Lancet*, 348, 1124, 1996.
51. Gore, S., Bird, A., and Ross, A., Prison rights: mandatory drug tests and performance indicators for prisons, *Br. Med. J.*, 312, 1411, 1966.
52. Gore, S. and Bird, A., Mandatory drug tests in prisons, *Br. Med. J.*, 310, 595, 1995.
53. Epstein, R., Urinalysis testing in correctional facilities, *Boston Univ. Law Rev.*, 67, 475, 1987.
54. Keyser, A., Feucht, T., and Flaherty, R., Keeping the prison clean: an update on pennsylvania's drug control strategy, *Corrections Today*, 68, August 2002.
55. Tominaga, M., Michiue, T., and Maeda, H., Evaluation of the on-site immunoassay drug-screening device Triage-TOX in routine forensic autopsy, *Leg Med. (Tokyo)* 17(6), 499, 2015.
56. Kim, S., Kim, H., Park, Y., Lim, J., Kim, J., Koo, S., and Kwon, G.C., Evaluation of an automated reader and color interprepation-based immunoassays for multiplexed drugs-of-abuse testing in urine, *J. Anal. Toxicol.*, 41, 412, 2017.
57. Scherer, J., Fiorentin, T., Marcelo, M., Sousa, T., Pechansky, F., Ferrão, M., and Limberger, ., Oral fluid testing for cocaine: Analytical evaluation of two point-of-collection drug screening devices, *J. Anal. Toxicol.*, 41, 392, 2017
58. Leno, A., Saarimies, J., Grönholm, M., and Lillsunde, P., Comparison of eight commercial on-site screening devices for drugs-of-abuse testing, Scand. J. Clin. Lab. Invest., 61, 325, 2001.
59. Crouch, D., Hersch, R.K., Cook, R.F., Frank, J.F., and Walsh, J.M., A field evaluation of five on-site drug-testing devices, *J. Anal. Toxicol.*, 26, 493, 2002.
60. Yacoubian, G.S., Wish, E.D., and Choyka, J.D., A comparison of the ONTRAK TesTcup-5 to laboratory urinalysis among arrestees, *J. Psychoactive Drugs*, 34(3), 325, 2002.
61. Willette, R. and Kadehjian, L., *Drugs-of-Abuse Test Devices, in On-Site Drug Testing*, Jenkins, A.J. and Goldberger, B.A., Eds., Humana Press, Totowa, NJ, 2002, chap. 17.
62. Kadehjian, L., Performance of five non-instrumented urine drug-testing devices with challenging near-cutoff specimens, *J. Anal. Toxicol.*, 25, 670, 2001.
63. Wiencek, J., Colby, J., and Nichols, J., Rapid assessment of drugs of abuse, *Adv. Clin.Chem.*, 80, 193, 2017.
64. Hayden, J., Schmeling, M., and Hoofnagle, A., Lot-to-lot variations in a qualitative lateral-flow immunoassay for chronic pain drug monitoring, *Clin. Chem.*, 60(6), 896, 2014.
65. Willette, R. and Kadehjian, L., Performance of drug abuse testing with POCT devices and onsite instruments in criminal justice settings, presentation at the Society of Forensic Toxicologists annual meeting, 2007.
66. Lin, C-N., Nelson, G., and McMillin, G., Evaluation of the NexScreen and DrugCheck Waive RT urine drug detection cups, *J. Anal. Toxicol.*, 37, 30, 2013.
67. Attema-de Jong, M., Peeters, S., and Franssen, E.F., Performance of three point-of-care urinalysis test devices for drugs of abuse and therapeutic drugs applied in the emergency department, *J. Emerg. Med.*, 42(6), 682, 2012.
68. Byrne, A., Evaluation of six point of care tests for drug of abuse in urine, *TIAFT Bulletin*, 33(4), 69, 2003.
69. Grönholm, M. and Lillsunde, P., A comparison between on-site immunoassay drug-testing devices and laboratory results, *For. Sci. Int.*, 121, 37, 2001.
70. Peace, M., Tarnai, L., and Poklis, A., Performance evaluation of four on-site drug-testing devices for detection of drugs of abuse in urine, *J. Anal. Toxicol.*, 24, 589, 2000.
71. Beck, O., Carlsson, S., Tusic, M., Olsson, R., Franzen, L., and Hulten, P., Laboratory and clinical evaluation of on-site urine drug testing, Scand. J. Clin. Lab. Invest., 74(8), 681, 2014.
72. *Proposed Revisions to Mandatory Guidelines for Federal Workplace Drug Testing Programs*, SAMHSA, Notice, 69 FR 19673, April 13, 2004.
73. Walsh, J., Flegel, R., Crouch, D., Cangianelli, L., and Baudys, J., An evaluation of rapid point-of-collection oral fluid drug-testing devices, *J. Anal. Toxicol.*, 27, 429, 2003.
74. Verstraete, A. and Raes, E., Eds., Roadside Testing and Assessment, ROSITA-2, Final Report, March 2006.
75. Blencowe, T., Pehrsson, A., and Lillsunde, P., Eds., Analytical Evaluation of Oral Fluid Screening Devices and Preceding Selection Procedures, Driving under the Influence of Drugs and Medicines, DRUID, March 30, 2010.
76. Walsh, J., Crouch, D., Danaceau, J., Cangianelli, L., Liddicoat, L., and Adkins, R., Evaluation of ten oral fluid point-of-collection drug-testing devices, *J. Anal.Toxicol.*, 31(1), 44, 2007.
77. Crouch, D., Walsh, J., Flegel, R., Cangianelli, L., Baudys, J., and Atkins, R., An evaluation of selected oral fluid point-of-collection drug-testing devices, *J. Anal. Toxicol.*, 29(4), 244, 2005.
78. Musshoff, F., Hokamp, E.G., Bott, U., and Madea, B., Performance evaluation of on-site oral fluid drug screening devices in normal police procedure in Germany, *For. Sci. Int.*, 238, 120, 2014.
79. Wille, S., Samyn, N., Ramirez-Fernandez, M., and De Boeck, G., Evaluation of on-site oral fluid screening using Drugwipe-5(+), RapidSTAT and Drug Test 5000 for the detection of drugs of abuse in drivers, *For. Sci. Int.*, 198(1–3), 2, 2010

80. Yacoubian, G.S., Wish, E.D., and Perez, D.M., A comparison of saliva testing to urinalysis in an arrestee population, *J. Psychoactive Drugs*, 33(3), 289, 2001.
81. *Mandatory Guidelines for Federal Workplace Drug Testing Programs—Oral Fluid*, SAMHSA, Issuance of Guidelines, 84 FR 57554, October 25, 2019
82. *Conforming Products List of Screening Devices To Measure Alcohol in Bodily Fluids*, National Highway Traffic Safety Adminsitrtaion, Department of Transportation, 77 FR 35745, June 14, 2012.
83. Mieczkowski, T., The utilization of ion mobility spectrometry in a criminal justice field application, in *Drug Testing Technology. Assessment of Field Applications*, T. Mieczkowski, Ed., CRC Press, Boca Raton, FL, 1999, Chapter 4.

6.3 REGULATORY CONCERNS FOR POINT OF COLLECTION TESTING IN THE WORKPLACE

Susan D. Crumpton, Jennifer A. Collins, Craig A. Sutheimer, and Michael R. Baylor

6.3.1 Introduction

Point of Collection (POC) testing has been used in the workplace and other areas of forensic drug testing for a number of years. As with laboratory-based workplace drug testing, POC test users must implement procedures that ensure accurate and reliable test results, while protecting donor rights to privacy and confidentiality. Many procedures for the collection, handling, and reporting of workplace drug test specimens are common to both POC testing and laboratory-based testing. However, some aspects of POC testing are unique and pose significant challenges to regulatory oversight.

In April 2004, the Department of Health and Human Services (HHS) issued proposed revisions to the Mandatory Guidelines for Federal Workplace Drug Testing Programs (HHS Guidelines) that included the use of POC testing for oral fluid and urine.[1] After considering the scientific literature and comments submitted by the public, HHS concluded that further investigation of POC testing – using the HHS Guidelines' analytes and cutoffs– was necessary in order to deem POC testing to be equivalent to HHS-certified laboratory initial testing. Because of the concerns raised by the public and federal agencies during the review process, the HHS did not include POC testing in the final HHS Guidelines[2] implemented in 2010, nor in the current HHS Guidelines for both urine and oral fluid testing.[3,4] Only laboratory-based drug testing is allowed for federally regulated workplace programs.

6.3.2 POC Testing Techniques

6.3.2.1 POC Testing Devices for Drugs of Abuse

POC testing devices for drugs of abuse were first available in the mid-1980s and early 1990s. POC devices include both non-instrumented devices with visually detected endpoints, as well as semi-automated or automated instrumented testing devices with instrument-read endpoints. The variety of devices include those that are cleared by the Food and Drug Administration (FDA) for in-vitro diagnostic use as well as those waived by the FDA under CLIA (Clinical Laboratory Improvement Amendments of 1988) that can be used outside a laboratory setting, in a workplace, or other collection site. The primary advantage of POC testing is that it is performed locally with a rapid turnaround of negative results that can be used to support decisions about hiring or continued employment. Most POC drug test devices utilize lateral flow or immunochromatography technology to perform tests similar to the competitive binding immunoassays currently used in laboratory-based initial testing. In general, the devices are comprised of a sample pad, a reagent pad, and a membrane or immunochromatography strip that facilitates the flow of the urine or oral fluid sample across test reaction/detection zones. These reaction zones consist of immobilized drug conjugates or antibodies that can react with components of a sample as it flows along the strip. Depending on the device format, the detection of drug in the sample can be either a negative-indicating reaction (i.e., the absence of a band indicates a presumptive positive result) or a positive-indicating reaction (i.e., the presence of a band indicates a presumptive positive result). Some POC devices are incorporated into the collection container.

There is a wide variation in the testing panels and cutoffs available for POC devices.[5–18] Although their ability to perform at some administrative cutoffs has been questioned over the course of the past decade, commercially available devices now appear to meet minimal technical requirements. As indicated previously, a number of the devices have been approved by the FDA. The FDA's Center for Devices and Radiological Health provides information on test categorization and approval/clearance of test devices (relevant searchable databases are available at www.fda.gov/MedicalDevices/DeviceRegulationandGuidance/Databases/default.htm).

Investigators, independent of the manufacturers, have evaluated non-instrumented POC devices for urine and oral fluid, and have found them to perform similarly to the instrumented immunoassay tests conducted in laboratories using the same cutoffs.[5,7,8] The investigators conducted tests on both drug-free urine and donor specimens. The drug-free urine was tested with and without added drug analytes. Donor specimens were selected from specimens that had previously been analyzed and determined to be drug-free or to contain varying amounts of the target analyte. Little performance difference was noted between the POC tests conducted by laboratory technicians and those conducted by non-laboratory personnel who had been trained in the proper procedures for conducting and reading the tests.[5,7]

A number of independent investigators[6,7,12,13,15–18] have evaluated non-instrumented POC devices for oral fluid. In some of these studies, fortified oral fluids at concentrations consistent with the 2004 proposed HHS cutoffs were analyzed.[12,13,16] These studies found device variability and noted that, while improved, the devices still had difficulty in reliably detecting cannabinoids. The investigators suggested that the rapid evolution of the device technology should be able to overcome any current problems relating to targeted analyte and manufacturer's cutoff, and that manufacturers should be able to provide assays consistent with proposed HHS cutoffs. In one study,[12] investigators concluded that "there is every reason to be optimistic about the future for drug testing using the oral fluid matrix."

6.3.2.2 POC Testing Devices for Specimen Validity

POC devices are widely used for specimen validity testing (SVT), and to identify synthetic urine or adulterated urine specimens. Specimen validity tests conducted with POC devices utilize technology similar to that employed by laboratories on instrumented testing equipment used for screening/initial SVT procedures.

Both independent investigators and manufacturers have evaluated urine non-instrumented SVT POC devices for the detection of abnormal urine specimens.[9–11] Additional information may be found in other subsections of this chapter. The studies evaluated drug-containing specimens to which adulterating chemicals or commercial adulterant products were added. Results from these preliminary studies were variable; however, the studies did demonstrate the ability of the various devices to measure creatinine, pH, and some oxidizing adulterants. These are the minimum initial SVT tests required by the current HHS Guidelines for urine specimens.

6.3.3 Regulatory Issues for POC Testing

6.3.3.1 Evidentiary Value

POC testing must be scientifically and forensically sound. POC test results alone (i.e., without confirmatory testing by an alternative analytical technique) do not meet the forensic and scientific standards that have been deemed necessary for regulated workplace drug testing. In April 2004, HHS proposed allowing POC testing for urine and oral fluid specimens to identify the absence of drugs or to identify a specimen as valid. Under those proposed HHS Guidelines, only specimens with valid negative POC test results could be reported from a POC testing site by a trained tester. Specimens with positive or invalid POC test results would be considered a presumptive or non-negative specimen (i.e., a specimen with a positive POC drug test response, an unacceptable POC SVT result, an abnormal POC drug test response, or an abnormal physical characteristic identified by the collector and/or trained tester). All presumptive (non-negative) specimens would be sent under chain-of-custody to an HHS-certified laboratory for initial and confirmatory testing.

As noted earlier, HHS did not include POC testing in the final HHS Guidelines implemented in 2010 or in subsequent HHS Guidelines for urine and oral fluid. However, the scientific and technical standards proposed for POC testing in April 2004 remain relevant and appropriate for workplace drug testing programs.

6.3.3.2 Regulatory Oversight

Because of the massive decentralized nature of POC testing, it is anticipated that monitoring POC testing would necessitate an extensive program that could not be easily managed by a single regulatory entity. While one regulatory body could retain overall responsibility for regulated testing, it might be practical for additional organizations to take an active part in the direct oversight of POC testing sites and trained testers. This chapter refers to such groups as POC Oversight Groups (POGs). Possible oversight groups could be accreditation bodies, individual federal agencies, non-Government training/certifying organizations, or industry groups such as the Drug and Alcohol Testing Industry Association (DATIA). In turn, the Regulatory Body could monitor the POG's procedures and records.

6.3.3.3 POC Devices

Laboratories are expected to validate their initial and confirmatory testing instruments and assays prior to use. Their validation studies should address variables that exist in, and among, laboratories. The variables include the instruments (e.g., manufacturer, model, condition, settings), analysts (e.g., variation in practices including measurement and pipetting techniques), quality control materials, and reagents (e.g., different materials and/or mixtures, as well as differences in preparation and/or storage conditions). Due to the multiple variables, the regulatory emphasis is on the user's validation, as well as the product manufacturer's validation.

The regulatory focus on POC test validation, at least in part, can be shifted from the user to the device manufacturer. POC testing involves discrete non-instrumented devices which have fewer testing variables than the instrumented assays used by laboratories. Unlike laboratory-based instrumented tests, an individual with little or no scientific/technical knowledge and experience can utilize a POC device, without extensive training. At least two published studies have documented comparable performance between individuals with non-scientific backgrounds and those with scientific/technical experience.[5,7] Non-instrumented POC devices are configured by the manufacturer and most include QC integrated into the device, as a process control that indicates that the device performed as designed (i.e., sufficient sample volume, sample migration occurred). Some manufacturers also provide QC samples or recommend QC samples from a certain vendor, and recommend QC frequency. The integrated and/or manufacturer-specified QC processes should reduce variability among testers, as opposed to QC samples prepared by individual users or purchased from various suppliers. POC devices require no specimen pre-treatment (e.g., extraction) and no user-prepared reagents. The validation of POC devices by manufacturer lot could be the basis for approved use in regulated drug testing programs.

To set a baseline level of performance, POC devices used in a regulated program should be cleared by the FDA through its regulatory processes. These processes include review and evaluation of the manufacturer's validation records for the device supporting the stated purpose (i.e., drug detection). The forensic requirements of workplace drug testing necessitate evaluation beyond that required by the FDA. This additional evaluation should involve review by the regulatory body or a POG designated by the body.

Under the described evaluation structure, the POC device manufacturer would submit an application to the regulatory body, including data that support the manufactured lot's performance at and around specified cutoffs, and data supporting the lot's specificity to detect the target analyte(s) in the presence of analogous compounds. The regulatory body could forward the application and supporting data to the POG for technical review. The manufacturer would participate in an appropriate performance testing (PT) program, and send its PT results to the POG for review. If the application, validation data, and PT performance are found to be acceptable, the POG would recommend approval of the device lot to the regulatory body and direct the manufacturer to retain a predetermined number of devices that could be used to assess problems that might arise during the life of the device lot. The regulatory body would issue a certificate of acceptability and place the device lot on a conforming products list (CPL) that would be published and updated periodically.

The relationships between the POC device manufacturer, POG, and regulatory body as described above are schematically depicted in Figure 6.3.1.

6.3.3.4 Trained Testers and POC Testing Sites

The regulatory body should specify training and performance requirements for POC testers. At a minimum, this training should address chain-of-custody documentation, confidentiality of test results and donor information, recordkeeping, and testing procedures that ensure proper

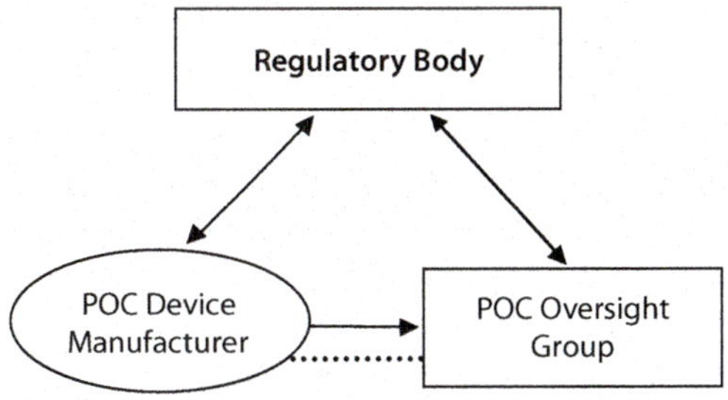

FIGURE 6.3.1 Regulatory issues: POC device manufacturer, regulatory body, and POC oversight group (POG). POC Manufacturer submits application and device lot validation data to the Regulatory Body; Regulatory Body forwards application and validation data to the POG for review; POG (or other agent) forwards Performance Testing (PT) set to the Manufacturer; Manufacturer reports PT results to POG for review; If PT results are acceptable, the POG recommends approval of the device lot to the Regulatory Body; Regulatory Body places approved device lot on conforming products list (CPL)

operation, storage, QC procedures, result interpretation, and any maintenance procedures for each type of POC device used.

Individuals seeking certification for testing regulated specimens should be required to submit an application and documentation of training to the Regulatory Body or its designated agent (e.g., the POG, a personnel certification body). Qualified applicants would be sent a set of proficiency samples on behalf of the regulatory body. Individuals reporting acceptable results would be issued a trained tester certificate with a specified expiration date (e.g., one year). Prior to the expiration date, a set of proficiency samples would be sent to the trained tester for certification renewal. Training records should be available for review, and should be maintained by the POG and updated as appropriate.

Ongoing compliance must also be monitored. Direct oversight of POC testing sites/trained testers could be accomplished by a POG, with periodic PT challenges for trained testers and onsite inspections of a sampling of POC testing sites.

As currently required of laboratories certified by HHS under the National Laboratory Certification Program (NLCP), the POC testing sites/trained testers should be required to have and follow a standard operating procedures (SOP) manual that incorporates procedures required for regulated workplace testing. To ensure consistency among the various POC testing sites/trained testers, it may be practical for entities under whose regulations testing is performed to write and distribute the SOP manuals.

Any procedural deficiencies or discrepant test results identified through the inspection or PT programs, or reported to the regulatory body or POG by a Medical Review Officer (MRO) could be addressed through remediation by the POG with the POC testing site. Remediation would involve investigation and corrective actions to correct identified problems. Based on identified deficiencies, a POC testing site or a trained tester could be suspended from testing regulated specimens. Any errors attributed to a POC device itself could be referred for remediation by the POG with the POC device manufacturer. Based on identified deficiencies, a device lot could be removed from the CPL. The timing of the suspension or device lot removal would be dependent on the degree and imminence of harm to the tested population and general public.

The relationships between the trained tester, POG, and regulatory body as described above are outlined in Figure 6.3.2.

6.3.3.5 Specimens

HHS published revised HHS Guidelines for urine (i.e., Mandatory Guidelines for Federal Workplace Drug Testing Programs using Urine, UrMG)[3] effective October 1, 2017, and new HHS Guidelines for oral fluid (i.e., Mandatory Guidelines for Federal Workplace Drug Testing Programs using Oral Fluid, OFMG)[4] effective January 1, 2020. Federal agencies and regulated employers are now allowed to test urine, oral fluid, or both specimen types in their

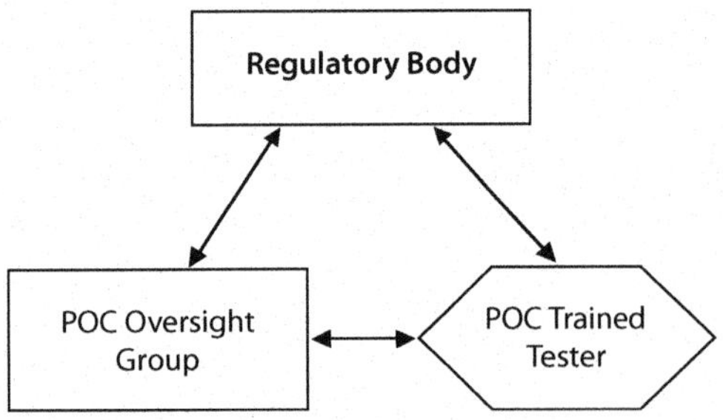

FIGURE 6.3.2 Regulatory issues: POC trained testers, regulatory body, and POC oversight group (POG). Trained tester submits an application and training documentation to the regulatory body which then forwards application and training documentation to the POG for review; If qualifications and training are acceptable, POG forwards the performance testing (PT) set to the trained tester; the trained tester reports PT results to the POG for review; If acceptable, the POG recommends certification of the trained tester to the regulatory body, which then issues certificate to trained tester and provides copy of certification to the POG

workplace drug testing programs. Oral fluid has been used for many years in nonregulated workplace drug testing programs. The choice of specimen depends on several factors, especially the drug detection time using a particular specimen matrix and the reason for the test (e.g., pre-employment, post-accident, reasonable suspicion, return to duty, follow-up, random). Currently, POC devices are available for testing urine or oral fluid specimens. Devices for other specimen matrices may be developed in the future. The history, technologies, analytes, and forensic applications of POC devices are detailed in other subsections of this chapter.

POC testing of urine is most suited for situations that require quick, negative results such as in emergency/crisis management and in pre-employment situations, particularly if the collection/test site performs only a few tests a day. With POC testing's high negative predictive value, it can save on transportation costs associated with the shipment of urine specimens to a laboratory. As with laboratory-based urine testing, POC urine testing can be used for random, reasonable suspicion/cause, and post-accident testing if drug use occurred more than three hours prior to the incident. POC urine testing may be least suited for return-to-duty and follow-up testing.

Similar to urine, POC testing of oral fluid also is suited for situations that require quick, negative results such as in emergency/crisis management or in pre-employment situations, when the collection/test site performs only a few tests a day. It can save on transportation costs associated with the shipment of oral fluid specimens to a laboratory. Drug analytes appear in oral fluid soon after use, and have a shorter detection time than drug analytes in urine. Therefore, in a workplace setting, oral fluid testing is most suited for reasonable suspicion/cause and post-accident testing. It may be least suited for random testing. Oral fluid may not be well suited for return-to-duty or follow-up testing.

6.3.3.6 Collection Sites and Specimen Collection

Specimen collection requirements should closely parallel those procedures already established for laboratory-based workplace drug testing, such as those required by HHS for federal workplace specimens and by the Department of Transportation (DOT) for their regulated industries' workplace specimens.[19,20] These procedures were developed to ensure a consistent, forensically defensible collection using strict chain-of-custody procedures, thereby ensuring that the integrity and identity of each specimen are maintained. A brief summary of specimen collection requirements follows.

A collection site may be a permanent or temporary facility. All sites where regulated specimens are collected must be equipped with security features limiting access to appropriate collection site personnel. A dedicated collection facility must be secured at all times. Temporary collection facilities, at a minimum, must be secured during collections.

Collection sites must tailor the facility and operations to the specimen type(s) collected. For example, urine specimen collections take place in a restroom and the facility must also enable observed collections. The collector must take additional measures to prevent specimen dilution, substitution, or adulteration (e.g., turning off the water supply or securing faucets, coloring the water in the toilet, preventing access to items that may be used to adulterate a specimen). Oral fluid collections do not require the same level of privacy as a urine collection. Because oral fluid collections are observed, the donor has limited opportunity to tamper with the specimen. The collector must inspect the donor's oral cavity prior to beginning the collection, and maintain visual contact with the donor until the collection is completed. If the collector identifies an item that could interfere with the collection when inspecting the donor's oral cavity, the collector directs the donor to remove the item, and provides water (e.g., up to four ounces) for the donor to drink and/or rinse his/her mouth. Once the oral cavity is clear of any interfering items, the collector waits ten minutes prior to starting the oral fluid specimen collection.

Essential elements of a proper collection include procedures for verifying donor identity; maintaining specimen identification and integrity throughout the collection process, subsequent storage, and transfers; documenting the collection and chain-of-custody using a standardized custody and control form (CCF); and examining the specimen for adequate volume and other characteristics (e.g., the temperature of a urine specimen). Specimen containers should be sealed in the presence of the donor. The seal must be tamper-evident and the container must prevent contamination of the specimen. Collection site procedures must ensure the accuracy, security, and confidentiality of drug test information.

6.3.3.7 POC Testing Procedures and Reporting Results

POC testing differs from laboratory-based testing in that the same individual may collect and test the specimen. To avoid confrontation, testing should not occur in the presence of the donor and the tester should not reveal any test results to the donor.

After completing testing, the tester should reseal presumptive non-negative primary specimens with a tamper-evident seal to ensure the integrity of the specimen. The split specimen must not be opened: the original seal must remain intact. Both primary and split specimens should be placed in a secondary container (e.g., bag, box, mailer) that is then sealed and kept in secured storage until the specimen package is transferred to a laboratory for initial and confirmatory testing.

The tester should report specimens with negative POC drug test results and acceptable responses for POC specimen validity tests to the MRO by sending a completed CCF and/or electronic report. Measures must be taken to ensure the security and confidentiality of donor information. The tester should discard valid negative specimens immediately after testing, unless the negative specimen is sent to a laboratory for quality assurance (QA) purposes.

The relationships between the trained testers, laboratory, MRO, and POG for reporting results from POC sites are depicted in Figure 6.3.3.

6.3.3.8 Quality Control/Quality Assurance

Due to the forensic aspects of workplace drug testing, quality control requirements for workplace POC testing may be more stringent than those for non-regulated on-site testing in clinical environments (i.e., "point of care testing").[21,22] However, quality control requirements for POC testing may also differ from those required for laboratory-based instrumented tests in a regulated workplace testing program.

HHS-certified laboratories are required to document the validity of results in each initial and confirmatory test batch by analyzing a specified type and percentage of QC samples. POC testing using discrete POC devices has fewer testing variables. In addition, many, if not most, devices include a test line or control line that indicates proper test performance. Therefore, it would appear sufficient to document acceptable performance for each trained tester on each day that the individual tests specimens with a specific test device. As previously noted, POC testing should be used only as a screening test, with any presumptive non-negative specimens forwarded to a laboratory for initial testing and reflexing to confirmatory testing as required, in accordance with stringent QC policies.

The HHS Guidelines include requirements for an external QA program. Federal agencies and regulated employers must submit blind proficiency samples to certified laboratories (i.e., a specified percentage of the donor specimens they submit for testing) to demonstrate the laboratory's ability to obtain and report results correctly. A QA program for POC testing sites/trained testers could require a specified percentage of POC test-negative donor specimens to be sent to a certified laboratory for testing (with donor identification and demographic information redacted). The laboratory would then report its results through the MRO to the POG for review.

This QA process involving the interactions of the trained tester, laboratory, MRO, and POG is incorporated into Figure 6.3.4.

6.3.4 POC Testing Advantages and Disadvantages

The major advantage of POC testing is the almost immediate identification of negative test results. POC testing is performed as a discrete analysis, not requiring batch configuration, so individual specimens can be analyzed without delay.

1. Employer costs for negative POC test specimens appear to be comparable to costs of laboratory-based testing. Due to the additional testing performed, the employer costs for non-negative specimens are predicted to be greater than costs

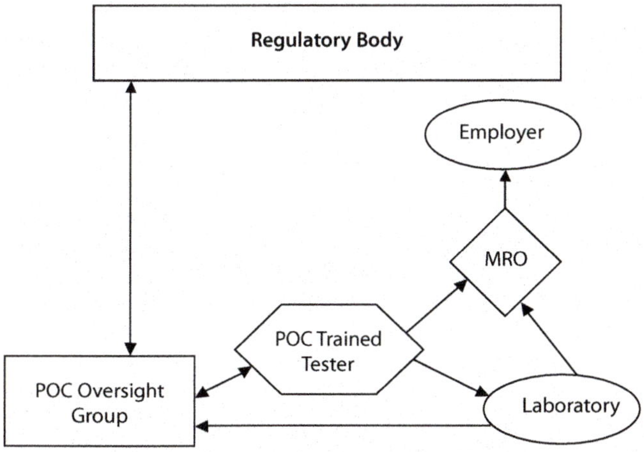

FIGURE 6.3.3 Regulatory issues: POC testing, laboratory testing, reporting results, and quality assurance (QA). Trained tester reports negative results to the MRO; the trained tester forwards non-negative specimens to the laboratory for testing; the trained tester forwards a percentage of negative specimens to the laboratory for QA testing; laboratory reports all specimen results to the MRO; laboratory reports QA results to the POG; MRO reports results to the employer

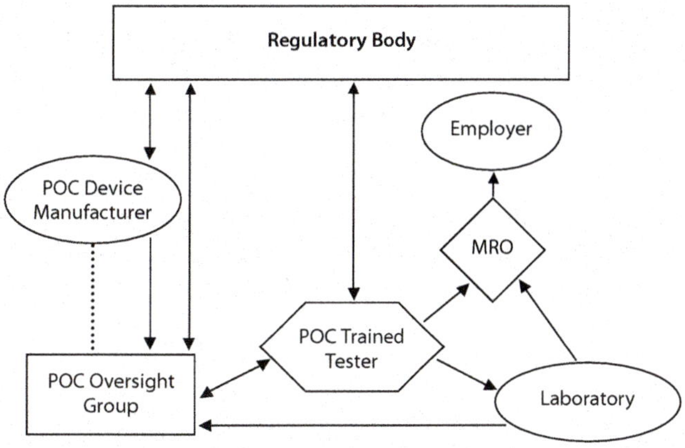

FIGURE 6.3.4 The regulatory oversight of POC testing: interaction of all components

for laboratory testing. POC test devices have a shelf-life of 12 to 18 months. This relatively short time may be a major disadvantage to testing sites with a limited specimen volume to be analyzed, as the tendency of manufacturers to package devices in multiples could result in a significant number of the devices expiring before use.

2. Another disadvantage of POC testing may be the costs associated with the complex oversight/regulatory program needed for an extremely decentralized population of sites/testers.
3. Procedural disadvantages that have been noted for POC testing in other fields, such as clinical testing,[23] would not appear to be of concern in a regulated workplace setting with POC testing used only as a screening method. For example, the potential for misinterpretation of results would be unlikely. A POC device that is prone to inconclusive results probably would not meet the criteria for placement on the regulatory body's CPL. Additionally, training requirements for testers and regulatory oversight as previously described (e.g., proficiency testing, QA program using POC test-negative specimens) should reveal systemic problems.

6.3.5 Role of the Medical Review Officer (MRO)

The MRO plays an essential part in regulated workplace drug testing.[1–4] In the described POC testing scheme, the MRO would provide the final interpretation of test results and serves as the liaison among the various parties involved in a drug test (e.g., the regulatory body, federal agency, the employer, the donor, the collection site, the POC testing site and POC trained tester, and the laboratory). The MRO must report negative drug test results from a POC testing site to the employer/agency in the same manner as results obtained from a laboratory. Non-negative specimens must be treated by the MRO in the same manner regardless of whether they were first tested using POC tests or tested only by a laboratory. These MRO interactions are depicted in Figures 6.3.3 and 6.3.4.

The MRO must be knowledgeable about the capabilities of the POC tests and laboratory-based test methods that were used for specimens that he/she reviews. The MRO must report any discrepant or erroneous test results to the regulatory body, so an investigation can be conducted to identify and address the cause(s) of the problem.

Due to conflict of interest concerns, some relationships between MROs and laboratories are considered inappropriate and should be prohibited (i.e., the MRO must not be an employee, agent of, or have any financial interest in a regulated laboratory). Similar prohibitions should be instituted for the relationship between MROs and POC device manufacturers and for the relationship between an MRO and a POC testing site for which the MRO reviews drug test results.

6.3.6 Regulatory Oversight

The unique challenges for the regulatory body are that the POC testing sites may be numerous, decentralized, and that many trained testers may have little forensic experience or training. As proposed, another oversight group (POG) could provide administrative and technical support to a regulatory body. It is conceived that delegated functions could include reviewing and approving POC devices, providing training (i.e., initial training for users or "train-the-trainer" courses), and maintaining administrative oversight of testers and POC testing sites. Records are an essential component in any forensic field. A POG could maintain the records for workplace drug testing programs, such as a registry of trained testers, records of results by a tester for each device as part of a QA program, and other documentation demonstrating the acceptability of testing, reporting, and recordkeeping.

POC testing has both technical/scientific issues and administrative/policy issues that must be addressed by regulators.[24] The Substance Abuse and Mental Health Services Administration (SAMHSA) within HHS accredits laboratories to perform federal workplace drug testing and monitors federal workplace drug testing through the NLCP via on-site inspections and quarterly PT challenges. Similar direct oversight may be required to ensure that regulated workplace drug testing using POC testing is conducted with the equivalent integrity and technical standards as testing in an accredited laboratory. With proper safeguards and regulatory oversight in place, it is envisioned that POC testing has the potential to become a significant part of workplace drug testing.

6.3.7 Acknowledgments

The authors would like to express their appreciation to Ron Flegel, M.S. (Division of Workplace Programs, Center for Substance Abuse Prevention, SAMHSA) for regulatory insight and to Lois Holliday, M.S. (RTI International) for research and editorial support.

REFERENCES

1. Proposed Mandatory Guidelines for Workplace Drug Testing Programs, Substance Abuse and Mental Health Services Administration, Department of Health and Human Services, 69 Federal Register (FR) 19673 (April 13, 2004).
2. Mandatory Guidelines for Workplace Drug Testing Programs, Substance Abuse and Mental Health Services Administration, Department of Health and Human Services, 73 Federal Register (FR) 71858 (November 25, 2008).
3. Mandatory Guidelines for Workplace Drug Testing Programs using Urine, Substance Abuse and Mental Health Services Administration, Department of Health and Human Services, 82 Federal Register (FR) 7920 (January 23, 2017).
4. Mandatory Guidelines for Workplace Drug Testing Programs using Oral Fluid, Substance Abuse and Mental Health Services Administration, Department of Health and Human Services, 84 Federal Register (FR) 57554 (October 25, 2019).

5. Kadehjian, L.J. Performance of five non-instrumented urine drug-testing devices with challenging near-cutoff specimens. *J Anal Toxicol*, 25, 670–679, 2001.
6. Barrett, C., et al. Comparison of point-of-collection screening of drugs of abuse in oral fluid with a laboratory-based urine screen. *Forensic Sci Int*, 122, 163–166, 2001.
7. Crouch, D.J., et al. A field evaluation of five on-site drug-testing devices. *J Anal Toxicol*, 26, 493–499, 2002.
8. Peace, M.R., et al. Performance evaluation of four on-site drug-testing devices for detection of drugs of abuse in urine. *J Anal Toxicol*, 24, 589–594, 2000.
9. Peace, M.R. and Tarnai, L.D. Performance evaluation of three on-site adulterant detection devices for urine specimens. *J Anal Toxicol*, 26, 464–470, 2002.
10. Wong, R. The effect of adulterants on urine screen for drugs of abuse: Detection by an on-site dipstick device. *Am Clin Lab*, 21, 37, 2002.
11. Wong, B., et al. Adulterants: Its detection and effects on urine drug screens. Abstract: Society of Forensic Toxicologists, 2003 Meeting.
12. Walsh, J.M., et al. An evaluation of rapid point-of-collection oral fluid drug-testing devices. *J Anal Toxicol*, 27, 429–439, 2003.
13. Crouch, D.J., et al. An evaluation of selected oral fluid point-of-collection devices. *J Anal Toxicol*, 29, 244–248, 2005.
14. Moody, D.E., et al. A comparative evaluation of the instant-view 5-panel test card with the OnTrak TesTcup Pro 5: comparison with gas chromatography-mass spectrometry. *J Anal Toxicol*, 30, 50–56, 2006.
15. Concheiro, M., et al. Confirmation by LC-MS of drugs in oral fluid obtained from roadside testing. *Forensic Sci Int*, 170, 156–162, 2007.
16. Walsh, J.M., et al. Evaluation of ten oral fluid point-of-collection drug-testing devices. *J Anal Toxicol*, 31, 44–54, 2007.
17. Crouch, D.J., et al. Laboratory evaluation and field application of roadside oral fluid collectors and drug testing devices. *Ther Drug Monit*, 30, 188–195, 2008.
18. Desrosiers, N.A., et al. On-site test for cannabis in oral fluid. *Clin Chem*, 58, 1418–1425, 2012.
19. HHS Urine Specimen Collection Handbook for Federal Agency Workplace Drug Testing Programs, downloaded August 2016 from http://www.samhsa.gov/workplace/resources
20. DOT Urine Specimen Collection Guidelines for the U.S. Department of Transportation Workplace Drug Testing Programs 49 CFR Part 40, downloaded August 2016 from https://www.transportation.gov/odapc/urine-specimen-collection-guidelines
21. Lewandrowski, K., et al. Implementation of point-of-care rapid urine testing for drugs of abuse in the emergency department of an academic medical center: impact on test utilization and ED length of stay. *Am J Clin Pathol, 129*, 796–801, 2008.
22. Wu, A.H.B. On-site tests for therapeutic drugs, in *On-Site Drug Testing*, Jenkins, A.J. and Goldberger, B.A., Eds., Humana Press, Totowa, NJ, 2002, chap. 2.
23. George, S. and Braithwaite, R. Use of on-site testing for drugs of abuse. *Clin Chem*, 48, 10, 2002.
24. Shults, T.F. and Caplan, Y.H. Program requirements, standards, and legal considerations for on-site drug testing devices in workplace testing programs, in *On-Site Drug Testing*, Jenkins, A.J. and Goldberger, B.A., Eds., Humana Press, Totowa, NJ, 2002, chap 4.

6.4 ALCOHOL DETERMINATION IN POINT OF COLLECTION TESTING

John Robert Zettl

This section is divided into five subsections: (1) Introduction; (2) Pharmacology of Alcohol; (3) APOCT Specimens; (4) APOCT Devices – Breath as a Specimen; (5) Oral Fluid/Saliva as a Specimen, and; (6) Oral Fluid/Saliva Devices. A comprehensive discussion of alcohol pharmacology and toxicology and evidentiary breath testing can be found in alternate sections of *The Drug Abuse Handbook*. The materials presented here, relating to areas covered by other authors, are to assist the reader in understanding this chapter.

Devices used for human subject alcohol determination/testing can be separated into four broad categories: (a) Law Enforcement – Driving Under the Influence; (b) Diagnostic for Treatment or Other Medical Purposes; (c) Pre-Employment and Workplace Compliance; and (d) For Cause and Random for Governmental Compliance. This chapter will focus on devices used in the latter two venues: Pre-Employment and for Workplace Compliance and For Cause and Random for Governmental Compliance.

6.4.1 Introduction

It is appropriate to have a brief discussion about how and why alcohol testing is important in Point of Collection Testing.

6.4.1.1 Alcohol Abuse in the United States

In 2014, 87.6% of people aged 18 or older reported they drank alcohol at some point in their lifetime; 71.0% reported that they drank in the past year; 56.9% reported that they drank in the past month;[1] and 6.7% of the people ages 18 or older reported they engaged in heavy drinking in the past month.[1]

Drinking too much can harm your health. Excessive alcohol use led to approximately 88,000 deaths and 2.5 million years of potential life lost annually in the United States from 2006–2010, shortening the lives of those who died by an average of 30 years.[1] Further, excessive drinking was responsible for one in ten deaths among working-age adults aged 20–64 years. The economic cost of excessive alcohol consumption in 2010 was estimated as $249 billion, or $2.05 a drink.[1]

In the United States, alcohol accounts for two-thirds of all workplace substance abuse complaints and depletes a similar percentage from industries' healthcare benefit budgets. The results of a 2002 study released by The Substance Abuse and Mental Health Services Administration (SAMHSA) showed drug use trends in the United States. Of interest is that most alcohol and drug users are employed.[1]

Alcohol abuse and its related problems cost society many billions of dollars each year.[1–5] Estimates of the economic costs of alcohol abuse attempt to assess in monetary terms the damage that results from the misuse of alcohol. These costs include expenditures on alcohol-related problems and opportunities that are lost because of alcohol. In a 1985 cost study,[6] Rice and co-workers estimated that the cost to society of alcohol abuse was $70.3 billion. By adjusting cost estimates for the effects of inflation and the growth of the population over time that cost today could be well over $ 100 billion.

According to the National Safety Council[7] $250 billion are lost annually from injuries sustained in motor vehicle accidents and of that number $40 billion is lost in alcohol-related crashes. Two out of every five automobile crashes are alcohol-related.[8] This is an economic loss to society of $90,000.00 from a single highway fatality and a total economic loss exceeding $4 billion annually. The drinking driver affects every one of us through increased taxes for additional law enforcement needs, medical facilities, incarceration, rehabilitation, and social security and welfare for survivors, as well as increased insurance rates.

6.4.2 Pharmacology of Alcohol

6.4.2.1 What is a "Standard Alcoholic Drink"?

In the United States, one "standard" drink contains roughly 14 grams of pure alcohol, which is found in 12 ounces of regular beer, usually about 5% alcohol, 5 ounces of wine, which is typically about 12% alcohol, and 1.5 ounces of distilled spirits, which is about 40% alcohol.

6.4.2.2 Alcohol in the Body

A complete discussion of the pharmacology and toxicology of alcohol testing can be found in an alternate chapter of this book.

Alcohol is a low molecular weight organic molecule that is sufficiently similar to water so as to be miscible with water in all proportions. Alcohol is able to cross cell membranes by a simple diffusion process; therefore, it can quickly achieve equilibrium throughout the body. The result of these properties is that alcohol rapidly becomes associated with all parts of the body, including oral fluid, and concentrations of alcohol will be found in proportion to body water content.

Alcohol is commonly ingested orally and passes from the mouth, through the esophagus, into the stomach, and then into the small intestine. From here, alcohol is absorbed into the body's blood and distributed by the circulatory system to all parts of the body. As alcohol is transported through the body by the blood flow, it passes through the liver, which is primarily responsible for its metabolism, then to the kidneys where it is eliminated into the urine, then to the brain where it elicits its primary symptomology effects, and finally to the lungs where some alcohol passes unaltered out of the body.

It is the quantity of alcohol present in the brain that affects a person's normal functioning. Practicality necessitates that a specimen that is in close equilibrium with the brain's alcohol concentration be used to reflect a person's alcohol concentration.

Most early studies centered on the use of blood to correlate the degree of alcohol impairment, however, over the last 50-plus years, breath testing has supplemented blood as the specimen of choice in many venues and, more recently, oral fluid/saliva for APOCT testing. Due to the difficulty in the collection of urine, its use as a specimen for APOCT testing may not be a facilities' first choice, and blood is more likely to be used in defining driving under the influence of alcohol, and blood and/or urine in defining driving under the influence of drugs.

Serum, or plasma, is more often used in clinical situations for alcohol analysis. Since the water content of serum/plasma is greater than that of whole blood, serum/plasma alcohol concentrations can be 10–20% greater than a corresponding collected blood specimen. Therefore, if serum/plasma tests are to be utilized where blood alcohol concentrations define legal penalties, the serum/plasma concentrations must be corrected. Serum to blood ratios vary from 1.12–1.17 while plasma averages 1.18. A ratio of 1.16 is commonly used to make the conversion.

For additional information and a more in-depth understanding of the pharmacology of alcohol refer to the *Forensic Science Handbook*, Vol. 1, 2nd Edition, Chapter 12, editor Richard Saferstein, "The Determination of Alcohol in Blood and Breath," by Yale H. Caplan and J. Robert Zettl; *The Drug Abuse Handbook*, 2nd Edition, Chapter 5, editor Steven Karch; and *Garriott's Medicolegal Aspects of Alcohol*, 6th Edition, Chapters 2, 3, 6, and 7, editors Yale H. Caplan and Bruce A. Goldberger.

6.4.3 APOCT Specimens and Devices

6.4.3.1 Specimens

Blood, serum, plasma, or urine is seldom used in Alcohol Point of Collection Testing (APOCT), due to issues that hinder their ease of collection. In most instances, existing regulations or statutes may dictate the choice of specimen. Breath and oral fluid/saliva are the specimens most likely to be used for APOCT venues.

With recent technological advances, oral fluid/saliva is now pressing breath as the preferred specimen of choice in certain venues. Oral fluid/saliva can, with appropriate care in specimen procurement and application of the accepted distribution ratios, be correlated with blood and a blood alcohol equivalent reported.

6.4.3.2 Oral Fluid – Saliva

Oral fluid/saliva testing has not been regularly employed due to the practical constraints of law enforcement for driving under the influence. It is, however, used extensively in the workplace environment. Oral fluid/saliva may not be practical for DUI enforcement since significant subject cooperation is needed to facilitate collection; however, recent advances in collection technology hold promise not only for alcohol, but for on-site (roadside) drug detection.[9]

6.4.3.3 Transdermal Alcohol Measurement – Sweat

Though Transdermal Alcohol Measurement (TAM) is not used in APOCT venues it is worth at least a minor discussion here because of its use in probation/parole settings and where subjects need to be monitored continuously to determine if they are continuing to abstain from alcohol consumption. Often, agencies involved in APOCT and other human alcohol-testing may transverse to other venues.

The body of scientific literature on TAM dates back almost 70 years.[10] Based on published research in this field, one can conclude that measuring alcohol transdermally (via sweat/perspiration) on a constant basis provides an effective screen for alcohol consumption and a reasonable approximation of the magnitude of that consumption.

Early research on the ability to measure transdermal perspiration (sweat) culminated in a White Paper titled "The Determination of Blood Alcohol Concentration by Transdermal Measurement" in 2002 by J. Robert Zettl.[10] The objective of that research was to compare the accuracy of readings using the Alcohol Monitoring Systems (AMS) SCRAM® bracelet to alcohol concentrations measured by conventional breath analysis. This was accomplished by establishing a series of objective scientific protocols, as specified in the Methodology section of the paper. The Zettl White Paper gives an overview of the science of transdermal alcohol testing, as well as an introduction to the AMS SCRAM® original product. Since this White Paper, AMS has conducted additional research and ongoing client monitoring using newer generation SCRAM® units.[11] See Figure 6.4.1 for the SCRAM unit and Figure 6.4.2 on how it attaches to the ankle of a person.

6.4.3.3.1 *Breath*

Breath tests to determine the alcohol concentration present in a person's body are by far the most frequently utilized test for Driving Under the Influence (DUI)/alcohol cases in the United States. At the time of writing, all but possibly two U.S. states have adopted legislation that permits reporting of a subject's alcohol concentration in breath units as alcohol per 210 L of breath. Breath-alcohol analysis is considered the method of choice used by law enforcement to enforce DUI statutes. It is also the method of choice in many other venues, due to 1) the non-invasive way a sample can be collected; 2) the operational simplicity of the new generation breath testing equipment; 3) the speed with which analyses may be conducted; 4) the convenience of being able to perform the analysis at or near the collection site, and; 5) the convenience of having the test results immediately available. A complete discussion of breath alcohol testing can be found in an alternate chapter of this book, as well as in the aforementioned writings in *The Forensic Science Handbook* and *Garriott's Medicolegal Aspects of Alcohol.*

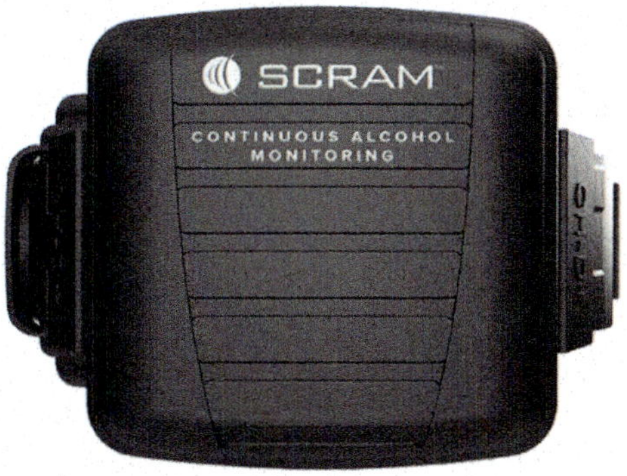

FIGURE 6.4.1 No caption

FIGURE 6.4.2 No caption

Breath-testing devices may be classified as Passive Alcohol devices (PAS/sniffers); Screening or Preliminary Breath Testers (PBTs); Alternate Uses; and Evidential Breath Test instruments (EBTs). The equipment and/or testing processes listed in this chapter may be incomplete due to devices and systems becoming obsolete or replaced with newer generation devices after 2017. The National Highway Traffic Administration has established a conforming products list for units in each of these categories, and those lists will be discussed under each section. A current list can be obtained by contacting the National Highway Traffic Safety Administration, Office of Alcohol and State Program, at 400 Seventh Street, S.W., Washington, D.C., 20590.[12,13]

This section considers devices that collect and sample breath specimens that are expiratory in composition.

6.4.4 APOCT Devices

6.4.4.1 General

The National Highway Traffic Administration (NHTSA) has established a conforming products list for instruments that conform to the Model Specifications for Devices to Measure Breath Alcohol. This list contains all devices currently approved to perform breath alcohol testing within the United States. While many of the devices found on the present Conforming Products List are no longer manufactured, some are still in use.[12]

In August 1994. the NHTSA published its first "Model Specification for Screening Devices to Measure Alcohol in Bodily Fluids." These specifications established performance criteria and methods for testing alcohol screening devices to measure alcohol content. The specifications supported state laws that targeted underage drinkers,

"Zero Tolerance," and the Department of Transportation's Workplace alcohol testing program. In December 1994, the NHTSA published its first Conforming Products List (CPL) of devices and, later that year, with corrections, identified additional devices that met NHTSA's Model Specifications for Screening Devices to Measure Alcohol in Bodily Fluids. Between 1994 and 2012, the NHTSA updated and revised the original CPL and in June 2012 it updated the CPL to where over 50 devices now appear on the present CPL.[13]

6.4.4.2 Breath Instrumentation – Evidential

Evidential Breath Testers (EBTs) employ a printer and data reduction capabilities and can be used in APOTC venues where precision, accuracy, and a saved record are needed. As previously stated, the National Highway Traffic Administration has established a conforming products list for evidential breath testing devices/instruments and another list for screening devices.[12,13]

It is not possible to list all the various instruments and manufactured equipment. The following is a list of the four companies that manufacture EBTs, generally for the law enforcement community to process DUIs, and the most recent units they market. These units can also be used for APOCT. Additional information on each of these units can be found by querying each manufacturer's website.

From left to right in Figures 6.4.3–6.4.7 are Intoximeters DMT; Dräger's Alcotest 9510; Intoximeters EC/IR II; Lifeloc's EV30T; and CMI's Intoxilyzer 9000.

FIGURE 6.4.3 Intoximeters DMT

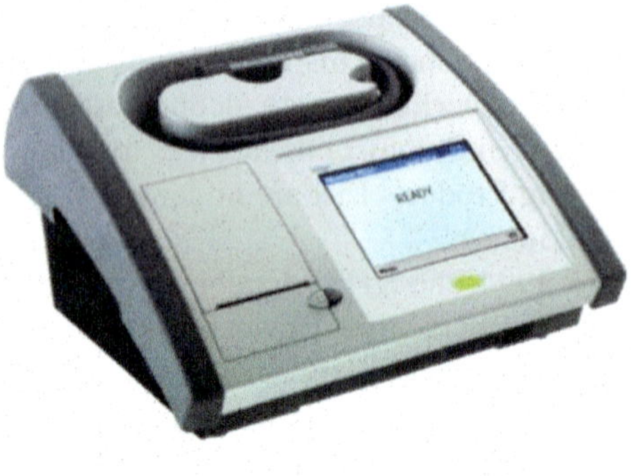

FIGURE 6.4.4 Draeger Alcotest 9510

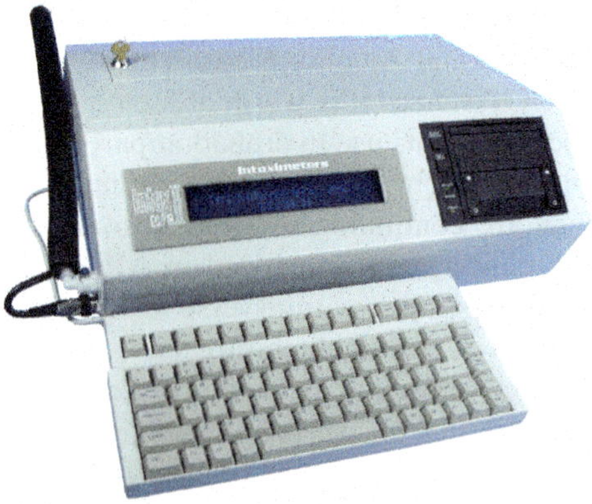

FIGURE 6.4.5 Intoximeters EC/IR IV

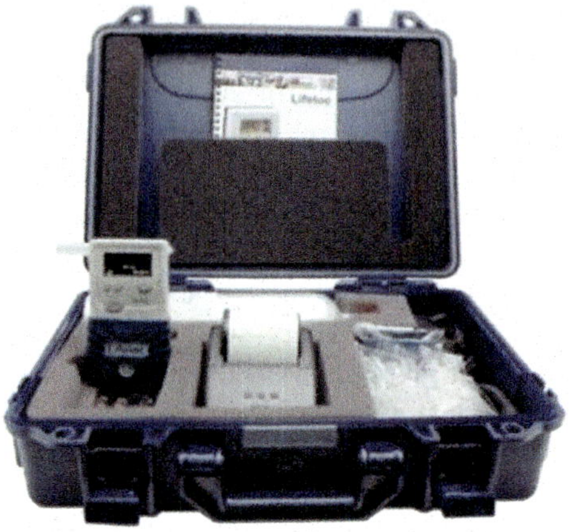

FIGURE 6.4.6 Lifeloc EV30T

FIGURE 6.4.7 CMI Intoxilzyer 9000

6.4.4.3 Breath Instrumentation – Evidential Screeners

Breath screening, or preliminary breath testers (PBTs), were originally intended to assist in quickly determining a person's approximate alcohol concentration and were not generally sufficiently accurate for APOCT purposes. Many of the former Screening Units now have become Evidential Breath Testers by employing an attachable printer and data reduction capabilities and can be used in APOTC venues where precision, accuracy, and a printed record are needed.

The NHTSA establishes which devices can be used for screening under its "Conforming Products List of Screening Devices to Measure Alcohol in Body Fluids."[13]

It should be noted some PBTs generally do not have Mouth Alcohol Detection and should be used with caution as Evidential Breath Testers. Additionally, many handheld PBTs do not have printers attached unless updated with Print Capability as an additional cost. Print capability should be used where authentication of test results needs to be maintained.

As previously stated it is not possible to list all the various instrument manufactures equipment for screening units that can be used in an evidentiary setting. Following is a list of the 4 companies that manufacture PBTs with data reduction and print capabilities. The market for these devices has been for the Law Enforcement community to process DUI's but can be used in an APOCT setting. Additional information on each of these units can be found by querying each manufactures web site.

From left to right are the Intoximeter Alco-Sensor RBT IV; Dräger's Alcotest 8610; Lifeloc's FC20BT; and CMI's Intoxilyzer 400PA (Figures 6.4.8–6.4.11).

6.4.4.4 Breath Instrumentation – Non-Evidentiary Screeners

Breath screening or Preliminary Breath Testers (PBTs) were originally marketed as a means for law enforcement officers to quickly determine a person's approximate alcohol concentration at the roadside. PBT's were not intended to be used as evidence in a legal proceeding. When used for APOCT purposes they have the same precision and accuracy as their big brothers but do have the capability to provide a printed record.

Again, it needs to be pointed out that most if not all PBTs do not have Mouth Alcohol Detection and should be used with caution. A deprivation period (waiting period) where the subject is observed to not place anything in their mouth is required. At least 15 minutes is sufficient. Other issues to be aware of are belching or in some way bringing stomach gases or fluids into the oral cavity prior to taking a

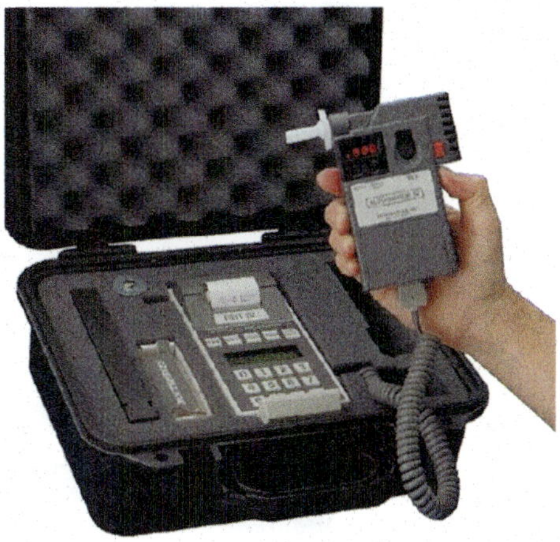

FIGURE 6.4.8 Alco-Sensor RBT IV

FIGURE 6.4.9 Drager Alcotest 8610

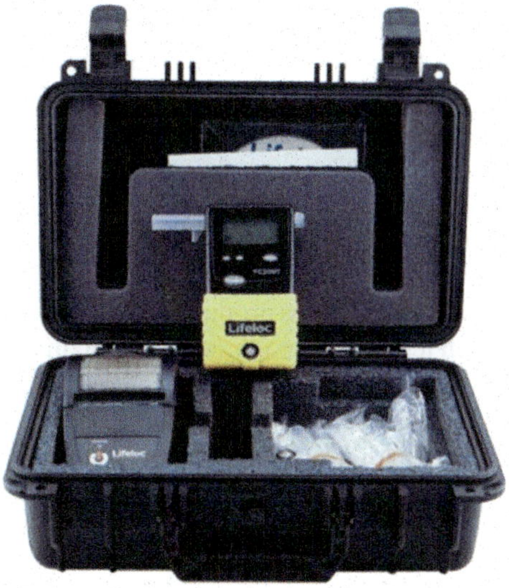

FIGURE 6.4.10 Lifeloc FC20BT

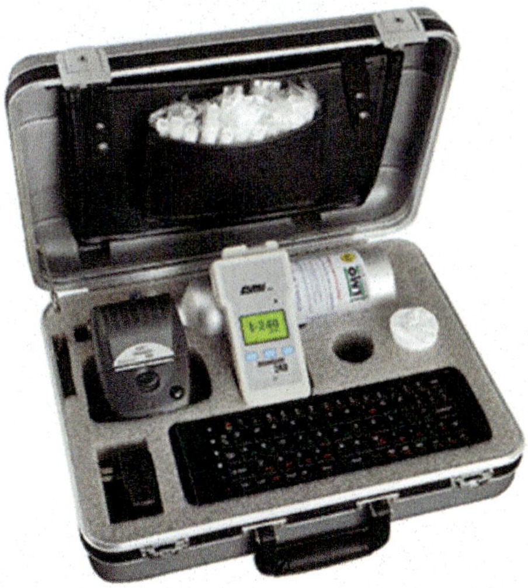

FIGURE 6.4.11 Intoxilyzer 400PA

sample that may contain alcohol and contaminate the testing procedure.

There are many companies that either manufacture their own units or sell additional breath-screening units from a few hundred dollars to over a thousand. There are other breath-test instruments costing as low as $40.00. If accuracy is not an issue, and the only concern is evaluating if the person tests positive (above a predetermined limit – which may be as low as 0.02%) or not, then the more expensive instruments could be excluded.

A list of four prominent companies that manufacture PBTs follows. Additional information on each of these units can be found by querying each manufacturer's website.

From left to right in Figures 6.4.12–6.4.15 are the Dräger Alcotest® 6820; Lifeloc's Phoenix 6.0BT; Intoximeter Alco-Sensor FST; and CMI's Intoxilyzer 400 (Figures 6.4.12–6.4.15).

6.4.4.5 Passive Alcohol Sensor Devices – PAS

"Passive" alcohol-sensing devices are designed to detect the presence of alcohol in a person's normal expelled breath, that is, the subject being tested is not required to blow into a mouthpiece as with conventional breath-test devices. Passive alcohol-sensing devices pull, by use of a fan or other mechanical means, the vapor from the subject's normal breath when the device is held in close proximity to his or her mouth.

The device can also be held over open containers of an alcoholic beverage to see if a product has alcohol in it. This is effective when testing underage subjects who may be drinking illegally. The present distributor of the PAS Systems is LLC, Fredericksburg, VA markets the PAS IV Passive Alcohol Sensor with LED Flashlight (Figure 6.4.16). It is a non-invasive alcohol-screening instrument, which has a built-in high-intensity flashlight. Their product information refers to the device as a "sniffer" for overt or covert alcohol detection.

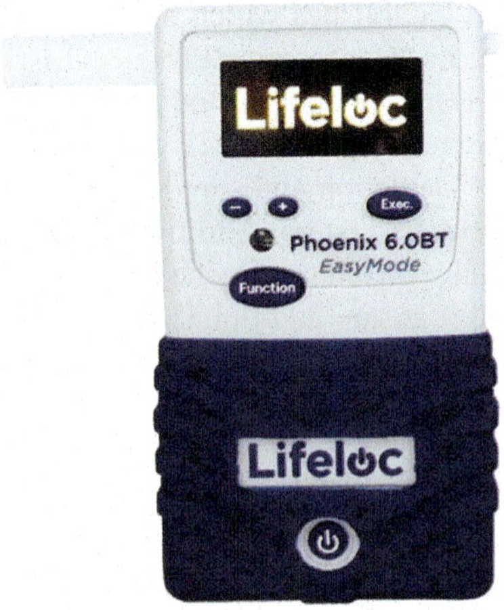

FIGURE 6.4.13 Lifeloc Phoenix 6.0BT

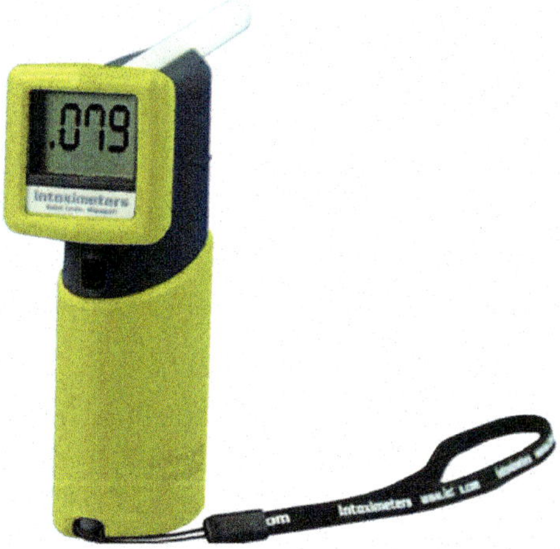

FIGURE 6.4.14 Intoximeters FST

FIGURE 6.4.12 Dräger Alcotest® 6820

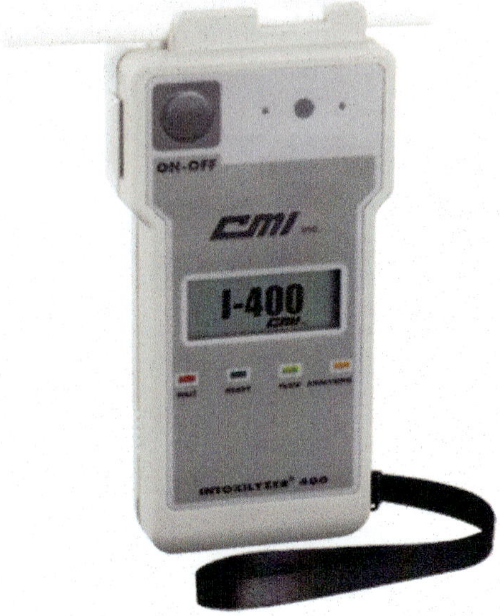

FIGURE 6.4.15 CMI Intoxilyzer 400

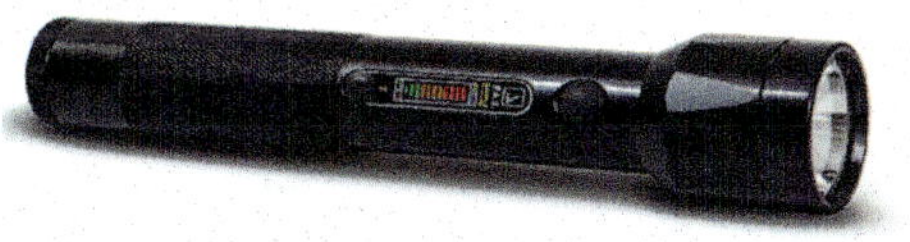

FIGURE 6.4.16 PAS V Passive Alcohol Sensor with LED Flashlight

6.4.5 APOCT Oral Fluid/Saliva

6.4.5.1 Analytical Principle

Oral fluid is primarily saliva mixed with other minor oral fluid secretions. Because the body produces saliva on a continual basis, drugs and metabolites that are secreted into saliva reflect what is in the bloodstream. The direct link between saliva and blood provides a dynamic means of testing individuals to determine their current drug status. Thus, oral fluid serves as a "window" into the body for most drugs. This description of Oral Fluid was excerpted from a paper by Dr. Edward Cone.[14]

6.4.5.2 Oral Fluid

The terms oral fluid and saliva are interchangeable in many texts and research grants, company marketing strategies, dissertations, and peer review articles. For this chapter, Oral Fluid will be used.

Oral fluid collection for alcohol testing is regularly employed in POCT facilities but is not used in DUI alcohol testing due to its practical constraints in court. There is ongoing research for the use of oral fluid in the evaluation of Driving Under the Influence of Drugs (DUID) cases. Though oral fluid may be impractical for DUI enforcement – because significant subject cooperation is needed to facilitate the collection – recent advances in collection technology hold great promise for its use in Point of Collection Testing for on-site (roadside) drug detection.[9]

Oral fluid alcohol results can be compared to the amount of alcohol contained in a person's blood. If collected properly by observing a waiting period after a person has consumed their last alcoholic beverage, usually 10 to 15 minutes, then any residual alcohol will have been absorbed, swallowed, or evaporated, and their mouth is "clear." According to one manufacturer's information, the relationship between the amount of saliva alcohol and blood alcohol is 1:1 while with breath it is, 000048:1, making saliva a more sensitive testing medium than breath.[15]

As previously stated, it is not possible to list all the various providers of oral fluid/saliva-based products that can be used for APOCT testing. There are numerous companies (including Alco Screen; Breath Scan; QED; and Saliva Confirm Premium) with products available, so depending upon one's workload and client base an online query will provide additional information to research the subject further.

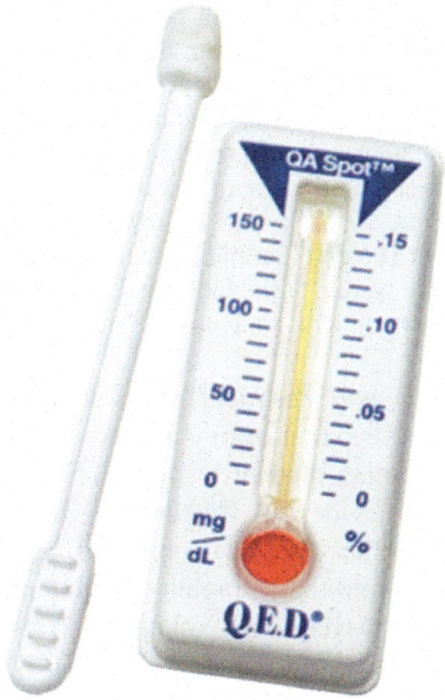

FIGURE 6.4.17 Q.E.D.

6.4.5.3 Saliva-Based Devices

6.4.5.3.1 Q.E.D.® Saliva Alcohol Test

The Q.E.D. is a quantitative test device for the rapid determination of Equivalent Blood Alcohol Content (BAC) using a non-invasive saliva sample. Approved by the Federal Department of Transportation (DOT) for commercial alcohol testing programs, the Q.E.D. uses a unique patented lateral flow method to rapidly determine alcohol presence in saliva expressed as % BAC and ml/dl concentration. As simple as reading a thermometer.[16]

The Q.E.D.® Saliva Alcohol test uses a pre-set chemical reactive process that requires no user intervention, a color bar rises to the level of alcohol present in the system in much the same way as a mercury thermometer (Figure 6.4.17). In extensive clinical trials, saliva alcohol levels measured by the Q.E.D.® Saliva Alcohol test demonstrated a high correlation rate of 98% (r = 0.98) to blood analyzed by sophisticated laboratory gas chromatography methods.[16]

The Q.E.D.® Saliva Alcohol Test is an easy-to-use diagnostic procedure with everything required contained in a sealed foil package. The total time required for the test is between three and five minutes.

According to product information from Ora-Sure Technologies, Inc. the Q.E.D.® Saliva Alcohol Test will accurately measure a range of blood alcohol concentration of 0-145 mg/dL or 0.000%–0.145% equivalent BAC.[16]

There are several prominent oral fluid–based alcohol test procedures. One the QED saliva alcohol test procedure[16] will not react with ketones often found in the saliva of diabetic patients. Unlike some breath analyzers and other oral fluid tests, the QED is specific to ethyl alcohol and will not cross-react with acetone and ketone produced by diabetic patients.

According to the manufactures information[16]

> The Q.E.D. Saliva Alcohol Test (the only DOT Approved and CLIA waived alcohol saliva test) is an on-site, low-cost alternative to breath or blood testing. The test is easy to operate and provides quantitative results as accurate as a blood test. The Q.E.D. test serves customers in workplace

> testing, criminal justice and in hospital, emergency, psychiatric and occupational health departments. The test is designed to be administered by professional users. The Q.E.D. test is to be administered by a certified Screening Test Technician or trained professional. The test is run on saliva by swabbing the mouth and then pressing the saturated swab into the red center. It will run like a thermometer, with both a control line and a line indicating the level of alcohol in the system of the individual detecting the blood alcohol level of an individual up to 15.

The technology and chemical reaction employed in the QED or the test strip technology is not as precise, accurate, or reliable as breath-alcohol testing. Saliva-based alcohol tests require an Evidential Breath Test (EBT) to confirm positive test results. Saliva alcohol testing is much less expensive to operate than a breath test and unless a POCT facility conducts a very high volume of tests in a central location then saliva testing instead of breath may be more cost-effective. Since most employees do not test positive for alcohol, simple screening is generally more cost-effective for POCT facilities.

6.4.5.3.2 Test Strip

The second type of disposable tester, strip test technology does not have a great correlation between a person's true blood alcohol concentration and saliva alcohol concentration. Strip-based saliva testers are treated with an enzyme called alcohol oxidize, which responds to alcohol in proportion to the concentration of alcohol in a mixed saliva sample. The user estimates the BAC by comparing the color change on the test strip patch to standard colors calibrated to correspond to different BACs. Although some saliva testers seem to indicate the presence of alcohol well, the enzyme alcohol oxidize used in these testers is easily affected by hot and cold temperatures. Hot temperatures will tend to indicate falsely high readings, while cold temperatures tend to indicate falsely low readings.

Exposure to temperatures above 80 degrees Fahrenheit, or to ambient air, will destroy the enzyme alcohol oxidize rendering the tester useless. Most saliva testers give no indication if contamination has occurred and, if it has, they may not work effectively. Saliva testers generally have a shelf life of one year or less.

6.4.5.3.3 ALCO-Screen (Test Strip)

The ALCO-Screen™ marketing by Chematics, Inc.[17] (Figure 6.4.18) saliva alcohol test is intended for use as a rapid, highly sensitive method to detect the presence of alcohol in saliva and to provide a semi-quantitative approximation of blood alcohol concentration. For applications where a quantitative determination of blood alcohol concentration is required, a positive ALCO-Screen™ result must be verified using an acceptable quantitative alcohol analysis procedure. ALCO-Screen™ requires no special training provided instructions are followed carefully. However, a qualified professional should perform quantitative follow-up testing for any positive screening result.

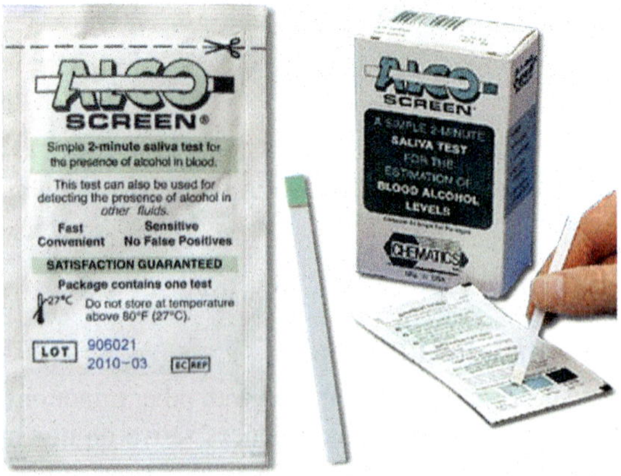

FIGURE 6.4.18 No caption

6.4.5.3.4 The ALCO-Screen™

ALCO-Screen™ is not intended as a measurement of mental or physical impairment but rather a screening test for the presence of alcohol in semi-quantitative amounts.

As with any saliva-based or breath-alcohol tester, a deprivation period of at least 15 minutes must be observed before beginning the test. This includes non-alcoholic drinks, tobacco products, coffee, breath mints, food, etc.

The ALCO-Screen is used by saturating a reactive pad with saliva from the test individual's mouth or sputum cup. At exactly two minutes, a change in color is observed in the reactive pad. A color change of green or blue indicates the presence of alcohol and a positive result. Results obtained after more than two minutes and 30 seconds (2.5 minutes) may be erroneous and should not be used. BAC is estimated by comparing the color of the reactive pad to the color chart on the back of the test package.

The ALCO-Screen™ produces a color change in the presence of saliva alcohol ranging from a light green-gray color at 0.02% blood alcohol concentration to a dark blue-gray color near 0.30% blood alcohol concentration. The product is designed and calibrated to be interpreted two minutes after saturation of the reactive pad. Waiting longer than two minutes to interpret the test can result in erroneous or false-positive results. ALCO-Screen™ is a visually interpreted test, as such; exact interpretation of results is not required in most cases. However, persons who are color blind or visually impaired may have trouble when a more specific interpretation is required. Furthermore, where test interpretation may be biased for whatever reason, it is suggested that another person's opinion of test results or color matching be obtained.

6.4.5.3.5 ALCO Screen 2

ALCO-Screen™ 2 is also marketed by Chematics, Inc.[17] is a simple and cost-effective method of monitoring for alcohol consumption in a ZERO TOLERANCE testing program (Figure 6.4.19). According to its product, information the ALCO-Screen™ 2 has been tested and approved by the US Department of Transportation (DOT) for required testing of all transportation and safety-sensitive employees for

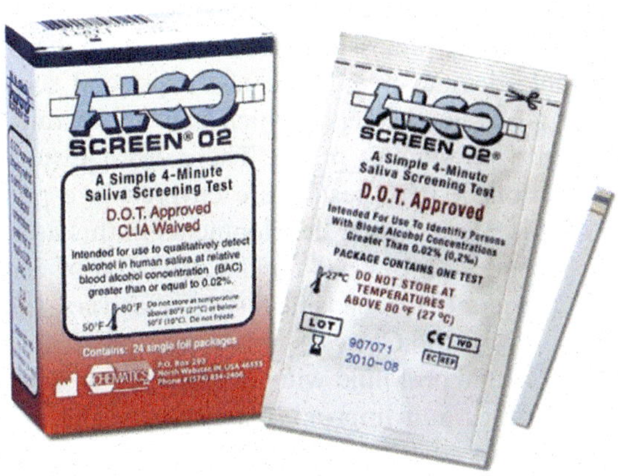

FIGURE 6.4.19 ALCO-Screen™ 2

blood alcohol concentrations above the federally mandated zero tolerance level of 0.02%.

ALCO-Screen™ 2 is a simple one-step saliva-screening test that works in a clean, non-invasive manner and provides results in four minutes. The product is highly sensitive and can be used for evidentiary purposes. The Alco-Screen 02 has been tested and approved by the US Department of Transportation (DOT) for required testing of all transportation and safety-sensitive employees for blood alcohol concentrations above the federally mandated zero tolerance level of 0.02%. Completed test results can be photocopied for permanent filing.

6.4.5.3.6 Chemical – Color Change–Based

Subcategories of screening devices, which are not electronic, make a determination of alcohol concentration by use of a chemical reaction

The device or process consists of either dichromate or permanganate salts in acid-impregnated crystals which are placed in glass tubes. The individual being tested blows into a balloon or plastic bag or through the tube. After a certain volume of air or time has transpired a measurement of the length of stain on the crystals in the tube (color change) is used to approximate the BrAC. The color change is a result of the chemical reaction occurring between alcohol and the chromate or permanganate salts in the crystals. The results obtained from using these devices should be read according to time requirements expressed by the manufacturer. Other oxidizable components of breath will continue to react with the chemicals and may produce false-positives.

Screening devices that utilize a color change reaction for alcohol detection are disposable and good for only one test whereas electronic devices have an extended life and can be used repeatedly after resetting, hence they may be more cost effective if an agency is doing multiple testing.

One of the more popular disposable screeners is the Breath Scan Alcohol Detector.[18] See the product below. According to the manufacturer's promotional materials, it is a disposable breath-alcohol indicator designed for one-time use and according to its manufacturer, it provides an accurate measure of the alcohol present in the exhaled breath of a test subject. By measuring the alcohol content in the breath, a reliable indication of the blood alcohol level is achieved. The Breath Scan® detector employs a new, patented technology for simple, on-the-spot screening for the presence of blood alcohol. The Breath Scan® tester can be used once and then disposed of, minimizing contamination associated with repeated use of non-disposable units (e.g. no AIDS cross-transmission). Its low cost and ease of use make the Breath Scan® tester ideal for screening to determine whether an individual should submit to a forensic-quality blood test for confirmation.

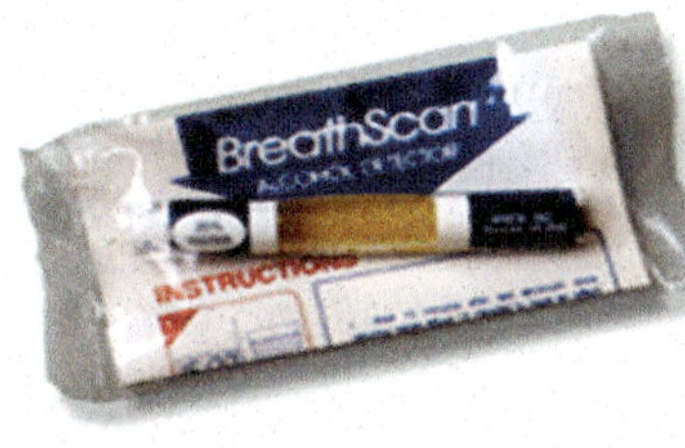

BreathScan

The Breath Scan's low cost and ease of use make it ideal for screening to determine whether an individual should submit to a forensic quality blood test for confirmation. Just break the internal capsule, shake, and blow hard into the test cylinder of Breath Alcohol Detector for a few seconds. Then read the color change of the chemical crystals within two minutes or less. Approved by the Department of Transportation (DOT), the Breath Alcohol Detector is available in 5 BAC levels for a complete range of sensitivity – .10%, .08%, .05%, .04%, and .02% (for zero tolerance testing) – and it is very light and easy to carry around, weighing 0.16 ounces.

6.4.5.3.7 Blood and Urine

Because this area (blood and urine) is not a subject of this chapter, the issue will be addressed only briefly. Other treatises and handbooks can be found to assist the reader in understanding this area of alcohol testing.

Blood or urine specimens must be collected in a suitable manner to maintain the chain of custody, as in any forensic case, if test results are to be used in punitive situations. However, additional precautions are required since the specimens are biological in nature, namely, removal of blood by qualified medical persons in an alcohol-free manner, preservation of the specimen to permit mailing, and long-term storage. Before establishing a system for collection, one should consult with their certifying state or other agency in control of specimen collection to prevent unnecessary problems.

For additional information and a more in-depth understanding of blood and urine alcohol pharmacology and toxicology and testing procedures refer to the *Forensic Science Handbook*, Vol. 1, 2nd Edition, Chapter 12, editor Richard Saferstein, "The Determination of Alcohol in Blood and Breath," by Yale H. Caplan and J. Robert Zettl and *Garriott's Medicolegal Aspects of Alcohol*, 6th Edition, Chapters 2, 3, 6, and 7, editors Yale H. Caplan and Bruce A. Goldberger.

REFERENCES

1. Substance Abuse and Mental Health Services Administration (SAMHSA). 2014 National Survey on Drug Use and Health (NSDUH). http://www.samhsa.gov.
2. *The Economic Cost of Alcohol Abuse: 1975.* Berry, R.E.; Boland, J.P.; Smart, C.; and Kanak, J. Policy Analysis, Inc., Brookline, MA, 1977.
3. *Economic Costs to Society of Alcohol and Drug Abuse and Mental Illness: 1977.* Cruze, A.M.; Harwood, H.J.; Kristiansen, P.L.; Collins, J.J.; and Jones, D.C. Research Triangle Institute, Research Triangle Park, N.C., 1981.
4. *Economic Costs to Society of Alcohol and Drug Abuse and Mental Illness: 1980.* Harwood, H.J.; Napolitano, D.M.; Kristiansen, P.L.; and Collins, J.J. Research Triangle Institute, Research Triangle Park, N.C., 1984.
5. *Estimating the Cost of Illness. Health Economics Series, No. 6. DHEW Pub. No. (PHS) 947-6, 1966.* Rice, D.P. U. S. Department of Health, Education and Welfare, Rockville, MD.
6. *The Economic Costs of Alcohol and Drug Abuse and Mental Illness: 1985.* Rice, D.P.; Kelman, S.; Miller, L.S.; and Dunmeyer, S. National Institute on Drug Abuse, Rockville, MD, 1990.
7. National Safety Council, 1121 Spring Lake Drive, Itasca, Illinois. 60143–3201.
8. National Highway Traffic Safety Administration, Traffic Safety Programs, Impaired Driving Division, 400 Seventh St., SW, NTS-11, Washington, DC, 20590.
9. Roadside Testing Assessment - ROSITA Project. http://www.transport-research.info/sites/default/files/project/documents/rositarep.pdf.
10. *The Determination of Blood Alcohol Concentration by Transdermal Measurement.* White Paper 2002. John Robert Zettl.
11. Alcohol Monitoring Systems, 7325 South Platte River Parkway, Littleton, CO. 80120. https://www.scramsystems.com.
12. U. S. Department of Transportation, National Highway Traffic Safety Administration. Highway safety programs: conforming products list of evidential breath alcohol measurement devices. *Federal Register*, 77: 35747–35751, 2012.
13. U. S. Department of Transportation, National Highway Traffic Safety Administration. Highway safety programs: conforming products list of screening devices to measure alcohol in bodily fluids. *Federal Register*, 77: 35745–35747, 2012.
14. Intercept Science of Oral Fluid Testing. Edward J. Cone, Ph.D. www.redplanettesting.com/docs.
15. Craig Medical Distribution, Inc. 185 Park Center Drive, Building P, Vista, CA. 92801.
16. OraSure Technologies, Inc. Bethlehem, PA (Formerly STC Technologies, Inc.).
17. Chematics, Inc. P. O. Box 293, North Webster, IN. 46555. 1-800348-5147.
18. Test Medical Symptoms at Home, Inc. 6633 Ashman Rd, Maria Stein, OH 45860. 1-888-595-3136.

6.5 POINT-OF-COLLECTION (POC) DRUG TESTING: NEW DEVELOPMENTS AND APPLICATIONS

6.5.1 Introduction

Devices for testing drugs in biological samples, predominantly urine, at the Point-of Collection or Point-of-Care (POC) have been available for many years. POC testing largely falls into two classifications. Firstly, smaller hand-held portable devices (e.g. urine test cups) and secondly, bench-top larger instruments which can be operated, for example, in a physician's office. The general history and mode of action of POC tests were covered in a previous edition of this book. Newer developments in this area have been associated with devices for the detection of drugs in oral fluid, especially for roadside testing of drivers, and programmable Bio-Nano Chip systems applicable to detecting drugs in urine and oral fluid with an emphasis on extending drug test profiles and improving sensitivity. While workplace testing has historically been the site for most POC tests, wider application of the devices has taken place within pain-management settings, rehabilitation clinics, and physician offices where drug test results can be produced during a patient visit. With improvements in sensitivity, technology, and instrumentation, POC tests that use oral fluid have also become commercially available; their utility in forensic applications such as identification of drugged drivers is increasing (Table 6.5.1).

6.5.2 New Developments in Rapid Drug Testing

The original lateral flow immunoassays built into cups or test strips, which are visually read and have a limited test profile (some are single drug tests), are simple, rapid, and inexpensive. Such lateral flow assays generally have antigens to the target antibodies immobilized as dried lines across a test strip along with a control line further along. Over the years, the devices have advanced, in particular with the expansion of the test profile; some visually read products are currently able to detect 14 drugs and adulterants (creatinine, specific gravity, and pH) and some have temperature indicators.

A typical 14 drug test panel for urine is likely to include:

1. cocaine (benzoylecgonine)
2. marijuana (carboxy-THC)
3. opiates (morphine)
4. amphetamine
5. methamphetamine
6. phencyclidine
7. benzodiazepines (target drug depends on manufacturer)
8. methadone
9. barbiturates (target drug depends on manufacturer)
10. tricyclic antidepressants (target drug depends on manufacturer)
11. oxycodone
12. propoxyphene
13. buprenorphine
14. MDMA (Ecstasy)

There are many commercially available products which vary in drug profile and cut-off concentrations, as well as FDA clearance (CLIA-waived) status, and consumers should be

TABLE 6.5.1
Comparison of POC and Laboratory Based Testing

	POC: Handheld devices	POC: Bench top Immunoassays	Laboratory-based testing
Collection	Rapid	Rapid	Rapid
Results	Minutes	Minutes – Hours	Days
Ease of use	Simple; minimal training required	More complex equipment; moderate training required	Complex instrumentation high level training required
Drug test panel	Limited to device design	Limited to immunoassay panels	Wide range
Result generation	Visually read	Instrumented	Instrumented
Result retention	None	Electronically retained	Electronically retained
Proficiency programs	None	Available	Available

aware of the specification of their chosen device. Of greater interest is the variation in cross-reactivity of incorporated antibodies to structurally similar drugs in the wider drug classes. For example, while the "opiates" class is likely targeted toward morphine, the extent to which the product detects 6-acetylmorphine (heroin metabolite) will be important in a criminal justice situation, but its cross-reactivity with hydrocodone may be more critical in a clinical setting. Similarly, the ability of a benzodiazepine antibody to detect alprazolam may be essential in North America, whereas in other locations it may not be as necessary.

While visually read urine test cups are inexpensive and readily available, technological improvements have been made in terms of reading the signal with an instrument to assist in interpreting the results particularly when close to a pre-established cut-off concentration. Generic strip readers are available, but many manufacturers have incorporated readers into an integrated sample processing system (e.g. eScreen; NetScan Drug Test Scanner). Result uploading to data systems and connectivity are also available.

Instrumented products incorporating a reader are considered more reliable because the decision (POS/NEG) is made electronically and can operate in adverse lighting conditions. While optical scanners may not offer improved sensitivity over the human eye, many readers incorporating fluorescent or chemiluminescent signal-enhancement allow lower concentrations of drug to be detected. When cut-offs are set by professional or regulatory bodies, this may not be considered an advantage, but as the field expands to the analysis of other biological fluids – such as oral fluid and blood – improved sensitivity will be required.

One of the more promising developments for improving sensitivity and quality in POC testing is the introduction of the programmable Bio Nano Chip (p-BNC) platform. The platforms have been successfully used in various areas of clinical diagnostics including cardiovascular and infectious disease detection (Christodoulides et al. 2012).

The so-called "Lab-on-a-chip" was described in 2015 by McRae et al. as

> a versatile multiplexed and multiclass chemical- and bio-sensing system for bioscience and clinical measurements. The system is comprised of two main components, a disposable cartridge and a portable analyzer. The customizable single-use plastic cartridges, which now can be manufactured in high volumes using injection molding, are designed for analytical performance, ease of use, reproducibility, and low cost.

In 2015, Christodoulides et al. published two papers describing the next generation programmable Bio-Nano-Chip system for on-site drug detection in oral fluids and its application to the detection of THC, morphine, cocaine, methadone, amphetamine, methamphetamine, and benzodiazepines in oral fluid. They claim the test runs within ten minutes and provides sensitive detection limits, but also claim that "when combined with concentration measurements from this and prior impairment studies, information about cocaine-induced impairment may be revealed." The relationship between drug concentrations in oral fluid and impairment has been widely discussed, and continues to be an area of research, but no correlations have yet been scientifically accepted.

6.5.3 Applications

6.5.3.1 Urine and Oral Fluid

6.5.3.1.1 Workplace

The convenience of producing a reliable drug test result within a few minutes is obviously useful in many areas of testing. POC testing is currently carried out in some workplace settings, especially in remote locations. While numerous urine POC devices are FDA-cleared and are able to achieve SAMHSA cut-offs for workplace testing, FDA cleared oral fluid POC devices are not at mandated workplace testing concentrations. In 2003, Walsh et al. evaluated four POC devices for drug detection in oral fluid on the premise that there were no national standards or accepted cut-offs available at the time. Overall, the performance of the rapid POC oral fluid devices was quite variable, and that has continued over the subsequent years, even as many more systems become commercially available. In 2007, the group repeated their experiments, adding devices which had more recently come to the market. With the exception of one device, false positive results did not occur. The devices were evaluated for their effectiveness to comply with proposed SAMHSA workplace cut-off concentrations (at the time); the results were varied. While the device performance was seen to be improving, none reached the proposed THC cut-off of 4 ng/mL.

Other individual drug test devices are also commercially available (e.g. cotinine/nicotine tests) that may be useful in workplace or insurance testing. Regardless of the specimen type or POC device implemented into a workplace testing program, policies encompassing sample collection, chain-of-custody and security, confirmation of presumptive positives, quality control procedures, data management, and result interpretation must also be in place.

6.5.3.2 Urine

6.5.3.2.1 Clinical Settings

POC devices for urine are widely used in clinical applications such as pain management clinics, rehabilitation centers, and physician offices. In an Emergency Department setting, Attema-de Jonge et al. reported screening 80 urine samples on three different devices. Amphetamines (n = 16), cocaine (n = 27), cannabis (n = 25), benzodiazepines (n = 25), and opiates (n = 8) were the most frequently found. The sensitivity and specificity of all three devices were higher than 93% for these compounds, with the exception of the sensitivity for cannabis with one device and the sensitivity for benzodiazepines with two of the devices.

In 2014, Bertholf and Reisfield presented a strong case for using CLIA-waived POC devices in medical practice, citing that immediate results can assist in patient-clinician interaction and discussion. Test results that agree with the expected patient dosing regimen indicate patient compliance with prescription drugs; conversely, the presence of illicit drugs or lack of prescribed medication can stimulate productive patient-physician interaction. While accepting that laboratory-based analysis provides more reliable results, economic and time-saving benefits and convenience and increased efficiency were considerable advantages. A shortage of qualified laboratory technicians has also contributed to the use of preliminary screening POC tests.

The authors encourage a fundamental awareness of the limitations of POC tests, specifically regarding immunoassay cross-reactivity; the possibility of apparent non-compliance from a patient when in fact the device does not detect a specific drug could be problematic.

There is considerable variation in the number of drugs and metabolites detected by different devices. In order to determine whether a specific drug of interest may be identified, the extent of cross-reactivity and potential for interfering compounds is important. Some device manufacturers provide extensive data, including information on predominant urinary metabolites, while others provide only limited profiles.

Opiates: A comparison of two currently available POC urine devices is shown in Table 6.5.2a and 6.5.2b for the opiates class (cutoff: 2000 ng/mL), with the target drug morphine (100%) and benzodiazepines.

TABLE 6.5.2A
Comparison of Opiate Cross-reactivity for Two POC Devices

	Opiates: 2000 ng/mL	
	NexScreen {1}	EZ-Screen {2}
	Cross-reactivity (%)	
Morphine	100	100
Codeine	100	250
6-acetylmorphine	100	66.7
Ethylmorphine	8	500
Hydrocodone	8	100
Hydromorphone	6.7	66.7
Morphine-3-glucuronide	No data	66.7
Dihydrocodeine	No data	66.7
Diacetylmorphine (heroin)	No data	100
Oxycodone	No data	<0.3
Oxymorphone	No data	<0.3

In a clinical setting, the EZ-Screen device may be preferable because of its superior ability to identify hydrocodone (Vicodin®; Lortab®, Norco®) which is widely prescribed as a pain medication. In order to identify compliance with a prescription, or identify abuse if not prescribed, then the higher cross-reactivity of the EZ-Screen device is an advantage. Neither device has the capability of identifying oxycodone (Oxycontin®, Percocet®, etc.), so an additional POC test should be used for its detection (Figure 6.5.1).

Benzodiazepines: A comparison of the two devices for the identification of benzodiazepines and their major urinary metabolites is shown. While both have the same cut-off concentration (300 ng/mL), the NexScreen target drug is oxazepam and the EZ-Screen target drug is nordiazepam.

The selection of a POC device for a specific purpose should be based on the extent of cross-reactivity to relevant drugs and metabolites.

Professional Societies: In 2016, the American Association for Clinical Chemistry (AACC) began to develop a guideline, the scope and purpose of which was to compile evidence-based recommendations for the use of laboratory and point-of-care (POC) urine drug tests for relevant over-the-counter medications, prescribed and non-prescribed drugs, and illicit substances in pain management (www.aacc.org).

The document notes that Point-of-Care testing devices developed for workplace screening use high cut-off thresholds, and, hence, offer low sensitivity.

Recommendation: POC (oral fluid/urine) qualitative presumptive assays offer similar performance characteristics to laboratory-based immunoassays for detecting some over-the-counter medications, prescribed and non-prescribed drugs, and illicit substances in pain-management patients. However, physicians using POC testing must reference the POC package

TABLE 6.5.2B
Comparison of Benzodiazepine Cross-reactivity for Two POC Devices

	Benzodiazepines: 300 ng/mL	
	NexScreen {1}	EZ-Screen {2}
	Cross-reactivity (%)	
Nordiazepam	60	100
Oxazepam	100	60
Alprazolam	75	120
Chlordiazepoxide	3.75	<0.3
Clobazam	75	600
Clonazepam	6	120
Diazepam	15	600
Flunitrazepam	30	400
Lorazepam	7.5	12
Nitrazepam	150	600
Temazepam	150	600
Triazolam	3.75	40
Estazolam	1.5	No data
Lormetazepam	6	No data
Oxazepam glucuronide	No data	12
α-hydroxy-alprazolam	No data	1.2
Lorazepam glucuronide	No data	30
Temazepam glucuronide	No data	40
α-hydroxy triazolam	No data	<3
Clorazepate	No data	120
Flurazepam	No data	<0.3
Desalkylflurazepam	No data	120
Desmethylchlordiazepoxide	No data	60
Desmethylflunitrazepam	No data	400
Midazolam	No data	6
7-aminoclonazepam	No data	<0.3
7-aminoflunitrazepam	No data	<0.3

insert and/or consult laboratory personnel to accurately determine the assay's capabilities (especially amphetamine, benzodiazepine, and opiate immunoassays), and understand the limitations for detecting specific medications within a drug class to prevent incorrect assumptions or interpretation and to determine when additional testing is necessary.

Recommendation: Appropriately performed and interpreted urine POC immunoassay testing can be cost-effective for detecting the use or inappropriate use of some over-the-counter medications, prescribed and non-prescribed drugs, and illicit substances in pain-management patients.

Literature reports: In addition to the determination of medication compliance in a patient population, another advantage of POC testing is to determine other drug uses that may be occurring, potentially enhancing the risks and increasing undesirable side effects. So, does random drug testing reduce illicit drug use in patients prescribed pain medications? Manchikanti et al. (2006) tested 50 patients prescribed opioids, by random drug testing with a rapid 9-drug test panel urine cup. Marijuana use was identified in 11% of patients, cocaine in 5%, and methamphetamine and/or amphetamines in 2% which was significantly lower than illicit drug use identified in previous data; they concluded that use of these random tests **deterred and reduced** illicit drug use in the pain population.

In subsequent research, the group also addressed the diagnostic accuracy of urine drug testing (UDT) using POC devices (Manchikanti et al. 2010, 2011). The results showed that the highest agreement for drug classes was with opioids (80.4%); false positive results for illicit substances were low. The group concluded that:

> The UDT with immunoassay in an office setting is appropriate, convenient, and cost-effective. Compared with laboratory testing for opioids and illicit drugs, immunoassay in-office testing had high specificity and agreement, demonstrating the value of immunoassay drug testing. Because of variable sensitivity, clinicians would be well-advised to take a cautious approach when interpreting the results.

In 2012, Mikel et al. looked specifically at the accuracy of using POC devices for the detection of benzodiazepines in 995 patients in a pain management facility. Urine specimens were analyzed using POC and LC-MS/MS. Point of care assays yielded false-negative results for patients prescribed benzodiazepines nearly 20% of the time (98 out of 498 patients), particularly when patients were taking lorazepam or clonazepam. Broad class POC immunoassays, specifically opiates and benzodiazepines, are more prone to manufacturing differences than tests for specific analytes (e.g. cocaine metabolite); therefore published results may not apply to a different product. The importance of identifying illicit or additional non-prescribed drug use in the pain and rehabilitation populations, as well as monitoring drug compliance were identified as critical components in the quality of patient care and pain management. Self-reported drug use is unreliable, even when there are no negative ramifications to illegal drug use.

Katz and Fanciullo (2002) reported evidence from various studies which suggest that monitoring the behavior alone of patients will fail to identify other drug use, and routine urine testing of these patients was instead appropriate. An alternate approach was taken by Lewandrowski et al. (2008) who reported on the impact of implementing a POC program in the emergency department of a major hospital regarding the impact on length of patient stay and drug test result turnaround time. The mean time from sample collection to result reporting decreased by 69.4% (108 to 33 min) and, the average length of patient stay fell by 27%. Further there was no clear preference for central laboratory analysis or POC, but following implementation of the program the volume of urine drug testing increased by 30%.

Unfortunately, POC testing has often been criticized as having high rates of false results (positive and negative) compared to laboratory-based testing. This description arises from a lack of education on the part of the consumer as to which drug(s) the device is designed to detect and at what concentration. POC urine cups with limited drug

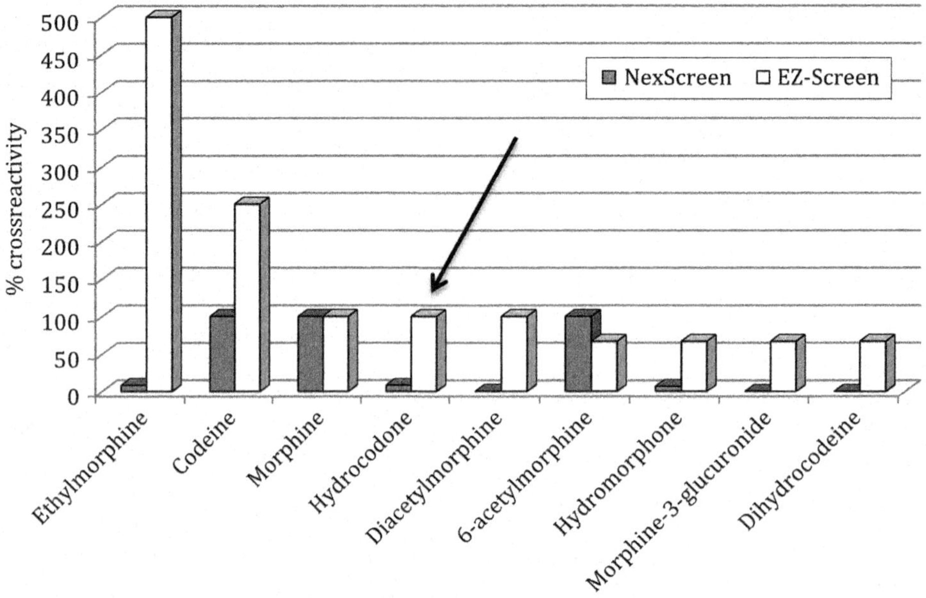

FIGURE 6.5.1 Cross-reactivity of opioid compounds with two different POC devices for urinalysis

panels and high cut-offs may cause false-negative results, so implementation of a POC testing protocol must include an understanding of target drugs, cross-reactivity to other compounds, and sensitivity (see cross-reactivity tables). In 2012, SAMHSA published an extensive Technical Assistance Publication TAP 32 entitled "Clinical Drug Testing in Primary Care" which encompasses many of the limitations and advantages of POC tests including how they should be selected. Within the last few years, smaller, bench-top analyzers are now being characterized as POC devices, where immunoassay drug testing can be carried out in a physician's office, often during the patient visit. The advantages of instrumentation over visual testing include the ability to routinely calibrate the instrument, include quality controls in the analyses, and participate in proficiency testing programs to assess accuracy and competence.

6.5.3.3 Oral fluid

6.5.3.3.1 Clinical Settings

Several publications have reported results from studies in which paired oral fluid and urine collected from patients were analyzed, to determine whether oral fluid provided similar information to urine in this particular population (Cao et al. 2014; Conermann et al. 2014). In 2015, Kunkel et al. reported that the analysis of oral fluid from an observed collection, detected illicit drug use as well as non-compliance more often than the urine specimens. However, all these publications use laboratory-based analysis, not POC devices; to date POC commercial products for oral fluid are not widely used in clinical applications such as pain management and rehabilitation testing.

6.5.3.3.2 Driving Under the Influence of Drugs (DUID)

In 2007, the National Roadside Survey included the collection and analysis of paired blood and oral fluid specimens from 3,276 drivers. From 326 positive pairs, 75.7% were an exact drug match across all classes and 21.4% had at least one drug class in common. Overall, a 97.1% correlation rate for paired specimens was obtained, indicating that oral fluid testing provides similar information to blood analysis (Kelley-Baker et al. 2014). The drug positivity rate in drivers was 16.3% with approximately half of those positive for marijuana.

In 2013–2014, the survey was repeated, showing that drug prevalence in drivers had increased to 20% overall, and marijuana detection increased from 8.6% in 2007 to 12.6% in 2014 www.nhtsa.gov). These numbers were based on laboratory analyses, but interest in evaluation of POC tests for this application has increased, particularly because oral fluid analysis was shown to be reliable for indicating drug intake.

The preferred specimen for analysis in drugged-driving identification is blood, as the active drug, if detected, is likely still circulating in the body. However, a medical professional is required to collect the sample, and sometimes a warrant is also necessary. These specifications take time to collate and drugs, in particular tetrahydrocannabinol, THC (the active compound in marijuana), is dissipated rapidly throughout the body. Oral fluid, a reflection of the free drug circulating in blood can be collected much more quickly, therefore, there is significant interest from the law enforcement community regarding an oral fluid analytical device which could be used by at the roadside or in a detention facility to identify drugs in drivers reliably, in a timely manner.

Cut-off Concentrations and Target Drugs: Many research groups have evaluated the predominantly visually read, handheld, portable POC oral fluid devices during the past several years, generally concluding that, for some drugs, they are specific and reliable, and for others, predominantly marijuana and benzodiazepines, improvements in sensitivity are necessary (Crouch et al. 2008; Perhsson et al. 2008; Strano-Rossi et al. 2012; Vanstechelman et al. 2012; Musshoff et al. 2014).

Several devices are currently commercially available; information on 15 devices is presented below. The identification of a cut-off concentration for drugs in oral fluid is problematic because research on saliva drug concentrations, while expanding, is more limited than information on urine or blood. Professional societies recommend drug test levels, but usually, these are for workplace testing and are not really relevant to either clinical or DUID applications. Therefore the commercially available devices are not particularly consistent in detection claims. Cut-off concentrations for PCP (10 ng/mL), amphetamines (50 ng/mL), and opiates (40 ng/mL) are similar with some devices showing improved sensitivity; other drug test levels are markedly different.

Test strips are often made by the same manufacturer and then implanted into different POC cassettes and test devices. Many of the oral fluid rapid tests are urine-based assays diluted to have the sensitivity and range required for saliva testing. This is particularly observed in the devices that claim wide test panels (ketamine; propoxyphene; oxycodone; barbiturates; buprenorphine; etc.). In oral fluid, the predominant drugs are the parent compounds – e.g. THC; cocaine, etc. and not the main urinary metabolites; 11-nor-9-carboxy-delta 9-tetrahydrocannabinol (THC-COOH); and benzoylecgonine (BZE), respectively. Using a modified urine assay for oral fluid analysis does not target the correct drug; as a result, true positives could be missed when these tests are implemented.

Marijuana: Several devices market their marijuana-detection level as relatively low (12 ng/mL); upon closer inspection, the target analyte is the metabolite THC-COOH, which is present in oral fluid at 1,000 times lower concentration than THC.

Cocaine: Based on the same concept, an antibody used for a cocaine urine assay will target its metabolite, BZE. An oral fluid assay using this antibody will not identify cocaine in saliva, which is more indicative of recent cocaine use than BZE. While the problem is not as severe as with marijuana detection, there is still a concern that recent use may be missed if cocaine is not included in the target antibody.

Benzodiazepines: The detection of benzodiazepines in oral fluid is problematic even in a laboratory-based analysis because of their weak acidity, poor distribution into oral fluid, and binding to proteins which result in extremely low accumulation of detectable drug in saliva. The overall sensitivity of POC testing devices for this drug class needs improvement.

Record retention: The majority of devices are read subjectively by observation for the presence or absence of a test strip indicating negative or positive results. Generally, there is no provision for the retention of a result, so the utility is aimed at areas where rapid results have limited impact (e.g. pre-employment screening at temporary hiring agencies). For DUID cases, the DDS®2 (Alere), now named Abbott SoToxa and the Drug Test 5000 (Draeger) demonstrate rapid analysis of oral fluid with instrumental detection and record retention. Each has been involved in published field studies and research projects with law enforcement applications (Moore et al. 2013; Logan et al. 2014).

As with clinical applications, some larger bench-top type instruments can be considered as POC tests; some automated immunoassay analyzers are small enough to be placed into jails or police stations for DUID purposes, and the major immunoassay manufacturers can provide oral fluid kits to be used with bench-top instruments. A different format is the Evidence Multistat (Randox, Northern Ireland) which uses biochip array technology with chemiluminescence detection to provide good sensitivity and detect a wide variety of drugs in oral fluid in 17 minutes.

For oral fluid POC testing, DUID will likely remain the area of most interest for the next few years. It should be noted that, in all cases, a second specimen must be collected for confirmation of presumptive drug classes present; the majority of POC tests do not have a sample remaining for further testing, so a separate specimen must be taken. As far back as 2001, Gronholm and Lillsunde reported on the comparison between urine and oral fluid based POC with laboratory testing, concluding that

> good results were obtained for the urine on-site devices, with accuracies of 93–99% for amphetamines, 97–99% for cannabinoids, 94–98% for opiates and 90–98% for benzodiazepines. However, differences in the ease of performance and interpretation of test result were observed. It was possible to detect amphetamines and opiates in oral fluid by the used on-site devices, but the benzodiazepines and cannabinoids did not fulfil the needs of sensitivity.

There are still similar concerns about POC oral fluid tests. However, while laboratory-based testing obviously provides more accurate results than POC, the convenience and relatively low cost of a reliable preliminary result are attractive factors in drug testing. POC oral fluid tests continue to improve, and reliable systems are increasingly commercially available.

6.5.4 Continuing Evolution and Future Trends

In 2014, St. John and Price published a review of existing and emerging technologies in POC testing, focusing on healthcare applications including glucose measurement, infectious disease testing, cardiac markers, hematology, and immunology analyzers. There has been a growth of POC urine tests in the primary care physician office to reduce expenses associated with large hospital analyses.

In drug testing, the same trend can be seen, especially in rehabilitation and medical monitoring situations, as

TABLE 6.5.3
Comparison of POC Devices

			Cut-off concentrations (ng/mL)						
Device	**Results**	**Drugs**	**THC** *THC-COOH*	**AMP METH**	**Morphine**	**Cocaine***BZE*	**Benzodiazepines**	**Methadone**	**PCP**
Drug Test 5000	Print/Electronic	7	5	50/35	20	20	15 Diazepam	20	
DDS2	Print/Electronic	6	25	50/50	40	30	20 Temazepam		
Drug Wipe 5	Visual/Reader	5	10	60	10	10	10 Diazepam		
OrAlert	Visual	7	100	50/50	40	20	10 Oxazepam		10
Oral-AQ 7	Visual	7	25	50/50	25	20	5		
Rapid STAT	Visual/Reader	6	15	25/25	25	12	25 Oxazepam	75	
iScreen	Visual	6	*12*	50/50	40	*20*			10
Oraline/SalivaConfirm	Visual	8	12	50/50	40	20	20	30	10
OralView	Visual	8	12	50/50	40	20	20	30	10
Oral fluid cassette *Also includes: Oxycodone (50); Barbiturates (50); Buprenorphine (10)*	Visual	11	12	50/50	40	20	50 Oxazepam	35	10
Stat Swab *Also includes: Oxycodone (50); Barbiturates (300); Buprenorphine (10)*	Visual	11	12	50/50	40	*20*	50 Oxazepam		10
Rapid Detect/ Saliva Scan / Oral Cube *Also includes: Cotinine (50); Ketamine (50); Propoxyphene (50); Oxycodone (20); Barbiturates (50); Buprenorphine (5)*	Visual	15	12 100 THC	50/50	40	20	10 Oxazepam	30 20 (EDDP)	10

described earlier. Instruments with biochip technology and/or enhanced detection techniques have been added to the marketplace in the last few years and this will continue.

Several commercial vendors are entering the space of POC or small instrument immunoassay analysis for urine, oral fluid, and even blood (Table 6.5.3).

REFERENCES

Attema-de Jonge, M.E., Peeters, S.Y., and Franssen, E.J., Performance of three point-of-care urinalysis test devices for drugs of abuse and therapeutic drugs applied in the emergency department. *J Emerg Med* 42(6):682–691, 2012.

Bertholf, R., and Reisfield, G.M., The case for point-of-care drug testing. *Medical Lab Manage* 3(2):6, 2014.

Cao, J.M., Ma, J.D., Morello, C.M., Atayee, R., and Best, B.M., Observations on hydrocodone and its metabolites in oral fluid specimens of the pain population: comparison with urine. *J Opioid Manag* 10(3):177–86, 2014. doi:10.5055/jom.2014.0206.

Christodoulides, N., Floriano, P.N., Sanchez, X., Li, L., Hocquard, K., Patton, A., Muldoon, R., Miller, C.S., Ebersole, J.L., Redding, S., Yeh, C.K., Furmaga, W.B., Wampler, D.A., Bozkurt, B., Ballantyne, C.M., and McDevitt, J.T., Programmable bio-nanochip technology for the diagnosis of cardiovascular disease at the point-of-care. *Methodist Debakey Cardiovasc J* 8(1):6–12, 2012.

Christodoulides, N., De La Garza, R., Simmons, G.W., McRae, M.P., Wong, J., Newton, T.F., Kosten, T.R., Haque, A., and McDevitt, J.T., Next generation programmable Bio-Nano-Chip system for on-site detection in oral fluids. *J Drug Abuse* 1(1):1–6, 2015a.

Christodoulides, N., De La Garza, R., Simmons, G.W., McRae, M.P., Wong, J., Newton, T.F., Smith, R., Mahoney, J.J., Hohenstein, J., Gomez, S., Floriano, P.N., Talavera, H., Sloan, D.J., Moody, D.E., Andrenyak, D.M., Kosten, T.R., Haque, A., and McDevitt, J.T., Application of programmable bio-nano-chip system for the quantitative detection of drugs of abuse in oral fluids. *Drug Alcohol Depend* 153:306–313, 2015b.

Conermann, T., Gosalia, A., Kabazie, A.J., Moore, C., Miller, K., Fetsch, M., and Irvan, D., Utility of oral fluid in compliance monitoring of opioid medications. *Pain Phys* 17:63–70, 2014.

Crouch, D.J., Walsh, J.M., Cangianelli, L., and Quintela, O., Laboratory evaluation and field application of roadside oral fluid collectors and drug testing devices. *Ther Drug Monit* 30(2):188–95, 2008.

Gronholm,M., and Lillsunde, P., A comparison between on-site immunoassay drug-testing devices and laboratory results. *Forensi Sci Int* 121(1–2):37–46, 2001.

Katz, N., Fanciullo G.J., Role of urine toxicology testing in the management of chronic opioid therapy. *Clin J Pain* 18(4 Suppl):S76–82, 2002.

Kelley-Baker, T., Moore, C., Lacey, J., and Yao, J., Comparing drug detection in oral fluid and blood: data from a national sample of nighttime drivers. *Traffic Inj Prev* 15(2):111–118, 2014.

Kunkel, F., Fey, E., Borg, D., Stripp, R., and Getto, C., Assessment of the use of oral fluid as a matrix for drug monitoring in patients undergoing treatment for opioid addiction. *J Opioid Manag* 11(5):435–42, 2015. doi:10.5055/jom.2015.0293.

Lewandrowski, K., Flood, J., Finn, C., Tannous, B., Farris, A.B., Benzer, T.I., and Lee-Lewandrowski, E., Implementation of point-of-care rapid urine testing for drugs of abuse in the emergency department of an academic medical center: impact on test utilization and ED length of stay. *Am J Clin Pathol* 129(5):796–801, 2008.

Logan, B.K., Mohr, A.L., and Talpins, S.K., Detection and prevalence of drug use in arrested drivers using the Dräger Drug Test 5000 and Affiniton DrugWipe oral fluid drug screening devices. *J Anal Toxicol* 38(7):444–450, 2014.

Manchikanti, L., Manchukonda, R., Pampati, V., Damron, K.S., Brandon, D.E., Cash, K.A., and McManus, C.D., Does random urine drug testing reduce illicit drug use in chronic pain patients receiving opioids? *Pain Physician* 9(2):123–129, 2006.

Manchikanti, L., Malla, Y., Wargo, B.W., Cash, K.A., Pampati, V., Damron, K.S., McManus, C.D., and Brandon, D.E., Protocol for accuracy of point of care (POC) or in-office urine drug testing (immunoassay) in chronic pain patients: a prospective analysis of immunoassay and liquid chromatography tandem mass spectrometry (LC/MS/MS). *Pain Physician* 13(1):E1–E22, 2010.

Manchikanti, L., Malla, Y., Wargo, B.W., and Fellows, B. Comparative evaluations of the accuracy of immunoassay with liquid chromatography tandem mass spectrometry (LC/MS/MS) of urine drug testing (UDT) opioids and illicit drugs in chronic pain patients. *Pain Phys* 14:175–187, 2011.

McRae, M.P., Simmons, G.W., Wong, J., Shadfan, B., Gopalkrishnan, S., Christodoulides, N., and McDevitt, J.T., Programmable bio-nano-chip system: a flexible point-of-care platform for bioscience and clinical measurements. *Lab Chip* 15(20):4020–31, 2015.

Mikel, C., Pesce, A.J., Rosenthal, M., and West, C., Therapeutic monitoring of benzodiazepines in the management of pain: current limitations of point of care immunoassays suggest testing by mass spectrometry to assure accuracy and improve patient safety. *Clin Chim Acta* 413(15–16):1199–202, 2012.

Moore C, Kelley-Baker T, Lacey J. Field testing of the Alere DDS2 mobile test system for drugs in oral fluid. *J Anal Toxicol* 37(5):305–307, 2013.

Musshoff, F., Hokamp, E.G., Bott, U., and Madea, B., Performance evaluation of on-site oral fluid drug screening devices in normal police procedure in Germany. *Forens Sci Int* 238:120–4, 2014.

Pehrsson, A., Gunnar, T., Engblom, C., Seppä, H., Jama, A., and Lillsunde, P., Roadside oral fluid testing: comparison of the results of drugwipe 5 and drugwipe benzodiazepines on-site tests with laboratory confirmation results of oral fluid and whole blood. *Forens Sci Int* 175(2–3):140–8, 2008.

Strano-Rossi, S., Castrignano, E., Anzillotti, L., Serpelloni, G., Mollica, R., Tagliaro, F., Pascali, J.P., di Stefano, D., Sgalla, R., and Chiarotti, M., Evaluation of four oral fluid devices (DDS®, Drugtest 5000®, Drugwipe 5+® and RapidSTAT®) for on-site monitoring drugged driving in comparison with UHPLC-MS/MS analysis. *Forens Sci Int* 221(1–3):70–76, 2012.

St. John, A., and Price, C.P., Existing and emerging technologies for point-of-care testing. *Clin Biochem Rev* 35(3):155–167, 2014.

Vanstechelman, S., Isalberti, C., Van der Linden, T., Pil, K., Legrand, S.A., and Verstraete, A.G., Analytical evaluation of four on-site oral fluid drug testing devices. *J Anal Toxicol* 36(2):136–140, 2012.

Walsh, J.M., Flegel, R., Crouch, D.J., Cangianelli, L., and Baudys J, An evaluation of rapid point-of-collection oral fluid drug testing devices. *J Anal Toxicol.* 27(7):429–439, 2003.

Walsh, J.M., Crouch, D.J., Danaceau, J.P., Cangianelli, L., Liddicoat, L., and Adkins, R., Evaluation of ten oral fluid point-of-collection drug-testing devices. *J Anal Toxicol* 31(1):44–54, 2007.

https://www.aacc.org/~/media/practice-guidelines/pain-management/rough-draft-pain-management-lmpg-v6aacc.pdf?la=en. Accessed July 1, 2016.

www.nhtsa.gov/staticfiles/nti/pdf/812118-Roadside_Survey_2014.pdf. Accessed August 17, 2016.

7 Post-Mortem Toxicology

Section Editor: Dimitri Gerostamoulos

CONTENTS

DOI: 10.4324/9781315155159-7

Due to the continuous increase in availability and use of pharmaceuticals and illicit drugs, post-mortem toxicology has become more and more important in death investigations. The introduction of new substances on the market requires higher awareness among pathologists and toxicologists and necessitates the development of methods that encompass the newcomers. Fortunately, many important achievements have been made in methodology. The application of novel techniques, such as modifications of solid phase extraction and liquid chromatography–mass spectrometry techniques, now offers better conditions for efficient and sensitive analyses of numerous substances.

Many important contributions regarding the impact of various post-mortem changes that may influence the toxicological results have been published. Pharmacogenetic analyses, such as those to identify poor metabolizers, may now be applied to post-mortem material and can assist in the determination of the manner of death. Studies on the post-mortem redistribution of drugs have resulted in a wide-spread appreciation of the influence of the specimen type on the drug concentrations.

In recent years, the specific detection of many compounds and their metabolites in various matrices has improved substantially. The interpretation of their concentrations, however, remains a difficult task. Therefore, despite the progress in post-mortem toxicology; information about previous drug use, the circumstances surrounding death, and the autopsy findings are still very important in deriving correct conclusions from the analytical results. An intimate collaboration between toxicologists and pathologists is therefore desirable.

7.1 INTRODUCTION TO POST-MORTEM TOXICOLOGY

7.1.1 Medicolegal Death Investigation

Coroners and medical examiners investigate unexpected, unnatural, or violent deaths (including homicides and suicides). Depending on the legal jurisdiction, the medical examiner, coroner, or pathologist is responsible for determining the cause and manner of death. The cause of death is the injury, intoxication, or disease that initiates a process leading to death; if that initial event had not occurred, the individual would not have died. Death may follow years after the causal event, and the manner of death is the circumstances in which the cause of death occurred. Five classifications are used to categorize the manner of death: homicide, suicide, accident, natural, and undetermined.

Medicolegal death investigations include a range of medical and scientific tests, which are conducted to assist in the determination of death.

Post-mortem toxicology involves the analysis of drugs and poisons in biological samples taken from deceased persons. This results in the production of medicolegal case reports and subsequently, the interpretation of these results, which can assist the pathologist or the coroner in determining the cause of death. The use of drugs may not always be obvious to case investigators; there are many instances where deaths may initially appear to be due to natural causes but are ultimately determined to be caused by drugs or poisons. The routine analysis of post-mortem specimens is therefore essential in cases reported to the coroner or medical examiner. The analysis of post-mortem tissues can be challenging for a variety of reasons. Often, there is a lack of information regarding the signs or symptoms prior to the death of an individual. The use of drugs, whether they are over-the-counter medications, prescribed preparations, or illicit drugs, may not be obvious to investigators such as police. Any delay in the collection of specimens can also be critical in a coronial investigation, as post-mortem changes can occur quite quickly after death. These changes will affect not only the concentration of drugs but also the type of drug that may be present. The testing of post-mortem biological specimens can be a complex process involving modern, scientific equipment and specialized staff; hence the need for a routine, systematic approach.

To determine the manner of death, all available information pertaining to a particular case, including the terminal events, scene investigation, police reports, social and medical history, autopsy findings, and results of histological and toxicological testing, must be considered.

7.1.1.1 The Role of Police and Medical Examiner/Coroner's Investigators

Cases requiring medicolegal death investigation may vary depending on the jurisdiction and legislative requirements. Local county laws and state and federal legislation will often explicitly state whether the case falls under the jurisdiction of the medical examiner or the coroner. In most instances, the following points need to be considered:

a. Any death where any form of violence, whether criminal, suicidal, or accidental, was directly responsible or contributory
b. Any death caused by an unlawful act or criminal neglect
c. Any death occurring in a suspicious, unusual, or unexplained fashion (including fires)
d. Any death where there is no attending physician
e. Any death of a person confined to a public institution
f. The death of any prisoner, even though both the cause and the manner appear to be natural
g. Any death caused by or contributed to by drugs or other chemical poisoning or overdose
h. Any sudden death of a person in apparent good health
i. Any death occurring during diagnostic or therapeutic procedures
j. Any fetal stillbirth in the absence of a physician
k. Any death where there is insufficient medical information to explain the individual's demise

An unnatural death is any death that is not a direct result of a natural, medically recognized disease process. Any death where an outside, intervening influence is either directly or indirectly contributory to the individual's demise, or accelerates and exacerbates an underlying disease process to such a degree as to cause death, would also fall into the category of unnatural death.

Investigators are the eyes and ears of the medical examiner/coroner, especially in cases where the body is removed prior to the pathologist's involvement. The importance of an adequate investigation into past social and medical history cannot be overemphasized.

Police reports and investigations provide scene documentation. Typically, a report will include a description and identification of the body, time and place of death, eyewitness accounts, drugs and paraphernalia present, and photographs. Investigators assigned by the medical examiner/coroner collect all items and information that pertain to establishing the cause and manner of death. Investigators contact the family and friends of the deceased for information regarding, for example, past medical and social history and prescribed medications. Many cases have histories of prescription drugs to guide the investigation. All medication bottles should be verified as to content and count in addition to performing a routine pharmacy check of the person's medication usage. Medical examiner investigators must also contact hospitals and treating physicians to obtain copies of medical records and police agencies to obtain arrest records. A file is progressively assembled that contains all the relevant background information to assist the pathologist in understanding the medical and social history of the deceased.

The medicolegal systems in countries outside the United States vary, but the selection of cases subjected to a forensic pathology examination is usually similar. In several countries, however, the police are responsible for the investigation even in noncriminal cases. It is therefore important that the pathologists and toxicologists stay in good contact with the investigating police officer to obtain all the relevant information outlined here.

7.1.1.2 Role of the Forensic Pathologist

The principal role of the forensic pathologist is to investigate sudden, unexpected, and violent deaths in order to determine the cause and manner of death. In suspected drug-related deaths or poisonings, the pathologist must exclude both traumatic or pathological mechanisms as possible causes of death and select and preserve appropriate specimens for toxicological analysis. After autopsy, cases can often be divided into two categories: those with an anatomical cause of death and those without. Few drugs leave tell-tale signs obvious enough that the pathologist can determine a manner and cause of death without additional testing. Obvious exceptions include liver necrosis caused by acetaminophen, severely hemorrhagic gastric mucosa and smell from cyanide exposure or coronary artery disease, and cardiac enlargement in a cocaine user. Negative findings require toxicological analyses. Approximately 10% of the cases submitted for toxicology do not have any guiding features. Many of the thousands of potential compounds that could have caused death will have already been eliminated after the history and autopsy results are correlated. Since the majority of drugs and poisons do not produce characteristic pathological lesions, their presence in the body can be demonstrated only by chemical methods.

Collection and preservation of appropriate specimens is a critical component of the autopsy examination [1–4]. What is collected depends, at least partly, on the policy and resources of the investigating organization. The utility of these specimens depends not only on the condition of the body but also on the pathologist's technique.

Specimen collection is the first link in the chain of custody. Sample integrity within the chain of custody is an essential requirement for the forensic investigation. In cases where an autopsy fails to determine a cause of death or where there is an incomplete investigation, it is imperative to collect an adequate variety of specimens. Subsequent findings may modify or narrow the field of search and make it unnecessary to examine each specimen, but they can always be discarded. Many toxins, however, are completely lost in the embalming process. If the appropriate specimens are not collected at the time of the initial post-mortem examination, therefore, the cause of death may never be adequately determined.

7.1.2 Certification of Death

The "certificate of death" is a medical and legal document, which must be filed with the Bureau of Vital Statistics (United States) or similar government registries in other parts of the world. The death certificate contains demographic information as well as the cause and manner of death as determined by the medical examiner. Five different classifications are internationally recognized: (1) homicide, (2) suicide, (3) accident, (4) natural, and (5) undetermined/unascertained. The results from toxicological analyses of post-mortem specimens (and sometimes ante-mortem specimens) are evaluated to determine whether drugs or poisons have contributed to or caused death. Negative toxicological results may be equally important as positive results, and sometimes even more meaningful, as in the case of antiepileptic medicine not detected in a suspected seizure death, or as compared with a positive cannabis test in the urine of a shooting victim.

7.1.3 The Role of Toxicology in Death Investigation

Most toxicology laboratories have established routines for specific types of cases, and the pathologist often provides some indication of what toxicological testing should be performed on each case. Cases of suspected homicide require much more thorough testing than obvious cases of accidental or natural death. However, this may not always be the case – for example, alcohol and other sedative hypnotic drugs are often detected in fire victims and may well have contributed to the cause of death (Figure 7.1.1).

7.1.3.1 Homicides

The relationship between intoxication and violence is well recognized [6–9]. Toxicological studies in cases of traumatic homicide should include tests for alcohol and a comprehensive range of prescription and illicit drugs. Toxicological findings may help explain how the victim became involved in a physical altercation. In addition, the results of drug screening provide information about the deceased's lifestyle, which may prove useful to police as they search for the murderer. Toxicological investigations may also reveal evidence that a victim was drugged to incapacitation and then murdered. Homicides are sometimes caused by the direct use of poison, e.g., cyanide, heroin, or insulin; compounds such as these need to be tested in either the source laboratory or a reference laboratory.

7.1.3.2 Suicides

In cases of suicide, investigators try to discover an explanation for the act [9–11]. People may be driven to suicide by failing health, financial problems, losing of a loved one, severe mental depression, and other causes. Drugs that can potentiate or exacerbate depression are commonly detected in suicides. A well-recognized drawback with antidepressants is that they neutralize passivity and inhibition before they affect the mood and thereby confer an increased risk for suicide during the first weeks of treatment [12, 13]. Drugs commonly found in suicide victims include alcohol, sedatives (particularly benzodiazepines), analgesics,

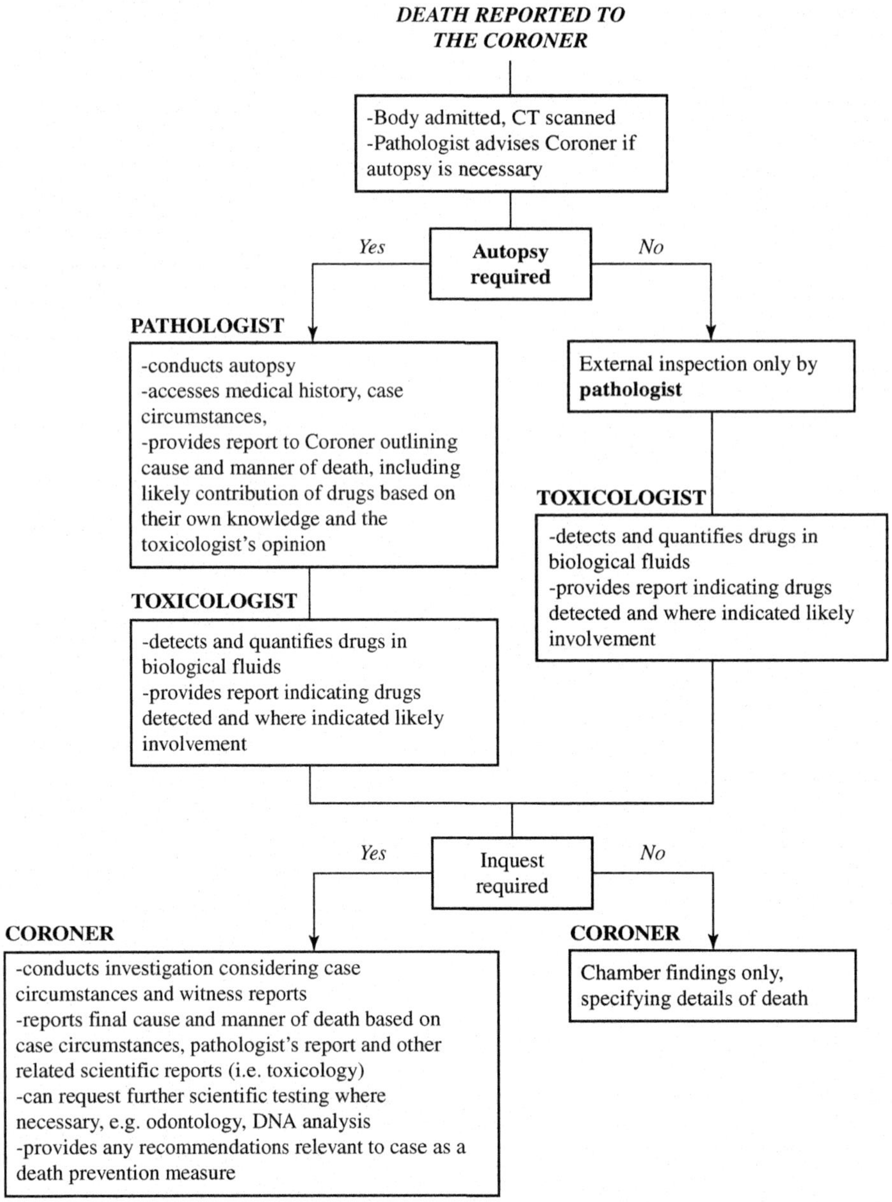

FIGURE 7.1.1 Flow-chart showing role and function of the pathologist, toxicologist, and coroner in the Victorian death investigation, Australia [5].

hypnotics, and sometimes even illicit drugs. Toxicological investigations should therefore encompass many intoxicants. Occasionally, a suicide victim employs multiple means to reduce the chances of survival, implying that an intake of drugs should not be overlooked even if another suicidal method is apparent. Toxic gases such as carbon monoxide or euthanasia-type drugs such as barbiturates [14] and other household chemicals are sometimes used in suicide cases [15].

7.1.3.3 Accidents

For fatal accidents, motor vehicle crashes immediately come to mind; however, accidental deaths occur in many other circumstances [16, 17]. Drowning, falls, fires, electrocutions, boating accidents, aircraft crashes, and accidental drug overdoses are included in this classification. Accidents often result from carelessness or the impairment of mental or motor function on the part of the victim or another person. In apparent cases of accidental death, it is important to confirm or rule out the use of common drugs such as alcohol or other drug-induced impairment. Many insurance policies exclude death or injury resulting from the misuse of intoxicating substances, although in some cases, quite the opposite is true. In those jurisdictions where drug deaths are considered accidents, double indemnity clauses may come into play. The sobriety or intoxication of the deceased can be a factor in efforts to assign blame. And of course, apparent accidental deaths may turn out to be suicides or natural deaths occurring in circumstances that suggest an accident.

For example, when a driver becomes incapacitated by a heart attack and subsequently loses control of the motor vehicle, toxicology may play a part in the investigation. Detection of intoxicants, together with other evidence, may indicate that an apparent accident was intentional. For example, finding large quantities of a drug in a deceased person's stomach suggests that an overdose was intentional (i.e., suicide) rather than accidental. If a post-mortem investigation fails to detect carbon monoxide in the blood of a burn victim or soot in the airway, it may be that the victim had already died when the fire started. Such cases may be deaths from natural causes or attempts to destroy evidence of a homicide. Further investigation may discover evidence of illness or trauma. Workplace accidents must always be investigated for the possible involvement of alcohol or other drugs, since there are likely to be insurance claims against the employer. Another aspect of workplace-related accidents concerns exposure to toxic chemicals. The potential for such exposures varies depending on the type of work undertaken. If exposure to a toxic chemical is alleged or suspected, investigators should obtain a list of chemicals in the workplace, and the toxicology laboratory should analyze for those chemicals whose toxicity is consistent with the circumstances of death.

7.1.3.4 Natural Deaths

Apparent natural deaths may or may not require toxicological study; however, this is increasingly not the case in a modern toxicology laboratory. If the autopsy clearly reveals the cause of death, and no history of drug or alcohol misuse is known, the pathologist may decide that further toxicological studies are not necessary. Sometimes, this decision can be overruled by the medical examiner or coroner based on other preventative aspects to an investigation or where the cause of death has been established by other means (e.g., post-mortem whole body computed tomography) [18–20].

The reason why toxicology is conducted in many natural deaths is that sometimes it is necessary to evaluate compliance with required pharmacotherapy, such as measurement of anticonvulsant drug levels in a person with epilepsy who has a seizure and then dies. When the apparent cause of death may be related to drug or alcohol misuse, testing should be done to determine whether relevant drugs are present. For example, acute myocardial infarctions, cerebral hemorrhages, ruptured brain aneurysms, and dissecting aortic aneurysms are often associated with recent cocaine use. Such cases should be tested for cocaine and other drugs, particularly when this occurs in young people or when there is a history of drug use. A diagnosis of alcoholism should call for a blood alcohol analysis.

The diagnosis of sudden infant death syndrome (SIDS) is a diagnosis of exclusion. All apparent SIDS cases should be tested for alcohol and other drugs. Child abuse can include drugging a restless infant, where even a small dose of a drug may be fatal. When there is any uncertainty regarding the cause of death, testing should be done to rule out an overdose. Terminally ill people sometimes commit suicide, and hospice patients are occasionally poisoned by their caregivers. When samples for apparent natural deaths are submitted to the toxicology laboratory for testing, unrecognized poisoning cases are sometimes discovered.

7.1.3.5 Unclassified, Undetermined/Unascertained, or Pending

When the cause or manner of death remains elusive at the completion of investigations and autopsy, the case is left unclassified/undetermined pending further studies [21–23]. Additional inquiries, microscopic examinations, and microbiological and toxicological studies are initiated to find sufficient evidence for a diagnosis. The primary goal for the toxicology laboratory is to determine whether substances are present in the deceased in sufficient quantities to contribute to or cause death. If a probable toxic cause of death is identified, the laboratory gathers additional evidence to assist the pathologist in deciding how it was administered, estimating how much was used (if possible) and how long before death. The results of toxicology testing are considered along with other evidence to formulate an opinion regarding the manner and cause of death. It is always preferable for the laboratory to communicate with the pathologist responsible for the case investigation so that all possible analyses are undertaken [24].

7.1.3.6 Pending Toxicology (Overdose)

Death by poisoning or overdose may be accidental, suicidal, or homicidal [25–29]. Various clues indicating poisoning may be observed during the autopsy. In some cases, a large number of partially degraded medicinal tablets are found in the stomach, esophagus, mouth, and nostrils, or a typically strong smell of alcohol is noticed. Other unusual odors or abnormal colors of stomach contents, urine, tissues, and specific lesions may suggest to the experienced forensic pathologist that a drug or poison was the cause of death. Evidence from the death scene, such as a suicide note or empty containers, may point to a poisoning or drug overdose in some cases. Most drug-related deaths, however, do not leave such tell-tale markers as those found in heart attacks, cancer, or trauma. Often, the only clue from the autopsy is pulmonary congestion and edema. The pathologist calls upon the toxicology laboratory to confirm the suspicion by identifying the poison or poisons and gathering enough quantitative data to support a conclusion that the detected poison was sufficient to contribute to or cause death.

In addition, the laboratory may sometimes be able to shed light on the issues of how much was taken and the route of administration. The assignment of manner of death is based on the totality of the evidence, including the pharmacology and toxicology of the substance, the route of administration and quantity taken, the social and medical history of the deceased, and evidence collected from the death scene. Drug-related death certification is by a process of compilation and evaluation of all findings during the death investigation, where elimination of a number of other possible causes of death is as important as the detection of a toxic substance in sufficient concentrations to have caused or contributed to the death [30, 31].

7.1.4 The Toxicology Examination

The toxicological investigation typically begins with the preliminary identification of drugs or chemicals present in post-mortem specimens [1–3, 32–36]. Confirmatory testing is then performed to conclusively identify the substance(s) present in the post-mortem specimens. In a forensic laboratory, positive identification must be established by at least two independent analyses, each based on a different analytic principle. The next step in the process is to determine the quantity of a substance in the specimens (if appropriate). Identifying drugs in waste fluids such as bile and urine is a useful undertaking, but quantifying drugs in these fluids usually has limited interpretive value. Drug quantification in peripheral blood, along with quantification in samples from liver, gastric contents, or other specimens as dictated by the case, provides more meaningful interpretive information. Therapeutic and toxic ranges have been established for many compounds [30], but it should be recognized that "therapeutic" concentrations can rarely be determined in the post-mortem setting [31, 37]. All cases cannot be tested for all drugs. A number of factors, some of which are not immediately obvious, determine what kind of and how many tests will be done. The importance of the medicolegal classification of death and specimen collection has already been mentioned. But other factors, such as geographic patterns of drug use and laboratory capabilities, must also be considered. Occasionally, mere detection of a drug or poison is sufficient. In the case of some prescription medications, however, the actual amount present must be quantified. A request for "therapeutic" drug analysis may be made even if the autopsy has already determined the cause of death. If a history of seizure is obtained, the pathologist may request an antiepileptic drug screen to determine whether or not the person was taking any such medication. The same holds true for other cases, such as theophylline in individuals with asthma. An individual who has committed suicide may have been prescribed therapeutic drugs for depression or other mental illness. A test for these drugs may indicate the degree of patient compliance.

7.1.4.1 Poisons

Often, the nature of a suspected toxin is unknown. This type of case is termed a "general unknown." In cases of this nature, a full analysis of all available specimens by as many techniques as possible may be required to reach a conclusion. The most common approach involves first testing for volatile agents, pesticides, and insecticides, followed by drug screens. The drug screen is usually confined to those drugs that are commonly seen in the casework [38]. When the most common substances have been ruled out, the laboratory proceeds to test for more exotic drugs and poisons.

7.1.4.2 Comprehensive Toxicology Screening

It is impossible to consider the topic of forensic toxicology without discussing analytical toxicology in detail [39]. Screening methods should provide presumptive identification, or at least class identification, while also giving an indication of concentration. An adequate screening protocol, which is capable of detecting or eliminating the majority of commonly encountered toxins, usually requires a combination of two or more chemically unrelated techniques. Some toxins are so common that no matter what type of case, they should always be included for analysis. These include ethanol, salicylate, acetaminophen, sedatives, hypnotics, and other drugs such as cocaine, opiates, and antidepressants. All screening tests that are positive for substances relevant to the case must then be confirmed and analytes of significance submitted for quantification in several tissues. Later sections in this chapter discuss testing methods and how they are combined to yield effective analytical strategies.

7.1.4.3 Case Review

During the toxicological investigation, each case is subjected to periodic review. Its status is evaluated, and the need for additional testing is determined. Based on what is known about the death and the specimens available, a panel of screening tests is designed to quickly detect or rule out the most common drugs and when appropriate, poisons. New tests may be ordered to expand the initial search or to confirm preliminary findings. Laboratory personnel must effectively communicate with the pathologist concerning the scope (and limitations) of the services they can provide, suggest the proper selection of specimens, and assist with interpretation of the results. In particular, when drug screens are used, the pathologist should know which drugs they cover and which drugs will go undetected. To operate effectively, the toxicologist must be provided with enough information about the history and autopsy findings to rationally select the most appropriate tests [24, 40].

Nowadays, most modern toxicology laboratories utilize multi-analyte methods and therefore have greater interrogating power from the initial point of analysis. The advent of liquid chromatography–tandem mass spectrometry (LC/MS/MS) technologies has enabled fast, high-throughput screening and confirmation for hundreds of drugs. Most drugs are captured by such testing regimes; however, laboratories must understand and accept that it is not possible to test for all forensically relevant compounds. As new compounds are identified and scheduled accordingly, laboratories must incorporate these into their drugs testing schemes.

7.1.4.4 Quality Assurance

Each laboratory must formulate and adhere to a quality assurance (QA) program. QA provides safeguards to ensure that the toxicology report contains results that are accurate and reproducible, and that the chain of custody has been preserved. A written QA plan sets out the procedures employed to ensure reliability and provides the means to document that those procedures were correctly followed. The laboratory's strict adherence to a proper QA program induces confidence in the laboratory's work product and prevents or overcomes potential legal challenges. Before a new or improved method is introduced into a laboratory, it must be selected with care, and its performance must be rigorously and impartially evaluated under laboratory conditions. There are many standards now that provide guidance for forensic toxicology laboratories to achieve best practice (OSAC, SWGTOX).

7.1.4.5 The Toxicology Report

When all toxicological testing is completed, the results are summarized in a report that is sent to the pathologist. This report becomes a part of the autopsy report. It specifies the name of the deceased, if known, the medical examiner case number, and usually one other identifier (this may be gender or age). The specimens tested, the substances detected in each specimen, and the measured concentrations of those substances are presented in tabular form. The report should also list substances tested for but not found, especially if they were named in the toxicology request. If any drug was detected but not confirmed, a note to that effect should be on the report. In addition, any information about the specimens, such as the date and time of collection of ante-mortem blood or any unusual condition of a specimen, should also be noted on the report. Because of the well-known difficulties associated with the post-mortem redistribution of many drugs, the report should always indicate where in the body the blood specimen was obtained. Toxicology reports are usually signed or initialed by the issuing toxicologist and in some jurisdictions, may be signed by the pathologist as well.

7.1.4.6 Toxicological Interpretation

Toxicological results are not easily interpreted. The significance of the reported results must be explained, often to a jury [41]. The pharmacology, toxicology, local patterns of drug abuse, and post-mortem changes can all affect the toxicological results. In any given case, a toxicologist may be asked the following questions (even though a definitive answer may not be possible in all instances):

1. What was taken, when, and how?
2. Was the drug or combination of drugs sufficient to kill or to affect behavior?
3. What are its effects on behavior?
4. Does the evidence indicate whether a substance was taken for therapeutic purposes, as a manifestation of drug misuse, for suicidal purposes, or was it administered homicidally?
5. Was the deceased intoxicated at the time of the incident that caused death?
6. How would intoxication by the particular drug manifest?
7. Is there any alternative explanation for the findings?
8. What additional tests might shed light on the questions?

ACKNOWLEDGMENTS

Much of this material has been updated since the last edition of this text – thanks to W. Lee Hearn and H. Chip Walls for their original and informative material.

REFERENCES

1. Drummer, O.H., Requirements for bioanalytical procedures in postmortem toxicology. *Analytical and Bioanalytical Chemistry*, 2007. **388**(7): p. 1495–1503.
2. Skopp, G., Postmortem toxicology. *Forensic Science, Medicine, and Pathology*, 2010. **6**(4): p. 314–325.
3. Dinis-Oliveira, R.J., F. Carvalho, J.A. Duarte, F. Remião, A. Marques, A. Santos, and T. Magalhães, Collection of biological samples in forensic toxicology. *Toxicology Mechanisms and Methods*, 2010. **20**(7): p. 363–414.
4. Cooper, G.A.A., A. Negrusz, and C. Ebooks, *Clarke's analytical forensic toxicology*. 2nd ed. 2013, London: Pharmaceutical Press.
5. Pilgrim, J.L., D. Gerostamoulos, and O.H. Drummer, The role of toxicology interpretations in prevention of sudden death. *Forensic Science, Medicine, and Pathology*, 2012. **8**(3): p. 263–269.
6. Garriott, J.C., Drug use among homicide victims. Changing patterns. *The American Journal of Forensic Medicine and Pathology*, 1993. **14**(3): p. 234.
7. Panczak, R., M. Geissbühler, M. Zwahlen, M. Killias, K. Tal, and M. Egger, Homicide-suicides compared to homicides and suicides: Systematic review and meta-analysis. *Forensic Science International*, 2013. **233**(1): p. 28–36.
8. Kuhns, J.B., D.B. Wilson, E.R. Maguire, S.A. Ainsworth, and T.A. Clodfelter, A meta-analysis of marijuana, cocaine and opiate toxicology study findings among homicide victims. *Addiction*, 2009. **104**(7): p. 1122–1131.
9. Darke, S., J. Duflou, and M. Torok, Drugs and violent death: Comparative toxicology of homicide and non-substance toxicity suicide victims. (Report). *Addiction*, 2009. **104**(6): p. 1000.
10. Värnik, A., M. Sisask, P. Värnik, J. Wu, K. Kõlves, E. Arensman, M. Maxwell, T. Reisch, R. Gusmão, C. van Audenhove, G. Scheerder, C. van Der Feltz-Cornelis, C. Coffey, M. Kopp, A. Szekely, S. Roskar, and U. Hegerl, Drug suicide: A sex-equal cause of death in 16 European countries. *BMC Public Health*, 2011. **11**(1): p. 61.
11. Sheehan, C., R. Rogers, and J. Boardman, Postmortem presence of drugs and method of violent suicide. *Journal of Drug Issues*, 2015. **45**(3): p. 249–262.
12. Stahl, S.M., A.A. Nierenberg, and J.M. Gorman, Evidence of early onset of antidepressant effect in randomized controlled trials. *Journal of Clinical Psychiatry*, 2001. **62**(Suppl 4): p. 17–23; discussion 37–40.
13. Licinio, J. and M.L. Wong, Depression, antidepressants and suicidality: A critical appraisal. *Nature Reviews Drug Discovery*, 2005. **4**(2): p. 165–171.
14. Castaing, N., L. Benali, D. Ducint, M. Molimard, S. Gromb, and K. Titier, Suicide with Cisatracurium and Thiopental: Forensic and analytical aspects. *Journal of Analytical Toxicology*, 2011. **35**(6): p. 375–380.
15. Osborne, N.J., R. Cairns, A.H. Dawson, K.M. Chitty, and N.A. Buckley, Epidemiology of coronial deaths from pesticide ingestion in Australia. *International Journal of Hygiene and Environmental Health*, 2017. **220**(2): p. 478–484.
16. Ahlner, J., A. Holmgren, and A.W. Jones, Demographics and post-mortem toxicology findings in deaths among people arrested multiple times for use of illicit drugs and/or impaired driving. *Forensic Science International*, 2016. **265**: p. 138–143.
17. Torjesen, I., Methadone is responsible for over half of accidental drug poisoning deaths in toddlers. *BMJ British Medical Journal (Online)*, 2016. **353**.

18. O'Donnell, C., An image of sudden death: Utility of routine post-mortem computed tomography scanning in medico-legal autopsy practice. *Diagnostic Histopathology*, 2010. **16**(12): p. 552–555.
19. Bedford, P.J., Routine CT scan combined with preliminary examination as a new method in determining the need for autopsy. *Forensic Science, Medicine, and Pathology*, 2012. **8**(4): p. 390–394.
20. Saunders, S.L., B. Morgan, V. Raj, and G.N. Rutty, Post-mortem computed tomography angiography: Past, present and future. *Forensic Science, Medicine, and Pathology*, 2011. **7**(3): p. 271–277.
21. Allebeck, P., C. Allgulander, L. Henningsohn, and S.W. Jakobsson, Causes of death in a cohort of 50 465 young men – Validity of recorded suicide as underlying cause of death. *Scandinavian Journal of Social Medicine*, 1991. **19**(4): p. 242–247.
22. Zhuo, L., Y. Zhang, H.R. Zielke, B. Levine, X. Zhang, L. Chang, D. Fowler, and L. Li, Sudden unexpected death in epilepsy: Evaluation of forensic autopsy cases. *Forensic Science International*, 2012. **223**(1): p. 171–175.
23. Puranik, R., C.K. Chow, J.A. Duflou, M.J. Kilborn, and M.A. McGuire, Sudden death in the young. *Heart Rhythm*, 2005. **2**(12): p. 1277–1282.
24. Pilgrim, J.L., D. Gerostamoulos, and O.H. Drummer, The role of toxicology interpretations in prevention of sudden death. *Forensic Science, Medicine, and Pathology*, 2012. **8**(3): p. 263–269.
25. Marzuk, P.M., K. Tardiff, and A.C. Leon, Increase in fatal suicidal poisonings and suffocations in the year final exit was published: A national study. *American Journal of Psychiatry*, 1994. **151**(12): p. 1813–4.
26. Hammersley, R., M.T. Cassidy, and J. Oliver, Drugs associated with drug-related deaths in Edinburgh and Glasgow, November 1990 to October 1992. *Addiction*, 1995. **90**(7): p. 959–65.
27. McGinnis, J.M. and W.H. Foege, Actual causes of death in the United States. *JAMA*, 1993. **270**(18): p. 2207–12.
28. Mokdad, A.H., J.S. Marks, D.F. Stroup, and J.L. Gerberding, Actual causes of death in the United States, 2000. *JAMA*, 2004. **291**(10): p. 1238–1245.
29. Finnberg, A., M. Junuzovic, L. Dragovic, R. Ortiz-Reyes, M. Hamel, J. Davis, and A. Eriksson, Homicide by poisoning. *American Journal of Forensic Medicine and Pathology*, 2013. **34**(1): p. 38–42.
30. Stead, A.H. and A.C. Moffat, A collection of therapeutic, toxic and fatal blood drug concentrations in man. *Human Toxicology*, 1983. **2**(3): p. 437–64.
31. Gill, J.R. and M. Stajíc, Classical mistakes in forensic toxicology made by forensic pathologists. *Academic Forensic Pathology*, 2012. **2**(3): p. 228–234.
32. Cina, S.J., K.A. Collins, and B.A. Goldberger, Toxicology: What is routine for medicolegal death investigation purposes? *Academic Forensic Pathology*, 2011. **1**(1): p. 28–31.
33. Davis, G.G., National association of medical examiners position paper: Recommendations for the investigation, diagnosis, and certification of deaths related to opioid drugs. *Academic Forensic Pathology*, 2013. **3**(1): p. 77–83.
34. Maurer, H.H., Current role of liquid chromatography–mass spectrometry in clinical and forensic toxicology. *Analytical and Bioanalytical Chemistry*, 2007. **388**(7): p. 1315–1325.
35. Drummer, O.H. and J. Gerostamoulos, Postmortem drug analysis: Analytical and toxicological aspects. *Therapeutic Drug Monitoring*, 2002. **24**(2): p. 199–209.
36. Bogusz, M.J., Liquid chromatography–mass spectrometry as a routine method in forensic sciences: A proof of maturity. *Journal of Chromatography*, 2000. **748**(1): p. 3–19.
37. Druid, H. and P. Holmgren, Compilations of therapeutic, toxic, and fatal concentrations of drugs. *Journal of Toxicology: Clinical Toxicology*, 1998. **36**(1–2): p. 133–4; author reply 135–136.
38. Peters, F.T., Recent advances of liquid chromatography–(tandem) mass spectrometry in clinical and forensic toxicology. *Clinical Biochemistry*, 2011. **44**(1): p. 54–65.
39. Remane, D., D.K. Wissenbach, and F.T. Peters, Recent advances of liquid chromatography–(tandem) mass spectrometry in clinical and forensic toxicology—An update. *Clinical Biochemistry*, 2016. **49**(13): p. 1051–1071.
40. Langlois, N.E.I., J.D. Gilbert, K.J. Heath, C. Winskog, and C. Kostakis, An audit of the toxicology findings in 555 medico-legal autopsies finds manner of death changed in 5 cases. *Forensic Science, Medicine, and Pathology*, 2013. **9**(1): p. 44–47.
41. Drummer, O.H., Good practices in forensic toxicology. *Current Pharmaceutical Design*, 2017. **23**(36): p. 5437–5441.

7.2 POST-MORTEM TOXICOLOGY SAMPLING

Specimen selection, collection, preservation, and exhibit security place unique demands on the post-mortem forensic toxicologist. Modern forensic toxicology laboratories now rely on high-throughput, extremely sensitive analytical equipment to provide detection of a wide range of substances and poisons that are often present in deceased persons. While not all people who die are subject to a medico-legal investigation, the prevalence of drugs in these deaths often mirrors what drugs are being consumed in the communities where these deaths occur. Local knowledge about what drugs are being ingested can often inform what toxicological analyses are most needed. The common utilization of broad screen multi-analyte methods now enables laboratories to detect a much larger range of compounds than ever before. However, it must be recognized that – even with technological advances – accurate, forensically defensible results are predicated on the quality and type of specimens provided and the documentation of each specimen's origin and history. Equally important are issues relating to security and evidence control during the collection and storage process. Finally, in considering data available from publications and databases, it is important to recognize that the quality and the "comparability" of data between institutions are only as good as the consistency of approach in specimen collection, storage, and analysis between these organizations.

Standard guidelines now exist for the standard collection of specimens for a post-mortem toxicology investigation. These can often be mandated by local organizations (e.g., UKIAFT, GtFCH, SWGTOX). Many major references have, each in their own manner, sought to provide information about specimen collection protocols and issues [1–4].

The issues of post-mortem release and/or redistribution of drugs from tissues into blood as mechanisms that can lead to legitimate debates about the meaning of a reported value continue to be a significant problem in the interpretation of forensic toxicology results [5–8]. Thus, even an analytically "accurate value" may be subject to misinterpretation when the drug concentration in a single blood specimen is used to explain the circumstances surrounding a drug intoxication death, particularly when the drug concentrations are not excessively high or low. This and other specimen collection and documentation issues are the subjects for discussion in this chapter.

7.2.1 Chain of Custody

One major difference between forensic and clinical toxicology is that institutions performing forensic work are held legally accountable for documenting the handling of specific evidence within the organization. This means that all evidence associated with a specific case must be kept in a secure area at all times and be accounted for during its lifetime by using a record or chain of custody (COC).

Documentation should include who handled the evidence, what evidence was handled, when and why the evidence was handled, and where the evidence was located at all times. This documentation is central to the demonstration that the evidence has remained intact and has not been adulterated, changed, mishandled, or misplaced in any fashion that would compromise its integrity. Evidence ties together people, places, actions, and things, which have an important impact on circumstances surrounding events in which individuals are held legally accountable. In criminal actions, the importance of the evidence may truly involve a "life or death" determination, while in civil litigation, large sums of money or property may be at stake.

The biological specimens collected during the autopsy are evidence and must be legally accounted for at all times. Specimens must be maintained in secure, limited-access areas with access restricted to only those individuals designated in the institution's standard operating procedure. Specimen handling has been, and will continue to be, legally scrutinized by the courts. Properly maintained COC documentation rules out any period of time in which a specimen may be left vulnerable to adulteration or tampering. Failure to properly document the COC may compromise not only the integrity of the specimen but also the credibility of the institution handling the specimen. The use of modern case management systems for documenting COC and other specimen transactions within the post-mortem forensic toxicology laboratory has become standard practice [3, 4].

7.2.1.1 Specimen Collection

7.2.1.1.1 Specimen Containers

There are several unique challenges to collecting post-mortem forensic toxicology specimens compared with specimen collection in other forensic toxicology disciplines such as human performance toxicology and employment drug testing. Post-mortem specimen quality can be quite variable, making specimen collection and subsequent reproducibility in aliquoting of the specimen difficult at times [8]. Specimen quantity, or availability, will vary considerably from one case to another, yet the laboratory must attempt to provide a comprehensive toxicological analysis for a general unknown [9, 10]. In the latter regard, detection limits are challenged, and trace findings may have a major bearing on issues of compliance and proper patient care in hospitalized or extended care facilities and the potential for civil litigation. The use of appropriate specimen containers and preservatives can be critical to the toxicologists' ability to ultimately identify a substance in a given specimen.

Usually, the best container to utilize when collecting and storing post-mortem biological fluids is glass [1]. Glass is inert, does not contain any plasticizer contaminants, and maximizes storage space. Plasticizer contamination is further reduced with Teflon-lined caps. If drug concentrations lower than 0.010 μg/mL are expected, silation of glassware may be indicated [1]. Disposable Pyrex glass culture tubes are suitable for long-term frozen storage and come in a variety of sizes. However, glass tubes are not commonly used and have largely been replaced by polypropylene tubes for ease of access and storage. It is important that the container size chosen for each specimen will allow it to be as close to full as possible in order to minimize concerns about oxidative losses due to air trapped in the top of the container, volatile drug evaporation, and "salting-out" effects from preservatives that may be added to the tube. Given the sensitivity of most modern instruments, 10 mL tubes represent the best choice for blood specimens. Most types of plastic containers are suitable for the collection of solid tissue specimens and gastric contents. The nature of solid tissue reduces direct contact with the plastic container, and the relative amount of drug(s) present in gastric contents will minimize the influence of plasticizer interference. Whether a facility chooses glass or plastic, it is important that the laboratory carefully evaluate the container before routinely collecting specimens in it. The nature and potential for contamination can be evaluated by analyzing drug-negative biological fluids stored over time in the container. In addition, the plastic must be chosen carefully to ensure that it does not crack when frozen. For example, polystyrene is subject to cracking under these conditions, whereas polypropylene is not.

7.2.1.1.2 Specimen Preservatives

The addition of preservatives to blood containers can limit bacterially mediated changes that can occur post collection [11]. In general, forensic blood specimens should be preserved by adding a minimum of 2% w/v sodium fluoride to the collection container. Sodium fluoride is added to inhibit conversion of glucose to ethanol by microorganisms [12–14], oxidation of ethanol by microorganisms [15, 16], post-mortem conversion of cocaine to ecgonine methyl ester by cholinesterases [15, 17], and enzymatic loss of other esters such as 6-acetylmorphine [1, 18]. A number of other drugs are also subject to post-mortem change, which can be due to bacterial or microbial effects or the inherent stability properties of the drug itself [19]. Best practice for forensic toxicology laboratories is to collect blood in tubes containing preservatives (sodium fluoride) and anticoagulants (potassium oxalate) [7, 8]; these are typically added to collection containers for blood ahead of time. However, if only a small amount of blood is collected, the excess fluoride may affect headspace volatile assays by altering the vapor pressure of the analyte [20]. Ideally, two preserved and one unpreserved blood specimen should be taken for a range of analyses to be undertaken.

Once collected, blood specimens should be stored in tightly sealed containers at low temperatures (4 °C short term and –20 °C long term). The low temperatures inhibit bacterial growth and generally slow reaction kinetics, such as the conversion of ethanol to acetaldehyde [15]. Some laboratories may choose to sub-sample an aliquot of preserved blood, sufficient in quantity to fill the secondary container. This should be removed from the primary specimen at the time of specimen accessioning and stored at –20 °C in a frost-free freezer. This aliquot should be saved for the quantitative confirmation of unstable analytes such as cocaine and olanzapine and for ethanol reanalysis, if needed. This will ultimately depend on the protocols established between the mortuary, pathologists, and the toxicology laboratory. The collection of sufficient blood for toxicological analyses will sometimes be dependent upon the case circumstances and the range of tests required.

Specimen preservatives are generally not required for other specimens (e.g., urine, bile, vitreous, tissues, etc.); however, sodium (or potassium) fluoride should be added to all samples subject to alcohol analysis. As for blood, these specimens should be stored sealed at 4 °C until testing is completed and then frozen at –20 °C if long-term storage is required. Additionally, a second sample of blood should be collected for general drug analysis, which is stored at –20 °C; a further unpreserved blood sample should also be collected, which then requires to be centrifuged to enable serum to be collected for a range of biochemical tests [21–23].

7.2.1.2 Sampling

Biological fluids are collected using new or chemically clean hypodermic syringes using appropriate needle gauges and lengths for the specimen to be collected. One needle and syringe should be used per specimen taken. If syringes and needles are to be reused, care must be taken to scrupulously clean and disinfect these devices between uses. A typical cleansing procedure should include a minimum of 30 min of soaking in a disinfectant, e.g., 10% solution of household bleach in water (0.5% w/v sodium hypochlorite in water), followed by washing with a non-ionic detergent and rinsing with copious amounts of clean water. Additional disinfection can be performed using an autoclave operated under proper quality control guidelines. The College of American Pathologists recommends that instruments be autoclaved at the usual steam autoclave pressure of 15 lb for 45 min. These conditions are suitable for most pathogens; however, higher pressures and temperatures for longer times (approximately 2 h) are necessary if the rare Creutzfeldt–Jakob disease is of concern. For all this effort, disposable needles and syringes are the easiest and most time-effective and efficient approach for sampling while reducing the possibility for specimen contamination. Additionally, autopsy staff must maintain the cleanliness of the specimen container as they collect the specimen. All spillage on the outside of the container should be rinsed off and decontaminated using 10% bleach solution or equivalent decontaminating agent/disinfectant.

Collection techniques are discussed in the following sub-sections by specimen type. Table 7.2.1 provides a summary of the information discussed in detail in the text.

7.2.1.2.1 Blood

The collection of blood will be dependent upon standard practices and resources; it will also be dependent upon whether a full or partial autopsy is conducted. Increasingly, many blood samples for toxicology are collected in the absence of an autopsy. Since post-mortem redistribution was first identified

TABLE 7.2.1
Post-Mortem Forensic Specimens for Toxicological Analysis

Specimen	Amount/volume	Storage	Use/application/comments
Blood (peripheral)	<10 mL (preserved)	+4 °C	Ethanol and volatile analysis
	<10 mL (preserved)	−20 °C	For general drug screening
	<10 mL (unpreserved)	−20 °C	Collected and centrifuged to obtain post-mortem serum, which can be used for biochemistry tests, e.g., insulin
Urine	30 mL minimum	−20 °C	General drug screening, confirmations
Bile	10 mL	−20 °C	Can be used for drug screening, e.g., opioids
Hair	100 mg	Room temperature, away from light	Used for general drugs screening; identify distal and proximal ends
Vitreous humor	All (combined)	−20 °C	Can be used for ethanol analysis, drug screening, electrolytes
Gastric contents	Al		Drug screening; useful in overdose situations
Liver	50 g	−20 °C	Useful for identifying redistribution issues; collect from deep right lobe (preferred)
Spleen	50 g	−20 °C	Useful in fire deaths when blood not available
Brain, fat	50 g	−20 °C	Optional but may be useful in infant drug deaths
Lung	50 g	+4 °C	Lung fluid useful for volatile poisons; collect in sealed container and analyze promptly

Note: biological specimens stored at 4 °C should be stored at −20 °C once analyzed.

as an issue in forensic toxicology [24, 25], the collection of peripheral blood has been preferred to central or cardiac blood [26]. However, many forensic organizations still collect cardiac blood in addition to peripheral blood. Cardiac or central blood can be utilized as a screening matrix, often because the concentration of drugs is typically higher than in peripheral specimens, thereby making the identification of some low-threshold drugs easier than if sampling peripheral blood alone. The use of heart blood for screening can now be disregarded, as modern instruments have sufficient sensitivity for the detection of drugs in very low concentrations. This procedure adds time to the analysis, as the central blood is first screened, and if drugs are detected, a peripheral specimen is used for quantitation. In high-throughput toxicology laboratories, this is not performed – femoral blood remains the specimen of choice, even though redistribution can still occur for many compounds [27–29].

If central blood specimens are collected, the blood sample should be taken by needle aspiration using a suitable hypodermic syringe. If there is any possibility that a second post-mortem examination may be required, duplicate samples must be collected [26].

Peripheral blood specimens are usually obtained from the femoral vein. Leg veins are preferred to veins of the head and neck due to the anatomical presence of a larger number of valves that resist blood movement from the intestines. The peripheral blood specimen should be taken using a clean or new 10- to 20-mL hypodermic syringe. Do not "milk" the leg in order to increase specimen volume [26]. If possible, up to 10 mL of peripheral blood should be collected. The source of the peripheral blood specimen should be noted on the specimen container. If peripheral blood cannot be collected, the site of collection of other specimens must be clearly stated on the collection tube.

7.2.1.2.2 Urine

During autopsy, urine specimens should be taken directly from the bladder by insertion of a clean/new hypodermic needle into the bladder. For non-autopsied cases, the needle may be inserted directly through the lower abdominal wall, just above the pubic symphysis [30]. If possible, up to 30 mL of urine should be acquired. In cases where the bladder appears to be empty, it is important to aspirate as much urine as possible from the bladder and the ureter.

7.2.1.2.3 Vitreous Humor

Vitreous humor specimens are obtained by direct aspiration from each eye using a 5- to 10-mL syringe and a 20-gauge needle. The needle should be inserted through the outer canthus until its tip is placed centrally in the globe. Vitreous humor can be aspirated from the globe by application of gentle suction. Vacuum tubes and heavy suction should be avoided to prevent specimen contamination with retinal fragments and other tissue. With proper technique, 2 to 3 mL of fluid can be removed from each eye in an adult, while up to about 1 mL of specimen may be removed from a newborn. Once the vitreous specimen has been removed from the eye, an appropriate amount of saline can be injected back into the eye in order to reproduce the cosmetic integrity of the eye. Vitreous humor specimens obtained from both eyes may be combined in one properly labelled specimen container.

7.2.1.2.4 Gastric Contents

Because gastric contents are not homogeneous, and because the total volume of gastric fluid is critical in the interpretation of positive findings, the entire contents of the stomach should be collected. If this is not possible, the total volume present must be noted and provided with the specimen to the laboratory. The pathologist should tie off the stomach ends before removing it from the organ block. The stomach should be opened away from other specimens and tissues in such a manner as to avoid contamination of other viscera.

7.2.1.2.5 Hair

Hair is preferably collected from the posterior vertex or the back of the skull, where the average hair growth rate is fairly constant and has been extensively studied [31]. The size of the sample to be collected is dependent on the purpose of the analysis. If a segmental analysis is desired, hair from a 1 × 2 cm area will typically yield about 50 mg of hair/cm segments, which is the amount used for many reported gas chromatography–mass spectrometry (GC/MS) or liquid chromatography–mass spectrometry (LC/MS) methods. Hair should be the first post-mortem specimen collected, as this minimizes contamination from the autopsy process. The sample is usually collected using aluminum foil and an envelope. The root ends must be noted and tied together to yield at least 50–100 mg. Hair will not always be available from the head; other sources of hair include axillary, pubic, and beard hair. This will depend on the toxicological information that is required of the investigation. Hair is particularly useful in pediatric deaths, especially when there is the suggestion of drug use by the parents or carers of the child as well as positive detection in post-mortem blood or urine or other solid tissues.

Hair that is contaminated with blood or other fluids should be noted and information provided to the toxicology laboratory. This can be common following road traffic accidents, violent assaults, and decomposition [31]. In such instances, the standard hair collection kit foil and envelope may be inappropriate, and an alternative, more robust collection vessel is required. Hair must be collected as close to the scalp as possible. The amount of hair that remains can often have consequences for estimating exposure times based on residual hair that is still on the scalp [32].

7.2.1.2.6 Liver

Liver is a useful specimen that should always be collected as a standard autopsy specimen. In death investigations, liver is a used by forensic toxicologists to supplement results obtained in blood. A portion of the right lobe of the liver (about 50 g) is preferred to avoid post-mortem transfer of unabsorbed drug from the intestines [33]. Often, liver can provide additional information regarding the degree of post-mortem redistribution [34]. The liver must be homogenized in water or neutral buffer to allow extraction of drugs for analysis.

7.2.1.2.7 Bile

Following the removal of the organ block during the autopsy process, bile is aspirated from the gallbladder using a clean/new hypodermic syringe. If there is any possibility of contamination, the gallbladder should be tied off and removed from the organ block so that the bile may be collected away from the potential source of contamination. Up to 15 mL of bile should be collected and placed into a properly labelled screw-capped glass culture tube. Additionally, bile should be collected prior to the liver specimen to prevent specimen contamination.

7.2.1.2.8 Other Tissues

When collecting other tissue (e.g., kidney, spleen, or muscle, and dependent on the nature of the investigation or the suspected poisoning agents), a minimum of 20 g should be collected [10]. Each specimen collected should be put into its own properly labelled airtight container. If inhalants are suspected, it is important to collect and seal the specimen in a container as soon as possible after the body has been opened. The measurement of drug content in a number of key organs and tissues (e.g., brain, fat, or muscle) is only useful in very limited cases, since there is little data to properly interpret the significance of a concentration in these tissues.

7.2.1.2.9 Labelling

The first step in the specimen collection process (including evidence collection) is ensuring that the specimen containers are labelled appropriately. Without attention to this detail, all other activities that occur with the specimen(s) are suspect. First, the collector must only be working with one specimen at a time. Second, specimens collected should never be placed into an unlabeled container. The collector must ensure that the container is labelled so that it can be read prior to the placement of the specimen into the container. The label should include a minimum of three unique identifiers, which satisfies all current international accreditation standards. Typically, these will include (1) institutional case number identifier; (2) name or other identifier; (3) date and time of collection; and (4) site of collection when applicable (femoral blood, etc.). Finally, tamper-resistant tape with the collector's initials and the collection date should be placed over the specimen lid and container to document specimen integrity. Alternatively, all the samples collected for a given case may be placed in a tamper-evident container labelled with the case number and name. This protocol is particularly useful in institutions with larger caseloads, where specimens may not immediately be transferred to the toxicology laboratory.

7.2.1.2.10 Non-Biological Evidence

Evidence found at a scene may provide additional information to assist in the toxicological investigation. Drug paraphernalia (cocaine spoons, cookers, bongs, syringes, poppers, butane lighters, etc.) is suggestive of a possible drug-related death or at least a history of drug abuse. Prescription drugs at a scene may be useful for compiling a list of suspected drugs, attending physicians, and pharmacy phone numbers. However, this evidence may be misleading, as drugs found a scene are frequently old, may not have been taken for years or due to patient compliance problems, or may be someone else's medication. Pain medication and tranquilizers, particularly important in drug deaths, are often prescribed to be taken on an as-needed basis and thus subject to being collected in medicine cabinets. Counting the number of tablets or capsules in a prescription vial for consistency with the date of the prescription and dosage instructions may be useful but has the potential for many variables, including compliance. Additionally, empty medicine vials are not necessarily indicative of a drug overdose. Nevertheless, it is important that for a potentially drug-related death, the role of the drugs found at the scene be ruled out by assaying for the agents of potential pharmacological significance. Whether prescription vials are submitted to the toxicology laboratory is largely a matter of choice in a given jurisdiction. Since these items are evidence, it is often best that the police maintain them and provide a list to the laboratory. Unless the toxicology laboratory has specific experience in analyzing powders and syringes, or has jurisdiction over them, these items are best left for the crime laboratory to analyze if needed. In cases where poisoning is suspected, household products at the scene may provide key evidence for the toxicologist. Examples include aerosol containers in suspected inhalation deaths, rat and pest killers, insecticides and pesticides, caustics, windshield washer solvents, anti-freeze, Freon, etc. The garage, basement, or under-sink cabinets are common storage places for many of these items. Unlabeled containers holding solids or liquids, or more importantly, labelled containers that clearly hold a different product, may be the key to a poisoning case. These items, or an aliquot of them, should be provided to the toxicology laboratory since they often contain analytes for which the toxicology laboratory does not test. The analysis of the product in question may provide mass spectral data and chromatographic information that can be correlated with findings in the biological matrix. Suicide notes are often critical in determining whether drug intoxication is determined to be an accident or a suicide. However, the toxicologist is cautioned that even if a suicide note identifies the suicidal agent or agents, toxicological analysis may reveal a different substance entirely.

ACKNOWLEDGMENTS

Much of this material has been updated since the last edition of this text – thanks to Bradford L. Hepler and Daniel S. Isenchmid for their original and informative material.

REFERENCES

1. Moffat, A.C., M.D. Osselton, B. Widdop, and J. Watts, *Clarke's analysis of drugs and poisons: In pharmaceuticals, body fluids and postmortem material*. 4th ed. 2011, London: Pharmaceutical Press. 2 volumes.
2. Spitz, W.U., D.J. Spitz, and R.S. Fisher, *Spitz and Fisher's medicolegal investigation of death: Guidelines for the application of pathology to crime investigation*. 4th ed. 2006, Springfield, IL: Charles C. Thomas. 1325 p.
3. Flanagan, R.J., *Fundamentals of analytical toxicology*. 2007, Chichester, England: John Wiley & Sons. 505 p.
4. Siegel, J.A., P.J. Saukko, and M.M. Houck, *Encyclopedia of forensic sciences*. 2nd ed. 2013, London: Elsevier, Academic Press. 4 volumes.
5. Jones, G.R. and D.J. Pounder, Site dependence of drug concentrations in postmortem blood--a case study. *Journal of Analytical Toxicology*, 1987. **11**(5): p. 186–190.
6. Gill, J.R., From death to death certificate: What do the dead say? *Journal of Medical Toxicology*, 2017. **13**(1): p. 111–116.
7. Drummer, O.H., Good practices in forensic toxicology. *Current Pharmaceutical Design*, 2017. **23**(36): p. 5437–5441.
8. Skopp, G., Postmortem toxicology. *Forensic Science, Medicine, and Pathology*, 2010. **6**(4): p. 314–325.
9. Drummer, O.H. and J. Gerostamoulos, Postmortem drug analysis: Analytical and toxicological aspects. *Therapeutic Drug Monitoring*, 2002. **24**(2): p. 199–209.
10. Dinis-Oliveira, R.J., F. Carvalho, J.A. Duarte, F. Remião, A. Marques, A. Santos, and T. Magalhães, Collection of biological samples in forensic toxicology. *Toxicology Mechanisms and Methods*, 2010. **20**(7): p. 363–414.
11. Castle, J.W., D.M. Butzbach, G.S. Walker, C.E. Lenehan, F. Reith, and K.P. Kirkbride, Microbial impacts in postmortem toxicology, in *Forensic microbiology*, David O. Carter, Jeffery K. Tomberlin, M. Eric Benbow, and Jessica L.Metcalf, Editor. 2017, Wiley. p. 212–244.
12. Caplan, Y.H., B.A. Goldberger, and E.H. Aguayo, *Garriott's medicolegal aspects of alcohol*. 6th ed. 2015, Tucson, AZ: Lawyers & Judges Publishing Company, Inc. xiv, 702 p.
13. Hunsaker, D.M. and J.C. Hunsaker, Postmortem alcohol interpretation, in *Forensic pathology reviews*, M. Tsokos, Editor. 2004, Totowa, NJ: Humana Press. p. 307–338.
14. Kugelberg, F.C. and A.W. Jones, Interpreting results of ethanol analysis in postmortem specimens: A review of the literature. *Forensic Science International*, 2007. **165**(1): p. 10–29.
15. Isenschmid, D.S., B.S. Levine, and Y.H. Caplan, A comprehensive study of the stability of cocaine and its metabolites. *Journal of Analytical Toxicology*, 1989. **13**(5): p. 250–256.
16. Tiscione, N.B., R.E. Vacha, I. Alford, D.T. Yeatman, and X. Shan, Long-term blood alcohol stability in forensic antemortem whole blood samples. *Journal of Analytical Toxicology*, 2015. **39**(6): p. 419–425.
17. Toennes, S.W. and G.F. Kauert, Importance of vacutainer selection in forensic toxicological analysis of drugs of abuse. *Journal of Analytical Toxicology*, 2001. **25**(5): p. 339–343.
18. Nakamura, G.R., J.I. Thornton, and T.T. Noguchi, Kinetics of heroin deacetylation in aqueous alkaline solution and in human serum and whole blood. *Journal of Chromatography*, 1975. **110**(1): p. 81–89.
19. Peters, F.T., Stability of analytes in biosamples-an important issue in clinical and forensic toxicology? *Analytical and Bioanalytical Chemistry*, 2007. **388**(7): p. 1505–1519.
20. Prouty, R.W. and W.H. Anderson, A comparison of postmortem heart blood and femoral blood ethyl alcohol concentrations. *Journal of Analytical Toxicology*, 1987. **11**(5): p. 191–197.
21. Coe, I.J., Postmortem chemistry update emphasis on forensic application. *American Journal of Forensic Medicine and Pathology*, 1993. **14**(2): p. 91–117.
22. Palmiere, C., M.d.M. Lesta, S. Sabatasso, P. Mangin, M. Augsburger, and F. Sporkert, Usefulness of postmortem biochemistry in forensic pathology: Illustrative case reports. *Legal Medicine*, 2012. **14**(1): p. 27–35.

23. Madea, B. and F. Musshoff, Postmortem biochemistry. *Forensic Science International*, 2007. **165**(2): p. 165–171.
24. Pounder, D.J. and G.R. Jones, Post-mortem drug redistribution—A toxicological nightmare. *Forensic Science International*, 1990. **45**(3): p. 253–263.
25. Jones, G.R. and D.J. Pounder, Site dependence of drug concentrations in postmortem blood—A case study*. *Journal of Analytical Toxicology*, 1987. **11**(5): p. 186–190.
26. Forrest, A.R., ACP broadsheet no 137: April 1993. Obtaining samples at post mortem examination for toxicological and biochemical analyses. *Journal of Clinical Pathology*, 1993. **46**(4): p. 292–296.
27. Gerostamoulos, D., J. Beyer, V. Staikos, P. Tayler, N. Woodford, and O.H. Drummer, The effect of the postmortem interval on the redistribution of drugs: A comparison of mortuary admission and autopsy blood specimens. *Forensic Science, Medicine, and Pathology*, 2012. **8**(4): p. 373–379.
28. Kennedy, M.C., Post-mortem drug concentrations. *Internal Medicine Journal*, 2010. **40**(3): p. 183–187.
29. Ferner, R.E., Post-mortem clinical pharmacology. *British Journal of Clinical Pharmacology*, 2008. **66**(4): p. 430–443.
30. Di Maio, V.J.M., *Forensic pathology*. 2nd ed. Ed. D.J. Di Maio. 2001, Boca Raton: CRC Press.
31. Cooper, G.A., Hair testing is taking root. *Annals of Clinical Biochemistry*, 2011. **48**(Pt 6): p. 516–530.
32. LeBeau, M.A., M.A. Montgomery, and J.D. Brewer, The role of variations in growth rate and sample collection on interpreting results of segmental analyses of hair. *Forensic Science International*, 2011. **210**(1–3): p. 110–116.
33. Drummer, O.H. and J. Gerostamoulos, Postmortem drug analysis: Analytical and toxicological aspects. *Therapeutic Drug Monitoring*, 2002. **24**(2): p. 199–209.
34. McIntyre, I., Liver and peripheral blood concentration ratio (L/P) as a marker of postmortem drug redistribution: A literature review. *Forensic Science, Medicine, and Pathology*, 2014. **10**(1): p. 91–96.

7.3 COMMON METHODS IN POST-MORTEM TOXICOLOGY

7.3.1 Analytical Chemistry in Post-Mortem Toxicology

Analytical toxicology is an applied science. Forensic toxicologists must be familiar not only with the effects and toxic mechanisms involved in poisoning but also with the metabolism of drugs, the chemical properties of parent drugs and their metabolites, and the composition of biological samples (especially in a post-mortem context). The detection and measurement of toxicologically relevant concentrations of potent new drugs requires the use of analytical techniques at the forefront of instrumental technology. Constantly developing techniques have now enabled toxicologists to retrospectively interrogate spectral data for new drugs and metabolites. The routine use of liquid chromatography (LC) coupled with mass spectrometry (MS) has transformed the ability of toxicology laboratories to detect hundreds of substances simultaneously, leading to improved analytical sensitivity, reduced sample volumes, higher throughput, and the replacement of older nonspecific techniques. However, the initial high-cost capital investment means that some laboratories still rely on established and arguably more affordable techniques such as immunoassays and gas chromatography (GC). Ultimately, the resources available to a forensic organization will determine the level of instrumentation and the technical expertise of the toxicology laboratory.

7.3.1.1 Immunoassays

The use of quick, reliable, automated, rapid tests has been useful in many drug testing environments. From point of care to laboratory settings, the use of immunoassays is relatively common. The advantages of such testing are the ease and rapid screening of samples for a range of drug classes. These usually are limited to drugs of abuse in urine, although applications now exist for a variety of matrices, including blood, oral fluid, and hair.

Immunoassays for post-mortem toxicology are sold commercially as kits. Often, they are exactly the same products as those used for urine drug screening in forensic urine drug testing programs [1, 2]. Such products are standardized and validated by the manufacturer and recommended for the analysis of particular specimen types, such as urine or serum. When urine cannot be obtained, other tissue may be used. A number of publications have described effective techniques for precipitating/extracting drugs from blood or tissue homogenates. Generally, the technique involves use of a solvent, such as acetone or acetonitrile, followed by evaporation of the solvent/water mixture and reconstitution in a suitable reagent for assay according to the procedure for urine. However, application to specimens other than urine requires validation; even kits that are designed for clinical blood cannot be used on post-mortem tissues without verification and validation of the efficacy of these kits. Post-mortem artefacts can interfere with certain chemistries (e.g., amphetamines) by the production of putrefactive amines [3, 4]. Immunoassays are based upon the principle of producing antibodies that recognize and bind to specific chemicals by interacting with unique structural features of their molecules. The interaction is analogous to that of a lock and key. Some antibodies are so selective that they bind to only one substance, such as methamphetamine. Others interact with a variety of compounds with similar structures, such as amphetamine, methamphetamine, phentermine, ephedrine, pseudoephedrine, and others, though not with structurally dissimilar compounds such as morphine. Therein lie some of the limitations of using immunoassays for post-mortem toxicology. They can be non-specific with a wide range of cross-reactivities to different drug chemistries [5, 6]. For post-mortem screening, assays utilizing antibodies with broad selectivity for drugs within a particular class, such as sympathomimetic amines, are preferred over those with antibodies sensitive to one specific drug, such as methamphetamine. Thus, a negative class-selective assay can exclude all drugs with which it interacts, albeit with differing sensitivity for individual drugs. Conversely, a positive result requires further testing to distinguish among the possibilities. With few exceptions, all cross-reacting substances are of potential interest to the post-mortem toxicology laboratory.

Immunoassays used for drug screening utilize a competitive interaction between the drug in the specimen and a labeled drug in the reagent for sites on an antibody specific to the drug being tested. The drug is detected by its ability to displace or block the binding of a fixed amount of chemically labeled drug molecules that are included in the reagent. The label can be an enzyme, a fluorescent molecule, a radioactive isotope, or some other substance that can be detected by instrumental means. The object of the assay is to measure either the amount of antibody-bound or the amount of free labeled drug, which is related to the concentration of the targeted drug in the sample.

Some assays can distinguish between bound and free labeled drug in a mixture and are referred to as *homogeneous immunoassays*. Others require physical separation of bound and free label prior to making the measurement. These are called *heterogeneous immunoassays*. In general, homogeneous immunoassays are more readily automated and thus, less labor intensive than heterogeneous immunoassays. Various types of immunoassays use different detection principles, such as enzyme immunoassay (EIA), fluorescence polarization immunoassay (FPIA), radioimmunoassay (RIA), kinetic interaction of microparticulates in solution (KIMS), and enzyme-linked immunosorbent assay (ELISA). Each type has advantages and disadvantages in terms of cost, throughput, and time for analysis in post-mortem drug screening. The detection limit for various members of a class of drugs (e.g., opiates) or the degree of cross-reactivity for similar drugs (e.g., sympathomimetic amines) varies. It has also been established that new drugs such as novel psychoactive substances (NPS) cannot be satisfactorily screened using immunoassays [7].

Each manufacturer of immunoassay reagents should be consulted for specific information regarding detection limits for various drugs within a class. These assays are easy to perform, the results are "semiquantitative" (higher or lower than a predetermined calibrator cut-off concentration) rather than subjective, and they generally have low detection limits (0.02 to 1.0 μg/mL). Several non-isotopic immunoassays (e.g., EMIT™, CEDIA®, and FPIA) have been automated for post-mortem drug screening. Immunoassays complement chromatographic procedures (GC and MS) because they detect those drugs that would require hydrolysis prior to chromatography (e.g., morphine-3-glucuronide and oxazepam glucuronide), a separate extraction (e.g., benzoylecgonine), or derivatization. For abused drugs, immunoassays have been methods of choice for initial screening; however, some laboratories are now replacing immunoassays with MS methods as they become more financially viable, enabling simultaneous screening and confirmation [8, 9]. For example in therapeutic drug monitoring, the adoption of LC-MS as a standard analytical technique for the measurement of immunosuppressant drugs is common practice and has replaced immunoassays entirely [10].

Some biochemical tests can be performed using immunoassays specific for certain poisons, such as insulin. These often require either ante-mortem and/or post-mortem serum samples for analysis.

7.3.1.2 Chromatography

Chromatographic drug screening techniques separate components of mixtures by partitioning them between a stationary phase, usually a solid or a viscous liquid, and a mobile phase consisting of a gas or liquid. Under a given set of chromatographic conditions, the time required for a substance to traverse the chromatographic column (retention time) is characteristic. Separated analytes are detected and identified by a variety of techniques, and often, quantitative measurements or semiquantitative estimates of analyte concentration may be made by reference to a standard curve. The most common forms of chromatography applicable to post-mortem analysis include GC-MS and LC-MS, although a number of different detectors other than MS can be used to identify compounds of interest [11–14]. Numerous papers have been published in relation to applicable techniques for forensic toxicology. A brief overview of the most common applications is provided in the following sub-sections.

7.3.1.3 Gas Chromatography

GC is widely used for qualitative and quantitative drug analysis. It is relatively rapid and capable of resolving a broad spectrum of drugs. Modern GC employs fused silica capillary columns that are coated on their inner wall with a liquid stationary phase consisting of a polymer chemically bonded to the silica [15]. The most common liquid phases are methyl silicones that contain 1, 5, or 50% phenyl side chains. The higher phenyl contents yield higher-polarity liquid phases. Other polymers are used for special purposes.

The mobile phase is a gas, i.e., the carrier gas. Usually, helium is used, although hydrogen, nitrogen, and gas mixtures may be preferred for some applications. The coiled column, which may be 10 to 60 m in length, is located in an oven having a precisely controlled programmable temperature capability. During a chromatographic analysis, the column temperature may be kept constant, raised at a selected constant rate, or programmed through a series of temperature ramps and isothermal intervals. The separation capabilities of GC are determined by the polarity of the liquid phase, the flow rate and composition of the carrier gas, and the temperature program. Compounds are separated as a consequence of their different vapor pressures at the column temperature and their affinity for the liquid phase, which is related to their polarity. In practice, the sample is injected manually or by an autosampler, either as an extract in a suitable organic solvent or as a vapor of volatile analytes mixed with air or carrier gas. The sample is volatilized in the heated injection port, and its constituents are swept into the column. As the analysis proceeds, some components move through the column faster than others, forming discrete bands that progress to the distal end and emerge into the detector, ideally in a pure state. GC detectors of various types recognize particular properties of substances, generating an electrical signal proportional to the quantity of the substance in the detector. The resulting signal is electronically amplified and recorded on a moving chart or more commonly, processed by a microcomputer to yield absolute and relative retention time, peak area, and height data for each detected component in the sample. Retention times of sample components, relative to a reference compound (internal standard) that is added to the sample, are constant for a given set of chromatographic conditions. Presumptive identifications are based on relative retention times corresponding with those produced by standards under identical conditions. For drug screening, some laboratories use dual column GCs with both columns originating at the same injection port [16, 17]. The sample is divided between the two columns and analyzed simultaneously on both. Agreement of relative retention times in two columns of differing polarities provides greater certainty of identification [18].

Some drugs do not chromatograph well with GC because they contain polar functional groups that adhere strongly to the liquid phase or depress the vapor pressure. Such problems can often be overcome by converting the active functional groups to less polar derivatives, such as esters from alcohols, phenols, or carboxylic acids, or amides from amines. Derivatives may be selected to give longer or shorter retention times while improving peak shape and sensitivity [19, 20]; derivatization techniques are also useful for chiral analysis of compounds [21, 22].

There are now many different types of detectors that are used in post-mortem toxicology laboratories. Each has characteristics that allow the detection and quantification of some of, but not all, the drugs and poisons that are of concern to the post-mortem toxicologist.

7.3.1.3.1 Flame Ionization Detector

The flame ionization detector (FID) uses a hydrogen/air flame to oxidize sample components that emerge from the column. Substances containing carbon yield a charged plasma. Electrodes produce a high-voltage field, which deflects the charged particles to a collector that produces an electric current with a magnitude proportional to the quantity of the component. The FID detects virtually all drugs that can be passed through the GC; however, lipids and other matrix-derived components interfere with the detection of drugs and limit practical sensitivity. The FID, once the mainstay of GC in toxicology laboratories, is still used for the analysis of alcohols, gamma hydroxy butyrate (GHB), and other volatile substances in a GC [23–25] equipped with an automated headspace sampler. Drugs other than volatiles can be determined with the use of FID; however, most GC basic drug screens typically employ nitrogen/phosphorus detectors (NPDs), which provide better sensitivity and selectivity than FID.

7.3.1.3.2 Nitrogen/Phosphorus Detector

The NPD has some similarities to the FID in that a hydrogen-air flame is used, but the collector is a ceramic bead coated with a rubidium salt. The NPD is insensitive to carbon when properly adjusted, but it responds with high sensitivity to compounds containing nitrogen or phosphorus. Furthermore, it can be tuned to maximize sensitivity to either element. The selectivity for nitrogen makes the NPD ideal for screening basic drugs, which all contain amine functions [26–29].

7.3.1.3.3 Electron Capture Detector

The electron capture detector (ECD) contains a radioactive nickel-63 foil that emits high-energy electrons (beta particles). The carrier gas is ionized by the radiation, forming anions that establish an ion current between two electrodes. Sample compounds emerging from the GC column extract electrons from the ionized gas, decreasing the current flow. The change in current is the signal produced by the detector. Most substances do not capture electrons and are not detected by the ECD. However, the presence of two or more halogen atoms or a nitro or nitroso group in the molecule allows the substance to be detected. The outstanding sensitivity of the ECD for most polyhalogenated compounds is the reason for its use in the analysis of benzodiazepines [30]; however, most benzodiazepine analysis these days is conducted using LC-MS. A laboratory possessing a GC with an ECD detector must have a radioactive materials license. A general license is sufficient for sealed detectors, but a specific license is required if the detector can be disassembled.

7.3.1.3.4 Gas Chromatography/Mass Spectrometry

GC-MS is a powerful analytical tool for identification of semi-volatile organic compounds. It combines the separation efficiency of GC with the structure-elucidating capabilities of MS. When it is used to identify unknown substances in a sample extract, the instrument may be programmed to automatically search for matches against a predefined library (target compound analysis), or it can acquire spectral data for later analysis. In the latter instance, the operator examines a chromatogram peak by peak, extracting background-subtracted spectra and searching spectral libraries by using a pattern-matching algorithm through the instrument's data system. If no acceptable match is found, the spectrum can be visually compared with printed compilations of mass spectral data. Considerable experience is required for effective and efficient substance identification by GC-MS. A chromatogram may consist of hundreds of peaks, most of which represent endogenous compounds. Recognition of frequently encountered patterns can save considerable time by avoiding unnecessary library searches. Conversely, the experienced operator will recognize the novel pattern as one that requires investigation. Nevertheless, a thorough search of a GC-MS data file can take an hour or more. When GC-MS is employed to identify unknown peaks from a GC analysis, the portion of the chromatogram that must be examined can be narrowed if the same type of column and same column temperature program are used in both instruments. The remaining extract from the GC analysis can be injected into the GC-MS. Knowing the relative retention time of the unknown, the operator can first locate the peak corresponding to the internal standard and then estimate the region of the GC-MS chromatogram where the unknown peak should be. That region is examined carefully to locate and identify a peak whose spectrum is inconsistent with expected endogenous compounds. With some instrumentation, it is possible to simultaneously inject extracts onto a system with both MS and NP detector systems. This may be done either by connecting two columns to a single injector or by splitting the effluent from one column into two detectors (one MS, one NP).

In the identification of substances, an extract of the sample is analyzed in the GC-MS with a column temperature program extending from below the boiling point of the solvent to 350 °C or higher. When the GC-MS run is complete, the entire chromatogram is examined. Time can be saved by initially examining the 20 or 30 largest peaks. GC-MS is often used to identify the drug, or drugs, giving rise to a positive result in a class-selective immunoassay test. Such analyses are most efficiently accomplished by methods that search an area of the chromatogram for patterns matching reference spectra in a computer library.

The library is generated by analyzing a standard of each of the targeted drugs and storing a representative spectrum in the data system [31–33]. The search can be programmed to take place automatically at the end of each data file acquisition. However, the data must be reviewed by the operator before reporting. GC-MS data can be used for both identification and confirmation in drug screening. However, for it to serve as a final confirmation test, the GC-MS analysis should be performed on a separate aliquot or a different specimen from that which yields the initial presumptive finding.

The typical combination is a GC combined with a single quadrupole mass spectrometer; however, there are many different iterations now possible. Two-dimensional

GC-MS (GCxGC-MS), which has been used in the analysis of petrochemicals for many years, has been used in forensic toxicology for drug screening and confirmation [34, 35]. GCxGC-MS involves the coupling of two columns connected sequentially with a modulator positioned between them. The modulator, located at the head of the second column, transfers fractions of the effluent from the primary column (generally nonpolar) to the secondary column (generally polar), providing enhanced peak capacity and separation power due to the orthogonal separation by the two differing properties of the columns [36]. This results in a two-dimensional chromatogram with the different parameters on the respective axes. The uptake of this method has been minimal due to the complexity of the data derived from the analysis and limitations regarding standardized methodology, data interpretation, and consistency of results [37]. The use of GC usually requires extensive sample clean-up and chemical derivatization of the analytes of interest to reduce polarity and increase volatility [38], which can often be time-consuming and not conducive to high-throughput laboratories. The use of additional mass spectrometers can lead to significant increases in sensitivity using GC-MS/MS [39–44].

7.3.1.4 High Performance Liquid Chromatography

HPLC utilizes a column filled with microscopic particles of silica or resin particles bonded with a polymer whose side chains have specific functional groups. The polymer is the stationary phase in HPLC, and the nature of the side chains determines the type of interactions the column will have with analytes. Various normal phases and reverse phases are available. Normal phases are characterized by polar side chains such as silica, diol, amino, and cyano, whereas reverse phases have nonpolar side chains such as 8 carbon (C-8) and 18 carbon (C-18) aliphatic and phenyl moieties. Anion and cation exchange phases are also available. The mobile phase in HPLC is a mixed solvent containing a buffer to suppress or induce ionization of analytes as required for the intended separation. The solvent composition may be kept constant (isocratic), or the percentages of components may be varied (gradient) during the analysis. For instance, in reverse-phase HPLC, the mobile phase will start at higher polarity. As the run proceeds, the polarity is decreased, enabling the removal of any remaining nonpolar substances from the nonpolar reverse-phase column while decreasing the tendency toward broad peaks near the end of a run (Figure 7.3.1).

7.3.1.4.1 Ultraviolet Absorption Detectors

One of the most common detection systems for HPLC is a UV absorption detector [11]. The less expensive detectors measure absorption at a single wavelength, which may be fixed (e.g., at 254 or 280 nm) or variable over a range of 190 to over 340 nm. The variable wavelength detectors are set to a desired wavelength by the operator, and some can be programmed to change wavelengths during the analysis. However, the time required to change wavelengths precludes using variable wavelength detectors for spectral scanning of peaks.

7.3.1.4.2 Diode Array Detectors

Photo diode array detectors simultaneously measure absorbance at many small wavelength increments over a broad wavelength band. The detector uses a diffraction grating to break the light beam into a spectrum that is focused onto an array of UV-sensitive photo diodes. Thus, UV spectra of individual peaks can be recorded. A data processing system enables the instrument to determine peak purity by

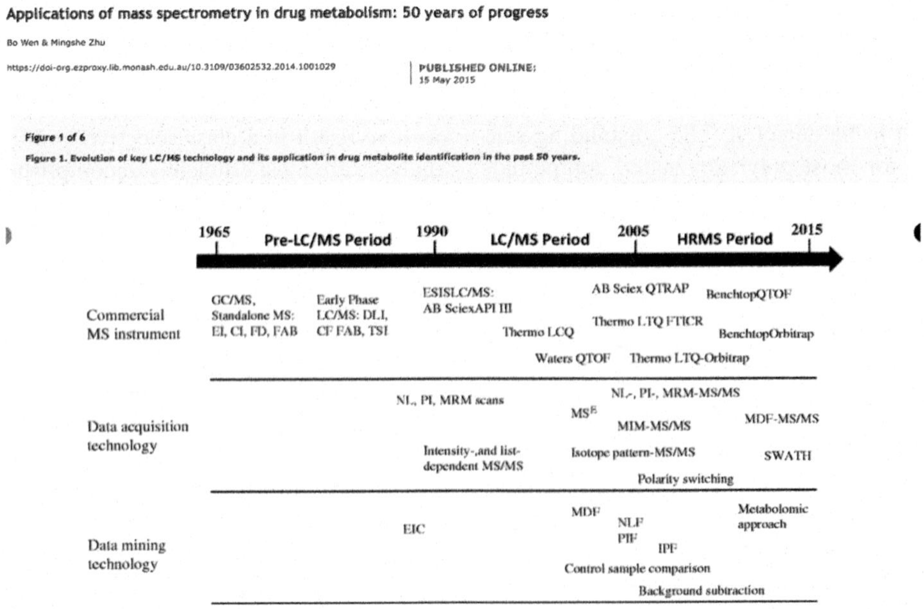

FIGURE 7.3.1 Evolution of LC-MS over the last 50 years [45].

comparing spectra at the leading and tailing ends of a peak and to create and search libraries of target analyte spectra. The sensitivity of the diode array detector is poorer than that of the fixed or variable wavelength detector, but the availability of spectral data makes it a valuable tool for drug screening [46, 47].

7.3.1.4.3 Fluorescence Detectors

Fluorescence detectors, with variable excitation and emission wavelengths, provide high sensitivity and specificity for the detection and quantification of fluorescent compounds, but they are more useful for quantification than for screening. Fluorescence detection could be used to provide a sensitive screen to target a single substance or a group of substances with similar fluorescence characteristics and different retention times [56–59].

All these hyphenated analytical techniques (HPLC-UV, HPLC-DAD, and HPLC-F) have slowly been superseded by LC-MS applications.

7.3.1.4.4 High Performance Liquid Chromatography/Mass Spectrometry

The rapid development in LC-MS instrumentation over the last 20 years has resulted in thousands of publications relating to toxicological applications of LC-MS drug identification and quantitation. A large number of reviews have been published, which summarize the bulk of applications to testing in clinical and post-mortem toxicology [10, 45, 48–53].

HPLC coupled to a single-stage MS (e.g., quadrupole or ion trap analyzers) can be used to separate and detect compounds using this form of separation; however, in practice, tandem MS is far more sensitive and powerful and has largely taken over single-stage LC-MS applications. Tandem MS is also used with GC (GC-MS/MS), although this combination is much less common than LC-MS/MS. In this approach (i.e., MS/MS), a target ion is selected by the first MS stage, followed by collisional-induced dissociation, which produces secondary fragments that are then analyzed by the second stage of the MS. Such a procedure involves the use of (1) selected reaction monitoring for preliminary screening of possible drugs, (2) neutral loss screening to indicate the presence of any member of a given class of drugs, and (3) the acquisition of complete product spectra for confirmation. Using the first-stage MS to isolate a specific ion not only saves time but also significantly improves the limits of detection by reducing chemical noise in the MS/MS spectrum. By removing the majority of interfering clutter in the first stage of MS, the MS/MS spectrum generated is often extremely clean. Thus, both detectability and specificity are increased with MS/MS.

Both electrospray ionization (ESI) and atmospheric pressure chemical ionization (APCI) modes of ionization are used as well as both negative and positive ion detection modes. ESI is useful for labile molecules that cannot be ionized by other techniques but does suffer from more interference from ion suppression compared with the APCI mode, which has similarities to the chemical ionization (CI) mode in GC-MS. LC-MS/MS procedures are now routinely employed for the rapid screening and confirmation of up to hundreds of drugs in a single sample, at drug levels often lower than several nanograms (ng) per milliliter (mL), using small sample sizes. The high sensitivity allows the use of very small sample sizes, including the detection of drugs in hair. LC-MS/MS is now widely used by forensic scientists in their casework for drug detection in biological samples, solid exhibits, and clandestine laboratory investigations, and in the detection of accelerants in arson cases.

A limitation of this form of MS is that in most cases, the method targets known compounds (drugs and possible metabolites, and perhaps other poisons). While hundreds of substances can be included in the targeted analysis, it cannot cover all possible substances that are eluting from the end of the column. Ideally, non-targeted screening is preferred, but this is more complex to achieve using tandem MS, requiring data-independent acquisition (DIA). This form of acquisition will reduce the sensitivity and increase the detection limit compared with targeted acquisition (MS spends more time looking for known ions in discrete time windows rather than all possible ions), and since chromatograms are rarely free of a host of endogenous-type substances, it will be time-consuming to examine all peaks. Specialist MS applications include the detection of nonvolatile ethanol metabolites (sulfate and glucuronide) in biological specimens, congeners of various alcoholic products in biological specimens to determine the source and possible time course of consumption of alcohol, and measuring the glucuronide conjugates of drugs to better estimate possible toxicity.

While the use of MS/MS spectra can be used to determine a structure from fragmentation patterns, the use of complementary techniques is advised to unequivocally determine chemical structures. These would include other ionization techniques, high-resolution MS (HR-MS), and/or nuclear magnetic resonance (NMR).

7.3.1.5 Other Applications of Mass Spectrometry

Another form of MS, inductively coupled plasma MS (ICP-MS), can be used to screen post-mortem samples for the presence of metals. Ion ratio MS (IR-MS) is another form of MS that is not widely used in forensic toxicology laboratories but utilized by other laboratories that are trying to determine the age of a substance through quantitative analyses of the isotopic patterns of characteristic elements. It has been used in forensic illicit drug laboratories to determine the source of a seizure based on its isotopic patterns, such as the region where cocaine or marijuana leaf material has grown, or whether testosterone detected in a doping situation has come from endogenous or synthetic sources (Table 7.3.1).

7.3.1.5.1 High-Resolution Mass Spectrometry

HR-MS developed over 50 years ago when double focusing MS (and the older magnetic sector instruments) became available; however, it was not until the last decade or so that

TABLE 7.3.1
Selected Types and Applications of Mass Spectrometry

GC-MS	Detection of volatile and thermally stable analytes (ethanol, many drugs, gases, solvents). Electron ionization (EI) and chemical ionization (CI)used.
LC-MS/MS	Targeted screening and quantification of most drugs and drug metabolites. Negative and positive ionization using electrospray ionization (ESI) and atmospheric pressure chemical ionization (APCI) modes.
HR-MS	Unknown screening of biological and non-biological exhibits for drugs and other chemicals. LC and GC are common hyphenated systems; also, matrix assisted laser desorption/ionization (MALDI) and desorption electrospray ionization (DESI) ionization modes are used for direct analysis.
ICP-MS	Detection of metals and other elements in biological and non-biological exhibits.
IR-MS	Determining the source of plants, drugs, and other chemicals through the use of changing isotopic patterns.

Abbreviations: HR-MS, high resolution mass spectrometry; ICP-MS, inductively coupled mass spectrometry; IR-MS, isotope ratio mass spectrometry.

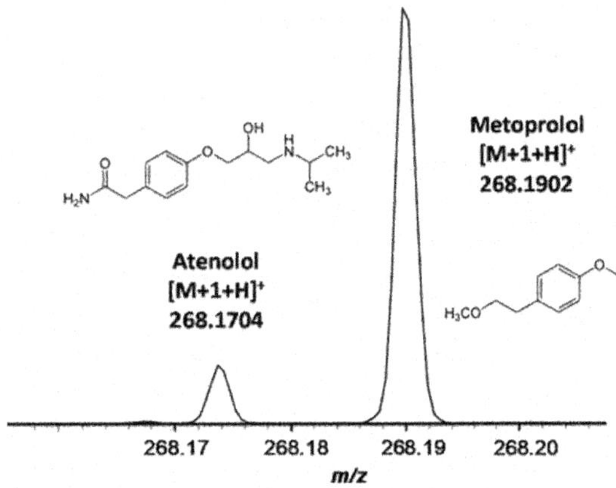

FIGURE 7.3.2 Mass separation by HR-MS of two beta-blockers with same integer molecular weight but quite different accurate weights.

affordable commercial "bench-top" instruments became available with coupling to LC and use of ESI with time-of-flight or Orbitrap mass analyzers. Hybrid instruments are available with quadrupole or ion trap analyzers before the HR analyzer. Accurate masses to a resolution of about 5 ppm, or to four decimal places, are possible. This enables analyzers to distinguish compounds with the same integer mass but with different chemical formulae. Libraries are used by analysts to provide formulae of likely matches. The use of retention time and ionization patterns further assists in identification.

An example of this is shown in Figure 7.3.2 for mass separation of two beta-blockers that have the same nominal mass.

Formal identification usually only occurs when complementary spectroscopic techniques are used, such as tandem MS, and then comparison with an authentic standard. The applications of HR-MS extend those of tandem MS for the analysis of samples that are likely to contain unusual or unknown molecules. The information obtained can be interrogated at any time to search for other substances not previously identified. These include multi-analyte approaches for the detection of NPS [54] and other drugs [55–57], higher–molecular weight poisons, such as amatoxins deriving from amanita mushroom poisoning [58–61] (Figure 7.3.3), a variety of plant-derived poisons, protein toxins from envenomation [62], and chemical warfare agents [63].

Analysis of wastewater in cities has enabled governments to quantify the extent of illicit and other drug use at a population level enabling evidence-based targeted public health and enforcement programs. Combining HR-MS with improved separation techniques, such as multi-dimensional chromatography, has further enhanced the ability to detect unknown molecules in complex matrices; this includes the use of two different-polarity GC or LC columns (GCxGC/TOF-MS, LCxLC/TOF-MS) to effect improved separation (Figure 7.3.4).

7.3.1.5.2 Inductively Coupled Plasma MS

Toxicologists should be prepared to support investigations that involve toxic exposure to metals and metalloids. Proper sample collection and rigorous state-of-the-art analytical techniques are critical to prevent exogenous contamination [65, 66]. Inductively coupled plasma MS (ICP-MS) is an ideal method to screen specimens (i.e., blood, hair, and urine) for the presence of heavy metals. ICP-MS differs from other forms of MS described thus far in that a vaporized sample is heated to atomize metal ions under extremely high temperature (up to about 10,000 °C), and the excited atoms and ions (plasma) are separated based on their mass and charge. This technique allows the detection of large numbers of elements at (often) sub-picogram per milliliter concentrations. Since most elements have naturally occurring isotopes, this further assists in identifying and quantifying metals in exhibits, including biological materials. An example might be to verify suspected arsenic poisoning or simply to check whether exposure to one or more heavy metals has occurred environmentally or occupationally. Elements such as arsenic, thallium, cadmium and lead, and others can easily be measured in one analysis.

7.3.1.5.3 Matrix Assisted Laser Desorption/Ionization (MALDI) and Desorption Electrospray Ionization (DESI)

Two types of MS not discussed before are MALDI and DESI. MALDI stands for matrix assisted laser desorption/

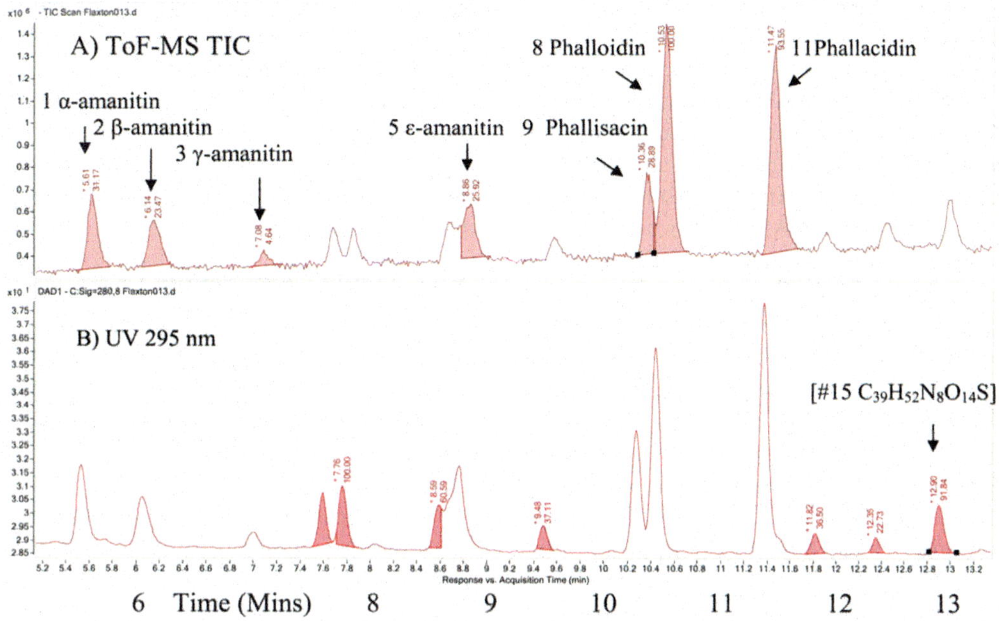

FIGURE 7.3.3 Example of TOF-MS applied to amatoxin analysis. (From Clarke, D. B., et al., ***Analytical Methods***, 4, 1298–1309, 2012 [60].)

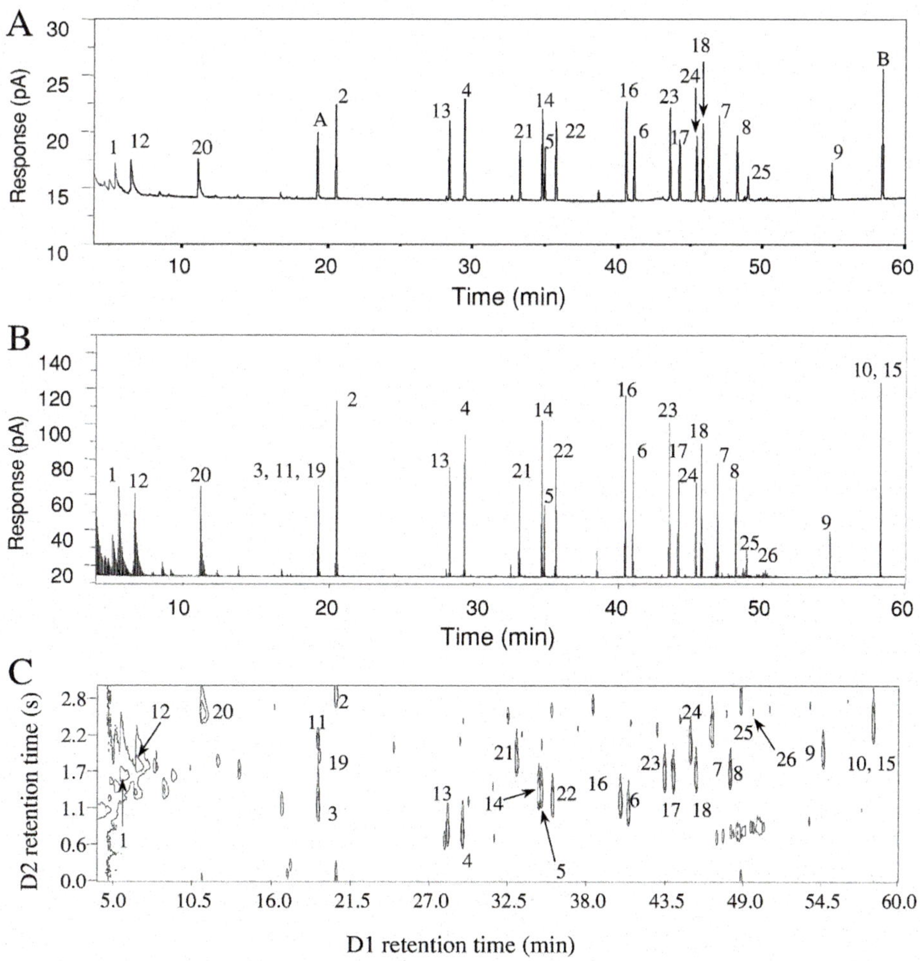

FIGURE 7.3.4 Analysis of a composite standard of 27 drugs. (A) Normal GC analysis, (B) pulsed GCxGC analysis, and (C) GCxGC contour plot. (Reproduced from Kueh, A. J., et al., ***Journal of Chromatography A***, 1000, 109, 2003 [64].)

ionization, in which the sample is mixed in a special matrix, and UV light of high energy from a laser converts it into a vapor. DESI stands for desorption electrospray ionization and uses a fast-moving charged solvent stream to extract analytes from the surfaces and propel the secondary ions produced toward the MS. MALDI and DESI can be used as a non-destructive way to analyze exhibits such as powders, pills, and trace residues [67]. HR-MS is typically used to identify ions produced by MALDI based on their accurate MW, while tandem MS is often used to identify specific transitions (specific ions produced by target ions). MALDI-HR-MS has also been used to visualize latent fingerprints and even to detect within the trace deposits the presence of drugs and other substances that may assist the investigation. Multi-dimensional LC-MS/MS has even been used to quantify intact human insulin and some recombinant analogues. This has the potential to provide more accurate monitoring of diabetic patients and detect potential doping with insulin in athletes.

LC-MS/MS is now commonly used for the analysis of smaller molecules with polar functional groups, especially drug metabolites and their conjugates. This approach can provide intact conjugate information not obtainable using parallel GC-MS approaches. It also bypasses the hydrolysis and chemical derivatization steps that are often required in GC-MS applications. A common application is the analysis of morphine and its two glucuronide metabolites in blood and urine. The screening of urine or other biological specimens for bio-markers of diseases (e.g., metabolomics) has become a significant research effort that has a forensic medical interest using tandem MS and HR-MS. These approaches are now possible with high-speed computers combined with chemical fragmentation libraries and sophisticated data-analysis algorithms. MALDI-MS is now being used to detect molecular changes in neurodegenerative and psychiatric disorders including Alzheimer's disease, Parkinson's disease, and schizophrenia.

7.3.1.6 Ultraviolet-Visible Spectrophotometry

Ultraviolet-visible (UV-Vis) spectrophotometry was one of the earliest instrumental techniques used in post-mortem forensic toxicology. The use of ultraviolet and visible spectrophotometry as a screening tool is based on the fact that many drugs contain aromatic nuclei that absorb light in the UV and visible regions. Such drugs have absorption spectra with maxima and minima at characteristic wavelengths. Furthermore, the spectrum often changes with the ionization state of the drug in acidic or basic solutions. UV absorption maxima and entire spectra of drugs and poisons are available from various references. Several limitations, however, affect the use of spectrophotometry. The major limitation is the lack of sensitivity required to detect many of today's therapeutic or misused drugs. Another drawback of spectrophotometry is the requirement that the drug be isolated in a form free from substances with overlapping spectra. Drug mixtures and impure extracts yield mixed spectra that may not be interpretable. In addition, spectrophotometry is not able to distinguish between the parent drug and metabolites. Some of a drug's metabolites may be active, while others are inactive, and there is a need to distinguish between these compounds. In spite of these deficiencies, a role remains for spectrophotometric methods for some drug and toxicant analyses. UV spectrometry is especially useful for purity and concentration checks of primary and stock standards.

7.3.1.7 Sample Preparation

7.3.1.7.1 Extraction Methods

There are now many approaches to the preparation of samples for drugs or poison analysis. One is the direct analysis of the specimen for the presence of a specific analyte or its class without isolation or purification. The other is isolation of the analyte from the sample followed by instrumental analysis of the concentrated extract [68].

The most common example of this is liquid–liquid extraction of an appropriately buffered sample with an immiscible organic solvent. The proper choice of sample, pH, and solvent will effectively remove the target analytes from the aqueous sample matrix. Adequate sample preparation increases the sensitivity and selectivity of a method and can reduce the background noise of matrix effects associated with different types of analysis.

Post-mortem matrices can be challenging to analyze. They can be degraded, hemolyzed, putrefied, and affected by a great number of changes that occur after death. Traditionally, specimens have been extracted using liquid–liquid techniques (LLE) or protein precipitation (PPT). While solid-phase extraction (SPE) techniques have been used for poor-quality post-mortem specimens, much better and more consistent recoveries are achieved using traditional LLE techniques. A great number of published papers exist documenting different applications for blood, urine, vitreous humor, and other solid tissues using either extraction technique. Dilute and shoot methods are not commonly used in forensic toxicology, as these are subject to large matrix interferences, ion suppression/enhancement, and contamination. Complex matrices often require a clean-up step to optimize the extract for injection on modern instrumentation. PPT methods are often used when the sensitivity is not a limiting factor but can be significantly improved when coupled to modern ultra-fast chromatography coupled with MS [69, 70].

7.3.1.7.2 Liquid–Liquid Extraction

The LLE technique dates to the mid-19th century, when Stas and Otto developed extraction schemes for nonvolatile organic compounds. The method utilizes differences in the pH and solubility characteristics of various analytes. A basic compound is in the non-ionized form in alkaline pH; an acidic compound is in the ionized form in a similar medium. A compound in its non-ionized form prefers the lipophilic environment of an organic solvent to the aqueous environment of the biologic sample. It is on this basis that the separation of drugs from the biologic matrix occurs.

The specimen is buffered according to the pH characteristics of the analyte of interest and mixed with an immiscible organic solvent. Commonly used solvents are hexane, toluene, diethyl ether, chlorobutane, dichloromethane, chloroform, or mixtures of these. Ionized compounds and many of the biologic components such as proteins remain in the aqueous layer, while the unionized drug molecules are transferred to the organic solvent. The extraction process can be illustrated by taking as an example a basic drug of pK 8 present in plasma. If the plasma is brought to pH 10 using a suitable alkali or alkaline buffer and is shaken with a suitable organic solvent, the drug will be removed from the aqueous into the organic phase. Unfortunately, many endogenous bases and neutral compounds will also be extracted if they are soluble in the organic solvent. The organic phase is then separated from the aqueous phase (using a Pasteur pipette, for example). This is usually done after centrifugation to completely separate the two phases. The organic phase is typically evaporated, derivatized (if required), reconstituted, and injected into a chromatographic system. Recoveries of compounds of interest can be increased by using mixed solvents such as 1-chlorobutane, hexane, and butyl acetate or solvent combinations such as chloroform/2-propanol or hexane/2-propanol. A solvent of high polarity will often give higher extraction efficiencies but much dirtier extracts. It should also be noted that extraction conditions should always be optimized using the relevant biological fluid. It should not be assumed that the extractability from water will exactly match that from blood or tissue homogenates.

LLE is generally a very efficient extraction technique and can now be automated to assist in rapid extractions of drugs from matrices such as oral fluid [71] and urine [72]. Sometimes, extraction techniques can be combined to improve efficiency and detectability [73]. For matrices such as hair, decontamination procedures are applied prior to any extraction, and the sample can then be extracted with LLE or SPE [74].

7.3.1.7.3 Solid-Phase Extraction

SPE techniques have existed for many years now and are routinely applied to "cleaner" matrices such as serum, plasma, urine, and vitreous humor. While there are novel applications for the use of SPE for solid tissues, these are specimens that are more amenable to LLE processes.

In SPE, the specimen is applied to a solid packing material, which is usually, but not exclusively, silica gel based. The sample is partitioned between the matrix and the solid phase, which provides the separation. The general process of SPE involves several steps: (1) column conditioning, (2) addition of specimen, (3) column washing with solvents to remove interfering substances, and (4) analyte elution. Each individual step depends on the analyte of interest or the type of extraction column, and method development frequently involves a significant amount of trial and error.

SPE is utilized in a vast number of analytical methods developed for drug detection in human post-mortem materials [75, 76]. The advantages of SPE procedures include decreased operator time, reduced solvent volumes, and increased extraction efficiency [77]. In post-mortem toxicology, the availability of automated SPE systems has made this extraction technique attractive to forensic laboratories with a high throughput of post-mortem samples, where several extraction programs adjusted for different analytical methods can be run on the same system.

Other derivations of SPE include techniques such solid-phase microextraction (SPME), a simple, rapid, efficient, and solventless extraction method useful for extraction of limited classes of drugs [78, 79]. Unfortunately, SPME is not an extraction technique that can routinely be used for a large range of drugs. A range of other SPE-based techniques are also available, including dispersive liquid–liquid microextraction (DLLME); liquid-phase microextraction (LPME); microextraction by packed sorbent (MEPS); and stir bar sorptive extraction (SBSE) [80].

Universal LLE procedures are preferable for general unknown analysis, because substances with very different physicochemical properties must be isolated from heterogeneous matrices. On the other hand, SPE is preferable if target compounds must be selectively isolated from relatively homogeneous samples, such as urine for confirmation of a single drug, or metabolite, or a group of drugs with similar extraction properties.

ACKNOWLEDGMENTS

Much of this material has been updated since the last edition of this text – thanks to toxicologists W. Lee Hearn and H. Chip Walls for their original and informative material.

REFERENCES

1. Kwong, T.C., B. Magnani, and C. Moore, Urine and oral fluid drug testing in support of pain management. *Critical Reviews in Clinical Laboratory Sciences*, 2017. **54**(6): p. 433–445.
2. Aziz, K., Drugs-of-abuse testing. Screening and confirmation. *Clinics in Laboratory Medicine*, 1990. **10**(3): p. 493–502.
3. Skopp, G., Postmortem toxicology. *Forensic Science, Medicine, and Pathology*, 2010. **6**(4): p. 314–25.
4. Swortwood, M.J., W.L. Hearn, and A.P. DeCaprio, Cross-reactivity of designer drugs, including cathinone derivatives, in commercial enzyme-linked immunosorbent assays. *Drug Testing and Analysis*, 2014. **6**(7–8): p. 716–27.
5. Phan, H.M., K. Yoshizuka, D.J. Murry, and P.J. Perry, Drug testing in the workplace. *Pharmacotherapy*, 2012. **32**(7): p. 649–56.
6. Saitman, A., H.-D. Park, and R.L. Fitzgerald, False-positive interferences of common urine drug screen immunoassays: A review. *Journal of Analytical Toxicology*, 2014. **38**(7): p. 387–396.
7. Sundström, M., A. Pelander, and I. Ojanperä, Comparison between drug screening by immunoassay and ultra-high performance liquid chromatography/high-resolution time-of-flight mass spectrometry in post-mortem urine. *Drug Testing and Analysis*, 2015. **7**(5): p. 420–427.

8. Stephanson, N.N., P. Signell, A. Helander, and O. Beck, Use of LC–HRMS in full scan-XIC mode for multi-analyte urine drug testing – A step towards a 'black-box' solution? *Journal of Mass Spectrometry*, 2017. **52**(8): p. 497–506.
9. Oyaert, M., N. Peersman, D. Kieffer, K. Deiteren, A. Smits, K. Allegaert, I. Spriet, J. Van Eldere, J. Verhaegen, P. Vermeersch, and S. Pauwels, Novel LC–MS/MS method for plasma vancomycin: Comparison with immunoassays and clinical impact. *Clinica Chimica Acta*, 2015. **441**: p. 63–70.
10. Taylor, P.J., C.-H. Tai, M.E. Franklin, and P.I. Pillans, The current role of liquid chromatography-tandem mass spectrometry in therapeutic drug monitoring of immunosuppressant and antiretroviral drugs. *Clinical Biochemistry*, 2011. **44**(1): p. 14–20.
11. Bogusz, M.J., Hyphenated liquid chromatographic techniques in forensic toxicology. *Journal of Chromatography. Part B, Biomedical Sciences and Applications*, 1999. **733**(1): p. 65–91.
12. Smith, M.L., S.P. Vorce, J.M. Holler, E. Shimomura, J. Magluilo, A.J. Jacobs, and M.A. Huestis, Modern instrumental methods in forensic toxicology*. *Journal of Analytical Toxicology*, 2007. **31**(5): p. 237–253.
13. Mogoll, N.G.S., C.D. Quiroz-Moreno, P.S. Prata, J.R. de Almeida, A.S. Cevallos, R. Torres-Gui, and F. Augusto, New advances in toxicological forensic analysis using mass spectrometry techniques. *Journal of Analytical Methods in Chemistry*, 2018. **2018**: p. 17.
14. Kostakis, C., P. Harpas, and P.C. Stockham, Chapter 11 - Forensic toxicology, in *Liquid chromatography*. 2nd ed., S. Fanali, et al., Editors. 2017, Elsevier. p. 301–358.
15. Bogusz, M. and R.A. de Zeeuw, An evaluation of fused silica capillary columns for the screening of basic drugs in postmortem blood: Qualitative and quantitative analysis. *Journal of Forensic Sciences*, 1986. **31**(3): p. 800–1.
16. Tiscione, N.B., I. Alford, D.T. Yeatman, and X. Shan, Ethanol analysis by headspace gas chromatography with simultaneous flame-ionization and mass spectrometry detection. *Journal of Analytical Toxicology*, 2011. **35**(7): p. 501–511.
17. Honey, D., C. Caylor, R. Luthi, and S. Kerrigan, Comparative alcohol concentrations in blood and vitreous fluid with illustrative case studies. *Journal of Analytical Toxicology*, 2005. **29**(5): p. 365–369.
18. Logan, B., G. Case, and E. Kiesel, Differentiation of diethyl ether/acetone and ethanol/acetonitrile solvent pairs, and other common volatiles by dual column headspace gas chromatography. *Journal of Forensic Sciences*, 1994. **39**(6): p. 1544–1551.
19. Drummer, O.H., Chromatographic screening techniques in systematic toxicological analysis. *Journal of Chromatography B Biomedical Sciences and Applications*, 1999. **733**(1–2): p. 27–45.
20. Lin, D.-L., S.-M. Wang, C.-H. Wu, B.-G. Chen, and R.H. Liu, Chemical derivatization for forensic drug analysis by GC-and LC-MS. *Forensic Science Review*, 2016. **28**: p. 17–35.
21. Schwaninger, A.E., M.R. Meyer, and H.H. Maurer, Chiral drug analysis using mass spectrometric detection relevant to research and practice in clinical and forensic toxicology. *Journal of Chromatography. Part A*, 2012. **1269**: p. 122–135.
22. Peters, F.T., T. Kraemer, and H.H. Maurer, Drug testing in blood: Validated negative-ion chemical ionization gas chromatographic–Mass spectrometric assay for determination of amphetamine and methamphetamine enantiomers and its application to toxicology cases. *Clinical Chemistry*, 2002. **48**(9): p. 1472.
23. Monteiro, C., J. Franco, P. Proença, A. Castañera, A. Claro, D. Vieira, and F. Corte-Real, Qualitative and quantitative analysis of a group of volatile organic compounds in biological samples by HS-GC/FID: Application in practical cases. *Forensic Science International*, 2014. **243**: p. 137–143.
24. Jones, A.W., A. Holmgren, and J. Ahlner, Toxicological analysis of blood and urine samples from female victims of alleged sexual assault. *Clinical Toxicology*, 2012. **50**(7): p. 555–561.
25. Monteiro, C., J.M. Franco, P. Proença, A. Castañera, A. Claro, D.N. Vieira, and F. Corte-Real, Qualitative and quantitative analysis of a group of volatile organic compounds in biological samples by HS-GC/FID: Application in practical cases. *Forensic Science International*, 2014. **243**: p. 137–143.
26. Drummer, O.H., S. Horomidis, S. Kourtis, M.L. Syrjanen, and P. Tippett, Capillary gas chromatographic drug screen for use in forensic toxicology. *Journal of Analytical Toxicology*, 1994. **18**(3): p. 134–8.
27. Cox, R.A., J.A. Crifasi, R.E. Dickey, S.C. Ketzler, and G.L. Pshak, A single-step extraction for screening whole blood for basic drugs by capillary GC/NPD. *Journal of Analytical Toxicology*, 1989. **13**(4): p. 224–8.
28. Fretthold, D., P. Jones, G. Sebrosky, and I. Sunshine, Testing for basic drugs in biological fluids by solvent extraction and dual capillary GC/NPD. *Journal of Analytical Toxicology*, 1986. **10**(1): p. 10–4.
29. Taylor, R.W., S.D. Le, S. Philip, and N.C. Jain, Simultaneous identification of amphetamine and methamphetamine using solid-phase extraction and gas chromatography/nitrogen phosphorous detection or gas chromatography/mass spectrometry. *Journal of Analytical Toxicology*, 1989. **13**(5): p. 293–5.
30. Schutz, H., Modern screening strategies in analytical toxicology with special regard to new benzodiazepines. *Z Rechtsmed*, 1988. **100**(1): p. 19–37.
31. Maurer, H., K. Pfleger, and A. Weber, *Mass spectral and GC data of drugs, poisons, pesticides, pollutants, and their metabolites*, 4th edition. 2017.
32. Maurer, H.H., Systematic toxicological analysis of drugs and their metabolites by gas chromatography-mass spectrometry. *Journal of Chromatography*, 1992. **580**(1–2): p. 3–41.
33. Maurer, H.H., Systematic toxicological analysis procedures for acidic drugs and/or metabolites relevant to clinical and forensic toxicology and/or doping control. *Journal of Chromatography B*, 1999. **733**(1–2): p. 3–25.
34. Song, S.M., P. Marriott, A. Kotsos, O.H. Drummer, and P. Wynne, Comprehensive two-dimensional gas chromatography with time-of-flight mass spectrometry (GC x GC-TOFMS) for drug screening and confirmation. *Forensic Science International*, 2004. **143**(2–3): p. 87–101.
35. Moore, C., S. Rana, C. Coulter, F. Feyerherm, and H. Prest, Application of two-dimensional gas chromatography with electron capture chemical ionization mass spectrometry to the detection of 11-nor-Δ9-tetrahydrocannabinol-9-ca rboxylic acid (THC-COOH) in hair. *Journal of Analytical Toxicology*, 2006. **30**(3): p. 171–177.
36. Alam, M.S. and R.M. Harrison, Recent advances in the application of 2-dimensional gas chromatography with soft and hard ionisation time-of-flight mass spectrometry in environmental analysis. *Chemical Science*, 2016. **7**(7): p. 3968–3977.

37. Gruber, B., B.A. Weggler, R. Jaramillo, K.A. Murrell, P.K. Piotrowski, and F.L. Dorman, Comprehensive two-dimensional gas chromatography in forensic science: A critical review of recent trends. *Trends in Analytical Chemistry*, 2018. **105**: p. 292–301.
38. Sampat, A., M. Lopatka, M. Sjerps, G. Vivo-Truyols, P. Schoenmakers, and A. van Asten, Forensic potential of comprehensive two-dimensional gas chromatography. *Trends in Analytical Chemistry*, 2016. **80**: p. 345–363.
39. Kintz, P., Value of hair analysis in postmortem toxicology. *Forensic Science International*, 2004. **142**(2–3): p. 127–134.
40. Barr, J.R., W.J. Driskell, L.S. Aston, and R.A. Martinez, Quantitation of metabolites of the nerve agents sarin, soman, cyclohexylsarin, VX, and Russian VX in human urine using isotope-dilution gas chromatography-tandem mass spectrometry. *Journal of Analytical Toxicology*, 2004. **28**(5): p. 372–8.
41. Huestis, M.A., R.A. Gustafson, E.T. Moolchan, A. Barnes, J.A. Bourland, S.A. Sweeney, E.F. Hayes, P.M. Carpenter, and M.L. Smith, Cannabinoid concentrations in hair from documented cannabis users. *Forensic Science International*, 2007. **169**(2–3): p. 129–36.
42. Kintz, P., M. Villain, V. Dumestre, and V. Cirimele, Evidence of addiction by anesthesiologists as documented by hair analysis. *Forensic Science International*, 2005. **153**(1): p. 81–4.
43. Niedbala, R.S., K.W. Kardos, D.F. Fritch, K.P. Kunsman, K.A. Blum, G.A. Newland, J. Waga, L. Kurtz, M. Bronsgeest, and E.J. Cone, Passive cannabis smoke exposure and oral fluid testing. II. Two studies of extreme cannabis smoke exposure in a motor vehicle. *Journal of Analytical Toxicology*, 2005. **29**(7): p. 607–15.
44. Niedbala, S., K. Kardos, S. Salamone, D. Fritch, M. Bronsgeest, and E.J. Cone, Passive cannabis smoke exposure and oral fluid testing. *Journal of Analytical Toxicology*, 2004. **28**(7): p. 546–52.
45. Wen, B. and M. Zhu, Applications of mass spectrometry in drug metabolism: 50 years of progress. *Drug Metabolism Reviews*, 2015. **47**(1): p. 71–87.
46. Li, S., P.J. Gemperline, K. Briley, and S. Kazmierczak, Identification and quantitation of drugs of abuse in urine using the generalized rank annihilation method of curve resolution. *Journal of Chromatography. Part B, Biomedical Sciences and Applications*, 1994. **655**(2): p. 213–223.
47. Herzler, M., S. Herre, and F. Pragst, Selectivity of substance identification by HPLC-DAD in toxicological analysis using a UV spectra library of 2682 compounds. *Journal of Analytical Toxicology*, 2003. **27**(4): p. 233–242.
48. Maurer, H.H., Current role of liquid chromatography–mass spectrometry in clinical and forensic toxicology. *Analytical and Bioanalytical Chemistry*, 2007. **388**(7): p. 1315–1325.
49. Peters, F.T., Recent advances of liquid chromatography–(tandem) mass spectrometry in clinical and forensic toxicology. *Clinical Biochemistry*, 2011. **44**(1): p. 54–65.
50. Maurer, H.H., What is the future of (ultra) high performance liquid chromatography coupled to low and high resolution mass spectrometry for toxicological drug screening? *Journal of Chromatography. Part A*, 2013. **1292**: p. 19–24.
51. Mbughuni, M.M., P.J. Jannetto, and L.J. Langman, Mass spectrometry applications for toxicology. *EJIFCC*, 2016. **27**(4): p. 272–287.
52. Ojanperä, I., M. Kolmonen, and A. Pelander, Current use of high-resolution mass spectrometry in drug screening relevant to clinical and forensic toxicology and doping control. *Analytical and Bioanalytical Chemistry*, 2012. **403**(5): p. 1203–1220.
53. Couchman, L. and P.E. Morgan, LC-MS in analytical toxicology: Some practical considerations. *Biomedical Chromatography*, 2011. **25**(1–2): p. 100–123.
54. Dei Cas, M., E. Casagni, S. Arnoldi, V. Gambaro, and G. Roda, Screening of new psychoactive substances (NPS) by gas-chromatography/time of flight mass spectrometry (GC/MS-TOF) and application to 63 cases of judicial seizure. *Forensic Science International: Synergy*, 2019. **1**: p. 71–78.
55. Broecker, S., S. Herre, B. Wust, J. Zweigenbaum, and F. Pragst, Development and practical application of a library of CID accurate mass spectra of more than 2,500 toxic compounds for systematic toxicological analysis by LC-QTOF-MS with data-dependent acquisition. *Analytical and Bioanalytical Chemistry*, 2011. **400**(1): p. 101–17.
56. Grapp, M., C. Kaufmann, F. Streit, and L. Binder, Systematic forensic toxicological analysis by liquid-chromatography-quadrupole-time-of-flight mass spectrometry in serum and comparison to gas chromatography-mass spectrometry. *Forensic Science International*, 2018. **287**: p. 63–73.
57. Telving, R., J.B. Hasselstrøm, and M.F. Andreasen, Targeted toxicological screening for acidic, neutral and basic substances in postmortem and antemortem whole blood using simple protein precipitation and UPLC-HR-TOF-MS. *Forensic Science International*, 2016. **266**: p. 453.
58. Gicquel, T., S. Lepage, M. Fradin, O. Tribut, B. Duretz, and I. Morel, Amatoxins (α- and β-amanitin) and phallotoxin (phalloidin) analyses in urines using high-resolution accurate mass LC–MS technology. *Journal of Analytical Toxicology*, 2014. **38**(6): p. 335–340.
59. Helfer, A.G., M.R. Meyer, J.A. Michely, and H.H. Maurer, Direct analysis of the mushroom poisons α- and β-amanitin in human urine using a novel on-line turbulent flow chromatography mode coupled to liquid chromatography–high resolution-mass spectrometry/mass spectrometry. *Journal of Chromatography. Part A*, 2014. **1325**: p. 92–98.
60. Clarke, D.B., A.S. Lloyd, and P. Robb, Application of liquid chromatography coupled to time-of-flight mass spectrometry separation for rapid assessment of toxins in Amanita mushrooms. *Analytical Methods*, 2012. **4**(5): p. 1298–1309.
61. Ahmed, W., K. Gonmori, M. Suzuki, K. Watanabe, and O. Suzuki, Simultaneous analysis of α-amanitin, β-amanitin, and phalloidin in toxic mushrooms by liquid chromatography coupled to time-of-flight mass spectrometry. *Forensic Toxicology*, 2010. **28**(2): p. 69–76.
62. Zhang, J., J. Peng, X. Chen, Y. Gong, L. Wan, F. Gao, S. Gan, F. Wei, S. Ma, J. Chen, and J. Nie, Rapid identification of bile acids in snake bile using ultrahigh-performance liquid chromatography with electrospray ionization quadrupole time-of-flight tandem mass spectrometry. *Journal of Chromatography. Part B*, 2016. **1036–1037**: p. 157–169.
63. Aleksenko, S.S., Liquid chromatography with mass-spectrometric detection for the determination of chemical warfare agents and their degradation products. *Journal of Analytical Chemistry*, 2012. **67**(2): p. 82–97.
64. Kueh, A.J., P.J. Marriott, P.M. Wynne, and J.H. Vine, Application of comprehensive two-dimensional gas chromatography to drugs analysis in doping control. *Journal of Chromatography A*, 2003. **1000**(1–2): p. 109–24.

65. Christensen, J.M., Human exposure to toxic metals: Factors influencing interpretation of biomonitoring results. *Science of the Total Environment*, 1995. **166**: p. 89–135.
66. Flanagan, R.J., The poisoned patient: The role of the laboratory. *British Journal of Biomedical Science*, 1995. **52**(3): p. 202–13.
67. Wojtowicz, A. and R. Wietecha-PosAuszny, DESI-MS analysis of human fluids and tissues for forensic applications. (Report). *Applied Physics. Part A, Materials Science & Processing*, 2019. **125**(5): p. 1.
68. Kataoka, H., Chapter 1 - Sample preparation for liquid chromatography, in *Liquid chromatography*. 2nd ed. S. Fanali, et al., Editors. 2017, Elsevier. p. 1–37.
69. Vincenti, M., D. Cavanna, E. Gerace, V. Pirro, M. Petrarulo, D. Di Corcia, and A. Salomone, Fast screening of 88 pharmaceutical drugs and metabolites in whole blood by ultra-high-performance liquid chromatography–tandem mass spectrometry. *Analytical and Bioanalytical Chemistry*, 2013. **405**(2): p. 863–879.
70. Di Rago, M., E. Saar, L.N. Rodda, S. Turfus, A. Kotsos, D. Gerostamoulos, and O.H. Drummer, Fast targeted analysis of 132 acidic and neutral drugs and poisons in whole blood using LC-MS/MS. *Forensic Science International*, 2014. **243**: p. 35–43.
71. Rositano, J., P. Harpas, C. Kostakis, and T. Scott, Supported liquid extraction (SLE) for the analysis of methylamphetamine, methylenedioxymethylamphetamine and delta-9-tetrahydrocannabinol in oral fluid and blood of drivers. *Forensic Science International*, 2016. **265**: p. 125–130.
72. Versace, F., F. Sporkert, P. Mangin, and C. Staub, Rapid sample pre-treatment prior to GC–MS and GC–MS/MS urinary toxicological screening. *Talanta*, 2012. **101**: p. 299–306.
73. Ferreirós Bouzas, N., S. Dresen, B. Munz, and W. Weinmann, Determination of basic drugs of abuse in human serum by online extraction and LC–MS/MS. *Analytical and Bioanalytical Chemistry*, 2009. **395**(8): p. 2499.
74. Vogliardi, S., M. Tucci, G. Stocchero, S.D. Ferrara, and D. Favretto, Sample preparation methods for determination of drugs of abuse in hair samples: A review. *Analytica Chimica Acta*, 2015. **857**: p. 1–27.
75. Scheurer, J. and C.M. Moore, Solid-phase extraction of drugs from biological tissues--a review. *Journal of Analytical Toxicology*, 1992. **16**(4): p. 264–269.
76. Holm, K.M.D. and K. Linnet, Chiral analysis of methadone and its main metabolite, EDDP, in postmortem brain and blood by automated SPE and liquid chromatography–mass spectrometry. *Journal of Analytical Toxicology*, 2012. **36**(7): p. 487–496.
77. Kumazawa, T., C. Hasegawa, X.-P. Lee, and K. Sato, New and unique methods of solid-phase extraction for use before instrumental analysis of xenobiotics in human specimens. *Forensic Toxicology*, 2010. **28**(2): p. 61–68.
78. Ulrich, S., Solid-phase microextraction in biomedical analysis. *Journal of Chromatography. Part A*, 2000. **902**(1): p. 167–194.
79. Mariotti, K.d.C., R.S. Schuh, P. Ferranti, R.S. Ortiz, D.Z. Souza, F. Pechansky, P.E. Froehlich, and R.P. Limberger, Simultaneous analysis of amphetamine-type stimulants in plasma by solid-phase microextraction and gas chromatography-mass spectrometry. *Journal of Analytical Toxicology*, 2014. **38**(7): p. 432.
80. Namera, A., Recent advances in unique sample preparation techniques for bioanalysis. *Bioanalysis*, 2013. **5**(8): p. 915–932.

7.4 STRATEGIES FOR POST-MORTEM TOXICOLOGY INVESTIGATION

7.4.1 SCREENING STRATEGY

The process of establishing which cases require which analytical tests in many laboratories is predetermined. Most medico-legal case investigations can be categorized as homicide or suspicious, accident, suicide, drug related, and natural. Depending on the case type, certain tests may be conducted to conduct as comprehensive an analysis as possible and to expedite the progress of a case. This also enables laboratories to batch tests and casework accordingly, resulting in high throughput. Ultimately, this will be dependent on the toxicology laboratory and the practices in place with the pathologist and the medical examiner or coroner.

The first step in any case is to review the case circumstances and medical information. Some forensic organizations utilize a triage process prior to any autopsy, which may include imaging from computerized tomography (CT) scanning, medical information, and rapid toxicology [1–3]. This enables discussion between medical and legal practitioners in determining the requirement for post-mortem examination. If the pathologist or coroner makes no specific requests for analysis, then responsibility for deciding which tests to do falls exclusively to the professional judgment of the toxicologist. The classic example is a person who has died under suspicious circumstances and where the history, scene, and autopsy fail to disclose a definitive cause of death. The laboratory must have a systematic toxicological approach (STA) for the investigation of cases [4–19]. This not only enables a simultaneous detection of wide range of compounds in different samples but assists in completing cases in a reasonable timeframe.

Obviously, cases of suspected drug intoxication require the most comprehensive testing, typically on samples of blood, liver, gastric contents, and urine [20, 21]. The extent of testing is dependent upon the resources of the toxicology laboratory as well as any jurisdictional agreements as to the degree of toxicology testing which is undertaken. Cases that are classified as homicides or suspicious will typically include a blood ethanol analysis and a standard drug-of-abuse screen in blood and/or urine, with the concentration of any identified drug being quantified in the blood. This is true for most medico-legal investigations, but laboratories will have their own documented policies for different case types. Fatalities involving motor vehicle drivers require a blood ethanol determination and a comprehensive drug screen, with any positive drug concentration quantified in the blood. Fatalities resulting from a fire require blood carbon monoxide and sometimes cyanide analyses in addition to alcohol and other drugs [22].

7.4.2 GENERAL CONCEPTS

Screening protocols should include tests capable of detecting as many drugs as possible within the constraints imposed by the available specimens, the laboratory's workload, and requirements specific to the case [23]. Most laboratories lack the resources required to treat every case as a general unknown, applying test after test until all possible drugs and poisons are ruled out. Such an approach may occasionally be warranted when there is a high suspicion of poisoning, but usually, several standardized protocols can be used to eliminate most of the substances that can realistically be expected in a sample.

A broad-spectrum screen, capable of detecting or eliminating most of the common drugs, usually requires a combination of three or more techniques. Additional tests can be combined with standardized screening protocols, thereby expanding the screening capability to encompass additional drugs of concern based upon the specifics of the case.

The most effective strategies employ a combination of immunoassays with chromatographic techniques and chemical tests in order to detect a wide range of substances. Immunoassays are used to test for classes of drugs with similar structures, while the chromatographic tests detect large groups of drugs with similar extraction characteristics, polarities, and detection characteristics. Chemical tests are selective for the chemical reactivity of substances with similar structures. The type of analysis required also depends on the type of biologic specimen to be analyzed. A putrefied liver specimen, for example, will require greater sample preparation than would a urine specimen. Some drugs are present in much smaller concentrations than others and thus, require more sophisticated detection techniques.

It is impossible to design a single analytical scheme that is capable of detecting all the available drugs and poisons while being suitable for the wide variety of specimen combinations that may be submitted. Therefore, the laboratory needs to have a number of screening methods, e.g., multi-analyte [24–28] supplemented with as many special methods as required [29, 30]. Because the main objective is qualitative detection rather than quantification, general screening methods are usually more flexible than special methods and can therefore be applied to a wider variety of materials. A good general method will provide a provisional identification, which can then be confirmed by the application of a quantitative directed analysis.

7.4.3 BASIC STRATEGIES

In laboratories with small caseloads, each case may be reviewed individually by the director, who assigns specific tests. Testing large numbers of samples proceeds more efficiently, and in a more organized fashion, when standardized assay panels are performed on batches of samples. Blood and urine are the specimens of choice to screen for drugs and poisons. Depending on the circumstances of the case, other samples include liver, stomach contents, hair, or bile. The blood volatiles screen detects and quantifies ethanol while simultaneously screening for methanol, isopropanol, and acetone as well as other volatiles, such as halogenated and non-halogenated hydrocarbons that are sometimes inhaled for purposes of intoxication [31, 32].

Each of the immunoassay tests is used to detect substances that cannot easily be included in one or two chromatographic procedures, or for which routine chromatographic tests may be too insensitive, or where specialized extraction or derivatization conditions may be required.

7.4.3.1 The General Unknown

Cases in which a toxic cause of death is suspected but where a specified toxic agent is not known are referred to as *general unknowns* and require an open-ended search for poisons. The first step in investigating a general unknown is to carefully examine the medical records, case history, autopsy findings, and scene observations for evidence of specific toxins or of a toxic mechanism. The case history and medical records may describe symptoms characteristic of a particular pharmacologic category. Cardiac rhythm disturbances, respiratory rate and pattern, pupil size and responsiveness, condition of reflexes, convulsions, and any other pre-mortem symptoms may suggest a toxic mechanism that excludes some toxins from a long list of possible agents. Autopsy findings may also provide guidance. The condition of the gastric and esophageal mucosa may suggest or exclude corrosive poisons. The presence of massive pulmonary edema may indicate pre-terminal respiratory depression. Hepatic necrosis may indicate acetaminophen or Amanita mushroom toxicity, among other agents. Needle punctures and, especially, "track marks" indicate possible intravenous drug overdose. These and other observations, properly interpreted, can narrow the focus of the analytical search. Consideration of the place where death occurred, or where the terminal symptoms appeared, may suggest toxic agents. Scene investigation can yield valuable clues. For example, the death of a jewelry store employee may have resulted from exposure to cyanide, which is used in jewelry manufacture. Other employment settings have associated chemical hazards that should be recognized when planning a strategy for investigation of a workplace death.

In the home, other toxic exposures are more likely. Drugs, pesticides, and other chemical products for household use are possible agents. Also, drug misuse at home can result in accidents or fatal intoxication. Reports of witnesses can also give valuable clues. What was the deceased doing at the onset of illness? When was the deceased last seen alive? Was the deceased behaving normally, or was intoxication indicated? Was there a complaint of feeling sick? Eliciting such observations may make it possible to shorten the list of possible drugs.

The volatiles screen by headspace gas chromatography (GC), while designed to test for the common alcohols and acetone, can also detect other volatile chemicals, such as toluene and other solvents and volatile anesthetics. Drug screening tests are essential to rule out drug intoxication, and chromatographic screens can detect many other chemical substances besides drugs. Gas chromatography-mass spectrometry (GC/MS) is a mainstay of screening protocols for general unknowns. Semi-volatile organic compounds can be identified by computerized comparison of their mass spectra with libraries containing over 50,000 spectra of pesticides, drugs, and industrial chemicals. Tests for drugs and poisons not detected by the basic strategy can be added to the protocol for general unknowns. Selective immunoassays are available to test for cardiac glycosides, LSD, fentanyls, haloperidol, aminoglycoside antibiotics, and anticonvulsants. Clinical laboratories can provide assistance with tests for potassium, lithium, iron, and insulin or C-peptide or other biochemical markers. Toxic metals and nonmetals can be detected by atomic absorption spectrophotometry, and classical inorganic qualitative tests can be used to screen for toxic anions on a dialysate of urine, blood, or stomach contents. Other drugs that do not chromatograph well by GC may be detected by high-performance liquid chromatography (HPLC).

The following guidelines should be observed in approaching the general unknown:

1. If specimen selection and quantity are not limiting factors, then the objective should be the broadest screen possible with available technology.
2. The blood and vitreous fluid alcohol content should be determined before or simultaneously with other analyses.
3. Blood alcohol analyses should be performed by headspace GC utilizing an internal standard. This does not preclude possible confirmation by some other procedure.
4. If carbon monoxide is to be determined, this should also be done prior to drug screening procedures.
5. In the absence of background information on a given case, the systematic toxicological analyses should provide the best chances of successfully finding a drug or poison. That is, the more commonly encountered drugs and poisons should be sought before the more rarely encountered ones are considered.
6. In the event that specimen selection and quantity are limited, it will be necessary to plan assays more carefully. Immunoassay procedures should be applied early in the scheme if proper samples are available.
7. All assays should be considered with the intent of subsequently confirming positive findings by another independent procedure. This means, for example, that if specimen size is a limiting factor, then different stages of a general screen should be performed sequentially rather than in parallel.

7.4.4 Screening

Screening or initial testing comprises preliminary or presumptive tests to determine whether a drug or class of drugs is present in a biological specimen. This is often followed by confirmation testing; which is the process to verify the detection of a specific drug from an initial or screening test. The common approach of screening and confirmation has long been used in forensic toxicology laboratories, where defined limits of reporting have been based on low-level concentrations of drugs. Sometimes, these are established based on lowest concentrations derived after therapeutic dosing (for legitimate drugs) as well as being part of the performance characteristics of the validated method. Improvements to instrument technology have also resulted in reduced background noise, hence improving signal-to-noise ratios and leading to measurable drug concentrations at low levels (sub-ng/mL/g to pg/mL/g levels) [33]. This capability, however, does not always mean that drugs were ingested; other factors such as passive exposure, endogenous substances, and absorption of drugs from food or the environment must also be considered. The measurement of trace amounts of drugs or chemicals in casework samples does not mean that these always have forensic significance. Caution must therefore be taken regarding the interpretation of "ingestion" or "exposure" to a drug or substance [34].

Screening often involves the incorporation of drug immunoassays as well as broad multi-analyte GC/MS or liquid chromatography-mass spectrometry (LC/MS) techniques. Numerous papers have been published describing these methods; however, these do not always suit all laboratories. Forensic laboratories will have targeted screens for compounds of interest supplemented by general unknown screening methods that are linked to libraries of spectral data [35, 36]. Forensic toxicology will at some stage approach a black box scenario whereby a biological sample will be placed into an instrument and an identification will be made as the possible drug or substance in that sample.

7.4.4.1 Screening by Immunoassay

Immunoassays are still used by a number of forensic laboratories as front line screening for drugs of abuse [37–40], some prescription drugs [41, 42], alcohol markers [43, 44] and a limited number of new psychoactive substances [45, 46]. These simple and rapid tests are widely used for screening in urine [43] but can also be applied to blood/serum [47], oral fluid [48, 49], and hair [50, 51].

Immunoassays are nonspecific tests for a particular drug or a class of drugs (e.g., opioids). Immunoassay screening techniques rely on the competition of the analyte and the labeled antigen with an antibody showing some selectivity and reasonable sensitivity; however, not all members of a class of drugs will be equally detectable [22]. For example, the common opioid test is designed to detect morphine and codeine but will have only limited sensitivity to some other synthetic opioids such as oxycodone and not at all to others (e.g., methadone and fentanyl) [52, 53]. Another example is that if an amphetamines immunoassay is used, it should be one of broad class selectivity, not one of the newer and more specific monoclonal antibody assays, so that it has the chance of detecting the maximum number of amphetamines and related drugs (e.g., ephedrine, pseudoephedrine).

7.4.4.2 Chromatographic Methods

Chromatographic methods are used to expand the range of a drug screen beyond those drugs detectable by the immunoassays. The extraction system should be selective for basic drugs, and neutral substances will also be extracted [54–60] (Table 7.4.1).

7.4.4.3 Screening with Gas Chromatography

GC for basic drugs in blood is more sensitive than a basic drug screen on gastric contents but is also more labor intensive. It may be included in a general drug screen whenever urine is not available, or it may be reserved for cases where intoxication is indicated by the investigation and gastric contents yield negative screening results.

Figure 12.4.1 illustrates general screening protocols for various combinations of post-mortem samples.

When initial chromatographic screening tests reveal an unidentified peak from GC that does not match any standard, extracts may be further screened by GC/MS in the full-scan electron impact (EI) ionization mode [60, 62–64]. Reconstructed ion chromatograms are inspected for spectra that indicate exogenous (i.e., xenobiotic) substances. Suspect spectra are compared with the instrument's computerized libraries of drugs, poisons, and their metabolites. In addition, spectra may be visually compared with published compilations of mass spectral data [65] or on-line libraries such as NIST[1] of ChemSpider.[2] Whenever a tentative identification is made, the unknown and reference spectra must be visually compared to verify their identity. Chromatographic analyses coupled with mass spectrometry are complex methods of screening for drugs and poisons. The analyst must have a considerable amount of training and experience to competently perform such tests.

TABLE 7.4.1
Comparison of mass spectrometry techniques used in toxicology [61]

	GC/MS	LC/MS/MS	LC/HRMS
Analyzer cost	Law	Expensive	Very expensive
Analyte chemistry/size	Small, volatile	Broad	Broad
Targeted vs. untargeted	Untargeted	Targeted	Untargeted/targeted
Sample preparation	Extensive	Minimal–extensive	Minimal–extensive
Turnaround time	Slow	Fast(er)	Fast(er)
Cost per sample	Moderate	Low–moderate	Low–moderate
Sensitivity	Good	Better	Good

To provide adequate support for a medical examiner's office, the toxicology laboratory should periodically assess the prevalence of drugs in the population served and adjust its offering of routine tests accordingly. Certain drugs are more prevalent in various localities due to supply routes, ethnic practices, and demand. Changing patterns of drug use may be identified through crime laboratory statistics and various epidemiological monitoring programs, such as the Drug Abuse Warning Network (DAWN), European Monitoring Centre for Drugs and Drug Addiction (EMCDDA), and United Nations of Drugs and Crime (UNODC). Professional organizations such as the Society of Forensic Toxicologists (SOFT) and the International Association of Forensic Toxicologists (TIAFT) also have sub-committees where drug detections are documented and shared across their membership.

7.4.4.4 Screening with Liquid Chromatography

Increasingly, many drugs that cannot be detected by GC can be detected by HPLC. HPLC separates analytes in solution, at or near ambient temperature, and therefore can be used for drugs that are too thermolabile or polar to be analyzed by GC. Furthermore, chemical derivatization is rarely, if ever, required prior to analysis of drugs by HPLC. While most, but not all, drugs absorb ultraviolet (UV) light sufficiently well to be detected by a UV detector, a UV spectrum usually does not give sufficient information on its own for a forensically valid identification. Therefore, the preferred detector in modern forensic toxicology laboratories is the mass spectrometer. LC/MS has now become widely accepted as the most useful screening technique in forensic toxicology. LC/MS can also be coupled to other detectors such as UV, which can provide a high degree of confidence in the identification of a compound. Large screening libraries, similar in concept to those available on GC, are also available for LC/MS. Product ion spectra libraries have been created by vendors, which are usually instrument specific and not easily transferable across different LC/MS platforms [66–70]. Many laboratories also create their own in-house libraries from reference materials or from exhibits or from illicit drug labs, which can often provide these from seized material.

7.4.5 Confirmation

7.4.5.1 What Confirmation Is Necessary and Why

Courts require that the opinions expressed by toxicologists be of a "reasonable scientific probability," that the identity of reported substances be known with "scientific certainty," and that quantitative values be accurate to a stated statistical probability. Screening tests provide tentative identification of drugs and poisons. The forensic standard for conclusive identification requires that their identity be confirmed by additional tests.

The confirmatory test must clearly identify the specific drug and/or its metabolite(s). Confirmatory methods may include gas chromatography with flame ionization (GC-FID), electron capture (GC-ECD), and nitrogen-phosphorus (GC-NPD) detectors, HPLC, UV spectroscopy, GC/MS, LC/MS, and other hyphenated techniques such as MS/MS coupled to a GC or LC sample introduction system. Any chemical test can be subject to errors that may cause a false-positive result. Immunoassays can cross-react with substances other than the target drug. Chromatographic methods can have interfering substances that produce a signal or spot at the same time and place as a target analyte. GC/MS and LC/MS can yield false-positive results if a sample is mislabeled or contaminated in process, or by carryover from a preceding injection, or if the spectrum does not have a unique fragmentation pattern. For example, amitriptyline and cyclobenzaprine have similar retention times (RTs) and yield fragmentation patterns that are nearly identical. They may be confused if the molecular ion cannot be discerned.

In recognition of the possibility of a false-positive result from a single test, it is necessary that all potentially significant results be confirmed. Confirmation requires at least one additional test based on a different chemical detection principle with high specificity and sensitivity at least equal to the initial test. The essence of confirmation is to assemble a sufficient body of evidence such that a technically competent independent reviewer would agree with the conclusion. The requirement for two or more chemically distinct methodologies is based on the concern that chemical similarity could cause a false-positive result in one type of test and may also influence another test with a similar chemical principle. A radioimmunoassay cannot confirm enzyme immunoassay results, since the chemical properties responsible for antibody binding may affect the antibodies in both tests similarly. Likewise, two similar GC columns such as 1% and 5% phenyl-methylsilicone (DB-1 and DB-5) would not serve to confirm one another, because the polarities of the two liquid phases and hence, the elution orders of most drugs are similar.

A combination of less specific chromatographic procedures (e.g., immunoassay, GC-NPD/ECD, or HPLC/MS) can be used to confirm screening results. A second chromatographic method based on a different chemical principle may be used to confirm a presumptive finding from a chromatographic screening test. Derivatization of the presumptively identified drug can alter its chromatographic behavior sufficiently to permit confirmation by reanalysis in the same chromatographic system. Some screening procedures, such as GC/MS, identify specific compounds. Even here, a second test on a separate aliquot should be performed to "verify" the analyte and ensure that no human error in sample handling or analyses has occurred. Re-injection of the same extract would not be sufficient. An exception to this rule would be limited sample volume precluding repeat analyses.

In post-mortem toxicology, confirmation tests are often applied to specimens other than the one used for screening. By employing a quantitative confirmatory method, the analyte is simultaneously confirmed and quantified. For example, a presumptive finding of THC-COOH in urine by immunoassay may be confirmed by a quantitative MS procedure applied to blood. Forensic toxicology laboratories must have specific criteria for the reporting of positive findings. These criteria may be dependent on the performance of the analytical methods or adhering to guidelines for best practice [71].

7.4.5.2 Gas Chromatography-Mass Spectrometry

GC/MS is generally accepted as unequivocal identification for most drugs, providing confirmatory information when performed correctly. However, GC/MS assays can be conducted in many ways, depending on the specific requirements and use of the results. Pharmacokinetic studies generally employ chemical ionization with single-ion monitoring to obtain optimum sensitivity. In such studies, the target drug is expected to be present, so criteria for identification need not be as rigorous, but single-ion monitoring is not usually considered sufficient for forensic purposes. GC/MS methods for the confirmation of illegal drugs of abuse in urine most often use EI ionization and multiple-ion monitoring to obtain conclusive results. The more traditional MS identification criterion calls for matching RTs and full-scan EI mass spectra of the unknown with a standard. Large transferable EI mass spectra libraries exist and are available for library searching of acquired spectra from any instruments [65]. Guidelines now exist for the mass spectral identification of compounds in forensic toxicology [72, 73].

Mass spectrometry in conjunction with chromatographic separation is an internationally accepted combination for identification of an analyte in the extract. To enable compound identification using chromatography, tolerances for acceptable RTs for compounds of interest for both gas and liquid chromatography must be defined. For GC/MS procedures, the chromatographic separation should be carried out using capillary columns. For LC/MS procedures, the chromatographic separation can be performed using any suitable LC column. In either case, the minimum acceptable RT for the analyte(s) under examination should be at least twice the retention time corresponding to the void volume of the column. The RT or relative retention time (RRT) of the analyte in the sample extract must match that of the contemporaneous standard within a specified window after taking into consideration the resolving power of the chromatographic system.

Forensic samples can be analyzed by full-scan data acquisition or by selected ion monitoring. A good-quality, full-scan mass spectrum that matches a reference spectrum clearly constitutes a more definitive identification than ion current profiles of a few selected ions at the correct RT.

Many factors can impact the specificity of GC/MS screening; these include the choice of internal standard, selectivity of the extraction procedure, choice of derivative (where appropriate), efficiency of the GS separation, method of ionization, mass spectrum ions to be monitored, and signal-to-noise ratio of the detected ions [74]. Using GC/MS in the scanning mode, as both a screening and a definitive identification methodology, has become quite common. If the drug is an unknown, full-scan mode is the method of choice. Further comparison of the unknown's full mass spectrum with reference spectra will be necessary. Mass spectra are tentatively identified by a computerized library search and visually compared by an experienced analyst [75, 76]. GC/MS with selected ion monitoring (GC/MS-SIM) is commonly used to confirm the presence of drugs and/or metabolites in post-mortem samples. A well-designed assay, involving the selected ion monitoring of three or more abundant and structurally diagnostic ions, combined with specific requirements for the analyte's RT relative to a suitable internal standard or calibrator, is regarded as a reliable identification. Even fewer ions can provide an acceptable identification if the assay employs a highly selective extraction procedure or selective mode of ionization, such as ammonia chemical ionization.

GC/MS-SIM assays are extremely useful to confirm or exclude the presence of a suspected analyte that may have been indicated by history or screening results. However, target compound analyses such as GC/MS-SIM will detect, or exclude, only a limited number of related chemical compounds or classes of drugs. A reference standard and control materials of the target analyte must be analyzed within the same batch. Selected ion monitoring typically provides signal intensities that are 10- to 100-fold greater than those from full-scan analysis performed on quadrupole instruments. SIM analyses are therefore better adapted for quantitative measurements. Selected ion monitoring is generally less susceptible to interferences from co-eluting compounds than an assay employing full-scan recording. However, unlike full-scan spectral acquisition, a selected ion monitoring assay will not detect unsuspected drugs that may be of toxicological significance.

Standards adopted for conclusive drug identification include (1) the appearance of the monitored ions at a correct RT and (2) acceptable intensity ratios among those ions. The RT and ion intensity ratios observed in the test sample are compared with those established from the calibrator(s) containing the target analyte, at a suitable concentration, incorporated in the same analytical batch.

7.4.5.3 Potential Problems with GC/MS Analyses

Several problems may be encountered in GC/MS analysis. The mass spectral library may give erroneous identifications when concentrations near the detection limit are analyzed, when chromatographically interfering substances are present, or when isomers are analyzed. Even MS with a full fragmentation pattern may not provide adequate confirmation, either because several drugs have very similar fragmentation patterns, such as the barbiturates, for example, or because the drug may exhibit only one major peak consisting of a low-mass fragment ion in its mass spectrum, such as the tricyclic antidepressants.

When using the SIM mode, a considerable gain in GC/MS sensitivity can be achieved by focusing on the most abundant ion and two or more other characteristic ions. However, many illegal drugs or metabolites (and numerous other commonly used drugs, e.g., antihistamines, local anesthetics, some beta-blocking agents, etc.) have similar El mass spectra, showing a common base peak and weak molecular ion signals. Many elute over a wide range of RTs; others may have closely related retention indices.

The complexity of biological matrices encountered in post-mortem cases, such as "blood," tissues, gastric contents, and hair/nails, necessitates well-designed, and often multistep, sample treatment procedures [77]. This is especially true when utilizing procedures based on physicochemical properties of drug/metabolites. Suitable sample preparation is the most important prerequisite in the GC/MS of typical post-mortem samples. It involves isolation and if necessary, cleavage of conjugates and/or derivatization of the drugs and their metabolites. Derivatization steps are necessary if relatively polar compounds such as metabolites are to be screened or confirmed.

7.4.5.4 Liquid Chromatography-Mass Spectrometry

LC/MS is arguably the most important technique in forensic toxicology [24, 78–83]. LC/MS has become increasingly popular both for screening purposes and for sensitive and specific confirmation analyses. Many drugs cannot be analyzed by GC/MS because they are either thermolabile or too polar or insufficiently volatile to chromatograph well, if at all. In contrast, virtually any drug can be analyzed by LC/MS after development of a suitable method. Other than the issue of cost, the only disadvantage of LC over GC is that LC separations usually require more development time than GC separations. As with GC/MS, so-called "hyphenated" techniques may be used, such as LC/MS/MS. Tandem MS-MS instruments have the enormous advantage of being able to provide a much higher degree of specificity than LC/MS alone. The first mass spectrometer in the LC/MS/MS system generates a conventional mass spectrum. One specific mass is then allowed to pass through into a separate collision cell, where it can be ionized further. Either the entire mass spectrum of that chosen ion may be displayed or a single ion isolated in SIM mode. Tandem MS techniques such as LC/MS/MS are particularly useful for post-mortem forensic work because they minimize interference from endogenous compounds such as putrefactive products. LC/MS/MS-TOF (time-of-flight) or high-resolution accurate mass instruments (LC/HRMS) offer a further degree of specificity because of the increased specificity imparted by the medium to high mass resolution of TOF instruments. The advantage of accurate mass instruments is the selective power of measuring m/z at four or five decimal places based on the empirical formula of a particular compound. For example, in LC/HRMS, the pseudo molecular ion (M+H) of methadone is 310.2165 (formula C27H21NO), and the M+H of fluoxetine is also 310.1413 (formula C17H18F3NO). "Low-resolution" MS would detect an M+H of 310 for either drug. The corresponding accurate masses for M+H (310.2165 and 310.1413, respectively) are distinguishable due to the high resolution of the instrument. However, there are issues if the empirical formula of two drugs is the same, as this results in identical accurate mass values. In this instance, RT separation or utilization of accurate mass fragmentation by introducing collision energy would be needed to distinguish between the two drugs [84]. Of course, the major drawbacks of LC/MS/MS and LC/MS/MS-TOF instruments are considerably increased cost and complexity of operation, often requiring a dedicated operator. Having stated that, the development of a method for a particular analyte is generally easier with LC/MS than with GC/MS because standards with reference compounds can be directly injected and calibration curves can readily be constructed. A special feature that the operator must keep in mind is that a change in pH to adjust the chromatography will also affect the charge of the compounds at the time for ionization and hence, influence the mass spectrometric detection.

Different interface systems are available. The most utilized alternative is atmospheric pressure-positive electrospray ionization (ESI), and several applications in forensic toxicology with this methodology have been reported. Alternatively, atmospheric pressure-chemical ionization (APCI) can be used. Both these variants of LC/MS instrumentation cover a wider spectrum of polar and nonpolar drugs than GC/MS analysis can offer, and ESI also allows the analysis of molecules with higher masses. Many new broad screen applications for LC/MS that have been reported in clinical toxicology can be applied to forensic laboratories [61, 85, 86]. Newer applications of LC/MS include paper MS, in which the biofluid sample is spotted onto a paper substrate, and extraction and ionization occur directly from the paper without any need for additional sample preparation [87].

ADVANTAGES AND DISADVANTAGES OF GC/MS COMPARED WITH LC/MS [84]

Advantages

- Ionization by GC/MS is not as affected by matrix components as LC/MS techniques
- GC/MS libraries are transferable between different systems, but LC/MS libraries generally are not
- More published methods using GC/MS
- GC/MS is generally cheaper than LC/MS

Disadvantages

- GC/MS is not applicable to as many compounds as LC/MS
- GC/MS may require derivatization to facilitate chromatography and/or mass spectral performance
- GC/MS cannot be coupled to UV to provide additional identification power
- GC/MS is generally a less sensitive technique than LC/MS (unless GC/MS/MS is used)

GC: Gas chromatography
LC: Liquid chromatography
MS: Mass spectrometry
MS/MS: Tandem mass spectrometry
UV: Ultraviolet light detectors or multi-wavelength detectors

7.4.6 Quantification of Drugs and Poisons

> When you can measure what you are speaking about and express it in numbers, you know something about it; but when you cannot express it in numbers, your knowledge is of meagre and unsatisfactory kind.
>
> **Lord Kelvin (1824–1907)**

Screening and confirmation (qualitative) tests establish the presence of a specific substance; quantitative tests measure the amount of that substance in a particular specimen. Qualitative information alone can demonstrate that the deceased was exposed to the substance before death and may even enable the toxicologist to offer an opinion regarding the ante-mortem interval in which the exposure probably took place. However, quantitative information is often required to form an opinion on whether or not the exposure was sufficient to cause behavioral toxicity or death. Drug concentrations in post-mortem tissues, or fluids, must be related to reference values derived from other cases [88].

7.4.6.1 What Should Be Quantified?

Substances should be quantified only when necessary for interpretation. Most quantitative assays are separate, labor-intensive procedures that measure only one drug or group of similar compounds. Quantifying substances that, by their nature, could have no conceivable bearing on the issues of the case is a waste of time and resources. For example, drugs with no psychoactivity, such as acetaminophen, should not be quantified in a motor vehicle accident driver victim, while diphenhydramine, an antihistamine with sedative side effects, should. On the other hand, if the victim was a passenger, diphenhydramine would not require quantification. In general, substances that can cause behavioral toxicity should be quantified. In most natural deaths, it is important to know that the concentration of a prescribed or therapeutic drug is not excessive. Semi-quantitative information, derived from blood screening tests, is often sufficient to make the assessment. Only if the concentration estimate indicates an excessive amount would a quantitative assay be required. Poisons such as carbon monoxide, cyanide, and heavy metals should always be quantified in appropriate specimens. Tests for ethanol usually yield both qualitative and quantitative data, which should be reported if higher than the laboratory's administrative cut-off (usually 0.01%).

Cocaine should always be quantified. Its concentration is usually important, and its instability in storage may prevent subsequent analysis if it is not quantified soon after detection. Other drugs or poisons that are unstable in storage should be quantified before their decomposition renders the analysis unreliable. In a case that is pending the outcome of toxicology testing, any detected drugs or poisons and their metabolites should be quantified, unless it is clear from the circumstances of the case that a particular substance did not play a role in the cause or manner of death. When resuscitation has been attempted, lidocaine, morphine, and atropine may be detected in post-mortem blood. Unless a medication error is suspected, or the quantity appears to be excessive, it is not necessary to quantify them. Nor is there any need to quantify caffeine and nicotine, unless toxicity is suspected or screening tests indicate that an abnormally large amount of either is present. In most cases, a drug's metabolites are just as important to quantify as the parent compound. The ratio of parent drug to its metabolite often indicates the state of pharmacokinetics in the individual case. For example, a ratio greater than 1 for amitriptyline/nortriptyline may indicate an acute ingestion or short interval from ingestion to death, while a ratio of 0.3 in a propoxyphene/nor-propoxyphene case may indicate chronic exposure. Active or toxic metabolites of a drug or poison are always measured, but inactive metabolites may also be important. Their presence may shed light on the pattern of drug use. High concentrations of benzoylecgonine indicate accumulations from multiple doses. Low concentrations suggest that only a few doses were taken or that there has been a long interval since the last dose. Furthermore, there is some evidence that benzoylecgonine may be a vasoconstrictor, so it may contribute to the hypertensive effects of cocaine use.

There is currently debate regarding the quantification of novel psychoactive substances (NPS) for forensic toxicology [89] and what the minimum quantifiable amount of drug is in a matrix. If an established minimum quantifiable limit is agreed to by toxicologists for NPS, this may lead to laboratories having a uniform approach in dealing with these analyses, may provide results that are defensible in the court, and may provide the bulk of data for national and international comparison for these drugs [90]. However NPS are challenging in many ways for laboratories in terms of not only detection of the substance(s) and metabolites(s) but also how pharmacologically active they may be as well as the relative toxicity. Qualitative determination of these substances is therefore sufficient for routine forensic purposes.

7.4.6.2 Specimens for Quantification of Drugs and Poisons

The choice of the sample for quantitative analysis is very important. Often, it is sufficient to quantify drugs or poisons in blood only. If toxicity is not suspected, a blood quantification can verify that the drug was present and that its concentration was consistent with therapeutic use. Also, when a drug concentration is clearly in the lethal range, and poisoning or overdose is suspected, a blood determination may be sufficient. It may not be necessary to quantify brain morphine levels in an intravenous heroin user, found dead with syringe, tourniquet, and "cooker" present, with autopsy evidence of pulmonary edema and a high concentration of morphine in the blood, to support a conclusion that death was caused by a heroin overdose. Likewise, a 15 mg/L blood amitriptyline concentration, in a case accompanied by a suicide note, is sufficient to define overt toxicity regardless of potential post-mortem diffusion. Carbon monoxide should be measured in blood, its site of action. Other specimens are likely to give negative results. One exception, not related to drug abuse, is the analysis of skeletal muscle specimens for carbon monoxide to assist in the differentiation between entrance and exit gunshot wounds.

Tissues that selectively take up a particular drug class may have a much higher concentration than that found in blood. For example, volatile anesthetics, cocaine, marijuana, tricyclic antidepressants, and other lipid-soluble substances are preferentially absorbed into the fatty tissues of the brain and liver, while digoxin and other cardiac glycosides are taken up by cardiac muscle.

7.4.6.3 The Toxicology Report

Individual cases should be reviewed periodically to assess the status of the investigation and the quality of the acquired data. Reassessment may suggest the need for additional tests. Before a report is issued, the entire case file must be reviewed to ensure that results are forensically acceptable and that sufficient data have been gathered to determine whether, and to what extent, drugs or poisons influenced the cause and manner of death. When testing has been completed, the toxicologist reviews the file one final time to ensure that nothing has been overlooked. In cases where the cause of death is not obvious, and determinations have been put on hold pending the results of toxicological testing, the toxicologist and pathologist together review the investigation, autopsy, and toxicology results. When both are satisfied that the toxicology results answer the questions pertinent to the case, a final toxicology report is issued. The need for communication and teamwork for an effective system cannot be overemphasized.

Once all tests have been completed, the laboratory will need to produce a report, which often, but not always, supplements a forensic autopsy report. The report must reference specific details of the deceased (Name, Date of Birth), the time and date of the collection of the specimens, the site of collection, and the time and date of delivery to the laboratory. The most important section, which contains the results, should be clear and unambiguous, describing the drug or poison in the specimen for which the measurement has been made, the concentration in standard units, and the analytical technique used.

It is imperative that the toxicologist considers the findings in consultation with the pathologist, especially in the case of a drug-related death. It has been established that if toxicologists make no comments on the findings, in many instances, neither do the subsequent pathologists or coroners/medical examiners make any comments in relation to the drugs detected [91]. Toxicologists should be more actively engaged in providing opinions on the possible role of drugs in deaths as well as highlighting probable adverse drug reactions rather than relying on others to identify the potential risks. However, this requires that the appropriate clinical and circumstantial information is made available to the toxicologist before they produce their report. Without this information, it is difficult to predict the consequences of toxicological results obtained in the laboratory.

ACKNOWLEDGMENTS

Much of this material has been updated since the last edition of this text – thanks to Hendrik Druid and W. Lee Hearn for their original and informative material.

NOTES

1. https://chemdata.nist.gov
2. www.chemspider.com/

REFERENCES

1. Bedford, P.J., Routine CT scan combined with preliminary examination as a new method in determining the need for autopsy. *Forensic Science, Medicine, and Pathology*, 2012. **8**(4): p. 390–394.
2. Winklhofer, S., E. Surer, G. Ampanozi, T. Ruder, P. Stolzmann, M. Elliott, A. Oestreich, T. Kraemer, M. Thali, H. Alkadhi, and W. Schweitzer, Post-mortem whole body computed tomography of opioid (heroin and methadone) fatalities: Frequent findings and comparison to autopsy. *European Radiology*, 2014. **24**(6): p. 1276–1282.
3. Leth, P., Computerized tomography used as a routine procedure at postmortem investigations. *American Journal of Forensic Medicine and Pathology*, 2009. **30**(3): p. 219–222.
4. Tracqui, A., P. Kintz, and P. Mangin, Systematic toxicological analysis using HPLC/DAD. *Journal of Forensic Sciences*, 1995. **40**(2): p. 254–262.
5. Polettini, A., A. Groppi, C. Vignali, and M. Montagna, Fully-automated systematic toxicological analysis of drugs, poisons, and metabolites in whole blood, urine, and plasma by gas chromatography-full scan mass spectrometry. *Journal of Chromatography B Biomedical Sciences and Applications*, 1998. **713**(1): p. 265–279.
6. Drummer, O.H., Chromatographic screening techniques in systematic toxicological analysis. *Journal of Chromatography B Biomedical Sciences and Applications*, 1999. **733**(1–2): p. 27–45.
7. Maurer, H.H., Systematic toxicological analysis procedures for acidic drugs and/or metabolites relevant to clinical and forensic toxicology and/or doping control. *Journal of Chromatography B*, 1999. **733**(1–2): p. 3–25.
8. Polettini, A., Systematic toxicological analysis of drugs and poisons in biosamples by hyphenated chromatographic and spectroscopic techniques. *Journal of Chromatography B Biomedical Sciences and Applications*, 1999. **733**(1–2): p. 47–63.
9. Stimpfl, T., W. Demuth, K. Varmuza, and W. Vycudilik, Systematic toxicological analysis: Computer-assisted identification of poisons in biological materials. *Journal of Chromatography B: Analytical Technologies in the Biomedical and Life Sciences*, 2003. **789**(1): p. 3–7.

10. Jansen, R., G. Lachatre, and P. Marquet, LC-MS/MS systematic toxicological analysis: Comparison of MS/MS spectra obtained with different instruments and settings. *Clinical Biochemistry*, 2005. **38**(4): p. 362–372.
11. Lee, H.K., C.S. Ho, Y.P.H. Iu, P.S.J. Lai, C.C. Shek, Y.-C. Lo, H.B. Klinke, and M. Wood, Development of a broad toxicological screening technique for urine using ultra-performance liquid chromatography and time-of-flight mass spectrometry. *Analytica Chimica Acta*, 2009. **649**(1): p. 80–90.
12. Peters, F.T., O. Drvarov, S. Lottner, A. Spellmeier, K. Rieger, W.E. Haefeli, and H.H. Maurer, A systematic comparison of four different workup procedures for systematic toxicological analysis of urine samples using gas chromatography-mass spectrometry. *Analytical and Bioanalytical Chemistry*, 2009. **393**(2): p. 735–745.
13. Broecker, S., F. Pragst, A. Bakdash, S. Herre, and M. Tsokos, Combined use of liquid chromatography-hybrid quadrupole time-of-flight mass spectrometry (LC-QTOF-MS) and high performance liquid chromatography with photodiode array detector (HPLC-DAD) in systematic toxicological analysis. *Forensic Science International*, 2011. **212**(1–3): p. 215–226.
14. Gottzein, A.K., F. Musshoff, and B. Madea, Systematic toxicological analysis revealing a rare case of captan ingestion. *Journal of Forensic Sciences*, 2013. **58**(4): p. 1099–103.
15. Maurer, H.H., What is the future of (ultra) high performance liquid chromatography coupled to low and high resolution mass spectrometry for toxicological drug screening? *Journal of Chromatography. Part A*, 2013. **1292**: p. 19–24.
16. Arnhard, K., A. Gottschall, F. Pitterl, and H. Oberacher, Applying 'sequential windowed acquisition of all theoretical fragment ion mass spectra' (SWATH) for systematic toxicological analysis with liquid chromatography-high-resolution tandem mass spectrometry. *Analytical and Bioanalytical Chemistry*, 2015. **407**(2): p. 405–14.
17. Grapp, M., H.H. Maurer, and H. Desel, Systematic forensic toxicological analysis by GC-MS in serum using automated mass spectral deconvolution and identification system. *Drug Testing and Analysis*, 2016. **8**(8): p. 816–25.
18. Grapp, M., C. Kaufmann, F. Streit, and L. Binder, Systematic forensic toxicological analysis by liquid-chromatograph y-quadrupole-time-of-flight mass spectrometry in serum and comparison to gas chromatography-mass spectrometry. *Forensic Science International*, 2018. **287**: p. 63–73.
19. Seither, J.Z., R. Hindle, L.E. Arroyo-Mora, and A.P. DeCaprio, Systematic analysis of novel psychoactive substances. I. Development of a compound database and HRMS spectral library. *Forensic Chemistry*, 2018. **9**: p. 12–20.
20. Drummer, O.H. and J. Gerostamoulos, Postmortem drug analysis: Analytical and toxicological aspects. *Therapeutic Drug Monitoring*, 2002. **24**(2): p. 199–209.
21. Skopp, G., Postmortem toxicology. *Forensic Science, Medicine, and Pathology*, 2010. **6**(4): p. 314–325
22. Drummer, O.H. and D. Gerostamoulos, *Forensic drug analysis*. 2013, London: Future Science Ltd.
23. Osselton, M.M. and A.C. Widdop, *Clarke's analysis of drugs and poisons: In pharmaceuticals, body fluids and postmortem material*. A.C. Moffat, et al., Editors. 2011, London: Pharmaceutical Press. 2 vols.
24. Maurer, H.H., Multi-analyte procedures for screening for and quantification of drugs in blood, plasma, or serum by liquid chromatography-single stage or tandem mass spectrometry (LC-MS or LC-MS/MS) relevant to clinical and forensic toxicology. *Clinical Biochemistry*, 2005. **38**(4): p. 310–318.
25. Montenarh, D., M. Hopf, S. Warth, H.H. Maurer, P. Schmidt, and A.H. Ewald, A simple extraction and LC-MS/MS approach for the screening and identification of over 100 analytes in eight different matrices. *Drug Testing and Analysis*, 2015. **7**(3): p. 214–240.
26. Mut, L., T. Grobosch, T. Binscheck-Domaß, and W. Frenzel, Toxicological screening of human plasma by on-line SPE-HPLC-DAD: Identification and quantification of basic drugs and metabolites. *Biomedical Chromatography*, 2015. **29**(6): p. 935–952.
27. Patteet, L., D. Cappelle, K.E. Maudens, C.L. Crunelle, B. Sabbe, and H. Neels, Advances in detection of antipsychotics in biological matrices. *Clinica Chimica Acta*, 2015. **441**: p. 11–22.
28. Remane, D., D.K. Wissenbach, and F.T. Peters, Recent advances of liquid chromatography–(tandem) mass spectrometry in clinical and forensic toxicology—An update. *Clinical Biochemistry*, 2016. **49**(13): p. 1051–1071.
29. Curry, A.S., *Analytical methods in human toxicology*. 1985, Weinheim: Verlag Chemie.
30. Dart, R.C., *Medical toxicology*. 3rd ed. 2004, Philadelphia, PA: Lippincott, Williams & Wilkins. xxix, 1914 p.
31. Tagliaro, F., G. Lubli, S. Ghielmi, D. Franchi, and M. Marigo, Chromatographic methods for blood alcohol determination. *Journal of Chromatography*, 1992. **580**(1–2): p. 161–90.
32. Garriott, J.C. and E.H. Aguayo, *Garriott's medicolegal aspects of alcohol*. 5th ed. 2008, Tucson, AZ: Lawyers & Judges Pub. Co. x, 534 p.
33. Heesun, C. and C. Sanggil, Overview of forensic toxicology, yesterday, today and in the future. *Current Pharmaceutical Design*, 2017. **23**(36): p. 5429–5436.
34. Logan, B.K.a.R.-M., and D. Jeri, Forensic toxicology: Scope, challenges, future directions and needs, in *Forensic science current issues, future directions*, S. American Academy of Forensic and D.H. Ubelaker, Editors. 2012, Chichester, West Sussex: Wiley-Blackwell.
35. Frank, T.P., K.W. Dirk, B.F. Paolo, M. Emilia, and P. Simona, Method development in forensic toxicology. *Current Pharmaceutical Design*, 2017. **23**(36): p. 5455–5467.
36. Rosano, T.G., M. Wood, and T.A. Swift, Postmortem drug screening by non-targeted and targeted ultra-performance liquid chromatography-mass spectrometry technology. *Journal of Analytical Toxicology*, 2011. **35**(7): p. 411–23.
37. McLaughlin, P., P.D. Maskell, D. Pounder, and D. Osselton, Use of the randox evidence investigator immunoassay system for near-body drug screening during post-mortem examination in 261 forensic cases. *Forensic Science International*, 2019. **294**: p. 211–215.
38. Winborn, J. and S. Kerrigan, Desomorphine screening using commercial enzyme-linked immunosorbent assays. *Journal of Analytical Toxicology*, 2017. **41**(5): p. 455–460.
39. Labay, L.M., C.P. Bitting, K.M. Legg, and B.K. Logan, The determination of insulin overdose in postmortem investigations. *Academic Forensic Pathology*, 2016. **6**(2): p. 174–183.
40. Tominaga, M., T. Michiue, and H. Maeda, Evaluation of the on-site immunoassay drug-screening device Triage-TOX in routine forensic autopsy. *Legal Medicine*, 2015. **17**(6): p. 499–502.
41. Milone, M.C., Laboratory testing for prescription opioids. *Journal of Medical Toxicology*, 2012. **8**(4): p. 408–416.

42. Tominaga, M., T. Michiue, O. Inamori-Kawamoto, A.M. Hishmat, S. Oritani, M. Takama, T. Ishikawa, and H. Maeda, Efficacy of drug screening in forensic autopsy: Retrospective investigation of routine toxicological findings. *Legal Medicine*, 2015. **17**(3): p. 172–176.
43. Köhler, K.M., R. Hammer, K. Riedy, V. Auwärter, and M.A. Neukamm, Evaluation of CEDIA and DRI drugs of abuse immunoassays for urine screening on a Thermo Indiko Plus Analyzer. *Journal of Clinical Laboratory Analysis*, 2017. **31**(1). e22021.
44. Sundström, M., A.W. Jones, and I. Ojanperä, Utility of urinary ethyl glucuronide analysis in post-mortem toxicology when investigating alcohol-related deaths. *Forensic Science International*, 2014. **241**: p. 178–182.
45. Regester, L.E., J.D. Chmiel, J.M. Holler, S.P. Vorce, B. Levine, and T.Z. Bosy, Determination of designer drug cross-reactivity on five commercial immunoassay screening kits. *Journal of Analytical Toxicology*, 2014. **39**(2): p. 144–151.
46. Ellefsen, K.N., M. Concheiro, and M.A. Huestis, Synthetic cathinone pharmacokinetics, analytical methods, and toxicological findings from human performance and postmortem cases. *Drug Metabolism Reviews*, 2016. **48**(2): p. 237–265.
47. Hino, Y., I. Ojanperä, I. Rasanen, and E. Vuori, Performance of immunoassays in screening for opiates, cannabinoids and amphetamines in post-mortem blood. *Forensic Science International (Online)*, 2003. **131**(2–3): p. 148–155.
48. Barrett, C., C. Good, and C. Moore, Comparison of point-of-collection screening of drugs of abuse in oral fluid with a laboratory-based urine screen. *Forensic Science International*, 2001. **122**(2–3): p. 163–166.
49. Townsend, S., L. Fanning, and R. O'Kennedy, Salivary analysis of drugs—Potential and difficulties. *Analytical Letters*, 2008. **41**(6): p. 925–948.
50. Kintz, P., A. Salomone, and M. Vincenti, *Hair analysis in clinical and forensic toxicology*. 2015, Boston, MA: Elsevier.
51. Rutty, G.N. and SpringerLink, *Essentials of autopsy practice: Reviews, updates, and advances*. 2017, Cham, Switzerland: Springer.
52. Saitman, A., H.-D. Park, and R.L. Fitzgerald, False-positive interferences of common urine drug screen immunoassays: A review. *Journal of Analytical Toxicology*, 2014. **38**(7): p. 387–396.
53. Brown, N.W., Toxicology in clinical laboratories: Challenging times. *British Journal of Biomedical Science*, 2017. 74(3): p. 110–120.
54. Cox, R.A., J.A. Crifasi, R.E. Dickey, S.C. Ketzler, and G.L. Pshak, A single-step extraction for screening whole blood for basic drugs by capillary GC/NPD. *Journal of Analytical Toxicology*, 1989. **13**(4): p. 224–8.
55. Chen, X.H., J.P. Franke, J. Wijsbeek, and R.A. de Zeeuw, Isolation of acidic, neutral, and basic drugs from whole blood using a single mixed-mode solid-phase extraction column. *Journal of Analytical Toxicology*, 1992. **16**(6): p. 351–5.
56. Drummer, O.H., S. Horomidis, S. Kourtis, M.L. Syrjanen, and P. Tippett, Capillary gas chromatographic drug screen for use in forensic toxicology. *Journal of Analytical Toxicology*, 1994. **18**(3): p. 134–8.
57. Watts, V.W. and T.F. Simonick, Screening of basic drugs in biological samples using dual column capillary chromatography and nitrogen-phosphorus detectors. *Journal of Analytical Toxicology*, 1986. **10**(5): p. 198–204.
58. Chen, X.H., J.P. Franke, J. Wijsbeek, and R.A. de Zeeuw, Determination of basic drugs extracted from biological matrices by means of solid-phase extraction and wide-bore capillary gas chromatography with nitrogen-phosphorus detection. *Journal of Analytical Toxicology*, 1994. **18**(3): p. 150–3.
59. Di Rago, M., E. Saar, L.N. Rodda, S. Turfus, A. Kotsos, D. Gerostamoulos, and O.H. Drummer, Fast targeted analysis of 132 acidic and neutral drugs and poisons in whole blood using LC–MS/MS. *Forensic Science International*, 2014. **243**: p. 35–43.
60. Moffat, A.C., M.D. Osselton, B. Widdop, and J. Watts, *Clarke's analysis of drugs and poisons: In pharmaceuticals, body fluids and postmortem material*. 4th ed. 2011, London: Pharmaceutical Press. 2 vols.
61. Van Wijk, X.M.R., R. Goodnough, and J.M. Colby, Mass spectrometry in emergency toxicology: Current state and future applications. *Critical Reviews in Clinical Laboratory Sciences*, 2019. **56**(4): p. 1–14.
62. Maurer, H.H., Systematic toxicological analysis of drugs and their metabolites by gas chromatography—mass spectrometry. *Journal of Chromatography B: Biomedical Sciences and Applications*, 1992. **580**(1–2): p. 3–41.
63. Maurer, H.H., Identification and differentiation of barbiturates, other sedative-hypnotics and their metabolites in urine integrated in a general screening procedure using computerized gas chromatography-mass spectrometry. *Journal of Chromatography*, 1990. **530**(2): p. 307–26.
64. Gibb, R.P., H. Cockerham, G.A. Goldfogel, G.M. Lawson, and V.A. Raisys, Substance abuse testing of urine by GC/MS in scanning mode evaluated by proficiency studies, TLC/GC, and EMIT. *Journal of Forensic Sciences*, 1993. **38**(1): p. 124–33.
65. Maurer, H., K. Pfleger, and A. Weber, *Mass spectral and GC data of drugs, poisons, pesticides, pollutants, and their metabolites*, 4th edition. 2017.
66. Milman, B.L., Towards a full reference library of MS(n) spectra. Testing of a library containing 3126 MS2 spectra of 1743 compounds. *Rapid Communications in Mass Spectrometry*, 2005. **19**(19): p. 2833–9.
67. Baumann, C., M.A. Cintora, M. Eichler, E. Lifante, M. Cooke, A. Przyborowska, and J.M. Halket, A library of atmospheric pressure ionization daughter ion mass spectra based on wideband excitation in an ion trap mass spectrometer. *Rapid Communications in Mass Spectrometry*, 2000. **14**(5): p. 349–56.
68. Dresen, S., J. Kempf, and W. Weinmann, Electrospray-ionization MS/MS library of drugs as database for method development and drug identification. *Forensic Science International*, 2006. **161**(2–3): p. 86–91.
69. Gergov, M., W. Weinmann, J. Meriluoto, J. Uusitalo, and I. Ojanpera, Comparison of product ion spectra obtained by liquid chromatography/triple-quadrupole mass spectrometry for library search. *Rapid Communications in Mass Spectrometry*, 2004. **18**(10): p. 1039–46.
70. Marquet, P., F. Saint-Marcoux, T.N. Gamble, and J.C. Leblanc, Comparison of a preliminary procedure for the general unknown screening of drugs and toxic compounds using a quadrupole-linear ion-trap mass spectrometer with a liquid chromatography-mass spectrometry reference technique. *Journal of Chromatography B*, 2003. **789**(1): p. 9–18.
71. LeBeau, M., W. Andollo, W.L. Hearn, R. Baselt, E. Cone, B. Finkle, D. Fraser, A. Jenkins, J. Mayer, A. Negrusz, A. Poklis, H.C. Walls, L. Raymon, M. Robertson, and J. Saady,

Recommendations for toxicological investigations of drug-facilitated sexual assaults. *Journal of Forensic Sciences*, 1999. **44**(1): p. 227–30.

72. Toxicology SAG, N.I.o.F.S., Australia, *MS identification guidelines in forensic toxicology - An Australian approach*, T. Bulletin, Editor. 2011, Melbourne, VIC: TIAFT. p. 52–55.
73. (GTFCh), S.o.T.a.F.C., *Guideline of GTFCh for quality assurance in forensic-toxicological investigations*, in *Toxichem Krimtech*. 2018, Germany: Society of Toxicological and Forensic Chemistry (GTFCh). p. 2–7.
74. Foltz, J.C., GC/MS analysis of body fluids for drugs of abuse, in *Forensic applications of mass spectrometry*, J. Yinon, Editor. 1995, Boca Raton, FL: CRC Press.
75. Maurer, H.H., Systematic toxicological analysis of drugs and their metabolites by gas chromatography-mass spectrometry. *Journal of Chromatography*, 1992. **580**(1–2): p. 3–41.
76. Moffat, A.C., *Clarke's analysis of drugs and poisons*. 4th ed. 2011, Pharmaceutical Press.
77. Bogusz, M., J. Wijsbeek, J.P. Franke, R.A. de Zeeuw, and J. Gierz, Impact of biological matrix, drug concentration, and method of isolation on detectability and variability of retention index values in gas chromatography. *Journal of Analytical Toxicology*, 1985. **9**(2): p. 49–54.
78. Polettini, A., *Applications of LC-MS in toxicology*. 2006, London: Pharmaceutical Press.
79. Peters, F.T., Recent advances of liquid chromatography–(tandem) mass spectrometry in clinical and forensic toxicology. *Clinical Biochemistry*, 2011. **44**(1): p. 54–65.
80. Maurer, H.H., Current role of liquid chromatography–mass spectrometry in clinical and forensic toxicology. *Analytical and Bioanalytical Chemistry*, 2007. **388**(7): p. 1315–1325.
81. Meyer, M.R., A.G. Helfer, and H.H. Maurer, Current position of high-resolution MS for drug quantification in clinical & forensic toxicology. *Bioanalysis*, 2014. **6**(17): p. 2275–2284.
82. Maurer, H.H., Mass spectrometry for research and application in therapeutic drug monitoring or clinical and forensic toxicology. *Therapeutic Drug Monitoring*, 2018. **40**(4): p. 389–393.
83. Mbughuni, M.M., P.J. Jannetto, and L.J. Langman, Mass spectrometry applications for toxicology. *EJIFCC*, 2016. **27**(4): p. 272–287.
84. Drummer, O.H. and D. Gerostamoulos, Forensic drug analysis. *Forensic Drug Analysis*, 2013. 1–125.
85. Thoren, K.L., J.M. Colby, S.B. Shugarts, A.H.B. Wu, and K.L. Lynch, Comparison of information-dependent acquisition on a tandem quadrupole TOF vs a triple quadrupole linear ion trap mass spectrometer for broad-spectrum drug screening. *Clinical Chemistry*, 2016. **62**(1): p. 170–178.
86. Whitman, J.D. and K.L. Lynch, Optimization and comparison of information-dependent acquisition (IDA) to sequential window acquisition of all theoretical fragment ion spectra (SWATH) for high-resolution mass spectrometry in clinical toxicology. *Clinical Chemistry*, 2019. **65**(7): p. 862–870.
87. McKenna, J., R. Jett, K. Shanks, and N.E. Manicke, Toxicological drug screening using paper spray high-resolution tandem mass spectrometry (HR-MS/MS). *Journal of Analytical Toxicology*, 2018. **42**(5): p. 300–310.
88. Baselt, R.C., *Disposition of toxic drugs and chemicals in man*. 2017.
89. Gerostamoulos, D., S. Elliott, H.C. Walls, F.T. Peters, M. Lynch, and O.H. Drummer, To measure or not to measure? That is the NPS question. *Journal of Analytical Toxicology*, 2016. **40**(4): p. 318–320.
90. Bogusz, M.J., Letter to the editor concerning the letter: Gerostamoulos D., Elliott S., Walls H.C., Peters F.T., Lynch M., Drummer O.H. (2016) to measure or not to measure? That is the NPS question. *Journal of Analytical Toxicology*, 2016. **40**(9): p. 767–768.
91. Pilgrim, J.L., D. Gerostamoulos, and O.H. Drummer, The role of toxicology interpretations in prevention of sudden death. *Forensic Science, Medicine, and Pathology*, 2012. **8**(3): p. 263–269.

7.5 QUALITY ASSURANCE IN POST-MORTEM TOXICOLOGY

7.5.1 Introduction

The essence of the post-mortem forensic analysis is to characterize a subject's biological tissue in terms of toxic chemical content. Based on the analytical result, an opinion can then be formed about the influence the toxic substance may have had on the subject. Since the result of any chemical analysis carries with it an uncertainty that is inherent in all measurements, an attempt must be made to control and measure the factors that influence that uncertainty. Only when these factors are measured and controlled can the analytical results be deemed reliable.

The quality assurance program is established to ensure the public that the results generated by the laboratory are reliable. This is crucial in a forensic toxicology laboratory, since the analytical results are closely scrutinized in a court of law, where truth and impartiality must be authenticated for the public good. A comprehensive quality assurance program will provide an expert witness with details concerning the measurable factors that affect the analytical result. These factors include personnel; the implements of measurement; the quality of materials used; the sample; the analytical method; the analytical instruments; data handling; and reporting.

The quality assurance program describes the steps taken to document the execution of the quality control procedures; the traceability of reported data to raw data; instrument status during analysis; quality control status; description of the analytical method; qualifications of the analysts; sample integrity and chain of custody; and the corrective actions undertaken for out-of-control situations. The quality control program sets forth the procedures to be taken to measure and control all sources of random and systematic errors so that limits of accuracy and precision can be established for all analytical methods. It also describes the technical operations undertaken to assure that the data obtained are within the established limits.

7.5.2 Accreditation

All modern laboratories are accredited to conduct post-mortem toxicology. Accreditation provides a means of determining, formally recognizing, and promoting that an organization is competent to perform specific types of assessment activities related to post-mortem toxicology. The activities for which accreditation is granted, which may not be all activities the facility performs, are described in a scope of accreditation. The International Laboratory Accreditation Cooperation (ILAC) is the international organization for accreditation bodies operating in accordance with ISO/IEC[1] standards and involved in the accreditation of conformity assessment bodies. Some countries are members of ILAC with the ultimate aim of developing and establishing a global network of accredited facilities that can be relied on to provide accurate results. Organizations such as the American Society of Crime Lab Directors (ASLCD), United Kingdom National External Quality Assessment Service (UK NEQAS), National Association of Testing Authorities (NATA, Australia), European Network of Forensic Science Institutes (ENSFI), and Hong Kong Accreditation Service (HKAS) are members of ILAC.

Each local accreditation organization will oversee the inspection and ultimately, the approval for laboratories to conduct post-mortem analytical testing in accordance with the requirements of the standard *ISO/IEC 17025 – General requirements for the competence of testing and calibration laboratories*. Laboratories will often have other forms of accreditation, which may be specific to modes of testing, e.g., urine or oral fluid for workplace or drugs and driver testing. The laboratory must maintain a quality framework approach, which includes the following sub-sections.

7.5.3 Standard Operating Procedures

The standard operating procedure is a written document that outlines in detail the mode of operation of the laboratory. It addresses the relationship of the laboratory with the institutions that it serves, the organizational structure of the laboratory, the quality assurance program, and the chemical hygiene plan. It must address every facet of the laboratory's operation and be available to all laboratory personnel and the public for consultation and review.

The standard operating procedures should address, as a minimum, the following aspects of the laboratory operation:

- Table of organization
- Personnel qualifications
- Precision implements
- Materials
- Sampling
- Analytical methods
- Instruments
- Data
- Reporting
- Proficiency program

The standard operating procedures manual is to be kept up to date and reviewed on a yearly basis to ensure that it typifies the actual operation and that it meets the needs of the laboratory. It is important to archive any old procedures, whether modified or omitted from the manual, so that they can be retrieved for future reference. The rest of this chapter is devoted to expanding on the subjects that are deemed indispensable in a comprehensive quality assurance program and standard operating procedure manual.

7.5.4 Personnel

The table of organization should be represented by means of a flowchart or schematic diagram. It should include all positions in order of hierarchy, names of persons occupying each position, and accountability of each individual.

A training folder for all individuals in the laboratory must be available with determined competencies and assessments. Evidence of court training and monitoring must also be included as a measure of competency for analysts who provide evidence in court. Analysts/examiners must have tertiary qualifications and/or demonstrated experience in the relevant discipline. The latest version of ISO/IEC 17025 has been revised to allow risk-based thinking, which has led to some reduction in prescriptive requirements and their replacement by performance-based outcomes; of note, there is greater flexibility in the requirements for processes, procedures, documented information, and organizational responsibilities.

7.5.5 Continuing Education

The laboratory director is responsible for providing access to continuing education for all employees. Continuing education is essential to the development of the laboratory in maintaining the reliability and integrity necessary in an ever-challenging field. New and more potent drugs are being continuously developed along with more advanced analytical techniques and equipment necessary for their detection and identification. Keeping abreast of the new information, be it pharmacological or analytical, is of the utmost importance for the subsistence of the forensic laboratory. Membership in professional forensic organizations, such as the American Academy of Forensic Sciences (AAFS), the Society of Forensic Toxicologists (SOFT), and the International Association of Forensic Toxicologists (TIAFT), provides the venue by which continuing education is not only available but relevant to the forensic laboratory. A training program must be available and include assessment of initial competency for all new staff in all applicable areas before such staff are authorized to work independently, including an evaluation of knowledge of existing literature and examination and identification of known and unknown materials.

7.5.6 Measuring Devices

Regardless of their simplicity, burets, pipettes, volumetric flasks, pipettors, pipettor-diluters, and the analytical balance are used in one way or another in nearly every chemical analysis. They impart the first sources of systematic errors in the analysis. For this reason, it is imperative that their quality, maintenance, and calibration be addressed in the standard operating procedures.

The selection and maintenance of chemical measuring devices and instruments is beyond the scope of this section but is covered in detail in textbooks of quantitative chemical analysis and instrumental analysis.

7.5.7 Reagents

Chemicals, reagents, solvents, and gases used in the process of executing the analytical procedures must meet minimum quality criteria as required by the analytical method. They should be properly stored, according to manufacturers' specifications or good chemical hygiene practice, in order to maintain their integrity and safety. Special care must be taken to record the receipt date and consider the stability of the reagent before use.

The determination of trace amounts of analytes in complex biological fluids or tissues often requires concentration of organic solvent extracts, which must be analyzed by very sensitive instruments. This circumstance creates a need for high-purity solvents, reagents, and gases to avoid introducing significant interferences during the analytical process. Commercially available solvents have been developed with special qualities applicable to specific purposes. Examples include solvents possessing low ultraviolet absorption, used in high-performance liquid chromatography and spectrophotometry, as well as solvents with negligible halogenated organic content, required for electron capture detectors or negative ion chemical ionization mass spectrometry. A post-mortem toxicology laboratory should procure the highest quality of reagent possible to minimize the potential for interferences with its analytical methods. The ability of newer instruments such as liquid chromatography-quadrupole time-of-flight mass spectrometry (LC/MS QTOF) means that sub-nanogram concentrations of drugs can now be routinely measured. Laboratories must ensure that any cross contamination is reduced or eliminated by segregating different analyses. For example, the analysis of drugs in hair should be isolated from the main toxicology laboratory to avoid any possible laboratory contamination. A different balance should be used from one that is used to weigh out drug stocks. Good laboratory practice is essential to ensuring the validity of test results.

The use of inert, high-purity gases for gas-liquid chromatography (GC) has been an essential part of its operation since its inception as an analytical tool. The fragile nature of liquid phases in the presence of oxygen (air) at high temperatures and the development of very sensitive detectors such as nitrogen-phosphorus, electron capture, and mass spectrometers, among others, have made the gas quality a priority issue in the operation of the laboratory. Gases with 99.999% purity containing sub-part-per-million quantities of air, moisture, and organic compounds are readily available at moderate cost. There are also a variety of products designed to remove or "scrub" contaminants from the gas stream before their introduction into the instrument, which can be utilized if high-purity gases are not readily available. These gas scrubbers should be monitored periodically for proper operation as part of the standard operating procedures.

The preparation of reagents, buffers, and mixtures should be conducted according to the specific instructions in the procedures manual. A reagent log book containing the preparation instructions for the most common solutions provides a convenient way to record their preparation with traceable information such as date of preparation, preparer, stock reagent lot number, and expiration date. This information should always be included in the reagent flask label along with the identification of the solution, its concentration, and any applicable safety recommendation.

7.5.8 Reference Materials

The accuracy of any quantitative analytical procedure depends directly on the purity of the standard used for calibrating the method. Therefore, the analyst must ascertain that the standards, or reference materials, used to prepare the calibrators are chemically pure. New reference materials for novel psychoactive substances (NPS) are not easily obtained. The cost of maintaining such reference standards is also prohibitive. New approaches to the identification of substances without reference materials have been documented [1–3]; however, they have yet to be evaluated and accepted by courts.

7.5.9 Calibrators

Calibrators are materials with which the sample is compared in order to determine the concentration or other quantity. Methods known to have acceptable accuracy because physical or matrix effects are negligible may be calibrated with certified reference solutions. However, procedural constraints and complex matrix effects of biological samples make the use of certified reference solutions impossible in many routine methods. The calibrators selected for such methods must simulate the physical and chemical properties of the samples in order to compensate for matrix effects during analysis and to be sensitive to important changes in analytical error conditions.

Assay values assigned to calibrators must be sufficiently accurate for the intended use. The uncertainty interval for the assigned concentration value must be small compared with the analytical precision of the method to be calibrated. That is, the absolute error calculated for the assigned value using dimensional analysis must be smaller than the absolute error obtained when the calibrator is analyzed multiple times by the method.

In the forensic laboratory, three types of calibrators may be encountered. The first is the use of a reference standard solution as a calibrator when the method has no procedural constraints and matrix effects are virtually non-existent. Certified standard solutions for this type of method can be obtained commercially or prepared in the laboratory with reference materials. However, these are usually restricted to the most commonly encountered drugs, such as ethanol, cocaine, methamphetamine, delta-9-tetrahydrocannabinol, and others. This type of method, although rare in the forensic laboratory, can best be exemplified by the analysis of volatiles using headspace techniques with gas chromatography and the percent purity determination of drug exhibits using ultraviolet spectrometry.

The second type of calibrators includes those obtained from commercial sources as kits to be used in self-contained analytical systems. They are matrix specific and manufactured in bulk under strict quality control. They are carefully designed to perform a specific task under rigorously controlled conditions and are provided with lot numbers and expiration dates. Assays of this type include quantitative techniques by radioactive, enzymatic, and fluorescent immunoassays.

The last type of calibrators encountered in the forensic laboratory is of most concern because they assume the most uncertainty. They are usually employed in analytical assays involving multistep extractions, concentration, derivatization, and complex instruments of analysis and data reduction. These working standards must be prepared in the laboratory from pure reference materials, be diluted with blank sample matrix to resemble the biological sample, and remain accurate enough to convey a reliable measurement when a sample is compared with them [4]. For this reason, every effort should be made to ensure the quality of reference material, the proper maintenance of volumetric implements and balances, and the application of good analytical skills. The preparation of a calibrator, or working standard, begins with the preparation of a stock solution from the reference drug material. A water-soluble organic solvent that readily dissolves the drug material without adverse reaction is the solvent of choice. Solvents that are not water soluble can be used, but they require additional steps to remove the solvent when further dilutions are made into aqueous biological fluids. A concentration of 1 mg of the unionized form of the drug per milliliter of solvent is convenient and adequate for most drugs analyzed. To keep the uncertainty of the calibrator below the variance of the method, it is desirable to know the exact concentration of the stock standard to at least three significant figures. The solutions, stored in capped amber vials at −20 °C, can have long shelf lives if care is taken to allow the solutions to reach room temperature before opening, thus avoiding moisture condensation in the solution. The stability of these solutions must be established periodically.

7.5.9.1 Multilevel Calibration

The calibration scheme used for the purpose of carrying out quantifications of unknown specimens is done with the preparation of a calibration graph that includes a minimum of five to eight concentration levels (including a blank). Typically, but not always, a linear relationship is obtained for reliable and reproducible quantitation. The mathematical model that adequately describes the relationship between analyte concentration in the samples and response, however, is not always linear [4]. When the order of magnitude in a calibration curve is equal to one, ordinary least squares regression models can be used. However, this is not normally the case in analytical toxicology, given that most methods span two or three orders of magnitude, which can be associated with significant variability across the calibration range. It is recommended in these instances that the data should be mathematically transformed to a weighted least squares model (e.g., $1/x$ or $1/x^2$), such that the variances are accounted for in the calibration range [4, 5].

To control for the influence of matrix effects, it is recommended to add the same volume of working stock solution to each aliquot of biological matrix when preparing the calibrators. To do this, a fresh set of working stock solutions is prepared by serial dilutions from the stock solution. Mixtures of drugs and metabolites can also be included in the working stock solution sets. The calibration graph is obtained by plotting the detector response against the assigned concentration of analyte in the working standard. Chromatographic assays that use internal standards are calibrated by plotting the detector response ratio of analyte to internal standard against the assigned concentration of analyte in the working standard. Using the statistical method of linear regression, the straight line that best fits the points can be determined. The slope of the line and the y-intercept are used to calculate the quantity of analyte in an unknown sample based on its detector response. Figure 7.5.1 shows a representative calibration curve for the analysis of fentanyl. Some calibrations are inherently nonlinear, and therefore, it is acceptable to apply a quadratic curve fit rather than force a linear fit to data that is clearly not linear. It is up to the analyst, or as a matter of policy the laboratory, to determine when the degree of nonlinearity is clearly unacceptable. Furthermore, it is good practice for evaluation of the calibration to include reading each calibrator against the established curve. Most calibrators should read within ±20% of the target with perhaps a wider margin as the calibration approaches the origin.

7.5.9.2 Method of Additions

The method of additions is a very powerful calibration technique because the accuracy is independent of matrix effects. The technique requires that replicates of the specimen, instead of blank matrix, be fortified with the different levels of calibrators, along with an unspiked replicate of the specimen serving as the "blank." All the samples are analyzed by the analytical method as usual. A calibration graph is generated by plotting the detector response of the analyte (or response ratio if using internal standard) against the concentration of the calibrators and plotting the response of the unfortified specimen on the y-axis (x = 0). Using the statistical method of linear regression, the straight line that best fits the points is determined, and the absolute value of the x-intercept represents the calculated concentration of the specimen. Figure 7.5.2 shows the calculation of azide in blood by the method of additions.

A disadvantage encountered in forensic analysis when using the method of additions is the requirement that multiple aliquots of the specimen be used when forensic samples are inherently limited in size. The use of this method of calibration, therefore, should be limited to situations where a rare analysis is being considered, when controls are not available, or when dealing with a particularly difficult matrix (e.g., liver).

7.5.9.3 Internal Standards

A suitable internal standard should be used in chromatographic assays. The internal standard can be defined as a substance that is added to all samples (specimens, standards, and controls) in a given assay before processing begins to correct for the many variations that occur in the manipulation of the samples during the entire analysis. Systematic errors affecting the quantity of analyte isolated from the sample will also affect the quantity of the internal standard in the same proportion. Therefore, the ratio of analyte to internal standard at the beginning of the procedure will remain unchanged throughout. For this concept to hold true, the internal standard must comply with certain qualifications. First, the internal standard must have chemical and physical characteristics very similar to those of the analyte

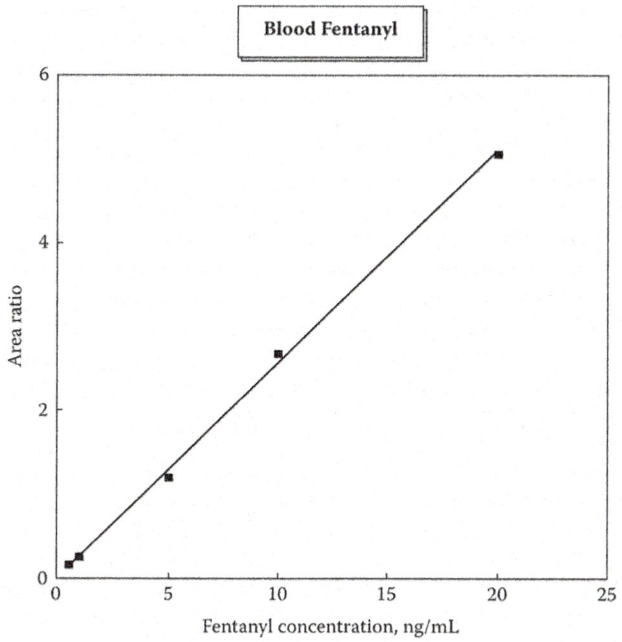

FIGURE 7.5.1 Multilevel calibration.

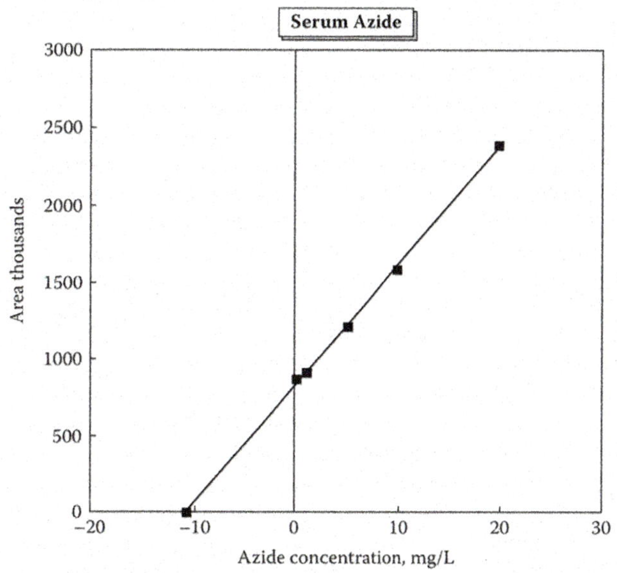

FIGURE 7.5.2 Calibration by method of additions.

of interest. This quality ensures that extraction partition coefficients, formation of derivatives, chromatographic characteristics, and detector response are similar enough not to alter their weight ratio significantly. A compound such as difluorococaine, for example, is not a good internal standard choice for cocaine because its enhanced lipophilicity imparts a very different extraction partition ratio, a different chromatographic characteristic, and a dissimilar response to a nitrogen-phosphorus detector. A compound such as propylbenzoylecgonine, an analogue of cocaine containing a propyl ester instead of a methyl ester, is chemically and physically more satisfactory.

From the point of view of extraction and derivatization properties, the most appropriate internal standard is an analogue of the analyte that has been labeled with a stable isotope. These substances have identical chemical and physical characteristics to the analyte, so their weight ratio is not affected during the analysis.

Isotopically labeled compounds may contain the nonlabeled compound as an impurity, or their mass spectrum may sometimes contain fragment ions with the same mass to charge ratio as the monitored irons of the target analyte [6].

In addition, it is important to add precisely the same amount of internal standard to each sample. It is not necessary to know exactly the weight amount added as long as it is exactly the same amount. The normal practice is to decide in advance the approximate quantity of internal standard to be added to each sample, since the ratio of analyte to internal standard can be measured most accurately when they are present in similar concentrations. The quantity of internal standard added to the samples, then, should give a concentration intermediate between the lowest and highest expected analyte concentrations. This concentration should be such that the lowest anticipated weight ratio of analyte to internal standard should approximately equal the inverse of the highest anticipated ratio. So, if one desires to measure concentrations of a drug over the range 1 to 1,000 ng/mL, the amount of internal standard added should give a concentration of approximately 32 ng/mL (1:32 ~ 32:1,000). Some analysts may favor the use of a lower concentration of internal standard to facilitate more accurate measurements of low levels of the drug, since low levels are more difficult to measure than high levels.

7.5.9.4 Controls

A control is a test sample of known concentration that is analyzed along with every batch of specimen to make certain that the analytical procedure performs within the expected limits of variation. Three types of controls can be defined: (1) the negative control, which is drug free and analyzed in qualitative and quantitative methods to show that the method is not introducing a contaminant that may construe a false positive; (2) a positive control, containing the drug at a concentration near the limit of detection and used in qualitative methods to demonstrate adequate performance; and (3) the analytical control(s), containing the drug at a meaningful level(s) and used to monitor the performance of the quantitative method. The intended use of controls is to monitor the performance of a method over a long period of time in an internal quality control program, never to calibrate a procedure. The level chosen for the analytical control should be of clinical and/or forensic importance, such as the significant therapeutic concentration of a drug or the legal intoxication level of ethanol. For assays where many samples are being analyzed, controls should be evenly distributed throughout the run, and one should be included at the end. Control materials are useful only if applicable to the analytical method used. As is the case with calibrators, the control must simulate the physical and chemical properties of the samples to compensate for matrix effects during analysis and to monitor the performance characteristics of the method. They must be homogeneous to be sensitive to analytical imprecision and stable enough to detect system errors for meaningful periods of time.

Control materials for post-mortem toxicology can be difficult to source and can often be expensive given the range of drugs required in a toxicological analysis. Often, commercially sourced clinical samples are used instead as quality controls, unless the laboratory can generate its own controls. This will often require drugs from different batches to ensure a degree of analytical separation from the primary drug stock used for the calibration curve. Laboratory-made controls are less likely nowadays, as the restriction on the use of human tissue prevents the use of collected specimens for other purposes (such as making up controls). Thus, the laboratory can only source clinical blood or urine that has been spiked with the drugs of interest at known concentrations. The complexity of other post-mortem specimens such as nails, hair, decomposed tissue, as well as detection of unstable analytes, can be challenging, for few controls actually exist. The use of validated methods ensures that variances between ante-mortem (clinical) and post-mortem matrices can be taken into consideration. However, the need to measure the quality of the method's performance during an analysis is still imperative, and these obstacles must be overcome with analytically sound ingenuity and thorough documentation.

Commercial immunoassays are provided with control materials specifically designed to be used for their intended purpose. These control materials are manufactured in bulk under strict quality control and are conveniently provided with the expected value, acceptable limits of variation, lot number, and expiration dates. However, it is good laboratory practice, where practical, to include at least one independently prepared positive control. These are usually supplied in the form of urine or lyophilized serum or plasma, with target concentrations, lot numbers, and expiration dates. Their stability may be short (5 to 30 days) once they have been reconstituted, but they remain stable for months if refrigerated in their lyophilized state. The drug selection available usually incorporates common drugs of abuse and drugs of clinical therapeutic interest, which albeit adequate, leaves the forensic laboratory with unaddressed needs.

A decision must be made as to whether to prepare batches of control material for future use or to prepare a working stock solution from which fresh controls can be fashioned at the time of analysis. The decision to prepare large batches of control material for future use rests on the requirements that (1) the drug be stable for a reasonable period of time in the appropriately preserved matrix of choice, and (2) the control be used frequently enough to merit the effort of establishing the limits of variation for the batch. For example, assays that are used frequently, such as blood ethanol, are good candidates for this type of control material. An assay that is performed about two or three times a year does not merit a batch preparation, even if the control material is deemed stable for a period of years in a frozen state.

A batch is simply prepared by making a proper dilution of the stock solution into the desired volume of biological fluid and adding the required preservatives as outlined in the procedures manual for the specimens being simulated. The control material can be dispensed into labeled vials containing working aliquots and stored until needed under the same protocols used for samples.

Control materials fashioned at the time of analysis are preferred for many post-mortem toxicology analyses. They are prepared fresh at the time of analysis by spiking an aliquot of a working stock solution into the required amount of blank matrix. Hence, any fluid or tissue homogenate can be fortified with the control before processing, allowing the performance of the assay to be monitored for any tissue. The working stock solutions may remain stable for long periods of time because they are prepared in organic solvents. Therefore, a single working stock solution may be used repeatedly to monitor performance even for infrequently performed analyses. However, precautions must be taken to prevent or minimize evaporation of the solvent. The working stock solution is prepared by diluting the stock solution to an intermediate concentration so that a small aliquot added to the required amount of blank matrix yields the desired control concentration. The solvent used must be water soluble, and care must be taken that the volume of control solution chosen to spike the blank does not affect the matrix significantly. Keeping the solvent concentration of the matrix well below 10% is advisable to avoid protein precipitation.

Once a control material has been procured, it is identified with a lot number and if applicable, an expiration date. Using control materials, the assay is evaluated to determine accuracy and precision expressed as standard deviation and coefficient of variation, which are evaluated by standard statistical methods. Where practical, this requires that the control be analyzed 20 to 30 times over a period of several days by all analysts who perform the assay using the variety of measuring devices that could conceivably be used to perform the assay. A smaller number of analyses may be more practical where the analyte is not routinely performed.

Occasionally, the forensic laboratory needs to perform a rare analysis for which a control has not been established (e.g., yohimbine, LSD) or one for which a control is impractical to maintain (e.g., toluene, cyanide). In these situations, one can perform a "spike recovery" study to verify that the calculated result was not influenced by matrix differences between the specimen and the calibrators. This is accomplished by spiking a replicate of the specimen with one of the working stock calibrator solutions. The solution is chosen so that the amount added is not lower than one-tenth the existing concentration and not more than ten times the existing concentration, and that the addition does not produce a concentration higher than the limits of linearity. The spiked sample is analyzed, and the result is used to calculate the percent recovery as follows. Recoveries that are outside the 20% margin allowed by this principle indicate that matrix effects are abnormally high and that the original concentration calculated for the specimen is inaccurate. If this is the case, the method of additions discussed in Section 7.5.9.2 can be pursued in the quest for an accurate result.

7.5.10 Samples and Sampling

Sampling is often called the basis of analysis because the analytical result is never better than the sample from which it is derived. The purpose of sampling is to provide the analyst with a representative part of the "object" that is suitable for the analysis. In forensic work, an appreciation of how the analytes may decompose and how contaminants may be introduced are important factors to consider [6].

7.5.11 Analytical Methods, Method Validation, and Standard Operating Procedures

The analytical method is the set of instructions detailing the entire procedure by which a particular analysis is performed. The instructions describe the preparation of reagents, standards, controls, and sample; the steps to isolate and concentrate the analyte; the instrumental requirements; and data manipulation and reporting. It is in the execution of the method that most of the sources of measurement uncertainty are introduced, so strict guidelines must be followed to control them. Guidelines for method development instituted in a comprehensive procedures manual provide an effective way to tackle the analytical challenges that are frequently encountered in the forensic laboratory.

7.5.11.1 Quality of an Analytical Procedure

An analytical challenge is approached by selecting the method that is most appropriate in terms of its quality features to tackle the chemical problem. The factors that govern the quality of an analytical procedure are the limit of detection, sensitivity, dynamic linear range, precision, accuracy, and selectivity. These have been extensively covered in the literature [4–7] as well as a standardized approach developed by the Scientific Working Group for Forensic Toxicology (SWGTOX) [8]. This standard reflects a minimum level of practice. A number of parameters have been defined for method validation in forensic toxicology; these include, for quantitative procedures, selectivity, calibration model (linearity), stability, accuracy (bias, precision), and limit of quantification. Additional parameters that might have to be evaluated include limit of detection, recovery, reproducibility, and ruggedness (robustness) [5]. The following is a short summation of those parameters and their relevance to modern forensic toxicology laboratories.

7.5.11.2 Limit of Detection (LOD), Limit of Quantification (LOQ), and Limit of Reporting (LOR)

The LOD can be defined as the smallest detector response given by the analyte that can be reliably differentiated from background noise produced by the instrument or the procedure. This signal is not necessarily quantifiable, since most detectors are not linear at low response levels. The classical determination for the method detection limit involves statistical analysis of the probability that the signal is produced by the analyte, and not the instrument, with given confidence limits.

In methodologies that render irregular background noise from sample to sample, it is commonly accepted that a signal-to-noise ratio of at least 3:1 [8] is needed to consider the signal as being produced by the analyte. The establishment of a higher signal-to-noise ratio as a decision guideline increases the confidence that the analyte is present at the expense of deciding that it is absent at lower ratios.

The LOQ is the lowest amount of an analyte in a sample that can be quantitatively determined with suitable precision and accuracy [5]. It often represents the lowest calibrator in the calibration curve. Quantification below the lowest calibrator is not recommended, and laboratories should refrain from reporting "trace detected." It is advisable that laboratories re-evaluate the lowest LOQ if concentrations are to be reported below this value. The LOR can be the LOQ but often is higher [9]. Sometimes, a laboratory may consider reporting drugs at levels higher than the LOQ to avoid having to report insignificant drugs at low concentrations, e.g., caffeine, nicotine, and cotinine.

7.5.11.3 Sensitivity and Linearity

The sensitivity of a method can be defined as the change in detector response given by a change in concentration. The detector response is composed of a part that depends on the concentration and a part that is independent of it (the blank). In addition, the detector response is not linearly proportional to the concentration over the entire range of possible values. The range of values for which the sensitivity is constant is called the "linear dynamic range," and methods should be developed so that this range is as large as possible. The linear dynamic range, or linearity, is limited at the lower level by concentration values whose detector response cannot be distinguished from the detector noise, or by ambiguous values of sensitivity. The linear range is limited at the upper level by saturation of the detector signal.

7.5.11.4 Accuracy, Precision, and Bias

Although the concept of accuracy is vague and difficult to interpret, it has been defined as the difference (error or bias) between an individual result, or the mean of a set of results, and the value that is accepted as the true or correct value for the quantity measured. An accurate measurement is one that is free of bias, does not scatter when repeated, and results in the "true value." The true value, however, is unknown, because it must be measured, and measurements are biased and imprecise. Nevertheless, the accuracy can be estimated by measuring properties that are related to the concept of "accurate."

Precision is a measure of the dispersion of results when an analytical procedure is repeated on one sample. Although the dispersion of results may be caused by many sources, it is usually implied that it is caused by random fluctuations in the procedure. If no bias exists, the results usually scatter around the expected value in a normal distribution, described by a Gaussian curve. The normal distribution of the population of results is characterized by the position of the mean (x) and the standard deviation (s). The precision of an analytical method is often expressed as the standard deviation or coefficient of variation (CV), and it is calculated and monitored by analysis of control materials.

7.5.11.5 Selectivity and Specificity

Selectivity refers to the ability of an analytical procedure to produce correct results for various components of a mixture without any mutual interference among the components. Specificity refers to the ability of an analytical procedure to discriminate between components in a mixture by their ability to produce a detector signal.

7.5.11.6 Qualitative Methods

Qualitative methods characterize the sample in terms of the identity of its toxic constituents. The identity can be specific, as produced by mass or infrared spectra, or nonspecific, as produced by immunoassays; however, it is recommended that mass spectrometry be used to confirm the compound(s) of interest in forensic casework unless it is internationally agreed that other methods (gas chromatography with flame ionization detector [GC-FID]) have the requisite specificity to identify a compound, e.g., ethanol. Qualitative methods require that all analytes that can be detected or ruled out in the analysis be known. With each assay, a negative control and a control representative of the analytes being tested should be analyzed. The positive control should contain the analytes near their respective LOD, and both should be prepared in a matrix similar to the samples. Interferences that can adversely affect the result should be determined and documented in the written procedure.

7.5.11.7 Quantitative Methods

Quantitative methods characterize the sample in terms of the quantity of its constituents. The measured quantity carries with it an inherent uncertainty that must be known in

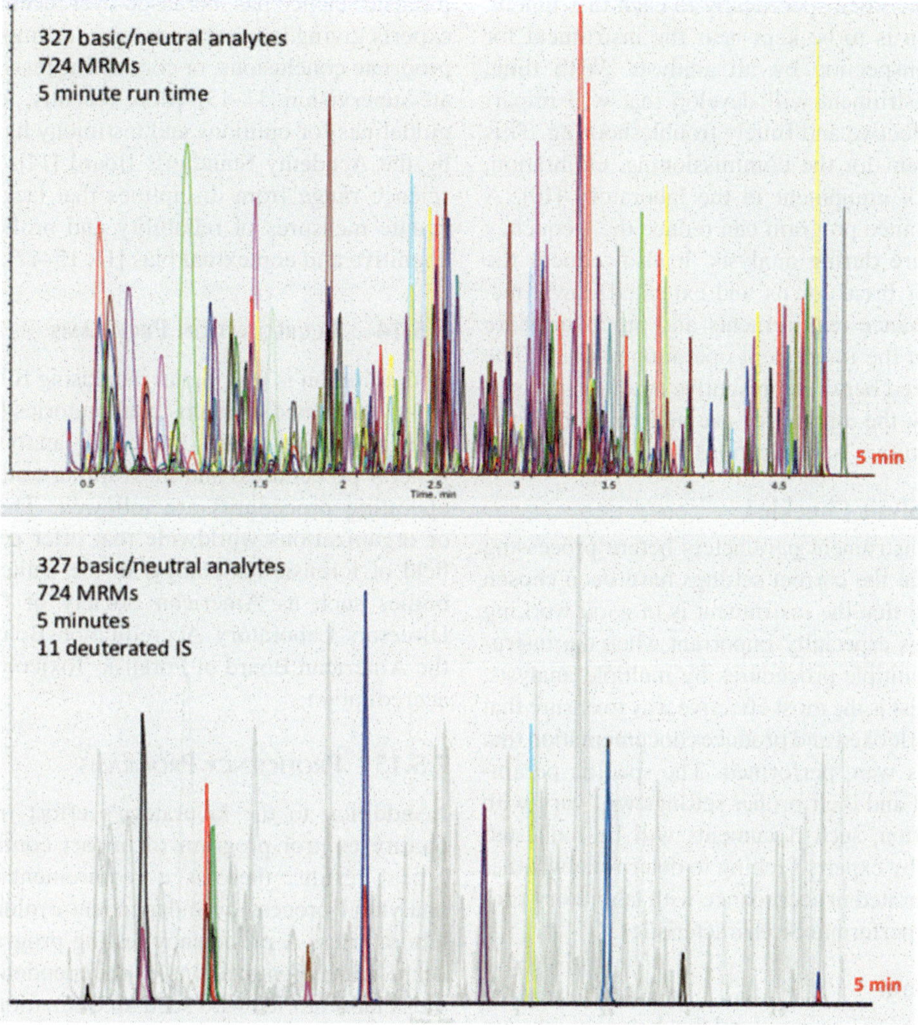

FIGURE 7.5.3 Multiple internal standards for multi-analyte assay using tandem LC/MS.

order to appraise its reliability. The accepted thresholds of uncertainty, or limits of variation, are determined by quantifying the factors that affect the quality of the method. Therefore, each quantitative technique must be validated by determining its LOD, dynamic linear range, precision, and accuracy.

7.5.12 Instruments

In analytical chemistry, information about the chemical composition of a sample is obtained by measuring some chemical or physical property that is characteristic of the component of interest. These measurements are made by various analytical instruments designed to measure specific properties. To apply instrumentation most efficiently to the problems, the analyst must understand the fundamental relations of chemical species to their physical and chemical properties. The analyst must know the scope, applicability, and limitations of physical property measurement with respect to qualitative and quantitative analysis. Knowing this, the analyst can call upon the instrumentation for the measurement of the desired properties with the needed accuracy and precision [6].

The instrument is a device that converts chemical information to a form that is more readily observable. It accomplishes this function in several steps, which may include (1) generation of a signal, (2) transduction (transformation of the signal to one of a different nature, such as electrical), (3) amplification of the transformed signal, and (4) presentation of the signal by a scale, recorder, integrator, or printout. Some instruments also prepare the sample into a form that can be analyzed or perform separation of components for increased specificity. It is common to find a combination of instruments working in tandem to produce the desired results.

To ensure that the instrumental data are reliable, steps must be taken to control the proper function of the instrument. This can be accomplished by establishing standard operating procedures that address proper installation guidelines, a preventive maintenance program, periodic performance evaluations, and pre-analysis checklists. All documentation concerning instrument maintenance and checks should be recorded specifically to each instrument. This documentation is to be kept near the instrument for easy access and inspection by all analysts. With time, a history of the instrument will develop that will impart great insight for effective and timely troubleshooting. This is also a requirement for the commissioning, calibration, and maintenance of equipment in the laboratory [10]. A preventive maintenance program can reduce the frequency of instrument failure during analysis. It also reduces the likelihood of major breakdowns and extended downtime. Preventive maintenance requirements and procedures are usually specified in the instrument operation manual. The time interval required between preventive maintenance services is dictated by the amount of use and environmental factors or manufacturers' specifications.

7.5.12.1 Pre-Analysis Checklist

A review of vital instrument parameters before processing samples ensures that the correct settings have been chosen for the analysis and that the instrument is in good working order. This becomes especially important when the instrument is used for multiple procedures by multiple analysts. The use of a checklist is the most effective way to ensure that no parameter is overlooked and produces documentation that pre-analysis checks were performed. The specific parameters to be checked and their proper settings will vary with the instrument. Often, such documents will be requested for court purposes by experts seeking to determine whether instruments are operated in accordance with laboratory procedures or defined performance characteristics.

7.5.12.2 Case Data

The AAFS and the SOFT recommend that before results are reported, each batch of analytical data should be reviewed by scientific personnel who are experienced with the analytical protocols used in the laboratory.

At a minimum, this review should include both an administrative and a technical review including chain of custody data, validity of analytical data and calculations, and quality control data. The review should be documented within the analytical record.

7.5.13 Toxicology Reports and Opinions

Post-mortem forensic laboratories are an integral part of, supported by, or associated with government agencies involved in medicolegal investigations. The laboratory must comply with the reporting requirements mandated by the agency to which the reports are submitted. Thus, a report format can be neither standardized nor recommended, since it will depend on the specific needs of the recipient. In general, however, the written report should include all information necessary to identify the case and its source, the test results, the methods used for analysis, and the signature of the individual responsible for its contents.

Toxicologists will be required to provide expert testimony in cases that proceed to court. The scrutiny of forensic science has increased over recent years, with some experts giving inaccurate or false testimony, reaching inappropriate conclusions, or conducting tests without appropriate supervision [11–13]. More recently, forensic toxicology guidelines for opinions and testimony have been published by the Academy Standards Board [14]. Issues in forensic science range from disciplines that lack validation, inadequate measures of reliability and proficiency, as well as cognitive and contextual bias [11, 15–17].

7.5.14 Accreditation Programs

Accreditation is playing an increasing role in the quality of work performed in forensic laboratories [10, 18]. It ensures that the laboratory has acceptable analytical methods and general procedures, and most important, that the standard operating procedures are followed. There are a number or organizations worldwide that offer accreditation in the field of forensic toxicology. In the United States, national bodies such as American Society of Crime Laboratory Directors Laboratory Accreditation Board (ASCLD[2]) and the American Board of Forensic Toxicology (ABFT[3]) offer accreditation.

7.5.15 Proficiency Programs

In addition to the laboratory's effort in implementing a quality control program to impart confidence to its analytical results, there is a requirement to scrutinize the analytical process by independent evaluation against peer laboratories. A proficiency testing program established by accrediting organizations or independent consultants provides laboratories with such an evaluation mechanism. The proficiency program provides laboratories with chemically fortified samples simulating those encountered routinely by the laboratory for analysis. The program derives statistical data on the results reported by the participating laboratories and issues a summary of useful information about the results. When the result of a chemical analysis is compared with the results obtained by other laboratories on the same sample, the laboratory can make a responsible determination of the strengths and weaknesses of its overall operation. This information can be used to focus resources on those areas that need improvement, be it personnel, training, equipment, method development, reference materials, or the like. It also builds confidence in the methods that yield reliable results. Forensic toxicology laboratories must participate in external proficiency testing programs that evaluate as many of the analytical tests in as many specimen types as possible. These programs are the only independent way to evaluate the reliability of the methods used and the overall operating procedures of the laboratory.

ACKNOWLEDGMENTS

Much of this material has been updated since the last edition of this text – thanks to Wilmo Andollo for his original and informative material.

NOTES

1. International Organization for Standardization (ISO) and the International Electrotechnical Commission (IEC).
2. American Society of Crime Laboratory Directors/ Laboratory Accreditation Board: www.ascld-lab.org.
3. American Board of Forensic Toxicology: www.abft.org.

REFERENCES

1. Laks, S., A. Pelander, E. Vuori, E. Ali-Tolppa, E. Sippola, and I. Ojanpera, Analysis of street drugs in seized material without primary reference standards.(Author Abstract). *Analytical Chemistry*, 2004. **76**(24): p. 7375.
2. Ojanperä, I., S. Mesihää, I. Rasanen, A. Pelander, and R.A. Ketola, Simultaneous identification and quantification of new psychoactive substances in blood by GC-APCI-QTOFMS coupled to nitrogen chemiluminescence detection without authentic reference standards. *Analytical and Bioanalytical Chemistry*, 2016. **408**(13): p. 3395.
3. Ojanperä, S., I. Rasanen, J. Sistonen, A. Pelander, E. Vuori, and I. Ojanperä, Quantification of drugs in plasma without primary reference standards by liquid chromatography-chemiluminescence nitrogen detection: Application to tramadol metabolite ratios. *Therapeutic Drug Monitoring*, 2007. **29**(4): p. 423–428.
4. Peters, F.T., O.H. Drummer, and F. Musshoff, Validation of new methods. *Forensic Science International*, 2007. **165** (2–3): p. 216–24.
5. Peters, F.T. and H.H. Maurer, Bioanalytical method validation and its implications for forensic and clinical toxicology – A review. *Journal for Quality, Comparability and Reliability in Chemical Measurement*, 2002. **7**(11): p. 441–449.
6. Moffat, A.C., *Clarke's analysis of drugs and poisons*. 4th ed. 2011, Pharmaceutical Press.
7. Peters, F.T., O. Drvarov, S. Lottner, A. Spellmeier, K. Rieger, W.E. Haefeli, and H.H. Maurer, A systematic comparison of four different workup procedures for systematic toxicological analysis of urine samples using gas chromatography-mass spectrometry. *Analytical and Bioanalytical Chemistry*, 2009. **393**(2): p. 735–45.
8. Scientific Working Group for Forensic Toxicology, Scientific Working Group for forensic toxicology (SWGTOX) standard practices for method validation in forensic toxicology. *Journal of Analytical Toxicology*, 2013. **37**(7): p. 452–474.
9. Cooper, G.A., S. Paterson, and M.D. Osselton, The United Kingdom and Ireland association of forensic toxicologists: Forensic toxicology laboratory guidelines (2010). *Science & Justice*, 2010. **50**(4): p. 166–176.
10. Wilson-Wilde, L., The international development of forensic science standards — A review. *Forensic Science International*, 2018. **288**: p. 1–9.
11. Bell, S., S. Sah, T.D. Albright, S.J. Gates, M.B. Denton, and A. Casadevall, A call for more science in forensic science. *Proceedings of the National Academy of Sciences*, 2018. **115**(18): p. 4541.
12. Drummer, O., A.R.W. Forrest, B. Goldberger, and S.B. Karch, Forensic science in the dock. *BMJ*, 2004. **329**(7467): p. 636–637.
13. Boyd, S., Gendered drug policy: Motherisk and the regulation of mothering in Canada. *International Journal of Drug Policy*, 2019. **68**: p. 109–116.
14. Board, A.S., *ANSI/ASB best practice recommendation 037, first edition 2019; guidelines for opinions and testimony in forensic toxicology*. 2019, AAFS Standards Board, LLC, Colorado Springs, CO.
15. Edmond, G., K. Martire, and R. Kemp, How to cross-examine forensic scientists: A guide for lawyers. *Australian Bar Review*, 2014. **39**(2): p. 174–197.
16. Edmond, G., B. Found, K. Martire, K. Ballantyne, D. Hamer, R. Searston, M. Thompson, E. Cunliffe, R. Kemp, M. San Roque, J. Tangen, R. Dioso-Villa, A. Ligertwood, D. Hibbert, D. White, G. Ribeiro, G. Porter, A. Towler, and A. Roberts, Model forensic science. *Australian Journal of Forensic Sciences*, 2016. **48**(5): p. 496–537.
17. Flanagan, R.J., Cut costs at all costs! *Forensic Science International*, 2018. **290**: p. e26–e28.
18. Scientific Working Group for Forensic Toxicology, Scientific Working Group for forensic toxicology (SWGTOX) standard for laboratory personnel. *Journal of Analytical Toxicology*, 2015. **39**(3): p. 241–250.

7.6 INTERPRETATION OF POST-MORTEM DRUG LEVELS

7.6.1 Introduction

In the early to mid-1900s, the practice of forensic toxicology was relatively limited in scope. Certainly, toxicologists could determine blood alcohol and a limited number of drugs with accuracy approaching that of today. However, the toxicological investigation was different in at least two respects. First, the sophistication of testing for drugs was limited, primarily relying on the efficiency of extraction techniques, followed by gravimetric and later spectrophotometric analysis. Second, with the exception of alcohol and a relatively limited number of drugs or poisons (e.g., salicylate, barbiturates, arsenic, heavy metals), there was a very limited database of reference drug concentrations available. The interpretation of quantitative results relied very heavily on the history and circumstances of the case, including the police investigation, witness accounts, and autopsy findings.

The development of gas chromatography (GC) and high-performance liquid chromatography (HPLC) during the early 1970s had a major influence on the development and growth of pharmacokinetics and therapeutic drug monitoring. As a result, the kinetics of drug absorption, distribution, metabolism, and excretion in clinical patients was easier to understand and predict. This coincided with a vast increase in the range of pure pharmaceuticals available, many of which were of lower absolute dosage compared with those previously available; for example, the replacement of barbiturates with low-dose benzodiazepines. It was logical that toxicologists started to use the pharmacokinetic data gained from living patients to interpret post-mortem blood concentrations, for example, to predict whether a given blood drug concentration was "in the therapeutic range" or whether the blood level was "fatal," or even to predict the amount ingested prior to death. Experience has since shown that post-mortem drug concentrations must be interpreted from a perspective very different from that for living patients. Many processes occur after death that can change drug and alcohol concentrations, sometimes to a very large extent.

Post-mortem changes must be considered when interpreting analytical toxicology results. It is no longer acceptable to interpret post-mortem toxicology results from tables of so-called therapeutic, toxic, and fatal ranges without taking into consideration the medical history, the immediate circumstances of the death, and the various processes that can affect drug concentrations both before and after death. It is probably fair to say that many toxicologists and pathologists are less confident about interpreting post-mortem drug concentrations today – and with good reason – than they may have been in the past.

It is important to remember that there are no "absolute" rules for the interpretation of toxicology results. The more information that is available to, and considered by, the interpreter, the more likely are the conclusions reached to be accurate. In the courtroom, lawyers, judges, and jurors often view all science, including the forensic subspecialties, in absolute terms. Certainly, if the toxicologist does his or her job properly, the laboratory findings will have the required accuracy. However, the subsequent interpretation is in part based on the scope of the toxicology testing (not least including the range of specimens tested), in part on the quantitative results, and perhaps most importantly, on the history and circumstances surrounding the death. Attempts to interpret toxicology findings solely on the basis of so-called normal or reference ranges are irresponsible.

It is not the purpose of this chapter to teach anyone how to interpret post-mortem drug concentrations but rather, to outline some of the pre-mortem and post-mortem factors that should be taken into account when doing so.

7.6.1.1 General Considerations

7.6.1.1.1 The Analytical Result

It should be obvious that the interpretation of any toxicology test result will be no more reliable than the analytical result itself. The interpreter must be satisfied that the analysis is sufficiently accurate for the purpose, or at least know the limitations of the testing. Was the standard material used to prepare the calibrators pure and correctly identified? F or example, was the salt or water of crystallization properly taken into account? Was the calibration properly prepared and valid in the range where the specimens were measured? Was the assay adequately verified by quality control samples? Was the assay sufficiently specific? Could endogenous substances or other drugs or metabolites have interfered with analysis of the specimen, either by obscuring the target analyte or by increasing the apparent concentration? If the specimen was analyzed only once, what was the potential for accidental contamination? Was there a matrix effect? For example, was recovery of the drug from the specimen the same, relatively, as from the calibrators? Using similar matrix calibrators (e.g., blood) is not necessarily a guarantee of that, since post-mortem blood, by its nature, is variable from case to case, or even from site to site within the same cadaver. The extraction efficiency of drug or metabolite or internal standard from animal or outdated blood bank blood may sometimes be markedly different from the efficiency for decomposed case blood. Although it is practically impossible to know the "absolute" or true concentration of drug in a post-mortem specimen, the degree of confidence increases with the specificity of the analysis, with replication, or in some cases, by applying multiple analytical methods of different physical or chemical principles.

The use of mass spectrometry with multiple ion monitoring and stable isotope (e.g., deuterated)–labeled internal standards will usually provide a higher degree of confidence in the accuracy of the analytical result than immunoassay procedures. The completeness of the analysis should also be considered. It is never possible to test for every single drug during routine screening tests. However, a careful review of the medications or other potential poisons available to the deceased should assist the laboratory in determining whether any of these substances would have been detected if present in significant concentrations.

7.6.1.1.2 Post-Mortem Specimens

Relying on a toxicology result from a single specimen can be misleading because of the post-mortem changes that can occur. The most commonly used specimen, blood, is not a homogeneous fluid. It is good forensic practice to have multiple specimens available, or at least blood specimens from different sites in the body, because of the potential difficulties in interpreting post-mortem toxicology results [1–10].

7.6.1.1.3 Blood

The concentrations of many drugs are affected by post-mortem redistribution (PMR) through the vascular system from the major organs, by direct post-mortem diffusion from organ to organ, and sometimes by incomplete distribution [11–25]. Sedimentation of blood after death may also affect the drug "blood" concentration obtained. For some drugs, the distribution between blood and plasma is markedly uneven during life. However, toxicologists should be cautious about applying factors to "correct" for blood:plasma distribution unless it is known that the distribution is maintained after death. It may be found that the blood:plasma distribution that exists during life, due to active processes, decays after death occurs, for example, due to changes in pH and therefore, protein binding.

Toxicologists should be cautious about inferring the exact source of a blood specimen from the labeled description. Blood, simply labeled as such, could come from almost anywhere, even collected as pooled blood at the scene. Most toxicologists and pathologists are well acquainted with the widely discouraged practice of drawing blood by a "blind stick" through the chest wall. Although such blood may be labeled as "heart blood," it may contain pericardial fluid or worse, may be from the pleural cavity and therefore potentially contaminated by gastric contents, particularly if the death was traumatic or decomposition severe [1]. Even blood drawn from the "heart" after opening the body cavity at autopsy may contain blood from a number of sources. So-called "heart" blood may contain blood from one or more of the cardiac chambers – the ventricles and atria. However, it may equally contain blood that has drained from the pulmonary vein and artery (and hence the lungs), from the inferior vena cava (and hence from the liver), and from the aorta and subclavian veins. As a result, so-called heart blood is potentially one of the most nonhomogeneous specimens in the body. As described later, PMR and other factors can cause the concentrations of many drugs to vary markedly from site to site [11–13]. Even drug concentrations in blood drawn from the same site, but simply placed into different collection vials, can also sometimes differ by severalfold [5].

It is generally recommended that to avoid the effects of PMR or diffusion from the major organs, femoral blood should be sampled wherever possible. While this is certainly a good practice, interpreters should be cautioned that there is no such thing as "pure femoral blood"; it is simply blood drawn from the site of the femoral vein. Certainly, if the proximal part of the femoral vein is ligated prior to sampling, it is likely that much of the blood will be "peripheral" and therefore relatively uncontaminated by blood from the major organs. However, this is rarely the case. Femoral blood is typically drawn by a "stick" to the unligated femoral vein in the groin area, such that blood will be drawn from above and below the site of sampling. If the volume drawn is relatively small (e.g., 2 to 5 mL), it is unlikely that much blood will be drawn down from the central body cavity. However, with some skill, it is often possible to draw 50 mL or more of blood from a "femoral stick." Even with a limited knowledge of anatomy, it does not require much thought to realize that at least some of this blood will have been drawn down from the inferior vena cava and hence, from the liver. An alternative sampling technique is to cut the iliac vein at the side of the pelvis during autopsy and only sample blood that is massaged out from the femoral vein directly into a test tube. Even if such a procedure ensures that the collected blood is from the femoral vein, some post-mortem changes may just as well have happened in this blood, too, e.g., diffusion from vessel walls and skeletal muscle. Since blood concentrations of some drugs have the potential for marked post-mortem change, it is good practice to analyze blood obtained from more than one site, plus tissue or other specimens where this may be useful. The use of popliteal blood has also been recently evaluated [2, 3], suggesting a lower degree of PMR.

7.6.1.1.4 Vitreous Humor

Vitreous humor, although limited in volume (e.g., 3 to 6 mL), is an extremely useful specimen. It has been used for years to verify post-mortem blood concentrations of ethanol, since post-mortem fermentation does not occur to any significant extent in the eye. However, vitreous humor has also been useful for a number of drugs [26–28], including alcohol [29] For example, it is well known that digoxin concentrations will rise after death in cardiac blood, due to PMR from myocardial tissue, and possibly other organs. Consequently, vitreous digoxin concentrations are more likely to reflect those in ante-mortem plasma [30]. Vitreous humor has been used to analyze a large number of other drugs, including barbiturates, cocaine, morphine, tricyclic antidepressants, and benzodiazepines [31, 32]. However, interpretation of vitreous drug concentrations is difficult, in part because very few studies have been published that relate blood concentrations to those in vitreous humor, and in part because the large ad hoc data on vitreous drug concentrations is fragmented in innumerable case reports.

In general, however, those drugs that tend to be somewhat hydrophilic at physiological pH (e.g., digoxin, benzoylecgonine, acetaminophen, salicylate) are more likely to have concentrations approaching those in blood or plasma than those drugs that are either highly protein bound (e.g., tricyclic antidepressants) or highly lipophilic (e.g., benzodiazepines). In fact, a significant negative correlation between the vitreous:blood concentration ratio and the degree of protein binding of different drugs has been reported [27]. Because the eye is remote from the central body cavity and the abdominal organs, it has been suggested that vitreous may be a useful fluid for the determination of drugs that are subject to PMR. That may hold true for many drugs, such as digoxin. However, others have shown that some drugs, notably cocaine, may increase in concentration in the vitreous humor after death [33, 34]. Post-mortem diffusion of drugs to the vitreous from the brain, particularly in bodies lying in a prone position for an extended time, may be a possible source of error and warrants systematic studies.

7.6.1.1.5 Liver

Many toxicologists rank the liver second only after blood in importance as a specimen of interpretive value in post-mortem toxicology [35]. It is particularly valuable for the tricyclic antidepressants and many other drugs that are very highly protein bound. It is useful for the phenothiazine neuroleptics, which have a very large dosage range and hence, range in "therapeutic" blood concentrations. Liver tissue is also of value for interpreting post-mortem concentrations of many other drugs where a sufficiently large database has been established, and particularly where blood is not available due to severe decomposition, fire, or exsanguination.

One other aspect of liver drug concentrations should be considered. It is known that post-mortem diffusion from the stomach may artifactually elevate concentrations of the drug proximal to the stomach – for example, after an overdose, where both the concentration and the absolute amount of drug in the stomach are high [36–38].

However, little appears to have been done to assess the kinetics of drugs in the liver after therapeutic doses [39]. For example, common sense would suggest that drug concentrations in the liver, particularly of drugs that are strongly protein bound, would increase dramatically in the period after a dose was taken compared with that at steady state. This might be particularly important for drugs with a relatively long half-life and those that are often taken in single night-time doses or divided with a large portion of the dose at night. As for other specimens, liver concentrations are extremely valuable for assessing the role of many drugs in a death, but only in conjunction with other analytical findings and history [40, 41]. The site of sampling may also be important in forensic toxicology [42, 43], and it has been suggested that passive diffusion from the gastric content into surrounding organs mainly concerns the lower lobe of the left lung, the left posterior margin of the liver, and to a lesser extent, the caudate lobe and when the corpse is in a supine position, the posterior part of the right lobe [44].

7.6.1.1.6 Gastric Contents

Interpretation of the analytical findings of drugs in the gastric contents is largely dictated by common sense. It is the amount of drug or poison remaining in the gastric contents that is important; the concentration of the drug is generally of far less importance. The tricyclic antidepressants offer a good example. Most forensic toxicologists regard total tricyclic concentrations greater than 2 to 3 mg/L, even in post-mortem "cardiac" blood, as at least potentially toxic or fatal. So, what does a gastric tricyclic concentration of 1,500 mg/L mean? The answer is, on its own, not much, except that the person may have consumed his or her medication a relatively short period prior to death. For example, 200 mg amitriptyline at night is a fairly common dosage. If the gastric volume was, say, 120 mL, then 1,500 mg/L would be completely consistent with the person taking the normal dosage just prior to death – probably from unrelated causes. However, if in our example the gastric volume at autopsy was 900 mL, then a concentration of 1,500 mg/L would calculate out to 1,350 mg/900 mL in the stomach, and therefore almost certainly consistent with an overdose. Conversely, a relatively low absolute amount of drug in the gastric contents, with or without a high concentration, does not rule out the possibility of an overdose. Numerous case histories have shown that it may take several hours for an individual to die from an intentional overdose, depending on the exact drugs or poisons ingested, the amounts, co-ingestion of alcohol, general state of health, and age. It is not unusual for people to die from an oral overdose with less than a single therapeutic dose remaining in the stomach, notwithstanding the fact that an overdose of drugs can be irritant to the stomach lining and therefore delay gastric emptying. Extensive vomiting before death can also reduce the amount of drug remaining in the stomach at the time death occurs.

Two other aspects of "gastric toxicology" should be mentioned. The simple presence of a drug in the gastric contents does not necessarily mean that the drug was recently consumed or even prove that the drug was taken orally. Most drugs will be re-excreted into the gastric contents through the gastric juice, maintaining an equilibrium between the gastric fluid and the blood. This is especially so for drugs that are basic (alkaline) in nature. This can readily be demonstrated where it is known that a drug has only been administered intravenously under controlled conditions and yet can be found later in small concentrations in the gastric contents. The same phenomenon can be seen with drug metabolites, where, invariably, concentrations can be found in the gastric fluid. While it could be argued that microbial metabolism could have occurred in the stomach, it is more likely that the majority of the metabolites found were secreted into the stomach via the gastric juice. Conversely, the presence of "ghost" tablets in gastric contents has been reported for at least one type of slow-release analgesic where overdose or abuse was not suspected. Apparently, the wax-resin matrix of these sustained release tablets may remain in the gastric contents long after the active ingredient has diffused out [38].

More commonly, significant amounts of conglomerated, unabsorbed tablet or capsule residue can be found in the stomach many hours, or even a day or two, after a large overdose was consumed. These masses can occur after overdoses when large amounts of capsules or tablets may form a gelatinous mass, which is not readily dissolved or broken up, and which may lie slowly dissolving; they are called *bezoars* [45]. While the term can apply to unabsorbed masses of almost anything (e.g., hair balls), it is also applied to unabsorbed drug formulations. They occur, at least in part, because gastric emptying time is delayed significantly by irritants, including large amounts of undissolved drug residue. However, the phenomenon is also occasionally seen in patients in whom overdosage is extremely unlikely (e.g., a controlled setting such as a hospital or nursing home) but where several unabsorbed tablets may be recovered from the stomach. This is more likely to occur where enteric- coated tablets are involved; these do not dissolve in the stomach but may stick together to form a small mass of tablets. It is also more likely to happen in elderly individuals or in other patients in whom gastric motility is abnormally slow.

7.6.1.1.7 Urine

It is almost universally accepted that with few exceptions, there is very little correlation between urine and blood drug concentrations, and even less correlation between urine drug concentrations and pharmacological effect. So many factors affect urine concentration, such as fluid intake, rate of metabolism, glomerular clearance, urine pH, and the times of voiding relative to the dose, that any attempt to predict or even estimate a blood concentration from a urine concentration is pure folly. As always, there are some exceptions. Urine alcohol concentrations can be used to estimate the approximate blood alcohol concentration, but only if the bladder is completely voided and the measurement made on the second void [46]. Estimates of the body burden of some heavy metals are still made on 24-h urine collections.

7.6.1.1.8 Brain

The brain is the primary site of action of many forensically important drugs, such as the antidepressants, benzodiazepines, and narcotics. It is potentially a very useful specimen for the measurement and interpretation of drugs because it is remote from the stomach and other major organs in the body and would not be expected to be affected by post-mortem diffusion and redistribution. However, although drug concentration data in brain tissue is not hard to find in the literature, it is largely fragmented into innumerable case reports, which seldom specify what anatomic region of brain tissue was analyzed. The brain is an anatomically diverse organ, such that concentrations of many drugs vary significantly from one region to another – up to about two-fold [11, 13].

7.6.1.1.9 Other Soft Tissues

Most of the major organs, such as the kidneys, lungs, spleen, and myocardial tissue, have at some time been analyzed to estimate the degree of drug or poison exposure. However, for most drugs, adequate reference databases are not available in the literature, so the interpretive value of these measurements may be limited. Skeletal muscle has the potential to be one of the most useful specimens for drug or poison determination, particularly where the body is severely decomposed, or where PMR or diffusion might affect measurement in blood or other organs. The problem is one of obtaining sufficient reference values for that drug in skeletal muscle in order to make a confident interpretation. Some studies have been published, but data is scattered and incomplete [11, 13, 47].

The potential usefulness of bone marrow for the determination of both drugs and alcohol has been explored. [48–52]. For drugs and other poisons at least, this could be very useful in cases where severe decomposition, fire, or the action of wild animals has made the major organs unavailable but where bone marrow can still be harvested and analyzed. As for many other specimens, the problem is again one of establishing an adequate and reliable database of reference values.

7.6.1.1.10 Other Fluids

Bile has been used for decades as one of the primary specimens analyzed in the forensic toxicology laboratory, but mainly for the detection and measurement of morphine. However, the usefulness of bile has decreased in the past few years as sensitive immunoassays and mass spectrometry–based assays have been developed for whole blood. For most drugs, including morphine, the interpretive value of bile is limited [53, 54]. Biliary drug concentrations may also be influenced by post-mortem diffusion from the liver and the stomach. Cerebrospinal fluid (CSF) is also a potentially useful specimen for the measurement and interpretation of drugs, since it is the fluid that "bathes" the central nervous system, the brain, and the spinal cord. Its limitation lies mainly in the fact that it is often more difficult to collect than blood post-mortem, and as for many other specimens, there is a very limited database of reference values [55]. As for the vitreous, drugs that are highly protein bound or those that are lipophilic will tend to have significantly lower concentrations than in the blood. Intraosseous fluid (IOF) may serve as an alternative matrix for drug testing [56].

7.6.1.1.11 Injection Sites, Nasal Swabs

Suspect injection sites are periodically excised and submitted for analysis to support evidence of that route of administration. However, the simple qualitative detection or even quantitative measurement of a drug in a piece of skin is evidence only that the drug was taken or used, not that it was necessarily injected, let alone at that site. Sometimes, it is forgotten that most drugs are distributed throughout the body from any route of administration, such that any piece of skin will contain some amount of the drug. For such measurements to be useful, a similar piece of skin from another part of the body, not suspected to be an injection site, must be analyzed for comparison. Only if the concentration in the suspect site is substantially higher than that in the reference site can meaningful conclusions be drawn. Even then, a perfect injection may not cause persistent elevated drug concentrations at the intravenous injection site, in contrast to an intramuscular or subcutaneous site. Similarly, the simple detection of a drug such as cocaine in a nasal swab does not prove that the drug was "snorted." Any fluid secreted by the body, including sweat, vaginal fluid, and nasal secretions, will contain some concentration of the drug. In this instance, quantitative determination is difficult and interpretation even more so, unless the concentration of drug in the nasal secretions is extremely high relative to the blood.

7.6.1.1.12 Hair

Most drugs and poisons will be absorbed by bone, nails, and hair. Hair has long been used for the determination of arsenic and heavy metals, and by cutting the hair into sequential sections, for estimating the duration of exposure to the poison [57].

Hair analysis has the potential to be useful in post-mortem analyses, for example, to estimate the duration of exposure to a drug or toxin, and hence, provide information about the subject's previous drug use [58–63]. While hair has been established as a routine matrix for forensic toxicology, the interpretation of hair results remain complex and is subject to many variables. Those variables include the degree of incorporation of drug into the hair due to melanin binding [64, 65]. Even if the melanin content in the hair is measured, there are different types of melanin, and besides, a correction for total melanin content can only be applied to drugs for which the drug–melanin binding characteristics have been firmly established. For most drugs, such information is lacking, and hence, the exact hair drug concentration per se is rarely informative.

Contamination of hair is also an issue post-mortem, as hair decontamination procedures cannot consistently remove external drug contamination to lower than reportable cut-offs for all analytes. Additionally, there is no consensus on the most effective decontamination procedure for forensic hair analysis, although future systematic studies may lead to a standardization. Ultimately, forensic toxicologists should limit their interpretation of drugs in hair to biological markers of exposure in cases where metabolites generated exclusively from biotransformation are lacking [66].

Hair analysis can be extremely useful in cases where children die unexpectedly and in which there is no positive toxicology even though drug use may be suspected as a risk factor [67]. The analysis of a child's hair will often reveal previous exposure to drugs [68, 69], which may assist in the death investigation [67] or in child poisoning cases [70].

7.6.1.1.13 Nails and Bone

One advantage of analysis of keratinized materials that should be emphasized is the stability of drugs in hair and nails, which means that such samples can be stored at room temperature for very long periods without major degradation of incorporated drugs. Drugs are incorporated into nails via both the root of the growing nail and the nail bed [71]. This implies that during the growth of the nail, drugs follow the movement of the keratinized matrix both upward and forward. In addition, the growth of nails is variable and generally slow. Hence, temporal mapping of previous drug intake using analysis of nails is unlikely to be possible. On the other hand, nails are almost always available for analysis [72], whereas hair is not; some subjects may present with alopecia totalis or have shaved the hair on many body parts. Despite the limitations regarding the growth rate of nails, this matrix has the potential to be a useful source for information about the drug use history of the decedent [73, 74].

Most drugs and poisons will be taken up in bone and therefore, unless volatile, will be detectable in skeletonized remains [75, 76]. The interpretation of concentrations of certain drugs or poisons is relatively easy, since either the normal or reference values are well established (e.g., arsenic or heavy metals) or the substance should not be present in any concentration (e.g., strychnine). However, the interpretation of specific concentrations of pharmaceutical drugs or drugs of abuse is problematic because of limited reference levels. In addition, it should be recognized that bone is continuously remodeled; hence, drugs incorporated in bone tissue over time will be liberated and re-delivered to the blood. This means that a negative detection in bone does not rule out an exposure, and a positive detection will not give very much information as to the time for exposure.

7.6.1.1.14 Exhibits

Most forensic toxicologists are willing to analyze potentially drug-related exhibits found at the scene of death. Syringes or spoons can provide a valuable confirmation of drugs that may have been used prior to death. For example, heroin is so rapidly broken down to morphine that little or no heroin, or even monoacetylmorphine, may be detectable in post-mortem blood. The finding of morphine in, for example, blood could indicate use of either heroin or a morphine salt (or codeine, if it was also found). However, it should be borne in mind that most addicts reuse syringes, and therefore, the presence of a drug in a syringe found in the same room as a body does not necessarily mean that drugs contained therein were involved in the death, although it may provide circumstantial evidence.

The use or abuse of insulin in a person without diabetes is exceptionally difficult to prove, since blood insulin concentrations are so variable, are difficult to determine accurately in post-mortem blood, and even during life, correlate poorly with blood glucose. The detection of insulin in a used syringe near someone who was not prescribed the drug can provide useful circumstantial evidence of abuse.

The presence of drug residues in drinking glasses or cups can provide evidence of at least the route of ingestion and in most cases assist with the determination of manner of death, especially if the drug residue is large and obvious. Care would obviously have to be taken to distinguish, say, a multiple drug overdose mixed in a glass of water from two or three hypnotic tablets introduced into an alcoholic beverage for the purposes of administering a "Mickey Finn."

Newer drugs such as novel psychoactive substances (NPS) can often be determined in exhibits submitted to the toxicology laboratory or to the illicit drug laboratory. Given the relatively small number of commercially available reference materials, exhibits found near the deceased can often provide vital information for subsequent biological sample analysis [77].

7.6.1.2 Pharmacokinetics

Although other parts of this book deal with the topic of pharmacokinetics in some detail, it is worth reviewing the basics as they relate to post-mortem interpretation. The kinetics of all drugs and poisons in the body are characterized by absorption, distribution, metabolism, and excretion. All these parameters affect the concentrations that will be found in the body after death and therefore, the interpretation of analytical toxicology results.

7.6.1.2.1 Absorption and Distribution

Absorption may be via the oral route, parenteral (e.g., intravenous, intramuscular, subcutaneous), pulmonary, dermal, and rarely, rectal. The route of absorption can be very important to the interpretation. For example, many drugs are extremely toxic via the intravenous route, especially if given rapidly. For example, heroin, barbiturates, and many other drugs can cause severe hypotension and may be fatal if given rapidly, even though the total dose given is within the range normally considered "therapeutic." The resulting post-mortem blood concentrations may be below those normally considered fatal. At the other extreme, dermal absorption of medication is probably the slowest, such that even therapeutic concentrations in blood may take several hours to reach. Moreover, absorption of the drug may continue for several hours after the source of the drug, for example, a transdermal patch, is removed due to the depot of medication that accumulates in the upper layers of the skin.

Morphine provides a good and common example of why the interpretation of blood concentrations alone in isolation from the case history is difficult. First, opiate tolerance can vary tremendously between individuals and even within the same individual over a relatively short time span (days or weeks). Tolerance is an important consideration both clinically, where opioids may be chronically administered for pain, and in abuse situations, where they are used for their euphoric effect. The form of the opioids will affect how rapidly the drug crosses the blood–brain barrier and therefore, how potent it is. For example, heroin (diacetylmorphine) is at least twice as potent as morphine, probably because it is more lipid soluble and reaches the central nervous system faster than the more hydrophilic drug morphine. It has been suggested that heroin may simply be a pro-drug for morphine but one that reaches the site of action more efficiently. As a result, blood concentrations of morphine seen in heroin abuse deaths are frequently lower than concentrations resulting from the therapeutic administration of oral or parenteral morphine in clinical situations. The situation is complicated further because morphine is extensively metabolized by conjugation with glucuronic acid. Originally, it was assumed that this resulted in exclusively water-soluble metabolites, which were pharmacologically inactive. However, while morphine-3-glucuronide is devoid of narcotic activity, morphine-6-glucuronide, which is typically present in blood at higher concentrations than unconjugated morphine, is more potent than morphine itself [78]. Furthermore, much of the case data published in the clinical and forensic toxicology literature does not even distinguish between unconjugated and "total" morphine, let alone the 3- and 6-glucuronides, which are seldom measured routinely. With all these variables, it is no wonder that unconjugated morphine blood concentrations correlate poorly with analgesic effect and central nervous system depression. A good example of this has been described, where prolonged respiratory depression was observed in three patients in renal failure, in whom morphine concentrations were extremely low but morphine-6-glucuronide had accumulated to toxic levels [79].

7.6.1.2.2 Metabolism and Pharmacogenetics

A detailed treatise on the mechanisms of drug metabolism and the accumulation of drugs or metabolites due to impaired metabolism is beyond the scope of this chapter. However, it is worth pointing out at least three different scenarios where impaired metabolism can have a significant impact on the interpretation of results. Metabolism can be impaired by liver disease, such as advanced cirrhosis. However, not all metabolic pathways will be impaired equally by liver disease, and indeed, some pathways may be affected little, if at all. Oxidative pathways, which are easily saturable, are likely to be affected more than others, such as glucuronidation. A person's metabolism may be genetically deficient, for example, in cytochrome P4502D6 (CYP2D6). This pathway is responsible for many oxidative transformations, such as ring hydroxylation of the tricyclic antidepressants, and genetically poor metabolizers can be identified post-mortem [80]. Third, co-ingested drugs can inhibit one or more drug metabolism pathways. For example, most or all of the selective serotonin-reuptake inhibitors (SSRIs) inhibit CYP2D6, and some are extremely potent in this regard. The degree of elevation of the drugs or metabolites affected depends very much on the respective dosages of the drugs involved and not least, on the "metabolic reserve" of the individual patient. Some drug–drug interactions or genetic polymorphisms may only result in slightly elevated drug or metabolite concentrations, perhaps necessitating lowering of dosage. However, in some circumstances, the increases may be so dramatic as to cause life-threatening toxicity or death, particularly where the side effects were not sufficiently severe to alert the physician or patient that cardiotoxicity might be a problem [81, 82].

7.6.1.2.3 Calculation of Total Body Burden

Calculations of the total amount of drug ingested in self- or homicidal poisonings have been attempted many times over the years. Calculations typically involve measurement of the drug or poison in the major organs, including, where possible, skeletal muscle, and then taking into account the organ weights to arrive at a total estimate of the amount in the body. In some cases, the amounts have correlated very well with the available physical evidence (e.g., amount of drug in an empty injection vial or amount prescribed).[83, 84]. Doubtless, in some other examples attempted by toxicologists, correlation with the physical evidence was less convincing or not possible. In order for such calculations to be meaningful, a number of factors must be assumed. Perhaps most importantly, the particular part of the tissue or blood sample analyzed must be representative of the remainder of the organ or tissue. Since most organs are not homogeneous, and because uneven post-mortem diffusion (as discussed later) can lead to non-homogeneity of concentration, being sure of the average concentration of drug within any one organ may be difficult without analyzing that entire organ. While it is easy to know the weight of individual organs such as the heart, lungs, liver, kidneys, and brain, it is very difficult to reliably estimate the total amount of tissue into which most drugs readily distribute, including the skeletal muscle. While the mass of skeletal muscle can be estimated from medical tables given a person's height and weight, there is no assurance that the concentration of drug measured in one or two portions of skeletal muscle is representative of that in muscle from all other parts of the body.

Similar arguments apply to adipose tissue, where it is more difficult to obtain representative samples and assay accurately. It should also be borne in mind that for a person chronically taking a drug with a very large volume of distribution and a long half-life, the equivalent of many times the total daily dose will be normally present in the body even after therapeutic doses. Estimation of the total body burden of a drug may not be without value in all cases; it must be done with caution and the variables well understood and acknowledged. It is the rare cases of homicidal poisoning where significant weight may be erroneously placed on such calculations and where the stakes are the highest.

7.6.1.2.4 Estimation of Amount Ingested from Blood Levels

Given the foregoing discussion, it should go without saying that using pharmacokinetic calculations to try to estimate dosage, given a post-mortem blood concentration, is of virtually no value and can be extremely misleading [85]. Several factors make such calculations invalid [86]. The blood drug concentration measured post-mortem must be representative of that present at the time of death. As discussed elsewhere in this chapter, that is often not the case, and it is very difficult to predict whether any given post-mortem drug concentration represents the concentration at the time of death, even for drugs for which PMR is thought to be minimal. Any toxicologist who has routinely analyzed drugs in multiple blood samples from the same case knows how often those concentrations unexpectedly vary from sample to sample. Also, the drug must be at steady state at the time the person dies. By the very nature of drug-related deaths, that is rarely the case. Even if the gastric contents contain relatively little drug, much of the drug could still be present in the ileum or at least, not have attained equilibrium with muscle, adipose tissue, and the major organs. Finally, the rate of absorption, bioavailability, volume of distribution, half-life, rate of metabolism, and clearance are seldom known for any specific individual and can vary tremendously between subjects. The estimation of dose from post-mortem blood concentrations should be avoided [87–89].

7.6.1.3 Post-Mortem Redistribution and Other Changes

One question should be asked before attempting to interpret post-mortem drug concentrations: is the concentration found likely to represent, at least approximately, that present at the time of death? Unfortunately, the answer is often a flat no, or at least not necessarily. A number of factors need to be considered.

7.6.1.3.1 Incomplete Distribution

It is often the case that sudden deaths involving drugs are caused by abuse or suicidal drug overdose. Death will therefore usually occur before steady state has been reached. If a person is actively absorbing an overdose, it is likely that the concentration of the drug in blood leaving the liver (i.e., the inferior vena cava and right atrium) will have a somewhat higher concentration than, for example, venous blood returning from the peripheral vessels (e.g., femoral vein), for no other reason than that a substantial amount of the drug will be absorbed during the course of circulation through the body. This has been demonstrated in living patients, with concentration differences up to about twofold recorded between arterial and venous blood [90, 91]. It is an open question whether this is a practical issue in post-mortem toxicology. In two cases of almost instantaneous death following heroin injection, the concentrations of morphine and codeine in blood collected from heart, brachial veins, and femoral veins were uniform, indicating a very rapid equilibrium [92].

7.6.1.3.2 Post-Mortem Redistribution and Post-Mortem Diffusion

PMR and post-mortem diffusion involve the movement of drug after death along a concentration gradient. Although the differentiation of these terms is not always clear in the literature, PMR generally refers to the release of drugs from areas of higher concentration in organ tissues and subsequent diffusion into and through the capillaries and larger blood vessels of those organs. Post-mortem diffusion generally refers to the diffusion of drug along a concentration gradient from an area of high concentration to an area of low concentration. The usual scenario is where a high concentration of drug in the stomach contents (e.g., after an overdose) causes elevated concentrations of the drug in nearby tissue (e.g., proximal lobe of the liver) or blood.

Much is still unknown about the extent to which post-mortem changes in drug concentration occur and the drugs affected; however, some generalizations can be made. PMR is likely to be most marked for drugs that are highly protein bound, but particularly those sequestered in the major organs such as the lungs and liver (e.g., tricyclic antidepressants, propoxyphene, chloroquine, cannabis). PMR starts to occur within an hour after death and continues as the post-mortem interval increases. The most important quantitative changes in blood drug concentration occur within the first 24 h and are highly site dependent. In general, increases will be greater in blood from "central" sites, such as the vessels near the major organs, than in more peripheral sites, such as the femoral veins. However, blood drug concentrations can vary fivefold or more between cardiac, hepatic, and pulmonary sites. Given the very close proximity of these major vessels to one another and the organs they serve, it is impossible to even estimate peri-mortem drug concentrations based on the post-mortem interval and site from which a blood sample was drawn. Even aside from the unpredictable nature of PMR per se, blood from the "heart," if labeled as such, could have come from either of the cardiac atria or ventricles, the pulmonary vein or artery, the aorta, or the inferior vena cava.

Since it is known that many drug concentrations change after death due to redistribution from the major organs, it is recommended that post-mortem blood for drug and alcohol analysis be taken from a peripheral site such as the femoral vein. However, it should be emphasized that even if a "good" femoral blood sample is obtained, it is no guarantee that the drug concentrations subsequently measured will represent those present at the moment of death [93]. In fact, it is well established that femoral blood concentrations of many drugs can increase twofold or more after death. While it is possible that some of this increase is due to diffusion of released drug down the major vessels to the groin, it should be borne in mind that drug concentrations in skeletal muscle are often twofold or higher than in the peri-mortem blood. Given the mass of muscle surrounding these relatively small peripheral vessels, diffusion of drug directly into the blood across the vessel wall is very likely to occur. While in many of the published studies on PMR, the vessels have been carefully ligated prior to taking blood samples, this is rarely done during routine medico-legal autopsies. Consequently, blood labeled as "femoral" may contain blood drawn down from the inferior vena cava. This is particularly likely to be the case where large volumes (e.g., 30 to 50 mL) have been obtained from a supposedly femoral site.

The mechanisms for PMR probably involve release of drug from protein-bound sites after death occurs, with subsequent diffusion into interstitial fluid, through the capillaries, and into the larger blood vessels. Since this process appears to start within an hour or so of death, decomposition or putrefaction per se is not likely to play a role, at least in the early stages. It is more likely that cessation of active cellular processes and the rapid fall in blood and tissue pH that occurs after death would lead to changes in the conformation of proteins and therefore, release of some proportion of drugs present from the protein-bound state. It is important to bear in mind that these changes start well before putrefaction and microbiological action are likely to play a role. Changes can be dependent upon the length of time of the post-mortem interval; these are unpredictable and can be significant if samples are not collected for days after admission to a forensic institution [94] (Figure 7.6.1).

Other types of post-mortem diffusion can occur. For example, it has been demonstrated that over a period of a day or more, significant changes in drug concentrations in the major organs can occur. This has been shown for the tricyclic antidepressants, where concentrations in the lungs tended to decrease commensurate with an increase in concentration in the liver [95]. This study was done in such a manner as to show that these changes can occur due to direct diffusion from one organ to the other independently of the residue of drug in the stomach. However, the magnitude of these changes is not likely to affect the interpretation of tissue drug concentrations to a significant extent. It has also been demonstrated that post-mortem diffusion of drug from the stomach can markedly increase drug concentrations in

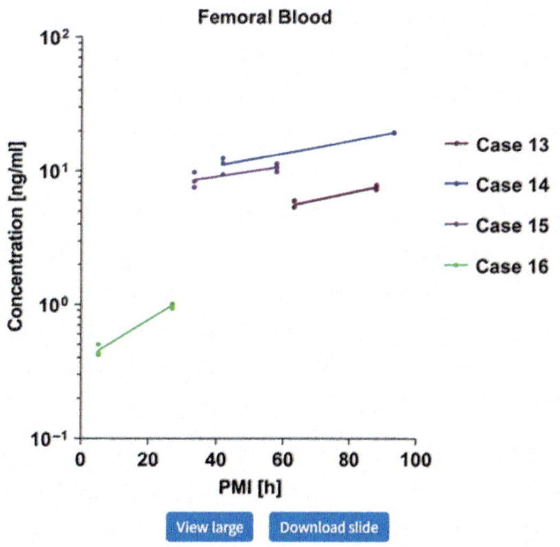

PMR of fentanyl in femoral blood displayed as concentration vs. postmortem interval (PMI). Each dot represents one sample of the triplicate measurements. The mean concentrations at each sampling time point were connected with a line in each case.

FIGURE 7.6.1 Post-mortem redistribution of fentanyl over time [94]. Each dot represents one sample of the triplicate measurements. The main concentrations at each sampling time point are connected with a line in each case.

proximal lobes of the liver and lungs as well as post-mortem blood in some of the central vessels [36, 38]. Ironically, when organ tissue was analyzed in previous decades, post-mortem diffusion into the liver or lungs might have been less important, since it was not uncommon to homogenize large amounts of organ tissue (e.g., 500 g), such that any local increases in concentration would be averaged out. However, today, the tendency in many laboratories is to homogenize small amounts of tissue (e.g., 2 to 10 g), which could lead to a gross overestimation of the amount of drug in the organ if the sampled tissue was taken close to the stomach. The potential for post-mortem diffusion of drugs in this manner has been known for decades, but recent work has brought the issue the attention it deserves and better quantified the potential changes.

Aspiration of gastric contents can provide one more important mechanism whereby post-mortem blood concentrations can be artificially elevated [96]. This can occur agonally, as death is occurring, or after death, during transportation of the body. It is a factor that may more commonly occur after overdosage, when the stomach contains a very concentrated cocktail of one or more drugs, with or without alcohol. However, it could also be very important to consider in deaths where therapeutic doses have been consumed and death occurs as a result of unrelated natural causes. It is not uncommon, for example, for tricyclic antidepressants to be taken as a single nightly dose, and in fact, large doses of many antipsychotic drugs are taken at night. This can result in drug concentrations in the stomach of the order of grams per liter, which if aspirated, could result in significant increases in some local post-mortem blood concentrations. Not surprisingly, the pulmonary vein and artery blood concentrations are elevated to the greatest extent following simulated aspiration. This is more significant than it might seem, because much of the so-called "heart blood," which is often sampled at autopsy, is in fact blood of pulmonary origin drawn from the major pulmonary vessels or the left atrium. A comprehensive discussion of the possible mechanisms for PMR has been published [97–100].

7.6.1.4 Other Considerations

7.6.1.4.1 Trauma

Severe trauma can affect the interpretation of both alcohol and drug concentrations [101]. For example, it is not uncommon for severe motor vehicle accidents to result in rupture of the stomach and diaphragm [102]. This can easily result in the release of gastric fluid into the body cavity. Because blood may be difficult to obtain from discrete vessels, pooled blood from the pleural cavity may be sampled. If an autopsy is performed, the origin and nature of the fluid so drawn should be obvious and hopefully noted. However, if an autopsy is not performed, and "blood" is sampled through the chest wall in an attempt to obtain cardiac blood, the coroner or medical examiner may be unaware that the sample is contaminated with gastric fluid. If even small, therapeutic amounts of drug remain unabsorbed in the gastric contents in these circumstances, it can result in what appears to be a grossly elevated "blood" drug (or alcohol) concentration. The release of microorganisms from the gastrointestinal tract and subsequent potential for fermentation is a well-recognized problem.

Trauma causing extended blood loss may also affect blood drug levels, since the physiological reactions include, in addition to increased heart rate and peripheral vasoconstriction, plasma volume refill. Hence, blood levels may increase or drop depending on their concentrations in the restoration fluid. Experimentally, codeine and morphine blood levels were found to increase significantly after controlled exsanguination in rats [103], and a similar study showed that the analgesic effect of morphine was elevated when given to rats with hemorrhagic shock [104]. Although further studies are needed to determine the impact of and conditions for such ante-mortem redistribution for several drugs with different pharmacokinetic properties, the phenomenon should be considered in trauma cases with longer duration of blood loss.

7.6.1.4.2 Artifacts of Medication Delivery

Artifacts of absorption and distribution must be recognized when interpreting post-mortem blood concentrations. For example, it is quite common to find grossly elevated concentrations of lidocaine in cases where resuscitation has been unsuccessfully attempted. Concentrations may be two to five times those normally considered therapeutic when lidocaine is given by intravenous infusion for the treatment of cardiac arrhythmias. If lidocaine is administered as a bolus intracardiac injection, and normal cardiac rhythm is never established, very high local concentrations will result in the cardiac blood. These could be interpreted as "fatal" unless all the circumstances are considered. Devices that automatically deliver medication by the parenteral route can lead to artificially high blood concentrations post-mortem. Most of these devices will continue to periodically dispense medication, usually narcotics, into the vein after a person dies, unless they are switched off and disconnected quickly. This can result in extremely high local concentrations of drug, which may be misinterpreted as an overdose.

Transdermal patches left on a body after death will give rise to locally high concentrations of the drug (e.g., fentanyl). Since these patches rely primarily on passive diffusion across a rate-limiting membrane for drug delivery, the concentration of the medication in the local area will continue to rise after death, albeit at a slower rate. Since blood circulation through the skin obviously stops after death, the drug will no longer be transported away except by diffusion, allowing a local build-up of drug. However, such a high concentration gradient exists between the gel containing the medication in the patch and the skin that even modest post-mortem diffusion might be expected to raise the post-mortem blood and tissue concentrations up to several inches away.

7.6.1.4.3 Additive and Synergistic Toxicity

When interpreting drug concentrations, it is important to take into account the sum of the effects of all the drugs detected. This is often an issue in drug abuse deaths, particularly those involving prescription drugs. Such deaths often involve multiple drugs of the same type (e.g., benzodiazepines or narcotics), individually present in "therapeutic" amounts and often in combination with alcohol. Interpretation of blood drug concentrations in these cases has to take into account disease that may be present and the total amounts of drugs and alcohol. In many cases, these effects may simply be additive, i.e., simply the sum of the individual effects of the drugs involved. In other cases, the effect may be truly synergistic, such that the toxicity is greater than would be expected based on the pharmacology and concentrations of the individual drugs. Cases where multiple drugs are present, with or without alcohol, are probably the most difficult to interpret and rely heavily on the experience of the interpreter and a reliable and complete case history.

7.6.1.4.4 Adverse Reactions

A death attributed to neuroleptic malignant syndrome (NMS) resulting from therapy with phenothiazine or some other neuroleptics is a good example of a fatal adverse drug reaction [105]. Combinations of drugs can result in similar syndromes, such as combination of a tricyclic antidepressant and a monoamine oxidase inhibitor (MAOI) causing serotonin syndrome [106–108]. Although not always fatal, a serotonin reaction can result in death and might be considered where there is no other reasonable cause of death and especially where there are elevated concentrations of MAOIs and either tricyclic antidepressants or SSRIs. It should be borne in mind that by the very nature of drug–drug or other adverse reactions, blood concentrations of the drug(s) involved are seldom predictive of the outcome and are often well within the range normally expected from therapeutic doses. In the absence of clinical observations, such fatalities can be very difficult to diagnose accurately.

7.6.1.4.5 Drug Instability

It should not be overlooked that many drugs are unstable in any biological fluid. Cocaine is probably the most notable example [109]. It is broken down in aqueous solution and enzymatically in blood or plasma to benzoylecgonine and methylecgonine, neither of which has much pharmacological activity. While cocaine may be stabilized to some extent by the addition of fluoride after the blood is collected, the extent of breakdown between death and autopsy must be considered. Unfortunately, there are many variables to consider. First, the toxicity of cocaine itself correlates only poorly with blood concentration, even in the living. There is good evidence that cocaine concentrations in post-mortem blood can increase or decrease depending on the exact site of collection [110, 111]. There are probably competing effects due to variable breakdown in different areas of the body and true PMR. The collection and measurement of cocaine in vitreous humor has been attempted to overcome these problems. However, it has been shown that cocaine will often, if irreproducibly, increase in concentration with time in the vitreous humor. The mechanism for this has not been proved, but it likely involves PMR from the brain, where cocaine is known to concentrate relative to the blood, into the eye via the optic nerve and other soft tissue. It is possible that time-dependent post-mortem increases in vitreous concentrations may occur for other drugs where those drugs attain higher concentrations in the brain.

7.6.1.4.6 Interpretation Using Tables of Values

There probably is not a forensic toxicologist or pathologist alive who has not used published tables as a reference when trying to interpret post-mortem blood concentrations [112, 113]. Tables of such values became a necessary evil due to the sheer volume of medical and forensic literature. However, they unfortunately perpetuate the myth that post-mortem toxicology results can be interpreted solely using, or heavily relying on, so-called "therapeutic," "toxic," and "fatal" ranges. Although tables of drug concentrations can serve as a useful reference point, it should be borne in mind that many of the values in these tables are derived from serum or plasma data from living patients, that the ranges are seldom referenced to published cases, and that they may not take into account or state other variables such as PMR, time of survival after intoxication, or the presence of other drugs, natural disease, or injury. Having stated that, one compilation has attempted to address some of these issues and indeed, bases the post-mortem values it lists exclusively on carefully collected femoral blood samples [114]. In that compilation, values are also provided for "controls," consisting of deceased subjects who with certainty died of causes other than intoxication and who were not incapacitated at the time of the demise. Such data are equally important as levels in fatal cases. and additional compilations using this approach are encouraged [112].

7.6.1.4.7 Conclusion

In the final analysis, post-mortem toxicology results must be interpreted with regard to all the available information, including medical history, information from the scene, autopsy findings, nature and exact location of the post-mortem samples collected, and the circumstances of the death. Only after weighing all of these variables can post-mortem results be reliably interpreted. Even then, it must be admitted that reliable interpretation of some results is simply not possible based on the available information. In many respects, the desirable underlying approach to the interpretation of post-mortem drug concentrations is not much different from that used a century ago: a good scene investigation, medical investigation, laboratory investigation, and the application of common sense.

ACKNOWLEDGMENTS

Much of this material has been updated since the last edition of this text – thanks to Graham Jones for his original and informative material.

REFERENCES

1. Brockbals, L., S.N. Staeheli, D. Gascho, L.C. Ebert, T. Kraemer, and A.E. Steuer, Time-dependent postmortem redistribution of opioids in blood and alternative matrices. *Journal of Analytical Toxicology*, 2018. **42**(6): p. 365–374.
2. Lemaire, E., C. Schmidt, N. Dubois, R. Denooz, C. Charlier, and P. Boxho, Site-, technique-, and time-related aspects of the postmortem redistribution of diazepam, methadone, morphine, and their metabolites: Interest of popliteal vein blood sampling. *Journal of Forensic Sciences*, 2017. **62**(6): p. 1559–1574.
3. Lemaire, E., C. Schmidt, R. Denooz, C. Charlier, and P. Boxho, Popliteal vein blood sampling and the postmortem redistribution of diazepam, methadone, and morphine. *Journal of Forensic Sciences*, 2016. **61**(4): p. 1017–1028.
4. Staeheli, S.N., D. Gascho, J. Fornaro, P. Laberke, L.C. Ebert, R.M. Martinez, M.J. Thali, T. Kraemer, and A.E. Steuer, Development of CT-guided biopsy sampling for time-dependent postmortem redistribution investigations in blood and alternative matrices--proof of concept and application on two cases. *Analytical and Bioanalytical Chemistry*, 2016. **408**(4): p. 1249–1258.
5. Gerostamoulos, D., J. Beyer, V. Staikos, P. Tayler, N. Woodford, and O.H. Drummer, The effect of the postmortem interval on the redistribution of drugs: A comparison of mortuary admission and autopsy blood specimens. *Forensic Science, Medicine, and Pathology*, 2012. **8**(4): p. 373–379.
6. Han, E., E. Kim, H. Hong, S. Jeong, J. Kim, S. In, H. Chung, and S. Lee, Evaluation of postmortem redistribution phenomena for commonly encountered drugs. *Forensic Science International*, 2012. **219**(1–3): p. 265–271.
7. Yarema, M.C. and C.E. Becker, Key concepts in postmortem drug redistribution. *Clinical Toxicology (Phila)*, 2005. **43**(4): p. 235–241.
8. Barnhart, F.E., H.J. Bonnell, and K.M. Rossum, Postmortem drug redistribution. *Forensic Science Review*, 2001. **13**(2): p. 101–129.
9. Gerostamoulos, J. and O.H. Drummer, Postmortem redistribution of morphine and its metabolites. *Journal of Forensic Sciences*, 2000. **45**(4): p. 843–845.
10. Langford, A.M. and D.J. Pounder, Possible markers for postmortem drug redistribution. *Journal of Forensic Sciences*, 1997. **42**(1): p. 88–92.
11. Jones, G.R. and D.J. Pounder, Site dependence of drug concentrations in postmortem blood--a case study. *Journal of Analytical Toxicology*, 1987. **11**(5): p. 186–190.
12. Prouty, R.W. and W.H. Anderson, A comparison of postmortem heart blood and femoral blood ethyl alcohol concentrations. *Journal of Analytical Toxicology*, 1987. **11**(5): p. 191–197.
13. Pounder, D.J. and G.R. Jones, Post-mortem drug redistribution - A toxicological nightmare. *Forensic Science International*, 1990. **45**(3): p. 253–263.
14. Prouty, R.W. and W.H. Anderson, The forensic science implications of site and temporal influences on postmortem blood-drug concentrations. *Journal of Forensic Sciences*, 1990. **35**(2): p. 243–270.
15. Hilberg, T., J. Mørland, and A. Bjørneboe, Postmortem release of amitriptyline from the lungs; A mechanism of postmortem drug redistribution. *Forensic Science International*, 1994. **64**(1): p. 47–55.
16. Hilberg, T., S. Rogde, and J. Mørland, Postmortem drug redistribution - Human cases related to results in experimental animals. *Journal of Forensic Sciences*, 1999. **44**(1): p. 3–9.
17. Leikin, J.B. and W.A. Watson, Post-mortem toxicology: What the dead can and cannot tell us. *Journal of Toxicology: Clinical Toxicology*, 2003. **41**(1): p. 47–56.
18. Drummer, O.H., Postmortem toxicology of drugs of abuse. *Forensic Science International*, 2004. **142**(2–3): p. 101–13.
19. Rodda, K.E. and O.H. Drummer, The redistribution of selected psychiatric drugs in post-mortem cases. *Forensic Science International*, 2006. **164**(2–3): p. 235–239.
20. Papavdi, A., E.F. Kranioti, P. Mylonakis, A. Papadomanolakis, and M. Michalodimitrakis, The use of postmortem forensic toxicology today. An alert for the pathologist. *International Journal of Medical Toxicology and Legal Medicine*, 2008. **10**(2): p. 1–4.
21. Dinis-Oliveira, R.J., F. Carvalho, J.A. Duarte, F. Remiao, A. Marques, A. Santos, and T. Magalhaes, Collection of biological samples in forensic toxicology. *Toxicology Mechanisms and Methods*, 2010. **20**(7): p. 363–414.
22. Kennedy, M.C., Post-mortem drug concentrations. *Journal of Internal Medicine*, 2010. **40**(3): p. 183–187.
23. Skopp, G., Postmortem toxicology. *Forensic Science, Medicine, and Pathology*, 2010**6**(4): p. 314–325.
24. Glicksberg, L., R. Winecker, C. Miller, and S. Kerrigan, Postmortem distribution and redistribution of synthetic cathinones. *Forensic Toxicology*, 2018. **36**(2): p. 291–303.
25. Concheiro, M., R. Chesser, J. Pardi, and G. Cooper, Postmortem toxicology of new synthetic opioids. *Frontiers in Pharmacology*, 2018. **9**(1210): p. 1–18.
26. Forrest, A.R., ACP broadsheet no 137: April 1993. Obtaining samples at post mortem examination for toxicological and biochemical analyses. *Journal of Clinical Pathology*, 1993. **46**(4): p. 292–296.
27. Holmgren, P., H. Druid, A. Holmgren, and J. Ahlner, Stability of drugs in stored postmortem femoral blood and vitreous humor. *Journal of Forensic Sciences*, 2004. **49**(4): p. 820–825.
28. Metushi, I.G., R.L. Fitzgerald, and I.M. McIntyre, Assessment and comparison of vitreous humor as an alternative matrix for forensic toxicology screening by GC-MS. *Journal of Analytical Toxicology*, 2016. **40**(4): p. 243–247.
29. Jones, A.W. and F.C. Kugelberg, Alcohol concentrations in post-mortem body fluids. *Human & Experimental Toxicology*, 2006. **25**(11): p. 623–624; author reply 625–626.
30. Vorpahl, T.E. and J.I. Coe, Correlation of antemortem and postmortem digoxin levels. *Journal of Forensic Sciences*, 1978. **23**(2): p. 329–334.
31. Bévalot, F., N. Cartiser, C. Bottinelli, L. Fanton, and J. Guitton, Vitreous humor analysis for the detection of xenobiotics in forensic toxicology: A review. *Forensic Toxicology*, 2016. **34**(1): p. 12–40.
32. Maskell, P.D., N.E. Wilson, L.N. Seetohul, M.L. Crichton, L.J. Beer, G. Drummond, and G. De Paoli, Postmortem tissue distribution of morphine and its metabolites in a series of heroin-related deaths. *Drug Testing and Analysis*, 2019. **11**(2): p. 292–304.
33. McKinney, P.E., S. Phillips, H.F. Gomez, J. Brent, M. MacIntyre, and W.A. Watson, Vitreous humor cocaine and metabolite concentrations: Do postmortem specimens reflect blood levels at the time of death? *Journal of Forensic Sciences*, 1995. **40**(1): p. 102–107.
34. Mackey-Bojack, S., J. Kloss, and F. Apple, Cocaine, cocaine metabolite, and ethanol concentrations in postmortem blood and vitreous humor. *Journal of Analytical Toxicology*, 2000. **24**(1): p. 59–65.
35. Drummer, O.H. and D. Gerostamoulos, Toxicological analysis: Drug screening and confirmation, in *Handbook of forensic medicine*. 2014. p. 866–872.

36. Pounder, D.J., E. Adams, C. Fuke, and A.M. Langford, Site to site variability of postmortem drug concentrations in liver and lung. *Journal of Forensic Sciences*, 1996. **41**(6): p. 927–932.
37. Pounder, D.J., C. Fuke, D.E. Cox, D. Smith, and N. Kuroda, Postmortem diffusion of drugs from gastric residue: An experimental study. *American Journal of Forensic Medicine and Pathology*, 1996. **17**(1): p. 1–7.
38. Anderson, D.T., K.L. Fritz, and J.J. Muto, Oxycontin: The concept of a "ghost pill" and the postmortem tissue distribution of oxycodone in 36 cases. *Journal of Analytical Toxicology*, 2002. **26**(7): p. 448–459.
39. McIntyre, I.M., Analytical data supporting the "theoretical" postmortem redistribution factor (Ft): A new model to evaluate postmortem redistribution. *Forensic Sciences Research*, 2016. **1**(1): p. 33–37.
40. McIntyre, I.M., Liver and peripheral blood concentration ratio (L/P) as a marker of postmortem drug redistribution: A literature review. *Forensic Science, Medicine, and Pathology*, 2014. **10**(1): p. 91–96.
41. Anastos, N., I.M. McIntyre, M.J. Lynch, and O.H. Drummer, Postmortem concentrations of citalopram. *Journal of Forensic Sciences*, 2002. **47**(4): p. 882–884.
42. Morley, S.R. and J. Bolton, Variation in postmortem liver sampling: Implications for postmortem toxicology interpretation. *Journal of Clinical Pathology*, 2012. **65**(12): p. 1136–1137.
43. Bierton, C., J.D. Gilbert, C. Kostakis, and N.E.I. Langlois, Route of drug administration may influence toxicological levels in the liver. *Journal of Clinical Pathology*, 2013. **66**(7): p. 630.
44. Pélissier-Alicot, A.-L., J.-M. Gaulier, P. Champsaur, and P. Marquet, Mechanisms underlying postmortem redistribution of drugs: A review. *Journal of Analytical Toxicology*, 2003. **27**(8): p. 533–544.
45. Simpson, S.-E., Pharmacobezoars described and demystified. *Clinical Toxicology*, 2011. **49**(2): p. 72–89.
46. Jones, A.W., Reference limits for urine/blood ratios of ethanol in two successive voids from drinking drivers. *Journal of Analytical Toxicology*, 2002. **26**(6): p. 333–339.
47. Christensen, H., A. Steentoft, and K. Worm, Muscle as an autopsy material for evaluation of fatal cases of drug overdose. *Journal of Forensic Sciences Soc*, 1985. **25**(3): p. 191–206.
48. Winek, C.L., E.M. Morris, and W.W. Wahba, The use of bone marrow in the study of postmortem redistribution of nortriptyline. *Journal of Analytical Toxicology*, 1993. **17**(2): p. 93–98.
49. Winek, C.L., S.E. Westwood, and W.W. Wahba, Plasma versus bone marrow desipramine: A comparative study. *Forensic Science International*, 1990. **48**(1): p. 49–57.
50. Vandenbosch, M., T. Somers, and E. Cuypers, Distribution of methadone and metabolites in skeletal tissue. *Journal of Analytical Toxicology*, 2018. **42**(6): p. 400–408.
51. Tominaga, M., T. Michiue, T. Ishikawa, O. Kawamoto, S. Oritani, K. Ikeda, M. Ogawa, and H. Maeda, Postmortem analyses of drugs in pericardial fluid and bone marrow aspirate. *Journal of Analytical Toxicology*, 2013. **37**(7): p. 423–429.
52. Cartiser, N., F. Bévalot, L. Fanton, Y. Gaillard, and J. Guitton, State-of-the-art of bone marrow analysis in forensic toxicology: A review. *International Journal of Legal Medicine*, 2011. **125**(2): p. 181–198.
53. Duflou, J., S. Darke, and J. Easson, Morphine concentrations in stomach contents of intravenous opioid overdose deaths. *Journal of Forensic Sciences*, 2009. **54**(5): p. 1181–1184.
54. Tassoni, G., C. Cacaci, M. Zampi, and R. Froldi, Bile analysis in heroin overdose. *Journal of Forensic Sciences*, 2007. **52**(6): p. 1405–1407.
55. Engelhart, D.A. and A.J. Jenkins, Comparison of drug concentrations in postmortem cerebrospinal fluid and blood specimens. *Journal of Analytical Toxicology*, 2007. **31**(9): p. 581–587.
56. Rodda, L.N., J.A. Volk, E. Moffat, C.M. Williams, K.L. Lynch, and A.H.B. Wu, Evaluation of intraosseous fluid as an alternative biological specimen in postmortem toxicology. *Journal of Analytical Toxicology*, 2017. **42**(3): p. 163–169.
57. Poklis, A. and J.J. Saady, Arsenic poisoning: Acute or chronic? Suicide or murder? *American Journal of Forensic Medicine and Pathology*, 1990. **11**(3): p. 226–232.
58. Druid, H., J.J. Strandberg, K. Alkass, I. Nystrom, F.C. Kugelberg, and R. Kronstrand, Evaluation of the role of abstinence in heroin overdose deaths using segmental hair analysis. *Forensic Science International*, 2007. **168**(2–3): p. 223–226.
59. Kronstrand, R., I. Nystrom, J. Strandberg, and H. Druid, Screening for drugs of abuse in hair with ion spray LC-MS-MS. *Forensic Science International*, 2004. **145**(2–3): p. 183–190.
60. Kronstrand, R., R. Grundin, and J. Jonsson, Incidence of opiates, amphetamines, and cocaine in hair and blood in fatal cases of heroin overdose. *Forensic Science International*, 1998. **92**(1): p. 29–38.
61. Tagliaro, F., Z. De Battisti, F.P. Smith, and M. Marigo, Death from heroin overdose: Findings from hair analysis. *Lancet*, 1998. **351**(9120): p. 1923–1925.
62. Darke, S., W. Hall, S. Kaye, J. Ross, and J. Duflou, Hair morphine concentrations of fatal heroin overdose cases and living heroin users. *Addiction*, 2002. **97**(8): p. 977–984.
63. Musshoff, F., K. Lachenmeier, H. Wollersen, D. Lichtermann, and B. Madea, Opiate concentrations in hair from subjects in a controlled heroin-maintenance program and from opiate-associated fatalities. *Journal of Analytical Toxicology*, 2005. **29**(5): p. 345–352.
64. Joseph, R.E., Jr., T.P. Su, and E.J. Cone, In vitro binding studies of drugs to hair: Influence of melanin and lipids on cocaine binding to Caucasoid and Africoid hair. *Journal of Analytical Toxicology*, 1996. **20**(6): p. 338–344.
65. Gygi, S.P., R.E. Joseph, Jr., E.J. Cone, D.G. Wilkins, and D.E. Rollins, Incorporation of codeine and metabolites into hair. Role of pigmentation. *Drug Metabolism and Disposition*, 1996. **24**(4): p. 495–501.
66. Mantinieks, D., D. Gerostamoulos, P. Wright, and O. Drummer, The effectiveness of decontamination procedures used in forensic hair analysis. *Forensic Science, Medicine, and Pathology*, 2018. **14**(3): p. 349–357.
67. Wang, X. and O.H. Drummer, Review: Interpretation of drug presence in the hair of children. *Forensic Science International*, 2015. **257**: p. 458–472.
68. Moosmann, B., N. Roth, M. Hastedt, A. Jacobsen-Bauer, F. Pragst, and V. Auwarter, Cannabinoid findings in children hair - What do they really tell us? An assessment in the light of three different analytical methods with focus on interpretation of Delta 9-tetrahydrocannabinolic acid A concentrations. *Drug Testing and Analysis*, 2015. **7**(5): p. 349–357.
69. Bassindale, T., Quantitative analysis of methamphetamine in hair of children removed from clandestine laboratories--evidence of passive exposure? *Forensic Science International*, 2012. **219**(1–3): p. 179–182.
70. Kintz, P., J. Evans, M. Villain, and V. Cirimele, Interpretation of hair findings in children after methadone poisoning. *Forensic Science International*, 2010. **196**(1–3): p. 51–54.

71. Palmeri, A., S. Pichini, R. Pacifici, P. Zuccaro, and A. Lopez, Drugs in nails: Physiology, pharmacokinetics and forensic toxicology. *Clinical Pharmacokinetics*, 2000. **38**(2): p. 95–110.
72. Suzuki, O., H. Hattori, and M. Asano, Nails as useful materials for detection of methamphetamine or amphetamine abuse. *Forensic Science International*, 1984. **24**(1): p. 9–16.
73. Krumbiegel, F., M. Hastedt, and M. Tsokos, Nails are a potential alternative matrix to hair for drug analysis in general unknown screenings by liquid-chromatography quadrupole time-of-flight mass spectrometry. *Forensic Science, Medicine, and Pathology*, 2014. **10**(4): p. 496–503.
74. Krumbiegel, F., M. Hastedt, L. Westendorf, A. Niebel, M. Methling, M.K. Parr, and M. Tsokos, The use of nails as an alternative matrix for the long-term detection of previous drug intake: Validation of sensitive UHPLC-MS/MS methods for the quantification of 76 substances and comparison of analytical results for drugs in nail and hair samples. (Report). *Forensic Science, Medicine, and Pathology*, 2016. **12**(4): p. 416.
75. Vardakou, I., S. Athanaselis, C. Pistos, S. Papadodima, C. Spiliopoulou, and K. Moraitis, The clavicle bone as an alternative matrix in forensic toxicological analysis. *Journal of Forensic and Legal Medicine*, 2014. **22**: p. 7–9.
76. McIntyre, M.I., V.C. King, H.M. Boratto, and H.O. Drummer, Post-mortem drug analyses in bone and bone marrow. *Therapeutic Drug Monitoring*, 2000. **22**(1): p. 79–83.
77. Araújo, A.M., M.J. Valente, M. Carvalho, D. Dias da Silva, H. Gaspar, F. Carvalho, M. de Lourdes Bastos, and P. Guedes de Pinho, Raising awareness of new psychoactive substances: Chemical analysis and in vitro toxicity screening of 'legal high' packages containing synthetic cathinones. *Archives of Toxicology*, 2015. **89**(5): p. 757–771.
78. Westerling, D., C. Persson, and P. Hoglund, Plasma concentrations of morphine, morphine-3-glucuronide, and morphine-6-glucuronide after intravenous and oral administration to healthy volunteers: Relationship to nonanalgesic actions. *Therapeutic Drug Monitoring*, 1995. **17**(3): p. 287–301.
79. Osborne, R.J., S.P. Joel, and M.L. Slevin, Morphine intoxication in renal failure: The role of morphine-6-glucuronide. *British Medical Journal (Clin Res Ed)*, 1986. **292**(6535): p. 1548–1549.
80. Druid, H., P. Holmgren, B. Carlsson, and J. Ahlner, Cytochrome P450 2D6 (CYP2D6) genotyping on postmortem blood as a supplementary tool for interpretation of forensic toxicological results. *Forensic Science International*, 1999. **99**(1): p. 25–34.
81. Swanson, J.R., G.R. Jones, W. Krasselt, L.N. Denmark, and F. Ratti, Death of two subjects due to imipramine and desipramine metabolite accumulation during chronic therapy: A review of the literature and possible mechanisms. *Journal of Forensic Sciences*, 1997. **42**(2): p. 335–339.
82. Pilgrim, J.L., D. Gerostamoulos, and O.H. Drummer, Review: Pharmacogenetic aspects of the effect of cytochrome P450 polymorphisms on serotonergic drug metabolism, response, interactions, and adverse effects. *Forensic Science, Medicine, and Pathology*, 2011. **7**(2): p. 162–184.
83. Saady, J.J., R.V. Blanke, and A. Poklis, Estimation of the body burden of arsenic in a child fatally poisoned by arsenite weedkiller. *Journal of Analytical Toxicology*, 1989. **13**(5): p. 310–312.
84. Pounder, D.J. and J.I. Davies, Zopiclone poisoning: Tissue distribution and potential for postmortem diffusion. *Forensic Science International*, 1994. **65**(3): p. 177–183.
85. Drummer, O., A.R.W. Forrest, B. Goldberger, and S.B. Karch, Forensic science in the dock. *BMJ*, 2004. **329**(7467): p. 636–637.
86. Chatterton, C.N. and G.R. Jones, Interpretative aspects of toxicological results, in *Forensic drug analysis*. p. 110–123.
87. Cook, D.S., R.A. Braithwaite, and K.A. Hale, Estimating antemortem drug concentrations from postmortem blood samples: The influence of postmortem redistribution. *Journal of Clinical Pathology*, 2000. **53**(4): p. 282.
88. Langford, N.J., S.R. Morley, and R.E. Ferner, The relationship between antemortem and postmortem morphine concentrations. *Clinical Toxicology*, 2019**57**(12): p. 1142–1145.
89. Tolliver, S.S., W.L. Hearn, and K.G. Furton, Evaluating the relationship between postmortem and antemortem morphine and codeine concentrations in whole blood. *Journal of Analytical Toxicology*, 2010. **34**(8): p. 491–497.
90. Sato, S., F.J. Baud, C. Bismuth, M. Galliot, E. Vicaut, and A. Buisine, Arterial-venous plasma concentration differences of meprobamate in acute human poisonings. *Human & Experimental Toxicology*, 1986. **5**(4): p. 243–8.
91. Baud, F., A. Buisine, C. Bismuth, M. Galliot, E. Vicaut, R. Bourdon, and P. Fournier, Arterio-venous plasma concentration differences in amitriptyline overdose. *Journal of Toxicology – Clinical Toxicology*, 1985. **23**(4–6): p. 391–406.
92. Druid, H. and P. Holmgren, Fatal injections of heroin. Interpretation of toxicological findings in multiple specimens. *International Journal of Legal Medicine*, 1998. **112**(1): p. 62–66.
93. Gerostamoulos, D., J. Beyer, V. Staikos, P. Tayler, N. Woodford, and O.H. Drummer, The effect of the postmortem interval on the redistribution of drugs: A comparison of mortuary admission and autopsy blood specimens. *Forensic Science, Medicine, and Pathology*, 2012. **8**(4): p. 373–379.
94. Brockbals, L., S.N. Staeheli, D. Gascho, L.C. Ebert, T. Kraemer, and A.E. Steuer, Time-dependent postmortem redistribution of opioids in blood and alternative matrices. *Journal of Analytical Toxicology*, 2018. **42**(6): p. 365–374.
95. Hilberg, T., J. Morland, and A. Bjorneboe, Postmortem release of amitriptyline from the lungs; a mechanism of postmortem drug redistribution. *Forensic Science International*, 1994. **64**(1): p. 47–55.
96. Pounder, D.J. and K. Yonemitsu, Postmortem absorption of drugs and ethanol from aspirated vomitus--an experimental model. *Forensic Science International*, 1991. **51**(2): p. 189–195.
97. Pélissier-Alicot, A.L., M.D. Pierccechi-Marti, G. Leonetti, P. Champsaur, J.M. Gaulier, and P. Marquet, Mechanisms underlying postmortem redistribution of drugs: About current knowledge. *La redistribution post-mortem des xénobiotiques: Le point sur l'état actuel des connaissances*, 2001. **44**(2): p. 133–141.
98. Rohrig, T.P., 13 postmortem redistribution, in *Postmortem toxicology*. 2019, Academic Press, London, p. 185–198.
99. Kennedy, M., Interpreting postmortem drug analysis and redistribution in determining cause of death: A review. *Pathology and Laboratory Medicine International*, 2015. **7**: p. 55–62.
100. Pounder, D.J., The nightmare of postmortem drug changes. *Legal Medicine*, 1993. p. 163–191.
101. Chaturvedi, A.K., Postmortem aviation forensic toxicology: An overview. *Journal of Analytical Toxicology*, 2010. **34**(4): p. 169–176.
102. Kugelberg, F.C. and A.W. Jones, Interpreting results of ethanol analysis in postmortem specimens: A review of the literature. *Forensic Science International*, 2007. **165**(1): p. 10–29.

103. Kugelberg, F.C., P. Holmgren, and H. Druid, Codeine and morphine blood concentrations increase during blood loss. *Journal of Forensic Sciences*, 2003. **48**(3): p. 664–667.
104. De Paepe, P., F.M. Belpaire, M.T. Rosseel, and W.A. Buylaert, The influence of hemorrhagic shock on the pharmacokinetics and the analgesic effect of morphine in the rat. *Fundamental & Clinical Pharmacology*, 1998. **12**(6): p. 624–630.
105. Laposata, E.A., P. Hale, Jr., and A. Poklis, Evaluation of sudden death in psychiatric patients with special reference to phenothiazine therapy: Forensic pathology. *Journal of Forensic Sciences*, 1988. **33**(2): p. 432–440.
106. Pilgrim, J.L., D. Gerostamoulos, N. Woodford, and O.H. Drummer, Serotonin toxicity involving MDMA (ecstasy) and moclobemide. *Forensic Science International*, 2012. **215**(1–3): p. 184–188.
107. Pilgrim, J.L., D. Gerostamoulos, and O.H. Drummer, Deaths involving contraindicated and inappropriate combinations of serotonergic drugs. *International Journal of Legal Medicine*, 2011. **125**(6): p. 803–815.
108. Pilgrim, J.L., D. Gerostamoulos, and O.H. Drummer, Deaths involving serotonergic drugs. *Forensic Science International*, 2010. **198**(1–3): p. 110–117.
109. Isenschmid, D.S., B.S. Levine, and Y.H. Caplan, A comprehensive study of the stability of cocaine and its metabolites. *Journal of Analytical Toxicology*, 1989. **13**(5): p. 250–6.
110. Hearn, W.L., E.E. Keran, H.A. Wei, and G. Hime, Site-dependent postmortem changes in blood cocaine concentrations. *Journal of Forensic Sciences*, 1991. **36**(3): p. 673–84.
111. Logan, B.K., D. Smirnow, and R.G. Gullberg, Lack of predictable site-dependent differences and time-dependent changes in postmortem concentrations of cocaine, benzoylecgonine, and cocaethylene in humans. *Journal of Analytical Toxicology*, 1997. **21**(1): p. 23–31.
112. Baselt, R.C., *Disposition of toxic drugs and chemicals in man*. 2017, Biomedical Publications, Seal Beach, CA.
113. Moffat, A.C., *Clarke's analysis of drugs and poisons*. 4th ed. 2011, Pharmaceutical Press, London.
114. Druid, H. and P. Holmgren, A compilation of fatal and control concentrations of drugs in postmortem femoral blood. *Journal of Forensic Sciences*, 1997. **42**(1): p. 79–87.

8 New Psychoactive Substances

Section Editors: Fintan Garavan, Brandi L. Bellissima and Steven B. Karch

CONTENTS

DOI: 10.4324/9781315155159-8

An array of new synthetic psychoactive products (designer drugs) first came to notice in the 2000s. The first were benzylpiperazine and methylone, but their creation has led to the production of a new category of abused drugs, referred to by most as New Psychoactive Substances (NPS). These new substances were designed to mimic Ecstasy/amphetamines yet circumvent both international and domestic drug controls at that time, which is why they became known as legal highs. As the 2000s progressed, more and more of these altered structures flooded the market and expanded to involve drugs that mimicked not only amphetamines but also cocaine, lysergic acid diethylamide (LSD), psilocin (magic mushrooms), and ketamine. The concomitant rise of the internet/darknet facilitated the purchase, sales, and transport of these chemicals and allowed the rapid spread of their use across the globe. By the end of 2018, the European Monitoring Centre for Drugs and Drug Addition (EMCDDA) was monitoring more than 730 NPS, 55 of which were detected for the first time in Europe [1]. The United States Drug Enforcement Administration (DEA) (www.deadiversion.usdoj.gov) reports that in the United States, over 300 NPS have been encountered [2]. Currently, in both Europe and the United States, seizures of NPS predominately consist of synthetic cannabinoids and cathinones, but diverse substances including synthetic opioids and synthetic benzodiazepines are becoming more prominent. These substances are found as powders, tablets, blotters, and liquids.

These chemicals/compounds are sold on the black markets as "legal highs," "bath salts," and "research chemicals." To promote clear terminology on this issue, the United Nations Office on Drug Crimes (UNODC) uses the term "new psychoactive substances," which are defined as "substances of abuse, either in a pure form or a preparation, that are not controlled by the 1961 Single Convention on Narcotic Drugs or the 1971 Convention on Psychotropic Substances, but which may pose a public health threat."

The term "new" does not exclusively refer to novel synthetic drugs, as there are several compounds included under this umbrella term that are well known to the general population. Some have even been used in various cultures long before modern times. The term "new" refers to the fact that although the chemicals are known, there are new modifications to the structures (both naturally occurring and synthetic structures), and they are "new" in terms of availability and abuse.

Confusion exists over the creation of this new category of drugs of abuse called "new psychoactive substances" because "old" drugs, such as naturally occurring psilocin and psilocybin, tryptamines such as *N,N*-dimethyltryptamine (DMT) and tetrahydroharmine (THH), cathinone, LSD, and 3,4-methylenedioxymethamphetamine (MDMA), are also included within this new category. For the purposes of this chapter, these drugs will not be discussed because they are described extensively in the literature. However, their history of use is important to the evolution of NPS.

Psilocin and psilocybin are derived from mushrooms, plants, and some species of animals; they have been used in ceremonial practices for centuries. LSD, first synthesized in 1938, was widely used in the 1960s–1970s and continues to be used today. Other drugs such as MDMA and 3,4 methylenedioxyamphetamine (MDA) became popular in the

1990s in the club/rave scene and also continue to be used. The Khat plant (*Catha edulis*) is an evergreen that grows in the higher mountains of East Africa, where it is a popular, socially acceptable stimulant; it is also grown in the southwest deserts of the United States. The Khat plant contains two principal psychoactive compounds – cathinone and cathine. Cathinone (S(–)-alpha-aminopropiophenone) is the more abundant and more potent. These compounds were identified in the late 1970s and have effects similar to amphetamine [3].

Ketamine abuse has been known since the 1980s, while the phenylethylamines and piperazines appeared in the 1990s and 2000s, respectively. In 2004, the synthetic cannabinoids arrived and were followed by the synthetic cathinones. In 2014, there were over 350 NPS reported under the European Union Early Warning System [1]. As of December 2018, 888 substances had been reported to the UNODC Early Warning Advisory by governments, laboratories, and public health and law enforcement agencies from 119 countries and territories [4].

One of the interesting things about these drugs is the multitude of colorful "brand" names that exist; none of these names give any indication as to the active ingredient(s). Another layer of complexity superimposed on the issue of nomenclature is that different countries/regions may have different street names for the same drug. The disparity is simply the result of the fact that the proper chemical names are so complex that they would never be recognized by users. Instead, more inventive and imaginative names are applied. The issue of naming is particularly important for the synthetic cannabinoids and the tryptamines.

The rapid and constant emergence of these compounds has led many countries to enact strict controls and outright bans [5]. Despite legal efforts, these drugs continue to persist on black markets, and therefore, it is necessary to be aware of them. That said, it is not possible to discuss all 880 plus compounds individually. This chapter will address the more prevalent categories of NPS.

Within the United States, under the Controlled Substances Act (CSA), the DEA, the Department of Health and Human Services, or other interested parties can add, delete, or change the schedule of a drug or other substances. An Eight-Factor Analysis as described by the CSA is used (www.dea.gov/controlled-substances-act).

The factors used to determine whether or not a substance should be controlled include:

- Its actual or relative potential for abuse
- Scientific evidence of its pharmacological effect, if known
- The state of current scientific knowledge regarding the drug or other substance
- Its history and current pattern of abuse
- The scope, duration, and significance of abuse
- What, if any, risk there is to the public health
- Its psychic or physiological dependence liability

There are scant data relating to the pharmacology and toxicology of these new drugs. While few controlled studies exist, increasing numbers of case reports involving NPS provide much needed insights into their clinical effects. While reading through various reports, it becomes apparent that many of the compounds produce similar effects through similar mechanisms. Speaking in broad terms, many of the drugs are considered stimulants and work through the adrenergic and serotonergic systems to cause activation and/or inhibition of reuptake of monoamines. Others are hallucinogenic and work through the serotonergic and dopaminergic pathways. All the drugs interact with different pathways to varying degrees, making it difficult to comprehend how they exert their effects and therefore, how toxicity manifests.

The paucity of pharmacology, pharmacokinetics, and pharmacodynamics studies limits not only clinical understanding but also postmortem analysis and interpretation. The existence of these drugs poses many challenges for forensic toxicologists and medical and legal professionals, and the information gaps are daunting.

8.1 SYNTHETIC CANNABINOIDS

Cannabis sativa is a plant that has long been used by humans for medicinal and recreational purposes. Cannabinoids are biologically active compounds found in *C. sativa* [6]. Despite the widespread use of *C sativa*, it was not until 1933 that the first biologically active secondary metabolite, cannabinol, was isolated from cannabis [7]. Cannabidiol, another active component, was isolated in 1940 [8]. Surprisingly, it was not until 1964 that the most psychoactive component of cannabis, Δ^9-tetrahydrocannabinol (THC), a terpenophenolic cannabinoid, was partially elucidated (Figure 8.1). Δ^9-THC is one of at least 50 biologically active compounds found in *C. sativa* [9] and is often used recreationally due to its psychoactive effects.

The synthetic cannabinoids (or cannabimimetics) are non-natural analogues of endo- and phytocannabinoids (such as Δ^9-THC) that were originally synthesized to study their use as pharmacotherapeutic agents and the endocannabinoid system in general [10]. Like Δ^9-THC, they bind to the cannabinoid receptors. Most are full agonists of CB_1 receptor subtype, unlike Δ^9-THC, which is a partial agonist. In 2004, several internet sites in European countries began to offer "herbal" blends with names such as "Spice," "Yucatan Fire," and "Skunk" for purchase; these products

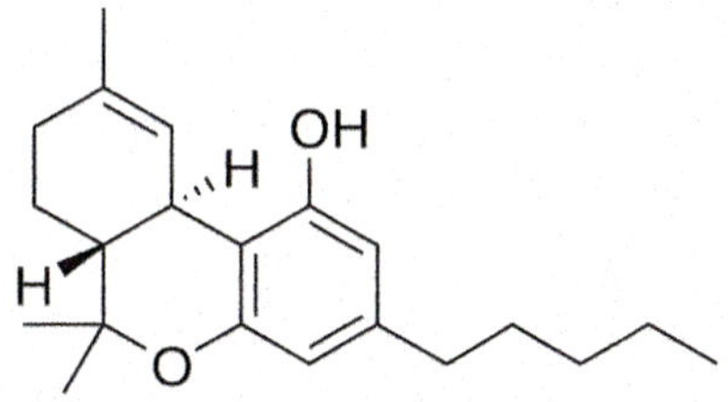

FIGURE 8.1 Chemical structure of Δ^9-tetrahydrocannabinol.

were promoted as legal blends of herbs for smoking [11]. In 2008, 1-Naphthyl(1-pentyl-1H-indol-3-yl)methanone (JWH-018) and 2-[(1S,3R)-3-Hydroxycyclohexyl]-5-(2-methyl-2-nonanyl)phenol (CP-47,497-C8, a homologue of CP-47,497) were just two of the synthetic cannabinoids identified in "herbal" blends. These blends are available for purchase not only via the internet [12, 13] but also in more traditional "smoke shops." On the streets, the product sold was found to contain various amounts and combinations of synthetic cannabinoids sprayed onto herbal mixtures and sold as "legal" cannabis alternatives [14]. The resulting effects are more pronounced than those observed with Δ^{9}-THC. They are, in short, a more potent drug. Synthetic cannabinoids are the largest group of NPS.

8.1.1 Nomenclature

The naming of synthetic cannabinoids is not harmonized. It is not uncommon for synthetic cannabinoids to be named after the individuals who first synthesized them, usually in the course of medical research. Perhaps the most well-known synthetic cannabinoids are the JWH compounds, named after John W. Huffman, a chemist at Clemson University [15]. Some synthetic cannabinoids take the name of the university in which they were discovered, as is the case for the HU series (the Hebrew University, Jerusalem) [16]. The CP series of synthetic cannabinoids was synthesized by Pfizer; CP are the initials of Charles Pfizer, who founded Pfizer. Illicit drug producers do not use a predictable naming system. For example, the synthetic cannabinoid AKB-48 is named after a Japanese punk rock band, and XLR-11 is a type of rocket fuel. With many new compounds being synthesized each year, abbreviated versions of the International Union of Pure and Applied Chemistry (IUPAC) nomenclature began to appear in the literature, although they are not consistent. For example, the IUPAC nomenclature of AKB-48 is *N*-(1-adamantyl)-1-pentyl-1H-indazole-3-carboxamide. An abbreviation of the IUPAC nomenclature for AKB-48 is APINACA. It is not uncommon for a compound to be referred to by multiple different names.

Chemists at the EMCDDA recognized that each of the new synthetic cannabinoids could be divided into four components consisting of a tail, core, linker, and linked group [17]. By giving each group a particular designation, the drug can be identified without using the actual long chemical name using the following arrangement: LinkedGroup – TailCoreLinker.

The drug sold as APICA is actually an EMCADDA abbreviation for the synthetic cannabinoid with the IUPAC nomenclature *N*-(adamantyl)-1-pentyl-3-1H-indole-3-carboxamide (Figure 8.2).

Using the letter "A" does not imply that it represents the first group; rather, it represents the linked group. "A" indicates that the linked group is an amide group and it is acting as the linker. In addition, the letters used to complete the sequence are listed in such a way as to conform to where they fit in the structure. Further, if a substituent is present on the tail group (i.e., 5-flouro), this is placed at the front of the name, while linked group substituents would be placed before the linked group. Finally, core substituents would be placed at the end of the code name. However, this system is not without flaws. Using this template, according to the EMCDDA, AB-FUBINACA (as it is often reported in the literature), with the IUPAC nomenclature *N*-(1-carbamoyl-2-methyl-propyl)-1-[(4-fluorophenyl)methyl] indazole-3-carboxamide, is called MABO-FUBINACA. Interestingly, the source of "MABO" is not clear.

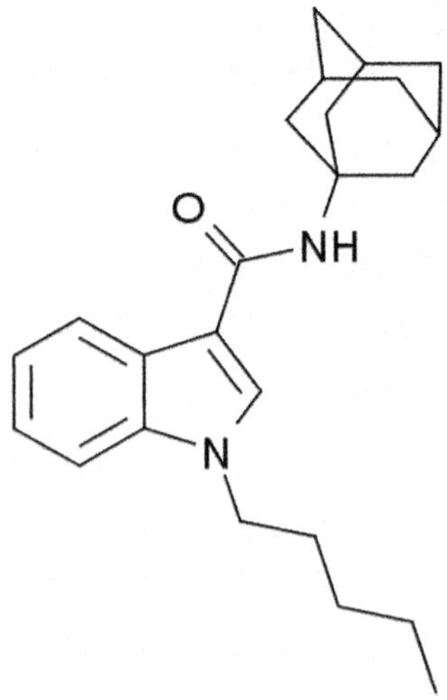

FIGURE 8.2 Chemical structure of *N*-(adamantyl)-1-pentyl-3-1H-indole-3-carboxamide (APICA), illustrating the EMCDDA group designations.

8.1.2 Chemistry

Cannabinoids are compounds with diverse chemical structures that are grouped according to key structural components. Most are lipophilic, readily crossing the blood–brain barrier, and volatile. A key structural feature is the side chain, usually containing between four and nine saturated carbon atoms, which lends to the activity of the molecule. Like their nomenclature, the system(s) used to classify synthetic cannabinoids varies among reports [18–21]. This is not surprising, given the growing list of synthetic cannabinoids; at least 180 different compounds have been reported by the EMCDDA over the last 10 years [22]. Classic cannabinoids such as Δ^{9}-THC are based on a dibenzopyran, while cyclohexylphenol cannabinoids are bicyclic derivatives of Δ^{9}-THC. Naphthoylindoles are often referred to as "first-generation" (e.g., many of the JWH compounds) synthetic cannabinoids. The indole derivatives comprise the largest group of synthetic cannabinoids, which is further divided into benzoyl, naphthoyl, phenylacetyl, alkoyl, carboxylate, and carboxamides. Table 8.1 details the structural classes of synthetic cannabinoids as well as representative members of each class; this table is not exhaustive.

TABLE 8.1
Structural Classes and Representative Examples of Synthetic Cannabinoids

Classification	Examples
Dibenzopyrans	Δ^9-THC, HU-210
Cyclohexylphenols	CP-47,497, CP-47,497-C6, CP47,497-C8, CP,55940
Napthoylindoles	AM-1220, AM-2201, JWH-007, JWH-015, JWH-018, JWH-019, JWH-022, JWH-071, JWH-073, JWH-081, JWH-122, JWH-122 (5-fluoropentyl), JWH-200, JWH-210, JWH-211, JWH-387, JWH-398, MAM-2201
Benzoylindoles	AM-679, AM-694, AM-694 (chloro), AM-2233, RCS-4, WIN-48,098
Phenylacetylindoles	JWH-167, JWH-201, JWH-203, JWH-204, JWH-206, JWH-207, JWH-208, JWH-209, JWH-249, JWH-250, JWH-251, JWH-253, JWH-302, JWH-305, JWH-306, JWH-311, JWH-312, JWH-316, RCS-8
Alkoylindoles	A-7962260, A-834,735, AB-001, AB-005, AM-1248, FUB-144, UR-144, XLR-11 (5-fluoro-UR-144), XLR-12
Indole carboxamides	5-fluoro-CUMYL-PICA, 5-fluoro-NNEI, AB-BICA, AB-CHMICA, AB-FUBICA, ADBICA, ADB-BICA, ADB-FUBICA, CUMYL-BICA, CUMYL-PICA, 5-fluoro-SDB-006, MDMB-CHMICA, MDMB-FUBICA, MMB-2201, MMB-FUBICA, NNEI (MN24), PX-1 (5-fluoro-APP-PICA), SDB-001 (APICA; 2-NEI), STB-006, STS-135
Indazole carboxamides	5-fluoro-AB-PINACA, 5-fluoro-ADB, 5-fluoro-ADB-PINACA, 5-fluoro-AEB (5-fluoro-EMBPINACA), 5-fluoro-AMB, 5-fluoro-CUMYL-PINACA, AB-CHMINACA, AB-CHMINACA, AB-PINACA, ADB-BINACA, ADB-CHMINACA (MAB-CHMINACA), ADB-FUBINACA, ADB-PINACA, ADB-PINACA, AMB, AMB, EMB-FUBINACA, FUB-AKB48 (FUBAPINACA), FUB-AKB48 (FUBAPINACA), MDMB-CHMINACA, MDMB-FUBINACA, MDMB-FUBINACA, PX-2, PX-3 (APP-CHMINACA), THJ

() = alternate name.

Adapted from Debruyne D and Le Boisselier R, *Substance Abuse and Rehabilitation*, 6, 113, 2015 and Abbate, ASM, et al., *Pure Applied Chemistry* 90, 1225, 2018.

8.1.3 Pharmacology

The endocannabinoid system has a role in regulating brain, endocrine, and immune function [23]. The endogenous cannabinoid receptors, subtypes CB_1 and CB_2, are found throughout this system; CB_1 receptors are abundant in the central nervous system [24], while the CB_2 receptors are primarily expressed in the immune system [25]. The endocannabinoid system is thought to act in a retrograde manner, whereby endocannabinoids are released post synapse and travel back across the synaptic cleft [26]. They are not the main neurotransmitters at the synapse but instead, regulate the release of other neurotransmitters, including gamma-aminobutyric acid (GABA) and glutamate, by coupling to G-proteins. Endocannabinoids such as anandamide [27] are natural ligands, but cannabinoids such as Δ^9-THC and synthetic cannabinoids also interact with cannabinoid receptors. CB_1 receptor stimulation inhibits neurotransmitter release, accounting for most neurobehavioral effects.

Synthetic cannabinoids vary in potency and binding affinity (*Ki*) at CB_1 and CB_2 receptors; this contributes to the overall effect experienced by users. In most displacement studies, the binding affinity of the synthetic cannabinoid is determined relative to Δ^9-THC. If the compound has a larger *Ki*, then this indicates a weaker affinity for the receptor. A smaller *Ki* is reflective of a stronger binding affinity. To put this in perspective, the *Ki* of Δ^9-THC at CB_1 is 39.5 nM, while the *Ki* of JWH-018 and HU-210 at CB_1 is 9.0 and 0.06 nM, respectively [28, 29].

The half maximal effect concentration (EC_{50}) is used to describe potency; it is the concentration at which 50% of the maximal effect is observed. Recent studies demonstrated that selected third-generation synthetic cannabinoids, such as 5F-PB-22 (K_i = 2.87 nM, EC_{50} 1.2 nM) and BB-22 (K_i = 0.88 nM, EC_{50} = 2.5 nM), retain greater CB_1 receptor agonist potency (five- and sevenfold, respectively) and efficacy, as well as a higher binding affinity (26- and 30-fold, respectively) at CB_1 than JWH-018 [30].

8.1.4 Analytical Techniques

The rapid emergence of new synthetic cannabinoids has posed many challenges for laboratory personnel in charge of screening, confirming, and quantifying these compounds in biological matrices. Immunoassay techniques such as enzyme-linked immunosorbent assay (ELISA) are used as a screening tool in most laboratories. Generally, they are compound specific with limited cross-reactivity. ELISA immunoassays targeted to the parent compound may not cross-react with metabolites and provide limited information regarding the structure of the compound. Therefore, ELISA may identify which class of drugs is present, but this technique generally lacks the ability to identify a specific member of the class.

Targeted liquid chromatography-tandem mass spectrometry (LC-MS-MS) is a high-throughput methodology, but if it is to be used to identify compounds that have not already been identified, certified reference standards are required for confirmation. In short, a targeted analytical technique will not identify new synthetic cannabinoids. Non-targeted MS screening is an ideal technique as it provides a measurement of the accurate mass, may identify and confirm fragment ions, and will provide structural as well as metabolite information [31].

8.1.5 Metabolism

The detection of synthetic cannabinoids in biological samples is challenging not only from an analytical perspective but also because these compounds are rapidly [32] and extensively metabolized. Due to a lack of preclinical safety data, there are limited controlled studies investigating synthetic cannabinoid metabolism in humans. Investigators often rely on *in vitro* incubations with human liver hepatocytes (HLH) or human liver microsomes (HLM) [19] and then confirm the results using authentic urine samples from known users or from self-administration. Incubations with HLH are reflective of the liver environment; they retain the activity of cytochrome P450 (CYP) enzymes, carboxylesterase (CES) enzymes, UDP-glucuronosyl-transferase (UGT) enzymes, cofactors, transporters, and binding proteins [31]. Inter-individual variations in liver enzyme activity are common; this issue is overcome *in vitro* using pooled HLM. The disadvantage of HLM incubation is the fact that CYP and UGT enzymes are often so enriched in the liver preparation that there is a lack of competition with other enzymes. Ultimately, the overall abundance of the metabolites may not reflect what would be observed *in vivo* [31]. Various CYP isoforms, including CYP2C9, CYP2C19, CYP1A2, CYP3A4, and CYP2B6 [33–36], CES enzymes, including CES1 [37], as well as several UGT enzymes, including UGT1A1, UGT1A9, and UGT2B7 [38], have been implicated in the metabolism of synthetic cannabinoids.

Synthetic cannabinoids are mainly hydroxylated, dealkylated, and carboxylated prior to conjugation. Hydroxylation occurs at various positions on the molecule, which may include the aliphatic chain, the indole, the naphthalene, or the substituted aromatic rings. These may be further metabolized to carboxylic acids, conjugated with glucuronic acid. and excreted into urine as glucuronic acid conjugates [37, 39, 40]. Urine is easy to collect, affords adequate sample volume, and provides longer detection windows than blood; it is the most common biological matrix for NPS metabolite analysis [41]. Typically, the concentrations of the parent compound (if detected) as well as the metabolites are low due to the lower doses required with the use of high-potency synthetic cannabinoids [42]. Identification of synthetic cannabinoid metabolites is important; not only are some metabolites active, for example, a hydroxylated metabolite of JWH-018 [43], but metabolites serve as markers of synthetic cannabinoid intake.

Many compounds, such as 1-Naphthyl 1-(4-fluorobenzyl)-1H-indole-3-carboxylate (FDU-PB-22) and 8-Quinolinyl 1-(4-fluorobenzyl)-1H-indole-3-carboxylate (FUB-PB-22), are structurally similar and share metabolites (Figure 8.3). Their metabolism was investigated *in vitro* using HLM and confirmed using authentic urine samples [44]. FDU-PB-22 and FUB-PB-22 underwent extensive ester hydrolysis when incubated with HLM, and both compounds shared the same carboxylic acid metabolite. The same metabolite was identified in authentic urine samples collected from drivers suspected of driving under the influence of FDU-PB-22 and FUB-PB-22. Both compounds were detected in blood samples (both FUB-PB-22 and FDU-PB-22 were detected in one driver, while only FUB-PB-22 was detected in the other); parent drug was not detected in urine specimens. The authors concluded that in urine, it is not possible to differentiate between FDU-PB-22 and FUB-PB-22 intake due to extensive ester hydrolysis. However, the carboxylic acid metabolite was a good marker of FDU-PB-22 and/or FUB-PB-22 intake.

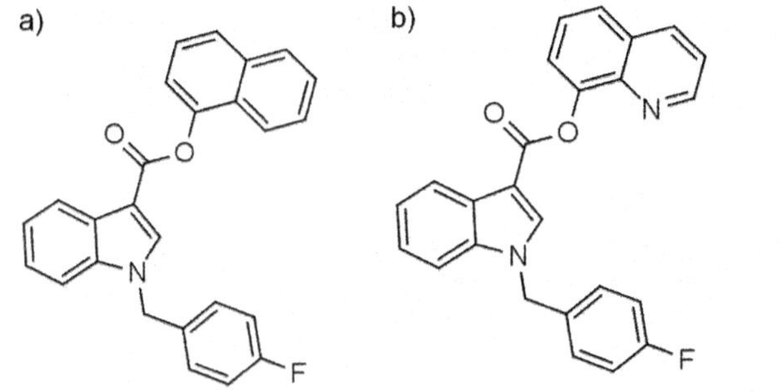

FIGURE 8.3 Chemical structure of (a) FDU-PB-22 and (b) FUB-PB-22.

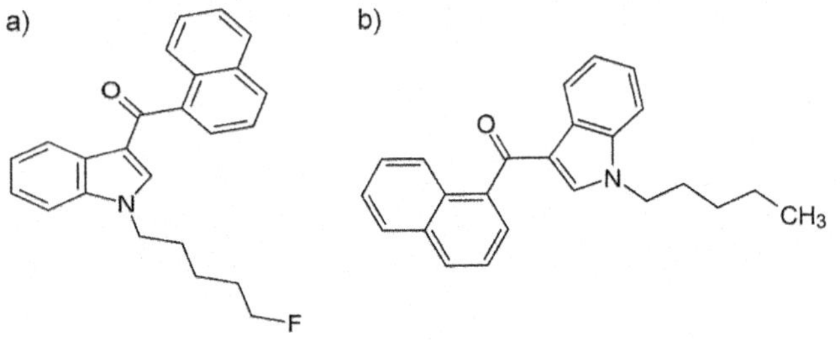

FIGURE 8.4 Chemical structure of (a) AM-2201 and (b) JWH-018.

In a human self-administration study, 5 mg of [1-(5-fluoropentyl)-1H-indazol-3-yl](naphthalen-1-yl)methanone (AM-2201) was ingested to identify urinary metabolites [45]. In urine, the major metabolites identified were JWH-018 *N*-(5-OH-pentyl), JWH-018 *N*-pentanoic acid, AM-2201 6-OH-indole, and AM-2201 *N*-(4-OH-pentyl). The highest concentrations were for JWH-018 *N*-pentanoic acid and JWH-018 *N*-(5-OH-pentyl). However, the investigator only ingested AM-2201, and it was therefore determined that AM-2201 and JWH-018 share metabolites. Similar findings were reported using HLM [46]. This is not surprising, as AM-2201 and JWH-018 are structurally similar (Figure 8.4). The authors concluded that the presence of AM-2201 6-OH-indole and AM-2201 *N*-(4-OH-pentyl) metabolites are required to confirm AM-2201 intake.

8.1.6 Pharmacokinetics and Toxicology

With over 180 synthetic cannabinoids now reported in the literature, the interpretation of clinical and postmortem concentrations offers significant challenges and must be done with caution. The main challenges arise from the paucity of pharmacologic data and the absence of controlled pharmacokinetic and pharmacodynamic studies. Synthetic cannabinoids produce common clinical signs and symptoms such as psychosis, agitation, hallucinations, seizures, hypertension, tachycardia, and in many cases, multiorgan failure and rhabdomyolysis [47]. In general, they display a sympathomimetic-type overdrive despite the apparent interaction with CB_1 and CB_2 receptors. This may suggest that their interaction with CB_1 and CB_2 receptors causes similar effects to sympathomimetics and/or that they have effects on sympathomimetic pathways.

In another human pharmacokinetic study, six subjects inhaled smoke from 2 and 3 mg of JWH-018, following which the drug and ten of its metabolites were measured in blood after 12 hours using LC-MS-MS [48]. The maximum concentration of JWH-018 ranged from 2.9 to 9.9 ng/mL approximately 5 min after inhalation, which markedly decreased during the next 1.5 hours, after which a multi-exponential decline ($t_{1/2}$ medians 1.3 and 5.7 h) was observed. The observation implies that gradual accumulation of the drug may be seen in chronic abusers. The authors of the study suggest that the observed multi-exponential decline leads to slow terminal elimination of JWH-018 and all its metabolites. Since it has been known for years that with prolonged use Δ^9-THC accumulates in adipose tissue, it should be no surprise that the analogues do as well [49].

In another study, forensic cases were analyzed for the presence of JWH-018 and two of its metabolites, JWH-018 *N*-(5-OH-pentyl) and JWH-018 *N*-pentanoic acid, using LC-MS-MS [50]. JWH-018 was detected in only 3 of the 600 blood samples (range 0.3–0.8 ng/mL; mean 0.6 ng/mL) and was not detected in any urine samples. JWH-018 *N*-(5-OH-pentyl) was detected in 92 blood samples (range 0.3–22.7 ng/mL; mean 2.5 ng/mL) and 63 urine samples (range 8.7–27.9 ng/mL; mean 15.4 ng/mL). Finally, JWH-018 *N*-pentanoic acid was detected in 145 blood samples (range 0.3–63.5 ng/mL; mean 6.4 ng/mL) and 93 urine samples (range 2.6–327.0 ng/mL; mean 65.4 ng/mL). This suggests that JWH-018 has a short half-life but also highlights the longer detection window for metabolites.

There is significant overlap in the concentrations of synthetic cannabinoids presented in human performance reports, clinical case reports, and postmortem reports [51–56]. When detected in blood, the majority of the concentrations reported were <1.0 ng/mL. This is not surprising as these compounds are extensively and rapidly metabolized.

The synthetic cannabinoids are known to be lipophilic, but their characteristics within biological matrices has not been studied. In cases where solid tissues such as adipose tissue and organs are simultaneously reported with blood values, the findings confirm the lipophilic nature of these compounds and support the idea that these compounds are prone to postmortem redistribution [57, 58]. Concentrations should be interpreted taking into account the total circumstances of the case. Given the lipophilic properties of these compounds, the ratio between central and peripheral blood together with the volume of distribution, the time between exposure and death, the route of administration, and the rate of decomposition must be considered. In isolation, any single blood value may be misleading. Further complicating the postmortem interpretation of synthetic cannabinoid concentrations is the fact that there is insufficient data regarding the stability of these compounds in blood and other tissues.

8.1.7 Legal Status

The regulation of synthetic cannabinoids continues to evolve as illicit manufacturers structurally modify compounds to evade legislation. The control status of a particular synthetic cannabinoid may vary between countries, although the rationale behind regulation is similar [20]. In general, there are two approaches to coping with the continuous influx of synthetic cannabinoids each year.

Some countries have taken the approach of listing the specific compounds by their chemical and common names. This method is clear and unambiguous, with the compound in concern clearly listed and clearly illegal. However, if the compound is not listed, then technically it is not illegal, and therein lies a problem. With the continual manufacture of structurally similar compounds, this approach is laborious and requires constant updating. Nonetheless, countries such as Russia, Switzerland, Austria, and Germany and several other European countries have taken this approach [59].

The second approach is a more circumspective method where legislation is scripted to cover entire classes of chemicals and their analogues. In the United States, for example, legislation was put forward by Congress using what is referred to as the "analogue principle." This incorporates chemicals that are substantially similar in structure and share similar pharmacological and toxicological activity with the psychoactive prototype [60]. This seems a sensible approach, as it offers a more dynamic legislation for dealing with an ever-changing market in a prospective manner, but there are limitations. There is no general agreement among experts as to what constitutes an analogue-based structural similarity, nor is there any agreement on what constitutes an analogue based on similarities in pharmacology and toxicology. The latter point is exceptionally challenging because controlled data for these compounds does not exist. Further, just because two chemicals are structurally similar, this does not mean that they will have similar pharmacology and exert similar toxicology outcomes.

A blanket generic approach was proposed in the United Kingdom, Luxembourg, and Ireland, whereby compounds that are structurally similar to substances previously identified in herbal blends are banned. The legislation listed some exceptions, such as alcohol, nicotine, and caffeine [20]. Japan has taken another approach that lists each and every compound under the "Designated Substances" classification [61].

8.2 PHENETHYLAMINES

Phenethylamines are primary amines; the amino group is attached to a benzene ring through a two-carbon ethyl

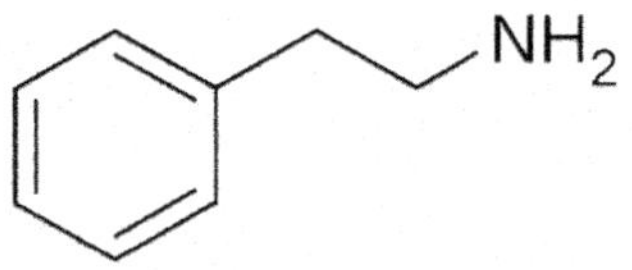

FIGURE 8.5 Chemical structure of phenethylamine.

group (Figure 8.5). All phenethylamines are colorless and liquid at room temperature. Members of this family have a fishy odor and are soluble in water, ethanol, and ether. Many other monoamine alkaloids exist, including MDMA, amphetamine, and methamphetamine, but are not considered here as they are not "new."

Most phenethylamines are stimulants, but some of the designer substitutions have additional psychoactive properties [62]. Table 8.2 is a simplified listing of the multitude of phenethylamines that are now available on the black market. It is not an exhaustive list, but it does list the major categories and some examples of each that will be discussed.

8.2.1 Methylated Phenethylamines

8.2.1.1 D-Series

This group is characterized by the presence of methoxy groups at positions 2 and 5 of the benzene ring with variation at the fourth position. As a result, these drugs have hallucinogenic properties due to their $5HT_{2a}$, $5\text{-}HT_{2b}$, and $5\text{-}HT_{2c}$ serotonergic receptor agonist activity. 2,5-dimethoxy-4-bromoamphetamine (DOB) and 2,5-dimethoxy-4-chloroamphetamine (DOC) are two examples of methylated phenethylamines. They have a slow onset (1 hour) yet are potent, requiring a small dose, which puts naïve users at risk, as they may overdose believing that the drug is not working. These compounds have a long period of action with effects lasting for days. A death has been reported from the use of 2,5-dimethoxy-4-bromoamphetamine (DOM) [63]. There is no human pharmacokinetic data available, and the limited toxicity data comes from very few case reports [64]. DOM does not enhance, and might attenuate, the positive reinforcing effects of the mu-opioid receptor agonist heroin.

8.2.1.2 Benzodifurans

This group of phenethylamines has members in both the ring-substituted amphetamines and the ring-substituted methylenedioxy-phenethylamines (Table 8.2). Benzodifurans (containing two heterocyclic rings), including bromo-dragonFLY and 2-CB-FLY, are ring-substituted phenylethylamines with potent $5HT_{2A}$ receptor agonist effects and predominant hallucinogenic effects. The effects can last for up to 2–3 days. Bromo-dragonFLY toxicity produces excess adrenergic activity and severe vasoconstriction, in some cases resulting in limb amputation, delayed onset of seizures, and toxicity [65]. Deaths secondary to bromo-dragonFLY have occurred in Europe and the United States [66].

Recently identified (6-(2-Aminopropyl)benzofuran) (6-APB) and (5-(2-Aminopropyl)benzofuran) (5-APB) are single–furan ring benzofuran compounds that can produce sympathetic system stimulation and euphoria. Similarly to most other stimulant members of this general group, they are believed to exert their effects by stimulation of monoamine pathways and as agonists at 5HT receptors. A fatal case of 5-APB reported a postmortem blood concentration of 2.9 mg/L with a trace of alcohol [67].

8.2.1.3 Aminoindanes

When mephedrone, piperazine derivatives, and other synthetic cathinones were banned between 2009 and 2010, a new class of synthetic drugs called the aminoindanes came to the market almost immediately (Figure 8.6). It is reported that these drugs are non-neurotoxic analogues of amphetamine and MDMA, causing serotonin release and inhibiting reuptake inhibition effects [68]. These were marketed as

TABLE 8.2
Structural Classes and Representative Examples of Phenethylamines

Sub-classification			Examples
Methylated phenethylamines			
	Ring-substituted amphetamines	D-series	DOB, DOC, DOI, DON, DOM
		Benzodifurans	DOB-DragonFly, 2C-B-Fly
		Aminoindanes	2AI, 2AT, MMAI
	Beta-ketonated amphetamines	Natural cathinone	
		Synthetic cathinones	Mephedrone, methedrone, bupropion, methcathinone
		Pyrrolidine derivatives	MOPP, MPPP, αPPP
Methylenedioxy-phenethylamines			
	Ring-substituted methylenedioxy-phenethylamines	Beta-ketonated	Ethylone, methylone, MDPV, MDPPP
		Aminoindanes	MDAI, 5IAI, MBDB, 6APB, 5APB
	N-benzyl derivatives (2C series)		2CB, 2CI, 2CD, 2C-NBOMe, 2CBFlyNBOM
Ring-substituted phenethylamines	Mescaline, dopamine, tyramine		

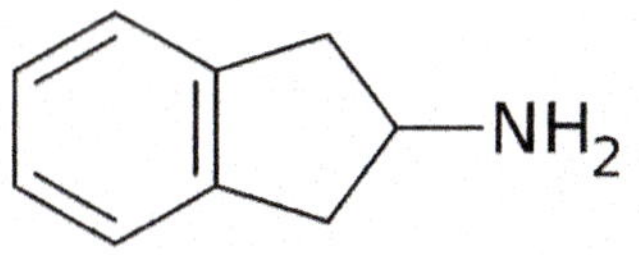

FIGURE 8.6 Chemical structure of aminoindane.

analogues of MDMA and supposedly were less neurotoxic. One of the first was 5,6-methylenedioxy-2-aminoindane (MDAI), and this was followed by 4,6-methylenedioxy-*N*-methyl-2-aminoindane (2-AI), 5-iodo-2-aminoindane (5-IAI), 5-methoxy-6-methyl-2-aminoindane (NMAI) and 5-methoxy-2-aminoindane (MEAI) [69].

Like other synthetic drugs, aminoindanes were originally investigated for possible clinical use for treatment of Parkinson's disease and psychotherapy. They are believed to act mainly through serotonergic pathways. Deaths have been reported, but in every reported case involving MDAI, other drugs or alcohol were present [70]. Single case reports exist for both 5-IAI and 2-AI [71].

8.2.2 Methylenedioxy-phenethylamines

8.2.2.1 *N*-benzyl derivatives (2C series)

25C-NBOMe: Numerous configurations of this molecule are possible, and there is a large family of analogues: 25I-NBOMe, 25B-NBOMe, and 25I-CBOMe, to name a few. These drugs act as 5-HT_{2A} receptor agonists (they are classified as type 2C agonists) and can produce typical serotonin syndrome with bizarre behavior and severe agitation. Only a small amount of drug is needed to produce symptoms that may persist for days. Because of their potency, members of the family are sold on impregnated blotter paper. The terminology "2C" is an acronym coined by Alexander Shulgin for the two carbon atoms between the benzene ring and the amino group on the analogue being synthesized [72]. Pharmacokinetic studies have not been performed, although postmortem tissue concentrations were measured in one case: an intoxicated 19-year old who fell/leaped from a balcony and died of multiple blunt force trauma. Autopsy was performed 7 hours after death, and it revealed essentially the same concentration in heart and peripheral blood (410 and 405 pg/mL, respectively) [73]. A fatal case of 25C-NBOMe toxicity is reported in which both antemortem and postmortem samples were analyzed. The young male died approximately 12 hours post ingestion, having presented with serotonin-type symptoms. Postmortem samples of peripheral blood (0.6 μg/kg), urine (2.9 μg/kg), vitreous humor (0.33 μg/kg), liver (0.82 μg/kg), and gastric contents (0.32 μg/kg) were quantified for 25C-NBOMe, and a blood sample (0.81 μg/kg) taken before death at 2–4 hours post ingestion was also available [74].

8.2.3 Legal Status

Most, if not all, members of this group are considered Schedule 1 or Class A drugs in the United States and are therefore illegal to possess or sell. In the United States, aminoindane is not scheduled but is considered an analogue of amphetamine, and therefore, possession of this drug may lead to prosecution. It was classified as a controlled substance in China in 2015. Aminoindanes are generally not well controlled within Europe, and different member states have placed these drugs in varied legal status.

8.3 SYNTHETIC CATHINONES

"Bath salts" is the most common name for substances that fall within a broad category of drugs called "synthetic cathinones," which are related to a naturally occurring stimulant found in the Khat plant. Synthetic cathinones are considered "euphoric stimulants" with a short duration of action and physical and psychological effects similar to those of other stimulants such as cocaine and amphetamine. They are beta-keto analogues of amphetamines; however, despite their commonalities in chemical structure, synthetic cathinones possess distinct neuropharmacological profiles that produce unique effects. In addition, the non-keto analogues of synthetic cathinones target monoamine systems, causing the release of neurotransmitters exhibiting stimulant properties, although some of the members of this group have hallucinogenic effects.

Synthetic cathinones can be administered by almost any route. In the absence of human pharmacokinetic studies, it is not known whether one route of administration is more advantageous than another. Effects are apparent 30–45 minutes after ingestion, and the desired effects last 1–3 hours. A number of deaths have occurred after the use of different cathinone derivatives, including alpha-pyrrolidinobutiophenone (α-PBP), alpha-pyrrolidinovalerophenone (α-PVP), 4-methoxy-alpha-pyrrolidinoheptanophenone (PV8), and 4-methoxy-alpha-pyrrolidinooctanophenone (PV9) [75–79].

A review study of 32 human performance and postmortem cases, involving six different synthetic cathinones, has been published. Blood concentrations were reported for 23 postmortem cases. The concentrations ranged from 10 to 729 ng/mL. The lowest concentration (10 ng/mL) was for 3,4-methylenedioxypyrovalerone (MDPV), while the highest concentration (729 ng/mL) corresponded to methylone. All the cases involved other drugs.

8.3.1 3,4-Methylenedioxypyrovalerone

MDVP is the 3,4-methylenedioxy ring-substituted analogue of pyrovalerone (Figure 8.7). It was first synthesized in 1969 but reappeared in 2007 in Germany as a NPS [1]. MDVP is also known as "Molly" and is the most common synthetic cathinone identified in blood and urine of patients admitted to emergency departments after taking "bath salts." The popularity of this drug may have to do with the fact that MDVP is the only synthetic cathinone that has no effect on serotonin receptors, making empathogenic feelings unlikely. MDVP acts primarily as a stimulant and can cause

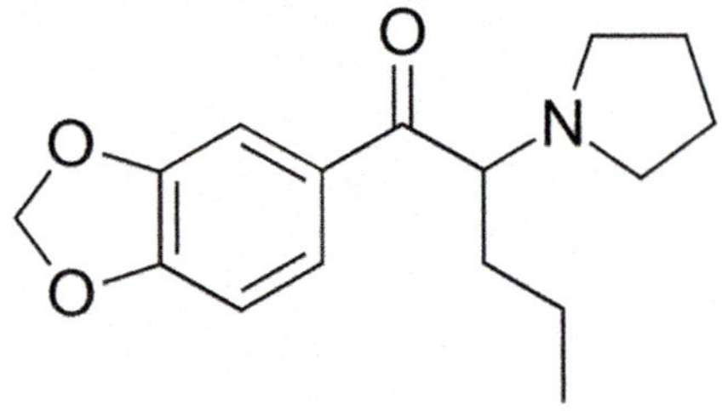

FIGURE 8.7 Chemical structure of MDVP.

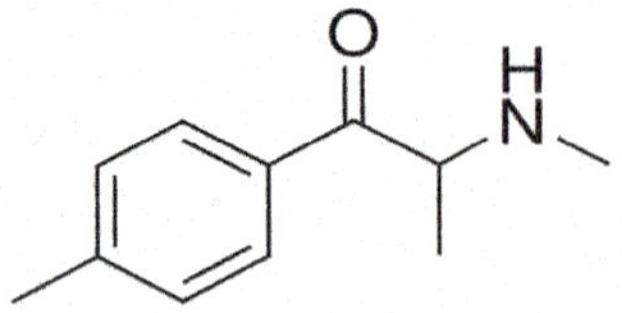

FIGURE 8.8 Chemical structure of mephedrone.

psychosis. It still retains the ability to prevent the reuptake of dopamine and noradrenaline, thereby increasing concentrations of both. In humans, dopamine accumulation and stimulation not only increases euphoria but also increases the probability of addiction, at least in experimental animals [78]. That said, given the number of years that MDVP has been on the market, MDVP addiction has yet to become a proven problem. A handful of MDVP deaths have been reported, but there is limited data to distinguish them from any other cause of excited delirium.

8.3.2 Mephedrone

Mephedrone is a synthetic cathinone with stimulant properties (Figure 8.8) and is often labeled as "plant food" or "bath salts." It is a beta-keto amphetamine; however, the beta group decreases the potency of the amphetamine-like activity but preserves its central and peripheral "empathogenic" activity. Its actions are similar to those of MDVP. In excess, mephedrone produces a typical hyperadrenergic syndrome. In very large doses, it can induce psychosis.

Mephedrone's predominant actions are on serotonin as opposed to dopamine transporters, suggesting that the newer analogues of mephedrone, such as 4-methyl amphetamine, may cause entactogenic effects similarly to MDMA. The analogue 3-methylmethcathinone (3-MMC) has more stimulant-type properties, like those of amphetamine. Because of pharmacological and structural similarities to mephedrone, similar health risks can be expected for these analogues [79]. A study of six male volunteers, all given a 150 mg dose of mephedrone, has been reported [80]. 4′-carboxy-mephedrone and nor-mephedrone were identified as the most common metabolites. *N*-succinyl-nor-mephedrone was the metabolite with the longest half-life (8.2 hours). In urine, 4′-carboxy-mephedrone was the main metabolite recovered.

In a report of 18 deaths involving mephedrone, 9 cases listed mephedrone toxicity as the cause of death. Postmortem blood concentrations ranged between 1.33 and 22 mg/L [81]. A further six cases of mephedrone combined with multiple other drugs had postmortem blood concentrations of mephedrone that ranged between 0.04 and 1.3 mg/L. An earlier report from 2010 indicated that multiple other drugs tend to be present with mephedrone [82]. A study carried out examining the stability of mephedrone over 6 months in whole blood in both antemortem and postmortem samples found that mephedrone was most stable when stored at −20 degrees Celsius [81].

8.3.3 Methylone

Methylone is a substituted cathinone and is an analogue of MDMA, first encountered in 2005 (Figure 8.9) [83]. Methylone is another beta-keto amphetamine popular in Europe and Asia but rarely used in the United States. It acts on catecholamine transporters and possibly on the vesicular monoamine transporter. In a report describing a case of sudden death, the blood concentration was 70 ng/mL [84]. There have been no human pharmacokinetic studies, but in four postmortem studies, heart blood concentrations ranged from 0.060 to 1.12 mg/L [85]. In the absence of further data, it would be fair to assume that its clinical effects generally resemble those of any other beta-keto amphetamine.

The clinical toxicity displayed in emergency room patients is mostly that of sympathetic stimulation with agitation, tachycardia, and systolic hypertension [86]. When death occurs, symptoms are mostly non-specific with pulmonary edema and some evidence of upper airway obstruction.

8.3.4 Butylone

Butylone is the beta-keto (substituted cathinone) analogue of methylbenzodioxolylbutanamine (MBDB) and the substituted methylenedioxyphenethylamine analogue of buphedron (Figure 8.10). Butylone shares the same common effects of "empathogens" (secondary to blockade of serotonin reuptake) and stimulation from minimally modified

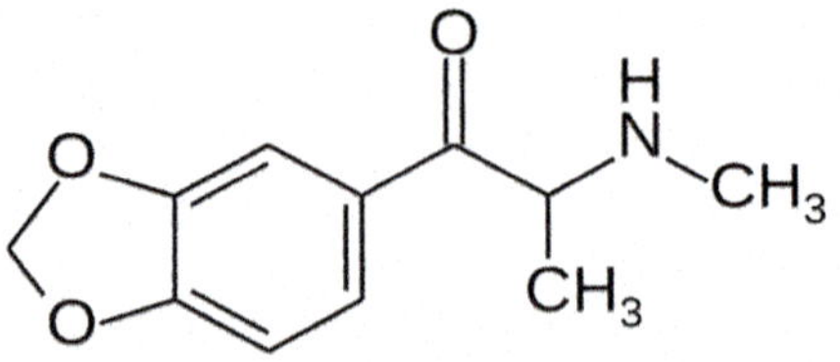

FIGURE 8.9 Chemical structure of methylone.

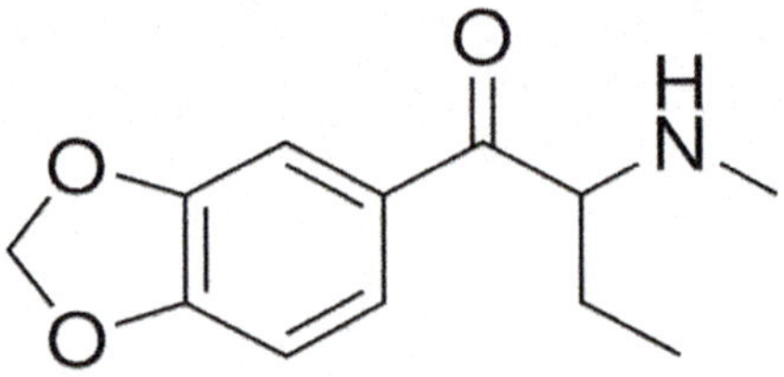

FIGURE 8.10 Chemical structure of butylone.

amphetamines. Other than the fact that it can be metabolized by any of three routes – demethylation followed by O-methylation, beta-keto reduction, and dealkylation [87] – nothing is known of the drug's pharmacokinetics, although an abundance of analytical techniques to identify butylone in tissue appear to be available [88].

8.3.5 Pyrrolidinovalerophenone

α-PVP is more commonly known as FLAKKA (Figure 8.11). Like the other members of its group, use is associated with hyperstimulation and agitation. α-PVP acts as a noradrenergic-dopamine reuptake inhibitor in a way that is similar to its methylenedioxy derivative MDPV [89]. Very little is known about this compound, although it certainly can cause psychosis. It achieved abundant publicity for causing "zombie"-like behavior in the United States. Nonetheless, this molecule appears to be especially toxic, probably as a consequence of combined dopamine toxicity, induced reactive oxygen and nitrogen species formation, and apoptosis. It is a beta-keto amphetamine, and it is reasonable to suppose that it shares similar modes of toxicity [90]. Human pharmacokinetic studies have not been reported, although one measurement of autopsy tissue distribution has been published [91]. Blood, urine, brain, kidney, liver, and gastric contents were reported as 174, 401, 292, 122, 190, and 606 ng/mL, respectively.

In the one reported postmortem study, analysis by LC-MS-MS (limit of detection 0.2 ng/mL for α-PVP and 0.5 ng/mL for α-pyrrolidinohexiophenone [PHP]), no α-PVP was detected in any tissue except hair, confirming early use but ostensibly excluding it as a cause of death. α-PHP is a longer-chain homologue of α-PVP. In one reported case, a large man and a known heavy user of α-PHP, α-PHP was present in all tissues examined. Interestingly, bile and urine concentrations (1.2 and 5.6 ng/mL, respectively) were lower than in blood collected in the thoracic cavity (15.3 ng/mL). Lung and spleen had the highest concentrations: lung was 71.1 ng/mL, and spleen was 83.8 ng/mL. Concentrations of 3.5, 7.9, 4.7, and 23.6 ng/mL were observed in the liver, kidney, brain, and heart, respectively [92].

8.3.6 Dibutylone

Dibutylone is a stimulant drug and a beta-keto amphetamine that is structurally related to butylone (Figure 8.12). It is one of the newer designer drugs that have been

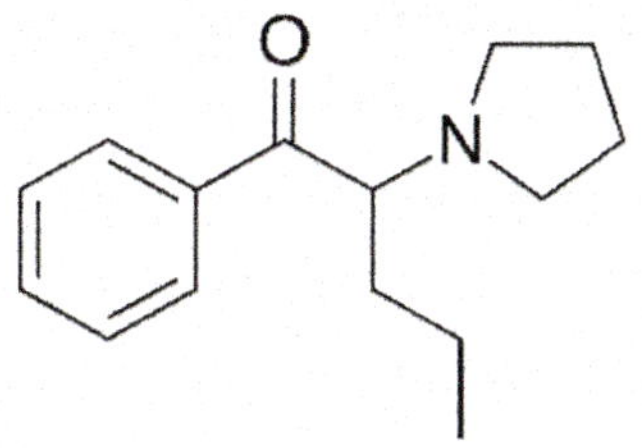

FIGURE 8.11 Chemical structure of α-PVP.

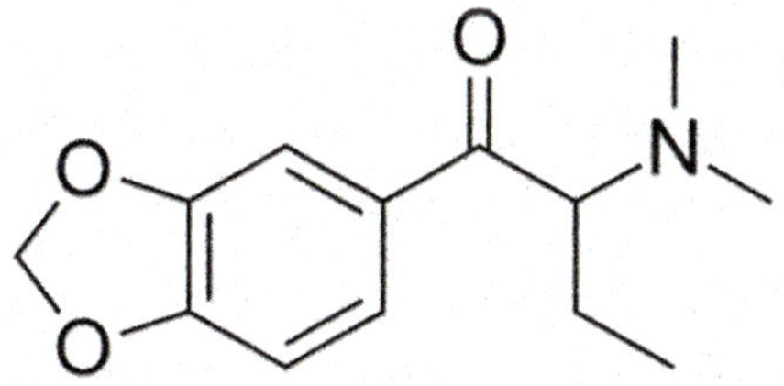

FIGURE 8.12 Chemical structure of dibutylone.

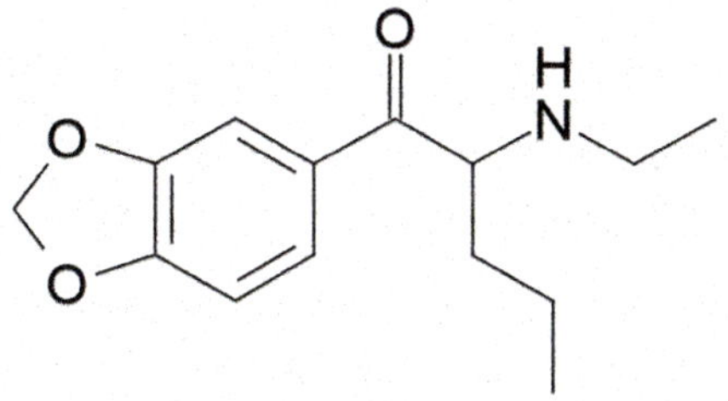

FIGURE 8.13 Chemical structure of *N*-ethyl pentylone.

detected in products marketed as bath salts or plant food. Its main metabolite is butylone. Five other metabolites have been identified when dibutylone is incubated with HLM. Dibutylone concentrations in tissues, including blood, urine, vitreous humor, and liver, ranged between 10 and 1,400 ng/mL [93].

8.3.7 *N*-Ethyl Pentylone

N-ethyl pentylone is a substituted cathinone (Figure 8.13), and like the other members of this group, it shares attenuated amphetamine-like activity with accompanying feelings of euphoria and agitation. Blood concentrations in four *N*-ethyl pentylone deaths were reported from Alabama with values ranging from 0.031 to 0.953 mg/L [94]. However, none of the deaths were solely due to *N*-ethyl pentylone toxicity. In specimens collected as part of death investigation cases (n = 17), the blood concentrations ranged from 12 to 790 ng/mL, while specimens from drugged drivers (n = 5) ranged from 21 to 87 ng/mL [95].

8.3.8 Legal Status

In the United States, numerous synthetic cathinones were placed under CSA [5] control between 1973 and 2018, with an emphasis on ten cathinones, which were placed into Schedule I in 2017 (butylone, naphyrone, pentylone, pentedrone, 3-fluoro-N-methylcathinone (FMC), 4-FMC, 4-methyl-N-ethylcathinone, 4-methyl-pyrrolidinopropiophenone, α-PBP, and α-PVP). Mephedrone was banned in Israel and Sweden in 2008 and in the European Union and the United States in 2012.

8.4 PIPERAZINES

Piperazines do not occur in nature; they are entirely synthetic and are a class of compounds that mimic the effects of Ecstasy (MDMA/MDA). Benzylpiperazines (BZP) and phenylpiperazine are the two main structural groups from which the derivatives are derived (Table 8.3, Figure 8.14). On the streets, these drugs carry various names that include "A2," "Bliss," "Herbal Ecstasy," "Legal X," "Bolts," "Frenzy," "Exodus," and "Good Stuff," to name a few. Although they were originally investigated as anti-helminthic agents for livestock in the 1940s–1950s, they were never developed for market due to their stimulant properties. Similarly, they were investigated in the 1970s as antidepressants, but likewise, as their amphetamine/stimulant properties became apparent, they were not pursued for treatment purposes. Cyclizine is a piperazine with a legitimate medical use as an anti-histamine with anti-nausea properties. In the 1990s, several piperazines, labeled as legal alternatives to Ecstasy, appeared on the rave or dance club circuit. They were commonly referred to as "party pills." Piperazines were popular in New Zealand as a legal party drug, and in 2007, an estimated five million BZP pills were sold in New Zealand [96]. They are considered to have approximately one-tenth the potency of amphetamine. At lower doses, they produce the stimulant effects, and at higher doses, they will produce hallucinations.

8.4.1 Pharmacology and Toxicology

BZP is thought to cause both the release of dopamine and noradrenaline and inhibition of monoamine reuptake. The elevated levels of noradrenaline readily explain the rise in blood pressure and heart rate associated with these drugs. The mild hallucinogenic effects of BZP at high doses are due to its binding with the $5HT_{2a}$ receptor. Activity through this receptor subtype in the gastrointestinal tract is thought to provide an explanation for the intense side effects, including stomach pains and nausea, caused by these drugs [97]. Phenylpiperazines are believed to act more directly post-synaptically at 5HT receptors and also act indirectly to release serotonin and/or decrease its reuptake. The phenylpiperazines have lower noradrenergic and dopaminergic activity [98]. The lack of dopaminergic activity may account for the reduced addictiveness [99].

The piperazine drugs are typically taken in tablet or powder form but are also known to be available in liquid form. Piperazine derivatives are rapidly absorbed in the gastrointestinal tract [100] and are mainly metabolized in the liver by the CYP enzymes [83]. The derivatives are known to cross the blood–brain barrier readily. The central effects of these compounds occur approximately 2 hours after oral

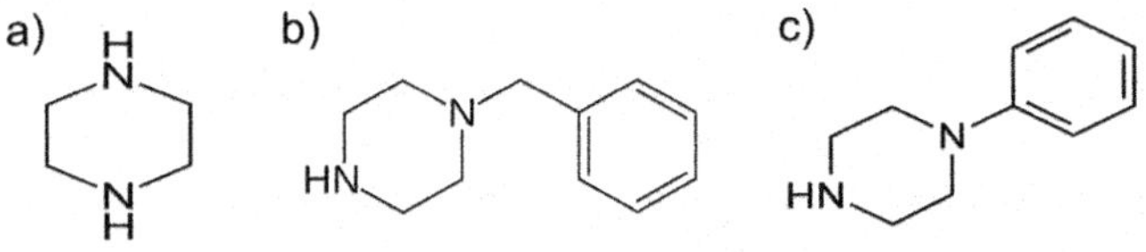

FIGURE 8.14 Chemical structure of a) piperazine, b) benzylpiperazine, and c) phenylpiperazine.

ingestion and will last 4–8 hours [101]. The metabolism of mCPP and 3-TFMPP involves hydroxylation by CYP2D6 with glucuronidation, sulfation, and acetylation [102, 103]. Inter-individual variation is probably the result of CYP2D6 polymorphism [104].

Several human studies have been performed. In one, seven volunteers took 200 mg of an oral form of BZP. The maximum mean plasma concentration was 262 ng/mL after 75 minutes. The major metabolites included 3-hydroxy benzylpiperazine and 4-hydroxy benzylpiperazine. The elimination half-life was 5.5 hours, with plasma levels detectable up to 30 hours post ingestion [100]. A study into the subjective effects on volunteers who took 100 or 200 mg BZP, 30 mg 3-3-TFMPP, or 60 mg TFMMP has also been performed [105]. BZP showed significant dexamphetamine-like stimulant effects, inducing euphoria, sociability, and drug-liking, whereas 3-TFMPP induced fewer stimulant-like effects, but increased anxiety, via its serotonergic effects. The combination of BZP and 3-TFMPP induced similar subjective effects along with well-characterized dexamphetamine and MDMA-like effects.

The piperazines have been sold as MDMA and as adulterants in cocaine, amphetamine, and Ecstasy. mCPP has an elimination half-life of 2.6–6.1 hours, but there is individual variation, with marked variation in peak concentrations [101]. Few deaths have been reported with piperazines: 19 postmortem cases involving piperazines (BZP and 3-TFMPP) have been reported, but in all cases, either an independent cause of death was determined or there were multiple other drugs present [106]. A single case of multi-organ failure due to BZP ingestion has been reported [107].

In a postmortem study of blood from three fatalities involving BZP and/or 3-TFMPP, blood concentrations of BZP ranged from <0.50 to 1.4 ng/L, and 3-TMFPP concentrations ranged from 0.05 to 0.15 mg/L. In each case, alcohol and/or other drugs were present [108]. Another report describes a woman who had taken BZP and developed the full spectrum of status epilepticus, disseminated intravascular coagulopathy, rhabdomyolysis, and renal failure. The concentration of BZP in her blood was 0.2 mg/L 10 hours post admission.

TABLE 8.3
Structural Classification and Representative Examples of Piprazines

Sub-classification	Examples
Benzylpiperazines	*N*-Benzylpiperazine1-(3,4-Methylenedioxybenzyl)-piperazine (MDBZP)
Phenylpiperazines	1-(3-Chlorophenyl)-piperazine (mCPP)1-(3-Trifluoromethylphenyl)-piperazine (3-TFMPP)1-(4-Methoxyphenyl)-piperazine (pMeOPP)1-(4-Fluorophenyl)-piperazine (pFPP)

A second individual reported in the same paper took three to four "party pills" and survived prolonged hospitalization (4 days) after ingesting a mix of BZP and MDMA. Blood concentrations 3 hours after admission were 2.23 mg/L (BZP) and 1.05 mg/L (MDMA) [108]. Still another report describes the postmortem blood concentrations in an individual who combined BZP and MDMA. The amount ingested is not known, nor is it known whether the concentrations were measured in central or peripheral blood. The BZP concentration was 1.7 mg/L blood; MDMA was not quantified [109]. All these patients displayed classic hyperadrenergic syndrome. BZP will not be detected by routine immuno-screening tests, though there is some evidence that high levels of BZP will cross-react to some degree with amphetamine screens, depending on the product used.

One death associated with mCPP use has been reported, but it is far from a clear-cut case, as the decedent died from an acute asthmatic attack and was known to have asthma. A cause and effect relationship between the mCPP and status asthmaticus is not established. Blood levels were not reported [110]. In stored blood samples, either at room temperature or at 4 degrees Celsius, piperazines as a group experience the highest rate of degradation between day 91 (~3 months) and day 182 (~6 months) but then remain fairly stable, with significant amounts still measurable at 1 year. BZP, methyl-BZP, and fluoro-BZP were generally more stable than phenyl piperazines over time under all storage conditions [111].

8.4.2 Piperazine Derivatives

1-cyclohexyl-4-(1,2-diphenylethyl)piperazine) (MT-45) was first reported in 2014 [112]. The first case was a 24-year-old man who was found dead in his chair with bags labeled "MT-45," "Methoxmetamine," and "Methoxphenidine" found in his room. No other history was available. MT-45 was detected in femoral blood, heart blood, liver, pericardial fluid, urine, vitreous humor, and stomach contents. The concentration in femoral blood was 450 μg/L. Specific ELISA kits are available for MT-45, 3,4-Dichloro-N-{[1-(dimethylamino)cyclohexyl]methyl}benzamide (AH-7921), and 3,4-Dichloro-N-[2-(dimethylamino)cyclohexyl]-N-met hylbenzamide (U-47700) (Randox Toxicology), but their use would still require verification with tandem MS. MT-45 first undergoes *N*-dealkylation, then hydroxylation and subsequent glucuronidation, though it appears that only small amounts undergo glucuronidation [113].

An observational study from Sweden describes 11 patients who presented independently, from 2013 to 2014, with severe but non-fatal MT-45 intoxication. In four of the cases, MT-45 was the only drug detected; the others were polydrug intoxications. All the patients were males aged 17–32 years; they commonly presented with opioid-like adverse symptoms, such as unconsciousness and respiratory depression. Naloxone was effective in some of the cases, but not all. Interestingly, three of the patients had transient hearing loss that resolved in a matter of weeks. Later in the same year that the first cases were reported, the same group reported three additional patients, also MT-45 users, with hair depigmentation and loss, widespread folliculitis and dermatitis, as well as painful intertriginous dermatitis, dry eyes, and elevated liver enzymes. Two of the patients also showed transverse white Mees' lines (leukonychia striata) on the fingernails and toenails, while two patients developed bilateral cataracts requiring surgery [114]. These findings remain unexplained.

While the parent compound MT-45 was first synthesized by the Dainippon Company more than 50 years ago, the fluorinated derivative 2F-MT-45 only appeared in 2014 [115]. Three additional fluorinated derivatives have been identified since. Metabolites of MT-45 inhibit mu-opioid receptor–mediated inhibition of cyclic adenosine monophosphate and also inhibit recruitment of beta-arrestin2 (an intracellular protein that helps modulate activity of the sympathetic nervous system) and binding to G- protein. It appears that the fluorinated derivates do not share these actions. Even non-fluorinated MT-45 has only a fraction of morphine's ability to alter beta-arrestin2 or G-proteins, which is probably the reason why Dainippon never bothered to put MT-45 through clinical trials [116].

8.4.3 Legal Status

BZP were classified as controlled substances in the United States in 2002 and in Sweden in 2003. In 2004, BZP were permanently placed on Schedule 1 by the United States DEA. In 2008, they became illegal in New Zealand, and also in 2008, the European Union requested that countries place BZP under control. Piperazines were classified as Class C drugs (under the Misuse of Drugs Act 1971) in the United Kingdom in 2009. MT-45 was scheduled by the United States DEA in 2017 when the first documented fatalities occurred.

8.5 PIPRADROL

Pipradrol was originally licensed as a medication for management of Attention Deficit Hyperactivity Disorder, obesity, and narcolepsy. The pipradrol derivatives desoxypipradrol (2-diphenylmethylpiperidine [2-DPMP]), diphenylprolinol (diphenyl-2-pyrrolidinemethanol [D2PM]), and diphenylmethylpyrrolidine (desoxy D2PM) have been reported as NPS or "legal highs" and produce amphetamine-like effects. On the streets, pipradol is sold as "Whack, Ivory Wave, Head Candy, and Neuroblast." However, undeclared D2PM was recently detected in slimming pills bought in Thailand and Hong Kong [117]. It is structurally related to methylphenidate (Ritalin®) (Figure 8.15).

8.5.1 Pharmacology and Toxicology

The pipradrol derivatives are potent and selective catecholamine transporter blockers without substrate releasing properties. Both D2PM and 2-DPMP lack serotonergic

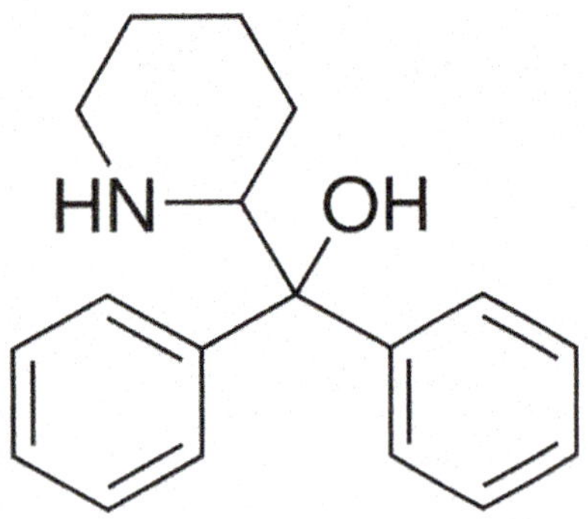

FIGURE 8.15 Chemical structure of pipradol.

activity and trace amine-associated receptor 1 (TAAR1) binding. Altogether, the pipradrol derivatives are potent and selective catecholamine uptake inhibitors, consistently with their prolonged psychostimulant actions. 2-DPMP is a long-acting noradrenaline-dopamine reuptake inhibitor with a half-life between 16 and 20 hours [118]. The pharmacological profile of D2PM is also likely associated with high abuse liability and an increased risk of psychiatric complications [119, 120].

Toxicity has been associated with the use of "Ivory Wave," which originally contained the pipradrol derivative 2-DPMP, but due to the undesirable psychiatric effects of 2-DPMP, it fell out of favor. Subsequently, D2PM use emerged as a replacement in 2010 [118]. The clinical toxicity of 2-DPMP and D2PM is long-lasting (24–72 hours) and involves sympathomimetic stimulation and predominantly psychiatric symptoms, including agitation, hallucinations, and insomnia.

There are no human toxicity studies for these compounds, and limited clinical information from clinical and poison information services is available. One report describes a cluster of 2-DPMP toxicity–related cases where patients presented with chest pain, palpitations, and increased blood pressure as well as increased psychosis and agitation [121]. An Irish case report from 2011 identified synthetic cocaine (fluorotropacocaine) and 2-DPMP in "Whack." In another case series (n = 26) where 2-DPMP was identified in the "Ivory Wave" used, 96% of patients who presented to emergency departments had neuropsychiatric features, while tachycardia, dystonia, and rhabdomyolysis were other common presentations up to 1 week after ingestion [122]. In Finland, over a 20-month period from October 2010 to May 2012, samples from human performance cases (driving under the influence: DUI) and samples from unrelated autopsies were analyzed for 2-DPMP [123]. The concentration range, for the DUI cases, of 2-DPMP was 0.06–0.89 mg/L (mean 0.073 mg/L); other drugs were present in the majority of cases. In total, 2-DPMP was identified in 1.7% of impaired drivers over this time period. In addition, 2-DPMP was identified in five autopsies, amounting to 0.05% of cases over the same time period. 2-DPMP was thought to contribute to the cause of death in 2 of the 5 autopsy cases. The blood concentration in both of these autopsy cases was reported as 1.4mg/L. No fatalities directly attributed to D2PM and 2-DPMP have been reported.

8.5.2 Legal Status

The pipradol derivatives (D2PM, desoxy D2PM, and 2-DPMP) were designated Class B in the United Kingdom in 2012. In Germany, they are controlled substances and are tradable but cannot be prescribed. The drugs are not controlled in Asia.

8.6 ARYLCYCLOHEXYLAMINES

Phencyclidine is believed to be the first arylcyclohexylamine with recognized anesthetic properties and serves as the prototype for arylcyclohexylamine derivatives (Figure 8.16) [124]. These NPS all exhibit dissociative effects due to their antagonism of N-methyl-D-aspartate (NMDA) receptors. Many have been studied as alternatives to traditional anesthetic agents but for the same reason, are prone to recreational abuse. On the streets, they are commonly referred to as "Special K" or "Super K."

8.6.1 Ketamine

Ketamine is not a "new" drug, and much is known about the pharmacology and toxicology of this drug due to its widespread clinical use and abuse (Figure 8.17). This provides useful insights as to how the analogues, which are new to the illegal market, achieve their pharmacological effects. Ketamine's actions were originally explained by its ability to bind to the classic mu-opioid receptors while at the same time blocking the NMDA receptor. In 2011, it was found to possess anti-inflammatory actions [125], and other data suggests an effect on muscarinic receptors [126]. Interestingly, sub-anesthetic doses appear to be of some value in the treatment of depression and anxiety [127]. It also activates the monoamine oxidase enzymatic system to produce cyclization of the catecholamine neurotransmitters; the cyclic derivatives are psychogenic and toxic. These modifications are the cause of the hallucinatory phenomena that can occur

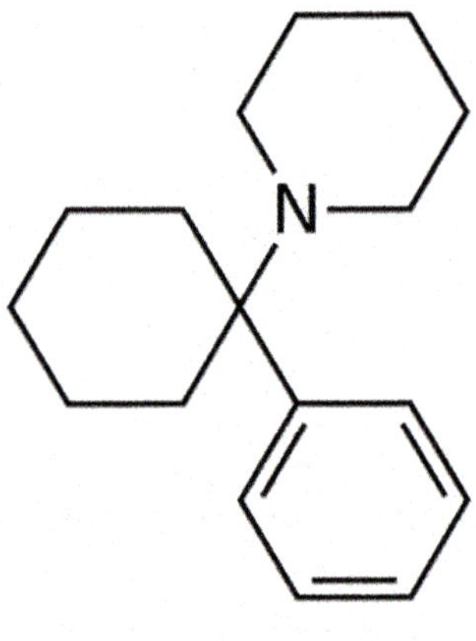

FIGURE 8.16 Chemical structure of phencyclidine.

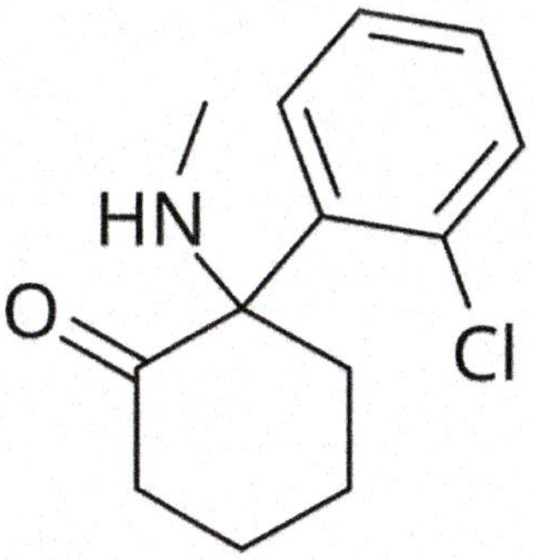

FIGURE 8.17 Chemical structure of ketamine.

upon awakening or are sought by recreational users [128]. New uses for this drug are regularly reported, and it seems to exert a disparate number of effects. There is also evidence that at sub-anesthetic doses, ketamine meets all the requirements for a party drug [129].

Until recently, ketamine was only produced as the (S) enantiomer, which has four times the affinity for the NMDA receptor compared with the racemic form. Ketamine is also thought to act on the $5HT_{2A}$ receptor and to show high affinity for opioid receptors [130]. The pharmacokinetic differences between the two isomers have never been studied. Ketamine is metabolized by CYP enzymes. In humans, CYP3A4 is responsible for *N*-demethylation of ketamine. Other CYP enzymes may make contributions, but they are minor [131]. The main metabolite is dehydroketamine with minor amounts of other conjugates.

Ketamine is lipid soluble and therefore, has a very high volume of distribution [132]. This is important for postmortem interpretation. First, ketamine will accumulate in the fat of heavy users and may well be detected at death even when use was remote. Second, drug redistribution is inevitable, and whatever concentration is determined in postmortem blood, it is unlikely to have any predictable relationship to the plasma concentration at the time of death. Its behavior is best described as that of an open two-compartment model. A third forensic consideration is worth mentioning. Compared with other anesthetics, ketamine seems to have little inherent toxicity. Even in the drug abuse setting, ketamine rarely causes fatalities, and if it does, the postmortem blood concentration is usually over 5 mg/L. The most recent evidence suggests that ketamine interacts with specific bacteria, which may account for its positive effect in patients with ulcerative colitis [133]. In addition, there is evidence that ketamine exerts toxic effects on the kidney, producing papillary necrosis and fibrosis [134].

8.6.2 Methoxetamine

Some refer to methoxetamine (MXE) as a phencyclidine analogue and some as a ketamine analogue, but the difference is largely academic (Figure 8.18). Sometimes it is referred to as 3-Me-2-Oxo-PCE. Methoxetamine was first encountered in Europe in 2012. It is a high-affinity NMDA receptor agonist and produces effects that are

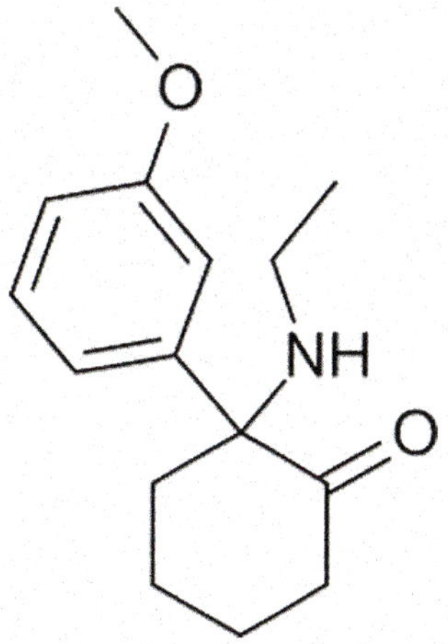

FIGURE 8.18 Chemical structure of methoxetamine.

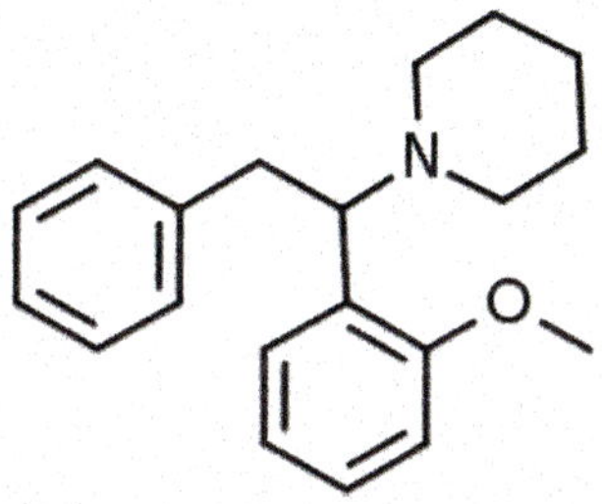

FIGURE 8.19 Chemical structure of methoxyphenidine.

essentially indistinguishable from those of ketamine [135, 136]. In addition to being a non-competitive NMDA receptor antagonist, it is also a dopamine reuptake inhibitor, an agonist at dopamine D2 receptors, and a serotonin agonist that also has antagonistic activity against muscarinic and opioid receptors [137]. Like ketamine, it produces dissociative anesthesia. Formal pharmacokinetic studies have not been published. Serum concentrations in one report of three intoxicated men ranged from 0.09 to 0.2 mg/L [138]. In a report describing a mixed fatal drug overdose, the blood MXE concentration was 0.064 mg/L [139].

8.6.3 Methoxyphenidine

Methoxyphenidine (MXP) is related to MXE and has been available as a "research chemical" since 2013 (Figure 8.19). It is reported to be an alternative to the "dissociative anesthetics" methoxetamine and ketamine. In three reported 2-MXP-related deaths, postmortem femoral blood levels were 24.0, 2.0, and 1.36 mg/L. The only case where the drug was not thought to be responsible for the death was the case with the lowest level [140]. Human pharmacokinetic studies have not been performed. Clinical presentations include tachycardia, nystagmus, hyperthermia, and coma. A further two fatal cases involving 3-MXP reported a wide range of postmortem concentrations ranging from 0.63 to 3.2 mg/L, but methamphetamine was present in one case, and alcohol was present in the other [141].

8.6.4 Legal Status

In the United States, ketamine is a Class B or a Schedule 3 drug by prescription only. MXE is a Schedule 1 drug in most countries in Europe. It is considered an analogue of PCP in most states in the United States and is treated in the same way as PCP, as a Schedule 1 drug.

8.7 TRYPTAMINES

Tryptamines are derived from the naturally occurring amino acid tryptophan (Figure 8.20). Naturally occurring tryptamines such as psilocybin (4-phosphoryloxy-*N*,*N*-dimethyltryptamine) and psilocin (4-hydroxy-*N*,*N*-dimethyltryptamine) are present in over 200 types of mushroom (genus *Psilocybe*), commonly called the "magic mushrooms." Serotonin and melatonin are members of the tryptamine family. Psilocybin is a prodrug rapidly converted to psilocin, which is primarily responsible for its hallucinogenic properties. Mushrooms containing these compounds have been used in various cultures, particularly in South America, for thousands of years but for reasons that are not clear, are still classified with other members of the NPS class. Other naturally occurring tryptamines such as bufotenin (5-hydroxy-*N*,*N*-dimethyltryptamine) and 5-MeO-DMT (5-methoxy-*N*,*N*-dimethyltryptamine) are found on toads, plants, and some mushrooms.

Although not discussed in this chapter, LSD is a synthetic tryptamine that was first introduced in 1938. Strangely, it is still considered an NPS. New synthetically produced tryptamine hallucinogens including alpha-methyltryptamine (AMT), 5-methoxy-*N*,*N*-dimethyltryptamine (5-MeO-DMT), 5-methoxy-*N*,*N*-diisopropyltryptamine (5-MeO-DiPT), 4-hydroxy-*N*,*N*-diethyltryptamine (4-HO-DET), and 4-hydroxy-*N*-isopropyl *N*-methyltryptamine (4-HO-MiPT) have emerged on the market. They are newer synthetic tryptamines designed as replacements for LSD ("legal" alternatives to LSD). On the streets, 5-MeO-DiPT is known as "Foxy-methoxy," while 5-MeO-DMT is known as "Foxy."

Tryptamines are further classified as "simple" or "ergolines" (Table 8.4). The simple tryptamines are further divided based on (1) no modification of the indole ring; (2) modification at the 4-position of the indole ring; and (3) modification at the 5-position of the indole ring (Figure 8.20). Only substitutions at the 4- and 5-positions are discussed, because modifications at position 6 or 7 result in reduced hallucinogenic activity [142].

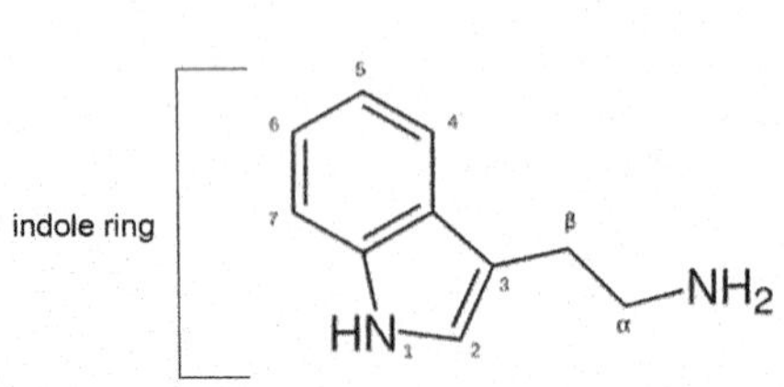

FIGURE 8.20 Chemical structure of tryptamine.

8.7.1 Pharmacology and Toxicology

The tryptamines induce their hallucinogenic effects mainly as agonists or partial agonists of serotonin 5-HT_{2a}, 5-HT_{2c}, and 5HT_{1a} [143]. As a result of these interactions, the tryptamines can cause serotonin-like syndromes, although most of this information comes from what is known of the naturally occurring tryptamines rather than the new synthetic forms, for which there is little data. It is believed that the naturally occurring tryptamines were not known to be directly associated with deaths, although they may have been indirectly involved in deaths by causing changes in behaviors that increased the likelihood of accidental deaths.

DMT is a simple unsubstituted natural tryptamine, and, for the most part, the pharmacology of this group mimics the behavior of DMT. It is not active when taken orally, as it is rapidly metabolized in first pass metabolism due to the action of monoamine oxidase [62]. Other simple unsubstituted synthetic tryptamines such as *N*,*N*-diallyltryptamine (DALT), dipropyltryptamine (DPT), diethyltryptamine (DET), and di-isopropyltryptamine (DiPT) are all active after oral ingestion. One death has been reported in association with AMT [144]. It is worth noting that AMT has stimulant properties [145].

There is little clinical information available with regard to new synthetic tryptamines that have a position 4 substitution; these include 4-HO-DET and 4-HO-MiPT, and deaths have been reported with the use of a position 5 substitution, 5-MeO-DALT [146, 147].

Tryptamine users exhibit vital sign abnormalities, namely, tachycardia, tachypnea, and hypertension. In severe intoxications, hyperthermia may also occur [148]. Reports of rhabdomyolysis and renal failure have also been described [149]. Other clinical effects include trismus, anxiety, euphoria, sweating, diarrhea, nausea, vomiting, abdominal pain, sialorrhea, diaphoresis, palpitations, drowsiness, dysphoria, and mydriasis [144].

8.7.2 Legal Status

All members of this class are considered controlled substances and are illegal to possess in the United States, Europe, China, and Japan.

8.8 PLANT-BASED SUBSTANCES

8.8.1 Kratom

Kratom is a tropical tree (*Mitragyna speciosa*) native to Southeast Asia. Its leaves contain compounds that can have psychotropic effects.

8.8.1.1 Pharmacology and Toxicology

At least one of the plant's components, the indole alkaloid mitragynine, is a potent opiate agonist, capable of producing analgesia comparably to morphine. Mitragynine accounts for 70% of the alkaloids found in Kratom leaves, but many other indoles are found there as well. Mitragynine is not

TABLE 8.4
Structural Classification and Representative Examples of Tryptamines

Sub-classification		Examples
Simple tryptamines		
	Ring-unsubstituted	DMT[a], DiPT, DALT, DET, AET, AMT
	Ring 4-substituted	Psilocybin[a], 4-OH-DET, 4-HODiPT, 4-HOMiPT
	Ring 5-substituted	5-MeO-DMT[a], 5-MeO-DiPT, 5-MeO-MiPT
Ergolines		LSD, Morning Glory[a]

[a] naturally occurring tryptamines.

the only active compound of Kratom, and at least 20–25 pharmacoactive alkaloids have been isolated. Mitragynine is metabolized in part to 7-hydroxymitragynine, and this compound (the main metabolite of mitragynine) is thought to be 4 times more potent than mitragynine and 17 times more potent than morphine [150].

Activity occurs through agonism at mu-opioid receptors and antagonism at delta-opioid receptors. This may provide an explanation as to why it is less of a respiratory depressant than heroin or oxycodone [151]. Kratom exerts opioid alpha2 receptor agonistic effects as well as anti-inflammatory and parasympathetic-impeding effects.

Some of the Kratom alkaloids, including mitragynine, are added to soft drinks that are popular with those who work long hours. At low doses, it has demonstrated a cocaine/stimulant-like effect. However, at higher doses, mitragynine induces sedation, feelings of pleasure, and pain relief [152]. Kratom can be administered by almost any route, although intravenous (IV) use has not been reported. The pharmacokinetics has been only partially investigated in man. One study measured the basic pharmacokinetic parameters in chronic users who had been held at a steady dose for 7 days. The time to reach the maximum plasma concentration was 0.83 ± 0.35 hours, the terminal half-life was 23.24 ± 16.07 hours, and the apparent volume of distribution was 38.04 ± 24 L/kg. Urinary excretion of unchanged mitragynine was 0.14%. Kratom pharmacokinetics followed an oral two-compartment model [153]. According to the United States Food and Drug Administration (FDA), there have been occasional reports of psychosis and liver damage, though it is not clear whether illness is actually due to Kratom or to adulterants [154].

Kratom has been studied from an addiction point of view, and considerable data exists from studies carried out in Asia, where it is commonly used. These studies indicate that Kratom can be addictive, and discontinuation leads to withdrawal symptoms [155].

Deaths have been attributed to Kratom use, with most cases involving other drugs. However, one case is cited with mitragynine only as the drug responsible for the death [156]. Similarly, a report from the United States Center for Disease Control (CDC), using data from 32 states and the District of Columbia comprised of 27,338 unintentional overdose deaths, showed that 0.56% or 152 cases were positive for Kratom on postmortem toxicology testing. In 91/152 cases, Kratom was listed as having contributed to the death, and in 7/152, Kratom was listed as the sole cause of death; however, the completeness of the toxicology testing is questioned [157].

8.8.1.2 Legal Status

Up to June 2019, Kratom was not scheduled as a controlled substance in the United States. However, since 2012, the United States FDA has taken a number of actions related to Kratom and in November 2017, issued a public health advisory; in addition, the DEA has identified Kratom as a drug of concern [157].

8.8.2 Salvia divinorum

Salvia divinorum is a mint-like plant native to Mexico and used with some frequency in both the United States and the European Union. Of the alkaloids it contains, Salvinorin A is a highly selective full agonist at the kappa-opioid receptor [158] but does not interact with serotonin receptors as all other known hallucinogens do [159]. It rivals LSD in potency [160].

8.8.2.1 Pharmacology and Toxicology

A study using six healthy volunteers examined the pharmacokinetics of Salvinorin A after inhalation. The data for the subjects show the time-dependent course of salvinorin in blood over 90 minutes. The study also reports a positive relationship between salvinorin and prolactin release [161]. Persistent psychosis is said to be a rare, but recognized, complication [162]; however, this is challenged by several studies in the peer-reviewed literature [149].

In addition to its hallucinogenic properties, the plant has possible medicinal value. There is evidence that Salvinorin interacts with the CB_1 cannabinoid receptor in the brain, exerting anti-inflammatory effects [163, 164]. The most recent studies show that Salvinorin A attenuates cardiovascular changes and alleviates brain injury after subarachnoid hemorrhage. The suspected mechanism is increased expression of endothelial nitric oxide synthase and nitric oxide content and at the same time, decreasing endothelin-1 concentration and aquaporin (AQP-4) protein expression [165]. There are no reports of postmortem-related results involving Salvinorin A and/or deaths due to Salvinorin A.

8.8.2.2 Legal Status

Salvinorin A is controlled in 35 states in the United States, and 27 nations have enacted various legislative controls [166].

8.9 FENTANYL

8.9.1 General Considerations

A Belgian corporation, Jensen Pharmaceuticals, first synthesized fentanyl and some of its derivatives in the 1950s. Jensen's goal was to produce a non-barbiturate IV anesthetic that was more potent and faster acting than the barbiturates. It was thought that a highly lipid-soluble agent would cross the blood–brain barrier more quickly than the barbiturates, producing analgesia more rapidly. Receptor binding was not a consideration, as the mu-opioid receptor had not yet been discovered. Both morphine and meperidine, the most potent agents then available, contain a central piperidine molecule, and it seemed logical to the Jensen chemists that piperidine must be the moiety responsible for effective analgesia (Figure 8.21).

Jensen researchers proceeded to synthesize a series of meperidine derivatives. Meperidine was chosen mainly because its piperidine moiety was chemically much more accessible than that of morphine, which is more complex molecule. It was already known that fat-soluble molecules were more effective analgesics than hydrophilic compounds. In their attempts to increase lipid solubility, various moieties were added and/or replaced at different positions on the piperidine ring (N benzene rings, methyl or ethyl groups) in hopes of producing a molecule that would be more adherent to the pain receptor, whatever and wherever it might prove to be [167]. Many of the derivatives that were created and discarded (such as carfentanil, also known as carfentanyl) have now returned to the illicit market, where they are contributing to the skyrocketing opioid death rates.

Fentanyl was introduced to the European market in 1960 and the United States market in 1963. FDA regulators were concerned that the drug might be dangerous and lead to needless complications during anesthesia. As a consequence, fentanyl was nearly a decade old before it was sold in the United States, and then only when compounded with droperidol (ratio of 50 to 1). Of the molecules experimentally created, fentanyl appeared to be the most desirable. It was 50–100 times more potent than morphine, was more lipid soluble than any opioid then on the market (octanol/water coefficient of 813), and had the most rapid onset of action and the highest therapeutic index (277 vs 4.7 for meperidine and morphine) [167].

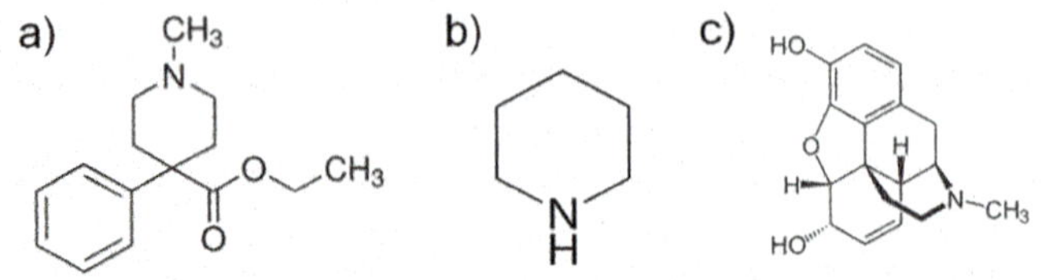

FIGURE 8.21 Chemical structure of a) meperidine, b) piperidine, and c) morphine.

Because the potency of fentanyl analogues is so great and the danger of overdose so high, human experimentation is severely restricted, and very little literature on the human pharmacology, pharmacokinetics, and toxicokinetics of fentanyl analogues is available. The information that is available is drawn from the animal literature (which may or may not be relevant) and from anecdotal case reports and observational cohorts. Even less is known about the postmortem toxicology of fentanyl analogues, save for what tissue concentrations have been reported in cases where a fentanyl or one of its analogues is the likely cause of death. The highest concentrations of fentanyl and its analogues are found in fat, liver, and brain, but these concentrations are likely to be relatively low. Virtually nothing is known about fentanyl redistribution after death, and the volume of distribution remains unknown for almost all the analogues. Nonetheless, overdose with one or another member of the fentanyl series should be easily recognized, as the fentanyls are only toxic to the extent that they bind to the mu-opioid receptor. In life, these drugs cause nausea, vomiting, respiratory depression, miosis, and ultimately, apnea. In death, there is nothing about the clinical presentation to distinguish a fentanyl death from a heroin death. The one exception might be the absence of skin excoriation: synthetic agents like fentanyl do not cause mast cell histamine release, but naturally occurring opiates do [168].

8.9.2 Introduction

Deaths due to drug overdose in the United States in 2017 amounted to approximately 72,000, an increase of 12% from the previous year, continuing the upward trend that began in 2013. In that year, a near tenfold increase in deaths involving synthetic opioids began, rising from 3,105 in 2013 to approximately 30,000 in 2017. Recent data from the United States CDC has identified fentanyl as the single drug most frequently involved in overdose deaths. In some states, the increase has been even more dramatic. In New York State, opioid-related overdose deaths increased by nearly 35% between 2015 and 2016, with fentanyl-related deaths increasing by 160% [169]. The variation seems likely to be the result of distribution networks, but dealer competition would be an equally possible cause.

The popularity of fentanyl and other synthetic opioids is also increasing in Europe. In 2017, law enforcement agencies reported approximately 1,300 seizures of new synthetic opioids to the European Union Early Warning System. The majority of these cases (70%) were seizures of fentanyl derivatives, but a number of other types of opioids (such as U-47,700 and U-51,754) were also reported. The total quantity of opioid powders and tablets reported in the European Union has seen a continued increase since 2012. Overall, seizures of new synthetic opioids in 2017 amounted to approximately 17 kilograms. According to the EMCDDA, the mortality rate due to overdoses in Europe in 2017 was estimated at 22.6 deaths per million population aged 15–64 years [170]. In the United States, figures from the first half of 2018 indicated that the total number of opiate deaths (in a population of 300 million) will be close to orders of magnitude higher than in Europe.

It is important to understand that most of the increase in fentanyl deaths is not attributable to prescription fentanyl but rather, related to illicitly manufactured fentanyl analogues. Occasionally, pure fentanyl is mixed with, or sold as, heroin, and it is sometimes added to counterfeit pills sold as oxycodone [171]. Carfentanil was just one of the many analogues produced in the quest for what we now call fentanyl. Of the analogues, carfentanil (a piperidine, a methyl ester, a tertiary amino compound, and a tertiary carboxamide) was developed and discarded in the 1950s because its potency was so great that it was thought to pose a clinical menace. With a potency estimated to be 10,000 times that of morphine and 100 times the potency of fentanyl [172], carfentanil is the most potent opioid ever seen in the United States. For reasons yet to be explained, carfentanil deaths tend to occur in clusters. Ohio and Florida seem to be the worst afflicted, with more than 400 and 500 deaths, respectively, reported in 2016 [173].

8.9.3 Synthesis

The original synthesis of fentanyl as devised by Jensen and his co-workers used *N*-benzyl-4-piperidone as the starting material. According to the United States DEA,

> [the] Janssen synthesis route is difficult to perform and is beyond the rudimentary skills of most clandestine laboratory operators. Only individuals who have acquired advanced chemistry knowledge and skills have successfully used this synthesis route. Forensic laboratories can verify whether fentanyl was manufactured illicitly by the Janssen route by detecting the impurity benzylfentanyl in the tested fentanyl drug exhibit [174].

The approach to making fentanyl used by clandestine chemists is referred to as the Siegfried method. The method requires *N*-phenethyl-4-piperidone (NPP) as the precursor. The alpha position of the phenethyl group is methylated along with the 3-position of the piperidine ring, forming alpha methyl phentyl, equal in potency to fentanyl itself. Clandestine chemists then attach different moieties to produce analogues. In its rulemaking notice, the DEA stated:

> The detection of the impurity 4-anilino-N-phenethyl-4-piperidine (4-ANPP) without the presence of benzylfentanyl in the fentanyl drug exhibit suggests that the fentanyl was manufactured by the Siegfried method (i.e., a small amount of 4-ANPP is not consumed in the last reaction in the synthesis and a trace amount of 4-ANPP can be found in the illicit fentanyl produced) [174].

The massive increase in fentanyl-related drug deaths is explained mainly by the prevalence and potency of the analogues, and the only sources for the analogues appear to be China and Mexico. Only four illicit fentanyl labs using 4-ANPP have ever been confiscated in the United States, presumably because 4-ANPP sales are regulated and must be reported to the DEA. Still, imports have more than met the demand.

The DEA reports seizing 800-gram equivalents of pure fentanyl and enough of unused 4-ANPP precursor to make an additional 5,000 grams of pure fentanyl in its four related seizures. Given the amount of illicit fentanyl and precursor chemicals found at these four domestic fentanyl laboratories, no matter which modifications of the Siegfried method were used, 5,800 mg of fentanyl could have been produced. Although the numbers are hard to grasp, 5.8 kg of fentanyl, once diluted for street sale, would yield over 45 million effective doses!

8.9.4 Physiochemical Properties and Pharmacokinetics

Chemical Name: N-Phenyl-N-[1-9phenylethyl0-4-piperidinyl]propanamide

Physical Properties

Structure and Form: Available as the citrate salt, soluble in water

CAS: 437-38-7

MW: 336.5

Vd: 3 L/Kg

pKa: 8.4

Protein binding: 84%

Synonyms: Street drug may be referred to as "China White." Fentanyl produced by Abbot Laboratories is called Actiq.

Pharmacokinetic Values:

Cmax

- IV: After 200 µg, 4.6 ± 1.87 h
- IM: Not Known
- Oral after 15 mg, 4 h
- Sublingual: 0.24–2.52 ng/mL
- Transdermal: 2.6 ± 1.3 h
- Effervescent: 800 µg, 11.7 h

Half-Life

- IV: After 219 µg, ± 10 min
- IM: Not Known
- Oral: after 200 µg, 200 minutes
- Sublingual: 3.2–6.4 h
- Transdermal: 21.9 ± 8.9 minutes
- Effervescent: 800 µg, 11.7 h

Tmax

- IV: After 0.4 h (35 ± 15 h)
- IM: Not Known
- Oral: After 39–57 minutes
- Sublingual: After 200 µg, 40 ng/mL (range 20–1,200)
- Transdermal: 20–40 h
- Effervescent: 800 µg, 35–45 min

8.9.5 Formulations

Until recently, fentanyl was most often encountered either in the operating room, as an anesthesia adjunct, or as a drug abused anesthesiologists, or on patients who die while wearing fentanyl patches for prolonged pain. Partially used transdermal patches, taken from bodies by families of decedents or funeral homes, are not rare. Abusers usually heat the patch gently to vaporize the fentanyl. Jensen markets two other fentanyl derivatives: alfentanil (Alfenta), which is an ultra-short-acting agent (5–10 minutes), and sufentanil (Sufenta), which is also short acting but five to ten times more potent than fentanyl. Sufentanil is used largely in cardiac surgery [175].

Sufenta is an effervescent tablet designed for buccal use only. It is to be put into the mouth and not swallowed. It is also short acting, and its effervescent formula accelerates absorption. Carfentanil, the most potent of the fentanyls, is also produced by Jensen, but only for veterinary use in large animals. It is frequently encountered in faux MDMA pills and even more frequently used to enhance the potency of illicit heroin. Fentanyl is also produced in the form of an adherent patch. Once a patch is applied to the skin, fentanyl is detected in the blood within 2 hours, and by the time 12 hours have elapsed, blood concentrations approximate those after fentanyl is given intravenously. Because of the time lag in absorption, Fentanyl is never used as the first analgesic [176]. Astra produces a combination of fentanyl and droperidol. Actiq is manufactured by Takeda Pharmaceuticals and sold in a dosage form like a lozenge, while Remifentanil is sold by GlaxoSmithKline. Remifentanil is twice as potent as fentanyl and 100–200 times as potent as morphine. Unlike other synthetic opioids, which the liver metabolizes, it possess an ester linkage that undergoes rapid hydrolysis by non-specific tissue and plasma esterases.

8.9.6 Genomics

The amount of fentanyl required to produce an acceptable level of analgesia varies greatly between individuals. The variation is explained by CYPA34 polymorphism. Variation is especially marked among the Chinese populations, where controlled studies have shown that CYP3A4*1G polymorphism is strongly associated with the analgesic efficacy of intraoperative fentanyl in patients undergoing hysteroscopy under general anesthesia [177].

A small observational study of Chinese female burn patients confirmed the initial studies. In this study, three patients, all with CYP slow-metabolizing genotypes, were identified as CYP2D6*9, CYP2D6*29, and CYP3A4*1B. All were found to have increased serum fentanyl concentrations due to impaired clearance. The variation could be of importance when trying to calculate the amount of fentanyl administered to polymorphic patients [178].

In a separate study of 35 healthy volunteers (19 men and 16 women), each person received a single 300 μg oral dose of fentanyl and was then genotyped using real-time polymerase chain reaction (PCR) for known polymorphisms of CYP3A4 and CYP3A5, ATP-binding cassette subfamily B member 1 (ABCB1), opioid receptor mu 1 (OPRM1), catechol-O-methyltransferase (COMT), and adrenoceptor beta 2 (ADRB2).

The results of the study show that fentanyl pharmacokinetics are affected by sex; carriers of the CYP3A4*22 allele, which is known to reduce the mRNA expression, showed a greater area under the concentration-time curve (AUC) and lower clearance in women; again, the results were found to be widely variable. Carriers of the ABCB1 C1236T T/T genotype were found to have a lower AUC and higher clearance as well as lower half-life. On the other hand, carriers of CYP3A5*3, ABCB1 C3435T, and ABCB1 G2677T/A were found to have unaltered pharmacokinetics and pharmacodynamics [179].

Finally, it has been suggested that a panel of 10 genes and 11 single nucleotide polymorphisms can be used to predict Addiction Severity Index for both alcohol and drugs of abuse (all opioids including fentanyl), though this suggestion has not been widely confirmed.

8.9.7 Pharmacology and Pharmacokinetics

Unlike some of the synthetic NPS, fentanyl and its analogues are unique in that all their actions are produced via the mu-opioid receptor. Fentanyl and its analogues bind only at the mu receptor, which means that this group of drugs only produces mu receptor–type effects: nausea, vomiting, drowsiness, miosis, and apnea. It also means that all their effects can be reversed with NARCAN®. Depending on how the fentanyl molecule has been modified, affinity for the mu receptor may vary (explaining why some of the analogues require only minute doses to produce the same effects as very large doses of morphine). It also explains why poisoning with certain analogues may require multiple doses of NARCAN® before the circulation is restored.

Rarely, fentanyls may interact with various tissues to increase muscle tone, which may make ventilation difficult ("wooden chest" syndrome), and even cause serotonin syndrome. Published case reports suggest that serotonin syndrome is rare when only fentanyl is administered [180] but more common when fentanyl is given to patients taking selective serotonin reuptake inhibitor (SSRI) and serotonin-norepinephrine (SNRI) [181] drugs. The mechanism has not been proven, but in animal studies, type 1A dopamine receptors seem to be involved [182].

Fentanyl treatment and treatment with analogues causes modest increases in intracranial pressure and small decreases in mean arterial pressure and cerebral perfusion pressure. When high doses of fentanyl were given for cardiac surgery, plasma concentrations averaged 34 ± 7 ng/mL [183], but respiratory depression is measurable at levels as low as 1–5 ng/mL [184]. Steady-state concentrations produced by fentanyl on the order of 2.5 ng/mL have been observed in cancer patients. The concentration range for conscious sedation adequate for surgery is, on average, 13 ng/mL [185]. When steady-state concentration is reached after patch application, mean plasma concentrations average 2.5 ng/mL, but this value cannot be used as the sole guide to therapy because there is so much intra-individual variation due to CY3A45 polymorphism (particularly CYP3A4*22 and CYP3A5*3) [186].

8.9.8 Metabolism

Piperidine *N*-dealkylation to form norpiperidine is the main metabolic route for parenterally administered fentanyl metabolism in man. Amide hydrolysis occurs, leading to the formation of desopropionylfentanyl, and alkyl hydroxylation yields hydroxylfentanyl [187]. When given orally, in the form of a lozenge, fentanyl is subject to hepatic first pass metabolism by CYP3A4 microsomes in the duodenum. In addition, very small amounts of hydroxynorfentanyl will, after *N*-dealkylation, yield hydroxyfentanyl [188]. Patients treated chronically with certain antiepileptic drugs such as carbamazepine require higher fentanyl doses to achieve adequate analgesia. The requirement for a higher dose in these patients has not been fully established but seems likely to be the result of increased hepatic metabolism [189]. Renal excretion accounts for up to 10% of the dose.

8.9.9 Tissue Concentrations

There are good reasons why tissue concentrations of fentanyl and presumably, fentanyl analogues are difficult to predict and even more difficult to interpret. The primary difficulty for clinicians is that the fentanyl molecule was designed for maximal lipid solubility, so it penetrates the blood–brain barrier rapidly.

Drugs with a high degree of lipid solubility inevitably have a high volume of distribution and redistribution (the reversible transfer of a drug from one location to another within the body). In the living, fentanyl redistribution is rightly regarded as the duration-limiting factor for analgesia after single or infrequent doses (analogous to thiopentone). Enormous variation in the pharmacokinetic constants reported for fentanyl can be seen even in healthy volunteers. Hence, estimates of fentanyl's apparent volume of distribution range from around 60 to over 300 L, estimates of terminal half-life range from about 1.5 to 6 hours (15 hours in geriatric patients), and total body clearance ranges from 0.4 to over 1.5 L/minute. Renal excretion accounts for up to 10% of the dose [190, 191]. Given the enormous range of values for volume of distribution that have been reported, it is difficult to design controlled pharmacokinetic studies.

The situation is even more complicated in the postmortem setting. Fentanyl's high volume of distribution virtually guarantees that the blood concentration measured at autopsy will bear no predictable relationship to what that level was in life, or for that matter, how that concentration relates to that of any other fentanyl-associated death. The issue had been debated for some years but was finally put to rest in 2010. Olson et al. measured fentanyl concentrations in postmortem specimens that had been collected from 20 medical examiner cases [192]. Femoral blood, heart blood, heart tissue, liver tissue, and skeletal muscle were all sampled and analyzed. In seven of the cases, femoral blood was obtained at two different postmortem intervals, the first just shortly after death (4 hours) and the second at autopsy (21.6 hours after death, mean value). Fentanyl concentrations in the first set of samples ranged from undetectable to 14.6 μg/L (mean, 4.6 μg/L). In the second set, the concentration was 2.0 μg/L in the 4-hour sample, rising to 52.5 μg/L (mean, 17.3 μg/L) in the second specimen. Corresponding mean fentanyl concentrations for the group of 20 in heart blood, liver tissue, and heart tissue were 29.8 μg/L, 109.7 mg/kg, and 103.4 mg/kg, respectively. What they would have been 6 hours later is anyone's guess.

Extreme variations in postmortem tissue concentrations have been reported over and over again [193]. German researchers analyzed whole blood from 118 decedents who had been receiving morphine and 27 decedents who were receiving therapeutic morphine and simultaneously wearing fentanyl patches. Fentanyl concentrations were over nine times higher at autopsy than they had been in life.

In another study of fentanyl patches, a group of researchers found so much variation, both intra- and inter-individual and also in manner of death, that they concluded:

> The very wide and overlapping ranges of postmortem fentanyl concentrations effectively nullify the utility of correlating the dose and expected postmortem concentration for any particular death. Based on the variable relationship between dose and blood concentration, the antemortem dose cannot be reliably predicted based on the postmortem concentration [194].

Obviously, postmortem concentrations of drugs with a high volume of distribution cannot be directly compared with *in vivo* serum concentrations. The terms "therapeutic" or "toxic" thresholds have no meaning in the setting of postmortem toxicology, nor does the term "subtherapeutic," at least in the postmortem setting. Drugs with any degree of lipophilicity may persist in deep tissue stores for days after they were consumed. THC is a good example [49]. It can be slowly released from decomposing tissue for days and may not have been present in the blood at all at the time of death. The practice of appending these "therapeutic concentration ranges" measured in life and comparing them with values measured in the blood after death only serves to complicate the situation. The practice should be discontinued, as it can only confuse the courts.

8.9.10 Clinical Mechanisms

Fentanyl and most of the NPS derived from fentanyl operate via the same mechanisms as morphine and other classical opiates. Their main effects include activation of mu-opioid receptors: analgesia, respiratory depression, euphoria, miosis, decreased intestinal motility, sedation, addiction, and dependence [195]. However, there are occasional exceptions to the rule. U-50488 is mainly a kappa-opioid receptor agonist. In animal models, it behaves as an analgesic, antitussive, diuretic, and anticonvulsant, and its side effects include dysphoria and hallucinations. At the same time, studies have shown that it is also a mu-opioid receptor agonist [196]. U-51754 (a non-fentanyl synthetic opioid [NOS]) is mainly a kappa-opioid receptor agonist that has been studied in animal models as an analgesic, antitussive, diuretic, and anticonvulsant. Its side effects include dysphoria and hallucinations, and it has been reported to possess μ-opioid receptor agonist effects. U-51754 is not as selective for kappa-opioid receptors as U-47700 [197].

8.9.11 Maternal Fetal Considerations

Literature on the subject is sparse and hard science rarer still. The little peer-reviewed evidence that has been published suggests that there is no need for fentanyl-using mothers to cease nursing. One report describes an infant who was born to a mother with chronic pain who was being treated with fentanyl 100 μg/h transdermal patches throughout her pregnancy and during lactation. On day of life 27, when the baby was feeding and gaining weight on maternal milk, analysis of the mother's milk found a fentanyl level of 6.4 ng/mL, while the infant's blood fentanyl level was undetectable [198]. In a second study of five lactating women who had received fentanyl during anesthesia, milk was collected 5, 7, 9, 11, and 24 hours after drug administration. Venous blood was collected at intervals up to 7 hours. Testing showed that between 0.006% and 0.073% of the administered fentanyl was detected in the infant, prompting the authors to conclude: "fentanyl excreted into milk within 24 hours of induction of anesthesia provides insufficient justification for interrupting breast-feeding" [199]. Toxnet lists a paper by Leuschen et al. that measured the concentrations of fentanyl in the breast milk of ten healthy women who had received 50 or 100 μg of fentanyl citrate as often as every hour during active labor [200]. At delivery, 5 mL of blood was taken from each mother's antecubital vein and the umbilical cord. A sample of breast milk (2–5 mL) was collected 4 and 24 hours after delivery. "Results showed a lack of substantial excretion in breast milk after short term maternal exposure which was consistent with the drug's short serum half-life of 219 min and its rapid renal clearance" [200].

8.9.12 Fentanyl Interactions

It is important to distinguish between drugs detected along with fentanyl in any apparent fentanyl-related deaths and cases where fentanyl is an incidental finding. The mere presence of other drugs, which is more often the case than not, does not prove that the second drug detected interacted in any way with fentanyl or exerted any sort of synergistic effect. On the other hand, drugs known to be CYP3A4 inhibitors (i.e., ketaconazole, erythromycin, or ritonavir) should be considered to have played a role in toxicity and/or death. Ritonavir, one of the strongest CYP3A4 inhibitors, reduces fentanyl clearance by 67%, resulting in more than doubling the excretion time. And because fentanyl is a weak base, fentanyl is also excreted in the acidic gastric juice and reabsorbed later from the small intestine, resulting in secondary elevations in fentanyl plasma concentrations [201]. Rare case reports describe the occurrence of serotonin syndrome in patients taking other serotonergic agents who have been treated with even small doses of fentanyl [202].

8.9.13 Autopsy Findings

There are no autopsy findings that would distinguish a fentanyl death from one due to any other narcotic. Transdermal patches may be present and will continue to release fentanyl long after death, resulting in extremely high postmortem blood fentanyl concentrations. It follows that antemortem drug levels cannot be inferred by extrapolating from the postmortem concentration, a fact that may make the cause of death determination problematic, if not impossible [194]. For example, suppose a decedent, wearing a fentanyl patch because of an orthopedic injury, died of some of cause, such as myocardial infarction. If the autopsy was not performed until 12 hours later, and an early myocardial infarct was discovered, death could be mistakenly attributed to the artifactual high concentrations of fentanyl detected. The situation is even worse if only an external autopsy is performed and drug concentrations measured in blood obtained from a "blind stick." Attributing death to the drug detected does simplify the process, but it certainly does not identify, with any certainty, the cause of death.

8.9.14 Occupational Exposure

Fentanyl and its analogues pose a significant risk from occupational exposure. The National Institute for Occupational Safety and Health (NIOSH) divides fentanyl exposures into three categories and suggests standard safe work practices. The recommendations include the use of personal protective equipment, which requires considerable advanced training. Excellent training materials and specific guidelines are available, at no charge, from the NIOSH web site at www.cdc.gov/niosh/topics/fentanyl/risk.html. Many of the NIOSH suggestions, particularly those having to do with protective masks and clothing, are actually legal requirements. All death investigators need to be aware of them.

- **Minimal:** Response to a situation where it is suspected that fentanyl may be present, but no fentanyl products are visible
  - Example: An emergency medical service (EMS) response to a suspected fentanyl overdose or law enforcement operation where intelligence indicates that fentanyl products are suspected, but they are not visible on scene
- **Moderate:** Response to a situation where small amounts of fentanyl products are visible

    - Example: An EMS response to a suspected fentanyl overdose or law enforcement operation where fentanyl products are suspected and small amounts are visible on scene
- **High:** Response to a situation where liquid fentanyl or large amounts of fentanyl products are visible
- Example: A fentanyl storage or distribution facility, fentanyl milling operation, or fentanyl production laboratory

8.10 FENTANYL ANALOGUES: METABOLISM AND DETECTION

It is difficult to identify the event or events, technical and political, that led to the current fentanyl epidemic. But the discovery of a simplified synthetic production method for fentanyl (Siegfried Method) surely contributed. The synthesis of pure fentanyl is a technically demanding and expensive process, explaining why only a handful of fentanyl labs have ever been seized in the United States. With the advent of cheaper, albeit less pure, fentanyl, made mostly in Mexico, as well as precursor chemicals made in China during the last decade, illegal labs began to produce countless fentanyl analogues. The analogues were almost always legal at the time of introduction; considerable time may pass before any new fentanyl analogue can be scheduled by the United States DEA. To get around this problem, the DEA has scheduled all fentanyl analogues not already scheduled in previous rulemaking as illegal [203].The move seems to make sense, because with hundreds of chemical manipulations possible, scheduling each new analogue becomes a Herculean task.

Many of the analogues are actually patented drugs already developed for the legal market, but then, for various reasons, the development process and clinical trials were abandoned. Still, even though the analogues were never produced, their synthetic formulas and production formulas still exist and can be found in publications available to anyone. These publications have proven fertile sources of information for the clandestine drug trade. Of the possible analogue precursors that can be produced, observational studies of opiate-like deaths have shown that the fentanyl phenylpiperidine (acetylfentanyl) is the most common. Depending on the individual's CYP3A4 status, fentanyl itself is partly metabolized to 4-ANPP. Individual variations in response to fentanyl administration are probably explained by this polymorphism, and so is the presence of 4-ANPP.

Fentanyl analogues are not the only synthetic opiates. Three drugs, fentanyl, methadone, and tramadol, are also synthetic and perfectly legal for medical use. More recently, three new classes of mu receptor binders, having nothing to do with fentanyl save for the shared ability to cause respiratory depression (benzamides, piperazines, and phenylpiperidines), have enjoyed some popularity. Like fentanyl itself, members of all three groups are potent mu agonists; in large doses, they also bind the kappa receptor. Binding by these mu agonists is tight and prolonged. As a consequence, respiratory depression may be difficult to reverse [204, 205]. Typical members of each class will be briefly discussed, mainly because so little is known about them. What little we do know about both non-fentanyl agents and fentanyl analogues is derived from case reports, animal studies, and autopsy materials. On the other hand, great strides have been made in the detection of these dangerous drugs. The reader is referred to specialty journals for the most current information on this subject.

A very large proportion of opiate-related deaths are attributed to fentanyl analogues, but just how large is not known. Multiple databases exist, but they have not been harmonized, and ultimately, they rely on subjective rulings made by the pathologist. The main reason for the increased number of fatalities is probably economic, as the required materials and equipment for producing these compounds have become much cheaper. Another reason is that in-depth training in chemistry is no longer required to manufacture illicit synthetic analogues. As additional analogues are identified, it should be borne in mind that some actually are much weaker agonists than fentanyl and may be unrelated to the cause of death [206].

Information on metabolism is limited, and detection of the metabolites is spotty. Fentanyl analogues all belong to the same family, the 4-anilinopiperidines [207]. With a few exceptions, standard clinical immunoassays do not detect synthetic opioids. The first immunoassay for fentanyl was introduced in 2011 [208], although it was unable to detect norfentanyl, an important active metabolite.

Other fentanyl assays claim to cross-react with 4-metylbutyryl fentanyl, acetylfentanyl, butyrylfentanyl, carfentanil, furanylfentanyl, isobutyrylfentanyl, trans-methylfentanyl, and valerylfentanyl. However, the cross-reactivity of these ELISA-based screening assays remains disputed [209], and in any event, verification is required by other methods, ideally with tandem MS.

Since 2011, many antibody companies have entered the market. The DRI® fentanyl assay from Thermo Scientific also cross-reacts with acetylfentanyl and hydroxypyridone, but it does not react with norfentanyl, presumably because the molecule lacks the alkylated piperidine shared by all the other members of the group [210, 211]. Fortunately, the number of new immunoassays is proliferating almost as quickly as the number of new analogues. Definitive identification is possible, but testing requires considerable expense and labor beyond the means of many medical examiners' laboratories [212].

The first illicit fentanyl analogue appeared in the winter of 1979, when multiple opioid overdoses occurred in California abusers who injected a substance called "China White" or synthetic heroin. However, postmortem testing in these cases failed to reveal heroin or any other known opioid. The causative agent was eventually identified as alpha-methylfentanyl (AMF) mixed with other analogues [213, 214)]. In the mid-1980s, ten new analogues were identified [214], and soon opioid fatalities began to reach epidemic proportions. This increase coincided with the appearance of acetylfentanyl, which is also thought to be the cause of many deaths, mainly on the east coast of the United States [215]. However, in the majority of deaths, fentanyl or fentanyl metabolites were present as well, and it may be that the role of acetylfentanyl was exaggerated.

Analogues like alpha-methylfentanyl, alfentanil, butyrfentanyl, carfentanil, and sufentanil are mainly metabolized in the liver by CYP3A4, yielding *N*-dealkylated inactive metabolites (note that sufentanil and alfentanil are dealkylated to the same product, which can be a forensic issue). As far as is known, furanylfentanyl is the only analogue that undergoes initial hydrolysis [216]. Within the group of analogues, a variety of lesser metabolites are formed via different routes, and the number of metabolites produced can be quite large. The majority of the metabolites are almost invariably inactive. For example, a total of 32 metabolites of acetylfentanyl have been identified to date [212]. Remifentanil has an accessible ester group, which is thought to explain why it is not, to any significant degree, metabolized by CYP enzymes [217].

8.10.1 Fentanyl Analogues: Individual Agents

Although the CDC data indicates that more than 70,000 overdose deaths will occur in the United States in 2019, a majority of the decedents will be polydrug users. Classification is often arbitrary, and it is often impossible to attribute death to just one drug. Another compounding difficulty in assigning a cause of death is that neither users nor their friends know exactly what drug they are taking, and they cannot relate what they are feeling to the drug they have taken [218].

One very large commercial forensic laboratory developed a method capable of detecting 19 different NPS and then applied it to 2,758 samples from suspected opiate-related deaths occurring all over the United States from October 16, 2016 to September 17, 2017. Carfentanil, 4-ANPP, and furanylfentanyl were the three most prevalent fentanyl-related compounds detected. More than half (56.1%) were positive for 4-ANPP, 44.5% were positive for furanylfentanyl, and 25.2% of cases were positive for carfentanil [219]. The universal distribution of these compounds suggests that the most commonly encountered fentanyl analogues are chiefly present as adulterants used to augment the potency of highly diluted heroin or as products of metabolism.

8.10.1.1 Acetylfentanyl

The United States DEA scheduled acetylfentanyl in 2017 [220]. Little is known of its history, but it was first encountered as an adulterant in European MDMA tablets in 2015. It is seen with some frequency as a heroin adulterant, and it appears to be widely available, though rarely seen in a pure form. It is a mu agonist but with only a fifth the potency of fentanyl and is even less effective than morphine or heroin. Lack of potency appears to explain why it is almost always used with other drugs, chiefly other opiates and benzodiazepines. In one study of samples from Rhode Island, blood levels ranged from 17 to 945 ng/mL. This confirms that acetylfentanyl is less potent than fentanyl itself. All the decedents were white males between the ages of 21 and 40 years [221].

In a study from Florida, 375 of 500 presumed opiate deaths were found to be a consequence of fentanyl or one of its analogues [221]. Researchers in Detroit measured postmortem acetylfentanyl concentrations in 2015 and compared them with results from 2016. The 2016 cases had a mean acetylfentanyl concentration of 0.9 ng/mL (range 0.1–5.3 ng/mL) and an associated higher concentration of fentanyl. Multiple other drugs were also present. The 2015 cases had higher concentrations of acetylfentanyl (mean 8.9 ng/mL; range 0.28–37 ng/mL) with lower, yet still toxic, concentrations of fentanyl. This led the researchers to conclude that the cause of death in these recent cases was likely multiple drug toxicity with fentanyl and that the consistently observed lower peripheral blood concentrations of acetylfentanyl were most likely an artifact in the manufacture of the consumed illicit fentanyl. This suggestion has never been confirmed [222] and is probably unjustified given that the human volume of distribution (and therefore the tendency to redistribution) is unknown.

8.10.1.2 4-anilino-N-phenethyl-4-piperidine

4-ANPP is a derivative of 4-piperidone used as an intermediate in the manufacture of fentanyl, which probably explains why it is detected with such frequency. Although it is also a metabolite of furanylfentanyl and fentanyl itself, 4-ANPP and furanylfentanyl bind to the mu receptor but exert only a fraction of the effect elicited by pure fentanyl. Nonetheless, 4-ANPP and furanylfentanyl have been ruled as the cause of death in both the United States [223] and the European Union. These rulings are probably mistaken, because it is known that 4-ANNP is a minor metabolite of fentanyl itself but, as described, has much lower potency than fentanyl itself. In any case, both drugs can be detected by ELISA. Neither of these compounds appears to be popularly used as a single agent, but when this occurs, it is usually in the form of faux MDMA.

8.10.1.3 Alpha-methylfentanyl

Alpha-methylfentanyl was first synthesized by Jensen Pharmaceuticals, just one of a series of drugs created in their attempts to produce a better opioid. It was first produced in the 1960s but never underwent clinical trials (United States Patent 3164600). It reappeared in 1976 as a component of "China White," which was responsible for two deaths in California. After 13 additional "China White" deaths were reported, alpha-methylfentanyl was finally identified as a component [224]. The drug was scheduled by the DEA 2 years following its identification but re-emerged in the early 1990s when a simplified synthetic method was introduced (the Siegfried method – see earlier for details). Except for the fact that major alpha-methylfentanyl metabolites in rats are norfentanyl and hydroxypropionyl, exactly the same as with fentanyl [225], nothing is known about this drug's pharmacokinetics, pharmacodynamics, or postmortem toxicology. Alpha-methylacetylfentanyl is also a Schedule I controlled substance that was briefly popular in the 1980s. It is made via the same synthetic route as alpha-methylfentanyl but by substituting the relatively common acetic anhydride for the more difficult to obtain chemical propionic anhydride in the synthesis. Even less is known about this compound than alpha-methylfentanyl.

8.10.1.4 Carfentanil

Carfentanil is an extremely potent opioid, first sold in 1986. It is produced by Jensen Pharmaceuticals and sold under the brand name "Wildnil." Jensen Pharmaceuticals is the same company that originally synthesized fentanyl. It was intended to be used in combination with an α2-adrenoreceptor agonist in large mammals (i.e., elephants). Because of its high therapeutic index, on an equimolar basis, the lethal dose of carfentanil is approximately the same as that of fentanyl, but its ability to bind to the mu receptor is much greater and more rapid [226], as is its ability to cross the blood–brain barrier. It is estimated that carfentanil is 100 times more potent than fentanyl and 10,000 times more potent than morphine.

Carfentanil became famous in 2012 when Russian police pumped it to end a hostage situation. Over 800 theater goers were held captive by 33 terrorists, several armed with a suicide bomb vest. A mixture of carfentanil and remifentanil was pumped into the ventilation system of an auditorium where hostages were being held. At least 33 terrorists and 129 hostages died during or shortly after the raid. The terrorists were shot dead after falling unconscious due to the effects of the aerosol. Their explosive vests' straps were removed, and a bomb in the auditorium was deactivated. Only 2 hostages were shot by the terrorists, while the other 125 died through a combination of the aerosol and, according to testimony given at the World Court, clearly demonstrated inadequate medical treatment following the rescue [227]. Sometime during 2016, carfentanil began to appear as an adulterant in heroin. Authorities were quick to identify China as the origin of the drug. If there were any doubts, a Canadian police action in 2018 interdicted a 1-kilogram parcel of carfentanil shipped from China. The parcel was labeled as toner cartridges [228]. Almost nothing is known about the pharmacokinetics of this drug, but its metabolism has recently been partially characterized, and the first preliminary pharmacokinetic information has also been reported.

A 2018 report describes a 34-year-old male recreational carfentanil user who survived after 31 hours of assisted ventilation. Blood was drawn at three points during his treatment, allowing some pharmacokinetic measurements. The elimination half-life was 5.7 hours for carfentanil and 11.8 hours for the norcarfentanil metabolite. By interpolation, it was calculated that the carfentanil concentration would have been 0.52 ng/mL when the patient awoke [229]

Using time-of-flight MS, Feasel et al. were able to identify 12 carfentanil metabolites [172]. *N*-Dealkylation and monohydroxylation of the piperidine ring were the dominant metabolic pathways. Two *N*-oxide metabolites and one glucuronide metabolite were observed. Surprisingly, hydrolysis played a minimal role in the drug's metabolism. Incubation of the drug with HLM demonstrated rapid clearance by CYP enzymes, but when incubated with hepatocytes, clearance was much lower. U.S. federal regulations limit the total national production of carfentanil to 19 grams.

8.10.1.5 Furanylfentanyl

Furanylfentanyl is a fairly common heroin adulterant, sometimes sold as faux MDMA. In mice, it has only one-fifth the potency (equivalent dose [ED50]) of fentanyl. It first appeared in the Baltic States early in the year 2000. It was scheduled by the United States DEA in November 2015. The U.S. supply of this drug appears to come entirely from China [230]. Unlike most of the other fentanyl analogues, furanylfentanyl's major metabolites are generated by amide hydrolysis and dihydrodiol formation. The normetabolite is not produced [231].

The first cluster of furanylfentanyl-related deaths was reported from Sweden, where there were 11 deaths over a 4-month period. Furanylfentanyl was present alone or in combination with other illicit drugs. Five of the decedents were known drug users. Femoral blood concentrations of furanylfentanyl ranged from 0.41 to 2.47 ng/mL. The authors of the report concluded that it was impossible to establish a lethal concentration from an incidental finding in the absence of pharmacokinetic and pharmacodynamic data [232].

A recent report described the findings of suspected fentanyl poisonings. Of the 84 deaths investigated, fentanyl and/or a fentanyl analogue was present in 40 (48%) of the decedents. A number of analogues were encountered, including carfentanil (n = 17), fentanyl (n = 9), carfentanil and fentanyl together (n = 12), and fentanyl, carfentanil, 4-fluorobutyrylfentanyl, and butyrylfentanyl together (n = 2). The median (range) postmortem blood fentanyl concentration was 2.66 (0.21–107) µg/L, and the median (range) carfentanil concentration was 0.24 (0.03–1.66) µg/L [233]. Interestingly, median blood free morphine concentrations were lower in deaths where fentanyl/fentanyl analogues were present, but there was too much overlap between cases where fentanyl was and was not the cause of death to reach conclusions based on isolated blood concentrations.

8.10.2 Synthetic Opioids

8.10.2.1 Benzamides

3,4-Dichloro-N-[2-(dimethylamino)cyclohexyl]-*N*-methylbenzamide (U-47700) was developed by the pharmaceutical company Allen & Hanburys. It is a strong opiate agonist and in high doses, a kappa agonist as well. Like fentanyl, it is not particularly difficult to make and requires no specialized equipment or skills to produce. Anecdotal information suggests that it is going out of fashion. New analogues keep turning up [234], mostly involving substitutions of one of the two rings contained in the molecule. It can be identified in blood, both from the living and from the dead, using LC-MS-MS; a specific antibody has been produced for U-47700 [235]. Studies show that U-47700 has 7.5 times the ability of morphine to block painful stimuli in mice [236]. While there is no evidence of addiction in experimental animals, there is anecdotal information on the internet that suggests at least scattered abuse [237]. Law enforcement reports suggest fairly widespread abuse. It is usually sold as a pill (often faux oxycodone or diazepam) [211]. Anecdotal reports of overdose death have been reported from scattered locations around the world [209, 238, 239]. The United States DEA reports that more than 15 U-47700 deaths have occurred. In a study reported by a commercial laboratory, retesting 20 cases where heroin was thought to be the cause of death, 5 of the deaths were actually found to be the result of U-47700 and furanylfentanyl. Other fatalities have also been reported from the EMCDDA.

REFERENCES

1. European Drug Report. European Drug Report 2019: trends and developments 2019, June Available from: http://www.emcdda.europa.eu/publications/edr/trends-developments/2019_en.
2. Administration DE. About synthetic drugs 2017 Available from: https://www.deadiversion.usdoj.gov/synthetic_drugs/about_sd.html.
3. Kalix P. Cathinone, a natural amphetamine. *Pharmacology & Toxicology*. 1992;70(2):77–86.
4. Crime UNOoDa. Early warning advisory on NPS 2018, June Available from: http://www.unodc.org/unodc/en/frontpage/2018/June/second-regional-meeting-on-new-psychoactive-substances-in-the-americas-takes-place-in-brazil.html.
5. Bonson KR, Dalton T, Chiapperino D. Scheduling synthetic cathinone substances under the controlled substances act. *Psychopharmacology (Berl)*. 2019;236(3):845–60.
6. ElSohly MA, Slade D. Chemical constituents of marijuana: the complex mixture of natural cannabinoids. *Life Sciences*. 2005;78(5):539–48.
7. Wood TB, Spivey W, Easterfield TH. The resin of Indian hemp. *Journal of the Chemical Society Transactions* 1896;69(0):539–46.
8. Adams R, Hunt M, Clark JH. Structure of cannabidiol, a product isolated from the marihuana extract of minnesota wild Hemp. I. *Journal of the American Chemical Society*. 1940;62(1):196–200.
9. Turner CE, Elsohly MA, Boeren EG. Constituents of Cannabis sativa L. XVII. A review of the natural constituents. *Journal of Natural Products*. 1980;43(2):169–234.
10. Castaneto MS, Gorelick DA, Desrosiers NA, Hartman RL, Pirard S, Huestis MA. Synthetic cannabinoids: epidemiology, pharmacodynamics, and clinical implications. *Drug and Alcohol Dependence*. 2014;144:12–41.
11. Shevyrin VA, Morzherin YY. Cannabinoids: structures, effects, and classification. *Russian Chemical Bulletin*. 2015;64(6):1249–66.
12. Auwärter V, Dresen S, Weinmann W, Müller M, Pütz M, Ferreirós N. 'Spice' and other herbal blends: harmless incense or cannabinoid designer drugs? *Journal of Mass Spectrometry*. 2009;44(5):832–7.
13. Uchiyama N, Kikura-Hanajiri R, Ogata J, Goda Y. Chemical analysis of synthetic cannabinoids as designer drugs in herbal products. *Forensic Science International*. 2010;198(1–3):31–8.
14. Dresen S, Ferreiros N, Putz M, Westphal F, Zimmermann R, Auwarter V. Monitoring of herbal mixtures potentially containing synthetic cannabinoids as psychoactive compounds. *J Mass Spectrom*. 2010;45(10):1186–94.
15. Huffman JW, Dai D, Martin BR, Compton DR. Design, synthesis and pharmacology of cannabimimetic indoles. *Bioorganic & Medicinal Chemistry Letters*. 1994;4(4):563–6.
16. Schuster J, Ates M, Brune K, Guhring H. The cannabinoids R(-)-7-hydroxy-delta-6-tetra-hydrocannabinol-dimethylheptyl (HU-210), 2-O-arachidonoylglycerylether (HU-310) and arachidonyl-2-chloroethylamide (ACEA) increase isoflurane provoked sleep duration by activation of cannabinoids 1 (CB1)-receptors in mice. *Neurosci Lett*. 2002;326(3):196–200.
17. Synthetic cannabinoids in Europe updated 6/6/2017 Available from: http://www.emcdda.europa.eu/system/files/publications/2753/POD_Synthetic%20cannabinoids_0.pdf.
18. Debruyne D, Le Boisselier R. Emerging drugs of abuse: current perspectives on synthetic cannabinoids. *Substance Abuse and Rehabilitation*. 2015;6:113–29.
19. Presley B, Smr G, Scott K, Sl K, Logan B. *Metabolism and Toxicological Analysis of Synthetic Cannabinoids in Biological Fluids and Tissues*. 2016. 103–69.
20. Abbate ASM, Presley BC, Uchiyama N. The ongoing challenge of novel psychoactive drugs of abuse. Part I. Synthetic cannabinoids (IUPAC Technical Report). *Pure Applied Chemistry* 2018;90(8):1225–82.
21. Vadim S, Vladimir M, Endres GW, Yuri S, Yuri M. On a new cannabinoid classification system: a sight on the illegal market of novel psychoactive substances. *Cannabis and Cannabinoid Research*. 2016;1(1):186–94.
22. Nichols DE, Barfknecht CF, Long JP, et al. Potential psychotomimetics. 2. Rigid analogs of 2,5-dimethoxy-4 -methylphenylisopropylamine (DOM, STP). *Journal of Medicinal Chemistry*. 1974;17(2):161–6.
23. Komorowski J, Stepień H. [The role of the endocannabinoid system in the regulation of endocrine function and in the control of energy balance in humans]. *Postepy Higieny i Medycyny Doswiadczalnej (Online)*. 2007;61:99–105.
24. Herkenham M, Lynn AB, Little MD, Johnson MR, Melvin LS, de Costa BR, et al. Cannabinoid receptor localization in brain. *Proceedings of the National Academy of Sciences*. 1990;87(5):1932–6.
25. Munro S, Thomas KL, Abu-Shaar M. Molecular characterization of a peripheral receptor for cannabinoids. *Nature*. 1993;365(6441):61–5.
26. Wilson RI, Nicoll RA. Endogenous cannabinoids mediate retrograde signalling at hippocampal synapses. *Nature*. 2001;410(6828):588–92.
27. Di Marzo V, Melck D, Bisogno T, De Petrocellis L. Endocannabinoids: endogenous cannabinoid receptor ligands with neuromodulatory action. *Trends in Neurosciences*. 1998;21(12):521–8.
28. Pertwee RG. The diverse CB1 and CB2 receptor pharmacology of three plant cannabinoids: Δ9-tetrahydrocannabinol, cannabidiol and Δ9-tetrahydrocannabivarin. *British Journal of Pharmacology*. 2008;153(2):199–215.

29. Spaderna M, Addy PH, D'Souza DC. Spicing things up: synthetic cannabinoids. *Psychopharmacology (Berl)*. 2013;228(4):525–40.
30. De Luca MA, Castelli MP, Loi B, Porcu A, Martorelli M, Miliano C, et al. Native CB1 receptor affinity, intrinsic activity and accumbens shell dopamine stimulant properties of third generation SPICE/K2 cannabinoids: BB-22, 5F-PB-22, 5F-AKB-48 and STS-135. *Neuropharmacology*. 2016;105:630–8.
31. Diao X, Huestis M. Approaches, challenges, and advances in metabolism of new synthetic cannabinoids and identification of optimal urinary marker metabolites. *Clinical Pharmacology & Therapeutics*. 2017;101(2):239–53.
32. Teske J, Weller J-P, Fieguth A, Rothämel T, Schulz Y, Tröger HD. Sensitive and rapid quantification of the cannabinoid receptor agonist naphthalen-1-yl-(1-pentylindol-3-yl)methanone (JWH-018) in human serum by liquid chromatography–tandem mass spectrometry. *Journal of Chromatography B*. 2010;878(27):2659–63.
33. Holm NB, Nielsen LM, Linnet K. CYP3A4 mediates oxidative metabolism of the synthetic cannabinoid AKB-48. *The AAPS Journal*. 2015;17(5):1237–45.
34. Maurer HH, Sauer C, Theobald DS. Toxicokinetics of drugs of abuse: current knowledge of the isoenzymes involved in the human metabolism of tetrahydrocannabinol, cocaine, heroin, morphine, and codeine. *Therapeutic Drug Monitoring*. 2006;28(3):447–53.
35. Rajasekaran M, Brents LK, Franks LN, Moran JH, Prather PL. Human metabolites of synthetic cannabinoids JWH-018 and JWH-073 bind with high affinity and act as potent agonists at cannabinoid type-2 receptors. *Toxicology and Applied Pharmacology*. 2013;269(2):100–8.
36. Erratico C, Negreira N, Norouzizadeh H, Covaci A, Neels H, Maudens K, et al. In vitro and in vivo human metabolism of the synthetic cannabinoid AB-CHMINACA. *Drug Testing and Analysis*. 2015;7(10):866–76.
37. Thomsen R, Nielsen LM, Holm NB, Rasmussen HB, Linnet K, Consortium tI. Synthetic cannabimimetic agents metabolized by carboxylesterases. *Drug Testing and Analysis*. 2015;7(7):565–76.
38. Chimalakonda KC, Bratton SM, Le V-H, Yiew KH, Dineva A, Moran CL, et al. Conjugation of synthetic cannabinoids JWH-018 and JWH-073, metabolites by human UDP-glucuronosyltransferases. *Drug Metabolism and Disposition: The Biological Fate of Chemicals*. 2011;39(10):1967–76.
39. Sobolevskii TG, Prasolov IS, Rodchenkov GM. Application of mass spectrometry to the structural identification of the metabolites of the synthetic cannabinoid JWH-018 and the determination of them in human urine. *Journal of Analytical Chemistry*. 2011;66(13):1314–23.
40. Wintermeyer A, Möller I, Thevis M, Jübner M, Beike J, Rothschild MA, et al. In vitro phase I metabolism of the synthetic cannabimimetic JWH-018. *Analytical and Bioanalytical Chemistry*. 2010;398(5):2141–53.
41. Hutter M, Broecker S, Kneisel S, Franz F, Brandt SD, Auwarter V. Metabolism of nine synthetic cannabinoid receptor agonists encountered in clinical casework: major in vivo Phase I Metabolites of AM-694, AM-2201, JWH-007, JWH-019, JWH-203, JWH-307, MAM-2201, UR-144 and XLR-11 in Human Urine Using LC-MS/MS. *Current Pharmaceutical Biotechnology*. 2018;19(2):144–62.
42. Castaneto MS, Wohlfarth A, Desrosiers NA, Hartman RL, Gorelick DA, Huestis MA. Synthetic cannabinoids pharmacokinetics and detection methods in biological matrices. *Drug Metabolism Reviews*. 2015;47(2):124–74.
43. Chimalakonda KC, Seely KA, Bratton SM, Brents LK, Moran CL, Endres GW, et al. Cytochrome P450-mediated oxidative metabolism of abused synthetic cannabinoids found in K2/Spice: identification of novel cannabinoid receptor ligands. *Drug Metabolism and Disposition*. 2012;40(11):2174–84.
44. Diao X, Scheidweiler K, Wohlfarth A, Pang S, Kronstrand R, Huestis M. In vitro and in vivo human metabolism of synthetic cannabinoids FDU-PB-22 and FUB-PB-222016.
45. Hutter M, Moosmann B, Kneisel S, Auwärter V. Characteristics of the designer drug and synthetic cannabinoid receptor agonist AM-2201 regarding its chemistry and metabolism. *Journal of Mass Spectrometry*. 2013;48(7):885–94.
46. Jang M, Yang W, Shin I, Choi H, Chang H, Kim E. Determination of AM-2201 metabolites in urine and comparison with JWH-018 abuse. *International Journal of Legal Medicine*. 2014;128(2):285–94.
47. Tournebize J, Gibaja V, Kahn J-P. Acute effects of synthetic cannabinoids: update 2015. *Substance Abuse*. 2016;38(3):344–66.
48. Toennes SW, Geraths A, Pogoda W, Paulke A, Wunder C, Theunissen EL, et al. Pharmacokinetic properties of the synthetic cannabinoid JWH-018 and of its metabolites in serum after inhalation. *Journal of Pharmaceutical and Biomedical Analysis*. 2017;140:215–22.
49. Levisky JA, Bowerman DL, Jenkins WW, Johnson DG, Karch SB. Drugs in postmortem adipose tissues: evidence of antemortem deposition. *Forensic Science International*. 2001;121(3):157–60.
50. Erol Öztürk Y, Yeter O, Alpertunga B. Validation of JWH-018 and its metabolites in blood and urine by UPLC–MS/MS: monitoring in forensic cases. *Forensic Science International*. 2015;248:88–93.
51. Kaneko S. Motor vehicle collisions caused by the 'super-strength' synthetic cannabinoids, MAM-2201, 5F-PB-22, 5F-AB-PINACA, 5F-AMB and 5F-ADB in Japan experienced from 2012 to 2014. *Forensic Toxicology*. 2017;35(2):244–51.
52. Karinen R, Tuv SS, Øiestad EL, Vindenes V. Concentrations of APINACA, 5F-APINACA, UR-144 and its degradant product in blood samples from six impaired drivers compared to previous reported concentrations of other synthetic cannabinoids. *Forensic Science International*. 2015;246:98–103.
53. Boland DM, Reidy LJ, Seither JM, Radtke JM, Lew EO. Forty-three fatalities involving the synthetic cannabinoid, 5-Fluoro-ADB: forensic pathology and toxicology implications. *Journal of Forensic Sciences*. 2020;65(1):170–182.
54. Reidy L, Seither J, Boland D. Identification of synthetic cannabinoid 5-fluoro-ADB in human performance and postmortem samples: a case series. *Journal of Forensic Toxicology and Pharmacology*. 2018;7(2):9.
55. Hermanns-Clausen M, Kneisel S, Hutter M, Szabo B, Auwärter V. Acute intoxication by synthetic cannabinoids – four case reports. *Drug Testing and Analysis*. 2013;5(9–10):790–4.
56. Kraemer M, Boehmer A, Madea B, Maas A. Death cases involving certain new psychoactive substances: a review of the literature. *Forensic Science International*. 2019;298:186–267.
57. Schaefer N, Peters B, Bregel D, Kneisel S, Auwärter V, Schmidt PH, et al. A fatal case involving several synthetic cannabinoids. *Toxichem Krimtech*. 2013;80(Spec Iss):248–51.

58. Hasegawa K, Wurita A, Minakata K, Gonmori K, Nozawa H, Yamagishi I, et al. Postmortem distribution of AB-CHMINACA, 5-fluoro-AMB, and diphenidine in body fluids and solid tissues in a fatal poisoning case: usefulness of adipose tissue for detection of the drugs in unchanged forms. *Forensic Toxicology.* 2014;33(1):45–53.
59. Grafinger KE, Bernhard W, Weinmann W. Scheduling of new psychoactive substance the Swiss way: a review and critical analysis. *Science & Justice.* 2019;59(4):459–66.
60. Presley BC, Jansen-Varnum SA, Logan BK. Analysis of synthetic cannabinoids in botanical material: a review of analytical methods and findings. *Forensic Science Review.* 2013;25(1–2):27–46.
61. Kikura-Hanajiri R, Kawamura NU, Goda Y. Changes in the prevalence of new psychoactive substances before and after the introduction of the generic scheduling of synthetic cannabinoids in Japan. *Drug Testing and Analysis.* 2014;6(7–8):832–9.
62. Hill SL, Thomas SHL. Clinical toxicology of newer recreational drugs. *Clinical Toxicology (Philadelphia, Pa).* 2011;49(8):705–19.
63. Balíková M. Nonfatal and fatal DOB (2,5-dimethoxy-4-bromoamphetamine) overdose. *Forensic Science International.* 2005;153(1):85–91.
64. Bowen JS, Davis GB, Kearney TE, Bardin J. Diffuse vascular spasm associated with 4-bromo-2,5-dimethoxyamphetamine ingestion. *JAMA.* 1983;249(11):1477–9.
65. Wood DM, Looker JJ, Shaikh L, Button J, Puchnarewicz M, Davies S, et al. Delayed onset of seizures and toxicity associated with recreational use of Bromo-dragonFLY. *Journal of Medical Toxicology.* 2009;5(4):226–9.
66. Andreasen MF, Telving R, Birkler RID, Schumacher B, Johannsen M. A fatal poisoning involving Bromo-Dragonfly. *Forensic Sci Int.* 2009;183(1–3):91–6.
67. McIntyre IM, Gary RD, Trochta A, Stolberg S, Stabley R. Acute 5-(2-aminopropyl)benzofuran (5-APB) intoxication and fatality: a case report with postmortem concentrations. *Journal of Analytical Toxicology.* 2015;39(2):156–9.
68. Sainsbury PD, Kicman AT, Archer RP, King LA, Braithwaite RA. Aminoindanes—the next wave of 'legal highs'? *Drug Testing and Analysis.* 2011;3(7–8):479–82.
69. Pinterova N, Horsley RR, Palenicek T. Synthetic aminoindanes: a summary of existing knowledge. *Frontiers in Psychiatry [Internet].* 2017;8:236. Available from: http://europepmc.org/abstract/MED/29204127; http://europepmc.org/articles/PMC5698283?pdf=render; http://europepmc.org/articles/PMC5698283; https://doi.org/10.3389/fpsyt.2017.00236.
70. Staeheli SN, Boxler MI, Oestreich A, Marti M, Gascho D, Bolliger SA, et al. Postmortem distribution and redistribution of MDAI and 2-MAPB in blood and alternative matrices. *Forensic Science International.* 2017;279:83–7.
71. Elliott S, Evans J. A 3-year review of new psychoactive substances in casework. *Forensic Science International.* 2014;243:55–60.
72. Nichols DE. Hallucinogens. *Pharmacology & Therapeutics.* 2004;101(2):131–81.
73. Poklis JL, Devers KG, Arbefeville EF, Pearson JM, Houston E, Poklis A. Postmortem detection of 25I-NBOMe [2-(4-iodo-2,5-dimethoxyphenyl)-N-[(2-methoxyphenyl)methyl]ethanamine] in fluids and tissues determined by high performance liquid chromatography with tandem mass spectrometry from a traumatic death. *Forensic Science International.* 2014;234:e14–20.
74. Andreasen MF, Telving R, Rosendal I, Eg MB, Hasselstrøm JB, Andersen LV. A fatal poisoning involving 25C-NBOMe. *Forensic Science International.* 2015;251:e1–8.
75. Majchrzak M, Celiński R, Kuś P, Kowalska T, Sajewicz M. The newest cathinone derivatives as designer drugs: an analytical and toxicological review. *Forensic Toxicology.* 2018;36(1):33–50.
76. Hasegawa K, Suzuki O, Wurita A, Minakata K, Yamagishi I, Nozawa H, et al. Postmortem distribution of α-pyrrolidinovalerophenone and its metabolite in body fluids and solid tissues in a fatal poisoning case measured by LC–MS–MS with the standard addition method. *Forensic Toxicology.* 2014;32(2):225–34.
77. Hasegawa K, Wurita A, Minakata K, Gonmori K, Nozawa H, Yamagishi I, et al. Postmortem distribution of PV9, a new cathinone derivative, in human solid tissues in a fatal poisoning case. *Forensic Toxicology.* 2015;33(1):141–7.
78. Baumann MH, Partilla JS, Lehner KR. Psychoactive "bath salts": not so soothing. *European Journal of Pharmacology.* 2013;698(1–3):1–5.
79. Luethi D, Kolaczynska KE, Docci L, Krähenbühl S, Hoener MC, Liechti ME. Pharmacological profile of mephedrone analogs and related new psychoactive substances. *Neuropharmacology.* 2018;134(Pt A):4–12.
80. Olesti E, Farré M, Papaseit E, Krotonoulas A, Pujadas M, de la Torre R, et al. Pharmacokinetics of mephedrone and its metabolites in human by LC-MS/MS. *The AAPS Journal.* 2017;19(6):1767–78.
81. Busardò FP, Kyriakou C, Tittarelli R, Mannocchi G, Pantano F, Santurro A, et al. Assessment of the stability of mephedrone in ante-mortem and post-mortem blood specimens. *Forensic Science International.* 2015;256:28–37.
82. Dickson AJ, Vorce SP, Levine B, Past MR. Multiple-drug toxicity caused by the coadministration of 4-methylmethcathinone (mephedrone) and heroin. *Journal of Analytical Toxicology.* 2010;34(3):162–8.
83. Addition EMCfDaD. New drugs and emerging trends 2009 [Available from: http://www.emcdda.europa.eu/publications/annual-report/2009_en.
84. Carbone PN, Carbone DL, Carstairs SD, Luzi SA. Sudden cardiac death associated with methylone use. *The American Journal of Forensic Medicine and Pathology.* 2013;34(1):26–8.
85. Cawrse BM, Levine B, Jufer RA, Fowler DR, Vorce SP, Dickson AJ, et al. Distribution of methylone in four postmortem cases. *Journal of Analytical Toxicology.* 2012;36(6):434–9.
86. Wood MR, Lalancette RA, Bernal I. Crystallographic investigations of select cathinones: emerging illicit street drugs known as `bath salts'. *Acta Crystallographica Section C, Structural Chemistry.* 2015;71(Pt 1):32–8.
87. Prosser JM, Nelson LS. The toxicology of bath salts: a review of synthetic cathinones. *Journal of Medical Toxicology.* 2012;8(1):33–42.
88. Grecco GG, Kisor DF, Magura JS, Sprague JE. Impact of common clandestine structural modifications on synthetic cathinone "bath salt" pharmacokinetics. *Toxicology and Applied Pharmacology.* 2017;328:18–24.
89. Watterson LR, Burrows BT, Hernandez RD, Moore KN, Grabenauer M, Marusich JA, et al. Effects of α-pyrrolidinopentiophenone and 4-methyl-N-ethylcathinone, two synthetic cathinones commonly found in second-generation "bath salts," on intracranial self-stimulation thresholds in rats. *The International Journal*

of *Neuropsychopharmacology [Internet].* 2014;18(1). Available from: http://europepmc.org/abstract/MED/25522379; http://europepmc.org/articles/PMC4368864?pdf=render; http://europepmc.org/articles/PMC4368864; https://doi.org/10.1093/ijnp/pyu014.
90. Páleníček T, Lhotková E, Žídková M, Balíková M, Kuchař M, Himl M, et al. Emerging toxicity of 5,6-methylenedioxy-2-aminoindane (MDAI): pharmacokinetics, behaviour, thermoregulation and LD50 in rats. *Progress in Neuro-psychopharmacology & Biological Psychiatry.* 2016;69:49–59.
91. Potocka-Banaś B, Janus T, Majdanik S, Banaś T, Dembińska T, Borowiak K. Fatal intoxication with α-PVP, a Synthetic cathinone derivative. *Journal of Forensic Sciences.* 2017;62(2):553–6.
92. Vignali C, Moretti M, Groppi A, Osculati AMM, Tajana L, Morini L. Distribution of the synthetic cathinone α-Pyrrolidinohexiophenone in biological specimens. *Journal of Analytical Toxicology.* 2018;43(1):el–e6.
93. Krotulski AJ, Mohr ALA, Papsun DM, Logan BK. Dibutylone (bk-DMBDB): intoxications, quantitative confirmations and metabolism in authentic biological specimens. *Journal of Analytical Toxicology.* 2018;42(7):437–45.
94. Atherton D, Dye D, Robinson CA, Beck R. n-Ethyl pentylone-related deaths in alabama. *Journal of Forensic Sciences.* 2019;64(1):304–8.
95. Krotulski AJ, Papsun DM, De Martinis BS, Mohr ALA, Logan BK. N-Ethyl pentylone (Ephylone) intoxications: quantitative confirmation and metabolite identification in authentic human biological specimens. *Journal of Analytical Toxicology.* 2018;42(7):467–75.
96. Gee P, Fountain J. Party on? BZP party pills in New Zealand. *The New Zealand Medical Journal [Internet].* 2007;120(1249):U2422. Available from: http://europepmc.org/abstract/MED/17308559.
97. Nikolova I, Danchev N. Piperazine based substances of abuse: a new party Pills on Bulgarian drug market. *Biotechnology & Biotechnological Equipment.* 2008;22(2):652–5.
98. Nelson ME, Bryant SM, Aks SE. Emerging drugs of abuse. *Emergency Medicine Clinics.* 2014;32(1):1–28.
99. Tancer M, Johanson C-E. Reinforcing, subjective, and physiological effects of MDMA in humans: a comparison with d-amphetamine and mCPP. *Drug and Alcohol Dependence.* 2003;72(1):33–44.
100. Antia U, Lee HS, Kydd RR, Tingle MD, Russell BR. Pharmacokinetics of 'party pill' drug N-benzylpiperazine (BZP) in healthy human participants. *Forensic Science International.* 2009;186(1–3):63–7.
101. Katz DP, Deruiter J, Bhattacharya D, Ahuja M, Bhattacharya S, Clark CR, et al. Benzylpiperazine: "A messy drug". *Drug and Alcohol Dependence.* 2016;164:1–7.
102. Staack RF, Fritschi G, Maurer HH. New designer drug 1-(3-trifluoromethylphenyl) piperazine (TFMPP): gas chromatography/mass spectrometry and liquid chromatography/mass spectrometry studies on its phase I and II metabolism and on its toxicological detection in rat urine. *Journal of Mass Spectrometry.* 2003;38(9):971–81.
103. Staack RF, Maurer HH. Piperazine-derived designer drug 1-(3-Chlorophenyl)piperazine (mCPP): GC-MS studies on its metabolism and its toxicological detection in rat urine including analytical differentiation from its precursor drugs trazodone and Nefazodone*. *Journal of Analytical Toxicology.* 2003;27(8):560–8.
104. Feuchtl A, Bagli M, Stephan R, Frahnert C, Kölsch H, Kühn KU, et al. Pharmacokinetics of m-chlorophenylpiperazine after intravenous and oral administration in healthy male volunteers: implication for the pharmacodynamic profile. *Pharmacopsychiatry.* 2004;37(4):180–8.
105. Lin JC, Jan RK, Kydd RR, Russell BR. Subjective effects in humans following administration of party pill drugs BZP and TFMPP alone and in combination. *Drug Testing and Analysis.* 2011;3(9):582–5.
106. Elliott S. Current awareness of piperazines: pharmacology and toxicology. *Drug Testing and Analysis.* 2011;3(7-8):430–8.
107. Gee P, Jerram T, Bowie D. Multiorgan failure from 1-benzylpiperazine ingestion—legal high or lethal high? *Clinical Toxicology (Philadelphia, Pa).* 2010;48(3):230–3.
108. Elliott S, Smith C. Investigation of the first deaths in the United Kingdom involving the detection and quantitation of the piperazines BZP and 3-TFMPP. *Journal of Analytical Toxicology.* 2008;32(2):172–7.
109. Wikström M, Holmgren P, Ahlner J. A2 (N-benzylpiperazine) a new drug of abuse in Sweden. *Journal of Analytical Toxicology.* 2004;28(1):67–70.
110. Gaillard YP, Cuquel AC, Boucher A, Romeuf L, Bevalot F, Prevosto JM, et al. A fatality following ingestion of the designer drug meta-chlorophenylpiperazine (mCPP) in an Asthmatic-HPLC-MS/MS detection in biofluids and hair. *Journal Forensic Sciences.* 2013;58(1):263–269.
111. Lau T, LeBlanc R, Botch-Jones S. Stability of synthetic piperazines in human whole blood. *Journal of Analytical Toxicology.* 2018;42(2):88–98.
112. Coppola M, Mondola R. MT-45: a new, dangerous legal high. *Journal of Opioid Management.* 2014;10(5):301–2.
113. McKenzie C, Sutcliffe OB, Read KD, Scullion P, Epemolu O, Fletcher D, et al. Chemical synthesis, characterisation and in vitro and in vivo metabolism of the synthetic opioid MT-45 and its newly identified fluorinated analogue 2F-MT-45 with metabolite confirmation in urine samples from known drug users. *Forensic Toxicology.* 2018;36(2):359–74.
114. Helander A, Bradley M, Hasselblad A, Norlen L, Vassilaki I, Backberg M, et al. Acute skin and hair symptoms followed by severe, delayed eye complications in subjects using the synthetic opioid MT-45. *British Journal of Dermatology.* 2017;176(4):1021–7.
115. McKenzie C, Sutcliffe OB, Read KD, et al. Chemical synthesis, characterization and *in vitro* and *in vivo* metabolism of the synthetic opioid MT-45 and its newly identified fluorinated analogue 2F-MT-45 with metabolite confirmation in urine samples from known drug users. *Forensic Toxicology.* 2018;36(2):359–74.
116. Smith M, Baptista-Hon D, Antonides L, et al. Activation of the mu-opioid receptor by MT-45 and its synthetic and metabolic derivatives. *British Journal of Anesthesia.* 2019;122(3):e51.
117. Lau NK, Chong YK, Tang MH, Ching CK, Mak TW. Desoxy-D2PM: a novel psychoactive substance in convenience stores. *Hong Kong Medical Journal = Xianggang yi xue za zhi.* 2016;22(5):515.
118. Corkery JM, Elliott S, Schifano F, Corazza O, Ghodse AH. 2-DPMP (desoxypipradrol, 2-benzhydrylpiperidine, 2-phenylmethylpiperidine) and D2PM (diphenyl-2-pyrrolidin-2-yl-methanol, diphenylprolinol): a preliminary review. *Progress in Neuro-psychopharmacology & Biological Psychiatry.* 2012;39(2):253–8.

119. Wood DM, Puchnarewicz M, Johnston A, Dargan PI. A case series of individuals with analytically confirmed acute diphenyl-2-pyrrolidinemethanol (D2PM) toxicity. *European Journal of Clinical Pharmacology.* 2012;68(4):349–53.
120. Simmler LD, Rickli A, Schramm Y, Hoener MC, Liechti ME. Pharmacological profiles of aminoindanes, piperazines, and pipradrol derivatives. *Biochemical Pharmacology.* 2014;88(2):237–44.
121. Murray DB, Potts S, Haxton C, Jackson G, Sandilands EA, Ramsey J, et al. 'Ivory wave' toxicity in recreational drug users; integration of clinical and poisons information services to manage legal high poisoning. *Clinical Toxicology (Philadelphia, Pa).* 2012;50(2):108–13.
122. Wood DM, Dargan PI. Use and acute toxicity associated with the novel psychoactive substances diphenylprolinol (D2PM) and desoxypipradrol (2-DPMP). *Clinical Toxicology (Philadelphia, Pa).* 2012;50(8):727–32.
123. Kriikku P, Wilhelm L, Rintatalo J, Hurme J, Kramer J, Ojanperä I. Prevalence and blood concentrations of desoxypipradrol (2-DPMP) in drivers suspected of driving under the influence of drugs and in post-mortem cases. *Forensic Science International.* 2013;226(1–3):146–51.
124. Bertron JL, Seto M, Lindsley CW. DARK classics in chemical neuroscience: phencyclidine (PCP). *ACS Chemistry Neurosciences.* 2018;9(10):2459–74.
125. Liu F-L, Chen T-L, Chen R-M. Mechanisms of ketamine-induced immunosuppression. *Acta Anaesthesiologica Taiwanica.* 2012;50(4):172–7.
126. Durieux ME. Inhibition by ketamine of muscarinic acetylcholine receptor function. *Anesthesia and Analgesia.* 1995;81(1):57–62.
127. Feifel D. Breaking sad: unleashing the breakthrough potential of ketamine's rapid antidepressant effects. *Drug Development Research.* 2016;77(8):489–94.
128. Idvall J, Ahlgren I, Aronsen KR, Stenberg P. Ketamine infusions: pharmacokinetics and clinical effects. *British Journal of Anaesthesia.* 1979;51(12):1167–73.
129. Vroegop MP, van Dongen RT, Vantroyen B, Kramers C. [Ketamine as a party drug]. *Ned Tijdschr Geneeskd.* 2007;151(37):2039–42.
130. Miliano C, Serpelloni G, Rimondo C, Mereu M, Marti M, De Luca MA. Neuropharmacology of New Psychoactive Substances (NPS): focus on the rewarding and reinforcing properties of cannabimimetics and amphetamine-like stimulants. *Frontiers in Neuroscience [Internet].* 2016;10:153. Available from: http://europepmc.org/abstract/MED/27147945; http://europepmc.org/articles/PMC4835722?pdf=render; http://europepmc.org/articles/PMC4835722; https://doi.org/10.3389/fnins.2016.00153.
131. Adams JD, Jr, Baillie TA, Trevor AJ, Castagnoli N, Jr. Studies on the biotransformation of ketamine. 1-Identification of metabolites produced in vitro from rat liver microsomal preparations. *Biomed Mass Spectrom.* 1981;8(11):527–38.
132. Moffatt, A, Osselton D, (eds). *Clarke's Analysis of Drugs and Poisons.* London: Pharmaceutical Press, 2004.
133. Getachew B, Aubee JI, Schottenfeld RS, Csoka AB, Thompson KM, Tizabi Y. Ketamine interactions with gut-microbiota in rats: relevance to its antidepressant and anti-inflammatory properties. *BMC Microbiology [Internet].* 2018;18(1):222. Available from: http://europepmc.org/abstract/MED/30579332; http://europepmc.org/articles/PMC6303954?pdf=render; http://europepmc.org/articles/PMC6303954; https://doi.org/10.1186/s12866-018-1373-7.
134. Ho CCK, Pezhman H, Praveen S, Goh EH, Lee BC, Zulkifli MZ, et al. Ketamine-associated ulcerative cystitis: a case report and literature review. *The Malaysian Journal of Medical Sciences.* 2010;17(2):61–5.
135. Zanda MT, Fadda P, Chiamulera C, Fratta W, Fattore L. Methoxetamine, a novel psychoactive substance with serious adverse pharmacological effects: a review of case reports and preclinical findings. *Behavioural Pharmacology.* 2016;27(6):489–96.
136. Hofer KE, Grager B, Müller DM, Rauber-Lüthy C, Kupferschmidt H, Rentsch KM, et al. Ketamine-like effects after recreational use of methoxetamine. *Annals of Emergency Medicine.* 2012;60(1):97–9.
137. Coppola M, Mondola R. Methoxetamine: from drug of abuse to rapid-acting antidepressant. *Medical Hypotheses.* 2012;79(4):504–7.
138. Wood DM, Davies S, Puchnarewicz M, Johnston A, Dargan PI. Acute toxicity associated with the recreational use of the ketamine derivative methoxetamine. *European Journal of Clinical Pharmacology.* 2012;68(5):853–6.
139. Karinen R, Tuv SS, Rogde S, Peres MD, Johansen U, Frost J, et al. Lethal poisonings with AH-7921 in combination with other substances. *Forensic Science International.* 2014;244:e21–4.
140. Elliott SP, Brandt SD, Wallach J, Morris H, Kavanagh PV. First reported fatalities associated with the 'research chemical' 2-methoxydiphenidine. *Journal of Analytical Toxicology.* 2015;39(4):287–93.
141. Mitchell-Mata C, Thomas B, Peterson B, Couper F. Two fatal intoxications involving 3-methoxyphencyclidine. *Journal of Analytical Toxicology.* 2017;41(6):503–7.
142. Araújo AM, Carvalho F, Bastos MdL, Guedes de Pinho P, Carvalho M. The hallucinogenic world of tryptamines: an updated review. *Archives of Toxicology.* 2015;89(8):1151–73.
143. Tittarelli R, Mannocchi G, Pantano F, Romolo FS. Recreational use, analysis and toxicity of tryptamines. *Current Neuropharmacology.* 2015;13(1):26–46.
144. Boland DM, Andollo W, Hime GW, Hearn WL. Fatality due to acute alpha-methyltryptamine intoxication. *Journal of Analytical Toxicology.* 2005;29(5):394–7.
145. Lessin AW, Long RF, Parkes MW. CENTRAL STIMULANT ACTIONS OF ALPHA-ALKYL SUBSTITUTED TRYPTAMINES IN MICE. *British Journal of Pharmacology and Chemotherapy.* 1965;24:49–67.
146. Corkery JM, Durkin E, Elliott S, Schifano F, Ghodse AH. The recreational tryptamine 5-MeO-DALT (N,N-diallyl-5-methoxytryptamine): a brief review. *Progress in Neuro-psychopharmacology & Biological Psychiatry.* 2012;39(2):259–62.
147. Tanaka E, Kamata T, Katagi M, Tsuchihashi H, Honda K. A fatal poisoning with 5-methoxy-N,N-diisopropyltryptamine, Foxy. *Forensic Science International.* 2006;163(1–2):152–4.
148. Täljemark J, Johansson BA. Drug-induced acute psychosis in an adolescent first-time user of 4-HO-MET. *European Child & Adolescent Psychiatry.* 2012;21(9):527–8.
149. Jovel A, Felthous A, Bhattacharyya A. Delirium due to intoxication from the novel synthetic tryptamine 5-MeO-DALT. *Journal of Forensic Sciences.* 2014;59(3):844–6.
150. Karinen R, Fosen JT, Rogde S, Vindenes V. An accidental poisoning with mitragynine. *Forensic Science International.* 2014;245:e29–32.
151. Váradi A, Marrone GF, Palmer TC, Narayan A, Szabó MR, Le Rouzic V, et al. Mitragynine/Corynantheidine pseudoindoxyls as opioid analgesics with Mu agonism and delta antagonism, which do not recruit β-Arrestin-2. *Journal of Medicinal Chemistry.* 2016;59(18):8381–97.

152. Jansen KL, Prast CJ. Ethnopharmacology of kratom and the Mitragyna alkaloids. *Journal of Ethnopharmacology.* 1988;23(1):115–9.
153. Trakulsrichai S, Sathirakul K, Auparakkitanon S, Krongvorakul J, Sueajai J, Noumjad N, et al. Pharmacokinetics of mitragynine in man. *Drug Design, Development and Therapy [Internet].* 2015;9:2421–9. Available from: http://europepmc.org/abstract/MED/25995615; http://europepmc.org/articles/PMC4425236?pdf=render; http://europepmc.org/articles/PMC4425236; https://doi.org/10.2147/DDDT.S79658.
154. Hassan Z, Bosch OG, Singh D, Narayanan S, Kasinather BV, Seifritz E, et al. Novel psychoactive substances-recent progress on neuropharmacological mechanisms of action for selected drugs. *Frontiers in Psychiatry [Internet].* 2017;8:152. Available from: http://europepmc.org/abstract/MED/28868040; http://europepmc.org/articles/PMC5563308?pdf=render; http://europepmc.org/articles/PMC5563308; https://doi.org/10.3389/fpsyt.2017.00152.
155. White CM. Pharmacologic and clinical assessment of kratom. *American Journal of Health-System Pharmacy.* 2018;75(5):261–7.
156. Gershman K, Timm K, Frank M, Lampi L, Melamed J, Gerona R, et al. Deaths in colorado attributed to Kratom. *The New England Journal of Medicine.* 2019;380(1):97–8.
157. Olsen EOM, O'Donnell J, Mattson CL, Schier JG, Wilson N. Notes from the field: unintentional drug overdose deaths with Kratom detected - 27 States, July 2016–December 2017. *MMWR Morbidity and Mortality Weekly Report [Internet].* 2019;68(14):326–7. Available from: http://europepmc.org/abstract/MED/30973850; http://europepmc.org/articles/PMC6459583?pdf=render; http://europepmc.org/articles/PMC6459583; https://doi.org/10.15585/mmwr.mm6814a2.
158. Roth BL, Baner K, Westkaemper R, Siebert D, Rice KC, Steinberg S, et al. Salvinorin A: a potent naturally occurring nonnitrogenous kappa opioid selective agonist. *Proceedings of the National Academy of Sciences of the United States of America.* 2002;99(18):11934–9.
159. Sheffler DJ, Roth BL. Salvinorin A: the "magic mint" hallucinogen finds a molecular target in the kappa opioid receptor. *Trends in Pharmacological Sciences.* 2003;24(3):107–9.
160. Teksin ZS, Lee IJ, Nemieboka NN, Othman AA, Upreti VV, Hassan HE, et al. Evaluation of the transport, in vitro metabolism and pharmacokinetics of Salvinorin A, a potent hallucinogen. *European Journal of Pharmaceutics and Biopharmaceutics.* 2009;72(2):471–7.
161. Johnson MW, MacLean KA, Caspers MJ, Prisinzano TE, Griffiths RR. Time course of pharmacokinetic and hormonal effects of inhaled high-dose salvinorin A in humans. *Journal of Psychopharmacology (Oxford, England).* 2016;30(4):323–9.
162. Przekop P, Lee T. Persistent psychosis associated with salvia divinorum use. *The American Journal of Psychiatry.* 2009;166(7):832.
163. Aviello G, Borrelli F, Guida F, Romano B, Lewellyn K, De Chiaro M, et al. Ultrapotent effects of salvinorin A, a hallucinogenic compound from Salvia divinorum, on LPS-stimulated murine macrophages and its anti-inflammatory action in vivo. *Journal of Molecular Medicine (Berlin, Germany).* 2011;89(9):891–902.
164. Fichna J, Dicay M, Hirota SA, Traboulsi D, Macdonald JA, Janecka A, et al. Differential effects of salvinorin A on endotoxin-induced hypermotility and neurogenic ion transport in mouse ileum. *Neurogastroenterology and Motility.* 2011;23(6):583-e212.
165. Sun J, Zhang Y, Lu J, Zhang W, Yan J, Yang L, et al. Salvinorin A ameliorates cerebral vasospasm through activation of endothelial nitric oxide synthase in a rat model of subarachnoid hemorrhage. *Microcirculation (New York, NY: 1994).* 2018;25(3):e12442.
166. Stogner J, Khey DN, Griffin OH, Miller BL, Boman JH. Regulating a novel drug: an evaluation of changes in use of Salvia divinorum in the first year of Florida's ban. *The International Journal on Drug Policy.* 2012;23(6):512–21.
167. Stanley TH. The fentanyl story. *Journal of Pain.* 2014;15(12):1215–26.
168. Karch S, Drummer O. *Karch's Pathology of Drug Abuse,* 5th edition. Karch SB, editor. Boca Raton: CRC Press, Taylor and Francis, 1995.
169. Vohra V, Hodgman M, Marraffa J, Barba K, Stoppacher R. Fentanyl- and fentanyl analog-related deaths across five counties in Central New York between 2013 and 2017. *Clinical Toxicology (Philadelphia, Pa).* 2019:1–5.
170. European Monitoring Centre for Drugs and Drug Addiction. *European Drug Report 2019: Trends and Developments.* Luxemberg: United Nations, 2019.
171. Prevention CfDCa. Reported law enforcement encounters testing positive for fentanyl increase across US. 2017. Available from: https://wwwcdcgov/drugoverdose/data/fentanyl-le-reportshtml.
172. Feasel M, Wohlfarth A, et al. Metabolism of carfentanil, an ultra-potent opioid, in human liver microsomes and human hepatocytes by high-resolution mass spectrometry. *AAPS Journal.* 2016;18(6):1489–99.
173. O'Donnell J, Gladden R, Mattson C, et al. Notes from the field: overdose deaths with carfentanil and other fentanyl analogs detected — 10 States, July 2016–June 2017. *MMWR: Morbidity and Mortality Weekly Report.* 2018;67(27):767–8.
174. Sannerud C. Control of a chemical precursor used in the illicit manufacture of fentanyl as a list i chemical. *Federal Register.* 1970;72(77):20039–47.
175. Schwartz JG, Garriott JC, Somerset JS, Igler EJ, Rodriguez R, Orr MD. Measurements of fentanyl and sufentanil in blood and urine after surgical application. Implication in detection of abuse. *American Journal of Forensic Medicine and Pathology.* 1994;15(3):236–41.
176. Calis KA, Kohler DR, Corso DM. Transdermally administered fentanyl for pain management. *Clinical Pharmacy.* 1992;11(1):22–36.
177. Yuan R, Zhang X, Deng Q, Wu Y, Xiang G. Impact of CYP3A4*1G polymorphism on metabolism of fentanyl in Chinese patients undergoing lower abdominal surgery. *Clinica Chimica Acta.* 2011;412(9–10):755–60.
178. Grimsrud K, Ivanova X, Herwin C, et al. Identification of cytochrome P450 polymorphisms in burn patients and impact on fentanyl pharmacokinetics: a pilot study. *J Burn Care Res.* 2019;40(1):91–6.
179. Saiz-Rodríguez M, Ochoa D, Herrador, C. Polymorphisms associated with fentanyl pharmacokinetics, pharmacodynamics and adverse effects. *Basic & Clinical Pharmacology and Toxicology.* 2019;124(3):321–9.
180. Kirschner R, Donovan JW. Serotonin syndrome precipitated by fentanyl during procedural sedation. *Journal of Emergency Medicine.* 2010;38(4):477–80.
181. Gaffney RR, Schreibman IR. Serotonin syndrome in a patient on trazodone and duloxetine who received fentanyl following a percutaneous liver biopsy. *Case Reports in Gastroenterology.* 2015;9(2):132–6.

182. Bassett KE, Anderson JL, Pribble CG, Guenther E. Propofol for procedural sedation in children in the emergency department. *Annals of Emergency Medicine.* 2003;42(6):773–82.
183. Lunn JK, Stanley TH, Eisele J, Webster L, Woodward A. High dose fentanyl anesthesia for coronary artery surgery: plasma fentanyl concentrations and influence of nitrous oxide on cardiovascular responses. *Anesthesia and Analgesia.* 1979;58(5):390–5.
184. Fung DL, Eisele JH. Fentanyl pharmacokinetics in awake volunteers. *Journal of Clinical Pharmacology.* 1980;20(11):652–8.
185. Cartwright P, Prys-Roberts C, Gill K, Dye A, Stafford M, Gray A. Ventilatory depression related to plasma fentanyl concentrations during and after anesthesia in humans. *Anesthesia and Analgesia.* 1983;62(11):966–74.
186. Barratt DT, Bandak B, Klepstad P, Dale O, Kaasa S, Christrup LL, et al. Genetic, pathological and physiological determinants of transdermal fentanyl pharmacokinetics in 620 cancer patients of the EPOS study. *Pharmacogenet Genomics.* 2014;24(4):185–94.
187. Kharasch ED, Hoffer C, Whittington D. Influence of age on the pharmacokinetics and pharmacodynamics of oral transmucosal fentanyl citrate. *Anesthesiology.* 2004;101(3):738–43.
188. Labroo RB, Paine MF, Thummel KE, Kharasch ED. Fentanyl metabolism by human hepatic and intestinal cytochrome P450 3A4: implications for interindividual variability in disposition, efficacy, and drug interactions. *Drug Metab Dispos.* 1997;25(9):1072–80.
189. Nozari;, Akeju O, Mirzakhani H. Prolonged therapy with the anticonvulsant carbamazepine leads to increased plasma clearance of fentanyl.Molecules. *Molecules.* 2019;19(24):4.
190. Pelissier-Alicot AL, Gaulier JM, Champsaur P, Marquet P. Mechanisms underlying postmortem redistribution of drugs: a review. *Journal of Analytical Toxicology.* 2003;27(8):533–44.
191. Mather LE. Clinical pharmacokinetics of fentanyl and its newer derivatives. *Clinical Pharmacokinetics.* 1983;8(5):422–46.
192. Olson KN, Luckenbill K, Thompson J, Middleton O, Geiselhart R, Mills KM, et al. Postmortem redistribution of fentanyl in blood. *American Journal of Clinical Pathology.* 2010;133(3):447–53.
193. Andresen H, Gullans A, Veselinovic M, Anders S, Schmoldt A, Iwersen-Bergmann S, et al. Fentanyl: toxic or therapeutic? Postmortem and antemortem blood concentrations after transdermal fentanyl application. *Journal of Analytical Toxicology.* 2012;36(3):182–94.
194. Gill JR, Lin PT, Nelson L. Reliability of postmortem fentanyl concentrations in determining the cause of death. *Journal of Medical Toxicology.* 2013;9(1):34–41.
195. Perez-Mana C, Papaseit E, Fonseca F, Farre A, Torrens M, Farre M. Drug interactions with new synthetic opioids. *Frontiers in Pharmacology.* 2018;9:1145.
196. Solimini R, Pichini S, Pacifici R, Busardo FP, Giorgetti R. Pharmacotoxicology of non-fentanyl derived new synthetic opioids. *Frontiers in Pharmacology.* 2018;9:654.
197. Fabregat-Safont D, Carb6n X, Ventura M, Fornís I, Guillam6n E, Sancho JV, et al. Updating the list of known opioids through identification and characterization of the new opioid derivative 3,4-dichloro-N-(2-(diethylamin o)cyclohexyl)-N-methylbenzamide (U-49900). *Sci Rep* [Internet]. 2017;7(1):6338. Available from: http://europepmc .org/abstract/MED/28740128; http://europepmc.org/articles /PMC5524693?pdf=render; http://europepmc.org/articles/ PMC5524693; https://doi.org/10.1038/s41598-017-06778-9.
198. Cohen RS. Fentanyl transdermal analgesia during pregnancy and lactation. *Journal of Human Lactation.* 2009;25(3):359–61.
199. Nitsun M, Szokol JW, Saleh HJ, Murphy GS, Vender JS, Luong L, et al. Pharmacokinetics of midazolam, propofol, and fentanyl transfer to human breast milk. *Clinical and Pharmacology Therapeutics.* 2006;79(6):549–57.
200. Leuschen M, Wolf L, Rayburn W. Fentanyl excretion in breast milk. *Clinical Pharmacokinetics.* 1990;9(May):336–7.
201. Olkkola KT, Palkama VJ, Neuvonen PJ. Ritonavir's role in reducing fentanyl clearance and prolonging its half-life. *Anesthesiology.* 1999;91(3):681–5.
202. Warner ME, Naranjo J, Pollard EM, Weingarten TN, Warner MA, Sprung J. Serotonergic medications, herbal supplements, and perioperative serotonin syndrome. *Canadian Journal of Anaesthesia.* 2017;64(9):940–6.
203. Drug Enforcement Administration DoJ. Schedules of controlled substances: temporary placement of fentanyl related substances in schedule. *Journal of Federal Register.* 2018;83:5188–92.
204. Patrick M, Yan ZY. Synthetic opioids. *Handbook of Experimental Pharmacology -New Psychoactive Substances.* 2018(252):353–81.
205. Casy AF, Parfitt RT. New York: Springer Science & Business Media, 1986.
206. Pichini S, Pacifici R, Marinelli E, Busardo FP. European drug users at risk from illicit fentanyls mix. *Frontiers in Pharmacology.* 2017;8:785.
207. Suzuki J, El-Haddad S. A review: fentanyl and non-pharmaceutical fentanyls. *Drug Alcohol Dependence.* 2017;171:107–16.
208. Wang G, Huynh K, Barhate R, Rodrigues W, Moore C, Coulter C, et al. Development of a homogeneous immunoassay for the detection of fentanyl in urine. *Forensic Science International.* 2011;206(1–3):127–31.
209. Armenian P, Olson A, Anaya A, Kurtz A, Ruegner R, Gerona RR. Fentanyl and a novel synthetic opioid U-47700 masquerading as street "Norco" in Central California: a case report. *Annals of Emergency Medicine.* 2017;69(1):87–90.
210. Wang BT, Colby JM, Wu AH, Lynch KL. Cross-reactivity of acetylfentanyl and risperidone with a fentanyl immunoassay. *Journal of Analytical Toxicology.* 2014;38(9):672–5.
211. (2016a) PS. U-47,7000. Drug trend bulletin. 2016(8).
212. Armenian P, Vo KT, Barr-Walker J, Lynch KL. Fentanyl, fentanyl analogs and novel synthetic opioids: a comprehensive review. *Neuropharmacology.* 2018;134(Pt A):121–32.
213. Kram TC, Cooper DA, Allen AC. Behind the identification of China White. *Analytical Chemistry.* 1981;53(12):1379A–86A.
214. Henderson GL. Fentanyl-related deaths: demographics, circumstances, and toxicology of 112 cases. *Journal of Forensic Sciences.* 1991;36(2):422–33.
215. Lozier MJ, Boyd M, Stanley C, Ogilvie L, King E, Martin C, et al. Acetyl fentanyl, a novel fentanyl analog, causes 14 overdose deaths in Rhode Island, March-May 2013. *Journal of Medical Toxicology.* 2015;11(2):208–17.
216. Guitton J, Buronfosse T, Desage M, Lepape A, Brazier JL, Beaune P. Possible involvement of multiple cytochrome P450S in fentanyl and sufentanil metabolism as opposed to alfentanil. *Biochemical Pharmacology.* 1997;53(11):1613–9.

217. Burkle H, Dunbar S, Van Aken H. Remifentanil: a novel, short-acting, mu-opioid. *Anesthesia and Analgesia.* 1996;83(3):646–51.
218. Miller JM, Stogner JM, Miller BL, Blough S. Exploring synthetic heroin: accounts of acetyl fentanyl use from a sample of dually diagnosed drug offenders. *Drug Alcohol Review.* 2018;37(1):121–7.
219. Moody MT, Diaz S, Shah P, Papsun D, Logan BK. Analysis of fentanyl analogs and novel synthetic opioids in blood, serum/plasma, and urine in forensic casework. *Drug Drug Testing and Analysis.* 2018;10(9):1358–67.
220. Drug Enforcement Administration DoJ. Schedules of controlled substances: placement of acetyl fentanyl into Schedule I. Final order. *Federal Register.* 2017;82(108):26349–51.
221. Finkelstein MJ, Chronister CW, Stanley C, Ogilvie LM, Goldberger BA. Analysis of acetyl fentanyl in postmortem specimens by gas chromatography-mass spectrometry (GC-MS): method validation and case report. *Journal of Analytical Toxicology.* 2019;43(5):392–8.
222. Avedschmidt S, Schmidt C, Isenschmid D, Kesha K, Moons D, Gupta A. Acetyl fentanyl: trends and concentrations in metro detroit. *Journal of Forensic Sciences.* 2019;64(1):149–53.
223. Fogarty MF, Papsun DM, Logan BK. Analysis of fentanyl and 18 novel fentanyl analogs and metabolites by LC-MS-MS, and report of fatalities associated with methoxyacetylfentanyl and cyclopropylfentanyl. *Journal of Analytical Toxicology.* 2018;42(9):592–604.
224. Gillespie TJ, Gandolfi AJ, Davis TP, Morano RA. Identification and quantification of alpha-methylfentanyl in post mortem specimens. *Journal of Analytical Toxicology.* 1982;6(3):139–42.
225. Sato S, Suzuki S, Lee X-P, Sato K. Studies on 1-(2-phene thyl)-4-(N-propionylanilino)piperidine (fentanyl) and related compounds VII. Quantification of alpha-methylfentanyl metabolites excreted in rat urine. *Forensic Science International.* 2010;195(1–3):68–72.
226. Jacobson E, Kollias G, Heard, DJ, et al. Immobilization of African elephants with carfentanil and antagonism with nalmefene and diprenorphine. *Journal of Zoo Animal Medicine.* 1988;19(1/2):1–7.
227. Riches JR, Read RW, Black RM, Cooper NJ, Timperley CM. Analysis of clothing and urine from Moscow theatre siege casualties reveals carfentanil and remifentanil use. *Journal of Analytical Toxicology.* 2012;36(9):647–56.
228. Kinetz E, Butler D. *Chemical Weapon for Sale: China's Unregulated Narcotic.* AP. 2018 October 7, 2016.
229. Uddayasankar U, Lee C, Oleschuk C, Eschun G, Ariano RE. The pharmacokinetics and pharmacodynamics of carfentanil after recreational exposure: a case report. *Pharmacotherapy.* 2018;38(6):e41–e5.
230. Welch A. Fentanyl:J what you need to know about it. *CBS News*, 2016.
231. Watanabe S, Vikingsson S, Roman M, Green H, Kronstrand R, Wohlfarth A. In vitro and in vivo metabolite identification studies for the new synthetic opioids acetylfentanyl, acrylfentanyl, furanylfentanyl, and 4-fluoro-isobutyrylfentanyl. *AAPS Journal.* 2017;19(4):1102–22.
232. Guerrieri D, Rapp E, Roman M, Druid H, Kronstrand R. Postmortem and toxicological findings in a series of furanylfentanyl-related deaths. *Journal of Analytical Toxicology.* 2017;41(3):242–9.
233. Rab E, Flanagan R, Hudson S. Detection of fentanyl and fentanyl analogues in biological samples using liquid chromatography-high resolution mass spectrometry. *Forensic Science International.* 2019;300:13–8.
234. Zhao S, Freeman JP, Bacon CL, Fox GB, O'Driscoll E, Foley AG, et al. Syntheses of 1,2-diamino and 1,2-aminoalcohol derivatives in the piperidine and pyrrolidine series as anti-amnesic agents. *Bioorganic and Medical Chemistry.* 1999;7(8):1647–54.
235. Krotulski AJ, Mohr ALA, Papsun DM, Logan BK. Dibutylone (bk-DMBDB): intoxications, quantitative confirmations and metabolism in authentic biological specimens. *Journal of Analytical Toxicology.* 2018;42(7): 437–45.
236. Cheney DL, Goldstein A. Tolerance to opioid narcotics: time course and reversibility of physical dependence in mice. *Nature.* 1971;232(5311):477–8.
237. Beardsley PM, Zhang Y. Synthetic opioids. *Handbook of Experimental Pharmacology.* 2018;252:353–81.
238. Schneir A, Metushi IG, Sloane C, Benaron DJ, Fitzgerald RL. Near death from a novel synthetic opioid labeled U-47700: emergence of a new opioid class. *Clinical Toxicology (Philadelphia, Pa).* 2017;55(1):51–4.
239. Coopman V, Blanckaert P, Van Parys G, Van Calenbergh S, Cordonnier J. A case of acute intoxication due to combined use of fentanyl and 3,4-dichloro-N-[2-(dimethylami no)cyclohexyl]-N-methylbenzamide (U-47700). *Forensic Science International.* 2016;266:68–72.

9 Legal Aspects of the Opioid Epidemic

Section Editors: Eric Lasker and Robert E. Johnston

CONTENTS

9.1 LEGAL ASPECTS OF THE OPIOID EPIDEMIC

Fern P. O'Brian, Esq., Kathryn S. Jensen, Esq., Robert E. Johnston, Esq., and Jessica Lu, Esq.[1]

9.1.1 Introduction

"The federal court is probably the least likely branch of government to try and tackle [the opioid epidemic], but candidly, the other branches of government, federal and state, have punted," Judge Dan Polster during the first hearing of the Opioid Multidistrict Litigation in January 2018.

The rise in prescriptions for opioid medications has created a public health crisis in the United States. By 2016, more people had died from opioid overdoses than died during the entire Vietnam War. Opioid overdose is the leading cause of death for Americans under 50. The crisis affects people

DOI: 10.4324/9781315155159-9

from all walks of life and shows no sign of slowing. At least 100 people die of opioid overdoses every day.

Federal and state governments have declared the opioid epidemic a national health emergency. The epidemic has given rise to legislation to mitigate the impact on Americans, government regulation and enforcement actions, and massive nationwide litigation involving an increasing number of corporate and individual defendants in the chain of distribution of opioids, from manufacturers to physicians. This chapter outlines the evolution of the opioid crisis, the government's efforts to combat its effects and hold those who allegedly contributed to the epidemic responsible, and the litigation arising from it. It also analyzes medical malpractice claims involving opioids and precautionary measures physicians can take to help avoid becoming embroiled in the multifaceted aspects of the opioid epidemic.

9.1.2 Opioid Overview

9.1.2.1 Medical Uses

Opioids have long been used to treat pain and other ailments. Poppy plants have been cultivated since as early as 3400 BC, leading to the development of morphine in the early 1800s.[2] Opioids are compounds that work by interacting with opioid receptors in brain cells to reduce the perception of pain, signaling to the brain that a person is not in pain.[3] Opioids can be derived from the poppy plant (e.g., morphine or codeine) or can be manufactured synthetically (e.g., hydrocodone, OxyContin, and fentanyl).[4]

Like other narcotics, opioids are used to manage chronic and acute pain and are regarded as among the most effective drugs for pain relief.[5] "Their use in the management of acute severe pain and chronic pain related to advanced medical illness is considered the standard of care in most of the world."[6]

Although opioids are commonly used to treat patients who have cancer or are approaching the end of life, they are also used for treatment of moderate to severe pain associated with other serious medical conditions. "Several medical professional organizations acknowledge the utility of opioid therapy and many case series and large surveys report satisfactory reductions in pain, improvement in function and minimal risk of addiction."[7] However, the overtreatment of patients and epidemic-level opioid abuse and addiction have caused public officials and medical practitioners to reconsider their widespread use.[8]

9.1.2.2 Risks of Adverse Effects

Despite their well-accepted benefits in relieving pain,[9] opioids may have serious adverse side effects requiring warning.[10] Common adverse effects include sedation, dizziness, nausea, vomiting, constipation, physical dependence, tolerance, and respiratory depression.[11] Extended use may cause increases in the amount of medication necessary to achieve the same pain-relieving effects. In turn, dependence may occur, and abrupt cessation of longer-term use often causes withdrawal symptoms. Withdrawal symptoms include diarrhea, nausea, vomiting, muscle pain, anxiety, and irritability.[12] In addition to these adverse effects, very high doses of opioids can slow a person's breathing and heart rate, which can lead to death.[13]

Among the most serious adverse effects are overdose and psychological addiction.[14] Addiction is characterized as an urge to use opioids even when they are no longer medically required.[15] One of the factors leading to addiction is the phenomenon of tolerance, which results when a particular dose of an opioid no longer provides the same pain-relieving effects, leading patients to seek higher doses to achieve the same analgesic effects.[16]

Awareness of these risks of opioid addiction has increased dramatically. When they were initially marketed, opioids were not regarded as addictive. Indeed, an early study of opioids' risk of addiction, performed by Dr Hershel Jick and Jane Porter, concluded that addiction was rare in patients treated with narcotics.[17] This study, which included nearly 12,000 patients, found "only four cases of reasonably well documented addiction in patients who had no history of addiction."[18] The study did not, however, identify how long the patients were treated with opioids, the purpose of the treatment, or dosage.[19] In 2017, Dr David Juurlink published a letter taking the position that the 1980 Jick and Porter Study had contributed to the opioid epidemic:

> The crisis arose in part because physicians were told that the risk of addiction was low when opioids were prescribed for chronic pain. A one-paragraph letter that was published in the *Journal* in 1980 was widely invoked in support of this claim, even though no evidence was provided by the correspondents. ... we found that a five-sentence letter published in the *Journal* in 1980 was heavily and uncritically cited as evidence that addiction was rare with long-term opioid therapy. We believe that this citation pattern contributed to the North American opioid crisis by helping to shape a narrative that allayed prescribers' concerns about the risk of addiction associated with long-term opioid therapy.[20]

Since the 1980s, the medical community and the public have become much more aware of the risk of opioid addiction. Thus, physicians are exercising more caution in prescribing increasing dosage or renewing patient prescriptions of opioids.[21] "The past several decades in the United States have been characterized by attitudes that have shifted repeatedly in response to clinical and epidemiological observations [regarding opioid use], and events in the legal and regulatory communities."[22] One unintended consequence of the reduction in opioid prescriptions is that opioid users may seek illegal and more powerful opioids, such as heroin and fentanyl, because of their addiction.[23]

9.1.2.3 Current Opioid Epidemic

In response to the rapid increase in the use of prescription and non-prescription opioids in the United States from the mid- to late 1990s to the present,[24] the director of the Center for Disease Control and Prevention (CDC) stated: "We have an emergency on our hands. The fast-moving opioid overdose epidemic ... is accelerating."[25] Although the causes of the crisis are multifaceted and complex, the statistics of the crisis demonstrate that opioid use is at crisis level. In 2016, more people died from opioid overdoses than all U.S. deaths during the entire course of the Vietnam War.[26] Opioid overdose is the leading cause of death for Americans under 50, and over 100 Americans die daily from an opioid overdose.[27] By 2016, "the number of overdose deaths involving opioids (including prescription opioids and illegal opioids like heroin and illicitly manufactured fentanyl) was five times higher than in 1999."[28] More troubling, as of 2018, 40% of all U.S. opioid overdose deaths involved a prescription opioid.[29] President Trump responded to the epidemic in late 2017 by declaring the problem a national health emergency.[30]

Government agencies such as the Department of Health and Human Services (HHS) and the CDC attribute the opioid crisis to multiple factors. According to the HHS, beginning in the mid- to late 1990s, pharmaceutical companies marketing opioids allegedly downplayed the risk of opioid addiction and sought to assure the medical community that opioids were both safe and effective pain relievers.[31] Dr David Juurlink noted that many of these companies relied upon the letter by Dr Jick and Ms Porter stating that opioids were not addictive in order to promote widespread marketing and sales of the drug. In turn, healthcare providers prescribed opioids at increasing rates.[32]

According to the HHS and the CDC, pharmaceutical distributors shipped and supplied massive quantities of opioids, often without reporting sales to authorities. Pharmacies often allegedly "turned a blind eye" to the large amount of opioids sold to the public and frequently did not question suspicious prescriptions from doctors.[33] Researchers report that the increases in opioid prescriptions were associated with dramatic increases in opioid-related overdose deaths and addiction.[34]

9.1.3 Government Efforts to Curb the Opioid Epidemic

Widespread concern about the opioid epidemic prompted state and federal governments to enact various prevention measures, including legislation, agency action, educational outreach, and increased accessibility to naloxone, an overdose-reversal drug.[35]

9.1.3.1 Legislation

Federal and state legislators have proposed and enacted legislation to combat the epidemic by investing in prevention, detection, surveillance, and treatment for the abuse of opioids. In 2016, Congress passed the Comprehensive Addiction Recovery Act (CARA) in its initial effort to curb the opioid epidemic. CARA increased federal funding to states for increased access to opioid treatment providers and to require federal and state agencies to disseminate more information to consumers about the risks of prescription opioid abuse.[36] Senator Robert Portman (R-OH), the author of the Senate version of CARA, stated:

> This is a historic moment, the first time in decades that Congress has passed comprehensive addiction legislation, and the first time Congress has ever supported long-term addiction recovery. This is also the first time that we've treated addiction like the disease that it is, which will help put an end to the stigma that has surrounded addiction for too long.[37]

Since 2016, similar legislation seeking to combat the epidemic by investing in prevention, detection, surveillance, and treatment of opioid addiction has been proposed.[38] In early 2018, both the House and the Senate introduced identical "CARA 2.0" bills, (S. 2456) and (H.R. 5311), which would include increased funding for national education campaigns, increased access to medication-assisted treatment, expanded first responder training, and increased access to naloxone.[39] On October 24, 2018, President Trump signed the SUPPORT for Patients and Communities Act (H.R. 6) (SUPPORT Act), which is a comprehensive opioid legislation based on the House and Senate's opioid bills, including elements of CARA 2.0. The SUPPORT Act focuses on "improving the federal response to the opioid epidemic via changes to Medicaid and Medicare, expansion of treatment resources for health care providers and enhancement of recovery supports for patients."[40]

In 2018, Congress introduced a variety of additional bills targeting opioid addiction, which were still pending as of this publication, including the Stop Counterfeit Drugs by Regulating and Enhancing Enforcement Now Act (SCREEN Act), sponsored by U.S. Representative Frank Pallone Jr. of New Jersey.[41] The Act would allow the U.S. Food and Drug Administration (FDA) to destroy and/or refuse to import drugs identified as "articles of concern," such as heroin and fentanyl. In addition, the bill would allow the FDA to use emergency recalls prohibiting the distribution of opioid drugs and debar companies that continue to import drugs illegally. The bill would also authorize $110 million in spending for innovation of new pain treatments and provide enhanced access to opioid abuse treatment.[42]

Another pending bipartisan bill introduced in early 2018 is the Durbin–Kennedy Opioid Quota Reform Act of 2018. The Drug Enforcement Agency (DEA) is responsible for establishing annual quotas determining the exact amount of each drug that is permitted to be produced in the United States each year. Currently, the DEA's manufacturing quotas are based upon the amount of the drug sold in the previous year and expected demand, but some consider the DEA's quota for opioids to be inflated because opioids are overprescribed.[43] The Act would require the DEA to consider public health factors, such as overdose and death rates, in setting opioid manufacturing quotas, thereby enabling the DEA to adjust manufacturing quotas to limit opioid diversion and abuse. [44]

Finally, the Senate Committee on Health, Education, Labor, & Pensions (HELP) released a draft bill that would, among other things, authorize grants for communities to set up comprehensive opioid recovery centers, require the HHS to issue guidance on best practices for operating recovery facilities, and allow the National Institutes of Health (NIH) to approach pharmaceutical companies and universities to conduct opioid-related research.[45] Some state legislatures have proposed the imposition of taxes on opioid sales in an effort to curb the epidemic.[46] It remains to be seen which, if any, of the proposed legislation described here will be enacted and whether the existing and proposed laws will be effective in tackling the opioid epidemic.

9.1.3.2 Regulatory Action

In addition to legislative changes, government agencies and the executive branch have taken steps to combat the epidemic. In 2018, President Trump emphasized that ending the epidemic is a national priority.[47] In late March 2018, he announced a four-point plan to combat the epidemic. First, the plan seeks to reduce the supply of opioids by requiring harsher punishment for manufacturers and criminally negligent doctors, pharmacies, and distributors, including making opioid trafficking a capital offense subject to the death penalty. Second, the plan would reduce demand and improper prescribing by utilizing advertising to help deter the use of opioids. Third, the plan would help addicts by enabling more people to obtain naloxone and creating more treatment programs. Finally, President Trump's plan would include measures to combat "the driving forces" of the opioid crisis by curbing overprescription and expanding addiction treatment systems.[48]

9.1.3.2.1 Department of Justice

The U.S. Department of Justice (DOJ), the HHS, the DEA, and other government agencies have also responded to the epidemic by participating in litigation, developing multistep plans, and creating task forces. DOJ officials have made numerous public statements regarding the crisis, and the DOJ's involvement in the consolidated multidistrict litigation against opioid manufacturers, distributors, and pharmacies, discussed in Section 9.4.2.1, indicates that it may play an even bigger role in opioid-related litigation, particularly litigation targeting opioid manufacturers and distributors. In April 2018, DOJ filed a motion to participate in settlement discussions and participate as friend of the court in the federal opioid litigation against pharmaceutical manufacturers and distributors.[49] DOJ contended:

> The United States has a unique interest and expertise regarding the subjects at issue in this litigation and can provide information and expertise to assist the parties and the Court in reaching a comprehensive and effective resolution of the issues in this case. The United States will lend its knowledge and understanding of the federal government and its agencies for the benefit of the litigation and provide the nationwide view of this crisis of national scope whenever it is called upon by the Court.[50]

In June 2018, the motion was granted as unopposed.[51] DOJ has also repeatedly stated its intention to utilize the False Claims Act to hold those responsible for the opioid epidemic accountable. For example, former Attorney General Sessions stated in 2017 that DOJ would "make it a high priority of the Department to root out and prosecute fraud in federal programs and to recover any monies lost due to fraud or false claims."[52]

9.1.3.2.1.1 DOJ's Opioid Fraud and Abuse Detection Unit In addition to expressing its goals and strategies to combat the opioid epidemic, DOJ has also taken action to curb the epidemic through the creation of specialized units and task forces, such as the Opioid Fraud and Abuse Detection Unit. In 2018, DOJ placed 12 prosecutors in geographic areas that experience high levels of opioid prescription abuse by healthcare providers. The prosecutors' primary stated goal is to curb the unlawful sale of opioids and in turn, alleviate the addiction problem in the United States.[53] DOJ adopted a hybrid approach to combatting the opioid crisis through prosecution of both drug traffickers and those participating in healthcare fraud, including physicians, drug treatment centers, and pharmacists. DOJ has partnered with the DEA, FBI, HHS, and other state and federal agencies to craft this program.[54]

DOJ asserts that although doctors and pharmacists have a license to dispense controlled substances, they are allowed to do so only within the bounds of a legitimate practice. Under the Controlled Substances Act (CSA), it is a crime for anyone to distribute controlled substances without registration.[55] Even if an entity has a registration, however, the registration allows prescriptions only for legitimate medical purposes that are consistent with the professional standard of care.[56] This initiative requires doctors to exercise due diligence in writing prescriptions. Prescribers who defraud healthcare benefit programs such as Medicare and Medicaid by charging for services that were not performed or overcharging for services related to opioids will also be identified and prosecuted.[57] For example, physicians who prescribe medically unnecessary opioid treatment to a Medicare beneficiary, which is then reimbursed by Medicare Part D, will be identified and prosecuted by the Opioid Fraud and Abuse Detection Unit.

DOJ's actions are based on reports that doctors often charge for medically unnecessary procedures, services not actually rendered, or "upcoded" services when evaluating patients to prescribe opioids.[58] Further, doctors may prescribe unnecessary services, such as magnetic resonance imaging, to their addicted patients to make more money.[59] DOJ plans to use "red flags" to identify doctors and physicians who violate federal statutes.[60] Physicians should be aware that these "red flags" include high patient numbers, cursory exams, high cash prices, high percentages of doctors' patients who are prescribed controlled substances, prescription of multiple controlled substances,[61] and treatment of out-of-state patients, among other factors.[62]

The CSA requires pharmacists to identify overprescribing. In prosecuting pharmacists, DOJ will look for similar red flags to those for physicians. Pharmacists must determine whether the prescription is for legitimate medical purposes and within the usual course of that practice.[63] In addition, other red flags for pharmacists include multiple patients with identical prescriptions, high percentages of pharmacies' prescriptions for controlled substances from a single doctor, prescriptions of high dosages/quantities compared with medical conditions, failure to use drug monitoring programs/data collection sites, or providing high volumes of prescriptions of controlled substances compared with peer pharmacies.[64] DOJ also looks for doctors or pharmacies providing "buffer drugs," which consists of ordering two drugs (only one of which is an opioid), or billing for improperly dispensed controlled substances.[65]

9.1.3.2.1.2 DOJ's Prescription Interdiction & Litigation Task Force DOJ is also creating another task force called the Prescription Interdiction & Litigation (PIL) Task Force. PIL will utilize both civil and criminal law enforcement tools, such as the False Claims Act (FCA), "to reverse the tide of opioid overdoses in the United States."[66] The task force will target opioid manufacturers and distributors. PIL will include senior officials from the offices of the Attorney General and Executive Office for U.S. Attorneys, the Civil Division, Criminal Division, and the DEA. In addition to the FCA, the task force plans to use the CSA to bring claims against responsible parties. PIL will also help investigate and support municipalities in bringing claims against manufacturers and distributors of opioids while expanding efforts by the Opioid Fraud and Abuse Unit through working with DEA and HHS to investigate illegal practices. The PIL aims to (1) improve the coordination of data sharing within the federal government to better identify fraud and violations of the law; (2) evaluate regulatory changes to the role governing opioid distribution; and (3) evaluate potential legislative changes.[67]

9.1.3.2.2 Drug Enforcement Administration

The DEA is also involved in combatting the epidemic by targeting opioid distributors for failure to report suspicious orders. The CSA requires drug distribution companies to report suspicious orders of narcotics to the DEA, including unusually large or unusually frequent orders. Distributors who fail to report may be fined or have their DEA registrations revoked. For example, Mallinckrodt Pharmaceuticals agreed to pay $35 million to resolve DEA probes into its monitoring and reporting of suspicious orders of controlled substances.[68] As discussed later, a rule was proposed in 2018 that would allow the DEA to place limits on pharmaceutical companies or distributors if it suspects opioid drugs are being siphoned to others in the chains of distribution who may sell them for illegal purposes.[69] The purpose of the rule is "to strengthen controls over diversion of controlled substances and make other improvements in the quota management regulatory system for the production, manufacturing, and procurement of controlled substances."[70] For example, in 2018, the DEA suspended opioid sales by a wholesale distributor for failing to identify suspicious orders to pharmacies. It was the first time in 6 years that the DEA had cut off sales by a narcotic distributor.[71]

9.1.3.2.3 Food and Drug Administration

The U.S. FDA has also been actively involved in combatting the opioid epidemic. The FDA requested in 2017 that Endo Pharmaceuticals remove its opioid pain medication, oxymorphone hydrochloride, from the market. The FDA indicated that the benefits of the drug may no longer outweigh its risks. This was the first time that the FDA had requested a manufacturer to remove a currently marketed opioid pain medication from the market due to public health concerns of possible addiction and abuse.[72]

FDA Commissioner Scott Gottlieb announced in 2018 that internet service providers and social media companies should take action to track and prevent illegal sales of opioids. Specifically, because fentanyl is frequently sold online, the FDA hopes to collaborate with online companies tracking data regarding sellers and purchases of the drug.[73] The FDA also released Draft Guidance in 2018 outlining proposed methods for drug companies to develop new medications to treat opioid addiction. The Draft Guidance focuses on the creation of modified-release drugs that can be implanted or injected.[74] The FDA announced in early April 2018 that it would spend $10 million in the fiscal year 2019 to expand access to naloxone by changing its status from prescription to over-the-counter.[75]

9.1.3.3 Criminal Prosecutions and Government Investigations

Federal prosecutors have charged opioid sales managers for violations of the Anti-Kickback Statute. For example, John Kapoor of Insys Therapeutics, Inc. was arrested and charged with racketeering and fraud in October 2017 for allegedly bribing doctors to prescribe a fentanyl-based painkiller spray for off-label uses.[76] Luzerne County (Pennsylvania) also filed a federal lawsuit alleging that Purdue Pharma, Endo Pharmaceuticals Inc., Janssen Pharmaceuticals, Teva Pharmaceutical Industries, and other opioid manufacturers violated the Racketeer Influenced and Corrupt Organizations Act (RICO) by illegally marketing the highly addictive fentanyl spray.[77] Congress has begun its own investigation of fentanyl distributors through the Subcommittee on Oversight and Investigations of the House Energy and Commerce Committee.[78] Witnesses from opioid distributors testified at a May 8, 2018 hearing regarding the excess availability of opioids in certain West Virginia counties.[79] Following the November 2018 elections, it is anticipated that Congress will engage in even more aggressive oversight.[80]

The federal government has also increased its prosecution of physicians under the CSA, which provides criminal sanctions for individuals who distribute or dispense Schedule I or II substances (most opioid drugs are Schedule II substances).[81] Physicians are generally provided with an exception from the applicability of section 841(a)(1), which provides for criminal sanctions, pursuant to 21 U.S.C. § 802(21), so long as their prescriptions are "for a legitimate medical purpose."[82] Where, however, a physician knowingly prescribes outside the course of professional practice or without a legitimate medical purpose, criminal sanctions may be imposed under the CSA.[83]

Based on a review of data contained in the National Practitioner Data Bank between 2011 and 2014, one commentator has determined that federal criminal cases against physicians increased from 88 cases in 2011 to 371 cases by 2014, a quadrupling of the number of cases brought against physicians under the CSA.[84] Many of these prosecutions have focused on prescribers of pain medicines.[85] Dr Paul Volkman, for example, received four life sentences based on the fact that four of his patients at the Tri-State Health Clinic in Portsmouth, Ohio died after taking pain medicines distributed by his dispensary at the clinic.[86] Dr Dewey MacKay was sentenced in 2013 to serve 240 months in prison for prescribing opioid pain medication that allegedly caused the death of one of his patients.[87] In 2010, Dr Stephen Schneider and his nurse/wife Linda were sentenced to 30 and 33 years in prison, respectively, for their prescription of pain medication allegedly resulting in numerous deaths at a pain management clinic in Kansas.[88]

The doctors in these examples were prosecuted under an enhanced sentencing provision added to the CSA in 1986 that provides mandatory minimum sentences of 20 years and mandatory maximum sentences of life for offenses in which "death or serious bodily injury results from" the distribution of the controlled substance.[89] In 2014, the United States Supreme Court determined that the enhancement statute could only be applied where a jury finds that there is evidence beyond a reasonable doubt that the controlled substance provided by the distributor was the "but-for" cause of death or injury.[90] The defendant in *Burrage* had provided illicit heroin to Joshua Banka, who died after a 24-hour "drug binge" that included marijuana, stolen oxycodone (which was "crushed, cooked and injected"), and heroin that he had procured from Burrage during the binge.[91] Alprazolam, clonazepam, and hydrocodone were also found in Banka's residence. Two experts testified for the prosecution that the heroin had played a contributing role with the other drugs to cause Banka's death, but neither would testify that Banka would have survived had he not taken the heroin.[92] The trial court instructed the jury that they could apply the enhancement statute if heroin had contributed to Banka's death, and Burrage was convicted and sentenced using the enhancement statute.[93] Justice Scalia, writing for the court and joined by all the Justices but Ginsburg and Sotomayor, who concurred, held that but-for causation was the background principle against which "Congress legislate[s]" and that the ordinary meaning of the phrase "results from" indicated a Congressional intention to require but-for causation.[94] Accordingly, the enhancement statute could not be applied where there was no evidence from which a jury could conclude beyond a reasonable doubt that the heroin the defendant supplied was the but-for cause of death.

As a result of the court's decision in *Burrage*, several of the convictions of physicians discussed here have been revisited. In the *MacKay* case, the physician's sentence of 240 months (20 years) was reduced to 36 months.[95] The impact on the Schneiders was even more significant. The trial court concluded that the enhanced sentence for all but one of the death counts had to be vacated because it could not conclude that the jury would have reached a different result if a "but-for" causation instruction had been given.[96] As to the other count, the court held that the evidence was sufficient for the jury to have found but-for causation beyond a reasonable doubt and conclude that the instruction error was, therefore, harmless.[97]

Several commentators have criticized the Supreme Court's *Burrage* decision. Some criticize Justice Scalia's view that the plain meaning of the "resulting from" language is, in fact, but-for causation and that many states have adopted a view that causation can be based on contributory effect, even if but-for causation cannot be shown.[98] Other commentators have bemoaned the fact that *Burrage* increases the prosecutorial burden for death "resulting from" cases such that an effective deterrent to overprescription of opioids has been removed from the government's arsenal.[99] It remains to be seen, however, whether *Burrage* has, in fact, trimmed prosecutorial zeal for charging physicians in opioid cases involving death. It also remains to be seen whether the mandatory enhancements under 841(b)(1)(C) will remain the law should civil justice reform wipe away the concepts of mandatory maximum and minimum sentences. It remains the law, however, that physicians can be prosecuted and punished under the CSA for their prescribing practices of opioids that are not in accord with professional standards. The only question is how long a sentence can be imposed.

9.1.4 Litigation

The opioid crisis has given rise to a wide variety of litigation, including lawsuits brought by state attorneys general, city mayors, Indian Nations, and private parties against pharmacies, doctors, manufacturers, distributors, and others. In August 2019, the first bench trial concluded in Oklahoma state court, resulting in the first ruling holding a drug company responsible for the opioid crisis. Judge Thad Balkman ordered that Johnson & Johnson pay the state over $572 million, which he calculated to be the cost of the first year of a plan to abate the public nuisance caused by the opioid crisis.[100] He later acknowledged that he had made a $107 million math error, which will be corrected in the future. Oklahoma's sole (and novel) claim for relief against the defendants was for causing a public nuisance pursuant to 50 O.S. 1981 § I et seq.[101] The state had sought over $17 billion to combat the epidemic over the next three decades, but the judge held that the state did not present sufficient evidence of the amount of time and costs necessary to abate the epidemic beyond the first year of an abatement plan. The case was originally brought by the state against Purdue, Teva, and Johnson & Johnson, but the state settled with other defendants before the case went to trial in May.[102] On September 25, Johnson & Johnson filed an appeal with the Oklahoma Supreme Court, arguing that the ruling "disregard[ed] a century of precedent."[103] As of November

2019, the appeal remains pending before the Oklahoma Supreme Court.

9.1.4.1 Overview of Allegations

Many of the claims in these cases are similar regardless of whether the defendant is a distributor or a manufacturer of opioids. Typical claims against manufacturers include unjust enrichment, negligence, false advertising, violations of public nuisance laws, fraud, deceptive marketing, racketeering, corruption, and violations of federal and state laws regarding controlled substances and unfair competition. Claims against distributors may additionally include diversion, failure to report suspicious orders to DEA, and violations of the RICO. Claims against pharmacies include, among others, violations of the CSA and FCA. As explained in more detail later, these claims show that the government and private parties are asserting a plethora of civil legal theories against numerous parties involved in the manufacture and distribution of opioids.

9.1.4.2 Manufacturers and Distributors

Private parties, along with cities, states, and Indian tribes, have sued manufacturers and distributors of opioids under a variety of theories, many of which overlap. At the most basic level, plaintiffs allege that opioid manufacturers and/or distributors failed to communicate to patients and doctors both (1) the efficacy of the drugs and (2) the risk of overdose, addiction, and death. Plaintiffs typically assert false advertising or misrepresentation as legal theories to support such claims.[104] Plaintiffs also allege that manufacturers, in particular, overstated the benefits and downplayed the risks of opioids for decades, which in turn led to overprescription of the drugs, overuse, addiction, and death.[105] Plaintiffs also assert violations of state consumer protection laws, alleging that manufacturers misled consumers regarding the safety and efficacy of their products.[106] Plaintiffs also claim fraud, including Medicaid fraud, based on allegations that manufacturers made false statements to obtain reimbursements.[107]

One of the more unusual claims that plaintiffs allege is public nuisance, as was the case in the first bench trial mentioned earlier. Generally, public nuisance is "an unreasonable interference with a right common to the general public," including conditions that endanger public health or safety.[108] This doctrine is typically used by a government entity in the context of interference with real property or infringement of public rights. Government entities bringing suit in the context of opioid litigation argue that because the opioid epidemic has resulted in harm to the community, subverts public order, and causes inconvenience to the public in general, public nuisance is an appropriate basis for their claims.[109] For example, the City of Miami sued manufacturers, distributors, and pharmacies in April 2018, alleging that the "Defendants … made fraudulent and negligent misrepresentations, were negligent and grossly negligent, created a public nuisance, and were unjustly enriched."[110] States, cities, and Native American tribes across the country have pled this legal theory in opioid-related litigation. Although Johnson & Johnson's appeal from the first bench trial remains pending, we may expect plaintiffs to bring more public nuisance claims in the future given Judge Balkman's ruling.

Plaintiffs often assert the additional legal theory of "diversion" against opioid distributors. Plaintiffs contend that distributors have allowed diversion of the drugs because they were aware (or should have been aware) that particularly high amounts of opioids were sold to particular communities, leading to oversupply and abuse. They claim that distributors should have noticed such diversion as a "red flag" and should have taken precautions to prevent the distribution to those communities.[111] This theory may be asserted as a violation of federal and state laws intended to prevent diversion.[112] The Cherokee Nation, for example, filed such a suit in April 2017 against distributors, including McKesson Corporation, Cardinal Health, AmerisourceBergen, CVS, Walgreens, and Walmart. The basis of the plaintiffs' diversion claim is that the distribution companies allegedly filled suspicious orders from retailers that were unusually large or unusually frequent and in violation of the FCA and state law. The complaint alleges that distributors allowed massive quantities of opioids to be diverted to the black market, which exacerbated the epidemic of opioid abuse in the Cherokee Nation.[113]

In addition to claims of diversion, plaintiffs, including Native American Nations and states, allege that both distributors and manufacturers should be held liable for unjust enrichment due to additional profits they made at the expense of plaintiffs.[114]

9.1.4.2.1 Multidistrict Litigation

Given the explosion of opioid lawsuits across the country, the Judicial Panel on Multidistrict Litigation (JPML) in late 2017 created a multidistrict litigation (MDL) in the Northern District of Ohio to handle pretrial matters in many similar opioid cases filed around the country in a consolidated fashion. The JPML tasked Judge Dan Polster of the Northern District of Ohio with structuring and managing about 300 lawsuits involving plaintiffs such as local governments, hospitals, unions, and Native American tribes with suits involving claims against drug manufacturers, distributors, and pharmacies. The allegations by plaintiffs in the MDL include that opioid manufacturers overstated benefits and understated risks in marketing the prescription medications to doctors. Plaintiffs also allege that distributors failed to monitor, detect, and/or investigate suspicious orders of opioids. Manufacturer defendants in the MDL include Actavis Generics, Allergan plc, Cephalon, Inc., Endo International plc, Janssen Pharmaceuticals, Johnson & Johnson, Purdue Pharma L.P., Teva Pharmaceutical Industries Ltd., and Watson Pharmaceuticals, Inc.[115] Distributor defendants include AmerisourceBergen Corporation, McKesson Corporation, and Cardinal Health, Inc., which together allegedly distributed more than 80% of the drugs at issue.

Despite defense objections to consolidation of these cases, the JPML held that the cases brought against opioid manufacturers and distributors shared common issues of fact, such as the manufacturers' and distributors' knowledge of alleged diversion and alleged improper marketing. The JPML concluded that MDL was an appropriate process for the complex cases.[116] Plaintiffs' lawyers argue that damages could amount to hundreds of billions of dollars.[117]

The Northern District of Ohio was chosen as the district to oversee the MDL because of its strong connection to the opioid epidemic as well as Judge Polster's experience with opioid litigation.[118] Judge Polster has aggressively advocated for early settlement. In late March 2018, Judge Polster compelled the disclosure of alleged competitive business information, which is normally protected from disclosure during the discovery phase of litigation, from AmerisourceBergen, Cardinal Health Inc., and McKesson Corporation. Judge Polster reasoned that the chances of early resolution of the MDL litigation would be enhanced by requiring these disclosures early. He directed the parties to prepare certain cases to proceed in the MDL and set three consolidated cases for a 3-week bellwether trial starting March 18, 2019. Plaintiffs' lawyers frankly noted: "We're very pleased because trial dates tend to force settlement – that's a truism in our world."[119]

Although the plaintiffs who initially moved to consolidate the litigation into an MDL were cities, states, and counties, plaintiffs in the MDL now include Native American tribes, hospitals, and private individuals. For example, the New York Attorney General sued Insys Therapeutics, Inc. for misrepresenting that its spray version of fentanyl was safe for non-cancer patients and appropriate for treating mild pain. Although Insys's product was approved by the FDA in 2012, the Attorney General claims that Insys encouraged sales representatives to recommend higher doses of the drug than were medically necessary.[120] Ohio's Attorney General also brought suit against opioid distributors McKesson, AmerisourceBergen, Cardinal Health, and Miami-Luken, Inc. for allegedly selling opioids in violation of state and federal laws meant to stop diversion. The Attorney General sued drug manufacturers in both state court and multidistrict litigation.[121]

In October 2019, the first MDL bellwether case settled hours before trial was set to begin.[122] Two Ohio counties, Summit and Cuyahoga, accepted a settlement deal of approximately $260 million from distributors AmerisourceBergen, Cardinal Health, and McKesson and manufacturer Teva Pharmaceuticals.[123] Other defendants had settled earlier. However, there remain thousands more plaintiffs in the MDL, and cases remain on track for trial. The deals still await final approval.

Ironically, a month prior to settlement, some of the drug companies had urged Judge Polster to recuse himself from presiding over the trial because of his encouragement for parties to settle and for commenting to the press about the litigation.[124] Once Judge Polster refused to recuse himself, the petitioners sought a writ of mandamus with the Sixth Circuit to compel him to step aside. The Sixth Circuit rejected the motion, explaining that Judge Polster "pushed for settlement not because he had prejudged the case, but because that was the most expedient way to conclude the dispute."[125] The Sixth Circuit provided some advice to MDL judges involved in high-profile litigation, however:

> Judge Polster's statements to the press and in court might call into question his impartiality. But we must take his statements in context. Judge Polster equally placed blame on all parties … While we may not have chosen to make the statements, grant the interviews, or participate in the programs that form the basis for this petition, particularly in a case of such enormous public interest and significance, and while we do not encourage Judge Polster to continue these actions, we nevertheless conclude that Petitioners have not established that they are entitled to a writ of mandamus requiring Judge Polster's recusal on the basis of this conduct.[126]

Judge Polster himself commented that he had been active in encouraging settlement, but explained:

> It goes without saying that if even a small fraction of the 2,000 cases in the MDL requires a months-long trial, the federal judiciary will be overwhelmed and most of the defendants would be forced into bankruptcy, simply because of litigation costs. … Ordinarily, the resolution of a social epidemic should be the responsibility of our other two branches of government, but these are not ordinary times.[127]

Further highlighting the extraordinary and novel nature of this litigation, Judge Polster approved plaintiffs' motion for a negotiation class, thereby permitting lawyers for a group of 49 cities and counties to negotiate class-wide settlements, on a voluntary basis, with defendants who make, distribute, or sell opioids nationwide.[128] This is the first time that Federal Rule of Civil Procedure 23 has been used to create such a class.[129] If 75% of voting class members support a proposed settlement, class counsel will ask the court to approve the settlement, which will then become binding on the class.[130] It remains to be seen whether such a class will achieve settlement more efficiently than through a bellwether trial process.

9.1.4.3 Prescribers and Pharmacies

Although manufacturers and distributors are the most significant targets of litigation, prescribers and pharmacies have not entirely avoided the opioid litigation. Plaintiffs have more recently brought claims against prescribers, pharmacies, and pharmacists for their role in the supply chain that facilitates people's access to prescription opioids.[131]

In 2018, Webb County, Texas sued the three largest pharmacy benefit management firms (PBMs) – CVS Caremark, Express Scripts, and OptumRx – as well as smaller PBMs that operate in Texas. Plaintiffs allege that the PBMs hid their financial relationships with drug makers, gave opioids better positions on their formularies, and purposely included more addictive opioids in their formularies to generate larger profits.[132] Plaintiffs also allege that PBMs drove the opioid epidemic on the basis of increasing profits from such drugs.[133] The defense refutes these claims, arguing that "PBMs play a less significant role and one that's harder to ascribe liability to under traditional tort principles."[134]

9.1.4.4 Medical Malpractice

Perhaps the most expected type of litigation in the opioid epidemic context is medical malpractice litigation. Medical malpractice occurs when a hospital, doctor, or other healthcare professional, through a negligent act or omission, causes an injury to a patient.[135] Medical negligence is commonly defined as the failure of a physician to exercise the skill, care, and diligence generally exercised by physicians in the same medical community and under the same or similar circumstances.[136] The plaintiff in a medical malpractice suit must establish 1) that there is a physician–provider relationship that gives rise to a duty of care; 2) the applicable standard of care; 3) that the physician breached that standard of care; 4) that the breach was the cause of the plaintiff's injury; and 5) that the plaintiff incurred damages.[137] The prescription of opioid medications by physicians as pain management carries with it a high risk of litigation. This section outlines standard-of-care practices that may help decrease the risk of a medical malpractice suit and discusses some common lawsuits involving the prescription of opioid medications.

9.1.4.4.1 Standard of Care in Medical Malpractice Cases Involving Prescription of Opioid Medications

In determining whether a physician has breached the standard of care in lawsuits involving the prescription of opioid medications, courts may look to generally accepted clinical practices. Examples of these clinical practices are outlined by the Federation of State Medical Board of the United States in the Model Guidelines for the Use of Controlled Substances for the Treatment of Pain and by the Substance Abuse and Mental Health Services Administration (SAMHSA).[138] The practices for prescribing opioid medications include evaluating the patient, developing a treatment plan, obtaining informed consent, conducting periodic review, and complying with controlled substances laws and regulations.[139]

9.1.4.4.1.1 Evaluation To reduce the risk of litigation, physicians should conduct a thorough patient evaluation before prescribing an opioid medication. The physician should question the patient regarding the nature and intensity of the pain, the effect that the pain has on the patient, and past and current treatments.[140] The physician should also obtain a thorough medical history, including the patient's past use of drugs – both illicit and prescribed.[141] Many states have developed Prescription Drug Monitoring Programs (PDMPs), which prescribers should check to determine whether a patient is obtaining prescriptions for drugs from multiple physicians.[142]

Courts consider the adequacy of the physician's evaluation a key component in determining whether the physician breached the standard of care. Courts have refused to find against physicians where the physician "spoke with [the] patient, took a detailed history, and on the basis of all the circumstances, prescribed medications accordingly."[143]

9.1.4.4.1.2 Developing a Treatment Plan Physicians prescribing opioid medications should develop written treatment plans with their patients.[144] The plan should clearly state realistic goals to be reached in terms of both pain relief and improved physical and psychosocial function.[145] Importantly, physicians should only prescribe opioid medications if the expected benefits for pain relief outweigh the risks to the patient.[146] In making this determination, the physician should consider the severity of the patient's pain, the patient's reliability in taking medications, and the dependence-producing potential of the medication.[147] At least one court has found a physician liable for a patient's addiction to morphine where there was evidence that other, non-addictive drugs would have been equally effective in treating the patient's condition.[148]

Once an appropriate medication is selected, the physician should also carefully consider the appropriate dosage and duration of the prescription.[149] Many organizations have released handbooks that include guidelines on safe opioid dosage.[150] If possible, the patient should only receive opioid prescriptions from one physician and one pharmacy throughout the treatment to reduce the risk of abuse.[151]

9.1.4.4.1.3 Informed Consent As with any treatment, physicians must obtain informed consent from their patients before proceeding with an opioid treatment, including discussion of the risks and benefits of the treatment.[152] Because the failure to obtain a patient's informed consent may be considered a breach of the standard of care, obtaining a patient's informed consent is critical in avoiding medical malpractice liability. The informed consent agreement should be in writing and should be signed by both the patient and the physician.[153] The agreement should include the risks of the medication, the need to adhere to a single treatment regimen, that the patient agrees to obtain the medication from only one physician and to take it as prescribed, that the patient is responsible for safeguarding the medication, and the consequences of failure to adhere to the treatment plan, which may include refusing to treat the patient further, referral to a rehabilitation center, or referral of the patient's identity to tracking agencies to prevent doctor-shopping.[154]

9.1.4.4.1.4 Monitoring the Patient Prescribing physicians must monitor patients throughout treatment with opioid prescriptions, which may include speaking with family members and other close contacts about patients' progress. Regular follow-up appointments should be required to monitor the therapy and its effect on the patient's health.[155]

Monitoring subjective symptoms as well as objective symptoms, including body weight, pulse rate, and temperature, can identify early warning signs of opioid abuse and allow necessary treatment modifications.[156]

Failure to monitor opioid patients may form the basis for medical malpractice lawsuits. Physicians across the country have faced both civil and criminal charges for failing to monitor patients and ignoring warning signs that patients were abusing opioid medications.[157] For example, a New Mexico jury found a physician guilty of malpractice for allowing his patient to become addicted to morphine when the physician failed to meet regularly with a patient while continuing to prescribe opioid medications.[158] The monitoring might have to continue even after the physician has stopped the prescription. A judge in Georgia found that physicians breached their duty of care by failing to monitor the patient's respiratory function after his last dose of opioid medication, ultimately leading to the patient's death.[159]

9.1.4.4.1.5 Complying with Controlled Substances Laws and Regulation Executing the prescription order correctly is vital to prevent manipulation of the opioid prescription. The CSA requires that prescriptions for controlled substances be signed and dated on the day they are issued, and that the prescription include details such as the name and address of the patient, the name and address of the physician, the name and quantity of the drug, and directions for use, among others.[160] There are additional federal requirements for Schedule II classified drugs – the category into which many prescription opioid drugs fall.[161] DOJ makes available a Practitioner's Manual, which sets out the requirements involved in prescribing opioid medications.[162] State regulations often impose additional requirements.[163] For example, one New Jersey state court found a physician liable for medical malpractice when he prescribed post-dated and undated prescriptions for narcotics in violation of federal regulations for Schedule II narcotics, which resulted in the patient's addiction.[164]

9.1.4.4.2 Types of Medical Malpractice Suits Involving Opioid Medications

In recent years, lawsuits involving the prescription of drugs have increased as the plaintiffs' bar broadened its circle of target defendants beyond pharmaceutical companies to include treating physicians as well.[165] Lawsuits involving the prescription of drugs are now the fourth most common kind of medical malpractice claim and often involve the prescription of opioids, even in some cases for a physician's failure to uncover fraud in obtaining the prescription.[166] The damages alleged in these lawsuits include overdose, addiction, and third party injury.[167] We may also see an increase in lawsuits involving the use of naloxone as it is becoming more readily available.

9.1.4.4.2.1 Overdose Cases Opioid-related medical malpractice claims cases against prescribing physicians often involve overdoses,[168] and the pool of potential plaintiffs is ever-increasing. The number of deaths resulting from opioid overdoses doubled from 21,089 in 2010 to 42,249 in 2016.[169] The media has reported on numerous cases involving doctors who allegedly negligently prescribed opioids, resulting in an overdose. For example, one suit against a Philadelphia area doctor resulted in a million-dollar settlement after the doctor prescribed nearly 200 narcotic pain and anxiety pills every week to a patient who ultimately overdosed and died.[170] The doctor testified that he did not perform routine physician checks such as ordering blood work or urine tests, reviewing records from other doctors, or properly diagnosing the patient's pain, nor did he take any measures to protect the patient when he suspected abuse of the drugs.[171] In a California case, a doctor was convicted of murder for recklessly prescribing drugs to patients after they disclosed their drug addictions and two admitted to dealing the drugs they were prescribed.[172] Notably, that physician was subject to both criminal and civil liability.[173]

9.1.4.4.2.2 Addiction Cases Patients also pursue malpractice actions against physicians when they become addicted to opioid medication. Under the learned intermediary doctrine, a drug manufacturer has a duty to warn of a drug's known dangerous propensities, including the risk of addiction, but it is the physician who has the duty to convey that warning to the patient.[174] Many manufacturers properly avoid liability because of this doctrine, making it more likely that physicians will be the targets of these suits.[175] For example, a Massachusetts jury found that a physician failed to meet the standard of skill and care required of him when he administered morphine to a patient over 3 years in increasing frequency until she became addicted.[176] The physician originally prescribed morphine without any physical examination of the patient or assessment of her pain and without conducting a medical history.[177] The jury found that the physician continuously increased the dosage and frequency of morphine, ultimately causing the patient to become addicted.[178] Similarly, a North Carolina court denied summary judgment for a defendant physician when there was evidence that a physician prescribed the narcotic pantopon, morphine, and other addictive drugs for over 12 years to a patient at increasing doses.[179] The physician did not evaluate the potential of using non-addictive substances to treat the patient's pain and failed to keep accurate records of the prescriptions.[180]

9.1.4.4.2.3 Fraud in Obtaining Prescriptions Cases Courts are split on whether a physician may be held liable for a patient's opioid addiction or overdose when a patient procures the drug by fraud. For example, a Mississippi court held that a patient could not maintain a malpractice action against a doctor for addiction to OxyContin when he obtained the drug "by misrepresenting his medical history and ongoing treatment to those from whom he sought care" and utilized ten doctors and seven pharmacies in multiple cities in order to obtain the drugs.[181]

In other jurisdictions, however, courts have held physicians liable for negligent behavior even when the patient engaged in fraudulent behavior. In a South Carolina case, a jury found that the physician was negligent and reckless in overprescribing narcotic painkillers to the patient and failing to monitor the patient for addiction, but the court subsequently reduced the punitive damages award, where the patient deliberately overdosed on the pain medication.[182]

9.1.4.4.2.4 Third Party Injury Cases Third parties may bring medical malpractice cases against physicians for negligently prescribing opioids to a patient, which resulted in the injury or death to the third party. For example, in West Virginia, plaintiffs sued the prescribing physician after an opioid patient caused a car accident under the influence of the medication, killing a man and injuring his wife and children.[183] Plaintiffs alleged that the doctor negligently prescribed codeine and other addictive drugs for 17 years, causing the patient to become addicted.[184] The court held that the physician breached his duty of care by continuing to prescribe opioids over several years in spite of knowledge that the patient was a drug and alcohol abuser instead of taking action to rehabilitate the patient.[185]

9.1.4.4.2.5 Naloxone Cases Narcan®, a form of naloxone, stops or reverses opioid overdoses when given in a timely manner.[186] Given the popularity of Narcan® to reverse opioid overdose, the recent FDA approval of a Narcan® nasal spray,[187] and the U.S. Surgeon General's public health advisory encouraging greater availability and awareness of Narcan,®[188] it is possible that more suits will be filed alleging that healthcare workers negligently administered, or negligently failed to administer, Narcan®. For example, in a California medical malpractice suit against a hospital and its doctors, plaintiffs alleged that the hospital was negligent in failing to administer sufficient Narcan® during their decedent's opioid overdose.[189] The court dismissed the case, holding that the plaintiffs could not show that the doctors failed to comply with the standard of care in administering Narcan® during the decedent's overdose.[190] Nonetheless, it is likely that more cases involving the administration of Narcan® will be brought in the future.

9.1.5 Conclusion

The opioid epidemic has given rise to legislation, government regulation and enforcement actions, and massive nationwide litigation. Individuals and state governments are increasingly turning to courts to hold doctors, pharmacists, pharmaceutical companies, and insurance companies liable for opioid misuse, abuse, addiction, and overdose, with varying degrees of success. It must be expected that the plaintiffs' bar will continue to seek out new legal theories and targets to compensate patients and others affected by opioid abuse.

NOTES

1. Fern, Kathryn, and Robert are partners and Jessica is an associate attorney at the law firm of Hollingsworth LLP. Their practice specializes in the areas of pharmaceutical products, toxic torts, and products liability litigation.
2. Rosenblum, A. et al., *Opioids and the Treatment of Chronic Pain: Controversies, Current Status, and Future Directions*, Exp. Clin. Psychopharmacol 405 (2008), *available at* https://www.ncbi.nlm.nih.gov/pmc/articles/PMC2711509/; Booth, M., *Opium: A History*, St. Martin's Press, 1986.
3. Carrie Krieger, *What Are Opioids and Why Are They Dangerous? available at* https://www.mayoclinic.org/diseases-conditions/prescription-drug-abuse/expert-answers/what-are-opioids/faq-20381270; https://www.webmd.com/pain-management/guide/narcotic-pain-medications#1; *Opioid Overdose: Commonly Used Terms*, Ctrs. for Disease Control & Prevention, *available at* https://www.cdc.gov/drugoverdose/opioids/terms.html.
4. Krieger, C., *What Are Opioids and Why Are They Dangerous?*, Mayo Clinic, (Mar. 21, 2018). *available at* https://www.mayoclinic.org/diseases-conditions/prescription-drug-abuse/expert-answers/what-are-opioids/faq-20381270.
5. Portenoy, R.K. et al., *Substance Abuse: A Comprehensive Textbook*, 4th ed. Philadelphia: Lippincott, Williams & Wilkens, 2004. Acute and Chronic Pain; at 863–904.
6. Rosenblum et al., *Opioids and the Treatment of Chronic Pain*, Exp. Clin. Psychopharmacol. 405 (2008) *available at* https://www.ncbi.nlm.nih.gov/pmc/articles/PMC2711509/.
7. *Id.*
8. *Id.*
9. Benyamin, R. et al., *Opioid Complications and Side Effects*, Pain Physician: S105 (2008), *available at* https://www.ncbi.nlm.nih.gov/pubmed/18443635.
10. Opioid (Narcotic) Pain Medications, *available at* https://www.webmd.com/pain-management/guide/narcotic-pain-medications#2.
11. Benyamin, R. et al., *Opioid Complications and Side Effects*, Pain Physician. S105 (1008), *available at* https://www.ncbi.nlm.nih.gov/pubmed/18443635.
12. Opioid (Narcotic) Pain Medications, *available at* https://www.webmd.com/pain-management/guide/narcotic-pain-medications#2.
13. Krieger, C., *What are Opioids and Why Are They Dangerous?*, Mayo Clinicm (March 21, 2018). *available at* https://www.mayoclinic.org/diseases-conditions/prescription-drug-abuse/expert-answers/what-are-opioids/faq-20381270.
14. Benyamin, R. et al., *Opioid Complications and Side Effects*, Pain Physician. S105 (2008), *available at* https://www.ncbi.nlm.nih.gov/pubmed/18443635.
15. National Institute of Health, Opioid addiction, *available at* https://ghr.nlm.nih.gov/condition/opioid-addiction#statistics.
16. Mayo Clinic Staff, *How Opioid Addiction Occurs*, Mayo Clinic (Feb. 16, 2018) *available at* https://www.mayoclinic.org/diseases-conditions/prescription-drug-abuse/in-depth/how-opioid-addiction-occurs/art-20360372.
17. Porter, J. et al., *Addiction Rare in Patients Treated with Narcotics*, 302 New Eng. J. Med. (1980), *available at* https://www.nejm.org/doi/10.1056/NEJM198001103020221.
18. *Id.*
19. Juurlink, D. et al., *A 1980 Letter on the Risk of Opioid Addiction*, 376 New Eng. J. Med. 2194 (2017), *available at* https://www.nejm.org/doi/full/10.1056/NEJMc1700150.
20. Juurlink, D. et al., *A 1980 Letter on the Risk of Opioid Addiction*, 376 New Eng. J. Med. 2194 (2017), *available at* https://www.nejm.org/doi/full/10.1056/NEJMc1700150.

21. Mayo Clinic Staff, *How Opioid Addiction Occurs*, Mayo Clinic (Feb. 16, 2018) *available at* https://www.mayoclinic.org/diseases-conditions/prescription-drug-abuse/in-depth/how-opioid-addiction-occurs/art-20360372.
22. Rosenblum, A. et al., *Opioids and the Treatment of Chronic Pain*, 16(5) Exper. Clin Psychopharmacol. 405 (2008), *available at* https://www.ncbi.nlm.nih.gov/pmc/articles/PMC2711509/.
23. Mayo Clinic Staff, *How Opioid Addiction Occurs*, Mayo Clinic (Feb 16, 2018) *available at* https://www.mayoclinic.org/diseases-conditions/prescription-drug-abuse/in-depth/how-opioid-addiction-occurs/art-20360372.
24. Department of Health and Human Services, *What Is the U.S. Opioid Epidemic?* U.S. Department of Health and Human Services (Sept. 19, 2018), *available at* https://www.hhs.gov/opioids/about-the-epidemic/index.html.
25. Stein, R., *Jump in Overdoses Shows Opioid Epidemic Has Worsened*, NPR (Mar. 6, 2018) *available at* https://www.npr.org/sections/health-shots/2018/03/06/590923149/jump-in-overdoses-shows-opioid-epidemic-has-worsened.
26. *See* Police Executive Research Forum, *The Unprecedented Opioid Epidemic* (Sept. 2017) *available at* https://www.policeforum.org/assets/opioids2017.pdf.
27. *See* Centers for Disease Control, *Opioid Overdose, Understanding the Epidemic*, CDC, *available at* https://www.cdc.gov/drugoverdose/epidemic/index.html.
28. Centers for Disease Control and Prevention, *Opioid Overdose: Understanding the Epidemic*, CDC, *available at* https://www.cdc.gov/drugoverdose/epidemic/index.html.
29. *See id.*
30. *See* Fact Sheet, *President Donald J. Trump is Taking Action on Drug Addiction and the Opioid Crisis*, The White House (Oct. 26, 2017), *available at* https://www.whitehouse.gov/briefings-statements/president-donald-j-trump-taking-action-drug-addiction-opioid-crisis/.
31. Department of Health and Human Services, *What Is the U.S. Opioid Epidemic?*, U.S. Department of Health and Human Services (Mar. 6, 2018), https://www.hhs.gov/opioids/about-the-epidemic/index.html.
32. *See generally* Behavioral Health Coordinating Committee, *Addressing Prescription Drug Abuse in the United States*, U.S. Department of Health and Human Services, *available at* https://www.cdc.gov/drugoverdose/pdf/hhs_prescription_drug_abuse_report_09.2013.pdf.
33. *See id.*
34. Frenk, SM et al., Nat'l Ctr. Health Statistics Data Brief No. 189, *Prescription Opioid Analgesic Use Among Adults: United States, 1999-2012* (Feb. 2015), https://www.cdc.gov/nchs/data/dataBriefs/db189.pdf.
35. Centers for Disease Control, Community-Based Opioid Overdose Prevention Programs Providing Naloxone – United States, 2010, 61(06) *Morbidity and Mortality Weekly Report* 101–105 at http://www.cdc.gov/mmwr/preview/mmwrhtml/mm6106a1.htm (Revised February 17, 2012) (Editorial Note).
36. Comprehensive Addiction and Recovery Act of 2016, Pub. L. No. 114-198, 2016 (130 Stat.) 695.
37. Press Release, Rob Portman, Portman, Whitehouse, Ayotte, Klobuchar Cheer Final Passage of Comprehensive Addiction and Recovery Act (July 13, 2016).
38. Combating the Opioid Epidemic Act, S. 204, 115 Cong. (2017-2018), *available at* https://www.congress.gov/bill/115th-congress/senate-bill/2004.
39. Bill to reauthorize and expand the Comprehensive Addiction and Recovery Act of 2016, S. ___, 115th Cong. 2d Session (2018)
40. Brankovic, V., *House and Senate Reach Agreement on Comprehensive Opioid Response Package*, NACo, (Nov. 2, 2018), *available at* https://www.naco.org/blog/house-and-senate-reach-agreement-comprehensive-opioid-response-package.
41. Stop Counterfeit Drugs by Regulating and Enhancing Enforcement Now Act, H.R. ___ 115th Cong. 2d Session (2018), https://democrats-energycommerce.house.gov/sites/democrats.energycommerce.house.gov/files/documents/SCREEN%20Act%20Legislative%20Text.pdf.
42. *Id.*
43. Press Release, John Kennedy, U.S. Sen. John Kennedy (R-La.) Introduces Bipartisan Opioid Quota Reform Bill (Mar. 12, 2018), *available at* https://www.kennedy.senate.gov/public/press-releases?ID=DE6208F4-18B4-4D86-AC07-94632D232D3F.
44. *Id.*
45. *The Opioid Crisis Response Act of 2018: Hearing before the U.S. Senate Committee on Health, Education, Labor & Pensions*, (2018), https://www.help.senate.gov/hearings/the-opioid-crisis-response-act-of-2018.
46. *See* Nesto, M., *State Opioid Taxes Seen as Well-Intentioned but Misguided*, Law360 (Mar. 23, 2018), *available at* https://www.law360.com/productliability/articles/1024624/state-opioid-taxes-seen-as-well-intentioned-but-misguided?nl_pk=14db981f-22fc-4624-b659-f75a03e68ca0&utm_source=newsletter&utm_medium=email&utm_campaign=productliability&read_more=1.
47. *See, e.g.*, Press Release, U.S. Department of Justice, Justice Department to File Statement of Interest in Opioid Case (Feb. 27, 2018), *available at* https://www.justice.gov/opa/pr/justice-department-file-statement-interest-opioid-case. *See also* Guarnaccia, M., *Trump May Do Some Litigation Against Opioid Cos.*, Law360 (Mar. 1, 2018), *available at* https://www.law360.com/articles/1017698/print?section=lifesciences.
48. Merica, D. et al., *Trump's Opioid plan to Take Three-Pronged Approach, Including Death Penalty for High-Volume Traffickers*, CNN (Mar. 19, 2018), *available at* https://www.cnn.com/2018/03/18/politics/trump-opioid-plan/index.html.
49. Refer to Section 4.2.1 for more information about the multi-district litigation.
50. *See* Brief in Support of Motion to Participate in Settlement Discussions and as a Friend of the Court at 2, *In re: National Prescription Opiate Litig.,* 1:17-md-02804, ECF No. 212-1 (N.D. Ohio Apr. 2, 2018).
51. Order, *In re Nat'l Prescription Opiate Litig.*, No. 1:17-md-02804-DAP (N.D. Ohio, June 19, 2018).
52. Testimony Transcript, *Jeff Sessions Opening Statement before the Senate Judiciary Committee*, Politico (June 13, 2017), *available at* https://www.politico.com/story/2017/01/full-text-jeff-sessions-opening-statement-before-the-senate-judiciary-committee-233396.
53. The DOJ'S Opioid Fraud and Abuse Detection Units, Presented by the American Bar Association Health Law Section and Center for Professional Development (Mar. 7 2018) (materials available through the American Bar Association, www.americanbar.org).
54. *See* Press Release, U.S. Department of Justice, Attorney General Sessions Announces Opioid Fraud and Abuse Detection Unit (Aug. 2, 2017), *available at* https://www.justice.gov/opa/pr/attorney-general-sessions-announces-opioid-fraud-and-abuse-detection-unit.
55. 21 U.S.C. §§ 801-904.
56. *See* § 21 C.F.R. 1306.04.

57. *See* 18 § U.S.C. 1347.
58. The DOJ'S Opioid Fraud and Abuse Detection Units, Presented by the American Bar Association Health Law Section and Center for Professional Development (Mar. 7 2018).
59. *Id.*
60. *Id.*
61. This is also known as a "cocktail" of opioids, and according to DOJ there are very few medical uses for adding drugs such as benzodiazepines or gabapentin.
62. The DOJ'S Opioid Fraud and Abuse Detection Units, Presented by the American Bar Association Health Law Section and Center for Professional Development (Mar. 7 2018).
63. *See id.*
64. *Id.*
65. *Id.*
66. Press Release, U.S. Department of Justice, Attorney General Sessions Announces New Prescription Interdiction & Litigation Task Force (Feb. 27, 2018), *available at* https://www.justice.gov/opa/pr/attorney-general-sessions-announces-new-prescription-interdiction-litigation-task-force.
67. *Id.*
68. Raymond, N., *Opioid Maker Mallinckrodt Agrees to $35 Million U.S. Drugs Probes Settlement*, Reuters (Apr. 3, 2017), *available at* https://www.reuters.com/article/us-mallinckrodt-settlement-idUSKBN1751JM.
69. *See* Field, E., *DEA Proposes Capping Opioid Quotas*, Law360 (Apr. 17, 2018), *available at* https://www.law360.com/productliability/articles/1034480/dea-proposes-capping-opioid-quotas?nl_pk=65455e4e-3409-4479-86e9-1fad4d866d82&utm_source=newsletter&utm_medium=email&utm_campaign=productliability.
70. Notice of Proposed Rulemaking re Controlled Substance Quotas, Drug Enforcement Administration, U.S. Department of Justice, 21 CFR Part 1303 [Docket No. DEA–480] RIN 1117–AB48, *available at* https://www.justice.gov/opa/press-release/file/1053681/download.
71. Bernstein, L. & Horowitz, S., *DEA Issues First Immediate Suspension of Opioid Sales to a Wholesaler since 2012*, *available at* http://www.standard.net/National/2018/05/06/DEA-issues-first-immediate-suspension-of-opioid-sales-to-a-wholesaler-since-2012.html?printFriendly=201805060133.
72. Press Release, U.S. Food & Drug Administration, *FDA Requests Removal of Opana ER for Risks Related to Abuse* (June 8, 2017), *available at* https://www.fda.gov/NewsEvents/Newsroom/PressAnnouncements/ucm562401.htm
73. *See* Field, E., *FDA Head Puts Spotlight on Internet's Role in Opioid Crisis*, Law360 (Apr. 4, 2018), *available at* https://www.law360.com/articles/1029836/print?section=lifesciences.
74. Field, E., *FDA Offers Guidance on Making Opioid Addiction Treatments*, Law360 (Apr. 20, 2018), *available at* https://www.law360.com/articles/1035756/fda-offers-guidance-on-making-opioid-addiction-treatments.
75. Department of Health and Human Services, U.S. Food and Drug Administration, *Justification of Estimates for Appropriations Committees (Fiscal Year 2019)*, at 11.
76. *See* Newsham, J., *Insys Founder Charged with Racketeering in Opioid Scheme*, Law360 (Oct. 26, 2017), *available at* https://www.law360.com/articles/978733/insys-founder-charged-with-racketeering-in-opioid-scheme.
77. *See Luzerne County v. Purdue Pharma L.P. et al., No. 3:17-cv-2043 (M.D. Pa. Nov. 8, 2017).*
78. *See* House Oversight and Investigations Committee, *Combatting the Opioid Crisis: Investigations*, *available at* https://energycommerce.house.gov/opioids-investigations/ (last visited May 3, 2018).
79. Press Release, U.S. House of Representatives, Energy and Commerce Committee, *SubOversight Announces Hearing to Press Distributors about Efforts in West Virginia in Midst of Opioid Crisis* (Apr. 12, 2018), *available at* https://energycommerce.house.gov/news/press-release/suboversight-announces-hearing-to-press-distributors-about-efforts-in-west-virginia-in-midst-of-opioid-crisis/.
80. *Statement of Ranking Member Nadler for the Hearing on "Challenges and Solutions in the Opioid Abuse Crisis"* (May 8, 2018), *available at* https://nadler.house.gov/press-release/statement-ranking-member-nadler-hearing-%E2%80%9Cchallenges-and-solutions-opioid-abuse-crisis%E2%80%9D.
81. 21 U.S.C. § 841(a)(1).
82. 21 C.F.R. § 1306.04(a).
83. *United States v. Moore*, 423 U.S. 122 (1975).
84. Yang, Tony et al., *Managing Increasing Liability Risks Related to Opioid Prescribing, The*, 130(3) Am. J. Med. 249 (2017).
85. *See generally* McClure, A., *Illegitimate Overprescription: How Burrage v. United States is Hindering Punishment of Physicians and Bolstering the Opioid Epidemic*, 93(4) Notre Dame L. Rev. 1747 (2018).
86. *United States v. Volkman*, 736 F.3d 1013, 1017 (6th Cir. 2013).
87. *United States v. MacKay*, 715 F.3d 807, 813 (10th Cir. 2013).
88. *United States v. Schneider*, No. 07-10234-01, 02, 2010 U.S. Dist. LEXIS 111968 at *21 (D. Kan. Oct. 20, 2010).
89. 21 U.S.C. § 841(b)(1)(C).
90. *Burrage v. United States*, 571 U.S. 204, 218-219 (2014).
91. *Id.* at 206.
92. *Id.* at 207.
93. *Id.* at 208.
94. *Id.* at 214.
95. *United States v. MacKay*, 20 F. Supp. 3d 1287, 1299 (D. Utah 2014).
96. *Id.* at 1217.
97. *Id.* at 1218.
98. *See* Johnson, E., *Cause-in-Fact After Burrage v. United States*, 68(6) Florida L. Rev. 1727 (2016).
99. McClure, A., *Illegitimate Overprescription: How Burrage v. United States Is Hindering Punishment of Physicians and Bolstering the Opioid Epidemic*, 93(4) Notre Dame L. Rev. 1747 (2018).
100. J. After Non-Jury Trial, *Oklahoma ex rel. Hunter v. Purdue Pharma L.P.*, No. CJ-2017-816 (Okla. Dist. Ct. Cleveland Cnty. Aug. 26, 2019).
101. *Id.*
102. Daniel Siegal, *Okla. Judge Rules J&J Caused Opioid Crisis, Owes $572M*, Law360 (Aug. 26, 2019), *available at* https://www.law360.com/articles/1187330/okla-judge-rules-j-j-caused-opioid-crisis-owes-572m
103. Pet. in Error, *Oklahoma ex rel. Hunter v. Purdue Pharma L.P.*, No. 118272 (Okla. Sept. 25, 2019).
104. *See, e.g.*, Complaint, *State of Ohio ex rel. DeWine v. Purdue Pharma L.P.*, No. 17CI000261 (C.P. Ross Cty. Ohio 2017).
105. *See, e.g.*, Complaint, State of Florida Office of the Attorney General, Department of Legal Affairs v. Purdue Pharma L.P. et al, No. 72158675 (6th Cir. 2018).
106. See, e.g., Complaint, Commonwealth of Massachusetts v. Purdue Pharma L.P. et al, (Mass. 2018) *available at* https://www.mass.gov/files/documents/2018/06/12/Purdue%20Complaint%20FILED.pdf). pp. 69-71.

107. *See, e.g.*, Complaint, *State of Ohio ex rel. DeWine v. Purdue Pharma L.P.*, No. 17CI000261 (C.P. Ross Cty. Ohio 2017). In May 2018, the City of Los Angeles sued opioid manufacturers and distributors Purdue Pharma LP., Teva Pharmaceuticals USA Inc., Janssen Pharmaceuticals Inc., Endo Pharmaceuticals Inc., Insys Therapeutics Inc., Mallinckrodt LLC, Cardinal Health Inc., McKesson Corp. and AmerisourceBergen Corp. alleging that the defendants' actions were negligent and created a public nuisance and that defendants violated the Racketeer Influenced and Corrupt Organizations Act. *See California, v. Purdue Pharma LP et al.*, 2:18-cv-03712 (C.D. Cal. May 3, 2018).
108. Restatement Second of Torts § 821B.
109. Complaint, State of Florida Office of the Attorney General, Department of Legal Affairs v. Purdue Pharma L.P. et al, No. 72158675 (6th Cir. 2018), *available at* http://myfloridalegal.com/webfiles.nsf/WF/KMAN-AYSNYR/$file/Complaint.pdf) and First Amended Complaint, Everett v. Purdue Pharma, L.P., No. 2:17-CV-00209-RSM (W.D. Wash. 2017), ECF No. 37, *available at*https://everettwa.gov/DocumentCenter/View/12717/First-Amended-Complaint?bidId); *City of Cleveland v. AmerisourceBergen Drug Corporation, et al.*, No. 1:18-op-45132 (N.D. Ohio Mar. 6, 2018).
110. *City of Miami v. Purdue Pharma L.P.* Complaint (filed 4/16/18 in the Circuit Court of the 11th Judicial Circuit and for Miami-Dade County, Florida).
111. Petition, Cherokee Nation v. McKesson Corp., No. 6:18CV00056 (E.D. Okla. 2017).
112. *See Ohio v. McKesson Corp.* (Filed 2/26/2018 in the Ohio Court of Common Pleas, No. CVH 20180055).
113. *See McKesson Corp. et al. v. Hembree et al.*, 4:17-cv-00323 (N.D. Okla. June 8, 2017).
114. See, e.g., Petition, Cherokee Nation v. McKesson Corp., No. 6:18CV00056 (E.D. Okla. 2017) at 48–49. For example, Chicago sued Purdue, Cephalon, Janssen, Endo, Allergan, and Depomed, Inc. claiming that the companies pushed prescriptions on people that were medically unnecessary despite knowing the dangers of addiction and that Chicago is entitled to reimbursement for costs it incurred in attempting to mitigate the epidemic. *City of Chicago v. Purdue Pharma LP et al.*, 1:14-cv-04361 (N.D. Ill. 2014).; *City of Birmingham v. AmerisourceBergen Drug Corp. et al.*, 2:17-cv-01360 (N.D. Ala. Aug. 14, 2017).; *See Navajo Nation v. Purdue Pharma LP et al.*, 1:18-cv-00338 (D.N.M. Apr. 11, 2018).
115. In September 2019, Purdue Pharma filed for bankruptcy in an attempt to settle the thousands of lawsuits brought against it. *See* John Bacon, *Purdue Pharma Files for Bankruptcy. Here's What it Means*, USA Today (Sept. 16, 2019), *available at* https://www.usatoday.com/story/news/nation/2019/09/16/purdue-pharma-files-bankruptcy-heres-what-means/2339353001/
116. *See* JPML Transfer Order (Doc. #1), In re Nat'l Prescription Opiate Litig., No. 2804 (N.D. Ohio, Dec. 5, 2017).
117. *See In re: National Prescription Opiate Litig.*, No. 1:17-md-2804 (N.D. Ohio Dec. 12, 2017).
118. *See* JPML Transfer Order (Doc. #1), In re Nat'l Prescription Opiate Litig., No. 2804 (N.D. Ohio, Dec. 5, 2017).
119. Overley, J., *Opioid MDL Judge Sets Litigation Plan, Bashes DEA*, Law360 (Apr. 11, 2018), *available at* https://www.law360.com/articles/1009123/opioid-mdl-judge-sets-litigation-plan-bashes-dea; *see also* Parloff, R., *Q&A: Opioid Plaintiffs' Lawyer Paul Hanly on What a Settlement Might Look Like*, The Opioid Institute (Jan. 31, 2018), *available at* https://opioidinstitute.org/2018/01/31/test/.
120. *Schneiderman v. Insys Therapeutics Inc.* (Filed 2/1/2018 in the Supreme Court of the State of New York, County of New York).
121. *See Ohio v. McKesson Corp.* (Filed 2/26/2018 in the Ohio Court of Common Pleas, No. CVH 20180055).
122. Aaron Cooper et al., *4 Pharmaceutical Companies Accused in the Opioid Epidemic Reach a $260 Million Settlement Just before Trial*, CNN, updated (Oct. 21, 2019), *available at* https://www.cnn.com/2019/10/21/health/ohio-opioid-settlement-monday/index.html
123. *Id.*
124. Order, *In re AmerisourceBergen Drug Corp.*, No. 19-3935 (6th Cir. Oct. 11, 2019), ECF No. 9-2, *available at* https://assets.documentcloud.org/documents/6467320/19-3935-Documents.pdf
125. *Id.*
126. *Id.*
127. Lenny Bernstein, *Judge in Landmark Opioid Trial Declines to Step Aside*, The Washington Post (Sept. 26, 2019), *available at* https://www.washingtonpost.com/health/judge-in-landmark-opioid-trial-declines-to-step-aside/2019/09/26/ddac54d4-e062-11e9-8dc8-498eabc129a0_story.html
128. In Re: National Prescritpion Opiates Litigation, MDL No. 2804 (N.D. Ohio), FAQs, https://www.opioidsnegotiationclass.info/Home/FAQ#faq1 (updated Nov. 1, 2019).
129. *Id.*
130. *Id.*
131. Toich, L., *Opioid Lawsuit Places Blame on Pharmacy Benefit Managers*, AJPB (Mar. 1, 2018), *available at* https://www.ajpb.com/news/opioid-lawsuit-places-blame-on-pharmacy-benefit-managers
132. Mueller, A., *Express Scripts among Pharmacy Benefit Firms Include in Opioid Lawsuit*, St. Louis Bus. J. (Feb. 26, 2018), *available at* https://www.bizjournals.com/stlouis/news/2018/02/26/express-scripts-among-pharmacy-benefit-firms.html
133. KGNS Staff, *Webb Counrt Joins Opioid Lawsuit*, KGNS (Mar. 2, 2018), *available at* https://www.kgns.tv/content/news/Opioid-lawsuit-webb-county-475680373.html; Haffajee, R.L., *Drug Companies' Liability for the Opioid Epidemic*, 377 New Eng. J. Med. 2301 (2017), *available at* https://www.nejm.org/doi/full/10.1056/NEJMp1710756?page=1&sort=oldest; https://www.forbes.com/sites/legalnewsline/2018/06/07/lets-blame-the-criminals-pharmacies-facing-opioid-litigation-say/#4664e8ae64b8.
134. Toich, L., *Opioid Lawsuit Places Blame on Pharmacy Benefit Managers*, AJPB (Mar. 1, 2018), *available at* https://www.ajpb.com/news/opioid-lawsuit-places-blame-on-pharmacy-benefit-managers.
135. American Board of Professional Liability Attorneys, *What Is Medical Malpractice?*, ABPLA, *available at* https://www.abpla.org/what-is-malpractice (last visited Nov. 20, 2018).
136. *See* 61 Am. Jur. 2d Physicians, Surgeons, Etc. § 187 (2018).
137. *See* 142 Am. Jur. 3d Proof of Facts § 149 (2014).
138. Federation of State Medical Boards of the United States, Inc., *Model Policy for the Use of Controlled Substances for the Treatment of Pain* (May 2004), *available at* https://www.ihs.gov/painmanagement/includes/themes/newihstheme/display_objects/documents/modelpolicytreatmentpain.pdf, [hereinafter *FSMB Model Policy*]; Substance

Abuse and Mental Health Services Administration, *Opioid Overdose Toolkit* (2013), *available at* https://store.samhsa.gov/system/files/sma18-4742.pdf [hereinafter *SAMHSA Toolkit*]; Substance Abuse and Mental Health Services Administration, *Opioid Overdose Prevention Toolkit: Information for Prescribers* (2013), *available at* https://www.integration.samhsa.gov/Opioid_Toolkit_Prescribers.pdf [hereinafter *SAMHSA Toolkit for Prescribers*].
139. *Id.*
140. FSMB Model Policy.
141. *Id.*
142. *See* Prescription Drug Monitoring Program Training and Technical Assistance Center, *Prescription Drug Monitoring Frequently Asked Questions (FAQ)*, *available at* http://www.pdmpassist.org/content/prescription-drug-monitoring-frequently-asked-questions-faq (last visited Nov. 20, 2018). Currently, 49 states, The District of Columbia, and Guam have legislation that authorizes the creation and operation of a PDMP and have a PDMP that is operational. *Id.*
143. *Dallaire v. HSU*, 23 A.3d 792, 798 (Conn. App. Ct. 2011).
144. FSMB Model Policy.
145. *Id.*
146. SAMHSA Toolkit. It has been recommended that the treatment should be combined with nonpharmacological therapy and non-opioid pharmacologic therapy. *Id.*
147. SAMHSA Toolkit for Prescribers.
148. *Ballenger v. Crowell*, 247 S.E.2d 287 (N.C. Ct. App. 1978).
149. SAMHSA Toolkit.
150. *See, e.g.*, Agency Medical Directors' Group, *Interagency Guideline on Opioid Dosing for Chronic Non-Cancer Pain: An Educational Aid to Improve Care and Safety with Opioid Therapy* (2010), *available at* http://www.agencymeddirectors.wa.gov/files/opioidgdline.pdf.
151. FSMB Model Policy.
152. *Id.*
153. SAMHSA Toolkit for Prescribers.
154. *Id.*
155. FSMB Model Policy.
156. SAMHSA Toolkit.
157. *See* Sapatkin, D., *Too Many Pills, Too Little Oversight*, The Philadelphia Inquirer (Oct. 19, 2015), http://articles.philly.com/2015-10-19/news/67591674_1_pain-pills-barone-prescription-drugs; Gerber, M. et al., *California Doctor Convicted of Murder in Overdose Deaths of Patients,* Los Angeles Times (Oct. 30, 2015), http://www.latimes.com/local/lanow/la-me-ln-doctor-prescription-drugs-murder-overdose-verdict-20151030-story.html; McCarty, J.F., *Two Cleveland Clinic Doctors Accused in Lawsuits of Contributing to Three Opioid Overdose Deaths*, Cleveland (Oct. 28, 2018), https://www.cleveland.com/metro/index.ssf/2018/10/two_cleveland_clinic_doctors_a.html.
158. *Los Alamos Med. Ctr. v. Coe*, 275 P.2d 175, 176 (N.M 1954).
159. *Mixon v. U.S.*, 58 F. Supp. 3d 1355 (M.D. Ga. 2014).
160. 21 C.F.R. § 1306.05.
161. *See* 21 C.F.R. § 1306.11.
162. U.S. Department of Justice, *Practitioner's Manual: An Informational Outline of the Controlled Substances Act*, U.S. Department of Justice (2006), *available at* https://www.deadiversion.usdoj.gov/pubs/manuals/pract/pract_manual012508.pdf.
163. SAMHSA Toolkit for Prescribers.
164. *Taglieri v. Moss*, 842 A.2d 280 (N.J. Super. Ct. App. Div. 2004) (affirming the lower court's finding that the doctor's "willful violations of the administrative regulations constituted negligence as a matter of law").
165. Cappelino, A., *Opioid Use Causes Increase in Medical Malpractice Litigation* (Nov. 30, 2017), *available at* https://www.theexpertinstitute.com/opioid-use-causes-increase-medical-malpractice-litigation/.
166. *Id.*
167. Poe, A.H., *What Does America's Painkiller Abuse Epidemic Mean for Attorneys – And What Can Be Done?* 42-OCT Mont. Law 26 (2016).
168. Cappellino, A., *Opioid Use Causes Increase in Medical Malpractice Litigation* (Nov. 30, 2017), *available at* https://www.theexpertinstitute.com/opioid-use-causes-increase-medical-malpractice-litigation/.
169. U.S. Dep't of Health & Human Services, *Surgeon General's Advisory on Naloxone and Opioid Overdose*, *available at* https://www.surgeongeneral.gov/priorities/opioid-overdose-prevention/naloxone-advisory.html (last visited Nov. 29, 2018).
170. *See* Sapatkin, D., *Too Many Pills, Too Little Oversight*, The Philadelphia Inquirer (Oct. 19, 2015), http://articles.philly.com/2015-10-19/news/67591674_1_pain-pills-barone-prescription-drugs.
171. *Id.*
172. Gerber, M. et al., *California Doctor Convicted of Murder in Overdose Deaths of Patients,* Los Angeles Times (Oct. 30, 2015), http://www.latimes.com/local/lanow/la-me-ln-doctor-prescription-drugs-murder-overdose-verdict-20151030-story.html.
173. *Id.*
174. Am. Jur. 2d Physicians, Surgeons, and Other Healers § 235.
175. *See Bodie v. Purdue Pharma Co.*, No. 05-13834, 2007 WL 1577964 (11th Cir. June 1, 2007); *Foister v. Purdue Pharma, L.P.*, 295 F. Supp. 2d (2003).
176. *King v. Solomon*, 81 N.E.2d 838, 839 (Mass. 1948).
177. *Id.*
178. *Id.*
179. *Ballenger v. Crowell*, 247 S.E.2d 287, 289 (N.C. Ct. App. 1978).
180. *Id.*
181. *Price v. Purdue Pharma Co.*, 920 So. 2d 479, 486 (Miss. 2006).
182. *Id.*
183. *Osborne v. U.S.*, 166 F. Supp. 2d 479 (S.D. W. Va. 2001).
184. *Id.* at 491.
185. *Id.* at 500.
186. *See* Drugs.com, *Naloxone*, available at http://www.drugs.com/pro/naloxone.html.
187. Gustin, B.E., *Narcan Nasal Spray to Counteract Narcotic Overdose* (Nov. 22, 2015), *available at* http://www.emergencymedicineexpert.com/dr.-gustin-39s-blog/narcan-nasal-spray-to-counteract-narcotic-overdose.html.
188. U.S. Dep't of Health & Human Services, *Surgeon General's Advisory on Naloxone and Opioid Overdose, available at* https://www.surgeongeneral.gov/priorities/opioid-overdose-prevention/naloxone-advisory.html (last visited Nov. 29, 2018).
189. *Richardson v. Contra Costa Cty.*, No. A131855, 2012 WL 1654959, at *1 (Cal. Ct. App. May 11, 2012).
190. *Id.*

9.2 DAUBERT AND TESTING CLAIMS OF ADVERSE DRUG EFFECTS IN THE COURTROOM

Eric G. Lasker and Tamara F. Barago[1]

> There is something fascinating about science. One gets such wholesale returns of conjecture out of such a trifling investment of fact.
>
> **Mark Twain, Life on the Mississippi (1874)**

In today's litigious society, no textbook on the potential adverse health effects of drugs would be complete without a discussion of how claims of alleged adverse drug reactions are evaluated in the courtroom. While there are many examples of licit and illicit drugs that have scientifically established adverse effects, there are also many examples of medically indicated drugs that have been pulled from the market, in whole or in part, based upon perceived risks that are not borne out by the objective scientific data. Over the past 30 years, the courts have been inundated with scientifically-unfounded claims that pharmaceuticals or medical devices caused adverse health effects, starting with the allegations in the 1980s that the morning sickness drug Bendectin caused birth defects and continuing in the 1990s, 2000s, and beyond with, for example, claims of autoimmune disease from silicone breast implants and claims of strokes and cardiovascular diseases from the postpartum lactation drug Parlodel®. These cases have led the courts to develop important evidentiary rules that – when properly applied – prevent such unfounded claims from reaching the jury.

Ever since the United States Supreme Court's landmark ruling in the Bendectin case *Daubert v. Merrell Dow Pharmaceuticals, Inc.*,[2] judges have been tasked with the obligation to serve as gatekeepers to keep scientifically unreliable and irrelevant expert testimony out of the courtroom. The standards set forth in *Daubert*, which the Supreme Court has described as "exacting,"[3] have had a significant impact on numerous areas of legal dispute, but perhaps no area has been more affected than toxic tort and pharmaceutical product liability litigation. Under *Daubert* and its progeny, *General Electric v. Joiner*[4] and *Kumho Tire Co., Ltd. v. Carmichael*,[5] a plaintiff can no longer get a product liability claim before a jury based solely on an expert's subjective opinion that the plaintiff's injury was caused by a particular drug. Rather, the plaintiff must demonstrate that the expert's opinion is scientifically valid, both on the general causation question of whether the drug could potentially cause the injury in any patient and the specific causation question of whether the drug in fact did cause the particular plaintiff's injury.[6]

Daubert has imposed a significant obligation on trial courts, and many judges have struggled to understand the scientific principles that they must follow in their new role.[7] In addition, there have been "consistent efforts by recalcitrant judges to stop or roll back" the "radical changes wrought by the 'Daubert revolution.'"[8] Plaintiffs' counsel and like-minded legal observers have sought to take advantage of this uncertainty by arguing that the Supreme Court provided ambiguous guidance regarding the admissibility of medical causation testimony and that courts should defer to the judgment of medical experts so long as they follow the same "differential diagnosis" reasoning in their expert testimony as they do in their clinical practice.[9] These arguments are wrong. The guidance provided by the Supreme Court is clear: expert testimony that a drug caused an adverse event is admissible only if it is based on the scientific method, *i.e.*, evidence properly derived through the generating and testing of hypotheses. This guidance provides a simple framework for courts considering the variety of evidence generally put forth by causation experts in drug product liability litigation, whether it be epidemiology, animal research, chemical analogies, anecdotal information, or differential diagnosis.

In this chapter, we review the Supreme Court's adoption of the scientific method as the standard for admissibility of expert testimony and analyze how a court's proper understanding of the scientific method can guide it in evaluating the different types of causation evidence presented in pharmaceutical product liability litigation, both with respect to general and specific causation. Throughout this discussion and in the concluding section, we will draw on our firm's experience as national defense counsel in a series of product liability cases involving the prescription drug Parlodel®, in which these evidentiary issues have been analyzed in depth in judicial opinions across the country. The Parlodel® litigation has been described in another textbook as "the first significant products liability causation debate of the 21st century" and one that "will serve as a guide to understanding the significant causation issues that will continue to be involved, at increased rates of complexity, in the 21st century products cases."[10]

9.2.1 The Supreme Court's Directive: Expert Testimony Must Be Derived by the Scientific Method

In *Daubert*, the Supreme Court held that scientific testimony is not admissible unless it satisfies the dual requirements of scientific reliability and relevance. Scholarly debate regarding *Daubert* has often focused on the four factors suggested by the Court in determining scientific reliability: (1) testing, (2) peer review, (3) error rate and standards, and (4) general acceptance. However, a rote discussion of these factors misses the point. These factors are relevant only insofar as they assist the trial court in applying the overarching directive of *Daubert* that expert testimony must be based on the scientific method. The Supreme Court explained that "in order to qualify as 'scientific knowledge' an inference must be derived by the scientific method."[11] The Court defined the scientific method as follows: "Scientific methodology today is based on generating hypotheses and testing them to see if they can be falsified; indeed, this methodology is what distinguishes science from other fields of human inquiry."[12] Moreover, "[s]cientific validity for one purpose is not necessarily scientific validity for other, unrelated purposes."[13] In other words, expert testimony is admissible only if empirical testing validates the specific theory to which the expert opines.[14]

Daubert also explains that while admissible expert testimony must be based on the scientific method, "there are important differences between the quest for truth in a courtroom and the quest for truth in the laboratory."[15] "[S]cientific conclusions are subject to perpetual revision. Law, on the other hand, must resolve disputes finally and quickly."[16] Accordingly, expert testimony must be judged based on the current state of scientific knowledge, not on the possibility that additional knowledge may emerge in the future. The Court recognized that the requirement of existing empirical evidence "on occasion will prevent the jury from learning of authentic insights and innovation" but held that this "is the balance struck by Rules of Evidence designed not for the exhaustive search for cosmic understanding but for particularized resolution of legal disputes."[17]

Four years after *Daubert*, the Supreme Court provided further guidance on how judges should use the scientific method in evaluating expert testimony. In *Joiner*, the plaintiffs' experts contended that their opinion (that PCBs can cause lung cancer) should be admitted because they relied on epidemiology and animal studies, which are standard tools used by scientists in testing causal hypotheses. The Court rejected this contention, explaining that a faithful application of the scientific method requires more: "whether animal studies can ever be the proper foundation for an expert's testimony was not the issue. The issue was whether *these* experts' opinions were sufficiently supported by the animal studies on which they purported to rely."[18] In other words, expert testimony must be based on empirical testing that *validates* the conclusions reached.[19]

The *Joiner* Court held that the research cited by plaintiffs' experts did not validate their conclusions because the epidemiological studies did not report a statistically significant causal link between PCBs and lung cancer, lacked proper controls, and examined substances other than PCBs, and because the animal studies involved massive doses of PCBs and a different type of cancer and could not be properly extrapolated to humans. Plaintiffs' experts could not support their opinions under the scientific method because their conclusions ultimately rested on subjective leaps from the scientific evidence. "[N]othing in either *Daubert* or the Federal Rules of Evidence requires a district court to admit evidence that is connected to existing data only by the *ipse dixit* of the expert. A court may conclude that there is simply too great an analytical gap between the data and opinion proffered."[20]

Two years later, in *Kumho Tire*, the Supreme Court held that the *Daubert* requirements of reliability and relevance apply to all expert testimony, including experience-based testimony. Even in areas where the four factors proposed in *Daubert* are inapplicable, the Court explained that the overarching question remains the same: "Is the expert's testimony supported by a methodology that has been objectively validated and supports the conclusions offered?"[21] In evaluating this question, the Court instructed that courts should consider whether the expert "employs in the courtroom the same level of intellectual rigor that characterizes the practice of the expert in the relevant field."[22]

9.2.2 Evaluating General Causation Evidence Under the Scientific Method

General causation opinions in drug product liability litigation may be based on a wide variety of evidence of differing scientific value, including, *inter alia*, epidemiology, animal studies, chemical analogies, case reports, and regulatory findings and other secondary sources. Some legal observers have argued that a medical expert's evaluation of this evidence involves a "complex inferential process" and that the expert accordingly should be allowed to simply lump this evidence together and reach "a subjective judgment about the strength of the evidence."[23] However, *Daubert* clearly requires more. Under *Daubert*, a trial court must consider each of these categories of evidence in light of the scientific method, and the expert's testimony may only be admitted if the expert can establish, through scientific evidence, that her causal hypothesis has been reliably tested and validated.

Further, a causation expert cannot satisfy her *Daubert* burden by arguing that the scientific research necessary to test her hypothesis has not been or cannot be performed. *Daubert* requires trial judges to evaluate expert testimony based on the science that exists at the time, not the possibility of new scientific discoveries in the future or guesswork as to what those discoveries might show.[24] As Judge Posner of the United States Court of Appeal for the Seventh Circuit explained, "the courtroom is not the place for scientific guesswork, even of the inspired sort. Law lags science, it does not lead it."[25]

9.2.2.1 Epidemiology

Controlled epidemiological studies are generally considered the most reliable evidence for testing a hypothesis that a particular substance causes a particular injury in humans.[26] Epidemiological studies can be especially important in cases where the drug or substance at issue is widely used or where there is a measurable background rate of the alleged injury regardless of exposure. In these situations, epidemiology may be the only way to test the hypothesis that observed injuries in exposed individuals are reflective of an increased risk and a causal connection rather than pure statistical chance.[27] While the absence of epidemiology may not be fatal to a plaintiff's case, numerous courts have held that a plaintiff seeking to establish causation without such evidence will face a high evidentiary hurdle.[28] A reliable causation opinion also cannot "simply ignore the epidemiology that exists."[29] Courts have also rejected expert testimony that is based upon a cherry-picking of isolated epidemiologic findings without explanation for the expert's failure to consider contrary epidemiologic findings.[30]

When a causation expert relies on epidemiological studies to support her opinions, a trial court must analyze those studies to determine whether they provide a proper foundation for the expert's testimony under the scientific method. The finding in an epidemiological study of an *association* between a substance and an injury is not equivalent of *causation*.[31] There are three reasons that a positive association may be observed in an epidemiological study: (1) chance, (2) bias, and (3) real effect.[32] As the Supreme Court recognized in *Joiner*, epidemiological research cannot provide a scientifically reliable basis for an affirmative causation opinion if it is statistically insignificant or inadequately controlled for bias.[33]

Epidemiologists attempt to account for the possibility of chance by calculating "confidence intervals" around point estimates of potential increased risk derived from epidemiological studies. An epidemiological study is considered to show a statistically significant association with an increased risk if the confidence interval of upper and lower bound estimates of risk does not include the possibility of no increased risk in the exposed population. The possibility of no increased risk is referred to as the "null" hypothesis, which is generally indicated by a relative risk or odds ratio of 1.0.[34] The generally accepted confidence interval in epidemiological studies is 95%, meaning that a study is not statistically significant unless the "null" hypothesis of no increased (or decreased) risk can be excluded with 95% confidence.[35] If an epidemiological study is not statistically significant, it cannot provide scientifically reliable evidence of an association, let alone causation.[36] Further, numerous courts have held that epidemiological evidence can only support a conclusion that a substance is more likely than not the cause of disease if it establishes a doubling of the risk of the disease.[37] The reasoning behind this requirement is that if exposure does not at least double the risk of injury, then more than half of the population suffering from injuries allegedly caused by the substance would have been injured anyway through pure chance (based on the background risk of injury) thereby disproving "more likely than not" legal causation. Courts have also cautioned against reliance on statistically significant subgroup analyses, given the likelihood that numerous subgroup analyses will result in spurious statistical associations in some endpoints through chance alone.[38]

Bias in epidemiology is any systematic error that makes the two groups being compared different in more ways than just the variable being studied.[39] Common sources of bias include confounding factors (other factors associated with the studied factor that might account for a perceived increased risk), selection bias (uncontrolled differences between the studied populations), and information bias (systematic error in measuring data that results in differential accuracy of information).[40] A court must consider each of these sources of bias in interpreting an epidemiological study because bias can produce an erroneous association.[41] Thus, for example, courts have excluded expert causation testimony based on purported statistically significant epidemiologic evidence where the study failed to account for other confounding exposures that could have accounted for the apparent association.[42] Courts have rejected expert opinions that relied upon epidemiological studies where the subjects were not blinded to the study hypothesis.[43] Courts have rejected expert testimony based on epidemiological studies that failed to adequately address the possibility that injured subjects would be more likely to recall a preceding exposure than healthy controls ("recall bias").[44] Courts have also rejected expert testimony that relied upon epidemiological studies that failed to articulate selection criteria for participants in the study and thus could not account for selection biases "that could lead to erroneous inferences regarding causation."[45]

The existence of a well-controlled epidemiological study that reports a statistically significant increased association with a specific injury does not, by itself, provide scientifically reliable evidence establishing causation.[46] "The strong consensus among epidemiologists is that conclusions about causation should not be drawn, if at all, until a number of criteria have been considered."[47] In analyzing the scientific reliability of epidemiological evidence under *Daubert*, a number of courts have been guided by a set of criteria published by the noted epidemiologist Sir Austin Bradford Hill in 1965 ("the Bradford Hill criteria").[48] The Bradford Hill criteria can be summarized as follows: (1) strength of association, (2) consistency and replication of findings, (3) specificity with respect to both the substance and injury at issue; (4) evidence of a dose-response relationship, (5) temporal relationship, (6) biological plausibility, and (7) consideration of alternative explanations.[49]

In light of these criteria, courts have rejected statistically significant epidemiological research under *Daubert* where the reported relative risk is only slightly elevated[50] and have suggested that epidemiological research reporting a relative increased risk of less than three times indicates only a weak association (strength of association).[51] Courts have also rejected isolated, statistically significant epidemiological findings that are not replicated in other epidemiological research (consistency).[52] Courts have rejected epidemiological studies reporting statistically significant associations with allegedly similar substances or allegedly similar injuries (specificity).[53] And courts have rejected alleged associations in epidemiological studies that did not demonstrate a dose response relationship (dose response).[54] Moreover, courts have not accepted the mere incantation of the name of Bradford Hill as establishing the reliability of a causation hypothesis.[55] These criteria must be applied faithfully or they can also generate unreliable conclusions,[56] as demonstrated by two review papers published in 1989–1990 that both purported to use the Bradford Hill criteria to assess the epidemiological evidence regarding an association between alcohol consumption and breast cancer, but reached dramatically different conclusions.[57] Courts also have excluded causation opinions where the expert applied the Bradford

Hill analysis without first establishing that an association existed between the specific drug and the injury at issue.[58]

Causation experts sometimes attempt to bolster individually weak epidemiological studies by relying on "meta-analyses" in which otherwise insignificant or inconsistent findings are pooled to generate a single purportedly significant finding. This approach was rejected by courts in the Bendectin litigation,[59] and rightfully so. While meta-analyses can provide useful information if conducted pursuant to proper scientific methodology, they have frequently reported causal relationships that do not survive scientific scrutiny.[60] By pooling data from different studies, meta-analyses can paper over biases and other weaknesses in the underlying studies, disregard inconsistent findings, and improperly combine divergent population groups. As one commentator has explained, "[m]eta-analyses begin with scientific studies, usually performed by academics or government agencies, and sometimes incomplete or disputed. The data from these studies are then run through computer models of bewildering complexity, which produces results of implausible precision."[61] After finding that meta-analyses were frequently contradicted by subsequent large, randomized controlled trials, another investigator cautioned: "The popularity of meta-analysis may at least partly come from the fact that it makes life simpler and easier for reviewers as well as readers. However, over simplification may lead to inappropriate conclusions."[62] Pursuant to *Daubert*, a court must look behind the "bewildering complexity" of meta-analysis and protect against "inappropriate conclusions" by requiring the expert to establish the reliability and relevance both of the different pieces of information going into the meta-analysis and the calculations used to combine the information into a single result.

9.2.2.2 Animal Research

Animal research may be a useful tool for raising suspicions that can then be tested in humans, but there are significant differences in humans and laboratory animals that limit the degree to which animal research can validate a causation hypothesis in humans.[63] There are numerous examples of apparent positive findings in animal studies that have subsequently been found inapplicable to humans. The most commonly cited example, perhaps, is saccharine, which was linked to bladder cancer in rats over 20 years ago but was later removed from the National Toxicology Program list of potential human carcinogens after years of subsequent research failed to find any health risk in humans. Similarly, scientists have determined that a common insecticide, carbaryl, causes fetal abnormalities in dogs because dogs lack a specific enzyme involved in metabolizing carbaryl. Humans have the enzyme at issue and are accordingly not believed to be at risk.[64] Because of numerous such problems of extrapolation, courts repeatedly have held that animal studies alone cannot prove causation in humans.[65]

At a minimum, extrapolations from animal studies to humans are not considered reliable in the absence of a credible scientific explanation why such extrapolation is warranted.[66] In evaluating whether animal studies can form a reliable foundation for a causation opinion, trial courts should consider such factors as: (1) whether the results followed a dose response curve; (2) whether the animal studies involved massive doses, (3) whether the studies involved different routes of administration, (4) whether the studies are conducted in intact animals (as opposed, *e.g.*, to isolated animal parts), (5) whether the results have been replicated in different animal species, and (6) whether the animal models have been shown to be reliable predictors of human experience.[67]

Animal toxicology studies are not designed to establish whether a substance is safe in humans but rather to allow scientists to study the types of effects a substance can produce under specified conditions.[68] Accordingly, animal studies are often conducted with the goal of inducing the greatest number of adverse effects. This is accomplished in a number of ways, including the use of extremely high doses and exposures through special routes designed to deliver the substance directly to a particular organ without allowing for normal absorption and metabolization.[69] While these models are useful and appropriate in the laboratory as a means to generate hypotheses for further testing, they create additional problems for extrapolating study findings to humans.

The existence of a dose-response relationship has been described as the most fundamental and pervasive concept in toxicology.[70] All substances, even water, become toxic at a high enough dose. Conversely, however, "it has long been recognized that acute toxicological responses are associated with thresholds; that is, there is some dose below which the probability of an individual responding is zero."[71] As stated by the oft-described father of chemical pharmacology, Paracelsus (1493-1541), "What is there that is not poison? All things are poison and nothing [is] without poison. Solely a dose determines that a thing is not a poison."[72] Accordingly, even leaving to one side the issue of interspecies variations, the fact that a high-dose study results in adverse effects in animals cannot be extrapolated into a scientifically reliable conclusion that the substance can cause such effects at normal exposure levels in humans.[73] To the contrary, because toxic effects in humans are generally expected to appear in the same range on the basis of dose per unit of body surface as in experimental animals, a finding of adverse events in animals at only very high doses may be more indicative of the safety of the substance in normal use.[74]

The route by which a substance enters the body can also have a significant effect on its toxicity. Animal researchers frequently administer chemical agents through special routes, including, *inter alia*, (1) intraperitoneal, (2) subcutaneous, (3) intramuscular, and (4) intravenous.[75] These routes of administration may bypass the normal mechanisms through which potential toxins are removed before reaching the general circulation. For example, many substances are biotransformed and detoxified by the liver; while these substances may demonstrate toxic effects when injected intravenously, intramuscularly, or subcutaneously, they are perfectly safe if ingested orally.[76] Likewise, animal researchers also use genetically designed or physically altered animals in which normal protective body mechanisms are removed.[77] These types of animal studies can be useful in studying how an animal's normal body mechanisms interact and how substances can affect isolated physiological systems, but they do not reflect real world risks, even in the species being studied.

In conducting its *Daubert* inquiry, a trial court also must determine whether the findings in the animal studies "fit" the opinions being offered in the case. Thus, an expert cannot rely on animal research that relates to a different injury than the one at issue. For example, animal carcinogenicity studies indicate that animals "react differently and in much more diverse ways than man" and that "compared to humans much more variation occurs in the cancer sites in animals."[78] However, in cases in which a chemical has been associated with cancers in both animal studies and epidemiological studies, "the target organ is usually identical."[79] In *Joiner*, the Supreme Court thus rejected animal research in part because the animals had developed a different type of cancer than the cancer at issue in the plaintiff.[80]

9.2.2.3 Chemical Analogies

Causation opinions derived from chemical analogies rely on the hypothesis that a substance's effects can be predicted based on the established effects of similarly structured compounds. Trial courts should be very wary of such "guilt-by-association" evidence,[81] particularly where there is scientific research involving the actual substance at issue that demonstrates differences between it and its purported chemical cousins. Because even small changes in molecular structure can radically change a particular substance's properties and propensities, research in analogous substances does not reliably test the causal hypothesis at issue.[82]

The difficulty in relying on chemical analogies has been demonstrated by attempts to create computerized programs to assess the toxicity of chemical agents based on structure-activity relationships ("SARs"). These computerized models are far more sophisticated than the simplistic chemical analogies often relied on by causation experts in toxic tort litigation, and often rely on additional information regarding a substance beyond its chemical structure. Even so, while these models ultimately may prove helpful in setting research priorities or generating hypotheses, they have failed to provide reliable predictions as to a chemical's toxic effect.[83] As reported in one survey article, two prediction toxicity exercises conducted under the aegis of the National Toxicology Program have found that models that attempt to predict carcinogenicity "based solely on information derived from chemical structure" have been particularly unreliable, with the first exercise reporting that "overall accuracy in terms of positive or negative predictions was in the range 50–65%" and the ongoing second exercise reporting even higher error rates in preliminary results.[84] Moreover, "[a] clear limitation of almost all the prediction systems ... was their excessive sensitivity, *i.e.*, incorrectly predicting many non-carcinogens as positive."[85] Efforts to predict toxicity based on structure activity relationships have resulted in similar problems.[86]

9.2.2.4 Case Reports/Case Series

Case reports and case series are anecdotal observations of adverse effects occurring in coincidence with exposure to a given substance. If a sufficient body of similar case reports appear in the literature, they can spur epidemiological or other controlled research to test the hypothesis that a causal link exists.[87] However, as most courts have properly recognized, case reports themselves do not test the causal hypothesis and accordingly cannot support a causation opinion under *Daubert*.[88] Case reports are merely anecdotal accounts of observations in particular individuals; they are not controlled tests, frequently lack analyses, and frequently make little attempt to screen out alternative causes for a patient's condition.[89] As discussed above, when the substance at issue is widely used, it is statistically certain given general background rates of injury that there will be case reports in which an exposure and an injury coincidentally coincide. Accordingly, the existence of such case reports is of little scientific value.[90]

Adverse drug experience reports ("ADEs") – reports made by third parties, usually physicians, concerning an adverse medical event in a patient taking a particular drug – are also widely rejected as scientifically reliable evidence of causation.[91] The spontaneous adverse event reports that a manufacturer may be required to submit to a federal or state regulator (for example, ADE reports required by the FDA) often have an even more attenuated "fit" with a plaintiff's alleged injury than case reports published in the literature. Spontaneous reports, such as those sent to the FDA, are required to be sent based on a temporal association between a reported event and the use of a substance, irrespective of whether there is a causal relationship involved. These reports are not reliable scientific evidence of medical causation, and their use by a regulator to carry out authorized regulatory purposes does not imbue them with any greater scientific reliability.[92]

In drug product liability cases, causation experts may rely on so-called "causality assessments" of individual case reports. Causality assessments are algorithms used in some European pharmacovigilance regulatory schemes that seek to impose some structure on evaluation of individual case reports by creating standardized questions to be used in the review of such reports, such as:

- Was the adverse event a known consequence of the drug?
- Did the event occur in temporal proximity to the use of the drug?
- Did the symptoms disappear upon withdrawal of the drug ("dechallenge")?
- Did the symptoms reappear following reintroduction of the drug ("rechallenge")?

- Are there alternative causes for the adverse event?

Reviewers then grade individual case reports using such terms as "not possible," "unlikely," "possible," and "probable."[93] Causality assessments are used by some regulatory agencies as a signaling tool, but "they have no objective reliability which would render them useful in a wider environment."[94] "None of the available causality assessment systems has been validated ... In other words the uncertainty [inherent in case reports] is not reduced, but categorized (at best in a semiquantitative way)."[95] Studies of standardized causality assessments have repeatedly found significant disagreements between graders using the same assessment methodology.[96] Accordingly, causality assessments carry no greater scientific weight than other case reports and likewise cannot provide the type of evidence required under *Daubert.*[97]

Some case reports include information regarding purported dechallenges or rechallenges, *i.e.*, reports that a patient's condition improved when the substance was removed or worsened when the substance was reintroduced. Where the dechallenge/rechallenge report is merely an after-the-fact account of an anecdotal observation, it suffers from similar reliability problems as other case reports. Many medical conditions result in fluctuations in symptomology in the ordinary course, and apparent temporal associations with exposure may be due to pure chance. Even if the dechallenge or rechallenge is conducted prospectively with the intent of testing a causal hypothesis, a perceived effect in one person has limited scientific value at best.[98] Because the data are limited to a single observation, a trial court must be particularly diligent in determining whether the dechallenge/rechallenge was conducted under strict controls to account for potential confounding influences. Prospective dechallenge/rechallenge experiments – sometimes referred to as "single subject" or "n of 1" experiments – have numerous limitations that preclude general causation conclusions.[99] "[W]ithout strong assumptions regarding how an intervention on one individual relates to its effects on others, the results from a single-subject design provide little useful information ... [and e]xamination of a single subject cannot verify those assumptions."[100] As courts have explained, a prospective dechallenge/rechallenge report "constitutes but one single, uncontrolled experiment."[101]

9.2.2.5 Secondary Source Materials

In addition to actual scientific or anecdotal data, causation experts will sometimes rely on secondary source materials that cite to the primary evidence, such as regulatory materials, textbooks, and internal company documents. These secondary materials do not add any additional scientific knowledge and are no more reliable than the evidence they cite.[102] They do not test a causal hypothesis; they merely report the findings of others.

In particular, regulatory findings do not provide relevant "peer review" for a causation opinion, because they are based on a risk-utility analysis that involves a much lower standard of proof than that which is demanded by a court of law.[103] For example, one article reported that the vast majority of regulatory withdrawals of approvals for drugs in Spain during the 1990s were based solely on case reports.[104] As one commentary observed, "law, societal considerations, costs, politics, and the likelihood of litigation challenging a given regulation all influence the level of scientific proof required by the regulator decision-maker in setting regulatory standards and make such standards problematic as reference points in litigation."[105]

9.2.2.6 The Scientific Method vs. Weight of the Evidence

One key issue in the assessment of general causation expert testimony is whether trial courts should defer to the expert's inchoate "weighing of the evidence" or instead require the expert to demonstrate that the individual lines of evidence upon which he relies are independently reliable evidence of causation. As a number of courts have noted, when predicated on individually unreliable pieces of evidence, the weight of the evidence methodology is inherently faulty because "[i]t amounts to a hollow whole of hollow parts."[106] Nonetheless, a number of courts have erroneously accepted "weight of the evidence" testimony.

In *Milward v. Acuity Specialty Products Group, Inc.*, the First Circuit Court of Appeals held that an expert witness could reliably opine as to whether benzene could cause a rare type of acute myeloid leukemia based upon his inchoate "weight of the evidence" assessment where none of the individual lines of evidence reliably supported a causation opinion.[107] The First Circuit explained that the plaintiffs' expert's "weight of the evidence" approach employed the methodology of abductive inference or inference to the best explanation, whereby – rather than drawing conclusions through logical inferences from known propositions or from a range of known particulars – conclusions "are drawn about a particular proposition or event by a process of eliminating all other possible conclusions to arrive at the most likely one, the one that best explains the available data."[108] The central flaw in the First Circuit's holding is that:

> [T] here is no way for a court to so evaluate the "weight of the evidence" approach followed by the Milwards' expert. An "inference to the best explanation" cannot be tested, it cannot be falsified, and it cannot be validated against known or potential rates of error. Ultimately, then, the court is left with nothing but the expert's self-serving assurances that he has weighed the evidence in a scientifically appropriate manner.[109]

In *Joiner*, the U.S. Supreme Court rejected a similar undefined weighing of evidence that was independently insufficient to support causation.[110] The Fifth and Tenth Circuits, along with numerous courts in other jurisdictions, also have expressly rejected causation opinions in which experts sought to aggregate individually unreliable lines of scientific evidence into a purportedly reliable "weight of the evidence."[111]

9.2.3 Causation Opinions Based On Clinical Reasoning

The question of whether clinical reasoning can reliably support a causation opinion must be considered separately with respect to general causation and specific causation. Doctors do not in their ordinary clinical practice reach scientifically reliable determinations regarding general causation; they make individualized treatment decisions based on the exigencies of the moment. Accordingly, clinical reasoning cannot reliably support a general causation opinion. On the other hand, clinical reasoning through a differential diagnosis may provide reliable support for a specific causation opinion, so long as the diagnosis is reached in a manner that it is faithful to the scientific method. Differential diagnoses conducted for tort litigation purposes raise unique issues of reliability, however, because they generally are conducted *post hoc* and not in the context of medical treatment.

9.2.3.1 Clinical Reasoning and General Causation

Doctors in their day-to-day practice are required to make treatment decisions for individual patients based upon the clinical information before them. These clinical judgments do not provide a reliable basis for a general causation opinion.[112] Courts have recognized that "[t]he ability to diagnose medical conditions is not remotely the same … as the ability to deduce … in a scientifically reliable manner, the causes of those medical conditions."[113] Doctors do not conduct scientific testing in their daily practice to determine whether particular substances can cause particular injuries. Indeed, few doctors have more than rudimentary training in the scientific methods used to determine causation.[114] Instead, they reach working diagnoses and make conservative medical judgments based on their Hippocratic oath to "first, do no harm."[115] Thus, for example, if a patient reports a recent exposure to a new medication or chemical substance, the doctor may order the patient to avoid further exposures based not on a scientific determination of causality but simply as a no-risk prophylactic measure.[116]

While doctors may reach tentative opinions regarding causation in the course of providing treatment, their opinions are not reached pursuant to the scientific method, but are instead based on inferential leaps that allow them to provide immediate therapeutic care. Clinical causation opinions based on differential diagnosis are "a mixture of science and art, far too complicated for its accuracy to be assessed quantitatively or for a meaningful error rate to be calculated."[117] Moreover, differential diagnosis only "follow[s] the causal stream up to a point where intervention is possible" because, typically, physicians "do not care about a disease's etiology ... unless understanding causation would assist in diagnosis and treatment."[118] As one court explained,

> Doctors in their day-to-day practices stumble upon coincidental occurrences and random events and often follow human nature, which is to confuse association and causation. They are programmed by human nature and the rigors and necessities of clinical practices to conclude that temporal association equals causation, or at least that it provides an adequate proxy in the chaotic and sometimes inconclusive world of medicine. This shortcut aids doctors in their clinical practices because the most important objective day-to-day is to help their patients and "first do no harm," as their Hippocratic oath requires. Consequently, they make leaps of faith. … [This type of] clinical impression is not the sort of scientific methodology that *Daubert* demands.[119]

Plaintiffs' counsel seeking to rely on clinical reasoning to support a general causation opinion will often cite to the language in *Kumho Tire* that an expert must "employ[] in the courtroom the same level of intellectual rigor that characterizes the practice of the expert in the relevant field."[120] This argument is misplaced, because, as explained above, "the relevant field[s]" for a general causation opinion are epidemiology and toxicology, not clinical medicine.[121] Plaintiffs' counsel will also argue that differential diagnosis is a well-recognized, scientifically reliable technique. But differential diagnosis is a reliable methodology only for "ruling out" alternative causes of injury from a list of possible causes; it does not "rule in" a substance as a potential cause in the first instance.[122] Courts therefore recognize that absent of a reliable general causation opinion, a differential diagnosis opinion is insufficient evidence of causation.[123]

9.2.3.2 Clinical Reasoning and Specific Causation

Although insufficient for purposes of general causation, a differential diagnosis may provide a scientifically reliable basis for a specific causation opinion – *i.e.*, that an established toxin in fact caused a plaintiff's injury. "In performing a differential diagnosis, a physician begins by 'ruling in' all scientifically plausible causes of the plaintiff's injury. The physician then 'rules out' the least plausible causes of injury until the most likely cause remains. The final result of a differential diagnosis is the expert's conclusion that a defendant's product caused (or did not cause) the plaintiff's injury."[124] However, an expert's bare assertion that he applied a differential diagnosis is not sufficient to satisfy *Daubert*. "[A]n expert does not establish the reliability of his techniques or the validity of his conclusions simply by claiming that he performed a differential diagnosis on a patient."[125] A trial court must determine whether the differential diagnosis is based on a reliable methodology. Accordingly, the expert must demonstrate that the differential diagnosis was based on a sufficient and valid clinical investigation.[126] The expert also must have a scientifically reliable basis for excluding alternative causes of the plaintiff's injury, including the possibility that the injury was idiopathic.[127] If the expert is the plaintiff's own treating physician, the same rigorous *Daubert* analysis applies to his or her proffered specific causation opinion.[128]

In analyzing the reliability of a specific causation opinion based on differential diagnosis, trial courts must ensure that the expert employs "the same level of intellectual rigor" in the courtroom as a treating physician would employ in the ordinary care of patients.[129] An expert cannot simply look for all possible causes of a person's illness from the universe of potential causes and declare that each of them – including the exposure at issue – should be considered actual but-for causes for purposes of tort liability.[130] Even if an expert can show reliable scientific evidence supporting some level of increased risk from a drug, the expert cannot reliably point to the drug as the cause of an individual plaintiff's injury if that plaintiff has other independent risk factors that are more strongly associated with the injury in question. For example, assume that there is scientifically reliable epidemiological evidence showing a 3 times statistically significant increased risk of stroke in patients who used a given drug X. That evidence may be sufficient to support an expert's specific causation opinion with regard to a plaintiff who has no other risk factor for stroke. However, it would not be sufficient to support a specific causation opinion with regard to a patient who also suffers from uncontrolled hypertension and has smoked a pack of cigarettes a day for the past 20 years given the greater risks posed by those co-morbid conditions. Where a plaintiff has other established risk factors that could have caused the plaintiff's injury, the expert must explain how he ruled out these other potential causes to reliably support an opinion that the injury was due instead to a drug exposure.[131]

A trial court also needs to evaluate an expert's differential diagnosis in light of the artificial circumstances in which it is reached. Unlike differential diagnoses conducted by doctors in their day-to-day practice, a differential diagnosis in a litigation context is often conducted in support of an already asserted legal claim of causation. This raises myriad possibilities of bias, both intentional and unintentional.

Consider a hypothetical example of typical large-scale drug product liability litigation. Based on anecdotal reports of adverse events and possibly pressure from special interest organizations like Public Citizen, the FDA recommends labeling changes or withdraws approval of a drug.[132] The same day, if not before, plaintiffs' firms will begin advertising for potential plaintiffs through various forms of media, including the internet, television, radio, and print media. Provided that the drug has been used by a relatively large number of patients, there will be a ready population of patients that had adverse events while taking the drug based solely on statistical chance due to the background rates of such events regardless of drug use. Accordingly, plaintiffs' counsel can quickly gather a large pool of potential plaintiffs.

Plaintiffs' counsel will then start weeding through that pool to exclude individuals with obvious alternative causes for their injuries and patients whose injury did not emerge in temporal proximity to their ingestion of the drug. At first blush, this might appear to be a reliable method for determining those individuals whose injuries were more likely due to the drug. That interpretation, however, is based on the false premise that medicine can always find a cause for an injury. In fact, there are many conditions for which medicine frequently cannot find a cause.[133] In other words, there is often a measurable background rate of *idiopathic* injuries, *i.e.*, injuries with unknown causes. In addition, "[t]emporal proximity is generally not a reliable indicator of a causal relationship."[134] Plaintiffs' counsel's weeding out process, accordingly, often merely identifies the statistically-expected population of patients who coincidentally had adverse events of unknown cause while taking the drug.

At the same time plaintiffs' counsel are reviewing their potential plaintiff population, they will also be looking for an expert witness to provide a specific causation opinion. Generally, plaintiffs' counsel will select an expert who is already prepared to offer a favorable general causation opinion. Plaintiffs' counsel will also select an expert witness who is pre-disposed towards providing a favorable specific causation opinion. This does not mean that the expert is intentionally biased or insincere in his opinion, but it does mean that the expert will enter the process with a preconceived assumption of causality.

By the time the expert and plaintiff are brought together for purposes of a differential diagnosis, the result is effectively preordained. The expert will start his examination from the premise that the substance at issue is dangerous and a likely cause of injury regardless of potential alternative causes. The plaintiff will not present with obvious alternative causes of injury sufficient to shake the expert from his initial presumption. Moreover, in cases where the expert is not the patient's treating physician, the expert will not test his initial diagnosis through ongoing observation and medical treatment.

This "differential diagnosis" bears little resemblance to a differential diagnosis conducted by treating physicians in their regular practice, and cannot provide the type of objective validation that *Daubert* requires for admissibility of an expert specific causation opinion. Trial courts must recognize that there is an inherent "selection bias" at work in mass drug product liability litigation and carefully evaluate the expert's specific causation opinion with this artificial background in mind.

9.2.4 The Parlodel® Litigation

During the 1990s and 2000s, a number of product liability cases involving the prescription drug Parlodel® worked their way through the courts. The Parlodel® litigation resulted in a body of *Daubert* case law that squarely addresses the issues of medical causation expert testimony discussed above and provides a detailed analysis of "all of the components of the 'causation' argument that are available to experts in the most contentious of products liability case[s]."[135]

A judicial consensus emerged that plaintiffs' experts' causation opinions in the Parlodel® litigation do not satisfy the requirements of *Daubert*. Three federal appellate courts, the Eighth, Tenth, and Eleventh Circuits, unanimously affirmed district court opinions excluding the causation opinions of plaintiffs' experts, and four other published district court opinions excluding this testimony were not appealed.[136] A few earlier district court opinions, two of which were drafted by the same magistrate judge, have gone the other way.[137] The Parlodel® opinions thus provide a useful *Daubert* case study of courts that properly evaluated medical causation testimony based on the scientific method and those that do not.

9.2.4.1 Plaintiffs' Allegations Regarding Parlodel®

Parlodel® (bromocriptine mesylate) is an FDA-approved drug used for a variety of indications, including Parkinson's Disease, amenorrhea/galactorrhea (lack of menses), infertility, and acromegaly (a growth disorder). From 1980 to 1994, Parlodel® was also approved for the prevention of postpartum lactation ("PPL") in women who elected not to breast-feed. The manufacturer of Parlodel® withdrew the drug from the market for this PPL indication following receipt of a number of case reports of strokes, seizures, and myocardial infarctions and an FDA advisory committee determination that there was limited need for pharmaceutical treatment for PPL. The FDA withdrew its approval of Parlodel® for the PPL indication in 1995, based on its conclusion that the limited utility of the drug for PPL did not outweigh the possible risks.[138]

Plaintiffs' experts allege that Parlodel® causes vasoconstriction (a narrowing of blood vessels) which they allege can cause stroke, seizures, and myocardial infarction. Plaintiffs' experts' concede that the epidemiological studies conducted on the drug have not established a causal link with these injuries and that there is a body of controlled clinical research in humans that has found that Parlodel® has the exact opposite effect of causing vasodilation (a widening of blood vessels). Plaintiffs' experts also concede that controlled intact animal research has not shown a causal link between Parlodel® and strokes, seizures, or myocardial infarctions in animals. Plaintiffs' experts base their causation opinion on anecdotal case reports (including alleged dechallenge/rechallenge reports), animal research involving limited endpoints, chemical analogies, a variety of secondary source materials, and differential diagnoses.[139]

9.2.4.2 Opinions Admitting Plaintiffs' Experts' Causation Opinions

The district courts that have admitted plaintiffs' experts' causation opinions have relied primarily on differential diagnoses and the determination that lesser scientific evidence of general causation should be accepted because it allegedly would not be possible to conduct an epidemiological study of sufficient strength to adequately test plaintiffs' experts' causation hypothesis. Thus, one magistrate judge dismissed the lack of any direct scientific evidence supporting plaintiffs' experts' causation opinion, reasoning that "[s]cience, like many other human endeavors, draws conclusions from circumstantial evidence, when other, better forms of evidence [are] not available."[140] In a subsequent opinion, the same magistrate judge sounded a similar theme: "In science, as in life, where there is smoke, fire can be inferred, subject to debate and further testing."[141] The court was similarly deferential in its review of plaintiffs' experts' specific causation opinions. While noting that there were a number of alternative causes for the injuries at issue, the court found that the "debate creates a question about the weight to be accorded the plaintiffs' experts' opinions, but it does not affect the admissibility."[142]

Missing in these opinions is any recognition of the requirement in *Daubert* that the experts' causation opinions be based on the scientific method of testing and validating hypotheses. *Daubert* does not permit expert testimony to be admitted based on the smoke of anecdotal reports and inferences, nor does it allow courts to lower the bar of scientific reliability based on a perceived lack of relevant scientific evidence. In accepting plaintiffs' experts' lower showing of evidence, these courts abdicated their gatekeeping responsibility.

9.2.4.3 Opinions Excluding Plaintiffs' Experts' Opinions

By contrast, in the Parlodel® cases in which courts have evaluated plaintiffs' experts' opinions based on the scientific method, the experts' testimony has been excluded. These courts have conducted detailed analyses of each of the different categories of evidence discussed above, and their reasoning and conclusions are incorporated in that discussion. The overarching theme in these opinions is the courts' recognition that medical causation opinions are not admissible unless they are based upon scientifically tested and validated hypotheses.

As these courts have explained, *Daubert* does not establish a "best efforts" test.[143] An expert cannot satisfy *Daubert* by arguing that he has "used the best methodology available under the circumstance,"[144] or that he has "done the best [he] could with the available data and the scientific literature."[145] Rather, the expert must answer the "key question," whether the "theory being advanced by the expert is testable or has been tested, the methodology of which is what distinguishes science from other fields of human inquiry."[146] "The hallmark of [*Daubert*'s] reliability prong is the scientific method, *i.e.*, the generation of testable hypotheses that are then subjected to the real world crucible of experimentation, falsification/validation, and replication."[147] The "testing of hypotheses" is "a critical aspect of the application of the scientific method."[148] Expert opinions "reposed in the realm of 'may cause' or 'possibly could cause'" must be excluded.[149] "While hypothesis is essential in the scientific community because it leads to advances in science, speculation in the courtroom cannot aid the fact finder in making a determination of whether liability exists."[150]

These Parlodel® cases forcefully answer critics of *Daubert* who argue for a lower standard based on deferential review of medical causation testimony:

> The *Daubert* trilogy, in shifting the focus to the kind of empirically supported, rationally explained reasoning

> required in science, has greatly improved the quality of the evidence upon which juries base their verdicts. Although making determinations of reliability may present the court with the difficult task of ruling on matters that are outside its field of expertise, this is less objectionable than dumping a barrage of scientific evidence on a jury, who would likely be less equipped than a judge to make reliability and relevancy determinations.[151]

The scientific method serves as a bulwark against subjective judgments and inspired guesswork masquerading as scientific knowledge. Courts that ignore the scientific method in their review of medical causation opinions do a disservice to the legal system and disregard the Supreme Court's mandate.

9.2.5 Conclusion

Faced with the exacting standards of *Daubert*, plaintiffs' causation experts will often respond with a spaghetti-on-the-wall strategy in the hope that something will stick. The Supreme Court's adoption of the scientific method as the central guide to admissibility provides district courts with the solution they need to untangle the mess. For each strand in plaintiffs' expert's analysis, the questions are the same: Is the expert relying on evidence that has been tested and validated, and does the evidence fit the question at issue? Unless an expert can answer both of these questions in the affirmative, he should not be allowed to serve up his opinions to a jury.

As Supreme Court Justice Breyer explained in his concurring opinion in *Joiner*, the evidentiary safeguards imposed by the courts against unreliable science provide an important bulwark against unfounded litigation that can threaten access to needed healthcare:

> [M]odern life, including good health as well as economic well-being, depends upon the use of artificial or manufactured substances ... [I]t may, therefore, prove particularly important to see that judges fulfill their *Daubert* gatekeeping function, so that they help assure that the powerful engine of tort liability, which can generate strong financial incentives to reduce, or to eliminate, production, points toward the right substances and does not destroy the wrong ones.[152]

While this textbook has focused primarily on the dangers of *drug abuse*, the potential dangers of *litigation abuse* on the availability of medically-indicated pharmaceutical products also pose a threat to patient health that must not be ignored.

NOTES

1. Mr. Lasker and Ms. Barago are attorneys in the Washington, D.C. law firm Hollingsworth LLP, where they specialize in pharmaceutical and toxic tort litigation.
2. 509 U.S. 579 (1993).
3. *Weisgram v. Marley Co.*, 528 U.S. 440, 455 (2000).
4. 522 U.S. 136 (1997).
5. 526 U.S. 137 (1999).
6. *See, e.g., Raynor v. Merrell Pharms. Inc.*, 104 F. 3d 1371, 1376 (D.C. Cir. 1997).
7. One survey of 400 state trial judges found that while a large majority of judges agreed that the role of "gatekeeper" was an appropriate one for a judge, most judges did not have a proper understanding of the scientific principles set forth in *Daubert. See* Sophia I. Gatowski, *et al., Asking the Gatekeepers: A National Survey of Judges on Judging Expert Evidence in a Post-Daubert World*, 25(5) Law and Human Behavior 433 (2001).
8. David E. Bernstein, *The Misbegotten Judicial Resistance to the Daubert Revolution*, 89 NOTRE DAME L. REV. 27, 29-30 (2013); see also David E. Bernstein & Eric G. Lasker, Defending Daubert: It's Time to Amend Federal Rule of Evidence 702, 57(1) W & M Law Rev. 1 (2015).
9. *See, e.g.*, J. Kassirer & J. Cecil, *Inconsistency in Evidentiary Standards for Medical Testimony: Disorder in the Courts*, 288(11) JAMA 1382-87 (Sept. 2002); M. Berger, *Upsetting the Balance Between Adverse Interests: The Impact of the Supreme Court's Trilogy on Expert Testimony in Toxic Tort Litigation*, 64 SUM Law & Contemp. Probs. 289 (Spring/Summer 2001).
10. Terence F. Kiely, Science and Litigation: Products Liability in Theory and Practice 177 (CRC Press 2002).
11. 509 U.S. at 590.
12. *Id.* at 593. The Supreme Court cited to two philosophical texts on the nature of scientific evidence. *See id.* (citing C. Hempel, The Philosophy of Natural Science 49 (1966) ("[T]he statements constituting a scientific explanation must be capable of an empirical test"); K. Popper, Conjectures and Refutations: The Growth of Scientific Knowledge 37 (5th ed. 1989) ("[T]he criterion of the scientific status of a theory is its falsifiability, or refutability, or testability")).
13. *Id.* at 591.
14. The four factors discussed in *Daubert* provide different methods by which an expert's opinion can be analyzed for adherence to the scientific method. Two of the factors, testing and error rates, are integral parts of the scientific method itself. The other two factors, peer review and general acceptance, can provide independent support that the opinion was properly derived by the scientific method. Peer review, however, should not be mindlessly equated with publication. As the Supreme Court noted, publication "is but one element of peer review." *Daubert*, 509 U.S. at 593. Peer review, like general acceptance, refers more broadly to the concept that the theory at issue has been subjected to and found valid through empirical testing by the broader scientific community. *See generally* W. Anderson, *et al., Daubert's Backwash: Litigation-Generated Science*, 34 U. Mich. J.L. Reform 619 (2001); E. Chan, *The "Brave New World" of Daubert: True Peer Review, Editorial Peer Review, and Scientific Validity*, 70 N.Y.U. L. Rev. 100 (1995).
15. *Daubert*, 509 U.S. at 596-97.
16. *Id.* at 597.
17. *Id.*
18. 522 U.S. at 145.
19. *See id.* at 146 ("conclusions and methodology are not entirely distinct from one another").
20. *Id.*
21. *See* 526 U.S. at 157 (noting with respect to challenged tire expert's testimony that "despite the prevalence of tire testing," plaintiffs did not "refer to any articles or papers that validate [the expert's] approach").

22. *Id.* at 152.
23. Kassirer & Cecil, *supra* note 9, at 1384, 1386; *see also* Berger, *supra* note 9.
24. 509 U.S. at 597.
25. *Rosen v. Ciba-Geigy Corp.*, 78 F.3d 316, 319 (7th Cir. 1996).
26. *See, e.g., Soldo v. Sandoz Pharms. Corp.*, 244 F. Supp. 2d 434, 532 (W.D. Pa. 2003) (epidemiology is "the primary generally accepted methodology for demonstrating a causal relation between a chemical compound and a set of symptoms or a disease") (quoting *Conde v. Velsicol Chem. Corp.*, 804 F. Supp. 972, 1025-26 (S.D. Ohio 1992), *aff'd*, 24 F.3d 809 (6th Cir. 1994)); *Hollander v. Sandoz Pharms. Corp.*, 95 F. Supp. 2d 1230, 1235, n.14 (W.D. Okla. 2000) ("In the absence of an understanding of the biological and pathological mechanisms by which disease develops, epidemiological evidence is the most valid type of scientific evidence of toxic causation"), *aff'd*, 289 F.3d 1193 (10th Cir. 2002); *Breast Implant Litig.*, 11 F. Supp. 2d 1217, 1224-25 (D. Colo. 1998) (same, citing cases).
27. There has been some controversy regarding whether certain types of epidemiological studies should be considered inherently more reliable than others in establishing causation. Historically, courts have understood that randomized controlled clinical trials are less likely to report erroneous associations than observational epidemiological studies, like cohort or case control studies. *See In re Rezulin Prod. Liab. Litig.*, 369 F. Supp. 2d 398, 406 (S.D.N.Y. 2005); *see also* David H. Kaye & David A. Freeman, *Reference Guide on Statistics*, Reference Manual on Scientific Evidence (2d ed. 2000) at 94-95. However, research suggests that this understanding may be mistaken, *see* John Concato, *et. al.*, *Randomized, Controlled Trials, Observational Studies, and the Hierarchy of Research Design*, 342(25) New Eng. J. Med. 1887 (2000); John Concato, *Observational Versus Experimental Studies: What's the Evidence for a Hierarchy*?, 1 J. Am. Soc. Experimental NeuroTherapeutics 341 (2004). In a review of the most highly cited clinical research (defined as studies cited more than 1,000 times in the literature), a scientist concluded that 16% of the top-cited clinical research studies relating to medical interventions had been contradicted within the following 15 years and another 16% were followed by subsequent research suggesting that the initial findings may have been overstated. John P.A. Ioannidis, *Contradicted and Initially Stronger Effects in Highly Cited Clinical Research*, 294(2) JAMA 218 (2005). While epidemiological evidence can provide the best evidence of causation, as explained below, even the best study cannot establish that causation in fact exists.
28. *See, e.g., Glastetter v. Novartis Pharms. Corp.*, 252 F.3d 986, 992 (8th Cir. 2001) (while not an absolute prerequisite, the lack of epidemiology "limited the available tools with which [plaintiff] could prove causation," and is a factor to be considered in evaluating the reliability of plaintiff's experts' methodology); *Siharath v. Sandoz Pharms. Corp.*, 131 F. Supp. 2d 1347, 1358 (N.D. Ga. 2001), *aff'd sub. nom Rider v. Sandoz Pharms. Corp.*, 295 F.3d 1194 (11th Cir. 2002).
29. *Perry v. Novartis Pharm. Corp.*, 564 F. Supp. 2d 452, 465 (E.D. Pa. 2008) (finding it "disquieting that [plaintiff's expert] fails to even mention [the only published epidemiology] study in his initial report."); *see also Gannon v. United States.*, 292 F. App'x 170, 174 (3d Cir. 2008) (expert testimony disallowed where expert, as well as Institute of Medicine, agreed epidemiologic evidence did not support causal relationship); *Norris v. Baxter Healthcare Corp.*, 397 F.3d 878, 882 (10th Cir. 2005) (where a large body of contrary epidemiological evidence exists, "it is necessary to at least address it with evidence that is based on medically reliable and scientifically valid methodology").
30. *See Arias v. DynCorp*, 928 F. Supp. 2d 10, 24-25 (D.D.C. 2013) (excluding opinion of expert who failed to explain why he credited one study and dismissed another); *Cano v. Everest Minerals Corp.*, 362 F. Supp. 2d 814, 850 (W.D. Tex. 2005) (rejecting testimony of expert who "sifted through the literature to pick and choose positive relative risks between ionizing radiation (of any type, source, and dose) and a particular Plaintiff's cancer").
31. *See* Michael D. Green, *Reference Guide on Epidemiology*, Reference Manual on Scientific Evidence (2d ed. 2000) at 336.
32. *See Magistrini v. One Hour Martinizing Dry Cleaning*, 180 F. Supp. 2d 584, 591 (D.N.J. 2002), *aff'd*, 68 Fed. Appx. 356 (3d Cir. 2003); *Caraker v. Sandoz Pharms. Corp.*, 188 F. Supp 2d 1026, 1032 (S.D. Ill 2001); *see also* Eddy A. Bresnitz, *Principles of Research Design* in Goldfrank's Toxicologic Emergencies 1827-28 (Goldfrank, *et al.* eds. 6th ed. 1998).
33. *See Joiner*, 522 U.S. at 145-46.
34. *See Turpin v. Merrell Dow Pharms., Inc.*, 959 F.2d 1349, 1353 n.1 (6th Cir. 1992).
35. *Id.*, at 723 (citing *DeLuca v. Merrell Dow Pharms., Inc.*, 791 F. Supp. 1042, 1046 (D.N.J. 1992), *aff'd*, 6 F.3d 778 (3d Cir. 1993)).
36. *See Joiner*, 522 U.S. at 145; *see also Wells v. SmithKline Beecham Corp.*, 601 F.3d 375, 380 (5th Cir. 2010) ("this court has frowned on causative conclusions bereft of statistically significant epidemiological support"); *Dunn v. Sandoz Pharms. Corp.*, 275 F. Supp. 2d 672, 681 (M.D.N.C. 2003) ("statistically insignificant results do not constitute proof" of causation); *Soldo*, 244 F. Supp. 2d at 533 ("Courts have emphasized that epidemiologic proof must be statistically significant.") (citing cases); *Caraker*, 188 F. Supp. 2d at 1034 (rejecting experts' causation opinions "inasmuch as they rely on selective use of statistically insignificant data from epidemiological studies"). Although some courts recently have questioned the necessity of statistically significant studies to support a causation opinion, they recognize that experts must adhere to the usual practice of their profession, which, for statisticians and epidemiologists, among others, entails finding a statistically significant association. *See In re Lipitor (Atorvastatin Calcium) Mktg., Sales Practices & Prods. Liab. Litig.*, 892 F. 3d 624, 642 (4th Cir. 2018) (district court correctly excluded opinion of statistician who did not adhere to the "norm" of first finding "a statistically significant association").
37. *See Magistrini*, 180 F. Supp. 2d at 591; *Siharath*, 131 F. Supp. 2d at 1356; *In re Breast Implant Litig.*, 11 F. Supp. 2d at 1225-26; *Hall v. Baxter Healthcare Corp.*, 947 F. Supp. 1387, 1403-04 (D. Or. 1996); *see also Daubert v. Merrell Dow Pharms., Inc*, 43 F.3d 1311, 1321 (9th Cir. 1995) ("*Daubert II*") ("A relative risk of less than two may suggest teratogenicity, but it actually tends to *dis*prove legal causation as it shows that Bendectin does not double the likelihood of birth defects"). *But cf. In re Hanford Nuclear Reservation Litig.*, 292 F.3d 1124, 1137 (9th Cir. 2002) (plaintiffs did not need to present epidemiological evidence showing a doubling of cancer risk from ionizing radiation at specific exposure levels because capability of ionizing radiation to cause cancer generally has been recognized by scientific and legal authority).

38. *See Newman v. Motorola, Inc.*, 218 F. Supp. 2d 769, 779 (D. Md. 2002), *aff'd* 62 Fed. R. Evid. Serv. 1289 (4th Cir. 2003).
39. *See Magistrini*, 180 F. Supp. 2d at 592.
40. *See Merrell Dow Pharms. v. Havner*, 953 S.W.2d 706, 719 (Tex. 1997); *see also* Bresnitz, *supra* note 32, at 1831-32; Michael D. Green, et al., *Reference Guide on Epidemiology*, Reference Manual on Scientific Evidence at 389, 392, & 395 (2d ed. 2000) (discussing sources of bias); David A. Grimes & Kenneth F. Schulz, *Bias and causal associations in observational research*, 359 The Lancet 248 (Jan. 19, 2002) (same, including real world examples of confounding errors).
41. *Magistrini*, 180 F. Supp. 2d at 591; *Caraker*, 188 F. Supp. 2d at 1032; *see also Havner*, 953 S.W.2d at 719 ("Bias can dramatically affect the scientific reliability of an epidemiological study.").
42. *See Nelson v. Tennessee Gas Pipeline Co.*, 243 F.3d 244, 252-54 (6th Cir. 2001) (expert's failure to account for confounding factors in cohort study or alleged PCB exposures rendered his opinion unreliable); *see also In re Bextra & Celebrex Mktg. Sales Practices & Prod. Liab. Litig.*, 524 F. Supp. 2d 1166, 1179 (N.D. Cal. 2007) (not scientifically reliable for expert to rely on study that failed to account for critical confounding factors).
43. *See Allison v McGhan Med. Corp.*, 184 F.3d 1300, 1315 (11th Cir. 1999) (noting that the women participating in the study at issue "were aware of the hypothesis, a factor which could have created bias, skewing the results and ultimately making the conclusions suspect").
44. *See Newman*, 218 F. Supp. 2d at 778; *see also Maras v. Avis Rent A Car Sys., Inc.*, 393 F. Supp. 2d 801, 808 (D. Minn. 2005) (rejecting expert testimony based on epidemiological study that, among other failures, may have been influenced by recall bias).
45. *In re TMI Litig.*, 193 F.3d 613, 707-08 (3d Cir. 1999); *see also Bouchard v. Am. Home Prods. Corp.*, 213 F. Supp. 2d 802, 809-10 (N.D. Ohio 2002) (excluding expert causation testimony to the extent based on epidemiological study tainted with selection bias).
46. *See, e.g., Amorgianos v. Nat'l R.R. Passenger Corp.*, 137 F. Supp. 2d 147, 168 (E.D.N.Y. 2001), *aff'd*, 303 F.3d 256 (2d Cir. 2002).
47. *Havner*, 953 S.W.2d at 718.
48. *See Dunn*, 275 F. Supp 2d at 677-78; *Magistrini*, 180 F. Supp. 2d at 592-93; *Amorgianos*, 137 F. Supp. 2d at 168; *Castellow v. Chevron* USA, 97 F. Supp. 2d 780, 786-87 & n.2 (S.D. Tex. 2000); *In re Breast Implants*, 11 F. Supp. 2d at 1233 n.5; *Havner*, 953 S.W.2d at 718 & n.2.
49. *Id.*; *see also* Bresnitz, supra note 32, at 1827-28 (describing Bradford Hill criteria in detail); Grimes & Schulz, *supra* note 40 (same); Douglas L. Weed, *Underdetermination and Incommensurability in Contemporary Epidemiology*, 7(2) Kennedy Institute of Ethics Journal 107, 113-15 (1997) (same).
50. *See Allison*, 184 F.3d at 1315 (noting that statistically significant epidemiological study reporting an increased risk of marker of disease of 1.24 times in patients with breast implants was so close to 1.0 that it "was not worth serious consideration for proving causation."); *In re Breast Implants Litig.*, 11 F. Supp. 2d at 1227 (same).
51. *See Havner*, 953 S.W.2d at 719.
52. *See, e.g., Miller v. Pfizer, Inc.*, 196 F. Supp. 2d 1062, (D. Kan. 2002) (expert failed to address "fact that other research is contrary to his conclusion), *aff'd*, 356 F.3d 1326 (10th Cir.), *cert denied*, 125 S. Ct. 40 (2004); *Havner*, 953 S.W.2d at 727 ("if scientific methodology is followed, a single study would not be viewed as indicating that it is 'more probable than not' that an association exists").
53. *See Joiner*, 522 U.S. at 145-46 (studies proffered as evidence of PCB-lung cancer link involved exposures to mineral oils or other potential carcinogens); *Burleson v. Tex. Dep't. of Criminal Justice*, 393 F.3d 577, 585-86 (5th Cir. 2004) (rejecting expert testimony where expert could not point to epidemiological studies demonstrating statistically significant link between thorium dioxide exposure and plaintiff's type of lung or throat cancer); *Allison*, 184 F.3d at 1315 (studies reported link to injuries not suffered by plaintiff); *Schudel v. Gen. Elec. Co.*, 120 F.3d 991, 997 (9th Cir. 1997) (studies involved exposures to organic solvents other than those at issue); *Magistrini*, 180 F. Supp. 2d at 603-04 (to same effect); *see also Wells*, 601 F.3d at 380 (rejecting as reliable causation evidence a study reporting "a class association, as opposed to a specific medication, finding"); *Jones v. Novartis Pharm. Corp.*, 235 F. Supp. 3d 1244, 1270 (N.D. Ala. 2017) (rejecting general causation opinion based on an association for an entire drug class, and not an association between the specific drug at issue and the injury alleged), *aff'd*, 720 F. App'x. 1006 (11th Cir. 2018).
54. *See Newman*, 218 F. Supp. 2d at 778 (no dose response relationship found in study involving cell phone use and cancer); *Kelley v. Am. Heyer-Schulte Corp.*, 957 F. Supp. 873, 879 (W.D. Tex. 1997).
55. *See Hollander,* 289 F.3d at 1204 (rejecting expert's causation testimony despite his claimed adherence to the Bradford Hill methodology): *Dunn,* 275 F. Supp. 2d at 677-78 (same).
56. *See Lust v. Merrell Dow Pharms. Inc.*, 89 F.3d 594, 598 (9th Cir 1996) ("the district court should be wary that the [expert's] method has not been faithfully applied"); *O'Conner v. Commonwealth Edison Co.*, 13 F.3d 1090, 1106-07 (7th Cir. 1994) (excluding opinion where expert did not follow his own expressed methodology for establishing causation); *Knight v. Kirby Inland Marine, Inc.*, 363 F. Supp. 2d 859, 864 (N.D. Miss. 2005) (expert's "Bradford-Hill analysis is only as reliable as the underlying data upon which it is based"); *Hall*, 947 F. Supp. at 1400 (quoting *Lust*).
57. *See* Weed (1997), *supra* note 49, at 115, 116-18 (discussing Robert A. Hiatt, *Alcohol Consumption and Breast Cancer*, 7 Medical Oncology Tumor Pharmacotherapy 143 (1990) (concluding that women with risk factors for breast cancer should limit alcohol use) and Ernst L. Wynder & Randall E. Harris, *Does Alcohol Consumption Influence the Risk of Developing Breast Cancer?* in Important Advances in Oncology 283 (V.T. Devita, S. Hellman, and S.A. Rosenberg eds. 1989) (concluding that there was no evidence of a causal link)).
58. *In re Lipitor*, 892 F. 3d at 642 (affirming exclusion of expert's general causation opinion where he deviated from the "norm" of relying on a statistically significant association before applying Bradford Hill analysis); *Jones*, 235 F. Supp. 3d at 1269 (holding that, before applying Bradford Hill criteria, expert needed to establish that an association "existed based on existing medical literature").
59. *See, e.g., DeLuca v. Merrell Dow Pharms., Inc.*, 791 F. Supp. 1042, 1046-59 (D.N.J. 1992), *aff'd without op.*, 6 F.3d 778 (3d Cir. 1993); *see also Knight*, 363 F. Supp. 2d at 866 (rejecting causation opinion based on meta-analyses of cancer risks to chemical industry employees).

60. For examples, see Douglas L. Weed, *Interpreting epidemiological evidence; how meta-analysis and causal inference methods are related*, 29 Int'l J. Epidemiol. 387 (2000); Jacques LeLorier, *et. al.*, *Discrepancies Between Meta-Analyses and Subsequent Large Randomized, Controlled Trials*, 337(8) New Eng. J. Med. 536 (1997); Samuel Shapiro, *Is Meta-Analysis a Valid Approach to the Evaluation of Small Effects in Observational Studies?* 50(3) J. Clin. Epidemiol. 223 (1997); Samuel Shapiro, *Meta-analysis/Shmeta-analysis*, 140(9) Am. J. Epid. 771 (Nov. 1994).
61. Shapiro (1994), *supra* note 60, at 771.
62. LeLorier (1997), *supra* note 60, at 541; *see also* J. Berlin et al., *The Use of Meta-Analysis in Pharmacoepidemiology*, in Pharmacoepidemiology at 726 (5th ed. 2012) ("Combining a group of poorly done studies can produce a precise summary result built on a very weak foundation.").
63. *See, e.g.*, Irva Hertz-Picciotto, *Epidemiology and Quantitative Risk Assessment: A Bridge from Science to Policy*, 85(4) Am. J. Public Health. 484, 485 (1995) ("The uncertainty stemming from interspecies extrapolation is far larger than the uncertainty resulting from uncontrolled bias or errors in exposure information in epidemiological studies").
64. *See* Bernard D. Goldstein & Mary Sue Henifen, *Reference Guide on Toxicology*, Reference Manual on Scientific Evidence 420 n.48 (2d ed. 2000). For additional examples of the often dramatic differences in responses among animal species and between animals and humans, see David L. Eaton & Curtis D. Klaassen, *Principles of Toxicology* in Casarett & Doull's Toxicology: The Basic Science of Poisons 25-26 (Curtis D. Klaassen ed., 6th ed. 2001); Elaine M. Faustman & Gilbert S. Omenn, *Risk Assessment*, in Casarett & Doull's Toxicology: The Basic Science of Poisons, *supra*, at 88-90; Lorenz Rhomberg, *Risk Assessment and the use of information on underlying biological mechanisms: A perspective*, 365 Mutation Research 175, 179-80 (1996); Jan M. M. Meijers, *et al.*, *The Predictive Value of Animal Data in Human Cancer Risk Assessment*, 25 Regulatory Toxicology & Pharmacology 94 (1997).
65. *See Chapman v. Procter & Gamble Distrib., LLC*, 766 F.3d 1296, 1308 (11th Cir. 2014); *Johnson v. Arkema, Inc.*, 685 F.3d 452, 463 (5th Cir. 2012) (there is "very limited usefulness of animal studies when confronted with questions of toxicity") (citations omitted); *Siharath*, 131 F. Supp. 2d at 1367; *Wade-Greaux v. Whitehall Labs.,Inc.*, 874 F. Supp. 1441, 1483-84 (D.V.I. 1994), *aff'd without op.*, 46 F.3d 1120 (3d Cir. 1994).
66. *See Soldo*, 244 F. Supp. 2d at 565; *Siharath*, 131 F. Supp. 2d at 1366-67 (citing cases); *see also Newkirk v. ConAgra Foods, Inc.*, 727 F. Supp. 2d 1006, 1026 (E.D. Wash. 2010) (excluding expert who "offers no explanation for how and why the results of [rat] studies can be extrapolated to humans"), *aff'd*, 438 F. App'x 607 (9th Cir. 2011).
67. *See, e.g.*, *Joiner*, 522 U.S. at 144; *Hollander*, 289 F.3d at 1209; *Turpin*, 959 F.2d at 1358-61; *In re Rezulin Prod. Liab. Litig.*, 369 F. Supp. 2d at 406-07; *Caraker*, 188 F. Supp. 2d at 1037; *Wade-Greaux*, 874 F. Supp. at 1477.
68. *See* Eaton & Klaassen, *supra* note 64, at 27.
69. *See id.*; Karl K. Rozman & Curtis D. Klaassen, *Absorption, Distribution, and Excretion of Toxicants*, in Casarett & Doull's Toxicology: The Basic Science of Poisons, at 111.
70. *See* Eaton & Klaassen, *supra* note 64, at 17-18.
71. *Id.* at 21.
72. *Id.* at 13.
73. *See, e.g.*, Meijers, *supra* note 64, at 100 (concluding based on a comparison of animal and epidemiological studies for specific chemicals that "chemicals with little or no cancer potential in humans have been tested at too high concentrations in rodents ... which resulted in the observed carcinogenic effect").
74. *Id.* at 27. Federal regulatory agencies such as the Environmental Protection Agency thus use high dose animal research as a basis for establishing conservative regulatory safe exposure levels for humans (albeit at levels several multiples below that found to have no effect in animals). *See, e.g.*, Faustman & Omenn, *supra* note 64, at 92-94.
75. *See* Rozman & Klaassen, *supra* note 69, at 111; *see also* Meijers, *supra* note 64, at 95-98; Hertz-Picciotto, *supra* note 63, at 485.
76. *See* Eaton & Klaassen, *supra* note 64, at 14; Rozman & Klaassen, *supra* note 69, at 111-14.
77. *See, e.g.*, Rhomberg, *supra* note 64, at 181-83 (discussing carcinogenicity testing in animals engineered to be more susceptible to tumors).
78. Meijers, *supra* note 64, at 98.
79. *Id.*
80. *See Joiner*, 522 U.S. at 145; *see also Glastetter*, 252 F.3d at 991; *In re Accutane Prods. Liab.*, 511 F. Supp. 2d 1288, 1294 (M.D. Fla. 2007) (rat studies involving high doses of different chemical cannot support opinion of expert who fails to show data can be properly extrapolated to humans and who fails to differentiate dog studies with contrary results); *In re Baycol Prods. Litig.*, 532 F. Supp. 2d 1029, 1057-58 (D. Minn. 2007) (rejecting expert reliance on animal studies that neither involved drug in question nor even drugs in same class),), *aff'd*, 596 F.3d 884 (8th Cir. 2010); *Dunn*, 275 F. Supp. 2d at 683 (rejecting animal studies as basis for expert's opinion where expert failed to explain how results of animal studies could be extrapolated to humans).
81. *Caraker*, 188 F. Supp. 2d at 1038; *see also Soldo*, 244 F. Supp. 2d at 549 ("Other federal courts facing proffered expert testimony based on the effects of allegedly similar compounds have reached the same conclusion and rejected such contentions: these courts have found that consideration of the effects of *other* drugs can only lead away from the truth.") (citing cases).
82. *See McClain v. Metabolife Int'l, Inc.*, 401 F.3d 1233, 1246 (11th Cir. 2005); *Rider*, 295 F.3d at 1200-01; *Glastetter*, 252 F.3d at 990; *Schudel*, 120 F.3d at 996-97; *see also Jones*, 235 F. Supp. 3d at 1271-72 (rejecting general causation opinion where expert admitted differences among drugs in the class); *In re Accutane Prods. Liab.*, 511 F. Supp. 2d at 1294 (rejecting expert testimony based on Vitamin A data in case involving Accutane, which is a derivative of Vitamin A).
83. *See, e.g.*, Faustman & Omenn, *supra* note 64, at 86-87; A.M. Richard & R. Benigni, *AI and SAR Approaches for Predicting Chemical Carcinogenicity: Survey and Status* Report, 13(1) SAR and QSAR in Environmental Research 1 (2002); J. Ashby & R.W. Tenant, *Prediction of rodent carcinogenicity for 44 chemicals: results*, 9(1) Mutagenisis 7 (1994).
84. *See* Richard & Benigni, *supra* note 83, at 8, 10.
85. *Id.* at 8; *see also* Ashby & Tenant, *supra* note 83, at abstract ("Carcinogenicity tends to be overpredicted by this integrated technique" of basing predictions on chemical structure, genotoxicity and rodent toxicity.).
86. *See* James D. McKinney, *et al.*, *Forum: The Practice of Structure Activity Relationships (SAR) in Toxicology*, 56 Toxicological Sciences 8, 15 (2000) ("Given the huge range

and variability of possible interactions of chemicals in biological systems, it is highly unlikely that SAR models will ever achieve absolute certainty in predicting a toxicity outcome, particularly in a whole-animal system.").

87. *See* Howard Hu & Frank E. Speizer, *Influence of Environmental and Occupational Hazards on Disease*, in Harrison's Principles of Internal Medicine 19 (Braunwald, *et al.* eds. 15th ed. 2001) ("Case reports either sent to local authorities or published in the literature often prompt follow-up studies that can lead to the identification of new hazards"); David A. Grimes & Kenneth F. Schulz, *Descriptive Studies: what they can and cannot do*, 359 The Lancet 145 (Jan. 12, 2002) ("epidemiologists and clinicians generally use descriptive reports to search for clues of cause of disease – *i.e.*, generation of hypotheses."); J.A. Arnaiz, *et al.*, *The use of evidence in pharmacovigilence: Case reports as the reference source for drug withdrawals*, 57 Eur. J. Clin. Pharmacol 89-91 (2001).
88. *See Chapman,* 766 F.3d at 1308; *Wells*, 601 F.3d at 380; *McClain*, 401 F.3d at 1253-54; *Norris v. Baxter Healthcare Corp.*, 397 F.3d 878, 885 (10th Cir. 2005); *Rider*, 295 F.3d at 1199; *Hollander*, 289 F.3d at 1211; *Glastetter*, 252 F.3d at 989-90; *Soldo*, 244 F. Supp. 2d at 541; *Caraker*, 188 F. Supp. 2d at 1034-35; *Brumbaugh v. Sandoz Pharm. Corp.*, 77 F. Supp. 2d 1153, 1156 (D. Mont. 1999); *see also Siharath*, 131 F. Supp. 2d at 1361-62 (citing cases).
89. *See Rider*, 295 F.3d at 1199; *Glastetter*, 252 F.3d at 989-90; *Soldo*, 244 F. Supp. 2d at 539-40; *see also* Ellenhorn's Medical Toxicology: Diagnosis and Treatment of Human Poisoning 1 (Ellenhorn ed. 2d ed. 1997) ("Case reports demonstrate a temporal but not necessarily causative relationship between exposure and health effects. This information is often confounded by the inability to exclude other causes of illness.").
90. *See* Grimes & Schulz, *supra* note 87, at 148 (case reports, case series, and other descriptive studies "do not allow conclusions about cause of disease").
91. *See, e.g., In re Baycol Prods. Litig.*, 532 F. Supp. 2d at1037-41 (rejecting meta-analysis of ADE data to prove relative toxicities of drugs); *In re Meridia Prods. Liab. Litig.*, 328 F. Supp. 2d 791, 807 (N.D. Ohio 2004) (rejecting plaintiffs' comparison of adverse cardiovascular events reported to FDA with respect to Meridia® and Xenical® and the conclusion that twice as many ADEs for Meridia® compared to Xenical® reflects a doubling of risk), *aff'd sub nom. Meridia Prods. Liab. Litig. v. Abbott Labs.*, 447 F.3d 861 (6th Cir. 2006); *Leathers v. Pfizer, Inc.*, 233 F.R.D. 687, 694 (N.D. Ga. 2006) ("[A]dverse incident reports generally do not, standing alone, render an expert's opinion reliable under *Daubert*.").
92. *See, e.g., McClain*, 401 F.3d at 1250, 1253-54 (reversing trial court's admission of expert testimony predicated on adverse event reports); *Swallow v. Emergency Med. of Idaho, P.A.*, 67 P.3d 68, 72-74 (Idaho 2003) (affirming trial court's exclusion of adverse event reports and expert testimony predicated on those reports under *Daubert* and the state court standard regarding the admissibility of expert testimony, as "speculation based on a temporal concurrence of events").
93. *See* M.N.G. Dukes, *et al.*, *Responsibility for Drug-Induced Injury: A Reference Book for Lawyers, the Health Professionals and manufacturers* 45-46 (2d ed. 1998); Ronald H.B. Meyboom, *et. al.*, *Causal or Casual? The Role of Causality Assessments in Pharmacovigilance*, 17(6) Drug Safety 374, 375-81 (1997).
94. M.N.G. Dukes, *supra* note 93 at 46.
95. Meyboom, *supra* note 93, at 382.
96. *See* Meyboom, *supra* note 93, at 381; G. Miremont, *et al.*, *Adverse drug reactions: physicians' opinions versus a causality assessment method*, 46 Eur. J. Clin. Pharmacol. 285, 288 (1994).
97. *See Glastetter v. Novartis Pharms. Corp.*, 107 F. Supp. 2d 1015, 1037 n. 21 (E.D. Mo. 2000) ("like case reports ... a causality assessment involves only one individual, and, in any event, is not sufficient to establish causation"), *aff'd*, 252 F.3d 986 (8th Cir. 2001); *Soldo*, 244 F. Supp. 2d at 545 (plaintiff has failed to show that the causality assessment "methodology – adopted for foreign regulatory purposes – meets any of the *Daubert* criteria, nor has plaintiff shown any other indicia of reliability.").
98. *See Dunn*, 275 F. Supp 2d at 683; *Soldo*, 244 F. Supp. 2d at 541-42; *Caraker*, 188 F. Supp. 2d at 1035-36; *see also Revels v. Novartis Pharms. Corp.*, No. 03-98-00231-CV, 1999 WL 644732, *5 (Tex. App. Aug. 26, 1999).
99. *See* David M. Reboussin & Timothy M. Morgan, *Statistical considerations in the use and analysis of single-subject designs*, Medicine and Science in Sports and Exercise 639, 640-642 (1996) (discussing limitations).
100. *Id.*, abstract.
101. *Soldo*, 244 F. Supp. 2d at 541 (quoting *Revels*, 1999 WL 644732, at *5); *see also McClain*, 401 F.3d at 1254-55 ("dechallenge/re-challenge tests are still case reports and do not purport to offer definitive conclusions as to causation") (quoting *Rider*, 295 F.3d at 1200).
102. *See Soldo*, 244 F. Supp. 2d at 513, 542; *Caraker*, 188 F. Supp. 2d at 1039; *Siharath*, 131 F. Supp. 2d at 1370; *Glastetter*, 107 F. Supp. 2d at 1034 n.18.
103. *See McLain*, 401 F.3d at 1248-50; *Rider*, 295 F.3d at 1201; *Glastetter*, 252 F.3d at 991; *Hollander*, 289 F.3d at 1215; *Conde*, 24 F.3d at 814; *Dunn*, 2003 WL 21856420, at * 10; *Soldo*, 244 F. Supp. 2d at 513; *see also* Richard A. Merrill, *Regulatory Toxicology*, in Casarett & Doull's Toxicology: The Basic Science of Poisons 1041-43 (1975), (discussing federal regulator's conservative risk-utility analysis); Joseph V. Rodricks & Susan H. Rieth, *Toxicological Risk Assessment in the Courtroom: Are Available Methodologies Suitable for Evaluating Toxic Tort and Product Liability Claims?* 27 Regulatory Toxicology and Pharmacology 21, 27 (1998) ("The public health-oriented resolution of scientific uncertainty [used by regulators] is not especially helpful to the problem faced by a court").
104. *See* Arnaiz, *supra* note 87.
105. Rodricks & Rieth, *supra* note 1038, at 30.
106. *Caraker v. Sandoz Pharm. Corp.*, 188 F. Supp. 2d 1026, 1040 (S.D. Ill. 2001); *see also Siharath*, 131 F. Supp. 2d at 1371 ("one cannot lump together lots of hollow evidence in an attempt to determine what caused a medical harm").
107. 639 F.3d 11, 23 (1st Cir. 2011).
108. *Id.* at 17 n.7.
109. Eric G. Lasker, *Manning the Daubert Gate: A Defense Primer in Response to Milward v. Acuity Specialty Products*, 79 DEF. COUNS. J. 128, 131 (April 2012).
110. 522 U.S. at 146.
111. *See, e.g., Hollander*, 289 F.3d at 1216 n.21 ("[Plaintiffs] maintain that even though each individual category of evidence may be insufficient, all of the evidence considered as a whole raises factual questions as to whether Parlodel® caused her stroke. [Plaintiffs] cite no legal authority in support of this approach, and in our view, this argument is

inconsistent with *Daubert*."); *Allen v. Pa. Eng'g Corp.*, 102 F.3d 194, 198 (5th Cir. 1996) ("We are also unpersuaded that the 'weight of the evidence' methodology these experts use is scientifically acceptable for demonstrating a medical link between Allen's EtO exposure and brain cancer."); *Magistrini*, 180 F. Supp. 2d at 608 ("Where, as here, elements of judgment pervade the methodology, it is essential that the expert set forth the method for weighing the evidence upon which his opinion is based. Absent that, this Court's role as gatekeeper to assess the reliability of the methodology applied in this case is nullified.").

112. *See Soldo*, 244 F. Supp. 2d at 508; *Siharath*, 131 F. Supp. 2d at 1362; *In re Breast Implant Litig.*, 11 F. Supp. 2d at 1230; *Hall*, 947 F. Supp. at 1413.
113. *Tamraz v. Lincoln Elec. Co.*, 620 F.3d 665, 673 (6th Cir. 2010) (plaintiff conflated proposed expert's expertise in diagnosis with expertise in etiology because "most treating physicians have more training in and experience with diagnosis than etiology" (citing Joe G. Hollingsworth & Eric G. Lasker, *The Case Against Differential Diagnosis: Daubert, Medical Causation Testimony, and the Scientific Method*, 37 J. Health L. 85, 98 (2004)).
114. *See* Hu & Speizer, *supra* note 87.
115. *See Siharath*, 131 F. Supp. 2d at 1371; *see also* Miremont, *supra* note 96, at 288 (explaining finding that physicians are more likely to attribute causation to a drug as being due to their "necessarily more pragmatic approach to patients and diseases").
116. *See* Kassirer & Cecil, *supra* note 9, at 1384.
117. John M. Conley & John B. Garver, III, *William C. Keady and the Law of Scientific Evidence*, 68 Miss. L.J. 39, 51 (1998).
118. Herbert A. Simon, *Artificial-Intelligence Approaches to Problem Solving and Clinical Diagnosis*, in Logic of Discovery and Diagnosis in Medicine 72, 87 (Kenneth F. Schaffner ed. 1985).
119. *Siharath*, 131 F. Supp. 2d at 1372.
120. 526 U.S. at 152.
121. *See Siharath*, 131 F. Supp. 2d at 1362; Michael B. Kent, Jr., *Daubert, Doctors and Differential Diagnosis: Treating Medical Causation Testimony as Evidence*, 66 Def. Couns. J. 525, 532-33 (1999); *see also Thomas v. Novartis Pharms. Corp.*, 443 F. App'x 58, 62 (6th Cir. 2011) (expertise in recognizing and treating an injury is not sufficient to establish a doctor is qualified to testify on the cause of an injury).
122. *See Norris*, 397 F.3d at 885; *Soldo*, 244 F. Supp. 2d at 524; *Siharath*, 131 F. Supp. 2d at 1362-63; *Glastetter*, 107 F. Supp. 2d at 1027.
123. *Chapman*, 766 F.3d at 1311 (differential diagnosis unreliable where expert "ruled-in and considered an etiology" that had not been established to cause plaintiff's disease); *Jones*, 235 F. Supp. 3d at 1277 (where there is no admissible general causation opinion in the case, "then an expert may not rely on a differential diagnosis to prove specific causation"); *In re Zoloft (Sertralinehydrochloride) Prods. Liab. Litig.*, 176 F.Supp.3d 483, 496 (E.D. Pa. 2016) ("the ruling-out process, by itself, cannot establish causation."), *aff'd*, 858 F.3d 787 (3d Cir. 2017).
124. *Glastetter,* 252 F.3d at 989 (differential diagnosis was invalid because the experts "lacked a proper basis for 'ruling in' [the drug] Parlodel as a potential cause of [stroke] in the first place").
125. *Guinn v. AstraZeneca Pharm. LP,* 602 F.3d 1245, 1253 (11th Cir. 2010).
126. *See Soldo*, 244 F. Supp. 2d at 551; *Garrison v. Novartis Pharm. Corp.*, 30 F. Supp.3d 1325, 1339 (M.D. Ala. 2014) (excluding specific causation testimony of plaintiff's expert where expert failed to conduct "a sufficiently thorough analysis to support his conclusive elimination of osteomyelitis as a specific cause of ONJ" and "glosses over" certain facts that "compromise the reliability of [expert's] firm conclusion that [plaintiff's] ONJ was solely caused by her exposure to bisphosphonates").
127. *See Daubert,* 43 F.3d at 1319; *Hall v. Conoco Inc.*, 886 F.3d 1308, 1311–12 (10th Cir. 2018); *Chapman*, 766 F.3d at 1311; *Soldo*, 244 F. Supp. 2d at 551-52; *Perry*, 564 F. Supp. 2d at 471; *Magistrini,* 180 F. Supp. 2d at 608-10; *Nelson v. Am. Home Prods. Corp.*, 92 F. Supp. 2d 954, 971 (W.D. Mo. 2000).
128. *Deutsch v. Novartis Pharm. Corp.*, 768 F. Supp. 2d 420, 472 (E.D.N.Y. 2011) ("[W]hen the treating physician seeks to opine on causation, that opinion 'is subject to the same standards of scientific reliability that govern the expert opinions of physicians hired solely for the purposes of litigation.'") (quoting *In re Aredia & Zometa Prods. Liab. Litig.*, 754 F. Supp. 2d 934, 936 (M.D. Tenn. 2010)).
129. *Kumho Tire*, 536 U.S. at 152.
130. *See Cano v. Everest Minerals Corp.*, 362 F. Supp. 2d 814, 846 (W.D. Tex. 2005).
131. *See In re Lipitor*, 892 F.3d at 645 (excluding specific causation opinion where expert failed to provide "a reasoned scientific analysis" for excluding other possible causes of plaintiff's diabetes); *Wills v. Amerada Hess Corp.*, 379 F.3d 32, 50 (2d Cir. 2004) (excluding expert's specific causation opinion that plaintiff's squamous cell carcinoma had been caused by polycyclic aromatic hydrocarbons where plaintiff was a smoker and heavy consumer of alcohol); *In re Trasylol Prods. Liab. Litig.*, No. 08-MD-1928, 2013 WL 3353833, at *9 (S.D. Fla. July 3, 2013) ("Where an expert testifies that a particular injury could have numerous causes and simply picks the cause that is most advantageous to a plaintiff's claim, such testimony is not admissible.") (quotations & alterations omitted); *Harvey v. Novartis Pharm. Corp.*, 895 F. Supp. 2d 1206, 1213 (N.D. Ala. 2012) ("Because [the expert] never offered a principled reason for ruling out osteomyelitis, his opinion that Zometa caused [plaintiff's] osteonecrosis would be nothing more than speculation and conjecture."); *Easter v. Aventis Pasteur, Inc.*, 358 F. Supp. 2d 574, 577 (E.D. Tex. 2005) (expert could not reliably point to thimerosal in vaccine as a cause of plaintiff's neurological injuries where plaintiff had autism that could not be linked to vaccine and was independently associated with such injuries).
132. As discussed *supra* at __, such regulatory action is not the equivalent of a finding of causation.
133. *See, e.g.*, Steven A. Kittner, *et al*, *Cerebral Infarction in Young Adults*, 50 Neurology 890-94 (1998) (despite neurologists' careful review, in 50.5% of cases, no probable cause of stroke in young adults could be identified).
134. *Guinn*, 602 F.3d at 1254 ("[t]he temporal connection between exposure to chemicals and an onset of symptoms, standing alone, is entitled to little weight in determining causation"); *Kilpatrick v. Breg, Inc.*, 613 F.3d 1329, 1343 (11th Cir. 2010) ("[P]roving a *temporal* relationship ... does not establish a *causal* relationship .... [S]imply because a person takes drugs and then suffers an injury does not show causation.").
135. Kiely, *supra* note 10. In addition to being used as a case study for legal scholars, the Parlodel® litigation was discussed in an article published in the Journal of the American Medical Association by an unsuccessful *amicus*

for plaintiffs appealing a Parlodel® *Daubert* exclusionary ruling to the Eleventh Circuit Court of Appeals in *Rider*. *See* J. Kassirer & J. Cecil, *supra* note 9.

136. *Rider*, 295 F.3d 1194; *Hollander*, 289 F.3d 1193; *Glastetter*, 252 F.3d 986; *Dunn*, 275 F. Supp. 2d 672; *Soldo*, 244 F. Supp. 2d 434; *Caraker*, 188 F. Supp. 2d 1026; *Brumbaugh*, 77 F. Supp. 2d 1153; *see also Revels*, 1999 WL 644732 (excluding Parlodel® causation opinions on Texas analog of *Daubert*).

137. *Brasher v. Sandoz Pharms. Corp.*, 160 F. Supp. 2d 1291 (N.D. Ala. 2001) (Putnam, M.J.); *Globetti v. Sandoz Pharms. Corp.*, 111 F. Supp. 2d 1174 (N.D. Ala. 2000) (Putnam, M.J.); *Eve v. Sandoz Pharms. Corp.*, 2001 U.S. Dist. LEXIS 4531 (S.D. Ind. Mar. 7, 2001); *see also Hyman & Armstrong, P.S.C. v. Gunderson*, 279 S.W.3d 93 (Ky. 2008).

138. *See Caraker*, 188 F. Supp. 2d at 1028, 1040.

139. *See generally Rider*, 295 F.3d 1194; *Glastetter*, 252 F.3d 986; *Caraker*, 188 F. Supp. 2d 1026.

140. *Globetti*, 111 F. Supp. 2d at 1180; *see also Eve*, 2001 U.S. Dist. LEXIS 4531, at *75 (quoting *Globetti*).

141. *Brasher*, 160 F. Supp. 2d at 1296; *see also id.* at 1297 ("Given the practical unavailability of other forms of scientific evidence, reliance on those that are available is all the more reasonable.").

142. *Id.* at 1299.

143. *Siharath*, 131 F. Supp. 2d at 1373.

144. *Id.* at 1371.

145. *Hollander*, 289 F.3d at 1213.

146. *Brumbaugh*, 77 F. Supp. 2d at 1156.

147. *Caraker*, 188 F. Supp. 2d at 1030.

148. *Soldo*, 244 F. Supp. 2d at 529.

149. *Glastetter*, 107 F. Supp. 2d at 1025.

150. *Dunn*, 275 F. Supp 2d at 684.

151. *Rider*, 295 F.3d at 1197.

152. *Joiner*, 522 U.S. at 148-49 (Breyer, J., concurring).

Appendix A
Conversion Formulas

Toxicology reports are not standardized. Depending on the units of measure used, what looks like a very large number may in fact be a very small one. Forensic toxicology laboratories report results in µg/mL.

CONVERTING UNITS OF MEASURE

A blood cocaine concentration of 1,200 ng/mL (approximately the plasma concentration after smoking one rock of cocaine) might be reported as

$$1,200 \text{ ng / mL} = 1.2 \text{ µg / mL} = 1,200 \text{ µg / L} = 1.2 \text{ mg / L}$$

The concentrations of hormones such as epinephrine are much lower than the concentrations of exogenous drugs and are usually expressed in picograms (pg). If the concentration of cocaine in the aforementioned example were expressed in picograms (which, as a practical matter, it never is), 1200 ng/mL would be equal to 1,200,000 pg/mL.

CONVERTING MOLES INTO GRAMS

Clinical laboratories express results in millimoles (mmol) or standard international (SI) units. To convert to standard concentration measurements, divide 1,000 by the molecular weight, and then divide that number into the concentration value expressed as µmol/L.

Example: In a research study of morphine pharmacokinetics, the maximum blood concentration after a 10 mg subcutaneous injection of morphine was given to a 70 kg man was reported as 262 ± 49 nmol/L. To convert that concentration into ng/mL,

1. Divide 1,000 by the molecular weight of morphine: 1,000/285.34 (the molecular weight of morphine) = 3.50.
2. Convert nanomoles (nmol) into micromoles (µmol): 262 nmol/L = 0.262 µmol/L.
3. Divide the number of mmol/L by 3.50: 0.262/3.50 = 0.0748 µg/mL = 74.8 ng/mL.

Appendix B
Blood Ethanol Concentrations

Individuals who take abused drugs often ingest ethanol at the same time. Widmark's formula is the standard method used by forensic toxicologists to calculate blood ethanol concentrations (BECs) and is universally recognized by the legal system. However, an approach first suggested by Charles Winek, from Duquesne University, works equally well and is easier to remember (*Forensic Sciences*, C.W. Wecht, Ed., Matthew Binder Press, New York, chapter 31B, 1984). Winek's formula is based on the observation that a 150 lb man will have a BEC of 0.025% after drinking 1 oz of 100 proof (50%) ethanol. Given that assumption (which is accurate under almost all circumstances), the formula for calculating the BEC is

$$\begin{aligned} \text{BEC} = &\left(150 / \text{body weight}\right)\left(\% \text{ ethanol} / 50\right) \\ &\times\left(\text{ounces consumed}\right)\left(0.025\right) \end{aligned}$$

Example: A 200 lb man drinks five 12 oz cans of beer. The beer contained 4% ethanol. The BEC would be given by the following equation:

$$\begin{aligned} \text{BEC} &= \left(150/200\right)\left(4/50\right)\left(60\right)\left(0.025\right)\text{BEC} \\ &= \left(0.75\right)\left(0.08\right)\left(60\right)\left(0.025\right) \\ \text{BEC} &= 0.090\% \end{aligned}$$

Remember when using this calculation that it assumes all the ethanol was ingested at one time.

Appendix C
Volume of Distribution Calculations

Some drugs, such as morphine, rapidly leave the blood and distribute widely throughout the body. Other drugs, such as morphine metabolites, stay mostly in the blood. The tendency for a molecule to remain in the blood or distribute into tissue can only be determined by actual measurement. The volume of distribution is the apparent volume needed to contain all the drugs injected into the body at the same concentration as observed in the blood. If, for example, 10 g of food coloring were dissolved in a 10 L aquarium, the resultant concentration would be 1 g/L, and the volume of distribution, abbreviated as V_{ss}, would be 10 L. The V_{ss} for drugs that remain mostly in the bloodstream, such as the morphine glucuronides, will be much lower than 1. The V_{ss} for drugs that penetrate widely into tissue, such as cocaine (V_{ss} = approximately 3), will be much greater than 1. V_{ss} calculations can be used to estimate the amount of drug administered:

$$\begin{aligned}\text{Dose} = &\left(\text{body weight}\left[\text{kg}\right]\right)\\ &\times\left(\text{volume of distribution}\left[\text{L/kg}\right]\right)\\ &\times\left(\text{blood concentration}\left[\text{mg/L}\right]\right)\end{aligned}$$

V_{ss} calculations apply *only to the living*. Postmortem redistribution and other postmortem changes make V_{ss} calculations in the deceased extremely unreliable. An example taken from an actual court case appears as follows. An individual was charged with accidentally administering a lethal dose of diphenhydramine (Benadryl). Witnesses observed that the accused administered one injection with a 10 cc syringe. The decedent weighed 72.6 kg and at autopsy had a blood diphenhydramine concentration of 5.1 mg/L. Thus, the accused would have to have injected:

$$\text{Dose} = 72.6\ \text{kg} \times 4.5V_{ss} \times 5.1\ \text{mg/L} = 1{,}666.2\ \text{mg}$$

The average 30 mL multidose vial of diphenhydramine contains only 500 mg. The accused had only a 10 cc syringe. If the V_{ss} calculation is to be believed, the accused would have to have injected the victim with more than three vials of diphenhydramine, a process that would have required at least ten separate injections!

The main utility of V_{ss} calculations in postmortem investigations is as a quality assurance check of reported blood concentrations. If the V_{ss} calculation suggests that an implausible amount of drug has been ingested, an error in laboratory or sampling methods may be indicated (the blood analyzed may, for example, have been scooped from the chest cavity).

Appendix D
Normal Organ Weights

The data are from a table included in a paper by Geoffroy Lorin de la Grandmaison et al. It was first published in October 2001 and is reproduced with permission (*Forensic Sci. Int.* 119(2): 149–154). Since the study was so recently published and was based on 684 autopsies, it no doubt reflects weights as they are observed today.

Comparative Data of Organ Weight (g) of Males and Females

	Males (n = 355)		Females (n = 329)	
	Mean ± SD	**Range**	**Mean ± SD**	**Range**
Heart	365 ± 71	90–630	312 ± 78	174–590
Right lung	663 ± 239	200–1593	546 ± 207	173–1700
Left lung	583 ± 216	206–1718	467 ± 174	178–1350
Liver	1677 ± 396	670–2900	1475 ± 362	508–3081
Spleen	156 ± 87	30–580	140 ± 78	33–481
Pancreas	144 ± 39	65–243	122 ± 35	60–250
Right kidney	162 ± 39	53–320	135 ± 39	45–360
Left kidney	160 ± 41	50–410	136 ± 37	40–300
Thyroid	25 ± 11	12–87	20 ± 9	5–88

Note: SD, standard deviation.

Mean and Standard Deviation of Organ Weight (g) according to Height (cm)

	Males			Females		
	144 ≤ H ≤ 165	**165 ≤ H ≤ 175**	**176 ≤ H ≤ 190**	**126 ≤ H ≤ 155**	**156 ≤ H ≤ 165**	**166 ≤ H ≤ 180**
Heart	344 ± 75	360 ± 75	381 ± 56	320 ± 88	308 ± 79	311 ± 67
Right lung	616 ± 210	625 ± 207	741 ± 274	494 ± 202	545 ± 183	597 ± 243
Left lung	523 ± 190	551 ± 178	658 ± 257	450 ± 146	472 ± 181	491 ± 204
Liver	1455 ± 370	1637 ± 369	1831 ± 384	1275 ± 321	1496 ± 331	1624 ± 380
Spleen	120 ± 51	150 ± 88	180 ± 90	122 ± 67	139 ± 79	160 ± 82
Pancreas	138 ± 35	143 ± 39	147 ± 39	111 ± 25	122 ± 35	138 ± 41
Right kidney	150 ± 49	157 ± 36	170 ± 37	117 ± 32	137 ± 40	148 ± 36
Left kidney	155 ± 53	164 ± 38	175 ± 38	120 ± 41	136 ± 35	148 ± 33
Thyroid	25 ± 7	25 ± 13	25 ± 9	20 ± 11	18 ± 6	20 ± 11

Note: H, height.

Index

Page numbers followed by 'n' refer to notes.

B

E

T

U